O

D1408704

THE INTERNATIONAL DICTIONARY OF
FILMS AND FILMMAKERS: VOLUME V

TITLE INDEX

THE INTERNATIONAL DICTIONARY OF FILMS AND FILMMAKERS

Volume I
FILMS

Volume II
DIRECTORS/FILMMAKERS

Volume III
ACTORS AND ACTRESSES

Volume IV
WRITERS AND PRODUCTION ARTISTS

Volume V
TITLE INDEX

THE INTERNATIONAL DICTIONARY OF FILMS AND FILMMAKERS: VOLUME V

TITLE INDEX

Editor:
James Vinson

Associate Editor:
Greg S. Faller

St J

ST. JAMES PRESS
CHICAGO AND LONDON

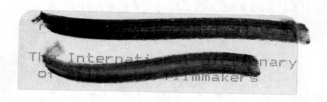

ST. JAMES PRESS
425 North Michigan Avenue
Chicago 60611, U.S.A.
or
3 Percy Street
London W1P 9FA, England

First published in the U.S.A. and U.K. in 1987

British Library Cataloguing in Publication Data

The International dictionary of films and filmmakers.
  Vol 5: Title Index
  I. Moving-pictures—Dictionaries
  I. Vinson, James   II. Faller, Greg S.
  791.43′03′21   PN1993.45

  ISBN 0 912289 86 4

Compiled and typeset by Florencetype Ltd., Kewstoke, Avon
Printed at The Bath Press, Avon.

CONTENTS

INTRODUCTION

The following list of titles cites all films included in the first four volumes of this series, including cross-references for alternative or English-language titles. The name(s) and number(s) in parenthesis following the title and date refer the reader to the appropriate entry or entries, where full information is given:

2 — Directors/Filmmakers
3 — Actors and Actresses
4 — Writers and Production Artists

Titles appearing in **bold** have separate entries in volume 1 — Films.

THE INTERNATIONAL DICTIONARY OF
FILMS AND FILMMAKERS: VOLUME V

TITLE INDEX

A

A, 1964 (Lenica 2, Delerue 4)
A 8a. Bienal de São Paulo, 1965 (Diegues 2)
A B C, 1950 (Hofman 4)
A belles dents, 1966 (Gélin 3)
A bientôt j'espère, 1969 (Marker 2)
A bon pied, bon ceil, 1972 (George, Ch. D. 3)
A bout de souffle, 1960 (Broca 2, Chabrol 2, Godard 2, Melville 2, Belmondo 3, Seberg 3, Coutard 4, de Beauregard 4)
A canção do berço, 1930 (Cavalcanti 2)
A cavallo della tigre, 1961 (Comencini 2, Monicelli 2, Manfredi 3, Volonté 3, Age and Scarpelli 4)
A českých mlýnu, 1929 (Stallich 4)
A chacun son enfer, 1977 (Cayatte 2, Girardot 3)
A cheval, 1950 (Decaë 4)
A ciascuno il suo, 1967 (Petri 2, Papas 3, Volonté 3)
A coeur joie, 1967 (Bardot 3)
A côté de nous. See Riadom s nami, 1931
A Couteaux tirés, 1962 (Dalio 3)
A Cruz de Ferro, 1968 (de Almeida 4)
A da veni . . . Don Calogero. See Filo d'erba, 1952
A donde van nuestros hijos, 1958 (Del Rio 3)
A doppia faccia. See Double Face, 1969
A double tour, 1959 (Broca 2, Chabrol 2, Belmondo 3, Decaë 4 Evein 4, Gégauff 4, Rabier 4)
A Estrangeira, 1982 (de Almeida 4)
A fleur d'eau, 1969 (Reichenbach 2, Braunberger 4)
A fleur de peau, 1962 (Kosma 4)
A Flor do Mar, 1986 (de Almeida 4)
A grande cidade, 1966 (Diegues 2)
A Hunting We Will Go, 1932 (Fleischer, M. and D. 2)
A Hunting We Won't Go, 1943 (Fleischer, M. and D. 2)
A Ilha dos Amores, 1982 (de Almeida 4)
A l'aube d'un monde, 1956 (Cocteau 2)
A l'aube du troisième jour, 1963 (Kosma 4)
A L'Horizon du Sud, 1924 (Modot 3)
A l'ombre d'un été, 1977 (Vanel 3)
A la belle etoile, 1966 (Prévert 4)
A la belle frégate, 1942 (Spaak 4)
A la Cabaret, 1916 (Sennett 2)
A la conquête du Pôle, 1912 (Méliès 2)
A la conquête de l'air, 1901 (Zecca 2)
A la culotte de zouave, 1947–51 (Verneuil 2)
A la française, 1962 (Dauphin 3)
A la mémoire du rock, 1962 (Reichenbach 2, Braunberger 4)
A la poursuite du vent, 1943 (Leenhardt 2)
A la recherche d'un appartement, 1906 (Guy 2)
A las cinco de la tarde, 1960 (Bardem 2, Rey 3)
A Lei da Terra—Alentejo 76, 1976 (de Almeida 4)
A media luz los tres, 1957 (Alcoriza 4)
A ménesgazda, 1978 (Madaras 3)
A mezzanotte va la ronda del piacere, 1975 (Cardinale 3, Gassman 3, Giannini 3, Vitti 3)
A mi Folkunk, 1959 (Madaras 3)
A mi-chemin du ciel, 1929 (Cavalcanti 2)
A nagy kék Jelzés, 1969 (Latinovits 3)
A noi piace freddo, 1960 (Tognazzi 3)
A nous deux, Madame la vie, 1936 (Barrault 3, Wakhévitch 4)
A nous deux, 1979 (Deneuve 3, Lai 4)
A nous la liberté, 1931 (Clair 2, Auric 4, Meerson 4, Périnal 4, Trauner 4)
A nous quatre, Cardinal, 1973 (Douy 4)
A nyní hraje dechovka, 1953 (Stallich 4)
A Paris . . . un jeudi, 1954 (Kosma 4)

A Paris tous les deux, 1957 (Fernandel 3)
A pied, à cheval, et en voiture, 1957 (Belmondo 3, Cassel 3)
A pied, à cheval, et un sputnik, 1958 (Auer 3)
. . . a pozdravuji vlaštovky, 1972 (Jires 2)
A propos d'une rivière, 1955 (Franju 2)
A propos de Jivago, 1962 (Alexeieff and Parker 2)
A propos de Nice, 1930 (Vigo 2, Kaufman 4)
A proposito Lucky Luciano, 1973 (Rosi 2, O'Brien, E. 3, Steiger 3, Volonté 3, Cristaldi 4, Guerra 4)
A qualsiasi prezzo, 1968 (Kinski 3, Pidgeon 3)
A qui le bébé?, 1947 (Verneuil 2)
A Sagrada Família, 1972 (de Almeida 4)
A shchastiya bylo tak vozmotzno, 1916 (Mozhukin 3)
A sud niente di nuovo, 1956 (Bertini 3)
A szarnok szive, 1981 (Madaras 3)
A téglafal mogott, 1979 (Kroner 3)
A to Z, 1956 (Snow 2)
A toda máquina, 1951 (Infante 3)
A toi de faire, Mignonne, 1963 (Constantine 3)
A tous les vents, 1945 (Decaë 4)
A tout casser, 1953 (Colpi 4, Decaë 4)
A tout casser. See Consortium, 1968
A tout prendre, 1963 (Jutra 2)
. . . à Valparaiso, 1963 (Ivens 2, Delerue 4)
A város peremén, 1957 (Jancsó 2, Madaras 3)
A Venise, une nuit, 1937 (Christian-Jaque 2)
A Votre santé!, 1950 (Fradetal 4)
A Voz do carnaval, 1933 (Miranda 3)
A 009 Mission to Hong Kong. See Gehemnis der drei Dschunken, 1965
A život jde dál, 1935 (Stallich 4)
A.B.C., 1958 (Lassally 4)
A.B.C.A., 1943 (Alwyn 4)
Aa furusato, 1938 (Mizoguchi 2, Yoda 4)
Aa, kaigun, 1969 (Mori 3)
Aa koe naki tomo, 1972 (Imai 2)
Aaamour, 1978 (Brdečka 4)
Aadha din aadhi raat, 1977 (Azmi 3)
Aag, 1948 (Kapoor 2)
Aage Badho, 1947 (Anand 3)
Aaghat, 1985 (Nihalani 4)
Aah, 1953 (Kapoor 2)
Aaj ka M.L.A. Ram Avtaar, 1984 (Azmi 3)
Aakash, 1953 (Biswas 4)
Aamua Kaupungissa, 1954 (Donner 2)
Aanasi yiğit doğurmus, 1966 (Guney 2)
Aandhiya, 1952 (Anand 3)
Aaram, 1951 (Anand 3, Biswas 4)
Aarohan, 1982 (Chandragupta 4)
Aaron Slick from Punkin Crick, 1952 (Seaton 2, Bumstead 4, Head 4, Lang 4)
Aashik, 1962 (Kapoor 2)
Aashiyana, 1952 (Kapoor 2)
Aasraa, 1941 (Biswas 4)
Aath Din, 1946 (Burman 4)
Ab Dilli Dur Nahin, 1957 (Kapoor 2)
Ab Mitternacht, 1938 (Hoffmann 4)
Ab Morgen sind wir reich und ehrlich, 1977 (Baker C. 3, Jurgens 3, Kennedy, A. 3)
Abajo el telón, 1954 (Cantinflas 3)
Abalone Industry, 1913 (Sennett 2)
Abandon Ship, 1956 (Zetterling 2, Power 3)
Abandonadas, 1944 (Fernández 2, Armendáriz 3, Del Rio 3, Figueroa 4)

1

Abandonado, 1949 (Armendáriz 3)
Abandoned, 1949 (Chandler 3, Boyle 4, Daniels 4)
Abare andon, 1956 (Kagawa 3)
Abare Goemon, 1966 (Mifune 3)
Abare Himatsuri, 1970 (Mori 3)
Abare-jishi, 1953 (Yamada 3)
Abarenbo kaido, 1957 (Yamada 3, Yoda 4)
Abarenbou taishou, 1960 (Yoda 4)
Abasheshey, 1962 (Sen 2)
Abastecimento, nova política, 1968 (Pereira Dos Santos 2)
Abbandano, 1940 (Stallich 4)
Abbasso la miseria, 1945 (Magnani 3)
Abbasso la ricchezza!, 1946 (De Sica 2, Magnani 3)
Abbasso lo zio, (Bellocchio 2)
Abbé Constantin, 1925 (Duvivier 2)
Abbé Constantin, 1933 (Dauphin 3, Rosay 3, Burel 4, Spaak 4)
Abbott and Costello Go to Mars, 1953 (Abbott and Costello 3,
    Boyle 4)
Abbott and Costello in Hollywood, 1945 (Walters 2, Abbott and
    Costello 3, Ball 3, Irene 4)
Abbott and Costello in the Foreign Legion, 1950 (Abbott and
    Costello 3)
Abbott and Costello Meet Captain Kidd, 1952 (Aldrich 2, Abbott and
    Costello 3, Laughton 3, Cortez 4)
Abbott and Costello Meet Dr. Jekyll and Mr. Hyde, 1953 (Abbott and
    Costello 3, Karloff 3, Salter 4, Westmore, F. 4)
Abbott and Costello Meet Frankenstein, 1948 (Abbott and Costello 3,
    Chaney Lon, Jr. 3, Lugosi 3, Price 3, Pierce 4)
Abbott and Costello Meet the Ghosts. See Abbott and Costello Meet
    Frankenstein, 1948
Abbott and Costello Meet the Invisible Man, 1951 (Abbott and
    Costello 3, Salter 4)
Abbott and Costello Meet the Keystone Kops, 1955 (Abbott and
    Costello 3, Abbott and Costello 3, Salter 4)
Abbott and Costello Meet the Killer, Boris Karloff, 1949 (Abbott and
    Costello 3, Karloff 3)
Abdication, 1974 (Cusack 3, Finch 3, Ullmann 3, Rota 4, Unsworth 4)
Abduction of St. Anne, 1975 (Wagner 3, Duning 4)
Abduction, 1975 (Malone 3)
Abductors, 1957 (McLaglen 3, La Shelle 4)
Abdul the Damned, 1935 (Kortner 3, Eisler 4)
Abdulla the Great, 1954 (Auric 4, Garmes 4)
Abdullah, 1981 (Kapoor 2)
Abdullah's Harem. See Abdulla the Great, 1954
Abe Gets Even With Father, 1911 (Sennett 2)
Abe Lincoln in Illinois, 1940 (Cromwell 2, Gordon 3, Massey 3,
    Howe 4, Plunkett 4, Polglase 4, Sherwood 4)
Abeille et les hommes, 1960 (Braunberger 4)
Abeilles, 1956 (Braunberger 4)
Abel Gance—The Charm of Dynamite, 1968 (Anderson 2)
Abend . . . Nacht . . . Morgen, 1920 (Murnau 2, Veidt 3)
Abenteuer der Sybille Brant, 1925 (Porten 3)
Abenteuer der Thea Roland, 1933 (Dagover 3)
Abenteuer des Dr. Kircheisen, 1920 (Wiene 2)
Abenteuer des Konigs Pausole, 1933 (Jannings 3)
Abenteuer des Prinzen Achmed, 1923–26 (Ruttmann 2)
Abenteuer des Prinzen Achmed. See Geschichte des Prinzen Achmed,
    1923–26
Abenteuer des Till Ulenspiegel, 1957 (Ivens 2, Geschonneck 3,
    Matras 4)
Abenteuer des Werner Holt, 1965 (Domrose 3)
Abenteuer einer schonen Frau. See Abenteuer der Thea Roland, 1933
Abenteuer eines Heimgekehrten. See Rinaldo Rinaldini, 1927
Abenteuer eines jungen Herrn in Polen, 1934 (Frohlich 3,
    Tschechowa 3)
Abenteuer eines Zehnmarkscheinen, 1927 (Homolka 3, Freund 4)
Abenteuer geht weiter, 1939 (Gallone 2)
Abenteuer in Wien. See Gefahrliches Abenteuer, 1953
Abenteurer, 1921 (Courant 4)
Aberglaube, 1940 (Ruttmann 2)
Abgrund der Seelen, 1920 (Gad 2)
Abhagin, 1938 (Roy 2)
Abhigyan, 1938 (Sircar 4)

Abhijan, 1962 (Ray, S. 2, Chatterjee 3, Chandragupta 4, Datta 4)
Abhilasha, 1938 (Biswas 4)
Abhiman, 1957 (Biswas 4)
Abhiman, 1973 (Bachchan 3, Burman 4)
Abhinetri, 1940 (Sircar 4)
Abidjan, port de pêche, 1962 (Rouch 2)
Abie's Irish Rose, 1929 (Fleming 2, Hersholt 3, Banton 4,
    Furthman 4, Mankiewicz 4, Rosson 4, Schulberg 4)
Abie's Irish Rose, 1946 (Sutherland 2)
Abilene Town, 1946 (Scott, R. 3)
Abismos de pasión, 1953 (Buñuel 2)
Abito Nero da sposa, 1943 (Zampa 2, Flaiano 4)
Able Man. See Karl fo sin hatt, 1940
Ableminded Lady, 1922 (Walthall 3)
Abominable Dr. Phibes, 1971 (Cotten 3, Price 3)
Abominable Homme des douanes, 1963 (Allégret 2, Brasseur 3,
    Dalio 3, Delerue 4)
Abominable Snow Rabbit, 1961 (Jones 2)
Abominable Snowman, 1957 (Cushing 3, Trumbo 4)
Abominable Snowman. See Jujin Yuki-Otoko, 1955
Abominable Snowman of the Himalayas. See Abominable Snowman,
    1957
About Face, 1942 (Dumont 3, Roach 4)
About Face, 1951 (Glennon 4, Prinz 4)
About Fakes. See F for Fake, 1975
About Mrs. Leslie, 1954 (Ryan 3, Head 4, Laszlo 4, Wallis 4,
    Young, V. 4)
About Puberty and Reproduction, 1974 (Patel 4)
About 'The White Bus', 1967 (Anderson 2)
About VD, 1974 (Patel 4)
Above All Law. See Indische Grabmal, 1921
Above and Beyond, 1953 (Taylor, R. 3, Frank and Panama 4,
    Friedhofer 4, Rose 4)
Above Suspicion, 1943 (Saville 2, Crawford, J. 3, MacMurray 3,
    Rathbone 3, Veidt 3, Irene 4, Kaper 4)
Above Us the Waves, 1955 (Mills 3)
Abracadabra, 1958 (Vukotić 4)
Abraham Bosse, 1972 (Leenhardt 2)
Abraham Lincoln, 1924 (Sutherland 2, Fazenda 3, Marion 4)
Abraham Lincoln, 1930 (Griffith 2, Bosworth 3, Huston 3, Merkel 3,
    Walthall 3, Menzies 4, Schenck 4, Struss 4)
Abrégeons les formalitiés!, 1917 (Feyder 2)
Abril de Giron, 1966 (Alvarez 2)
Abril de Vietnam en el año del gato, 1975 (Alvarez 2)
Abroad with 2 Yanks, 1944 (Dwan 2, Bendix 3)
Abschied, 1930 (Siodmak 2, Schufftan 4)
Abschied vom Frieden, 1979 (Domrose 3, Geschonneck 3,
    Hoffmann 3)
Abschied von Gestern, 1966 (Kluge 2)
Abseits vom Gluck, 1914 (Porten 3, Freund 4, Messter 4)
Absence, 1976 (Brakhage 2)
Absence of Malice, 1981 (Pollack 2, Field 3, Newman 3, Roizman 4)
Absent-Minded Bootblack, 1903 (Hepworth 2)
Absent-Minded Professor, 1961 (Disney 2, MacMurray 3, Wynn 3,
    Ellenshaw 4)
Absent-Minded Waiter, 1979 (Henry 4)
Absinthe, 1914 (Brenon 2)
Absolute Quiet, 1936 (Waxman 4)
Absolution, 1978 (Burton 3)
Absturz, 1922 (Nielsen 3)
Abuelita, 1942 (García 3)
Abus de confiance, 1937 (Darrieux 3, Vanel 3, Burel 4)
Abused Confidence. See Abus de confiance, 1937
Abwege, 1928 (Pabst 2)
Abyss, 1914 (Selig 4)
Abyss. See Afgrunden, 1910
Ac kurtlar, 1969 (Guney 2)
Acá las tortas, 1951 (García 3)
Academician Ivan Pavlov, 1949 (Enei 4)
Academician Ivan Pavlov. See Akademik Ivan Pavlov, 1949
Academy Awards Film, 1951 (Clarke, C.C. 4)
Acadie, l'Acadie!, 1970 (Perrault 2)
Acapulco, 1951 (Fernández 2)

Adventures of a Brown Man in Search of Civilization, 1972 (Ivory 2, Lassally 4)
Adventures of a Millionaire's Son, 1913 (Holger-Madsen 2)
Adventures of a Young Man, 1962 (Ritt 2, Kennedy, A. 3)
Adventures of an Old Flirt, 1909 (Porter 2)
Adventures of Arsène Lupin. See Aventures d'Arsène Lupin, 1956
Adventures of *, 1957 (Hubley 4)
Adventures of Barrie MacKenzie, 1972 (Beresford 2)
Adventures of Billy, 1911 (Griffith 2, Crisp 3, Bitzer 4)
Adventures of Bullwhip Griffin, 1967 (Disney 2, Malden 3, McDowall 3, Ellenshaw 4)
Adventures of Captain Africa, 1954 (Katzman 4)
Adventures of Captain Fabian, 1951 (Flynn 3, Moorehead 3, Price 3, Douy 4, Lourié 4)
Adventures of Casanova, 1948 (Friedhofer 4)
Adventures of Dr. Dolittle. See Doktor Dolittle und seine Tiere, 1928
Adventures of Dolly, 1908 (Griffith 2)
Adventures of Don Juan, 1949 (Florey 2, Flynn 3, Kurnitz 4, Steiner 4, Wald 4)
Adventures of Don Quixote, 1973 (Harrison 3, Legrand 4)
Adventures of Frank and Jesse James, 1948 (Canutt 4)
Adventures of Gerard, 1970 (Skolimowski 2, Cardinale 3, Hawkins 3, Wallach 3)
Adventures of Goopi and Bagha. See Goopy Gyne Bagha Byne, 1969
Adventures of Hajji Baba, 1954 (Tiomkin 4, Wanger 4)
Adventures of Huckleberry Finn, 1939 (Mankiewicz 2, Rooney 3, Waxman 4)
Adventures of Huckleberry Finn, 1960 (Curtiz 2, Keaton 2, Carradine 3, Hall 4, McCord 4)
Adventures of Huckleberry Finn, 1985 (Lassally 4)
Adventures of Ichabod and Mr. Toad, (Crosby 3)
Adventures of Ichabod and Mr. Toad. See Ichabod and Mr. Toad, 1949
Adventures of Jimmy, 1950 (Broughton 2)
Adventures of Kathlyn, 1914 (Selig 4)
Adventures of King Pausole. See Aventures du roi Pausole, 1933
Adventures of Marco Polo, 1938 (Cooper, Gary 3, Rathbone 3, Turner, L. 3, Basevi 4, Day 4, Friedhofer 4, Glennon 4, Goldwyn 4, Maté 4, Newman 4, Sherwood 4)
Adventures of Mark Twain, 1944 (Carradine 3, Crisp 3, March 3, Lasky 4, Polito 4, Steiner 4)
Adventures of Mark Twain, 1986 (Vinton 4)
Adventures of Martin Eden, 1942 (Ford, G. 3, Trevor 3, Planer 4, Schulberg 4)
Adventures of Mr. Wonderful, 1959 (Ustinov 3)
Adventures of Nick Carter, 1972 (Crawford, B. 3, O'Brien, P. 3, Winters 3, Bumstead 4)
Adventures of Pinocchio. See Pinocchiova dobrodružstvi, 1971
Adventures of Prince Achmed. See Abenteuer des Prinzen Achmed, 1923–26
Adventures of Quentin Durward, 1955 (Junge 4, Kaper 4)
Adventures of Quentin Durward. See Quentin Durward, 1955
Adventures of Red Ryder, 1938 (Farnum 3)
Adventures of Rex and Rinty, 1935 (Auer 3, Eason 4)
Adventures of Robin Hood, 1938 (Curtiz 2, De Havilland 3, Flynn 3, Rains 3, Rathbone 3, Blanke 4, Eason 4, Friedhofer 4, Gaudio 4, Korngold 4, Miller, S. 4, Polito 4, Raine 4, Wallis 4)
Adventures of Robinson Crusoe, 1922 (Johnson, N. 3)
Adventures of Robinson Crusoe. See Aventuras de Robinson Crusoe, 1952
Adventures of Sadie. See Our Girl Friday, 1953
Adventures of Sherlock Holmes, 1939 (Bruce 3, Lupino 3, Rathbone 3, Day 4, Raksin 4, Shamroy 4)
Adventures of Sherlock Holmes' Smarter Brother, 1975 (Finney 3, Wilder 3, Fisher 4)
Adventures of Shorty, 1914 (Ince 4)
Adventures of Sir Galahad, 1950 (Katzman 4)
Adventures of Takla Makan. See Kiganjo no boken, 1966
Adventures of Tartu, 1943 (Donat 3, Mahin 4)
Adventures of the Queen, 1975 (Bellamy 3)
Adventures of Till Eulenspiegel. See Abenteuer des Till Ulenspiegel, 1957
Adventures of Tom Sawyer, 1938 (Taurog 2, Brennan 3, Meek 3, Howe 4, Menzies 4, Plunkett 4, Selznick 4, Steiner 4, Wheeler 4)

Adventures of Werner Holt. See Abenteuer des Werner Holt, 1965
Adventuress, 1920 (Valentino 3)
Adventuress. See I See a Dark Stranger, 1946
Adventurous Automobile Trip. See Raid Paris-Monte Carlo en deux heures, 1905
Adventurous Sex, 1925 (Bow 3)
Adversary. See Pratidwandi, 1970
Advice to the Lovelorn, 1933 (Newman 4, Zanuck 4)
Advise and Consent, 1962 (Preminger 2, Ayres 3, Fonda, H. 3, Laughton 3, Meredith 3, Pidgeon 3, Tierney 3, Bass 4, Wheeler 4)
Adviser of the World's Adviser. See Tenka no goikenban o Ikensuru otoko, 1947
Aedel Daad, 1911 (Gad 2)
Aegteskab og Pigesjov, 1914 (Blom 2)
Aelita, 1924 (Protazanov 2)
Aereløse, 1916 (Holger-Madsen 2)
Aeresoprejsning, 1915 (Holger-Madsen 2)
Aerial Gunner, 1943 (Arlen 3, Gable 3, Mitchum 3)
Aeriel Joyride, 1916 (Hardy 3)
Aero-Engine, 1933 (Grierson 2)
Aerograd, 1935 (Dovzhenko 2, Tisse 4)
Aeroplane Inventor. See Opfinders Skaebne, 1911
Aeropuerto, 1953 (Rey 3)
Aesop's Fable: Foiling the Fox, 1950 (Terry 4)
Aesop's Fable: Golden Egg Goosie, 1951 (Terry 4)
Aesop's Fable: The Mosquito, 1945 (Terry 4)
Aeventyrersken, 1914 (Blom 2)
Af Elskovs Naade, 1913 (Blom 2)
Afanasi Nikitin, 1957 (Biswas 4)
Aféra plukovníka Redla, 1931 (Vích 4)
Affair, 1973 (Wagner 3, Wood 3)
Affair in Havana, 1957 (Armendáriz 3)
Affair in Monte Carlo. See 24 Hours of a Woman's Life, 1952
Affair in Trinidad, 1952 (Ford, G. 3, Hayworth 3, Duning 4, Walker 4)
Affair Lafont. See Conflit, 1938
Affair Maurizius, 1953 (Gélin 3)
Affair of Hearts, 1910 (Griffith 2, Sennett 2)
Affair of Susan, 1935 (Pitts 3, Waxman 4)
Affair of the Follies, 1927 (Stone 3, Gaudio 4, Wilson, C. 4)
Affair of the Heart. See Ljubavni Slučaj, tragedija sluzbenice PTT, 1967
Affair of the Skin, 1963 (Strick 2, Grant, L. 3, Fields 4, Maddow 4)
Affair to Remember, 1957 (Daves 2, McCarey 2, Grant, C. 3, Kerr 3, Friedhofer 4, Krasner 4, Lemaire 4, Smith, J.M. 4, Wald 4, Wheeler 4)
Affair with a Stranger, 1953 (Darwell 3, Mature 3, Simmons 3)
Affaire classée, 1932 (Spaak 4)
Affaire Clémenceau, 1918 (Bertini 3)
Affaire Clémenceau. See Processo Clémenceau, 1918
Affaire Coquelet, 1934 (Matras 4)
Affaire d'une nuit, 1960 (Verneuil 2, Bardot 3, Aurenche 4)
Affaire de la Rue de Lourcine, 1923 (Chevalier 3)
Affaire des poisons, 1955 (Darrieux 3, D'Eaubonne 4)
Affaire des poissons, 1965 (Braunberger 4)
Affaire Dominici, 1972 (Depardieu 3, Gabin 3)
Affaire Dreyfus, 1899 (Méliès 2)
Affaire Dreyfus, 1902 (Zecca, 2)
Affaire du collier de la reine, 1946 (L'Herbier 2, Annenkov 4, Douy 4, Ibert 4, Spaak 4)
Affaire du courrier de Lyon, 1937 (Autant-Lara 2, Aurenche 4)
Affaire est dans le sac, 1932 (Jaubert 4, Prévert 4, Trauner 4)
Affaire Lafarge, 1937 (Von Stroheim 2, Dalio 3, Aurenche 4, Auric 4, Fradetal 4, Lourié 4)
Affaire Manet, 1950 (Astruc 2)
Affaire Maurizius, 1954 (Duvivier 2, Vanel 3, Walbrook 3, Douy 4)
Affaire Nina B, 1962 (Siodmak 2, D'Eaubonne 4, Delerue 4)
Affaire personnelle. See Personal Affair, 1932
Affaires de coeur, 1909 (Cohl 2)
Affaires publiques, 1934 (Bresson 2, Dalio 3)
Affaires sont les affaires, 1943 (Vanel 3)
Affairs of a Gentleman, 1934 (Lukas 3)
Affairs of a Rogue. See First Gentleman, 1948

Affairs of Anatol, 1921 (DeMille 2, Daniels 3, Reid 3, Swanson 3, Macpherson 4, Struss 4)
Affairs of Annabel, 1938 (Ball 3, Polglase 4)
Affairs of Cappy Ricks, 1937 (Brennan 3)
Affairs of Cellini, 1934 (La Cava 2, Ball 3, Bennett C. 3, Calhern 3, March 3, Wray 3, Day 4, Meredyth 4, Newman 4, Rosher 4, Zanuck 4)
Affairs of Dobie Gillis, 1953 (Fosse 2, Reynolds, D. 3)
Affairs of Geraldine, 1946 (Meek 3, Alton, J. 4)
Affairs of Hearts. See Affaires de coeur, 1909
Affairs of Jimmy Valentine, 1942 (Alton, J. 4)
Affairs of Julie. See Zurcher Verlobung, 1957
Affairs of Martha, 1942 (Dassin 2, Kaper 4, Lennart 4, Schary 4)
Affairs of Maupassant, 1938 (Sakall 3)
Affairs of Messalina. See Messalina, 1951
Affairs of Sally. See Fuller Brush Girl, 1950
Affairs of Susan, 1945 (Brent 3, Fontaine 3, Dreier 4, Head 4, Wallis 4)
Affectionately Yours, 1941 (Bacon 2, Bellamy 3, Hayworth 3, McDaniel 3, McQueen, B. 3, Oberon 3, Gaudio 4, Grot 4, Orry-Kelly 4, Wallis 4)
Affiche, 1924 (Epstein 2)
Affiches en goguette, 1906 (Méliès 2)
Affinities, 1922 (Moore, C. 3)
Affreux, 1959 (Allégret, M. 2, Fresnay 3)
Afgrunden, 1910 (Gad 2, Nielsen 3)
Aflame in the Sky, 1927 (Walker 4)
Afraid to Love, 1927 (Brook 3, Schulberg 4)
Afraid to Talk, 1932 (Calhern 3, Freund 4)
Africa, 1930 (Lantz 4)
Africa, 1967 (North 4)
Africa Before Dark, 1928 (Disney 2)
Africa Express, 1975 (Palance 3)
Africa Screams, 1949 (Abbott and Costello 3, Howard, S. 3)
Africa sotto i mari, 1952 (Loren 3)
Africa Squawks, 1939 (Terry 4)
Africa Squeaks, 1932 (Iwerks 4)
Africa Squeaks, 1939 (Clampett 4)
Africa—Texas Style!, 1967 (Mills 3, Arnold 4)
Africa under the Seas. See Africa sotto i mari, 1952
Africain, 1983 (Broca 2, Deneuve 3)
African. See Africain, 1983
African Fury. See Cry, The Beloved Country, 1951
African in London, 1941 (Pearson 2)
African Jungle, 1924 (Lantz 4)
African Lion, 1955 (Iwerks 4)
African Queen, 1952 (Huston 2, Bogart 3, Hepburn, K. 3, Cardiff 4, Spiegel 4)
African Queen, 1977 (Oates 3)
African Treasure, 1952 (Mirisch 4)
Afro-American Artist, 1976 (Moss 4)
Afsar, 1950 (Anand 3, Burman 4)
Afskedens timme, 1973 (Andersson B. 3)
Aftenlandet, 1977 (Watkins 2)
After a Lifetime, 1971 (Loach 2)
After All, 1912 (Lawrence 3)
After Five, 1915 (Darwell 3, Hayakawa 3)
After Giorgione, 1975 (Le Grice 2)
After Laughter, 1981 (Vanderbeek 2)
After Leonardo, 1973 (Le Grice 2)
After Leslie Wheeler, 1973 (Le Grice 2)
After Life, 1978 (Patel 4)
After Lumiere, 1974 (Le Grice 2)
After Manet, 1975 (Le Grice 2)
After Many Years, 1908 (Griffith 2, Lawrence 3, Bitzer 4)
After Midnight, 1927 (Shearer 3, Day 4, Gibbons 4)
After Midnight. See Captain Carey U.S.A., 1950
After My Last Move. See Nach Meinem letzten Umzug, 1970
After Office Hours, 1935 (Bennett C. 3, Burke 3, Gable 3, Adrian 4, Mankiewicz 4, Rosher 4)
After School, 1912 (Dwan 2)
After the Ball, 1929 (Fleischer, M. and D. 2)
After the Ball, 1932 (Balcon 4, Junge 4)
After the Ball, 1957 (Harvey 3, Mathieson 4)

After the Ball. See Après le bal, 1897
After the Dance, 1935 (August 4)
After the Earthquake, 1935 (Sircar 4)
After the Fall, 1974 (Dunaway 3)
After the Fox, 1966 (Sellers 3)
After the Fox. See Caccia alla volpe, 1966
After the Rehearsal, 1984 (Thulin 3)
After the Storm, 1915 (Eason 4)
After the Storm, 1928 (Bosworth 3, Walker 4)
After the Thin Man, 1936 (Van Dyke, W.S. 2, Loy 3, Powell, W. 3, Stewart 3, Brown, N. 4, Freed 4, Goodrich and Hackett 4, Stothart 4, Stromberg 4)
After the Verdict, 1929 (Tschechowa 3, Galeen 4, Reville 4)
After Tomorrow, 1932 (Borzage 2, Howe 4, Levien 4)
After Tonight, 1933 (Auer 3, Bennett C. 3, Cooper 4, Murfin 4, Polglase 4, Rosher 4, Steiner 4)
After Your Own Heart, 1921 (Mix 3)
Aftermath, 1914 (Eason 4)
Aftermath, 1980 (Brakhage 2)
Aftermath. See Madchen ohne Heimat, 1926
Afternoon, 1965 (Warhol 2)
Afterwards. See Their Big Moment, 1934
Afurika monogatari, 1981
Again One Night. See Aruyo futatabi, 1956
Against a Crooked Sky, 1976 (Boone 3)
Against All. See Proti všem, 1957
Against All Flags, 1952 (Flynn 3, O'Hara 3, Quinn 3, Salter 4)
Against All Odds, 1984 (Bridges 3, Widmark 3)
Against the Law, 1934 (Bond 3)
Against the Wind, 1948 (Crichton 2, Signoret 3, Balcon 4, Clarke, T.E.B. 4)
Agatha, 1977 (Hoffman 3, Redgrave, V. 3, Russell 4, Storaro 4)
Agatha. See Agatha et les lectures illimitées, 1981
Agatha Christie's Ordeal by Innocence, 1984 (Donaggio 4, Golan and Globus 4)
Agatha et les lectures illimitées, 1981 (Duras 2)
Agaton and Fina. See Agaton och Fina, 1912
Agaton och Fina, 1912 (Jaenzon 4)
Age d'or, 1930 (Buñuel 2, Modot 3, Braunberger 4)
Age de la terre. See Idade da terra, 1980
Age des artères, 1959 (Delerue 4)
Age for Love, 1931 (Newman 4, Seitz 4, Sherwood 4)
Age ingrat, 1964 (Fernandel 3, Gabin 3, Delerue 4)
Age of Bamboo at Mentawei. See Bambuåldern på Mentawei, 1937–38
Age of Consent, 1932 (La Cava 2, Berman 4, Hunt 4, Selznick 4)
Age of Consent, 1969 (Powell 2, Mason 3)
Age of Curiosity, 1963 (Farrow 3)
Age of Daydreaming. See Álmodozások kora, 1964
Age of Desire, 1923 (Borzage 2, Coffee 4)
Age of Indiscretion, 1935 (Lukas 3, Coffee 4, Haller 4)
Age of Infidelity. See Muerte de un ciclista, 1955
Age of Innocence, 1924 (Ruggles 2)
Age of Innocence, 1934 (Dunne 3, Berman 4, Heerman 4, Plunkett 4, Steiner 4)
Age of Love, 1931 (Horton 3)
Age of the Earth. See Idade da terra, 1980
Age tendre, 1974 (Guillemot 4)
Age Versus Youth, 1911 (Lawrence 3)
Agence Cacahuete, 1912–14 (Raimu 3)
Agence matrimoniale, 1951 (Blier 3, Noiret 3, Douy 4, Kosma 4)
Agency, 1901 (Mitchum 3)
Agent de poche, 1909 (Cohl 2)
Agent 8¾. See Hot Enough for June, 1963
Agent et le violoniste. See Violoniste, 1908
Agent plongeur, 1901 (Zecca 3)
Agents tels qu'on nous les présente, 1908 (Feuillade 2)
Agget ar lost, 1974 (Von Sydow 3)
Aggie Appleby, Maker of Men, 1933 (Sandrich 2, Pitts 3, Hunt 4, Plunkett 4, Steiner 4)
Aggressor, 1911 (Ince 4)
Aggrippés à la terre, 1968 (Ivens 2)
Agguato a Tangeri, 1958 (Cervi 3)

Ağit, 1971 (Guney 2)

Agitator, 1912 (Emerson 4)

Agitpoezd VTsIK, 1921 (Vertov 2)

Agnes of God, 1985 (Bancroft 3, Fonda, J. 3, Adam 4, Delerue 4, Nykvist 4)

Agnese va a morire, 1976 (Age and Scarpelli 4, Morricone 4)

Agnese Visconti, 1910 (Pastrone 2)

Agnus Dei. *See* Egi bárány, 1970

Agonie de Byzance, 1913 (Feuillade 2)

Agonie de Jerusalem, 1926 (Duvivier 2)

Agonie des aigles, 1920 (Duvivier 2)

Agonie des aigles, 1933 (Pagnol 2, Wakhévitch 4)

Agonies of Agnes, 1918 (Dressler 3)

Agonizing Adventure. *See* Angoissante Aventure, 1919

Agony and the Ecstasy, 1965 (Reed 2, Harrison 3, Heston 3, Dunne 4, Goldsmith 4, North 4, Shamroy 4, Smith, J.M. 4)

Agosta, 1986 (Branco 4, de Almeida 4)

Agostino, 1962 (Bolognini 2, Thulin 3)

Agostino di Ippona, 1972 (Rossellini 2)

Agression, 1965 (Foldès 4)

Agression, 1975 (Deneuve 3, Trintignant 3, Braunberger 4)

Aguila o sol, 1937 (Cantinflas 3)

Aguirre, der Zorn Gottes, 1972 (Guerra 2, Herzog 2, Kinski 3)

Aguirre, the Wrath of God. *See* Aguirre, der Zorn Gottes, 1972

Ah! My Friends without Voice. *See* Aa koe naki tomo, 1972

Ah, My Home Town. *See* Aa furusato, 1938

Ah! Nango shosa, 1938 (Tsuburaya 4)

Ah Nurture, 1948 (Peterson 2)

Ah, Wilderness!, 1935 (Brown 2, Barrymore L. 3, Beery 3, Rooney 3, Goodrich and Hackett 4, Stothart 4, Stromberg 4)

Ahasin Polawatha, 1978 (Peries 2)

A-Hauntin We Will Go, 1942 (Cook 3, Laurel & Hardy 3, Day 4)

A-Haunting We Will Go, 1966 (McKimson 4)

Ahava Ilemeth, 1982 (Golan and Globus 4)

Ahen senso, 1943 (Shindo 3, Takamine 3)

Ahí está el detalle, 1940 (Cantinflas 3, García 3)

Ahí viene Martín Corona, 1951 (Infante 3, Figueroa 4)

Ahijado de la muerte, 1946 (Negrete 3, Alcoriza 4)

Ahora soy rico, 1952 (Infante 3)

Ahora te vamos a llamar hermano, 1971 (Ruiz 2)

Ai, 1954 (Mori 3)

Ai futatabi, 1972 (Ichikawa 2)

Ai margini della metropoli, 1952 (Di Venanzo 4)

Ai ni yomigaeru hi, 1923 (Mizoguchi 2)

Ai no borei, 1978 (Oshima 2, Takemitsu 4, Toda 4)

Ai no corrida, 1976 (Oshima 2, Toda 4)

Ai no kane, 1959 (Kagawa 3)

Ai no onimotsu, 1955 (Yamada 3, Yamamura 3)

Ai no rekishi, 1955 (Tsukasa 3)

Ai no sanga, 1950 (Yamamura 3, Miyagawa 4)

Ai no sekai, 1943 (Takamine 3)

Ai to chikai, 1945 (Imai 2)

Ai to honoho to, 1961 (Mori 3, Shimura 3)

Ai to kibo no machi, 1959 (Oshima 2)

Ai to nikushimi no kanata e, 1951 (Kurosawa 2, Mifune 3)

Ai to shi no tanima, 1954 (Gosho 2)

Ai vostri ordini, signora!, 1938 (De Sica 2)

Ai wa chikara da, 1930 (Naruse 2)

Ai wa dokomaremo, 1932 (Yamada 3)

Ai wa furu hoshi no kanata ni, 1956 (Mori 3)

Ai yo hoshi to tomoni, 1947 (Takamine 3, Hayasaka 4)

Ai yo jinrui to tomo ni are, 1931 (Takamine 3, Tanaka 3)

Aid to the Nation, 1947 (DeMille 2)

Aida, 1953 (Loren 3)

Aide-toi, 1918 (Feuillade 2)

Aido, 1969 (Hani 2)

Aido, Slave of Love. *See* Aido, 1969

Aienkyo, 1937 (Mizoguchi 2, Yoda 4)

Aigle à deux têtes, 1947 (Cocteau 2, Feuillère 3, Marais 3, Auric 4, Matras 4, Wakhévitch 4)

Aigle noir. *See* Vendicatore, 1959 (Dieterle 2)

Aiglon, 1931 (Burel 4, Planer 4)

Aigrette Hunter, 1910 (Olcott 2)

Aiguille rouge, 1950 (Wakhévitch 4)

Ai-jin, 1953 (Ichikawa 2)

Aijo fudo, 1959 (Kagawa 3)

Aijo no keifu, 1961 (Gosho 2, Yamamura 3)

Aijo no kessan, 1956 (Mifune 3)

Aijo no miyako, 1958 (Tsukasa 3)

Aijo shindansho, 1948 (Takamine 3)

Aijo-fudo, 1959 (Yamada 3)

Aijou dudou, 1959 (Yoda 4)

Aile ou la cuisse, 1976 (Dalio 3, Renoir 4)

Ailes de la colombe, 1981 (Huppert 3)

Aime le bruit, 1912–14 (Cohl 2)

Aimez-vous Brahms?, 1961 (Litvak 2, Bergman 3, Montand 3, Auric 4, Trauner 4)

Aimez-vous Brahms?. *See* Goodbye Again, 1961

Aimez-vous les femmes?, 1964 (Feuillère 3, Evein 4, Vierny 4)

Aimless Walk. *See* Bezúčelná procházka, 1930

Ain't It the Truth, 1914 (Beery 3)

Ain't Love Funny?, 1926 (Plunkett 4)

Ain't Misbehavin', 1955 (Cahn 4)

Ain't She Sweet, 1931 (Fleischer, M. and D. 2)

Ain't She Tweet, 1951 (Freleng 4)

Ain't That Ducky, 1945 (Freleng 4)

Ain't We Got Fun, 1937 (Avery 2)

Ainé des Ferchaux, 1963 (Melville 2, Belmondo 3, Vanel 3, Decaë 4, Delerue 4)

Ainsi finit la nuit, 1948 (Dauphin 3)

Air, 1972 (Driessen 4)

Air Cadet, 1951 (Hudson 3)

Air Circus, 1928 (Hawks 2, Carré 4, Miller, S. 4)

Air City. *See* Aerograd, 1935

Air Crew, 1943 (Fleischer, R. 2)

Air de Paris, 1954 (Carné 2, Arletty 3, Gabin 3)

Air Express, 1937 (Lantz 4)

Air Force, 1943 (Hawks 2, Carey 3, Garfield 3, Kennedy, A. 3, Young, G. 3, Howe 4, Nichols 4, Wald 4, Wallis 4, Waxman 4)

Air Fright, 1933 (Roach 4)

Air Hawks, 1935 (Bellamy 3)

Air Hostess, 1933 (Darwell 3, Walker 4)

Air Legion, 1929 (Glennon 4, Plunkett 4)

Air Mail, 1925 (Baxter W. 3, Fairbanks, D. Jr. 3)

Air Mail, 1932 (Bellamy 3, O'Brien, P. 3, Summerville 3, Freund 4, Laemmle 4)

Air Outpost, 1937 (Alwyn 4)

Air pur, 1940 (Clair 2, Douy 4, Lourié 4)

Air Raid Wardens, 1943 (Laurel & Hardy 3, Meek 3)

Air Tonic, 1933 (Grable 3)

Air Waves, 1939 (Vorkapich 4)

Airborne, 1973 (Jarre 4)

Airman's Letter to His Mother, 1941 (Gielgud 3)

Airplane, 1980 (Bernstein 4)

Airplane II: The Sequel, 1982 (Torn 3, Bernstein 4, Biroc 4)

Airport, 1970 (Hathaway 2, Seaton 2, Bisset 3, Heflin 3, Kennedy, G. 3, Lancaster 3, Martin, D. 3, Seberg 3, Ames 4, Dunn 4, Head 4, Hunter 4, Laszlo 4, Newman 4, Westmore, B. 4)

Airport '77, 1977 (Cotten 3, De Havilland 3, Grant, L. 3, Kennedy, G. 3, Lee, C. 3, Lemmon 3, Stewart 3, Head 4, Whitlock 4)

Airport '80—The Concorde. *See* Concorde—Airport '79, 1979

Airport 1975, 1974 (Andrews D. 3, Black 3, Heston 3, Kennedy, G. 3, Loy 3, Swanson 3, Head 4)

Airs, 1976 (Brakhage 2)

Aisai monogatari, 1951 (Shindo 2)

Aisai-ki, 1959 (Tsukasa 3)

Aisureba koso, 1955 (Imai 2, Yoshimura 2, Kagawa 3, Yamada 3, Yamamura 3)

Aiyoku no ki, 1930 (Gosho 2, Tanaka 3)

Aiyoku no sabaki, 1953 (Kagawa 3)

Aizen katsura, 1938 (Tanaka 3)

Aizen katsura, 1954 (Kyo 3)

Aizen katsura: Kanketsu-hen, 1939 (Tanaka 3)

Aizen tsubaki, 1940 (Tanaka 3)

Aizen-bashi, 1951 (Tanaka 3, Yoda 4)

Aizome-gasa, 1956 (Hasegawa 3)
Aizo-toge, 1934 (Mizoguchi 2, Yamada 3)
Ajantrik, 1958 (Ghatak 4)
Ajia no musume, 1938 (Yoda 4)
Ajos vandados, 1978 (Chaplin 3)
Akademik Ivan Pavlov, 1949 (Cherkassov 3)
Akadou Suzunosuke, 1958 (Miyagawa 4)
Akage, 1969 (Iwashita 3, Mifune 3)
Akahige, 1965 (Kurosawa 2, Kagawa 3, Mifune 3, Ryu 3, Shimura 3,
    Tanaka 3, Muraki 4)
Akai jinbaori, 1958 (Kagawa 3)
Akai satsui, 1964 (Imamura 2)
Akai shuriken, 1965 (Miyagawa 4)
Akai yuhi ni terasarete, 1925 (Mizoguchi 2)
Akaler Sandhane, 1980 (Sen 2)
Akanegumo, 1967 (Shinoda 2, Iwashita 3, Takemitsu 4, Toda 4)
Akanishi Kakita, 1936 (Shimura 3)
Akasen chitai, 1956 (Mizoguchi 2, Kyo 3, Shindo 3, Miyagawa 4)
Akasen no hi wa kiezu, 1958 (Kyo 3)
Akash Kusum, 1965 (Sen 2, Mitra 4)
Akatsuki ni inoru, 1940 (Tanaka 3)
Akatsuki no dasso, 1950 (Kurosawa 2, Hayasaka 4)
Akatsuki no Gassho, 1955 (Kagawa 3)
Akatsuki no gassho, 1963 (Yamamura 3)
Akatsuki no hatakaze, 1938 (Yoda 4)
Akatsuki no shi, 1924 (Mizoguchi 2)
Akatsuki no tsuiseki, 1950 (Ichikawa 2)
Akatsuki no yushi, 1926 (Kinugasa 2, Hasegawa 3)
Akatsuki wa tokedo, 1937 (Tanaka 3)
Akce B, 1951 (Fric 2, Kroner 3)
Akcja pod Arsenalem, 1977 (Stawinsky 4)
Aken senso, 1943 (Tsuburaya 4)
Aki futatabi, 1937 (Takamine 3)
Aki tachinu, 1960 (Naruse 2)
Akibiyori, 1960 (Ozu 2, Hara 3, Iwashita 3, Ryu 3, Tsukasa 3)
Akit ketten szeretnek, 1915 (Curtiz 2)
Akitsu onsen, 1962 (Yamamura 3)
Akkara Paha, 1969 (Peries 2)
Akogare, 1935 (Gosho 2)
Akogare, 1966 (Takemitsu 4)
Ako-jo, 1952 (Yamada 3)
Ako-roshi, 1953 (Yamada 3)
Akrobat na hrazdě, 1953 (Stallich 4)
Akrobat scho-o-on, 1943 (Staudte 2)
Akrosh, 1980 (Patil 3, Nihalani 4)
Akt, 1961 (Skolimowski 2)
Aktenskapabrottaren, 1964 (Bjornstrand 3)
Äktenskapsbrydån, 1913 (Sjostrom 2, Jaenzon 4)
Äktenskapsleken, 1935 (Jaenzon 4)
Aktrisa, 1943 (Babochkin 3, Moskvin 4)
Aku no monsho, 1964 (Kishida 3)
Aku no tanoshisa, 1954 (Mori 3)
Akujo no kisetsu, 1958 (Yamada 3)
Akuma no kanpai, 1947 (Miyagawa 4)
Akuma no temari-uta, 1977 (Ichikawa 2)
Akuma-to, 1980 (Shinoda 2, Miyagawa 4)
Akumyo series, 1961–1974 (Yoda 4)
Akumyo, 1961 (Miyagawa 4)
Akumyo muteki, 1965 (Miyagawa 4)
Akumyo nawabari arashi, 1974 (Miyagawa 4)
Akumyo niwaka, 1965 (Miyagawa 4)
Akumyo zakura, 1966 (Miyagawa 4)
Akuto, 1965 (Shindo 2, Kishida 3)
Al caer de la tarde, 1948 (Armendáriz 3)
Al Capone, 1959 (Steiger 3, Ballard 4, Raksin 4)
Al Capone im deutschen Wald, 1969 (Fassbinder 2)
Al di là del bene e del male, 1980 (Donaggio 4)
Al di là della legge, 1968 (Van Cleef 3)
Al diavolo la celebrità, 1949 (Monicelli 2, Auer 3)
Al Jennings of Oklahoma, 1951 (Duryea 3)
Al otro lado de la ciudad, 1962 (Valli 3)
Al piacere di rivederla, 1976 (Fabian 3)
Al sole, 1935 (Gallone 2)

Al Treleor Muscle Exercises, 1905 (Bitzer 4)
Ala Mode, 1958 (Vanderbeek 2)
Alaap, 1977 (Bachchan 3)
Alabama—Two Thousand Light Years, 1969 (Wenders 2)
Aladdin, 1953 (Reiniger 2)
Aladdin, 1958 (Merkel 3, Porter 4)
Aladdin and His Lamp, 1952 (Wanger 4)
Aladdin and His Wonderful Lamp, 1939 (Fleischer, M. and D. 2)
Aladdin and the Wonderful Lamp, 1934 (Iwerks 4)
Aladdin and the Wonderful Lamp, 1917 (Franklin 2)
Aladdin's Lamp, 1931 (Terry 4)
Aladdin's Lamp, 1935 (Terry 4)
Aladdin's Lamp, 1943 (Terry 4)
Aladdin's Lamp, 1947 (Terry 4)
Alageyik, 1958 (Guney 2)
Alamo, 1960 (Boone 3, Harvey 3, Wayne 3, Widmark 3, Clothier 4,
    Tiomkin 4)
Alarcosbal, 1918 (Lugosi 3)
Alarm, 1914 (Sennett 2, Arbuckle 3, Normand 3)
Alarm, 1941 (Rasp 3)
Alarm, 1969 (Fassbinder 2)
Alarm auf Gleis B. See Gleisdreieck, 1936
Alarm aus Station III, 1939 (Frohlich 3)
Alarm Clock Andy, 1919 (Ince 4)
Alarm im Zirkus, 1954 (Geschonneck 3)
Alarm in Peking, 1937 (Frohlich 3)
Alarme!, 1943 (Ivens 2)
Alarmstufe V, 1941 (Hoffmann 4)
Alas and Alack, 1915 (Chaney Lon 3)
Alas, Poor Yorick, 1913 (Bosworth 3)
Alaska, 1930 (Lantz 4)
Alaska, 1944 (Carradine 3)
Alaska Highway, 1943 (Arlen 3)
Alaska Love, 1932 (Sennett 2)
Alaska Seas, 1954 (Ryan 3, Head 4)
Alaska Sweepstakes, 1936 (Lantz 4)
Alaskafuchse, 1964 (Mueller-Stahl 3)
Alaskan, 1924 (Brenon 2, Wong 3, Howe 4)
Alauddin Khan, 1963 (Ghatak 4)
Alazatosan jelentem, 1960 (Gabór 3)
Alba, 1917 (Bertini 3)
Alba Regia, 1961 (Gabór 3, Samoilova 3)
Albany Bunch, 1931 (Sennett 2)
Albergo Luna, Camera 34, 1947 (Rota 4)
Albero degli zoccoli, 1978 (Olmi 2)
Albero di natale, 1969 (Bourvil 3)
Alberobello, 'Au pays des trulli', 1957 (Braunberger 4)
Albert 1er, Roi des Belges, 1950 (Spaak 4)
Albert Pinto ko gussa kyon aata hai, 1981 (Azmi 3, Patil 3)
Albert Schweitzer, 1957 (March 3, Meredith 3)
Albert, R.N., 1953 (Arnold 4)
Albertfalvai történet, 1955 (Mészáros 2)
Albigeois, 1964 (Braunberger 4)
Albur de amor, 1946 (Armendáriz 3)
Alby's Delight. See Over the Brooklyn Bridge, 1984
Alcalde de Zalamea, 1953 (Rey 3)
Alcatraz Island, 1938 (Sheridan 3)
Alchimie, 1966 (Delerue 4)
Alchimiste Prarafaragamus ou la Cornue infernale, 1906 (Méliès 2)
Alcofrisbas, the Master Magician. See Enchanteur Alcofrisbas,
    1903
Alcohol Abuse: The Early Warning Signs, 1977 (Fonda, H. 3)
Alcool tue, 1947 (Resnais 2)
Aldebaran, 1935 (Blasetti 2, Cervi 3)
Aldrig i livet, 1957 (Thulin 3)
Ale doktore, 1978 (Brejchová 3)
Alejandra, 1941 (García 3)
Alena, 1947 (Hrušínský 3)
Alenka, 1962 (Shukshin 3)
Alerte au sud, 1953 (Von Stroheim 2, Kosma 4)
Alerte en Méditerranée, 1938 (Fresnay 3)
Alex and the Gypsy, 1976 (Bujold 3, Lemmon 3, Mancini 4)

Alex in Wonderland, 1970 (Fellini 2, Mazursky 2, Burstyn 3, Moreau 3, Sutherland 3, Kovacs 4)
Alex the Great, 1928 (Miller, V. 4)
Alexander Calder, 1963 (Richter 2)
Alexander den Store, 1917 (Stiller 2, Madsen 3, Jaenzon 4)
Alexander Hamilton, 1931 (Arliss 3)
Alexander Nevsky. See Alexandr Nevskii, 1938
Alexander Parkhomenko, 1942 (Dovzhenko 2)
Alexander Popov, 1949 (Cherkassov 3)
Alexander the Great, 1955 (Rossen 2, Baker S. 3, Bloom 3, Burton 3, Cushing 3, Darrieux 3, March 3, Andrejew 3, Krasker 4)
Alexander the Great. See Alexander den Store, 1917
Alexander's Ragtime Band, 1931 (Fleischer, M. and D. 2)
Alexander's Ragtime Band, 1938 (King 2, Ameche 3, Carradine 3, Chaney Lon, Jr. 3, Faye 3, Hersholt 3, Power 3, Brown, Harry Joe 4, Leven 4, Newman 4, Trotti 4, Zanuck 4)
Alexandr Nevskii, 1938 (Eisenstein 2, Cherkassov 3, Prokofiev 4, Tisse 4)
Alexandra, 1914 (Porten 3, Messter 4)
Alexandre i Chanakya, 1967 (Tyszkiewicz 3)
Alexandre le bienheureux, 1968 (Noiret 3)
Alexandria . . . Why?. See Iskindria . . . Leh?, 1978
Alf, Bill, and Fred, 1964 (Godfrey 4)
Alfabeto notturno, 1951 (Birri 2)
Alfa-Romeo és Jula, 1969 (Latinovits 3)
Alfie, 1966 (Caine 3, Winters 3)
Alfred noćni čuvar, 1971 (Grgić 4)
Alfred the Great, 1969 (York, M. 3)
Alfredo!, 1940 (Gallone 2)
Alfredo, Alfredo, 1972 (Germi 2, Hoffman 3, Pinelli 4)
Alf's Button, 1920 (Hepworth 2)
Alf's Button, 1930 (Oberon 3)
Alf's Button Afloat, 1938 (Sim 3)
Algie on the Force, 1913 (Sennett 2)
Algiers, 1938 (Cromwell 2, Boyer 3, Lamarr 3, Howe 4, Irene 4, Reynolds 4, Wanger 4)
Algol, 1920 (Jannings 3)
Algy, the Watchman, 1911 (Sennett 2)
Ali Baba, 1936 (Iwerks 4)
Ali Baba. See Ali Baba et les quarante voleurs, 1954
Ali Baba and the 40 Thieves, 1918 (Franklin 2)
Ali Baba Bound, 1939 (Clampett 4)
Ali Baba Bunny, 1957 (Jones 2)
Ali Baba et les 40 voleurs, 1902 (Zecca, 2)
Ali Baba et les quarante voleurs, 1954 (Becker 2, Fernandel 3, Wakhévitch 4)
Ali Baba Goes to Town, 1937 (Carradine 3, Cobb 3, Del Rio 3, Canutt 4)
Ali Baba Nights, 1953 (Wong 3)
Ali Barbouyou et Ali Bouf à l'huile, 1907 (Méliès 2)
Alia en el bajia, 1941 (Armendáriz 3)
Alias a Gentleman, 1948 (Beery 3)
Alias Aladdin, 1920 (Roach 4)
Alias Bulldog Drummond, 1935 (Wray 3)
Alias Bulldog Drummond. See Bulldog Jack, 1935
Alias French Gertie, 1930 (Daniels 3, Hunt 4)
Alias Jesse James, 1959 (McLeod 2, Bond 3, Cody 3, Cooper, Gary 3, Crosby 3, Hope 3, Rogers, R. 3, Head 4)
Alias Jimmy Valentine, 1915 (Tourneur, M. 2, Carré 4)
Alias Jimmy Valentine, 1920 (Polito 4)
Alias Jimmy Valentine, 1929 (Barrymore L. 3, Gibbons 4)
Alias John Preston, 1956 (Lee, C. 3)
Alias Ladyfingers. See Ladyfingers, 1921
Alias Mary Dow, 1935 (Carradine 3, Milland 3, Muse 3)
Alias Mary Flynn, 1925 (Berman 4)
Alias Mary Smith, 1932 (Walthall 3)
Alias Mike Moran, 1919 (Cruze 2, Reid 3)
Alias Mr. Twilight, 1947 (Sturges, J. 2)
Alias Nick Beal, 1949 (Milland 3, Dreier 4, Waxman 4)
Alias Texas Pete Owens. See Sell 'em Cowboy, 1924
Alias the Deacon, 1928 (Hersholt 3)
Alias the Deacon, 1940 (Auer 3, Cortez 4, Salter 4)

Alias the Deacon. See Half a Sinner, 1934
Alias the Doctor, 1932 (Bacon 2, Curtiz 2, Barthelmess 3, Karloff 3, Grot 4)
Alibaba, 1940 (Biswas 4)
Alibi, 1929 (Menzies 4, Schenck 4, Sullivan 4)
Alibi, 1937 (Von Stroheim 2, Dalio 3, Jouvet 3, Achard 4, Auric 4, Fradetal 4, Lourié 4)
Alibi, 1942 (Mason 3)
Alibi, 1968 (Morricone 4)
Alibi, 1969 (Gassman 3)
Alibi Ike, 1935 (Brown 3, De Havilland 3)
Alice series, 1924–27 (Disney 2)
Alice. See Alicja, 1979
Alice Adams, 1923 (Barnes 4)
Alice Adams, 1935 (Stevens 2, Hepburn, K. 3, MacMurray 3, McDaniel 3, Berman 4, Murfin 4, Plunkett 4, Polglase 4, Steiner 4)
Alice au pays des merveilles, 1948 (Renoir 4)
Alice Be Good, 1926 (Sennett 2)
Alice Doesn't Live Here Anymore, 1974 (Scorsese 2, Burstyn 3, Keitel 3)
Alice in den Stadten, 1973 (Wenders 2, Vogler 3)
Alice in Switzerland, 1939 (Cavalcanti 2)
Alice in the Cities. See Alice in den Stadten, 1974
Alice in Wonderland, 1903 (Hepworth 2)
Alice in Wonderland, 1933 (Mankiewicz 2, McLeod 2, Arlen 3, Cooper, Gary 3, Fazenda 3, Fields, W.C. 3, Grant, C. 3, Horton 3, Marsh 3, Edouart 4, Glennon 4, Menzies 4, Tiomkin 4, Westmore, W. 4)
Alice in Wonderland, 1951 (Disney 2, Lewin 4)
Alice in Wonderland. See Alice au pays des merveilles, 1948
Alice or the Last Escapade. See Alice ou La Dernière Fugue, 1977
Alice, ou La Dernière Fugue, 1977 (Chabrol 2, Vanel 3, Rabier 4)
Alice's Adventures in Wonderland, 1972 (Moore, D. 3, Richardson 3, Sellers 3, Barry 4, Shankar 4, Unsworth 4)
Alice's Restaurant, 1969 (Penn 2, Allen, D. 4)
Alice's Wonderland, 1923 (Disney 2)
Alicja, 1979 (Cassel 3)
Alien, 1915 (Ince 4)
Alien, 1979 (Hurt, J. 3, Stanton 3, Goldsmith 4)
Alien Encounter, 1976 (Lee, C. 3)
Alien Oro, 1982 (Trumbull 4)
Alien Souls, 1916 (Hayakawa 3)
Alien Thunder, 1975 (George, Ch. D. 3, Sutherland 3)
Alien's Invasion, 1905 (Hepworth 2)
Aliéniste. See Asilo muito louco, 1969
Aliki, 1962 (Maté 4)
Aliki in the Navy. See Aliki sto naftiko, 1960
Aliki sto naftiko, 1960 (Lassally 4)
Aliki, My Love. See Aliki, 1962
Alimony, 1918 (Valentino 3)
Alimony, 1924 (Baxter W. 3)
Alimony Madness, 1933 (Eason 4)
Aline, 1950 (Lollobrigida 3, Delli Colli 4)
Alitet Leaves for the Hills. See Alitet ukhodit v gory, 1949
Alitet ukhodit v gory, 1949 (Donskoi 2)
Alive and Kicking, 1958 (Holloway 3)
Alkali Ike's Boarding House, 1912 (Anderson G. 3)
Alkali Ike's Misfortunes, 1912 (Anderson G. 3)
Alkony, 1971 (Szabó 2)
Alkonyok és hajnalok, 1961 (Jancsó 2)
All a bir-r-rd, 1949 (Freleng 4)
All Aboard, 1917 (Daniels 3, Lloyd 3, Roach 4)
All about Dogs, 1942 (Terry 4)
All about Eve, 1950 (Mankiewicz 2, Baxter A. 3, Davis 3, Monroe 3, Ritter 3, Sanders 3, Head 4, Krasner 4, Lemaire 4, Newman 4, Wheeler 4, Zanuck 4)
All about People, 1967 (Fonda, H. 3, Heston 3, Lancaster 3)
All American, 1932 (Arlen 3, Brennan 3)
All American Chump, 1936 (Clarke, C.C. 4)
All American Co-ed, 1941 (Langdon 3, Prinz 4, Roach 4)
All American Kickback, 1931 (Sennett 2)
All American Toothache, 1936 (Roach 4)
All Ashore, 1953 (Edwards 2, Rooney 3, Duning 4)

All at Sea, 1914 (Sennett 2)
All at Sea, 1919 (Roach 4)
All at Sea, 1929 (Gibbons 4)
All at Sea, 1935 (Harrison 3)
All at Sea. *See* Barnacle Bill, 1957
All by Myself, 1943 (Beavers 3)
All Creatures Great and Small, 1974 (Hopkins, A. 3)
All Dressed Up, 1920 (Roach 4)
All Fall Down, 1962 (Frankenheimer 2, Beatty 3, Lansbury 3, Malden 3, Saint 3, Ames 4, Houseman 4, Jeakins 4, North 4)
All for a Girl, 1916 (Hardy 3)
All for a Woman. *See* Danton, 1920
All for Her, 1912 (Brenon 2)
All for Love, 1912 (Lawrence 3)
All for Love. *See* Vše pro lásku, 1930
All for Old Ireland, 1915 (Olcott 2)
All for Peggy, 1915 (Chaney Lon 3)
All Fowled Up, 1955 (McKimson 4)
All God's Children, 1980 (Widmark 3)
All Good Countrymen. *See* Všichni dobři rodáci, 1968
All Gummed Up, 1947 (Three Stooges 3)
All Hands, 1940 (Mills 3, Balcon 4)
All Hands on Deck, 1961 (Taurog 2, Smith, J.M. 4)
All I Desire, 1953 (Sirk 2, O'Sullivan 3, Stanwyck 3, Hunter 4, Westmore, F. 4)
All In, 1936 (Balcon 4)
All in a Day, 1920 (Roach 4)
All in a Night's Work, 1961 (MacLaine 3, Martin, D. 3, Robertson 3, Head 4, La Shelle 4, Previn 4, Wallis 4)
All Is Confusion. *See* Riding on Air, 1937
All Is Well. *See* Tenka taihai, 1955
All It Is in Life, 1910 (Griffith 2)
All Lit Up, 1920 (Roach 4)
All Lit Up, 1959 (Halas and Batchelor 2)
All Man, 1916 (Marion 4)
All Men Are Enemies, 1934 (Hoffenstein 4, Seitz 4)
All Mine to Give, 1956 (Jaffe 3, Steiner 4)
All My Darling Daughters, 1972 (Massey 3, Young, R. 3)
All My Life, 166 (Baillie 2)
All My Sons, 1948 (Lancaster 3, Robinson, E. 3)
All Night, 1918 (Valentino 3)
All Night Long, 1924 (Capra 2, Sennett 2, Langdon 3)
All Night Long, 1961 (Dearden 2, Attenborough 3)
All Night Long, 1981 (Girardot 3, Hackman 3, Streisand 3)
All of a Sudden Peggy, 1920 (Sutherland 2)
All of Me, 1934 (Hopkins, M. 3, March 3, Raft 3, Banton 4, Buchman 4)
All of Myself. *See* Watashi no subete o, 1954
All on Account of a Laundry Mark, 1910 (Porter 2)
All on Account of the Milk, 1910 (Sennett 2, Pickford 3, Sweet 3)
All One Night. *See* Love Begins at Twenty, 1936
All Out. *See* Tutto per tutto, 1968
All Out for 'V', 1942 (Terry 4)
All Over the Top, 1949 (Cusack 3)
All Over the Town, 1949 (Baker S. 3)
All Over Town, 1937 (Ladd 3)
All Quiet on the Western Front, 1930 (Cukor 2, Milestone 2, Zinnemann 2, Ayres 3, Pitts 3, Summerville 3, Edeson 4, Freund 4, Laemmle 4)
All Quiet on the Western Front, 1979 (Neal 3, Pleasance 3)
All Russian Elder Kalinin. *See* Vserusski starets Kalinin, 1920
All Screwed Up. *See* Tutto a posto e niente in ordine, 1974
All Square. *See* Gang War, 1928
All Star Bond Rally, 1945 (Crain 3, Crosby 3, Hope 3, Sinatra 3)
All Star Production of Patriotic Episodes for the Second Liberty Loan, 1917 (Hart 3)
All Teed Up, 1930 (Roach 4)
All That Heaven Allows, 1955 (Sirk 2, Hudson 3, Moorehead 3, Wyman 3, Hunter 4)
All That I Have, 1951 (Biroc 4)
All That Jazz, 1979 (Fosse 2, Lange 3, Scheider 3)

All That Money Can Buy, 1941 (Dieterle 2, Darwell 3, Huston 3, Simon, S. 3, August 4, Herrmann 4, Polglase 4)
All the Brothers Were Valiant, 1923 (Chaney Lon 3)
All the Brothers Were Valiant, 1953 (Granger 3, Stone 3, Taylor, R. 3, Wynn 3, Berman 4, Brown, Harry 4, Plunkett 4, Rozsa 4)
All the Drawings of the Town, 1959 (Vukotić 4)
All The Fine Young Cannibals, 1960 (Beavers 3, Wagner 3, Wood 3, Berman 4, Daniels 4, Rose 4)
All the Kind Strangers, 1974 (Keach 3)
All the King's Horses, 1935 (Horton 3, Wyman 3, Banton 4, Prinz 4)
All the King's Men, 1949 (Rossen 2, Crawford, B. 3, Ireland 3, McCambridge 3, Guffey 4)
All the Marbles, 1981 (Aldrich 2, Falk 3, Biroc 4)
All the President's Men, 1976 (Pakula 2, Hoffman 3, Redford 3, Robards 3, Warden 3, Goldman, W. 4, Jenkins 4, Willis 4)
All the Right Noises, 1969 (Fisher 4)
All the Way. *See* Joker is Wild, 1957
All the Way Boys. *See* Piu forte ragazzi!, 1972
All the Way Home, 1963 (Smith, D. , Preston 3, Simmons 3, Kaufman 4, Sylbert 4)
All the World to Nothing, 1918 (Furthman 4)
All The World's a Stage, 1910 (Lawrence 3)
All the World's a Stage, 1979 (Moss 4)
All the World's a Stooge, 1941 (Three Stooges 3)
All the Young Men, 1960 (Ladd 3, Poitier 3, Duning 4)
All These Women. *See* For att inte tala om all dessa kvinnor, 1964
All Things Flow. *See* Panta Rhei, 1951
All This, and Heaven Too, 1940 (Litvak 2, Boyer 3, Davis 3, Friedhofer 4, Haller 4, Orry-Kelly 4, Robinson 4, Steiner 4, Wallis 4)
All This and Money Too. *See* Love Is a Ball, 1963
All This and Rabbit Stew, 1941 (Avery 2)
All This and Rabbit Stew, 1950 (Terry 4)
All Through the Night, 1942 (Anderson J. 3, Bogart 3, Darwell 3, Lorre 3, Veidt 3, Deutsch 4, Mercer 4, Wald 4)
All Wet, 1924 (McCarey 2, Roach 4)
All Wet, 1927 (Disney 2)
All Woman, 1918 (Baxter W. 3, Marsh 3)
All Women Have Secrets, 1939 (Lake 3, Head 4)
All Wool, 1925 (Roach 4)
All'ombra delle fanciulle in fiore, 1952 (Delli Colli 4)
All's Fair at the Fair, 1938 (Fleischer, M. and D. 2)
All's Well, 1941 (Fleischer, M. and D. 2)
All's Well That Ends Well, 1940 (Terry 4)
Allá en el Rancho Grande, 1936 (De Fuentes 2, Fernández 2, Figueroa 4)
Allá en el Rancho Grande, 1948 (De Fuentes 2, Negrete 3)
Allá en el trópico, 1940 (De Fuentes 2, García 3, Figueroa 4)
Alla ricerca di Tadzio, 1970 (Visconti 2)
All-American, 1953 (Curtis 3)
All-American Boy, 1973 (Voight 3)
Allami áruház, 1952 (Gábor 3)
Alle man på post, 1940 (Bjornstrand 3)
Allegheny Uprising, 1939 (Sanders 3, Trevor 3, Wayne 3, Musuraca 4, Plunkett 4, Polglase 4)
Allegretto, 1936 (Fischinger 2)
Allegro barbaro. *See* Allegro barbaro: Magyar rapszödia 2, 1978
Allegro barbaro: Magyar rapszödia 2, 1978 (Jancsó 2)
Allegro non troppo, 1976 (Bozzetto 4)
Allegro squadrone, 1954 (De Sica 2, Gélin 3, Sordi 3, D'Amico 4, Vích 4)
Allegro squadrone. *See* Gaités de l'escadron, 1954
Alleman, 1963 (Haanstra 2)
Aller et retour, 1948 (Astruc 2)
Aller simple, 1971 (Giannini 3)
Allergic to Love, 1944 (Salter 4)
Aller-retour. *See* Aller et retour, 1948
Alles dreht sich alles bewegt sich, 1928–29 (Richter 2)
Alles fur Geld, 1923 (Jannings 3, Kraly 4)
Alles fur Papa, 1953 (Jurgens 3, Tschechowa 3)
Alles Schwindel, 1940 (Frohlich 3)
Alley of the World. *See* Ukiyo kouji, 1939

Allez Oop, 1934 (Keaton 2)
Alliance, 1970 (Karina 3, Carrière 4)
Alligator, 1980 (Sayles 4)
Alligator Named Daisy, 1955 (Holloway 3, Rutherford 3)
Alligator People, 1959 (Chaney Lon, Jr. 3, Struss 4)
Alligators. See Fiume de grande caimano, 1980
Alljon meg á menet!, 1973 (Madaras 3)
Allo Berlin? Ici Paris!, 1931 (Duvivier 2)
Allo! Hallo! Alo!, 1962 (Popescu-Gopo 4)
Allons z'enfants, 1980 (Aumont 3)
Allonsanfan, 1974 (Taviani, P. and V. 2, Mastroianni 3, Morricone 4)
Allotment Wives, 1945 (Francis, K. 3)
Allotria, 1936 (Walbrook 3)
All-Star Bond Rally, 1945 (Darnell 3, Grable 3)
All-Star Musical Revue, 1945 (Pan 4, Prinz 4)
Alltagliche Geschichte, 1944 (Frohlich 3)
Allumettes animées, 1908 (Cohl 2)
Allumettes fantaisies, 1912 (Cohl 2)
Allumettes magiques. See Allumettes fantaisies, 1912
Allumorphoses, 1960 (Delerue 4)
Allvarsamma leken, 1945 (Dahlbeck 3)
Alma de bronce, 1944 (Armendáriz 3)
Alma de Gaucho, 1930 (Shamroy 4)
Almas encontradas, 1933 (Figueroa 4)
Álmatlan évek, 1959 (Torocsik 3)
Almodozasok kora, 1964 (Szabó 2, Gabór 3)
Almonds and Raisins, 1983 (Mankowitz 4)
Almost a Gentleman, 1939 (Hunt 4)
Almost a Hero, 1910 (Porter 2)
Almost a Husband, 1919 (Rogers, W. 3)
Almost a Lady, 1926 (Rosson 4)
Almost a Wild Man, 1913 (Gish, D. 3)
Almost an Actress, 1913 (Chaney Lon 3, Fazenda 3)
Almost Angels, 1962 (Disney 2)
Almost Human, 1927 (Adrian 4, Buckland 4)
Almost Human. See Shock Waves, 1975
Almost Married, 1932 (Bellamy 3, Friedhofer 4, Menzies 4)
Almost Perfect Affair, 1979 (Ritchie 2, Vitti 3, Decaë 4, Delerue 4)
Alô, alô, Brasil!, 1935 (Miranda 3)
Alô, alô, carnaval!, 1936 (Miranda 3)
Alochaya, 1940 (Sircar 4)
Aloha Bobby and Rose, 1975 (Fraker 4)
Aloha Hooey, 1941 (Avery 2)
Aloha Oe, 1915 (Ince 4)
Aloha Oe, 1931 (Fleischer, M. and D. 2)
Aloha ou Le Chant des iles, 1937 (Arletty 3, Spaak 4)
Aloise, 1974 (Huppert 3, Seyrig 3)
Alom a házrol, 1971 (Szabó 2)
Aloma of the South Seas, 1926 (Tourneur, M. 2, Baxter W. 3, Johnson, N. 3, Powell, W. 3)
Aloma of the South Seas, 1941 (Johnson, N. 3, Lamour 3, Dreier 4, Edouart 4, Head 4, Siodmak 4, Struss 4, Young, V. 4)
Alone. See Odna, 1931
Alone. See Samac, 1958
Alone at Last. See Endelig Alene, 1914
Alone in a City. See Sam pósród miasta, 1965
Alone in the Dark, 1982 (Palance 3, Pleasance 3)
Alone in the Jungle, 1913 (Selig 4)
Alone in the World, 1916 (Weber 2)
Alone on the Pacific. See Taiheiyo hitoribotchi, 1963
Alone with the Monsters, 1958 (Lassally 4)
Along Came Auntie, 1926 (Hardy 3, Roach 4)
Along Came Daffy, 1946 (Freleng 4)
Along Came Jones, 1945 (Cooper, Gary 3, Duryea 3, Young, L. 3, Fields 4, Friedhofer 4, Johnson 4, Krasner 4, Plunkett 4)
Along Came Sally. See Aunt Sally, 1933
Along Came Youth, 1930 (McLeod 2, Head 4)
Along Flirtation Walk, 1935 (Freleng 4)
Along the Border, 1916 (Mix 3)
Along the Galgu River. See Galga mentén, 1954
Along the Great Divide, 1951 (Walsh 2, Brennan 3, Douglas, K. 3, Mayo 3, Veiller 4)
Along the Mohawk Trail, 1956 (Chaney Lon, Jr. 3)

Along the Navajo Trail, 1945 (Rogers, R. 3)
Along the River Nile, 1912 (Olcott 2)
Alpagueur, 1976 (Evein 4)
Alpentragodie, 1927 (Kortner 3, Andrejew 4)
Alpha Beta, 1976 (Finney 3, Roberts 3)
Alpha Caper, 1973 (Fonda, H. 3)
Alpha Omega, 1961 (Bozzetto 4)
Alphabet Murders, 1965 (Tashlin 2, Rutherford 3)
Alphaville, 1965 (Godard 2, Constantine 3, Karina 3, Léaud 3, Coutard 4, Guillemot 4)
Alpine Yodeler, 1936 (Terry 4)
Alraune, 1918 (Curtiz 2)
Alraune, 1927 (Wegener 3, Galeen 4, Planer 4)
Alraune, 1930 (Basserman 3, Oswald 2, Kaper 4)
Alraune, 1952 (Knef 3, Von Stroheim 2, Herlth 4)
Als ich wiederkam, 1926 (Oswald 2)
Als twee druppels water, 1963 (Rademakers 2, Coutard 4)
Alsace, 1915 (Burel 4)
Alsino and the Condor. See Alsino y el condór, 1982
Alsino y el condór, 1982 (Littin 2)
Alskande par, 1964 (Zetterling 2, Andersson H. 3, Bjornstrand 3, Dahlbeck 3, Nykvist 4)
Alskarinnan, 1962 (Sjoman 2, Andersson B. 3, Von Sydow 3)
Alskling, jag ger mig, 1943 (Molander 2)
Alskling på vågen, 1956 (Nykvist 4)
Also es war so . . ., 1976 (Karina 3)
'Alt, oo Goes Theer?, 1936 (Holloway 3)
Alt paa et Kort, 1912 (Blom 2)
Alta infedeltà, 1964 (Monicelli 2, Petri 2, Scola 2, Blier 3, Bloom 3, Cassel 3, Manfredi 3, Tognazzi 3, Vitti 3, Age and Scarpelli 4, Di Venanzo 4, Gherardi 4)
Altar of Death, 1912 (Ince 4, Sullivan 4)
Altar of Love, 1915 (Costello, M. 3)
Altar of the Aztecs, 1913 (Bosworth 3)
Altar Stairs, 1922 (Karloff 3)
Altars of Desire, 1927 (Daniels 4, Gibbons 4, Gillespie 4)
Altars of the East, 1955 (Ayres 3)
Altars of the World, 1976 (Ayres 3)
Alte Balhaus, 1925 (Tschechowa 3)
Alte Gesetz, 1923 (Dupont 2, Krauss 3, Porten 3, Junge 4)
Alte Herzen, neue Zeiten, 1926 (Pick 2)
Alte Lied, 1930 (Dagover 3)
Alte und der junge Konig, 1935 (Jannings 3, Von Harbou 4)
Altered Message, 1911 (Guy 2)
Altered States, 1979 (Russell 2, Hurt, W. 3, Chayefsky 4, Smith, D. 4)
Altes Herz wird wieder jung, 1943 (Jannings 3, Wagner 4)
Altgermanische Bauernkultur, 1934 (Ruttmann 2)
Alt-Heidelberg, 1923 (Krauss 3, Metzner 4)
Although There Are Millions of Women. See Onna wa ikuman aritotemo, 1966
Altitude 42625, 1964 (Braunberger 4)
Altitude 3200, 1938 (Benoit-Lévy 2, Barrault 3, Blier 3, Jaubert 4)
Altra, 1947 (Amidei 4)
Altri, gli altri e noi, 1967 (De Sica 2)
Altri tempi, 1952 (Blasetti 2, De Sica 2, Fabrizi 3, Lollobrigida 3, D'Amico 4)
Alum and Eve, 1932 (Pitts 3, Roach 4)
Aluminité, 1910 (Gance 2)
Alvarez Kelly, 1966 (Dmytryk 2, Holden 3, Widmark 3, Green, J. 4, Mercer 4)
Always a Way, 1911 (Lawrence 3)
Always Audacious, 1920 (Cruze 2, Reid 3)
Always Faithful, 1927 (Sweet 3)
Always Goodbye, 1931 (Stone 3, Edeson 4, Friedhofer 4, Menzies 4)
Always Goodbye, 1938 (Marshall 3, Stanwyck 3)
Always in My Heart, 1942 (Francis, K. 3, Huston 3)
Always Kickin', 1939 (Fleischer, M. and D. 2)
Always Leave Them Laughing, 1949 (Lahr 3, Mayo 3, Cahn 4, Haller 4, Mercer 4, Wald 4)
Always on Sunday, 1963 (Aumont 3)
Always on Sunday, 1965 (Russell 2)
Always Tell Your Wife, 1923 (Hitchcock 2)

Always Together, 1947 (Bogart 3, Flynn 3, Diamond 4)
Alye parusa, 1961 (Ptushko 2)
Am Abend auf der Heide, 1941 (Von Harbou 4)
Am Meer, 1924 (Nielsen 3)
Am Rande der Gross-stadt, 1922 (Kortner 3)
Am Rande der Welt, 1927 (Dieterle 2, Wagner 4)
Am roten Kliff, 1921 (Kortner 3)
Am seidenen Faden, no date (Staudte 2)
Am Tor des Lebens, 1918 (Wiene 2)
Am Tor des Todes. See Am Tor des Lebens, 1918
Am Webstuhl der Zeit, 1921 (Holger-Madsen 2)
Ama a tu prójimo, 1958 (Cantinflas 3)
Ama no yuhgao, 1948 (Hayasaka 4)
Amadeus, 1983 (Smith, D. , Forman 2, Ondricek 4)
Amagi kara kita otoko, 1950 (Yamada 3)
Amai himitsu, 1971 (Yoshimura 2)
Amai shiru, 1964 (Kyo 3)
Amakusa shiro tokisada, 1962 (Oshima 2)
Amami, 1940 (Gallone 2)
Amanat, 1955 (Roy 2)
Amant de Bornéo, 1942 (Arletty 3)
Amant de cinq jours, 1961 (Broca 2, Cassel 3, Presle 3, Seberg 3, Delerue 4, Evein 4)
Amant de Lady Chatterley, 1955 (Allégret, M. 2, Darrieux 3, Kosma 4, Périnal 4, Trauner 4)
Amant de Madame Vidal, 1936 (D'Eaubonne 4)
Amant de paille, 1950 (Aumont 3)
Amante della città Sepolta. See Atlantide, 1960
Amante di Paride, 1953 (Allégret, M. 2)
Amante italiana. See Sultans, 1966
Amante segreta, 1941 (Gallone 2, Valli 3, Vích 4)
Amanti, 1968 (De Sica 2, Dunaway 3, Mastroianni 3, Guerra 4, Ponti 4, van Runkle 4, Zavattini 4)
Amanti d'oltretomba, 1965 (Morricone 4)
Amanti del deserto, 1956 (Cervi 3)
Amanti del mostro, 1974 (Kinski 3)
Amanti di Gramigna, 1969 (Volonté 3)
Amanti di Ravello, 1950 (Baarová 3)
Amanti senza amore, 1947 (Gherardi 4, Rota 4)
Amantia Pestilens, 1963 (Bujold 3)
Amants, 1958 (Malle 2, Cuny 3, Modot 3, Moreau 3, Decaë 4, Evein 4)
Amants de Bras-Mort, 1950 (Auric 4)
Amants de demain, 1957 (Brasseur 3, Manès 3)
Amants de la Villa Borghese, 1954 (Philipe 3)
Amants de minuit, 1931 (Allégret, M. 2, Allégret, Y. 2, Braunberger 4)
Amants de Teruel, 1961 (Renoir 4, Theodorakis 4)
Amants de Tolède, 1952 (Armendáriz 3, Valli 3, Barsacq 4)
Amants de Vérone, 1949 (Cayatte 2, Aimée 3, Brasseur 3, Dalio 3, Reggiani 3, Alekan 4, Kosma 4, Prévert 4)
Amants de villa Borghese. See Villa Borghese, 1953
Amants du Pont Saint-Jean, 1947 (Simon, M. 3, Aurenche 4)
Amants du Tage, 1955 (Verneuil 2, Armendáriz 3, Dalio 3, Gélin 3, Howard, T. 3, D'Eaubonne 4, Legrand 4)
Amants et voleurs, 1935 (Arletty 3, Simon, M. 3)
Amants terribles, 1936 (Allégret, M. 2)
Amants terribles, 1984 (Branco 4)
Amapola del Camino, 1937 (Armendáriz 3)
Amar Akbar Anthony, 1977 (Azmi 3, Bachchan 3)
Amar Deep, 1958 (Anand 3)
Amar Lenin, 1970 (Ghatak 4)
Amarcord, 1974 (Fellini 2, Cristaldi 4, Donati 4, Guerra 4, Rota 4)
Amardeep, 1979 (Azmi 3)
Amarilly of Clothes-Line Alley, 1918 (Neilan 2, Pickford 3, Marion 4)
Amarrando el cordon, 1968 (Alvarez 2)
Amateur Broadcast, 1935 (Lantz 4)
Amateur Daddy, 1932 (Baxter W. 3, Friedhofer 4, Howe 4)
Amateur Film. See Parlorna, 1922
Amateur Gentleman, 1926 (Olcott 2, Barthelmess 3)
Amateur Gentleman, 1936 (Fairbanks, D. Jr. 3)
Amateur Night, 1927 (Love 3)
Amateur Night, 1935 (Terry 4)
Amator, 1978 (Zanussi 2)

Amature Nite, 1929 (Lantz 4)
Amazing Captain Nemo, 1978 (Ferrer, J. 3, Meredith 3)
Amazing Colossal Man, 1957 (Biroc 4)
Amazing Dobermans, 1977 (Astaire 3)
Amazing Dr. Clitterhouse, 1938 (Huston 2, Litvak 2, Bogart 3, Bond 3, Crisp 3, Hayward 3, Robinson, E. 3, Trevor 3, Gaudio 4, Steiner 4)
Amazing Dr. G, 1965 (Rey 3)
Amazing Grace, 1974 (Fetchit 3, McQueen, B. 3)
Amazing Mr. Blunden, 1972 (Bernstein 4, Fisher 4)
Amazing Mr. Forrest. See Gang's All Here, 1939
Amazing Mr. Williams, 1939 (Blondell 3, Douglas, M. 3)
Amazing Mr. X. See Spiritualist, 1948
Amazing Mrs. Holliday, 1943 (Durbin 3, Fitzgerald 3, O'Brien, E. 3, Levien 4, Salter 4)
Amazing Monsieur Fabre. See Monsieur Fabre, 1951
Amazing Quest of Ernest Bliss, 1936 (Grant, C. 3)
Amazing Transparent Man, 1959 (Ulmer 2, Pierce 4)
Amazing Vagabond, 1929 (Miller, V. 4, Plunkett 4)
Amazing What Color Can Do, 1954 (Kaufman 4)
Amazonas, 1965 (Rocha 2)
Amazons, 1917 (Menjou 3, Marion 4)
Amazons of Rome. See Vergine di Roma, 1961
Amazzone mascherata, 1914 (Bertini 3)
Ambar, 1952 (Kapoor 2)
Ambassador, 1984 (Burstyn 3, Mitchum 3, Golan and Globus 4)
Ambassador at Large, 1964 (Homolka 3)
Ambassador Bill, 1931 (Milland 3, Rogers, W. 3)
Ambassadors, 1977 (Remick 3)
Ambassador's Daughter, 1956 (De Havilland 3, Loy 3, Menjou 3, Barsacq 4, Krasna 4)
Ambassador's Despatch. See Valise diplomatique, 1909
Ambassador's Disappearance, 1913 (Costello, M. 3)
Ambassador's Envoy, 1914 (Hayakawa 3, Ince 4)
Ambiciosos, 1959 (Félix 3)
Ambiciosos. See Fièvre monte à El Pao, 1959
Ambitieuse, 1959 (Allégret, Y. 2, O'Brien, E. 3, Wakhévitch 4)
Ambition of the Baron, 1915 (Bushman 3, Swanson 3)
Ambitious. See Bakumatsu, 1970
Ambitious Butler, 1912 (Sennett 2, Normand 3)
Ambitious Ethel, 1916 (Hardy 3)
Ambrose's Cup of Woe, 1916 (Sennett 2)
Ambrose's First Falsehood, 1914 (Sennett 2)
Ambrose's Fury, 1915 (Sennett 2, Fazenda 3)
Ambrose's Little Hatchet, 1915 (Sennett 2, Fazenda 3)
Ambrose's Lofty Perch, 1915 (Sennett 2, Fazenda 3)
Ambrose's Nasty Temper, 1915 (Sennett 2)
Ambrose's Rapid Rise, 1916 (Sennett 2)
Ambrose's Sour Grapes, 1915 (Sennett 2)
Ambulance Corps Drill, 1899 (Bitzer 4)
Ambush, 1939 (Crawford, B. 3)
Ambush, 1949 (Wood 2, Taylor, R. 3, Plunkett 4)
Ambush. See Machibuse, 1970
Ambush at Cimarron Pass, 1957 (Eastwood 3)
Ambush Bay, 1966 (Rooney 3)
Ambushers, 1967 (Martin, D. 3, Guffey 4)
Ame d'argile, 1955 (Delerue 4)
Ame d'artiste, 1925 (Dulac 2, Manès 3, Vanel 3)
Ame de bronze, 1918 (Baur 3)
Ame de clown, 1933 (Fresnay 3, D'Eaubonne 4)
Ame de Pierre, 1912 (Modot 3)
Amelia and the Angel, 1957 (Russell 2)
Amère victoire, 1957 (Burton 3, D'Eaubonne 4)
America, 1924 (Griffith 2, Barrymore L. 3, Bitzer 4)
America, America, 1964 (Kazan 2, Allen, D. 4, Wexler 4)
America and Lewis Hine, 1984 (Robards 3)
America at the Movies, 1977 (Delon 3, Heston 3)
America Can Give It, 1942 (Huston 3)
America Is Hard to See, 1969 (de Antonio 2)
America Is Waiting, 1981 (Conner 2)
America Revisited, 1971 (Ophuls 2)
Américain, 1970 (Fabian 3, Signoret 3)
Américain, 1979 (Trintignant 3)
Américain. See Chemin d'Ernoa, 1921

Américain se détend, 1957 (Reichenbach 2, Braunberger 4)
American, 1919 (Karloff 3)
American, 1927 (Love 3)
American Aristocracy, 1916 (Fleming 2, Fairbanks, D. 3, Loos 4)
American Beauty, 1927 (Wilson, C. 4)
American Boy, 1978 (Scorsese 2)
American Christmas Carol, 1979 (Baker 4)
American Citizen, 1914 (Barrymore J. 3)
American Creed, 1946 (Jones, J. 3)
American Dream, 1966 (Leigh, J. 3)
American Dream. See Drömmen om Amerika, 1976
American Dreamer, 1971 (Kovacs 4)
American Dreamer, 1984 (Giannini 3)
American Empire, 1942 (Farnum 3)
American Film, 1967 (Heston 3)
American Friend, 1976 (Fuller 2, Ray, N. 2)
American Friend. See Amerikanische Freund, 1977
American Gigolo, 1979 (Schrader 2, Gere 3)
American Girls, 1978 (Andrews D. 3)
American Graffiti, 1973 (Coppola 2, Lucas 2, Dreyfuss 3, Ford, H. 3, Fields 4, Murch 4, Wexler 4)
American Guerilla in the Philippines, 1950 (Lang 2, Elam 3, Power 3, Presle 3, Lemaire 4, Trotti 4, Wheeler 4)
American Heiress, 1917 (Hepworth 2)
American Hot Wax, 1977 (Fraker 4)
American in Paris, 1951 (Minnelli 2, Caron 3, Kelly, Gene 3, Nilsson 3, Alton, J. 4, Ames 4, Edens 4, Freed 4, Gibbons 4, Green, J. 4, Orry-Kelly 4, Plunkett 4, Sharaff 4, Smith, J.M. 4)
American Madness, 1932 (Capra 2, Huston 3, O'Brien, P. 3, Riskin 4, Walker 4)
American March, 1941 (Fischinger 2)
American Matchmaker. See Americaner Schadchen, 1939
American Methods, 1917 (Farnum 3)
American People, 1945 (Huston 3)
American Playhouse, 1982 (Demme 2)
American Pop, 1981 (Bakshi 2)
American Portrait, 1949 (Ladd 3)
American Prisoner, 1929 (Carroll M. 3)
American Raspberry. See Prime Time, 1977
American Road, 1954 (North 4)
American Romance, 1944 (Vidor, K. 2, Irene 4, Rosson 4)
American Soldier. See Amerikanische Soldat, 1970
American Soldier in Love and War, 1903 (Bitzer 4)
American Success Company, 1979 (Bridges 3, Jarre 4)
American Success. See American Success Company, 1979
American Tragedy, 1931 (Von Sternberg 2, Sidney 3, Banton 4, Dreier 4, Garmes 4, Hoffenstein 4)
American Venus, 1926 (Brooks 3, Fairbanks, D. Jr. 3, Hunt 4)
American Way, 1961 (Emshwiller 2)
American Werewolf in London, 1981 (Baker 4, Bernstein 4)
American West of John Ford, 1971 (Stewart 3)
American Widow, 1917 (Barrymore E. 3)
American Years, 1976 (Hammid 2)
Americaner Schadchen, 1939 (Ulmer 2)
Americanization of Emily, 1964 (Hiller 2, Andrews, J. 3, Coburn, J. 3, Douglas, M. 3, Wynn 3, Chayefsky 4, Mercer 4)
Americano, 1916 (Fleming 2, Fairbanks, D. 3, Emerson 4, Loos 4)
Americano, 1954 (Ford, G. 3)
Americano a Roma, 1954 (Scola 2, Sordi 3, Ponti 4)
Americano in vacanza, 1945 (Zampa 2, Cortese 3, Ponti 4, Rota 4)
America's Cup Race, 1899 (Porter 2)
America's Sweetheart: The Mary Pickford Story, 1978 (Fonda, H. 3)
Americathon, 1979 (George, Ch. D. 3)
Amerikanische Freund, 1977 (Wenders 2, Ganz 3, Hopper 3)
Amerikanische Soldat, 1970 (Fassbinder 2, Von Trotta 2)
Amérique insolite, 1960 (Reichenbach 2, Braunberger 4, Legrand 4)
Amérique lunaire, 1962 (Reichenbach 2, Braunberger 4)
Amérique vue par un franǐ.ais. See Amérique insolite, 1960
Ames d'enfants, 1928 (Benoit-Lévy 2)
Ames de fous, 1917 (Dulac 2, Francis, E. 3)
Ametralladora, 1943 (Infante 3)
Ami de Vincent, 1983 (Fabian 3, Karina 3)
Ami Fritz, 1933 (D'Eaubonne 4)

Ami viendra ce soir, 1945 (Gélin 3, Simon, M. 3, Honegger 4)
Amica, 1969 (Lattuada 2)
Amiche, 1955 (Antonioni 2, Cortese 3, D'Amico 4, Di Venanzo 4, Fusco 4)
Amici di Nick Hezard, 1976 (Cortese 3)
Amici miei, 1975 (Germi 2, Monicelli 2, Blier 3, Noiret 3, Tognazzi 3, Pinelli 4)
Amici miei atto II, 1982 (Monicelli 2, Tognazzi 3, Pinelli 4)
Amici per la pelle, 1955 (Rota 4)
Amico del giaguaro, 1958 (Delli Colli 4)
Amigos, 1972 (Delli Colli 4)
Amiral Nakhimov, 1946 (Pudovkin 2, Golovnya 4)
Amiral Tempête. See Admiral Ushakov, 1953
Amitie noire, 1946 (Cocteau 2)
Amitiés particulières, 1964 (Delannoy 2, Aurenche 4, Bost 4, Matras 4)
Amityville Horror, 1979 (Steiger 3, Schifrin 4)
Amityville II: The Possession, 1982 (Schifrin 4)
Amleto e il suo clown, 1920 (Gallone 2)
Amo non amo, 1978 (Bisset 3, Schell, Maximilian 3, Stamp 3)
Amo te sola, 1935 (De Sica 2)
Amok, 1933 (Courant 4, Meerson 4, Trauner 4)
Amok, 1944 (Félix 3)
Amokfutds, 1974 (Darvas 3)
Among People. See Vlyudyakh, 1939
Among the Living, 1941 (Carey 3, Farmer 3, Hayward 3, Muse 3, Fort 4, Head 4)
Among the Missing, 1934 (August 4)
Among the Mourners, 1914 (Sennett 2, Arbuckle 3)
Among Those Present, 1921 (Sennett 2, Lloyd 3, Roach 4)
Among Vultures. See Unter Geiern, 1964
Amoozin' But Confoozin', 1944 (Fleischer, M. and D. 2)
Amor, amor, amor, 1965 (Figueroa 4)
Amor de Don Juan, 1956 (Bardem 2, Rey 3)
Amor de perdição, 1978 (Oliveira 2, Branco 4)
Amor en el aire, 1967 (Rey 3)
Amor non ho . . . pero . . . pero, 1951 (Lollobrigida 3)
Amor tiene cara de mujer, 1973 (Figueroa 4)
Amor und das standhafte Liebespaar, 1920 (Reiniger 2)
Amor y sexo, 1963 (Félix 3)
Amore, 1923 (Gallone 2)
Amore, 1935 (Cervi 3, Feuillère 3)
Amore, 1948 (Fellini 2, Rossellini 2, Magnana 3, Pinelli 4)
Amore, 1965 (Brazzi 3)
Amore a Roma, 1960 (De Sica 2, Risi 2, Flaiano 4)
Amore audaz. See Enigmatique Monsieur Parkes, 1930
Amore canta, 1941 (De Laurentiis 4)
Amore difficile, 1962 (Scola 2, Wicki 2, Gassman 3, Manfredi 3)
Amore e chiacchiere, 1957 (Blasetti 2, De Sica 2, Cervi 3, Zavattini 4)
Amore e ginnastica, 1973 (D'Amico 4)
Amore e guai, 1958 (Cortese 3, Mastroianni 3)
Amore e rabbia, 1969 (Bellocchio 2, Bertolucci 2, Godard 2, Pasolini 2, Fusco 4, Guillemot 4)
Amore in città, 1953 (Antonioni 2, Fellini 2, Ferreri 2, Lattuada 2, Risi 2, Tognazzi 3, Di Venanzo 4, Pinelli 4, Zavattini 4)
Amore in Italia, 1978 (Comencini 2)
Amore in quattro dimensioni, 1963 (Delli Colli 4)
Amore mio, aiutami, 1969 (Sordi 3, Vitti 3)
Amore mio non farmi male, 1974 (Cortese 3)
Amore, piombo, e furore, 1978 (Oates 3, Donaggio 4)
Amore primitivo, 1964 (Mansfield 3)
Amore vince amore, 1921 (Bertini 3)
Amores de una viuda, 1948 (Alcoriza 4)
Amori di Ercole, 1960 (Mansfield 3)
Amori di Manon Lescaut, 1954 (Pinelli 4)
Amori di mezzo secolo, 1954 (Rossellini 2, Sordi 3, Delli Colli 4)
Amori pericolosi, 1964 (Delli Colli 4)
Amorosa menzogna, 1949 (Antonioni 2, Fusco 4)
Amorous Adventures of Moll Flanders, 1965 (De Sica 2, Lansbury 3, Novak 3, Sanders 3, Addison 4)
Amorous General. See Waltz of the Toreadors, 1962
Amorous Mr. Prawn. See Amorous Prawn, 1962
Amorous Prawn, 1962 (Greenwood 3, Barry 4)
Amos, 1985 (Douglas, K. 3)

Amour, 1973 (Warhol/Morrissey 2, Vangelis 4)
Amour. *See* Lamuru, 1933
Amour à l'américaine, 1931 (Allégret, M. 2, Allégret, Y. 2, Fejos 2, Braunberger 4)
Amour à la chaîne, 1964 (Delerue 4)
Amour à la mer, 1964 (Delon 3)
Amour à mort, 1984 (Vierny 4)
Amour à tous les étages, 1902 (Zecca, 2)
Amour à vingt ans, 1962 (Ophuls 2, Truffaut 2, Wajda 2, Cybulski 3, Léaud 3, Coutard 4, Delerue 4, Stawinsky 4, Takemitsu 4)
Amour autour de la maison, 1946 (Brasseur 3, Kosma 4)
Amour avec des si . . ., 1963 (Braunberger 4)
Amour blessé, 1975 (Lefebvre 2)
Amour c'est gai, l'amour c'est triste, 1968 (Dalio 3)
Amour chante, 1930 (Allégret, M. 2, Florey 2, Braunberger 4)
Amour d'automne, 1912 (Feuillade 2)
Amour d'un métier, 1950 (Colpi 4)
Amour d'une femme, 1954 (Grémillon 2, Presle 3)
Amour de Jeanne Ney. *See* Liebe der Jeanne Ney, 1927
Amour de pluie, 1974 (Schneider 3, Carrière 4, Lai 4)
Amour de poche, 1957 (Melville 2, Marais 3, Cloquet 4)
Amour de Swann, 1983 (Carrière 4, Nykvist 4)
Amour de Swann. *See* Swann in Love, 1983
Amour en Allemagne, 1983 (Mueller-Stahl 3)
Amour en fuite, 1979 (Truffaut 2, Léaud 3, Almendros 4, Delerue 4)
Amour en question, 1978 (Cayatte 2, Andersson B. 3, Girardot 3)
Amour est en jeu, 1957 (Girardot 3)
Amour est un jeu. *See* Ma Femme, mon gosse et moi, 1957
Amour et discipline, 1931 (D'Eaubonne 4)
Amour et la veine, 1932 (D'Eaubonne 4)
Amour existe, 1961 (Braunberger 4, Delerue 4)
Amour fou, 1968 (Rivette 2, de Beauregard 4)
Amour l'après-midi, 1972 (Rohmer 2, Fabian 3, Almendros 4)
Amour, madame . . ., 1951 (Arletty 3)
Amour par terre, 1984 (Rivette 2, Chaplin 3)
Amour tenace, 1912 (Linders 3)
Amoureux. *See* Epervier, 1933
Amoureux du France, 1962 (Reichenbach 2, Legrand 4)
Amoureux sont seuls au monde, 1948 (Jouvet 3, Jeanson 4)
Amours célèbres, 1961 (Bardot 3, Belmondo 3, Brasseur 3, Delon 3, Feuillère 3, Girardot 3, Noiret 3, Signoret 3, Achard 4, Audiard 4, Jarre 4, Prévert 4, Wakhévitch 4)
Amours de Casanova, 1933 (Mozhukin 3)
Amours de Lady Hamilton. *See* Lady Hamilton, 1968
Amours de Toni. *See* Toni, 1935
Amours, délices et orgues. *See* Collège swing, 1946
Amours finissent à l'aube, 1953 (Alekan 4)
Ampélopède, 1974 (Huppert 3)
Amphitryon, 1935 (Herlth 4, Rohrig 4, Wagner 4)
Amposter, 1914 (August 4)
Amsterdam Affair, 1968 (Fisher 4)
Amsterdam Kill, 1977 (Mitchum 3)
Amulet of Ogum. *See* Amuleta de ogum, 1974
Amuleta de ogum, 1974 (Pereira Dos Santos 2)
Amuletten, 1911 (Magnusson 4)
Amy, 1981 (O'Brien, M. 3)
Amy Goes to Buy Some Bread, 1979 (Vukotić 4)
An der schonen blauen Donau, 1926 (Albers 3, Andrejew 4)
An einem Freitag um halb zwolf . . ., 1961 (Vích 4)
An franzosischen Kaminen, 1963 (Domrose 3)
An jedem Finger zehn, 1954 (Albers 3)
An klingenden Ufern, 1949 (Jurgens 3)
An quarante, 1940 (Berry 3)
An uns glaubt Gott nicht mehr, 1981 (Mueller-Stahl 3)
Ana, 1957 (Ichikawa 2, Kyo 3, Yamamura 3)
Ana, 1981 (Branco 4, de Almeida 4)
Ana and the Wolves. *See* Ana y los lobos, 1973
Aña y los lobos, 1973 (Saura 2, Chaplin 3)
Anadi, 1959 (Kapoor 2)
Analfabeto, 1960 (Cantinflas 3, García 3)
Anam, 1956 (Sharif 3)
Anand, 1971 (Bachchan 3)
Anand Aur Anand, 1984 (Anand 3, Patil 3)

Anaparastassi, 1970 (Angelopoulos 2)
Anarchie chez Guignol, 1906 (Méliès 2)
Anarchist, 1913 (Brenon 2)
Anarchistes ou La Bande à Bonnot, 1967 (Girardot 3)
Anastasia, 1956 (Litvak 2, Bergman 3, Brynner 3, Andrejew 4, Newman 4)
Anastasia nio fratello, 1973 (Amidei 4)
Anata kaimasu, 1956 (Kobayashi 2)
Anata no biru, 1954 (Hani 2)
Anata to watashi no ai-kotoba, 1959 (Kyo 3)
Anatahan, 1953 (Von Sternberg 2, Tsuburaya 4)
Anath Ashram, 1937 (Sircar 4)
Anatolian Smile. *See* America, America, 1964
Anatomie stunde, 1977 (Zanussi 2)
Anatomist, 1961 (Sim 3)
Anatomy Lesson. *See* Anatomie stunde, 1977
Anatomy of a Marriage. *See* Vie conjugale, 1964
Anatomy of a Murder, 1959 (Preminger 2, Arden 3, Remick 3, Scott, G. 3, Stewart 3, Bass 4, Leven 4)
Anatomy of an Illness, 1983 (Wallach 3)
Anatomy of Cindy Fink, 1965 (Leacock 2)
Anatomy of Love, 1972 (Nowicki 3)
Anatomy of Love. *See* Tempi nostri, 1953
Anatra all'arancia, 1976 (Tognazzi 3, Vitti 3)
Anche se volessi lavorare che faccio?, 1972 (Morricone 4)
Anchors Aweigh, 1945 (Donen 2, Sidney 2, Grayson 3, Kelly, Gene 3, Sinatra 3, Cahn 4, Hanna and Barbera 4, Irene 4, Lennart 4, Pasternak 4)
Anciens de Saint-Loup, 1950 (Blier 3, Reggiani 3)
Ancient City. *See* Koto, 1980
Ancient Law. *See* Alte Gesetz, 1923
Ancient Mariner, 1926 (Bow 3, August 4)
Ancient Temples of Egypt, 1912 (Olcott 2)
And a Little Child Shall Lead Them, 1909 (Griffith 2)
And a Still Small Voice, 1918 (Walthall 3)
And at Last. *See* Abasheshey, 1962
And Baby Makes Six, 1979 (Oates 3)
And Baby Makes Three, 1949 (Burke 3, Young, R. 3, Duning 4, Guffey 4)
And God Created Woman. *See* Et Dieu créa la femme, 1956
And God Said to Cain. *See* E Dio disse a Caino . . ., 1969
And Happiness Will Be Possible. *See* A shchastiya bylo tak vozmotzno, 1916
And His Wife Came Back, 1913 (Bunny 3)
And Hope to Die. *See* Course du lièvre à travers les champs, 1972
And Justice for All, 1979 (Jewison 2, Pacino 3, Warden 3)
And No One Could Save Her, 1973 (Remick 3)
And Nothing But the Truth, 1984 (Jackson 3)
And Now for Something Completely Different, 1971 (Godfrey 4)
And Now My Love. *See* Toute une vie, 1974
And Now the Screaming Starts, 1973 (Cushing 3)
And Now Tomorrow, 1944 (Bondi 3, Hayward 3, Ladd 3, Young, L. 3, Chandler 4, Dreier 4, Head 4, Young, V. 4)
And One Was Beautiful, 1940 (Cummings 3)
And Quiet Flows the Don. *See* Tikhy Don, 1957–58
And Quiet Rolls the Dawn. *See* Ek Din Pratidin, 1979
And So They Were Married, 1936 (Astor 3, Douglas, M. 3, Meek 3, Schulberg 4)
And So to Bed. *See* Grosse Liebesspiel, 1963
And Suddenly it's Murder. *See* Crimen, 1960
And the Angels Sing, 1944 (Hutton 3, Lamour 3, MacMurray 3, Dreier 4, Frank and Panama 4, Head 4, Struss 4, Young, V. 4)
And the Earth Shall Give Back Life, 1953 (Kaufman 4)
And the Green Grass Grew All Around, 1931 (Fleischer, M. and D. 2)
And the Ship Sailed On. *See* E la nave va, 1983
And the Wild Wild Women. *See* Nella città l'inferno, 1958
And Then There Were None, 1945 (Clair 2, Anderson J. 3, Auer 3, Fitzgerald 3, Huston 3, Nichols 4)
And Then There Were None, 1974 (Attenborough 3)
And There Came a Man. *See* . . . e venne un uomo, 1965
And There Was No More Sea. *See* En de zee was niet meer, 1955
And to Think That I Saw It on Mulberry Street, 1944 (Pal 2)
And Yet They Go. *See* Shikamo karera wa yuku, 1931

And Yet We Live. *See* Dokkoi ikiteiru, 1951
Andagine su un cittadino al di spora di ogni sopetto, 1970 (Volonté 3)
Andaz, 1949 (Kapoor 2)
Andechser Gefühl, 1975 (Von Trotta 2)
Andel blažene smrti, 1965 (Marković 3)
Andělský kabát, 1948 (Brdečka 4, Hofman 4)
Andere, 1913 (Basserman 3, George, H. 3, Warm 4)
Andere, 1924 (Hoffmann 4)
Andere, 1930 (Wiene 2, George, H. 3, Kortner 3)
Andere Ich, 1918 (Kortner 3)
Andere Seite, 1931 (Veidt 3)
Anders als die Andern, 1919 (Oswald 2, Veidt 3)
Andersen hos fotografen, 1975 (Roos 2)
Andersens hemmelighed, 1971 (Roos 2)
Anderson Tapes, 1971 (Lumet 2, Cannon 3, Connery 3, Jones 4)
Anderssonskans Kalle, 1950 (Andersson H. 3)
Andesu no hanayome, 1966 (Hani 2)
Andhaa Kaanoon, 1983 (Bachchan 3)
Andhi, 1940 (Sircar 4)
Ando volando bajo, 1957 (Armendáriz 3)
André Masson et les quatre éléments, 1958 (Grémillon 2, Delerue 4)
Andreas Hofer, 1909 (Porten 3, Messter 4)
Andreas Schluter, 1942 (George, H. 3, Tschechowa 3, Herlth 4)
Andrei Kozhukhov, 1917 (Protazanov 2, Mozhukin 3)
Andrei Rublev. *See* Andrei Rubliov, 1965
Andrei Rubliov, 1965 (Mikhalkov-Konchalovski 2, Tarkovsky 2)
Andreina, 1917 (Bertini 3)
Andremo in città, 1966 (Chaplin 3, Delli Colli 4, Stawinsky 4, Zavattini 4)
Andrew Jackson, 1913 (Dwan 2)
Andriesh, 1954 (Paradzhanov 2)
Androclès, 1912 (Feuillade 2)
Androcles and the Lion, 1952 (Lanchester 3, Martin, S. 3, Mature 3, Simmons 3, D'Agostino 4, Dunn 4, Horner 4, Stradling 4)
Android, 1983 (Kinski 3)
Andromeda Strain, 1970 (Wise 2, Leven 4, Trumbull 4)
Andy Clyde Gets Spring Chicken, 1939 (Bruckman 4)
Andy Hardy Comes Home, 1958 (Rooney 3, Stone 3)
Andy Hardy Gets Spring Fever, 1939 (Van Dyke, W.S. 2, Rooney 3, Stone 3)
Andy Hardy Meets Debutante, 1940 (Garland 3, Rooney 3, Stone 3)
Andy Hardy Steps Out. *See* Andy Hardy's Double Life, 1942
Andy Hardy's Blonde Trouble, 1944 (Marshall 3, Stone 3, Irene 4)
Andy Hardy's Double Life, 1942 (Rooney 3, Stone 3, Williams 3)
Andy Hardy's Double Trouble, 1944 (Rooney 3)
Andy Hardy's Private Secretary, 1941 (Grayson 3, Rooney 3, Stone 3, Murfin 4, Stothart 4)
Andy of the Royal Mounted, 1915 (Anderson G. 3)
Andy Plays Hookey, 1946 (Bruckman 4)
Andy Warhol Films Jack Smith Filming Normal Love, 1963 (Warhol 2)
Andy Warhol's Bad, 1977 (Warhol/Morrissey 2, Baker C. 3, Corman 4)
Andy Warhol's Dracula, 1974 (De Sica 2, Warhol/Morrissey 2)
Andy Warhol's Frankenstein, 1974 (Warhol/Morrissey 2)
Andy Warhol's Frankenstein. *See* Carne per Frankenstein, 1974
Ane de Bruidan, 1932 (Douy 4)
Ane no shussei, 1940 (Takamine 3)
Ane to imoto, 1965 (Iwashita 3, Yamamura 3)
Anema e core, 1951 (Manfredi 3)
Anfisa, 1912 (Protazanov 2)
Angarey, 1954 (Burman 4)
Ange de la nuit, 1943 (Barrault 3, Signoret 3)
Ange de minuit. *See* Bouclette, 1917
Ange gardien, 1933 (Meerson 4)
Ange que j'ai vendu, 1938 (Barsacq 4)
Angeklagt nach N.218, 1966 (Ford, A. 2, Lomnicki 3, Schüfftan 4)
Angel, 1937 (Lubitsch 2, Dietrich 3, Douglas, M. 3, Horton 3, Marshall 3, Banton 4, Dreier 4, Lang 4, Raphaelson 4)
Angel and Sinner. *See* Boule de suif, 1945
Angel and the Badman, 1947 (Carey 3, Wayne 3, Canutt 4)
Angel, Angel, Down We Go, 1969 (McDowall 3, Katzman 4)
Angel, Angel, Down We Go. *See* Cult of the Damned, 1969
Angel Baby, 1961 (Blondell 3, McCambridge 3, Reynolds, B. 3, Wexler 4)

Angel Child, 1908 (Porter 2)
Angel Dust, 1980 (Woodward 3)
Angel Esquire, 1919 (Pearson 2)
Ángel exterminador, 1962 (Buñuel 2, Alcoriza 4, Figueroa 4)
Angel Face, 1952 (Preminger 2, Marshall 3, Mitchum 3, Simmons 3, D'Agostino 4, Nugent 4, Stradling 4, Tiomkin 4)
Angel from Texas, 1940 (Reagan 3, Wyman 3)
Angel in Exile, 1948 (Dwan 2)
Angel Levine, 1970 (Kadár 2, Wallach 3, Jenkins 4)
Angel of Broadway, 1927 (Weber 2, Adrian 4, Coffee 4, Miller, A. 4)
Angel of Contention, 1914 (Gish, L. 3)
Angel of Darkness. *See* Donne proibite, 1953
Angel of Death, 1913 (Brenon 2)
Angel of Death. *See* Egy Barany, 1970
Angel of Happy Death. *See* Angel blažene smrti, 1965
Angel of Paradise Ranch, 1911 (Dwan 2)
Angel of the Canyons, 1913 (Dwan 2)
Angel of the Studio, 1912 (Lawrence 3)
Angel on Earth. *See* Engel auf Erden, 1959
Angel on My Shoulder, 1946 (Baxter A. 3, Muni 3, Rains 3, Tiomkin 4)
Angel on the Amazon, 1948 (Bennett C. 3, Brent 3)
Angel Out of the Slums, 1911 (White 3)
Angel over Brooklyn. *See* Angel paso sobre Brooklyn, 1957
Angel paso sobre Brooklyn, 1957 (Ustinov 3)
Angel Puss, 1944 (Jones 2)
Angel Street. *See* Gaslight, 1940
Angel with the Trumpet, 1951 (Schell, Maria 3, Werner 3, Krasker 4)
Angel Wore Red, 1960 (De Sica 2, Bogarde 3, Cotten 3, Gardner 3, Johnson 4, Kaper 4)
Angela, 1954 (Brazzi 3)
Angela, 1977 (Huston 2, Loren 3, Delerue 4, Mancini 4)
Angela. *See* Tarots, 1972
Angèle, 1934 (Pagnol 2, Fernandel 3, Honegger 4)
Angeles de Puebla, 1966 (Figueroa 4)
Angeli dalle mani bendate, 1975 (Brazzi 3)
Angelic Attitude, 1916 (Mix 3)
Angelica, 1939 (Ibert 4)
Angelika, 1940 (Tschechowa 3)
Angelika, 1954 (Schell, Maria 3)
Angelina. *See* Onorevole Angelina, 1947
Angelitos negros, 1948 (Infante 3)
Angelo bianco, 1942 (Cortese 3)
Angelo bianco, 1955 (Delli Colli 4)
Angelo e il diavolo, 1946 (Cervi 3, Zavattini 4)
Angels and the Pirates. *See* Angels in the Outfield, 1951
Angels Brigade, 1979 (Palance 3)
Angel's Coat. *See* Andělský kabát, 1948
Angels Die Hard!, 1970 (Corman 4)
Angels' Door, 1971 (Brakhage 2)
Angels Hard as They Come, 1971 (Demme 2, Corman 4)
Angel's Holiday, 1937 (Chaney Lon, Jr. 3)
Angels in the Outfield, 1951 (Brown 2, Crosby 3, Douglas, P. 3, Leigh, J. 3, Stone 3, Wynn 3)
Angels of Darkness. *See* Donne proibite, 1953
Angels of Mercy, 1942 (Crosby 3)
Angels of the Streets. *See* Anges du péché, 1943
Angels One Five, 1951 (Hawkins 3, Francis 4)
Angels over Broadway, 1940 (Fairbanks, D. Jr. 3, Hayworth 3, Garmes 4, Hecht 4)
Angels Wash Their Faces, 1939 (Reagan 3, Sheridan 3, Buckner 4, Deutsch 4)
Angels with Dirty Faces, 1938 (Curtiz 2, Bogart 3, Cagney 3, O'Brien, P. 3, Sheridan 3, Friedhofer 4, Orry-Kelly 4, Polito 4, Steiner 4)
Angélus, 1899–1900 (Guy 2)
Angelus, 1922 (Astor 3)
Anger in His Eyes. *See* Con la rabbia agli occhi, 1976
Anges du péché, 1943 (Bresson 2)
Anges gardiens, 1964 (Reichenbach 2)
Angkor. *See* Grande Cité, 1954
Anglers, 1914 (Sennett 2)
Angoissante Aventure, 1919 (Mozhukin 3)
Angoisse, 1913 (Feuillade 2)
Angoisse au foyer, 1915 (Feuillade 2)

Angola, 1984 (Branco 4)
Angora Love, 1929 (Laurel and Hardy 3, Roach 4)
Angriff der Gegenwart auf der ubrige Zeit, 1985 (Hoffmann 3, Mueller-Stahl 3)
Angry Boy, 1950 (Hammid 2)
Angry Hills, 1959 (Aldrich 2, Baker S. 3, Mitchum 3, Adam 4)
Angry Man. See Homme en colère, 1979
Angry Red Planet, 1960 (Cortez 4)
Angry Sea. See Chino hate ni ikiru mono, 1960
Angry Sea. See Ikari no umi, 1944
Angry Silence, 1960 (Reed, O. 3, Arnold 4, Green, G. 4)
Angry Street. See Ikari no machi, 1949
Angst, 1928 (Frohlich 3)
Angst, 1954 (Rossellini 2, Bergman 3, Amidei 4)
Angst des Tormanns beim Elfmeter, 1971 (Wenders 2, Vogler 3)
Angst essen Seele auf, 1973 (Fassbinder 2)
Angst vor der Angst, 1975 (Fassbinder 2)
Angulimaal, 1960 (Biswas 4)
Angyalföldi fiatalok, 1955 (Jancsó 2)
Angyelok foldje, 1962 (Madaras 3)
Anhonee, 1952 (Kapoor 2)
Ani imoto, 1953 (Naruse 2, Kyo 3, Mori 3)
Ani imoto, 1976 (Imai 2)
Ani no hanayome, 1941 (Yamada 3)
Ani Ohev Otach Rosa, 1971 (Golan and Globus 4)
Ani to sono imoto, 1956 (Tsukasa 3)
Aničko vrat se!, 1926 (Ondra 3)
Aniki-Bóbó, 1942 (Oliveira 2)
Anikti epistoli, 1968 (Lassally 4)
Anillo de compromiso, 1951 (Alcoriza 4)
Anima allegra, 1918 (Bertini 3)
Anima del demi-monde, 1913 (Bertini 3)
Anima nera, 1962 (Rossellini 2, Gassman 3)
Anima persa, 1976 (Risi 2, Deneuve 3, Gassman 3, Delli Colli 4, Lai 4)
Anima redenta, 1917 (Bertini 3)
Anima selvaggia, 1920 (Bertini 3)
Animal, 1913 (Dwan 2, Reid 3)
Animal, 1977 (Belmondo 3, Welch 3, Audiard 4, Renoir 4)
Animal Crackers, 1930 (Dumont 3, Marx Brothers 3, Green, J. 4, Heerman 4, Ryskind 4)
Animal Farm, 1954 (Halas and Batchelor 2, de Rochemont 4)
Animal Kingdom, 1932 (Cukor 2, Howard, L. 3, Loy 3, Glazer 4, Irene 4, Mandell 4, Selznick 4, Steiner 4)
Animal Vegetable Mineral, 1955 (Halas and Batchelor 2)
Animal Within, 1912 (Dwan 2)
Animal World, 1955 (Harryhausen 4, O'Brien 4)
Animals, 1972 (Wynn 3)
Animals and the Brigands. See Zvířátka a Petrovští, 1946
Animals Film, 1981 (Christie 3)
Animals of Eden and After, 1970 (Brakhage 2)
Animas Trujano, 1961 (Mifune 3, Figueroa 4)
Animated Genesis, 1951 (Foldès 4)
Animated Luncheon, 1900 (Porter 2)
Animated Matches. See Allumettes animées, 1908
Animated Poster, 1903 (Porter 2)
Animaux, 1963 (Jarre 4)
Anita Garibaldi. See Camicie rosse, 1952
Anjangarh, 1948 (Roy 2, Sircar 4)
Anjo-ke no butokai, 1947 (Shindo 2, Yoshimura 2, Hara 3, Mori 3)
Anjou, 1977 (Leenhardt 2)
Anju to Zushio-maru, 1961 (Yamada 3, Yamamura 3)
Anjuta, The Dancer. See Balettprimadonnan, 1916
Ankara, Heart of Turkey. See Ankara—serdche Turkiye, 1934
Ankara—serdche Turkiye, 1934 (Yutkevich 2)
Ankoku-gai, 1956 (Mifune 3)
Ankokugai no kaoyaku, 1959 (Mifune 3)
Ankokugai no taiketsu, 1960 (Mifune 3, Tsukasa 3)
Ankur, 1974 (Benegal 2, Azmi 3, Nihalani 4)
An-Magritt, 1968 (Ullmann 3)
Ann Carver's Profession, 1933 (Wray 3, Riskin 4)
Ann Vickers, 1933 (Dunne 3, Huston 3, Berman 4, Cooper 4, Murfin 4, Plunkett 4, Polglase 4, Steiner 4)

Anna, 1952 (Lattuada 2, Risi 2, Gassman 3, Loren 3, Mangano 3, De Laurentiis 4, Ponti 4, Rota 4)
Anna, 1965 (Karina 3)
Anna, 1970 (Donner 2, Andersson H. 3)
Anna. See Anuschka, 1955
Anna. See Édes Anna, 1958
Anna and the King of Siam, 1946 (Cromwell 2, Cobb 3, Darnell 3, Dunne 3, Harrison 3, Day 4, Herrmann 4, Jennings 4, Miller, A. 4, Wheeler 4)
Anna Ascends, 1922 (Fleming 2, Brady 3)
Anna Boleyn, 1920 (Lubitsch 2, Jannings 3, Porten 3, Kraly 4, Messter 4)
Anna Christie, 1923 (Sweet 3, Ince 4)
Anna Christie, 1930 (Brown 2, Feyder 2, Florey 2, Dressler 3, Garbo 3, Adrian 4, Daniels 4, Day 4, Gibbons 4, Marion 4, Shearer 4, Thalberg 4)
Anna di Brooklyn, 1958 (De Sica 2, Lollobrigida 3)
Anna i komandor, 1974 (Smoktunovsky 3)
Anna Karenina, 1927 (Gibbons 4)
Anna Karenina, 1935 (Brown 2, Von Stroheim 2, Garbo 3, March 3, O'Sullivan 3, Rathbone 3, Adrian 4, Behrman 4, Daniels 4, Gibbons 4, Levien 4, Selznick 4, Stothart 4)
Anna Karenina, 1948 (Duvivier 2, Cervi 3, Leigh, V. 3, Richardson 3, Alekan 4, Andrejew 4, Beaton 4)
Anna Karenina, 1968 (Samoilova 3)
Anna Karenina. See Love, 1927
Anna Karénine. See Anna Karenina, 1948
Anna la bonne, 1959 (Cocteau 2, Jutra 2)
Anna Lucasta, 1949 (Crawford, B. 3, Goddard 3, Homolka 3, Ireland 3, Cahn 4, Polito 4)
Anna Lucasta, 1958 (Ballard 4, Bernstein 4)
Anna the Adventuress, 1920 (Hepworth 2, Colman 3)
Annabel Takes a Tour, 1939 (Ball 3)
Annabelle Lee, 1972 (O'Brien, M. 3)
Annabelle's Affairs, 1931 (Beavers 3, MacDonald 3, McLaglen 3, Clarke, C.C. 4)
Annabel's Romance, 1916 (White 3)
Annapolis, 1928 (Bosworth 3, Miller, A. 4)
Annapolis Farewell, 1935 (Beavers 3)
Annapolis Salute, 1937 (Carey 3, Heflin 3)
Annapolis Story, 1955 (Siegel 2, Mirisch 4)
Anna-Clara och hennes broder, 1923 (Borgstrom 3)
Anne Against the World, 1929 (Karloff 3)
Anne and Muriel. See Deux Anglaises et le continent, 1971
Anne of Green Gables, 1919 (Hackett 4, Marion 4)
Anne of Green Gables, 1934 (MacGowan 4, Plunkett 4, Steiner 4)
Anne of the Golden Heart, 1914 (Daniels 3)
Anne of the Indies, 1951 (Tourneur, J. 2, Jourdan 3, Marshall 3, Dunne 4, Lemaire 4, Waxman 4, Wheeler 4)
Anne of the Thousand Days, 1969 (Bujold 3, Burton 3, Papas 3, Quayle 3, Taylor, E. 3, Delerue 4, Wallis 4)
Anne of Windy Poplars, 1940 (Summerville 3)
Anneau fatal, 1912 (Feuillade 2)
Anneaux d'or, 1956 (Cardinale 3)
Année dernière à Marienbad, 1961 (Resnais 2, Seyrig 3, Colpi 4, Evein 4, Robbe-Grillet 4, Vierny 4)
Année prochaine si tout va bien, 1981 (Adjani 3)
Année sainte, 1976 (Darrieux 3, Gabin 3)
Année se meurt, 1951 (Fradetal 4)
Années 80, 1983 (Akerman 2)
Années lumières. See Light Years Away, 1981
Annelie, 1941 (Krauss 3, Von Harbou 4)
Anne-Marie, 1936 (D'Eaubonne 4, Honegger 4, Ibert 4)
Anni difficili, 1948 (Zampa 2, Amidei 4)
Anni facili, 1953 (Zampa 2, Amidei 4, De Laurentiis 4, Gherardi 4, Ponti 4, Rota 4)
Anni più belli. See Giorni più belli, 1956
Anni ruggenti, 1962 (Scola 2, Cervi 3, Manfredi 3, Amidei 4)
Annibale, 1960 (Mature 3)
Annie, 1982 (Huston 2, Finney 3, Booth 4, Stark 4)
Annie Bell. See Merke Punkt, 1911

Annie Get Your Gun, 1950 (Sidney 2, Calhern 3, Hutton 3, Keel 3, Wynn 3, Alton, R. 4, Deutsch 4, Edens 4, Freed 4, Gibbons 4, Plunkett 4, Rose 4, Rose 4, Rosher 4)

Annie Hall, 1977 (Allen 2, Duvall, S. 3, Keaton 3, Rosenblum 4, Willis 4)

Annie Laurie, 1916 (Hepworth 2)

Annie Laurie, 1927 (Bosworth 3, Gish, L. 3, Gibbons 4)

Annie Moved Away, 1934 (Lantz 4)

Annie Oakley, 1935 (Stevens 2, Douglas, M. 3, Stanwyck 3, Hunt 4, Plunkett 4, Polglase 4)

Anniversary, 1963 (Pidgeon 3)

Anniversary, 1968 (Davis 3, Sangster 4)

Anniversary of the Revolution. See Godovshchina revoliutsiya, 1919

Anniversary Trouble, 1935 (Roach 4)

Anno Domini 1573. See Seljačka buna 1573, 1975

Anno uno, 1975 (Rossellini 2)

Ano hashi no tamoto de, Part III: Ano hito was ima, 1963 (Yamamura 3)

Ano hata oute, 1944 (Hayasaka 4, Tsuburaya 4)

Ano kumo no hate ni hoshi wa matataku, 1962 (Yamamura 3)

Ano nami no hate made, 1961 (Iwashita 3)

Año Siete, 1966 (Alvarez 2)

Ano te kono te, 1952 (Ichikawa 2)

Ano uno, 1972 (Gomez, S. 2)

Anohito wa ima, 1963 (Iwashita 3)

Anokha bandhan, 1982 (Azmi 3)

Anokha Pyar, 1948 (Biswas 4)

Anónimo, 1966 (Alvarez 2)

Anonyme, 1957 (Alexeieff and Parker 2)

Anonymes du ciel, 1951 (Kosma 4)

Anote konote, 1952 (Mori 3)

Another Air. See Jiný vzduch, 1939

Another Bottle, Doctor, 1926 (Fleischer, M. and D. 2)

Another Chance, 1914 (Reid 3)

Another Dawn, 1937 (Dieterle 2, Flynn 3, Francis, K. 3, Brown, Harry Joe 4, Friedhofer 4, Gaudio 4, Korngold 4, Orry-Kelly 4)

Another Face, 1935 (McDaniel 3, Plunkett 4)

Another Fine Mess, 1930 (Laurel and Hardy 3)

Another Language, 1933 (Farnum 3, Montgomery 3, Adrian 4, Mankiewicz 4, Stewart 4, Wanger 4)

Another Man, Another Chance, 1977 (Lelouch 2)

Another Man, Another Chance. See Autre Homme, une autre chance, 1977

Another Man's Poison, 1951 (Davis 3, Fairbanks, D. Jr. 3, Krasker 4)

Another Man's Wife, 1913 (Dwan 2)

Another Man's Wife, 1924 (Beery 3)

Another Part of the Forest, 1948 (Duryea 3, March 3, O'Brien, E. 3, Boyle 4)

Another Shore, 1948 (Crichton 2, Holloway 3, Auric 4, Balcon 4, Slocombe 4)

Another Sky, 1955 (Lassally 4)

Another Thin Man, 1939 (Van Dyke, W.S. 2, Loy 3, Powell, W. 3, Daniels 4, Gibbons 4, Goodrich and Hackett 4, Stromberg 4)

Another Time, Another Place, 1958 (Connery 3, Turner, L. 3)

Another to Conquer, 1941 (Ulmer 2)

Another Way of Life. See O něčem jiném, 1963

Another Wild Idea, 1934 (Roach 4)

Ansatsu, 1964 (Shinoda 2, Iwashita 3, Okada 3, Takemitsu 4)

Ansichten eines Clowns, 1975 (Schygulla 3, Lassally 4)

Ansiedad, 1952 (Infante 3, Figueroa 4)

Ansigtet. See Stjaalne Ansigt, 1914

Ansikte mot ansikte, 1976 (Bergman 2, Bjornstrand 3, Ullmann 3, Nykvist 4)

Ansiktet, 1958 (Bergman 2, Andersson B. 3, Bjornstrand 3, Thulin 3, Von Sydow 3, Fischer 4)

Answer to Violence. See Zamach, 1958

Ant and the Aardvark, 1968 (Freleng 4)

Ant Pasted, 1952 (Freleng 4)

Antarctica. See Nankyoku monogatari, 1983

Anthony Adverse, 1936 (Leroy 2, De Havilland 3, Gwenn 3, March 3, Rains 3, Blanke 4, Gaudio 4, Grot 4, Korngold 4, Wallis 4)

Anthony and Cleopatra, 1908 (Costello, M. 3)

Anthony of Padua. See Antonio di Padova, 1949

Anthony's Broken Mirror. See Antonijevo razbijeno ogledalo, 1957

Anthropo-cynical Farce, 1970 (Kawamoto 4)

Anti-Cats, 1950 (Terry 4)

Antichrist. See Anticristo, 1974

Anticipation of the Night, 1958 (Brakhage 2)

Anticristo, 1974 (Ferrer, M. 3, Kennedy, A. 3, Valli 3, Morricone 4)

Anti-Darwin. See Co zizala netusila, 1969

Antigone, 1960 (Papas 3)

Antimiracolo, 1965 (Cristaldi 4)

Antinea, 1961 (Trintignant 3, Volonté 3)

Antinea. See Atlantide, 1961

Antionette Sabrier, 1926 (Francis, E. 3)

Antiquités de l'Asie occidentale, 1943 (Honegger 4)

Antoine et Antoinette, 1947 (Becker 2, Modot 3)

Antoinette Sabrier, 1926 (Dulac 2)

Anton der Zauberer, 1978 (Geschonneck 3)

Anton Ivanovic serdisya, 1941 (Ermler 2)

Anton Ivanovich Gets Mad. See Anton Ivanovic serditsya, 1941

Anton the Terrible, 1916 (Rosher 4)

Antonieta, 1982 (Saura 2, Adjani 3)

Antonijevo razbijeno ogledalo, 1957 (Makavejev 2)

Antônio das Mortes, 1969 (Rocha 2)

Antonio di Padova, 1949 (Fabrizi 3)

Antonio Gaudi, 1961 (Russell 2)

Antonio Gaudi, 1985 (Takemitsu 4)

Antonito, 1961 (Finch 3)

Antony and Cleopatra, 1972 (Rey 3)

Ants in His Pants, 1939 (Finch 3, Rafferty 3)

Ants in the Pantry, 1936 (Three Stooges 3)

Ants in the Plants, 1940 (Fleischer, M. and D. 2)

Ants in Your Pantry, 1945 (Terry 4)

Anugraham, 1979 (Patil 3)

Anuraag, 1972 (Burman 4)

Anuradha, 1960 (Shankar 4)

Anuschka, 1955 (Babochkin 3)

Anvil Chorus, 1922 (Roach 4)

Anwalt des Herzens, 1927 (Dagover 3)

Anxiety. See Endise, 1974

Anxious Years. See Dark Journey, 1937

Any Bonds Today, 1942 (Clampett 4)

Any Little Girl That's a Nice Little Girl, 1931 (Fleischer, M. and D. 2)

Any Man's Wife. See Michael O'Halloran, 1937

Any Night, 1922 (Anderson G. 3)

Any Number Can Play, 1949 (Brooks, R. 2, Leroy 2, Astor 3, Gable 3, Stone 3, Freed 4, Rosson 4)

Any Number Can Win. See Melodie en sous-sol, 1962

Any Old Port, 1920 (Roach 4)

Any Old Port, 1932 (Laurel & Hardy 3)

Any Rags, 1932 (Fleischer, M. and D. 2)

Any Second Now, 1969 (Granger 3)

Any Temporary Father. See Moj tata na otredjeno vreme, 1983

Any Wednesday, 1966 (Fonda, J. 3, Robards 3, Duning 4, Epstein, J. & P. 4, Jeakins 4)

Any Which Way You Can, 1980 (Eastwood 3, Gordon 3)

Any Wife, 1922, (Brenon 2)

Any Woman, 1925 (King 2, Furthman 4, Haller 4)

Any Woman's Choice, 1914 (Bushman 3)

Anya és leánya, 1981 (Mészáros 2)

Anybody Here Seen Kelly, 1928 (Wyler 2)

Anybody's Blonde, 1931 (Walthall 3)

Anybody's Goat, 1932 (Arbuckle 3)

Anybody's Woman, 1930 (Arzner 2, Brook 3, Lukas 3, Akins 4, Lang 4)

Anyone Can Kill Me. See Tous peuvent me tuer, 1957

Anyone Can Play. See Dolci signori, 1967

Anything Can Happen, 1952 (Seaton 2, Ferrer, J. 3, Head 4, Young, V. 4)

Anything Goes, 1936 (Milestone 2, Carradine 3, Crosby 3, Dumont 3, Lupino 3, Wyman 3, Carmichael 4, Dreier 4, Glazer 4, Struss 4, Young, V. 4)

Anything Goes, 1955 (Crosby 3, O'Connor 3, Cahn 4, Head 4)

Anything Once, 1917 (Chaney Lon 3)

Anything Once, 1927 (Normand 3)

Anzio, 1968 (Mitchum 3)
Anzio. *See* Sbarco di Anzio, 1968
Anzukko, 1958 (Naruse 2, Kagawa 3, Yamamura 3)
Aoba-jo no oni, 1962 (Hasegawa 3)
Aogashima no kodomotachi, 1955 (Kagawa 3)
Aoi me, 1956 (Tsukasa 3, Muraki 4)
Aoi sanmyaku, 1949 (Imai 2, Hara 3)
Aoi sanmyaku: enpen, 1957 (Tsukasa 3)
Aoi yaju, 1960 (Tsukasa 3)
Aoiro kakumei, 1953 (Ichikawa 2)
Aos, 1964 (Kuri 4)
Aozora ni naku, 1932 (Naruse 2)
Aozora roshi, 1936 (Yamada 3)
Apa, 1966 (Szabó 2, Gabór 3, Madaras 3)
Apache, 1928 (Johnson, N. 3)
Apache, 1954 (Aldrich 2, Bronson 3, Lancaster 3, Laszlo 4, Raksin 4)
Apache Country, 1952 (Autry 3, Bushman 3)
Apache Drums, 1951 (Muse 3, Lewton 4, Salter 4)
Apache Rifles, 1964 (Murphy 3)
Apache Rose, 1947 (Rogers, R. 3)
Apache Trail, 1942 (Reed, D. 3, Schary 4)
Apache Uprising, 1966 (Arlen 3, Chaney Lon, Jr. 3)
Apache War Smoke, 1952 (Alton, J. 4)
Apache Woman, 1955 (Corman 4, Crosby 4)
Apache's Gratitude, 1913 (Mix 3)
Apachen, 1919 (Dupont 2)
Apachen von Paris. *See* Apachenliebe, 1928
Apachenliebe, 1928 (Dieterle 2)
Apachentanz, 1906 (Porten 3, Messter 4)
Apaches pas veinards, 1903 (Guy 2)
Apám néhány boldog éve, 1977 (Madaras 3)
Aparadhi Kaun, 1957 (Roy 2)
Aparajito, 1956 (Ray, S. 2, Chandragupta 4, Datta 4, Mitra 4, Shankar 4)
Apart from You. *See* Kimi to wakarete, 1933
Apartment, 1960 (Wilder 2, Lemmon 3, MacLaine 3, MacMurray 3, Deutsch 4, Diamond 4, La Shelle 4, Mandell 4, Trauner 4)
Apartment for Peggy, 1948 (Seaton 2, Crain 3, Gwenn 3, Holden 3, Lemaire 4, Raksin 4)
Ape, 1940 (Karloff 3, Siodmak 4)
Ape and Super Ape. *See* Bij de beesten af, 1972
Ape Man, 1943 (Lugosi 3, Brown, K. 4, Katzman 4)
Ape regina, the Conjugal Bed. *See* Storia moderna, 1963
Ape Woman. *See* Donna scimmia, 1964
Apes of Wrath, 1959 (Freleng 4)
Apna Haath Jaganath, 1960 (Burman 4)
Apna Paraya, 1942 (Biswas 4)
Apne paraye, 1980 (Azmi 3)
Apocalisse sull fiume giallo. *See* Herrin der Welt, 1960
Apocalypse des animaux, 1973 (Vangelis 4)
Apocalypse Now, 1979 (Coppola 2, Milius 2, Brando 3, Duvall, R. 3, Ford, H. 3, Forrest 3, Hopper 3, Sheen 3, Storaro 4, Tavoularis 4)
Apokalypse, 1918 (Reiniger 2)
Apólogo, 1939 (Mauro 2)
Apostasy. *See* Hakai, 1948
Apostle of Vengeance, 1916 (Gilbert 3, Hart 3, August 4)
Apothecary. *See* Medikus, 1916
Appaloosa, 1966 (Fernández 2, Brando 3)
Appare binanshi, 1928 (Tanaka 3)
Appare Isshin Tasuke, 1945 (Kurosawa 2)
Apparences, 1964 (Delerue 4)
Apparition. *See* Revenant, 1903
Apparitions fugitives, 1904 (Méliès 2)
Apparizione, 1943 (Fellini 2, Valli 3)
Appassionata, 1944 (Bjornstrand 3, Borgstrom 3)
Appassionata, 1974 (Cortese 3)
Appassionata. *See* Taková láska, 1959
Appât. *See* Koder, 1975
Appearances, 1921 (Hitchcock 2, Crisp 3)
Appel de la nuit. *See* Voix du métal, 1933
Appel du sang, 1920 (Novello 3)
Appelez-moi Mathilde, 1968 (Blier 3)
Appelkriget, 1971 (Von Sydow 3)

Appetit d'oiseau, 1964 (Foldès 4)
Applause, 1929 (Mamoulian 2, Fort 4, Ruttenberg 4, Wanger 4)
Apple, 1962 (Dunning 4)
Apple, 1963 (Dinov 4)
Apple, 1980 (Golan and Globus 4)
Apple Dumpling Gang Rides Again, 1979 (Elam 3)
Apple Game, 1977 (Chytilová 2, Menzel 2)
Apple Tree Maiden. *See* Jabloňová panna, 1974
Apple Tree with Golden Apples. *See* Jabluňka se zlatými jablky, 1952
Apple War. *See* Appelkriget, 1971
Apples and Oranges, 1962 (Bass 4)
Apples to You!, 1934 (Roach 4)
Apple-Tree Girl, 1917 (Crosland 2)
Appointment, 1969 (Lumet 2, Aimée 3, Sharif 3, Barry 4, Gherardi 4)
Appointment for Love, 1941 (Boyer 3, Sullavan 3)
Appointment in Berlin, 1943 (Sanders 3, Planer 4)
Appointment in Honduras, 1953 (Tourneur, J. 2, Elam 3, Ford, G. 3, Sheridan 3, Biroc 4)
Appointment in London, 1952 (Bogarde 3)
Appointment with a Shadow, 1957 (Salter 4)
Appointment with a Shadow. *See* Midnight Story, 1957
Appointment with Danger, 1951 (Ladd 3, Dreier 4, Seitz 4, Young, V. 4)
Appointment with Venus, 1951 (More 3, Niven 3)
Apprenez à soulever une charge, 1949 (Decaë 4)
Apprenticeship of Duddy Kravitz, 1974 (Dreyfuss 3, Warden 3)
Apprentis, 1964 (Tanner 2)
Apprentis sorciers, 1977 (Hopper 3)
Apprezzato professionista di sicuro avvenire, 1972 (De Santis 2)
Approach of Autumn. *See* Aki tachinu, 1960
Approach to Science, 1947 (Alwyn 4)
Appuntamente col disonore, 1970 (Kinski 3, Sanders 3)
Appuntamento per le spie, 1965 (Andrews D. 3)
Appunti per un film indiano, 1969 (Pasolini 2)
Appunti per una Orestiade africana, 1969 (Pasolini 2)
Appunti su un fatto di cronaca, 1951 (Visconti 2)
Apres l'amour, 1947 (Tourneur, M. 2)
Après l'orage, 1942 (Berry 3)
Après le bal, 1897 (Méliès 2)
Après le vent des sables, 1974 (Lassally 4)
April, 1961 (Ioseliani 2)
April, April. *See* 't Was een April, 1935
April Folly, 1920 (Davies 3)
April Fool, 1924 (Roach 4)
April Fools, 1969 (Boyer 3, Deneuve 3, Loy 3, Sylbert 4)
April in Paris, 1952 (Dauphin 3, Day 3, Cahn 4, Prinz 4)
April in Portugal, 1954 (Howard, T. 3)
April Love, 1957 (Jones S. 3, Lemaire 4, Newman 4)
April Showers, 1923 (Moore, C. 3, Schulberg 4)
April Showers, 1926 (Jolson 3)
April Showers, 1948 (Sakall 3, Sothern 3, Prinz 4)
Apunte sobre Ana, 1971 (García Berlanga 2)
Apur Sansar, 1959 (Ray, S. 2, Chatterjee 3, Chandragupta 4, Datta 4, Mitra 4, Shankar 4)
Aqua, 1960 (Almendros 4)
Aqua Duck, 1963 (McKimson 4)
Aquarians, 1970 (Ferrer, J. 3, Schifrin 4)
Aquarien, 1974 (Brakhage 3)
Aquarium, 1895 (Lumière 2)
Aquasex. *See* Mermaids of Tiburon, 1961
Aquella casa en las afueras, 1980 (Valli 3)
Aquí está Heraclio Bernal, 1957 (Figueroa 4)
Aqui llegó el valenton, 1938 (Negrete 3)
Aquila Nera, 1946 (Monicelli 2, Brazzi 3, Cervi 3, Lollobrigida 3)
Ar aldrig for sent, 1956 (Bjornstrand 3)
Ar med Henry, 1967 (Roos 2)
Ara nonkida ne, 1926 (Tanaka 3)
Arab, 1915 (DeMille 2, Buckland 4)
Arab, 1924 (Ingram 2, Novarro 3, Seitz 4)
Arabe. *See* Arab, 1924
Arabella, 1916 (Negri 3)
Arabella, 1924 (Marsh 3, Rasp 3, Metzner 4)

Arabella, 1967 (Bolognini 2, Giannini 3, Marsh 3, Rutherford 3, Morricone 4)
Arabesque, 1966 (Donen 2, Loren 3, Peck 3, Mancini 4)
Arabian Adventure, 1979 (Cushing 3, Lee, C. 3, Rooney 3)
Arabian Bazaar, 1937–40 (Cardiff 4)
Arabian Jewish Dance, 1903 (Porter 2)
Arabian Knight, 1920 (Hayakawa 3)
Arabian Love, 1922 (Gilbert 3, August 4, Furthman 4)
Arabian Nights, 1942 (Howard, S. 3, Krasner 4, Wanger 4)
Arabian Tights, 1933 (Roach 4)
Arabian Tragedy, 1912 (Olcott 2)
Arabics, from 1980 (Brakhage 2)
Arabie interdite, 1937 (Clément 2)
Arab's Bride, 1912 (Cruze 2)
Aradhana, 1969 (Burman 4)
Araignées rouges, 1955 (Rabier 4)
Arakawa no Sakichi, 1936 (Hasegawa 3)
Araki Mataemon, 1931 (Yamada 3)
Araki Mataemon, 1955 (Yamada 3)
Arakure daimyo, 1960 (Kagawa 3)
Arakure, 1957 (Naruse 2, Mori 3, Takamine 3)
Aranyak, 1963 (Ghatak 4)
Aranyar din Ratri, 1970 (Chatterjee 3)
Aranyáso, 1914 (Curtiz 2)
Aranyember, 1918 (Korda 2)
Aranyember, 1962 (Latinovits 3)
Aranyer Din Ratri, 1970 (Ray, S. 2, Chandragupta 4, Datta 4)
Aranyfey, 1963 (Darvas 3)
Arashi, 1956 (Tanaka 3)
Arashi nisaku hana, 1940 (Yamada 3)
Arashi no naka no haha, 1952 (Kagawa 3)
Arashi no naka no otoko, 1957 (Kagawa 3, Mifune 3)
Arat az Oroszházi Dözsa, 1953 (Jancsó 2)
Arbeitstag, 1965 (Zavattini 4)
Arbejdet kalder, 1941 (Henning-Jensen 2)
Arboles de Buenos-Aires, 1957 (Torre-Nilsson 2)
Arbor Day, 1936 (Krasner 4, Roach 4)
Arbre de Noël, 1969 (Alekan 4)
Arbre de Noël. See Albero di natale, 1969
Arbres aux champignons, 1951 (Markopoulos 2)
Arc, 1970 (Madaras 3)
Arcadian Maid, 1910 (Griffith 2, Sennett 2, Pickford 3, Bitzer 4)
Arcadians, 1927 (Saville 2)
Arcangelo, 1969 (Gassman 3)
Arch of Triumph, 1948 (Aldrich 2, Milestone 2, Bergman 3, Boyer 3, Calhern 3, Laughton 3, Alekan 4, Brown, Harry 4, Head 4, Menzies 4)
Arch of Triumph, 1985 (Hopkins, A. 3, Pleasance 3)
Archanděl Gabriel a paní Husa, 1964 (Trnka 2)
Archangel Gabriel and Mistress Goose. See Archanděl Gabriel a paní Husa, 1964
Arche, 1919 (Oswald 2, Freund 4)
Arche de Noé, 1946 (Brasseur 3, Kosma 4, Prévert 4)
Arche de Noé, 1967 (Grimault 4, Laguionie 4)
Archer and the Sorceress, 1981 (Kennedy, G. 3)
Archer: Fugitive From the Empire, 1981 (Kennedy, G. 3)
Archimède le clochard, 1959 (Blier 3, Gabin 3, Audiard 4)
Archipel des amours, 1982 (Fabian 3)
Architects of England, 1941 (Alwyn 4)
Architectural Millinery, 1954 (Peterson 2)
Architecture, art de l'espace, 1961 (Barrault 3)
Architecture de lumière, 1953 (Colpi 4)
Architecture et chauffage d'aujourd'hui, 1960 (Delerue 4)
Architecture of Entertainment, 1960 (Russell 2)
Arcidiavolo, 1966 (Scola 2, Gassman 3)
Arctic Rivals, 1954 (Terry 4)
Ard, 1969 (Chahine 2)
Ard el Salam, 1955 (Sharif 3)
Ardha Satya, 1983 (Patil 3, Nihalani 4)
Arditi civili, 1940 (Amidei 4)
Are Blond Men Bashful?, 1924 (Roach 4)
Are Brunettes Safe?, 1927 (Roach 4)
Are Crooks Dishonest?, 1918 (Daniels 3, Lloyd 3, Roach 4)

Are ga minato no hikari da, 1961 (Imai 2)
Are ga minato no tomoshibi da, 1961 (Kishida 3, Yamamura 3)
Are Husbands Human?, 1925 (Roach 4)
Are Husbands Necessary?, 1942 (Taurog 2, Milland 3, Head 4, Lang 4)
Are Parents People?, 1925 (Menjou 3, Glennon 4)
Are Parents Pickles?, 1925 (Roach 4)
Are These Our Children?, 1931 (Ruggles 2, Steiner 4)
Are These Our Children? See Age of Consent, 1932
Are Waitresses Safe?, 1917 (Sennett 2)
Are We Civilized?, 1934 (Farnum 3)
Are Witnesses Safe?, 1917 (Summerville 3)
Are Women to Blame?, 1928 (Negri 3)
Are You a Failure?, 1923 (Lang 4, Schulberg 4)
Are You a Mason?, 1915 (Barrymore J. 3)
Are You Afraid. See Er i bange, 1971
Are You Legally Married?, 1919 (Polito 4)
Are You Listening?, 1932 (Hersholt 3, Rosson 4)
Are You with It?, 1948 (O'Connor 3)
Aren't We All, 1932 (Oberon 3)
Arena, 1953 (Fleischer, R. 2, Van Cleef 3, Young, G. 3)
Arena, 1973 (Corman 4)
Arendás zsidó, 1917 (Curtiz 2)
Arènes joyeuses, 1935 (Stradling 4)
Argent, 1928 (L'Herbier 2, Artaud 3, Berry 3, Meerson 4)
Argent, 1936 (Matras 4)
Argent, 1983 (Bresson 2)
Argent de poche, 1976 (Truffaut 2)
Argent des autres, 1978 (Deneuve 3, Trintignant 3)
Argentine Love, 1924 (Dwan 2, Daniels 3, Hunt 4)
Argentine Nights, 1940 (Cahn 4)
Argila, 1940 (Mauro 2)
Argine, 1938 (Cervi 3, Vích 4)
Argyle Case, 1929 (Pitts 3)
Ari no Machi no Maria, 1958 (Gosho 2)
Aria dla atlety, 1979 (Pszoniak 3)
Ariane, 1931 (Czinner 2, Bergner 3, Mayer 4)
Arie prérie, 1949 (Trnka 2, Brdečka 4)
Arise My Love, 1940 (Leisen 2, Wilder 2, Colbert 3, Milland 3, Brackett, C. 4, Dreier 4, Glazer 4, Head 4, Irene 4, Lang 4, Young, V. 4)
Aristo, 1934 (D'Eaubonne 4)
Aristo Cat, 1943 (Jones 2)
Aristocats, 1970 (Chevalier 3)
Aristocrates, 1955 (Fresnay 3)
Aristocrat's Stairs. See Kizoku no kaidan, 1959
Arizona, 1919 (Fairbanks, D. 3)
Arizona, 1940 (Ruggles 2, Arthur 3, Holden 3, Walker 4, Young, V. 4)
Arizona. See Men Are Like That, 1931
Arizona Bound, 1927 (Cooper, Gary 3)
Arizona Bushwhackers, 1968 (Cagney 3, De Carlo 3, Ireland 3, Keel 3)
Arizona Cyclone, 1941 (Salter 4)
Arizona Escapade, 1912 (Anderson G. 3)
Arizona Kid, 1930 (Baxter W. 3, Lombard 3)
Arizona Kid, 1939 (Rogers, R. 3)
Arizona Mahoney, 1936 (Crabbe 3, Cummings 3, Head 4)
Arizona Mission. See Gun the Man Down, 1956
Arizona Raiders, 1936 (Crabbe 3)
Arizona Raiders, 1965 (Murphy 3)
Arizona Ranger, 1948 (Hunt 4)
Arizona Slim, 1975 (De Carlo 3)
Arizona to Broadway, 1933 (Bennett J. 3)
Arizona Trail, 1943 (Salter 4)
Arizona Wildcat, 1927 (Mix 3)
Arizona Wooing, 1915 (Mix 3)
Arizonian, 1935 (Vidor, C. 2, Calhern 3, Nichols 4, Plunkett 4)
Arjun Pandit, 1976 (Burman 4)
Arjun Sardar, 1958 (Ghatak 4)
Arkadas, 1974 (Guney 2)
Arkansas Judge, 1941 (Rogers, R. 3, Lardner 4)
Arkansas Traveler, 1938 (Bainter 3, Dreier 4, Head 4)
Arlésienne, 1922 (Duvivier 2, Burel 4)
Arlésienne, 1930 (Vanel 3)
Arlésienne, 1942 (Allégret, M. 2, Jourdan 3, Raimu 3, Achard 4)

Arlette et ses papas, 1933 (Berry 3)
Arm Drenthe, 1929–30 (Ivens 2)
Arm of the Law, 1932 (O'Brien, P. 3)
Arm of Vengeance, 1914 (Anderson G. 3)
Arm wie eine Kirchenmaus, 1931 (Oswald 2)
Arma, 1978 (Cardinale 3)
Arma dei vigliacchi, 1913 (Bertini 3)
Armageddon, 1977 (Delon 3)
Arman, 1953 (Anand 3, Burman 4)
Armand and Michaela Denis series, 1955 (Balcon 4)
Armata assura, 1932 (Cervi 3)
Armata Brancaleone, 1966 (Monicelli 2, Gassman 3, Volonté 3, Age
    and Scarpelli 4, Gherardi 4)
Arme à gauche, 1965 (Sautet 2)
Arme Eva. See Frau Eva, 1915
Arme Jenny, 1912 (Gad 2, Nielsen 3)
Arme kleine Sif, 1927 (Wegener 3)
Arme Marie, 1914 (Lubitsch 2, Wiene 2)
Arme Sunderin, 1923 (Kortner 3)
Arme Violetta, 1920 (Negri 3, Kraly 4, Wagner 4)
Armed Intervention, 1913 (Eason 4)
Armed Nation. See Pueblos en armas, 1961
Armed Police Force. See Busou keikantai, 1948
Armée d'Agenor, 1909 (Cohl 2)
Armée des ombres, 1969 (Melville 2, Cassel 3, Reggiani 3, Signoret 3)
Armée populaire arme le peuple, 1969 (Ivens 2)
Armes kleines Madchen, 1924 (Kortner 3)
Armistice, 1929 (Balcon 4)
Armoire, 1969 (Braunberger 4)
Armoire volante, 1948 (Fernandel 3, Modot 3)
Armonie pucciniane, 1938 (Fusco 4)
Armored Attack. See North Star, 1943
Armored Car, 1937 (Cortez 4)
Armored Car Robbery, 1950 (Fleischer, R. 2)
Armored Command, 1961 (Keel 3, Reynolds, B. 3, Haller 4)
Armored Vault. See Panzergewoble, 1926
Arms and the Girl, 1917 (Burke 3)
Arms and the Gringo, 1914 (Gish, D. 3, Reid 3)
Arms and the Man. See Helden, 1959
Arms and the Woman, 1916 (Grot 4, Miller, A. 4)
Arms and the Woman. See Mr. Winkle Goes to War,
    1944
Armstrong's Wife, 1915 (Cruze 2)
Army. See Rikugun, 1944
Army Girl, 1938 (Eason 4, Young, V. 4)
Army Surgeon, 1912 (Sullivan 4)
Army Surgeon, 1942 (Sutherland 2)
Arnaud, 1967 (Bourvil 3)
Arnelo Affair, 1947 (Arden 3, Irene 4)
Arnold, 1974 (Lanchester 3, McDowall 3, Duning 4)
Arnulf Rainer, 1958–60 (Kubelka 2)
Arohan, 1982 (Benegal 2)
Aroma of the South Seas, 1931 (Balcon 4)
Around is Around, 1950–51 (McLaren 2)
Around Sennichimae. See Sennichimae fukin, 1945
Around the Corner, 1930 (Glennon 4, Walker 4)
Around the World, 1931 (Terry 4)
Around the World, 1943 (Dwan 2, Auer 3)
Around the World, 1967 (Kapoor 2)
Around the World in Eighteen Days, 1923 (Eason 4)
Around the World in 80 Days. See Reise um die Erde in 80 Tagen, 1919
Around the World in 80 Days, 1956 (Keaton 2, Boyer 3, Brown 3,
    Cantinflas 3, Carradine 3, Coburn, C. 3, Colman 3, Dietrich 3,
    Fernandel 3, Gielgud 3, Hardwicke 3, Howard, T. 3, Lorre 3,
    MacLaine 3, McLaglen 3, Mills 3, Niven 3, Raft 3, Sinatra 3,
    Adam 4, Bass 4, Coward 4, Menzies 4, Young, V. 4)
Around the World in Eighty Minutes with Douglas Fairbanks, 1931
    (Fleming 2, Fairbanks, D. 3, Newman 4, Sherwood 4)
Around the World under the Sea, 1966 (Wynn 3)
Around the World with Orson, 1956 (Constantine 3)
Arouse and Beware. See Man from Dakota, 1940
Arousers. See Sweet Kill, 1972
Arrah-na-Pogue, 1911 (Olcott 2)

Arrangement, 1969 (Kazan 2, Boone 3, Douglas, K. 3, Dunaway 3,
    Kerr 3, Surtees 4, van Runkle 4, Westmore, P. 4)
Arrangiatevi!, 1959 (Bolognini 2)
Arrest Bulldog Drummond, 1939 (Dreier 4, Head 4)
Arrêtez les tambours, 1961 (Blier 3, Delerue 4)
Arriba las mujeres, 1943 (Infante 3)
'Arriet's Baby, 1913 (Talmadge, N. 3)
Arrivano i dollari!, 1957 (Sordi 3)
Arrivano i nostri, 1951 (Age and Scarpelli 4)
Arrivano i Titani, 1962 (Cristaldi 4)
Arrivederci, Baby, 1966 (Auer 3, Curtis 3)
Arrivederci, Baby. See Drop Dead, Darling, 1966
Arrivederci, Papà!, 1948 (Rota 4, Vích 4)
Arrivée d'un bateau à vapeur, 1896-97 (Lumière 2)
Arrivée d'un train à La Ciotat, 1895 (Lumière 2)
Arrivée d'un train en gare de La Ciotat, 1936 (Lumière 2)
Arrivista, 1913 (Bertini 3)
Arrivistes, 1959 (Barsacq 4)
Arrivistes. See Trube Wasser, 1959
Arroseur arrosé, 1897–98 (Guy 2)
Arroseur Arrose, 1974 (Le Grice 2)
Arroseur arrosé, 1895 (Lumière 2)
Arrow in the Dust, 1954 (Cody 3, Hayden 3, Van Cleef 3)
Arrowhead, 1953 (Cody 3, Heston 3, Palance 3, Head 4)
Arrowsmith, 1931 (Ford, J. 2, Bondi 3, Colman 3, Loy 3, Day 4,
    Goldwyn 4, Howard 4, Newman 4)
Arruza, 1971 (Boetticher 2, Quinn 3, Ballard 4)
Ars, 1959 (Demy 2)
Ars Amandi. See Art d'aimer, 1983
Ars Gratia Artis, 1970 (Vukotić 4)
Arsén Lupin utolsó kalandja, 1921 (Fejos 2)
Arsenal, 1929 (Dovzhenko 2)
Arsenal Stadium Mystery, 1939 (Dickinson 2)
Arsenal: The January Uprising in Kiev in 1918. See Arsenal, 1929
Arsene Lupin, 1932 (Auer 3, Barrymore J. 3, Barrymore L. 3,
    Adrian 4, Coffee 4, Wilson, C. 4)
Arsène Lupin contre Arsène Lupin, 1962 (Cassel 3)
Arsène Lupin, detective, 1937 (Berry 3, Fradetal 4)
Arsène Lupin et la toison d'or, 1959 (Valli 3)
Arsene Lupin Returns, 1938 (Douglas, M. 3, Gibbons 4, Waxman 4)
Arsenic and Old Lace, 1944 (Capra 2, Grant, C. 3, Horton 3, Lorre 3,
    Massey 3, Epstein, J. & P. 4, Friedhofer 4, Mandell 4, Orry-
    Kelly 4, Polito 4, Steiner 4)
Art d'aimer, 1983 (Borowczyk 4)
Art d'être courtier, 1947–51 (Verneuil 2)
Art d'etre Papa, 1956 (Fernandel 3)
Art de la turlutte, 1969 (Braunberger 4)
Art de vivre, 1961 (Fabian 3)
Art Director, 1948 (Wheeler 4)
Art of Crime, 1975 (Clayburgh 3, Ferrer, J. 3)
Art of Love, 1965 (Jewison 2, Dickinson 3, Hunter 4)
Art of Love. See Prinzessin Olala, 1928
Art of Revival. See Eladás müvészete, 1960
Art of Salesmanship. See Eladás müvészete, 1960
Art of the English Craftsman, 1933 (Flaherty 2)
Art of Vision, 1965 (Brakhage 2)
Art pour l'art, 1965 (Godfrey 4)
Art Scene USA, 1966 (Emshwiller 2)
Art Versus Music, 1911 (Lawrence 3)
Art Works one: Academic Still Life, 1977 (Le Grice 2)
Art Works two: Time and Motion Study, 1977 (Le Grice 2)
Artamonov Affair. See Delo Artamonovykh, 1941
Arte del tobaco, 1974 (Gutiérrez 2)
Arte di arrangiarsi, 1954 (Zampa 2, Sordi 3)
Arte e realtà, 1950 (Delli Colli 4)
Arte in Sicilia, 1948 (Fusco 4)
Arteres de France, 1939 (Epstein 2)
Artesania popular, 1966 (Guzmán 2)
Artful Kate, 1911 (Pickford 3, Gaudio 4, Ince 4)
Arth, 1983 (Azmi 3, Patil 3)
Arthur, 1959 (Hitchcock 2)
Arthur, 1981 (Gielgud 3, Minnelli 3, Moore, D. 3)

Arthur Arthur, 1969 (Pleasance 3, Winters 3)
Arthur Honegger, 1955 (Demy 2)
Arthur Miller on Home Ground, 1979 (Cobb 3, Dunaway 3, Lancaster 3, Robinson, E. 3, Scott, G. 3)
Arthur Penn, 1970 (Bancroft 3, Hoffman 3)
Arthur Penn Films 'Little Big Man', 1970 (Hoffman 3)
Arthur Rubinstein, l'amour de la vie, 1968 (Reichenbach 2)
Arthur Rubinstein, 1979 (Reichenbach 2)
Arthur's Island. See Isola di Arturo, 1962
Article 330, 1934 (Pagnol 2)
Article 55, 1952 (Ferrer, J. 3)
Artifices, 1963 (Reichenbach 2, Braunberger 4)
Artificial Light, 1969 (Frampton 2)
Artist, 1918 (Hardy 3)
Artist, 1972 (Wynn 3)
Artist and the Brute, 1913 (Bosworth 3)
Artist's Dream, 1900 (Porter 2)
Artist's Great Madonna, 1913 (Ingram 2)
Artisten in der Zirkuskuppel: Ratlos, 1967 (Kluge 2, Jurgens 3)
Artistes at the Top of the Big Top—Disoriented. See Artisten in der Zirkuskuppel, 1967
Artistic Atmosphere, 1916 (Hardy 3)
Artists and Models, 1915 (Hardy 3)
Artists and Models, 1937 (Walsh 2, Arlen 3, Lupino 3, Meek 3, Banton 4, Dreier 4, Head 4, Prinz 4, Young, V. 4)
Artists and Models, 1955 (Lewis 2, Tashlin 2, Elam 3, MacLaine 3, Malone 3, Martin, D. 3, Edouart 4, Fulton 4, Head 4, Wallis 4)
Artists and Models Abroad, 1938 (Leisen 2, Bennett J. 3, Dreier 4, Head 4, Prinz 4)
Arts and Flowers. See Rodedanska priča, 1969
Arts et arbres, 1978 (Reichenbach 2)
Arturo's Island. See Isola di Arturo, 1962
Artzt von St. Pauli, 1968 (Jurgens 3)
Aru eiga kantoku no shogai, 1975 (Shindo 2, Tanaka 3)
Aru fujinkai no kokuhaku, 1950 (Yoda 4)
Aru kengo no shogai, 1959 (Mifune 3, Tsukasa 3)
Aru koroshiya no kagi, 1967 (Miyagawa 4)
Aru koroshiya, 1967 (Miyagawa 4)
Aru Onna, 1942 (Tanaka 3)
Aru onna, 1954 (Kyo 3, Mori 3)
Aru Osaka no onna, 1962 (Yoda 4)
Aru rakujitsu, 1959 (Mori 3)
Aru sonan, 1961 (Kagawa 3)
Aru to sono no baai, 1956 (Tsukasa 3)
Aru yo no tonosama, 1946 (Kinugasa 2, Hasegawa 3, Takamine 3, Yamada 3)
Aruba, Bonaire, Curazao. See A.B.C., 1958
Aruhi watashi wa, 1959 (Muraki 4)
Arupusu no wakadaisho, 1966 (Tanaka 3)
Aruyo futatabi, 1956 (Gosho 2)
Aruyo no tonosama, 1946 (Shindo 3)
Arvácska, 1975 (Madaras 3)
Aryan, 1916 (Hart 3, Hersholt 3, Love 3, August 4, Sullivan 4)
Arzoo, 1950 (Biswas 4)
Arzt aus Halberstadt, 1969 (Kluge 2)
Arzte, 1962 (Hoffmann 3)
Arztinner, 1984 (Hoppe 3)
As a Father Spareth His Son, 1913 (Bosworth 3)
As a Wife, As a Woman. See Tsuma to shite haha to shite, 1961
As Armas e o Povo, 1975 (de Almeida 4)
As des as, 1982 (Belmondo 3)
As Fate Ordained. See Enoch Arden, 1915
As Good as Married, 1937 (Pidgeon 3, Krasna 4, Raksin 4)
As Husbands Go, 1934 (Baxter W. 3, Oland 3, Behrman 4, Friedhofer 4, Lasky 4, Levien 4)
As in a Looking Glass, 1911 (Griffith 2, Bitzer 4)
As It Is in Life, 1910 (Pickford 3, Bitzer 4)
As Long As They're Happy, 1955 (Buchanan 3)
As Long as We Live. See Inochi aru kagiri, 1947
As Man Made Her, 1917 (Marion 4)
As negro, 1944 (Figueroa 4)
As Old as the Hills, 1950 (Halas and Batchelor 2)
As the Bells Rang Out, 1910 (Griffith 2, Bitzer 4)

As the Clouds Scatter. See Kumo ga chigireru toki, 1961
As the Devil Commands, 1932 (August 4)
As the Earth Turns, 1934 (Orry-Kelly 4)
As the Sea Rages, 1960 (Robertson 3)
As the Sea Rages. See Hellas, 1959
As the Sun Went Down, 1919 (Pitts 3)
As Told by Princess Bess, 1912 (Bosworth 3)
As Ye Sow, 1914 (Brady 3)
As You Desire Me, 1932 (Von Stroheim 2, Douglas, M. 3, Garbo 3, Adrian 4, Daniels 4)
As You Like It, 1912 (Costello, M. 3)
As You Like It, 1936 (Czinner 2, Lean 2, Bergner 3, Olivier 3, Cardiff 4, Meerson 4, Rosson 4, Schenck 4)
As Young as You Are, 1958 (Bumstead 4, Head 4)
As Young as You Feel, 1951 (Bennett C. 3, Monroe 3, Ritter 3, Chayefsky 4, Lemaire 4)
Asa no hamon, 1952 (Gosho 2, Kagawa 3, Takamine 3)
Asa no namikimichi, 1936 (Naruse 2)
Asa-Hanna, 1946 (Borgstrom 3)
Asahi wa kagayaku, 1929 (Mizoguchi 2)
Asakusa kurenai-dan, 1952 (Kyo 3)
Asakusa monogatari, 1953 (Mori 3)
Asakusa no hada, 1950 (Kyo 3)
Asakusa no yoru, 1954 (Kyo 3)
Asakusa yonin shimai, 1952 (Yamamura 3)
Asama no mozu, 1953 (Hasegawa 3)
Asani Sanket, 1973 (Ray, S. 2, Chatterjee 3, Datta 4)
Ascending Scale. See Aarohan, 1982
Ascenseur pour l'échafaud, 1958 (Malle 2, Moreau 3, Denner 3, Decaë 4)
Aschenbrodel, 1914 (Gad 2, Nielsen 3)
Aschenputtel, 1922 (Reiniger 2)
Asemblea General, 1960 (Gutiérrez 2, Almendros 4)
Asesino se embarca, 1966 (Figueroa 4)
Asfalttilampaat, 1968 (Donner 2)
Asfour, 1973 (Chahine 2)
Ash Can Fleet, 1939 (Zinnemann 2)
Ash Can, or Little Dick's First Adventure, 1915 (Franklin 2)
Ash Wednesday, 1973 (Fonda, H. 3, Taylor, E. 3, Head 4, Jarre 4)
Ashanti, 1979 (Fleischer, R. 2, Caine 3, Harrison 3, Sharif 3, Ustinov 3)
Ashanti, 1982 (Azmi 3)
Ashes, 1922 (Anderson G. 3)
Ashes, 1930 (Balcon 4)
Ashes. See Popioly, 1965
Ashes and Diamonds. See Popiól i diament, 1958
Ashes of Desire, 1919 (Borzage 2)
Ashes of Hope, 1914 (Bushman 3)
Ashes of the Past, 1914 (Sweet 3)
Ashes of Three, 1913 (Dwan 2)
Ashes of Vengeance, 1923 (Beery 3, Talmadge, N. 3, Gaudio 4, Schenck 4)
Ashi ni sawatta koun, 1930 (Ozu 2)
Ashi ni sawatta onna, 1952 (Ichikawa 2, Yamamura 3)
Ashi ni sawatta onna, 1960 (Kyo 3)
Ashi o arrata otoko, 1949 (Hasegawa 3)
Ashibi, 1928 (Tsuburaya 4)
Ashita kuru hito, 1955 (Yamamura 3)
Ashizuri misaki, 1954 (Yoshimura 2)
Ashura hangan, 1951 (Hasegawa 3)
Así era mi madre. See Bello recuerdo, 1961
Así era Pancho Villa, 1957 (Armendáriz 3)
Así es mi tierra, 1937 (Cantinflas 3)
Así se quiere en Jalisco, 1942 (De Fuentes 2, Negrete 3)
Asilo muito louco, 1969 (Pereira Dos Santos 2)
Asino y el condor, 1981 (Herrera 4)
Ask a Policeman, 1939 (Gilliat 4)
Ask Any Girl, 1959 (Walters 2, MacLaine 3, Niven 3, Young, G. 3, Pasternak 4, Rose 4)
Ask Father, 1918 (Daniels 3, Lloyd 3, Roach 4)
Ask Grandma, 1925 (Roach 4)
Aslan bey, 1968 (Guney 2)
Aslanlarin donusu, 1966 (Guney 2)

Asleep at the Switch, 1923 (Sennett 2)
Asleep in the Feet, 1933 (Pitts 3, Roach 4)
Asli Nagli, 1962 (Anand 3)
Aspern, 1982 (Valli 3, Branco 4, de Almeida 4)
Asphalt, 1929 (Frohlich 3, Herlth 4, Pommer 4, Rohrig 4)
Asphalt Jungle, 1950 (Huston 2, Calhern 3, Hayden 3, Jaffe 3,
    Martin, S. 3, Monroe 3, Warden 3, Maddow 4, Rosson 4, Rozsa 4)
Asphalt Lambs. See Asfalttilampaat, 1968
Ass and the Stick, 1974 (Halas and Batchelor 2)
Assam Garden, 1985 (Kerr 3)
Assassin. See Ansatsu, 1964
Assassin. See Assassino, 1961
Assassin. See Venetian Bird, 1952
Assassin a peur la nuit, 1942 (Delannoy 2, Berry 3, Auric 4)
Assassin connait la musique, 1963 (Schell, Maria 3)
Assassin est dans l'annuaire, 1961 (Fernandel 3)
Assassin habite au 21, 1942 (Clouzot 2, Fresnay 3, Gélin 3,
    Andrejew 4)
Assassin musicien, 1975 (Karina 3)
Assassin n'est pas coupable, 1946 (Berry 3)
Assassinat de la rue du Temple, 1904 (Guy 2)
Assassinat de McKinley, 1901 (Zecca, 2)
Assassinat de Trotsky, 1972 (Cortese 3, Delon 3)
Assassinat du Courrier de Lyon, 1904 (Guy 2)
Assassinat du Père Noël, 1941 (Christian-Jaque 2, Baur 3, Blier 3,
    Spaak 4)
Assassination. See Ansatsu, 1964
Assassination. See Assassination at Sarajevo, 1975
Assassination at Sarajevo, 1975 (Schell, Maximilian 3)
Assassination Bureau, 1969 (Dearden 2, Jurgens 3, Noiret 3,
    Reed, O. 3, Mankowitz 4, Unsworth 4)
Assassination of Trotsky, 1972 (Losey 2, Burton 3, Schneider 3)
Assassination of Trotsky. See Assassinat de Trotsky, 1972
Assassino, 1961 (Petri 2, Mastroianni 3, Presle 3, Cristaldi 4, Guerra 4)
Assassinio made in Italy. See Segreto del vestito rosso, 1963
Assassins de l'ordre, 1971 (Carné 2, Denner 3)
Assassins et voleurs, 1957 (Guitry 2)
Assault and Peppered, 1965 (McKimson 4)
Assault Force. See Ffolkes, 1980
Assault in the Park, 1959 (Wieland 2)
Assault on a Queen, 1966 (Sinatra 3, Daniels 4, Head 4)
Assault on Paradise. See Maniac, 1977
Assault on Precinct 13, 1977 (Carpenter 2)
Assault on the Wayne, 1970 (Cotten 3, Wynn 3)
Assaut, 1936 (Vanel 3)
Assayer of Lone Gap, 1915 (Eason 4)
Assedio dell'Alcazar, 1940 (Stallich 4)
Assedio di Siracusa, 1960 (Brazzi 3, Cervi 3)
Assenza ingiustificata, 1939 (Valli 3, Vích 4)
Assi alla ribalta, 1954 (Tognazzi 3)
Assiettes tournantes, 1895 (Lumière 2)
Assigned to Danger, 1948 (Boetticher 2)
Assignment, 1978 (Rey 3)
Assignment Children, 1954 (Kaye 3)
Assignment in Brittany, 1943 (Aumont 3, Irene 4, Rosher 4, Veiller 4)
Assignment K, 1968 (Redgrave, M. 3)
Assignment Munich, 1972 (Scheider 3, Wynn 3)
Assignment Paris, 1952 (Andrews D. 3, Sanders 3, Duning 4, Guffey 4)
Assignment Skybolt, 1966 (Lassally 4)
Assignment to Kill, 1967 (Gielgud 3, Homolka 3)
Assisi Underground, 1984 (Mason 3, Papas 3, Schell, Maximilian 3)
Assistance. See Jóember, 1970
Assistant Wives, 1927 (Hardy 3, Roach 4)
Assisted Elopement, 1912 (Dwan 2)
Associate. See Associé, 1979
Associé, 1979 (Carrière 4)
Assoluto naturale, 1969 (Bolognini 2, Harvey 3, Schell, Maximilian 3,
    Morricone 4)
Assommoir, 1910 (Baur 3)
Assunta spina, 1915 (Bertini 3)
Assunta spina, 1947 (Magnani)
Asszony elindul, 1949 (Darvas 3)
Asta, mein Engelchen, 1981 (Geschonneck 3)

****, 1967 (Warhol 2)
Astonished Heart, 1949 (Fisher 2, Johnson, C. 3, Coward 4)
Astragale, 1968 (Braunberger 4)
Astral Man, 1957 (Vanderbeek 2)
Astray from the Steerage. See Away from the Steerage, 1921
Astroduck, 1966 (McKimson 4)
Astrologie ou Le Miroir de la vie, 1952 (Grémillon 2)
Astromutts, 1963 (Vukotić 4)
Astronautes, 1959 (Marker 2, Borowczyk 4)
Astronauts. See Astronautes, 1959
Astronomer's Dream. See Lune à un mètre, 1898
Astro-Zombies, 1968 (Carradine 3)
Asu aru kagiri, 1962 (Kagawa 3)
Asu e no seiso, 1959 (Takemitsu 4)
Asu no odoriko, 1939 (Yoshimura 2)
Asu no taiyo, 1959 (Oshima 2)
Asu o tsukuru hitobito, 1946 (Kurosawa 2, Mori 3)
Asu wa docchi da, 1953 (Kagawa 3, Takamine 3)
Asunaro monogatari, 1955 (Hayasaka 4)
Aswa medher ghora, 1981 (Patil 3)
Asya's Happiness. See Istoriya Asi Klyachinoy, 1966
Asylum, 1972 (Cushing 3)
Asymvivastos, 1979 (Theodorakis 4)
@, 1979 (Brakhage 2)
At a Quarter to Two, 1911 (Pickford 3, Gaudio 4)
At avrat silah, 1966 (Guney 2)
At Bay, 1915 (Miller, A. 4)
At Breakneck Speed, 1900 (Bitzer 4)
At Coney Island, 1912 (Sennett 2, Sennett 2)
At Cripple Creek, 1912 (Reid 3)
At Dawn, 1914 (Reid 3)
At Dawn We Die. See Tomorrow We Live, 1942
At First Sight, 1917 (Rosher 4)
At First Sight, 1923 (Roach 4)
At 5:40. See Öt óra 40, 1939
At Great Cost. See Dorogoi tsenoi, 1957
At Gunpoint, 1955 (Brennan 3, MacMurray 3, Malone 3)
At hirsizi banus, 1967 (Guney 2)
At It Again, 1912 (Sennett 2, Normand 3)
At It Again. See Caught in the Rain, 1914
At Land, 1944 (Deren 2, Hammid 2)
At Long Last Love, 1975 (Bogdanovich 2, Reynolds, B. 3, Kovacs 4)
At Midnight, 1913 (Meredyth 4)
At Midnight in the Tomb. See V polnotch na kladbische, 1914
At Scrogginses' Corner, 1912 (Bunny 3)
At Sea Ashore, 1936 (Roach 4)
At Sword's Point, 1952 (Cooper, Gladys 3, O'Hara 3, Wilde 3)
At the 11th Hour. See Hvem var Forbryderen?, 1912
At the Altar, 1909 (Griffith 2, Bitzer 4)
At the Bottom of the Swimming Pool. See In fondo ala piscina, 1971
At the Break of Dawn, 1911 (Anderson G. 3)
At the Circus, 1939 (Leroy 2, Arden 3, Dumont 3, Marx Brothers 3,
    Waxman 4)
At the Circus, 1944 (Terry 4)
At the Duke's Command, 1911 (Pickford 3, Gaudio 4)
At the Earth's Core, 1976 (Cushing 3)
At the End of a Perfect Day, 1915 (Swanson 3)
At the End of the Trail, 1912 (Bushman 3)
At the French Ball, 1908 (Bitzer 4)
At the Front, 1943 (Zanuck 4)
At the Grey House, 1925 (Von Harbou 4)
At the Grey House. See Zur Chronik von Grieshuus, 1925
At the Lake. See U ozera, 1969
At the Lariat's End, 1913 (Anderson G. 3)
At the Lorinc Spinnery. See Lorinci fonóban, 1971
At the Mercy of Men, 1918 (Brady 3)
At the Monkey House, 1906 (Bitzer 4)
At the Old Maid's Ball, 1913 (Beery 3)
At the Old Stage Door, 1919 (Daniels 3, Lloyd 3, Roach 4)
At the Phone, 1912 (Guy 2)
At the Photographer's. See Kod fotografa, 1959
At the Ringside, 1921 (Roach 4)
At the Risk of My Life. See Inochi bo ni furo, 1971

At the River Galga. *See* Galga mentén, 1954

At 12:00, 1913 (Sennett 2)

At War with the Army, 1950 (Lewis 2, Martin, D. 3, Jenkins 4)

At Whose Door?, 1952 (Lassally 4)

At Yale. *See* Hold 'em Yale, 1928

At Your Service, 1935 (Lantz 4)

At Your Service Madame, 1936 (Freleng 4)

At žije nebožtik, 1935 (Fric 2, Haas 3, Stallich 4)

Ataka-ke no hitobito, 1952 (Tanaka 3, Yamamura 3)

Atala, 1912 (Bosworth 3)

Atalante, 1934 (Vigo 2, Simon, M. 3, Douy 4, Grimault 4, Jaubert 4, Kaufman 4)

Atarashiki tsuchi, 1937 (Hara 3, Hayakawa 3, Tsuburaya 4)

Atelier de Fernand Léger, 1954 (Borowczyk 4)

Ateliers de La Ciotat, 1895 (Lumière 2)

Atencion prenatal, 1972 (Gomez, S. 2)

Atentat u Sarajevu. *See* Assassination at Sarajevo, 1975

Athena, 1954 (Calhern 3, Reynolds, D. 3, Pasternak 4, Plunkett 4, Rose 4)

Athlète, 1931 (Fairbanks, D. Jr. 3)

Athlete, 1932 (Lantz 4)

Athlète incomplet, 1932 (Autant-Lara 2)

Athlète malgré lui. *See* Athlète, 1931

Athleten, 1925 (Nielsen 3, Junge 4)

Athletic Ambitions, 1915 (Mix 3)

Athletic Girl and Burglar, 1905 (Bitzer 4)

Atithee, 1978 (Azmi 3)

Atividades políticas em São Paulo, 1950 (Pereira Dos Santos 2)

Atlantic, 1929 (Dupont 2, Carroll M. 3, Rosher 4)

Atlantic Adventure, 1935 (Langdon 3)

Atlantic City, 1944 (Dandridge 3, Alton, J. 4)

Atlantic City, 1981 (Malle 2, Lancaster 3, Piccoli 3, Sarandon 3, Legrand 4)

Atlantic Episode. *See* Catch as Catch Can, 1937

Atlantic Ferry, 1941 (Fisher 2, Love 3, Redgrave, M. 3)

Atlantic Wall. *See* Mur de l'Atlantique, 1970

Atlantide, 1921 (Feyder 2)

Atlantide, 1932 (Pabst 2, Metzner 4, Schufftan 4)

Atlantide, 1961 (Ulmer 2)

Atlantide. *See* Antinea, 1961

Atlantik, 1929 (Dupont 2, Kortner 3)

Atlantis, 1913 (Blom 2, Curtiz 2)

Atlantis, 1930 (Dupont 2)

Atlantis, The Lost Continent, 1960 (Pal 2, Gillespie 4)

Atlas, 1960 (Corman 2)

Ato ni tsuzuku o shinzu, 1945 (Hasegawa 3)

Atoll K, 1950 (Laurel & Hardy 3)

Atom, 1918 (Borzage 2)

Atom Man vs. Superman, 1950 (Katzman 4)

Atomic City, 1952 (Lang 4)

Atomic Kid, 1954 (Edwards 2, Rooney 3)

Atonement, 1914 (Anderson G. 3)

Atonement of Gosta Berling. *See* Gosta Berlings saga, 1923

Atout coeur à Tokyo pour OSS 117, 1966 (Douy 4)

Atragon. *See* Kaitei gunkan, 1964

Atre, 1920 (Gance 2, Vanel 3)

Atroce menace, 1934 (Christian-Jaque 2)

Atsui yoru, 1968 (Yoshimura 2)

Att alska, 1964 (Donner 2, Andersson H. 3, Cybulski 3, Nykvist 4)

Att Segla ar Nodvandigt, 1937–38 (Fejos 2)

Atta Boy, 1925 (Laurel 3)

Atta Boy's Last Race, 1916 (Browning 2, Gish, D. 3)

Attack!, 1956 (Aldrich 2, Martin, S. 3, Marvin 3, Palance 3, Bass 4, Biroc 4)

Attack and Retreat. *See* Italiani brava gente, 1964

Attack Force, 1980 (Gibson 3)

Attack from the Sea. *See* Korabli shturmuiut bastioni, 1953

Attack in the Pacific, 1945 (Raksin 4)

Attack of the Crab Monsters, 1957 (Corman 4, Crosby 4)

Attack of the Enemy Planes. *See* Tekki kushu, 1943

Attack of the Giant Leeches, 1959 (Corman 4)

Attack of the Puppet People, 1958 (Laszlo 4)

Attack of the Robots, 1967 (Rey 3)

Attack on Terror: The FBI vs. the Ku Klux Klan, 1975 (Torn 3)

Attack Squadron. *See* Taiheiyo no tsubasa, 1963

Attaque d'un diligence, 1904 (Guy 2)

Attaque nocturne, 1931 (Fernandel 3)

Attendenti, 1961 (De Sica 2, Cervi 3)

Attentat, 1972 (Noiret 3, Piccoli 3, Scheider 3, Seberg 3, Trintignant 3, Volonté 3, Morricone 4)

Attenti al buffone!, 1975 (Manfredi 3, Wallach 3, Morricone 4)

Attention les enfants regardent, 1977 (Delon 3, Renoir 4)

Attention les yeux, 1975 (Braunberger 4)

Attention, Tortoise!. *See* Vnimanie, cherpakha!, 1969

Attention. *See* Pozor!, 1959

Atti degli apostoli, 1968 (Rossellini 2)

Attic, 1980 (Milland 3)

Attila. *See* Attila flagello di dio, 1955

Attila flagello di dio, 1955 (Loren 3, Papas 3, Quinn 3, Ponti 4, Struss 4)

Attila the Hun. *See* Attila flagello di dio, 1955

Atto di accusa, 1951 (Mastroianni 3)

Attong. *See* Young and the Brave, 1963

Attore Scomparso, 1941 (Zampa 2)

Attorney for the Defense, 1932 (Muse 3)

Attrait du bouge, 1912 (Feuillade 2)

Au bal de flore series, 1900 (Guy 2)

Au bonheur des dames, 1921 (Christian-Jaque 2)

Au bonheur des dames, 1929 (Duvivier 2)

Au bonheur des dames, 1943 (Cayatte 2, Simon, M. 3, Andrejew 4)

Au bout du monde, 1933 (Gabin 3, Vanel 3)

Au cabaret, 1899–1900 (Guy 2)

Au carrefour de la vie, 1949 (Storck 2)

Au champ de vapeur, 1969 (Braunberger 4)

Au Clair de la lune ou Pierrot malheureux, 1904 (Méliès 2)

Au coeur de l'Ile de France, 1954 (Grémillon 2)

Au coeur de la Casbah, 1951 (Decaë 4)

Au coeur de la ville, 1969 (Jutra 2)

Au deuil du Harem, 1922 (Modot 3)

Au fil de l'eau, 1932 (Matras 4)

Au Fou!, 1966 (Kuri 4)

Au grand balcon, 1949 (Fresnay 3, Kosma 4)

Au gré des flots, 1913 (Feuillade 2)

Au Guadalquiviz, 1965 (Braunberger 4)

Au hasard Balthazar, 1966 (Bresson 2, Cloquet 4)

Au joli coin, 1932 (Vanel 3)

Au nom de la loi, 1932 (Tourneur, M. 2, Vanel 3, Douy 4)

Au pays de George Sand, 1926 (Epstein 2, Périnal 4)

Au pays de Guillaume le Conquérant, 1954 (Delerue 4)

Au Pays de Porgy and Bess, 1957 (Reichenbach 2, Braunberger 4)

Au pays des grandes causses, 1951 (Fradetal 4)

Au pays des jouets, 1908 (Méliès 2)

Au pays des lions, 1912 (Feuillade 2)

Au pays des mages noirs, 1947 (Rouch 2)

Au pays du Roi Lépreux, 1927 (Feyder 2)

Au pays du scalp, 1931 (Cavalcanti 2, Jaubert 4)

Au pays noir, 1904–05 (Zecca 2)

Au péril de la mer, 1968 (Braunberger 4, Coutard 4)

Au petit bonheur, 1945 (L'Herbier 2, Darrieux 3)

Au Poulailler!, 1905 (Guy 2)

Au réfectoire, 1897–98 (Guy 2)

Au rendez-vous de la mort joyeuse, 1972 (Dauphin 3, Depardieu 3, Fabian 3, Cloquet 4)

Au royaume des cieux, 1949 (Duvivier 2, Reggiani 3)

Au rythme du siècle, 1953 (Delerue 4)

Au secours!, 1923 (Gance 2, Linders 3)

Au service du Tsar. *See* Adjudant des Zaren, 1929

Au verre de l'amitié, 1970 (Delerue 4)

Auberge du bon repos, 1903 (Méliès 2)

Auberge du Petit Dragon, 1934 (Modot 3, Burel 4)

Auberge ensorcelée, 1897 (Méliès 2)

Auberge rouge, 1910 (Gance 2)

Auberge rouge, 1923 (Epstein 2, Manès 3)

Auberge rouge, 1951 (Autant-Lara 2, Fernandel 3, Rosay 3, Aurenche 4, Bost 4, Douy 4)

Avanti la musica, 1962 (Cervi 3)
Avanti la musica. *See* En avant la musique, 1962
Avanti!, 1972 (Wilder 2, Lemmon 3, Diamond 4)
Avanti, c'e posto, 1942 (Fellini 2)
Avant-veille du grand soir, 1969 (Braunberger 4)
Avanzi di galera, 1954 (Constantine 3, Cortese 3, Fusco 4)
Avarice. *See* Yoku, 1958
Avatar, 1915 (Gallone 2)
Avatar botanique de Mlle. Flora, 1964 (Braunberger 4, Coutard 4)
Ave Caesar!, 1919 (Korda 2)
Ave Maria, 1936 (Ophuls 2, Planer 4)
Avec amour et avec rage. *See* Costanza della ragione, 1964
Avec André Gide, 1952 (Allégret, M. 2, Philipe 3, Braunberger 4)
Avec Claude Monet, 1966 (Gélin 3)
Avec le sourire, 1936 (Tourneur, M. 2, Chevalier 3)
Avec les gens du voyage, 1953 (Decaë 4)
Avec les peau des autres, 1966 (D'Eaubonne 4)
Avec les pilotes de porte-avions, 1953 (Delerue 4)
Avedis Aharonian, le dernier président arménien, 1947–51 (Verneuil 2)
Avenger. *See* Hamnaren, 1915
Avenger. *See* Mstitel, 1959
Avengers. *See* Day Will Dawn, 1942
Avenging Arrow, 1921 (Van Dyke, W.S. 2)
Avenging Bill, 1915 (Hardy 3)
Avenging Conscience, 1914 (Griffith 2, Crisp 3, Marsh 3, Sweet 3, Walthall 3, Bitzer 4, Brown, K. 4)
Avenging Rider, 1928 (Musuraca 4)
Avenging Rider, 1942 (Hunt 4)
Avenging Trail, 1917 (Gaudio 4)
Avenging Waters, 1936 (Bond 3)
Avenir d'Emilie, 1984 (Knef 3, Vierny 4)
Avenir devoile par les lignes des pieds, 1917 (Cohl 2)
Aventura de Gil Blas, 1956 (Rey 3)
Aventura de Musidora en España, 1922 (Musidora 3)
Aventuras de Juan Lucas, 1949 (Rey 3)
Aventuras de Robinson Crusoe, 1952 (Buñuel 2)
Aventure à Paris, 1936 (Allégret, M. 2, Arletty 3, Berry 3, Lourié 4)
Aventure à Pigalle, 1949 (Dalio 3)
Aventure c'est l'aventure, 1972 (Lelouch 2, Denner 3, Lai 4)
Aventure de Billy le Kid, 1973 (Léaud 3)
Aventure de Cabassou, 1946 (Fernandel 3)
Aventure de Moutonne. *See* Moutonnet, 1936
Aventure des millions, 1916 (Feuillade 2)
Aventure est au coin de la rue, 1943 (Renoir 4)
'Aventure' et ses Terre-Nuevas, 1953 (Delerue 4)
Aventure Malgache, 1944 (Hitchcock 2)
Aventures d'Arsène Lupin, 1956 (Becker 2, Cloquet 4)
Aventures d'un bout de papier, 1911 (Cohl 2)
Aventures d'un voyageur trop pressé, 1903 (Guy 2)
Aventures de Clementine, 1916 (Cohl 2)
Aventures de Holly and Wood, 1978 (Vierny 4)
Aventures de la famille Carre French language teaching series, 1964 (Halas and Batchelor 2)
Aventures de Rabbi Jacob, 1973 (Dalio 3, Decaë 4)
Aventures de Robert Macaire, 1925 (Epstein 2, Meerson 4)
Aventures de Till L'Espiègle, 1956 (Fabian 3, Philipe 3, Auric 4, Barsacq 4)
Aventures des Pieds-Nickelés, 1948 (Braunberger 4)
Aventures des Pieds-Nickles, 1916 (Cohl 2)
Aventures du roi Pausole, 1933 (Delannoy 2, Baranovskaya 3, Feuillère 3, Amidei 4, Jeanson 4, Maté 4)
Aventures en Laponie, 1960 (Braunberger 4)
Aventurier, 1934 (L'Herbier 2)
Aventurière, 1912 (Feuillade 2)
Aventurière, dame de compagnie, 1911 (Feuillade 2)
Aventurière des Champs-Elysées, 1956 (Fabian 3)
Aventuriers, 1966 (Delon 3, Reggiani 3)
Aventyrare, 1942 (Bjornstrand 3)

Aventyret, 1936 (Fischer 4, Jaenzon 4)
Avenue de l'Opera, 1900 (Guy 2)
Average Husband, 1930 (Sennett 2)
Average Man. *See* Borghese piccolo piccolo, 1977
Aveu, 1970 (Costa-Gavras 2, Marker 2, Montand 3, Signoret 3, Coutard 4, Evein 4)
Aveugle, 1897 (Guy 2)
Aveugle de Jérusalem, 1909 (Feuillade 2)
Aveux les plus doux, 1971 (Noiret 3, Coutard 4, Delerue 4)
Aviateur, 1931 (Fairbanks, D. Jr. 3)
Aviatikeren og Journalistens Hustru. *See* Lektion, 1911
Aviation Vacation, 1941 (Avery 2)
Aviator, 1929 (Horton 3)
Aviator, 1985 (Warden 3)
Aviator and the Journalist's Wife. *See* Lektion, 1911
Aviator's Wife, 1980 (Rohmer 2)
Avignon, bastion de la provence, 1951 (Philipe 3)
Avion de miniut, 1938 (Berry 3)
Avisen, 1954 (Roos 2)
Avoir seize ans, 1978 (Lefebvre 2)
Avtaar, 1983 (Azmi 3)
Avventura, 1959 (Antonioni 2, Vitti 3, Fusco 4, Guerra 4)
Avventura a Capri, 1958 (Vích 4)
Avventura di Annabella, 1943 (Magnani 3)
Avventura di Salvator Rosa, 1940 (Blasetti 2, Castellani 2, Cervi 3, Vích 4)
Avventure di Benvenuto Cellini. *See* Magnifico avventuriero, 1963
Avventure di Pinocchio, 1947 (Gassman 3)
Avventure di Pinocchio, 1971 (Comencini 2, Lollobrigida 3, Manfredi 3, Gherardi 4)
Avventure e gli amori di Miguel Cervantes, 1968 (Ferrer, J. 3)
Avventure nell'arcipelago, 1958 (Fusco 4)
Avventuriera del piano di sopra, 1941 (De Sica 2)
Avventuriero. *See* Rover, 1967
Avventurosa fuga. *See* Ultimi angeli, 1977
Avvocato della mala, 1977 (Ferrer, M. 3)
Avvoltoio nero, 1913 (Bertini 3)
Awa no odoriko, 1941 (Hasegawa 3, Takamine 3)
Awakening, 1909 (Griffith 2, Pickford 3, Bitzer 4)
Awakening, 1928 (Fleming 2, Banky 3, Barnes 4, Goldwyn 4, Marion 4, Menzies 4, Wilson, C. 4)
Awakening, 1980 (Heston 2, York, S. 3)
Awakening. *See* Probuzeni, 1959
Awakening. *See* Przebudzenie, 1934
Awakening. *See* Suor Letizia, 1956
Awakening of Bess, 1909 (Lawrence 3)
Awakening of Helena Richie, 1916 (Barrymore E. 3)
Awakening of Jones, 1912 (Bunny 3)
Awara, 1951 (Kapoor 2)
Award Presentation to Andy Warhol, 1964 (Mekas 2)
Away All Boats, 1956 (Boone 3, Chandler 3, Daniels 4)
Away from the Steerage, 1921 (Sennett 2)
Away Goes Prudence, 1920 (Burke 3)
Away Out West, 1910 (Anderson G. 3)
Awdat al Ibn al Dal, 1976 (Chahine 2)
Awful Moment, 1908 (Griffith 2, Lawrence 3)
Awful Orphan, 1948 (Jones 2)
Awful Skate, 1907 (Anderson G. 3)
Awful Truth, 1925 (Baxter W. 3)
Awful Truth, 1929 (Neilan 2)
Awful Truth, 1937 (McCarey 2, Bellamy 3, Dunne 3, Grant, C. 3, Walker 4)
Axe and the Lamp, 1963 (Halas and Batchelor 2)
Axe Me Another, 1934 (Fleischer, M. and D. 2)
Axel Munthe, der Arzt von San Michele, 1962 (Cortese 3)
Ay, Jalisco no te rajes!, 1941 (Negrete 3)
Ay qué rechulo es Puebla!, 1945 (García 3)
Ay qué tiempos, señor don Simón, 1941 (Figueroa 4)
Aya ni kanashiki, 1956 (Tanaka 3)
Ayako. *See* Aru Osaka no onna, 1962
Ayamna el Hilwa, 1954 (Sharif 3)
Až přidje kocour, 1963 (Brodský 3)

Až přijde kocour, 1963 (Brdečka 4, Kučera 4)
Azahares para tu boda, 1950 (García 3)
Azais, 1930 (D'Eaubonne 4)
Azonositás, 1975 (Madaras 3)

Azrail benim, 1968 (Guney 2)
Azredes, 1917 (Lugosi 3)
Aztecas, 1976 (Figueroa 4)
Azyllo muito louco. See Asilo muito louco, 1969

B

B Must Die. See Hay que matar a B, 1974
B.F.'s Daughter, 1948 (Coburn, C. 3, Heflin 3, Stanwyck 3, Wynn 3, Irene 4, Kaper 4, Ruttenberg 4)
B.J. Lang Presents, 1971 (Rooney 3, Wynn 3)
Baag ki Jyoti, 1953 (Biswas 4)
Baaji, 1951 (Burman 4)
Baal, 1969 (Fassbinder 2, Schlondorff 2, Von Trotta 2, Schygulla 3)
Baap Beti, 1954 (Roy 2)
Baat Ek Raat Ki, 1962 (Anand 3, Burman 4)
Baazi, 1951 (Anand 3)
Bab el Haded, 1958 (Chahine 2)
Baba, 1971 (Guney 2)
Baba Amine, 1950 (Chahine 2)
Baba Yaga—Devil Witch, 1973 (Baker C. 3)
Baba-Ali, 1952 (Colpi 4)
Babatu, 1976 (Rouch 2)
Babbitt, 1934 (Orry-Kelly 4)
Babe, 1975 (Ames 4, Goldsmith 4)
Babe Comes Home, 1927 (Fazenda 3, Nilsson 3, Struss 4)
Babe Ruth Story, 1948 (Bendix 3, Trevor 3)
Babel Yemen, 1977 (Howard, T. 3)
Babes in Arms, 1939 (Berkeley 2, Garland 3, Brown, N. 4, Edens 4, Freed 4)
Babes in Bagdad, 1952 (Ulmer 2, Goddard 3, Lee, C. 3)
Babes in the Goods, 1934 (Roach 4)
Babes in the Wood. See Perníková chaloupka, 1927
Babes in the Woods, 1917 (Franklin 2)
Babes in Toyland, 1934 (Laurel & Hardy 3, Roach 4)
Babes in Toyland, 1961 (Disney 2)
Babes on Broadway, 1941 (Berkeley 2, Bainter 3, Garland 3, Meek 3, O'Brien, M. 3, Reed, D. 3, Rooney 3, Edens 4, Freed 4)
Babe's School Days, 1915 (Hardy 3)
Babette Goes to War. See Babette s'en va-t-en guerre, 1959
Babette s'en va-t-en guerre, 1959 (Christian-Jaque 2, Bardot 3, Audiard 4)
Babies for Sale, 1940 (Ford, G. 3)
Babla, 1953 (Burman 4)
Bab's Burglar, 1917 (Barthelmess 3)
Bab's Diary, 1917 (Barthelmess 3)
Baby, 1915 (Franklin 2, Hardy 3)
Baby, 1932 (Ondra 3, Walbrook 3)
Baby. See Bebek, 1973
Baby and the Battleship, 1956 (Attenborough 3, Mills 3)
Baby and the Stork, 1911 (Griffith 2, Bitzer 4)
Baby Be Good, 1935 (Fleischer, M. and D. 2)
Baby Be Good. See Brother Rat and a Baby, 1940
Baby Blue Marine, 1976 (Gere 3, Kovacs 4)
Baby Bottleneck, 1945 (Clampett 4)
Baby Buggy Bunny, 1955 (Jones 2)
Baby Butch, 1953 (Hanna and Barbera 4)
Baby Carriage. See Barnvagnen, 1963
Baby Clothes, 1926 (Roach 4)
Baby Cyclone, 1928 (Sutherland 2, Gibbons 4)
Baby Day, 1913 (Sennett 2, Normand 3)
Baby Doll, 1916 (Hardy 3)
Baby Doll, 1956 (Kazan 2, Baker C. 3, Malden 3, Wallach 3, Kaufman 4, Sylbert 4)
Baby Face, 1933 (Brennan 3, Brent 3, Stanwyck 3, Wayne 3, Grot 4, Orry-Kelly 4, Zanuck 4)

Baby Face Harrington, 1935 (Walsh 2, Meek 3, Merkel 3, Johnson 4)
Baby Face Harrington. See Baby Face, 1933
Baby Face Nelson, 1957 (Siegel 2, Cook 3, Elam 3, Hardwicke 3, Rooney 3)
Baby It's You, 1983 (Sayles 4)
Baby l'indiavolate. See My Little Baby, 1916
Baby Love. See Roman Zair, 1983
Baby Mine, 1917 (Edeson 4)
Baby Mine, 1928 (Gibbons 4)
Baby on the Barge, 1915 (Hepworth 2)
Baby Puss, 1943 (Hanna and Barbera 4)
Baby Review, 1903 (Porter 2)
Baby Seal, 1941 (Terry 4)
Baby—Secret of the Lost Legend, 1984 (Goldsmith 4)
Baby Sitters' Jitters, 1951 (Three Stooges 3)
Baby Story, 1978 (Bozzetto 4)
Baby, Take a Bow, 1934 (Temple 3, Trevor 3)
Baby the Rain Must Fall, 1964 (Mulligan 2, Pakula 2, McQueen, S. 3, Remick 3, Bernstein 4, Laszlo 4)
Baby Wants a Bottleship, 1942 (Fleischer, M. and D. 2)
Baby's Birthday, 1929 (Sennett 2)
Baby's Pets, 1926 (Sennett 2)
Baby's Ride, 1914 (Reid 3)
Baby's Shoe, 1909 (Griffith 2, Lawrence 3, Bitzer 4)
Baby-Sitter, 1975 (Clément 2, Lai 4, Ponti 4)
Babysitter, 1980 (Houseman 4)
Bacall to Arms, 1946 (Clampett 4)
Baccanali di Tiberio, 1959 (Tognazzi 3)
Baccara, 1936 (Berry 3, Lourié 4)
Bacchantin, 1924 (Tschechowa 3)
Bacciamo le mani, 1973 (Kennedy, A. 3)
Bach Millionnaire, 1933 (Jeanson 4)
Bach to Bach, 1967 (Rosenblum 4)
Bachelor and the Bobby-soxer, 1947 (Grant, C. 3, Loy 3, Temple 3, Musuraca 4, Schary 4)
Bachelor Apartment, 1931 (Dunne 3)
Bachelor Bait, 1934 (Stevens 2, Plunkett 4, Polglase 4, Steiner 4)
Bachelor Brides, 1926 (Hathaway 2, Howard 2, Fort 4, Sullivan 4)
Bachelor Butt-in, 1926 (Sennett 2)
Bachelor Buttons, 1912 (Bunny 3)
Bachelor Daddy, 1941 (Horton 3, Krasner 4, Salter 4)
Bachelor Father, 1931 (Davies 3, Milland 3, Adrian 4)
Bachelor Father. See Ungkarlspappan, 1934
Bachelor Flat, 1962 (Tashlin 2, Weld 3, Smith, J.M. 4, Williams, J. 4)
Bachelor Girl Apartment. See Any Wednesday, 1966
Bachelor in Paradise, 1961 (Hope 3, Moorehead 3, Turner, L. 3, Mancini 4, Rose 4, Ruttenberg 4)
Bachelor in Paris. See Song of Paris, 1952
Bachelor Knight. See Bachelor and the Bobby Soxer, 1947
Bachelor Mother, 1939 (Coburn, C. 3, Niven 3, Rogers, G. 3, Irene 4, Kanin 4, Krasna 4, Polglase 4)
Bachelor of Arts, 1934 (Fetchit 3, Marsh 3, Walthall 3, Trotti 4)
Bachelor of Hearts, 1958 (Raphael 4, Unsworth 4)
Bachelor Party, 1957 (Warden 3, Chayefsky 4, La Shelle 4, North 4)
Bachelor's Affairs, 1932 (Menjou 3)
Bachelor's Baby, 1915 (Anderson G. 3)
Bachelor's Baby, 1927 (Fort 4)
Bachelors Beware. See Dokushinsha goyojin, 1930

Bachelor's Brides. *See* Bachelor Brides, 1926
Bachelor's Burglar, 1915 (Anderson G. 3)
Bachelor's Daughter, 1946 (Burke 3, Menjou 3, Trevor 3)
Bachelor's Folly. *See* Calendar, 1931
Bacio, 1973 (Cortese 3)
Bacio del sole, 1958 (Manfredi 3)
Bacio di Cirano, 1913 (Gallone 2)
Bacio di Cirano, 1920 (Gallone 2)
Back Alley Oprear, 1947 (Freleng 4)
Back at the Front, 1952 (Boyle 4)
Back Door to Heaven, 1939 (Howard 2, Heflin 3, Head 4)
Back Door to Hell, 1964 (Nicholson 3)
Back for Christmas, 1956 (Hitchcock 2)
Back from Eternity, 1956 (Bondi 3, Ryan 3, Steiger 3, D'Agostino 4, Waxman 4)
Back from the Dead, 1957 (Haller 4)
Back From the Front, 1943 (Three Stooges 3)
Back in Circulation, 1937 (Blondell 3, O'Brien, P. 3, Miller, S. 4, Wallis 4)
Back in the Saddle, 1941 (Autry 3)
Back of the Man, 1917 (Ince 4)
Back Page, 1931 (Arbuckle 3)
Back Pay, 1922 (Borzage 2, Marion 4)
Back Pay, 1930 (Beavers 3, Seitz 4)
Back Roads, 1981 (Ritt 2, Field 3, Alonzo 4, Mancini 4)
Back Stage, 1917 (Hardy 3)
Back Stage, 1919 (Keaton 2, Arbuckle 3)
Back Stage, 1923 (Roach 4)
Back Street, 1932 (Stahl 2, Darwell 3, Dunne 3, Pitts 3, Freund 4, Laemmle 4)
Back Street, 1941 (Boyer 3, Sullavan 3, Daniels 4)
Back Street, 1961 (Hayward 3, Cortez 4, Hunter 4, Lourié 4)
Back Streets of Paris. *See* Macadam, 1946
Back to Bataan, 1945 (Dmytryk 2, Bondi 3, Quinn 3, Wayne 3, D'Agostino 4, Musuraca 4)
Back to God's Country, 1919 (Cody 3, Walker 4)
Back to God's Country, 1927 (Adorée 3)
Back to God's Country, 1953 (Hudson 3)
Back to Life, 1913 (Dwan 2, Chaney Lon 3)
Back to the Farm, 1914 (Hardy 3)
Back to the Kitchen, 1914 (Gish, D. 3)
Back to the Kitchen, 1919 (Sennett 2, Fazenda 3)
Back to the Primitive, 1911 (Mix 3)
Back to the Soil, 1911 (Pickford 3, Gaudio 4)
Back to the Soil, 1941 (Terry 4)
Back to the Wall. *See* Dos au mur, 1958
Back to the Woods, 1919 (Daniels 3, Lloyd 3, Normand 3, Roach 4)
Back to the Woods, 1937 (Three Stooges 3)
Back Yard, 1920 (Hardy 3)
Back Yard Theater, 1914 (Sennett 2)
Backbiters. *See* Catherine, 1927
Backfire, 1950 (Mayo 3, O'Brien, E. 3, Grot 4, Veiller 4)
Backfire. *See* Echappement libre, 1964
Background to Danger, 1943 (Walsh 2, Greenstreet 3, Lorre 3, Raft 3, Burnett 4, Gaudio 4, Wald 4)
Backlash, 1956 (Sturges, J. 2, Reed, D. 3, Van Cleef 3, Widmark 3, Chase 4)
Backs to Nature, 1933 (Roach 4)
Backstage. *See* Limelight, 1935
Backstairs. *See* Hintertreppe, 1921
Backtrack, 1969 (Lupino 3, Chase 4)
Backwoods Bunny, 1959 (McKimson 4)
Backwoodsman's Suspicions, 1911 (Anderson G. 3)
Backyard. *See* Två trappor over gården, 1950
Bacon Grabbers, 1929 (Harlow 3, Laurel and Hardy 3, Roach 4)
Bacquet de Mesmer, 1905 (Méliès 2)
Bad and the Beautiful, 1952 (Minnelli 2, Bushman 3, Calhern 3, Carroll L. 3, Douglas, K. 3, Grahame 3, Pidgeon 3, Powell, D. 3, Turner, L. 3, Gibbons 4, Houseman 4, Raksin 4, Rose 4, Schnee 4, Surtees 4)
Bad Bascomb, 1946 (Beery 3, O'Brien, M. 3, Irene 4)
Bad Blood. *See* First Offence, 1936
Bad Boy, 1917 (Moore, C. 3)

Bad Boy, 1925 (McCarey 2, Roach 4)
Bad Boy, 1935 (Bondi 3, Carradine 3, Fazenda 3, Glennon 4)
Bad Boy, 1949 (Murphy 3, Struss 4)
Bad Boys. *See* Furyo shonen, 1960
'Bad Buck' of Santa Ynez, 1915 (Hart 3)
Bad Charleston Charlie, 1973 (Carradine 3)
Bad Company, 1931 (Garnett 2, Carey 3, Miller, A. 4)
Bad Company, 1972 (Bridges 3, Rosenblum 4, Willis 4)
Bad Company. *See* Mauvaises Fréquentations, 1967
Bad Day at Black Rock, 1954 (Sturges, J. 2, Borgnine 3, Brennan 3, Marvin 3, Ryan 3, Tracy 3, Previn 4, Schary 4)
Bad Eggs. *See* Rotagg, 1946
Bad for Each Other, 1953 (Heston 3, Planer 4, Wald 4)
Bad Game, 1913 (Sennett 2)
Bad Girl, 1931 (Borzage 2)
Bad Girls Don't Cry. *See* Notte brava, 1959
Bad Investment, 1912 (Dwan 2)
Bad Lands, 1925 (Carey 3, Polito 4, Stromberg 4)
Bad Little Angel, 1939 (Seitz 4)
Bad Lord Byron, 1948 (Zetterling 2, Greenwood 3)
Bad Luck. *See* Zezowate szczeście, 1960
Bad Luck Blackie, 1949 (Avery 2)
Bad Man, 1930 (Huston 3, Estabrook 4, Seitz 4)
Bad Man, 1941 (Beery 3, Reagan 3, Waxman 4)
Bad Man. *See* 'Bad Buck' of Santa Ynez, 1915
Bad Man and Others, 1915 (Walsh 2)
Bad Man and the Ranger, 1912 (Dwan 2)
Bad Man Bobbs, 1915 (Mix 3)
Bad Man From Cheyenne, (Johnson, N. 3)
Bad Man of Brimstone, 1938 (Beery 3, Stone 3)
Bad Man of Deadwood, 1941 (Rogers, R. 3, Canutt 4)
Bad Man of Wyoming. *See* Wyoming, 1940
Bad Man's Christmas Gift, 1910 (Anderson G. 3)
Bad Man's Downfall, 1911 (Anderson G. 3)
Bad Man's First Prayer, 1911 (Anderson G. 3)
Bad Man's Last Deed, 1910 (Anderson G. 3)
Bad Man's River, 1972 (Mason 3)
Bad Medicine, 1985 (Arkin 3)
Bad Men, 1941 (Barrymore L. 3)
Bad Men of Missouri, 1941 (Kennedy, A. 3, Wyman 3)
Bad Men of Tombstone, 1948 (Crawford, B. 3)
Bad Men's Money, 1929 (Canutt 4)
Bad Names. *See* Akumyo series, 1961–1974
Bad News Bears, 1976 (Ritchie 2, Matthau 3, Alonzo 4)
Bad News Bears Go to Japan, 1978 (Curtis 3)
Bad ol' Putty Tat, 1948 (Freleng 4)
Bad One, 1930 (Del Rio 3, Karloff 3, Menzies 4, Schenck 4, Struss 4, Wilson, C. 4)
Bad One. *See* Sorority Girl, 1957
Bad Seed, 1956 (Leroy 2, Mahin 4, North 4, Rosson 4)
Bad Sister, 1931 (Bogart 3, Davis 3, Pitts 3, Summerville 3, Freund 4, Laemmle 4)
Bad Sister. *See* White Unicorn, 1947
Bad Sleep Well. *See* Warui yatsu hodo yoku nemuru, 1960
Bad Son. *See* Mauvais Fils, 1980
Bad Timber, 1931 (Bosworth 3)
Bad Timing, 1980 (Roeg 2, Keitel 3)
Badarna, 1968 (Thulin 3)
Badban, 1954 (Anand 3)
Baddegama, 1980 (Peries 2)
Badge 373, 1973 (Duvall, R. 3)
Badge of Honor, 1934 (Crabbe 3)
Badge of Marshall Brennan, 1957 (Van Cleef 3)
Badge or the Cross, 1971 (Kennedy, G. 3)
Badger. *See* Tanuki, 1956
Badger General. *See* Tanuki no taishou, 1965
Badger's Holiday. *See* Tanuki no kyujitsu, 1966
Badger's Tea Pot. *See* Bunbuku chagama, 1939
Badi Bahu, 1951 (Biswas 4)
Badi Didi, 1939 (Roy 2)
Badlanders, 1958 (Daves 2, Borgnine 3, Ladd 3, Seitz 4)
Badlands, 1973 (Malick 2, Oates 3, Sheen 3, Spacek 3)

Balloon. *See* Fusen, 1956
Balloon Explosion. *See* Balloneksplosionen, 1913
Balloonatic, 1923 (Keaton 2)
Balloonland, 1935 (Iwerks 4)
Balloons, 1923 (Fleischer, M. and D. 2)
Ballot Box Bunny, 1950 (Freleng 4)
Ballroom Tragedy, 1905 (Bitzer 4)
Ballroom Buster, 1928 (Brennan 3)
Ballyhoo Buster, 1928 (Brennan 3)
Balthasar. *See* Au hasard, Balthazar, 1966
Balthazar, 1938 (Berry 3)
Baltic Deputy. *See* Deputat Baltiki, 1936
Baltic Express. *See* Pociag, 1959
Baltiiskoe nebo, 1960 (Ulyanov 3)
Baltimore Bullet, 1979 (Coburn, J. 3, Sharif 3)
Baltiyskoe niebo, 1961 (Gurchenko 3)
Balún Canán, 1976 (Figueroa 4)
Bálvány, 1963 (Madaras 3, Törőcsik 3)
Bambai Ka Babu, 1960 (Anand 3)
Bambi, 1942 (Disney 2, Franklin 3)
Bambina. *See* Faró da padre, 1974
Bambini chiedono perchè, 1972 (Morricone 4)
Bambini ci guardano, 1943 (De Sica 2, Mastroianni 3, Zavattini 4)
Bambini e noi, 1970 (Comencini 2)
Bambini in città, 1946 (Comencini 2)
Bambole, 1964 (Bolognini 2, Comencini 2, Risi 2, Lollobrigida 3, Manfredi 3, Vitti 3, Gherardi 4, Pinelli 4)
Bamboo Blonde, 1946 (Mann 2)
Bamboo Cross, 1953 (Ford, J. 2)
Bamboo Doll of Echizen. *See* Echizen take ningyo, 1963
Bamboo Leaf Flute of No Return. *See* Kaeranu sasabue, 1926
Bamboo Prison, 1954 (Guffey 4)
Bamboo Saucer, 1968 (Duryea 3)
Bambuåldern på Mentawei, 1937–38 (Fejos 2)
Bana kursun islemez, 1967 (Guney 2)
Banana da terra, 1939 (Miranda 3)
Banana Peel. *See* Peau de banane, 1963
Bananas, 1971 (Allen 2, Stallone 3, Rosenblum 4)
Banarasi Babu, 1973 (Anand 3)
Banba no Chutaro, 1955 (Yamada 3)
Bancho sarayashiki, 1937 (Hasegawa 3, Tanaka 3)
Banco de prince, 1950 (Burel 4)
Band Master, 1917 (Hardy 3)
Band Master, 1931 (Lantz 4)
Band of Angels, 1957 (Walsh 2, De Carlo 3, Gable 3, Poitier 3, Ballard 4, Steiner 4)
Band of Assassins. *See* Shinsen-gumi, 1969
Band of Ninja. *See* Ninja bugeicho, 1967
Band of Ninja. *See* Shinobi no mono, 1962
Band of Outsiders. *See* Band à part, 1964
Band Plays On, 1934 (Young, R. 3)
Band Wagon, 1953 (Minnelli 2, Astaire 3, Buchanan 3, Charisse 3, Gardner 3, Ames 4, Comden & Green 4, Deutsch 4, Edens 4, Freed 4, Gibbons 4, Kidd 4)
Banda de Jaider. *See* Verflucht dies Amerika, 1973
Banda degli onesti, 1956 (Age and Scarpelli 4, De Laurentiis 4)
Banda J & S, 1972 (Morricone 4)
Bande à Bébel, 1967 (Belmondo 3)
Bande à part, 1964 (Godard 2, Karina 3, Coutard 4, Guillemot 4, Legrand 4)
Bande von Hoheneck, no date (Staudte 2)
Bandeau sur les yeux, 1917 (Feuillade 2)
Bandeirantes, 1940 (Mauro 2)
Bandera, 1935 (Duvivier 2, Gabin 3, Modot 3, Spaak 4)
Bandhe Haath, 1972 (Bachchan 3)
Bandida, 1962 (Armendáriz 3, Félix 3, Figueroa 4)
Bandido, 1956 (Fleischer, R. 2, Mitchum 3, Laszlo 4, Smith, J.M. 4, Steiner 4)
Bandini, 1963 (Roy 2, Burman 4)
Bandit, 1913 (Sennett 2, Arbuckle 3)
Bandit. *See* Cucaracha, 1958
Bandit and the Preacher. *See* On the Night Stage, 1914
Bandit General. *See* Del odio nació el amor, 1949
Bandit General. *See* Torch, 1949

Bandit Island of Karabei. *See* Return to Treasure Island, 1954
Bandit King, 1907 (Anderson G. 3)
Bandit Makes Good, 1907 (Anderson G. 3)
Bandit of Point Loma, 1912 (Dwan 2)
Bandit of Sherwood Forest, 1946 (Wilde 3, Friedhofer 4, Gaudio 4)
Bandit of Zhobe, 1959 (Mature 3)
Bandit Trail, 1941 (Polglase 4)
Banditi a Milano, 1968 (Volonté 3, De Laurentiis 4)
Banditi a Roma. *See* Roma come Chicago, 1968
Bandito, 1946 (Lattuada 2, Magnani 3, De Laurentiis 4)
Bandit's Child, 1912 (Anderson G. 3)
Bandits in Rome. *See* Roma coma Chicago, 1969
Bandits of Corsica, 1954 (Van Cleef 3)
Bandits on the Wind. *See* Yato kaze no naka o hashiru, 1961
Bandit's Son, 1927 (Plunkett 4)
Bandit's Wager, 1916 (Ford, J. 2)
Bandit's Waterloo, 1908 (Griffith 2, Lawrence 3)
Bandit's Wife, 1910 (Anderson G. 3)
Bandolero!, 1968 (Kennedy, G. 3, Martin, D. 3, Stewart 3, Welch 3, Cahn 4, Clothier 4, Goldsmith 4, Needham 4, Smith, J.M. 4)
Bandolero, 1924 (Adorée 3)
Bang, 1967 (Godfrey 4)
Bang!, 1977 (Troell 2)
Bang! Bang! You're Dead. *See* Our Man in Marrakesh, 1966
Bang the Drum Slowly, 1973 (De Niro 3)
Bang! You're Dead, 1961 (Hitchcock 2)
Bangiku, 1954 (Naruse 2)
Bangville Police, 1913 (Sennett 2)
Banished. *See* Hanare-goze Orin, 1977
Banished Orin. *See* Hanare goze Orin, 1977
Banjo, 1947 (Fleischer, R. 2, Beavers 3)
Banjo on My Knee, 1936 (Cromwell 2, Brennan 3, McCrea 3, Stanwyck 3, Johnson 4)
Banjun no santo-kocho, 1959 (Yamada 3)
Bank, 1915 (Bacon 2, Chaplin 2, Purviance 3)
Bánk Bán, 1914 (Curtiz 2)
Bank Book. *See* Vildledt Elskov, 1911
Bank Breaker. *See* Kaleidoscope, 1966
Bank Detective. *See* Bank Dick, 1940
Bank Dick, 1940 (Fields, W.C. 3, Howard, S. 3, Merkel 3, Krasner 4)
Bank Director. *See* Karneval, 1908
Bank Holiday, 1938 (Reed 2)
Bank of Departure. *See* Ruri no kishi, 1956
Bank Robbery. *See* Skok, 1969
Bank Shot, 1974 (Scott, G. 3)
Banka, 1957 (Gosho 2, Mori 3)
Banker's Daughter, 1927 (Disney 2)
Banker's Daughter, 1933 (Terry 4)
Banker's Daughters, 1910 (Griffith 2, Walsh 2, Bitzer 4)
Bankett der Schmuggler. *See* Banquet des fraudeurs, 1952
Bankett fur Achilles, 1975 (Geschonneck 3)
Banketten, 1948 (Borgstrom 3)
Bankkrasch Unter den Linden, 1925 (Albers 3)
Bankokku no yuro, 1966 (Shimura 3)
Bankraub in der Rue Latour, 1961 (Kinski 3)
Bankrun. *See* Pressens Magt, 1913
Bankrupt Honeymoon, 1926 (Hardy 3)
Banner of Youth. *See* Sztandar mlodych, 1957
Bannerline, 1951 (Barrymore L. 3, Stone 3, Schnee 4)
Banning, 1967 (Hackman 3, Wagner 3, Bumstead 4, Jones 4)
Banović Strahinja, 1981 (Mimica 4)
Banque, 1955 (Rabier 4)
Banque Nemo, 1934 (Meerson 4)
Banquet des fraudeurs, 1952 (Storck 2, Rosay 3, Schufftan 4, Spaak 4)
Banquière, 1980 (Schneider 3, Trintignant 3)
Banquo's Chair, 1959 (Hitchcock 2)
Banshun, 1949 (Ozu 2, Hara 3, Ryu 3)
Bansi Birju, 1972 (Bachchan 3)
Bantam Cowboy, 1928 (Plunkett 4)
Banty Raids, 1963 (McKimson 4)
Banwara, 1950 (Kapoor 2)
Banware Nayan, 1950 (Kapoor 2)
Banya, 1962 (Yutkevich 2)

Banyon, 1971 (Ferrer, J. 3)
Banzai, 1913 (Ince 4)
Baptism. See Keresztelo, 1967
Bar de la fourche, 1972 (Huppert 3, de Beauregard 4)
Bar du Sud, 1938 (Vanel 3)
Bar Fly, 1924 (Roach 4)
Bar L Ranch, 1930 (Canutt 4)
Bar Sinister. See It's a Dog's Life, 1955
Bar 20, 1943 (Boyd 3, Mitchum 3, Wilson, M. 4)
Bar 20 Justice, 1938 (Boyd 3, O'Brien, P. 3, Head 4)
Bar 20 Rides Again, 1935 (Boyd 3)
Bara en danserska, 1927 (Albers 3, Dagover 3)
Bara en mor, 1949 (Sjoberg 2, Dahlbeck 3, Von Sydow 3)
Bara gassen, 1949 (Naruse 2)
Bara ikutabi, 1955 (Kinugasa 2)
Bara ikutabika, 1955 (Kyo 3)
Bara wa ikutabika, 1955 (Hasegawa 3)
Barabba, 1961 (Fleischer, R. 2, Borgnine 3, Cortese 3, Gassman 3,
    Kennedy, A. 3, Mangano 3, Palance 3, Quinn 3, De Laurentiis 4)
Barabbas, 1953 (Sjoberg 2, Dahlbeck 3, Nykvist 4)
Barabbas. See Barabba, 1961
Barajas, aeropuerto internacional, 1950 (Bardem 2)
Barátságos arcot kérek, 1935 (Sakall 3)
Barbara, 1961 (Andersson H. 3)
Barbara Frietchie, 1915 (Guy 2, Nilsson 3)
Barbara Frietchie, 1924 (Ince 4)
Barbara's Blindness, 1965 (Wieland 2)
Barbarella, 1968 (Vadim 2, Dauphin 3, Fonda, J. 3, Tognazzi 3, De
    Laurentiis 4, Jarre 4, Renoir 4)
Barbarian, 1921 (Crisp 3)
Barbarian, 1933 (Wood 2, Loy 3, Novarro 3, Adrian 4, Brown, N. 4,
    Freed 4, Loos 4, Rosson 4, Stothart 4)
Barbarian and the Geisha, 1958 (Huston 2, Jaffe 3, Wayne 3, Clarke,
    C.C. 4, Friedhofer 4, Lemaire 4, Smith, J.M. 4, Wheeler 4)
Barbarian, Ingomar, 1908 (Griffith 2, Lawrence 3, Bitzer 4)
Barbarians. See Revak, lo schiavo di Cartagine, 1960
Barbaro del ritmo, 1963 (Alvarez 2)
Barbary Coast, 1935 (Hawks 2, Brennan 3, Carey 3, Hopkins, M. 3,
    McCrea 3, Meek 3, Niven 3, Robinson, E. 3, Day 4, Goldwyn 4,
    Hecht 4, Newman 4)
Barbary Coast Bunny, 1956 (Jones 2)
Barbary Coast Gent, 1944 (Beavers 3, Beery 3, Carradine 3, Meek 3)
Barbary Pirate, 1949 (Katzman 4)
Barbary Sheep, 1917 (Tourneur, M. 2, Carré 4)
Barbe-Bleue, 1901 (Méliès 2)
Barbe-Bleue, 1935 (Jaubert 4)
Barbe-Bleue, 1951 (Christian-Jaque 2, Brasseur 3, Jeanson 4,
    Matras 4, Wakhévitch 4)
Barbe-Bleue, 1972 (Dmytryk 2, Burton 3, Legrand 4, Morricone 4)
Barbed Water, 1969 (Welles 2)
Barbed Wire, 1927 (Stiller 2, Brook 3, Negri 3, Banton 4, Furthman 4,
    Glennon 4, Pommer 4, Schulberg 4)
Barbed Wire, 1952 (Autry 3)
Barbeque Brawl, 1956 (Hanna and Barbera 4)
Barber, 1918 (Hardy 3)
Barber Shop, 1933 (Sennett 2, Fields, W.C. 3)
Barberina, die Tanzerin von Sanssouci. See Tanzerin von Sanssouci,
    1933
Barberousse, 1916 (Gance 2, Burel 4)
Barber's Daughter, 1929 (Sennett 2)
Barboni, 1946 (Risi 2)
Barbora Hlavsová, 1942 (Fric 2, Hrušínský 3)
Barbouzes, 1964 (Blier 3, Audiard 4)
Barca de oro, 1947 (Infante 3)
Barcarole, 1935 (Baarová 3, Feuillère 3, Frohlich 3, Manès 3, Herlth 4,
    Rohrig 4)
Barcarole. See Brand in der Oper, 1930
Barcarolle d'amour, 1929 (Boyer 3)
Barchante Neguib, 1945 (García 3)
Bardame, 1922 (Wagner 4)
Bardelys the Magnificent, 1926 (Florey 2, Vidor, K. 2, Gilbert 3,
    Daniels 4, Day 4, Gibbons 4)
Bardidi, 1939 (Sircar 4)

Bare Essence, 1982 (Ames 4)
Bare Fists, 1919 (Ford, J. 2, Carey 3)
Bare Knees, 1928 (Robinson 4)
Barefaced Flatfoot, 1950 (Burness 4, Hubley 4)
Barefoot Battalion, 1953 (Theodorakis 4)
Barefoot Boy, 1938 (Brown, K. 4)
Barefoot Contessa, 1954 (Mankiewicz 2, Bogart 3, Brazzi 3, Cortese 3,
    Gardner 3, Love 3, O'Brien, E. 3, Cardiff 4, Hornbeck 4)
Barefoot in the Park, 1967 (Boyer 3, Fonda, J. 3, Redford 3,
    Edouart 4, Head 4, La Shelle 4, Mercer 4, Wallis 4,
    Westmore, W. 4)
Barefoot Mailman, 1951 (Cummings 3, Duning 4)
Bargain, 1914 (Hart 3, Sullivan 4)
Bargain, 1931 (Merkel 3, Stone 3, Polito 4)
Bargain Daze, 1953 (Terry 4)
Bargain Hunt, 1928 (Sennett 2)
Bargain Hunters, 1914 (Beery 3)
Bargain of the Century, 1933 (Pitts 3, Roach 4)
Bari Theke Palive, 1959 (Ghatak 4)
Barier, 1978 (Smoktunovsky 3)
Bariera, 1966 (Skolimowski 2, Lomnicki 3, Nowicki 3)
Bariri, 1958 (Olmi 2)
Barish, 1956 (Anand 3)
Barker, 1928 (Fairbanks, D. Jr. 3, Garmes 4, Glazer 4, Grot 4,
    Mankiewicz 4)
Barkhatnyi sezon, 1978 (Smoktunovsky 3)
Barking-Donkey Sonichi. See Shiriboe Sonichi, 1969
Barkleys of Broadway, 1949 (Walters 2, Astaire 3, Burke 3, Rogers, G.
    3, Alton, R. 4, Comden and Green 4, Freed 4, Irene 4, Pan 4,
    Stradling 4)
Barn Dance, 1929 (Disney 2, Iwerks 4)
Barnabé, 1938 (Fernandel 3)
Barnaby—Father Dear Father, 1962 (Halas and Batchelor 2)
Barnaby—Overdue Dues Blues, 1962 (Halas and Batchelor 2)
Barnacle Bill, 1930 (Fleischer, M. and D. 2)
Barnacle Bill, 1941 (Beery 3, Meek 3, Gibbons 4, Kaper 4)
Barnacle Bill, 1957 (Guinness 3, Pleasance 3, Addison 4,
    Clarke, T.E.B. 4, Slocombe 4)
Barnen från Frostmofjallet, 1945 (Nykvist 4)
Barnet, 1909 (Blom 2)
Barnet, 1912 (Sjostrom 2, Stiller 2, Jaenzon 4, Magnusson 4)
Barnet, 1940 (Christensen 2)
Barnet. See Barnets Magt, 1914
Barnets Magt, 1914 (Holger-Madsen 2)
Barney Oldfield's Race for a Life, 1913 (Sennett 2, Sennett 2, Normand
    3)
Barnforbjudet, 1979 (Andersson B. 3)
Barnstormers, 1905 (Bitzer 4)
Barnum and Ringling Inc., 1927 (Hardy 3, Roach 4)
Barnum Was Right, 1929 (Beavers 3)
Barnvagnen, 1963 (Troell 2, Widerberg 2)
Barnyard Actor, 1955 (Terry 4)
Barnyard Amateurs, 1936 (Terry 4)
Barnyard Baseball, 1939 (Terry 4)
Barnyard Battle, 1929 (Disney 2, Iwerks 4)
Barnyard Blackout, 1943 (Terry 4)
Barnyard Boss, 1937 (Terry 4)
Barnyard Brat, 1939 (Fleischer, M. and D. 2)
Barnyard Concert, 1930 (Disney 2)
Barnyard Eggcitement, 1939 (Terry 4)
Barnyard Five, 1936 (Lantz 4)
Barnyard Flirtation. See Barnyard Flirtations, 1914
Barnyard Flirtations, 1914 (Sennett 2, Arbuckle 3)
Barnyard WAAC, 1942 (Terry 4)
Barocco, 1925 (Vanel 3)
Barocco, 1976 (Adjani 3, Depardieu 3, Sarde 4)
Baromètre de la fidélité, 1909 (Linders 3)
Baron, 1911 (Sennett 2)
Baron Blood. See Orrori del castello di Norimberga, 1972
Baron de Crac. See Monsieur de Crac, 1910
Baron de l'Ecluse, 1951 (Presle 3)
Baron de l'écluse, 1959 (Delannoy 2, Gabin 3, Audiard 4)
Baron fantôme, 1942 (Cocteau 2, Cuny 3)

Baron Munchausen's Dream. *See* Hallucinations du Baron Munchausen, 1911

Baron Munchhausen. *See* Baron Prášil, 1961

Baron of Arizona, 1950 (Fuller 2, Bondi 3, Price 3, Howe 4)

Baron Prášil, 1940 (Fric 2)

Baron Prášil, 1961 (Zeman 2, Brejchová 3, Kopecký 3, Brdečka 4)

Baroness and the Butler, 1938 (Bruce 3, Powell, W. 3, Schildkraut 3, La Shelle 4, Miller, A. 4, Trotti 4)

Baronesschen auf Strafurlaub, 1918 (Albers 3)

Baroni, 1974 (Fabrizi 3)

Barood, 1976 (Burman 4)

Baroud, 1931 (Ingram 2, Henreid 3, Burel 4, Wakhévitch 4)

Barque en mer, 1896-97 (Lumière 2)

Barque sortant du port, 1895 (Lumière 2)

Barquero, 1970 (Oates 3, Van Cleef 3)

Barrabas, 1919 (Feuillade 2)

Barrage contre le Pacifique, 1958 (Clément 2, Perkins 3, Valli 3, De Laurentiis 4, Rota 4)

Barrage de l'Aigle, 1946 (Leenhardt 2)

Barrage du Châtelot, 1953 (Colpi 4, Fradetal 4)

Barrandovské nocturno, aneb Jak film tančil a zpíval, 1984 (Švankmajer 4)

Barravento, 1962 (Rocha 2)

Barrel Full of Dollars. *See* Per una bara piena di dollari, 1970

Barren Gain, 1915 (Eason 4)

Barretts of Wimpole Street, 1934 (Franklin 2, Carroll L. 3, Laughton 3, March 3, O'Sullivan 3, Shearer 3, Adrian 4, Booth 4, Daniels 4, Gibbons 4, Stewart 4, Stothart 4, Thalberg 4, Vajda 4)

Barretts of Wimpole Street, 1956 (Franklin 2, Gielgud 3, Jones, J. 3, Junge 4, Kaper 4, Young, F. 4)

Barricade, 1939 (Baxter W. 3, Faye 3, Freund 4, Newman 4, Veiller 4)

Barricade, 1950 (Massey 3)

Barricade du point du jour, 1978 (Noiret 3)

Barrie MacKenzie Holds His Own, 1974 (Beresford 2, Pleasance 3)

Barrier, 1926 (Barrymore L. 3, Walthall 3)

Barrier, 1937 (Head 4)

Barrier. *See* Barier, 1978

Barrier. *See* Bariera, 1966

Barrier of Faith, 1915 (Talmadge, N. 3)

Barrière, 1915 (Feuillade 2, Musidora 3)

Barriere delle legge, 1953 (Brazzi 3)

Barrières, 1949 (Christian-Jaque 2)

Barriers Burned Away. *See* Chicago Fire, 1925

Barriers Swept Aside, 1915 (Nilsson 3)

Barrings, 1955 (Dagover 3, Tschechowa 3)

Barry, 1948 (Fresnay 3)

Barry Lyndon, 1975 (Kubrick 2, Adam 4, Rosenman 4)

Barsaat, 1949 (Kapoor 2)

Barsaat Ki Ek Raat, 1981 (Bachchan 3)

Bartered Bride. *See* Prodaná nevésta, 1933

Bartered Bride. *See* Verkaufte Braut, 1932

Bartholomew vs. the Wheel, 1964 (McKimson 4)

Bartok, 1964 (Russell 2)

Bartók Béla: az éjszaka zenéje, 1970 (Gaál 2)

Baruch. *See* Alte Gesetz, 1923

Baruffe chiozzotte. *See* Paese senza pace, 1943

Baruffe choizzotte, 1943 (Brazzi 3)

Baruten Bukvar, 1977 (Dinov 4)

Barwy ochronne, 1976 (Zanussi 2)

Baryshnya i chuligan. *See* Poet na ekrane, 1973

Bas de laine, 1911 (Feuillade 2)

Basant, 1943 (Biswas 4)

Baseball Bugs, 1945 (Freleng 4)

Baseball Madness, 1917 (Swanson 3)

Bas-fonds, 1936 (Becker 2, Renoir 2, Visconti 2, Gabin 3, Jouvet 3, Lourié 4, Spaak 4)

Bashful, 1917 (Roach 4)

Bashful Bachelor, 1941 (Pitts 3)

Bashful Buccaneer, 1925 (Brown, Harry Joe 4)

Bashful Buzzard, 1945 (Clampett 4)

Bashful Jim, 1925 (Sennett 2)

Bashful Suitor, 1921 (Astor 3)

Basic Training, 1971 (Wiseman 2)

Basilischi, 1963 (Wertmüller 2, Di Venanzo 4, Morricone 4)

Basilisk, 1914 (Hepworth 2)

Basketball Fix, 1951 (Ireland 3, Cortez 4, Leven 4)

Bassae, 1964 (Astruc 2)

Basta che non si sappia in giro, 1976 (Comencini 2, Manfredi 3, Age and Scarpelli 4)

Bastard. *See* Vildmarkens sång, 1940

Bastardi, 1968 (Kinski 3)

Bastardi. *See* Sons of Satan, 1968

Bastion Promenade 74. *See* Bástyasétány 74, 1974

Bástyasétány 74, 1974 (Schorm 2)

Bat, 1926 (Fazenda 3, Edeson 4, Menzies 4)

Bat, 1959 (Moorehead 3, Price 3, Biroc 4)

Bat Whispers, 1930 (Merkel 3, Schenck 4)

Bataan, 1943 (Garnett 2, Taylor, R. 3, Walker 3, Gibbons 4, Gillespie 4, Kaper 4, Schary 4, Wheeler 4)

Bataille, 1923 (Hayakawa 3)

Bataille, 1933 (L'Herbier 2, Boyer 3)

Bataille d'Austerlitz, 1909 (Cohl 2)

Bataille de boules de neige, 1899–1900 (Guy 2)

Bataille de l'eau lourde, 1948 (Epstein 2)

Bataille de San Sébastian, 1967 (Verneuil 2, Bronson 3, Morricone 4)

Bataille des dix millions, 1970 (Marker 2)

Bataille d'oreillers, 1899–1900 (Guy 2)

Bataille du rail, 1945 (Clément 2, Alekan 4)

Bataille silencieuse, 1937 (Fresnay 3, Simon, M. 3)

Bataille sur le grand fleuve, 1951 (Rouch 2)

Batailles de l'argent. *See* Trust, 1911

Bataillon du ciel, 1946 (Dalio 3)

Batalia pentru Roma. *See* Kampf um Rom, 1968-69

Batalla de Chile, 1975–76 (Guzmán 2, Marker 2)

Batavernas trohetsed, 1957 (Fischer 4)

Batavians' Oath of Fidelity. *See* Batavernas trohetsed, 1957

Bateau à soupe, 1946 (Vanel 3)

Bateau d'Emile, 1961 (Brasseur 3, Girardot 3, Simon, M. 3, Audiard 4)

Bateau de verre, 1928 (Rosay 3)

Bateau ivre, 1949 (Barrault 3)

Bateau sur l'herbe, 1971 (Cassel 3, Cortese 3, Evein 4)

Bateliers de la Volga, 1936 (Vanel 3)

Bateliers de la Volga, 1959 (Vanel 3)

Baten, 1961 (Troell 2)

Bath. *See* Banya, 1962

Bath Harem. *See* Ukiyo-buro, 1929

Bath of the Transitory World. *See* Ukiyo-buro, 1929

Bathers, 1900 (Hepworth 2)

Bathhouse Beauty. *See* Bathing Beauty, 1914

Bathhouse Blunder, 1916 (Sennett 2)

Bathhouse Scandal, 1918 (Beery 3)

Bathing Beauty, 1914 (Sennett 2, Arbuckle 3)

Bathing Beauty, 1944 (Sidney 2, Dumont 3, Meek 3, Rathbone 3, Williams 3, Alton, R. 4, Green, J. 4, Irene 4, Sharaff 4, Stradling 4)

Bathroom, 1970 (Kuri 4)

Bathtub Perils, 1916 (Sennett 2)

Bâtir à notre âge, 1956 (Leenhardt 2)

Bâtisseurs, 1938 (Epstein 2, Honegger 4)

Batman, 1966 (Meredith 3, Semple 4, Smith, J.M. 4)

Batman and Robin, 1949 (Katzman 4)

Batman Dracula, 1964 (Warhol 2)

Bato no zeni: Kesho-bosatsu no maki, 1931 (Hasegawa 3)

Bato no zeni: Ogon oni ranbu no maki, 1931 (Hasegawa 3)

Baton Bunny, 1959 (Jones 2)

Bâton, 1946 (Braunberger 4)

Battaglia d'Inghilterra, 1969 (Johnson, V. 3)

Battaglia del Sinai, 1969 (Fusco 4)

Battaglia di Algeri, 1966 (Pontecorvo 2, Morricone 4, Solinas 4)

Battaglia di Maratona, 1959 (Tourneur, J. 2)

Battaglia di Mareth. *See* Grande attacco, 1977

Battant, 1982 (Delon 3)

Battement de coeur, 1939 (Darrieux 3, Dauphin 3, Barsacq 4)

Battered!. *See* Intimate Strangers, 1977

Battered, 1978 (Blondell 3)

Batticuore, 1938 (Castellani 2)

Battle, 1911 (Griffith 2, Barrymore L. 3, Crisp 3, Sweet 3, Bitzer 4)

Beach Comber. *See* Under Crimson Skies, 1920
Beach Combers, 1936 (Lantz 4)
Beach Nut, 1919 (Beery 3)
Beach Nuts, 1918 (Lloyd 3, Roach 4)
Beach Pajamas, 1931 (Arbuckle 3)
Beach Party, 1963 (Cummings 3, Malone 3, Price 3)
Beach Red, 1967 (Torn 3, Wilde 3)
Beachcomber, 1915 (Bosworth 3)
Beachcomber, 1939 (Head 4)
Beachcomber, 1954 (Pleasance 3)
Beachcomber. *See* Vessel of Wrath, 1938
Beached and Bleached, 1915 (Talmadge, C. 3)
Beachhead, 1954 (Curtis 3)
Bead Game, 1977 (Patel 4)
Beaded Buckskin Bag, 1913 (Bosworth 3)
Beaks to the Grindstone, 1985 (Godfrey 4)
Beanstalk Bunny, 1955 (Jones 2)
Beanstalk Jack, 1933 (Terry 4)
Beanstalk Jack, 1946 (Terry 4)
Bear, 1984 (Stanton 3)
Bear. *See* Medvěd, 1961
Bear Affair, 1915 (Sennett 2, Fazenda 3)
Bear Escape, 1912 (Sennett 2, Sennett 2)
Bear Feat, 1949 (Jones 2)
Bear for Punishment, 1951 (Jones 2)
Bear Hug, 1963 (Hanna and Barbera 4)
Bear Island, 1979 (Lee, C. 3, Redgrave, V. 3, Sutherland 3,
    Widmark 3)
Bear Knuckles, 1963 (Hanna and Barbera 4)
Bear of a Story, 1916 (Mix 3)
Bear That Wasn't, 1967 (Jones 2)
Bear Up, 1963 (Hanna and Barbera 4)
Bear Ye One Another's Burden, 1910 (Lawrence 3)
Bearded Bandit, 1910 (Anderson G. 3)
Bearded Youth, 1911 (Sennett 2)
Bearer of the Golden Star. *See* Knight of the Gold Star, 1950
Bearly Able, 1962 (Hanna and Barbera 4)
Bears and Bad Men, 1918 (Laurel 3)
Bear's Tale, 1940 (Avery 2)
Bear's Wedding. *See* Medvezhya svadba, 1926
Beast. *See* Bête, 1974
Beast Alley. *See* Kemonomichi, 1965
Beast at Bay, 1912 (Griffith 2, Pickford 3, Bitzer 4)
Beast from a Haunted Cave, 1959 (Corman 4)
Beast from 20,000 Fathoms, 1953 (Van Cleef 3, Boyle 4,
    Harryhausen 4, Lourié 4)
Beast Must Die, 1974 (Cushing 3)
Beast of Hollow Mountain, 1956 (O'Brien 4)
Beast of the City, 1932 (Harlow 3, Hersholt 3, Huston 3, Rooney 3,
    Burnett 4, Mahin 4)
Beast with Five Fingers, 1947 (Florey 2, Lorre 3, Friedhofer 4,
    Siodmak 4, Steiner 4)
Beast with 1,000,000 Eyes, 1955 (Corman 4)
Beastmaster, 1982 (Torn 3)
Beasts of Berlin. *See* Hitler, Beast of Berlin, 1939
Beasts of Marseilles. *See* 7 Thunders, 1957
Beasts of Prey. *See* Dravci, 1948
Beasts of the Jungle, 1913 (Guy 2)
Beat Generation, 1958 (Coogan 3)
Beat Girl, 1960 (Lee, C. 3, Reed, O. 3, Barry 4, Lassally 4)
Beat It, 1918 (Daniels 3, Lloyd 3, Roach 4)
Beat Me Daddy, Eight to the Bar!, 1940 (Krasner 4)
Beat the Devil, 1954 (Clayton 2, Huston 2, Bogart 3, Jones, J. 3,
    Lollobrigida 3, Lorre 3, Francis 4, Morris 4)
Beat the Retreat, 1936 (Holloway 3)
Beat Thirteen. *See* 13. revír, 1945
Béata és az ordog, 1940 (Gabór 3)
Beating He Needed, 1912 (Sennett 2)
Beating Hearts and Carpets, 1915 (Sennett 2)
Beating the Game, 1921 (Gibbons 4)
Beatnik et le minet, 1967 (Leenhardt 2, Depardieu 3)
Beato Loro, 1975 (Cristaldi 4)
Beatrice, 1919 (Bertini 3)

Beatrice Cenci, 1926 (Amidei 4)
Beatrice Cenci, 1941 (Stallich 4)
Beatrice Cenci, 1956 (Cervi 3, Presle 3)
Beatrice devant le désir, 1944 (Berry 3, Signoret 3, Wakhévitch 4)
Béatrice ou La servante folle, 1959 (Cortese 3)
Beau and Arrows, 1932 (Lantz 4)
Beau Beste, 1933 (Lantz 4)
Beau Broadway, 1928 (Gibbons 4)
Beau Brummel, 1913 (Ingram 2)
Beau Brummell, 1924 (Astor 3, Barrymore J. 3)
Beau Brummell, 1954 (Granger 3, Love 3, Taylor, E. 3, Ustinov 3,
    Francis 4, Junge 4, Morris 4)
Beau Chumps. *See* Beau Hunks, 1931
Beau fixe, 1953 (Legrand 4)
Beau Geste, 1926 (Brenon 2, Colman 3, McLaglen 3, Powell, W. 3,
    Hunt 4)
Beau Geste, 1939 (Wellman 2, Cooper, Gary 3, Crawford, B. 3,
    Hayward 3, Milland 3, O'Connor 3, Preston 3, Dreier 4, Head 4,
    Newman 4)
Beau Geste, 1966 (Bumstead 4, Needham 4, Salter 4, Whitlock 4)
Beau Hunks, 1931 (Laurel & Hardy 3, Roach 4)
Beau Ideal, 1931 (Brenon 2, Young, L. 3, Hunt 4, Steiner 4)
Beau James, 1957 (Douglas, P. 3, Durante 3, Hope 3, Cahn 4, Head 4)
Beau Jour de noces, 1932 (Fernandel 3)
Beau Mariage, 1982 (Rohmer 2)
Beau Plaisir, 1969 (Perrault 2)
Beau Revel, 1921 (Stone 3, Ince 4)
Beau Sabreur, 1928 (Cooper, Gary 3, Powell, W. 3, Banton 4)
Beau Serge, 1958 (Broca 2, Chabrol 2, Decaë 3)
Beau Voyage, 1947 (Matras 4)
Beaubourg, 1977 (Almendros 4)
Beau-père, 1981 (Blier 2, Baye 3, Sarde 4, Vierny 4)
Beauté de l'effort, 1953 (Decaë 4)
Beauté du diable, 1949 (Clair 2, Modot 3, Philipe 3, Simon, M. 3,
    Barsacq 4, Di Venanzo 4)
Beauties of the Night. *See* Belles de nuit, 1952
Beautiful and Damned, 1922 (Fazenda 3)
Beautiful Banff and Lake Louise, 1935 (Hoch 4)
Beautiful Blonde from Bashful Bend, 1949 (Sturges, P. 2, Grable 3,
    Trumbo 4)
Beautiful Budapest, 1938 (Hoch 4)
Beautiful But Dangerous. *See* Donna piu bella del mondo, 1955
Beautiful But Dangerous. *See* She Couldn't Say No, 1954
Beautiful But Deadly. *See* Don is Dead, 1973
Beautiful But Poor. *See* Belle ma povere, 1957
Beautiful Cheat, 1945 (Banton 4)
Beautiful City, 1925 (Goulding 2, Barthelmess 3, Gish, D. 3, Powell,
    W. 3)
Beautiful Days. *See* Uruwashiki saigetsu, 1955
Beautiful Gambler, 1921 (Barnes 4)
Beautiful Liar, 1921 (Schulberg 4)
Beautiful Margaret. *See* Tout Petit Faust, 1910
Beautiful Nuisance. *See* On peut le dire sans se fâcher!, 1978
Beautiful Rebel. *See* Janice Meredith, 1924
Beautiful Sinner, 1924 (Van Dyke, W.S. 2)
Beautiful Stranger, 1954 (Baker S. 3, Ferrer, J. 3, Arnold 4)
Beautiful Swindlers. *See* Plus Belles Escroqueries du monde, 1964
Beautiful Voice, 1911 (Sennett 2)
Beauty. *See* Beauty for Sale, 1933
Beauty. *See* Reijin, 1946
Beauty and the Barge, 1937 (Hawkins 3, Rutherford 3)
Beauty and the Beast, 1934 (Freleng 4)
Beauty and the Beast, 1962 (Friedhofer 4, Pierce 4)
Beauty and the Beast, 1976 (Scott, G. 3)
Beauty and the Beast. *See* Belle et la bête, 1946
Beauty and the Bus, 1933 (Roach 4)
Beauty and the Devil. *See* Beauté du diable, 1949
Beauty and the Dragon. *See* Bijo to Kairyu, 1955
Beauty and the Robot. *See* Sex Kittens Go to College, 1960
Beauty and the Rogue, 1918 (King 2, Seitz 4)
Beauty Bunglers, 1915 (Sennett 2)
Beauty Capital. *See* Bibou no miyako, 1957
Beauty Care in the Jungle. *See* Skonhetsvård i djungeln, 1935–36

Beauty for Sale, 1933 (Brady 3, Merkel 3, Adrian 4, Howe 4)
Beauty for the Asking, 1939 (Ball 3)
Beauty on the Beach, 1950 (Terry 4)
Beauty Parlor, 1932 (Auer 3)
Beauty Prize. *See* Prix de beauté, 1930
Beauty Shop, 1922 (Fazenda 3)
Beauty Shop, 1950 (Terry 4)
Beauty Shop. *See* Schonheitspflasterchen, 1937
Beauty Shoppe, 1936 (Lantz 4)
Beauty's Daughter, 1935 (Bellamy 3, Trevor 3, Maté 4, Seitz 4)
Beauty's Daughter. *See* Navy Wife, 1935
Beauty's Worth, 1922 (Davies 3)
Beaux Arts mysterieux, 1910 (Cohl 2)
Beaux Jours, 1935 (Allégret, M. 2, Aumont 3, Barrault 3, Simon, S. 3, D'Eaubonne 4, Meerson 4, Spaak 4)
Beaux-Arts de Jocko, 1909 (Cohl 2)
Beaver Trouble, 1951 (Terry 4)
Bébé de l'escadron, 1935 (Brasseur 3, Douy 4, Lourié 4)
Bébé de l'Escadron. *See* Quand la vie était belle, 1935
Bébé embarrassant, 1905 (Guy 2)
Bebek, 1973 (Andersson H. 3)
Bebo's Girl. *See* Ragazza di Bube, 1963
Because He Loved Her, 1916 (Sennett 2)
Because He's My Friend, 1978 (Black 3)
Because I Love. *See* Aisureba koso, 1955
Because I Love. *See* Sukinareba koso, 1928
Because I Loved You. *See* Dich hab' ich geliebt, 1929
Because of Him, 1946 (Durbin 3, Laughton 3, Meek 3, Plunkett 4, Rozsa 4)
Because of the Cats, 1973 (Rademakers 2)
Because of You, 1952 (Chandler 3, Young, L. 3)
Because They're Young, 1960 (Weld 3, Williams, J. 4)
Because You're Mine, 1952 (Cahn 4, Green, J. 4, Pasternak 4, Rose 4, Rose 4, Ruttenberg 4)
Becket, 1964 (Burton 3, Cervi 3, Gielgud 3, O'Toole 3, Anhalt 4, Mathieson 4, Unsworth 4, Wallis 4)
Beckoning Flame, 1916 (Sullivan 4)
Becky, 1927 (Gibbons 4)
Becky Sharp, 1935 (Mamoulian 2, Bruce 3, Burke 3, Hardwicke 3, Hopkins, M. 3, Cooper 4, MacGowan 4, Steiner 4)
Becsapott újságíró, 1914 (Korda 2)
Bed, 1968 (Broughton 2)
Bed. *See* Secrets d'alcove, 1954
Bed and Board. *See* Domicile conjugal, 1970
Bed of Roses, 1922 (Roach 4)
Bed of Roses, 1933 (La Cava 2, Bennett C. 3, Darwell 3, McCrea 3, Cooper 4, Polglase 4, Rosher 4, Steiner 4)
Bed Sitting Room, 1969 (Lester 2, Moore, D. 3, Richardson 3, Watkin 4)
Bedazzled, 1967 (Donen 2, Moore, D. 3, Welch 3)
Bedelia, 1930 (Fleischer, M. and D. 2)
Bedelia, 1946 (Young, F. 4)
Bedevilled, 1955 (Leisen 2, Baxter A. 3, Dauphin 3, Alwyn 4, Junge 4, Rose 4)
Bedevilled Rabbit, 1957 (McKimson 4)
Bedford Incident, 1965 (Poitier 3, Sutherland 3, Widmark 3)
Bedingung—Kein Anhang!, 1914 (Lubitsch 2)
Bedknobs and Broomsticks, 1971 (Jaffe 3, Lansbury 3, McDowall 3, Ellenshaw 4)
Bedlam, 1946 (Robson 2, Karloff 3, D'Agostino 4, Lewton 4, Musuraca 4)
Bedlam in Paradise, 1955 (Three Stooges 3)
Bednijat Luka, 1979 (Paskaleva 3)
Bedroom Blunder, 1917 (Sennett 2)
Bedside, 1934 (Florey 2, Beavers 3, Meek 3, Orry-Kelly 4)
Bedstemoders Vuggevise. *See* Operabranden, 1912
Bedtime, 1923 (Fleischer, M. and D. 2)
Bedtime for Bonzo, 1951 (Fleischer, M. and D. 2, Reagan 3)
Bedtime for Sniffles, 1940 (Jones 2)
Bedtime Story, 1933 (Taurog 2, Chevalier 3, Horton 3, Glazer 4, Johnson 4, Lang 4, Young, W. 4)
Bedtime Story, 1941 (Seaton 2, Arden 3, March 3, Young, L. 3, Irene 4, Schulberg 4, Walker 4)

Bedtime Story, 1964 (Brando 3, Dern 3, Jones S. 3, Niven 3, Salter 4)
Bedtime Worries, 1933 (Roach 4)
Bee and the Dove, 1950 (Popescu-Gopo 4)
Bee-Deviled Bruin, 1948 (Jones 2)
Beef and the Banana. *See* Biffen och Bananen, 1951
Beef-for and After, 1962 (Hanna and Barbera 4)
Beekeeper's Scrapbook. *See* Slikovnica pčelara, 1958
Beelzebub's Daughters. *See* Filles du Diable, 1903
Beep Beep, 1952 (Jones 2)
Beep Prepared, 1962 (Jones 2)
Beer and Pretzels, 1933 (Three Stooges 3)
Beer Baron. *See* Song of the Eagle, 1933
Beer Barrel Polecats, 1946 (Three Stooges 3)
Bees, 1978 (Carradine 3, Corman 4)
Bee's Buzz, 1929 (Sennett 2)
Bees in His Bonnet, 1918 (Daniels 3, Lloyd 3, Roach 4)
Beethoven, 1927 (Kortner 3)
Beethoven, le voleur de femmes. *See* Grand Amour de Beethoven, 1937
Beethoven—Tage aus einem Leben, 1976 (Hoppe 3)
Before Breakfast, 1919 (Daniels 3, Lloyd 3, Roach 4)
Before Dawn, 1933 (Darwell 3, Oland 3, Fort 4, Steiner 4)
Before Dawn. *See* Reimei izen, 1931
Before Election. *See* Választás elótt, 1953
Before Him All Rome Trembled. *See* Devanti a lui tremava tutta Roma, 1946
Before I Hang, 1940 (Karloff 3, Brown, K. 4)
Before Midnight, 1925 (Furthman 4)
Before Midnight, 1934 (Bellamy 3)
Before Spring, 1958 (Ivens 2)
Before the Dawn. *See* Yoake mae, 1953
Before the Judgment of History. *See* Pered sudom istorii, 1967
Before the Public, 1922 (Roach 4)
Before the Raid, 1943 (Weiss 2, Dalrymple 4)
Before the Revolution. *See* Prima della rivoluzione, 1964
Before the White Man Came, 1912 (Reid 3)
Before Winter Comes, 1969 (Hurt, J. 3, Karina 3, Niven 3, Quayle 3, Topol 3)
Befriete Hande, 1939 (Hoffmann 4)
Beg, 1971 (Batalov 3, Ulyanov 3)
Beg, Borrow, or Steal, 1937 (Daniels 4)
Begar, 1946 (Borgstrom 3)
Begegnung in Rom. *See* Parigina a Roma, 1954
Begegnung in Salzburg, 1964 (Jurgens 3)
Begegnung mit Fritz Lang, 1963 (Godard 2)
Beggar. *See* Tainstvennie nekto, 1914
Beggar Life. *See* Svet, kde se žebrá, 1938
Beggar Maid, 1921 (Astor 3)
Beggar Man of Paris. *See* Smil, 1916
Beggar of Cawnpore, 1916 (Sullivan 4)
Beggar on Horseback, 1925 (Cruze 2, Horton 3, Brown, K. 4)
Beggar Prince, 1920 (Hayakawa 3)
Beggar Princess. *See* Grevinde Hjerteløs, 1915
Beggar's Deceit, 1900 (Hepworth 2)
Beggars in Ermine, 1934 (Walthall 3)
Beggars of Life, 1928 (Wellman 2, Arlen 3, Beery 3, Brooks 3, Glazer 4)
Beggar's Opera, 1953 (Holloway 3, Olivier 3, Green, G. 4, Wakhévitch 4)
Beggar's Opera. *See* Dreigroschenoper, 1931
Begierde. *See* Abwege, 1928
Beginning of the End, 1947 (Edwards 2, Taurog 2, Walker 3, Gillespie 4, Irene 4)
Begone Dull Care, 1949 (McLaren 2)
Begreite Hande, 1939 (Tschechowa 3)
Begstvo Mistera Makkinli, 1976 (Babochkin 3)
Begstvo Puankare, 1932 (Ptushko 2)
Beguiled, 1971 (Siegel 2, Eastwood 3, Page 3, Schifrin 4, Westmore, F. 4)
Behave Yourself!, 1951 (Chaney Lon, Jr. 3, Cook 3, Winters 3, Howe 4, Krasna 4, Orry-Kelly 4, Wald 4)
Behemoth, The Sea Monster. *See* Giant Behemoth, 1959
Behind Closed Doors, 1931 (Wilson, C. 4)

Behind Closed Doors. *See* Porte Chiuse, 1960
Behind Closed Shutters. *See* Persiane chiuse, 1951
Behind Green Lights, 1946 (Ireland 3)
Behind Jury Doors, 1932 (Eason 4)
Behind Locked Doors, 1948 (Boetticher 2)
Behind Office Doors, 1931 (Astor 3, Hunt 4)
Behind That Curtain, 1929 (Baxter W. 3, Karloff 3, Levien 4)
Behind the Altar. *See* Geheimnis des Abbe, 1927
Behind the Bars. *See* Rács, 1970
Behind the Closed Shutters. *See* Persiane chiuse, 1951
Behind the Counter, 1927 (Horton 3)
Behind the Door, 1919 (Beery 3, Bosworth 3, Ince 4)
Behind the Door. *See* Man with Nine Lives, 1940
Behind the Door. *See* Oltre la porta, 1982
Behind the Front, 1926 (Sutherland 2, Arlen 3, Beery 3)
Behind the Headlines, 1937 (Meek 3)
Behind the High Wall, 1956 (Sidney 3)
Behind the Iron Mask, 1977 (De Havilland 3)
Behind the Iron Mask. *See* Fifth Musketeer, 1979
Behind the Lines, (Johnson, N. 3)
Behind the Make-Up, 1930 (Arzner 2, Francis, K. 3, Lukas 3,
    Powell, W. 3, Wray 3, Estabrook 4, Lang 4, Miller, A. 4)
Behind the Map, 1917 (Pitts 3)
Behind the Mask, 1917 (Guy 2)
Behind the Mask, 1932 (Karloff 3, Swerling 4)
Behind the Mask, 1958 (Redgrave, M. 3, Redgrave, V. 3, Krasker 4)
Behind the News, 1940 (Schary 4)
Behind the Rising Sun, 1943 (Dmytryk 2, Ryan 3)
Behind the Scenes, 1908 (Griffith 2, Lawrence 3)
Behind the Scenes, 1914 (Pickford 3)
Behind the Screen, 1916 (Bacon 2, Chaplin 2, Purviance 3)
Behind the Screen. *See* Kulissi ekrana, 1916
Behind the Shutters, 1973 (Bardem 2)
Behind the Shutters. *See* Corrupcion de Chris Miller, 1973
Behind the Silence. *See* Detras del silencio, 1972
Behind the Spanish Lines, 1938 (Dickinson 2)
Behind the Stockade, 1911 (Ince 4)
Behind the Veil, 1914 (Weber 2)
Behind the Wall. *See* Za sciana, 1971
Behinderte Zukunft, 1970 (Herzog 2)
Behold a Pale Horse, 1964 (Zinnemann 2, Peck 3, Quinn 3, Sharif 3,
    Jarre 4, Trauner 4)
Behold My Wife, 1935 (Leisen 2, Sheridan 3, Sidney 3, Schulberg 4,
    Shamroy 4)
Behold This Woman, 1924 (Blackton 2)
Behold Thy Son. *See* Kiiroi karasu, 1957
Behold We Live. *See* If I Were Free, 1933
Beichte einer Toten, 1920 (Krauss 3)
Beiden Gatten der Frau Ruth, 1919 (Galeen 4)
Beiden Rivalen, 1914 (Warm 4)
Beil von Wandsbek, 1949 (Staudte 2, Geschonneck 3)
Being, 1983 (Ferrer, J. 3, Malone 3)
Being Respectable, 1924 (Fazenda 3)
Being There, 1979 (Ashby 2, Douglas, M. 3, MacLaine 3, Sellers 3,
    Warden 3)
Being Two Isn't Easy. *See* Watashi wa ni-sai, 1962
Beispiellose Verteidigung der Festung Deutschkreuz, 1966 (Herzog 2)
Béke utja, 1917 (Curtiz 2)
Bekenntnis der Ina Kahr, 1954 (Pabst 2, Jurgens 3)
Bekenntnisse des Hochstaplers Felix Krull, 1957 (Dagover 3, Herlth 4)
Bekotott szemmel, 1975 (Kovács 2, Madaras 3)
Bekstvo sa robija, 1978 (Samardžić 3)
Bel Age, 1958 (Cloquet 4, Delerue 4, Vierny 4)
Bel ami, 1939 (Tschechowa 3)
Bel Ami, 1954 (Barsacq 4, Eisler 4)
Bel Indifférent, 1957 (Cocteau 2, Demy 2, Evein 4, Fradetal 4, Jarre 4)
Bel ouvrage, 1943 (Alekan 4)
Béla Bartók: The Music of the Night. *See* Bartók Béla, 1970
Bela Lugosi Meets a Brooklyn Gorilla, 1952 (Lugosi 3)
Bela Trave, 1976 (Samardžić 3)
Belanin yedi turlusu, 1969 (Guney 2)
Belaya vorona, 1941 (Yutkevich 2)
Belges et la mer, 1954 (Storck 2)

Belgian, 1918 (Olcott 2)
Belgian Grand Prix, 1955 (Haanstra 2)
Belgique nouvelle, 1937 (Storck 2)
Belgique profonde, 1980 (Reichenbach 2)
Believe in Me, 1971 (Bisset 3)
Believe It or Else, 1939 (Avery 2)
Believe Me Xanthippe. *See* Believe Me Xantippe, 1918
Believe Me Xantippe, 1918 (Cruze 2, Crisp 3, Reid 3)
Belinski, 1953 (Kozintsev 2, Moskvin 4, Shostakovich 4)
Bell' Antonio, 1960 (Bolognini 2, Pasolini 2, Brasseur 3, Cardinale 3,
    Mastroianni 3)
Bell, Book, and Candle, 1958 (Lanchester 3, Lemmon 3, Novak 3,
    Stewart 3, Duning 4, Howe 4, Taradash 4)
Bell Boy, 1918 (Keaton 2, Arbuckle 3)
Bell for Adano, 1945 (King 2, Bendix 3, Dalio 3, Haas 3, Tierney 3,
    La Shelle 4, Newman 4, Raine 4, Trotti 4)
Bell Hoppy, 1954 (McKimson 4)
Bell of Austi, 1914 (Ince 4)
Bella di Lodi, 1962 (Delli Colli 4)
Bella di Roma, 1955 (Comencini 2, Sordi 3, Rota 4)
Bella Donna, 1915 (Porter 2)
Bella Donna, 1923 (Menjou 3, Negri 3, Miller, A. 4)
Bella Donna, 1934 (Hardwicke 3, Veidt 3)
Bella donna, 1983 (Janda 3)
Bella mugnaia, 1955 (De Sica 2, Loren 3, Mastroianni 3, De Laurentiis
    4, Ponti 4)
Bellamy Trial, 1929 (Gibbons 4, Miller, A. 4)
Bella's Beau, 1912–13 (White 3)
Bella's Elopement, 1914 (Costello, M. 3)
Bell-Bottom George, 1943 (Formby 3)
Bellboy, 1960 (Lewis 2, Bumstead 4, Head 4)
Belle, 1973 (Cloquet 4)
Belle Américaine, 1961 (Cloquet 4)
Belle au bois dormant, 1935 (Alexeieff and Parker 2)
Belle au bois dormant. *See* Sleeping Beauty, 1930
Belle Aventure, 1942 (Allégret, M. 2, Dauphin 3, Jourdan 3, Presle 3,
    Achard 4, Auric 4, Burel 4)
Belle Aventure. *See* Schone Abenteuer, 1932
Belle Captive, 1983 (Alekan 4, Robbe-Grillet 4)
Belle cérébrale, 1968 (Foldès 4)
Belle Dame sans merci, 1920 (Dulac 2)
Belle de jour, 1966 (Buñuel 2, Deneuve 3, Fabian 3, Piccoli 3,
    Carrière 4, Vierny 4)
Belle de Paris. *See* Under My Skin, 1949
Belle della notte, 1952 (Lollobrigida 3)
Belle dell'aria, 1958 (Cervi 3)
Belle Emmerdeuse. *See* On peut le dire sans se fâcher!, 1978
Belle Equipe, 1936 (Duvivier 2, Gabin 3, Vanel 3, Spaak 4)
Belle et la bête, 1946 (Cocteau 2, Marais 3, Alekan 4, Auric 4)
Belle et le corsaire. *See* Corsaro della mezzaluna, 1956
Belle et l'empereur, 1959 (Matras 4)
Belle Etoile, 1938 (Aumont 3, Simon, M. 3, Wakhévitch 4)
Belle famiglie, 1964 (Girardot 3)
Belle Fille comme moi, 1972 (Truffaut 2, Denner 3, Delerue 4)
Belle Garce, 1930 (Manès 3)
Belle Garce, 1947 (Spaak 4)
Belle Journée, 1954 (Cloquet 4)
Belle Journée, 1972 (Colpi 4)
Belle le Grand, 1951 (Dwan 2, Young, V. 4)
Belle ma povere, 1957 (Risi 2, Delli Colli 4)
Belle Marinière, 1932 (Delannoy 2, Gabin 3, Achard 4, Maté 4)
Belle Marinière, 1963 (Cloquet 4)
Belle Meunière, 1948 (Pagnol 2)
Belle Nivernaise, 1923 (Epstein 2)
Belle of New York, 1919 (Davies 3)
Belle of New York, 1952 (Walters 2, Astaire 3, Wynn 3, Alton, R. 4,
    Deutsch 4, Freed 4, Mercer 4, Rose 4, Rose 4, Smith, J.M. 4)
Belle of Siskiyou, 1913 (Anderson G. 3)
Belle of the Nineties, 1934 (Dmytryk 2, McCarey 2, West 3, Banton 4,
    Dreier 4, Struss 4)
Belle of the Yukon, 1944 (Scott, R. 3, Fields 4)
Belle of Yorktown, 1913 (Ince 4)

Belle Otéro, 1954 (Félix 3)
Belle que voilà, 1949 (Morgan 3, Douy 4, Kosma 4)
Belle Russe, 1919 (Bara 3)
Belle Starr, 1941 (Andrews D. 3, Beavers 3, Muse 3, Scott, R. 3, Tierney 3, Banton 4, Day 4, MacGowan 4, Newman 4, Trotti 4)
Belle Starr, 1980 (Alonzo 4)
Belle Starr's Daughter, 1948 (Burnett 4)
Belles de nuit, 1952 (Clair 2, Philipe 3, Barsacq 4)
Belles de nuit. See Belle della notte, 1952
Belles of St. Clement's, 1936 (Havelock-Allan 4)
Belles of St. Trinian's, 1954 (Sim 3, Arnold 4, Gilliat 4)
Belles on Their Toes, 1952 (Crain 3, Hunter 3, Loy 3, Carmichael 4, Jeakins 4, Lemaire 4)
Bellezza del mondo, 1926 (De Sica 2)
Bellissima, 1951 (Rosi 2, Visconti 2, Magnani 3, D'Amico 4, Zavattini 4)
Bellissimo novembre, 1968 (Bolognini 2, Lollobrigida 3, Morricone 4)
Bellman. See Sortilèges, 1944
Bello onesto emigrato Australia sposerebbe compaesana illibata, 1971 (Zampa 2, Cardinale 3)
Bello recuerdo, 1961 (García 3)
Bells, 1926 (Barrymore L. 3, Johnson, N. 3, Karloff 3)
Bells, 1982 (Houseman 4)
Bells Are Ringing, 1960 (Minnelli 2, Holliday 3, Martin, D. 3, Ames 4, Comden and Green 4, Freed 4, Krasner 4, Plunkett 4, Previn 4)
Bells Go Down, 1943 (Dearden 2, Mason 3, Balcon 4)
Bells Have Gone to Rome. See Harangok Rómabá mentek, 1958
Bells of Capistrano, 1942 (Autry 3)
Bells of Colorado, 1950 (Rogers, R. 3)
Bells of Rosarita, 1945 (Rogers, R. 3)
Bells of St. Mary's, 1945 (McCarey 2, Bergman 3, Crosby 3, D'Agostino 4, Head 4, Nichols 4)
Bells of San Angelo, 1947 (Rogers, R. 3)
Beloe solntse pustiny, 1969 (Yankovsky 3)
Beloved, 1934 (Rooney 3)
Beloved, 1971 (Hawkins 3)
Beloved. See Del odio nació el amor, 1949
Beloved. See Restless, 1978
Beloved Adventuress, 1917 (Marion 4)
Beloved Bachelor, 1931 (Lukas 3, Buchman 4, Rosher 4)
Beloved Bozo, 1925 (Sennett 2)
Beloved Brat, 1938 (Negulesco 2, Costello, D. 3, Crisp 3)
Beloved Brute, 1924 (Blackton 2, McLaglen 3)
Beloved Enemy, 1936 (Crisp 3, Niven 3, Oberon 3, Balderston 4, Day 4, Goldwyn 4, Newman 4, Toland 4)
Beloved Infidel, 1959 (King 2, Kerr 3, Peck 3, Reynolds 4, Shamroy 4, Wald 4, Waxman 4)
Beloved Jim, 1917 (Carey 3)
Beloved Rogue, 1927 (Crosland 2, Barrymore J. 3, Summerville 3, Veidt 3, August 4, Menzies 4)
Beloved Traitor, 1918 (Marsh 3)
Beloved Vagabond, 1923 (Matthews 3)
Beloved Vagabond, 1936 (Chevalier 3, Andrejew 4, Planer 4, Wimperis 4)
Below the Sea, 1933 (Bellamy 3, Wray 3, Swerling 4, Walker 4)
Below the Surface, 1920 (Bosworth 3)
Below Zero, 1930 (Laurel and Hardy 3, Roach 4)
Belstone Fox, 1973 (Roberts 3)
Belt Girls and the Playboy, 1961 (Coppola 2)
Belva, 1970 (Kinski 3)
Belyi Bim Chernoe Ukho, 1977 (Tikhonov 3)
Bemisal, 1982 (Bachchan 3)
Ben Bolt, 1913 (Guy 2)
Ben Hur, 1907 (Olcott 2)
Ben Hur, 1959 (Wyler 2, Hawkins 3, Jaffe 3, Heston 3, Adam 4, Canutt 4, Gillespie 4, Rozsa 4)
Ben oldukce yasarim, 1965 (Guney 2)
Benaam, 1974 (Bachchan 3)
Benazir, 1964 (Roy 2, Burman 4)
Bend of the River, 1952 (Mann 2, Fetchit 3, Hudson 3, Kennedy, A. 3, Stewart 3, Chase 4, Salter 4)
Bendix. See Bain d'X, 1956
Beneath the Czar, 1914 (Guy 2)

Beneath the Planet of the Apes, 1970 (Heston 3, McDowall 3, Dehn 4, Krasner 4, Rosenman 4, Smith, J.M. 4)
Beneath the 12-Mile Reef, 1953 (Boone 3, Wagner 3, Cronjager 4, Herrmann 4, Jeakins 4, Lemaire 4, Reynolds 4)
Benefis, 1979 (Gurchenko 3)
Benefit of the Doubt, 1965 (Jackson 3)
Benefits. See Benefis, 1979
Bengal Brigade, 1954 (Hudson 3, Miller, S. 4, Salter 4)
Bengal Famine, 1943 (Roy 2)
Bengazi, 1955 (McLaglen 3, Biroc 4)
Ben-Hur, 1926 (Niblo 2, Bushman 3, Johnson, N. 3, Loy 3, Novarro 3, Eason 4, Gibbons 4, Gillespie 4, Goldwyn 4, Mathis 4, Meredyth 4, Struss 4, Thalberg 4, Wilson, C. 4)
Beni komori, 1951 (Kinugasa 2, Hasegawa 3)
Benikmori, 1931 (Tsuburaya 4)
Benilde ou a Virgem Mãe, 1975 (Oliveira 2)
Benilde: Virgin and Mother. See Benilde ou a Virgem Mãe, 1975
Benim adim Kerim, 1967 (Guney 2)
Benito Cereno, 1969 (Guerra 2)
Benito Mussolini, 1961 (Rossellini 2)
Benjamin, 1968 (Deneuve 3, Morgan 3, Piccoli 3, Cloquet 4)
Benjy, 1951 (Zinnemann 2, Fonda, H. 3)
Benny from Panama, 1934 (Roach 4)
Benny Goodman Story, 1955 (Reed, D. 3, Daniels 4, Mancini 4)
Benny's Place, 1982 (Gossett 3)
Benson Murder Case, 1930 (Auer 3, Boyd 3, Lukas 3, Powell, W. 3)
Benten Boy. See Benten kozou, 1958
Benten Kozo, 1928 (Kinugasa 2, Hasegawa 3)
Benten kozou, 1958 (Miyagawa 4)
Benvenuta, 1983 (Fabian 3, Gassman 3)
Benvenuto Cellini, or a Curious Evasion. See Benvenutto Cellini ou une curieuse évasion, 1904
Benvenuto Cellini, 1910 (Feuillade 2)
Benvenuto reverendo!, 1950 (Fabrizi 3)
Benvenutto Cellini ou une curieuse évasion, 1904 (Méliès 2)
Beqasoor, 1950 (Biswas 4)
Bequest to the Nation, 1973 (Finch 3, Jackson 3, Quayle 3, Fisher 4, Legrand 4, Wallis 4)
Bequest to the Nation. See Nelson Affair, 1973
Berammee geisha makaridoru, 1961 (Yamamura 3)
Bercail, 1919 (L'Herbier 2)
Berceau de Dieu, 1926 (Musidora 3)
Berceaux, 1932 (Epstein 2)
Beregis avtomobilia, 1964 (Smoktunovsky 3)
Bérénice, 1954 (Rohmer 2)
Bergadler. See Mountain Eagle, 1926
Berg-Ejvind och hans hustru, 1918 (Sjostrom 2, Jaenzon 4, Magnusson 4)
Bergère et le ramoneur, 1952 (Aimée 3, Brasseur 3, Reggiani 3, Kosma 4)
Berget pa månens baksida, 1982 (Andersson B. 3)
Bergkatze, 1921 (Lubitsch 2, Negri 3, Kraly 4)
Berkeley Square, 1933 (Howard, L. 3, Balderston 4, Lasky 4, Levien 4)
Berlin Affair, 1970 (Dauphin 3, Lai 4)
Berlin Affair, 1985 (Donaggio 4, Golan and Globus 4)
Berlin—Alexanderplatz, 1931 (George, H. 3)
Berlin Alexanderplatz, 1980 (Fassbinder 2)
Berlin Conference, 1945 (Gerasimov 2)
Berlin Correspondent, 1942 (Andrews D. 3, Day 4, Miller, V. 4)
Berlin—Die Symphonie einer Grossstadt, 1927 (Freund 4, Mayer 4)
Berlin Express, 1948 (Tourneur, J. 2, Kortner 3, Lukas 3, Oberon 3, Ryan 3, Ballard 4, D'Agostino 4, Orry-Kelly 4, Siodmak 4)
Berlin Horse, 1970 (Le Grice 2)
Berlin Tunnel 21, 1981 (Ferrer, J. 3)
Berlin W., 1920 (Albers 3)
Berlingot et Cie, 1939 (Fernandel 3)
Berlinguer ti voglio bene, 1977 (Valli 3)
Bermuda Affair, 1956 (Sutherland 2)
Bermuda: la fossa maledetta, 1978 (Kennedy, A. 3)
Bermuda Mystery, 1944 (Basevi 4, La Shelle 4)
Bernard Miles on Gun Dogs, 1948 (Wright 2)
Bernard Shaw's Village, 1951 (Kaye 3)
Bernardine, 1957 (Gaynor 3, Lemaire 4, Mercer 4)

Between Two Women, 1944 (Barrymore L. 3, Johnson, V. 3, Wynn 3, Irene 4, Rosson 4, Wilson, C. 4)

Between Two Worlds, 1944 (Garfield 3, Greenstreet 3, Gwenn 3, Henreid 3, Friedhofer 4, Korngold 4)

Between 2 Worlds. *See* Delovak Athara, 1966

Between Two Worlds. *See* Mude Tod, 1921

Between Us Girls, 1942 (Cummings 3, Francis, K. 3)

Between Us Thieves. *See* Oss tjuvar emellan eller En burk ananas, 1945

Between Women and Wives. *See* Tsuma to onna no aida, 1976

Between Your Hands. *See* Bayn Ideak, 1960

Betwixt Love and Fire, 1913 (Sennett 2)

Beute der Erinnyen, 1921 (Krauss 3)

Beverly Hills Madam, 1986 (Schifrin 4)

Beverly of Graustark, 1926 (Franklin 2, Davies 3, Day 4, Gibbons 4)

Bewafa, 1952 (Kapoor 2)

Bewaqoof, 1960 (Burman 4)

Beware My Lovely, 1952 (Lupino 3, Ryan 3, D'Agostino 4, Horner 4)

Beware of a Holy Whore. *See* Warnung vor einer heiligen Nutte, 1970

Beware of Barnacle Bill, 1935 (Fleischer, M. and D. 2)

Beware of Blondes, 1928 (Walker 4)

Beware of Children. *See* No Kidding, 1960

Beware of Married Men, 1928 (Loy 3)

Beware of Pity, 1946 (Cooper, Gladys 3, Hardwicke 3, Beaton 4)

Beware of the Dog, 1923 (La Cava 2)

Beware of Widows, 1927 (Ruggles 2)

Beware Spooks!, 1939 (Brown 3)

Beware the Boarders, 1918 (Sennett 2)

Bewitched, 1945 (Gwenn 3, Kaper 4)

Bewitched Bunny, 1954 (Jones 2)

Bewitched Inn. *See* Auberge ensorcelée, 1897

Bewitched Matches, 1912–14 (Cohl 2)

Bewitched Trunk. *See* Coffre enchanté, 1904

Beyaz atli adam, 1965 (Guney 2)

Beyoğlu canavari, 1968 (Guney 2)

Beyond a Reasonable Doubt, 1956 (Lang 2, Andrews D. 3, Fontaine 3)

Beyond All Limits. *See* Flor de mayo, 1957

Beyond Decay. *See* Choraku no kanata, 1924

Beyond Evil. *See* Al di là del bene E del male, 1980

Beyond Glory, 1948 (Ladd 3, Murphy 3, Reed, D. 3, Dreier 4, Head 4, Seitz 4)

Beyond London, 1928 (Berman 4)

Beyond Love and Hate. *See* Ai to nikushimi no kanata e, 1951

Beyond Mombasa, 1956 (Lee, C. 3, Reed, D. 3, Wilde 3)

Beyond Price, 1921 (Ruttenberg 4)

Beyond the Barricade. *See* Har jeg Ret til at tage mit eget Liv, 1919

Beyond the Bermuda Triangle, 1975 (MacMurray 3)

Beyond the Blue Horizon, 1942 (Lamour 3, Dreier 4, Head 4, Westmore, F. 4, Young, V. 4)

Beyond the Border, 1925 (Carey 3, Polito 4, Stromberg 4)

Beyond the City, 1914 (Eason 4)

Beyond the Door. *See* Oltre la porta, 1982

Beyond the Forest, 1949 (Vidor, K. 2, Cotten 3, Davis 3, Blanke 4, Coffee 4, Head 4, Steiner 4)

Beyond the Forest. *See* Tam za lesem, 1962

Beyond the Last Frontier, 1943 (Mitchum 3)

Beyond the Law, 1968 (Torn 3)

Beyond the Law. *See* Al di là della legge, 1968

Beyond the Limit, 1983 (Gere 3)

Beyond the Limit. *See* Honorary Consul, 1983

Beyond the Mountains. *See* Más allá de las montañas, 1967

Beyond the Poseidon Adventure, 1979 (Caine 3, Field 3, Jones S. 3, Malden 3, Warden 3, Ames 4)

Beyond the Purple Hills, 1950 (Autry 3)

Beyond the Rainbow, 1922 (Bow 3)

Beyond the Reef, 1981 (Lai 4)

Beyond the River. *See* Bottom of the Bottle, 1956

Beyond the Rockies, 1932 (McCord 4)

Beyond the Rocks, 1922 (Wood 2, Swanson 3, Valentino 3)

Beyond the Square. *See* Tul a Kálvin-téren, 1955

Beyond the Time Barrier, 1960 (Ulmer 2, Pierce 4)

Beyond the Valley of the Dolls, 1970 (Smith, J.M. 4)

Beyond the Wall. *See* Mude Tod, 1921

Beyond the Wood. *See* Tam za lesem, 1962

Beyond This Place, 1959 (Johnson, V. 3, Adam 4, Cardiff 4)

Beyond Time. *See* Nince ido, 1973

Beyond Tomorrow, 1940 (Sutherland 2, Carey 3, Ouspenskaya 3, Garmes 4)

Beyond Victory, 1931 (Boyd 3, Pitts 3, Mandell 4)

Bez svidetelei, 1983 (Ulyanov 3)

Bez znieczulenia, 1978 (Wajda 2, Janda 3)

Bezhin Lug, 1966 (Eisenstein 2)

Bezhin Meadow. *See* Bezhin Lug, 1966

Bezúčelná procházka, 1930 (Hammid 2)

Bhagyachakra, 1935 (Sircar 4)

Bhavna, 1984 (Azmi 3)

Bhavni bhavai, 1981 (Patil 3)

Bhookh, 1947 (Biswas 4)

Bhowani Junction, 1956 (Cukor 2, Gardner 3, Granger 3, Berman 4, Levien 4, Rozsa 4, Young, F. 4)

Bhumika, 1977 (Benegal 2, Patil 3, Nihalani 4)

Bhuvan Shome, 1969 (Sen 2)

Bianchi cavalli d'Agosto, 1975 (Seberg 3)

Bianco, il giallo, il nero, 1975 (Wallach 3)

Bianco, rosso, e . . ., 1972 (Lattuada 2, Loren 3, Rey 3, Guerra 4, Ponti 4)

Bianco, rosso, e verdone, 1981 (Morricone 4)

Bibbia, 1965 (Huston 2, Gardner 3, O'Toole 3, Scott, G. 3, De Laurentiis 4, Dunn 4)

Biberpelz, 1937 (George, H. 3)

Biberpelz, 1949 (Geschonneck 3)

Bible, 1976 (Carné 2)

Bible. *See* Bibbia, 1965

Bible for Girls, 1934 (Zhao 3)

Bible Stories, 1980 (Halas and Batchelor 2)

Bibliothèques, 1963 (Borowczyk 4)

Bibo no miyako, 1957 (Tsukasa 3, Muraki 4)

Bibo no umi, 1950 (Kyo 3)

Bice skoro propast sveta, 1968 (Girardot 3)

Biches, 1968 (Chabrol 2, Audran 3, Trintignant 3, Gégauff 4, Rabier 4)

Biciklisti, 1970 (Marković 3, Samardžić 3)

Bicycle. *See* Rower, 1955

Bicycle Flirt, 1928 (Sennett 2, Lombard 3)

Bicycle Thief. *See* Ladri de biciclette, 1948

Bidapesti tavasz, 1955 (Gabór 3)

Bidaya wa Nihaya, 1960 (Sharif 3)

Bidon d'or, 1931 (Christian-Jaque 2)

Bidone, 1955 (Fellini 2, Crawford, B. 3, Masina 3, Flaiano 4, Pinelli 4, Rota 4)

Bidrohi, 1935 (Burman 4)

Biely vsriv, 1970 (Gurchenko 3)

Bien amada, 1951 (Fernández 2, Figueroa 4)

Bien-aimée, 1967 (Morgan 3)

Bienamados, 1965 (Figueroa 4)

Bienfaiteur, 1941 (Raimu 3)

Bienfaits du cinématographe, 1904 (Guy 2)

Bienvenido, Mr. Marshall!, 1952 (Bardem 2, García Berlanga 2, Rey 3)

Bière, 1924 (Grémillon 2, Périnal 4)

Bièvre, fille perdue, 1939 (Clément 2)

Biff Bang Buddy, 1924 (Arthur 3)

Biffen and the Banana. *See* Biffen och bananen, 1951

Biffen och Bananen, 1951 (Andersson H. 3, Fischer 4)

Big Adventure, 1921 (Eason 4, Miller, V. 4)

Big Bad Mama, 1974 (Dickinson 3, Corman 4)

Big Barrier. *See* Schloss Hubertus: Der Fischer von Heiligensee, 1955

Big Beat, 1957 (Mancini 4)

Big Bird Cage, 1972 (Corman 4)

Big Blockade, 1942 (Cavalcanti 2, Crichton 2, Mills 3, Redgrave, M. 3, Balcon 4)

Big Bonanza, 1944 (Arlen 3)

Big Boodle, 1957 (Armendáriz 3, Flynn 3, Garmes 4)

Big Boss. *See* Ankokugai no kaoyaku, 1959

Big Boss. *See* Fists of Fury, 1971

Big Bounce, 1968 (Grant, L. 3)

Big Boy, 1930 (Crosland 2, Jolson 3)

Big Brain, 1933 (Wray 3, Edeson 4)

Big Brawl, 1980 (Ferrer, J. 3, Schifrin 4)

Big Break, 1953 (Strick 2)

Big Broadcast, 1932 (Crosby 3, Head 4)

Big Broadcast of 1936, 1935 (Taurog 2, Crosby 3, Robinson, B. 3, Glazer 4, Head 4, Prinz 4)

Big Broadcast of 1937, 1936 (Leisen 2, Milland 3, Banton 4, Dreier 4, Head 4, Young, V. 4)

Big Broadcast of 1938, 1938 (Leisen 2, Fields, W.C. 3, Hope 3, Lamour 3, Dreier 4, Head 4)

Big Brother, 1923 (Dwan 2)

Big Brown Eyes, 1936 (Walsh 2, Bennett J. 3, Grant, C. 3, Pidgeon 3, Reynolds 4, Wanger 4)

Big Build-Up, 1942 (Terry 4)

Big Bus, 1976 (Ferrer, J. 3, Gordon 3)

Big Business, 1924 (Roach 4)

Big Business, 1929 (Stevens 2, Laurel and Hardy 3, Roach 4)

Big Business Girl, 1931 (Blondell 3, Young, L. 3, Polito 4)

Big Cage, 1933 (Rooney 3)

Big Calibre, 1937 (Katzman 4)

Big Carnival, 1951 (Douglas, K. 3, Head 4)

Big Carnival. See Ace in the Hole, 1951

Big Cats and How They Came to Be, 1976 (Giersz 4)

Big Chance, 1933 (Rooney 3)

Big Chase, 1954 (Chaney Lon, Jr. 3)

Big Chief. See Grand chef, 1959

Big Chief Ko-Ko, 1925 (Fleischer, M. and D. 2)

Big Chief Ugh-Amugh-Ugh, 1938 (Fleischer, M. and D. 2)

Big Chill, 1983 (Hurt, W. 3)

Big Circus, 1951 (Hoch 4)

Big Circus, 1959 (Lorre 3, Mature 3, Price 3, Bennett 4)

Big City, 1928 (Browning 2, Chaney Lon 3, Day 4, Gibbons 4, Young, W. 4)

Big City, 1937 (Borzage 2, Rainer 3, Tracy 3, Gibbons 4, Krasna 4, Ruttenberg 4, Schary 4)

Big City, 1948 (Donen 2, Taurog 2, O'Brien, M. 3, Preston 3, Ames 4, Pasternak 4, Surtees 4)

Big City. See A grande cidade, 1966

Big City. See Mahanagar, 1963

Big City Blues, 1932 (Leroy 2, Blondell 3, Bogart 3, Grot 4)

Big Clock, 1948 (Lanchester 3, Laughton 3, Milland 3, O'Sullivan 3, Dreier 4, Head 4, Seitz 4, Young, V. 4)

Big Combo, 1955 (Van Cleef 3, Wilde 3, Alton, J. 4, Raksin 4)

Big Country, 1958 (Ashby 2, Wyler 2, Baker C. 3, Heston 3, Peck 3, Simmons 3, Bass 4, Planer 4)

Big Crash. See Stora skrallen, 1943

Big Cube, 1969 (Turner, L. 3, Figueroa 4)

Big Dan, 1923 (Wellman 2, August 4)

Big Day, 1960 (Pleasance 3)

Big Day in Bogo, 1958 (Dickinson 2)

Big Deal at Dodge City. See Big Hand for the Little Lady, 1966

Big Deal on Madonna Street. See Soliti ignoti, 1958

Big Decision. See Basketball Fix, 1951

Big Diamond, 1929 (Mix 3)

Big Diamond Robbery, 1929 (Plunkett 4)

Big Doll House, 1971 (Corman 4)

Big Ears, 1931 (Roach 4)

Big Fella, 1937 (Rutherford 3)

Big Fibber, 1933 (Sennett 2)

Big Fight, 1930 (Fetchit 3)

Big Fisherman, 1959 (Borzage 2, Bondi 3, Keel 3, Estabrook 4, Garmes 4)

Big Fix, 1947 (Miller, V. 4)

Big Fix, 1978 (Dreyfuss 3, Head 4)

Big Flame, 1969 (Loach 2)

Big Flash, 1932 (Langdon 3)

Big Gamble, 1931 (Niblo 2, Boyd 3, Oland 3, Pitts 3)

Big Gamble, 1960 (Fleischer, R. 2, D'Eaubonne 4, Jarre 4, Zanuck 4)

Big Game, 1921 (Roach 4)

Big Game, 1936 (Berman 4, Polglase 4)

Big Game, 1972 (Milland 3)

Big Game Hunt, 1937 (Terry 4)

Big Gundown. See Resa dei conti, 1967

Big Guns, 1973 (Delon 3)

Big Guy, 1939 (Cooper, J 3, McLaglen 3, Salter 4)

Big Hand for the Little Lady, 1966 (Fonda, H. 3, Meredith 3, Robards 3, Woodward 3, Garmes 4, Mercer 4, Raksin 4)

Big Hangover, 1950 (Johnson, V. 3, Nilsson 3, Taylor, E. 3, Deutsch 4, Krasna 4, Rose 4, Rose 4)

Big Heart. See Miracle on 34th Street, 1947

Big Hearted Herbert, 1934 (Orry-Kelly 4)

Big Heat, 1953 (Lang 2, Ford, G. 3, Grahame 3, Marvin 3, Lang 4, Wald 4)

Big Heel-watha, 1944 (Avery 2)

Big House, 1930 (Fejos 2, Beery 3, Montgomery 3, Stone 3, Gibbons 4, Marion 4, Shearer 4, Thalberg 4)

Big House Bunny, 1948 (Freleng 4)

Big House, U.S.A., 1955 (Bronson 3, Chaney Lon, Jr. 3, Crawford, B. 3)

Big Hug. See Stora famnen, 1939

Big Idea, 1918 (Daniels 3, Lloyd 3, Roach 4)

Big Idea, 1923 (Roach 4)

Big Idea, 1934 (Three Stooges 3)

Big Jack, 1949 (Beery 3, Stothart 4, Surtees 4)

Big Jake, 1971 (Boone 3, O'Hara 3, Wayne 3, Bernstein 4, Clothier 4)

Big Jim Garrity, 1916 (Miller, A. 4)

Big Jim McLain, 1952 (Wayne 3)

Big Joe. See Veli Jože, 1980

Big Kick, 1925 (Roach 4)

Big Kick, 1930 (Langdon 3, Roach 4)

Big Killing, 1928 (Beery 3, Mankiewicz 4, Schulberg 4)

Big Knife, 1955 (Aldrich 2, Boone 3, Lupino 3, Martin, S. 3, Palance 3, Sloane 3, Steiger 3, Winters 3, Bass 4, Laszlo 4)

Big Land, 1957 (Ladd 3, Mayo 3, O'Brien, E. 3, Seitz 4)

Big Leaguer, 1953 (Aldrich 2, Robinson, E. 3)

Big Lift, 1950 (Seaton 2, Clift 3, Douglas, P. 3, Clarke, C.C. 4, Newman 4, Reynolds 4)

Big Little Person, 1919 (Valentino 3)

Big Moments from Little Pictures, 1924 (Rogers, W. 3, Roach 4)

Big Money, 1937 (Cavalcanti 2, Watt 2)

Big Mouse-Take, 1963 (Hanna and Barbera 4)

Big Mouth, 1967 (Lewis 2, Wheeler 4)

Big News, 1929 (La Cava 2, Lombard 3, Miller, A. 4)

Big Night, 1951 (Losey 2, Lardner 4)

Big Noise, 1928 (Dwan 2, Hecht 4)

Big Noise, 1936 (Sim 3)

Big Noise, 1944 (Laurel & Hardy 3)

Big Operator, 1959 (Rooney 3, Ames 4)

Big Pal, 1925 (Furthman 4)

Big Palooka, 1929 (Sennett 2)

Big Parade, 1925 (Vidor, K. 2, Adorée 3, Bosworth 3, Gilbert 3, Basevi 4, Gibbons 4, Thalberg 4)

Big Parade, 1952 (Godfrey 4)

Big Pond, 1930 (Sturges, P. 2, Chevalier 3, Colbert 3, Fort 4, Green, J. 4)

Big Punch, 1920 (Ford, J. 2, Furthman 4)

Big Race, 1937 (Lantz 4)

Big Race. See Texan, 1930

Big Rally, 1950 (Dovniković 4, Vukotić 4)

Big Red, 1962 (Disney 2, Pidgeon 3)

Big Red One, 1980 (Fuller 2, Audran 3, Marvin 3)

Big Red Riding Hood, 1925 (McCarey 2, Roach 4)

Big Ripoff. See Controrapina, 1978

Big Rip-Off, 1975 (Curtis 3)

Big Risk. See Classe tous risques, 1960

Big Rose, 1974 (Winters 3)

Big Sam. See Great Scout and Cathouse Thursday, 1976

Big Shakedown, 1934 (Davis 3)

Big Shave, 1967 (Scorsese 2)

Big Shot, 1931 (O'Sullivan 3, Miller, A. 4)

Big Shot, 1937 (Musuraca 4, Polglase 4)

Big Shot, 1942 (Bogart 3, Deutsch 4)

Big Show, 1923 (Roach 4)

Big Show, 1936 (Autry 3, Rogers, R. 3, Canutt 4)

Big Show, 1961 (Robertson 3, Williams 3)

Big Sky, 1952 (Hawks 2, Douglas, K. 3, D'Agostino 4, Jeakins 4, Nichols 4, Tiomkin 4)

Big Sleep, 1946 (Hawks 2, Bacall 3, Bogart 3, Cook 3, Malone 3, Brackett, L. 4, Furthman 4, Steiner 4)
Big Sleep, 1978 (Boone 3, Mills 3, Mitchum 3, Reed, O. 3, Stewart 3)
Big Snatch. *See* Mélodie en sous-sol, 1962
Big Sombrero, 1949 (Autry 3)
Big Spree. *See* Grande Vadrouille, 1966
Big Squawk, 1929 (Roach 4)
Big Stampede, 1932 (Wayne 3, McCord 4)
Big Steal, 1949 (Siegel 2, Bendix 3, Mitchum 3, Novarro 3)
Big Store, 1941 (Dumont 3, Marx Brothers 3)
Big Street, 1942 (Ball 3, Beavers 3, Fonda, H. 3, Moorehead 3)
Big Timber, 1917 (Reid 3)
Big Time, 1929 (Ford, J. 2, Fetchit 3)
Big Time Operators. *See* Smallest Show on Earth, 1957
Big Time Vaudeville Reels, 1936 (McDaniel 3)
Big Timer, 1932 (Riskin 4)
Big Top, 1938 (Terry 4)
Big Top Bunny, 1951 (McKimson 4)
Big Town, 1924 (Roach 4)
Big Town Czar, 1939 (Arden 3)
Big Town Girl, 1937 (Trevor 3)
Big Town Round-up, 1921 (Mix 3)
Big Trail, 1930 (Walsh 2, Bond 3, Wayne 3, Edeson 4, Friedhofer 4)
Big Trees, 1952 (Douglas, K. 3, Glennon 4)
Big Tremaine, 1916 (Gaudio 4)
Big Wave, 1962 (Hayakawa 3)
Big Wednesday, 1978 (Milius 2)
Big Wheel, 1949 (McDaniel 3, Rooney 3, Laszlo 4)
Big Yellow Schooner to Byzantium, 1978 (Fonda, H. 3)
Bigamie, 1927 (George, H. 3)
Bigamist, 1953 (Darwell 3, Fontaine 3, Gwenn 3, Lupino 3, O'Brien, E. 3)
Bigamist. *See* Bigamo, 1955
Bigamo, 1955 (De Sica 2, Mastroianni 3, Age and Scarpelli 4, Amidei 4)
Bigfoot, 1973 (Carradine 3)
Bigger and Better Blondes, 1927 (Arthur 3, Roach 4)
Bigger than Life, 1956 (Ray, N. 2, Mason 3, Matthau 3, Lemaire 4, Raksin 4, Smith, J.M. 4, Wheeler 4)
Biggest Bank Robbery. *See* Nightingale Sang in Berkeley Square, 1980
Biggest Battle. *See* Grande Battle
Biggest Bundle of Them All, 1968 (De Sica 2, Wagner 3, Welch 3)
Biggest Fight on Earth. *See* Sandai kaiju chikyu saidai no kessen, 1965
Biggest Show on Earth, 1918 (Barnes 4)
Bij de beesten af, 1972 (Haanstra 2)
Bijin aishu, 1931 (Ozu 2)
Bijo no tokudane, 1952 (Kyo 3)
Bijo to ekitai ningen, 1958 (Tsuburaya 4)
Bijo to kairyu, 1955 (Yoshimura 2)
Bijo to tozoku, 1952 (Kyo 3, Mori 3)
Bijo to yaju, 1952 (Shimura 3)
Bijobu Sakyo, 1931 (Hasegawa 3)
Bijoutiers du clair de lune, 1958 (Vadim 2, Bardot 3, Rey 3, Valli 3, Auric 4)
Bijoya, 1935 (Sircar 4)
Bike Boy, 1967 (Warhol 2)
Bike Bug, 1921 (Roach 4)
Bikini Beach, 1964 (Karloff 3, Wynn 3, Crosby 4)
Bikini Paradise, 1964 (Lourié 4)
Bila jednom jedna točka, 1964 (Dragić 4)
Bila nemoc, 1937 (Haas 3)
Bílá paní, 1965 (Hrušínský 3, Kopecký 3)
Bílá spona, 1960 (Fric 2)
Bilans kwartalny, 1975 (Zanussi 2, Komorowska 3)
Bild der Zeit. *See* Dr. Mabuse, der Spieler, 1921–22
Bildnis, 1925 (Banky 3)
Bildnis des Dorian Gray, 1917 (Oswald 2)
Bilet powrotny, 1978 (Stawinsky 4)
Biliár, 1964 (Pojar 4)
Bilitis, 1977 (Lai 4)
Biljett till paradiset, 1962 (Dahlbeck 3)
Bill series, 1914–15 (Browning 2)
Bill Apperson's Boy, 1919 (Polito 4)

Bill Bumper's Bargain, 1911 (Bushman 3)
Bill Haywood, Producer, 1915 (Mix 3)
Bill of Divorcement, 1932 (Cukor 2, Barrymore J. 3, Burke 3, Hepburn, K. 3, Estabrook 4, Selznick 4, Steiner 4, Westmore, E. 4)
Bill of Divorcement, 1940 (Bainter 3, Marshall 3, Menjou 3, O'Hara 3, Musuraca 4, Trumbo 4)
Bill of Hare, 1962 (McKimson 4)
Bill: On His Own, 1983 (Rooney 3)
Bill Sharkley's Last Game, 1909 (Carey 3)
Billard cassé, 1917 (Feyder 2)
Billboard Frolics, 1936 (Freleng 4)
Billboard Girl, 1932 (Sennett 2, Crosby 3, Hornbeck 4)
Bille de clown, 1950 (Burel 4)
Billet de banque, 1906 (Feuillade 2)
Billet de mille, 1932 (Dauphin 3, Rosay 3, Matras 4)
Billiards. *See* Biliár, 1964
Billion Dollar Brain, 1967 (De Toth 2, Russell 2, Caine 3, Homolka 3, Malden 3, Russell 4)
Billion Dollar Scandal, 1933 (Brown, Harry Joe 4)
Billion Dollar Threat, 1979 (Bellamy 3, Wynn 3)
Billionaire. *See* Okuman-choja, 1954
Billions, 1920 (Nazimova 3)
Billy and the Butler, 1912 (Bushman 3)
Billy Blazes, Esq., 1919 (Daniels 3, Lloyd 3, Roach 4)
Billy Boy, 1954 (Avery 2)
Billy Budd, 1962 (Douglas, M. 3, Ryan 3, Stamp 3, Ustinov 3, Bodeen 4, Krasker 4)
Billy Dodges Bills, 1913 (Sennett 2)
Billy Gets Her Man, 1948 (Burke 3)
Billy Goat Whiskers, 1937 (Terry 4)
Billy Jack Goes to Washington, 1977 (Bernstein 4)
Billy Jim, 1922 (Borzage 2)
Billy Liar, 1963 (Schlesinger 2, Christie 3)
Billy Mouse's Akwakade, 1940 (Terry 4)
Billy Rose's Casa Manana Review, 1938 (Sidney 2)
Billy Rose's Diamond Horseshoe, 1945 (Seaton 2, Dumont 3, Grable 3, Newman 4, Pan 4, Raksin 4)
Billy Rose's Jumbo, 1962 (Walters 2, Day 3)
Billy Rose's Jumbo. *See* Jumbo, 1962
Billy the Bear Tamer, 1915 (Talmadge, C. 3)
Billy the Kid, 1930 (Vidor, K. 2, Beery 3, Hart 3, Gibbons 4, MacArthur 4)
Billy the Kid, 1941 (Chaney Lon, Jr. 3, Taylor, R. 3)
Billy the Kid Returns, 1938 (Rogers, R. 3)
Billy the Kid Trapped, 1942 (Crabbe 3)
Billy the Kid vs. Dracula, 1966 (Carradine 3)
Billy the Kid Wanted, 1941 (Crabbe 3)
Billy the Kid's Roundup, 1941 (Crabbe 3)
Billy the Kid's Smoking Gun, 1942 (Crabbe 3)
Billy Two Hats, 1973 (Jewison 2, Peck 3)
Billy Two Hats. *See* Lady and the Outlaw, 1973
Billy's Rival, 1914 (Loos 4)
Billy's Stratagem, 1911 (Griffith 2, Bitzer 4)
Billy's Wager, 1915 (Talmadge, C. 3)
Bilocation, 1973 (Lassally 4)
Bilý Raj, 1924 (Ondra 3)
Bim, Bam, Bum. *See* Bim-bum, 1972
Bim, le petit âne, 1951 (Prévert 4)
Bimbo's Express, 1931 (Fleischer, M. and D. 2)
Bimbo's Initiation, 1931 (Fleischer, M. and D. 2)
Bim-bum, 1972 (Grgić 4)
Bimi. *See* King of the Wild, 1930
Bin defa olurum, 1969 (Guney 2)
Binding Sentiments. *See* 'Holdudvar', 1968
Binettoscope, 1910 (Cohl 2)
Bing Crosby in Cinerama's Russian Adventure. *See* Cinerama's Russian Adventure, 1965
Bing Crosby's Washington State, 1968 (Crosby 3)
Bing Presents Oreste, 1955 (Dmytryk 2, Crosby 3)
Bingo Crosbyana, 1936 (Freleng 4)
Bingo Long Traveling All-Stars and Motor Kings, 1976 (Jones, J.E. 3, Pryor 3)

Bink Runs Away. *See* Bink's Vacation, 1913
Bink's Vacation, 1913 (Loos 4)
Bio Woman, 1980 (Godfrey 4)
Biography of a Bachelor Girl, 1935 (Auer 3, Horton 3, Meek 3,
    Merkel 3, Montgomery 3, Howe 4, Loos 4, Stothart 4, Thalberg 4)
Bionda sottochiave, 1939 (Zavattini 4)
Bip Goes to Town, 1941 (Ivens 2)
Bir cirkin adam, 1969 (Guney 2)
Bir gun mutlaka, 1975 (Guney 2)
Biraghin, 1946 (Gallone 2)
Biraj Bahu, 1954 (Roy 2)
Biraj Bou, 1946 (Sircar 4)
Birch Interval, 1976 (Torn 3, Rosenman 4)
Bird, 1978 (Brakhage 2)
Bird and the Worm. *See* Ptica i crvek, 1977
Bird Came C.O.D., 1941 (Jones 2)
Bird in a Bonnet, 1958 (Freleng 4)
Bird in a Guilty Cage, 1951 (Freleng 4)
Bird in the Head, 1946 (Three Stooges 3)
Bird Missing Spring. *See* Sekishun-cho, 1959
Bird of Paradise, 1932 (Berkeley 2, Vidor, K. 2, Chaney Lon, Jr. 3,
    Del Rio 3, McCrea 3, Dunn 4, Selznick 4, Steiner 4)
Bird of Paradise, 1951 (Daves 2, Chandler 3, Elam 3, Jourdan 3,
    Sloane 3, Hoch 4, Lemaire 4, Wheeler 4)
Bird of Prey. *See* Epervier, 1933
Bird of Springs Past. *See* Sekishun-cho, 1959
Bird Symphony, 1955 (Terry 4)
Bird Tower, 1941 (Terry 4)
Bird with the Crystal Plumage. *See* Uccello dalle piume di cristallo,
    1969
Birdcall. *See* Lockfågeln, 1971
Birdland, 1935 (Terry 4)
Birdman of Alcatraz, 1962 (Frankenheimer 2, Lancaster 3, Malden 3,
    O'Brien, E. 3, Ritter 3, Bernstein 4, Guffey 4)
**Birds, 1963 (Hitchcock 2, Hedren 3, Boyle 4, Head 4, Herrmann 4,
    Iwerks 4, Whitlock 4)**
Bird's a Bird, 1915 (Sennett 2)
Birds and the Bees, 1956 (Sturges, P. 2, Taurog 2, Niven 3, Head 4)
Birds Anonymous, 1957 (Freleng 4)
Birds at Sunrise, 1972 (Wieland 2)
Birds in Peru. *See* Oiseaux vont mourir au Pérou, 1968
Birds of a Father, 1961 (McKimson 4)
Birds of a Feather, 1917 (Daniels 3, Lloyd 3, Roach 4)
Birds of a Feather. *See* Cage aux folles, 1979
Birds of Passage. *See* Tažní ptáci, 1961
Birds of Prey, 1930 (Bruce 3, Hawkins 3, Dean 4)
Birds, The Bees, and the Italians. *See* Signore e signori, 1966
Birdy and the Beast, 1944 (Clampett 4)
Birgitt Haas Must Be Killed. *See* Il Faut tuer Birgitt Haas, 1981
Birha Ki Baat, 1950 (Anand 3)
Biribi, 1971 (Aumont 3, Theodorakis 4)
Birichino di Papà, 1943 (Rota 4, Zavattini 4)
Birth of a Flivver, 1916 (O'Brien 4)
**Birth of a Nation, 1915 (Ford, J. 2, Griffith 2, Von Stroheim 2, Walsh 2,
    Crisp 3, Gish, L. 3, Marsh 3, Reid 3, Walthall 3, Bitzer 4,
    Brown, K. 4)**
Birth of a Notion, 1947 (McKimson 4)
Birth of a Robot, 1936 (Jennings 2, Lye 2)
Birth of a Star, 1944 (Kaye 3)
Birth of Mankind, 1946 (Lee, B. 3)
Birth of the Blues, 1941 (Crosby 3, Dreier 4, Head 4, Mercer 4)
Birth of the Year, 1938 (Alwyn 4)
Birthday, 1922 (Fleischer, M. and D. 2)
Birthday Gift. *See* Fødselsdagsgaven, 1912
Birthday Party, 1937 (Lantz 4)
Birthday Party, 1968 (Friedkin 2, Shaw 3, Pinter 4)
Birthright, 1924 (Micheaux 2)
Birthright, 1939 (Micheaux 2)
Biruma no tategato, 1956 (Ichikawa 2)
Bis das der Tod euch scheidet, 1979 (Domrose 3)
Bis wir uns Wiedersehen, 1953 (Schell, Maria 3)
Bisarca, 1950 (Baarová 3)
Bisbetica domata, 1942 (Amidei 4)

Biscuit Eater, 1940 (Dreier 4, Head 4)
Biscuit Eater, 1972 (Ayres 3)
Bishop Misbehaves, 1935 (Dupont 2, Gwenn 3, O'Sullivan 3)
Bishop Murder Case, 1930 (Daves 2, Rathbone 3, Coffee 4, Gibbons 4)
Bishop of the Ozarks, 1923 (Polito 4)
Bishop's Candlesticks, 1929 (Huston 3)
Bishop's Misadventures. *See* Bishop Misbehaves, 1935
Bishop's Room. *See* Stanza del vescovo, 1977
Bishop's Wife, 1947 (Cooper, Gladys 3, Grant, C. 3, Lanchester 3,
    Niven 3, Young, L. 3, Friedhofer 4, Goldwyn 4, Jenkins 4,
    Sharaff 4, Sherwood 4, Toland 4)
Bismarck, 1940 (Dagover 3)
Bisschen Liebe fur dich, 1932 (Metzner 4)
Bist du es lachendes Gluck. *See* Mascottchen, 1929
Bisturi: La mafia bianca, 1973 (Zampa 2)
Bit of Blarney, 1946 (Fleischer, M. and D. 2)
Bitch, 1965 (Warhol 2)
Bite and Run. *See* Mordi e fuggi, 1973
Bite the Bullet, 1975 (Brooks, R. 2, Coburn, J. 3, Hackman 3,
    Johnson, B. 3, Boyle 4, North 4)
Bite the Dust, 1969 (Van Cleef 3)
Bite to Eat. *See* Sousto, 1960
Bitka na Neretvi, 1969 (Welles 2, Bondarchuk 3, Brynner 3, Jurgens 3,
    Samardžić 3, Herrmann 4)
Bits of Life, 1921 (Neilan 2, Chaney Lon 3, Wong 3)
Bitter Apples, 1927 (Loy 3)
Bitter Grass. *See* Gorge trave, 1965
Bitter Reunion. *See* Beau Serge, 1958
Bitter Rice. *See* Riso amaro, 1948
Bitter Spirit. *See* Eien no hito, 1961
Bitter Springs, 1950 (Rafferty 3, Balcon 4)
Bitter Sweet, 1933 (Wilcox 2, Neagle 3, Young, F. 4)
Bitter Sweet, 1940 (Saville 2, Van Dyke, W.S. 2, Eddy 3,
    MacDonald 3, Sanders 3, Adrian 4, Stothart 4)
Bitter Sweets, 1928 (Shamroy 4)
Bitter Tea of General Yen, 1933 (Capra 2, Stanwyck 3, Walker 4,
    Wanger 4)
Bitter Tears of Petra von Kant. *See* Bitteren Tranen der Petra von
    Kant, 1972
Bitter Victory, 1957 (Ray, N. 2, Jurgens 3, Lee, C. 3)
Bitter Victory. *See* Amère victoire, 1957
Bitteren Tranen der Petra von Kant, 1972 (Fassbinder 2, Schygulla 3)
Bittersweet Love, 1976 (Turner, L. 3)
Bitva v puti, 1961 (Ulyanov 3)
Bitwa pod Lenino, 1943 (Ford, A. 2)
Bivio, 1950 (Vanel 3)
Biwi O Biwi, 1981 (Kapoor 2)
Bizalom, 1979 (Szabó 2)
Bizarre Bizarre. *See* Drôle de drama, 1937
Bjalata odiseja, 1973 (Paskaleva 3)
Bjalata Staja, 1968 (Karamitev 3)
Bla undulator, 1965 (Henning-Jensen, 2) 2)
Blaa Natviol, 1911 (Blom 2)
Black Abbot. *See* Schwarze Abt, 1963
Black Ace, 1928 (Johnson, N. 3)
Black and White. *See* Fantasmagorie, 1908
Black and White Like Day and Night. *See* Schwarz und Weiss wie Tage
    und Nacht, 1978
Black Angel, 1946 (Crawford, B. 3, Duryea 3, Lorre 3)
Black Angel. *See* Paroxismus, 1969
Black Bag, 1922 (Miller, V. 4)
Black Bart, Highwayman. *See* Black Bart, 1948
Black Bart, 1948 (De Carlo 3, Duryea 3, Friedhofer 4)
Black Beauty, 1946 (Hunt 4, Tiomkin 4)
Black Beauty, 1971 (Mankowitz 4)
Black Belt History of Three Countries. *See* Kuroobi sangoku-shi, 1956
Black Bird, 1926 (Browning 2, Gibbons 4, Gillespie 4, Young, W. 4)
Black Bird, 1975 (Audran 3, Cook 3, Segal 3, Booth 4, Horner 4)
Black Book, 1949 (Cummings 3)
Black Book. *See* Reign of Terror, 1949
Black Buccaneer. *See* Gordon, il Pirato Nero, 1961
Black Camel, 1931 (Lugosi 3, Oland 3, Young, R. 3, Carré 4)

Black Captain. *See* Fekete Kapitany, 1921
Black Castle, 1952 (Chaney Lon, Jr. 3, Karloff 3, Salter 4)
Black Cat, 1934 (Ulmer 2, Carradine 3, Karloff 3, Lugosi 3)
Black Cat, 1941 (Cooper, Gladys 3, Crawford, B. 3, Ladd 3, Lugosi 3, Rathbone 3, Cortez 4, Salter 4)
Black Cat. *See* Gatto nero, 1981
Black Cat in the Bush. *See* Yabu no naka no kuroneko, 1968
Black Cauldron, 1985 (Hurt, J. 3)
Black Chancellor. *See* Sorte Kansler, 1912
Black Coin, 1936 (Canutt 4)
Black Crows. *See* Svarte fugler, 1983
Black Cyclone, 1925 (Stevens 2, Roach 4)
Black Diamond, 1915 (Selig 4)
Black Diamond. *See* Cerný démant, 1955
Black Diamond Express, 1927 (Zanuck 4)
Black Diamonds, 1940 (Arlen 3, Salter 4)
Black Doll, 1938 (Cortez 4)
Black Dragons, 1942 (Lugosi 3, Katzman 4)
Black Eagle. *See* Aquila Nera, 1946
Black Eyes, 1939 (Brenon 2)
Black Eyes and Blues, 1941 (Bruckman 4)
Black Feather, 1928 (Costello, M. 3)
Black Flame. *See* Černý plamen, 1930
Black Flowers for the Bride. *See* Something for Everyone, 1970
Black Fox, 1962 (Dietrich 3)
Black Friday, 1940 (Karloff 3, Lugosi 3, Salter 4, Siodmak 4)
Black Fury, 1935 (Curtiz 2, Bond 3, Marsh 3, Muni 3)
Black Fury. *See* Mitsuyu-sen, 1954
Black Genesis: The Art of Tribal Africa, 1970 (Moss 4)
Black Ghost. *See* Last Frontier, 1932
Black Ghost Bandit, 1915 (Eason 4)
Black Girl from . . . *See* Noire de . . ., 1966
Black Glove. *See* Face the Music, 1954
Black God and the Blond Devil. *See* Deus e o diabo na terra do sol, 1964
Black Gold, 1947 (Quinn 3, Eason 4)
Black Gold, 1963 (Cody 3)
Black Hand, 1906 (Bitzer 4)
Black Hand, 1950 (Kelly, Gene 3, Plunkett 4)
Black Hand Blues, 1925 (Roach 4)
Black Hole, 1979 (Borgnine 3, Perkins 3, Schell, Maximilian 3, Barry 4, Ellenshaw 4)
Black Horse Canyon, 1954 (McCrea 3, Salter 4)
Black Hussar. *See* Schwarze Husar, 1932
Black Imp. *See* Diable noir, 1905
Black Is White, 1920 (White 3)
Black Jack, 1950 (Duvivier 2, Dalio 3, Marshall 3, Kosma 4, Spaak 4)
Black Jack, 1979 (Loach 2, Cushing 3)
Black Jack. *See* Wild in the Sky, 1972
Black Jack's Treasure. *See* Skarb Czarnego Jacka, 1961
Black Jesus. *See* Seduto alla sua destra, 1968
Black Journal. *See* Signora degli Orrori, 1977
Black Killer, 1971 (Kinski 3)
Black Knight, 1954 (Garnett 2, Cushing 3, Ladd 3, Addison 4, Box 4)
Black Legend, 1948 (Schlesinger 2)
Black Legion, 1937 (Bogart 3, Sheridan 3, Barnes 4)
Black Lightning, 1924 (Bow 3)
Black Limelight, 1939 (Massey 3)
Black Magic, 1929 (Walthall 3)
Black Magic, 1949 (Welles 2, Cortese 3, Annenkov 4, Bennett 4, D'Eaubonne 4)
Black Magic. *See* Cagliostro, 1949
Black Marble, 1980 (Stanton 3, Jarre 4, Roizman 4)
Black Masks. *See* Svarta makerna, 1912
Black Midnight, 1949 (Boetticher 2, McDowall 3)
Black Moon, 1934 (Muse 3, Wray 3, August 4)
Black Moon, 1975 (Malle 2, Nykvist 4)
Black Narcissus, 1947 (Powell and Pressburger 2, Kerr 3, Simmons 3, Cardiff 4, Ellenshaw 4, Junge 4)
Black Noon, 1971 (Grahame 3, Milland 3, Duning 4)
Black Oak Conspiracy, 1977 (Corman 4)
Black on White, 1954 (Alwyn 4)
Black on White. *See* Mustaa Valkoisella, 1968

Black Orchid, 1916 (Selig 4)
Black Orchid, 1959 (Ritt 2, Loren 3, Quinn 3, Head 4, Ponti 4)
Black Orchid. *See* Trifling Woman, 1922
Black Orchids, 1916 (Ingram 2)
Black Oxen, 1924 (Bow 3, Kraly 4)
Black Oxfords, 1924 (Sennett 2)
Black Palm Trees. *See* Svarta palmkronor, 1968
Black Panthers, 1968 (Varda 2)
Black Parachute, 1944 (Carradine 3)
Black Patch, 1957 (Martin, S. 3, Goldsmith 4)
Black Peter. *See* Cerný Petr, 1963
Black Pirate, 1926 (Crisp 3, Fairbanks, D. 3)
Black Pirates, 1954 (Chaney Lon, Jr. 3)
Black Rainbow. *See* Fekete szivarvany, 1916
Black River. *See* Kuroi kawa, 1957
Black Room, 1935 (Karloff 3)
Black Rose, 1950 (Hathaway 2, Welles 2, Harvey 3, Hawkins 3, Power 3, Cardiff 4, Jennings 4, Mathieson 4)
Black Roses, 1921 (Hayakawa 3)
Black Roses. *See* Svarta rosor, 1932
Black Sabbath, 1964 (Karloff 3)
Black Sail. *See* Chornyi parus, 1929
Black Scorpion, 1957 (O'Brien 4)
Black Sea Fighters, 1942 (March 3)
Black Secret, 1919 (White 3)
Black Sheep, 1909 (Anderson G. 3)
Black Sheep, 1912 (Griffith 2, Bitzer 4)
Black Sheep, 1934 (Terry 4)
Black Sheep, 1935 (Dwan 2, Trevor 3, Miller, A. 4)
Black Sheep, 1956 (Carradine 3, Chaney Lon, Jr. 3)
Black Sheep of Whitehall, 1941 (Dearden 2, Mills 3, Balcon 4)
Black Shield of Falworth, 1954 (Curtis 3, Leigh, J. 3, Marshall 3, Maté 4, Salter 4)
Black Sleep, 1956 (Lugosi 3, Rathbone 3)
Black Spider, 1920 (Colman 3)
Black Spider, 1931 (Terry 4)
Black Spurs, 1965 (Arlen 3, Chaney Lon, Jr. 3, Darnell 3)
Black Stallion, 1979 (Coppola 2, Rooney 3)
Black Stallion. *See* Return of Wildfire, 1948
Black Stallion Returns, 1982 (Rooney 3, Delerue 4)
Black Sunday, 1977 (Frankenheimer 2, Dern 3, Shaw 3, Alonzo 4, Lehman 4, Williams, J. 4)
Black Swan, 1942 (King 2, Muse 3, O'Hara 3, Power 3, Quinn 3, Sanders 3, Basevi 4, Day 4, Hecht 4, Miller, S. 4, Newman 4, Shamroy 4)
Black Tent, 1956 (Pleasance 3, Alwyn 4)
Black Tide. *See* Kuroi ushio, 1954
Black Tide. *See* Stormy Crossing, 1958
Black Tights. *See* Collants noirs, 1960
Black Tuesday, 1954 (Robinson, E. 3, Cortez 4)
Black Tulip. *See* Tulipe noire, 1963
Black Veil for Lisa. *See* Morte non ha sesso, 1969
Black Viper, 1908 (Bitzer 4)
Black Vision, 1965 (Brakhage 2)
Black Watch, 1929 (Ford, J. 2, Loy 3, McLaglen 3, Scott, R. 3, August 4)
Black Waters, 1929 (Neilan 2, Johnson, N. 3)
Black Whip, 1956 (Dickinson 3, Martin, S. 3, Biroc 4)
Black Widow, 1954 (Heflin 3, Raft 3, Rogers, G. 3, Tierney 3, Clarke, C.C. 4, Johnson 4, Lemaire 4)
Black Windmill, 1974 (Siegel 2, Caine 3, Pleasance 3, Seyrig 3)
Black Zoo, 1963 (Cook 3, Crosby 4)
Blackbeard, 1911 (Bosworth 3)
Blackbeard the Pirate, 1952 (Walsh 2, Bendix 3, Darnell 3, Young, V. 4)
Blackbeard's Ghost, 1968 (Lanchester 3, Ustinov 3, Ellenshaw 4)
Blackbird, 1926 (Adorée 3, Chaney Lon 3)
Blackbird Descending, 1977 (Le Grice 2)
Blackbirds, 1916 (Rosher 4)
Blackboard Jungle, 1955 (Brooks, R. 2, Mazursky 2, Calhern 3, Ford, G. 3, Poitier 3, Berman 4, Gibbons 4)
Blackboard Revue, 1940 (Iwerks 4)
Blackened Hills, 1912 (Dwan 2)

Blackguard, 1925 (Hitchcock 2, Balcon 4)
Blackjack Ketchum Desperado, 1956 (Katzman 4)
Blacklist, 1916 (Sweet 3, Rosher 4)
Blackmail, 1929 (Hitchcock 2, Ondra 3, Bennett 4)
Blackmail, 1939 (Robinson, E. 3)
Blackmailed, 1952 (Allégret, M. 2, Zetterling 2, Bogarde 3)
Blackout, 1978 (Allyson 3, Aumont 3, Milland 3)
Blackout, 1985 (Widmark 3)
Blackout. *See* Contraband, 1940
Blackout. *See* Murder by Proxy, 1955
Blacks and Whites in Days and Nights, 1960 (Vanderbeek 2)
Blacksmith, 1922 (Keaton 2)
Blackwell's Island, 1939 (Garfield 3)
Blacula, 1972 (Cook 3)
Blade af Satans Bog, 1921 (Dreyer 2)
Blade Runner, 1982 (Ford, H. 3, Trumbull 4, Vangelis 4)
Blague dans le coin, 1963 (Fernandel 3, Spaak 4)
Blaho lásky, 1966 (Trnka 2, Brdečka 4)
Blaise Pascal, 1975 (Rossellini 2)
Blåjackor, 1945 (Fischer 4)
Blake of Scotland Yard, 1937 (Katzman 4)
Blame It on Father, 1953 (Lee, B. 3)
Blame it on Love, 1940 (Ladd 3)
Blame It on Rio, 1984 (Caine 3)
Blame the Woman, 1932 (Niblo 2, Menjou 3)
Blanande hav, 1956 (Nykvist 4)
Blanc comme neige, 1947 (Bourvil 3, Cloquet 4)
Blanc et le noir, 1931 (Allégret, M. 2, Florey 2, Guitry 2, Fernandel 3,
    Raimu 3, Braunberger 4)
Blanche, 1970 (Simon, M. 3, Borowczyk 4)
Blanche comme neige, 1908 (Cohl 2)
Blanche Fury, 1947 (Allégret, M. 2, Granger 3, Green, G. 4,
    Havelock-Allan 4, Unsworth 4)
Blanchisserie américaine, 1915 (Cohl 2)
Blandt mange, 1961 (Henning-Jensen 2)
Blarney, 1926 (Adorée 3, Gibbons 4, Lewin 4)
Blarney Stone, 1913 (Bunny 3)
Blason, 1915 (Feuillade 2)
Blast, 1976 (Corman 4)
Blaubart, 1951 (Albers 3, Kortner 3)
Blaubart. *See* Barbe-Bleue, 1951
**Blaue Engel, 1930 (Von Sternberg 2, Albers 3, Dietrich 3, Jannings 3,
    Pommer 4, Waxman 4)**
Blaue Hand, 1967 (Kinski 3)
Blaue Laterne, 1918 (Porten 3, Messter 4)
Blaue Licht, 1932 (Riefenstahl 2)
Blaue Maus, 1913 (Warm 4)
Blaue von Himmel, 1932 (Wilder 2)
Blauvogel, 1979 (Hoffmann 3)
Blaze Away, 1922 (Roach 4)
Blaze o' Glory, 1929 (Walthall 3)
Blaze of Noon, 1947 (Baxter A. 3, Bendix 3, Hayden 3, Holden 3,
    Deutsch 4, Dreier 4, Head 4)
Blazes, 1961 (Breer 2)
Blazing Days, 1927 (Wyler 2)
Blazing Forest, 1952 (Arlen 3, Moorehead 3)
Blazing Frontier, 1943 (Crabbe 3)
Blazing Guns, 1934 (Canutt 4)
Blazing Saddles, 1974 (Brooks, M. 2, Pryor 3, Wilder 3, Biroc 4)
Blazing Stewardesses, 1976 (De Carlo 3)
Blazing Sun, 1950 (Autry 3)
Blázni, vodníci, a podvodníci, 1980 (Švankmajer 4)
Bláznova kronika, 1964 (Zeman 2)
Blé en herbe, 1953 (Autant-Lara 2, Feuillère 3, Aurenche 4, Bost 4,
    Douy 4)
Blé en liasses, 1969 (Dalio 3)
Blechtrommel, 1979 (Schlondorff 2, Olbrychski 3, Pszoniak 3,
    Winkler 3, Jarre 4)
Bled, 1929 (Becker 2, Renoir 2)
Bleierne Zeit, 1981 (Von Trotta 2, Vogler 3)
Blekitny krzyż, 1955 (Munk 2)
Bless the Beasts and Children, 1971 (Kramer, S. 2, Wheeler 4)
Bless the Children, 1953 (Zhao 3)

Blessed Event, 1932 (Powell, D. 3, Polito 4)
Blessure, 1921 (Bertini 3)
Bleu gang . . ., 1972 (Storaro 4)
Bleu perdu, 1972 (Driessen 4)
Bleuets dans la tête, 1969 (Almendros 4)
Bleus de la marine, 1934 (Fernandel 3)
Bleus de l'amour, 1932 (Wakhévitch 4)
Blick zuruck, 1944 (Jurgens 3, Stallich 4)
Blighty, 1927 (Balcon 4)
Blind Adventure, 1918 (Ruggles 2)
Blind Adventure, 1933 (Schoedsack 2, Bellamy 3, Plunkett 4,
    Steiner 4)
Blind Alibi, 1938 (Musuraca 4)
Blind Alley, 1939 (Vidor, C. 2, Bellamy 3, Ballard 4)
Blind Bargain, 1922 (Chaney Lon 3)
Blind Date, 1934 (Darwell 3, Rooney 3, Sothern 3)
Blind Date, 1954 (Terry 4)
Blind Date, 1959 (Losey 2, Baker S. 3, Presle 3)
Blind Deception, 1911 (Lawrence 3)
Blind Desire. *See* Part de l'ombre, 1945
Blind Director. *See* Angriff der Gegenwart auf der ubrige Zeit, 1985
Blind Fate, 1914 (Hepworth 2)
Blind Fate. *See* Lotteriseddel No. 22152, 1915
Blind Goddess, 1926 (Fleming 2, Banton 4)
Blind Goddess, 1948 (Bloom 3)
Blind Hearts, 1921 (Bosworth 3)
Blind Husbands, 1918 (Von Stroheim 2, Carey 3, Daniels 4, Day 4)
Blind Justice, 1934 (Mills 3)
Blind Justice. *See* Haevnens Nat, 1915
Blind Love, 1912 (Sweet 3)
Blind Love, 1979 (Legrand 4)
Blind Man's Bluff, 1936 (Mason 3)
Blind Man's Bluff, 1971 (Karloff 3)
Blind Man's Bluff. *See* Coleccionista de cadeveras, 1971
Blind Man's Tact, 1910 (Lawrence 3)
Blind Passion. *See* V boynoi slepote strastei, 1916
Blind Princess and the Poet, 1911 (Griffith 2, Sweet 3, Bitzer 4)
Blind Spot, 1958 (Caine 3)
Blind Spot. *See* Flusternde Tod, 1975
Blind Terror, 1971 (Fleischer, R. 2, Farrow 3, Bernstein 4, Fisher 4)
Blind White Duration, 1967 (Le Grice 2)
Blinde, 1911 (Porten 3, Messter 4)
Blinde Skaebne. *See* Lotteriseddel No. 22152, 1915
Blinded by the Light, 1980 (Alonzo 4)
Blindfold, 1966 (Cardinale 3, Hudson 3, Warden 3, Bumstead 4,
    Dunne 4, Schifrin 4, Whitlock 4)
Blindfold. *See* Bekotott szemmel, 1974
Blinding Sentiments. *See* Holdudvar, 1968
Blindkuh, 1914 (Lubitsch 2)
Blindness of Devotion, 1915 (Ingram 2)
Blindness of Fortune, 1918 (Hepworth 2)
Blinkeyes, 1926 (Pearson 2, Balfour 3)
Blinkity Blank, 1954–55 (McLaren 2)
Blinky, 1923 (Miller, V. 4)
Blisniezy, 1945 (Orlova 3)
Bliss, 1917 (Daniels 3, Lloyd 3)
Bliss, 1967 (Markopoulos 2)
Bliss, 1984 (Kennedy, G. 3)
Bliss of Love. *See* Blaho lásky, 1966
Bliss of Mrs. Blossom, 1968 (Attenborough 3, MacLaine 3, Godfrey 4,
    Unsworth 4)
Blithe Spirit, 1945 (Lean 2, Harrison 3, Rutherford 3, Coward 4,
    Havelock-Allan 4)
Blithe Spirit, 1966 (Bogarde 3)
Blitz on the Fritz, 1943 (Langdon 3, Bruckman 4)
Blitz Wolf, 1942 (Avery 2)
Blitzzug der Liebe, 1925 (Hoffmann 4)
Blixt och dunder, 1938 (Fischer 4)
Blizzard, 1921 (Hardy 3)
Blob, 1958 (McQueen, S. 3)
Block Busters, 1944 (Langdon 3, Katzman 4)
Block 15. *See* Blok 15, 1959
Block Signal, 1926 (Arthur 3)

Blockade, 1928 (Nilsson 3)
Blockade, 1938 (Dieterle 2, Carroll M. 3, Fonda, H. 3, Basevi 4, Irene 4, Maté 4, Wanger 4)
Blockade. *See* Bloko, 1964
Block-Heads, 1938 (Langdon 3, Laurel & Hardy 3, Roach 4)
Blockhouse, 1973 (Sellers 3)
Block-notes di un regista, 1969 (Fellini 2, Mastroianni 3)
Blodets rost, 1913 (Sjostrom 2, Jaenzon 4)
Blok 15, 1959 (Schorm 2)
Blokasa, 1974 (Ulyanov 3)
Bloko, 1964 (Theodorakis 4)
Blomstertid, 1940 (Sjoberg 2)
Blonde Alibi, 1946 (Cook 3)
Blonde and Groom, 1943 (Langdon 3)
Blonde Blackmailer. *See* Stolen Time, 1955
Blonde Bombshell. *See* Bombshell, 1933
Blonde Cheat, 1938 (Fontaine 3, Hunt 4)
Blonde Crazy, 1931 (Blondell 3, Cagney 3, Calhern 3, Milland 3, Haller 4)
Blonde de Pekin, 1968 (Robinson, E. 3)
Blonde Dream. *See* Blonder Traum, 1932
Blonde Dynamite. *See* She's Dangerous, 1936
Blonde Fever, 1944 (Astor 3, Gardner 3, Grahame 3, Irene 4)
Blonde for Danger. *See* Sois belle et tais toi, 1958
Blonde from Brooklyn, 1945 (Guffey 4)
Blonde from Buenos Aires. *See* Carnival of Crime, 1964
Blonde from Peking. *See* Blonde de Pekin, 1968
Blonde from Singapore, 1941 (Dmytryk 2)
Blonde in Love. *See* Lásky jedné plavovlásky, 1965
Blonde Inspiration, 1941 (Berkeley 2, Meek 3, Kaper 4)
Blonde Menace. *See* Scattergood Meets Broadway, 1941
Blonde or Brunette, 1927 (Menjou 3, Schulberg 4)
Blonde Saint, 1926 (Stone 3, Gaudio 4)
Blonde Trouble, 1937 (Head 4)
Blonde Venus, 1932 (Von Sternberg 2, Dietrich 3, Grant, C. 3, Marshall 3, McDaniel 3, Banton 4, Furthman 4, Glennon 4)
Blonder Traum, 1932 (Wilder 2, Pommer 4, Reisch 4)
Blondes for Danger, 1938 (Wilcox 2)
Blonde's Revenge, 1926 (Sennett 2)
Blondie Goes to College, 1942 (Bruckman 4, Cahn 4)
Blondie Johnson, 1933 (Blondell 3, Gaudio 4, Orry-Kelly 4)
Blondie Knows Best, 1946 (Howard, S. 3)
Blondie of the Follies, 1932 (Goulding 2, Davies 3, Durante 3, Montgomery 3, Pitts 3, Barnes 4, Freed 4, Loos 4, Marion 4)
Blondie on a Budget, 1940 (Hayworth 3)
Blondie Plays Cupid, 1940 (Ford, G. 3)
Blondie Takes a Vacation, 1939 (Meek 3)
Blondie's Blessed Event, 1942 (Cahn 4)
Blondy, 1975 (Andersson B. 3)
Blood. *See* Occhio nel labarinto, 1970
Blood Alley, 1955 (Wellman 2, Bacall 3, Wayne 3, Clothier 4)
Blood and Lace, 1970 (Grahame 3)
Blood and Roses. *See* Et mourir de plaisir, 1960
Blood and Sand, 1922 (Arzner 2, Niblo 2, Valentino 3, Mathis 4, Westmore, M. 4)
Blood and Sand, 1941 (Mamoulian 2, Carradine 3, Darnell 3, Hayworth 3, Nazimova 3, Power 3, Quinn 3, Banton 4, Day 4, Newman 4, Swerling 4, Zanuck 4)
Blood and Soul. *See* Chi to rei, 1923
Blood and Steel, 1959 (Crosby 4)
Blood and Water, 1913 (Guy 2)
Blood Barrier, 1920 (Blackton 2)
Blood Bath, 1965 (Corman 4)
Blood Beast Terror, 1968 (Cushing 3)
Blood Brother. *See* Rodnoi brat, 1929
Blood Brothers, 1978 (Mulligan 2, Gere 3, Bernstein 4, Surtees 4)
Blood Demon. *See* Schlangengrube und das Pendel, 1967
Blood Feast. *See* Fin de fiesta, 1959
Blood Feud, 1935 (Sircar 4)
Blood Feud, 1983 (Borgnine 3)
Blood Fiend. *See* Theatre of Death, 1967
Blood for Blood, Death for Death. *See* Krov'za krov', smert'za smert', 1941

Blood for Dracula, 1974 (Polanski 2)
Blood for Dracula. *See* Andy Warhol's Dracula, 1974
Blood Holiday, 1968 (Wynn 3)
Blood in the Streets, 1976 (Reed, O. 3)
Blood Kin, 1969 (Coburn, J. 3, Howe 4, Jones 4)
Blood Money, 1933 (Anderson J. 3, Ball 3, D'Agostino 4, Newman 4, Zanuck 4)
Blood Money. *See* Moneda sangrienta, 1974
Blood Need Not Be Spilled. *See* Ne nado krovi, 1917
Blood of a Poet. *See* Sang d'un poète, 1930
Blood of Dracula's Castle, 1967 (Carradine 3, Kovacs 4)
Blood of Frankenstein. *See* Dracula Vs. Frankenstein, 1969
Blood of Fu Manchu, 1968 (Lee, C. 3)
Blood of Ghastly Horror, 1965 (Carradine 3)
Blood of Hussain, 1980 (Lassally 4)
Blood of Minas. *See* Sangue Mineiro, 1929
Blood of Others, 1983 (Chabrol 2, Audran 3, Aumont 3)
Blood of the Children, 1915 (Meredyth 4)
Blood of the Iron Maiden, 1970 (Carradine 3)
Blood of the Man Devil. *See* House of the Black Death, 1965
Blood of the Vampire, 1958 (Sangster 4)
Blood on My Hands. *See* Kiss the Blood Off My Hands, 1948
Blood on the Arrow, 1964 (Cook 3)
Blood on the Balcony. *See* Benito Mussolini, 1961
Blood on the Moon, 1948 (Wise 2, Brennan 3, Cody 3, Mitchum 3, Preston 3, D'Agostino 4, Musuraca 4)
Blood on the Sun, 1945 (Cagney 3, Sidney 3, Rozsa 4)
Blood Orange, 1953 (Fisher 2)
Blood Relative. *See* Liens du sang, 1978
Blood Ruby, 1914 (Costello, M. 3)
Blood Seekers. *See* Dracula Vs. Frankenstein, 1969
Blood Ship, 1927 (Arlen 3, Bosworth 3)
Blood Sisters. *See* Sisters, 1972
Blood Suckers. *See* Dr. Terror's Gallery of Horrors, 1967
Blood, Sweat and Fear. *See* Mark il poliziotta, 1975
Blood Tide, 1982 (Ferrer, J. 3, Jones, J.E. 3)
Blood Wedding. *See* Bodas de sangre, 1981
Blood Will Tell, 1912 (Ince 4)
Blood Will Tell, 1914 (Bushman 3)
Bloodbath at the House of Death, 1983 (Price 3)
Bloodhounds of Broadway, 1952 (Bronson 3, Cronjager 4, Lemaire 4)
Bloodhounds of the North, 1913 (Dwan 2, Chaney Lon 3)
Bloodline, 1979 (Hepburn, A. 3, Papas 3, Schneider 3, Sharif 3, Morricone 4, Young, F. 4)
Blood's Tone, 1965 (Brakhage 2)
Bloodsport, 1973 (Johnson, B. 3)
Bloodstain, 1912 (Guy 2)
Bloodsuckers. *See* Incense for the Damned, 1970
Bloody Brood, 1959 (Falk 3, Schufftan 4)
Bloody Bushido Blade. *See* Bushido Blade, 1978
Bloody Chamber, 1982 (Stamp 3)
Bloody Hands of the Law. *See* Mano spietat della legge, 1973
Bloody Judge. *See* Processo de las brujas, 1970
Bloody Mama, 1970 (De Niro 3, Dern 3, Winters 3, Alonzo 4)
Bloomfield, 1970 (Schneider 3, Mankowitz 4)
Blooming at Night. See Yoru hiraku, 1931
Blossom Time. *See* Blomstertid, 1940
Blossoming Port. *See* Hanasaku minato, 1943
Blossoms in the Dust, 1941 (Leroy 2, Garson 3, Pidgeon 3, Adrian 4, Freund 4, Gibbons 4, Loos 4, Stothart 4)
Blossoms on Broadway, 1937 (Head 4, Schulberg 4, Shamroy 4)
Blot, 1921 (Weber 2, Calhern 3)
Blot on the Scutcheon, 1911 (Griffith 2, Bitzer 4)
Blot on the Shield, 1915 (Eason 4)
Blotted Brand, 1911 (Dwan 2)
Blotto, 1930 (Laurel and Hardy 3, Roach 4)
Bloudĕni, 1965 (Brejchová 3)
Blow!. *See* Fukeyo harukaze, 1953
Blow by Blow, 1928 (McCarey 2, Roach 4)
Blow 'em Up, 1922 (Roach 4)
Blow Job, 1963 (Warhol 2)
Blow, Love Wind. *See* Fukeyo koikaze, 1935
Blow Me Down, 1931 (Fleischer, M. and D. 2)

Blow to the Heart. *See* Colpa al cuore, 1982
Blow Your Own Horn, 1923 (Baxter W. 3)
Blow-Ball. *See* Bóbita, 1964
Blowing Wild, 1953 (Bond 3, Cooper, Gary 3, Quinn 3, Stanwyck 3, Tiomkin 4)
Blow-Out, 1936 (Avery 2)
Blow-Out, 1981 (De Palma 2, Donaggio 4, Zsigmond 4)
Blow-Out. *See* Grande Bouffe, 1973
Blow-Up, 1966 (Antonioni 2, Redgrave, V. 3, Guerra 4, Ponti 4)
Bludiště moci, 1969 (Schorm 2)
Blue, 1968 (Malden 3, Stamp 3, Cortez 4)
Blue and the Gold. *See* Annapolis Story, 1955
Blue Angel, 1959 (Dmytryk 2, Jurgens 3, Friedhofer 4, Shamroy 4)
Blue Angel. *See* Blaue Engel, 1930
Blue Beard. *See* Barbe-Bleue, 1901
Blue Beast. *See* Aoi yaju, 1960
Blue Bird, 1918 (Tourneur, M. 2, Carré 4)
Blue Bird, 1940 (Bruce 3, Temple 3, Day 4, Miller, A. 4, Newman 4, Zanuck 4)
Blue Blazes, 1936 (Keaton 2)
Blue Blazes Rawden, 1918 (Hart 3, August 4)
Blue Blood, 1973 (Reed, O. 3)
Blue Blood and Red, 1916 (Walsh 2)
Blue Bud. *See* Aoi me, 1956
Blue Canadian Rockies, 1952 (Autry 3)
Blue Cat Blues, 1956 (Hanna and Barbera 4)
Blue Collar, 1978 (Schrader 2, Keitel 3, Pryor 3)
Blue Dahlia, 1946 (Bendix 3, Ladd 3, Lake 3, Chandler 4, Dreier 4, Head 4, Houseman 4, Young, V. 4)
Blue Danube, 1928 (Schildkraut 3, Adrian 4, Grot 4, Miller, A. 4)
Blue Danube, 1931 (Wilcox 2, Young, F. 4)
Blue Danube, 1934 (Schildkraut 3)
Blue Denim, 1959 (Brackett, C. 4, Dunne 4, Herrmann 4, Reynolds 4, Wheeler 4)
Blue Eagle, 1926 (Ford, J. 2, Gaynor 3)
Blue Envelope Mystery, 1916 (Menjou 3)
Blue Field Duration, 1972 (Le Grice 2)
Blue from Heaven. *See* Modré z nebe, 1962
Blue Gardenia, 1953 (Lang 2, Baxter A. 3, Sothern 3, Musuraca 4)
Blue Grass Romance, 1913 (Ince 4)
Blue Hawaii, 1961 (Taurog 2, Lansbury 3, Presley 3, Edouart 4, Fulton 4, Head 4, Lang 4, Wallis 4)
Blue Jeans. *See* Blue Denim, 1959
Blue Knight, 1975 (Holden 3, Kennedy, G. 3, Mancini 4)
Blue Lagoon, 1949 (Cusack 3, Simmons 3, Gilliat 4, Unsworth 4)
Blue Lagoon, 1979 (Almendros 4)
Blue Lamp, 1950 (Dearden 2, Bogarde 3, Balcon 4, Clarke, T.E.B. 4)
Blue Light. *See* Blaue Licht, 1932
Blue Max, 1966 (Mason 3, Goldsmith 4, Slocombe 4)
Blue Monday, 1938 (Hanna and Barbera 4)
Blue Montana Skies, 1939 (Autry 3, Eason 4)
Blue Moon Murder Case, 1932 (Florey 2)
Blue Moses, 1962 (Brakhage 2)
Blue Mountains. *See* Aoi sanmyaku, 1949
Blue Movie, 1968 (Warhol 2)
Blue Murder at St. Trinian's, 1957 (Sim 3, Arnold 4, Gilliat 4)
Blue of the Night, 1933 (Sennett 2, Crosby 3)
Blue or the Gray, 1913 (Gish, D. 3, Gish, L. 3)
Blue Peter, 1958 (Lassally 4)
Blue Plate Symphony, 1954 (Terry 4)
Blue Revolution. *See* Aoiro kakumei, 1953
Blue Rose, 1913 (Talmadge, N. 3)
Blue Skies, 1946 (Astaire 3, Crosby 3, Head 4, Lang 4, Pan 4)
Blue Smoke, 1935 (Bennett 4)
Blue Steel, 1934 (Wayne 3, Canutt 4)
Blue Streak McCoy, 1920 (Carey 3, Eason 4)
Blue Thunder, 1983 (McDowell 3, Oates 3, Scheider 3, Alonzo 4)
Blue Vanguard, 1957 (Dickinson 2)
Blue Veil, 1951 (Blondell 3, Cusack 3, Laughton 3, Moorehead 3, Sloane 3, Wood 3, Wyman 3, Krasna 4, Planer 4, Wald 4, Waxman 4, Westmore, P. 4)
Blue Water, 1924 (Shearer 3)
Blue White, 1965 (Brakhage 2)

Blue, White, and Perfect, 1941 (Marsh 3, Chase 4)
Bluebeard, 1944 (Ulmer 2, Carradine 3)
Bluebeard, 1972 (Welch 3)
Bluebeard. *See* Barbe-Bleue, 1972
Bluebeard. *See* Landru, 1963
Bluebeard's Brother, 1932 (Terry 4)
Bluebeard's Castle, 1964 (Powell 2)
Bluebeard's Eighth Wife, 1923 (Swanson 3)
Bluebeard's Eighth Wife, 1938 (Guitry 2, Lubitsch 2, Wilder 2, Colbert 3, Cooper, Gary 3, Horton 3, Niven 3, Banton 4, Brackett, C. 4, Dreier 4, Prinz 4)
Bluebeard's Seven Wives, 1926 (Sweet 3, Haller 4)
Bluebeard's Six Wives. *See* Sei mogli di Barbablu', 1950
Bluebeard's Ten Honeymoons, 1960 (Sanders 3)
Bluebird, 1976 (Cukor 2, Fonda, J. 3, Gardner 3, Taylor, E. 3, Head 4, Young, F. 4)
Bluebottles, 1928 (Lanchester 3, Laughton 3)
Bluejackets. *See* Blåjackor, 1945
Blueprint for Murder, 1953 (Cotten 3, Marsh 3, Lemaire 4)
Blues, 1931 (Terry 4)
Blues Brothers, 1980 (Whitlock 4)
Blues della domenica, 1952 (Zurlini 2)
Blues for Lovers. *See* Ballad in Blue, 1964
Blues in the Night, 1941 (Kazan 2, Litvak 2, Rossen 2, Blanke 4, Haller 4, Mercer 4)
Bluff, 1916 (Feyder 2)
Bluff, 1924 (Wood 2)
Bluff, 1976 (Quinn 3)
Bluff Stop, 1978 (Donner 2)
Bluffer, 1930 (Sennett 2)
Bluffers, 1915 (Eason 4)
Blume in Love, 1973 (Mazursky 2, Segal 3, Winters 3)
Blume von Hawaii, 1933 (Oswald 2)
Blumenfrau vom Potsdamer Platz, 1925 (Dieterle 2)
Blumenfrau von Lindenau, 1931 (Lamarr 3)
Blunden Harbor, 1952 (Peterson 2)
Blunder Below, 1942 (Fleischer, M. and D. 2)
Blunder Boys, 1955 (Three Stooges 3)
Blundering Boob. *See* New Janitor, 1914
Blusen Konig, 1917 (Lubitsch 2, Kraly 4)
Blushing Bride, 1921 (Furthman 4)
Blushing Charlie. *See* Lyckliga skitar, 1970
Blut der Ahnen, 1920 (Wiene 2, Dagover 3, Warm 4)
Blut und Boden, 1933 (Ruttmann 2)
Blutsbruderschaft, (Staudte 2)
Blutschande die 173 St. G.B., 1929 (Tschechowa 3)
Bly jednou jeden Král, 1955 (Brdečka 4)
Boadicea, 1928 (Asquith 2)
Boarding House Feud, 1915 (Talmadge, C. 3)
Boardwalk, 1979 (Gordon 3, Leigh, J. 3)
Boat, 1921 (Keaton 2)
Boatniks, 1970 (Ameche 3)
Boats under Oars, 1901 (Bitzer 4)
Bob and Carol and Ted and Alice, 1969 (Mazursky 2, Cannon 3, Gould 3, Wood 3, Jones 4, Lang 4)
Bob and the Pirates, 1960 (Haller 4)
Bob Hampton of Placer, 1921 (Neilan 2, Carré 4)
Bob Hope Reports to the Nation, 1947 (Kaye 3)
Bob Kick the Mischievous Kid. *See* Bob Kick, l'enfant terrible, 1903
Bob Kick, l'enfant terrible, 1903 (Méliès 2)
Bob le Flambeur, 1956 (Melville 2, Decaë 4)
Bob Mathias Story, 1954 (Bond 3)
Bob, Son of Battle. *See* Thunder in the Valley, 1947
Bobbed Hair, 1922 (Boyd 3)
Bobbed Hair, 1925 (Crosland 2, Costello, D. 3, Fazenda 3)
Bobbie of the Ballet, 1916 (Chaney Lon 3)
Bobbikins, 1960 (Jones S. 3)
Bobby, 1974 (Kapoor 2)
Bobby Deerfield, 1977 (Pollack 2, Pacino 3, Decaë 4, Sargent 4)
Bobby the Coward, 1911 (Bitzer 4)
Bobby's Kodak, 1908 (Bitzer 4)
Bóbita, 1964 (Mészáros 2)
Bobo, 1967 (Brazzi 3, Sellers 3, Cahn 4, Lai 4)

Bobo Jacco, 1979 (Girardot 3)
Bobosse, 1958 (Presle 3)
Bobs, 1928 (Grémillon 2)
Bôca de Ouro, 1962 (Pereira Dos Santos 2)
Bocal aux poissons-rouges, 1895 (Lumière 2)
Boccaccio, 1920 (Curtiz 2)
Boccaccio, 1972 (Blier 3)
Boccaccio '70, 1962 (De Sica 2, Fellini 2, Monicelli 2, Visconti 2,
    Loren 3, Schneider 3, D'Amico 4, Flaiano 4, Gherardi 4, Ponti 4,
    Rota 4, Zavattini 4, Pinelli 4)
Bocchan dohyo-iri, 1943 (Tanaka 3)
Bocchan kisha, 1955 (Yamamura 3)
Bodakunden, 1920 (Molander 2)
Bodas de Fuego, 1949 (Armendáriz 3)
Bodas de sangre, 1976 (Papas 3)
Bodas de sangre, 1981 (Saura 2)
Bodes der for. See Haevnet, 1911
Bødes der for. See Haevnet, 1911
Body. See Ratai, 1962
Body. See Take This—My Body, 1974
Body and Soul, 1925 (Micheaux 2, Robeson 3)
Body and Soul, 1927 (Barrymore L. 3, Gibbons 4, Gillespie 4)
Body and Soul, 1931 (Bogart 3, Loy 3, Furthman 4, Grot 4)
Body and Soul, 1947 (Aldrich 2, Polonsky 2, Rossen 2, Garfield 3,
    Friedhofer 4, Howe 4)
Body and Soul, 1981 (Golan and Globus 4)
Body and Soul. See Pride of the Marines, 1945
Body Disappears, 1942 (Horton 3, Wyman 3)
Body Double, 1984 (Donaggio 4)
Body Heat, 1981 (Hurt, W. 3, Turner, K. 3, Barry 4)
Body of My Enemy. See Corps de mon ennemi, 1976
Body Snatcher, 1945 (Wise 2, Karloff 3, Lugosi 3, D'Agostino 4,
    Lewton 4)
Body Stealers, 1969 (Sanders 3)
Bodyguard, 1944 (Hanna and Barbera 4)
Bodyguard, 1948 (Fleischer, R. 2)
Bodyguard. See Yojimbo, 1961
Boefje, 1939 (Sirk 2)
Boeing Boeing, 1965 (Lewis 2, Curtis 3, Ritter 3, Anhalt 4, Ballard 4,
    Head 4, Wallis 4)
Boer Pietersen schiet in de roos, 1949 (Haanstra 2)
Boeuf sur la langue, 1933 (Christian-Jaque 2)
Boevi kinosbornik, 1942 (Donskoi 2)
Bof, 1970 (Vierny 4)
Bofers Gun, 1968 (Williamson 3)
Bofuu no bara, 1931 (Takamine 3)
Bogie, 1980 (Taradash 4)
Bohdan Khmelnytsky, 1941 (Dovzhenko 2)
Boheme, 1915 (Brady 3)
Boheme, 1923 (Dreier 4, Kraly 4)
Boheme, 1926 (Florey 2, Vidor, K. 2, Adorée 3, Gilbert 3, Gish, L. 3,
    Horton 4, Carré 4, Gibbons 4, Gillespie 4)
Boheme—Künstlerliebe, 1923 (Dieterle 2)
Bohemian Dancer, 1929 (Young, W. 4)
Bohemian Girl, 1922 (Cooper, Gladys 3, Novello 3)
Bohemian Girl, 1936 (Laurel & Hardy 3, Roach 4)
Bohus bataljon, 1949 (Nykvist 4)
Bohuslav Martinu, 1980 (Jires 2)
Boi pod Tsaritsinom, 1920 (Vertov 2)
Boia di Lilla, 1952 (Brazzi 3)
Boilesk, 1931 (Fleischer, M. and D. 2)
Bois des amants, 1960 (Autant-Lara 2, Rosay 3, Douy 4)
Bois et cuivres, 1958 (Decaë 4)
Bois sacré, 1939 (Dalio 3)
Boîte à malice, 1903 (Méliès 2)
Boite aux rêves, 1943 (Allégret, Y. 2, Philipe 3, Signoret 3,
    Wakhévitch 4)
Boite diabolique, 1911 (Cohl 2)
Boje sanjaju, 1958 (Makavejev 2)
Bojo, 1950 (Yamada 3)
Bojo no hito, 1961 (Hara 3)
Boks, 1961 (Skolimowski 2)
Bokser, 1966 (Olbrychski 3)

Bokseri idu u raj, 1967 (Samardžić 3)
Boku no marumage, 1933 (Naruse 2)
Boku wa san-nin mae, 1958 (Kagawa 3)
Bokul, 1954 (Sircar 4)
Bokura no otouto, 1933 (Yoda 4)
Bokuto kidan, 1960 (Kishida 3)
Bokyaku no hanabira: Kanketsu-hen, 1957 (Tsukasa 3)
Bol d'air à Loué. See Douceur du village, 1963
Bold and the Brave, 1956 (Rooney 3)
Bold Caballero, 1937 (Canutt 4)
Bold Cavalier. See Bold Caballero, 1937
Bold Emmett, 1915 (Olcott 2)
Bold Seven. See Semero smelykh, 1936
Bolero, 1934 (Ruggles 2, Lombard 3, Milland 3, Raft 3, Sheridan 3,
    Banton 4, Prinz 4, Wilson, C. 4)
Boléro, 1942 (Arletty 3, Signoret 3)
Bolero, 1984 (Kennedy, G. 3, Bernstein 4, Golan and Globus 4)
Bolero. See Uns et les autres, 1981
Bolero de Raquel, 1956 (Cantinflas 3, Figueroa 4)
Bolivar 63-29, 1963 (Gélin 3)
Bolivia, 1946 (Ferrer, J. 3)
Bolly, 1968 (Halas and Batchelor 2)
Bolond április, 1957 (Fábri 2)
Bolschye Kryla, 1937 (Babochkin 3)
Bolshaya semya, 1955 (Batalov 3)
Bolshoi Ballet, 1957 (Czinner 2)
Bolwieser, 1977 (Fassbinder 2)
Bom Povo Português, 1980 (de Almeida 4)
Bom the Flyer. See Flyg-Bom, 1952
Boman på utstallningen, 1923 (Magnusson 4)
Bomarzo, 1949 (Antonioni 2)
Bomb at 10:10. See Bomba u 10.10, 1967
Bomb by Accident. See Bombe par hasard, 1969
Bomb for a Dictator. See Fanatiques, 1957
Bomb Mania. See Bombománie, 1959
Bomb Was Stolen. See S-a furat o bomba, 1961
Bomba and the African Treasure. See African Treasure, 1952
Bomba and the Elephant Stampede. See Elephant Stampede, 1951
Bomba and the Hidden City. See Hidden City, 1950
Bomba and the Jungle Girl, 1952 (Mirisch 4)
Bomba and the Lion Hunters. See Lion Hunters, 1952
Bomba Kemal, 1967 (Guney 2)
Bomba on Panther Island, 1950 (Mirisch 4)
Bomba the Jungle Boy, 1949 (Mirisch 4)
Bomba u 10.10, 1967 (Marković 3)
Bombai Ka Babu, 1960 (Burman 4)
Bombardier, 1943 (O'Brien, P. 3, Ryan 3, Scott, R. 3, Dunn 4,
    Musuraca 4)
Bombardment of Monte Carlo. See Bomben auf Monte Carlo, 1931
Bombay Clipper, 1941 (Cortez 4, Salter 4)
Bombay Talkie, 1970 (Ivory 2, Jhabvala 4, Mitra 4)
Bombay to Goa, 1972 (Bachchan 3)
Bombe par hasard, 1969 (Grimault 4, Laguionie 4)
Bomben auf Monte Carlo, 1931 (Albers 3, Lorre 3, Pommer 4)
Bomben auf Monte Carlo, 1960 (Constantine 3)
Bombero atómico, 1950 (Cantinflas 3, Figueroa 4)
Bombers B-52, 1957 (Malden 3, Wood 3, Clothier 4, Rosenman 4)
Bomber's Moon, 1943 (Florey 2, Ballard 4, Basevi 4)
Bombomania. See Bombománie, 1959
Bombománie, 1959 (Trnka 2, Brdečka 4, Pojar 4)
Bombs, 1916 (Sennett 2, Fazenda 3)
Bombs and Bangs, 1914 (Sennett 2)
Bombs and Banknotes, 1916 (Beery 3)
Bombs over Burma, 1942 (Wong 3)
Bombs over Japan. See Wild Blue Yonder, 1951
Bombs over London. See Midnight Menace, 1936
Bombshell, 1933 (Fleming 2, Beavers 3, Harlow 3, Merkel 3, O'Brien,
    P. 3, Adrian 4, Booth 4, Furthman 4, Mahin 4, Rosson 4,
    Stromberg 4)
Bombsight Stolen. See Cottage to Let, 1941
Bon Allumeur. See Saturnin, 1921
Bon baisers de Hong Kong, 1975 (Rooney 3)
Bon Dieu sans confession, 1953 (Autant-Lara 2, Darrieux 3, Douy 4)

Bon et les méchants, 1976 (Lelouch 2, Reggiani 3, Lai 4)
Bon Plaisir, 1983 (Trintignant 3)
Bon propriétaire, 1913 (Feuillade 2)
Bon Roi Dagobert, 1963 (Cervi 3, Fernandel 3)
Bon Voyage, 1944 (Hitchcock 2)
Bon Voyage, 1962 (Disney 2, MacMurray 3, Wyman 3)
Bon Voyage. See Schastlivogo plavaniya, 1949
Bon voyage Amédée, 1956 (Fabian 3)
Bona, 1980 (Brocka 2)
Bonanza Bunny, 1959 (McKimson 4)
Bonaparte et la révolution, 1971 (Gance 2)
Bonaventure. See Thunder on the Hill, 1951
Bonbon, 1947 (Hasegawa 3)
Bonchi, 1960 (Ichikawa 2, Kyo 3, Yamada 3, Miyagawa 4)
Bond, 1918 (Chaplin 2, Purviance 3)
Bond Between, 1917 (Crisp 3)
Bond Boy, 1922 (King 2, Barthelmess 3)
Bond Street, 1948 (Clayton 2)
Bondage, 1917 (Chaney Lon 3)
Bondage, 1933 (Darwell 3, Friedhofer 4)
Bondage of Barbara, 1919 (Marsh 3)
Bondman, 1916 (Farnum 3)
Bondman, 1929 (Wilcox 2, Steiner 4)
Bonds of Hate. See Prometheus I-II, 1919
Bonds of Honor, 1919 (Hayakawa 3)
Bone Dry, 1922 (Roach 4)
Bone for a Bone, 1949 (Freleng 4)
Bonehead. See His Favorite Pastime, 1914
Bongo Fuego—Forms—Petit matin, 1967 (Foldès 4)
Bonheur, 1934 (L'Herbier 2, Boyer 3, Francis, E. 3, Marais 3,
    Simon, M. 3, Douy 4, Stradling 4)
Bonheur, 1965 (Varda 2, Rabier 4)
Bonheur des autres, 1918 (Dulac 2)
Bonheur d'être aimée, 1962 (Storck 2)
Bonheur est pour demain, 1962 (Delerue 4)
Boniface somnambule, 1950 (Fernandel 3)
Bonita of El Cajon, 1911 (Dwan 2)
Bonjour, Monsieur La Bruyère, 1958 (Braunberger 4)
Bonjour, New York!, 1928 (Florey 2, Chevalier 3)
Bonjour sourire, 1956 (Sautet 2, Burel 4)
Bonjour Tristesse, 1957 (Preminger 2, Kerr 3, Niven 3, Seberg 3,
    Auric 4, Bass 4, Périnal 4)
Bonne à tout faire. See Difficulté d'être infidèle, 1963
Bonne Absinthe, 1899–1900 (Guy 2)
Bonne Année, 1913 (Feuillade 2)
Bonne Année, 1972 (Lelouch 2, Fabian 3, Lai 4)
Bonne Aventure, 1932 (Fradetal 4)
Bonne Bergère et la méchante princesse, 1908 (Méliès 2)
Bonne chance, 1935 (Guitry 2)
Bonne Chance, Charlie, 1962 (Constantine 3)
Bonne Etoile, 1942 (Fernandel 3)
Bonne Farce avec ma tête, 1904 (Méliès 2)
Bonne Occase, 1965 (Trintignant 3)
Bonne pour Monsieur, un domestique pour Madame, 1910 (Linders 3)
Bonne Soupe, 1964 (Blier 3, Gélin 3, Girardot 3)
Bonne Tisane, 1957 (Audran 3, Blier 3)
Bonnes à tuer, 1954 (Darrieux 3, D'Eaubonne 4)
Bonnes Causes, 1963 (Christian-Jaque 2, Bourvil 3, Brasseur 3,
    Jeanson 4)
Bonnes Femmes, 1960 (Chabrol 2, Audran 3, Decaë 4, Gégauff 4)
**Bonnie and Clyde, 1967 (Penn 2, Beatty 3, Dunaway 3, Hackman 3,
    Wilder 3, Allen, D. 4, Guffey 4, Tavoularis 4, Towne 4,
    van Runkle 4)**
Bonnie, Bonnie Lassie, 1919 (Browning 2)
Bonnie Brier Bush. See Beside the Bonnie Brier Bush, 1921
Bonnie of the Hills, 1913 (Anderson G. 3)
Bonnie Prince Charlie, 1923 (Cooper, Gladys 3, Novello 3)
Bonnie Prince Charlie, 1948 (Hawkins 3, Niven 3, Korda 4, Krasker 4)
Bonnie Scotland, 1935 (Laurel & Hardy 3, Roach 4)
Bonny May, 1920 (Love 3)
Bons baisers à lundi, 1974 (Blier 3, Audiard 4)
Bons baisers de Dinard, 1949 (Decaë 4)
Bons Vivants, 1965 (Blier 3, Audiard 4)

Bonsoir mesdames, bonsoir messieurs, 1943 (Renoir 4)
Bonsoir Paris, bonjour l'amour, 1956 (Gélin 3, D'Eaubonne 4)
Bonsoirs, 1910 (Cohl 2)
Bonsoirs Russes, 1910 (Cohl 2)
Bonzo Goes to College, 1952 (Gwenn 3, O'Sullivan 3)
Boo, Boo, Theme Song, 1931 (Fleischer, M. and D. 2)
Boob, 1926 (Wellman 2, Crawford, J. 3, Carré 4, Daniels 4, Gibbons 4)
Boobs and Bricks, 1913 (Dwan 2)
Boobs in Arms, 1940 (Three Stooges 3)
Boobs in the Woods, 1925 (Capra 2, Sennett 2, Langdon 3)
Boobs in the Woods, 1949 (McKimson 4)
Booby Dupes, 1945 (Three Stooges 3)
Booby Traps, 1943 (Clampett 4)
Boogey Man, 1980 (Carradine 3)
Boogie Doodle, 1939–41 (McLaren 2)
Boogie Man Will Get You, 1942 (Karloff 3, Lorre 3)
Boogie Woogie Bugle Boy of Company B, 1941 (Lantz 4)
Boogie Woogie Dream, 1942 (Horne 3)
Book Agents, 1912–13 (White 3)
Book Agent's Romance, 1916 (Anderson G. 3)
Book Bargain, 1935 (Cavalcanti 2)
Book Bargain, 1937–39 (McLaren 2)
Book Revue, 1945 (Clampett 4)
Book Shop, 1937 (Terry 4)
Bookworm, 1939 (Freleng 4)
Bookworms, 1920 (Howard, L. 3)
Booloo, 1938 (Head 4)
Boom, 1963 (De Sica 2, Sordi 3, De Laurentiis 4, Zavattini 4)
Boom!, 1968 (Losey 2, Burton 3, Taylor, E. 3, Barry 4, Coward 4,
    Slocombe 4)
Boom. See Bum, 1979
Boom Town, 1940 (Colbert 3, Gable 3, Lamarr 3, Tracy 3, Adrian 4,
    Canutt 4, Gibbons 4, Gillespie 4, Mahin 4, Rosson 4, Waxman 4)
Boomerang, 1913 (Ince 4)
Boomerang, 1919 (Walthall 3)
Boomerang, 1925 (Schulberg 4)
Boomerang, 1947 (Kazan 2, Andrews D. 3, Cobb 3, Kennedy, A. 3,
    Malden 3, Basevi 4, Day 4, de Rochemont 4, Lemaire 4,
    Newman 4, Zanuck 4)
Boomerang Bill, 1922 (Barrymore L. 3)
Boon. See Anugraham, 1979
Boon. See Kondura, 1977
Boop-Oop-a-Doop, 1932 (Fleischer, M. and D. 2)
Booster, 1928 (Roach 4)
Boot Polish, 1954 (Kapoor 2)
Bootlegger, 1911 (Bosworth 3)
Bootlegger, 1922 (Laurel 3)
Bootleggers, 1922 (Shearer 3)
Boots, 1919 (Barthelmess 3, Gish, D. 3)
Boots and Saddles, 1937 (Autry 3)
Boots! Boots!, 1934 (Formby 3)
Boots Malone, 1952 (Dieterle 2, Holden 3, Bernstein 4, Guffey 4)
Booty and the Beast, 1953 (Three Stooges 3)
Boquetière des Innocents, 1922 (Modot 3)
Boquitas pintadas, 1974 (Torre-Nilsson 2)
Border, 1982 (Richardson 2, Keitel 3, Nicholson 3, Oates 3,
    Zsigmond 4)
Border Badmen, 1945 (Crabbe 3)
Border Cafe, 1937 (Carey 3, Musuraca 4)
Border Cavalier, 1927 (Wyler 2)
Border Devils, 1932 (Carey 3)
Border Feud. See Gransfolken, 1913
Border Flight, 1936 (Cummings 3, Farmer 3, Dreier 4, Head 4)
Border G-Man, 1938 (August 4)
Border Incident, 1949 (Mann 2, Alton, J. 4, Previn 4)
Border Justice, 1925 (Eason 4)
Border Legion, 1919 (Bosworth 3)
Border Legion, 1924 (Hathaway 2, Howard 2)
Border Legion, 1930 (Arlen 3, Wray 3)
Border Legion, 1940 (Rogers, R. 3)
Border Patrol, 1928 (Carey 3, Polito 4)
Border Patrol, 1943 (Boyd 3, Mitchum 3, Wilson, M. 4)
Border Ranger, 1911 (Anderson G. 3)

Border River, 1954 (Armendáriz 3, De Carlo 3, McCrea 3)
Border Street. *See* Ulica graniczna, 1949
Border Treasure, 1950 (Hunt 4)
Border Vigilantes, 1941 (Boyd 3, Head 4)
Border Weave, 1942 (Alwyn 4, Cardiff 4)
Border Wireless, 1918 (Hart 3, August 4, Sullivan 4)
Borderland, 1937 (Boyd 3, Head 4)
Borderline, 1925 (Robeson 3)
Borderline, 1950 (MacMurray 3, Trevor 3, Cahn 4, Salter 4)
Borderline, 1980 (Bronson 3)
Borderlines. *See* Caretakers, 1963
Bordertown, 1935 (Armendáriz 3, Davis 3, Muni 3, Gaudio 4, Orry-
    Kelly 4, Westmore, P. 4)
Bored of Education, 1936 (Roach 4)
Borghese piccolo piccolo, 1977 (Monicelli 2, Sordi 3, Winters 3,
    Amidei 4)
Borgne, 1981 (Ruiz 2)
Borinage. *See* Misère au Borinage, 1934
Boring Afternoon. *See* Fádní odpoledne, 1965
Born Again, 1978 (Andrews D. 3, Brent 3)
Born for Glory. *See* Brown on Resolution, 1935
Born for Glory. *See* Forever England, 1935
Born for Trouble. *See* Murder in the Big House, 1942
Born Free, 1966 (Barry 4, Foreman 4)
Born in Sin. *See* Kawano hotoride, 1962
Born Losers, 1967 (Russell, J. 3)
Born Lucky, 1932 (Powell 2)
Born Reckless, 1930 (Ford, J. 2, Bond 3, Brown 3, Nichols 4)
Born Reckless, 1937 (Carey 3, Chaney Lon, Jr. 3)
Born Reckless, 1959 (Biroc 4)
Born to Battle, 1926 (Arthur 3)
Born to Be Bad, 1934 (Grant, C. 3, Young, L. 3, Day 4, Newman 4,
    Zanuck 4)
Born to Be Bad, 1950 (Ray, N. 2, Ferrer, M. 3, Fontaine 3, Ryan 3,
    Musuraca 4, Schnee 4)
Born to Be Loved, 1959 (Haas 3)
Born to Be Wild, 1938 (Bond 3)
Born to Buck, 1968 (Fonda, H. 3)
Born to Dance, 1936 (Merkel 3, Powell, E. 3, Stewart 3, Adrian 4,
    Edens 4, Newman 4, Porter 4)
Born to Kill, 1947 (Wise 2, Cook 3, Trevor 3)
Born to Kill. *See* Cockfighter, 1974
Born to Love, 1931 (Bennett C. 3, McCrea 3)
Born to Peck, 1952 (Lantz 4)
Born to Sing, 1941 (Berkeley 2, Dumont 3)
Born to Sing. *See* Almost Angels, 1962
Born to the West, 1938 (Wayne 3, Head 4)
Born to Win, 1971 (Passer 2, Black 3, De Niro 3, Segal 3,
    Rosenblum 4)
Born Yesterday, 1950 (Cukor 2, Crawford, B. 3, Holden 3, Holliday 3,
    Horner 4, Walker 4)
Born Yesterday, 1956 (Kanin 4)
Børnenes Synd, 1916 (Holger-Madsen 2)
Børnevennerne, 1914 (Holger-Madsen 2)
Boro no kesshitai, 1943 (Imai 2, Hara 3)
Borom Sarret, 1963 (Sembene 2)
Borrasca humana, 1939 (Armendáriz 3)
Borrowed Babies. *See* Kölcsönkért csecsemök, 1914
Borrowed Clothes, 1918 (Weber 2)
Borrowed Finery, 1914 (Ingram 2)
Borrowed Identity, 1913 (Anderson G. 3)
Borrowed Trouble, 1948 (Boyd 3)
Borrowers, 1973 (Allen, J. 4, Trumbull 4)
Borsalino, 1970 (Belmondo 3, Delon 3, Carrière 4)
Borsalino & Co., 1974 (Delon 3)
Börsenkonigin, 1917 (Nielsen 3)
Borsós Miklós, 1965 (Mészáros 2)
Boryoku, 1952 (Yoshimura 2)
Borza, 1935 (Van Dongen 2)
Bosambo. *See* Sanders of the River, 1935
Bösewichter mussen dran, 1975 (Hoppe 3)
Boško Buha, 1978 (Samardžić 3)
Bosko in Dutch, 1933 (Freleng 4)

Bosphore, 1963 (Delerue 4)
Boss, 1915 (Brady 3, Carré 4)
Boss, 1956 (Trumbo 4)
Boss of Boomtown, 1944 (Salter 4)
Boss of Camp 4, 1922 (Van Dyke, W.S. 2)
Boss of Hangtown Mesa, 1942 (Farnum 3, Salter 4)
Boss of the Katy Mine, 1912 (Anderson G. 3)
Boss Said No. *See* Blondie Goes to College, 1942
Boss Tweed, 1933 (Coburn, C. 3)
Bossu, 1934 (Lourié 4)
Bossu, 1944 (Delannoy 2, Modot 3, Annenkov 4, Auric 4, Matras 4)
Bossu, 1959 (Bourvil 3)
Bossu de Rome. *See* Gobbo, 1960
Boston Quackie, 1957 (McKimson 4)
Boston Strangler, 1968 (Fleischer, R. 2, Curtis 3, Fonda, H. 3,
    Kennedy, G. 3, Anhalt 4, Day 4, Smith, J.M. 4)
Boston Tea Party, 1908 (Porter 2)
Bostonians, 1984 (Redgrave, V. 3, Jhabvala 4, Lassally 4)
Botab dourou, 1968 (Yoda 4)
Botany Bay, 1953 (Hardwicke 3, Ladd 3, Mason 3, Seitz 4, Waxman 4)
Both Ends of the Candle. *See* Helen Morgan Story, 1957
Both You and I. *See* Ore mo omae mo, 1946
Botostroj, 1954 (Hrušínský 3)
Botschafterin, 1960 (Warm 4)
Botta e risposta, 1949 (Fernandel 3, De Laurentiis 4)
Bottle, 1915 (Hepworth 2)
Bottle Babies, 1924 (Roach 4)
Bottle Imp, 1917 (Neilan 2, Hayakawa 3)
Bottleneck. *See* Ingorgo, 1979
Bottom Line. *See* On aura tout vu!, 1976
Bottom of the Bottle, 1956 (Hathaway 2, Cotten 3, Johnson, V. 3,
    Garmes 4, Lemaire 4, Wheeler 4)
Bottoms Up, 1934 (Ball 3, Tracy 3, Miller, A. 4)
Boucher, 1970 (Chabrol 2, Audran 3)
Boucher, la star, et l'orpheline, 1973 (Presle 3, Cloquet 4)
Boucher, la star, et l'orpheline. *See* Evlalie quitte les champs, 1973
Bouclette, 1917 (L'Herbier 2)
Boudoir Brothers, 1932 (Sennett 2)
Boudoir Diplomat, 1930 (Freund 4, Glazer 4, Laemmle 4)
Boudu sauvé des eaux, 1932 (Becker 2, Renoir 2, Simon, M. 3, Renoir 4)
Boudu Saved from Drowning. *See* Boudu sauvé des eaux, 1932
Bought, 1931 (Bennett C. 3, Milland 3)
Bought and Paid For, 1916 (Brady 3, Edeson 4, Marion 4)
Boulanger de Valorgue, 1952 (Verneuil 2, Fernandel 3)
Boulangerie de Monceau, 1963 (Rohmer 2)
Boule de suif, 1945 (Christian-Jaque 2, Presle 3, Barsacq 4, Jeanson 4,
    Matras 4)
Boule de suif. *See* Pyshka, 1934
Boulevard, 1960 (Duvivier 2)
Boulevard des assassins, 1982 (Audran 3)
Boulevard du Rhum, 1971 (Bardot 3, Douy 4)
Boulevard Nights, 1979 (Schifrin 4)
Boulevardier from the Bronx, 1936 (Freleng 4)
Boulez, 1965 (Reichenbach 2)
Boulot aviateur, 1937 (Simon, M. 3)
Bouncer, 1925 (Roach 4)
Bouncing Babies, 1929 (Roach 4)
Bound and Gagged, 1919 (Grot 4)
Bound for Glory, 1976 (Ashby 2, Rosenman 4, Wexler 4, Whitlock 4)
Bound in Morocco, 1918 (Dwan 2, Fairbanks, D. 3)
Bound on the Wheel, 1915 (Chaney Lon 3, Furthman 4)
Boundary House, 1918 (Hepworth 2)
Bounty, 1984 (Gibson 3, Hopkins, A. 3, Olivier 3, Vangelis 4)
Bounty Hunter, 1954 (De Toth 2, Borgnine 3, Scott, R. 3)
Bounty Hunters. *See* Indio Black, sai che ti dico, 1970
Bounty Killer, 1919 (Anderson G. 3)
Bounty Killer, 1965 (Arlen 3, Crabbe 3, Duryea 3)
Bouquet, 1915 (Beery 3)
Bouquetière des Catalans, 1915 (Musidora 3)
Bourbon Street Blues, 1978 (Fassbinder 2)
Bourdelle, 1950 (Honegger 4)
Bourdelle, sculpteur monumental, 1962 (Contard 4)
Boure nad Tatrami, 1932 (Stallich 4, Vich 4)

Bourgeois Gentilhomme, 1958 (Alekan 4)
Bourgogne, 1936 (Epstein 2)
Bourreau turc, 1904 (Méliès 2)
Bourse. See Valise diplomatique, 1909
Bourse et la vie, 1965 (Fernandel 3)
Bourse ou la vie. See Piednadze, 1961
Bout de Zan et le poilu, 1915 (Musidora 3)
Bout de Zan et l'espion, 1915 (Musidora 3)
Bout-de-chou, 1935 (Brasseur 3)
Bout-de-Zan et la torpille, 1916 (Feuillade 2)
Bout-de-Zan revient du cirque, 1912 (Feuillade 2)
Boutique des miracles. See Tenda dos milagres, 1977
Bow Bells, 1954 (Lassally 4)
Bow Wow, 1922 (Sennett 2, Fazenda 3)
Bow Wows, 1922 (Roach 4)
Bowery, 1914 (Walsh 2)
Bowery, 1933 (Walsh 2, Ball 3, Beery 3, Cooper, J 3, Raft 3, Wray 3,
    Day 4, Estabrook 4, Newman 4, Zanuck 4)
Bowery at Midnight, 1942 (Lugosi 3, Katzman 4)
Bowery Bimboes, 1930 (Lantz 4)
Bowery Bishop, 1924 (Walthall 3)
Bowery Blitzkrieg, 1941 (Katzman 4)
Bowery Boy, 1940 (Fuller 2)
Bowery Boys, 1914 (Sennett 2, Arbuckle 3)
Bowery Buckaroos, 1947 (Cody 3)
Bowery Champs, 1944 (Katzman 4)
Bowery to Broadway, 1944 (O'Connor 3)
Bowled Over, 1923 (Roach 4, Roach 4)
Bowling Bimboes, 1930 (Lantz 4)
Bowling Match, 1913 (Sennett 2, Normand 3)
Bowling-Alley Cat, 1942 (Hanna and Barbera 4)
Boxcar Bertha, 1972 (Scorsese 2, Carradine 3, Corman 4)
Boxe de la France, 1943 (Honegger 4)
Boxer. See Bokser, 1966
Boxer. See Uomo dalle pelle dura, 1971
Boxing. See Boks, 1961
Boxing Gloves, 1929 (Roach 4)
Boxing Kangaroo, 1920 (Fleischer, M. and D. 2)
Boy. See Shonen, 1969
Boy and a Bike, 1951 (Buchanan 3)
Boy and His Dog, 1948 (Prinz 4)
Boy and His Dog, 1976 (Robards 3)
Boy and the Kite. See Pojken och draken, 1962
Boy and the Law, 1914 (Stahl 2)
Boy and the Pigeon. See Malchik i golub, 1961
Boy and the Sea, 1953 (Brakhage 2)
Boy Crazy, 1922 (Stromberg 4)
Boy Detective, 1908 (Bitzer 4)
Boy, Did I Get a Wrong Number!, 1966 (Hope 3, Lewin 4)
Boy Friend, 1926 (Gibbons 4)
Boy Friend, 1928 (McCarey 2, Roach 4)
Boy Friend, 1971 (Russell 2, Jackson 3, Russell 4, Watkin 4)
Boy From Barnado's. See Lord Jeff, 1938
Boy from Indiana, 1950 (Burke 3)
Boy from Oklahoma, 1954 (Curtiz 2, Chaney Lon, Jr. 3, Steiner 4)
Boy in Blue. See Knabe in Blau, 1919
Boy in the Barrel, 1903 (Bitzer 4)
Boy in the Plastic Bubble, 1976 (Bellamy 3)
Boy in the Tree. See Pojken i tradet, 1961
Boy Meets Girl, 1938 (Bacon 2, Bellamy 3, Cagney 3, O'Brien, P. 3,
    Reagan 3, Edeson 4, Polito 4, Wallis 4)
Boy of Flanders, 1924 (Coogan 3)
Boy of Mine, 1923 (Walthall 3)
Boy of the Revolution, 1911 (Cruze 2)
Boy of the Sea. See Kaikoku danji, 1926
Boy of the Streets, 1937 (Cooper, J 3)
Boy of Two Worlds. See Paw, 1959
Boy on a Dolphin, 1957 (Negulesco 2, Ladd 3, Loren 3, Webb 3,
    Friedhofer 4, Krasner 4, Smith, J.M. 4)
Boy Rider, 1927 (Plunkett 4)
Boy Slaves, 1939 (Berman 4, Hunt 4)
Boy Ten Feet Tall, 1965 (Robinson, E. 3)
Boy Ten Feet Tall. See Sammy Going South, 1963

Boy Trouble, 1939 (O'Connor 3, Head 4)
Boy Who Stole a Million, 1960 (Crichton 2, Slocombe 4)
Boy Who Turned Yellow, 1972 (Powell and Pressburger 2)
Boy with Green Hair, 1948 (Losey 2, Nilsson 3, O'Brien, P. 3, Ryan 3,
    D'Agostino 4, Schary 4)
Boycotted Baby, 1917 (Hardy 3)
Boyevoye kinosbornik n. 7, 1941 (Yutkevich 2)*
Boyhood Daze, 1957 (Jones 2)
Boykott, 1930 (Dagover 3)
Boy's Day, 1964 (Attenborough 3)
Boys from Brazil, 1978 (Schaffner 2, Ganz 3, Mason 3, Olivier 3,
    Peck 3, Decaë 4, Goldsmith 4)
Boys from Brooklyn. See Bela Lugosi Meets a Brooklyn Gorilla, 1952
Boys from Syracuse, 1940 (Sutherland 2)
Boys from the West Coast. See Vesterhavsdrenge, 1950
Boys in Brown, 1949 (Attenborough 3, Bogarde 3)
Boys in the Band, 1970 (Friedkin 2)
Boys' Night Out, 1962 (Bendix 3, Homolka 3, Novak 3, Cahn 4)
Boys of Paul Street. See Pál utcai fiúk, 1968
Boys of the City, 1940 (Katzman 4)
Boys' Ranch, 1946 (Irene 4)
Boys School. See Disparus de Saint-Agil, 1938
Boys to Board, 1923 (Roach 4)
Boys Town, 1938 (Taurog 2, Rooney 3, Tracy 3, Schary 4)
Boys Will Be Boys, 1921 (Rogers, W. 3)
Boys Will Be Boys, 1932 (Stevens 2)
Boys Will Be Boys, 1935 (Balcon 2)
Boys Will Be Joys, 1925 (Roach 4)
Božská Ema, 1979 (Kopecký 3)
Bra flicka reder sig sjalv, 1914 (Sjostrom 2)
Braccia aperte, 1922 (Gallone 2)
Braccio violento della mala. See Dinero Maldito, 1978
Braconniers, 1903 (Guy 2)
Bracos de Sologne, 1933 (Aurenche 4)
Brahim, 1956 (Cloquet 4)
Brahma Diamond, 1909 (Griffith 2, Lawrence 3, Bitzer 4)
Brahmane et le papillon, 1901 (Méliès 2)
Brahmin and the Butterfly. See Brahmane et le papillon, 1901
Brain, 1969 (Niven 3)
Brain. See Cerveau, 1969
Brain. See Vengeance, 1962
Brain Eaters, 1958 (Corman 4)
Brain Snatcher. See Man Who Changed His Mind, 1936
Brains Repaired. See Retapeur de Cervelles, 1911
Brainsnatcher. See Man Who Lived Again, 1936
Brainstorm, 1965 (Andrews D. 3, Hunter 3, Martin, S. 3, Duning 4)
Brainstorm, 1983 (Robertson 3, Wood 3, Serafine 4, Trumbull 4)
Brainwashed. See Droit d'aimer, 1972
Brainwashed. See Schachnovelle, 1960
Brainwaves, 1982 (Curtis 3)
Bramble Bush, 1960 (Burton 3, Dickinson 3, Ballard 4, Rosenman 4)
Bramy raju, 1967 (Wajda 2)
Brancaleone alla crusada. See Brancaleone alle Crociate, 1970
Brancaleone alle Crociate, 1970 (Monicelli 2, Gassman 3, Age and
    Scarpelli 4, Gherardi 4)
Branches, 1970 (Emshwiller 2)
Branco di vigliacchi, 1962 (Moore, R. 3)
Brand, 1912 (Dwan 2)
Brand im Ozean, no date (Staudte 2)
Brand in der Oper, 1930 (Frohlich 3, Grundgens 3, Reisch 4,
    Wagner 4)
Brand New Hero, 1914 (Sennett 2, Arbuckle 3)
Brand of Cowardice, 1916 (Barrymore L. 3)
Brand of Evil. See Aku no monsho, 1964
Brand of Fear, 1911 (Dwan 2)
Brand of Hate, 1934 (Katzman 4)
Brand of Lopez, 1920 (Hayakawa 3)
Branded, 1950 (Ladd 3, Dreier 4, Head 4, Lang 4, Maté 4)
Branded a Bandit, 1924 (Canutt 4)
Branded Woman, 1920 (Talmadge, N. 3, Emerson 4, Hunt 4, Loos 4)
Brandende straal, or Wigwam, 1911 (Ivens 2)
Brandherd. See Verlogene Moral, 1921
Branding, 1929 (Ivens 2)

Branding a Bad Man, 1911 (Dwan 2)
Branding Broadway, 1918 (Hart 3, August 4, Sullivan 4)
Brandos Costumes, 1974 (de Almeida 4)
Brandsoldaten, 1916 (Borgstrom 3)
Brandstifter, 1969 (Von Trotta 2)
Brandy, el sheriff de Losatumba, 1963 (Borau 2)
Brandy for the Parson, 1951 (Grierson 2, More 3, Addison 4)
Brandy, the Sheriff of Losatumba. See Brandy, el sheriff de
    Losatumba, 1963
Branle-bas de combat, 1936 (Ibert 4)
Brannigan, 1975 (Attenborough 3, Ferrer, M. 3, Wayne 3, Fisher 4)
Branningar, 1912 (Jaenzon 4, Magnusson 4)
Branningar, 1935 (Bergman 3, Jaenzon 4)
Braque, 1950 (Cloquet 4)
Bras de la nuit, 1961 (Darrieux 3)
Brasa dormida, 1928 (Mauro 2)
Brasher Doubloon, 1947 (Kortner 3, Basevi 4)
Brasier ardent, 1923 (Mozhukin 3)
Brasilianas, 1945-56 (Mauro 2)
Brass, 1923 (Franklin 2)
Brass Bottle, 1923 (Tourneur, M. 2)
Brass Bottle, 1964 (Bumstead 4)
Brass Buttons, 1919 (King 2, Furthman 4)
Brass Check, 1918 (Bushman 3)
Brass Commandments, 1923 (Farnum 3)
Brass Knuckles, 1927 (Bacon 2, Blanke 4)
Brass Monkey, 1917 (Selig 4)
Brass Monkey. See Lucky Mascot, 1948
Brass Target, 1978 (Kennedy, G. 3, Loren 3, Von Sydow 3)
Brat, 1919 (Guy 2, Nazimova 3, Mathis 4)
Brat, 1931 (Ford, J. 2, Balfour 3, August 4, Behrman 4, Levien 4)
Brat geroya, 1940 (Donskoi 2)
Bratichka, 1927 (Gerasimov 2, Kozintsev 2, Enei 4, Moskvin 4)
Brats, 1930 (Roach 4)
Bratya, 1912 (Mozhukin 3)
Bratya Karamazovy, 1968 (Ulyanov 3)
Bratya razbotchniki, 1912 (Mozhukin 3)
Brautigam, die Komodiantin und der Zuhalter, 1968 (Fassbinder 2)
Bravados, 1958 (King 2, Peck 3, Van Cleef 3, Friedhofer 4, Lemaire 4,
    Newman 4, Shamroy 4, Wheeler 4)
Brave and Bold, 1911 (Sennett 2)
Brave and the Beautiful. See Magnificent Matador, 1955
Brave Bulls, 1951 (Rossen 2, Ferrer, M. 3, Quinn 3, Crosby 4, Howe 4,
    Trumbo 4)
Brave Deserve the Fair, 1915 (Mix 3)
Brave Dog, 1951 (Macskássy 4)
Brave Don't Cry, 1952 (Grierson 2)
Brave Hare, 1955 (Ivanov-vano 4)
Brave Hunter, 1912 (Sennett 2, Sennett 2, Normand 3)
Brave Little Bat, 1941 (Jones 2)
Brave One, 1956 (Cardiff 4, Trumbo 4, Young, V. 4)
Brave Ones, 1916 (Hardy 3)
Brave Rifles, 1966 (Kennedy, A. 3)
Brave Soldier at Dawn. See Akatsuki no yushi, 1926
Brave Sunder, 1931 (Kortner 3)
Brave Tin Soldier, 1934 (Iwerks 4)
Brave Warrior, 1952 (Katzman 4)
Braver Than the Bravest, 1916 (Roach 4)
Braves gens, 1912 (Feuillade 2)
Braves Petits Soldats de plomb, 1915 (Cohl 2)
Bravest Girl in the South, 1910 (Olcott 2)
Bravest Way, 1918 (Hayakawa 3)
Bravissimo, 1955 (Sordi 3, Age and Scarpelli 4)
Bravo Alpha, 1957 (Jarre 4)
Bravo di Venezia, 1941 (Brazzi 3, Cortese 3)
Bravo for Billy, 1979 (Halas and Batchelor 2)
Bravo, Mr. Strauss, 1943 (Pal 2)
Brawn of the North, 1922 (Murfin 4)
Brazen Beauty, 1918 (Browning 2)
Brazen Bell, 1962 (Cobb 3)
Brazil, 1944 (Horton 3, Rogers, R. 3)
Brazil: A Report on Torture, 1971 (Wexler 4)
Breach of Promise, 1932 (Miller, A. 4, Veiller 4)

Breach of Promise, 1941 (Brook 3)
Bread, 1924 (Bosworth 3, Coffee 4, Lewin 4)
Bread. See Pão, 1959
Bread and Chocolate. See Pane e cioccolata, 1973
Bread Cast upon the Water, 1913 (Ince 4)
Bread, Love and Dreams. See Pane, amore e fantasia, 1953
Bread of the Border, 1924 (Arzner 2)
Breadline. See Heros for Sale, 1933
Break, Break, Break, 1914 (Eason 4)
Break of Hearts, 1935 (Boyer 3, Hepburn, K. 3, Hersholt 3, Berman 4,
    Biroc 4, Heerman 4, Polglase 4, Steiner 4, Veiller 4)
Break the Chains. See Springt die Ketten, 1930
Break the News, 1937 (Clair 2, Buchanan 3, Chevalier 3, Meerson 4)
Break to Freedom. See Albert, R.N., 1953
Break Up the Dance. See Rozbijemy zabawe, 1957
Breakaway, 1966 (Conner 2)
Breakdance 2: Electric Boogaloo, 1984 (Golan and Globus 4)
Breakdown, 1955 (Hitchcock 2)
Breakdown. See Si j'etais un espion, 1967
Breaker Morant, 1980 (Beresford 2)
Breakers. See Branding, 1929
Breakers. See Branningar, 1912
Breakers Ahead, 1935 (Green, G. 4)
Breakfast, 1972 and 1976 (Snow 2)
Breakfast at Sunrise, 1927 (Dressler 3, Talmadge, C. 3, Schenck 4)
Breakfast at Tiffany's, 1961 (Edwards 2, Hepburn, A. 3, Neal 3,
    Rooney 3, Axelrod 4, Edouart 4, Fulton 4, Head 4, Mancini 4,
    Mercer 4, Planer 4, Westmore, W. 4)
Breakfast Club, 1985 (Allen, D. 4)
Breakfast for Two, 1937 (Marshall 3, Meek 3, Stanwyck 3, Hunt 4)
Breakfast in Hollywood, 1946 (Bondi 3, Burke 3, Pitts 3)
Breakheart Pass, 1975 (Bronson 3, Johnson, B. 3, Ballard 4, Canutt 4,
    Goldsmith 4)
Breaking Away, 1979 (Yates 2, Tesich 4)
Breaking Branches Is Forbidden, 1968 (Kawamoto 4)
Breaking into Society, 1923 (Stromberg 4)
Breaking Point, 1924 (Brenon 2, Howe 4)
Breaking Point, 1950 (Curtiz 2, Garfield 3, Neal 3, McCord 4, Wald 4)
Breaking the Ice, 1925 (Sennett 2)
Breaking the Ice, 1938 (Costello, D. 3, Young, V. 4)
Breaking the Sound Barrier. See Sound Barrier, 1952
Breaking Up, 1978 (Remick 3)
Breakout, 1975 (Huston 2, Bronson 3, Duvall, R. 3, Ballard 4,
    Goldsmith 4)
Breakout. See Danger Within, 1959
Breakthrough, 1979 (Mitchum 3, Steiger 3)
Breakthrough. See Cross of Iron II, 1979
Breakthrough Steiner, 1979 (Burton 3)
Break-Up, 1968 (Ferreri 2)
Breakup. See Rupture, 1970
Breath of Scandal, 1913 (Nilsson 3)
Breath of Scandal, 1924 (Schulberg 4)
Breath of Scandal, 1925 (Nilsson 3)
Breath of Scandal, 1960 (Curtiz 2, Chevalier 3, Lansbury 3, Loren 3,
    Head 4, Lardner 4, Ponti 4)
Breathdeath, 1964 (Vanderbeek 2)
Breathing, 1963 (Breer 2)
Breathless, 1983 (Gere 3, Lourié 4, Sylbert 4)
Breathless. See A bout de souffle, 1959
Bred in the Bone, 1915 (Crisp 3, Gish, D. 3)
Breed o' the North, 1914 (Ince 4)
Breed of Men, 1919 (Hart 3, August 4)
Breed of the Mountains, 1914 (Reid 3)
Breezes of Love. See Fukeyo koikaze, 1935
Breezing Home, 1937 (Cook 3, Dunne 4)
Breezy, 1973 (Eastwood 3, Holden 3, Legrand 4)
Breite Weg, 1917 (Gad 2)
Brelan d'as, 1952 (Verneuil 2, Simon, M. 3)
Bremen Freedom. See Bremer Freiheit, 1972
Bremen Town Musicians, 1935 (Iwerks 4)
Bremer Freiheit, 1972 (Fassbinder 2, Schygulla 3)
Brenda Starr, 1976 (Schifrin 4)

Bright Leaf, 1950 (Curtiz 2, Bacall 3, Cooper, Gary 3, Crisp 3, Neal 3, Blanke 4, Freund 4, Young, V. 4)
Bright Lights, 1916 (Sennett 2, Arbuckle 3, Normand 3)
Bright Lights, 1925 (Day 4, Gibbons 4)
Bright Lights, 1928 (Disney 2)
Bright Lights, 1930 (Curtiz 2, Carradine 3, Garmes 4, Grot 4)
Bright Lights, 1935 (Berkeley 2, Brown 3, Brown, Harry Joe 4, Grot 4, Orry-Kelly 4)
Bright Lights and Shadows. See Bright Lights of Broadway, 1923
Bright Lights of Broadway, 1923 (Goulding 2)
Bright Prospects. See Ljusnande framtid, 1940
Bright Road, 1953 (Dandridge 3)
Bright Road. See Sretlyi put, 1940
Bright Shawl, 1923 (Goulding 2, Astor 3, Barthelmess 3, Gish, D. 3, Powell, W. 3, Robinson, E. 3)
Bright Skies, 1920 (Pitts 3)
Bright Victory, 1951 (Robson 2, Hudson 3, Kennedy, A. 3, Buckner 4, Daniels 4)
Brighton Rock, 1947 (Boulting 2, Attenborough 3)
Brighton Story, 1956 (Lassally 4)
Brighton Strangler, 1945 (D'Agostino 4, Hunt 4)
Brighty of the Grand Canyon, 1967 (Cotten 3)
Brigitte et Brigitte, 1965 (Chabrol 2, Fuller 2)
Brigitte Horney, 1977 (Zanussi 2)
Brillanten, 1937 (Rohrig 4)
Brillantstjernen, 1912 (Blom 2)
Brilliant Murder. See Kenran taru satsujin, 1951
Brillianty dlya diktatury proletariata, 1976 (Samoilova 3)
Brimade dans une caserne. See Saut à la couverture, 1895
Brimstone, 1949 (Brennan 3)
Bring Back 'em Sober, 1932 (Sennett 2)
Bring Himself Back Alive, 1940 (Fleischer, M. and D. 2)
Bring Home the Turkey, 1927 (Roach 4)
Bring Me the Head of Alfredo Garcia, 1974 (Fernández 2, Peckinpah 2, Oates 3, Young, G. 3)
Bring on the Girls, 1945 (De Carlo 3, Lake 3, Head 4, Struss 4)
Bring Your Smile Along, 1955 (Edwards 2)
Bringin' Home the Bacon, 1924 (Arthur 3)
Bringing Home the Bacon, 1941 (Terry 4)
Bringing Up Baby, 1938 (Hawks 2, Bond 3, Fitzgerald 3, Grant, C. 3, Hepburn, K. 3, Dunn 4, Nichols 4, Polglase 4)
Bringing Up Father, 1928 (Dressler 3, Booth 4, Daniels 4, Gibbons 4, Marion 4)
Brink of Hell. See Toward the Unknown, 1956
Brink of Life. See Nara livet, 1958
Brink's Job, 1978 (Friedkin 2, Falk 3, Oates 3, Rowlands 3, De Laurentiis 4, Tavoularis 4)
Briseur de chaînes, 1941 (Fresnay 3, Matras 4)
Bristet Lykke, 1913 (Blom 2)
Brita i grosshandlarhuset, 1946 (Borgstrom 3, Dahlbeck 3)
Brita in the Wholesaler's House. See Brita i grosshandlarhuset, 1946
Britain at Bay, 1940 (Watt 2)
Britain Now series, 1973 (Halas and Batchelor 2)
Britannia Hospital, 1981 (Anderson 2, McDowell 3)
Britannia Mews, 1949 (Andrews D. 3, Arnold 4)
Britannia Mews. See Forbidden Street, 1949
Britannia of Billingsgate, 1933 (Mills 3, Balcon 4, Junge 4)
British Agent, 1934 (Curtiz 2, Francis, K. 3, Howard, L. 3, Blanke 4, Grot 4, Haller 4, Orry-Kelly 4)
British—Are They Artistic?, 1947 (Donat 3)
British Family in Peace and War, 1940 (Pearson 2)
British Intelligence, 1940 (Karloff 3)
British Sounds, 1969 (Godard 2)
British Youth, 1941 (Pearson 2)
Briton and Boer, 1910 (Mix 3)
Broadcast. See Ekpombi, 1968
Broad-Minded, 1930 (Leroy 2, Brown 3, Lugosi 3)
Broadway, 1929 (Fejos 2, Laemmle 4)
Broadway, 1942 (Crawford, B. 3, O'Brien, P. 3, Raft 3, Sakall 3)
Broadway after Dark, 1924 (Leroy 2, Menjou 3, Nilsson 3, Shearer 3)
Broadway Ahead. See Sweetheart of the Campus, 1941
Broadway and Home, 1920 (Crosland 2)
Broadway Babies, 1929 (Leroy 2, Polito 4)

Broadway Bad, 1933 (Blondell 3, Crisp 3, Rogers, G. 3, Barnes 4, Friedhofer 4)
Broadway Bill, 1918 (Gaudio 4)
Broadway Bill, 1934 (Capra 2, Ball 3, Baxter W. 3, Bond 3, Loy 3, Muse 3, Buchman 4, Riskin 4, Walker 4)
Broadway Billy, 1926 (Brown, Harry Joe 4)
Broadway Blues, 1929 (Sennett 2)
Broadway Butterfly, 1925 (Fazenda 3)
Broadway by Light, 1957 (Resnais 2)
Broadway Daddies. See Broadway Babies, 1929
Broadway Danny Rose, 1984 (Farrow 3, Willis 4)
Broadway Folly, 1930 (Lantz 4)
Broadway Gold, 1923 (Gibbons 4)
Broadway Gondolier, 1935 (Bacon 2, Blondell 3, Fazenda 3, Menjou 3, Powell, D. 3, Barnes 4, Epstein, J. & P. 4, Grot 4, Kraly 4, Orry-Kelly 4, Wald 4)
Broadway Hoofer, 1929 (Fazenda 3, Walker 4)
Broadway Hostess, 1935 (Orry-Kelly 4)
Broadway Lady, 1925 (Ruggles 2)
Broadway Limited, 1941 (McLaglen 3, Pitts 3, Roach 4)
Broadway Love, 1918 (Chaney Lon 3)
Broadway Melody, 1929 (Goulding 2, Love 3, Brown, N. 4, Freed 4, Gibbons 4, Shearer 4)
Broadway Melody of 1936, 1935 (Merkel 3, Powell, E. 3, Taylor, R. 3, Adrian 4, Brown, N. 4, Edens 4, Freed 4, Newman 4, Rosher 4)
Broadway Melody of 1938, 1937 (Garland 3, Powell, E. 3, Taylor, R. 3, Adrian 4, Brown, N. 4, Daniels 4, Edens 4, Freed 4, Gibbons 4, Vorkapich 4)
Broadway Melody of 1940, 1940 (Taurog 2, Astaire 3, Powell, E. 3, Adrian 4, Newman 4, Porter 4, Ruttenberg 4, Schary 4)
Broadway Musketeers, 1938 (Sheridan 3, Deutsch 4)
Broadway Nights, 1927 (Sothern 3, Stanwyck 3, Haller 4)
Broadway or Bust, 1924 (Miller, V. 4)
Broadway Rhythm, 1944 (Walters 2, Horne 3, Alton, R. 4, Green, J. 4, Irene 4, Sharaff 4)
Broadway Rose, 1922 (Goulding 2)
Broadway Scandal, 1918 (Chaney Lon 3)
Broadway Serenade, 1939 (Berkeley 2, Ayres 3, MacDonald 3, Adrian 4, Kraly 4, Lederer 4, Stothart 4)
Broadway Singer. See Torch Singer, 1933
Broadway Thru a Keyhole, 1933 (Ball 3, Sothern 3, Newman 4, Zanuck 4)
Broadway to Hollywood, 1933 (Brady 3, Cooper, J 3, Durante 3, Eddy 3, Merkel 3, Rooney 3, Daniels 4, Tiomkin 4)
Broadway's Like That, 1930 (Blondell 3, Bogart 3)
Broceliande, 1969 (Jarre 4)
Brock's Last Case, 1973 (Widmark 3)
Broder emellan, 1946 (Borgstrom 3)
Broderna, 1913 (Stiller 2, Jaenzon 4)
Broderna Karlsson, 1972 (Sjoman 2)
Broke in China, 1927 (Sennett 2)
Broken Arrow, 1950 (Daves 2, Chandler 3, Cody 3, Stewart 3, Friedhofer 4, Newman 4, Wheeler 4)
Broken Barriers, 1924 (Menjou 3, Shearer 3)
Broken Blossoms, 1919 (Griffith 2, Barthelmess 3, Crisp 3, Gish, L. 3, Bitzer 4, Brown, K. 4)
Broken Blossoms, 1936 (Courant 4)
Broken Butterfly, 1919 (Tourneur, M. 2, Carré 4)
Broken Chains, 1922 (Garnett 2, Moore, C. 3, Wilson, C. 4)
Broken Chains. See Yevo prizyv, 1925
Broken Cloud, 1915 (Eason 4)
Broken Coin, 1915 (Ford, J. 2)
Broken Commandment. See Hakai, 1962
Broken Cross, 1911 (Griffith 2, Bitzer 4)
Broken Doll, 1910 (Griffith 2, Bitzer 4)
Broken Doll, 1921 (Dwan 2)
Broken Dreams, 1933 (Scott, R. 3)
Broken Drum. See Yabure daiko, 1949
Broken Earth, 1940 (Muse 3)
Broken Fetters, 1916 (Ingram 2)
Broken Gate, 1927 (Arthur 3)
Broken Hearts of Broadway, 1921 (Moore, C. 3)

Broken Hearts of Hollywood, 1926 (Bacon 2, Fairbanks, D. Jr. 3, Miller, V. 4)
Broken in the Wars, 1918 (Hepworth 2)
Broken Jug. See Zerbrochene Krug, 1937
Broken Lance, 1954 (Dmytryk 2, Cody 3, Tracy 3, Wagner 3, Widmark 3, Lemaire 4)
Broken Land, 1961 (Nicholson 3, Crosby 4)
Broken Law, 1915 (Farnum 3)
Broken Leghorn, 1959 (McKimson 4)
Broken Locket, 1909 (Griffith 2, Pickford 3, Bitzer 4)
Broken Lullaby, 1932 (Pitts 3, Raphaelson 4, Vajda 4)
Broken Lullaby. See Man I Killed, 1932
Broken Melody, 1934 (Oberon 3)
Broken Oath, 1910 (Lawrence 3)
Broken Parole, 1913 (Anderson G. 3)
Broken Pledge, 1915 (Beery 3, Swanson 3)
Broken Sabre, 1966 (Carradine 3)
Broken Sky. See Brusten Himmel, 1982
Broken Spell, 1910 (Costello, M. 3, Talmadge, N. 3)
Broken Spell, 1912–13 (White 3)
Broken Spur, 1912 (Bosworth 3)
Broken Strings, 1940 (Muse 3)
Broken Ties, 1912 (Dwan 2)
Broken Violin. See Lulli ou le violon brisé, 1908
Broken Ways, 1913 (Griffith 2, Carey 3, Sweet 3, Bitzer 4)
Broken Wing, 1923 (Schulberg 4)
Broken Wing, 1932 (Douglas, M. 3, Velez 3)
Broken Wings, 1913 (Walthall 3)
Brollopet på Ulfasa, 1909 (Magnusson 4)
Brollopet på Ulfåsa, 1911 (Jaenzon 4)
Brolloppsnatt. See Noc postlubna, 1959
Brollopsdagen, 1960 (Andersson B. 3, Von Sydow 3)
Brollopsresan, 1935 (Molander 2, Jaenzon 4)
Brolly. See Parapličko, 1957
Bromo and Juliet, 1926 (McCarey 2, Roach 4)
Broncho Billy series, 1910–1916 (Anderson, G. 3)
Broncho Buster's Bride, 1911 (Dwan 2)
Broncho Busting for Flying A Pictures, 1912 (Dwan 2)
Broncho Twister, 1927 (Mix 3)
Bronco Billy, 1980 (Eastwood 3, Lourié 4)
Bronco Buster, 1935 (Lantz 4)
Bronco Buster, 1952 (Boetticher 2, Boyle 4)
Bronenosets Potemkin, 1925 (Eisenstein 2, Tisse 4)
Brontë Sisters. See Soeurs Brontë, 1979
Bronze Bell, 1921 (Johnson, N. 3, Barnes 4)
Bronze Venus. See Duke Is Tops, 1938
Brood, 1979 (Reed, O. 3)
Brooding Eyes, 1926 (Barrymore L. 3)
Brookfield Recreation Center, 1964 (Baillie 2)
Brooklyn Orchid, 1942 (Bendix 3, Roach 4)
Broom. See Metla, 1972
Broth of a Boy, 1959 (Fitzgerald 3)
Brother Brigands. See Bratya razbotchniki, 1912
Brother, Can You Spare a Dime?, 1975 (Cagney 3)
Brother from Another Planet, 1984 (Sayles 4)
Brother John, 1950 (Fleischer, M. and D. 2)
Brother John, 1971 (Poitier 3, Jones 4)
Brother of a Hero. See Brat geroya, 1940
Brother of the Bear, 1921 (Astor 3)
Brother Orchid, 1940 (Bacon 2, Bellamy 3, Bogart 3, Crisp 3, Robinson, E. 3, Sothern 3, Gaudio 4, Wallis 4)
Brother Rat, 1938 (Beavers 3, Reagan 3, Wyman 3, Haller 4, Wald 4, Wallis 4)
Brother Rat and a Baby, 1940 (Ladd 3, Reagan 3, Wyman 3, Rosher 4, Wald 4, Wallis 4)
Brother Sun, Sister Moon. See Fratello sole, sorella luna, 1972
Brother, the Sister, and the Cowpuncher, 1910 (Anderson G. 3)
Brotherhood, 1968 (Ritt 2, Douglas, K. 3, Papas 3, Kaufman 4, Schifrin 4)
Brotherhood of Man, 1946 (Hubley 4, Lardner 4)
Brotherhood of Satan, 1971 (Martin, S. 3)
Brotherhood of the Bell, 1970 (Ford, G. 3, Goldsmith 4)
Brotherly Love, 1928 (Arthur 3, Gibbons 4)

Brotherly Love, 1936 (Fleischer, M. and D. 2)
Brotherly Love. See Country Dance, 1969
Brothers, 1912 (Griffith 2, Carey 3, Reid 3, Bitzer 4)
Brothers, 1913 (Dwan 2)
Brothers. See Bratya, 1912
Brothers. See Broderna, 1913
Brothers and Sisters of the Toda Family. See Toda-ke no kyodai, 1941
Brothers in Law, 1957 (Boulting 2)
Brothers in the Saddle, 1949 (Hunt 4)
Brothers Karamazov, 1958 (Brooks, R. 2, Bloom 3, Brynner 3, Cobb 3, Schell, Maria 3, Alton, J. 4, Berman 4, Epstein, J. & P. 4, Kaper 4, Plunkett 4)
Brothers Karamazov. See Bruder Karamasoff, 1920
Brother's Keeper, 1939 (McDowall 3)
Brother's Loyalty, 1913 (Bushman 3)
Brothers Rico, 1957 (Boyle 4, Duning 4, Guffey 4)
Brother's Sacrifice, 1917 (Selig 4)
Brothers under the Chin, 1924 (Laurel 3, Roach 4)
Brothers Wood. See Freres Boutdebois, 1908
Brother's Wrong, 1909 (Olcott 2)
Brothers-in-Law, 1956 (Schlesinger 2, Attenborough 3)
Brott i Paradiset, 1959 (Andersson H. 3, Bjornstrand 3)
Brouillard sur la ville. See Gaz mortels, 1916
Brown Bomber. See Spirit of Youth, 1937
Brown of Harvard, 1926 (Wayne 3, Gibbons 4, Gillespie 4, Stewart 4)
Brown on Resolution, 1935 (Fisher 2, Balfour 3, Mills 3, Junge 4)
Brown Wallet, 1936 (Powell 2, Dalrymple 4)
Browning, 1913 (Feuillade 2)
Browning Version, 1951 (Asquith 2, Redgrave, M. 3, Dillon 4)
Brown's Seance, 1912 (Sennett 2, Normand 3)
Brsna, 1979 (Grgić 4)
Brubaker, 1980 (Rafelson 2, Redford 3, Schifrin 4)
Bruce Gentry, 1949 (Katzman 4)
Bruciati da cocente passione, 1976 (Lattuada 2)
Brucke, 1949 (Wagner 4)
Brucke, 1959 (Wicki 2)
Bruden kom genom taket, 1947 (Bjornstrand 3)
Bruder Karamasoff, 1920 (Jannings 3, Kortner 3, Krauss 3)
Bruder Lautensack, 1973 (Domrose 3, Hoppe 3)
Bruder Schellenberg, 1926 (Veidt 3)
Bruder Schellenberg, 1926 (Dagover 3)
Bruder von Zaarden, 1918 (Basserman 3)
Bruegel, 1967 (Gélin 3)
Brug, 1928 (Ivens 2, Van Dongen 4)
Bruja sin escoba, 1966 (Hunter 3)
Bruna indiavolata, 1951 (Tognazzi 3, Age and Scarpelli 4)
Brune piquante, 1932 (Fernandel 3)
Brune que violà, 1960 (Fabian 3)
Brunes ou blondes, 1950 (Audiard 4)
Brunkul, 1941 (Henning-Jensen 2)
Brunnen des Wahnsinns, 1921 (Planer 4)
Brushfire, 1962 (Ireland 3, Sloane 3)
Brussels 'Loops', 1958 (Clarke 2)
Brusten Himmel, 1982 (Thulin 3)
Brutal Justice. See Roma a mano armato, 1976
Brutalität in Stein, 1960 (Kluge 2)
Brutality, 1912 (Griffith 2, Barrymore L. 3, Bitzer 4)
Brute, 1914 (Olcott 2)
Brute. See Bruto, 1953
Brute. See Dúvad, 1959
Brute Force, 1912 (Marsh 3)
Brute Force, 1914 (Barrymore L. 3)
Brute Force, 1947 (Brooks, R. 2, Dassin 2, De Carlo 3, Lancaster 3, Daniels 4, Rozsa 4)
Brute Force. See In Prehistoric Days, 1913
Brute Island. See McVeagh of the South Seas, 1914
Brute Man, 1946 (Salter 4)
Brute Master, 1920 (Bosworth 3, Nilsson 3)
Bruto, 1952 (Buñuel 2, Armendáriz 3, Alcoriza 4)
Brutti, sporchi, cattivi, 1976 (Manfredi 3, Ponti 4)
Bruyère, 1964–69 (Rohmer 2)
Bryggerens Datter, 1912 (Dreyer 2)

Brzezina, 1970 (Wajda 2, Olbrychski 3)
Brzina, ali oprez, 1968 (Dragić 4)
Bu vatanin cocuklari, 1958 (Guney 2)
Bubble Trouble, 1953 (Three Stooges 3)
Bubbles, 1922 (Fleischer, M. and D. 2)
Bubbles of Song, 1951 (Fleischer, M. and D. 2)
Bubbling Over, 1921 (Roach 4)
Bubú, 1970 (Bolognini 2)
Buccaneer Bunny, 1947 (Freleng 4)
Buccaneer, 1938 (DeMille 2, Bondi 3, Brennan 3, March 3, Quinn 3,
    Quinn 3, Dreier 4, Head 4, Macpherson 4, Prinz 4, Sullivan 4)
Buccaneer, 1958 (DeMille 2, Bloom 3, Boyer 3, Brynner 3, Heston 3,
    Bernstein 4, Head 4, Westmore, F. 4)
Buccaneers, 1911 (Bosworth 3)
Buccaneers, 1924 (Roach 4)
Buccaneer's Girl, 1950 (De Carlo 3, Lanchester 3, Boyle 4)
Buch des Lasters, 1917 (Hoffmann 4)
Buchanan Rides Alone, 1958 (Boetticher 2, Scott, R. 3, Ballard 4,
    Boyle 4, Brown, Harry Joe 4)
Buchhalterin, 1918 (Dupont 2)
Buchse des Pandora, 1929 (Pabst 2, Brooks 3, Kortner 3, Andrejev 4,
    Vajda 4)
Buck and the Preacher, 1972 (Muse 3, Poitier 3)
Buck Benny Rides Again, 1940 (Sandrich 2, Bond 3, Dreier 4, Head 4,
    Lang 4, Young, V. 4)
Buck Privates, 1928 (Pitts 3)
Buck Privates, 1941 (Abbott and Costello 3, Howard, S. 3, Krasner 4)
Buck Privates Come Home, 1947 (Abbott and Costello 3)
Buck Richard's Bride, 1913 (Bosworth 3)
Buck Rogers, 1939 (Crabbe 3)
Buck Rogers in the 25th Century, 1979 (Palance 3)
Buckaroo Bugs, 1944 (Clampett 4)
Bucket of Blood, 1959 (Corman 4)
Bucking Broadway, 1917 (Ford, J. 2, Carey 3)
Bucking Society, 1916 (Sennett 2, Summerville 3)
Bucklige und die Tanzerin, 1920 (Murnau 2, Krauss 3, Freund 4,
    Mayer 4)
Buckskin, 1968 (Arlen 3, Chaney Lon, Jr. 3)
Buckskin Frontier, 1943 (Cobb 3, Young, V. 4)
Bucovina-Ukrainian Land. See Bukovyna-Zemlya Ukrayinska, 1940
Budapest, amiért szeretem, 1971 (Szabó 2)
Budapest Tales. See Budapesti mesék, 1976
Budapest, Why I Love It. See Budapest, amiért szeretem, 1971
Budapesti mesék, 1976 (Szabó 2, Madaras 3)
Budapesti tavasz, 1956 (Darvas 3)
Budd Doble Comes Back, 1913 (Mix 3)
Buddenbrooks, 1959 (Dagover 3, Herlth 4)
Buddenbrooks, 1984 (Gielgud 3)
Buddha. See Shaka, 1961
Buddy and Towser, 1933 (Freleng 4)
Buddy Buddy, 1981 (Kinski 3, Lemmon 3, Matthau 3, Diamond 4,
    Schifrin 4)
Buddy System, 1983 (Dreyfuss 3, Sarandon 3)
Buddy the Gob, 1934 (Freleng 4)
Buddy's Downfall, 1914 (Talmadge, C. 3)
Buddy's First Call, 1914 (Talmadge, C. 3)
Buddy's Trolley Troubles, 1934 (Freleng 4)
Budo kagami, 1934 (Yamada 3)
Budo sen-ichi-ya, 1938 (Yamada 3)
Budskab til Napoleon paa Elba, 1909 (Blom 2)
Buena suerte, 1960 (García 3)
Buenos dias, Buenos Aires, 1960 (Birri 2)
Bufera, 1913 (Bertini 3)
Bufere, 1952 (Gabin 3, Reggiani 3)
Buffalo Bill, 1944 (Wellman 2, Darnell 3, McCrea 3, O'Hara 3,
    Quinn 3, Basevi 4, Shamroy 4)
Buffalo Bill and the Indians, or Sitting Bull's History Lesson, 1976
    (Altman 2, Chaplin 3, Duvall, S. 3, Keitel 3, Lancaster 3,
    Newman 3)
Buffalo Bill on the U.P. Trail, 1926 (Pierce 4)
Buffalo Hunting, 1914 (Mix 3)
Buffer Zone. See Cserepek, 1981
Bufferin, 1966 (Warhol 2)

Buffet froid, 1979 (Blier 2, Blier 3, Depardieu 3)
Bug, 1975 (Smith, J.M. 4)
Bug Carnival, 1937 (Terry 4)
Bug Parade, 1941 (Avery 2)
Bugambilia, 1944 (Fernández 2, Armendáriz 3, Del Rio 3, Figueroa 4)
Bugged by a Bee, 1969 (McKimson 4)
Bughouse Bell Hops, 1915 (Lloyd 3, Roach 4)
Bugiarda, 1965 (Comencini 2)
Bugle Call, 1916 (Sullivan 4)
Bugle Call, 1927 (Coogan 3, Gibbons 4, Sullivan 4)
Bugle Sounds, 1941 (Beery 3, Reed, D. 3, Stone 3)
Bugles in the Afternoon, 1951 (Milland 3, Brown, Harry 4, Tiomkin 4)
Bugs and Thugs, 1953 (Freleng 4)
Bugs Beetle and His Orchestra, 1938 (Terry 4)
Bug's Bonnets, 1956 (Jones 2)
Bugs Bunny series, from 1944 (Freleng 4)
Bugs Bunny and the 3 Bears, 1944 (Jones 2)
Bugs Bunny Gets the Boid, 1942 (Clampett 4)
Bugs Bunny Superstar, 1975 (Welles 2, Clampett 4)
Bugsy and Mugsy, 1957 (Freleng 4)
Build Me a World, 1979 (Jackson 3)
Build My Gallows High. See Out of the Past, 1947
Build Thy House, 1920 (Rains 3)
Builders, 1954 (Altman 2)
Building the Great Los Angeles Aqueduct, 1913 (Dwan 2)
Buio in sala, 1950 (Risi 2)
Buisson ardent, 1955 (Alexeieff and Parker 2)
Buki naki tatakai, 1960 (Yoda 4)
Bukovyna-Zemlya Ukrayinska, 1940 (Dovzhenko 2)
Bull and Sand, 1924 (Sennett 2)
Bull Dog, 1937 (Biswas 4)
Bull Fighter, 1927 (Sennett 2)
Bull of the West, 1965 (Kennedy, G. 3)
Bull Rushes, 1931 (Balcon 4)
Bulldog Breed, 1960 (Caine 3, Reed, O. 3)
Bulldog Courage, 1925 (Love 3)
Bulldog Drummond, 1929 (Ball 3, Bennett J. 3, Colman 3, Barnes 4,
    Goldwyn 4, Howard 4, Menzies 4, Toland 4)
Bulldog Drummond Comes Back, 1937 (Barrymore J. 3, Dreier 4,
    Head 4)
Bulldog Drummond Escapes, 1937 (Milland 3, Head 4)
Bulldog Drummond in Africa, 1938 (Quinn 3, Dreier 4, Head 4)
Bulldog Drummond Strikes Back, 1934 (Auer 3, Ball 3, Colman 3,
    Merkel 3, Oland 3, Young, L. 3, Day 4, Johnson 4, Newman 4,
    Zanuck 4)
Bulldog Drummond Strikes Back, 1947 (Anhalt 4)
Bulldog Drummond's Bride, 1939 (Dreier 4, Head 4)
Bulldog Drummond's Peril, 1938 (Dmytryk 2, Barrymore J. 3,
    Dreier 4, Head 4)
Bulldog Drummond's Revenge, 1937 (Barrymore J. 3, Head 4)
Bulldog Drummond's Secret Police, 1939 (Carroll L. 3, Head 4)
Bulldog Drummond's Third Round, 1925 (Buchanan 3)
Bulldog Jack, 1935 (Richardson 3, Balcon 4, Gilliat 4, Junge 4)
Bulldog Jack. See Alias Bulldog Drummond, 1935
Bulldog Sees It Through, 1940 (Buchanan 3)
Bulldozing the Bull, 1938 (Fleischer, M. and D. 2)
Bulldozing the Bull, 1951 (Terry 4)
Bull-ero, 1932 (Terry 4)
Bulles de savon animées, 1906 (Méliès 2)
Bulles de Savon, 1934 (Dudow 2)
Bullet, 1978 (Anand 3)
Bullet for a Badman, 1964 (Murphy 3, Biroc 4, Bumstead 4)
Bullet for Berlin, 1918 (Hart 3)
Bullet for Joey, 1955 (Raft 3, Robinson, E. 3)
Bullet for Sandoval. See Desperados, 1970
Bullet for Stefano. See Passatore, 1947
Bullet for the General. See Quien sabe?, 1967
Bullet Is Waiting, 1954 (Simmons 3, Planer 4, Robinson 4, Tiomkin 4)
Bullet Proof, 1920 (Carey 3)
Bullet Scars, 1942 (Bosworth 3, McCord 4)
Bullet Wound. See Dankon, 1969
Bullets and Brown Eyes, 1916 (Gilbert 3, Hersholt 3)
Bullets Cannot Pierce Me. See Bana kursun islemez, 1967

Bullets for O'Hara, 1941 (Howard 2, Bosworth 3, McCord 4)
Bullets or Ballots, 1921 (Astor 3)
Bullets or Ballots, 1936 (Beavers 3, Blondell 3, Bogart 3, Cook 3, Robinson, E. 3, Miller, S. 4)
Bullets, Sin, and Bathtub Gin. *See* Lady in Red, 1979
Bullfight, 1935 (Terry 4)
Bullfight, 1955 (Clarke 2)
Bullfight. *See* Course de tauraux, 1951
Bullfight at Málaga, 1958 (Leacock 2)
Bullfighter and the Lady, 1951 (Boetticher 2, Young, V. 4)
Bullfighters, 1945 (Laurel & Hardy 3)
Bullitt, 1968 (Yates 2, Bisset 3, Duvall, R. 3, McQueen, S. 3, Fraker 4, Schifrin 4, van Runkle 4)
Bulloney, 1933 (Iwerks 4)
Bulls and Bears, 1930 (Sennett 2)
Bull's Eye, 1918 (Johnson, N. 3)
Bull's Eye for Farmer Pietersen. *See* Boer Pietersen schiet in de roos, 1949
Bully, 1932 (Iwerks 4)
Bully Beef, 1930 (Terry 4)
Bully for Bugs, 1953 (Jones 2)
Bully Frog, 1936 (Terry 4)
Bully Romance, 1939 (Terry 4)
Bum, 1979 (Pojar 4)
Bum Bandit, 1931 (Fleischer, M. and D. 2)
Bum Voyage, 1934 (Roach 4)
Bumerang, 1979 (Paskaleva 3)
Bummelstudenten, 1917 (Freund 4)
Bump, 1920 (Howard, L. 3)
Bumping into Broadway, 1919 (Daniels 3, Lloyd 3, Roach 4)
Bunbuku chagama, 1939 (Yoda 4)
Bunch of Flowers, 1914 (Loos 4)
Bunch That Failed, 1912–13 (White 3)
Bunco Bill's Visit, 1914 (Bunny 3)
Bunco Game at Lizardhead, 1911 (Anderson G. 3)
Buncoed Stage Johnnie, 1908 (Méliès 2)
Bundle of Joy, 1956 (Taurog 2, Merkel 3, Reynolds, D. 3, Krasna 4)
Bungalow Boobs, 1924 (McCarey 2, Roach 4)
Bungalow Troubles, 1920 (Sennett 2)
Bungawan Solo, 1951 (Ichikawa 2)
Bungle Uncle, 1961 (Hanna and Barbera 4)
Bungled Bungalow, 1950 (Burness 4)
Bungles' Elopement, 1916 (Hardy 3)
Bungles Enforces the Law, 1916 (Hardy 3)
Bungles Lands a Job, 1916 (Hardy 3)
Bungles' Rainy Day, 1916 (Hardy 3)
Bungs and Bunglers, 1919 (Hardy 3)
Bunker, 1981 (Hopkins, A. 3)
Bunker Bean, 1936 (Ball 3)
Bunker-Hill Bunny, 1949 (Freleng 4)
Bunkie, 1912 (Bosworth 3)
Bunnies Abundant, 1962 (Hanna and Barbera 4)
Bunny series, 1912–14 (Bunny 3)
Bunny and Claude, 1968 (McKimson 4)
Bunny Hugged, 1951 (Jones 2)
Bunny Lake is Missing, 1965 (Preminger 2, Olivier 3, Bass 4, Coward 4, Fisher 4)
Bunny O'Hare, 1971 (Borgnine 3, Davis 3)
Bunny-mooning, 1937 (Fleischer, M. and D. 2)
Buon appetito, 1956 (Delli Colli 4)
Buona Sera, Mrs. Campbell, 1968 (Grant, L. 3, Lollobrigida 3, Winters 3, Frank 4)
Buone notizie, 1979 (Petri 2, Morricone 4)
Buongiorno elefante!, 1952 (De Sica 2, D'Amico 4, Zavattini 4)
Buongiorno natura, 1955 (Olmi 2)
Buono, il brutto il cattivo, 1966 (Leone 2, Van Cleef 3, Wallach 3, Age and Scarpelli 4, Delli Colli 4, Morricone 4)
Buono, il brutto, il cattivo. *See* Good, the Bad, and the Ugly, 1966
Buraikan, 1970 (Shinoda 2, Iwashita 3, Toda 4)
Burari burabura monogatari, 1962 (Takamine 3)
Burcak tarlasi, 1966 (Guney 2)
Burden of Dreams, 1982 (Cardinale 3, Kinski 3, Robards 3)
Burden of Fate. *See* Gnet roke, 1917

Burden of Life. *See* Jinsei ni onimotsu, 1935
Burden of Proof, 1917 (Davies 3)
Bureau des mariages, 1962 (Delerue 4)
Bureau of Missing Persons, 1933 (Davis 3, O'Brien, P. 3, Stone 3, Blanke 4)
Burglar, 1920 (Capra 2)
Burglar, 1928 (Sennett 2, Hornbeck 4)
Burglar, 1957 (Duryea 3, Mansfield 3)
Burglar by Proxy, 1919 (Polito 4)
Burglar Godfather, 1915 (Anderson G. 3)
Burglar on the Roof, 1898 (Blackton 2)
Burglarious Billy, 1915 (Talmadge, C. 3)
Burglarized Burglar, 1911 (Bushman 3)
Burglars, 1972 (Cannon 3)
Burglars. *See* Casse, 1971
Burglars Bold, 1921 (Roach 4)
Burglar's Dilemma, 1912 (Griffith 2, Barrymore L. 3, Gish, L. 3, Walthall 3, Bitzer 4)
Burglar's Mistake, 1909 (Bitzer 4)
Burgtheater, 1936 (Krauss 3, Tschechowa 3)
Burial Path, 1978 (Brakhage 2)
Buried Hand, 1915 (Walsh 2)
Buried Loot, 1935 (Taylor, R. 3)
Buried Secret. *See* Unge Blod, 1915
Buried Treasure, 1921 (Davies 3, Rosson 4)
Buried Treasure, 1926 (Roach 4)
Burlesque, 1928 (Brown 3)
Burlesque, 1932 (Terry 4)
Burlesque, 1944 (Brown 3)
Burlesque on Carmen, 1915 (Purviance 3)
Burlesque Suicide, 1902 (Porter 2)
Burma Convoy, 1941 (Salter 4)
Burma Victory, 1945 (Boulting 2)
Burmese Harp. *See* Biruma no tategoto, 1956
Burn!, 1969 (Brando 3)
Burn! See Queimada!, 1969
Burn 'em Up O'Connor, 1939 (Carey 3)
Burn, Witch, Burn. *See* Night of the Eagle, 1961
Burned Hand, 1915 (Browning 2)
Burn-'em-Up Barnes, 1934 (Canutt 4)
Burning Autumn. *See* Moeru aki, 1978
Burning Bridges, 1928 (Carey 3, Polito 4)
Burning Court. *See* Chambre ardente, 1962
Burning Daylight, 1914 (Franklin 2, Bosworth 3)
Burning Daylight, 1928 (Polito 4)
Burning Gold, 1936 (Boyd 3)
Burning Heart. *See* Brennende Herz, 1929
Burning Hills, 1956 (Wood 3, McCord 4)
Burning Sands, 1922 (Clarke, C.C. 4, Glennon 4, Howe 4, Young, W. 4)
Burning Secret. *See* Brennendes Geheimnis, 1933
Burning Soil. *See* Brennende Acker, 1922
Burning Stable, 1900 (Hepworth 2)
Burning the Candle, 1917 (Walthall 3)
Burning the Wind, 1929 (Karloff 3)
Burning Up, 1930 (Sutherland 2, Arlen 3)
Burning Words, 1923 (Johnson, N. 3)
Burning Youth. *See* Moyuru wakamonotachi, 1962
Burning Youth. *See* Yama no sanka: Moyuru wakamono-tachi, 1962
Burnt Cork, 1912 (Bunny 3)
Burnt Fingers, 1927 (Stradling 4)
Burnt Offering. *See* Passport to Hell, 1932
Burnt Offerings, 1976 (Smith, D. , Black 3, Davis 3, Meredith 3, Reed, O. 3, Lourié 4)
Burnt Offerings. *See* Passport to Hell, 1932
Burschenlied aus Heidelberg, 1930 (Herlth 4, Hoffmann 4, Rohrig 4)
Bury Me Dead, 1947 (Alton, J. 4)
Bus, 1965 (Fields 4, Wexler 4)
Bus Stop, 1956 (Logan 2, Monroe 3, Axelrod 4, Krasner 4, Lemaire 4, Newman 4, Reynolds 4, Wheeler 4)
Bus Terminal. *See* Florence 13.30, 1957
Bush Christmas, 1947 (Rafferty 3)
Bushbaby, 1970 (Gossett 3)

Busher, 1919 (Gilbert 3, Moore, C. 3, Ince 4)
Bushido. *See* Bushido zankoku monogatari, 1963
Bushido Blade, 1978 (Boone 3, Jones, J.E. 3, Mifune 3, Wynn 3)
Bushido: Samurai Saga. *See* Bushido zankoku monogatari, 1963
Bushido zankoku monogatari, 1963 (Imai 2, Kishida 3, Mori 3, Yoda 4)
Bushwackers, 1951 (Chaney Lon, Jr. 3, Elam 3, Ireland 3, Biroc 4)
Bushy Hare, 1950 (McKimson 4)
Business and Pleasure, 1932 (Karloff 3, McCrea 3, Rogers, W. 3)
Business Is a Pleasure, 1934 (Grable 3)
Business Must Not Interfere, 1912–14 (Cohl 2)
Business of Love, 1925 (Horton 3, Pitts 3)
Busman's Holiday, 1940 (Young, F. 4)
Busman's Honeymoon, 1940 (Junge 4)
Busou keikantai, 1948 (Yoda 4)
Bussende Magdalena, 1915 (Wiene 2)
Busted Blossoms, 1934 (Terry 4)
Busted Hearts, 1916 (Hardy 3)
Busted Hearts. *See* Those Love Pangs, 1914
Busted Johnny. *See* Making a Living, 1914
Buster Keaton Rides Again, 1965 (Keaton 2)
Buster Keaton Story, 1957 (DeMille 2, Coogan 3, Lorre 3, O'Connor 3, Head 4, Westmore, F. 4, Young, V. 4)
Buster se marie, 1930 (Autant-Lara 2, Rosay 3)
Bustin' Loose, 1981 (Pryor 3)
Busting, 1973 (Gould 3)
Busting the Beanery, 1916 (Roach 4)
Busy Barber, 1932 (Lantz 4)
Busy Bee, 1936 (Terry 4)
Busy Bees, 1922 (Roach 4)
Busy Bodies, 1933 (Laurel & Hardy 3, Roach 4)
Busy Body, 1967 (Baxter A. 3, Pryor 3, Ryan 3, Green, J. 4)
Busy Buddies, 1944 (Three Stooges 3)
Busy Buddies, 1956 (Hanna and Barbera 4)
Busy Day, 1914 (Chaplin 2, Sennett 2)
Busybody, 1923 (La Cava 2)
But I Don't Want to Get Married, 1970 (Jones S. 3, Duning 4)
But Not for Me, 1959 (Seaton 2, Baker C. 3, Cobb 3, Gable 3, Hayes 4, Head 4)
But the Flesh Is Weak, 1932 (Horton 3, Montgomery 3, Adrian 4)
But the Greatest of These Is Charity, 1912 (Cruze 2)
Buta to gunkan, 1961 (Imamura 2)
Butai sugata, 1940 (Tanaka 3)
Butch and Sundance, 1979 (Lester 2, Kovacs 4)
Butch Cassidy and the Sundance Kid, 1969 (Hill, G.R. 2, Martin, S. 3, Newman 3, Redford 3, Goldman, W. 4, Hall 4, Head 4, Smith, J.M. 4)
Butch Minds the Baby, 1942 (Crawford, B. 3, Howard, S. 3)
Butcher Boy, 1917 (Keaton 2, Arbuckle 3, Schenck 4)
Butcher Boy, 1932 (Lantz 4)
Butcher of Seville, 1944 (Terry 4)
Butley, 1973 (Bates 3, Dillon 4, Fisher 4, Pinter 4)
Butter Fingers, 1925 (Sennett 2)
Buttercup Chain, 1970 (Slocombe 4)
Butterfield 8, 1960 (Harvey 3, Taylor, E. 3, Berman 4, Hayes 4, Kaper 4, Rose 4, Ruttenberg 4, Schnee 4)
Butterflies Are Free, 1972 (Hawn 3, Lang 4)
Butterfly, 1924 (Brown 2)
Butterfly, 1981 (Welles 2, Keach 3, Morricone 4)
Butterfly. *See* Harakiri, 1919
Butterfly Ball, 1974 (Halas and Batchelor 2)
Butterfly Ball, 1976 (Price 3)
Butterfly Net, 1912 (Bushman 3)

Butterfly of Night. *See* Yoru no cho, 1957
Butterfly on the Wheel, 1915 (Tourneur, M. 2, Carré 4)
Button My Back, 1929 (Sennett 2, Hornbeck 4)
Buttons, 1915 (Pearson 2)
Buttons, 1927 (Coogan 3, Gibbons 4, Gillespie 4)
Buwana Toshi no uta, 1965 (Takemitsu 4)
Buy Me That Town, 1941 (Dreier 4, Head 4)
Büyuk cellatlar, 1967 (Guney 2)
Buzie Bianche. *See* Professione Figlio, 1980
Buzzin' Around, 1933 (Arbuckle 3)
Bwana Devil, 1952 (Bruce 3, Biroc 4, Clampett 4)
Bwana Toshi. *See* Buwana Toshi no uta, 1965
Bwana Toshi no uta, 1965 (Hani 2)
By Candlelight, 1934 (Whale 2, Lukas 3, Kraly 4, Laemmle 4)
By Design, 1980 (Jutra 2)
By Divine Right, 1919 (Von Sternberg 2)
By Golly, 1920 (Sennett 2)
By Heck, 1922 (Sennett 2)
By Hook or By Crook. *See* I Dood It, 1943
By Indian Post, 1919 (Ford, J. 2, Carey 3)
By Love Possessed, 1961 (Sturges, J. 2, Robards 3, Sloane 3, Turner, L. 3, Bernstein 4, Cahn 4, Mirisch 4)
By Right of Purchase, 1918 (Talmadge, N. 3)
By Rocket to the Moon. *See* Frau im Mond, 1929
By St. Anthony. *See* U svetého Antoníčka, 1933
By St. Matthias. *See* U sv. Matĕje, 1928
By Stork Delivery, 1916 (Sennett 2)
By the Beautiful Sea, 1931 (Fleischer, M. and D. 2)
By the Governor's Order, 1914 (Costello, M. 3)
By the Lake. *See* U ozera, 1969
By the Law. *See* Po zakonu, 1926
By the Light of the Moon, 1911 (Porter 2)
By the Light of the Silvery Moon, 1926 (Fleischer, M. and D. 2)
By the Light of the Silvery Moon, 1931 (Fleischer, M. and D. 2)
By the Light of the Silvery Moon, 1953 (Day 3, Steiner 4)
By the Sad Sea Waves, 1917 (Daniels 3, Lloyd 3, Roach 4)
By the Sea, 1915 (Chaplin 2, Purviance 3)
By the Sea, 1931 (Terry 4)
By the Shortest of Heads, 1915 (Formby 3)
By the Sun's Rays, 1914 (Chaney Lon 3)
By ved navn København, 1960 (Roos 2)
By Whose Hand?, 1932 (Walker 4)
By Word of Mouse, 1954 (Freleng 4)
By Your Leave, 1934 (Grable 3, Berman 4, Musuraca 4, Plunkett 4, Steiner 4)
Byakko-tai, 1927 (Tanaka 3)
Byakuran no uta, 1939 (Hasegawa 3)
Byakuya no kyoen, 1932 (Yamada 3)
Bye Bye Birdie, 1963 (Sidney 2, Leigh, J. 3, Biroc 4, Green, J. 4)
Bye Bye Brasil, 1980 (Diegues 2)
Bye Bye Braverman, 1968 (Lumet 2, Segal 3, Warden 3, Kaufman 4, Rosenblum 4)
Bye Bye Monkey, 1978 (Ferreri 2, Depardieu 3, Mastroianni 3)
Bye Bye Monkey. *See* Ciao maschio, 1978
Byelyi orel, 1928 (Protazanov 2)
Byl jednou jeden král, 1954 (Trnka 2, Kopecký 3)
Byl sobie raz, 1957 (Lenica 2, Borowczyk 4)
Byn vid den Trivsamma Brunnen, 1937–38 (Fejos 2)
Byosai monogatari, 1956 (Tanaka 3, Yamada 3)
Byt, 1968 (Švankmajer 4)
Bytva za nashu Radyansku Ukrayinu, 1943 (Dovzhenko 2)

C

C. a K. polní maršálek, 1930 (Vích 4)
C.A.S.H. *See* Whiffs, 1975
C.I.D., 1956 (Anand 3)
C.O.D., 1932 (Powell 2)
Ça aussi c'est Paris, 1930 (Fresnay 3)
Ça colle, 1933 (Christian-Jaque 2, Fernandel 3)
Ça n'arrive qu'aux autres, 1971 (Deneuve 3, Mastroianni 3)
Ça va barder!, 1955 (Constantine 3)
Ça va etre ta fête, 1961 (Constantine 3)
Cab No. 519. *See* Droske 519, 1909
Caballero a la medida, 1953 (Cantinflas 3)
Caballo blanco, 1961 (García 3)
Cabane aux souvenirs, 1946 (Vanel 3)
Cabaret, 1953 (Rey 3)
Cabaret, 1972 (Fosse 2, Minnelli 3, York, M. 3, Allen, J. 4, Unsworth 4)
Cabaret du grand large, 1946 (Hayakawa 3)
Cabaret Singer, 1912–13 (White 3)
Cabbage Fairy. *See* Fée aux choux, 1896
Cabezas cortadas, 1970 (Rocha 2)
Cabin in the Cotton, 1932 (Curtiz 2, Barthelmess 3, Davis 3, Muse 3, Walthall 3, Orry-Kelly 4)
Cabin in the Sky, 1943 (Minnelli 2, Horne 3, McQueen, B. 3, Edens 4, Freed 4, Gibbons 4, Irene 4, Lewin 4)
Cabina, 1973 (Bozzetto 4)
Cabinet des Dr. Caligari. *See* Kabinett des Dr. Caligari, 1920
Cabinets de physique au XVIIIème siècle, 1964–69 (Rohmer 2)
Cabiria, 1914 (Pastrone 2)
Cabiria. *See* Notti di Cabiria, 1956
Cable Car Murder, 1971 (Goldsmith 4)
Cable Car Murders. *See* Cross Current, 1971
Cable Car Mystery, 1971 (Wagner 3)
Cable Laying, 1940 (Balcon 4)
Cabo Blanco, 1979 (Bronson 3, Rey 3, Robards 3, Sanda 3, Goldsmith 4)
Cabos Blancos, 1954 (Van Dyke, W. 2)
Cabriola, 1965 (Ferrer, M. 3)
Cabrioles ou la journée d'une danseuse, 1963 (Cassel 3)
Caça, 1963 (Oliveira 2)
Caccia alla volpe, 1938 (Blasetti 2)
Caccia alla volpe, 1966 (De Sica 2, Mature 3, Zavattini 4)
Caccia in brughiera, 1949 (Risi 2)
Caccia tragica, 1947 (De Santis 2, Zavattini 4)
Cache. *See* Battant, 1982
Cactus Cure, 1925 (Canutt 4)
Cactus Flower, 1969 (Bergman 3, Hawn 3, Matthau 3, Diamond 4, Jones 4, Lang 4)
Cactus Jack. *See* Villain, 1979
Cactus Jack Heartbreaker, 1914 (Mix 3)
Cactus Jim's Shopgirl, 1915 (Mix 3)
Cactus Kid, 1930 (Disney 2)
Cactus Makes Perfect, 1942 (Three Stooges 3)
Cactus Nell, 1917 (Sennett 2, Beery 3)
Cadaveri eccellenti, 1976 (Rosi 2, Cuny 3, Rey 3, Vanel 3, Von Sydow 3, Guerra 4)
Cadavres exquis. *See* Cadaveri eccelenti, 1976
Caddy, 1953 (Lewis 2, Taurog 2, Martin, D. 3, Reed, D. 3, Head 4)
Caddy's Dream, 1911 (Pickford 3)
Cadeau, 1982 (Cardinale 3, Legrand 4)
Cadena de Amor, 1971–73 (Brocka 2)
Cadet Girl, 1941 (Ladd 3, Clarke, C.C. 4)
Cadet Rousselle, 1946 (Dunning 4)
Cadet Rousselle, 1954 (Bourvil 3)

Cadets de l'océan, 1941 (Gélin 3)
Cadetti di guascogna, 1950 (Tognazzi 3, Age and Scarpelli 4)
Cadres fleuris, 1910 (Cohl 2)
Caduta degli angeli ribelli, 1981 (Valli 3)
Caduta degli dei, 1969 (Visconti 2, Bogarde 3, Thulin 3, Jarre 4)
Caduta di Troia, 1910 (Pastrone 2)
Caesar and Cleopatra, 1946 (Granger 3, Holloway 3, Leigh, V. 3, Moore, R. 3, Rains 3, Simmons 3, Auric 4, Cardiff 4, Krasker 4, Mathieson 4, Young, F. 4)
Cafajestes, 1962 (Guerra 2)
Caf'Conc, 1954 (Chevalier 3)
Café Chantani, 1953 (Tognazzi 3)
Café Colón, 1958 (Félix 3, Figueroa 4)
Café Colón de la Cerna, 1958 (Armendáriz 3)
Café de Paris, 1938 (Berry 3, Brasseur 3, Matras 4)
Café du Cadran, 1946 (Blier 3)
Café Electric, 1927 (Dietrich 3)
Café Express, 1980 (Manfredi 3, Cristaldi 4)
Cafe in Cairo, 1924 (Polito 4, Stromberg 4)
Cafe in the Main Street. *See* Kavárna na hlavní třídě, 1954
Cafe Metropole, 1937 (Menjou 3, Power 3, Young, L. 3, Johnson 4)
Cafe Society, 1939 (Carroll M. 3, MacMurray 3, Dreier 4, Head 4)
Café tabac, 1965 (Piccoli 3)
Cafe Waiter's Dream. *See* Songe d'un garçon de café, 1910
Cage, 1947 (Peterson 2)
Cage, 1975 (Thulin 3, Sarde 4)
Cage aux folles, 1979 (Tognazzi 3, Morricone 4)
Cage aux folles II, 1981 (Tognazzi 3, Morricone 4)
Cage of Doom. *See* Terror from the Year Five Thousand, 1958
Cage of Gold, 1950 (Dearden 2, Simmons 3, Auric 4, Balcon 4, Slocombe 4)
Caged, 1950 (Cromwell 2, Darwell 3, Moorehead 3, Steiner 4, Wald 4)
Caged Fury, 1948 (Crabbe 3)
Caged Heat, 1974 (Demme 2, Corman 4)
Cagey Canary, 1941 (Avery 2, Clampett 4)
Cagliostro, 1928 (Oswald 2, Meerson 4)
Cagliostro, 1949 (Mangano 3)
Cagliostro, 1974 (Jurgens 3)
Cagliostro. *See* Black Magic, 1947
Cagna, 1972 (Ferreri 2, Mastroianni 3, Carrière 4)
Cagna. *See* Liza, 1972
Cahill, United States Marshal, 1973 (Coogan 3, Kennedy, G. 3, Wayne 3, Bernstein 4, Biroc 4)
Caicara, 1950 (Cavalcanti 2)
Caid, 1960 (Fernandel 3)
Caída, 1959 (Torre-Nilsson 2)
Caids, 1972 (Reggiani 3, Douy 4)
Caimano del Piave, 1950 (Cervi 3)
Cain and Mabel, 1936 (Bacon 2, Davies 3, Gable 3, Wyman 3, Barnes 4, Orry-Kelly 4, Westmore, P. 4)
Cain at Abel, 1982 (Brocka 2)
Caine, 1967 (Fuller 2)
Caine Mutiny, 1954 (Dmytryk 2, Kramer, S. 2, Bogart 3, Ferrer, J. 3, Johnson, V. 3, MacMurray 3, Marvin 3, Planer 4, Steiner 4, Wald 4)
Cain's Cutthroats, 1970 (Carradine 3)
Cain's Way. *See* Cain's Cutthroats, 1970
Cairo, 1942 (Mankiewicz 2, Van Dyke, W.S. 2, MacDonald 3, Young, R. 3, Stothart 4, Wheeler 4)
Cairo, 1963 (Sanders 3)
Cairo Road, 1950 (Harvey 3, Morris 4)
Cairo Station. *See* Bab el Haded, 1958
Caissière du Grand Cafe, 1946 (Fernandel 3)

Caissounbouw Rotterdam, 1929 (Ivens 2)
Cake Eater, 1924 (Rogers, W. 3, Roach 4)
Cake-Walk de la pendule, 1903 (Guy 2)
Cake-walk infernal, 1903 (Méliès 2)
Cala naprzód, 1966 (Cybulski 3)
Calaboose, 1942 (Roach 4)
Calabuch, 1956 (García Berlanga 2, Cortese 3, Gwenn 3, Flaiano 4)
Calais-Douvres, 1931 (Planer 4)
Calais-Douvres. See Nie wieder Liebe, 1931
Calamitous Elopement, 1908 (Griffith 2, Lawrence 3, Bitzer 4)
Calamity. See Kalamita, 1982
Calamity Anne, Detective, 1913 (Dwan 2)
Calamity Anne Parcel Post, 1913 (Dwan 2)
Calamity Anne's Beauty, 1913 (Dwan 2)
Calamity Anne's Inheritance, 1913 (Dwan 2)
Calamity Anne's Trust, 1913 (Dwan 2)
Calamity Anne's Vanity, 1913 (Dwan 2)
Calamity Anne's Ward, 1912 (Dwan 2)
Calamity Jane, 1953 (Day 3, Keel 3)
Calamity Jane, 1984 (Forrest 3)
Calamity Jane and Sam Bass, 1949 (De Carlo 3)
Calamity Jane's Love Affair, 1914 (Eason 4)
Calamity the Cow, 1967 (Dalrymple 4)
Calandria, 1933 (De Fuentes 2)
Calaveras, 1969 (Grimault 4)
Calaveras del terror, 1943 (Armendáriz 3)
Calcutta, 1947 (Bendix 3, Ladd 3, Dreier 4, Head 4, Miller, S. 4,
    Seitz 4, Young, V. 4)
Calcutta, 1969 (Malle 2)
Calcutta Cruel City. See Do Digha Zamin, 1953
Calcutta 71, 1972 (Sen 2)
Calendar, 1931 (Bruce 3, Marshall 3, Balcon 4)
Calendar Girl, 1947 (Dwan 2, McLaglen 3)
Calendar of the Year, 1936 (Cavalcanti 2)
Calender of the Year, 1937 (Grierson 2)
Calibre 44, 1959 (Armendáriz 3)
Calico Vampire, 1916 (Loos 4)
Caliente Love, 1933 (Sennett 2)
Califfa, 1971 (Schneider 3, Tognazzi 3, Morricone 4)
California, 1927 (Van Dyke, W.S. 2)
California, 1947 (Fitzgerald 3, Milland 3, Quinn 3, Stanwyck 3,
    Dreier 4, Head 4, Miller, S. 4, Young, V. 4)
California Conquest, 1952 (Wilde 3, Wright 3, Katzman 4)
California in '49. See Days of '49, 1924
California Kid, 1974 (Nolte 3, Sheen 3)
California Mail, 1929 (Brown, Harry Joe 4)
California or Bust, 1923 (Roach 4)
California Passage, 1950 (Cody 3)
California Romance, 1922 (Gilbert 3, August 4, Furthman 4)
California Split, 1974 (Altman 2, Gould 3, Segal 3)
California Straight Ahead, 1925 (Mandell 4)
California Straight Ahead, 1937 (Wayne 3)
California Suite, 1978 (Caine 3, Coburn, J. 3, Fonda, J. 3, Matthau 3,
    Pryor 3, Smith 3, Booth 4, Stark 4)
Caligula, 1980 (Gielgud 3, McDowell 3, O'Toole 3, Donati 4)
Caliph Storch, 1954 (Reiniger 2)
Call, 1909 (Griffith 2, Walthall 3, Bitzer 4)
Call a Cop!, 1931 (Stevens 2, Roach 4)
Call a Cop, 1921 (Sennett 2)
Call a Messenger, 1939 (Crabbe 3, Salter 4)
Call a Taxi, 1920 (Roach 4)
Call for Mr. Caveman, 1919 (Roach 4)
Call from Home, 1912–13 (White 3)
Call Girl. See Models, Inc., 1952
Call Harry Crown. See 99 44/100%, 1974
Call Her Mom, 1971 (Charisse 3, Johnson, V. 3)
Call Her Savage, 1932 (Auer 3, Bow 3, Garmes 4)
Call Him Mr. Shatter, 1975 (Cushing 3)
Call It a Day, 1937 (Brady 3, De Havilland 3, Blanke 4, Haller 4,
    Orry-Kelly 4, Robinson 4, Wallis 4)
Call It Luck, 1934 (Nichols 4, Trotti 4)
Call me Bwana, 1963 (Hope 3)
Call Me Genius. See Rebel, 1961

Call Me Madam, 1953 (O'Connor 3, Sanders 3, Alton, R. 4,
    Newman 4, Shamroy 4, Sharaff 4, Wheeler 4)
Call Me Mister, 1951 (Bacon 2, Berkeley 2, Boone 3, Dailey 3,
    Grable 3, Hunter 3, Lemaire 4, Lewin 4, Newman 4, Wheeler 4)
Call Northside 777, 1948 (Hathaway 2, Cobb 3, Ritter 3, Stewart 3,
    Lemaire 4, Newman 4, Wheeler 4, Zanuck 4)
Call of Flesh. See Jotai, 1964
Call of Her People, 1917 (Barrymore E. 3)
Call of the Blood. See Appel du sang, 1920
Call of the Canyon, 1923 (Fleming 2, Leroy 2, Howe 4)
Call of the Canyon, 1942 (Autry 3)
Call of the Circus, 1910 (Lawrence 3)
Call of the Circus, 1930 (Bushman 3)
Call of the Cuckoo, 1927 (Laurel and Hardy 3, Bruckman 4, Roach 4)
Call of the East, 1917 (Cruze 2, Hayakawa 3)
Call of the Flesh, 1930 (Adorée 3, Dressler 3, Novarro 3, Gibbons 4,
    Shearer 4, Stothart 4)
Call of the Mate, 1924 (Furthman 4)
Call of the North, 1914 (DeMille 2, Buckland 4)
Call of the Open Range, 1911 (Dwan 2)
Call of the Plains, 1913 (Anderson G. 3)
Call of the Prairie, 1936 (Boyd 3)
Call of the Road, 1920 (McLaglen 3)
Call of the Song, 1911 (Pickford 3, Gaudio 4)
Call of the Wild, 1908 (Griffith 2, Lawrence 3)
Call of the Wild, 1923 (Roach 4)
Call of the Wild, 1935 (Wellman 2, Gable 3, Young, L. 3, Day 4,
    Newman 4, Rosher 4, Zanuck 4)
Call of the Wild, 1972 (Heston 3)
Call of the Yukon, 1938 (Arlen 3, Eason 4)
Call of Youth, 1920 (Hitchcock 2)
Call Out the Marines, 1942 (McLaglen 3, Hunt 4, Musuraca 4)
Call the Witness, 1921 (Roach 4)
Call to Arms, 1902 (Hepworth 2)
Call to Arms, 1910 (Griffith 2, Sennett 2, Pickford 3, Bitzer 4)
Call to Arms, 1913 (Dwan 2)
Call to Glory, 1966 (Van Cleef 3)
Callahans and the Murphys, 1927 (Dressler 3, Gibbons 4, Marion 4)
Callaway Went Thataway, 1952 (Gable 3, Keel 3, MacMurray 3,
    Taylor, E. 3, Williams 3, Frank and Panama 4, Rose 4)
Calle Mayor, 1956 (Bardem 2, de Beauregard 4, Kosma 4)
Called Back, 1912 (Cruze 2)
Calligraphie japonaise, 1961 (Braunberger 4)
Calling All Curs, 1939 (Three Stooges 3)
Calling All Husbands, 1940 (McCord 4)
Calling All Tars, 1936 (Hope 3)
Calling Bulldog Drummond, 1951 (Saville 2, Pidgeon 3, Junge 4,
    Wimperis 4)
Calling Dr. Death, 1943 (Miller, V. 4, Salter 4)
Calling Dr. Gillespie, 1942 (Barrymore L. 3, Gardner 3, Reed, D. 3)
Calling Dr. Kildare, 1939 (Ayres 3, Barrymore L. 3, Turner, L. 3)
Calling Hubby's Bluff, 1929 (Sennett 2)
Calling Mr. Death, 1943 (Chaney Lon, Jr. 3)
Calling of Dan Matthews, 1936 (Arlen 3, Brown, K. 4)
Calling of Jim Barton, 1914 (Anderson G. 3)
Calling the Tune, 1936 (Dickinson 2, Hardwicke 3)
Calling Wild Bill Hickok, 1943 (Canutt 4)
Callisto, 1943 (Honegger 4)
Calm Yourself, 1935 (Young, R. 3)
Calmos, 1975 (Blier 2, Blier 3, Delerue 4, Renoir 4)
Calumet. See Lula mira, 1962
Columnia, 1939 (García 3)
Calvaire, 1914 (Feuillade 2, Musidora 3)
Calvert's Folly. See Calvert's Valley, 1922
Calvert's Valley, 1922 (Gilbert 3, Furthman 4)
Calypso Heat Wave, 1957 (Katzman 4)
Calypso Joe, 1957 (Dickinson 3)
Camacchio, 1942 (Fusco 4)
Camada Negra, 1977 (Borau 2)
Cambiale, 1959 (Gassman 3, Tognazzi 3)
Cambio de sexo, 1976 (Almendros 4)
Cambio della guardia, 1962 (Cervi 3)
Cambrick Mask, 1919 (Costello, M. 3)

Cambrioleur et agent, 1904 (Guy 2)
Cambrioleurs, 1897–98 (Guy 2)
Cambrioleurs de Paris, 1904 (Guy 2)
Came the Brawn, 1938 (Roach 4)
Came the Dawn, 1928 (McCarey 2, Roach 4)
Camee, 1913 (Tourneur, M. 2)
Camela è una bambola, 1959 (Manfredi 3)
Camelia, 1953 (Félix 3, Figueroa 4)
Camelot, 1967 (Logan 2, Redgrave, V. 3, Newman 4)
Camels Are Coming, 1934 (Balcon 4)
Camels West. See Southwest Passage, 1954
Cameo Kirby, 1914 (DeMille 2)
Cameo Kirby, 1923 (Ford, J. 2, Arthur 3, Gilbert 3, Johnson, N. 3)
Cameo Kirby, 1930 (Fetchit 3, Loy 3)
Camera Buff. See Amator, 1978
Camera d'albergo, 1980 (Monicelli 2, Gassman 3)
Camera Makes Woopee, 1934–35 (McLaren 2)
Cameraman, 1928 (Keaton 2, Bruckman 4)
Cameramen at War, 1944 (Lye 2)
Cameriera bella presenza offresi, 1951 (De Sica 2, Fellini 2, Cervi 3, Fabrizi 3, Sordi 3, Pinelli 4)
Cameriere, 1959 (Tognazzi 3, Delli Colli 4)
Camicie rosse, 1952 (Rosi 2, Cuny 3, Magnani 3, Reggiani 3, Gherardi 4)
Camilla, 1954 (Flaiano 4)
Camilla, 1955 (Cristaldi 4)
Camille, 1915 (Gordon 3, Carré 4, Marion 4)
Camille, 1917 (Bara 3)
Camille, 1919 (Negri 3)
Camille, 1921 (Nazimova 3, Valentino 3, Mathis 4)
Camille, 1927 (Niblo 2, Costello, M. 3, Talmadge, N. 3, Menzies 4, Schenck 4)
Camille, 1937 (Cukor 2, Barrymore L. 3, Garbo 3, Taylor, R. 3, Adrian 4, Akins 4, Booth 4, Daniels 4, Freund 4, Gibbons 4, Marion 4, Stothart 4, Thalberg 4)
Camille, 1984 (Gielgud 3)
Camille. See Dame aux camélias, 1934
Camille Without Camelias. See Signora senza camelie, 1953
Caminito alegre, 1943 (García 3)
Camino de infierno, 1950 (Armendáriz 3)
Camino de Sacramento, 1945 (Negrete 3)
Caminos de ayer, 1938 (Negrete 3)
Camion, 1977 (Duras 2, Depardieu 3)
Camion blanc, 1942 (Cayatte 2, Berry 3)
Camisards, 1970 (Allio 2)
Camminacammina, 1983 (Olmi 2)
Cammino degli eroi, 1936 (Fusco 4)
Cammino della speranza, 1950 (Fellini 2, Germi 2, Pinelli 4)
Camorra, 1972 (Seberg 3, Vanel 3)
Camouflage, 1943 (Terry 4)
Camouflage. See Barwy ochronne, 1976
Camouflage Kiss, 1918 (Furthman 4)
Camp, 1965 (Warhol 2)
Camp Followers. See Soldatesse, 1965
Campagne de France 1814-(?), 1916 (Cohl 2)
Campagne electorale, 1909 (Linders 3)
Campana de mi pueble, 1944 (Armendáriz 3)
Campane a Martello, 1949 (Zampa 2, Lollobrigida 3, Gherardi 4, Ponti 4, Rota 4)
Campbell Soups, 1912 (Cohl 2)
Campbell's Kingdom, 1957 (Baker S. 3, Bogarde 3)
Campement treize, 1938 (Alekan 4)
Campi sperimentali, 1957 (Olmi 2)
Camping, 1957 (Zeffirelli 2, Manfredi 3, Ponti 4)
Campo dei fiori, 1943 (Fellini 2, Fabrizi 3, Magnani 3)
Campus a Go-Go. See Eriki no wakadaisho, 1966
Campus Carmen, 1928 (Sennett 2, Lombard 3)
Campus Cinderella, 1930 (Hayward 3)
Campus Confessions, 1938 (Grable 3, Dreier 4, Head 4)
Campus Crushes, 1930 (Sennett 2)
Campus Flirt, 1926 (Daniels 3)
Campus Sweetheart, 1922 (Rogers, G. 3)
Campus Sweetheart, 1931 (Newman 4)

Campus Vamp, 1928 (Sennett 2)
Can Horses Sing?, 1971 (Lassally 4)
Can pazari, 1968 (Guney 2)
Can She Bake A Cherry Pie?, 1983 (Black 3)
Can This Be Dixie?, 1936 (McDaniel 3, Summerville 3, Glennon 4, Trotti 4)
Can We Escape. See Har jeg Ret til at tage mit eget Liv, 1919
Can You Beat It?, 1915 (Talmadge, C. 3)
Can You Take It?, 1934 (Fleischer, M. and D. 2)
Canada Is My Piano, 1967 (Dunning 4)
Canadian Capers, 1931 (Terry 4)
Canadian Moonshiners, 1910 (Olcott 2)
Canadian Officers in the Making, 1917 (Pearson 2)
Canadian Pacific, 1949 (Scott, R. 3, Tiomkin 4)
Canadian Pacific Railroad Shots, 1899 (Bitzer 4)
Canadians, 1961 (Ryan 3, Mathieson 4)
Canaima, 1945 (Negrete 3)
Canal Zone, 1942 (Planer 4)
Canal Zone, 1977 (Wiseman 2)
Canale, 1965–66 (Bertolucci 2)
Cananea, 1976 (Figueroa 4)
Canard aux cérises, 1951 (Kosma 4)
Canary Bananas, 1935 (Leacock 2)
Canary Murder Case, 1929 (Arthur 3, Brooks 3, Powell, W. 3, Banton 4, Mankiewicz 4)
Canary Row, 1949 (Freleng 4)
Canasta de cuentos mexicanos, 1956 (Armendáriz 3, Félix 3, Figueroa 4)
Canasta uruguaya, 1951 (Alcoriza 4)
Canby Hill Outlaws, 1916 (Mix 3)
Can-Can, 1960 (Chevalier 3, Dalio 3, Jourdan 3, MacLaine 3, Sinatra 3, Daniels 4, Lederer 4, Pan 4, Sharaff 4, Smith, J.M. 4, Wheeler 4)
Canção de Lisboa, 1933 (Oliveira 2)
Cancel My Reservation, 1972 (Bellamy 3, Crosby 3, George, Ch. D. 3, Hope 3, Saint 3, Wayne 3, Wynn 3)
Canción de cuna, 1952 (De Fuentes 2)
Canción del alma, 1938 (Figueroa 4)
Canción del milagro, 1940 (Figueroa 4)
Candid Camera, 1932 (Sennett 2)
Candid Candidate, 1937 (Fleischer, M. and D. 2)
Candidate, 1972 (Ritchie 2, Crawford, B. 3, Douglas, M. 3, Redford 3, Wood 3)
Candidate. See Kandidat, 1980
Candidate for a Killing. See Candidato per un assassino, 1969
Candidato per un assassino, 1969 (Rey 3)
Candide, 1960 (Brasseur 3, Cassel 3, Simon, M. 3)
Candle and the Moth. See Evangeliemandens Liv, 1914
Candle in the Wind. See Fuzen no tomoshibi, 1957
Candlelight in Algeria, 1943 (Fisher 2, Mason 3)
Candlemaker, 1956 (Halas and Batchelor 2)
Candles at Nine, 1944 (Matthews 3)
Candleshoe, 1978 (Niven 3)
Candy, 1968 (Huston 2, Brando 3, Burton 3, Coburn, J. 3, Matthau 3, Henry 4, Tavoularis 4, Trumbull 4)
Candy House, 1934 (Lantz 4)
Candy Kid, 1917 (Hardy 3)
Candy Lamb, 1935 (Lantz 4)
Candy Man, 1969 (Sanders 3)
Candy Stripe Nurses, 1974 (Corman 4)
Candy Trail, 1916 (Hardy 3)
Cani del Sinai. See Fortini/Cani, 1976
Canicule, 1983 (Marvin 3, Audiard 4, Lai 4)
Canker of Jealousy, 1915 (Hepworth 2)
Cannabis, 1969 (Jurgens 3)
Canned Feud, 1949 (Freleng 4)
Canned Fishing, 1938 (Roach 4)
Cannery Row, 1982 (Huston 2, Nolte 3, Nykvist 4)
Cannery Woe, 1961 (McKimson 4)
Cannibal Attack, 1954 (Weissmuller 3, Katzman 4)
Cannibal King, 1915 (Hardy 3)
Cannibal Orgy or the Maddest Story Ever Told. See Spider Baby, 1968
Cannibali, 1970 (Morricone 4)
Canning the Cannibal King, 1917 (Pitts 3)

Cannon, 1971 (Wynn 3)
Cannon Ball, 1915 (Sennett 2)
Cannon Ball Express, 1924 (Sennett 2)
Cannon for Cordoba, 1970 (Bernstein 4)
Cannonball, 1931 (Sennett 2)
Cannonball, 1976 (Scorsese 2, Corman 4)
Cannonball Carquake. See Death Race 2000, 1975
Cannonball Run, 1981 (Elam 3, Fonda, P. 3, Martin, D. 3,
    Moore, R. 3, Reynolds, B. 3, Needham 4)
Cannonball Run II, 1984 (Reynolds, B. 3, Needham 4)
Canon, 1964 (McLaren 2)
Canon City, 1948 (Alton, J. 4)
Can't Help Singing, 1944 (Durbin 3, Plunkett 4, Salter 4)
Canta delle marane, 1960 (Pasolini 2)
Canta mi corazon, 1964 (García 3)
Cantaclaro, 1945 (Figueroa 4)
Cantata. See Oldás és kotés, 1963
Cantata de Chile, 1975 (Solás 2, Villagra 3, Herrera 4)
Canterbury Tale, 1944 (Powell and Pressburger 2, Junge 4)
Canterbury Tales. See Racconti di Canterbury, 1972
Canterville Ghost, 1944 (Dassin 2, Laughton 3, O'Brien, M. 3,
    Young, R. 3)
Cantiere d'inverno, 1955 (Olmi 2)
Cantiflas boxeador, 1940 (Cantinflas 3)
Cantiflas ruletero, 1940 (Cantinflas 3)
Canto a mi tierra, 1938 (Armendáriz 3)
Canto da saudade, 1952 (Mauro 2)
Canto della vita, 1945 (Gallone 2, Valli 3)
Canto ma sottovoce, 1945 (Zavattini 4)
Cantoria d'Angeli, 1949 (Di Venanzo 4)
Canyon Dweller, 1912 (Dwan 2)
Canyon Hawks, 1930 (Canutt 4)
Canyon of Adventure, 1928 (Brown, Harry Joe 4, McCord 4)
Canyon of Light, 1926 (Mix 3)
Canyon of the Fools, 1923 (Carey 3)
Canyon Pass. See Raton Pass, 1951
Canyon Passage, 1946 (Tourneur, J. 2, Andrews D. 3, Bond 3,
    Hayward 3, Banton 4, Carmichael 4, Cronjager 4, Wanger 4)
Canzone appasionata, 1953 (Bolognini 2)
Canzone del sole, 1933 (De Sica 2)
Canzone di Werner, 1914 (Bertini 3)
Canzoni a due voci, 1953 (Fusco 4)
Canzoni, canzoni, canzoni, 1953 (Manfredi 3, Sordi 3, Flaiano 4)
Cap. See Kapa, 1971
Cap de l'Espérance, 1951 (Feuillère 3, Kosma 4)
Cap du sud, 1935 (Storck 2)
Cap perdu, 1930 (Dupont 2, Baur 3)
Canable Lady Cook, 1916 (Beery 3)
Cape Ashizuri. See Ashizuri misaki, 1954
Cape Fear, 1962 (Mitchum 3, Peck 3, Boyle 4, Herrmann 4)
Cape Forlorn, 1930 (Dupont 2, Junge 4)
Cape Town Affair, 1967 (Fuller 2, Bisset 3, Trevor 3)
Capello a tre punte, 1935 (Valli 3)
Caper of the Golden Bulls, 1967 (Head 4)
Capestro degli Asburgo, 1915 (Bertini 3)
Capiano degli ussari, 1939 (Zampa 2)
Capitaine Corsaire. See Mollenard, 1938
Capitaine Fracasse, 1928 (Cavalcanti 2, Boyer 3)
Capitaine Fracasse, 1942 (Gance 2, Honegger 4)
Capitaine Fracasse, 1961 (Marais 3, Noiret 3)
Capitaine jaune, 1930 (Vanel 3)
Capitaine Mollenard. See Mollenard, 1938
Capitaine Singrid, 1968 (Tavernier 2)
Capital Punishment, 1925 (Bow 3, Schulberg 4)
Capital Story, 1945 (Kaufman 4)
Capital versus Labor, 1909 (Porter 2)
Capitan, 1960 (Bourvil 3, Marais 3)
Capitán aventurero, 1938 (García 3)
Capitan Fantasma, 1953 (Age and Scarpelli 4)
Capitan Fracassa, 1940 (Stallich 4, Zavattini 4)
Capitan Malacara, 1944 (Armendáriz 3)
Capitana Allegria. See Pour Don Carlos, 1921
Capitano di Venezia, 1951 (Di Venanzo 4)

Capitol Affair, 1971 (McCambridge 3)
Capitu, 1968 (Diegues 2)
Capkovy povídky, 1947 (Fric 2, Trnka 2)
Cap'n Abe's Niece, 1917 (Costello, M. 3)
Cap'n Jericho. See Hell and High Water, 1933
Capone, 1975 (Stallone 2, Corman 4)
Caporal épinglé, 1962 (Renoir 2, Cassel 3, Kosma 4, Spaak 4)
Caporale do giornata, 1958 (Manfredi 3)
Cappello da prete, 1945 (Baarová 3, Amidei 4)
Cappotto, 1952 (Ferreri 2, Lattuada 2, Zavattini 4)
Cappucetto rosso, Cenerentola . . . et voi ci credete, 1972 (Brazzi 3)
Cappy Ricks, 1921 (Young, W. 4)
Caprelles et pantopodes, 1930 (Jaubert 4)
Capriccio, 1938 (Rohrig 4)
Capriccio all'italiana, 1968 (Bolognini 2, Monicelli 2, Pasolini 2,
    Mangano 3, Age and Scarpelli 4, Delli Colli 4, Zavattini 4)
Capriccio Espagnol. See Spanish Fiesta, 1941
Caprice, 1913 (Pickford 3)
Caprice, 1967 (Tashlin 2, Day 3, Shamroy 4, Smith, J.M. 4)
Caprice de Noël, 1963 (McLaren 2)
Caprice de princesse, 1933 (Clouzot 2, Planer 4)
Caprices, 1941 (Cayatte 2, Blier 3, Darrieux 3, Andrejew 4)
Caprices de Marie, 1969 (Broca 2, Cortese 3, Noiret 3, Delerue 4)
Caprices of Kitty, 1915 (Bosworth 3, Marion 4)
Capricious Summer. See Rozmarné léto, 1968
Capricorn One, 1977 (Black 3, Gould 3, Goldsmith 4)
Capriolen, 1937 (Grundgens 3, Planer 4)
Captain Apache, 1971 (Baker C. 3, Van Cleef 3)
Captain Barnacle's Baby, 1911 (Bunny 3)
Captain Barnacle's Courtship, 1911 (Bunny 3)
Captain Barnacle's Messmate, 1912 (Bunny 3, Talmadge, N. 3)
Captain Black Jack, 1950 (Duvivier 2, Moorehead 3, Sanders 3)
Captain Blood, 1935 (Curtiz 2, De Havilland 3, Flynn 3, Meek 3,
    Rathbone 3, Brown, Harry Joe 4, Friedhofer 4, Grot 4, Haller 4,
    Korngold 4, Robinson 4, Wallis 4, Westmore, P. 4)
Captain Blood. See Captain Pirate, 1952
Captain Boycott, 1947 (Donat 3, Granger 3, Sim 3, Alwyn 4, Gilliat 4,
    Morris 4)
Captain Cap, 1963 (Braunberger 4)
Captain Careless, 1928 (Miller, V. 4, Plunkett 4)
Captain Carey, U.S.A., 1950 (Leisen 2, Ladd 3, Dreier 4, Friedhofer 4,
    Seitz 4)
Captain Caution, 1940 (Ladd 3, Mature 3, Plunkett 4, Roach 4)
Captain China, 1950 (Chaney Lon, Jr. 3, Alton, J. 4)
Captain Clegg, 1962 (Cushing 3, Reed, O. 3)
Captain Courageous, 1937 (Hawks 2)
Captain Courageous, 1952 (Burness 4)
Captain Courtesy, 1915 (Bosworth 3, Marion 4)
Captain Cowboy, 1929 (Canutt 4)
Captain Eddie, 1945 (Bacon 2, MacMurray 3)
Captain Fly-by-Night, 1922 (Howard 2)
Captain from Castile, 1947 (King 2, Cobb 3, Power 3, Basevi 4,
    Clarke, C.C. 4, Day 4, Lemaire 4, Newman 4, Trotti 4)
Captain Fury, 1939 (Carradine 3, Lukas 3, McLaglen 3, Canutt 4,
    Roach 4)
Captain Grant's Children. See Detti kapitana Granta, 1936
Captain Hareblower, 1953 (Freleng 4)
Captain Hates the Sea, 1934 (Milestone 2, Gilbert 3, McLaglen 3,
    Meek 3, Three Stooges 3, August 4)
Captain Horatio Hornblower, 1951 (Walsh 2, Baker S. 3, Lee, C. 3,
    Mayo 3, Peck 3, Green, G. 4)
Captain Hurricane, 1935 (Chaney Lon, Jr. 3, Plunkett 4)
Captain Is a Lady, 1940 (Bondi 3, Burke 3, Coburn, C. 3, Dailey 3,
    Kaper 4)
Captain Jack's Dilemma, 1912 (Bunny 3)
Captain Jack's Diplomacy, 1912 (Bunny 3)
Captain January, 1924 (Bosworth 3)
Captain January, 1936 (Carradine 3, Darwell 3, Summerville 3,
    Temple 3, Seitz 4, Zanuck 4)
Captain Kate, 1911 (Mix 3)
Captain Kidd, 1945 (Carradine 3, Farnum 3, Laughton 3, Scott, R. 3,
    Raine 4)
Captain Kidd, Jr., 1919 (Pickford 3, Marion 4, Rosher 4)

Captain Kidd's Kids, 1919 (Daniels 3, Lloyd 3, Roach 4)
Captain Kleinschmidt's Adventures in the Far North. *See* Adventures
   in the Far North, 1923
Captain Lash, 1929 (McLaglen 3)
Captain Lightfoot, 1955 (Sirk 2, Hudson 3, Burnett 4, Hunter 4,
   Salter 4)
Captain Macklin, 1915 (Gish, L. 3)
Captain McLean, 1914 (Von Stroheim 2)
Captain Moonlight. *See* D'ye Ken John Peel?, 1935
Captain Nemo and the Underwater City, 1970 (Ryan 3)
Captain Newman, M.D., 1963 (Curtis 3, Dickinson 3, Duvall, R. 3,
   Peck 3, Westmore, B. 4, Whitlock 4)
Captain of Koepenick, 1941 (Oswald 2)
Captain of Koepenick. *See* Modern Hero, 1941
Captain of the Guard, 1930 (Fejos 2)
Captain Pirate, 1952 (Brown, Harry Joe 4, Duning 4)
Captain Salvation, 1927 (Daniels 4, Gibbons 4)
Captain Sinbad, 1963 (Armendáriz 3, Schufftan 4)
Captain Thunder, 1930 (Crosland 2, Wray 3)
Captain Tugboat Annie, 1945 (Darwell 3)
Captain Video, 1951 (Katzman 4)
Captain's Captain, 1918 (Costello, M. 3)
Captains Courageous, 1937 (Fleming 2, Barrymore L. 3, Carradine 3,
   Douglas, M. 3, Rooney 3, Tracy 3, Gibbons 4, Gillespie 4,
   Mahin 4, Rosson 4, Waxman 4)
Captains Courageous, 1977 (Malden 3)
Captain's Kid, 1936 (Haller 4)
Captains of the Clouds, 1942 (Curtiz 2, Cagney 3, Young, G. 3,
   Hoch 4, Mercer 4, Polito 4, Raine 4, Steiner 4, Wallis 4)
Captain's Paradise, 1953 (De Carlo 3, Guinness 3, Johnson, C. 3,
   Arnold 4)
Captivating Mary Carstairs, 1915 (Talmadge, C. 3, Talmadge, N. 3)
Captive, 1915 (DeMille 2, Sweet 3, Buckland 4, Macpherson 4)
Captive City, 1952 (Garmes 4)
Captive City. *See* Citta prigioniera, 1962
Captive Girl, 1950 (Crabbe 3, Weissmuller 3, Katzman 4)
Captive God, 1916 (Hart 3, August 4)
Captive Heart, 1946 (Dearden 2, Redgrave, M. 3, Balcon 4,
   Slocombe 4)
Captive Soul. *See* Rablélek, 1913
Captive Wild Woman, 1943 (Dmytryk 2, Carradine 3, Pierce 4,
   Salter 4)
Captive's Island. *See* Shokei no shima, 1966
Capture, 1950 (Sturges, J. 2, Ayres 3, Wright 3, Cronjager 4)
Capture of Aquinaldo, 1913 (Darwell 3)
Capture of the Biddle Brothers, 1902 (Porter 2)
Capture of Yegg Bank Burglars, 1904 (Porter 2)
Captured!, 1933 (Fairbanks, D. Jr. 3, Howard, L. 3, Lukas 3,
   Orry-Kelly 4)
Captured by Bedouins, 1912 (Olcott 2)
Car, 1977 (Rosenman 4, Whitlock 4)
Car 99, 1935 (MacMurray 3, Sheridan 3, Head 4, Sullivan 4)
Car of Chance, 1917 (Young, W. 4)
Car of Dreams, 1935 (Mills 3, Balcon 4, Junge 4)
Car of Tomorrow, 1951 (Avery 2)
Car Wash, 1976 (Muse 3, Pryor 3)
Cara del terror, 1962 (Rey 3)
Carabina 30-30, 1958 (Figueroa 4)
Carabiniere, 1963 (Rossellini 2)
Carabiniere a cavallo, 1961 (Manfredi 3, Di Venanzo 4, Gherardi 4)
Carabiniers, 1963 (Godard 2, Coutard 4, de Beauregard 4,
   Guillemot 4, Ponti 4)
Carambolages, 1962 (Delon 3, Audiard 4)
Caravaggio, 1940 (Stallich 4)
Caravan, 1934 (Boyer 3, Fazenda 3, Johnson, N. 3, Young, L. 3,
   Raphaelson 4)
Caravan, 1946 (Granger 3)
Caravan pour Zagora. *See* Secret des hommes bleus, 1960
Caravane, 1934 (Brasseur 3)
Caravane d'amour, 1970 (Reichenbach 2)
Caravane de la lumière, 1947 (Fradetal 4)
Caravans, 1978 (Cotten 3, Lee, C. 3, Quinn 3, Slocombe 4)
Carbine Williams, 1952 (Stewart 3, Plunkett 4)

Carbon Arc Projection, 1947 (Hoch 4)
Carbon Copy, 1981 (Segal 3, Warden 3)
Carbunara, 1955–59 (Taviani, P. and V. 2)
Carcasse et le Tord-Cou, 1947 (Simon, M. 3)
Cárcel de Cananca, 1960 (Armendáriz 3)
Card, 1952 (Guinness 3, Alwyn 4, Morris 4)
Card Game. *See* Poker, 1920
Cardboard Baby, 1909 (Olcott 2)
Cardboard Cavalier, 1949 (Dillon 4)
Cardboard City, 1934 (Barrymore L. 3)
Cardboard City. *See* Ciudad de carton, 1932
Cardboard Lover, 1928 (Gibbons 4, Wilson, C. 4)
Cardenal, 1951 (Bennett 4)
Cardeuse de Matelas, 1906 (Méliès 2)
Cardigan's Last Case. *See* State's Attorney, 1932
Cardinal, 1963 (Smith, D. , Huston 2, Preminger 2, Gish, D. 3,
   Meredith 3, Schneider 3, Bass 4, Shamroy 4, Wheeler 4)
Cardinal Richelieu, 1935 (Arliss 3, Carradine 3, O'Sullivan 3, Day 4,
   Johnson 4, Newman 4, Zanuck 4)
Cardinal Richelieu's Ward, 1914 (Cruze 2)
Cardinal's Conspiracy, 1909 (Griffith 2, Lawrence 3, Pickford 3,
   Bitzer 4, Ince 4)
Cardinal's Visit, from 1981 (Baillie 2)
Cardinale Lambertini, 1955 (Cervi 3)
Card-Index. *See* Kartoteka, 1966
Cards on the Table. *See* Cartas Boca arriba, 1965
Care and Affection. *See* Szeretet, 1963
Career, 1939 (Trumbo 4)
Career, 1959 (MacLaine 3, Martin, D. 3, Cahn 4, Head 4, La Shelle 4,
   Wallis 4, Waxman 4)
Career. *See* Kariera, 1955
Career: Medical Technologists, 1954 (Bernstein 4)
Career of a Chambermaid. *See* Telefoni bianchi, 1975
Career of Dima. *See* Dimy Gorina, 1961
Career of Pavel Camrda. *See* Kariéra Pavla Camrdy, 1931
Career Woman, 1936 (Trevor 3, Trotti 4)
Careers, 1929 (Seitz 4)
Carefree, 1938 (Sandrich 2, Astaire 3, Bellamy 3, Rogers, G. 3,
   Berman 4, Nichols 4, Pan 4, Polglase 4)
Careful, Soft Shoulders, 1942 (Clarke, C.C. 4, Day 4)
Careless Age, 1929 (Fairbanks, D. Jr. 3, Young, L. 3)
Careless Lady, 1932 (Bennett J. 3, Friedhofer 4, Seitz 4)
Careless Love. *See* Bonne Soupe, 1964
Careless Years, 1957 (Hiller 2)
Careless Youth. *See* Leichtsinnige Jugend, 1931
Caretaker, 1963 (Roeg 2, Bates 3, Pleasance 3, Shaw 3, Pinter 4)
Caretakers, 1963 (Crawford, J. 3, Marshall 3, Ballard 4, Bernstein 4)
Caretaker's Daughter, 1925 (McCarey 2, Roach 4)
Caretaker's Daughter, 1934 (Roach 4)
Carey Treatment, 1972 (Edwards 2, Coburn, J. 3)
Cargaison blanche, 1937 (Siodmak 2, Berry 3, Dalio 3)
Cargaison blanche, 1957 (Broca 2)
Cargamento prohibibo, 1965 (Figueroa 4)
Cargo from Jamaica, 1933 (Grierson 2, Wright 2)
Cargo of Innocents. *See* Stand By for Action, 1942
Cargo to Capetown, 1950 (Crawford, B. 3, Ireland 3, Duning 4)
Caribbean, 1952 (Hardwicke 3, Muse 3, Head 4)
Caribbean Gold. *See* Caribbean, 1952
Cariboo Trail, 1950 (Scott, R. 3)
Carillons, 1936 (Storck 2)
Carillons sans joie, 1962 (Auric 4, Cloquet 4)
Cariñoso, 1958 (Alcoriza 4)
Carl Dreyer, 1965 (Rohmer 2)
Carl Nielsen 1865–1931, 1978 (Roos 2)
Carl Th. Dreyer, 1966 (Roos 2)
Carlo Pisacane, 1955–59 (Taviani, P. and V. 2)
Carlos Monzon, 1974 (Reichenbach 2)
Carlos und Elisabeth, 1924 (Dieterle 2, Oswald 2, Veidt 3)
Carlton-Browne of the F.O., 1958 (Boulting 2, Sellers 3, Addison 4)
Carmen, 1900–07 (Guy 2)
Carmen, 1915 (DeMille 2, Walsh 2, Bara 3, Reid 3, Buckland 4,
   Macpherson 4)
Carmen, 1916 (Chaplin 2)

Carmen, 1918 (Lubitsch 2, Negri 3, Kraly 4)
Carmen, 1926 (Feyder 2, Modot 3, Meerson 4)
Carmen, 1933 (Reiniger 2)
Carmen, 1943 (Christian-Jaque 2, Marais 3, Jeanson 4, Spaak 4)
Carmen, 1960 (Gassman 3)
Carmen, 1967 (Wakhévitch 4)
Carmen, 1983 (Saura 2)
Carmen, 1984 (Guerra 4)
Carmen, Baby, 1967 (Kinski 3)
Carmen Comes Home. See Karumen kokyo no kaeru, 1951
Carmen di Trastavere, 1962 (Gallone 2)
Carmen fra i rossi, 1939 (Stallich 4)
Carmen Jones, 1954 (Preminger 2, Dandridge 3, Bass 4)
Carmen nejen podle Bizeta, 1968 (Schorm 2)
Carmen, Not According to Bizet. See Carmen nejen podle Bizeta, 1968
Carmen von St. Pauli, 1928 (Rasp 3, Junge 4)
Carmenita the Faithful, 1911 (Anderson G. 3)
Carmen's Pure Love. See Karumen junjo su, 1952
Carmen's Veranda, 1944 (Terry 4)
Carnal Circuit. See Insaziabili, 1969
Carnal Knowledge, 1971 (Nichols 2, Nicholson 3, Sylbert 4)
Carnaval, 1953 (Pagnol 2, Verneuil 2)
Carnaval à La Nouvelle-Orléans, 1957 (Reichenbach 2, Braunberger 4)
Carnaval des vérités, 1919 (Autant-Lara 2, L'Herbier 2)
Carnavals, 1950 (Storck 2)
Carne de horca, 1954 (Brazzi 3)
Carne de presidio, 1951 (Armendáriz 3, Alcoriza 4)
Carne inquieta, 1952 (Baarová 3)
Carne per Frankenstein, 1973 (Guerra 4, Ponti 4)
Carnegie Hall, 1947 (Ulmer 2, Schufftan 4)
Carnet de bal, 1937 (Duvivier 2, Baur 3, Fernandel 3, Jouvet 3, Raimu 3, Rosay 3, Jaubert 4, Jeanson 4)
Carnet de viaje, 1961 (Ivens 2)
Carnets du Major Thompson, 1957 (Sturges, P. 2, Matras 4)
Carnevale di Venezia, 1927 (Amidei 4)
Carnival, 1911 (Olcott 2)
Carnival, 1921 (McLaglen 3, Novello 3)
Carnival, 1931 (Wilcox 2, Schildkraut 3)
Carnival, 1935 (Ball 3, Durante 3, Riskin 4)
Carnival, 1946 (Holloway 3, Dillon 4, Green, G. 4)
Carnival, 1953 (Fernandel 3)
Carnival. See Karneval, 1908
Carnival. See Karneval, 1961
Carnival Boat, 1932 (Bosworth 3, Boyd 3, Rogers, G. 3, McCord 4)
Carnival Capers, 1932 (Lantz 4)
Carnival Girl, 1926 (Garmes 4)
Carnival in Costa Rica, 1947 (Cobb 3, Basevi 4, Hoffenstein 4, Reynolds 4)
Carnival in Flanders. See Kermesse héroïque, 1935
Carnival in the Clothes Cupboard, 1940 (Halas and Batchelor 2)
Carnival Man, 1929 (Huston 3)
Carnival Night. See Karnavalnaya noch, 1956
Carnival of Crime, 1964 (Aumont 3)
Carnival of Killers. See Spie contro il mondo, 1966
Carnival of Sinners. See Main du diable, 1942
Carnival Rock, 1957 (Corman 4, Crosby 4)
Carnival Story, 1954 (Baxter A. 3, Haller 4, Trumbo 4)
Carnival Story. See Rummelplatz der Liebe, 1954
Carnival Week, 1927 (Terry 4)
Carny, 1980 (Cook 3, North 4)
Caro Michele, 1976 (Monicelli 2, Seyrig 3, D'Amico 4, Delli Colli 4, Guerra 4, Rota 4)
Caro Papà, 1979 (Risi 2, Gassman 3, Delli Colli 4)
Carobni zvuci, 1957 (Vukotić 4)
Carodějuv učen, 1977 (Zeman 2)
Carol, 1970 (Emshwiller 2)
Carol for Another Christmas, 1964 (Hayden 3, Saint 3)
Carola, 1975 (Caron 3, Lourié 4)
Carola Lamberti—Eine vom Zirkus, 1954 (Porten 3)
Carolina, 1934 (King 2, Barrymore L. 3, Fetchit 3, Gaynor 3, Temple 3, Young, R. 3)

Carolina Blues, 1944 (Miller 3, Cahn 4, Duning 4, Planer 4)
Carolina Moon, 1940 (Autry 3)
Carolina Rediviva, 1920 (Borgstrom 3, Magnusson 4)
Caroline au pays natal, 1951 (Decaë 4)
Caroline chérie, 1950 (Auric 4)
Caroline chérie, 1967 (De Sica 2, Blier 3, Vierny 4)
Caroline du Sud, 1952 (Decaë 4)
Carolyn of the Corners, 1918 (Love 3)
Caronna nera. See Corona negra, 1952
Carosello di varietà, 1955 (Fabrizi 3)
Carosello napoletano, 1954 (Rosi 2, Loren 3)
Carousel, 1956 (King 2, Jones S. 3, Clarke, C.C. 4, Glazer 4, Newman 4, Reynolds 4, Smith, J.M. 4, Wheeler 4)
Carpenter, 1922 (Laurel 3)
Carpetbaggers, 1964 (Dmytryk 2, Ayres 3, Baker C. 3, Cummings 3, Ladd 3, Bernstein 4, Edouart 4, Hayes 4, Head 4, Westmore, W. 4)
Carpocapse des pommes, 1955 (Rabier 4)
Carquake. See Cannonball, 1976
Carradines in Concert, 1980 (Carradine 3)
Carrara, 1950 (Di Venanzo 4)
Carré de valets, 1947 (Jeanson 4)
Carrefour, 1938 (Berry 3, Vanel 3, Burel 4, D'Eaubonne 4)
Carrefour des enfants perdus, 1943 (Reggiani 3)
Carrefour des passion. See Uomini sono nemici, 1948
Carrefour des passions, 1948 (Cortese 3, Kosma 4)
Carrefour du crime, 1947 (Burel 4)
Carriage to Vienna. See Kočár do Vídně, 1966
Carrie, 1951 (Wyler 2, Hopkins, M. 3, Jones, J. 3, Olivier 3, Head 4, Raksin 4)
Carrie, 1976 (De Palma 2, Spacek 3, Donaggio 4)
Carrière de Suzanne, 1963 (Rohmer 2)
Carrington, V.C., 1956 (Asquith 2, Niven 3)
Carro armato dell otto settembre, 1960 (Pasolini 2, Guerra 4)
Carrosse d'or, 1953 (Magnani 3, Renoir 4)
Carrots and Peas, 1969 (Frampton 2)
Carry Harry, 1942 (Langdon 3)
Carry on Constable, 1960 (Dillon 4)
Carry on Cruising, 1962 (Dillon 4)
Carry On George, 1939 (Formby 3)
Carry On Milkmaids, 1974 (Halas and Batchelor 2)
Carrying the Mail, 1934 (Canutt 4)
Cars That Ate Paris, 1974 (Weir 2)
Carson City, 1952 (De Toth 2, Massey 3, Scott, R. 3)
Carson City Kid, 1940 (Rogers, R. 3)
Carson City Raiders, 1948 (Canutt 4)
Carta, 1930 (Fort 4)
Carta de amor, 1943 (Negrete 3)
Cartagine in fiamme, 1959 (Gallone 2, Brasseur 3, Cervi 3, Gélin 3)
Cartas Boca arriba, 1965 (Rey 3)
Cartas marcadas, 1947 (Infante 3)
Carte a Sara, 1956 (Bardem 2)
Carte américaine, 1912–14 (Cohl 2)
Carter's Army, 1970 (Pryor 3)
Carters of Greenwood English language teaching series, 1964 (Halas and Batchelor 2)
Cartes sur table, 1965 (Constantine 3, Carrière 4, D'Eaubonne 4)
Cartes vivants, 1905 (Méliès 2)
Carthage in Flames. See Cartagine in fiamme, 1959
Carthusian. See Karthauzi, 1916
Cartoon Factory, 1925 (Fleischer, M. and D. 2)
Cartoonland, 1921 (Fleischer, M. and D. 2)
Cartouche, 1934 (Fradetal 4)
Cartouche, 1962 (Broca 2, Belmondo 3, Cardinale 3, Dalio 3, Delerue 4, Matras 4, Spaak 4)
Car-Tune Portrait, 1937 (Fleischer, M. and D. 2)
Carve Her Name with Pride, 1958 (Aimée 3, Caine 3, Alwyn 4)
Carved in Ivory, 1974 (Lassally 4)
Cas de conscience, 1939 (Berry 3)
Cas du Docteur Laurent, 1956 (Gabin 3, Alekan 4, Kosma 4)
Casa chica, 1950 (Del Rio 3)
Casa colorado, 1947 (Armendáriz 3, Figueroa 4)
Casa de cristal, 1967 (Alcoriza 4)
Casa de mujeres, 1966 (Del Rio 3)

Casa del ángel, 1957 (Torre-Nilsson 2)
Casa del ogro, 1938 (De Fuentes 2, Figueroa 4)
Casa del peccato, 1938 (Valli 3)
Casa del pelicano, 1977 (Figueroa 4)
Casa del rencor, 1941 (Figueroa 4)
Casa del terror, 1959 (Chaney Lon, Jr. 3)
Casa Ricordi, 1954 (Gallone 2, Mastroianni 3, Presle 3, Age and Scarpelli 4)
Casa sin fronteras, 1972 (Chaplin 3)
Casablanca, 1942 (Curtiz 2, Bergman 3, Bogart 3, Dalio 3, Greenstreet 3, Henreid 3, Lorre 3, Rains 3, Sakall 3, Veidt 3, Edeson 4, Epstein, J. & P. 4, Friedhofer 4, Koch 4, Orry-Kelly 4, Steiner 4, Wallis 4, Westmore, P. 4)
Casablanca, 1961 (Solás 2)
Casanova, 1927 (Delannoy 2, Litvak 2, Mozhukin 3, Simon, M. 3, Burel 4)
Casanova, 1976 (Fellini 2, Sutherland 3, De Laurentiis 4, Donati 4, Rota 4)
Casanova & Co., 1977 (Curtis 3)
Casanova '70, 1965 (Ferreri 2, Monicelli 2, Mastroianni 3, Age and Scarpelli 4, D'Amico 4, Guerra 4, Ponti 4)
Casanova Brown, 1944 (Wood 2, Cook 3, Cooper, Gary 3, Wright 3, Fields 4, Johnson 4, Seitz 4)
Casanova Cat, 1950 (Hanna and Barbera 4)
Casanova di Federico Fellini. See Casanova, 1976
Casanova farebbe cosi, 1942 (Sordi 3)
Casanova's Big Night, 1954 (McLeod 2, Carradine 3, Chaney Lon, Jr. 3, Fontaine 3, Hope 3, Price 3, Rathbone 3)
Casanove wider willen, 1931 (Rosay 3)
Casbah, 1948 (De Carlo 3, Haas 3, Lorre 3)
Cascade de feu, 1904 (Méliès 2)
Case Against Ferro, 1976 (Signoret 3)
Case Against Mrs. Ames, 1936 (Bondi 3, Brent 3, Carroll M. 3, Wanger 4)
Case Dismissed, 1924 (Arthur 3)
Case is Closed. See Kharij, 1982
Case of Becky, 1915 (Sweet 3)
Case of Colonel Redl. See Fall des Generalstabsoberst Redl, 1931
Case of Jonathan Drew. See Lodger, 1926
Case of Lena Smith, 1929 (Von Sternberg 2, Banton 4, Dreier 4, Furthman 4, Rosson 4)
Case of Marcel Duchamp, 1983 (Lassally 4)
Case of Mr. Pelham, 1955 (Hitchcock 2)
Case of Sergeant Grischa, 1930 (Brenon 2, Hersholt 3, Hunt 4, Plunkett 4)
Case of the Black Parrot, 1941 (McCord 4)
Case of the Curious Bride, 1935 (Curtiz 2, Flynn 3, Brown, Harry Joe 4, Grot 4, Laszlo 4, Orry-Kelly 4)
Case of the Evil Mouse, 1961 (Dovniković 4)
Case of the Howling Dog, 1934 (Crosland 2, Astor 3, Orry-Kelly 4)
Case of the Lost Sheep, 1935 (Lantz 4)
Case of the Lucky Legs, 1935 (Gaudio 4)
Case of the Missing Blonde. See Lady in the Morgue, 1938
Case of the Missing Hare, 1942 (Jones 2)
Case of the Mukkinese Battlehorn, 1955 (Sellers 3)
Case of the Sleepy Boxer. See Slučaj pospanog boksera, 1961
Case of the Velvet Claw, 1936 (Blanke 4)
Casey and His Neighbor's Goat, 1903 (Porter 2)
Casey at the Bat, 1912 (Talmadge, N. 3)
Casey at the Bat, 1927 (Beery 3, Pitts 3, Furthman 4)
Casey's Frightful Dream, 1904 (Porter 2)
Casey's Shadow, 1978 (Ritt 2, Matthau 3, Alonzo 4, Stark 4)
Casey's Vendetta, 1914 (Browning 2)
Cash, 1933 (Crichton 2, Donat 3, Gwenn 3, Wimperis 4)
Cash and Carry, 1937 (Three Stooges 3, Bruckman 4)
Cash Customers, 1921 (Roach 4)
Cash McCall, 1960 (Wood 3, Blanke 4, Coffee 4, Steiner 4)
Cash on Delivery. See To Dorothy, a Son, 1954
Cash on Demand, 1961 (Cushing 3)
Cash on the Barrel Head, 1962 (Bendix 3)
Cash Parrish's Pal, 1915 (Hart 3, August 4)
Cash Register, 1982 (Grgić 4)
Casimir, 1950 (Fernandel 3)

Casino de Paree. See Go into Your Dance, 1935
Casino de Paris, 1957 (De Sica 2)
Casino Murder Case, 1935 (Carroll L. 3, Fazenda 3, Lukas 3, Russell, R. 3, Clarke, C.C. 4, Tiomkin 4)
Casino Royale, 1967 (Allen 2, Huston 2, Roeg 2, Welles 2, Belmondo 3, Bisset 3, Boyer 3, Holden 3, Kerr 3, Niven 3, O'Toole 3, Raft 3, Sellers 3, Fisher 4, Mankowitz 4, Williams, R. 4)
Casket for Living. See Tosei tamatebako, 1925
Caso Haller, 1933 (Blasetti 2)
Caso Mattei, 1972 (Rosi 2, Volonté 3, Cristaldi 4, Guerra 4)
Caso Raoul, 1975 (Valli 3)
Casotto, 1977 (Deneuve 3)
Casque d'or, 1952 (Becker 2, Dauphin 3, Modot 3, Reggiani 3, Signoret 3, D'Eaubonne 4)
Cass Timberlane, 1947 (Sidney 2, Astor 3, Pidgeon 3, Tracy 3, Turner, L. 3, Irene 4, Levien 4, Stewart 4)
Cassandra Crossing, 1977 (Gardner 3, Lancaster 3, Loren 3, Sheen 3, Thulin 3, Valli 3, Goldsmith 4, Ponti 4)
Casse, 1971 (Verneuil 2, Belmondo 3, Sharif 3, Morricone 4, Renoir 4)
Casse-pieds, 1948 (Blier 3, Burel 4)
Cassette de l'émigrée, 1912 (Feuillade 2)
Cassidy of Bar 20, 1938 (Boyd 3, Head 4)
Cassis, 1966 (Mekas 2)
Cassis Colank, 1958–59 (Breer 2)
Cassowary. See Hikuidori, 1926
Cast a Dark Shadow, 1955 (Bogarde 3)
Cast a Giant Shadow, 1966 (Brynner 3, Dickinson 3, Douglas, K. 3, Sinatra 3, Topol 3, Wayne 3, Bernstein 4)
Cast a Long Shadow, 1959 (Murphy 3, Mirisch 4)
Cast Iron. See Virtuous Sin, 1930
Cast of the Die, 1914 (Anderson G. 3)
Casta Diva, 1935 (Gallone 2, Planer 4)
Casta Diva, 1955 (Gallone 2, Age and Scarpelli 4)
Castagne sono buone, 1970 (Germi 2)
Castagnino, diario romano, 1966 (Birri 2)
Castaways. See Rozbitkowie, 1969
Castel Sant'Angelo, 1946 (Blasetti 2)
Castelli in aria, 1938 (Castellani 2, De Sica 2)
Castello dei morti vivi, 1964 (Lee, C. 3, Sutherland 3)
Castello di paura, 1972 (Brazzi 3)
Castiglione, 1954 (Brazzi 3, De Carlo 3)
Castilian, 1963 (Crawford, B. 3)
Castilian. See Valle de las espadas, 1963
Cast-Iron, 1964 (Ioseliani 2)
Castle series, 1966–68, (Le Grice 2)
Castle. See Schloss, 1968
Castle in the Air, 1952 (Rutherford 3)
Castle in the Desert, 1942 (Miller, V. 4)
Castle Keep, 1969 (Pollack 2, Aumont 3, Dern 3, Falk 3, Lancaster 3, Decaë 4, Douy 4, Legrand 4, Taradash 4)
Castle of Evil, 1966 (Mayo 3)
Castle of Fu Manchu, 1970 (Lee, C. 3)
Castle of Otranto. See Otrantský zámek, 1977
Castle of Terror. See Vergine de Norimberga, 1964
Castle of the Living Dead. See Castello dei morti vivi, 1964
Castle of the Spider's Web. See Kumonosu-jo, 1957
Castle on the Hudson, 1940 (Litvak 2, Garfield 3, Meredith 3, O'Brien, P. 3, Sheridan 3, Deutsch 4, Edeson 4, Miller, S. 4)
Castle within a Castle. See Slot I Et Slot, 1954
Castle Without a Name, 1920 (Lukas 3)
Castles in the Sky and Rhinestones. See Wolkenbau und Flimmerstern, 1919
Castro Street, 1966 (Baillie 2)
Cat. See Chatte, 1958
Cat and Duplicat, 1967 (Jones 2)
Cat and Mouse. See Chat et la souris, 1975
Cat and Mouse. See Mousey, 1974
Cat and the Canary, 1927 (Leni 2)
Cat and the Canary, 1939 (Goddard 3, Hope 3, Dreier 4, Head 4, Lang 4)
Cat and the Canary, 1978 (Hiller 3)
Cat and the Fiddle, 1934 (Howard 2, Hersholt 3, MacDonald 3, Novarro 3, Adrian 4, Clarke, C.C. 4, Rosson 4, Stothart 4)

Cat and the Mermouse, 1949 (Hanna and Barbera 4)
Cat Ballou, 1965 (Fonda, J. 3, Marvin 3)
Cat Came Back, 1936 (Freleng 4)
Cat Came Back, 1944 (Terry 4)
Cat Concerto, 1946 (Hanna and Barbera 4)
Cat Creature, 1973 (Carradine 3)
Cat Creeps, 1930 (Hersholt 3)
Cat, Dog, & Co., 1929 (Roach 4)
Cat Feud, 1959 (Jones 2)
Cat Fishin', 1946 (Hanna and Barbera 4)
Cat from Outer Space, 1978 (McDowall 3, McDowell 3, Ames 4,
    Schifrin 4)
Cat Happy, 1950 (Terry 4)
Cat Meets Mouse, 1942 (Terry 4)
Cat Napping, 1951 (Hanna and Barbera 4)
Cat Nipped, 1932 (Lantz 4)
Cat 'o Nine Tails. See Gatto a nove code, 1969
Cat of the Night. See Yoru no mesuneko, 1929
Cat on a Hot Tin Roof, 1958 (Brooks, R. 2, Anderson J. 3, Newman 3,
    Taylor, E. 3, Daniels 4, Rose 4)
Cat on a Hot Tin Roof, 1976 (Olivier 3, Wagner 3, Wood 3)
Cat on a Hot Tin Roof, 1984 (Lange 3, Torn 3)
**Cat People, 1942 (Tourneur, J. 2, Simon, S. 3, Bodeen 4, D'Agostino 4,
    Dunn 4, Lewton 4, Musuraca 4)**
Cat People, 1982 (Schrader 2, McDowell 3, Whitlock 4)
Cat, Shozo, and the Two Women. See Neko to Shozo to futari no onna,
    1956
Cat That Hated People, 1948 (Avery 2)
Cat Trouble, 1947 (Terry 4)
Cat Women of the Moon, 1953 (Bernstein 4)
Catacombs. See Katacomby, 1940
Catalina, Here I Come, 1927 (Sennett 2)
Catalina Rowboat Race. See Smith series, 1926–28
Catamount Killing, 1974 (Zanussi 2)
Catapult and the Kite. See Prak a drak, 1960
Cat-astrophe, 1916 (Terry 4)
Catastrophe de la Martinique, 1902 (Zecca, 2)
Catch. See Shiiku, 1961
Catch As Catch Can, 1927 (Shamroy 4)
Catch as Catch Can, 1937 (Mason 3, Rutherford 3)
Catch as Catch Can. See Scatenato, 1967
Catch Me a Spy, 1971 (Blier 3, Douglas, K. 3, Howard, T. 3,
    Braunberger 4, Dillon 4)
Catch Meow, 1961 (Hanna and Barbera 4)
Catch My Smoke, 1922 (Mix 3)
Catch My Soul, 1973 (Hall 4)
Catch Us If You Can, 1965 (Boorman 2)
Catch-as-Catch-Can, 1931 (Pitts 3, Roach 4)
Catcher, 1971 (Baxter A. 3)
Catching a Coon, 1921 (Roach 4)
Catch-22, 1970 (Nichols 2, Welles 2, Arkin 3, Dalio 3, Perkins 3,
    Sheen 3, Voight 3, Henry 4, Sylbert 4, Watkin 4, Whitlock 4)
Catene invisibili, 1942 (Valli 3)
Catered Affair, 1956 (Brooks, R. 2, Borgnine 3, Davis 3, Fitzgerald 3,
    Reynolds, D. 3, Alton, J. 4, Previn 4, Westmore, P. 4)
Caterina de Russia, 1962 (Knef 3)
Catfood, 1968 (Wieland 2)
Cathédrale, 1947 (Braunberger 4)
Cathédrale de Chartres. See Chartres, 1923
Catherine, 1927 (Renoir 2)
Catherine, 1964 (Loach 2)
Catherine & Co. See Catherine et Cie, 1975
Catherine and I. See Io e Caterina, 1980
Catherine et Cie, 1975 (Aumont 3)
Catherine, il suffit d'un amour, 1969 (Douy 4)
Catherine the Great, 1934 (Czinner 2, Bergner 3, Fairbanks, D. Jr. 3,
    Biro 4, Korda 4, Krasker 4, Mathieson 4, Périnal 4, Wimperis 4)
Catherine the Great. See Katharina die Grosse, 1920
Catholics, 1973 (Cusack 3, Howard, T. 3, Sheen 3, Fisher 4)
Cathy Come Home, 1966 (Loach 2)
Catlow, 1971 (Brynner 3, Love 3)
Catnip Capers, 1940 (Terry 4)
Catnip Gang, 1949 (Terry 4)

Cats, 1956 (Breer 2)
Cats. See Bastardi, 1968
Cats. See Kattorna, 1965
Cats. See Sons of Satan, 1971
Cats and Bruises, 1965 (Freleng 4)
Cats and Dogs, 1932 (Lantz 4)
Cats A-Weigh, 1953 (McKimson 4)
Cat's Bah, 1955 (Jones 2)
Cat's Cradle, 1959 (Brakhage 2)
Cat's Cradle, 1974 (Driessen 2)
Cat's Eye, 1985 (Cardiff 4)
Cats in the Bag, 1936 (Terry 4)
Cat's Meow, 1924 (Capra 2, Sennett 2, Langdon 3)
Cat's Meow, 1956 (Avery 2)
Cat's Nine Lives, 1927 (Lantz 4)
Cat's Pajamas, 1926 (Wellman 2, Banton 4, Vajda 4)
Cat's Paw, 1914 (Cruze 2)
Cat's Paw, 1934 (Lloyd 3, Merkel 3, Newman 4)
Cat's Revenge, 1954 (Terry 4)
Cat's Tale, 1940 (Freleng 4)
Cat's Tale, 1951 (Terry 4)
Cat's Whiskers, 1923 (Terry 4)
Cat's Whiskers, 1926 (Lantz 4)
Cat's Word of Honor. See Kočičí siovo, 1960
Cat-Tails for Two, 1953 (McKimson 4)
Cattivo soggetto, 1933 (De Sica 2)
Cattle Annie and Little Britches, 1979 (Lancaster 3, Steiger 3)
Cattle Drive, 1951 (McCrea 3)
Cattle Empire, 1958 (McCrea 3)
Cattle, Gold and Oil, 1911 (Dwan 2)
Cattle King, 1963 (Garnett 2, Taylor, R. 3)
Cattle King's Daughter, 1912 (Anderson G. 3)
Cattle Queen of Montana, 1954 (Dwan 2, Elam 3, Reagan 3,
    Stanwyck 3, Alton, J. 4, Estabrook 4, Polglase 4)
Cattle Rustler's End, 1911 (Dwan 2)
Cattle Rustler's Father, 1911 (Anderson G. 3)
Cattle Stampede, 1943 (Crabbe 3)
Cattle Station. See Phantom Stockman, 1953
Cattle Thief, 1936 (Bond 3)
Cattle Thief's Brand, 1911 (Dwan 2)
Cattle Thieves, 1909 (Olcott 2)
Cattle Town, 1952 (McCord 4)
Cattleman's Daughter, 1911 (Anderson G. 3)
Catty Cornered, 1952 (Freleng 4)
Cauchemar du Fantoche, 1908 (Cohl 2)
Caught, 1931 (Arlen 3, Lang 4)
Caught, 1949 (Ophuls 2, Mason 3, Ryan 3, Garmes 4)
Caught by Television. See Trapped by Television, 1936
Caught by Wireless, 1908 (Bitzer 4)
Caught Courting, 1913 (Costello, M. 3)
Caught in a Cabaret, 1914 (Chaplin 2, Sennett 2, Normand 3)
Caught in a Flue, 1914 (Sennett 2, Arbuckle 3)
Caught in a Jam, 1916 (Roach 4)
Caught in a Taxi, 1929 (Sennett 2, Hornbeck 4)
Caught in His Own Net. See Medbejlerens Haevn, 1910
Caught in His Own Trap. See Direktørens Datter, 1912
Caught in the Act, 1912–13 (White 3)
Caught in the Act, 1915 (Sennett 2, Summerville 3)
Caught in the Draft, 1941 (Hope 3, Lamour 3, Dreier 4, Head 4,
    Struss 4, Young, V. 4)
Caught in the End, 1917 (Sutherland 2)
Caught in the Kitchen, 1928 (Sennett 2, Hornbeck 4)
Caught in the Park, 1915 (Sennett 2)
Caught in the Rain, 1914 (Chaplin 2, Sennett 2)
Caught in the Toils. See Hvide Djaevel, 1915
Caught in Tights, 1914 (Sennett 2)
Caught Short, 1930 (Dressler 3, Gibbons 4)
Caught with the Goods, 1911 (Sennett 2, Sennett 2)
Cauldron of Blood. See Coleccionista de cadeveras, 1971
Causa králík, 1979 (Jires 2, Kopecký 3)
Cause commune, 1940 (Cavalcanti 2, Hamer 2)
Cause for Alarm, 1951 (Garnett 2, Young, L. 3, Previn 4,
    Ruttenberg 4)

Cause for Concern, 1974 (Howard, T. 3)
Cause of the Great European War, 1914 (Pearson 2)
Cause toujours . . . tu m'intéresses!, 1979 (Girardot 3)
Cause toujours, mon lapin, 1961 (Constantine 3, Legrand 4)
Cautionary Tale, 1944 (Holloway 3)
Cautiva del recuerdo, 1955 (Figueroa 4)
Cavalcade, 1933 (Brook 3, Grable 3, Behrman 4, Levien 4, Menzies 4)
Cavalcade, 1955 (Coward 4)
Cavalcade d'amour, 1939 (Dauphin 3, Simon, M. 3, Annenkov 4, Aurenche 4, Honegger 4)
Cavalcade des heures, 1943 (Fernandel 3)
Cavalcade of Stars, 1935 (Buchanan 3)
Cavalcade of the Academy Awards, 1940 (Barrymore L. 3, Jolson 3, Wilson, C. 4)
Cavalcade of the Movies. See Film Parade, 1933
Cavalcata ardente, 1927 (Gallone 2)
Cavale, 1971 (Braunberger 4, Douy 4)
Cavaleur, 1978 (Broca 2, Darrieux 3, Girardot 3, Audiard 4, Delerue 4)
Cavalier Lafleur, 1934 (Fernandel 3)
Cavalier of the Streets, 1937 (Havelock-Allan 4)
Cavalier of the West, 1932 (Carey 3)
Cavaliere Costante Nicosia indemontiato ovvero Dracula in Brianza, 1975 (Brazzi 3, Cortese 3)
Cavaliere di ferro. See Conte Ugolino, 1949
Cavaliere misterioso, 1948 (Monicelli 2, Gassman 3)
Cavalieri della regina, 1954 (Bolognini 2)
Cavaliers on the Road. See Motokavalierer, 1950
Cavalleria, 1936 (Magnani 3, Vích 4)
Cavalleria rusticana, 1953 (Gallone 2, Quinn 3, Struss 4)
Cavallina storna, 1956 (Cervi 3, Zavattini 4)
Cavalo de Oxumaire, 1961 (Guerra 2)
Cavalry Command, 1963 (Arlen 3)
Cavalry Scout, 1951 (Mirisch 4)
Cavar un foso, 1966 (Torre-Nilsson 2)
Cave Girl, 1921 (Karloff 3)
Cave In!, 1979 (Milland 3)
Cave Man, 1926 (Loy 3)
Cave Man, 1934 (Iwerks 4)
Cave of Sharks. See Bermuda: la fossa maledetta, 1978
Cave se rebiffe, 1961 (Blier 3, Gabin 3, Rosay 3, Audiard 4, Legrand 4)
Caveman, 1926 (Milestone 2)
Caveman, 1981 (Schifrin 4)
Caveman. See His Prehistoric Past, 1914
Caveman Inki, 1950 (Jones 2)
Cavern, 1965 (Ulmer 2)
Caves du Majestic, 1944 (Spaak 4)
Caves of La Jolla, 1911 (Dwan 2)
Caves of Steel, 1967 (Cushing 3)
Caviar, 1930 (Terry 4)
Cavo olio fludio 220.000 volt, 1959 (Olmi 2)
Caxambu!, 1967 (Ireland 3)
Caza, 1966 (Saura 2)
Cazadores. See Open Season, 1974
Ce cher Victor, 1975 (Blier 3)
Ce cochon de Morin, 1933 (Spaak 4, Wakhévitch 4)
Ce Coquin d'Anatole, 1951 (Modot 3)
Ce corps tant désiré, 1957 (Gélin 3)
Ce monde banal, 1960 (Decaë 4)
Ce n'est pas moi, 1941 (Douy 4)
Ce pays dont les frontières ne sont que fleurs, 1968 (Auric 4)
Ce que je vois dans mon telescope, 1902 (Zecca, 2)
Ce que les flots racontent, 1916 (Gance 2, Burel 4)
Ce que savait Morgan, 1974 (Duras 2)
Ce qu'on dit, ce qu'on pense, 1930 (Brasseur 3)
Ce sacré Amédée. See Bon Voyage Amédée, 1956
Ce sacre grandpère, 1967 (Simon, M. 3)
Ce sacré Amédée. See Bon Voyage Amédée, 1956
C'è sempre un ma, 1942 (Zampa 2, Zavattini 4)
Ce siècle a cinquante ans, 1950 (Cocteau 2, Fresnay 3, Achard 4, Auric 4)
Ce soir . . . le cirque, 1951 (Colpi 4)
Ce soir ou jamais, 1961 (Karina 3)
Cease Fire!, 1953 (Tiomkin 4, Wallis 4)

Cecile est morte, 1943 (Tourneur, M. 2)
Cecilia, 1982 (Granados 3)
Cecilia of the Pink Roses, 1917 (Davies 3)
Cecilia Valdés, 1982 (Solás 2, Villagra 3)
Ceddo, 1977 (Sembene 2)
Ceiling. See Strop, 1962
Ceiling Hero, 1940 (Avery 2)
Ceiling Zero, 1935 (Hawks 2, Cagney 3, O'Brien, P. 3, Brown, Harry Joe 4, Edeson 4, Orry-Kelly 4)
Ceiling Zero, 1936 (Brown, Harry Joe 4)
Cekání na déšt, 1978 (Kachyna 2)
Cela s'appelle l'aurore, 1955 (Buñuel 2, Modot 3, Douy 4, Kosma 4)
Celebrity, 1928 (Garnett 2)
Celebrity Art Portfolio, 1974 (Novak 3)
Celestial Code, 1915 (Walsh 2)
Celimene, Poupee de Montmartre, 1925 (Curtiz 2)
Céline and Julie Go Boating. See Céline et Julie vont en bateau, 1974
Céline et Julie vont en bateau, 1974 (Rivette 2)
Cell 2455, Death Row, 1955 (Wald 4)
Cellbound, 1955 (Avery 2)
Celle qui domine, 1927 (Gallone 2)
Celle qui n'était plus, 1957 (Fradetal 4)
Celluloid et la marbre, 1965 (Rohmer 2)
Cellulose. See Celuloza, 1954
Celui qui doit mourir, 1958 (Dassin 2, Mercouri 3, Auric 4, Douy 4)
Celui qui reste, 1915 (Feuillade 2, Musidora 3)
Celuloza, 1954 (Kawalerowicz 2)
Cementerio de las águilas, 1938 (Negrete 3)
Cena delle beffe, 1941 (Blasetti 2, Castellani 2, Cortese 3)
Cendrillon ou la pantoufle mystérieuse, 1912 (Méliès 2)
Cenpa, 1939 (Alexeieff and Parker 2)
Cent ans de mission, 1948 (Cloquet 4)
Cent Dollars mort ou vif, 1909 (Modot 3)
Cent Francs par second, 1952 (Bourvil 3)
Cent mille dollars au soleil, 1963 (Verneuil 2, Belmondo 3, Blier 3, Audiard 4, Delerue 4)
Cent pour cent, 1957 (Alexeieff and Parker 2)
125, Rue Montmartre, 1959 (Audiard 4)
122 rue de Provence, 1978 (Morricone 4)
Centaurs, c. 1918-21 (McCay 2)
Centennial Summer, 1946 (Preminger 2, Bennett C. 3, Brennan 3, Crain 3, Darnell 3, Gish, D. 3, Wilde 3, Mercer 4, Newman 4, Wheeler 4)
Centinela alerta!, 1936 (Buñuel 2, Grémillon 2)
Cento anni d'amore, 1953 (De Sica 2, Chevalier 3, Fabrizi 3, D'Amico 4)
Centomila dollari, 1940 (Castellani 2)
Centomila dollari per Ringo, 1965 (Morricone 4)
Central Airport, 1933 (Wellman 2, Barthelmess 3, Wayne 3, Orry-Kelly 4)
Central Park, 1932 (Blondell 3, Walthall 3)
Central Region. See Region centrale, 1970-71
Centrales de la mine, 1958 (Delerue 4)
Centre, 1978 (Brakhage 2)
Century Next Door, 1970 (Keach 3)
Century Turns, 1971 (Boone 3)
C'era una volta, 1967 (Rosi 2, Del Rio 3, Loren 3, Sharif 3, Guerra 4, Ponti 4)
C'era una volta Angelo Musco, 1968 (Brazzi 3)
C'era una volta il West, 1968 (Bertolucci 2, Leone 2, Bronson 3, Cardinale 3, Elam 3, Fonda, H. 3, Argento 4, Delli Colli 4, Morricone 4)
Ceramika Ilzecka, 1951 (Wajda 2)
Cerasella, 1959 (Vích 4)
C'eravamo tanto amati, 1974 (De Sica 2, Fellini 2, Scola 2, Fabrizi 3, Gassman 3, Manfredi 3, Mastroianni 3, Age and Scarpelli 4)
Cercasi Gesù, 1982 (Comencini 2)
Cerceau magique, 1908 (Cohl 2)
Cercle des passions, 1982 (Fabian 3, de Almeida 4)
Cercle enchanté, 1955 (Rabier 4)

Cercle rouge, 1970 (Melville 2, Bourvil 3, Delon 3, Montand 3, Volonté 3, Decaë 4)
Cerco, 1970 (de Almeida 4)
Ceremony, 1963 (Harvey 3, Ireland 3, Rey 3, Morris 4)
Ceremony, 1965 (Dovniković 4)
Ceremony. See Gishiki, 1971
Cerf-volant du bout du monde, 1958 (Alekan 4)
Cerná sobota, 1960 (Brdečka 4)
Cerni andělé, 1969 (Danailov 3)
Cernite angeli. See Cerni andělé, 1969
Cerný démant, 1955 (Zeman 2)
Cerný Petr, 1963 (Forman 2, Passer 2)
Černý plamen, 1930 (Stallich 4)
Cerro Pelado, 1966 (Alvarez 2)
Čert nespí, 1957 (Kroner 3)
Certain Monsieur, 1941 (Cloquet 4)
Certain M. Jo, 1957 (Simon, M. 3, Kosma 4)
Certain Rich Man, 1921 (Hersholt 3)
Certain Smile, 1958 (Negulesco 2, Brazzi 3, Fontaine 3, Goodrich and Hackett 4, Krasner 4, Newman 4, Wheeler 4)
Certain Young Man, 1928 (Adorée 3, Novarro 3, Gibbons 4)
Certaines nouvelles, 1976 (Presle 3)
Certo certissimo . . . anzi probabile, 1970 (Cardinale 3)
Certo giorno, 1968 (Olmi 2)
Certosa di Parma. See Chartreuse de Parma, 1947
Certuv mlýn, 1950 (Trnka 2, Pojar 4)
Ceruza és radír, 1960 (Macskássy 4)
Cervantes, 1968 (Jourdan 3, Lollobrigida 3, Rey 3)
Cerveau, 1969 (Belmondo 3, Bourvil 3, Wallach 3, Delerue 4)
Cerveau. See Brain, 1969
Cervená aerovka, 1960 (Hofman 4)
Ces dames aux chapeaux verts, 1929 (Périnal 4)
Ces dames aux chapeaux verts, 1937 (Douy 4, Jaubert 4)
Ces dames preferent le Mambo, 1958 (Constantine 3)
Ces Dames s'en melent, 1965 (Constantine 3)
Ces gens de Paris, 1958 (Braunberger 4)
Ces messieurs de la santé, 1933 (Feuillère 3, Raimu 3, Courant 4, Douy 4)
César, 1936 (Pagnol 2, Fresnay 3, Raimu 3)
Cesar and Rosalie. See César et Rosalie, 1972
César et Rosalie, 1972 (Lenica 2, Sautet 2, Huppert 3, Montand 3, Sarde 4)
Cesare Zavattini e il 'Campo di grano dei corvi' di Van Gogh, 1972 (Zavattini 4)
Cesarée, 1978 (Duras 2)
Cessez le feu, 1934 (Honegger 4)
Cest a sláva, 1969 (Hrušínský 3)
C'est arrivé à Paris, 1952 (Audiard 4)
C'est dur pour tout le monde, 1975 (Blier 3)
C'est l'aviron, 1944 (McLaren 2)
C'est le printemps, 1916 (Feuillade 2)
C'est Papa qui prend la purge, 1906 (Feuillade 2)
C'est pas parce qu'on a rien à dire qu'il fermer sa gueule, 1974 (Blier 3)
C'est pour les orphelins!, 1917 (Musidora 3)
Cesta do hlubin studákovy duse, 1939 (Hrušínský 3)
Cesta do Prahy Vincence Moštek a Simona Pešla z Vlčnova l.p. 1969, 1969 (Jires 2)
Cesta do pravěku, 1955 (Zeman 2)
Cesta duga godinu dana, 1958 (De Santis 2, Petri 2, Guerra 4)
Cesta k barikádám, 1945 (Stallich 4)
Cet homme est dangereux, 1953 (Constantine 3, D'Eaubonne 4)
Cet obscur objet de désir, 1977 (Buñuel 2, Carrière 4)
C'était moi. See Ernest le rebelle, 1938
C'était un jour commes les autres, 1970 (Cloquet 4)
C'était un musicien, 1933 (Bresson 2)
C'était un Québécois en Bretagne, madame!, 1977 (Perrault 2)
Cette nuit-là, 1958 (Burel 4)
Cette sacrée gamine, 1955 (Auer 3, Bardot 3, Fabian 3)
Cette vieille canaille, 1933 (Litvak 2, Baur 3, Andrejew 4, Courant 4)
Ceux de chez nous, 1915 (Guitry 3)
Ceux du ballon rond, 1948 (Fradetal 4)
Ceux du deuxième bureau. See Homme à abattre, 1937
Ceux du rail, 1942 (Clément 2, Alekan 4)

Cézanne. See Art Works one: Academic Still Life, 1977
Chacal de Nahueltoro, 1969 (Littin 2, Villagra 3)
Chacals, 1917 (Musidora 3)
Cha-Cha-Cha Boom!, 1956 (Katzman 4)
Chaco Legacy, 1978 (Keach 3)
Chacun sa chance, 1931 (Gabin 3)
Chad Hanna, 1940 (King 2, Carradine 3, Darnell 3, Darwell 3, Fonda, H. 3, Lamour 3, Banton 4, Day 4, Johnson 4, Zanuck 4)
Chadwick Family, 1974 (MacMurray 3)
Chagall, 1953 (Braunberger 4, Kosma 4)
Chagell, 1963 (Price 3)
Chagrin d'amour, 1901 (Zecca, 2)
Chagrin et la pitié, 1969 (Ophuls 2)
Chai, 1924 (Ermler 2)
Chaim—to Life!, 1974 (Wallach 3)
Chain Gang, 1950 (Katzman 4)
Chain Letters, 1935 (Terry 4)
Chain Lightning, 1950 (Bogart 3, Massey 3, Haller 4, Veiller 4)
Chain Reaction, 1971 (Dinov 4)
Chain Reaction, 1980 (Miller 2)
Chained, 1934 (Brown 2, Crawford, J. 3, Gable 3, Rooney 3, Wynn 3, Mahin 4, Stothart 4, Stromberg 4)
Chaines, 1910 (Cohl 2)
Chaines. See Geschlecht in Fesseln—Die Sexualnot der Gefangenen, 1928
Chaînes d'or. See Anneaux d'or, 1956
Chains, 1912 (Bushman 3)
Chains of Evidence, 1920 (Brenon 2)
Chair, 1962 (Leacock 2)
Chair, 1963 (Kuri 4)
Chair, 1967 (Dunning 4)
Chair de l'orchidée, 1974 (Cortese 3, Feuillère 3, Signoret 3, Valli 3, Carrière 4)
Chair de poule, 1963 (Duvivier 2, Burel 4, Delerue 4)
Chair et le diable, 1953 (Auric 4, Wakhévitch 4)
Chair et le diable. See Fuco nelle vene, 1953
Chairman, 1969 (Maddow 3)
Chairman. See Most Dangerous Man in the World, 1969
Chairy Tale, 1957 (Jutra 2, McLaren 2, Shankar 4)
Chaise à porteurs enchantée, 1905 (Méliès 2)
Chakkari fujin to ukkari fujin, 1952 (Kagawa 3)
Chakra, 1981 (Patil 3)
Chalachitra, 1981 (Sen 2)
Chaleur du foyer, 1955 (Auric 4)
Chaleur du sein, 1938 (Arletty 3, Simon, M. 3)
Chaliapin, 1972 (Donskoi 2)
Chalice of Sorrow, 1916 (Ingram 2)
Chalis Baba Ek Chor, 1954 (Burman 4)
Chaliya, 1960 (Kapoor 2)
Chalk Garden. 1964 (Evans 3, Kerr 3, Mills 3, Arnold 4, Dillon 4, Hayes 4, Hunter 4)
Chalk Line, 1972 (Emshwiller 2)
Chalk Marks, 1924 (Walker 4)
Challenge, 1922 (Fleischer, M. and D. 2)
Challenge, 1938 (Korda 4, Krasker 4, Périnal 4)
Challenge, 1960 (Quayle 3)
Challenge, 1970 (Crawford, B. 3, Lukas 3, Smith, J.M. 4)
Challenge, 1982 (Frankenheimer 2, Mifune 3, Goldsmith 4, Sayles 4)
Challenge. See It Takes a Thief, 1960
Challenge. See Sfida, 1958
Challenge: A Tribute to Modern Art, 1976 (Kline 2)
Challenge of Greatness, 1976 (Welles 2)
Challenge of the Mackennas. See Sfida dei Mackenna, 1970
Challenge—Science Against Cancer, 1950 (Massey 3)
Challenge to Be Free, 1975 (Garnett 2)
Challenge to Lassie, 1949 (Crisp 3, Gwenn 3, Previn 4)
Challenge to Live. See Ai to honoho to, 1961
Challenge to Live. See 'Chosen' yoi: Ali to honoo to, 1961
Challenger. See Lady and Gent, 1932
Challengers, 1970 (Baxter A. 3, Mineo 3)
Chalti Ka Naam Gaddi, 1958 (Burman 4)
Chamade, 1968 (Deneuve 3, Piccoli 3)
Chambara fufu, 1930 (Naruse 2)

Chamber Harmony. *See* Komorní harmonie, 1963
Chamber of Horrors, 1966 (Curtis 3)
Chamberlain. *See* Kammarjunkaren, 1914
Chambre, 1964 (Cloquet 4)
Chambre, 1972 (Akerman 2)
Chambre ardente, 1962 (Duvivier 2, Auric 4, Spaak 4)
Chambre blanche, 1969 (Lefebvre 2)
Chambre de bonne, 1970 (Braunberger 4)
Chambre en ville, 1982 (Demy 2, Piccoli 3, Sanda 3, Evein 4)
Chambre obscure. *See* Laughter in the Dark, 1969
Chambre 34, 1945 (Braunberger 4)
Chambre verte, 1978 (Truffaut 2, Baye 3, Almendros 4)
Champ, 1931 (Vidor, K. 2, Beery 3, Cooper, J 3, Marion 4, Terry 4)
Champ, 1979 (Zeffirelli 2, Blondell 3, Cook 3, Dunaway 3,
    Martin, S. 3, Voight 3, Warden 3)
Champ du possible, 1962 (Delerue 4)
Champagne, 1928 (Hitchcock 2, Balfour 3)
Champagne Charlie, 1944 (Cavalcanti 2, Holloway 3, Balcon 4,
    Clarke, T.E.B. 4)
Champagne Charlie. *See* Night Out, 1915 (Chaplin 2)
Champagne for Caesar, 1950 (Colman 3, Price 3, Tiomkin 4)
Champagne Murders. *See* Scandale, 1967
Champagne Safari, 1951 (Hayworth 3)
Champagne Waltz, 1937 (Sutherland 2, Wilder 2, MacMurray 3,
    Banton 4, Prinz 4, Young, V. 4)
Champeen, 1922 (Roach 4)
Champignon, 1969 (Valli 3)
Champion, 1913 (Sennett 2, Normand 3)
Champion, 1915 (Bacon 2, Chaplin 2, Anderson G. 3, Purviance 3)
Champion, 1949 (Kramer, S. 2, Robson 2, Douglas, K. 3,
    Kennedy, A. 3, Foreman 4, Planer 4, Tiomkin 4)
Champion du jeu à la mode, 1910 (Cohl 2)
Champion of Justice, 1944 (Terry 4)
Champions, 1983 (Hurt, J. 3, Johnson, B. 3)
Champions: A Love Story, 1979 (Alonzo 4)
Champions juniors, 1950 (Fradetal 4, Kosma 4)
Champs-Elysées, 1928 (Kaufman 4)
Chamsin, 1972 (Schell, Maria 3)
Chance, 1931 (Rosay 3)
Chance at Heaven, 1933 (McCrea 3, Rogers, G. 3, Cooper 4,
    Musuraca 4, Plunkett 4, Polglase 4, Steiner 4)
Chance Deception, 1912 (Griffith 2, Sweet 3, Bitzer 4)
Chance et l'amour, 1964 (Chabrol 2, Tavernier 2, Blier 3, Chevalier 3,
    Piccoli 3, de Beauregard 4)
Chance Meeting. *See* Blind Date, 1959
Chance Meeting. *See* Young Lovers, 1954
Chance Meeting on the Ocean. *See* Spotkanie na Atlantyku, 1979
Chance of a Lifetime, 1950 (More 3)
Chance of a Night Time, 1931 (Wilcox 2)
Chance Shot, 1912 (Lawrence 3)
Chances, 1931 (Dwan 2, Fairbanks, D. Jr. 3, Haller 4, Young, W. 4)
Chandi Sona, 1977 (Kapoor 2)
Chandidas, 1932 (Sircar 4)
Chandler, 1971 (Caron 3, Grahame 3, Oates 3)
Chandu the Magician, 1932 (Lugosi 3, Walthall 3, Howe 4, Menzies 4)
Chanel solitaire, 1981 (Black 3, Caron 3)
Chang, 1927 (Schoedsack 2, Cooper 4)
Change, 1974 (Schell, Maria 3)
Change in Baggage, 1914 (Bunny 3)
Change of Habit, 1969 (Presley 3)
Change of Heart, 1909 (Griffith 2, Bitzer 4)
Change of Heart, 1934 (Auer 3, Darwell 3, Gaynor 3, Rogers, G. 3,
    Temple 3, Friedhofer 4, Hoffenstein 4, Levien 4)
Change of Heart, 1938 (Darwell 3)
Change of Heart. *See* Two and Two Make Six, 1962
Change of Seasons, 1980 (Hopkins, A. 3, MacLaine 3)
Change of Spirit, 1912 (Griffith 2, Sweet 3, Walthall 3)
Change the Needle, 1925 (Roach 4)
Changeling, 1979 (Douglas, M. 3, Scott, G. 3)
Changes for the Better, 1948 (Holloway 3)
Changes in the Village. *See* Gamperaliya, 1964
Changing Earth. *See* Ont staan en vergaan, 1954
Changing Husbands, 1924 (Boyd 3, Pitts 3, Glennon 4)

Channel Crossing, 1933 (Bruce 3, Gwenn 3, Junge 4)
Channel Incident, 1940 (Asquith 2)
Channing of the Northwest, 1922 (Shearer 3)
Chanson d'armor, 1934 (Epstein 2)
Chanson de gestes, 1966 (Braunberger 4)
Chanson de Roland, 1978 (Kinski 3)
Chanson de rue, 1945 (Decaë 4)
Chanson des peupliers, 1931 (Epstein 2)
Chanson du pavé, 1951 (Colpi 4)
Chanson du souvenir, 1936 (Sirk 2)
Chanson d'une nuit, 1932 (Clouzot 2, Brasseur 3)
Chanson d'une nuit. *See* Lied einer Nacht, 1932
Chansons de Paris, 1934 (Barsacq 4)
Chansons s'envolent, 1947–51 (Verneuil 2)
Chant de l'amour, 1935 (D'Eaubonne 4)
Chant des ondes, 1943 (Leenhardt 2)
Chant du départ. *See* Desert Song, 1943
Chant du marin, 1932 (Gallone 2, Planer 4)
Chant du monde, 1965 (Deneuve 3, Vanel 3)
Chant du Styrène, 1958 (Resnais 2, Braunberger 4, Delerue 4)
Chantelouve, 1921 (Boyer 3)
Chanteur de Mexico, 1956 (Bourvil 3)
Chanteur de minuit, 1937 (Matras 4, Renoir 4, Wakhévitch 4)
Chanteur de Seville, 1930 (Novarro 3)
Chanteur inconnu, 1931 (Clouzot 2, Simon, S. 3, Courant 4,
    Wakhévitch 4)
Chanteur inconnu, 1947 (Cayatte 2, Barsacq 4)
Chantier en ruines, 1945 (Leenhardt 2)
Chantons sous l'Occupation, 1976 (Rouch 2, Colpi 4)
Chants populaires, 1943–46 (Dunning 4)
Chants retrouvés, 1948 (Colpi 4)
Chaos. *See* Kaos, 1984
Chapayev, 1934 (Vasiliev 2, Babochkin 3)
Chapayev is with Us, 1941 (Gerasimov 2)
Chapayev Is with Us. *See* Chapayev s nami, 1941
Chapayev s nami, 1941 (Babochkin 3)
Chapeau. *See* Coup de vent, 1905
Chapeau de paille d'Italie, 1927 (Clair 2, Tschechowa 3, Meerson 4)
Chapeau de paille d'Italie, 1940 (Fernandel 3)
Chapeau-Claqué, 1909 (Linders 3)
Chapeaux à transformations, 1895 (Lumière 2)
Chapeaux des belles dames, 1909 (Cohl 2)
Chaperon, 1916 (Van Dyke, W.S. 2)
Chaplin Revue, 1959 (Chaplin 2)
Chapman Report, 1962 (Cukor 2, Bloom 3, Fonda, J. 3, Winters 3,
    Orry-Kelly 4, Rosenman 4)
Chappaqua, 1966 (Barrault 3, Schufftan 4, Shankar 4)
Chapter in Her Life, 1923 (Weber 2)
Chapter Two, 1979 (Caan 3, Booth 4, Stark 4)
Chaque jour à son secret, 1957 (Fabian 3)
Char Ankhen, 1944 (Biswas 4)
Char Dil Char Rahen, 1959 (Kapoor 2, Biswas 4)
Charade, 1953 (Mason 3, Biroc 4)
Charade, 1963 (Donen 2, Coburn, J. 3, Grant, C. 3, Hepburn, A. 3,
    Kennedy, G. 3, Matthau 3, D'Eaubonne 4, Lang 4, Mancini 4,
    Mercer 4)
Charandas Chor, 1975 (Benegal 2, Nihalani 4)
Charandas the Thief. *See* Charandas Chor, 1975
Charcuterie mécanique, 1895 (Lumière 2)
Charcutier de Machonville, 1946 (Decaë 4, Fradetal 4)
Charge at Feather River, 1953 (Steiner 4)
Charge Is Murder. *See* Twilight of Honor, 1963
Charge of the Gauchos, 1928 (Bushman 3, Musuraca 4)
Charge of the Lancers, 1954 (Aumont 3, Goddard 3, Katzman 4)
Charge of the Light Brigade, 1936 (Curtiz 2, Bruce 3, Crisp 3,
    De Havilland 3, Flynn 3, Niven 3, Canutt 4, Eason 4, Friedhofer 4,
    Polito 4, Steiner 4, Wallis 4)
Charge of the Light Brigade, 1968 (Richardson 2, Gielgud 3,
    Howard, T. 3, Redgrave, V. 3, Addison 4, Watkin 4,
    Williams, R. 4)
Charing Cross Road, 1935 (Mills 3)
Chariot de Thespis, 1941 (Alekan 4)
Chariots of Fire, 1981 (Anderson 2, Gielgud 3, Vangelis 4, Watkin 4)

Charité, 1927 (Vanel 3)
Charité du prestidigitateur, 1905 (Guy 2)
Charlatan, 1901 (Méliès 2)
Charlatan. *See* Kuruzslo, 1917
Charlemagne, 1933 (Raimu 3, Douy 4)
Charles and Diana: A Royal Love Story, 1982 (Addison 4)
Charles, Dead or Alive. *See* Charles mort ou vif, 1969
Charles mort ou vif, 1969 (Tanner 2)
Charleston, 1979 (Bernstein 4)
Charleston. *See* Sur un air de Charleston, 1927
Charleston Chain Gang, 1902 (Porter 2)
Charleston-Parade. *See* Sur un air de Charleston, 1927
Charley series, 1946–47 (Halas and Batchelor 2)
Charley and the Angel, 1973 (MacMurray 3)
Charley My Boy, 1926 (McCarey 2, Roach 4)
Charley Varrick, 1973 (Siegel 2, Matthau 3, Schifrin 4)
Charley's American Aunt. *See* Charley's Aunt, 1941
Charley's Aunt, 1915 (Hardy 3)
Charley's Aunt, 1941 (Seaton 2, Baxter A. 3, Francis, K. 3, Gwenn 3,
    Banton 4, Day 4, Newman 4)
Charley's Tante, 1934 (Rasp 3)
Charlie and the Sausages. *See* Mabel's Busy Day, 1914
Charlie and the Umbrella. *See* Between Showers, 1914
Charlie at the Races. *See* Gentleman of Nerve, 1914
Charlie at the Studio. *See* Film Johnnie, 1914
Charlie Bubbles, 1967 (Finney 3, Minnelli 3)
Charlie Cann in Reno, 1939 (Summerville 3)
Charlie Chan and the Curse of the Dragon Queen, 1981 (Dickinson 3,
    Grant, L. 3, McDowall 3, Roberts 3, Ustinov 3)
Charlie Chan at Monte Carlo, 1938 (Oland 3)
Charlie Chan at the Circus, 1936 (Oland 3)
Charlie Chan at the Olympics, 1937 (Oland 3, Miller, V. 4)
Charlie Chan at the Opera, 1936 (Karloff 3, Oland 3, Meredyth 4)
Charlie Chan at the Race Track, 1936 (Oland 3)
Charlie Chan at the Wax Museum, 1940 (Day 4, Miller, V. 4)
Charlie Chan at Treasure Island, 1939 (Day 4, Miller, V. 4)
Charlie Chan Carries On, 1931 (Brent 3, Oland 3)
Charlie Chan in Egypt, 1935 (Fetchit 3, Hayworth 3, Oland 3)
Charlie Chan in Honolulu, 1938 (Clarke, C.C. 4, Day 4)
Charlie Chan in London, 1934 (Milland 3, Oland 3)
Charlie Chan in Panama, 1940 (Day 4, Miller, V. 4)
Charlie Chan in Paris, 1935 (Oland 3)
Charlie Chan in Reno, 1939 (Miller, V. 4)
Charlie Chan in Rio, 1941 (Day 4)
Charlie Chan in Shanghai, 1935 (Oland 3)
Charlie Chan in the City of Darkness, 1939 (Carroll L. 3, Chaney Lon,
    Jr. 3, Miller, V. 4)
Charlie Chan on Broadway, 1937 (Chaney Lon, Jr. 3, Oland 3)
Charlie Chan's Chance, 1932 (Oland 3, August 4)
Charlie Chan's Courage, 1934 (Oland 3, Miller, S. 4)
Charlie Chan's Greatest Case, 1933 (Oland 3)
Charlie Chan's Murder Cruise, 1940 (Carroll L. 3, Miller, V. 4)
Charlie Chan's Secret, 1936 (Oland 3, Maté 4)
Charlie Chaplin's Burlesque on Carmen. *See* Carmen, 1916
Charlie Cobb: Nice Night for a Hanging, 1977 (Bellamy 3)
Charlie et ses deux nénettes, 1973 (Sarde 4)
Charlie McCarthy, Detective, 1939 (Calhern 3, Cummings 3)
Charlie on the Ocean. *See* Shanghaied, 1915
Charlie on the Spree. *See* In the Park, 1915
Charlie the Burglar. *See* Police!, 1916
Charlie the Hobo. *See* Tramp, 1915
Charlie the Sailor. *See* Shanghaied, 1915
Charlie's Day Out. *See* By the Sea, 1915
Charlie's Recreation. *See* Tango Tangles, 1914
Charlotte. *See* Jeune Fille assassinée, 1974
Charlotte and Her Steak. *See* Présentation ou Charlotte et son steak,
    1951
Charlotte et son Jules, 1958 (Cocteau 2, Godard 2, Belmondo 3,
    Braunberger 4)
Charlotte et Véronique, 1957 (Godard 2)
Charlotte Lowenskjold, 1930 (Molander 2, Jaenzon 4)
Charlotte Lowenskold. *See* Charlotte Lowenskjold,
    1930

Charlotte's Web, 1972 (Moorehead 3, Reynolds, D. 3, Hanna and
    Barbera 4)
Charly, 1968 (Bloom 3, Robertson 3, Shankar 4)
Charm of Life, 1953 (Harrison 3)
Charm School, 1920 (Cruze 2, Reid 3)
Charm School. *See* Collegiate, 1936
Charmant FrouFrou, 1901 (Guy 2)
Charmants garçons, 1957 (Broca 2, Gélin 3, Legrand 4, Spaak 4)
**Charme discret de la bourgeoisie, 1972 (Buñuel 2, Audran 3, Cassel 3,
    Piccoli 3, Rey 3, Seyrig 3, Carrière 4)**
Charmer, 1915 (Johnson, N. 3)
Charmer, 1925 (Olcott 2, Negri 3, Howe 4)
Charmer. *See* Moonlight Sonata, 1937
Charmes de l'existence, 1949 (Grémillon 2)
Charming Sinners, 1929 (Arzner 2, Brook 3, Powell, W. 3, Banton 4)
Charrette fantôme, 1939 (Duvivier 2, Epstein 2, Fresnay 3, Jouvet 3,
    Ibert 4)
Charro!, 1969 (Presley 3)
Charro negro, 1940 (Armendáriz 3)
Chartres, 1923 (Grémillon 2, Périnal 4)
Chartreuse de Parme, 1948 (Christian-Jaque 2, Philipe 3, Annenkov 4,
    D'Eaubonne 4)
**Charulata, 1964 (Ray, S. 2, Chatterjee 3, Chandragupta 4, Datta 4,
    Mitra 4)**
Chase, 1913 (Dwan 2)
Chase, 1946 (Cummings 3, Lorre 3, Morgan 3, Planer 4)
Chase, 1966 (Penn 2, Brando 3, Dickinson 3, Duvall, R. 3, Fonda, J. 3,
    Hopkins, M. 3, Redford 3, Barry 4, Day 4, La Shelle 4, Spiegel 4)
Chase. *See* Caza, 1966
Chase a Crooked Shadow, 1957 (Baxter A. 3, Fairbanks, D. Jr. 3)
Chase after Adam. *See* Pogón za Adamem, 1970
Chase for the Golden Needles. *See* Golden Needles, 1974
Chased by Bloodhounds, 1912 (Bunny 3)
Chaser, 1928 (Langdon 3)
Chaser, 1938 (Stone 3, Turner, L. 3)
Chasers. *See* Dragueurs, 1959
Chases of Pimple Street, 1935 (Roach 4)
Chashar Meye, 1931 (Sircar 4)
Chasing Danger, 1939 (Miller, V. 4)
Chasing Rainbows, 1930 (Dressler 3, Love 3, Gibbons 4, Meredyth 4)
Chasing the Chaser, 1925 (Roach 4)
Chasing the Limited, 1915 (Furthman 4)
Chasing the Moon, 1922 (Mix 3)
Chasing Yesterday, 1935 (Plunkett 4)
Chasse à l'hippopotame, 1946 (Rouch 2)
Chasse à l'homme, 1964 (Belmondo 3, Blier 3, Deneuve 3, Presle 3,
    Audiard 4)
Chasse au cambrioleur, 1903–04 (Guy 2)
Chasse au lion à l'arc, 1965 (Rouch 2, Braunberger 4)
Chassé-croisé, 1931 (Fradetal 4)
Chasseur, 1970 (Reichenbach 2, Braunberger 4)
Chasseur de chez Maxim's, 1927 (Meerson 4)
Chasseurs de lions, 1913 (Feuillade 2)
Chaste Suzanne, 1937 (Raimu 3, D'Eaubonne 4)
Chastity, 1923 (Schulberg 4)
Chastity Belt. *See* Cintura di castita, 1967
Chastnaia zhizn, 1982 (Ulyanov 3)
Chat, 1971 (Gabin 3, Signoret 3, Sarde 4)
Chat botte, 1903 (Zecca 2)
Chat et la souris, 1975 (Lelouch 2, Aumont 3, Morgan 3, Reggiani 3,
    Lai 4)
Chateau de la peur, 1912 (Feuillade 2)
Château de rêve, 1933 (Clouzot 2, Darrieux 3)
Château de verre, 1950 (Clément 2, Marais 3, Morgan 3, Barsacq 4,
    Bost 4)
Chateau des amants maudits. *See* Beatrice Cenci, 1956
Château du passé, 1958 (Decaë 4, Rabier 4)
Château en Suède, 1963 (Vadim 2, Jurgens 3, Trintignant 3, Vitti 3)
Châteaux de France, 1940 (Resnais 2)
Châteaux en Espagne, 1953 (Darrieux 3)
Chateaux stop . . . sur la Loire, 1962 (Delerue 4)
Châtelaine du Liban, 1926 (Modot 3)
Chatelaine du Liban, 1933 (Epstein 2, Matras 4)

Chatollets Hemmelighed, 1913 (Dreyer 2)
Chato's Land, 1971 (Bronson 3, Palance 3)
Chatpatee, 1983 (Patil 3)
Chatte, 1958 (Wicki 2, Blier 3, Kosma 4)
Chatte métamorphosée en femme, 1909 (Feuillade 2)
Chatte sort ses griffes, 1959 (Kosma 4)
Chatte sur un doigt brûlant, 1974 (Dalio 3)
Chatterbox, 1936 (Ball 3, Plunkett 4)
Chatterbox, 1943 (Brown 3)
Chaudron infernal, 1903 (Méliès 2)
Chaudronnier, 1949 (Fradetal 4)
Chauncey Explains, 1905 (Bitzer 4)
Chaussette, 1906 (Guy 2)
Chaussette surprise, 1978 (Dalio 3, Karina 3, Carrière 4)
Chaussures matrimoniales, 1909 (Cohl 2)
Che!, 1969 (Fleischer, R. 2, Palance 3, Sharif 3, Schifrin 4,
    Smith, J.M. 4, Wilson, M. 4)
Che?, 1972 (Mastroianni 3, Ponti 4)
Che?. See What?, 1972
Che, Buenos Aires, 1962 (Birri 2)
Che c'entriamo noi con la rivoluzione?, 1972 (Gassman 3, Morricone 4)
Che distinta famiglia, 1943 (Cervi 3)
Che gioia vivere, 1961 (Clément 2, Cervi 3, Delon 3, Bost 4, Decaë 4)
'Che' Guevara, 1968 (Ireland 3)
Che si dice a Roma, 1979 (Scola 2)
Che Tempi!, 1948 (Sordi 3)
Cheap, 1974 (Corman 4)
Cheap Detective, 1978 (Falk 3, Williamson 3, Alonzo 4, Booth 4,
    Houseman 4, Stark 4)
Cheap Kisses, 1924 (Hersholt 3, Sullivan 4)
Cheaper by the Dozen, 1950 (Crain 3, Loy 3, Webb 3, Lemaire 4,
    Shamroy 4, Trotti 4, Wheeler 4)
Cheaper to Marry, 1925 (Fazenda 3, Stone 3, Gibbons 4)
Cheat, 1915 (DeMille 2, Hayakawa 3, Buckland 4)
Cheat, 1923 (Negri 3, Miller, A. 4)
Cheat. See Manèges, 1950
Cheated Hearts, 1921 (Baxter W. 3, Karloff 3, Miller, V. 4)
Cheated Love, 1921 (Glennon 4, Levien 4)
Cheater, 1920 (Valentino 3)
Cheater Reformed, 1921 (Furthman 4)
Cheaters, 1934 (Beavers 3, Boyd 3)
Cheaters, 1945 (Burke 3, Schildkraut 3)
Cheaters. See Tricheurs, 1958
Cheating Cheaters, 1919 (Dwan 2, Nilsson 3, Edeson 4)
Cheating Cheaters, 1934 (Wray 3)
Check and Double Check, 1930 (Crosby 3, Steiner 4)
Check Your Baggage, 1918 (Roach 4)
Checkered Flag or Crash, 1978 (Sarandon 3)
Checkers, 1937 (Merkel 3)
Checkmate, 1912 (Dwan 2)
Checkmate, 1935 (Pearson 2, Havelock-Allan 4)
Checkpoint, 1956 (Baker S. 3, Dillon 4)
Checkpoint Charley. See Warum die Ufos unseren Salat klauen, 1980
Cheech and Chong's Next Movie, 1980 (Whitlock 4)
Cheech & Chong's Nice Dreams, 1981 (Keach 3)
Cheer Boys Cheer, 1939 (Gwenn 3, Balcon 4)
Cheer Up and Smile, 1930 (Wayne 3)
Cheerful Alley. See Yokina uramachi, 1939
Cheerful Canary. See Vessiolaia Kanaireika, 1929
Cheerful Givers, 1917 (Love 3)
Cheering a Husband, 1914 (Beery 3)
Cheering Town. See Kanko no machi, 1944
Cheers for Miss Bishop, 1941 (Garnett 2, Farnum 3, Gwenn 3)
Cheers of the Crowd, 1935 (Krasner 4)
Cheese Chasers, 1951 (Jones 2)
Cheese It, The Cat!, 1957 (McKimson 4)
Cheese Special, 1913 (Fazenda 3)
Chef at Circle G, 1915 (Mix 3)
Chef schickt seinen besten Mann. See Requiem per un agent segreto,
    1967
Chef-lieu de Canton, 1911 (Feuillade 2)
Chefs d'oeuvres de Bébé, 1910 (Cohl 2)
Chefs de demain, 1944 (Clément 2, Alekan 4)

Chelovek, drama nachidnya, 1912 (Mozhukin 3)
Chelovek iz restorana, 1929 (Golovnya 4)
Chelovek niotkuda, 1961 (Gurchenko 3)
Chelovek No. 217, 1944 (Romm 2)
Chelovek s drugoi storoni, 1972 (Andersson B. 3, Tikhonov 3)
Chelovek s kinoapparatom, 1929 (Vertov 2)
Chelovek s ruzhyom, 1938 (Yutkevich 2, Cherkassov 3,
    Shostakovich 4)
Chelsea Girls, 1966 (Warhol 2)
Chemin de bonheur, 1933 (Kaufman 4)
Chemin de Damas, 1952 (Simon, M. 3, Schufftan 4)
Chemin de l'honneur, 1939 (Brasseur 3)
Chemin de la terre, 1962 (Delerue 4)
Chemin de Rio, 1937 (Aumont 3, Jeanson 4)
Chemin de Rio. See Cargaison blanche, 1937
Chemin d'Ernoa, 1921 (Delluc 2, Francis, E. 3)
Chemin des écoliers, 1959 (Bourvil 3, Delon 3, Aurenche 4, Barsacq 4,
    Bost 4, Matras 4)
Chemin du paradis, 1930 (Planer 4)
Chemin perdu, 1979 (Seyrig 3, Vanel 3, Vierny 4)
Chemins de Katmandou, 1969 (Cayatte 2)
Chemins de l'exil ou Les Dernières Années de Jean-Jacques Rousseau,
    1978 (Goretta 2)
Chemist, 1936 (Keaton 2)
Cher Inconnu, 1981 (Seyrig 3, Signoret 3, Cloquet 4, Evein 4, Sarde 4)
Cher Victor, 1975 (Valli 3)
Cher vieux Paris!, 1950 (Decaë 4)
Cherchez la femme, 1921 (Curtiz 2)
Chère Louise, 1972 (Broca 2, Moreau 3, Delerue 4)
Chères vieilles choses, 1957 (Colpi 4, Delerue 4)
Chéri Bibi, 1954 (Auric 4)
Cheri de sa concierge, 1934 (Fernandel 3)
Chéri-Bibi, 1938 (Aumont 3, Dalio 3, Fresnay 3)
Chernyi barak, 1933 (Maretskaya 3)
Cherokee Kid, 1927 (Musuraca 4)
Cherokee Strip, 1940 (Head 4)
Cherokee Uprising, 1950 (Cody 3)
Cherry Blossom Chorus. See Sakura Ondo, 1934
Cherry Blossoms, 1971–73 (Brocka 2)
Cheryomushki, 1963 (Shostakovich 4)
Chess Fever. See Shakhmatnaya goryachka, 1925
Chess Player. See Joueur d'échecs, 1938
Chess Players, 1977 (Attenborough 3)
Chess Players. See Shatranj Ke Khilari, 1977
Chess-nuts, 1932 (Fleischer, M. and D. 2)
Chesty: A Tribute to a Legend, 1970 (Ford, J. 2, Wayne 3)
Chetniks!, 1943 (Day 4, Friedhofer 4)
Chetyre vizity Samuelya Vulfa, 1934 (Maretskaya 3)
Chev, 1974 (Yankovsky 3)
Cheval d'orgueil, 1980 (de Beauregard 4, Rabier 4)
Chevalier de Gaby, 1920 (Modot 3)
Chevalier de Ménilmontant, 1953 (Chevalier 3)
Chevalier des neiges, 1912 (Méliès 2)
Chevaliers de la nuit. See Ritter der Nacht, 1928
Chevaux d'acier. See Moissons d'aujourd'hui, 1949
Chevaux de Vaugirard, 1961 (Delerue 4)
Chevaux du Vercors, 1942 (Alekan 4)
Cheveaux d'Hollywood, 1964 (Reichenbach 2)
Chevelure, 1961 (Piccoli 3)
Chèvre, 1961 (Fradetal 4)
Chèvre, 1981 (Depardieu 3)
Chèvre d'or, 1942 (Bost 4)
Chewin' Bruin, 1940 (Clampett 4)
Cheyenne, 1929 (Brown, Harry Joe 4)
Cheyenne, 1947 (Walsh 2, Kennedy, A. 3, Wyman 3, Buckner 4,
    Friedhofer 4, Steiner 4)
Cheyenne Autumn, 1964 (Ford, J. 2, Baker C. 3, Carradine 3,
    Del Rio 3, Johnson, B. 3, Kennedy, A. 3, Malden 3, Marsh 3,
    Mineo 3, Robinson, E. 3, Stewart 3, Widmark 3, Clothier 4, Day 4,
    North 4)
Cheyenne Cyclone, 1932 (Canutt 4)
Cheyenne Kid, 1933 (Musuraca 4, Steiner 4)
Cheyenne Rides Again, 1937 (Chaney Lon, Jr. 3)

Cheyenne Roundup, 1943 (Salter 4)
Cheyenne Social Club, 1970 (Fonda, H. 3, Jones S. 3, Kelly, Gene 3, Stewart 3, Clothier 4)
Cheyenne's Pal, 1917 (Ford, J. 2)
Chez le magnétiseur, 1897–98 (Guy 2)
Chez le Maréchal-Ferrant, 1899–1900 (Guy 2)
Chez le photographe, 1900 (Guy 2)
Chhota Bhai, 1949 (Sircar 4)
Chhoti Chhoti Baten, 1965 (Biswas 4)
Chhou Dance of Puralia, 1970 (Ghatak 4)
Chhupa Rustom, 1973 (Anand 3, Burman 4)
Chi dice donna dice . . . donna, 1975 (Audran 3, Fabian 3)
Chi è senza peccato, 1952 (Rosay 3)
Chi l'ha vista morire?, 1972 (Morricone 4)
Chi l'ha visto?, 1942 (Fellini 2, Cortese 3, Sordi 3)
Chi legge? Viaggio lungo il Tirreno, 1960 (Zavattini 4)
Chi ni somuku mono, 1929 (Hasegawa 3)
Chi to rei, 1923 (Mizoguchi 2)
Chi to suna, 1965 (Mifune 3)
Chiamavano Cosetta, 1917 (Gallone 2)
Chiave, 1983 (Morricone 4)
Chica del lunes, 1966 (Torre-Nilsson 2, Kennedy, A. 3)
Chica del molino rojo, 1973 (Ferrer, M. 3)
Chicago, 1927 (Adrian 4, Coffee 4)
Chicago after Midnight, 1928 (Plunkett 4)
Chicago Calling, 1951 (Duryea 3)
Chicago, Chicago. See Gaily, Gaily, 1969
Chicago Confidential, 1957 (Cook 3)
Chicago Deadline, 1949 (Kennedy, A. 3, Ladd 3, Reed, D. 3, Seitz 4, Young, V. 4)
Chicago Fire, 1925 (Van Dyke, W.S. 2)
Chicago Kid, 1945 (Brown, K. 4)
Chicago Story, 1981 (Schifrin 4)
Chicago-Digest, 1950 (Gélin 3, Piccoli 3)
Chicas de club, 1972 (Rey 3)
Chichi, 1930 (Takamine 3)
Chichi ariki, 1942 (Ozu 2, Ryu 3)
Chichi kaeru haha no kokoro, 1935 (Yamada 3)
Chichiko-daka, 1956 (Yoda 4)
Chicken, 1928 (Sennett 2)
Chicken a la King, 1919 (Garmes 4)
Chicken a la King, 1937 (Fleischer, M. and D. 2)
Chicken Chaser, 1914 (Sennett 2, Arbuckle 3)
Chicken Every Sunday, 1949 (Seaton 2, Dailey 3, Wood 3, Epstein, J. & P. 4, Lemaire 4, Newman 4, Wheeler 4)
Chicken Feed, 1927 (Roach 4)
Chicken Fracas-see, 1962 (Hanna and Barbera 4)
Chicken in the Case, 1921 (Heerman 4)
Chicken Jitters, 1939 (Clampett 4)
Chicken Reel, 1934 (Lantz 4)
Chicken Thief, 1904 (Bitzer 4)
Chicken-Hearted Jim, 1916 (Ford, J. 2)
Chicken-Hearted Wolf, 1962 (Hanna and Barbera 4)
Chickens, 1916 (Hardy 3)
Chickens Come Home, 1931 (Laurel and Hardy 3)
Chicken-Wagon Family, 1939 (Cronjager 4)
Chickie, 1925 (Bosworth 3)
Chicos, 1959 (Ferreri 2)
Chiedo asilo, 1979 (Ferreri 2, Sarde 4)
Chief, 1933 (Rooney 3)
Chief Cook, 1917 (Hardy 3)
Chief Crazy Horse, 1955 (Mature 3, Boyle 4)
Chief from Goinge. See Goingehovdingen, 1953
Chief of the Horse Farm. See Ménesgazda, 1978
Chiefs, 1969 (Leacock 2)
Chief's Blanket, 1912 (Barrymore L. 3, Sweet 3)
Chief's Daughter, 1911 (Griffith 2, Bosworth 3, Bitzer 4)
Chief's Predicament, 1913 (Sennett 2, Normand 3)
Chief's Son Is Dead. See Hovdingens Son ar dod, 1937–38
Chieko Story. See Chieko-sho, 1957
Chieko-sho, 1957 (Hara 3, Yamamura 3)
Chieko-sho, 1967 (Iwashita 3, Okada 3)
Chiemi no haihiiru, 1956 (Muraki 4)

Chiemi no hatsukoi chaccha musume, 1956 (Tsukasa 3)
Chiemi's High Heeled Shoes. See Chiemi no haihiiru, 1956
Chien andalou, 1929 (Buñuel 2, Braunberger 4)
Chien dans un jeu de quilles, 1962 (Gégauff 4)
Chien de pique, 1960 (Allégret, Y. 2, Constantine 3, Legrand 4)
Chien fou, 1966 (Guillemot 4)
Chien jouant à la balle, 1905 (Guy 2)
Chien Mélomane, 1973 (Grimault 4)
Chien qui rapporte, 1909 (Linders 3)
Chien qui rapporte, 1931 (Arletty 3)
Chienne, 1931 (Allégret, Y. 2, Renoir 2, Simon, M. 3, Braunberger 4)
Chiens, 1966 (Fabian 3)
Chiens, 1978 (Depardieu 3)
Chiens perdus sans collier, 1955 (Delannoy 2, Guerra 2, Gabin 3, Aurenche 4, Bost 4)
Chiens savants, 1902 (Guy 2)
Chiffonier, 1899–1900 (Guy 2)
Chiffonniers d'Emmaus, 1954 (Kosma 4)
Chigo no kenpo, 1927 (Hasegawa 3, Tsuburaya 4)
Chiisai tobosha, 1966 (Kyo 3)
Chiisaki tabigeinin, 1925 (Tanaka 3)
Chiisana boken ryoko, 1964 (Oshima 2)
Chiisana tobosha, 1967 (Kinugasa 2, Miyagawa 4)
Chijin no ai, 1949 (Kyo 3, Mori 3)
Chijo, 1957 (Yoshimura 2, Kagawa 3, Tanaka 3)
Chijo no seiza, 1934 (Tanaka 3)
Chijo-hen, 1934 (Tanaka 3)
Chikagai 24-jikan, 1947 (Hayasaka 4)
Chikagai nijuyo-jikan, 1947 (Imai 2)
Chika-gai no dankon, 1949 (Kyo 3)
Chikagai no nijuyo-jikan, 1947 (Yamamura 3)
Chikamatsu monogatari, 1954 (Mizoguchi 2, Hasegawa 3, Kagawa 3, Shindo 3, Hayasaka 4, Miyagawa 4, Yoda 4)
Chikashitsu, 1927 (Tanaka 3)
Chikita, 1961 (Ganz 3)
Chikuzan hitori-tabi, 1977 (Shindo 2)
Chikyu boeigun, 1957 (Tsuburaya 4)
Child, 1954 (Mason 3)
Child. See Barnet, 1912
Child. See Barnets Magt, 1914
Child and the Killer, 1958 (Roeg 2)
Child Crusoes, 1911 (Costello, D. 3, Talmadge, N. 3)
Child in the House, 1956 (Baker S. 3, Adam 4)
Child Influence, 1912–13 (White 3)
Child is Born, 1940 (Bacon 2, Rossen 2, Arden 3, Rosher 4, Wallis 4)
Child Is Waiting, 1962 (Cassavetes 2, Kramer, S. 2, Garland 3, Lancaster 3, Rowlands 3, La Shelle 4)
Child of Divorce, 1946 (Fleischer, R. 2)
Child of Manhattan, 1933 (Sturges, P. 2, Darwell 3, Grable 3)
Child of the Ghetto, 1910 (Griffith 2, Bitzer 4)
Child of the Paris Streets, 1916 (Marsh 3)
Child of the Prairie, 1913 (Mix 3)
Child of the Prairie, 1915 (Mix 3)
Child of the Purple Sage, 1912 (Anderson G. 3)
Child of the Streets, 1967 (Benegal 2)
Child of the West, 1912 (Anderson G. 3)
Child of the Wilderness, 1912 (Bosworth 3)
Child Psykolojiky, 1941 (Fleischer, M. and D. 2)
Child Sock-ology, 1961 (Hanna and Barbera 4)
Child, The Dog, and the Villain, 1915 (Mix 3)
Child Thou Gavest Me, 1920 (Stahl 2, Stone 3)
Child under a Leaf, 1974 (Cannon 3, Lai 4)
Child Went Forth, 1941 (Losey 2, Eisler 4)
Childhood of Gorky. See Detstvo Gorkovo, 1938
Childhood of Ivan. See Ivanovo detstvo, 1962
Childhood of Maxim Gorki. See Detstvo Gorkovo, 1938
Childhood's Vows, 1900 (Bitzer 4)
Children. See Enfants, 1985
Children and Cars, 1971 (Halas and Batchelor 2)
Children at School, 1937 (Grierson 2, Wright 2)
Children, Books. See Gyermekek, konyvek, 1962
Children Feeding Ducklings, 1899 (Bitzer 4)
Children Galore, 1954 (Fisher 2)

Children Hand in Hand. *See* Te o tsunagu kora, 1962
Children in the Classroom. *See* Kyoshitsu no kodomotachi, 1954
Children in the Crossfire, 1984 (Lassally 4)
Children in the House, 1916 (Franklin 2, Talmadge, N. 3)
Children in the Surf, 1904 (Bitzer 4)
Children in Traffic. *See* Djeva u saobračaju, 1968
Children Making Cartoons, 1973 (Halas and Batchelor 2)
Children Must Learn, 1940 (Van Dyke, W. 2)
Children of An Lac, 1980 (Jones S. 3)
Children of Angyalfold. *See* Angyalföldi fiatalok, 1955
Children of Change. *See* Campane a martello, 1949
Children of Chaos, 1950 (Reggiani 3)
Children of Chaos. *See* Carrefour des enfants perdus, 1943
Children of China, 1939 (Zhao 3)
Children of Darkness. *See* Kinder der Finsternis, 1922
Children of Divorce, 1927 (Von Sternberg 2, Bow 3, Cooper, Gary 3, Banton 4)
Children of Dreams, 1931 (Crosland 2)
Children of Mata Hari. *See* Peau de Torpédo, 1969
Children of Paradise. *See* Enfants du paradis, 1945
Children of Pleasure, 1930 (Gibbons 4)
Children of Rage, 1975 (Cusack 3)
Children of Sanchez, 1978 (Davis 3, Del Rio 3, Quinn 3, Figueroa 4, Zavattini 4)
Children of the Atomic Bomb. *See* Genbakuno-ko, 1952
Children of the Century, 1933 (Zhao 3)
Children of the City. *See* Ditya bolchogo goroda, 1914
Children of the Damned, 1963 (Love 3)
Children of the Dust, 1923 (Borzage 2)
Children of the Feud, 1916 (Gish, D. 3)
Children of the Forest, 1913 (Anderson G. 3)
Children of the Night. *See* Nattbarn, 1956
Children of the Soviet Arctic. *See* Romantiki, 1941
Children of the Storm. *See* Deti buri, 1926
Children of the Street. *See* Gatans barn, 1914
Children of the Sun, 1960 (Hubley 4)
Children of the Whirlwind, 1925 (Barrymore L. 3)
Children of Theatre Street, 1977 (Kelly, Grace 3)
Children of This Country. *See* Bu vatanin cocuklari, 1958
Children Pay, 1916 (Gish, L. 3)
Children Upstairs, 1955 (Anderson 2, Lassally 4)
Children Were Watching, 1961 (Leacock 2)
Children Who Draw. *See* Eo kaku kodomotachi, 1955
Children's Corner, 1939 (L'Herbier 2)
Children's Corner, 1956 (Lassally 4)
Children's Friend, 1909 (Griffith 2, Bitzer 4)
Children's Hour, 1962 (Ashby 2, Wyler 2, Bainter 3, Hepburn, A. 3, Hopkins, M. 3, MacLaine 3, Hayes 4, Jeakins 4, North 4, Planer 4)
Child's Faith, 1910 (Griffith 2, Bitzer 4)
Child's First Adventure. *See* Chiisana boken ryoko, 1964
Child's Impulse, 1910 (Griffith 2, Pickford 3, Bitzer 4)
Child's Love. *See* Barnet, 1909
Child's Play, 1972 (Lumet 2, Mason 3, Preston 3)
Child's Remorse, 1912 (Griffith 2, Bitzer 4)
Child's Sacrifice, 1910 (Guy 2)
Child's Stratagem, 1910 (Griffith 2, Bitzer 4)
Chile con Carmen, 1930 (Lantz 4)
Chile, Land of Charm, 1937 (Hoch 4)
Chili con Corny, 1965 (McKimson 4)
Chili Weather, 1963 (Freleng 4)
Chilly Scenes of Winter. *See* Head Over Heels, 1979
Chilly Willy in the Legend of Rockabye Point, 1955 (Avery 2)
Chiltern Country, 1938 (Cavalcanti 2)
Chimatsuri, 1929 (Tsuburaya 4)
Chimes at Midnight. *See* Falstaff, 1966
Chimes at Midnight, 1966 (Welles 2, Gielgud 3, Moreau 3, Richardson 3, Rutherford 3)
Chimmie Fadden, 1915 (DeMille 2, Buckland 4)
Chimmie Fadden Out West, 1915 (DeMille 2, Buckland 4, Macpherson 4)
Chimney's Secret, 1915 (Chaney Lon 3)
Chimp, 1932 (Laurel & Hardy 3, Roach 4)
China, 1931 (Lantz 4, Terry 4)

China, 1943 (Bendix 3, Ladd 3, Young, L. 3, Dreier 4, Head 4, Young, V. 4)
China Bound, 1929 (Gibbons 4)
China Clipper, 1936 (Bogart 3, O'Brien, P. 3, Walthall 3, Edeson 4, Orry-Kelly 4)
China Corsair, 1951 (Borgnine 3)
China Doll, 1958 (Borzage 2, Bond 3, Mature 3, Clothier 4)
China Fights, 1942 (Eisler 4)
China Gate, 1957 (Fuller 2, Dalio 3, Dickinson 3, Van Cleef 3, Biroc 4, Steiner 4, Young, V. 4)
China Girl, 1942 (Hathaway 2, McLaglen 3, Tierney 3, Basevi 4, Day 4, Friedhofer 4, Garmes 4, Hecht 4, Newman 4, Zanuck 4)
China hilaria, 1939 (Armendáriz 3)
China Is Near. *See* Cina è vicina, 1967
China Jones, 1959 (McKimson 4)
China Memoir, 1974 (MacLaine 3)
China 9, Liberty 37. *See* Amore, piombo, e furore, 1978
China Passage, 1937 (Musuraca 4)
China poblana, 1943 (Félix 3)
China Rose, 1983 (Scott, G. 3)
China Seas, 1935 (Garnett 2, Beery 3, Gable 3, Harlow 3, McDaniel 3, Meek 3, Russell, R. 3, Stone 3, Adrian 4, Brown, N. 4, Freed 4, Furthman 4, Gibbons 4, Lewin 4, Stothart 4, Thalberg 4)
China Sky, 1945 (Quinn 3, Scott, R. 3, Musuraca 4)
China Story. *See* Satan Never Sleeps, 1961
China Strikes Back, 1937 (Maddow 4)
China Syndrome, 1979 (Fonda, J. 3, Lemmon 3, Jenkins 4)
China Tea, 1966 (Le Grice 2)
China Venture, 1953 (Siegel 2, O'Brien, E. 3)
Chinaman, 1920 (Fleischer, M. and D. 2)
Chinaman's Chance, 1933 (Iwerks 4)
China's 400 Million. *See* 400 Million, 1938
China's 400,000,000, 1939 (March 3)
China's Little Devils, 1945 (Carey 3, Tiomkin 4)
Chinatown, 1974 (Huston 2, Polanski 2, Dunaway 3, Nicholson 3, Alonzo 4, Goldsmith 4, Sylbert 4, Towne 4)
Chinatown at Midnight, 1949 (Katzman 4)
Chinatown Charlie, 1928 (Wong 3)
Chinatown My Chinatown, 1929 (Fleischer, M. and D. 2)
Chinatown Mystery, 1915 (Hayakawa 3)
Chinatown Nights, 1929 (Wellman 2, Beery 3, Oland 3, Selznick 4)
Chinatown Squad, 1935 (Schary 4)
Chinchoge, 1933 (Tanaka 3)
Chinese Adventures in China. *See* Tribulations d'un chinois en Chine, 1965
Chinese Bungalow, 1931 (Neagle 3)
Chinese Bungalow, 1941 (Lukas 3)
Chinese Connection, 1971 (Lee, B. 3)
Chinese Den. *See* Chinese Bungalow, 1941
Chinese Parrot, 1927 (Leni 2, Bosworth 3, Summerville 3, Wong 3)
Chinese Prime Minister, 1974 (Anderson J. 3)
Chinese Room, 1966 (Figueroa 4)
Chinese Roulette. *See* Chinesisches Roulette, 1976
Chinese Shadows. *See* Ombres chinoises, 1982
Chinese Vase. *See* Vasens Hemmelighed, 1913
Chinesischen Gotze. *See* Unheimliche Haus, 1916
Chinesisches Roulette, 1976 (Fassbinder 2, Karina 3)
Ching Lin Foo Outdone, 1900 (Porter 2)
Chinjara monogatari, 1962 (Iwashita 3)
Chink, 1921 (Roach 4)
Chinmoku, 1971 (Shinoda 2, Iwashita 3, Miyagawa 4, Takemitsu 4)
Chino. *See* Valdez il mezzosangue, 1973
Chino hate ni ikiru mono, 1960 (Tsukasa 3)
Chinois à Paris, 1974 (Blier 3)
Chinoise, 1967 (Léaud 3, Coutard 4, Guillemot 4)
Chinoise ou Plutôt à la chinoise, 1966 (Godard 2)
Chintao yosai bakugeki merrei, 1963 (Tsuburaya 4)
Chiny i liudi, 1929 (Protazanov 2)
Chip of the Flying U, 1914 (Mix 3)
Chip Off the Old Block, 1913 (Sennett 2)
Chip Off the Old Block, 1944 (O'Connor 3)
Chips Are Down. *See* Jeux sont faits, 1947
Chiqué, 1930 (Vanel 3)

Chira Kumar Sabha, 1932 (Sircar 4)
Chiriakhana, 1967 (Ray, S. 2, Datta 4)
Chirimen kuyo, 1934 (Yamada 3)
Chirurgie fin de siècle, 1900 (Guy 2)
Chirurgien distrait, 1909 (Cohl 2)
Chiseler, 1931 (Sennett 2)
Chisto angliskoe ubiistvo, 1973 (Batalov 3)
Chisum, 1970 (Johnson, B. 3, Wayne 3, Clothier 4)
Chithod Vijay, 1947 (Kapoor 2)
Chittor Vijay, 1947 (Burman 4)
Chitty Chitty Bang Bang, 1968 (Adam 4)
Chiuzoi pidzak, 1927 (Enei 4)
Chivas rayadas, 1962 (García 3)
Chivato, 1961 (Haller 4)
Chiyoda Castle on Fire. See Chiyoda-jo enjo, 1959
Chiyoda no ninjo, 1930 (Hasegawa 3)
Chiyoda-jo enjo, 1959 (Yoda 4)
Chlen pravitelstva, 1939 (Maretskaya 3)
Chloe, 1934 (Neilan 2)
Chloe in the Afternoon. See Amour l'après-midi, 1972
Chlopcy, 1973 (Komorowska 3)
Choc, 1982 (Audran 3, Delon 3, Deneuve 3)
Choc en retour, 1937 (Simon, M. 3)
Choca, 1973 (Fernández 2)
Chocolate Factory, 1952 (Peterson 2)
Chocolate Girl. See Chokoreito garu, 1932
Chocolate Soldier, 1941 (Saville 2, Bruce 3, Eddy 3, Freund 4,
    Gibbons 4, Kaper 4, Stothart 4)
Chohichiro matsudaira, 1930 (Tsuburaya 4)
Choice. See Ekhtiar, 1970
Choice Chance Woman Dance, 1971 (Emshwiller 2)
Choice of a Goal, 1975 (Bondarchuk 3)
Choice of Arms. See Choix des Armes, 1981
Choice of Weapons. See Trial by Combat, 1976
Choices of the Heart, 1983 (Sheen 3, Houseman 4)
Choirboys, 1977 (Aldrich 2, Gossett 3, Biroc 4)
Choito neesan omoide yanagi, 1952 (Yamamura 3)
Choix d'assassins, 1966 (de Beauregard 4)
Choix des armes, 1981 (Deneuve 3, Depardieu 3, Montand 3, Sarde 4)
Chokon yasha, 1928 (Kinugasa 2, Hasegawa 3)
Chokoreito garu, 1932 (Naruse 2)
Chokoreito to heitai, 1938 (Takamine 3)
Cholly Polly, 1942 (Fleischer, M. and D. 2)
Chômeur de Clochemerle, 1957 (Fernandel 3)
Choo Choo Swing, 1948 (Fleischer, M. and D. 2)
Choo-Choo, 1932 (Roach 3)
Choose Me, 1984 (Bujold 3)
Choose Your Partner. See Two Girls on Broadway, 1940
Choose Your Weppins, 1935 (Fleischer, M. and D. 2)
Choosing a Husband, 1909 (Griffith 2, Bitzer 4)
Chop Suey, 1930 (Terry 4)
Chop Suey and Co., 1919 (Daniels 3, Lloyd 3, Roach 4)
Chopin, 1958 (Cloquet 4)
Chor Kanta, 1931 (Sircar 4)
Choraku no kanata, 1924 (Kinugasa 2)
Choral von Leuthen, 1933 (Staudte 2, Tschechowa 3, Planer 4)
Chori Chori, 1956 (Kapoor 2)
Chornyi parus, 1929 (Enei 4)
Chorus, 1974 (Sen 2)
Chorus Girl, 1912–13 (White 3)
Chorus Girls, 1978 (Ferrer, M. 3)
Chorus Kid, 1928 (Robinson 4)
Chorus Lady, 1915 (Reid 3)
Chorus Lady, 1924 (Leroy 2)
Chosen, 1978 (Quayle 3)
Chosen, 1982 (Douglas, K. 3, Schell, Maximilian 3, Steiger 3,
    Bernstein 4)
Chosen Survivors, 1974 (Cooper, J 3)
'Chosen' yoi: Ali to honoo to, 1961 (Tsukasa 3)
Choses de la vie, 1970 (Sautet 2, Piccoli 3, Schneider 3, Sarde 4)
Chotard et Cie., 1933 (Becker 2, Renoir 2, Douy 4)
Chouans, 1946 (Marais 3, Kosma 4, Renoir 4, Spaak 4)
Chouchou Yuji no meoto zenzai, 1965 (Yoda 4)

Chouki the Bar Owner. See Izakaya Chouji, 1983
Chow Hound, 1951 (Jones 2)
Chr. IV som Bygherre, 1941 (Henning-Jensen 2)
Chrezvychainoe proisshestvie, 1958 (Tikhonov 3)
Chris and the Wonderful Lamp, 1917 (Crosland 2)
Chris Columbo, 1938 (Terry 4)
Chris Columbus, Jr., 1934 (Lantz 4)
Christ en croix, 1910 (Feuillade 2)
Christ Stopped at Eboli. See Cristo si è fermato a Eboli, 1979
Christa, 1970 (Gélin 3)
Christa Hartungen, 1917 (Freund 4)
Christening Party. See Keresztelo, 1967
Christening Party. See Křtiny, 1981
Christian, 1923 (Tourneur, M. 2)
Christian. See Kristián, 1939
Christian Dior, 1969 (Reichenbach 2)
Christian IVur: Master Builder. See Chr. IV som Bygherre, 1941
Christian Licorice Store, 1971 (Renoir 2)
Christian Wahnschaffe, 1921 (Gad 2, Krauss 3, Veidt 3)
Christie Johnson, 1921 (Brook 3)
Christina, 1929 (Howard 2, Gaynor 3)
Christine, 1958 (Delon 3, Presle 3, Schneider 3, Auric 4, D'Eaubonne
    4, Matras 4, Spaak 4)
Christine, 1983 (Stanton 3)
Christine of the Big Tops, 1926 (Levien 4)
Christine of the Hungry Heart, 1924 (Baxter W. 3, Brook 3)
Christmas at the Brothel. See Natale in Casa di Appuntamento, 1976
Christmas Burglars, 1908 (Griffith 2, Lawrence 3, Bitzer 4)
Christmas Carol, 1938 (Mankiewicz 2, Carroll L. 3, Waxman 4)
Christmas Carol, 1965 (Depardieu 3)
Christmas Carol, 1971 (Jones 2, Williams, R. 4)
Christmas Carol, 1984 (Scott, G. 3, York, S. 3)
Christmas Carol. See Scrooge, 1951
Christmas Coal Mine Miracle, 1977 (Carradine 3)
Christmas Comes But Once a Year, 1936 (Fleischer, M. and D. 2)
Christmas Crackers. See Caprice de Noël, 1963
Christmas Day in the Workhouse, 1914 (Pearson 2)
Christmas Dream. See Rêve de Noël, 1900
Christmas Dream. See Vánočni, 1946
Christmas Eve, 1947 (Brent 3, Raft 3, Scott, R. 3)
Christmas Eve. See Notch pered Rozdestvom, 1913
Christmas Eve. See Przedświateczny wieczór, 1966
Christmas Feast, 1974 (Halas and Batchelor 2)
Christmas Gift, 1980 (Vinton 4)
Christmas Holiday, 1944 (Siodmak 2, Durbin 3, Kelly, Gene 3,
    Mankiewicz 4, Salter 4)
Christmas in Connecticut, 1945 (Greenstreet 3, Sakall 3, Stanwyck 3,
    Head 4)
Christmas in July, 1940 (Sturges, P. 2, Powell, D. 3, Dreier 4, Head 4)
Christmas Kid. See Joe Navidad, 1966
Christmas Lilies of the Field, 1979 (Schell, Maria 3)
Christmas Memories, 1915 (Daves 2)
Christmas Miracle in Caufield, U.S.A. See Christmas Coal Mine
    Miracle, 1977
Christmas Party, 1931 (Davies 3, Gable 3)
Christmas Party. See Jackie Cooper's Christmas, 1932
Christmas Revenge, 1915 (Anderson G. 3)
Christmas That Almost Wasn't. See Natale che quasi non fu,
    1966
Christmas to Remember, 1978 (Robards 3, Saint 3, Woodward 3)
Christmas Tree, 1969 (Holden 3, Auric 4)
Christmas Tree. See Albero di natale, 1969
Christmas under Fire, 1941 (Watt 2, Dalrymple 4)
Christmas Visitor, 1958 (Halas and Batchelor 2)
Christmas with Elizabeth. See Vánoce s Alžbětou, 1968
Christmas Without Snow, 1980 (Houseman 4)
Christoph Columbus, 1922 (Basserman 3)
Christopher Bean, 1933 (Wood 2, Barrymore L. 3, Bondi 3, Dressler 3,
    Daniels 4)
Christopher Bean. See Late Christopher Bean, 1933
Christopher Columbus, 1949 (Cusack 3, March 3,
    Mathieson 4)
Christopher Columbus, 1983 (Lattuada 2)

Christopher Strong, 1933 (Arzner 2, Burke 3, Hepburn, K. 3, Akins 4, Berman 4, Glennon 4, Plunkett 4, Polglase 4, Selznick 4, Steiner 4, Vorkapich 4)
Christo's Valley Curtain, 1972 (Maysles A. and D. 2)
Christus, 1919 (Krauss 3)
Chronicle. See Krónika, 1967
Chronicle of Anna Magdalena Bach. See Chronik der Anna Magdalena Bach, 1968
Chronicle of Flaming Years. See Povest plamennykh let, 1961
Chronicle of May Rain. See Samidare zoshi, 1924
Chronicles of the Grey House. See Zur Chronik von Grieshuus, 1925 (Dagover 3)
Chronik der Anna Magdalena Bach, 1968 (Straub and Huillet 2)
Chronik eines Mordes, 1965 (Domrose 3)
Chronique d'un été, 1960 (Rivette 2, Rouch 2, Coutard 4)
Chronique provinciale, 1958 (Jarre 4, Rappeneau 4)
Chrysalis, 1973 (Emshwiller 2)
Chrysanthemums. See Krisantemi, 1914
Chto delat', 1928 (Ptushko 2)
Chu Chin Chow, 1934 (Kortner 3, Wong 3)
Chu Chu and the Philly Flash, 1981 (Arkin 3, Warden 3, Jarre 4)
Chubasco, 1968 (Sothern 3)
Chu-Chin-Chow, 1923 (Wilcox 2)
Chu-Chin-Chow, 1934 (Balcon 4, Gilliat 4, Metzner 4)
Chudá holka, 1929 (Fric 2, Stallich 4)
Chudí lidé, 1939 (Hammid 2)
Chuji uridasu, 1935 (Shimura 3)
Chuka, 1967 (Borgnine 3, Mills 3, Head 4)
Chump at Oxford, 1940 (Cushing 3, Langdon 3, Laurel & Hardy 3, Roach 4)
Chump Champ, 1950 (Avery 2)
Chumps, 1912 (Bunny 3, Reid 3)
Chumps, 1930 (Sennett 2)
Chung Kuo, 1972 (Antonioni 2)
Chung lieh t'u, 1975 (King Hu 2)
Chung-shen ta shih, 1981 (King Hu 2)
Chupke Chupke, 1975 (Bachchan 3, Burman 4)
Churchill and the Generals, 1979 (Cotten 3)
Churchill the Man, 1973 (Fairbanks, D. Jr. 3)
Churetsu nikudan sanyushi, 1936 (Shimura 3)
Churning. See Manthan, 1976
Chushingura, 1932 (Kinugasa 2, Hasegawa 3, Tanaka 3)
Chushingura, 1939 (Hasegawa 3, Takamine 3)
Chushingura, 1954 (Yamada 3, Yoda 4)
Chushingura, 1958 (Hasegawa 3, Kyo 3, Shimura 3, Shindo 3, Yamamura 3)
Chushingura, 1962 (Hara 3, Mifune 3, Shimura 3)
Chushingura: Hana no maki, Yuki no maki, 1962 (Tsukasa 3)
Chushingura: Ninjo-hen, Fukusku-hen, 1934 (Yamada 3)
Chushingura, Part II, 1939 (Yamada 3)
Chute. See Queda, 1978
Chute dans le bonheur. See Chacun sa chance, 1931
Chute de cinq étages, 1906 (Méliès 2)
Chute de la maison Usher, 1928 (Buñuel 2, Epstein 2)
Chute d'un corps, 1973 (Buñuel 2, Rey 3, Carrière 4)
Chutes de pierres, danger du mort, 1958–59 (Breer 2)
Chuvas de verao, 1977 (Diegues 2)
Chuzhie pisma, 1975 (Yankovsky 3)
Chuzhoy pidzhak, 1927 (Moskvin 4)
Chuzoi bereg, 1930 (Donskoi 2)
Chwila pokoju, 1965 (Konwicki 4)
Chyorni parus, 1929 (Yutkevich 2)
Chyortovo koleso, 1926 (Gerasimov 2, Kozintsev 2, Enei 4, Moskvin 4)
Chytte ho, 1924 (Ondra 3)
Ci risiamo, vero Provvidenza?, 1973 (Morricone 4)
Ci troviamo in galleria, 1953 (Bolognini 2, Loren 3, Sordi 3)
Ciao Gulliver, 1970 (Ferreri 2)
Ciao maschio, 1978 (Depardieu 3, Mastroianni 3, Sarde 4)
Ciao maschio. See Bye Bye Monkey, 1978
Cible humaine, 1904 (Guy 2)
Ciboulette, 1933 (Allégret, Y. 2, Autant-Lara 2, Courant 4, Meerson 4, Prévert 4, Trauner 4)
Cicala, 1980 (Lattuada 2)

Ciclon, 1963 (Alvarez 2)
Ciclon, 1977 (Baker C. 3, Kennedy, A. 3)
Cidade mulher, 1934 (Mauro 2)
Cieca di Sorrento, 1934 (Magnani 3)
Ciel est à vous, 1944 (Grémillon 2, Vanel 3, Douy 4, Spaak 4)
Ciel est par-dessus le toit, 1956 (Cloquet 4)
Ciel, la terre, 1966 (Ivens 2)
Ciel partagé. See Geteilte Himmel, 1964
Cielito lindo, 1936 (Figueroa 4)
Cielo è rosso, 1950 (Auer 3, Cervi 3, Vích 4, Zavattini 4)
Cielo negro, 1951 (Rey 3)
Cielo sulla palude, 1949 (Aldo 4, D'Amico 4)
Cién, 1956 (Kawalerowicz 2)
Cien Metros con Charlot, 1967 (Guzmán 2)
Cifte tabancali kabadayi, 1969 (Guney 2)
Cifte yurekli, 1970 (Guney 2)
Cigale et la fourmi, 1909 (Feuillade 2)
Cigale et la fourmi, 1953 (Kosma 4)
Cigalon, 1935 (Pagnol 2)
Cigány, 1941 (Gabór 3)
Cigányok, 1962 (Gaál 2)
Cigar. See Cigara, 1975
Cigara, 1975 (Grgić 4)
Cigaretpigen, 1915 (Holger-Madsen 2)
Cigarette, 1919 (Dulac 2)
Cigarette Maker. See Cigaretpigen, 1915
Cigarette Tests, 1934 (Fischinger 2)
Cigarette, That's All, 1915 (Weber 2)
Cigarettes Bastos, 1938 (Alexeieff and Parker 2)
Ciklámen, 1916 (Korda 2)
Cimarron, 1930 (Ruggles 2, Cody 3, Dunne 3, Clothier 4, Cronjager 4, Dunn 4, Eason 4, Estabrook 4, Plunkett 4, Steiner 4, Westmore, E. 4)
Cimarron, 1960 (Mann 2, Baxter A. 3, Ford, G. 3, McCambridge 3, Schell, Maria 3, Gillespie 4, Plunkett 4, Surtees 4, Waxman 4)
Cimarron Kid, 1951 (Boetticher 2, Murphy 3)
Cimego. See San Massenza, 1955
Cimetière dans la falaise, 1951 (Rouch 2)
Cina. See Chung Kuo, 1972
Cina è vicina, 1967 (Bellocchio 2, Cristaldi 4, Delli Colli 4, Morricone 4)
Cinch for the Gander, 1925 (Wray 3)
Cincinnati Kid, 1965 (Ashby 2, Jewison 2, Blondell 3, Malden 3, McQueen, S. 3, Robinson, E. 3, Torn 3, Weld 3, Lardner 4, Schifrin 4)
Cinco vêzes Favela, 1962 (Diegues 2)
58–59, 1959 (Almendros 4)
Cinderella, 1911 (Selig 4)
Cinderella, 1914 (Pickford 3)
Cinderella, 1922 (Disney 2)
Cinderella, 1925 (Lantz 4)
Cinderella, 1933 (Terry 4)
Cinderella, 1937 (Kaufman 4)
Cinderella, 1950 (Disney 2, Iwerks 4)
Cinderella, 1963 (Reiniger 2)
Cinderella. See Pepeljuga, 1979
Cinderella Italian Style. See C'era una volta, 1967
Cinderella Jones, 1946 (Berkeley 2, Cook 3, Horton 3, Sakall 3, Cahn 4, Polito 4)
Cinderella Liberty, 1973 (Caan 3, Wallach 3, Williams, J. 4, Zsigmond 4)
Cinderella Man, 1917 (Marsh 3)
Cinderella Meets Fella, 1938 (Avery 2)
Cinderella or the Glass Slipper. See Cendrillon ou la pantoufle mystérieuse, 1912
Cinderfella, 1960 (Lewis 2, Tashlin 2, Anderson J. 3, Bumstead 4, Head 4)
Cinders, 1926 (Balfour 3)
Cinders in Love, 1916 (Summerville 3)
Cinders of Love, 1916 (Sennett 2)
Cinegiornale della pace, 1963 (Zavattini 4)
Cinema According to Bertolucci, 1977 (Sutherland 3, Valli 3)
Cinéma au service de l'histoire, 1927 (Dulac 2)

Cinéma cinéma, 1969 (Braunberger 4)
Cinema d'altri tempi, 1953 (Age and Scarpelli 4, Gherardi 4)
Cinéma de papa, 1970 (Broca 2)
Cinéma du diable, 1967 (L'Herbier 2)
Cinema Girl's Romance, 1915 (Pearson 2)
Cinema Murder, 1919 (Davies 3, Marion 4, Rosson 4)
Cinema secondo Bertolucci. See Bertolucci secondo il cinema, 1975
Cinema-Truth. See Kino-pravda, 1922–23
Cinerama's Russian Adventure, 1965 (Crosby 3)
Cinétracts, 1968 (Godard 2)
Cinq cents balles, 1961 (Braunberger 4)
Cinq gars pour Singapour, 1967 (Amidei 4)
Cinq Gentlemen maudits, 1931 (Duvivier 2, Baur 3, Walbrook 3, Ibert 4, Meerson 4)
5% des risques, 1979 (Cassel 3)
Cinq sous de Lavarède, 1938 (Fernandel 3)
Cinquième soleil, 1965 (Reichenbach 2)
50 Ans de Don Juan, 1922 (Vanel 3)
Cinque giornate, 1973 (Argento 4)
Cinque marines per cento ragazze, 1961 (Tognazzi 3)
Cinque ore in contanti, 1961 (Sanders 3)
Cinque per l'inferno, 1968 (Kinski 3)
Cinque pistole di violenca. See Mio nome è Shanghai Joe, 1973
Cinque poveri in automobile, 1952 (Fabrizi 3, Zavattini 4)
Cintura di castità, 1949 (Flaiano 4)
Cintura di castità, 1968 (Curtis 3, Vitti 3, Donati 4)
Ciociara, 1960 (De Sica 2, Belmondo 3, Loren 3, Ponti 4, Zavattini 4)
Ciphers. See Číslice, 1966
Cipola Colt, 1975 (Hayden 3)
Circe the Enchantress, 1924 (Gibbons 4)
Circle, 1925 (Borzage 2, Crawford, J. 3, Basevi 4, Gibbons 4)
Circle, 1957 (Mills 3)
Circle, 1976 (Hayworth 3, Houseman 4)
Circle C Ranch Wedding Present, 1910 (Anderson G. 3)
Circle of Children, 1977 (Roberts 3)
Circle of Danger, 1951 (Tourneur, J. 2, Milland 3, Harrison 3, Morris 4)
Circle of Death, 1935 (Canutt 4)
Circle of Deceit, 1981 (Schlondorff 2)
Circle of Deceit. See Falschung, 1981
Circle of Iron, 1978 (Coburn, J. 3, Wallach 3)
Circle of Iron. See Silent Flute, 1977
Circle of Love. See Ronde, 1950
Circle of Love. See Ronde, 1964
Circle of Two, 1979 (Dassin 2, Burton 3)
Circo, 1942 (Cantinflas 3, Figueroa 4)
Circo, 1948 (García Berlanga 2)
Circo equestre Za-Bum, 1944 (Fabrizi 3, Sordi 3, Valli 3)
Circo mas pequeño, 1963 (Ivens 2)
Circoncision, 1949 (Rouch 2)
Circonstances atténuantes, 1939 (Arletty 3, Simon, M. 3)
Circostanza, 1974 (Olmi 2)
Circular Fence, 1911 (Dwan 2)
Circular Panorama of the Electric Tower, 1901 (Porter 2)
Circular Path, 1915 (Walthall 3)
Circular Tensions, 1950 (Smith 2)
Circulez!, 1931 (Brasseur 3)
Circumstance. See Circostanza, 1974
Circumstantial Evidence, 1919 (Micheaux 2)
Circus, 1920 (Fleischer, M. and D. 2)
Circus, 1927 (Chaplin 2)
Circus, 1932 (Iwerks 4)
Circus. See Tsirk, 1936
Circus Ace, 1927 (Mix 3)
Circus and the Boy, 1914 (Ingram 2)
Circus Arrives. See Danserindens Haevn, 1915
Circus Clown, 1934 (Brown 3, Orry-Kelly 4)
Circus Comes to Town. See Under the Big Top, 1938
Circus Cowboy, 1924 (Wellman 2)
Circus Days, 1923 (Coogan 3)
Circus Days, 1935 (Terry 4)
Circus Drawings, 1964 (Williams, R. 4)
Circus Fever, 1925 (Roach 4)

Circus Hoodoo, 1934 (Langdon 3)
Circus Kid, 1928 (Brown 3, Plunkett 4)
Circus King. See Zirkuskonig, 1924
Circus Man, 1914 (DeMille 2)
Circus Maximus, 1980 (Gabór 3, Geschonneck 3)
Circus of Fear, 1967 (Kinski 3, Lee, C. 3)
Circus of Horrors, 1960 (Pleasance 3, Mathieson 4, Slocombe 4)
Circus of Love. See Rummelplatz der Liebe, 1954
Circus of Sin. See Salto mortale, 1931
Circus Queen Murder, 1933 (Menjou 3, August 4)
Circus Rookies, 1928 (Day 4, Gibbons 4)
Circus Shadow. See Shadow, 1937
Circus Today, 1926 (Sennett 2)
Circus Today, 1940 (Avery 2)
Circus World, 1964 (Hathaway 2, Cardinale 3, Hayworth 3, Wayne 3, Fisher 4, Hecht 4, Renoir 4, Tiomkin 4)
Circusfarm, 1956 (Carlsen 2)
Cirkin kiral, 1966 (Guney 2)
Cirkin kiral affetmez, 1967 (Guney 2)
Cirkin ve cesur, 1971 (Guney 2)
Cirkus bude, 1954 (Hrušínský 3, Kopecký 3)
Cirkus Hurvínek, 1955 (Trnka 2)
Cirkus v cirkuse, 1975 (Kučera 4)
Cirque de la mort, 1918 (Florey 2)
Císařuv pekař a Pekařuv pekař, 1951 (Fric 2, Trnka 2, Brdečka 4)
Císařuv slavík, 1948 (Trnka 2, Brdečka 4, Pojar 4)
Cisco Kid, 1931 (Baxter W. 3)
Cisco Kid and the Lady, 1940 (Bond 3)
Cisco Pike, 1971 (Black 3, Hackman 3, Stanton 3)
Ciske—A Child Wants Love. See Ciske—Ein Kind braucht Liebe, 1955
Ciske de Rat. See Ciske—Ein Kind braucht Liebe, 1955
Ciske—Ein Kind braucht Liebe, 1955 (Staudte 2)
Číslice, 1966 (Švankmajer 4)
Cita de amor, 1956 (Fernández 2, Figueroa 4)
Citadel, 1938 (Saville 2, Vidor, K. 2, Donat 3, Harrison 3, Richardson 3, Russell, R. 3, Dalrymple 4, Junge 4, Meerson 4, Stradling 4)
Citadel of Crime. See Man Betrayed, 1941
Citadel of Silence. See Citadelle du silence, 1937
Citadelle du silence, 1937 (L'Herbier 2, Francis, E. 3, Andrejew 4, Honegger 4)
Cité d'argent, 1955 (Delerue 4)
Cité de l'indicible peur. See Grande frousse, 1964
Cités du ciel, 1959 (Fradetal 4)
Citizen. See Nagarik, 1982
Citizen Kane, 1941 (Welles 2, Cotten 3, Ladd 3, Moorehead 3, Sloane 3, Dunn 4, Herrmann 4, Mankiewicz 4, Polglase 4, Toland 4)
Citizen Karel Havlíček. See Občan Karel Havlíček, 1966
Citizen of Tomorrow, 1942 (Alwyn 4)
Citizens Band. See Handle with Care, 1977
Città dei traffici, 1949 (Risi 2)
Città delle donne, 1980 (Fellini 2, Mastroianni 3)
Città di notte, 1958 (Rota 4)
Città di Stendhal, 1949 (Fusco 4)
Città dolente, 1948 (Fellini 2, Delli Colli 4)
Citta prigioniera, 1962 (Niven 3)
Città sconvolta—caccia spietata ai rapitori, 1975 (Cortese 3)
Città si difende, 1951 (Fellini 2, Germi 2, Lollobrigida 3, Pinelli 4)
Città violenta, 1970 (Bronson 3, Morricone 4)
City, 1914 (Ince 4)
City, 1939 (Cavalcanti 2, Lorentz 2, Van Dyke, W. 2, Copland 4)
City, 1971 (Quinn 3)
City Across the River, 1949 (Curtis 3, Ritter 3)
City Beautiful, 1914 (Gish, D. 3, Reid 3)
City Beneath the Sea, 1953 (Boetticher 2, Quinn 3, Ryan 3)
City Beneath the Sea, 1970 (Cotten 3, Wagner 3)
City Butterfly. See Grosstadt Schmetterling, 1929
City Called Copenhagen. See By ved navn København, 1960
City for Conquest, 1940 (Kazan 3, Litvak 2, Cagney 3, Crisp 3, Kennedy, A. 3, Quinn 3, Sheridan 3, Friedhofer 4, Howe 4, Polito 4, Steiner 4, Wallis 4)
City Girl, 1930 (Brown 3, Carré 4)
City Girl, 1938 (Chaney Lon, Jr. 3)

City Gone Wild, 1927 (Cruze 2, Brooks 3, Furthman 4, Glennon 4, Mankiewicz 4)
City Government. See City Speaks, 1947
City Hall to Harlem in 15 Seconds via the Subway Route, 1904 (Porter 2)
City Has Your Face. See Městomä svou tvář, 1958
City Heat, 1984 (Eastwood 3, Reynolds, B. 3, Torn 3)
City in Darkness. See Charlie Chan in City in Darkness, 1939
City in Fear, 1980 (Rosenman 4)
City in the Sea, 1965 (Price 3)
City Is Dark. See Crime Wave, 1954
City Jungle. See Dzungle velkoměsta, 1929
City Jungle. See Young Philadelphians, 1959
City Lights, 1931 (Chaplin 2, Harlow 3, Newman 4)
City Limits, 1984 (Jones, J.E. 3)
City Map. See Várostérkép, 1977
City of Bad Men, 1953 (Boone 3, Crain 3, Clarke, C.C. 4, Jeakins 4, Lemaire 4)
City of Chance, 1939 (Day 4)
City of Darkness, 1915 (August 4, Ince 4)
City of Darkness, 1939 (Day 4)
City of Darkness. See Charlie Chan in the City of Darkness, 1939
City of Desire. See Joen no chimata, 1923
City of Dim Faces, 1918 (Hayakawa 3, Marion 4)
City of Fear, 1958 (Ballard 4, Goldsmith 4)
City of Live Water. See Město živé vody, 1934
City of Masks, 1920 (Brown, K. 4)
City of Pirates. See Ville de pirates, 1984
City of Play, 1929 (Balcon 4)
City of Secrets. See Stadt ist voller Geheimnisse, 1955
City of Shadows, 1955 (McLaglen 3)
City of Song, 1931 (Gallone 2)
City of the Dead, 1960 (Lee, C. 3)
City of Torment. See Und uber uns der Himmel, 1947
City of Women. See Città delle donne, 1980
City on Fire, 1979 (Gardner 3, Winters 3)
City on Trial. See Processo alla città, 1951
City Out of Wilderness, 1973 (Hammid 2)
City Park, 1934 (Walthall 3, Brown, K. 4)
City Prepares. See First Days, 1939
City Slicker, 1918 (Daniels 3, Lloyd 3, Roach 4)
City Slicker, 1952 (Terry 4)
City Sparrow, 1920 (Wood 3)
City Speaks, 1947 (Alwyn 4)
City Story, 1954 (Ford, G. 3)
City Streets, 1931 (Mamoulian 2, Cooper, Gary 3, Goddard 3, Lukas 3, Sidney 3, Garmes 4)
City That Never Sleeps, 1924 (Cruze 2, Brown, K. 4)
City That Never Sleeps, 1953 (Young, G. 3)
City Tramp. See Stadtstreicher, 1965
City under the Sea, 1965 (Bennett 4)
City Under the Sea. See War Gods of the Deep, 1965
City Vamp, 1915 (Marion 4)
City Without Men, 1943 (Darnell 3, Raksin 4, Schulberg 4)
Ciudad de carton, 1932 (Gaynor 3, Young, R. 3)
Ciudad de los Niños, 1956 (García 3)
Civilforsvaret, 1950 (Carlsen 2)
Civilian, 1912 (Ince 4)
Civilization, 1916 (Ince 4, Sullivan 4)
Civilization's Child, 1916 (August 4, Sullivan 4)
Claim Jumper, 1913 (Ince 4)
Claim Jumpers, 1911 (Dwan 2)
Clair de femme, 1979 (Costa-Gavras 2, Montand 3, Schneider 3)
Clair de lune, 1932 (Fradetal 4)
Clair de lune à Maubege, 1962 (Bourvil 3)
Clair de lune espagnol, 1909 (Cohl 2)
Clair de lune sous Richelieu, 1911 (Gance 2)
Clair de terre, 1970 (Feuillère 3, Girardot 3, Presle 3)
Claire's Knee. See Genou de Claire, 1970
Clairvoyant, 1935 (Rains 3, Wray 3, Balcon 4, Bennett 4, Junge 4)
Clambake, 1967 (Presley 3)
Clan de los immorales, 1973 (Ferrer, J. 3)

Clan des Siciliens, 1969 (Verneuil 2, Delon 3, Gabin 3, Decaë 4, Morricone 4)
Clan of the Cave Bear, 1986 (Sayles 4)
Clancy, 1974 (Brakhage 2)
Clancy at the Bat, 1929 (Sennett 2)
Clancy Street Boys, 1943 (Katzman 4)
Clancy's Kosher Wedding, 1927 (Plunkett 4)
Clap Your Hands, 1948 (Fleischer, M. and D. 2)
Claque, 1932 (Fernandel 3)
Clara and Her Mysterious Toys, 1912–14 (Cohl 2)
Clara Cleans Her Teeth, 1926 (Disney 2)
Clara de Montargis, 1950 (Renoir 4)
Clara et les chics types, 1980 (Adjani 3)
Clara et les méchants, 1957 (Wakhévitch 4)
Clarence, 1922 (Menjou 3, Reid 3)
Clarence, 1937 (Head 4)
Claretta and Ben. See Permettete che ami vostre figlia?, 1974
Clarissa, 1941 (Frohlich 3)
Claro, 1975 (Rocha 2)
Clash by Night, 1952 (Lang 2, Douglas, P. 3, Monroe 3, Ryan 3, Stanwyck 3, D'Agostino 4, Krasna 4, Musuraca 4, Wald 4)
Clash of the Titans, 1981 (Bloom 3, Meredith 3, Olivier 3, Smith 3, Harryhausen 4)
Clash of the Wolves, 1925 (Walker 4)
Class, 1983 (Bisset 3, Robertson 3, Bernstein 4)
Class. See You Never Can Tell, 1920
Class of 1984, 1983 (McDowall 3, Schifrin 4)
Class of Miss MacMichael, 1979 (Jackson 3, Reed, O. 3)
Classe d'histoire, 1953 (Cloquet 4)
Classe de lettres, 1953 (Cloquet 4)
Classe de mathematiques, 1953 (Cloquet 4)
Classe operaia va in paradiso, 1971 (Petri 2, Volonté 3, Morricone 4)
Classe tous risques, 1960 (Sautet 2, Belmondo 3, Dalio 3, Cloquet 4, Delerue 4)
Classic Fairy Tales series, 1965 (Halas and Batchelor 2)
Classification des plantes, 1982 (Ruiz 2)
Classification of Plants. See Classification de plantes, 1982
Classified, 1925 (Mathis 4, Rosson 4)
Classmates, 1908 (Bitzer 4)
Classmates, 1913 (Barrymore L. 3, Sweet 3, Walthall 3, Gaudio 4)
Classmates, 1924 (Barthelmess 3, Seitz 4)
Claudelle Inglish, 1961 (Kennedy, A. 3)
Claudi vom Geisterhof, 1915 (Veidt 3, Messter 4)
Claudia, 1943 (Goulding 2, Young, R. 3, Basevi 4, Newman 4, Ryskind 4, Shamroy 4)
Claudia and David, 1946 (Astor 3, Young, R. 3, Basevi 4, La Shelle 4)
Claudine, 1974 (Jones, J.E. 3)
Claudine. See Claudine à l'école, 1938
Claudine à l'école, 1938 (Brasseur 3)
Clavigo, 1970 (Ophuls 2)
Claw, 1927 (Olcott 2)
Claws for Alarm, 1955 (Jones 2)
Claws in the Lease, 1963 (McKimson 4)
Clay. See Argila, 1940
Clay. See Korkarlen, 1921
Clay Heart. See Guldets Gift, 1916
Clay Pigeon, 1949 (Fleischer, R. 2, Foreman 4)
Clay Pigeon, 1971 (Meredith 3)
Claymation, 1978 (Vinton 4)
Clé sur la porte, 1978 (Girardot 3, Sarde 4)
Clean Heart, 1924 (Blackton 2)
Clean Pastures, 1937 (Freleng 4)
Clean Shaven Man, 1936 (Fleischer, M. and D. 2)
Clean Slate. See Coup de torchon, 1981
Cleaning Time, 1915 (Hardy 3)
Cleaning Up, 1926 (Arbuckle 3)
Clean-Up, 1917 (Young, W. 4)
Clear All Wires, 1933 (Daves 2, Marshall 3, Merkel 3)
Clear the Decks for Action. See Klart till drabbning, 1937
Clearing the Trail, 1928 (Eason 4)
Clemenceau Case, 1915 (Brenon 2, Bara 3)
Clémentine Chérie, 1963 (Noiret 3)

Cléo de 5 à 7, 1961 (Godard 2, Varda 2, Constantine 3, Karina 3, de Beauregard 4, Evein 4, Legrand 4, Ponti 4, Rabier 4)
Cleo from 5 to 7. *See* Cléo de 5 à 7, 1961
Cleopatra, 1917 (Bara 3)
Cleopatra, 1934 (DeMille 2, Carradine 3, Colbert 3, Farnum 3, Schildkraut 3, Banton 4, Dreier 4, Prinz 4, Young, W. 4)
Cleopatra, 1963 (Mankiewicz 2, Burton 3, Harrison 3, McDowall 3, Taylor, E. 3, Buchman 4, North 4, Pan 4, Renoir 4, Shamroy 4, Sharaff 4, Smith, J.M. 4, Wanger 4, Zanuck 4)
Cleopatra Jones, 1973 (Winters 3)
Cléopâtre, 1899 (Méliès 2)
Cleopatsy, 1918 (Roach 4)
Clérambard, 1969 (Noiret 3)
Clever Dummy, 1917 (Sennett 2, Beery 3)
Clever Girl. *See* Okos lány, 1955
Clever Girl Takes Care of Herself. *See* Bra flicka reder sig sjalv, 1914
Clever Mrs. Carfax, 1917 (Crisp 3)
Client sérieux, 1932 (Autant-Lara 2)
Cliente seductor, 1931 (Chevalier 3)
Cliff. *See* Shiroi gake, 1960
Climats, 1962 (Piccoli 3, Fusco 4, Vierny 4)
Climax, 1930 (Hersholt 3)
Climax, 1944 (Costello, M. 3, Karloff 3, Siodmak 4)
Climax. *See* Immorale, 1967
Climb an Angry Mountain, 1972 (Duning 4)
Climber, 1917 (King 2)
Climbers, 1927 (Loy 3)
Climbers. *See* Ambitieuse, 1959
Climbing High, 1939 (Reed 2, Matthews 3, Redgrave, M. 3, Sim 3, Junge 4)
Clinging Vine, 1926 (Miller, A. 4, Sullivan 4)
Clinic. *See* Sanitarium, 1910
Clinic of Stumble, 1947 (Peterson 2)
Clive of India, 1935 (Auer 3, Carradine 3, Carroll L. 3, Colman 3, Young, L. 3, Day 4, Guffey 4, Newman 4, Zanuck 4)
Cloak. *See* Shinel, 1926
Cloak and Dagger, 1946 (Lang 2, Cooper, Gary 3, Friedhofer 4, Lardner 4, Polito 4, Steiner 4)
Cloches de Paques, 1912 (Feuillade 2)
Clock, 1945 (Minnelli 2, Garland 3, Walker 3, Wynn 3, Freed 4, Gillespie 4, Irene 4)
Clock Strikes Eight. *See* College Scandal, 1935
Clockmaker. *See* Horloger de Saint-Paul, 1974
Clockmaker's Dream. *See* Rêve d'horloger, 1904
Clockwork Orange, 1971 (Kubrick 2, McDowell 3, Barry 4)
Clod, 1912 (Ince 4)
Clodo et les vicieuses, 1970 (Bourvil 3)
Clodoche, 1938 (Berry 3)
Cloister's Touch, 1909 (Griffith 2, Walthall 3, Bitzer 4)
Clone Master, 1978 (Bellamy 3, Biroc 4)
Clonus Horror, 1979 (Wynn 3)
Cloportes, 1966 (Rosay 3)
Cloportes. *See* Métamorphose des cloportes, 1966
Close Call, 1911 (Sennett 2)
Close Call, 1916 (Mix 3)
Close Call for Boston Blackie, 1946 (Guffey 4)
Close Encounters of the Third Kind, 1977 (Schrader 2, Spielberg 2, Truffaut 2, Dreyfuss 3, Alonzo 4, Fraker 4, Kovacs 4, Slocombe 4, Trumbull 4, Williams, J. 4, Zsigmond 4)
Close Harmony, 1929 (Cromwell 2, Sutherland 2, Harlow 3, Hunt 4)
Close Quarters, 1943 (Dalrymple 4)
Close Relations, 1933 (Arbuckle 3)
Close Shave, 1929 (Sennett 2, Hornbeck 4)
Close Shave, 1937 (Terry 4)
Close to My Heart, 1951 (Bainter 3, Milland 3, Tierney 3, Steiner 4)
Close to Nature, 1968 (Benegal 2)
Closed Circuit. *See* System ohne Schatten, 1983
Closed Door, 1912 (Lawrence 3)
Closed Doors. *See* S vyloučením veřejnosti, 1933
Closed Mondays, 1974 (Vinton 4)
Closed Road, 1916 (Tourneur, M. 2, Carré 4)
Closely Watched Trains. *See* Ostře sledované vlaky, 1966
Closet, 1965 (Warhol 2)

Close-up: The Blood. *See* Közelrölia: a ver, 1965
Clothes, 1929 (Bennett C. 3)
Clothes and the Woman, 1937 (Sim 3)
Clothes Make the Man, 1915 (Hardy 3)
Clothes Make the Pirate, 1925 (Tourneur, M. 2, Gish, D. 3)
Clothes Make the Woman, 1928 (Pidgeon 3)
Clothes of Deception. *See* Itsuwareru seiso, 1951
Cloud and Clear. *See* Oblačna priča, 1972
Cloud in the Sky, 1940 (Ulmer 2)
Cloudburst, 1951 (Baker S. 3, Preston 3)
Cloud-Capped Star. *See* Meghe Dhaka Tara, 1960
Clouded Name, 1923 (Shearer 3)
Clouded Yellow, 1950 (Howard, T. 3, More 3, Simmons 3, Unsworth 4)
Clouds, 1917 (Van Dyke, W.S. 2)
Clouds at Sunset. *See* Akanegumo, 1967
Clouds at Twilight. *See* Yuyake-gumo, 1956
Clouds of Glory, 1978 (Russell 4)
Clouds over Europe. *See* Q Planes, 1939
Clouds will Roll Away. *See* Není stále zamrečeno, 1950
Clověk pod vodou, 1961 (Brdečka 4)
Clown, 1916 (Rosher 4)
Clown, 1931 (Lantz 4)
Clown and Policeman, 1900 (Hepworth 2)
Clown and the Alchemist, 1900 (Porter 2)
Clown and the Primadonna, 1913 (Costello, M. 3)
Clown Bux, 1935 (Modot 3, D'Eaubonne 4, Douy 4)
Clown en sac, 1904 (Guy 2)
Clown Must Laugh. *See* Pagliacci, 1936
Clown Princes, 1939 (Sidney 2, Roach 4)
Clowning, 1931 (Terry 4)
Clowns, 1902 (Guy 2)
Clowns, 1970 (Fellini 2, Donati 4, Rota 4)
Clowns. *See* Ansichten eines Clowns, 1975
Clown's Little Brother, 1920 (Fleischer, M. and D. 2)
Clown's Pup, 1919 (Fleischer, M. and D. 2)
Clown's Triumph, 1912 (Brenon 2)
Club, 1980 (Beresford 2)
Club de femmes, 1936 (Delannoy 2, Darrieux 3, Francis, E. 3)
Club de femmes, 1956 (Trintignant 3)
Club des aristocrates, 1937 (Berry 3)
Club des soupirants, 1941 (Cayatte 2, Fernandel 3, Burel 4, Wakhévitch 4)
Club Havana, 1946 (Ulmer 2)
Club Life in Stone Age, 1940 (Terry 4)
Club Méditerranée, 1976 (Reichenbach 2)
Club of the Big Deed. *See* S.V.D, 1927
Club Sandwich, 1931 (Terry 4)
Clubman and the Tramp, 1908 (Griffith 2, Lawrence 3, Bitzer 4)
Clubs Are Trumps, 1917 (Lloyd 3, Roach 4)
Clue, 1915 (Hayakawa 3, Sweet 3)
Clue, 1985 (Whitlock 4)
Clue of the New Pin, 1929 (Gielgud 3)
Clum perdesi, 1960 (Guney 2)
Clunked on the Corner, 1929 (Sennett 2, Hornbeck 4)
Cluny Brown, 1946 (Lubitsch 2, Boyer 3, Jones, J. 3, Hoffenstein 4, La Shelle 4, Wheeler 4)
Clutching Hand, 1936 (Farnum 3, Canutt 4)
Co se septa, 1938 (Haas 3)
Co to bouchlo?, 1970 (Pojar 4)
Co zizala netusila, 1969 (Pojar 4)
Coach, 1978 (Wynn 3)
Coal Black and de Sebben Dwarfs, 1943 (Clampett 4)
Coal Miner's Daughter, 1980 (Spacek 3)
Coalface, 1935 (Cavalcanti 2, Grierson 2)
Coals of Fire, 1911 (Bosworth 3)
Coals of Fire, 1918 (Niblo 2)
Coartada en disco rojo, 1970 (Rey 3)
Coast Guard, 1939 (Bellamy 3, Scott, R. 3, Ballard 4)
Coast of Folly, 1925 (Dwan 2, Swanson 3)
Coast Patrol, 1925 (Wray 3)
Coast to Coast, 1980 (Cannon 3)
Coastal Command, 1942 (Dalrymple 4)

Coat's Tale, 1914 (Sennett 2)
Cobbler, 1923 (Roach 4)
Cobbler Stay at Your Bench. *See* Skomakare bliv vid din last, 1915
Cobra, 1925 (Valentino 3, Adrian 4, Menzies 4, Westmore, M. 4)
Cobra, 1967 (Andrews D. 3)
Cobra, 1986 (Golan and Globus 4)
Cobra. *See* Saut de l'ange, 1971
Cobra Woman, 1944 (Brooks, R. 2, Siodmak 2, Chaney Lon, Jr. 3)
Cobweb, 1916 (Hepworth 2)
Cobweb, 1955 (Minnelli 2, Bacall 3, Boyer 3, Gish, L. 3, Grahame 3, Widmark 3, Wray 3, Houseman 4, Paxton 4, Rosenman 4)
Cobweb. *See* Pókháló, 1973
Cobweb Castle. *See* Kumonosu-jo, 1957
Cobweb Hotel, 1936 (Fleischer, M. and D. 2)
Cocagne, 1960 (Fernandel 3)
Cocaine Cowboys, 1979 (Palance 3)
Cocardiers, 1967 (Carrière 4)
Cochecito, 1960 (Ferreri 2)
Cocher de fiacre endormi, 1897–98 (Guy 2)
Cock Crows Twice. *See* Niwatori wa futatabi naku, 1954
Cock o' the Walk, 1930 (Loy 3, Schildkraut 3)
Cock of the Air, 1932 (Lederer 4, Newman 4, Sherwood 4)
Cockaboody, 1973 (Hubley 4)
Cock-a-Doodle Deaux Deaux, 1966 (McKimson 4)
Cock-a-Doodle Dog, 1951 (Avery 2)
Cockeyed Cavaliers, 1934 (Sandrich 2, Plunkett 4)
Cockeyed Cowboys of Calico County, 1970 (Cody 3, Elam 3, Rooney 3)
Cockeyed Miracle, 1946 (Seaton 2, Cooper, Gladys 3, Wynn 3)
Cock-Eyed World, 1929 (Walsh 2, Brown 3, McLaglen 3, Carré 4, Edeson 4)
Cockfighter, 1974 (Oates 3, Stanton 3, Almendros 4, Corman 4)
Cockleshell Heroes, 1955 (Ferrer, J. 3, Howard, T. 3, Lee, C. 3, Addison 4, Box 4)
Cockoo Cavaliers, 1940 (Three Stooges 3)
Cockroach. *See* Sváb, 1947
Cocktail, 1937 (Henning-Jensen 2)
Cocktail Hour, 1933 (Daniels 3, Scott, R. 3, August 4)
Cocktails for Three, 1978 (Cardinale 3)
Cocktails in the Kitchen. *See* For Better, For Worse, 1954
Cocky Bantam, 1943 (Fleischer, M. and D. 2)
Cocky Cockroach, 1932 (Terry 4)
Cocoanut Grove, 1938 (Arden 3, MacMurray 3, Head 4)
Cocoanuts, 1929 (Florey 2, Dumont 3, Francis, K. 3, Marx Brothers 3, Lemaire 4, Ruttenberg 4, Ryskind 4, Wanger 4)
Cocoon, 1985 (Ameche 3)
Cocorico Monsieur Poulet, 1977 (Rouch 2)
Cocotiers, 1963 (Rouch 2)
Cocotte d'azur, 1959 (Kosma 4)
Cocu magnifique, 1946 (Barrault 3)
Code. *See* Szyfry, 1966
Code Name Heraclitus, 1965 (Baker S. 3)
Code of Honor, 1911 (Bosworth 3)
Code of Honor, 1916 (Borzage 2)
Code of Scotland Yard. *See* Shop at Sly Corner, 1946
Code of the Scarlet, 1928 (Brown, Harry Joe 4, McCord 4)
Code of the Sea, 1924 (Fleming 2)
Code of the Secret Service, 1939 (Reagan 3, McCord 4)
Code of the Streets, 1938 (Carey 3)
Code of the West, 1925 (Howard 2, Bennett C. 3)
Code 7, Victim 5. *See* Victim 5, 1964
Code Two, 1953 (Wynn 3)
Codename Wildgeese, 1984 (Kinski 3)
Codfish Balls, 1930 (Terry 4)
Codine, 1963 (Colpi 4)
Cody of the Pony Express, 1950 (Katzman 4)
Coeur à l'envers, 1980 (Girardot 3)
Coeur battant, 1961 (Trintignant 3, Legrand 4, Matras 4)
Coeur de coq, 1946 (Fernandel 3)
Coeur de Gueux, 1936 (Epstein 2)
Coeur de la France, 1962 (Leenhardt 2)
Coeur de Lilas, 1932 (Litvak 2, Fernandel 3, Gabin 3, Courant 4)
Coeur de Paris, 1931 (Benoit-Lévy 2, Fradetal 4)

Coeur de Tzigane, 1909 (Modot 3)
Coeur des pierres, 1967 (Colpi 4)
Coeur et l'argent, 1912 (Feuillade 2)
Coeur fidèle, 1923 (Epstein 2, Manès 3)
Coeur fragile, 1916 (Musidora 3)
Coeur gros comme ça, 1961 (Reichenbach 2, Morgan 3, Braunberger 4)
Coeur joyeaux, 1931 (Gabin 3)
Coeur sur la main, 1948 (Bourvil 3)
Coeurs farouches, 1924 (Duvivier 2)
Coffee House. *See* Kaffeehaus, 1971
Coffee, Tea, or Me, 1973 (Frank 4)
Coffre enchanté, 1904 (Méliès 2)
Coffre-fort, 1908 (Cohl 2)
Coffret de laque, 1932 (Darrieux 3)
Coffret de Tolède, 1914 (Feuillade 2)
Cohen at Coney Island, 1912 (Normand 3)
Cohen Collects a Debt, 1912 (Sennett 2)
Cohen Collects a Debt. *See* Cohen at Coney Island, 1912
Cohen Saves the Flag, 1913 (Sennett 2, Normand 3)
Cohen's Advertising Scheme, 1904 (Porter 2)
Cohens and Kellys in Hollywood, 1932 (Ayres 3, Karloff 3)
Cohens and the Kellys, 1927 (Florey 2)
Cohens and the Kellys in Trouble, 1933 (Stevens 2, O'Sullivan 3)
Cohen's Outing, 1913 (Sennett 2)
Coiffeur pour dames, 1952 (Fernandel 3)
Coincidences, 1946 (Reggiani 3)
Col cuore in gola, 1967 (Trintignant 3)
Col ferro e col fuoco, 1964 (Crain 3, Fusco 4)
Cold Comfort, 1957 (Sellers 3)
Cold Days. *See* Hideg napok, 1966
Cold Deck, 1917 (Hart 3, August 4)
Cold Feet, 1930 (Lantz 4)
Cold Journey, 1972 (George, Ch. D. 3)
Cold Night's Death, 1973 (Wallach 3)
Cold Romance, 1949 (Terry 4)
Cold Room, 1984 (Segal 3)
Cold Sweat, 1970 (Ullmann 3)
Cold Sweat. *See* De la part des copains, 1970
Cold Sweat. *See* Uomo dalle due ombre, 1971
Cold Turkey, 1925 (Sennett 2)
Cold Turkey, 1929 (Lantz 4)
Cold Turkey, 1940 (Langdon 3)
Cold Turkey, 1971 (Horton 3)
Cold Wind in August, 1961 (Crosby 4)
Cold-blooded Beast. *See* Bestia uccide a sangue freddo, 1971
Colditz Story, 1955 (Mills 3)
Coleccionista de cadeveras, 1971 (Aumont 3)
Cólera del viente, 1970 (Rey 3)
Colère des dieux, 1947 (Annenkov 4, Burel 4)
Colette, 1950 (Cocteau 2)
Collage, 1961 (Hammid 2)
Collants noirs, 1960 (Charisse 3, Alekan 4, Wakhévitch 4)
Collars and Cuffs, 1923 (Laurel 3, Roach 4)
Colle universelle, 1907 (Méliès 2)
Collection particulière, 1973 (Borowczyk 4)
Collectionneuse, 1967 (Rohmer 2, Almendros 4, de Beauregard 4)
Collections privées, 1979 (Borowczyk 4, Braunberger 4)
Collector, 1965 (Wyler 2, Stamp 3, Jarre 4, Krasker 4, Surtees 4)
Colleen, 1936 (Blondell 3, Fazenda 3, Keeler 3, Powell, D. 3, Orry-Kelly 4, Polito 4)
Colleen Bawn, 1911 (Olcott 2)
College, 1927 (Keaton 2, Schenck 4)
College, 1931 (Lantz 4)
College Boob, 1926 (Arthur 3)
College Chums, 1912–13 (White 3)
College Coach, 1933 (Wellman 2, Meek 3, O'Brien, P. 3, Powell, D. 3, Wayne 3, Freed 4, Mercer 4, Orry-Kelly 4)
College Confidential, 1960 (Cook 3, Marshall 3)
College Days, 1926 (Montgomery 3)
College Hero, 1927 (Walker 4)
College Holiday, 1936 (Head 4, Prinz 4, Young, V. 4)
College Humor, 1933 (Ruggles 2, Arlen 3, Crosby 3)
College Is a Nice Place. *See* Daigaku yoi toko, 1936

College Kiddo, 1927 (Sennett 2)
College Love, 1929 (Laemmle 4)
College Rhythm, 1934 (Dmytryk 2, Taurog 2, Sheridan 3, Wyman 3, Prinz 4)
College Scandal, 1935 (Brackett, C. 4)
College Spirit, 1932 (Terry 4)
College Swing, 1938 (Walsh 2, Coogan 3, Cummings 3, Grable 3, Hope 3, Horton 3, Carmichael 4, Dreier 4, Head 4, Prinz 4)
Collège swing, 1946 (Duvivier 2)
College to You. *See* Pedagogical Institution, 1940
College Vamp (remake), 1931 (Sennett 2)
College Widow, 1927 (Costello, D. 3, Blanke 4)
Collegians, 1926 (Gable 3)
Collegiate, 1936 (Grable 3, Head 4, Prinz 4)
Collégiennes, 1956 (Deneuve 3)
Collier de la reine, 1909 (Feuillade 2)
Collier de perles, 1915 (Feuillade 2, Musidora 3)
Collier vivant, 1909 (Modot 3)
Collisions, 1976 (Emshwiller 2)
Colloids, 1969 (Godfrey 4)
Colloque de chiens, 1977 (Ruiz 2)
Colomba, 1918 (Veidt 3)
Colomba, 1933 (Modot 3)
Colombine, 1920 (Jannings 3)
Colombo Plan, 1967 (Halas and Batchelor 2)
Colonel. *See* Ezredes, 1917
Colonel Blimp. *See* Life and Death of Colonel Blimp, 1943
Colonel Bogey, 1948 (Fisher 2)
Colonel Bontemps, 1915 (Feuillade 2, Musidora 3)
Colonel Chabert, 1943 (Raimu 3)
Colonel Effingham's Raid, 1945 (Bennett J. 3, Coburn, C. 3, Meek 3, Cronjager 4, Trotti 4)
Col. Heeza Liar series, 1924 (Lantz 4)
Colonel March Investigates, 1953 (Karloff 3)
Colonel March of Scotland Yard. *See* Colonel March Investigates, 1953
Colonel Redl, 1985 (Mueller-Stahl 3)
Colonello Chabert, 1920 (Gallone 2)
Colonel's Cup. *See* Sports Day, 1945
Colonel's Ward, 1912 (Ince 4)
Colonia penal, 1971 (Ruiz 2, Villagra 3)
Colonialskandal, 1927 (Warm 4)
Colonie Sicedison, 1958 (Olmi 2)
Colonna di ferro, 1940 (Mastroianni 3)
Color Box, 1935 (Lye 2)
Color Cry, 1953 (Lye 2)
Color Fields, 1977 (Vanderbeek 2)
Color of Pomegranates. *See* Sayat nova, 1972
Color Purple, 1985 (Jones 4)
Color Rhythm, 1942 (Fischinger 2)
Colorado, 1915 (Bosworth 3)
Colorado, 1921 (Eason 4, Miller, V. 4)
Colorado, 1940 (Rogers, R. 3)
Colorado Jim. *See* Colorado Pluck, 1921
Colorado Pluck, 1921 (Furthman 4)
Colorado Sundown, 1952 (Beavers 3)
Colorado Sunset, 1939 (Autry 3, Crabbe 3, Farnum 3)
Colorado Territory, 1949 (Walsh 2, Malone 3, Mayo 3, McCrea 3, Veiller 4)
Colored Girl's Love, 1914 (Sennett 2)
Colored Villainy, 1915 (Sennett 2)
Colorful Bombay, 1937 (Hoch 4)
Colorful China. *See* Színfoltok Kínából, 1957
Colorful Islands—Madagascar and Seychelles, 1936 (Hoch 4)
Colors Are Dreaming. *See* Boje sanjaju, 1958
Colors of China. *See* Színfoltok Kínából, 1957
Colors of Vásárhely. *See* Vásárhelyi szinek, 1961
Colosseum and Juicy Lucy, 1970 (Baker S. 3)
Colosso di Rodi, 1961 (Leone 2)
Colossus of New York, 1958 (Edouart 4, Lourié 4)
Colossus of Rhodes. *See* Colosso di Rodi, 1961
Colossus: The Forbin Project, 1970 (Head 4)
Colour Box. *See* Color Box, 1935
Colour Cocktail, 1934–35 (McLaren 2)

Colour Flight, 1938 (Lye 2)
Colour in Clay, 1942 (Cardiff 4)
Coloured Villainy, 1915 (Arbuckle 3)
Colpa al cuore, 1982 (Trintignant 3)
Colpa altrui, 1914 (Bertini 3)
Colpa e la pena, (Bellocchio 2)
Colpevoli, 1957 (De Sica 2)
Colpo di pistola, 1941 (Castellani 2)
Colpo di sole, 1968 (Amidei 4)
Colpo di vento, 1936 (Berry 3)
Colpo rovente, 1969 (Flaiano 4)
Colt 45, 1950 (Scott, R. 3)
Colt Comrades, 1943 (Boyd 3, Mitchum 3, Wilson, M. 4)
Coltello di ghiaccio, 1972 (Baker C. 3)
Colter Craven Story, 1960 (Ford, J. 2)
Columbus Discovers America, 1956 (Peterson 2)
Column South, 1953 (Murphy 3)
Coma, 1978 (Bujold 3, Torn 3, Widmark 3, Goldsmith 4)
Comanche, 1956 (Andrews D. 3, Cody 3)
Comanche Station, 1960 (Boetticher 2, Scott, R. 3, Brown, Harry Joe 4)
Comanche Territory, 1950 (Cody 3, O'Hara 3)
Comancheros, 1961 (Curtiz 2, Elam 3, Marvin 3, Wayne 3, Bernstein 4, Clothier 4, Smith, J.M. 4)
Comancho blanco, 1969 (Cotten 3)
Comandamenti per un gangster, 1968 (Argento 4, Morricone 4)
Comandos comunales, 1972 (Guzmán 2)
Comata, the Sioux, 1909 (Griffith 2, Bitzer 4)
Combat America, 1944 (Gable 3)
Combat dans l'île, 1961 (Schneider 3, Trintignant 3, Evein 4, Rappeneau 4)
Combat Squad, 1953 (Ireland 3)
Combats sans haine, 1948 (Spaak 4)
Combourg, visage de pierre, 1948 (Fresnay 3)
Come and Get It, 1929 (Miller, V. 4, Plunkett 4)
Come and Get It, 1936 (Hawks 2, Wyler 2, Brennan 3, Farmer 3, McCrea 3, Day 4, Furthman 4, Goldwyn 4, Maté 4, Murfin 4, Newman 4, Toland 4)
Come and Play, Sir! See Pojdte, pane, budeme si hrát!, 1965-67
Come Back Charleston Blue, 1972 (Jones 4)
Come Back, Little Sheba, 1952 (Lancaster 3, Bumstead 4, Head 4, Howe 4, Wallis 4, Waxman 4)
Come Back, Little Sheba, 1977 (Olivier 3, Woodward 3)
Come Back, Little Shicksa, 1949 (Lewis 2)
Come Back to Erin, 1914 (Olcott 2)
Come Back to Me. *See* Doll Face, 1946
Come Back to the Five and Dime, Jimmy Dean, Jimmy Dean, 1982 (Altman 2, Black 3)
Come Blow Your Horn, 1963 (Cobb 3, Martin, D. 3, Sinatra 3, Cahn 4, Daniels 4, Head 4)
Come Clean, 1931 (Laurel and Hardy 3, Roach 4)
Come Dance with Me. *See* Voulez-vous danser avec moi?, 1959
Come Drink With Me. *See* Ta tsui hsia, 1965
Come Fill the Cup, 1951 (Cagney 3, Massey 3, Young, G. 3, Blanke 4, Steiner 4)
Come Fly with Me, 1963 (Malden 3, Cahn 4, Morris 4)
Come Live with Me, 1941 (Brown 2, Lamarr 3, Meek 3, Stewart 3, Stothart 4)
Come Next Spring, 1956 (Brennan 3, Sheridan 3, Steiner 4)
Come of Age, 1954 (Anderson J. 3)
Come On Cowboys, 1937 (Canutt 4)
Come on Danger, 1932 (Musuraca 4)
Come On, George!, 1939 (Dearden 2)
Come On In, 1918 (Emerson 4, Loos 4)
Come On Leathernecks, 1938 (Cruze 2, Ladd 3)
Come on Marines!, 1934 (Hathaway 2, Arlen 3, Lupino 3, Sheridan 3, Prinz 4)
Come on Out, about 1961 (Coppola 2)
Come On Over, 1922 (Moore, C. 3, Gibbons 4)
Come On, Rangers, 1938 (Rogers, R. 3)
Come Out Fighting, 1945 (Katzman 4)
Come Out of the Kitchen, 1919 (Hackett 4)
Come Out of the Pantry, 1935 (Buchanan 3, Wray 3)

Come persi la guerra, 1948 (Pinelli 4, Rota 4)
Come Play with Me. *See* Grazia, zia, 1968
Come September, 1961 (Mulligan 2, Hudson 3, Lollobrigida 3, Bumstead 4, Daniels 4, Salter 4)
Come Take a Trip in My Airship, 1924 (Fleischer, M. and D. 2)
Come Take a Trip in My Airship, 1930 (Fleischer, M. and D. 2)
Come to My House, 1927 (August 4)
Come to the Stable, 1949 (Lanchester 3, Young, L. 3, La Shelle 4, Lemaire 4, Newman 4, Reynolds 4)
Come una rosa al naso, 1976 (Gassman 3)
Come Up Smiling. *See* Ants in His Pants, 1939
Come Up Smiling. *See* Sing Me a Love Song, 1936
Come with Us. *See* Pojdře námi, 1938
Comeback, 1970 (Hopkins, M. 3)
Comedians, 1967 (Burton 3, Gish, L. 3, Guinness 3, Jones, J.E. 3, Taylor, E. 3, Ustinov 3, Decaë 4)
Comedians. *See* Cómicos, 1954
Comedians in Africa, 1967 (Burton 3, Gish, L. 3, Guinness 3)
Comédie du bonheur, 1940 (Cocteau 2, L'Herbier 2, Francis, E. 3, Jourdan 3, Novarro 3, Presle 3, Simon, M. 3, Ibert 4)
Comédie Française, 1934 (Fradetal 4)
Comédien, 1948 (Guitry 2)
Comédians, 1964 (Brasseur 3)
Comédiens ambulants, 1950 (Fernandel 3, Jouvet 3)
Comedy Man, 1963 (More 3)
Comedy of Death. *See* Komedia smerti, 1915
Comedy of Terrors, 1963 (Tourneur, J. 2, Brown 3, Karloff 3, Lorre 3, Price 3, Rathbone 3, Crosby 4)
Comedy Tale of Fanny Hill, 1963 (Cortez 4)
Comedy-Graph. *See* Binettoscope, 1910
Come-On, 1956 (Baxter A. 3, Hayden 3, Haller 4, Head 4)
Comes a Horseman, 1978 (Pakula 2, Caan 3, Fonda, J. 3, Robards 3, Jenkins 4, Willis 4)
Comet over Broadway, 1938 (Berkeley 2, Crisp 3, Francis, K. 3, Hayward 3, Buckner 4, Howe 4, Orry-Kelly 4)
Cometogether, 1971 (Delli Colli 4)
Comets, 1929 (Lanchester 3)
Comic, 1969 (Rooney 3, Wilde 3)
Comic Book Land, 1950 (Terry 4)
Comic Grimacer, 1901 (Hepworth 2)
Comic History of Aviation. *See* Jak se člověk naučil létat, 1958
Comical Sculpture. *See* Jodai no chokoku, 1950
Cómicos, 1954 (Bardem 2, Rey 3)
Comin' Round the Mountain, 1936 (Autry 3)
Comin' round the Mountain, 1940 (Merkel 3, Dreier 4, Head 4)
Comin' Round the Mountain, 1951 (Abbott and Costello 3)
Comin' Thro' the Rye, 1916 (Hepworth 2)
Comin' Thro' the Rye, 1922 (Hepworth 2)
Comin' Through the Rye, 1926 (Fleischer, M. and D. 2)
Coming Apart, 1969 (Torn 3)
Coming Home, 1978 (Ashby 2, Dern 3, Fonda, J. 3, Voight 3, Salt 4, Wexler 4)
Coming of Amos, 1925 (Fort 4, Miller, A. 4)
Coming of Angelo, 1913 (Griffith 2, Sweet 3, Bitzer 4)
Coming of Columbus, 1912 (Selig 4)
Coming of the Dial, 1933 (Grierson 2)
Coming of the Law, 1919 (Mix 3)
Coming Out of the Ice, 1982 (Jarre 4)
Coming Out Party, 1934 (Bruce 3, Friedhofer 4, Lasky 4, Seitz 4)
Coming Out Party, 1965 (Loach 2)
Coming Through, 1925 (Sutherland 2, Beery 3)
Comizi d'amore, 1964 (Pasolini 2, Delli Colli 4)
Command, 1953 (Fuller 2, Tiomkin 4)
Command Decision, 1948 (Franklin 2, Wood 2, Gable 3, Johnson, V. 3, Pidgeon 3, Gibbons 4, Gillespie 4, Rosson 4, Rozsa 4)
Command Performance, 1931 (Auer 3, Merkel 3)
Command Performance, 1937 (Pearson 2)
Commander of the Navy. *See* Flottans overman, 1958
Commanding Officer, 1915 (Dwan 2, Crisp 3)
Commando. *See* Marcia o crepa, 1963
Commando Attack. *See* Leopardi di Churchill, 1970
Commandos, 1968 (Van Cleef 3, Argento 4)

Commandos Strike at Dawn, 1942 (Gish, L. 3, Hardwicke 3, Muni 3, Plunkett 4)
Commare secca, 1962 (Bertolucci 2, Pasolini 2)
Comme il est bon mon français. *See* Como é gostoso o meu francês, 1971
Comme je te veux, 1969 (Braunberger 4)
Comme on fait son lit on se couche, 1903–04 (Guy 2)
Comme s'il en pleuvait, 1963 (Constantine 3)
Comme un boomerang, 1976 (Delon 3, Vanel 3, Fisher 4)
Comme un éclair, 1968 (Dauphin 3)
Comme un poisson dans l'eau, 1962 (Noiret 3, Legrand 4)
Comme un pot de fraises, 1974 (Braunberger 4, Coutard 4)
Comme une carpe, 1932 (Fernandel 3, Prévert 4)
Comme une lettre à la poste, 1938 (Storck 2)
Commencement Day, 1924 (Roach 4)
Comment ça va, 1976 (Godard 2, de Beauregard 4)
Comment épouser un premier ministre, 1964 (Evein 4)
Comment Fabien devient architecte, 1900 (Zecca 2)
Comment monsieur prend son bain, 1903 (Guy 2)
Comment on disperse les foules, 1903–04 (Guy 2)
Comment on dort à Paris!, 1905 (Guy 2)
Comment qu'elle est!, 1960 (Constantine 3)
Comment réussir quand on est con et pleurnichard, 1974 (Audran 3, Audiard 4, Braunberger 4)
Comment savoir, 1966 (Jutra 2)
Comment Yukong déplaça les montagnes, 1976 (Ivens 2)
Commissaire est bon enfant, le gendarme est sans pitie, 1935 (Becker 2)
Commissario, 1962 (Comencini 2, Sordi 3, Age and Scarpelli 4)
Commissario Pepe, 1968 (Scola 2)
Common Cause, 1918 (Blackton 2)
Common Clay, 1919 (Miller, A. 4)
Common Clay, 1930 (Fleming 2, Ayres 3, Bennett C. 3, Furthman 4)
Common Enemy, 1910 (Daniels 3)
Common Ground, 1916 (Rosher 4)
Common Heritage, 1940 (Howard, L. 3)
Common Law, 1923 (Bosworth 3)
Common Law, 1931 (Bennett C. 3, McCrea 3)
Common Property, 1919 (Moore, C. 3)
Common Scents, 1962 (Hanna and Barbera 4)
Common Sin, 1920 (Haller 4)
Commonwealth, 1967 (Halas and Batchelor 2)
Commotion on the Ocean, 1956 (Three Stooges 3)
Communal Organization. *See* Comandos comunales, 1972
Communale, 1965 (Auric 4)
Commune. *See* Gromada, 1952
Commune de Paris, 1951 (Kosma 4)
Commune senso del pudore, 1976 (Noiret 3, Sordi 3)
Communicants. *See* Nattsvardsgasterna, 1963
Communion solennelle, 1976 (Baye 3, Dalio 3)
Communo senso del pudore, 1976 (Cardinale 3)
Como é gostoso o meu francês, 1971 (Pereira Dos Santos 2)
Como por que y para que asesina a un general?, 1971 (Alvarez 2)
Como yo te quería, 1944 (García 3)
Compact, 1911 (White 3)
Compact with Death. *See* Daŕbuján a Pandrhola, 1960
Compadre Mendoza, 1933 (De Fuentes 2)
Compagni, 1963 (Monicelli 2, Blier 3, Girardot 3, Mastroianni 3, Age and Scarpelli 4, Cristaldi 4)
Compagnia dei matti, 1928 (De Sica 2, Amidei 4)
Compagnie des fous. *See* Compagnia dei matti, 1928
Compagno Don Camillo, 1964 (Comencini 2, Cervi 3)
Compagnons de la marguerite, 1966 (Burel 4)
Compagnons de voyage encombrants, 1903 (Guy 2)
Compañero Presidente, 1971 (Littin 2)
Compañeros. *See* Vamos a matar, compañeros!, 1970
Companion, 1977 (Friedhofer 4)
Companions in Nightmare, 1968 (Baxter A. 3, Douglas, M. 3, Gossett 3, Young, G. 3, Herrmann 4)
Company of Cowards. *See* Advance to the Rear, 1963
Company of Killers, 1970 (Johnson, V. 3, Milland 3)
Company of Wolves, 1984 (Lansbury 3)

Company She Keeps, 1951 (Cromwell 2, Bridges 3, Houseman 4, Musuraca 4)
Comparison of Heights. *See* Takekurabe, 1955
Compartiment pour dames seules, 1934 (Christian-Jaque 2, Stradling 4)
Compartiment tueurs, 1965 (Costa-Gavras 2, Dauphin 3, Denner 3, Gélin 3, Montand 3, Piccoli 3, Reggiani 3, Signoret 3, Trintignant 3)
Compassionate Marriage, 1928 (Robinson 4)
Compères, 1983 (Depardieu 3)
Competition, 1915 (Eason 4)
Competition, 1980 (Dreyfuss 3, Remick 3, Schifrin 4)
Compleat Beatles, 1982 (McDowell 3)
Complessi, 1965 (Risi 2, Manfredi 3, Sordi 3, Tognazzi 3, Age and Scarpelli 4)
Complexes. *See* Complessi, 1965
Compliments of Mister Flow. *See* Mister Flow, 1936
Complot petrolero: La cabeza de la hidra, 1981 (Leduc 2)
Compositeur toqué, 1905 (Méliès 2)
Compositeurs et chansons de Paris, 1947–51 (Verneuil 2)
Composition in Blue. *See* Komposition in Blau, 1935
Compressed Hare, 1961 (Jones 2)
Compromis, 1978 (Blier 3)
Compromise, 1925 (Crosland 2, Brook 3, Fazenda 3)
Compromised, 1931 (Haller 4, Young, W. 4)
Compromising Fable. *See* Bajka knomprmisni, 1959
Compromising Positions, 1985 (Sarandon 3)
Comptes à rebours, 1970 (Moreau 3, Reggiani 3, Signoret 3, Vanel 3, Delerue 4)
Compulsion, 1959 (Fleischer, R. 2, Welles 2, Lemaire 4, Reynolds 4, Wheeler 4)
Computer Generation, 1973 (Vanderbeek 2)
Computer Glossary, 1967 (Bernstein 4)
Computer Graphics No. 1, 1972 (Emshwiller 2)
Computers. *See* Komputery, 1967
Comrade X, 1940 (Vidor, K. 2, Arden 3, Gable 3, Homolka 3, Lamarr 3, Adrian 4, Gillespie 4, Hecht 4, Kaper 4, Lederer 4, Reisch 4, Ruttenberg 4)
Comrades, 1911 (Sennett 2)
Comrades. *See* Drugarčine, 1979
Comrades of 1918. *See* Westfront 1918, 1930
Comradeship. *See* Kamaradschaft, 1931
Comte de Monte Cristo, 1942 (Spaak 4)
Comte de Monte Cristo, 1961 (Autant-Lara 2, Jourdan 3, Douy 4)
Comte de Monte-Cristo, 1914 (Modot 3)
Comte de Monte-Cristo, 1953 (Marais 3)
Comte Kostia, 1925 (Veidt 3)
Comtesse Doddy, 1919 (Negri 3, Kraly 4)
Comtesse Maria, 1928 (Meerson 4)
Con Artists, 1981 (Quinn 3)
Con il cuore fermo, Sicilia, 1965 (Zavattini 4)
Con la División del Norte. *See* Los de abajo, 1940
Con la rabbia agli occhi, 1976 (Brynner 3)
Con los dorados de Pancho Villa, 1939 (Fernández 2, Armendáriz 3)
Con su amable permiso, 1940 (Figueroa 4)
Conan the Barbarian, 1982 (Milius 2, Jones, J.E. 3, Von Sydow 3)
Conan the Destroyer, 1984 (Cardiff 4)
Concealing a Burglar, 1908 (Griffith 2, Lawrence 3, Bitzer 4)
Concealment. *See* Secret Bride, 1934
Conceit, 1921 (Costello, M. 3)
Concept Films series, 1961–69 (Halas and Batchelor 2)
Conception and Contraception, 1972 (Patel 4)
Concert, 1921 (Stone 3)
Concert, 1962 (Borowczyk 4)
Concert. *See* Koncert, 1962
Concert for Students. *See* Koncert pro studenty, 1970
Concerto. *See* I've Always Loved You, 1946
Concerto Brandenbourgeois, 1967 (Reichenbach 2, Braunberger 4, Coutard 4)
Concerto for Sub-Machine Gun. *See* Koncert za mašinsku pušku, 1958
Concerto in X Minor, 1968 (Kuri 4)
Concerto per pistola solista, 1970 (Valli 3)
Concierge, 1900 (Guy 2)

Concierge revient de suite, 1978 (Guillemot 4)
Concorde affaire, 1979 (Cotten 3)
Concorde—Airport '79, 1979 (Andersson B. 3, Delon 3, McCambridge 3, Wagner 3, Bumstead 4, Schifrin 4)
Concours de bébés, 1904 (Guy 2)
Concours de boules, 1896-97 (Lumière 2)
Concrete Cowboys, 1979 (Sangster 4)
Concrete Jungle. *See* Criminal, 1960
Condamné à mort s'est échappé, 1956 (Bresson 2, Burel 4)
Condamnés, 1947 (Fresnay 3)
Condé, 1970 (Fabian 3)
Conde Dracula, 1970 (Kinski 3, Lee, C. 3)
Condemned, 1923 (Furthman 4)
Condemned, 1929 (Ruggles 2, Colman 3, Barnes 4, Goldwyn 4, Howard 4, Menzies 4, Toland 4)
Condemned. *See* Danserindens Kaerlighedsdrøm, 1915
Condemned Man Escapes. *See* Condamné a mort s'est échappé, 1956
Condemned of Altona, 1962 (March 3)
Condemned of Altona. *See* Sequestri di Altona, 1962
Condemned to Death, 1932 (Gwenn 3)
Condemned to Live, 1935 (Auer 3)
Condemned Women, 1938 (Musuraca 4, Polglase 4)
Condition of Man series, 1971 (Halas and Batchelor 2)
Condominium, 1979 (Bellamy 3)
Condor, 1970 (De Toth 2, Cody 3, Cook 3, Van Cleef 3, Jarre 4)
Condorman, 1981 (Reed, O. 3, Mancini 4)
Conduct Unbecoming, 1975 (Attenborough 3, Howard, T. 3, Keach 3, York, M. 3, York, S. 3)
Conductor, 1979 (Gielgud 3)
Conductor. *See* Dyrygent, 1979
Conduisez-moi madame, 1932 (Meerson 4)
Cone of Silence, 1960 (Cushing 3, Sanders 3)
Coney Island Police Patrol, 1904 (Bitzer 4)
Coney Island, 1943 (Seaton 2, Grable 3, Day 4, Newman 4, Pan 4, Rose 4)
Coney Island, 1950 (Rosenblum 4)
Coney Island. *See* Fatty at Coney Island, 1917
Confederate Ironclad, 1912 (Nilsson 3)
Confederate's Honey, 1940 (Freleng 4)
Confession, 1965 (Gould 3)
Confession, 1918 (Franklin 2)
Confession, 1920 (Walthall 3)
Confession, 1929 (Barrymore L. 3)
Confession, 1937 (Crisp 3, Francis, K. 3, Rathbone 3, Blanke 4, Epstein, J. & P. 4, Grot 4, Orry-Kelly 4, Wallis 4)
Confession, 1965 (Dieterle 2, Rogers, G. 3)
Confession. *See* Aveu, 1970
Confessions. *See* Confessions of Boston Blackie, 1941
Confessions of a Co-ed, 1931 (Crosby 3, Sidney 3, Garmes 4)
Confessions of a Counterspy. *See* Man on a String, 1960
Confessions of a Frustrated Housewife. *See* Moglie di mio padre, 1976
Confessions of a Loving Couple, 1967 (York, M. 3)
Confessions of a Nazi Spy, 1939 (Litvak 2, Lukas 3, Robinson, E. 3, Sanders 3, Steiner 4)
Confessions of a Queen, 1925 (Sjostrom 2, Stone 3, Basevi 4, Gibbons 4)
Confessions of an Opium Eater, 1962 (Price 3, Biroc 4, Lourié 4)
Confessions of Boston Blackie, 1941 (Dmytryk 2)
Confessions of Felix Krull. *See* Bekenntnisse des Hochstaplers Felix Krull, 1957
Confessions of Gynecologist. *See* Aru fujinkai no kokuhaku, 1950
Confessions of Ina Kahr. *See* Bekenntnis der Ina Kahr, 1954
Confetti, 1927 (Buchanan 3)
Confidence, 1909 (Griffith 2, Lawrence 3, Bitzer 4)
Confidence, 1933 (Lantz 4)
Confidence. *See* Bizalom, 1979
Confidence Girl, 1952 (Clothier 4)
Confidence Man, 1924 (Heerman 4)
Confidences d'un piano, 1957 (Decaë 4)
Confident de ces dames, 1959 (Fernandel 3, Tognazzi 3)
Confidential Agent, 1945 (Bacall 3, Boyer 3, Lorre 3, Buckner 4, Howe 4, Waxman 4)
Confidential Report, 1955 (Redgrave, M. 3)

Contract on Cherry Street, 1977 (Sinatra 3, Anhalt 4, Goldsmith 4)
Contrebandiers, 1906 (Linders 3)
Contrebasse, 1962 (Delerue 4)
Contro la legge, 1950 (Mastroianni 3)
Contrôleur des wagon-lits, 1935 (Darrieux 3)
Controrapina, 1978 (Black 3, Van Cleef 3)
Controsesso, 1964 (Castellani 2, Ferreri 2, Manfredi 3, Tognazzi 3, Guerra 4, Zavattini 4)
Controversy. See Sostyazanie, 1964
Convenient Burglar, 1911 (Sennett 2)
Convention City, 1933 (Astor 3, Blondell 3, Menjou 3, Powell, D. 3, Blanke 4, Orry-Kelly 4)
Conversa Acabada, 1980 (Branco 4, de Almeida 4)
Conversation, 1974 (Coppola 2, Duvall, R. 3, Ford, H. 3, Forrest 3, Hackman 3, Murch 4, Tavoularis 4)
Conversation Piece. See Gruppo di famiglia in un interno, 1974
Conversation with Arnold Toynbee, 1954 (Hammid 2)
Conversations with Willard Van Dyke, 1981 (Ivens 2)
Conversion d'Irma, 1913 (Feuillade 2)
Conversion of Ferdys Pistora. See Obrácení Ferdýše Pištory, 1931
Conversion of Frosty Blake, 1915 (Hart 3, August 4)
Conversion of Smiling Tom, 1915 (Mix 3)
Convert. See Conversion of Frosty Blake, 1915
Convert of San Clemente, 1911 (Bosworth 3)
Converts, 1910 (Griffith 2, Walthall 3, Bitzer 4)
Convict 993, 1918 (Miller, A. 4)
Convict 99, 1938 (McDowall 3)
Convict No. 113. See Fange no. 113, 1916
Convict 13, 1920 (Keaton 2)
Convicted, 1938 (Hayworth 3)
Convicted, 1950 (Crawford, B. 3, Ford, G. 3, Malone 3, Duning 4, Guffey 4, Miller, S. 4)
Convicted Woman, 1940 (Farnum 3, Ford, G. 3)
Convicts, 1982 (Steiger 3)
Convict's Daughter, 1912–13 (White 3)
Convicts Four, 1962 (Crawford, B. 3, Price 3, Biroc 4, Rosenman 4)
Convicts No. 10 and No. 13. See Politimesteren, 1911
Convict's Sacrifice, 1909 (Griffith 2, Walthall 3, Bitzer 4)
Convict's Threat, 1915 (Anderson G. 3)
Convoy, 1927 (Haller 4)
Convoy, 1940 (Brook 3, Granger 3, Balcon 4)
Convoy, 1978 (Peckinpah 2, Borgnine 3, Coburn, J. 3)
Conway the Kerry Dancer, 1912 (Olcott 2)
Coo Coo Nut Grove, 1936 (Freleng 4)
Coocoo Murder Case, 1931 (Iwerks 4)
Coo-Coo the Magician, 1933 (Iwerks 4)
Coogan's Bluff, 1968 (Siegel 2, Cobb 3, Eastwood 3, Schifrin 4)
Cook, 1918 (Keaton 2, Arbuckle 3)
Cook. See Dough and Dynamite, 1914
Cook and Peary: The Race to the North Pole, 1983 (Steiger 3)
Cook in Trouble. See Sorcellerie culinaire, 1904
Cook of Canyon Camp, 1917 (Crisp 3)
Cool Hand Luke, 1967 (Hopper 3, Kennedy, G. 3, Martin, S. 3, Newman 3, Stanton 3, Hall 4, Schifrin 4)
Cool Million, 1972 (Coogan 3)
Cool of the Day, 1962 (Finch 3)
Cool Ones, 1967 (McDowall 3, Cahn 4, Crosby 4)
Cool World, 1964 (Clarke 2, Wiseman 2)
Coolie, 1983 (Bachchan 3)
Coonskin, 1975 (Bakshi 2, Fraker 4)
Cooperativas agricolas! El Agua, 1960 (Gómez, M. 2)
Co-Operette, 1939 (Holloway 3)
Coopertivas agropecurias, 1960 (Almendros 4)
Co-Optimists, 1930 (Holloway 3)
Cop, 1928 (Garnett 2, Boyd 3, Crisp 3, Miller, A. 4)
Cop. See Condé, 1970
Cop. See Ripoux, 1984
Cop Fools the Sergeant, 1904 (Porter 2)
Cop Killer. See Order of Death, 1983
Cop or Hood. See Flic ou voyou, 1979
Copacabana, 1947 (Marx Brothers 3, Miranda 3, Glennon 4)
Copacabana Palace, 1962 (Amidei 4)
Copains, 1964 (Noiret 3)

Copains du dimanche, 1958 (Belmondo 3)
Copenhagen, 1956 (Carlsen 2)
Copenhagen Ballet, 1960 (Robinson 4)
Copie conforme, 1946 (Jouvet 3, Jeanson 4)
Coplan ouvrte le feu a Mexico, 1967 (Tavernier 2)
Coplan sauve sa peau, 1967 (Blier 3, Kinski 3)
Cop-Out. See Stranger in the House, 1967
Copper Canyon, 1950 (Lamarr 3, Milland 3, Dreier 4, Head 4, Lang 4)
Copper Coin King. See Doka o, 1926
Copper Sky, 1957 (Martin, S. 3)
Copperhead, 1920 (Barrymore L. 3)
Coppie, 1970 (De Sica 2, Monicelli 2, Sordi 3, Vitti 3, Zavattini 4)
Cops, 1922 (Keaton 2)
Cops and Robbers, 1973 (Legrand 4)
Cops and Robbers. See Guardie e ladri, 1951
Cops and Robin, 1978 (Borgnine 3)
Cops and Watches. See Twenty Minutes of Love, 1914
Cops Is a Business, 1912–13 (White 3)
Cops Is Always Right, 1938 (Fleischer, M. and D. 2)
Copy Cat, 1941 (Fleischer, M. and D. 2)
Coq du regiment, 1933 (Fernandel 3)
Coquecigrole, 1932 (Darrieux 3, D'Eaubonne 4)
Coquette, 1929 (Beavers 3, Pickford 3, Menzies 4, Struss 4)
Coquette's Suitors, 1910 (Lawrence 3)
Coquille et le clergyman, 1927 (Dulac 2, Artaud 3)
Cor, 1931 (Epstein 2)
Coracão, 1960 (Oliveira 2)
Coraggio, 1955 (Cervi 3, De Laurentiis 4)
Coralie et Cie., 1933 (Cavalcanti 2, Rosay 3, Burel 4, D'Eaubonne 4)
Corazón bandolero, 1934 (Fernández 2)
Corazón de la noche, 1983 (Figueroa 4)
Corazón salvaje, 1968 (Figueroa 4)
Corbeau, 1943 (Clouzot 2, Fresnay 3, Andrejew 4, Warm 4)
Corbeille enchantée, 1903 (Méliès 2)
Corbusier, d'architecte du bonheur, 1956 (Delerue 4)
Cord of Life, 1909 (Griffith 2, Bitzer 4)
Corde raide, 1960 (Girardot 3, Jarre 4)
Cordon-bleu, 1931 (Feuillère 3)
Corinthian Jack, 1921 (McLaglen 3)
Coriolan, 1950 (Cocteau 2)
Cork and Vicinity, 1912 (Bunny 3)
Corky, 1972 (Johnson, B. 3, McDowall 3, Willis 4)
Corleone, 1978 (Cardinale 3, Morricone 4)
Corn. See Korn, 1943
Corn Is Green, 1945 (Bruce 3, Davis 3, Friedhofer 4, Orry-Kelly 4, Polito 4, Robinson 4, Steiner 4)
Corn Is Green, 1979 (Cukor 2, Hepburn, K. 3, Barry 4, Dillon 4, Slocombe 4)
Corn Plastered, 1951 (McKimson 4)
Corne d'or, 1963 (Delerue 4)
Corner in Colleens, 1916 (Sullivan 4)
Corner in Cotton, 1916 (Loos 4)
Corner in Hats, 1914 (Browning 2, Loos 4)
Corner in Water, 1916 (Mix 3)
Corner in Wheat, 1909 (Griffith 2, Sweet 3, Walthall 3, Bitzer 4, Macpherson 4)
Corner of Great Tokyo. See Dai-Tokyo no ikkaku, 1930
Corner Pocket, 1921 (Roach 4)
Cornered, 1932 (Eason 4)
Cornered, 1945 (Dmytryk 2, Powell, D. 3, D'Agostino 4, Paxton 4)
Cornet, 1955 (Rasp 3, Reisch 4)
Corniaud, 1964 (Bourvil 3, Decaë 4, Delerue 4)
Corny Casanovas, 1952 (Three Stooges 3)
Corny Concerto, 1943 (Clampett 4)
Corona di ferro, 1941 (Blasetti 2, Castellani 2, Cervi 3, Vích 4)
Corona negra, 1950 (Brazzi 3, Félix 3, Gassman 3)
Coronación, 1975 (Figueroa 4)
Coronado, 1935 (McLeod 2, Prinz 4)
Coronation of Edward VII. See Sacré d'Édouard VII, 1902
Coronation of King Edward VII, 1901 (Hepworth 2)
Coronation Parade, 1953 (Hathaway 2, Clarke, C.C. 4)
Coroner Creek, 1948 (Scott, R. 3, Brown, Harry Joe 4)
Corot, 1965 (Leenhardt 2)

Corpo. *See* Take This—My Body, 1974
Corpo d'amore, 1971 (Storaro 4)
Corporal Kate, 1926 (Sullivan 4)
Corporation and the Ranch Girl, 1911 (Anderson G. 3)
Corps célestes, 1973 (Sarde 4)
Corps de Diane, 1968 (Denner 3, Moreau 3)
Corps de mon ennemi, 1976 (Verneuil 2, Belmondo 3, Blier 3, Audiard 4, Lai 4)
Corpse Came C.O.D., 1947 (Blondell 3, Brent 3, Duning 4)
Corpse Vanished. *See* Revenge of the Zombies, 1944
Corpse Vanishes, 1942 (Lugosi 3, Katzman 4)
Corregidor, 1943 (Ulmer 2)
Correva l'anno di grazia 1870 . . ., 1972 (Morricone 4)
Corri, uomo, corri, 1968 (Ireland 3, Morricone 4)
Corrida d'hier et d'aujourd'hui, 1965 (Braunberger 4)
Corridor of Mirrors, 1948 (Lee, B. 3, Auric 4)
Corridors of Blood, 1963 (Karloff 3, Lee, C. 3)
Corriere del re, 1947 (Brazzi 3, Cortese 3)
Corrupción de Chris Miller, 1973 (Bardem 2, Seberg 3)
Corruption, 1933 (Auer 3)
Corruption, 1968 (Cushing 3)
Corruption. *See* Going Straight, 1916
Corruption in the Halls of Justice. *See* Corrozione a Palazzo di Giustizia, 1975
Corruption of Chris Miller. *See* Corrupcion de Chris Miller, 1973
Corruzione, 1963 (Bolognini 2, Fusco 4)
Corruzione a Palazzo di Giustizia, 1975 (Donaggio 4)
Corsair, 1931 (Newman 4)
Corsaire, 1939 (Allégret, M. 2, Dalio 3, Jourdan 3)
Corsario negro, 1944 (Armendáriz 3, Figueroa 4)
Corsaro, 1924 (Gallone 2)
Corsaro della mezzaluna, 1956 (Fabian 3)
Corsaro nero, 1937 (Vích 4)
Corsaro nero, 1976 (Ferrer, M. 3)
Corsican Brothers, 1941 (Fairbanks, D. Jr. 3, Farnum 3, Estabrook 4, Plunkett 4, Stradling 4, Tiomkin 4)
Corsican Brothers, 1985 (Chaplin 3, Pleasance 3)
Corsican Brothers. *See* Frères corses, 1939
Corso rouge, 1913 (Tourneur, M. 2)
Corta notte delle bambole di vetro, 1971 (Morricone 4)
Cortili, 1947 (Risi 2)
Corvette K-225, 1943 (Hawks 2, Fitzgerald 3, Mitchum 3, Scott, R. 3, Gaudio 4)
Corvette Port Arthur. *See* Alarme!, 1943
Corvette Summer, 1978 (Lucas 2)
Coryphee, 1914 (Lawrence 3)
Cosa avete fatto a Solange, 1972 (Morricone 4)
Cosa buffa, 1973 (Morricone 4)
Cosa Nostra: An Arch Enemy of the FBI, 1967 (Duvall, R. 3, Pidgeon 3)
Cosacchi, 1959 (Fusco 4)
Cose da pazzi, 1953 (Pabst 2, Fabrizi 3)
Cose dell'altro mondo, 1939 (Amidei 4)
Cose di Cosa Nostra, 1970 (De Sica 2, Fabrizi 3)
Cosi come sei, 1978 (Lattuada 2, Mastroianni 3, Morricone 4)
Cosi dolce cosi perversa, 1969 (Baker C. 3, Trintignant 3)
Cosi fan tutte, 1970 (Stallich 4)
Cosmic Man, 1959 (Carradine 3)
Cosmic Ray, 1960–62 (Conner 2)
Cossacks, 1928 (Adorée 3, Gilbert 3, Gibbons 4, Marion 4)
Cossacks Across the Danube. *See* Zaporosch Sa Dunayem, 1938
Cossacks in Exile. *See* Zaporosch Sa Dunayem, 1938
Cost of Dying. *See* Quanto costa morire, 1968
Costa azzurra, 1959 (Sordi 3)
Costanza della ragione, 1964 (Deneuve 3)
Coster Bill of Paris. *See* Crainquebille, 1933
Costly Exchange, 1915 (Browning 2)
Costumi e bellezze d'Italia, 1948 (Risi 2)
Côté d'Adam, 1963 (Grimault 4)
Côté d'Azur, 1948 (Leenhardt 2)
Coton, 1935 (Storck 4)
Cottage on Dartmoor, 1929 (Asquith 2)
Cottage to Let, 1941 (Asquith 2, Mills 3, Sim 3)

Cotton Club, 1984 (Gere 3, Barry 4, Sylbert 4)
Cotton Queen, 1937 (Holloway 3)
Couch, 1961 (Edwards 2)
Couch, 1964 (Warhol 2)
Coucher d'une Parisienne, 1900 (Guy 2)
Coucher d'Yvette, 1897 (Guy 2)
Cough and Sneeze. *See* Kašlání a kýchani, 1950
Could I But Live. *See* Ware hitotsubu no mugi naredo, 1965
Couleur chair, 1978 (Hopper 3, Ullmann 3)
Couleur de feu, 1957 (Storck 2)
Couleur de temps. *See* Demons de midi, 1978
Couleurs de Venise, 1945 (Aldo 4)
Coulomb's Law, 1959 (Leacock 2)
Council Bluffs to Omaha—Train Scenic, 1900 (Bitzer 4)
Counsel for the Defense, 1912 (Costello, M. 3, Talmadge, N. 3)
Counsel on De Fence, 1934 (Langdon 3)
Counsellor-at-Law, 1933 (Wyler 2, Barrymore J. 3, Daniels 3, Douglas, M. 3, Mandell 4)
Counsel's Opinion, 1933 (Dwan 2)
Count, 1916 (Chaplin 2, Purviance 3)
Count and the Cowboys, 1911 (Anderson G. 3)
Count Down Clown, 1960 (Hanna and Barbera 4)
Count Downe. *See* Son of Dracula, 1974
Count Dracula. *See* Conde Dracula, 1970
Count Dracula and His Vampire Bride. *See* Satanic Rites of Dracula, 1973
Count Five and Die, 1958 (Hunter 3)
Count of Monk's Bridge. *See* Munkbrogreven, 1934
Count of Monte Cristo, 1908 (Selig 4)
Count of Monte Cristo, 1913 (Porter 2, Bosworth 3)
Count of Monte Cristo, 1934 (Calhern 3, Donat 3, Muse 3, Dunne 4, Newman 4)
Count of Monte Cristo, 1975 (Curtis 3, Howard, T. 3, Jourdan 3, Pleasance 3)
Count of Monte Cristo. *See* Comte de Monte Cristo, 1961
Count of Ten, 1928 (Miller, V. 4)
Count Takes the Count, 1936 (Roach 4)
Count the Hours, 1953 (Siegel 2, Elam 3, Wright 3, Alton, J. 4)
Count the Votes, 1919 (Daniels 3, Lloyd 3)
Count Three and Pray, 1955 (Heflin 3, Woodward 3, Duning 4, Guffey 4)
Count Vim's Last Exercise, 1967 (Weir 2)
Count Your Blessings, 1959 (Negulesco 2, Brazzi 3, Chevalier 3, Kerr 3, Krasner 4, Rose 4, Waxman 4)
Count Your Change, 1919 (Daniels 3, Lloyd 3, Roach 4)
Countdown, 1967 (Altman 2, Caan 3, Duvall, R. 3, Rosenman 4)
Countdown. *See* Comptes à rebours, 1970
Counted Out. *See* Knock Out, 1914
Counter Jumper, 1922 (Hardy 3)
Counter-Attack, 1945 (Muni 3, Howe 4)
Counter-Espionage, 1942 (Dmytryk 2)
Counterfeit, 1919 (Miller, A. 4)
Counterfeit, 1936 (Schulberg 4)
Counterfeit Cat, 1949 (Avery 2)
Counterfeit Killer, 1968 (McCambridge 3, Jones 4)
Counterfeit Lady, 1937 (Bellamy 3)
Counterfeit Traitor, 1962 (Seaton 2, Dahlbeck 3, Holden 3, Kinski 3, Head 4, Newman 4)
Counterfeiter, 1913 (Ince 4)
Counterfeiters, 1914 (Lawrence 3)
Counterfeiters, 1948 (Chaney Lon, Jr. 3)
Counterfeiter's Confederate, 1913 (Nilsson 3)
Counterfeiters of Paris. *See* Cave se rebiffe, 1961
Counterplan. *See* Vstrechnyi, 1932
Counterplot, 1959 (Struss 4)
Counterpoint, 1968 (Heston 3, Schell, Maximilian 3, Kaper 4, Whitlock 4)
Countess, 1914 (Bushman 3)
Countess Betty's Mine, 1914 (Reid 3)
Countess Charming, 1917 (Crisp 3)
Countess Donelli. *See* Grafin Donelli, 1924
Countess from Hong Kong, 1967 (Chaplin 2, Brando 3, Chaplin 3, Hedren 3, Loren 3, Rutherford 3)

Countess of Monte Cristo, 1934 (Lukas 3, Wray 3, Freund 4, Laemmle 4)
Countess of Monte Cristo, 1948 (Henie 3, Cronjager 4, Reisch 4)
Countess's Honor. *See* Grevindens Aere, 1919
Country, 1984 (Lange 3)
Country Beyond, 1936 (Trotti 4)
Country Boy, 1915 (DeMille 2)
Country Boy, 1934 (Freleng 4)
Country Boy, 1966 (Fields 4)
Country Bumpkin. *See* All American Chump, 1936
Country Chairman, 1914 (Dwan 2)
Country Comes to Town, 1931 (Grierson 2, Wright 2)
Country Courtship, 1905 (Bitzer 4)
Country Cousin, 1919 (Crosland 2)
Country Cupid, 1911 (Griffith 2, Bitzer 4)
Country Dance, 1969 (Cusack 3, O'Toole 3, York, S. 3, Addison 4)
Country Doctor, 1909 (Griffith 2, Lawrence 3, Pickford 3, Bitzer 4)
Country Doctor, 1927 (Adrian 4, Grot 4)
Country Doctor, 1936 (King 2, Darwell 3, Hersholt 3, Summerville 3, Johnson 4, Levien 4, Seitz 4, Zanuck 4)
Country Doctor. *See* Fundoshi isha, 1960
Country Doctor. *See* Pouta, 1961
Country Doctor. *See* Selskiy vrach, 1951
Country Excursion. *See* Partie de campagne, 1946
Country Fair, 1934 (Lantz 4)
Country Flapper, 1922 (Gish, D. 3, Hackett 4)
Country Girl, 1954 (Seaton 2, Crosby 3, Holden 3, Kelly, Grace 3, Alton, R. 4, Head 4, Young, V. 4)
Country Hero, 1917 (Keaton 2, Arbuckle 3)
Country Life series, 1917 (Blackton 2)
Country Lovers, 1911 (Sennett 2, Sweet 3)
Country Mouse, 1914 (Bosworth 3)
Country Mouse, 1935 (Freleng 4)
Country Mouse and the City Mouse, 1921 (Terry 4)
Country Music Holiday, 1958 (Rosenblum 4)
Country Music U.S.A. *See* Las Vegas Hillbillies, 1966
Country of Bells. *See* Paese dei campanelli, 1953
Country of the Soviets. *See* Strana Sovietov, 1937
Country School, 1931 (Lantz 4)
Country Schoolmaster, 1906 (Bitzer 4)
Country Store, 1937 (Lantz 4)
Country That God Forgot, 1916 (Neilan 2)
Country to Country. *See* Země zemi, 1962
Country Town, 1944 (Alwyn 4)
Countrywomen, 1942 (Alwyn 4)
Counts of Pocci. *See* Grafen Pocci, 1967
County Chairman, 1935 (Fetchit 3, Rooney 3)
County Fair, 1920 (Tourneur, M. 2)
County Fair, 1932 (Bosworth 3)
County Fair, 1950 (Muse 3, Mirisch 4)
County Hospital, 1932 (Laurel & Hardy 3, Roach 4)
Coup de bambou, 1962 (Presle 3, Matras 4)
Coup de berger, 1956 (Chabrol 2, Braunberger 4)
Coup de foudre, 1976 (Deneuve 3, Noiret 3)
Coup de grâce, 1965 (Darrieux 3, Piccoli 3)
Coup de grâce. *See* Fangschuss, 1976
Coup de Jarnac, 1909 (Cohl 2)
Coup de roulis, 1931 (D'Eaubonne 4)
Coup de téléphone, 1931 (Lourié 4, Meerson 4, Spaak 4)
Coup de torchon, 1981 (Tavernier 2, Audran 3, Huppert 3, Noiret 3, Aurenche 4, Sarde 4, Trauner 4)
Coup de vent, 1905 (Feuillade 2)
Coup du berger, 1956 (Godard 2, Rivette 2)
Coup du fakir, 1915 (Feuillade 2, Musidora 3)
Coup du parapluie, 1980 (Decaë 4)
Coup pur pour rien, 1970 (Braunberger 4)
Coupable, 1936 (Barsacq 4, Ibert 4)
Couple, 1951 (Zhao 3)
Couple, 1960 (Schüfftan 4)
Couple idéal, 1945 (Cayatte 2, Signoret 3, Renoir 4)
Couple Takes a Wife, 1972 (Loy 3)
Couple témoin, 1977 (Constantine 3)
Couples. *See* Coppie, 1970

Couple's Drum. *See* Meoto daiko, 1941
Coups de feu à l'aube, 1932 (Artaud 3, Modot 3)
Cour des miracles, 1902 (Guy 2)
Courage, 1921 (Franklin 2, Menjou 3)
Courage for Every Day, 1964 (Menzel 2)
Courage for Every Day. *See* Každý den odvahu, 1964
Courage, fuyons, 1980 (Deneuve 3)
Courage of Black Beauty, 1957 (Leven 4)
Courage of Kavik the Wolf Dog. *See* Kavik the Wolf Dog, 1978
Courage of Lassie, 1946 (Taylor, E. 3, Irene 4, Kaper 4)
Courage of Marge O'Doone, 1919 (Karloff 3)
Courageous Coward, 1919 (Hayakawa 3)
Courageous Dr. Christian, 1940 (Hersholt 3, Alton, J. 4, Lardner 4)
Courageous Mr. Penn. *See* Penn of Pennsylvania, 1942
Coureurs de brousse, 1956 (Decaë 4)
Courier of Lyon. *See* Affaire du courrier de Lyon, 1937
Courier to the Tsar. *See* Strogoff, 1968
Couronne noire, 1952 (Cocteau 2)
Couronnes, 1909 (Cohl 2)
Courrier Sud, 1936 (Bresson 2, Vanel 3, Barsacq 4, Ibert 4)
Cours après moi que je t'attrape, 1976 (Girardot 3)
Cours d'une vie, 1966 (Delerue 4)
Course a l'abîme, 1915 (Feuillade 2)
Course à l'échalote, 1975 (Dauphin 3, Decaë 4)
Course au pétrole, 1938 (Leenhardt 2)
Course au potiron, 1906 (Feuillade 2, Carré 4)
Course aux millions, 1912 (Feuillade 2)
Course de taureaux, 1951 (Braunberger 4, Decaë 4)
Course de taureaux à Nîmes, 1906 (Guy 2)
Course des belles-mères, 1907 (Feuillade 2)
Course du lièvre à travers les champs, 1972 (Clément 2, Ryan 3, Trintignant 3, Lai 4)
Course en sac, 1895 (Lumière 2)
Courses d'obstacles, 1957 (Delerue 4)
Court House Crooks, 1915 (Sennett 2)
Court Intrigue. *See* Hofintrige, 1912
Court Jester, 1956 (Carradine 3, Kaye 3, Lansbury 3, Rathbone 3, Cahn 4, Frank and Panama 4, Head 4)
Court Martial, 1928 (Walker 4)
Court Martial. *See* Carrington, V.C., 1954
Court Martial of Billy Mitchell, 1955 (Preminger 2, Bellamy 3, Cooper Gary 3, Steiger 3, Tiomkin 4)
Courte échelle, 1899–1900 (Guy 2)
Courte tête, 1956 (Audiard 4)
Courtes Jambes, 1938 (Dalio 3)
Courtesans of Bombay, 1982 (Ivory 2, Jhabvala 4)
Courtin' of Calliope Clew, 1916 (Borzage 2)
Courting. *See* Námluvy, 1961
Courting of Mary, 1911 (Pickford 3)
Courting Trouble, 1932 (Sennett 2)
Court-Martialled, 1915 (Hepworth 2)
Courtneys of Curzon Street, 1947 (Wilcox 2, Neagle 3)
Courtship of Andy Hardy, 1942 (Reed, D. 3, Rooney 3)
Courtship of Eddie's Father, 1963 (Minnelli 2, Ford, G. 3, Jones S. 3, Krasner 4, Pasternak 4, Rose 4)
Courtship of Judge Hardy, 1942 (Stone 3)
Courtship of Miles Sandwich, 1923 (Roach 4)
Courtship of Miles Standish, 1910 (Bosworth 3)
Courtship of Miles Standish, 1923 (Johnson, N. 3)
Courtship of O San, 1914 (Ince 4)
Courtship of O'Sann. *See* O Mimi san, 1914
Cousin Angélica. *See* Prima Angélica, 1974
Cousin cousine, 1975 (Guillemot 4)
Cousin de Callao, 1962 (Delerue 4)
Cousin Pons, 1923 (Modot 3)
Cousin Wilbur, 1939 (Sidney 2, Roach 4)
Cousins, 1959 (Broca 2, Chabrol 2, Audran 3, Decaë 4, Evein 4, Gégauff 4, Rabier 4)
Couteau dans la plaie, 1962 (Litvak 2, Loren 3, Alekan 4, Theodorakis 4, Trauner 4)
Couturier de ces dames, 1956 (Fabian 3, Fernandel 3)
Couturière de Lineville, 1931 (Maté 4)
Covek nije tica, 1966 (Makavejev 2)

Covenant with Death, 1967 (Fernández 2, Hackman 3, Rosenman 4)
Cover Girl, 1944 (Donen 2, Vidor, C. 2, Arden 3, Hayworth 3, Kelly, Gene 3, Banton 4, Cole 4, Guffey 4, Maté 4)
Cover Girl Models, 1975 (Corman 4)
Cover Me, Babe, 1970 (Smith, J.M. 4)
Covered Pushcart, 1949 (Terry 4)
Covered Wagon, 1923 (Arzner 2, Cruze 2, Cody 3, Brown, K. 4)
Covert Action. *See* Sono stato un'agente CIA, 1978
Cover-Up, 1949 (Bendix 3, Laszlo 4, Salter 4)
Covjek koji je morao pjevati, 1970 (Dragić 4)
Cow and I. *See* Vache et le prisonnier, 1959
Cow Country, 1953 (O'Brien, E. 3)
Cow on the Moon. *See* Krava na mjesecu, 1959
Cow Town, 1950 (Autry 3)
Coward, 1911 (White 3)
Coward, 1912 (Dwan 2)
Coward, 1915 (August 4, Ince 4, Sullivan 4)
Coward, 1927 (Baxter W. 3)
Coward. *See* Zbabělec, 1962
Coward and the Holy Man. *See* Kapurush-o-Mahapurush, 1965
Coward and the Saint. *See* Kapurush-o-Mahapurush, 1965
Cowboy, 1958 (Daves 2, Ford, G. 3, Lemmon 3, Martin, S. 3, Bass 4, Duning 4, Trumbo 4)
Cowboy and the Artist, 1911 (Dwan 2)
Cowboy and the Blonde, 1941 (Clarke, C.C. 4, Day 4)
Cowboy and the Girl. *See* Lady Takes a Chance, 1943
Cowboy and the Indians, 1949 (Autry 3)
Cowboy and the Lady, 1922 (Johnson, N. 3)
Cowboy and the Lady, 1938 (McCarey 2, Brennan 3, Cooper, Gary 3, Oberon 3, Basevi 4, Behrman 4, Day 4, Goldwyn 4, Levien 4, Newman 4, Toland 4)
Cowboy and the Outlaw, 1911 (Dwan 2)
Cowboy and the Senorita, 1944 (Rogers, R. 3)
Cowboy and the Squaw, 1910 (Anderson G. 3)
Cowboy Commandos, 1943 (Bond 3)
Cowboy Cop, 1926 (Arthur 3)
Cowboy Coward, 1911 (Anderson G. 3)
Cowboy from Brooklyn, 1938 (Bacon 2, O'Brien, P. 3, Powell, D. 3, Reagan 3, Sheridan 3, Deutsch 4, Edeson 4, Mercer 4, Wallis 4)
Cowboy in Manhattan, 1943 (Salter 4)
Cowboy Jimmy, 1957 (Mimica 4, Vukotić 4)
Cowboy Kid, 1928 (Miller, S. 4)
Cowboy Quarterback, 1939 (McCord 4)
Cowboy Samaritan, 1913 (Anderson G. 3)
Cowboy Serenade, 1942 (Autry 3)
Cowboy Sheik, 1924 (Roach 4, Rogers, W. 3)
Cowboy Socialist, 1912 (Dwan 2)
Cowboys, 1971 (Dern 3, Wayne 3, Ravetch 4, Surtees 4, Williams, J. 4)
Cowboys Cry for It, 1923 (Laurel 3)
Cowboy's Deliverance, 1911 (Dwan 2)
Cow-boys français, 1953 (Decaë 4)
Cowboys from Texas, 1939 (Canutt 4)
Cowboy's Mother-in-Law, 1910 (Anderson G. 3)
Cowboy's Ruse, 1911 (Dwan 2)
Cowboy's Sweetheart, 1910 (Anderson G. 3)
Cowboy's Vindication, 1910 (Anderson G. 3)
Cowcatcher's Daughter, 1931 (Sennett 2)
Cowpuncher's Law, 1911 (Anderson G. 3)
Cowpuncher's Peril, 1916 (Mix 3)
Cowpuncher's Ward, 1910 (Anderson G. 3)
Cow's Husband, 1931 (Fleischer, M. and D. 2)
Cow's Kimono, 1926 (Roach 4)
Coy Decoy, 1941 (Clampett 4)
Crabe-Tambour, 1977 (Coutard 4, de Beauregard 4, Sarde 4)
Crack in the Mirror, 1960 (Fleischer, R. 2, Welles 2, D'Eaubonne 4, Jarre 4, Zanuck 4)
Crack in the World, 1965 (Andrews D. 3, Lourié 4)
Crack o' Dawn, 1925 (Garmes 4)
Crack Your Heels, 1919 (Daniels 3, Lloyd 3, Roach 4)
Cracked Ice Man, 1933 (Roach 4)
Cracked Nuts, 1931 (Karloff 3, Musuraca 4, Steiner 4)
Cracked Nuts, 1941 (Auer 3, Merkel 3)
Cracked Quack, 1951 (Freleng 4)

Cracked Wedding Bells, 1920 (Roach 4)
Cracker Factory, 1979 (Wood 3)
Crackers, 1984 (Sutherland 3, Warden 3, Kovacs 4)
Crackpot King, 1946 (Terry 4)
Crackpot Quail, 1941 (Avery 2)
Cracks, 1967 (Bourvil 3, Delerue 4)
Cracksman, 1963 (Sanders 3)
Cracksman Santa Claus, 1913 (Reid 3)
Crack-up, 1937 (Lorre 3)
Crack-Up, 1946 (Marshall 3, O'Brien 3, Trevor 3, Paxton 4)
Cradle, 1922 (Rosson 4)
Cradle of Courage, 1920 (Hart 3, Hayakawa 3, August 4)
Cradle of Genius, 1959 (Fitzgerald 3)
Cradle Robbers, 1924 (Roach 4)
Cradle Snatchers, 1927 (Hawks 2, Fazenda 3)
Cradle Song, 1933 (Leisen 2, Auer 3, Head 4, Lang 4)
Crafty Selim. *See* Tilki Selim, 1966
Craig's Wife, 1928 (Baxter W. 3)
Craig's Wife, 1936 (Arzner 2, Burke 3, Darwell 3, Russell, R. 3, Ballard 4)
Crainquebille, 1922 (Feyder 2, Rosay 3, Burel 4)
Crainquebille, 1933 (Modot 3)
Cranes Are Flying. *See* Letiat zhuravli, 1957
Cranks at Work, 1960 (Russell 2)
Crash, 1928 (McCord 4)
Crash, 1932 (Dieterle 2, Brent 3, Haller 4, Orry-Kelly 4)
Crash, 1976 (Carradine 3, Ferrer, J. 3)
Crash Dive, 1943 (Andrews D. 3, Baxter A. 3, Power 3, Burnett 4, Day 4, Shamroy 4, Swerling 4)
Crash Donovan, 1936 (Bond 3, Krasner 4)
Crash Goes the Hash, 1944 (Three Stooges 3)
Crash Landing, 1958 (Katzman 4)
Crash of Silence. *See* Mandy, 1952
Crashin' Thru, 1939 (Cody 3)
Crashing Hollywood, 1931 (Arbuckle 3, Grable 3)
Crashing Hollywood, 1938 (Musuraca 4)
Crashout, 1955 (Bendix 3, Kennedy, A. 3)
Craven, 1915 (Reid 3)
Crawling Eye. *See* Trollenberg Terror, 1958
Crawling Hand, 1963 (Arlen 3)
Crawlspace, 1971 (Kennedy, A. 3, Wright 3, Goldsmith 4)
Crawlspace, 1986 (Donaggio 4)
Crayon and the Eraser. *See* Ceruza és radír, 1960
Crayono, 1907 (Bitzer 4)
Craze, 1974 (Evans 3, Howard, T. 3, Palance 3, Francis 4)
Crazed Fruit. *See* Kurutta kajitsu, 1956
Crazies, 1973 (Romero 2)
Crazy Composer. *See* Compositeur toqué, 1905
Crazy Cruise, 1941 (Avery 2, Clampett 4)
Crazy Day. *See* Giornata balorda, 1960
Crazy Desire. *See* Voglia matta, 1962
Crazy Feet, 1929 (Roach 4)
Crazy for Love. *See* Trou normand, 1952
Crazy House, 1928 (Roach 4)
Crazy House, 1940 (Lantz 4)
Crazy House, 1943 (Bruce 3, Chaney Lon, Jr. 3, Howard, S. 3, Rathbone 3, Cahn 4)
Crazy House. *See* House in Nightmare Park, 1973
Crazy Joe, 1973 (Torn 3, Wallach 3)
Crazy Knights, 1944 (Katzman 4)
Crazy Like a Fox, 1926 (McCarey 2, Hardy 3, Roach 4)
Crazy Mama, 1975 (Demme 2, Sothern 3, Corman 4)
Crazy Mixed-Up Pup, 1954 (Avery 2)
Crazy Page. *See* Kurutta ippeiji, 1926
Crazy Prospector, 1913 (Anderson G. 3)
Crazy Quilt, 1966 (Meredith 3)
Crazy That Way, 1930 (Bennett J. 3)
Crazy to Act, 1927 (Sennett 2, Hardy 3)
Crazy to Marry, 1921 (Cruze 2, Arbuckle 3, Brown, K. 4)
Crazy Town, 1932 (Fleischer, M. and D. 2)
Crazy World, 1968 (Kuri 4)
Crazy World of Julius Vrooder, 1974 (Hiller 2)
Crazy World of Laurel and Hardy, 1967 (Roach 4)

Crazy Years. *See* Lude godini, 1978
Crazylegs, 1953 (Miller, V. 4)
Cream Puff Romance, 1916 (Sennett 2, Arbuckle 3)
Creation, 1979 (Brakhage 2)
Creation, 1982 (Vinton 4)
Création d'ulcères artificiels chez le chien, 1934 (Storck 2)
Creation of the Humanoids, 1962 (Pierce 4)
Creation of the World. *See* Stvoření světa, 1957
Creator, 1985 (O'Toole 3)
Creature. *See* Titan Find, 1984
Creature from Black Lake, 1976 (Elam 3)
Creature from the Black Lagoon, 1954 (Mancini 4, Salter 4, Westmore, B. 4)
Creature from the Haunted Sea, 1960 (Corman 4)
Creature Walks among Us, 1956 (Mancini 4, Salter 4, Westmore, B. 4)
Creature with the Atom Brain, 1955 (Siodmak 4)
Creature with the Blue Hand. *See* Blaue Hand, 1967
Créatures, 1966 (Varda 2, Dahlbeck 3, Deneuve 3, Piccoli 3)
Creatures of the Prehistoric Planet. *See* Horror of the Blood Monsters, 1970
Creatures of the Red Planet. *See* Horror of the Blood Monsters, 1970
Credo ou La Tragédie de Lourdes, 1924 (Duvivier 2)
Creed of Violence, 1969 (Van Cleef 3)
Creep Show, 1982 (Romero 2)
Creepers. *See* Phenomena, 1984
Creeping Flesh, 1972 (Cushing 3, Lee, C. 3, Francis 4)
Creeping Unknown. *See* Quatermass Experiment, 1955
Creeps, 1956 (Three Stooges 3)
Creepy Time Pal, 1960 (Hanna and Barbera 4)
Cremators. *See* Spaľovači mrtvol, 1968
Crème Simon, 1937 (Alexeieff and Parker 2)
Creo en Dios, 1940 (De Fuentes 2, Figueroa 4)
Creosoot, 1931 (Ivens 2, Van Dongen 4)
Creosote. *See* Creosoot, 1931
Crepúscolo de un Dios, 1968 (Fernández 2)
Crépuscule d'épouvante, 1921 (Duvivier 2, Vanel 3)
Crescendo, 1969 (Sangster 4)
Crescete e moltiplicatevi, 1973 (Morricone 4)
Crest of the Wave, 1954 (Kelly, Gene 3)
Crest of the Wave. *See* Seagulls Over Sorrento, 1954
Crésus, 1960 (Fernandel 3, Kosma 4)
Crève-Coeur, 1954 (Decaë 4, Rabier 4)
Cri de coeur, 1974 (Audran 3, Seyrig 3)
Cri du cormoran le soir au-dessus des jonques, 1970 (Blier 3, Depardieu 3, Audiard 4, D'Eaubonne 4)
Cria! *See* Cría cuervos, 1976
Cría cuervos, 1976 (Saura 2, Chaplin 3)
Cricca dorata, 1913 (Bertini 3)
Cricket in Times Square, 1971 (Jones 2)
Cricket on the Hearth, 1909 (Griffith 2, Bitzer 4)
Cricket on the Hearth, 1914 (Guy 2, Gaudio 4)
Cricket on the Hearth. *See* Sverchok na Pechia, 1915
Cries and Whispers. *See* Viskningar och rop, 1973
Crime. *See* Morderstwo, 1957
Crime and Passion, 1966 (Wicki 2)
Crime and Passion, 1976 (Passer 2, Black 3, Sharif 3)
Crime and Punishment, 1935 (Von Sternberg 2, Lorre 3, Ballard 4, Schulberg 4)
Crime and Punishment. *See* Crime et châtiment, 1935
Crime and Punishment. *See* Crime et châtiment, 1956
Crime and Punishment. *See* Prestuplenie i nakazanie, 1968
Crime and Punishment. *See* Raskolnikov, 1923
Crime and Punishment, U.S.A., 1959 (Corman 4, Crosby 4)
Crime at a Girls' School. *See* Zločin v dívčí škole, 1965
Crime au concert Mayol, 1954 (Manès 3)
Crime by Night, 1944 (Wyman 3)
Crime Club, 1973 (Sheen 3)
Crime de Grand-père, 1910 (Gance 2)
Crime de la rue du Temple. *See* Assassinat de la rue du Temple, 1904
Crime de Monsieur Lange, 1936 (Becker 2, Renoir 2, Berry 3, Grimault 4, Kosma 4, Prévert 4)
Crime de Monsieur Pégotte, 1935 (Berry 3)
Crime Doctor, 1934 (Crisp 3, Murfin 4, Plunkett 4, Steiner 4)

Crime Doctor's Courage, 1945 (Baxter W. 3)
Crime Doctor's Diary, 1949 (Baxter W. 3, Anhalt 4)
Crime Doctor's Gamble, 1947 (Baxter W. 3)
Crime Doctor's Manhunt, 1946 (Baxter W. 3, Brackett, L. 4)
Crime Doctor's Strangest Case, 1943 (Baxter W. 3)
Crime Doctor's Warning, 1945 (Baxter W. 3)
Crime Does Not Pay. *See* Crime ne paie pas, 1962
Crime du Bouif, 1951 (Braunberger 4)
Crime et châtiment, 1935 (Baur 3, Honegger 4, Lourié 4)
Crime et châtiment, 1956 (Blier 3, Gabin 3, Renoir 4, Spaak 4)
Crime in a Night Club. *See* Zločin v šantánu, 1968
Crime in Paradise. *See* Brott i Paradiset, 1959
Crime in the Streets, 1956 (Cassavetes 2, Siegel 2, Mineo 3, Waxman 4
Crime ne paie pas, 1962 (Brasseur 3, Cervi 3, Darrieux 3, Feuillère 3, Girardot 3, Morgan 3, Noiret 3, Aurenche 4, Bost 4, Delerue 4, Jeanson 4, Matras 4, Wakhévitch 4)
Crime Nobody Saw, 1937 (Ayres 3, McDaniel 3, Head 4)
Crime of Cain, 1914 (Ingram 2)
Crime of Dr. Crespi, 1935 (Von Stroheim 2)
Crime of Dr. Hallet, 1938 (Bellamy 3, Krasner 4)
Crime of Helen Stanley, 1934 (Bellamy 3, Bond 3)
Crime of Monsieur Lange. *See* Crime de Monsieur Lange, 1936
Crime of Passion, 1957 (Hayden 3, Stanwyck 3, Wray 3, La Shelle 4)
Crime of the Century, 1933 (Hersholt 3, Banton 4, Head 4)
Crime of the Century. *See* Walk East on Beacon, 1952
Crime on a Summer Morning. *See* Par un beau matin d'été, 1965
Crime on Their Hands, 1948 (Three Stooges 3)
Crime School, 1938 (Bogart 3, Friedhofer 4, Steiner 4)
Crime Wave, 1954 (De Toth 2, Bronson 3, Hayden 3, Glennon 4)
Crime Without Passion, 1934 (Rains 3, Garmes 4, Hecht 4, MacArthur 4, Vorkapich 4)
Crimebusters, 1961 (Dern 3)
Crimen, 1960 (Blier 3, Manfredi 3, Mangano 3, Sordi 3, De Laurentiis 4, Di Venanzo 4, Gherardi 4)
Crimen de doble filo, 1964 (Borau 2)
Crimen de Oribe, 1949 (Torre-Nilsson 2)
Crimen y castigo, 1950 (De Fuentes 2)
Crimes de l'amour. *See* Rideau cramoisi, 1952
Crime's End. *See* My Son is Guilty, 1939
Crimes of Passion, 1984 (Perkins 3, Turner, K. 3)
Criminal, 1915 (Costello, M. 3, Talmadge, N. 3, Sullivan 4)
Criminal, 1960 (Losey 2, Baker S. 3, Krasker 4, Sangster 4)
Criminal at Large. *See* Frightened Lady, 1932
Criminal Code, 1931 (Hawks 2, Huston 3, Karloff 3, Howe 4, Miller, S. 4)
Criminal Court, 1946 (Wise 2)
Criminal Hypnotist, 1908 (Griffith 2, Bitzer 4)
Criminal Lawyer, 1951 (O'Brien, P. 3)
Criminal Life of Archibaldo de la Cruz. *See* Ensayo de un crimen, 19
Criminals, 1913 (Dwan 2)
Criminals of the Air, 1937 (Hayworth 3)
Criminel, 1932 (Baur 3)
Crimson City, 1928 (Loy 3, Wong 3)
Crimson Cult, 1970 (Karloff 3)
Crimson Cult. *See* Curse of the Crimson Altar, 1968
Crimson Curtain. *See* Rideau cramoisi, 1953
Crimson Dove, 1917 (Marion 4)
Crimson Dynasty. *See* Koenigsmark, 1936
Crimson Kimono, 1959 (Fuller 2, Boyle 4)
Crimson Pirate, 1952 (Siodmak 2, Lancaster 3, Lee, C. 3, Adam 4, Alwyn 4, Mathieson 4)
Crimson Romance, 1934 (Von Stroheim 2)
Crimson Runner, 1925 (Polito 4, Stromberg 4)
Crimson Stain Mystery, 1916 (Costello, M. 3)
Crimson Trail, 1935 (Bond 3)
Crinoline, 1906 (Guy 2)
Cripple Girl. *See* Kaerligheds Laengsel, 1915
Cripta de l'incubo, 1963 (Lee, C. 3)
Crise est finie, 1934 (Siodmak 2, Darrieux 3, Schufftan 4, Siodmak
Crisis, 1912 (Ince 4)
Crisis, 1950 (Brooks, R. 2, Ferrer, J. 3, Grant, C. 3, Novarro 3, Ames 4, Freed 4, Rozsa 4)
Crisis, 1963 (Leacock 2)

Crisis. *See* Kris, 1946
Crisis: A Film of 'The Nazi Way', 1938 (Hammid 2, Kline 2)
Crisis at Central High, 1981 (Woodward 3)
Crisis en el Caribe, 1962 (Alvarez 2)
Criss Cross, 1949 (Siodmak 2, Curtis 3, De Carlo 3, Duryea 3, Lancaster 3, Leven 4, Planer 4, Rozsa 4)
Cristeaux, 1928 (Gance 2)
Cristeros, 1946 (García 3)
Cristo proibito, 1951 (Cervi 3, Cuny 3)
Cristo si è fermato a Eboli, 1979 (Rosi 2, Cuny 3, Papas 3, Volonté 3, Cristaldi 4, Guerra 4)
Critic, 1906 (Bitzer 4)
Critic, 1963 (Brooks, M. 2)
Critical List, 1978 (Gossett 3, Wagner 3)
Critic's Choice, 1963 (Ball 3, Hope 3, Torn 3, Duning 4, Head 4, Lang 4)
Crockett Doodle-Do, 1960 (McKimson 4)
Croisée des chemins, 1942 (Brasseur 3)
Croisière de L'Atalante, 1926 (Grémillon 2)
Croisière pour l'inconnu, 1947 (Brasseur 3, Dauphin 3)
Croisières sidérales, 1941 (Bourvil 3, Bost 4)
Croissance de Paris, 1954 (Braunberger 4)
Croix de bois, 1931 (Artaud 3, Vanel 3, Douy 4)
Croix des vivants, 1962 (Cuny 3, Barsacq 4)
Croix du Sud, 1931 (Christian-Jaque 2)
Cromwell, 1911 (Berry 3)
Cromwell, 1970 (Guinness 3, Unsworth 4)
Cronaca criminale del Far West. *See* Banda J & S, 1972
Cronaca di un amore, 1950 (Antonioni 2, Fusco 4)
Cronaca familiare, 1962 (Zurlini 2, Mastroianni 3)
Cronaca nera, 1947 (Cervi 3, Amidei 4)
Cronache di poveri amanti, 1954 (Mastroianni 3, Amidei 4, Di Venanzo 4)
Crónica Cubana, 1963 (Corrieri 3)
Crook. *See* Voyou, 1970
Crook Buster, 1925 (Wyler 2)
Crook That Cried Wolf, 1963 (Hanna and Barbera 4)
Crooked Billet, 1930 (Carroll M. 3, Balcon 4)
Crooked Circle, 1932 (Pitts 3)
Crooked Hearts, 1972 (Fairbanks, D. Jr. 3, O'Sullivan 3, Russell, R. 3, Biroc 4)
Crooked Mirror. *See* Křivé zrcadlo, 1956
Crooked Road, 1911 (Griffith 2, Bitzer 4)
Crooked Road, 1965 (Granger 3, Ryan 3)
Crooked to the End, 1915 (Sennett 2)
Crooked Trails, 1916 (Mix 3)
Crooked Way, 1949 (Florey 2, Alton, J. 4, Polglase 4)
Crooks and Coronets, 1969 (Evans 3, Oates 3)
Crooks Anonymous, 1962 (Christie 3)
Crooks Can't Win, 1928 (Brown 3)
Crooks in Clover. *See* Penthouse, 1933
Crook's Tour, 1933 (Roach 4)
Crooner, 1932 (Bacon 2, Orry-Kelly 4)
Crop Chasers, 1939 (Iwerks 4)
Croquemitaine et Rosalie, 1916 (Cohl 2)
Croquette, 1927 (Balfour 3)
Crorepati, 1936 (Sircar 4)
Crosby Case, 1934 (Auer 3)
Cross Country Cruise, 1934 (Ayres 3)
Cross Country Detours, 1940 (Avery 2)
Cross Country Romance, 1940 (Ladd 3, Hunt 4)
Cross Creek, 1983 (McDowell 3, Steenburgen 3, Torn 3, Alonzo 4)
Cross Current, 1971 (Ferrer, J. 3)
Cross Currents, 1935 (Havelock-Allan 4)
Cross Fire, 1933 (Musuraca 4, Plunkett 4)
Cross My Heart, 1937 (Havelock-Allan 4)
Cross My Heart, 1947 (Hutton 3, Head 4, Lang 4, Schnee 4)
Cross of Iron, 1977 (Peckinpah 2, Burton 3, Coburn, J. 3, Schell, Maximilian 3)
Cross of Iron II, 1979 (Jurgens 3)
Cross of Lorraine, 1943 (Garnett 2, Aumont 3, Hardwicke 3, Kelly, Gene 3, Lorre 3, Freund 4, Gibbons 4, Kaper 4, Lardner 4)
Cross of the Living. *See* Croix des vivants, 1960

Cross of Valour. *See* Krzyz walecznych, 1959
Cross Purposes, 1913 (Reid 3)
Cross Red Nurse, 1918 (Dressler 3)
Cross Shot, 1976 (Cobb 3)
'Cross the Mexican Line, 1914 (Reid 3)
Cross Your Heart, 1912 (Cruze 2)
Crossbar, 1979 (Ireland 3)
Crossbeam. *See* Tvärbalk, 1967
Cross-Country original, 1909 (Linders 3)
Crosscurrent. *See* Cable Car Mystery, 1971
Crossed Love and Swords, 1915 (Sennett 2, Fazenda 3)
Crossed Swords, 1978 (Reed, O. 3, Welch 3)
Crossed Swords. *See* Maestro di Don Giovanni, 1953
Crossed Swords. *See* Prince and the Pauper, 1978
Crossfire, 1947 (Dmytryk 2, Grahame 3, Mitchum 3, Ryan 3, Young, R. 3, D'Agostino 4, Hunt 4, Paxton 4, Schary 4)
Crossing Fox River, 1976
Crossing of Paris. *See* Traversée de Paris, 1956
Crossings and Meetings, 1974 (Emshwiller 2)
Crossplot, 1969 (Moore, R. 3)
Crossroads, 1942 (Lamarr 3, Nilsson 3, Powell, W. 3, Rathbone 3, Trevor 3, Kaper 4, Ruttenberg 4)
Crossroads, 1955 (Lee, C. 3)
Crossroads, 1976 (Conner 2)
Crossroads. *See* Carrefour, 1939
Crossroads. *See* Jujiro, 1928
Crossroads. *See* Shizi jietou, 1937
Crossroads of Life. *See* I Livets Braending, 1915
Crossroads of New York, 1922 (Sennett 2, Hornbeck 4)
Crossways. *See* Jujiro, 1928
Crosswinds, 1951 (Head 4)
Crouching Beast, 1935 (Kortner 3)
Croulants se portent bien, 1961 (Auric 4)
Crow, 1919 (Eason 4)
Crow on a Moonlit Night. *See* Tsukiyo garasu, 1939
Crowd, 1928 (Vidor, K. 2, Gibbons 4, Gillespie 4, Thalberg 4)
Crowd Roars, 1932 (Hawks 2, Blondell 3, Cagney 3, Miller, S. 4, Zanuck 4)
Crowd Roars, 1938 (Fleming 2, O'Sullivan 3, Taylor, R. 3, Wyman 3, Seitz 4)
Crowd Snores, 1932 (Lantz 4)
Crowded Day, 1954 (Roberts 3)
Crowded Hour, 1925 (Daniels 3, Hunt 4)
Crowded Paradise, 1956 (Kaufman 4, Sylbert 4)
Crowded Sky, 1960 (Andrews D. 3, Rosenman 4, Schnee 4, Stradling 4)
Crowded Streetcar. *See* Manin densha, 1957
Crowing Pains, 1947 (McKimson 4)
Crown of Lies, 1926 (Negri 3, Glennon 4, Vajda 4)
Crown of the Year, 1943 (Alwyn 4)
Crown of Thorns. *See* I.N.R.I., 1923
Crown Prince's Double, 1916 (Costello, M. 3, Talmadge, N. 3)
Crown Versus Stevens, 1936 (Powell 2)
Crows and Sparrows. *See* Wuya yu Maque, 1948
Crow's Feat, 1961 (Freleng 4)
Crow's Fete, 1963 (Hanna and Barbera 4)
Crucial Test, 1912 (Bosworth 3)
Crucial Test, 1916 (Menjou 3, Marion 4)
Crucible. *See* Sorcières de Salem, 1957
Crucified Lovers. *See* Chikamatsu monogatari, 1954
Crucifijo de piedra, 1954 (García 3)
Crudeli, 1966 (Cotten 3, Morricone 4)
Cruel, Cruel Love, 1914 (Chaplin 2, Sennett 2)
Cruel Sea, 1953 (Baker S. 3, Hawkins 3)
Cruel Story of the Samurai's Way. *See* Bushido zankoku monogatari, 1963
Cruel Story of Youth. *See* Seishun zankoku monogatari, 1960
Cruel Tower, 1956 (Haller 4)
Cruise, 1967 (Hubley 4)
Cruise Cat, 1951 (Hanna and Barbera 4)
Cruise into Terror, 1978 (Milland 3)
Cruise Missile. *See* Teheran Incident, 1979
Cruise of the Jasper B., 1926 (Garnett 2)

Cruise of the Zaca, 1952 (Flynn 3)
Cruisin' Down the River, 1953 (Edwards 2)
Cruising, 1980 (Friedkin 2, Pacino 3)
Crusader, 1922 (Howard 2)
Crusades, 1935 (DeMille 2, Auer 3, Bosworth 3, Carradine 3,
    Farnum 3, Schildkraut 3, Sheridan 3, Young, L. 3, Banton 4,
    Brackett, C. 4, Dreier 4, Head 4, Nichols 4, Prinz 4, Young, W. 4)
Crush Proof, 1971 (Hopper 3)
Crushin' Thru, 1923 (Carey 3)
Cruz diablo, 1934 (De Fuentes 2, Fernández 2, Hayworth 3)
Cruz na praça, 1958 (Rocha 2)
Cruzada ABC, 1966 (Pereira Dos Santos 2)
Crvena zemlja, 1975 (Samardžić 3)
Cry. See Křik, 1963
Cry Baby, 1958 (Corman 4)
Cry Baby Killer, 1958 (Nicholson 3, Crosby 4)
Cry Blood, Apache, 1970 (McCrea 3)
Cry Danger, 1951 (Powell, D. 3, Biroc 4, Day 4)
Cry for Happy, 1961 (Ford, G. 3, O'Connor 3, Duning 4, Guffey 4)
Cry for Help, 1912 (Griffith 2, Barrymore L. 3, Carey 3, Gish, D. 3,
    Gish, L. 3, Bitzer 4)
Cry from the Streets, 1958 (Dalrymple 4)
Cry from the Wilderness, 1909 (Porter 2)
Cry Havoc, 1943 (Bainter 3, Blondell 3, Mitchum 3, Nilsson 3,
    Sothern 3, Sullavan 3, Freund 4, Irene 4)
Cry in the Night, 1956 (Ladd 3, O'Brien, E. 3, Wood 3, Seitz 4)
Cry in the Wilderness, 1973 (Kennedy, G. 3)
Cry of Battle, 1963 (Heflin 3, Fields 4)
Cry of the Banshee, 1970 (Bergner 3, Price 3)
Cry of the Children, 1912 (Cruze 2)
Cry of the City, 1948 (Siodmak 2, Mature 3, Winters 3, Lemaire 4,
    Newman 4, Wheeler 4)
Cry of the Hunted, 1953 (Gassman 3)
Cry of the Innocent, 1978 (Cusack 3)
Cry of the Penguins. See Mr. Forbush and the Penguins, 1971
Cry of the Weak, 1919 (Miller, A. 4)
Cry of the World, 1933 (de Rochemont 4)
Cry of Triumph. See Hempas bar, 1977
Cry Onion. See Cipola Colt, 1975
Cry Terror, 1958 (Dickinson 3, Marsh 3, Mason 3, Steiger 3)
Cry, The Beloved Country, 1952 (Poitier 3, Krasker 4)
Cry Wolf, 1947 (Flynn 3, Stanwyck 3, Blanke 4, Head 4, Waxman 4)
Cry Wolf, 1980 (Krasker 4)
Crying and Laughing. See Gens qui pleurent et gens qui rient, 1900
Crying Out Loud. See Cotton Queen, 1937
Crying to the Blue Sky. See Aozora ni naku, 1932
Crying Wolf, 1947 (Terry 4)
Cryptogramme rouge, 1915 (Feuillade 2)
Crystal Ball, 1943 (Bendix 3, De Carlo 3, Goddard 3, Milland 3,
    Dreier 4, Head 4, Young, V. 4)
Crystal Trench, 1959 (Hitchcock 2)
Crystals, 1959 (Leacock 2)
Csak egy telefon, 1970 (Gabór 3, Gabór 3, Gabór 3, Gabór 3)
Csardasfurstin, 1934 (Herlth 4)
Csend és kiáltás, 1968 (Jancsó 2, Torocsik 3)
Cserepek, 1981 (Gaál 2)
Csillagosok, katonák, 1967 (Jancsó 2)
Csunya fiu, 1918 (Curtiz 2)
Ctyřikrát o Bulharsku, 1958 (Kachyna 2)
Cuando crezcas, querido Adam, 1965 (Granados 3)
Cuando el amor rie. See Ladron de amor, 1930
Cuando habla el corazón, 1943 (Infante 3)
Cuando levanta la niebla, 1952 (Fernández 2, Figueroa 4)
Cuando los hijos nos juzgan, 1951 (Buñuel 2)
Cuando los hijos se van, 1941 (García 3)
Cuando quiere un mexicano, 1944 (Negrete 3)
Cuando viajan las estrellas, 1942 (Negrete 3, Figueroa 4)
Cuando viva villa es la muerte, 1958 (Armendáriz 3)
Cuandolloran los valientes, 1945 (Infante 3)
Cuatro Juanes, 1964 (Figueroa 4)
Cuatro milpas, 1937 (Fernández 2, Armendáriz 3)
Cuatro Puentes, 1974 (Alvarez 2)
Cuatro Robinsones, 1940 (Rey 3)

Cub, 1915 (Tourneur, M. 2)
Cub, 1917 (Carré 4)
Cuba, 1979 (Lester 2, Connery 3)
Cuba à Montmartre, 1947–51 (Verneuil 2)
Cuba baila, 1960 (Zavattini 4)
Cuba: Battle of the 10,000,000. See Bataille des dix millions, 1970
Cuba Cabana, 1952 (Warm 4)
Cuba Dos de Enero, 1965 (Alvarez 2)
Cuba '58, 1962 (Corrieri 3)
Cuba 1958. See Cuba '58, 1962
Cuba, pueblo armado. See Pueblos en armas, 1961
Cuba Si!, 1961 (Marker 2, Braunberger 4, Grimault 4)
Cuban Love Song, 1931 (Van Dyke, W.S. 2, Durante 3, Fazenda 3,
    Velez 3, Booth 4, Lewin 4, Meredyth 4, Rosson 4, Sullivan 4)
Cuban Rebel Girls, 1959 (Flynn 3)
Cuban Struggle Against the Demons. See Pelea cubana contra los
    demonios, 1971
Cuba's 10 Years. See Tiz éves Kuba, 1969
Cubisme. See Statues d'épouvante, 1953
Cucaracha, 1934 (Cooper 4, MacGowan 4)
Cucaracha, 1958 (Fernández 2, Armendáriz 3, Del Rio 3, Félix 3,
    Figueroa 4)
Cuccagna, 1962 (Tognazzi 3, Morricone 4)
Cuckoo. See Hototogisu, 1932
Cuckoo. See Jihi shincho, 1927
Cuckoo Bird, 1939 (Terry 4)
Cuckoo Clock, 1950 (Avery 2)
Cuckoo in a Choo Choo, 1952 (Three Stooges 3)
Cuckoo in the Nest, 1933 (Junge 4)
Cuckoo Love, 1925 (Roach 4)
Cuckoos, 1930 (Musuraca 4, Plunkett 4)
Cudotvorni mác, 1950 (Marković 3)
Cue Ball Cat, 1950 (Hanna and Barbera 4)
Cuenca, 1958 (Saura 2)
Cuentos del alhamnara: Guancanayabo, 1963 (Gómez, M. 2)
Cuentos eróticos, 1979 (García Berlanga 2)
Cuerpo de mujer, 1949 (Alcoriza 4, Figueroa 4)
Cuerpo repartido y el mundo al revés, 1975 (Ruiz 2)
Cueva de los tiburones. See Bermuda: la fossa maledetta, 1978
Cugina, 1974 (Morricone 4)
Cuidado con el amor, 1954 (Infante 3)
Cuidado con el ser, 1954 (Infante 3)
Cuisine au buerre, 1963 (Bourvil 3, Fernandel 3)
Cuivres à la voix d'or, 1958 (Decaë 4)
Cukrová bouda, 1980 (Kachyna 2)
Culastrice nobile veneziano, 1976 (Mastroianni 3)
Cul-de-sac, 1966 (Lenica 2, Polanski 2, Bisset 3, Bisset 3, Pleasance 3)
Culloden, 1964 (Watkins 2)
Culottes rouges, 1962 (Bourvil 3, Bourvil 3)
Culpables, 1958 (Rey 3)
Culpepper Cattle Company, 1972 (Goldsmith 4, Needham 4,
    Smith, J.M. 4)
Cult of the Damned, 1969 (Jones, J. 3)
Cult of the Damned. See Angel, Angel, Down We Go, 1969
Cultural Lisbon. See Lisboa Cultural, 1983
Culture intensive ou Le Vieux Mari, 1904 (Guy 2)
Cumberland Story, 1947 (Jennings 2)
Cumbite, 1964 (Gutiérrez 2)
Cumbre que nos une, 1979 (Alvarez 2)
Cumbres borrascoses. See Abismos de pasión, 1953
Cummington Story, 1945 (Copland 4)
Cumplimos, 1962 (Alvarez 2)
Cunegonde, 1932 (Fernandel 3)
Cunning Little Vixen. See Liška bystrouška, 1954
Cuore, 1948 (De Sica 2)
Cuore di cane, 1976 (Lattuada 2, Von Sydow 3)
Cuore di mamma, 1969 (Morricone 4)
Cuore rivelatore, 1935 (Monicelli 2)
Cuore rivelatore, 1948 (Risi 2)
Cuore semplice, 1977 (Valli 3, Zavattini 4)
Cuori infranti, 1963 (Manfredi 3)
Cuori nella tormenta, 1940 (Sordi 3, Amidei 4)
Cuori senza frontiere, 1950 (Zampa 2, Lollobrigida 3, Ponti 4)

Czardas-Konig, 1958 (Wagner 4)
Czarina. *See* Royal Scandal, 1945
Czarna Ksiazka, 1915 (Negri 3)
Czarne skrzydla, 1962 (Tyszkiewicz 3)
Czas przeszly, 1961 (Lomnicki 3)
Czech Connection, 1975 (Nemec 2)

Czech Year. *See* Spalicek, 1947
Czechoslovakia on Parade, 1938 (Hoch 4)
Czerwone i czarne, 1963 (Giersz 4)
Czlowiek na torze, 1956 (Munk 2, Stawinsky 4)
Człowiek z marmuru, 1978 (Wajda 2, Lomnicki 3)
Człowiek z zelaza, 1981 (Wajda 2)

D

D.F., 1978 (Figueroa 4)
D.O.A., 1950 (O'Brien, E. 3, Laszlo 4, Maté 4, Tiomkin 4)
Da Berlino l'apocalisse, 1967 (Dauphin 3)
Da Geheimnis der gelben Narzissen. *See* Devil's Daffodil, 1962
Da halt die Welt dem Atem an, 1927 (Krauss 3, Junge 4)
Da qui all'eredità, 1956 (Sordi 3)
Da Svante forsvandt, 1975 (Carlsen 2)
Da uomo a uomo, 1967 (Van Cleef 3, Morricone 4)
Dabbling in Art, 1921 (Sennett 2)
Dábelské libánky, 1970 (Brejchová 3)
Dach uberem Chopf, 1962 (Ganz 3)
Dacha, 1973 (Gurchenko 3)
Dactylo se marie, 1934 (Douy 4, Planer 4)
Dad, 1982 (Grgić 4)
Dad and Dave Come to Town, 1938 (Finch 3)
Dad Rudd, M.P., 1940 (Rafferty 3)
Dadascope, 1956–61 (Richter 2)
Daddies, 1924 (Marsh 3)
Daddy, 1923 (Coogan 3)
Daddy Boy, 1927 (Sennett 2)
Daddy Goes a Grunting, 1925 (Roach 4)
Daddy Knows Best, 1933 (Sennett 2)
Daddy Long Legs, 1919 (Neilan 2, Pickford 3, Rosher 4)
Daddy Long Legs, 1931 (Baxter W. 3, Gaynor 3, Merkel 3, Behrman 4, Friedhofer 4, Levien 4)
Daddy Long Legs, 1955 (Negulesco 2, Astaire 3, Caron 3, Ritter 3, Lemaire 4, Mercer 4, Newman 4, Reynolds 4, Shamroy 4, Wheeler 4)
Daddy Wanted. *See* Pappa sokes, 1947
Daddy's Gone A-Hunting, 1925 (Borzage 2, Gibbons 4)
Daddy's Gone A-Hunting, 1969 (Robson 2, Laszlo 4, Semple 4, Williams, J. 4)
Dad's Choice, 1927 (Horton 3)
Dad's Day, 1929 (McCarey 2, Roach 4)
Dad's Downfall, 1917 (Sutherland 2)
Daesh radio!, (Yutkevich 2)
Daesh vozkukh, 1924 (Vertov 2)
Daffodil Killer. *See* Geheimnis der gelben Narzissen, 1961
Daffy Dilly, 1948 (Jones 2)
Daffy Doc, 1938 (Clampett 4)
Daffy Doodles, 1946 (McKimson 4)
Daffy Duck and Egghead, 1937 (Avery 2)
Daffy Duck and the Dinosaur, 1939 (Jones 2)
Daffy Duck Hunt, 1949 (McKimson 4)
Daffy Duck in Hollywood, 1938 (Avery 2)
Daffy Duck Slept Here, 1948 (McKimson 4)
Daffy Rents, 1966 (McKimson 4)
Daffy the Commando, 1943 (Freleng 4)
Daffy's Dinner, 1967 (McKimson 4)
Daffy's Inn Trouble, 1961 (McKimson 4)
Daffy's Romance, 1938 (Avery 2)
Dag skall gry, 1944 (Borgstrom 3)
Dagfin, 1926 (Wegener 3, Schufftan 4)
Dagger. *See* Dolken, 1915
Dagger. *See* Kortik, 1954
Daggers of Blood. *See* Col ferro e col fuoco, 1964
Dağlarin kurdu Kocero, 1964 (Guney 2)

Dağlarin oğlu, 1965 (Guney 2)
Dagny, 1976 (Olbrychski 3)
Daguerre ou la naissance de la photographie, 1964 (Leenhardt 2)
Daguerrotypes, 1975 (Varda 2)
Dai Chushingura, 1957 (Yamada 3)
Dai go fukuryu-maru, 1959 (Shindo 2)
Dai kusen, 1966 (Tsuburaya 4)
Dai tatsumaki, 1964 (Tsuburaya 4)
Daiboken, 1965 (Tsuburaya 4)
Daibosatsu toge, 1966 (Mifune 3)
Daibutsu kaigen, 1952 (Kinugasa 2, Hasegawa 3, Kyo 3)
Daichi no komoriuta, 1976 (Okada 3, Tanaka 3)
Daichi wa hohoemu, 1925 (Mizoguchi 2)
Dai-Chushingura, 1930 (Yamada 3)
Daigaku no kotengu, 1952 (Kagawa 3)
Daigaku no nijuhachi-nin shu, 1959 (Tsukasa 3)
Daigaku no oneichan, 1959 (Tsukasa 3, Muraki 4)
Daigaku wa detakeredo, 1929 (Ozu 2, Tanaka 3)
Daigaku yoi toko, 1936 (Ozu 2, Ryu 3)
Daigaky no samuri-tachi, 1957 (Tsukasa 3)
Daikaiju Baran, 1958 (Tsuburaya 4)
Daikon to ninjin, 1965 (Iwashita 3, Ryu 3, Tsukasa 3)
Dainah la métisse, 1931 (Grémillon 2, Vanel 3, Périnal 4, Spaak 4)
Dai-ni no jinsei, 1948 (Yamamura 3)
Dai-ni no seppun, 1954 (Takamine 3)
Daisan no Akumyo, 1963 (Miyagawa 4)
Dai-san no shikaku, 1959 (Mori 3)
Daisies. *See* Sedmikrásky, 1966
Daisy, 1965 (Dinov 4)
Daisy Bell, 1925 (Fleischer, M. and D. 2)
Daisy Bell, 1929 (Fleischer, M. and D. 2)
Daisy Kenyon, 1947 (Preminger 2, Andrews D. 3, Crawford, J. 3, Fonda, H. 3, Lemaire 4, Raksin 4, Shamroy 4, Wheeler 4)
Daisy Miller, 1974 (Bogdanovich 2, Fields 4, Raphael 4)
Dai-tatsumaki, 1964 (Mifune 3)
Daitokai: Bakuhatsu-hen, 1929 (Tanaka 3)
Daitokai no kao, 1949 (Yamamura 3)
Dai-tokai no ushimitsu-doki, 1949 (Mori 3)
Dai-Tokyo bi ikkaku, 1930 (Gosho 2, Takamine 3)
Dai-Tokyo tanjo: Oedo no kane, 1958 (Yamada 3)
Daitozoku, 1964 (Mifune 3, Shimura 3, Tsuburaya 4)
Dakota, 1945 (Bond 3, Brennan 3, Haas 3, Wayne 3, Canutt 4, Foreman 4)
Dakota Dan. *See* Tools of Providence, 1915
Dakota Incident, 1956 (Bond 3, Darnell 3, Haller 4)
Dakota Lil, 1950 (Leven 4, Tiomkin 4)
Daktar, 1940 (Sircar 4)
Daku Mansoor, 1934 (Roy 2, Sircar 4)
Daleko e sunce, 1953 (Marković 3)
Daleko ot voiny, 1969 (Yankovsky 3)
Daleks—Invasion Earth AD 2150, 1966 (Cushing 3)
Dallas, 1950 (Cooper, Gary 3, Massey 3, Eason 4, Haller 4, Steiner 4, Veiller 4)
Dalle Ardenne all'inferno, 1968 (Ireland 3, Jurgens 3, Morricone 4)
Daltons Ride Again, 1945 (Chaney Lon, Jr. 3)
Dam Busters, 1955 (Redgrave, M. 3, Shaw 3)
Dam the Delta, 1958 (Halas and Batchelor 2)

Dama del Alba, 1966 (Del Rio 3)
Dáma s malou nožkou, 1919 (Ondra 3)
Dama s sobachkoi, 1960 (Batalov 3, Moskvin 4)
Damaged Lives, 1933 (Ulmer 2)
Damals, 1942 (Brazzi 3)
Dame à la longue vue, 1963 (Braunberger 4)
Dame aus Berlin, 1925 (Dieterle 2, Krauss 3)
Dame aus der Cottage-Villa. See Villa im Tiergarten, 1926
Dame aux camélias, 1934 (Gance 2, Fresnay 3, Stradling 4)
Dame aux camélias, 1952 (Cervi 3, Presle 3, Barsacq 4)
Dame aux camélias, 1962 (Pagnol 2)
Dame aux camélias, 1980 (Ganz 3)
Dame blonde, 1914 (Francis, E. 3)
Dame dans l'auto avec des lunettes et un fusil, 1970 (Audran 3)
Dame dans l'auto avec des lunettes et un fusil. See Lady in a Car with
    Glasses and a Gun, 1970
Dame de Chez Maxim's, 1934 (Korda 2, Jeanson 4)
Dame de Chez Maxim's, 1950 (D'Eaubonne 4)
Dame de Haut-le-Bois, 1946 (Rosay 3)
Dame de l'ouest, 1942 (Simon, M. 3)
Dame de Malacca, 1937 (Allégret, M. 2, Blier 3, Feuillère 3,
    Trauner 4)
Dame de Monsoreau, 1923 (Manès 3)
Dame de Montsoreau, 1913 (Tourneur, M. 2)
Dame, der Teufel, und die Probiermamsell, 1917 (Wiene 2, Porten 3,
    Messter 4)
Dame d'onze heures, 1947 (Kosma 4)
Dame mit den schwarzen Handschuh, 1919 (Curtiz 2)
Dame mit den Sonnenblum, 1920 (Curtiz 2)
Dame mit der Maske, 1928 (George, H. 3, Galeen 4)
Dame vraiment bien, 1908 (Feuillade 2)
Damen i svart, 1958 (Nykvist 4)
Damen med de lyse Handsker, 1942 (Christensen 2, Henning-Jensen 2)
Damen med kameliorna, 1925 (Borgstrom 3)
Damernes Blad, 1911 (Blom 2)
Dames, 1934 (Berkeley 2, Daves 2, Blondell 3, Keeler 3, Pitts 3,
    Powell, D. 3, Barnes 4, Orry-Kelly 4)
Dames and Dentists, 1920 (Hardy 3)
**Dames du Bois de Boulogne, 1945 (Bresson 2, Cocteau 2, Melville 2,
    Douy 4)**
Dami kanjat. See Dámská volenka, 1980
Damien—Omen II, 1978 (Ayres 3, Grant, L. 3, Holden 3, Sidney 3,
    Goldsmith 4)
Damme in Glashaus, 1921 (Negri 3)
Damn Citizen, 1958 (Mancini 4)
Damn the Defiant!. See H.M.S. Defiant, 1962
Damn Yankees, 1958 (Donen 2, Fosse 4)
Damnation Alley, 1977 (Sanda 3, Ames 4, Goldsmith 4)
Damnation du Docteur Faust, 1904 (Méliès 2)
Damnation of Faust. See Faust aux enfers, 1903
Damned, 1963 (Losey 2, Reed, O. 3, Bernard 4)
Damned. See Caduta degli dei, 1969
Damned. See Maudits, 1947
Damned Don't Cry, 1950 (Crawford, J. 3, Martin, S. 3, McCord 4,
    Wald 4)
Damned Holiday. See Prokleti praznik, 1958
Damned in Venice. See Nero Veneziamo, 1978
Damoi, 1949 (Kagawa 3)
Damon der Frauen. See Rasputin, 1932
Damon des Himalaya, 1935 (Honegger 4)
Damon des Meeres, 1930 (Curtiz 2, Dieterle 2)
Damon the Mower, 1972 (Dunning 4)
Damon und Mensch, 1915 (Oswald 2)
Damonische Liebe, 1950 (Herlth 4)
D'amore si muore, 1972 (Mangano 3, Morricone 4)
D'amour et d'eau fraîche, 1934 (Dauphin 3, Fernandel 3)
D'amour et d'eau fraîche, 1975 (Girardot 3)
Dams and Waterways, 1911 (Dwan 2)
Damsel in Distress, 1937 (Stevens 2, Astaire 3, Fontaine 3, August 4,
    Berman 4, Pan 4, Polglase 4)
Dámská volenka, 1980 (Danailov 3)
Damy, 1955 (Gerasimov 2)
Dan Candy's Law. See Alien Thunder, 1975

Dan chez les gentlemen. See Residencia fpara espias, 1967
Dan Cupid, Assayer, 1914 (Anderson G. 3)
Dan the Dandy, 1911 (Griffith 2, Bitzer 4)
Dance at Eagle Pass, 1913 (Anderson G. 3)
Dance at Silver Gulch, 1912 (Anderson G. 3)
Dance Chromatic, 1959 (Emshwiller 2)
Dance Contest, 1934 (Fleischer, M. and D. 2)
Dance Contest in Esira. See Danstavlingen i Esira, 1935–36
Dance, Fools, Dance, 1931 (Crawford, J. 3, Gable 3, Rosher 4)
Dance, Girl, Dance, 1940 (Arzner 2, Ball 3, Bellamy 3, O'Hara 3,
    Ouspenskaya 3, Polglase 4, Pommer 4)
Dance Hall, 1929 (Murfin 4, Plunkett 4)
Dance Hall, 1941 (Day 4)
Dance Hall, 1950 (Crichton 2, Slocombe 4)
Dance Hall Hostess, 1933 (Eason 4)
Dance Hall Marge, 1931 (Sennett 2)
Dance in the Rain. See Ples v dezju, 1961
Dance in the Sun, 1954 (Clarke 2)
Dance Little Lady, 1954 (Zetterling 3)
Dance Madness, 1926 (Florey 2, Basevi 4, Daniels 4, Gibbons 4)
Dance Movie, 1963 (Warhol 2)
Dance Music, 1927 (Haller 4)
Dance of Death, 1969 (Olivier 3, Unsworth 4)
Dance of Death. See Totentanz, 1919
Dance of Life, 1929 (Cromwell 2, Cromwell 2, Sutherland 2, Banton 4,
    Glazer 4, Hunt 4, Selznick 4)
Dance of the Dwarfs, 1984 (Fonda, P. 3)
Dance of the Heron, 1966 (Vierny 4)
Dance of the Heron. See Dans van de reiger, 1966
Dance of the Looney Spoons, 1959 (Vanderbeek 2)
Dance of the 7 Veils, 1970 (Russell 2)
Dance of the Vampires, 1967 (Slocombe 4)
Dance of the Vampires. See Fearless Vampire Killers, 1967
Dance Pretty Lady, 1931 (Asquith 2)
Dance—Steigler & Steigler, 1981 (Lee, C. 3)
Dance Team, 1931 (Howe 4)
Dance Training. See Kyoren no buto, 1924
Dance with Me, Henry, 1956 (Abbott and Costello 3)
Dance with My Doll. See Dansa min docka, 1953
Dancer of Izu. See Izu no odoriko, 1933
Dancer of Paris, 1926 (Haller 4)
Dancers, 1925 (Goulding 2, Johnson, N. 3)
Dancers, 1930 (Friedhofer 4)
Dancers in the Dark, 1932 (Hopkins, M. 3, Raft 3, Mankiewicz 4,
    Struss 4)
Dancers of Tomorrow. See Asu no odoriko, 1939
Dancer's Peril, 1917 (Brady 3)
Dancer's Revenge. See Danserindens Haevn, 1915
Dancer's Strange Dream. See Danserindens Kaerlighedsdrøm, 1915
Dances in Japan. See Nihon no buyo, 1958
Danchi nanatsu-no taizai, 1964 (Tsukasa 3)
Dancin' Fool, 1920 (Daniels 3, Reid 3)
Dancing Bear, 1937 (Terry 4)
Dancing Co-Ed, 1939 (Turner, L. 3, Walker 3)
Dancing Craze, 1912–13 (White 3)
Dancing Dynamite, 1931 (Brennan 3)
Dancing Fool, 1920 (Wood 2)
Dancing Fool, 1932 (Fleischer, M. and D. 2)
Dancing Fool. See Harold Teen, 1933
Dancing Girl, 1915 (Dwan 2)
Dancing Girl. See Maihime, 1951
Dancing Girl of Butte, 1909 (Griffith 2, Sennett 2, Bitzer 4)
Dancing Girls of Izu. See Izu no odoriko, 1933
Dancing in a Harem. See Danse au sérail, 1897
Dancing in the Dark, 1949 (Hersholt 3, Menjou 3, Powell, W. 3,
    Lemaire 4, Newman 4, Wheeler 4)
Dancing Instructor, 1929 (Brown 3)
Dancing Lady, 1933 (Arden 3, Astaire 3, Crawford, J. 3, Eddy 3,
    Gable 3, Three Stooges 3, Adrian 4, Booth 4, Selznick 4,
    Vorkapich 4)
Dancing Mad. See Tänzer meiner Frau, 1925
Dancing Masters, 1943 (Dumont 3, Laurel & Hardy 3, Mitchum 3,
    Basevi 4)

Dancing Mothers, 1926 (Brenon 2, Goulding 2, Bow 3, Banton 4, Hunt 4)
Dancing on a Dime, 1940 (Head 4, Lang 4, Young, V. 4)
Dancing on the Moon, 1935 (Fleischer, M. and D. 2)
Dancing Pirate, 1936 (Cooper 4, Newman 4, O'Brien 4, Raksin 4)
Dancing Shoes, 1949 (Terry 4)
Dancing with Crime, 1947 (Attenborough 3, Bogarde 3, Lassally 4)
Dandy in Aspic, 1968 (Mann 2, Farrow 3, Harvey 3, Dillon 4, Jones 4)
Dandy Lion, 1940 (Fleischer, M. and D. 2)
Dandy, the All-American Girl, 1976 (Schatzberg 2)
Danfoss—jorden rundt døgnet rundt, 1959 (Carlsen 2)
Danger, 1923 (Walker 4)
Danger Ahead, 1923 (Howard 2)
Danger Ahead, 1935 (Katzman 4)
Danger: Diabolik, 1968 (Piccoli 3)
Danger: Diabolik. See Diabolik, 1968
Danger Girl, 1916 (Sennett 2, Swanson 3)
Danger—Go Slow, 1918 (Chaney Lon 3)
Danger Grows Wild, 1966 (Brynner 3, Dickinson 3, Hawkins 3, Howard, T. 3, Alekan 4, Auric 4)
Danger Grows Wild. See Poppy Is Also a Flower, 1966
Danger in the Pacific, 1942 (Salter 4)
Danger Island, 1939 (Lorre 3)
Danger Lights, 1930 (Arthur 3, Dunn 4, Struss 4)
Danger Line. See Bataille, 1923
Danger, Love at Work, 1937 (Preminger 2, Carradine 3, Cook 3, Horton 3, Sothern 3, Miller, V. 4)
Danger on the Air, 1938 (Cobb 3, Cortez 4)
Danger on Wheels, 1940 (Arlen 3)
Danger Patrol, 1937 (Carey 3, Musuraca 4)
Danger Quest, 1926 (Brown, Harry Joe 4)
Danger Rider, 1928 (Eason 4)
Danger Rides the Range. See Three Texas Steers, 1939
Danger Signal, 1945 (Florey 2, Deutsch 4, Howe 4)
Danger Stalks Near. See Fuzen no tomoshibi, 1957
Danger Street, 1928 (Baxter W. 3)
Danger Within, 1959 (Caine 3)
Danger! Women at Work, 1943 (Ulmer 2)
Dangerous, 1935 (Davis 3, Brown, Harry Joe 4, Haller 4, Orry-Kelly 4)
Dangerous Age, 1922 (Stahl 2, Stone 3, Meredyth 4)
Dangerous Age. See Beloved Brat, 1938
Dangerous Business, 1921 (Talmadge, C. 3, Emerson 4, Loos 4)
Dangerous Business, 1946 (Howard, S. 3)
Dangerous Cargo. See Forbidden Cargo, 1925
Dangerous Comment, 1940 (Mills 3, Balcon 4)
Dangerous Corner, 1934 (Douglas, M. 3, Hunt 4, Plunkett 4, Steiner 4)
Dangerous Coward, 1924 (Brown, Harry Joe 4)
Dangerous Crossing, 1953 (Crain 3, La Shelle 4, Lemaire 4, Reynolds 4, Wheeler 4)
Dangerous Curves, 1929 (Arlen 3, Bow 3, Francis, K. 3)
Dangerous Curves Behind, 1925 (Sennett 2)
Dangerous Dan McFoo, 1939 (Avery 2)
Dangerous Dude, 1926 (Brown, Harry Joe 4)
Dangerous Exile, 1957 (Jourdan 3, Auric 4, Unsworth 4)
Dangerous Females, 1929 (Dressler 3)
Dangerous Flirt, 1924 (Browning 2)
Dangerous Game, 1941 (Arlen 3, Cortez 4, Salter 4)
Dangerous Hero. See Kiken no eiyu, 1957
Dangerous Hours, 1919 (Niblo 2, Barnes 4, Sullivan 4)
Dangerous Inheritance. See Girls' School, 1950
Dangerous Innocence, 1925 (Hersholt 3)
Dangerous Intrigue, 1936 (Bellamy 3)
Dangerous Lies, 1921 (Hitchcock 2)
Dangerous Maid, 1923 (Talmadge, C. 3, Heerman 4, Schenck 4, Sullivan 4)
Dangerous Mission, 1954 (Bendix 3, Mature 3, Price 3, Bennett 4, Burnett 4)
Dangerous Mists. See U-Boat Prisoner, 1944
Dangerous Moment, 1921 (Glennon 4)
Dangerous Money, 1924 (Daniels 3, Powell, W. 3, Hunt 4)
Dangerous Moonlight, 1941 (Beaton 4, Krasker 4, Mathieson 4)
Dangerous Moves. See Diagonale du fou, 1984
Dangerous Nan McGrew, 1930 (Fort 4)

Dangerous Number, 1937 (Sothern 3, Young, R. 3, Wilson, C. 4)
Dangerous Paradise, 1920 (Goulding 2)
Dangerous Paradise, 1930 (Wellman 2, Arlen 3, Oland 3)
Dangerous Partners, 1945 (Gwenn 3, Freund 4, Irene 4)
Dangerous Profession, 1949 (O'Brien, P. 3, Raft 3)
Dangerous Secrets, 1938 (Lukas 3)
Dangerous to Know, 1938 (Florey 2, Quinn 3, Wong 3, Head 4)
Dangerous Toys, 1921 (Goulding 2)
Dangerous Venture, 1947 (Boyd 3)
Dangerous When Wet, 1953 (Walters 2, Williams 3, Hanna and Barbera 4, Mercer 4, Rose 4, Rose 4, Rosson 4, Smith, J.M. 4)
Dangerous Woman, 1929 (Brook 3, Dreier 4)
Dangerous Years, 1948 (Monroe 3)
Dangerous Years of Kiowa Jones, 1966 (Mineo 3)
Dangerously They Live, 1941 (Florey 2, Garfield 3, Massey 3)
Dangerously Yours, 1933 (Auer 3, Baxter W. 3, Friedhofer 4, Seitz 4)
Dangerously Yours, 1937 (Darwell 3)
Dangers de l'alcoolisme, 1899–1900 (Guy 2)
Dangers of a Bride, 1917 (Sennett 2, Swanson 3)
Dangers of the Canadian Mounted, 1948 (Canutt 4)
Dani, 1963 (Samardžić 3)
Daniel, 1967 (Bergman 2)
Daniel and the Devil. See All That Money Can Buy, 1941
Daniel Boone, 1907 (Porter 2, Lawrence 3)
Daniel Boone, 1936 (Carradine 3, Muse 3)
Daniel Boone, Trail Blazer, 1956 (Chaney Lon, Jr. 3)
Daniel Deronda, 1921 (Brook 3)
Daniel Druskat, 1976 (Domrose 3)
Daniele Cortis, 1947 (Cervi 3, Gassman 3, Gherardi 4, Rota 4, Vích 4)
Danish Brigade in Sweden. See Brigaden i Sverige, 1945
Danish Design, 1960 (Roos 2)
Danish Island. See Danske Sydhavsøer, 1944
Danish Motorboat Story, 1953 (Carlsen 2)
Danish Village Church. See Landsbykirken, 1947
Danites, 1912 (Bosworth 2)
Danjuro sandai, 1944 (Mizoguchi 2, Kyo 3, Tanaka 3)
Dankon, 1969 (Okada 3, Muraki 4, Takemitsu 4)
Dann schon lieber Lebertran, 1930 (Ophuls 2, Schufftan 4)
Danny Kaye Story. See Birth of a Star, 1944
Danny Travis. See Last Word, 1979
Danryu, 1939 (Yoshimura 2)
Dans Arles où sont les Alyscamps, 1966 (Braunberger 4)
Dans la brousse, 1912 (Feuillade 2)
Dans la gueule du loup, 1961 (Bourvil 3)
Dans la nuit, 1929 (Vanel 3)
Dans la poussière du soleil, 1971 (Schell, Maria 3, Lai 4)
Dans la réserve africaine, 1961 (Braunberger 4)
Dans la Vallée d'Ossau, 1912 (Cohl 2)
Dans la vie, 1911 (Feuillade 2)
Dans la vie tout s'arrange, 1950 (Henreid 3, Kosma 4)
Dans la ville blanche, 1983 (Tanner 2, Ganz 3, Branco 4, de Almeida 4)
Dans les coulisses, 1900 (Guy 2)
Dans les rues, 1933 (Aumont 3, Andrejew 4, Eisler 4, Maté 4)
Dans l'ouragan de la vie, 1916 (Dulac 2)
Dans un miroir, 1985 (de Almeida 4)
Dans une île perdue, 1930 (Cavalcanti 2)
Dans van de reiger, 1966 (Rademakers 2)
Dansa min docka, 1953 (Bjornstrand 3)
Dansai Hyoe issho-tabi, 1933 (Yamada 3)
Danse au sérail, 1897 (Méliès 2)
Danse basque, 1901 (Guy 2)
Danse de l'ivresse, 1900 (Guy 2)
Danse de mort, 1947 (Von Stroheim 2, Wakhévitch 4)
Danse des saisons series, 1900 (Guy 2)
Danse du papillon, 1900 (Guy 2)
Danse du pas des foulards par des almées, 1900 (Guy 2)
Danse du ventre, 1900–01 (Guy 2)
Danse fleur de lotus, 1897 (Guy 2)
Danse Macabre. See Tanyets smerti, 1916
Danse mauresque, 1902 (Guy 2)
Danse serpentine, 1900 (Guy 2)
Danse serpentine par Mme Bob Walter, 1899–1900 (Guy 2)
Dansei No. 1, 1955 (Mifune 3)

Darling of the Rich, 1922 (Hackett 4)
Darling, How Could You, 1951 (Leisen 2, Fontaine 3, Head 4)
Darò un millione, 1935 (De Sica 2, Zavattini 4)
Daroga pravdy, 1956 (Gurchenko 3)
Dartozoku, 1963 (Tsuburaya 4)
Dårskapens hus, 1951 (Andersson H. 3)
Dášenku, 1975 (Pojar 4)
Dash for Liberty. See Højt Spil, 1913
Dash, Love and Splash, 1914 (Sennett 2)
Dash of Courage, 1916 (Sennett 2, Beery 3, Swanson 3)
Dash Through the Clouds, 1911 (Sennett 2, Normand 3)
Dashenka. See Dášenku, 1975
Dashing Girls. See Szikrázó lányok, 1973
Dastaan, 1950 (Kapoor 2)
Date, 1971 (Cortez 4)
Date for Dinner, 1947 (Terry 4)
Date to Skate, 1938 (Fleischer, M. and D. 2)
Date with a Lonely Girl. See T.R. Baskin, 1971
Date with Destiny. See Mad Doctor, 1940
Date with Destiny. See Return of October, 1949
Date with Dizzy, 1957 (Hubley 4)
Date with Duke, 1947 (Pal 2)
Date with Judy, 1948 (Donen 2, Beery 3, Miranda 3, Taylor, E. 3,
    Pasternak 4, Rose 4, Surtees 4)
Date with the Falcon, 1941 (Sanders 3)
Dates and Nuts, 1937 (Allyson 3)
Datsugoku, 1950 (Mifune 3)
Daughter. See Musume, 1926
Daughter of Asia. See Ajia no musume, 1938
Daughter of Brahma. See Maharadjaens Yndlingshustru II, 1918
Daughter of Deceit. See Hija del a engaño, 1951
Daughter of Destiny. See Alraune, 1927
Daughter of Dr Jekyll, 1957 (Ulmer 4)
Daughter of Eve, 1919 (Colman 3)
Daughter of Israel, 1914 (Talmadge, N. 3)
Daughter of Israel. See Dots Izrila, 1917
Daughter of Liberty, 1911 (Dwan 2)
Daughter of Luxury, 1922 (Pitts 3)
Daughter of Luxury. See Five and Ten, 1931
Daughter of MacGregor, 1916 (Olcott 2)
Daughter of Rosie O'Grady, 1950 (Darwell 3, Reynolds, D. 3,
    Sakall 3)
Daughter of Shanghai, 1937 (Florey 2, Crabbe 3, Quinn 3, Wong 3,
    Head 4)
Daughter of the City, 1915 (Van Dyke, W.S. 2)
Daughter of the Confederacy, 1913 (Olcott 2)
Daughter of the Congo, 1930 (Micheaux 2)
Daughter of the Dragon, 1931 (Hayakawa 3, Oland 3, Wong 3,
    Buchman 4)
Daughter of the Fortune Teller. See Blaa Natviol, 1911
Daughter of the Gods, 1916 (Brenon 2, Hunt 4)
Daughter of the Law, 1921 (Glennon 4)
Daughter of the Mind, 1969 (Carradine 3, Milland 3, Tierney 3,
    Smith, J.M. 4)
Daughter of the Mountains. See Hogfjallets dotter, 1914
Daughter of the Navajos, 1911 (Guy 2)
Daughter of the Night. See Tanz auf dem Vulkan, 1921
Daughter of the Orient. See Daughter of Shanghai, 1937
Daughter of the Poor, 1917 (Love 3)
Daughter of the Railway. See Jernbanens Datter, 1911
Daughter of the Regiment. See Regimentstochter, 1928
Daughter of the Sheriff, 1913 (Anderson G. 3)
Daughter of the South, 1911 (White 3)
Daughter of the West, 1949 (Farnum 3)
Daughter of 2 Worlds, 1920 (Goulding 2, Talmadge, N. 3)
Daughter-in-Law. See Snotchak, 1912
Daughters Courageous, 1939 (Curtiz 2, Bainter 3, Crisp 3, Garfield 3,
    Rains 3, Blanke 4, Epstein, J. & P. 4, Howe 4, Steiner 4, Wallis 4)
Daughters of Darkness. See Rouge aux lèvres, 1971
Daughters of Destiny. See Destinées, 1952
Daughters of Joshua Cabe, 1972 (Elam 3)
Daughters of Joshua Cabe Return, 1974 (Dailey 3)
Daughters of Pleasure, 1924 (Bow 3)

Daughters of Senor Lopez, 1912 (Dwan 2)
Daughters of the Rich, 1923 (Schulberg 4, Struss 4)
Daughters of Today, 1924 (Pitts 3)
Daughters of Yoshiwara. See Takekurabe, 1955
Daughter's Strange Inheritance, 1915 (Talmadge, N. 3)
Daughters Who Pay, 1925 (Lugosi 3)
Daughters, Wives, and a Mother. See Musume tsuma haha, 1960
Daumier, 1958 (Leenhardt 2)
Dauphine Java, 1960 (Alexeieff and Parker 2)
Dave's Love Affair, 1911 (Sennett 2)
David, 1977 (Driessen 4)
David and Bathsheba, 1951 (King 2, King 2, Bushman 3, Hayward 3,
    Massey 3, Peck 3, Cole 4, Dunne 4, Lemaire 4, Newman 4,
    Shamroy 4, Wheeler 4, Zanuck 4)
David and Lisa, 1962 (Perry 4)
David Copperfield, 1935 (Cukor 2, Barrymore L. 3, Fields, W.C. 3,
    Lanchester 3, O'Sullivan 3, Rathbone 3, Stone 3, Estabrook 4,
    Gibbons 4, Selznick 4, Stothart 4, Vorkapich 4)
David Copperfield, 1970 (Attenborough 3, Cusack 3, Evans 3, Hiller 3,
    Olivier 3, Redgrave, M. 3, Richardson 3, Arnold 4)
David e Golia, 1959 (Welles 3)
David Garrick, 1914 (Ingram 2)
David Golder, 1930 (Duvivier 2, Baur 3, Meerson 4, Périnal 4,
    Trauner 4)
David Harum, 1915 (Dwan 2, Rosson 4)
David Harum, 1934 (Cruze 2, Darwell 3, Fetchit 3, Rogers, W. 3)
David Lynn's Sculpture, 1961 (Baillie 2)
Davolja posla, 1965 (Grgić 4)
Davudo, 1965 (Guney 2)
Davy, 1957 (Dearden 2, Slocombe 4)
Davy Crockett, 1910 (Bosworth 3, Selig 4)
Davy Crockett and the River Pirates, 1955 (Disney 2, Glennon 4)
Davy Crockett at the Fall of the Alamo, 1926 (Pierce 4)
Davy Crockett, King of the Wild Frontier, 1955 (Cody 3, Ellenshaw 4)
Davy Jones' Locker, 1934 (Iwerks 4)
Dawn, 1914 (Crisp 3, Selig 4)
Dawn, 1919 (Blackton 2)
Dawn, 1928 (Marshall 3)
Dawn. See Gryning, 1945
Dawn. See Hajnal, 1971
Dawn. See Raat Bhore, 1956
Dawn. See Svítání, 1933
Dawn All Night. See Svítalo celou noc, 1980
Dawn and Twilight, 1914 (Bushman 3)
Dawn at Socorro, 1954 (Van Cleef 3)
Dawn Guard, 1941 (Boulting 2)
Dawn Maker, 1916 (Hart 3, Sullivan 4)
Dawn of a New Day. See Fajr Yum Jadid, 1964
Dawn of a Tomorrow, 1924 (Clarke, C.C. 4)
Dawn of Manchukuo and Mongolia. See Mammo Kenkoku no Reimei,
    1932
Dawn of Passion, 1912 (Dwan 2)
Dawn of the Dead. See Zombie, 1978
Dawn of the East, 1921 (Brady 3)
Dawn of Tomorrow, 1915 (Pickford 3)
Dawn of Understanding, 1918 (Gilbert 3, Love 3)
Dawn Patrol, 1930 (Hawks 2, Barthelmess 3, Fairbanks, D. Jr. 3,
    Haller 4, Miller, S. 4, Saunders 4, Wallis 4)
Dawn Patrol, 1938 (Goulding 2, Crisp 3, Fitzgerald 3, Flynn 3, Niven 3,
    Rathbone 3, Friedhofer 4, Miller, S. 4, Saunders 4, Steiner 4,
    Wallis 4)
Dawn Rider, 1935 (Wayne 3, Canutt 4)
Dawn Trail, 1930 (McCord 4)
Day. See Antonito, 1961
Day After, 1909 (Sweet 3)
Day After, 1983 (Robards 3, Raksin 4, Serafine 4)
Day After. See Up from the Beach, 1965
Day After Tomorrow. See Strange Holiday, 1946
Day and the Hour. See Jour et l'heure, 1962
Day at Santa Anita, 1936 (De Havilland 3)
Day at School, 1916 (Hardy 3)
Day at the Beach, 1938 (Freleng 4)
Day at the Beach, 1969 (Polanski 2, Sellers 3)

Day at the Circus, 1901 (Porter 2)
Day at the Races, 1937 (Seaton 2, Wood 2, Dandridge 3, Dumont 3, Marx Brothers 3, O'Sullivan 3, Edens 4, Gibbons 4, Kaper 4, Pirosh 4, Ruttenberg 4, Waxman 4)
Day at the Zoo, 1939 (Avery 2)
Day by Day, 1913 (Beery 3)
Day Christ Died, 1980 (Anhalt 4)
Day Dreams, 1922 (Keaton 2)
Day for Night, 1973 (Aumont 3, Cortese 3)
Day for Night. See Nuit américaine, 1973
Day I Stopped Smoking, 1982 (Dragić 4)
Day in Court. See Giorno in pretura, 1953
Day in Jerusalem, 1912 (Olcott 2)
Day in June, 1944 (Terry 4)
Day in the Country. See Partie de campagne, 1946
Day in the Death of Joe Egg, 1971 (Bates 3)
Day Nurse, 1932 (Lantz 4)
Day of a Man of Affairs, 1929 (Rogers, G. 3)
Day of Anger. See Giorno dell'ira, 1967
Day of Faith, 1923 (Browning 2)
Day of Fury, 1956 (Boyle 4)
Day of Happiness. See Den stchastia, 1964
Day of Joy. See Glaedens Dag, 1918
Day of Marriage. See Totsuguhi, 1956
Day of Reckoning, 1915 (Eason 4)
Day of Reckoning, 1933 (Merkel 3)
Day of the Animals, 1976 (Schifrin 4)
Day of the Bad Man, 1958 (MacMurray 3, Van Cleef 3, Salter 4)
Day of the Dolphin, 1973 (Nichols 2, Scott, G. 3, Delerue 4, Fraker 4, Henry 4, Sylbert 4)
Day of the Evil Gun, 1968 (Ford, G. 3, Kennedy, A. 3, Stanton 3)
Day of the Fight, 1950 (Kubrick 2)
Day of the Fox, 1956 (Peterson 2)
Day of the Jackal, 1973 (Zinnemann 2, Cusack 3, Seyrig 3, Delerue 4)
Day of the Locust, 1975 (Schlesinger 2, Black 3, Meredith 3, Page 3, Sutherland 3, Barry 4, Hall 4, Salt 4, Whitlock 4)
Day of the Outlaw, 1959 (De Toth 2, Cook 3, Ryan 3)
Day of the Triffids, 1963 (Keel 3)
Day of Triumph, 1955 (Cobb 3)
Day of Wrath. See Vredens Dag, 1943
Day Our Lives Shine. See Waga shogai no kagayakeru hi, 1948
Day Shall Dawn. See Jago hua savera, 1958
Day She Paid, 1919 (Ingram 2)
Day That Shook the World. See Assassination at Sarajevo, 1975
Day the Bookies Wept, 1939 (Grable 3)
Day the Clown Cried, 1972 (Lewis 2)
Day the Earth Caught Fire, 1961 (Caine 3, Mankowitz 4)
Day the Earth Moved, 1974 (Cooper, J 3)
Day the Earth Stood Still, 1951 (Wise 2, Jaffe 3, Neal 3, Herrmann 4, Lemaire 4, Reynolds 4, Wheeler 4)
Day the Fish Came Out, 1967 (Lassally 4, Theodorakis 4)
Day the Hot Line Got Hot, 1969 (Boyer 3, Taylor, R. 3)
Day the Sun Rose. See Gion matsuri, 1968
Day the World Ended, 1955 (Corman 4)
Day They Gave Babies Away. See All Mine to Give, 1956
Day They Robbed the Bank of England, 1960 (O'Toole 3, Périnal 4)
Day Time Ended, 1980 (Malone 3)
Day to Live, 1931 (Terry 4)
Day to Remember, 1953 (Holloway 3)
Day to Wed. See Totsuguhi, 1956
Day Will Come. See Es kommt ein Tag, 1950
Day Will Dawn, 1942 (Kerr 3, Richardson 3)
Day with the Boys, 1969 (Kovacs 4)
Daybreak, 1931 (Feyder 2, Hersholt 3, Novarro 3)
Daybreak. See Jour se lève, 1939
Daybreak and Whiteye, 1957 (Brakhage 2)
Daybreak in Udi, 1949 (Alwyn 4)
Daydreamer, 1966 (Hayakawa 3, Karloff 3)
Daydreams, 1928 (Lanchester 3, Laughton 3)
Daylight Burglar, 1913 (Crisp 3)
Days and Nights in the Forest. See Aranyer din Ratri, 1970
Days in the Trees. See Journées entières dans les arbres, 1976
Days of '49, 1913 (Ince 4, Sullivan 4)

Days of '49, 1924 (Canutt 4)
Days of Fury, 1978 (Price 3)
Days of Fury. See Giorno del furore, 1973
Days of Glory, 1944 (Tourneur, J. 2, Haas 3, Peck 3, Dunn 4, Gaudio 4, Robinson 4)
Days of Hate. See Dias de odio, 1954
Days of Heaven, 1978 (Malick 2, Gere 3, Almendros 4, Morricone 4, Wexler 4)
Days of Hope, 1976 (Loach 2)
Days of Jesse James, 1939 (Rogers, R. 3)
Days of Love. See Giorni d'amore, 1954
Days of October. See Oktiabr' dni, 1958
Days of Old, 1922 (Roach 4)
Days of the Pony Express, 1913 (Anderson G. 3)
Days of '36. See Mères tou 36, 1972
Days of Volochayev. See Volochayevskiye dni, 1937
Days of Water, 1972 (Gómez, M. 2)
Days of Wilfred Owen, 1965 (Burton 3)
Days of Wine and Roses, 1962 (Edwards 2, Lemmon 3, Remick 3, Mancini 4, Mercer 4)
Days of Youth. See Jeugddag, 1929–30
Day's Pleasure, 1919 (Chaplin 2, Coogan 3, Purviance 3)
Daytime Wife, 1939 (Darnell 3, Power 3, Day 4, Zanuck 4)
Daytime Wives, 1923 (Coffee 4)
Dayu san yori, 1957 (Tanaka 3)
Daze in the West, 1927 (Wyler 2)
D-Day, The Sixth of June, 1956 (O'Brien, E. 3, Taylor, R. 3, Brackett, C. 4, Brown, Harry 4, Garmes 4, Lemaire 4)
De aire y fuego, 1972 (Brazzi 3)
De America soy hijo . . . y a ella me debo, 1972 (Alvarez 2)
De Babord à Tribord, 1926 (Matras 4)
De bouche à oreille, 1957 (Decaë 4)
De cierta manera, 1977 (Gomez, S. 2)
De Grands Evènements et des gens ordinaires, 1979 (Ruiz 2)
De haut à bas, 1933 (Lorre 3)
De kalte ham Skarven, 1965 (Ullmann 3)
De keder sig på landet. See Et sommereventyr, 1919
De la ferraille à l'acier victorieux, 1940 (Auric 4)
De la guerra americana, 1969 (Granados 3)
De la Légion, 1936 (Fernandel 3)
De la part des copains, 1970 (Bronson 3)
De la poudre et des balles. See Bonne Chance, Charlie, 1962
De la veine a revendre. See Zezowate szczeście, 1960
De l'amour, 1964 (Karina 3, Piccoli 3, Braunberger 4, Guillemot 4)
De l'autre côté de l'eau, 1951 (Cortez 4)
De Mayerling à Sarajevo, 1940 (Ophuls 2, Feuillère 3, Courant 4, D'Eaubonne 4)
De Pisis, 1957 (Fusco 4)
De Renoir à Picasso, 1950 (Brasseur 3)
De Sade, 1969 (Huston 3, Corman 4)
Dea del mare, 1907 (Bertini 3)
Deacon Outwitted, 1913 (Sennett 2)
Deacon's Troubles, 1912 (Sennett 2, Normand 3)
Deacon's Whiskers, 1915 (Loos 4)
Dead, 1960 (Brakhage 2)
Dead Cert, 1973 (Richardson 2)
Dead Country. See Holt vidék, 1971
Dead Don't Die, 1975 (Milland 3)
Dead Don't Dream, 1948 (Boyd 3)
Dead Don't Scream, 1975 (Blondell 3)
Dead End, 1937 (Wyler 2, Bogart 3, Bond 3, McCrea 3, Sidney 3, Trevor 3, Basevi 4, Day 4, Goldwyn 4, Mandell 4, Newman 4, Toland 4, Westmore, P. 4)
Dead Eyes of London. See Toten Augen von London, 1961
Dead Heat on a Merry-Go-Round, 1966 (Coburn, J. 3, Ford, H. 3)
Dead Image. See Dead Ringer, 1964
Dead Landscape. See Holt vidék, 1971
Dead Letter, 1915 (Hardy 3)
Dead Line. See Gray Horizon, 1919
Dead Man's Claim, 1912 (Anderson G. 3)
Dead Man's Curve, 1928 (Fairbanks, D. Jr. 3)
Dead Man's Eyes, 1944 (Chaney Lon, Jr. 3)
Dead Man's Shoes, 1913 (Reid 3)

Dead Men Don't Wear Plaid, 1982 (Head 4, Rozsa 4)
Dead Men Tell, 1941 (Clarke, C.C. 4, Raksin 4)
Dead Men Tell No Tales, 1920 (Haller 4)
Dead Men's Shoes, 1939 (McDowall 3)
Dead of Night, 1945 (Cavalcanti 2, Crichton 2, Dearden 2, Hamer 2,
    Redgrave, M. 3, Auric 4, Balcon 4, Clarke, T.E.B. 4, Slocombe 4)
Dead of Summer. See Ondata di calore, 1970
Dead on Arrival, 1979 (Palance 3)
Dead on Course. See Wings of Danger, 1952
Dead Ones, 1948 (Markopoulos 2)
Dead Only Perish. See Ölume yalniz gidilar, 1963
Dead or Alive. See Minuto per pregare, un instante per morire, 1968
Dead Pays, 1912 (Ince 4)
Dead Pigeon on Beethoven Street, 1973 (Fuller 2, Audran 3)
Dead Reckoning, 1947 (Cromwell 2, Bogart 3)
Dead Ringer, 1964 (Davis 3, Henreid 3, Malden 3, Haller 4, Previn 4)
Dead Run. See Deux Billets pour Mexico, 1967
Dead Yesterday, 1937 (Darwell 3)
Dead Zone, 1983 (Sheen 3)
Deadend Cats, 1947 (Terry 4)
Deadfall, 1968 (Caine 3, Barry 4)
Deadhead Miles, 1972 (Arkin 3, Lupino 3, Raft 3)
Deadlier Sex, 1920 (Karloff 3, Sweet 3)
Deadlier Than the Male, 1966 (Sangster 4)
Deadliest Season, 1977 (Streep 3)
Deadline. See Deadline U.S.A., 1952
Deadline at Dawn, 1946 (Hayward 3, Lukas 3, Eisler 4, Musuraca 4)
Deadline at Eleven, 1920 (Costello, M. 3)
Deadline U.S.A., 1952 (Brooks, R. 2, Barrymore E. 3, Bogart 3,
    Krasner 4, Lemaire 4, Wheeler 4)
Deadlock, 1931 (Bennett 4)
Deadlock, 1965 (Halas and Batchelor 2)
Deadlock. See Sikátor, 1966
Deadly Affair, 1967 (Lumet 2, Andersson H. 3, Mason 3, Schell,
    Maximilian 3, Signoret 3, Dehn 4, Jones 4, Young, F. 4)
Deadly Bees, 1966 (Francis 4)
Deadly Blessing, 1981 (Borgnine 3)
Deadly Companions, 1961 (Peckinpah 2, Martin, S. 3, O'Hara 3,
    Clothier 4)
Deadly Dreams, 1971 (Leigh, J. 3)
Deadly Game, 1982 (Howard, T. 3)
Deadly Glass of Beer, 1916 (Browning 2)
Deadly Harvest, 1972 (Boone 3)
Deadly Hero, 1976 (Jones, J.E. 3)
Deadly Honeymoon, 1972 (Bernstein 4)
Deadly Is the Female, 1949 (Young, V. 4)
Deadly Lessons, 1983 (Reed, D. 3)
Deadly Mantis, 1957 (Westmore, B. 4)
Deadly Ray from Mars. See Flash Gordon's Trip to Mars, 1938
Deadly Roulette, 1967 (Pidgeon 3, Wagner 3, Schifrin 4)
Deadly Strangers, 1974 (Hayden 3)
Deadly Sweet. See Col cuore in gola, 1967
Deadly Trap. See Maison sous les arbres, 1971
Deadwood Coach, 1924 (Mix 3)
Deadwood Dick, 1940 (Canutt 4)
Deadwood '76, 1965 (Zsigmond 4)
Deadwood Sleeper, 1905 (Bitzer 4)
Deaf Burglar, 1913 (Sennett 2)
Deaf, Dumb, and Daffy, 1924 (Roach 4)
Deaf Smith and Johnny Ears, 1972 (Quinn 3)
Deaf Smith and Johnny Ears. See Amigos, 1972
Deaf-Mutes Ball, 1907 (Bitzer 4)
Deal of the Century, 1983 (Friedkin 2)
Deal with the Devil. See Mystike Fremmede, 1914
Dealing for Daisy. See Mr. 'Silent'Haskins, 1915
Dear Brat, 1951 (Wood 3, Ames 4, Head 4, Seitz 4)
Dear Brigitte, 1965 (Bardot 3, Stewart 3, Ballard 4, Duning 4,
    Smith, J.M. 4)
Dear Dead Delilah, 1972 (Moorehead 3)
Dear Departed, 1920 (Roach 4)
Dear Detective, 1978 (Girardot 3)
Dear Detective. See Tendre poulet, 1978
Dear Father. See Caro Papà, 1979

Dear Heart, 1964 (Ford, G. 3, Lansbury 3, Page 3, Mancini 4)
Dear Hearts. See Mrs. Soffel, 1985
Dear Inspector. See Dear Detective, 1978
Dear Inspector. See Tendre poulet, 1978
Dear Margery Boobs, 1977 (Godfrey 4)
Dear Mr. Prohack, 1949 (Bogarde 3, Dalrymple 4)
Dear Murderer, 1947 (Mathieson 4)
Dear Octopus, 1943 (Johnson, C. 3)
Dear Old Girl, 1913 (Bushman 3)
Dear Old Switzerland, 1944 (Terry 4)
Dear Relatives. See Kara slakten, 1933
Dear Ruth, 1947 (Holden 3, Dreier 4, Head 4, Laszlo 4, Mercer 4)
Dear Summer Sister. See Natsu no imoto, 1972
Dear Wife, 1949 (Holden 3, Dreier 4)
Dearie, 1927 (Blanke 4)
Dearly Purchased Friendship. See Dyrekøbt Venskab, 1912
De-as fi Harap Alb, 1965 (Popescu-Gopo 4)
Death among Friends, 1975 (Henreid 3)
Death and the Maiden. See Hawkins on Murder, 1973
Death at Broadcasting House, 1934 (Hawkins 3)
Death at Dawn. See Akatsuki no shi, 1924
Death at 45 RPM. See Meurtre en 45 tour, 1960
Death at Love House, 1976 (Blondell 3, Carradine 3, Lamour 3,
    Sidney 3, Wagner 3)
Death Bell. See Halálcsengö, 1917
Death Bite, 1982 (Fonda, P. 3, Reed, O. 3)
Death by Hanging. See Koshikei, 1968
Death Cliff. See Shi no dangai, 1951
Death Command of the Tower. See Boro no kesshitai, 1943
Death Corps. See Shock Waves, 1977
Death Dance, 1918 (Brady 3)
Death Day, 1933 (Eisenstein 2)
Death Dice, 1915 (Walsh 2)
Death Disk, 1909 (Griffith 2, Bitzer 4)
Death Drives Through, 1935 (Huston 2)
Death Flight. See SST—Death Flight, 1977
Death Hunt, 1981 (Bronson 3, Dickinson 3, Marvin 3)
Death in Canaan, 1978 (Richardson 2, Addison 4)
Death in Persepolis, 1974 (Attenborough 3)
Death in the Doll's House. See Shadow on the Wall, 1950
Death in the Garden. See Mort en ce jardin, 1956
Death in the Snow. See Echigo tsutsuishi oyashirazu, 1964
Death in the Sun. See Flusternde Tod, 1975
Death in the Vatican. See Morte in Vaticano, 1982
Death in Venice. See Morte a Venezia, 1971
Death Is Called Engelchen. See Smrt si říká Engelchen, 1963
Death Kiss, 1933 (Lugosi 3)
Death Line, 1972 (Lee, C. 3, Pleasance 3)
Death of a Bureaucrat. See Muerte de un burócrata, 1966
Death of a Champion, 1939 (Florey 2, O'Connor 3, Head 4)
Death of a Corrupt Man. See Morte di un operatore, 1978
Death of a Cyclist. See Muerte de un ciclista, 1955
Death of a Gunfighter, 1969 (Siegel 2, Horne 3, Widmark 3,
    Westmore, B. 4)
Death of a Maiden. See Shojo no shi, 1927
Death of a Provincial. See Smierc prowincjala, 1966
Death of a Salesman, 1951 (Kramer, S. 2, March 3, North 4, Planer 4)
Death of a Salesman, 1957 (Sellers 3)
Death of a Salesman, 1985 (Hoffman 3)
Death of a Scoundrel, 1956 (Brent 3, De Carlo 3, Sanders 3, Howe 4,
    Steiner 4)
Death of a Virgin. See Shojo no shi, 1927
Death of Hemingway, 1965 (Markopoulos 2)
Death of Her Innocence. See Our Time, 1974
Death of Innocence, 1971 (Kennedy, A. 3, Sothern 3, Winters 3)
Death of Mario Ricci, 1983 (Goretta 2)
Death of Mario Ricci. See Mort de Mario Ricci, 1984
Death of Michael Turbin, 1954 (Fairbanks, D. Jr. 3)
Death of Mr. Baltisberger. See Smrt pana Baltisbergra, 1965
Death of My Sister. See Imoto no shi, 1921
Death of Siegfried. See Nibelungen, 1924
Death of Tarzan. See Tarzanova smrt, 1963
Death of the Fly. See Smrt mouchy, 1975

Death on the Diamond, 1934 (Rooney 3, Young, R. 3, Krasner 4)
Death on the Freeway, 1979 (Needham 4)
Death on the Mountain. *See* Aru sonan, 1916
Death on the Nile, 1978 (Davis 3, Farrow 3, Kennedy, G. 3, Lansbury 3, Niven 3, Smith 3, Ustinov 3, Warden 3, Cardiff 4, Rota 4)
Death Race 2000, 1975 (Stallone 3, Baker 4, Corman 4)
Death Rage. *See* Con la rabbia agli occhi, 1976
Death Ray. *See* Luch smerti, 1925
Death Rides a Horse. *See* Da uomo a uoma, 1967
Death Sentence, 1974 (Nolte 3)
Death Ship, 1980 (Kennedy, G. 3)
Death Squad, 1974 (Douglas, M. 3)
Death Takes a Holiday, 1934 (Leisen 2, March 3, Banton 4, Lang 4)
Death Takes a Holiday, 1971 (Douglas, M. 3, Loy 3, Lourié 4)
Death Trap. *See* Eaten Alive, 1977
Death Travels Too Much. *See* Humour noir, 1965
Death Valley, 1927 (Walker 4)
Death Watch, 1979 (Tavernier 2, Stanton 3)
Death Watch. *See* Mort en direct, 1979
Death Wheelers. *See* Living Dead, 1972
Death Wish, 1974 (Bronson 3, De Laurentiis 4)
Death Wish II, 1981 (Bronson 3)
Death Wish III, 1985 (Bronson 3)
Death Woman. *See* Senora Muerte, 1967
Death's Marathon, 1913 (Griffith 2, Barrymore L. 3, Sweet 3, Walthall 3, Bitzer 4)
Deathsport, 1978 (Corman 4)
Deathtrap, 1982 (Lumet 2, Caine 3, Cannon 3, Allen, J. 4)
Deathwatch, 1966 (Mazursky 2, Fields 4)
Débarquement, 1895 (Lumière 2)
Debauchery Is Wrong. *See* Doraku shinan, 1928
Debdas, 1935 (Sircar 4)
Débrouille-toi, 1917 (Feuillade 2, Musidora 3)
Débroussaillage chimique, 1955 (Rabier 4)
Debt, 1910 (Lawrence 3)
Debt. *See* His Debt, 1919
Debt of Honor, 1918 (Ruttenberg 4)
Debt of Honour, 1922 (Brook 3)
Deburau, 1951 (Guitry 2)
Debussy Film, 1965 (Russell 2)
Début du siècle, 1968 (Allégret, M. 2, Braunberger 4)
Debut in the Secret Service, 1914 (Cruze 2)
Débuts. *See* Nacala, 1970
Débuts d'un patineur, 1908 (Linders 3)
Débuts d'un yachtman, 1909 (Linders 3)
Décade prodigieuse, 1972 (Chabrol 2, Welles 2, Perkins 3, Piccoli 3, Gégauff 4)
Decameron, 1971 (Pasolini 2, Donati 4, Morricone 4)
Decameron. *See* Decamerone, 1971
Decameron Nights, 1924 (Wilcox 2, Barrymore L. 3)
Decameron Nights, 1953 (Fontaine 3, Jourdan 3, Green, G. 4)
Decameron Nights. *See* Dekameron-Nachte, 1924
Decamerone, 1971 (Mangano 3, Delli Colli 4)
Deceit, 1921 (Micheaux 2)
Deceived Slumming Party, 1908 (Bitzer 4)
Deceiver, 1914 (Loos 4)
Deceiver, 1921 (Hersholt 3)
Deceiver, 1931 (Wayne 3)
Deceivers, 1914 (Browning 2)
Deceiving Costume. *See* Itsuwareru seiso, 1951
December 7th, 1943 (Ford, J. 2, Andrews D. 3, Huston 3, Newman 4, Toland 4)
Décembre, mois des enfants, 1956 (Franju 2, Storck 2)
Deception, 1909 (Griffith 2, Lawrence 3, Bitzer 4)
Deception, 1946 (Davis 3, Henreid 3, Rains 3, Blanke 4, Grot 4, Haller 4, Korngold 4)
Deception, 1956 (Howard, T. 3)
Deception. *See* Anna Boleyn, 1920
Deception. *See* Richter und sein Henker, 1975
Deception Against Time. *See* Man in the Sky, 1957
Deceptions, 1985 (Lollobrigida 3)
Déchaînés, 1950 (Colpi 4)

Décharge, 1970 (Cloquet 4, Legrand 4)
Deciding Kiss, 1918 (Browning 2)
Decima vittima, 1965 (Petri 2, Mastroianni 3, Di Venanzo 4, Flaiano 4, Guerra 4, Ponti 4)
Decimals of Love. *See* Karlekens decimaler, 1960
Decisión, 1964 (Granados 3)
Decision Against Time. *See* Man in the Sky, 1956
Decision at Sundown, 1957 (Boetticher 2, Scott, R. 3, Brown, Harry Joe 4, Guffey 4)
Decision Before Dawn, 1951 (Litvak 2, Kinski 3, Knef 3, Malden 3, Werner 3, Planer 4, Waxman 4)
Decision of Christopher Blake, 1948 (Freund 4, Steiner 4)
Decisions! Decisions!, 1972 (Carradine 3)
Decisive Battle. *See* Kessen, 1944
Decks Ran Red, 1958 (Crawford, B. 3, Dandridge 3, Mason 3)
Declassée, 1925 (Brook 3, Fazenda 3, Gable 3, Gaudio 4)
Declic et des claques, 1965 (Girardot 3)
Décolleté dans le dos, 1975 (Nemec 2)
Decorator, 1920 (Hardy 3)
Decree of Destiny, 1910 (Griffith 2, Pickford 3, Bitzer 4)
Dédé la tendresse, 1972 (Dalio 3)
Dědéček, 1968 (Jires 2)
Dědeček automobil, 1955 (Forman 2, Kopecký 3)
Dědečkem proti své vuli, 1939 (Stallich 4)
Dédée, 1934 (Darrieux 3, Dauphin 3)
Dédée. *See* Dédée d'Anvers, 1948
Dédée d'Anvers, 1948 (Allégret, Y. 2, Blier 3, Dalio 3, Signoret 3, Wakhévitch 4)
Dedicated to the Kinks. *See* Summer in the City, 1970
Dedication of the Great Buddha. *See* Daibutsu kaigen, 1952
Dedicato al mare Eglo, 1979 (Morricone 4)
Deduce You Say, 1957 (Jones 2)
Deep, 1931 (Bennett C. 3)
Deep, 1970 (Welles 2)
Deep, 1977 (Yates 2, Bisset 3, Gossett 3, Nolte 3, Shaw 3, Wallach 3, Barry 4)
Deep Blue Sea, 1955 (Litvak 2, Leigh, V. 3, More 3, Arnold 4, Korda 4)
Deep End, 1970 (Skolimowski 2)
Deep in My Heart, 1954 (Donen 2, Astaire 3, Charisse 3, Ferrer, J. 3, Henreid 3, Keel 3, Kelly, Gene 3, Miller 3, Oberon 3, Pidgeon 3, Deutsch 4, Edens 4, Friedhofer 4, Plunkett 4, Rose 4)
Deep in the Heart of Texas, 1942 (Farnum 3, Salter 4)
Deep in the Pool, 1958 (Hitchcock 2)
Deep Purple, 1916 (Carré 4, Edeson 4)
Deep Purple, 1920 (Walsh 2, Menzies 4)
Deep Red. *See* Profondo rosso, 1976
Deep Sea Fishing, 1952 (Flynn 3)
Deep Six, 1958 (Bendix 3, Ladd 3, Wynn 3, Brown, Harry 4, Maté 4, Seitz 4)
Deep Threat. *See* Mer mère, 1975
Deep Valley, 1947 (Negulesco 2, Bainter 3, Lupino 3, Blanke 4, McCord 4, Steiner 4)
Deep Waters, 1920 (Tourneur, M. 2, Gilbert 3)
Deep Waters, 1948 (King 2, Andrews D. 3, Marsh 3, La Shelle 4, Lemaire 4, Lemaire 4)
Deer Hunter, 1978 (Smith, D. , Cimino 2, De Niro 3, Streep 3, Zsigmond 4)
Deer Stalking with Camera, 1905 (Bitzer 4)
Deerslayer, 1913 (Reid 3)
Deerslayer, 1943 (De Carlo 3)
Deerslayer, 1957 (Struss 3)
Deerslayer. *See* Lederstrumpf, 1920
Deewaar, 1975 (Bachchan 3)
Deewanjee, 1976 (Burman 4)
Defeated People, 1946 (Jennings 2)
Defection of Simas Kudirka, 1978 (Arkin 3, Pleasance 3)
Defective Detectives, 1944 (Langdon 3)
Defector, 1966 (Clift 3)
Defector. *See* Espion, 1966
Defence of Tsaritsin. *See* Oborona Tsartsina, 1942
Defend My Love. *See* Difendo il mio amore, 1956
Defendant, 1964 (Menzel 2)

Defendant. *See* Obžalovaný, 1964
Défense de fumer, 1961 (Delerue 4)
Défense de savoir, 1973 (Denner 3, Trintignant 3)
Défense de Tsaritsyne. *See* Oborona Tsaritsina, 1942
Defense of Madrid, 1936–37 (McLaren 2)
Defense of Sebastopol. *See* Oborona Sevastopolya, 1911
Defense of Tsaritsyn. *See* Oborona Tsaritsina, 1942
Defense Rests, 1934 (Arthur 3, Bond 3, Meek 3, August 4, Swerling 4)
Défenseur, 1930 (D'Eaubonne 4)
Defiance. *See* Trots, 1952
Defiant Ones, 1958 (Kramer, S. 2, Chaney Lon, Jr. 3, Curtis 3, Poitier 3)
Definitive afslag på anmodningen om et kys, 1949 (Roos 2)
Defizit, 1917 (Hoffmann 4)
Défroqué, 1953 (Fresnay 3)
Defying the Law, 1924 (Adorée 3)
Degenhardts, 1944 (George, H. 3)
Dégourdis de la onzième, 1937 (Christian-Jaque 2, Fernandel 3, Aurenche 4)
Degree of Murder. *See* Mord und Totschlag, 1967
Dein Herz ist meine Heimat, 1953 (Von Harbou 4)
Dein Schicksal, 1928 (Fischinger 2, Metzner 4)
Deine Zärtlichkeiten, 1969 (Wicki 2)
Déjà vu, 1984 (Donaggio 4, Golan and Globus 4)
Déjeuner de Bébé. *See* Repas de Bébé, 1895
Déjeuner de soleil, 1937 (Berry 3, Auric 4, D'Eaubonne 4)
Déjeuner des enfants, 1899–1900 (Guy 2)
Dejeuner du chat, 1895 (Lumière 2)
Déjeuner sur l'herbe, 1959 (Renoir 2, Kosma 4)
Dejeuner sur l'herbe, 1975 (Le Grice 2)
Dekameron-Nachte, 1924 (Krauss 3, Pommer 4)
Dekigokoro, 1933 (Ozu 2)
Dekkai dekkai yaro, 1969 (Iwashita 3)
Del mismo barro, 1930 (Furthman 4)
Del odio nació el amor, 1949 (Fernández 2, Armendáriz 3, Figueroa 4)
Del odio nació el amor. *See* Torch, 1949
Del ranco a la capital, 1941 (Armendáriz 3)
Dela i lyudi, 1932 (Romm 2)
Delancey Street: The Crisis Within, 1975 (Gossett 3, Schifrin 4)
Delayed Proposal, 1911 (Sennett 2)
Delessi Affair, 1979 (More 3)
Delfini, 1960 (Cardinale 3, Cristaldi 4, Di Venanzo 4, Fusco 4)
Delhi, 1937–40 (Cardiff 4)
Delhi Way, 1964 (Ivory 2)
Delicate Balance, 1973 (Richardson 2, Cotten 3, Hepburn, K. 3, Remick 3, Watkin 4)
Delicate Delinquent, 1957 (Lewis 2, Head 4)
Delicious, 1931 (Auer 3, Gaynor 3, Behrman 4, Levien 4)
Delicious Little Devil, 1919 (Valentino 3)
Delightful Rogue, 1929 (Plunkett 4)
Delightfully Dangerous, 1945 (Tashlin 2, Beavers 3, Bellamy 3, Krasner 4)
Delinquent Girl. *See* Furyo shojo, 1949
Delinquents, 1955 (Altman 2)
Delirium in a Studio. *See* Ali Barbouyou et Ali Bouf à l'huile, 1907
Délit de fuite, 1958 (Renoir 4)
Delitto al circolo del tennis, 1969 (Storaro 4)
Delitto d'amore, 1974 (Comencini 2)
Delitto di Giovanni Episcopo, 1947 (Fellini 2, Lattuada 2, Fabrizi 3, Lollobrigida 3, Mangano 3, Sordi 3, D'Amico 4, Rota 4)
Delitto Matteotti, 1973 (De Sica 2)
Delitto quasi perfetto, 1966 (Blier 3)
Deliver Us from Evil, 1973 (Kennedy, G. 3)
Deliverance, 1972 (Boorman 2, Reynolds, B. 3, Voight 3, Zsigmond 4)
Deliverance. *See* Sadgati, 1981
Dél-Kína tájain, 1957 (Jancsó 2)
Della nube alla resistenza, 1979 (Straub and Huillet 2)
Delo Artamonovykh, 1941 (Maretskaya 3, Orlova 3)
Delo bylo v Penkove, 1957 (Tikhonov 3)
Delo Rumiantseva, 1956 (Batalov 3)
Delovak Athara, 1966 (Peries 2)
Delphi Bureau, 1972 (Lourié 4)
Delphica, 1962 (Braunberger 4)

Delphine, 1968 (Gégauff 4)
Delta de sel, 1967 (Braunberger 4)
Delta Factor, 1970 (Garnett 2, De Carlo 3)
Delta Force, 1986 (Golan and Globus 4)
Delta Fox, 1976 (Ireland 3)
Delta Phase I, 1962 (Haanstra 2)
Déltol hajnalig, 1964 (Madaras 3)
Deluded Wife, 1916 (Eason 4)
Deluge. *See* Potop, 1915
Deluge. *See* Potop, 1974
Delusion, 1980 (Cotten 3)
Delusions of Grandeur. *See* Folie des grandeurs, 1971
Deluxe Annie, 1918 (Talmadge, N. 3)
Demain à Nanguila, 1960 (Ivens 2)
Demain Paris, 1964 (Leenhardt 2)
Demande en mariage mal engagée, 1901 (Zecca, 2)
Démanty noci, 1964 (Nemec 2, Kučera 4, Ondricek 4)
Demaskierung. *See* Nacht der Verwandlung, 1935
Déménagement à la cloche de bois, 1897–98 (Guy 2)
Déménagement à la cloche de bois, 1907 (Guy 2)
Dément du Lac Jean Jeune, 1947 (Jutra 2)
Dementia 13, 1963 (Coppola 2, Corman 4)
Demetrius and the Gladiators, 1954 (Daves 2, Bancroft 3, Borgnine 3, Burton 3, Hayward 3, Mature 3, Dunne 4, Krasner 4, Lemaire 4, Waxman 4, Wheeler 4)
Demi-Bride, 1927 (Shearer 3, Gibbons 4, Gillespie 4)
Demi-Paradise, 1943 (Asquith 2, Olivier 3, Rutherford 3, Dillon 4)
Demise of Father Mouret. *See* Faute de l'Abbé Mouret, 1970
Demoiselle du notaire, 1912 (Feuillade 2)
Demoiselle et le violoncelliste, 1965 (Grimault 4, Laguionie 4)
Demoiselle et son revenant, 1951 (Allégret, M. 2, Burel 4)
Demoiselles de Rochefort, 1967 (Demy 2, Darrieux 3, Deneuve 3, Piccoli 3, Cloquet 4, Evein 4, Legrand 4)
Démolition d'un mur, 1895 (Lumière 2)
Demon, 1972 (Kawamoto 4)
Demon. *See* God Told Me To, 1976
Demon Doctor. *See* Juggernaut, 1936
Demon for Trouble, 1934 (Katzman 4)
Demon of Fear, 1916 (Borzage 2)
Demon Pond. *See* Yashagaike, 1979
Demon Seed, 1977 (Christie 3)
Demoni, 1985 (Argento 4)
Demoniaque. *See* Louves, 1957
Demonio y carne. *See* Susana, 1950
Demons. *See* Demoni, 1985
Démons de l'aube, 1946 (Allégret, Y. 2, Signoret 3, Honegger 4, Wakhévitch 4)
Démons de midi, 1978 (Presle 3)
Démons de minuit, 1961 (Allégret, M. 2, Boyer 3)
Demons of the Swamp. *See* Attack of the Giant Leeches, 1959
Demonstration of Proletarian Solidarity. *See* Demostratie van proletarische solidariteit, 1930
Demostratie van proletarische solidariteit, 1930 (Ivens 2)
Demutiger und die Sangerin, 1925 (Dupont 2, Dagover 3)
Den, der sejrer. *See* Syndens Datter, 1915
Den of Beasts. *See* Kedamono no yado, 1951
Den of Thieves, 1905 (Hepworth 2)
Den of Thieves, 1914 (Reid 3)
Den pervyi, 1958 (Ermler 2, Smoktunovsky 3, Enei 4)
Den sedmý, osmá noc, 1969 (Schorm 2)
Den stchastia, 1964 (Batalov 3)
Dena Paona, 1931 (Sircar 4)
Dendai inchiki monogatari, 1963 (Kyo 3)
Denen kokyogaku, 1938 (Hara 3)
Dengeki Shutsudo, 1944 (Mori 3)
Denial, 1925 (Gibbons 4)
Denmark Grows Up, 1947 (Henning-Jensen 2)
Dénonciation, 1961 (Braunberger 4, Delerue 4)
Denso ningen, 1960 (Tsuburaya 4)
Dent récalcitrante, 1902 (Guy 2)
Dentellière, 1977 (Goretta 2, Huppert 3)
Dentist, 1919 (Sennett 2)
Dentist, 1932 (Sennett 2, Fields, W.C. 3)

Deserto rosso, 1964 (Antonioni 2, Vitti 3, Fusco 4, Guerra 4)
Desert's Price, 1925 (Van Dyke, W.S. 2)
Desert's Sting, 1914 (Macpherson 4, Meredyth 4)
Desert's Toll, 1926 (Stevens 2, Wong 3)
Desh Premee, 1982 (Bachchan 3)
Deshermati, 1938 (Sircar 4)
Desiderio, 1943 (De Santis 2, Rossellini 2)
Desiderio, la vita interiore, 1980 (Donaggio 4)
Design for Death, 1947 (Fleischer, R. 2)
Design for Leaving, 1954 (McKimson 4)
Design for Living, 1933 (Lubitsch 2, Cooper, Gary 3, Darwell 3,
    Hopkins, M. 3, Horton 3, March 3, Banton 4, Dreier 4, Hecht 4)
Design for Scandal, 1941 (Taurog 2, Pidgeon 3, Russell, R. 3,
    Daniels 4, Waxman 4)
Design of a Human Being. *See* Ningen moyo, 1949
Designing Woman, 1941 (Cole 4)
Designing Woman, 1957 (Minnelli 2, Bacall 3, Peck 3, Alton, J. 4,
    Ames 4, Previn 4, Rose 4, Schary 4)
Designs on Jerry, 1953 (Hanna and Barbera 4)
Désir mène les hommes, 1957 (Decaë 4)
Desirable, 1934 (Brennan 3, Brent 3, Darwell 3, Haller 4,
    Orry-Kelly 4)
Desire, 1923 (Barnes 4)
Desire, 1936 (Borzage 2, Lubitsch 2, Cooper, Gary 3, Dietrich 3,
    Banton 4, Dreier 4, Hoffenstein 4, Lang 4, Young, W. 4)
Désiré, 1937 (Guitry 2, Arletty 3)
Desire. *See* Touha, 1958
Desire. *See* Yoku, 1958
Desire. *See* Yokubo, 1953
Desire in the Dust, 1960 (Bennett J. 3, Ballard 4)
Desire Me, 1947 (Cukor 2, Leroy 2, Garson 3, Mitchum 3, Akins 4,
    Irene 4, Robinson 4, Ruttenberg 4, Stothart 4)
Desire of Night. *See* Aiyoku no ki, 1930
Desire, The Interior Life. *See* Desiderio, la vita interiore, 1980
Desire under the Elms, 1958 (Loren 3, Perkins 3, Bernstein 4)
Desired Woman, 1927 (Curtiz 2, Blanke 4, Zanuck 4)
Desirée, 1954 (Brando 3, Oberon 3, Simmons 3, Krasner 4, Lemaire 4,
    Newman 4, North 4, Reynolds 4, Taradash 4, Wheeler 4)
Desistfilm, 1954 (Brakhage 2)
Desk Set, 1957 (Blondell 3, Hepburn, K. 3, Tracy 3, Young, G. 3,
    Lemaire 4, Shamroy 4)
Desordre, 1951 (Cocteau 2)
Désordre, 1961 (Welles 2)
Désordre et la nuit, 1958 (Cassel 3, Darrieux 3, Gabin 3, Audiard 4)
Despair, 1979 (Bogarde 3)
Despair. *See* Eine Reise ins Licht, 1977
Despegue a las 18:00, 1969 (Alvarez 2)
Desperado, 1910 (Anderson G. 3)
Desperado, 1954 (Van Cleef 3)
Desperado Outpost. *See* Dokuritsu gurenta, 1959
Desperadoes, 1943 (Vidor, C. 2, Ford, G. 3, Scott, R. 3, Trevor 3,
    Brown, Harry Joe 4)
Desperadoes, 1970 (Borgnine 3, Palance 3)
Desperate, 1947 (Mann 2)
Desperate Adventure, 1938 (Novarro 3)
Desperate Case, 1981 (Lee, C. 3)
Desperate Chance. *See* 'Bad Buck' of Santa Ynez, 1915
Desperate Characters, 1971 (MacLaine 3)
Desperate Crime. *See* Histoire d'un crime, 1906
Desperate Decision. *See* Jeune Folle, 1952
Desperate Hero, 1920 (Ruggles 2)
Desperate Hours, 1955 (Wyler 2, Bogart 3, Kennedy, A. 3, March 3,
    Young, G. 3, Garmes 4, Head 4)
Desperate Journey, 1942 (Walsh 2, Basserman 3, Flynn 3, Kennedy,
    A. 3, Massey 3, Reagan 3, Friedhofer 4, Glennon 4, Steiner 4,
    Wald 4, Wallis 4)
Desperate Lives, 1982 (Biroc 4)
Desperate Lover, 1912 (Sennett 2, Normand 3)
Desperate Moment, 1953 (Zetterling 2, Bogarde 3)
Desperate Ones. *See* Más allá de las montañas, 1967
Desperate Search, 1952 (Keel 3, Wynn 3)
Desperate Trails, 1921 (Ford, J. 2, Carey 3)
Despertar da redentora, 1942 (Mauro 2)

Dessin de perspective. *See* Perspective, 1949
Dessous des cartes, 1948 (Cayatte 2, Reggiani 3, Spaak 4)
Destin des mères, 1911 (Feuillade 2)
Destin fabuleux de Desirée Clary, 1941 (Guitry 2, Barrault 3)
Destination Fury. *See* En pleine bagarre, 1961
Destination Gobi, 1952 (Wise 2, Widmark 3, Clarke, C.C. 4,
    Lemaire 4, Newman 4)
Destination Meatball, 1951 (Lantz 4)
Destination Milan, 1954 (Fairbanks, D. Jr. 3)
Destination Moon, 1950 (Pal 2)
Destination Murder, 1950 (Leven 4)
Destination Tokyo, 1944 (Daves 2, Garfield 3, Grant, C. 3, Glennon 4,
    Wald 4, Waxman 4)
Destination Unknown, 1933 (Garnett 2, Bellamy 3, O'Brien, P. 3)
Destination Unknown, 1942 (Salter 4)
Destinées, 1952 (Christian-Jacque 2, Delannoy 2, Colbert 3,
    Morgan 3, Piccoli 3, Aurenche 4, Bost 4, D'Eaubonne 4, Jeanson 4,
    Matras 4)
Destini di donne, 1953 (Amidei 4, Flaiano 4)
Destino e il timoniere, 1919 (Gallone 2)
Destins de Manoel, 1984 (Branco 4, de Almeida 4)
Destiny, 1943 (Ouspenskaya 3)
Destiny. *See* Mude Tod, 1921
Destiny of a Man. *See* Sudba cheloveka, 1959
Destiny of a Spy, 1969 (Quayle 3, Roberts 3)
Deštivý den, 1963 (Kučera 4)
Destroy All Monsters. *See* Kaiju soshingeki, 1968
Destroy, she said. *See* Détruire, dit-elle, 1969
Destroyer, 1915 (Nilsson 3)
Destroyer, 1943 (Ford, G. 3, Robinson, E. 3, Chase 4, Planer 4)
Destroying Angel, 1923 (Van Dyke, W.S. 2)
Destruction, 1916 (Bara 3, Oland 3)
Destruction of Sakura Jim. *See* Wrath of the Gods, 1914
Destruction of Sakura-Jima. *See* Wrath of the Gods, 1914
Destructors. *See* Marseilles Contract, 1974
Destry, 1955 (Murphy 3)
Destry Rides Again, 1932 (Mix 3, Pitts 3)
Destry Rides Again, 1939 (Auer 3, Dietrich 3, Merkel 3, Stewart 3,
    Pasternak 4)
Det ar min modell, 1946 (Molander 2)
Det ar min musik, 1942 (Fischer 4)
Det brinner en eld, 1943 (Molander 2, Sjostrom 2)
Det regnar på vår karlek, 1946 (Bergman 2, Bjornstrand 3)
Det svanger på slottet, 1959 (Fischer 4)
Det var i Maj, 1914 (Sjostrom 2)
Detained, 1924 (Laurel 3)
Detained While Waiting for Justice, Why?. *See* Detenuto i attesa di
    giudizio, 1971
Detective, 1930 (Lantz 4)
Detective, 1968 (Bisset 3, Duvall, R. 3, Remick 3, Sinatra 3, Biroc 4,
    Goldsmith 4, Smith, J.M. 4)
Détective, 1985 (Léaud 3)
Detective. *See* Father Brown, 1954
Detective Clive, Bart. *See* Scotland Yard, 1930
Detective Craig's Coup, 1914 (White 3)
Detective Lloyd. *See* Lloyd of the CID, 1931
Detective Story, 1951 (Wyler 2, Bendix 3, Douglas, K. 3, Grant, L. 3,
    Garmes 4, Head 4)
Detective Swift, 1914 (White 3)
Detektiv des Kaisers, 1930 (Tschechowa 3)
Detenuto in attesa di giudizio, 1971 (Sordi 3, Amidei 4)
Determination, 1922 (Costello, M. 3)
Determination, 1929 (O'Brien, P. 3)
Determined Woman, 1910 (Lawrence 3)
Déterminés à vaincre, 1968 (Ivens 2)
Deti buri, 1926 (Ermler 2)
Deti vaniushina, 1973 (Gurchenko 3)
Deti Vanyousina, 1915 (Mozhukin 3)
Detour, 1945 (Ulmer 2)
Detour, 1978 (Cushing 3)
Detouring America, 1939 (Avery 2)
Detras de esa puerta, 1972 (Fernández 2, Brazzi 3)
Detras del silencio, 1972 (Baker C. 3)

Détruire, dit-elle, 1969 (Duras 2, Gélin 3, Colpi 4)
Detstvo Gorkovo, 1938 (Donskoi 2)
Detti kapitana Granta, 1936 (Cherkassov 3)
Deuce of Spades, 1922 (Buckland 4)
Deus e o diabo na terra do sol, 1964 (Rocha 2)
Deus, Pátria, Autoridade, 1975 (de Almeida 4)
Deuses e os mortes, 1970 (Guerra 2)
Deutsche Herzen am Deutschen Rhein, 1925 (Albers 3)
Deutsche Panzer, 1940 (Ruttmann 2)
Deutsche Waffenschmiede, 1940 (Ruttmann 2)
Deutscher Traum. See Hitler. Ein Film aus Deutschland, 1977
Deutschland im Herbst, 1978 (Fassbinder 2, Kluge 2, Schlondorff 2, Winkler 3)
Deutschmeister, 1955 (Schneider 3)
Deux Anglaises et le continent, 1971 (Truffaut 2, Léaud 3, Almendros 4, Delerue 4)
Deux Billets pour Mexico, 1967 (Christian-Jaque 2)
Deux bobines et un fil, 1955 (Cloquet 4)
Deux Canards, 1933 (Douy 4)
Deux Combinards, 1937 (Berry 3)
Deux couverts, 1935 (Guitry 2, Fradetal 4)
Deux Françaises, 1915 (Feuillade 2, Musidora 3)
Deux Gamines, 1920 (Clair 2, Feuillade 2)
Deux Gosses, 1906 (Feuillade 2)
Deux grandes filles dans un pyjama, 1974 (Presle 3)
Deux heures à tuer, 1965 (Brasseur 3, Simon, M. 3)
Deux Heures moins le quart avant Jésus-Christ, 1982 (Fabian 3)
Deux hommes dans la ville, 1973 (Delon 3, Depardieu 3, Gabin 3, Sarde 4)
Deux hommes dans Manhattan, 1959 (Melville 2)
Deux Mondes, 1930 (Dupont 2)
Deux 'Monsieur' de Madame, 1933 (Burel 4)
Deux Orphelines, 1933 (Tourneur, M. 2, Douy 4, Ibert 4)
Deux ou trois choses que je sais d'elle, 1967 (Godard 2, Coutard 4)
Deux Rivaux, 1903–04 (Guy 2)
Deux Saisons de la vie, 1972 (Morricone 4)
Deux sous de violettes, 1951 (Barsacq 4)
Deux Timides, 1928 (Clair 2, Rosay 3, Meerson 4)
Deux Timides, 1942 (Allégret, Y. 2, Brasseur 3, Dauphin 3, Achard 4, Alekan 4)
Deux Verités, 1950 (Simon, M. 3)
2 Août 1914, 1914 (Linders 3)
Deuxième Ciel, 1969 (Braunberger 4)
Deuxième Procès d'Artur London, 1969 (Montand 3)
Deuxième Souffle, 1966 (Melville 2)
90 minut prekvapeni, 1953 (Haas 3)
Devanti a lui tremava tutta Roma, 1946 (Gallone 2, Magnani 3)
Devata, 1978 (Azmi 3)
Devcata, nedijte se!, 1937 (Haas 3)
Děvčátko, neříkej nel, 1932 (Stallich 4)
Děvče z hor, 1924 (Vích 4)
Devdas, 1935 (Roy 2)
Devdas, 1955 (Roy 2, Burman 4)
Development of the Stalk and the Root. See Szár és a gyokér fejlodése, 1961
Devi, 1960 (Ray, S. 2, Chatterjee 3, Chandragupta 4, Datta 4, Mitra 4)
Deviat dnei odnogo goda, 1962 (Romm 2, Batalov 3, Smoktunovsky 3)
Deviatoe yanvaria, 1926 (Moskvin 4)
Devil, 1908 (Griffith 2, Lawrence 3, Bitzer 4)
Devil, 1920 (Goulding 2, Arliss 3)
Devil. See Ordög, 1918
Devil and Daniel Webster. See All That Money Can Buy, 1941
Devil and Max Devlin, 1981 (Gould 3, Sangster 4)
Devil and Miss Jones, 1941 (Wood 2, Arthur 3, Coburn, C. 3, Cummings 3, Gwenn 3, Sakall 3, Krasna 4, Menzies 4, Stradling 4)
Devil and the Deep, 1932 (Cooper, Gary 3, Grant, C. 3, Laughton 3, Lang 4)
Devil and the 10 Commandments. See Diable et les dix commandements, 1962
Devil at 4 O'Clock, 1961 (Leroy 2, Aumont 3, Dalio 3, Sinatra 3, Tracy 3, Biroc 4, Duning 4)
Devil at His Elbow, 1916 (Menjou 3)
Devil Bat, 1941 (Lugosi 3)

Devil by the Tail. See Diable par la queue, 1968
Devil Commands, 1941 (Dmytryk 2, Karloff 3)
Devil Crag. See Seytan kayaliklari, 1970
Devil Dancer, 1927 (Niblo 2, Brook 3, Wong 3, Barnes 4, Goldwyn 4)
Devil Dodger, 1917 (Gilbert 3)
Devil Dogs of the Air, 1935 (Bacon 2, Bond 3, Cagney 3, O'Brien, P. 3, Edeson 4, Saunders 4)
Devil Doll, 1936 (Browning 2, Von Stroheim 2, Barrymore L. 3, O'Sullivan 3, Walthall 3, Fort 4, Gibbons 4, Waxman 4)
Devil Goddess, 1955 (Weissmuller 3, Katzman 4)
Devil Has Seven Faces. See Diavolo a sette face, 1971
Devil Horse, 1926 (Stevens 2, Canutt 4, Roach 4)
Devil Horse, 1932 (Carey 3, Canutt 4)
Devil in Evening Dress, 1973 (Miller 2)
Devil in Love. See Arcidiavolo, 1966
Devil in Love. See Diavolo innamorato, 1966
Devil in Silk. See Teufel in Seide, 1956
Devil in the Brain. See Diavolo nel cervello, 1972
Devil in the Flesh. See Diable au corps, 1947
Devil Is a Sissy, 1936 (Van Dyke, W.S. 2, Cooper, J 3, Rooney 3, Brown, N. 4, Freed 4, Mahin 4, Rosson 4, Stothart 4)
Devil Is a Woman, 1935 (Von Sternberg 2, Dietrich 3, Horton 3, Ballard 4, Banton 4, Dreier 4)
Devil Is a Woman. See Soriso del grande tentatore, 1973
Devil is an Empress, 1938 (Modot 3)
Devil Is an Empress. See Joueur d'échecs, 1938
Devil is Driving, 1937 (Cook 2)
Devil Makes Three, 1952 (Kelly, Gene 3, Vích 4)
Devil May Care, 1929 (Franklin 2, Day 4)
Devil May Hare, 1954 (McKimson 4)
Devil Never Sleeps, 1962 (Mathieson 4)
Devil Never Sleeps. See Satan Never Sleeps, 1962
Devil of a Fellow. See Teufelskerl, 1935
Devil of the Deep, 1938 (Terry 4)
Devil of the Desert. See Shaitan el Sahara, 1954
Devil on Horseback, 1936 (Miller 3)
Devil on Wheels. See Indianapolis Speedway, 1939
Devil Pays Off, 1941 (Alton, J. 4)
Devil, Probably. See Diable, probablement, 1977
Devil Riders, 1943 (Crabbe 3)
Devil Rides Out, 1968 (Fisher 2, Lee, C. 3, Bernard 4)
Devil Stone, 1917 (DeMille 2, Reid 3, Macpherson 4)
Devil Strikes at Night. See Nachts wann der Teufel kam, 1957
Devil Takes the Count. See Devil Is a Sissy, 1936
Devil Thumbs a Ride, 1947 (Hunt 4)
Devil to Pay, 1930 (Colman 3, Loy 3, Young, L. 3, Barnes 4, Day 4, Goldwyn 4, Newman 4, Toland 4)
Devil with Hitler, 1942 (Roach 4)
Devil with Women, 1930 (Bogart 3, McLaglen 3, Friedhofer 4, Nichols 4)
Devil Within Her. See I Don't Want to be Born, 1975
Devilish Honeymoon. See Kam čert nemuže, 1970
Devil-May-Care, 1929 (Novarro 3, Adrian 4, Gibbons 4, Kraly 4, Lewin 4, Shearer 4, Stothart 4, Tiomkin 4)
Devils, 1971 (Russell 2, Redgrave, V. 3, Reed, O. 3, Russell 4, Watkin 4)
Devil's Advocate, 1977 (Mills 3)
Devil's Advocate. See Des Teufels Advokat, 1977
Devil's Agent, 1962 (Cushing 3, Lee, C. 3)
Devil's Angels, 1967 (Cassavetes 2, Corman 4)
Devil's Bait, 1959 (Alwyn 4)
Devil's Bouncing Ball Song. See Akuma no temari-uta, 1977
Devil's Bride. See Devil Rides Out, 1968
Devil's Brigade, 1968 (Andrews D. 3, Holden 3, Robertson 3, Clothier 4, Needham 4, North 4)
Devil's Brother. See Fra Diavolo, 1933
Devil's Canyon, 1953 (Arlen 3, Mayo 3, D'Agostino 4, Musuraca 4)
Devil's Cargo, 1925 (Fleming 2, Beery 3)
Devil's Chaplain, 1929 (Karloff 3)
Devil's Circus, 1926 (Christensen 2, Shearer 3)
Devil's Claim, 1920 (Hayakawa 3, Moore, C. 3)
Devil's Cross. See Cruz diablo, 1934
Devil's Daffodil, 1961 (Lee, C. 3)

Devil's Daffodil. *See* Geheimnis der gelben Narzissen, 1961
Devil's Daughter, 1915 (Bara 3)
Devil's Daughter, 1972 (Cotten 3, Winters 3)
Devil's Daughter. *See* Fille du diable, 1945
Devil's Disciple, 1959 (Douglas, K. 3, Lancaster 3, Olivier 3, Fisher 4)
Devil's Doorway, 1950 (Mann 2, Calhern 3, Cody 3, Taylor, R. 3, Alton, J. 4, Canutt 4, Plunkett 4)
Devil's Double, 1916 (Hart 3, August 4)
Devil's 8, 1969 (Milius 2)
Devil's Envoy. *See* Visiteurs du soir, 1942
Devil's Eye. *See* Djävulens öga, 1960
Devil's Feud Cake, 1962 (Freleng 4)
Devil's Garden, 1920 (Barrymore L. 3, Stradling 4)
Devil's Garden. *See* Coplan sauve sa peau, 1967
Devil's General. *See* Teufels General, 1955
Devil's Hairpin, 1957 (Astor 3, Wilde 3, Head 4)
Devil's Hand, 1961 (Pierce 4)
Devil's Harbour, 1955 (Arlen 3)
Devil's Henchman, 1949 (Baxter W. 3)
Devil's Holiday, 1930 (Goulding 2, Bosworth 3, Lukas 3, Pitts 3)
Devil's Imposter. *See* Pope Joan, 1972
Devil's in Love, 1933 (Dieterle 2, Lugosi 3, Young, L. 3)
Devil's Instrument. *See* Djavulens instrument, 1967
Devil's Island, 1940 (Karloff 3)
Devil's Island. *See* Akuma-to, 1980
Devil's Island. *See* Gokumon-to, 1977
Devil's Lottery, 1932 (McLaglen 3, Friedhofer 4)
Devil's Men, 1976 (Cushing 3, Pleasance 3)
Devil's Messenger, 1962 (Chaney Lon, Jr. 3, Siodmak 4)
Devil's Mill. *See* Certuv mlýn, 1950
Devil's Needle, 1916 (Talmadge, N. 3)
Devil's Own. *See* Witches, 1966
Devil's Own Envoy. *See* Visiteurs du soir, 1942
Devil's Partner, 1923 (Shearer 3)
Devil's Partner, 1958 (Cronjager 4)
Devil's Party, 1938 (McLaglen 3, Krasner 4)
Devil's Pass, 1957 (Adam 4)
Devil's Pass. *See* Czarci źleb, 1948
Devil's Passkey, 1919 (Von Stroheim 2, Daniels 4, Day 4)
Devil's Pipeline, 1940 (Arlen 3, Salter 4)
Devil's Playground, 1937 (Bond 3, Del Rio 3, Ballard 4, Trumbo 4)
Devil's Playground, 1946 (Boyd 3)
Devil's Playground. *See* Lady Who Dared, 1931
Devil's Protegé. *See* Hvide Djaevel, 1915
Devil's Rain, 1975 (Borgnine 3, Lupino 3, Wynn 3)
Devil's Skipper, 1928 (Fetchit 3)
Devil's Temple. *See* Oni no sumu yakata, 1969
Devil's Toast. *See* Akuma no kanpai, 1947
Devil's Toy, 1916 (Edeson 4)
Devil's Toy. *See* Rouli-Roulant, 1966
Devil's Triangle, 1974 (Price 3)
Devil's Wanton. *See* Fängelse, 1949
Devil's Wheel. *See* Chyortovo koleso, 1926
Devil's Widow, 1971 (Gardner 3)
Devil's Widow. *See* Tam Lin, 1971
Devil's Work. *See* Davolja posla, 1965
Devil-Ship Pirates, 1964 (Lee, C. 3, Sangster 4)
Devil-Stone, 1917 (Bosworth 3, Buckland 4)
Devoir de Zouzou, 1955 (Kosma 4)
Devonsville Terror, 1983 (Pleasance 3)
Devoradora, 1946 (De Fuentes 2, Félix 3)
Devotee. *See* Puran Bhagat, 1933
Devotion, 1913 (Ince 4)
Devotion, 1931 (Howard, L. 3, Mandell 4, Stewart 4)
Devotion, 1946 (De Havilland 3, Greenstreet 3, Henreid 3, Kennedy, A. 3, Lupino 3, Buckner 4, Friedhofer 4, Haller 4, Korngold 4)
Devushka s dalekoi reki, 1928 (Enei 4)
Devushka s gitaroy, 1958 (Gurchenko 3)
Dezerter, 1958 (Stawinsky 4)
Dezertér, 1965 (Brdečka 4)
Dezertir, 1933 (Gerasimov 2, Pudovkin 2, Golovnya 4)
D'Fightin' Ones, 1961 (Freleng 4)

Dhadram Karam, 1975 (Kapoor 2)
Dharam Ki Devi, 1935 (Biswas 4)
Dharati Mata, 1938 (Sircar 4)
Dharti Ke Lal, 1945 (Shankar 4)
D'homme à hommes, 1948 (Christian-Jaque 2, Barrault 3, Blier 3, Kosma 4, Matras 4, Spaak 4)
Dhoon, 1953 (Kapoor 2)
Di quelle, 1953 (Fabrizi 3)
Día con el diablo, 1945 (Cantinflas 3, Figueroa 4)
Dia de Noviembre, 1972 (Solás 2)
Dia de vida, 1950 (Fernández 2, Figueroa 4)
Dia na rampa, 1957 (Rocha 2)
Diabel, 1972 (Pszoniak 3)
Diable au coeur, 1927 (Autant-Lara 2, L'Herbier 2, Balfour 3)
Diable au corps, 1947 (Autant-Lara 2, Tati 2, Philipe 3, Presle 3, Aurenche 4, Bost 4, Douy 4)
Diable boiteux, 1949 (Guitry 2)
Diable dans la boîte, 1976 (Presle 3, Carrière 4, Vierny 4)
Diable dans la ville, 1924 (Dulac 2)
Diable et les dix commandements, 1962 (Duvivier 2, Dalio 3, Darrieux 3, Dauphin 3, Delon 3, Fernandel 3, Ferrer, M. 3, Modot 3, Presle 3, Simon, M. 3, Audiard 4, Jeanson 4)
Diable noir, 1905 (Méliès 2)
Diable par la queue, 1968 (Broca 2, Montand 3, Schell, Maria 3, Delerue 4)
Diable probablement, 1977 (Bresson 2, Sarde 4)
Diable souffle, 1947 (Vanel 3, Alekan 4)
Diablo bajo la Almohada, 1969 (Thulin 3)
Diablo del desierto, 1954 (Armendáriz 3)
Diablo no es tan diablo, 1949 (García 3)
Diabolic Tenant. *See* Locataire diabolique, 1910
Diabolical Dr. Z.. *See* Miss Muerte, 1966
Diabolical Honeymoon. *See* Dábelské líbánky, 1970
Diabolical Wedding, 1971 (O'Brien, M. 3)
Diabolically Yours. *See* Diaboliquement votre, 1967
Diabolik, 1968 (De Laurentiis 4, Gherardi 4, Morricone 4)
Diabolik. *See* Danger: Diabolik, 1968
Diabolique. *See* Diaboliques, 1954
Diaboliquement vôtre, 1967 (Duvivier 2, Delon 3, Barsacq 4, Decaë 4, Gégauff 4)
Diaboliques, 1954 (Clouzot 2, Signoret 3, Vanel 3, Barsacq 4)
Diadalmas elet, 1923 (Lukas 3)
Diadiouskina kvartira, 1913 (Mozhukin 3)
Diagnosis for Murder. *See* Diagnosis: Murder, 1975
Diagnosis: Murder, 1975 (Lee, C. 3)
Diagnostic C.I.V., 1960 (Delerue 4)
Diagnoza X, 1933 (Stallich 4)
Diagonal Sinfonie, 1925 (Eggeling 2)
Diagonal Symphony. *See* Diagonal Sinfonie, 1925
Diagonale du fou, 1984 (Caron 3, Olbrychski 3, Piccoli 3, Pszoniak 3, Ullmann 3, Coutard 4, Guillemot 4)
Dial 1119, 1950 (Previn 4)
Dial M for Murder, 1954 (Hitchcock 2, Cummings 3, Kelly, Grace 3, Milland 3, Tiomkin 4)
Dial M for Murder, 1981 (Dickinson 3)
Dial 'P' for Pink, 1965 (Freleng 4)
Dialectique, 1966 (Guillemot 4)
Dialog, 1968 (Skolimowski 2, Kroner 3, Léaud 3)
Dialog, 1977 (Tikhonov 3)
Diálogo de exilados, 1974 (Ruiz 2)
Dialogo de exilados. *See* Dialogue d'exilés, 1974
Dialogue des Carmélites, 1960 (Barrault 3, Brasseur 3, Moreau 3, Valli 3)
Dialogue d'exilés, 1974 (Gélin 3)
Dialogue of Exiles. *See* Diálogo de exilados, 1974
Dialogue. *See* Dialog, 1968
Dialogues. *See* Rozhovory, 1969
Diamant, 1969 (Grimault 4)
Diamant du Sénéchal, 1914 (Feuillade 2)
Diamant noir, 1922 (Fresnay 3)
Diamant noir, 1940 (Delannoy 2, Vanel 3)
Diamanti che nessuno voleva rubare, 1968 (Andrews D. 3)
Diamond Cut Diamond, 1912 (Bunny 3, Reid 3)

Diamond Cut Diamond, 1932 (Niblo 2)
Diamond Cut Diamond. *See* Blame the Woman, 1932
Diamond Frontier, 1940 (McLaglen 3, Krasner 4, Salter 4)
Diamond Handcuffs, 1928 (Johnson, N. 3, Wilson, C. 4)
Diamond Head, 1962 (Heston 3, Green, G. 4, Williams, J. 4)
Diamond Horseshoe. *See* Billy Rose's Diamond Horseshoe, 1945
Diamond in the Rough, 1914 (Nilsson 3)
Diamond Jim, 1935 (Sturges, P. 2, Sutherland 2, Arthur 3, Mandell 4, Waxman 4)
Diamond Mercenaries, 1975 (Fonda, P. 3, Palance 3)
Diamond Mercenaries. *See* Killer Force, 1975
Diamond of the Little Cockerel. *See* Kiskakas gyémánt félkrajcárja, 1950
Diamond Queen, 1953 (Cortez 4, Lourié 4)
Diamond Ship. *See* Spinnen, 1919–20
Diamond Star, 1910 (Griffith 2, Bitzer 4)
Diamonds, 1976 (Shaw 3, Winters 3, Golan and Globus 4)
Diamonds Are Brittle. *See* Millard un billard, 1965
Diamonds Are Forever, 1971 (Connery 3, Barry 4, Whitlock 4)
Diamonds for Breakfast, 1968 (Mastroianni 3)
Diamonds of the Night. *See* Demanty noci, 1964
Diana, 1956 (Armendáriz 3)
Diana l'affascinatrice, 1915 (Bertini 3)
Diane, 1929 (Tschechowa 3, Andrejew 4)
Diane, 1955 (Hardwicke 3, Moore, R. 3, Turner, L. 3, Plunkett 4, Rozsa 4)
Diane of the Follies, 1916 (Gish, L. 3)
Diaries, Notes & Sketches, 1975 (Bogdanovich 2)
Diaries, Notes, and Sketches. *See* Walden, 1968
Diario de la guerra del cerdo, 1975 (Torre-Nilsson 2)
Diario di un italiano, 1973 (Valli 3)
Diary, 1981 (Vinton 4)
Diary. *See* Dvevnik, 1974
Diary for Timothy, 1946 (Jennings 2, Gielgud 3)
Diary of a Chambermaid, 1946 (Renoir 2, Anderson J. 3, Goddard 3, Meredith 3, Lourié 4)
Diary of a Chambermaid. *See* Journal d'une femme de chambre, 1964
Diary of a Country Priest. *See* Journal d'un curé de campagne, 1950
Diary of a Lost Girl. *See* Tagebuch einer Verlorenen, 1929
Diary of a Lost Woman. *See* Tagebuch einer Verlorenen, 1918
Diary of a Lover. *See* Tagebuch einer Verliebten, 1953
Diary of a Mad Housewife, 1970 (Perry 4)
Diary of a Madman, 1963 (Price 3, Williams, R. 4)
Diary of a Madman. *See* Para gnedych, 1915
Diary of a Nobody, 1964 (Russell 2)
Diary of a Shinjuku Burglar. *See* Shinjuku dorobo nikki, 1969
Diary of a Young Comic, 1979 (Keach 3)
Diary of an Unknown Soldier, 1959 (Watkins 2)
Diary of Anne Frank, 1959 (Ashby 2, Stevens 2, Schildkraut 3, Winters 3, Cardiff 4, Goodrich and Hackett 4, Lemaire 4, Newman 4, Wheeler 4)
Diary of Anne Frank, 1980 (Schell, Maximilian 3, Goodrich and Hackett 4)
Diary of Forbidden Dreams. *See* Che?, 1972
Diary of Major Thompson. *See* French They Are a funny Race, 1956
Diary of One Who Disappeared. *See* Zápisiník zmizeleho, 1979
Diary of Sueko. *See* Nianchan, 1959
Diary of the Pig War. *See* Diario de la guerra del cerdo, 1975
Diary of Yunbogi. *See* Yunbogi no nikki, 1965
Dias de odio, 1954 (Torre-Nilsson 2)
Días de otoño, 1962 (Figueroa 4)
Dias del agua, 1971 (Herrera 4)
Diavolo, 1963 (Sordi 3, De Laurentiis 4)
Diavolo a sette face, 1971 (Baker C. 3)
Diavolo bianco, 1947 (Brazzi 3)
Diavolo innamorato, 1966 (Rooney 3)
Diavolo innamorato. *See* Arcidiavolo, 1966
Diavolo nel cervello, 1972 (Presle 3, D'Amico 4, Morricone 4)
Dice. *See* Kocka, 1972
Dice of Destiny, 1920 (King 2)
Dicen que soy mujeriego, 1948 (García 3, Infante 3)
Dich hab' ich geliebt, 1929 (Reisch 4)
Diciotteni al sole, 1962 (Morricone 4)

Diciottenni, 1956 (Ponti 4)
Dick Barton Strikes Back, 1949 (Adam 4)
Dick Tracy, 1937 (Bushman 3)
Dick Tracy Meets Gruesome, 1947 (Karloff 3, D'Agostino 4)
Dick Tracy Returns, 1938 (Canutt 4)
Dick Tracy's Amazing Adventure. *See* Dick Tracy Meets Gruesome, 1947
Dick Tracy's G-Men, 1939 (Jones, J. 3)
Dick Turpin, 1925 (Cooper, Gary 3, Lombard 3, Mix 3)
Dick Turpin, 1933 (McLaglen 3)
Dick Whittington and His Cat, 1913 (Guy 2)
Dick Whittington's Cat, 1936 (Iwerks 4)
Dictator, 1922 (Cruze 2, Reid 3, Brown, K. 4)
Dictator, 1935 (Saville 2, Carroll M. 3, Andrejew 4, Planer 4)
Dictator. *See* Love Affair of the Dictator, 1935
Dictionnaire de Joachim, 1965 (Borowczyk 4)
Dictionnaire des pin-up girls, 1951 (Braunberger 4)
Did Mother Get Her Wash, 1911 (Sennett 2)
Did You Ever See a Dream Walking?, 1943 (Balcon 4)
Dida Ibsens Geschichte, 1918 (Veidt 3)
Didi, 1937 (Sircar 4)
Die! Die! My Darling. *See* Fanatic, 1968
Die Laughing, 1980 (Lanchester 3)
Die, Monster, Die!, 1965 (Karloff 3)
Die—oder Keine, 1932 (Courant 4)
Diebe, 1928 (Dieterle 2)
Diebe von Günsterburg. *See* Springende Hirsch, 1915
Dieci bianchi uccidi da un piccolo indiano, 1974 (Ireland 3)
Dieci comandamenti, 1945 (Germi 2, Brazzi 3)
Dieci italiani per un Tedesco, 1062 (Cervi 3)
Dieci minuti di vita, 1943 (De Sica 2)
Die-Hard Shoemakers. *See* Skalní ševci, 1931
Diese Mann gehort mir, 1950 (Frohlich 3)
Diese Nacht vergess' ich nie, 1949 (Frohlich 3)
Diesel, 1942 (Wegener 3)
Dieses Leid bliebt bei dir. *See* Kabarett, 1954
Dieu a besoin des hommes, 1950 (Delannoy 2, Fresnay 3, Gélin 3, Aurenche 4, Bost 4)
Dieu a choisi Paris, 1969 (Belmondo 3)
Dieux du feu, 1961 (Storck 2)
Dieux et les morts. *See* Deuses e os mortes, 1970
Difanzati della morte, 1956 (Solinas 4)
Difendo il mio amore, 1956 (Gassman 3, Di Venanzo 4)
Different Man, 1914 (Crisp 3)
Different Sons. *See* Futari no musuko, 1962
Difficile morire, 1977 (Jancsó 2)
Difficult Life. *See* Vita difficile, 1961
Difficult People. *See* Nehéz emberek, 1964
Difficult Years, 1950 (Garfield 3)
Difficult Years. *See* Anni difficili, 1948
Difficulté d'être infidèle, 1963 (Braunberger 4, Coutard 4)
Dig Up, 1922 (Roach 4)
Diga sul Pacifico, 1958 (Mangano 3)
Diga sul Pacifico. *See* Barrage contre le Pacifique, 1958
Digging for Victory, 1942 (Halas and Batchelor 2)
Digi sul ghiaccio, 1953 (Olmi 2)
Digital Dreams, 1983 (Coburn, J. 3)
Digterkongen. *See* Gudernes Yndling, 1919
Digue, ou Pour sauver la Hollande, 1911 (Gance 2)
Dijkbouw, 1952 (Haanstra 2)
Dike Builders. *See* Dijkbouw, 1952
Dikshul Wapas, 1943 (Sircar 4)
Dil e Naadan, 1982 (Patil 3)
Dil Hi To Hai, 1963 (Kapoor 2)
Dil Ki Rani, 1947 (Kapoor 2, Burman 4)
Dilemma, 1962 (Carlsen 2)
Dillinger, 1945 (Cook 3, Tiomkin 4)
Dillinger, 1973 (Milius 2, Dreyfuss 3, Johnson, B. 3, Oates 3, Stanton 4)
Dillinger è morto, 1968 (Ferreri 2, Girardot 3, Piccoli 3)
Dillinger est morte. *See* Dillinger è morto, 1968
Dillinger Is Dead. *See* Dillinger è morto, 1968
Dilruba, 1950 (Anand 3)

Dim Little Island, 1949 (Jennings 2)
Dimanche à Pekin, 1956 (Marker 2, Delerue 4)
Dimanche d'été. See Domenica d'estate, 1961
Dimanche de la vie, 1965 (Darrieux 3)
Dimanche de mai, 1963 (Goretta 2)
Dimanche Matin. See Niedzielny poranek, 1955
Dimanche nous volerons, 1956 (Belmondo 3)
Dime a Dance, 1937 (Allyson 3, Kaye 3)
Dime to Retire, 1955 (McKimson 4)
Dimension 5, 1966 (Hunter 3)
Dimensions of Dialogue. See Možnosti dialogu, 1982
Dimentica il mio passata, 1956 (Cortese 3)
Dimmi che fai tutto per mei, 1976 (D'Amico 4)
Dimples, 1936 (Carradine 3, Fetchit 3, Robinson, B. 3, Temple 3, Glennon 4, Johnson 4)
Dimy Gorina, 1961 (Gerasimov 2)
Din stund på jorden, 1972 (Fischer 4)
Din tillvaros land, 1940 (Sucksdorff 2)
Dina chez les lois, 1967 (Arletty 3)
Dina e Django, 1981 (de Almeida 4)
Dinah, 1931 (Fleischer, M. and D. 2)
Dinamiteros, 1962 (García 3)
Dinero Maldito, 1978 (Widmark 3)
Ding Dong Daddy, 1941 (Freleng 4)
Ding Dong Doggie, 1937 (Fleischer, M. and D. 2)
Dingaka, 1965 (Baker S. 3)
Dingbat Land, 1949 (Terry 4)
Ding-Dong. See Ručak, 1972
Dinky, 1935 (Astor 3, Cooper, J 3, Edeson 4)
Dinky Doodle Series, 1925–26 (Lantz 4)
Dinky Finds a Home, 1946 (Terry 4)
Dinner at Eight, 1933 (Cukor 2, Barrymore J. 3, Barrymore L. 3, Beery 3, Burke 3, Dressler 3, Harlow 3, Hersholt 3, Adrian 4, Daniels 4, Gibbons 4, Mankiewicz 4, Marion 4, Selznick 4, Stewart 4)
Dinner at the Ritz, 1937 (Lukas 3, Niven 3)
Dinner Hour, 1920 (Roach 4)
Dinner Jest, 1926 (Sennett 2)
Dinner Under Difficulties. See Salle à manger fantastique, 1898
Dino, 1957 (Mineo 3, Waxman 4)
Dinosaur, 1980 (Vinton 4)
Dinosaur and the Missing Link, 1914 (O'Brien 4)
Dinosaurs. See Dinozaury, 1961
Dinosaurus!, 1960 (Cortez 4)
Dinozaury, 1961 (Giersz 4)
Dinty, 1920 (Neilan 2, Moore, C. 3, Wong 3, Carré 4)
Dio, sei proprio un padreterno, 1973 (Van Cleef 3)
Diogenes Perhaps. See Možda Diogen, 1967
Dion Brothers. See Gravy Train, 1974
Dionysus in '69, 1970 (De Palma 2)
Dios eligió sus viajeros, 1963 (Rey 3)
Diosa arrodillada, 1947 (Félix 3)
Diplomacy, 1926 (Neilan 2, Sweet 3, Glazer 4)
Diplomaniacs, 1933 (Mankiewicz 2, Calhern 3, Cronjager 4, Steiner 4)
Diplomatic Courier, 1952 (Hathaway 2, Bronson 3, Knef 3, Malden 3, Marvin 3, Neal 3, Power 3, Ballard 4, Robinson 4, Wheeler 4)
Diplomatic Flo, 1914 (Lawrence 3)
Diplomatic Pouch. See Teka dypkuryera, 1927
Diplomat's Mansion. See Tokyo yowa, 1961
Diploteratology or Bardo Folly, 1967 (Landow 2)
Dippy Daughter, 1918 (Roach 4)
Dippy Dentist, 1920 (Roach 4)
Dipsy Gypsy, 1941 (Pal 2)
Diptyque, 1967 (Borowczyk 4)
Dir gehort mein Herz. See Marionette, 1938
Direct au coeur, 1933 (Pagnol 2)
Directed by John Ford, 1971 (Bogdanovich 2, Welles 2, Fonda, H. 3, Stewart 3, Wayne 3, Kovacs 4)
Direction d'acteurs par Jean Renoir, 1966 (Braunberger 4)
Director, 1915 (Barrymore J. 3)
Director's Notebook. See Block-Notes di un regista, 1969
Directors, 1963 (Germi 2, Godard 2, Hitchcock 2, Huston 2)
Direktørens Datter, 1912 (Blom 2)

Dirigible, 1931 (Capra 2, Bosworth 3, Karloff 3, Muse 3, Wray 3, Swerling 4, Walker 4)
Dirnenlied. See Ich glaub' nie mehr an eine Frau, 1929
Dirnenmorder von London. See Jack the Ripper, 1976
Dirnentragodie, 1927 (Homolka 3, Nielsen 3)
Dirnentragodie. See Zwischen Nacht under Morgen, 1931
Dirt, 1939 (McDowall 3)
Dirty Agents. See Guerre secrète, 1966
Dirty Angels. See Vergogna schifosi, 1968
Dirty Dingus Magee, 1970 (Elam 3, Kennedy, G. 3, Sinatra 3)
Dirty Dozen, 1967 (Aldrich 2, Cassavetes 2, Borgnine 3, Bronson 3, Kennedy, G. 3, Marvin 3, Ryan 3, Sutherland 3, Johnson 4)
Dirty Dozen—The Next Mission, 1985 (Borgnine 3, Marvin 3)
Dirty Duck, 1977 (Corman 4)
Dirty Face Dan, 1915 (Franklin 2)
Dirty Game. See Guerre secrète, 1966
Dirty Hands. See Innocents aux mains sales, 1975
Dirty Hands. See Mains sales, 1951
Dirty Harry, 1971 (Milius 2, Siegel 2, Eastwood 3, Schifrin 4)
Dirty Heroes. See Dalle Ardenne all'inferno, 1968
Dirty Knight's Work. See Trial by Combat, 1976
Dirty Knights' Work, 1976 (Pleasance 3)
Dirty Mary Crazy Larry, 1974 (Fonda, P. 3)
Dirty Money. See Flic, 1972
Dirty Tricks, 1981 (Gould 3)
Dirty Two. See Dito nell piaga, 1969
Dirty Weekend. See Mordi e fuggi, 1972
Dirty Work, 1933 (Laurel & Hardy 3, Roach 4)
Dirty Work, 1934 (Johnson, C. 3, Balcon 4, Junge 4)
Dirty Work in a Laundry, 1915 (Sennett 2)
Disappearance, 1977 (Hurt, J. 3, Sutherland 3)
Disappearance of Aimee, 1976 (Davis 3, Dunaway 3, Head 4)
Disappearance of Flight 412, 1974 (Ford, G. 3)
Disbarred, 1939 (Florey 2, Preston 3, Dreier 4, Head 4)
Discard, 1916 (Van Dyke, W.S. 2)
Discarded Woman, 1920 (Haller 4)
Disciple, 1915 (Hart 3, Hersholt 3, August 4)
Disco volante, 1965 (Mangano 3, Sordi 3, Vitti 3)
Discontent, 1916 (Weber 2)
Discord. See Hans engelska fru, 1926
Discord. See Roztržka, 1956
Discord and Harmony, 1914 (Dwan 2, Chaney Lon 3)
Discours de bienvenue de McLaren. See Opening Speech, 1960
Discover America, 1967 (Meredith 3)
Discovery, 1913 (Bushman 3)
Discovery of Zero, 1963 (Kuri 4)
Discovery on the Shaggy Mountain. See Objev na střapaté hurce, 1962
Discreet Charm of the Bourgeoisie. See Charme discret de la bourgeoisie, 1972
Discussion, 1895 (Lumière 2)
Discussion de M. Janssen et de M. Lagrange, 1895 (Lumière 2)
Discussion politique, 1901 (Zecca, 2)
Disenchantment, 1914 (Lawrence 3)
Disgraced, 1933 (Banton 4, Struss 4)
Dishevelled Hair. See Midare-gami, 1961
Dishonor Bright, 1936 (Sanders 3)
Dishonorable Discharge. See Ces dames preferent le Mambo, 1958
Dishonored, 1931 (Hathaway 2, Von Sternberg 2, Dietrich 3, McLaglen 3, Oland 3, Banton 4, Dreier 4, Garmes 4)
Dishonored Lady, 1947 (De Toth 2, Lamarr 3, Stromberg 4)
Disillusioned, 1912 (Bosworth 3)
Disillusioned Bluebird, 1944 (Fleischer, M. and D. 2)
Dislocations mystérieuses, 1901 (Méliès 2)
Dismissal, 1982 (Miller 2)
Dis-moi qui tuer, 1965 (Morgan 3)
Disobedient Robot. See Playful Robot, 1956
Disons, un soir à diner. See Metti, una sera a cena, 1969
Disorder. See Disordine, 1962
Disorder in the Court, 1936 (Three Stooges 3)
Disorderly Conduct, 1932 (Bellamy 3, Tracy 3)
Disorderly Orderly, 1964 (Lewis 2, Tashlin 2, Sloane 3, Edouart 4, Fulton 4, Head 4)
Disordine, 1962 (Jourdan 3, Jurgens 3, Valli 3)

Dlinnoe, dlinnoe delo, 1976 (Yankovsky 3)
Dlugoszewski Concert, 1965 (Emshwiller 2)
DM—Killer, 1964 (Jurgens 3)
Dnes naposled, 1958 (Fric 2)
Dnes večer všechno skončí, 1955 (Kachyna 2, Kučera 4)
Dnevnik direktora shkoly, 1975 (Gurchenko 3)
Do a Good Deed, 1935 (Lantz 4)
Do and Dare, 1922 (Mix 3)
Do Anjaane, 1976 (Bachchan 3)
Do Aur Do Paanch, 1980 (Bachchan 3)
Do Bhai, 1947 (Burman 4)
Do Bigha Zamin, 1953 (Roy 2)
Do budushchei vesny, 1961 (Smoktunovsky 3)
Do Detectives Think?, 1927 (Laurel and Hardy 3, Roach 4)
Do Do series, 1964 (Halas and Batchelor 2)
Do Dooni Char, 1968 (Roy 2)
Do Gentlemen Snore?, 1928 (McCarey 2, Roach 4)
Do Husbands Deceive?, 1918 (Roach 4)
Do I Love You?, 1934 (Gerasimov 2)
Do I Love You? See Lyubliu tebya?, 1934
Do Jasoos, 1975 (Kapoor 2)
Do lesíčka na čekanou, 1966 (Brdečka 4)
Do Me a Favor, 1922 (Roach 4)
Do Not Disturb, 1965 (Day 3, Welch 3, Boyle 4, Shamroy 4,
    Smith, J.M. 4)
Do Not Fold, Spindle, or Mutilate, 1971 (Loy 3, Sidney 3, Cortez 4,
    Goldsmith 4)
Do Not Judge. See Domen icke, 1914
Do panského stavu, 1925 (Ondra 3, Vích 4)
Do pivnice, 1982 (Švankmajer 4)
Do Raha, 1952 (Biswas 4)
Do Sitare, 1951 (Anand 3, Biswas 4)
Do Ustad, 1959 (Kapoor 2)
Do Widzenia Do Jutra, 1960 (Polanski 2, Cybulski 3)
Do You Know This Voice?, 1963
Do You Love Me?, 1946 (Grable 3, O'Hara 3, Cronjager 4)
Do You Love Your Wife?, 1919 (Laurel 3, Roach 4)
Do You Remember Love, 1985 (Woodward 3)
Do you remember? See Ty pomnis li?, 1914
Do You Take This Stranger?, 1970 (Cotten 3)
Do Your Duty, 1926 (Roach 4)
Do Your Duty, 1928 (Robinson 4)
Do Your Stuff, 1923 (Roach 4)
Do Yourself Some Good, 1975 (Hurt, J. 3)
Dobře placená procházka, 1965 (Forman 2)
Dobrodružstvi na Zlaté zátoce, 1955 (Pojar 4)
Dobrovoltsy, 1958 (Ulyanov 3)
Dobrý voják Svejk, 1931 (Fric 2, Haas 3, Stallich 4)
Dobrý voják Svejk, 1957 (Hrušínský 3, Kopecký 3)
Dobu, 1954 (Shindo 2, Yamamura 3)
Dobutsuen nikki, 1956 (Hani 2)
Doc, 1971 (Dunaway 3)
Doc Savage, the Man of Bronze, 1975 (Pal 2)
Doce mujeres, 1939 (Alton, J. 4)
Doce sillas, 1962 (Gutiérrez 2)
Dochki-materi, 1974 (Smoktunovsky 3)
Dochu sugoruku bune, 1926 (Kinugasa 2)
Dochu sugoruku kago, 1926 (Kinugasa 2)
Dock Brief, 1962 (Attenborough 3, Sellers 3)
Docks of New York, 1928 (Von Sternberg 2, Banton 4, Dreier 4,
    Furthman 4, Rosson 4, Saunders 4)
Docks of New York, 1945 (Katzman 4)
Docteur Carnaval, 1909 (Cohl 2)
Docteur Françoise Gailland, 1975 (Cassel 3, Girardot 3, Huppert 3,
    Renoir 4)
Docteur Jekyll et les femmes, 1981 (Borowczyk 4)
Docteur Laënnac, 1948 (Renoir 4)
Docteur Popaul, 1972 (Chabrol 2, Belmondo 3, Farrow 3, Gégauff 4,
    Rabier 4)
Doctor. See Doktor ur, 1916
Doctor and the Debutante. See Dr. Kildare's Victory,
    1941
Doctor and the Devils, 1985 (Francis 4)

Doctor and the Girl, 1949 (Coburn, C. 3, Ford, G. 3, Leigh, J. 3,
    Ames 4, Berman 4)
Doctor and the Woman, 1918 (Weber 2)
Doctor at Large, 1957 (Bogarde 3)
Doctor at Sea, 1955 (Bardot 3, Bogarde 3, Dillon 4)
Dr. Bessels Verwandlung, 1927 (Oswald 2)
Doctor Bridget, 1912 (Bunny 3)
Dr. Broadway, 1942 (Mann 2, Dreier 4)
Doctor Bull, 1933 (Ford, J. 2, Rogers, W. 3)
Dr. Cadman's Secret. See Black Sheep, 1956
Dr. Christian Meets the Women, 1940 (Hersholt 3, Alton, J. 4)
Dr. Cook's Garden, 1971 (Crosby 3)
Dr. Crippen, 1962 (Roeg 2, Pleasance 3)
Doctor Cupid, 1911 (Bunny 3)
Dr. Cyclops, 1940 (Schoedsack 2, Dreier 4, Edouart 4, Head 4,
    Hoch 4)
Doctor Death, Seeker of Souls, 1973 (Howard, M. 3)
Doctor Detroit, 1983 (Schifrin 4)
Dr. Devil and Mr. Hare, 1964 (McKimson 4)
Dr. Dippy's Sanitarium, 1906 (Bitzer 4)
Doctor Dolittle, 1967 (Fleischer, R. 2, Attenborough 3, Harrison 3,
    Smith, J.M. 4, Surtees 4)
Doctor Don'tlittle. See Doktor za životinje, 1972
Dr. Ehrlich's Magic Bullet, 1940 (Dieterle 2, Basserman 3, Meek 3,
    Ouspenskaya 3, Robinson, E. 3, Steiner 4, Wallis 4)
Dr. Ehrlich's Magic Bullet. See Story of Dr. Ehrlich's Magic Bullet,
    1940
Doctor Eva, 1970 (Nowicki 3)
Dr. Evans' Silence, 1973 (Bondarchuk 3)
Doctor Faustus, 1966 (Burton 3, Taylor, E. 3)
Dr. Fischer of Geneva, 1984 (Bates 3, Cusack 3, Mason 3)
Doctor for Animals. See Doktor za životinje, 1972
Dr. Gillespie's Criminal Case, 1943 (Barrymore L. 3, Johnson, V. 3,
    O'Brien, M. 3, Reed, D. 3, Irene 4)
Dr. Gillespie's New Assistant, 1942 (Barrymore L. 3, Johnson, V. 3)
Dr. Goldfoot and the Bikini Machine, 1965 (Taurog 2, Price 3)
Dr. Goldfoot and the Girl Bombs, 1966 (Price 3)
Dr. Heckyl and Mr. Hype, 1980 (Reed, O. 3)
Dr. Holl, 1951 (Herlth 4, Von Harbou 4)
Doctor in Distress, 1963 (Bogarde 3)
Doctor in the House, 1954 (Bogarde 3, More 3, Dillon 4)
Dr. Jack, 1922 (Lloyd 3, Roach 4)
Dr. Jekyll and Mr. Hyde, 1908 (Olcott 2, Selig 4)
Dr. Jekyll and Mr. Hyde, 1912 (Cruze 2)
**Dr. Jekyll and Mr. Hyde, 1932 (Mamoulian 2, Hopkins, M. 3, March 3,
    Banton 4, Dreier 4, Hoffenstein 4, Struss 4, Westmore, W. 4)**
Dr. Jekyll and Mr. Hyde, 1941 (Fleming 2, Saville 2, Bergman 3, Crisp
    3, Tracy 3, Turner, L. 3, Adrian 4, Mahin 4, Ruttenberg 4,
    Waxman 4)
Dr. Jekyll and Mr. Hyde, 1972 (Palance 3)
Dr. Jekyll and Mr. Hyde. See Skaebnesvangre Opfindelse, 1910
Dr. Jekyll and Mr. Hyde. See Januskopf, 1920
Dr. Jekyll and Mr. Mouse, 1946 (Hanna and Barbera 4)
Dr. Jerkyl's Hyde, 1953 (Freleng 4)
Dr. Justice, 1975 (Christian-Jaque 2)
Dr. Kildare Goes Home, 1940 (Ayres 3, Barrymore L. 3, Rosson 4)
Dr. Kildare's Crisis, 1940 (Ayres 3, Barrymore L. 3, Young, R. 3,
    Seitz 4)
Dr. Kildare's Strange Case, 1940 (Ayres 3, Barrymore L. 3, Seitz 4)
Dr. Kildare's Victory, 1941 (Van Dyke, W.S. 2, Ayres 3,
    Barrymore L. 3, Daniels 4)
Dr. Kildare's Wedding Day, 1941 (Ayres 3, Barrymore L. 3, Kaper 4)
Dr. Le Fleur's Theory, 1907 (Costello, M. 3)
**Dr. Mabuse, der Spieler, 1922 (Lang 2, Dagover 3, Hoffman 4,
    Pommer 4, Von Harbou 4)**
Dr. Mabuse, The Gambler. See Dr. Mabuse, der Spieler, 1922
Doctor Maniac. See Man Who Changed His Mind, 1936
Dr. Max, 1974 (Cobb 3)
Dr. Med. Hiob Preaetorius, 1963 (Rasp 3)
Dr. Med. Sommer, 1970 (Hoffmann 3)
Doctor Monica, 1934 (Dieterle 2, Beavers 3, Francis, K. 3, Blanke 4,
    Grot 4, Orry-Kelly 4, Polito 4)
Dr. Neighbor, 1916 (Bosworth 3)

Dr. Nicola, 1909 (Blom 2)
Dr. Nicola I, 1909 (Blom 2)
Dr. Nicola III, 1909 (Blom 2)
Dr. Nicola in Tibet. *See* Dr. Nicola III, 1909
Dr. No, 1962 (Connery 3, Adam 4, Barry 4)
Doctor of Seven Dials. *See* Corridors of Blood, 1963
Doctor Oswald, 1935 (Lantz 4)
Dr. Phibes Rises Again, 1972 (Cushing 3, Price 3)
Dr. Phil Doderlein, 1945 (George, H. 3, Wegener 3)
Dr. Pickle and Mr. Pryde, 1925 (Laurel 3)
Dr. Pulder Sows Poppies. *See* Dokter Pulder zaait papavers, 1975
Dr. Renault's Secret, 1942 (Day 4, Miller, V. 4, Raksin 4)
Doctor Rhythm, 1938 (Crosby 3, Crosby 4, Head 4, Lang 4, Swerling 4)
Doctor Says. *See* Angeklagt nach N.218, 1966
Dr. Schluter, 1965 (Hoppe 3)
Dr. Schotte, 1918 (Basserman 3)
Dr. Skinum, 1907 (Bitzer 4)
Dr. Smith's Baby, 1914 (Costello, M. 3)
Dr. Socrates, 1935 (Dieterle 2, Muni 3, Gaudio 4, Grot 4)
Dr. Strangelove, 1964 (Kubrick 2, Hayden 3, Jones, J.E. 3, Scott, G. 3, Sellers 3, Wynn 3, Adam 4)
Dr. Syn, 1937 (Arliss 3)
Doctor Takes a Wife, 1940 (Seaton 2, Gwenn 3, Milland 3, Young, L. 3)
Dr. Terror's Gallery of Horrors, 1967 (Carradine 3, Chaney Lon., Jr. 3)
Dr. Terror's House of Horrors, 1964 (Cushing 3, Lee, C. 3, Sutherland 3)
Dr. Vidya, 1962 (Burman 4)
Dr. Who and the Daleks, 1965 (Cushing 3)
Dr. Wislizenus, 1924 (Kortner 3)
Doctor X, 1932 (Curtiz 2, Wray 3, Grot 4)
Doctor Zhivago, 1965 (Lean 2, Chaplin 3, Christie 3, Guinness 3, Kinski 3, Richardson 3, Steiger 3, Jarre 4, Ponti 4, Young, F. 4)
Doctored Affair, 1913 (Sennett 2, Normand 3)
Doctors. *See* Hommes en blanc, 1955
Doctors at War, 1943 (Goodrich and Hackett 4)
Doctor's Courage. *See* Crime Doctor's Courage, 1945
Doctor's Diary, 1937 (Vidor, C. 2, D'Agostino 4, Head 4, Schulberg 4)
Doctor's Dilemma, 1959 (Asquith 2, Bogarde 3, Caron 3, Sim 3, Beaton 4, Kosma 4, Krasker 4)
Doctors Don't Tell, 1941 (Tourneur, J. 2, Bond 3)
Doctor's Duty, 1913 (Anderson G. 3)
Doctor's Gamble. *See* Crime Doctor's Gamble, 1947
Doctor's Legacy. *See* Ensom Kvinde, 1914
Doctor's Orders, 1934 (Mills 3)
Doctor's Perfidy, 1910 (Lawrence 3)
Doctor's Round. *See* Vizita, 1981
Doctor's Secret, 1913 (Talmadge, N. 3)
Doctor's Secret, 1929 (Hunt 4)
Doctor's Secret. *See* Hydrothérapie fantastique, 1910
Doctor's Tale. *See* Doktorká pohádka, 1963
Doctor's Testimony, 1914 (Lawrence 3)
Doctor's Trouble, 1912 (Ince 4)
Doctor's Warning. *See* Crime Doctor's Warning, 1945
Doctors' Wives, 1931 (Borzage 2, Baxter, W. 3, Bennett J. 3, Edeson 4)
Doctors' Wives, 1971 (Bellamy 3, Cannon 3, Hackman 3, Roberts 3, Bernstein 4, Lang 4, Taradash 4, Wheeler 4)
Documental a proposito del transito, 1971 (Gomez, S. 2)
Documenteur: An Emotion Picture, 1981 (Varda 2)
Documento, 1939 (Castellani 2)
Documento mensile, 1951 (Ferreri 2)
Documento mensile. *See* Appunti su un fatto di cronaca, 1951
Documento Z3, 1941 (Fellini 2)
Documents secrets, 1940 (Haas 3)
Dodatek k zákonu na ochranu státu, 1976 (Danailov 3)
Dødens Brud, 1911 (Blom 2)
Dødens Kontrakt. *See* Hendes Moders Løfte, 1916
Dødes Halsbaand, 1910 (Blom 2)
Dødes Røst. *See* Testamentets Hemmelighed, 1916
Dødes Sjael. *See* Kunstners Gennembrud, 1915
Dodes'ka-den, 1970 (Ichikawa 2)

Dodeskaden. *See* Dodesukaden, 1970
Dodesukaden, 1970 (Kurosawa 2, Muraki 4, Takemitsu 4)
Dodge City, 1939 (Curtiz 2, Bond 3, De Havilland 3, Flynn 3, Sheridan 3, Buckner 4, Canutt 4, Friedhofer 4, Polito 4, Steiner 4)
Dodge Your Debts, 1921 (Roach 4)
Dodging a Million, 1918 (Normand 3)
Dodging His Doom, 1917 (Sennett 2)
12 dicembre, 1972 (Pasolini 2, Volonté 3)
Dødsdømte. *See* Danserindens Kaerlighedsdrøm, 1915
Dødsdrømmen, 1911 (Blom 2)
Dodshoppet från cirkuskupolen, 1912 (Magnusson 4)
Dodskyssen, 1917 (Sjostrom 2, Jaenzon 4, Jaenzon 4)
Dødssejleren, 1911 (Holger-Madsen 2)
Dodsworth, 1936 (Wyler 2, Astor 3, Huston 3, Lukas 3, Niven 3, Ouspenskaya 3, Day 4, Goldwyn 4, Howard 4, Mandell 4, Maté 4, Newman 4)
Does. *See* Biches, 1968
Does It Pay, 1923 (Ruttenberg 4)
Dog, 1977 (Bardem 2)
Dog, A Mouse, and a Sputnik. *See* A pied, à cheval, et un sputnik, 1958
Dog and the Bone, 1937 (Terry 4)
Dog Catcher. *See* Dog Catcher's Love, 1917
Dog Catcher's Love, 1917 (Sennett 2, Summerville 3)
Dog Collared, 1950 (McKimson 4)
Dog Day. *See* Canicule, 1983
Dog Day Afternoon, 1975 (Lumet 2, Pacino 3, Allen, D. 4)
Dog Days, 1925 (Roach 4)
Dog Daze, 1937 (Freleng 4)
Dog Daze, 1939 (Sidney 2, Roach 4)
Dog Doctor, 1931 (Sennett 2)
Dog Eat Dog. *See* Einer frisst den anderern, 1964
Dog Gone It, 1927 (Lantz 4)
Dog Gone Modern, 1938 (Jones 2)
Dog Gone South, 1950 (Jones 2)
Dog Heaven, 1929 (Roach 4)
Dog in a Mansion, 1940 (Terry 4)
Dog Justice, 1928 (Musuraca 4)
Dog of Flanders, 1935 (Hunt 4, Plunkett 4)
Dog of Flanders, 1959 (Crisp 3)
Dog Pounded, 1953 (Freleng 4)
Dog Show, 1934 (Terry 4)
Dog Show, 1950 (Terry 4)
Dog Shy, 1926 (McCarey 2)
Dog Snatcher, 1952 (Burness 4)
Dog Soldiers. *See* Who'll Stop the Rain, 1978
Dog Star Man, 1964 (Brakhage 2)
Dog Tales, 1958 (McKimson 4)
Dog Tired, 1941 (Jones 2)
Dog Trouble, 1942 (Hanna and Barbera 4)
Dogadaj, 1969 (Mimica 4)
Doggone Mixup, 1938 (Langdon 3)
Doggone People, 1960 (McKimson 4)
Doggone Tired, 1949 (Avery 2)
Doggy and the 4. *See* Punt'a a čtyřlístek, 1954
Dog-Heads. *See* Psohlavci, 1931
Dog-Heads. *See* Psohlavci, 1954
Dog-House, 1952 (Hanna and Barbera 4)
Dogo no kishi, 1932 (Hasegawa 3)
Do-Good Wolf, 1960 (Hanna and Barbera 4)
Dogora—The Space Monster. *See* Uchu daikaiju Dogora, 1964
Dogpound Shuffle, 1974 (Fisher 4)
Dogs and People. *See* Psi a lidé, 1970
Dog's Dialogue. *See* Colloque de chiens, 1977
Dog's Dream, 1941 (Terry 4)
Dogs Is Dogs, 1931 (Roach 4)
Dog's Life, 1918 (Chaplin 2, Purviance 3)
Dog's Life. *See* Zivot je pes, 1933
Dogs of War, 1923 (Roach 4)
Dogs of War, 1981 (Smith, D. , Cardiff 4)
Dog's Tale. *See* Psí pohádka, 1959
Dogsday. *See* Canicule, 1983
Dohyo-matsuri, 1944 (Kurosawa 2, Miyagawa 4)

Doigts de lumière, 1947 (Fradetal 4)
Doigts qui voient, 1911 (Feuillade 2)
Doing Her Bit, 1917 (Gilbert 3)
Doing His Best. *See* Making a Living, 1914
Doing Imposikible Stunts, 1940 (Fleischer, M. and D. 2)
Doing Their Bit, 1918 (Ruttenberg 4)
Doing Their Bit, 1942 (Terry 4)
Doing Time, 1920 (Roach 4)
Do-It-Yourself Cartoon Kit, 1959 (Godfrey 4)
Do-It-Yourself Democracy, 1963 (Zetterling 2)
Dojoji Temple, 1976 (Kawamoto 4)
Dojoyaburi, 1964 (Iwashita 3)
Doka o, 1926 (Mizoguchi 2)
Dokkoi ikiteiru, 1951 (Imai 2)
Dokoku, 1952 (Hayasaka 4)
Doktar Glas, 1942 (Borgstrom 3)
Dokter Pulder zaait papavers, 1975 (Haanstra 2)
Doktor Dolittle und seine Tiere, 1928 (Reiniger 2)
Doktor Glas, 1967 (Zetterling 2)
Doktor Mabuze—Igrok, 1924 (Eisenstein 2)
Doktor Satansohn, 1915 (Lubitsch 2)
Doktor Toporkov. *See* Tzveti Zepozclaliye, 1917
Doktor ur, 1916 (Curtiz 2)
Doktor za životinje, 1972 (Grgić 4)
Doktorká pohádka, 1963 (Hofman 4)
Doku azami, 1927 (Hasegawa 3)
Dokud máš maminku, 1934 (Vích 4)
Dokuga, 1950 (Yamamura 3)
Dokuritsu bijin-tai, 1963 (Kagawa 3)
Dokuritsu gurenta, 1959 (Mifune 3)
Dokushinsha goyojin, 1930 (Gosho 2)
Dolandiricilar, 1961 (Guney 2)
Dolandiricilar sahi, 1961 (Guney 2)
Dolce corpo di Deborah, 1968 (Baker C. 3)
Dolce vita, 1960 (Fellini 2, Aimée 3, Cuny 3, Mastroianni 3, Flaiano 4, Gherardi 4, Pinelli 4, Rota 4)
Dolci signore, 1967 (Scola 2, Zampa 2, Cassel 3)
Doldertal 7, 1971 (Markopoulos 2)
Dole plotovi, 1962 (Makavejev 2)
Dolina Issy, 1982 (Konwicki 4)
Dolken, 1915 (Stiller 2, Jaenzon 4)
Doll, 1961 (Vukotić 4)
Doll. *See* Child's Sacrifice, 1910
Doll. *See* Lalka, 1968
Doll. *See* Puppe, 1919
Doll Face, 1946 (Miranda 3, La Shelle 4, Leven 4)
Doll Hospital, 1952 (Peterson 2)
Doll That Took the Town. *See* Donna del giorno, 1957
Dollar, 1937 (Molander 2, Bergman 3)
Dollar Dance, 1943 (McLaren 2)
Dollar Did It, 1913 (Sennett 2)
Dollar Down, 1925 (Browning 2, Walthall 3)
Dollar Mark, 1914 (Carré 4, Edeson 4)
Dollar-a-Year Man, 1921 (Cruze 2, Sutherland 2, Arbuckle 3, Brown, K. 4)
Dollaro a testa, 1966 (Rey 3, Reynolds, B. 3, Morricone 4)
Dollaro di fifa, 1960 (Tognazzi 3)
Dollarprinzessin und ihre sechs Freier, 1927 (Albers 3, Reisch 4)
$, 1971 (Brooks, R. 2, Beatty 3, Hawn 3, Jones 4)
Dollars of Dross, 1916 (Borzage 2)
Doll-house Mystery, 1915 (Franklin 2)
Dollmaker, 1984 (Fonda, J. 3, Jenkins 4)
Dolls. *See* Bambole, 1964
Doll's House, 1916 (Chaney Lon 3)
Doll's House, 1918 (Tourneur, M. 2, Carré 4)
Doll's House, 1922 (Nazimova 3)
Doll's House, 1973 (Bloom 3, Evans 3, Hopkins, A. 3, Richardson 3, Barry 4)
Doll's House, 1973 (Losey 2, Fonda, J. 3, Howard, T. 3, Seyrig 3, Fisher 4, Head 4, Legrand 4)
Dolly macht Karriere, 1930 (Litvak 2, Wagner 4)
Dolly Put the Kettle On, 1947 (Halas and Batchelor 2)

Dolly Sisters, 1945 (Grable 3, Sakall 3, Newman 4, Orry-Kelly 4, Wheeler 4)
Dolly Who Shed Real Tears. *See* Panence, která tence plakala, 1954
Dolly's Papa, 1907 (Selig 4)
Dolly's Scoop, 1916 (Chaney Lon 3)
Dolores. *See* Light Woman, 1928
Dolorosa, 1934 (Grémillon 2)
Dolwyn. *See* Last Days of Dolwyn, 1948
Dom, 1958 (Lenica 2, Borowczyk 4)
Dom, kotoryi postroil svift, 1982 (Yankovsky 3)
Dom na Trubnoi, 1928 (Maretskaya 3)
Dom, v kotorov ya zhivu, 1957 (Ulyanov 3)
Dom v sugribakh, 1928 (Ermler 2, Enei 4)
Domain of the Moment, 1977 (Brakhage 2)
Domani e un altro giorno, 1951 (Aldo 4)
Domani è troppo tardi, 1950 (De Sica 2)
Domani non siamo piú qui, 1967 (Thulin 3, Fusco 4)
Domaren, 1960 (Sjoberg 2, Nykvist 4)
Domburi-ike, 1963 (Tsukasa 3)
Domen icke, 1914 (Sjostrom 2, Borgstrom 3)
Domenica d'agosto, 1950 (Rosi 2, Mastroianni 3, Amidei 4, Zavattini 4)
Domenica della buona gente, 1954 (Loren 3, Manfredi 3, Rota 4)
Domenica d'estate, 1961 (Aumont 3, Fabian 3, Tognazzi 3, Amidei 4)
Domenica è sempre domenica, 1958 (De Sica 2, Sordi 3, Tognazzi 3)
Domestic Relations, 1922 (Glennon 4, Schulberg 4)
Domestic Troubles, 1928 (Fazenda 3)
Domicile conjugal, 1970 (Truffaut 2, Léaud 3, Almendros 4, Guillemot 4)
Domik v Kolomna, 1913 (Mozhukin 3)
Dominant Sex, 1937 (Brenon 2)
Dominatore dei sette mari, 1960 (Maté 4)
Domingo, 1961 (Diegues 2)
Domingo à Tarde, 1965 (de Almeida 4)
Domingo salvaje, 1966 (Figueroa 4)
Dominika's Name Day. *See* Když má svátek Dominika, 1967
Dominion, 1974 (Brakhage 2)
Dominique, 1978 (Robertson 3, Simmons 3)
Domino, 1943 (Blier 3, Achard 4, Aurenche 4)
Domino Killings. *See* Domino Principle, 1976
Domino Principle, 1976 (Kramer, S. 2, Hackman 3, Wallach 3, Widmark 3, Laszlo 4)
Domino vert, 1935 (Darrieux 3, Vanel 3)
Domyaku retto, 1975 (Yamamura 3)
Don, 1978 (Bachchan 3)
Don Bosco, 1935 (Amidei 4)
Don Camillo à Moscou. *See* Don Camillo en Russie, 1965
Don Camillo e i giovani d'oggi, 1972 (Cervi 3)
Don Camillo e l'onorevole Peppone, 1955 (Gallone 2, Cervi 3)
Don Camillo en Russie, 1965 (Fernandel 3)
Don Camillo et les contestataires, 1970 (Christian-Jaque 2)
Don Camillo Monsignore, 1961 (Gallone 2, Cervi 3, Fernandel 3)
Don Cesar de Bazan, 1957 (Enei 4)
Don Cesare di Bazan, 1942 (Cervi 3, Amidei 4, Zavattini 4)
Don Diego and Pelagea. *See* Dondiego i Pelaguya, 1928
Don Giovanni, 1955 (Czinner 2)
Don Giovanni, 1979 (Losey 2, Fisher 4, Trauner 4)
Don Giovanni della Costa Azzurra, 1962 (Belmondo 3, Jurgens 3)
Don Giovanni in Sicilia, 1967 (Lattuada 2)
Don Is Dead, 1973 (Fleischer, R. 2, Forrest 3, Quinn 3, Ames 4, Goldsmith 4, Head 4, Wallis 4)
Don Juan, 1922 (Metzner 4)
Don Juan, 1926 (Crosland 2, Astor 3, Barrymore J. 3, Loy 3, Oland 3, Carré 4, Meredyth 4)
Don Juan, 1955 (Fernandel 3, Wakhévitch 4)
Don Juan. *See* Amór de Don Juan, 1956
Don Juan. *See* Don Juan 1973, 1973
Don Juan. *See* Don Šajn, 1970
Don Juan et Faust, 1922 (Autant-Lara 2, L'Herbier 2)
Don Juan 1973, 1973 (Vadim 2, Bardot 3, Decaë 4)
Don Juan Quilligan, 1945 (Bendix 3, Blondell 3, Raksin 4)
Don Juan 68, 1968 (Jires 2)
Don Juan's Three Nights, 1926 (Stone 3)

Don Key, Son of Burro, 1926 (Roach 4)
Don Kikhot, 1957 (Cherkassov 3)
Don Lucio y el harmano pio, 1960 (Rey 3)
Don Pasquale, 1940 (De Santis 2)
Don Pietro Caruso, 1917 (Bertini 3)
Don Q, Son of Zorro, 1925 (Astor 3, Crisp 3, Fairbanks, D. 3,
    Hersholt 3, Oland 3, Grot 4)
Don Quichotte, 1903 (Zecca 2)
Don Quichotte, 1909 (Cohl 2)
Don Quichotte, 1933 (Pabst 2, Reiniger 2, Andrejew 4, Ibert 4,
    Wakhévitch 4)
Don Quichotte, 1964–69 (Rohmer 2)
Don Quichottes Kinder, 1981 (Domrose 3)
Don Quijote cabalga de nuevo, 1972 (Cantinflas 3)
Don Quintín el amargao, 1935 (Buñuel 2)
Don Quintín el amargao. See Hija del engaño, 1951
Don Quixote, 1934 (Iwerks 4)
Don Quixote, 1955 (Welles 2)
Don Quixote, 1957 (Kozintsev 2, Enei 4, Moskvin 4)
Don Quixote, 1966 (Rey 3)
Don Quixote. See Don Kikhot, 1957
Don Quixote. See Don Quichotte, 1909
Don Quixote. See Don Quichotte, 1933
Don Quixote de la Mancha, 1947 (Rey 3)
Don Šajn, 1970 (Švankmajer 4)
Don Winslow of the Coast Guard, 1943 (Brooks, R. 2)
Doña Barbara, 1943 (De Fuentes 2, Félix 3)
Doña Clarines, 1950 (García 3)
Doña Diabla, 1949 (Félix 3)
Dona Juana, 1927 (Czinner 2, Bergner 3, Freund 4)
Dona mentiras, 1930 (Fort 4)
Doña Perfecta, 1951 (Del Rio 3)
Donatella, 1956 (Monicelli 2, Fabrizi 3, Delli Colli 4)
Donauwalzer, 1930 (Reisch 4)
Doncella de piedra, 1955 (Figueroa 4)
Dondiego i Pelaguya, 1928 (Protazanov 2)
Done in Oil, 1934 (Roach 4)
Done in Wax, 1915 (Beery 3)
Dong Kingman, 1955 (Howe 4)
Donkey Skin. See Peau d'âne, 1971
Donkey Skin. See Szamárbör, 1918
Donna!, 1914 (Bertini 3)
Donna alla frontiera. See Frauen, die durch die Holle gehen, 1966
Donna che inventà l'amore, 1952 (Brazzi 3)
Donna che venne del mare, 1957 (De Sica 2)
Donna degli altri è sempre piú bella, 1963 (Tognazzi 3)
Donna dei Faraoni, 1960 (Fusco 4)
Donna del fiume, 1954 (Pasolini 2, Loren 3, De Laurentiis 4, Flaiano 4,
    Ponti 4)
Donna del giorno, 1957 (Reggiani 3, Zavattini 4)
Donna del lago, 1965 (Cortese 3)
Donna del mondo, 1963 (Ustinov 3)
Donna della domenica, 1975 (Comencini 2, Bisset 3, Mastroianni 3,
    Trintignant 3, Age and Scarpelli 4, Morricone 4)
Donna della montagna, 1943 (Castellani 2, De Laurentiis 4)
Donna di una notte, 1930 (Bertini 3)
Donna d'una notte. See Femme d'une nuit, 1930
Donna è una cosa meravigliosa, 1964 (Bolognini 2, Fabrizi 3,
    Di Venanzo 4, Guerra 4)
Donna, il diavolo, il tempo, 1921 (Bertini 3)
Donna invisibile, 1969 (Morricone 4)
Donna libera, 1953 (Cervi 3)
Donna nuda, 1913 (Gallone 2)
Donna nuda, 1918 (Bertini 3)
Donna piú bella del mondo, 1955 (Gassman 3, Lollobrigida 3,
    Solinas 4)
Donna scimmia, 1964 (Ferreri 2, Girardot 3, Tognazzi 3, Ponti 4)
Donnaren, 1960 (Thulin 3)
Donne e briganti, 1950 (Rota 4)
Donne e soldati, 1954 (Ferreri 2, Di Venanzo 4)
Donne proibite, 1953 (De Santis 2, Cortese 3, Darnell 3, Masina 3,
    Quinn 3, Zavattini 4)
Donne senza nome, 1949 (Cervi 3, Cortese 3, Rosay 3, Simon, S. 3)

Donne-moi la main, 1958 (Jarre 4)
Donne-moi tes yeux, 1943 (Guitry 2)
Donogoo Tonka, 1936 (Ondra 3)
Donovan Affair, 1929 (Capra 2)
Donovan's Brain, 1953 (Ayres 3, Biroc 4, Leven 4)
Donovan's Kid, 1931 (Niblo 2, Cooper, J 3)
Donovan's Kid, 1979 (Rooney 3)
Donovan's Kid. See Young Donovan's Kid, 1931
Donovan's Reef, 1963 (Ford, J. 2, Dalio 3, Lamour 3, Marsh 3,
    Marvin 3, Warden 3, Wayne 3, Clothier 4, Edouart 4, Head 4,
    Nugent 4)
Don's Party, 1975 (Beresford 2)
Don't Axe Me, 1958 (McKimson 4)
Don't Be Blue. See Tout peut arriver, 1969
Don't Be Jealous, 1928 (Brown 3)
Don't Believe in Monuments. See Spomenicima ne treba verovati, 1958
Don't Bet on Blonds, 1935 (Florey 2, Flynn 3)
Don't Bet on Love, 1933 (Ayres 3, Rogers, G. 3, Laemmle 4)
Don't Bet on Women, 1931 (Howard 2, MacDonald 3, Merkel 3)
Don't Bite your Dentist, 1930 (Sennett 2)
Don't Bother to Knock, 1952 (Bancroft 3, Cook 3, Monroe 3,
    Widmark 3, Ballard 4, Lemaire 4, Taradash 4)
Don't Bother to Knock, 1961 (Anderson J. 3, Raphael 4, Unsworth 4)
Don't Call Me Vasick. See Nerikej mi va siku, 1972
Don't Change Your Husband, 1919 (DeMille 2, Swanson 3,
    Buckland 4, Macpherson 4)
Don't Cry, It's Only Thunder, 1982 (Jarre 4)
Don't Cry, Pretty Girls. See Szép lányok, ne sirjatok, 1970
Don't Drink the Water, 1969 (Allen 2, Rosenblum 4, Williams, R. 4)
Don't Ever Marry, 1920 (Neilan 2, Carré 4, Heerman 4)
Don't Fence Me In, 1945 (Rogers, R. 3)
Don't Flirt, 1923 (Roach 4)
Don't Forget, 1924 (Roach 4)
Don't Gamble with Love, 1936 (Sothern 3)
Don't Get Gay with Your Manicure, 1903 (Bitzer 4)
Don't Get Jealous, 1929 (Sennett 2, Hornbeck 4)
Don't Get Personal, 1936 (Waxman 4)
Don't Get Personal, 1942 (Auer 3)
Don't Give Up. See Tappa inte sugen, 1947
Don't Give Up the Sheep, 1952 (Jones 2)
Don't Give Up the Ship, 1959 (Lewis 2, Taurog 2, Head 4, Wallis 4)
Don't Go Near the Water, 1957 (Walters 2, Ford, G. 3, Wynn 3,
    Cahn 4, Kaper 4, Rose 4)
Don't Go to Sleep, 1982 (Gordon 3)
Don't Hook Now, 1938 (Crosby 3, Hope 3)
Don't Just Stand There, 1968 (Wagner 3, Krasner 4)
Don't Kill Yourself. See Ongyilkos, 1970
Don't Knock the Rock, 1957 (Katzman 4)
Don't Knock the Twist, 1962 (Katzman 4)
Don't Leave Your Husband. See Dangerous Toys, 1921
Don't Let It Kill You. See Il ne faut pas mourir pour ça, 1967
Don't Look Back, 1981 (Gossett 3)
Don't Look Now, 1936 (Avery 2)
Don't Look Now, 1973 (Roeg 2, Christie 3, Sutherland 3, Donaggio 4)
Don't Look Now. See Grande Vadrouille, 1966
Don't Make Me Laugh, 1968 (Attenborough 3)
Don't Make Waves, 1967 (Mackendrick 2, Cardinale 3, Curtis 3)
Don't Marry, 1928 (August 4)
Don't Marry for Money, 1923 (Brown 2)
Don't Neglect Your Wife, 1921 (Stone 3)
Don't Open the Window. See Fin de semana para los muertos, 1974
Don't Park There!, 1924 (Garnett 2, Rogers, W. 3, Roach 4)
Don't Play Bridge with Your Wife, 1933 (Sennett 2)
Don't Play with Love. See Man spielt nicht mit der Liebe, 1926
Don't Pull Your Punches. See Kid Comes Back, 1937
Don't Push, I'll Charge When I'm Ready, 1977 (Bumstead 4)
Don't Raise the Bridge, Lower the River, 1967 (Lewis 2)
Don't Rock the Boat, 1920 (Roach 4)
Don't Say, 1973 (Le Grice 2)
Don't Say Die, 1923 (Roach 4)
Don't Shoot, 1922 (Miller, V. 4)
Don't Shoot, 1926 (Wyler 2)
Don't Shoot the Composer, 1966 (Russell 2)

Don't Shove, 1919 (Daniels 3, Lloyd 3, Roach 4)
Don't Tease the Mosquito. *See* Non stuzzicate la zanzara, 1967
Don't Tell Dad, 1925 (Sennett 2)
Don't Tell Everything, 1921 (DeMille 2, Wood 2, Reid 3, Swanson 3)
Don't Tell Everything, 1927 (Roach 4)
Don't Tell the Wife, 1927 (Blanke 4)
Don't Tell the Wife, 1937 (Ball 3, McDaniel 3, Merkel 3)
Don't Tempt the Devil. *See* Bonnes Causes, 1963
Don't Throw That Knife, 1951 (Three Stooges 3)
Don't Trust Your Husband, 1948 (Bacon 2, Carroll M. 3,
    MacMurray 3, Cronjager 4, Salter 4)
Don't Turn 'em Loose, 1936 (Grable 3, Stone 3)
Don't Turn the Other Cheek. *See* Viva la muerte . . . tua!, 1972
Don't Weaken, 1920 (Sennett 2, Roach 4)
Don't Worry, We'll Think of a Title, 1966 (Howard, M. 3)
Don't You Hear the Dogs Bark?. *See* Entends-tu les chiens aboyer?,
    1972
Donto okoze, 1959 (Oshima 2)
Donzoko, 1957 (Kurosawa 2, Kagawa 3, Mifune 3, Yamada 3,
    Muraki 4)
Dooley Scheme, 1911 (Sennett 2)
Doolhan, 1983 (Azmi 3)
Doolins of Oklahoma, 1949 (Ireland 3, Scott, R. 3, Brown,
    Harry Joe 4, Canutt 4, Duning 4)
Doomed Battalion, 1931 (Fulton 4)
Doomed Caravan, 1941 (Boyd 3, Head 4)
Doomed Cargo. *See* Seven Sinners, 1936
Doomed to Die, 1940 (Karloff 3)
Doomsday, 1928 (Cooper, Gary 3, Banton 4)
Doomsday, 1938 (Terry 4)
Doomsday Flight, 1966 (Johnson, V. 3, O'Brien, E. 3, Schifrin 4)
Doomsday Voyage, 1972 (Cotten 3)
Doomwatch, 1972 (Sanders 3)
Door, 1970 (Dragić 4)
Door. *See* Vrata, 1971
Door in the Wall, 1956 (Bernard 4)
Door Will Open, 1939 (Sidney 2)
Doorbell Rang, 1977 (Baxter A. 3)
Doorway of Destruction, 1915 (Ford, J. 2)
Doorway to Hell, 1930 (Ayres 3, Cagney 3, Zanuck 4)
Doosri, 1983 (Azmi 3)
Dopey Dicks, 1950 (Three Stooges 3)
Doplnenie kam SSD. *See* Dodatek k zákonu na ochranu státu, 1976
Doplnenie kam zakona za zaštitu na državata. *See* Dodatek k
    zákonu na ochranu státu, 1976
Doppelgangerin, 1925 (Dagover 3)
Doppelte Lottchen, 1950 (Herlth 4)
Doppia taglia per Monnesota Stinky, 1972 (Kinski 3)
Doppio delitto, 1978 (Mastroianni 3, Ustinov 3)
Dora, 1909 (Olcott 2)
Dora, 1943 (Bertini 3)
Dora Brandes, 1916 (Nielsen 3)
Dora Nelson, 1939 (Zampa 2)
Dora Thorne, 1915 (Barrymore L. 3)
Dora's Dunkin' Doughnuts, 1933 (Temple 3)
Dorado de Pancho Villa, 1967 (Fernández 2)
Doraku shinan, 1928 (Gosho 2)
Do-Re-Mi-Fa, 1915 (Sennett 2)
Dorf unterm Himmel, 1953 (Herlth 4)
Dorfen wir schweigen, 1926 (Kortner 3)
Dorian's Divorce, 1916 (Barrymore L. 3)
Dormeuse, 1962 (Rabier 4)
Dornenweg einer Furstin, 1928 (Albers 3)
Dornroschen, 1918 (Leni 2, Wegener 3)
Dornroschen, 1922 (Reiniger 2)
Doroga na Rubezal, 1971 (Gurchenko 3)
Dorogoi bessmertia, 1958 (Smoktunovsky 3)
Dorogoi moi chelovek, 1958 (Batalov 3)
Dorogoi tsenoi, 1957 (Donskoi 2)
Dorothea, 1974 (Sarde 4)
Dorothea Angermann, 1959 (Siodmak 2, Herlth 4)
Dorothea Tanning, ou le regard ébloui, 1960 (Delerue 4)
Dorotheas Rache, 1974 (Carrière 4)

Dorothée cherche l'amour, 1945 (Berry 3, Dauphin 3)
Dorothy Vernon of Haddon Hall, 1924 (Neilan 2, Pickford 3, Grot 4,
    Rosher 4, Young, W. 4)
Dorothys Bekenntnis, 1921 (Curtiz 2)
Dorp aan de rivier, 1958 (Rademakers 2)
Dortoir des grandes, 1953 (Marais 3, Moreau 3)
Dos apostoles, 1964 (García 3)
Dos au mur, 1958 (Moreau 3)
Dos cadetes, 1938 (García 3)
Dos de la Mafia. *See* Due mafiosi contro Goldginger, 1965
Dos hijos desobedientes, 1960 (Armendáriz 3)
Dos mexicanos en Sevilla, 1941 (García 3)
Dos mundos y un amor, 1954 (Armendáriz 3)
Dos pesos dejada, 1949 (García 3)
Dos tipos de cuidado, 1952 (Infante 3, Negrete 3, Figueroa 4)
Dos y media y venuno, 1959 (Rey 3)
Doshaburi, 1957 (Yamamura 3, Takemitsu 4)
Dossier noir, 1955 (Cayatte 2, Blier 3, Spaak 4)
Dostana, 1980 (Bachchan 3)
Dot and the Line, 1965 (Jones 2)
Dotanba, 1957 (Shimura 3)
Dotanuki, 1963 (Kyo 3)
Doto ichi man kairi, 1966 (Mifune 3)
Dots, 1939–41 (McLaren 2)
Dots Izrila, 1917 (Mozhukin 3)
Dottor Antonio, 1937 (Fusco 4)
Dotty World of James Lloyd, 1964 (Russell 2)
Douaniers et contrebandiers, 1905 (Guy 2)
Double Adventure, 1921 (Van Dyke, W.S. 2)
Double Amour, 1925 (Epstein 2)
Double Bed. *See* Lit à deux places, 1965
Double Chaser, 1942 (Freleng 4)
Double Confession, 1950 (Lorre 3, Unsworth 4)
Double Crime sur la Ligne Maginot, 1938 (Blier 3, Fradetal 4)
Double Cross Roads, 1930 (August 4, Estabrook 4)
Double Crossbones, 1951 (O'Connor 3)
Double Crossed. *See* Cash Parrish's Pal, 1915
Double Danger, 1938 (Meek 3)
Double Daring, 1926 (Arthur 3)
Double Date, 1941 (Merkel 3, Salter 4)
Double Deception. *See* Magiciennes, 1960
Double Destin, 1954 (Simon, S. 3)
Double Destiny. *See* Zweite Leben, 1954
Double Door, 1934 (Vidor, C. 2)
Double Dynamite, 1951 (Marx, G. 3, Russell, J. 3, Sinatra 3, Cahn 4)
Double Exposure, 1935 (Hope 3)
Double Face, 1969 (Kinski 3)
Double Harness, 1933 (Powell, W. 3, Cooper 4, Hunt 4, MacGowan 4,
    Murfin 4, Plunkett 4, Steiner 4)
**Double Indemnity, 1944 (Wilder 2, Darwell 3, MacMurray 3, Muse 3,
    Robinson, E. 3, Stanwyck 3, Chandler 4, Dreier 4, Head 4, Rozsa 4,
    Seitz 4)**
Double Indemnity, 1974 (Cobb 3, Winters 3)
Double jeu, 1916 (Feuillade 2)
Double Knot, 1913 (Walsh 2)
Double Life, 1947 (Cukor 2, Colman 3, Gordon 3, O'Brien, E. 3,
    Winters 3, Banton 4, Horner 4, Kanin 4, Krasner 4, Rozsa 4)
Double Man, 1967 (Schaffner 2, Brynner 3)
Double McGuffin, 1979 (Borgnine 3, Kennedy, G. 3)
Double Murders. *See* Doppio delitto, 1978
Double Negative, 1979 (Perkins 3)
Double or Mutton, 1955 (Jones 2)
Double or Nothing, 1937 (Dmytryk 2, Crosby 3, Glazer 4, Head 4,
    Lederer 4, Prinz 4, Struss 4, Young, V. 4)
Double Reward, 1912 (Ince 4)
Double Sixes, 1931 (Carey 3)
Double Speed, 1920 (Leroy 2, Wood 2, Reid 3)
Double Suicide. *See* Shinju ten no Amijima, 1969
Double Suicide of Sonezaki. *See* Sonezaki shinjuh, 1981
Double Trouble, 1915 (Fairbanks, D. 3)
Double Trouble, 1941 (Langdon 3)
Double Trouble, 1967 (Taurog 2, Presley 3, Rafferty 3)
Double Trouble. *See* Izvrnuta priča, 1972

Double Wedding, 1913 (Sennett 2)
Double Wedding, 1937 (Mankiewicz 2, Loy 3, Meek 3, Powell, W. 3, Adrian 4, Daniels 4, Swerling 4)
Double Whoopee, 1929 (Harlow 3, Laurel and Hardy 3, Roach 4)
Double-edged Murder. *See* Crimen de doble filo, 1964
Doubling for Romeo, 1921 (Rogers, W. 3)
Doubling in the Quickies, 1932 (Sennett 2)
Doubting Thomas, 1935 (Burke 3, Rogers, W. 3)
Douce, 1943 (Autant-Lara 2, Aurenche 4, Bost 4)
Doucement les basses!, 1971 (Delon 3)
Douceur d'aimer, 1930 (Arletty 3)
Douceur du village, 1963 (Reichenbach 2, Braunberger 4)
Douche après le bain, 1896-97 (Lumière 2)
Douche d'eau bouillante, 1907 (Méliès 2)
Dough and Dynamite, 1914 (Chaplin 2, Sennett 2, Summerville 2)
Doughboys, 1930 (Keaton 2, Sothern 3, Gibbons 4)
Doughboys in Ireland, 1943 (Mitchum 3)
Doughgirls, 1944 (Arden 3, Sheridan 3, Wyman 3, Deutsch 4, Haller 4)
Doughnut Designer. *See* Dough and Dynamite, 1914
Dough-Nuts, 1917 (Hardy 3)
Doughnuts and Society. *See* Stepping into Society, 1936
Doulos, 1963 (Melville 2, Belmondo 3, Piccoli 3, Reggiani 3, de Beauregard 4, Ponti 4)
Dourman, 1912 (Mozhukin 3)
Douro, faina fluvial, 1931 (Oliveira 2)
Douze heures d'horloge, 1959 (Alekan 4)
Douze heures de bonheur, 1952 (Evein 4)
Douze mois en France, 1970 (Leenhardt 2)
Douze Travaux d'Hercule, 1910 (Cohl 2)
Dove, 1927 (Talmadge, N. 3, Menzies 4, Schenck 4)
Dove, 1974 (Peck 3, Barry 4, Nykvist 4)
Dove in a Cottage, 1940 (Terry 4)
Dove in the Eagle's Nest, 1913 (Cruze 2)
Dov'è la libertà?, 1953 (Rossellini 2, De Laurentiis 4, Delli Colli 4, Flaiano 4)
Dove scenda il sole. *See* Unter Geiern, 1964
Dove vai in vacanza?, 1978 (Bolognini 2, Sordi 3, Morricone 4)
Dove vai tutta nuda?, 1969 (Gassman 3)
Dover Boys, 1942 (Jones 2)
Dover Revisited, 1942 (Watt 2)
Dover Road. *See* Little Adventuress, 1927
Dover Road. *See* Where Sinners Meet, 1934
Doverie, 1976 (Yankovsky 3)
Dovolená s andělem, 1952 (Stallich 4)
Down a Long Way, 1954 (Halas and Batchelor 2)
Down among the Sheltering Palms, 1952 (Goulding 2, Marvin 3, Lemaire 4, Lewin 4, Shamroy 4)
Down Among the Sugar Cane, 1932 (Fleischer, M. and D. 2)
Down among the Z Men, 1952 (Sellers 3)
Down and Dirty. *See* Brutti, sporchi, cattivi, 1976
Down and Out, 1922 (Roach 4)
Down Argentine Way, 1940 (Ameche 3, Grable 3, Miranda 3, Banton 4, Brown, Harry Joe 4, Day 4, Shamroy 4, Zanuck 4)
Down Beat Bear, 1956 (Hanna and Barbera 4)
Down by the Old Mill Stream, 1931 (Fleischer, M. and D. 2)
Down by the Sounding Sea, 1914 (Reid 3)
Down Dakota Way, 1949 (Rogers, R. 3)
Down in San Diego, 1941 (Dailey 3)
Down Memory Lane, 1949 (Sennett 2)
Down Mexico Way, 1941 (Autry 3)
Down Missouri Way, 1946 (Carradine 3)
Down on the Farm, 1920 (Sennett 2, Fazenda 3)
Down on the Farm, 1938 (Fazenda 3)
Down on the Levee, 1933 (Terry 4)
Down River, 1931 (Laughton 3)
Down the Ancient Stairs. *See* Per le antiche scale, 1976
Down the Hill to Creditville, 1914 (Crisp 3, Gish, D. 3, Reid 3)
Down the River, 1951 (Fleischer, M. and D. 2)
Down the Stretch, 1936 (Rooney 3)
Down Three Dark Streets, 1954 (Crawford, B. 3)
Down to Earth, 1917 (Fleming 2, Fairbanks, D. 3, Emerson 4, Loos 4)
Down to Earth, 1932 (Rogers, W. 3)

Down to Earth, 1947 (Hayworth 3, Horton 3, Cole 4, Duning 4, Maté 4)
Down to the Cellar. *See* Do pivnice, 1982
Down to the Sea in Ships, 1923 (Bow 3)
Down to the Sea in Ships, 1949 (Hathaway 2, Barrymore L. 3, Widmark 3, Lemaire 4, Mahin 4, Newman 4, Wheeler 4)
Down to the Sea in Shoes, 1923 (Sennett 2)
Down to Their Last Yacht, 1934 (Cronjager 4, Dunn 4, Plunkett 4, Steiner 4)
Down with Cats, 1943 (Terry 4)
Down with the Fences. *See* Dole plotovi, 1962
Downey Girl. *See* Dunungen, 1920
Downfall of Osen. *See* Orizuru osen, 1934
Downhearted Duckling, 1953 (Hanna and Barbera 4)
Downhill, 1927 (Hitchcock 2, Novello 3, Balcon 4)
Downhill Racer, 1969 (Ritchie 2, Hackman 3, Redford 3, Head 4)
Downstairs, 1932 (Gilbert 3, Lukas 3, Rosson 4)
Downtown. *See* Shitamachi, 1957
Downy Girl. *See* Dunungen, 1941
Dozen Daddies. *See* Tucet Mých tatínku, 1959
Dozen Socks, 1927 (Sennett 2)
Dozhivem do ponedelnika, 1968 (Tikhonov 3)
Dracula, 1931 (Browning 2, Lugosi 3, Fort 4, Freund 4, Laemmle 4, Pierce 4)
Dracula, 1958 (Fisher 2, Cushing 3, Lee, C. 3, Bernard 4, Sangster 4)
Dracula, 1974 (Palance 3)
Dracula, 1979 (Olivier 3, Pleasance 3, Mirisch 4, Whitlock 4, Williams, J. 4)
Dracula AD 1972, 1972 (Cushing 3, Lee, C. 3)
Dracula cerca sangue di vergine e . . . morì di sete!!, 1974 (Ponti 4)
Dracula Has Risen from the Grave, 1968 (Lee, C. 3, Bernard 4, Francis 4)
Dracula im Schloss des Schreckens. *See* Nell stretta morsa del ragno, 1971
Dracula, père et fils. *See* Dracula's Son, 1975
Dracula—Prince of Darkness, 1965 (Fisher 2, Lee, C. 3, Bernard 4)
Dracula Vs. Frankenstein, 1969 (Carradine 3, Chaney Lon, Jr. 3)
Dracula's Daughter, 1936 (D'Agostino 4, Fort 4)
Dracula's Dog. *See* Zoltan . . . Hound of Dracula, 1977
Dracula's Son, 1975 (Lee, C. 3)
Draft Horse, 1941 (Jones 2)
Draftee Daffy, 1944 (Clampett 4)
Drag, 1929 (Barthelmess 3, Haller 4)
Drag Harlan, 1920 (Farnum 3)
Drag-A-Long Droopy, 1953 (Avery 2)
Dragée haute, 1959 (Piccoli 3)
Dragées au poivre, 1963 (Belmondo 3, Karina 3, Signoret 3, Vitti 3, Decaë 4)
Dragnet, 1928 (Von Sternberg 2, Powell, W. 3, Dreier 4, Furthman 4, Mankiewicz 4, Rosson 4)
Dragnet, 1954 (Boone 3)
Dragnet Girl. *See* Hijosen no onna, 1933
Dragon de Komodo, 1958 (Delerue 4)
Dragon Gate. *See* Lung men feng-yün, 1976
Dragon Gate Inn. *See* Lung men k'o-chan, 1966
Dragon Inn. *See* Lung men k'o-chan, 1966
Dragon Murder Case, 1934 (Blanke 4, Gaudio 4, Orry-Kelly 4)
Dragon of Komodo. *See* Draken på Komodo, 1937–38
Dragon Painter, 1919 (Hayakawa 3)
Dragon Seed, 1944 (Van Dyke, W.S. 2, Barrymore L. 3, Hepburn, K. 3, Huston 3, Moorehead 3, Berman 4, Murfin 4, Stothart 4, Wheeler 4)
Dragonen, 1925 (Blom 2)
Dragonerliebchen, 1928 (Reisch 4)
Dragones de Ha-Long, 1976 (Alvarez 2)
Dragons de Villars, 1900–07 (Guy 2)
Dragon's Gold, 1953 (Cortez 4)
Dragonslayer, 1981 (Richardson 3, North 4)
Dragonwyck, 1946 (Mankiewicz 2, Bruce 3, Huston 3, Price 3, Tierney 3, Miller, A. 4, Newman 4, Wheeler 4, Zanuck 4)
Dragoon Wells Massacre, 1957 (Elam 3, Clothier 4)
Dragstrip Riot, 1958 (Wray 3)
Dragueurs, 1959 (Aimée 3, Douy 4, Jarre 4)

Drahoušek Klementýna, 1959 (Brdečka 4)
Draken på Komodo, 1937–38 (Fejos 2)
Drama of Jealousy. See Dramma della gelosia, 1970
Drama von Mayerling. See Tragödie im Hause Habsburg, 1924
Drama's Dreadful Deal, 1917 (Lloyd 3)
Dramatic Life of Abraham Lincoln. See Abraham Lincoln, 1924
Dramatic School, 1938 (Leroy 2, Dumont 3, Goddard 3, Rainer 3, Turner, L. 3, Adrian 4, Daniels 4, Vajda 4, Waxman 4)
Drame à Venise, 1907 (Zecca 2)
Drame au Château d'Acre, 1915 (Gance 2)
Drame au fond de la mer, 1900 (Zecca 2)
Drame au pays basque, 1913 (Feuillade 2)
Drame chez les fantoches, 1908 (Cohl 2)
Drame de Shanghai, 1938 (Pabst 2, Jouvet 3, Annenkov 4, Alekan 4, Andrejew 4, Courant 4, Jeanson 4, Schufftan 4)
Drame du taureau, 1965 (Braunberger 4)
Drame sur la planche a chaussures, 1915 (Cohl 2)
Drames du Bois de Boulogne, 1947 (Decaë 4)
Dramma al circo. See Manège, 1938
Dramma della Casbah, 1953 (Papas 3)
Dramma della gelosia, 1970 (Scola 2, Giannini 3, Mastroianni 3, Vitti 3, Age and Scarpelli 4)
Dranem series, 1900–07 (Guy 2)
Drango, 1957 (Chandler 3, Crisp 3, Bernstein 4, Howe 4)
Drapeau noir flotte sur la marmite, 1971 (Gabin 3, Audiard 4, D'Eaubonne 4)
Drastic Demise, 1945 (Anger 2)
Drátenícek, 1920 (Ondra 3)
Draufganger, 1931 (Albers 3)
Dravci, 1948 (Weiss 2)
Draw, 1984 (Coburn, J. 3, Douglas, K. 3)
Drawing for Cats. See Malovani pro kocku, 1961
Drawing Lesson. See Statue animée, 1903
Drawing the Line, 1915 (Eason 4)
Drawings from Life: Charles White, 1980 (Moss 4)
Dream, 1911 (Pickford 3, Gaudio 4, Ince 4)
Dream. See His Prehistoric Past, 1914
Dream. See Metshta, 1943
Dream. See San, 1966
Dream About a House. See Alom a házrol, 1971
Dream Called Anada. See Touha zvaná Anada, 1971
Dream Child, 1914 (Eason 4)
Dream Circus, 1939 (Reiniger 2)
Dream Doll, 1979 (Halas and Batchelor 2, Godfrey 4, Grgić 4)
Dream Flights. See Polety vo sne i nayavu, 1982
Dream Girl, 1916 (DeMille 2, Buckland 4, Macpherson 4)
Dream Girl, 1948 (Leisen 2, Hutton 3, Dreier 4, Head 4, Young, V. 4)
Dream House, 1932 (Sennett 2, Crosby 3, Hornbeck 4)
Dream Kids, 1944 (Fleischer, M. and D. 2)
Dream, NYC, The Return, The Flower, 1976 (Brakhage 2)
Dream of a Rarebit Fiend, 1906 (Porter 2)
Dream of Allan Gray. See Vampyr, 1932
Dream of an Opium Fiend. See Rêve d'un fumeur d'opium, 1908
Dream of Death. See Dødsdrømmen, 1911
Dream of Happiness. See Lyckodrommen, 1963
Dream of Kings, 1969 (Papas 3, Quinn 3, Leven 4, North 4)
Dream of Love, 1928 (Niblo 2, Crawford, J. 3, Oland 3, Adrian 4, Daniels 4, Gibbons 4)
Dream of Passion, 1978 (Dassin 2, Burstyn 3, Mercouri 3)
Dream of the Racetrack Fiend, 1905 (Bitzer 4)
Dream of Zorro. See Sogno di Zorro, 1951
Dream Path of Youth. See Seishun no yumeji, 1923
Dream Speaker, 1976 (Jutra 2)
Dream Street, 1921 (Griffith 2)
Dream Stuff, 1933 (Sennett 2)
Dream Valley. See Dromda dalen, 1947
Dream Walking, 1934 (Fleischer, M. and D. 2)
Dream Walking, 1950 (Terry 4)
Dream Wife, 1953 (Grant, C. 3, Kerr 3, Pidgeon 3, Krasner 4, Rose 4, Schary 4)
Dream Woman, 1914 (Guy 2)
Dreamboat, 1952 (Hunter 3, Lanchester 3, Rogers, G. 3, Webb 3, Krasner 4, Lemaire 4)

Dreamer, 1979 (Warden 3)
Dreamer. See Sanjar, 1960
Dreamer's Walk. See Drommares vandring, 1957
Dreaming, 1980 (Vanderbeek 2)
Dreaming Lips, 1937 (Czinner 2, Lean 2, Bergner 3, Massey 3, Andrejew 4, Garmes 4, Mayer 4)
Dreaming Lips. See Traumende Mund, 1932
Dreaming Lips. See Traumende Mund, 1953
Dreams, 1940 (Cushing 3)
Dreams. See Kvinnodrom, 1955
Dreams of a Rarebit Fiend, 1921 (McCay 2)
Dreams of Monte Carlo. See Monte Carlo, 1926
Dreams of Youth. See Wakoudo no yume, 1928
Dreams That Money Can Buy, 1954–57 (Richter 2)
Dreamscape, 1984 (Von Sydow 3, Jarre 4)
Dreamwood, 1972 (Broughton 2)
Dreamy Knights, 1916 (Hardy 3)
Drei amerikanische LPs, 1969 (Wenders 2)*
Drei Haselnusse fur Aschenbrodel, 1974 (Hoppe 3)
Drei Kuckucksuhren, 1926 (Wagner 4)
Drei machen ihr Gluck. See Teure Heimat, 1929
Drei Mannequins, 1926 (Albers 3)
Drei Probiermamsells. See Drei Mannequins, 1926
Drei Seelen und ein Gedanke, 1927 (Albers 3)
Drei Tage Liebe, 1931 (Albers 3)
Drei Tänze der Mary Wilford, 1920 (Wiene 2)
Drei um Edith, 1929 (Rasp 3, Junge 4)
Drei Unteroffiziere, (Staudte 2)
Drei van Hells, 1918 (Kraly 4)
Drei von der Stempelstelle, 1932 (Walbrook 3)
Drei von der Tankstelle, 1930 (Tschechowa 3, Pommer 4)
Drei von der Tankstelle. See Chemin du paradis, 1930
Dreigroschenoper, 1931 (Pabst 2, Artaud 3, Rasp 3, Andrejew 4, Wagner 4)
Dreigroschenoper, 1963 (Staudte 2, Jurgens 3, Knef 3)
Dreiklang, 1938 (Sirk 2, Dagover 3)
Dreimaderlhaus, 1918 (Oswald 2, Veidt 3)
Dreizehn, 1918 (Albers 3)
Dreizehn alte Esel, 1958 (Albers 3)
Dresden Doll, 1922 (Fleischer, M. and D. 2)
Dress. See Klanningen, 1964
Dress Parade, 1927 (Boyd 3, Crisp 3, Love 3, Adrian 4)
Dress Returns to Glory, 1947 (Zhao 3)
Dressage de chevaux sauvages, 1970 (Braunberger 4)
Dressed to Kill, 1928 (Astor 3, Brown 3, Estabrook 4)
Dressed to Kill, 1941 (Day 4)
Dressed to Kill, 1946 (Bruce 3, Rathbone 3, Salter 4)
Dressed to Kill, 1980 (De Palma 2, Caine 3, Dickinson 3, Donaggio 4)
Dressed to Thrill, 1935 (Brook 3, Maté 4, Raphaelson 4)
Dresser, 1984 (Yates 2, Finney 3)
Dressmaker from Paris, 1925 (Hawks 2, Banton 4, Glennon 4)
Dressmaker's Bill, 1910–11 (White 3)
Drevená dedina, 1954 (Kroner 3)
Dreyfus, 1930 (Oswald 2, Basserman 3, George, H. 3, Hardwicke 3, Homolka 3, Kortner 3, Rasp 3, Warm 4)
Dreyfus Affair. See Affaire Dreyfus, 1899
Dreyfus Case. See Dreyfus, 1930
Drift Fence, 1936 (Crabbe 3, Miller, V. 4)
Drifter, 1929 (Mix 3)
Drifter, 1932 (Farnum 3)
Drifter, 1944 (Crabbe 3)
Drifters, 1929 (Grierson 2)
Driftin' Thru, 1926 (Carey 3, Polito 4)
Drifting, 1923 (Browning 2, Beery 3, Wong 3)
Drifting Clouds. See Wakare-gumo, 1951
Drifting Souls, 1932 (Auer 3)
Driftwood, 1912 (Dwan 2)
Driftwood, 1928 (Walker 4)
Driftwood, 1947 (Dwan 2, Brennan 3, Wood 3, Alton, J. 4)
Drink Hearty, 1920 (Roach 4)
Drink's Lure, 1912 (Griffith 2, Crisp 3, Bitzer 4)
Drip-Along Daffy, 1951 (Jones 2)
Dripping Water, 1969 (Snow 2, Wieland 2)

Ducking They Did Go, 1939 (Three Stooges 3)
Ducks and Drakes, 1921 (Daniels 3)
Ducksters, 1950 (Jones 2)
Dude and the Burglar, 1903 (Bitzer 4)
Dude Goes West, 1948 (Struss 4, Tiomkin 4)
Dude Wrangler, 1930 (Bushman 3)
Dudes Are Pretty People, 1942 (Roach 4)
Due castelli, 1963 (Bozzetto 4)
Due colonelli, 1962 (Pidgeon 3)
Due compari, 1955 (Fabrizi 3)
Due cuori felici, 1932 (De Sica 2)
Due cuori sotto sequestro, 1941 (Fusco 4)
Due Foscari, 1942 (Brazzi 3)
Due gondolieri. See Venezia, la luna e tu, 1958
Due lettere anonime, 1944 (Ponti 4)
Due madri, 1938 (De Sica 2)
Due mafiosi contro Goldginger, 1965 (Rey 3)
Due marescialli, 1961 (De Sica 2)
Due Marines e un Generale, 1967 (Keaton 2)
Due milioni per un sorriso, 1939 (Castellani 2)
Due mogli sono troppe, 1951 (D'Amico 4, Rota 4)
Due nemici, 1961 (Sordi 3, Age and Scarpelli 4, D'Amico 4,
    De Laurentiis 4)
Due notti con Cleopatra, 1954 (Scola 2, Loren 3, Sordi 3, Struss 4)
Due orfanelle, 1942 (Gallone 2, Valli 3, Stallich 4)
Due orfanelle, 1947 (Age 4)
Due orfanelle, 1954 (Rota 4)
Due pezzi di pane, 1979 (Gassman 3, Noiret 3)
Due sergenti, 1936 (Cervi 3, Valli 3)
Due soldi di speranza, 1951 (Castellani 2, Rota 4)
Due volte Giuda, 1968 (Kinski 3)
Due volti della paura. See Coartada en disco rojo, 1970
Duel, 1912 (Sennett 2, Normand 3)
Duel, 1939 (Clouzot 2, Fresnay 3, Raimu 3, Matras 4)
Duel, 1971 (Spielberg 2)
Duel. See Párbaj, 1960
Duel à mort, 1950 (Keaton 2)
Duel à travers les âges, 1952 (Audiard 4)
Duel at Diablo, 1966 (Andersson B. 3, Poitier 3)
Duel at Ichijoji Temple. See Zoko Miyamoto Musashi, 1955
Duel at Kagiya Corner. See Ketto Kagiya no tsuji, 1951
Duel at Silver Creek, 1952 (Siegel 2, Marvin 3, Murphy 3, Salter 4)
Duel at the Rio Grande. See Segno di Zorro, 1963
Duel de Monsieur Myope, 1908 (Linders 3)
Duel in the Forest. See Schinderhannes, 1958
Duel in the Jungle, 1954 (Andrews D. 3, Crain 3)
Duel in the Sun, 1946 (Dieterle 2, Vidor, K. 2, Von Sternberg 2,
    Welles 2, Barrymore L. 3, Carey 3, Cotten 3, Gish, L. 3, Huston 3,
    Jones, J. 3, Marshall 3, McQueen, B. 3, Peck 3, Basevi 4, Eason 4,
    Garmes 4, Menzies 4, Plunkett 4, Rosson 4, Selznick 4, Tiomkin 4)
Duel of a Snowy Night. See Yuki no yo ketto, 1954
Duel of Champions. See Orazi e Curiazi, 1962
Duel of the Candles, 1911 (Dwan 2)
Duel Personalities, 1939 (Sidney 2)
Duel tragique, 1904 (Guy 2)
Duelle, 1976 (Rivette 2)
Duellists, 1977 (Finney 3, Keach 3, Keitel 3)
Duello nel mundo, 1966 (Blier 3)
Duelo en las montañas, 1949 (Fernández 2, Figueroa 4)
Dueña y señora, 1948 (García 3, Figueroa 4)
Duffy, 1968 (Coburn, J. 3, Mason 3, York, S. 3)
Duffy of San Quentin, 1954 (O'Sullivan 3, Alton, J. 4)
Duffy's Tavern, 1945 (Crosby 3, Fitzgerald 3, Goddard 3, Hutton 3,
    Ladd 3, Lake 3, Lamour 3, Dreier 4, Frank and Panama 4, Head 4)
Duhovita priča, 1978 (Grgić 4)
Dui Purush, 1945 (Sircar 4)
Duke de Ribbon Counter, 1911 (Lawrence 3)
Duke for a Day, 1934 (Roach 4)
Duke is Tops, 1938 (Horne 3)
Duke of Chimney Butte, 1921 (Borzage 2)
Duke of West Point, 1939 (Fontaine 3)
Duke Steps Out, 1929 (Cruze 2, Daves 2, Crawford, J. 3, Gibbons 4)
Duke's Plan, 1909 (Griffith 2, Bitzer 4)

Dukhiyari, 1937 (Biswas 4)
Dukkestuen, 1950 (Carlsen 2)
Dulces horas, 1981 (Saura 2)
Dulcima, 1971 (Mills 3)
Dulcimer Street. See London Belongs to Me, 1948
Dulcinea, 1962 (Fusco 4)
Dulcinea del Toboso, 1966 (Rey 3)
Dulcy, 1923 (Franklin 2, Talmadge, C. 3, Emerson 4, Loos 4,
    Sullivan 4)
Dulcy, 1940 (Burke 3, Dailey 3, Sothern 3, Kaper 4)
Dulha Dulhan, 1964 (Kapoor 2)
Dum bramborové natě, (Hrušínský 3)
Dum na předměstí, 1933 (Haas 3, Stallich 4, Vích 4)
Dum v Kaprové ulici, 1967 (Brejchová 3)
Dumb Cluck, 1937 (Lantz 4)
Dumb Daddies, 1928 (McCarey 2, Roach 4)
Dumb Girl of Portici, 1916 (Weber 2, Karloff 3, Rosher 4)
Dumb Half Breed's Defense, 1910 (Anderson G. 3)
Dumb Waiter, 1928 (Sennett 2, Hornbeck 4)
Dumb-Bell, 1922 (Roach 4)
Dumbbell. See Corniaud, 1965
Dumbconscious Mind, 1942 (Fleischer, M. and D. 2, Hubley 4)
Dumb-Hounded, 1942 (Avery 2)
Dumbo, 1941 (Disney 2)
Dum-Bom, 1953 (Andersson B. 3)
Dumka, 1964 (Paradzhanov 3)
Dummkopf, 1920 (Pick 2, Mayer 4)
Dummy, 1929 (Cromwell 2, March 3, Pitts 3, Hunt 4, Mankiewicz 4)
Duna—halak—madarak, 1971 (Szabó 2)
Dunaj hajós, 1974 (Madaras 3)
Dune, 1984 (Ferrer, J. 3, Mangano 3, Von Sydow 3, Francis 4,
    Whitlock 4)
Dung-Aw, 1981 (Brocka 2)
Dungeon, 1922 (Micheaux 2)
Dungeon. See Scarf, 1951
Duniya, 1968 (Anand 3)
Dunked in the Deep, 1949 (Three Stooges 3)
Dunkel bei Tageslicht. See Nappali sotétség, 1963
Dunkirk, 1958 (Attenborough 3, Mills 3, Arnold 4)
Dunoyer de Segonzac, 1965 (Reichenbach 2, Braunberger 4)
Dunungen, 1920 (Jaenzon 4, Magnusson 4)
Dunungen, 1941 (Borgstrom 3, Fischer 4)
Dunwich Horror, 1970 (Jaffe 3, Corman 4)
Duomo di Milano, 1946 (Blasetti 2)
Dupe, 1916 (Sweet 3)
Duplicity, 1978 (Brakhage 2)
Duplicity II, 1978 (Brakhage 2)
Duplicity III, 1980 (Brakhage 2)
Duplizitat der Ereignisse, 1919 (Basserman 3, Dreier 4)
Dupont Lajoie, 1974 (Huppert 3)
Dupont-Barbès, 1951 (Kosma 4)
Duquesa del Tepetate, 1951 (García 3)
Dura Lex. See Po zakonu, 1926
Durand of the Bad Lands, 1917 (Mix 3)
Durand of the Badlands, 1925 (Lombard 3)
Durante l'estate, 1971 (Olmi 2)
Duration. See Whitchurch Down, 1972
Durbargati Padma, 1971 (Ghatak 4)
Durch die Walder, durch die Auen, 1956 (Pabst 2)
Durfen wir schweigen?, 1926 (Oswald 2, Kortner 3,
    Veidt 3)
During Cherry Time, 1911 (Lawrence 3)
During the Plague. See Mens Pesten raserr, 1913
During the Round-Up, 1913 (Griffith 2, Gish, L. 3, Walthall 3,
    Bitzer 4)
During the Summer. See Durante l'estate, 1971
Durs à cuire, 1964 (Chabrol 2, Audran 3)
Dushman, 1938 (Sircar 4)
Dushman, 1956 (Anand 3)
Dusk to Dawn, 1922 (Vidor, K. 2, Barnes 4)
Dusks and Dawns. See Alkonyok és hajnalok, 1961
Dusman, 1979 (Guney 2)
Dust, 1985 (Howard, T. 3)

ust Be My Destiny, 1939 (Rossen 2, Bond 3, Garfield 3, Howe 4,
   Steiner 4)
ust Fever, 1962 (Watkins 2)
ust of Desire. See Song of Love, 1923
ustbin Parade, 1941 (Halas and Batchelor 2)
usty and Sweets McGee, 1970 (Fraker 4)
usty Ermine, 1936 (Rutherford 3, Courant 4)
utch at the Double. See Nederland in 7 Lessen, 1948
utch Gold Mine, 1911 (Sennett 2)
utch Treat, 1930 (Terry 4)
utchman, 1966 (Barry 4)
utiful But Dumb, 1941 (Three Stooges 3)
utiful Dub, 1919 (Daniels 3, Lloyd 3, Roach 4)
uty and the Beast, 1943 (Fleischer, M. and D. 2)
úvad, 1959 (Fábri 2)
va Fedora, 1959 (Shukshin 3)
va mrazíci, 1954 (Trnka 2)
va z onoho světa, 1962 (Kopecký 3)
va-Buldi-Dva, 1929 (Kuleshov 2, Maretskaya 3)
vadsat' let sovetskogo kino. See Kino za XX liet, 1940
vadtsat' chetyr'e Tschasa daschd, 1982 (Danailov 3)
vadzatdva neshchastia, 1930 (Enei 4)
vakrát kayček, 1939-40 (Hammid 2)
vama pod Nebeto, 1962 (Karamitev 3)
vanáct křesel, 1933 (Fric 2)
vanácti měsíčkách, 1960 (Hofman 4)
vaschdy roschdjonny, 1934 (Babochkin 3)
vatsat dnei bez voiny, 1976 (Gurchenko 3)
ve zhizni, 1960 (Tikhonov 3)
ver bez zamka, 1973 (Gurchenko 3)
vevnik, 1974 (Dragić 4)
vojí život, 1924 (Vích 4)
voryanskoye gnezdo, 1969 (Mikhalkov-Konchalovski 2,
   Tyszkiewicz 3)

Dwaj ludzie z szasa, 1958 (Polanski 2)
Dwarf's Spring Adventures. See Wiosenne przygody krasnala,
   1959
Dweller in the Desert. See Burning Sands, 1922
Dwie brygady, 1948 (Lomnicki 3)
Dyadya Vanya, 1970 (Mikhalkov-Konchalovski 2, Bondarchuk 3,
   Smoktunovsky 3)
D'ye Ken John Peel?, 1935 (Holloway 3)
Dying for a Smoke, 1965 (Halas and Batchelor 2)
Dylan Thomas, 1961 (Burton 3)
Dýmky, 1966 (Brejchová 3)
Dynamit, 1947 (Borgstrom 3)
Dynamitattentatet paa Fyrtaarnet. See Dødssejleren,
   1911
Dynamite, 1929 (DeMille 2, Lombard 3, McCrea 3, Scott, R. 3,
   Adrian 4, Gibbons 4, Macpherson 4, Shearer 4, Stothart 4)
Dynamite, 1938 (Biswas 4)
Dynamite Anchorage. See Murder Is My Beat, 1955
Dynamite Chicken, 1971 (Pryor 3)
Dynamite Dan, 1924 (Karloff 3)
Dynamite Girl, 1963 (Auer 3)
Dynamite Jack, 1960 (Fernandel 3)
Dynamite Man from Glory Jail. See Fools' Parade, 1971
Dynamite Pass, 1950 (Musuraca 4)
Dynamite Smith, 1924 (Beery 3, Love 3, Sullivan 4)
Dynamite Women, 1976 (Corman 4)
Dynasty, 1976 (Ford, H. 3, Keach 3)
Dyrekøbt Glimmer. See Hulda Rasmussen, 1911
Dyrekøbt Venskab, 1912 (Blom 2)
Dyrygent, 1979 (Wajda 2, Janda 3)
Dzieje grzechu, 1975 (Borowczyk 4)
Dzis w nocy umrze miastro, 1961 (Tyszkiewicz 3)
Dziura w ziemi, 1969 (Nowicki 3)
Dzungle velkoměsta, 1929 (Vích 4)

E

arrivato il cavaliere, 1950 (Monicelli 2, Ponti 4)
arrivato l'accordatore, 1952 (Loren 3, Sordi 3)
caduta una donna, 1941 (Brazzi 3, Zavattini 4)
. e continuavano a fregarsi il milione di dollari, 1970 (Lollobrigida 3,
   Van Cleef 3)
Dio disse a Caino . . ., 1969 (Kinski 3)
la donna crea l'amore, 1976 (Audran 3, Fabian 3)
la nave va, 1983 (Fellini 2, Guerra 4)
'Lollipop, 1975 (Ferrer, J. 3)
più facile che un cammello, 1950 (Zampa 2, Gabin 3, D'Amico 4,
   Rota 4, Zavattini 4)
primavera, 1950 (Castellani 2, D'Amico 4, Rota 4,
   Zavattini 4)
ropeya del camino, 1941 (Armendáriz 3)
.T.—The Extra-Terrestrial, 1982 (Spielberg 2, Burtt 4,
   Williams, J. 4)
tanta paura, 1976 (Wallach 3)
tornato Sabata . . . hai chiuso, 1972 (Van Cleef 3)
venne l'ora della vendetta, 1970 (Cotten 3)
. . e venne un uomo, 1965 (Olmi 2, Steiger 3)
ach Dawn I Crow, 1948 (Freleng 4)
ach Dawn I Die, 1939 (Cagney 3, Holden 3, Raft 3, Edeson 4,
   Raine 4, Steiner 4)
ach for All, 1946 (Alwyn 4)
ach to His Kind, 1917 (Hayakawa 3)
ach to His Own Way. See Var sin vag, 1948
adie Was a Lady, 1945 (Miller 3, Guffey 4)
ager Beaver, 1945 (Jones 2)

Eagle, 1925 (Brown 2, Banky 3, Cooper, Gary 3, Valentino 3,
   Adrian 4, Barnes 4, Kraly 4, Menzies 4, Westmore, M. 4)
Eagle and the Hawk, 1933 (Leisen 2, Grant, C. 3, Lombard 3, March 3,
   Banton 4, Miller, S. 4, Saunders 4)
Eagle and the Hawk, 1950 (Howe 4)
Eagle Has Landed, 1976 (Sturges, J. 2, Caine 3, Duvall, R. 3,
   Pleasance 3, Quayle 3, Sutherland 3, Schifrin 4)
Eagle in a Cage, 1970 (Gielgud 3, Richardson 3)
Eagle of the Night, 1928 (Costello, M. 3)
Eagle of the Pacific. See Taiheiyo no washi, [#2]1953
Eagle of the Sea, 1926 (Karloff 3, Schulberg 4)
Eagle Squadron, 1942 (Bruce 3, Cooper, Gladys 3, Cooper 4, Cortez 4,
   Raine 4, Wanger 4)
Eagle with Two Heads. See Aigle à deux têtes, 1947
Eagle's Brood, 1935 (Boyd 3, Farnum 3)
Eagle's Mate, 1914 (Pickford 3)
Eagles of the Fleet. See Flat Top, 1952
Eagles over Britain. See Battaglia d'Inghilterra, 1969
Eagle's Wing, 1978 (Audran 3, Keitel 3, Sheen 3)
Eagle's Wings, (Johnson, N. 3)
Eames Lounge Chair, 1956 (Bernstein 4)
Earl Carroll Sketchbook, 1946 (Horton 3, Cahn 4)
Earl Carroll Vanities, 1945 (Arden 3)
Earl of Chicago, 1940 (Saville 2, Gwenn 3, Montgomery 3)
Early Autumn. See Kohayagawa-ke no aki, 1961
Early Bird Dood It, 1942 (Avery 2)
Early Days, 1979 (Lester 2, Richardson 3)
Early Days of Communication, 1958 (Halas and Batchelor 2)

Early Days Out West, 1912 (Rosher 4)
Early Frost, 1985 (Rowlands 3, Sidney 3)
Early Spring. *See* Before Spring, 1958
Early Spring. *See* Shoshun, 1956
Early Summer, 1951 (Ryu 3)
Early Summer. *See* Bakushu, 1951
Early to Bed, 1928 (Laurel and Hardy 3, Roach 4)
Early to Bed, 1933 (Gwenn 3)
Early to Bed, 1936 (McLeod 2)
Early to Bed. *See* Ich bei Tag und Du bei Nacht, 1932
Early to Bet, 1951 (McKimson 4)
Early to Wed, 1926 (Borzage 2, Pitts 3)
Early Worm Gets the Bird, 1939 (Avery 2)
Earrings of Madame De. *See* Madame de . . ., 1953
Earth. *See* Zemlya, 1930
Earth Dies Screaming, 1964 (Fisher 2)
Earth Entranced. *See* Terra em transe, 1967
Earth in Labour, 1950 (Halas and Batchelor 2)
Earth Sings. *See* Zem spieva, 1933
Earth Smiles. *See* Daichi wa hohoemu, 1925
Earth Spirit. *See* Erdgeist, 1923
Earth II, 1971 (Schifrin 4)
Earth vs. the Flying Saucers, 1956 (Harryhausen 4, Katzman 4, Siodmak 4)
Earthbottom, 1954–56 (Romero 2)
Earthbound, 1940 (Baxter W. 3, Day 4, Newman 4)
Earthling, 1981 (Holden 3)
Earthquake, 1974 (Robson 2, Bujold 3, Gardner 3, Heston 3, Kennedy, G. 3, Matthau 3, Ames 4, Whitlock 4, Williams, J. 4)
Earth's Final Fury. *See* When Time Ran Out, 1980
Earth's Revenge. *See* Omstridte Jord, 1915
Earthworm Tractors, 1936 (Brown 3)
Easiest Profession. *See* Chômeur de Clochemerle, 1957
Easiest Way, 1931 (Bennett C. 3, Gable 3, Menjou 3, Montgomery 3)
Easiest Way. *See* Quand on est belle, 1931
East African Safari, 1965 (Reichenbach 2)
East China Sea. *See* Higashi Shinaki, 1968
East Is East, 1916 (Evans 3)
East Is West, 1922 (Franklin 2, Oland 3, Talmadge, C. 3, Gaudio 4, Marion 4, Schenck 4)
East Is West, 1930 (Ayres 3, Robinson, E. 3, Velez 3)
East Lynne, 1912 (Cruze 2)
East Lynne, 1916 (Bara 3)
East Lynne, 1925 (Coffee 4)
East Lynne, 1931 (Brook 3, Seitz 4)
East Lynne in Bugville, 1912–13 (White 3)
East Lynne on the Western Front, 1931 (Pearson 2)
East Lynne with Variations, 1919 (Sennett 2)
East Meets West, 1936 (Arliss 3, Balcon 4)
East of Borneo, 1931 (Johnson, N. 3, Fulton 4)
East of Broadway, 1924 (Howard 2)
East of Eden, 1955 (Kazan 2, Dean 3, Massey 3, Basevi 4, McCord 4, Rosenman 4)
East of Elephant Rock, 1976 (Hurt, J. 3)
East of Java, 1935 (Muse 3, Waxman 4)
East of Java. *See* South Sea Sinner, 1950
East of Shanghai. *See* Rich and Strange, 1931
East of Sudan, 1964 (Quayle 3)
East of Suez, 1925 (Walsh 2, Negri 3, Dreier 4)
East of Sumatra, 1953 (Boetticher 2, Chandler 3, Quinn 3, Boyle 4)
East of the Rising Sun. *See* Malaya, 1949
East of the River, 1940 (Garfield 3, Deutsch 4)
East of the Water Plug, 1924 (Sennett 2)
East Side Kids, 1940 (Katzman 4)
East Side of Heaven, 1939 (Auer 3, Blondell 3, Crosby 3)
East Side, West Side, 1927 (Dwan 2, Fleischer, M. and D. 2)
East Side, West Side, 1949 (Leroy 2, Charisse 3, Gardner 3, Heflin 3, Mason 3, Stanwyck 3, Lennart 4, Rose 4, Rosher 4, Rozsa 4)
Easter Celebration at Jerusalem, 1912 (Olcott 2)
Easter Parade, 1948 (Walters 2, Astaire 3, Garland 3, Miller 3, Alton, R. 4, Edens 4, Freed 4, Goodrich and Hackett 4, Green, J. 4, Irene 4, Smith, J.M. 4, Stradling 4)
Easter Yeggs, 1948 (McKimson 4)

Eastern Cowboy, 1911 (Dwan 2)
Eastern Flower, 1913 (Dwan 2)
Eastern Girl, 1912 (Dwan 2)
Eastern Westerner, 1920 (Lloyd 3, Roach 4)
Easy Come, Easy Go, 1928 (Arthur 3, Cronjager 4)
Easy Come, Easy Go, 1947 (Fitzgerald 3, Dreier 4, Head 4, MacGowan 4)
Easy Come, Easy Go, 1967 (Lanchester 3, Presley 3, Head 4, Wallis 4)
Easy Go. *See* Free & Easy, 1930
Easy Life. *See* Snadný život, 1957
Easy Life. *See* Sorpasso, 1962
Easy Living, 1937 (Leisen 2, Sturges, P. 2, Arthur 3, Milland 3, Dreier 4, Head 4)
Easy Living, 1949 (Tourneur, J. 2, Ball 3, Mature 3, Schnee 4)
Easy Money, 1912–13 (White 3)
Easy Money, 1925 (Brown, Harry Joe 4)
Easy on the Eyes, 1933 (Sennett 2)
Easy Peckin's, 1953 (McKimson 4)
Easy Pickings, 1927 (Nilsson 3)
Easy Rider, 1969 (Rafelson 2, Black 3, Fonda, P. 3, Hopper 3, Nicholson 3, Kovacs 4)
Easy Road. *See* Asymvivastos, 1979
Easy Street, 1917 (Chaplin 2, Purviance 3)
Easy Street, 1928 (Micheaux 2)
Easy to Look At, 1945 (Salter 4)
Easy to Love, 1934 (Astor 3, Horton 3, Menjou 3, Grot 4, Haller 4, Orry-Kelly 4)
Easy to Love, 1953 (Berkeley 2, Walters 2, Baker C. 3, Charisse 3, Johnson, V. 3, Williams 3, Pasternak 4, Rose 4, Rose 4, Smith, J.M. 4)
Easy to Take, 1936 (Dmytryk 2)
Easy to Wed, 1946 (Ball 3, Johnson, V. 3, Williams 3, Wynn 3, Green, J. 4, Irene 4, Stradling 4)
Easy Virtue, 1927 (Hitchcock 2, Balcon 4)
Easy Years. *See* Anni facili, 1953
Eat Me, Kitty, Eight to the Bar, 1942 (Terry 4)
Eat My Dust!, 1976 (Corman 4)
Eaten Alive, 1977 (Ferrer, M. 3)
Eatin' on the Cuff, 1942 (Clampett 4)
Eating Raoul, 1982 (Henry 4)
Eating Season, 1951 (Tierney 3)
Eating Too Fast, 1966 (Warhol 2)
Eau, 1966 (Alexeieff and Parker 2)
Eau à la bouche, 1959 (Braunberger 4)
Eau d'Evian, 1938 (Alexeieff and Parker 2)
Eau vive, 1938 (Epstein 2, Jaubert 4)
Eau vive, 1941 (Decaë 4)
Eaux d'artifice, 1953 (Anger 2)
Eaux profondes, 1981 (Huppert 3, Trintignant 3)
Eaux troublés, 1949 (Kosma 4)
Eaux vives. *See* Fleuve: Le Tarn, 1951
Eaux vives, eaux mortes, 1966 (Gélin 3)
Eavesdropper, 1909 (Griffith 2, Bitzer 4)
Eavesdropper, 1914 (Sennett 2)
Eavesdropper. *See* Ojo de la cerradura, 1964
Ebb Tide, 1922 (Clarke, C.C. 4, Glennon 4, Young, W. 4)
Ebb Tide, 1932 (Oberon 3)
Ebb Tide, 1937 (Farmer 3, Fitzgerald 3, Homolka 3, Milland 3, Head 4, Young, V. 4)
Ebirah—Terror of the Deep. *See* Nankai no daiketto, 1966
Ebony, Ivory, and Jade, 1979 (Sangster 4)
Ebony Parade, 1947 (Dandridge 3)
Ebreo errante, 1947 (Fellini 2, Cortese 3, Gassman 3, Vích 4)
Ecce Homo, 1915 (Gance 2)
Ecce homo, 1966 (Fresnay 3)
Ecce Homo, 1968 (Papas 3, Morricone 4)
Eccentric Dancer, 1900 (Hepworth 2)
Ecco. *See* Mondo di notte, 1963
Echappement libre, 1964 (Belmondo 3, Rey 3, Seberg 3, Wakhévitch 4)
Echec au porteur, 1957 (Moreau 3, Reggiani 3)
Echec au roi, ou Le Roi s'ennui, 1931 (Rosay 3)
Echec au roy, 1943 (Alekan 4)

Egy szerelem három éjszaka, 1967 (Latinovits 3)
Egy tukor, 1971 (Szabó 2)
Egymásra nézve, 1982 (Kroner 3)
Egymillió fontos bankó, 1916 (Korda 2)
Egypt, 1912 (Olcott 2)
Egypt by Three, 1953 (Constantine 3, Cotten 3)
Egypt the Mysterious, 1912 (Olcott 2)
Egypte eternelle, 1953 (Decaë 4)
Egyptian, 1954 (Curtiz 2, Carradine 3, Mature 3, Simmons 3,
    Tierney 3, Ustinov 3, Dunne 4, Herrmann 4, Lemaire 4,
    Newman 4, Robinson 4, Shamroy 4, Wheeler 4, Zanuck 4)
Egyptian Mummy, 1914 (Talmadge, C. 3)
Egyptian Sports, 1912 (Olcott 2)
Egyptian Story. See Hadota Misreya, 1982
Egyptologists, 1965 (Heston 3)
Együtt Károlyi Mihállyal—Beszélgetés Károlyi1973 (Kovács 2)
Ehe, 1929 (Dagover 3)
Ehe der Luise Rohrbach, 1917 (Jannings 3, Porten 3, Freund 4,
    Messter 4)
Ehe der Maria Braun, 1978 (Fassbinder 2, Schygulla 3)
Ehe des Dr. Med. Danwitz, 1956 (Schell, Maximilian 3)
Ehe fur eine Nacht, 1953 (Frohlich 3)
Ehe in Not, 1929 (Oswald 2)
Ehegeheimnisse. See Wie bliebe ich jung und schön, 1926
Ehen zu Dritt. See Ehe in Not, 1929
Ehi, amico . . . c'e Sabata, hai chiuso?, 1969 (Van Cleef 3)
Ehne el Talamza, 1959 (Sharif 3)
Ehrengard, 1982 (Cassel 3)
Ei gerochsky podvig, 1914 (Mozhukin 3)
Eid des Fursten Ulrich. See Spitzen, 1926
Eien no hito, 1961 (Kinoshita 2, Takamine 3)
Eien no kokoro, 1928 (Tanaka 3)
Eifélkor, 1957 (Gábor 3)
Eifersucht, 1925 (Czinner 2, Krauss 3, Schufftan 4)
Eiger Sanction, 1975 (Eastwood 3, Kennedy, G. 3, Williams, J. 4)
8½. See Otto e mezzo, 1963
Eight Bells, 1935 (Bellamy 3, Sothern 3, Walker 4)
Eight Cylinder Bull, 1926 (Arthur 3)
Eight Girls in a Boat, 1934 (Robinson 4)
8 Hours Don't Make a Day. See Acht Stunden sind kein Tag, 1972
813: The Adventures of Arsène Lupin. See Happyacu, 1923
Eight Iron Men, 1952 (Dmytryk 2, Kramer, S. 2, Marvin 3, Anhalt 4,
    Brown, Harry 4, Hunt 4)
Eight O'Clock Walk, 1953 (Attenborough 3)
Eight on the Lam, 1967 (Hope 3, Lewin 4)
8 x 8, 1952 (Cocteau 2)
8 x 8, 1954–57 (Richter 2)
8-Ball Bunny, 1950 (Jones 2)
1848, 1948 (Risi 2)
Eighteen in the Sun. See Diciotteni al sole, 1962
Eighteen-Year Old Girl. See Osmnáctiletá, 1939
8th Day of the Week. See Osmy dzien tygodnia, 1957
8th Free May Day. See 8. szabad Május 1, 1952
Eight-Thirteen, 1920 (Beery 3)
80 Days, 1944 (Jennings 2)
80 Huszar, 1977 (Madaras 3)
80 Steps to Jonah, 1969 (Mineo 3, Rooney 3, Wynn 3, La Shelle 4)
80,000 Suspects, 1963 (Cusack 3)
Eijanaika, 1980 (Imamura 2)
Eiko eno 5000 kiro, 1969 (Mifune 3)
Eiko eno kurohyo, 1969 (Ryu 3)
Eikyu no ai, 1935 (Tanaka 3)
Eileen of the Trees. See Glorious Youth, 1929
Einbrecher, 1930 (Pommer 4)
Einbruch, 1927 (Planer 4)
Eindringling, 1911 (Porten 3, Messter 4)
Eine Dubarry von heute, 1926 (Albers 3)
Eine Libesgeschichte, 1954 (Knef 3)
Eine Nacht der Liebe. See Liebesnachte, 1929
Eine Nacht im Grandhotel, 1931 (Metzner 4)
Eine Stunde glück, 1930 (Dieterle 2)
Einer frisst den anderen, 1964 (Mansfield 3)
Einer zuviel an Bord, 1935 (Baarová 3)

Einleitung zu Arnold Schoenberg Begleit Musik zu einer
    Lichtspielscene, 1969 (Straub and Huillet 2)
Einmal ist keinmal, 1955 (Wolf 2)
Einmal werd'ich Dir gefallende, 1937 (Rasp 3)
Eins Berlin-Harlem, 1974 (Fassbinder 2)
Eins x Eins der Ehe, 1949 (Herlth 4)
Einsichten eines Clowns, 1976 (Schell, Maximilian 3)
Einspänner Nr. 13. See Fiaker Nr. 13, 1926
Einstein Theory of Relativity, 1923 (Fleischer, M. and D. 2)
Eisenbahnkonig, 1921 (Kortner 3)
Eisenstein in Mexico, 1933 (Eisenstein 2)
Eisenstein's Mexican Project, 1958 (Eisenstein 2)
Eiserne Kreuz, 1915 (Oswald 2)
Eiserne Wille, 1917 (Basserman 3)
Ejszaka rabjai, 1914 (Curtiz 2)
Ek Adhuri Kahani, 1972 (Sen 2)
Ek baar kaho, 1980 (Azmi 3)
Ek Dil Sou Afsane, 1963 (Kapoor 2)
Ek Din Pratidin, 1979 (Sen 2)
Ek hi bhool, 1981 (Azmi 3)
Ek Hi Raasta, 1939 (Biswas 4)
Ek hi rasta, 1977 (Azmi 3)
Ek Ke Baad Ek, 1960 (Anand 3, Burman 4)
Ek Naujawan, 1951 (Burman 4)
Ek Nazar, 1972 (Bachchan 3)
Ekaterina Voronina, 1957 (Ulyanov 3)
Ekel, 1931 (Schufftan 4)
Ekezet, 1976 (Madaras 3)
Ekhtiar, 1970 (Chahine 2)
Ekimae onsen, 1962 (Tsukasa 3)
Ekpombi, 1968 (Angelopoulos 2)
Ekspeditricen, 1911 (Blom 2)
Eksploatacija, 1971 (Dragić 4)
El, 1952 (Buñuel 2, Figueroa 4)
El Cid, 1961 (Mann 2, Heston 3, Loren 3, Canutt 4, Fields 4,
    Krasker 4, Rozsa 4)
El Cordobès, 1966 (Reichenbach 2)
El Dorado, 1921 (L'Herbier 2, Francis, E. 3)
El Dorado, 1967 (Hawks 2, Caan 3, Mitchum 3, Wayne 3, Brackett,
    L. 4, Edouart 4, Rosson 4)
El Greco, 1965 (Ferrer, M. 3, Rey 3, Morricone 4)
El Paso, 1949 (Hayden 3)
Eladás muvészete, 1960 (Jancsó 2, Mészáros 2)
Elastic Affair, 1930 (Hitchcock 2)
Elbowing, 1980 (Driessen 4)
Eld ombord, 1923 (Sjostrom 2, Jaenzon 4, Magnusson 4)
Elder Brother, 1914 (Bushman 3)
Elder Vasili Gryaznov. See Starets Vasili Gryaznov, 1924
Eldora, 1953 (Markopoulos 2)
Eldorado, 1921 (Autant-Lara 2)
Eldorado, 1963 (Topol 3, Golan and Globus 4)
Eleagabl Kuperus. See Nachtgestalten, 1921
Eleanor and Franklin: The White House Years, 1977 (Barry 4)
Eleanor, First Lady of the World, 1982 (Addison 4)
Eleanora Duse, 1947 (Brazzi 3)
Elecciones municipales, 1970 (Guzmán 2)
Electra, 1962 (Papas 3, Lassally 4, Theodorakis 4)
Electra. See Lektro, 1927
Electra Glide in Blue, 1973 (Cook 3, Hall 4)
Electric Alarm, 1915 (Browning 2)
Electric Horseman, 1979 (Pollack 2, Fonda, J. 3, Redford 3,
    Roizman 4, Sargent 4, Stark 4)
Electric House, 1922 (Keaton 2)
Electric Man. See Man Made Monster, 1940
Electricity Cure, 1900 (Hepworth 2)
Electrification de la ligne Bruxelles-Anvers, 1935 (Storck 2)
Electrification de la ligne Paris-Vierzon, 1925 (Grémillon 2)
Electrocuté, 1911 (Gance 2)
Electrocuté, 1904 (Guy 2)
Electronic Mouse Trap, 1946 (Terry 4)
Electron's Tale, 1970 (Godfrey 4)
Electrorytmes, 1967 (Foldès 4)
Electroshow, 1966 (Guzmán 2)

Emma, 1932 (Brown 2, Dressler 3, Hersholt 3, Loy 3, Rooney 3, Adrian 4, Marion 4)
Emma Hamilton. *See* Lady Hamilton, 1968
Emmanuelle, 1974 (Cuny 3, Lai 4)
Emmanuelle on Taboo Island. *See* Spiaggia del desiderio, 1976
Emmanuelle II—Joys of a Woman. *See* Emmanuelle II: L'Anti-vierge, 1975
Emmanuelle II: L'Anti-vierge, 1975 (Lai 4)
Emmerdeur, 1973 (Coutard 4)
Emotional Education. *See* Selskaya uchitelnitsa, 1947
Empereur de Perou, 1981 (Rooney 3)
Emperor, 1965 (Lucas 2)
Emperor and a General. *See* Nippon no ichiban nagai hi, 1967
Emperor Jones, 1925 (Robeson 3)
Emperor Jones, 1933 (Haller 4)
Emperor of Peru. *See* Empereur de Perou, 1981
Emperor of Portugal. *See* Kejsaren av Portugallien, 1944
Emperor of the North, 1973 (Aldrich 2, Biroc 4)
Emperor of the North. *See* Emperor of the North Pole, 1973
Emperor of the North Pole, 1973 (Borgnine 3, Cook 3, Marvin 3, Smith, J.M. 4)
Emperor Waltz, 1948 (Wilder 2, Crosby 3, Fontaine 3, Brackett, C. 4, Dreier 4, Edouart 4, Head 4, Young, V. 4)
Emperor's Baker and the Baker's Emperor. *See* Císařuv pekař a Pekařuv pekař, 1951
Emperor's Candlesticks, 1937 (O'Sullivan 3, Powell, W. 3, Rainer 3, Young, R. 3, Gibbons 4, Rosson 4, Waxman 4)
Emperor's New Clothes, 1966 (Carradine 3)
Emperor's Nightingale, 1951 (Karloff 3)
Emperor's Nightingale. *See* Císařuv slavík, 1948
Empire, 1964 (Warhol 2)
Empire de la nuit, 1962 (Constantine 3, Legrand 4)
Empire of Passion. *See* Ai no borei, 1978
Empire of the Senses. *See* Ai no corrida, 1976
Empire Sonrai. *See* Songhays, 1963
Empire Strikes Back, 1980 (Kershner 2, Lucas 2, Ford, H. 3, Guinness 3, Jones, J.E. 3, Brackett, L. 4, Burtt 4, Edlund 4, Williams, J. 4)
Emploi du temps, 1967 (Braunberger 4)
Employees Entrance, 1932 (Young, L. 3, Orry-Kelly 4)
Empreinte des géants, 1980 (Reggiani 3)
Empreinte du Dieu, 1940 (Spaak 4)
Empress, 1917 (Guy 2)
Emptied-out Grocer's Shop. *See* U snědeného krámu, 1933
Empty Canvas. *See* Noia, 1963
Empty Gun, 1917 (Chaney Lon 3)
Empty Hands, 1924 (Fleming 2, Shearer 3, Wilson, C. 4)
Empty Hearts, 1924 (Bow 3, Haller 4)
Empty Holsters, 1937 (Eason 4)
Empty Pockets, 1917 (Brenon 2)
Empty Saddles, 1936 (Brooks 3)
Empty Socks, 1927 (Disney 2)
Empty Star. *See* Estrella vacia, 1958
En attendant l'auto, 1970 (Braunberger 4)
En av de många, 1915 (Sjostrom 2)
En avant la musique, 1962 (Fernandel 3)
En bombe, 1909 (Linders 3)
En bombe après l'obtention de son bachot. *See* En bombe, 1909
En cas de malheur, 1958 (Autant-Lara 2, Bardot 3, Cassel 3, Feuillère 3, Gabin 3, Aurenche 4, Bost 4, Douy 4)
En classe, 1897–98 (Guy 2)
En cours de route. *See* Utkozben, 1979
En Crète sans les dieux, 1934 (Leenhardt 2, Jaubert 4)
En de zee was niet meer, 1955 (Haanstra 2)
En effeuillant la Marguerite, 1956 (Allégret, M. 2, Auer 3, Bardot 3, Gélin 3, Trauner 4)
En el rio, 1961 (Borau 2)
En este pueblo no hay ladrones, 1964 (Buñuel 2)
En faction, 1902 (Guy 2)
En fastman i taget, 1952 (Bjornstrand 3)
En fluga gor ingen sommar, 1947 (Bjornstrand 3)
En kvinnas ansikte, 1938 (Borgstrom 3)
En la hacienda de la flor, 1948 (Armendáriz 3)

En la mitad del mundo, 1963 (Figueroa 4)
En la otra isla, 1968 (Gomez, S. 2)
En légitime défense, 1958 (Blier 3)
En lisant le journal, 1932 (Cavalcanti 2)
En, men ett lejon, 1940 (Molander 2, Jaenzon 4)
En natt, 1931 (Molander 2)
En och en, 1978 (Thulin 3, Nykvist 4)
En passant, 1943 (Alexeieff and Parker 2)
En passant par la Lorraine, 1950 (Franju 2, Fradetal 4, Kosma 4)
En plein cirage, 1961 (Delerue 4)
En plein Midi, 1957 (Leenhardt 2)
En pleine bagarre, 1961 (Constantine 3)
En quête de Marie, 1952 (Braunberger 4)
En rade, 1927 (Cavalcanti 2, Braunberger 4)
En route, 1910 (Cohl 2)
En souvenir de moi. *See* Vie de Jésus, 1951
En tiempos de la Inquisición, 1946 (Negrete 3)
En to iu onna, 1971 (Iwashita 3)
En to iu onna, 1971 (Imai 2)
Enamorada, 1946 (Fernández 2, Armendáriz 3, Félix 3, Figueroa 4)
Enamorado, 1951 (Infante 3, Figueroa 4)
Enchanted April, 1935 (Cronjager 4, Hoffenstein 4, MacGowan 4, Plunkett 4, Steiner 4)
Enchanted Barn, 1919 (Love 3)
Enchanted Basket. *See* Corbeille enchantée, 1903
Enchanted Castle in Dudinci, 1952 (Vukotić 4)
Enchanted Cottage, 1924 (Barthelmess 3)
Enchanted Cottage, 1945 (Cromwell 2, Marshall 3, Young, R. 3, Bodeen 4, Mankiewicz 4)
Enchanted Desna. *See* Zacharovannaya Desna, 1965
Enchanted Drawing, 1900 (Blackton 2, Porter 2)
Enchanted Forest, 1945 (D'Agostino 4)
Enchanted Hill, 1926 (Arlen 3, Cooper, Gary 3)
Enchanted Island, 1927 (Walthall 3)
Enchanted Island, 1958 (Dwan 2, Andrews D. 3)
Enchanted Island. *See* Madol Duwa, 1976
Enchanted Sedan Chair. *See* Chaise à porteurs enchantée, 1905
Enchanted Well. *See* Puits fantastique, 1903
Enchanteur Alcofrisbas, 1903 (Méliès 2)
Enchantment, 1916 (Borzage 2)
Enchantment, 1921 (Davies 3)
Enchantment, 1948 (Carroll L. 3, Niven 3, Wright 3, Friedhofer 4, Goldwyn 4, Head 4, Jenkins 4, Mandell 4, Toland 4)
Encore, 1951 (Clarke, T.E.B. 4)
Encore Paris, 1965 (Jarre 4)
Encounter. *See* Imbarco a mezzanotte, 1952
Encounter. *See* Stranger on the Prowl, 1952
Encounter at the Elbe. *See* Vstrecha na Elbe, 1949
Encrucijada para una monja, 1967 (Fusco 4)
Encuentro: la salacion, 1965 (Gómez, M. 2)
Encyclopédie filmée—Alchimie, Azur, Absence, 1952 (Grémillon 2)
End, 1978 (Field 3, Loy 3, Martin, S. 3, O'Brien, P. 3, Reynolds, B. 3 Woodward 3, Williams, J. 4)
End. *See* Slut, 1966
End as a Man, 1957 (Spiegel 4)
End as a Man. *See* Strange One, 1957
End of a Circle, 1913 (Anderson G. 3)
End of a Clairvoyant. *See* Konec jasnovidce, 1958
End of a Day. *See* Fin du jour, 1939
End of a Priest. *See* Farářuv konec, 1968
End of a Prolonged Journey. *See* Hana no nagadosu, 1954
End of an Era. *See* Yuganthayo, 1983
End of Arthur's Marriage, 1965 (Loach 2)
End of Battle Fire. *See* Senka no hate, 1950
End Of Dawn, 1964 (Warhol 2)
End of Day. *See* Fin du jour, 1938
End of Desire. *See* Vie, 1958
End of Innocence. *See* Casa del ángel, 1957
End of St. Petersburg. *See* Konyets Sankt-Peterburga, 1927
End of Summer. *See* Kohayagawa-ke no aki, 1961
End of the Affair, 1955 (Dmytryk 2, Cushing 3, Johnson, V. 3, Kerr Mills 3, Coffee 4)
End of the Chieftain, 1970 (Mikhalkov-Konchalovski 2)

End of the Feud, 1912 (Dwan 2, Bushman 3)
End of the Feud, 1914 (Dwan 2, Chaney Lon 3)
End of the Game. See Richter und sein Henker, 1975
End of the Night. See Koniec nocy, 1957
End of the Rainbow. See Northwest Outpost, 1947
End of the Road, 1954 (Addison 4)
End of the Road, 1969 (Jones, J.E. 3, Keach 3, Willis 4)
End of the Romance, 1912 (Bosworth 3)
End of the Tour, 1917 (Barrymore L. 3)
End of the Trail, 1916 (Farnum 3)
End of the World, 1924 (Edeson 4)
End of the World, 1978 (Lee, C. 3)
End of the World in Our Usual Bed in a Night Full of Rain, 1978
  (Wertmüller 2, Giannini 3)
Enda natt, 1938 (Molander 2, Bergman 3)
Ende eines Wintermarchens. See Hitler. Ein Film aus Deutschland,
  1977
Ende vom Lied, 1914 (Porten 3, Messter 4)
Ende von Liede, 1919 (Nielsen 3)
Endelig Alene, 1914 (Holger-Madsen 2)
Endise, 1974 (Guney 2)
Endless Desire. See Hateshinaki yokubo, 1958
Endless Deviltry. See Zrak, 1978
Endless Love, 1981 (Zeffirelli 2, Watkin 4)
Endless Night, 1972 (Sanders 3, Gilliat 4, Herrmann 4)
Endless Passion. See Hateshinaki jonetsu, 1949
Endormi, 1963 (Braunberger 4)
Endowing Your Future, 1957 (Allen, D. 4)
Endstation Freiheit, 1980 (Hauff 2)
Eneide, 1970 (Storaro 4)
Enemies. See Vragi, 1977
Enemies of Children, 1923 (Boyd 3, Nilsson 3)
Enemies of Society. See Big Brain, 1933
Enemies of the People. See Public Enemy, 1931
Enemies of Women, 1923 (Crosland 2, Barrymore L. 3, Bow 3)
Enemy, 1927 (Niblo 2, Gish, L. 3, McCrea 3, Booth 4, Day 4,
  Gibbons 4)
Enemy. See Dusman, 1979
Enemy Agent, 1940 (Salter 4)
Enemy Agent. See British Intelligence, 1940
Enemy Air Attack. See Tekki kushu, 1943
Enemy Below, 1957 (Jurgens 3, Mitchum 3, Powell, D. 3, Lemaire 4,
  Rosson 4)
Enemy from Space. See Quatermass II, 1957
Enemy General, 1960 (Aumont 3, Johnson, V. 3, Katzman 4)
Enemy Mine, 1985 (Gossett 3)
Enemy of Soap, 1918 (Roach 4)
Enemy of the People, 1977 (Andersson B. 3, McQueen, S. 3, Lourié 4,
  Rosenman 4)
Enemy of the People. See Minshu no teki, 1946
Enemy of Women, 1944 (Alton, J. 4)
Enemy Sex, 1924 (Cruze 2, Brown, K. 4)
Energie et vous, 1961 (Storck 2)
Energy First, 1955 (Anderson 2)
Energy Picture, 1959 (Halas and Batchelor 2)
Enez Eussa, 1961 (Delerue 4)
Enfance de l'art, 1910 (Cohl 2)
Enfant aimé, 1971 (Akerman 2)
Enfant au fennec, 1956 (Decaë 4)
Enfant de l'amour, 1929 (L'Herbier 2, Simon, M. 3)
Enfant de la barricade. See Sur la barricade, 1907
Enfant de la roulotte, 1914 (Feuillade 2)
Enfant de la tourmente. See Retour au bonheur, 1939
Enfant de ma soeur, 1932 (Artaud 3)
Enfant du carnaval, 1921 (Mozhukin 3, Vanel 3)
Enfant du carnaval, 1934 (Mozhukin 3)
Enfant du miracle, 1932 (Fradetal 4)
Enfant et chien, 1896-7 (Lumière 2)
Enfant sauvage, 1969 (Truffaut 2, Almendros 4, Guillemot 4)
Enfants, 1985 (Gélin 3)
Enfants au bord de la mer, 1896-97 (Lumière 2)
Enfants aux jouets, 1895 (Lumière 2)
Enfants de l'amour, 1953 (Kosma 4)

Enfants de la peur. See Os filhos do medo, 1978
Enfants dorment la nuit, 1948 (Colpi 4)
Enfants du miracle, 1903–04 (Guy 2)
**Enfants du paradis, 1945 (Carné 2, Arletty 3, Barrault 3, Brasseur 3,
  Modot 3, Barsacq 4, Kosma 4, Prévert 4, Trauner 4)**
Enfants du silence, 1963 (Jutra 2)
Enfants gâtés, 1977 (Tavernier 2, Huppert 3, Piccoli 3, Sarde 4)
Enfants terribles, 1950 (Cocteau 2, Melville 2, Decaë 4)
Enfer de Dien Bien Phu. See Jump Into Hell, 1955
Enfer de Rodin, 1957 (Alekan 4)
Enfer des anges, 1939 (Christian-Jaque 2, Blier 3, D'Eaubonne 4,
  Renoir 4)
Enfer du jeu, 1939 (Douy 4)
Enforcer, 1951 (Walsh 2, Bogart 3, Sloane 3)
Enforcer, 1975 (Eastwood 3)
Engagement. See Fidanzati, 1963
Engagement Italiano, 1965 (Brazzi 3)
Engagement Italiano. See Ragazza in prestito, 1965
Engagement Ring, 1911 (Sennett 2)
Engagement Ring. See Konyaku yubiwa, 1950
Engeiji ringu, 1950 (Tanaka 3)
Engeiji ringu. See Konyaku yubiwa, 1950
Engel auf Erden, 1959 (Schneider 3, Braunberger 4, D'Eaubonne 4)
Engel auf Erden. See Mademoiselle Ange, 1959
Engel aus Eisen, 1981 (Lassally 4)
Engel mit der Posaune, 1948 (Jurgens 3, Schell, Maria 3, Werner 3)
Engelein, 1913 (Gad 2, Nielsen 3, Freund 4, Kraly 4)
Engeleins Hochzeit, 1914 (Gad 2, Nielsen 3, Freund 4)
Engineer Kochin's Mistake. See Oshibka inzheneva Kochina, 1939
Engineer Prite's Project. See Proyekt inzhenera Praita, 1918
England Made Me, 1972 (Finch 3, York, M. 3)
Englische Heirat, 1934 (Walbrook 3)
English Potter, 1933 (Flaherty 2)
English Without Tears, 1944 (Dauphin 3, Rutherford 3)
Englishman and the Girl, 1910 (Griffith 2, Sennett 2, Pickford 3,
  Bitzer 4, Ince 4)
Englishman's Home, 1939 (Gwenn 3, Henreid 3)
Engrenage, 1919 (Feuillade 2)
Enhorningen, 1955 (Molander 2)
Enigma, 1983 (Sheen 3)
Enigmatique Monsieur Parkes, 1930 (Colbert 3, Menjou 3)
Enigme, 1919 (Feuillade 2)
Enigme de dix heures, 1916 (Gance 2, Burel 4)
Enjo, 1958 (Ichikawa 2, Miyagawa 4)
Enlevement de Dejanire Goldebois, 1917 (Cohl 2)
Enlèvement en automobile et mariage précipité, 1903 (Guy 2)
Enlèvement en hydroplane, 1913 (Linders 3)
Enlevez-moi, 1932 (Arletty 3, Douy 4)
Enlisted Man's Honor, 1911 (Guy 2)
Enmeiin no semushiotoko, 1924 (Tsuburaya 4)
Ennemi public, 1937 (Storck 2)
Ennemi public no. 1, 1953 (Verneuil 2, Fernandel 3, Audiard 4,
  Rota 4)
Ennemis, 1960 (Brasseur 3)
Enoch Arden, 1911 (Griffith 2, Bitzer 4, Macpherson 4)
Enoch Arden, 1915 (Gish, L. 3, Reid 3)
Enola Gay: The Men, The Mission, The Atomic Bomb, 1980 (Jarre 4)
Enormous Changes at the Last Minute, 1985 (Sayles 4)
Enough of It. See Huskors, 1914
Enough Rope. See Meurtrier, 1963
Enough to Do, 1925 (Hardy 3, Laurel 3)
Enquête aboutit, 1954 (Colpi 4)
Enquête de l'inspecteur Morgan. See Blind Date,
  1959
Enquête sur le 58, 1944 (Gélin 3, Vanel 3)
Enquiry into General Practice, 1959 (Lassally 4)
Enredate y veras, 1948 (Alcoriza 4)
Enredos de papá, 1938 (García 3)
Enredos de una gallega, 1951 (Alcoriza 4)
Enrico Caruso, leggenda di una voce, 1951 (Lollobrigida 3)
Enrico cuisinier, 1955 (Grimault 4)
Enrico IV, 1984 (Mastroianni 3)
Ensayo de un crimen, 1955 (Buñuel 2)

Ensign Pulver, 1964 (Logan 2, Matthau 3, Nicholson 3, Duning 4, Jeakins 4, Reynolds 4)
Ensom Kvinde, 1914 (Blom 2)
Entanglement. *See* Karami-ai, 1962
Entebbe. *See* Operation Thunderbolt, 1977
Entebbe: Operation Thunderbolt, 1977 (Kinski 3)
Entends-tu les chiens aboyer?, 1974 (Reichenbach 2, Vangelis 4)
Entente cordiale, 1939 (L'Herbier 2, Fradetal 4)
Enter Laughing, 1966 (Ferrer, J. 3, Winters 3, Biroc 4, Jones 4)
Enter Madam!, 1935 (Grant, C. 3, Sheridan 3, Banton 4, Brackett, C. 4, Dreier 4, Glazer 4)
Enter the Dragon, 1973 (Lee, B. 3, Schifrin 4)
Enter the Ninja, 1981 (Golan and Globus 4)
Enterrement de Kennedy, 1963 (Reichenbach 2)
Entertainer, 1960 (Richardson 2, Yates 2, Bates 3, Finney 3, Olivier 3, Addison 4, Morris 4)
Entertainer, 1976 (Lemmon 3, Reynolds 4)
Entfesselte Wein. *See* Seine Hoheit, der Eintanzer, 1927
Entfuhrung, 1936 (Frohlich 3)
Enthusiasm: Symphony of the Don Basin. *See* Entuziazm: Simfoniia Donbassa, 1931
Enticement, 1925 (Astor 3, Brook 3, Ince 4)
Entire Days in the Trees. *See* Des Journées entières dans les arbres, 1976
Entity, 1983 (Bernstein 4)
Entlassung, 1942 (Jannings 3, Krauss 3, Wagner 4)
Entlassung auf Bewarung, 1965 (Domrose 3)
Entotsu no mieru basho, 1953 (Gosho 2, Takamine 3, Tanaka 3)
Entr'acte, 1924 (Clair 2, Braunberger 4)
Entrainement du toréro, 1968 (Braunberger 4)
Entraîneuse, 1938 (Morgan 3, Spaak 4)
Entre Calais et Douvres, 1897 (Méliès 2)
Entre ciel et terre, 1977 (Reichenbach 2)
Entre deux trains, 1947–51 (Verneuil 2)
Entre Hermanos, 1944 (Armendáriz 3)
Entre Kampuchea y Vietnam, 1978 (Alvarez 2)
Entre la mer et l'eau douce, 1967 (Bujold 3)
Entre la terre et le ciel, 1959 (Delerue 4, Rappeneau 4)
Entre monjas anda el diablo, 1972 (García 3)
Entre nous, 1983 (Huppert 3)
Entre onze heures et minuit, 1948 (Jouvet 3, Jeanson 4)
Entre Seine et mer, 1960 (Leenhardt 2)
Entrée des artistes, 1938 (Allégret, M. 2, Cayatte 2, Blier 3, Dalio 3, Dauphin 3, Jouvet 3, Auric 4, Jeanson 4, Matras 4, Trauner 4)
Entrega immediata, 1963 (Cantinflas 3, Figueroa 4)
Entres angen, ur Dollarprinsessan, 1910 (Magnusson 4)
Entuziazm: Simfoniia Donbassa, 1931 (Vertov 2)
Envers du paradis, 1953 (Von Stroheim 2, Burel 4)
Eo kaku kodomotachi, 1955 (Hani 2)
Eolomea, 1972 (Hoppe 3)
Epatozoides, 1968 (Foldès 4)
Eperon d'or, 1930 (Matras 4)
Epervier, 1933 (L'Herbier 2, Boyer 3, Marais 3)
Epic That Never Was, 1963 (Bogarde 3)
Epidemic, 1914 (Beery 3)
Epidemic. *See* Járvány, 1975
Epilepsy, 1976 (Benegal 2)
Epilog, 1950 (Kortner 3)
Episode, 1935 (Reisch 4, Stradling 4)
Episode of Cloudy Canyon, 1913 (Anderson G. 3)
Epistemology of Jean Piaget. *See* Jean Piaget, 1977
Epitaph to My Love. *See* Waga koi no tabiji, 1961
Epitome. *See* Shukuzu, 1953
Epoch of Loyalty. *See* Kinno jidai, 1926
Epouse infernale, 1963 (Braunberger 4)
Epouvantail, 1943 (Aurenche 4, Grimault 4)
Epoux célibataires, 1933 (Robison 2)
Epoux scandaleux, 1935 (Spaak 4)
Epreuve, 1914 (Feuillade 2)
Equilibre, 1952 (Ibert 4)
Equilibriste, 1902 (Guy 2)

Equine Spy, 1912 (Guy 2)
Equinox Flower. *See* Higanbana, 1958
Equipage, 1927 (Tourneur, M. 2, Burel 4)
Equipage, 1935 (Litvak 2, Aumont 3, Vanel 3, Honegger 4, Jaubert 4)
Equivoque 1900, 1966 (Braunberger 4)
Equus, 1977 (Lumet 2, Burton 3, Morris 4)
Er du grønlaender. *See* Kaláliuvit, 1970
Er i bange, 1971 (Carlsen 2, Roos 2)
Er oder Dich. *See* Seine grosster Bluff, 1927
Er oder ich. *See* Seine grosster Bluff, 1927
Er tilladt at vaere åndssvag, 1969 (Roos 2)
Er und seine Schwester, 1931 (Ondra 3)
Era di venerdi 17, 1956 (Sordi 3, Zavattini 4)
Era lui, si! si!, 1951 (Loren 3, Delli Colli 4, Rota 4)
Era notte a Roma, 1960 (Rossellini 2, Bondarchuk 3)
Eradicating Auntie, 1909 (Griffith 2, Bitzer 4)
Eraku nare, 1932 (Naruse 2)
Eran trecento, 1952 (Brazzi 3)
Erbe der Van Diemen, 1921 (Hoffmann 4)
Erbe von Pretoria, 1934 (Grundgens 3)
Erbföster, 1915 (Dieterle 2)
Ercole al centro della terra, 1961 (Lee, C. 3)
Ercole alla conquista di Alantide, 1961 (Volonté 3)
Erdei sportverseny, 1951 (Macskássy 4)
Erdgeist, 1923 (Basserman 3, George, H. 3, Nielsen 3, Mayer 4)
Eredità Ferramonti, 1976 (Bolognini 2, Quinn 3, Sanda 3, Morricone 4)
Ereji, 1951 (Mifune 3)
Eremitten. *See* Syndig Kaerlighed, 1915
Erendira, 1983 (Guerra 2, Papas 3)
Erfinder, 1980 (Ganz 3)
Eric, 1975 (Neal 3)
Eric the Great. *See* Last Performance, 1928
Eric Winstone's Coach, 1957 (Unsworth 4)
Eriki no wakadaisho, 1966 (Tanaka 3)
Eriko to tomoni, 1951 (Yamamura 3)
Erkel, 1952 (Darvas 3, Gábor 3)
Erlebnisse einer Nacht, 1930 (Baranovskaya 3, Warm 4)
Ernani, 1911 (Bertini 3)
Ernest Hemingway's Adventures of a Young Man, 1962 (Garmes 4)
Ernest le rebelle, 1938 (Christian-Jaque 2, Fernandel 3, Prévert 4)
Ernst Fuchs, 1976 (Lassally 4)
Ernst Thalman Fuhrer seiner Klasse, 1955 (Piccoli 3)
Eroberung der Zitadelle, 1977 (Wicki 2)
Eroe dei nostri tempi, 1955 (Lattuada 2, Monicelli 2, Sordi 3, Cristaldi 4, Fusco 4, Rota 4)
Eroe sono io, 1951 (Age and Scarpelli 4)
Erogami no onryo, 1930 (Ozu 2)
Erogeny, 1976 (Broughton 2)
Eroi della domenica, 1952 (Risi 2, Mastroianni 3, Solinas 4)
Eroica, 1949 (Werner 3)
Eroica, 1957 (Munk 2, Lomnicki 3, Stawinsky 4)
Eroica, 1960 (Lassally 4)
Eroica—Polen 44. *See* Eroica, 1957
Eroismo d'amore, 1914 (Bertini 3)
Eroit mousquetairè. *See* Three Must-Get-Theres, 1922
Eros, O Basileus, 1967 (Markopoulos 2)
Erotic Tales. *See* Cuentos eróticos, 1979
Erotica. *See* Amore difficile, 1960
Erotikon, 1920 (Stiller 2, Magnusson 4)
Erotikon, 1929 (Hammid 2, Vích 4)
Erotique. *See* Erotyk, 1960
Erotissimo, 1968 (Girardot 3, Braunberger 4)
Erotyk, 1960 (Skolimowski 2)
Errand Boy, 1961 (Lewis 2, Head 4)
Erreur de poivrot, 1904 (Guy 2)
Erreur judiciaire, 1899–1900 (Guy 2)
Erreur judiciaire, 1947 (Dalio 3)
Erreur tragique, 1913 (Feuillade 2)
Ersatz, 1961 (Vukotić 4)
Ersbsunde. *See* Vererbte Triebe: Der Kampf ums neue Geschlecht, 1929
Erste April 2000, 1952 (Jurgens 3)

Erste Fruhlingstag, 1956 (Frohlich 3)
Erste Kuss, 1928 (Ondra 3)
Erste Liebe, 1970 (Sanda 3, Schell, Maximilian 3, Nykvist 4)
Erste Liebe. See First Love, 1970
Erste Polka, 1979 (Schell, Maria 3)
Erste Recht des Kindes, 1932 (Planer 4, Von Harbou 4)
Erteil des Arztes, 1914 (Basserman 3)
Eruption of Mount Pelée. See Eruption volcanique à la Martinique, 1902
Eruption volcanique à la Martinique, 1902 (Méliès 2)
Erzieherin gesucht, 1950 (Von Harbou 4)
Es akkor a pasas . . ., 1966 (Torocsik 3)
Es blasen die Trompetten, 1926 (Albers 3)
Es flustert die liebe, 1935 (Frohlich 3)
Es flustert die Nacht, 1929 (Dagover 3)
Es geschah am 20 Juli, 1955 (Pabst 2, Wicki 2)
Es geschah am hellichten Tag, 1959 (Simon, M. 3)
Es geschehen noch Wunder, 1952 (Knef 3, Vích 4)
Es gibt eine Frau, die Dich niemals vergisst, 1930 (Dagover 3)
Es kommt alle Tage vor . . ., 1930 (Warm 4)
Es kommt ein Tag, 1950 (Dagover 3, Schell, Maria 3, Von Harbou 4)
Es leuchten die Sterne, 1938 (Tschechowa 3)
Es leuchtet meine Liebe, 1922 (Dieterle 2)
Es nálunk lehtetlen, 1965 (Macskássy 4)
Es war eine rauschende Ballnacht, 1939 (Rasp 3)
Es war einmal ein Walzer, 1932 (Wilder 2)
Es werde Licht, 1917–18 (Dupont 2, Oswald 2, Pick 2, Krauss 3)
Es wird alles wieder gut, 1957 (Wicki 2)
Es wird schon wieder besser, 1932 (Kaper 4, Wagner 4)
Es zogen drei Burschen, 1927 (Albers 3)
Esa pareja feliz, 1951 (Bardem 2, García Berlanga 2, Rey 3)
Escalada del chantaje, 1965 (Alvarez 2)
Escalation, 1968 (Morricone 4)
Escale, 1959 (Delerue 4)
Escale à Paris, 1951 (Decaë 4)
Escale au soleil, 1947 (Verneuil 2, Fernandel 3)
Escalier de service, 1955 (Auer 3, Darrieux 3)
Escalier sans fin, 1943 (Fresnay 3, Matras 4, Spaak 4)
Escambray, 1961 (Alvarez 2)
Escamotage d'une dame chez Robert-Houdin, 1896 (Méliès 2)
Escándalo, 1934 (Figueroa 4)
Escándalo de estrellas, 1944 (Infante 3)
Escapade, 1935 (Powell, W. 3, Rainer 3, Kaper 4, Mankiewicz 4, Reisch 4)
Escapade, 1955 (Mills 3, Sim 3, Stewart 4)
Escapade, 1957 (Jourdan 3, Wakhévitch 4)
Escapade, 1974 (Trintignant 3)
Escapade de Filoche, 1915 (Feuillade 2, Musidora 3)
Escapade in Japan, 1957 (Eastwood 3, Wright 3, Steiner 4)
Escapades of Eva. See Eva tropí hlouposti, 1939
Escape, 1914 (Griffith 2, Crisp 3, Gish, L. 3, Marsh 3, Sweet 3, Bitzer 4)
Escape, 1925 (Florey 2)
Escape, 1930 (Bruce 3, Carroll M. 3, Dean 4)
Escape, 1940 (Leroy 2, Basserman 3, Nazimova 3, Shearer 3, Taylor, R. 3, Veidt 3, Adrian 4, Cronjager 4, Day 4, Waxman 4)
Escape, 1948 (Mankiewicz 2, Cusack 3, Harrison 3, Alwyn 4, Dunne 4, Lemaire 4, Young, F. 4)
Escape, 1971 (Grahame 3, Schifrin 4)
Escape Artist, 1982 (Coogan 3, Delerue 4, Tavoularis 4)
Escape at Dawn. See Akatsuki no dasso, 1950
Escape at Dawn. See Red Sky at Morning, 1945
Escape by Night, 1937 (Bond 3)
Escape Episode, 1944 (Anger 2)
Escape Episode, 1946 (Anger 2)
Escape from Alcatraz, 1979 (Siegel 2, Eastwood 3)
Escape from Andersonville, 1909 (Olcott 2)
Escape from Captivity. See Bekstvo sa robija, 1978
Escape From Dartmoor. See Cottage on Dartmoor, 1929
Escape from Devil's Island, 1935 (Johnson, N. 3)
Escape from East Berlin. See Tunnel 28, 1962
Escape from Fort Bravo, 1953 (Sturges, J. 2, Holden 3, Surtees 4)
Escape from Japan. See Nihon dashutsu, 1964

Escape from New York, 1981 (Carpenter 2, Borgnine 3, Pleasance 3, Stanton 3, Van Cleef 3)
Escape from Prison. See Datsugoku, 1950
Escape from San Quentin, 1957 (Katzman 4)
Escape from the Dark, 1975 (Sim 3)
Escape from the Planet of the Apes, 1971 (McDowall 3, Mineo 3, Biroc 4, Dehn 4, Goldsmith 4, Smith, J.M. 4)
Escape From Yesterday. See Bandera, 1935
Escape from Zahrain, 1962 (Brynner 3, Mason 3, Mineo 3, Warden 3, Fulton 4, Head 4)
Escape in the Desert, 1944 (Florey 2, Deutsch 4)
Escape into Dreams. See Natale al campo 119, 1948
Escape Me Never, 1935 (Czinner 2, Lean 2, Bergner 3, Périnal 4)
Escape Me Never, 1947 (Basserman 3, Flynn 3, Lupino 3, Young, G. 3, Blanke 4, Friedhofer 4, Korngold 4, Polito 4, Prinz 4)
Escape of Jim Dolan, 1913 (Mix 3)
Escape of Nicholas and Alexandra, 1973 (Fontaine 3)
Escape on the Fog, 1945 (Boetticher 2)
Escape to Athena, 1979 (Cardinale 3, Gould 3, Moore, R. 3, Niven 3, Anhalt 4, Schifrin 4)
Escape to Bermuda, 1955 (Ryan 3)
Escape to Burma, 1955 (Dwan 2, Stanwyck 3, Alton, J. 4, Jennings 4, Polglase 4)
Escape to Danger, 1943 (Alwyn 4, Green, G. 4)
Escape to Glory, 1940 (O'Brien, P. 3, Irene 4, Planer 4)
Escape to Glory. See Submarine Zone, 1940
Escape to Happiness. See Intermezzo, 1939
Escape to Paradise, 1939 (Young, V. 4)
Escape to the Sun, 1972 (Golan and Globus 4)
Escape to the Sun. See Habrichka el hashemersh, 1972
Escape to Victory. See Victory, 1981
Escape to Witch Mountain, 1975 (Milland 3, Pleasance 3)
Escaped the Law, But . . . . See Største Kaerlighed, 1914
Escapes Home. See Útěky domu, 1980
Escapulario, 1966 (Figueroa 4)
Esclave, 1923 (Boyer 3)
Esclave, 1953 (Gélin 3, Auric 4)
Esclave blanche, 1927 (Vanel 3)
Esclave blanche, 1938 (Dalio 3, Alekan 4, Andrejew 4, Jaubert 4)
Escondida, 1955 (Armendáriz 3, Félix 3, Figueroa 4)
Escondido, 1968 (Ryan 3)
Escondido. See Minuto per pregare, un instante per morire, 1968
Esconocido. See Playa prohibida, 1955
Escopeta nacional, 1978 (García Berlanga 2)
Escort West, 1959 (Mature 3, Clothier 4)
Escuadró de la muerte, 1966 (Crawford, B. 3)
Escuela de música, 1955 (Infante 3)
Escuela de rateros, 1956 (Infante 3, Alcoriza 4)
Escuela de sordomudos, 1967 (Guzmán 2)
Escuela de vagabundos, 1954 (Infante 3)
Escuela para solteras, 1964 (García 3, Figueroa 4)
Escuela rural, 1960 (Almendros 4)
Esecutori, 1976 (Keach 3, Moore, R. 3)
Esercito di cinque uomini, 1969 (Argento 4, Morricone 4)
Esfinge de cristal, 1968 (Taylor, R. 3)
Eshaet Hub, 1960 (Sharif 3)
Eskapade, 1936 (Von Harbou 4)
Eskimo, 1933 (Van Dyke, W.S. 2, Gillespie 4, Mahin 4)
Eskimo Limon, 1977 (Golan and Globus 4)
Eskimo Limon 6. See Eskimo Ohgen, 1985
Eskimo Ohgen, 1985 (Golan and Globus 4)
Eskimo Village, 1933 (Grierson 2)
Eskimo-Baby, 1917 (Nielsen 3)
Eskiya celladi, 1967 (Guney 2)
Esleuchten die Sterne, 1938 (Tschechowa 3)
Esli khochesh byt schastlivym, 1974 (Shukshin 3)
Esli var vrag ne sdaetsia, 1982 (Ulyanov 3)
Esmeralda, 1905 (Guy 2)
Esmerelda, 1915 (Pickford 3)
Espagne 1937, 1937 (Buñuel 2)
España insolita, 1965 (Rey 3)
Espectro de la novia, 1943 (Figueroa 4)
Esperanza, 1972 (Alcoriza 4)

Esperienza del cubismo, 1949 (Delli Colli 4)
Espion, 1966 (Godard 2, McDowall 3, Coutard 4)
Espion. *See* Defector, 1966
Espion, lève-toi, 1981 (Janda 3, Piccoli 3, Audiard 4, Morricone 4)
Espionage, 1937 (Lukas 3)
Espionage Agent, 1939 (Bacon 2, McCrea 3, Buckner 4, Deutsch 4, Rosher 4)
Espions, 1957 (Clouzot 2, Jaffe 3, Jurgens 3, Ustinov 3, Auric 4, Matras 4)
Espions. *See* Spione, 1928
Espoir au village, 1950 (Cloquet 4)
Espontánes, 1963 (Rey 3)
Esquadrón 201, 1945 (García 3)
Esqueleto de la señora Morales, 1959 (Alcoriza 4)
Esrefpasali, 1966 (Guney 2)
Essay on Rehearsing. *See* Etude o zkoušce, 1976
Essene, 1972 (Wiseman 2)
Esso, 1954 (Alexeïeff and Parker 2)
Essor, 1920 (Fresnay 3)
Esta tierra nuestra, 1959 (Gutiérrez 2)
Estafa de amor, 1954 (Figueroa 4)
Estambul 65, 1965 (Kinski 3)
Estampida, 1971 (Alvarez 2)
Estate in quattro, 1969 (Andersson B. 3, Bjornstrand 3)
Estate violenta, 1959 (Zurlini 2, Trintignant 3, D'Amico 4)
Est-ce bien raisonnable, 1980 (Audiard 4, Decaë 4)
Esther, 1910 (Feuillade 2)
Esther, 1962 (Eisler 4)
Esther and the King, 1960 (Walsh 2)
Esther Waters, 1948 (Bogarde 3, Cusack 3, Dalrymple 4)
Estouffade à la Carabei, 1967 (Seberg 3)
Estrangeira, 1981 (Branco 4)
Estrella vacia, 1958 (Félix 3)
Estudantes, 1935 (Miranda 3)
Et cetera, 1966 (Švankmajer 4)
Et crac!, 1969 (Chabrol 2)
Et Dieu créa la femme, 1956 (Vadim 2, Bardot 3, Jurgens 3, Trintignant 3)
Et moi j'te dis qu'elle t'a fait de l'oeil, 1935 (Berry 3)
Et mourir de plaisir, 1960 (Allégret, M. 2, Vadim 2, Ferrer, M. 3, Renoir 4)
Et per tetto un cielo di stelle, 1968 (Morricone 4)
Et quand vient le soir, 1969 (Braunberger 4)
. . . Et Satan conduit le bal, 1962 (Deneuve 3, Coutard 4)
Et si nous buvions un coup, 1908 (Cohl 2)
Et si on faisait l'amour. *See* Scusi, facciamo l'amore, 1968
Et sommereventyr, 1919 (Schenstrom 3)
Et ta soeur?, 1958 (Arletty 3, Cassel 3, Fresnay 3)
Eta del ferro, 1964 (Rossellini 2)
Età dell'amore, 1953 (Fabrizi 3)
Etait une chaise. *See* Chairy Tale, 1957 (Jutra 2)
Etalon, 1969 (Bourvil 3)
Etat de siège, 1972 (Costa-Gavras 2, Montand 3, Solinas 4, Theodorakis 4)
Etat sauvage, 1978 (Piccoli 3)
Etc., 1975 (Breer 2)
Eté indien, 1957 (Reichenbach 2, Braunberger 4)
Eté meurtrier, 1983 (Adjani 3, Delerue 4)
Eterna agonía, 1949 (García 3)
Eterna femmina, 1953 (Lamarr 3)
Eterna femmina. *See* Femmina, 1953
Eternal City, 1915 (Porter 2)
Eternal City, 1923 (Barrymore L. 3, Colman 3, Goldwyn 4, Miller, A. 4)
Eternal Fire, 1937–40 (Cardiff 4)
Eternal Flame, 1922 (Menjou 3, Talmadge, N. 3, Gaudio 4, Marion 4, Schenck 4)
Eternal Grind, 1916 (Pickford 3)
Eternal Love, 1929 (Lubitsch 2, Barrymore J. 3, Bosworth 3, Kraly 4, Schenck 4)
Eternal Love. *See* Elet, halál, szerelem, 1929
Eternal Love. *See* Liang Shan-po yü Chu Ying-t'ai, 1963
Eternal Melodies. *See* Melodie eterne, 1940

Eternal Mother, 1911 (Griffith 2, Normand 3, Sweet 3, Bitzer 4)
Eternal Mother, 1917 (Barrymore E. 3)
Eternal Prague, 1941 (Weiss 2)
Eternal Question, 1916 (Oland 3)
Eternal Rainbow. *See* Kono ten no niji, 1958
Eternal Sappho, 1916 (Bara 3)
Eternal Sea, 1955 (Hayden 3, Bernstein 4)
Eternal Sin, 1917 (Brenon 2, Barthelmess 3, Hunt 4)
Eternal Struggle, 1923 (Adorée 3, Beery 3)
Eternal Three, 1923 (Neilan 2, Bosworth 3, Love 3, Wilson, C. 4)
Eternal Triangle, 1910 (Lawrence 3)
Eternal Triangle, 1922 (Terry 4)
Eternal Waltz. *See* Ewiger Walzer, 1954
Eternal Woman, 1929 (Walker 4)
Eternally Yours, 1939 (Garnett 2, Arden 3, Burke 3, Crawford, B. 3, Niven 3, Pitts 3, Young, L. 3, Banton 4, Irene 4, Wanger 4)
Eternel conflit, 1947 (Modot 3, Barsacq 4, Matras 4, Spaak 4)
Eternel Retour, 1943 (Cocteau 2, Delannoy 2, Marais 3, Annenkov 4, Auric 4, Wakhévitch 4)
Eternity of Love. *See* Wakarete ikirutokimo, 1961
Etes-vous fiancée à un marin grec ou à un pilote de ligne?, 1970 (Fabian 3, Braunberger 4, Coutard 4)
Etes-vous jalouse?, 1937 (Kaufman 4)
Ethel Gets Consent, 1914–15 (Browning 2)
Ethel's Romeos, 1915 (Hardy 3)
Ethel's Teacher, 1914 (Browning 2)
Ethnographical Museum. *See* Skansen, 1978
Etienne of the Glad Heart, 1914 (Mix 3)
Etirage des ampoules électriques, 1924 (Grémillon 2)
Etnocidio: notas sobre el Mezquital, 1978 (Leduc 2)
Eto sluchilos v militsii, 1963 (Ulyanov 3)
Etoile au soleil, 1942 (Bost 4)
Etoile de mer, 1926 (Artaud 3)
Etoile de mer, 1959 (Delerue 4)
Etoile de mer, 1967 (Braunberger 4)
Etoile de Valencia, 1933 (Gabin 3, Simon, S. 3)
Etoile disparait, 1932 (Delannoy 2)
Etoile disparaît, 1932 (Delannoy 2)
Etoile du nord, 1982 (Noiret 3, Signoret 3, Aurenche 4, Sarde 4)
Etoile du sud, 1969 (Segal 3, Coutard 4)
Etoile filant, 1930 (Brasseur 3)
Etoile sans lumière, 1945 (Berry 3, Montand 3, Reggiani 3, D'Eaubonne 4)
Etoiles. *See* Sterne, 1959
Etoiles de Midi, 1959 (Jarre 4)
Etoiles ne meurent jamais, 1957 (Raimu 3)
Etrange Affaire, 1981 (Baye 3, Piccoli 3)
Etrange aventure de Lemmy Caution. *See* Alphaville, 1965
Etrange Désir de M. Bard, 1953 (Simon, M. 3, Burel 4)
Etrange destin, 1945 (Burel 4)
Etrange Madame X, 1951 (Grémillon 2, Morgan 3)
Etrange Mr. Steve, 1957 (Moreau 3)
Etrange Monsieur Victor, 1938 (Grémillon 2, Raimu 3, Achard 4, Spaak 4)
Etrange Suzy, 1941 (Dauphin 3)
Etranger. *See* Straniero, 1967
Etrangère, 1930 (Burel 4, Meerson 4)
Etruscologia (profanatori di tombe), 1961 (Storaro 4)
Etsuraku, 1965 (Oshima 2)
Ett brott, 1940 (Borgstrom 3)
Ett hemligt giftermål eller Bekannelsen på dodsbadden, 1912 (Borgstrom 3)
Etta of the Footlights, 1914 (Costello, D. 3, Costello, M. 3)
Ettaro di cielo, 1958 (Mastroianni 3, Cristaldi 4, Di Venanzo 4, Flaiano 4, Guerra 4, Rota 4)
Ettore Fieramosca, 1938 (Blasetti 2, Cervi 3, Vích 4)
Ettore lo fusto, 1972 (De Sica 2, Giannini 3)
Etuda, 1962 (Hofman 4)
Etuda o zkoušce, 1976 (Schorm 2)
Etude, 1961 (Gaál 2)
Etude cinégraphique sur une arabesque, 1929 (Dulac 2)
Etudes de mouvements, 1928 (Ivens 2)
Etudiante d'aujourd'hui, 1966 (Rohmer 2)

Everything Happens at Night, 1939 (Cummings 3, Henie 3, Milland 3, Brown, Harry Joe 4, Cronjager 4, Day 4)
Everything I Have Is Yours, 1953 (Mercer 4)
Everything Is Thunder, 1936 (Bennett C. 3, Homolka 3, Balcon 4, Junge 4)
Everything Remains for the People. *See* Vse ostaetsia lyudyam, 1963
Everything That Lives. *See* Ikitoshi Ikerumono, 1934
Everything Turns, Everything Revolves. *See* Alles dreht sich, alles bewegt sich, 1928–29
Everything You Always Wanted to Know About Sex, 1972 (Allen 2, Carradine 3, Quayle 3, Reynolds, B. 3, Wilder 3)
Everything's Ducky, 1962 (Cooper, J 3, Rooney 3)
Everything's Rosie, 1931 (Bruckman 4, Musuraca 4)
Everywoman, 1919 (Daniels 3)
Everywoman's Husband, 1918 (Swanson 3)
Everywoman's Man. *See* Prizefighter and the Lady, 1933
Eve's Daughter, 1914 (Ingram 2)
Eve's Daughter, 1918 (Burke 3)
Eves futures, 1963 (Delerue 4)
Eve's Leaves, 1926 (Boyd 3, Miller, A. 4)
Eve's Love Letters, 1926 (Laurel 3, Roach 4)
Eve's Lover, 1925 (Bow 3)
Evette, 1965 (Warhol 2)
Evidence, 1922 (Bennett C. 3)
Evidence, 1929 (Loy 3)
Evidence Enclosed. *See* Settled Out of Court, 1925
Evidence in Camera. *See* Headline Shooter, 1933
Eviga lankar, 1947 (Borgstrom 3)
Evil Eden. *See* Mort en ce jardin, 1956
Evil Eye, 1917 (Sweet 3)
Evil Eye. *See* Ragazza che sapeva troppo, 1962
Evil Genius. *See* Truet Lykke, 1915
Evil Inheritance, 1912 (Dwan 2)
Evil Men Do, 1914 (Ingram 2, Costello, D. 3, Costello, M. 3)
Evil Mind. *See* Clairvoyant, 1935
Evil of Frankenstein, 1964 (Cushing 3, Francis 4)
Evil Roy Slade, 1972 (Rooney 3)
Evil That Men Do, 1985 (Bronson 3, Ferrer, J. 3)
Evil under the Sun, 1981 (Mason 3, McDowall 3, Smith 3, Ustinov 3)
Evil Village. *See* Falu rossza, 1937
Evils of Chinatown. *See* Confessions of an Opium Eater, 1962
Evintrude: Die Geschichte eines Abenteuers, 1914 (Wegener 3)
Eviny Evas Tochter, 1928 (Ondra 3)
Evita Peron, 1981 (Dunaway 3, Ferrer, J. 3)
Evitez le désordre, 1949 (Decaë 4)
Evlalie quitte les champs, 1973 (Lee, C. 3, Seyrig 3, Simon, M. 3)
Evolution, 1925 (Fleischer, M. and D. 2)
Evolution of Fashion,, 1917 (Laurel 3)
Evolution of Life series, 1964 (Halas and Batchelor 2)
Evolution of Percival, 1914 (Talmadge, C. 3)
Ewige Fluch, 1921 (Warm 4)
Ewige Klang, 1943 (Tschechowa 3)
Ewige Maske, 1935 (Tschechowa 3)
Ewige Nacht, 1914 (Gad 2, Nielsen 3, Freund 4, Kraly 4)
Ewige Spiel, 1951 (Warm 4)
Ewiger Walzer, 1954 (Wicki 2)
Ewigkeit von Gestern. *See* Brutalität in Stein, 1960
Exalted Flapper, 1929 (Clarke, C.C. 4)
Examination. *See* Zaliczenie, 1969
Examination Day at School, 1910 (Griffith 2, Pickford 3, Bitzer 4)
Example. *See* Ibret, 1971
Ex-Bad Boy, 1931 (Arthur 3, Brent 3)
Excalibur, 1981 (Boorman 2, Williamson 3)
Excess Baggage, 1928 (Cruze 2, Daves 2, Day 4, Gibbons 4, Marion 4)
Ex-Champ, 1939 (McLaglen 3)
Exchange Is No Robbery, 1898 (Hepworth 2)
Exchange of Wives, 1925 (Adorée 3, Gibbons 4)
Excitement of a Young Day. *See* Wakaki hi no kangeki, 1931
Exciters, 1923 (Daniels 3, Levien 4)
Exciting Adventure. *See* Kouzelné dobrodružství, 1982
Exciting Courtship, 1914 (Browning 2)
Exclusive, 1937 (Farmer 3, MacMurray 3, Glazer 4, Head 4)
Exclusive Story, 1935 (Gillespie 4)

Ex-Convict, 1904 (Porter 2)
Ex-Convict, 1914 (Nilsson 3)
Excursion a Vueltabajo, 1965 (Gomez, S. 2)
Excursion House, 1954 (Van Dyke, W. 2)
Excuse Me, 1925 (Gibbons 4)
Excuse Me . . . *See* Scusi, lei e favorevole o contrario, 1967
Excuse My Dust, 1920 (Wood 2, Reid 3)
Excuse My Dust, 1951 (Darwell 3, Pan 4, Rose 4, Rose 4)
Excuse My Glove, 1925 (Roach 4)
Exécution, 1960 (Cloquet 4)
Execution, 1972 (Robards 3)
Execution, 1985 (Torn 3)
Execution of Private Slovik, 1974 (Sheen 3)
Execution Squad. *See* Mano spietata della legge, 1976
Executioner, 1970 (Homolka 3)
Executioner. *See* Azrail benim, 1968
Executioner. *See* Verdugo, 1963
Executioner's Song, 1982 (Wallach 3)
Executive Action, 1973 (Lancaster 3, Ryan 3, Trumbo 4)
Executive Suite, 1954 (Wise 2, Allyson 3, Calhern 3, Douglas, P. 3, Holden 3, March 3, Pidgeon 3, Stanwyck 3, Winters 3, Gibbons 4, Houseman 4, Lehman 4, Rose 4)
Exemple Etretat, 1962 (Braunberger 4, Delerue 4)
Exile, 1917 (Tourneur, M. 2, Carré 4)
Exile, 1931 (Micheaux 2)
Exile, 1947 (Ophuls 2, Bruce 3, Fairbanks, D. Jr. 3, Planer 4)
Exile of 'Bar-K' Ranch, 1915 (Eason 4)
Exiled. *See* Aeventyrersken, 1914
Exiles, 1923 (Gilbert 3)
Exiles. *See* Landsflyktiga, 1921
Existentialist, 1964 (Emshwiller 2)
Exit Smiling, 1926 (Gibbons 4)
Exit the Vamp, 1921 (Boyd 3)
Ex-Lady, 1933 (Florey 2, Davis 3, Gaudio 4, Orry-Kelly 4, Riskin 4)
Ex-Mrs. Bradford, 1936 (Arthur 3, Powell, W. 3, Hunt 4, Polglase 4, Veiller 4)
Exode, 1910 (Feuillade 2)
Exodus, 1960 (Preminger 2, Cobb 3, Mineo 3, Newman 3, Richardson 3, Saint 3, Bass 4, Day 4, Trumbo 4)
Exo-Man, 1977 (Ferrer, J. 3)
Exorcist, 1973 (Smith, D. , Friedkin 2, Burstyn 3, Cobb 3, McCambridge 3, Von Sydow 3, Baker 4, Roizman 4)
Exorcist II: The Heretic, 1977 (Smith, D. , Boorman 2, Burton 3, Henreid 3, Jones, J.E. 3, Von Sydow 3, Morricone 4, Whitlock
Expectation. *See* Oczekiwanie, 1961
Expedition. *See* Abhijan, 1962
Expensive Husbands, 1937 (Negulesco 2)
Expensive Visit, 1915 (Hardy 3)
Expensive Women, 1931 (Costello, D. 3)
Experience, 1921 (Barthelmess 3, Miller, A. 4, Young, W. 4)
Experiment, 1922 (Brook 3)
Experiment, 1943 (Fric 2)
Experiment in Evil. *See* Testament du Docteur Cordelier, 1959
Experiment in Terror, 1962 (Edwards 2, Ford, G. 3, Remick 3, Mancini 4)
Experiment Perilous, 1944 (Tourneur, J. 2, Brent 3, Lamarr 3, Lukas 3, Dunn 4, Gaudio 4)
Experimental Animation: Peanut Vendor, 1933 (Lye 2)
Experimental Marriage, 1919 (Talmadge, C. 3)
Expert, 1932 (Beavers 3)
Expert's Opinion, 1935 (Havelock-Allan 4)
Expiated Innocence. *See* Sonad oskuld, 1915
Expiation, 1909 (Griffith 2, Bitzer 4)
Expiation, 1915 (Feuillade 2)
Exploit on the Ice. *See* Podvig vo idach, 1928
Exploitation. *See* Eksploatacija, 1971
Exploits de Farfadet, 1916 (Cohl 2)
Exploits de feu-follet, 1912 (Cohl 2)
Exploits of Elaine, 1915 (Barrymore L. 3, White 3)
Explorers, 1931 (Terry 4)
Explosion, 1971 (Coutard 4)
Explosion of a Motor Car, 1900 (Hepworth 2)
Explosive Generation, 1961 (Crosby 4)

Ex-Plumber, 1931 (Arbuckle 3)
Exposed, 1938 (Cortez 4)
Exposed, 1983 (Andersson B. 3, Keitel 3, Decaë 4, Delerue 4)
Exposition de Caricatures. *See* Unforeseen Metamorphosis, 1912–14
Exposition de 1900, 1900 (Méliès 2)
Exposition 1900, 1967 (Allégret, M. 2, Braunberger 4)
Exposition française à Moscou, 1962 (Delerue 4)
Expostulations, 1960–62 (Romero 2)
Exposure, 1958 (Dickinson 2)
Express Sedan. *See* Suttobi kago, 1952
Express Train in a Railway Cutting, 1899 (Hepworth 2)
Expresso Bongo, 1959 (Harvey 3, Mankowitz 4)
Expropriación, 1972–73 (Ruiz 2)
Expropriation. *See* Expropriación, 1972–73
Exquisite Sinner, 1926 (Florey 2, Von Sternberg 2, Adorée 3, Loy 3, Gibbons 4)
Exquisite Thief, 1919 (Browning 2)
Ex-Sweeties, 1931 (Sennett 2, Grable 3)
Extase, 1933 (Lamarr 3, Stallich 4)
Extázis 7-töl 10-ig, 1969 (Kovács 2)
Extenuating Circumstances. *See* Circonstances atténuantes, 1939
Exterminating Angel. *See* Angel exterminador, 1962
Exterminator, 1945 (Terry 4)
Exterminator I, 1984 (Golan and Globus 4)
Extinguished Cinders. *See* Brasa dormida, 1928
Extra, 1962 (Cantinflas 3)
Extra Day, 1956 (Simon, S. 3)
Extra Dollars, 1954 (Holliday 3)
Extra! Extra!, 1922 (Howard 2)
Extra Girl, 1923 (Sennett 2, Normand 3, Hornbeck 4)
Extraconiugale, 1964 (Delli Colli 4)
Extraordinaires Exercices de la famille Coeur-de-Bois, 1912 (Cohl 2)
Extraordinary Child, 1954 (Brakhage 2)
Extraordinary Illusions. *See* Dislocations mystérieuses, 1901
Extraordinary Illusions. *See* Illusions funambulesques, 1903
Extraordinary Incident. *See* Chrezvychainoe proisshestvie, 1958
Extraordinary Seaman, 1968 (Frankenheimer 2, Dunaway 3, Niven 3, Rooney 3, Jarre 4)
Extraordinary Years. *See* Neobyčejná léta, 1952
Extravagante Mission, 1945 (Renoir 4)
Extremities, 1913 (Costello, M. 3, Talmadge, N. 3)
Ex-voto, 1919 (Autant-Lara 2)
Ex-Voto. *See* Diable au coeur, 1927

Eye for an Eye, 1918 (Nazimova 3, Mathis 4)
Eye for an Eye, 1966 (Martin, S. 3, Ballard 4)
Eye for an Eye, 1981 (Lee, C. 3)
Eye for an Eye. *See* Oeil pour oeil, 1957
Eye Myth, 1972 (Brakhage 2)
Eye Myth, 1981 (Brakhage 2)
Eye of Conscience, 1911 (Bosworth 3)
Eye of the Cat, 1969 (Head 4, Schifrin 4)
Eye of the Cat. *See* Attenti al buffone!, 1975
Eye of the Devil, 1966 (Hiller 2, Kerr 3, Niven 3, Pleasance 3)
Eye of the Government, 1914 (Olcott 2)
Eye of the Needle, 1981 (Sutherland 3, Rozsa 4)
Eye of the Needle. *See* Smania addosso, 1963
Eye of the Night, 1916 (Gilbert 3, Sullivan 4)
Eye of the Spider. *See* Occhio del ragno, 1971
Eye on Emily, 1964 (Kanin 4)
Eye That Never Sleeps, 1912 (Bushman 3)
Eye Witness. *See* Your Witness, 1950
Eyes. *See* Desa Nisa, 1972
Eyes in the Night, 1942 (Zinnemann 2, Reed, D. 3, Schary 4)
Eyes of Charles Sand, 1972 (Bennett J. 3)
Eyes of God, 1913 (Weber 2)
Eyes of Hell. *See* Mask, 1961
Eyes of Hollywood, 1949 (Ladd 3)
Eyes of Laura Mars, 1978 (Carpenter 2, Kershner 2, Dunaway 3)
Eyes of Mystery, 1918 (Browning 2)
Eyes of Texas, 1948 (Rogers, R. 3)
Eyes of the Forest, 1923 (Mix 3)
Eyes of the Mummy. *See* Augen der Mumie Ma, 1918
Eyes of the Totem, 1926 (Van Dyke, W.S. 2)
Eyes of the Underworld, 1942 (Chaney Lon, Jr. 3, Salter 4)
Eyes of the World, 1930 (King 2, Merkel 3, Fulton 4)
Eyes of Youth, 1919 (Valentino 3, Edeson 4)
Eyes that Could Not Close, 1913 (Guy 2)
Eyes That See Not, 1912 (Porter 2)
Eyes, The Mouth. *See* Occhi, la bocca, 1983
Eyes Without a Face. *See* Yeux sans visage, 1960
Eyewash, 1959 (Breer 2)
Eyewitness, 1980 (Yates 2, Hurt, W. 3, Tesich 4)
Eygalières, commune de France, 1957 (Braunberger 4)
Ezerkilencszázötvenketto. *See* 8. szabad Május 1, 1952
Ezredes, 1917 (Curtiz 2)
Ezust kecske, 1916 (Curtiz 2)

F

F comme Fairbanks, 1976 (Piccoli 3)
F for Fake, 1975 (Bogdanovich 2, Reichenbach 2, Welles 2, Cotten 3, Harvey 3, Legrand 4)
F. Scott Fitzgerald and the Last of the Belles, 1974 (Sarandon 3)
F. Scott Fitzgerald in Hollywood, 1976 (Weld 3)
F.I.S.T., 1978 (Jewison 2, Stallone 3, Steiger 3, Kovacs 4)
F.P.1 antwortet nicht, 1932 (Albers 3, Lorre 3, Veidt 3, Pommer 4, Reisch 4, Siodmak 4)
F.P.1. *See* F.P. 1 antwortet nicht, 1932
F.P.1 Does Not Answer. *See* F.P. 1 antwortet nicht, 1932
F.P.1 Does Not Reply. *See* F.P.1 antwortet nicht, 1932
F.P.1 ne répond plus, 1932 (Boyer 3, Brasseur 3)
F.T.A., 1972 (Fonda, J. 3, Trumbo 4)
F.T.A. *See* FTA Show, 1972
Fabbrica del Duomo, 1948 (Risi 2)
Fábián Bálint találkozása Istennel, 1979 (Fábri 2)
Fabiola, 1948 (Blasetti 2, Cervi 3, Morgan 3, Simon, M. 3, D'Amico 4, Zavattini 4)
Fabiola, 1960 (Rey 3)
Fable. *See* Brsna, 1979

Fable of Elvira and Farina and the Meal Ticket, 1915 (Swanson 3)
Fable of Napoleon and the Bumpkin, 1914 (Beery 3)
Fable of the Brash Drummer and the Nectarine, 1914 (Beery 3)
Fable of the Bush League Lover Who Failed to Qualify, 1914 (Beery 3, Bushman 3)
Fable of the Business Boy and the Droppers-in, 1914 (Beery 3)
Fable of the Coming Champion Who Was Delayed, 1914 (Beery 3)
Fable of the Roystering Blades, 1915 (Beery 3)
Fabrication du ciment artificiel, 1924 (Grémillon 2)
Fabrication du fil, 1924 (Grémillon 2)
Fabrication industrielle des solutés injectables, 1951 (Colpi 4)
Fabrication industrielle des comprimés et dragées, 1952 (Colpi 4)
Fabuleuse Aventure de Marco Polo, 1965 (Welles 2, Quinn 3, Sharif 3, Rappeneau 4)
Fabuleuse Aventure de Marco Polo. *See* Echiquier de Dieu, 1964
Fabulous Adventures of the Legendary Baron Munchausen, 1979 (Legrand 4)
Fabulous Joe, 1947 (Daniels 3, Meek 3, Roach 4)
Fabulous World of Jules Verne. *See* Vynález zkásy, 1958
Fabulously Lucky Man. *See* Báječní muži s klikou, 1978

Faccia a faccia, 1967 (Volonté 3, Morricone 4)
Faccia da mascalzone, 1955 (Cortese 3)
Face, 1963 (Kuri 4)
Face, 1965 (Warhol 2)
Face. See Ansiktet, 1958
Face. See Arc, 1970
Face. See Tvář, 1973
Face at the Window, 1910 (Griffith 2, Walthall 3, Bitzer 4)
Face at the Window, 1912 (Guy 2)
Face at the Window, 1915 (Mix 3)
Face au destin, 1941 (Berry 3)
Face Behind the Mask, 1941 (Florey 2, Lorre 3, Planer 4)
Face Between, 1922 (Coffee 4)
Face from the Past. See Natsukashi no kao, 1941
Face in the Crowd, 1957 (Kazan 2, Neilan 2, Matthau 3, Neal 3, Remick 3, Stradling 4, Sylbert 4)
Face in the Dark, 1918 (Marsh 3)
Face in the Fog, 1922 (Crosland 2, Barrymore L. 3)
Face in the Fog, 1936 (Katzman 4)
Face in the Rain, 1963 (Kershner 2, Fields 4, Wexler 4)
Face in the Sky, 1933 (Tracy 3, Friedhofer 4, Garmes 4)
Face of a Fugitive, 1959 (Coburn, J. 3, MacMurray 3, Goldsmith 4)
Face of a Murderer. See Satsujinsha no kao, 1949
Face of Another. See Tanin no kao, 1966
Face of Eve, 1968 (Lee, C. 3)
Face of Fear, 1971 (Warden 3)
Face of Fu Manchu, 1965 (Lee, C. 3)
Face of Marble, 1946 (Carradine 3)
Face of Scotland, 1938 (Grierson 2, Wright 2)
Face of Terror. See Cara del terror, 1962
Face of the Enemy. See Fashizm budet razbit, 1941
Face of the Screaming Werewolf. See Casa del terror, 1959
Face Off, 1977 (Emshwiller 2)
Face on the Bar-Room Floor, 1914 (Chaplin 2, Sennett 2)
Face on the Barroom Floor, 1908 (Porter 2)
Face on the Barroom Floor, 1923 (Ford, J. 2, Walthall 3)
Face on the Ceiling, 1915 (Ince 4)
Face That Launched a 1000 Ships. See Amante di Paride, 1953
Face That Launched a Thousand Ships. See Eterna femmina, 1953
Face the Camera, 1922 (Roach 4)
Face the Music, 1954 (Fisher 2)
Face to Face, 1952 (Mason 3, Preston 3, Friedhofer 4, Struss 4)
Face to Face. See Ansikte mot ansikte, 1976
Face to Face. See Faccia a faccia, 1967
Face to Face. See Twarza w twarz, 1968
Face Value, 1927 (Florey 2)
Faceless Man. See Counterfeit Killer, 1968
Faces, 1968 (Cassavetes 2, Rowlands 3)
Faces in the Dark, 1960 (Zetterling 2, Ireland 3, Theodorakis 4)
Faces of America, 1965 (Emshwiller 2)
Faces of Children. See Visages d'enfants, 1925
Faces of Love. See Repérages, 1977
Facing the Music, 1933 (Gilliat 4)
Facteur trop ferré, 1907 (Feuillade 2)
Factory Front, 1940 (Cavalcanti 2)
Factory Front. See Cause commune, 1940
Factory Girl, 1909 (Olcott 2)
Facts of Life, 1960 (Ball 3, Beavers 3, Hope 3, Bass 4, Frank and Panama 4, Head 4, Lang 4, Mercer 4)
Facts of Love. See Twenty Nine Acacia Avenue, 1936
Fada, 1932 (Burel 4)
Fade In, 1968 (Reynolds, B. 3, Fraker 4)
Fadeaway, 1926 (Fleischer, M. and D. 2)
Faded Lilies, 1909 (Griffith 2, Pickford 3, Bitzer 4)
Fader og Søn, 1911 (Blom 2)
Faderen, 1909 (Blom 2)
Fadern, 1969 (Sjoberg 2)
Faderulla, ur Goteborgssystemet I . . ., 1910 (Magnusson 4)
Fádní odpoledne, 1965 (Passer 2, Kučera 4)
Faedrenes Synd, 1914 (Blom 2)
Fahlstrom, 1980 (Ruiz 2)
Fahne von Kriwoi Rog, 1968 (Geschonneck 3)
Fahrendes Volk, 1921 (Dreier 4)

Fahrendes Volk, 1938 (Feyder 2, Albers 3, Rosay 3)
Fahrenheit 451, 1966 (Roeg 2, Truffaut 2, Christie 3, Cusack 3, Werner 3, Herrmann 4)
Fahrt ins Abenteuer, 1926 (Courant 4)
Fahrt ins Blaue, 1919 (Kraly 4)
Fahrt ins Gluck, 1945 (Knef 3, Von Harbou 4)
Fai in fretta ad ucidermi . . . ho Freddo!, 1965 (Vitti 3)
Faibles femmes, 1959 (Delon 3)
Fail Safe, 1964 (Lumet 2, Fonda, H. 3, Matthau 3, Rosenblum 4)
Failing of Raymond, 1971 (Henreid 3, Wyman 3)
Faille, 1975 (Piccoli 3, Carrière 4, Morricone 4)
Failure, 1911 (Griffith 2, Crisp 3, Bitzer 4)
Failure's Song is Sad. See Haizan no uta wa kanashi, 1923
Faim, 1973 (Foldès 4)
Faim de loup, 1932 (Brasseur 3)
Faim du monde, 1958 (Grimault 4, Prévert 4)
Faim . . . L'occasion . . . L'herbe tendre, 1904 (Guy 2)
Faint Heart, 1922 (La Cava 2)
Faint Heart, 1929 (Lahr 3)
Faint Perfume, 1925 (Powell, W. 3)
Fainting Lover, 1931 (Sennett 2)
Fair and Muddy, 1928 (Roach 3)
Fair and Worm-er, 1946 (Jones 2)
Fair Co-ed, 1927 (Tourneur, J. 2, Wood 2, Gibbons 4, Gillespie 4, Seitz 4)
Fair Co-ed, 1927 (Davies 3, McCrea 3)
Fair Dentist, 1911 (Pickford 3, Gaudio 4)
Fair Exchange, 1909 (Griffith 2, Bitzer 4)
Fair Exchange. See Getting Acquainted, 1914
Fair Lady, 1922 (Stradling 4)
Fair Rebel, 1914 (Gish, D. 3)
Fair Sussex, 1913 (Pearson 2)
Fair Today, 1941 (Lantz 4)
Fair Warning, 1931 (Brent 3)
Fair Week, 1922 (Roach 4)
Fair Wind to Java, 1953 (MacMurray 3, McLaglen 3, Young, V. 4)
Fairfax Avenue, 1949 (Lewis 2)
Fair-Haired Hare, 1951 (Freleng 4)
Faisons le point sur les Spoutniks, 1957 (Gélin 3)
Faisons un rêve, 1936 (Guitry 2, Arletty 3, Dauphin 3, Raimu 3, Simon, M. 3)
Fait divers, 1922 (Artaud 3)
Faites soigner vos égratignures, 1949 (Decaë 4)
Faites vos jeux, Mesdames. See Feu à volonté, 1964
Faith Healer, 1921 (Menjou 3)
Faith, Hope and Hogan, 1953 (Crosby 3)
Faithful, 1910 (Griffith 2, Bitzer 4)
Faithful Heart, 1932 (Saville 2, Marshall 3, Balcon 4, Biro 4)
Faithful Hearts. See Faithful Heart, 1932
Faithful in My Fashion, 1946 (Reed, D. 3, Irene 4)
Faithful Indian, 1911 (Anderson G. 3)
Faithful Servant, 1913 (Costello, M. 3)
Faithful Taxicab, 1913 (Sennett 2)
Faithful Unto Death. See Hjertets Guld, 1912
Faithfully in My Fashion, 1946 (Horton 3)
Faithless, 1932 (Montgomery 3, Adrian 4, Wilson, C. 4)
Faits d'hiver, 1951 (Decaë 4)
Faits divers, 1923 (Autant-Lara 2, Honegger 4)
Faits divers à Paris, 1949 (Fradetal 4)
Fajr Yum Jadid, 1964 (Chahine 2)
Fake Girl. See Karakuri musume, 1927
Fake Isabella. See Hamis Isabella, 1968
Faker, 1929 (Oland 3)
Fakers. See Hell's Bloody Devils, 1970
Faking with Society. See Caught in a Cabaret, 1914
Fakir de Singapoure, 1908 (Méliès 2)
Fakir du Grand Hotel, 1933 (Burel 4)
Fakira, 1976 (Azmi 3)
Fakty minurshego dnia, 1981 (Ulyanov 3)
Fala, Brasilia, 1965 (Pereira Dos Santos 2)
Falak, 1968 (Kovács 2, Gábor 3, Latinovits 3, Theodorakis 4)
Falbalas, 1945 (Becker 2, Presle 3, Douy 4)
Falchivi koupon, 1912 (Mozhukin 3)

alcon and the Co-Eds, 1943 (Malone 3, Hunt 4)
alcon in Hollywood, 1944 (Musuraca 4)
alcon in San Francisco, 1945 (Miller, V. 4)
alcon Strikes Back, 1943 (Dmytryk 2)
alcon Takes Over, 1942 (Bond 3)
alcons. *See* Magasiskola, 1970
alcon's Adventure, 1946 (D'Agostino 4)
alcon's Alibi, 1946 (Cook 3)
alcon's Brother, 1942 (Sanders 3)
alcon's Gold, 1982 (Schifrin 4)
alena, 1916 (Gallone 2)
all. *See* Caída, 1959
all. *See* Queda, 1978
all des Generalstabsoberst Redl, 1931 (Dagover 3)
all Guy, 1921 (Hardy 3)
all Guy, 1930 (Plunkett 4)
all Guy, 1947 (Cook 3, Mirisch 4)
all In, 1942 (Roach 4)
all Molander, 1944 (Pabst 2, Wegener 3)
all of Berlin. *See* Padeniye Berlina, 1949
all of Eve, 1929 (Emerson 4, Loos 4)
all of Lola Montès. *See* Lola Montès, 1955
all of Montezuma, 1912 (Bushman 3)
all of the House of Usher, 1960 (Corman 4, Crosby 4)
all of the House of Usher. *See* Zánik domu Usheru, 1981
all of the House of Usher. *See* House of Usher, 1960
all of the Rebel Angels. *See* Caduta degli angeli ribelli, 1981
all of the Roman Empire, 1964 (Mann 2, Ferrer, M. 3, Guinness 3,
    Ireland 3, Loren 3, Mason 3, Quayle 3, Sharif 3, Krasker 4,
    Tiomkin 4)
all of the Romanoffs, 1917 (Brenon 2, Hunt 4)
all of the Romanov Dynasty. *See* Padenye dinastii romanovykh, 1927
all Rainer, 1942 (Wagner 4)
all River, Mass. *See* At Breakneck Speed, 1900
all Rosentopf, 1918 (Lubitsch 2)
all Tokeramo. *See* Polizeiakte 909, 1933
alle. *See* Salon Dora Green, 1933
allen, 1975 (Watkins 2)
allen Angel, 1945 (Preminger 2, Andrews D. 3, Carradine 3,
    Darnell 3, Faye 3, La Shelle 4, Raksin 4, Wheeler 4)
allen Arches, 1933 (Roach 4)
allen Hero, 1913 (Browning 2, Gish, D. 3, Loos 4)
allen Idol, 1919 (Ruttenberg 4)
allen Idol, 1948 (Reed 2, Hawkins 3, Morgan 3, Richardson 3,
    Alwyn 4, Korda 4, Périnal 4)
allen Sparrow, 1943 (Garfield 3, O'Hara 3, Musuraca 4, Polglase 4)
allen Star, 1917 (Hepworth 2, Sutherland 2)
allen Woman. *See* Daraku suru onna, 1967
allende Stern, 1950 (Wicki 2, Krauss 3)
allible Fable, 1962 (Hanna and Barbera 4)
alling for You, 1933 (Balcon 4, Gilliat 4)
alling Hare, 1943 (Clampett 4)
alling in Love, 1984 (De Niro 3, Keitel 3, Streep 3)
alling in Love Again, 1980 (Gould 3, York, S. 3, Legrand 4)
alling Leaves, 1912 (Guy 2)
alling Leaves. *See* Listopad, 1966
alling Man, 1971 (Wynn 3)
allow Land. *See* Magyar ugaraon, 1972
ALN, 1965 (Kramer, R. 2)
alsche Arzt. *See* Namenlos, 1923
alsche Bewegung, 1974 (Wenders 2, Schygulla 3, Vogler 3)
alsche Dimitry, 1922, (Albers 3)
alsche Ehemann, 1931 (Wilder 2, Herlth 4, Hoffmann 4, Rohrig 4)
alsche Gewicht, 1971 (Wicki 2)
alschspieler, 1920 (Albers 3)
alschung, 1981 (Schlondorff 2, Ganz 3, Schygulla 3, Carrière 4,
    Jarre 4)
alse Alarm, 1923 (Fleischer, M. and D. 2)
alse Alarms, 1936 (Three Stooges 3)
alse Bride, 1914 (Lawrence 3)
alse Colors, 1914 (Weber 2, Bosworth 3, Marion 4)
alse Colors, 1943 (Boyd 3, Mitchum 3)
alse Evidence. *See* For sin Faders Skyld, 1916

False Faces, 1919 (Chaney Lon 3, Walthall 3)
False Faces, 1932 (McCord 4)
False Faces, 1943 (Siodmak 4)
False Faces. *See* Let 'em Have It, 1935
False Hare, 1964 (McKimson 4)
False Idol. *See* False Madonna, 1932
False Impressions, 1932 (Sennett 2)
False Madonna, 1932 (Francis, K. 3)
False Millionaire. *See* Pour mon coeur et ses millions, 1931
False Note. *See* Falchivi koupon, 1912
False Paradise, 1948 (Boyd 3)
False Road, 1920 (Niblo 2, Barnes 4, Sullivan 4)
False Step. *See* Schritt vom Wege, 1939
False Suspicion, 1911 (Bushman 3)
False Witness. *See* Arkansas Judge, 1941
False Witness. *See* Transient Lady, 1935
False Witness. *See* Zig Zag, 1970
Falsely Accused, 1905 (Hepworth 2)
Falsely Accused, 1907 (Bitzer 4)
Falstaff, 1913 (Rosay 3)
Falstaff, 1966 (Rey 3)
Falstaff. *See* Chimes at Midnight, 1966
Falu rossza, 1937 (De Toth 2)
Fama, 1921 (Bertini 3)
Famalicão, 1940 (Oliveira 2)
Fame, 1936 (Wilcox 2)
Fame. *See* Sláva, 1960
Fame and Fortune, 1918 (Mix 3)
Fame and the Devil, 1929 (Auer 3)
Fame and the Devil. *See* Al diavolo la celebrita, 1949
Fame Is the Name of the Game, 1966 (Duvall, R. 3, Wagner 3,
    Warden 3)
Fame Is the Spur, 1947 (Boulting 2)
Fame Street, 1932 (Walthall 3)
Famiglia impossibile, 1940 (Zavattini 4)
Famiglia Passaguai, 1951 (Fabrizi 3)
Famiglia Passaguai fa fortuna, 1952 (Fabrizi 3)
Familia Dressel, 1935 (De Fuentes 2)
Familia Pérez, 1948 (García 3)
Familia Pichilin, 1978 (Solanas and Getino 2)
Familia provisional, 1955 (García Berlanga 2)
Familiar, 1973 (Solanas and Getino 2)
Familie Benthin, 1950 (Dudow 2)
Familie Buchholz, 1944 (Frohlich 3, Porten 3)
Familie Raffke, 1923 (Albers 3)
Familie Schimeck, 1926 (Dieterle 2, Tschechowa 3)
Familiebilleder, 1964 (Carlsen 2)
Familienparade, 1936 (Jurgens 3)
Familientag im Hause Prellstein, 1927 (Courant 4)
Familjen Andersson, 1937 (Borgstrom 3)
Familjens hemlighet, 1936 (Molander 2)
Familjens traditioner, 1920 (Magnusson 4)
Famille Duraton, 1939 (Berry 3)
Famille Lefrançais, 1939 (Basserman 3)
Famille Pont-Biquet, 1935 (Christian-Jaque 2)
Family, 1976 (Kovacs 4)
Family. *See* Città violenta, 1970
Family. *See* Kareinaru Ichizoku, 1974
Family Affair, 1937 (Barrymore L. 3, Rooney 3)
Family Affair, 1955 (Kaufman 4)
Family Affair. *See* Life with the Lyons, 1954
Family Centered Maternity Care, 1961 (Hammid 2)
Family Diary. *See* Cronaca familiare, 1962
Family Entrance, 1925 (McCarey 2, Roach 4)
Family Feud, 1943 (Darwell 3)
Family Focus, 1975 (Emshwiller 2)
Family Group, 1928 (Roach 4)
Family Happiness. *See* Semeinoe schaste, 1970
Family Home. *See* His Trysting Place, 1914
Family Honeymoon, 1948 (Colbert 3, MacMurray 3, McDaniel 3,
    Daniels 4, Orry-Kelly 4)
Family Honor, 1920 (Vidor, K. 2)
Family Jewels, 1965 (Lewis 2, Baxter, A. 3, Head 4)

Family Life, 1971 (Loach 2)
Family Life. See Zycie rodzinne, 1970
Family Mixup, 1912 (Sennett 2)
Family Next Door, 1939 (Krasner 4)
Family Nobody Wanted, 1975 (Jones S. 3)
Family of Women. See Jokei kazoku, 1963
Family Plot, 1976 (Hitchcock 2, Black 3, Dern 3, Bumstead 4, Head 4,
    Lehman 4, Williams, J. 4)
Family Portrait, 1950 (Jennings 2)
Family Reunion, 1981 (Davis 3)
Family Rico, 1972 (Mineo 3)
Family Secret, 1951 (Cobb 3, Duning 4, Guffey 4)
Family Secret. See Familjens hemlighet, 1936
Family Secrets, 1979 (Blondell 3)
Family Swedenhielms. See Swedenhielms, 1935
Family Tree, 1948 (Dunning 4)
Family Troubles, 1932 (Stevens 2)
Family Upside Down, 1978 (Astaire 3, Ames 4, Biroc 4, Hunter 4,
    Mancini 4)
Family Way, 1966 (Boulting 2, Mills 3)
Family Without a Dinner Table. See Shokutaku no nai ie, 1985
Family's Honor, 1913 (Ingram 2)
Family's Situation. See Kazoku no jijo, 1962
Famine, 1915 (Hayakawa 3)
Famous Box Trick. See Illusions fantasmagoriques, 1898
Famous Escape, 1908 (Bitzer 4)
Famous Ferguson Case, 1932 (Bacon 2, Blondell 3)
Famous Mrs. Fair, 1923 (Niblo 2, Marion 4)
Famous Soviet Heroes. See Slava Sovetskim Geroiniam, 1938
Famous Sword Bijomaru. See Meito Bijomaru, 1945
FAMU Newsreel. See Zurnál FAMU, 1961
Fan, 1949 (Preminger 2, Carroll M. 3, Crain 3, Sanders 3, La Shelle 4,
    Lemaire 4, Reisch 4, Wheeler 4)
Fan, 1981 (Smith, D. , Bacall 3, Donaggio 4)
Fan Fan, 1918 (Franklin 2)
Fanatic, 1968 (Sutherland 3)
Fanatiques, 1957 (Fabian 3, Fresnay 3, Burel 4)
Fanatisme, 1934 (Negri 3)
Fanchon, the Cricket, 1915 (Pickford 3)
Fanciulla di Amalfi, 1921 (Bertini 3)
Fanciulla di portici, 1940 (Amidei 4, Delli Colli 4)
Fanciulla, il poeta e la laguna, 1920 (Gallone 2)
Fanciulle di lusso, 1952 (Flaiano 4, Rota 4)
Fancy Answers, 1941 (Gardner 3)
Fancy Baggage, 1929 (Loy 3)
Fancy Pants, 1950 (Ball 3, Hope 3, Dreier 4, Head 4, Lang 4)
Fandy ó Fandy, 1982 (Kachyna 2)
Fanfan la Tulipe, 1951 (Christian-Jaque 2, Lollobrigida 3, Philipe 3,
    Jeanson 4, Matras 4)
Fanfan the Tulip. See Fanfan la Tulipe, 1951
Fanfare, 1958 (Haanstra 2)
Fanfare d'amour, 1935 (Fradetal 4)
Fanfaron, mali klaun, 1968 (Pojar 4)
Fanfaron, The Little Clown. See Fanfaron, mali klaun, 1968
Fanfulla da lodi, 1939 (Vích 4)
Fange nr. 1, 1935 (Fejos 2)
Fange Nr. 113, 1917 (Dreyer 2, Holger-Madsen 2)
Fangelse, 1949 (Bergman 2)
Fangerfamilie i Thuledistriktet, 1967 (Roos 2)
Fango sulla metropoli, 1965 (Giannini 3)
Fangs of the Wild, 1928 (Berman 4)
Fangschuss, 1976 (Schlondorff 2, Von Trotta 2)
Fanny, 1932 (Allégret, M. 2, Pagnol 2, Fresnay 3, Raimu 3)
Fanny, 1961 (Logan 2, Boyer 3, Caron 3, Chevalier 3, Cardiff 4,
    Epstein, J. & P. 4)
Fanny and Alexander. See Fanny och Alexander, 1982
Fanny by Gaslight, 1944 (Asquith 2, Granger 3, Mason 3)
Fanny Foley Herself, 1931 (Steiner 4, Wilson, C. 4)
Fanny Foley Herself. See Top of the Bill, 1931
Fanny Hill, 1964 (Hopkins, M. 3)
Fanny Hill, 1983 (Reed, O. 3)
Fanny Hill: Memoirs of a Woman of Pleasure. See Fanny Hill, 1964
Fanny in the Lion's Den, 1933 (Terry 4)

Fanny och Alexander, 1982 (Bergman 2, Andersson H. 3,
    Bjornstrand 3, Nykvist 4)
Fanny's Conspiracy, 1913 (Talmadge, N. 3)
Fanny's Wedding Day, 1933 (Terry 4)
Fanrik Stals sagner, 1909 (Magnusson 4)
Fan's Note, 1972 (Meredith 3)
Fantaisie d'un jour, 1954 (Kosma 4)
Fantaisie sur quatre cordes, 1957 (Braunberger 4)
Fantaisies d'Agenor maltrace, 1911 (Cohl 2)
Fantaisies pour clarinette, 1947–51 (Verneuil 2)
Fantaisies truquées, 1915 (Cohl 2)
Fantasia, 1940 (Disney 2, Fischinger 2)
Fantasia chez les ploucs, 1971 (Delon 3, Braunberger 4)
Fantasia sottomarina, 1939 (Rossellini 2)
Fantasia II, 1957 (Peterson 2)
Fantasma d'amore, 1981 (Risi 2, Mastroianni 3, Schneider 3)
Fantasma del convento, 1934 (De Fuentes 2)
FANTASMAGORIE, 1908 (Cohl 2)
Fantasmi a Roma, 1961 (Scola 2, Gassman 3, Mastroianni 3, Amidei
    Cristaldi 4, Flaiano 4, Rota 4)
Fantasmi e ladri, 1958 (Tognazzi 3)
Fantassin Guignard, 1905 (Guy 2)
Fantastic Tale of Naruto. See Naruto hicho, 1957
Fantastic Voyage, 1966 (Fleischer, R. 2, Kennedy, A. 3, O'Brien, E.
    Pleasance 3, Welch 3, Laszlo 4, Rosenman 4, Smith, J.M. 4)
Fantastica, 1980 (Reggiani 3)
Fantasy for Piano, 1972 (Kuri 4)
Fantoche cherche un logement. See Maison du Fantoche, 1916
Fantômas, 1913 (Feuillade 2)
Fantômas, 1931 (Allégret, Y. 2, Fejos 2, Modot 3, Braunberger 4)
Fantômas, 1947 (Signoret 3)
Fantômas, 1964 (Marais 3)
Fantômas contre Fantômas, 1914 (Feuillade 2)
Fantômas contre Scotland Yard, 1967 (Marais 3, Douy 4)
Fantômas se déchaine, 1965 (Marais 3, Douy 4)
Fantôme de bonheur, 1929 (Modot 3)
Fantôme de la liberté, 1974 (Buñuel 2, Piccoli 3, Vitti 3, Carrière 4)
Fantôme du Moulin Rouge, 1924 (Clair 2)
Fantômes du chapelier, 1982 (Chabrol 2)
Fantorro, le dernier justicier, 1972 (Lenica 2)
Fantorro, the Last Just Man. See Fantorro, le dernier justicier, 1972
Far Call, 1929 (Dwan 2, Baxter W. 3, Scott, R. 3, Miller, S. 4, Rosse
    4)
Far Country, 1955 (Mann 2, Brennan 3, Elam 3, Stewart 3, Chase 4,
    Daniels 4, Salter 4)
Far Cry, 1926 (Bosworth 3, Sweet 3)
Far Cry, 1959 (Finch 3)
Far East. See Volochayevskiye dni, 1937
Far East Martial Court. See Tokyo saiban, 1983
Far from Dallas, 1972 (Gélin 3)
Far from the Madding Crowd, 1967 (Roeg 2, Schlesinger 2, Bates 3,
    Christie 3, Finch 3, Stamp 3, Raphael 4)
Far from Vietnam. See Loin du Viêtnam, 1967
Far Frontier, 1948 (Rogers, R. 3)
Far Horizons, 1955 (Heston 3, MacMurray 3, Reed, D. 3, Canutt 4,
    Head 4, Maté 4, Salter 4)
Får jag låna din fru?, 1959 (Nykvist 4)
Far Out West, 1967 (Chaney Lon, Jr. 3, Sheridan 3)
Far Shore, 1976 (Wieland 2)
Far West Story. See Banda J & S, 1972
Fara, 1954 (Anand 3)
Faraar, 1975 (Bachchan 3)
Farandole, 1945 (Cayatte 2, Blier 3, Auric 4, Jeanson 4)
Faraon, 1965 (Kawalerowicz 2, Konwicki 4)
Farar, 1955 (Biswas 4)
Faráťuv konec, 1968 (Schorm 2, Brejchová 3, Brodský 3)
Faraway Love, 1947 (Zhao 3)
Farbror Johannes ankomst till Stockholm, 1912 (Jaenzon 4)
Farces de cuisinière, 1902 (Guy 2)
Farces de Jocko, 1897–98 (Guy 2)
Farceur, 1961 (Broca 2, Aimée 3, Cassel 3, Delerue 4)
Farewell Again, 1937 (Howe 4, Pommer 4)
Farewell Friend. See Adieu l'ami, 1968

Fear o' God. *See* Mountain Eagle, 1926
Fear of Fear. *See* Angst vor der Angst, 1975
Fear on Trial, 1975 (Scott, G. 3, Houseman 4)
Fear over the City. *See* Peur sur la ville, 1975
Fear Strikes Out, 1957 (Mulligan 2, Pakula 2, Malden 3, Perkins 3, Bernstein 4, Head 4)
Fearless Fagan, 1952 (Donen 2, Leigh, J. 3, Wynn 3, Lederer 4)
Fearless Frank. *See* Frank's Greatest Adventure, 1967
Fearless Vampire Killers, or Pardon Me, But Your Teeth Are in My Neck, 1967 (Polanski 2, Godfrey 4)
Fearless Vampire Killers. *See* Dance of the Vampires, 1967
Fearmakers, 1958 (Tourneur, J. 2, Andrews D. 3)
Feast. *See* Utage, 1967
Feast and Famine, 1914 (Eason 4)
Feast at Zhirmunka. *See* Pir v Girmunka, 1941
Feast of Life, 1916 (Marion 4)
Feast or Famine, 1965 (Van Dyke, W. 2)
Feather Bluster, 1958 (McKimson 4)
Feather Dusted, 1955 (McKimson 4)
Feather Finger, 1966 (McKimson 4)
Feather Gets in the Game, 1908 (Lawrence 3)
Feather in Her Hat, 1935 (Burke 3, Rathbone 3, Walker 4)
Feather in Her Heart, 1935 (Niven 3)
Feather in His Hare, 1946 (Jones 2)
Feather Your Nest, 1937 (Formby 3, Dean 4)
Feathered Nest, 1916 (Fazenda 3)
Featherweight Champ, 1953 (Terry 4)
Febbre di vivere, 1953 (Mastroianni 3, D'Amico 4)
Fede, 1916 (Gallone 2)
Federal Agent, 1936 (Boyd 3)
Federal Bullets, 1937 (Brown, K. 4)
Federal Man-Hunt, 1938 (Fuller 2)
Federal Operator 99, 1945 (Canutt 4)
Federale, 1961 (Tognazzi 3, Morricone 4)
Fediha fil Zamalek, 1958 (Sharif 3)
Fedora, 1916 (Bertini 3)
Fedora, 1978 (Wilder 2, Ferrer, J. 3, Fonda, H. 3, Holden 3, Knef 3, York, M. 3, Diamond 4, Fisher 4, Rozsa 4, Trauner 4)
Fedora. *See* Fehér éjszakák, 1916
Fée au printemps, 1906 (Guy 2)
Fée aux choux, 1896 (Guy 2)
Fée caraboose ou le Poignard fatal, 1906 (Méliès 2)
Fee Fie Foes, 1961 (Hanna and Barbera 4)
Feed 'em and Weep, 1929 (Roach 4)
Feed 'em and Weep, 1938 (Roach 4)
Feed the Kitty, 1952 (Jones 2)
Feedback, 1965 (Vanderbeek 2)
Feeder de l'est. *See* Chaleur du foyer, 1955
Feedin' the Kiddie, 1957 (Hanna and Barbera 4)
Feeding Time, 1913 (Sennett 2)
Feel My Pulse, 1928 (La Cava 2, Arlen 3, Daniels 3, Powell, W. 3, Hunt 4)
Feenhande, 1912 (Messter 4)
Feet First, 1930 (Lloyd 3, Bruckman 4)
Feet of Clay, 1924 (DeMille 2)
Feet of Mud, 1924 (Capra 2, Sennett 2, Langdon 3)
Fegyver, 1971 (Macskássy 4)
Fehér éjszakák, 1916 (Korda 2)
Fehér rózsa, 1919 (Korda 2)
Feind im Blut, 1931 (Ruttmann 2)
Feinde, 1940 (Wagner 4)
Feine Gesellschaft—Beschrankte Haftung, 1982 (Bergner 3)
Fekete Kapitany, 1921 (Fejos 2)
Fekete szivarvany, 1916 (Curtiz 2)
Feldgrau. *See* Mann aus dem jenseits, 1925
Feldherrenhugel, 1926 (Tschechowa 3)
Feldobott ko, 1968 (Madaras 3)
Felices Pascuas, 1954 (Bardem 2)
Félicie Nanteuil, 1942 (Allégret, M. 2, Dauphin 3, Jourdan 3, Presle 3, Achard 4, Ibert 4)
Felicità perduta, 1946 (Delli Colli 4)
Feline Frame-Up, 1953 (Jones 2)

Félins, 1964 (Clément 2, Delon 3, Fonda, J. 3, Borowczyk 4, Decaë 4, Schifrin 4)
Félix Leclerc, troubadour, 1959 (Jutra 2)
Felix on the Job, 1916 (Chaney Lon 3)
Felix the Fox, 1948 (Terry 4)
Fella with the Fiddle, 1937 (Freleng 4)
Fellini: A Director's Notebook. *See* Block-notes di un regista, 1969
Fellini Roma, 1972 (Mastroianni 3)
Fellini Roma. *See* Roma, 1972
Fellini Satyricon, 1969 (Cuny 3, Rey 3)
Fellini Satyricon. *See* Satyricon, 1969
Fellini's Casanova. *See* Casanova, 1976
Fellow Americans, 1942 (Stewart 3, Kanin 4)
Fellow Citizens, 1920 (Roach 4)
Fellow Countrymen. *See* Zemliaka, 1975
Fellow Romans, 1921 (Roach 4)
Fellow Voyagers, 1913 (Costello, M. 3)
Fellows Who Ate the Elephant. *See* Zo o kutta renchu, 1947
Fem Kopier, 1913 (Blom 2)
Female, 1924 (Wood 2, Baxter W. 3)
Female, 1933 (Curtiz 2, Dieterle 2, Brennan 3, Brent 3, Blanke 4, Orry-Kelly 4)
Female. *See* Femme et le pantin, 1958
Female Animal, 1957 (Lamarr 3, Salter 4)
Female Artillery, 1973 (Lupino 3)
Female Bunch, 1969 (Chaney Lon, Jr. 3)
Female Cop, 1914 (Hardy 3)
Female Demon. *See* Chokon yasha, 1928
Female Highwayman, 1906 (Selig 4)
Female Impersonator. *See* Masquerader, 1914
Female Instinct. *See* Snoop Sisters, 1972
Female Jungle, 1956 (Carradine 3, Mansfield 3)
Female of the Species, 1912 (Griffith 2, Weber 2, Pickford 3, Bitzer 4)
Female on the Beach, 1955 (Chandler 3, Crawford, J. 3, Lang 4)
Female: 70 Times 7. *See* Setente veces siete, 1962
Females is Fickle, 1940 (Fleischer, M. and D. 2)
Feme, 1927 (Oswald 2)
Femeile zilelor noastre, 1958 (Mészáros 2)
Feminine Touch, 1941 (Mankiewicz 2, Van Dyke, W.S. 2, Ameche 3, Francis, K. 3, Heflin 3, Meek 3, Adrian 4, Waxman 4)
Feminine Touch, 1956 (Balcon 4)
Femme à sa fenêtre, 1976 (Noiret 3, Schneider 3)
Femme au volant, 1933 (Maté 4)
Femme aux bottes rouges, 1974 (Deneuve 3, Carrière 4)
Femme blonde. *See* Dame blonde, 1914
Femme chipée, 1934 (Berry 3)
Femme coquette, 1955 (Godard 2)
Femme coupée en morceaux, 1945 (Dauphin 3)
Femme d'une nuit, 1930 (L'Herbier 2)
Femme d'à côté, 1981 (Depardieu 3, Delerue 4)
Femme dans la nuit, 1941 (Dauphin 3, Alekan 4, Kosma 4)
Femme de Jean, 1973 (Delerue 4)
Femme de l'aviateur, 1980 (Rohmer 2)
Femme de nulle part, 1922 (Delluc 2, Francis, E. 3)
Femme disparaît, 1942 (Feyder 2, Dauphin 3, Rosay 3, D'Eaubonne 4)
Femme douce, 1969 (Bresson 2, Sanda 3, Cloquet 4)
Femme du boulanger, 1938 (Pagnol 2, Raimu 3)
Femme du bout du monde, 1937 (Epstein 2, Aumont 3, Vanel 3)
Femme du Ganges, 1974 (Duras 2, Depardieu 3)
Femme d'une nuit, 1930 (Artaud 3, Bertini 3, Burel 4)
Femme écarlate, 1968 (Chabrol 2, Vitti 3, Gégauff 4)
Femme en blanc se révolte. *See* Nouveau Journal d'une femme en blanc, 1966
Femme en bleu, 1972 (Piccoli 3, Simon, S. 3)
Femme en homme, 1932 (Rosay 3, Meerson 4, Périnal 4)
Femme en rouge, 1946 (Gélin 3)
Femme enfant, 1982 (Kinski 3)
Femme est passée. *See* Nunca pasa mada, 1963
Femme est une femme, 1961 (Godard 2, Belmondo 3, Karina 3, Moreau 3, Coutard 4, de Beauregard 4, Evein 4, Guillemot 4, Legrand 4, Ponti 4)
Femme et le fauve, 1955 (Auric 4)

Femme et le pantin, 1958 (Duvivier 2, Bardot 3, Achard 4, Aurenche 4, Wakhévitch 4)
Femme et le rossignol, 1930 (Christian-Jaque 2)
Femme fatale, 1917 (Feuillade 2)
Femme fatale, 1945 (Brasseur 3)
Femme fidèle, 1976 (Vadim 2, Renoir 4)
Femme idéale, 1933 (D'Eaubonne 4)
Femme inconnue, 1923 (Burel 4)
Femme infidèle, 1969 (Chabrol 2, Audran 3, Rabier 4)
Femme invisible, 1933 (Meerson 4)
Femme mariée, 1964 (Godard 2, Leenhardt 2, Léaud 3, Coutard 4, Guillemot 4)
Femme noire, femme nue, 1969 (Colpi 4)
Femme nue, 1932 (Burel 4, Meerson 4)
Femme nue et Satan, 1959 (Simon, M. 3)
Femme que j'ai assassinée, 1949 (Vanel 3)
Femme que j'ai le plus aimée, 1942 (Arletty 3, Blier 3)
Femme qui se partage, 1936 (Brasseur 3)
Femme rêvée, 1927 (Vanel 3)
Femme sans importance, 1937 (Spaak 4)
Femme singe. See Donna scimmia, 1963
Femme spectacle, 1960 (Lelouch 2, Braunberger 4)
Femme sur la lune. See Frau im Mond, 1929
Femme-Fleur, 1965 (Lenica 2)
Femmemariée, 1964 (Leenhardt 2)
Femmes, 1969 (Bardot 3)
Femmes au soleil, 1973 (Almendros 4)
Femmes d'abord, 1963 (Auer 3, Constantine 3)
Femmes de Paris, 1952 (Simon, M. 3)
Femmes de personne, 1984 (Delerue 4)
Femmes et des fleurs, 1963 (Leenhardt 2)
Femmes fatales. See Calmos, 1975
Femmes savantes, 1963 (Fabian 3)
Femmes s'en balancent, 1954 (Constantine 3)
Femmes sont marrantes, 1957 (Presle 3)
Femmina, 1953 (Allégret, M. 2)
Femmina. See Grande Sauterelle, 1967
Femmine di lusso, 1960 (Cervi 3, Tognazzi 3)
Femmine insaziabili. See Insaziabili, 1969
Femmine tre volte, 1957 (Manfredi 3, Delli Colli 4, Ponti 4)
Fence at Bar Z Ranch, 1910 (Anderson G. 3)
Fencing Master, 1907 (Bitzer 4)
Fencing Master, 1915 (Walsh 2)
Fencing Master. See Tateshi danpei, 1950
Fenêtre ouverte, 1952 (Storck 2)
Fenómos del futbol, 1962 (García 3)
Fényes szelek, 1969 (Jancsó 2, Madaras 3)
Fer à cheval, 1915 (Feuillade 2, Musidora 3)
Ferdinand Lassalle, 1918 (Dupont 2)
Ferdinand le noceur, 1935 (Fernandel 3)
Ferdinando I, re di Napoli, 1959 (De Sica 2, Fabrizi 3, Mastroianni 3)
Férfiarckép, 1964 (Gaál 2)
Ferghana Canal, 1939 (Eisenstein 2, Tisse 4)
Feri, 1954 (Anand 3)
Feria de las flores, 1942 (Infante 3)
Feriebørn, 1952 (Roos 2)
Ferien auf Immenhof, 1957 (Wagner 4)
Ferita, 1921 (Bertini 3)
Fermata Etna, 1981 (Ganz 3)
Ferme aux loups, 1943 (Andrejew 4)
Ferme des sept péchés, 1949 (Kosma 4)
Ferme du pendu, 1945 (Bourvil 3, Vanel 3, Douy 4)
Fermière à Montfaucon, 1967 (Rohmer 2)
Fernandel the Dressmaker. See Couturier de ces dames, 1956
Fernández de Peralvillo, 1953 (García 3)
Fernes Jamaica, 1969 (Fassbinder 2)
Feroce Saladino, 1937 (Valli 3)
Ferrente. See Bacciamo le mani, 1973
Ferréol, 1916 (Bertini 3)
Ferroviere, 1956 (Germi 2, Ponti 4)
Ferry Pilot, 1941 (Dalrymple 4)
Ferry to Hong Kong, 1959 (Welles 2, Jurgens 3, Mathieson 4)
Fertilizzanti complessi, 1956 (Olmi 2)

Fertiluzzanti produtti dalla Societá del Gruppo Edison, 1959 (Olmi 2)
Fès, 1950 (Auric 4)
Fesche Erzherzog, 1927 (Courant 4)
Fessée, 1937 (Dauphin 3, Fradetal 4)
Festa di maggio, 1957 (Fabrizi 3)
Festin de Balthazar, 1910 (Feuillade 2, Carré 4)
Festin des mots, 1965 (Cuny 3)
Festival, 1952 (Lassally 4)
Festival acrobatique, 1951 (Kosma 4)
Festival dans le désert, 1969 (Reichenbach 2)
Festival Game, 1969 (Heston 3, Hopper 3)
Festival of Nyan-nyan-myan. See Nyan-nyan-myan-hoi, 1940
Festok városa—Szentendre, 1964 (Mészáros 2)
Fête à Henriette, 1952 (Duvivier 2, Knef 3, Auric 4, D'Eaubonne 4, Jeanson 4)
Fête des mères, 1969 (Braunberger 4)
Fête des morts, 1969 (Reichenbach 2, Braunberger 4)
Fête des pères. See Mords pas, on t'aime, 1975
Fête espagnole, 1919 (Delluc 2, Dulac 2, Francis, E. 3, Modot 3)
Fête sauvage, 1975 (Vangelis 4)
Fêtes de Belgiques, 1969–72 (Storck 2)
Fêtes de France, 1939 (Leenhardt 2)
Fêtes du centenaire, 1930 (Storck 2)
Fêtes galantes, 1965 (Clair 2, Cassel 3, Matras 4, Wakhévitch 4)
Fetita mincinoasa, 1953 (Popescu-Gopo 4)
Fetters. See Pouta, 1961
Feu!, 1926 (Brasseur 3, Vanel 3)
Feu!, 1937 (Delannoy 2, Feuillère 3, Ibert 4, Wakhévitch 4)
Feu. See Forêt calcinée, 1971
Feu à volonté, 1964 (Ophuls 2, Constantine 3)
Feu aux poudres, 1957 (Fabian 3, Vanel 3)
Feu d'artifice improvisé, 1905 (Méliès 2)
Feu de paille, 1939 (Benoit-Lévy 2)
Feu follet, 1963 (Malle 2, Moreau 3, Cloquet 4, Evein 4)
Feu la mère de madame, 1936 (Arletty 3)
Feu Mathias Pascal, 1925 (Cavalcanti 2, L'Herbier 2, Mozhukin 3, Simon, M. 3, Burel 4, Meerson 4)
Feu Nicolas, 1943 (Douy 4)
Feu quelque part, 1952 (Audiard 4)
Feu sacré, 1920 (Linders 3)
Feu sacré, 1942 (Burel 4)
Feud, 1910 (Olcott 2)
Feud, 1919 (Mix 3)
Feud, 1936 (Terry 4)
Feud and the Turkey, 1908 (Griffith 2, Lawrence 3, Bitzer 4)
Feud in the Kentucky Hills, 1912 (Griffith 2, Pickford 3, Walthall 3, Bitzer 4)
Feud of the West, 1936 (McCord 4)
Feud There Was, 1938 (Avery 2)
Feudin', Fussin', and A-Fightin', 1948 (O'Connor 3)
Feuding Hillbillies, 1948 (Terry 4)
Feudists, 1913 (Bunny 3)
Feuer, 1914 (Gad 2, Nielsen 3, Freund 4, Kraly 4)
Feuerlöscher E.A. Winterstein, 1968 (Kluge 2)
Feuerwerk, 1954 (Schneider 3)
Feulin' Around, 1949 (Three Stooges 3)
Feux de la chandeleur, 1972 (Girardot 3, Legrand 4)
Feux de la mer, 1948 (Epstein 2)
Feux Follets, 1928 (Vanel 3)
Fever. See Horečka, 1958
Fever in the Blood, 1961 (Ameche 3, Dickinson 3, Marshall 3)
Fever Pitch, 1985 (Giannini 3)
Fevralskii veter, 1981 (Ulyanov 3)
Few Words of Introduction. See Uvodní slovo pronese, 1964
Ffolkes, 1980 (Mason 3, Moore, R. 3, Perkins 3)
Fi Baitina Rajul, 1961 (Sharif 3)
Fiacre nr. 13, 1941 (Stallich 4)
Fiaker Nr. 13, 1926 (Curtiz 2, Leni 2)
Fiamma che no si spegne, 1949 (Cervi 3)
Fiammata, 1924 (Gallone 2)
Fiammata, 1952 (Blasetti 2)
Fiançailles d'Agénor, 1916 (Feuillade 2, Musidora 3)
Fiançailles de Flambeau, 1916 (Cohl 2)

Fighting Dervishes, 1912 (Olcott 2)
Fighting Dude, 1926 (Arbuckle 3)
Fighting Eagle, 1927 (Crisp 3, Lombard 3, Adrian 4, Miller, A. 4, Sullivan 4)
Fighting Engineers, 1943 (Eason 4)
Fighting Father Dunne, 1948 (Nilsson 3, O'Brien, P. 3)
Fighting Fathers, 1927 (Roach 4)
Fighting Film Album. *See* Boevi kinosbornik, 1942
Fighting Film Album No. 7. *See* Boyevoye kinosbornik n. 7, 1941
Fighting Fluid, 1925 (McCarey 2, Roach 4)
Fighting for Gold, 1919 (Mix 3)
Fighting for Justice, 1933 (Brennan 3)
Fighting for Love, 1917 (Hersholt 3)
Fighting for Love, 1919 (Johnson, N. 3)
Fighting Gringo, 1917 (Carey 3)
Fighting Guardsman, 1945 (Guffey 4)
Fighting Heart, 1919 (Eason 4)
Fighting Heart, 1925 (Ford, J. 2, McLaglen 3, August 4)
Fighting Instinct. *See* Manden, der sejrede, 1918
Fighting Kentuckian, 1949 (Haas 3, Hardy 3, Marsh 3, Wayne 3, Garmes 4)
Fighting Lady, 1944 (Taylor, R. 3, de Rochemont 4, Newman 4)
Fighting Legion, 1930 (Brown, Harry Joe 4, McCord 4)
Fighting Line, 1919 (Eason 4)
Fighting Love, 1927 (Walthall 3)
Fighting Mad, 1976 (Demme 2, Fonda, P. 3, Corman 4)
Fighting Man of the Plains, 1949 (Scott, R. 3)
Fighting Marine, 1935 (Canutt 4, Eason 4)
Fighting Odds, 1917 (Dwan 2)
Fighting O'Flynn, 1948 (Fairbanks, D. Jr. 3, Edeson 4)
Fighting Parson, 1930 (Langdon 3, Roach 4)
Fighting Pimpernel. *See* Elusive Pimpernel, 1950
Fighting Prince of Donegal, 1966 (Disney 2, Ellenshaw 4)
Fighting Rangers, 1934 (Bond 3)
Fighting Rats of Tobruk. *See* Rats of Tobruk, 1944
Fighting Sap, 1924 (Brown, Harry Joe 4)
Fighting Seabees, 1944 (Hayward 3, Wayne 3, Chase 4)
Fighting Shadows, 1935 (Bond 3)
Fighting Shepherdess, 1920 (Gaudio 4)
Fighting Sheriff, 1931 (Muse 3)
Fighting Smile, 1925 (Arthur 3, Brown, Harry Joe 4)
Fighting Stallion, 1926 (Canutt 4)
Fighting Stock, 1935 (Balcon 4)
Fighting Stranger, 1921 (Selig 4)
Fighting Streak, 1922 (Mix 3)
Fighting Sullivans. *See* Sullivans, 1944
Fighting Test, 1931 (Canutt 4)
Fighting Texans, 1933 (Canutt 4)
Fighting the Flames, 1925 (Eason 4)
Fighting Thorobreds, 1926 (Brown, Harry Joe 4)
Fighting Through, 1934 (Canutt 4)
Fighting Westerner. *See* Rocky Mountain Mystery, 1935
Fighting with Kit Carson, 1933 (Canutt 4)
Fighting Youth, 1925 (Eason 4)
Fighting Youth, 1935 (Sheridan 3)
Fights of Nations, 1907 (Bitzer 4)
Figli chiedono perche, 1972 (D'Amico 4)
Figli del marchese Lucera, 1938 (Cervi 3)
Figli di nessuno, 1951 (Rosay 3)
Figlia del capitano, 1947 (Gassman 3, De Laurentiis 4, Pinelli 4)
Figlia del corsaro verde, 1940 (Stallich 4)
Figlia del tempesta, 1920 (Gallone 2)
Figlia di Frankenstein, 1971 (Cotten 3)
Figlia di Mata Hari, 1955 (Gallone 2)
Figlie del mare, 1919 (Gallone 2)
Figlio del Capitano Blood, 1962 (Brown, Harry Joe 4, Robinson 4)
Figlio del corsaro rosso, 1942 (Amidei 4)
Figlio di Lagardere, 1952 (Brazzi 3)
Figlio d'oggi, 1961 (Cervi 3)
Figuration, 1931 (Dauphin 3)
Figurehead, 1920 (Nilsson 3)
Figures de cire, 1912 (Tourneur, M. 2)
Figures de cire et têtes de bois, 1916 (Cohl 2)

Figures Don't Lie, 1927 (Sutherland 2, Arlen 3, Mankiewicz 4, Schulberg 4)
Figures in a Landscape, 1970 (Losey 2, McDowell 3, Shaw 3, Alekan 4)
Fil à la patte, 1955 (Bourvil 3)
File of the Golden Goose, 1969 (Brynner 3)
File on Thelma Jordan, 1950 (Siodmak 2, Stanwyck 3, Dreier 4, Head 4, Wallis 4)
Fill It Up, Premium! See Plein de super, 1976
Fille à croquer, 1950 (Reggiani 3)
Fille à la dérive, 1964 (Guillemot 4)
Fille à papa, 1936 (Morgan 3)
Fille au fouet, 1952 (Simon, M. 3)
Fille bien gardée, 1924 (Feuillade 2)
Fille consue de fil blanc, 1977 (Reggiani 3)
Fille dangereuse. *See* Bufere, 1952
Fille dans la montagne, 1964 (Leenhardt 2)
Fille de Hambourg, 1958 (Allégret, Y. 2, Gélin 3)
Fille de Jephté, 1910 (Feuillade 2)
Fille de l'eau, 1925 (Renoir 2, Braunberger 4)
Fille de la mer morte, 1966 (Brasseur 3, Golan and Globus 4)
Fille de Madame Angot, 1935 (Arletty 3)
Fille des chiffonniers, (Baur 3)
Fille d'Eve, 1916 (Musidora 3)
Fille du diable, 1945 (Fresnay 3)
Fille du margrave, 1912 (Feuillade 2)
Fille du puisatier, 1940 (Pagnol 2, Fernandel 3, Raimu 3)
Fille du régiment, 1932 (Dauphin 3)
Fille du samourai. *See* Tochter des Samurai, 1937
Fille du torrent, 1960 (Valli 3)
Fille et des fusils, 1964 (Lelouch 2, Braunberger 4)
Fille nommée Madeleine, 1953 (Bost 4)
Fille pour l'été, 1959 (Presle 3, Delerue 4)
Fille prodigue, 1980 (Piccoli 3)
Fille sage, 1963 (Borowczyk 4)
Filles de la concierge, 1934 (Tourneur, J. 2, Wakhévitch 4)
Filles du cantonnier, 1909 (Feuillade 2)
Filles du Diable, 1903 (Méliès 2)
Filles du Rhone, 1938 (Burel 4, Jaubert 4)
Filling the Gap, 1941 (Halas and Batchelor 2)
Film, 1965 (Keaton 2, Kaufman 4)
Film About a Woman Who . . ., 1974 (Rainer 2)
Film about the Book. *See* Film o knjizi A.B.C., 1962
Film and Reality, 1952 (Cavalcanti 2)
Film comme les autres, 1968 (Godard 2)
Film Concert No. 1. *See* Koncert na ekrane, 1939
Film d'amore e d'anarchia, 1973 (Wertmuller 2, Giannini 3, Rota 4)
Film de Jean, 1953 (Allégret, M. 2)
Film den Niemand sieht, 1964 (Thulin 3)
Film der Menschlichkeit. *See* I.N.R.I., 1923
Film Elation of Spejbl. *See* Spejblovo filmové opojení, 1931
Film Fan, 1939 (Clampett 4)
Film Form, 1970 (Vanderbeek 2)
Film gegen die Volkskrankheit Krebs—jeder Achte . . ., 1941 (Ruttmann 2)
Film in Which There Appear Sprocket Holes, Edge Lettering, Dirt Particles, Etc., 1965 (Landow 2)
Film ist Rhythmus. *See* Rhythmus, 1921–24
Film Johnnie, 1914 (Chaplin 2, Sennett 2, Arbuckle 3)
Film Magazine No. 1, 1963 (Emshwiller 2)
Film Magazine of the Arts, 1963 (Mekas 2)
Film Making Techniques: Acting, 1973 (Fonda, H. 3)
Film o knjizi A.B.C., 1962 (Makavejev 2)
Film of Love and Anarchy. *See* Film d'Amore e d'anarchia, 1973
Film ohne Titel, 1947 (Knef 3, Herlth 4)
Film Parade, 1933 (Blackton 2)
Film That Rises to the Surface of Clarified Butter, 1968 (Landow 2)
Film with 3 Dancers, 1970 (Emshwiller 2)
Film Without Title. *See* Film ohne Titel, 1947
Film-Concert Dedicated to the 25th Anniversary of the Red Army, 1941 (Gerasimov 2)
Filmnotities uit de Sovjet-Unie, 1930 (Ivens 2)
Filmprimadonna, 1913 (Gad 2, Nielsen 3, Freund 4, Kraly 4)

Fire Raisers, 1933 (Powell 2, Balcon 4, Junge 4)
Fire Sale, 1977 (Arkin 3)
Fire the Cook, 1918 (Roach 4)
Fire the Fireman, 1922 (Roach 4)
Fire the Flag! See Ano hata o ute, 1944
Fire the Kaiser, 1918 (Fairbanks, D. 3)
Fire Within. See Feu follet, 1963
Fireball, 1950 (Garnett 2, Monroe 3, O'Brien, P. 3, Rooney 3, Polglase 4, Young, V. 4)
Fireball 500, 1966 (Crosby 4)
Fireball Forward, 1972 (Smith, J.M. 4)
Fireball Jungle, 1969 (Chaney Lon, Jr. 3)
Firebird, 1934 (Dieterle 2, Darwell 3, Blanke 4, Grot 4, Haller 4, Orry-Kelly 4)
Firebrand, 1962 (Crosby 4)
Firebrand Jordan, 1930 (Canutt 4)
Firebug, 1905 (Bitzer 4)
Firebugs, 1913 (Sennett 2)
Firecreek, 1967 (Elam 3, Fonda, H. 3, Stewart 3, Clothier 4, Newman 4)
Firecreek, 1968 (Fonda, H. 3, Stewart 3)
Fired, 1918 (Dressler 3)
Fired Man, 1940 (Hunt 4)
Firefall. See Cascade de feu, 1904
Firefly, 1937 (MacDonald 3, Adrian 4, Gibbons 4, Goodrich and Hackett 4, Stothart 4, Stromberg 4, Vorkapich 4)
Firefly Light. See Hotaru-bi, 1958
Firefly of France, 1918 (Crisp 3, Reid 3)
Firefly's Light. See Hotaru-bi, 1958
Firefox, 1982 (Eastwood 3, Jarre 4)
Fireman, 1916 (Bacon 2, Chaplin 2, Purviance 3)
Fireman, 1931 (Lantz 4)
Fireman, Save My Child, 1918 (Daniels 3, Lloyd 3, Roach 4)
Fireman, Save My Child, 1927 (Sutherland 2, Beery 3, Schulberg 4)
Fireman Save My Child, 1932 (Bacon 2, Brown 3, Polito 4)
Fireman Save My Child, 1935 (Terry 4)
Fireman to the Rescue, 1903 (Hepworth 2)
Fireman's Bride, 1931 (Terry 4)
Fireman's Picnic, 1937 (Lantz 4)
Firemen's Ball. See Hoří, má panenko, 1967
Firepower, 1979 (Coburn, J. 3, Loren 3, Mature 3, Wallach 3)
Fires of Conscience, 1914 (Reid 3)
Fires of Conscience, 1916 (Farnum 3)
Fires of Fate, 1913 (Reid 3)
Fires of Rebellion, 1916 (Chaney Lon 3)
Fires of Youth. See Up for Murder, 1931
Fires on the Plain. See Nobi, 1959
Fires Were Started, 1943 (Jennings 2, Alwyn 4)
Fireside Brewer, 1920 (Sennett 2, Fazenda 3)
Firestarter, 1984 (Scott, G. 3, Sheen 3)
Fireworks, 1947 (Anger 2)
Fireworks over the Sea. See Umi no hanabi, 1951
Firma Heiratet, 1914 (Lubitsch 2, Freund 4)
Firma heiratet, 1930 (Metzner 4)
First a Girl, 1935 (Saville 2, Matthews 3, Balcon 4)
First and the Last, 1937 (Dean 4, Stallich 4)
First and the Last. See 21 Days, 1937
1st April 2000, 1952 (Wagner 4)
First Auto, 1927 (Zanuck 4)
First Baby, 1904 (Bitzer 4)
First Baby, 1936 (Darwell 3, McDaniel 3, Trotti 4)
1st Bad Man, 1955 (Avery 2)
First Blood, 1982 (Stallone 3)
First Born, 1921 (Hayakawa 3, Wong 3)
First Born, 1928 (Carroll M. 3, Balcon 4, Reville 4)
First Charge of the Machete. See Primera carga al machete, 1969
First Circle, 1974 (Ford, A. 2)
First Comes Courage, 1943 (Arzner 2, Oberon 3, Brown, Harry Joe 4, Walker 4)
First Day. See Den pervyi, 1958
First Day of Freedom. See Pierszwy dzien wolnosci, 1964
1st Days, 1939 (Cavalcanti 2, Jennings 2, Watt 2)
First Deadly Sin, 1980 (Dunaway 3, Sinatra 3)

First Echelon. See Pervye eshelon, 1956
First Family, 1980 (Torn 3, Henry 4)
First Flying Fish, 1955 (Terry 4)
1st Gentleman, 1948 (Cavalcanti 2, Aumont 3)
First Great Train Robbery. See Great Train Robbery, 1978
First Great Train Robbery, 1979 (Goldsmith 4)
First Hundred Years, 1924 (Capra 2, Sennett 2, Langdon 3)
First Hundred Years, 1938 (Montgomery 3, Krasna 4, Ruttenberg 4)
First in War, 1932 (Roach 4)
First Kiss, 1928 (Cooper, Gary 3, Wray 3)
First Kiss. See První políbení, 1935
First Lad. See Pervyi paren, 1958
First Lady, 1937 (Fazenda 3, Francis, K. 3, Brown, Harry Joe 4, Orry-Kelly 4, Steiner 4, Wallis 4)
First Legion, 1951 (Sirk 2, Boyer 3, Carroll L. 3)
First Line of Defence, 1947 (Halas and Batchelor 2)
First Love, 1921 (Baxter W. 3, Levien 4)
First Love, 1939 (Durbin 3, Pasternak 4, Salter 4)
First Love, 1970 (Cortese 3)
First Love, 1977 (Barry 4)
First Love. See Hatsukoi, 1926
First Love. See Erste Liebe, 1970
First Love. See Pervaya liubov, 1968
First Love. See Pervaya lyubov, 1933
First Love. See Primo amore, 1978
First Man to the Moon, 1921 (Fleischer, M. and D. 2)
First Men in the Moon, 1964 (Finch 3, Harryhausen 4)
First Mrs. Fraser, 1932 (Dickinson 2)
First Misunderstanding, 1911 (Pickford 3)
First Monday in October, 1981 (Clayburgh 3, Matthau 3)
First Name Carmen. See Prénom Carmen, 1983
First 99, 1958 (Halas and Batchelor 2)
First of the Few, 1942 (Howard, L. 3, Niven 3, Dillon 4, Mathieson 4, Périnal 4)
First Offence, 1936 (Mills 3, Balcon 4)
First Piano Quartet, 1954 (La Shelle 4)
First Prize. See Hogsta vinsten, 1915
First Rebel. See Allegheny Uprising, 1939
First Robin, 1939 (Terry 4)
First Round-Up, 1934 (Roach 4)
First Seven Years, 1930 (Roach 4)
First Snow, 1935 (Terry 4)
First Snow, 1947 (Terry 4)
First Teacher. See Pyervy uchityel, 1965
First Texan, 1956 (McCrea 3, Mirisch 4)
First Time, 1952 (Tashlin 2, Cummings 3, Laszlo 4)
First Time, 1969 (Bisset 3, Laszlo 4)
First to Fight, 1967 (Hackman 3)
First Travelling Saleslady, 1956 (Eastwood 3, Rogers, G. 3)
First Violin, 1912 (Bunny 3, Costello, M. 3, Talmadge, N. 3)
First Woman Jury in America, 1912 (Bunny 3)
First World War, 1934 (de Rochemont 4)
First Year, 1926 (Borzage 2, Marion 4)
First Year, 1932 (Howard 2, Gaynor 3, Friedhofer 4)
First Year. See Primer año, 1970
First Years. See Pierwsze lata, 1949
First, You Cry, 1978 (Perkins 3)
Fischio al naso, 1967 (Ferreri 2)
Fish, 1922 (Fleischer, M. and D. 2)
Fish. See Riba, 1976
Fish Men, 1978 (Cotten 3)
Fish 'n' Slips, 1962 (McKimson 4)
Fishe da Krin. See Tlatsche, 1939
Fisher Folks, 1911 (Griffith 2, Bitzer 4, Macpherson 4)
Fisherboy's Faith, 1912 (Bosworth 3)
Fishergirl's Folly, 1914 (Pearson 2)
Fisher-Maid, 1911 (Pickford 3, Gaudio 4, Ince 4)
Fishermaid of Bally David, 1911 (Olcott 2)
Fisherman, 1931 (Lantz 4)
Fisherman's Luck, 1945 (Terry 4)
Fisherman's Wharf, 1939 (Young, V. 4)
Fishing, 1921 (Fleischer, M. and D. 2)
Fishing by the Sea, 1947 (Terry 4)

Fishing Made Easy, 1941 (Terry 4)
Fishing Trip. See Ribolov, 1972
Fishing Village. See Fiskebyn, 1919
Fishy Affair, 1913 (Sennett 2)
Fishy Tales, 1937 (Roach 4)
Fiskarvals från Bohuslan, 1909 (Magnusson 4)
Fiskebyn, 1919 (Stiller 2, Magnusson 4)
Fiskelivets favor, 1908 (Jaenzon 4)
Fist Fight, 1964 (Breer 2)
Fist in His Pocket. See Pugni in tasca, 1965
Fist of Fury. See Chinese Connection, 1971
Fistful of Dollars, 1964 (Eastwood 3)
Fistful of Dollars. See Per un pugno di dollari, 1964
Fistful of Dynamite. See Giù la testa, 1971
Fistic Mystic, 1968 (McKimson 4)
Fists and Fodder, 1920 (Hardy 3)
Fists of Fury, 1971 (Lee, B. 3)
Fit for a King, 1937 (Brown 3)
Fit to be Tied, 1952 (Hanna and Barbera 4)
Fitilj, 1971 (Grgić 4)
Fitzcarraldo, 1982 (Herzog 2, Cardinale 3, Kinski 3)
Fitzwilly, 1967 (Evans 3, Biroc 4, Boyle 4, Lennart 4, Mirisch 4,
    Williams, J. 4)
Fitzwilly Strikes Back. See Fitzwilly, 1967
Fiuk a térrol, 1967 (Darvas 3)
Fiume de grande caimano, 1980 (Ferrer, M. 3)
Fiume di dollari, 1966 (Duryea 3, Morricone 4)
Five, 1970 (Halas and Batchelor 2)
5 Acres of Land. See Akkara Paha, 1969
Five Against the House, 1955 (Novak 3, Duning 4, Wald 4)
Five and Dime, 1933 (Lantz 4)
Five and Ten, 1931 (Davies 3, Howard, L. 3, Adrian 4, Barnes 4,
    Booth 4)
Five and Ten Cent Annie, 1928 (Fazenda 3)
5 Angles on Murder. See Woman in Question, 1950
Five Bloody Days to Tombstone. See Five Bloody Graves, 1970
Five Bloody Graves, 1970 (Carradine 3, Zsigmond 4)
Five Bold Women, 1959 (Wexler 4)
5 Boys of Barska Street. See Piatka z ulicy Barskiej, 1954
Five Branded Women, 1960 (Moreau 3)
Five Branded Women. See Giovanna e le altre, 1960
5 Branded Women. See Jovanka e le altri, 1960
Five Brothers and Sisters. See Gonin no kyodai, 1939
Five Came Back, 1939 (Ball 3, Carradine 3, Musuraca 4, Polglase 4,
    Trumbo 4)
5 Card Stud, 1968 (Hathaway 2, Martin, D. 3, McDowall 3, Mitchum 3,
    Jarre 4, Wallis 4)
Five Cent's Trick Book. See Chacho ninpo-cho, 1965
Five Cities of June, 1963 (Heston 3)
5 Copies. See Fem Kopier, 1913
Five Day Lover. See Amant de cinq jours, 1961
Five Days—Five Nights. See Pyat dney—pyat nochey, 1960
Five Days One Summer, 1982 (Zinnemann 2, Connery 3, Bernstein 4)
Five Days to Live, 1922 (Hayakawa 3, Fort 4)
Five Easy Pieces, 1970 (Rafelson 2, Black 3, Nicholson 3, Kovacs 4)
Five Finger Exercise, 1962 (Hawkins 3, Russell, R. 3, Schell,
    Maximilian 3, Goodrich and Hackett 4, Orry-Kelly 4, Stradling 4)
Five Fingers, 1952 (Mankiewicz 2, Darrieux 3, Mason 3,
    Herrmann 4, Lemaire 4, Wheeler 4, Wilson, M. 4, Zanuck 4)
Five for Four, 1942 (McLaren 2)
Five for Hell. See Cinque per l'inferno, 1968
Five Gents on the Spot. See Zoku shacho gyogo-ki, 1966
Five Girls to Cope With. See Pět holek na krku, 1966
Five Golden Dragons, 1967 (Cummings 3, Duryea 3, Kinski 3,
    Lee, C. 3, Raft 3)
Five Golden Hours, 1961 (Charisse 3)
Five Golden Hours. See Cinque ore in contanti, 1961
Five Graves to Cairo, 1943 (Von Stroheim 2, Wilder 2, Baxter A. 3,
    Biro 4, Brackett, C. 4, Dreier 4, Head 4, Rozsa 4, Seitz 4)
Five Guns West, 1954 (Malone 3, Corman 4, Crosby 4)
500 Hats of Bartholomew Cubbins, 1943 (Pal 2)
$500,000 Reward, 1911 (Sennett 2)
Five into Hell. See Cinque per l'inferno, 1968

Five Man Army. See Esercito di 5 uomini, 1969
5 Men in the Circus. See Sakasu gonin-gumi, 1935
Five Men of Great Edo. See Oh-Edo gonon otoko, 1951
Five Miles to Midnight, 1962 (Aumont 3, Perkins 3, Young, G. 3)
Five Miles to Midnight. See Couteau dans la plaie, 1962
Five Minutes to the Duel. See Kettou gofun-mar, 1953
Five O'Clock Girl, 1929 (Davies 3)
Five of a Kind, 1938 (Darwell 3, Hersholt 3, Summerville 3, Trevor 3)
Five of the Jazzband. See Funf von der Jazzband, 1932
Five Pennies, 1959 (Hope 3, Kaye 3, Weld 3, Head 4)
Five People Are Lost. See Petorica odpisani, 1974
Five Pound Man, 1937 (Dillon 4)
Five Pound Reward, 1920 (Howard, L. 3)
Five Puplets, 1935 (Terry 4)
Five Savage Men. See Animals, 1972
Five Star Final, 1931 (Leroy 2, Karloff 3, Robinson, E. 3, Polito 4,
    Wallis 4, Zanuck 4)
Five Steps to Danger, 1956 (Hayden 3)
5,000 Dollars Reward—Dead or Alive, 1911 (Dwan 2)
5,000 Fingers of Dr. T, 1953 (Kramer, S. 2, Planer 4, Salter 4)
Five Weeks in a Balloon, 1962 (Hardwicke 3, Lorre 3, Marshall 3,
    Bennett 4, Hoch 4, Smith, J.M. 4)
Five Witnesses. See Gonin no mokugekisha, 1948
5:48, 1979 (Ivory 2)
5-Storied Pagoda. See Goju-no to, 1944
Five-Thousand Elopement, 1916 (Mix 3)
Fixed Bayonets, 1951 (Fuller 2, Dean 3, Ballard 4, Lemaire 4,
    Wheeler 4)
Fixer, 1968 (Frankenheimer 2, Bates 3, Bogarde 3, Jarre 4, Jeakins 4,
    Trumbo 4)
Fixer Dugan, 1939 (Hunt 4)
Fixer-Uppers, 1935 (Laurel & Hardy 3, Roach 4)
Fjols til Fjells, 1957 (Ullmann 3)
Fjorten dage i jernalderen, 1977 (Roos 2)*
Flaaende Stern, 1950 (Wicki 2)
Flag, 1926 (Bushman 3)
Flag Lieutenant, 1926 (Young, F. 4)
Flag Lieutenant, 1932 (Wilcox 2, Neagle 3)
Flag Maker. See American, 1927
Flag nazii, 1929 (Enei 4)
Flag Wind of Dawn. See Akatsuki no hatakaze, 1938
Flagpole Jitters, 1956 (Three Stooges 3)
Flám, 1966 (Kopecký 3)
Flamands Roses de Camargue, 1969 (Braunberger 4)
Flambeau au pays des surprises, 1916 (Cohl 2)
Flambeau aux lignes. See Flambeau au pays des surprises, 1916
Flambeau, chien perdu. See Journée de Flambeau, 1916
Flambée des rêves, 1924 (Vanel 3)
Flame, 1947 (Crawford, B. 3, McDaniel 3)
Flame and the Arrow, 1950 (Tourneur, J. 2, Lancaster 3, Mayo 3,
    Haller 4, Salt 4, Steiner 4)
Flame and the Flesh, 1954 (Brooks, R. 2, Turner, L. 3, Junge 4,
    Pasternak 4)
Flame in the Ashes, 1913 (Ince 4)
Flame in the Streets, 1962 (Mills 3)
Flame of Araby, 1951 (Chandler 3, Chaney Lon, Jr. 3, O'Hara 3,
    Hunter 4)
Flame of Barbary Coast, 1945 (McQueen, B. 3, Canutt 4)
Flame of Calcutta, 1953 (Katzman 4)
Flame of Life, 1923 (Beery 3, Miller, V. 4)
Flame of Life. See Sången om den eldroda blomman, 1918
Flame of Love, 1930 (Wong 3)
Flame of New Orleans, 1941 (Clair 2, Auer 3, Dietrich 3, Muse 3,
    Krasna 4, Maté 4, Pasternak 4)
Flame of the Barbary Coast, 1945 (Schildkraut 3, Wayne 3, Chase 4)
Flame of the Islands, 1955 (De Carlo 3)
Flame of the Yukon, 1926 (La Shelle 4)
Flame over India, 1959 (Bacall 3, Nugent 4)
Flame over India. See Northwest Frontier, 1959
Flame Within, 1935 (Goulding 2, Marshall 3, O'Sullivan 3, Howe 4)
Flames, 1926 (Hersholt 3, Karloff 3)
Flames, 1932 (Brown, K. 4)
Flames of '49. See Half Breed, 1916

Flames of Passion, 1922 (Wilcox 2, Marsh 3)
Flaming Arrow, 1911 (White 3)
Flaming Arrow. *See* Brandende straal, or Wigwam, 1911
Flaming Barriers, 1924 (Clarke, C.C. 4)
Flaming Fathers, 1927 (Roach 4)
Flaming Feather, 1951 (Arlen 3, Hayden 3)
Flaming Flappers, 1925 (Roach 4)
Flaming Forest, 1926 (Adorée 3, Gibbons 4, Young, W. 4)
Flaming Forties, 1924 (Carey 3, Marion 4, Polito 4, Stromberg 4)
Flaming Frontier, 1926 (Johnson, N. 3, Miller, V. 4)
Flaming Frontier, 1965 (Granger 3)
Flaming Frontiers, 1938 (Cody 3)
Flaming Fury, 1926 (Karloff 3)
Flaming Gold, 1934 (Boyd 3, O'Brien, P. 3, Rosher 4)
Flaming Guns, 1932 (Farnum 3, Mix 3)
Flaming Hearts, 1913 (Bunny 3)
Flaming Signal, 1933 (Auer 3, Walthall 3)
Flaming Sky. *See* Moyuru oozora, 1940
Flaming Star, 1960 (Siegel 2, Del Rio 3, Presley 3, Clarke, C.C. 4, Johnson 4)
Flaming Sword, 1915 (Barrymore L. 3)
Flaming Sword. *See* Verdens Undergang, 1915
Flaming Torch. *See* Bob Mathias Story, 1954
Flaming Years. *See* Povest plamennykh let, 1961
Flaming Youth, 1923 (Moore, C. 3)
Flamingo, 1947 (Dandridge 3)
Flamingo Road, 1949 (Curtiz 2, Crawford, J. 3, Greenstreet 3, McCord 4, Steiner 4, Wald 4)
Flamme, 1923 (Lubitsch 2, Negri 3, Kraly 4)
Flamme, 1925 (Vanel 3)
Flamme, 1936 (Vanel 3, D'Eaubonne 4)
Flamme cachée, 1920 (Musidora 3)
Flamme lugen, 1926 (Porten 3)
Flamme merveilleuse, 1903 (Méliès 2)
Flammen, 1927 (Tschechowa 3)
Flammende Volker, 1921 (Wegener 3)
Flammes sur l'Adriatique, 1968 (Astruc 2)
Flammesvaerdet. *See* Verdens Undergang, 1915
Flap, 1970 (Reed 2, Quinn 3, Winters 3)
Flapper, 1920 (Crosland 2, Shearer 3, Marion 4)
Flapper Wives, 1924 (Horton 3, Murfin 4)
Flareup, 1969 (Welch 3)
Flash Back, 1975 (Huppert 3)
Flash Gordon, 1936 (Crabbe 3)
Flash Gordon, 1980 (Topol 3, Von Sydow 3, Donati 4, Semple 4)
Flash Gordon Conquers the Universe, 1940 (Crabbe 3)
Flash Gordon's Trip to Mars, 1938 (Crabbe 3)
Flash in the Dark, 1914 (Reid 3)
Flash of Fate, 1918 (Young, W. 4)
Flash of Light, 1910 (Griffith 2, Bitzer 4)
Flashes Festivals, 1965 (Harrison 3)
Flashing Spikes, 1962 (Ford, J. 2, Wayne 3)
Flashing Spurs, 1924 (Eason 4)
Flashlight Girl, 1916 (Chaney Lon 3)
Flashpoint, 1984 (Torn 3)
Flat. *See* Byt, 1968
Flat Broke, 1920 (Roach 4)
Flat Foot Fledgling, 1952 (Terry 4)
Flat Foot Stooges, 1938 (Three Stooges 3)
Flat Hatting, 1946 (Hubley 4)
Flat Top, 1952 (Hayden 3, Mirisch 4)
Flatbed Annie and Sweetiepie: Lady Truckers, 1979 (Stanton 3)
Flavor of Green Tea over Rice. *See* Ochazuke no aji, 1952
Flaw, 1955 (Fisher 2)
Flaxy Martin, 1949 (Cook 3, Mayo 3)
Flea Circus, 1954 (Avery 2)
Flea in Her Ear, 1968 (Harrison 3, Jourdan 3, Roberts 3, Cahn 4, Kaper 4, Lang 4)
Flea in Her Ear. *See* Puce à l'oreille, 1968
Fledermaus, 1931 (Ondra 3)
Fledermaus, 1937 (Baarová 3)
Fledermaus, 1946 (Herlth 4)
Fledermaus '55. *See* Oh! Rosalinda, 1955

Fledged Shadows. *See* Opeřené stíny, 1930
Fleet Air Arm, 1943 (Balcon 4)
Fleet That Came to Stay, 1946 (Boetticher 2)
Fleet's In, 1928 (Bow 3, Banton 4)
Fleet's In, 1942 (Holden 3, Hutton 3, Lamour 3, Head 4, Mercer 4, Young, V. 4)
Fleets of Stren'th, 1942 (Fleischer, M. and D. 2)
Fleming Faloon, 1963 (Landow 2)
Flemish Farm, 1943 (Brook 3)
Flesh, 1932 (Ford, J. 2, Goulding 2, Beery 3, Hersholt 3, Edeson 4)
Flesh, 1968 (Warhol/Morrissey 2)
Flesh and Blood, 1912 (Guy 2)
Flesh and Blood, 1922 (Chaney Lon 3)
Flesh and Blood, 1951 (Clayton 2, Greenwood 3)
Flesh and Desire. *See* Fuco nelle vene, 1953
Flesh and Fantasy, 1943 (Duvivier 2, Boyer 3, Cummings 3, Muse 3, Robinson, E. 3, Stanwyck 3, Boyle 4, Cortez 4, Head 4, Hoffenstein 4)
Flesh and Fury, 1951 (Curtis 3, Salter 4)
Flesh and the Devil, 1926 (Brown 2, Garbo 3, Gilbert 3, Daniels 4, Gibbons 4, Glazer 4, Thalberg 4)
Flesh and the Fiends, 1960 (Cushing 3, Pleasance 3)
Flesh and Woman. *See* Grand Jeu, 1954
Flesh Creatures. *See* Horror of the Blood Monsters, 1970
Flesh Creatures of the Red Planet. *See* Horror of the Blood Monsters, 1970
Flesh Feast, 1973 (Lake 3)
Flesh for Frankenstein. *See* Carne per Frankenstein, 1973
Flesh is Hot. *See* Buta no gunkan, 1961
Flesh of Morning, 1956 (Brakhage 2)
Flesh Will Surrender. *See* Delitto di Giovanni Episcopo, 1947
Fletch, 1985 (Leven 2)
Fleur au fusil, 1959 (Rosay 3)
Fleur d'oseille, 1967 (Audiard 4, D'Eaubonne 4)
Fleur de l'âge, 1947 (Carné 2, Aimée 3, Reggiani 3, Trauner 4)
Fleur de l'âge, 1964 (Rouch 2, Teshigahara 2, Bujold 3, Braunberger 4, Takemitsu 4)
Fleur des ruines, 1916 (Gance 2, Burel 4)
Fleur Lafontaine, 1978 (Domrose 3, Hoffmann 3)
Fleurs sauvages, 1981 (Lefebvre 2)
Fleuve Dieu, 1956 (Fresnay 3)
Fleuve invisible, 1960 (Delerue 4)
Fleuve: Le Tarn, 1951 (Fradetal 4)
Flic, 1972 (Melville 2, Delon 3, Deneuve 3)
Flic ou voyou, 1978 (Belmondo 3, Audiard 4, Decaë 4, Sarde 4)
Flic Story, 1975 (Delon 3, Trintignant 3)
Flicka for mej, 1943 (Borgstrom 3)
Flickan ar ett fynd, 1943 (Borgstrom 3)
Flickan från fjallbyn, 1948 (Dahlbeck 3)
Flickan från Paradiset, 1924 (Borgstrom 3)
Flickan från tredje raden, 1949 (Bjornstrand 3, Borgstrom 3)
Flickan i fonstret mittemot, 1942 (Fischer 4)
Flickan i frack, 1956 (Nykvist 4)
Flickan i regnet, 1955 (Andersson B. 3)
Flickan och djavulen, 1944 (Borgstrom 3)
Flicker Fever, 1935 (Sennett 2)
Flickering Youth, 1924 (Capra 2, Sennett 2)
Flickorna, 1968 (Zetterling 2, Andersson B. 3, Andersson H. 3, Bjornstrand 3)
Flickornas Alfred, 1935 (Borgstrom 3)
Fliegende Klassenzimmer, 1954 (Herlth 4)
Fliegende Koffer, 1921 (Reiniger 2)
Fliegenden Ärzte von Ostafrika, 1970 (Herzog 2)
Fliegenden Briganten, 1921 (Warm 4)
Fliehende Schatten, 1922 (Pick 2)
Flies, 1923 (Fleischer, M. and D. 2)
Flies. *See* Mouchy, 1950
Flies Ain't Human, 1941 (Fleischer, M. and D. 2)
Flight, 1929 (Capra 2, Walker 4)
Flight, 1974 (Brakhage 2)
Flight. *See* Beg, 1971
Flight. *See* Flugten, 1942
Flight Angels, 1940 (Bellamy 3, Wyman 3, Wald 4)

Flusternde Tod, 1975 (Howard, T. 3)
Flûte à six schtroumpfs, 1976 (Legrand 4)
Flute and the Arrow. *See* Djungelsaga, 1957
Flute Concert at Sans Souci. *See* Flotenkonzert von Sanssouci, 1930
Flute magique, 1946 (Grimault 4)
Flûte merveilleuse, 1910 (Linders 3)
Fluttering Hearts, 1927 (Hardy 3, Roach 4)
Fly, 1958 (Marshall 3, Price 3, Lemaire 4, Struss 4)
Fly. *See* Muha, 1966
Fly About the House, 1949 (Halas and Batchelor 2)
Fly by Night, 1942 (Siodmak 2, Basserman 3, Seitz 4)
Fly Cop, 1917 (Hardy 3)
Fly in the Ointment, 1943 (Fleischer, M. and D. 2)
Fly Me, 1972 (Corman 4)
Fly with Money. *See* Musca cu bani, 1954
Flyg-Bom, 1952 (Bjornstrand 3)
Flyin' Cowboy, 1928 (Eason 4)
Flying Blind, 1941 (Arlen 3, Head 4, Tiomkin 4)
Flying Cadets, 1941 (Salter 4)
Flying Cat, 1951 (Hanna and Barbera 4)
Flying Colors, 1917 (Borzage 2)
Flying Cups and Saucers, 1949 (Terry 4)
Flying Deuces, 1939 (Sutherland 2, Langdon 3, Laurel & Hardy 3)
Flying Devils, 1933 (Bellamy 3, Musuraca 4, Steiner 4)
Flying Doctor, 1936 (Balcon 4)
Flying Doctors of East Africa. *See* Fliegenden Ärzte von Ostafrika 1970
Flying Down to Rio, 1933 (Astaire 3, Del Rio 3, Muse 3, Rogers, G. 3, Cooper 4, Dunn 4, Hunt 4, Irene 4, Pan 4, Plunkett 4, Polglase 4, Steiner 4)
Flying Dragon, 1978 (Jurgens 3)
Flying Dutchman. *See* Rotterdam—Europoort, 1966
Flying Elephants, 1927 (Laurel and Hardy 3, Roach 4)
Flying Fabian. *See* Leteći Fabijan, 1968
Flying Fever, 1941 (Terry 4)
Flying Fists, 1931 (Iwerks 4)
Flying Fists, 1938 (Katzman 4)
Flying Fleet, 1929 (Novarro 3, Gibbons 4)
Flying Fontaines, 1959 (Katzman 4)
Flying Fool, 1929 (Garnett 2, Boyd 3, Miller, A. 4)
Flying Fool, 1931 (Wilson, C. 4)
Flying Fortress, 1942 (Fisher 2)
Flying Fury, 1926 (Walker 4)
Flying High, 1931 (Berkeley 2, Lahr 3, O'Brien, P. 3, Adrian 4)
Flying Horseman, 1926 (August 4)
Flying Irishman, 1939 (Berman 4, Hunt 4, Trumbo 4)
Flying Leathernecks, 1951 (Ray, N. 2, Ryan 3, Wayne 3)
Flying Luck, 1927 (Arthur 3)
Flying Man, 1962 (Dunning 4)
Flying Missile, 1950 (Ford, G. 3, Duning 4)
Flying News. *See* Lucky Devils, 1941
Flying Oil, 1935 (Terry 4)
Flying Padre, 1951 (Kubrick 2)
Flying Pat, 1920 (Gish, D. 3)
Flying Romeos, 1928 (Leroy 2)
Flying Saucer. *See* Disco Volante, 1965
Flying Saucer Daffy, 1958 (Three Stooges 3)
Flying Saucers Coming!. *See* Talíře nad Velkým Malíkovem1977
Flying Saucers Over Our Town. *See* Talíře nad Velkým Malíkoven, 1977
Flying Scotsman, 1929 (Milland 3)
Flying Skyscraper, 1949 (Mills 3)
Flying Sorceress, 1955 (Hanna and Barbera 4)
Flying South, 1937 (Terry 4)
Flying South, 1947 (Terry 4)
Flying Squad, 1940 (Hawkins 3)
Flying Squad. *See* Flying Squadron, 1940
Flying Squadron, 1940 (Brenon 2)
Flying Tigers, 1942 (Wayne 3, Young, V. 4)
Flying to Fortune, 1912 (Cruze 2)
Flying Torpedo, 1916 (Love 3, Brown, K. 4)
Flying U Ranch, 1927 (Walker 4)
Flying Wild, 1941 (Katzman 4)

Flying with Music, 1942 (Roach 4)
Flyktingar finner en hamn, 1945 (Henning-Jensen 2)
FM, 1978 (Alonzo 4)
F-Man, 1936 (Dreier 4)
Focal Point. *See* Point de mire, 1977
Fodselsdagsgaven, 1912 (Blom 2)
Fog, 1923 (Fazenda 3)
Fog, 1933 (Schary 4)
Fog, 1980 (Carpenter 2, Leigh, J. 3, Bottin 4, Houseman 4, Serafine 4)
Fog. *See* Study in Terror, 1965
Fog and Rain. *See* Kire no ame, 1924
Fog Bound, 1923 (Costello, M. 3)
Fog Over Frisco, 1934 (Dieterle 2, Davis 3, Blanke 4, Gaudio 4, Orry-Kelly 4)
Fogadó az orok világossághoz, 1981 (Torocsik 3)
Foggy Harbor. *See* Kiri no minato, 1923
Foghorn. *See* Muteki, 1952
Foghorn Leghorn, 1948 (McKimson 4)
Fohn, 1950 (Albers 3)
Foiled Again, 1914 (Browning 2)
Foiled Again, 1935 (Terry 4)
Foiled by Fido, 1915 (Sennett 2)
Foiling Fickle Father, 1913 (Sennett 2)
Foire aux Cancres, 1963 (Bourvil 3, Grimault 4)
Foire aux chimères, 1946 (D'Eaubonne 4)
Foire internationale de Bruxelles, 1940 (Storck 2)
Folchetto di Narbonne, 1911 (Bertini 3)
Fold embere, 1917 (Curtiz 2)
Foldámadott a tenger, 1953 (Darvas 3)
Folie des grandeurs, 1971 (Montand 3, Decaë 4, Wakhévitch 4)
Folie des vaillants, 1925 (Dulac 2)
Folie du Docteur Tube, 1916 (Gance 2)
Folies Bergere, 1935 (Chevalier 3, Oberon 3, Sothern 3, Achard 4, Day 4, Meredyth 4, Newman 4, Zanuck 4)
Folies bourgeoises, 1976 (Chabrol 2, Audran 3, Cassel 3, Dern 3, Jurgens 3, Schell, Maria 3, Rabier 4)
Folies d'Elodie, 1981 (Gégauff 4)
Folies douces, 1978 (Guillemot 4)
Folies masquées series, 1901 (Guy 2)
Folies-Bergère, 1957 (Constantine 3)
Folk Tale. *See* Bhavni bhavai, 1981
Folket i Simlångsdalen, 1947 (Dahlbeck 3)
Folket på Hogbogården, 1939 (Borgstrom 3)
Folketingsvalg 1945, 1945 (Henning-Jensen 2)
Folkets Ven, 1918 (Holger-Madsen 2)
Folle à tuer, 1975 (Sarde 4)
Folle Aventure, 1930 (Planer 4)
Follet, 1943 (Henning-Jensen 2)
Follie d'estate, 1966 (Scola 2)
Follie per l'opera, 1948 (Lollobrigida 3, Fusco 4)
Follies Girl, 1943 (Mayo 3)
Follow Me, 1972 (Reed 2, Farrow 3, Topol 3, Barry 4, Wallis 4)
Follow Me, Boys!, 1966 (Disney 2, Gish, L. 3, MacMurray 3)
Follow Me Quietly, 1949 (Fleischer, R. 2)
Follow That Car, 1964 (Halas and Batchelor 2)
Follow That Dream, 1962 (Presley 3, Lederer 4, Salter 4)
Follow the Band, 1943 (Mitchum 3)
Follow the Boys, 1944 (Sutherland 2, Welles 2, Beavers 3, Bruce 3, Chaney Lon, Jr. 3, Dietrich 3, Fields, W.C. 3, MacDonald 3, Muse 3, O'Connor 3, Raft 3, Cahn 4)
Follow the Crowd, 1918 (Daniels 3, Lloyd 3, Roach 4)
Follow the Fleet, 1936 (Sandrich 2, Astaire 3, Ball 3, Grable 3, Rogers, G. 3, Scott, R. 3, Berman 4, Pan 4, Polglase 4, Steiner 4)
Follow the Leader, 1930 (Taurog 2, Rogers, G. 3, Green, J. 4, Head 4)
Follow the Leader, 1944 (Katzman 4)
Follow the Sun, 1951 (Baxter A. 3, Ford, G. 3, Lemaire 4)
Follow Thru, 1930 (Banton 4)
Follow Your Heart, 1936 (Bruce 3, Muse 3)
Follow Your Star, 1938 (Pearson 2)
Folly of Anne, 1914 (Gish, L. 3)
Folly of Vanity, 1924 (August 4)
Folly to Be Wise, 1952 (Sim 3, Gilliat 4)
Foma Gordeyev, 1959 (Donskoi 2)

Fome de amor, 1968 (Pereira Dos Santos 2)
Fond de l'air est rouge, 1977 (Marker 2)
Fonderies Martin, 1938 (Alexeieff and Parker 2)
Foney Fables, 1942 (Freleng 4)
Fontane Effi Briest, 1974 (Fassbinder 2, Schygulla 3)
Food for Scandal, 1920 (Cruze 2)
Food of the Gods, 1976 (Lupino 3)
Foo-Foo series, 1960 (Halas and Batchelor 2)
Fool, 1913 (Pearson 2)
Fool, 1924 (Goulding 2, Ruttenberg 4)
Fool and His Money, 1914 (Weber 2)
Fool Coverage, 1952 (McKimson 4)
Fool for Love, 1985 (Stanton 3)
Fool Killer, 1965 (Perkins 3, Jeakins 4, Rosenblum 4)
Fool There Was, 1915 (Bara 3)
Fool There Was, 1922 (Stone 3)
Foolish Age, 1919 (Sennett 2, Fazenda 3)
Foolish Age, 1921 (Stromberg 4)
Foolish Duckling, 1952 (Terry 4)
Foolish Husbands, 1929 (Sennett 2, Hornbeck 4)
Foolish Husbands. See Histoire de rire, 1941
Foolish Matrons, 1921 (Brown 2, Tourneur, M. 2, Bosworth 3)
Foolish Wives, 1922 (Von Stroheim 2, Brown, Harry Joe 4, Daniels 4, Day 4, Mandell 4)
Fools, 1970 (Robards 3)
Fools First, 1922 (Neilan 2, Struss 4)
Fools for Luck, 1928 (Fields, W.C. 3)
Fools for Scandal, 1938 (Leroy 2, Bellamy 3, Lombard 3, Wyman 3, Banton 4, Deutsch 4, Grot 4)
Fools' Gold, 1946 (Boyd 3)
Fool's Gold. See Krakguldet, 1969
Fools' Highway, 1924 (Coffee 4)
Fool's Luck, 1926 (Arbuckle 3)
Fools of Fate, 1909 (Griffith 2, Bitzer 4)
Fools' Parade, 1971 (Baxter A. 3, Kennedy, G. 3, Martin, S. 3)
Fool's Paradise, 1921 (DeMille 2, Struss 4)
Fool's Paradise, 1971 (Stewart 3, Westmore, F. 4)
Fool's Revenge, 1909 (Griffith 2, Bitzer 4)
Fool's Revenge, 1916 (Oland 3)
Fools Rush In, 1949 (Unsworth 4)
Fools, Water Sprites, and Imposters. See Blázni, vodníci, a podvodníci, 1980
Foot and Mouth, 1955 (Anderson 2, Lassally 4)
Foot Film. See Volleyball, 1967
Foot of Romance, 1914 (Beery 3)
Football, 1935 (Terry 4)
Football, 1962 (Decaë 4)
Football Coach. See College Coach, 1933
Football Fever, 1937 (Lantz 4)
Football Freaks, 1971 (Halas and Batchelor 2)
Football Romeo, 1938 (Sidney 2, Roach 4)
Football Toucher Downer, 1937 (Fleischer, M. and D. 2)
Footlight Glamour. See Upstream, 1926
Footlight Parade, 1933 (Bacon 2, Berkeley 2, Blondell 3, Cagney 3, Garfield 3, Keeler 3, Powell, D. 3, Barnes 4, Grot 4, Wallis 4)
Footlight Serenade, 1942 (Grable 3, Mature 3, Wyman 3, Day 4, Garmes 4, Pan 4)
Footlight Varieties, 1951 (Hunt 4)
Footlights. See Sunny Side Up, 1926
Footlights and Fools, 1929 (March 3, Moore, C. 3, Grot 4, Wilson, C. 4)
Footloose, 1979 (Von Sydow 2)
Footloose Heiress, 1937 (Sheridan 3, Edeson 4)
Footloose Widows, 1926 (Fazenda 3, Zanuck 4)
Footprints. See Orme, 1974
Footprints. See Slady, 1974
Footprints. See Stopy, 1960
Footsteps in the Dark, 1941 (Bacon 2, Bellamy 3, Flynn 3, Haller 4, Wallis 4)
Footsteps in the Fog, 1955 (Granger 3, Simmons 3, Coffee 4)
Footsteps in the Night. See Honeymoon Adventure, 1931
Footsteps in the Snow, 1966 (Lake 3)
Foozle at a Tea Party, 1914 (Roach 4)

Fop. See Pizhon, 1929
For a Cop's Hide. See Pour la peau d'un flic, 1970
For a Few Dollars More. See Per qualche dollaro in piú, 1966
For a Joyful Life. See Za život radostný, 1951
For a Wife's Honor, 1908 (Griffith 2)
For a Woman's Honor, 1910 (Olcott 2)
For Alimony Only, 1926 (Brook 3, Adrian 4, Coffee 4, Miller, A. 4)
For Art's Sake, 1923 (Roach 4)
For att inte tala om alla dessa kvinnor, 1964 (Bergman 2, Andersson B. 3, Andersson H. 3, Dahlbeck 3, Nykvist 4)
For Auld Lang Syne, 1937 (Cagney 3)
For Beauty's Sake, 1941 (Dumont 3, Clarke, C.C. 4, Day 4)
For Better—But Worse, 1915 (Sennett 2)
For Better, For Worse, 1919 (DeMille 2, Swanson 3, Buckland 4, Howe 4, Macpherson 4)
For Better, For Worse, 1954 (Bogarde 3, Green, G. 4)
For Better for Worse, 1959 (Halas and Batchelor 2)
For Better . . . For Worse. See That Little Band of Gold, 1915
For Better or Worse. See That Little Band of Gold, 1915
For Better or Worser, 1935 (Fleischer, M. and D. 2)
For Big Stakes, 1922 (Mix 3)
For Cash, 1915 (Chaney Lon 3)
For Crimin' Out Loud, 1956 (Three Stooges 3)
For de Andre. See Du skal elske din Naeste, 1915
For France, 1917 (Ruggles 2, Von Stroheim 2)
For Freedom, 1918 (Farnum 3)
For Freedom of Cuba, 1912 (Ince 4)
For Friendship. See For vanskaps skull, 1963
For God and Country, 1943 (Huston 3)
For Guests Only, 1923 (Roach 4)
For Heaven's Sake, 1926 (Lloyd 3, Bruckman 4)
For Heaven's Sake, 1950 (Seaton 2, Bennett J. 3, Blondell 3, Cummings 3, Gwenn 3, Webb 3, Lemaire 4, Newman 4)
For hennes skull, 1930 (Jaenzon 4)
For Her Boy's Sake, 1913 (Cruze 2)
For Her Brother's Sake, 1911 (Pickford 3, Gaudio 4, Ince 4)
For Her Brother's Sake, 1914 (Ince 4)
For Her Father's Sins, 1914 (Reid 3, Sweet 3, Loos 4)
For Her Sake. See For hennes skull, 1930
For Her Sister's Sake. See Brillantstjernen, 1912
For His Country's Honor. See For sit Lands Aere, 1915
For His Son, 1911 (Griffith 2, Sweet 3, Bitzer 4)
For Honor of the Name, 1911 (White 3)
For Husbands Only, 1917 (Weber 2)
For Ladies Only, 1981 (Grant, L. 3)
For Lizzie's Sake, 1913 (Sennett 2, Normand 3)
For Love . . . For Magic. See Per amore . . . per magia, 1966
For Love of a Queen. See Dictator, 1935
For Love of Gold, 1908 (Griffith 2)
For Love of Ivy, 1968 (Poitier 3, Jones 4)
For Love of You, 1933 (Dickinson 2, Gallone 2)
For Love or Money, 1939 (Cortez 4, Taradash 4)
For Love or Money, 1963 (Bendix 3, Douglas, K. 3, Ritter 3, Young, G. 3)
For Love or Money. See Crossroads of New York, 1922
For Love or Money. See Cash, 1933
For Massa's Sake, 1911 (White 3)
For Me and My Gal, 1942 (Berkeley 2, Garland 3, Kelly, Gene 3, Wynn 3, Daniels 4, Freed 4)
For Me and My Girl. See For Me and My Gal, 1942
For Men Only, 1951 (Henreid 3)
For Native Soil. See Za rodnou hroudu, 1930
For Old Times Sake, 1913 (Bushman 3)
For Peace, 1956 (Zhao 3)
For Pete's Sake, 1934 (Roach 4)
For Pete's Sake, 1974 (Yates 2, Streisand 3, Kovacs 4)
For Safe Keeping, 1923 (Roach 4)
For Sale, 1924 (Menjou 3, McCord 4)
For Sale a Bungalow, 1927 (Sennett 2)
For Sale—A Life, 1912 (Cruze 2)
For Scent-imental Reasons, 1949 (Jones 2)
For sin Faders Skyld, 1916 (Holger-Madsen 2)
For sin karleks skull, 1914 (Sjostrom 2, Stiller 2)

For Singles Only, 1960 (Katzman 4)
For sit Lands Aere, 1915 (Blom 2)
For the Defense, 1922 (Pitts 3, Rosson 4)
For the Defense, 1930 (Cromwell 2, Francis, K. 3, Powell, W. 3, Banton 4, Lang 4)
For the Empire, 1915 (Pearson 2)
For the First Time. See Serenade einer grossen Liebe, 1958
For the Good of Her Men, 1912 (Dwan 2)
For the Honor of the 7th, 1912 (Ince 4)
For the Love o' Pete, 1926 (Lantz 4)
For the Love of It, 1980 (Arden 3)
For the Love of Ludwig, 1932 (Sennett 2)
For the Love of Man. See Lyubit cheloveka, 1972
For the Love of Mary, 1948 (Beavers 3, Durbin 3, Haas 3, O'Brien, E. 3, Boyle 4, Daniels 4, Orry-Kelly 4)
For the Love of Mike, 1927 (Capra 2, Colbert 3, Haller 4)
For the Love of Mike, 1932 (Oberon 3)
For the Love of Rusty, 1947 (Sturges, J. 2)
For the Love of Tillie. See Tillie's Punctured Romance, 1914
For the Queen's Honor, 1911 (Pickford 3, Gaudio 4)
For the Son of the House, 1913 (Gish, D. 3)
For the Soul of Rafael, 1920 (Carré 4, Edeson 4)
For the Soviet Homeland. See Ka sovetskuyu rodinyu, 1937
For Them That Trespass, 1949 (Cavalcanti 2)
For Those in Peril, 1944 (Crichton 2, Balcon 4, Clarke, T.E.B. 4)
For Those Unborn, 1914 (Sweet 3)
For Those We Love, 1921 (Chaney Lon 3)
For Those Who Dare. See Lust for Gold, 1949
For Those Who Think Young, 1964 (Burstyn 3, Raft 3)
For Valour, 1917 (Barthelmess 3)
For vanskaps skull, 1963 (Andersson H. 3, Fischer 4)
For Whom Do We Love? See Dare no tame ni aisuruka, 1971
For Whom the Bell Tolls, 1943 (Wood 2, Bergman 3, Cooper, Gary 3, De Carlo 3, Canutt 4, Dreier 4, Head 4, Menzies 4, Nichols 4, Struss 4, Young, V. 4)
For Wives Only, 1926 (Heerman 4, Rosson 4)
For You Alone. See When You're in Love, 1937
For You at the Front: The Kazakhstan Front. See Tebe, Front, 1943
For You I Die, 1947 (Auer 3, Clothier 4)
For Your Daughter's Sake. See Common Sin, 1920
For Your Eyes Only, 1981 (Moore, R. 3, Topol 3)
Forager, 1910 (Olcott 2)
Forayer Faeroerne, 1961 (Roos 2)
Forbid Them Not, 1961 (Ferrer, J. 3, Fraker 4)
Forbidden, 1919 (Weber 2)
Forbidden, 1932 (Capra 2, Bellamy 3, Menjou 3, Stanwyck 3, Swerling 4, Walker 4)
Forbidden, 1953 (Curtis 3, Daniels 4, Maté 4)
Forbidden. See Proibito, 1955
Forbidden Adventure, 1931 (Fazenda 3, Lang 4)
Forbidden Adventure. See Newly Rich, 1931
Forbidden Cargo, 1925 (Karloff 3)
Forbidden Christ. See Cristo proibito, 1951
Forbidden City, 1910 (Franklin 3)
Forbidden City, 1918 (Talmadge, N. 3, Schenck 4)
Forbidden Country, 1934 (Reville 4)
Forbidden Fruit, 1921 (DeMille 2, Macpherson 4)
Forbidden Fruit. See Fruit défendu, 1952
Forbidden Games. See Jeux interdits, 1951
Forbidden Heaven, 1935 (Krasner 4)
Forbidden Hours, 1928 (Adorée 3, Novarro 3, Day 4, Gibbons 4)
Forbidden Love. See Homme du Niger, 1940
Forbidden Music. See Land Without Music, 1936
Forbidden Paradise, 1924 (Lubitsch 2, Gable 3, Menjou 3, Negri 3, Dreier 4, Kraly 4)
Forbidden Passage, 1941 (Zinnemann 2)
Forbidden Path, 1918 (Bara 3)
Forbidden Paths, 1917 (Hayakawa 3)
Forbidden Planet, 1956 (Pidgeon 3, Gibbons 4, Gillespie 4, Plunkett 4, Rose 4)
Forbidden Range, 1923 (Canutt 4)
Forbidden Relations. See Visszaesők, 1983
Forbidden Room, 1914 (Dwan 2, Chaney Lon 3, Meredyth 4)

Forbidden Songs. See Zakazane piosenki, 1947
Forbidden Street, 1949 (Negulesco 2, O'Hara 3, Lardner 4, Périnal 4)
Forbidden Street. See Britannia Mews, 1949
Forbidden Thing, 1920 (Dwan 2, Gaudio 4)
Forbidden to Know. See Defense de savoir, 1973
Forbidden Valley, 1920 (Blackton 2)
Forbidden Way. See Cytherea, 1924
Forbidden Woman, 1920 (Edeson 3)
Forbidden Woman, 1927 (Schildkraut 3, Adrian 4, Buckland 4)
Forbidden Women. See Donne proibite, 1953
Forbidden World, 1982 (Corman 4)
Forbin Project, 1970 (Westmore, B. 4, Whitlock 4)
Forbryders Liv og Levned, 1916 (Dreyer 2)
Forbryders Memoirer. See Forbryders Liv og Levned, 1916
Forbush and the Penguins, 1971 (Sucksdorff 2)
Force de l'enfant, 1908 (Cohl 2)
Force of Arms, 1951 (Curtiz 2, Holden 3, McCord 4, Steiner 4, Veiller 4)
Force of Evil, 1948 (Aldrich 2, Polonsky 2, Garfield 3, Day 4, Raksin 4)
Force Ten from Navarone, 1978 (Ford, H. 3, Shaw 3, Foreman 4)
Forced Bravery, 1913 (Sennett 2)
Forced Landing, 1941 (Arlen 3, Alton, J. 4, Head 4, Tiomkin 4)
Forcing Dad's Consent, 1914 (Talmadge, C. 3)
Foreclosure, 1912 (Dwan 2)
Foreign Affair, 1948 (Wilder 2, Arthur 3, Dietrich 3, Brackett, C. 4, Dreier 4, Head 4, Lang 4)
Foreign Affairs, 1935 (Balcon 4)
Foreign Correspondent, 1940 (Hitchcock 2, Basserman 3, Gwenn 3, Marshall 3, McCrea 3, Sanders 3, Bennett 4, Guffey 4, Harrison 4, Maté 4, Menzies 4, Newman 4, Wanger 4)
Foreign Devils, 1927 (Van Dyke, W.S. 2, Gibbons 4)
Foreign Exchange, 1970 (Sangster 4)
Foreign Intrigue, 1956 (Mitchum 3, Thulin 3)
Foreign Legion, 1928 (Stone 3)
Foreign Spy, 1913 (Reid 3)
Foreigner's Okichi. See Toujin Okichi, 1955
Foreman and the Jury, 1913 (Sennett 2)
Foreman of Bar Z Ranch, 1915 (Mix 3)
Foreman Went to France, 1941 (Cavalcanti 2, Hamer 2, Balcon 4)
Foreman's Choice, 1915 (Mix 3)
Foreman's Cousin, 1912 (Anderson G. 3)
Forest, 1931 (Gerasimov 2)
Forest Murmurs, 1947 (Vorkapich 4)
Forest on the Hill, 1919 (Hepworth 2)
Forest Ranger, 1910 (Anderson G. 3)
Forest Rangers, 1942 (Goddard 3, Hayward 3, MacMurray 3, Dreier 4, Lang 4, Young, V. 4)
Forest Ranger's Daughter, 1909 (Lawrence 3)
Forester's Plea, 1911 (Anderson G. 3)
Forester's Song. See Do lesíčka na čekanou, 1966
Forêt calcinée, 1971 (Braunberger 4)
Forêt sacrée, 1950 (Philipe 3)
Forêt secrète d'Afrique, 1968 (Storck 2)
Forever, 1922 (Reid 3, Miller, A. 4)
Forever After, 1926 (Astor 3, Struss 4)
Forever Amber, 1947 (Preminger 2, Stahl 2, Carroll L. 3, Darnell 3, Sanders 3, Wilde 3, Dunne 4, Lardner 4, Lemaire 4, Raksin 4, Shamroy 4, Wheeler 4)
Forever and a Day, 1943 (Clair 2, Goulding 2, Keaton 2, Saville 2, Wilcox 2, Bruce 3, Cooper, Gladys 3, Crisp 3, Cummings 3, Gwenn 3, Hardwicke 3, Horton 3, Lanchester 3, Laughton 3, Lupino 3, Marshall 3, Matthews 3, Milland 3, Neagle 3, Oberon 3, Rains 3, Bennett 4, Garmes 4, Musuraca 4, Stewart 4)
Forever, Darling, 1956 (Ball 3, Calhern 3, Mason 3, Cahn 4, Kaper 4)
Forever England, 1935 (Balcon 4)
Forever England. See Brown on Resolution, 1935
Forever Female, 1953 (Douglas, P. 3, Holden 3, Rogers, G. 3, Epstein, J. & P. 4, Head 4, Stradling 4, Young, V. 4)
Forever Free, 1983 (Moss 4)
Forever in Love. See Pride of the Marines, 1945
Forever My Heart, 1954 (Aimée 3, Fairbanks, D. Jr. 3)
Forever My Love, 1962 (Schneider 3)
Forever Young, Forever Free. See E 'Lollipop, 1975

Forever Yours, 1944 (Tiomkin 4)
Forever Yours. *See* Forget-Me-Not, 1936
Forever Yours. *See* Hub illal Abad, 1959
Forfaiture, 1937 (Allégret, Y. 2, L'Herbier 2, Francis, E. 3, Hayakawa 3, Jouvet 3, Braunberger 4, Schufftan 4)
Forfejlet Spring. *See* Højt Spil, 1913
Forgerons, 1895 (Lumière 2)
Forgery. *See* Falschung, 1981
Forget Me Not, 1922 (Van Dyke, W.S. 2, Love 3)
Forget Mozart, 1985 (Mueller-Stahl 3)
Forget-Me-Not, 1917 (Marion 4)
Forget-Me-Not, 1936 (Hornbeck 4, Krasker 4, Wimperis 4)
Forgiven in Death, 1911 (Anderson G. 3)
Forgotten. *See* Olvidados, 1950
Forgotten Babies, 1933 (Roach 4)
Forgotten Commandments, 1932 (Carradine 3, Struss 4)
Forgotten Faces, 1928 (Brook 3, Powell, W. 3, Estabrook 4, Hunt 4, Selznick 4)
Forgotten Faces, 1936 (Dupont 2, Cummings 3, Marshall 3)
Forgotten Faces, 1961 (Watkins 2)
Forgotten Prayer, 1916 (Borzage 2)
Forgotten Sweeties, 1927 (Roach 4)
Forgotten Victory, 1939 (Zinnemann 2)
Forgotten Village, 1940 (Hammid 2, Kline 2, Meredith 3, Eisler 4)
Forgotten Woman, 1939 (Arden 3, Cortez 4)
Forgotten Women. *See* Mad Parade, 1931
Forjadores de la paz, 1962 (Alvarez 2)
Forked Trails, 1915 (Mix 3)
Forlorn River, 1937 (Crabbe 3, Head 4)
Form Phases, 1952–54 (Breer 2)
Formal Kimono. *See* Harekosode, 1940
Formation, 1952 (Godfrey 4)
Formerly, You Had a Big Time. *See* Vroeger kon je lachen, 1983
Formula, 1980 (Brando 3, Gielgud 3, Scott, G. 3)
Formula I, febbre della velocità, 1978 (Hackman 3)
Fornaretto di Venezia, 1964 (Morgan 3)
Fornarina, 1942 (Baarová 3)
Forraederen, 1910 (Blom 2)
Forsaking All Others, 1922 (Moore, C. 3)
Forsaking All Others, 1934 (Mankiewicz 2, Van Dyke, W.S. 2, Burke 3, Crawford, J. 3, Gable 3, Montgomery 3, Russell, R. 3, Adrian 4, Toland 4)
Forseglade loppar, 1927 (Molander 2, Jaenzon 4)
Forsok inte med mej, 1946 (Borgstrom 3)
Forsta alskarinnan. *See* I livets vår, 1912
Forste Honorar, 1912 (Blom 2)
Forste Kaerlighed, 1912 (Blom 2)
Forsterchristel, 1926 (Dieterle 2, Andrejew 4)
Forsterchristl, 1952 (Herlth 4)
Forsyte Saga. *See* That Forsyte Woman, 1949
Fort Algiers, 1953 (De Carlo 3)
Fort Apache, 1948 (Ford, J. 2, Armendáriz 3, Bond 3, Cody 3, Fonda, H. 3, McLaglen 3, Temple 3, Wayne 3, Basevi 4, Clothier 4, Cooper 4, Nugent 4)
Fort Apache, the Bronx, 1981 (Newman 3)
Fort Bowie, 1957 (Johnson, B. 3)
Fort Defiance, 1951 (Cody 3, Johnson, B. 3, Cortez 4)
Fort Dobbs, 1958 (Mayo 3, Clothier 4, Steiner 4)
Fort Graveyard. *See* Chi to suna, 1965
Fort Massacre, 1958 (McCrea 3, Mirisch 4)
Fort Osage, 1952 (Cody 3, Mirisch 4)
Fort Saganne, 1983 (Deneuve 3, Depardieu 3, Noiret 3)
Fort Ti, 1953 (Katzman 4)
Fort Utah, 1967 (Arlen 3, Ireland 3, Mayo 3)
Fort Vengeance, 1953 (Wanger 4)
Fort Worth, 1951 (Scott, R. 3)
Fort-Dolorès, 1938 (Kaufman 4)
Forth Door, 1921 (Van Dyke, W.S. 2)
Forth Door, 1924 (Wong 3)
Fortini/Cani, 1976 (Straub and Huillet 2)
Fortress on the Volga. *See* Oborona Tsartsina, 1942
Fortuna, 1973 (Stawinsky 4)

Fortuna di essere donna, 1955 (Blasetti 2, Boyer 3, Loren 3, Mastroianni 3, D'Amico 4, Flaiano 4)
Fortuna viene dal cielo, 1943 (Magnani 3)
Fortunat, 1960 (Bourvil 3, Morgan 3)
Fortune, 1913 (Bunny 3)
Fortune, 1931 (Dauphin 3)
Fortune, 1975 (Nichols 2, Nicholson 3, Alonzo 4, Sylbert 4)
Fortune Cookie, 1966 (Wilder 2, Lemmon 3, Matthau 3, Diamond 4, La Shelle 4, Mandell 4, Previn 4)
Fortune Hunter. *See* Lyckoriddare, 1921
Fortune Hunters, 1913 (Guy 2)
Fortune Hunters, 1946 (Terry 4)
Fortune in Diamonds. *See* Adventurers, 1951
Fortune Is a Woman, 1957 (Hawkins 3, Lee, C. 3, Alwyn 4, Gilliat 4)
Fortune Teller, 1923 (Fleischer, M. and D. 2)
Fortune Teller. *See* Maid Mad, 1916
Fortunella, 1958 (Fellini 2, Douglas, P. 3, Masina 3, Sordi 3, De Laurentiis 4, Flaiano 4, Pinelli 4, Rota 4)
Fortunella, 1958 (Douglas, P. 3, Masina 3, Sordi 3)
Fortune's Fool. *See* Alles fur Geld, 1923
Fortune's Mask, 1922 (Hardy 3)
Fortunes of a Composer, 1912 (Talmadge, N. 3)
Fortunes of War, 1914 (Ince 4)
Forty Carats, 1973 (Kelly, Gene 3, Ullmann 3, Lang 4, Legrand 4)
48 Hour Prison Break. *See* Shutsugoku yonjuhachi jikan, 1969
48 Hours. *See* Went the Day Well?, 1942
48 Hrs., 1982 (Hill, W. 2, Nolte 3)
48-Year-Old Rebel. *See* Yonjuhachi-sai no teiko, 1956
41st. *See* Sorok pervyi, 1927
45 Fathers, 1937 (McDaniel 3)
45 Minutes from Hollywood, 1926 (Laurel and Hardy 3, Roach 4)
Forty Guns, 1957 (Fuller 2, Stanwyck 3, Biroc 4, Lemaire 4)
Forty Guns to Apache Pass, 1967 (Murphy 3)
40 Hearts, 1931 (Kuleshov 2)
40 Leagues from Paradise, 1970 (Peries 2)
Forty Little Mothers, 1940 (Berkeley 2, Anderson J. 3, Lake 3)
Forty Little Mothers. *See* Mioche, 1936
40 Million People. *See* Health of a Nation, 1939
Forty Naughty Girls, 1937 (Pitts 3, Polglase 4)
4917, 1917 (Hersholt 3)
49th Man, 1953 (Ireland 3, Katzman 4)
49th Parallel, 1941 (Powell and Pressburger 2, Howard, L. 3, Massey 3, Olivier 3, Mathieson 4, Young, F. 4)
49th Parallel. *See* Invaders, 1942
40 Pounds of Trouble, 1963 (Jewison 2, Curtis 3)
42nd Street, 1933 (Bacon 2, Berkeley 2, Baxter W. 3, Brent 3, Daniels 3, Keeler 3, Merkel 3, Powell, D. 3, Rogers, G. 3, Walthall 3, Orry-Kelly 4, Polito 4, Zanuck 4)
47 Loyal Ronin. *See* Chushingura, 1954
Forty Thieves, 1932 (Terry 4)
Forty Thieves, 1944 (Boyd 3, Wilson, M. 4)
Forty Thousand Horsemen, 1940 (Rafferty 3)
Forty Winks, 1925 (Boyd 3, Wong 3)
Forty Years of Experiment, 1928–29 (Richter 2)
40-Horse Hawkins, 1924 (Miller, V. 4)
Forviste, 1914 (Holger-Madsen 2)
Forward a Century, 1951 (Lassally 4)
Forward Flag of Independence. *See* Susume dokuritsuki, 1943
Forward into the Future, 1964 (Peries 2)
Forward March Hare, 1953 (Jones 2)
Forward Pass, 1929 (Fairbanks, D. Jr. 3, Young, L. 3)
Forza bruta, 1940 (Brazzi 3)
Forza del destino, 1950 (Gallone 2)
Forza G, 1971 (Morricone 4)
Forza Italia!, 1978 (Morricone 4)
Fossils. *See* Kaseki, 1975
Foster and Laurie, 1975 (Schifrin 4)
Fotó Háber, 1963 (Latinovits 3)
Foto proibite di una signora per bene, 1971 (Morricone 4)
Fou, 1970 (Goretta 2)
Fou de la falaise, 1916 (Gance 2, Burel 4)
Fou de Labo 4, 1967 (Blier 3, Brasseur 3)
Fougères bleues, 1975 (Fabian 3, de Beauregard 4)

Foul Ball Player, 1940 (Fleischer, M. and D. 2)
Foul Play, 1976 (Bardem 2)
Foul Play, 1978 (Hawn 3, Meredith 3, Moore, D. 3, Roberts 3)
Foule hurle, 1932 (Gabin 3)
Found Film, 1968-70 (Vanderbeek 2)
Foundation of Ordination. *See* Seishoku no ishizue, 1978
Foundations of Progress, 1972 (Benegal 2)
Foundling, 1915 (Dwan 2, Crisp 3, Pickford 3)
Foundling, 1916 (Marion 4)
Foundling of Fate. *See* Hittebarnet, 1916
Fountain, 1934 (Cromwell 2, Hersholt 3, Lukas 3, Berman 4,
    Hoffenstein 4, Murfin 4, Plunkett 4, Polglase 4, Steiner 4)
Fountainhead, 1949 (Vidor, K. 2, Cooper, Gary 3, Massey 3, Neal 3,
    Blanke 4, Steiner 4)
Fountainhead. *See* Izumi, 1956
Fountains of Bakhisarai, 1909 (Protazanov 2)
Four Around a Woman. *See* Kampfende Herzen, 1920
Four Bags Full. *See* Traversée de Paris, 1956
4 Barriers, 1937 (Cavalcanti 2, Grierson 2, Watt 2)
4 Chimneys. *See* Entotsu no mieru basho, 1953
Four Companions. *See* Vier gesellen, 1938
4 Dark Hours. *See* Green Cockatoo, 1937
Four Daughters, 1938 (Curtiz 2, Garfield 3, Rains 3, Blanke 4,
    Coffee 4, Epstein, J. & P. 4, Friedhofer 4, Haller 4, Orry-Kelly 4,
    Steiner 4, Wallis 4)
Four Days in November, 1964 (Bernstein 4)
Four Days Leave, 1949 (Signoret 3, Wilde 3, Lardner 4, Siodmak 4)
Four Days of Naples. *See* Quattro giornate de Napoli, 1962
Four Days' Wonder, 1936 (Cortez 4)
Four Deuces, 1975 (Palance 3)
Four Devils, 1928 (Murnau 2, Gaynor 3, Mayer 4)
Four Faces West, 1947 (McCrea 3)
Four Feathers, 1929 (Schoedsack 2, Arlen 3, Brook 3, Johnson, N. 3,
    Powell, W. 3, Wray 3, Banton 4, Cooper 4, Estabrook 4,
    Selznick 4)
Four Feathers, 1939 (Richardson 3, Biro 4, Hornbeck 4, Krasker 4,
    Périnal 4, Rozsa 4, Unsworth 4, Wimperis 4)
4 Flights to Love. *See* Paradis perdu, 1939
Four for Texas, 1963 (Aldrich 2, Bronson 3, Elam 3, Martin, D. 3,
    Sinatra 3, Three Stooges 3, Biroc 4, Cahn 4, Guffey 4, Laszlo 4)
Four Friends, 1981 (Penn 2, Cloquet 4, Tesich 4)
Four Frightened People, 1934 (DeMille 2, Colbert 3, Marshall 3,
    Coffee 4, Struss 4)
Four Girls in Town, 1956 (Hudson 3, North 4)
Four Girls in White, 1939 (Merkel 3)
Four Guns to the Border, 1954 (Brennan 3, Mancini 4, Salter 4)
Four Horsemen of the Apocalypse, 1921 (Ingram 2, Beery 3,
    Hersholt 3, Johnson, N. 3, Novarro 3, Valentino 3, Mathis 4,
    Seitz 4)
Four Horsemen of the Apocalypse, 1962 (Minnelli 2, Boyer 3, Cobb 3,
    Ford, G. 3, Henreid 3, Lansbury 3, Lukas 3, Thulin 3, Gillespie 4,
    Krasner 4, Orry-Kelly 4, Périnal 4, Plunkett 4, Previn 4)
Four Hours to Kill, 1935 (Leisen 2, Barthelmess 3, Milland 3, Head 4,
    Krasna 4)
400 Blows. *See* Quatre Cents Coup, 1959
400 Million, 1939 (Ivens 2, Eisler 4, Nichols 4, Van Dongen 4)
4 in the Afternoon, 1951 (Broughton 2)
Four in the Morning, 1953 (Ivory 2)
Four in the Morning, 1965 (Barry 4)
Four Jills in a Jeep, 1944 (Niblo 2, Faye 3, Francis, K. 3, Grable 3,
    Miranda 3, Basevi 4, Friedhofer 4)
Four Just Men, 1939 (Balcon 4)
Four Kinds of Love. *See* Bambole, 1965
4 Little Tailors. *See* 4 Petits Tailleurs, 1910
Four Love Stories. *See* Yottsu no koi no monogatari, 1947
4 Masked Men, 1934 (Pearson 2)
Four Men and a Girl. *See* Kentucky Moonshine, 1938
Four Men and a Prayer, 1938 (Ford, J. 2, Carradine 3, Fitzgerald 3,
    Niven 3, Sanders 3, Young, L. 3, Levien 4, MacGowan 4)
Four Minutes Late, 1914 (Mix 3)
4 Moods. *See* Hsi nu ai le, 1970
Four Mothers, 1941 (Rains 3, Blanke 4, Rosher 4)
4 Musicians of Bremen, 1922 (Disney 2)

Four Musketeers, 1974 (Lester 2, Cassel 3, Chaplin 3, Dunaway 3,
    Heston 3, Lee, C. 3, Reed, O. 3, Welch 3, York, M. 3, Schifrin 4
    Watkin 4)
4 Nights of a Dreamer. *See* Quatre Nuits d'un rêveur, 1971
Four o'Clock, 1957 (Hitchcock 2)
4 Orphans, 1923 (La Cava 2)
Four Parts, 1934 (Roach 4)
Four Poster, 1952 (Kramer, S. 2, Harrison 3, Hubley 4, Tiomkin 4)
4 Seasons of Tateshina. *See* Tateshina no shiki, 1966
Four Shall Die, 1940 (Dandridge 3)
4 Sided Triangle, 1953 (Fisher 2)
Four Sons, 1928 (Ford, J. 2, Clarke, C.C. 4)
Four Sons, 1940 (Ameche 3, Brown, Harry Joe 4, Day 4, Shamroy 4,
    Zanuck 4)
Four Star Boarder, 1935 (Roach 4)
4 Steps in the Clouds. *See* Quattro passi fra le nuvole, 1942
4 Times About Bulgaria. *See* Ctyřikrát o Bulharsku, 1958
4 Troublesome Heads. *See* Homme de tête, 1898
Four Wall Duration, 1973 (Le Grice 2)
Four Walls, 1928 (Crawford, J. 3, Gilbert 3, Gibbons 4, Howe 4)
4 Ways Out. *See* Città si difende, 1951
Four Wives, 1939 (Curtiz 2, Rains 3, Blanke 4, Epstein, J. & P. 4,
    Polito 4, Steiner 4, Wallis 4)
Fourberies de Pingouin, 1916 (Feuillade 2, Musidora 3)
Four-Bit Man, 1919 (Eason 4)
Fourchambault, 1929 (Vanel 3)
Fourflusher, 1928 (Ruggles 2)
Four's a Crowd, 1938 (De Havilland 3, Flynn 3, Russell, R. 3,
    Deutsch 4, Haller 4, Orry-Kelly 4, Robinson 4)
Four's a Crowd. *See* Four Daughters, 1938
Fourteen Carrot Rabbit, 1950 (Freleng 4)
Fourteen Hours, 1951 (Cassavetes 2, Hathaway 2, Darwell 3,
    Douglas, P. 3, Hunter 3, Kelly, Grace 3, Moorehead 3, Lemaire 4
    Newman 4, Paxton 4, Wheeler 4)
14 Year Old Girl. *See* Hedy, 1965
Fourteenth Man, 1920 (Daniels 3, Brown, K. 4)
Fourth Alarm, 1926 (Roach 4)
Fourth Estate, 1940 (Mayer 4)
Fourth Horseman, 1932 (Mix 3)
4th Marriage of Dame Margaret. *See* Prästänkan, 1920
Fourth Mrs. Anderson, 1971 (Baker C. 3)
Fourth Musketeer, 1923 (Howard 2)
Fourvière, 1948 (Colpi 4)
Fowl Ball, 1930 (Lantz 4)
Fowl Play, 1937 (Fleischer, M. and D. 2)
Fowl Play, 1973 (McKimson 4)
Fowl Weather, 1952 (Freleng 4)
Fox, 1921 (Carey 3)
Fox, 1967 (Fraker 4, Koch 4, Schifrin 4)
Fox. *See* Faustrecht der Freiheit, 1974
Fox and the Duck, 1945 (Terry 4)
Fox and the Grapes, 1921 (Terry 4)
Fox and the Hound, 1981 (Rooney 3)
Fox and the Jug. *See* Liška a džbán, 1947
Fox and the Rabbit, 1935 (Lantz 4)
Fox Chase, 1928 (Disney 2)
Fox Chase, 1952 (Lye 2)
Fox Hunt, 1906 (Bitzer 4)
Fox Hunt, 1925 (Roach 4)
Fox Hunt, 1950 (Terry 4)
Fox Hunting the Roman Campagna, 1937–40 (Cardiff 4)
Fox in a Fix, 1951 (McKimson 4)
Fox Movietone Follies of 1929, 1929 (Cooper, J 3, Fetchit 3)
Fox Movietone Follies of 1930, 1930 (Grable 3)
Fox Pop, 1942 (Jones 2)
Fox Talent Movietone, 1928 (Gaynor 3)
Fox Terror, 1957 (McKimson 4)
Foxed by a Fox, 1955 (Terry 4)
Foxes of Harrow, 1947 (Stahl 2, Haas 3, Harrison 3, McLaglen 3,
    O'Hara 3, La Shelle 4, Lemaire 4, Newman 4, Wheeler 4)
Foxfire, 1955 (Chandler 3, Duryea 3, Russell, J. 3, Daniels 4)
Foxfire Childwatch, 1971 (Brakhage 2)
Foxhole in Cairo, 1960 (Caine 3)

Frauen am Abgrund, 1929 (Planer 4)
Frauen aus der Wiener Vorstadt, 1925 (Reisch 4)
Frauen, die durch die Holle gehen, 1966 (Baxter A. 3)
Frauen in New York, 1977 (Fassbinder 2)
Frauen sind keine Engel, 1943 (Jurgens 3, Stallich 4)
Frauen von Folies Bergères, 1926 (Warm 4)
Frauen von Gnadenstein, 1921 (Von Harbou 4)
Frauenarzt Dr. Pratorius, 1950 (Wagner 4)
Frauenarzt Dr. Schafer, 1927 (Albers 3)
Frauenehre, 1918 (Kortner 3)
Frauengasse von Algier, 1927 (Hoffmann 4)
Frauenhaus von Brescia, 1920 (Dreier 4)
Frauenhaus von Rio, 1927 (Planer 4)
Frauennot-Frauengluck, 1930 (Tisse 4)
Frauenopfer, 1922 (Dieterle 2, Leni 2, Basserman 3, Porten 3)
Frauenschicksal, 1929 (Robison 2)
Frauenschicksale, 1952 (Dudow 2, Eisler 4)
Fraulein, 1958 (Ferrer, M. 3)
Fraulein aus Argentinien, 1928 (Albers 3)
Fraulein Barbier, 1915 (Wiene 2)
Fraulein Doktor, 1968 (Lattuada 2, Giannini 3, More 3, De
   Laurentiis 4, Morricone 4)
Fraulein Else, 1929 (Czinner 2, Basserman 3, Bergner 3, Freund 4)
Fraulein Fahnrich, 1929 (Reisch 4)
Fraulein Hoffmanns Erzahlungen, 1933 (Ondra 3)
Fraulein Josette, meine Frau, 1926 (Warm 4)
Fraulein Julie, 1922 (Dieterle 2, Nielsen 3, Herlth 4, Rohrig 4)
Fraulein Pfiffikus, 1919 (Krauss 3)
Fraulein Piccolo, 1914 (Lubitsch 2)
Fraulein Raffke, 1923 (Krauss 3)
Fraulein Seifenschaum, 1914 (Lubitsch 2)
Fraulein vom Amt, 1925 (Galeen 4, Wagner 4)
Fraulein von Barnhelm, 1940 (Hoffmann 4)
Fraulein von Scuderi, 1955 (Porten 3)
Frayle, 1959 (Olmi 2)
Freaks, 1932 (Browning 2, Beavers 3, Gibbons 4, Thalberg 4)
Freaks of the Deep, 1932 (Sennett 2)
Freccia nel fianco, 1945 (Lattuada 2, Flaiano 4, Ponti 4, Rota 4,
   Zavattini 4)
Freckled Fish, 1919 (Hardy 3)
Freckled Rascal, 1929 (O'Brien, P. 3, Musuraca 4, Plunkett 4)
Freckles, 1912 (Bunny 3)
Freckles, 1917 (Neilan 2, Bosworth 3)
Freckles, 1928 (Bosworth 3)
Freckles, 1935 (Berman 4, Plunkett 4)
Freckles, 1960 (Crosby 4)
Fred Barry, comédien, 1959 (Jutra 2)
Fredaines de pierrette series, 1900 (Guy 2)
Freddie Steps Out, 1946 (Katzman 4)
Frederick Douglass: The House on Cedar Hill, 1977 (Moss 4)
Free and Easy, 1930 (DeMille 2, Keaton 2, Niblo 2, Barrymore L. 3,
   Coogan 3, Montgomery 3, Gibbons 4)
Free and Easy, 1941 (Sidney 2, Anderson J. 3, Bruce 3, Cummings 3)
Free Breathing. See Szabad lélegzet, 1973
Free Eats, 1932 (Roach 4)
Free Enterprise, 1948 (Terry 4)
Free Fall, 1967 (Vanderbeek 2)
Free for All, 1949 (Cummings 3, Buckner 4)
Free Love, 1930 (Pitts 3, Summerville 3)
Free Man. See Homme libre, 1973
Free Radicals, 1957 (Lye 2)
Free School. See Jiyu gakko, 1951
Free Soul, 1931 (Brown 2, Barrymore L. 3, Gable 3, Howard, L. 3,
   Shearer 3, Adrian 4, Daniels 4)
Free Spirit. See Belstone Fox, 1973
Free the Army. See F.T.A., 1972
Free to Live. See Holiday, 1938
Free to Love, 1925 (Bow 3, Schulberg 4)
Free Wheeling, 1932 (Roach 4)
Free Woman. See Strohfeuer, 1971
Freebie and the Bean, 1974 (Arkin 3, Caan 3, Kovacs 4, Lourié 4)
Freed 'em and Weep, 1929 (McCarey 2)
Freedom, 1970 (Black 3)

Freedom Committee. See Frihedsfonden, 1945
Freedom Must Have Wings, 1941 (Balcon 4)
Freedom of the Press, 1928 (Stone 3, Walthall 3)
Freedom Radio, 1940 (Asquith 2, Brook 3, Dillon 4)
Freedom Road, 1978 (Kadár 2)
Freehande, 1912 (Porten 3)
Freeze Out, 1921 (Ford, J. 2, Carey 3)
Frei bis zum nachsten Mal, 1969 (Fassbinder 2)
Freie Fahrt, 1928 (Metzner 4)
Freight Prepaid. See Fast Freight, 1921
Freighters of Destiny, 1931 (McCord 4)
Freiheit in Fesseln, 1929 (Warm 4)
Freiwild, 1928 (Holger-Madsen 2)
Frelsende Film, 1915 (Holger-Madsen 2)
Fremde, 1917 (Pick 2, Krauss 3, Hoffmann 4)
Fremde, 1930 (Burel 4)
Fremde Frau, (Staudte 2)
Fremde Furst, 1918 (Wegener 3)
Fremde Vogel, 1911 (Gad 2, Nielsen 3, Freund 4)
Fremdenlegionar. See Wenn die Schwalben heimwarts ziehn, 1928
French Cancan, 1955 (Renoir 2, Félix 3, Gabin 3, Modot 3, Piccoli 3,
   Douy 4)
French Communique, 1940 (Hamer 2)
French Connection, 1971 (Friedkin 2, Hackman 3, Rey 3, Scheider 3,
   Roizman 4)
French Connection II, 1975 (Frankenheimer 2, Hackman 3, Rey 3,
   Renoir 4)
French Conspiracy. See Attentat, 1972
French Cops Learning English, 1908 (Méliès 2)
French Doll, 1923 (Marion 4)
French Downstairs, 1916 (Weber 2)
French Dressing, 1927 (Dwan 2, Brook 3, Haller 4)
French Dressing, 1963 (Russell 2, Delerue 4, Russell 4)
French Duel, 1909 (Griffith 2, Bitzer 4)
French Fried, 1930 (Terry 4)
French Game. See Coeur battant, 1961
French Key, 1946 (Arlen 3)
French Kiss, 1981 (Douglas, M. 3)
French Leave, 1930 (Carroll M. 3)
French Leave, 1948 (Coogan 3, Cooper, J 3)
French Leave. See Poudre d'escampette, 1971
French Lieutenant's Woman, 1981 (Reisz 2, Streep 3, Francis 4,
   Pinter 4)
French Line, 1954 (Bacon 2, Novak 3, Russell, J. 3, D'Agostino 4,
   Dunn 4)
French Lunch, 1969 (Douglas, K. 3)
French Maid, 1907 (Crisp 3)
French Milliner, 1916 (Loos 4)
French Mistress, 1960 (Boulting 2, Addison 4)
French Provincial. See Souvenirs d'en France, 1975
French Quarter, 1978 (Mayo 3)
French Rarebit, 1951 (McKimson 4)
French, They Are a Funny Race. See Carnets du Major Thompson,
   1957
French Touch. See Coiffeur pour dames, 1952
French Town, September 1944, 1944 (Hardwicke 3, Alwyn 4)
French Way. See Mouton enragé, 1974
French White Cargo. See Cargaison blanche, 1937
French Without Tears, 1939 (Asquith 2, Lean 2, Milland 3,
   Dalrymple 4, Dillon 4, Head 4)
Frenchie, 1950 (Lanchester 3, McCrea 3, Winters 3, Salter 4)
Frenchman's Creek, 1944 (Leisen 2, Bruce 3, Fontaine 3, Rathbone 3,
   Dreier 4, Jennings 4, Young, V. 4)
Frenchy, 1914 (Crisp 3)
Frenesia dell'estate, 1963 (Zampa 2, Gassman 3, Age and Scarpelli
Frenzied Finance, 1916 (Hardy 3)
Frenzy, 1972 (Hitchcock 2)
Frenzy. See Hets, 1944
Frère de lait, 1916 (Feyder 2)
Freres Boutdebois, 1908 (Cohl 2)
Frères corses, 1939 (Brasseur 3)
Frères d'Afrique, 1939 (Brasseur 3)
Frères Karamazov. See Morder Dimitri Karamasoff, 1931

From the Cloud to the Resistance. *See* Della nube alla resistenza, 1979
From the Czech Mills. *See* A českých mlýnu, 1929
From the Earth to the Moon, 1958 (Cotten 3, Sanders 3)
From the Four Corners, 1941 (Howard, L. 3, Havelock-Allan 4)
From the 400 to the Herd, 1912 (Dwan 2)
From the Life of the Marionettes. *See* Aus dem Leben der Marionetten, 1980
From the Manger to the Cross, 1912 (Olcott 2)
From the Mixed-Up Files of Mrs. Basil E. Frankweiler, 1973 (Bergman 3)
From the Other Side of the Water. *See* De l'autre côté de l'eau, 1951
From the Police, with Thanks. *See* Polizia ringrazia, 1972
From the Shadows, 1913 (August 4)
From the Terrace, 1960 (Robson 2, Loy 3, Newman 3, Woodward 3, Bernstein 4, Lehman 4, Wheeler 4)
From the World of Wood Cottages. *See* Ze světa lesních samot, 1933
From This Day Forward, 1946 (Fontaine 3, D'Agostino 4, Kanin 4)
From Wash to Washington, 1914 (Cruze 2)
From Whom Cometh My Help, 1949 (Poitier 3)
Fromme Luge, 1938 (Negri 3)
Front, 1943 (Vasiliev 2)
Front, 1976 (Allen 2, Ritt 2)
Front at the Enemy's Rear. *See* Front v tylu vraga, 1981
Front Behind the Front. *See* Front za liniei, 1977
Front bex flangov, 1975 (Tikhonov 3)
Front de mer, 1951 (Auric 4)
Front Line, 1940 (Watt 2)
Front Page, 1931 (Milestone 2, Horton 3, Menjou 3, O'Brien, P. 3, Summerville 3, Day 4, Lederer 4)
Front Page, 1974 (Wilder 2, Lemmon 3, Matthau 3, Sarandon 3, Bumstead 4, Diamond 4)
Front Page Story, 1922 (Horton 3)
Front Page Story, 1953 (Hawkins 3)
Front Page Woman, 1935 (Curtiz 2, Brent 3, Davis 3, Gaudio 4, Orry-Kelly 4)
Front v tylu vraga, 1981 (Tikhonov 3)
Front Without Flanks. *See* Front bex flangov, 1975
Front za liniei, 1977 (Tikhonov 3)
Frontier, 1935 (Gerasimov 2)
Frontier. *See* Aerogard, 1935
Frontier. *See* Granica, 1977
Frontier Badmen, 1943 (Chaney Lon, Jr. 3, Farnum 3, Salter 4)
Frontier Doctor, 1911 (Anderson G. 3)
Frontier Gal, 1945 (De Carlo 3, Banton 4)
Frontier Girl's Courage, 1911 (Bosworth 3)
Frontier Hellcat. *See* Unter Geiern, 1964
Frontier Horizon. *See* New Frontier, 1939
Frontier Marshal, 1934 (Bond 3)
Frontier Marshal, 1939 (Dwan 2, Bond 3, Carradine 3, Chaney Lon, Jr. 3, Scott, R. 3, Clarke, C.C. 4, Day 4, Raksin 4)
Frontier Outlaws, 1944 (Crabbe 3)
Frontier Pony Express, 1939 (Johnson, N. 3, Rogers, R. 3)
Frontier Rangers, 1959 (Tourneur, J. 2, Dickinson 3)
Frontier Scout. *See* Quincannon, Frontier Scout, 1956
Frontier Trail, 1926 (Carey 3, Polito 4)
Frontier Vengeance, 1940 (Canutt 4)
Frontier Wife, 1913 (Ince 4)
Frontiere, 1934 (Cervi 3)
Frontière, 1961 (Braunberger 4)
Frontiers. *See* Grens, 1984
Frontiers of News, 1964 (Van Dyke, W. 2)
Frontiersman, 1938 (Boyd 3, Head 4)
Frontiersman. *See* Buckskin, 1968
Frontline Cameras 1935-1965, 1965 (Van Dyke, W. 2)
Frosch mit der Maske, 1959 (Rasp 3)
Frou Frou, 1914 (Cruze 2)
Frou Frou, 1918 (Bertini 3)
Frou Frou. *See* Toy Wife, 1938
Frou-Frou, 1955 (Auer 3, Cervi 3, Alekan 4)
Frozen Dead, 1967 (Andrews D. 3)
Frozen Feet, 1939 (Terry 4)
Frozen Ghost, 1945 (Chaney Lon, Jr. 3, Salter 4)
Frozen Hearts, 1923 (Laurel 3, Roach 4)

Frozen Justice, 1929 (Dwan 2, Carré 4, Levien 4, Rosson 4)
Frozen Logger. *See* Zmrzly dřevař, 1962
Frozen North, 1922 (Keaton 2)
Frozen North, 1941 (Terry 4)
FRPS, 1973 (Le Grice 2)
Fru Kristina, 1917 (Borgstrom 3)
Fru Potifar, 1911 (Blom 2)
Frucht ohne Liebe, 1956 (Wicki 2)
Fruchten, 1933 (Pasternak 4)
Fruhjahrsparade, 1934 (Pasternak 4)
Fruhling auf Immenhof, 1974 (Tschechowa 3)
Fruhling braucht Zeit, 1965 (Hoppe 3)
Fruhlingserwachen, 1929 (Oswald 2, Rasp 3)
Fruhlingsrauschen, 1929 (Dieterle 2)
Fruhlingsstimmen, 1933 (Fejos 2, Sakall 3)
Fruit défendu, 1952 (Verneuil 2, Fernandel 3, Alekan 4)
Fruit of Evil, 1914 (Reid 3)
Fruit of Paradise. *See* Ovoce stromů rajských jíme, 1969
Fruit of the Trees of Paradise. *See* Ovoce stromů rajských jíme, 1969
Fruitful Vine, 1921 (Rathbone 3)
Fruits amers, 1966 (Kosma 4)
Fruits communs, 1960 (Delerue 4)
Fruits de l'été, 1954 (Feuillère 3, Barsacq 4)
Fruits de la passion, 1982 (Colpi 4)
Fruits de saison, 1902 (Guy 2)
Fruits et légumes animés, 1915 (Cohl 2)
Fruits et légumes vivants, 1912 (Cohl 2)
Fruits of Passion, 1982 (Kinski 3)
Fruits of Passion. *See* Fruits de la passion, 1982
Fruits of the Faith, 1922 (Rogers, W. 3, Roach 4)
Fruits sauvages, 1953 (Kosma 4)
Frumento, 1958 (Olmi 2)
Frusta e il corpo, 1963 (Lee, C. 3)
Frustrated Future. *See* Behinderte Zukunfte, 1970
Frustration. *See* Lady, 1964
FTA Show, 1972 (Sutherland 3)
Fubuki ni sakebu ookami, 1931 (Hasegawa 3)
Fubuki to tomo ni keiyukinu, 1959 (Mori 3, Yamada 3)
Fubuki-toge, 1929 (Hasegawa 3)
Fuchs von Glenarvon, 1940 (Tschechowa 3, Wagner 4)
Fuck. *See* Blue Movie, 1968
Fuck Off! Images of Finland. *See* Perkele! Kuvia Suomesta, 1971
Fuck the Army. *See* F.T.A., 1972
Fuco nelle vene, 1953 (Brazzi 3)
Fuddy Duddy Buddy, 1951 (Hubley 4)
Fuefuki-gawa, 1960 (Kinoshita 2, Iwashita 3, Takamine 3)
Fuente magica, 1961 (Williams 3)
Fuentovejuna, 1947 (Rey 3)
Fuerzas vivas, 1974 (Alcoriza 4)
Fufu, 1953 (Naruse 2)
Fuga, 1960 (Diegues 2)
Fuga, 1964 (Aimée 3, Amidei 4)
Fuga in città, 1950 (Risi 2)
Fuga in Francia, 1948 (Germi 2, Flaiano 4, Gherardi 4, Ponti 4, Rota 4)
Fuggitiva, 1941 (Magnani 3)
Fugitif, 1946 (Burel 4)
Fugitive, 1910 (Griffith 2, Bitzer 4)
Fugitive, 1913 (Dwan 2)
Fugitive, 1915 (August 4)
Fugitive, 1935 (Shamroy 4)
Fugitive, 1947 (Ford, J. 2, Armendáriz 3, Bond 3, Del Rio 3, Fonda, H. 3, Cooper 4, Figueroa 4, Nichols 4)
Fugitive. *See* Captain Pirate, 1952
Fugitive. *See* On the Night of the Fire, 1939
Fugitive. *See* Return of Draw Egan, 1916
Fugitive. *See* Taking of Luke McVane, 1915
Fugitive Apparitions. *See* Apparitions fugitives, 1904
Fugitive Family, 1980 (Ferrer, M. 3, Wallach 3)
Fugitive for a Night, 1938 (Trumbo 4)
Fugitive from Chicago. *See* Fluchtling aus Chicago, 1934
Fugitive from Montreal. *See* Inconnue de Montréal, 1950
Fugitive in 6B. *See* Brigante Musolino, 1950
Fugitive in the Sky, 1937 (McCord 4)

Fugitive Kind, 1960 (Lumet 2, Brando 3, Magnani 3, Woodward 3, Kaufman 4, Sylbert 4)
Fugitive Lady, 1934 (Ball 3)
Fugitive Lady. *See* Strada, 1949
Fugitive Lovers, 1934 (Montgomery 3, Three Stooges 3, Gillespie 4, Goodrich and Hackett 4)
Fugitive of the Prairies, 1943 (Crabbe 3)
Fugitive Road, 1934 (Von Stroheim 2, McCord 4)
Fugitives, 1929 (Harlow 3)
Fugitives. *See* Kacaklar, 1971
Fugitives. *See* Sande Kaerlighed, 1912
Fugitives Find Shelter. *See* Flyktinger finner en hamn, 1945
Fugue de Jim Baxter. *See* Son Oncle de Normandie, 1939
Fugue de Lily, 1917 (Feuillade 2)
Fugue de Mahmoud, 1950 (Leenhardt 2)
Fuite de gaz, 1912 (Linders 3)
Fuji, 1974 (Breer 2)
Fuji sancho, 1948 (Hayasaka 4)
Fujicho, 1947 (Kinoshita 2, Tanaka 3)
Fujinkai no himitsu, 1959 (Hara 3)
Fujinka-i no kokuhaku, 1957 (Yamamura 3)
Fukeiki jidai, 1930 (Naruse 2)
Fukei-zu, 1934 (Tanaka 3)
Fukei-zu, 1942 (Hasegawa 3, Takamine 3, Yamada 3)
Fukei-zu, 1949 (Hasegawa 3)
Fukeizu, 1962 (Yoda 4)
Fukeyo harukaze, 1953 (Mifune 3, Yamamura 3)
Fukeyo koikaze, 1935 (Gosho 2)
Fukkatsu, 1950 (Kyo 3, Yoda 4)
Fukushu no shichikamen, 1955 (Yamamura 3)
Fukushu suruwa wareni ari, 1979 (Imamura 2)
Full Ahead. *See* Cala naprzód, 1966
Full Circle, 1976 (Farrow 3)
Full Confession, 1939 (Fitzgerald 3, McLaglen 3, Hunt 4)
Full Fathom Five, 1934 (Gielgud 3)
Full House, 1920 (Cruze 2)
Full House. *See* O. Henry's Full House, 1952
Full Life. *See* Mitasareta seikatsu, 1962
Full o' Pep, 1922 (Roach 3)
Full of Life, 1956 (Holliday 3, Duning 4)
Full Rich Life. *See* Cynthia, 1947
Full Treatment, 1961 (Rosay 3)
Full Treatment. *See* Stop Me Before I Kill, 1961
Full Value, 1912 (Dwan 2)
Fulla Bluff Man, 1940 (Fleischer, M. and D. 2)
Fuller Brush Girl, 1950 (Bacon 2, Tashlin 2, Ball 3)
Fuller Brush Man, 1947 (Tashlin 2)
Fully Insured, 1923 (Roach 4)
Fultah Fisher's Boarding House, 1922 (Capra 2)
Fumée, historie et fantaisie, 1962 (Piccoli 3)
Fumée noire, 1920 (Delluc 2, Francis, E. 3)
Fumées, 1951 (Alexeieff and Parker 2)
Fumeria d'oppio, 1947 (Fellini 2)
Fumetsu no nekkyu, 1955 (Tsukasa 3)
Fumetsu so ai, 1928 (Tanaka 3)
Fumo di Londra, 1966 (Sordi 3, Amidei 4)
Fun and Fancy Free, 1947 (Disney 2, Iwerks 4)
Fun from the Press, 1923 (Fleischer, M. and D. 2)
Fun House, 1936 (Lantz 4)
Fun in a Bakery Shop, 1902 (Porter 2)
Fun in Acapulco, 1963 (Lukas 3, Presley 3, Head 4, Wallis 4)
Fun of Your Life, 1949 (Heston 3)
Fun on the Joy Line, 1905 (Bitzer 4)
Fun with Dick and Jane, 1977 (Fonda, J. 3, Segal 3)
Functions and Relations, 1968 (Halas and Batchelor 2)
Fund im Neubau, 1915 (Oswald 2)
Fundoshi isha, 1960 (Hara 3, Yamamura 3)
Fundvogel, 1930 (Wegener 3, Warm 4)
Funebrak, 1932 (Stallich 4)
Funeral, 1985 (Ryu 3)
Funeral in Berlin, 1966 (Caine 3, Homolka 3, Adam 4)
Funeral of Queen Victoria, 1901 (Hepworth 2)
Funeral Rites. *See* Ososhiki, 1985 (Ryu 3)

Funf Patronenhulsen, 1960 (Geschonneck 3, Mueller-Stahl 3)
5% de risque, 1979 (Ganz 3)
Funf verfluchten Gentlemen, 1931 (Duvivier 2)
Funf von der Jazzband, 1932 (Lorre 3)
Funf von Titan. *See* Vor uns liegt das Leben, 1948
Funfter Akt, siebte Szene. Fritz Kortner probt Kabale und Liebe, 1965 (Syberberg 2)
Funfuhrtee in der Ackerstrasse, 1926 (Planer 4)
15 Jahre schweren Kerker. *See* Frauen aus der Wiener Vorstadt, 1925
Funhouse, 1981 (Baker 4)
Funivia del Faloria, 1950 (Antonioni 2)
Funkzauber, 1927 (Oswald 2, Krauss 3)
Funniest Man in the World, 1967 (Fairbanks, D. Jr. 3)
Funny Bunny Business, 1942 (Terry 4)
Funny Face, 1933 (Iwerks 4)
Funny Face, 1957 (Donen 2, Astaire 3, Hepburn, A. 3, Deutsch 4, Edens 4, Head 4)
Funny Face. *See* Bright Lights, 1935
Funny Girl, 1968 (Wyler 2, Pidgeon 3, Sharif 3, Streisand 3, Lennart 4, Sharaff 4, Stark 4, Stradling 4)
Funny Lady, 1975 (Caan 3, McDowall 3, Sharif 3, Streisand 3, Allen, J. 4, Howe 4, Jenkins 4, Stark 4)
Funny Old Man. *See* Smešný pán, 1969
Funny Thing Happened on the Way to the Forum, 1966 (Keaton 2, Lester 2, Roeg 2, Frank 4, Williams, R. 4)
Funny Thing Happened on the Way to the Crusades. *See* Cintura di castità, 1967
Funnymooners, 1926 (Sennett 2)
Funtoosh, 1956 (Anand 3, Burman 4)
Fuoco, 1915 (Pastrone 2)
Fuorilegge, 1949 (Gassman 3)
Fuorilegge del matrimonio, 1963 (Taviani, P. and V. 2, Girardot 3, Tognazzi 3, Fusco 4)
Furai monogatari: Abare Hisha, 1960 (Hasegawa 3, Yamada 3)
Furai monogatari: Ninkyo-hen, 1959 (Hasegawa 3, Yamada 3)
Furankenshutain no kaiju—Sanda tai Gailah, 1966 (Tsuburaya 4)
Furankenshutain tai Baragon, 1966 (Shimura 3, Tsuburaya 4)
Furcht, 1917 (Veidt 3)
Furia, 1947 (Brazzi 3, Cervi 3)
Furie des S.S. *See* Dieci italiani per un Tedesco, 1962
Furie du désir, 1975 (Ireland 3)
Furies, 1930 (Crosland 2)
Furies, 1950 (Mann 2, Anderson J. 3, Bondi 3, Huston 3, Stanwyck 3, Bumstead 4, Dreier 4, Head 4, Schnee 4, Wallis 4, Waxman 4)
Furin kaza, 1969 (Mifune 3, Shimura 3)
Furisode kenpo, 1955 (Yamada 3)
Furisode kyojo, 1952 (Hasegawa 3)
Furniture Movers, 1918 (Roach 4)
Furoncle, 1915 (Feuillade 2)
Furs, 1911 (Sennett 2)
Furst der Nacht, 1919 (Albers 3)
Furst oder Clown, 1927 (Homolka 3)
Furst Woronzeff, 1934 (Robison 2)
Furstin Woronzoff, 1920 (Dreier 4)
Further Adventures of the Girl Spy, 1910 (Olcott 2)
Furtivos, 1975 (Borau 2)
Furto e l'anima del commercio, 1971 (Blier 3)
Furto su misura, 1962 (Valli 3)
Furusato, 1923 (Mizoguchi 2)
Furusato, 1930 (Mizoguchi 2)
Furusato no uta, 1925 (Mizoguchi 2)
Fury, 1922 (Goulding 2, King 2, Barthelmess 3, Gish, D. 3)
Fury, 1936 (Lang 2, Mankiewicz 2, Bond 3, Brennan 3, Sidney 3, Tracy 3, Gibbons 4, Krasna 4, Ruttenberg 4, Waxman 4)
Fury, 1978 (Smith, D. , Cassavetes 2, De Palma 2, Douglas, K. 3, Baker 4, Williams, J. 4)
Fury at Furnace Creek, 1948 (Mature 3, Newman 4, Raksin 4)
Fury at Showdown, 1956 (La Shelle 4)
Fury at Smuggler's Bay, 1961 (Cushing 3)
Fury is a Woman. *See* Sibirska Ledi Magbet, 1962
Fury of the Congo, 1951 (Weissmuller 3, Katzman 4)
Fury of the Jungle, 1933 (Muse 3, Schary 4)
Fury of the Tropics. *See* Tropic Fury, 1939

Fury of the Wild, 1929 (O'Brien, P. 3)
Fury Unleashed. *See* Hot Rod Gang, 1958
Furyo shojo, 1949 (Naruse 2)
Furyo shojo, 1960 (Yamamura 3)
Furyo shonen, 1960 (Hani 2, Takemitsu 4)
Furyu Fukagawa uta, 1960 (Yamada 3, Yamamura 3)
Furyu katsujin-ken, 1934 (Yamada 3)
Furyu onsen nikki, 1958 (Tsukasa 3)
Furyu onsen: banto nikki, 1962 (Tsukasa 3)
Fuse. *See* Fitilj, 1971
Fusée, 1933 (Tourneur, J. 2)
Fusen, 1956 (Imamura 2, Mori 3)
Fusetsu ni ju-nen, 1951 (Okada 3)
Fushin no toki, 1968 (Imai 2, Kishida 3)
Fusils. *See* Fuzis, 1964
Fusion, 1967 (Emshwiller 2)
Fuss and Feathers, 1909 (Porter 2)
Fuss and Feathers, 1918 (Niblo 2, Barnes 4)
Fussganger, 1974 (Bergner 3, Dagover 3, Rosay 3, Schell,
  Maximilian 3)
Fust, 1970 (Jancsó 2)
Futamabatu, 1933 (Tanaka 3)
Futari de aruita iku-haru-aki, 1962 (Kinoshita 2)
Futari de aruita ikutoshitsuki, 1962 (Takamine 3)
Futari no Iida, 1976 (Takamine 3)

Futari no Musashi, 1960 (Hasegawa 3)
Futari no musuko, 1962 (Shimura 3)
Futatsu doro, 1933 (Kinugasa 2, Hasegawa 3)
Future of Emily. *See* Avenir d'Emilie, 1984
Future Women. *See* Rio '70, 1970
Future's in the Air, 1936 (Alwyn 4)
Futures vedettes, 1954 (Allégret, M. 2, Auer 3, Bardot 3, Marais 3)
Futureworld, 1976 (Brynner 3, Fonda, P. 3)
Futz, 1969 (Forrest 3, Zsigmond 4)
Fuun Konpira-san, 1950 (Yamada 3)
Fuun senryo-bune, 1952 (Hasegawa 3)
Fuun tenman-zoshi, 1930 (Yamada 3)
Fuunji: Oda Nobunaga, 1959 (Kagawa 3)
Fuunjo-shi, 1928 (Hasegawa 3, Tsuburaya 4)
Fuyaki shinju, 1934 (Kinugasa 2)
Fuyuki shinju, 1931 (Hasegawa 3, Yamada 3)
Fuzen no tomoshibi, 1957 (Kinoshita 2, Takamine 3)
Fuzis, 1964 (Guerra 2)
Fuzz, 1972 (Brynner 3, Reynolds, B. 3, Welch 3, Jeakins 4)
Fuzzy Pink Nightgown, 1957 (Taurog 2, Menjou 3, Merkel 3,
  Russell, J. 3, Wynn 3, La Shelle 4)
Fuzzy Settles Down, 1944 (Crabbe 3)
Fy og Bi series, 1921–1940, (Madsen and Schenstrom 3)
400 nyttio ett, 1964 (Sjoman 2, Fischer 4)
4 x 4, 1965 (Troell 2, Von Sydow 3)

G

G.I. Blues, 1960 (Taurog 2, Presley 3, Head 4, Wallis 4)
G.I. Joe, 1945 (Mitchum 3)
G.I. Wanna Go Home, 1946 (Three Stooges 3)
G.m.b.H Tenor, 1916 (Lubitsch 2)
G-Man Jitters, 1939 (Terry 4)
G-Man's Wife. *See* Public Enemy Wife, 1936
G-Men, 1935 (Cagney 3, Canutt 4, Fusco 4, Miller, S. 4, Orry-Kelly 4,
  Polito 4, Wallis 4, Zanuck 4)
G-Men Never Forget, 1947 (Canutt, 4)
G.P.U., 1942 (Rohrig 4)
G.S.O., 1958 (Kosma 4)
Gaa med mig hjem, 1941 (Christensen 2)
Gabbiano, 1977 (Bellocchio 2)
Gabbiano volano basso, 1977 (Ferrer, M. 3)
Gabby Goes Fishing, 1941 (Fleischer, M. and D. 2)
Gable and Lombard, 1976 (Clayburgh 3, Head 4, Legrand 4)
Gabriel over the White House, 1933 (La Cava 2, Huston 3, Adrian 4,
  Glennon 4, Wanger 4, Wilson, C. 4)
Gabriel Schillings Flucht, 1962 (Dieterle 2)
Gabriela, 1983 (Mastroianni 3)
Gabriele ein, zwei, drei, 1937 (Frohlich 3)
Gabrielle, 1954 (Bjornstrand 3, Fischer 4)
Gab's nur einmal, 1958 (Albers 3)
Gaby, 1956 (Caron 3, Hardwicke 3, Goodrich and Hackett 4,
  Lederer 4, Rose 4)
Gadflies, 1976 (Brakhage 2)
Gadfly. *See* Ovod, 1955
Gadfly. *See* Poprigunya, 1955
Gaest fra en anden Verden. *See* Tugthusfange No. 97, 1914
Gaétan ou le commis audacieux, 1922 (Feuillade 2)
Gage d'amour, 1904 (Guy 2)
Gagnant, 1935 (Allégret, Y. 2, Fradetal 4)
Gagnant, 1979 (Audran 3)
Gai Dimanche, 1935 (Tati 2)
Gai Savoir, 1968 (Godard 2, Léaud 3)
Gaiety George, 1946 (Moore, R. 3)
Gaiety Girls. *See* Paradise for Two, 1937
Gaijo no suketchi, 1925 (Mizoguchi 2)

Gaily, Gaily, 1969 (Ashby 2, Jewison 2, Kennedy, G. 3, Mercouri 3,
  Boyle 4, Mancini 4)
Gaines Roussel, 1939 (Alexeieff and Parker 2)
Gaite Parisienne. *See* Gay Parisian, 1941
Gaités de l'escadron, 1913 (Tourneur, M. 2)
Gaités de l'escadron, 1932 (Tourneur, M. 2, Fernandel 3, Gabin 3,
  Raimu 3, Douy 4)
Gaités de l'escadron, 1954 (Audiard 4)
Gaités de l'exposition, 1938 (Kaufman 4)
Gaités de la finance, 1935 (Fernandel 3, Spaak 4)
Gajre, 1948 (Biswas 4)
Gakusei geisha, 1962 (Iwashita 3)
Gakuso o idete, 1925 (Mizoguchi 2)
Gal Who Took the West, 1949 (Coburn, C. 3, De Carlo 3, Boyle 4,
  Daniels 4, Salter 4)
Galápagos Islands, 1938 (Leacock 2)
Galathea, 1921 (Banky 3)
Galathea, 1935 (Reiniger 2)
Galaxie, 1966 (Markopoulos 2)
Galaxy of Terror, 1981 (Corman 4)
Galeerenstrafling, 1918 (Wegener 3, Wagner 4)
Galerie des monstres, 1924 (Cavalcanti 2)
Galeries Lévy et Cie, 1931 (Christian-Jaque 2)
Galettes de Pont Aven, 1975 (Sarde 4)
Galga mentén, 1954 (Jancsó 2)
Galgamannen, 1945 (Molander 2, Borgstrom 3)
Galia, 1966 (D'Eaubonne 4)
Galileo, 1968 (Cusack 3, Morricone 4, Pinelli 4)
Galileo, 1975 (Losey 2, Gielgud 3, Topol 3)
Gallant Blade, 1948 (Duning 4, Guffey 4)
Gallant Defender, 1935 (Rogers, H. 3)
Gallant Gringo. *See* Adventurer, 1927
Gallant Hours, 1960 (Cagney 3, Montgomery 3)
Gallant Hussar, 1928 (Novello 3)
Gallant Journey, 1946 (Wellman 2, Ford, G. 3, Guffey 4)
Gallant Lady, 1933 (La Cava 2, Brook 3, Day 4, Newman 4, Zanuck 4)
Gallant Legion, 1948 (Schildkraut 3)
Gallant Little Tailor, 1954 (Reiniger 2)

Garçonne, 1957 (Achard 4)
Garçonnière, 1960 (De Santis 2, Petri 2)
Garde à vue, 1980 (Schneider 3, Audiard 4, Delerue 4)
Garde-chasse, 1951 (Decaë 4)
Garden. *See* Zahrada, 1968
Garden. *See* Zahradu, 1975
Garden Gopher, 1950 (Avery 2)
Garden Murder Case, 1936 (Walthall 3, Clarke, C.C. 4)
Garden of Allah, 1916 (Selig 4)
Garden of Allah, 1927 (Ingram 2, Garmes 4)
Garden of Allah, 1936 (Logan 2, Boyer 3, Carradine 3, Dietrich 3,
    Rathbone 3, Schildkraut 3, Miller, V. 4, Rosson 4, Selznick 4,
    Steiner 4, Wheeler 4)
Garden of Delights. *See* Jardín de las delicias, 1970
Garden of Earthly Delights, 1981 (Brakhage 2)
Garden of Eden, 1928 (Milestone 2, Kraly 4, Menzies 4)
Garden of Eden, 1954 (Kaufman 4)
Garden of Evil, 1954 (Hathaway 2, Cooper, Gary 3, Hayward 3,
    Widmark 3, Brackett, C. 4, Herrmann 4, Krasner 4, Lemaire 4,
    Wheeler 4)
Garden of the Finzi-Continis. *See* Giardino dei Finzi Contini, 1971
Garden of the Moon, 1938 (Berkeley 2, O'Brien, P. 3, Gaudio 4,
    Mercer 4, Wald 4)
Garden of Venus, 1981 (Ireland 3)
Garden of Weeds, 1924 (Cruze 2, Baxter W. 3, Brown, K. 4)
Garden of Women. *See* Onna no sono, 1954
Gardener, 1922 (Laurel 3)
Gardener. *See* Tradgårdsmastaren, 1912
Gardener of Eden, 1981 (Broughton 2)
Gardens of England, 1942 (Unsworth 4)
Gardeoffizier. *See* Leibgardist, 1925
Gardez le sourire. *See* Sonnenstrahl, 1933
Gardien de la nuit, 1985 (Branco 4)
Gardienne du feu, 1913 (Feuillade 2)
Gardiens de phare, 1929 (Feyder 2, Grémillon 2, Périnal 4)
Gare centrale. *See* Bab el Haded, 1958
Gareeb, 1942 (Biswas 4)
Gargousse, 1938 (Jeanson 4)
Gargoyles, 1971 (Wilde 3)
Garib, 1974 (Anand 3)
Garibaldino al convento, 1942 (De Sica 2)
Garment Center, 1957 (Boone 3)
Garment Jungle, 1957 (Aldrich 2, Cobb 3, Biroc 4)
Garment Jungle. *See* Garment Center, 1957
Garnison amoureuse, 1933 (Brasseur 3, Fernandel 3, Planer 4)
Garou-Garou, le passe-muraille, 1950 (Greenwood 3, Audiard 4)
Garou-Garou. *See* Passe-Muraille, 1950
Garrison's Finish, 1914 (Mix 3)
Garrison's Finish, 1923 (Pickford 3, Rosson 4)
Garryowen, 1920 (Pearson 2)
Gars des vues, 1975 (Lefebvre 2)
Gas, 1981 (Hayden 3, Sutherland 3)
Gas and Air, 1923 (Laurel 3, Roach 4)
Gaslight, 1940 (Dickinson 2, Walbrook 3, Junge 4)
Gaslight, 1944 (Cukor 2, Bergman 3, Boyer 3, Cotten 3, Lansbury 3,
    Balderston 4, Gibbons 4, Irene 4, Kaper 4, Reisch 4, Ruttenberg 4)
Gaslight Ridge, 1957 (Raksin 4)
Gasmann, 1941 (Ondra 3)
Gas-Oil, 1955 (Gabin 3, Moreau 3, Audiard 4)
Gasoline Engagement, 1911 (Pickford 3, Gaudio 4)
Gasoline Gus, 1921 (Cruze 2, Arbuckle 3, Brown, K. 4)
Gasoline Lover, 1923 (Wray 3)
Gasoline Wedding, 1918 (Lloyd 3, Roach 4)
Gaspard a un rendez-vous, 1963 (Braunberger 4)
Gaspard de Besse, 1935 (Raimu 3)
Gaspard fait du cheval, 1963 (Braunberger 4)
Gaspard se marie, 1964 (Braunberger 4)
Gaspards, 1973 (Denner 3, Depardieu 3, Noiret 3)
Gasparone, 1955 (Eisler 4)
Gassenhauer, 1931 (Pick 2, Staudte 2, Schufftan 4)
Gassi, 1960 (Delerue 4)
Gas-s-s-s, or It Became Necessary to Destroy the World in Order to
    Save It, 1970 (Corman 4)

Gast i eget hus, 1957 (Nykvist 4)
Gastone, 1959 (De Sica 2, Sordi 3)
Gasu ningen daiichigo, 1960 (Tsuburaya 4)
Gatans barn, 1914 (Sjostrom 2, Magnusson 4)
Gate of Hell. *See* Jigokumon, 1953
Gate of Youth. *See* Seishun no mon, 1975
Gate of Youth: Independence. *See* Seishun no mon: Jiritsu hen, 1977
Gates of Heaven. *See* Bramy raju, 1967
Gates of Paris. *See* Porte de Lilas, 1957
Gates of the Forest, 1980 (Ullmann 3)
Gates of the Night. *See* Portes de la nuit, 1946
Gates to Paradise. *See* Bramy raju, 1967
Gateway, 1938 (Ameche 3, Carey 3, Carradine 3, Cronjager 4,
    Reisch 4, Trotti 4)
Gateway of the Moon, 1928 (Del Rio 3, Johnson, N. 3, Pidgeon 3)
Gateway to Glory. *See* Aa, kaigun, 1969
Gateway to the Catskills, 1906 (Bitzer 4)
Gathering, 1977 (Barry 4)
Gathering of Eagles, 1963 (Hudson 3, Bumstead 4, Goldsmith 4,
    Irene 4, Pirosh 4)
Gatling Gun, 1973 (Carradine 3)
Gator, 1976 (Reynolds, B. 3, Fraker 4)
Gatti. *See* Bastardi, 1968
Gatti. *See* Sons of Satan, 1971
Gattin, 1943 (Von Harbou 4)
Gatto, 1977 (Comencini 2, Leone 2, Morricone 4)
Gatto a nove code, 1971 (Malden 3, Argento 4, Morricone 4)
Gatto nero, 1981 (Donaggio 4)
Gattopardo, 1963 (Pollack 2, Visconti 2, Cardinale 3, Delon 3,
    Lancaster 3, Reggiani 3, D'Amico 4, Rota 4)
Gaucho, 1928 (Fairbanks, D. 3, Velez 3, Gaudio 4)
Gaucho, 1964 (Risi 2, Scola 2, Gassman 3, Manfredi 3)
Gaucho Serenade, 1940 (Autry 3)
Gauchos judíos, 1975 (Torre-Nilsson 2)
Gauchos of Eldorado, 1941 (Canutt 4)
Gauguin, 1950 (Resnais 2, Braunberger 4)
Gauguin the Savage, 1980 (Lassally 4)
Gauloises bleues, 1968 (Girardot 3, Guillemot 4)
Gaunt Stranger, 1938 (Balcon 4, Gilliat 4)
Gaunt Woman. *See* Destiny of a Spy, 1969
Gauntlet, 1975 (Eastwood 3)
Gautama the Buddha, 1967 (Roy 2)
Gaven. *See* Fødselsdagsgaven, 1912
Gavilán pollero, 1950 (Infante 3, Figueroa 4)
Gavilanes, 1954 (Infante 3)
Gavotte, 1902 (Guy 2)
Gavotte, 1967 (Borowczyk 4)
Gay Adventure, 1953 (Meredith 3)
Gay Adventure. *See* Golden Arrow, 1949
Gay and Devilish, 1922 (Fort 4)
Gay Antics, 1946 (Freleng 4)
Gay Back Alley. *See* Yokina uramachi, 1939
Gay Bride, 1935 (Lombard 3, Pitts 3)
Gay Caballero, 1932 (McLaglen 3)
Gay Caballero, 1940 (Cronjager 4, Day 4)
Gay Canary, 1929 (Kuleshov 2)
Gay Corinthian, 1925 (McLaglen 3)
Gay Deceiver, 1926 (Stahl 2, Booth 4, Gaudio 4, Gibbons 4, Glazer 4
Gay Deception, 1935 (Wyler 2, Lasky 4, Reynolds 4)
Gay Defender, 1927 (La Cava 2, Cronjager 4, Mankiewicz 4)
Gay Desperado, 1936 (Mamoulian 2, Auer 3, Lupino 3, Day 4,
    Lasky 4, Newman 4)
Gay Diplomat, 1931 (Berman 4, Steiner 4)
Gay Divorce. *See* Gay Divorcee, 1934
Gay Divorcee, 1934 (Sandrich 2, Astaire 3, Brady 3, Grable 3,
    Horton 3, Rogers, G. 3, Berman 4, Biroc 4, Pan 4, Plunkett 4,
    Polglase 4, Steiner 4)
Gay Duellist. *See* Meet Me at Dawn, 1947
Gay Falcon, 1941 (Cooper, Gladys 3, Sanders 3, Musuraca 4,
    Polglase 4)
Gay Huskies. *See* Lykkehjulet, 1926
Gay Knighties, 1941 (Pal 2)
Gay Lady. *See* Battle of Paris, 1929

Generation. *See* Pokolenie, 1954
Génération du désert, 1958 (Jarre 4)
Génération spontanée, 1909 (Cohl 2)
Générations comiques. *See* Génération spontanée, 1909
Generela, 1970 (Félix 3)
Generosity. *See* Aedel Daad, 1911
Genesis,1968 (Carradine 3)
Genesung, 1956 (Wolf 2)
Genevieve, 1953 (More 3)
Genghis Khan, 1965 (Mason 3, Wallach 3, Mathieson 4, Unsworth 4)
Genie, 1953 (Fairbanks, D. Jr. 3)
Génie de feu, 1908 (Méliès 2)
Genii of Fire. *See* Génie de feu, 1908
Genitori in blue-jeans, 1960 (Tognazzi 3)
Genius, 1917 (Hardy 3)
Genius, 1970 (Markopoulos 2)
Genius at Work, 1946 (Lugosi 3)
Genius in the Family. *See* So Goes My Love, 1946
Genji monogatari, 1951 (Shindo 2, Yoshimura 2, Hasegawa 3, Kyo 3, Shindo 3)
Genji monogatari: Ukifune, 1957 (Hasegawa 3)
Genki de ikauyo, 1941 (Tanaka 3)
Gennem Kamp til Sejr, 1911 (Gad 2)
Genocide, 1981 (Taylor, E. 3)
Genopstandelsen. *See* Opstandelse, 1914
Genou de Claire, 1970 (Rohmer 2, Almendros 4)
Genroku bushido, 1940 (Shimura 3)
Genroku chushingura, 1941–2 (Yoda 4)
Genroku onna, 1924 (Tanaka 3)
Gens d'Abitibi, 1979 (Perrault 2)
Gens du mil, 1951 (Rouch 2)
Gens du voyage, 1938 (Feyder 2, Rosay 3, D'Eaubonne 4)
Gens qui pleurent et gens qui rient, 1900 (Méliès 2)
Gens sans importance, 1955 (Verneuil 2, Gabin 3)
Gente da Praia da Vieira, 1975 (de Almeida 4)
Gente del Po, 1947 (Antonioni 2)
Gente dell'aria, 1942 (Cervi 3)
Gente di rispetto, 1975 (Zampa 2, Morricone 4)
Gente en la playa, 1961 (Almendros 4)
Genti così, 1949 (Fusco 4)
Gentilhomme des bas-fonds. *See* Ritter der Nacht, 1928
Gentle Annie, 1944 (Reed, D. 3)
Gentle Art of Seduction. *See* Chasse à l'homme, 1964
Gentle Corsican, 1956 (Lassally 4)
Gentle Creature. *See* Femme douce, 1970
Gentle Cyclone, 1926 (Van Dyke, W.S. 2, Hardy 3)
Gentle Gunman, 1952 (Dearden 2, Bogarde 3, Mills 3)
Gentle Julia, 1923 (Love 3)
Gentle Julia, 1936 (McDaniel 3)
Gentle Sergeant. *See* Three Stripes in the Sun, 1955
Gentle Sex, 1943 (Dauphin 3, Greenwood 3, Howard, L. 3, Dillon 4, Krasker 4)
Gentle Touch. *See* Feminine Touch, 1956
Gentleman after Dark, 1942 (Hopkins, M. 3, Krasner 4, Tiomkin 4)
Gentleman at Heart, 1942 (Cook 3, Clarke, C.C. 4)
Gentleman Burglar, 1908 (Porter 2)
Gentleman Cracksman, 1914 (Cooper, Gladys 3)
Gentleman Daku, 1937 (Biswas 4)
Gentleman de Cocody, 1964 (Christian-Jaque 2, Marais 3)
Gentleman d'Epsom, 1962 (Gabin 3, Audiard 4, Legrand 4)
Gentleman for a Day. *See* Union Depot, 1931
Gentleman from America, 1923 (Karloff 3, Miller, V. 4)
Gentleman from Blue Gulch. *See* Conversion of Frosty Blake, 1915
Gentleman from Dixie, 1941 (Muse 3)
Gentleman from Mississippi, 1914 (Edeson 4)
Gentleman from Nowhere, 1948 (Baxter W. 3, Anhalt 4)
Gentleman in Room Six, 1951 (Kaufman 4)
Gentleman Jim, 1942 (Walsh 2, Bond 3, Flynn 3, Buckner 4)
Gentleman Jo . . . uccidi, 1967 (Morricone 4)
Gentleman Misbehaves, 1946 (Howard, S. 3)
Gentleman of Fashion, 1913 (Bunny 3)
Gentleman of Leisure, 1915 (DeMille 2)
Gentleman of Nerve, 1914 (Normand 3)

Gentleman of Paris, 1927 (d'Arrast 2, Menjou 3, Glazer 4, Mankiewicz 4, Rosson 4)
Gentleman of Paris, 1931 (Gilliat 4)
Gentleman of the Room. *See* Kammarjunkaren, 1913
Gentleman or Thief, 1913 (Loos 4)
Gentleman Tramp, 1975 (Bogdanovich 2, Chaplin 3, Harrison 3, Matthau 3, Almendros 4)
Gentleman's Agreement, 1935 (Pearson 2, Leigh, V. 3, Havelock-Allan 4)
Gentleman's Agreement, 1947 (Kazan 2, Garfield 3, Jaffe 3, Peck 3, Lemaire 4, Miller, A. 4, Newman 4, Wheeler 4, Zanuck 4)
Gentleman's Fate, 1931 (Gilbert 3)
Gentlemen Are Born, 1934 (Darwell 3, Orry-Kelly 4)
Gentlemen from Blue Gulch. *See* Roughneck, 1915
Gentlemen, I Have Killed Einstein. *See* Zabil jsem Einsteina pánové, 1969
Gentlemen in Room 8, 1951 (Hammid 2)
Gentlemen Marry Brunettes, 1955 (Crain 3, Russell, J. 3, Cole 4)
Gentlemen of Nerve, 1914 (Chaplin 2, Sennett 2, Summerville 3)
Gentlemen of the Press, 1929 (Francis, K. 3, Huston 3)
Gentlemen Prefer Blondes, 1928 (Emerson 4, Loos 4, Mankiewicz 4, Rosson 4)
Gentlemen Prefer Blondes, 1953 (Hawks 2, Coburn, C. 3, Dalio 3, Monroe 3, Russell, J. 3, Carmichael 4, Cole 4, Lederer 4, Lemaire 4, Wheeler 4)
Gentlemen with Guns, 1946 (Crabbe 3)
Gents in a Jam, 1952 (Three Stooges 3)
Gents Without Cents, 1944 (Three Stooges 3)
Genuine, 1920 (Wiene 2, Mayer 4)
Genzaburo ihen: Hissatsu-ken oni no maki, 1934 (Hasegawa 3)
Genzaburo ihen: Shokuran renbo no maki, 1934 (Hasegawa 3)
Geo le mystérieux, 1916 (Dulac 2)
Geography Films Series, 1944–49 (Leacock 2)
Geole, 1921 (Musidora 3)
Geordie, 1955 (Sim 3, Alwyn 4, Gilliat 4)
George and Margaret, 1940 (Fisher 2)
George Bernard Shaw, 1957 (Lassally 4)
George Dumpson's Place, 1964 (Emshwiller 2)
George in Civvie Street, 1946 (Formby 3)
George Raft Story, 1961 (Mansfield 3)
George Takes the Air. *See* It's in the Air, 1938
George Washington Carver, 1959 (Moss 4)
George Washington Slept Here, 1942 (Coburn, C. 3, McDaniel 3, Sheridan 3, Deutsch 4, Haller 4, Orry-Kelly 4, Wald 4)
George Washington's Escape, 1911 (Bosworth 3)
George White's 1935 Scandals, 1935 (Faye 3, Powell, E. 3, Friedhofer 4, Lemaire 4)
George White's Scandals, 1934 (Durante 3, Faye 3, Friedhofer 4, Garmes 4, Lemaire 4)
Georgia O'Keeffe, 1947 (Hammid 2)
Georgia's Friends. *See* Four Friends, 1981
Georgie and the Dragon, 1951 (Hubley 4)
Georginas Grunde, 1975 (Schlondorff 2, Von Trotta 2)
Georgina's Reasons. *See* Georginas Grunde, 1975
Georgy Girl, 1966 (Bates 3, Mason 3)
Gerald Cranston's Lady, 1924 (Goulding 2)
Geraldine, 1929 (Wilson, C. 4)
Geranium, 1911 (Costello, D. 3)
Gerarchi si muore, 1962 (Fabrizi 3)
Gerard Malanga Reads Poetry. *See* Bufferin, 1966
Gerechten von Kummerow, 1982 (Hoppe 3)
Gerechtigkeit, 1920 (Kortner 3)
Gerechtigkeit, 1925 (Dieterle 2)
German Calling, 1942 (Lye 2)
German Manpower, 1943 (Kanin 4)
German Sisters. *See* Bleierne Zeit, 1981
Germania, anno zero, 1947 (Rossellini 2, Amidei 4)
Germanin, 1943 (Stallich 4)
Germany in Autumn. *See* Deutschland im Herbst, 1978
Germany, Year Zero. *See* Germania, anno zero, 1947
Germinal, 1963 (Allégret, Y. 2, Blier 3, Spaak 4)
Germination d'un haricot, 1928 (Dulac 2)
Gern hab' ich die Frau'n gekillt. *See* Spie contro il mondo, 1966

Geroite na Shipka, 1954 (Vasiliev 2, Karamitev 3)
Gerolsteini kaland, 1957 (Darvas 3)
Geronimo, 1939 (Dreier 4, Head 4)
Geronimo, 1962 (Friedhofer 4)
Geronimo's Last Raid, 1912 (Emerson 4)
Gertie on Tour, c. 1918-21 (McCay 2)
Gertie the Dinosaur, 1914 (McCay 2)
Gertie the Trained Dinosaur. *See* Gertie the Dinosaur, 1914
Gertrud, 1964 (Dreyer 2)
Gervaise, 1955 (Clément 2, Schell, Maria 3, Aurenche 4, Auric 4, Bost 4)
Geschaft, 1917 (Jannings 3)
Geschichte der stillen Muhle, 1914 (Oswald 2, Warm 4)
Geschichte des kleinen Muck, 1953 (Staudte 2)
Geschichte des Prinzen Achmed, 1923–26 (Reiniger 2)
Geschichte einer Leidenschaft. *See* Weib in Flammen, 1928
Geschichte einer Liebe, 1981 (Ganz 3)
Geschichte eines Lebens. *See* Annelie, 1941
Geschichte vom armen Hassan, 1959 (Geschonneck 3)
Geschichten aus dem Wienerwald, 1981 (Dagover 3, Schell, Maximilian 3)
Geschichten jener Nacht, 1967 (Geschonneck 3)
Geschichtsunterricht, 1972 (Straub and Huillet 2)
Geschiedene Frau, 1953 (Herlth 4)
Geschlecht derer von Ringwall, 1918 (Wiene 2, Freund 4)
Geschlecht in Fesseln—Die Sexualnot der Gefangenen, 1928 (Dieterle 2)
Geschlossene Kette, 1920 (Negri 3, Wagner 4)
Geschwader Fledermaus, 1958 (Eisler 4)
Gesicht im Dunkeln. *See* Double Face, 1969
Gespensterschiff, 1921 (Leni 2)
Gespensterstunde, 1917 (Gad 2)
Gestandnis unter vier Augen, 1954 (Knef 3)
Gestartes Rendez-vous, 1897 (Messter 4)
Gestes de France, 1963 (Braunberger 4)
Gestes du silence, 1960 (Storck 2)
Gestohlene Gesicht, 1930 (Schufftan 4)
Gestohlene Herz, 1934 (Reiniger 2)
Gestohlene Jahr, 1951 (Werner 3)
Gestorte Hochzeitsnacht, 1950 (Jurgens 3)
Gestos e Fragmentos, 1982 (de Almeida 4)
Gesù di Nazareth, 1977 (Zeffirelli 2)
Gesù di Nazareth. *See* Jesus of Nazareth, 1977
Gesunkenen, 1925 (Dieterle 2, Albers 3, Nielsen 3, Tschechowa 3)
Gesuzza la sposa Garibaldina. *See* Mille otto cento sessanta, 1934
Get Busy, 1924 (Roach 4)
Get Carter, 1970 (Caine 3)
Get Charlie Tully. *See* Ooh . . . You Are Awful, 1972
Get Cracking, 1943 (Formby 3)
Get Crazy, 1983 (McDowell 3)
Get 'em All. *See* Kenju yo saraba, 1960
Get 'em Young, 1926 (Laurel 3, Roach 4)
Get Going, 1943 (Salter 4)
Get Hep to Love, 1942 (O'Connor 3)
Get Married Mother. *See* Kachan kekkon shiroyo, 1962
Get Off My Back. *See* Synanon, 1965
Get Out and Get Under, 1920 (Lloyd 3)
Get Out Your Handkerchiefs. *See* Préparez vos mouchoirs, 1978
Get Rich Quick, 1913 (Sennett 2)
Get That Venus, 1933 (Arthur 3)
Get to Know Your Rabbit, 1972 (De Palma 2, Welles 2, Alonzo 4)
Get Your Man, 1921 (Howard 2)
Get Your Man, 1923 (Roach 4)
Get Your Man, 1927 (Arzner 2, Bow 3, Schulberg 4)
Get Your Man, 1934 (Harrison 3)
Get Yourself a College Girl, 1964 (Katzman 4)
Get-Away, 1941 (Dailey 3, Reed, D. 3, Burnett 4)
Getaway, 1972 (Hill, W. 2, Peckinpah 2, Johnson, B. 3, McQueen, S. 3, Ballard 4, Jones 4)
Geteilte Himmel, 1964 (Wolf 2)
Get-Rich-Quick Wallingford, 1915 (Niblo 2)
Get-Rich-Quick Wallingford, 1921 (Borzage 2)
Getting a Start in Life, 1915 (Mix 3)

Getting Acquainted, 1914 (Chaplin 2, Sennett 2, Normand 3)
Getting an Eyeful, 1938 (Kaye 3)
Getting Atmosphere, 1912 (Bosworth 3)
Getting Away from It All, 1972 (Meredith 3)
Getting Even, 1909 (Griffith 2, Pickford 3, Bitzer 4)
Getting Gertie's Garter, 1927 (Garnett 2, Rosson 4)
Getting Gertie's Garter, 1945 (Dwan 2, Friedhofer 4)
Getting His Goat, 1920 (Roach 4)
Getting His Goat. *See* Property Man, 1914
Getting Married, 1978 (Johnson, V. 3)
Getting Mary Married, 1919 (Dwan 2, Davies 3, Emerson 4, Loos 4)
Getting of Wisdom, 1977 (Beresford 2)
Getting Reuben Back, 1912–13 (White 3)
Getting Straight, 1970 (Ford, H. 3, Gould 3, Kovacs 4)
Gewehr uber (Staudte 2)
Gewissen in Aufruhr, 1961 (Geschonneck 3)
Gewisser Herr Gran, 1933 (Albers 3, Basserman 3, Tschechowa 3)
Gewisser Judas, 1958 (Herlth 4)
Gewitter im Mai, 1919 (Veidt 3)
Gewitterflug zu Claudia, 1937 (Tschechowa 3)
Gezeichneten, 1922 (Dreyer 2)
Ghaltit Habibi, 1957 (Sharif 3)
Gharam el Asyad, 1960 (Sharif 3)
Ghare Bahire, 1982 (Ray, S. 2, Chatterjee 3, Datta 4)
Ghidrah, The Three Headed Monster. *See* Sandai kaiju chikyu saidai no kessen, 1965
Ghosks in the Bunk, 1939 (Fleischer, M. and D. 2)
Ghost, 1911 (Sennett 2)
Ghost and Mrs. Muir, 1947 (Mankiewicz 2, Harrison 3, Sanders 3, Tierney 3, Wood 3, Day 4, Dunne 4, Herrmann 4, Lang 4, Lemaire 4)
Ghost Breaker, 1914 (DeMille 2, Buckland 4, Macpherson 4)
Ghost Breaker, 1922 (Leroy 2, Johnson, N. 3, Reid 3)
Ghost Breakers, 1940 (Goddard 3, Hope 3, Johnson, N. 3, Lukas 3, Quinn 3, Dreier 4, Head 4, Lang 4)
Ghost Camera, 1933 (Lupino 3, Mills 3)
Ghost Catchers, 1944 (Chaney Lon, Jr. 3)
Ghost Comes Home, 1940 (Burke 3, Meek 3)
Ghost Flower, 1918 (Borzage 2)
Ghost Goes West, 1935 (Clair 2, Donat 3, Lanchester 3, Cardiff 4, Hornbeck 4, Korda 4, Mathieson 4, Rosson 4, Sherwood 4)
Ghost Goes Wild, 1947 (Horton 3, Alton, J. 4)
Ghost in the Garret, 1920 (Gish, D. 3)
Ghost in the Invisible Bikini, 1966 (Bushman 3, Karloff 3, Rathbone 3, Cortez 4)
Ghost in the Noonday Sun, 1974 (Sellers 3)
Ghost of Flight 401, 1978 (Raksin 3)
Ghost of Folly, 1926 (Sennett 2)
Ghost of Frankenstein, 1942 (Bellamy 3, Chaney Lon, Jr. 3, Hardwicke 3, Lugosi 3, Krasner 4, Pierce 4, Salter 4)
Ghost of Hidden Valley, 1946 (Crabbe 3)
Ghost of Love. *See* Fantasma d'amore, 1981
Ghost of Slumber Mountain, 1918 (O'Brien 4)
Ghost of St. Michael's, 1941 (Balcon 4)
Ghost of the Twisted Oaks, 1915 (Olcott 2)
Ghost of the Variety. *See* Spøgelset i Gravkaelderen, 1910
Ghost Parade, 1931 (Sennett 2)
Ghost Patrol, 1923 (Love 3)
Ghost Ship, 1943 (Robson 2, D'Agostino 4, Lewton 4, Musuraca 4)
Ghost Steps Out, 1946 (Abbott 3)
Ghost Story, 1981 (Smith, D. , Astaire 3, Douglas, M. 3, Fairbanks, D. Jr. 3, Neal 3, Cardiff 4, Houseman 4, Sarde 4, Whitlock 4)
Ghost Story of Youth. *See* Seishun kaidan, 1955
Ghost Talks, 1929 (Brown 3, Fetchit 3)
Ghost Talks, 1949 (Three Stooges 3)
Ghost Town, 1937 (Carey 3)
Ghost Town, 1944 (Terry 4)
Ghost Town, 1955 (Biroc 4)
Ghost Town Gold, 1936 (Canutt 4)
Ghost Train, 1931 (Balcon 4, Biro 4)
Ghost Train. *See* Yuhrei ressha, 1949
Ghost Valley, 1932 (McCord 4)

Ghost Valley Raiders, 1940 (Canutt 4)
Ghost Wanted, 1940 (Jones 2)
Ghostbusters, 1984 (Bernstein 4, Edlund 4, Kovacs 4)
Ghosts, 1915 (Von Stroheim 2, Walthall 3, Emerson 4)
Ghosts Before Breakfast. See Vormittagsspuk, 1927–28
Ghosts in the Night. See Ghosts on the Loose, 1943
Ghosts Italian Style. See Questi fantasmi, 1967
Ghosts of Rome. See Fantasmi a Roma, 1961
Ghosts of Yesterday, 1918 (Talmadge, N. 3)
Ghosts on the Loose, 1943 (Gardner 3, Lugosi 3, Katzman 4)
Ghoul, 1933 (Hardwicke 3, Karloff 3, Richardson 3, Balcon 4, Junge 4)
Ghoul, 1975 (Cushing 3, Hurt, J. 3, Francis 4)
Ghum Bhangaar Gaan, 1964 (Shankar 4)
Ghungroo, 1983 (Patil 3)
Giacomo l'idealista, 1942 (Lattuada 2, Risi 2, Ponti 4)
Giallo automatico, 1980 (Bozzetto 4)
Giallo napoletano, 1979 (Mastroianni 3, Piccoli 3)
Gian Burrasca, 1943 (Zavattini 4)
Giant, 1956 (Stevens 2, Baker C. 3, Dean 3, Hopper 3, Hudson 3, McCambridge 3, Mineo 3, Taylor, E. 3, Hornbeck 4, Leven 4, Tiomkin 4)
Giant Behemoth, 1959 (Lourié 4, O'Brien 4)
Giant Claw, 1957 (Katzman 4)
Giant Killer, 1924 (Lantz 4)
Giants vs. Yanks, 1923 (Roach 4)
Giarabub, 1942 (Sordi 3)
Giardino dei Finzi Contini, 1971 (De Sica 2, Sanda 3)
Giardino delle delizie, 1967 (Morricone 4)
Giarrettiera Colt, 1968 (Fusco 4)
Gibier de potence, 1951 (Arletty 3, Aurenche 4)
Gibraltar, 1932 (Wright 2)
Gibraltar, 1938 (Von Stroheim 2, Fradetal 4, Wakhévitch 4)
Gibson Goddess, 1909 (Griffith 2, Sennett 2, Pickford 3, Bitzer 4)
Giddap, 1925 (Sennett 2)
Giddy Age, 1932 (Sennett 2)
Giddy, Gay and Ticklish, 1915 (Sennett 2)
Giddyap, 1950 (Raksin 4)
Giddy-yapping, 1944 (Fleischer, M. and D. 2)
Gideon of Scotland Yard, 1958 (Ford, J. 2, Adam 4, Young, F. 4)
Gideon of Scotland Yard. See Gideon's Day, 1958
Gideon's Day, 1958 (Cusack 3, Hawkins 3, Clarke, T.E.B. 4)
Gideon's Trumpet, 1980 (Houseman 4)
Gidget, 1959 (Robertson 3, Duning 4, Guffey 4, Williams, J. 4)
Gidget Gets Married, 1972 (Bennett J. 3, Biroc 4)
Gidget Goes Hawaiian, 1961 (Duning 4)
Gidget Goes to Rome, 1963 (Williams, J. 4)
Gidget Grows Up, 1969 (Cummings 3)
Gidslet, 1913 (Christensen 2)
Gifle, 1974 (Adjani 3, Girardot 3, Delerue 4)
Gift, 1973 (Brakhage 2)
Gift, 1979 (Ford, G. 3)
Gift. See Cadeau, 1982
Gift. See Dárek, 1946
Gift Horse, 1952 (Attenborough 3, Howard, T. 3)
Gift of Gab, 1934 (Karloff 3, Lugosi 3, Lukas 3, Freund 4, Wald 4)
Gift of Green, 1946 (Van Dongen 4)
Gift of Love, 1958 (Negulesco 2, Bacall 3, Brackett, C. 4, Krasner 4, Lemaire 4)
Gift of Love: A Christmas Story, 1983 (Lansbury 3, Remick 3)
Gift of the Black Folk, 1977 (Moss 4)
Gift O'Gab, 1917 (Van Dyke, W.S. 2)
Gift Supreme, 1920 (Chaney Lon 3)
Gift Wrapped, 1951 (Freleng 4)
Giftas, 1926 (Borgstrom 3)
Giftas, 1956 (Zetterling 2)
Giftasvuxnar dottrar, 1933 (Jaenzon 4)
Giftgas, 1929 (Baranovskaya 3, Kortner 3)
Giftpilen, 1915 (Blom 2)
Giganti della Tessaglia, 1960 (Vích 4)
Gigantis the Fire Monster. See Gojira no gyakushu, 1955
Gigi, 1948 (Noiret 3)
Gigi, 1958 (Minnelli 2, Caron 3, Chevalier 3, Jourdan 3, Ames 4, Beaton 4, Freed 4, Previn 4, Ruttenberg 4)

Gigolette, 1935 (Bellamy 3, Ruttenberg 4)
Gigolette, 1937 (Morgan 3)
Gigolettes, 1932 (Arbuckle 3)
Gigolo, 1926 (Howard 2, Adrian 4, Fort 4, Sullivan 4)
Gigolo, 1960 (Valli 3)
Gigot, 1962 (Kelly, Gene 3, Cahn 4)
Gilbert and Sullivan. See Story of Gilbert and Sullivan, 1953
Gilda, 1946 (Vidor, C. 2, Ford, G. 3, Hayworth 3, Cole 4, Friedhofer 4, Maté 4, Polglase 4)
Gilda Live, 1980 (Nichols 2)
Gilded Cage, 1916 (Brady 3, Edeson 4, Marion 4)
Gilded Fool, 1915 (Farnum 3)
Gilded Highway, 1926 (Blackton 2, Loy 3, Musuraca 4)
Gilded Lily, 1921 (Haller 4)
Gilded Lily, 1935 (Ruggles 2, Colbert 3, MacMurray 3, Meek 3, Milland 3, Banton 4)
Gilded Spider, 1916 (Chaney Lon 3)
Gildersleeve on Broadway, 1943 (Burke 3)
Gildersleeve's Bad Day, 1943 (Darwell 3)
Gillekop, 1919 (Blom 2, Dreyer 2)
Gill-Women of Venus. See Voyage to the Planet of the Prehistoric Women, 1966
Gilly y Praze, 1920 (Ondra 3)
Gimme, 1923 (Walthall 3, Gibbons 4)
Gimme Shelter, 1970 (Maysles A. and D. 2, Murch 4, Wexler 4)
Gina. See Mort en ce jardin, 1956
Ginecologo della mutua, 1977 (Fabrizi 3)
Ginepro fatto uomo, (Bellocchio 2)
Ginger, 1935 (Glennon 4)
Ginger Bread Boy, 1934 (Lantz 4)
Ginger e Fred, 1986 (Masina 3, Mastroianni 3)
Ginger in the Morning, 1973 (Spacek 3)
Gingerbread Hut. See Perníková chalupka, 1951
Gingham Girl, 1920 (Sennett 2)
Gingham Girl, 1927 (Plunkett 4)
Gink at the Sink, 1952 (Bruckman 4)
Ginpei from Koina. See Toina no Ginpei, 1933
Ginpei the Outlaw. See Muhoumono Ginpei, 1938
Ginrei no hate, 1947 (Kurosawa 2, Mifune 3, Shimura 3)
Ginrin, 1955 (Takemitsu 4)
Ginsberg the Great, 1927 (Blanke 4)
Gin-Shinju, 1956 (Shindo 2)
Ginza Cosmetics. See Ginza gesho, 1951
Ginza gesho, 1951 (Naruse 2, Kagawa 3, Tanaka 3)
Ginza kankan musume, 1949 (Takamine 3)
Ginza no onna, 1955 (Yoshimura 2)
Ginza no yanagi, 1932 (Gosho 2, Tanaka 3)
Ginza Sanshiro, 1950 (Ichikawa 2)
Gioccattolo, 1979 (Manfredi 3, Morricone 4)
Giochi di Colonia, 1958 (Olmi 2)
Giochi particolari, 1970 (Mastroianni 3, Guerra 4, Morricone 4)
Gioco pericoloso, 1942 (Amidei 4)
Gioconda Smile. See Woman's Vengeance, 1948
Gion bayashi, 1953 (Mizoguchi 2, Shindo 3, Miyagawa 4, Yoda 4)
Gion Festival. See Gion matsuri, 1933
Gion Festival Music. See Gion bayashi, 1953
Gion matsuri, 1933 (Mizoguchi 2)
Gion matsuri, 1968 (Iwashita 3, Mifune 3, Shimura 3)
Gion no shimai, 1936 (Mizoguchi 2, Yamada 3, Yoda 4)
Gion no shimai, 1956 (Yoda 3)
Giordano Bruno, 1973 (Volonté 3, Morricone 4, Storaro 4)
Giornata balorda, 1960 (Bolognini 2, Pasolini 2)
Giornata nera per l'ariete, 1971 (Morricone 4, Storaro 4)
Giornata particolare, 1977 (Ponti 4)
Giornata speciale, 1977 (Loren 3, Mastroianni 3)
Giorni contati, 1962 (Petri 2, Guerra 4)
Giorni d'amore, 1954 (De Santis 2, Petri 2, Mastroianni 3)
Giorni di fuoco. See Winnetou: Il Teil, 1964
Giorni di gloria, 1945 (De Santis 2, Visconti 2)
Giorni felici, 1942 (Cortese 3)
Giorni più bella, 1956 (De Sica 2)
Giorno da leone, 1961 (Cristaldi 4)
Giorno del furore, 1973 (Cardinale 3, Reed, O. 3)

Girl Loves Boy, 1937 (Brown, K. 4)
Girl Missing, 1932 (Florey 2, Beavers 3)
Girl Most Likely, 1957 (Leisen 2, Merkel 3, Robertson 3)
Girl Must Live, 1939 (Reed 2)
Girl Named Sooner, 1975 (Remick 3, Goldsmith 4)
Girl Named Tamiko, 1962 (Sturges, J. 2, Harvey 3, Anhalt 4, Bernstein 4, Head 4, Lang 4, Wallis 4)
Girl Next Door, 1923 (Van Dyke, W.S. 2)
Girl Next Door, 1953 (Dailey 3, Kidd 4, Lemaire 4, Lennart 4, Shamroy 4)
Girl Next Room, 1910–11 (White 3)
Girl No. 217. See Chelovek No. 217, 1944
Girl O' My Dreams, 1934 (Chaney Lon, Jr. 3)
Girl o' the Woods, 1913 (Lawrence 3)
Girl of Gold Gulch, 1916 (Mix 3)
Girl of My Dreams. See Sweetheart of Sigma Chi, 1933
Girl of the Golden West, 1915 (DeMille 2, Buckland 4, Macpherson 4)
Girl of the Golden West, 1923 (Polito 4)
Girl of the Golden West, 1930 (Polito 4, Young, W. 4)
Girl of the Golden West, 1938 (Eddy 3, MacDonald 3, Pidgeon 3, Adrian 4, Canutt 4, Gibbons 4, Stothart 4, Vorkapich 4)
Girl of the Lighthouse, 1912 (Bosworth 3)
Girl of the Limberlost, 1934 (Walthall 3)
Girl of the Limberlost, 1945 (Ferrer, M. 3, Guffey 4)
Girl of the Meiji Period. See Meiji haruaki, 1968
Girl of the Mountains, 1912 (Bosworth 3)
Girl of the Night, 1915 (Chaney Lon 3)
Girl of the Ozarks, 1936 (Dreier 4)
Girl of the Port, 1930 (Glennon 4)
Girl of the Rio, 1932 (Brenon 2, Del Rio 3, Steiner 4)
Girl of the Timber Claims, 1917 (Talmadge, C. 3)
Girl of the West, 1911 (Anderson G. 3)
Girl of Vaniousine. See Deti Vanyousina, 1915
Girl of Yesterday, 1915 (Dwan 2, Crisp 3, Pickford 3, Marion 4)
Girl on a Motorcycle, 1968 (Delon 3, Cardiff 4, D'Eaubonne 4)
Girl on Approval, 1962 (Roberts 3)
Girl on the Barge, 1929 (Hersholt 3)
Girl on the Bridge, 1951 (Haas 3)
Girl on the Canal. See Painted Boats, 1945
Girl on the Front Page, 1936 (Krasner 4)
Girl on the Late, Late Show, 1974 (De Carlo 3, Grahame 3, Ireland 3, Johnson, V. 3, Pidgeon 3)
Girl on the Stairs, 1924 (Walker 4)
Girl on the Subway, 1958 (Furthman 4)
Girl on Triple X Ranch. See Girl from the Triple X, 1910
Girl Overboard, 1929 (Ruggles 2)
Girl Overboard, 1936 (Pidgeon 3)
Girl Reporter, 1912–13 (White 3)
Girl Rush, 1944 (Mitchum 3, Musuraca 4)
Girl Rush, 1955 (Russell, R. 3, Alton, R. 4, Daniels 4, Head 4, Hornbeck 4, Pirosh 4)
Girl Said No, 1930 (Wood 2, Dressler 3, Gibbons 4, MacArthur 4)
Girl Scout, 1909 (Olcott 2)
Girl Shy, 1924 (Lloyd 3, Roach 4)
Girl Spy Before Vicksburg, 1910 (Olcott 2)
Girl Stroke Boy, 1971 (Greenwood 3)
Girl Swappers. See Two and Two Make Six, 1962
Girl That I Love. See Waga koiseshi otome, 1946
Girl Thief. See Love at Second Sight, 1934
Girl Trouble, 1942 (Ameche 3, Bennett J. 3, Burke 3, Cronjager 4, Day 4, Newman 4)
Girl Was Young, 1937 (Harrison 4)
Girl Was Young. See Young and Innocent, 1937
Girl Who Came Back, 1923 (Pitts 3, Schulberg 4)
Girl Who Couldn't Say No, 1968 (Segal 3)
Girl Who Had Everything, 1953 (Powell, W. 3, Taylor, E. 3, Young, G. 3, Previn 4)
Girl Who Stayed at Home, 1919 (Griffith 2, Barthelmess 3, Bitzer 4)
Girl Who Won, 1914 (Lawrence 3)
Girl Who Wouldn't Work, 1925 (Barrymore L. 3, Walthall 3)
Girl with a Gun. See Ragazza con la pistola, 1968
Girl with a Suitcase. See Ragazza con la valigia, 1961
Girl with Green Eyes, 1964 (Richardson 2, Finch 3, Addison 4)

Girl with Ideas, 1937 (Pidgeon 3, Krasner 4)
Girl with the Green Eyes, 1916 (Guy 2)
Girl with the Guitar. See Devushka s gitaroy, 1958
Girl with the Pistol. See Ragazza con la pistola, 1968
Girl Without a Room, 1933 (Auer 3, Banton 4)
Girl Woman, 1919 (Costello, M. 3)
Girl Worth While, 1913 (Cruze 2)
Girlfriends, 1978 (Wallach 3)
Girlfriends. See Amiche, 1955
Girlfriends. See Biches, 1968
Girlish Impulse, 1911 (Lawrence 3)
Girls. See Flickorna, 1968
Girls about Town, 1931 (Cukor 2, Beavers 3, Francis, K. 3, McCrea 3, Banton 4, Haller 4, Vorkapich 4)
Girls and a Daddy, 1908 (Griffith 2, Bitzer 4)
Girls Can Play, 1937 (Hayworth 3, Ballard 4)
Girls Demand Excitement, 1931 (Wayne 3, Clarke, C.C. 4)
Girl's Desire, 1922 (Baxter W. 3)
Girls' Dormitory, 1936 (Marshall 3, Power 3, Simon, S. 3)
Girl's Folly, 1917 (Tourneur, M. 2, Carré 4, Marion 4)
Girls from Wilko. See Panny z Wilka, 1979
Girls! Girls! Girls!, 1962 (Taurog 2, Presley 3, Anhalt 4, Head 4, Wallis 4)
Girls Gone Wild, 1929 (MacMurray 3, Edeson 4)
Girls Growing Up, 1967 (Halas and Batchelor 2)
Girls He Left Behind. See Gang's All Here, 1943
Girls in Chains, 1943 (Ulmer 2)
Girls in Prison, 1956 (Darwell 3, Marsh 3)
Girls in the Night, 1953 (Boyle 4)
Girls Marked Danger. See Tratta della bianche, 1952
Girls of France. See Jeunes Filles de France, 1938
Girls of Huntington House, 1973 (Jones S. 3, McCambridge 3, Spacek 3)
Girls of Izu. See Izu no musumetachi, 1945
Girls of Pleasure Island, 1953 (Lanchester 3)
Girls of the Big House, 1945 (Alton, J. 4)
Girls on Probation, 1938 (Hayward 3, Reagan 3)
Girls on the Beach, 1965 (Corman 4)
Girls on the Loose, 1958 (Henreid 3)
Girl's School, 1938 (Bellamy 3, Planer 4)
Girls' School, 1949 (Biswas 4)
Girl's School, 1950 (Beavers 3)
Girl's Stratagem, 1913 (Griffith 2, Barrymore L. 3, Marsh 3, Bitzer 4)
Girls Town, 1942 (Nilsson 3)
Girl's Way, 1923 (Lukas 3)
Girls Will Be Boys, 1912–13 (White 3)
Girls Will Be Boys, 1934 (Siodmak 4)
Girl-Shy Cowboy, 1928 (Miller, S. 4)
Giro City, 1982 (Jackson 3)
Giro del monde degli innamorati di Paynet, 1974 (Morricone 4)
Girovaghi, 1956 (Ustinov 3)
Gisants, 1949 (Fresnay 3)
Giselle, 1952 (Buchanan 3)
Giselle, 1970 (Alekan 4)
Gishi shimatsu-ki, 1962 (Iwashita 3, Yamamura 3)
Gishiki, 1971 (Oshima 2, Takemitsu 4, Toda 4)
Git Along, Little Dogies, 1937 (Autry 3, Farnum 3)
Gitan, 1975 (Delon 3, Girardot 3)
Gitana tenias que ser, 1953 (Infante 3, Alcoriza 4)
Gitanella, 1914 (Feuillade 2)
Gitanes, 1932 (Vanel 3)
Gitanilla, 1940 (Rey 3)
Gitans d'Espagne, 1945 (Braunberger 4)
Gitta entdeckt ihr Herz, 1932 (Frohlich 3, Courant 4)
Giù la testa, 1972 (Leone 2, Coburn, J. 3, Steiger 3, Morricone 4)
Giù le mani . . . carogna, 1970 (Kinski 3)
Giudizio di Michelangelo, 1949 (Fusco 4)
Giudizio universale, 1961 (De Sica 2, Aimée 3, Borgnine 3, Durante 3, Fernandel 3, Gassman 3, Manfredi 3, Mangano 3, Mercouri 3, Palance 3, Sordi 3, De Laurentiis 4, Zavattini 4)
Giulietta degli spiriti, 1965 (Fellini 2, Cortese 3, Masina 3, Di Venanzo 4, Flaiano 4, Gherardi 4, Pinelli 4, Rota 4)
Giulietta e Romeo, 1911 (Bertini 3)

Giulietta e Romeo, 1954 (Castellani 2)
Giulietta e Romeo. *See* Romeo and Juliet, 1954
Giungla, 1942 (Amidei 4)
Giuseppe Verdi, 1938 (Gallone 2, Brasseur 3)
Giuseppe w Warszawie, 1964 (Cybulski 3)
Giustiziere sfida la città, 1975 (Cotten 3)
Give a Girl a Break, 1953 (Donen 2, Fosse 2, Reynolds, D. 3, Goodrich and Hackett 4, Previn 4)
Give and Take, 1928 (Hersholt 3)
Give and Take, 1956 (Hanna and Barbera 4)
Give and Take. *See* Singing in the Corn, 1946
Give Her a Ring, 1934 (Granger 3)
Give Her the Moon. *See* Caprices de Maria, 1969
Give Me a Sailor, 1938 (Grable 3, Hope 3, Dreier 4, Head 4, Prinz 4)
Give Me Liberty, 1937 (Eason 4)
Give Me Your Heart, 1936 (Brent 3, Francis, K. 3, Orry-Kelly 4, Robinson 4)
Give My Regards to Broad Street, 1984 (Richardson 3)
Give My Regards to Broadway, 1948 (Bacon 2, Bainter 3, Dailey 3, Hoffenstein 4, Lemaire 4, Reynolds 4, Wheeler 4)
Give Out, Sisters, 1942 (Dailey 3, O'Connor 3)
Give Us Air. *See* Daesh vozkukh, 1924
Give Us Radio!. *See* Daesh radio!
Give Us the Moon, 1944 (Simmons 3)
Give Us This Day, 1949 (Dmytryk 2)
Give Us This Day. *See* Ingeborg Holm, 1913
Give Us This Night, 1936 (Dreier 4, Korngold 4)
Give Us Wings, 1936 (Weiss 2)
Give Us Wings, 1940 (Howard, S. 4, Salter 4)
Giving the Bride Away, 1919 (Roach 4)
Giving Them Fits, 1915 (Daniels 3, Lloyd 3, Roach 4)
Givoi troup, 1912 (Mozhukin 3)
Giwaku, 1982 (Iwashita 3)
Glace a trois faces, 1927 (Epstein 2)
Glaciers, 1942 (Decaë 4)
Glad dig i din ungdom, 1939 (Borgstrom 3)
Glad Eye, 1927 (Saville 2)
Glad Rag Doll, 1929 (Curtiz 2, Beavers 3, Costello, D. 3)
Glad Rags, 1923 (Bruckman 4)
Glad Rags to Riches, 1932 (Temple 3)
Gladiator, 1938 (Brown 3, D'Agostino 4, Young, V. 4)
Gladiatorerna, 1969 (Watkins 2)
Gladiators. *See* Gladiatorerna, 1969
Glaedens Dag, 1918 (Dreyer 2)
Glaive et la balance, 1963 (Cayatte 2, Perkins 3, Jeanson 4, Spaak 4)
Glamour, 1934 (Wyler 2, Beavers 3, Lukas 3, Laemmle 4)
Glamour Boy, 1941 (Cooper, J 3, Dreier 4, Head 4, Young, V. 4)
Glamour for Sale, 1940 (Planer 4)
Glamour Girl, 1948 (Katzman 4)
Glanz gegen Gluck, 1923 (Veidt 3)
Glanz und Elend der Kurtisanen, 1927 (Wegener 3, Planer 4)
Glas, 1958 (Haanstra 2)
Glas du Père Césaire, 1909 (Gance 2)
Glas Wasser, 1922 (Pommer 4)
Glas Wasser, 1960 (Grundgens 3)
Glas Wasser. *See* Spiel der Konigin, 1923
Glasberget, 1953 (Molander 2, Bjornstrand 3)
Glass. *See* Glas, 1958
Glass Bottom Boat, 1966 (Tashlin 2, Day 3, Shamroy 4)
Glass Cage, 1955 (Ireland 3)
Glass Cage, 1964 (Cook 3)
Glass Houses, 1970 (Raksin 4)
Glass Key, 1935 (Milland 3, Raft 3, Sheridan 3, Head 4)
Glass Key, 1942 (Bendix 3, Ladd 3, Lake 3, Dreier 4, Head 4, Young, V. 4)
Glass Menagerie, 1950 (Douglas, K. 3, Kennedy, A. 3, Wyman, Steiner 4, Wald 4)
Glass Menagerie, 1973 (Hepburn, K. 3, Barry 4)
Glass Mountain, 1948 (Cortese 3, Rota 4)
Glass of Water. *See* Glas Wasser, 1960
Glass of Wine. *See* Glass vin, 1960
Glass Slipper, 1938 (Terry 4)

Glass Slipper, 1955 (Walters 2, Caron 3, Lanchester 3, Pidgeon 3, Wynn 3, Kaper 4, Plunkett 4, Rose 4)
Glass Sphinx. *See* Esfinge de cristal, 1968
Glass Tomb. *See* Glass Cage, 1955
Glass vin, 1960 (Fischer 4)
Glass Wall, 1953 (Gassman 3, Grahame 3, Biroc 4)
Glass Web, 1953 (Robinson, E. 3)
Glassmakers of England, 1933 (Flaherty 2)
Gleam O'Dawn, 1922 (Gilbert 3, Furthman 4)
Glee Quartette, 1930 (Buchanan 3)
Gleisdreieck, 1936 (Staudte 2, Frohlich 3)
Glen or Glenda?, 1952 (Lugosi 3)
Glenn Miller Story, 1954 (Mann 2, Allyson 3, Stewart 3, Daniels 4, Mancini 4)
Gli anni ruggenti, 1962 (Zampa 2)
Glimpse of Austria, 1938 (Hoch 4)
Glimpse of Los Angeles, 1914 (Sennett 2, Normand 3)
Glimpse of the San Diego Exposition, 1915 (Sennett 2)
Glimpses of Java and Ceylon, 1937 (Hoch 4)
Glimpses of New Brunswick, 1938 (Hoch 4)
Glimpses of Peru, 1937 (Hoch 4)
Glimpses of the Moon, 1923 (Dwan 2, Costello, D. 3, Costello, M. 3, Daniels 3, Rosson 4)
Glimpses of the U.S.A., 1959 (Bernstein 4)
Glimpses of West Bengal, 1978 (Chandragupta 4)
Glinka. *See* Kompozitor Glinka, 1952
Glissements progressifs du plaisir, 1974 (Huppert 3, Robbe-Grillet 4)
Glitter. *See* Drop Kick, 1927
Gljiva, 1972 (Grgić 4)
Global Affair, 1964 (De Carlo 3, Hope 3, Ames 4, Lederer 4, Ruttenberg 4)
Glomdalsbruden, 1926 (Dreyer 2)
Gloria, 1913 (Bertini 3)
Gloria, 1931 (Frohlich 3, Gabin 3)
Gloria, 1977 (Autant-Lara 2)
Gloria, 1980 (Cassavetes 2, Rowlands 3, Henry 4)
Gloria Alley, 1952 (Caron 3)
Gloria's Romance, 1916 (Barthelmess 3, Burke 3)
Glorifying the American Girl, 1929 (Burke 3)
Glorious Adventure, 1918 (Marsh 3)
Glorious Adventure, 1922 (Blackton 2, McLaglen 3)
Glorious Betsy, 1928 (Crosland 2, Costello, D. 3)
Glorious Campaign. *See* Spanilá jízda, 1963
Glorious Days. *See* Lilacs in the Spring, 1955
Glorious Fourth, 1927 (Roach 4)
Glorious Lady, 1919 (Goulding 2)
Glorious Life, 1923 (Lukas 3)
Glorious Musketeers, 1973 (Halas and Batchelor 2)
Glorious 6th of June, 1934 (Jennings 2)
Glorious Youth, 1929 (Ondra 3)
Glory, 1956 (Brennan 3, O'Brien, M. 3)
Glory Alley, 1952 (Daniels 4, Rose 4, Rose 4)
Glory at Sea. *See* Gift Horse, 1952
Glory Boy. *See* My Old Man's Place, 1971
Glory Brigade, 1953 (Marvin 3, Mature 3)
Glory Guys, 1965 (Caan 3, Howe 4)
Glory of Love. *See* While Paris Sleeps, 1923
Glory on the Summit. *See* Moyuru wakamonotachi, 1962
Glory on the Summit. *See* Yama no sanka: Moyuru wakamono-tachi, 1962
Glory Stompers, 1967 (Hopper 3)
Glory to Me, Death to the Enemy! See Slava nam, smert vragam!, 1914
Glove, 1978 (Blondell 3, Wynn 3)
Glove Birds, 1942 (Bruckman 4)
Glove Taps, 1937 (Roach 4)
Glow Worm, 1930 (Fleischer, M. and D. 2)
Glowa, 1953 (Borowczyk 4)
Glu uber Nacht, 1932 (Sakall 3)
Gluck auf der Alm, 1958 (Schell, Maximilian 3)
Gluck bei Frauen, 1944 (Stallich 4)
Glucklichen Jahre der Thorwalds, 1962 (Staudte 2, Bergner 3)
Glucklicher Mensch, 1943 (Jurgens 3, Wagner 4)
Glucklicke Mutter, 1928 (Dietrich 3)

Gluhende Gasse, 1927 (ALBers 3)
Glurumov's Film Diary. *See* Kinodnevik Glumova, 1923
Glut, 1983 (Mueller-Stahl 3)
Glutton's Nightmare, 1901 (Hepworth 2)
Gnet roka, 1917 (Baranovskaya 3)
Gniazdo, 1974 (Pszoniak 3)
Gnome-Mobile, 1967 (Disney 2, Brennan 3, Ellenshaw 4)
Go and Get It, 1920 (Neilan 2, Carré 4)
Go As You Please, 1920 (Roach 4)
Go Chase Yourself, 1938 (Ball 3)
Gô chez les oiseaux, 1939 (Grimault 4)
Go Fly a Kit, 1957 (Jones 2)
Go for Broke, 1951 (Johnson, V. 3, Pirosh 4, Schary 4)
Go Getter, 1937 (Berkeley 2, Daves 2, Brent 3, Edeson 4,
    Orry-Kelly 4, Wallis 4)
Go Go Amigo, 1965 (McKimson 4)
Go Go Mania. *See* Pop Gear, 1965
Go Into Your Dance, 1935 (Berkeley 2, Florey 2, Jolson 3, Keeler 3,
    Gaudio 4, Polito 4)
Go, Man, Go, 1954 (Poitier 3, Howe 4, North 4)
Go Naked in the World, 1961 (Borgnine 3, Lollobrigida 3, Deutsch 4,
    Krasner 4, Rose 4)
Go See Mother . . . Father Is Working. *See* Va voir Maman, 1977
Go Tell the Spartans, 1978 (Lancaster 3)
Go to Blazes, 1942 (Balcon 4)
Go to Blazes, 1962 (Smith 3, Addison 4)
Go to Nowhere, 1966 (Ivanov-vano 4)
Go West, 1925 (Keaton 2, Arbuckle 3, Roach 4, Schenck 4)
Go West, 1940 (Marx Brothers 3, Edens 4, Kaper 4)
Go West, Big Boy, 1931 (Terry 4)
Go West, Young Lady, 1941 (Ford, G. 3, Miller 3, Cahn 4, Plunkett 4)
Go West, Young Man, 1936 (Hathaway 2, Brady 3, Scott, R. 3, West 3,
    Banton 4, Dreier 4, Struss 4)
Goal Rush, 1932 (Iwerks 4)
Goalie's Anxiety at the Penalty Kick. *See* Angst des Tormanns beim
    Elfmeter, 1971
Goat, 1918 (Crisp 3, Hardy 3, Novarro 3, Marion 4)
Goat, 1921 (Keaton 2)
Goat Getter, 1925 (Garmes 4)
Gobbo, 1960 (Pasolini 2, Blier 3, De Laurentiis 4, Gherardi 4)
Goben no tsubaki, 1965 (Iwashita 3, Okada 3)
Go-Between, 1971 (Losey 2, Bates 3, Christie 3, Redgrave, M. 3,
    Dillon 4, Fisher 4, Legrand 4, Pinter 4)
Gobu no tamashii, 1938 (Shindo 3)
God Created Woman. *See* Et Dieu créa la femme, 1956
God Gave Me 20 Cents, 1926 (Brenon 2)
God Is My Co-Pilot, 1945 (Florey 2, Massey 3, Buckner 4, Waxman 4)
God is My Partner, 1957 (Brennan 3)
God King, 1975 (Peries 2)
God Needs Men. *See* Dieu a besoin des hommes, 1950
God Shiva, 1955 (Haanstra 2)
God Told Me To, 1976 (Corman 4)
God Within, 1912 (Griffith 2, Barrymore L. 3, Sweet 3, Walthall 3,
    Bitzer 4)
Goda vanner, trogna grannar, 1938 (Fischer 4)
Godan, 1962 (Shankar 4)
Godchild, 1974 (Palance 3, Warden 3)
Goddag børn!, 1953 (Roos 2)
Goddag Dyr!, 1947 (Roos 2)
Goddess, 1958 (Cromwell 2, Beavers 3, Chayefsky 4)
Goddess. *See* Devi, 1960
Goddess of Sagebrush Gulch, 1912 (Griffith 2, Sweet 3, Bitzer 4)
Godelureaux, 1961 (Chabrol 2, Audran 3, Gégauff 4, Rabier 4)
**Godfather, 1972 (Smith, D. , Coppola 2, Brando 3, Caan 3,
    Duvall, R. 3, Hayden 3, Keaton 3, Pacino 3, Murch 4, Reynolds 4,
    Rota 4, Tavoularis 4, Willis 4)**
**Godfather, Part II, 1974 (Smith, D. , Coppola 2, Caan 3, De Niro 3,
    Duvall, R. 3, Keaton 3, Pacino 3, Stanton 3, Corman 4, Murch 4,
    Rota 4, Tavoularis 4, van Runkle 4, Willis 4)**
Godina ot ponedelnici. *See* Rok ze samých pondělku, 1977
Godless Girl, 1929 (DeMille 2, Adrian 4, Grot 4, Macpherson 4)
Godmothers, 1973 (Rooney 3)
Godovshchina revoliutsiya, 1919 (Vertov 2)

Gods and the Dead. *See* Deuses e os mortes, 1970
God's Clay, 1928 (Ondra 3)
God's Country, 1946 (Keaton 2)
God's Country and the Law, 1921 (Olcott 2)
God's Country and the Woman, 1936 (Brent 3, Friedhofer 4, Gaudio 4,
    Raine 4, Steiner 4, Wallis 4)
God's Gift to Women, 1931 (Curtiz 2, Blondell 3, Brooks 3)
God's Gun, 1978 (Boone 3, Palance 3, Van Cleef 3)
God's Inn by the Sea, 1911 (Bushman 3)
God's Little Acre, 1958 (Mann 2, Ryan 3, Bernstein 4, Haller 4,
    Maddow 4)
Gods of the Plague. *See* Gotter der Pest, 1969
God's Outlaw, 1919 (Bushman 3)
God's Stepchildren, 1938 (Micheaux 2)
God's Unfortunate, 1912 (Dwan 2)
Godson. *See* Cose di Cosa Nostra, 1971
Goduria, 1976 (Monicelli 2)
Godzilla. *See* Gojira, 1954
Godzilla vs. the Thing. *See* Gojira tai Mosura, 1964
Godzina szczytu, 1973 (Stawinsky 4)
Godzina W, 1979 (Stawinsky 4)
Goethe lebt, 1932 (George, H. 3)
Gog, 1954 (Marshall 3)
Go-Get-'em Haines, 1936 (Boyd 3)
Goglerblod. *See* Troløs, 1913
Gogleren. *See* Elskovs Magt, 1912
Goha, 1958 (Cardinale 3, Sharif 3)
Goiken Gomuyo, 1925 (Tanaka 3)
Goin' South, 1978 (Nicholson 3, Steenburgen 3, Almendros 4)
Goin' to Heaven on a Mule, 1934 (Freleng 4)
Goin' to Town, 1935 (West 3, Banton 4, Dreier 4, Struss 4)
Going and Coming Back, 1985 (Fabian 3)
Going and Coming Back. *See* Partir, Revenir, 1985
Going Ape!, 1981 (Bernstein 4)
Going Ashore. *See* Strandhugg, 1950
Going Bye-Bye, 1934 (Laurel & Hardy 3, Roach 4)
Going Crooked, 1926 (Love 3, Clarke, C.C. 4)
Going Ga-ga, 1928 (McCarey 2)
Going Gay, 1933 (Dickinson 2, Gallone 2)
Going! Going! Gone!, 1918 (Daniels 3, Lloyd 3, Roach 4)
Going! Going! Gosh!, 1952 (Jones 2)
Going Highbrow, 1935 (Florey 2, Horton 3, Pitts 3, Edeson 4,
    Orry-Kelly 4)
Going Hollywood, 1933 (Walsh 2, Crosby 3, Davies 3, Adrian 4,
    Brown, N. 4, Freed 4, Marion 4, Stewart 4, Stothart 4, Wanger 4)
Going Home, 1972 (Mitchum 3)
Going My Way, 1944 (McCarey 2, Crosby 3, Fitzgerald 3, Dreier 4,
    Head 4)
Going of the White Swan, 1914 (Mix 3)
Going Places, 1938 (Dandridge 3, Powell, D. 3, Reagan 3, Glazer 4,
    Mercer 4, Wald 4, Wallis 4)
Going Places, 1939 (Reagan 3)
Going Places. *See* Valseuses, 1973
Going Some, 1912–13 (White 3)
Going Spanish, 1934 (Hope 3)
Going Steady, 1958 (Katzman 4)
Going Steady. *See* Yotz 'im Kavua, 1971
Going Straight, 1917 (Franklin 2, Talmadge, N. 3)
Going to Blazes, 1933 (Lantz 4)
Going to Congress, 1924 (Rogers, W. 3, Roach 4)
Going Up, 1923 (Leroy 2)
Going West to Make Good, 1916 (Mix 3)
Going Wild, 1931 (Brown 3, Pidgeon 3, Polito 4)
Going Wild. *See* Aviateur, 1931
Goingehov dingen, 1953 (Dahlbeck 3, Thulin 3)
Gojira, 1954 (Shimura 3, Tsuburaya 4)
Gojira no gyakushu, 1955 (Tsuburaya 4)
Gojira no musuko, 1967 (Tsuburaya 4)
Gojira tai Mosura, 1964 (Tsuburaya 4)
Goju man-nin no isan, 1963 (Mifune 3, Muraki 4)
Goju-no to, 1944 (Gosho 2)
Gokumoncho, 1955 (Kagawa 3)
Gokumonto, 1977 (Ichikawa 2, Tsukasa 3)

Goldie Gets Along, 1933 (Irene 4)
Goldie Locks and the 3 Bears, 1922 (Disney 2)
Goldielocks and the Three Bears, 1934 (Lantz 4)
Goldilocks and the Jivin' Bears, 1944 (Freleng 4)
Goldimouse and the Three Cats, 1959 (Freleng 4)
Goldpuppen. *See* Pleasure Girls, 1965
Goldtown Ghost Raiders, 1953 (Autry 3)
Goldwyn Follies, 1938 (Ladd 3, Menjou 3, Day 4, Goldwyn 4, Hecht 4, Newman 4, Toland 4)
Golem, 1914 (Wegener 3, Galeen 4)
Golem, 1920 (Rohrig 4)
Golem, 1936 (Duvivier 2, Baur 3, Andrejew 4, Stallich 4, Vích 4)
Golem, 1979 (Janda 3, Pszoniak 3)
Golem. *See* Golem, wie er in die Welt kam, 1920
Golem und die Tanzerin, 1917 (Wegener 3)
Golem, wie er in die Welt kam, 1920 (Wegener 3, Freund 4, Galeen 4)
Golf, 1922 (Hardy 3)
Golf Bug, 1922 (Roach 4)
Golf Game and the Bonnet, 1913 (Bunny 3)
Golf Nut, 1927 (Sennett 2)
Golf Nuts, 1930 (Terry 4)
Golfa, 1957 (Figueroa 4)
Golfers, 1929 (Sennett 2)
Golfers, 1937 (Lantz 4)
Golfos, 1962 (Saura 2)
Golf's Golden Years, 1970 (Crosby 3)
Golgotha, 1935 (Duvivier 2, Baur 3, Feuillère 3, Gabin 3, Ibert 4)
Goli čovek, 1968 (Samardžić 3)
Goliat contra los gigantes, 1961 (Rey 3)
Goliath Against the Giants. *See* Goliat contra los gigantes, 1961
Goliath and the Dragon. *See* Vendetta di Ercole, 1960
Goliath and the Vampire. *See* Maciste contre il vampiro, 1961
Goljamata pobeda, 1973 (Paskaleva 3)
Golod . . . golod . . . golod, 1921 (Pudovkin 2, Tisse 4)
Golowin geht durch die Stadt, 1940 (Hoffmann 4)
Golpeando en la selva, 1967 (Alvarez 2)
Golu Hadawatha, 1968 (Peries 2)
Gólyakalifa, 1917 (Korda 2)
Gommes, 1968 (Delerue 4)
Gommes, 1972 (Robbe-Grillet 4)
Gomorron Bill, 1945 (Borgstrom 3, Nykvist 4)
Gondole delle chimers, 1936 (Burel 4)
Gone Are the Days!, 1963 (Kaufman 4, Rosenblum 4)
Gone Batty, 1954 (McKimson 4)
Gone to Earth, 1950 (Powell and Pressburger 2, Cotten 3, Cusack 3, Jones, J. 3, Francis 4, Selznick 4)
Gone to the Country, 1921 (Roach 4)
Gone with the West, 1975 (Caan 3)
Gone with the Wind, 1939 (Cukor 2, Fleming 2, Hawks 2, Bond 3, Darwell 3, De Havilland 3, Gable 3, Howard, L. 3, Leigh, V. 3, McDaniel 3, McQueen, B. 3, Canutt 4, Eason 4, Friedhofer 4, Garmes 4, Haller 4, Howard 4, Menzies 4, Plunkett 4, Rosson 4, Selznick 4, Steiner 4, Westmore, M. 4, Wheeler 4)
Gonin no kyodai, 1939 (Yoshimura 2)
Gonin no mokugekisha, 1948 (Yoda 4)
Gonin no totsugekitai, 1961 (Yamamura 3)
Gonshchiki, 1972 (Yankovsky 3)
Gonul kusu, 1965 (Guney 2)
Gonza the Spearman. *See* Yari no Gonza, 1985
Gonzague ou L'Accordeur, 1933 (Grémillon 2)
Gonzales Tamales, 1957 (Freleng 4)
Gonzaque, 1923 (Chevalier 3)
Good Against Evil, 1977 (Sangster 4, Schifrin 4)
Good and Naughty, 1926 (Negri 3, Glennon 4)
Good and the Bad. *See* Bon et les méchants, 1976
Good Bad Girl. *See* Inez from Hollywood, 1924
Good Bad Man, 1916 (Dwan 2, Fleming 2, Fairbanks, D. 3, Johnson, N. 3, Love 3)
Good Bad Wife, 1921 (Hackett 4)
Good Business Deal, 1915 (Eason 4)
Good Catch, 1912 (Bushman 3)
Good Causes. *See* Bonnes Causes, 1962
Good Cheer, 1926 (Roach 4)

Good Companions, 1933 (Pearson 2, Saville 2, Gielgud 3, Gwenn 3, Hawkins 3, Matthews 3, Balcon 4, Dalrymple 4, Friedhofer 4, Junge 4)
Good Companions, 1957 (Johnson, C. 3, Roberts 3)
Good Dame, 1934 (Brennan 3, Farnum 3, March 3, Sidney 3, Schulberg 4, Shamroy 4)
Good Day for a Hanging, 1958 (MacMurray 3)
Good Day for Fighting. *See* Custer of the West, 1968
Good Deed Daily, 1955 (Terry 4)
Good Die Young, 1954 (Clayton 2, Baker S. 3, Grahame 3, Harvey 3, Ireland 3, Auric 4)
Good Earth, 1937 (Fleming 2, Franklin 2, Muni 3, Rainer 3, Freund 4, Gibbons 4, Gillespie 4, Jennings 4, Lewin 4, Stothart 4, Thalberg 4, Vorkapich 4)
Good Egg, 1939 (Jones 2)
Good Fairy, 1935 (Sturges, P. 2, Bondi 3, Marshall 3, Sullavan 3, Laemmle 4, Mandell 4)
Good Fairy. *See* Zemma, 1951
Good Fellows, 1943 (Dreier 4, Head 4)
Good Financial Situation. *See* Hidari uchiwa, 1935
Good Friends and Faithful Neighbors. *See* Goda vanner, trogna grannar, 1938
Good Girls Go to Paris, 1939 (Blondell 3, Douglas, M. 3, Coffee 4)
Good Glue Sticks. *See* Colle universelle, 1907
Good Gracious Annabelle, 1919 (Burke 3)
Good Guys and the Bad Guys, 1969 (Carradine 3, Kennedy, G. 3, Mitchum 3)
Good Guys Wear Black, 1977 (Andrews D. 3)
Good Housekeeping, 1933 (Darwell 3)
Good Humor Man, 1950 (Bacon 2, Tashlin 2)
Good Indian, 1913 (Mix 3)
Good Intentions, 1930 (Howard 2)
Good Little Devil, 1913 (Porter 2, Pickford 3)
Good Love and the Bad, 1912 (Dwan 2)
Good Luck, Miss Wyckoff, 1979 (Pleasance 3)
Good Luck Mr. Yates, 1943 (Basserman 3, Trevor 3)
Good Luck of a Souse. *See* Il y a un dieu pour les ivrognes, 1908
Good Medicine, 1929 (Horton 3)
Good Men and True, 1922 (Carey 3)
Good Morning. *See* Ohayo, 1959
Good Morning Doctor. *See* You Belong to Me, 1941
Good Morning, Judge, 1913 (Cruze 2)
Good Morning, Judge, 1922 (Roach 4)
Good Morning, Judge, 1943 (Beavers 3, Boyle 4)
Good Morning, Madam, 1925 (Sennett 2)
Good Morning, Miss Dove, 1955 (Jones, J. 3, Reynolds 4, Shamroy 4)
Good Morning, Nurse!, 1925 (Sennett 2)
Good Mothers. *See* Mødrehjaelpen, 1942
Good Mouse Keeping, 1952 (Terry 4)
Good Neighbor Sam, 1964 (Lemmon 3, Robinson, E. 3, Schneider 3, Guffey 4)
Good News, 1930 (Daves 2, Crabbe 3, Love 3, Brown, N. 4, Freed 4, Gibbons 4, Marion 4)
Good News, 1947 (Walters 2, Allyson 3, Comden and Green 4, Edens 4, Freed 4, Rose 4)
Good Night Elmer, 1940 (Jones 2)
Good Night Nurse, 1918 (Keaton 2, Arbuckle 3)
Good Night, Rusty, 1943 (Pal 2)
Good Noose, 1962 (McKimson 4)
Good Old Irish Tunes, 1941 (Terry 4)
Good Old School Days. *See* Those Were the Days, 1940
Good Old Soak, 1937 (Beery 3, Merkel 3)
Good People's Sunday. *See* Domenica della buona gente, 1953
Good Provider, 1922 (Borzage 2)
Good References, 1920 (Talmadge, C. 3)
Good Riddance, 1923 (Roach 4)
Good Sam, 1948 (McCarey 2, Beavers 3, Cooper, Gary 3, Sheridan 3)
Good Scout, 1934 (Iwerks 4)
Good Shepherdess and the Evil Princess. *See* Bonne Bergère et la méchante princesse, 1908
Good Soldier Schweik. *See* Dobrý voják Svejk, 1931
Good Soldier Schweik. *See* Dobrý voják Švejk, 1957
Good Soldier Schweik. *See* Osudy dobrého vojáka Svejkova, 1955

Grande Mare, 1930 (Chevalier 3, Colbert 3, Fort 4)
Grande paese d'Acciaio, 1960 (Olmi 2)
Grande Passion, 1929 (Christian-Jaque 2, Delannoy 2, Dagover 3)
Grande Pastorale, 1943 (Clément 2, Alekan 4)
Grande Sauterelle, 1967 (Audiard 4)
Grande scrofa nera, 1972 (Cuny 3)
Grande silenzio, 1968 (Kinski 3, Trintignant 3, Morricone 4)
Grande speranza, 1954 (Rota 4)
Grande strada azzurra, 1957 (Pontecorvo 2, Valli 3, Gherardi 4, Solinas 4)
Grande Terre, 1955 (Decaë 4)
Grande tormenta, 1920 (Gallone 2)
Grande Trouille, 1974 (Cushing 3, Valli 3)
Grande Trouille. See Tendre Dracula, 1974
Grande Vadrouille, 1966 (Bourvil 3, Auric 4, Renoir 4)
Grande Vie, 1960 (Masina 3)
Grande Vie. See Kunstseidene Madchen, 1960
Grande Voliere, 1947 (Renoir 4)
Grande-Bretagne et les Etats-Unis de 1896 à 1900, 1968 (Allégret, M. 2, Braunberger 4)
Grandes Familles, 1958 (Brasseur 3, Gabin 3, Audiard 4)
Grandes Gueules, 1965 (Bourvil 3)
Grandes Manoeuvres, 1955 (Clair 2, Bardot 3, Morgan 3, Philipe 3, Barsacq 4)
Grandes Personnes, 1960 (Presle 3, Seberg 3, Coutard 4, Evein 4)
Grandeur nature, 1974 (Piccoli 3, Carrière 4, Jarre 4, Trauner 4)
Grandeur nature. See Tamaño natural, 1974
Grandhotel Nevada, 1934 (Vích 4)
Grandi condottieri, 1965 (Guerra 4)
Grandi magazzini, 1939 (Castellani 2, De Sica 2)
Grandi naif jugoslavi, 1973 (Storaro 4)
Grandma's Boy, 1922 (Lloyd 3, Roach 4)
Grandma's Girl, 1930 (Sennett 2)
Grandma's Pet, 1932 (Lantz 4)
Grandmother Sabella. See Nonna Sabella, 1957
Grandmother's Story. See Au pays des jouets, 1908
Grandmother's War Story, 1911 (Olcott 2)
Grandpa Involuntarily. See Dědečkem proti své vuli, 1939
Grandpa Planted a Beet. See Zasadil dědek řepu, 1945
Grands, 1936 (Vanel 3)
Grands Chemins, 1962 (Aimée 3, Gégauff 4)
Grands Feux, 1937 (Alexeieff and Parker 2)
Grands Moments, 1965 (Lelouch 2, Braunberger 4)
Grands Seigneurs. See Gentleman d'Epsom, 1962
Granges brûlées, 1973 (Delon 3, Signoret 3, Vierny 4)
Granica, 1977 (Janda 3, Lomnicki 3)
Granite Hotel, 1940 (Fleischer, M. and D. 2)
Granitsa, 1935 (Cherkassov 3)
Granny, 1914 (Gish, D. 3)
Granny Takes Over. See Páté kolo u vozu, 1958
Granpa. See Dědáček, 1968
Gransfolken, 1913 (Stiller 2, Jaenzon 4, Magnusson 4)
Grant Wood, 1950 (Fonda, H. 3)
Granton Trawler, 1934 (Cavalcanti 2, Grierson 2)
Grapes of Wrath, 1940 (Ford, J. 2, Bond 3, Carradine 3, Darwell 3, Fonda, H. 3, Marsh 3, Day 4, Johnson 4, Newman 4, Toland 4, Zanuck 4)
Graset sjunger. See Grass Is Singing, 1981
Grasp of Greed, 1916 (Chaney Lon 3)
Grass, 1925 (Schoedsack 2, Cooper 4)
Grass, 1968 (Le Grice 2)
Grass Country Goes Dry, 1914 (Beery 3)
Grass Is Greener, 1960 (Donen 2, Grant, C. 3, Kerr 3, Mitchum 3, Simmons 3)
Grass Is Singing, 1981 (Black 3)
Grasshopper, 1970 (Bisset 3, Cotten 3)
Grasshopper, 1975 (Vukotića 4)
Grasshopper. See Poprigunya, 1955
Grasshopper and the Ant, 1954 (Reiniger 2)
Grassy Shires, 1944 (Alwyn 4)
Grateful Outcast, 1912–13 (White 3)
Gratitude of Wanda, 1913 (Reid 3)
Gratuités, 1927 (Grémillon 2, Périnal 4)

Grausame Freundin, 1932 (Ondra 3, Rasp 3)
Grausame Job. See Peau d'espion, 1967
Grausige Nachte, 1921 (Pick 2, Krauss 3, Mayer 4)
Graustark, 1915 (Bushman 3)
Graustark, 1925 (Talmadge, N. 3, Gaudio 4, Marion 4, Menzies 4, Schenck 4)
Graveside Story. See Comedy of Terrors, 1963
Gravy Train, 1974 (Forrest 3, Keach 3)
Gray Dame. See Graa Dame, 1909
Gray Dawn, 1922 (Hersholt 3)
Gray Ghost, (Johnson, N. 3)
Gray Horizon, 1919 (Hayakawa 3)
Gray Lady Down, 1978 (Heston 3, Keach 3, Mirisch 4)
Grayeagle, 1977 (Cody 3, Elam 3, Johnson, B. 3)
Grazia, zia, 1968 (Morricone 4)
Graziella, 1925 (Artaud 3)
Graziella, 1954 (D'Amico 4)
Grease, 1978 (Arden 3, Blondell 3)
Grease II, 1982 (Arden 3)
Greased Lightning, 1977 (Van Peebles 2, Pryor 3)
Greaser, 1915 (Walsh 2)
Greaser and the Weakling, 1912 (Dwan 2)
Greaser's Gauntlet, 1908 (Griffith 2)
Great, 1975 (Godfrey 4)
Great Adventure, 1918 (Guy 2)
Great Adventure, 1921 (Barrymore L. 3, Stradling 4)
Great Adventure. See Adventurers, 1950
Great Adventure. See Stora aventyret, 1953
Great Adventure. See Velké dobrodružství, 1952
Great American Beauty Contest, 1973 (Cummings 3, Jourdan 3)
Great American Broadcast, 1941 (Faye 3, Banton 4, Day 4, MacGowan 4, Newman 4, Shamroy 4)
Great American Cowboy, 1974 (McCrea 3)
Great American Pastime, 1956 (Miller 3, Berman 4)
Great American Tragedy, 1972 (Kennedy, G. 3, Duning 4)
Great Awakening, 1941 (Basserman 3)
Great Balloon Adventure. See Olly Olly Oxen Free, 1977
Great Bank Hoax. See Shenanigans, 1977
Great Bank Robbery, 1969 (Cook 3, Jaffe 3, Novak 3, Cahn 4)
Great Barrier, 1937 (Balcon 4)
Great Barrier. See Silent Barriers, 1937
Great Battle. See Grande attacco, 1977
Great Big Thing, 1967 (Rosenblum 4)
Great Carrot Train Robbery, 1969 (McKimson 4)
Great Caruso, 1951 (Green, J. 4, Levien 4, Pasternak 4, Rose 4, Ruttenberg 4, Shearer 4)
Great Catherine, 1968 (Hawkins 3, Moreau 3, O'Toole 3, Morris 4, Tiomkin 4)
Great Citizen. See Velikii grazhdanin, 1938-39
Great Clown. See Muharraj el Kabir, 1951
Great Cognito, 1982 (Vinton 4)
Great Commandment, 1939 (Banton 4, Salter 4)
Great Consoler. See Velikii uteshitel, 1933
Great Dan Patch, 1949 (Brennan 3, Muse 3)
Great Dawn. See Grande aurora, 1946
Great Day, 1920 (Hitchcock 2)
Great Day, 1945 (Alwyn 4)
Great Day in the Morning, 1956 (Tourneur, J. 2, Mayo 3, D'Agostino 4)
Great Deception, 1926 (Rathbone 3, Haller 4)
Great Decision. See Men of America, 1932
Great Diamond Robbery, 1953 (Nilsson 3, Ruttenberg 4)
Great Dictator, 1940 (Chaplin 2, Goddard 3, Struss 4)
Great Divide, 1925 (Beery 3, Pitts 3, Gibbons 4, Glazer 4, Thalberg 4, Young, W. 4)
Great Divide, 1930 (Loy 3, Garmes 4)
Great Ecstasy of the Sculptor Steiner. See Große Ekstase des Bildschnitzers Steiner, 1974
Great Escape, 1963 (Sturges, J. 2, Attenborough 3, Bronson 3, Coburn, J. 3, McQueen, S. 3, Pleasance 3, Bernstein 4, Burnett 4)
Great Event, 1979 (Mancini 4)
Great Expectations, 1946 (Lean 2, Guinness 3, Mills 3, Simmons 3, Green, G. 4, Havelock-Allan 4)

Great Ziegfeld, 1936 (Loy 3, Powell, W. 3, Rainer 3, Adrian 4, Edens 4, Freund 4, Gibbons 4, Stromberg 4)
Greater Claim, 1921 (Ruggles 2)
Greater Devotion, 1914 (Reid 3)
Greater Glory, 1926 (Hersholt 3, Karloff 3, Lawrence 3, Nilsson 3, Mathis 4)
Greater Influence, 1912–13 (White 3)
Greater Law, 1917 (Hersholt 3)
Greater Love, 1913 (Dwan 2)
Greater Love Hath No Man, 1915 (Guy 2)
Greater Than a Crown, 1925 (Costello, D. 3, August 4)
Greater Than Fame, 1920 (Crosland 2)
Greater Than Love, 1921 (Niblo 2, Stahl 2, Sullivan 4)
Greater Wealth, 1913 (Bosworth 3)
Greatest, 1977 (Borgnine 3, Duvall, R. 3, Johnson, B. 3, Jones, J.E. 3, Lardner 4)
Greatest Battle on Earth. See Sandai kaiju chikyu saidai no kessen, 1965
Greatest Gift, 1974 (Ford, G. 3)
Greatest in the World. See Største i Verden, 1919
Greatest Love. See Europa '51, 1952
Greatest Power, 1917 (Barrymore E. 3)
Greatest Question, 1919 (Griffith 2, Gish, L. 3, Bitzer 4)
Greatest Show on Earth, 1952 (DeMille 2, Boyd 3, Crosby 3, Grahame 3, Heston 3, Hope 3, Hutton 3, Lamour 3, O'Brien, E. 3, Stewart 3, Wilde 3, Head 4, Jeakins 4, Young, V. 4)
Greatest Story Ever Told, 1965 (Ashby 2, Stevens 2, Baker C. 3, Ferrer, J. 3, Heflin 3, Heston 3, Lansbury 3, McDowall 3, Mineo 3, Pleasance 3, Poitier 3, Rains 3, Schildkraut 3, Von Sydow 3, Wayne 3, Winters 3, Day 4, Friedhofer 4, Gillespie 4, Newman 4)
Greatest Thing in Life, 1918 (Griffith 2, Gish, L. 3, Bitzer 4)
Greatest Thing That Almost Happened, 1977 (Jones, J.E. 3)
Greco, 1966 (Donati 4)
Greed, 1925 (Ingram 2, Von Stroheim 2, Hersholt 3, Pitts 3, Daniels 4, Day 4, Gibbons 4, Mathis 4)
Greed for Gold, 1913 (Anderson G. 3)
Greed in the Sun. See Cent mille dollars au soleil, 1963
Greed of Gold. See Desert Greed, 1926
Greedy for Tweety, 1957 (Freleng 4)
Greedy Humpty Dumpty, 1936 (Fleischer, M. and D. 2)
Greek Meets Greek, 1921 (Roach 4)
Greek Sculpture, 1959 (Wright 2)
Greek Testament, 1942 (Cavalcanti 2, Crichton 2)
Greek Tycoon, 1978 (Bisset 3, Quinn 3)
Greeks Had a Word for Them, 1932 (Blondell 3, Grable 3, Barnes 4, Day 4, Goldwyn 4, Howard 4, Newman 4)
Greeks Take Troy, 1956 (Peterson 2)
Green and Pleasant Land, 1955 (Anderson 2, Lassally 4)
Green Berets, 1968 (Leroy 2, Wayne 3, Hoch 4, Rozsa 4)
Green Bird. See Grune Vogel, 1979
Green Book. See Zelená knízka, 1948
Green Carnation. See Trials of Oscar Wilde, 1960
Green Cat, 1915 (Talmadge, C. 3)
Green Cat, 1922 (Roach 4)
Green Cockatoo, 1937 (Howard 2, Mills 3, Menzies 4, Rozsa 4, Wimperis 4)
Green Dolphin Street, 1947 (Saville 2, Cooper, Gladys 3, Gwenn 3, Heflin 3, Reed, D. 3, Turner, L. 3, Gillespie 4, Irene 4, Kaper 4, Plunkett 4, Raphaelson 4, Shearer 4, Wilson, C. 4)
Green Earth. See Midori no daichi, 1942
Green Eyed Monster, 1912 (Dwan 2)
Green Eyed Woman. See Take a Letter, Darling, 1942
Green Fields, 1937 (Ulmer 2)
Green Fire, 1954 (Douglas, P. 3, Granger 3, Kelly, Grace 3, Gillespie 4, Rose 4, Rozsa 4)
Green Flood. See Zoldár, 1965
Green for Danger, 1946 (Howard, T. 3, Sim 3, Alwyn 4, Gilliat 4, Mathieson 4)
Green Ghost. See Spectre vert, 1929
Green Ghost. See Unholy Night, 1929
Green Girdle, 1941 (Cardiff 4)
Green Glove, 1951 (Ford, G. 3, Hardwicke 3, Bennett 4, Cloquet 4, Kosma 4, Maté 4, Renoir 4, Trauner 4)

Green Goddess, 1923 (Olcott 2, Arliss 3)
Green Goddess, 1930 (Arliss 3)
Green Grass of Wyoming, 1948 (Coburn, C. 3, McDowall 3, Clarke, C.C. 4, Lemaire 4)
Green Grow the Rushes, 1951 (Burton 3)
Green Hell, 1940 (Whale 2, Bennett J. 3, Cody 3, Fairbanks, D. Jr. 3, Price 3, Sanders 3, Freund 4, Marion 4)
Green Horizons. See Zelené obzory, 1962
Green Hornet, 1939 (Ladd 3)
Green Hornet, 1974 (Lee, B. 3)
Green Ice, 1981 (Anhalt 4)
Green Light, 1937 (Borzage 2, Flynn 3, Hardwicke 3, Blanke 4, Friedhofer 4, Orry-Kelly 4, Steiner 4, Wallis 4)
Green Line, 1944 (Terry 4)
Green Man, 1956 (Dearden 2, Sim 3, Gilliat 4)
Green Mansions, 1959 (Cobb 3, Ferrer, M. 3, Hayakawa 3, Hepburn, A. 3, Perkins 3, Ames 4, Jeakins 4, Kaper 4, Ruttenberg 4)
Green Manuela. See Grune Manuela, 1923
Green Mare. See Jument verte, 1959
Green Mountain Land, 1950 (Flaherty 2)
Green Mountains. See Aoi sanmyaku, 1949
Green Murder Case, 1929 (Powell, W. 3)
Green Native Country. See Midorino furusato, 1946
Green Necklace. See Grona halsbandet, 1912
Green Pastures, 1936 (Blanke 4, Friedhofer 4, Korngold 4, Wallis 4)
Green Promise, 1949 (Brennan 3, Wood 3)
Green Queen. See Reine verte, 1964
Green Room. See Chambre verte, 1978
Green Scarf, 1954 (Redgrave, M. 3)
Green Shadow, 1913 (Ince 4)
Green Swamp, 1916 (Sullivan 4)
Green Temptation, 1922 (Arlen 3)
Green Years, 1946 (Saville 2, Coburn, C. 3, Cooper, Gladys 3, Gibbons 4, Gillespie 4, Irene 4, Levien 4, Stothart 4)
Green Years. See Zoldár, 1965
Greene Murder Case, 1929 (Arthur 3)
Greene Murder Case. See Night of Mystery, 1937
Green-Eyed Blonde, 1957 (Trumbo 4)
Green-Eyed Devil, 1914 (Gish, L. 3)
Greengage Summer, 1961 (Saville 2, Darrieux 3, Love 3, More 3, York, S. 3, Koch 4, Young, F. 4)
Greenhorn, 1913 (Ince 4)
Greenwich Village, 1944 (Ameche 3, Bendix 3, Holliday 3, Miranda 3, Basevi 4, Brown, N. 4, Green 4, Shamroy 4)
Greetings, 1969 (De Palma 2, De Niro 3)
Greetings Bait!, 1943 (Freleng 4)
Greetings Moscow!. See Zdravstuvy Moskva!, 1945
Greetings to the Swallows. See . . . a pozdravuji vlaštovky, 1972
Gregor Marold, 1918 (Kortner 3)
Greifer, 1930 (Albers 3)
Greifer, 1958 (Albers 3)
Grekh, 1916 (Protazanov 2, Mozhukin 3)
Greluchon delicat, 1934 (Baur 3)
Gremlins, 1984 (Goldsmith 4)
Grendel, Grendel, Grendel, 1981 (Ustinov 3)
Grenoble. See Treize Jours en France, 1968
Grens, 1984 (Branco 4)
Grenzfeuer, 1934 (Rasp 3)
Gretchen the Greenhorn, 1916 (Franklin 2, Gish, D. 3)
Grève, 1904–05 (Zecca 2)
Grève, 1911 (Feuillade 2)
Grève des apaches, 1908 (Feuillade 2)
Grevinde Hjerteløs, 1915 (Holger-Madsen 2)
Grevindens Aere, 1919 (Blom 2, Dreyer 2)
Grey Gardens, 1975 (Maysles A. and D. 2)
Grey Gold. See Or gris, 1980
Grey Sentinel, 1913 (Ince 4)
Greyfriars Bobby, 1961 (Disney 2, Crisp 3, Whitlock 4)
Greyhounded Hare, 1949 (McKimson 4)
Greystoke: The Legend of Tarzan, Lord of the Apes, 1984 (Richardson 3, Baker 4, Russell 4, Towne 4, Whitlock 4)
Gribiche, 1925 (Feyder 2, Rosay 3, Meerson 4)

Gribouille, 1937 (Allégret, M. 2, Blier 3, Dalio 3, Morgan 3, Raimu 3, Achard 4, Auric 4, Trauner 4)
Gricheux, 1909 (Cohl 2)
Gridiron Flash, 1934 (Dumont 3, Berman 4, Plunkett 4, Steiner 4)
Grido, 1957 (Antonioni 2, Valli 3, Di Venanzo 4, Fusco 4)
Grido della città, 1950 (Risi 2)
Grief in Bagdad, 1925 (Roach 4)
Grierson, 1972 (Haanstra 2, Ivens 2)
Griffin and Phoenix: A Love Story, 1976 (Clayburgh 3, Falk 3)
Grihadah, 1936 (Roy 2, Sircar 4)
Grillon du foyer, 1923 (Boyer 3)
Grim Comedian, 1921 (Meredyth 4)
Grim Game, 1919 (Buckland 4)
Grim Pastures, or The Fight for Fodder, 1944 (Dunning 4)
Grim Reaper. See Commare secca, 1962
Grim Tale of War, 1913 (Nilsson 3)
Grimace, 1966 (Blier 2)
Grimaldi, 1956 (Peterson 2)
Grin and Bear It, 1933 (Stevens 2)
Grind, 1915 (Chaney Lon 3)
Gringalet, 1946 (Vanel 3)
Gringuita en Mexico, 1951 (Alcoriza 4)
Grip of Fear. See Experiment in Terror, 1962
Grip of Jealousy, 1916 (Chaney Lon 3)
Grip of the Strangler. See Haunted Strangler, 1958
Grip of the Yukon, 1928 (Bushman 3)
Grips, Grunts, and Groans, 1937 (Three Stooges 3, Bruckman 4)
Grisbi. See Touchez pas au Grisbi, 1954
Grisou, 1938 (Blier 3, Brasseur 3)
Grissom Gang, 1971 (Aldrich 2, Biroc 4)
Grit, 1915 (August 4)
Grit, 1924 (Bow 3)
Grit of the Girl Telegrapher, 1912 (Nilsson 3)
Grizzly Golfer, 1951 (Burness 4, Hubley 4)
Grizzly Gulch Chariot Race, 1915 (Mix 3)
Grocery Clerk's Romance, 1912 (Sennett 2, Normand 3)
Gromada, 1952 (Kawalerowicz 2)
Gromaire, 1970 (Reichenbach 2, Braunberger 4)
Grona halsbandet, 1912 (Jaenzon 4, Magnusson 4)
Gronland, 1980 (Roos 2)
Gronlandske dialektoptagelser og trommedanse fra Thuledistriktet, 1967 (Roos 2)
Groom Wore Spurs, 1951 (Rogers, G. 3)
Gros Câlin, 1979 (Manfredi 3)
Gros Coup, 1964 (Delerue 4, Gégauff 4)
Gros et le maigre, 1961 (Polanski 2)
Gros Lot, 1933 (Fernandel 3)
Gross Fog, 1973 (Le Grice 2)
Gross Paris, 1973 (de Beauregard 4)
Grosse Abenteuerin, 1928 (Wiene 2)
Grosse Atlantik, 1962 (Welles 2)
Grosse Attraktion, 1931 (Kaper 4)
Grosse Caisse, 1965 (Bourvil 3)
Grosse Ekstase des Bildschnitzers Steiner, 1974 (Herzog 2)
Grosse Fall, 1944 (Frohlich 3)
Grosse Freiheit Nr. 7, 1944, (Albers 3)
Grosse Gefahr, 1915 (Kortner 3)
Grosse Konig, 1942 (Frohlich 3, Wegener 3)
Grosse Licht, 1920 (Jannings 3)
Grosse Liebe, 1931 (Preminger 2)
Grosse Liebesspiel, 1963 (Knef 3)
Grosse Mandarin, 1949 (Wegener 3)
Grosse Pause, 1927 (Porten 3)
Grosse Reise, 1961 (Dieterle 2)
Grosse Schatten, 1942 (George, H. 3)
Grosse Schweigen, 1922 (Porten 3)
Grosse Sehnsucht, 1930 (Dagover 3, Kortner 3, Ondra 3, Rasp 3, Tschechowa 3, Veidt 3, Pasternak 4)
Grosse Spiel (Staudte 2)
Grosse Sprung, 1927 (Riefenstahl 2)
Grosse Sunderin, 1913 (Porten 3, Messter 4)
Grosse Tête, 1962 (Constantine 3, Guillemot 4, Legrand 4)
Grosse Unbekannte, 1927 (Planer 4)

Grosse und die kleine Welt, 1921 (Albers 3, Dreier 4)
Grosse und kleine Welt, 1936 (George, H. 3)
Grosse Verhau, 1970 (Kluge 2)
Grosse Zapfenstreich, 1952 (Herlth 4)
Grossfurstin Alexandra, 1933 (Sakall 3)
Grossindustrielle, 1923 (Wagner 4)
Grossreinemachen, 1935 (Ondra 3)
Grossstadt Schmetterling, 1929 (Sakall 3, Wong 3)
Grossstadtkavaliere. See Kleine aus der Kongektion, 1925
Grosste Gauner des Jahrhunderts, 1927 (Albers 3)
Grotesque Chicken. See Spatně namalovaná slepice, 1963
Grounds for Divorce, 1925 (Fazenda 3, Banton 4)
Grounds for Marriage, 1950 (Grayson 3, Johnson, V. 3, Nilsson 3, Stone 3, Alton, J. 4, Kaper 4, Raksin 4, Rose 4)
Group, 1966 (Lumet 2, Buchman 4, Kaufman 4, Rosenblum 4)
Group Instruction. See Group no shido, 1956
Group no shido, 1956 (Hani 2)
Group Picture with Lady. See Gruppenbild mit Dame, 1977
Grov Spøg, 1908 (Holger-Madsen 2)
Growing Pains, 1928 (Roach 4)
Growing Pains, 1953 (Terry 4)
Growing Up. See Asunaro monogatari, 1955
Growing Up. See Takekurabe, 1955
Growing Years, 1951 (Fonda, H. 3)
Grub Stake, 1923 (Walker 4)
Grubstake Mortgage, 1912 (Dwan 2)
Grudge, 1915 (Hart 3)
Gruesome Twosome, 1945 (Clampett 4)
Gruft mit dem Raselschloss, 1964 (Kinski 3)
Grumpy, 1930 (Cukor 2, Lukas 3)
Grune Manuela, 1923 (Dieterle 2, Dupont 2, Junge 4)
Grune Vogel, 1979 (Szabó 2)
Gruppenbild mit Dame, 1977 (Schneider 3)
Gruppo di famiglia in un interno, 1974 (Visconti 2, Cardinale 3, Lancaster 3, Mangano 3, Sanda 3, D'Amico 4)
Grüss und kuss Veronika, 1934 (Pasternak 4, Waxman 4)
Gryning, 1945 (Sucksdorff 2)
Guadalajara, 1943 (Armendáriz 3)
Guadalcanal Diary, 1943 (Bendix 3, Quinn 3, Basevi 4, Clarke, C.C. 4, Trotti 4)
Guaglio. See Proibito rubare, 1948
Guantes de Oro, 1959 (Alcoriza 4)
Guapo del 900, 1960 (Torre-Nilsson 2)
Guappi, 1973 (Cardinale 3)
Guard. See Stracena varta, 1956
Guard That Girl, 1935 (Bond 3)
Guardatele, ma non toccatele!, 1959 (Tognazzi 3)
Guardia del corpo, 1942 (De Sica 2)
Guardia, guardia scelta, brigadiere e maresciallo, 1956 (Bolognini 2, Cervi 3, Fabrizi 3, Manfredi 3, Sordi 3)
Guardia, ladro e cameriera, 1958 (Manfredi 3)
Guardian, 1984 (Gossett 3, Sheen 3)
Guardians of the Wild, 1928 (Miller, V. 4)
Guardie e ladri, 1951 (Monicelli 2, Fabrizi 3, De Laurentiis 4, Flaiano 4)
Guardsman, 1931 (Franklin 2, Pitts 3, Adrian 4, Lewin 4, Vajda 4)
Guayana: Crime of the Century. See Guayana: Cult of the Damned, 1979
Guayana: Cult of the Damned, 1979 (Cotten 3)
Gubben Kommer, 1939 (Sjostrom 2)
Gubecziana, 1974 (Vukotić 4)
Gubijinso, 1935 (Mizoguchi 2)
Gubijinso, 1941 (Hayasaka 4)
Guddobai, 1948 (Mori 3, Takamine 3)
Gudernes Yndling, 1919 (Holger-Madsen 2)
Guemes, 1970 (Torre-Nilsson 2)
Guendalina, 1956 (Lattuada 2, De Laurentiis 4, Ponti 4)
Guêpes, 1961 (Braunberger 4, Delerue 4)
Guerillas. See American Guerila in the Philippines, 1950
Guérillera, 1982 (Cassel 3)
Guerilleros. See Briganti italiani, 1961
Guérisseur, 1954 (Marais 3, Bost 4)
Guérité. See Douaniers et contrabandiers, 1905

Guernica, 1950 (Resnais 2, Braunberger 4)
Guerra alla guerra, 1946 (Zavattini 4)
Guerra continua, 1961 (Palance 3, Reggiani 3)
Guerra de los pasteles, 1943 (Armendáriz 3)
Guerra del cerdo. *See* Diario de la guerra del cerdo, 1975
Guerra e pace. *See* War and Peace, 1956
Guerra olvidada, 1967 (Alvarez 2)
Guerra segreta, 1965 (Gassman 3)
Guerra segreta. *See* Guerre Secrète, 1965
Guerre comme à la guerre, 1971 (Jurgens 3)
Guerre des karts. *See* Grosse Tête, 1962
Guerre des valses. *See* Walzerkrieg, 1933
Guerre du feu, 1981 (Sarde 4)
Guerre du silence, 1959 (Lelouch 2)
Guerre est finie, 1966 (Resnais 2, Bujold 3, Montand 3, Piccoli 3, Thulin 3, Fusco 4, Vierny 4)
Guerre populaire au Laos, 1969 (Ivens 2)
Guerre secrète, 1965 (Christian-Jaque 2, Bourvil 3, Fonda, H. 3, Girardot 3, Kinski 3, Ryan 3)
Guerrilla, 1908 (Griffith 2, Bitzer 4)
Guerrilla Fighter. *See* Padatik, 1973
Guess Who's Coming to Dinner?, 1967 (Kramer, S. 2, Hepburn, K. 3, Poitier 3, Tracy 3)
Guest, 1951 (Newman 4)
Guest. *See* Caretaker, 1963
Guest in the House, 1944 (De Toth 2, Baxter A. 3, Bellamy 3, Wilde 3, Garmes 4, Stromberg 4)
Guest Wife, 1945 (Wood 2, Ameche 3, Colbert 3)
Guestless Dinner Party. *See* Store Middag, 1914
Guests of Honour, 1941 (Cavalcanti 2, Crichton 2)
Guests of the Nation, 1934 (Cusack 3)
Guet-apens, 1913 (Feuillade 2)
Gueule d'amour, 1937 (Grémillon 2, Gabin 3, Spaak 4)
Gueule de l'autre, 1979 (Jurgens 3)
Gueule de l'emploi, 1973 (Gélin 3, Presle 3)
Gueule ouverte, 1974 (Baye 3, Almendros 4)
Gueux au paradis, 1945 (Fernandel 3, Raimu 3)
Guglielmo Tell, 1949 (Cervi 3)
Guidance to the Indulgent. *See* Doraku shinan, 1928
Guide, 1965 (Anand 3, Burman 4)
Guide for the Married Man, 1967 (Ball 3, Hunter 3, Jaffe 3, Kelly, Gene 3, Mansfield 3, Matthau 3, Smith, J.M. 4, Williams, J. 4)
Guided Muscle, 1955 (Jones 2)
Guiding Conscience. *See* Lykken, 1916
Guignol, marionnette de France, 1943 (Fernandel 3)
Guignolo, 1979 (Belmondo 3, Audiard 4, Decaë 4)
Guile of Women, 1921 (Rogers, W. 3)
Guillaume Apollinaire, 1955 (Kosma 4)
Guillotine, 1924 (Albers 3)
Guilt Is Not Mine. *See* Ingiusta condanna, 1952
Guilt of Janet Ames, 1947 (Douglas, M. 3, Russell, R. 3, Coffee 4, Duning 4, Walker 4)
Guilt of Vladimir Olmer. *See* Vina Vladimira Olmera, 1956
Guilty?, 1930 (Muse 3)
Guilty as Charged, 1932 (McLaglen 3)
Guilty as Charged. *See* Guilty as Hell, 1932
Guilty as Hell, 1932 (Arlen 3, Struss 4)
Guilty Bystander, 1950 (Tiomkin 4)
Guilty Conscience, 1985 (Hopkins, A. 3)
Guilty Generation, 1931 (Karloff 3, Young, R. 3)
Guilty Hands, 1931 (Van Dyke, W.S. 2, Barrymore L. 3, Francis, K. 3, Stromberg 4)
Guilty Melody, 1936 (Stallich 4)
Guilty of Treason, 1950 (Friedhofer 4)
Guilty Ones, 1916 (Hardy 3)
Guilty or Innocent: The Sam Sheppard Murder Case, 1975 (Schifrin 4)
Guinea Pig, 1948 (Boulting 2, Attenborough 3)
Guinguette, 1958 (Delannoy 2, Jeanson 4)
Guirlande merveilleuse, 1903 (Méliès 2)
Guitar Craze, 1959 (Russell 2)
Gulag, 1985 (McDowell 3)
Guldet og vort Hjerte, 1913 (Holger-Madsen 2)
Guldets Gift, 1915 (Dreyer 2, Holger-Madsen 2)

Guldmønten. *See* Alt paa et Kort, 1912
Guldspindeln, 1914 (Sjostrom 2)
Gulf Stream, 1939 (Alexeieff and Parker 2)
Gull!. *See* Trut!, 1944
Gullible Canary, 1942 (Fleischer, M. and D. 2)
Gulliver's Travels, 1939 (Young, V. 4)
Gulliver's Travels, 1977 (Love 3, Legrand 4)
Gulls and Buoys, 1972 (Breer 2)
Gulvbehandling, 1955 (Carlsen 2)
Gulyashchaya, 1961 (Gurchenko 3)
Gumshoe, 1971 (Finney 3)
Gun. *See* Dio, sei proprio un padreterno, 1973
Gun Battle at Monterey, 1957 (Hayden 3, Van Cleef 3)
Gun Before Butter, 1972 (Lassally 4)
Gun Belt, 1953 (Elam 3)
Gun Brothers, 1956 (Crabbe 3)
Gun Crazy, 1949 (Trumbo 4)
Gun Crazy. *See* Deadly Is the Female, 1949
Gun Fever, 1958 (Cody 3)
Gun Fightin' Gentleman, 1919 (Ford, J. 2, Carey 3)
Gun for a Coward, 1957 (Cody 3, Hunter 3, MacMurray 3)
Gun Fury, 1953 (Walsh 2, Marvin 3, Reed, D. 3, Wald 4)
Gun Glory, 1957 (Granger 3, Plunkett 4)
Gun Gospel, 1927 (Brown, Harry Joe 4, Polito 4)
Gun in His Hand, 1945 (Losey 2)
Gun Justice, 1927 (Wyler 2)
Gun Justice, 1934 (McCord 4)
Gun Law, 1919 (Ford, J. 2, Carey 3)
Gun Law, 1929 (Musuraca 4, Plunkett 4)
Gun Law, 1938 (Bond 3, August 4)
Gun Moll. *See* Poopsie, 1974
Gun o' Gunga Din, 1911 (White 3)
Gun Packer, 1919 (Ford, J. 2, Carey 3)
Gun Play, 1951 (Hunt 4)
Gun Pusher. *See* Gun Packer, 1919
Gun Riders. *See* Five Bloody Graves, 1970
Gun Runner. *See* Santiago, 1956
Gun Runners, 1958 (Siegel 2, Elam 3, Murphy 3, Sloane 3)
Gun Smoke, 1931 (Arlen 3, Fazenda 3)
Gun Smugglers, 1948 (Hunt 4)
Gun That Won the West, 1955 (Katzman 4)
Gun the Man Down, 1956 (Dickinson 3, Clothier 4)
Gun Woman, 1918 (Borzage 2)
Gunbatsu, 1970 (Mifune 3, Shimura 3)
Guney olum saciyor, 1969 (Guney 2)
Gunfight, 1971 (Black 3, Douglas, K. 3)
Gunfight at Comanche Creek, 1962 (Biroc 4)
Gunfight at Commanche Creek, 1962 (Murphy 3)
Gunfight at Dodge City, 1959 (McCrea 3, Mirisch 4, Salter 4)
Gunfight at Sandoval, 1959 (Duryea 3)
Gunfight at the O.K. Corral, 1957 (Sturges, J. 2, Douglas, K. 3, Elam 3, Hopper 3, Ireland 3, Lancaster 3, Van Cleef 3, Head 4, Lang 4, Tiomkin 4, Wallis 4)
Gunfighter, 1917 (Hart 3, August 4)
Gunfighter, 1923 (Farnum 3)
Gunfighter, 1950 (De Toth 2, King 2, Malden 3, Marsh 3, Peck 3, Johnson 4, Lemaire 4, Miller, A. 4, Newman 4, Zanuck 4)
Gunfighters, 1947 (Scott, R. 3, Brown, Harry Joe 4)
Gunfighters of Abilene, 1960 (Crabbe 3)
Gunfighters of Casa Grande. *See* Pistoleros de Casa Grande, 1965
Gung Ho!, 1943 (Mitchum 3, Scott, R. 3, Krasner 4, Salter 4, Wanger 4)
Gunga Din, 1939 (Hawks 2, Stevens 2, Fairbanks, D. Jr. 3, Fontaine 3, Grant, C. 3, Jaffe 3, McLaglen 3, August 4, Berman 4, Clothier 4, Dunn 4, Hecht 4, MacArthur 4, Newman 4, Polglase 4)
Gunkan sudeni kemuri nashi, 1950 (Yamamura 3)
Gunki hatameku shitani, 1972 (Shindo 2)
Gunless Bad Man, 1926 (Wyler 2)
Gunman, 1911 (Dwan 2)
Gunman, 1914 (Walsh 2)
Gunman in the Streets. *See* Traqué, 1950
Gunman's Walk, 1958 (Heflin 3, Duning 4, Nugent 4)
Gunn, 1967 (Edwards 2, Mancini 4)

Gunnar Hedes saga, 1922 (Stiller 2, Jaenzon 4, Magnusson 4)
Gunnar Hede's Saga. *See* Gunnar Hedes saga, 1922
Gunpoint, 1966 (Murphy 3, Bumstead 4, Salter 4)
Gunpoint!. *See* At Gunpoint!, 1955
Gunpowder Plot, 1900 (Hepworth 2)
Gunro no machi, 1952 (Yamamura 3)
Guns, 1980 (Kramer, R. 2)
Guns. *See* Fuzis, 1964
Guns and Guitars, 1936 (Autry 3)
Guns A-Poppin', 1957 (Three Stooges 3)
Guns at Batasi, 1964 (Attenborough 3, Farrow 3, Hawkins 3,
    Addison 4, Fisher 4, Slocombe 4)
Guns for San Sebastian, 1968 (Jaffe 3, Quinn 3)
Guns for San Sebastian. *See* Bataille de San Sebastian, 1967
Guns for the Dictator. *See* Arme à gauche, 1965
Guns, Girls, and Gangsters, 1959 (Van Cleef 3)
Guns in the Afternoon. *See* Ride the High Country, 1962
Guns of Darkness, 1962 (Asquith 2, Caron 3, Niven 3, Fisher 4,
    Krasker 4)
Guns of Diablo, 1964 (Bronson 3)
Guns of Fort Petticoat, 1957 (Murphy 3, Brown, Harry Joe 4)
Guns of Loos, 1928 (Carroll M. 3)
Guns of Navarone, 1961 (Halas and Batchelor 2, Yates 2, Baker S. 3,
    Niven 3, Papas 3, Peck 3, Quayle 3, Quinn 3, Foreman 4, Morris 4,
    Tiomkin 4)
Guns of the Magnificent Seven, 1968 (Kennedy, G. 3, Rey 3,
    Bernstein 4)
Guns of the Pecos, 1937 (McCord 4)
Guns of the Timberland, 1960 (Crain 3, Ladd 3, Seitz 4)
Guns of the Trees, 1961 (Mekas 2)
Guns of Wyoming. *See* Cattle King, 1963
Guns of Zangara, 1960 (Van Cleef 3)
Gunsaulus Mystery, 1921 (Micheaux 2)
Gunsight Ridge, 1957 (McCrea 3, Jennings 4, Laszlo 4)
Gunslinger, 1956 (Ireland 3, Corman 4)
Gunsmoke, 1953 (Murphy 3, Boyle 4)
Gunsmoke Ranch, 1937 (Canutt 4)
Gunstling von Schonbrunn, 1929 (Dagover 3, Junge 4)
Guraida, 1943 (Tsuburaya 4)
Gurentai no uta, 1934 (Yoda 4)
Guru, 1968 (Ivory 2, York, M. 3, Jhabvala 4, Mitra 4)
Gus and the Anarchists, 1915 (Hardy 3)
Gus Edwards' Song Revue, 1929 (Day 4)
Gusher, 1913 (Sennett 2, Normand 3)
Gussie Rivals Jonah, 1915 (Sennett 2)
Gussie the Golfer, 1914 (Sennett 2, Summerville 3)
Gussie Tied to Trouble, 1915 (Sennett 2)
Gussie's Backward Way, 1915 (Sennett 2)
Gussie's Day of Rest, 1915 (Sennett 2, Summerville 3)
Gussie's Wayward Path, 1915 (Sennett 2)
Gustav Adolfs Page, 1960 (Jurgens 3, Herlth 4)
Gustave est médium, 1921 (Feuillade 2)

Gutei kenkei, 1931 (Gosho 2)
Gutter. *See* Dobu, 1954
Guvernørens Datter, 1912 (Blom 2)
Guv'nor, 1935 (Arliss 3, Balcon 4, Junge 4)
Guy, a Gal, and a Pal, 1945 (Boetticher 2, Edwards 2, Hunter 4)
Guy Could Change, 1946 (Howard 2, Alton, J. 4)
Guy de Maupassant, 1978 (Gélin 3)
Guy Named Joe, 1943 (Edwards 2, Fleming 2, Barrymore L. 3, Bond 3,
    Dunne 3, Johnson, V. 3, Tracy 3, Williams 3, Freund 4, Gibbons 4,
    Irene 4, Stothart 4, Trumbo 4)
Guy Upstairs, 1915 (Eason 4)
Guy Who Came Back, 1951 (Bennett J. 3, Darnell 3, Douglas, P. 3,
    La Shelle 4, Lemaire 4, Wheeler 4)
Guyana: Crime of the Century. *See* Guyana: Cult of the Damned,
    1979
Guyana: Cult of the Damned, 1979 (De Carlo 3)
Guyana: el crimen del siglo, 1979 (Ferrer, M. 3, Ireland 3)
Guyrkoviscarna, 1920 (Magnusson 4)
Guys and Dolls, 1955 (Mankiewicz 2, Brando 3, Simmons 3, Sinatra 3,
    Goldwyn 4, Kidd 4, Mandell 4, Sharaff 4, Stradling 4)
Guys of the Sea. *See* Umi no yarodomo, 1957
Gwen, ou le livre de sable, 1984 (Laguionie 2)
Gwiazdy musza plonać, 1954 (Munk 2)
Gyalog a mennyországba, 1959 (Latinovits 3, Torocsik 3)
Gyangu chushingura, 1963 (Yamamura 3)
Gyarmat a fold alatt, 1951 (Fábri 2)
Gycklarnas afton, 1953 (Bergman 2, Andersson H. 3, Bjornstrand 3,
    Fischer 4, Nykvist 4)
Gyermekek, konyvek, 1962 (Mészáros 2)
Gyldne Smil, 1935 (Fejos 2)
Gymnasium Jim, 1922 (Sennett 2)
Gymnasts, 1961 (Baillie 2)
Gypped in the Penthouse, 1955 (Three Stooges 3)
Gypsies. *See* Cigányok, 1962
Gypsy, 1911 (Lawrence 3)
Gypsy, 1962 (Leroy 2, Malden 3, Russell, R. 3, Wood 3, Orry-Kelly 4,
    Stradling 4)
Gypsy and the Gentleman, 1958 (Losey 2, Mercouri 3)
Gypsy Blood. *See* Carmen, 1918
Gypsy Blood. *See* Zigeunerblut, 1911
Gypsy Blood. *See* Zugelloses Blut, 1917
Gypsy Cavalier, 1922 (Blackton 2)
Gypsy Colt, 1954 (Bond 3, Van Cleef 3)
Gypsy Fiddler, 1933 (Terry 4)
Gypsy Girl. *See* Sky West and Crooked, 1966
Gypsy Life, 1945 (Terry 4)
Gypsy Melody, 1936 (Velez 3)
Gypsy Moths, 1969 (Frankenheimer 2, Hackman 3, Kerr 3,
    Lancaster 3, Bernstein 4)
Gypsy Queen, 1913 (Sennett 2, Arbuckle 3, Normand 3)
Gypsy Romance, 1914 (Reid 3)
Gypsy Wildcat, 1944 (Bruce 3)

H

H + 2, 1971 (Lancaster 3)
H. 2 S., 1968 (Morricone 4)
H.G. Wells' The Shape of Things to Come. *See* Shape of Things to
    Come, 1979
H.M. Pulham, Esq., 1941 (Vidor, K. 2, Coburn, C. 3, Heflin 3,
    Lamarr 3, Young, R. 3, Gibbons 4, Kaper 4)
H.M.S. Defiant, 1962 (Bogarde 3, Guinness 3, Mathieson 4)
H-Man. *See* Bijo to ekitai ningen, 1958
Ha egyszer husz év mulva . . ., 1964 (Gabór 3)
Ha fatto tredici!, 1951 (Fusco 4)
Ha fatto una signora, 1939 (Valli 3)

Ha! Ha! Ha!, 1934 (Fleischer, M. and D. 2)
Haadsaa, 1983 (Patil 3)
Haakon VII, 1952 (Carlsen 2)
Haar Jeet, 1939 (Roy 2)
Habanera, 1937 (Sirk 2)
Habañeras, 1983 (Granados 3)
Habatales series, 1960 (Halas and Batchelor 2)
Habeas Corpus, 1928 (Laurel and Hardy 3, Roach 4)
Habit of Happiness, 1916 (Dwan 2, Fleming 2, Fairbanks, D. 3,
    Menjou 3)
Habit Rabbit, 1963 (Hanna and Barbera 4)

Habit vert, 1937 (Berry 3, Blier 3, D'Eaubonne 4)
Habitantes de la casa deshabitada, 1958 (Rey 3)
Habrichka el hashemersh, 1972 (Harvey 3, Hawkins 3, Ireland 3)
Haceldama ou Le Prix du Sang, 1919 (Duvivier 2)
Hachyyuhachinenme no taiyo, 1941 (Tsuburaya 4)
Hadaka no jukyu-sai, 1970 (Shindo 2)
Hadaka no shima, 1960 (Shindo 2)
Hadaka no taiyo, 1958 (Shindo 2)
Hadota Misreya, 1982 (Chahine 2)
Haevnens Nat, 1915 (Christensen 2)
Haevnet, 1911 (Blom 2)
Hafenmelodie, 1949 (Geschonneck 3)
Hagen Girl, 1947 (Temple 3)
Hagiographia, 1971 (Markopoulos 2)
Haha, 1929 (Takamine 3)
Haha, 1958 (Kyo 3)
Haha, 1963 (Shindo 2)
Haha nareba onna nareba, 1952 (Yamada 3)
Haha no ai, 1935 (Hasegawa 3, Takamine 3)
Haha no chizu, 1942 (Mori 3, Hayasaka 4)
Haha no hatsukoi, 1954 (Kagawa 3)
Haha no saigetsu, 1965 (Tanaka 3)
Haha no uta, 1938 (Tanaka 3)
Haha o kowazu-ya, 1934 (Ozu 2)
Haha san-nin, 1958 (Yamada 3)
Haha shirayuki, 1956 (Yoda 4)
Haha to ko, 1938 (Tanaka 3)
Haha wa shinazu, 1942 (Naruse 2)
Haha yo, kimi no na o kegasu nakare, 1928 (Gosho 2, Tanaka 3)
Haha yo ko yo, 1933 (Yoda 4)
Hahakogusa, 1959 (Tanaka 3, Yamamura 3)
Hahako-zo, 1956 (Yamada 3)
Haha-tsubaki, 1950 (Yamamura 3)
Hahayo koishi, 1926 (Gosho 2)
Hahn im Korb, 1925 (Dieterle 2)
Hai hun, 1957 (Zhao 3)
Haikyo no naka, 1923 (Mizoguchi 2)
Hail Hero, 1969 (Kennedy, A. 3, Wright 3)
Hail Mafia! See Je vous salue, Maffia, 1965
Hail the Conquering Hero, 1944 (Sturges, P. 2, Dreier 4, Head 4, Seitz 4)
Hail the Woman, 1921 (Ince 4, Sullivan 4)
Hail to Freedom. See Viva la libertad, 1965
Haim Soutine, 1959 (Delerue 4)
Haine, 1979 (Kinski 3)
Hair, 1979 (Forman 2, Ray, N. 2, Ondricek 4)
Hair Cut-Ups, 1953 (Terry 4)
Hair Raising Hare, 1945 (Jones 2)
Hair Trigger Baxter, 1926 (Haller 4)
Hair Trigger Casey, 1922 (Borzage 2)
Hair Trigger Casey. See Immediate Lee, 1916
Hair Trigger Stuff, 1920 (Eason 4)
Haircut, 1963 (Warhol 2)
Hairless Hector, 1941 (Terry 4)
Hairpins, 1920 (Niblo 2, Barnes 4, Sullivan 4)
Hairy Ape, 1944 (Bendix 3, Hayward 3)
Hairyozuma shimatsu-ki, 1967 (Tsukasa 3)
Haitoku no mesu, 1961 (Yamamura 3)
Haizan no uta wa kanashi, 1923 (Mizoguchi 2)
Hajduk, 1974 (Madaras 3)
Hajduška Kletva, 1958 (Karamitev 3)
Hajnal, 1971 (Szabó 2)
Hakai, 1948 (Kinoshita 2, Mori 3)
Hakai, 1962 (Ichikawa 2, Kishida 3, Miyagawa 4)
Hakarka ha a dom, 1954 (Dickinson 2)
Hakoiri musume, 1935 (Ozu 2, Tanaka 3)
Hakone fuun-roku, 1952 (Yamada 3)
Hakuchi, 1951 (Kurosawa 2, Hara 3, Mifune 3, Mori 3, Shimura 3, Hayasaka 4)
Hakuchu no ketto, 1950 (Yamamura 3)
Hakuchu no torima, 1966 (Oshima 2, Toda 4)
Hakufujin no yoren, 1956 (Tsuburaya 4)
Hakugy, 1953 (Hara 3)

Hakuji no hito, 1957 (Yamamura 3)
Hakuro no kamen, Jigokudani no taiketsu, 1954 (Yamada 3)
Hal Roach Comedy Carnival, 1947 (Meek 3)
Halálcsengö, 1917 (Curtiz 2)
Halbblut, 1919 (Lang 2, Hoffmann 4, Pommer 4)
Halbseide, 1925 (Oswald 2, Albers 3)
Halbzart, 1959 (Schneider 3)
Hale and Hearty, 1922 (Roach 4)
Half a Bride, 1928 (La Cava 2, Cooper, Gary 3, Lombard 3)
Half a Dollar Bill, 1924 (Nilsson 3)
Half a Man, 1925 (Garnett 2, Laurel 3)
Half a Sinner, 1934 (Brennan 3, McCrea 3, Rooney 3)
Half a Sinner, 1940 (Trumbo 4)
Half a Sixpence, 1968 (Sidney 2, Unsworth 4)
Half Angel, 1936 (Carradine 3, Glennon 4, MacGowan 4, Meredyth 4, Zanuck 4)
Half Angel, 1951 (Cotten 3, Young, L. 3, Krasner 4, Newman 4, Riskin 4)
Half Breed, 1922 (Clarke, C.C. 4)
Half Breed. See Halvblod, 1913
Half Caste. See Halbblut, 1919
Half Holiday, 1931 (Sennett 2)
Half Human, 1957 (Carradine 3)
Half Marriage, 1929 (Murfin 4, Plunkett 4)
Half Shot at Sunrise, 1930 (Plunkett 4, Musuraca 4, Steiner 4)
Half Way to Shanghai, 1942 (Salter 4)
Half-a-Dollar Bill, 1923 (Van Dyke, W.S. 2)
Half-Back of Notre Dame, 1924 (Sennett 2)
Half-Breed, 1916 (Dwan 2, Fleming 2, Fairbanks, D. 3, Loos 4)
Half-Breed, 1952 (Cody 3, Young, R. 3, Eason 4)
Half-Fare Hare, 1956 (McKimson 4)
Half-Naked Truth, 1932 (La Cava 2, Velez 3, Berman 4, Glennon 4, Selznick 4, Steiner 4)
Half-Pint Pygmy, 1948 (Avery 2)
Half-shot Shooters, 1936 (Three Stooges 3, Bruckman 4)
Half-Way Girl, 1925 (Bosworth 3)
Halfway House, 1944 (Cavalcanti 2, Dearden 2, Rosay 3, Balcon 4, Clarke, T.E.B. 4)
Half-Way to Heaven, 1929 (Arthur 3, Lukas 3, Lang 4)
Half-Wit's Holiday, 1947 (Three Stooges 3)
Halhatatlanság, 1959 (Jancsó 2)
Halil, the Crow-Man. See Kargaci Halil, 1968
Halimeden mektup var, 1964 (Guney 2)
Halkas Gelobnis, 1918 (Albers 3)
Hall of Lost Steps. See Sál ztracených kroku, 1960
Hallelujah, 1929 (Vidor, K. 2, Gibbons 4, Shearer 4, Thalberg 4)
Hallelujah, I'm a Bum, 1933 (Milestone 2, Jolson 3, Langdon 3, Behrman 4, Day 4, Hecht 4, Newman 4)
Hallelujah, I'm a Tramp. See Hallelujah I'm a Bum!, 1933
Hallelujah the Hills, 1963 (Emshwiller 2)
Hallelujah Trail, 1965 (Sturges, J. 2, Lancaster 3, Pleasance 3, Remick 3, Bernstein 4, Head 4, Surtees 4)
Halles, 1929 (Kaufman 4)
Halliday Brand, 1957 (Bond 3, Cotten 3)
Hallo! Hallo! Hier spricht Berlin. See Allo Berlin? Ici Paris!, 1931
Halloween, 1978 (Carpenter 2, Pleasance 3)
Halloween II, 1980 (Pleasance 3)
Hallroom Boys, 1906 (Bitzer 4)
Hallroom Girls, 1912–13 (White 3)
Halls of Anger, 1970 (Bridges 3, Guffey 4, Mirisch 4)
Halls of Montezuma, 1951 (Milestone 2, Boone 3, Malden 3, Palance 3, Wagner 3, Widmark 3, Hoch 4, Lemaire 4, Reynolds 4, Wheeler 4)
Hallucination. See Lidércnyomás, 1920
Hallucinations du Baron Munchausen, 1911 (Méliès 2)
Hallucinations pharmaceutiques, 1908 (Méliès 2)
Hallucinations sadiques, 1969 (Gélin 3)
Hallucinators. See Naked Zoo, 1971
Halvblod, 1913 (Sjostrom 2, Magnusson 4)
Ham and Eggs, 1927 (Fazenda 3)
Ham and Eggs, 1933 (Lantz 4)
Ham and Eggs. See Ham and Eggs at the Front, 1927
Ham and Eggs at the Front, 1927 (Loy 3, Clarke, C.C. 4)

Ham Artist. *See* Face on the Bar-Room Floor, 1914
Ham Dard, 1953 (Biswas 4)
Ham in a Role, 1949 (McKimson 4)
Hamagure no komoriuta, 1973 (Yoshimura 2)
Hamari Baat, 1943 (Kapoor 2, Biswas 4)
Hamateur Night, 1938 (Avery 2)
Hambone and Hillie, 1984 (Gish, L. 3)
Hamburg, 1961 (Roos 2)
Hamburger Hamlet, 1975 (Keach 3)
Hame Khelne Do, 1962 (Biswas 4)
Hamilton in the Music Festival, 1961 (Halas and Batchelor 2)
Hamilton the Musical Elephant, 1961 (Halas and Batchelor 2)
Hamis Isabella, 1968 (Madaras 3)
Hamles, 1960 (Skolimowski 2)
Hamlet, 1910 (Blom 2)
Hamlet, 1920 (Nielsen 3, Courant 4)
Hamlet, 1939 (Gielgud 3, Hawkins 3)
Hamlet, 1948 (Cushing 3, Holloway 3, Lee, C. 3, Olivier 3, Quayle 3, Simmons 3, Dillon 4, Mathieson 4)
Hamlet, 1960 (Schell, Maximilian 3)
Hamlet, 1963 (Kozintsev 2, Smoktunovsky 3, Enei 4, Moskvin 4, Shostakovich 4)
Hamlet, 1964 (Burton 3, Gielgud 3)
Hamlet, 1969 (Dmytryk 2, Richardson 2, Hopkins, A. 3, Williamson 3, Addison 4, Fisher 4)
Hamlet's Castle. *See* Shakespeare og Kronborg, 1950
Hammersmith Is Out, 1972 (Burton 3, Raft 3, Taylor, E. 3, Ustinov 3, Head 4)
Hammett, 1982 (Coppola 2, Wenders 2, Cook 3, Forrest 3, Sidney 3, Barry 4, Biroc 4, Tavoularis 4)
Hammond Mystery. *See* Undying Monster, 1942
Hamnaren, 1915 (Stiller 2)
Hamnstad, 1948 (Bergman 2, Fischer 4)
Hampelmann, 1930 (Sakall 3, Courant 4)
Hampels Abenteuer, 1915 (Oswald 2)
Hampi, 1960 (Rouch 2)
Hamrahi, 1945 (Roy 2, Sircar 4)
Hams That Couldn't Be Cured, 1942 (Lantz 4)
Hamster. *See* Křeček, 1946
Hamusse Hanussen, 1955 (Warm 4)
Hana, 1941 (Yoshimura 2, Tanaka 3)
Hana aru zasso, 1939 (Tanaka 3)
Hana futatabi, 1956 (Yamamura 3)
Hana hiraku, 1948 (Ichikawa 2, Hayasaka 4)
Hana hiraku, 1955 (Yamada 3)
Hana no Banzui-in, 1959 (Yamada 3)
Hana no bojo, 1958 (Tsukasa 3)
Hana no kenka-jo, 1953 (Hasegawa 3)
Hana no Kodo-kan, 1953 (Hasegawa 3)
Hana no maki, Arashi no maki, 1956 (Yamamura 3)
Hana no nagadosu, 1954 (Kinugasa 2)
Hana no nagawakizashi, 1954 (Hasegawa 3)
Hana no Oedo no musekinin, 1964 (Shindo 3)
Hana no saku ie, 1963 (Iwashita 3, Yamamura 3)
Hana no sugao, 1949 (Okada 3, Yamamura 3)
Hana no tsukihi, 1949 (Yamada 3)
Hana no wataridori, 1956 (Hasegawa 3)
Hana no Yoshiwara hyakunin-giri, 1960 (Yoda 4)
Hana no yukyo-den, 1958 (Hasegawa 3)
Hanahagi sensei to Santa, 1952 (Yamada 3)
Hanakago no uta, 1937 (Gosho 2, Takamine 3, Tanaka 3)
Hanako-sen, 1943 (Takamine 3)
Hanakurabe tanuki-goten, 1949 (Kyo 3)
Hanamuko no negoto, 1935 (Gosho 2)
Hanamuko Taiheiki, 1945 (Yoda 4)
Hanano sando-gasa, 1954 (Hasegawa 3)
Hananoren, 1959 (Tsukasa 3)
Hanaoka Seishu no tsuma, 1967 (Shindo 2, Takamine 3)
Hanare goze Orin, 1977 (Shinoda 2, Iwashita 3, Miyagawa 4, Takemitsu 4)
Hanasake jijii, 1923 (Kinugasa 2)
Hanasaku minato, 1943 (Kinoshita 2)
Hanataba no yume, 1938 (Takamine 3)

Hanatsumi nikki, 1939 (Shindo 3)
Hanauta ojosan, 1938 (Tanaka 3)
Hanayome kaigi, 1956 (Tsukasa 3)
Hanayome karuta, 1937 (Takamine 3)
Hanayome kurabe, 1935 (Tanaka 3)
Hanayome no negoto, 1933 (Gosho 2, Hasegawa 3, Tanaka 3)
Hanayome san wa sekai-ichi, 1959 (Shindo 2)
Hand, 1981 (Caine 3)
Hand. *See* Ruka, 1965
Hand in the Trap. *See* Mano en la trampa, 1961
Hand Movie, 1968 (Rainer 2)
Hand of Death, 1961 (Crosby 4)
Hand of Destiny, 1914 (White 3)
Hand of Fate, 1912 (Bosworth 3)
Hand of Peril, 1916 (Tourneur, M. 2, Carré 4)
Hand Organ Man, 1909 (Olcott 2)
Hand Painted Abstraction, 1934–35 (McLaren 2)
Hand That Rocks the Cradle, 1917 (Weber 2)
Handcuffs or Kisses, 1921 (Colman 3)
Handful of Clouds. *See* Doorway to Hell, 1930
Handful of Love. *See* Handfull karlek, 1974
Handful of Rice. *See* Handfull Ris, 1938
Handfull karlek, 1974 (Sjoman 2, Thulin 3)
Handfull Ris, 1938 (Fejos 2)
Handle with Care, 1965 (Lancaster 3)
Handle with Care, 1977 (Demme 2)
Handler der vier Jahreszeiten, 1971 (Fassbinder 2, Schygulla 3)
Handling Ships, 1944–45 (Halas and Batchelor 2)
Hands Across the Border, 1943 (Rogers, R. 3)
Hands Across the Table, 1935 (Leisen 2, Bellamy 3, Lombard 3, MacMurray 3, Krasna 4)
Hands, Knees, and Bumps a Daisy, 1969 (Dunning 4)
Hands of Cormac Joyce, 1972 (Cusack 3)
Hands of Orlac, 1960 (Lee, C. 3, Pleasance 3)
Hands of Orlac. *See* Mad Love, 1935
Hands of Orlac. *See* Orlacs Hande, 1924
Hands Off, 1921 (Mix 3)
Hands over the City. *See* Mani sulla citta, 1963
Hands Up!, 1917 (Browning 2, Moore, C. 3)
Hands Up!, 1926 (Johnson, N. 3)
Hands Up!. *See* Rece do gory, 1967
Handsome Boy Trying to Rule the World. *See* Tenka o nerau bishounen, 1955
Hand-tinting, 1967–68 (Wieland 2)
Handy Andy, 1934 (Rogers, W. 3, Taylor, R. 3, Miller, A. 4)
Handy Man, 1918 (Hardy 3)
Handy Man, 1923 (Laurel 3)
Hang 'em High, 1967 (Dern 3, Eastwood 3, Hopper 3, Johnson, B. 3)
Hanged Man, 1964 (Siegel 2, O'Brien, E. 3)
Hanging Out—Yonkers, 1973 (Akerman 2)
Hanging Tree, 1959 (Daves 2, Cooper, Gary 3, Malden 3, Schell, Maria 3, Scott, G. 3, McCord 4, Orry-Kelly 4, Steiner 4)
Hangivelse, 1965 (Thulin 3)
Hangman, 1959 (Curtiz 2, Taylor, R. 3, Bumstead 4, Head 4, Nichols 4)
Hangman's House, 1928 (Ford, J. 2, Bosworth 3, McLaglen 3, Wayne 3)
Hangman's Knot, 1952 (Marvin 3, Reed, D. 3, Scott, R. 3, Brown, Harry Joe 4, Canutt 4)
Hangmen Also Die!, 1943 (Lang 2, Brennan 3, Farnum 3, Eisler 4, Howe 4)
Hangover. *See* Baksmalla, 1973
Hangover. *See* Female Jungle, 1956
Hangover Square, 1945 (Darnell 3, McDowall 3, Sanders 3, Herrmann 4, La Shelle 4, Wheeler 4)
Hangup, 1974 (Hathaway 2)
Hangyaboly, 1971 (Fábri 2, Torocsik 3)
Hangyaku-ji, 1961 (Shindo 3)
Hanibalove Alpe, 1969 (Grgić 4)
Hanjo, 1961 (Yamamura 3, Takemitsu 4)
Hanka, 1955 (Vorkapich 4)
Hanky Panky, 1982 (Poitier 3, Widmark 3, Wilder 3)

Hara-Kiri, 1919 (Lang 2, Dagover 3, Hoffmann 4)
Hara-Kiri. *See* Battle, 1934
Harakiri. *See* Seppuku, 1962
Harangok Rómába mentek, 1958 (Jancsá 2, Gabór 3, Madaras 3)
Harangok városa—Veszprém, 1965 (Mészáros 2)
Harbor in the Heart of Europe. *See* Přístav v srdci Europy, 1939–40
Harbor Island, 1912 (Bosworth 3)
Harbor Scenes, 1935 (Maddow 4)
Hard Boiled, 1925 (McCarey 2, Roach 4)
Hard Boiled Egg, 1948 (Terry 4)
Hard Boiled Mahoney, 1948 (Johnson, N. 3)
Hard Cash, 1913 (Ingram 2)
Hard Cider, 1914 (Sennett 2)
Hard Contract, 1969 (Black 3, Coburn, J. 3, Dauphin 3, Hayden 3, Meredith 3, Remick 3, North 4)
Hard Day's Night, 1964 (Lester 2)
Hard, Fast, and Beautiful, 1951 (Lupino 3, Trevor 3)
Hard Fists, 1927 (Wyler 2)
Hard Guy, 1930 (Tracy 3)
Hard klang, 1952 (Sjostrom 2)
Hard Knocks, 1924 (Roach 4)
Hard Knocks and Love Taps, 1921 (Sennett 2)
Hard Labor on the River Douro. *See* Douro, faina fluvial, 1931
Hard Luck, 1921 (Keaton 2)
Hard Summer. *See* Vizivárosi nyár, 1965
Hard Times, 1975 (Hill, W. 2, Bronson 3, Coburn, J. 3, Martin, S. 3)
Hard Times. *See* Fukeiki jidai, 1930
Hard Times for Vampires. *See* Tempi duri vampiri, 1959
Hard to Beat, 1909 (Porter 2)
Hard to Get, 1929 (Fazenda 3, Seitz 4)
Hard to Get, 1938 (De Havilland 3, Powell, D. 3, Grot 4, Mercer 4, Rosher 4, Wald 4, Wallis 4)
Hard to Handle, 1933 (Leroy 2, Cagney 3, Orry-Kelly 4)
Hard Wash, 1896 (Bitzer 4)
Hard Way, 1942 (Lupino 3, Howe 4, Orry-Kelly 4, Prinz 4, Wald 4)
Hard Way, 1979 (Van Cleef 3, Decae 4)
Harda leken, 1955 (Fischer 4)
Harda viljor, 1923 (Magnusson 4)
Hard-Boiled, 1926 (Mix 3)
Hard-Boiled, 1929 (Plunkett 4)
Hard-Boiled Haggerty, 1927 (Plunkett 4, Polito 4, Wilson, C. 4)
Hardboiled Rose, 1929 (Loy 3)
Hard-Boiled Tenderfoot, 1924 (Roach 4)
Hardcore, 1979 (Schrader 2, Scott, G. 3)
Harder They Fall, 1956 (Robson 2, Bogart 3, Steiger 3, Friedhofer 4, Guffey 4, Wald 4)
Hardhat and Legs, 1980 (Kanin 4)
Hardly Working, 1980 (Lewis 2)
Hardship of Miles Standish, 1940 (Freleng 4)
Hardys Ride Again, 1939 (Stone 3)
Hardys Ride High, 1939 (Rooney 3)
Hare and the Hounds, 1940 (Terry 4)
Hare Brush, 1954 (Freleng 4)
Hare Conditioned, 1945 (Jones 2)
Hare Do, 1947 (Freleng 4)
Hare Force, 1944 (Freleng 4)
Hare Grows in Manhattan, 1947 (Freleng 4)
Hare Krishna, 1966 (Mekas 2)
Hare Life, 1951 (Freleng 4)
Hare Mail, 1931 (Lantz 4)
Hare Ribbin', 1944 (Clampett 4)
Hare Splitter, 1947 (Freleng 4)
Hare Tonic, 1945 (Jones 2)
Hare Trigger, 1945 (Freleng 4)
Hare Trimmed, 1952 (Freleng 4)
Hare We Go, 1949 (Freleng 4)
Hare-Brained Hypnotist, 1942 (Freleng 4)
Hare-Breadth Hurry, 1963 (Jones 2)
Haredevil Hare, 1947 (Jones 2)
Harekosode, 1940 (Yoda 4)
Hare-kosode, 1961 (Hasegawa 3, Yoda 4)
Hare-less Wolf, 1957 (Freleng 4)
Harem, 1967 (Ferreri 2, Baker C. 3, Tognazzi 3, Morricone 4)

Harem Knight, 1926 (Sennett 2)
Harem Scarem, 1927 (Disney 2)
Haremseventyr, 1914 (Holger-Madsen 2)
Hare-Way to the Stars, 1958 (Jones 2)
Hari Hondal Bargadar, 1980 (Benegal 2, Nihalani 4)
Harikiri shacho, 1956 (Tsukasa 3)
Harikomi, 1958 (Takamine 3)
Harjeet, 1940 (Sircar 4)
Harlekin, 1931 (Reiniger 2)
Harlem, 1942 (Gallone 2, Amidei 4)
Harlem Globetrotters, 1951 (Dandridge 3)
Harlem Hotshots, 1940 (Horne 3)
Harlem in Heaven, 1938 (Robinson, B. 3)
Harlem on Parade, 1942 (Horne 3)
Harlem Wednesday, 1958 (Hubley 4)
Harlequin, 1980 (Crawford, B. 3)
Harlot, 1964 (Warhol 2)
Harlow, 1965 (Baker C. 3, Lansbury 3, Rogers, G. 3, Hayes 4, Head Ruttenberg 4, Westmore, W. 4)
Harmadik nekifutás, 1973 (Madaras 3)
Harminkét nevem volt, 1972 (Latinovits 3, Torocsik 3)
Harmonikář, 1953 (Stallich 4)
Harmony at Home, 1930 (Miller, S. 4)
Harmony Heaven, 1930 (Wimperis 4)
Harmony Lane, 1935 (Muse 3)
Harmony Parade. *See* Pigskin Parade, 1936
Harold and Maude, 1971 (Ashby 2, Cusack 3, Gordon 3, Alonzo 4)
Harold Lloyd's Funny Side of Life, 1966 (Lloyd 3)
Harold Lloyd's World of Comedy, 1962 (Lloyd 3)
Harold Teen, 1928 (Leroy 2, Haller 4)
Harold Teen, 1933 (Orry-Kelly 4)
Harold's Bad Man, 1915 (Mix 3)
Harom csillag, 1960 (Jancsó 2, Gabór 3, Karamitev 3, Torocsik 3)
Harom és jél muskétás, 1935 (Sakall 3)
Harp in Hock, 1927 (Love 3, Levien 4)
Harp of Burma. *See* Biruma no tategoto, 1956
Harp of Tara, 1914 (Ince 4)
Harper, 1966 (Bacall 3, Leigh, J. 3, Martin, S. 3, Newman 3, Wagner Winters 3, Goldman, W. 4, Hall 4, Previn 4)
Harrad Experiment, 1973 (Hedren 3)
Harri! Harri!. *See* Hemât i Natten, 1977
Harriet Craig, 1950 (Crawford, J. 3, Duning 4, Walker 4)
Harrigan's Kid, 1943 (Chase 4, Schary 4)
Harrison és Barrison, 1917 (Korda 2)
Harry & Son, 1984 (Newman 3, Woodward 3, Allen, D. 4, Bumstead 4, Mancini 4)
Harry and Tonto, 1974 (Mazursky 2, Burstyn 3, George, Ch. D. 3)
Harry and Walter Go to New York, 1976 (Caan 3, Caine 3, Gould 3, Horner 4, Kovacs 4)
Harry Black, 1958 (Granger 3)
Harry Black and the Tiger. *See* Harry Black, 1958
Harry in Your Pocket, 1973 (Coburn, J. 3, Pidgeon 3, Schifrin 4)
Harry Lauder Songs series, 1931 (Balcon 4)
Harry Never Holds. *See* Harry in Your Pocket, 1973
Harry Tracy, 1982 (Dern 3)
Harry's War, 1981 (Cook 3, Page 3)
Hart to Hart, 1979 (McDowall 3, Wagner 3)
Haru ichiban, 1966 (Iwashita 3)
Haru kitareba, 1937 (Takamine 3)
Haru koro no hana no en, 1958 (Kinugasa 2)
Haru no mezame, 1947 (Naruse 2)
Haru no mizuumi, 1956 (Yamamura 3)
Haru no tawamure, 1949 (Takamine 3, Hayasaka 4)
Haru no uzumaki, 1954 (Kyo 3)
Haru no yume, 1960 (Kinoshita 2)
Haru o matsu hitobito, 1959 (Takemitsu 4)
Haru ramman, 1966 (Mori 3, Tsukasa 3)
Haru wa gofujin kara, 1932 (Ozu 2)
Harubiyori, 1967 (Iwashita 3)
Haruka nari haha no kuni, 1950 (Kyo 3, Yamada 3, Yoda 4)
Harukanaru soro, 1980 (Tsukasa 3)
Harum Scarum, 1965 (Presley 3, Katzman 4)
Harun al Raschid, 1924 (Curtiz 2)

Harusugata gonin-otoko, 1936 (Hasegawa 3)
Harvard, Here I Come, 1942 (De Carlo 3, Brown, K. 4, Planer 4)
Harvest, 1962 (Van Dyke, W. 2)
Harvest. *See* Regain, 1937
Harvest Hands, 1923 (Roach 4)
Harvest Help, 1940 (Wright 2)
Harvest in the Cooperative 'Dosza'. *See* Arat az Oroshází Dözsa, 1953
Harvest of Flame, 1913 (Reid 3)
Harvest of My Lai, 1970 (Ophuls 2)
Harvest of Sin, 1913 (Ince 4)
Harvest of Tears. *See* Pressens Magt, 1913
Harvest Shall Come, 1942 (Alwyn 4)
Harvest Time, 1940 (Terry 4)
Harvester, 1936 (Brady 3)
Harvey, 1950 (Stewart 3, Daniels 4, Orry-Kelly 4)
Harvey Girls, 1946 (Sidney 2, Walters 2, Charisse 3, Garland 3,
    Lansbury 3, Alton, R. 4, Edens 4, Freed 4, Irene 4, Mercer 4,
    Raphaelson 4, Rose 4)
Harvey Middleman, Fireman, 1965 (Smith, D.)
Has Anybody Here Seen Kelly?, 1926 (Fleischer, M. and D. 2)
Has Anybody Seen My Gal?, 1929 (Love 3)
Has Anybody Seen My Gal?, 1952 (Sirk 2, Coburn, C. 3, Dean 3,
    Hudson 3)
Hasard et la violence, 1974 (Montand 3, Evein 4)
Hasard et l'amour, 1913 (Linders 3)
Hasegawa Roppa no Iemitsu to Hikosa, 1941 (Hasegawa 3)
Hasenaginica, 1967 (Markoviá 3)
Hash House Fraud, 1915 (Sennett 2, Fazenda 3)
Hash House Mashers, 1915 (Sennett 2)
Hash Shop, 1930 (Lantz 4)
Hasher's Delirium. *See* Songe d'un garçon de café, 1910
Hash-House Hero. *See* Star Boarder, 1914
Hashi no nai kawa, 1969–70 (Imai 2)
Hasimura Togo, 1917 (Hayakawa 3) (Rosher 4)
Haskovy povídky, 1952 (Hrušínský 3)
Hasshu kyokakujin, 1936 (Shimura 3)
Hasta la victoria siempre, 1967 (Alvarez 2)
Hasta que perdió Jalisco, 1945 (De Fuentes 2, Negrete 3)
Hasty Hare, 1952 (Jones 2)
Hasty Heart, 1950 (Neal 3, Reagan 3)
Hasty Marriage, 1931 (Roach 4)
Hat, 1964 (Moore, D. 3, Hubley 4)
Hat. *See* Sešir, 1976
Hat Check Girl, 1932 (Rogers, G. 3)
Hat Check Honey, 1944 (Krasner 4, Salter 4)
Hat, Coat, and Glove, 1934 (Beavers 3, Hunt 4, MacGowan 4,
    Plunkett 4, Steiner 4)
Hat hét boldogság, 1939 (De Toth 2)
Hatamoto kenka-daka, 1961 (Yamamura 3)
Hatamoto taikutsu otoko, 1956 (Shindo 3)
Hatamoto to Banshiin, 1960 (Yamamura 3)
Hataoka junsa, 1940 (Yoda 4)
Hataraku ikka, 1939 (Naruse 2)
Hatari!, 1962 (Hawks 2, Wayne 3, Brackett, L. 4, Fulton 4, Head 4,
    Mancini 4, Mercer 4)
Hatarnegol, 1971 (Topol 3)
Hatch Up Your Troubles, 1948 (Hanna and Barbera 4)
Hatchet Man, 1932 (Wellman 2, Robinson, E. 3, Young, L. 3, Grot 4)
Hate, 1922 (Mathis 4)
Hate for Hate. *See* Odio per odio, 1967
Hater of Men, 1917 (Gilbert 3)
Haters, 1912 (Dwan 2)
Haters. *See* Grudge, 1915
Hateshinaki jonetsu, 1949 (Ichikawa 2)
Hateshinaki yokubo, 1958 (Imamura 2)
Hatfields and the McCoys, 1975 (Palance 3)
Hatful of Dreams, 1945 (Pal 2)
Hatful of Rain, 1957 (Zinnemann 2, Saint 3, Herrmann 4, Lemaire 4,
    Wheeler 4)
Hatmaker. *See* Fantômes du chapelier, 1982
Hatred. *See* Mollenard, 1938
Hats Off, 1927 (Laurel and Hardy 3, Roach 4)
Hats Off, 1936 (Fuller 2)

Hatsugaro-ondo, 1936 (Shimura 3)
Hatsukoi, 1926 (Gosho 2)
Hatsukoi jigokuhen, 1968 (Hani 2, Takemitsu 4)
Hatsukoi no haru, 1933 (Takamine 3)
Hatsukoi san-nin masuko, 1955 (Tsukasa 3)
Hatta Marri, 1932 (Sennett 2)
Hatter's Castle, 1941 (Kerr 3, Mason 3)
Haunted, 1977 (Mayo 3)
Haunted and the Hunted. *See* Dementia, 1963
Haunted Bedroom, 1919 (Niblo 2, Barnes 4, Sullivan 4)
Haunted Castle. *See* Schloss Vogelod, 1921
Haunted Cat, 1951 (Terry 4)
Haunted Gold, 1932 (Wayne 3, Musuraca 4)
Haunted Hat, 1915 (Hardy 3)
Haunted Homestead, 1927 (Wyler 2)
Haunted Honeymoon, 1925 (Roach 4)
Haunted Honeymoon, 1940 (Montgomery 3)
Haunted Honeymoon. *See* Busman's Holiday, 1940
Haunted Hotel, 1907 (Blackton 2)
Haunted House, 1921 (Keaton 2)
Haunted House, 1928 (Christensen 2, Biro 4, Polito 4)
Haunted House, 1929 (Disney 2, Iwerks 4)
Haunted House of Wild Isle, 1915 (Nilsson 3)
Haunted Lady, 1929 (Ruggles 2)
Haunted Mouse, 1941 (Avery 2)
Haunted Pajamas, 1917 (Gaudio 4)
Haunted Palace, 1963 (Chaney Lon, Jr. 3, Cook 3, Price 3, Corman 4,
    Crosby 4)
Haunted Spooks, 1920 (Lloyd 3, Roach 4)
Haunted Strangler, 1958 (Karloff 3)
Haunted World. *See* Ercole al centro della terra, 1961
Haunting, 1963 (Wise 2, Bloom 3)
Haunting Fear, 1915 (Nilsson 3)
Haunting of Julia, 1981 (Farrow 3)
Haunting of Rosalind, 1973 (Sarandon 3)
Haunts of the Very Rich, 1972 (Lourié 4)
Haupt des Juarez, 1920 (Warm 4)
Hauptdarsteller, 1977 (Hauff 2)
Hauptmann Florian von der Muhle, 1968 (Hoppe 3)
Hauptmann von Koln, 1956 (Dudow 2, Geschonneck 3)
Hauptmann von Kopenick, 1907 (Freund 4)
Hauptmann von Kopenick, 1931 (Oswald 2)
Haus am Meer, 1972 (Hauff 2, Schygulla 3)
Haus der Frauen, 1977 (Zanussi 2)
Haus der Luge, 1925 (Pick 2, Krauss 3, Rasp 3)
Haus der Luge. *See* Wildentes, 1925
Haus der tausend Freuden, 1967 (Price 3)
Haus der Unseligen, 1922 (Tschechowa 3)
Haus des Lebens, 1952 (Frohlich 3, Jurgens 3, Rasp 3)
Haus in der Dragonergasse, 1921 (Oswald 2)
Haus in der Karpfengasse, 1964 (Brejchová 3)
Haus ohne Lachen, 1923 (Galeen 4)
Haus zum Mond, 1920 (Kortner 3, Hoffmann 4)
Hauser's Memory, 1970 (Siodmak 4)
Haut les mains!, 1912 (Feuillade 2)
Haut les mains!. *See* En pleine bagarre, 1961
Haut sur ces montagnes, 1945 (McLaren 2)
Haute Lisse, 1956 (Grémillon 2)
Hautes solitudes, 1974 (Seberg 3)
Haut-le-Vent, 1944 (Vanel 3)
Havana Widows, 1933 (Blondell 3, Barnes 4)
Have a Heart, 1934 (Merkel 3, Howe 4)
Have Rocket, Will Travel, 1959 (Three Stooges 3)
Have You Thought of Talking to the Director?, 1962 (Baillie 2)
Havets Djavul, 1935–36 (Fejos 2)
Havets husmaend, 1954 (Carlsen 2)
Havets Son, 1949 (Thulin 3)
Having a Wonderful Crime, 1945 (Sutherland 2, O'Brien, P. 3)
Having It All, 1982 (Cannon 3)
Having Wonderful Time, 1938 (Arden 3, Ball 3, Fairbanks, D. Jr. 3,
    Meek 3, Miller 3, Rogers, G. 3, Berman 4, Polglase 4)
Havoc, 1916 (Stone 3)
Havoc, 1924 (Goulding 2)

Havre sac, 1963 (Braunberger 4)
Havsbandet, 1971 (Andersson H. 3)
Havsgammar. *See* Rosen på Tistelon, 1916
Hawaii, 1966 (Hill, G.R. 2, Andrews, J. 3, Hackman 3, Von Sydow 3, Bernstein 4, Dunn 4, Jeakins 4, Mirisch 4, Taradash 4, Trumbo 4)
Hawaii Calls, 1938 (Bond 3)
Hawaiian Birds, 1936 (Fleischer, M. and D. 2)
Hawaiian Nights, 1939 (Cortez 4)
Hawaiian Nights. *See* Down to Their Last Yacht, 1934
Hawaiian Pineapple, 1930 (Terry 4)
Hawaiians, 1970 (Chaplin 3, Heston 3, Ballard 4, Mancini 4, Mirisch 4)
Hawai-Marei oki kaisen, 1942 (Shindo 3, Tsuburaya 4)
Hawk, 1935 (Dmytryk 2)
Hawk. *See* Ride Him Cowboy, 1932
Hawk the Slayer, 1980 (Palance 3)
Hawkins and Watkins, 1932 (Sennett 2)
Hawkins on Murder, 1973 (Martin, S. 3, Stewart 3, Goldsmith 4)
Hawks and the Sparrows. *See* Uccelacci e uccellini, 1966
Hawk's Nest, 1928 (Christensen 2, Polito 4, Robinson 4)
Hawk's Trail, 1920 (Van Dyke, W.S. 2)
Hawleys of High Street, 1933 (Bennett 4)
Hawmps, 1976 (Elam 3)
Hawthorne of the U.S.A., 1919 (Cruze 2, Reid 3)
Haxan, 1922 (Christensen 2)
Hay Foot, 1941 (Roach 4)
Hay que matar a B, 1973 (Borau 2, Audran 3, Meredith 3, Neal 3)
Hay Ride, 1937 (Terry 4)
Hay un niño en su futuro, 1951 (Negrete 3, Figueroa 4)
Hayabusa daimyo, 1961 (Yamamura 3)
Hayfoot, Strawfoot, 1926 (Sennett 2)
Hayl-Moskau, 1932 (Moskvin 4)
Hayseed, 1919 (Keaton 2, Arbuckle 3)
Hayseed Romance, 1935 (Keaton 2)
Haystack. *See* Meule, 1963
Haystacks and Steeples, 1916 (Sennett 2, Swanson 3)
Haywire, 1980 (Remick 3, Robards 3)
Hazai pályán, 1968 (Latinovits 3)
Hazard, 1948 (Goddard 3, Dreier 4)
Hazards of Helen, 1915 (Nilsson 3)
Hazard's People, 1976 (Houseman 4)
Hazasodik az uram, 1913 (Curtiz 2)
Házasságból elégséges, 1962 (Torocsik 3)
Hazel Kirke, 1916 (White 3)
Hazel's People. *See* Happy As the Grass was Green, 1973
Hazukashii yume, 1927 (Gosho 2, Tanaka 3)
He. *See* Rosier de Madame Husson, 1932
He and His Sister. *See* On a jeho sestra, 1931
He and She. *See* Assoluto naturale, 1969
He and She. *See* Kanojo to kare, 1963
He Answered the Ad, 1913 (Bunny 3)
He Called Her In, 1913 (Dwan 2)
He Can't Make It Stick, 1943 (Fleischer, M. and D. 2, Hubley 4)
He Comes Up Smiling, 1918 (Dwan 2, Fairbanks, D. 3, August 4, Marion 4)
He Cooked His Goose, 1952 (Three Stooges 3)
He Couldn't Take It, 1933 (Darwell 3, Schary 4)
He Did and He Didn't, 1916 (Sennett 2, Arbuckle 3, Normand 3)
He Died after the War. *See* Tokyo senso sengo kiwa, 1970
He Died with His Eyes Open. *See* On ne meurt que deux foix, 1985
He Doesn't Care to Be Photographed, 1912–14 (Cohl 2)
He Dood it Again, 1943 (Terry 4)
He Forgot to Remember, 1926 (Roach 4)
He Fought for the U.S.A., 1911 (Bushman 3)
He Found a Star, 1941 (Greenwood 3, Junge 4)
He Had 'em Buffaloed, 1917 (Pitts 3)
He Hired the Boss, 1943 (Day 4)
He Is My Brother, 1976 (Dmytryk 2)
He Knew Women, 1930 (Cronjager 4)
He Laughed Last, 1956 (Edwards 2)
He Laughs Last, 1920 (Hardy 3)
He Leads, Others Follow, 1919 (Daniels 3, Lloyd 3, Roach 4)
He Learned about Women, 1932 (Banton 4, Head 4, Lang 4)
He Likes Things Upside-Down, 1912–14 (Cohl 2)

He Loved an Actress, 1938 (Langdon 3)
He Loved Her So. *See* Twenty Minutes of Love, 1914
He Loved the Ladies, 1914 (Sennett 2)
He Loves To Be Amused, 1912–14 (Cohl 2)
He Loves to Watch the Flight of Time, 1912–14 (Cohl 2)
He Married His Wife, 1940 (Cook 3, McCrea 3, Day 4, Zanuck 4)
He Poses For His Portrait, 1912–14 (Cohl 2)
He Ran All the Way, 1951 (Garfield 3, Winters 3, Horner 4, Howe 3, Trumbo 4, Waxman 4)
He Rides Tall, 1963 (Duryea 3)
He Ruins His Family Reputation, 1912–14 (Cohl 2)
He Slept Well, 1912–14 (Cohl 2)
He Snoops to Conquer, 1944 (Formby 3)
He Stayed for Breakfast, 1940 (Douglas, M. 3, Young, L. 3, Vajda 4, Walker 4)
He Trumped Her Ace, 1930 (Sennett 2)
He Walked by Night, 1948 (Mann 2, Alton, J. 4)
He Wants What He Wants When He Wants It, 1912–14 (Cohl 2)
he was born, he suffered, he died, 1974 (Brakhage 2)
He Was Her Man, 1934 (Bacon 2, Blondell 3, Cagney 3, Barnes 4, Grot 4, Orry-Kelly 4)
He Was Her Man, 1937 (Freleng 4)
He Was Not Ill, Only Unhappy, 1912–14 (Cohl 2)
He Who Gets Slapped, 1924 (Sjostrom 2, Chaney Lon 3, Gilbert 3, Shearer 3, Gibbons 4, Thalberg 4, Wilson, C. 4)
He Who Gets Smacked, 1925 (Sennett 2)
He who Laughs Last, 1910 (Bunny 3)
He Who Must Die. *See* Celui qui doit mourir, 1958
He Who Rides a Tiger, 1965 (Crichton 2)
He Winked and Won, 1917 (Hardy 3)
He Would a Hunting Go, 1913 (Sennett 2, Arbuckle 3)
He Wouldn't Stay Down, 1915 (Sennett 2)
He's a Cockeyed Wonder, 1950 (Rooney 3)
He, She, and the Money. *See* Hans, hon, och pengarna, 1936
He, She, or It. *See* Poupée, 1962
Head, 1968 (Rafelson 2, Hopper 3, Mature 3, Nicholson 3)
Head. *See* Femme nue et Satan, 1959
Head. *See* Nackte und der Satan, 1959
Head for Business, 1911 (Lawrence 3)
Head Guy, 1930 (Langdon 3, Roach 4)
Head Man, 1928 (Young, L. 3)
Head of the Family, 1928 (Robinson 4)
Head of the Family. *See* Padre di famiglia, 1968
Head of the House, 1916 (Eason 4)
Head of the House, 1952 (Leacock 2)
Head On, 1980 (Huston 2)
Head over Heels, 1922 (Menjou 3, Normand 3)
Head over Heels, 1937 (Matthews 3, Balcon 4, Junge 4)
Head over Heels, 1979 (Grahame 3)
Head over Heels in Love. *See* Head over Heels, 1937
Headdresses of Different Periods. *See* Histoire de chapeaux, 1910
Headin' East, 1937 (Howard, S. 3)
Headin' for Danger, 1928 (Miller, V. 4, Plunkett 4)
Headin' for God's Country, 1943 (Nilsson 3)
Headin' South, 1918 (Fairbanks, D. 3)
Headless Horseman, 1922 (Rogers, W. 3)
Headless Horseman, 1934 (Iwerks 4)
Headleys at Home, 1938 (Beavers 3)
Headline Bands, 1939 (Hutton 3)
Headline Shooter, 1933 (Bellamy 3, Walthall 3, D'Agostino 4, Musuraca 4, Polglase 4, Steiner 4)
Headline Woman, 1935 (Bond 3)
Headlines of Destruction. *See* Je suis un sentimental, 1955
Heads or Tails. *See* Pile ou face, 1979
Heads Up, 1930 (Green, J. 4)
Heads Up, Charly. *See* Kopf hoch, Charly!, 1926
Healer, 1935 (Bellamy 3, Rooney 3)
Health, 1979 (Altman 2, Bacall 3, Jackson 3)
Health Farm, 1936 (Terry 4)
Health for the Nation, 1940 (Richardson 3)
Health for the Nation. *See* Health of a Nation, 1939
Health in Industry, 1938 (Watt 2)
Health of a Nation, 1939 (Cavalcanti 2)

Health-Giving Waters of Tisza. *See* Élteto Tisza-viz, 1954
Healthy and Happy, 1919 (Hardy 3)
Healthy Neighborhood, 1913 (Sennett 2)
Healthy, Wealthy, and Dumb, 1938 (Three Stooges 3)
Heap Big Chief, 1919 (Daniels 3, Lloyd 3, Roach 4)
Hear 'em Rave, 1918 (Daniels 3, Lloyd 3, Roach 4)
Hear Me Good, 1957 (Head 4)
Hearse, 1980 (Cotten 3)
Hearst and Davies Affair, 1985 (Mitchum 3)
Heart. *See* Coracão, 1960
Heart. *See* Kokoro, 1955
Heart. *See* Kokoro, 1973
Heart and Soul, 1917 (Bara 3)
Heart are Trumps, 1920 (Ingram 2)
Heart Beat, 1980 (Nolte 3, Spacek 3, Kovacs 4)
Heart Beats Again. *See* Serdtze betsya vnov, 1956
Heart Beats of Long Ago, 1910 (Griffith 2, Bitzer 4)
Heart Buster, 1924 (Mix 3)
Heart for a Song. *See* Srdce za písničku, 1933
Heart in Pawn, 1919 (Hayakawa 3)
Heart Is a Lonely Hunter, 1968 (Arkin 3, Keach 3, Howe 4)
Heart Line, 1921 (Barnes 4)
Heart o' the Hills, 1919 (Franklin 2, Gilbert 3, Pickford 3, Rosher 4)
Heart of a Child, 1920 (Nazimova 3)
Heart of a Child, 1958 (Pleasance 3)
Heart of a Cowboy, 1909 (Anderson G. 3)
Heart of a Cracksman, 1913 (Reid 3)
Heart of a Gambler, 1913 (Anderson G. 3)
Heart of a Lion, 1917 (Farnum 3)
Heart of a Man, 1959 (Wilcox 2, Neagle 3)
Heart of a Mother. *See* Serdtse materi, 1966
Heart of a Nation. *See* Untel Pere et Fils, 1943
Heart of a Painted Woman, 1915 (Guy 2)
Heart of a Siren, 1925 (Webb 3, Lemaire 4)
Heart of a Texan, 1922 (Canutt 4)
Heart of a Tigress, (Johnson, N. 3)
Heart of Alaska, 1924 (Costello, M. 3)
Heart of Arizona, 1938 (Boyd 3, Head 4)
Heart of Britain, 1941 (Jennings 2)
Heart of Flame, 1915 (Eason 4)
Heart of Glass. *See* Herz aus Glas, 1976
Heart of Gold, 1915 (Eason 4)
Heart of Jim Brice, 1913 (Costello, M. 3)
Heart of Maryland, 1915 (Brenon 2)
Heart of Maryland, 1927 (Bacon 2, Costello, D. 3, Loy 3)
Heart of New York, 1932 (Leroy 2)
Heart of Nora Flynn, 1916 (DeMille 2, Buckland 4, Macpherson 4)
Heart of Oyama, 1908 (Griffith 2, Lawrence 3)
Heart of Paris. *See* Gribouille, 1937
Heart of Princess Mitsari, 1915 (Cruze 2)
Heart of Salome, 1926 (Pidgeon 3)
Heart of Scotland, 1961-62 (Grierson 2)
Heart of Show Business, 1957 (DeMille 2, Chevalier 3, Crosby 3, Horne 3, Lancaster 3)
Heart of Spain, 1937 (Kline 2, Maddow 4, North 4)
Heart of Texas Ryan, 1917 (Mix 3)
Heart of the Golden West, 1942 (Rogers, R. 3)
Heart of the Hills, 1914 (Reid 3)
Heart of the Matter, 1953 (Finch 3, Howard, T. 3, Schell, Maria 3, Dalrymple 4)
Heart of the Mountains. *See* Kokoro no sanmyaku, 1966
Heart of the North, 1938 (Deutsch 4)
Heart of the Rio Grande, 1942 (Autry 3)
Heart of the Rockies, 1938 (Canutt 4)
Heart of the Rockies, 1951 (Rogers, R. 3)
Heart of the Sheriff, 1915 (Mix 3)
Heart of the Sunset, 1918 (Nilsson 3)
Heart of the Tyrant. *See* A szarnok szive, 1981
Heart of the West, 1936 (Boyd 3)
Heart of the West, 1975 (Pleasance 3)
Heart of the Wilds, 1918 (Neilan 2)
Heart of the Yukon, 1926 (Van Dyke, W.S. 2)
Heart of Twenty, 1920 (Pitts 3)

Heart of Variety, 1969 (Heston 3)
Heart of Wetona, 1918 (Franklin 2, Talmadge, N. 3)
Heart Punch, 1932 (Eason 4)
Heart Raider, 1923 (Ruggles 2)
Heart Song. *See* Ich und die Kaiserin, 1933
Heart Song. *See* Only Girl, 1933
Heart Strategy, 1916 (Sutherland 2)
Heart Strings, 1920 (Farnum 3)
Heart Thief, 1927 (Schildkraut 3, Levien 4)
Heart to Heart, 1928 (Astor 3, Fazenda 3, Polito 4)
Heart Trouble, 1928 (Langdon 3)
Heartbeat, 1946 (Wood 2, Aumont 3, Menjou 3, Rathbone 3, Rogers, G. 3, Ryskind 4)
Heartbeat. *See* Schpountz, 1937
Heartbeat. *See* Szivdobogás, 1961
Heartbeeps, 1981 (van Runkle 4, Whitlock 4, Williams, J. 4)
Heartbreak, 1931 (August 4, Friedhofer 4, Grot 4)
Heartbreak Kid, 1972 (Cahn 4, Roizman 4, Sylbert 4)
Heartburn, 1986 (Almendros 4)
Hearth Fires. *See* Feux de la chandeleur, 1972
Heartland, 1979 (Torn 3)
Hearts Adrift, 1914 (Porter 2, Pickford 3)
Hearts Afire. *See* Hearts in Exile, 1915
Hearts Aflame, 1923 (Nilsson 3)
Hearts and Diamonds, 1914 (Bunny 3)
Hearts and Dollars, 1924 (Litvak 2)
Hearts and Flowers, 1914 (Bushman 3)
Hearts and Flowers, 1919 (Sennett 2, Fazenda 3)
Hearts and Horses, 1913 (Dwan 2, Reid 3)
Hearts and Masks, 1914 (Mix 3)
Hearts and Minds. *See* Uomo da rispettare, 1973
Hearts and Planets, 1915 (Sennett 2)
Hearts and Saddles, 1917 (Mix 3)
Hearts and Sparks, 1916 (Sennett 2, Swanson 3)
Hearts and Spurs, 1925 (Van Dyke, W.S. 2, Lombard 3)
Hearts Are Thumps, 1937 (Roach 4)
Hearts Are Trumps, 1920 (Mathis 4, Seitz 4)
Heart's Desire, 1915 (Mix 3)
Hearts Divided, 1936 (Borzage 2, Bondi 3, Davies 3, Horton 3, McDaniel 3, Powell, D. 3, Rains 3, Brown, Harry Joe 4, Korngold 4, Orry-Kelly 4, Robinson 4)
Heart's Haven, 1922 (Hersholt 3)
Hearts in Bondage, 1936 (Ayres 3, Walthall 3, Brown, K. 4)
Hearts in Dixie, 1929 (Muse 3)
Hearts in Exile, 1915 (Carré 4, Edeson 4)
Hearts in Exile, 1929 (Curtiz 2, Costello, D. 3, Sothern 3)
Hearts in Shadow, 1915 (Eason 4)
Hearts in Springtime. *See* Glamour Boy, 1941
Heart's Music. *See* Hudba srdcí, 1934
Hearts of Age, 1934 (Welles 2)
Hearts of Dixie, 1929 (Fetchit 3)
Hearts of Humanity, 1932 (Hersholt 3)
Hearts of Lieutenants. *See* Lojtnantshjartan, 1941
Hearts of Oak, 1924 (Ford, J. 2, Bosworth 3)
Hearts of the Jungle, 1915 (Mix 3)
Hearts of the West, 1975 (Arkin 3, Bridges 3, Cody 3)
Hearts of the World, 1918 (Griffith 2, Von Stroheim 2, Gish, D. 3, Gish, L. 3, Bitzer 4, Coward 4)
Hearts or Diamonds, 1918 (King 2)
Hearts Up, 1921 (Carey 3)
Hearts Upon the Sea. *See* Cuori su mare, 1950
Heart's Voice. *See* Guldet og vort Hjerte, 1913
Heat, 1972 (Warhol/Morrissey 2)
Heat and Dust, 1982 (Ivory 2, Christie 3, Jhabvala 4, Lassally 4)
Heat and Mud. *See* Netsudeichi, 1950
Heat Haze. *See* Kagero, 1969
Heat Lightning, 1934 (Leroy 2, Darwell 3, Orry-Kelly 4)
Heat of Anger, 1971 (Cobb 3, Hayward 3)
Heat's On, 1943 (West 3, Cahn 4, Planer 4, Plunkett 4)
Heave Away My Johnny, 1948 (Halas and Batchelor 2)
Heave-ho. *See* Hej rup!, 1934
Heaven and Earth, 1956 (Slocombe 4)
Heaven and Earth Magic, from 1943 (Smith 2)

Heaven and Hell. *See* Tengoku to jigoku, 1963
Heaven and Pancakes. *See* Himmel och pannkaka, 1959
Heaven Avenges, 1912 (Griffith 2, Bitzer 4)
Heaven Can Wait, 1943 (Lubitsch 2, Ameche 3, Calhern 3,
    Coburn, C. 3, Muse 3, Tierney 3, Basevi 4, Cronjager 4,
    Newman 4, Raphaelson 4)
Heaven Can Wait, 1978 (Beatty 3, Cannon 3, Christie 3, Mason 3,
    Warden 3, Fraker 4, Henry 4, van Runkle 4)
Heaven Fell That Night. *See* Bijoutiers du clair de lune, 1958
Heaven Help Us, 1985 (Sutherland 3)
Heaven Knows, Mr. Allison, 1957 (Huston 2, Kerr 3, Mitchum 3,
    Auric 4, Mahin 4, Morris 4)
Heaven Linked with Love. *See* Tengoku ni musubi koi, 1932
Heaven on Earth, 1927 (Adorée 3, Gibbons 4, Gillespie 4)
Heaven on Earth, 1931 (Ayres 3, Carradine 3, Summerville 3)
Heaven Only Knows, 1947 (Cummings 3, Struss 4)
Heaven Scent, 1956 (Jones 2)
Heaven With a Barbed Wire Fence, 1939 (Bond 3, Ford, G. 3,
    Cronjager 4, Trumbo 4)
Heaven with a Gun, 1969 (Ford, G. 3)
Heavenly Body, 1943 (Bainter 3, Lamarr 3, Powell, W. 3, Gillespie 4,
    Irene 4, Kaper 4, Kurnitz 4, Reisch 4)
Heavenly Days, 1944 (Estabrook 4, Hunt 4)
Heavenly Daze, 1948 (Three Stooges 3)
Heavenly Puss, 1948 (Hanna and Barbera 4)
Heavens Above, 1963 (Boulting 2, Sellers 3)
Heaven's Call. *See* Battle Beyond the Sun, 1962
Heaven's Gate, 1980 (Cimino 2, Bridges 3, Cotten 3, Huppert 3,
    Hurt, J. 3, Zsigmond 4)
Heavens! My Husband!, 1932 (Sennett 2)
Heavy Seas, 1923 (Roach 4)
Heavy Traffic, 1973 (Bakshi 2)
Hebihime dochuh, 1949–50 (Hasegawa 3, Kyo 3, Yamada 3,
    Miyagawa 4, Yoda 4)
Hebihime-sama, 1940 (Kinugasa 2, Hasegawa 3, Yamada 3)
Hebihime-sama, 1951 (Hasegawa 3)
Hebrew Lesson, 1972 (Mankowitz 4)
Hec Ramsey. *See* Century Turns, 1971
Hecklers, 1966 (Strick 2)
Heckling Hare, 1941 (Avery 2)
Hectic Days. *See* Goryachie dyenechki, 1935
Hedda, 1975 (Jackson 3, Slocombe 4)
Hedda Gabler, 1919 (Pastrone 2)
Hedda Gabler, 1924 (Nielsen 3)
Hedena, 1924 (Basserman 3)
Hedgehog in the Mist, 1976 (Norstein 4)
Hedy, 1965 (Warhol 2)
Hedy the Shoplifter. *See* Hedy, 1965
Heel of Italy. *See* Yellow Caesar, 1940
Heer, 1956 (Biswas 4)
Heera Panna, 1974 (Anand 3)
Heerak Rajar Deshe, 1979 (Ray, S. 2, Datta 4)
Heideschulmeister Uwe Karsten, 1933 (Tschechowa 3)
Heideschulmeister Uwe Karsten, 1954 (Wagner 4)
Heidi, 1937 (Dwan 2, Hersholt 3, Temple 3, Miller, A. 4)
Heidi, 1952 (Comencini 2)
Heidi, 1968 (Redgrave, M. 3, Schell, Maximilian 3, Simmons 3)
Heidi's Song, 1982 (Cahn 4, Hanna and Barbera 4)
Heien, 1929 (Ivens 2)
Height of Battle. *See* Senka no hate, 1950
Height of Glory. *See* Na viershina slavy, 1916
Heiji happy-aku-ya-cho, 1949 (Hasegawa 3)
Heilige Berg, 1926 (Riefenstahl 2)
Heilige Flamme, 1931 (Dieterle 2, Frohlich 3)
Heilige Luge, 1927 (Holger-Madsen 2, Homolka 3)
Heilige Simplizie, 1920 (Von Harbou 4)
Heilige und ihr Narr, 1928 (Dieterle 2, Manès 3, Andrejew 4)
Heimat, 1938 (George, H. 3)
Heimkehr, 1928 (Frohlich 3, Pommer 4)
Heimkehr, 1941 (Rohrig 4)
Heimkehr des alten Herrn, 1977 (Schygulla 3)
Heimkehr des Odysseus, 1918 (Wiene 2)
Heimkehr ins Gluck (Staudte 2)

Heimlich nach St. Pauli, 1964 (Mansfield 3)
Heimliche Ehen, 1956 (Mueller-Stahl 3)
Heimlichkeiten, 1968 (Staudte 2, Karamitev 3)
Heimweh, 1927 (Dieterle 2)
Heinrich der Vierte, 1926 (Courant 4)
Heinze's Resurrection, 1913 (Sennett 2, Normand 3)
Heir to Genghis Khan. *See* Potomok Chingis-khan, 1928
Heiratsnest, 1927 (Reisch 4)
Heir-Conditioned, 1955 (Freleng 4)
Heiress, 1949 (Wyler 2, Clift 3, De Havilland 3, Hopkins, M. 3,
    Richardson 3, Copland 4, Head 4, Hornbeck 4, Horner 4)
Heiress at Coffee Dan's, 1917 (Love 3)
Heiresses. *See* Orokség, 1980
Heirs. *See* Herederos, 1969
Heirs. *See* Örökösök, 1970
Heisse Ernte, 1956 (Herlth 4)
Heisses Blut, 1911 (Gad 2, Nielsen 3, Freund 4)
Heisses Spiel fur Hart Manner. *See* Rebus, 1968
Heist. *See* $, 1971
Hej rup!, 1934 (Fric 2)
Hej, te eleven Fa . . ., 1963 (Jancsó 2)
Heja Roland, 1966 (Widerberg 2)
Held aller Madchentraume, 1929 (Reisch 4)
Held by the Enemy, 1920 (Crisp 3, Stone 3)
Held Up for the Makin's, 1920 (Eason 4)
Helden, 1959 (Warm 4)
Heldorado, 1946 (Rogers, R. 3)
Helen la Belle, 1957 (Reiniger 2)
Helen Morgan Story, 1957 (Curtiz 2, Newman 3, McCord 4, Prinz 4)
Helen of Four Gates, 1920 (Hepworth 2)
Helen of Troy, 1955 (Wise 2, Baker S. 3, Bardot 3, Hardwicke 3,
    Adam 4, Steiner 4, Stradling 4)
Helen of Troy. *See* Skona Helena, 1951
Helen, Queen of the Nautch Girls, 1972 (Ivory 2)
Hélène, 1936 (Benoit-Lévy 2, Barrault 3, Burel 4)
Hélène, ou le malentendu, 1972 (Laguionie 4)
Helen's Babies, 1924 (Bow 3, Horton 3, Daniels 4)
Helen's Marriage, 1911 (Sennett 2)
Helicopter, 1944 (Terry 4)
Helicopter Spies, 1968 (Carradine 3, Carroll L. 3)
Heliotrope, 1921 (Rosson 4)
Hell and High Water, 1933 (Arlen 3)
Hell and High Water, 1954 (Fuller 2, Lemaire 4, Newman 4,
    Wheeler 4)
Hell Below, 1933 (Durante 3, Huston 3, Montgomery 3, Young, R. 3
    Mahin 4, Rosson 4)
Hell Below Zero, 1954 (Robson 2, Baker, S. 3, Ladd 3)
Hell Bent, 1918 (Ford, J. 2, Carey 3)
Hell Bent for Glory. *See* Lafayette Escadrille, 1957
Hell Bent for Heaven, 1926 (Blackton 2, Musuraca 4)
Hell Bent for Leather, 1960 (Murphy 3)
Hell Canyon, 1957 (Crosby 4)
Hell Cat, 1934 (Sothern 3)
Hell Diggers, 1921 (Reid 3)
Hell Divers, 1931 (Beery 3, Gable 3, Gillespie 4)
Hell Drivers, 1957 (Baker S. 3, Connery 3, Unsworth 4)
Hell Harbor, 1930 (King 2, Hersholt 3, Velez 3, Fulton 4)
Hell, Heaven, and Hoboken. *See* I Was Monty's Double, 1958
Hell Hound of Alaska. *See* Darkening Trail, 1915
Hell in Korea. *See* Hill in Korea, 1956
Hell in the City. *See* Nella città l'inferno, 1958
Hell in the Heavens, 1934 (Baxter W. 3, Glennon 4)
Hell in the Pacific, 1968 (Boorman 2, Marvin 3, Mifune 3, Hall 4,
    Schifrin 4)
Hell Is a City, 1960 (Baker S. 3, Pleasance 3)
Hell Is for Heroes, 1962 (Siegel 2, Coburn, J. 3, McQueen, S. 3,
    Blanke 4, Pirosh 4, Rosenman 4)
Hell Is Sold Out, 1951 (Attenborough 3)
Hell Morgan's Girl, 1916 (Chaney Lon 3)
Hell on Devil's Island, 1957 (Haller 4)
Hell on Frisco Bay, 1956 (Ladd 3, Mansfield 3, Robinson, E. 3,
    Wray 3, Seitz 4, Steiner 4)
Hell or High Water, 1954 (Widmark 3)

ell River. *See* Partizani, 1974
ell Ship Mutiny, 1957 (Carradine 3, Lorre 3)
ell to Eternity, 1960 (Hayakawa 3, Hunter 3)
ell Unlimited, 1936–37 (McLaren 2)
ell with Heroes, 1968 (Cardinale 3, Jones 4)
ellbenders. *See* Crudeli, 1966 (Cotten 3)
ell-Bent for Election, 1944 (Hubley 4)
ellcats of the Navy, 1957 (Reagan 3)
elldorado, 1935 (Cruze 2, Arlen 3, Bellamy 3, Fetchit 3, Walthall 3, Lasky 4, Seitz 4)
ellé, 1972 (Vadim 2, Gégauff 4, Renoir 4)
eller in Pink Tights, 1960 (Cukor 2, Cody 3, Loren 3, Novarro 3, O'Brien, M. 3, Quinn 3, Head 4, Nichols 4, Ponti 4)
eller Wahn, 1982 (Von Trotta 2, Schygulla 3, Winkler 3)
ellfighters, 1968 (Wayne 3, Clothier 4, Head 4, Needham 4, Rosenman 4, Whitlock 4)
ellfire, 1949 (Canutt 4)
ell-Fire Austin, 1932, (McCord 4)
ellfire Club, 1961 (Cushing 3, Sangster 4)
ellgate, 1952 (Bond 3, Hayden 3)
ellhound of the Plains, 1926 (Canutt 4)
ellion, 1924 (Karloff 3)
ellions, 1961 (Adam 4)
ello Baby, 1925 (McCarey 2, Roach 4)
ello Beautiful. *See* Powers Girl, 1943
ello Charlie, 1959 (Hecht 4)
ello Cheyenne, 1928 (Mix 3)
ello Children. *See* Zdravstvuitye deti, 1962
ello, Dolly!, 1969 (Kelly, Gene 3, Matthau 3, Streisand 3, Edens 4, Kidd 4, Lehman 4, Reynolds 4, Sharaff 4, Smith, J.M. 4, Stradling 4)
ello Down There, 1968 (Dreyfuss 3, Leigh, J. 3, McDowall 3)
ello Elephant! See Buongiorno, elefante!, 1952
ello Everybody!, 1933 (Scott, R. 3, Head 4)
ello, Frisco, Hello, 1943 (Bond 3, Faye 3, Basevi 4, Clarke, C.C. 4, Leven 4, Pan 4, Rose 4)
ello God, 1958 (Flynn 3)
ello, How Am I?, 1939 (Fleischer, M. and D. 2)
ello Lafayette, 1926 (Arthur 3)
ello London, 1958 (Henie 3, Holloway 3)
ello Pop, 1933 (Three Stooges 3)
ello Sister, 1930 (Rosson 4)
ello, Sister, 1933 (Crosland 2, Pitts 3, Howe 4)
ello Sucker, 1941 (Salter 4)
ello Teacher, 1918 (Roach 4)
ello Television, 1930 (Sennett 2)
ello Trouble, 1913 (Beery 3)
ello, Trouble, 1932 (Bond 3)
ello Uncle, 1920 (Roach 4)
ello-Goodbye, 1970 (Negulesco 2, Jurgens 3, Decaë 4, Lai 4, Zanuck 4)
ell-Roarin' Reform, 1919 (Mix 3)
ell's Angels, 1930 (Harlow 3, Estabrook 4, Gaudio 4)
ell's Angels on Wheels, 1967 (Nicholson 3, Kovacs 4)
ell's Bells, 1929 (Iwerks 4)
ell's Bloody Devils, 1970 (Carradine 3, Crawford, B. 3, Kovacs 4)
ell's Boss. *See* Meido no kaoyaku, 1957
ell's Devils. *See* Hitler, Beast of Berlin, 1939
ell's Fire, 1934 (Iwerks 4)
ell's Five Hours, 1958 (Haller 4)
ell's Four Hundred, 1926 (Struss 4)
ell's Half Acre, 1954 (Lanchester 3)
ell's Heels, 1930 (Lantz 4)
ell's Heroes, 1930 (Huston 2, Wyler 2)
ell's Highroad, 1925 (Coffee 4)
ell's Highway, 1932 (Muse 3, Cronjager 4)
ell's Hinges, 1916 (Gilbert 3, Hart 3, Hersholt 3, Sullivan 4)
ell's Horizon, 1955 (Ireland 3, Crosby 4)
ell's House, 1932 (Davis 3, O'Brien, P. 3)
ell's Island, 1930 (Swerling 4)
ell's Island, 1955 (Head 4)
ell's Kitchen, 1939 (Dupont 2, Reagan 3, Rosher 4)

Hell's Worm. *See* Jigoku no mushi, 1938
Hell-Ship Morgan, 1936 (Sothern 3)
Hell-to-Pay Austin, 1916 (Love 3)
Hellyys, 1972 (Donner 2)
Hellzapoppin', 1941 (Auer 3, Howard, S. 3)
Help. *See* Segítseg, 1970
Help!, 1965 (Lester 2, Watkin 4)
Help, Help, 1911 (Sennett 2)
Help! Help! Hydrophobia!, 1913 (Sennett 2, Arbuckle 3)
Help One Another, 1924 (Roach 4)
Help Wanted, 1915 (Bosworth 3)
Help Wanted!, 1939 (Zinnemann 2)
Help Wanted—Male, 1920 (King 2, Sweet 3)
Help Yourself, 1920 (Hunt 4)
Helpful Genie, 1951 (Terry 4)
Helpful Hogan, 1923 (La Cava 2)
Helpful Sisterhood, 1914 (Talmadge, N. 3)
Helping Hand, 1908 (Griffith 2, Lawrence 3)
Helping Him Out, 1911 (White 3)
Helping Himself. *See* His New Profession, 1914
Helpless Hippo, 1954 (Terry 4)
Helpmates, 1931 (Laurel & Hardy 3, Roach 4)
Helsinki 62. *See* Helsinky 62, 1962
Helsinky 62, 1962 (Schorm 2)
Helyet az oregeknek, 1934 (Sakall 3)
Hem från Babylon, 1941 (Sjoberg 2)
Hemåt i Natten, 1977 (Donner 2)
Hemingway's Adventures of a Young Man, 1962 (Dailey 3, Wallach 3, Smith, J.M. 4, Wald 4, Waxman 4)
Hemligt giftermål, 1912 (Sjostrom 2, Magnusson 4)
Hemmelighedsfulde X, 1913 (Christensen 2)
Hemo the Magnificent, 1957 (Capra 2)
Hempas bar, 1977 (Andersson H. 3)
Hen Fruit, 1930 (Lantz 4)
Hen Hop, 1942 (McLaren 2)
Hen in the Wind. *See* Kaze no naka no mendori, 1948
Hen Will Squawk Again. *See* Niwatori wa futatabi naku, 1954
Hendes Aere. *See* For sit Lands Aere, 1915
Hendes Helt, 1917 (Holger-Madsen 2)
Hendes Moders Løfte, 1916 (Holger-Madsen 2)
Hendes Naade, 1925 (Blom 2)
Henkel, ein deutsches Werk in seiner Arbeit, 1938 (Ruttmann 2)
Henker, Frauen und Soldaten, 1935 (Albers 3)
Hennes melodi, 1940 (Bjornstrand 3, Borgstrom 3)
Hennessy, 1975 (Howard, T. 3, Remick 3, Steiger 3)
Henpecked Duck, 1941 (Clampett 4)
Henpecked Hoboes, 1946 (Avery 2)
Henpecked Husband, 1905 (Bitzer 4)
Henri Langlois, 1970 (Bergman 3, Deneuve 3, Gish, L. 3)
Henri Matisse, ou le talent du bonheur, 1961 (Kosma 4)
Henriette Jacoby, 1918 (Oswald 2, Veidt 3)
Henry, 1955 (Anderson 2, Lassally 4)
Henry Aldrich, Boy Scout, 1944 (Dreier 4)
Henry Aldrich, Editor, 1942 (Dreier 4, Head 4)
Henry Aldrich for President, 1941 (Dreier 4, Head 4)
Henry Aldrich Gets Glamour, 1943 (Dreier 4, Head 4)
Henry Aldrich Haunts a House, 1943 (Dreier 4, Head 4)
Henry Aldrich Plays Cupid, 1944 (Dreier 4)
Henry Aldrich Swings It, 1943 (Dreier 4)
Henry Aldrich's Little Secret, 1944 (Dreier 4, Head 4)
Henry Cotton: This Game of Golf, 1974 (Lassally 4)
Henry VIII, 1911 (Goulding 2)
Henry Geldzahler, 1964 (Warhol 2)
Henry Goes to Arizona, 1940 (Summerville 3)
Henry Moore, 1951 (Alwyn 4)
Henry Moore at the Tate Gallery, 1970 (Lassally 4)
Henry 9 'til 5, 1970 (Godfrey 4)
Henry V, 1945 (Olivier 3, Dillon 4, Krasker 4, Mathieson 4)
Henry VIII and His Six Wives, 1972 (Pleasance 3)
Hep Cat, 1942 (Clampett 4)
Hepcat, 1946 (Terry 4)
Her Actor Friend, 1926 (Sennett 2)
Her Adventurous Night, 1946 (Salter 4)

Her Sister's Children, 1911 (Bunny 3)
Her Sister's Secret, 1913 (Cruze 2)
Her Sister's Secret, 1946 (Ulmer 2, Planer 4)
Her Slight Mistake, 1915 (Mix 3)
Her Soldier Sweetheart, 1910 (Olcott 2)
Her Son. See Sønnen, 1914
Her Splendid Folly, 1933 (Beavers 3)
Her Strange Desire. See Potiphar's Wife, 1931
Her Summer Hero, 1927 (Plunkett 4)
Her Surrender, 1916 (Nilsson 3)
Her Sweetheart. See Christopher Bean, 1933
Her Terrible Ordeal, 1909 (Griffith 2, Bitzer 4)
Her Torpedoed Love, 1917 (Sennett 2, Fazenda 3)
Her Twelve Men, 1954 (Garson 3, Ryan 3, Houseman 4, Kaper 4,
   Rose 4, Ruttenberg 4)
Her Twin Brother, 1912–13 (White 3)
Her Twin Brother, 1914 (Meredyth 4)
Her Two Sons, 1911 (Lawrence 3)
Her Unborn Child, 1930 (Cook 3)
Her Unwilling Husband, 1920 (Sweet 3)
Her Wedding Bell, 1913 (Sweet 3)
Her Wedding Night, 1930 (Bow 3)
Her Wild Oat, 1927 (Neilan 2, Moore, C. 3, Young, L. 3, Robinson 4)
Her Winning Punch, 1915 (Summerville 3)
Her Wonderful Lie. See Addio Mimi, 1951
Hera Pheri, 1976 (Bachchan 3)
Héraclite l'obscur, 1967 (Denner 3)
Herakles, 1962 (Herzog 2)
Herb Alpert and the Tijuana Brass Double Feature, 1966 (Hubley 4)
Herbert von Karajan, 1966 (Reichenbach 2)
Herbie Anyone Lived in a Pretty Hometown, 1965 (Lucas 2)
Herbie Rides Again, 1974 (Wynn 3)
Herbstsonate, 1978 (Bergman 2, Bjornstrand 3, Ullmann 3, Nykvist 4)
Hercegno Pongyolában, 1914 (Curtiz 2)
Hercule, 1938 (Berry 3, Brasseur 3, Fernandel 3)
Hercules, 1983 (Donaggio 4, Golan and Globus 4)
Hercules and the Big Stick. See 12 Travaux d'Hercule, 1910
Hercules and the Captive Women. See Ercole alla conquista di
   Alantide, 1961
Hercules at the Center of the Earth. See Ercole al centro della terra,
   1961
Hercules the Athlete. See Verdens Herkules, 1908
Herd. See Suru, 1978
Here and There, 1961 (Kuri 4)
Here Come the Co-eds, 1945 (Abbott and Costello 3,
   Chaney Lon, Jr. 3)
Here Come the Girls, 1918 (Daniels 3, Lloyd 3, Roach 4)
Here Come the Girls, 1953 (Hope 3, Head 4)
Here Come the Jets, 1959 (Struss 4)
Here Come the Nelsons, 1952 (Hudson 3)
Here Come the Waves, 1944 (Sandrich 2, Crosby 3, De Carlo 3,
   Hutton 3, Dreier 4, Head 4, Lang 4, Mercer 4)
Here Comes Carter, 1936 (Orry-Kelly 4)
Here Comes Cookie, 1935 (McLeod 2, Head 4)
Here Comes Mr. Jordan, 1941 (Costello, M. 3, Horton 3,
   Montgomery 3, Rains 3, Buchman 4, Head 4, Miller, S. 4,
   Walker 4)
Here Comes Mr. Zerk, 1943 (Langdon 3)
Here Comes Santa Claus. See J'ai recontré le Père Noël, 1984
Here Comes the Bride, 1919 (Barrymore J. 3)
Here Comes the Cavalry, 1941 (Young, G. 3)
Here Comes the Groom, 1934 (Bond 3, Brown, Harry Joe 4,
   Robinson 4)
Here Comes the Groom, 1951 (Capra 2, Crosby 3, Lamour 3,
   Wyman 3, Carmichael 4, Head 4, Mercer 4, Riskin 4)
Here Comes the Navy, 1934 (Bacon 2, Cagney 3, O'Brien, P. 3,
   Edeson 4, Orry-Kelly 4)
Here Comes Trouble, 1936 (Auer 3)
Here Comes Troubles, 1948 (Roach 4)
Here I Am, 1962 (Baillie 2)
Here I Am a Stranger, 1939 (Brown, Harry Joe 4, Miller, A. 4)
Here I Come. See Harvard, Here I Come, 1941
Here is a Fountain. See Koko ni izumi ari, 1955

Here Is a Man. See All That Money Can Buy, 1941
Here is a Spring. See Koko ni izumi ari, 1955
Here Is My Heart, 1934 (Crosby 3, Banton 4, Struss 4)
Here Is Tomorrow, 1941 (Maddow 4)
Here Is Your Life. See Har har du ditt liv, 1966
Here Kiddie Kiddie, 1960 (Hanna and Barbera 4)
Here Today, Gome Tamale, 1959 (Freleng 4)
Here We Come. See Har kommer vi, 1947
Here We Go, 1951 (McKimson 4)
Here We Go Again, 1942 (Dwan 2)
Herederos, 1969 (Léaud 3)
Heredity, 1912 (Griffith 2, Carey 3, Bitzer 4)
Here's Las Vegas. See Spree, 1967
Here's to Good Old Jail, 1938 (Terry 4)
Here's to Romance, 1935 (Friedhofer 4, Lasky 4, Levien 4)
Here's to the Girls. See Ojosan kampai, 1949
Heretic, 1977 (Boorman 2, Von Sydow 3)
Hergun olmektense, 1964 (Guney 2)
Heritage, 1953 (Hubley 4)
Heritage. See Odkaz, 1965
Heritage. See Orokség, 1980
Héritage du croissant, 1950 (Leenhardt 2)
Heritage of Eve, 1913 (August 4)
Heritage of Five Hundred Thousand People. See Gojuman-nin no isan,
   1963
Heritage of the Desert, 1924 (Hathaway 2, Daniels 3)
Heritage of the Desert, 1932 (Hathaway 2, Scott, R. 3)
Heritage of the Desert, 1939 (Head 4, Young, V. 4)
Héritier, 1973 (Denner 3)
Héritier des Mondésir, 1939 (Becker 2, Berry 3, Fernandel 3,
   Aurenche 4, Bost 4)
Herman Teirlinck, 1953 (Storck 2)
Hermann und Dorothea von heute. See Liebesleute, 1935
Hermanos del hierro, 1963 (Armendáriz 3, Figueroa 4)
Hermes Bird, 1979 (Broughton 2)
Hermine und die sieben Aufrechten, 1935 (George, H. 3)
Hermit, 1914 (Eason 4)
Hermit. See Syndig Kaerlighed, 1915
Hermit's Gold, 1911 (Dwan 2)
Hero, 1917 (Hardy 3)
Hero, 1923 (Schulberg 4, Struss 4)
Hero. See Bloomfield, 1970
Hero. See Nayak, 1966
Hero Ain't Nothin' But a Sandwich, 1977 (Corman 4)
Hero for a Day, 1953 (Terry 4)
Hero for a Night. See Hrdina jedné noci, 1935
Hero of Liao Yang, 1904 (Bitzer 4)
Hero of Little Italy, 1913 (Griffith 2, Carey 3, Sweet 3, Bitzer 4)
Hero of the Hour, (Johnson, N. 3)
Hero with a Knife. See Kamali zeybek, 1964
Hero-Captain Korkoran. See Hrdinný kapitán Korkorán, 1934
Héroe a la fuerza, 1963 (García 3)
Héroe desconocido, 1981 (Figueroa 4)
Heroes, 1916 (Hardy 3)
Heroes, 1970 (Negulesco 2)
Heroes, 1977 (Field 3, Ford, H. 3)
Heroes and Husbands, 1922 (Schulberg 4)
Heroes and Sinners. See Héros sont fatigués, 1955
Heroes Are Made. See Kak zakalyalas stal, 1942
Heroes Are Tired. See Héros sont fatigués, 1955
Heroes for Sale, 1933 (Wellman 2, Barthelmess 3, Bond 3,
   Young, L. 3, Orry-Kelly 4)
Heroes in Yellow and Blue. See Hjaltar i gult och blått, 1940
Heroes of Shipka. See Geroite na Shipka, 1954
Heroes of Telemark, 1965 (Mann 2, Douglas, K. 3, Redgrave, M. 3,
   Arnold 4, Fulton 4)
Heroes of the Hills, 1938 (Canutt 4)
Heroes of the Marne. See Famille Lefrançais, 1939
Heroes of the Mine, 1913 (Pearson 2)
Heroes of the Street, 1922 (Goulding 2)
Heroic Harold, 1912–13 (White 3)
Heroine of Mons, 1914 (Howard, L. 3)
Héroïnes du mal, 1978 (Borowczyk 4, Braunberger 4)

Héroïque Monsieur Boniface, 1949 (Fernandel 3)
Héroïsme de Paddy, 1916 (Gance 2, Burel 4)
Heroismus einer Franzosin, 1913 (Porten 3, Messter 4)
Heron and the Crane, 1975 (Norstein 4)
Héros de Chipka. *See* Geroite na Shipka, 1954
Héros de l'air, 1962 (Delerue 4)
Héros de la Marne, 1938 (Raimu 3, Ibert 4)
Hero's Island, 1962 (Mason 3, Oates 3, Stanton 3, Torn 3, McCord 4)
Héros sont fatigués, 1955 (Félix 3, Jurgens 3, Montand 3, Alekan 4)
Herr Arnes pengar, 1919 (Molander 2, Stiller 2, Jaenzon 4, Magnusson 4)
Herr Arnes pengar, 1954 (Molander 2, Andersson B. 3)
Herr auf Bestellung, 1930 (Reisch 4)
Herr Burovorsteher, 1931 (Planer 4)
Herr der Bestien, 1921 (Hoffmann 4)
Herr der Galgenleiter. *See* Bankkrasch Unter den Linden, 1925
Herr der Liebe, 1919 (Lang 2, Hoffmann 4, Pommer 4)
Herr Doktor, 1917 (Feuillade 2)
Herr Generaldirektor, 1925 (Basserman 3)
Herr Meets Hare, 1944 (Freleng 4)
Herr Meister und Frau Meisterin, 1928 (Albers 3)
Herr och fru Stockholm, 1921 (Garbo 3)
Herr Puntila und sein Knecht Matti, 1955 (Cavalcanti 2, Eisler 4)
Herr Sanders lebt gefahrlich, 1943 (Wagner 4)
Herr Storms første Monocle. *See* Min første Monocle, 1911
Herr Tartuff. *See* Tartuff, 1925
Herr uber Leben und Tod, 1919 (Pick 2)
Herr uber Leben und Tod, 1955 (Schell, Maria 3)
Herr und diener, 1917 (Basserman 3)
Herr und Hund, 1963 (Herlth 4)
Herren der Meere, 1922 (Korda 2)
Herren mit der weissen Weste, 1970 (Staudte 2)
Herrenpartie, 1964 (Staudte 2)
Herrin der Welt, 1918 (Lang 2)
Herrin der Welt, 1960 (Dieterle 2, Cervi 3, Presle 3)
Herrin und ihr Knecht, 1929 (Oswald 2)
Herrin von Atlantis. *See* Atlantide, 1932
Herring Murder Case, 1931 (Fleischer, M. and D. 2)
Herring Murder Mystery, 1944 (Fleischer, M. and D. 2)
Herringbone Clouds. *See* Iwashigumo, 1958
Herrliches Dasein, 1974 (Staudte 2)
Herrscher, 1937 (Jannings 3, Herlth 4, Von Harbou 4)
Hers to Hold, 1943 (Cotten 3, Durbin 3, Adrian 4)
Herz aus Glas, 1976 (Herzog 2)
Herz der Welt, 1952 (Herlth 4, Warm 4)
Herz des Konigin, 1940 (Rohrig 4)
Herz geht vor Anker, 1940 (Frohlich 3)
Herz kehrt Heim, 1956 (Schell, Maximilian 3)
Herz modern mobliert, 1940 (Frohlich 3)
Herz ohne Heimat, 1940 (Jurgens 3)
Herz vom Hochland, 1920 (Hoffmann 4)
Herz von St. Pauli, 1957 (Albers 3)
Herzbube, 1972 (Lollobrigida 3)
Herzbube. *See* King, Queen, Knave, 1972
Herzensphotograph, 1928 (Andrejew 4)
Herzog Ferrantes Ende, 1922 (Wegener 3, Freund 4)
Herzog von Reichstadt, 1931 (Planer 4)
Herzogin Satanella, 1920 (Curtiz 2)
Herzogin von Langeais. *See* Liebe, 1926
Herztrumpt, 1920 (Dupont 2)
Hesitating Houses, 1926 (Sennett 2)
Hesokuri shacho, 1956 (Tsukasa 3)
Hessian Renegades. *See* 1776, 1909
Hest på sommerferie, 1959 (Henning-Jensen 2)
Hesten paa Kongens Nytorv, 1941 (Henning-Jensen 2)
Hesten, 1943 (Henning-Jensen 2)
Hét tonna dollar, 1973 (Darvas 3)
Heterodyne, 1967 (Frampton 2)
Hets, 1944 (Bergman 2, Sjoberg 2, Zetterling 2, Bjornstrand 3)
Hetszàzeves szerelem, 1921 (Lukas 3)
Hetty King—Performer, 1970 (Anderson 2)
Heure de rêve, 1930 (Brasseur 3)
Heure exquise. *See* Nuit de Décembre, 1939

Heures, 1909 (Feuillade 2)
Heureuse Intervention, 1919 (Florey 2)
Heureux anniversaire, 1961 (Carrière 4)
Heureux qui comme Ulysse, 1970 (Fernandel 3, Colpi 4, Delerue 4)
Heut' kommt's drauf an, 1933 (Albers 3, Rainer 3, Kaper 4)
Heut spielt der Strauss, 1928 (Wiene 2, Planer 4)
Heut tanzt Mariett, 1928 (Andrejew 4)
Heut war ich bei der Frieda, 1928 (Albers 3)
Heute hieratet mein Mann, 1956 (Herlth 4)
Heute ist der schonste Tag in meinem Leben, 1936 (Oswald 2)
Heute Nacht—Eventuell, 1930 (Planer 4)
Heute nacht passiert's, 1953 (Tschechowa 3)
Hex, 1973 (Carradine 3)
Hex on Fogg's Millions, 1914 (Talmadge, N. 3)
Hexen, 1949 (Jurgens 3)
Hexer, 1932 (Rasp 3)
Hey Diddle Diddle, 1935 (Terry 4)
Hey Good Lookin', 1982 (Bakshi 2)
Hey Hey Cowboy, 1927 (Summerville 3)
Hey! Hey! USA!, 1938 (McDowall 3)
Hey, Pop!, 1932 (Arbuckle 3)
Hey Rookie, 1944 (Donen 2, Miller 3)
Hey Rube!, 1928 (Plunkett 4)
Hey There, 1918 (Daniels 3, Lloyd 3, Roach 4)
Hey There, It's Yogi Bear, 1963 (Hanna and Barbera 4)
Hi, Beautiful, 1944 (McDaniel 3)
Hi Diddle Diddle, 1943 (Burke 3, Menjou 3, Negri 3, Adrian 4)
Hi Gang, 1941 (Daniels 3, Green, G. 4)
Hi, Gaucho!, 1935 (Plunkett 4)
Hi, Good Lookin', 1944 (Salter 4)
Hi mo tsuki mo, 1969 (Iwashita 3, Mori 3)
Hi, Mom!, 1970 (De Palma 2, De Niro 3)
Hi Neighbor!, 1934 (Roach 4)
Hi, Nellie!, 1934 (Leroy 2, Meek 3, Muni 3, Orry-Kelly 4, Polito 4)
Hi no tori, 1950 (Hasegawa 3, Kyo 3)
Hi no tori, 1980 (Ichikawa 2)
Hi Ya, Chum, 1943 (Salter 4)
Hi Ya, Sailor, 1943 (Salter 4)
Hiawatha, 1952 (Mirisch 4)
Hiawatha's Rabbit Hunt, 1941 (Freleng 4)
Hibana, 1922 (Kinugasa 2)
Hibana, 1956 (Kinugasa 2)
Hibari no hanagata tantei gassen, 1958 (Yamamura 3)
Hibari no komori-uta, 1951 (Yamamura 3)
Hibari no zoku beranmee geisha, 1960 (Yamamura 3)
Hibernatus, 1969 (Delerue 4)
Hic-Cup Pup, 1952 (Hanna and Barbera 4)
Hick Chick, 1946 (Avery 3)
Hickey and Boggs, 1972 (Hill, W. 2)
Hickory Hill, 1968 (Leacock 2)
Hickory Hiram, 1918 (Laurel 3)
Hicksville Epicure, 1913 (Loos 4)
Hicksville's Finest, 1914 (Loos 4)
Hidari uchiwa, 1935 (Gosho 2)
Hidden Aces, 1927 (Shamroy 4)
Hidden Children, 1917 (Gaudio 4)
Hidden City, 1915 (Ford, J. 2)
Hidden City, 1950 (Mirisch 4)
Hidden City. *See* Darkest Africa, 1936
Hidden Eye, 1945 (Irene 4)
Hidden Fear, 1957 (De Toth 2)
Hidden Fires, 1918 (Marsh 3)
Hidden Fortress. *See* Kakushi toride no sanakunin, 1958
Hidden Gold, 1932 (Mix 3)
Hidden Gold, 1940 (Boyd 3, Head 4)
Hidden Guns, 1956 (Arlen 3, Carradine 3, Dickinson 3)
Hidden in the Fog. *See* I dimma dold, 1952
Hidden Letters, 1914 (Talmadge, N. 3)
Hidden Master, 1940 (Cushing 3)
Hidden Menace. *See* Star of the Circus, 1938
Hidden Mine, 1911 (Anderson G. 3)
Hidden Pearls, 1918 (Cruze 2, Hayakawa 3)
Hidden Power. *See* Woman Alone, 1937

Hijo-toshi, 1960 (Tsukasa 3)
Hikage no musume, 1957 (Kagawa 3, Yamada 3)
Hikaritokage, 1946 (Hara 3)
Hikaru umi, 1963 (Mori 3, Tanaka 3)
Hikinige, 1966 (Naruse 2, Takamine 3, Tsukasa 3)
Hikkoshi fufu, 1928 (Ozu 2)
Hikoki wa naze tobuka, 1943 (Tsuburaya 4)
Hikuidori, 1926 (Kinugasa 2)
Hilarious Posters. *See* Affiches en goguette, 1906
Hilda Crane, 1956 (Aumont 3, Simmons 3, Dunne 4, Lemaire 4, Raksin 4)
Hilde Warren and Death. *See* Hilde Warren und der Tod, 1917
Hilde Warren und der Tod, 1917 (Lang 2, Courant 4, Hoffmann 4)
Hildegard, 1948 (Zetterling 2)
Hill, 1965 (Lumet 2, Connery 3, Redgrave, M. 3, Morris 4)
Hill Billy, 1924 (Young, W. 4)
Hill in Korea, 1956 (Baker S. 3, Caine 3, Shaw 3, Dalrymple 4, Francis 4)
Hill Tillies, 1936 (Roach 4)
Hill 24 Doesn't Answer, 1955 (Dickinson 2)
Hillbilly, 1935 (Lantz 4)
Hillbilly Hare, 1950 (McKimson 4)
Hillbillys in a Haunted House, 1967 (Carradine 3, Chaney Lon, Jr. 3, Rathbone 3)
Hillcrest Mystery, 1918 (Miller, A. 4)
Hills Are Calling, 1914 (Hepworth 2)
Hills of Home, 1948 (Crisp 3, Gwenn 3, Leigh, J. 3, Stothart 4)
Hills of Old Wyomin', 1936 (Fleischer, M. and D. 2)
Hills of Old Wyoming, 1937 (Boyd 3, Head 4)
Hills of Peace, 1914 (Anderson G. 3)
Hills of Utah, 1951 (Autry 3)
Hills Run Red. *See* Fiume di dollari, 1966
Hilly Billy, 1951 (Fleischer, M. and D. 2)
Himatsuri, 1984 (Takemitsu 4)
Himawari-musume, 1953 (Mifune 3)
Himegimi to ronin, 1953 (Kagawa 3)
Himetaru kakugo, 1943 (Hasegawa 3, Yamada 3)
Hime-yasha gyojo-ki, 1959 (Yamada 3)
Himeyuri Lily Tower. *See* Himeyuri no to, 1953
Himeyuri Lily Tower. *See* Himeyuri no to, 1982
Himeyuri no to, 1953 (Imai 2, Kagawa 3, Okada 3)
Himeyuri no to, 1982 (Imai 2)
Himiko, 1974 (Shinoda 2, Iwashita 3, Takemitsu 4)
Himitsu, 1952 (Tanaka 3)
Himlaspelet, 1942 (Sjoberg 2)
Himmel och pannkaka, 1959 (Bjornstrand 3)
Himmel, wir erben ein Schloss, 1943 (Ondra 3)
Himmelskibet, 1917 (Holger-Madsen 2)
Himmliche Walzer, 1948 (Jurgens 3)
Himself as Herself, 1967 (Markopoulos 2)
Hin och smålanningen, 1949 (Nykvist 4)
Hin under Her, 1950 (Jurgens 3)
Hinarai naku sato, 1929 (Tanaka 3)
Hind. *See* Alageyik, 1958
Hindenburg, 1975 (Wise 2, Bancroft 3, Meredith 3, Scott, G. 3, Young, G. 3, Jeakins 4, Surtees 4, Whitlock 4)
Hindle Wakes, 1931 (Saville 2, Gwenn 3, Balcon 4)
Hindoo Charm, 1913 (Costello, D. 3, Costello, M. 3)
Hindoo Dagger, 1908 (Griffith 2, Bitzer 4)
Hindu, 1953 (Karloff 3)
Hindu Tomb. *See* Indische Grabmal, 1959
Hindustan Hamara, 1950 (Anand 3)
Hinoki butai, 1946 (Hasegawa 3, Yamada 3)
Hinotori, 1977 (Legrand 4)
Hinter Klostermann, 1952 (Tschechowa 3, Herlth 4)
Hintertreppe, 1921 (Dieterle 2, Leni 2, Kortner 3, Porten 3, Junge 4, Mayer 4)
Hip Action, 1933 (Fields, W.C. 3)
Hip Hip Hurry!, 1959 (Jones 2)
Hipólito el de Santa, 1949 (De Fuentes 2)
Hipoteza, 1972 (Zanussi 2)
Hippodrome, 1943 (Buchanan 3)
Hips, Hips, Hooray!, 1934 (Sandrich 2, Grable 3, Steiner 4)

Hira aur Patthar, 1977 (Azmi 3)
Hiram's Bride, 1909 (Olcott 2)
Hirameku yaiba, 1926 (Tanaka 3)
Hirate Miki, 1951 (Yamada 3, Yamamura 3)
Hired and Fired, 1916 (Hardy 3)
Hired and Fired, 1922 (Roach 4)
Hired Hand, 1971 (Fonda, P. 3, Oates 3, Zsigmond 4)
Hired Wife, 1940 (Russell, R. 3, Krasner 4)
Hireling, 1973 (Shaw 3, Mankowitz 4)
Hiren hikui-zuka, 1931 (Hasegawa 3)
Hi-Riders, 1974 (Ferrer, M. 3)
Hirondelle et la mésange, 1921 (Burel 4)
Hirondelle et la mésange, 1983 (Colpi 4)
Hiroshima, 1953 (Yamada 3)
Hiroshima mon amour, 1959 (Duras 2, Resnais 2, Okada 3, Colpi 4, Delerue 4, Fusco 4, Vierny 4)
Hirt von Maria Schnee, 1919 (Hoffmann 4)
Hiryuh no ken, 1937 (Miyagawa 4)
His Affair. *See* This Is My Affair, 1937
His Alibi, 1916 (Sennett 2, Arbuckle 3)
His and Hers, 1961 (Reed, O. 3)
His Athletic Wife, 1913 (Beery 3)
His Aunt Emma, 1912–13 (White 3)
His Auto Ruination, 1916 (Sennett 2)
His Awful Daughter, 1912–13 (White 3)
His Awful Vengeance, 1914 (Loos 4)
His Best Girl, 1921 (Roach 4)
His Better Self, 1911 (Guy 2, Ince 4)
His Birth Right, 1918 (Hayakawa 3)
His Birthday, 1910–11 (White 3)
His Bitter Half, 1949 (Freleng 4)
His Bitter Pill, 1916 (Sennett 2)
His Bogus Uncle, 1911 (Lawrence 3)
His Bread and Butter, 1916 (Sennett 2, Summerville 3)
His Bridal Night, 1919 (Brady 3)
His Bridal Sweet, 1935 (Langdon 3)
His Brother's Ghost, 1945 (Crabbe 3)
His Brother's Wife, 1936 (Van Dyke, W.S. 2, Hersholt 3, Stanwyck 3, Taylor, R. 3, Waxman 4)
His Busted Trust, 1916 (Sennett 2, Summerville 3)
His Busy Day, 1918 (Roach 4)
His Butler's Sister, 1943 (Borzage 2, Durbin 3, O'Brien, P. 3, Adrian 4, Hoffenstein 4, Salter 4)
His Call. *See* Yevo prizyv, 1925
His Captive Woman, 1929 (Garmes 4, Wilson, C. 4)
His Children's Children, 1923 (Wood 2, Daniels 3, Oland 3)
His Chorus Girl Wife, 1911 (Lawrence 3)
His Chum, the Baron, 1913 (Sennett 2)
His Cool Nerve, 1917 (Sutherland 3)
His Country. *See* Ship Comes in, 1928
His Country's Bidding, 1914 (Hepworth 2)
His Crooked Career, 1913 (Sennett 2)
His Daredevil Queen. *See* Mabel at the Wheel, 1914
His Daughter, 1911 (Griffith 2, Bitzer 4)
His Day of Rest, 1908 (Bitzer 4)
His Day Out, 1918 (Hardy 3)
His Debt, 1919 (Hayakawa 3)
His Diving Beauty. *See* Sea Nymphs, 1914
His Dog, 1927 (Schildkraut 3, Adrian 4, Brown, K. 4)
His Double Life, 1933 (Gish, L. 3, Edeson 4)
His Dress Shirt, 1911 (Pickford 3, Gaudio 4)
His Duty, 1909 (Griffith 2, Bitzer 4)
His Duty. *See* Man from Nowhere, 1915
His English Wife. *See* Hans engelska fru, 1926
His Ex Marks the Spot, 1940 (Keaton 2)
His Excellency, 1951 (Hamer 2, Slocombe 4)
His Excellency. *See* Yevo prevosoditelstvo, 1927
His Family Tree, 1935 (Vidor, C. 2, Plunkett 4)
His Fatal Beauty, 1917 (Pitts 3)
His Father's Deputy, 1913 (Mix 3)
His Father's Footsteps, 1915 (Sennett 2)
His Father's Son, 1917 (Barrymore L. 3)
His Favorite Pastime, 1914 (Chaplin 2, Sennett 2, Arbuckle 3)

is Feathered Nest. *See* Feathered Nest, 1916
is Fight, 1914 (Mix 3)
is First Command, 1929 (La Cava 2, Boyd 3, Miller, A. 4)
is 1st False Step, 1916 (Sennett 2)
is 1st Flame, 1927 (Sennett 2, Langdon 3, Hornbeck 4)
is First Job, 1908 (Méliès 2)
is First Love. *See* I livets vår, 1912
is First Monocle. *See* Min første Monocle, 1911
is First Patient. *See* Første Honorar, 1912
is Foothill Folly, 1917 (Sutherland 2)
is Forgotten Wife, 1924 (Baxter W. 3)
is Friend, The Burglar, 1911 (Lawrence 3)
is Friend's Wife, 1911 (Bushman 3)
is Girl Friday, 1940 (Hawks 2, Bellamy 3, Grant, C. 3, Russell, R. 3, Lederer 4, Walker 4)
is Glorious Night, 1929 (Barrymore L. 3, Gilbert 3, Gibbons 4)
is Glorious Night. *See* Si l'empereur savait ça!, 1930
is Greatest Bluff. *See* Seine grosster Bluff, 1927
is Greatest Gamble, 1934 (Buchman 4, Plunkett 4, Steiner 4)
is Greatest Sacrifice, 1921 (Farnum 3)
is Guardian Angel. *See* Hans gode Genius, 1920
is Guardian Auto, 1915 (Cruze 2)
is Halted Career, 1914 (Sennett 2)
is Hare Raising Tale, 1950 (Freleng 4)
is Hereafter, 1916 (Sennett 2, Fazenda 3)
is Heroic Action. *See* Ei gerochsky podvig, 1914
is Hidden Purpose, 1918 (Sennett 2)
is Honor, The Mayor, 1913 (Bunny 3)
is Hoodoo, 1913 (Loos 4)
is Hour, 1924 (Vidor, K. 2, Gilbert 3, Gibbons 4)
is Hour of Manhood, 1914 (Hart 3, August 4, Ince 4)
is House in Order, 1920 (Miller, A. 4)
is Innocent Dupe. *See* Sjaeletyven, 1915
is Inspiration, 1913 (Barrymore L. 3)
is Jonah Day, 1920 (Hardy 3)
is Kind of Woman, 1951 (Mitchum 3, Price 3, Russell, J. 3)
is Lady. *See* When a Man Loves, 1927
is Last Adventure. *See* Battling Buckaroos, 1933
is Last Burglary, 1910 (Griffith 2, Walthall 3, Bitzer 4)
is Last False Step, 1919 (Sennett 2)
is Last Haul, 1928 (Neilan 2)
is Last Laugh, 1916 (Sennett 2)
is Last Race, 1923 (Eason 4)
is Last Scent, 1916 (Sennett 2)
is Last 12 Hours. *See* E piú facile che un cammello, 1950
is Last Twelve Hours. *See* Mondo le condanna, 1952
is Late Excellency. *See* Selige Excellenz, 1926
is Lesson, 1912 (Griffith 2, Bitzer 4)
is Lesson, 1914 (Crisp 3, Gish, D. 3, Gish, L. 3)
s Little Page, 1913 (Talmadge, N. 3)
is Lordship, 1932 (Powell 2)
is Lordship, 1936 (Arliss 3, Balcon 4, Junge 4)
s Lordship's Dilemma, 1915 (Fields, W.C. 3)
is Lordship's White Feather, 1912 (Guy 2)
is Lost Love, 1909 (Griffith 2, Pickford 3, Bitzer 4)
is Luckless Love, 1915 (Sennett 2)
is Lying Heart, 1916 (Sennett 2)
is Majesty, 1919 (Karloff 3)
is Majesty Bunker Bean. *See* Bunker Bean, 1936
is Majesty O'Keefe, 1954 (Lancaster 3, Chase 4, Tiomkin 4)
s Majesty, King Ballyhoo. *See* Man braucht kein Geld, 1931
is Majesty, the American, 1919 (Fleming 2, Fairbanks, D. 3)
is Majesty's Field Marshall. *See* C. a K. polní maršálek, 1930
is Marriage Mixup, 1935 (Langdon 3)
is Marriage Wow, 1925 (Capra 2, Sennett 2)
s Master's Voice, 1936 (Horton 3)
s Most Difficult Part. *See* Hans vanskeligste Rolle, 1912
s Mother, 1912 (Olcott 2)
s Mother-in-Law, 1912 (Bunny 3)
s Mother's Picture, 1912 (Nilsson 3)
s Mother's Scarf, 1911 (Griffith 2, Bitzer 4)
s Mother's Son, 1913 (Griffith 2, Reid 3, Bitzer 4)
s Mother's Trust, 1914 (Crisp 3)

His Mouse Friday, 1951 (Hanna and Barbera 4)
His Move, 1905 (Bitzer 4)
His Musical Career, 1914 (Chaplin 2, Sennett 2)
His Mysterious Adventure. *See* Seine Frau, die Unbekannte, 1923
His Name Is Sukhe-Bator. *See* Ego zovat Sukhe-Bator, 1942
His Naughty Thoughts, 1917 (Sennett 2)
His Neighbor's Wife, 1913 (Porter 2)
His Nemesis, 1912 (Ince 4)
His New Job, 1915 (Chaplin 2, Swanson 3)
His New Lid, 1910 (Ince 4)
His New Mama, 1924 (Capra 2, Sennett 2, Langdon 3)
His New Profession, 1914 (Chaplin 2, Sennett 2)
His New Stenographer, 1928 (Sennett 2, Hornbeck 4)
His New York Wife, 1926 (Musuraca 4)
His Nibs, 1922 (La Cava 2, Moore, C. 3)
His Night Out, 1915 (Purviance 3)
His Night Out, 1935 (Bond 3, Horton 3, Mandell 4, Waxman 4)
His Off Day, 1938 (Terry 4)
His Official Appointment, 1913 (Talmadge, N. 3)
His Old-Fashioned Mother, 1913 (Dwan 2)
His Only Father, 1919 (Daniels 3, Lloyd 3, Roach 4)
His Only Son, 1912 (Reid 3)
His Other Woman. *See* Desk Set, 1957
His Own Fault, 1911 (Sennett 2)
His Own Law, 1920 (Bosworth 3)
His Picture in the Papers, 1916 (Fleming 2, Von Stroheim 2, Fairbanks, D. 3, Emerson 4, Loos 4)
His Precious Life, 1917 (Sennett 2, Fazenda 3, Summerville 3)
His Prehistoric Past, 1914 (Chaplin 2, Sennett 2)
His Pride and Shame, 1916 (Sennett 2)
His Private Life, 1926 (Arbuckle 3)
His Private Life, 1928 (Menjou 3, Vajda 4)
His Private Secretary, 1933 (Wayne 3)
His Real Wife. *See* Hans Rigtige Kone, 1917
His Reckless Fling. *See* His Favorite Pastime, 1914
His Reformation, 1909 (Anderson G. 3)
His Regeneration, 1914 (Chaplin 2)
His Regeneration, 1915 (Anderson G. 3)
His Return, 1915 (Walsh 2)
His Rich Uncle, 1912–13 (White 3)
His Robe of Honor, 1918 (Ingram 2, Walthall 3)
His Royal Flush. *See* Mr. 'Silent' Haskins, 1915
His Royal Shyness, 1932 (Sennett 2)
His Royal Slyness, 1919 (Lloyd 3, Roach 4)
His Saving Grace, 1917 (Sutherland 2)
His Second Childhood, 1914 (Sennett 2)
His Secretary, 1925 (Shearer 3, Day 4, Gibbons 4, Wilson, C. 4)
His Sense of Duty, 1912 (Ince 4)
His Sick Friend, 1910 (Lawrence 3)
His Silver Bachelorhood, 1913 (Talmadge, N. 3)
His Sister from Paris, 1925 (Kraly 4)
His Sister-in-law, 1910 (Griffith 2, Bitzer 4)
His Sister's Children, 1911 (Costello, D. 3)
His Sister's Kids, 1913 (Sennett 2, Arbuckle 3)
His Sister's Sweetheart, 1911 (Guy 2)
His Smothered Love, 1918 (Sennett 2)
His Squaw, 1912 (Ince 4)
His Stolen Fortune, 1914 (Bushman 3)
His Supreme Moment, 1925 (Colman 3, Sweet 3, Wong 3, Goldwyn 4, Marion 4, Miller, A. 4)
His Sweetheart, 1917 (Crisp 3)
His Taking Ways, 1914 (Sennett 2)
His Talented Wife, 1914 (Sennett 2)
His Tiger Lady, 1928 (Banton 4, Mankiewicz 4, Vajda 4)
His Tiger Wife, 1928 (Menjou 3)
His Tired Uncle, 1913 (Bunny 3)
His Trust, 1910 (Griffith 2, Bitzer 4)
His Trust Fulfilled, 1910 (Griffith 2, Bitzer 4)
His Trysting Place, 1914 (Chaplin 2, Sennett 2, Normand 3)
His Uncle Dudley, 1917 (Sennett 2)
His Unlucky Night, 1928 (Sennett 2, Lombard 3, Hornbeck 4)
His Ups and Downs, 1913 (Sennett 2)
His Ward's Love, 1909 (Griffith 2, Bitzer 4)

His Wedded Wife, 1914 (Ingram 2)
His Wedding Night, 1917 (Keaton 2, Arbuckle 3)
His Wedding Night. See Hans brollopsnatt, 1915
His Wife's Child, 1913 (Lawrence 3)
His Wife's Friend, 1918 (Sennett 2)
His Wife's Husband, 1922 (Stradling 4)
His Wife's Mistake, 1916 (Sennett 2, Arbuckle 3)
His Wife's Mother, 1909 (Griffith 2, Lawrence 3)
His Wife's Past. See Hans hustrus forflutna, 1915
His Wife's Stratagem, 1912–13 (White 3)
His Wife's Visitor, 1909 (Griffith 2, Pickford 3, Bitzer 4)
His Wild Oats, 1916 (Sennett 2)
His Winning Punch, 1915 (Sennett 2)
His Woman, 1931 (Colbert 3, Cooper, Gary 3)
His Wooden Wedding, 1925 (McCarey 2, Roach 4)
His Young Wife. See Miserie del signor Travet, 1946
His Younger Sister. See Ani imoto, 1976
His Youthful Fancy, 1920 (Sennett 2)
Hi-sen-ryo, 1960 (Hasegawa 3, Kagawa 3)
Hiss and Make Up, 1943 (Freleng 4)
Hissatsu shikakenin, 1973 (Iwashita 3, Yamamura 3)
Hisshoka, 1945 (Mizoguchi 2, Tanaka 3)
Histérica, 1952 (Figueroa 2)
Histoire comique. See Félicie Nanteuil, 1942
Histoire d'Adèle H., 1975 (Truffaut 2, Adjani 3, Almendros 4)
Histoire d'amour, 1933 (Ophuls 2)
Histoire d'amour, 1951 (Gélin 3, Jouvet 3, Audiard 4)
Histoire d'amour. See Tavaszi zápor, 1932
Histoire de chapeaux, 1910 (Cohl 2)
Histoire de pin-up girls, 1950 (Braunberger 4)
Histoire de puce, 1909 (Feuillade 2)
Histoire de rire, 1941 (L'Herbier 2, Presle 3)
Histoire de una traición, 1970 (Rey 3)
Histoire d'eau, 1958 (Godard 2, Truffaut 2, Braunberger 4)
Histoire du soldat inconnu, 1932 (Storck 2)
Histoire d'un crime, 1906 (Méliès 2)
Histoire d'un petit garçon devenu grand, 1963 (Reichenbach 2, Braunberger 4)
Histoire d'un Pierrot, 1913 (Bertini 3)
Histoire d'une crime, 1901 (Zecca, 2)
Histoire simple, 1978 (Sautet 2, Schneider 3, Sarde 4)
Histoire très bonne et très joyeuse de Colinot Trousse-Chemise, 1973 (Bardot 3, Cloquet 4)
Histoires extraordinaires, 1949 (Berry 3)
Histoires extraordinaires, 1968 (Fellini 2, Malle 2, Vadim 2, Bardot 3, Fonda, J. 3, Fonda, P. 3, Price 3, Stamp 3, Delli Colli 4, Renoir 4, Rota 4)
Histoires extraordinaires. See Tre passi nel delirio, 1968
Histoires insolites, 1974 (Chabrol 2)
Historia de un amor, 1955 (Figueroa 4)
Historia de un gran amor, 1942 (García 3, Negrete 3, Figueroa 4)
Historia de una batalla, 1962 (Gómez, M. 2)
Historia de una mala mujer, 1948 (Del Rio 3)
Historia naturae, 1967 (Švankmajer 2)
Historia wspólczesna, 1961 (Stawinsky 4)
Historias de la revolucion, 1961 (Gutiérrez 2, Zavattini 4)
Historias prohibidas de Pulgarcito, 1979 (Leduc 2)
Histórias Selvagems, 1978 (de Almeida 4)
Historical Fan. See Eventail animé, 1909
Historie blechatého psa, 1958 (Brdečka 4)
Historie fikového listu, 1938 (Hammid 2)
Historien om en Mand, 1944 (Roos 2)
Historien om en Moder, 1912 (Blom 2)
Historien om en moder, 1979 (Karina 3, Gégauff 4)
Historien om et slot, J.F. Willumsen, 1951 (Roos 2)
History, 1970 (Gehr 2)
History and Romance of Transportation, 1939 (Maddow 4)
History Is Made at Night, 1937 (Borzage 2, Logan 2, Arthur 3, Boyer 3, Basevi 4, Newman 4, Toland 4)
History Lessons. See Geschichtsunterricht, 1972
History of a Battle. See Historia de una batalla, 1962
History of Adventure, 1964 (Bass 4)
History of Albertfalva. See Albertfalvai történet, 1955

History of Beer, 1956 (Kawamoto 4)
History of Inventions, 1960 (Halas and Batchelor 2)
History of Motion in Motion, 1967 (Vanderbeek 2)
History of Mr. Polly, 1949 (Mills 3, Alwyn 4)
History of Numbers. See Számok története, 1962
History of Postwar Japan as Told by a Bar Hostess. See Nippon sengoshi, 1970
History of the Cinema, 1957 (Halas and Batchelor 2)
History of the Civil War. See Istoriia grazhdenskoi voini, 1922
History of the Fig Leaf. See Historie fikového listu, 1938
History of the Vatican. See Vaticano de Pio XII, 1940
History of the World, Part I, 1981 (Brooks, M. 2, Hurt, J. 3, Whitlock 4)
Hit, 1973 (Pryor 3, Schifrin 4)
Hit, 1984 (Hurt, J. 3, Rey 3, Stamp 3)
Hit and Run, 1924 (Miller, V. 4)
Hit and Run, 1957 (Haas 3)
Hit and Run. See Hikinige, 1966
Hit Him Again, 1918 (Lloyd 3, Roach 4)
Hit Him Again. See Fatal Mallet, 1914
Hit Lady, 1973 (Wynn 3)
Hit Me Again. See Smarty, 1934
Hit of the Show, 1928 (Brown 3, Plunkett 4)
Hit Parade of 1941, 1940 (Miller 3)
Hit Parade of 1943, 1943 (Arden 3, Dandridge 3, Hayward 3)
Hit Parade of 1947, 1947 (Rogers, R. 3, Alton, J. 4)
Hit the Deck, 1930 (Clothier 4)
Hit the Deck, 1955 (Darwell 3, Miller 3, Pidgeon 3, Reynolds, D. 3, Levien 4, Pan 4, Pasternak 4, Rose 4)
Hit the Hay, 1946 (Hunter 4)
Hit the High Spots, 1924 (Roach 4)
Hit the Ice, 1943 (Abbott and Costello 3)
Hit the Road, 1941 (Howard, S. 3, Salter 4)
Hit the Saddle, 1937 (Hayworth 3, Canutt 4)
Hitch Hiker, 1933 (Langdon 3)
Hitch Hikers, 1947 (Terry 4)
Hitch in Time, 1978 (Clarke, T.E.B. 4)
Hitched, 1971 (Field 3)
Hitchhiker, 1939 (Terry 4)
Hitch-Hiker, 1953 (Lupino 3, O'Brien, E. 3, D'Agostino 4, Musuraca 4)
Hitchin' Posts, 1920 (Ford, J. 2, Carey 3)
Hitler, 1962 (Biroc 4, Salter 4)
Hitler, a Film from Germany. See Hitler. Ein Film aus Deutschland, 1977
Hitler, Beast of Berlin, 1939 (Ladd 3)
Hitler? Connais pas!, 1963 (Blier 2, Delerue 4)
Hitler—Dead or Alive, 1943 (Bond 3, Brown, K. 4)
Hitler. Ein Film aus Deutschland, 1977 (Syberberg 2)
Hitler Gang, 1944 (Kortner 3, Dreier 4, Goodrich and Hackett 4, Head 4, Laszlo 4)
Hitler Lives, 1945 (Siegel 2)
Hitler: the Last Ten Days, 1973 (Guinness 3)
Hitler's Children, 1943 (Dmytryk 2)
Hitler's Hangman. See Hitler's Madman, 1943
Hitler's Madman, 1943 (Sirk 2, Carradine 3, Gardner 3)
Hitler's Son, 1978 (Cushing 3)
Hitlerjunge Quex, 1933 (George, H. 3)
Hito hada Kannon, 1937 (Kinugasa 2)
Hito no issho, 1928 (Mizoguchi 2)
Hito no yo no sugata, 1928 (Gosho 2, Tanaka 3)
Hitokiri Hikosai, 1955 (Yamamura 3)
Hitori musuko, 1936 (Ozu 2, Ryu 3)
Hitorine, 1961 (Yamada 3)
Hitotsubu no mugi, 1958 (Yoshimura 2)
Hits of the Nineties, 1948 (Fleischer, M. and D. 2)
Hittebarnet, 1916 (Holger-Madsen 2)
Hit-the-Trail Holliday, 1918 (Neilan 2, Barthelmess 3, Emerson 4, Loos 4)
Hitting a New High, 1937 (Walsh 2, Horton 3, Hunt 4, Lasky 4, Polglase 4)
Hiun no maki, 1952 (Hasegawa 3)
Hi-Yo Silver, 1940 (Farnum 3)

Holland Days, 1934 (Terry 4)
Holland Submarine Torpedo Boat, 1904 (Bitzer 4)
Holle der Jungfrauen, 1927 (Krauss 3)
Holle der Liebe—Erlebnisse aus einem Tanzpalais, 1926 (Dieterle 2)
Hollenspuk in 6 Akten. See Kurfurstendamm, 1920
Hollische Macht, 1922 (Wiene 2)
Hollow Triumph, 1948 (Bennett J. 3, Henreid 3, Alton, J. 4)
Holly and the Ivy, 1952 (Johnson, C. 3, Richardson 3, Korda 4)
Hollywood, 1923 (Cruze 2, DeMille 2, Arbuckle 3, Astor 3, Boyd 3, Hart 3, Negri 3, Nilsson 3, Pitts 3, Rogers, W. 3, Brown, K. 4)
Hollywood Blue, 1970 (Rooney 3)
Hollywood Boulevard, 1936 (Florey 2, Bushman 3, Cooper, Gary 3, Costello, M. 3, Cummings 3, Marsh 3, Dreier 4, Head 4, Struss 4)
Hollywood Boulevard, 1976 (Corman 4)
Hollywood Bowl, 1950 (Hanna and Barbera 4)
Hollywood Canine Canteen, 1946 (McKimson 4)
Hollywood Canteen, 1944 (Daves 2, Brown 3, Crawford, J. 3, Davis 3, Garfield 3, Greenstreet 3, Henreid 3, Lorre 3, Lupino 3, Malone 3, Rogers, R. 3, Sakall 3, Stanwyck 3, Wyman 3, Glennon 4, Prinz 4)
Hollywood Cavalcade, 1939 (Keaton 2, Sennett 2, Ameche 3, Faye 3, Jolson 3, Meek 3, Brown, Harry Joe 4, Day 4, Raksin 4, Zanuck 4)
Hollywood Cowboys. See Hearts of the West, 1975
Hollywood Daffy, 1946 (Freleng 4)
Hollywood Diet, 1932 (Terry 4)
Hollywood Double, 1932 (Sennett 2)
Hollywood Extra Girl, 1935 (DeMille 2)
Hollywood Fathers, 1955 (Brown 3, Fairbanks, D. Jr. 3)
Hollywood Gad-About, 1934 (Astor 3, Cagney 3, Hart 3)
Hollywood Goes A-Fishing, 1956 (Andrews D. 3)
Hollywood Goes to Church, 1949 (Ford, G. 3)
Hollywood Handicap, 1932 (Wayne 3)
Hollywood Handicap, 1938 (Keaton 2)
Hollywood Happenings, 1931 (Sennett 2)
Hollywood Hero, 1927 (Sennett 2)
Hollywood Hobbies, 1939 (Sidney 2)
Hollywood Hoodlum, 1934 (Eason 4)
Hollywood Horror House. See Comeback, 1970
Hollywood Hotel, 1937 (Berkeley 2, Hayward 3, Powell, D. 3, Reagan 3, Mercer 4, Orry-Kelly 4, Rosher 4, Wald 4, Wallis 4)
Hollywood in Uniform, 1943 (Ford, G. 3, Gable 3, Heflin 3)
Hollywood Kid, 1924 (Sennett 2)
Hollywood Knight, 1973 (Wynn 3)
Hollywood Knights, 1980 (Fraker 4)
Hollywood Lights, 1932 (Arbuckle 3, Grable 3)
Hollywood Luck, 1932 (Arbuckle 3, Grable 3)
Hollywood Matador, 1942 (Lantz 4)
Hollywood on Parade No. 13, 1934 (Del Rio 3, Dressler 3)
Hollywood on Parade No. 8, 1933 (Brown 3)
Hollywood on Parade Nos. 3–4, 1932 (Mix 3)
Hollywood on Parade, 1932 (Rogers, G. 3)
Hollywood on Parade, 1933 (Cagney 3, Crabbe 3, Three Stooges 3)
Hollywood on Trial, 1976 (Dmytryk 2)
Hollywood or Bust, 1956 (Lewis 2, Tashlin 2, Martin, D. 3, Bumstead 4, Head 4, Wallis 4)
Hollywood Park, 1946 (Grable 3)
Hollywood Party, 1934 (Dwan 2, Goulding 2, Durante 3, Laurel & Hardy 3, Three Stooges 3, Velez 3, Young, R. 3, Brown, N. 4, Freed 4, Howe 4)
Hollywood Revue of 1929, 1929 (Keaton 2, Barrymore L. 3, Crawford, J. 3, Davies 3, Dressler 3, Gilbert 3, Laurel & Hardy 3, Love 3, Shearer 3, Brown, N. 4, Day 4, Freed 4, Gibbons 4)
Hollywood Rodeo, 1949 (Wayne 3)
Hollywood Roundup, 1938 (Howard, S. 3)
Hollywood Shower of Stars, 1955 (Bendix 3)
Hollywood Speaks, 1932 (O'Brien, P. 3, Krasna 4)
Hollywood Star, 1929 (Sennett 2)
Hollywood Steps Out, 1941 (Avery 2)
Hollywood Story, 1951 (Farnum 3, McCrea 3)
Hollywood Ten, 1950 (Dmytryk 2, Lardner 4)
Hollywood Theme Song, 1930 (Sennett 2)
Hollywood Today No. 4, 1928 (Mix 3)

Hollywood Victory Caravan, 1945 (Crosby 3, Hope 3, Hutton 3, Ladd 3)
Hollywood You Never See, 1935 (DeMille 2)
Hollywood's Wild Angel, 1979 (Scorsese 2)
Holocaust Two Thousand, 1977 (Morricone 4)*
Holt vidék, 1971 (Gaál 2, Torocsik 3)
Holy Apes. See Bramy raju, 1967
Holy Matrimony, 1943 (Stahl 2, Fields, G. 3, Ballard 4, Basevi 4, Johnson 4)
Holy Smoke, 1963 (Borowczyk 4)
Holy Terror, 1929 (Roach 4)
Holy Terror, 1931 (Bogart 3)
Holy Veil. See Voile sacré, 1926
Homage at Siesta Time. See Homenaje a la hora de la siesta, 1962
Homage to Jean Tinguely's 'Homage to N.Y.', 1960 (Breer 2)
Homard flambé. See Bateau d'Emile, 1961
Hombori, 1949 (Rouch 2)
Hombre, 1966 (Ritt 2, Boone 3, March 3, Newman 3, Howe 4, Ravetch 4, Smith, J.M. 4)
Hombre de Alazan, 1958 (Alcoriza 4)
Hombre de Maisinicú, 1973 (Corrieri 3)
Hombre de papel, 1963 (Figueroa 4)
Hombre inquieto, 1954 (García 3)
Hombre nuestro de Cada Dia, 1959 (Armendáriz 3, Alcoriza 4)
Hombres en mi vida, 1932 (Velez 3)
Home, 1916 (Ince 4, Sullivan 4)
Home, 1919 (Weber 2)
Home Again, 1958 (Kaufman 4)
Home and Refuge. See Hemåt i Natten, 1977
Home and School, 1946 (Alwyn 4)
Home at Seven, 1952 (Hawkins 3, Richardson 3, Korda 4)
Home Before Dark, 1958 (Leroy 2, Simmons 3, Biroc 4, Cahn 4, Waxman 4)
Home Breakers, 1915 (Sennett 2, Summerville 3)
Home Breaking Hound, 1915 (Sennett 2)
Home Brew. See Fireside Brewer, 1920
Home Cured, 1926 (Arbuckle 3)
Home Folks, 1912 (Griffith 2, Barrymore L. 3, Pickford 3, Bitzer 4)
Home for the Holidays, 1972 (Brennan 3, Field 3)
Home from Babylon. See Hem från Babylon, 1941
Home from the Hill, 1960 (Minnelli 2, Mitchum 3, Sloane 3, Ames 4, Kaper 4, Krasner 4, Plunkett 4, Ravetch 4)
Home from the Sea, 1915 (Walsh 2)
Home from the Sea, 1962 (Peries 2)
Home Girl, 1928 (Hopkins, M. 3)
Home Guard, 1941 (Terry 4)
Home in Indiana, 1944 (Hathaway 2, Bond 3, Brennan 3, Crain 3, Basevi 4, Cronjager 4, Friedhofer 4)
Home in Oklahoma, 1946 (Rogers, R. 3)
Home in Wyomin', 1942 (Autry 3)
Home Is the Hero, 1959 (Kennedy, A. 3)
Home Maker, 1925 (Brook 3)
Home Movies, 1979 (De Palma 2, Douglas, K. 3, Donaggio 4)
Home of the Brave, 1949 (Kramer, S. 2, Robson 2, Foreman 4, Tiomkin 4)
Home of the Hopeless, 1950 (Fonda, H. 3)
Home on the Prairie, 1939 (Autry 3)
Home on the Rails, 1982 (Driessen 4)
Home on the Range, 1935 (Coogan 3, Scott, R. 3, Sheridan 3)
Home on the Range, 1938 (Ballard 4)
Home Stretch, 1920 (Roach 4)
Home Stretch, 1947 (Lemaire 4)
Home Sweet Home, 1910–11 (White 3)
Home Sweet Home, 1914 (Griffith 2, Crisp 3, Gish, D. 3, Gish, L. 3, Marsh 3, Sweet 3, Walthall 3, Bitzer 4)
Home Sweet Homicide, 1946 (Bacon 2, Scott, R. 3, Basevi 4, Leven 4, Seitz 4)
Home Talent, 1921 (Sennett 2, Hornbeck 4)
Home to Danger, 1951 (Fisher 2, Baker S. 3)
Home to Stay, 1978 (Fonda, H. 3)
Home Town. See Furusato, 1930
Home Town Story, 1951 (Crisp 3)
Home Trail, 1927 (Wyler 2)

Honeymoon Hate, 1927 (Mankiewicz 4)
Honeymoon Hotel, 1964 (Lanchester 3, Wynn 3, Berman 4, Cahn 4)
Honeymoon in Bali, 1939 (Carroll M. 3, MacMurray 3, Head 4, Reynolds 4)
Honeymoon Limited, 1935 (Krasner 4)
Honeymoon Lodge, 1943 (Muse 3, Bruckman 4)
Honeymoon Machine, 1961 (McQueen, S. 3, Ames 4, La Shelle 4, Rose 4)
Honeymoon Trio, 1931 (Arbuckle 3)
Honeymoon Trip. See Brollopsresan, 1935
Honeymoon Trip. See Jalousie 1976, 1976
Honeymoon with a Stranger, 1969 (Leigh, J. 3)
Honeymoon Zeppelin, 1930 (Sennett 2)
Honeymoon's Over, 1939 (Day 4, Miller, V. 4)
Honeymooners, 1914 (Blackton 2, Bunny 3, Lawrence 3)
Honeymoons. See Voyage des noces, 1975
Honeymousers, 1956 (McKimson 4)
Honey's Money, 1962 (Freleng 4)
Honeysuckle Rose, 1980 (Pollack 2, Schatzberg 2, Cannon 3)
Hong Kong, 1951 (Bruce 3, Reagan 3, Head 4)
Hong Kong un addio, 1962 (Flaiano 4)
Honkers, 1972 (Coburn, J. 3)
Honkon no hoshi, 1962 (Yamamura 3)
Honkon no yoru, 1961 (Tsukasa 3)
Honky, 1971 (Jones 4)
Honky Tonk, 1929 (Bacon 2)
Honky Tonk, 1941 (Gable 3, Trevor 3, Turner, L. 3, Berman 4, Gibbons 4, Rosson 4, Waxman 4)
Honky Tonk, 1974 (Biroc 4, Bumstead 4)
Honky Tonk Freeway, 1981 (Schlesinger 2, Page 3, Bernstein 4)
Honky-Donkey, 1934 (Roach 4)
Honkytonk Man, 1982 (Eastwood 3)
Honneur du Corse, 1906 (Guy 2)
Honneur d'un capitaine, 1982 (de Beauregard 4)
Honneurs de la guerre, 1960 (Cloquet 4)
Honno, 1966 (Shindo 2)
Honolulu, 1939 (Powell, E. 3, Young, R. 3, Waxman 4)
Honolulu Lu, 1942 (Cahn 4, Planer 4)
Honoo no hada, 1951 (Yamamura 3)
Honor among Lovers, 1931 (Arzner 2, Colbert 3, March 3, O'Brien, P. 3, Rogers, G. 3)
Honor Bound, 1928 (August 4)
Honor First, 1922 (Adorée 3, Gilbert 3, August 4)
Honor of His Family, 1909 (Griffith 2, Walthall 3, Bitzer 4)
Honor of His House, 1918 (Hayakawa 3, Rosher 4)
Honor of the District Attorney, 1915 (Eason 4)
Honor of the Family, 1931 (Bacon 2, Daniels 3, Grot 4, Haller 4)
Honor of the Humble, 1914 (Lawrence 3)
Honor of the Mounted, 1914 (Dwan 2, Chaney Lon 3)
Honor of the Nation. See Ei gerochsky podvig, 1914
Honor of the Press, 1932 (Eason 4)
Honor of the Regiment, 1913 (Meredyth 4)
Honor of Thieves, 1908 (Griffith 2, Bitzer 4)
Honor System, 1917 (Walsh 2)
Honor Thy Father, 1912 (Pickford 3)
Honor Thy Father, 1973 (Duning 4)
Honorable Algernon, 1913 (Talmadge, N. 3)
Honorable Billy. See Society For Sale, 1918
Honorable Catherine, 1942 (L'Herbier 2, Feuillère 3, Barsacq 4, Jeanson 4)
Honorable Event. See Pickwick Papers, 1913
Honorable Friend, 1916 (Hayakawa 3)
Honorable Mr. Buggs, 1927 (Hardy 3, Roach 4)
Honorable Société, 1978 (Dalio 3, Gélin 3)
Honorable Stanislas, agent secret, 1963 (Delerue 4)
Honorary Consul, 1983 (Caine 3, Gere 3)
Honoré de Marseilles, 1956 (Fernandel 3)
Honoring a Hero, 1911 (White 3)
Honor's Altar, 1916 (Stone 3, Sullivan 4)
Honour above All, 1928 (Grot 4)
Honour Redeemed. See Victoria Cross, 1917
Honourable Mr. Wong. See Hatchet Man, 1932
Honours Easy, 1935 (Brenon 2)

Honradez es un estorbo, 1937 (García 3)
Honryu, 1926 (Gosho 2, Tanaka 3)
Hoodlum, 1919 (Franklin 2, Pickford 3, Rosher 4)
Hoodlum Empire, 1952 (Trevor 3)
Hoodlum Priest, 1961 (Kershner 2, Wexler 4)
Hoodlum Saint, 1946 (Taurog 2, Lansbury 3, Powell, W. 3, Stone 3, Summerville 3, Williams 3)
Hoodlum's Honor. See Ganovenehre, 1966
Hoodman Blind, 1923 (Ford, J. 2)
Hoodoo, 1910–11 (White 3)
Hoodoo Ann, 1916 (Marsh 3)
Hoofs and Goofs, 1957 (Three Stooges 3)
Hook, 1963 (Seaton 2, Douglas, K. 3, Ruttenberg 4)
Hook and Hand, 1914 (Guy 2)
Hook and Ladder, 1924 (Miller, V. 4)
Hook and Ladder, 1932 (Roach 4)
Hook and Ladder Number One, 1932 (Terry 4)
Hook, Line, and Sinker, 1922 (Roach 4)
Hook, Line, and Sinker, 1930 (Musuraca 4)
Hook, Line, and Sinker, 1939 (Terry 4)
Hook, Line and Sinker, 1969 (Lewis 2)
Hook, Line and Stinker, 1958 (Jones 2)
Hooked at the Altar, 1926 (Sennett 2)
Hookibi, 1928 (Hasegawa 3)
Hooks and Jabs, 1933 (Langdon 3)
Hoola Boola, 1941 (Pal 2)
Hooligans. See Golfos, 1962
Hooper, 1978 (Field 3, Reynolds, B. 3, Needham 4)
Hoopla, 1933 (Bow 3)
Hooray for Love, 1935 (Robinson, B. 3, Sothern 3, Plunkett 4)
Hoose-Gow, 1929 (Laurel and Hardy 3, Roach 4)
Hoosier Romance, 1918 (Moore, C. 3, Selig 4)
Hoosier Schoolboy, 1937 (Rooney 3)
Hoot Mon, 1919 (Laurel 3, Roach 4)
Hootenanny Hoot, 1963 (Katzman 4)
Hop, Look, and Listen, 1948 (McKimson 4)
Hop Pickers. See Starci na chmelu, 1964
Hop, Skip, and a Chump, 1941 (Freleng 4)
Hop the Bell-Hop, 1919 (Hardy 3)
Hop, the Devil's Brew, 1916 (Weber 2)
Hop to It, 1925 (Hardy 3)
Hopalong Cassidy series, (Boyd 3)
Hopalong Casualty, 1961 (Jones 2)
Hopalong Rides Again, 1937 (Head 4)
Hope, 1922 (Astor 3)
Hope. See Naděje, 1963
Hope. See Umut, 1970
Hope Avenue. See Viale della speranza, 1953
Hope Chest, 1918 (Barthelmess 3, Gish, D. 3, Garmes 4)
Hope Diamond Mystery, 1921 (Karloff 3)
Hope Is Not Dead Yet. See Nozomi naki ni arazu, 1949
Hope of Blue Sky. See Kibo no aozora, 1960
Hope to Die. See Course du lièvre à travers ces champs, 1972
Hopeful Donkey, 1943 (Terry 4)
Hopeless. See Szegénylegények, 1965
Hopeless Ones. See Umutsuzlar, 1971
Hopes of Blind Alley, 1914 (Dwan 2)
Hopi Legend, 1913 , (Reid 3)
Hoppity Pop, 1946 (McLaren 2)
Hoppla, jetzt kommt Eddie!, 1958 (Constantine 3)
Hoppsan!, 1955 (Andersson H. 3, Thulin 3)
Hoppy Daze, 1961 (McKimson 4)
Hoppy Go Lucky, 1952 (McKimson 4)
Hoppy Serves a Writ, 1943 (Boyd 3, Mitchum 3)
Hoppy's Holiday, 1947 (Boyd 3)
Hopscotch, 1980 (Jackson 3, Matthau 3)
Hor, var der ikke én, som lo, 1978 (Carlsen 2)
Hora de los hornos, 1968 (Alvarez 2, Solanas and Getino 2)
Horace '62, 1962 (Trintignant 3)
Horace Greeley, Jr., 1925 (Capra 2, Langdon 3)
Horacijev uspon i pad, 1969 (Grgić 4)
Horde, 1928 (Tschechowa 3)
Hordubalové, 1937 (Fric 2)

Hordubals. *See* Hordubalové, 1937
Horečka, 1958 (Jires 2)
Hoří, má panenko, 1967 (Forman 2, Passer 2, Ondricek 4)
Horizon, 1932 (Kuleshov 2)
Horizon, 1966 (Coutard 4)
Horizon. *See* Horizont, 1970
Horizons noirs series. *See* Svarta Horisonter series, from 1935
Horizons nouveaux, 1961 (Delerue 4)
Horizons West, 1952 (Boetticher 2, Hudson 3, Ryan 3)
Horizont, 1970 (Madaras 3)
Horizontal Lieutenant, 1962 (Gillespie 4, Pasternak 4)
Horizontal-Vertical Orchestra. *See* Horizontal-Vertikal Orchester, 1923
Horizontal-Vertikal Orchester, 1923 (Eggeling 2)
Horká zima, 1972 (Kachyna 2)
Horloger de Saint-Paul, 1974 (Tavernier 2, Noiret 3, Aurenche 4, Bost 4, Sarde 4)
Horn Blows at Midnight, 1945 (Walsh 2, Dumont 3, Waxman 4)
Horn i norr, 1950 (Sucksdorff 2)
Hornets' Nest, 1970 (Hudson 3, Morricone 4)
Horns and Hoofs. *See* Pinto Ben, 1915 (Hart 3)
Horoki, 1954 (Okada 3)
Horoki, 1962 (Naruse 2, Takamine 3, Tanaka 3, Tsukasa 3)
Horoscope for a Child, 1970 (Benegal 2)
Horror Castle. *See* Vergine de Norimberga, 1964
Horror Chamber of Dr. Faustus. *See* Yeux sans visage, 1960
Horror Dream, 1947 (Peterson 2)
Horror Express, 1974 (Lee, C. 3)
Horror Film series, 1970–72 (Le Grice 2)
Horror Hotel. *See* City of the Dead, 1960
Horror Island, 1941 (Salter 4)
Horror of Dracula. *See* Dracula, 1958
Horror of Frankenstein, 1970 (Bernard 4, Sangster 4)
Horror of It All, 1964 (Fisher 2)
Horror of the Blood Monsters, 1970 (Carradine 3, Zsigmond 4)
Horror Show, 1979 (Perkins 3)
Horse, 1965 (Warhol 2)
Horse, 1970 (Gabin 3)
Horse. *See* Koń, 1967
Horse. *See* Uma, 1941
Horse Collars, 1935 (Bruckman 4)
Horse Feathers, 1932 (McLeod 2, Marx Brothers 3, Mankiewicz 4)
Horse Fly Opera, 1941 (Terry 4)
Horse Hare, 1959 (Freleng 4)
Horse Hoofs, 1931 (Carey 3)
Horse of Oxumaire. *See* Cavalo de Oxumaire, 1961
Horse on Bill, 1913 (Loos 4)
Horse on Holiday, 1959 (Greenwood 3)
Horse on the Merry-Go-Round, 1938 (Iwerks 4)
Horse Over Tea Kettle, 1962 (Breer 2)
Horse Play, 1924 (Lantz 4)
Horse Race Fever. *See* Rennfieber, 1917
Horse Shoes, 1927 (Arthur 3, Bruckman 4)
Horse Shoo, 1964 (Hanna and Barbera 4)
Horse Soldiers, 1959 (Ford, J. 2, Holden 3, Martin, S. 3, Wayne 3, Clothier 4, Mahin 4, Mirisch 4)
Horse That Cried. *See* Dorogoi tsenoi, 1957
Horse, the Woman, and the Gun. *See* At avrat silah, 1966
Horse Thief, 1905 (Bitzer 4)
Horse Thief, 1912 (Dwan 2)
Horse Thief, 1913 (Sennett 2)
Horse Thief's Bigamy, 1911 (Dwan 2)
Horse Trader, 1927 (Wyler 2)
Horse Without a Head, 1963 (Aumont 3, Clarke, T.E.B. 4)
Horsefly Fleas, 1947 (McKimson 4)
Horseman, 1971 (Sharif 3)
Horseman of the Plains, 1928 (Mix 3)
Horseman, The Woman and The Moth, 1968 (Brakhage 2)
Horsemasters, 1961 (Pleasance 3, Francis 4)
Horsemen, 1970 (Frankenheimer 2, Palance 3, Delerue 4, Renoir 4, Trumbo 2)
Horsemen of the Wind. *See* Vsadniki vetra, 1930
Horseplayer, 1961 (Hitchcock 2)

Horse-Race and Wife. *See* Kyouba to nyoubou, 1932
Horses. *See* Hesten, 1943
Horses and Their Ancestors, 1962 (Hubley 4)
Horses Collars, 1935 (Three Stooges 3)
Horse's Mouth, 1958 (Guinness 3)
Horses of Death, 1972 (Dunning 4)
Horseshoe for Luck. *See* Podkova pro štěsti, 1946
Horseshoe Nail, 1940 (Dickinson 2)
Horsing Around, 1957 (Three Stooges 3)
Horské volání SOS, 1929 (Stallich 4)
Horst Wessel. *See* Hans Westmar, 1933
Horton Hatches the Egg, 1942 (Clampett 4)
Horton Hears a Who, 1971 (Jones 2)
Horyu Temple. *See* Horyu-ji, 1958
Horyu-ji, 1958 (Hani 2)
Hose, 1927 (Krauss 3)
Hosen des Ritters von Bredow, 1973 (Hoppe 3, Mueller-Stahl 3)
Hospital, 1970 (Wiseman 2)
Hospital, 1971 (Hiller 2, Scott, G. 3, Chayefsky 4)
Hospital Guard. *See* Kveska, 1923
Hospital Massacre, 1982 (Golan and Globus 4)
Hospitaliky, 1937 (Fleischer, M. and D. 2)
Hostage, 1917 (Novarro 3, Reid 3)
Hostage, 1967 (Carradine 3, Stanton 3)
Hostage of the Embassy. *See* Mystiske Selskabsdame, 1917
Hostage Tower, 1980 (Fairbanks, D. Jr. 3, Johnson, C. 3, Roberts 3)
Hostages, 1943 (Bendix 3, Homolka 3, Lukas 3, Rainer 3, Dreier 4, Head 4, Young, V. 4)
Hostile Guns, 1967 (Arlen 3, De Carlo 3)
Hostile Witness, 1967 (Milland 3)
Hostinec 'U kamenného stolu', 1949 (Hrušínský 3)
Hot Air Salesman, 1937 (Fleischer, M. and D. 2)
Hot and Cold, 1933 (Lantz 4)
Hot Angel, 1958 (Struss 4)
Hot Blood, 1956 (Ray, N. 2, Russell, J. 3, Wilde 3)
Hot Box, 1972 (Demme 2, Corman 4)
Hot Cakes for 2, 1926 (Sennett 2)
Hot Car Girl, 1958 (Corman 4)
Hot Curves, 1930 (Taurog 2)
Hot Dog, 1928 (Disney 2)
Hot Dogs. *See* Mabel's Busy Day, 1914
Hot Enough for June, 1963 (Bogarde 3)
Hot Feet, 1931 (Lantz 4)
Hot Finish. *See* Mabel at the Wheel, 1914
Hot for Hollywood, 1930 (Lantz 4)
Hot for Paris, 1929 (Walsh 2, McLaglen 3, Carré 4)
Hot Heels, 1924 (Roach 4)
Hot Heir, 1931 (Balcon 4)
Hot Heiress, 1931 (Pidgeon 3, Polito 4)
Hot Ice, 1955 (Three Stooges 3)
Hot Lead, 1951 (Musuraca 4)
Hot Lead and Cold Feet, 1978 (Elam 3)
Hot Marshland. *See* Netsudeichi, 1950
Hot Millions, 1968 (Malden 3, Smith 3, Ustinov 3)
Hot Money, 1935 (Roach 4)
Hot Money, 1936 (Edeson 4)
Hot Money Girls. *See* Treasure of San Teresa, 1959
Hot News, 1928 (Daniels 3, Lukas 3)
Hot Night. *See* Atsui yoru, 1968
Hot Off the Press, 1922 (Roach 4)
Hot Off the Press, 1934 (Katzman 4)
Hot Pearls. *See* Blonde from Singapore, 1941
Hot Pepper, 1933 (McLaglen 3, Velez 3, Clarke, C.C. 4, Nichols 4)
Hot Resort, 1984 (Golan and Globus 4)
Hot Rhythm, 1944 (Langdon 3)
Hot Rock, 1972 (Yates 2, Redford 3, Segal 3, Goldman, W. 4, Jones 3)
Hot Rod Action, 1969 (Zsigmond 4)
Hot Rod and Reel, 1959 (Jones 2)
Hot Rod Gang, 1958 (Crosby 4)
Hot Rods, 1953 (Terry 4)
Hot Rods to Hell, 1967 (Andrews D. 3, Crain 3, Katzman 4)
Hot Sands, 1934 (Terry 4)

Hot Saturday, 1932 (Arlen 3, Darwell 3, Grant, C. 3, Scott, R. 3, Head 4)
Hot Scots, 1948 (Three Stooges 3)
Hot Spell, 1936 (Terry 4)
Hot Spell, 1958 (Cukor 2, MacLaine 3, Quinn 3, Head 4, North 4, Wallis 4, Westmore, F. 4)
Hot Spot, 1932 (Roach 4)
Hot Spot, 1941 (Grable 3, Mature 3, Cronjager 4)
Hot Spot. See I Wake Up Screaming, 1941
Hot Steel, 1940 (Arlen 3)
Hot Stuff, 1911 (Sennett 2)
Hot Stuff, 1924 (Roach 4)
Hot Stuff, 1929 (Leroy 2, Fazenda 3)
Hot Stuff, 1956 (Three Stooges 3)
Hot Stuff, 1971 (Grgić 4)
Hot Summer Game, 1965 (Zsigmond 4)
Hot Summer Night, 1957 (Previn 4)
Hot Time in the Old Town Tonight, 1930 (Fleischer, M. and D. 2)
Hot Tip, 1935 (Pitts 3, Plunkett 4)
Hot Touch, 1980 (Vadim 2)
Hot Turkey, 1930 (Terry 4)
Hot Water, 1924 (Lloyd 3, Roach 4)
Hot Wind. See Neppu, 1943 (Hara 3)
Hot Winter. See Horká zima, 1972
Hot Wire, 1980 (Kennedy, G. 3, Martin, S. 3)
Hotaru-bi, 1958 (Gosho 2)
Hot-Cross Bunny, 1948 (McKimson 4)
Hotel, 1967 (Douglas, M. 3, Malden 3, Oberon 3, Head 4, Lang 4)
Hotel Adlon, 1955 (Wagner 4)
Hotel at Osaka. See Osaka no yado, 1954
Hotel Berlin, 1945 (Lorre 3, Massey 3, Waxman 4)
Hotel Blue Star. See Hotel Modrá hvězda, 1941
Hotel Continental, 1931 (Walthall 3)
Hôtel de la gare, 1914 (Feuillade 2)
Hotel des Amériques, 1982 (Deneuve 3)
Hotel des étudiants, 1932 (Périnal 4)
Hôtel des Invalides, 1951 (Franju 2, Fradetal 4, Jarre 4)
Hôtel des voyageurs de commerce, 1906 (Méliès 2)
Hôtel du libre échange, 1934 (Allégret, M. 2, Fernandel 3, Grimault 4, Meerson 4, Prévert 4, Trauner 4)
Hôtel du Nord, 1938 (Carné 2, Arletty 3, Aumont 3, Blier 3, Jouvet 3, Aurenche 4, Jaubert 4, Jeanson 4, Trauner 4)
Hôtel du silence, 1908 (Cohl 2)
Hotel for Strangers. See Hotel pro cizince, 1966
Hotel for Women, 1939 (Darnell 3, Sothern 3, Zanuck 4)
Hotel Haywire, 1937 (Sturges, P. 2, Head 4)
Hotel Honeymoon, 1912 (Guy 2)
Hotel Imperial, 1927 (Stiller 2, Negri 3, Furthman 4, Glennon 4, Pommer 4)
Hotel Imperial, 1939 (Florey 2, Milland 3, Head 4)
Hotel Mixup. See Mabel's Strange Predicament, 1914
Hotel Modrá hvězda, 1941 (Fric 2)
Hotel Monterey, 1972 (Akerman 2)
Hotel New Hampshire, 1984 (Richardson 2, Watkin 4)
Hotel of the Americas. See Hotel des Amériques, 1982
Hotel Paradis, 1917 (Dreyer 2)
Hotel Paradiso, 1966 (Guinness 3, Lollobrigida 3, Carrière 4, Decaë 4)
Hotel Paradiso. See Hotel Paradis, 1917
Hotel Potemkin, 1924 (Banky 3)
Hotel pro cizince, 1966 (Schorm 2)
Hotel Reserve, 1944 (Mason 3)
Hotel Sahara, 1951 (De Carlo 3, Ustinov 3)
Hotel Splendide, 1932 (Powell 2)
Hotelgeheimnisse, 1928 (Metzner 4)
Hothouse, 1981 (Pinter 4)
Hototogisu, 1932 (Gosho 2, Hasegawa 3, Takamine 3)
Hotovo, jedem, 1947 (Hofman 4, Pojar 4)
Hotsy Footsy, 1952 (Burness 4)
Hotsy Toty, 1925 (Sennett 2)
Hottentot, 1922 (Garnett 2)
Hottentot, 1929 (Horton 3)
Hotter Than Hot, 1929 (Langdon 3, Roach 4)
Houat, 1963 (Fradetal 4)

Houdini, 1953 (Pal 2, Curtis 3, Leigh, J. 3, Head 4, Laszlo 4)
Hound Dog Man, 1959 (Siegel 2, Darwell 3, Clarke, C.C. 4, Wald 4, Wheeler 4)
Hound for Trouble, 1951 (Jones 2)
Hound Hunters, 1947 (Avery 2)
Hound of the Baskervilles, 1939 (Bruce 3, Carradine 3, Rathbone 3, Day 4)
Hound of the Baskervilles, 1959 (Fisher 2, Cushing 3, Lee, C. 3, Bernard 4)
Hound of the Baskervilles, 1969 (Granger 3)
Hound of the Baskervilles, 1977 (Warhol/Morrissey 2, Greenwood 3, Matthews 3, Moore, D. 3)
Hounded. See Johnny Allegro, 1949
Hounding the Hares, 1948 (Terry 4)
Hounds of Zaroff. See Most Dangerous Game, 1932
Hour after Hour, 1974 (Nowicki 3)
Hour and the Man, 1914 (Bushman 3)
Hour Before the Dawn, 1944 (Lake 3, Dreier 4, Head 4, Rozsa 4, Seitz 4)
Hour Glass, 1972 (Popescu-Gopo 4)
Hour of Glory. See Small Back Room, 1949
Hour of Parting. See Afskedens timme, 1973
Hour of Terror, 1912–13 (White 3)
Hour of the Furnaces. See Hora de los hornos, 1968
Hour of the Gun, 1967 (Sturges, J. 2, Robards 3, Ryan 3, Voight 3, Anhalt 4, Ballard 4, Goldsmith 4)
Hour of the Trial. See I Provningens stund, 1916
Hour of the Wolf. See Vargtimmen, 1968
Hour of 13, 1952 (Addison 4, Green, G. 4, Junge 4)
Hours Between. See 24 Hours, 1931
Hours by Air, 1936 (Pitts 3)
Hours of Love. See Le ore dell'amore, 1963
House. See Dom, 1958
House. See Kuća, 1975
House Across the Bay, 1940 (Hitchcock 2, Bennett J. 3, Pidgeon 3, Raft 3, Irene 4, Wanger 4)
House, after Five Years of Living, 1955 (Bernstein 4)
House at the End of the World. See Die, Monster, Die!, 1965
House at the Terminus. See Tam na konečné, 1957
House Behind the Cedars, mid–1920s (Micheaux 2)
House Broken, 1936 (Havelock-Allan 4)
House Builder-Upper, 1938 (Fleischer, M. and D. 2)
House Built Upon Sand, 1917 (Gish, L. 3)
House Busters, 1952 (Terry 4)
House by the River, 1950 (Lang 2, Cronjager 4, Leven 4)
House Calls, 1978 (Jackson 3, Matthau 3, Bumstead 4, Epstein, J. & P. 4, Mancini 4)
House Cleaning Blues, 1937 (Fleischer, M. and D. 2)
House Divided, 1919 (Blackton 2)
House Divided, 1931 (Huston 2, Wyler 2, Huston 3, Fulton 4)
House Hunting Mice, 1947 (Jones 2)
House I Live In, 1945 (Leroy 2, Sinatra 3)
House in Bayswater, 1960 (Russell 2)
House in Nightmare Park, 1973 (Milland 3)
House in the Snow-Drifts. See Dom v sugribakh, 1928
House in the Square, 1951 (Alwyn 4)
House Is Not a Home, 1964 (Crawford, B. 3, Taylor, R. 3, Welch 3, Winters 3, Head 4)
House No. 44, 1955 (Burman 4)
House of a Thousand Candles, 1915 (Selig 4)
House of a Thousand Candles, 1936 (Auer 3)
House of a Thousand Dolls. See Haus der tausend Freuden, 1967
House of Bamboo, 1955 (Fuller 2, Hayakawa 3, Ryan 3, Lemaire 4, Wheeler 4)
House of Blackmail, 1953 (Lassally 4)
House of Bondage, 1913 (Ince 4)
House of Cards, 1916 (Guy 2)
House of Cards, 1969 (Welles 2, Head 4, Lai 4, Ravetch 4)
House of Connelly. See Carolina, 1934
House of Dark Shadows, 1970 (Smith, D. , Bennett J. 3)
House of Darkness, 1913 (Griffith 2, Barrymore L. 3, Gish, L. 3, Bitzer 4)
House of Darkness, 1948 (Harvey 3)

House of Death. *See* Smerti doma, 1915
House of Discord, 1913 (Barrymore L. 3, Gish, D. 3, Sweet 3)
House of Doom. *See* Black Cat, 1934
House of Dracula, 1945 (Carradine 3, Chaney Lon, Jr. 3, Pierce 4, Salter 4)
House of Dracula's Daughter, 1973 (Carradine 3, Crawford, B. 3)
House of Errors, 1942 (Langdon 3)
House of Evil, 1972 (Karloff 3)
House of Evil. *See* House on Sorority Row, 1982
House of Exorcism. *See* Lisa e il diavolo, 1972
House of Fate. *See* Muss 'em Up, 1936
House of Fear, 1939 (Krasner 4)
House of Fear, 1945 (Bruce 3, Rathbone 3, Lourié 4, Miller, V. 4, Salter 4)
House of Flame, 1979 (Kawamoto 4)
House of Folly. *See* Dårskapens hus, 1951
House of Frankenstein, 1944 (Carradine 3, Chaney Lon, Jr. 3, Karloff 3, Fulton 4, Pierce 4, Salter 4, Siodmak 4)
House of Freaks, 1973 (Brazzi 3)
House of Fright. *See* Two Faces of Doctor Jekyll, 1960
House of Hate, 1918 (White 3)
House of Horror, 1929 (Christensen 2, Fazenda 3, Haller 4, Polito 4)
House of Horror, 1946 (Salter 4)
House of Intrigue. *See* Londra chiama Polo Nord, 1956
House of Light. *See* Chambre blanche, 1969
House of Lovers. *See* Pot bouille, 1957
House of Magic, 1937 (Lantz 4)
House of Marney, 1927 (Hepworth 2)
House of Mystery, 1914 (White 3)
House of Numbers, 1957 (Palance 3, Previn 4, Schnee 4)
House of Pleasure. *See* Plaisir, 1952
House of Pride, 1912 (Bushman 3)
House of Ricordi. *See* Casa Ricordi, 1954
House of Rothschild, 1934 (Arliss 3, Karloff 3, Young, L. 3, Young, R. 3, Day 4, Johnson 4, Newman 4, Westmore, M. 4, Zanuck 4)
House of Secrets, 1956 (Green, G. 4)
House of Settlement. *See* Mr. Soft Touch, 1949
House of Silence, 1918 (Crisp 3, Reid 3)
House of Silence, 1962 (Bernstein 4)
House of Strangers, 1949 (Mankiewicz 2, Hayward 3, Krasner 4, Lemaire 4, Wheeler 4)
House of Terror. *See* Casa del terror, 1959
House of the Angel. *See* Casa del ángel, 1957
House of the Arrow, 1953 (Homolka 3)
House of the Black Death, 1965 (Carradine 3, Chaney Lon, Jr. 3)
House of the Long Shadows, 1983 (Carradine 3, Cushing 3, Lee, C. 3, Price 3, Golan and Globus 4)
House of the Seven Corpses, 1973 (Carradine 3, Ireland 3)
House of the Seven Gables, 1940 (Price 3, Sanders 3, Krasner 4)
House of the Seven Hawks, 1959 (Taylor, R. 3)
House of the Sleeping Virgins. *See* Nemureru bijo, 1968
House of the Spaniard, 1936 (Dickinson 2)
House of the Tolling Bell, 1920 (Blackton 2)
House of Tomorrow, 1949 (Avery 2)
House of Trent, 1933 (Bennett 4)
House of Usher, 1960 (Price 3)
House of Usher. *See* Fall of the House of Usher, 1960
House of Wax, 1953 (De Toth 2, Bronson 3, Price 3, Glennon 4)
House of Women. *See* Haus der Frauen, 1977
House of Women. *See* Kvinnohuset, 1953
House of Wrath, 1924 (Sullivan 4)
House on Chelouche Street, 1973 (Golan and Globus 4)
House on 56th Street, 1933 (Florey 2, Francis, K. 3, Haller 4, Orry-Kelly 4)
House on Garibaldi Street, 1979 (Topol 3)
House on Greenapple Road, 1970 (Leigh, J. 3, Pidgeon 3, Wynn 3)
House on Haunted Hill, 1959 (Cook 3, Price 3)
House on 92nd Street, 1945 (Hathaway 2, Carroll L. 3, de Rochemont 4, Wheeler 4, Zanuck 4)
House on Sorority Row, 1982 (Goldsmith 4)
House on Telegraph Hill, 1951 (Wise 2, Cortese 3, Ballard 4, Lemaire 4, Newman 4, Wheeler 4)

House That Dinky Built, 1925 (Lantz 4)
House That Dripped Blood, 1970 (Cushing 3, Lee, C. 3)
House that Jack Built, 1912 (Dwan 2)
House That Wouldn't Die, 1970 (Stanwyck 3)
House with the Closed Shutters, 1910 (Griffith 2, Walthall 3, Bitzer 4)
House with the Golden Windows, 1916 (Reid 3)
House Without a Christmas Tree, 1972 (Robards 3)
Houseboat, 1916 (Sennett 2)
Houseboat, 1958 (Grant, C. 3, Loren 3, Duning 4, Edouart 4, Fulton 4, Head 4, Westmore, F. 4)
Housebreakers, 1914 (Browning 2)
Household Pest, 1910 (Talmadge, N. 3)
Householder, 1963 (Ivory 2, Jhabvala 4, Mitra 4)
Housekeeper of Circle C, 1913 (Anderson G. 3)
Housekeeper's Daughter, 1939 (Bennett J. 3, Mature 3, Meek 3, Menjou 3, Irene 4, Roach 4)
Housemaster, 1938 (Brenon 2)
Housewife, 1934 (Brennan 3, Brent 3, Orry-Kelly 4)
Housewife Herman, 1938 (Terry 4)
Housing Problem, 1946 (Terry 4)
Houslový koncert, 1962 (Jires 2)
Houston Story, 1956 (Katzman 4)
Houston Texas, 1956 (Reichenbach 2, Braunberger 4)
Houston Texas, 1980 (Reichenbach 2)
Hovdingens Son ar dod, 1937–38 (Fejos 2)
How a Man Loves. *See* Woman He Loved, 1922
How a Mosquito Operates, 1912 (McCay 2)
How Awful about Allan, 1970 (Perkins 3)
How Bridget's Lover Escaped. *See* Mariage de Victorine, 1907
How Cissy Made Good, 1915 (Bunny 3)
How Could William Tell?, 1919 (La Cava 2)
How Could You, Caroline?, 1918 (Love 3)
How Could You, Jean?, 1918 (Pickford 3, Pitts 3, Marion 4, Rosher 4)
How Death Came to Earth, 1971 (Patel 4)
How Do I Know It's Sunday, 1934 (Freleng 4)
How Do I Love Thee?, 1970 (O'Hara 3, Winters 3)
How Dr. Nicola Procured the Chinese Cane. *See* Dr. Nicola, 1909
How Dry I Am, 1920 (Roach 4)
How Ducks Are Fattened, 1899 (Bitzer 4)
How Funny Can Sex Be? See Sesso matto, 1973
How Green Was My Valley, 1941 (Ford, J. 2, Crisp 3, Fitzgerald 3, McDowall 3, O'Hara 3, Pidgeon 3, Banton 4, Day 4, Dunne 4, La Shelle 4, Miller, A. 4, Newman 4, Zanuck 4)
How Hazel Got Even, 1915 (Crisp 3, Gish, D. 3)
How He Lied to Her Husband, 1931 (Gwenn 3)
How He Prepared the Room, 1912 (Bunny 3)
How Heroes Are Made, 1914 (Sennett 2)
How High Is Up?, 1940 (Three Stooges 3)
How Hiram Won Out, 1913 (Sennett 2, Arbuckle 3)
How I Play Golf, 1931 (Cagney 3)
How I Play Golf No. 7: The Spoon, 1933 (Huston 3)
How I Spent My Summer Vacation, 1967 (Pidgeon 3, Wagner 3, Schifrin 4)
How I Won the War, 1967 (Lester 2, Watkin 4)
How It Feels to be Run Over, 1900 (Hepworth 2)
How It Happened, 1913 (Mix 3)
How Jones Lost His Roll, 1905 (Porter 2)
How Kico Was Born, 1951 (Vukotić 4)
How Man Learned to Fly. *See* Jak se člověk naučil létat, 1958
How Mike Got the Soap in His Eyes, 1903 (Bitzer 4)
How Motion Pictures Are Made, 1914 (Sennett 2)
How Much Do You Owe?. *See* Jackpot, 1950
How Much Wood Would a Woodchuck Chuck, 1976 (Herzog 2)
How Nerves Are Made, 1914 (Normand 3)
How Not to Dress. *See* Herr och fru Stockholm, 1921
How Not to Lose Your Head While Shotfiring, 1973 (Dunning 4)
How Not to Succeed in Business, 1975 (Halas and Batchelor 2)
How Rastus Gets His Turkey, 1910–11 (White 3)
How Romeo and Juliet Loved Each Other. *See* Kako su se voleli Romeo i Juliet, 1967
How She Triumphed, 1911 (Griffith 2, Sweet 3, Bitzer 4)
How Sweet It Is!, 1968 (Dalio 3, Reynolds, D. 3, Ballard 4, Rose 4)

How Tasty Was My Little Frenchman. *See* Como é gostoso o meu francês, 1971
How the Burglar Tricked the Bobby, 1901 (Hepworth 2)
How the Day Was Saved, 1913 (Loos 4)
How the Elector Will Vote. *See* Kak budet golosovat 'izbiratel', 1937
How the F-100 Got Its Tail, 1955 (Leacock 2)
How the Grinch Stole Christmas, 1970 (Jones 2)
How the Puppy Tore His Trousers. *See* Jak si pejsek roztrhl kalhoty, 1951
How the Steel Was Tempered. *See* Kak zakalyalas stal, 1942
How the West Was Won, 1963 (Ford, J. 2, Hathaway 2, Baker C. 3, Brennan 3, Cobb 3, Fonda, H. 3, Malden 3, Massey 3, Moorehead 3, Peck 3, Preston 3, Reynolds, D. 3, Ritter 3, Stewart 3, Tracy 3, Van Cleef 3, Wallach 3, Wayne 3, Widmark 3, Cahn 4, Canutt 4, Daniels 4, Gillespie 4, Krasner 4, La Shelle 4, Lang 4, Mercer 4, Newman 4, Plunkett 4)
How the World Works. *See* Jak je svět zařízen, 1956
How to Be a Hostess, 1959 (Halas and Batchelor 2)
How to Be Loved. *See* Jak być kochana, 1962
How to Be Very, Very Popular, 1955 (Coburn, C. 3, Cummings 3, Grable 3, Cahn 4, Johnson 4, Krasner 4, Lemaire 4)
How to Beat the High Cost of Living, 1980 (Lange 3)
How to Commit Marriage, 1969 (Hope 3, Wyman 3, Lang 4, Panama 4)
How to Destroy the Reputation of the Greatest Secret Agent. *See* Magnifique, 1973
How to Fill a Wild Bikini. *See* How to Stuff a Wild Bikini, 1965
How to Fire a Lewis Gun, 1918 (Fleischer, M. and D. 2)
How to Fire a Stokes Mortar, 1918 (Fleischer, M. and D. 2)
How to Furnish an Apartment. *See* Jak zariditi byt, 1959
How to Handle Women, 1928 (Lugosi 3)
How to Keep a Husband, 1914 (Loos 4)
How to Keep Cool, 1953 (Terry 4)
How to Keep Slim. *See* Jak na to, 1963
How to Marry a Millionaire, 1953 (Negulesco 2, Bacall 3, Grable 3, Monroe 3, Powell, W. 3, Johnson 4, Lemaire 4, Newman 4, Wheeler 4)
How to Murder a Rich Uncle, 1957 (Caine 3, Coburn, C. 3, Hiller 3, Box 4, Paxton 4)
How to Murder Your Wife, 1965 (Lemmon 3, Trevor 3, Axelrod 4, Stradling 4, Sylbert 4)
How to Read an Army Map, 1918 (Fleischer, M. and D. 2)
How to Relax, 1954 (Terry 4)
How to Save a Marriage—and Ruin Your Life, 1968 (Martin, D. 3, Wallach 3, Garmes 4, Legrand 4)
How to Score a Movie, 1978 (Howard, T. 3)
How to Steal a Diamond in Four Uneasy Lessons. *See* Hot Rock, 1972
How to Steal a Million, 1966 (Wyler 2, Boyer 3, Dalio 3, Hepburn, A. 3, O'Toole 3, Wallach 3, Kurnitz 4, Lang 4, Trauner 4, Williams, J. 4)
How to Steal a Million. *See* Jak jsem ukradl milioń, 1966
How to Steal an Airplane, 1970 (Mineo 3)
How to Steal the World, 1968 (Carroll L. 3)
How to Stop a Motor Car, 1902 (Hepworth 2)
How to Stuff a Wild Bikini, 1965 (Keaton 2, Rooney 3, Crosby 4)
How to Succeed in Business Without Really Trying, 1967 (Boyle 4, Guffey 4)
How to Succeed with Sex, 1972 (Katzman 4)
How Villains Are Made. *See* Race, 1914
How Weary Went Wooing, 1915 (Mix 3)
How Wet Was My Ocean, 1940 (Terry 4)
How Women Love, 1922 (Stradling 4)
Howard the Duck, 1986 (Barry 4)
Howards of Virginia, 1940 (Grant, C. 3, Hardwicke 3, Ladd 3, Buchman 4, Glennon 4, Vorkapich 4)
Howling, 1980 (Carradine 3, Baker 4, Bottin 4, Donaggio 4, Sayles 4)
Howling Success, 1954 (Terry 4)
How's About It?, 1943 (Howard, S. 3)
How've You Been, 1933 (Arbuckle 3)
Hoyden, 1911 (Lawrence 3)
Hoyden's Awakening, 1913 (Franklin 2)
Hoyo, 1953 (Mifune 3)
Hra na krále, 1967 (Jires 2)

Hra oživot, 1956 (Weiss 2)
Hraběnka z Podskali, 1925 (Ondra 3)
Hrabina Cosel, 1968 (Olbrychski 3)
Hrajeme si, 1957 (Hofman 4)
Hranjenik, 1970 (Mimica 4)
Hrátky s čertem, 1956 (Stallich 4)
Hrdiná jedné noci, 1935 (Stallich 4)
Hrdina jedné noci, 1935 (Fric 2)
Hrdinný kapitán Korkorán, 1934 (Vích 4)
Hřichy v manželstvi, 1924 (Ondra 3)
Hříšná krev, 1929 (Vích 4)
Hrnec nafoukanec, 1961 (Hofman 4)
Hry lásky šálivé, 1971 (Kopecký 3)
Hsi nu ai le, 1970 (King Hu 2)
Hsia nü, 1969 (King Hu 2)
Hu Man, 1974 (Moreau 3, Stamp 3)
Hua t'ien-t'so, 1961 (King Hu 2)
Hub illal Abad, 1959 (Chahine 2)
Hubbi el Wahid, 1960 (Sharif 3)
Hubby Buys a Baby, 1913 (Bunny 3)
Hubby to the Rescue, 1914 (Browning 2)
Hubby's Cure, 1914 (Fazenda 3)
Hubby's Job, 1913 (Sennett 2, Normand 3)
Hubby's Latest Alibi, 1928 (Sennett 2, Hornbeck 4)
Hubby's Quiet Little Game, 1926 (Sennett 2)
Hubby's Toothache, 1913 (Bunny 3)
Hubby's Week-end Trip, 1928 (Sennett 2, Hornbeck 4)
Huckleberry Finn, 1931 (Taurog 2, Coogan 3, Darwell 3, Muse 3)
Huckleberry Finn, 1939 (Seitz 4)
Huckleberry Finn, 1975 (Elam 3, Kovacs 4)
Huckleberry Finn. *See* Adventures of Huckleberry Finn, 1939
Hucksters, 1947 (Gable 3, Gardner 3, Greenstreet 3, Kerr 3, Menjou 3, Wynn 3, Irene 4, Rosson 4)
Hud, 1963 (Ritt 2, Douglas, M. 3, Neal 3, Newman 3, Bernstein 4, Edouart 4, Head 4, Howe 4, Ravetch 4, Westmore, W. 4)
Hudba srdcí, 1934 (Vích 4)
Hudba z Marsu, 1954 (Kadár 2)
Huddle, 1932 (Wood 2, Merkel 3, Novarro 3, Adrian 4, Gillespie 4, Sullivan 4)
Hudson's Bay, 1940 (Bruce 3, Muni 3, Price 3, Tierney 3, Banton 4, Day 4, MacGowan 4, Newman 4, Trotti 4)
Hudutlarin kanunu, 1966 (Guney 2)
Hue and Cry, 1947 (Crichton 2, Sim 3, Auric 4, Balcon 4, Clarke, T.E.B. 4, Slocombe 4)
Huellas del pasado, 1950 (Alcoriza 4)
Huey. *See* Black Panthers, 1968
Hug Bug, 1926 (Roach 4)
Hughie at the Victory Derby, 1919 (Pearson 2)
Hugo architecte, 1964–69 (Rohmer 2)
Hugs and Mugs, 1950 (Three Stooges 3)
Huguenot, 1909 (Feuillade 2, Carré 4)
Huilor, 1938 (Alexeieff and Parker 2, Auric 4)
Huis clos, 1954 (Arletty 3, Kosma 4)
Huit hommes dans un château, 1942 (Aurenche 4, Honegger 4)
Huit Jours de bonheur. *See* Liebesexpress, 1931
Huitième Jour, 1960 (Fradetal 4, Kosma 4)
Hula, 1927 (Fleming 2, Hathaway 2, Bow 3, Brook 3, Schulberg 4)
Hula from Hollywood, 1954 (Kaye 3)
Hula Hula Land, 1917 (Sennett 2)
Hula Hula Land, 1949 (Terry 4)
Hula La La, 1951 (Three Stooges 3)
Hulda from Holland, 1916 (Pickford 3)
Hulda Rasmussen, 1911 (Gad 2)
Hulda's Lovers, 1908 (Bitzer 4)
Hullabaloo, 1940 (Burke 3, Dailey 3, Meek 3)
Hullabaloo over Georgie and Bonnie's Pictures, 1978 (Ivory 2, Jhabvala 4, Lassally 4)
Hullo Everbody. *See* Getting Acquainted, 1914
Hullo Fame, 1941 (Ustinov 3)
Hum Bhi Insaan Hai, 1948 (Anand 3)
Hum Dono, 1961 (Anand 3)
Hum Ek Hai, 1946 (Anand 3)
Hum paanch, 1981 (Azmi 3)

Hurricane, 1979 (Troell 2, Farrow 3, Howard, T. 3, Robards 3, Von Sydow 3, De Laurentiis 4, Donati 4, Nykvist 4, Rota 4, Semple 4)
Hurricane Express, 1932 (Wayne 3, Canutt 4)
Hurricane Horseman, 1925 (Arthur 3)
Hurricane Horseman, 1931 (Canutt 4)
Hurricane Hutch, 1921 (Oland 3)
Hurricane Island, 1951 (Katzman 4)
Hurricane Kid, 1925 (Miller, V. 4)
Hurricane Rider, 1931 (Carey 3)
Hurricane Smith, 1952 (Arlen 3, De Carlo 3, Ireland 3, Head 4)
Hurricane's Girl, 1922 (Beery 3)
Hurry Call, 1932 (Hunt 4)
Hurry, Charlie, Hurry, 1941 (Johnson, N. 3, Musuraca 4)
Hurry, Doctor, 1925 (Sennett 2)
Hurry Doctor, 1931 (Fleischer, M. and D. 2)
Hurry, Hurry. See Deprisa, deprisa, 1980
Hurry Sundown, 1966 (Preminger 2, Caine 3, Dunaway 3, Fonda, J. 3, Kennedy, G. 3, Meredith 3, Krasner 4)
Hurry West, 1921 (Roach 4)
Hurvínek's Circus. See Cirkus Hurvínek, 1955
Husarenliebe. See Es blasen die Trompetten, 1926
Husassistenten, 1914 (Holger-Madsen 2)
Husband and Wife. See Fufu, 1953
Husband for Anna. See Marito per Anna Zaccheo, 1953
Husband Hunters, 1927 (Arthur 3)
Husbands, 1970 (Cassavetes 2, Falk 3)
Husbands and Lovers, 1924 (Stahl 2, Stone 3, Booth 4, Gaudio 4)
Husbands Beware, 1956 (Three Stooges 3, Bruckman 4)
Husband's Holiday, 1931 (Brook 3)
Husbands or Lovers. See Honeymoon in Bali, 1939
Husbands or Lovers. See Nju, 1924
Husband's Reunion, 1933 (Sennett 2)
Huse til mennesker, 1972 (Roos 2)
Hush, 1920 (Edeson 4)
Hush . . . Hush, Sweet Charlotte, 1964 (Aldrich 2, Astor 3, Cotten 3, Davis 3, De Havilland 3, Dern 3, Kennedy, G. 3, Moorehead 3, Biroc 4)
Hush Money, 1921 (Brady 3)
Hush Money, 1931 (Bennett J. 3, Loy 3, Raft 3, Nichols 4, Seitz 4)
Hush My Mouse, 1945 (Jones 2)
Hushed Hour, 1919 (Sweet 3, Edeson 4)
Hushing the Scandal, 1915 (Sennett 2)
Huskors, 1914 (Holger-Madsen 2)
Hussards, 1955 (Blier 3, Bourvil 3, Auric 4)
Hussards et grisettes, 1901 (Guy 2)
Hussite Warrior. See Jan Žižka, 1955
Hustle, 1975 (Aldrich 2, Borgnine 3, Deneuve 3, Johnson, B. 3, Reynolds, B. 3, Biroc 4)
Hustler, 1921 (Roach 4)

Hustler, 1961 (Rossen 2, Newman 3, Scott, G. 3, Allen, D. 4, Horner 4, Schufftan 4)
Hustlin' Hawk, 1923 (Rogers, W. 3, Roach 4)
Hustling, 1975 (Clayburgh 3, Remick 3)
Hustling for Health, 1919 (Laurel 3, Roach 4)
Húsz óra, 1964 (Fábri 2)
Hvad med os?, 1963 (Carlsen 2)
Hvem er Gentlemantyven, 1915 (Holger-Madsen 2)
Hvem er han?. See Ensom Kvinde, 1914
Hvem var Forbryderen?, 1912 (Blom 2)
Hvězda jede na jih, 1958 (Kopecký 3)
Hvězda zvaná Pelyněk, 1964 (Fric 2)
Hvide Dame, 1913 (Holger-Madsen 2)
Hvide Djaevel, 1916 (Dreyer 2, Holger-Madsen 2)
Hvide Slavehandel I, 1910 (Blom 2)
Hvide Slavehandel II, 1911 (Blom 2)
Hvide Slavehandel III, 1912 (Gad 2)
Hvo som elsker sin Fader or Faklen, 1915 (Holger-Madsen 2)
Hvor bjergene sejler, 1955 (Henning-Jensen 2)
Hvor er magten blevet af?, 1968 (Carlsen 2)
Hvor Sorgerne glemmes, 1916 (Holger-Madsen 2)
Hvorledes Dr. Nicola erhvervede den kinesiske Stok. See Dr. Nicola, 1909
Hy Rutabaga, 1973 (Pojar 4)
Hyakumanin no musumetachi, 1963 (Gosho 2, Iwashita 3)
Hyas, 1930 (Jaubert 4)
Hyde and Hare, 1955 (Freleng 4)
Hyde-and-Go Tweet, 1959 (Freleng 4)
Hydrothérapie fantastique, 1910 (Méliès 2)
Hyena's Laugh, 1927 (Lantz 4)
Hymn of Nations, 1946 (Meredith 3)
Hymn to a Tired Man. See Nihon no seishun, 1968
Hymn to Her, 1974 (Brakhage 2)
Hyoroku yume monogatari, 1943 (Takamine 3, Tsuburaya 4)
Hypnosis. See Nur tote Zeugen schweigen, 1963
Hypnotic Eyes, 1933 (Terry 4)
Hypnotist, 1922 (Fleischer, M. and D. 2)
Hypnotist's Revenge, 1907 (Bitzer 4)
Hypnotized, 1932 (Sennett 2, McDaniel 3, Hornbeck 4)
Hypnotized, 1952 (Terry 4)
Hypnotizing the Hypnotist, 1911 (Bunny 3)
Hyp-nut-tist, 1935 (Fleischer, M. and D. 2)
Hypochondriac. See Malato imaginario, 1979
Hypo-Chondri-Cat, 1950 (Jones 2)
Hypocrites, 1914 (Weber 2, Bosworth 3, Marion 4)
Hypothèse du tableau volé, 1978 (Ruiz 2, Vierny 4)
Hypothesis. See Hipoteza, 1972
Hypothesis of a Stolen Painting. See Hypothèse du tableau volé, 1978
Hysteria, 1964 (Francis 4, Sangster 4)
Hysterical, 1982 (Wynn 3)
Hysterical High Spots in American History, 1941 (Lantz 4)

I

I.N.R.I., 1923 (Wiene 2, Krauss 3, Nielsen 3, Porten 3, Metzner 4)
I, a Man, 1967 (Warhol 2)
I, a Virgin. See Badarna, 1968
I Accuse!, 1957 (Ferrer, J. 3, Walbrook 3, Alwyn 4)
I Aim at the Stars, 1960 (Jurgens 3)
I Ain't Got Nobody, 1932 (Fleischer, M. and D. 2)
I Am a Camera, 1955 (Clayton 2, Harvey 3, Winters 3, Arnold 4, Dehn 4, Green, G. 4, Mathieson 4)
I Am a Cat. See Wagahai wa neko de aru, 1975
I Am a Fugitive from a Chain Gang, 1932 (Leroy 2, Muni 3, Orry-Kelly 4, Polito 4, Wallis 4, Zanuck 4)

I Am a Girl with the Devil in My Body. See Jsem děvče s čertem v těle, 1933
I Am a Thief, 1934 (Florey 2, Astor 3, Blanke 4, Orry-Kelly 4)
I Am Blushing, 1982 (Sjoman 2)
I Am Curious—Blue. See Jag ar nyfiken—blå, 1968
I Am Curious—Yellow. See Jag ar nyfiken—gul, 1967
I Am Photogenic. See Sono fotogenico, 1980
I am Poor, But Angry. See Siroma sam, al sam besan, 1969
I Am Suzanne, 1934 (Garmes 4, Lasky 4)
I Am the Cheese, 1983 (Wagner 3)
I Am the Law, 1922 (Beery 3)

I Am the Law, 1938 (Robinson, E. 3, Swerling 4)

I Am the Man, 1924 (Barrymore L. 3)

I Am Tokichiro. See Baku wa Toukichiroh, 1955

I Am Two. See Watashi wa ni-sai, 1962

I and My Lovers. See Galia, 1966

I Ask for the Floor. See Ja prasu slova, 1976

I Became a Criminal. See They Made Me a Fugitive, 1947

I Beg a Word. See Proshu slova, 1976

I Believe in You, 1951 (Dearden 2, Harvey 3, Johnson, C. 3)

I Believed in You, 1934 (Beavers 3)

I Blush. See Jag rodfnar, 1981

I Bombed Pearl Harbor. See Taiheiyo no arashi, 1960

I Bury the Living, 1958 (Boone 3)

I Call First. See Who's That Knocking at My Door, 1968

I Can Get It for You Wholesale, 1951 (Polonsky 2, Dailey 3, Hayward 3, Jaffe 3, Sanders 3, Krasner 4, Lemaire 4)

I Can Hardly Wait, 1943 (Three Stooges 3, Bruckman 4)

I Cannot Say That Person's Name. See Sono hito no na wa ienai, 1951

I Can't Escape from You, 1936 (Fleischer, M. and D. 2)

I Can't Give You Anything But Love, Baby, 1940 (Crawford, B. 3, Salter 4)

I Changed My Sex. See Glen or Glenda?, 1952

I, Claudius, 1937 (Laughton 3, Korda 4, Krasker 4, Périnal 4)

I . . . comme Icare, 1979 (Verneuil 2, Morricone 4)

I Confess, 1953 (Hitchcock 2, Baxter A. 3, Clift 3, Malden 3, Orry-Kelly 4, Reville 4, Tiomkin 4)

I corpi presentano tracce di violenza carnale, 1973 (Ponti 4)

I Could Go On Singing, 1963 (Bogarde 3, Garland 3, Head 4)

I Cover the Underworld, 1955 (Van Cleef 3)

I Cover the War, 1937 (Wayne 3)

I Cover the Waterfront, 1933 (Cruze 2, Colbert 3, D'Agostino 4, Newman 4)

I Deal in Danger, 1966 (Schifrin 4, Smith, J.M. 4)

I den store pyramide, 1974 (Roos 2)

I Did It, Mama, 1909 (Griffith 2, Bitzer 4)

I Didn't Do It, 1945 (Formby 3)

I Died a Thousand Times, 1955 (Chaney Lon., Jr. 3, Hopper 3, Marvin 3, Palance 3, Winters 3, Burnett 4, McCord 4)

I dimma dold, 1952 (Fischer 4)

I Do, 1921 (Lloyd 3, Roach 4)

I dolci inganni, 1960 (Lattuada 2)

I Don't Care Girl, 1953 (Bacon 2, Cole 4, Wheeler 4)

I Don't Remember, 1935 (Langdon 3)

I Don't Want to be Born, 1975 (Pleasance 3)

I Don't Want to Make History, 1936 (Fleischer, M. and D. 2)

I Dood It, 1943 (Minnelli 2, Horne 3, McQueen, B. 3, Powell, E. 3, Sharaff 4)

I Dream of Jeannie, 1952 (Dwan 2, Beavers 3)

I Dream Too Much, 1935 (Cromwell 2, Auer 3, Ball 3, Fonda, H. 3, Berman 4, Pan 4, Polglase 4, Steiner 4)

I drugie ofitsialnye litsa, 1976 (Tikhonov 3)

I Eats My Spinach, 1931 (Fleischer, M. and D. 2)

I Escaped from Devil's Island, 1973 (Corman 4)

I Escaped from the Gestapo, 1943 (Carradine 3)

I Feel Like a Feather in the Breeze, 1936 (Fleischer, M. and D. 2)

'I' Film. See Ik-Film, 1929

I Flunked, But . . . See Radkudai wa shita keredo, 1930

I formerlaere, 1949 (Carlsen 2)

I Found Stella Parish, 1935 (Leroy 2, Francis, K. 3, Lukas 3, Brown, Harry Joe 4, Orry-Kelly 4, Saunders 4)

I Found Stella Parish. See Stella Parish, 1935

I Give My Heart, 1936 (Siodmak 4)

I Give My Life, 1936 (Walbrook 3)

I Give My Life. See Port Arthur, 1936

I Give My Love, 1934 (Beavers 3, Lukas 3, Freund 4)

I Gopher You, 1953 (Freleng 4)

I Graduated, But . . . See Daigaku wa detakeredo, 1929

I Hate Your Guts. See Intruder, 1961

I Have a New Master. See Ecole buissonnière, 1949

I Haven't Got a Hat, 1935 (Freleng 4)

I havsbandet, 1971 (Von Sydow 3)

I Heard, 1931 (Fleischer, M. and D. 2)

I, I, I . . . and the Others. See Io, io, io . . . e gli altri, 1966

I Kill You and Commend You to God. See T'ammazzo! Raccomandanti a Dio, 1968

I Killed. See Jag drapte, 1943

I Killed Rasputin. See J'ai tué Raspoutine, 1967

I Kiss Your Hand, Madame. See Ich kusse Ihre Hand, Madame, 1929

I Knew Her Well. See Io la conoscevo bene, 1965

I Know That You Know That I Know. See Io so che tu sai che io so, 1982

I Know Where I'm Going, 1945 (Powell and Pressburger 2, Hiller 3, Junge 4)

I Kynighi, 1977 (Angelopoulos 2)

I Like Babies and Infinks, 1937 (Fleischer, M. and D. 2)

I Like It That Way, 1934 (Rooney 3)

I Like Mike, (Topol 3)

I Like Mountain Music, 1931 (Fleischer, M. and D. 2)

I Like Your Nerve, 1931 (Fairbanks, D. Jr. 3, Karloff 3, Young, L. 3, Haller 4)

I Live Again, 1936 (Love 3)

I Live for Love, 1935 (Berkeley 2, Del Rio 3, Barnes 4, Epstein, J. & P. 4, Orry-Kelly 4, Wald 4)

I Live for You. See I Live for Love, 1935

I Live in Fear. See Ikimono no kiroku, 1955

I Live in Grosvenor Square, 1945 (Wilcox 2, Harrison 3, Neagle 3)

I Live in Grosvenor Square. See Yank in London, 1945

I Live My Life, 1935 (Mankiewicz 2, Van Dyke, W.S. 2, Crawford, J. 3, Adrian 4, Tiomkin 4)

I Live on Danger, 1942 (Nilsson 3)

I Lived With You, 1933 (Lupino 3, Novello 3)

I Lived Without You, 1933 (Hawkins 3)

I Livets Braending, 1915 (Holger-Madsen 2)

I livets vår, 1912 (Sjostrom 3, Jaenzon 4, Magnusson 4)

I Liza kai i alli, 1961 (Lassally 4)

I Look at You, 1941 (Ladd 3)

I Love a Bandleader, 1945 (Planer 4)

I Love a Lassie, 1925 (Fleischer, M. and D. 2)

I Love a Mystery, 1945 (Guffey 4)

I Love a Mystery, 1973 (Lupino 3)

I Love a Soldier, 1944 (Sandrich 2, Bondi 3, Fitzgerald 3, Goddard 3, Head 4, Lang 4)

I Love Melvin, 1953 (Merkel 3, O'Connor 3, Reynolds, D. 3, Taylor, R. 3, Alton, R. 4, Rose 4, Rosson 4, Smith, J.M. 4)

I Love My Wife, 1970 (Gould 3, Schifrin 4)

I Love That Man, 1933 (Brown, Harry Joe 4, Krasner 4, Robinson 4)

I Love to Singa, 1936 (Avery 2)

I Love Trouble, 1947 (Ireland 3, Duning 4)

I Love You Again, 1940 (Van Dyke, W.S. 2, Loy 3, Powell, W. 3, Kurnitz 4, Lederer 4, Waxman 4)

I Love You, Alice B. Toklas!, 1968 (Sellers 3, Bernstein 4, van Runkle 4)

I Love You, I Love You Not. See Amo non Amo, 1978

I Love, You Love. See Io amo, tu ami, 1961

I Love, You Love. See Jag alskar, du alskar, 1968

I Love You, Rosa. See Ani Ohev Otach Rosa, 1971

I Loved a Soldier, 1936 (Hathaway 2, Dietrich 3)

I Loved a Woman, 1933 (Francis, K. 3, Robinson, E. 3, Blanke 4)

I Loved You Wednesday, 1933 (King 2, Baxter, W. 3, Menzies 4)

I Married a Communist. See Woman on Pier 13, 1950

I Married a Doctor, 1936 (Fazenda 3, O'Brien, P. 3, Brown, Harry Joe 4, Orry-Kelly 4, Robinson 4)

I Married a Monster from Outer Space, 1958 (Bumstead 4, Fulton 4, Head 4)

I Married a Shadow. See J'ai épousé une ombre, 1983

I Married a Witch, 1942 (Clair 2, Hayward 3, Lake 3, March 3, Dreier 4, Head 4, Pirosh 4, Waxman 4)

I Married a Woman, 1958 (Dickinson 3, Menjou 3, Wayne 3, Ballard 4, D'Agostino 4)

I Married an Angel, 1942 (Van Dyke, W.S. 2, Eddy 3, Horton 3, MacDonald 3, Loos 4, Stothart 4, Stromberg 4)

I Married Too Young. See Married Too Young, 1961

I Married You for Fun. See Ti ho sposato per allegria, 1967

I Met a Girl Who . . . . See Cintura di Castità, 1969

I Met a Murderer, 1939 (Mason 3)

I Met Him in Paris, 1937 (Ruggles 2, Colbert 3, Douglas, M. 3, Young, R. 3, Banton 4, Dreier 4)

I Met My Love Again, 1938 (Logan 2, Bennett J. 3, Fonda, H. 3, Wanger 4)

I, Mobster, 1958 (Corman 4, Crosby 4)

I, Mobster, 1970 (Cushing 3, Lee, C. 3)

I natt eller aldrig, 1941 (Molander 2)

I Need a Woman. See Adamson i Sverige, 1966

I Never Changes My Altitude, 1937 (Fleischer, M. and D. 2)

I Never Promised You a Rose Garden, 1977 (Andersson B. 3, Sidney 3, Corman 4)

I Never Sang for My Father, 1969 (Douglas, M. 3, Hackman 3)

I Only Have Eyes for You, 1937 (Avery 2)

I Only Want You to Love Me. See Ich will doch nur, dass Ihr mich liebt, 1976

I Ought to be in Pictures, 1982 (Matthau 3)

I Passed for White, 1960 (Williams, J. 4)

I Promise to Pay, 1937 (Ballard 4)

I Provningens stund, 1916 (Sjostrom 2)

I Remember Mama, 1948 (Stevens 2, Dunne 3, Hardwicke 3, Homolka 3, Bodeen 4, D'Agostino 4, Musuraca 4)

I Rok och Dans, 1954 (Thulin 3)

I Saw the New World Born, 1982 (Bondarchuk 3)

I Saw the Whole Thing, 1962 (Hitchcock 2)

I Saw What You Did, 1965 (Crawford, J. 3, Ireland 3, Biroc 4, Westmore, B. 4)

I See a Dark Stranger, 1946 (Howard, T. 3, Kerr 3, Alwyn 4, Gilliat 4)

I See Everybody Naked. See Vedo Nudo, 1969

I See Ice, 1938 (Formby 3, McDowall 3, Dean 4)

I Sell Anything, 1934 (Florey 2, O'Brien, P. 3, Orry-Kelly 4)

I Sent a Letter to My Love. See Cher Inconnu, 1981

I Shall Return. See American Guerilla in the Philippines, 1950

I Shot Jesse James, 1949 (Fuller 2, Ireland 3)

I Should Have Stood in Bedlam, 1949 (Lewis 2)

I Sign in Blood. See Imzam kanla yazilir, 1970

I som har intraden . . ., 1945 (Bjornstrand 3)

I Spy. See Morning After, 1934

I Stand Accused, 1938 (Cummings 3)

I Stand Condemned. See Moscow Nights, 1935

I Stole a Million, 1939 (Raft 3, Trevor 3, Krasner 4)

I Surrender Dear, 1931 (Sennett 2, Crosby 3, Hornbeck 4)

I Surrender Dear, 1948 (Katzman 4)

I Survived Certain Death. See Přežil isem svou smrt, 1960

I Take This Woman, 1931 (Von Sternberg 2, Cooper, Gary 3, Lombard 3, Vorkapich 4)

I Take This Woman, 1940 (Ruggles 2, Van Dyke, W.S. 2, Calhern 3, Lamarr 3, Tracy 3, Kaper 4, MacArthur 4, Rosson 4)

I Taw a Putty Tat, 1947 (Freleng 4)

I Thank a Fool, 1962 (Cusack 3, Finch 3, Hayward 3)

I, the Jury, 1953 (Saville 2, Cook 3, Alton, J. 4, Waxman 4)

I Think They Call Him John, 1964 (Love 3)

I Vor Pittfalks, 1967 (Williams, R. 4)

I Wake Up Screaming, 1941 (Cook 3, Mature 3)

I Wake up Screaming. See Hot Spot, 1941

I Walk Alone, 1947 (Douglas, K. 3, Lancaster 3, Dreier 4, Head 4, Schnee 4, Wallis 4, Young, V. 4)

I Walk the Line, 1970 (Frankenheimer 2, Peck 3, Weld 3, Sargent 4)

I Walked with a Zombie, 1943 (Tourneur, J. 2, D'Agostino 4, Hunt 4, Lewton 4, Siodmak 4)

I Wanna Be a Life Guard, 1936 (Fleischer, M. and D. 2)

I Wanna Be a Sailor, 1937 (Avery 2)

I Wanna Play House with You, 1936 (Freleng 4)

I Want a Divorce, 1940 (Beavers 3, Blondell 3, Powell, D. 3, Dreier 4, Head 4, Young, V. 4)

I Want My Dinner, 1903 (Bitzer 4)

I Want My Hat!. See Mrs. Jones' Lover, 1909

I Want to Be a Shellfish. See Watashi wa kai ni naritai, 1959

I Want to Hold Your Hand, 1978 (Spielberg 2)

I Want to Live, 1958 (Wise 2, Hayward 3, Hornbeck 4, Wanger 4)

I Want to Live, 1983 (Stanton 3)

I Want You, 1951 (Robson 2, Andrews D. 3, Day 4, Goldwyn 4, Mandell 4, Stradling 4)

I Wanted Wings, 1941 (Leisen 2, Holden 3, Lake 3, Milland 3, Dreier 4, Edouart 4, Head 4, Young, V. 4)

I Was a Communist for the FBI, 1951 (Steiner 4)

I Was a Criminal. See Captain of Koepenick, 1941

I Was a Criminal. See Passport to Heaven, 1943

I Was a Fireman. See Fires Were Started, 1943

I Was a Mail Order Bride, 1901 (Addison 4)

I Was a Male War Bride, 1949 (Hawks 2, Grant, C. 3, Sheridan 3, Lederer 4, Wheeler 4)

I Was a Prisoner on Devil's Island, 1941 (Brown, K. 4)

I Was a Shoplifter, 1950 (Curtis 3, Hudson 3)

I Was a Spy, 1933 (Saville 2, Bruce 3, Carroll M. 3, Gwenn 3, Marshall 3, Veidt 3, Balcon 4, Junge 4)

I Was a Teenage Thumb, 1963 (Jones 2)

I Was a Teenage Werewolf, 1957 (La Shelle 4)

I Was an Adventuress, 1940 (Von Stroheim 2, Lorre 3, Cronjager 4, Day 4, Johnson 4, Shamroy 4, Zanuck 4)

I Was Born, But . . . See Umarete wa mita karedo, 1932

I Was Framed, 1942 (Bosworth 3, McCord 4)

I Was Happy Here, 1966 (Addison 4)

I Was Happy Here. See Passage of Love, 1965

I Was Monty's Double, 1958 (Mills 3, Addison 4)

I Was 19. See Ich war neunzehn, 1967

I Will, I Will . . . for Now, 1976 (Gould 3, Keaton 3, Alonzo 4, Cahn 4, Panama 4)

I Will If You Will. See Infermiera, 1975

I Wished on the Moon, 1935 (Fleischer, M. and D. 2)

I Wonder Who's Kissing Her Now, 1931 (Fleischer, M. and D. 2)

I Wonder Who's Kissing Her Now, 1947 (Bacon 2, Day 4, Lemaire 4, Leven 4, Newman 4, Pan 4)

I Won't Forget That Night. See Sono yo wa wasurenai, 1962

I Wouldn't Be in Your Shoes, 1948 (Mirisch 4)

I Yam Love Sick, 1938 (Fleischer, M. and D. 2)

I Yam What I Yam, 1931 (Fleischer, M. and D. 2)

Ibañez' Torrent. See Torrent, 1926

Ibaragi Ukon, 1939 (Miyagawa 4)

Ibis rouge, 1975 (Simon, M. 3)

IBM at the Fair, 1965 (Bernstein 4)

IBM Mathematics Peep Show, 1961 (Bernstein 4)

IBM Puppet Show, 1965 (Bernstein 4)

Ibn el Nil, 1951 (Chahine 2)

Ibo-kyodai, 1957 (Tanaka 3, Yoda 4)

Ibret, 1971 (Guney 2)

Ibun sarutobi sasuke, 1965 (Shinoda 2, Takemitsu 4)

Icarus, 1960 (De Palma 2)

Ice, 1970 (Kramer, R. 2)

Ice. See Is, 1970

Ice Capades Revue, 1942 (Alton, J. 4)

Ice Carnival, 1941 (Terry 4)

Ice Cold Cocos, 1926 (Sennett 2)

Ice Cold in Alex, 1958 (Mills 3, Quayle 3)

Ice Flood, 1927 (Walthall 3)

Ice Follies of 1939, 1939 (Ayres 3, Crawford, J. 3, Stewart 3, Stone 3, Adrian 4, Brown, N. 4, Freed 4, Ruttenberg 4, Waxman 4)

Ice Man's Luck, 1929 (Lantz 4)

Ice Palace, 1960 (Burton 3, Ryan 3, Biroc 4, Blanke 4, Steiner 4)

Ice Pirates, 1983 (Carradine 3, Serafine 4)

Ice Pond, 1939 (Terry 4)

Ice Station Zebra, 1968 (Sturges, J. 2, Borgnine 3, Hudson 3, Legrand 4)

Icebound, 1924 (Buckland 4)

Ice-Breaker Krassnin. See Podvig vo idach, 1928

Iced Bullet, 1917 (Sullivan 4)

Iceland, 1942 (Henie 3, Day 4, Miller, A. 4)

Iceman Cometh, 1973 (Frankenheimer 2, Bridges 3, Marvin 3, Ryan 3, Jeakins 4)

Iceman's Ball, 1932 (Brennan 3)

Icepick. See Coltello di ghiaccio, 1972

Ich—Axel Casar Springer, 1970 (Hoppe 3)

Ich bei Tag und Du bei Nacht, 1932 (Pommer 4)

Ich bin auch nur eine Frau, 1962 (Schell, Maria 3)

Ich bin du, 1934 (Rohrig 4)

Ich bin Sebastian Ott, 1939 (Hoffmann 4)

If It Were Raining. *See* Comme s'il en pleuvait, 1963
If It's Tuesday, This Must Be Belgium, 1969 (Cassavetes 2, De Sica 2)
If Marriage Fails, 1925 (Brook 3, Hersholt 3, Sullivan 4)
If My Country Should Call, 1916 (Chaney Lon 3)
If One Thousand Clarinets, 1964 (Menzel 2)
'If Only' Jim, 1921 (Carey 3)
If This Be Sin. *See* That Dangerous Age, 1950
If Tomorrow Comes, 1971 (Baxter A. 3)
If We Only Knew, 1913 (Sweet 3, Walthall 3)
If Winter Comes, 1923 (Ruttenberg 4)
If Winter Comes, 1947 (Saville 2, Kerr 3, Lansbury 3, Leigh, J. 3,
    Pidgeon 3, Berman 4, Irene 4, Stothart 4, Wimperis 4)
If You Believe It, It's So, 1922 (Young, W. 4)
If You Could Only Cook, 1935 (Arthur 3, Marshall 3)
If You Feel Like Singing. *See* Summer Stock, 1950
If You Had a Wife Like This, 1907 (Bitzer 4)
If You Like It. *See* Sukinareba koso, 1928
If You Love. *See* Aisureba koso, 1955
If You Want to Be Happy. *See* Esli khochesh byt schastlivym, 1974
Iga Kottou gunryu, 1941 (Yoda 4)
Iga Kottou Military Style. *See* Iga Kottou gunryu, 1941
Igano minatsuki, 1958 (Hasegawa 3)
Igen, 1964 (Darvas 3)
Igéret foldje, 1961 (Torocsik 3)
Igloo for Two, 1955 (Terry 4)
Ignace, 1937 (Fernandel 3)
Igor Bulichov and the Others. *See* Igor Bulichov i drugie, 1973
Igor Bulichov i drugie, 1953 (Ulyanov 3)
Igor Bulichov i drugie, 1973 (Tikhonov 3, Ulyanov 3)
Igrok, 1972 (Batalov 3)
Iguana dalla lingua di fuoco, 1972 (Cortese 3)
Igy jottem, 1964 (Jancsó 2, Madaras 3)
Ihr grosse Fall. *See* Grosse Fall, 1944
Ihr Junge, 1931 (Sakall 3)
Ihr Privatsekretar, 1940 (Frohlich 3)
Ihr Sport, 1919 (Wiene 2)
Ihre Durchlaucht, die Verkauferin, 1933 (Planer 4)
Ihre Hoheit befiehlt, 1931 (Wilder 2, Pommer 4)
Ihre Majestat die Liebe, 1931 (Sakall 3, Andrejew 4)
Iikagen baka, 1964 (Iwashita 3)
Ikari no machi, 1949 (Naruse 2)
Ikari no umi, 1944 (Imai 2, Tsuburaya 4)
Ikarus, 1975 (Hoppe 3)
Ike, 1979 (Duvall, R. 3)
Ikebana, 1953–57 (Teshigahara 2)
Ikeru shikabane, 1920 (Kinugasa 2)
Ik-Film, 1929 (Ivens 2)
Ikimono no kiroku, 1955 (Kurosawa 2, Mifune 3, Shimura 3,
    Hayasaka 4, Muraki 4)
Ikinokata Shinsengumi, 1932 (Kinugasa 2)
Ikiru, 1952 (Kurosawa 2, Shimura 3, Hayasaka 4)
Ikisi de cesurdu, 1963 (Guney 2)
Ikiteiru gazo, 1948 (Hayasaka 4)
Ikite-iru Magoroku, 1943 (Kinoshita 2)
Ikiteiru ningyo, 1957 (Yamada 3)
Ikitoshi ikeru mono, 1955 (Yamamura 3)
Ikitoshi Ikerumono, 1934 (Gosho 2)
Ikonostast, 1969 (Dinov 4)
Il a été perdu une mariée, 1932 (Burel 4, Meerson 4, Spaak 4)
Il est charmant, 1931 (Stradling 4)
Il est minuit, Docteur Schweitzer, 1952 (Fresnay 3, Moreau 3,
    Cloquet 4)
Il était une chaise. *See* Chairy Tale, 1957
Il était une fois, 1933 (Douy 4)
Il était une fois la révolution. *See* Giù la testa, 1972
Il était une fois un flic, 1972 (Delon 3)
Il faut tuer Birgitt Haas, 1981 (Noiret 3, Sarde 3)
Il faut vivre dangereusement, 1975 (Girardot 3)
Il ne faut pas mourir pour ça, 1967 (Lefebvre 2)
Il n'y a pas de fumée sans feu, 1973 (Cayatte 2, Girardot 3)
Il pleut sur Santiago, 1975 (Andersson B. 3, Girardot 3)
Il suffit d'une fois, 1946 (Matras 4)
Il y a des pieds au plafond, 1912 (Gance 2)

Il y a longtemps que je t'aime, 1979 (Guillemot 4)
Il y a un dieu pour les ivrognes, 1908 (Méliès 2)
Ildprøve, 1915 (Holger-Madsen 2)
Ile au trésor, 1985 (Branco 4, de Almeida 4)
Ile de Pâques, 1935 (Storck 2, Jaubert 4)
Ile de sein, 1958 (Delerue 4)
Ile d'Ouessant. *See* Enez Eussa, 1961
Ile Maurice, 1960 (Braunberger 4)
Ile mystérieuse, 1973 (Colpi 4)
Ile mystérieuse. *See* Mystery Island, 1973
Iles enchantées, 1965 (Rabier 4)
Ilhas Encantadas, 1965 (de Almeida 4)
Iliac Passion, 1967 (Markopoulos 2)
I'll Be Glad When You're Dead, You Rascal, 1932 (Fleischer, M.
    and D. 2)
I'll Be Seeing You, 1944 (Cukor 2, Dieterle 2, Cotten 3, Rogers, G. 3,
    Temple 3, Gaudio 4, Head 4, Schary 4)
I'll Be Suing You, 1934 (Roach 4)
I'll Be Yours, 1947 (Sturges, P. 2, Bendix 3, Durbin 3, Menjou 3,
    Banton 4)
I'll Buy You. *See* Anata kaimasu, 1956
I'll Cry Tomorrow, 1955 (Hayward 3, Gibbons 4, Mercer 4, North 4,
    Rose 4)
I'll Defend You My Love. *See* Difendo il mio amore, 1956
I'll Dig Your Grave. *See* Sono Sartana, il vostro bechino, 1969
I'll Get By, 1950 (Crain 3, Dailey 3, Mature 3, Ritter 3, Clarke, C.C. 4,
    Lemaire 4)
I'll Get Him Yet, 1919 (Barthelmess 3, Gish, D. 3, Garmes 4)
I'll Get You, 1951 (Raft 3)
I'll Give a Million, 1938 (Baxter W. 3, Carradine 3, Hersholt 3,
    Lorre 3, MacGowan 4, Zanuck 4)
I'll Give My Life, 1960 (Dickinson 3)
I'll Love You Always, 1935 (August 4, Buchman 4)
Ill Met by Moonlight, 1957 (Powell and Pressburger 2, Bogarde 3,
    Cusack 3, Lee, C. 3, Theodorakis 4)
I'll Never Crow Again, 1941 (Fleischer, M. and D. 2)
I'll Never Forget What's 'is Name, 1967 (Welles 2, Love 3, Reed, O. 3,
    Lai 4)
I'll Never Forget You, 1951 (Power 3, Balderston 4, Périnal 4)
I'll Never Forget You. *See* House in the Square, 1951
I'll Never Heil Again, 1941 (Three Stooges 3, Bruckman 4)
I'll Say So, 1918 (Walsh 2)
I'll See You in My Dreams, 1952 (Curtiz 2, Day 3, McCord 4, Prinz 4)
I'll Take Romance, 1937 (Douglas, M. 3, Murfin 4)
I'll Take Sweden, 1965 (Hope 3, Weld 3)
I'll Take Vanilla, 1922 (Roach 4)
I'll Take Vanilla, 1934 (Roach 4)
I'll Tell the World, 1934 (Mandell 4)
I'll Tell the World, 1945 (Salter 4)
I'll Wait for You, 1941 (Kaper 4)
Illegal, 1955 (Mansfield 3, Burnett 4, Steiner 4)
Illegal Divorce. *See* Second Hand Wife, 1932
Illegal Entry, 1949 (Brent 3, Daniels 3)
Illegal Traffic, 1938 (Crabbe 3, Preston 3, Dreier 4, Head 4)
Ill-Fated Love. *See* Amor di perdição, 1978
Illicit, 1931 (Blondell 3, Stanwyck 3, Zanuck 4)
Illicit Interlude. *See* Sommarlek, 1951
Illuminacja, 1973 (Zanussi 2)
Illumination, 1912 (Reid 3)
Illumination, 1963 (Reichenbach 2)
Illumination. *See* Illuminacja, 1973
Illuminations, 1963 (Braunberger 4)
Illusion, 1929 (Francis, K. 3, Lukas 3, Schulberg 4)
Illusion, 1947 (Braunberger 4)
Illusion. *See* Maya, 1936
Illusion in Moll, 1952 (Knef 3, Pommer 4, Vích 4)
Illusion of Blood. *See* Yotsuya kaidan, 1965
Illusioniste mondain, 1901 (Zecca, 2)
Illusioniste renversant, 1903 (Guy 2)
Illusions. *See* Time Out of Mind, 1947
Illusions fantaisistes, 1910 (Méliès 2)
Illusions fantasmagoriques, 1898 (Méliès 2)
Illusions funambulesques, 1903 (Méliès 2)

Impossible Object, 1973 (Legrand 4)
Impossible Object. *See* Impossible objet, 1973
Impossible Objet, 1973 (Frankenheimer 2, Bates 3, Sanda 3, Renoir 4, Trauner 4)
Impossible Voyage. *See* Voyage à travers l'impossible, 1904
Impossible Years, 1968 (Niven 3, Ames 4, Daniels 4)
Imposter, 1918 (Polito 4)
Imposter, 1944 (Duvivier 2, Gabin 3, Lourié 4)
Impostor, 1931 (Fort 4)
Impostor, 1944 (Tiomkin 4)
Impostor, 1956 (Armendáriz 3)
Impotence. *See* Xala, 1974
Impractical Joker, 1937 (Fleischer, M. and D. 2)
Imprécateur, 1977 (Piccoli 3)
Impression of John Steinbeck—Writer, 1969 (Fonda, H. 3)
Impressionable Years, 1952 (Fonda, H. 3)
Impressioniste fin de siècle, 1899 (Méliès 2)
Impressions de New York, 1955 (Reichenbach 2, Braunberger 4)
Impressions de Paris, 1966 (Reichenbach 2)
Imprevisto, 1961 (Lattuada 2, Aimée 3)
Imprint of Giants. *See* Empreinte des géants, 1980
Improper Channels, 1981 (Arkin 3)
Improper Conduct. *See* Mauvaise conduite, 1984
Impulse, 1954 (Kennedy, A. 3)
Impures, 1954 (Presle 3, Alekan 4)
Imputazione di omicidio per uno studente, 1971 (Bolognini 2, Cortese 3)
Imus, 1973 (Kuri 4)
Imzam kanla yazilir, 1970 (Guney 2)
In a Fantastic Vision. *See* V Blouzněni, 1928
In a Hempen Bag, 1909 (Griffith 2, Bitzer 4)
In a Lonely Place, 1950 (Ray, N. 2, Bogart 3, Grahame 3, Guffey 4)
In a Monastery Garden, 1929 (Balcon 4)
In a Year with 13 Moons. *See* In einem Jahr mit 13 Monden, 1978
In Again—Out Again, 1917 (Von Stroheim 2, Fairbanks, D. 3, Edeson 4, Emerson 4, Loos 4)
In and Out, 1914 (Beery 3)
In Anfang war das Wort, 1928 (Metzner 4)
In Another's Nest, 1913 (Dwan 2)
In Bermuda, 1914 (Rosher 4)
In Between, 1955 (Brakhage 2)
In Between, 1978 (Mekas 2)
In Blossom Time, 1911 (Olcott 2)
In Bridal Attire, 1914 (Talmadge, C. 3)
In Broad Daylight, 1971 (Boone 3)
In Caliente, 1935 (Bacon 2, Berkeley 2, Del Rio 3, Horton 3, O'Brien, P. 3, Barnes 4, Epstein, J. & P. 4, Orry-Kelly 4, Polito 4, Wald 4)
In Celebration, 1974 (Anderson 2, Bates 3)
In Cold Blood, 1967 (Brooks, R. 2, Boyle 4, Hall 4, Jones 4)
In Conference, 1931 (Sennett 2)
In Cupid's Realm, or, A Game of Hearts, 1908 (Lawrence 3)
In Dalarna and Jerusalem. *See* Ingmarsarvet, 1925
In Defiance of the Law, 1914 (Mix 3)
In dem grossen Augenblick, 1911 (Gad 2)
In der Nacht, 1931 (Ruttmann 2)
In Dickens Land, 1913 (Pearson 2)
In einem Jahr mit 13 Monden, 1978 (Fassbinder 2)
In einer Freeden Stadt, 1963 (Herlth 4)
In Enemy Country, 1968 (Anhalt 4, Head 4, Whitlock 4)
In faccia al destino, 1913 (Bertini 3)
In Fast Company, 1924 (Fort 4)
In fondo ala piscina, 1971 (Baker C. 3)
In Gay Madrid, 1930 (Novarro 3, Adrian 4, Day 4, Gibbons 4, Meredyth 4, Stothart 4)
In Gefahr und grösster Not bringt der Mittelweg den Tod, 1974 (Kluge 2, Jurgens 3)
In geheimer Mission, 1938 (Frohlich 3, Wegener 3)
In God We Trust, 1913 (Bosworth 3)
In God We Trust, 1980 (Pryor 3)
In Harm's Way, 1965 (Preminger 2, Andrews D. 3, Douglas, K. 3, Fonda, H. 3, Holloway 3, Kennedy, G. 3, Meredith 3, Neal 3, Wayne 3, Bass 4, Edouart 4, Goldsmith 4, Wheeler 4)

In His Steps, 1936 (Brown, K. 4)
In Hollywood with Potash and Perlmutter, 1924 (Leroy 2, Talmadge, C. 3, Carré 4, Goldwyn 4, Marion 4, Miller, A. 4)
In jenen Tagen, 1947 (Geschonneck 3)
In Judgement Of, 1918 (Nilsson 3)
In Life's Cycle, 1910 (Griffith 2, Walthall 3, Bitzer 4)
In Like Flint, 1967 (Cobb 3, Coburn, J. 3, Daniels 4, Goldsmith 4, Smith, J.M. 4)
In Line of Duty, 1931 (Glennon 4)
In Little Italy, 1909 (Griffith 2, Walthall 3, Bitzer 4)
In Little Italy, 1912 (Bosworth 3)
In Love and War, 1913 (Reid 3)
In Love and War, 1958 (Hunter 3, Wagner 3, Anhalt 4, Canutt 4, Dunne 4, Friedhofer 4, Lemaire 4, Reynolds 4, Wald 4)
In Many Fields, 1967 (Godfrey 4)
In Memoriam, 1977 (Borau 2, Chaplin 3)
In Memoriam László Mészáros. *See* Mészáros László emlékére, 1968
In My Merry Oldsmobile, 1931 (Fleischer, M. and D. 2)
In Name Only, 1939 (Cromwell 2, Coburn, C. 3, Francis, K. 3, Grant, C. 3, Lombard 3, Banton 4, Berman 4, Hunt 4, Polglase 4)
In Name Only, 1969 (Lancaster 3)
In Neighboring Kingdoms, 1911 (Talmadge, N. 3)
In nome del Papa Re, 1978 (Manfredi 3)
In nome del popolo italiano, 1972 (Risi 2, Gassmann 3, Age and Scarpelli 4)
In nome della legge, 1949 (Fellini 2, Germi 2, Monicelli 2, Pinelli 4, Rota 4)
In Old Amarillo, 1951 (Rogers, R. 3)
In Old Arizona, 1929 (Walsh 2, Baxter W. 3, Brown 3, Edeson 4)
In Old Caliente, 1939 (Rogers, R. 3)
In Old California, 1910 (Griffith 2, Walthall 3, Bitzer 4)
In Old California, 1929 (Walthall 3)
In Old California, 1942 (Wayne 3)
In Old California When the Gringos Came, 1911 (Mix 3)
In Old Cheyenne, 1941 (Rogers, R. 3)
In Old Chicago, 1938 (King 2, Ameche 3, Brady 3, Faye 3, Power 3, Canutt 4, Levien 4, MacGowan 4, Trotti 4, Zanuck 4)
In Old Colorado, 1941 (Boyd 3, Head 4)
In Old Florida, 1911 (Olcott 2)
In Old Heidelberg, 1915 (Emerson 4)
In Old Kentucky, 1909 (Griffith 2, Pickford 3, Walthall 3, Bitzer 4)
In Old Kentucky, 1920 (Neilan 2, Carré 4, Gaudio 4)
In Old Kentucky, 1927 (Stahl 2, Fetchit 3, Booth 4, Gibbons 4)
In Old Kentucky, 1935 (Robinson, B. 3, Rogers, W. 3)
In Old Madrid, 1911 (Pickford 3, Gaudio 4, Ince 4)
In Old Mexico, 1938 (Boyd 3, Head 4)
In Old Missouri, 1940 (Ladd 3)
In Old Monterey, 1939 (Autry 3)
In Old Oklahoma, 1943 (Wayne 3, Canutt 4, Plunkett 4)
In Old Santa Fe, 1934 (Autry 3)
In Olden Days. *See* Altri tempi, 1952
In Our Hands, 1959 (Dickinson 2)
In Peaceful Days. *See* V mirnye dni, 1950
In Person, 1935 (Brent 3, Rogers, G. 3, Berman 4, Cronjager 4, Pan 4, Polglase 4)
In Praise of Older Women, 1977 (Black 3)
In Prehistoric Days, 1913 (Griffith 2, Bitzer 4)
In Pursuit of Polly, 1918 (Burke 3)
In Search of a Sinner, 1920 (Talmadge, C. 3, Emerson 4, Loos 4)
In Search of a Thrill, 1924 (Baxter W. 3)
In Search of America, 1971 (Bridges 3, Mineo 3)
In Search of Dracula, 1971 (Lee, C. 3)
In Search of Famine. *See* Akaler Sandhane, 1980
In Search of Gregory, 1969 (Christie 3, Hurt, J. 3, Guerra 4)
In Search of the Castaways, 1962 (Disney 2, Chevalier 3, Sanders 3, Alwyn 4, Ellenshaw 4)
In Society, 1944 (Abbott and Costello 3, Lourié 4)
In Soft in a Studio, 1916 (Roach 4)
In Swift Waters, 1912 (Lawrence 3)
In the Beginning, 1975 (Lassally 4)

In the Aisles of the Wild, 1912 (Griffith 2, Carey 3, Gish, L. 3, Walthall 3, Bitzer 4)
In the Arctic Night, 1911 (Bunny 3)
In the Barber Shop. *See* Salon de coiffure, 1908
In the Big City. *See* V bolshom gorode, 1927
In the Bishop's Carriage, 1913 (Porter 2, Pickford 3)
In the Blood, 1923 (McLaglen 3)
In the Bonds of Passion. *See* Skaebnes Veje, 1913
In the Border States, 1910 (Griffith 2, Bitzer 4)
In the Candlelight, 1914 (Eason 4)
In The Clutches of a Vapor Bath, 1911 (Bunny 3)
In the Clutches of the Gang, 1914 (Sennett 2, Arbuckle 3, Normand 3)
In the Cool of the Day, 1963 (Fonda, J. 3, Lansbury 3, Houseman 4, Orry-Kelly 4)
In the Cool of the Night, 1962 (Adam 4)
In the Country, 1966 (Kramer, R. 2)
In the Course of Time. *See* Im Lauf der Zeit, 1976
In the Days of Daring, 1916 (Mix 3)
In the Days of '49, 1911 (Griffith 2, Bitzer 4)
In the Days of Gold, 1911 (Bosworth 3, Mix 3)
In the Days of Struggle. *See* V dni borbi, 1920
In the Days of the Thundering Herd, 1914 (Mix 3)
In the Days of Witchcraft, 1913 (Bosworth 3)
In the Diplomatic Service, 1916 (Bushman 3)
In the Dough, 1933 (Arbuckle 3)
In the Employ of the Secret Service. *See* Im Geheimdienst, 1931
In the Face of Demolition, 1953 (Lee, B. 3)
In the French Style, 1963 (Baker S. 3, Seberg 3, Kosma 4)
In the Glare of the Lights, 1914 (Bushman 3)
In the Good Old Summer Time, 1930 (Fleischer, M. and D. 2)
In the Good Old Summertime, 1926 (Fleischer, M. and D. 2)
In the Good Old Summertime, 1949 (Keaton 2, Garland 3, Johnson, V. 3, Minnelli 3, Nilsson 3, Sakall 3, Alton, R. 4, Goodrich and Hackett 4, Irene 4, Pasternak 4, Stradling 4)
In the Grazing Country, 1901 (Bitzer 4)
In the Grease!, 1925 (Roach 4)
In the Hands of a Pitiless Destiny. *See* V roukatch bespotchadnogo roka, 1914
In the Hands of Impostors. *See* Hvide Slavehandel II, 1911
In the Hands of the Jury, 1915 (Nilsson 3)
In the Haunts of Rip Van Winkle, 1906 (Bitzer 4)
In the Heart of a Fool, 1921 (Dwan 2, Nilsson 3)
In the Heart of the Catskills, 1906 (Bitzer 4)
In the Heat of the Night, 1967 (Ashby 2, Jewison 2, Grant, L. 3, Oates 3, Poitier 3, Steiger 3, Jones 4, Mirisch 4, Wexler 4)
In the Hollow of Her Hand, 1918 (Brady 3)
In the Jungle. *See* W dżungli, 1957
In the King of Prussia, 1982 (de Antonio 2)
In the Land of the Setting Sun, 1919 (Hersholt 3)
In the Latin Quarter, 1915 (Talmadge, C. 3)
In the Little House under Emauzy. *See* V tom domečku pod Emauzy, 1933
In the Maiden's Room. *See* Diadiouskina kvartira, 1913
In the Meantime, Darling, 1944 (Edwards 2, Preminger 2, Crain 3, Muse 3, Basevi 4)
In the Midst of the Jungle. *See* In the Midst of the Wilds, 1913
In the Midst of the Wilds, 1913 (Bosworth 3)
In the Money, 1934 (Beavers 3)
In the Moonlight, 1914 (Eason 4)
In the Mountains of Ala-Tau. *See* V gorakh Ala–Tau, 1944
In the Mountains of Yugoslavia, 1946 (Tisse 4)
In the Name of Life. *See* Vo imya zhizni, 1946
In the Name of Love, 1925 (Arlen 3, Beery 3)
In the Name of the Father. *See* Nel nome del padre, 1971
In the Name of the Fatherland. *See* Vo imya rodini, 1943
In the Name of the Italian People. *See* In nome del popolo italiano, 1972
In the Name of the Law. *See* In nome della legge, 1949
In the Navy, 1941 (Abbott and Costello 3, Howard, S. 3, Powell, D. 3)
In the Next Room, 1930 (Seitz 4)
In the Nick, 1959 (Adam 4)
In the Night. *See* In der Nacht, 1931
In the N.Y. Subway, 1903 (Bitzer 4)

In the Open, 1914 (Eason 4)
In the Outskirts of the City. *See* A város peremén, 1957
In the Palace of the King, 1923 (Bosworth 3, Johnson, N. 3, Sweet 3, Mathis 4)
In the Park, 1915 (Bacon 2, Chaplin 2, Purviance 3)
In the Power of the Ku-Klux-Klan, 1913 (Olcott 2)
In the Prime of Life. *See* Ekspeditricen, 1911
In the Purple Hills, 1915 (Eason 4)
In the Ranks, 1913 (Ince 4)
In the Realm of the Senses. *See* Ai no corrida, 1976
In the River. *See* En el rio, 1961
In the Ruins. *See* Haikyo no naka, 1923
In the Sage Brush Country, 1914 (Hart 3)
In the Sands of the Desert. *See* W piaskach pustyni, 1963
In the Season of Buds, 1910 (Griffith 2, Pickford 3, Bitzer 4)
In the Shade of the Old Apple Sauce, 1931 (Fleischer, M. and D. 2)
In the Shade of the Old Apple Tree, 1930 (Fleischer, M. and D. 2)
In the Shadow of the Pines, 1911 (Bosworth 3)
In the South China Countryside. *See* Dél-Kína tájain, 1957
In the Spring of Life. *See* I livets vår, 1912
In the Springtime of Life. *See* Na primavera da vida, 1926
In the Storm. *See* U oluji, 1952
In the Sultan's Garden, 1911 (Pickford 3, Gaudio 4, Ince 4)
In the Sultan's Power, 1909 (Bosworth 3, Selig 4)
In the Summertime. *See* Durante l'estate, 1971
In the Sweet Pie and Pie, 1941 (Three Stooges 3, Bruckman 4)
In the Tents of the Assa, 1912 (Bosworth 3)
In the Twilight, 1915 (Eason 4)
In the Villain's Power, 1917 (O'Brien 4)
In the Wake of the Bounty, 1933 (Flynn 3)
In the Watches of the Night, 1909 (Griffith 2, Pickford 3, Bitzer 4)
In the White City. *See* Dans la ville blanche, 1983
In the Window Recess, 1909 (Griffith 2, Bitzer 4)
In the Year 2000, 1912 (Guy 2)
In the Year of the Pig, 1968 (de Antonio 2)
In These Days. *See* Näinä Päivinä, 1955
In This House of Brede, 1975 (Dillon 4)
In This Our Life, 1942 (Huston 2, Astor 3, Bogart 3, Bond 3, Brent 3, Burke 3, Coburn, C. 3, Cook 3, Davis 3, De Havilland 3, Huston 3, McDaniel 3, Friedhofer 4, Haller 4, Koch 4, Orry-Kelly 4, Steiner 4, Wallis 4)
In Time with Industry. *See* Trade Tattoo, 1937
In Town Tonight, 1935 (Holloway 3)
In Trust, 1915 (Eason 4)
In 2 Minds, 1967 (Loach 2)
In una notte piena di Pioggia, 1977 (Giannini 3)
In Venice, 1933 (Terry 4)
In Walked Charley, 1932 (Roach 4)
In Which We Serve, 1942 (Lean 2, Attenborough 3, Howard, L. 3, Johnson, C. 3, Mills 3, Coward 4, Green, G. 4)
In Wrong, 1919 (Gaudio 4)
In Wrong. *See* Between Showers, 1914
Ina no Kantaro, 1943 (Hasegawa 3, Yamada 3)
Ina Song. *See* Ina-bushi, 1940
Ina-bushi, 1940 (Hayasaka 4)
Ina-bushi jinji. *See* Ina no Kantaro, 1943
Inadmissible Evidence, 1968 (Anderson 2, Moore, D. 3, Williamson 3)
Inauguration de l'Exposition universelle, 1900 (Lumière 2)
Inauguration of the Pleasure Dome, 1954 (Anger 2)
Inay, 1977 (Brocka 2)
Inazuma, 1952 (Naruse 2, Kagawa 3, Takamine 3)
Inazuma-zoshi, 1951 (Tanaka 3)
Inbad the Sailor, 1923 (Sennett 2)
Incantesimo tragico, 1951 (Brazzi 3, Félix 3, Vanel 3)
Incantevole nemica, 1953 (Keaton 2, Sordi 3, Tognazzi 3, Age and Scarpelli 4)
Incanto di mezzanotte, 1940 (Vích 4)
Ince cumali, 1967 (Guney 2)
Incendiary Blonde, 1945 (Fitzgerald 3, Hutton 3, Dreier 4, Head 4)
Incense for the Damned, 1970 (Cushing 3)
Incensurati, 1960 (De Sica 2, Tognazzi 3)
Incertaine Vocation de Médéric de Plougastel, 1966 (Braunberger 4)
Inchiesa, 1971 (Bertolucci 2)

Inchon, 1981 (Bisset 3, Mifune 3, Olivier 3, Sharif 3, Goldsmith 4)
Incident, 1967 (Ritter 3, Sheen 3)
Incident at a Corner, 1960 (Hitchcock 2)
Incident at Blood Pass. *See* Machibuse, 1970
Incident at Phantom Hill, 1966 (Duryea 3, Nugent 4, Salter 4)
Incident at Vichy, 1973 (Keach 3)
Incident in a Volcano, 1941 (Kuleshov 2)
Incident in Shanghai, 1938 (Havelock-Allan 4)
Incident on a Dark Street, 1973 (Bernstein 4)
Incidents in the Great European War, 1914 (Pearson 2)
Incognito, 1933 (Brasseur 3)
Incognito, 1958 (Constantine 3)
Income Tax, 1976 (Patel 4)
Income Tax Sappy, 1953 (Three Stooges 3)
Incompetent Hero, 1914 (Sennett 2, Arbuckle 3)
Incompreso, 1967 (Comencini 2, Quayle 3)
Inconnue d'un soir, 1948 (Dauphin 3)
Inconnue de Monte-Carlo, 1938 (Berry 3)
Inconnue de Montréal, 1950 (Kosma 4)
Inconnue des six jours, 1926 (Simon, M. 3)
Inconnus dans la maison, 1941 (Clouzot 2, Fresnay 3, Raimu 3)
Incontro, 1971 (Morricone 4)
Incorrigible, 1975 (Broca 2, Belmondo 3, Bujold 3, Audiard 4,
    Delerue 4)
Incorrigible Dukane, 1915 (Barrymore J. 3)
Incorruptible. *See* Hercule, 1937
Incredible Floridas, 1972 (Weir 2)
Incredible Invasion, 1971 (Karloff 3)
Incredible Journey, 1963 (Disney 2)
Incredible Journey of Dr. Meg Laurel, 1979 (Wyman 3, Green, G. 4)
Incredible Melting Man, 1977 (Baker 4)
Incredible Mr. Limpet, 1963 (McKimson 4)
Incredible Sarah, 1976 (Fleischer, R. 2, Jackson 3, Bernstein 4)
Incredible Shrinking Man, 1957 (Salter 4)
Incredible Shrinking Woman, 1981 (Baker 4)
Incredible Two-Headed Transplant, 1970 (Dern 3)
Incredibly Strange Creatures Who Stopped Living and Became Crazy
    Mixed-Up Zombies, 1964 (Zsigmond 4)
Incubo sulla città contaminata, 1980 (Ferrer, M. 3)
Incubus, 1965 (Hall 4)
Incubus, 1981 (Ireland 3)
Indagine su un cittadino al di sopra di ogni sospetto, 1970 (Petri 2,
    Morricone 4)
Inde fantôme, 1969 (Malle 2)
Indée d'apache, 1907 (Linders 3)
Independence, 1976 (Huston 2, Wallach 3)
Indestructible Man, 1956 (Chaney Lon, Jr. 3)
Indestructible Wife, 1919 (Brady 3)
Index Hans Richter, 1969 (Markopoulos 2)
India, 1958 (Rossellini 2)
India, 1972 (de Almeida 4)
India favolosa, 1954 (Renoir 4)
India on Parade, 1937 (Hoch 4)
India Song, 1975 (Duras 2, Seyrig 3)
India vista da Rossellini, 1958 (Rossellini 2)
Indian Adventure. *See* Indiántörténet, 1961
Indian Agent, 1948 (Cody 3, Hunt 4)
Indian and the Child, 1912 (Anderson G. 3)
Indian Brothers, 1911 (Griffith 2, Bitzer 4)
Indian Chief and the Seidlitz Powder, 1901 (Hepworth 2)
Indian Durbar, 1937–40 (Cardiff 4)
Indian Fighter, 1955 (De Toth 2, Chaney Lon, Jr. 3, Cook 3,
    Douglas, K. 3, Matthau 3, Hecht 4, Waxman 4)
Indian Friendship, 1912 (Anderson G. 3)
Indian Girl's Love, 1910 (Anderson G. 3)
Indian Jealousy, 1912 (Dwan 2)
Indian Legend, 1912 (Ince 4)
Indian Maiden's Lesson, 1911 (Anderson G. 3)
Indian Massacre, 1912 (Ince 4)
Indian Mother, 1910 (Olcott 2)
Indian Paint, 1964 (Crosby 4)
Indian Pudding, 1930 (Terry 4)
Indian Raiders, 1912 (Reid 3)

Indian Romeo and Juliet, 1912 (Reid 3)
Indian Runner's Romance, 1909 (Griffith 2, Pickford 3, Bitzer 4)
Indian Sorcerer. *See* Fakir de Singapoure, 1908
Indian Story. *See* Indiántörténet, 1961
Indian Summer, 1912 (Griffith 2, Pickford 3, Bitzer 4)
Indian Summer, 1978 (Delon 3, Giannini 3)
Indian Summer. *See* Barkhatnyi sezon, 1978
Indian Sunbeam, 1912 (Anderson G. 3)
Indian Temples, 1937–40 (Cardiff 4)
Indian Territory, 1950 (Autry 3)
Indian Tomb. *See* Indische Grabmal, 1921
Indian Trailer, 1909 (Anderson G. 3)
Indian Vestal, 1911 (Bosworth 3)
Indian Village. *See* Indisk by, 1951
Indian Wife's Devotion, 1910 (Mix 3)
Indian Youth—An Exploration, 1968 (Benegal 2)
Indiana Jones and the Temple of Doom, 1984 (Lucas 2, Spielberg 2,
    Ford, H. 3, Slocombe 4, Williams, J. 4)
Indianapolis Speedway, 1939 (Bacon 2, O'Brien, P. 3, Sheridan 3,
    Deutsch 4, Orry-Kelly 4)
Indian's Gratitude, 1913 (Ince 4)
Indian's Lament, (Johnson, N. 3)
Indian's Loyalty, 1913 (Griffith 2, Gish, L. 3, Bitzer 4)
Indian's Narrow Escape, 1915 (Anderson G. 3)
Indian's Sacrifice, 1911 (Anderson G. 3)
Indiántörténet, 1961 (Jancsó 2)
Indict and Convict, 1974 (Loy 3, Wallach 3, Goldsmith 4)
Indiens sont encore loin, 1977 (Huppert 3)
Indifferenti, 1963 (Cardinale 3, Goddard 3, Steiger 3, Winters 3,
    Cristaldi 4, D'Amico 4, Di Venanzo 4, Fusco 4)
Indio, 1939 (Armendáriz 3)
Indio Black, sai che ti dico: sei un gran figlio di . . ., 1970 (Brynner 3)
Indische Grabmal, 1921 (Lang 2, Veidt 3, Von Harbou 4)
Indische Grabmal, 1959 (Lang 2)
Indische Tuch, 1963 (Kinski 3)
Indiscreet, 1931 (McCarey 2, Swanson 3, Day 4, Newman 4, Toland 4)
Indiscreet, 1958 (Donen 2, Bergman 3, Grant, C. 3, Cahn 4, Krasna 4,
    Young, F. 4)
Indiscret, 1969 (Reichenbach 2)
Indiscretion. *See* Christmas in Connecticut, 1945
Indiscretion. *See* Stazione Termini, 1953
Indiscretion of an American Wife. *See* Stazione Termini, 1953
Indiscretion of an American Wife, 1953 (Clift 3)
Indisk by, 1951 (Sucksdorff 2)
Indiskrete Frau, 1927 (Reisch 4)
Indonesia Calling, 1946 (Ivens 2, Finch 3)
Indonesian Family. *See* Rodzina indonezyjska, 1973
Induito, 1960 (Armendáriz 3)
Industrial Britain, 1931-32 (Grierson 2)
Industrial Britain, 1933 (Flaherty 2)
Industrial Symphony. *See* Philips-Radio, 1931
Industrie de la tapisserie et du meuble sculpté, 1935 (Storck 2)
Industrie du verre, 1913 (Burel 4)
Inesorabilia, 1951 (Brazzi 3, Vanel 3)
Inevitable, 1917 (Nilsson 3)
Inez from Hollywood, 1924 (Arzner 2, Astor 3, Nilsson 3, Stone 3,
    Edeson 4)
Infamous. *See* Aereløse, 1916
Infant at Snakeville, 1911 (Anderson G. 3)
Infanzia, vocazione, e prime esperienze di Giacomo Casanova,
    veneziano, 1969 (Comencini 2, D'Amico 4, Gherardi 4)
Infatuation, 1926 (Oland 3, Rosson 4)
Infedeli, 1953 (Monicelli 2, Lollobrigida 3)
Inferior Sex, 1919 (Gaudio 4)
Infermiera, 1975 (Ponti 4)
Infernal Cake Walk. *See* Cake-walk infernal, 1903
Infernal Cauldron. *See* Chaudron infernal, 1903
Infernal Machine, 1933 (Auer 3)
Infernal Triangle, 1935 (Roach 4)
Infernal Trio. *See* Trio infernal, 1973
Inferno, 1920 (Czinner 2)
Inferno, 1953 (Ryan 3, Jeakins 4, Lemaire 4)
Inferno, 1979 (Valli 3, Argento 4)

nferno dell'amore. *See* Liebesholle, 1927
nferno des Verbrechens. *See* Dr. Mabuse, der Spieler, 1921–22
nferno—Men of the Time. *See* Dr. Mabuse, der Spieler, 1921–22
nferno—Menschen der Zeit. *See* Dr. Mabuse, der Spieler, 1921–22
nferno of First Love. *See* Haysuoki jigokuhen, 1968
nfidel, 1922 (Karloff 3, Schulberg 4)
nfideli, 1953 (Papas 3)
nfideli, 1917 (Nilsson 3)
nfidelity. *See* Altri tempi, 1952
nfidelity. *See* Amant de cinq jours, 1960
nfinity, 1977 (Popescu-Gopo 4)
nfirmière, 1914 (Gance 2)
nflation, 1927–28 (Richter 2)
nfluence of Sympathy, 1913 (Lawrence 3)
nformation, 1966 (Frampton 2)
nformation Kid. *See* Fast Companions, 1932
nformation Machine, 1957 (Bernstein 4)
nformation Please, 1940 (Gordon 3)
nformation Please, 1942 (Carradine 3)
nformation Please No. 8, 1941 (Karloff 3)
nformation Please No. 12, 1941 (Karloff 3)
nformation Received, 1963 (Roeg 2)
nformer, 1912 (Griffith 2, Barrymore L. 3, Carey 3, Gish, D. 3,
    Pickford 3, Walthall 3, Bitzer 4)
nformer, 1929 (Robison 2, Milland 3, Cardiff 4, Herlth 4, Rohrig 4)
**nformer, 1935 (Ford, J. 2, Bond 3, McLaglen 3, Meek 3, August 4,
    Guffey 4, Nichols 4, Plunkett 4, Polglase 4, Steiner 4)**
nformer. *See* Zinker, 1931
nge bliver voksen, 1954 (Roos 2)
nge Larsen, 1924 (Albers 3, Porten 3)
nge und die Millionen, 1933 (Wegener 3, Hoffmann 4)
ngeborg Holm, 1913 (Sjostrom 2, Borgstrom 3, Magnusson 4)
ngen dans på rosor. *See* I Never Promised You a Rose Garden, 1977
ngénieurs de la mer, 1952 (Delerue 4)
ngénieux Attendat, 1909 (Linders 3)
ngenjor Andrées luftfard, 1981 (Troell 2, Von Sydow 3)
ngens Mans Kvinna, 1953 (Von Sydow 3)
ngénu, 1971 (Delerue 4)
ngiusta condanna, 1952 (Brazzi 3)
ngmar Bergman, 1971 (Andersson B. 3, Gould 3)
ngmar Inheritance. *See* Ingmarsarvet, 1925
ngmarsarvet, 1925 (Molander 2, Veidt 3, Jaenzon 4, Magnusson 4)
ngmarsonerna, 1919 (Sjostrom 2, Jaenzon 4, Magnusson 4)
ngomar of the Hills, 1915 (Anderson G. 3)
ngorgo, 1979 (Comencini 2, Cardinale 3, Depardieu 3, Girardot 3,
    Mastroianni 3, Rey 3, Sordi 3, Tognazzi 3)
ngrate, 1908 (Griffith 2, Lawrence 3, Bitzer 4)
nherit the Wind, 1960 (Kramer, S. 2, Kelly, Gene 3, March 3, Tracy 3,
    Laszlo 4)
nheritance, 1963 (Burton 3, Ryan 3)
nheritance. *See* Eredità Ferramonti, 1976
nheritance. *See* Karamiai, 1962
nheritance. *See* Uncle Silas, 1947
nheritor. *See* Héritier, 1973
nheritors. *See* Os herdeiros, 1969
nhumaine, 1923 (Autant-Lara 2, Cavalcanti 2, L'Herbier 2)
nitiation à la danse des Possédés, 1949 (Rouch 2)
nitiation à la mort. *See* Magiciens, 1975
nitiation of Sarah, 1978 (Winters 3)
niwa Hachiro, 1933 (Yamada 3)
njun Trouble, 1937 (Clampett 4)
njun Trouble, 1951 (Terry 4)
njun Trouble, 1969 (McKimson 4)
nki and the Lion, 1941 (Jones 2)
nki and the Mynah Bird, 1943 (Jones 2)
nki at the Circus, 1947 (Jones 2)
nklings, 1927 (Fleischer, M. and D. 2)
nkognito, 1936 (Frohlich 3)
n-Laws, 1979 (Hiller 2, Arkin 3, Falk 3)
nmaan Dharam, 1977 (Bachchan 3)
nmates: A Love Story, 1981 (Curtis 3, Jones S. 3)
nn at Osaka. *See* Osaka no yado, 1954
nn of Evil. *See* Inochi bo ni furo, 1971

Inn of Osaka. *See* Osaka no yado, 1954
Inn of the Damned, 1974 (Anderson J. 3)
Inn of the Sixth Happiness, 1958 (Robson 2, Bergman 3, Donat 3,
    Jurgens 3, Arnold 4, Box 4, Lennart 4, Young, F. 4)
Inn Where No Man Rests. *See* Auberge du bon repos, 1903
Innamorati, 1955 (Bolognini 2, Cervi 3, Manfredi 3)
Inner and Outer Space, 1960 (Breer 2)
Inner Circle, 1912 (Griffith 2, Pickford 3, Bitzer 4)
Inner Eye, 1972 (Ray, S. 2, Datta 4)
Inner Shrine, 1917 (Bosworth 3)
Inner Voice, 1920 (Haller 4)
Innocence, 1923 (Nilsson 3)
Innocence Is Bliss. *See* Miss Grant Takes Richmond, 1949
Innocence Unprotected. *See* Nevinost bez zaštite, 1968
Innocent, 1918 (Menzies 4)
Innocent, 1921 (Rathbone 3)
Innocent. *See* Innocente, 1976
Innocent Affair. *See* Don't Trust Your Husband, 1948
Innocent Bystanders, 1972 (Andrews D. 3, Baker S. 3, Chaplin 3,
    Pleasance 3)
Innocent Grafter, 1912 (Dwan 2)
Innocent Husbands, 1925 (McCarey 2, Roach 4)
Innocent Lie, 1916 (Olcott 2)
Innocent Magdalene, 1916 (Dwan 2, Fleming 2, Gish, L. 3)
Innocent Sinner, 1917 (Sutherland 2, Walsh 2)
Innocent Sorcerers. *See* Niewinni czarodzieje, 1960
Innocent Witch. *See* Osore-zan no onna, 1964
Innocente, 1976 (Visconti 2, Giannini 3, D'Amico 4)
Innocente Casimiro, 1945 (Sordi 3)
Innocenti pagano, 1953 (Baarová 3)
Innocents, 1961 (Clayton 2, Kerr 3, Redgrave, M. 3, Auric 4, Dehn 4,
    Francis 4)
Innocents. *See* Neviňátka, 1929
Innocents aux mains sales, 1975 (Chabrol 2, Schneider 3, Steiger 3,
    Rabier 4)
Innocents in Paris, 1953 (Bloom 3, Dauphin 3, Harvey 3, Lee, C. 3,
    Rutherford 3, Sim 3, Kosma 4, Wakhévitch 4)
Innocents of Paris, 1929 (Chevalier 3, Lang 4, Vajda 4)
Innocent's Progress, 1918 (Borzage 2)
Innocents with Dirty Hands. *See* Innocents aux mains sales, 1975
Inocente, 1955 (García 3, Infante 3, Alcoriza 4)
Inocente, 1970 (García 3)
Inocentes, 1962 (Bardem 2)
Inochi aru kagiri, 1946 (Yamamura 3, Hayasaka 4)
Inochi bo ni furo, 1971 (Kobayashi 2, Takemitsu 4)
Inochi hateru hi made, 1966 (Iwashita 3)
Inochi no mando, 1944 (Hasegawa 3)
Inochi o kakeru otoko, 1958 (Hasegawa 3)
Inondation, 1923 (Cavalcanti 2, Delluc 2, Francis, E. 3)
Inquest, 1940 (Boulting 2)
Inquest. *See* Voruntersuchung, 1931
Inquilaab, 1984 (Bachchan 3)
Inquilab, 1935 (Kapoor 2)
Insaan Jag Utha, 1959 (Burman 4)
Insaf, 1937 (Biswas 4)
Insaniyat, 1954 (Anand 3)
Insatiable Bee. *See* Telhetetlen méhecske, 1958
Insaziabili, 1969 (Ireland 3, Malone 3)
Insect Woman. *See* Nippon konchuki, 1963
Insel, 1934 (Rosay 3)
Insel, 1974 (Wenders 2)
Insel der Traume, 1926 (Courant 4)
Insel der verbotenen Kusse, 1926 (Warm 4)
Insel der Verschollenen, 1921 (Gad 2)
Inserts, 1975 (Dreyfuss 3, Russell 4)
Insh'Allah, 1965 (Bates 3)
Insiang, 1976 (Brocka 2)
Inside a Girls' Dormitory. *See* Dortoir des grandes, 1953
Inside Daisy Clover, 1965 (Mulligan 2, Pakula 2, Gordon 3,
    McDowall 3, Redford 3, Wood 3, Head 4, Lang 4, Previn 4,
    Tavoularis 4)
Inside Detroit, 1955 (O'Brien, P. 3)
Inside Edges, 1975 (Emshwiller 2)

Inside Information, 1939 (Carey 3)
Inside Job, 1946 (Browning 2)
Inside Job. *See* Alpha Caper, 1973
Inside Moves, 1980 (Barry 4, Kovacs 4)
Inside Story, 1938 (Darwell 3, Miller, V. 4)
Inside Story, 1948 (Dwan 2, Lehman 4)
Inside Straight, 1950 (Chaney Lon, Jr. 3, McCambridge 3)
Inside the Gelatin Factory, 1972 (Emshwiller 2)
Inside the Lines, 1918 (Stone 3)
Inside the Lines, 1930 (Auer 3, Musuraca 4)
Inside the Third Reich, 1981 (Gielgud 3)
Inside the Underworld. *See* Storm over Lisbon, 1944
Insignificance, 1985 (Curtis 3)
Insolent, 1972 (Douy 4)
Insomnia Is Good for You, 1957 (Sellers 3)
Insomniac at the Bridge. *See* Eveillé du Pont de l'Alma, 1985
Insomnie, 1963 (Carrière 4)
Insoumis, 1964 (Delon 3, Delerue 4, Evein 4, Renoir 4)
Inspecteur aime la bagarre, 1956 (Kosma 4)
Inspecteur la Bavure, 1980 (Depardieu 3, Decaë 4)
Inspector, 1962 (Robson 2, Pleasance 3, Arnold 4)
Inspector. *See* Revisor, 1933
Inspector Calls, 1954 (Sim 3)
Inspector Clouseau, 1968 (Edwards 2, Arkin 3)
Inspector General, 1949 (Kaye 3, Lanchester 3, Green, J. 4, Kurnitz 4, Wald 4)
Inspector Goes Home. *See* Inspektor se vraća kući, 1959
Inspector Hornleigh, 1939 (Sim 3)
Inspector Hornleigh Goes to It, 1941 (Cusack 3, Sim 3)
Inspector Hornleigh on Holiday, 1939 (Sim 3, Gilliat 4)
Inspector Maigret. *See* Maigret tend un piège, 1957
Inspector Mask, 1962 (Dragić 4)
Inspektor, 1965 (Samardžić 3)
Inspektor a noc, 1963 (Danailov 3)
Inspektor se vraća kući, 1959 (Mimica 4)
Inspektorat i nošta. *See* Inspektor a noc, 1963
Inspirace, 1949 (Zeman 2)
Inspiration, 1931 (Brown 2, Garbo 3, Montgomery 3, Stone 3, Adrian 4, Daniels 4)
Inspiration. *See* Inspirace, 1949
Instant de la paix. *See* Augenblick des Friedens, 1965
Instant Sex, 1979 (Godfrey 4)
Instinct. *See* Honno, 1966
Instinct est maître, 1917 (Feyder 2)
Institute for Revenge, 1979 (Schifrin 4)
Institutional Quality, 1969 (Landow 2)
Instructional Steamer 'Red Star'. *See* Instruktorii Parokhod 'Krasnaia Zvezda', 1920
Instructive Story. *See* Shido monogatari, 1941
Instruktorii Parokhod 'Krasnaia Zvezda', 1920 (Vertov 2)
Instruments of the Orchestra, 1946 (Mathieson 4)
Insult, 1932 (Gielgud 3)
Insultin' the Sultan, 1934 (Iwerks 4)
Insulting the Sultan, 1920 (Roach 4)
Inta Habibi, 1956 (Chahine 2)
Intelektualista, 1969 (Giersz 4)
Intellectual. *See* Intelektualista, 1969
Intelligence Men, 1965 (Dillon 4)
Intelligence Service. *See* Ill Met By Moonlight, 1956
Intent to Kill, 1958 (Cardiff 4, Sangster 4)
Intentions of Murder. *See* Akai satsui, 1964
Intercourse, 1959 (Brakhage 2)
Interdit de séjour, 1953 (Piccoli 3)
Interference, 1929 (Brook 3, Powell, W. 3, Banton 4, Hunt 4)
Interim, 1952 (Brakhage 2)
Interim Balance. *See* Věrni zustaneme, 1945
Interior of a Railway Carriage, 1901 (Hepworth 2)
Interiors, 1978 (Allen 2, Keaton 3, Page 3, Rosenblum 4, Willis 4)
Interlude, 1957 (Sirk 2, Allyson 3, Brazzi 3, Rosay 3, Daniels 4, Hunter 4)
Interlude, 1968 (Sutherland 3, Werner 3, Delerue 4, Fisher 4)
Intermezzo, 1936 (Molander 2, Bergman 3)

Intermezzo, 1939 (Bergman 3, Howard, L. 3, Irene 4, Menzies 4, Selznick 4, Steiner 4, Toland 4, Westmore, M. 4, Wheeler 4)
Intermezzo, 1974 (Popescu-Gopo 4)
Intermezzo einer Ehe in sieben Tagen, 1925 (Banky 3)
Intermezzo einer Ehe in sieben Tagen. *See* Soll man heiraten?, 1925
International House, 1933 (Sutherland 2, Fields, W.C. 3, Lugosi 3, Banton 4, Haller 4)
International Lady, 1941 (Brent 3, Rathbone 3, Estabrook 4)
International Settlement, 1938 (Carradine 3, Del Rio 3, Sanders 3)
International Settlement, 1954 (Fairbanks, D. Jr. 3)
International Sneak, 1917 (Sennett 2)
International Squadron, 1941 (Reagan 3)
International Velvet, 1978 (Hopkins, A. 3, Lai 4)
Internecine Project, 1974 (Coburn, J. 3, Grant, L. 3, Wynn 3, Unsworth 4)
Interno di un convento, 1977 (Borowczyk 4)
Interns, 1962 (Robertson 3)
Interns Can't Take Money, 1937 (McCrea 3, Stanwyck 3, Dreier 4, Head 4)
Interpol, 1957 (Howard, T. 3, Mature 3, Paxton 4)
Interrupted Elopement, 1911 (Sennett 2)
Interrupted Game, 1911 (Sennett 2)
Interrupted Journey, 1949 (Havelock-Allan 4)
Interrupted Melody, 1955 (Ford, G. 3, Moore, R. 3, Deutsch 4, Levien 4, Rose 4, Ruttenberg 4)
Interrupted Message, 1900 (Bitzer 4)
Interrupted Picnic, 1898 (Hepworth 2)
Interrupted Solitude, 1974 (Emshwiller 2)
Interval, 1973 (Oberon 3, Figueroa 4)
Intervention in the Far East. *See* Volochayevskiye dni, 1937
Interview, 1971 (Sen 2)
Interview with Joseph Welch, 1954 (Van Dyke, W. 2)
Interview with President Allende, 1971 (Wexler 4)
Interviews with My Lai Veterans, 1970 (Strick 2, Wexler 4)
Intimate Dream. *See* Hazukashii yume, 1927
Intimate Interview, 1930 (Cagney 3)
Intimate Lighting. *See* Intimni osvetleni, 1965
Intimate Moments. *See* Madame Claude 2, 1981
Intimate Stranger, 1956 (Losey 2, Koch 4)
Intimate Strangers, 1977 (Douglas, M. 3)
Intimate Strangers, 1985 (Keach 3, Taylor, E. 3)
Intimita proibite di una giovane sposa, 1970 (Brazzi 3)
Intimní osvětlení, 1965 (Passer 2, Ondricek 4)
Into Her Kingdom, 1926 (Wilson, C. 4)
Into the Blue, 1951 (Wilcox 2)
Into the Desert, 1912 (Cruze 2)
Into the Light. *See* Wise Guy, 1926
Into the Net, 1924 (Bennett C. 3)
Into the Night, 1985 (Papas 3)
Into Thin Air, 1985 (Burstyn 3)
Into Your Dance, 1935 (Freleng 4)
Intoccabili, 1968 (Cassavetes 2, Falk 3, Rowlands 3, Morricone 4)
Intolerance, 1916 (Browning 2, Griffith 2, Van Dyke, W.S. 2, Von Stroheim 2, Crisp 3, Fairbanks, D. 3, Gish, L. 3, Johnson, N. 3, Love 3, Marsh 3, Talmadge, C. 3, Bitzer 4, Brown, K. 4, Loos 4)
Intrepid Davy, 1911 (Bunny 3)
Intrepid Mr. Twigg, 1968 (Francis 4)
Intriguantes, 1954 (Moreau 3)
Intrigue, 1948 (Raft 3)
Intrigue, 1964 (Brazzi 3)
Intrigue and Love. *See* Úklady a láska, 1972
Intriguen der Madame de la Pommeraye, 1921 (Herlth 4, Hoffmann 4, Rohrig 4)
Introducing Audrey Hepburn, 1953 (Hepburn, A. 3)
Introducing the Dial, 1935 (Grierson 2)
Introduction to Feedback, 1960 (Bernstein 4)
Introduction to the Enemy, 1974 (Fonda, J. 3, Wexler 4)
Intruder, 1913 (Costello, M. 3)
Intruder, 1914 (Reid 3)
Intruder, 1933 (Auer 3)
Intruder, 1953 (Hawkins 3, Adam 4, Mathieson 4)
Intruder, 1961 (Corman 4)
Intruder. *See* Invader, 1935

Intruder in the Dust, 1949 (Brown 2, Deutsch 4, Maddow 4, Surtees 4)
Intruders, 1947 (Terry 4)
Intruders, 1970 (Ford, H. 3, O'Brien, E. 3)
Intrusa, 1955 (Delli Colli 4)
Intruse, 1913 (Feuillade 2)
Intrusion at Lompoc, 1912 (Dwan 2)
Inubue, 1978 (Yamamura 3)
Inugami Family. See Inugami-ke no ichizoku, 1976
Inugami-ke no ichizoku, 1976 (Ichikawa 2, Kishida 3)
Inundados, 1961 (Birri 2)
Invader, 1935 (Keaton 2, Spiegel 4)
Invaders, 1912 (Ince 4, Sullivan 4)
Invaders, 1942 (Lean 2, Walbrook 3)
Invaders. See 49th Parallel, 1941
Invaders from Mars, 1953 (Leven 4, Menzies 4, Seitz 4)
Invaders from Mars, 1986 (Golan and Globus 4)
Invasion, 1970 (Allégret, Y. 2, Piccoli 3)
Invasion. See Tatárjárás, 1917
Invasion of the Animal People, 1962 (Carradine 3)
Invasion of the Astros. See Kaiju daisenso, 1966
Invasion of the Astro-Monsters. See Kaiju daisenso, 1966
Invasion of the Body Snatchers, 1956 (Peckinpah 2, Siegel 2, Wanger 4)
Invasion of the Body Snatchers, 1978 (Siegel 2, Duvall, R. 3, Sutherland 3)
Invasion of the Body Stealers. See Body Stealers, 1969
Invasion pacifique. See Québec-USA, 1962
Invasion 1700. See Col ferro e col fuoco, 1964
Invasion U.S.A., 1985 (Golan and Globus 4)
Invasore, 1943 (Rossellini 2)
Inventiamo l'amore, 1938 (Cervi 3)
Invention for Destruction. See Vynález zkázy, 1958
Inventive Love. See Elskovs Opfindsomhed, 1913
Inventor. See Erfinder, 1980
Inventor of Shoes. See Izumitelj cipela, 1967
Inventor's Secret, 1911 (Sennett 2)
Invenzione di Morel, 1974 (Karina 3)
Investigation of a Citizen above Suspicion. See Indagine su un cittadino al di sopra di ogni sospetto, 1970
Investigation of Murder. See Laughing Policeman, 1973
Inviati speciali, 1943 (Flaiano 4)
Invincibili sette, 1964 (Guerra 4)
Invincible, 1943 (Gerasimov 2)
Invincible. See Njepobedimye, 1943
Invincible Bad Names. See Akumyo muteki, 1965
Invincible Six, 1970 (Jurgens 3)
Invincible Six. See Heroes, 1970
Invisible Agent, 1942 (Basserman 3, Hardwicke 3, Lorre 3, Salter 4, Siodmak 4)
Invisible Avenger, 1958 (Howe 4)
Invisible Enemy, 1931 (Buchanan 3)
Invisible Enemy. See Neviditelní nepřátelé, 1950
Invisible Fluid, 1908 (Bitzer 4)
Invisible Ghost, 1941 (Lugosi 3, Muse 3, Katzman 4)
Invisible Ink, 1921 (Fleischer, M. and D. 2)
Invisible Invaders, 1959 (Carradine 3)
Invisible Man, 1933 (Whale 2, Carradine 3, Rains 3, Edeson 4, Fulton 4, Laemmle 4, Pierce 4)
Invisible Man, 1975 (Cooper, J 3)
Invisible Man. See Nevidimi chelovek, 1935
Invisible Man. See Tomei ningen, 1954
Invisible Man Returns, 1940 (Hardwicke 3, Price 3, Fulton 4, Krasner 4, Salter 4, Siodmak 4)
Invisible Man's Revenge, 1944 (Carradine 3, Fulton 4, Krasner 4, Salter 4)
Invisible Menace, 1938 (Karloff 3)
Invisible Mouse, 1947 (Hanna and Barbera 4)
Invisible Moustache of Raoul Dufy, 1954–55 (Peterson 2)
Invisible Opponent. See Unsichtbare Gegner, 1933
Invisible Power, 1921 (Gibbons 4)
Invisible Power. See Washington Merry-Go-Round, 1932
Invisible Ray, 1936 (Bondi 3, Karloff 3, Lugosi 3, D'Agostino 4, Fulton 4, Waxman 4)

Invisible Stripes, 1940 (Bacon 2, Bogart 3, Holden 3, Raft 3, Haller 4, Wallis 4)
Invisible Wall, 1947 (Chandler 3)
Invisible Wall. See Osynliga muren, 1944
Invisible Woman, 1941 (Sutherland 2, Barrymore J. 3, Homolka 3, Howard, S. 3, Fulton 4, Siodmak 4)
Invitata, 1969 (Piccoli 3)
Invitation, 1952 (Calhern 3, Johnson, V. 3, Kaper 4, Rose 4)
Invitation, 1973 (Goretta 2)
Invitation à la chasse, 1974 (Von Trotta 2, Gégauff 4)
Invitation au voyage, 1927 (Dulac 2)
Invitation to a Gunfighter, 1964 (Kramer, S. 2, Brynner 3, Martin, S. 3, Segal 3, Raksin 4)
Invitation to a Wedding, 1982 (Gielgud 3)
Invitation to Happiness, 1939 (Ruggles 2, Dunne 3, MacMurray 3, Dreier 4, Head 4)
Invitation to Monte Carlo, 1959 (Sinatra 3)
Invitation to the Dance, 1956 (Charisse 3, Kelly, Gene 3, Freed 4, Hanna and Barbera 4, Ibert 4, Junge 4, Previn 4, Ruttenberg 4, Young, F. 4)
Invitation to the Inside. See Zaproszenie do wnetrza, 1978
Invitation to the Wedding, 1983 (Young, F. 4)
Invité de la 11e, 1945 (Wakhévitch 4)
Invité du Mardi, 1949 (Blier 3)
Invite Monsieur à dîner, 1932 (Autant-Lara 2)
Invitée, 1969 (Guerra 4)
Invocation of My Demon Brother, 1969 (Anger 2)
Io amo, tu ami, 1961 (Blasetti 2, De Laurentiis 4)
Io e Caterina, 1980 (Sordi 3)
Io, io, io . . . e gli altri, 1966 (Blasetti 2, De Sica 2, Lollobrigida 3, Manfredi 3, Mangano 3, Mastroianni 3, Age and Scarpelli 4, D'Amico 4, Flaiano 4)
Io la conoscevo bene, 1965 (Scola 2, Manfredi 3, Tognazzi 3, Salter 4)
Io non vedo, tu non parli, lui non sente, 1971 (De Sica 2)
Io piaccio, 1955 (Fabrizi 3)
Io so che tu sai che io so, 1982 (Sordi 3, Vitti 3)
Io sono il Capataz!, 1950 (Loren 3, Delli Colli 4)
Io uccido, tu uccidi, 1965 (Trintignant 3)
Iola's Promise, 1912 (Griffith 2, Pickford 3, Bitzer 4)
Iolanda la figlia del corsaro nero, 1951 (Gherardi 4)
Ipcress File, 1965 (Caine 3, Adam 4, Barry 4)
Iphigenia, 1977 (Papas 3, Theodorakis 4)
Ipotesi, 1970 (Petri 2)
Ippocampo, 1943 (De Sica 2, Baarová 3, Zavattini 4)
Ippodromi all'Alba, 1950 (Blasetti 2)
Ippon-gatana dohyo-iri, 1934 (Kinugasa 2, Hasegawa 3)
Ippon-gatana dohyo-iri, 1960 (Hasegawa 3)
Ire a Santiago, 1964 (Gomez, S. 2)
Ireland or Bust, 1932 (Terry 4)
Ireland the Oppressed, 1912 (Olcott 2)
Ireland, The Tear and the Smile, 1960 (Van Dyke, W. 2)
Ireland's Martyr, 1915 (Olcott 2)
Irene, 1926 (Leroy 2, Moore, C. 3, Mathis 4, McCord 4)
Irene, 1940 (Wilcox 2, Burke 3, Milland 3, Neagle 3)
Irene, Irene, 1976 (Cuny 3)
Irene's Infatuation, 1912 (Bunny 3)
Irezumi, 1966 (Miyagawa 4)
Irezumi chohan, 1936 (Shimura 3)
Irezumi hangan, 1933 (Hasegawa 3)
Irezumi hangan: Hyaku-san kiki no maki, 1933 (Hasegawa 3)
Irezumi hangan: Kanketsu-hen, 1933 (Hasegawa 3)
Irgendwo in Berlin, 1946 (Rasp 3)
Iris, 1915 (Hepworth 2)
Iris and the Lieutenant. See Iris och lojtnantshjarta, 1946
Iris och lojtnantshjarta, 1946 (Sjoberg 2, Zetterling 2)
Irish Eyes Are Smiling, 1944 (Quinn 3, Newman 4, Pan 4)
Irish Girl's Love, 1912 (Olcott 2)
Irish Hearts, 1927 (Meredyth 4, Miller, V. 4, Zanuck 4)
Irish Honeymoon, 1911 (Olcott 2)
Irish in America, 1915 (Olcott 2)
Irish in Us, 1935 (Bacon 2, Cagney 3, De Havilland 3, O'Brien, P. 3, Barnes 4, Orry-Kelly 4)
Irish Luck, 1925 (Heerman 4)

Irish Stew, 1930 (Terry 4)
Irish Sweepstakes, 1934 (Terry 4)
Irma La Douce, 1963 (Wilder 2, Caan 3, Lemmon 3, MacLaine 3, Diamond 4, La Shelle 4, Mandell 4, Orry-Kelly 4, Previn 4, Trauner 4, Westmore, F. 4)
Irma la voyante, 1945 (Fernandel 3)
Iron and Steel, 1914 (Costello, M. 3)
Iron Claw, 1916 (White 3)
Iron Crown. See Corona di ferro, 1941
Iron Curtain, 1948 (Wellman 2, Andrews D. 3, Tierney 3, Clarke, C.C. 4, Lemaire 4, Newman 4, Wheeler 4)
Iron Duke, 1934 (Saville 2, Arliss 3, Cooper, Gladys 3, Balcon 4, Courant 4, Junge 4)
Iron Gate. See Bab el Haded, 1958
Iron Glove, 1954 (Katzman 4)
Iron Hand, 1916 (Bosworth 3)
Iron Heart, 1917 (Grot 4, Miller, A. 4)
Iron Heel, 1912 (Bushman 3)
Iron Horse, 1924 (Ford, J. 2, Cody 3)
Iron Maiden, 1963 (Dillon 4)
Iron Major, 1943 (O'Brien, P. 3, Ryan 3)
Iron Man, 1931 (Browning 2, Ayres 3, Harlow 3)
Iron Man, 1951 (Chandler 3, Hudson 3, Boyle 4, Chase 4)
Iron Mask, 1929 (Dwan 2, Fairbanks, D. 3, Carré 4, Menzies 4)
Iron Mask, 1954 (Fairbanks, D. Jr. 3)
Iron Master, 1913 (August 4)
Iron Mistress, 1952 (Ladd 3, Mayo 3, Blanke 4, Seitz 4, Steiner 4)
Iron Nag, 1925 (Sennett 2)
Iron Petticoat, 1956 (Hepburn, K. 3, Hope 3, Dillon 4, Hecht 4)
Iron Rider, 1920 (Furthman 4)
Iron Ring. See Kanawa, 1972
Iron Road, 1925 (Barrymore L. 3)
Iron Road, 1943 (Cobb 3)
Iron Sheriff, 1957 (Hayden 3)
Iron Strain, 1915 (August 4, Ince 4, Sullivan 4)
Iron Trail, 1921 (Haller 4)
Iron-Carrier. See Jarnbararen, 1911
Ironside, 1967 (Jones 4)
Irony of Fate, 1910 (Lawrence 3)
Iro-zange, 1956 (Mori 3, Tanaka 3)
Irrashaimase, 1955 (Kagawa 3)
Irreconcilable Differences, 1984 (Fraker 4)
Irrende Seelen, 1920 (Herlth 4, Rohrig 4)
Irrende Seelen. See Sklaven der Sinne, 1921
Irrepressible Brightness of Spring, 1948 (Zhao 3)
Irresistible. See Belle ma povere, 1957
Irresistible Lover, 1927 (Laemmle 4)
Irresistible Man. See Unwiderstehliche, 1937
Irrfahrt ins Gluck, 1914 (Hoffmann 4)
Irrgarten der Leidenschaft. See Pleasure Garden, 1926
Irrungen, 1918 (Porten 3)
Irrwege der Liebe, 1918 (Albers 3)
Is, 1970 (Fischer 4)
Is Everybody Happy?, 1928 (Roach 4)
Is Life Worth Living?, 1921 (Crosland 2)
Is Marriage the Bunk?, 1925 (McCarey 2, Hardy 3, Roach 4)
Is Matrimony a Failure?, 1922 (Cruze 2, Menjou 3, Pitts 3, Brown, K. 4)
Is My Face Red, 1932 (Muse 3, Pitts 3, Krasner 4, Robinson 4, Steiner 4)
Is My Palm Read, 1931 (Fleischer, M. and D. 2)
Is Paris Burning?, 1966 (Coppola 2, Welles 2, Boyer 3)
Is Paris Burning?. See Paris brûle-t-il?, 1966
Is There Justice?, 1931 (Walthall 3)
Is There Sex After Death, 1971 (Henry 4)
Is This a Record?, 1973 (Godfrey 4)
Is This Trip Really Necessary?. See Blood of the Iron Maiden, 1970
Is Zat So?, 1927 (Fairbanks, D. Jr. 3)
Isabel, 1968 (Bujold 3)
Isabelle, 1951 (Kosma 4)
Isabelle devant le désir, 1974 (Decaë 4)
Isadora, 1968 (Reisz 2, Love 3, Redgrave, V. 3, Robards 3, Jarre 4)
Isadora Duncan, The Biggest Dancer in the World, 1966 (Russell 2)

Ise ondo, 1929 (Hasegawa 3)
Isen brydes, 1947 (Roos 2)
Ishi, The Last of His Tribe, 1978 (Jarre 4, Trumbo 4)
Ishi-gassen, 1955 (Yamada 3)
Ishii Tsuneemon, 1934 (Hasegawa 3)
Ishimatsu of Mori. See Mori no Ishimatsu, 1949
Ishimatsu of the Forest. See Mori no Ishimatsu, 1949
Ishin no uta, 1938 (Yoda 4)
Ishinaka sensei gyojoki, 1949 (Naruse 2)
Ishinaka-sensei gyojoki datsugoko, 1950 (Mifune 3)
Ishq, Ishq, Ishq, 1974 (Anand 3, Azmi 3)
Ishq par Zor Nahin, 1970 (Burman 4)
Isidore a la deveine, 1919 (Florey 2)
Isidore sur le lac, 1919 (Florey 2)
I-ski Love-ski You-ski, 1936 (Fleischer, M. and D. 2)
Iskindria . . . Leh?, 1978 (Chahine 2)
Isla de la pasión, 1941 (Fernández 2, Armendáriz 3)
Isla de mujeres, 1952 (Alcoriza 4)
Isla del tesoro, 1969 (Gomez, S. 2)
Isla misteriosa. See Mysterious Island, 1973
Isla para dos, 1958 (Figueroa 4)
Island, 1976 (Hurt, J. 3)
Island, 1980 (Ritchie 2, Caine 3, Decaë 4, Morricone 4)
Island. See Hadaka no shima, 1960
Island. See Ile au trésor, 1985
Island. See On, 1966
Island at the Top of the World, 1973 (Ellenshaw 4, Jarre 4)
Island in the Sky, 1938 (Cronjager 4)
Island in the Sky, 1953 (Wellman 2, Wayne 3, Basevi 4, Clothier 4, Friedhofer 4)
Island in the Sun, 1957 (Rossen 2, Dandridge 3, Fontaine 3, Mason 3, Arnold 4, Young, F. 4, Zanuck 4)
Island of Desire, 1952 (Darnell 3)
Island of Despair. See 99 mujeres, 1969
Island of Doomed Men, 1940 (Lorre 3)
Island of Dr. Moreau, 1977 (Lancaster 3, York, M. 3, Fisher 4)
Island of Dr. Moreau. See Island of Lost Souls, 1933
Island of Horrors. See Gokumon-to, 1977
Island of Lost Men, 1939 (Crawford, B. 3, Quinn 3, Wong 3, Head 4, Raine 4, Struss 4)
Island of Lost Souls, 1933 (Arlen 3, Laughton 3, Lugosi 3, Scott, R. 3, Struss 4, Young, W. 4)
Island of Lost Women, 1959 (Seitz 4)
Island of Lost Women. See 99 mujeres, 1969
Island of Love, 1963 (Matthau 3, Preston 3, Duning 4, Stradling 4)
Island of Mutations. See Isola degli uomini pesci, 1979
Island of Naked Scandal. See Shima to ratai jiken, 1931
Island of Silver Herons. See Ostrov stříbrných volavek, 1976
Island of Terror, 1966 (Fisher 2, Cushing 3)
Island of the Blue Dolphins, 1964 (Kennedy, G. 3, Whitlock 4)
Island of the Burning Damned. See Night of the Big Heat, 1967
Island of Treasure, 1965 (Welles 2)
Island Rescue. See Appointment with Venus, 1951
Island Unknown, 1971 (Quayle 3)
Islands in the Stream, 1977 (Schaffner 2, Bloom 3, Scott, G. 3, Goldsmith 4)
Islas Marías, 1950 (Fernández 2, Infante 3, Figueroa 4)
Isle of Conquest, 1919 (Talmadge, N. 3, Emerson 4, Loos 4)
Isle of Escape, 1930 (Johnson, N. 3, Loy 3)
Isle of Forgotten Sins, 1943 (Ulmer 2, Carradine 3)
Isle of Forgotten Women, 1927 (Walker 4)
Isle of Fury, 1936 (Bogart 3, Orry-Kelly 4)
Isle of Lost Ships, 1923 (Tourneur, M. 2, Nilsson 3)
Isle of Lost Ships, 1929 (Polito 4)
Isle of Lost Women. See 99 mujeres, 1969
Isle of Missing Men, 1942 (Oswald 2)
Isle of Missing Men. See Devil's Pipeline, 1940
Isle of Pingo Pongo, 1938 (Avery 2)
Isle of Retribution, 1926 (McLaglen 3)
Isle of the Dead, 1945 (Robson 2, Karloff 3, D'Agostino 4, Lewton 4)
Isle of the Lion. See Oroszlán ugrani készul, 1969
Isle of the Snake People, 1970 (Karloff 3)
Isn't It Romantic?, 1948 (McLeod 2, Lake 3, Dreier 4, Head 4)

It's a Big Country, 1951 (Brown 2, Sturges, J. 2, Vidor, C. 2, Wellman 2, Barrymore E. 3, Calhern 3, Cooper, Gary 3, Kelly, Gene 3, Johnson, V. 3, Leigh, J. 3, March 3, Powell, W. 3, Sakall 3, Stone 3, Wynn 3, Alton, J. 4, Kaper 4, Lennart 4, Raksin 4, Schary 4)

It's a Boy, 1918 (Fazenda 3)

It's a Boy, 1920 (Sennett 2)

It's a Boy, 1923 (Roach 4)

It's a Boy, 1933 (Horton 3, Balcon 4)

It's a Cinch, 1932 (Arbuckle 3)

It's a Date, 1940 (Durbin 3, Francis, K. 3, Pidgeon 3, Sakall 3, Krasna 4, Pasternak 4)

It's a Dog's Life, 1955 (Gwenn 3, Bernstein 4, Hayes 4)

It's a Dog's Life. See Vita di cani, 1950

It's a Funny, Funny World, 1978 (Golan and Globus 4)

It's a Gift, 1923 (Roach 4)

It's a Gift, 1934 (McLeod 2, Fields, W.C. 3, Dreier 4, Schulberg 4)

It's a Good Day, 1969 (Fields 4)

It's a Grand Old Nag, 1947 (Clampett 4)

It's A Great Feeling, 1949 (Cooper, Gary 3, Crawford, J. 3, Day 3, Flynn 3, Greenstreet 3, Kaye 3, Neal 3, Reagan 3, Robinson, E. 3, Sakall 3, Wyman 3, Cahn 4, Diamond 4, Prinz 4)

It's a Great Life, 1929 (Wood 2, Gibbons 4)

It's a Great Life. See Toller hecht auf krummer tour, 1962

It's a Hap-hap-happy Day, 1941 (Fleischer, M. and D. 2)

It's a Hard Life, 1919 (Roach 4)

It's a Joke, Son, 1947 (Merkel 3)

It's a Mad, Mad, Mad, Mad World, 1963 (Smith, D. , Keaton 2, Kramer, S. 2, Lewis 2, Brown 3, Durante 3, Falk 3, Horton 3, Pitts 3, Rooney 3, Three Stooges 3, Tracy 3, Dunn 4, Edouart 4, Laszlo 4, O'Brien 4)

It's a Pleasure, 1945 (Henie 3)

It's a Small World, 1935 (Tracy 3, La Shelle 4, Miller, A. 4)

It's a Small World, 1950 (Struss 4)

It's a 2ft 6in above the Ground World, 1972 (Godfrey 4)

It's a Wild Life, 1918 (Daniels 3, Lloyd 3, Roach 4)

It's a Wise Child, 1931 (Davies 3, Booth 4)

It's a Wonderful Life, 1946 (Capra 2, Barrymore L. 3, Bond 3, Bondi 3, Grahame 3, Reed, D. 3, Stewart 3, Biroc 4, Goodrich and Hackett 4, Hornbeck 4, Swerling 4, Tiomkin 4, Walker 4)

It's a Wonderful World, 1939 (Van Dyke, W.S. 2, Colbert 3, Stewart 3, Adrian 4, Hecht 4, Mankiewicz 4)

It's Alive, 1974 (Baker 4, Herrmann 4)

It's All in the Stars, 1946 (Terry 4)

It's All True, 1942 (Welles 2)

It's All Yours, 1938 (Auer 3, Carroll M. 3)

It's Always Fair Weather, 1955 (Donen 2, Charisse 3, Dailey 3, Kelly, Gene 3, Comden and Green 4, Freed 4, Kidd 4, Previn 4, Rose 4)

It's Always Now, 1965 (Allen, D. 4)

It's Always Sunday, 1955 (Dwan 2)

It's Because of Good Weather. See Youki no seidayo, 1932

It's Better to Pull at the Same End. See Ve dvou se to lépe táhne, 1928

It's Easy to Remember, 1935 (Fleischer, M. and D. 2)

It's Forever Springtime. See E primavera, 1950

It's Good to Be Alive, 1974 (Gossett 3, Legrand 4)

It's Great to Be Alive, 1933 (Friedhofer 4)

It's Great to Be Crazy, 1918 (Laurel 3)

It's Great to Be Young, 1956 (Mills 3, Addison 4)

It's Him, Yes! Yes!,. See Era lui, si! si!, 1951

It's Hot in Hell. See Singe en hiver, 1962

It's Hummer Time, 1950 (McKimson 4)

It's In the Air, 1935 (Merkel 3)

It's in the Air, 1938 (Dearden 2, Formby 3, Dean 4)

It's in the Bag, 1945 (Ameche 3, Bendix 3, Carradine 3, Reville 4, Ryskind 4)

It's in the Bag. See Affaire est dans le sac, 1932

It's Love Again, 1936 (Saville 2, Matthews 3, Young, R. 3, Balcon 4, Junge 4)

It's Love I'm After, 1937 (Davis 3, De Havilland 3, Howard, L. 3, Orry-Kelly 4, Robinson 4, Wallis 4)

It's Magic. See Romance on the High Seas, 1948

It's Morning. See Už je ráno, 1956

It's My Model. See Det ar min modell, 1946

It's My Turn, 1980 (Clayburgh 3, Allen, J. 4)

It's Never Too Late. See Är aldrig for sent, 1956

It's Nice to Have a Mouse Around the House, 1964 (Freleng 4)

It's No Laughing Matter, 1914 (Weber 2, Bosworth 3, Marion 4)

It's Not Just You, Murray, 1964 (Scorsese 2)

It's Not the Size That Counts. See Percy's Progress, 1974

It's Nothing, Only a Game. See No es nada mama, solo un juego, 1973

It's Only Money, 1962 (Lewis 2, Tashlin 2, Head 4)

It's Pink But Is It Mink?, 1975 (McKimson 4)

It's the Cat's, 1926 (Fleischer, M. and D. 2)

It's the Natural Thing to Do, 1939 (Fleischer, M. and D. 2)

It's the Old Army Game, 1926 (Sutherland 2, Brooks 3, Fields, W.C. 3)

It's Tough to Be Famous, 1932 (Beavers 3, Fairbanks, D. Jr. 3, Polito 4)

It's Trad, Dad, 1962 (Lester 2)

It's Up to You, 1941 (Kazan 2)

Itsuwareru seiso, 1950 (Yoshimura 2, Kyo 3, Shindo 3)

Itto, 1934 (Benoit-Lévy 2)

Itto d'Afrique, 1934 (Clouzot 2)

Ittouryu shinan, 1936 (Miyagawa 4)

Iumoreski, 1924 (Vertov 2)

Ivan, 1932 (Dovzhenko 2)

Ivan Franko, 1956 (Bondarchuk 3)

Ivan Grozny, 1944 (Eisenstein 2, Pudovkin 2, Cherkassov 3, Moskvin 4, Prokofiev 4, Tisse 4)

Ivan Grozny II: Boyarskii Zagovor, 1958 (Eisenstein 2, Cherkassov 3, Moskvin 4, Prokofiev 4, Tisse 4)

Ivan, il figlio del diavolo bianco, 1953 (Age and Scarpelli 4)

Ivan Kondarev, 1973 (Paskaleva 3)

Ivan Kondarev. See Jménem Zivota, 1973

Ivan Rybakov, 1961 (Babochkin 3)

Ivan the Terrible, Part I. See Ivan Grozny, 1944

Ivan the Terrible, Part II: The Boyars' Plot. See Ivan Grozny II: Boyarskii Zagovor, 1958

Ivanhoe, 1913 (Brenon 2)

Ivanhoe, 1952 (Fontaine 3, Sanders 3, Taylor, E. 3, Taylor, R. 3, Canutt 4, Junge 4, Rozsa 4, Young, F. 4)

Ivanhoe, 1982 (Mason 3)

Ivanovo detstvo, 1962 (Tarkovsky 2)

Ivan's Childhood. See Ivanovo detstvo, 1962

I've Always Loved You, 1946 (Borzage 2, Ouspenskaya 3, Chase 4, Gaudio 4)

I've Got Rings on My Fingers, 1929 (Fleischer, M. and D. 2)

I've Got Your Number, 1934 (Beavers 3, Blondell 3, O'Brien, P. 3, Orry-Kelly 4)

Ivica i Marica, 1979 (Grgić 4)

Ivonne, 1915 (Bertini 3)

Ivory Ape, 1980 (Palance 3)

Ivory Hunter. See Where No Vultures Fly, 1951

Ivory Snuff Box, 1915 (Tourneur, M. 2, Carré 4)

Ivy, 1947 (Wood 2, Fontaine 3, Hardwicke 3, Marshall 3, Bennett 4, Menzies 4, Orry-Kelly 4)

Ivy and John, 1965 (Warhol 2)

Iwan Koschula, 1914 (Oswald 2)

Iwashigumo, 1958 (Naruse 2, Tsukasa 3)

Iz Lebiazhego soobshchaiut, 1960 (Shukshin 3)

Izakaya Chouji, 1983 (Muraki 4)

Izin, 1975 (Guney 2)

Izo no odoriko, 1967 (Takemitsu 4)

Izotöpok a gyogyászatban, 1959 (Jancsó 2)

Izu no musumetachi, 1945 (Gosho 2)

Izu no odoriko, 1933 (Gosho 2, Tanaka 3)

Izumi, 1956 (Kobayashi 2)

Izumitelj cipela, 1967 (Grgić 4)

Izvrnuta priča, 1972 (Grgić 4)

Izzy and His Rival. See Billy's Rival, 1914

Izzy and Moe, 1985 (Cooper, J 3)

J

Jailed, 1916 (Roach 4)
Jailed and Bailed, 1923 (Roach 4)
Jailhouse Rock, 1957 (Presley 3, Berman 4)
J'aime toutes les femmes, 1935 (Darrieux 3)
Jajauma narashi, 1966 (Muraki 4)
Jaje, 1959 (Mimica 4)
Jaje, 1973 (Grgić 4)
Jak być kochana, 1962 (Cybulski 3)
Jak daleko stad, jak blisko, 1971 (Komorowska 3, Konwicki 4)
Jak je svět zařízen, 1956 (Hofman 4)
Jak jsem ukradl milioń, 1966 (Hrušínský 3)
Jak na to, 1963 (Brdečka 4)
Jak napálit advokáta, 1980 (Kopecký 3)
Jak pejsek a kočička myli podlahu, 1950 (Hofman 4)
Jak pejsek a kočičkou psali psaní, 1954 (Hofman 4)
Jak pejsek s kočičkou dělali dort, 1951 (Hofman 4)
Jak se člověk naučil létat, 1958 (Brdečka 4)
Jak se moudrý Aristoteles stal jěstě moudřejšim, 1970 (Brdečka 4)
Jak si pejsek roztrhl kalhoty, 1951 (Hofman 4)
Jak stařeček měnil až vyměnil, 1953 (Trnka 2)
Jak zařídit byt, 1959 (Brdečka 4, Pojar 4)
Jako yashiki, 1955 (Hasegawa 3)
Jakob der Lugner, 1975 (Brodský 3, Geschonneck 3, Mueller-Stahl 3)
Jako-man to Tetsu, 1948 (Shindo 3)
Jal, 1952 (Anand 3)
Jali Note, 1960 (Anand 3)
Jalisco canta en Sevilla, 1948 (De Fuentes 2, Negrete 3)
Jalisco nunca pierde, 1937 (Armendáriz 3, Figueroa 4)
Jalna, 1935 (Cromwell 2, Bruce 3, Cronjager 4, Fort 4, MacGowan 4, Plunkett 4, Polglase 4, Veiller 4)
Jalousie, 1975 (Baye 3, Legrand 4)
Jalousie du barbouillé, 1928 (Cavalcanti 2)
Jalsaghar, 1958 (Ray, S. 2, Chandragupta 4, Datta 4, Mitra 4)
Jalti Nishani, 1957 (Biswas 4)
Jam Session, 1944 (Donen 2, Miller 3, Muse 3, Cahn 4)
Jamaica Inn, 1939 (Hamer 2, Hitchcock 2, Laughton 3, O'Hara 3, Gilliat 4, Harrison 4, Pommer 4, Reville 4, Stradling 4)
Jamaica Run, 1953 (Milland 3, Muse 3, Head 4)
Jamais plus toujours, 1975 (Delerue 4)
Jambon d'Ardenne, 1977 (Girardot 3)
Jambul, 1952 (Enei 4)
James Brothers. See True Story of Jesse James, 1957
James Dean Story, 1957 (Altman 2)
James Dean—The First American Teenager, 1975 (Baker C. 3, Caron 3, Hopper 3, Keach 3)
James Wong Howe, 1974 (Lancaster 3)
Jamestown Baloos, 1957 (Breer 2)
Jamestown Exposition, 1907 (Bitzer 4)
Jammin' the Blues, 1944 (Cole 4)
Jamuna, 1949 (Anand 3)
Jan Hus, 1955 (Trnka 2, Hrušínský 3, Kopecký 3)
Jan Knukke's Wedding. See Zhenitba Jana Knukke, 1934
Jan Konstantin, 1961 (Schorm 2)
Jan Roháč z Dubé, 1946 (Kopecký 3, Stallich 4)
Jan Žižka, 1956 (Trnka 2, Hrušínský 3, Kopecký 3)
Jana Aranya, 1975 (Ray, S. 2, Datta 4)
Jane and the Stranger, 1910 (Lawrence 3)
Jane Austen in Manhattan, 1980 (Ivory 2, Baxter A. 3, Jhabvala 4)
Jane Doe, 1983 (Saint 3)
Jane Eyre, 1944 (Welles 2, Fontaine 3, Marsh 3, Moorehead 3, O'Brien, M. 3, Taylor, E. 3, Basevi 4, Herrmann 4, MacGowan 4)
Jane Eyre, 1971 (Hawkins 3, Scott, G. 3, York, S. 3, Williams, J. 4)
Jan-E-Man, 1976 (Anand 3)
Janes gode Ven. See Største i Verden, 1919
Janet of the Chorus, 1915 (Talmadge, N. 3)
Jangadero, 1961 (Wexler 4)
Janice Meredith, 1924 (Davies 3, Fields, W.C. 3, Barnes 4)
Janie, 1944 (Curtiz 2, McDaniel 3, Cahn 4)
Janie Gets Married, 1946 (Malone 3, McDaniel 3, Meek 3)
Janitor, 1913 (Sennett 2)
Janitor, 1916 (Beery 3)
Janitor. See Eyewitness, 1980
Janitor's Joyful Job, 1915 (Hardy 3)

Janitor's Vacation, 1916 (Beery 3)
Janitor's Wife's Temptation, 1915 (Sennett 2)
Janitzio, 1934 (Fernández 2)
János Tornayi. See Tornyai János, 1962
Jánošík, 1935 (Fric 2)
Janošík, 1962 (Kroner 3)
Janus-Faced. See Januskopf, 1920
Januskopf, 1920 (Murnau 2, Lugosi 3, Veidt 3, Freund 4, Hoffmann 4)
Januskopf, 1972 (Mueller-Stahl 3)
Jaokman to Tetsu, 1949 (Mifune 3)
Japan and the Japanese. See Nihon to Nihonjin, 1970
Japanerin, 1918 (Dupont 2, Veidt 3)
Japanese Fantasy. See Japon de fantaisie, 1909
Japanese Grandmothers. See Nippon no obachan, 1962
Japanese House, 1955 (Peterson 2)
Japanese Magic. See Japon de fantaisie, 1909
Japanese Nightingale, 1918 (Furthman 4, Miller, A. 4)
Japanese Summer: Double Suicide. See Muri-shinju: Nihon no natsu, 1967
Japanese Swords: The Work of Kouhei Miyairi. See Nihontou, 1976
Japanese Tragedy. See Nihon no higeki, 1953
Japanese Youth. See Nihon no seishun, 1968
Japon de fantaisie, 1909 (Cohl 2)
Japon insolite, 1981 (Reichenbach 2)
Jaquar, 1967 (Braunberger 4)
Jardín de las delicias, 1970 (Saura 2, Chaplin 3)
Jardin des supplices, 1976 (Carrière 4)
Jardin qui bascule, 1974 (Moreau 3, Seyrig 3)
Jardinier, 1973 (Fresnay 3)
Jardinier. See Arroseur arrosé, 1895
Jardinier d'Argenteuil, 1966 (Gabin 3, Jurgens 3)
Jardins de Paris, 1948 (Resnais 2)
Jardins de Paris, 1961 (Fradetal 4)
Jardins du diable. See Coplan sauve sa peau, 1967
Jarnac's Treacherous Blow. See Coup de Jarnac, 1909
Jarnbararen, 1911 (Jaenzon 4, Magnusson 4)
Jarní píseň, 1944 (Hrušínský 3)
Jarov Praze, 1934 (Hammid 2)
Jarrett, 1973 (Ford, G. 3, Quayle 3)
Jarvány, 1975 (Madaras 3)
Jascha Heifetz Master Class, 1962 (Hammid 2)
Jashumon no onna, 1924 (Kinugasa 2)
Jason and the Argonauts, 1963 (Harryhausen 4, Herrmann 4)
Jasper, 1942–46 (Pal 2)
Jassy, 1947 (Unsworth 4)
Jatagan Mala, 1953 (Makavejev 2)
Jaték a muzeumban, 1965 (Gabór 3)
Jaune de soleil, 1971 (Duras 2)
Java Head, 1923 (Glennon 4, Young, W. 4)
Java Head, 1934 (Dickinson 2, Gwenn 3, Richardson 3, Wong 3, Dean 4)
Java Seas. See East of Java, 1935
J'avais sept filles, 1955 (Chevalier 3)
Jawaharlal Nehru, 1982 (Benegal 2)
Jawani, 1942 (Biswas 4)
Jawani-Ki-Raat, 1939 (Sircar 4)
Jaws, 1975 (Spielberg 2, Dreyfuss 3, Scheider 3, Shaw 3, Fields 4, Williams, J. 4)
Jaws of Hell. See Balaclava, 1930
Jaws 3-D, 1983 (Gossett 3)
Jaws II, 1978 (Scheider 3, Williams, J. 4)
Jayhawkers, 1959 (Chandler 3, Head 4)
Jazz Age, 1929 (Fairbanks, D. Jr. 3, McCrea 3, Walthall 3, Plunkett
Jazz Boat, 1960 (Roeg 2)
Jazz Comedy. See Veselye rebiate, 1934
Jazz Fool, 1929 (Disney 2, Iwerks 4)
Jazz Mad, 1928 (Hersholt 3)
Jazz Mad, 1931 (Terry 4)
Jazz Mamas, 1929 (Sennett 2)
Jazz River, 1934 (Toland 4)
Jazz Singer, 1927 (Crosland 2, Jolson 3, Loy 3, Oland 3, Carré 4, Zanuck 4)
Jazz Singer, 1953 (Curtiz 2, Prinz 4, Steiner 4)

Jazz Singer, 1980 (Fleischer, R. 2, Olivier 3, Horner 4)
Jazz Waiter. *See* Caught in a Cabaret, 1914
Jazzed Honeymoon, 1919 (Daniels 3, Lloyd 3, Roach 4)
Jazzmania, 1923 (Goulding 2, Hersholt 3, Gibbons 4)
Je bridge au plafond, 1909 (Linders 3)
Je chante, 1938 (Presle 3, Matras 4)
Je l'ai été trois fois, 1952 (Guitry 2, Blier 3)
Je m'appellerai Guillaume Apollinaire. *See* Guillaume Apollinaire, 1955
Je n'aime que toi, 1949 (D'Eaubonne 4)
Je reviendrai à Kandara, 1956 (Gélin 3, Kosma 4)
Je sais rien, mais je dirai tout, 1973 (Blier 3)
Je serai seule après minuit, 1931 (Clouzot 2)
Je suis avec toi, 1943 (Blier 3, Fresnay 3)
Je suis de la revue. *See* Botta e risposta, 1949
Je suis Pierre Rivière, 1975 (Huppert 3, Vierny 4)
Je suis un as, 1930 (Brasseur 3)
Je suis un homme perdu, 1932 (Dauphin 3)
Je suis un sentimental, 1955 (Constantine 3)
Je t'aime, 1973 (Moreau 3)
Je t'aime, je t'aime, 1968 (Resnais 2)
Je t'aime, moi non plus, 1975 (Depardieu 3)
Je t'aime, tu danses, 1975 (Seyrig 3)
Je t'attendrai. *See* Deserteur, 1938
Je te confie ma femme, 1933 (Arletty 3)
Je te tiens, tu me tiens par la barbichette, 1978 (Presle 3)
Je tire chemin, 1968 (Barrault 3)
Je, tu, elles, 1971 (Braunberger 4, Foldès 4)
Je, tu, il, elles, 1974 (Akerman 2)
Je vais craquer, 1979 (Baye 3)
Je voudrais un enfant, 1909 (Linders 3)
Je vous aime, 1980 (Deneuve 3, Depardieu 3)
Je vous ferai aimer la vie, 1979 (Legrand 4)
Je vous salue, Mafia, 1965 (Constantine 3, Presle 3, Coutard 4)
Je vous salue, Paris, 1968 (Braunberger 4)
Je vous y prrrrends!, 1897–98 (Guy 2)
Jealous Husband, 1911 (Griffith 2, Sennett 2, Bitzer 4)
Jealous Husbands, 1923 (Tourneur, M. 2)
Jealous Lover, 1933 (Terry 4)
Jealous Rage, 1912 (Dwan 2)
Jealous Waiter, 1913 (Sennett 2)
Jealousy, 1929 (March 3, Fort 4)
Jealousy, 1934 (Ball 3)
Jealousy, 1945 (Haas 3, Eisler 4, Trumbo 4)
Jealousy, 1963 (Dinov 4)
Jealousy. *See* Eifersucht, 1925
Jealousy. *See* Emergency Wedding, 1950
Jealousy. *See* Revnost, 1914
Jealousy. *See* Shitto, 1949
Jealousy and the Man, 1909 (Griffith 2, Bitzer 4)
Jealousy—Italian Style. *See* Dramma della gelosia, 1970
Jean Cocteau, 1949 (Roos 2)
Jean Cocteau fait du cinéma, 1925 (Cocteau 2)
Jean Coton, 1953 (Allégret, M. 2)
Jean de la Lune, 1931 (Aumont 3, Simon, M. 3, Achard 4, Meerson 4, Périnal 4, Trauner 4)
Jean de la Lune, 1948 (Astruc 2, Darrieux 3, Dauphin 3, Achard 4)
Jean de la lune, 1977 (Guillemot 4)
Jean Effel, 1948 (Resnais 2)
Jean Intervenes, 1912 (Reid 3)
Jean la poudre, 1912 (Tourneur, M. 2)
Jean o' the Heather, 1916 (Olcott 2)
Jean Piaget, 1977 (Goretta 2)
Jean Renoir, le patron, 1966 (Rivette 2)
Jean Taris champion de natation. *See* Taris, 1931
Jean-Jacques Rousseau, 1957 (Leenhardt 2)
Jean-Luc persecuté, 1965 (Goretta 2)
Jean-Marc. *See* Vie conjugale, 1964
Jeanne, 1934 (Fradetal 4, Lourié 4, Stradling 4)
Jeanne Dielman, 23 Quai du Commerce, 1080 Bruxelles, 1975 (Akerman 2, Seyrig 3)
Jeanne Eagels, 1957 (Sidney 2, Chandler 3, Moorehead 3, Novak 3, Duning 4, Levien 4)

Jeanne la française. *See* Joana a Francesa, 1973
Jeanne Moreau, 1966 (Reichenbach 2)
Jeannie, 1941 (Redgrave, M. 3)
Jean-Paul Belmondo, 1965 (Lelouch 2)
Jedenacte prikazani, 1925 (Haas 3)
Jedenacte prikazani, 1935 (Fric 2)
Jeder fur sich und Gott gegen alle, 1974 (Herzog 2)
Jeder stirbt fur sich allein, 1970 (Geschonneck 3, Hoppe 3)
Jeder stirbt fur sich allein, 1976 (Knef 3)
Jedermanns Frau, 1924 (Korda 2)
Jedermanns Weib. *See* Jedermanns Frau, 1924
Jedna z milionu, 1935 (Stallich 4)
Jeena yahan, 1981 (Azmi 3)
Jeep, 1938 (Fleischer, M. and D. 2)
Jeepers Creepers, 1939 (Rogers, R. 3, Clampett 4)
Jeet, 1949 (Anand 3, Biswas 4)
Jeevan Sathi, 1939 (Biswas 4)
Jeewan Jyoti, 1953 (Burman 4)
Jefe máximo, 1940 (De Fuentes 2, Armendáriz 3, Figueroa 4)
Jeff, 1969 (Delon 3)
Jeffries, Jr., 1924 (McCarey 2, Roach 4)
Jeffries-Corbett Fight, 1903 (Bitzer 4)
Jeg et hus mig bygge vil, 1955 (Carlsen 2)
Jego Ostatni Czyn, 1916 (Negri 3)
Její lékař, 1933 (Baarová 3, Haas 3, Stallich 4)
Jelbeszéd, 1974 (Brejchová 3)
Jelenlét, 1965 (Jancsó 2)
Jengibre contra dinamita, 1939 (Cantinflas 3)
Jennie, 1940 (Day 4)
Jennie. *See* Portrait of Jennie, 1948
Jennie Gerhardt, 1933 (Astor 3, Darwell 3, Sidney 3, Schulberg 4, Shamroy 4)
Jennie, Wife/Child, 1968 (Zsigmond 4)
Jennifer, 1953 (Lupino 3, Howe 4)
Jennifer, 1964 (De Palma 2)
Jennifer: A Woman's Story, 1979 (Green, G. 4)
Jennifer on My Mind, 1971 (De Niro 3)
Jenny, 1936 (Carné 2, Barrault 3, Rosay 3, Vanel 3, D'Eaubonne 4, Kosma 4, Prévert 4)
Jenny Is a Good Thing, 1969 (Lancaster 3)
Jenny Lamour. *See* Quai des orfèvres, 1947
Jenny Lind, 1930 (Robison 2, Rosay 3)
Jenny Lind. *See* Lady's Morals, 1930
Jenny's Pearls, 1913 (Sennett 2)
Jens Langkniv, 1940 (Henning-Jensen 2)
Jens Månsson i Amerika, 1947 (DeMille 2)
Jens Månsson in America. *See* Jens Månsson i Amerika, 1947
Jeopardy, 1953 (Sturges, J. 2, Stanwyck 3, Rose 4, Schnee 4, Tiomkin 4)
Jeremiah Johnson, 1972 (Milius 2, Pollack 2, Redford 3, Anhalt 4)
Jerguš Lapin, 1960 (Kroner 3)
Jericho, 1937 (Robeson 3)
Jéricho, 1945 (Brasseur 3, Renoir 4, Spaak 4)
Jerk, 1979 (van Runkle 4)
Jerk, Too, 1984 (Biroc 4)
Jerky Turkey, 1945 (Avery 2)
Jernbanens Datter, 1911 (Blom 2)
Jérôme Bosch, 1963 (Guillemot 4)
Jérome Perreau, héros des barricades, 1936 (Gance 2)
Jerry, 1924 (Gallone 2)
Jerry series, 1951 (Hanna and Barbera 4)
Jerusalem, 1937–40 (Cardiff 4)
Jerusalem File, 1972 (Pleasance 3, Williamson 3, Coutard 4)
Jesien, 1955 (Borowczyk 4)
Jess, 1912 (Cruze 2)
Jesse and James, 1931 (Terry 4)
Jesse James, 1939 (King 2, Carradine 3, Chaney Lon, Jr. 3, Darwell 3, Fonda, H. 3, Meek 3, Power 3, Scott, R. 3, Summerville 3, Canutt 4, Johnson 4, Zanuck 4)
Jesse James at Bay, 1941 (Rogers, R. 3)
Jesse James vs. the Daltons, 1954 (Katzman 4)
Jessica, 1962 (Negulesco 2, Chevalier 3, Dalio 3, Dickinson 3, Moorehead 3)

Jester's Tale. *See* Bláznova kronika, 1964
Jesus Christ Superstar, 1973 (Jewison 2, Previn 4, Slocombe 4)
Jesus of Nazareth, 1977 (Bancroft 3, Cardinale 3, Cortese 3)
Jesus of Nazareth. *See* Gesú di Nazareth, 1977
Jesusita en Chihuahua, 1942 (Infante 3)
Jet Cage, 1962 (Freleng 4)
Jet Carrier, 1954 (La Shelle 4)
Jet over the Atlantic, 1959 (Mayo 3, Raft 3)
Jet Pilot, 1957 (Von Sternberg 2, Leigh, J. 3, Wayne 3, D'Agostino 4, Furthman 4, Hoch 4, Kaper 4)
Jet Storm, 1959 (Zetterling 2, Attenborough 3, Baker S. 3)
J'étais une aventurière, 1938 (Feuillère 3, Barsacq 4)
Jetée, 1964 (Marker 2)
Jettchen Gebert, 1918 (Oswald 2, Veidt 3)
Jetzt und in der Stunde des Todes, 1963 (Hoppe 3)
Jeu avec le feu, 1974 (Noiret 3, Trintignant 3, Robbe-Grillet 4)
Jeu de la puce, 1969 (Delerue 4)
Jeu de la vérité, 1961 (Trintignant 3, Matras 4)
Jeu de l'oie, 1980 (Ruiz 2)
Jeu de massacre, 1967 (Cassel 3)
Jeu de solitaire, 1976 (Valli 3, Carrière 4)
Jeu 1, 1962 (Reichenbach 2, Braunberger 4)
Jeudi on chantera comme dimanche, 1966 (Storck 2, Delerue 4)
Jeugddag, 1929–30 (Ivens 2)
Jeune Fille. *See* Young One, 1960
Jeune Fille assassinée, 1974 (Vadim 2)
Jeune Fille et l'étoile, 1960 (Braunberger 4)
Jeune Fille et un million, 1932 (Dauphin 3)
Jeune Fille la plus méritante de France, 1922 (Musidora 3)
Jeune Fille romanesque, 1909 (Linders 3)
Jeune Fille un seul amour. *See* Katya, 1960
Jeune Folle, 1952 (Allégret, Y. 2, Trauner 4)
Jeune Homme et la mort, 1953 (Anger 2)
Jeune Morte. *See* Chiens, 1966
Jeunes Filles à marier, 1935 (Berry 3)
Jeunes filles dans la nuit, 1943 (Berry 3)
Jeunes filles d'aujourd'hui. *See* Maturareise, 1943
Jeunes Filles de France, 1940 (Allégret, M. 2)
Jeunes filles de Paris, 1936 (Simon, M. 3)
Jeunes Filles d'hier et d'aujourd'hui, 1916 (Musidora 3)
Jeunes filles en détresse, 1939 (Pabst 2, Presle 3, Andrejew 4)
Jeunes Gens a marier, 1912 (Cohl 2)
Jeunes Loups, 1967 (Carné 2)
Jeunes mariés, 1953 (D'Eaubonne 4, Spaak 4)
Jeunes Timides. *See* Deux Timides, 1942
Jeunesse, 1934 (Stradling 4)
Jeunesse d'abord, 1935 (Brasseur 3, Prévert 4)
Jeunesse de France, 1968 (Braunberger 4)
Jeunesses musicales, 1956 (Jutra 2)
Jeux, 1979 (Ruiz 2)
Jeux. *See* Jeu 1, 1962
Jeux dangereux, 1958 (Wakhévitch 4)
Jeux de cartes, 1916 (Cohl 2)
Jeux de l'amour, 1959 (Broca 2, Chabrol 2, Cassel 3, Delerue 4, Evein 4)
Jeux de l'été et de la mer, 1936 (Storck 2)
Jeux d'enfants, 1946 (Fradetal 4)
Jeux des anges, 1964 (Borowczyk 4)
Jeux interdits, 1951 (Clément 2, Aurenche 4, Bost 4)
Jeux sont faits, 1947 (Delannoy 2, Presle 3, Auric 4, Bost 4, Colpi 4, Matras 4)
Jew Suss, 1934 (Hardwicke 3, Veidt 3, Balcon 4, Junge 4)
Jewel, 1933 (Hawkins 3)
Jewel Case. *See* Sølvdaasen med Juvelerne, 1910
Jewel of the Nile, 1985 (Turner, K. 3)
Jewel Robbery, 1932 (Dieterle 2, Francis, K. 3, Powell, W. 3)
Jewel Thief, 1966 (Anand 3, Burman 4)
Jeweller's Terror. *See* Juvelernes Skroek, 1915
Jewels in Our Hearts. *See* Tokyo no koibito, 1952
Jewels of a Sacrifice, 1913 (Dwan 2)
Jewish Gauchos. *See* Gauchos judíos, 1975
Jewish Prudence, 1927 (Roach 4)
Jew's Christmas, 1913 (Weber 2)

Jezebel, 1938 (Huston 2, Wyler 2, Bainter 3, Brent 3, Crisp 3, Davis, Fonda, H. 3, Blanke 4, Friedhofer 4, Haller 4, Orry-Kelly 4, Steiner 4, Wallis 4)
Jhansi ri-rani, 1952 (Haller 4)
Jiban Maran, 1939 (Sircar 4)
Jidosha dorobo, 1964 (Takemitsu 4)
Jigoku, 1979 (Kishida 3)
Jigoku kaido, 1929 (Hasegawa 3)
Jigoku no kifujin, 1949 (Kurosawa 2)
Jigoku no mon, 1952 (Hasegawa 3)
Jigoku no mushi, 1938 (Shimura 3, Miyagawa 4)
Jigoku no soko made tsukiauze, 1959 (Yamamura 3)
Jigokubana, 1957 (Kyo 3, Yamamura 3)
Jigokumon, 1953 (Kinugasa 2, Hasegawa 3, Kyo 3)
Jigokuno magarikago, 1959 (Imamura 2)
Jigsaw, 1949 (Dietrich 3, Fonda, H. 3, Garfield 3, Meredith 3)
Jigsaw, 1968 (Jones 4)
Jigsaw, 1972 (O'Brien, E. 3)
Jigsaw. *See* Homme en colère, 1979
Jigsaw Man, 1984 (Caine 3, Olivier 3, Francis 4)
Jihi shincho, 1927 (Mizoguchi 2)
Jihishincho, 1954 (Kagawa 3)
Jikizamurai, 1930 (Hasegawa 3)
Jilt, 1909 (Griffith 2, Bitzer 4)
Jim, 1914 (Mix 3)
Jim Bludso, 1917 (Browning 2)
Jim Bougne, boxeur, 1923 (Chevalier 3)
Jim Cameron's Wife, 1914 (Hart 3)
Jim Crow, 1912 (Vanel 3)
Jim Jam Janitor, 1928 (Sennett 2, Hornbeck 4)
Jim Jeffries-Jim Sharkey Fight, 1899 (Bitzer 4)
Jim la houlette, 1935 (Fernandel 3)
Jim the Conqueror, 1927 (Boyd 3, Rosson 4)
Jim the Penman, 1921 (Barrymore L. 3, Stradling 4)
Jim Thorpe—All American, 1951 (Curtiz 2, Lancaster 3, Haller 4, Steiner 4)
Jimmy and Sally, 1933 (Trevor 3)
Jimmy bruiteur, 1930 (Benoit-Lévy 2)
Jimmy Hayes and Muriel, 1914 (Mix 3)
Jimmy the Gent, 1934 (Curtiz 2, Cagney 3, Darwell 3, Davis 3, Orry-Kelly 4)
Jimmy the Kid, 1983 (Gordon 3)
Jimpu Group. *See* Jimpuren, 1933
Jimpuren, 1933 (Mizoguchi 2)
Jinanbou garasu, 1955 (Miyagawa 4)
Jinchoge, 1966 (Kyo 3, Tsukasa 3)
Jinete fantasma, 1967 (Figueroa 4)
Jingle Bells, 1927 (Lantz 4)
Jingle Bells, 1931 (Terry 4)
Jinks Joins the Temperance Club, 1911 (Sennett 2)
Jinkyo, 1924 (Mizoguchi 2)
Jinpinin, 1928 (Hasegawa 3)
Jinruigaku nyumon, 1966 (Imamura 2)
Jinsei gekijo, 1952 (Hayasaka 4)
Jinsei gekijo seishun-hen, 1958 (Mifune 3)
Jinsei no onimotsu, 1935 (Gosho 2, Tanaka 3)
Jinsei o Mitsumete, 1923 (Kinugasa 2)
Jinsei tohbo-gaeri, 1955 (Yamada 3)
Jinsei tonbo-gaeri, 1946 (Imai 2)
Jinx, 1919 (Normand 3)
Jinxed, 1982 (Siegel 2, Elam 3, Torn 3, Zsigmond 4)
Jiný vzduch, 1939 (Stallich 4)
Jinya no Shotaro, 1934 (Yamada 3)
Jirocho Fuji, 1959 (Hasegawa 3, Kyo 3)
Jirocho goshi, 1952 (Shindo 3)
Jirokichi goshi, 1952 (Hasegawa 3)
Jiruba no Tetsu, 1950 (Kurosawa 2)
Jis Desh Me Ganga Behti Hai, 1960 (Kapoor 2)
Jisei wa umai, 1930 (Hasegawa 3)
Jitney Elopement, 1915 (Bacon 2, Chaplin 2, Purviance 3)
Jitterbugs, 1943 (Laurel & Hardy 3, Basevi 4)
Jivaro, 1954 (Chaney Lon, Jr. 3, Head 4)
Jive Junction, 1943 (Ulmer 2)

Jiyu gakko, 1951 (Yoshimura 2, Kyo 3, Yamamura 3)
Jménem Zivota, 1973 (Danailov 3)
Jmenuji se Fifinka, 1953 (Stallich 4)
Jo, 1971 (Blier 3, Decaë 4)
Jo as oreg a Haznal, 1935 (Sakall 3)
Joachim, Put It in the Machine. *See* Jáchyme hod to do stroje, 1973
Joan at the Stake. *See* Giovanna d'Arco al rogo, 1954 (Bergman 3)
Joan of Arc, 1948 (Fleming 2, Bergman 3, Bond 3, Ferrer, J. 3, Day 4,
    Friedhofer 4, Hoch 4, Jeakins 4, Vorkapich 4, Wanger 4)
Joan of Arc at the Stake. *See* Giovanna d'Arco al rogo, 1954
Joan of Paris, 1942 (Dalio 3, Henreid 3, Ladd 3, Morgan 3, Bennett 4)
Joan of Plattsburg, 1918 (Normand 3)
Joan of the Angels?. *See* Matka Joanna od Aniolów, 1961
Joan of the Ozarks, 1942 (Brown 3)
Joan the Woman, 1917 (DeMille 2, Bosworth 3, Crisp 3, Novarro 3,
    Reid 3, Buckland 4, Macpherson 4)
Joana a Francesa, 1973 (Diegues 2, Moreau 3)
Joanna, 1925 (Del Rio 3)
Joanna, 1968 (Sutherland 3, Lassally 4)
Joaquin Murieta, 1964 (Hunter 3, Kennedy, A. 3)
Joaquin Murieta, 1969 (Goldsmith 4)
Job. *See* Posto, 1961
Job in a Million, 1937 (Grierson 2)
Jo-bachi, 1978 (Ichikawa 2)
Jobard series, (Cohl 2)
Jocelyn, 1951 (Braunberger 4)
Jocko musicien, 1903 (Guy 2)
Joconde, 1957 (Delerue 4)
Jocular Winds, 1913 (Dwan 2)
Jodai no chokoku, 1950 (Hayasaka 4)
Joe, 1970 (Sarandon 3)
Joe and Ethel Turp Call on the President, 1939 (Brennan 3, Sothern 3,
    Stone 3)
Joe Butterfly, 1957 (Meredith 3, Murphy 3, Wynn 3)
Joe . . . cercati un posto per morire, 1969 (Hunter 3)
Joe Dakota, 1957 (Van Cleef 3, Salter 4)
Joe Debbs, 1917 (Lang 2)
Joe Glow the Fire Fly, 1941 (Jones 2)
Joe Hill, 1971 (Widerberg 2)
Joe il Rosso, 1936 (Fusco 4)
Joe Kidd, 1972 (Sturges, J. 2, Duvall, R. 3, Eastwood 3, Bumstead 4,
    Schifrin 4)
Joe Macbeth, 1955 (Douglas, P. 3)
Joe Navidad, 1966 (Hunter 3)
Joe Palooka—Champ, 1946 (Cook 3)
Joe Palooka in the Knock-Out, 1947 (Muse 3)
Joe Smith, American, 1942 (Gardner 3, Young, R. 3, Schary 4)
Joe Valachi: I segreti di Cosa Nostra, 1972 (De Laurentiis 4)
Joe Valachi: I segreti di Cosa Nostra. *See* Valachi Papers, 1972
Jóember, 1970 (Macskássy 4)
Joen, 1959 (Kinugasa 2)
Joen no chimata, 1923 (Mizoguchi 2)
Joen no hatoba, 1951 (Kyo 3)
Joe's Lunch Wagon, 1934 (Terry 4)
Joey Boy, 1965 (Gilliat 4)
Jofroi, 1934 (Pagnol 2)
Jofusei, 1927 (Hasegawa 3)
Jogakusei-ki, 1941 (Takamine 3, Yamada 3)
Jogashima no ame, 1950 (Hasegawa 3)
Johan, 1920 (Stiller 2, Magnusson 4)
Johan Ekberg, 1964 (Troell 2)
Johan Ulfstjerna, 1923 (Magnusson 4)
Johan Ulfstjerna, 1936 (Fischer 4, Jaenzon 4)
Johanes Kepler, 1974 (Hoppe 3)
Johann Hopkins der Dritte, 1921 (Lugosi 3)
Johann Mouse, 1952 (Hanna and Barbera 4)
Johann Sebastian Bach: Fantasia G-Moll, 1965 (Švankmajer 4)
Johann Strauss. *See* Kaiserwalzer, 1932
Johann the Coffin Maker, 1927 (Florey 2)
Johanna Enlists, 1918 (Beery 3, Pickford 3, Marion 4, Rosher 4)
Johannes fils de Johannes, 1918 (Musidora 3)
Johannes Goth, 1920 (Krauss 3, Mayer 4)
Johannes Jørgensen i Assissi, 1950 (Roos 2)

Johannes Jørgensen i Svendborg, 1954 (Roos 2)
Johannes Larsen, 1957 (Roos 2)
Johannes V. Jensen, 1947 (Roos 2)
Johannestraum, 1919 (Hoffmann 4)
Johannisnacht, 1933 (Dagover 3)
John and Julie, 1955 (Sellers 3)
John and Mary, 1969 (Yates 2, Farrow 3, Hoffman 3, Jones 4)
John Barleycorn, 1914 (Bosworth 3)
John Burns of Gettysburg, 1913 (Nilsson 3)
John Colter's Escape, 1912 (Bosworth 3)
John Ericsson, 1937 (Sjostrom 2, Borgstrom 3)
John F. Kennedy: Years of Lightning, Day of Drums, 1966 (Schell,
    Maximilian 3, Peck 3)
John Gilpin's Ride, 1908 (Hepworth 2)
John Goldfarb, Please Come Home, 1965 (Coogan 3, MacLaine 3,
    Ustinov 3, Head 4, Shamroy 4, Smith, J.M. 4, Williams, J. 4)
John Halifax Gentleman, 1915 (Pearson 2)
John Halifax, Gentleman, 1938 (McDowall 3)
John Henry and the Inky Poo, 1946 (Pal 2)
John Loves Mary, 1949 (Neal 3, Reagan 3, Wald 4)
John Meade's Woman, 1937 (D'Agostino 4, Head 4, Mankiewicz 4,
    Reynolds 4, Schulberg 4)
John Needham's Double, 1916 (Weber 2)
John Oakhurst, Gambler, 1911 (Bosworth 3)
John Paul Jones, 1959 (Aumont 3, Coburn, C. 3, Cushing 3, Davis 3,
    Farrow 3, Adam 4, Steiner 4)
John Petticoats, 1919 (Hart 3, August 4, Sullivan 4)
John Rance—Gentleman, 1914 (Talmadge, N. 3)
John Smith—1922 (Astor 3, Heerman 4)
John Smith Wakes Up, 1940 (Greenwood 3)
John, the Tenant. *See* Arendás zsidó, 1917
John the Younger Brother. *See* Jön az öcsem, 1919
John Tobin's Sweetheart, 1913 (Bunny 3)
Johnny Allegro, 1949 (Raft 3, Biroc 4, Duning 4)
Johnny Angel, 1945 (Raft 3, Trevor 3, Carmichael 4)
Johnny Apollo, 1940 (Hathaway 2, Lamour 3, Power 3, Brown,
    Harry Joe 4, Day 4, Dunne 4, Miller, A. 4, Zanuck 4)
Johnny Banco, 1966 (Allégret, Y. 2, D'Eaubonne 4)
Johnny Belinda, 1948 (Negulesco 2, Ayres 3, Moorehead 3, Wyman 3,
    McCord 4, Steiner 4, Wald 4)
Johnny Belinda, 1967 (Farrow 3)
Johnny Come Lately, 1943 (Howard 2, Cagney 3, McDaniel 3, Muse 3)
Johnny Comes Flying Home, 1946 (Basevi 4)
Johnny Concho, 1956 (Martin, S. 3, Sinatra 3, Wynn 3)
Johnny Cool, 1963 (Cook 3, Cahn 4)
Johnny Dark, 1954 (Curtis 3, Boyle 4, Salter 4)
Johnny Doesn't Live Here Anymore, 1944 (Mitchum 3, Simon, S. 3)
Johnny Doughboy, 1942 (Alton, J. 4, Cahn 4)
Johnny Eager, 1941 (Leroy 2, Heflin 3, Taylor, R. 3, Turner, L. 3,
    Kaper 4, Mahin 4, Rosson 4)
Johnny Frenchman, 1945 (Rosay 3, Balcon 4, Clarke, T.E.B. 4)
Johnny Get Your Gun, 1919 (Cruze 2, Crisp 3, Stone 3)
Johnny Get Your Hair Cut, 1927 (Coogan 3, Costello, M. 3, Eason 4)
**Johnny Got His Gun, 1971 (Robards 3, Sutherland 3, Trumbo 4,
    van Runkle 4)**
**Johnny Guitar, 1954 (Ray, N. 2, Bond 3, Borgnine 3, Carradine 3,
    Crawford, J. 3, Hayden 3, McCambridge 3, Maddow 4, Stradling 4,
    Young, V. 4)**
Johnny haute-couture, 1934 (Brasseur 3)
Johnny Holiday, 1950 (Bendix 3, Carmichael 4, Waxman 4)
Johnny in the Clouds. *See* Way to the Stars, 1945
Johnny le Fligueur, 1973 (Van Cleef 3)
Johnny March. *See* Identity Unknown, 1945
Johnny Mera Naam, 1970 (Anand 3)
Johnny Nobody, 1961 (Bendix 3, Cusack 3)
Johnny O'Clock, 1947 (Rossen 2, Chandler 3, Cobb 3, Powell, D. 3,
    Duning 4, Guffey 4)
Johnny One-Eye, 1950 (Florey 2, O'Brien, P. 3, Polglase 4)
Johnny Reno, 1966 (Andrews D. 3, Arlen 3, Russell, J. 3)
Johnny rettet Nebrador, 1953 (Albers 3)
Johnny Smith and Poker-Huntas, 1938 (Avery 2)
Johnny Stool Pigeon, 1949 (Curtis 3, Duryea 3, Winters 3,
    Orry-Kelly 4)

Johnny Tiger, 1966 (Taylor, R. 3, Green, J. 4, Mercer 4)
Johnny Tremain, 1957 (Disney 2, Ellenshaw 4, Iwerks 4)
Johnny Trouble, 1957 (Barrymore E. 3)
Johnny Vagabond. See Johnny Come Lately, 1943
Johnny, We Hardly Knew Ye, 1977 (Meredith 3)
Johnny's Days. See J'ai tout donné, 1971
Johnstown Flood, 1926 (Gable 3, Gaynor 3, Lawrence 3)
Johnstown Flood, 1946 (Terry 4)
Joi Baba Felunath, 1978 (Ray, S. 2, Chatterjee 3, Datta 4)
Joi Kinuyo sensei, 1936 (Tanaka 3)
Joi no Kiroku, 1941 (Tanaka 3)
Joie de revivre, 1947 (Storck 2)
Join the Circus, 1923 (Roach 4)
Join the Marines, 1937 (Brown, K. 4)
Joi-uchi, 1967 (Kobayashi 2, Mifune 3, Takemitsu 4)
Joka, 1952 (Yamamura 3)
Joke. See Zert, 1968
Joke of Destiny, 1984 (Tognazzi 3)
Joke on the Joker, 1911 (Sennett 2)
Jokei, 1960 (Yoshimura 2, Kyo 3, Miyagawa 4)
Jokei kazoku, 1963 (Kyo 3, Miyagawa 4, Yoda 4)
Joker. See Farceur, 1961
Joker Is Wild, 1957 (Vidor, C. 2, Coogan 3, Crain 3, Sinatra 3, Cahn 4,
    Head 4, Westmore, F. 4)
Jokyo II: Mono o takaku uritsukeru onna, 1959 (Ichikawa 2)
Jokyu aishi, 1931 (Gosho 2)
Jolanda, la figlia del corsaro nero, 1952 (De Laurentiis 4, Delli Colli 4)
Jolanta—den gackande suggan, 1945 (Jaenzon 4)
Jolanta—The Elusive Sow. See Jolanta—den gackande suggan, 1945
Joli Mai, 1963 (Marker 2, Karina 3, Montand 3, Signoret 3, Legrand 4)
Jolly Bad Fellow, 1963 (Hamer 2, Barry 4)
Jolly Green, 1970 (Coutard 4)
Jolly Jilter, 1927 (Sennett 2)
Jolly Little Elves, 1934 (Lantz 4)
Jolly Whirl. See Singeries humaines, 1910
Jolson Sings Again, 1949 (Jolson 3, Buchman 4, Duning 4)
Jolson Story, 1946 (Jolson 3, Cole 4, Walker 4)
Jolt for General Germ, 1931 (Fleischer, M. and D. 2)
Jomai, 1961 (Iwashita 3)
Jon az ocsem, 1919 (Curtiz 2)
Jonah Man, 1904 (Hepworth 2)
Jonah Who Will Be 25 in the Year 2000. See Jonas qui aura vingt cinq
    ans en l'an 2000, 1976
Jonan no Yoemon, 1931 (Hasegawa 3)
Jonas qui aura vingt cinq ans en l'an 2000, 1976 (Tanner 2)
Jonathan Livingston Seagull, 1973 (Leven 4)
Jones and His New Neighbors, 1909 (Griffith 2, Lawrence 3, Bitzer 4)
Jones and the Lady Book Agent, 1909 (Griffith 2, Lawrence 3,
    Bitzer 4)
Jones Family in Hollywood, 1939 (Keaton 2)
Jones Family in Quick Millions, 1939 (Keaton 2)
Jones Have Amateur Theatricals, 1909 (Griffith 2, Lawrence 3,
    Bitzer 4)
Jonetsu, 1932 (Takamine 3)
Jonetsu no rumuba, 1950 (Yamamura 3)
Jonque, 1964 (Guillemot 4)
Joobachi, 1952 (Mori 3)
Joobachi, 1978 (Tsukasa 3)
Jordan is a Hard Road, 1915 (Dwan 2, Gish, D. 3)
Jordens Haevn. See Omstridte Jord, 1915
Jorg Ratgeb—Maler, 1978 (Hoppe 3)
Jorobado, 1943 (Negrete 3)
José Torres, 1960 (Teshigahara 2, Takemitsu 4)
José Torres, Part II, 1965 (Teshigahara 2, Takemitsu 4)
Josef und seine Bruder, 1922 (Krauss 3)
Josei ni kansuru juni-sho, 1954 (Ichikawa 2)
Josei no kakugo, 1940 (Tanaka 3)
Josei no shori, 1946 (Mizoguchi 2, Shindo 2, Tanaka 3)
Josei tai dansei, 1950 (Yamamura 3)
Josei wa tsuyoshi, 1924 (Mizoguchi 2)
Joselito vagabundo, 1965 (García 3)
Joseph Andrews, 1977 (Richardson 2, Gielgud 3, Addison 4, Watkin 4)
Joseph Balsamo, 1971 (Douy 4)

Joseph in the Land of Egypt, 1914 (Cruze 2)
Joseph Mánes, 1951 (Pojar 4)
Josephine and Men, 1955 (Boulting 2, Buchanan 3, Finch 3, Addison 4)
Josette, 1936 (Christian-Jaque 2, Fernandel 3)
Josette, 1938 (Dwan 2, Ameche 3, Chaney Lon, Jr. 3, Lahr 3,
    Simon, S. 3, Young, R. 3, Zanuck 4)
Josh's Suicide, 1911 (Sennett 2)
Joshila, 1973 (Anand 3)
Joshu to tomoni, 1956 (Hara 3, Kagawa 3, Tanaka 3)
Joshua Then and Now, 1985 (Arkin 3, Sarde 4)
Jóslat, 1920 (Fejos 2)
Jotai, 1964 (Takemitsu 4)
Jotai, 1969 (Kishida 3, Okada 3)
Jotai wa kanashiku, 1957 (Tanaka 3)
Joue avec Dodo, 1912–14 (Cohl 2)
Jouet, 1976 (Evein 4)
Jouets animés, 1912 (Cohl 2)
Joueur, 1948 (Rosay 3)
Joueur, 1958 (Autant-Lara 2, Blier 3, Philipe 3, Aurenche 4, Bost 4,
    Douy 4)
Joueur d'echecs, 1938 (Modot 3, Rosay 3, Veidt 3)
Jougasaki no ame, 1950 (Miyagawa 4)
Jougasaki's Rain. See Jougasaki no ame, 1950
Jouiuchi, 1967 (Muraki 4)
Joujoux savants. See Jouets animés, 1912
Jouons le jeu, 1952 (Brasseur 3, Chevalier 3)
Jour à Paris, 1965 (Trintignant 3)
Jour de fête, 1949 (Strick 2, Tati 2)
Jour de fête, 1974 (Baye 3)
Jour de tournage, 1969 (Montand 3)
Jour des noces, 1970 (Goretta 2)
Jour des parques. See Rupture, 1970
Jour du frotteur, 1932 (Cavalcanti 2)
Jour du terme, 1904 (Guy 2)
Jour et l'heure, 1962 (Clément 2, Piccoli 3, Signoret 3, Decaë 4,
    Evein 4)
Jour peut-être à San Pedro ou ailleurs, 1977 (Cardinale 3)
**Jour se lève, 1939 (Carné 2, Arletty 3, Berry 3, Blier 3, Gabin 3,
    Reggiani 3, Courant 4, Jaubert 4, Prévert 4, Trauner 4)**
Jour viendra, 1933 (Aumont 3)
Journal animé, 1908 (Cohl 2)
Journal de la résistance, 1945 (Coward 4)
Journal d'un combat, 1964 (Delon 3)
Journal d'un curé de campagne, 1950 (Bresson 2, Burel 4)
Journal d'un fou, 1963 (Delerue 4)
Journal d'un scélérat, 1950 (Rohmer 2, Gégauff 4)
Journal d'un suicide, 1972 (Seyrig 3)
Journal d'une femme de chambre, 1963 (Buñuel 2, Moreau 3, Piccoli 3,
    Carrière 4, Wakhévitch 4)
Journal d'une femme en blanc, 1965 (Autant-Lara 2, Aurenche 4,
    Douy 4)
Journal masculin, 1948 (Braunberger 4)
Journal of a Crime, 1934 (Darwell 3, Menjou 3, Pidgeon 3, Blanke 4,
    Haller 4, Orry-Kelly 4)
Journal of Resistance, 1944 (Balcon 4)
Journal of the Orange Flower. See Karatachi nikki, 1959
Journal Out of the City. See Wycieczka za miasto, 1968
Journal tombe à cinq heures, 1942 (Blier 3, Fresnay 3, Honegger 4)
Journalist. See Vasha znakomaya, 1927
Journalist. See Zhurnalist, 1967
Journalist's Tale, 1985 (Godfrey 4)
Journée avec Jacques Hélian et son orchestre, 1947–51 (Verneuil 2)
Journée bien remplie, 1972 (Trintignant 3)
Journée de Flambeau, 1916 (Cohl 2)
Journée naturelle, 1947 (Resnais 2)
Journées entières dans les arbres, 1976 (Duras 2, Almendros 4)
Journey, 1954 (Fairbanks, D. Jr. 3)
Journey, 1959 (Litvak 2, Aimée 3, Brynner 3, Kerr 3, Robards 3,
    Auric 4, Fisher 4)
Journey, 1972 (Bujold 3)
Journey. See Viaggio, 1974
Journey Back to Oz, 1973 (Minnelli 3, Rooney 3, Cahn 4)
Journey Beneath the Desert. See Antinea, 1961

Juif errant, 1904 (Méliès 2)
Juif errant, 1926 (Artaud 3)
Juif polonais, 1931 (Baur 3, D'Eaubonne 4)
Jujin Yukiotoko, 1957 (Tsuburaya 4)
Jujin Yukiotoko. See Half Human, 1957
Jujiro, 1928 (Kinugasa 2)
Juke Box Rhythm, 1958 (Katzman 4)
Juke Girl, 1942 (Reagan 3, Sheridan 3, Deutsch 4, Glennon 4, Wald 4, Wallis 4)
Jukti, Takke Aar Gappo, 1974 (Ghatak 4)
Jukyu no hanayome, 1955 (Yamamura 3)
Jukyu-sai no haru, 1933 (Gosho 2, Takamine 3)
Jules and Jim. See Jules et Jim, 1961
Jules et Jim, 1961 (Truffaut 2, Moreau 3, Werner 3, Coutard 4, Delerue 4)
Jules of the Strong Heart, 1918 (Crisp 3)
Julia, 1977 (Zinnemann 2, Fonda, J. 3, Redgrave, V. 3, Robards 3, Schell, Maximilian 3, Streep 3, Delerue 4, Dillon 4, Murch 4, Sargent 4, Slocombe 4)
Julia lebt, 1963 (Domrose 3, Hoffmann 3)
Julia Misbehaves, 1948 (Bruce 3, Garson 3, Pidgeon 3, Taylor, E. 3, Deutsch 4, Irene 4, Ruttenberg 4, Wimperis 4)
Juliana in Seventy Turbulent Years. See Juliana in zeventig bewogen jaren, 1979
Juliana in zeventig bewogen jaren, 1979 (Haanstra 2)
Julianwale, 1953 (Biswas 4)
Julie, 1956 (Day 3, Jourdan 3, Marsh 3)
Julie de Carneilhan, 1950 (Brasseur 3, Feuillère 3)
Julie la Rousse, 1959 (Gélin 3)
Julie Pot de Colle, 1977 (Broca 2, Carrière 4, Delerue 4)
Julie the Redhead. See Julie la Rousse, 1959
Julie Vrevská, 1977 (Danailov 3)
Juliet of the Spirits. See Giulietta degli spiriti, 1965
Julietta, 1953 (Allégret, M. 2, Marais 3, Moreau 3, Alekan 4, Braunberger 4, D'Eaubonne 4)
Juliette et Juliette, 1973 (Girardot 3)
Juliette ou la clé des songes, 1951 (Carné 2, Philipe 3, Alekan 4, Kosma 4, Trauner 4)
Julija Vrevskaja. See Julie Vrevská, 1977
Julius Caesar, 1908 (Costello, M. 3)
Julius Caesar, 1950 (Heston 3, Hunter 3)
Julius Caesar, 1953 (Mankiewicz 2, Brando 3, Calhern 3, Garson 3, Gielgud 3, Kerr 3, O'Brien, E. 3, Gibbons 4, Houseman 4, Rozsa 4, Ruttenberg 4)
Julius Caesar, 1970 (Gielgud 3, Heston 3, Lee, C. 3, Robards 3)
July Days, 1923 (Roach 4)
July 14th. See Quatorze Juillet, 1933
Jumbo, 1962 (Berkeley 2, Durante 3, Ames 4, Daniels 4, Edens 4, Gillespie 4, Pasternak 4)
Jumeaux de Brighton, 1936 (Bresson 2, Raimu 3, Simon, M. 3)
Jument verte, 1959 (Autant-Lara 2, Bourvil 3, Aurenche 4, Bost 4, Douy 4)
Jump. See Salto, 1965
Jump for Glory, 1937 (Fairbanks, D. Jr. 3)
Jump Into Hell, 1955 (Dalio 3)
Jump Your Job, 1922 (Roach 4)
Jumpin' Jupiter, 1955 (Jones 2)
Jumping Beans, 1922 (Fleischer, M. and D. 2)
Jumping Beans, 1930 (Terry 4)
Jumping for Joy, 1956 (Holloway 3)
Jumping Jacks, 1952 (Lewis 2, Taurog 2, Martin, D. 3, Bumstead 4, Head 4, Wallis 4)
Junai monogatari, 1957 (Imai 2)
Junak Markos, 1953 (Dinov 4)
June Bride, 1935 (Terry 4)
June Bride, 1948 (Bainter 3, Davis 3, Montgomery 3, Reynolds, D. 3, Blanke 4, Grot 4, Head 4, McCord 4)
June Madness, 1920 (Roach 4)
June Moon, 1931 (Mankiewicz 2, Sutherland 2)
June Night. See Juninatt, 1965
Junge Baron Neuhaus, 1934 (Herlth 4, Rohrig 4)
Junge Frau von 1914, 1970 (Hoffmann 3)
Junge Graf, 1935 (Ondra 3)

Junge Mann—was nun?, 1967 (Hoffmann 3)
Junge Medardus, 1923 (Curtiz 2)
Junge Torless, 1966 (Schlondorff 2)
Jungens (Staudte 2)
Junges Herz voll Liebe, 1953 (Wicki 2)
Jungfer, 1969 (Hoppe 3)
Jungfrukallen, 1960 (Bergman 2, Von Sydow 3, Nykvist 4)
Jungle, 1937–40 (Cardiff 4)
Jungle Book, 1942 (Johnson, N. 3, Cooper 4, Garmes 4, Hornbeck 4, Korda 4, Wheeler 4)
Jungle Book, 1967 (Disney 2, Sanders 3)
Jungle Book. See Rudyard Kipling's Jungle Book, 1942
Jungle Cat, 1959 (Iwerks 4)
Jungle Fighters. See Long and the Short and the Tall, 1961
Jungle Girl, 1941 (Canutt 4)
Jungle Jim, 1948 (Weissmuller 3, Katzman 4)
Jungle Jim in the Forbidden Land, 1952 (Weissmuller 3, Katzman 4)
Jungle Jingles, 1929 (Lantz 4)
Jungle Jitters, 1934 (Iwerks 4)
Jungle Jitters, 1938 (Freleng 4)
Jungle Jumble, 1932 (Lantz 4)
Jungle Man, 1941 (Crabbe 3)
Jungle Maneaters, 1954 (Katzman 4)
Jungle Manhunt, 1951 (Weissmuller 3, Katzman 4)
Jungle Moon-Men, 1955 (Weissmuller 3, Katzman 4)
Jungle Patrol, 1944 (Finch 3)
Jungle Princess, 1936 (Lamour 3, Milland 3, Head 4)
Jungle Rhythm, 1929 (Disney 2, Iwerks 4)
Jungle Siren, 1942 (Crabbe 3)
Jungle Terror. See Fireball Jungle, 1969
Jungle Trail, 1919 (Farnum 3)
Jungle Trail of the Son of the Tarzan. See Son of Tarzan, 1921
Jungle Warfare, 1943 (Halas and Batchelor 2)
Jungle Woman, 1944 (Salter 4)
Jungle Woman. See Nabonga, 1944
Juninatt, 1965 (Andersson B. 3, Fischer 4)
Juninatten, 1940 (Bergman 3, Bjornstrand 3)
Juninin no shashin-ka, 1953–57 (Teshigahara 2)
Junior Bonner, 1972 (Peckinpah 2, Johnson, B. 3, Lupino 3, McQueen, S. 3, Preston 3, Ballard 4)
Junior Jive Bomber, 1944 (Prinz 4)
Junior Miss, 1945 (Seaton 2, Clarke, C.C. 4)
Junior Officer, 1912 (Bosworth 3)
Junjo, 1930 (Naruse 2)
Junkman, 1918 (Roach 4)
Juno and the Paycock, 1929 (Hitchcock 2, Fitzgerald 3, Reville 4)
Junoon, 1978 (Benegal 2, Azmi 3, Nihalani 4)
Junpaku no yoru, 1951 (Mori 3)
Juntos, pero no revueltos, 1938 (Negrete 3)
Jupiter. See Douze heures de bonheur, 1952
Jupiter's Darling, 1955 (Sidney 2, Keel 3, Sanders 3, Williams 3, Gibbons 4, Pan 4, Plunkett 4, Rose 4, Rosher 4)
Jupiter's Thigh. See On a volé la cuisse de Jupiter, 1980
Jupiter's Thunderbolts. See Tonnerre de Jupiter, 1903
Jurébavard, 1947–51 (Verneuil 2)
Jurmana, 1979 (Bachchan 3)
Jurokuya seishin, 1931 (Hasegawa 3)
Jury of Fate, 1917 (Browning 2)
Jury of One. See Testament, 1974
Jury's Evidence, 1936 (Dalrymple 4)
Jury's Secret, 1938 (Darwell 3, Wray 3, Krasner 4)
Jus' Passin' Through, 1923 (Rogers, W. 3, Roach 4)
Jusan nichi no kinyobi, 1959 (Oshima 2)
Jusqu'à la nuit, 1984 (Branco 4, de Almeida 4)
Jusqu'à la victoire, 1970 (Godard 2)
Jusqu'au bout du monde, 1962 (Delerue 4)
Jusqu'au coeur, 1968 (Lefebvre 2)
Jusqu'au dernier, 1956 (Moreau 3, Audiard 4, D'Eaubonne 4)
Jusqu'au feu exclusivement, 1971 (Fradetal 4)
Just a Bear, 1931 (Sennett 2)
Just a Clown, 1934 (Terry 4)
Just a Few Little Things, 1916 (Beery 3)
Just a Gigolo, 1931 (Milland 3)

K

Kaettekita yopparai, 1968 (Oshima 2, Toda 4)
Kaffeehaus, 1971 (Fassbinder 2, Schygulla 3)
Kafuku, 1937 (Naruse 2)
Kagaj Ke Phool, 1959 (Burman 4)
Kaga-sodo, 1953 (Yamada 3)
Kagayake nihon no josei, 1932 (Tanaka 3)
Kagayaku Showa, 1929 (Tanaka 3)
Kage no kuruma, 1970 (Iwashita 3)
Kage no Tsume, 1972 (Iwashita 3)
Kage o matoite, 1949 (Kagawa 3)
Kageboshi, 1950 (Yamada 3, Yamamura 3)
Kagemusha, 1980 (Kurosawa 2, Miyagawa 4, Muraki 4)
Kagero, 1969 (Shindo 2)
Kagero ezu, 1959 (Kinugasa 2)
Kagero-gasa, 1959 (Hasegawa 3, Kagawa 3)
Kagi, 1959 (Ichikawa 2, Kyo 3, Miyagawa 4)
Kagirinaki hodo, 1934 (Naruse 2)
Kagoya Dainagon, 1931 (Hasegawa 3)
Kagoya hangan, 1935 (Hasegawa 3)
Kaguyahimi, 1935 (Tsuburaya 3)
Kahin Aur Chal, 1968 (Anand 3)
Kahreden kursun, 1965 (Guney 2)
Kaidan, 1964 (Kobayashi 2, Kishida 3, Shimura 3, Takemitsu 4,
Toda 4)
Kaido no kishi, 1928 (Gosho 2)
Kaigun bakugekitai, 1940 (Hayasaka 4, Tsuburaya 4)
Kaigun tokubetsu shonen hei, 1972 (Imai 2, Muraki 4)
Kaiju daisenso, 1966 (Tsuburaya 4)
Kaiju soshingeki, 1968 (Tsuburaya 4)
Kaiketsu, 1941 (Yamada 3)
Kaikoku danji, 1926 (Mizoguchi 2)
Kaikokuki, 1928 (Kinugasa 2, Hasegawa 3, Tanaka 3)
Kaikyou, 1982 (Muraki 4)
Kainszeichen, 1919 (Oswald 2)
Kaintuck, 1912 (Reid 3)
Kaise Kahoon, 1964 (Burman 4)
Kaisen no zenya, 1943 (Tanaka 3)
Kaiser, The Beast of Berlin, 1918 (Chaney Lon 3)
Kaiserwalzer, 1932 (Frohlich 3, Sakall 3)
Kaisha-in seikatsu, 1929 (Ozu 2)
Kaitchka, 1915 (Mozhukin 3)
Kaitei gunkan, 1964 (Tsuburaya 4)
Kaito Sayamaro, 1928 (Hasegawa 3, Tsuburaya 4)
Kaizoki-sen, 1950 (Mifune 3)
Kak budet golosovat' izbiratel', 1937 (Yutkevich 2)
Kak khoroshi, kak svezhi byli rozi, 1913 (Protazanov 2)
Kak on lgal eyo muzhu, 1957 (Smoktunovsky 3)
Kak zakalyalas stal, 1942 (Donskoi 2)
Kakedashi jidai, 1947 (Hayasaka 4)
Kakka, 1940 (Imai 2)
Kako, 1961 (Yamamura 3)
Kako su se voleli Romeo i Julija, 1967 (Marković 3)
Kakoe, ono, more?, 1965 (Shukshin 3)
Kakubei-jishi, 1951 (Yamada 3)
Kakureta ninkimono, 1959 (Yoda 4)
Kakushi toride no san-akunin, 1958 (Kurosawa 2, Mifune 3, Shimura 3,
Muraki 4)
Kakute kamikaze wa fuku, 1944 (Miyagawa 4)
Kakute yume ari, 1954 (Yamamura 3)
Kal, Aaj Aur Kal, 1972 (Kapoor 2)
Kala Baaz, 1977 (Anand 3)
Kala Bazar, 1960 (Anand 3, Burman 4)
Kala Pani, 1958 (Anand 3, Burman 4)
Kaláliuvit, 1970 (Roos 2)
Kalamita, 1982 (Chytilová 2)
Kaleidoscope, 1935 (Lye 2)
Kaleidoscope, 1966 (Beatty 3, York, S. 3)
Kaleidoscope. See Chalachitra, 1981
Kalemites Visit Gibraltar, 1912 (Olcott 2)
Kalina krasnaya, 1974 (Shukshin 3)
Kali-Yug, Goddess of Vengeance, 1963 (Kinski 3)
Kaliyugaya, 1982 (Peries 2)
Kalkmalerier, 1954 (Roos 2)

Kalle Karlsson från Jularbo, 1952 (Thulin 3)
Kallelsen, 1974 (Bergman 2, Andersson H. 3)
Kalte Herz, 1950 (Geschonneck 3)
Kalyug, 1981 (Benegal 2, Nihalani 4)
Kam čert nemuže, 1970 (Brodský 3)
Kam s ním, 1956 (Kopecký 3)
Kama Sutra Rides Again, 1971 (Godfrey 4)
Kamaeleonen. See Maaneprinsessen, 1916
Kamal, 1949 (Burman 4)
Kamali zeybek, 1964 (Guney 2)
Kamaszváros, 1962 (Mészáros 2)
Kamenny tsvetok, 1946 (Ptushko 2)
Kameradschaft, 1931 (Pabst 2, Metzner 4, Wagner 4)
Kami e no michi, 1928 (Gosho 2)
Kamienne niebo, 1959 (Lomnicki 3)
Kamigami no fukaki yokubo, 1968 (Imamura 2)
Kaminari oyaji, 1937 (Takamine 3)
Kaminingyo haru no sayaki, 1926 (Mizoguchi 2)
Kamiyui Shinza, 1932 (Hasegawa 3)
Kamla, 1984 (Azmi 3)
Kammarjunkaren, 1913 (Stiller 2, Jaenzon 4)
Kammermusik, 1924 (Porten 3)
Kamo to negi, 1966 (Mori 3)
Kamouraska, 1973 (Jutra 2, Bujold 3)
Kampen Mod Kraeften, 1947 (Dreyer 2)
Kampen om hans hjarta, 1916 (Stiller 2)
Kampen om tungtvannet. See Bataille de l'eau lourde, 1948
Kampf des Donald Westhof, 1927 (Homolka 3, Courant 4)
Kampf gegen Berlin, 1925 (Junge 4)
Kampf um Karthago. See Salammbo, 1924
Kampf um Rom, 1968 (Siodmak 2, Welles 2, Andersson H. 3,
Harvey 3)
Kampf um Rom II, 1969 (Harvey 3)
Kampf uns ich, 1922 (Tschechowa 3)
Kampfende Herzen, 1920 (Lang 2, Von Harbou 4, Warm 4)
Kampfende Welten, 1922 (Dupont 2)
Kamyaab, 1984 (Azmi 3)
Kan Govdeyi goturdu, 1965 (Guney 2)
Kan su gibi akacak, 1969 (Guney 2)
Kanal, 1957 (Wajda 2, Stawinsky 4)
Kanashiki hakuchi, 1924 (Mizoguchi 2)
Kanashimi wa onna dakeni, 1958 (Shindo 2, Kyo 3, Tanaka 3)
Kanawa, 1972 (Shindo 2)
Kanchanjanga, 1962 (Ray, S. 2, Datta 4, Mitra 4)
Kancho mada shinazu, 1942 (Yoshimura 2)
Kandidat, 1980 (Kluge 2, Schlondorff 2)
Kandy Perahera, 1971 (Peries 2)
Kane, 1926 (Mizoguchi 2)
Kanetsu-hen, 1961 (Takamine 3)
Kangaroo, 1952 (Milestone 2, Boone 3, O'Hara 3, Rafferty 3,
Clarke, C.C. 4, Newman 4)
Kangaroo Steak, 1930 (Terry 4)
Kangaroom Courting, 1954 (Burness 4)
Kangeki jidai, 1928 (Tanaka 3)
Kanhaiya, 1959 (Kapoor 3)
Kanigliche Bettler, 1917 (Oswald 2)
Kani-ko sen, 1953 (Mori 3, Yamamura 3)
Kanimin son damlasina kadar, 1970 (Guney 2)
Kanketsu Sasaki Kojiro, 1951 (Mifune 3)
Kanko no machi, 1944 (Kinoshita 2)
Kanli buğday, 1965 (Guney 2)
Kann dej som Hemma, 1948 (Thulin 3)
Kanojo, 1926 (Gosho 2, Tanaka 3)
Kanojo no hatsugen, 1946 (Tanaka 3)
Kanojo to kare, 1963 (Hani 2, Okada 3, Takemitsu 4)
Kanojo to unmei, 1924 (Kinugasa 2)
Kanonenserenade, 1958 (De Sica 2, Staudte 2)
Kanpai! Miai-kekkon, 1958 (Kagawa 3)
Kanraku no onna, 1924 (Mizoguchi 2)
Kansas City Bomber, 1972 (Welch 3)
Kansas City Confidential, 1952 (Elam 3, Van Cleef 3)
Kansas City Kitty, 1944 (Donen 2, Guffey 4)
Kansas City Princess, 1934 (Blondell 3, Barnes 4, Orry-Kelly 4)

Kawano hotoride, 1962 (Yamamura 3)
Kaya. *See* Paja ubit ču te!, 1967
Kaya, I'll Kill You. *See* Paja ubit ču te!, 1967
Kazabana, 1959 (Kinoshita 2)
Kazablan, 1973 (Golan and Globus 4)
Kazaks—Minorité nationale—Sinkiang, 1977 (Ivens 2)
Kazan, 1921 (Selig 4)
Kazan-myaku, 1950 (Mori 3)
Každá koruna dobrá, 1961 (Kopecký 3)
Každý den odvahu, 1964 (Schorm 2, Brejchová 3, Brodský 3)
Kaze futatabi, 1952 (Yamamura 3)
Kaze no naka no mendori, 1948 (Ozu 2, Ryu 3, Tanaka 3)
Kaze no shisen, 1963 (Iwashita 3)
Kaze tachinu, 1954 (Yamamura 3)
Kazoku, 1942 (Tanaka 3)
Kazoku no jijo, 1962 (Yoshimura 2)
Kde je Míša?, 1954 (Hofman 4)
Kdo hledá zlaté dno, 1975 (Menzel 2)
Kdo šetří, ten jede, 1954 (Hofman 4)
Kdo své nebe neunese, 1959 (Schorm 2)
Kdyby tisic karinetu, 1964 (Brejchová 3)
Kdybych byl tátou, 1939 (Stallich 4)
Když má svátek Dominika, 1967 (Kopecký 3, Stallich 4)
Když struny Ikají, 1930 (Haas 3, Vích 4)
Kean, 1910 (Blom 2)
Kean, 1921 (George, H. 3)
Kean, 1924 (Mozhukin 3)
Kean, 1940 (Brazzi 3)
Kean, 1956 (Rosi 2, Gassman 3, Cristaldi 4, D'Amico 4, Di Venanzo 4)
Kedamono no yado, 1951 (Kurosawa 2)
Keep, 1983 (Box 4)
Keep 'Em Flying, 1941 (Abbott and Costello 3)
Keep 'em Growing, 1943 (Terry 4)
Keep 'em Rolling, 1934 (Huston 3, Huston 3, Plunkett 4, Steiner 4)
Keep 'em Slugging, 1943 (Howard, S. 3, Salter 4)
Keep Fit, 1937 (Formby 3)
Keep in Style, 1934 (Fleischer, M. and D. 2)
Keep Laughing, 1932 (Arbuckle 3)
Keep On Rockin', 1971 (Leacock 2)
Keep Smiling, 1925 (Bruckman 4, Garmes 4)
Keep Smiling, 1938 (Fields, G. 3, Cronjager 4)
Keep Your Mouth Shut, 1944 (McLaren 2, Dunning 4)
Keep Your Powder Dry, 1945 (Moorehead 3, Turner, L. 3, Irene 4)
Keep Your Seats Please, 1936 (Formby 3, Sim 3)
Keeper, 1983 (Lee, C. 3)
Keeper of the Bees, 1925 (Bow 3)
Keeper of the Bees, 1935 (Bosworth 3)
Keeper of the Bees, 1947 (Sturges, J. 2, Darwell 3)
Keeper of the Flame, 1942 (Cukor 2, Saville 2, Hepburn, K. 3, Meek 3, Tracy 3, Adrian 4, Daniels 4, Kaper 4, Stewart 4, Wheeler 4)
Keeper of the Lions, 1937 (Lantz 4)
Keepers. *See* Tête contre les murs, 1958
Keeping Company, 1940 (Freund 4, Mankiewicz 4)
Keeping Fit, 1942 (Crawford, B. 3)
Keeps Rainin' All the Time, 1934 (Fleischer, M. and D. 2)
Kegyelet, 1967 (Szabó 2)
Keian hi-cho, 1952 (Yamamura 3)
Keimendes Leben, 1918–19 (Jannings 3)
Kein Engel ist so rein, 1950 (Tschechowa 3, Herlth 4)
Kein Engel ist so rein, 1960 (Albers 3)
Keine Angst vor Liebe, 1933 (Walbrook 3)
Keiraku hichu, 1928 (Kinugasa 2)
Keirin shonin gyojoki, 1964 (Imamura 2)
Keishicho monogatari, 1960 (Yamamura 3)
Kejsaren av Portugallien, 1944 (Molander 2, Sjostrom 2, Borgstrom 3)
Kekkon, 1947 (Kinoshita 2, Tanaka 3)
Kekkon he no michi, 1937 (Yamada 3)
Kekkon kaido, 1933 (Tanaka 3)
Kekkon koshinkyoku, 1951 (Ichikawa 2)
Kekkon no seitai, 1941 (Imai 2)
Kekkon no sekkei, 1963 (Iwashita 3)
Kekkon-gaku nyumon, 1930 (Ozu 2)
Kekkonshiki, kekkonshiki, 1963 (Iwashita 3, Tanaka 3)

Kelly and Me, 1957 (Johnson, V. 3)
Kelly From the Emerald Isle, 1913 (Guy 2)
Kelly Gets His Man, 1927 (Wyler 2)
Kelly of the Secret Service, 1936 (Katzman 4)
Kelly the Second, 1936 (Roach 4)
Kelly's Heroes, 1970 (Eastwood 3, Stanton 3, Sutherland 3, Figueroa 4, Schifrin 4)
Kelp Industry, 1913 (Sennett 2)
Kemono no Ken, 1965 (Iwashita 3)
Kemonomichi, 1965 (Muraki 4, Takemitsu 4)
Kempy. *See* Wise Girls, 1929
Ken Murray's Hollywood, 1965 (Grant, C. 3)
Ken to hana, 1972 (Mori 3)
Kenju jigoku, 1952 (Yamamura 3)
Kenju yo saraba, 1960 (Kishida 3)
Kenka-tobi, 1939 (Hasegawa 3, Yamada 3)
Kennedy the Great, 1939 (Hunt 4)
Kennel Murder Case, 1933 (Curtiz 2, Astor 3, Powell, W. 3, Orry-Kelly 4)
Kenny Rogers as the Gambler, 1980 (Biroc 4)
Keno Bates, Liar, 1915 (Hart 3, August 4)
Kenran taru satsujin, 1951 (Miyagawa 4)
Kensetsu no hitobito, 1934 (Yamada 3)
Kentish Industries, 1913 (Pearson 2)
Kentuckian, 1908 (Bitzer 4)
Kentuckian, 1955 (Carradine 3, Lancaster 3, Matthau 3, Merkel 3, Van Cleef 3, Herrmann 4, Laszlo 4)
Kentucky, 1938 (Brennan 3, Young, L. 3, Trotti 4, Zanuck 4)
Kentucky Bells, 1931 (Lantz 4)
Kentucky Colonel, 1920 (Glennon 4)
Kentucky Feud, 1905 (Bitzer 4)
Kentucky Fried Movie, 1977 (Sutherland 3)
Kentucky Handicap, 1926 (Brown, Harry Joe 4)
Kentucky Kernels, 1934 (Stevens 2, Dumont 3, Cronjager 4, Plunkett 4, Steiner 4)
Kentucky Moonshine, 1938 (Carradine 3, Summerville 3, MacGowan 4)
Kentucky Pride, 1925 (Ford, J. 2, Walthall 3)
Kenun Naruto shibuki. *See* Awa no odoriko, 1941
Kenya, South Africa, 1962 (Leacock 2)
Képi, 1905 (Guy 2)
Kept Husbands, 1931 (Bacon 2, McCrea 3, Steiner 4)
Keresztello, 1967 (Gaál 2, Latinovits 3)
Kermes. *See* Kirmes, 1960
Kermesse aux chansons, 1947–51 (Verneuil 2)
Kermesse fantastique, 1951 (Auric 4)
Kermesse héroïque, 1935 (Feyder 2, Jouvet 3, Rosay 3, Meerson 4, Spaak 4, Stradling 4, Trauner 4)
Kernels of Corn, 1947 (Fleischer, M. and D. 2)
Kerry Gow, 1912 (Olcott 2)
Kertes kázak utcájá, 1963 (Gabór 3, Latinovits 3)
Kes, 1969 (Loach 2)
Kesa and Moritou. *See* Kesa to Moritou, 1939
Kesa to Moritou, 1939 (Miyagawa 4)
Keshoyuki, 1940 (Yamada 3)
Kessen, 1944 (Yoshimura 4)
Kessen no osorae, 1943 (Hara 3, Tsuburaya 4)
Két arckép, 1965 (Kovács 2)
Két bors okrocske, 1955 (Macskássy 4)
Két emelet boldogsag, 1960 (Torocsik 3)
Két félido a pokolban, 1961 (Fábri 2)
Két lány az utcán, 1939 (De Toth 2)
Két vallomas, 1957 (Torocsik 3)
Kétszívu férfi, 1916 (Korda 2)
Kettles in the Ozarks, 1956 (Merkel 3)
Ketto Ganryu-Jima, 1956 (Mifune 3, Shimura 3)
Ketto Kagiya no tsuji, 1952 (Kurosawa 2, Mifune 3, Shimura 3)
Kettou gofun-mar, 1953 (Yoda 4)
Key, 1934 (Curtiz 2, Crisp 3, Powell, W. 3, Haller 4, Orry-Kelly 4)
Key, 1953 (Lancaster 3)
Key, 1958 (Reed 2, Caine 3, Holden 3, Homolka 3, Howard, T. 3, Loren 3, Arnold 4, Foreman 4, Morris 4)
Key, 1976 (Godfrey 4)

Kill a Dragon, 1967 (Palance 3)
Kill Me Tomorrow, 1957 (Fisher 2, O'Brien, P. 3)
Kill or Be Killed, 1942 (Lye 2)
Kill or Be Killed, 1949 (Hunt 4)
Kill or Cure, 1923 (Laurel 3, Roach 4)
Kill Patrice, un shérif pas comme les autres, 1969 (Reichenbach 2, Braunberger 4)
Kill the Killer. See Koroshiya o barase, 1969
Kill the Nerve, 1922 (Roach 4)
Kill the Umpire, 1950 (Bacon 2, Tashlin 2, Bendix 3, Merkel 3)
Killdozer, 1974 (Burtt 4, Whitlock 4)
Killer!. See Que la bête meure, 1969
Killer Ape, 1953 (Weissmuller 3, Katzman 4)
Killer at Large, 1936 (Chaney Lon, Jr. 3)
Killer Bees, 1974 (Swanson 3)
Killer by Night, 1971 (McCambridge 3, Wagner 3, Jones 4)
Killer Cop. See Polizia ha le mani legate, 1974
Killer Diller, 1948 (McQueen, B. 3)
Killer Elite, 1975 (Peckinpah 2, Caan 3, Duvall, R. 3, Young, G. 3)
Killer Fish, 1978 (Black 3)
Killer Force, 1975 (Lee, C. 3)
Killer Force. See Diamond Mercenaries, 1975
Killer from Yuma. See Viva la muerte . . . tua!, 1972
Killer in the Family, 1983 (Mitchum 3)
Killer Inside Me, 1975 (Carradine 3, Keach 3, Wynn 3, Fraker 4)
Killer Is Loose, 1956 (Boetticher 2, Cotten 3, Ballard 4)
Killer McCoy, 1947 (Donen 2, Rooney 3, Ruttenberg 4)
Killer Nun. See Suor omicidi, 1978
Killer on a Horse. See Welcome to Hard Times, 1967
Killer Shark, 1950 (Boetticher 2)
Killer That Stalked New York, 1950 (Malone 3, Biroc 4, Salter 4)
Killer Walks, 1952 (Harvey 3)
Killers, 1946 (Brooks, R. 2, Huston 2, Siodmak 2, Gardner 3, Lancaster 3, O'Brien, E. 3, Rozsa 4, Veiller 4)
Killers, 1964 (Cassavetes 2, Siegel 2, Dickinson 3, Marvin 3, Reagan 3, Mancini 4, Williams, J. 4)
Killers. See Verano sangriento, 1977
Killer's Carnival. See Spie contro il mondo, 1966
Killers from Space, 1953 (Clothier 4)
Killer's Kiss, 1955 (Kubrick 2)
Killers of Kilimanjaro, 1959 (Pleasance 3, Taylor, R. 3, Alwyn 4)
Killers on Parade. See Yuhi ni akai ore no kao, 1961
Killing, 1956 (Kubrick 2, Cook 3, Hayden 3, Ballard 4)
Killing Hearts, 1914 (Sennett 2)
Killing Horace, 1914 (Arbuckle 3)
Killing in Monte Carlo. See Crimen, 1960
Killing Kind, 1973 (Sothern 3)
Killing of a Chinese Bookie, 1976 (Cassavetes 2)
Killing of an Egg, 1977 (Driessen 4)
Killing of Sister George, 1968 (Aldrich 2, York, S. 3, Biroc 4)
Kilroy on Deck. See French Leave, 1948
Kilroy Was Here, 1947 (Coogan 3, Cooper, J 3)
Kim, 1950 (Saville 2, Flynn 3, Lukas 3, Previn 4)
Kim, 1984 (O'Toole 3)
Kimi shinitamou koto nakare, 1954 (Tsukasa 3, Hayasaka 4)
Kimi to iku michi, 1936 (Naruse 2)
Kimi to wakarete, 1933 (Naruse 2)
Kimi to yuku amerika-kogo, 1950 (Kagawa 3)
Kimiko, Wife! Be Like a Rose. See Tsuma yo bara no yo ni, 1935
Kin no tamago, 1952 (Kagawa 3)
Kína vendégei voltunk, 1957 (Jancsó 2)
Kinare Kinare, 1962 (Anand 3)
Kind Hearts and Coronets, 1949 (Hamer 2, Greenwood 3, Guinness 3, Balcon 4, Slocombe 4)
Kind Lady, 1935 (Meek 3, Rathbone 3)
Kind Lady, 1951 (Sturges, J. 2, Barrymore E. 3, Lansbury 3, Wynn 3, Bennett 4, Plunkett 4, Raksin 4, Ruttenberg 4)
Kind Millionaire. See Pytlákova schovanka, 1949
Kind of Loving, 1962 (Schlesinger 2, Bates 3)
Kind ruft, 1914 (Gad 2, Nielsen 3, Freund 4)
Kindai musha shugyo, 1928 (Tanaka 3)
Kinder der Finsternis, 1922 (Dupont 2, Leni 2, Freund 4)
Kinder der Holle. See Hitler. Ein Film aus Deutschland, 1977

Kinder der Strasse, 1929 (George, H. 3)
Kinder des Generals, 1912 (Gad 2, Nielsen 3, Kraly 4)
Kinder, Mutter, und ein General, 1955 (Wicki 2, Kinski 3, Schell, Maximilian 3, Pommer 4)
Kinderarzt, 1910 (Porten 3, Messter 4)
Kinderseelen klagen euch an, 1927 (Rasp 3)
Kindled Courage, 1923 (Miller, V. 4)
Kindling, 1915 (DeMille 2, Buckland 4)
Kindly Scram, 1943 (Fleischer, M. and D. 2)
Kindred of the Dust, 1923 (Walsh 2, Menzies 4)
Kinegraphy, 1955 (Takemitsu 4)
Kinek a torvénye?, 1978 (Torocsik 3)
Kinesiske Vase. See Vasens Hemmelighed, 1913
Kinetic Art Show—Stockholm, 1961 (Breer 2)
King, 1930 (Langdon 3, Roach 4)
King, 1970 (Jones, J.E. 3)
King: A Filmed Record . . . Montgomery to Memphis, 1970 (Lumet 2, Heston 3, Lancaster 3, Quinn 3, Woodward 3)
King and Country, 1964 (Losey 2, Bogarde 3)
King and Four Queens, 1956 (Walsh 2, Gable 3, Ballard 4, North 4)
King and I, 1956 (Brynner 3, Kerr 3, Kerr 3, Brackett, C. 4, Lehman 4, Newman 4, Shamroy 4, Sharaff 4, Wheeler 4)
King and the Bird. See Roi et l'oiseau, 1980
King and the Chorus Girl, 1937 (Leroy 2, Blondell 3, Horton 3, Wyman 3, Gaudio 4, Krasna 4, Orry-Kelly 4)
King and the Woman. See Král a žena, 1967
King Charlie. See His Prehistoric Past, 1914
King Cowboy, 1928 (Mix 3)
King Creole, 1958 (Curtiz 2, Matthau 3, Presley 3, Head 4, Wallis 4)
King David, 1985 (Gere 3, Adam 4)
King for a Day, 1940 (Fleischer, M. and D. 2)
King Game. See Hra na krále, 1967
King Gun. See Gatling Gun, 1973
King in New York, 1957 (Chaplin 2, Colpi 4, Périnal 4)
King Klunk, 1933 (Lantz 4)
King Kong, 1933 (Schoedsack 2, Johnson, N. 3, Wray 3, Clothier 4, Cooper 4, Dunn 4, O'Brien 4, Selznick 4, Steiner 4)
King Kong, 1976 (Bridges 3, Lange 3, Baker 4, Barry 4, De Laurentiis 4, Dunn 4, Semple 4)
King Kong Escapes. See Kingu Kongu no gyakushu, 1967
King Kong tai Gojira, 1962 (Tsuburaya 4)
King Kong vs. Godzilla. See King Kong tai Gojira, 1962
King Lavra. See Král Lávra, 1950
King Lear, 1909 (Costello, M. 3)
King Lear, 1970 (Cusack 3, Wakhévitch 4)
King Lear, 1983 (Hurt, J. 3)
King Lear. See Karol Lear, 1971
King Log, 1932 (Grierson 2)
King Looney XIV, 1935 (Terry 4)
King Midas, Junior, 1942 (Fleischer, M. and D. 2, Hubley 4)
King of Alcatraz, 1938 (Florey 2, Carey 3, Preston 3, Quinn 3, Head 4)
King of Boda. See Bodakunden, 1920
King of Burlesque, 1936 (Baxter W. 3, Faye 3, Wyman 3, MacGowan 4, Zanuck 4)
King of Chinatown, 1939 (Quinn 3, Wong 3, Head 4)
King of Comedy, 1982 (Lewis 2, Scorsese 2, De Niro 3, Leven 4)
King of Gamblers, 1937 (Florey 2, Brooks 3, Crabbe 3, Trevor 3, Dreier 4, Head 4)
King of Hearts, 1966 (Bates 3, Brasseur 3)
King of Hearts. See Roi de coeur, 1966
King of Jazz, 1930 (Brennan 3, Crosby 3, Summerville 3, Laemmle 4, MacArthur 4)
King of Kings, 1927 (DeMille 2, Boyd 3, Johnson, N. 3, Schildkraut 3 Carré 4, Grot 4, Macpherson 4, Westmore, M. 4)
King of Kings, 1961 (Ray, N. 2, Welles 2, Hunter 3, Ryan 3, Torn 3, Krasner 4, Planer 4, Rozsa 4, Wakhévitch 4)
King of Kings. See Kirallar kirali, 1965
King of Kings. See Krák Králu, 1963
King of Marvin Gardens, 1972 (Rafelson 2, Burstyn 3, Dern 3, Nicholson 3, Kovacs 4)
King of Paris, 1934 (Hardwicke 3, Richardson 3)
King of Soho. See Street of Sin, 1928
King of the Arena, 1933 (McCord 4)

King of the Cannibal Islands, 1908 (Bitzer 4)
King of the Circus. *See* Zirkuskonig, 1924
King of the Congo, 1952 (Crabbe 3, Katzman 4)
King of the Coral Sea, 1954 (Rafferty 3)
King of the Cowboys, 1943 (Rogers, R. 3, Canutt 4)
King of the Damned, 1936 (Veidt 3, Balcon 4, Bennett 4, Gilliat 4)
King of the Gypsies, 1978 (Hayden 3, Sarandon 3, Winters 3,
    De Laurentiis 4, Nykvist 4)
King of the Jungle, 1933 (Crabbe 3, Haller 4)
King of the Khyber Rifles, 1953 (King 2, Herrmann 4, Lemaire 4,
    Shamroy 4, Wheeler 4)
King of the Khyber Rifles. *See* Black Watch, 1929
King of the Mardi Gras, 1935 (Fleischer, M. and D. 2)
King of the Mountain, 1981 (Hopper 3)
King of the Newsboys, 1938 (Ayres 3)
King of the Pecos, 1936 (Wayne 3, Canutt 4)
King of the Ritz, 1933 (Gallone 2, Balcon 4)
King of the Roaring Twenties, 1961 (Rooney 3, Schildkraut 3, Wynn 3,
    Swerling 4, Waxman 4)
King of the Rodeo, 1929 (Summerville 3)
King of the Stallions, 1942 (Cody 3)
King of the Street. *See* Král ulice, 1935
King of the Sumava. *See* Král Sumavy, 1959
King of the Texas Rangers, 1941 (Canutt 4)
King of the Turf, 1939 (Costello, D. 3, Menjou 3)
King of the Underworld, 1939 (Bogart 3, Francis, K. 3, Orry-Kelly 4)
King of the Wild, 1931 (Karloff 3, Karloff 3, Eason 4)
King of Thieves. *See* Dolandiricilar, 1961
King of Wild Horses, 1924 (Roach 4)
King on Main Street, 1925 (Love 3, Menjou 3, Howe 4)
King, Queen, Knave, 1972 (Skolimowski 2, Niven 3)
King, Queen, Knave. *See* Herzbube, 1972
King Rat, 1965 (Mills 3, Segal 3, Barry 4, Guffey 4)
King Richard and the Crusaders, 1954 (Harrison 3, Harvey 3, Mayo 3,
    Sanders 3, Blanke 4, Steiner 4)
King Richard the Lion-Hearted, 1923 (Beery 3)
King Solomon, 1918 (Hardy 3)
King Solomon of Broadway, 1935 (Crosland 2, D'Agostino 4,
    Mandell 4)
King Solomon's Mines, 1937 (Hardwicke 3, Robeson 3, Balcon 4,
    Bennett 4, Junge 4)
King Solomon's Mines, 1950 (Granger 3, Haas 3, Kerr 3, Plunkett 4,
    Surtees 4)
King Solomon's Mines, 1985 (Golan and Globus 4, Goldsmith 4)
King Steps Out, 1936 (Von Sternberg 2, Ballard 4, Buchman 4)
King Street War, 1970 (Brazzi 3)
King Tut's Tomb, 1950 (Terry 4)
King Ubu. *See* Ubu Roi, 1976
King Zilch, 1933 (Terry 4)
Kingdom of Islands, 1956 (Carlsen 2)
Kingdom of the Fairies. *See* Royaume des Fées,
    1903
Kings and Queens, 1956 (Czinner 2)
King's Breakfast, 1936 (Reiniger 2)
King's Breakfast, 1962 (Auer 3)
King's Cup, 1932 (Wilcox 2)
King's Dancer. *See* Tanzerin von Sanssouci, 1933
King's Daughter, 1934 (Terry 4)
King's Game, 1916 (White 3)
Kings Go Forth, 1958 (Daves 2, Curtis 3, Sinatra 3, Wood 3,
    Bernstein 4, Cahn 4)
King's Jester. *See* Re si diverte, 1941
King's Messenger, 1908 (Bitzer 4)
Kings of the Forest, 1912 (Selig 4)
Kings of the Road. *See* Im Lauf der Zeit, 1976
Kings of the Sun, 1963 (Brynner 3, Bernstein 4, Reynolds 4)
King's Pirate, 1967 (Whitlock 4)
King's Rhapsody, 1955 (Wilcox 2, Flynn 3, Neagle 3)
Kings Row, 1941 (Wood 2, Anderson J. 3, Coburn, C. 3, Cummings 3,
    Ouspenskaya 3, Rains 3, Reagan 3, Sheridan 3, Friedhofer 4,
    Howe 4, Korngold 4, Menzies 4, Orry-Kelly 4, Robinson 4,
    Wallis 4, Westmore, P. 4)
King's Story, 1965 (Welles 2)

King's Thief, 1955 (Moore, R. 3, Niven 3, Sanders 3, Plunkett 4,
    Rozsa 4)
King's Vacation, 1933 (Arliss 3, Powell, D. 3, Grot 4, Orry-Kelly 4)
King-Size Canary, 1947 (Avery 2)
Kingu Kongu no gyakushu, 1967 (Tsuburaya 4)
Kinkaid Gambler, 1916 (Hersholt 3, Johnson, N. 3)
Kinkan-shoku, 1975 (Kyo 3)
Kinno inaka-zamurai, 1932 (Yamada 3)
Kinno inaka-zamurai, 1937 (Yamada 3)
Kinno jidai, 1926 (Kinugasa 2, Hasegawa 3)
Kino, The Padre on Horseback, 1977 (Ireland 3)
Kino v derevne, 1930 (Ptushko 2)
Kino za XX liet, 1940 (Pudovkin 2, Shub 2)
Kinodnevik Glumova, 1923 (Eisenstein 2)
Kino-Eye. *See* Kino-glaz, 1924
Kino-glaz, 1924 (Vertov 2)
Kinokawa, 1966 (Iwashita 3, Tsukasa 3)
Kino-Nedelia, 1918–19 (Vertov 2)
Kino-pravda, 1922–23 (Vertov 2)
Kinsei Meishobu monogatari: Ogongai no hosha, 1954 (Yamada 3)
Kinuyo monogatari, 1930 (Gosho 2, Tanaka 3)
Kinuyo no hatsukoi, 1940 (Tanaka 3)
Kinuyo Story. *See* Kinuyo monogatari, 1930
Kipps, 1941 (Reed 2, Redgrave, M. 3, Beaton 4, Gilliat 4)
Kirallar kirali, 1965 (Guney 2)
Kirare no Senta, 1949 (Yamamura 3)
Kirare Yosa, 1928 (Hasegawa 3)
Kirare Yosaburou, 1960 (Miyagawa 4)
Kire no ame, 1924 (Kinugasa 2)
Kiri no minato, 1923 (Mizoguchi 2)
Kiri no minato no akai hana, 1962 (Kagawa 3)
Kiri no oto, 1956 (Yoda 3)
Kiri no yobanashi, 1946 (Hasegawa 3)
Kirinji, 1926 (Kinugasa 2)
Kirmes, 1960 (Staudte 2)
Kirpitchiki, 1925 (Pudovkin 2, Golovnya 4)
Kis ember, nagy varos, 1967 (Macskássy 4)
Kis Katalin Házasság, 1950 (Gabór 3)
Kisenga. *See* Men of 2 Worlds, 1946
Kishin yuri keiji, 1924 (Kinugasa 2)
Kiskakas gyémánt félkrajcárja, 1950 (Macskássy 4)
Kismat, 1943 (Biswas 4)
Kismet, 1917 (Brenon 2)
Kismet, 1920 (Gaudio 4)
Kismet, 1930 (Dieterle 2, Frohlich 3, Johnson, N. 3, Young, L. 3,
    Estabrook 4, Seitz 4)
Kismet, 1944 (Dieterle 2, Colman 3, De Carlo 3, Dietrich 3, Cole 4,
    Gibbons 4, Irene 4, Rosher 4, Stothart 4)
Kismet, 1955 (Minnelli 2, Elam 3, Keel 3, Ames 4, Cole 4, Freed 4,
    Gibbons 4, Lederer 4, Previn 4, Ruttenberg 4)
Kisoji no tabigasa, 1937 (Shimura 3)
Kisoshinju, 1927 (Tanaka 3)
Kiss, 1900 (Hepworth 2)
Kiss, 1913 (Reid 3)
Kiss, 1916 (Menjou 3)
Kiss, 1921 (Glennon 4)
Kiss, 1929 (Feyder 2, Ayres 3, Garbo 3, Daniels 4, Day 4, Gibbons 4,
    Kraly 4, Lewin 4)
Kiss, 1963 (Warhol 2)
Kiss, 1969 (Popescu-Gopo 4)
Kiss and Kill. *See* Blood of Fu Manchu, 1968
Kiss and Make Up, 1934 (Grant, C. 3, Horton 3, Sheridan 3, Banton 4,
    Dreier 4, Schulberg 4, Shamroy 4)
Kiss and Tell, 1945 (Temple 3, Polglase 4)
Kiss Before Dying, 1956 (Astor 3, Hunter 3, Wagner 3, Woodward 3,
    Ballard 4)
Kiss Before the Mirror, 1933 (Whale 2, Lukas 3, Pidgeon 3, Freund 4)
Kiss for Cinderella, 1922 (Brenon 2)
Kiss for Cinderella, 1926 (Hunt 4)
Kiss for Corliss, 1949 (Aldrich 2, Niven 3, Temple 3)
Kiss from Stadium. *See* Polibek ze stadionu, 1948
Kiss in a Taxi, 1927 (Daniels 3)
Kiss in the Dark, 1925 (Menjou 3, Polglase 4)

Kiss in the Dark, 1949 (Daves 2, Crawford, B. 3, Niven 3, Ouspenskaya 3, Wyman 3, Kurnitz 4, Steiner 4)
Kiss Me Again, 1925 (Lubitsch 2, Bow 3, Kraly 4)
Kiss Me Again, 1931 (Horton 3, Pidgeon 3, Garmes 4)
Kiss Me and Die. *See* Lady in Red, 1979
Kiss Me Cat, 1952 (Jones 2)
Kiss Me Deadly, 1955 (Aldrich 2, Saville 2, Elam 3, Martin, S. 3, Laszlo 4)
Kiss Me Goodbye, 1982 (Mulligan 2, Bridges 3, Caan 3, Field 3, Trevor 3)
Kiss Me Goodbye. *See* Going Gay, 1933
Kiss Me Kate, 1953 (Fosse 2, Sidney 2, Grayson 3, Keel 3, Keel 3, Miller 3, Wynn 3, Pan 4, Plunkett 4, Previn 4, Rosher 4)
Kiss Me, Kill Me, 1976 (O'Brien, P. 3)
Kiss Me, Stupid, 1964 (Wilder 2, Martin, D. 3, Novak 3, Diamond 4, La Shelle 4, Mandell 4, Previn 4, Trauner 4)
Kiss My Hand. *See* Bacciamo le mani, 1973
Kiss of Death, 1947 (Hathaway 2, Malden 3, Mature 3, Widmark 3, Hecht 4, Lederer 4, Lemaire 4, Wheeler 4, Zanuck 4)
Kiss of Death. *See* Dodskyssen, 1917
Kiss of Evil. *See* Kiss of the Vampire, 1963
Kiss of Fire, 1954 (Palance 3, Boyle 4, Salter 4)
Kiss of Fire. *See* Naples au baiser de feu, 1937
Kiss of Hate, 1916 (Barrymore E. 3)
Kiss of the Spider Woman, 1985 (Hurt, W. 3)
Kiss of the Vampire, 1963 (Bernard 4)
Kiss on the Cruise. *See* Kyssen på kryssen, 1950
Kiss, Part III: Women's Ways. *See* Kuchizuke, III: Onna doshi, 1955
Kiss the Blood Off My Hands, 1948 (Fontaine 3, Lancaster 3, Maddow 4, Rozsa 4)
Kiss the Boys Goodbye, 1941 (Ameche 3, Head 4, Young, V. 4)
Kiss the Bride Goodbye, 1944 (Simmons 3)
Kiss the Girls and Make Them Die. *See* Se tutte le donne del mondo, 1966
Kiss the Other Sheik. *See* Oggi, domani, dopodomani, 1965
Kiss Them for Me, 1957 (Donen 2, Grant, C. 3, Mansfield 3, Epstein, J. & P. 4, Krasner 4, Lemaire 4, Wald 4, Wheeler 4)
Kiss Tomorrow Goodbye, 1950 (Bond 3, Cagney 3, Brown, Harry 4)
Kisses, 1922 (Mathis 4)
Kisses and Kurses, 1930 (Lantz 4)
Kisses for Breakfast, 1941 (Muse 3, Wilde 3, Deutsch 4, Edeson 4)
Kisses for My President, 1964 (MacMurray 3, Wallach 3, Kaper 4, Surtees 4)
Kissin' Cousins, 1964 (Presley 3, Katzman 4)
Kissing Bandit, 1948 (Donen 2, Charisse 3, Grayson 3, Miller 3, Sinatra 3, Alton, R. 4, Brown, N. 4, Lennart 4, Pasternak 4, Plunkett 4, Surtees 4)
Kissing Cup's Race, 1920 (Brook 3)
Kissing Cup's Race, 1930 (Carroll M. 3)
Kisuka, 1965 (Tsuburaya 4)
Kit & Co., 1974 (Hoppe 3, Hoppe 3, Mueller-Stahl 3)
Kit Carson, 1940 (Andrews, D. 3, Bond 3, Cody 3, Farnum 3)
Kit Carson over the Great Divide, 1925 (Walthall 3)
Kit Carson's Wooing, 1911 (Mix 3)
Kit for Cat, 1947 (Freleng 4)
Kita no misaki, 1976 (Tanaka 3)
Kita no san-nin, 1946 (Takamine 3, Hayasaka 4)
Kitchen, 1966 (Warhol 2)
Kitchen Lady, 1918 (Sennett 2, Fazenda 3)
Kitchen Think, 1974 (Halas and Batchelor 2)
Kitsch, 1919 (Pick 2)
Kitten Sitter, 1949 (Terry 4)
Kitten with a Whip, 1964 (Biroc 4)
Kitty, 1929 (Saville 2)
Kitty, 1945 (Leisen 2, Goddard 3, Milland 3, Dreier 4, Young, V. 4)
Kitty. *See* Katka, 1950
Kitty and the Cowboys, 1911 (Bunny 3)
Kitty Foiled, 1947 (Hanna and Barbera 4)
Kitty Foyle, 1940 (Wood 2, Cooper, Gladys 3, Rogers, G. 3, Polglase 4, Stewart 4, Trumbo 4)
Kitty from Kansas City, 1931 (Fleischer, M. and D. 2)
Kitty from Killarney, 1927 (Sennett 2)
Kitty Kornered, 1946 (Clampett 4)

Kitty und die grosse Welt, 1956 (Schneider 3)
Kíváncsiság, 1970 (Macskássy 4)
Kiyen ryoko, 1959 (Takemitsu 4)
Kizil vazo, 1961 (Guney 2)
Kizilirmak-Karakoyun, 1967 (Guney 2)
Kizoku no kaidan, 1959 (Yoshimura 2, Mori 3)
Kizudarake no otoko, 1950 (Hasegawa 3)
Kizudarake no sanga, 1964 (Shindo 2, Yamamura 3)
Klabautermanden, 1969 (Carlsen 2)
Klabzuba's Eleven. *See* Klapzubova jedenáctka, 1938
Klanningen, 1964 (Sjoman 2, Bjornstrand 3)
Klansman, 1974 (Fuller 2, Burton 3, Marvin 3)
Klapzubova jedenáctka, 1938 (Stallich 4)
Klart till drabbning, 1937 (Fischer 4, Jaenzon 4)
Kleider machen Leute, 1940 (Herlth 4)
Klein Dorrit, 1934 (Ondra 3, Rasp 3)
Kleine aus der Kongektion, 1925 (Junge 4)
Kleine Chaos, 1966 (Fassbinder 2)
Kleine Dagmar, 1921 (Basserman 3)
Kleine Fernsehspiel, 1975 (Lenica 2)
Kleine Freundin braucht jeder Mann, 1927 (Albers 3)
Kleine Grenzverkehr, 1943 (Rohrig 4)
Kleine Hofkonzert, 1945 (Wagner 4)
Kleine Mutter, 1935 (Pasternak 4)
Kleine Napoleon. *See* So sind die Manner, 1922
Kleine Prinz, 1966 (Wolf 2)
Kleine Residenz, 1942 (Dagover 3)
Kleine Schornsteinfeger, 1935 (Reiniger 2)
Kleine Seitensprung, 1931 (Herlth 4, Rohrig 4)
Kleine Stadt will schlafen gehen, 1954 (Frohlich 3)
Kleine und die grosse Liebe, 1938 (Frohlich 3)
Kleine vom Variété, 1926 (Courant 4)
Kleiner Film einer grossen Stadt—Die Stadt Dusseldorf am Rhein, 1935 (Ruttmann 2)
Kleiner Mann—was nun?, 1967 (Hoppe 3)
Kleinstadtsunder, 1927 (Nielsen 3)
Klepsydra, 1972 (Nowicki 3)
Kleptomaniac, 1905 (Porter 2)
Kleptomanin, 1918 (Gad 2)
Kliatva molodikh, 1944 (Vertov 2)
Klizi-puzi, 1968 (Grgić 4)
Klockan på Ronneberga, 1944 (Borgstrom 3)
Klondike, 1932 (Walthall 3)
Klondike Annie, 1936 (Walsh 2, McLaglen 3, West 3, Dreier 4, Young, V. 4)
Klondike Fever, 1980 (Dickinson 3)
Klondike Fury, 1942 (Howard 2)
Klopka za generala, 1970 (Marković 3)
Klopoty z cieplem, 1964 (Giersz 4)
Klosterfriede, 1917 (Gad 2)
Klosterjager, 1920 (Planer 4)
Klostret I Sendomir, 1920 (Sjostrom 2, Magnusson 4)
Klown aus Liebe. *See* Zirkuskonig, 1925
Klub nravstvennosti, 1915 (Mozhukin 3)
Klubvennen. *See* Nattens Mysterium, 1916
Klugen Frauen, 1936 (Feyder 2)
Klupko, 1972 (Grgić 4)
Klute, 1971 (Pakula 2, Fonda, J. 3, Scheider 3, Sutherland 3, Jenkins 4, Willis 4)
Kluven varld, 1948 (Sucksdorff 2)
Klyuchi shchastya, 1913 (Protazanov 2)
Knabe in Blau, 1919 (Murnau 2, Hoffmann 4)
Knack, 1965 (Lester 2, Bisset 3, Barry 4, Watkin 4)
Knack . . . and How To Get It. *See* Knack, 1965
Knall und Fall als Hochstapler, 1951 (Jurgens 3)
Knave of Hearts, 1954 (Greenwood 3)
Knave of Hearts. *See* Monsieur Ripois, 1954
Kňazat, 1970 (Danailov 3)
Knickerbocker Buckaroo, 1919 (Wellman 2, Fairbanks, D. 3)
Knickerbocker Holiday, 1944 (Coburn, C. 3, Eddy 3, Winters 3, Brown, Harry Joe 4, Cahn 4, Plunkett 4)
Knife, 1918 (Brady 3)
Knife. *See* Mes, 1961

Knife. *See* Nož, 1967
Knife for the Ladies, 1974 (Elam 3)
Knife in the Head. *See* Messer im Kopf, 1978
Knife in the Water. *See* Nóz w wodzie, 1962
Kniga v derevne, 1929 (Ptushko 2)
Knight Duty, 1933 (Langdon 3)
Knight Errant, 1911 (Bosworth 3)
Knight in London, 1928 (Freund 4)
Knight of the Black Art. *See* Tambourin fantastique, 1908
Knight of the Gold Star, 1950 (Bondarchuk 3)
Knight of the Road, 1911 (Griffith 2, Bitzer 4)
Knight of the Snows. *See* Chevalier des neiges, 1912
Knight of the Street. *See* Kaido no kishi, 1928
Knight of the Sword. *See* Santo de la espada, 1969
Knight of the Trails, 1915 (Hart 3)
Knight Riders, 1979 (Romero 2)
Knight Without Armour, 1937 (Feyder 2, Dietrich 3, Donat 3, Biro 4,
    Cardiff 4, Hornbeck 4, Marion 4, Mathieson 4, Meerson 4,
    Rozsa 4, Stradling 4, Wimperis 4)
Knight-Mare Hare, 1955 (Jones 2)
Knights and Ladies, 1912–13 (White 3)
Knights for a Day, 1936 (Lantz 4)
Knights Must Fall, 1948 (Freleng 4)
Knights of the Range, 1940 (Head 4)
Knights of the Round Table, 1953 (Baker S. 3, Ferrer, M. 3,
    Gardner 3, Taylor, R. 3, Berman 4, Jennings 4, Junge 4, Rozsa 4,
    Young, F. 4)
Knights of the Square Table, or The Grail, 1917 (Crosland 2)
Knights of the Teutonic Order. *See* Krzyzacy, 1960
Knighty Knight Bugs, 1957 (Freleng 4)
Kniplinger. *See* Grevindens Aere, 1918
Knitting Pretty. *See* Tetke pletke, 1969
Knive, 1954 (Carlsen 2)
Knivstikkeren. *See* Farlig Forbryder, 1913
Knock, 1950 (Renoir 4)
Knock, Knock, 1940 (Lantz 4)
Knock on Any Door, 1949 (Ray, N. 2, Bogart 3, Guffey 4, Taradash 4)
Knock on Wood, 1954 (Zetterling 2, Kaye 3, Bumstead 4, Frank and
    Panama 4, Head 4, Kidd 4, Young, V. 4)
Knock ou Le Triomphe de la médecine, 1950 (Jouvet 3)
Knock, ou Le Triomphe de la médecine, 1933 (Jouvet 3)
Knocknagow, 1918 (Cusack 3)
Knockout, 1914 (Chaplin 2, Sennett 2, Arbuckle 3, Summerville 3)
Knockout, 1923 (Roach 4)
Knockout, 1932 (Roach 4)
Knockout, 1935 (Ondra 3)
Knockout, 1941 (Kennedy, A. 3, 3, Quinn 3, McCord 4)
Knock-Out. *See* Joe Palooka in the Knock-Out, 1947
Knockout. *See* Right to the Heart, 1942
Knockout Kisses, 1933 (Sennett 2)
Knockout Reilly, 1927 (Cronjager 4)
Knocturne, 1972 (Wieland 2)
Know Your Ally: Britain, 1944 (Capra 2, Hornbeck 4)
Know Your Enemy: Germany, 1945 (Capra 2)
Know Your Enemy: Japan, 1943 (Capra 2, Andrews D. 3,
    Huston 3)
Know Your Men, 1921 (White 3, Ruttenberg 4)
Knowing Men, 1930 (Rosher 4)
Knowing to Learn. *See* Comment savoir, 1966
Knud, 1966 (Roos 2)
Knud Rasmussens mindeekspedition til Kap Seddon, 1982
    (Roos 2)
Knudeproblem, 1959 (Carlsen 2)
Knute Rockne — All American, 1940 (Bacon 2, Howard 2,
    Basserman 3, Crisp 3, O'Brien, P. 3, Reagan 3, Buckner 4,
    Gaudio 4, Wallis 4)
Knutzy Knights, 1954 (Three Stooges 3)
Kobanzame, 1949 (Kinugasa 2, Yamada 3)
Koban-zame: Aizo-hen, 1949 (Hasegawa 3)
Koban-zame: Dogo-hen, 1948 (Hasegawa 3)
Kobayashi Takiji, 1974 (Imai 2)
Kobenhavn, Kalundborg og?, 1934 (Holger-Madsen 2)
Kobo no seishun, 1942 (Takamine 3)

Kobo Shinsen-gumi: Zen-shi, Ko-shi, 1930 (Yamada 3)
Kocaoğlan, 1964 (Guney 2)
Kočár do Vídně, 1966 (Kachyna 2)
Kocero, Mountain Wolf. *See* Dağlarin kurdu Kocero, 1964
Kočičí siovo, 1960 (Pojar 4)
Kočičí škola, 1961 (Pojar 4)
Kocka, 1972 (Grgić 4)
Kod fotografa, 1959 (Mimica 4)
Kodachi o tsukau onna, 1944 (Miyagawa 4, Yoda 4)
Kodachi o tsukau onna, 1961 (Kyo 3, Yoda 4)
Koder, 1975 (Baker C. 3)
Kodo nipon, 1940 (Tsuburaya 4)
Kodomo no me, 1956 (Takamine 3)
Koenigsmark, 1936 (Artaud 3, Fresnay 3, Ibert 4)
Koenigsmark, 1952 (Christian-Jaque 2, Aumont 3)
Koffer des Herrn O.F., 1931 (Lamarr 3, Lorre 3)
Kofukigo shuppo, 1980 (Kishida 3)
Kofuku, 1982 (Ichikawa 2)
Kofuku he no shotai, 1947 (Takamine 3)
Kofuku no isu, 1948 (Mori 3)
Kofuku sezu, 1959 (Tsuburaya 4)
Koga Mansion. *See* Koga yashiki, 1949
Koga yashiki, 1949 (Kinugasa 2, Hasegawa 3, Yamada 3)
Kogda derevya byli bolshimi, 1962 (Shukshin 3)
Koge, 1964 (Kinoshita 2, Tanaka 3)
Kogen no eki yo sayounara, 1951 (Kagawa 3)
Koharu kyogen, 1942 (Hayasaka 4)
Koharu's Performance. *See* Koharu kyogen, 1942
Kohayagawa-ke no aki, 1961 (Ozu 2, Hara 3, Ryu 3, Tsukasa 3)
Kohlberg, 1945 (Wegener 3)
Kohlhiesels Tochter, 1920 (Lubitsch 2, Jannings 3, Porten 3, Kraly 4)
Kohlhiesels Tochter, 1930 (Porten 3)
Koho jsem včera líbal, 1935 (Stallich 4, Vích 4)
Koi, 1924 (Kinugasa 2)
Koi moyo, 1930 (Yamada 3)
Koi no ikuji, 1926 (Tanaka 3)
Koi no katamichi kippu, 1960 (Shinoda 2)
Koi no Oranda-zaka, 1951 (Kyo 3)
Koi no Tokyo, 1932 (Gosho 2, Tanaka 3)
Koi no torinawa, 1925 (Tanaka 3)
Koi okami-bi, 1948 (Yamada 3)
Koi to bushi, 1925 (Kinugasa 2)
Koi to kenka, 1962 (Iwashita 3)
Koi ya koinasuna koi, 1962 (Yoda 4)
Koibito, 1951 (Ichikawa 2)
Koibumi, 1953 (Kagawa 3, Mori 3, Tanaka 3)
Koiguruma, 1930 (Yamada 3)
Koiguruma no maki, 1940 (Takamine 3)
Koikaze gojusan-tsugi, 1952 (Yoda 4)
Koina no Ginpei, 1933 (Hasegawa 3)
Koisuru tsuma, 1947 (Hayasaka 4)
Kojak and the Marcus-Nelson Murders. *See* Marcus-Nelson Murders,
    1973
Kojak: The Belarus File, 1985 (Von Sydow 3)
Kojin Kojitsu, 1961 (Iwashita 3)
Kojiro. *See* Sasaki Kojiro, 1967
Kojiro Sasaki. *See* Kanketsu Sasaki Kojiro, 1951
Kokila, 1937 (Biswas 4)
Kokkyo no uta, 1927 (Tanaka 3)
Koko, 1977 (Almendros 4)
Ko-Ko series, 1924–29 (Fleischer, M. and D. 2)
Koko ni izumi ari, 1955 (Imai 2, Okada 3)
Kokokara hajimaru, 1965 (Tsukasa 3)
Kokoro, 1955 (Ichikawa 2)
Kokoro, 1973 (Shindo 2)
Kokoro no sanmyaku, 1966 (Yoshimura 2)
Kokotsu no hito, 1973 (Takamine 3)
Kokur, 1955 (Mori 3)
Kokushi muso, 1932 (Yamada 3)
Kolberg, 1945 (George, H. 3)
Kolcsonkért csecsemok, 1914 (Curtiz 2)
Kolejarskie slowo, 1953 (Munk 2)
Koleskabe, 1954 (Carlsen 2)

Kolibel'naya, 1937 (Vertov 2)
Kolik slov stačí lásce, 1961 (Brejchová 3, Kopecký 3)
Kolingens galoscher, 1912 (Jaenzon 4, Magnusson 4)
Koloraturen, 1932 (Fischinger 2)
Kolyok, 1959 (Torocsik 3)
Kom tillbaka, 1962 (Troell 2)
Komal Gandhar, 1961 (Ghatak 4)
Komandirovka, 1962 (Shukshin 3)
Kombina, 1982 (Ivanov 3)
Kome, 1957 (Imai 2)
Komedia smerti, 1915 (Mozhukin 3)
Komedianti, 1954 (Hrušínský 3)
Komedie om Geld, 1936 (Ophuls 2)
Komm' zu mir zum Rendezvous, 1930 (Florey 2)
Kommunisti, 1976 (Lomnicki 3)
Komodianten, 1912 (Gad 2, Nielsen 3)
Komodianten, 1924 (Rasp 3)
Komodianten, 1941 (Pabst 2, Porten 3)
Komodianten des Lebens, 1924 (Courant 4, Kraly 4)
Komodiantenemil, 1980 (Hoppe 3)
Komodie der Leidenschaften, 1921 (Leni 2)
Komodie des Herzens, 1924 (Dagover 3, Herlth 4, Rohrig 4)
Komori zoshi, 1927 (Hasegawa 3, Tsuburaya 4)
Komoriuta Bushu-dako, 1935 (Miyagawa 4)
Komorní harmonie, 1963 (Schorm 2)
Komposition in Blau, 1935 (Fischinger 2)
Kompozitor Glinka, 1952 (Orlova 3, Tisse 4)
Komputery, 1967 (Zanussi 2)
Komsomol. See Pesn o geroyazh, 1932
Komsomol—Leader of Electrification. See K–SH–E, 1932
Komsomol—The Guide to Electrification. See K–SH–E, 1932
Komsomolsk, 1938 (Gerasimov 2)
Koń, 1967 (Giersz 4)
Kona Coast, 1968 (Blondell 3, Boone 3, Rafferty 3, La Shelle 4)
Koncert, 1961 (Szabó 2)
Koncert na ekrane, 1939 (Cherkassov 3)
Koncert pro studenty, 1970 (Schorm 2)
Koncert za mašinsku pušku, 1958 (Vukotić 4)
Kondelik—Father, Vejvara—Bridegroom. See Otec Kondelík a
    ženich Vejvara, 1926
Kondelik—Father-in-Law, Vejvara—Son-in-Law. See Tchán Kondelík
    a zet Vejvara, 1929
Kondura, 1977 (Benegal 2, Nihalani 4)
Konec cesty, 1959 (Kopecký 3)
Konec jasnovidce, 1958 (Chytilová 2, Kopecký 3)
Konga roja, 1943 (Armendáriz 3)
Konga-Yo. See Terreur sur la savane, 1962
Kongen bød, 1938 (Henning-Jensen 2)
Kongo, 1932 (Huston 3, Velez 3, Rosson 4)
Kongres kombatantów, 1949 (Munk 2)
Kongress amusiert sich, 1965 (Jurgens 3)
Kongress tanzt, 1931 (Dagover 3, Veidt 3, Herlth 4, Hoffmann 4,
    Pommer 4, Rohrig 4)
Koniec nocy, 1957 (Cybulski 3)
Koniec wojny, 1956 (Polanski 2)
Konig, 1913 (Basserman 3, Warm 4)
Konig fur eine Nacht, 1950 (Walbrook 3)
Konig Pausole. See Abenteuer des Konigs Pausole, 1933
Konig und die kleinen Madchen, 1925 (Albers 3)
Konig von Paris, 1930 (Courant 4)
Konigin einer Nacht, 1930 (Burel 4)
Konigin Louise. See Queen Louise, 1928
Konigin Luise, 1927 (Schufftan 4)
Konigin Luise, 1957 (Wicki 2)
Konigin vom Moulin-Rouge, 1925 (Wiene 2)
Konigliche Bettler, 1917 (Oswald 2)
Konigliche Hoheit, 1953 (Dagover 3)
Konigskinder, 1950 (Warm 4)
Konigskinder, 1962 (Mueller-Stahl 3)
Konigsliebchen, 1924 (Warm 4)
Konigsmark, 1936 (Tourneur, M. 2)
Konigswalzer, 1935 (Jurgens 3, Herlth 4, Rohrig 4)

Konigswalzer, 1955 (Warm 4)
Konjiki yasha, 1923 (Kinugasa 2)
Konjiki-yasha, 1933 (Hasegawa 3, Tanaka 3, Yamada 3)
Konketsuji Rika, 1973 (Yoshimura 2)
Konki, 1961 (Yoshimura 2, Kyo 3, Miyagawa 4)
Konkurs, 1963 (Forman 2, Passer 2, Ondricek 4)
Konna watashi ja nakattani, 1952 (Yamamura 3)
Kono futari ni sachi are, 1957 (Mifune 3)
Kono hiroi sora no dokoka ni, 1954 (Kobayashi 2, Takamine 3)
Kono sora no aru kagiri, 1964 (Tanaka 3)
Kono ten no niji, 1958 (Kinoshita 2, Tanaka 3)
Konohi uruwashi, 1962 (Iwashita 3)
Konoko o nokoshite, 1983 (Kinoshita 2)
Konrad Albert Pocci, der Fussballgraf vom Ammerland, 1967
    (Syberberg 3)
Konrad Albert Pocci, the Football Count from the Ammerland. See
    Konrad Albert Pocci, der Fussballgraf vom Ammerland, 1967
Konservanbraut, 1915 (Wiene 2)
Kontrakt, 1981 (Zanussi 2, Caron 3, Komorowska 3, Lomnicki 3)
Kontrybucja, 1967 (Lomnicki 3)
Konveyer smerti, 1933 (Romm 2)
Konyakci, 1965 (Guney 2)
Konyaku sanba-garasu, 1956 (Tsukasa 3)
Konyaku yubiwa, 1950 (Kinoshita 2, Mifune 3)
Konyaku yubiwa. See Engeiji ringu, 1950
**Konyets Sankt-Peterburga, 1927 (Pudovkin 2, Baranovskaya 3,
    Golovnya 4, Stothart 4)**
Konzert, 1931 (Tschechowa 3)
Konzert, 1944 (Frohlich 3)
Kooky Loopy, 1961 (Hanna and Barbera 4)
Ko-on, 1927 (Mizoguchi 2)
Kopf hoch, Charly!, 1926 (Dietrich 3)
Kopfuber ins Gluck, 1930 (Sakall 3, Douy 4)
Kopjások, 1974 (Madaras 3)
Korabli shturmuiut bastioni, 1953 (Romm 2)
Korea, 1959 (Ford, J. 2)
Korhinta, 1955 (Fábri 2, Torocsik 3)
Korkarlen, 1921 (Sjostrom 2, Borgstrom 3, Jaenzon 4, Magnusson 4)
Korkuszlar, 1965 (Guney 2)
Korn, 1943 (Henning-Jensen 2)
Korona rossiyskoy imperii, 1970 (Gurchenko 3)
Koroshiya o barase, 1969 (Miyagawa 4)
Kort ar sommaren, 1962 (Henning-Jensen 2, Andersson B. 3,
    Ullmann 3, Fischer 4)
Kortik, 1954 (Ermler 2)
Korube no taiyo, 1968 (Mifune 3)
Korui, 1927 (Hasegawa 3)
Korvettenkapitan, 1930 (Kaper 4)
Korzeń, 1965 (Giersz 4)
Kosenie jastrabej lúky, 1981 (Kroner 3)
Koshiben gambare, 1931 (Naruse 2)
Koshikei, 1968 (Oshima 2, Toda 4)
Kostnice, 1970 (Švankmajer 4)
Kotan no kuchibue, 1959 (Naruse 2, Mori 3, Shimura 3)
Kotch, 1971 (Lemmon 3, Matthau 3, Mercer 4, Paxton 4)
Koto, 1963 (Iwashita 3, Takemitsu 4)
Koto, 1980 (Ichikawa 2)
Kotoshi no koi, 1962 (Kinoshita 2)
Kotovsky, 1942 (Maretskaya 3, Prokofiev 4)
Koudoukan hamonjou, 1968 (Miyagawa 4)
Koukousei to onna kyoushi: hijou no seishun, 1962 (Muraki 4)
Koumiko Mystery. See Mystère Koumiko, 1965
Koushoku gonin onna, 1948 (Miyagawa 4)
Koutareki, 1936 (Tsuburaya 4)
Kouzelná Praha Rudolfa II, 1982 (Jires 2)
Kouzelné dobrodružství, 1982 (Kučera 4)
Kouzelný cirkus, 1977 (Schorm 2)
Kovboy Ali, 1966 (Guney 2)
Kovčeg, 1968 (Grgić 4)
Koya no ka, 1933 (Yamada 3)
Kozanoğlu, 1967 (Guney 2)
Kozara, 1962 (Samardžić 3)
Kozelkép, 1983 (Kovács 2)

Kurohyo, 1953 (Kyo 3)
Kuroi Gashu: Aru sogu, 1961 (Kagawa 3)
Kuroi junin no onna, 1961 (Ichikawa 2, Kishida 3)
Kuroi kawa, 1957 (Kobayashi 2, Yamada 3)
Kuroi sando-gasa, 1961 (Hasegawa 3)
Kuroi ushio, 1954 (Imamura 2, Yamamura 3)
Kuroobi sangokushi, 1956 (Kagawa 3, Mifune 3, Muraki 4)
Kurosawa. See Dodes'ka-den, 1970
Kurotokage, 1962 (Kyo 3)
Kuroun kaidou, 1948 (Miyagawa 4)
Kursunlarin kanunu, 1969 (Guney 2)
Kuruheru meikun, 1929 (Hasegawa 3)
Kurutta ippeiji, 1926 (Kinugasa 2, Tsuburaya 4)
Kurutta kajitsu, 1956 (Takemitsu 4)
Kuruzslo, 1917 (Curtiz 2)
Kusama no Hanjiro: Kiri no naka no wataridori, 1960 (Yamada 3)
Kuss des Fursten, 1912 (Porten 3, Messter 4)
Kussen, die man in Dunkeln stiehlt, 1917 (Negri 3)
Kussen ist keine Sund, 1926 (Albers 3, Reisch 4)
Kussen ist keine Sund, 1950 (Jurgens 3)
Kustom Kar Kommandos, 1965 (Anger 2)
Kuřásek a Kutilka, jak ráno vstávali, 1954 (Trnka 2)
Kuřásek and Kutilka. See Kuřásek a Kutilka, 1954
Kutsukake Tokijiro, 1934 (Kinugasa 2, Hasegawa 3, Yamada 3)
Kutsukake Tokojiro, 1961 (Miyagawa 4)
Kuwa no mi wa akai, 1939 (Tanaka 3)
Kuzdelem a letert, 1918 (Lugosi 3)
Kvarnen, 1921 (Magnusson 4)
Kvarteret Korpen, 1963 (Widerberg 2)
Kvartetten som sprangdes, 1950 (Molander 2, Sjostrom 2, Bjornstrand 3)
Kveska, 1923 (Ouspenskaya 3)
Kvet Sumavy, 1927 (Ondra 3)
Kvinde af Folket, 1909 (Blom 2)
Kvinna i leopard, 1958 (Andersson H. 3)
Kvinna i vitt, 1949 (Dahlbeck 3)
Kvinna utan ansikte, 1947 (Bergman 2, Molander 2)
Kvinnas ansikte, 1938 (Molander 2, Bergman 3)
Kvinnas morgondag. See Devil's Holiday, 1930

Kvinnodrom, 1955 (Bergman 2, Andersson H. 3, Bjornstrand 3, Dahlbeck 3)
Kvinnohuset, 1953 (Dahlbeck 3)
Kvinnor i fångelskap, 1943 (Borgstrom 3)
Kvinnors vantan, 1952 (Bergman 2, Bjornstrand 3, Dahlbeck 3, Fischer 4)
Kvocna, 1937 (Haas 3)
Kwaidan. See Kaidan, 1964
Kwaidan yanagi zoshi, 1932 (Tsuburaya 4)
Kybernetická babička, 1962 (Trnka 2)
Kybernetický dědeček, 1964 (Hofman 4)
Kyo, 1968 (Takemitsu 4)
Kyo mo mata kakute arinan, 1959 (Kinoshita 2)
Kyo no inochi, 1957 (Mori 3)
Kyo ware ren-ai su, 1949 (Mori 3)
Kyoen koigassen, 1930 (Yamada 3)
Kyofu no kuchu satsujin, 1957 (Yamamura 3)
Kyo-gesyo, 1961 (Iwashita 3)
Kyohubadan no joo, 1925 (Mizoguchi 2)
Kyokaku harusame-gasa, 1933 (Hasegawa 3)
Kyokaku harusame-gasa, 1960 (Hasegawa 3)
Kyokaku Soga, 1934 (Hasegawa 3)
Kyoko no hatsukoi, 1962 (Iwashita 3)
Kyoraku hicho, 1928 (Hasegawa 3)
Kyoraku yonin otoko, 1956 (Yamada 3)
Kyoren no buto, 1924 (Kinugasa 2)
Kyoren no onna shisho, 1926 (Mizoguchi 2)
Kyoshiro Nemuri's Swastika-Slash. See Nemuri Kyoshiro no manji-giri, 1969
Kyoshitsu no kodomotachi, 1954 (Hani 2)
Kyoto, 1969 (Ichikawa 2)
Kyoto. See Kyo, 1968
Kyouba to nyoubou, 1932 (Yoda 4)
Kyouenroku, 1939 (Yoda 4)
Kyrelor, bandit par amour, 1909 (Linders 3)
Kys og Kaerlighed, 1914 (Holger-Madsen 2)
Kyssen på kryssen, 1950 (Bjornstrand 3)
Kyujo hiroba, 1951 (Mori 3)
Kyupora no aru machi, 1962 (Imamura 2)
Kyvadlo, jáma, a naděje, 1983 (Švankmajer 4)

L

L.B.J., 1968 (Alvarez 2)
Laban Petterqvist Training for the Olympic Games. See Laban Petterqvist tranar for Olympiska spelen, 1912
Laban Petterqvist tranar for Olympiska spelen, 1912 (Jaenzon 4)
Labbra di lurido blu, 1976 (Morricone 4)
Labda varásza, 1962 (Mészáros 2)
Labios sem beijos, 1930 (Mauro 2)
Labirintus, 1976 (Kovács 2)
Labirynt, 1962 (Lenica 2)
Labor Goes to School, 1951 (Cloquet 4)
Laboratoire de l'angoisse, 1971 (Braunberger 4)
Laborinto, 1966 (Storaro 4)
Laburnum Grove, 1936 (Reed 2, Gwenn 3, Hardwicke 3)
Labyrint srdce, 1961 (Brejchová 3)
Labyrinth, 1967 (Lassally 4)
Labyrinth. See Labirintus, 1976
Labyrinth. See Labirynt, 1962
Labyrinth des Grauens. See Wege des Schreckens, 1921
Labyrinth of Power. See Bludiště moci, 1969
Labyrinth of the Heart. See Labyrint srdce, 1961
Labyrinthe, 1977 (Dickinson 3)
Labyrinths. See Labyrinthe, 1977

Lac-aux-Dames, 1934 (Allégret, M. 2, Allégret, Y. 2, Aumont 3, Simon, M. 3, Simon, S. 3, Auric 4, Meerson 4)
Lace. See Grevindens Aere, 1918
Lace. See Kruzheva, 1928
Lacemaker. See Dentellière, 1977
Lache Bajazzo, 1943 (Wagner 4)
Lache, Bajazzo, 1914 (Oswald 2)
Lacheln im Sturm. See Sourire dans la tempête, 1951
Lachende Ehemann, 1926 (Albers 3)
Lachende Erben, 1933 (Ophuls 2)
Lachende Grauen, 1920 (Krauss 3, Herlth 4)
Lachende Grille, 1926 (Andrejew 4)
Lachte man gerne, 1920 (Rasp 3)
Lackey and the Lady, 1919 (Howard, L. 3)
Lacombe, Lucien, 1973 (Malle 2, Cristaldi 4, Delli Colli 4)
Lacrimae rerum, 1917 (Bertini 3)
Lacy and the Mississippi Queen, 1978 (Elam 3, Lourié 4)
Lad—A Dog, 1961 (Glennon 4)
Lad an' a Lamp, 1932 (Roach 4)
Lad from Old Ireland, 1910 (Olcott 2)
Lad in His Lamp, 1948 (McKimson 4)
Ladali, 1949 (Biswas 4)
Ladder, 1964 (Dunning 4)

Ladder Jinx, 1922 (Horton 3)
Laddie, 1935 (Stevens 2, Crisp 3, Berman 4, Biroc 4, Polglase 4, Steiner 4)
Laddie, 1940 (Cushing 3, Polglase 4)
Ladenprinz, 1928 (Andrejew 4)
Ladies and Gentlemen, 1964 (Giersz 4)
Ladies at Play, 1926 (Fazenda 3, Wilson, C. 4)
Ladies, Be Careful of Your Sleeves. See Onna wa tamoto o goyojin, 1932
Ladies Courageous, 1944 (Edwards 2, Young, L. 3, Raine 4, Tiomkin 4, Wanger 4)
Ladies Doctor. See Ginecologo della mutua, 1977
Ladies First, 1918 (Sennett 2)
Ladies First. See Femmes d'abord, 1963
Ladies in Love, 1936 (Ameche 3, Bennett C. 3, Gaynor 3, Lukas 3, Power 3, Simon, S. 3, Young, L. 3)
Ladies in Retirement, 1941 (Vidor, C. 2, Lupino 3, Fort 4, Plunkett 4)
Ladies' Journal. See Damernes Blad, 1911
Ladies Love Brutes, 1930 (Astor 3, March 3, Mankiewicz 4, Young, W. 4)
Ladies Love Danger, 1935 (Raphaelson 4)
Ladies' Man, 1922 (Stromberg 4)
Ladies' Man, 1931 (Francis, K. 3, Lombard 3, Powell, W. 3, Banton 4, Mankiewicz 4)
Ladies' Man, 1947 (Cahn 4, Dreier 4)
Ladies' Man, 1961 (Lewis 2, Raft 3, Head 4)
Ladies Must Dress, 1927 (Heerman 4)
Ladies Must Eat, 1929 (Sennett 2, Hornbeck 4)
Ladies Must Live, 1921 (Arlen 3, Gilbert 3)
Ladies Must Live, 1940 (Cahn 4, McCord 4)
Ladies Must Love, 1933 (Dupont 2, Gaudio 4)
Ladies Must Play, 1930 (Walker 4)
Ladies of Leisure, 1926 (Lewin 4)
Ladies of Leisure, 1930 (Capra 2, Stanwyck 3, Swerling 4, Walker 4)
Ladies of Retirement, 1941 (Lanchester 3)
Ladies of the Big House, 1932 (Beavers 3, Darwell 3, Sidney 3)
Ladies of the Bois de Boulogne. See Dames du Bois de Boulogne, 1945
Ladies of the Chorus, 1948 (Monroe 3)
Ladies of the Jury, 1932 (Steiner 4)
Ladies of the Mob, 1928 (Wellman 2, Arlen 3, Bow 3)
Ladies of the Night. See Onna dake no yuro, 1947
Ladies of Washington, 1944 (Quinn 3, Basevi 4, Clarke, C.C. 4)
Ladies Past, 1930 (Stevens 2)
Ladies Should Listen, 1934 (Grant, C. 3, Horton 3, Sheridan 3, Dreier 4, Head 4)
Ladies They Talk About, 1933 (Stanwyck 3, Orry-Kelly 4, Seitz 4)
Ladies to Board, 1924 (Mix 3)
Ladri di biciclette, 1948 (De Sica 2, Amidei 4, D'Amico 4, Zavattini 4)
Ladro di Bagdad, 1960 (Delli Colli 4)
Ladro lui, ladra lei, 1958 (Zampa 2, Sordi 3)
Ladron de amor, 1930 (Furthman 4)
Ladrone, 1979 (Morricone 4)
Lady, 1925 (Borzage 2, Talmadge, N. 3, Gaudio 4, Marion 4, Menzies 4, Schenck 4)
Lady, 1964 (Thulin 3)
Lady and Gent, 1932 (Wayne 3)
Lady and the Bandit, 1951 (Brown, Harry Joe 4, Duning 4)
Lady and the Doctor. See Lady and the Monster, 1944
Lady and the Lynchings, 1977 (Carradine 3)
Lady and the Mob, 1939 (Bainter 3, Lupino 3)
Lady and the Monster, 1944 (Von Stroheim 2, Arlen 3, Alton, J. 4)
Lady and the Mouse, 1913 (Griffith 2, Barrymore L. 3, Gish, D. 3, Gish, L. 3, Bitzer 4)
Lady and the Outlaw, 1973 (Warden 3)
Lady and the Tramp, 1955 (Disney 2, Iwerks 4)
Lady Audley's Secret, 1915 (Bara 3)
Lady Barber, 1924 (Sennett 2)
Lady Be Careful, 1936 (Ayres 3, Crabbe 3, Dreier 4, Glazer 4, Head 4)
Lady Be Gay. See Laugh It Off, 1939
Lady Be Good, 1941 (Berkeley 2, McLeod 2, Barrymore L. 3, Dailey 3, Powell, E. 3, Sothern 3, Young, R. 3, Adrian 4, Edens 4, Freed 4)
Lady Bodyguard, 1943 (Dreier 4, Head 4)

Lady by Choice, 1934 (Lombard 3, Swerling 4)
Lady Caroline Lamb, 1972 (Mills 3, Olivier 3, Richardson 3, Cristaldi 4, Dillon 4, Morris 4)
Lady Charlie. See Busy Day, 1914
Lady Chatterley's Lover, 1981 (Russell 4)
Lady Chatterley's Lover. See Amant de Lady Chatterley, 1955
Lady Consents, 1936 (Marshall 3, Hunt 4, Polglase 4, Veiller 4)
Lady Doctor, 1912–13 (White 3)
Lady Escapes, 1937 (Chaney Lon, Jr. 3, Sanders 3)
Lady Eve, 1941 (Sturges, P. 2, Coburn, C. 3, Fonda, H. 3, Stanwyck 3, Head 4)
Lady Fights Back, 1937 (Krasner 4)
Lady for a Day, 1933 (Capra 2, Bosworth 3, Riskin 4, Walker 4)
Lady for a Night, 1941 (Blondell 3, Wayne 3, Plunkett 4)
Lady Frankenstein. See Figlia di Frankenstein, 1971
Lady from Boston. See Pardon My French, 1950
Lady from Cheyenne, 1941 (Preston 3, Young, L. 3, Krasner 4)
Lady from Chunking, 1942 (Wong 3)
Lady from Frisco. See Rebellion, 1936
Lady from Hell, 1926 (Sweet 3)
Lady from Hell. See Jigoku no kifujin, 1949
Lady from Louisiana, 1941 (Costello, M. 3, Dandridge 3, Wayne 3)
Lady from Nowhere, 1931 (Auer 3)
Lady from Nowhere, 1936 (Astor 3)
Lady from Paris. See Schone Abenteuer, 1924
Lady from Shanghai, 1948 (Welles 2, Hayworth 3, Sloane 3)
Lady from the Sea, 1929 (Milland 3)
Lady Gambles, 1949 (Curtis 3, Preston 3, Stanwyck 3, Orry-Kelly 4)
Lady Gangster, 1941 (Florey 2)
Lady Godiva, 1920 (Dreier 4)
Lady Godiva, 1955 (Peterson 2, Eastwood 3, McLaglen 3, O'Hara 3, Boyle 4, Salter 4)
Lady Godiva of Coventry. See Lady Godiva, 1956
Lady Godiva Rides Again, 1951 (Holloway 3, Howard, T. 3, Sim 3, Alwyn 4, Gilliat 4)
Lady Hamilton, 1921 (Oswald 2, George, H. 3, Krauss 3, Veidt 3, Dreier 4, Hoffmann 4)
Lady Hamilton, 1941 (Cooper, Gladys 3, Leigh, V. 3, Olivier 3, Maté 4)
Lady Hamilton, 1968 (Christian-Jaque 2)
Lady Hamilton. See That Hamilton Woman, 1941
Lady Hamilton—zwischen Smach und Liebe, 1969 (Mills 3)
Lady Has Plans, 1942 (Goddard 3, Milland 3, Head 4, Lang 4)
Lady Helen's Escapade, 1909 (Griffith 2, Lawrence 3, Bitzer 4)
Lady Ice, 1973 (Duvall, R. 3, Sutherland 3)
Lady in a Cage, 1964 (Caan 3, De Havilland 3, Sothern 3, Garmes 4, Head 4, Westmore, W. 4)
Lady in a Jam, 1942 (La Cava 2, Bellamy 3, Dunne 3)
Lady in Black, 1913 (Gish, D. 3, Loos 4)
Lady in Black. See Damen i svart, 1958
Lady in Cement, 1968 (Sinatra 3, Welch 3, Biroc 4)
Lady in Danger, 1934 (Balcon 4, Junge 4)
Lady in Distress, 1912–13 (White 3)
Lady in Distress, 1939 (Lukas 3)
Lady in Distress. See Window in London, 1939
Lady in Ermine, 1927 (Bushman 3, Glazer 4)
Lady in Grey, 1922 (Lukas 3)
Lady in Love, 1930 (Adrian 4)
Lady in Question, 1940 (Vidor, C. 2, Ford, G. 3, Hayworth 3)
Lady in Red, 1935 (Freleng 4)
Lady in Red, 1979 (Sayles 4)
Lady in the Car with Glasses and a Gun, 1970 (Litvak 2, Reed, O. 3, Legrand 4, Perry 4, Renoir 4)
Lady in the Dark, 1944 (Leisen 2, Auer 3, Baxter W. 3, Milland 3, Rogers, G. 3, Dreier 4, Goodrich and Hackett 4, Head 4)
Lady in the Iron Mask, 1952 (Laszlo 4, Tiomkin 4, Wanger 4)
Lady in the Lake, 1946 (Montgomery 3, Ames 4, Gibbons 4, Irene 4)
Lady in the Morgue, 1938 (Cortez 4)
Lady in the Train. See Sayidet el Kitar, 1952
Lady is a Square, 1959 (Wilcox 2, Neagle 3)
Lady Is Willing, 1934 (Bruce 3, Hardwicke 3, Howard, L. 3, Walker 4)
Lady Is Willing, 1942 (Leisen 2, Dietrich 3, MacMurray 3, Irene 4)

Lady Jane's Flight, 1908 (Lawrence 3)
Lady Killer, 1933 (Cagney 3, Blanke 4, Gaudio 4, Orry-Kelly 4)
Lady Killer of Rome. See Assassino, 1961
Lady Killers, 1916 (Roach 4)
Lady L, 1965 (Dalio 3, Dauphin 3, Loren 3, Newman 3, Niven 3, Noiret 3, Piccoli 3, Ustinov 3, Alekan 4, D'Eaubonne 4, Orry-Kelly 4, Ponti 4)
Lady Leone, 1912 (Lawrence 3)
Lady Liberty, 1971 (Sarandon 3)
Lady Liberty. See Mortadella, 1971
Lady Lies, 1929 (Colbert 3, Huston 3, Fort 4)
Lady Luck, 1946 (Young, R. 3, D'Agostino 4)
Lady Macbeth of Mtsensk. See Sibirska Ledi Magbet, 1962
Lady Marions sommarflirt, 1913 (Sjostrom 2, Borgstrom 3, Jaenzon 4, Magnusson 4)
Lady Marion's Summer Flirtation. See Lady Marions sommarflirt, 1913
Lady Mary's Love. See Naadige Frøken, 1911
Lady Musachino. See Musachino Fujin, 1951
Lady o' the Pines, 1921 (Astor 3)
Lady of Burlesque, 1943 (Wellman 2, Stanwyck 3, Cahn 4, Head 4, Stromberg 4)
Lady of Chance, 1928 (Goulding 2, Shearer 3, Adrian 4, Booth 4, Daniels 4, Gibbons 4)
Lady of Monza. See Monaca di Monza, 1969
Lady of Mystery. See Close Call for Boston Blackie, 1946
Lady of Quality, 1923 (Mandell 4)
Lady of Scandal, 1930 (Franklin 2, Rathbone 3, Adrian 4, Booth 4, Gibbons 4, Kraly 4, Miller, A. 4)
Lady of Secrets, 1936 (Akins 4, Schulberg 4)
Lady of Shalott, 1915 (Talmadge, C. 3)
Lady of the Boulevards. See Nana, 1934
Lady of the Dugouts, 1919 (Van Dyke, W.S. 2)
Lady of the Harem, 1926 (Walsh 2, Fazenda 3, Johnson, N. 3)
Lady of the House, 1978 (Cannon 3)
Lady of the Lake, 1931 (Balcon 4)
Lady of the Night, 1925 (Crawford, J. 3, Shearer 3, Gibbons 4)
Lady of the Night. See Lady of the Pavements, 1929
Lady of the Night. See Midnight Mary, 1933
Lady of the Pavements, 1929 (Griffith 2, Boyd 3, Velez 3, Bitzer 4, Menzies 4, Schenck 4, Struss 4)
Lady of the Sea, (Johnson, N. 3)
Lady of the Tropics, 1939 (Lamarr 3, Schildkraut 3, Taylor, R. 3, Hecht 4, Waxman 4)
Lady of the Tropics. See His Brother's Wife, 1936
Lady on a Train, 1945 (Bellamy 3, Durbin 3, Duryea 3, Horton 3, Rozsa 4)
Lady or the Tiger?, 1942 (Zinnemann 2)
Lady Oscar, 1978 (Demy 2, Varda 2, Evein 4, Legrand 4)
Lady Paname, 1950 (Jouvet 3, Annenkov 4, D'Eaubonne 4, Jeanson 4)
Lady Pays Off, 1951 (Sirk 2, Darnell 3, Boyle 4, Daniels 4)
Lady Peggy's Escape, 1913 (Olcott 2)
Lady! Please!, 1932 (Sennett 2, Grable 3)
Lady Possessed, 1952 (Mason 3, Struss 4)
Lady Raffles, 1928 (Walker 4)
Lady Robin Hood, 1925 (Karloff 3, Berman 4)
Lady Rose's Daughter, 1920 (Miller, A. 4)
Lady Says No!, 1951 (Niven 3, Howe 4, Orry-Kelly 4)
Lady Scarface, 1941 (Anderson J. 3, Musuraca 4)
Lady Sen. See Sen-hime, 1954
Lady Sings the Blues, 1972 (Pryor 3, Alonzo 4, Legrand 4)
Lady Surrenders, 1930 (Stahl 2, Rathbone 3, Laemmle 4)
Lady Surrenders. See Love Story, 1944
Lady Takes a Chance, 1943 (Arthur 3, Wayne 3, Swerling 4)
Lady Takes a Flyer, 1958 (Chandler 3, Turner, L. 3)
Lady Takes a Sailor, 1949 (Curtiz 2, Arden 3, Wyman 3, McCord 4, Steiner 4)
Lady to Love, 1930 (Sjostrom 2, Banky 3, Robinson, E. 3, Gibbons 4, Howard 4)
Lady to Love. See Sehnsucht jeder Frau, 1930
Lady Tubbs, 1935 (Crosland 2, Brady 3, Brennan 3)
Lady Vanishes, 1938 (Hitchcock 2, Lukas 3, Redgrave, M. 3, Gilliat 4, Reville 4)
Lady Vanishes, 1979 (Gould 3, Axelrod 4, Slocombe 4)

Lady Violette, 1922 (Lukas 3)
Lady Wants Mink, 1953 (Arden 3)
Lady Who Dared, 1931 (Gaudio 4)
Lady Who Lied, 1925 (Stone 3)
Lady Windermeres Facher, 1935 (Dagover 3)
Lady Windermere's Fan, 1925 (Lubitsch 2, Colman 3)
Lady Windermere's Fan. See Lady Windermeres Facher, 1935
Lady Windermere's Fan. See Fan, 1949
Lady with a Lamp, 1951 (Wilcox 2, Neagle 3)
Lady with a Past, 1932 (Bennett C. 3, Steiner 4)
Lady with a Ribbon. See Ribon o musubu fujin, 1939
Lady with Red Hair, 1940 (Hopkins, M. 3, Rains 3, Wilde 3, Edeson 4)
Lady with Sunflowers. See Napraforgós hölgy, 1918
Lady with the Black Glove. See Dame mit dem schwarzen Handschuh, 1919
Lady with the Dog. See Dama s sobachkoi, 1960
Lady Without Camelias. See Signora senza camelie, 1952
Lady Without Passport, 1950 (Lamarr 3)
Ladybug, Ladybug, 1963 (Perry 4)
Ladyfingers, 1921 (Coffee 4)
Ladyfingers, 1980 (Palance 3)
Ladyhawke, 1985 (Storaro 4)
Ladykillers, 1955 (Mackendrick 2, Guinness 3, Sellers 3, Balcon 4)
Lady's from Kentucky, 1939 (Beavers 3, Pitts 3, Raft 3, Head 4)
Lady's Morals, 1930 (Franklin 2, Beery 3, Adrian 4, Barnes 4, Booth 4, Freed 4, Gibbons 4, Kraly 4, Stothart 4)
Lady's Morals. See Jenny Lind, 1930
Lady's Name, 1918 (Pitts 3, Talmadge, C. 3)
Lady's Profession, 1933 (McLeod 2, Banton 4)
Lady's Tailor, 1919 (Sennett 2)
Laegens Hustru. See Mens Pesten raserr, 1913
Laereaar, 1914 (Blom 2)
Lafayette, 1961 (Welles 2, Hawkins 3, Renoir 4)
Lafayette Escadrille, 1957 (Wellman 2, Dalio 3, Eastwood 3, Clothier 4, Rosenman 4)
Lafayette, Where Are We?. See Hello Lafayette, 1926
Lagan, 1940 (Sircar 4)
Lage landen, 1960 (Haanstra 2)
Lagor i dunklet, 1942 (Borgstrom 3)
Lagourdette, gentleman cambrioleur, 1916 (Feuillade 2, Musidora 3)
Lagrime e sorrisi, 1912 (Bertini 3)
Laguna negra, 1952 (Rey 3)
Lahire ou le valet de cœur, 1922 (Feuillade 2)
Lahu ke do rang, 1979 (Azmi 3)
Laila—Liebe unter der Mitternachtssonne, 1958 (Nykvist 4)
Lair of Love. See Bestiare d'amour, 1964
Laisen no zenya, 1943 (Yoshimura 2)
Laisse aller, c'est une valse, 1970 (Blier 2, Blier 3, D'Eaubonne 4)
Laissez tirer les tireurs, 1964 (Constantine 3, Delerue 4)
Lajawab, 1950 (Biswas 4)
Lajwanti, 1958 (Burman 4)
Lake of Illusion. See Maboroshi no mizuumi, 1982
Lake Placid Serenade, 1944 (Alton, J. 4)
Lal Kunwar, 1952 (Burman 4)
Lalka, 1968 (Tyszkiewicz 3)
Lalquerida, 1949 (Armendáriz 3)
Lamb, 1915 (Fairbanks, D. 3)
Lamb, 1918 (Lloyd 3, Roach 4)
Lamb. See Lamm, 1964
Lamb, The Woman, The Wolf, 1914 (Dwan 2, Chaney Lon 3)
Lamb to the Slaughter, 1958 (Hitchcock 2)
Lamber fuhlt sich bedroht, 1950 (Jurgens 3)
Lambertville Story, 1949 (Kaufman 4)
Lambeth Walk, 1939 (Havelock-Allan 4)
Lament for a Bandit. See Llanto por un bandido, 1964
Lamentations. See Dung-Aw, 1981
Lamiel, 1967 (Dauphin 3, Karina 3, de Beauregard 4)
Lamjata, 1971 (Dinov 4)
Lamm, 1964 (Staudte 2)
Lamp. See Lampa, 1959
Lamp Post Favorites, 1948 (Fleischer, M. and D. 2)
Lamp Still Burns, 1943 (Granger 3, Howard, L. 3, Krasker 4)
Lampa, 1959 (Polanski 2)

Lampada alla finestra, 1940 (Magnani 3)
Lampe qui file, 1909 (Cohl 2)
Lampenfieber, 1951 (Jurgens 3)
Lampenfieber, 1960 (Wicki 2)
Lamuru, 1933 (Gosho 2)
Lancashire Luck, 1937 (Hiller 3, Havelock-Allan 4)
Lancelot and Guinevere, 1963 (Wilde 3)
Lancelot du Lac, 1974 (Bresson 2, Sarde 4)
Lancelot of the Lake. *See* Lancelot du Lac, 1974
Lancement d'un navire à La Ciotat, 1895 (Lumière 2)
Lancer Spy, 1937 (Del Rio 3, Lorre 3, Sanders 3, Schildkraut 3,
    Dunne 4, Zanuck 4)
Lancieri neri, 1961 (Ferrer, M. 3)
Land, 1942 (Flaherty 2, Crosby 4, Van Dongen 4)
Land. *See* Ard, 1969
Land and Freedom, 1941 (Eisenstein 2)
Land Baron of San Tee, 1912 (Dwan 2)
Land Beyond the Law, 1927 (Brown, Harry Joe 4, Polito 4)
Land Beyond the Law, 1937 (Eason 4)
Land des Schweigens und der Dunkelheit, 1971 (Herzog 2)
Land in Trance. *See* Terra em transe, 1967
Land is Forever Land. *See* Terra sempere terra, 1951
Land o' Lizards, 1916 (Borzage 2)
Land of Angels. *See* Angyelok foldje, 1962
Land of Dead Things, 1913 (Ince 4)
Land of Death, 1912 (Dwan 2)
Land of Desire. *See* Skepp till Indialand, 1947
Land of Enchantment: Southwest U.S.A. *See* Southwest, 1945
Land of Fate. *See* Praesten i Vejlby, 1920
Land of Fury. *See* Seekers, 1954
Land of Hope, 1921 (Brady 3)
Land of Jazz, 1920 (Furthman 4)
Land of Liberty, 1939 (Macpherson 4)
Land of Long Shadows, 1917 (Van Dyke, W.S. 2)
Land of Promise, 1917 (Burke 3)
Land of Promise, 1946 (Mills 3, Alwyn 4)
Land of Silence and Darkness. *See* Land des Schweigens und der
    Dunkelheit, 1971
Land of the Incas, 1937 (Hoch 4)
Land of the Lawless, 1927 (Fejos 2, Shamroy 4)
Land of the Midnight Fun, 1939 (Avery 2)
Land of the Minotaur. *See* Devil's Men, 1976
Land of the Pharaohs, 1955 (Hawks 2, Hawkins 3, Garmes 4,
    Kurnitz 4, Tiomkin 4, Trauner 4)
Land of the Soviets. *See* Strana Sovietov, 1937
Land of Water, 1940 (Pearson 2)
Land of White Alice, 1959 (Van Dyke, W. 2)
Land ohne Frauen, 1929 (Gallone 2, Veidt 3)
Land Raiders, 1970 (Rey 3)
Land Salesman, 1913 (Sennett 2)
Land Sharks Vs. Sea Dogs, 1912 (Bosworth 3)
Land Thieves, 1911 (Dwan 2)
Land Unknown, 1957 (Salter 4, Westmore, B. 4)
Land We Love. *See* Hero's Island, 1961
Land Without Bread. *See* Hurdes—Tierra sin pan, 1932
Land Without Music, 1936 (Durante 3)
Landfall, 1949 (Harvey 3)
Landing of the Pilgrims, 1940 (Terry 4)
Landlady, 1938 (Boulting 2)
Landloper, 1918 (Gaudio 4)
Landlord, 1970 (Ashby 2, Jewison 2, Gossett 3, Grant, L. 3, Boyle 4,
    Willis 4)
Landlord's Troubled, 1913 (Sennett 2)
Landlubber, 1922 (Roach 4)
Landru, 1963 (Chabrol 2, Melville 2, Audran 3, Darrieux 3, Denner 3,
    Knef 3, Morgan 3, de Beauregard 4, Ponti 4, Rabier 4)
Landsbykirken, 1947 (Dreyer 2)
Landscape, 1974 (Lenica 2)
Landscape after the Battle. *See* Krajobraz po bitwie, 1970
Landscapes of Southern China. *See* Dél-Kína tájain, 1957
Landsflyktige, 1921 (Stiller 2, Magnusson 4)
Landshovdingens dottrar, 1916 (Sjostrom 2, Jaenzon 4)
Landstrasse und Gross-stadt, 1921 (Kortner 3, Veidt 3, Hoffmann 4)

Lane That Had No Turning, 1922 (Fleming 2)
Lang ist der Weg, 1948 (Pommer 4)
Lang-Lasse i Delsbo, 1949 (Nykvist 4)
Langrevin père et fils, 1930 (Dauphin 3)
Langste Sekunde, 1977 (Mueller-Stahl 3)
Langt Borta och Nära, 1976 (Donner 2)
Language All My Own, 1935 (Fleischer, M. and D. 2)
Languedocienne, 1976 (Leenhardt 2)
Lantern Under a Full Moon. *See* Meigatsu somato, 1951
Lanterne magique, 1903 (Méliès 2)
Lanz und Elend eines Konigs. *See* Ludwig II, 1954
Laos, the Forgotten War. *See* Guerra olvidada, 1967
Lapicque, 1965 (Reichenbach 2)
Lapin 360, 1972 (Baxter A. 3)
Lapland, 1957 (Iwerks 4)
Lararinna på vift, 1941 (Fischer 4)
Larceny, 1948 (Duryea 3, Winters 3, Orry-Kelly 4)
Larceny, Inc., 1942 (Bacon 2, Crawford, B. 3, Quinn 3,
    Robinson, E. 3, Wyman 3, Deutsch 4, Gaudio 4, Wald 4, Wallis 4)
Larceny Lane. *See* Blonde Crazy, 1931
Large Family. *See* Bolshaya semya, 1955
Largest Boat Ever Launched Sidewalks, 1913 (Sennett 2)
Lariat Kid, 1929 (Brennan 3, Eason 4)
Larks on a String. *See* Skřivánci na niti, 1969
Lark's Song. *See* Skřiváncí píseň, 1933
Larry, 1974 (Forrest 3)
Larry's Recent Behaviour, 1963 (Wieland 2)
Lars Hård, 1948 (Dahlbeck 3)
Las Vegas 500 millones, 1968 (Palance 3)
Las Vegas 500 millones. *See* They Came to Rob Las Vegas, 1968
Las Vegas Hillbillies, 1966 (Mansfield 3)
Las Vegas Nights, 1941 (Sinatra 3, Head 4, Prinz 4, Young, V. 4)
Las Vegas Story, 1952 (Mature 3, Price 3, Russell, J. 3, Carmichael 4)
Lasca of the Rio Grande, 1931 (Summerville 3)
Laserblast, 1977 (McDowall 3, Wynn 3)
Lash, 1930 (Astor 3, Barthelmess 3, Haller 4)
Lash, 1934 (Mills 3)
Láska, 1972 (Kachyna 2)
Láska mezi kapkami deště, 1979 (Kachyna 2)
Láska v barvách karnevalu, 1974 (Schorm 2)
Lásky Alexandra Dumase St., 1970 (Kachyna 2)
Lásky jedné plavovlásky, 1965 (Forman 2, Passer 2, Ondricek 4)
Lass from the Stormy Croft. *See* Tosen från stormyrtorpet, 1918
Lasse-Maja, 1941 (Zetterling 2)
Lassie Come Home, 1943 (Bruce 3, Crisp 3, Gwenn 3, Lanchester 3,
    McDowall 3, Taylor, E. 3, Gibbons 4, Schary 4)
Last Act, 1916 (August 4)
Last Adventure. *See* Aventuriers, 1966
Last Adventure of Arsène Lupin. *See* Arsén Lupin utolsó kalandja,
    1921
Last Adventure of the Skeleton's Hand. *See* Juvelernes Skroek, 1915
Last Alarm, 1900 (Bitzer 4)
Last Alarm, 1926 (Costello, M. 3)
Last American Hero, 1973 (Bridges 3)
Last American Virgin, 1982 (Golan and Globus 4)
Last Angels. *See* Ultimi angeli, 1977
Last Angry Man, 1959 (Muni 3, Duning 4, Howe 4)
Last Betrothal. *See* Dernières Fiançailles, 1973
Last Blitzkrieg, 1959 (Johnson, V. 3, Katzman 4)
Last Bohemian. *See* Poslední bohém, 1931
Last Bohemian. *See* Utolsó bohém, 1912
Last Bridge. *See* Letzte Brucke, 1954
Last Card. *See* Keno Bates, Liar, 1915
Last Challenge, 1967 (Dickinson 3, Elam 3, Ford, G. 3)
Last Chance, 1921 (Selig 4)
Last Chance. *See* Harmadik nekifutás, 1973
Last Chance Motel. *See* Ultima chance, 1973
Last Chase, 1981 (Meredith 3)
Last Child, 1971 (Heflin 3)
Last Circus Show, 1975 (Cobb 3)
Last Command, 1928 (Hathaway 2, Von Sternberg 2, Jannings 3,
    Powell, W. 3, Biro 4, Clothier 4, Dreier 4, Glennon 4,
    Mankiewicz 4, Schulberg 4)

Last Command, 1955 (Borgnine 3, Hayden 3, Steiner 4)
Last Company. *See* Letzte Kompagnie, 1930
Last Convertible, 1979 (Houseman 4)
Last Couple Out. *See* Sista paret ut, 1956
Last Cry for Help, 1979 (Jones S. 3)
Last Curtain, 1937 (Havelock-Allan 4)
Last Dawn. *See* Utolsó hajnal, 1917
Last Day, 1975 (Widmark 3)
Last Day of the War. *See* Ultimo dia de la guerra, 1969
Last Days of Dolwyn, 1948 (Burton 3, Evans 3)
Last Days of Man on Earth. *See* Final Program, 1973
Last Days of Pompeii, 1935 (Schoedsack 2, Calhern 3, Rathbone 3, Cooper 4, Dunn 4, Hunt 4, O'Brien 4, Polglase 4)
Last Days of Pompeii. *See* Derniers Jours de Pompéi, 1948
Last Days of Pompeii. *See* Ultimi giorni di Pompeii, 1926
Last Days of Pompeii. *See* Ultimi giorni di Pompei, 1959
Last Days of Sodom and Gomorrah. *See* Sodoma e Gomorra, 1962
Last Deal, 1909 (Griffith 2, Bitzer 4)
Last Desire. *See* Dernière jeunesse, 1939
Last Detail, 1973 (Ashby 2, Nicholson 3, Towne 4)
Last Dinosaur, 1978 (Boone 3)
Last Drink of Whiskey, 1914 (Browning 2, Loos 4)
Last Drop of Water, 1911 (Griffith 2, Sennett 2, Sweet 3, Bitzer 4)
Last Embrace, 1979 (Demme 2, Scheider 3, Schneider 3, Rozsa 4)
Last Embrace. *See* Hoyo, 1953
Last Express, 1938 (Cortez 4)
Last 5 Minutes. *See* Ultimi cinque minuti, 1955
Last Flight, 1931 (Dieterle 2, Barthelmess 3, Saunders 4)
Last Flight of Noah's Ark, 1980 (Bujold 3, Gould 3, Jarre 4)
Last Four Days. *See* Mussolini: ultimo atto, 1974
Last Frontier, 1926 (Boyd 3, Johnson, N. 3)
Last Frontier, 1932 (Chaney Lon, Jr. 3, Canutt 4)
Last Frontier, 1955 (Mann 2, Bancroft 3, Mature 3, Preston 3, Wald 4)
Last Gangster. *See* Roger Touhy, Gangster, 1944
Last Gangster, 1937 (Beavers 3, Carradine 3, Robinson, E. 3, Stewart 3, Adrian 4, Daniels 4, Mahin 4, Vorkapich 4)
Last Generation, 1971 (McCambridge 3)
Last Gentleman, 1934 (Arliss 3, Meek 3, Day 4, Newman 4, Zanuck 4)
Last Goal. *See* Két félido a pokolban, 1961
Last Grenade, 1970 (Attenborough 3, Baker S. 3)
Last Gunfight. *See* Ankokugai no taiketsu, 1960
Last Hard Men, 1976 (Coburn, J. 3, Heston 3)
Last Holiday, 1950 (Guinness 3)
Last Hour, 1930 (Bennett 4, Gilliat 4)
Last Hours Before Morning, 1975 (Sylbert 4)
Last Hungry Cat, 1961 (Freleng 4)
Last Hunt, 1956 (Brooks, R. 2, Granger 3, Taylor, R. 3, Schary 4)
Last Hurrah, 1958 (Ford, J. 2, Carradine 3, Crisp 3, Darwell 3, Hunter 3, O'Brien, P. 3, Rathbone 3, Tracy 3, Nugent 4)
Last Hurrah, 1977 (Meredith 3)
Last Illusion. *See* Ruf, 1949
Last Indian, 1938 (Terry 4)
Last Judgement. *See* Giudizio universale, 1961
Last Lap, 1928 (Musuraca 4)
Last Laugh. *See* Letzte Mann, 1924
Last Lion, 1973 (Hawkins 3)
Last Love. *See* Letzte Liebe, 1938
Last Man. *See* Poslední muž, 1934
Last Man on Earth. *See* Ultimo uomo della terra, 1964
Last Man to Hang?, 1956 (Fisher 2)
Last Married Couple in America, 1980 (Segal 3, Wood 3, Head 4)
Last Metro. *See* Dernier Métro, 1980
Last Mile, 1932 (Edeson 4, Miller, S. 4)
Last Mile, 1959 (Rooney 3, Miller, S. 4)
Last Mohican, 1963 (Arkin 3)
Last Moment, 1923 (Calhern 3)
Last Moment, 1928 (Fejos 2, Shamroy 4)
Last Moment, 1954 (Cusack 3, Fairbanks, D. Jr. 3)
Last Moments. *See* Venditore di Palloncini, 1974
Last Mouse of Hamlin, 1955 (Terry 4)
Last Movie, 1971 (Fuller 2, Fonda, P. 3, Hopper 3, Kovacs 4)
Last Night. *See* Revolutionshochzeit, 1927 (Kortner 3)
Last NO, 1979 (Dovniković 4)

Last Notch, 1911 (Dwan 2)
Last of Mrs. Cheyney, 1929 (Franklin 2, Rathbone 3, Shearer 3, Adrian 4, Daniels 4, Gibbons 4, Kraly 4)
Last of Mrs. Cheyney, 1937 (Arzner 2, Bruce 3, Crawford, J. 3, Montgomery 3, Powell, W. 3, Gibbons 4, Raphaelson 4)
Last of Sheila, 1973 (Cannon 3, Coburn, J. 3, Mason 3, Perkins 3, Welch 3, Adam 4)
Last of Summer. *See* Kohayagawa-ke no aki, 1961
Last of the Buccaneers, 1950 (Henreid 3, Katzman 4)
Last of the Cavalry. *See* Army Girl, 1938
Last of the Clintons, 1935 (Carey 3)
Last of the Comanches, 1952 (De Toth 2, Crawford, B. 3, Canutt 4, Duning 4)
Last of the Cowboys, 1978 (Fonda, H. 3)
Last of the Cowboys. *See* Great Smokey Roadblock, 1978
Last of the Duanes, 1919 (Farnum 3)
Last of the Duanes, 1924 (Mix 3)
Last of the Duanes, 1930 (Loy 3)
Last of the Duanes, 1941 (Arden 3, Farnum 3, Clarke, C.C. 4, Day 4)
Last of the Line, 1914 (Hayakawa 3, Ince 4, Sullivan 4)
Last of the Mobile Hot-Shots, 1969 (Lumet 2)
Last of the Mobile Hot-Shots. *See* Blood Kin, 1969
Last of the Mohicans, 1920 (Brown 2, Tourneur, M. 2, Beery 3, Karloff 3)
Last of the Mohicans, 1932 (Bosworth 3, Carey 3, Canutt 4, Eason 4)
Last of the Mohicans, 1936 (Scott, R. 3, Balderston 4, Dunne 4)
Last of the Night Riders, (Johnson, N. 3)
Last of the Outlaws. *See* Last Outlaw, 1936
Last of the Pagans, 1935 (Friedhofer 4, Gillespie 4, Kaper 4)
Last of the Pony Riders, 1953 (Autry 3)
Last of the Powerseekers, 1971 (Turner, L. 3)
Last of the Red Hot Lovers, 1972 (Arkin 3)
Last of the Redmen, 1947 (Crabbe 3, Katzman 4)
Last of the Redskins. *See* Last of the Redmen, 1947
Last of the Renegades. *See* Winnetou: II Teil, 1964
Last of the Secret Agents, 1966 (Head 4)
Last Outlaw, 1919 (Ford, J. 2, Carey 3)
Last Outlaw, 1927 (Cooper, Gary 3)
Last Outlaw, 1936 (Carey 3, Walthall 3)
Last Outpost, 1935 (Grant, C. 3, Rains 3, Dreier 4, Head 4)
Last Outpost, 1951 (Cody 3, Reagan 3, Head 4)
Last Outpost. *See* Lost Outpost, 1935
Last Page, 1952 (Fisher 2, Brent 3)
Last Pair Out. *See* Sista paret ut, 1956
Last Parade, 1931 (Karloff 3, Muse 3, Robinson 4, Swerling 4)
Last Party of Chauvinists. *See* Siago no joui-tou, 1945
Last Performance, 1929 (Fejos 2, Veidt 3, Laemmle 4)
Last Picture Show, 1971 (Bogdanovich 2, Rafelson 2, Bridges 3, Burstyn 3, Johnson, B. 3, Surtees 4)
Last Posse, 1953 (Crawford, B. 3, Brown, Harry Joe 4)
Last Rebel, 1971 (Elam 3)
Last Remake of Beau Geste, 1977 (Howard, T. 3, Jones, J.E. 3, Ustinov 3, York, M. 3, Fisher 4)
Last Ride of the Dalton Gang, 1979 (Palance 3)
Last Romantic Lover, 1979 (Rey 3)
Last Round-Up, 1911 (Anderson G. 3)
Last Round-Up, 1934 (Hathaway 2, Scott, R. 3)
Last Round-Up, 1943 (Terry 4)
Last Roundup, 1947 (Autry 3)
Last Run, 1971 (Fleischer, R. 2, Huston 2, Scott, G. 3, Goldsmith 4, Nykvist 4)
Last Safari, 1967 (Hathaway 2, Granger 3)
Last Shot, 1913 (Anderson G. 3)
Last Shot. *See* Poslední výstřel, 1950
Last Squadron, 1932 (McCrea 3)
Last Stage. *See* Ostatni etap, 1947
Last Stage to Santa Cruz. *See* Letzte Ritt nach Santa Cruz, 1964 (Kinski 3)
Last Stagecoach West, 1957 (Van Cleef 3)
Last Starfighter, 1984 (Preston 3)
Last Straw, 1934 (Terry 4)
Last Summer, 1969 (Perry 4)
Last Summer. *See* Poslední léto, 1937

Law and the Woman, 1921 (Struss 4)
Law Beyond the Range, 1935 (Brennan 3)
Law Enforcers. *See* Polizia ringrazia, 1972
Law in Her Hands, 1936 (Orry-Kelly 4)
Law is the law. *See* Loi . . . c'est la loi, 1958
Law of Compensation, 1917 (Talmadge, N. 3)
Law of God, 1912 (Dwan 2)
Law of Men, 1919 (Barnes 4)
Law of Nature, 1918 (Johnson, N. 3)
Law of Smuggling. *See* Hudutlarin kanunu, 1966
Law of the Land, 1917 (Tourneur, M. 2, Carré 4)
Law of the Lawless, 1923 (Fleming 2)
Law of the Lawless, 1964 (Arlen 3, Bendix 3, Chaney Lon, Jr. 3, De Carlo 3)
Law of the Mountains, 1909 (Olcott 2)
Law of the Pampas, 1939 (Boyd 3, Head 4)
Law of the Range, 1928 (Crawford, J. 3)
Law of the Sierras. *See* Salomy Jane, 1923
Law of the Snow Country, 1926 (Johnson, N. 3)
Law of the Tropics, 1941 (Bennett C. 3, Bosworth 3)
Law of the Underworld, 1938 (Musuraca 4)
Law of the West, 1912 (Ince 2)
Law of the Wild, 1934 (Canutt 4, Eason 4)
Law of the Wilds, 1915 (Eason 4)
Law Rides West. *See* Santa Fe Trail, 1930
Law vs. Billy the Kid, 1954 (Katzman 4)
Law West of Tombstone, 1938 (Bond 3, Carey 3, Hunt 4, Polglase 4)
Lawaris, 1981 (Bachchan 3)
Lawbreakers, 1960 (Burnett 4)
Lawful Cheaters, 1925 (Bow 3)
Lawful Holdup, 1911 (Dwan 2)
Lawful Larceny, 1923 (Dwan 2, Costello, D. 3, Rosson 4)
Lawful Larceny, 1930 (Daniels 3, Hunt 4, Murfin 4, Plunkett 4)
Lawgiver. *See* Moses, 1975
Lawine, 1923 (Curtiz 2)
Lawless, 1950 (Losey 2, Hunt 4)
Lawless Breed, 1952 (Walsh 2, Hudson 3, Van Cleef 3)
Lawless Eighties, 1957 (Crabbe 3)
Lawless Frontier, 1934 (Wayne 3, Canutt 4)
Lawless Legion, 1929 (Brown, Harry Joe 4)
Lawless Nineties, 1936 (Wayne 3, Canutt 4)
Lawless Range, 1935 (Wayne 3, Canutt 4)
Lawless Rider, 1954 (Canutt 4)
Lawless Street, 1955 (Lansbury 3, Scott, R. 3, Brown, Harry Joe 4)
Lawman, 1971 (Cobb 3, Duvall, R. 3, Lancaster 3, Ryan 3)
Lawrence of Arabia, 1962 (Lean 2, Roeg 2, Cusack 3, Ferrer, J. 3, Guinness 3, Hawkins 3, Kennedy, A. 3, O'Toole 3, Quayle 3, Quinn 3, Rains 3, Sharif 3, Box 4, Jarre 4, Spiegel 4, Wilson, M. 4, Young, F. 4)
Law's Decree, 1914 (Lawrence 3)
Lawyer Man, 1932 (Dieterle 2, Blondell 3, Powell, W. 3, Grot 4, Orry-Kelly 4)
Lawyer's Secret, 1931 (Arlen 3, Arthur 3, Brook 3, Wray 3)
Laxdale Hall, 1952 (Grierson 2)
Lay Down Your Arms, 1914 (Holger-Madsen 2)
Lay Down Your Arms. *See* Ned Med Vabnene, 1914
Lazarus Syndrome, 1979 (Gossett 3)
Lazni car, 1955 (Marković 3)
Lazy Bones. *See* Hallelujah, I'm a Bum, 1933
Lazy Days, 1929 (Roach 4)
Lazy Lightning, 1926 (Wyler 2, Wray 3)
Lazy Little Beaver, 1947 (Terry 4)
Lazy River, 1934 (Young, R. 3)
Lazy River, 1968 (Dunning 4)
Lazy Wagon, 1956 (Wheeler 4)
Lazybones, 1925 (Borzage 2, Pitts 3, Marion 4)
Lazybones, 1934 (Fleischer, M. and D. 2)
Lazybones, 1935 (Powell 2)
Lazybones. *See* Lenora, 1949
Le Mans, 1971 (McQueen, S. 3, LeGrand 4)
Le Quiet Squad, 1967 (McKimson 4)
Lead Shoes, 1949 (Peterson 2)
Leadbelly, 1976 (Boyle 4, Sangster 4)

Leaden Bread. *See* Olověný chléb, 1954
Leaden Times. *See* Bleierne Zeit, 1981
Leader, 1964 (Conner 2)
Leading Lady, 1911 (Bunny 3, Reid 3)
Leading Lizzie Astray, 1914 (Sennett 2, Arbuckle 3)
Leading Man, 1911 (Sennett 2)
League of Gentlemen, 1959 (Dearden 2, Attenborough 3, Hawkins 3, Reed, O. 3)
League of Nations, 1924 (Fleischer, M. and D. 2)
Leah the Forsaken, 1912 (Brenon 2)
Leak in the Foreign Office, 1914 (Cruze 2)
Leányportre, 1971 (Szabó 2)
Leap Frog Railway, 1905 (Bitzer 4)
Leap in the Dark. *See* Salto nel vuoto, 1980
Leap into the Void. *See* Salto nel vuoto, 1979
Leap Year, 1922 (Cruze 2, Arbuckle 3)
Leap Year Cowboy, 1912 (Dwan 2)
Leap Year Proposals, 1912 (Bunny 3)
Leapfrog as Seen by the Frog, 1900 (Hepworth 2)
Leaping Love, 1929 (Roach 4)
Learn from Experience. *See* Kafuku, 1937
Learn Polikeness, 1938 (Fleischer, M. and D. 2)
Learning Modules for Rural Children, 1974–75 (Benegal 2)
Learning to Love, 1925 (Franklin 2, Talmadge, C. 3, Emerson 4, Loos 4, Schenck 4)
Learning to Walk, 1978 (Dovnikovic 4)
Learning Tree, 1969 (Guffey 4, Whitlock 4)
Lease of Life, 1954 (Donat 3, Balcon 4, Slocombe 4)
Leather and Nylon. *See* Soleil des voyous, 1967
Leather Burners, 1943 (Boyd 3, Mitchum 3)
Leather Gloves, 1948 (Edwards 2)
Leather Necker, 1935 (Langdon 3)
Leather Pushers, 1922 (Shearer 3)
Leather Saint, 1956 (Douglas, P. 3, Bumstead 4, Head 4)
Leather Stocking, 1909 (Bitzer 4)
Leather Stockings, 1909 (Griffith 2)
Leatherneck, 1929 (Boyd 3)
Leathernecking, 1930 (Dunne 3, Fazenda 3, Hunt 4, Murfin 4, Plunkett 4)
Leathernecks Have Landed, 1936 (Ayres 3, Bond 3, Miller, S. 4)
Leatherpushers, 1940 (Arlen 3, Howard, S. 3, Cortez 4, Salter 4)
Leave. *See* Izin, 1975
Leave All Fair, 1985 (Gielgud 3)
Leave 'em Laughing, 1928 (Stevens 2, Laurel and Hardy 3, Bruckman 4)
Leave 'em Laughing, 1981 (Cook 3, Cooper, J 3, Rooney 3)
Leave Her to Heaven, 1945 (Stahl 2, Crain 3, Price 3, Tierney 3, Wilde 3, Newman 4, Shamroy 4, Swerling 4, Wheeler 4)
Leave it to Blanche, 1934 (Harrison 3)
Leave It to Blondie, 1945 (Planer 4)
Leave It to Dad, 1933 (Langdon 3)
Leave It to John, 1936 (Iwerks 4)
Leave It to Lester, 1930 (Green, J. 4)
Leave It to Me, 1920 (Furthman 4)
Leave It to Me, 1922 (Roach 4)
Leave It to Me. *See* Nechte to na mně, 1955
Leave It to Smiley, 1914 (Browning 2)
Leave Well Enough Alone, 1939 (Fleischer, M. and D. 2)
Leaves from Satan's Book. *See* Blade af Satans Bog, 1921
Leaving This Child. *See* Konoko o nokoshite, 1983
Leb' wohl Christina, 1945 (Frohlich 3)
Lebbra bianca, 1951 (Loren 3)
Leben—ein Traum, 1917 (Wiene 2)
Leben geht weiter, 1945 (George, H. 3)
Leben mit Uwe, 1974 (Hoppe 3)
Leben unserer Prasidenten, 1951 (Eisler 4)
Leben Wilhelm Piecks. *See* Leben unserer Prasidenten, 1951
Lebende Buddhas, 1923 (Nielsen 2, Wegener 3)
Lebende Leichnam, 1918 (Oswald 2)
Lebende Tote, 1919 (Wiene 2, Porten 3)
Lebende Ware, 1966 (Hoppe 3)
Lebende Ware. *See* Gehetzte Frauen, 1927
Lebender Schatten. *See* Schatten, 1918

Léon Morin, prêtre, 1963 (Melville 2, Belmondo 3, de Beauregard 4, Decae 4)
Leon Morin, Priest. *See* Léon Morin, prêtre, 1963
Leonardo da Vinci, 1952 (Kaufman 4)
Leonardo da Vinci, 1972 (Castellani 2)
Leonardo's Diary. *See* Leonarduv deník, 1972
Leonarduv deník, 1972 (Švankmajer 4)
Leone di Amalfi, 1950 (Gassman 3)
Leone have sept cabecas, 1970 (Rocha 2, Léaud 3)
Leones del ring, 1972 (García 3)
Leones del ring versus la cosa nostra, 1972 (García 3)
Leonor, 1975 (Piccoli 3, Carrière 4, Morricone 4)
Leontines Ehemänner, 1928 (Wiene 2)
Leopard, 1917 (Lugosi 3)
Leopard. *See* Gattopardo, 1963
Leopard in the Snow, 1977 (More 3)
Leopard Man, 1943 (Tourneur, J. 2, D'Agostino 4, Lewton 4)
Leopard Woman, 1920 (Ruggles 2, Johnson, N. 3)
Leopardess, 1923 (Brady 3)
Leopardi di Churchill, 1970 (Kinski 3)
Leopard's Foundling, 1914 (Mix 3)
Léopold le bien-aimé, 1933 (Simon, M. 3, Douy 4)
Leoš Janáč ek, 1974 (Jires 2)
Lepke, 1974 (Curtis 3, Golan and Globus 4)
Lepší pán, 1971 (Schorm 2)
Lerhjertet. *See* Guldets Gift, 1916
Lermontov, 1941 (Prokofiev 4)
Les Collants noirs. *See* Un, deux, trois, quatre, 1960
Les Girls, 1957 (Cukor 2, Kelly, Gene 3, Cole 4, Deutsch 4, Orry-Kelly 4, Porter 4, Surtees 4)
Less Than Dust, 1916 (Von Stroheim 2, Pickford 3, Emerson 4)
Less Than Kin, 1918 (Crisp 3, Reid 3, Buckland 4)
Lesser Evil, 1912 (Griffith 2, Marsh 3, Sweet 3, Bitzer 4)
Lesson, 1910 (Griffith 2, Bitzer 4)
Lesson, 1918 (Talmadge, C. 3)
Lesson. *See* Lekce, 1972
Lesson. *See* Tsena cheloveka, 1928
Lesson for Life, 1916 (Eason 4)
Lesson in Love. *See* Lektion i karlek, 1954
Lesson in Mechanics, 1914 (Gish, D. 3)
Lessons for Wives. *See* French Dressing, 1927
Lessons in Love, 1921 (Talmadge, C. 3, Schenck 4)
Lest We Forget, 1909 (Lawrence 3)
Lest We Forget, 1937 (Hathaway 2, Cooper, Gary 3, Taylor, R. 3)
Lester Persky Story, 1964 (Warhol 2)
Let 'em Have It, 1935 (Wood 2, Arlen 3, Brady 3)
Let 'er Buck, 1925 (Miller, V. 4)
Let 'er Go, 1920 (Sennett 2)
Let 'er Go Gallagher, 1928 (Adrian 4)
Let Freedom Ring, 1939 (Barrymore L. 3, Eddy 3, McLaglen 3, Hecht 4)
Let George Do It, 1940 (Dearden 2, Formby 3, Balcon 4)
Let It Be Me, 1936 (Freleng 4)
Let It Rain, 1927 (Karloff 3)
Let Joy Reign Surpreme. *See* Que la fête commence, 1975
Let Katie Do It, 1916 (Franklin 3)
Let Me Call You Sweetheart, 1932 (Fleischer, M. and D. 2)
Let My People Go, 1960 (Anderson 2, Lassally 4)
Let My People Live, 1939 (Ulmer 2)
Let No Man Put Asunder, 1913 (Bushman 3)
Let No Man Put Asunder, 1924 (Blackton 2, Costello, M. 3, Webb 3)
Let No Man Write My Epitaph, 1959 (Seberg 3, Winters 3, Duning 4, Guffey 4)
Let the People Sing, 1942 (Sim 3, Ustinov 3)
Let Them Live!, 1937 (Raksin 4)
Let There Be Light, 1946 (Huston 3)
Let There Be Light. *See* Es Werde Licht, 1918
Let Us Be Gay, 1930 (Dressler 3, Shearer 3, Adrian 4, Gibbons 4, Marion 4, Shearer 4)
Let Us Be Gay. *See* Soyons gai, 1931
Let Us Live, 1939 (Bellamy 3, Fonda, H. 3, O'Sullivan 3, Ballard 4, Veiller 4)
Let Women Alone, 1925 (Beery 3, Walker 4)

Leteći Fabijan, 1968 (Grgić 4)
Letnie sny, 1972 (Gurchenko 3)
Léto, 1949 (Stallich 4)
Let's All Sing Like the Birdies Sing, 1934 (Fleischer, M. and D. 2)
Let's Be Famous, 1939 (Balcon 4)
Let's Be Ritzy, 1934 (Ayres 3)
Let's Build, 1923 (Roach 4)
Let's Celebrake, 1938 (Fleischer, M. and D. 2)
Let's Dance, 1950 (McLeod 2, Astaire 3, Hutton 3, Dreier 4, Head 4, Pan 4)
Let's Do It Again, 1953 (Milland 3, Wyman 3)
Let's Do It Again, 1975 (Poitier 3)
Let's Do Things, 1931 (Pitts 3, Roach 4)
Let's Eat, 1932 (Lantz 4)
Let's Face It, 1943 (Arden 3, De Carlo 3, Hope 3, Hutton 3, Pitts 3, Cahn 4, Head 4)
Let's Fall in Love, 1934 (Sothern 3)
Let's Get a Divorce, 1918 (Burke 3, Emerson 4, Loos 4)
Let's Get Married, 1926 (La Cava 2, Cronjager 4)
Let's Get Married, 1937 (Bellamy 3, Lupino 3)
Let's Get Married, 1960 (Adam 4)
Let's Get Movin', 1936 (Fleischer, M. and D. 2)
Let's Get Tough!, 1942 (Katzman 4)
Let's Go, 1918 (Daniels 3, Lloyd 3, Roach 4)
Let's Go, 1923 (Howard 2)
Let's Go, 1961 (Walsh 2)
Let's Go Crazy, 1951 (Sellers 3)
Let's Go Hunting in the Woods. *See* Do lesíčka na čekanou, 1966
Let's Go Latin, 1947 (Fleischer, M. and D. 2)
Let's go Native, 1930 (Francis, K. 3, MacDonald 3, Banton 4)
Let's Go Places, 1929 (Grable 3)
Let's Go to the Movies, 1948 (Foreman 4)
Let's Live a Little, 1948 (Cummings 3, Lamarr 3, Laszlo 4, Westmore, F. 4)
Let's Live Tonight, 1935 (Walker 4)
Let's Make a Million, 1937 (Horton 3, Head 4, Struss 4)
Let's Make It Legal, 1951 (Colbert 3, Monroe 3, Wagner 3, Ballard 4, Diamond 4, Lemaire 4)
Let's Make Love, 1960 (Cukor 2, Crosby 3, Kelly, Gene 3, Monroe 3, Montand 3, Cahn 4, Cole 4, Jeakins 4, Krasna 4, Wald 4)
Let's Make Music, 1941 (Mercer 4, Polglase 4)
Let's Make Up. *See* Lilacs in the Spring, 1955
Let's Play. *See* Hrajeme si, 1957
Let's Pretend and Come Up Smiling. *See* Sing Me a Love Song, 1936
Let's Sing a College Song, 1947 (Fleischer, M. and D. 2)
Let's Sing a Love Song, 1948 (Fleischer, M. and D. 2)
Let's Sing a Western Song, 1947 (Fleischer, M. and D. 2)
Let's Sing Again, 1936 (Carré 4)
Let's Talk about Men. *See* Questa volta parliamo di uomini, 1965
Let's Talk About Women. *See* Se permette parliamo di donne, 1964
Let's Talk It Over, 1934 (Darwell 3, Schary 4)
Let's Try Again, 1934 (Brook 3, Steiner 4)
Let's You and Him Fight, 1934 (Fleischer, M. and D. 2)
Letter, 1929 (Marshall 3, Fort 4)
Letter, 1940 (Wyler 2, Davis 3, Marshall 3, Friedhofer 4, Gaudio 4, Koch 4, Orry-Kelly 4, Steiner 4, Wallis 4)
Letter, 1982 (Remick 3)
Letter for Evie, 1946 (Dassin 2, Freund 4)
Letter from an Unknown Woman, 1948 (Ophuls 2, Fontaine 3, Jourdan 3, Banton 4, Houseman 4, Koch 4, Planer 4)
Letter From Bataan, 1942 (Hayward 3)
Letter from Home, 1941 (Reed 2, Johnson, C. 3)
Letter from Siberia, 1982 (Vierny 3)
Letter from Siberia. *See* Lettre de Sibérie, 1958
Letter M. *See* Slóvce M, 1964
Letter of Introduction, 1938 (Stahl 2, Arden 3, Menjou 3, Sheridan 3, Freund 4)
Letter to Jane or Investigation About a Still, 1971 (Godard 2)
Letter to Three Wives, 1949 (Mankiewicz 2, Crain 3, Darnell 3, Douglas, K. 3, Douglas, P. 3, Marsh 3, Ritter 3, Sothern 3, Lemaire 4, Miller, A. 4, Newman 4, Wheeler 4, Zanuck 4)
Letter to Three Wives, 1985 (Sothern 3)
Lettera all'Alba, 1948 (Vích 4)

Liebelei, 1933 (Ophuls 2, Grundgens 3, Tschechowa 3, Planer 4)
Liebensnest, 1922 (Wegener 3)
Liebersymphonie, 1983 (Hoppe 3)
Liebes A.B.C., 1916 (Nielsen 3)
Liebesbrief der Konigin, 1916 (Wiene 2, Messter 4)
Liebesbriefe. *See* Liebesnachte, 1929
Liebesbriefe der Baronin von S., 1924 (Galeen 4)
Liebesexpress, 1931 (Wiene 2)
Liebesfeuer, 1925 (Courant 4)
Liebesgeschichte, 1943 (Rohrig 4)
Liebesgeschichte, 1954 (Pommer 4)
Liebesgeschichten. *See* Madels von heute, 1925
Liebesgluck einer Blinden, 1909 (Porten 3, Messter 4)
Liebeshandel, 1926 (Junge 4, Wagner 4)
Liebesholle, 1927 (Gallone 2, Tschechowa 3)
Liebeskarussell, 1965 (Deneuve 3, Jurgens 3)
Liebeskommando, 1931 (Frohlich 3, Andrejew 4)
Liebes-Korridor, 1920 (Gad 2)
Liebesleute, 1935 (Frohlich 3)
Liebeslied, 1931 (Frohlich 3)
Liebesnachte, 1929 (Dietrich 3)
Liebesreigen, 1927 (Dieterle 2)
Liebesroman im Hause Hapsburg, 1936 (Wegener 3)
Liebesspiel, 1931 (Fischinger 2)
Liebesspiele im Schnee, 1967 (Siodmak 4, Stallich 4)
Liebestaumel, 1920 (Veidt 3)
Liebestraume, 1935 (Tschechowa 3)
Liebeswalzer, 1930 (Pommer 4)
Liebeszentrale. *See* Dollarprinzessin und ihre 6 Freier, 1927
Liebfrauenmilch, 1929 (Porten 3)
Liebling der Frauen, 1911 (Freund 4)
Liebling der Frauen, 1921 (Hoffmann 4)
Liebling der Gotter, 1930 (Jannings 3, Tschechowa 3)
Liebling der Matrosen, 1937 (Sirk 2)
Lieblingsfrau des Maharadscha, 1920 (Kortner 3)
Liebschaften des Hektor Dalmore, 1921 (Oswald 2, Veidt 3, Dreier 4)
Lied der Mutter, 1918 (Hoffmann 4)
Lied der Strome, 1954 (Ivens 2, Robeson 3, Shostakovich 4)
Lied, ein Kuss, ein Madel, 1932 (Frohlich 3)
Lied einer Nacht, 1932 (Litvak 2, Wagner 4)
Lied fur Dich, 1933 (Kaper 4)
Lied geht um die Welt, 1933 (Oswald 2)
Lied ist aus, 1930 (Reisch 4)
Lied vom Leben, 1930 (Eisler 4)
Lied von der Glocke, 1907 (Freund 4)
Liens du sang, 1978 (Chabrol 2, Audran 3, Pleasance 3, Sutherland 3, Rabier 4)
Lies. *See* Uso, 1963
Lies My Father Told Me, 1975 (Kadár 2)
Lieut. Danny, U.S.A., 1916 (Ince 4)
Lt. Kije. *See* Poruchik Kizhe, 1934
Lt. Robin Crusoe, U.S.N., 1966 (Disney 2)
Lt. Robin Crusoe, U.S.N., 1966 (Ellenshaw 4)
Lieutenant Schuster's Wife, 1972 (Grant, L. 3, Warden 3)
Lieutenant Smith, 1943 (Vorkapich 4)
Lieutenant souriant, 1931 (Colbert 3)
Lieutenant souriant. *See* Smiling Lieutenant, 1931
Lieutenant Wore Skirts, 1955 (Tashlin 2, Lemaire 4, Wheeler 4)
Lieutenant's Last Fight, 1912 (Ince 4)
Life. *See* Zhizn, 1927
Life and Adventures of Nicholas Nickleby, 1947 (Cavalcanti 2, Périnal 4)
Life and Adventures of Nicholas Nickleby. *See* Nicholas Nickleby, 1947
Life and Death of a Hollywood Extra, 1927 (Florey 2, Vorkapich 4)
Life and Death of Colonel Blimp, 1943 (Powell and Pressburger 2, Kerr 3, Walbrook 3, Cardiff 4, Junge 4, Périnal 4, Unsworth 4)
Life and Death of 9413—A Hollywood Extra. *See* Life and Death of a Hollywood Extra, 1927
Life and Loves of Beethoven. *See* Grand Amour de Beethoven, 1936
Life and Loves of Mozart. *See* Mozart, 1955
Life and Message of Swani Vivekananda, 1964 (Roy 2)
Life and Times of a Criminal. *See* Forbryders Liv og Levned, 1916

Life and Times of Judge Roy Bean, 1972 (Huston 2, Milius 2, Bisset 3, Gardner 3, Keach 3, McDowall 3, Newman 3, Perkins 3, Head 4, Jarre 4)
Life and Times of the Rev. Buck Shotte, 1968 (Weir 2)
Life at Forsbyholm, 1948 (Jaenzon 4)
Life at Stake, 1954 (Darwell 3)
Life At Stake. *See* Hra o život, 1956
Life at Stake. *See* Key Man, 1954
Life at the Top, 1965 (Harvey 3, Simmons 3, Morris 4)
Life Begins, 1932 (Young, L. 3)
Life Begins Again, 1942 (Alwyn 4)
Life Begins Anew. *See* Vita recominicia, 1945
Life Begins at College, 1937 (Chaney Lon, Jr. 3)
Life Begins at 8:30, 1942 (Lupino 3, Wilde 3, Cronjager 4, Day 4, Johnson 4, Leven 4, Newman 4)
Life Begins at 40, 1935 (Darwell 3, Rogers, W. 3, Summerville 3, Trotti 4)
Life Begins at 17, 1958 (Katzman 4)
Life Begins for Andy Hardy, 1941 (Garland 3, Rooney 3, Stone 3)
Life Begins in College, 1937 (Cook 3)
Life Begins in College. *See* Life Begins at College, 1937
Life Begins Now. *See* Nu borjar livet, 1948
Life Begins Tomorrow. *See* Vie commence demain, 1950
Life Begins with Love, 1937 (Ballard 4)
Life Behind a Mask. *See* Vsyou zhizn pod maskoi, 1915
Life Continues. *See* A život jde dál, 1935
Life for a Kiss, 1912 (Dwan 2)
Life for Ruth, 1962 (Dearden 2, Alwyn 4)
Life for the Czar. *See* Zhizn na Tzarya, 1911
Life Goes On, 1938 (Beavers 3)
Life Goes On. *See* Élet megy tovább, 1959
Life Hesitates at Forty, 1935 (Roach 4)
Life in Death. *See* Zhizn na smerti, 1914
Life in Hollywood No. 4, 1927 (Mix 3)
Life in Sometown, U.S.A., 1938 (Keaton 2)
Life in the Balance, 1913 (Sennett 2)
Life in the Balance, 1954 (Bancroft 3, Marvin 3, Horner 4)
Life in the Citadel. *See* Zhizn v tsitadel, 1947
Life in the Country. *See* Livet på landet, 1924
Life in the Raw, 1933 (Trevor 3)
Life in Your Hands, 1975 (Lancaster 3)
Life Insurance Training Film, 1975 (Halas and Batchelor 2)
Life Is a Bed of Roses. *See* Vie est un roman, 1984
Life is Like a Somersault. *See* Jinsei tonbo-gaeri, 1946
Life Is Nothing Without Music, 1947 (Matthews 3)
Life is Rising from the Ruins, 1948 (Kadár 2)
Life Is Short But Art Is Eternal. *See* Zhizn mig iskusstvo vetchno, 1916
Life Line, 1919 (Tourneur, M. 2, Beery 3, Carré 4)
Life Love Death. *See* Vie, l'amour, la mort, 1968
Life of a Communist Writer. *See* Kobayashi Takiji, 1974
Life of a Country Doctor. *See* Fundoshi isha, 1960
Life of a Cowboy, 1906 (Porter 2)
Life of a Film Director. *See* Mizoguchi Kenji no kiroku, 1975
Life of a Horse Dealer. *See* Bakuro ichidai, 1951
Life of a London Shopgirl, 1914 (Goulding 2)
Life of a Mother. *See* Historien om en Moder, 1912
Life of a Woman, 1953 (Shindo 2)
Life of an Actor. *See* Geidou ichidai otoko, 1941
Life of an American Cowboy, 1905 (Anderson G. 3)
Life of an American Fireman, 1903 (Porter 2)
Life of an American Policeman, 1905 (Porter 2)
Life of Beethoven. *See* Beethoven, 1927
Life of Buffalo Bill, 1910 (White 3)
Life of Chikuzan. *See* Chikuzan hitori-tabi, 1977
Life of Emile Zola, 1937 (De Toth 2, Dieterle 2, Calhern 3, Crisp 3, Muni 3, Schildkraut 3, Blanke 4, Friedhofer 4, Gaudio 4, Grot 4, Raine 4, Steiner 4, Wallis 4, Westmore, P. 4)
Life of General Villa, 1912 (Walsh 2)
Life of Her Own, 1950 (Cukor 2, Calhern 3, Milland 3, Turner, L. 3, Kaper 4, Lennart 4, Rose 4)
Life of Jimmy Dolan, 1933 (Fairbanks, D. Jr. 3, Rooney 3, Wayne 3, Young, L. 3, Edeson 4, Orry-Kelly 4)
Life of John Bunyan: Pilgrim's Progress, 1912 (Oland 3)

Lili, 1918 (Lugosi 3)
Lili, 1953 (Walters 2, Aumont 3, Caron 3, Ferrer, M. 3, Kaper 4)
Lili Marleen, 1980 (Fassbinder 2, Ferrer, M. 3, Giannini 3, Schygulla 3)
Lili Marlene, 1950 (Baker S. 3)
Lilies of the Field, 1924 (Wong 3)
Lilies of the Field, 1930 (Korda 2, Garmes 4, Grot 4)
Lilies of the Field, 1963 (Poitier 3, Goldsmith 4, Haller 4)
Liliom, 1919 (Curtiz 2)
Liliom, 1930 (Borzage 2, Behrman 4, Levien 4)
Liliom, 1934 (Lang 2, Artaud 3, Boyer 3, Maté 4, Pommer 4, Waxman 4)
Liliomfi, 1955 (Darvas 3)
Lilith, 1964 (Rossen 2, Beatty 3, Fonda, P. 3, Hackman 3, Seberg 3, Schufftan 4, Sylbert 4)
Lilith und Ly, 1919 (Lang 2)
Lilla Marta kommer tilbaka, 1948 (Bjornstrand 3)
Lille Chauffør, 1914 (Blom 2)
Lillian Gish, 1984 (Moreau 3)
Lillian Russell, 1940 (Ameche 3, Bruce 3, Faye 3, Fonda, H. 3, Banton 4, Day 4, Kaper 4, Newman 4, Shamroy 4, Zanuck 4)
Lilliputian Minuet. See Menuet lilliputien, 1905
Lilliput-put, 1980 (Bozzetto 4)
Lillis Ehe, 1919 (Dreier 4)
Lilly Turner, 1933 (Wellman 2, Brennan 3, Brent 3, Orry-Kelly 4)
Lily and the Rose, 1915 (Gish, L. 3)
Lily in Love, 1985 (Smith 3)
Lily of Killarney, 1934 (Holloway 3)
Lily of the Dust, 1924 (Negri 3)
Lily of the Tenements, 1910 (Griffith 2, Bitzer 4)
Lily's Lovers, 1911 (Sennett 2)
Limbo, 1972 (Robson 2)
Limehouse Blues, 1934 (Raft 3, Sheridan 3, Wong 3)
Limelight, 1936 (Wilcox 2, Buchanan 3, Neagle 3)
Limelight, 1952 (Aldrich 2, Chaplin 2, Keaton 2, Bloom 3, Bruce 3, Chaplin 3, Purviance 3, Lourié 4, Struss 4)
Limfjorden, 1961 (Carlsen 2)
Limit. See Granica, 1977
Limited Mail, 1925 (Zanuck 4)
Limonádový Joe, 1964 (Kopecký 3, Brdečka 4, Pojar 4)
Limousine Love, 1928 (Roach 4)
Limping Man, 1953 (Roberts 3)
Limuzyna Daimler-Benz, 1981 (Pszoniak 3)
Lin zexu, 1959 (Zhao 3)
Lina Braake, 1976 (Rasp 3)
Linarès, le jeune toréro, 1966 (Braunberger 4)
Linceul n'a pas de poches, 1974 (Gélin 3)
Lincoln Cycle, 1917 (Stahl 2)
Lincoln Highwayman, 1919 (Furthman 4)
Lincoln's Gettysburg Address, 1973 (Heston 3)
Linda, 1929 (Baxter W. 3, Laszlo 4)
Lindbergh Kidnapping Case, 1976 (Cotten 3, Hopkins, A. 3, Pidgeon 3, Wynn 3)
Line, 1969 (Rainer 4)
Line Cruising South, 1933 (Grierson 2)
Line of Black Clouds. See Kuroun kaidou, 1948
Line of Demarcation. See Ligne de démarcation, 1966
Line of Destiny. See Rekava, 1956
Line of Life. See Rekava, 1956
Line to Tschierva Hut, 1937 (Cavalcanti 2, Grierson 2)
Linea del fiume, 1976 (Hurt, J. 3)
Linear Accelerator, 1952 (Halas and Batchelor 2)
Linear Programming, 1965 (Halas and Batchelor 2)
Liner Cruising South, 1933 (Wright 2)
Lines Horizontal. See Lignes horizontales, 1962
Lines of White on the Sullen Sea, 1909 (Griffith 2, Bitzer 4)
Lines Vertical. See Lignes verticales, 1960
Line-Up, 1958 (Siegel 2, Wallach 3)
Linge turbulent, 1909 (Cohl 2)
Lingner Werke, 1936 (Alexeieff and Parker 2)
Linkshandige Frau, 1977 (Wicki 2, Depardieu 3, Ganz 3, Vogler 3, Winkler 3)
Linus, 1979 (Sjoman 2, Andersson H. 3)

Liolà, 1964 (Blasetti 2, Aimée 3, Brasseur 3, Tognazzi 3, Amidei 4, Delli Colli 4)
Lion, 1962 (Holden 3, Howard, T. 3, Arnold 4, Cardiff 4)
Lion and Albert, 1937 (Holloway 3)
Lion and the Girl, 1916 (Sennett 2)
Lion and the Horse, 1952 (Steiner 4)
Lion and the House, 1932 (Sennett 2)
Lion and the Mouse, 1928 (Bacon 2, Barrymore L. 3)
Lion and the Mouse, 1943 (Terry 4)
Lion and the Song. See Ley a písnička, 1958
Lion and the Souse, 1924 (Sennett 2)
Lion des Mogols, 1924 (Epstein 2, Mozhukin 3)
Lion Has 7 Heads. See Leone have sept cabecas, 1970
Lion Has Wings, 1939 (Powell and Pressburger 2, Oberon 3, Richardson 3, Dalrymple 4, Hornbeck 4, Korda 4, Stradling 4)
Lion Hunt, 1938 (Terry 4)
Lion Hunt, 1949 (Terry 4)
Lion Hunters, 1952 (Mirisch 4)
Lion Hunters. See Chasse au lion a l'arc, 1965
Lion in Winter, 1968 (Hepburn, K. 3, Hopkins, A. 3, O'Toole 3, Barry 4, Slocombe 4)
Lion Is in the Streets, 1953 (Walsh 2, Cagney 3, Chaney Lon, Jr. 3, Stradling 4, Waxman 4)
Lion nommé L'Américain, 1970 (Braunberger 4)
Lion of Sparta, 1961 (Maté 4, Unsworth 4)
Lion of the Desert, 1981 (Gielgud 3, Quinn 3, Reed, O. 3, Steiger 3, Jarre 4)
Lion savant, 1902 (Guy 2)
Lion Tamer, 1961 (Vukotić 4)
Lion, The Lamb, The Man, 1914 (Chaney Lon 3)
Lionel Lion, 1944 (Fleischer, M. and D. 2)
Lions and Ladies, 1919 (Hardy 3)
Lion's Busy, 1948 (Freleng 4)
Lion's Friend, 1934 (Terry 4)
Lion's Love, 1969 (Bogdanovich 2, Clarke 2, Varda 2, Constantine 3)
Lion's Roar, 1928 (Sennett 2)
Lions sont lâchés, 1961 (Verneuil 2, Cardinale 3, Darrieux 3, Morgan 3, Audiard 4, Matras 4)
Lion's Ward, (Johnson, N. 3)
Lion's Whiskers, 1925 (Sennett 2)
Lips without Kisses. See Labios sem beijos, 1930
Lipstick, 1976 (Bancroft 3, Fraker 4)
Lipstick. See Rossetto, 1960
Liqueur du couvent, 1903 (Guy 2)
Liquid Sunshine, 1921 (Balcon 4)
Liquidator, 1965 (Howard, T. 3, Cardiff 4, Schifrin 4, Williams, R. 4)
Lisa, 1962 (Dunne 4)
Lisa. See Inspector, 1962
Lisa and the Devil. See Lisa e il diavolo, 1972
Lisa Bright and Dark, 1972 (Baxter A. 3)
Lisa e il diavolo, 1972 (Valli 3)
Lisboa Cultural, 1983 (Oliveira 2)
Lisbon, 1956 (Milland 3, O'Hara 3, Rains 3)
Lise Fleron, 1919 (Bertini 3)
Lisetta, 1933 (De Sica 2)
Liška a džbán, 1947 (Trnka 2)
Liška bystrouška, 1954 (Hofman 4)
Lissy, 1957 (Wolf 2)
List of Adrian Messenger, 1963 (Huston 2, Cooper, Gladys 3, Curtis Dalio 3, Douglas, K. 3, Lancaster 3, Marshall 3, Mitchum 3, Scott, G. 3, Sinatra 3, Goldsmith 4, Veiller 4, Westmore, B. 4)
Listen, Darling, 1938 (Astor 3, Garland 3, Pidgeon 3)
Listen, Judge, 1952 (Three Stooges 3)
Listen Lester, 1924 (Fazenda 3)
Listen, Let's Make Love. See Scusi, facciamo l'amore?, 1968
Listen to Britain, 1942 (Jennings 2, Dalrymple 4)
Listening In, 1932 (Sennett 2)
Listopad, 1934 (Hammid 2)
Listopad, 1966 (Ioseliani 2)
Liszt, 1949 (Delli Colli 4)
Lisztomania, 1975 (Russell 2, Russell 4)
Lit à Colonne, 1942 (Marais 3, Spaak 4)
Lit à deux places, 1965 (Delannoy 2, Delli Colli 4)

Lito vilovito, 1964 (Samardžić 3)

Ltost, 1970 (Schorm 2)

Little Accident, 1930 (Fairbanks, D. Jr. 3, Pitts 3, Summerville 3)

Little Accident, 1939 (Krasner 4)

Little Adventuress, 1927 (Adrian 4, Grot 4)

Little American, 1917 (DeMille 2, Beery 3, Bosworth 3, Novarro 3, Buckland 4, Macpherson 4)

Little and Big. See Mali i veliki, 1966

Little Angels of Luck, 1910 (Griffith 2, Bitzer 4)

Little Anglers, 1952 (Terry 4)

Little Annie Rooney, 1925 (Pickford 3, Rosher 4)

Little Annie Rooney, 1931 (Fleischer, M. and D. 2)

Little Autogomobile, 1914 (Meredyth 4)

Little Beau Pepe, 1952 (Jones 2)

Little Big Horn, 1951 (Ireland 3)

Little Big Man, 1970 (Smith, D. , Penn 2, Dunaway 3, George, Ch. D. 3, Hoffman 3, Allen, D. 4, Jeakins 4, Needham 4, Tavoularis 4)

Little Big Shot, 1935 (Curtiz 2, Bond 3, Horton 3, Epstein, J. & P. 4, Gaudio 4, Orry-Kelly 4, Wald 4)

Little Billy Triumphs, 1914 (Sennett 2)

Little Billy's City Cousin, 1914 (Sennett 2)

Little Billy's Strategy, 1914 (Sennett 2)

Little Bit of Fluff, 1928 (Balfour 3)

Little Bit of Heaven, 1940 (Costello, M. 3, Pasternak 4, Seitz 4, Taradash 4)

Little Blabbermouse, 1940 (Freleng 4)

Little Black Sambo, 1935 (Iwerks 4)

Little Black Sambo, 1957-59 (Kawamoto 4)

Little Blonde in Black, 1915 (Furthman 4)

Little Bo Bopped, 1958 (Hanna and Barbera 4)

Little Boss, 1919 (Love 3)

Little Boy Blue, 1933 (Terry 4)

Little Boy Blue, 1936 (Iwerks 4)

Little Boy Boo, 1954 (McKimson 4)

Little Boy Lost, 1953 (Seaton 2, Crosby 3, Dauphin 3, Head 4, Young, V. 4)

Little Bricks. See Kirpitchiki, 1925

Little Broadcast, 1942 (Pal 2)

Little Brother. See Bratichka, 1927

Little Brother of the Rich, 1915 (Bosworth 3)

Little Brother Rat, 1939 (Jones 2)

Little Caesar, 1930 (Leroy 2, Fairbanks, D. Jr. 3, Robinson, E. 3, Gaudio 4, Grot 4, Wallis 4, Zanuck 4)

Little Catamount, 1915 (Gish, D. 3)

Little Chaos. See Kleine Chaos, 1966

Little Chauffeur. See Lille Chauffør, 1914

Little Chevalier, 1917 (Crosland 2)

Little Child Shall Lead Them, 1909 (Bitzer 4)

Little Chimney Sweep. See Kleine Schornsteinfeger, 1935

Little Church Around the Corner, 1923 (Bosworth 3)

Little Circus Rider, 1911 (Bosworth 3)

Little Colonel, 1935 (Barrymore L. 3, McDaniel 3, Robinson, B. 3, Temple 3, Friedhofer 4, La Shelle 4, Miller, A. 4)

Little Country Mouse, 1914 (Reid 3, Sweet 3)

Little Crane. See Zhuravushka, 1969

Little Cupids, 1915 (Franklin 2)

Little Damozel, 1932 (Wilcox 2, Neagle 3, Young, F. 4)

Little Darling, 1909 (Griffith 2, Pickford 3, Bitzer 4)

Little Dick's First Case, 1915 (Franklin 2)

Little Dog for Roger, 1967 (Le Grice 2)

Little Doll, 1961 (Dovniković 4)

Little Dragons, 1980 (Sothern 3)

Little Drummer Boy, 1969 (Ferrer, J. 3)

Little Drummer Girl, 1984 (Keaton 3, Kinski 3, Bumstead 4, Reynolds 4)

Little Dutch Mill, 1934 (Fleischer, M. and D. 2)

Little Dutch Plate, 1935 (Freleng 4)

Little Fairground Swing. See Korhinta, 1955

Little Fauss and Big Halsy, 1970 (Redford 3)

Little Fox, 1920 (Lukas 3)

Little Foxes, 1941 (Wyler 2, Davis 3, Duryea 3, Marshall 3, Wright 3, Goldwyn 4, Horner 4, Mandell 4, Orry-Kelly 4, Toland 4)

Little 'fraid Lady, 1920 (Marsh 3)

Little French Girl, 1925 (Brenon 2, Banton 4, Rosson 4)

Little Friend, 1934 (Balcon 4, Junge 4)

Little Giant, 1933 (Astor 3, Robinson, E. 3, Orry-Kelly 4)

Little Giant, 1946 (Abbott and Costello 3, Dumont 3)

Little Girl, Don't Say No! See Děvčátko, neříkej, ne!, 1932

Little Girl in Blue Velvet. See Petite Fille en velours bleu, 1978

Little Girl Next Door, 1916 (Van Dyke, W.S. 2)

Little Girl Who Lives Down the Lane, 1977 (Sheen 3)

Little Gloria . . . Happy at Last, 1982 (Lansbury 3)

Little Gold Bird. See Zlaté ptáče, 1932

Little Guardian Angel, 1956 (Dinov 4)

Little Hero, 1913 (Sennett 2, Normand 3)

Little House in Kolomn. See Domik v Kolomna, 1913

Little Hump-backed Horse, 1947 (Ivanov-vano 4)

Little Hut, 1956 (Robson 2, Gardner 3, Granger 3, Niven 3)

Little Injun, 1911 (Bosworth 3)

Little Irish Girl, 1926 (Costello, D. 3, Zanuck 4)

Little Island, 1958 (Williams, R. 4)

Little Island, 1969 (Kuri 4)

Little Italy, 1921 (Brady 3)

Little Italy. See Squadra antimafia, 1978

Little Joe, the Wrangler, 1942 (Salter 4)

Little Johnny Jet, 1953 (Avery 2)

Little Johnny Jones, 1923 (Leroy 2)

Little Johnny Jones, 1929 (Leroy 2)

Little Journey, 1927 (Carey 3, Gibbons 4, Lewin 4)

Little Ladies of the Night, 1976 (Gossett 3, Malone 3)

Little Lady Next Door, 1915 (Eason 4)

Little Lambkin, 1940 (Fleischer, M. and D. 2)

Little Lamby, 1937 (Fleischer, M. and D. 2)

Little Laura and Big John, 1973 (Black 3)

Little Liar, 1916 (Marsh 3, Loos 4)

Little Liar. See Fetita mincinoasa, 1953

Little Lion Hunter, 1939 (Jones 2)

Little Lord Fauntleroy, 1921 (Pickford 3, Rosher 4)

Little Lord Fauntleroy, 1936 (Cromwell 2, Costello, D. 3, Rooney 3, Miller, V. 4, Rosher 4, Selznick 4, Steiner 4)

Little Lord Fauntleroy, 1980 (Guinness 3)

Little Mail Carrier, 1914 (Lawrence 3)

Little Malcolm and His Struggle Against the Eunuchs, 1974 (Hurt, J. 3)

Little Man, 1941 (Musuraca 4)

Little Man, Big City. See Kis ember, nagy varos, 1967

Little Man, What Now?, 1934 (Borzage 2, Ulmer 2, Marsh 3, Sullavan 3, Laemmle 4)

Little Marie, 1915 (Browning 2)

Little Marta Returns. See Lilla Marta kommer tilbaka, 1948

Little Mary Sunshine, 1916 (King 2, Eason 4)

Little Match Girl. See Petite Marchande d'allumettes, 1928

Little Meena's Romance, 1916 (Fleming 2, Gish, D. 3)

Little Men, 1934 (McDaniel 3)

Little Men, 1940 (McLeod 2, Francis, K. 3)

Little Mermaid. See Malá mořská víla, 1976

Little Minister, 1934 (Crisp 3, Hepburn, K. 3, Nilsson 3, Berman 4, Heerman 4, Murfin 4, Plunkett 4, Polglase 4, Steiner 4)

Little Miss Big, 1946 (Salter 4)

Little Miss Broadway, 1938 (Darwell 3, Durante 3, Meek 3, Temple 3, Miller, A. 4, Zanuck 4)

Little Miss Broadway, 1947 (Katzman 4)

Little Miss Jazz, 1920 (Roach 4)

Little Miss Marker, 1934 (Menjou 3, Temple 3, Head 4, Schulberg 4)

Little Miss Marker, 1980 (Andrews J. 3, Curtis 3, Grant, L. 3, Matthau 3, Mancini 4)

Little Miss Nobody, 1936 (Carey 3, Darwell 3, Glennon 4)

Little Miss Rebellion, 1920 (Gish, D. 3)

Little Miss Smiles, 1922 (Ford, J. 2)

Little Miss Thoroughbred, 1938 (Sheridan 3)

Little Mr. Jim, 1945 (Zinnemann 2, Irene 4)

Little Mo, 1978 (Baxter A. 3)

Little Moon of Alban, 1965 (Bogarde 3)

Little Mother, 1929 (Roach 4)

Little Murders, 1971 (Arkin 3, Gould 3, Sutherland 3, Willis 4)

Little Murmurs, 1966 (Kuri 4)

Little Napoleon. See So sind die Manner, 1922

Little Nell's Tobacco, 1910 (Ince 4)
Little Nellie Kelly, 1940 (Taurog 2, Garland 3, Edens 4, Freed 4)
Little Nemo, 1909 (McCay 2)
Little Night Music, 1978 (Taylor, E. 3)
Little Nobody, 1935 (Fleischer, M. and D. 2)
Little Nuns. See Monachine, 1963
Little Old New York, 1923 (Olcott 2, Davies 3)
Little Old New York, 1940 (King 2, Bond 3, Faye 3, MacMurray 3,
    Balderston 4, Day 4, Newman 4, Shamroy 4, Zanuck 4)
Little Old World. See Piccolo mondo antico, 1941
Little Orphan, 1948 (Hanna and Barbera 4)
Little Orphan Airedale, 1947 (Jones 2)
Little Orphan Annie, 1919 (Moore, C. 3)
Little Orphan Annie, 1932 (Steiner 4)
Little Orphan Annie, 1938 (Head 4)
Little Orphan Willie, 1931 (Iwerks 4)
Little Owl. See Uhuka, a kis bagoly, 1969
Little Pal, 1915 (Pickford 3)
Little Pal. See Healer, 1935
Little Papa, 1935 (Roach 4)
Little People, 1926 (Cavalcanti 2, Dickinson 2, Pearson 2, Balfour 3)
Little Phantasy, 1946 (McLaren 2)
Little Prince, 1974 (Donen 2, Fosse 2, Wilder 3, Barry 4, Russell 4)
Little Prince, 1979 (Vinton 2)
Little Prince. See Kleine Prinz, 1966
Little Princess, 1917 (Hawks 2, Neilan 2, Pickford 3, Pitts 3, Marion 4,
    Rosher 4)
Little Princess, 1939 (Temple 3, Day 4, Miller, A. 4, Zanuck 4)
Little Problems, 1951 (Terry 4)
Little Prospector, 1910 (Anderson G. 3)
Little Puritan, 1915 (Talmadge, C. 3)
Little Quacker, 1950 (Hanna and Barbera 4)
Little Rebel, 1911 (Lawrence 3)
Little Rebel, 1913 (Olcott 2)
Little Red Hen, 1934 (Iwerks 4)
Little Red Hen, 1955 (Terry 4)
Little Red Riding Hood, 1911 (Pickford 3)
Little Red Riding Hood, 1922 (Disney 2)
Little Red Riding Hood, 1925 (Lantz 4)
Little Red Riding Rabbit, 1943 (Freleng 4)
Little Red Rodent Hood, 1951 (Freleng 4)
Little Red Walking Hood, 1937 (Avery 2)
Little Robinson Corkscrew, 1924 (Sennett 2)
Little Robinson Crusoe, 1924 (Coogan 3, Johnson, N. 3)
Little Romance, 1979 (Hill, G.R. 2, Crawford, B. 3, Olivier 3,
    Bumstead 4, Delerue 4)
Little Runaway, 1952 (Hanna and Barbera 4)
Little Runaway. See Chiisana tobosha, 1967
Little Rural Riding Hood, 1949 (Avery 2)
Little Savage, 1929 (Miller, V. 4, Plunkett 4)
Little School Mouse, 1952 (Hanna and Barbera 4)
Little Schoolma'am, 1916 (Franklin 2, Gish, D. 3)
Little Sea Nymph. See Malá mořská víla, 1976
Little Sex, 1982 (Delerue 4)
Little Shepherd of Bargain Row, 1916 (Van Dyke, W.S. 2)
Little Shepherd of Kingdom Come, 1928 (Barthelmess 3, Garmes 4,
    Meredyth 4)
Little Shepherd of Kingdom Come, 1960 (Kennedy, G. 3, Crosby 4)
Little Sheriff, 1912 (Anderson G. 3)
Little Shoes, 1917 (Walthall 3)
Little Shop of Horrors, 1960 (Nicholson 3, Corman 4)
Little Sinner, 1935 (Roach 4)
Little Sister, 1911 (Olcott 2)
Little Sister, 1914 (Mix 3)
Little Soap and Water, 1935 (Fleischer, M. and D. 2)
Little Soldier of '64, 1911 (Olcott 2)
Little Spreewald Maiden, 1910 (Olcott 2)
Little Story. See Mala kronika, 1962
Little Stranger, 1936 (Fleischer, M. and D. 2)
Little Substitute, 1913 (Bushman 3)
Little Sugar House. See Cukrová bouda, 1980
Little Sunset, 1914 (Bosworth 3)
Little Swee' Pea, 1936 (Fleischer, M. and D. 2)

Little Teacher, 1909 (Griffith 2, Pickford 3, Bitzer 4)
Little Teacher, 1915 (Sennett 2, Arbuckle 3, Normand 3)
Little Tease, 1913 (Griffith 2, Walthall 3, Bitzer 4)
Little Terror, 1917 (Ingram 2)
Little Theatre of Jean Renoir. See Petit Théâtre de Jean Renoir, 197
Little Tinker, 1947 (Avery 2)
Little Tokyo, U.S.A., 1942 (Day 4)
Little Tough Guys in Society, 1938 (Auer 3, Horton 3)
Little Train Robbery, 1905 (Porter 2)
Little Treasure, 1985 (Lancaster 3)
Little Turncoat, 1913 (Ince 4)
Little Western. See Maly western, 1960
Little White Dove. See Palomita blanca, 1972–73
Little White Savage, 1919 (Young, W. 4)
Little Widow, 1919 (Sennett 2)
Little Wild Girl, 1928 (Karloff 3)
Little Wildcat, 1922 (Hardy 3)
Little Window. See Okénko, 1933
Little Women, 1933 (Cukor 2, Bennett J. 3, Hepburn, K. 3, Lukas 3,
    Cooper 4, Heerman 4, MacGowan 4, Murfin 4, Plunkett 4,
    Polglase 4, Selznick 4, Steiner 4)
Little Women, 1949 (Leroy 2, Allyson 3, Astor 3, Brazzi 3, Leigh, J.
    O'Brien, M. 3, Taylor, E. 3, Deutsch 4, Gibbons 4, Jenkins 4,
    Plunkett 4)
Little Women, 1978 (Young, R. 3)
Little World of Don Camillo. See Petit Monde de Don Camillo, 195
Little Yank, 1917 (Gish, D. 3)
Little-Big-Cosmos. See Mikromakrokosmos, 1960
Littlest Horse Thieves. See Escape from the Dark, 1975
Littlest Outlaw, 1954 (Disney 2, Armendáriz 3)
Littlest Rebel, 1935 (Robinson, B. 3, Temple 3, Seitz 4)
Liubimaya shenshchina mekhanika Gavrilova, 1981 (Gurchenko 3)
Liv Ullman's Norway. See Look at Liv, 1977
Live a Little, Love a Little, 1968 (Presley 3, Ames 4)
Live Again, Die Again, 1974 (Page 3, Pidgeon 3)
Live and Learn, 1920 (Roach 4)
Live and Let Die, 1973 (Moore, R. 3, Baker 4)
Live Dangerously. See Lev farlight, 1944
Live Fast, Die Young, 1958 (Henreid 3)
Live for Life. See Vivre pour vivre, 1967
Live Ghost, 1934 (Laurel & Hardy 3, Roach 4)
Live, Love, and Believe, 1911 (Bushman 3)
Live, Love, and Learn, 1937 (Montgomery 3, Rooney 3, Russell, R.
    Brackett, C. 4)
Live Now, Pay Later, 1962 (Fisher 4)
Live to Love. See Devil's Hand, 1961
Live Today for Tomorrow, 1948 (March 3, Muse 3)
Live Today for Tomorrow. See Act of Murder, 1948
Live Wire, 1914 (Pearson 2)
Live Wire, 1937 (Brenon 2)
Live Wires, 1923 (Roach 4)
Liver Eaters. See Spider Baby, 1968
Lives of a Bengal Lancer, 1935 (Hathaway 2, Auer 3, Cooper, Gary
    Johnson, N. 3, Balderston 4, Banton 4, Dreier 4, Edouart 4,
    Head 4, Lang 4, Young, W. 4)
Lives of Jenny Dolan, 1975 (Ames 4, Hunter 4)
Lives of Performers, 1972 (Rainer 2)
Livet måste levas, 1943 (Borgstrom 3)
Livet på en pinne, 1942 (Borgstrom 3)
Livet på landet, 1924 (Jaenzon 4)
Livets Gøglespil, 1916 (Holger-Madsen 2)
Livets konflikter, 1913 (Sjostrom 2, Stiller 2, Jaenzon 4)
Livets Storme, 1910 (Blom 2)
Livid Flame, 1914 (Mix 3)
Living. See Ikiru, 1952
Living. See Ikitoshi Ikerumono, 1934
Living Between Two Worlds, 1963 (Zsigmond 4)
Living Blackboard. See Cauchemar du Fantoche, 1908
Living City, 1955 (Wexler 4)
Living Corpse. See Givoi troup, 1912
Living Corpse. See Ikeru shikabane, 1920
Living Corpse. See Nuits de feu, 1936
Living Corpse. See Zhivoi trup, 1928

Living Corpse. *See* Zhivoi trup, 1968
Living Dangerously, 1936 (Brenon 2)
Living Dead, 1972 (Sanders 3)
Living Dead. *See* Unheimliche Geschichten, 1932
Living Dead at the Manchester Morgue. *See* Fin de semana para los muertos, 1974
Living Dead Man. *See* Feu Mathias Pascal, 1925
Living Death, 1915 (Browning 2)
Living Desert, 1953 (Iwerks 4)
Living Earth, 1978 (Hammid 2)
Living Free, 1971 (Foreman 4)
Living Idol, 1957 (Lewin 4)
Living in a Big Way, 1947 (Donen 2, La Cava 2, Kelly, Gene 3, Winters 3, Berman 4, Irene 4, Ravetch 4, Rosson 4)
Living It Up, 1954 (Lewis 2, Taurog 2, Leigh, J. 3, Martin, D. 3, Head 4)
Living Magoroku. *See* Ikite-iru Magoroku, 1943
Living Mummy. *See* Levande mumien, 1916
Living on Love, 1937 (Musuraca 4, Polglase 4)
Living on Velvet, 1935 (Borzage 2, Brent 3, Francis, K. 3, Epstein, J. & P. 4, Orry-Kelly 4, Wald 4)
Living One's Life. *See* Zít svuj život, 1963
Living Playing Cards. *See* Cartes vivants, 1905
Living Portrait. *See* Ikiteiru gazo, 1948
Living Sea. *See* Umi wa ikiteiru, 1958
Living Stream. *See* Horn i norr, 1950
Living Tree . . .. *See* Hej, te eleven Fa . . ., 1963
Liza, 1972 (Ferreri 2, Deneuve 3, Piccoli 3, Flaiano 4, Sarde 4)
Liza. *See* Cagna, 1972
Liza and Her Double. *See* I Liza kai i alli, 1961
Lizard with a Woman's Skin. *See* Lucertola con la pelle di donna, 1971
Lizards. *See* Basilischi, 1963
Lizin let do nebe, 1937 (Hrušínský 3)
Lizino stestí, 1939 (Hrušínský 3)
Lizzie, 1957 (Blondell 3, Boone 3, Haas 3)
Lizzie and the Iceman, 1912–13 (White 3)
Lizzies of the Field, 1924 (Sennett 2)
Ljepotica 62, 1962 (Makavejev 2)
Ljubavni Slučaj, tragedija sluzbenice PTT, 1967 (Makavejev 2)
Ljubavni život Budimira Trajkovića, 1977 (Samardžić 3)
Ljubimec 13, 1958 (Karamitev 3)
Ljubitelj cveća, 1970 (Dovniković 4, Dragić 4)
Ljusnande framtid, 1940 (Molander 2, Jaenzon 4)
Llano Kid, 1939 (Head 4, Young, V. 4)
Llanto de la tortuga, 1974 (Figueroa 4)
Llanto por un bandido, 1964 (Buñuel 2, Saura 2)
Llevame en tus brazos, 1953 (Figueroa 4)
Lloyd of the CID, 1931 (Dickinson 2)
Lloyds of London, 1936 (King 2, Carroll M. 3, Power 3, Sanders 3, Glennon 4, MacGowan 4, Zanuck 4)
Lluvia roja, 1949 (Negrete 3)
LMNO, 1978 (Breer 2)
Lo chiamavano King . . ., 1971 (Kinski 3)
Lo chiameremo Andrea, 1972 (De Sica 2, Manfredi 3, Zavattini 4)
Lo mejor es reir, 1930 (d'Arrast 2)
Loaded Door, 1922 (Sutherland 2, Johnson, N. 3, Polito 2)
Loaded Pistols, 1949 (Autry 3)
Loaf. *See* Sousto, 1960
Loaf of Bread. *See* Sousto, 1960
Loafer, 1912 (Anderson G. 3)
Loafer. *See* Caicara, 1950
Loafers. *See* Vitelloni, 1953
Loafer's Mother, 1912 (Anderson G. 3)
Loan Shark, 1952 (Raft 3, Biroc 4)
Loan Shark King, 1914 (Talmadge, N. 3)
Local Boy Makes Good, 1931 (Brown 3, Polito 4)
Local Boy Makes Good. *See* Athlète, 1931
Local Color, 1913 (Mix 3)
Local Color, 1916 (Mix 3)
Local Hero, 1983 (Lancaster 3)
Local Romance. *See* Zižkovská romance, 1957
Locandiera, 1943 (Cervi 3)
Locataire, 1976 (Polanski 2, Adjani 3, Nykvist 4, Sarde 4)

Locataire. *See* Tenant, 1976
Locataire diabolique, 1910 (Méliès 2)
Locataires d'à côte, 1909 (Cohl 2)
Locations. *See* Schauplätze, 1967
Lock, Stock, and Barrel, 1971 (Meredith 3)
Lock Up Your Daughters, 1969 (York, S. 3)
Lock Your Doors. *See* Ape Man, 1943
Locked Door, 1929 (Boyd 3, Goddard 3, Pitts 3, Stanwyck 3, Menzies 4, Sullivan 4)
Locked Heart, 1918 (King 2)
Locked House, 1914 (Bunny 3)
Locked Out, 1911 (White 3)
Locket, 1912 (Dwan 2)
Locket, 1913 (Bunny 3)
Locket, 1946 (Mitchum 3, D'Agostino 4, Musuraca 4)
Lockfågeln, 1971 (Bjornstrand 3)
Locksmith and Chancellor. *See* Slesar i kantzler, 1923
Lockspitzel Asew, 1935 (Rasp 3, Tschechowa 3)
Lockvogel, 1934 (Rasp 3)
Loco Boy Makes Good, 1942 (Three Stooges 3, Bruckman 4)
Loco Luck, 1927 (Wray 3)
Locomotive No. 1000, 1926 (Kuleshov 2)
Locomotives, 1935 (Jennings 2)
Locura de amor, 1948 (Rey 3)
Locus, 1963 (Kuri 4)
Locusts, 1974 (Johnson, B. 3)
Lodge Nights, 1923 (Roach 4)
Lodger, 1926 (Hitchcock 2, Novello 3, Balcon 4)
Lodger, 1932 (Hawkins 3, Novello 3)
Lodger, 1944 (Hardwicke 3, Oberon 3, Sanders 3, Ballard 4, Basevi 4, Friedhofer 4)
Lodging for the Night, 1912 (Griffith 2, Pickford 3, Bitzer 4)
Loffe blir polis, 1950 (Nykvist 4)
Log Cabin. *See* Srub, 1965
Log kya kahenge, 1983 (Azmi 3)
Log of the Black Pearl, 1974 (Bellamy 3)
Log Rollers, 1953 (Terry 4)
Loga de la casa, 1950 (Armendáriz 3)
Logan's Run, 1976 (Ustinov 3, York, M. 3, Goldsmith 4, Laszlo 4)
Logik des Gefuhls, 1982 (Ganz 3, Vogler 3)
Logis de l'horreur. *See* Unheimliche Gast, 1922
Lohengrin, 1907 (Porten 3, Messter 4)
Lohengrin, 1936 (De Sica 2)
Loi, 1959 (Brasseur 3, Lollobrigida 3, Mercouri 3, Montand 3)
Loi. *See* Legge, 1959
Loi . . . c'est la loi, 1958 (Christian-Jaque 2, Fernandel 3, Age and Scarpelli 4, Cristaldi 4, Di Venanzo 4, Rota 4)
Loi des hommes, 1962 (Arletty 3, Dalio 3, Presle 3)
Loi des rues, 1956 (Manès 3, Trintignant 3)
Loi du 21 juin 1907, 1942 (Arletty 3)
Loi du nord, 1942 (Feyder 2, Morgan 3, Vanel 3, D'Eaubonne 4)
Loi du printemps, 1942 (Matras 4)
Loin de Manhattan, 1980 (Branco 4)
Loin du Viêt-nam, 1967 (Godard 2, Guerra 2, Ivens 2, Lelouch 2, Marker 2, Resnais 2, Varda 2, Cloquet 4)
Lojen och tårar, 1913 (Sjostrom 2, Jaenzon 4, Magnusson 4)
Lojtnantshjartan, 1941 (Jaenzon 4)
Lola, 1961 (Demy 2, Aimée 3, Coutard 4, de Beauregard 4, Evein 4, Legrand 4, Ponti 4)
Lola, 1981 (Fassbinder 2, Mueller-Stahl 3)
Lola. *See* Lola Montès, 1955
Lola. *See* Twinky, 1969
Lola Montès, 1955 (Ophuls 2, Ophuls 2, Ustinov 3, Werner 3, Annenkov 4, Auric 4, D'Eaubonne 4, Matras 4)
Lola Montez, 1919 (Albers 3)
Lola Montez. *See* Lola Montès, 1955
Lola, the Rat, 1914 (Costello, M. 3)
Lola Triana, 1936 (Clothier 4)
Lolas de Lola, 1976 (Léaud 3)
Lolita, 1962 (Kubrick 2, Mason 3, Sellers 3, Winters 3, Morris 4)
Lolly Madonna XXX, 1973 (Bridges 3, Ryan 3)
Lolly Madonna XXX. *See* Lolly-Madonna War, 1973
Lolly-Madonna War, 1973 (Steiger 3)

Longest Hunt. *See* Spara, gringo, spara, 1968
Longest Night, 1936 (Young, R. 3)
Longest Yard, 1974 (Aldrich 2, Reynolds, B. 3, Biroc 4)
Long-Haired Hare, 1948 (Jones 2)
Longing. *See* Akogare, 1935
Longue Marche, 1966 (Astruc 2, Trintignant 3)
Longue Nuit, 1965 (Braunberger 4)
Look at Life Freiheit, 1965 (Lucas 2)
Look at Liv, 1979 (Bergman 2, Andersson B. 3, Finch 3, Hackman 3, Ullmann 3, Von Sydow 3)
Look Back in Anger, 1959 (Richardson 2, Bloom 3, Burton 3, Evans 3, Pleasance 3, Addison 4, Morris 4)
Look for the Silver Lining, 1949 (Sakall 3, Prinz 4)
Look Out!. *See* Pozor!, 1959
Look Out Below, 1918 (Daniels 3, Lloyd 3, Roach 4)
Look Pleasant Please, 1918 (Daniels 3, Lloyd 3, Roach 4)
Look Up and Laugh, 1935 (Fields, G. 3, Leigh, V. 3, More 3, Dean 4)
Look What's Happened to Rosemary's Baby, 1976 (Crawford, B. 3, Gordon 3, Milland 3)
Look Who's Laughing, 1941 (Dwan 2, Ball 3, Polglase 4)
Look Your Best, 1923 (Moore, C. 3, Gibbons 4)
Looker, 1981 (Coburn, J. 3, Finney 3)
Lookin' to Get Out, 1982 (Ashby 2, Voight 3, Wexler 4)
Looking at the Bright Side, 1932 (Dean 4)
Looking for a Flat. *See* Nevité o bytě?, 1947
Looking for his Murderer. *See* Mann der seinen Morder sucht, 1931
Looking for Love, 1964 (Cahn 4, Krasner 4, Pasternak 4)
Looking for Mr. Goodbar, 1977 (Brooks, R. 2, Gere 3, Keaton 3, Weld 3, Fraker 4)
Looking for Mushrooms, 1961–67 (Conner 2)
Looking for Sally, 1925 (McCarey 2, Roach 4)
Looking for Trouble, 1914 (Beery 3)
Looking for Trouble, 1920 (Roach 4)
Looking for Trouble, 1934 (Wellman 2, Tracy 3, Day 4, Newman 4, Zanuck 4)
Looking Forward, 1933 (Brown 2, Barrymore L. 3, Stone 3, Adrian 4, Meredyth 4)
Looking Glass War, 1969 (Hopkins, A. 3, Richardson 3, Box 4)
Looking Good. *See* Corky, 1972
Looking on the Bright Side, 1932 (Fields, G. 3)
Looks and Smiles, 1981 (Loach 2)
Loony Tom, the Happy Lover, 1951 (Broughton 2)
Loophole, 1954 (Malone 3)
Loophole, 1980 (Finney 3, Sheen 3, York, S. 3, Schifrin 4)
Looping, 1975 (Geschonneck 3)
Looping the Loop, 1928 (Robison 2, Krauss 3, Manès 3, Herlth 4, Hoffmann 4, Rohrig 4)
Loops, 1939–41 (McLaren 2)
Loopy's Hare-Do, 1961 (Hanna and Barbera 4)
Loose Ankles, 1930 (Fairbanks, D. Jr. 3, Fazenda 3, Young, L. 3)
Loose Change, 1921 (Roach 4)
Loose Ends, 1930 (Cardiff 4)
Loose Loot, 1953 (Three Stooges 3)
Loose Tightwad, 1923 (Roach 4)
Loot, 1970 (Attenborough 3, Remick 3)
Loot Maar, 1980 (Anand 3)
Looters. *See* Estouffade à la Carabei, 1967
Lord am Alexanderplatz, 1967 (Domrose 3, Geschonneck 3, Mueller-Stahl 3)
Lord Arthur Saville's Crime. *See* Lidércnyomás, 1920
Lord Babs, 1932 (Balcon 4)
Lord Byron, 1922 (Veidt 3)
Lord Byron of Broadway, 1930 (Brown, N. 4, Freed 4, Gibbons 4, Shearer 4, Tiomkin 4)
Lord Camber's Ladies, 1932 (Hitchcock 2, Bruce 3)
Lord Chumley, 1914 (Gish, L. 3)
Lord Feathertop, 1908 (Porter 2)
Lord for a Night. *See* Aru yo no tonosama, 1946
Lord Jeff, 1938 (Wood 2, Coburn, C. 3, Rooney 3, Gibbons 4, Seitz 4)
Lord Jim, 1925 (Fleming 2)
Lord Jim, 1965 (Brooks, R. 2, Hawkins 3, Jurgens 3, Lukas 3, Mason 3, O'Toole 3, Wallach 3, Kaper 4, Mathieson 4, Young, F. 4)

Lord Love a Duck, 1966 (Gordon 3, McDowall 3, Weld 3, Axelrod 4)
Lord of the Rings, 1978 (Bakshi 2, Hurt, J. 3, Rosenman 4)
Lords of Flatbush, 1974 (Stallone 3)
Lords of Little Egypt, 1961 (Zetterling 2)
Lorelei, 1931 (Terry 4)
Lorenzaccio, 1977 (Jarre 4)
Lorenzo Burghardt, 1918 (Basserman 3)
Lorenzo il Magnifico, 1911 (Bertini 3)
Lorgnon accusateur, 1905 (Guy 2)
Lorie, 1984 (Azmi 3)
Lorinci fonóban, 1971 (Mészáros 2)
Lorna Doone, 1922 (Tourneur, M. 2, Ince 4)
Lorna Doone, 1935 (Dean 4)
Lorna Doone, 1951 (Duning 4)
Lorraine of the Lions, 1925 (Miller, V. 4)
Los Angeles Harbour, 1913 (Sennett 2)
Los de abajo, 1940 (Figueroa 4)
Los que no deben nacer, 1953 (García 3)
Los que volvieron, 1946 (García 3)
Los vom Mann. *See* Miss Hobbs, 1921
Lose No Time, 1921 (Roach 4)
Loser Take All. *See* Leather Gloves, 1948
Loser Takes All, 1956 (Brazzi 3, Périnal 4)
Losing Fame. *See* Pay Off, 1930
Losing Fight, 1914 (Mix 3)
Loss of Innocence. *See* Greengage Summer, 1961
Lost, 1955 (Green, G. 4)
Lost a Cook, 1917 (Sennett 2)
Lost—A Wife, 1925 (Menjou 3)
Lost and Found, 1979 (Jackson 3, Segal 3, Frank 4, Slocombe 4)
Lost and Found on a South Sea Island, 1923 (Walsh 2, Wilson, C. 4)
Lost and Foundling, 1944 (Jones 2)
Lost and Foundry, 1937 (Fleischer, M. and D. 2)
Lost and Won, 1917 (DeMille 2)
Lost Angel, 1943 (Gardner 3, Meek 3, O'Brien, M. 3, Wynn 3, Irene 4, Lennart 4, Schary 4, Surtees 4)
Lost Bag. *See* Naar Fruen gaar paa Eventyr, 1913
Lost Boundaries, 1949 (Ferrer, M. 3, de Rochemont 4)
Lost Bridegroom, 1916 (Barrymore J. 3)
Lost Canyon, 1943 (Boyd 3)
Lost Child, 1904 (Bitzer 4)
Lost Chord, 1933 (Hawkins 3)
Lost Combination, 1913 (Cruze 2)
Lost Command, 1966 (Robson 2, Cardinale 3, Delon 3, Morgan 3, Quinn 3, Segal 3, Surtees 4, Waxman 4)
Lost Continent, 1968 (Knef 3)
Lost Dog, 1924 (Roach 4)
Lost Empire, 1929 (Cooper 4)
Lost Face. *See* Ztracená tvář, 1965
Lost Honor of Katharina Blum. *See* Verlorene Ehre der Katharina Blum, 1975
Lost Horizon, 1937 (Capra 2, Colman 3, Horton 3, Jaffe 3, Riskin 4, Tiomkin 4, Walker 4, Westmore, E. 4)
Lost Horizon, 1972 (Boyer 3, Finch 3, Gielgud 3, Kennedy, G. 3, Ullmann 3, York, M. 3, Ames 4, Hunter 4, Pan 4, Surtees 4)
Lost House, 1915 (Gish, L. 3, Reid 3)
Lost Illusion. *See* Fallen Idol, 1948
Lost Illusions, 1911 (Porter 2)
Lost in a Harem, 1944 (Abbott and Costello 3)
Lost in Alaska, 1952 (Abbott and Costello 3, Boyle 4)
Lost in Prague. *See* Návrat domu, 1948
Lost in the Alps, 1907 (Porter 2)
Lost in the Arctic, 1911 (Mix 3)
Lost in the Garden of the World, 1975 (Hoffman 3)
Lost in the Jungle, 1911 (Mix 3, Selig 4)
Lost in the Stars, 1974 (North 4)
Lost in the Stratosphere, 1934 (McDaniel 3)
Lost in Transit, 1917 (Crisp 3)
Lost Jools. *See* Stolen Jools, 1931
Lost Jungle, 1934 (Rooney 3, Canutt 4)
Lost Kingdom. *See* Antinea, 1961
Lost Lady, 1934 (Johnson, N. 3, Stanwyck 3, Orry-Kelly 4)
Lost Letters, 1966 (Romm 2)

Lost Lord Lovell, 1915 (Gish, D. 3)
Lost Lost Lost, 1975 (Bogdanovich 2, Mekas 2)
Lost Man, 1969 (Poitier 3, Head 4, Jones 4)
Lost Moment, 1947 (Cummings 3, Hayward 3, Moorehead 3,
  Banton 4, Wanger 4)
Lost Necklace, 1911 (White 3)
Lost on the Western Front. See Romance of Flanders, 1937
Lost One. See Signora delle camelie, 1948
Lost One. See Verlorene, 1951
Lost Outpost, 1935 (Brackett, C. 4)
Lost Patrol, 1934 (Ford, J. 2, Karloff 3, McLaglen 3, Cooper 4, Fort 4,
  Nichols 4, Polglase 4, Steiner 4)
Lost People, 1949 (Zetterling 2, Attenborough 3)
Lost Planet, 1953 (Katzman 4)
Lost Sentry. See Ztracená varta, 1956
Lost Sermon, 1914 (Eason 4)
Lost Shadow. See Velorene Schatten, 1921
Lost Son, 1974 (Reiniger 2)
Lost Soul. See Anima persa, 1976
Lost Squadron, 1932 (Von Stroheim 2, Astor 3, Cronjager 4,
  Mankiewicz 4, Selznick 4, Steiner 4)
Lost Track. See Ztracená stopa, 1956
Lost Trail. See Ztracená stopa, 1956
Lost Treasure, 1914 (Eason 4)
Lost Treasure. See Thesouro perdido, 1927
Lost Tribe, 1949 (Weissmuller 3, Katzman 4)
Lost Volcano, 1950 (Mirisch 4)
Lost Weekend, 1945 (Wilder 2, Milland 3, Muse 3, Wyman 3,
  Brackett, C. 4, Dreier 4, Head 4, Rozsa 4, Seitz 4)
Lost World, 1925 (Beery 3, Love 3, Stone 3, Edeson 4, O'Brien 4,
  Westmore, P. 4)
Lost World, 1960 (Rains 3, Bennett 4, Hoch 4, O'Brien 4)
Lost World of Sinbad. See Daitozoku, 1964
Lost Years, 1911 (Bushman 3)
Lost Youth. See Gioventú perduta, 1947
Lotna, 1959 (Polanski 2, Wajda 2)
Lotta dell'uomo per la sua sopravvivenza, 1967 (Rossellini 2)
Lotte, 1928 (Porten 3)
Lotte in Italia, 1969 (Godard 2)
Lotte in Weimar, 1975 (Hoffmann 3)
Lotte Lenya Sings Kurt Weill, 1962 (Russell 2)
Lotte nell'ombra, 1939 (Amidei 4)
Lottekens Feldzug, 1915 (Wiene 2)
Lotterieschwede, 1959 (Geschonneck 3)
Lotteriseddel No. 22152, 1915 (Blom 2)
Lottery Bride, 1930 (Brown 3, MacDonald 3, Pitts 3, Menzies 4,
  Schenck 4)
Lottery Lover, 1935 (Wilder 2, Ayres 3, Glennon 4)
Lottery Man, 1919 (Cruze 2, Reid 3)
Lotus Eater, 1921 (Neilan 2, Barrymore J. 3, Moore, C. 3, Nilsson 3)
Loud Soup, 1929 (Roach 4)
Loudest Whisper. See Children's Hour, 1962
Loudest Whisper. See These Three, 1936
Loudwater Mystery, 1921 (Brook 3)
Louis Capet, 1954 (Leenhardt 2)
Louis Lecoin, 1966 (Delerue 4)
Louis Lumière, 1964–69 (Rohmer 2)
Louis Lumière. See Lumière et l'invention du cinématographe, 1953
Louisa, 1950 (Coburn, C. 3, Gwenn 3, Reagan 3, Boyle 4)
Louise, 1939 (Gance 2, Courant 4, Wakhévitch 4)
Louise de Lavallière, 1921 (Freund 4)
Louisiana Hayride, 1944 (Hunter 4)
Louisiana Purchase, 1941 (Hope 3, Dreier 4)
Louisiana Serenade, 1941 (Ryskind 4)
**Louisiana Story, 1948 (Flaherty 2, Leacock 2, Rosenblum 4,
  Van Dongen 4)**
Loulou, 1980 (Depardieu 3, Huppert 3)
Loup des Malveneur, 1943 (L'Herbier 2)
Loup et l'agneau, 1953 (Kosma 4)
Loup y es-tu?, 1983 (Rohmer 2)
Loupe de gran'maman, 1900 (Zecca 2)
Loupežnická pohádka, 1964 (Hofman 4)
Loupežník, 1931 (Vích 4)

Loups chassent la nuit, 1951 (Aumont 3, Kosma 4)
Loups entre eux, 1936 (Berry 3, Spaak 4)
Lourdes, 1958 (Russell 2)
Lourdes, 1965 (Braunberger 4)
Lourdes et ses miracles, 1954 (Demy 2)
Louve solitaire, 1967 (Lai 4)
Louves, 1957 (Moreau 3, Presle 3, Kosma 4)
Louvre Come Back to Me, 1962 (Jones 2)
Louvre Museum. See Musée du Louvre, 1979
Lov na mamuta, 1964 (Kopecký 3)
Lovable Cheat, 1949 (Oswald 2, Leven 4)
Love, 1919 (Arbuckle 3)
Love, 1920 (Ruggles 2)
Love, 1927 (Goulding 2, Tourneur, J. 2, Barrymore L. 3, Garbo 3,
  Gilbert 3, Adrian 4, Daniels 4, Gibbons 4, Marion 4)
Love, 1955 (Lee, B. 3)
Love, 1963 (Kuri 4)
Love. See Karlek, 1952
Love. See Koi, 1924
Love. See Láska, 1972
Love. See Liebe, 1956
Love. See Mirsu, 1924
Love. See Szerelem, 1970
Love à la Carte. See Adua e le compagne, 1960
Love Affair, 1932 (Bogart 3)
Love Affair, 1939 (Daves 2, Dmytryk 2, McCarey 2, Boyer 3, Dunne 3,
  Ouspenskaya 3, Berman 4, Maté 4, Polglase 4, Stewart 4)
Love Affair. See Ljubavni Slučaj, tragedija sluzbenice PTT, 1967
Love Affair in Toyland. See Drame chez les fantoches, 1908
Love Affair of the Dictator, 1935 (Brook 3)
Love Affair of the Dictator. See Dictator, 1935
Love Affair: The Eleanor and Lou Gehrig Story, 1978 (Neal 3)
Love Aflame, 1917 (Hersholt 3, Johnson, N. 3)
Love among the Millionaires, 1930 (Bow 3, Mankiewicz 4)
Love Among the Roses, 1910 (Griffith 2, Pickford 3)
Love among the Ruins, 1975 (Cukor 2, Hepburn, K. 3, Olivier 3,
  Barry 4, Dillon 4, Slocombe 4)
Love and a Warrior. See Koi to bushi, 1925
Love and a Whirlwind, 1922 (Brook 3)
Love and Anarchy. See Film d'amore e d'anarchia, 1973
Love and Anger. See Amore e rabbia, 1967
Love and Bullets, 1914 (Sennett 2)
Love and Bullets, 1979 (Bronson 3, Martin, S. 3, Steiger 3, Schifrin 4)
Love and Courage, 1913 (Sennett 2, Arbuckle 3)
Love and Death, 1975 (Allen 2, Keaton 3, Cloquet 4, Rosenblum 4)
Love and Death of Ogin. See Ogin Sawa, 1979
Love and Deficit. See Karlek och kassabrist, 1932
Love and Doughnuts, 1922 (Sennett 2)
Love and Downhill Skiing. See Karlek och stortlopp, 1946
Love and Duty, 1916 (Hardy 3)
Love and Dynamite, 1914 (Sennett 2)
Love and Fascination. See Bojo no hito, 1961
Love and Gasoline, 1914 (Sennett 2)
Love and Graft, 1914 (Fazenda 3)
Love and Hisses, 1937 (Chaney Lon, Jr. 3, Lahr 3, Simon, S. 3,
  MacGowan 4)
Love and Kisses, 1925 (Sennett 2)
Love and Larceny. See Mattatore, 1960
Love and Learn, 1928 (Mankiewicz 4)
Love and Learn, 1946 (Diamond 4, Steiner 4)
Love and Lemons, 1912 (Dwan 2)
Love and Lobsters. See He Did and He Didn't, 1916
Love and Lunch. See Mabel's Busy Day, 1914
Love (and) Marriage, 1958 (Anand 3)
Love and Marriage, 1970 (Godfrey 4)
Love and Money, 1982 (Kinski 3)
Love and Other Crimes. See Alex and the Gypsy, 1976
Love and Pain, 1913 (Sennett 2)
Love and Pain and the Whole Damn Thing, 1972 (Pakula 2, Smith 3,
  Sargent 4, Unsworth 4)
Love and Pledge. See Ai to chikai, 1945
Love and Rubbish, 1913 (Sennett 2)
Love and Salt Water, 1914 (Sennett 2)

Love and Separation in Sri Lanka. *See* Suri Lanka no ai to wakare, 1976

Love and Soda, 1914 (Beery 3)

Love and the Devil, 1929 (Korda 2, Garmes 4)

Love and the Frenchwoman. *See* Française et l'amour, 1960

Love and the Journalist. *See* Karlek och journalistik, 1916

Love and the Law, 1913 (Anderson G. 3, Reid 3)

Love and the Midnight Auto Supply, 1977 (Ireland 3)

Love and the Zeppelin. *See* Vzuchold a láska, 1947

Love and Trouble, 1915 (Beery 3)

Love and War. *See* Kys og Kaerlighed, 1914

Love As Disorder. *See* Affair of the Skin, 1963

Love at First Bite, 1950 (Three Stooges 3)

Love at First Flight, 1928 (Hornbeck 4)

Love at 1st Sight, 1928 (Sennett 2)

Love at Sea, 1936 (Havelock-Allan 4)

Love at Second Sight, 1934 (Holloway 3)

Love at the Top. *See* Mouton enragé, 1974

Love at Twenty. *See* Amour à vingt ans, 1962

Love Ban. *See* It's a 2ft 6in above the Ground World, 1972

Love Before Breakfast, 1936 (Lombard 3, Banton 4, D'Agostino 4, Waxman 4)

Love Begins at Twenty, 1936 (Barnes 4, Trumbo 4)

Love Between the Raindrops. *See* Láska mezi kapkami deště, 1979

Love Birds, 1934 (Pitts 3, Rooney 3, Summerville 3, Mandell 4)

Love Brand, 1923 (Laemmle 4)

Love Bug, 1925 (Roach 4)

Love Bug, 1969 (Ellenshaw 4)

Love Bugs, 1917 (Hardy 3)

Love Burglar, 1919 (Cruze 2, Beery 3, Nilsson 3, Reid 3)

Love by the Light of the Moon, 1901 (Porter 2)

Love Cage. *See* Félins, 1964

Love Charm, 1922 (Baxter W. 3)

Love Circle. *See* Metti, una sera a cena, 1969

Love Comes Along, 1930 (Daniels 3, Hunt 4, Plunkett 4)

Love Comet, 1916 (Sennett 2)

Love Contract, 1932 (Wilcox 2)

Love Crazy, 1941 (Cook 3, Loy 3, Muse 3, Powell, W. 3, Berman 4, Gibbons 4, Lederer 4)

Love Defender, 1919 (Polito 4)

Love Detectives, 1934 (Grable 3)

Love Doctor, 1930 (Cronjager 4, Mankiewicz 4)

Love Doll. *See* Life Size, 1976

Love 'em and Feed 'em, 1927 (Hardy 3, Bruckman 4, Roach 4)

Love 'em and Leave 'em, 1926 (Brooks 3, Banton 4)

Love 'em and Weep, 1927 (Laurel and Hardy 3, Roach 4)

Love Eterne. *See* Liang Shan-po yü Chu Ying-t'ai, 1963

Love Expert, 1920 (Talmadge, C. 3, Emerson 4, Loos 4)

Love Express. *See* Renai tokkyu, 1954

Love Film. *See* Szerelmesfilm, 1970

Love Finds a Way, 1908 (Griffith 2, Bitzer 4)

Love Finds a Way. *See* Alias French Gertie, 1930

Love Finds Andy Hardy, 1938 (Garland 3, Rooney 3, Stone 3, Turner, L. 3, Edens 4)

Love Flower, 1920 (Griffith 2, Barthelmess 3, Bitzer 4)

Love from a Stranger, 1937 (Rathbone 3, Marion 4)

Love from a Stranger, 1947 (Sidney 3, Gaudio 4, Salter 4)

Love Gambler, 1922 (Gilbert 3, August 4, Furthman 4)

Love Game. *See* Jeux de l'amour, 1960

Love Game. *See* Kara leken, 1959

Love God?, 1969 (O'Brien, E. 3)

Love Habit, 1931 (Lanchester 3)

Love Happy, 1949 (Tashlin 2, Marx Brothers 3, Monroe 3)

Love Has Many Faces, 1965 (Robertson 3, Turner, L. 3, Head 4, Raksin 4, Ruttenberg 4)

Love Heeds Not the Showers, 1911 (Pickford 3)

Love, Honor, and Behave, 1920 (Sennett 2)

Love, Honor, and Behave, 1938 (Buckner 4, Wallis 4)

Love, Honor, and Goodbye, 1945 (Alton, J. 4)

Love, Honor, and Oh, Baby!, 1933 (Meek 3, Pitts 3, Summerville 3, Krasna 4)

Love, Honor, and Oh, Baby!, 1940 (Cortez 4, Salter 4)

Love Hour, 1925 (Fazenda 3, Meredyth 4)

Love Hungry, 1928 (Heerman 4)

Love in a Bungalow, 1937 (Beavers 3, Krasner 4)

Love in a Goldfish Bowl, 1961 (Head 4)

Love in a Hammock, 1901 (Porter 2)

Love in a Police Station, 1927 (Sennett 2)

Love in a Teacup. *See* Himawari-musume, 1953

Love in an Apartment Hotel, 1912 (Griffith 2, Barrymore L. 3, Carey 3, Marsh 3, Sweet 3, Walthall 3, Bitzer 4)

Love in Armor, 1915 (Sennett 2, Arbuckle 3)

Love in Bloom, 1935 (Glazer 4)

Love in Exile, 1936 (Brook 3)

Love in Germany. *See* Liebe in Deutschland, 1983

Love in Las Vegas. *See* Viva Las Vegas, 1963

Love in Mardi Gras Colors. *See* Láska v barvách karnevalu, 1974

Love in Morocco. *See* Baroud, 1931

Love in Rome. *See* Amore a Roma, 1960

Love in Stunt Flying. *See* Liebe in Gleitflug, 1938

Love in the Afternoon, 1957 (Wilder 2, Chevalier 3, Cooper, Gary 3, Hepburn, A. 3, Diamond 4, Mercer 4, Trauner 4, Waxman 4)

Love in the City. *See* Amore in città, 1953

Love in the Desert, 1929 (Plunkett 4)

Love in the Hills, 1911 (Griffith 2, Sweet 3, Bitzer 4)

Love in the Rough, 1930 (Montgomery 3, Gibbons 4)

Love in the Suburbs, 1900 (Bitzer 4)

Love in the Tropics. *See* Tropisk Kaerlighed, 1911

Love in the West. *See* Hell-to-Pay Austin, 1916

Love in Tokyo. *See* Koi no Tokyo, 1932

Love Insurance, 1919 (Crisp 3)

Love is a Ball, 1963 (Boyer 3, Ford, G. 3, D'Eaubonne 4, Legrand 4)

Love Is a Funny Thing. *See* Homme qui me plait, 1969

Love Is a Headache, 1938 (Rooney 3, Adrian 4, Seitz 4)

Love Is a Many-Splendored Thing, 1955 (King 2, Holden 3, Jones, J. 3, Lemaire 4, Newman 4, Reynolds 4, Shamroy 4, Wheeler 4)

Love is a Racket, 1932 (Wellman 2, Fairbanks, D. Jr. 3, Raft 3)

Love Is an Awful Thing, 1922 (Heerman 4)

Love Is Better Than Ever, 1952 (Donen 2, Taylor, E. 3, Rose 4, Rosson 4)

Love Is Blind, 1909 (Porter 2)

Love is Blind, 1913 (Dwan 2)

Love is Blind. *See* Kaerlighed gør blind, 1912

Love Is Blind. *See* Liebe macht Blind, 1925

Love Is Colder Than Death. *See* Liebe ist kalter als der Tod, 1969

Love Is Everything, 1920 (Haller 4)

Love Is in the Air, 1937 (Reagan 3)

Love Is My Profession. *See* En cas de malheur, 1958

Love Is News, 1937 (Garnett 2, Ameche 3, Chaney Lon, Jr. 3, Cook 3, Darwell 3, Fetchit 3, Power 3, Sanders 3, Summerville 3, Young, L. 3)

Love Is Strength. *See* Ai wa chikara da, 1930

Love Kiss, 1930 (Meek 3)

Love, Laughs, and Lather, 1917 (Daniels 3, Lloyd 3, Roach 4)

Love Laughs at Andy Hardy, 1946 (Rooney 3, Stone 3, Irene 4)

Love Laughs at Locksmiths, 1908 (Lawrence 3)

Love Leads the Way, 1984 (Neal 3, Saint 3)

Love Lesson, 1921 (Roach 4)

Love Letters, 1945 (Dieterle 2, Cotten 3, Jones, J. 3, Dreier 4, Garmes 4, Head 4, Wallis 4, Young, V. 4)

Love Letters, 1984 (Corman 2)

Love Letters. *See* Liebesnachte, 1929

Love Letters of a Star, 1936 (Krasner 4)

Love, Life, and Laughter, 1923 (Pearson 2, Balfour 3)

Love, Life, and Laughter, 1934 (Fields, G. 3, Dean 4)

Love Light, 1921 (Pickford 3, Marion 4, Rosher 4)

Love, Live and Laugh, 1929 (Howard 2)

Love, Live with the Stars. *See* Ai yo hoshi to tomoni, 1947

Love Loops the Loop, 1918 (Sennett 2)

Love, Loot and Crash, 1915 (Sennett 2)

Love Lottery, 1953 (Crichton 2, Bogart 3, Niven 3, Slocombe 4)

Love, Luck and Gasoline, 1914 (Blackton 2)

Love Machine, 1971 (Cannon 3, Cooper, J 3, Ryan 3, Lang 4, Wheeler 4)

Love Madness, 1920 (Sullivan 4)

Love Makers. *See* Viaccia, 1960

Love Makes Us Blind. *See* Liebe macht Blind, 1923
Love Maniac. *See* Blood of Ghastly Horror, 1972
Love Mart, 1927 (Karloff 3, Garmes 4, Glazer 4)
Love Mask, 1916 (DeMille 2, Reid 3)
Love Master, 1924 (Murfin 4)
Love Match. *See* Partie de plaisir, 1975
Love Me, 1918 (Sullivan 4)
Love Me and the World Is Mine, 1928 (Dupont 2, Walthall 3, Mandell 4)
Love Me Forever, 1935 (Buchman 4, Swerling 4, Walker 4)
Love Me, Love Me, Love Me, 1962 (Williams, R. 4)
Love Me or Leave Me, 1955 (Vidor, C. 2, Cagney 3, Day 3, Cahn 4, Gibbons 4, Lennart 4, Pasternak 4, Rose 4)
Love Me Tender, 1956 (Presley 3, Buckner 4)
Love Me Tonight, 1932 (Mamoulian 2, Chevalier 3, Loy 3, MacDonald 3, Dreier 4, Head 4, Hoffenstein 4, Young, W. 4)
Love Microbe, 1907 (Bitzer 4)
Love Molds Labor, 1911 (White 3)
Love My Dog, 1927 (Roach 4)
Love Nest, 1923 (Keaton 2)
Love Nest, 1951 (Monroe 3, Diamond 4, Lemaire 4, Wheeler 4)
Love Nest on Wheels, 1937 (Keaton 2)
Love Never Dies, 1921 (Vidor, K. 2)
Love, Not Loving Love. *See* Koi ya koinasuna koi, 1962
Love Now, Pay Later. *See* Wahrheit uber Rosemarie, 1951
Love of a Judo Player. *See* Judo senshu no koi, 1934
Love of a Patriot. *See* Barbara Frietchie, 1924
Love of an Island Maid, 1912 (Bosworth 3)
Love of Chrysanthemum, 1910 (Talmadge, N. 3)
Love of Jeanne Ney. *See* Liebe der Jeanne Ney, 1927
Love of Penelope, 1913 (Bosworth 3)
Love of Sumako. *See* Joyu Sumako no koi, 1947
Love of Sunya, 1927 (Swanson 3)
Love of the Blind Girl. *See* Liebesgluck einer Blinden, 1909
Love of the 18th Century, 1921 (Lukas 3)
Love of the West, 1911 (Dwan 2)
Love of Tojuro. *See* Tojuro no koi, 1955
Love of Women, 1924 (Costello, M. 3)
Love Old and New. *See* Shamisen to otobai, 1961
Love on a Bet, 1936 (Epstein, J. & P. 4)
Love on a Budget. *See* Play Girl, 1932
Love on a Pillow. *See* Repos du guerrier, 1962
Love on Credit. *See* Kaerlighed på kredit, 1955
Love on Skates, 1916 (Sennett 2, Swanson 3)
Love on Tap, 1939 (Sidney 2)
Love on the Dole, 1941 (Kerr 3)
Love on the Ground. *See* Amour par terre, 1984
Love on the Riviera. *See* Racconti d'estate, 1958
Love on the Run, 1936 (Mankiewicz 2, Van Dyke, W.S. 2, Crawford, J. 3, Gable 3, Meek 3, Adrian 4, Mahin 4, Waxman 4)
Love on the Run. *See* Amour en fuite, 1979
Love on the Spot, 1932 (Dean 4)
Love on the Wing, 1937–39 (McLaren 2)
Love on Toast, 1937 (Dupont 2, Head 4)
Love on Tough Luck Ranch, 1912 (Anderson G. 3)
Love on Wheels, 1932 (Saville 2, Gwenn 3, Balcon 4)
Love One Another. *See* Gezeichneten, 1922
Love or Hate. *See* Passion Flower, 1920
Love Pains, 1932 (Roach 4)
Love Parade, 1929 (Lubitsch 2, Chevalier 3, Harlow 3, MacDonald 3, Banton 4, Dreier 4, Vajda 4)
Love Piker, 1923 (Barnes 4, Marion 4)
Love Required. *See* Nagrodzone uczucie, 1957
Love Riot, 1916 (Sennett 2, Fazenda 3)
Love Romance of the Girl Spy, 1910 (Olcott 2)
Love Root. *See* Mandragola, 1965
Love Route, 1915 (Dwan 2, Crisp 3)
Love Sickness at Sea, 1913 (Sennett 2, Normand 3)
Love 65. *See* Karlek 65, 1965
Love Slaves of the Amazon, 1957 (Siodmak 4)
Love, Soldiers, and Women. *See* Destinées, 1954
Love Song. *See* Valencia, 1926
Love Song of Barney Kempinski, 1966 (Rosenblum 4)

Love Special, 1921 (Reid 3)
Love Specialist. *See* Ragazza del palio, 1957
Love, Speed, and Thrills, 1915 (Sennett 2)
Love Storm. *See* Cape Forlorn, 1930
Love Storm. *See* Menschen in Kafig, 1930
Love Story, 1944 (Granger 3)
Love Story, 1970 (Hiller 2, Milland 3, Lai 4)
Love Story. *See* Douce, 1943
Love Story. *See* Intermezzo, 1939
Love Story series, 1971–72 (Le Grice 2)
Love Streams, 1984 (Rowlands 3, Golan and Globus 4)
Love Stronger Than Hatred. *See* Karlek starkare an hat, 1914
Love Sublime, 1917 (Browning 2)
Love Sundae, 1926 (Sennett 2)
Love Test, 1935 (Powell 3)
Love That Brute, 1950 (Douglas, P. 3, Elam 3, Wynn 3, Mahin 4)
Love That Lives. *See* Det Største i Verden, 1919
Love That Pup, 1949 (Hanna and Barbera 4)
Love That Whirls, 1949 (Anger 2)
Love the Clairvoyant, 1914 (Costello, M. 3)
Love the Italian Way. *See* Femmine di lusso, 1960
Love Thief, 1914 (Sennett 2)
Love Thief. *See* Rounders, 1914
Love Thy Neighbor, 1934 (Fleischer, M. and D. 2)
Love Thy Neighbor, 1940 (Sandrich 2, Dreier 4, Head 4, Young, V. 4)
Love Thy Neighbor, 1984 (Delerue 4)
Love Time, 1934 (Walthall 3, Miller, A. 4)
Love Toy, 1926 (Levien 4)
Love Trader, 1931 (Walthall 3)
Love Trap, 1929 (Wyler 2)
Love Under Cover, 1916 (Sutherland 2)
Love Under Fire, 1937 (Ameche 3, Carradine 3, Young, L. 3, Johnson 4)
Love under the Crucifix. *See* O-gin Sama, 1960
Love unto Death. *See* Amour à mort, 1984
Love Victorious, 1914 (Meredyth 4)
Love vs. Duty, 1914 (Ince 4)
Love War, 1970 (Dickinson 3)
Love Will Conquer, 1916 (Sennett 2)
Love Will Conquer. *See* Karleken segrar, 1949
Love Will Find a Way, 1908 (Porter 2)
Love with the Proper Stranger, 1963 (Mulligan 2, Pakula 2, McQueen, S. 3, Wood 3, Bernstein 4, Head 4, Krasner 4, Mercer 4)
Love Without Words. *See* Kolik slov staci lásce, 1961
Love Your Landlord, 1944 (Hunt 4)
Loveable Cheat, 1949 (Keaton 2)
Lovebound, 1923 (Furthman 4)
Loved By 2. *See* Akit ketten szeretnek, 1915
Loved Life. *See* Kanal, 1957
Loved One, 1965 (Ashby 2, Richardson 2, Andrews D. 3, Coburn, J. 3, Gielgud 3, McDowall 3, Steiger 3, Addison 4, Wexler 4)
Love-Ins, 1967 (Katzman 4)
Lovelorn, 1927 (Gibbons 4)
Lovelorn Leghorn, 1951 (McKimson 4)
Lovely Flute and Drum. *See* Natsukashiki fue ya taiko, 1967
Lovely Mary, 1926 (Love 3)
Lovely to Look At, 1952 (Leroy 2, Minnelli 2, Dalio 3, Grayson 3, Keel 3, Miller 3, Adrian 4, Berman 4, Gibbons 4, Pan 4)
Lovely to Look At. *See* Thin Ice, 1937
Lovely Way to Die, 1968 (Douglas, K. 3, Wallach 3)
Lovely Way to Go. *See* Lovely Way to Die, 1968
Lovemaker. *See* Calle Mayor, 1956
Lovemaking, 1968 (Brakhage 2)
Lover. *See* Ai-jin, 1953
Lover. *See* Koibito, 1951
Lover Boy. *See* Knave of Hearts, 1954
Lover Come Back, 1946 (Ball 3, Beavers 3, Brent 3, Salter 4)
Lover Come Back, 1962 (Day 3, Hudson 3, Irene 4, Westmore, B. 4)
Lovers?, 1927 (Stahl 2, Novarro 3, Booth 4, Gibbons 4)
Lovers. *See* Amants, 1958
Lovers and Liars, 1980 (Giannini 3, Hawn 3)
Lovers and Other Strangers, 1970 (Keaton 3, Young, G. 3)

Lover's Call. *See* Nedaa el Ochak, 1961
Lovers Courageous, 1932 (Montgomery 3, Adrian 4, Booth 4, Daniels 4)
Lovers, Happy Lovers. *See* Knave of Hearts, 1954
Lovers, Happy Lovers. *See* Monsieur Ripois, 1954
Lovers in Quarantine, 1925 (Daniels 3, Hunt 4, Polglase 4)
Lovers Like Us. *See* Sauvage, 1975
Lover's Lost Control, 1915 (Sennett 2)
Lover's Luck, 1914 (Sennett 2, Arbuckle 3)
Lovers Must Learn, 1962 (Steiner 4)
Lovers Must Learn. *See* Rome Adventure, 1962
Lovers' Net. *See* Amants du Tage, 1955
Lover's Oath, 1925 (Novarro 3)
Lovers of Lisbon. *See* Amants du Tage, 1955
Lovers of Teruel. *See* Amants de Teruel, 1962
Lovers of Toledo. *See* Amants de Tolède, 1952
Lovers of Verona. *See* Amants de Vérone, 1949
Lovers on a Tightrope. *See* Corde raide, 1960
Lovers' Post Office, 1914 (Sennett 2, Arbuckle 3, Normand 3)
Lover's Return. *See* Revenant, 1946
Lover's Romance. *See* Romans o uljublennyh, 1974
Lovers Three, 1912–13 (White 3)
Love's A-Poppin', 1953 (Bruckman 4)
Love's Berry. *See* Yahidka kokhannya, 1926
Love's Blindness, 1926 (Basevi 4, Gibbons 4)
Love's Boomerang. *See* Perpetua, 1922
Love's Command. *See* Liebeskommando, 1931
Love's Crucible. *See* Vem domer, 1922
Love's Detour, 1924 (Roach 4)
Love's Devotee. *See* Elskovsleg, 1913
Love's False Faces, 1919 (Sennett 2)
Love's Family Tree. *See* Aijo no keifu, 1961
Love's Greatest Mistake, 1927 (Sutherland 2, Powell, W. 3)
Love's Intrigue, 1924 (Sennett 2)
Love's Labor Won, 1948 (Terry 4)
Love's Languid Lure, 1927 (Sennett 2)
Love's Last Laugh, 1926 (Sennett 2)
Love's Miracle, 1912 (Cruze 2)
Loves of a Blonde. *See* Lásky jedné plavovlásky, 1965
Loves of a Dictator. *See* Dictator, 1934
Loves of a Pharaoh. *See* Weib des Pharao, 1922
Loves of Alexander Dumas Sr. *See* Lásky Alexandra Dumase St., 1970
Loves of an Actress, 1928 (Lukas 3, Negri 3, Vajda 4)
Loves of Ariane, 1931 (Czinner 2)
Loves of Ariane. *See* Ariane, 1931
Loves of Carmen, 1927 (Walsh 2, Del Rio 3, McLaglen 3)
Loves of Carmen, 1948 (Vidor, C. 2, Ford, G. 3, Hayworth 3)
Loves of Casanova, 1927
Loves of Colette. *See* Vie en rose, 1948
Loves of Edgar Allan Poe, 1942 (Darnell 3, Darwell 3, Day 4, Hoffenstein 4)
Loves of Hercules. *See* Amori di Ercole, 1960
Loves of Isadora. *See* Isadora, 1968
Loves of Joanna Godden, 1947 (Hamer 2, Rafferty 3, Balcon 4, Slocombe 4)
Loves of Madame Du Barry. *See* I Give My Heart, 1936
Loves of Omar Khayyam, 1957 (Dieterle 2)
Loves of Omar Khayyam. *See* Omar Khayyam, 1957 (Laszlo 4)
Loves of Ondine, 1967 (Warhol 2)
Loves of Pharaoh. *See* Weib des Pharao, 1922
Loves of Robert Burns, 1920 (Wilcox 2)
Loves of Three Queens. *See* Amante di Paride, 1953
Loves of Three Queens. *See* Eterna femmina, 1954
Loves of Zero, 1927 (Florey 2, Menzies 4)
Love's Old Dream, 1914 (Bunny 3)
Love's Old Sweet Song, 1924 (Merkel 3)
Love's Option, 1928 (Dickinson 2, Pearson 2)
Love's Outcast, 1921 (Sennett 2)
Love's Quarantine, 1913 (Bunny 3)
Love's Redemption, 1921 (Talmadge, N. 3, Hunt 4, Schenck 4)
Love's Renunciation, 1910–11 (White 3)
Love's Reward, 1924 (Roach 4)
Love's Sacrifice, 1914 (Ince 4)

Love's Savage Fury, 1971 (Addison 4)
Love's Stategem, 1909 (Lawrence 3)
Love's Sweet Piffle, 1924 (Sennett 2)
Love's Western Flight, 1914 (Reid 3)
Love's Young Scream, 1919 (Roach 4)
Lovesick, 1937 (Lantz 4)
Lovesick, 1983 (Huston 2, Guinness 3, Moore, D. 3, Sarde 4)
Lovesick Maidens of Cuddleton, 1912 (Bunny 3, Talmadge, N. 3)
Lovey Dovey, 1923 (Roach 4)
Lovey Mary, 1926 (Gibbons 4, Gillespie 4)
Lovin' Molly, 1974 (Lumet 2, Perkins 3, Sarandon 3)
Lovin' the Ladies, 1930 (Cronjager 4)
Loving, 1957 (Brakhage 2)
Loving, 1970 (Kershner 2, Hayden 3, Saint 3, Scheider 3, Segal 3, Wynn 3, Willis 4)
Loving Couples, 1980 (Coburn, J. 3, MacLaine 3, Sarandon 3)
Loving Couples. *See* Alskande par, 1964
Loving in the Rain. *See* Amour de pluie, 1974
Loving Lies, 1924 (Van Dyke, W.S. 2)
Loving You, 1957 (Presley 3, Head 4, Lang 4, Wallis 4)
Low of the Sea. *See* Mer mère, 1975
Lowat el Hub, 1960 (Sharif 3)
Lower Depths. *See* Bas-fonds, 1936
Lower Depths. *See* Donzoko, 1957
Lower the Boom, 1950 (Fleischer, M. and D. 2)
Lowland. *See* Tiefland, 1954
Low-Rank Soldiers. *See* Zouhei monogatari, 1963
Loyal 47 Ronin. *See* Chushingura, 1932
Loyal 47 Ronin. *See* Chushingura, 1962
Loyal 47 Ronin. *See* Genroku chushingura, 1941–2
Loyal Soldier of Pancho Villa. *See* Dorado de Pancho Villa, 1967
Loyalties, 1933 (Dickinson 2, Rathbone 3, Dean 4)
Loyalty of Sylvia, 1912 (Costello, M. 3)
L-Shaped Room, 1962 (Attenborough 3, Caron 3, Barry 4, Mathieson 4, Slocombe 4)
Lu, a kokott, 1918 (Curtiz 2)
Lu, the Cocotte. *See* Lu, a kokott, 1918
Luanda ya no es de San Pablo, 1976 (Alvarez 2)
Luce nelle tenebre, 1941 (Valli 3)
Lucenrna, 1925 (Ondra 3)
Lucertola con la pelle di donna, 1971 (Baker S. 3, Morricone 4)
Lucette, 1924 (Feuillade 2)
Luch smerti, 1925 (Kuleshov 2, Pudovkin 2, Golovnya 4)
Luci del varietà, 1950 (Fellini 2, Lattuada 2, Masina 3, Flaiano 4, Pinelli 4)
Lucía, 1968 (Solás 2, Herrera 4)
Lucia di Lammermoor, 1946 (Lollobrigida 3)
Luciano Serra, pilota, 1938 (Rossellini 2)
Lucien chez les barbares, 1981 (Moreau 3)
Lucien Leuwen, 1973 (Autant-Lara 2)
Lucifer Complex, 1978 (Wynn 3)
Lucifer Rising, 1974 (Anger 2)
Lucifer Rising, 1980 (Anger 2)
Lucile, 1912 (Cruze 2)
Lucille Love, the Girl of Mystery, 1914 (Ford, J. 2)
Luck o' the Foolish, 1924 (Capra 2, Sennett 2, Langdon 3)
Luck of Ginger Coffey, 1964 (Kershner 2, Shaw 3, Horner 4)
Luck of the Game. *See* Gridiron Flash, 1935
Luck of the Irish, 1920 (Dwan 2, Nilsson 3)
Luck of the Irish, 1948 (Baxter A. 3, Cobb 3, Power 3, Dunne 4, La Shelle 4, Lemaire 4)
Luck That Jealousy Brought, 1917 (Mix 3)
Luckiest Girl in the World, 1936 (Ryskind 4)
Lucky Beginners, 1935 (Roach 4)
Lucky Boy, 1929 (Taurog 2, Jolson 3)
Lucky Card, 1911 (Anderson G. 3)
Lucky Cisco Kid, 1940 (Andrews D. 3)
Lucky Dan, 1922 (Howard 2)
Lucky Day. *See* Den stchastia, 1964
Lucky Days, 1935 (Havelock-Allan 4)
Lucky Deal, 1915 (Mix 3)
Lucky Devils, 1933 (Boyd 3, Chaney Lon, Jr. 3, Cooper 4, Hunt 4, Plunkett 4, Robinson 4, Steiner 4)

Lucky Devils, 1941 (Arlen 3, Salter 4)
Lucky Dog, 1917 (Laurel and Hardy 3)
Lucky Duck, 1940 (Terry 4)
Lucky Ducky, 1948 (Avery 2)
Lucky Five. See Cinque povere in automobile, 1952
Lucky Horseshoe, 1911 (Sennett 2)
Lucky Horseshoe, 1925 (Cooper, Gary 3, Mix 3)
Lucky in Love, 1929 (Stradling 4)
Lucky Jim, 1909 (Griffith 2, Bitzer 4)
Lucky Jim, 1957 (Boulting 2, Addison 4)
Lucky Jo, 1964 (Brasseur 3, Constantine 3, Delerue 4)
Lucky Jordan, 1942 (De Carlo 3, Ladd 3, Deutsch 4, Dreier 4, Head 4, Seitz 4)
Lucky Lady, 1926 (Walsh 2, Barrymore L. 3, Sherwood 4)
Lucky Lady, 1975 (Donen 2, Fernández 2, Hackman 3, Minnelli 3, Reynolds, B. 3, Unsworth 4)
Lucky Larkin, 1930 (Brown, Harry Joe 4, McCord 4)
Lucky Leap, 1915 (Sennett 2)
Lucky Legs, 1942 (Edwards 2)
Lucky Luciano. See A proposito Lucky Luciano, 1973
Lucky Mascot, 1948 (Adam 4)
Lucky Me, 1954 (Cummings 3, Dalio 3, Day 3, Dickinson 3, Blanke 4)
Lucky Nick Cain, 1951 (Raft 3)
Lucky Night, 1939 (Taurog 2, Loy 3, Taylor, R. 3)
Lucky Number, 1921 (Roach 4)
Lucky Number, 1933 (Asquith 2, Balcon 4)
Lucky Number, 1961 (Biswas 4)
Lucky Partners, 1940 (Milestone 2, Colman 3, Rogers, G. 3, Irene 4, Polglase 4, Tiomkin 4)
Lucky Pigs, 1970 (Le Grice 2)
Lucky Star, 1929 (Borzage 2, Gaynor 3, Levien 4)
Lucky Star, 1982 (Steiger 3)
Lucky Stars, 1925 (Capra 2, Sennett 2, Langdon 3)
Lucky Stiff, 1949 (Lamour 3, Trevor 3, Laszlo 4)
Lucky Strike, 1915 (Hardy 3)
Lucky Texan, 1934 (Wayne 3, Canutt 4)
Lucky to Be a Woman. See Fortuna di essere donna, 1955
Lucky Toothache, 1910 (Sennett 2, Sennett 2, Pickford 3)
Lucky Touch. See Veinard, 1975
Lucky Transfer, 1915 (Browning 2)
Lucrèce, 1943 (Feuillère 3, Matras 4)
Lucrèce Borgia, 1935 (Gance 2, Artaud 3, Feuillère 3, Modot 3, Kaufman 4)
Lucrèce Borgia, 1952 (Christian-Jaque 2, Armendáriz 3, Matras 4)
Lucretia Borgia. See Lucrèce Borgia, 1953
Lucretia Lombard, 1923 (Shearer 3)
Lucrezia Borgia, 1922 (Dieterle 2, Oswald 2, Basserman 3, George, H. 3, Veidt 3, Wegener 3, Freund 4)
Lucrezia Borgia. See Lucrèce Borgia, 1952
Lucy Gallant, 1955 (Heston 3, Ritter 3, Trevor 3, Wyman 3, Bumstead 4, Head 4, Mahin 4)
Lude godini, 1978 (Samardžić 3)
Ludlow's Aeroplane, 1905 (Bitzer 4)
Ludo srce, 1959 (Mimica 4)
Ludwig, 1973 (Visconti 2, Howard, T. 3, Mangano 3, Schneider 3, D'Amico 4)
Ludwig der Zweite, König von Bayern, 1930 (Dieterle 2)
Ludwig II, 1954 (Kinski 3, Slocombe 4)
Ludwig—Requiem for a Virgin King. See Ludwig—Requiem fur einen jungfraulichen Konig, 1972
Ludwig—Requiem fur einen jungfraulichen Konig, 1972 (Syberberg 2)
Ludwig's Cook. See Theodor Hierneis oder: Wie man ehem. Hofkoch wird, 1972
Ludzie wisly, 1937 (Ford, A. 2)
Luffar-Petter, 1922 (Garbo 3)
Lugar do morto, 1982 (Branco 4)
Luge, 1950 (Frohlich 3)
Lugner und die Nonne, 1967 (Jurgens 3)
Lui per lei, 1971 (Ferreri 2, Morricone 4)
Luisa Sanfelice, 1942 (Vích 4)
Luise, Konigin von Preussen, 1931 (Grundgens 3, Porten 3)
Luise Millerin, 1922 (Dagover 3, Kortner 3, Krauss 3, Herlth 4, Pommer 4, Rohrig 4)

Luk královny Dorotky, povikovy, 1970 (Brejchová 3)
Luke series, 1916–17 (Daniels 3, Lloyd 3, Roach 4)
Lula mira, 1962 (Grgić 4)
Lullaby. See Kolibel'naya, 1937
Lullaby. See Sin of Madelon Claudet, 1931
Lullaby Bushu's Kite. See Komoriuta Bushu-dako, 1935
Lullaby of Broadway, 1951 (Day 3, Sakall 3)
Lullaby of Hamagure. See Hamagure no komoriuta, 1973
Lulli ou le violon brisé, 1908 (Méliès 2)
Lulu, 1918 (Curtiz 2, Jannings 3)
Lulu, 1953 (Cortese 3, Mastroianni 3)
Lulu, 1962 (Knef 3)
Lulu, 1967 (Leacock 2)
Lulu, 1980 (Borowczyk 4)
Lulu Belle, 1948 (Lamour 3, Laszlo 4, MacArthur 4)
Lulu the Fool. See Classe operaia va in paradiso, 1971
Lulu's Doctor, 1912 (Costello, M. 3)
Lumber Camp, 1937 (Lantz 4)
Lumber Chumps, 1933 (Lantz 4)
Lumber Jack Rabbit, 1955 (Jones 2)
Lumber Jerks, 1954 (Freleng 4)
Lumber Yard Gang, 1916 (Ford, J. 2)
Lumberjack, 1944 (Boyd 3)
Lumière, 1967 (Allégret, M. 2, Braunberger 4)
Lumière, 1976 (Ganz 3, Moreau 3)
Lumière d'en face, 1955 (Bardot 3)
Lumière d'été, 1943 (Grémillon 2, Barrault 3, Brasseur 3, Barsacq 4, Douy 4, Prévert 4, Trauner 4)
Lumière et l'invention du cinématographe, 1953 (Gance 2, Cloquet 4, Kosma 4)
Lumières de Paris, 1938 (Andrejew 4, Courant 4, Jaubert 4, Renoir 4)
Lummox, 1930 (Brenon 2, Menzies 4, Schenck 4, Struss 4)
Lumpaci Vagabundus, 1922 (Albers 3)
Lumpen und Seide, 1925 (Oswald 2)
Lumuha Pati Mga Anghel, 1971–73 (Brocka 2)
Luna, 1979 (Bertolucci 2, Clayburgh 3, Valli 3, Morricone 4, Storaro 4)
Luna de miel, 1959 (Powell 2, Theodorakis 4)
Luna di miele, 1963 (Tognazzi 3)
Luna sleva, 1928 (Cherkassov 3)
Lunar de la familia, 1952 (García 3)
Lunch, 1899–1900 (Guy 2)
Lunch. See Ručak, 1972
Lunch Hound, 1927 (Lantz 4)
Lunch on the Grass. See Déjeuner sur l'herbe, 1959
Luncheon at Twelve, 1933 (Roach 4)
Lune à un mètre, 1898 (Méliès 2)
Lune dans le caniveau, 1982 (Depardieu 3)
Lune dans son tablier, 1909 (Cohl 2)
Lune des Lapins, 1950 (Anger 2)
Lunegarde, 1945 (Allégret, M. 2, Achard 4)
Lunes, Martes, Myerkoles . . ., 1976 (Brocka 2)
Lunettes féeriques, 1909 (Cohl 2)
Lung men feng-yün, 1976 (King Hu 2)
Lung men k'o-chan, 1966 (King Hu 2)
Lunga calza verde, 1961 (Zavattini 4)
Lunga manica, 1947 (Delli Colli 4)
Lunga notte del '43, 1960 (Pasolini 2, Cervi 3)
Lunga strada azzurra, 1957 (Montand 3)
Lunga strada azzurra. See Grande strada azzurra, 1957
Lunga strada senza polvere, 1975 (Jurgens 3)
Lunkhead, 1929 (Sennett 2)
Lupa, 1953 (Lattuada 2, De Laurentiis 4)
Lupe. 1965 (Warhol 2)
Lupinek Case. See Případ Lupínek, 1960
Lupo, 1970 (Golan and Globus 2)
Lupo della Sila, 1949 (Gassman 3, Mangano 3, De Laurentiis 4)
Lupo e l'agnello, 1980 (Audiard 4)
Lure, 1914 (Guy 2)
Lure. See Koder, 1975
Lure of Ambition, 1919 (Bara 3)
Lure of Broadway. See Bright Lights, 1916
Lure of Hollywood, 1931 (Arbuckle 3)
Lure of the Circus, 1919 (Johnson, N. 3)

Lure of the Gown, 1909 (Griffith 2, Lawrence 3, Bitzer 4)
Lure of the Jungle. *See* Paw, 1959
Lure of the Sila. *See* Lupo della Sila, 1949
Lure of the Swamp, 1957 (Elam 3)
Lure of the Wilderness, 1952 (Negulesco 2, Brennan 3, Elam 3, Hunter 3, Cronjager 4, Jeakins 4, Lemaire 4, Waxman 4)
Lure of the Windigo, 1914 (Mix 3)
Lure of Woman, 1915 (Brady 3)
Lured, 1947 (Sirk 2, Ball 3, Coburn, C. 3, Hardwicke 3, Karloff 3, Sanders 3, Daniels 4, Stromberg 4)
Luring Lips, 1921 (Miller, V. 4)
Lust for a Vampire, 1970 (Sangster 4)
Lust for Evil. *See* Plein soleil, 1959
Lust for Gold, 1949 (Ford, G. 3, Lupino 3, Young, G. 3, Duning 4)
Lust for Life, 1956 (Minnelli 2, Douglas, K. 3, Quinn 3, Sloane 3, Ames 4, Gibbons 4, Houseman 4, Plunkett 4, Rozsa 4, Young, F. 4)
Lust in the Sun. *See* Dans la poussière du soleil, 1971
Lustgården, 1961 (Bergman 2, Andersson B. 3, Bjornstrand 3, Fischer 4)
Lustige Ehemann, 1919 (Lubitsch 2)
Lustige Witwer, 1929 (Reisch 4)
Lustigen Weiber, 1934 (Hoffmann 4)
Lustigen Weiber von Wien, 1931 (Andrejew 4, Reisch 4)
Lusty Men, 1952 (Ray, N. 2, Hayward 3, Kennedy, A. 3, Mitchum 3, D'Agostino 4, Garmes 4, Krasna 4, Wald 4)
Luther, 1927 (Herlth 4, Rohrig 4)
Luther, 1973 (Keach 3, Addison 4, Anhalt 4, Green, G. 4, Young, F. 4)
Lutte, 1961 (Jutra 2)
Lutte contre le gaspillage, 1951 (Decaë 4)
Luttes en Italie. *See* Lotte in Italia, 1969
Lutteurs américains, 1903 (Guy 2)
Lutzows wilde verwegene Jagd, 1927 (Oswald 2)
Luv, 1967 (Falk 3, Ford, H. 3, Lemmon 3, Laszlo 4)
Luxury Girls. *See* Fanciulle di lusso, 1952
Luxury Liner, 1933 (Brent 3)
Luxury Liner, 1948 (Brent 3, Pasternak 4, Rose 4)
Luxusweibchen, 1925 (Albers 3)

Luz del fin del mundo, 1971 (Douglas, K. 3, Brynner 3, Decaë 4)
Luz en mi camino, 1938 (Negrete 3)
Lyautey, bâtisseur d'empire, 1947 (Ibert 4)
Lycée sur la colline, 1952 (Fradetal 4)
Lyckliga skitar, 1970 (Sjoman 2)
Lyckodrommen, 1963 (Andersson H. 3, Bjornstrand 3)
Lyckonalen, 1915 (Stiller 2)
Lyckoriddare, 1921 (Garbo 3)
Lyda Ssanin, 1922 (Albers 3)
Lydia, 1916 (Holger-Madsen 2)
Lydia, 1918 (Dreyer 2)
Lydia, 1941 (De Toth 2, Duvivier 2, Cotten 3, Oberon 3, Garmes 4, Hecht 4, Hoffenstein 4, Hornbeck 4, Plunkett 4, Rozsa 4)
Lydia Bailey, 1952 (Negulesco 2, Dunne 4, Friedhofer 4, Lemaire 4)
Lydia Gilmore, 1916 (Porter 2)
Lydis, 1941 (Korda 4)
Lyin' Lion, 1949 (Terry 4)
Lyin' Mouse, 1937 (Freleng 4)
Lyin' Tamer, 1925 (Lantz 4)
Lying Lips, 1921 (Ince 4)
Lying Lips, 1939 (Micheaux 2)
Lykkehjulet, 1926 (Gad 2)
Lykken, 1916 (Holger-Madsen 2)
Lynet, 1933 (Holger-Madsen 2)
Lynmouth, 1913 (Pearson 2)
Lyon Lea, 1915 (Korda 2)
Lyon, place Bellecour, 1895 (Lumière 2)
Lyon, place des Cordeliers, 1895 (Lumière 2)
Lyons in Paris, 1956 (Daniels 3)
Lyric of a Port. *See* Minato no jojoushi, 1932
Lys de la Vie, 1920 (Clair 2)
Lyset i natten, 1953 (Roos 2)
Lysten styret. *See* Huskors, 1914
Lyubit cheloveka, 1972 (Gerasimov 2)
Lyubliu tebya?, 1934 (Cherkassov 3)
Lyubov i nenavist, 1935 (Maretskaya 3)
Lyubov silna na strastyou potseluya, 1916 (Mozhukin 3)
Lyubov Yarovaya, 1977 (Churikova 3)

M

M, 1931 (Lang 2, Grundgens 3, Lorre 3, Von Harbou 4, Wagner 4)
M, 1951 (Aldrich 2, Losey 2, Hubley 4, Laszlo 4, Raine 4, Salt 4)
M. Scrupule, ganster, 1953 (Dalio 3)
MBKS, 1973 (Le Grice 2)
M.G.M. Story, 1951 (Barrymore L. 3)
MGM Studio Tour, 1925 (Daniels 4)
M.P. Case. *See* Zaak M.P., 1960
Ma and Pa, 1922 (Sennett 2)
Ma and Pa Kettle at Home, 1954 (Boyle 4)
Ma and Pa Kettle at the Fair, 1951 (Eason 4)
Ma and Pa Kettle on Vacation, 1953 (Boyle 4)
Ma come fanno a farli cosi belli?, 1980 (Bozzetto 4)
Ma Cousine de Varsovie, 1931 (Clouzot 2, Gallone 2)
Ma cousine de Varsovie. *See* Meine Cousine aus Warschau, 1931
Ma es holnap, 1912 (Curtiz 2)
Ma Famille et mon toit. *See* Ciel est par-dessus le toit, 1956
Ma femme est une panthère, 1960 (Matras 4)
Ma Femme, mon gosse et moi, 1957 (Allégret, M. 2)
Ma femme, mon gosse, et moi. *See* Amour est en jeu, 1957
Ma Hermano Fidel, 1977 (Alvarez 2)
Ma Jeannette et mes copains, 1954 (Kosma 4)
Ma l'amore mio non muore, 1938 (Valli 3)
Ma mère l'eau. *See* Mamy Water, 1955
Ma no ike, 1923 (Kinugasa 2)

Ma no kisetsu, 1956 (Yamamura 3)
Ma no ogon, 1950 (Mori 3)
Ma non è una cosa seria!, 1936 (De Sica 2)
Ma nuit chez Maud, 1969 (Rohmer 2, Fabian 3, Trintignant 3, Almendros 4, Braunberger 4)
Ma Pomme, 1950 (Chevalier 3, Alekan 4, D'Eaubonne 4)
Ma tante d'Honfleur, 1931 (Fradetal 4)
Ma vagy holnap, 1965 (Kovács 2)
Maa, 1952 (Roy 2)
Maan, 1954 (Biswas 4)
Maaneprinsessen, 1916 (Holger-Madsen 2)
Mabel series, 1912–1922 (Normand 3)
Mabel series, 1913–16 (Arbuckle 3)
Mabel series, 1914 (Chaplin 2)
Mabel's Adventures series, from 1912 (Sennett 2)
Mabel's Busy Day, 1914 (Summerville 3)
Mabel's Flirtation. *See* Her Friend the Bandit, 1914
Maboroshi fujin, 1949 (Yamamura 3)
Maboroshi no mizuumi, 1982 (Muraki 4)
Maboroshi-jo, 1940 (Shimura 3)
Mabuta no haha, 1931 (Yamada 3)
Mabuta no haha, 1938 (Hasegawa 3)
Macabre. *See* Macabro, 1980
Macabro, 1980 (Delli Colli 4)

Macadam, 1946 (Feyder 2, Rosay 3, Signoret 3, D'Eaubonne 4)
Macahans, 1976 (Saint 3)
Macao, 1952 (Von Sternberg 2, Bendix 3, Grahame 3, Mitchum 3, Russell, J. 3, D'Agostino 4)
Macao, l'enfer du jeu, 1939 (Delannoy 2, Von Stroheim 2, Hayakawa 3, Auric 4)
Macao, l'enfer du jeu. See Enfer du jeu, 1939
Macario, 1959 (Figueroa 4)
Macaroni, 1985 (Lemmon 3, Mastroianni 3)
MacArthur, 1977 (Peck 3, Goldsmith 4, Whitlock 4)
MacArthur's Children. See Setouchi shounen yakyu-dan, 1984
Macbeth, 1908 (Lawrence 3, Ince 4)
Macbeth, 1916 (Fleming 2, Von Stroheim 2, Emerson 4, Loos 4)
Macbeth, 1948 (Welles 2, McDowall 3, Ibert 4)
Macbeth, 1960 (Anderson J. 3, Mathieson 4, Young, F. 4)
Macbeth, 1969 (Keach 3)
Macbeth, 1971 (Polanski 2)
Macbeth. See Makbet, 1969
Macchia rosa, 1969 (Giannini 3)
Macchie solari, 1974 (Morricone 4)
Macchina ammazzacattivi, 1948 (Rossellini 2, Amidei 4)
MacDonald's Farm, 1951 (Fleischer, M. and D. 2)
Macédoine, 1970 (Brasseur 3)
Mach' mich glucklich, 1935 (Robison 2)
Mach' mir die Wely zum Paradies, 1930 (Reisch 4)
Machete, 1958 (Van Cleef 3, Struss 4)
Machi no bofu, 1934 (Tanaka 3)
Machi no hitobito, 1926 (Gosho 2, Tanaka 3)
Machi to gesui, 1953 (Hani 2)
Machiboke no onna, 1946 (Shindo 2)
Machibuse, 1970 (Mifune 3)
'Machiko' yori: Hana hiraku, 1948 (Takamine 3)
Machine à parler d'amour, 1961 (Braunberger 4, Fradetal 4)
Machine à refaire la vie, 1924 (Duvivier 2)
Machine Age. See Kalyug, 1981
Machine Gun Kelly, 1958 (Bronson 3, Corman 4, Crosby 4)
Machine Gun McCain. See Intoccabili, 1968
Machine of Eden, 1970 (Brakhage 2)
Macho Callahan, 1970 (Cobb 3, Seberg 3, Fisher 4)
Machorka-Muff, 1963 (Straub and Huillet 2)
Macht der Finsternis, 1923 (Wiene 2, Andrejew 4)
Macht der Versuchung, 1922 (Dagover 3)
Macht des Goldes, 1912 (Gad 2)
Maciste, 1915 (Pastrone 2)
Maciste all'inferno, 1926 (Amidei 4)
Maciste alpino, 1916 (Pastrone 2)
Maciste contre il vampiro, 1961 (De Laurentiis 4)
Maciste nella gabbia dei Leoni, 1926 (Amidei 4)
Mack, 1973 (Pryor 3)
Mack at It Again, 1914 (Sennett 2, Sennett 2, Normand 3)
MacKenna's Gold, 1969 (Cobb 3, Massey 3, Meredith 3, Peck 3, Quayle 3, Robinson, E. 3, Sharif 3, Wallach 3, Wynn 3, Foreman 4, Jones 4, Tiomkin 4)
MacKintosh and T.J., 1975 (Rogers, R. 3)
Mackintosh Man, 1973 (Hill, W. 2, Huston 2, Mason 3, Newman 3, Sanda 3, Jarre 4, Morris 4)
Maclovia, 1948 (Fernández 2, Armendáriz 3, Félix 3, Figueroa 4)
Macomber Affair, 1947 (Bennett J. 3, Peck 3, Preston 3, Francis 4, Metzner 4, Robinson 4, Rozsa 4, Struss 4)
Maçons, 1905 (Guy 2)
Macskajáték, 1974 (Torocsik 3)
Mad about Men, 1954 (Rutherford 3)
Mad about Money, 1938 (Velez 3)
Mad About Music, 1938 (Taurog 2, Durbin 3, Marshall 3, Pasternak 4)
Mad Adventures of Rabbi Jacob. See Aventures de Rabbi Jacob, 1973
Mad Atlantic. See Doto ichi man kairi, 1966
Mad Bull, 1977 (Cook 3)
Mad Butcher. See Wuger kommt auf leisen Socken, 1972
Mad Checkmate. See Scacco tutto matto, 1968
Mad Doctor, 1941 (Rathbone 3, Head 4, Young, V. 4)
Mad Doctor of Market Street, 1942 (Johnson, N. 3, Merkel 3, Salter 4)
Mad Dog. See Mad Dog Morgan, 1976
Mad Dog Coll, 1961 (Hackman 3, Rosenblum 4, Sylbert 4)

Mad Dog Morgan, 1976 (Hopper 3)
Mad Emperor. See Patriote, 1938
Mad Emperor. See Tragédie impériale, 1938
Mad Game, 1933 (Tracy 3, Trevor 3, Miller, A. 4)
Mad Genius, 1931 (Curtiz 2, Barrymore J. 3, Karloff 3, Grot 4)
Mad Genius. See Coeur de Lilas, 1931
Mad Ghoul, 1943 (Kraly 4, Krasner 4, Salter 4)
Mad Hatter. See Breakfast in Hollywood, 1945
Mad Hatters, 1935 (Havelock-Allan 4)
Mad Holiday, 1936 (Gwenn 3, Pitts 3, Ruttenberg 4)
Mad Hour, 1928 (Haller 4, Robinson 4)
Mad House, 1934 (Terry 4)
Mad King, 1932 (Terry 4)
Mad Little Island. See Rockets Galore, 1958
Mad Love, 1935 (Lorre 3, Balderston 4, Freund 4, Gibbons 4, Tiomkin 4, Toland 4)
Mad Love. See Mania, 1918
Mad Magician, 1954 (Price 3, Glennon 4)
Mad Maid of the Forest, 1915 (Rosher 4)
Mad Man's Money. See Bad Men's Money, 1929
Mad Man's Ward, 1914 (Lawrence 3)
Mad Marriage, 1925 (Costello, M. 3)
Mad Masquerade. See Washington Masquerade, 1932
Mad Max, 1979 (Miller 2, Gibson 3)
Mad Max 2, 1981 (Miller 2, Gibson 3)
Mad Max Beyond Thunderdome, 1985 (Gibson 3, Jarre 4)
Mad Men of Europe, 1940 (Gwenn 3)
Mad Miss Manton, 1938 (Fonda, H. 3, McDaniel 3, Stanwyck 3, Berman 4, Epstein, J. & P. 4)
Mad Monk. See Rasputin and the Empress, 1933
Mad Monster Party, 1967 (Karloff 3)
Mad Night. See Egy orult éiszaka, 1969
Mad Parade, 1931 (Fazenda 3, Banton 4)
Mad Queen. See Locura de amor, 1948
Mad Racer, 1926 (Arthur 3)
Mad Room, 1968 (Winters 3)
Mad Sex. See Sesso matto, 1973
Mad Wednesday, 1947 (Sturges, P. 2, Lloyd 3)
Madagascar, 1954 (Delerue 4)
Madalena, 1960 (Lassally 4)
Madam Kitty. See Salon Kitty, 1976
Madam, Permit Me to Love Your Daughter. See Permettete che ami vostre fanciulla, 1974
Madam wunscht keine Kinder, 1926 (Freund 4)
Madama Butterfly, 1955 (Gallone 2)
Madame. See Madame Sans-Gêne, 1961
Madame and Wife. See Madamu to nyobo, 1931
Madame Blaubart. See Schicksal einer schonen Frau, 1932
Madame Bovary, 1934 (Becker 2, Renoir 2, Lourié 4, Wakhévitch 4)
Madame Bovary, 1937 (Negri 3)
Madame Bovary, 1949 (Minnelli 2, Cooper, Gladys 3, Heflin 3, Jones, J. 3, Jourdan 3, Mason 3, Berman 4, Gibbons 4, Plunkett 4, Rozsa 4, Smith, J.M. 4)
Madame Bovary—That's Me. See Pani Bovary—to ja, 1977
Madame Butterfly, 1915 (Olcott 2, Pickford 3)
Madame Butterfly, 1933 (Grant, C. 3, Sidney 3)
Madame Butterfly, 1955 (Renoir 4)
Madame Claude, 1976 (Dalio 3, Fabian 3, Kinski 3)
Madame Claude 2, 1981 (Lai 4)
Madame Curie, 1943 (Franklin 2, Leroy 2, Basserman 3, Garson 3, Johnson, V. 3, O'Brien, M. 3, Pidgeon 3, Walker 3, Gibbons 4, Irene 4, Ruttenberg 4, Sharaff 4, Stothart 4)
Madame De . . ., 1953 (De Sica 2, Ophuls 2, Boyer 3, Darrieux 3, Achard 4, Annenkov 4, D'Eaubonne 4, Matras 4)
Madame de Thèbes, 1915 (Stiller 2, Jaenzon 4, Magnusson 4)
Madame Double X, 1914 (Beery 3)
Madame Du Barry, 1934 (Dieterle 2, Del Rio 3, Blanke 4, Orry-Kelly 4, Polito 4)
Madame Du Barry, 1954 (Christian-Jaque 2, Jeanson 4, Matras 4)
Madame DuBarry, 1919 (Lubitsch 2, Bara 3, Jannings 3, Negri 3, Kraly 4)
Madame et le mort, 1942 (Bost 4)
Madame Guillotine, 1931 (Carroll M. 3)

Madame Julie. *See* Woman Between, 1931
Madame Mystery, 1926 (Bara 3, Hardy 3, Laurel 3, Roach 4)
Madame Nicotine, 1908 (Gaudio 4)
Madame of the Jury, 1930 (Anderson J. 3)
Madame Peacock, 1920 (Nazimova 3)
Madame Pimpernel. *See* Paris Underground, 1945
Madame Pompadour, 1927 (Dupont 2, Wilcox 2, Gish, D. 3, Marion 4)
Madame Q, 1929 (McCarey 2, Roach 4)
Madame Racketeer, 1932 (Raft 3)
Madame Récamier, 1928 (Rosay 3)
Madame Rex, 1911 (Griffith 2, Bitzer 4)
Madame Rosa, 1977 (Dauphin 3, Signoret 3)
Madame Rosa. *See* Vie devant soi, 1977
Madame Sans Gêne, 1909 (Blom 2)
Madame Sans Jane, 1925 (Roach 4)
Madame Sans-Gêne, 1925 (Brasseur 3, Swanson 3)
Madame Sans-Gêne, 1941 (Arletty 3, Cuny 3, Aurenche 4)
Madame Sans-Gêne, 1961 (Christian-Jaque 2, Loren 3, D'Eaubonne 4, Jeanson 4, Solinas 4)
Madame Satan, 1930 (DeMille 2, Adrian 4, Day 4, Gibbons 4, Macpherson 4, Prinz 4, Rosson 4, Shearer 4, Stothart 4)
Madame Sin, 1972 (Davis 3, Wagner 3)
Madame Soprani, 1963 (Giersz 4)
Madame Spy, 1918 (Hersholt 3)
Madame Spy, 1934 (Wray 3, Freund 4)
Madame Spy, 1942 (Bennett C. 3, Salter 4)
Madame Wants No Children. *See* Madam wunscht keine Kinder, 1926
Madame wunscht keine Kinder, 1926 (Korda 2, Dietrich 3)
Madame wunscht keine Kinder, 1933 (Wilder 2, Kaper 4)
Madame X, 1929 (Barrymore L. 3, Stone 3, Gibbons 4)
Madame X, 1937 (Wood 2, Gibbons 4, Seitz 4)
Madame X, 1966 (Bennett C. 3, Meredith 3, Turner, L. 3, Hunter 4, Westmore, B. 4)
Madame X, 1981 (Weld 3, Anhalt 4)
Madame Yuki. *See* Yuki-funjin ezu, 1950
Madamigella di Maupin, 1965 (Bolognini 2, Gherardi 4)
Madamu to nyobo, 1931 (Gosho 2, Tanaka 3)
Madchen Argentinien. *See* Fraulein aus Argentinien, 1928
Madchen aus der Ackerstrasse, 1920 (Courant 4)
Madchen aus Flandern, 1956 (Schell, Maximilian 3)
Madchen hinter gittern, 1949 (Wagner 4)
Madchen in Uniform, 1958 (Schneider 3)
Madchen Irene, 1936 (Dagover 3)
Madchen Johanna, 1935 (George, H. 3, Grundgens 3, Herlth 4, Rohrig 4)
Madchen mit dem guten Ruf, 1938 (Tschechowa 3, Wagner 4)
Madchen ohne Heimat, 1926 (Homolka 3)
Madchen ohne Vaterland, 1912 (Gad 2, Nielsen 3)
Madchen Schicksal, 1928 (Manès 3)
Madchen und die Manner, 1919 (Krauss 3)
Madchen vom Moorhof, 1935 (Sirk 2)
Madchen von Fano, 1940 (Wegener 3, Hoffmann 4)
Madchenjahre einer Konigin, 1936 (Warm 4)
Madchenjahre einer Konigin, 1954 (Schneider 3)
Maddalena, 1953 (Cervi 3, Vanel 3, Renoir 4)
Maddalena, 1970 (Kawalerowicz 2, Morricone 4)
Maddalena. *See* Fille nommée Madeleine, 1953
Maddalena Ferat, 1921 (Bertini 3)
Maddalena zero in condotta, 1941 (De Sica 2)
Made a Coward, 1913 (Mix 3)
Made for Each Other, 1939 (Cromwell 2, Beavers 3, Bond 3, Coburn, C. 3, Lombard 3, Stewart 3, Banton 4, Friedhofer 4, Menzies 4, Selznick 4, Shamroy 4, Swerling 4, Wheeler 4)
Made for Love, 1926 (Fort 4, Miller, A. 4)
Made in Heaven, 1921 (Adorée 3, Gibbons 4)
Made in Heaven, 1952 (Unsworth 4)
Made in Italy, 1965 (Scola 2, Fabrizi 3, Magnani 3, Manfredi 3, Sordi 3)
Made in Paris, 1966 (Dalio 3, Jourdan 3, Ames 4, Jones 4, Krasner 4, Pasternak 4, Rose 4)
Made in Sweden, 1968 (Von Sydow 3, Fischer 4)
Made in the Kitchen, 1921 (Sennett 2)

Made in U.S.A., 1966 (Godard 2, Karina 3, Léaud 3, Coutard 4, de Beauregard 4, Guillemot 4)
Made Manifest, 1980 (Brakhage 2)
Made on Broadway, 1933 (Montgomery 3, Adrian 4)
Madel aus dem Volke, 1927 (Reisch 4)
Madel aus USA, 1930 (Ondra 3)
Madel vom Ballett, 1918 (Lubitsch 2, Kraly 4)
Madel vom Ballett, 1936 (Ondra 3)
Madel vom Piccadilly, 1921 (Courant 4)
Madel von der Reeperbahn, 1930 (Tschechowa 3)
Madel von Nebenan, 1917 (Hoffmann 4)
Madeleine, 1921 (Albers 3)
Madeleine, 1950 (Lean 2, Alwyn 4, Green, G. 4)
Madeleine und der Legionar, 1958 (Staudte 2, Wicki 2, Knef 3, Vích 4)
Madeline, 1952 (Raksin 4)
Madels von heute, 1925 (Tschechowa 3, Warm 4)
Mademoiselle, 1965 (Richardson 2, Moreau 3)
Mademoiselle Ange, 1959 (Belmondo 3)
Mademoiselle cent millions, 1913 (Tourneur, M. 2)
Mademoiselle de la Ferté, 1948 (Cloquet 4)
Mademoiselle de la seigliere, 1921 (Burel 4)
Mademoiselle de Paris, 1955 (Aumont 3)
Mademoiselle Docteur, 1937 (Pabst 2, Von Stroheim 2, Barrault 3, Fresnay 3, Jouvet 3, Modot 3, Achard 4, Alekan 4, Annenkov 4, Honegger 4, Schufftan 4)
Mademoiselle Fifi, 1944 (Wise 2, Simon, S. 3, D'Agostino 4, Lewton 4)
Mademoiselle France. *See* Reunion in France, 1942
Mademoiselle from Armentieres, 1926 (Saville 2)
Mademoiselle Gobette. *See* Presidentessa, 1952
Mlle. Irene the Great, 1931 (Johnson 4)
Mademoiselle Josette, ma femme. *See* Fraulein Josette, meine Frau, 1926
Mademoiselle Josette, ma femme, 1933 (D'Eaubonne 4)
Mademoiselle ma mère, 1937 (Brasseur 3, Darrieux 3, Burel 4)
Mademoiselle Modiste, 1926 (Barnes 4)
Mademoiselle Modiste, 1952 (Dauphin 3)
Mademoiselle Mozart, 1936 (Darrieux 3, Morgan 3)
Mademoiselle Porte-bonheur. *See* Lucky Me, 1954
Mademoiselle X, 1945 (Achard 4, Matras 4, Wakhévitch 4)
Madge of the Mountains, 1911 (Bunny 3)
Madh Bhare Nain, 1955 (Burman 4)
Madhouse, 1974 (Cushing 3, Price 3)
Madhubala, 1950 (Anand 3)
Madhumati, 1955 (Ghatak 4)
Madhumati, 1958 (Roy 2)
Madigan, 1968 (Polonsky 2, Siegel 2, Fonda, H. 3, Widmark 3, Head 4, Westmore, B. 4)
Madigan: Park Avenue Beat, 1973 (Widmark 3)
Madigan: The Lisbon Beat, 1973 (Widmark 3)
Madigan: The Naples Beat, 1973 (Widmark 3)
Madigan's Millions. *See* Un Dollaro per 7 vigliacchi, 1967
Madison Avenue, 1962 (Andrews D. 3, Crain 3, Clarke, C.C. 4)
Madison Square Garden, 1932 (Pitts 3, Brown, Harry Joe 4)
Madla from the Brick-Kiln. *See* Madla z cihelny, 1933
Madla z cihelny, 1933 (Baarová 3, Haas 3, Stallich 4)
Madly, 1969 (Cortese 3, Delon 3, Lai 4)
Madman, 1911 (Bushman 3)
Madman. *See* Fou, 1970
Madman in the Dark. *See* Krok do tmy, 1938
Madman's Defence. *See* Dåres forsvarstal, 1976
Madmen of Europe. *See* Englishman's Home, 1939
Madmen of Mandoras, 1962 (Cortez 4)
Madness of the Heart, 1949 (Bennett 4)
Madness of Youth, 1923 (Gilbert 3, August 4)
Mado, 1927 (Tanaka 3)
Mado, 1976 (Sautet 2, Baye 3, Dauphin 3, Denner 3, Piccoli 3, Schneider 3, Sarde 4)
Mado kara tobidase, 1950 (Kagawa 3)
Madol Duwa, 1976 (Peries 2)
Madone des sleepings, 1955 (Von Stroheim 2, Burel 4)
Madonna Grazia, 1917 (Gallone 2)
Madonna of Avenue A, 1929 (Curtiz 2, Costello, D. 3, Zanuck 4)
Madonna of the Seven Moons, 1944 (Granger 3)

Madonna of the Storm, 1913 (Gish, L. 3)
Madonna of the Streets, 1924 (Beery 3, Nazimova 3)
Madonna of the Streets, 1930 (Polito 4)
Madonna's Secret, 1946 (Alton, J. 4)
Madre, 1913 (Bertini 3)
Madre folle, 1922 (Gallone 2)
Madriguera, 1969 (Saura 2, Chaplin 3)
Madrina del diablo, 1937 (Negrete 3)
Madron, 1970 (Boone 3, Caron 3)
Madwoman of Chaillot, 1969 (Boyer 3, Brynner 3, Dauphin 3, Evans 3,
    Henreid 3, Hepburn, K. 3, Homolka 3, Kaye 3, Masina 3,
    Pleasance 3, Anhalt 4, Guffey 4, Renoir 4)
Mae West, 1982 (McDowall 3)
Maelkehygiejne, 1954 (Carlsen 2)
Maelstrom, 1910 (Lawrence 3)
Maelstrom, 1913 (Ince 4)
Maestrina, 1913 (Bertini 3)
Maestro, 1958 (Fabrizi 3)
Maestro, 1979 (Cassel 3)
Maestro d'amore, 1977 (Brazzi 3)
Maestro di Don Giovanni, 1953 (Flynn 3, Lollobrigida 3, Cardiff 4)
Maestro di Vigevano, 1963 (Petri 2, Bloom 3, Sordi 3, Age and
    Scarpelli 4, Rota 4)
Maestro e Margarita, 1972 (Cuny 3, Tognazzi 3, Morricone 4)
Maestro Koko, 1969 (Grgić 4)
Maffia, 1972 (Torre-Nilsson 2)
Mafia, 1949 (Vanel 3)
Mafia. See Giorno della civetta, 1968
Mafia. See In nome della legge, 1949
Mafia. See Maffia, 1972
Mafia War. See Bacciamo le mani, 1973
Mafioso, 1962 (Ferreri 2, Lattuada 2, Sordi 3, Age and Scarpelli 4,
    De Laurentais 4, Rota 4)
Mafu Cage, 1979 (Grant, L. 3)
Magasins du XIXe siècle. See Strogoscopes, 1963
Magasiskola, 1970 (Gaál 2)
Magd, 1911 (Porten 3, Messter 4)
Magdalene, 1908 (Holger-Madsen 2)
Magee, 1970 (Sinatra 3)
Magellan, from 1972 (Frampton 2)
Maggie, 1954 (Mackendrick 2, Douglas, P. 3, Addison 4)
Maggie's First False Step, 1917 (Sennett 2, Beery 3, Fazenda 3)
Maggot, 1973 (Dunning 4)
Mágia, 1917 (Korda 2)
Magic, 1978 (Attenborough 3, Hopkins, A. 3, Meredith 3,
    Goldman, W. 4, Goldsmith 4)
Magic Bow, 1946 (Granger 3)
Magic Box, 1951 (Boulting 2, Attenborough 3, Donat 3, Holloway 3,
    Love 3, Olivier 3, Rutherford 3, Schell, Maria 3, Ustinov 3,
    Alwyn 4, Cardiff 4, Mathieson 4)
Magic Bullet. See Dr. Ehrlich's Magic Bullet, 1940
Magic Canvas, 1948 (Halas and Batchelor 2)
Magic Carpet, 1925 (Lantz 4)
Magic Carpet, 1951 (Ball 3, Katzman 4)
Magic Cartoons. See Génération spontanée, 1909
Magic Catalogue, 1956 (Vukotić 4)
Magic Christian, 1970 (Polanski 2, Attenborough 3, Brynner 3,
    Harvey 3, Lee, C. 3, Sellers 3, Welch 3, Unsworth 4)
Magic Circus. See Kouzelný cirkus, 1977
Magic Donkey. See Peau d'âne, 1970
Magic Dram, 1957-59 (Kawamoto 4)
Magic Eggs. See Omelette fantastique, 1909
Magic Fan. See Eventail animé, 1909
Magic Feature, from 1943 (Smith 2)
Magic Fire, 1956 (Dieterle 2, Dupont 2, Cushing 3, De Carlo 3, Rasp 3,
    Haller 4, Herlth 4, Korngold 4)
Magic Fish, 1934 (Terry 4)
Magic Flame, 1927 (Florey 2, King 2, Banky 3, Colman 3, Barnes 4,
    Goldwyn 4, Mathis 4, Meredyth 4)
Magic Fluke, 1948 (Hubley 4)
Magic Flute. See Trollflojten, 1975
Magic Fountain, 1961 (Hardwicke 3)
Magic Fountain. See Fuente magica, 1961

Magic Fountain Pen, 1909 (Blackton 2)
Magic Garden, 1927 (Plunkett 4)
Magic Garden of Stanley Sweetheart, 1970 (Goldsmith 4)
Magic Hoop. See Cerceau magique, 1908
Magic Horse, 1953 (Reiniger 2)
Magic Lamp, 1924 (Lantz 4)
Magic Lantern. See Lanterne magique, 1903
Magic Mountain, 1982 (Steiger 3)
Magic Night. See Goodnight Vienna, 1932
Magic of Lassie, 1978 (Faye 3, Rooney 3, Stewart 3)
Magic of the Diamond. See Magie du diamant, 1958
Magic on Broadway, 1937 (Fleischer, M. and D. 2)
Magic Pencil, 1940 (Terry 4)
Magic Prague of Rudolph II. See Kouzelná Praha Rudolfa II, 1982
Magic Shell, 1941 (Terry 4)
Magic Shoes, 1935 (Finch 3)
Magic Slipper, 1948 (Terry 4)
Magic Sounds. See Carobni zvuci, 1957
Magic Statue. See Mazou, 1938
Magic Strength, 1944 (Fleischer, M. and D. 2)
Magic Sword, 1962 (Rathbone 3)
Magic Town, 1947 (Wellman 2, Meek 3, Stewart 3, Wyman 3, Biroc 4,
    Hornbeck 4, Riskin 4)
Magic Voyage of Sinbad, 1962 (Coppola 2, Corman 4)
Magic Waltz. See Varázskeringö, 1918
Magic Wand, 1912 (Bushman 3)
Magical Maestro, 1951 (Avery 2)
Magician, 1926 (Ingram 2, Seitz 4)
Magician. See Ansiktet, 1958
Magician. See Magicien, 1927
Magician in Spite of Himself, 1951 (Loren 3)
Magician of Lublin, 1979 (Arkin 3, Winters 3)
Magician of Lublin. See Magier, 1979
Magicians of the Silver Screen. See Báječní muži s klikou, 1979
Magicien, 1898 (Méliès 2)
Magicien, 1927 (Wegener 3)
Magiciennes, 1960 (D'Eaubonne 4, Matras 4)
Magiciens, 1975 (Chabrol 2, Gégauff 4, Rabier 4)
Magiciens de Wanzerbé, 1949 (Rouch 2)
Magie du diamant, 1958 (Roos 2, Kosma 4)
Magie noire, 1904 (Guy 2)
Magier, 1979 (Golan and Globus 4, Jarre 4)
Magique Image, 1950 (Musidora 3)
Magirama, 1956 (Gance 2)
Magistral, 1983 (Gurchenko 3)
Magistrate. See Magistrato, 1959
Magistrato, 1959 (Zampa 2, Cardinale 3)
Magliari, 1959 (Rosi 2, Sordi 3, Cristaldi 4, D'Amico 4, Di
    Venanzo 4)
Mágnás Miska, 1916 (Korda 2)
Mágnás Miska, 1948 (Gabór 3)
Magnate, 1973 (Cassel 3)
Magnet, 1914 (Meredyth 4)
Magnet, 1950 (Alwyn 4, Balcon 4, Clarke, T.E.B. 4)
Magnet Laboratory, 1959 (Leacock 2)
Magnetic Monster, 1953 (Martin, S. 3, Siodmak 4)
Magnificent, 1926 (Vidor, K. 2)
**Magnificent Ambersons, 1942 (Welles 2, Baxter A. 3, Costello, D. 3,
    Cotten 3, Moorehead 3, Cortez 4, Herrmann 4)**
Magnificent Brute, 1936 (McLaglen 3)
Magnificent Cuckold. See Magnifico cornuto, 1964
Magnificent Doll, 1946 (Borzage 2, Meredith 3, Niven 3, Rogers, G. 3,
    Banton 4, Salter 4)
Magnificent Dope, 1942 (Seaton 2, Ameche 3, Fonda, H. 3, Horton 3,
    Day 4, Raksin 4)
Magnificent Flirt, 1928 (d'Arrast 2, Young, L. 3, Mankiewicz 4,
    Polglase 4)
Magnificent Fraud, 1939 (Florey 2, Head 4)
Magnificent Lie, 1931 (Bellamy 3, Boyer 3, Lang 4, Rosay 3,
    Raphaelson 4)
Magnificent March. See Wspanialu marsz, 1970
Magnificent Matador, 1955 (Boetticher 2, O'Hara 3, Quinn 3,
    Ballard 4)

Magnificent Obsession, 1935 (Stahl 2, Dunne 3, Taylor, R. 3, Heerman 4, Waxman 4)
Magnificent Obsession, 1954 (Sirk 2, Hudson 3, Moorehead 3, Wyman 3, Hunter 4)
Magnificent Outcast. *See* Almost a Gentleman, 1939
Magnificent Rogue, 1946 (Alton, J. 4)
Magnificent Roughnecks, 1956 (Rooney 3)
Magnificent Seven, 1960 (Sturges, J. 2, Bronson 3, Brynner 3, Coburn, J. 3, McQueen, S. 3, Wallach 3, Bernstein 4, Lang 4, Mirisch 4)
Magnificent Seven Deadly Sins, 1971 (Godfrey 4)
Magnificent Seven Ride!, 1972 (Van Cleef 3, Bernstein 4)
Magnificent Showman, 1964 (Hathaway 2)
Magnificent Showman. *See* Circus World, 1964
Magnificent Sinner. *See* Katya, 1960
Magnificent Tramp. *See* Archimède le clochard, 1959
Magnificent Yankee, 1950 (Sturges, J. 2, Calhern 3, Plunkett 4, Raksin 4, Ruttenberg 4)
Magnifici tre, 1961 (Tognazzi 3)
Magnifico avventuriero, 1963 (Blier 3, Fabian 3)
Magnifico cornuto, 1964 (Scola 2, Blier 3, Cardinale 3, Tognazzi 3, Volonté 3)
Magnifique, 1973 (Broca 2, Belmondo 3, Bisset 3)
Magnum Force, 1973 (Cimino 2, Milius 2, Eastwood 3, Schifrin 4)
Magoichi Saga. *See* Shirikurae Magoichi, 1969
Magokoro, 1939 (Naruse 2)
Magokoro, 1953 (Kobayashi 2, Tanaka 3)
Magot de Joséfa, 1964 (Autant-Lara 2, Bourvil 3, Brasseur 3, Magnani 3, Aurenche 4, Bost 4, Douy 4)
Magpie Madness, 1948 (Terry 4)
Magus, 1968 (Caine 3, Karina 3, Quinn 3, Green, G. 4)
Magyar fold ereje, 1916 (Curtiz 2)
Magyar nabob Zoltan Karpáthy, 1966 (Darvas 3)
Magyar Rhapszóia, 1978 (Madaras 3)
Magyar ugaraon, 1972 (Kovács 2, Latinovits 3)
Magyarenfurstin, 1923 (Wagner 4)
Magyarok, 1977 (Fábri 2)
Maha Geet, 1937 (Biswas 4)
Maha Prasthaner Pathey, 1952 (Sircar 4)
Mahaan, 1983 (Bachchan 3)
Mahal, 1970 (Anand 3)
Mahanagar, 1963 (Ray, S. 2, Chandragupta 4, Datta 4, Mitra 4)
Maharadjaens Yndlingshustru II, 1918 (Blom 2)
Maharadscha wider Willen, 1950 (Tschechowa 3)
Maharlika, 1970 (Crawford, B. 3)
Mahatma Kabir Munna, 1954 (Biswas 4)
Mahiru no ankoku, 1956 (Imai 2, Yamamura 3)
Mahiru no enbukyoku, 1949 (Yoshimura 2, Tanaka 3)
Mahiru no wana, 1960 (Iwashita 3)
Mahler, 1974 (Russell 2, Russell 4)
Mahlia la métisse, 1942 (Matras 4)
Mahogany, 1975 (Aumont 3, Perkins 3, Watkin 4)
Mahua, 1934 (Sircar 4)
Maid and the Man, 1921 (Dwan 2)
Maid at the Helm, 1911 (Bosworth 3)
Maid for Murder. *See* She'll Have to Go, 1961
Maid from Sweden, 1914 (Talmadge, C. 3)
Maid in China, 1938 (Terry 4)
Maid in Hollywood, 1934 (Roach 4)
Maid Mad, 1916 (Sennett 2, Fazenda 3)
Maid of Belgium, 1917 (Brady 3)
Maid of Niagara, 1910 (White 3)
Maid of Salem, 1937 (Bondi 3, Colbert 3, Farnum 3, MacMurray 3, Meek 3, Banton 4, Estabrook 4, Young, V. 4)
Maid of the Mist, 1915 (Chaney Lon 3)
Maid of the Mountains, 1909 (Anderson G. 3)
Maid of War, 1914 (Beery 3)
Maid or Man, 1911 (Pickford 3, Gaudio 4, Ince 4)
Maid to Order, 1916 (Hardy 3)
Maiden and Men, 1912 (Dwan 2)
Maiden Lane, 1936 (Trevor 3)
Maidens from Wilko. *See* Panny z Wilka, 1979
Maiden's Trust, 1917 (Sennett 2)

Maids, 1974 (Jackson 3, York, S. 3, Slocombe 4)
Maids a la Mode, 1933 (Pitts 3, Roach 4)
Maids and Muslin, 1920 (Hardy 3)
Maid's Night Out, 1911 (Normand 3)
Maid's Night Out, 1938 (Fontaine 3)
Maidstone, 1971 (Leacock 2, Torn 3)
Maigret à Pigalle, 1967 (Cervi 3, Amidei 4)
Maigret dirige l'enquête, 1955 (Kosma 4)
Maigret et l'affaire Saint-Fiacre, 1958 (Delannoy 2, Gabin 3, Audiard 4)
Maigret tend un piège, 1957 (Delannoy 2, Gabin 3, Girardot 3, Audiard 4)
Maigret voit rouge, 1963 (Fabian 3, Gabin 3)
Maihime, 1951 (Naruse 2, Yamamura 3)
Maiko sanjushi, 1955 (Yoda 4)
Mail and Female, 1937 (Roach 4)
Mail Call, 1944 (Vorkapich 4)
Mail Early, 1941 (McLaren 2)
Mail Early for Christmas, 1959 (McLaren 2)
Mail Order Bride, 1912 (Bushman 3)
Mail Order Bride, 1963 (Oates 3)
Mail Train. *See* Inspector Hornleigh Goes to It, 1941
Maillot noir, 1917 (Musidora 3)
Main, 1969 (Vierny 4)
Main à couper, 1974 (Blier 3, Spaak 4)
Main Actor. *See* Hauptdarstellar, 1977
Main Attraction, 1962 (Zetterling 2, Unsworth 4)
Main chaude, 1959 (Jarre 4)
Main du diable, 1942 (Tourneur, M. 2, Fresnay 3, Andrejew 4)
Main du professeur Hamilton ou Le Rou des dollars, 1903 (Guy 2)
Main Event, 1927 (Howard 2, Adrian 4)
Main Event, 1979 (Streisand 3)
Main mystérieuse, 1916 (Cohl 2)
Main Nashe Me Hoon, 1959 (Kapoor 2)
Main Street, 1923 (Fazenda 3)
Main Street after Dark, 1944 (Duryea 3)
Main Street of Paris, 1939 (Cardiff 4)
Main Street to Broadway, 1953 (Garnett 2, Logan 2, Barrymore E. 3, Barrymore L. 3, Calhern 3, Harrison 3, Moorehead 3, Wilde 3, Howe 4, Raphaelson 4, Sherwood 4)
Maine-Océan, 1984 (Branco 4, de Almeida 4)
Mainland. *See* Great Land, 1944
Mains d'Orlac, 1960 (Ferrer, M. 3)
Mains d'Orlac. *See* Hands of Orlac, 1960
Mains du futur, 1969 (Reichenbach 2)
Mains negatives, 1978 (Duras 2)
Mains Nettes, 1958 (Jutra 2)
Mains sales, 1951 (Brasseur 3, Gélin 3)
Mainspring, 1917 (King 2)
Mais n'te promène donc pas toute nue, 1936 (Arletty 3)
Mais où et donc ornicar?, 1978 (Chaplin 3)
Mais où sont les nègres d'antan?, 1962 (Delerue 4)
Maisen, 1936 (Shimura 3)
Maisie, 1939 (Sothern 3, Young, R. 3, Gibbons 4)
Maisie Gets Her Man, 1942 (Meek 3, Sothern 3, Stradling 4)
Maisie Goes to Reno, 1944 (Gardner 3, Meek 3, Sothern 3, Irene 4)
Maisie Was a Lady, 1941 (Ayres 3, O'Sullivan 3, Sothern 3)
Maiskie zvezdy, 1959 (Tikhonov 3)
Maison, 1970 (Simon, M. 3)
Maison aux images, 1955 (Grémillon 2)
Maison Bonnadieu, 1951 (Blier 3, Darrieux 3)
Maison dans la dune, 1934 (Matras 4, Spaak 4)
Maison de campagne, 1969 (Darrieux 3)
Maison de danses, 1931 (Tourneur, M. 2, Vanel 3)
Maison de Molière, 1980 (Reichenbach 2)
Maison d'en face, 1936 (Christian-Jaque 2)
Maison des Bories, 1969 (Cloquet 4)
Maison des lions, 1912 (Feuillade 2)
Maison des sept jeunes filles, 1941 (Douy 4, Spaak 4)
Maison du Fantoche, 1916 (Cohl 2)
Maison du Maltais, 1938 (Dalio 3, Jouvet 3, Courant 4, Ibert 4, Wakhévitch 4)
Maison du mystère, 1922 (Mozhukin 3, Vanel 3)

Maison du passeur, 1965 (Prévert 4)
Maison du silence, 1952 (Gélin 3)
Maison du souvenir. *See* Casa Ricordi, 1954
Maison jaune de Rio, 1930 (Vanel 3)
Maison sous la mer, 1946 (Aimée 3, Renoir 4)
Maison sous les arbres, 1971 (Clément 2, Dunaway 3, Buchman 4, Perry 4)
Maisons de la misère, 1937 (Storck 2, Jaubert 4)
Maître après Dieu, 1950 (Brasseur 3)
Maître Bolbec et son mari, 1934 (D'Eaubonne 4)
Maître chez soi, 1932 (Dauphin 3)
Maître de forges, 1933 (Gance 2, Strading 4)
Maître de la foudre, 1916 (Feuillade 2)
Maître de Montpellier, 1960 (Leenhardt 2)
Maître du temps, 1970 (Guerra 2)
Maître nageur, 1979 (Trintignant 3)
Maîtres fous, 1955 (Rouch 2, Braunberger 4)
Maitres-Nageurs, 1950 (Berry 3)
Maîtresse, 1975 (Depardieu 3, Almendros 4)
Maj på Malo, 1947 (Nykvist 4)
Maja desnuda, 1958 (Cervi 3)
Maja desnuda. *See* Naked Maba, 1958
Maja zwischen zwei Ehen, 1938 (Dagover 3)
Majboor, 1974 (Bachchan 3)
Majdanek—Cmentarzysko Europy, 1944 (Ford, A. 2)
Majesty of the Law, 1915 (Bosworth 3)
Major and the Minor, 1942 (Wilder 2, Milland 3, Rogers, G. 3, Brackett, C. 4, Dreier 4, Head 4, Laszlo 4)
Major Barbara, 1941 (Lean 2, Harrison 3, Hiller 3, Holloway 3, Kerr 3, Beaton 4, Korda 4, Mayer 4)
Major Bowes' Amateur Theatre of the Air, 1935 (Sinatra 3)
Major Dundee, 1964 (Peckinpah 2, Coburn 3, Heston 3, Johnson, B. 3, Oates 3)
Major from Ireland, 1912 (Olcott 2)
Major que no tuvo infancia, 1956 (Armendáriz 3)
Majordôme, 1964 (Delannoy 2, Bourvil 3, Jeanson 4)
Majority of One, 1961 (Leroy 2, Guinness 3, Russell, R. 3, Orry-Kelly 4, Steiner 4, Stradling 4)
Májové hvězdy, 1959 (Brejchová 3)
Makan No. 44, 1954 (Anand 3)
Makbet, 1969 (Wajda 2)
Make a Wish, 1937 (Meek 3, Rathbone 3)
Make Believe Ballroom, 1949 (Mercer 4)
Make Fruitful the Land, 1945 (Unsworth 4)
Make Haste to Live, 1954 (Bernstein 4)
Make It Real, 1948 (Ford, G. 3)
Make It Snappy, 1921 (Roach 4)
Make Love, Not War. *See* Volite se, a ne ratujte, 1970
Make Me a Star, 1932 (Blondell 3, Brook 3, Chevalier 3, Cooper, Gary 3, March 3, Pitts 3, Sidney 3)
Make Me an Offer, 1954 (Finch 3, Addison 4, Mankowitz 4)
Make Mine Laughs, 1949 (Fleischer, R. 2)
Make Mine Mink, 1960 (Dillon 4)
Make Mine Music, 1946 (Disney 2, Eddy 3, Iwerks 4)
Make Way for a Lady, 1936 (Bruce 3, Marshall 3)
Make Way for Lila. *See* Laila—Liebe unter der Mitternachtssonne, 1958
Make Way for Tomorrow, 1937 (McCarey 2, Bainter 3, Beavers 3, Bondi 3, Dreier 4, Head 4, Young, V. 4)
Make Your Own Bed, 1944 (Wyman 3)
Make-Believe Wife, 1918 (Burke 3)
Makedonskiot del od pekolot, 1971 (Mimica 4)
Maker of Men, 1931 (Wayne 3)
Makin' It, 1970 (Hitchcock 2)
Making a Living, 1914 (Chaplin 2, Sennett 2)
Making a Man of Him, 1911 (Bosworth 3)
Making Friends, 1936 (Fleischer, M. and D. 2)
Making Good, 1912 (Reid 3)
Making Good, 1932 (Lantz 4)
Making It Move, 1977 (Halas and Batchelor 2)
Making Love, 1981 (Hiller 2, Hiller 3, Reynolds 4)
Making Music Together, 1973 (Halas and Batchelor 2)
Making of a Lady. *See* Lady Hamilton, 1968

Making of a Man, 1911 (Griffith 2, Sweet 3, Bitzer 4)
Making of a 'Local Hero' (with a Little Help from His Friends), 1983 (Lancaster 3)
Making of an Automobile Tire, 1913 (Sennett 2)
Making of Superman: The Movie, 1980 (Hackman 3)
Making Photoplays in Egypt, 1912 (Olcott 2)
Making Stars, 1935 (Fleischer, M. and D. 2)
Making the Grade, 1947 (Matthews 3)
Makioka Sisters. *See* Sasame-yuki, 1950
Makkers staakt uw wild geraas, 1960 (Rademakers 2)
Makkhetes, 1916 (Curtiz 2)
Maksimenko brigád, 1950 (Jancsó 2)
Mal. *See* Rage, 1966
Mal de mer, 1912 (Linders 3)
Mal des autres, 1959 (Delerue 4)
Mal du siècle, 1953 (Lelouch 2)
Mala hembre, 1950 (Alcoriza 4)
Mala hierra, 1940 (Armendáriz 3)
Mala kronika, 1962 (Mimica 4)
Malá mořská víla, 1976 (Kachyna 2, Kučera 4)
'Mala' ordine, 1972 (Cusack 3)
Mala the Magnificent. *See* Eskimo, 1933
Malachi's Cove. *See* Seaweed Children, 1973
Malade hydrophobe, 1900 (Méliès 2)
Malade imaginaire. *See* Malato imaginario, 1979
Malaga, 1954 (O'Hara 3, Korda 4)
Malaga, 1960 (Stewart 4)
Malaga. *See* Moment of Danger, 1960
Malaire, 1950 (Vanel 3)
Malamondo, 1964 (Morricone 4)
Malaria, 1941 (Hayakawa 3)
Malarpirater, 1923 (Molander 2, Magnusson 4)
Malarpirater, 1959 (Bjornstrand 3)
Malatesta, 1970 (Constantine 3)
Malato imaginario, 1979 (Blier 3)
Malaya, 1949 (Barrymore L. 3, Cortese 3, Greenstreet 3, Nilsson 3, Stewart 3, Tracy 3, Head 4, Irene 4, Kaper 4)
Malchik i golub, 1961 (Mikhalkov-Konchalovski 2)
Malcolm X, 1972 (Jones, J.E. 3)
Malditas sean las mujeres, 1936 (García 3)
Maldone, 1927 (Grémillon 2, Honegger 4, Matras 4, Périnal 4)
Maldonne, 1947–51 (Verneuil 2)
Maldoror, 1951–52 (Anger 2)
Male and Female, 1919 (DeMille 2, Daniels 3, Swanson 3, Buckland 4 Howe 4, Macpherson 4)
Male Animal, 1942 (De Havilland 3, Fonda, H. 3, McDaniel 3, Young, G. 3, Edeson 4, Epstein, J. & P. 4, Wallis 4)
Male Companion. *See* Monsieur de compagnie, 1964
Mâle du siècle, 1975 (Forman 2)
Male Hunt. *See* Chasse à l'homme, 1964
Male Man, 1931 (Fleischer, M. and D. 2)
Maledetto imbroglio, 1959 (Cardinale 3)
Maléfice, 1912 (Feuillade 2)
Malencontre, 1920 (Dulac 2)
Malenkie tragedii, 1979 (Smoktunovsky 3)
Maleta, 1960 (Ruiz 2)
Malevil, 1981 (Trintignant 2)
Malfray, 1948 (Resnais 2)
Malgache Adventure. *See* Aventure Malgache, 1944
Malheur n'arrive jamais seul, 1903 (Méliès 2)
Malheur qui passe, 1916 (Feuillade 2)
Malheurs de la guerre, 1962 (Storck 2)
Malheurs de Sophie, 1945 (Trauner 4)
Mali i veliki, 1966 (Grgić 4)
Malia, 1918 (Bertini 3)
Malia, 1945 (Castellani 2, Brazzi 3, Cervi 3)
Malibran, 1944 (Cocteau 2, Guitry 2)
Malibu, 1983 (Coburn, J. 3, Novak 3, Saint 3)
Malibu Beach, 1939 (Freleng 4)
Malice in Slumberland, 1942 (Fleischer, M. and D. 2)
Malice in the Palace, 1949 (Three Stooges 3)
Malice in Wonderland, 1985 (Taylor, E. 3)
Malizia, 1973 (Storaro 4)

Mallarmé, 1964–69 (Rohmer 2)
Malle au mariage, 1912 (Linders 3)
Malmaison, 1963 (Fresnay 3)
Malombra, 1916 (Gallone 2)
Malombra, 1942 (Castellani 2, De Laurentiis 4)
Malovani pro kocku, 1961 (Pojar 4)
Malpertuis, 1972 (Welles 2, Cassel 3, Delerue 4, Fisher 4)
Malquerida, 1949 (Fernández 2, Del Rio 3, Figueroa 4)
Malrif, aigle royal, 1960 (Jarre 4)
Malstrømmen. See Store Fald, 1911
Malta Story, 1953 (Guinness 3, Hawkins 3, Alwyn 4, Krasker 4)
Maltese Bippy, 1969 (Daniels 4, Panama 4)
Maltese Falcon, 1931 (Daniels 3, Merkel 3)
Maltese Falcon, 1941 (Huston 2, Astor 3, Bogart 3, Bond 3, Cook 3, Greenstreet 3, Huston 3, Lorre 3, Blanke 4, Deutsch 4, Edeson 4, Orry-Kelly 4, Wallis 4)
Malu tianshi, 1937 (Zhao 3)
Malvado carabel, 1960 (García 3)
Maly western, 1960 (Giersz 4)
Malzenstwo z rozsadki, 1967 (Olbrychski 3)
Mama, 1976 (Gurchenko 3)
Mama Behave, 1926 (McCarey 2, Roach 4)
Mama cumple cien años, 1979 (Saura 2, Chaplin 3)
Mama ich lebe, 1977 (Wolf 2)
Mamá Inés, 1945 (García 3)
Mama Loves Papa, 1933 (McLeod 2, Stevens 2, Johnson 4)
Mama no shinkon-ryoko, 1954 (Yamada 3, Yamamura 3)
Mama Steps Out, 1937 (Brady 3, Emerson 4, Loos 4)
Mamaia, 1966 (Braunberger 4)
Maman Colibri, 1929 (Christian-Jaque 2, Duvivier 2)
Maman Colibri, 1937 (Aumont 3)
Maman et la putain, 1973 (Léaud 3)
Maman Popee, 1919 (Gallone 2)
Mama's Affair, 1921 (Fleming 2, Talmadge, C. 3, Emerson 4, Loos 4, Schenck 4)
Mama's Dirty Girls, 1974 (Grahame 3)
Mama's Little Pirate, 1935 (Roach 4)
Mama's New Hat, 1939 (Freleng 4)
Mamba, 1930 (Hersholt 3, Johnson, N. 3)
Mambo, 1954 (Rossen 2, Gassman 3, Mangano 3, Winters 3, Andrejew 4, De Laurentiis 4, Ponti 4, Rosson 4, Rota 4)
Mame, 1974 (Ball 3, Preston 3, Boyle 4, van Runkle 4)
Mamie Rose. See Mørke Punkt, 1911
Mamma mia, che impressione, 1951 (Sordi 3, Zavattini 4)
Mamma Roma, 1962 (Pasolini 2, Magnani 3, Delli Colli 4)
Mammals. See Ssaki, 1962
Mammame, 1986 (de Almeida 2)
Mamma's Boy, 1920 (Roach 4)
Mamma's Boys, 1916 (Hardy 3)
Mammo Kenkoku no Reimei, 1932 (Mizoguchi 2)
Mammy, 1930 (Curtiz 2, Bosworth 3, Jolson 3)
Mammy Water, 1965 (Rouch 2)
Mammy's Rose, 1916 (Borzage 2)
Mamouret. See Briseur de chaînes, 1941
Mampou hattenshi: Umi no gouzoku, 1942 (Miyagawa 4)
Mamsell Josabeth, 1963 (Fischer 4)
Mamy Water, 1955 (Braunberger 4)
Mam'zelle Bonaparte, 1941 (Tourneur, M. 2, Feuillère 3)
Mam'zelle Chiffon, 1919 (Musidora 3)
Mam'zelle Cricri. See Deutschmeister, 1955
Mam'zelle Nitouche, 1931 (Allégret, M. 2, Allégret, Y. 2, Feuillère 3, Ondra 3, Raimu 3, Simon, S. 3, Braunberger 4)
Mam'zelle Nitouche, 1953 (Allégret, Y. 2, Fernandel 3, Achard 4, Aurenche 4, D'Eaubonne 4, Wakhévitch 4)
Mam'zelle Pigalle. See Cette sacrée gamine, 1955
Mam'zelle Souris, 1958 (Delerue 4)
Mam'zelle Spahi, 1934 (Douy 4)
Mam'zelle Striptease. See En effeuillant la marguerite, 1956
Man, 1910 (Griffith 2, Bitzer 4)
Man, 1972 (Ayres 3, Jones, J.E. 3, Meredith 3, Goldsmith 4)
Man: A Modern Drama. See Chelovek, drama nachidnya, 1912
Man, A Woman, and a Bank. See Very Big Withdrawal, 1979

Man about the House, 1946 (Périnal 4)
Man About the House. See Vendetta nel sole, 1947
Man About Town, 1923 (Laurel 3, Roach 4)
Man About Town, 1932 (Baxter W. 3, Howe 4)
Man about Town, 1939 (Sandrich 2, Grable 3, Lamour 3, Dreier 4, Head 4, Prinz 4, Ryskind 4, Young, V. 4)
Man About Town. See Silence est d'or, 1947
Man Afraid, 1957 (Mancini 4)
Man Against Man. See Mr. 'Silent' Haskins, 1915
Man Against Man. See Otoko tai otoko, 1960
Man Against Woman, 1932 (Muse 3)
Man Alive, 1945 (Menjou 3, O'Brien, P. 3)
Man Alone, 1923 (Bosworth 3)
Man Alone, 1955 (Bond 3, Milland 3, Van Cleef 3, Young, V. 4)
Man among Men. See Dansei No. 1, 1955
Man and a Woman. See Homme et une femme, 1966
Man and Boy, 1971 (Jones 3)
Man and His Dog Out for Air, 1958 (Breer 2)
Man and His Mate. See One Million B.C., 1940
Man and His Soul, 1916 (Bushman 3)
Man and His Tools, 1962 (Hubley 4)
Man and His World, 1967 (Vanderbeek 2, Dovniković 4, Vukotić 4)
Man and Maid, 1925 (Adorée 3, Gibbons 4)
Man and the Girl, 1909 (Olcott 2)
Man and the Moment, 1929 (Grot 4, Polito 4)
Man and the Snake, 1972 (Fisher 4)
Man and the Stars. See Homem das estrelas, 1971
Man and the Woman, 1908 (Griffith 2, Bitzer 4)
Man and the Woman, 1917 (Guy 2)
Man and Wife, 1923 (Costello, M. 3, Shearer 3)
Man at Large, 1941 (Cook 3, Day 4, Miller, V. 4)
Man Bait, 1926 (Crisp 3, Fairbanks, D. Jr. 3, Rosson 4)
Man Behind the Door, 1914 (Menjou 3)
Man Behind the Gun, 1952 (Scott, R. 3, Buckner 4, Glennon 4)
Man Behind the Mask, 1936 (Powell 2, Carey 3)
Man Beneath, 1919 (Hayakawa 3)
Man Betrayed, 1941 (Bond 3, Wayne 3)
Man Between, 1953 (Reed 2, Bloom 3, Knef 3, Mason 3, Addison 4, Andrejew 4, Kurnitz 4)
Man braucht kein Geld, 1931 (Lamarr 3)
Man By the Roadside. See Mensch am Wege, 1923
Man Called Back, 1932 (Florey 2)
Man Called Dagger, 1967 (Kovacs 4)
Man Called Flintstone, 1966 (Hanna and Barbera 4)
Man Called Gannon, 1969 (Bumstead 4, Chase 4)
Man Called Horse, 1970 (Anderson J. 3, Cody 3, Rosenman 4)
Man Called John. See . . . e venne un uomo, 1965
Man Called Peter, 1955 (Newman 4)
Man Called Sullivan. See Great John L., 1944
Man Cannot Be Raped. See Manrape, 1978
Man Could Get Killed, 1966 (Mercouri 3, Clarke, T.E.B. 4)
Man Crazy, 1953 (Crosby 4)
Man die zijn haar kort liet knippen, 1966 (Tyszkiewicz 3, Cloquet 4)
Man for A' That, 1914 (Bushman 3)
Man for All Seasons, 1966 (Welles 2, Zinnemann 2, Hiller 3, Hurt, J. 3, Redgrave, V. 3, Shaw 3, York, S. 3, Box 4, Delerue 4)
Man for All That, 1915 (Walsh 2)
Man for Burning. See Un uomo da bruciare, 1962
Man Friday, 1975 (O'Toole 3)
Man from Bitter Roots, 1916 (Farnum 3)
Man from Blankley's, 1930 (Barrymore J. 3, Young, L. 3)
Man from Blankley's. See Fourteenth Man, 1920
Man from Button Willow, 1965 (Keel 3)
Man from Cairo, 1953 (Raft 3)
Man from Cheyenne, 1942 (Rogers, R. 3)
Man from Cocody. See Gentleman de Cocody, 1964
Man from Colorado, 1948 (Ford, G. 3, Holden 3, Chase 4, Duning 4, Maddow 4)
Man from C.O.T.T.O.N. See Gone Are the Days!, 1963
Man from Dakota, 1940 (Beery 3, Del Rio 3, Meek 3)
Man from Del Rio, 1956 (Quinn 3, Cortez 4, Horner 4)
Man from Down Under, 1943 (Laughton 3, Reed, D. 3, Irene 4)
Man from Downing Street, 1922 (Karloff 3)

Man from Far Away. *See* Uomo che viene de lontano, 1968

Man from Frisco, 1943 (Florey 2, Duryea 3)

Man from Funeral Range, 1918 (Reid 3)

Man from Galveston, 1963 (Coburn, J. 3, Hunter 3, Glennon 4)

Man from Hell, 1934 (Canutt 4)

Man from Hell's River, 1922 (Beery 3)

Man from Home, 1914 (DeMille 2, Buckland 4)

Man from Home, 1922 (Hitchcock 2, Nilsson 3, Miller, A. 4)

Man from Independence, 1974 (Bernstein 4)

Man From Kangaroo, 1920 (Glennon 4, Meredyth 4)

Man from Laramie, 1955 (Mann 2, Crisp 3, Elam 3, Kennedy, A. 3, Stewart 3, Duning 4, Lang 4)

Man from Mexico, 1914 (Barrymore J. 3)

Man From Monterey, 1933 (Wayne 3, McCord 4)

Man from Montreal, 1940 (Arlen 3, Krasner 4)

Man from Morocco, 1944 (Walbrook 3)

Man from Music Mountain, 1938 (Autry 3)

Man from Music Mountain, 1943 (Rogers, R. 3)

Man from Naples. *See* Mann aus Neapel, 1922

Man from Nowhere, 1915 (Hart 3)

Man from Oklahoma, 1945 (Rogers, R. 3)

Man from Painted Post, 1917 (Fleming 2, Fairbanks, D. 3)

Man from Planet X, 1951 (Ulmer 2)

Man from Red Gulch, 1925 (Carey 3, Stromberg 4)

Man from Snowy River, 1982 (Douglas, K. 3)

Man from Texas, 1915 (Mix 3)

Man from Texas, 1924 (Carey 3)

Man from Texas, 1948 (Merkel 3)

Man from the Alamo, 1953 (Boetticher 2, Ford, G. 3)

Man from the Diners' Club, 1963 (Tashlin 2, Kaye 3, Kennedy, G. 3, Sloane 3, Stanton 3)

Man from the East, 1912 (Dwan 2)

Man from the East, 1914 (Mix 3)

Man from the Folies Bergere. *See* Folies Bergere, 1935

Man From the Meteor, 1954–56 (Romero 2)

Man From the Other Side. *See* Chelovek s drugoi storoni, 1972

Man From the Restaurant, 1929 (Protazanov 2)

Man from the Restaurant. *See* Chelovek iz restorana, 1929

Man from Toronto, 1933 (Matthews 3, Balcon 4)

Man from Utah, 1934 (Wayne 3, Canutt 4)

Man from Wyoming, 1930 (Cooper, Gary 3)

Man from Yesterday, 1932 (Zinnemann 2, Boyer 3, Brook 3, Colbert 3, Banton 4, Struss 4)

Man from Yesterday, 1949 (Harvey 3)

Man Haters, 1922 (Roach 4)

Man Higher Up, 1913 (Bunny 3)

Man Hunt, 1911 (Dwan 2)

Man Hunt, 1935 (Ruttenberg 4)

Man Hunt, 1941 (Lang 2, Bennett J. 3, Carradine 3, McDowall 3, Pidgeon 3, Sanders 3, Banton 4, Day 4, MacGowan 4, Miller, A. 4, Newman 4, Nichols 4)

Man Hunter, 1919 (Farnum 3)

Man I Killed, 1932 (Lubitsch 2, Barrymore L. 3, Dreier 4)

Man I Killed. *See* Broken Lullaby, 1932

Man I Like. *See* Homme qui me plait, 1969

Man I Love, 1929 (Wellman 2, Arlen 3, Banton 4, Mankiewicz 4, Selznick 4)

Man I Love, 1946 (Walsh 2, Lupino 3, Friedhofer 4, Steiner 4)

Man I Married, 1940 (Bennett J. 3, Ouspenskaya 3, Day 4, Zanuck 4)

Man I Marry, 1936 (Bruce 3)

Man in a Bubble, 1980–82 (Peterson 2)

Man in a Cocked Hat. *See* Carlton-Browne of the F.O., 1958

Man in Demand, 1955 (Lee, C. 3)

Man in Grey, 1943 (Granger 3, Mason 3)

Man in Half Moon Street, 1944 (Dreier 4, Fort 4, Head 4, Rozsa 4)

Man in Hiding. *See* Mantrap, 1953

Man in Him, 1916 (Anderson G. 3)

Man in My Life. *See* Rajolfi Hayati, 1961

Man in Polar Regions, 1967 (Clarke 2)

Man in Possession, 1931 (Montgomery 3)

Man in Possession. *See* Personal Property, 1937

Man in Silence, 1959 (Halas and Batchelor 2)

Man in the Attic, 1953 (Palance 3, Lemaire 4, Wheeler 4)

Man in the Box, 1908 (Bitzer 4)

Man in the Cabin, 1913 (Anderson G. 3)

Man in the Couch, 1914 (Browning 2)

Man in the Dark, 1953 (O'Brien, E. 3, Crosby 4)

Man in the Glass Booth, 1975 (Hiller 2, Schell, Maximilian 3, Anhalt 4)

Man in the Gray Flannel Suit, 1956 (Cobb 3, Jones, J. 3, March 3, Peck 3, Wynn 3, Clarke, C.C. 4, Herrmann 4, Johnson 4, Lemaire 4, Smith, J.M. 4, Wheeler 4, Zanuck 4)

Man in the Iron Mask, 1939 (Whale 2, Bennett J. 3, Cushing 3, Schildkraut 3)

Man in the Iron Mask, 1977 (Aumont 3, Jourdan 3, Richardson 3, Young, F. 4)

Man in the Middle, 1964 (Howard, T. 3, Mitchum 3, Wynn 3, Barry 4)

Man in the Mirror, 1936 (Horton 3, Sim 3, Courant 4)

Man in the Moon, 1960 (Dearden 2, More 3)

Man in the Moon. *See* Clair de lune espagnol, 1909

Man in the Moonlight, 1919 (Moore, C. 3)

Man in the Net, 1959 (Curtiz 2, Ladd 3, Mirisch 4, Salter 4, Seitz 4)

Man in the Raincoat. *See* Homme à l'imperméable, 1957

Man in the Road, 1957 (Cusack 3)

Man in the Saddle, 1926 (Karloff 3, Wray 3)

Man in the Saddle, 1951 (De Toth 2, Scott, R. 3, Brown, Harry Joe 4, Duning 4)

Man in the Santa Claus Suit, 1980 (Astaire 3)

Man in the Shadow, 1958 (Chandler 3, Salter 4)

Man in the Sky, 1956 (Crichton 2, Hawkins 3, Pleasance 3, Slocombe 4)

Man in the Storm. *See* Arashi no naka no otoko, 1957

Man in the Trunk, 1942 (Day 4)

Man in the Vault, 1914 (Nilsson 3)

Man in the Vault, 1956 (Clothier 4)

Man in the White Suit, 1951 (Mackendrick 2, Greenwood 3, Guinness 3, Balcon 4, Slocombe 4)

Man in the Wilderness, 1971 (Huston 2, Fisher 4)

Man Inside, 1958 (Roeg 2, Palance 3, Pleasance 3)

Man is Dead. *See* Homme est mort, 1973

Man Is Not a Bird. *See* Covek nije tica, 1966

Man Is Ten Feet Tall. *See* Edge of the City, 1957

Man Is to Man . . ., 1962 (Brynner 3)

Man Life Passed By, 1923 (Bosworth 3)

Man Mad. *See* No Place to Land, 1958

Man Made Monster, 1941 (Chaney Lon, Jr. 3, Fulton 4, Salter 4)

Man Must Live, 1925 (Rosson 4)

Man Named John. *See* . . . e venne un uomo, 1965

Man Next Door, 1913 (Sennett 2)

Man Next Door, 1965 (Kuri 4)

Man och Kvinna, 1938 (Fejos 2)

Man of a Thousand Faces, 1957 (Cagney 3, Malone 3)

Man of Action, 1933 (Brennan 3)

Man of Affairs. *See* His Lordship, 1936

Man of Africa, 1953 (Grierson 2)

Man of Africa. *See* Men of 2 Worlds, 1946

Man of Aran, 1934 (Flaherty 2, Balcon 4)

Man of Bronze, 1918 (Stone 3)

Man of Bronze. *See* Jim Thorpe—All American, 1951

Man of Conquest, 1939 (Fontaine 3, August 4, Canutt 4, Eason 4, Head 4, Young, V. 4)

Man of Evil. *See* Fanny By Gaslight, 1944

Man of Honor, 1919 (Gaudio 4)

Man of Iron, 1935 (Astor 3)

Man of Iron, 1981 (Janda 3)

Man of Iron. *See* Czlowiek z zelaza, 1981

Man of Iron. *See* Ferroviere, 1956

Man of Iron. *See* Iron Road, 1925

Man of La Mancha, 1972 (Hiller 2, Loren 3, O'Toole 3)

Man of Marble. *See* Czlowiek z marmaru, 1978

Man of Mayfair, 1931 (Buchanan 3)

Man of Music. *See* Kompositor Glinka, 1952

Man of Nerve, 1925 (Arthur 3)

Man of Peace, 1928 (Bosworth 3)

Man of Quality, 1926 (Ruggles 2)

Man of Sorrow, 1916 (Farnum 3)

Man of Stone, 1921 (Goulding 2)

Man of the Earth, 1915 (Lukas 3)

Man of the Forest, 1921 (Hersholt 3)
Man of the Forest, 1926 (Hathaway 2, Oland 3, Schulberg 4)
Man of the Forest, 1933 (Hathaway 2, Carey 3, Crabbe 3, Scott, R. 3)
Man of the Hour, 1914 (Tourneur, M. 2, Carré 4)
Man of the Hour. *See* Colonel Effingham's Raid, 1945
Man of the Hour. *See* Homme du jour, 1936
Man of the Moment, 1935 (Fairbanks, D. Jr. 3)
Man of the Moment. *See* Toki no ujigami, 1932
Man of the People, 1937 (Clarke, C. C. 4)
Man of the Soil. *See* Föld embere, 1917
Man of the West, 1958 (Mann 2, Cobb 3, Cooper, Gary 3, Haller 4, Mirisch 4)
Man of the World, 1931 (Lombard 3, Powell, W. 3, Mankiewicz 4)
Man of the Year. *See* Homo eroticus, 1971
Man of Two Worlds, 1934 (Plunkett 4, Steiner 4)
Man of Wrath. *See* Wedding Group, 1936
Man on a Bus, 1955 (Crawford, B. 3)
Man on a String, 1960 (De Toth 2, Borgnine 3, de Rochemont 4, Duning 4)
Man on a String, 1972 (Warden 3)
Man on a Swing, 1973 (Robertson 3, Schifrin 4)
Man on a Tightrope, 1953 (Kazan 2, Boone 3, Grahame 3, March 3, Menjou 3, Lemaire 4, Sherwood 4, Waxman 4)
Man on America's Conscience. *See* Tennessee Johnson, 1942
Man on Fire, 1957 (Crosby 3, Raksin 4, Ruttenberg 4)
Man on the Beach, 1955 (Losey 2, Sangster 4)
Man on the Box, 1914 (DeMille 2, Buckland 4)
Man on the Case, 1914 (Dwan 2)
Man on the Eiffel Tower, 1949 (Laughton 3, Meredith 3, Brown, Harry 4, Cortez 4)
Man on the Flying Trapeze, 1934 (Fleischer, M. and D. 2)
Man on the Flying Trapeze, 1935 (Brennan 3, Fields, W.C. 3, Bruckman 4, Head 4)
Man on the Prowl, 1957 (Musuraca 4)
Man on the Roof, 1977 (Widerberg 2)
Man on the Run, 1949 (Harvey 3, More 3)
Man on the Run. *See* Kidnappers, 1964
Man on the Track. *See* Czlowiek na torze, 1956
Man Outside, 1967 (Heflin 3)
Man Pasand, 1980 (Anand 3)
Man Pays, 1924 (Roach 4)
Man Power, 1927 (Cronjager 4, Schulberg 4)
Man, Pride, and Vengeance. *See* Uomo, L'orgoglio, la vendetta, 1967
Man sku' vaere noget ved musikken, 1972 (Carlsen 2)
Man spielt nicht mit der Liebe, 1926 (Pabst 2, Krauss 3)
Man spielt nicht mit der Liebe, 1949 (Dagover 3)
Man steigt nach, 1927 (Metzner 4)
Man Taking Off His Gloves. *See* Tebukuro o nugasu otoko, 1946
Man There Was. *See* Terje Vigen, 1917
Man They Could Not Arrest, 1931 (Balcon 4, Wimperis 4)
Man They Could Not Hang, 1939 (Karloff 3, Brown, K. 4)
Man to Kill. *See* Homme à abattre, 1967
Man to Man, 1922 (Carey 3)
Man to Man, 1930 (Dwan 2)
Man to Men. *See* D'homme à hommes, 1948
Man to Remember, 1938 (Hunt 4, Kanin 4, Polglase 4, Trumbo 4)
Man to Respect. *See* Uomo da rispettare, 1973
Man Trap, 1917 (Young, W. 4)
Man Trouble, 1930 (Zinnemann 2, August 4)
Man Under Cover, 1922 (Browning 2, Miller, V. 4)
Man Under Suspicion, 1984 (Schell, Maximilian 3)
Man Under Water. *See* Clověk pod vodou, 1961
Man Upstairs, 1958 (Attenborough 3)
Man Vanishes. *See* Ningen johatsu, 1967
Man vs. Man. *See* Otoko tai otoko, 1960
Man Wanted, 1932 (Dieterle 2, Francis, K. 3, Merkel 3, Toland 4)
Man Who Broke the Bank at Monte Carlo, 1935 (Bennett J. 3, Bruce 3, Carradine 3, Colman 3, Johnson 4, Zanuck 4)
Man Who Came Back, 1924 (Goulding 2)
Man Who Came Back, 1930 (Walsh 2, Gaynor 3, Edeson 4, Friedhofer 4)
Man Who Came Back. *See* Swamp Water, 1941

Man Who Came to Dinner, 1941 (Burke 3, Davis 3, Durante 3, Sheridan 3, Young, G. 3, Epstein, J. & P. 4, Gaudio 4, Orry-Kelly 4, Wald 4, Wallis 4)
Man Who Came to the Port. *See* Minato e kita otoko, 1952
Man Who Changed His Mind, 1936 (Balcon 4, Gilliat 4)
Man Who Changed His Mind. *See* Man Who Lived Again, 1936
Man Who Cheated Himself, 1950 (Cobb 3, Miller, S. 4, Polglase 4)
Man Who Cheated Life. *See* Student von Prag, 1926
Man Who Committed Murder. *See* Mann, der den Mord beging, 1931
Man Who Could Cheat Death, 1959 (Fisher 2, Lee, C. 3, Sangster 4)
Man Who Could Work Miracles, 1936 (Richardson 3, Sanders 3, Biro 4, Hornbeck 4, Korda 4, Krasker 4, Rosson 4)
Man Who Could Work Miracles, 1937 (Richardson 3)
Man Who Couldn't Beat God, 1915 (Costello, M. 3)
Man Who Cried Wolf, 1937 (Stone 3)
Man Who Dared, 1920 (Furthman 4)
Man Who Dared, 1933 (Miller, A. 4, Nichols 4, Trotti 4)
Man Who Dared, 1946 (Sturges, J. 2)
Man Who Dared God, 1917 (Weber 2)
Man Who Fell to Earth, 1976 (Roeg 2, Torn 3, Henry 4)
Man Who Fights Alone, 1924 (Farnum 3, Horton 3)
Man Who Finally Died, 1962 (Zetterling 2, Baker S. 3, Cushing 3)
Man Who Found Himself, 1937 (Fontaine 3, Hunt 4)
Man Who Found Out, 1915 (Stone 3)
Man Who Had His Hair Cut Short. *See* Man die zijn haar kort liet knippen, 1966
Man Who Had to Sing. *See* Covjek koji je morao pjevati, 1970
Man Who Haunted Himself, 1970 (Dearden 2, Moore, R. 3)
Man Who Knew Too Much, 1934 (Hitchcock 2, Fresnay 3, Lorre 3, Balcon 4, Bennett 4, Courant 4, Junge 4)
Man Who Knew Too Much, 1955 (Hitchcock 2, Day 3, Gélin 3, Stewart 3, Bennett 4, Bumstead 4, Hayes 4, Head 4, Herrmann 4, Whitlock 4)
Man Who Laughed Last, 1929 (Hayakawa 3)
Man Who Laughs, 1928 (Leni 2, Veidt 3)
Man Who Left His Will on Film. *See* Tokyo senso sengo hiwa, 1970
Man Who Lies. *See* Homme qui ment, 1968
Man Who Lies. *See* Muž, ktory luže, 1968
Man Who Lived Again, 1936 (Karloff 3, Balderston 4)
Man Who Lived Again. *See* Man Who Changed His Mind, 1936
Man Who Lived Twice, 1936 (Bellamy 3, Bond 3)
Man Who Lost Himself, 1941 (Francis, K. 3, Sakall 3, Salter 4)
Man Who Loved Cat Dancing, 1973 (Cobb 3, Reynolds, B. 3, Warden 3, Perry 4, Williams, J. 4)
Man Who Loved Redheads, 1955 (Cooper, Gladys 3, Périnal 4)
Man Who Loved Women, 1983 (Andrews J. 3, Reynolds, B. 3, Mancini 4, Wexler 4)
Man Who Loved Women. *See* Homme qui aimait les femmes, 1977
Man Who Made the Army, 1917 (Pearson 2)
Man Who Murdered. *See* Mann, der den Mord beging, 1931
Man Who Never Was, 1956 (Cusack 3, Grahame 3, Sellers 3, Webb 3, Mathieson 4, Morris 4)
Man Who Paid, 1922 (Shearer 3)
Man Who Played God, 1922 (Arliss 3, Astor 3)
Man Who Played God, 1932 (Arliss 3, Davis 3, Milland 3)
Man Who Reclaimed His Head, 1934 (Bennett J. 3, Rains 3, D'Agostino 4)
Man Who Shot Liberty Valance, 1962 (Ford, J. 2, Carradine 3, Martin, S. 3, Marvin 3, O'Brien, E. 3, Stewart 3, Van Cleef 3, Wayne 3, Clothier 4, Head 4, Westmore, W. 4)
Man Who Stayed at Home, 1915 (Hepworth 2)
Man Who Talked Too Much, 1940 (Barthelmess 3, Brent 3)
Man Who Tamed the Victors. *See* Manden, der sejrede, 1918
Man Who Turned to Stone, 1957 (Katzman 4)
Man Who Understood Women, 1959 (Caron 3, Dalio 3, Fonda, H. 3, Johnson 4, Krasner 4, Wheeler 4)
Man Who Wagged His Tail. *See* Angel paso sobre Brooklyn, 1957
Man Who Waited, 1922 (Pierce 4)
Man Who Watched Trains Go By. *See* Paris Express, 1953
Man Who Went Out, 1913 (August 4)
Man Who Won, 1919 (Costello, M. 3)
Man Who Won, 1923 (Wellman 2, August 4)

Man Who Would Be King, 1975 (Huston 2, Caine 3, Connery 3, Head 4, Jarre 4, Morris 4, Trauner 4, Whitlock 4)
Man Who Would Not Die, 1975 (Malone 3, Wynn 3)
Man Who Wouldn't Die, 1942 (Day 4, Raksin 4)
Man Who Wouldn't Talk, 1940 (Marsh 3, Day 4, Miller, V. 4)
Man Who Wouldn't Talk, 1958 (Wilcox 2, Neagle 3, Quayle 3)
Man with a Cloak, 1951 (Calhern 3, Caron 3, Cotten 3, Stanwyck 3, Plunkett 4, Raksin 4)
Man with a Gun. See Chelovek s ruzhyom, 1938
Man with a Married Woman's Hairdo. See Boku no marumage, 1933
Man with a Million. See Million Pound Note, 1953
Man with a Movie Camera. See Chelovek s kinoapparatom, 1929
Man with an Umbrella. See Det regnar på vår karlek, 1946
Man with Bogart's Face, 1978 (De Carlo 3, Raft 3, Duning 4)
Man with My Face, 1951 (Warden 3)
Man with Nine Lives, 1940 (Karloff 3, Brown, K. 4)
Man with the Albatross, 1969 (Hedren 3)
Man with the Axe. See Parashuram, 1978
Man with the Balloons. See Oggi, domani, dopodomani, 1965
Man with the Deadly Lens. See Wrong is Right, 1982
Man with the Electric Voice. See Fifteen Wives, 1935
Man with the Glove, 1914 (Nilsson 3)
Man with the Golden Arm, 1955 (Preminger 2, Novak 3, Sinatra 3, Bass 4, Bernstein 4)
Man with the Golden Gun, 1974 (Lee, C. 3, Moore, R. 3, Barry 4)
Man with the Green Carnation. See Trials of Oscar Wilde, 1960
Man With the Gun, 1955 (Dickinson 3, Mitchum 3, Garmes 4, North 4)
Man With the Rubber Head. See Homme à la tête de caoutchouc, 1902
Man with the Scar. See Scar Hanan, 1925
Man with the Synthetic Brain. See Blood of Ghastly Horror, 1972
Man with the X-Ray Eyes. See X, 1963
Man with Thirty Sons. See Magnificent Yankee, 1950
Man with Three Wives, 1909 (Sweet 3)
Man With Two Brains, 1983 (Turner, K. 3)
Man with Two Faces, 1934 (Astor 3, Calhern 3, Robinson, E. 3, Gaudio 4)
Man with Wheels in His Head. See Malade hydrophobe, 1900
Man Within, 1914 (Reid 3)
Man Within, 1916 (Mix 3)
Man Within, 1947 (Attenborough 3, Greenwood 3, Redgrave, M. 3, Unsworth 4)
Man Without a Country, 1973 (Robertson 3)
Man Without a Face, 1935 (Cusack 3)
Man without a Future. See Manden uden Fremtid, 1915
Man Without a Map. See Moetikuta chizu, 1968
Man Without a Name. See Mann ohne Namen, 1920
Man Without a Name. See Mensch ohne Namen, 1932
Man without a Nationality. See Mukokuseki-sha, 1951
Man Without a Soul. See Man Without Desire, 1923
Man Without a Star, 1955 (Vidor, K. 2, Boone 3, Crain 3, Douglas, K. 3, Elam 3, Trevor 3, Van Cleef 3, Chase 4, Salter 4)
Man Without Desire, 1923 (Novello 3)
Man Without Mercy. See Gone with the West, 1975
Man, Woman, and Child, 1983 (Sheen 3, Delerue 4)
Man, Woman, and Dog, 1964 (Kuri 4)
Man, Woman, and Marriage, 1921 (Carré 4)
Man, Woman, and Sin, 1927 (Gilbert 3, Gibbons 4)
Man, Woman, and Wife, 1929 (Mandell 4)
Managed Money, 1934 (Temple 3)
Manbait. See Last Page, 1952
Manbeast! Myth or Monster, 1978 (Bottin 4)
Manche et la belle, 1957 (Verneuil 2, D'Eaubonne 4, Matras 4)
Manchu Eagle Murder Caper Mystery, 1975 (Coogan 3)
Manchurian Candidate, 1962 (Frankenheimer 2, Harvey 3, Lansbury 3, Leigh, J. 3, Sinatra 3, Axelrod 4, Sylbert 4)
Mandabi, 1968 (Sembene 2)
Mandacaru vermelho, 1961 (Pereira Dos Santos 2)
Mandalay, 1934 (Curtiz 2, Francis, K. 3, Oland 3, Temple 3, Gaudio 4, Grot 4)
Mandarin, bandit gentilhomme, 1962 (Douy 4)
Mandarin Mix-Up, 1924 (Laurel 3)
Mandarine, 1972 (Girardot 3, Noiret 3)
Mandarino per Teo, 1960 (Di Venanzo 4)

Mandarin's Gold, 1919 (Oland 3)
Mandate of Heaven, 1979 (Carradine 3)
Manden, der sejrede, 1918 (Holger-Madsen 2)
Manden uden Fremtid, 1915 (Holger-Madsen 2)
Manden uden Smil, 1916 (Holger-Madsen 2)
Mandi, 1983 (Azmi 3, Patil 3)
Mandingo, 1975 (Fleischer, R. 2, Mason 3, De Laurentiis 4, Jarre 4, Leven 4)
Mandragola, 1965 (Lattuada 2, Delli Colli 4, Donati 4)
Mandragora. See Galgamannen, 1945
Mandragore. See Alraune, 1950
Mandrake. See Alraune, 1927
Mandy, 1952 (Mackendrick 2, Hawkins 3, Alwyn 4, Slocombe 4)
Maneater, 1973 (Sangster 4)
Man-Eater of Kumaon, 1948 (Salter 4)
Man-Eating Sharks, 1932 (Sennett 2)
Manège, 1938 (Gallone 2)
Manèges, 1950 (Allégret, Y. 2, Blier 3, Signoret 3, Trauner 4)
Manet ou le novateur malgré lui, 1980 (Leenhardt 2)
Manfish, 1956 (Chaney Lon, Jr. 3)
Mangetsu sanju-koku-sen, 1952 (Yamada 3)
Mangiala, 1969 (Morricone 4)
Mangiati vivi, 1979 (Ferrer, M. 3)
Manhandled, 1924 (Dwan 2, Swanson 3, Rosson 4)
Manhandled, 1949 (Duryea 3, Hayden 3, Lamour 3, Head 4, Laszlo 4)
Manhattan, 1924 (Rosson 4)
Manhattan, 1979 (Allen 2, Keaton 3, Streep 3, Willis 4)
Manhattan Angel, 1949 (Katzman 4)
Manhattan Cocktail, 1928 (Arzner 2, Arlen 3, Lukas 3, Vajda 4)
Manhattan Cowboy, 1928 (Vajda 4)
Manhattan Heartbeat, 1940 (Day 4, Miller, V. 4)
Manhattan Knights, 1928 (Johnson, N. 3)
Manhattan Madness, 1916 (Dwan 2, Fleming 2, Fairbanks, D. 3, Menjou 3, Emerson 4, Loos 4)
Manhattan Madness. See Adventure in Manhattan, 1936
Manhattan Madness. See Woman Wanted, 1935
Manhattan Melodrama, 1934 (Mankiewicz 2, Van Dyke, W.S. 2, Gable 3, Loy 3, Powell, W. 3, Rooney 3, Howe 4, Selznick 4, Vorkapich 4)
Manhattan Memories, 1947 (Fleischer, M. and D. 2)
Manhattan Merry-Go-Round, 1937 (Autry 3)
Manhattan Monkey Business, 1935 (Roach 4)
Manhattan Moon, 1935 (D'Agostino 4)
Manhattan Parade, 1932 (Bacon 2)
Manhole Covers, 1954 (Peterson 2)
Manhunt. See From Hell to Texas, 1958
Manhunt in Milan. See 'Mala' Ordina, 1972
Manhunt of Mystery Island, 1945 (Canutt 4)
Mani sporche, 1978 (Petri 2, Mastroianni 3, Morricone 4)
Mani sulla città, 1963 (Rosi 2, Steiger 3, Di Venanzo 4)
Mania, 1918 (Negri 3)
Mania. See Flesh and the Fiends, 1960
Maniac, 1911 (Lawrence 3)
Maniac, 1962 (Sangster 4)
Maniac, 1977 (Ireland 3, Reed, O. 3, Corman 4)
Maniac Cook, 1908 (Griffith 2, Bitzer 4)
Maniac on Wheels. See Once a Jolly Swagman, 1948
Maniac's Desire, 1912–13 (White 3)
Manicure Girl, 1925 (Daniels 3, Hunt 4)
Manicure Lady, 1911 (Sennett 2, Sennett 2)
Manicurist, 1916 (Sennett 2)
Manila Calling, 1942 (Cook 3, Wilde 3, Day 4, Raksin 4)
Manila in the Claws of Light. See Maynila sa Kuko nig Liwanag, 1975
Manin densha, 1957 (Ichikawa 2)
Manina, la fille sans voiles, 1952 (Bardot 3)
Manitas de Plata, 1966 (Reichenbach 2)
Manitou, 1977 (Curtis 3, Meredith 3, Sothern 3, Schifrin 4)
Manja Walewska, 1936 (Tschechowa 3)
Manji, 1964 (Kishida 3)
Manjudhar, 1947 (Biswas 4)
Mankinda, 1957 (Vanderbeek 2)
Manly Man, 1911 (Pickford 3, Gaudio 4, Ince 4)
Mann auf Abwegen, 1939 (Albers 3)

Mann auf den Schienen. *See* Czlowiek na torze, 1956
Mann auf der Mauer, 1982 (Hauff 2)
Mann aus dem Jenseits, 1925 (Albers 3, Tschechowa 3, Wegener 3)
Mann aus Neapel, 1922 (Dupont 2)
Mann, dem man den Namen stahl, 1945 (Staudte 2)
Mann, der den Mord beging, 1931 (George, H. 3, Veidt 3, Courant 4, Warm 4)
Mann, der nicht lieben darf. *See* Geheimnis des Abbé X, 1927
Mann, der seinen Morder sucht, 1931 (Siodmak 2, Wilder 2, Herlth 4, Rohrig 4, Siodmak 4)
Mann, der Sherlock Holmes war, 1937 (Albers 3, Wagner 4)
Mann der Tat, 1919 (Jannings 3)
Mann der zweimal Leben wollte, 1950 (Tschechowa 3)
Mann, die sich verkaufte, 1959 (Knef 3)
Mann im Feuer, 1926 (Tschechowa 3)
Mann im Spiegel, 1916 (Wiene 2, Freund 4, Messter 4)
Mann im Strom, 1958 (Albers 3)
Mann mit dem Laubfrosch, 1929 (George, H. 3)
Mann mit den sieben Masken, 1918 (Messter 4)
Mann mit der Pranke, 1935 (Wegener 3, Von Harbou 4)
Mann mit Grundsaltzen?, 1943 (Herlth 4)
Mann mit Herz, 1932 (Frohlich 3)
Mann nennt es Amore, 1961 (Fusco 4)
Mann nennt es Liebe, 1953 (Jurgens 3)
Mann ohne Namen, 1920 (Krauss 3)
Mann seiner Frau, 1925 (Planer 4)
Mann um Mitternacht, 1924 (Holger-Madsen 2, Junge 4)
Mann von der Cap Arcona, 1982 (Geschonneck 3)
Mann will nach Deutschland, 1934 (Wegener 3, Wagner 4)
Mannekangen, 1913 (Stiller 2, Jaenzon 4)
Mannequin, 1926 (Cruze 2, Baxter W. 3, Costello, D. 3, Pidgeon 3, Pitts 3, Brown, K. 4)
Mannequin, 1933 (Bennett 4)
Mannequin, 1938 (Borzage 2, Mankiewicz 2, Crawford, J. 3, Tracy 3, Adrian 4)
Mannequin assassiné, 1947 (Gélin 3)
Mannequins, 1933 (D'Eaubonne 4)
Mannequins de Paris, 1956 (Auer 3, Audiard 4)
Manner ohne Bart, 1971 (Hoppe 3)
Manner sind zum Lieben da, 1960 (Warm 4)
Manner um Lucie, 1931 (d'Arrast 2, Korda 2, Stradling 4)
Manner vom blauen Kreuz. *See* Blekitny krzyź, 1955
Mannesmann, 1937 (Ruttmann 2)
Manniskor i stad, 1947 (Sucksdorff 2)
Manniskor motas och ljuv musik uppstår a hjartat. *See* Mennesker modes og sod musik opstår i hjertet, 1967
Mano che nutre la morte, 1973 (Kinski 3)
Mano dello straniero, 1953 (Howard, T. 3, Valli 3, Rota 4)
Mano en la trampa, 1961 (Torre-Nilsson 2)
Mano nascosta di Dio, 1971 (Kinski 3)
Mano spietat della legge, 1973 (Cusack 3, Kinski 3)
Manoeuvres, 1968 (Dovniković 4)
Manolescu, 1929 (George, H. 3, Mozhukin 3, Herlth 4, Hoffmann 4, Rohrig 4)
Manolescus Memoiren, 1920 (Oswald 2, Dreier 4)
Manolete, 1944 (Gance 2)
Manolis, 1962 (Theodorakis 4)
Manon, 1948 (Clouzot 2, Reggiani 3, Douy 4)
Manon 70, 1968 (Deneuve 3)
Manon de Montmartre, 1914 (Feuillade 2)
Manon des sources, 1952 (Pagnol 2)
Manon Lescaut, 1926 (Leni 2, Robison 2, Dietrich 3, Johnson, N. 3, Pommer 4)
Manon Lescaut, 1940 (De Sica 2, Gallone 2, Valli 3)
Manovre d'amore, 1939 (Zampa 2)
Manpower, 1941 (Walsh 2, Arden 3, Bond 3, Dietrich 3, Raft 3, Robinson, E. 3, Deutsch 4, Haller 4, Wald 4, Wallis 4)
Man-Proof, 1938 (Loy 3, Pidgeon 3, Russell, R. 3, Freund 4, Waxman 4, Young, W. 4)
Manque de mémoire, 1929 (Maté 4)
Manrape, 1978 (Donner 2)
Man's Best Friend, 1941 (Lantz 4)
Man's Calling, 1912 (Dwan 2)

Man's Castle, 1933 (Borzage 2, Tracy 3, Young, L. 3, August 4, Swerling 4)
Man's Country, 1919 (Chaney Lon 3)
Man's Desire, 1919 (Stone 3)
Man's Duty, 1912 (Reid 3)
Man's Duty, 1913 (Dwan 2)
Man's Enemy, 1914 (Gish, D. 3, Gish, L. 3)
Man's Favorite Sport?, 1964 (Hawks 2, Hudson 3, Head 4, Mancini 4, Mercer 4)
Man's Game, 1934 (Bond 3)
Man's Genesis, 1912 (Griffith 2, Marsh 3, Bitzer 4)
Man's Great Adversary. *See* Elskovs Magt, 1912
Man's Heart. *See* Otokogokoro, 1925
Man's Life. *See* Hito no issho, 1928
Man's Lust for Gold, 1912 (Griffith 2, Sweet 3, Bitzer 4)
Man's Man, 1929 (Cruze 2, Daves 2, Garbo 3, Gilbert 3, Day 4, Gibbons 4)
Man's Mate, 1924 (Adorée 3, Gilbert 3, Johnson, N. 3)
Man's Past, 1927 (Veidt 3)
Man's Value. *See* Tsena cheloveka, 1928
Man's Worldly Appearance. *See* Hito no yo no sugata, 1928
Mansarda, 1963 (Lomnicki 3)
Mansion of the Doomed, 1975 (Grahame 3)
Manslaughter, 1922 (DeMille 2, Boyd 3, Gillespie 4, Macpherson 4)
Manslaughter, 1930 (Colbert 3, March 3)
Mantan Messes Up, 1946 (Horne 3)
Mantango, 1963 (Tsuburaya 4)
Mantango—Fungus of Terror. *See* Mantango, 1963
Mantenuto, 1961 (Tognazzi 3)
Manthan, 1976 (Benegal 2, Patil 3, Nihalani 4)
Mantle of Charity, 1918 (Furthman 4)
Mantra-Mughdha, 1949 (Roy 2, Sircar 4)
Mantrap, 1926 (Fleming 2, Hathaway 2, Bow 3, Head 4, Howe 4, Schulberg 4)
Mantrap, 1943 (Siodmak 4)
Mantrap, 1953 (Fisher 2, Henreid 3)
Mantrap, 1961 (O'Brien, E. 3, Head 4, Hunter 4)
Manual of Arms, 1966 (Frampton 2)
Manuel Rodriguez, 1972 (Guzmán 2)
Manuela, 1957 (Armendáriz 3, Howard, T. 3, Pleasance 3, Alwyn 4)
Manuela, 1965 (Solás 2, Herrera 4)
Manuscript Found in Saragossa. *See* Rekopis znaleziony w Saragossie, 1964
Manxman, 1928 (Hitchcock 2, Ondra 3)
Many a Slip, 1931 (Ayres 3, Bennett J. 3, Summerville 3)
Many Happy Returns, 1922 (Roach 4)
Many Happy Returns, 1934 (McLeod 2, Milland 3, Head 4)
Many Rivers to Cross, 1955 (McLaglen 3, Taylor, R. 3, Brown, Harry 4, Plunkett 4, Seitz 4)
Many Scrappy Returns, 1926 (Roach 4)
Many Tanks, 1942 (Fleischer, M. and D. 2)
Many Voices, 1956 (Heston 3)
Manya, die Turkin, 1915 (Kortner 3)
Manzil, 1936 (Roy 2)
Manzil, 1960 (Anand 3, Burman 4)
Manzil, 1979 (Bachchan 3)
Manzil Maya, 1936 (Sircar 4)
Manzoor, 1949 (Sircar 4)
Mao le veut, 1965 (Lassally 4)
Maputo: Meridiano novo, 1976 (Alvarez 2)
Maquillage, 1927 (Vanel 3)
Maquillage, 1932 (Feuillère 3)
Maquillage. *See* Da halt die Welt den Aten an, 1927
Már nem olyan idoket élunk, 1964 (Gabór 3)
Mar y tú, 1951 (Fernández 2, Figueroa 4)
Mara Maru, 1952 (Flynn 3, Steiner 4)
Maracaibo, 1958 (Wilde 3, Head 4)
Maranhâo, 1965 (Rocha 2)
Marat Sade, 1967 (Jackson 3, Watkin 4)
Marathon, 1919 (Daniels 3, Lloyd 3, Roach 4)
Marathon. *See* Maraton, 1967
Marathon Man, 1976 (Schlesinger 2, Hoffman 3, Olivier 3, Scheider 3, Goldman, W. 4, Hall 4, Smith, D. 4)

Marathon Runner. *See* Laufer von Marathon, 1933
Maraton, 1967 (Brejchová 3)
Marâtre, 1906 (Guy 2)
Marauders, 1912 (Dwan 2)
Marauders, 1947 (Boyd 3)
Marauders, 1955 (Duryea 3, Wynn 3)
Marble Heart, 1913 (Cruze 2)
Marble Heart, 1916 (Brenon 2)
Marcel, ta mère t'appelle, 1962 (Grimault 4)
Marcelino, 1956 (Rey 3)
Marcelino, pan y vino, 1954 (Rey 3)
Marcella, 1920 (Gallone 2)
Marcella, 1940 (Gallone 2)
Marcellini Millions, 1917 (Crisp 3)
March Hare, 1921 (Daniels 3)
March Hare, 1956 (Cusack 3)
March of Dimes, 1942 (Gable 3)
March of the Movies. *See* Film Parade, 1933
March of Time series, 1940-51 (Lye 2)
March of Time. *See* Show Business at War, 1943
March of Time. *See* Wir um schalten auf Hollywood, 1931
March on Marines, 1940 (Eason 4)
March or Die, 1977 (Deneuve 3, Hackman 3, Von Sydow 3, Jarre 4)
March to Aldermaston, 1958 (Anderson 2, Burton 3)
March to Rome. *See* Marcia su Roma, 1962
Marchand d'amour, 1935 (Rosay 3, Jeanson 4)
Marchand de ballons, 1902 (Guy 2)
Marchand de coco, 1899–1900 (Guy 2)
Marchand de notes, 1942 (Aurenche 4, Grimault 4)
Marchand de plaisir, 1923 (Autant-Lara 2)
Marchande de sable, 1931 (Christian-Jaque 2)
Marchandes d'illusions, 1954 (Manès 3)
Marchands de rien, 1958 (Audiard 4)
Marché, 1896-97 (Lumière 2)
Marché à la volaille, 1899–1900 (Guy 2)
Marche de la faim, 1935 (Kosma 4)
Marche des machines, 1927 (Zinnemann 2, Kaufman 4)
Marche des rois, 1913 (Feuillade 2)
Marche française, 1956 (Delerue 4)
Marche nuptiale, 1928 (Christian-Baque 2)
Marche ou crève, 1959 (Blier 3, Delerue 4)
Marchesa d'Arminiani, 1920 (Negri 3)
Marchese del Grillo, 1982 (Monicelli 2)
Marcheurs de Sainte Rolende, 1974–75 (Storck 2)
Marching Along. *See* Stars and Stripes Forever, 1952
Marcia nuziale, 1966 (Ferreri 2, Tognazzi 3)
Marcia o crepa, 1963 (Granger 3)
Marcia su Roma, 1962 (Risi 2, Gassman 3, Tognazzi 3, Age and Scarpelli 4)
Marcia trionfale, 1976 (Bellocchio 2)
Marco Polo, 1962 (Christian-Jaque 2)
Marco the Magnificent, 1964 (Smith, D. 4)
Marco the Magnificent. *See* Fabuleuse Aventure de Marco Polo, 1965
Marcus Welby, M.D., 1969 (Young, R. 3)
Marcus-Nelson Murders, 1973 (Ferrer, J. 3)
Mardi Gras, 1958 (Goulding 2, Lemaire 4, Wald 4)
Mare, 1962 (Fusco 4)
Mare di guai, 1939 (Zampa 2)
Mare di Napoli, 1919 (Gallone 2)
Mare matto, 1963 (Castellani 2, Belmondo 3, Lollobrigida 3, Cristaldi 4, Rota 4)
Mare Nostrum, 1926 (Ingram 2, Carré 4, Seitz 4)
Mare Nostrum, 1950 (Félix 3, Rey 3)
Maréchal-ferrant, 1895 (Lumière 2)
Maresi, 1948 (Schell, Maria 3)
Marge, 1976 (Borowczyk 4)
Margherita fra i tre, 1942 (De Laurentiis 4)
Margie, 1940 (Auer 3, Cortez 4, Salter 4)
Margie, 1946 (King 2, Crain 3, McDaniel 3, Basevi 4, Clarke, C.C. 4, Newman 4)
Margin for Error, 1943 (Preminger 2, Bennett J. 3, Cronjager 4, Day 4)
Marginal, 1983 (Belmondo 3, Audiard 4)
Margo, 1970 (Golan and Globus 4)

Marguerite de la nuit, 1956 (Autant-Lara 2, Montand 3, Morgan 3, Douy 4, Jeanson 4)
Mari à prix fixe, 1963 (Karina 3)
Mari en laisse. *See* If a Man Answers, 1962
Mari rêve, 1936 (Arletty 3, Brasseur 3)
María, 1971 (Figueroa 4)
Maria and Napoleon. *See* Marysia i Napoleon, 1966
Maria Antonieta Rivas Mercado, 1982 (Schygulla 3)
María Candelaria, 1943 (Fernández 2, Armendáriz 3, Del Rio 3, Figueroa 4)
Maria Chapdelaine, 1934 (Duvivier 2, Aumont 3, Gabin 3, Périnal 4)
Maria Chapdelaine, 1950 (Morgan 3, Rosay 3)
Maria Chapdelaine. *See* Naked Heart, 1950
Maria Dabrowska, 1966 (Zanussi 2)
María de la O, 1948 (Figueroa 4)
María Elena, 1935 (Fernández 2, Armendáriz 3, Clothier 4, Figueroa 4)
María Eugenia, 1942 (Félix 3)
Maria Ilona, 1939 (Herlth 4)
Maria Magdalena, 1919 (Dreier 4)
Maria, matricula de Bilbao, 1961 (Vanel 3)
Maria no Oyuki, 1935 (Mizoguchi 2, Yamada 3)
Maria of the Ant Village. *See* Ari no Machi no Maria, 1958
Maria of the Street of Ants. *See* Ari no Machi no Maria, 1958
Maria Rosa, 1916 (DeMille 2, Reid 3, Buckland 4, Macpherson 4)
Maria Stuart, 1927 (Kortner 3)
Maria Tudor, 1920 (Dreier 4)
Mariage, 1974 (Lelouch 2, Lai 4)
Mariage à l'américaine, 1909 (Linders 3)
Mariage à la mode, 1974 (Chaplin 3, Sarde 4)
Mariage à responsabilité limité, 1933 (Burel 4, Jeanson 4, Spiegel 4)
Mariage au puzzle, 1909 (Linders 3)
Mariage au téléphone, 1912 (Linders 3)
Mariage d'amour, 1907 (Linders 3)
Mariage de chiffon, 1942 (Autant-Lara 2, Blier 3, Aurenche 4)
Mariage de Figaro, 1959 (Alekan 4)
Mariage de l'aînée, 1911 (Feuillade 2)
Mariage de Mademoiselle Beulemans, 1927 (Duvivier 2)
Mariage de Miss Nelly, 1913 (Feuillade 2)
Mariage de raison, 1916 (Feuillade 2)
Mariage de Victorine, 1907 (Méliès 2)
Mariage des dieux, 1969 (Braunberger 4)
Mariage forcé, 1909 (Linders 3)
Mariage imprévu, 1913 (Linders 3)
Mariage par suggestion, 1916 (Cohl 2)
Mariana, 1967 (Figueroa 4)
Marianne, 1929 (Davies 3, Adrian 4, Brown, N. 4, Freed 4, Gibbons 4)
Marianne and Julianne. *See* Bleierne Zeit, 1981
Marianne de ma jeunesse, 1955 (Duvivier 2, Ophuls 2, Burel 4, D'Eaubonne 4, Ibert 4, Schufftan 4, Wakhévitch 4)
Maria-Pilar. *See* Au coeur de la Casbah, 1951
Maria's Lovers, 1984 (Mitchum 3)
Maricruz, 1957 (Figueroa 4)
Marido de ida y vuelta, 1955 (Rey 3)
Marie, 1985 (Spacek 3, De Laurentiis 4, Lai 4)
Marie a mal aux dents, 1912 (Cohl 2)
Marie Antoinette, 1938 (Duvivier 2, Franklin 2, Van Dyke, W.S. 2, Barrymore J. 3, Fitzgerald 3, Power 3, Schildkraut 3, Shearer 3, Adrian 4, Daniels 4, Gibbons 4, Jennings 4, Stewart 4, Stothart 4, Stromberg 4, Vajda 4, Vorkapich 4)
Marie Chantal Against Dr. Kha. *See* Marie-Chantal contre le docteur Kha, 1965
Marie des angoisses, 1935 (Rosay 3, D'Eaubonne 4)
Marie du port, 1949 (Carné 2, Gabin 3, Alekan 4, Kosma 4, Trauner 4)
Marie Galante, 1934 (King 2, Fetchit 3, Tracy 3, Hoffenstein 4, Seitz 4)
Marie, legende hongroise. *See* Tavaszi zápor, 1932
Marie, Ltd., 1919 (Brady 3)
Marie poupée, 1976 (Sarde 4)
Marié qui se fait attendre, 1910 (Chevalier 3)
Marie Rambert Remembers, 1960 (Russell 2)
Marie Soleil, 1964 (Bardot 3)
Marie the Doll. *See* Marie poupée, 1976
Marie Walewska. *See* Conquest, 1937

Marriage Playground, 1929 (Francis, K. 3, March 3)
Marriage Ring, 1918 (Niblo 2, Barnes 4)
Marriage Rows, 1931 (Arbuckle 3)
Marriage Symphony. *See* Let's Try Again, 1934
Marriage Time. *See* Konki, 1961
Marriage Wow, 1925 (Langdon 3)
Marriage Wows, 1930 (Fleischer, M. and D. 2)
Marriage Wrestler. *See* Aktenskapabrottaren, 1964
Marriage: Year One, 1971 (Field 3, Moorehead 3)
Marriageable Daughters. *See* Giftasvuxnar dottrar, 1933
Marriage-Go-Round, 1960 (Hayward 3, Mason 3, Lemaire 4)
Married?, 1925 (Bennett C. 3)
Married and in Love, 1940 (Polglase 4)
Married Bachelor, 1941 (Schary 4)
Married Before Breakfast, 1937 (Young, R. 3)
Married But Single. *See* This Thing Called Love, 1941
Married by the Stork. *See* Storch hat uns getraut, 1933
Married Flirts, 1924 (Shearer 3)
Married for Millions, 1906 (Bitzer 4)
Married in Haste, 1929 (O'Brien, P. 3)
Married in Haste. *See* Consolation Marriage, 1931
Married in Haste. *See* Jitney Elopement, 1915
Married Lady Borrows Money. *See* Okusama shakuyosho, 1936
Married Life, 1920 (Sennett 2, Fazenda 3)
Married Life. *See* Kekkon no seitai, 1941
Married to a Mormon, 1922 (Brook 3)
Married Too Young, 1961 (Haller 4)
Married Virgin, 1920 (Valentino 3)
Married Woman. *See* Femme mariée, 1964
Marry Me, 1925 (Cruze 2, Horton 3, Brown, K. 4)
Marry Me, 1932 (Asquith 2, Balcon 4)
Marry Me, 1949 (Fisher 2)
Marry Me Again, 1953 (Tashlin 2, Cummings 3)
Marry the Boss's Daughter, 1941 (Clarke, C.C. 4)
Marry the Girl, 1937 (Auer 3, Brown, Harry Joe 4, Raksin 4, Wallis 4)
Marrying Kind, 1952 (Cukor 2, Bronson 3, Gordon 3, Holliday 3, Friedhofer 4, Horner 4, Kanin 4, Walker 4)
Mars, 1930 (Lantz 4)
Marschall Vorwarts, 1932 (Wegener 3)
Marseillaise, 1912 (Cohl 2)
Marseillaise, 1938 (Becker 2, Reiniger 2, Renoir 2, Jouvet 3, Modot 3, Barsacq 4, Kosma 4, Renoir 4, Wakhévitch 4)
Marseillaise. *See* Captain of the Guard, 1930
Marseille, premier port de France, 1945 (Decaë 4)
Marseilles Contract, 1974 (Caine 3, Mason 3, Slobomce 4)
Marshal of Gunsmoke, 1944 (Salter 4)
Marshal of Reno, 1944 (Edwards 2)
Marshal's Capture, 1913 (Mix 3)
Marshmallow Moon. *See* Aaron Slick from Punkin Crick, 1951
Marter der Liebe, 1927 (Gallone 2, Tschechowa 3)
Martha, 1923 (Disney 2)
Martha, 1973 (Fassbinder 2)
Martha's Rebellion, 1912 (Bunny 3)
Martha's Vindication, 1916 (Franklin 2, Talmadge, N. 3)
Marthe Richard, 1937 (Von Stroheim 2, Dalio 3, Feuillère 3, Honegger 4)
Martian in Moscow Russian language teaching series, 1964 (Halas and Batchelor 2)
Martian Thru Georgia, 1963 (Jones 2)
Martiens, 1973 (Vanel 3)
Martin, 1977 (Romero 2)
Martin Andersen Nexos sidste rejse, 1954 (Roos 2)
Martin Eden, 1914 (Bosworth 3)
Martin Fierro, 1968 (Torre-Nilsson 2)
Martin Luther, 1953 (de Rochemont 4)
Martin Makes It to the Top. *See* Martin na vrhu, 1969
Martin na vrhu, 1969 (Grgić 4)
Martin of the Mounted, 1926 (Wyler 2)
Martin Roumagnac, 1946 (Dietrich 3, Gabin 3, Gélin 3, Wakhévitch 4)
Martin Soldat, 1966 (Braunberger 4)
Martin the Cobbler, 1976 (Vinton 4)
Marty, 1955 (Borgnine 3, Chayefsky 4, La Shelle 4)
Martyr, 1973 (Ford, A. 2)

Martyre, 1924 (Vanel 3)
Martyre de l'obèse, 1932 (L'Herbier 2, Spaak 4)
Martyred Presidents, 1901 (Porter 2)
Martyrium, 1920 (Negri 3, Wagner 4)
Martyrs of Love. *See* Mucedníci lásky, 1967
Maruche, 1932 (Fernandel 3)
Marvellous Wreath. *See* Guirlande merveilleuse, 1903
Marx for Beginners, 1978 (Godfrey 4)
Mary, 1931 (Hitchcock 2, Tschechowa 3)
Mary Ann, 1918 (Korda 2)
Mary Burns, Fugitive, 1935 (Howard 2, Douglas, M. 3, Sidney 3, Wanger 4)
Mary Ellen Comes to Town, 1920 (Gish, D. 3)
Mary Find-the-Gold, 1921 (Pearson 2, Balfour 3)
Mary Jane's Pa, 1935 (Haller 4)
Mary Lou, 1928 (Andrejew 4)
Mary Magdalene. *See* Spade e la croce, 1958
Mary, Mary, 1963 (Leroy 2, Reynolds, D. 3, Stradling 4)
Mary, Mary, Bloody Mary, 1974 (Carradine 3)
Mary of Scotland, 1936 (Ford, J. 2, Carradine 3, Crisp 3, Hepburn, K. 3, March 3, August 4, Berman 4, Nichols 4, Plunkett 4, Polglase 4)
Mary of the Mines, 1912 (Ince 4)
Mary of the Movies, 1923 (Ingram 2, Fazenda 3, Pitts 3)
Mary Poppins, 1964 (Disney 2, Andrews J. 3, Darwell 3, Lanchester 3, Ellenshaw 4)
Mary, Queen of Scots, 1971 (Howard, T. 3, Jackson 3, Redgrave, V. 3, Barry 4, Wallis 4)
Mary, Queen of Tots, 1925 (Roach 4)
Mary Regan, 1919 (Weber 2)
Mary Stevens, M.D., 1933 (Bacon 2, Francis, K. 3, Orry-Kelly 4)
Marya Sklodowska-Curie. Ein Madchen, das die Welt verandert, 1972 (Staudte 2)
Maryland, 1940 (King 2, Bainter 3, Brennan 3, McDaniel 3, Muse 3, Day 4, Newman 4, Zanuck 4)
Mary's Birthday, 1951 (Reiniger 2)
Mary's Little Lamb, 1935 (Iwerks 4)
Mary's Romance, 1912–13 (White 3)
Marysia i krasnoludki, 1960 (Komorowska 3)
Marysia i Napoleon, 1966 (Tyszkiewicz 3)
Marzia nuziale, 1915 (Gallone 2)
Más allá de las montañas, 1967 (Papas 3, Rey 3, Schell, Maximilian 3, Matras 4)
Más allá del amor, 1945 (Figueroa 4)
Ma's Apron Strings, 1913 (Bunny 3)
Ma's Girls, 1915 (Mix 3)
Masamod, 1920 (Lukas 3)
Máscaras, 1976 (de Almeida 4)
Maschera di Cesare Borgia, 1941 (Stallich 4)
Mascot, 1914 (Browning 2)
Mascot. *See* Mascotte, 1930
Mascot of Troop 'C', 1911 (Guy 2)
Mascottchen, 1929 (Albers 3)
Mascotte, 1930 (Ford, A. 2)
Masculine Feminine. *See* Masculin-féminin, 1966
Masculin-féminin, 1966 (Godard 2, Bardot 3, Léaud 3, Guillemot 4, Lai 4)
Másfél millió, 1964 (Gabór 3)
M*A*S*H, 1970 (Altman 2, Duvall, R. 3, Gould 3, Sutherland 3, Lardner 4, Smith, J.M. 4)
Mashal, 1950 (Burman 4)
Masher, 1910 (Sennett 2, Sennett 2, Pickford 3)
Masher, 1912–13 (White 3)
Mask, 1918 (Gilbert 3)
Mask, 1921 (Selig 4)
Mask, 1961 (Vorkapich 4)
Mask, 1985 (Kovacs 4)
Mask and the Sword. *See* Singoalla, 1949
Mask of Comedy. *See* Gay Deceiver, 1926
Mask of Dijon, 1945 (Von Stroheim 3)
Mask of Dimitrios, 1944 (Negulesco 2, Greenstreet 3, Lorre 3, Blanke 4, Deutsch 4, Edeson 4)
Mask of Dust, 1954 (Fisher 2)

Mask of Fu Manchu, 1932 (Vidor, C. 2, Hersholt 3, Karloff 3, Loy 3, Stone 3, Adrian 4, Gaudio 4)
Mask of Lopez, 1924 (Brown, Harry Joe 4)
Mask of Love, 1916 (Chaney Lon 3)
Mask of Marcella. See Cool Million, 1972
Mask of Riches See Mask, 1918
Mask of Sheba, 1969 (Pidgeon 3, Schifrin 4)
Mask of the Avenger, 1951 (Quinn 3, Stromberg 4)
Mask-a-Raid, 1931 (Fleischer, M. and D. 2)
Maske, 1919 (Dupont 2)
Maske fällt, 1930 (Dieterle 2)
Masked Bride, 1925 (Florey 2, Von Sternberg 2, Bushman 3, Rathbone 3, Carré 4, Gibbons 4)
Masked Bride, 1978 (Chaplin 3)
Masked Mamas, 1926 (Sennett 2)
Masked Menace, 1927 (Arthur 3)
Masked Raider, 1919 (Karloff 3)
Masked Rider, 1916 (Gaudio 4)
Masked Woman, 1927 (Nilsson 3, Mathis 4)
Masked Wrestler, 1914 (Bushman 3)
Masken, 1920 (Basserman 3, Rohrig 4, Warm 4)
Masken, 1929 (Homolka 3, Warm 4)
Maskenfest der Liebe, 1918 (Messter 4)
Maskerade, 1934 (Tschechowa 3, Walbrook 3, Planer 4, Reisch 4)
Maskierte Liebe, 1912 (Porten 3)
Masková milenka, 1940 (Baarová 3)
Masks and Faces, 1917 (Cooper, Gladys 3)
Masks of the Devil, 1928 (Sjostrom 2, Gilbert 3, Adrian 4, Gibbons 4, Marion 4)
Masoom, 1983 (Azmi 3)
Masque de fer, 1962 (Marais 3)
Masque d'horreur, 1912 (Gance 2)
Masque du diable, 1976 (Laguionie 4)
Masque of the Red Death, 1964 (Roeg 2, Price 3, Corman 4)
Masquerada, 1949 (Armendáriz 3)
Masquerade, 1924 (Fleischer, M. and D. 2)
Masquerade, 1929 (Clarke, C.C. 4, Pierce 4)
Masquerade, 1931 (Robinson 4)
Masquerade, 1941 (Gerasimov 2)
Masquerade, 1964 (Dearden 2, Hawkins 3, Piccoli 3, Robertson 3, Goldman, W. 4)
Masquerade. See Masquerader, 1914
Masquerade in Mexico, 1945 (Leisen 2, Lamour 3, Dreier 4, Head 4, Young, V. 4)
Masquerade in Vienna. See Maskerade, 1934
Masquerader, 1914 (Chaplin 2, Sennett 2, Arbuckle 3)
Masquerader, 1922 (Buckland 4)
Masquerader, 1933 (Colman 3, Day 4, Estabrook 4, Goldwyn 4, Newman 4, Toland 4)
Masqueraders, 1906 (Bitzer 4)
Masques, 1952 (Alexeieff and Parker 2)
Mass Appeal, 1985 (Lemmon 3)
Mass for the Dakota Sioux, 1964 (Baillie 2)
Mass Mouse Meeting, 1943 (Fleischer, M. and D. 2)
Mass Production of Eggs. See Nagyuzemi tojástermelés, 1962
Massacre, 1912 (Griffith 2, Barrymore L. 3, Sweet 3, Bitzer 4)
Massacre, 1934 (Crosland 2, Barthelmess 3, Muse 3, Barnes 4, Orry-Kelly 4)
Massacre, 1969 (Reichenbach 2)
Massacre en dentelles, 1951 (Audiard 4)
Massacre Hill. See Eureka Stockade, 1949
Massacre in Rome. See Rappresaglia, 1973
Massacre of Sante Fe Trail, 1912 (Ince 4)
Massacre River, 1949 (Cody 3)
Massaggiatrici, 1962 (Noiret 3)
Massnahmen gegen Fanatiker, 1970 (Herzog 2)
Master. See Roda tornet, 1914
Master and Margherite. See Maestro e Margerita, 1972
Master and the Man, 1911 (Pickford 3, Gaudio 4)
Master Gunfighter, 1975 (Reynolds 4, Schifrin 4)
Master Hand, 1917 (Edeson 4)
Master Ideál. See Kantor Ideál, 1932
Master Mind, 1914 (DeMille 2, Darwell 3)

Master of Ballantrae, 1953 (Flynn 3, Adam 4, Alwyn 4, Cardiff 4)
Master of Ballantrae, 1984 (York, M. 3)
Master of Bankdam, 1947 (Fisher 2)
Master of His House, 1915 (Talmadge, C. 3)
Master of Lassie. See Hills of Home, 1948
Master of Love. See Herr der Liebe, 1919
Master of Love. See Maestro d'amore, 1977
Master of Men, 1933 (Wray 3, August 4)
Master of the House. See Du Skal Aere Din Hustru, 1925
Master of the Islands. See Hawaiians, 1970
Master of the Sea, 1941 (Hamer 2)
Master of the Vineyard, 1911 (Dwan 2)
Master of the World, 1961 (Bronson 3, Price 3)
Master Samuel. See Masterman, 1920
Master Touch. See Uomo da rispettare, 1973
Master V. See 'Pimpernel' Smith, 1941
Master Will Shakespeare, 1936 (Howard, L. 3)
Master Zoard. See Zoárd Mester, 1917
Masterman, 1920 (Sjostrom 2, Jaenzon 4, Magnusson 4)
Mastermind, 1920 (Barrymore L. 3)
Master's Wife, (Johnson, N. 3)
Masterson of Kansas, 1954 (Katzman 4)
Mastertjuven, 1915 (Stiller 2, Zaenzon 4)
Mastery of the Sea, 1941 (Cavalcanti 2)
Mat, 1926 (Pudovkin 2, Baranovskaya 3, Golovnya 4)
Mat, 1956 (Donskoi 2, Batalov 3, Maretskaya 3)
Mata au hi made, 1932 (Ozu 2)
Mata au hi made, 1950 (Imai 2, Okada 3)
Mata Hari, 1927 (Kortner 3, Junge 4)
Mata Hari, 1932 (Auer 3, Barrymore L. 3, Garbo 3, Novarro 3, Stone 3, Daniels 4, Glazer 4)
Mata Hari, 1984 (Golan and Globus 4)
Mata Hari, the Red Dancer. See Mata Hari, 1927
Mata Hari. See Spionin, 1921
Mata-Hari, Agent H-21, 1964 (Denner 3, Léaud 3, Moreau 3, Trintignant 3)
Matatabi, 1973 (Ichikawa 2)
Match Breaker, 1921 (Mandell 4)
Match Criqui-Ledoux, 1922 (Chevalier 3)
Match de boxe entre patineurs à roulettes, 1912 (Linders 3)
Match de catch, 1961 (Braunberger 4)
Match des Goldes, 1912 (Nielsen 3)
Match King, 1932 (Grot 4, Orry-Kelly 4)
Match Play, 1930 (Sennett 2)
Matches, 1913 (Dwan 2)
Matching Dreams, 1916 (Eason 4)
Matchless, 1966 (Lattuada 2, Pleasance 3, Morricone 4)
Matchmaker, 1911 (Lawrence 3)
Matchmaker, 1958 (MacLaine 3, Perkins 3, Deutsch 4, Hayes 4, Head 4, Lang 4, Westmore, F. 4)
Matchmaking Mamas, 1929 (Sennett 2, Lombard 3, Hornbeck 4)
Mate a la vida, 1953 (Armendáriz 3)
Mate of the Alden Bessie, 1912 (Bosworth 3)
Mate of the Sally Ann, 1917 (King 2)
Matelas alcoolique, 1906 (Guy 2)
Maten al león, 1975 (Figueroa 4)
Matenuto, 1961 (Tognazzi 3)
Mater dolorosa, 1910 (Feuillade 2)
Mater Dolorosa, 1917 (Gance 2, Modot 3, Burel 4)
Mater Dolorosa, 1923 (Walbrook 3)
Mater Dolorosa, 1933 (Gance 2, Artaud 3)
Materi i docheri, 1974 (Gerasimov 2)
Matériaux nouveaux, demeures nouvelles, 1956 (Colpi 4)
Maternelle, 1933 (Benoit-Lévy 2, Fradetal 4)
Maternité, 1927 (Benoit-Lévy 2)
Maternité, 1935 (Rosay 3, Ibert 4, Matras 4)
Maternity, 1917 (Brady 3)
Maternity. See Maternité, 1927
Maternity Hospital, 1971 (Vukotić 4)
Mates and Models, 1919 (Hardy 3)
Mathias Sandorf, 1921 (Modot 3)
Mathias Sandorf, 1962 (Blier 3, Jourdan 3, Spaak 4)
Matières nouvelles, 1964 (Storck 2)

Matilda, 1978 (Gould 3, Mitchum 3, Leven 4)
Matilda's Legacy, 1915 (Hardy 3)
Matinee Idol, 1920 (Capra 2)
Matinee Idol, 1928 (Love 3)
Matinee Idol, 1933 (Bennett 4)
Matinee Ladies, 1927 (Blanke 4, Buchman 4)
Matinee Scandal. *See* One Rainy Afternoon, 1936
Mating Call, 1928 (Cruze 2, Adorée 3, Mankiewicz 4)
Mating Game, 1959 (Douglas, P. 3, Merkel 3, Reynolds, D. 3, Rose 4)
Mating of Millie, 1948 (Ford, G. 3, Walker 4)
Mating Season, 1951 (Leisen 2, Hopkins, M. 3, Ritter 3, Brackett, C. 4, Lang 4, Reisch 4)
Matira Manisha, 1967 (Sen 2)
Matisse, or The Talent for Happiness, 1960 (Ophuls 2, Dauphin 3)
Matka Joanna od Aniolów, 1961 (Kawalerowicz 2, Konwicki 4)
Matka Kráčmerka, 1934 (Vích 4)
Matous the Shoemaker. *See* O ševci Matoušovi, 1948
Matrero, 1939 (Alton, J. 4)
Matriarca, 1969 (Trintignant 3)
Matriarhat, 1977 (Paskaleva 3)
Matrices, 1965 (Halas and Batchelor 2)
Matricule 33, 1933 (Feuillère 3)
Matrimaniac, 1916 (Fleming 2, Fairbanks, D. 3, Talmadge, C. 3, Emerson 4, Loos 4)
Matrimonial Bed, 1930 (Curtiz 2)
Matrimonial Boomerang, 1915 (Mix 3)
Matrimonial Maneuvers, 1913 (Costello, M. 3)
Matrimonial Problem. *See* Matrimonial Bed, 1930
Matrimonio, 1953 (De Sica 2, Cortese 3, Sordi 3, Vích 4)
Matrimonio all'italiana, 1964 (Castellani 2, De Sica 2, Loren 3, Mastroianni 3, Guerra 4, Ponti 4)
Matrimonio di Caterina, 1982 (Comencini 2)
Matrimony, 1915 (Ince 4, Sullivan 4)
Matri-Phony, 1942 (Three Stooges 3)
Matrix and Joseph's Coat, 1973 (Le Grice 2)
Matsudaira Choshichiro, 1930 (Hasegawa 3)
Matsui-uta Mitokichi goroshi, 1932 (Hasegawa 3)
Mattatore, 1960 (Risi 2, Scola 2, Gassman 3, Age and Scarpelli 4)
Mattei Affair. *See* Caso Mattei, 1972
Matteita otoko, 1942 (Hasegawa 3, Takamine 3, Yamada 3)
Matter of Dignity. *See* To telefteo psema, 1957
Matter of Humanities. *See* Marcus Welby, M.D., 1969
Matter of Innocence. *See* Pretty Polly, 1967
Matter of Life and Death, 1946 (Powell and Pressburger 2, Attenborough 3, Massey 3, Niven 3, Cardiff 4, Ellenshaw 4, Junge 4, Unsworth 4)
Matter of Morals. *See* Sista stegen, 1960
Matter of Resistance. *See* Vie de château, 1966
Matter of Time, 1976 (Minnelli 2, Bergman 3, Boyer 3, Minnelli 3, Rey 3, Unsworth 4)
Matthias Kneissel, 1970 (Fassbinder 2, Hauff 2, Schygulla 3)
Matto Grosso, 1932 (Crosby 4)
Matura, 1965 (Konwicki 4)
Maturareise, 1943 (Feyder 2, Schell, Maria 3)
Maudite soit la guerre, 1910 (Feuillade 2)
Maudits, 1947 (Clément 2, Dalio 3, Alekan 4, Jeanson 4)
Maudits sauvages, 1971 (Lefebvre 2)
Maulkorb, 1937 (Herlth 4)
Maulkorb, 1958 (Staudte 2)
Mauprat, 1926 (Buñuel 2, Epstein 2)
Mauvais coeur puni, 1904 (Guy 2)
Mauvais Coups, 1960 (Signoret 3)
Mauvais Fils, 1980 (Sautet 2)
Mauvais Garçon, 1922 (Chevalier 3)
Mauvais Garçon, 1936 (Darrieux 3)
Mauvaise conduite, 1984 (Almendros 4)
Mauvaise Graine, 1933 (Wilder 2, Darrieux 3)
Mauvaise Soupe, 1899–1900 (Guy 2)
Mauvaise Vie, 1907 (Linders 3)
Mauvaises Fréquentations, 1967 (Léaud 3)
Mauvaises Rencontres, 1955 (Astruc 2, Aimée 3, Dauphin 3, Piccoli 3, Douy 4)
Maverick Queen, 1956 (Stanwyck 3, Young, V. 4)

Max series, from 1910 (Linders 3)
Max and Moritz, 1978 (Halas and Batchelor 2)
Max Beckmann, 1961 (Fusco 4)
Max, der Vielgeprufte, 1920 (Dreier 4)
Max Dugan Returns, 1982 (Robards 3, Sutherland 3)
Max et les ferrailleurs, 1971 (Sautet 2, Piccoli 3, Schneider 3, Sarde 4)
Max Havelaar, 1976 (Rademakers 2)
Max, My Love, 1986 (Carrière 4)
Maxie, 1985 (Gordon 3)
Maxim. *See* Maximka, 1952
Maxime, 1958 (Verneuil 2, Arletty 3, Boyer 3, Morgan 3, Jeanson 4, Matras 4)
Maximenko Brigade. *See* Maksimenko brigád, 1950
Maximka, 1952 (Tikhonov 3)
Maxplatte, Maxplatten, 1965 (Trnka 2)
Max's Feet Are Pinched. *See* Soulier trop petit, 1909
Maxwell's Demon, 1968 (Frampton 2)
May and December, 1910 (Pickford 3)
May Blossom, 1915 (Dwan 2, Crisp 3)
May Stars. *See* Májové hvězdy, 1959
Maya Darpan, 1972 (Chandragupta 4)
Maya, 1936 (Roy 2, Sircar 4)
Maya, 1949 (Dalio 3, Auric 4, Barsacq 4)
Maya, 1961 (Anand 3)
Mayakovski Laughs. *See* Mayakovski smeyetsia, 1975
Mayakovski smeyetsia, 1975 (Yutkevich 2)
Maybe. *See* Chai, 1924
Maybe Darwin Was Right, 1942 (Eason 4)
Maybe I'll Come Home in the Spring, 1971 (Cooper, J 3, Field 3)
Maybe It's Love, 1930 (Wellman 2, Bennett J. 3, Brown 3)
Maybe It's Love, 1934 (Brown, Harry Joe 4, Edeson 4, Orry-Kelly 4, Wald 4)
Mayblossom, 1910–11 (White 3)
Mayday at 40,000 Feet, 1976 (Crawford, B. 3, Milland 3)
Mayerling, 1936 (Litvak 2, Boyer 3, Darrieux 3, Manès 3, Achard 4, Andrejew 4, Annenkov 4, Honegger 4, Jaubert 4)
Mayerling, 1957 (Litvak 2, Ferrer, M. 3)
Mayerling, 1968 (Deneuve 3, Gardner 3, Mason 3, Sharif 3, Alekan 4, Lai 4, Wakhévitch 4)
Mayerling to Sarajevo. *See* De Mayerling à Sarajevo, 1940
Mayflower, 1935 (Terry 4)
Mayflower: The Pilgrim's Adventure, 1979 (Hopkins, A. 3)
May-Fly. *See* Maaneprinsessen, 1916
Maynila sa Kuko nig Liwanag, 1975 (Brocka 2)
Mayol series, 1900–07 (Guy 2)
Mayor of 44th St., 1942 (Barthelmess 3)
Mayor of Hell, 1933 (Cagney 3, Orry-Kelly 4)
Maytime, 1923 (Bow 3, Schulberg 4, Struss 4)
Maytime, 1937 (Barrymore J. 3, Eddy 3, MacDonald 3, Adrian 4, Stothart 4, Stromberg 4, Vorkapich 4)
Maytime in Mayfair, 1949 (Wilcox 2, Neagle 3)
Maytime Tale. *See* Pohádka máje, 1926
Maze, 1953 (Menzies 4, Mirisch 4)
Maze bez rabota, 1973 (Paskaleva 3)
Mazel tov ou le mariage, 1968 (Cloquet 4)
Mazlíček, 1934 (Fric 2, Haas 3, Vích 4)
Mazo, 1952 (Yamada 3)
Mazo kaiketsu-hen, 1931 (Yamada 3)
Mazou, 1938 (Miyagawa 4)
Mazurka, 1935 (Negri 3, Warm 4)
Mazurka di papà, 1938 (De Sica 2)
Mazzabubu . . . quante come stanno quaggiu?, 1971 (Giannini 3)
Mazzetta, 1978 (Manfredi 3)
McCabe and Mrs. Miller, 1971 (Altman 2, Beatty 3, Christie 3, Duvall, S. 3, Zsigmond 4)
McCloud: Who Killed Miss U.S.A.?, 1970 (Bumstead 4)
McConnell Story, 1955 (Allyson 3, Ladd 3, Blanke 4, Seitz 4, Steiner 4
McDougal's Rest Farm, 1947 (Terry 4)
McFadden's Flats, 1927 (Edeson 4)
McFadden's Flats, 1935 (Darwell 3, Robinson 4)
McGuerins from Brooklyn, 1942 (Bendix 3, Roach 4)
McGuire Go Home. *See* High Bright Sun, 1964
McHale's Navy, 1964 (Borgnine 3, Kennedy, G. 3)

McKee Rankin's '49', 1911 (Bosworth 3)
McLintock!, 1963 (De Carlo 3, Martin, S. 3, O'Hara 3, Wayne 3, Clothier 4, Needham 4)
McMasters, 1970 (Carradine 3, Palance 3)
McNaughton's Daughter, 1976 (Bellamy 3)
McQ, 1974 (Sturges, J. 2, Wayne 3, Bernstein 4)
McVeagh of the South Seas, 1914 (Carey 3)
Me an' Bill, 1914 (Mix 3)
Me and Marlborough, 1935 (Saville 2, Balcon 4, Junge 4)
Me and My Gal, 1932 (Walsh 2, Bennett J. 3, Tracy 3, Walthall 3, Miller, A. 4)
Me and My Girl. See Mord Em'ly, 1922
Me and My Pal, 1933 (Laurel & Hardy 3)
Me and the Colonel, 1958 (Jurgens 3, Kaye 3, Rosay 3, Behrman 4, Cloquet 4, Duning 4, Guffey 4, Head 4, Wakhévitch 4)
Me and You. See Mig og dig, 1969
Me faire ça à moi!, 1961 (Constantine 3, Legrand 4)
Me, Gangster, 1928 (Walsh 2, Brown 3, Lombard 3, Edeson 4)
Me gustan valentones, 1958 (Alcoriza 4)
Me he de comer esa tuna, 1944 (Negrete 3)
Me, Natalie, 1969 (Lanchester 3, Pacino 3, Jenkins 4, Mancini 4, Smith, D. 4)
Meadow. See Prato, 1979
Meal Ticket, 1914 (Loos 4)
Mean Dog Blues, 1978 (Kennedy, G. 3)
Mean Frank and Crazy Tony. See Johnny le Fligueur, 1973 (Van Cleef 3)
Mean Johnny Barrows, 1975 (Gould 3, McDowall 3)
Mean Machine. See Longest Yard, 1974
Mean Season, 1984 (Schifrin 4)
Mean Streets, 1973 (Scorsese 2, De Niro 3, Keitel 3)
Meanest Gal in Town, 1934 (Carradine 3, Pitts 3, Hunt 4, Plunkett 4, Steiner 4)
Meanest Man in the World, 1923 (Sweet 3)
Meanest Man in the World, 1943 (Seaton 2, Gwenn 3, Day 4)
Measure of a Man, 1915 (Chaney Lon 3)
Measure of Man, 1969 (Halas and Batchelor 2)
Meat, 1975 (Wiseman 2)
Meat and Romance, 1940 (Ladd 3)
Meatcleaver Massacre, 1977 (Lee, C. 3)
Meatless Flyday, 1943 (Freleng 4)
Mecánica nacional, 1971 (García 3, Alcoriza 4)
Mécaniciens de l'armée de l'air, 1959 (Lelouch 2)
Mechanic, 1972 (Bronson 3, Wynn 3)
Mechanical Bird, 1952 (Terry 4)
Mechanical Cow, 1927 (Disney 2)
Mechanical Cow, 1937 (Terry 4)
Mechanical Flea, 1964 (Ivanov-vano 4)
Mechanical Handy Man, 1937 (Lantz 4)
Mechanical Man, 1932 (Lantz 4)
Mechanics of the Brain. See Mekhanikha golovnovo mozga, 1926
Med folket for fosterlandet, 1938 (Borgstrom 3)
Med fuld musik, 1933 (Schenstrom 3)
Med livet som insats, 1940 (Sjoberg 2)
Med mord i bagaget, 1961 (Ireland 3)
Medal for Benny, 1945 (Lamour 3, Dreier 4, Head 4, Young, V. 4)
Medal for the General, 1944 (Alwyn 4)
Medals. See Seven Days Leave, 1930
Medan porten var stangd, 1946 (Bjornstrand 3)
Medan staden sover, 1950 (Bergman 2, Andersson H. 3)
Medbejlerens Haevn, 1910 (Blom 2)
Meddlers, 1912 (Dwan 2)
Meddling Women, 1924 (Barrymore L. 3)
Medea, 1920 (Negri 3, Wegener 3)
Medea, 1969 (Pasolini 2, Mangano 3, Donati 4)
Médécin de service, 1933 (Brasseur 3)
Meden mesac, 1982 (Samardžić 3)
Media tono. See A donde van nuestros hijos, 1958
Medianoche, 1949 (Figueroa 4)
Mediante de Saint-Sulpice, 1923 (Modot 3)
Medic. See Toubib, 1979
Medical Story, 1975 (Ferrer, J. 3)
Medicine Ball Caravan, 1970 (Braunberger 4)

Medicine Ball Caravan. See Caravane d'amour, 1970
Medicine Bottle, 1909 (Griffith 2, Lawrence 3, Bitzer 4)
Medico della Mutua, 1968 (Zampa 2, Sordi 3, Amidei 4)
Medico e lo stregone, 1957 (De Sica 2, Monicelli 2, Mastroianni 3, Sordi 3, Age and Scarpelli 4, Gherardi 4, Rota 4)
Medikus, 1916 (Curtiz 2)
Meditation on Violence, 1948 (Deren 2)
Mediterranean Holiday, 1964 (Kelly, Grace 3)
Méditerranéenne, 1969 (Braunberger 4)
Medium, 1921 (Dagover 3, Krauss 3)
Medium, 1951 (Hammid 2, Wakhévitch 4)
Medium Cool, 1969 (Fields 4, Wexler 4)
Medusa Touch, 1978 (Burton 3, Remick 3)
Medvěd, 1961 (Fric 2)
Medvezhya svadba, 1926 (Tisse 4)
Meenakshi, 1942 (Roy 2, Sircar 4)
Meer, 1927 (George, H. 3, Tschechowa 3)
Meer ruft, 1933 (George, H. 3, Metzner 4)
Meerabai, 1933 (Sircar 4)
Meet Boston Blackie, 1940 (Florey 2, Planer 4)
Meet Danny Wilson, 1951 (Sinatra 3, Winters 3)
Meet Dr. Christian, 1939 (Hersholt 3, Lardner 4)
Meet John Doe, 1941 (Capra 2, Brennan 3, Cooper, Gary 3, Stanwyck 3, Mandell 4, Riskin 4, Tiomkin 4, Vorkapich 4)
Meet John Doughboy, 1941 (Clampett 4)
Meet Marlon Brando, 1965 (Maysles A. and D. 2)
Meet Me after the Show, 1951 (Grable 3, Cole 4, Lemaire 4)
Meet Me at Dawn, 1947 (Litvak 2, Holloway 3, Rutherford 3)
Meet Me at the Fair, 1952 (Sirk 2, Dailey 3)
Meet Me in Las Vegas, 1956 (Charisse 3, Dailey 3, Henreid 3, Horne 3, Lorre 3, Moorehead 3, Reynolds, D. 3, Sinatra 3, Cahn 4, Lennart 4, Pan 4, Pasternak 4, Rose 4)
Meet Me in St. Louis, 1944 (Minnelli 2, Walters 2, Astor 3, Garland 3, O'Brien, M. 3, Edens 4, Freed 4, Gibbons 4, Irene 4, Sharaff 4, Smith, J.M. 4)
Meet Me on Broadway, 1946 (Guffey 4)
Meet Me Tonight, 1952 (Holloway 3, Coward 4, Dillon 4, Havelock-Allan 4)
Meet Mr. Joad, 1942 (Balcon 4)
Meet Mr. Lucifer, 1953 (Holloway 3)
Meet My Girl, 1926 (Sennett 2)
Meet Nero Wolfe, 1936 (Hayworth 3, Schulberg 4)
Meet Sexton Blake, 1944 (Simmons 3)
Meet the Baron, 1933 (Durante 3, Pitts 3, Three Stooges 3, Krasna 4, Mankiewicz 4, Selznick 4)
Meet the Chump, 1941 (Howard, S. 3, Salter 4)
Meet the Fleet, 1940 (Eason 4)
Meet the Missus, 1924 (Roach 4)
Meet the Missus, 1937 (Polglase 4)
Meet the Missus, 1940 (Ladd 3)
Meet the Mob, 1942 (Pitts 3)
Meet the Navy, 1946 (Unsworth 4)
Meet the Nelsons. See Here Come the Nelsons, 1952
Meet the People, 1944 (Allyson 3, Ball 3, Lahr 3, Powell, D. 3, Irene 4, Surtees 4)
Meet the Pioneers, 1948 (Anderson 2)
Meet the Prince, 1926 (Schildkraut 3, Murfin 4, Struss 4)
Meet the Stars No. 4, 1941 (Abbott and Costello 3)
Meet the Stewarts, 1942 (Holden 3)
Meet the Wildcat, 1940 (Bellamy 3, Schildkraut 3, Cortez 4, Salter 4)
Meet Whiplash Willie. See Fortune Cookie, 1966
Meeting Again. See Sakai, 1953
Meeting György Lukács. See Találkozás Lukács György, 1972
Meeting Hearts. See Hjartan som motas, 1914
Meeting in Bucharest. See Setkání v Bukurešti, 1954
Meeting in July. See Setkání v červenci, 1977
Meeting in Leipzig. See Setkání v Lipsku, 1959
Meeting in the Night. See Mote i natten, 1946
Meeting of the Fashion Show, 1965 (Dovniković 4)
Meeting of the Ghost of Après Guerre. See Sengo-ha obake taikai, 1951
Meeting of the Ways, 1912 (Costello, D. 3)
Meeting on the Atlantic. See Spotkanie na Atlantyku, 1979

Merrily We Go to —. *See* Merrily We Go to Hell, 1932
Merrily We Go to Hell, 1932 (Arzner 2, Grant, C. 3, March 3,
    Sidney 3)
Merrily We Live, 1938 (McLeod 2, Bennett C. 3, Burke 3, Irene 4,
    Roach 4)
Merrily We Sing, 1946 (Fleischer, M. and D. 2)
Merrily Yours, 1933 (Temple 3)
Merry Andrew, 1958 (Kaye 3, Diamond 4, Kidd 4, Lennart 4,
    Mercer 4, Plunkett 4, Surtees 4)
Merry Chase, 1950 (Terry 4)
Merry Chase. *See* Resa di Titi, 1945
Merry Christmas, Mr. Lawrence, 1983 (Oshima 2)
Merry Christmas, Mr. Lawrence. *See* Senjo no merii kurisumasu, 1983
Merry Circus. *See* Veselý cirkus, 1950
Merry Comes to Town, 1937 (Pitts 3)
Merry Dog, 1933 (Lantz 4)
Merry Dwarfs, 1929 (Disney 2)
Merry Frinks, 1934 (Beavers 3, Edeson 4, Orry-Kelly 4)
Merry Frolics of Satan. *See* 400 Farces du Diable, 1906
Merry Mannequins, 1937 (Iwerks 4)
Merry Mavericks, 1951 (Three Stooges 3)
Merry Microbes. *See* Joyeux Microbes, 1909
Merry Mix-Up, 1957 (Three Stooges 3)
Merry Monahans, 1944 (O'Connor 3, Salter 4)
Merry Monarch. *See* Abenteuer des Konigs Pausole, 1933
Merry Old Soul, 1933 (Lantz 4)
Merry Old Soul, 1935 (Freleng 4)
**Merry Widow, 1925 (Von Stroheim 2, Gable 3, Gilbert 3, Daniels 4,
    Day 4, Gibbons 4, Glazer 4, Thalberg 4)**
Merry Widow, 1934 (Lubitsch 2, Chevalier 3, Horton 3, MacDonald 3,
    Meek 3, Merkel 3, Adrian 4, Gibbons 4, Raphaelson 4, Stothart 4,
    Thalberg 4, Vajda 4)
Merry Widow, 1952 (Dalio 3, Merkel 3, Turner, L. 3, Cole 4, Levien 4,
    Pasternak 4, Rose 4, Surtees 4)
Merry Widow. *See* Vig özvegy, 1918
Merry Widow Waltz Craze, 1908 (Porter 2)
Merry Widower, 1926 (Laurel 3, Roach 4)
Merry Wives of Gotham. *See* Lights of Old Broadway, 1925
Merry Wives of Reno, 1934 (Beavers 3, Haller 4, Orry-Kelly 4)
Merry Wives of Windsor, 1910 (Selig 4)
Merry-Go-Round, 1923 (Von Stroheim 2, Daniels 4, Day 4,
    Thalberg 4)
Merry-Go-Round, 1979 (Rivette 2)
Merry-Go-Round. *See* Korhinta, 1955
Merry-Go-Round in the Jungle, 1956 (Peterson 2)
Merry-Go-Round of 1938, 1937 (Auer 3, Brady 3, Fazenda 3, Lahr 3)
Mérsékelt égov, 1970 (Torocsik 3)
Merton of the Movies, 1924 (Cruze 2, Brown, K. 4)
Merton of the Movies, 1947 (Grahame 3, Haas 3, Alton, R. 4, Irene 4,
    Rose 4)
Merveilleuse Angélique, 1964 (Trintignant 3)
Merveilleuse Journée, 1981 (Evein 4)
Merveilleuse Tragédie de Lourdes, 1932 (Aumont 3)
Merveilleuse Vie de Jeanne d'Arc, 1928 (Modot 3)
Merveilleuse Visite, 1974 (Carné 2, Evein 4)
Merveilleux éventail vivant, 1904 (Méliès 2)
Merveilleux Parfum d'oseille, 1969 (Rosay 3)
Mes, 1961 (Rademakers 2)
Mes Petites Amoureuses, 1974 (Almendros 4)
Mes tantes et moi, 1936 (Morgan 3)
Mes voisins me font danser, 1909 (Linders 3)
Mesa of Lost Women, 1952 (Struss 4)
Mésaventure d'un charbonnier, 1899–1900 (Guy 2)
Mesék az frógéprol, 1916 (Korda 2)
Meshes of the Afternoon, 1943 (Deren 2, Hammid 2)
Meshi, 1951 (Naruse 2, Hara 3, Yamamura 3, Hayasaka 4)
Mesmerian Experiment. *See* Bacquet de Mesmer, 1905
Message, 1909 (Griffith 2, Bitzer 4)
Message, 1976 (Papas 3, Quinn 3)
Message. *See* Sandesaya, 1960
Message from Geneva, 1936 (Cavalcanti 2)
Message from the Moon, 1911 (Sennett 2)
Message in the Bottle, 1911 (Pickford 3, Gaudio 4, Ince 4)

Message of the Arrow, 1911 (White 3)
Message of the Mouse, 1917 (Blackton 2)
Message of the Violin, 1910 (Griffith 2, Bitzer 4)
Message to Buckshot John, 1915 (Bosworth 3)
Message to Garcia, 1936 (Beery 3, Carradine 3, Hayworth 3,
    Stanwyck 3, Maté 4, Zanuck 4)
Message to Gracias, 1963 (McKimson 4)
Message to Headquarters, 1913 (Cruze 2)
Message to My Daughter, 1973 (Sheen 3)
Message to Napoleon. *See* Budskab til Napoleon paa Elba, 1909
Messager, 1937 (Aumont 3, Blier 3, Gabin 3, Achard 4, Auric 4,
    Lourié 4)
Messager de la lumière, 1938 (Grimault 4)
Messalina, 1951 (Gallone 2, Félix 3)
Messe de minuit, 1906 (Guy 2)
Messenger, 1918 (Hardy 3)
Messenger Boy's Mistake, 1903 (Porter 2, Anderson G. 3)
Messenger to Kearney, 1912 (Bosworth 3)
Messer im Kopf, 1978 (Hauff 2, Ganz 3, Winkler 3)
Messia, 1978 (Rossellini 2)
Messiah. *See* Messia, 1978
Messiah of Evil, 1975 (Cook 3)
Messidor, 1978 (Tanner 2)
Messieurs les ronds-de-cuir, 1959 (Brasseur 3)
Messieurs Ludovic, 1946 (Berry 3, Blier 3, Kosma 4)
Messire Wolodyjowski, 1968 (Nowicki 3)
Město mé naděje, 1978 (Schorm 2)
Město živé vody, 1934 (Hammid 2)
Městomä svou tvář, 1958 (Kachyna 2)
Mesuinu, 1951 (Kyo 3, Shimura 3)
Mészáros László emlékére, 1968 (Mészáros 2)
Metadata, 1971 (Foldès 2)
Metall des Himmels, 1934 (Ruttmann 2)
Metamorfeus, 1969 (Brdečka 4)
Métamorphose des cloportes, 1965 (Brasseur 3, Audiard 4)
Metamorphoses comiques, 1912 (Cohl 2)
Métamorphoses du paysage industriel, 1964–69 (Rohmer 2)
Metamorphosis, 1975 (Nemec 2)
Metamorphosis. *See* FANTASMAGORIE, 1908
Metello, 1969 (Bolognini 2, D'Amico 4, Morricone 4)
Metempsychose, 1907 (Zecca 2)
Meteor, 1979 (Connery 3, Fonda, H. 3, Howard, T. 3, Malden 3,
    Wood 3)
Métier de fous, 1948 (Burel 4)
Metla, 1972 (Grgić 4)
Metro, 1934 (Franju 2)
Métro, 1950 (Leenhardt 2)
Metro By Night. *See* Moskva stroit metro, 1934
Metro lungo cinque, 1961 (Olmi 2)
**Metropolis, 1927 (Lang 2, Frohlich 3, George, H. 3, Rasp 3, Freund 4,
    Pommer 4, Schufftan 4, Von Harbou 4)**
Metropolitan, 1935 (Brady 3, Brennan 3, Darwell 3, Day 4, Maté 4,
    Meredyth 4, Newman 4, Zanuck 4)
Metropolitan Symphony. *See* Tokai kokyogaku, 1929
Metshta, 1943 (Romm 2)
Metti, una sera a cena, 1969 (Girardot 3, Trintignant 3, Argento 4,
    Delli Colli 4, Morricone 4)
Meule, 1963 (Allio 2)
Meunière débauchée, 1934 (d'Arrast 2)
Meurtre en 45 tour, 1960 (Darrieux 3)
Meurtre est un meurtre, 1972 (Chabrol 2, Audran 3)
Meurtres, 1950 (Fernandel 3, Moreau 3, Jeanson 4)
Meurtrier, 1963 (Autant-Lara 2, Aurenche 4, Bost 4, Douy 4)
Meurtrière. *See* Demutige und die Sangerin, 1925
Meus Amigos, 1974 (de Almeida 4)
Meus oito anos, 1956 (Mauro 2)
Mexicali Rose, 1929 (Stanwyck 3, Westmore, M. 4)
Mexicali Rose, 1939 (Autry 3, Farnum 3)
Mexicali Shmoes, 1958 (Freleng 4)
Mexican, 1911 (Dwan 2)
Mexican, 1914 (Mix 3)
Mexican. *See* Hurricane Horseman, 1931
Mexican. *See* Meksikanets, 1955

Mexican Affair. *See* Flor de mayo, 1957
Mexican Baseball, 1947 (Terry 4)
Mexican Boarders, 1961 (Freleng 4)
Mexican Cat Dance, 1962 (Freleng 4)
Mexican Hayride, 1948 (Abbott and Costello 3)
Mexican Manhunt, 1953 (Brent 3)
Mexican Mousepiece, 1966 (McKimson 4)
Mexican Spitfire, 1939 (Velez 3, Polglase 4)
Mexican Spitfire at Sea, 1942 (Pitts 3)
Mexican Spitfire Out West, 1940 (Velez 3, Polglase 4)
Mexican Spitfire's Baby, 1941 (Pitts 3)
Mexican Spitfire's Blessed Event, 1943 (Velez 3)
Mexican Sweethearts, 1909 (Griffith 2, Pickford 3, Bitzer 4)
Mexican Symphony, 1941 (Eisenstein 2)
Mexican Tragedy, 1912 (Ince 4)
Mexicanerin, 1919 (Veidt 3)
Mexicanos al grito de guerra, 1943 (Infante 3)
Mexican's Faith, 1910, (Anderson G. 3)
Mexican's Gratitude, 1909 (Anderson G. 3)
Mexico, 1930 (Lantz 4)
Mexico in Flames, 1982 (Bondarchuk 3)
México mágico, 1980 (Figueroa 4)
Mexico Marches, 1941 (Eisenstein 2)
Mexico, Mexico, 1967 (Reichenbach 2)
Mexico nuevo, 1964 (Reichenbach 2)
Mexico Soon. *See* Jutra Meksyk, 1965
México 2000, 1981 (Figueroa 4)
Meyer als Soldat, 1914 (Lubitsch 2)
Meyer auf der Alm, 1913 (Lubitsch 2)
Meyer aus Berlin, 1919 (Lubitsch 2)
Mezi nebem a zemí, 1958 (Brodský 3, Kopecký 3)
Mezzogiorno di fuoco par Lin-Hao. *See* Mio nome è Shanghai Joe, 1973
Mi candidato, 1938 (Armendáriz 3, Figueroa 4)
Mi madre adorada, 1948 (García 3)
Mi madrecita, 1940 (García 3)
Mi negra o su negra. *See* Bestia negra, 1939
Mi permette babbo, 1956 (Fabrizi 3, Sordi 3)
Mi preferida, 1950 (García 3)
Mi Querida señorita, 1972 (Borau 2)
Mi querido capitán, 1950 (García 3)
Mi viuda alegre, 1941 (Figueroa 4)
Mia signora, 1964 (Bolognini 2, Comencini 2, Mangano 3, Sordi 3)
Mia valle, 1955 (Olmi 2)
Miami, 1924 (Crosland 2)
Miami Exposé, 1956 (Cobb 3, Katzman 4)
Miami Story, 1954 (Katzman 4)
Miarka, Daughter of the Bear. *See* Miarka, fille l'ours, 1920
Miarka, fille l'ours, 1920 (Novello 3)
Miarka, la fille à l'ourse, 1923 (Vanel 3)
Miarka, la fille à l'ours, 1937 (Dalio 3, Honegger 4)
Mice Follies, 1953 (Hanna and Barbera 4)
Mice Follies, 1960 (McKimson 4)
Mice in Council, 1934 (Terry 4)
Mice Will Play, 1938 (Avery 2)
Michael, 1924 (Christensen 2, Dreyer 2, Freund 4, Maté 4, Pommer 4, Von Harbou 4)
Michael and Mary, 1931 (Saville 2, Marshall 3, Balcon 4, Biro 4)
Michael Carmichael, 1972 (Cushing 3)
Michael Kohlhaas—Der Rebell, 1969 (Schlondorff 2, Karina 3)
Michael Kohlhaas—The Rebel. *See* Michael Kohlhaas—Der Rebell, 1969
Michael McShane, Matchmaker, 1912 (Bunny 3)
Michael O'Halloran, 1923 (Boyd 3)
Michael O'Halloran, 1937 (Brown, K. 4)
Michael O'Hara the Fourth, 1972 (Dailey 3)
Michael Shayne, Private Detective, 1940 (Day 4)
Michael Strogoff, 1914 (Guy 2)
Michael Strogoff, 1936 (Walbrook 3)
Michael Strogoff. *See* Michel Strogoff, 1926
Michael Strogoff. *See* Soldier and the Lady, 1936
Michael the Brave, 1969 (Welles 2)
Michel Strogoff, 1926 (Mozhukin 3, Burel 4)

Michel Strogoff, 1935 (Delannoy 2, Vanel 3)
Michel Strogoff, 1956 (Gallone 2, Fabian 3, Jurgens 3, Barsacq 4)
Michelino la B, 1956 (Olmi 2)
Michigan Kid, 1928 (Adorée 3, Fulton 4)
Michigan Kid, 1946 (Miller, V. 4, Salter 4)
Michki protiv Youdenitsa, 1925 (Gerasimov 2, Kozintsev 2)
Michman Panin, 1960 (Tikhonov 3)
Michurin, 1948 (Dovzhenko 2, Bondarchuk 3, Shostakovich 4)
Mickey, 1918 (Sennett 2, Normand 3)
Mickey, 1948 (McDaniel 3)
Mickey series, 1927–34 (Rooney 3)
Mickey and His Goat, 1917 (O'Brien 4)
Mickey One, 1965 (Penn 2, Beatty 3, Cloquet 4, Jenkins 4)
Mickey Rooney, Then and Now, 1953 (Rooney 3)
Mickey, the Kid, 1939 (Pitts 3)
Mickey's Choo Choo, 1929 (Disney 2, Iwerks 4)
Mickey's Follies, 1929 (Iwerks 4)
Mickey's Naughty Nightmares, 1917 (O'Brien 4)
Mickey's Pal, 1912 (Guy 2)
Micki and Maude, 1985 (Moore, D. 3, Legrand 4)
Micro-Phonies, 1945 (Three Stooges 3)
Microscope Mystery, 1916 (Talmadge, C. 3)
Mid Channel, 1920 (Edeson 4)
Midareboshi Aragami-yama, 1950 (Yamada 3)
Midare-gami, 1961 (Kinugasa 2)
Midaregumo, 1967 (Naruse 2, Mori 3, Tsukasa 3, Takemitsu 4)
Midareru, 1964 (Naruse 2, Takamine 3)
Midas Run, 1969 (Astaire 3, McDowall 3, Richardson 3, Bernstein 4)
Midas Valley, 1985 (Simmons 3)
Middies Shortening Sail, 1901 (Bitzer 4)
Middle Age Crazy, 1980 (Dern 3)
Middle of the Night, 1959 (Grant, L. 3, March 3, Novak 3, Chayefsky 4)
Middle of the Road Is a Very Dead End. *See* In Gefahr und grösster Not bringt der Mittelweg den Tod, 1974
Middle Watch, 1939 (Buchanan 3)
Middleman. *See* Jana Aranya, 1975
Middlin' Stranger, 1927 (Karloff 3)
Midget's Revenge, 1912 (Talmadge, N. 3)
Midi à quatorze heures, 1972 (Foldès 4)
Midlanders, 1920 (Love 3)
Midnight, 1931 (Bennett 4)
Midnight, 1934 (Bogart 3)
Midnight, 1939 (Leisen 2, Wilder 2, Ameche 3, Astor 3, Barrymore J. 3, Colbert 3, Brackett, C. 4, Dreier 4, Head 4, Irene 4, Lang 4)
Midnight Adventure, 1909 (Griffith 2, Pickford 3, Bitzer 4)
Midnight Alibi, 1934 (Crosland 2, Barthelmess 3, Orry-Kelly 4)
Midnight Angel, 1941 (Siodmak 4)
Midnight at Madame Tussaud's, 1937 (Pearson 2)
Midnight Club, 1933 (Brook 3, Raft 3, Banton 4)
Midnight Court, 1937 (Raksin 4)
Midnight Cowboy, 1969 (Schlesinger 2, Hoffman 3, Voight 3, Barry 4, Salt 4, Smith, D. 4)
Midnight Cupid, 1910 (Griffith 2, Bitzer 4)
Midnight Daddies, 1929 (Sennett 2, Hornbeck 4)
Midnight Elopement, 1912 (Sennett 2, Normand 3)
Midnight Episode, 1950 (Holloway 3)
Midnight Event. *See* Pulnoční příhoda, 1960
Midnight Express, 1924 (Johnson, N. 3)
Midnight Express, 1978 (Hurt, J. 3)
Midnight Frolics, 1938 (Iwerks 4)
Midnight Girl, 1925 (Lugosi 3, Fort 4)
Midnight Intruder, 1938 (Krasner 4)
Midnight Kiss, 1926 (Gaynor 3)
Midnight Lace, 1960 (Day 3) (Harrison 3, Loy 3, Marshall 3, McDowall 3, Hunter 4, Irene 4)
Midnight Life, 1928 (Bushman 3)
Midnight Lovers, 1926 (Nilsson 3, Stone 3, Wilson, C. 4)
Midnight Madness, 1928 (Brook 3, Adrian 4)
Midnight Madonna, 1937 (Head 4)
Midnight Man, 1917 (Meredyth 4)
Midnight Man, 1974 (Lancaster 3)

Midnight Mary, 1933 (Wellman 2, Merkel 3, Young, L. 3, Adrian 4, Loos 4)
Midnight Menace, 1936 (Kortner 3)
Midnight Molly, 1925 (Berman 4)
Midnight Mystery, 1930 (Plunkett 4, Walker 4)
Midnight Parasites, 1972 (Kuri 4)
Midnight Patrol, 1918 (Ince 4)
Midnight Patrol, 1932 (Auer 3)
Midnight Patrol, 1933 (Laurel & Hardy 3, Roach 4)
Midnight Ride of Paul Revere, 1907 (Porter 2)
Midnight Romance, 1919 (Weber 2)
Midnight Snack, 1941 (Hanna and Barbera 4)
Midnight Story, 1957 (Curtis 3, Salter 4)
Midnight Supper, 1909 (Porter 2)
Midnight Taxi, 1928 (Loy 3, Zanuck 4)
Midnight Taxi, 1937 (Chaney Lon, Jr. 3)
Midori naki shima, 1948 (Yamamura 3)
Midori no daichi, 1941 (Shindo 3, Hayasaka 4)
Midori no nakama, 1954 (Mori 3)
Midorino furusato, 1946 (Hara 3)
Midshipmaid, 1932 (Bruce 3, Matthews 3, Mills 3)
Midshipmaid Gob. See Midshipmaid, 1932
Midshipman, 1925 (Boyd 3, Novarro 3, Wilson, C. 4)
Midshipman, 1932 (Balcon 4, Junge 4)
Midshipman Easy, 1935 (Dickinson 2, Reed 2, Dean 4)
Midshipman Jack, 1933 (D'Agostino 4, Plunkett 4, Polglase 4, Steiner 4)
Midsommer. See Gamle Købmandshus, 1911
Midsummer Day's Work, 1939 (Cavalcanti 2)
Midsummer Mush, 1933 (Roach 4)
Midsummer Music, 1960 (Lassally 4)
Midsummer Night's Dream, 1909 (Costello, M. 3)
Midsummer Night's Dream, 1935 (Dieterle 2, Brown 3, Cagney 3, De Havilland 3, Powell, D. 3, Rooney 3, Blanke 4, Grot 4, Korngold 4, Wallis 4, Westmore, P. 4)
Midsummer Night's Dream, 1961 (Burton 3)
Midsummer Night's Dream. See Sommernachtstraum, 1924
Midsummer Night's Dream. See Sen noci svatojánske, 1959
Midsummer Night's Sex Comedy, 1982 (Allen 2, Farrow 3, Ferrer, J. 3, Steenburgen 3, Willis 4)
Midsummer Nightmare, 1957 (Halas and Batchelor 2)
Midsummer-Time. See Gamle Kobmandshus, 1911
Midvinterblot, 1946 (Bjornstrand 3)
Midway, 1976 (Coburn, J. 3, Fonda, H. 3, Ford, G. 3, Heston 3, Mifune 3, Mitchum 3, Robertson 3, Wagner 3, Mirisch 4, Williams, J. 4)
Midwinter Blood. See Midvinterblot, 1946
Midwinter Trip to Los Angeles, 1912 (Dwan 2)
Miel se fue de la luna, 1951 (García 3, Alcoriza 4)
Miente y serás feliz, 1939 (García 3)
Mientras México duerme, 1938 (Figueroa 4)
Miércoles de ceniza, 1958 (Félix 3)
Miért rosszak a magyar filmek?, 1964 (Gabór 3)
Mig og dig, 1969 (Henning-Jensen 2)
Mighty, 1929 (Cromwell 2, Auer 3, Oland 3, Hunt 4, Mankiewicz 4)
Mighty Barnum, 1934 (Beery 3, Menjou 3, Day 4, Meredyth 4, Newman 4, Zanuck 4)
Mighty Hunters, 1940 (Jones 2)
Mighty Joe Young, 1949 (Schoedsack 2, Johnson, B. 3, Basevi 4, Cooper 4, Dunn 4, Harryhausen 4, Hunt 4, O'Brien 4)
Mighty Lak a Goat, 1942 (Gardner 3)
Mighty Lak a Rose, 1923 (Polito 4)
Mighty Like a Moose, 1926 (McCarey 2, Roach 4)
Mighty McGurk, 1947 (Beery 3, Irene 4)
Mighty Mouse series, 1944 (Terry 4)
Mighty Navy, 1941 (Fleischer, M. and D. 2)
Mighty Penny, 1942 (Balcon 4)
Mighty Treve, 1937 (Raksin 4)
Mignon, 1900–07 (Guy 2)
Mignon or The Child of Fate, 1912 (Guy 2)
Migrants, 1974 (Spacek 3)
Migratory Birds Under the Moon. See Tsuki no watari-dori, 1951
Mikado, 1939 (Dickinson 2, Dillon 4)

Mikado, 1967 (Fisher 4, Havelock-Allan 4)
Mike, 1926 (Neilan 2)
Mike and Jake at the Beach, 1913 (Fazenda 3)
Mike Fright, 1934 (Roach 4)
Mike's Murder, 1984 (Allen, D. 4, Barry 4)
Mikey and Nicky, 1976 (Falk 3, Ballard 4)
Mikis Theodorakis: A Profile of Greatness, 1974 (Bates 3)
Mikkel, 1948 (Roos 2)
Miklós Borsós. See Borsós Miklós, 1965
Mikolás Aleš, 1951 (Kopecký 3)
Mikosch ruckt ein, 1928 (Metzner 4)
Mikromakrokosmos, 1960 (Brdečka 4)
Mikti, 1937 (Sircar 4)
Mil, 1962 (Rouch 2)
Mil Amores, 1954 (Infante 3)
Mil huit cent quatorze, 1910 (Feuillade 2)
Miláček pluku, 1931 (Vích 4)
Milan, 1946 (Biswas 4)
Milana the Millionairess. See Milano miliardaria, 1951
Milanesi a Napoli, 1954 (Tognazzi 3)
Milano miliardaria, 1951 (Loren 3, Delli Colli 4)
Milano nera, 1963 (Fusco 4)
Milano odia: la polizia no puo sparare, 1974 (Morricone 4)
Milap, 1954 (Anand 3)
Milczenie, 1963 (Cybulski 3)
Mildred Pierce, 1945 (Curtiz 2, Arden 3, Crawford, J. 3, McQueen, B. 3, Friedhofer 4, Grot 4, Haller 4, Steiner 4, Wald
Mile de Jules Ladoumègue, 1932 (Kaufman 4)
Mile-a-Minute Romeo, 1923 (Mix 3)
Milenky starého kriminálnika, 1927 (Ondra 3)
Milestones, 1920 (Stone 3)
Milestones, 1975 (Kramer, R. 2)
Milestones of the Movies, 1966 (Clarke, C.C. 4)
Mili, 1975 (Bachchan 3, Burman 4)
Milieu du monde, 1974 (Tanner 2)
Militaire et nourrice, 1904 (Guy 2)
Militant School Ma'am, 1914 (Mix 3)
Militant Suffragette, 1912 (Cruze 2)
Militant Suffragette. See Busy Day, 1914
Militare e mezzo, 1960 (Fabrizi 3)
Militarists. See Gunbatsu, 1970
Military Academy, 1940 (Brown, K. 4)
Military Judas, 1913 (Ince 4)
Military Life, Pleasant Life. See Život vojenský, život veselý, 1934
Military Policemen. See Off Limits, 1952
Milk and Money, 1936 (Avery 2)
Milk for Baby, 1938 (Terry 4)
Milk We Drink, 1913 (Sennett 2)
Milkfed Boy, 1914 (Crisp 3)
Milkman, 1932 (Iwerks 4)
Milkman, 1950 (Durante 3, O'Connor 3, Boyle 4)
Milky Waif, 1946 (Hanna and Barbera 4)
Milky Way, 1922 (Van Dyke, W.S. 2)
Milky Way, 1936 (McCarey 2, Lloyd 3, Menjou 3, Head 4)
Milky Way. See Voie lactée, 1969
Mill Buyers, 1912 (Lawrence 3)
Mill of Life, 1914 (Costello, M. 3, Talmadge, N. 3)
Mill on the Floss, 1937 (Mason 3)
Mill on the Po. See Mulino del Po, 1949
Millard un billard, 1965 (Seberg 3)
Mille et Deuxième Nuit, 1933 (Modot 3, Mozhukin 3, Maté 4)
Mille et un millions, 1955 (Burel 4)
Mille et une nuits, 1922 (Modot 3)
Mille et une nuits. See Meraviglie di Aladino, 1961
Mille lire al mese, 1939 (Zampa 2, Valli 3)
Mille milliards de dollars, 1981 (Verneuil 2, Ferrer, M. 3, Moreau 3)
Mille villages, 1960 (Rabier 4)
1860, 1934 (Blasetti 2)
Miller Karafiat. See Pan otec Karafiat, 1935
Miller's Beautiful Daughter. See Bella mugnaia, 1955
Miller's Beautiful Wife. See Bella mugnaia, 1955
Miller's Daughter, 1934 (Freleng 4)

Minute to Pray, a Second to Die. *See* Minuto per pregare, un instante per morire, 1968
Minuteros, 1972–73 (Ruiz 2)
Minuto per pregare, un instante per morire, 1968 (Kennedy, A. 3)
Mio, 1970 (Hani 2)
Mio amico Jekyll, 1960 (Tognazzi 3)
Mio caro assassino, 1972 (Morricone 4)
Mio Dio, come sono caduta in basso!, 1974 (Comencini 2, Delli Colli 4)
Mio figlio Nerone, 1956 (De Sica 2, Bardot 3, Sordi 3, Swanson 3, Cristaldi 4)
Mio figlio professore, 1946 (Castellani 2, Fabrizi 3, D'Amico 4, Rota 4)
Mio nome e nessuno, 1974 (Fonda, H. 3, Morricone 4)
Mio nome è Shanghai Joe, 1973 (Kinski 3)
Mio Padre Monsignore, 1971 (Giannini 3)
Mioche, 1936 (Morgan 3, Spaak 4)
Miquette. *See* Miquette et sa mère, 1949
Miquette et sa mère, 1933 (Simon, M. 3, Fradetal 4)
Miquette et sa mère, 1940 (Gélin 3)
Miquette et sa mère, 1949 (Clouzot 2, Bourvil 3, Jouvet 3, Wakhévitch 4)
Mira, 1971 (Rademakers 2, Delerue 4)
Mira, 1977 (Shankar 4)
Mira ka Chitra, 1960 (Biswas 4)
Miracle, 1954 (Breer 2)
Miracle, 1958 (Cooper, Gladys 3)
Miracle, 1959 (Baker C. 3, Cooper, Gladys 3, Gassman 3, Moore, R. 3, Bernstein 4, Blanke 4, Haller 4)
Miracle. *See* Miracolo, 1948
Miracle. *See* Miraklet, 1913
Miracle Baby, 1923 (Carey 3)
Miracle Can Happen, 1947 (Huston 2, Goddard 3, Biroc 4, Cronjager 4, Laszlo 4, Seitz 4)
Miracle Can Happen. *See* On Our Merry Way, 1947
Miracle des loups, 1924 (Modot 3)
Miracle des loups, 1961 (Barrault 3)
Miracle des roses, 1908 (Cohl 4)
Miracle in Harlem, 1937 (Micheaux 2)
Miracle in Harlem, 1947 (Fetchit 3)
Miracle in Milan. *See* Miracolo a Milano, 1950
Miracle in Soho, 1957 (Cusack 3, Dillon 4)
Miracle in the Rain, 1956 (Dalio 3, Johnson, V. 3, Wyman 3, Hecht 4, Maté 4, Waxman 4)
Miracle Makers, 1923 (Van Dyke, W.S. 2)
Miracle Man, 1919 (Chaney Lon 3)
Miracle Man, 1932 (McLeod 2, Bosworth 3, Karloff 3, Sidney 3, Laszlo 4, Young, W. 4)
Miracle of Father Malachias. *See* Wunder des Malachias, 1961
Miracle of Hickory, 1944 (Garson 3)
Miracle of Morgan's Creek, 1944 (Sturges, P. 2, Hutton 3, Dreier 4, Head 4, Seitz 4)
Miracle of Our Lady of Fatima, 1952 (Steiner 4)
Miracle of the Bells, 1948 (Cobb 3, MacMurray 3, Sinatra 3, Valli 3, Cahn 4, Hecht 4, Lasky 4)
Miracle of the White Stallions, 1963 (Disney 2, Hiller 2, Jurgens 3, Taylor, R. 3)
Miracle of the Wolves. *See* Miracle des loups, 1924
Miracle on Ice, 1981 (Malden 3)
Miracle on Main Street, 1939 (Darwell 3, Salter 4)
Miracle on 34th Street, 1947 (Seaton 2, Gwenn 3, O'Hara 3, Ritter 3, Wood 3, Clarke, C.C. 4, Day 4, Lemaire 4, Zanuck 4, Newman 4)
Miracle on 34th Street, 1974 (McDowall 3)
Miracle Rider, 1935 (Mix 3, Eason 4)
Miracle sous l'inquisition, 1904 (Méliès 2)
Miracle Under the Inquisition. *See* Miracle sous l'inquisition, 1904
Miracle Woman, 1931 (Capra 2, Stanwyck 3, Swerling 4, Walker 4)
Miracle Worker, 1962 (Penn 2, Bancroft 3, Jenkins 4)
Miracles de Brahmane, 1900 (Méliès 2)
Miracles for Sale, 1939 (Browning 2, Young, R. 3)
Miracles n'ont lieu qu'une fois, 1951 (Allégret, Y. 2, Marais 3, Valli 3, Trauner 4)
Miracles of Brahmin. *See* Miracles de Brahmane, 1900
Miracles Still Happen. *See* Es geschehen noch Wunder, 1952
Miracolo, 1948 (Rossellini 2)
Miracolo a Loreto, 1949 (Zavattini 4)

Miracolo a Milano, 1950 (De Sica 2, Aldo 4, D'Amico 4, Di Venanzo 4, Korda 4, Zavattini 4)
Mirage, 1924 (Brook 3, Sullivan 4)
Mirage, 1965 (Dmytryk 2, Kennedy, G. 3, Matthau 3, Peck 3, Jones 4, Whitlock 4)
Mirage, 1981 (Gehr 2)
Mirage in the North. *See* Severnoe siianie, 1926
Mirages, 1937 (Barrault 3, Burel 4)
Mirages. *See* Si tu m'aimes, 1937
Mirages de Paris, 1932 (Andrejew 4, Douy 4, Jaubert 4)
Mirakel der Liebe, 1926 (George, H. 3)
Miraklet, 1913 (Sjostrom 2, Jaenzon 4, Magnusson 4)
Miramar praia das rosas, 1939 (Oliveira 2)
Miranda, 1948 (Rutherford 3)
Mircha, 1936 (Sakall 3)
Mireille, 1900–07 (Guy 2)
Mireille, 1906 (Feuillade 2)
Mireille Mathieu, 1966 (Reichenbach 2)
Mirele Efros, 1912 (Mozhukin 3)
Miren, 1963 (Takemitsu 4)
Miris poljskog cveća, 1977 (Samardžić 3)
Miroir, 1947 (Gabin 3, Gélin 3, Wakhévitch 4)
Miroir à deux faces, 1958 (Cayatte 2, Bourvil 3, Morgan 3)
Miroir aux alouettes, 1934 (Brasseur 3, Feuillère 3)
Mirror, 1911 (Pickford 3, Gaudio 4)
Mirror. *See* Egy tukor, 1971
Mirror. *See* Ogledalo, 1971
Mirror. *See* Zerkalo, 1975
Mirror Animations, 1956 (Smith 2)
Mirror Crack'd, 1980 (Chaplin 3, Curtis 3, Hudson 3, Lansbury 3, Novak 3, Taylor, E. 3)
Mirror from India, 1971 (Anderson 2)
Mirror Has Two Faces. *See* Miroir à deux faces, 1958
Mirror, Mirror, 1980 (Leigh, J. 3)
Mirror of Holland. *See* Spiegel van Holland, 1950
Mirrored Reason, 1980 (Vanderbeek 2)
Mirrors, 1985 (Wynn 3)
Mirsu, 1924 (Kinugasa 2)
Mirth and Melody. *See* Let's go Places, 1929
Mis abuelitas . . . nomás, 1959 (García 3)
Mis hijos, 1944 (García 3)
Míša Kulička, 1947 (Hofman 4)
Misadventures of a Claim Agent, 1912 (Dwan 2)
Misadventures of a Mighty Monarch, 1914 (Bunny 3)
Misadventures of Buster Keaton, 1955 (Keaton 2)
Misadventures of Merlin Jones, 1963 (Disney 2)
Misanthrope, 1966 (Braunberger 4)
Misappropriated Turkey, 1912 (Griffith 2, Bitzer 4)
Misbehaving Husbands, 1940 (Langdon 3, Young, G. 3)
Misbehaving Ladies, 1931 (Fazenda 3, Seitz 4)
Misc. Happenings, 1961-62 (Vanderbeek 2)
Mischances of a Photographer, 1908 (Méliès 2)
Mischief Maker, 1916 (Bosworth 3)
Mischievous Hedgehog, 1952 (Popescu-Gopo 4)
Misemono okoku, 1937 (Takamine 3)
Miser, 1913 (August 4)
Miser Murphy's Wedding Present, 1914 (Talmadge, N. 3)
Miser Punished. *See* Au Clair de la lune ou Pierrot malheureux, 190
Miserabili, 1947 (Monicelli 2, Cervi 3, Cortese 3, Mastroianni 3, Ponti 4)
Miserables, 1917 (Farnum 3)
Misérables, 1934 (Baur 3, Vanel 3, Douy 4, Honegger 4, Jaubert 4)
Miserables, 1935 (Carradine 3, Hardwicke 3, Laughton 3, March 3, Newman 4, Toland 4, Zanuck 4)
Miserables, 1950 (Hayakawa 3)
Miserables, 1952 (Milestone 2, Gwenn 3, Lanchester 3, Sidney 3, Jeakins 4, La Shelle 4, Lemaire 4, Newman 4, North 4)
Misérables, 1957 (Blier 3, Bourvil 3, Gabin 3, Reggiani 3, Audiard 4)
Misérables, 1978 (Cusack 3, Dauphin 3, Gielgud 3, Johnson, C. 3, Perkins 3)
Miserables. *See* Miserabili, 1947
Miseraretaru tamashii, 1953 (Yamada 3)
Misère au Borinage, 1934 (Ivens 2, Storck 2, Van Dongen 4)

Mr. Barnes of New York, 1922 (Novarro 3)
Mr. Belvedere Goes to College, 1949 (Chandler 3, Temple 3, Webb 3, Lemaire 4, Newman 4)
Mr. Belvedere Rings the Bell, 1951 (Webb 3, La Shelle 4, Lang 4, Lemaire 4)
Mister Big, 1943 (O'Connor 3)
Mr. Bigman. See Nagyember, 1968
Mr. Billings Spends His Dime, 1923 (Ruggles 2)
Mr. Blanchard's Secret, 1956 (Hitchcock 2)
Mr. Blandings Builds His Dream House, 1948 (Beavers 3, Douglas, M. 3, Grant, C. 3, Loy 3, McDaniel 3, Frank and Panama 4, Howe 4, Schary 4)
Mr. Bolter's Infatuation, 1912 (Bunny 3)
Mr. Bolter's Niece, 1913 (Bunny 3)
Mr. Bragg, A Fugitive, 1911 (Sennett 2)
Mr. Broadway, 1933 (Ulmer 2, Lahr 3, Velez 3)
Mister Buddwing, 1966 (Lansbury 3, Simmons 3, Rose 4)
Mr. Bug Goes to Town, 1942 (Carmichael 4)
Mr. Bunny in Disguise, 1914 (Bunny 3)
Mr. Bunnyhug Buys a Hat for His Bride, 1914 (Bunny 3)
Mr. Butler Buttles, 1912 (Talmadge, N. 3)
Mr. Butt-In, 1906 (Bitzer 4)
Mr. Carlson From Arizona, (Johnson, N. 3)
Mr. Casanova, 1954 (Head 4)
Mr. Celebrity, 1937 (Bushman 3)
Mr. Chedworth Steps Out, 1939 (Finch 3)
Mr. Chesher's Traction Engines, 1962 (Russell 2)
Mr. Chump, 1938 (Edeson 4)
Mister Cinderella, 1936 (Krasner 4, Roach 4)
Mister Cory, 1957 (Curtis 3)
Mr. Deeds Goes to Town, 1936 (Capra 2, Arthur 3, Cooper, Gary 3, Deutsch 4, Riskin 4, Tiomkin 4, Walker 4)
Mr. Denning Drives North, 1951 (Mills 3)
Mr. Dippy Dipped, 1913 (Beery 3)
Mr. District Attorney, 1941 (Lorre 3, Brown, K. 4)
Mr. District Attorney, 1947 (Glennon 4)
Mr. District Attorney in the Carter Case, 1941 (Alton, J. 4)
Mr. Dodd Takes the Air, 1937 (Brady 3, Wyman 3, Deutsch 4, Edeson 4)
Mr. Dolan of New York, (Johnson, N. 3)
Mister Drake's Duck, 1951 (Fairbanks, D. Jr. 3)
Mister Dynamite, 1935 (Crosland 3)
Mr. Dynamite, 1941 (Howard, S. 3, Salter 4)
Mister 880, 1950 (Goulding 2, Gwenn 3, Lancaster 3, La Shelle 4, Lemaire 4, Riskin 4, Zanuck 4)
Mr. Emmanuel, 1944 (Simmons 3)
Mr. Fix-It, 1912 (Sennett 2, Normand 3)
Mr. Fix-It, 1918 (Dwan 2, Fairbanks, D. 3, Edeson 4)
Mister Flow, 1936 (Siodmak 2, Feuillère 3, Jouvet 3, Jeanson 4)
Mr. Forbush and the Penguins, 1971 (Hurt, J. 3, Addison 4)
Mister 44, 1916 (Gaudio 4)
Mister 420. See Shri 420, 1955
Mister Freedom, 1969 (Montand 3, Noiret 3, Pleasance 3, Seyrig 3, Signoret 3)
Mr. Frenhofer and the Minotaur, 1948 (Peterson 2)
Mr. Gallagher and Mr. Shean, 1931 (Fleischer, M. and D. 2)
Mr. Griggs Returns. See Cockeyed Miracle, 1946
Mr. Grouch at the Seashore, 1911 (Sennett 2)
Mr. Halpern and Mr. Johnson, 1983 (Olivier 3)
Mr. Hayashi, 1961 (Baillie 2)
Mr. Head. See Monsieur Tête, 1959
Mr. Henpeck's Dilemma, 1913 (Pearson 2)
Mr. Hobbs Takes a Vacation, 1962 (O'Hara 3, Stewart 3, Johnson 4, Mancini 4, Mercer 4, Smith, J.M. 4, Wald 4)
Mister Hobo. See Guv'nor, 1935
Mr. Horn, 1979 (Black 3, Widmark 3, Goldman, W. 4)
Mr. Hulot's Holiday. See Vacances de M. Hulot, 1953
Mr. Hurry-Up, 1906 (Bitzer 4)
Mr. Hyppo, 1923 (Roach 4)
Mr. Ikla's Jubilee. See Jubilej gospodina Ikla, 1955
Mr. Imperium, 1951 (Hardwicke 3, Reynolds, D. 3, Turner, L. 3, Kaper 4, Plunkett 4)
Mister Jefferson Green, 1913 (Barrymore L. 3)

Mr. Jones at the Ball, 1908 (Griffith 2, Sennett 2, Lawrence 3, Bitzer Macpherson 4)
Mr. Jones Has a Card Party, 1909 (Griffith 2, Sennett 2, Lawrence 3, Bitzer 4)
Mr. King paa Eventyr. See Aegteskab og Pigesjov, 1914
Mr. Kingstreet's War, 1973 (Hedren 3)
Mr. Kinky. See Profeta, 1967
Mr. Klein, 1977 (Losey 2, Delon 3, Moreau 3, Fisher 4, Solinas 4, Trauner 4)
Mr. Know–How in Hot Water, 1962 (Dunning 4)
Mr. Lemon of Orange, 1931 (August 4)
Mr. Logan, U.S.A., 1918 (Mix 3)
Mr. Lord Says No. See Happy Family, 1952
Mr. Lucky, 1943 (Cooper, Gladys 3, Grant, C. 3, Menzies 4)
Mr. Lucky. See Rakkii-san, 1952
Mr. Magoo series, from 1953 (Burness 4)
Mr. Magoo, 1949 (Hubley 4)
Mr. Majestyk, 1974 (Fleischer, R. 2, Bronson 3, Mirisch 4)
Mr. Marzipan's Marriage. See Zenida gospodina Marcipana, 1963
Mr. Moses, 1965 (Baker C. 3, Mitchum 3, Barry 4, Morris 4)
Mr. Moto in Danger Island, 1939 (Bond 3, Hersholt 3)
Mr. Moto Takes a Chance, 1938 (Lorre 3, Miller, V. 4)
Mr. Moto Takes a Vacation, 1939 (Lorre 3, Schildkraut 3, Clarke, C.C. 4)
Mr. Moto's Gamble, 1938 (Bond 3, Chaney Lon, Jr. 3, Lorre 3)
Mr. Moto's Last Warning, 1939 (Carradine 3, Lorre 3, Sanders 3, Miller, V. 4, Raksin 4)
Mr. Muggs Rides Again, 1945 (Katzman 4)
Mr. Muggs Steps Out, 1943 (Katzman 4)
Mr. Music, 1950 (Coburn, C. 3, Crosby 3, Marx, G. 3, Dreier 4, Head 4)
Mr. Natwarlal, 1979 (Bachchan 3)
Mr. Nobody. See In the Sage Brush Country, 1914
Mr. Orchid. See Père tranquille, 1946
Mr. Patman, 1980 (Coburn, J. 3)
Mr. Peabody and the Mermaid, 1948 (Powell, W. 3, Johnson 4, Leven 4, Mercer 4, Westmore, B. 4)
Mr. Peck Goes Calling, 1911 (Sennett 2)
Mr. Peek-a-boo. See Garou-Garou, le passe-muraille, 1950
Mr. Potts Goes to Moscow. See Top Secret, 1952
Mr. Prokouk series. See Pan Prokouk series, 1947–72
Mr. Proudfoot Shows a Light, 1941 (Gilliat 4)
Mr. Pu. See Puu-san, 1953
Mister Quilp, 1974 (Bernstein 4)
Mr. Ricco, 1975 (Martin, D. 3, Westmore, F. 4)
Mister Roberts, 1955 (Ford, J. 2, Leroy 2, Logan 2, Bond 3, Cagney 3, Fonda, H. 3, Lemmon 3, Powell, W. 3, Hoch 4, Nugent 4, Waxman 4)
Mr. Robinson Crusoe, 1932 (Sutherland 2, Fairbanks, D. 3, Farnum 3, Newman 4)
Mr. Sardonicus, 1961 (Homolka 3, Guffey 4)
Mr. Satan, 1938 (Fisher 2)
Mr. Scarface. See Padroni della città, 1977
Mister Scoutmaster, 1953 (Gwenn 3, Webb 3, La Shelle 4, Lemaire 4)
Mr. Sebastian, 1967 (Gielgud 3)
Mr. Shome. See Bhuvan Shome, 1969
Mr. 'Silent' Haskins, 1915 (Hart 3)
Mr. Skeffington, 1944 (Davis 2, Rains 3, Epstein, J. & P. 4, Haller 4, Orry-Kelly 4, Waxman 4)
Mr. Skitch, 1933 (Cruze 2, Pitts 3, Rogers, W. 3, Levien 4, Seitz 4)
Mr. Slotter's Jubilee. See Pak slaag, 1979
Mr. Smith Carries On, 1937 (Havelock-Allan 4)
Mr. Smith Goes to Washington, 1939 (Capra 2, Arthur 3, Bondi 3, Carey 3, Costello, M. 3, Rains 3, Stewart 3, Buchman 4, Tiomkin 4, Vorkapich 4, Walker 4)
Mr. Smith Wakes Up, 1929 (Lanchester 3)
Mr. Soft Touch, 1949 (Bondi 3, Ford, G. 3, Ireland 3, Walker 4)
Mr. Strauss Takes a Walk, 1942 (Pal 2)
Mr. Sweeney's Masterpiece, 1912–13 (White 3)
Mr. Sycamore, 1975 (Simmons 3, Jarre 4)
Mister Topaz, 1961 (Sellers 3)
Mr. Universe, 1951 (Lahr 3, Tiomkin 4)
Mister V. See 'Pimpernel' Smith, 1941

Model Shop, 1969 (Demy 2, Aimée 3)
Model Wife, 1941 (Blondell 3, Powell, D. 3, Salter 4)
Modelage express, 1903 (Guy 2)
Modeling, 1923 (Fleischer, M. and D. 2)
Models, Inc., 1952 (Cortez 4)
Model's Ma, 1907 (Bitzer 4)
Moderato cantabile, 1960 (Duras 2, Belmondo 3, Moreau 3)
Moderca zostawia ślad, 1967 (Cybulski 3)
Moderens Ojne, 1917 (Borgstrom 3)
Modern DuBarry. See DuBarry von Heute, 1927
Modern Enoch Arden, 1916 (Sennett 2)
Modern Guide to Health, 1946 (Halas and Batchelor 2)
Modern Hero, 1934 (Pabst 2, Barthelmess 3, Beavers 3, Orry-Kelly 4)
Modern Hero, 1941 (Basserman 3)
Modern Hero. See Knute Rockne—All American, 1940
Modern Husbands, 1919 (Walthall 3)
Modern Jack the Ripper. See Farlig Forbryder, 1913
Modern Love, 1929 (Hersholt 3)
Modern Magdalen, 1915 (Barrymore L. 3)
Modern Marriage, 1920 (Bushman 3)
Modern Matrimony, 1923 (Heerman 4)
Modern Miracle. See Story of Alexander Graham Bell, 1939
Modern Mothers, 1928 (Fairbanks, D. Jr. 3, Walker 4)
Modern Musketeer, 1917 (Dwan 2, Fleming 2, Fairbanks, D. 3, Pitts 3)
Modern Prodigal, 1910 (Griffith 2, Bitzer 4)
Modern Red Riding Hood, 1935 (Terry 4)
Modern Rip, 1911 (Bosworth 3)
Modern Rip Van Winkle, 1914 (Eason 4)
Modern Rip Van Winkle. See Modern Rip, 1911
Modern Snare, 1913 (Reid 3)
Modern Times, 1936 (Chaplin 2, Goddard 3, Newman 4, Raksin 4)
Moderna suffragetten, 1913 (Stiller 2)
Moderne Ecole, 1909 (Cohl 2)
Moderne Ehen, 1924 (Dieterle 2, Kortner 3)
Moderner Don Juan, 1927 (Dagover 3)
Moderno Barba azul, 1946 (Keaton 2)
Moders Kaerlighed. See Historien om en Moder, 1912
Moders Kaerlighed. See Største Kaerlighed, 1914
Moderu to wakatono, 1947 (Yoda 4)
Modest Hero, 1913 (Gish, L. 3)
Modesty Blaise, 1966 (Losey 2, Bogarde 3, Stamp 3, Vitti 3, Fisher 4)
Modification, 1969 (Lai 4)
Modigliani of Montparnasse. See Montparnasse 19, 1957
Modiste, 1917 (Hardy 3)
Modré s nebe, 1983 (Brejchová 3)
Modré z nebe, 1962 (Hofman 4)
Modrehjaelpen, 1942 (Dreyer 2)
Moeru aki, 1978 (Takemitsu 4)
Moeru Shanhai, 1954 (Mori 3, Yamamura 3)
Moetikuta chizu, 1968 (Teshigahara 2, Takemitsu 4)
Mogambo, 1953 (Ford, J. 2, Gable 3, Gardner 3, Kelly, Grace 3, Junge 4, Mahin 4, Rose 4, Surtees 4, Young, F. 4)
Mogli pericolose, 1958 (Comencini 2)
Mogliamante, 1977 (Mastroianni 3)
Moglie americana, 1965 (Tognazzi 3, Flaiano 4)
Moglie del prete, 1970 (Risi 2, Loren 3, Mastroianni 3, Ponti 4)
Moglie di mio padre, 1976 (Baker C. 3)
Moglie e buoi . . ., 1956 (Cervi 3)
Moglie è uguale per tutti, 1955 (Tognazzi 3)
Moglie per una notte, 1952 (Cervi 3, Lollobrigida 3)
Moglie più bella, 1970 (Morricone 4)
Moglie virgine, 1976 (Baker C. 3)
Mogotona musume, 1956 (Tsukasa 3)
Mohabbat Ke Ansu, 1932 (Sircar 4)
Mohammad, Messenger of God, 1976 (Jarre 4)
Mohammad, Messenger of God. See Message, 1976
Mohammedan Conspiracy, 1914 (Cruze 2)
Mohan, 1947 (Anand 3)
Mohawk, 1955 (Struss 4)
Mohawk's Way, 1910 (Griffith 2, Bitzer 4)
Moi et l'impératrice, 1933 (Boyer 3, Brasseur 3)
Moi laskovyi i nezhnyi zver, 1978 (Yankovsky 3)

Moi, Pierre Rivière, ayant égorgé ma mère, ma soeur et mon frère, 1976 (Allio 2)
Moi syn, 1928 (Cherkassov 3)
Moi, un noir, 1958 (Rouch 2, Braunberger 4)
Moi universiteti, 1940 (Donskoi 2)
Moi y'en a vouloir des sous, 1973 (Blier 3)
Moine, 1972 (Buñuel 2, Carrière 4, Douy 4, Vierny 4)
Moineaux de Paris, 1953 (Aumont 3)
Mois le plus beau, 1968 (Gélin 3)
Moisson de l'espoir, 1969 (Reichenbach 2)
Moisson sera belle, 1954 (Fradetal 4)
Moissons d'aujourd'hui, 1949 (Cloquet 4)
Moissons de l'espoir, 1969 (Braunberger 4)
Moj tata na otredjeno vreme, 1983 (Samardžić 3)
Moje láska, 1964 (Hofman 4)
Moje žena Penelopa, 1955 (Hofman 4)
Mokey, 1942 (Dailey 3, Reed, D. 3, Rosher 4)
Moko raishu: Tekikoku kofuku, 1937 (Hasegawa 3)
Mokuseki, 1940 (Gosho 2)
Moldavian Fairy Tale. See Moldavskaia skazka, 1951
Moldavskaia skazka, 1951 (Paradzhanov 2)
Mole People, 1956 (Salter 4, Westmore, B. 4)
Molière, 1909 (Gance 2)
Molière, 1955 (Hamer 2, Belmondo 3)
Molière, 1978 (Lelouch 2)
Mollenard, 1938 (Siodmak 2, Baur 3, Dalio 3, Manès 3, Alekan 4, Schufftan 4, Spaak 4, Trauner 4)
Molly and Me, 1929 (Brown 3)
Molly and Me, 1945 (Fields, G. 3, McDowall 3, Clarke, C.C. 4)
Molly Bawn, 1916 (Hepworth 2)
Molly Maguires, 1970 (Ritt 2, Connery 3, Jeakins 4, Mancini 4, Westmore, W. 4)
Molly O', 1921 (Sennett 2, Normand 3, Hackett 4, Hornbeck 4)
Molly Pitcher, 1911 (Nilsson 3)
Mollycoddle, 1920 (Fleming 2, Beery 3, Fairbanks, D. 3)
Moloch, 1978 (Nowicki 3)
Molodaya gvardiya, 1947 (Gerasimov 2, Tikhonov 3, Shostakovich 4)
Molodost nashei strany, 1945 (Yutkevich 2)
Molodo-zeleno, 1962 (Ulyanov 3)
Molti sogni per le strade, 1948 (Magnani 3, De Laurentiis 4, Rota 4)
Mom, the Wolfman, and Me, 1980 (Wynn 3)
Môme vert-de-gris, 1953 (Constantine 3, Modot 3)
Moment. See Øjeblikket, 1980
Moment by Moment, 1978 (Horner 4)
Moment in Love, 1957 (Clarke 2)
Moment of Danger, 1960 (Dandridge 3, Fairbanks, D. Jr. 3, Howard, T. 3)
Moment of Danger. See Malaga, 1960
Moment of Darkness, 1915 (Hepworth 2)
Moment of Indiscretion, 1958 (Roeg 2)
Moment of Terror. See Hikinige, 1966
Moment of Truth. See Minute de vérité, 1952
Moment of Truth. See Momento della verità, 1965
Moment to Moment, 1966 (Leroy 2, Seberg 3, Mahin 4, Mancini 4, Mercer 4, Stradling 4)
Momento della verità, 1965 (Rosi 2, Di Venanzo 4)
Momento piú bello, 1957 (Mastroianni 3, Amidei 4, Rota 4)
Momentos de la vida de Martí. See Rosa blanca, 1953
Momma Don't Allow, 1956 (Reisz 2, Richardson 2, Lassally 4)
Mommie Dearest, 1981 (Dunaway 3, Mancini 4, Sharaff 4)
Mommilan Veriteot 1917, 1973 (Donner 2)
Mommilla Murders. See Mommilan Veriteot 1917, 1973
Mommy Loves Puppy, 1940 (Fleischer, M. and D. 2)
Mon ami Pierre, 1951 (Kosma 4)
Mon ami Victor, 1932 (Brasseur 3, Périnal 4)
Mon Amie Pierrette, 1967 (Lefebvre 2)
Mon amie Sylvie, 1972 (Reichenbach 2)
Mon amour est près de toi, 1943 (Andrejew 4)
Mon amour, mon amour, 1967 (Piccoli 3, Trintignant 3, Lai 4)
Mon and Ino. See Ani imoto, 1976
Mon cas, 1986 (Branco 4)
Mon Chapeau, 1933 (Dalio 3)
Mon chien, 1955 (Franju 2)

Monsieur Beaucaire, 1924 (Olcott 2, Daniels 3, Valentino 3, Braunberger 4, Westmore, M. 4)
Monsieur Beaucaire, 1946 (Crosby 3, Hope 3, Schildkraut 3, Dreier 4, Frank and Panama 4, Head 4)
Monsieur Bébé. *See* Bedtime Story, 1933
Monsieur Bibi. *See* Faut ce qu'il faut, 1940
Monsieur Brotonneau, 1939 (Pagnol 2, Raimu 3, Courant 4)
Monsieur Clown chez les Lilliputiens, 1909 (Cohl 2)
Monsieur Cordon, 1933 (Aurenche 4)
Monsieur de compagnie, 1964 (Broca 2, Cassel 3, Dalio 3, Deneuve 3, Girardot 3, Coutard 4, Delerue 4)
Monsieur de Crac, 1910 (Cohl 2)
Monsieur de minuit, 1931 (Maté 4, Meerson 4)
Monsieur de Voltaire, 1963 (Leenhardt 2)
Monsieur Don't-Care, 1924 (Laurel 3)
Monsieur et Madame Curie, 1953 (Franju 2, Fradetal 4)
Monsieur Fabre, 1951 (Fresnay 3, Renoir 4)
Monsieur Gregoire s'évadé, 1946 (Berry 3, Blier 3)
Monsieur Hector, 1940 (Fernandel 3)
Monsieur Ingres, 1967 (Leenhardt 2)
Monsieur La Bruyère, 1956 (Colpi 4)
M'sieur la caille, 1955 (Moreau 3, Kosma 4)
Monsieur la Souris, 1942 (Raimu 3, Achard 4, Auric 4)
Monsieur le Duc, 1932 (Autant-Lara 2)
Monsieur le marquis, 1933 (Robison 2)
Monsieur Lecocq, 1914 (Tourneur, M. 2)
Monsieur Papa, 1977 (Baye 3)
Monsieur Personne, 1936 (Christian-Jaque 2, Berry 3)
Monsieur Pinson, policier, 1915 (Feyder 2)
Monsieur Ripois, 1954 (Clément 2, Philipe 3, Francis 4, Morris 4)
Monsieur Ripois. *See* Knave of Hearts, 1954
Monsieur Stop, 1910 (Cohl 2)
Monsieur Taxi, 1952 (Simon, M. 3)
Monsieur Tête, 1959 (Lenica 2, Borowczyk 4, Colpi 4)
Monsieur Verdoux, 1947 (Chaplin 2, Florey 2, Purviance 3, Courant 4)
Monsieur Vincent, 1947 (Fresnay 2, Renoir 4)
Monsignor, 1982 (Bujold 3, Rey 3, Williams, J. 4)
Monsoon, 1953 (Haller 4, Jenkins 4)
Monster, 1925 (Chaney Lon 3, Sullivan 4)
Monster, 1979 (Carradine 3, Wynn 3)
Monster. *See* Monstre, 1903
Monster and the Girl, 1914 (Guy 2)
Monster and the Girl, 1941 (Lukas 3, Head 4)
Monster and Tiger Man. *See* Lady and the Monster, 1944
Monster Club, 1980 (Carradine 3, Pleasance 3, Price 3)
Monster from Galaxy 27, 1958 (Corman 4)
Monster from the Ocean Floor, 1954 (Corman 4, Crosby 4)
Monster Island. *See* Misterio en la isla de los monstruos, 1980
Monster Meets the Gorilla. *See* Bela Lugosi Meets a Brooklyn Gorilla, 1952
Monster of Highgate Ponds, 1961 (Cavalcanti 2, Halas and Batchelor 2)
Monster of Terror. *See* Die, Monster, Die!, 1965
Monster of the Island, 1953 (Karloff 3)
Monster Walks, 1932 (Auer 3)
Monster Zero. *See* Kaiju daisenso, 1966
Monsters. *See* Mostri, 1963
Monsters. *See* Nuovi mostri, 1977
Monsters from the Arcane Galaxy. *See* Monstrum z galaxie Arkana, 1981
Monsters in the Night. *See* Navy Versus the Night Monsters, 1965
Monstre, 1903 (Méliès 2)
Monstrum z galaxie Arkana, 1981 (Švankmajer 4, Vukotić 4)
Monstruo de la sombra, 1954 (Figueroa 4)
Montagna del dio cannibale, 1978 (Keach 3)
Montagna di cristalo. *See* Glass Mountain, 1948
Montagna di luce, 1949 (Risi 2)
Montagne aux météores, 1958 (Braunberger 4)
Montagne infidèle, 1923 (Epstein 2)
Montagne vivante, 1964 (Delerue 4)
Montana, 1930 (Daniels 4)
Montana, 1950 (Walsh 2, Flynn 3, Sakall 3, Chase 4, Freund 4)
Montana Belle, 1952 (Dwan 2, Brent 3, Cody 3, Russell, J. 3)

Montana Mix-Up, 1913 (Anderson G. 3)
Montana Moon, 1930 (Crawford, J. 3, Adrian 4, Brown, N. 4, Freed 4, Gibbons 4, Stothart 4)
Montana Territory, 1952 (Elam 3)
Monte Carlo, 1925 (Balfour 3)
Monte Carlo, 1926 (Florey 2, Pitts 3, Daniels 4, Gibbons 4, Wilson, C. 4)
Monte Carlo, 1928 (Bertini 3)
Monte Carlo, 1930 (Lubitsch 2, Buchanan 3, MacDonald 3, Pitts 3, Banton 4, Dreier 4, Vajda 4)
Monte Carlo. *See* Monte Carlo Story, 1957
Monte Carlo Baby, 1951 (Hepburn, A. 3)
Monte Carlo Madness. *See* Bomben auf Monte Carlo, 1931
Monte Carlo Nights, 1934 (Canutt 4)
Monte Carlo or Bust!, 1969 (Bourvil 3, Curtis 3, Hawkins 3, Moore, D. 3)
Monte Carlo Story, 1956 (De Sica 2, Auer 3, Dietrich 3)
Monte Cassino, 1946 (Germi 2)
Monte Cristo, 1922 (Florey 2, Adorée 3, Gilbert 3)
Monte Cristo, 1928 (Dagover 3, Modot 3)
Monte Walsh, 1970 (Marvin 3, Moreau 3, Palance 3, Barry 4, Fraker 4)
Montecarlo, 1956 (Risi 2)
Monte-Carlo, 1972 (Reichenbach 2)
Montecarlo. *See* Monte Carlo Story, 1956
Monte-charge, 1962 (Delerue 4)
Montenegro, 1981 (Makavejev 2)
Montenruba no yo wa hukete, 1952 (Kagawa 3)
Monterey Pop, 1967 (Leacock 2)
Montiel's Widow. *See* Viuda de Montiel, 1979
Montmartre, 1950 (Cardiff 4)
Montmartre. *See* Flamme, 1923
Montmartre Nocturne, 1951 (Cardiff 4)
Montmartre sur Seine, 1941 (Cayatte 2, Barrault 3)
Montonnet, 1936 (Prévert 4)
Montparnasse 19, 1957 (Becker 2, Aimée 3, Audran 3, Philipe 3, Annenkov 4, D'Eaubonne 4, Jeanson 4, Matras 4)
Montre, 1933 (Christian-Jaque 2)
Montreur d'ombre. *See* Schatten, 1923
Montreur d'ombres, 1959 (Delerue 4)
Monument of Totsuseki. *See* Totsuseki iseki, 1966
Mony a Pickle, 1937–39 (McLaren 2)
Mony a Pickle, 1938 (Cavalcanti 2)
Monzaburo no Hide, 1931 (Hasegawa 3)
Moo Cow Boogie, 1943 (Dandridge 3)
Moochin' Through Georgia, 1939 (Keaton 2, Bruckman 4)
Moods of the Sea, 1942 (Vorkapich 4)
Moon and Sixpence, 1942 (Basserman 3, Marshall 3, Sanders 3, Lewin 4, Seitz 4, Tiomkin 4)
Moon for Your Love. *See* Lune dans son tablier, 1909
Moon in the Gutter. *See* Lune dans le caniveau, 1982
Moon is Blue, 1953 (Preminger 2, Holden 3, Niven 3, Laszlo 4)
Moon Is Down, 1943 (Cobb 3, Hardwicke 3, Basevi 4, Johnson 4, Miller, A. 4, Newman 4)
Moon is to the Left. *See* Luna sleva, 1928
Moon of Israel. *See* Slavenkönigin, 1924
Moon over Burma, 1940 (Basserman 3, Lamour 3, Preston 3, Head 4, Young, V. 4)
Moon Over Harlem, 1939 (Ulmer 2)
Moon Over Her Shoulder, 1941 (Dailey 3)
Moon over Las Vegas, 1944 (Bruckman 4)
Moon over Miami, 1941 (Seaton 2, Ameche 3, Cummings 3, Grable . Banton 4, Brown, Harry Joe 4, Cole 4, Day 4, Newman 4, Pan 4 Shamroy 4)
Moon Pilot, 1962 (Disney 2, O'Brien, E. 3, Buckner 4)
Moon Riders, 1920 (Eason 4)
Moon Rises. *See* Tsukiwa noborinu, 1955
Moon Rock, 1970 (Dunning 4)
Moonbird, 1959 (Hubley 4)
Moonchild, 1974 (Carradine 3)
Mooncussers, 1962 (Homolka 3)
Moon-Faced. *See* Okame, 1927
Moonfleet, 1955 (Lang 2, Elam 3, Granger 3, Greenwood 3, Sanders Houseman 4, Plunkett 4, Rozsa 4)

oonflower of Heaven. *See* Ten no yugao, 1948
oonlight and Cactus, 1932 (Arbuckle 3)
oonlight and Cactus, 1944 (Howard, S. 3)
oonlight and Honeysuckle, 1921 (Boyd 3)
oonlight and Melody. *See* Moonlight and Pretzels, 1933
oonlight and Noses, 1925 (Laurel 3, Roach 4)
oonlight and Pretzels, 1933 (Freund 4)
oonlight Follies, 1921 (Glennon 4)
oonlight in Havana, 1942 (Mann 2)
oonlight in Hawaii, 1941 (Auer 3, Cortez 4)
oonlight Madness. *See* Gekka no kyojin, 1926
oonlight Masquerade, 1942 (Alton, J. 4)
oonlight Murder, 1936 (Clarke, C.C. 4, Stothart 4)
oonlight Serenade. *See* Au Clair de la lune ou Pierrot malheureux, 1904
oonlight Sonata, 1937 (Stallich 4)
oonlighter, 1953 (Bond 3, Elam 3, MacMurray 3, Stanwyck 3, Glennon 4)
oonlighting, 1982 (Skolimowski 2)
oonraker, 1979 (Moore, R. 3, Adam 4, Barry 4)
oonrise, 1949 (Borzage 2, Barrymore E. 3)
oonrise. *See* Tsukiwa noborinu, 1955
oon's Our Home, 1936 (Bondi 3, Brennan 3, Fonda, H. 3, Sullavan 3, Wanger 4)
oon's Ray, 1914 (Bushman 3)
oonshine, 1918 (Keaton 2, Arbuckle 3)
oonshine County Express, 1977 (Corman 4)
oonshine Maid and the Man, 1914 (Ingram 2)
oonshine Molly, 1914 (Reid 3)
oonshine Trail, 1919 (Blackton 2)
oonshine Valley, 1922 (Brenon 2, Farnum 3)
oonshine War, 1970 (Widmark 3)
oonshiner, 1913 (Dwan 2)
oonshiners, 1904 (Bitzer 4)
oonshiners, 1916 (Sennett 2, Arbuckle 3)
oonshiner's Heart, 1912 (Anderson G. 3)
oon-Spinners, 1964 (Disney 2, Greenwood 3, Negri 3, Papas 3, Wallach 3)
oonstone of Fez, 1914 (Costello, M. 3, Talmadge, C. 3)
oon-Struck Matador. *See* Clair de lune espagnol, 1909
oontide, 1942 (Lang 2, Gabin 3, Lupino 3, Rains 3, Basevi 4, Clarke, C.C. 4, Day 4, Newman 4, Reynolds 4)
oose Hunt in Canada, 1905 (Bitzer 4)
oose on the Loose, 1952 (Terry 4)
opey Dope, 1944 (Langdon 3)
opping Up, 1943 (Terry 4)
or defter, 1964 (Guney 2)
or och dotter, 1912 (Stiller 2, Jaenzon 4, Magnusson 4)
oral Code, 1917 (Barthelmess 3, Nilsson 3)
oral der Gasse, 1925 (Krauss 3)
oral der Ruth Halbfass, 1971 (Schlondorff 2, Von Trotta 2)
oral Fabric, 1916 (Ince 4, Sullivan 4)
oral of Ruth Halbfass. *See* Moral der Ruth Halbfass, 1971
oral und Liebe, 1933 (Homolka 3)
oralist. *See* Moralista, 1959
oralista, 1959 (De Sica 2, Sordi 3)
orálka pani Dulské, 1958 (Brejchová 3)
orals for Women, 1931 (Love 3)
orals of Marcus, 1935 (Velez 3)
oran of the Lady Letty, 1922 (Valentino 3, Glennon 4)
oran of the Marines, 1928 (Harlow 3, Cronjager 4)
oran of the Mounted, 1926 (Brown, Harry Joe 4)
oravia, 1955–59 (Taviani, P. and V. 2)
orbidone, 1965 (Aimée 3, Di Venanzo 4)
ord Em'ly, 1922 (Pearson 2, Balfour 3)
ord ohne Täter, 1920 (Dupont 2)
ord und Totschlag, 1967 (Schlondorff 2)
order Dmitri Karamasoff, 1931 (Kortner 3, Rasp 3)
order sind unter uns, 1946 (Staudte 2, Knef 3)
orderstwo, 1957 (Polanski 2)
ordi e fuggi, 1972 (Risi 2, Mastroianni 3, Reed, O. 3)
ordprozess Mary Dugan, 1931 (Robison 2)
ords pas, on t'aime, 1976 (Allégret, Y. 2, Presle 3)

Mordsache Holm, (Staudte 2)
More, 1969 (Almendros 4, Gégauff 4)
More American Graffiti, 1979 (Lucas 2)
More Dead Than Alive, 1968 (Price 3)
More Milk, 1965 (Warhol 2)
More Pep, 1936 (Fleischer, M. and D. 2)
More than a Kiss. *See* Don't Bet on Women, 1931
More than a Miracle. *See* C'era una volta, 1967
More Than a Secretary, 1936 (Arthur 3, Brent 3)
More Than Murder, 1984 (Keach 3)
More the Merrier, 1943 (Stevens 2, Arthur 3, Coburn, C. 3, McCrea 3)
More Trouble, 1918 (Gilbert 3, Furthman 4)
More yogne, 1972 (Ulyanov 3)
Moreto, 1967 (Danailov 3)
Morfalous, 1983 (Belmondo 3, Audiard 4)
Morgan, 1966 (Reisz 2, Redgrave, V. 3)
Morgan il pirata, 1961 (De Toth 2, Delli Colli 4)
Morgan the Pirate. *See* Morgan il pirata, 1961
Morgane la Sirène, 1927 (Burel 4)
Morgen beginnt das Leben, 1961 (Vích 4)
Morgen werde ich verhaftet, 1939 (Herlth 4)
Morgenrot, 1933 (Herlth 4, Hoffmann 4, Rohrig 4)
Morgensterne, 1977 (Lassally 4)
Mori no Ishimatsu, 1949 (Shindo 2, Yoshimura 2)
Mori Ranmaru, 1955 (Yamamura 3)
Mori to mizuumi no matsuri, 1958 (Kagawa 3)
Morianerna, 1965 (Dahlbeck 3)
Morianna. *See* Morianerna, 1965
Moriarty. *See* Sherlock Holmes, 1922
Móricz Zsigmond, 1956 (Jancsó 2)
Morir por la patria es vivir, 1976 (Alvarez 2)
Morishaige yo doko e iku, 1956 (Kagawa 3)
Moritori, 1948 (Kinski 3, Pommer 4, Warm 4)
Morituri, 1965 (Wicki 2, Brando 3, Brynner 3, Howard, T. 3, Fraker 4, Goldsmith 4, Hall 4, Smith, J.M. 4)
Moriturus, 1920 (Veidt 3)
Morke Punkt, 1913 (Blom 2, Holger-Madsen 2)
Mormon, 1912 (Dwan 2)
Mormon Main, 1917 (Rosher 4)
Mormonens Offer, 1911 (Blom 2)
Morning, 1968 (Gehr 2)
Morning. *See* Jutro, 1967
Morning. *See* Subah, 1983
Morning After, 1921 (Roach 4)
Morning After, 1934 (Dwan 2)
Morning After, 1986 (Allen, J. 4)
Morning Conflicts. *See* Asa no hamon, 1952
Morning Departure, 1950 (Attenborough 3, Mills 3, More 3, Alwyn 4)
Morning for the Osone Family. *See* Osone-ke no asa, 1946
Morning Glory, 1933 (Fairbanks, D. Jr. 3, Hepburn, K. 3, Menjou 3, Berman 4, Cooper 4, Glennon 4, Plunkett 4, Polglase 4, Steiner 4)
Morning in the City. *See* Aamua Kaupungissa, 1954
Morning Judge, 1926 (Fleischer, M. and D. 2)
Morning, Noon, and Night, 1931 (Fleischer, M. and D. 2)
Morning, Noon, and Night Club, 1937 (Fleischer, M. and D. 2)
Morning Papers, 1914 (Sennett 2)
Morning Premiere. *See* Jutro premiera, 1946
Morning Schedule. *See* Gozenchu no jikanwari, 1972
Morning Sun Shines. *See* Asahi wa kagayaku, 1929
Morning's Tree-lined Street. *See* Asa no namikimichi, 1936
Moro Naba, 1957 (Rouch 2)
Morocco, 1930 (Hathaway 2, Von Sternberg 2, Cooper, Gary 3, Dietrich 3, Menjou 3, Ballard 4, Banton 4, Dreier 4, Furthman 4, Garmes 4)
Morozko, 1965 (Churikova 3)
Morpheus Mike, 1917 (O'Brien 4)
Morphia the Death Drug, 1914 (Hepworth 2)
Mors aux dents, 1979 (Tavernier 2, Piccoli 3)
Morse Code Melody, 1963 (Godfrey 4)
Morsel. *See* Sousto, 1960
Mort, 1909 (Feuillade 2)
Mort de Belle, 1960 (Delerue 4)
Mort de Lucrèce, 1913 (Feuillade 2)

Mort de Mario Ricci, 1984 (Volonté 3)
Mort de Mozart, 1909 (Feuillade 2, Carré 4)
Mort de Robert Macaire et Bertrand, 1905 (Guy 2)
Mort de Vénus, 1930 (Storck 2)
Mort du cygne, 1937 (Benoit-Lévy 2, Burel 4)
Mort du Duc d'Enghien, 1912 (Gance 2)
Mort du soleil, 1921 (Dulac 2)
Mort d'un pourri, 1977 (Audran 3, Delon 3, Kinski 3, Audiard 4,
     Decaë 4, Sarde 4)
Mort d'un toréador, 1907 (Linders 3)
Mort en ce jardin, 1956 (Buñuel 2, Piccoli 3, Signoret 3, Vanel 3,
     Alcoriza 4)
Mort en direct, 1979 (Keitel 3, Noiret 3, Schneider 3, Von Sydow 3)
Mort en direct. See Death Watch, 1979
Mort en fraude, 1956 (Gélin 3, Audiard 4)
Mort en fuite, 1936 (Berry 3, Simon, M. 3)
Mort ne reçoit plus, 1944 (Berry 3, Wakhévitch 4)
Mort ne tue jamais personne, 1971 (Braunberger 4)
Mort, où est ta victoire?, 1964 (Noiret 3, Jarre 4)
Mort qui tue, 1913 (Feuillade 2)
Mort vivant, 1912 (Feuillade 2)
Mortadella, 1971 (Monicelli 2, Loren 3, D'Amico 4, Lardner 4,
     Ponti 4)
Mortadella. See Lady Liberty, 1972
Mortal Storm, 1940 (Borzage 2, Saville 2, Bond 3, Dailey 3,
     Ouspenskaya 3, Stewart 3, Sullavan 3, Young, R. 3, Adrian 4,
     Daniels 4, Kaper 4)
Morte a Venezia, 1971 (Visconti 2, Bogarde 3, Mangano 3)
Morte civile, 1912 (Bertini 3)
Morte di un amico, 1960 (Pasolini 2)
Morte di un operatore, 1978 (Sarde 4)
Morte ha fatto l'uovo, 1967 (Lollobrigida 3, Trintignant 3)
Morte in Vaticano, 1982 (Stamp 3, Donaggio 4)
Morte non ha sesso, 1969 (Mills 3, Fusco 4)
Morte sorride all'assassino, 1973 (Kinski 3)
Morte sospetta di una minorenne, 1975 (Ferrer, M. 3)
Mortelle randonnée, 1983 (Adjani 3, Audiard 4)
Morte-Saison des amours, 1960 (Gélin 3, Delerue 4, Vierny 4)
Morts en vitrine, 1957 (Colpi 4, Delerue 4)
Morts reviennent-ils? See Drame au Château d'Acre, 1915
Mor-Vran, 1931 (Epstein 2)
Mosaic, 1965 (McLaren 2)
Mosaic in Confidence. See Mosaik im Vertrauen, 1954–55
Mosaic Law, 1913 (Ince 4)
Mosaik im Vertrauen, 1954–55 (Kubelka 2)
Mosaique. See Mosaic, 1965
Moscow Builds the Subway. See Moskva stroit metro, 1934
Moscow Doesn't Believe in Tears. See Moskva slezam ne verit, 1980
Moscow Laughs. See Veselye rebiate, 1934
Moscow Nights, 1935 (Asquith 2, Baur 3, Olivier 3, Quayle 3,
     Hornbeck 4, Korda 4)
Moscow Nights. See Nuits moscovites, 1934
Moscow Strikes Back, 1942 (Vorkapich 4)
Mose, 1972 (Lancaster 3)
Moses, 1975 (Papas 3, Quayle 3, Thulin 3)
Moses. See Mose, 1972
Moses and Aaron. See Moses und Aron, 1975
Moses und Aron, 1975 (Straub and Huillet 2)
Moshimo kanojo ga, 1928 (Tanaka 3)
Moskau-Shanghai, 1936 (Negri 3, Wegener 3)
Moskva slezam ne verit, 1980 (Batalov 3, Smoktunovsky 3)
Moskva stroit metro, 1934 (Shub 2)
Moskva-Kassiopeia, 1974 (Smoktunovsky 3)
Mosquito, 1922 (Fleischer, M. and D. 2)
Moss Rose, 1947 (Barrymore E. 3, Mature 3, Price 3, Day 4,
     Furthman 4, Lemaire 4, Newman 4)
Most Beautiful. See Ichiban utsukushiku, 1944
Most Dangerous Game, 1932 (Schoedsack 2, Crabbe 3, Johnson, N. 3,
     McCrea 3, Wray 3, Cooper 4, Dunn 4, Steiner 4)
Most Dangerous Man Alive, 1961 (Dwan 2)
Most Dangerous Man in the World, 1969 (Peck 3, Goldsmith 4)
Most Dangerous Sin. See Crime et châtiment, 1956
Most Immoral Lady, 1929 (Pidgeon 3, Seitz 4)

Most Important Thing: Love. See Important c'est d'aimer, 1974
Most Precious Thing in Life, 1934 (Arthur 3, Bond 3, Darwell 3,
     Schary 4)
Most Useful Tree in the World. See Varldens mest Anvandbara Trad,
     1935–36
Most Wanted Man. See Ennemi public No 1, 1953
Most Wonderful Moment. See Momento piú bello, 1957
Mostri, 1963 (Risi 2, Scola 2, Gassman 3, Tognazzi 3, Age and
     Scarpelli 4)
Mostri di Roma, 1972 (Manfredi 3)
Mostro, 1977 (Zampa 2, Morricone 4)
Mostro dell'isola. See Monster of the Island, 1953
Mosura, 1961 (Kagawa 3, Shimura 3, Tsuburaya 4)
Mot de Cambronne, 1937 (Guitry 2)
Mot de l'. See Énigme, 1919
Mot nya tider, 1939 (Sjostrom 2, Bjornstrand 3)
Mote i natten, 1946 (Dahlbeck 3)
Mote med Livet, 1952 (Thulin 3)
Moten i skymningen, 1957 (Dahlbeck 3, Fischer 4)
Moth, 1917 (Menjou 3, Talmadge, N. 3)
Moth and the Flame, 1914 (Olcott 2)
Moth and the Spider, 1935 (Terry 4)
Motheaten Spring. See Mushibameru haru, 1932
Mother, 1913 (Loos 4)
Mother, 1914 (Tourneur, M. 2, Carré 4)
Mother. See Haha, 1963
Mother. See Mat, 1926
Mother. See Mat, 1956
Mother. See Okasan, 1952
Mother and Child. See Haha yo ko yo, 1933
Mother and Daughter. See Anya és leánya, 1981
Mother and Daughter. See Mor och dotter, 1945
Mother and Daughter. See Sredi dobrykh lyudei, 1962
Mother and Daughter—The Loving War, 1980 (Weld 3)
Mother and 11 Children. See Kachan to Juichi-nin no Kodomo, 1966
Mother and Son, 1967 (Nemec 2)
Mother and the Law, 1919 (Marsh 3)
Mother and the Whore. See Maman et la putain, 1973
Mother Carey's Chickens, 1938 (Bainter 3, Brennan 3, Keeler 3,
     Berman 4, Hunt 4)
Mother Didn't Tell Me, 1950 (La Shelle 4, Lemaire 4)
Mother, Do Not Shame Your Name. See Haha yo kimi no na o kegasu
     nakare, 1928
Mother, Get Married. See Kachan kekkon shiroyo, 1962
Mother Goose Land, 1925 (Fleischer, M. and D. 2)
Mother Goose Land, 1931 (Fleischer, M. and D. 2)
Mother Goose Nightmare, 1945 (Terry 4)
Mother Goose on the Loose, 1942 (Lantz 4)
Mother Goose Presents series, from 1946 (Harryhausen 4)
Mother Goose's Birthday Party, 1950 (Terry 4)
Mother Hulda, 1915 (Ince 4)
Mother, I Miss You. See Hahayo koishi, 1926
Mother Instinct, 1917 (Gilbert 3)
Mother Is a Freshman, 1949 (Bacon 2, Johnson, V. 3, Young, L. 3,
     Newman 4, Reynolds 4, Wheeler 4)
Mother Joan of the Angels. See Matka Joanna od Aniolów, 1961
Mother, Jugs and Speed, 1976 (Yates 2, Keitel 3, Jones 4)
Mother Kracmerka. See Matka Kráčmerka, 1934
Mother Kuster's Trip to Heaven. See Mutter Kusters Fahrt zum
     Himmel, 1975
Mother Lode, 1983 (Heston 3)
Mother Love, 1910 (Lawrence 3)
Mother Love. See Mutterliebe, 1929
Mother Machree, 1928 (Ford, J. 2, McLaglen 3, Wayne 3)
Mother, Mother, Mother, Pin a Rose on Me, 1924 (Fleischer, M.
     and D. 2)
Mother Never Dies. See Haha wa shinazu, 1942
Mother o' Mine, 1921 (Niblo 2, Sullivan 4)
Mother of Men, 1914 (Olcott 2)
Mother of Men, 1938 (Pearson 2)
Mother of Mine. See Gribiche, 1925
Mother of the Ranch, 1911 (Dwan 2, Anderson G. 3)
Mother Pin a Rose on Me, 1929 (Fleischer, M. and D. 2)

Mother—Sir!. *See* Navy Wife, 1956
Mother Was a Rooster, 1962 (McKimson 4)
Mother Wore Tights, 1947 (Baxter A. 3, Dailey 3, Grable 3, Day 4, Lemaire 4, Newman 4, Orry-Kelly 4, Trotti 4)
Mothering Heart, 1913 (Griffith 2, Gish, L. 3, Bitzer 4)
Mother-in-Law Is Coming. *See* Svarmor kommer, 1930
Mother-in-Law's Day, 1945 (Hunt 4)
Mothers and Daughters. *See* Materi i docheri, 1974
Mothers and Fathers, 1967 (Halas and Batchelor 2)
Mother's Atonement, 1915 (Chaney Lon 3)
Mother's Boy, 1913 (Sennett 2, Arbuckle 3)
Mother's Boy, 1929 (Stradling 4)
Mother's Boy. *See* Percy, 1925
Mother's Child, 1916 (Hardy 3)
Mother's Country Is Far. *See* Haruka narishi haha no kuni, 1950
Mothers Cry, 1930 (Karloff 3, Coffee 4)
Mother's Day, 1948 (Broughton 2)
Mother's Devotion. *See* Vernost materi, 1967
Mother's Heart. *See* Serdtse materi, 1966
Mother's Holiday, 1932 (Arbuckle 3)
Mother's Influence, 1914 (Reid 3)
Mother's Joy, 1923 (Laurel 3, Roach 4)
Mother's Love, 1910 (Walsh 2)
Mother's Love. *See* Hahayo koishi, 1926
Mother's Loyalty. *See* Vernost materi, 1967
Mother's Map. *See* Haha no chizu, 1942
Mother's Ordeal, 1917 (Van Dyke, W.S. 2)
Mother's Tears, 1953 (Lee, B. 3)
Mother's White Snow. *See* Haha shirayuki, 1956
Mothers-in-Law, 1923 (Schulberg 4, Struss 4)
Mothlight, 1963 (Brakhage 2)
Mothra. *See* Mosura, 1961
Motion Painting No. 1, 1947 (Fischinger 2)
Motion Pictures, 1956 (Breer 2)
Motiv pro vraždu, 1974 (Brejchová 3)
Motor Boat Mamas, 1928 (Sennett 2, Hornbeck 4)
Motor Buccaneers, 1913 (Bushman 3)
Motor Friend, 1910–11 (White 3)
Motorcar Apaches. *See* Lyckonalen, 1915
Motorcart. *See* Cochecito, 1960
Motorcycles. *See* Pětistovka, 1949
Motorcyclette. *See* Girl on a Motorcycle, 1968
Motoring Mamas, 1929 (Sennett 2, Hornbeck 4)
Motorizzati, 1962 (Manfredi 3, Tognazzi 3)
Motorkavalierer, 1950 (Andersson H. 3)
Mots ont un sens, 1970 (Marker 2)
Motylem jestem czyli romans czterdziestolatka, 1976 (Pszoniak 3)
Mouche, 1903–04 (Guy 2)
Mouchette, 1967 (Bresson 2, Cloquet 4)
Mouchy, 1950 (Brdečka 4)
Mouettes, 1916 (Burel 4)
Mouid maa el Maghoul, 1958 (Sharif 3)
Moulai Hafid et Alphonse XIII, 1912 (Cohl 2)
Moule, 1936 (Delannoy 2)
Moulin Rouge, 1928 (Dupont 2, Tschechowa 3, Junge 4)
Moulin Rouge, 1934 (Ball 3, Bennett C. 3, Day 4, Johnson 4, Newman 4, Rosher 4, Zanuck 4)
Moulin Rouge, 1953 (Clayton 2, Huston 2, Ophuls 2, Cushing 3, Ferrer, J. 3, Lee, C. 3, Auric 4, Dehn 4, Francis 4, Morris 4, Veiller 4)
Mount Vernon, 1949 (Van Dyke, W. 2)
Mountain, 1956 (Dmytryk 2, Arlen 3, Tracy 3, Trevor 3, Wagner 3, Edouart 4, Fulton 4, Head 4, Planer 4, Westmore, F. 4)
Mountain and River of Love. *See* Ai no sanga, 1950
Mountain Eagle, 1926 (Hitchcock 2, Balcon 4)
Mountain Fighters, 1943 (Eason 4)
Mountain Girl, 1915 (Gish, D. 3)
Mountain Justice, 1915 (Chaney Lon 3, Furthman 4)
Mountain Justice, 1930 (Brown, Harry Joe 4, McCord 4)
Mountain Justice, 1937 (Curtiz 2, Brent 3, Haller 4, Raine 4)
Mountain King. *See* Yedi Dağın aslani, 1966
Mountain Law, 1911 (Anderson G. 3)
Mountain Mary, 1915 (Eason 4)

Mountain Men, 1980 (Heston 3)
Mountain Music, 1937 (Florey 2, Fazenda 3, Dreier 4, Glazer 4, Head 4, Lederer 4, Prinz 4, Struss 4, Young, V. 4)
Mountain Music, 1976 (Vinton 4)
Mountain Pass. *See* Passe-Montagne, 1978
Mountain Pass of Love and Hate. *See* Aizo toge, 1934
Mountain Rat, 1914 (Crisp 3, Gish, D. 3)
Mountain Rhythm, 1939 (Autry 3, Eason 4)
Mountain Road, 1960 (Stewart 3)
Mountain Romance, 1938 (Terry 4)
Mountain Woman, 1921 (White 3, Ruttenberg 4)
Mountaineer, 1914 (Reid 3)
Mountaineer's Honor, 1909 (Griffith 2, Pickford 3, Bitzer 4)
Mountains and Rivers with Scars. *See* Kizudarake no sanga, 1964
Mountains at Dusk. *See* Gory o zmierzchu, 1970
Mountains of Mourne, 1930 (Wilcox 4)
Mountains of the Moon, 1958 (Van Dyke, W. 2)
Mounties Are Coming. *See* Vigilantes Are Coming, 1936
Mourir à Madrid, 1962 (Grimault 4, Jarre 4)
Mourir d'aimer, 1970 (Cayatte 2, Girardot 3)
Mourning Becomes Electra, 1947 (Douglas, K. 3, Massey 3, Redgrave, M. 3, Russell, R. 3, D'Agostino 4, Nichols 4)
Mouse and Garden, 1950 (Terry 4)
Mouse and Garden, 1959 (Freleng 4)
Mouse and His Child, 1978 (Ustinov 3)
Mouse and the Lion, 1913 (Grot 4)
Mouse and the Lion. *See* Egér és oroszlan, 1957
Mouse Cleaning, 1948 (Hanna and Barbera 4)
Mouse Comes to Dinner, 1945 (Hanna and Barbera 4)
Mouse Divided, 1951 (Freleng 4)
Mouse for Sale, 1953 (Hanna and Barbera 4)
Mouse in Manhattan, 1945 (Hanna and Barbera 4)
Mouse in the House, 1947 (Hanna and Barbera 4)
Mouse Mazurka, 1948 (Freleng 4)
Mouse Meets Bird, 1953 (Terry 4)
Mouse Menace, 1953 (Terry 4)
Mouse of Tomorrow, 1942 (Terry 4)
Mouse on 57th Street, 1961 (Jones 2)
Mouse on the Moon, 1963 (Lester 2, Rutherford 3)
Mouse That Jack Built, 1959 (McKimson 4)
Mouse That Roared, 1959 (Seberg 3, Sellers 3, Foreman 4)
Mouse Trouble, 1944 (Hanna and Barbera 4)
Mouse Wreckers, 1948 (Jones 2)
Mousemerized Cat, 1946 (McKimson 4)
Mouse-placed Kitten, 1959 (McKimson 4)
Mouse-taken Identity, 1957 (McKimson 4)
Mousetrap. *See* Mišolovka, 1972
Mousewarming, 1952 (Jones 2)
Mousey, 1974 (Douglas, K. 3, Love 3, Seberg 3)
Moussaillon, 1943 (Aurenche 4)
Moutarde me monte au nez, 1974 (Decaë 4)
Mouth Agape. *See* Gueule ouverte, 1974
Mouthpiece, 1932 (Goddard 3, Zanuck 4)
Mouton à cinq pattes, 1954 (Verneuil 2, Fernandel 3)
Mouton enragé, 1908 (Cohl 2)
Mouton enragé, 1974 (Cassel 3, Schneider 3, Trintignant 3)
Moutonnet, 1936 (Simon, M. 3)
Moutonnet à Paris. *See* Moutonnet, 1936
Moutons de Praxos. *See* A l'aube du troisième jour, 1963
Mouvement image par image, 1976–78 (McLaren 2)
Mouvement perpétuel, 1949 (Jutra 2)
Move, 1970 (Gould 3, Berman 4, Daniels 4, Smith, J.M. 4)
Move On, 1917 (Roach 4)
Move Over, Darling, 1963 (Day 3, Ritter 3, Smith, J.M. 4)
Movers and Shakers, 1985 (Matthau 3)
Movie, 1922 (Roach 4)
Movie, 1958 (Conner 2)
Movie Crazy, 1932 (Lloyd 3, Bruckman 4)
Movie Daze, 1934 (Roach 4)
Movie Dummy, 1918 (Roach 4)
Movie Experience: A Matter of Choice, 1968 (Heston 3)
Movie Fans, 1920 (Sennett 2)
Movie Mad, 1931 (Iwerks 4)

Movie Madness, 1952 (Terry 4)
Movie Maniacs, 1936 (Three Stooges 3)
Movie Movie, 1978 (Donen 2, Scott, G. 3, Wallach 3, Kidd 4)
Movie Murderer, 1970 (Cook 3, Kennedy, A. 3, Oates 3, Bumstead 4)
Movie Night, 1929 (Roach 4)
Movie Nut. See Film Johnnie, 1914
Movie Star, 1916 (Sennett 2)
Movie Stunt Pilot, 1954 (La Shelle 4)
Movies, 1925 (Arbuckle 3)
Movie-Town, 1931 (Sennett 2)
Moving Perspectives, 1967 (Sen 2)
Moving Picture Cowboy, 1914 (Mix 3)
Moving Spirit, 1951 (Halas and Batchelor 2)
Moving Target. See Harper, 1966
Moving Violation, 1976 (Corman 4)
Moving World series, from 1912 (Cohl 2)
Moviola: The Scarlett O'Hara War, 1980 (Curtis 3)
Moviola: This Year's Blonde, 1980 (Bernstein 4)
Moy dobry papa, 1971 (Gurchenko 3)
Moyuru daichi, 1940 (Hasegawa 3)
Moyuru ozora, 1940 (Hayasaka 4, Tsuburaya 4)
Moyuru wakamono-tachi, 1962 (Iwashita 3, Yamamura 3)
Mozambique, 1965 (Knef 3)
Mozart, 1955 (Werner 3)
Mozart. See Whom the Gods Love, 1936
Mozart i Salieri, 1962 (Smoktunovsky 3)
Mozart Story. See Wenn die Gotter Lieben, 1942
Možda Diogen, 1967 (Dragić 4)
Možnosti dialogu, 1982 (Švankmajer 4)
Mozu, 1940 (Yamada 3)
Mozu, 1961 (Yamada 3, Takemitsu 4)
Mravnost nade vse, 1937 (Haas 3)
Mrigaya, 1976 (Sen 2)
Ms. Don Juan. See Don Juan 1973, 1973
Mstitel, 1959 (Stallich 4)
Mučedníci lásky, 1967 (Anderson 2, Nemec 2, Ondricek 4)
Much Ado about Nothing, 1940 (Terry 4)
Much Ado About Nutting, 1953 (Jones 2)
Much Too Shy, 1942 (Formby 3)
Muchacha, 1960 (Figueroa 4)
Muchly Engaged, 1912–13 (White 3)
Mucho Locos, 1966 (McKimson 4)
Mucho Mouse, 1956 (Hanna and Barbera 4)
Mucke, 1954 (Wicki 2, Reisch 4)
Mud and Sand, 1922 (Laurel 3)
Mudata, 1953 (Armendáriz 3)
Muddle in Horse Thieves, 1913 (Mix 3)
Muddy Romance, 1913 (Sennett 2)
Muddy Water. See Nigorie, 1953
Mude Tod, 1921 (Lang 2, Dagover 3, Herlth 4, Pommer 4, Rohrig 4, Von Harbou 4, Wagner 4, Warm 4)
Mudlark, 1950 (Negulesco 2, Dunne 3, Guinness 3, Alwyn 4, Johnson 4, Périnal 4)
Mueda, memória e massacre, 1979 (Guerra 2)
Mueda, Memory and Massacre. See Mueda, memória e massacre, 1979
Muerta viaje demasiado. See Humour noir, 1965
Muerte al invasor, 1961 (Alvarez 2, Gutiérrez 2)
Muerte de Pio Baroja, 1957 (Bardem 2)
Muerte de un burócrata, 1966 (Gutiérrez 2)
Muerte de un presidente, 1951 (Rey 3)
Muerte di un ciclista, 1955 (Bardem 2, de Beauregard 4)
Muerte en este jardin. See Mort en ce jardin, 1956
Muet mélomane, 1899 (Zecca 2)
Mug Town, 1943 (Salter 4)
Mugaddar Ka Sikandar, 1978 (Bachchan 3)
Muggsy Becomes a Hero, 1910 (Pickford 3)
Muggsy's First Sweetheart, 1910 (Griffith 2, Pickford 3, Bitzer 4)
Mugsy's Girls, 1984 (Gordon 3)
Muha, 1966 (Mimica 4)
Muharraj el Kabir, 1951 (Chahine 2)
Muhle im Schwarzwaldertal, 1952 (Rasp 3)
Muhle von Sanssouci, 1926 (Dieterle 2, Tschechowa 3, Andrejew 4)
Muhomachi no yarodomo, 1959 (Yamamura 3)

Muhomatsu no issho, 1958 (Mifune 3, Takamine 3)
Muhoumatsu no issho, 1943 (Miyagawa 4)
Muhoumono Ginpei, 1938 (Miyagawa 4)
Muiderkring herleeft, 1948 (Haanstra 2)
Muj přítel Fabián, 1953 (Weiss 2)
Mujer cualquiera, 1949 (Félix 3)
Mujer de todos, 1945 (Félix 3)
Mujer en condominio, 1956 (Figueroa 4)
Mujer que yo perdi, 1949 (Infante 3)
Mujer sin alma, 1943 (De Fuentes 2, Félix 3)
Mujer sin amor. See Cuando los hijos nos juzgan, 1951
Mujer sin cabeza, 1944 (Figueroa 4)
Mujer, un hombre, una ciudad, 1978 (Gómez, M. 2)
Mujer X, 1954 (Figueroa 4)
Mujeres mandan, 1936 (De Fuentes 2, García 3, Figueroa 4)
Mujers de mi general, 1950 (Infante 3)
Mukl in transport z ráje, 1963 (Brodský 3)
Mukokuseki-sha, 1951 (Ichikawa 2)
Mukti, 1937 (Roy 2)
Mulata, 1953 (Armendáriz 3)
Mule Train, 1950 (Autry 3)
Mules and Mortgages, 1919 (Hardy 3)
Mule's Disposition, 1926 (Lantz 4)
Mulhall's Great Catch, 1926 (Brown, Harry Joe 4)
Mulher de verdade, 1954 (Cavalcanti 2)
Mulino del Po, 1949 (Fellini 2, Lattuada 2, Pinelli 4, Ponti 4)
Mumise, 1927 (Marshall 3)
Mummy, 1932 (Johnson, N. 3, Karloff 3, Balderston 4, Freund 4, Fulton 4, Pierce 4)
Mummy, 1959 (Fisher 2, Cushing 3, Lee, C. 3, Sangster 4)
Mummy's Boys, 1936 (Polglase 4)
Mummy's Curse, 1945 (Chaney Lon, Jr. 3, Farnum 3, Pierce 4)
Mummy's Dummies, 1948 (Three Stooges 3)
Mummy's Ghost, 1944 (Carradine 3, Chaney Lon, Jr. 3, Pierce 4, Salter 4)
Mummy's Hand, 1940 (Salter 4)
Mummy's Shroud, 1967 (Cushing 3)
Mummy's Tomb, 1942 (Chaney Lon, Jr. 3, Pierce 4, Salter 4)
Mum's the Word, 1926 (McCarey 2, Roach 4)
Mumsie, 1927 (Wilcox 2)
Mumsy, Nanny, Sonny, and Girly, 1969 (Francis 4)
Mumyo-yumyo, 1939 (Shimura 3)
Munchen-Berlin Wanderung, 1927 (Fischinger 2)
Munchener Bilderbogen, 1924–26 (Fischinger 2)
Munekata shimai, 1950 (Ozu 2, Ryu 3, Takamine 3, Tanaka 3, Yamamura 3)
Munekata Sisters. See Munekata shimai, 1950
Munich, or Peace in Our Time. See Munich, ou La Paix pour cent ans, 1967
Munich, ou La Paix pour cent ans, 1967 (Ophuls 2)
Municipal Bandwagon, 1931 (Astaire 3)
Municipal Elections. See Elecciones municipales, 1970
Munimji, 1954 (Anand 3, Burman 4)
Munition Conspiracy. See Krigens Fjende, 1915
Munka vagy hivatás?, 1963 (Mészáros 2)
Munkbrogreven, 1934 (Bergman 3)
Munster, Go Home!, 1966 (Carradine 3, De Carlo 3, Westmore, P. 4, Whitlock 4)
Muppet Movie, 1979 (Welles 2, Coburn, J. 3, Gould 3, Hope 3, Pryor 3)
Mur, 1970 (Guerra 2)
Mur, 1982 (Guney 2)
Mur. See Démolition d'un mur, 1895
Mur de l'Atlantique, 1970 (Bourvil 3, de Beauregard 4)
Mur Murs, 1980 (Varda 2)
Mura di Malapaga, 1949 (D'Amico 4)
Mura di Malapaga. See Au-delà des grilles, 1949
Mura hachibu, 1953 (Yamamura 3)
Mura no bukujo, 1924 (Tanaka 3)
Mura no hanayome, 1928 (Gosho 2, Tanaka 3)
Mura no kajiya, 1929 (Tanaka 3)
Mural Murals. See Mur Murs, 1980

Murasaki zukin, 1958 (Yamamura 3)
Muratti greift ein, 1934 (Fischinger 2)
Muratti Privat, 1935 (Fischinger 2)
Murder, 1930 (Hitchcock 2, Marshall 3, Reville 4)
Murder à la Carte. *See* Voici le temps des assassins, 1955
Murder à la Mod, 1967 (De Palma 2)
Murder Ahoy, 1964 (Rutherford 3)
Murder Among Friends, 1941 (Clarke, C.C. 4)
Murder at Dawn, 1932 (Auer 3)
Murder at Monte Carlo, 1935 (Flynn 3)
Murder at the Gallop, 1963 (Rutherford 3)
Murder at the Vanities, 1934 (Leisen 2, McLaglen 3, Meek 3,
    Sheridan 3, Prinz 4, Wilson, C. 4)
Murder at the World Series, 1977 (Leigh, J. 3)
Murder Attempt. *See* Pokus o vraždu, 1973
Murder by Agreement. *See* Journey into Nowhere, 1963
Murder by an Aristocrat, 1936 (Orry-Kelly 4)
Murder by Contract, 1958 (Ballard 4)
Murder by Death, 1976 (Falk 3, Guinness 3, Lanchester 3, Sellers 3,
    Smith 3, Booth 4, Stark 4)
Murder by Decree, 1979 (Bujold 3, Gielgud 3, Mason 3, Quayle 3,
    Sutherland 3)
Murder by Phone, 1982 (Barry 4)
Murder by Phone. *See* Bells, 1982
Murder by Proxy, 1955 (Fisher 2)
Murder: By Reason of Insanity, 1985 (Wallach 3)
Murder by Rope, 1936 (Pearson 2, Havelock-Allan 4)
Murder by Television, 1935 (Lugosi 3)
Murder by the Clock, 1931 (Struss 4)
Murder Czech Style. *See* Vražda po česku, 1966
Murder for Sale. *See* Temporary Widow, 1930
Murder Goes to College, 1937 (Dmytryk 2, Crabbe 3, Head 4)
Murder, He Says, 1945 (MacMurray 3, Dreier 4, Head 4)
Murder in Aspic, 1978 (Demme 2)
Murder in Bergen. *See* Let George Do It, 1940
Murder in Greenwich Village, 1937 (Arlen 3, Wray 3)
Murder in Island Street. *See* Vražda v Ostrovní ulici, 1933
Murder in Music City, 1979 (Sangster 4)
Murder in Peyton Place, 1977 (Malone 3)
Murder in the Air, 1940 (Reagan 3, McCord 4)
Murder in the Big House, 1942 (Johnson, V. 3, Eason 4, McCord 4)
Murder in the Big House. *See* Jailbreak, 1936
Murder in the Blue Room, 1944 (Diamond 4)
Murder in the Clouds, 1934 (Orry-Kelly 4, Schary 4)
Murder in the Family, 1938 (McDowall 3)
Murder in the Fleet, 1935 (Auer 3, Bond 3, Hersholt 3, Merkel 3,
    Taylor, R. 3, Krasner 4)
Murder in the Museum, 1934 (Walthall 3)
Murder in the Music Hall, 1946 (Alton, J. 4)
Murder in the Private Car, 1934 (Merkel 3)
Murder in Thornton Square. *See* Gaslight, 1944
Murder in Trinidad, 1934 (Bruce 3, Johnson, N. 3)
Murder, Inc., 1960 (Falk 3, Rosenblum 4, Sylbert 4)
Murder Is Easy, 1982 (De Havilland 3)
Murder Is My Beat, 1955 (Ulmer 2)
Murder Man, 1935 (Stewart 3, Tracy 3)
Murder Men, 1962 (Coburn, J. 3, Dandridge 3)
Murder Most Foul, 1964 (Rutherford 3)
Murder, My Sweet, 1944 (Powell, D. 3, Trevor 3, D'Agostino 4,
    Paxton 4)
Murder, My Sweet. *See* Farewell, My Lovely, 1944
Murder of Dr. Harrigan, 1936 (Astor 3)
Murder of Otsuya. *See* Otsuya goroshi, 1951
Murder on a Bridle Path, 1936 (Musuraca 4)
Murder on a Honeymoon, 1935 (Carroll L. 3, MacGowan 4,
    Musuraca 4, Plunkett 4)
Murder on Dante Street. *See* Ubiistvo na ulize Dante,
    1956
Murder on Diamond Row. *See* Squeaker, 1937
Murder on Flight 502, 1975 (Bellamy 3, Pidgeon 3)
Murder on Monday. *See* Home at Seven, 1952
Murder on the Blackboard, 1934 (MacGowan 4, Musuraca 4, Steiner 4)
Murder on the Bridge. *See* Richter und sein Henker, 1975

Murder on the Orient Express, 1974 (Lumet 2, Bacall 3, Bergman 3,
    Bisset 3, Cassel 3, Connery 3, Finney 3, Gielgud 3, Hiller 3,
    Perkins 3, Redgrave, V. 3, Roberts 3, Widmark 3, York, M. 3,
    Dehn 4, Unsworth 4)
Murder on the Roof, 1930 (Walker 4)
Murder on the Waterfront, 1943 (Eason 4)
Murder or Mercy, 1974 (Douglas, M. 3)
Murder Our Style. *See* Vražda po našem, 1966
Murder over New York, 1940 (Muse 3, Day 4, Miller, V. 4)
Murder Party. *See* Night of the Party, 1934
Murder Psalm, 1980 (Brakhage 2)
Murder She Said, 1961 (Kennedy, A. 3, Rutherford 3)
Murder that Wouldn't Die, 1980 (Ferrer, J. 3)
Murder Will Out, 1930 (Seitz 4)
Murder Will Out, 1939 (Hawkins 3)
Murder with Pictures, 1936 (Ayres 3, Head 4)
Murder Without Cause. *See* Mord ohne Täter, 1920
Murder Without Tears, 1953 (Miller, V. 4)
Murderer. *See* Aru koroshiya, 1967
Murderer and the Girl. *See* Zbrodniarz i panna, 1963
Murderer Dimitri Karamazov. *See* Morder Dmitri Karamasoff, 1931
Murderer Leaves a Clue. *See* Moderca zostawia ślad, 1967
Murderer Lives at Number 21. *See* Assassin habite au 21, 1942
Murderer Made in Italy. *See* Segreto del vestito rosso, 1963
Murderers Among Us. *See* Morder sind unter uns, 1946 (Knef 3)
Murderers Are on Their Way. *See* Ubitzi vykhodyat na dorogu, 1942
Murderers' Row, 1966 (Martin, D. 3, Malden 3, Schifrin 4)
Murders in the Rue Morgue, 1932 (Florey 2, Huston 2, Johnson, N. 3,
    Lugosi 3, Freund 4, Laemmle 4)
Murders in the Rue Morgue, 1971 (Robards 3)
Murders in the Zoo, 1933 (Sutherland 2, Darwell 3, Scott, R. 3,
    Haller 4)
Murdoch's Gang, 1973 (Leigh, J. 3)
Muriel, 1963 (Resnais 2, Seyrig 3, Braunberger 4, Delerue 4, Vierny 4)
Muri-shinju: Nihon no natsu, 1967 (Oshima 2, Toda 4)
Murmur of the Heart. *See* Souffle au coeur, 1971
Muro, 1947 (Torre-Nilsson 2)
Muro de silencio, 1972 (Alcoriza 4)
Murphy's I.O.U., 1913 (Sennett 2)
Murphy's Romance, 1985 (Fraker 4, Ravetch 4)
Murphy's War, 1971 (Yates 2, Noiret 3, O'Toole 3, Barry 4,
    Slocombe 4)
Murray's Mix-Up. *See* His Hereafter, 1916
Murri Affair. *See* Fatti di gente perbene, 1974
Musachino Fujin, 1951 (Hayasaka 4)
Musafir, 1955 (Ghatak 4)
Musasabi no Sankichi, 1927 (Tanaka 3)
Musashi and Kojiro. *See* Ketto ganryu-jima, 1956
Musashi Miyamoto, 1944 (Tanaka 3)
Musashi Miyamoto. *See* Miyamoto Musashi, 1944
Musashibo Benkei, 1942 (Takamine 3, Yamada 3)
Musashino fujin, 1951 (Mizoguchi 2, Mori 3, Shindo 3, Tanaka 3,
    Yamamura 3, Yoda 4)
Musca cu bani, 1954 (Popescu-Gopo 4)
Muscle Beach, 1948 (Strick 2)
Muscle Beach Party, 1964 (Lorre 3)
Muscle Beach Tom, 1956 (Hanna and Barbera 4)
Muscle Tussle, 1953 (McKimson 4)
Muscle Up a Little Closer, 1957 (Three Stooges 3)
Muscle-Bound Music, 1926 (Sennett 2)
Musée, 1964 (Borowczyk 4)
Musée des grotesques, 1911 (Cohl 2)
Musée du Louvre, 1979 (Takemitsu 4)
Musée Grevin, 1958 (Cocteau 2, Demy 2, Fradetal 4)
Musée vivant, 1965 (Storck 2)
Musen fusen, 1924 (Mizoguchi 2)
Museo dei sogni, 1948 (Comencini 2)
Museo dell'amore, 1935 (Lattuada 2)
Museum Mystery, 1937 (Havelock-Allan 4)
Museumsmysteriet, 1909 (Blom 2)
Mush and Milk, 1933 (Roach 4)
Mushibameru haru, 1932 (Naruse 2)
Mushukunin Mikoshin no Joukichi, 1972 (Miyagawa 4)

Music Box, 1932 (Laurel & Hardy 3, Roach 4)
Music for Madame, 1937 (Fontaine 3, August 4, Lasky 4, Polglase 4)
Music for Millions, 1944 (Allyson 3, Durante 3, Gardner 3, O'Brien, M. 3, Irene 4, Surtees 4)
Music for Millions, 1945 (Pasternak 4)
Music from Mars. See Hudba z Marsu, 1954
Music Goes 'round, 1936 (Buchman 4, Swerling 4, Walker 4)
Music Hall. See Tango Tangles, 1914
Music Hall Star. See Lydia, 1916
Music Hath Charms, 1936 (Lantz 4)
Music Hath Its Charms, 1915 (Browning 2)
Music in Darkness. See Musik i morker, 1948
Music in Manhattan, 1944 (Darwell 3)
Music in My Heart, 1939 (Hayworth 3)
Music in the Air, 1934 (Wilder 2, Bosworth 3, Swanson 3, Pommer 4, Waxman 4)
Music in Your Hair, 1934 (Roach 4)
Music Is Magic, 1935 (Daniels 3, Faye 3, McDaniel 3)
Music Lesson, 1932 (Iwerks 4)
Music Lovers, 1970 (Russell 2, Jackson 3, Previn 4, Russell 4, Slocombe 4)
Music Man, 1938 (Halas and Batchelor 2)
Music Man, 1962 (Jones S. 3, Preston 3, Jeakins 4)
Music Master, 1908 (Bitzer 4)
Music Master, 1927 (Dwan 2)
Music Room. See Jalsaghar, 1958
Musica, 1966 (Duras 2, Seyrig 3, Vierny 4)
Musical Madness, 1951 (Terry 4)
Musical Memories, 1935 (Fleischer, M. and D. 2)
Musical Mountaineers, 1939 (Fleischer, M. and D. 2)
Musical Pig. See Muzikalno prase, 1965
Musical Poster No. 1, 1940 (Lye 2)
Musical Tramps. See His Musical Career, 1914
Musicians' Girl. See Muzikantská Liduška, 1940
Musiciens de la mine, 1950 (Cloquet 4)
Musiciens du ciel, 1939 (Morgan 3, Simon, M. 3, Alekan 4, Andrejew 4, Honegger 4, Schufftan 4)
Musicomanie, 1910 (Cohl 2)
Musidora en Espagne. See Aventura de Musidora en España, 1922
Musik bei Nacht, 1953 (Jurgens 3, Herlth 4)
Musik i morker, 1948 (Bergman 2, Zetterling 2, Bjornstrand 3, Borgstrom 3)
Musik im Blut, 1934 (Warm 4)
Musik in Salzburg, 1944 (Dagover 3)
Musique en Méditerranée, 1968 (Reichenbach 2)
Musique tropicale, 1947–51 (Verneuil 4)
Musketeers of Little Side. See Malostranští mušketýři, 1932
Musketeers of Pig Alley, 1912 (Griffith 2, Barrymore L. 3, Carey 3, Gish, D. 3, Gish, L. 3, Bitzer 4)
Musodoro, 1954 (Rota 4)
Muss 'em Up, 1936 (Vidor, C. 2, Bond 3, Muse 3, August 4, Berman 4, Hunt 4, Polglase 4)
Muss Man sich gleich scheiden lassen?, 1932 (Sakall 3)
Mussolini: Last Days. See Mussolini: ultimo atto, 1974
Mussolini: ultimo atto, 1974 (Fonda, H. 3, Steiger 3, Morricone 4)
Mussorgsky, 1950 (Cherkassov 3, Orlova 3)
Mustaa Valkoisella, 1968 (Donner 2)
Mustang Country, 1977 (McCrea 3)
Mustang Pete's Love Affair, 1911 (Anderson G. 3)
Musterknaben, 1959 (Geschonneck 3)
Musty Musketeers, 1954 (Three Stooges 3)
Musuko no seishun, 1952 (Kobayashi 2)
Musume, 1926 (Gosho 2)
Musume Dojoji, 1946 (Ichikawa 2)
Musume no boken, 1958 (Kyo 3)
Musume no naka no musume, 1958 (Yamamura 3)
Musume tabigeinin, 1941 (Yoda 4)
Musume to watashi, 1962 (Hara 3, Yamamura 3)
Musume tsuma haha, 1960 (Naruse 2, Hara 3, Mori 3, Takamine 3)
Mut zur Sunde, 1918 (Albers 3)
Muta di Portici, 1954 (Mastroianni 3)
Mutations, 1974 (Pleasance 3, Cardiff 4)
Mute Witness, 1913 (Dwan 2)

Muteki, 1952 (Mifune 3, Shimura 3)
Mutineers, 1949 (Katzman 4)
Mutinés de l'Elseneur, 1936 (Honegger 4, Matras 4)
Mutiny, 1952 (Dmytryk 2, Lansbury 3, Laszlo 4, Tiomkin 4)
Mutiny Ain't Nice, 1938 (Fleischer, M. and D. 2)
Mutiny at Fort Sharp. See Escuadró de la muerte, 1966
Mutiny in the Arctic, 1941 (Arlen 3, Salter 4)
Mutiny on the Blackhawk, 1939 (Arlen 3)
Mutiny on the Bounty, 1935 (Crisp 3, Gable 3, Laughton 3, Booth 4, Clarke, C.C. 4, Edeson 4, Furthman 4, Gibbons 4, Gillespie 4, Jennings 4, Kaper 4, Lewin 4, Stothart 4, Thalberg 4, Westmore, M. 4, Wilson, C. 4)
Mutiny on the Bounty, 1962 (Milestone 2, Brando 3, Howard, T. 3, Rafferty 3, Gillespie 4, Hall 4, Kaper 4, Lederer 4, Surtees 4)
Mutiny on the Bunny, 1948 (Freleng 4)
Mutiny on the Elsinore, 1938 (Lukas 3)
Mutoscope Shorts, 1897 (Bitzer 4)
Mutt in a Rut, 1959 (McKimson 4)
Mutter Courage und ihre Kinder, 1955 (Douy 4)
Mutter Kusters Fahrt zum Himmel, 1975 (Fassbinder 2)
Mutter und Kind, 1924 (Dieterle 2, Porten 3)
Mutter und Kind, 1933 (Porten 3)
Mutter, verzaget nicht!, 1911 (Messter 4)
Mutterliebe, 1929 (Porten 3)
Mutterlied, 1937 (Von Harbou 4)
Mutts to You, 1938 (Three Stooges 3)
Muyder Circle Lives Again. See Muiderkring herleeft, 1948
Muž bez srdce, 1923 (Ondra 3)
Muž, který rozdával smích, 1970 (Kopecký 3)
Muž, který stoupl v ceně, 1967 (Kroner 3)
Muž, ktory luže, 1968 (Kroner 3)
Muž s orlem a slepici, 1978 (Brejchová 3)
Muz v povetri, 1955 (Hrusínský 3)
Muž z neznáma, 1939 (Fric 2)
Muž z prvního století, 1961 (Kopecký 3)
Muzhskoi Razgovor, 1969 (Shukshin 3)
Muži bez křídel, 1945 (Stallich 4)
Muži v offsidu, 1931 (Haas 3)
Muži v ofsajdu, 1931 (Vích 4)
Muzikalno prase, 1965 (Grgić 4)
Muzikantská Liduška, 1940 (Fric 2)
Muzzle. See Kanonen-Serenade, 1958
Muzzle Tough, 1953 (Freleng 4)
My American Uncle. See Mon oncle américaine, 1980
My American Wife, 1923 (Wood 2, Swanson 3)
My American Wife, 1936 (Burke 3, Sothern 3)
My Apprenticeship. See Vlyudyakh, 1939
My Artistical Temperature, 1937 (Fleischer, M. and D. 2)
My Asylum. See Chiedo asilo, 1979
My Aunt's Millions. See Fasters miljoner, 1934
My Baby, 1912 (Griffith 2, Barrymore L. 3, Gish, L. 3, Pickford 3, Walthall 3, Bitzer 4)
My Baby Just Cares for Me, 1931 (Fleischer, M. and D. 2)
My Beloved. See Dorogio moi chelovek, 1958
My Beloved Child. See Itoshi no wagako, 1926
My Best Friend's Girl, 1982 (Huppert 3)
My Best Gal, 1943 (Brooks, R. 2, Mann 2)
My Best Girl, 1927 (Bosworth 3, Pickford 3, Rosher 4)
My Bill, 1938 (Francis, K. 3, Orry-Kelly 4)
My Blood Runs Cold, 1965 (Duning 4)
My Blue Heaven, 1950 (Beavers 3, Dailey 3, Grable 3, Merkel 3, Lemaire 4, Newman 4, Trotti 4)
My Body, My Child, 1982 (Redgrave, V. 3)
My Bodyguard, 1980 (Gordon 3, Houseman 4)
My Bonnie, 1925 (Fleischer, M. and D. 2)
My Boy, 1922 (Coogan 3, Heerman 4)
My Boy Johnny, 1944 (Terry 4)
My Boys Are Good Boys, 1978 (Lupino 3)
My Brother Down There. See Running Target, 1956
My Brother Talks to Horses, 1946 (Zinnemann 2, Irene 4, Plunkett 4, Rosson 4)
My Brother's Keeper, 1948 (Lee, C. 3)
My Buddy, 1944 (Edwards 2)

My Bunny Lies Over the Sea, 1948 (Jones 2)

My Child. *See* Mein Kind, 1956

My City. *See* Orasul meu, 1967

My Cousin Rachel, 1952 (Burton 3, De Havilland 3, Jeakins 4, Johnson 4, La Shelle 4, Lemaire 4, Waxman 4, Wheeler 4)

My Crimes. *See* Mein Kampf, 1941

My Darling Clementine, 1946 (Ford, J. 2, Bond 3, Brennan 3, Darnell 3, Darwell 3, Fonda, H. 3, Ireland 3, Newman 4, Wheeler 4, Zanuck 4)

My Darling Clementine. *See* Drahoušek Klementýna, 1959

My Darling Daughters' Anniversary, 1973 (Massey 3, Young, R. 3)

My Daughter and I. *See* Musume to watashi, 1962

My Daughter Joy, 1950 (Robinson, E. 3, Périnal 4)

My Days with Jean Marc. *See* Anatomy of a Marriage, 1964

My Dear Bodyguard. *See* Sevgili muhafizin, 1970

My Dear Fellow! See Dorogio moi chelovek, 1958

My Dear Miss Aldrich, 1937 (O'Sullivan 3, Pidgeon 3, Mankiewicz 4)

My Dear Secretary, 1948 (Douglas, K. 3, Wynn 3, Biroc 4)

My Dearest Señorita. *See* Mi Querida señorita, 1972

My Dinner with Andre, 1981 (Malle 2)

My Dream is Yours, 1949 (Curtiz 2, Arden 3, Day 3, Menjou 3, Sakall 3, Haller 4, Kurnitz 4, Prinz 4)

My, dvoe muzhchin, 1963 (Shukshin 3)

My Enemy, the Sea. *See* Taiheiyo hitoribotchi, 1963

My Eye. *See* Mon Oeil, 1966

My Face Red in the Sunset. *See* Yuhi ni akai ore no kao, 1961

My Fair Lady, 1964 (Cukor 2, Cooper, Gladys 3, Harrison 3, Hepburn, A. 3, Holloway 3, Beaton 4, Pan 4, Previn 4, Stradling 4)

My Father's Happy Years. *See* Apám néhány boldog éve, 1977

My Father's House, 1947 (Kline 2, Crosby 4)

My Father's House, 1975 (Preston 3, Robertson 3)

My Fault. *See* Shin ono ga tsumi, 1926

My Favorite Blonde, 1942 (Carroll M. 3, Crosby 3, Hope 3, Dreier 4, Frank and Panama 4, Head 4)

My Favorite Brunette, 1947 (Chaney Lon, Jr. 3, Crosby 3, Hope 3, Ladd 3, Lamour 3, Lorre 3, Dreier 4, Head 4)

My Favorite Duck, 1942 (Jones 2)

My Favorite Spy, 1942 (Garnett 2, Lloyd 3, Wyman 3)

My Favorite Spy, 1951 (McLeod 2, Hope 3, Lamarr 3, Head 4, Mercer 4, Young, V. 4)

My Favorite Wife, 1940 (McCarey 2, Dunne 3, Grant, C. 3, Scott, R. 3, Kanin 4, Maté 4, Polglase 4)

My Favorite Year, 1982 (O'Toole 3)

My Feelin's Is Hurt, 1940 (Fleischer, M. and D. 2)

My Foolish Heart, 1949 (Robson 2, Andrews D. 3, Hayward 3, Day 4, Epstein, J. & P. 4, Garmes 4, Goldwyn 4, Head 4, Mandell 4, Young, V. 4)

My Forbidden Past, 1951 (Douglas, M. 3, Gardner 3, Mitchum 3, Muse 3)

My Friend, 1979 (Rademakers 2)

My Friend Dr. Jekyll. *See* Mio amico Jekyll, 1960

My Friend Fabian. *See* Muj přítel Fabián, 1953

My Friend Flicka, 1943 (McDowall 3, Day 4, Newman 4)

My Friend from India, 1927 (Adrian 4)

My Friend Irma, 1949 (Lewis 2, Martin, D. 3, Bumstead 4, Dreier 4, Head 4, Wallis 4)

My Friend Irma Goes West, 1950 (Lewis 2, Martin, D. 3, Bumstead 4, Dreier 4, Garmes 4, Head 4, Wallis 4)

My Friend Levy. *See* Min Ven Levy, 1914

My Friend Nicholas, 1961 (Brynner 3)

My Friend the Devil, 1922 (Ruttenberg 4)

My Friend the Gypsy. *See* Muj přítel Fabián, 1953

My Friend the King, 1931 (Powell 2)

My Friend the Monkey, 1939 (Fleischer, M. and D. 2)

My Friends. *See* Amici miei, 1975

My Friends Act II. *See* Amici miei atto II, 1982

My Gal Sal, 1930 (Fleischer, M. and D. 2)

My Gal Sal, 1942 (Hayworth 3, Mature 3, Day 4, Miller, S. 4, Newman 4, Pan 4)

My Geisha, 1962 (Cummings 3, MacLaine 3, Montand 3, Robinson, E. 3, Cardiff 4, Head 4, Krasna 4, Kurnitz 4, Waxman 4, Westmore, F. 4)

My Girl Tisa, 1948 (Haas 3, Haller 4, Steiner 4)

My Goodness, 1920 (Sennett 2)

My Green Fedora, 1935 (Freleng 4)

My Gun is Quick, 1957 (Leven 4)

My Heart Belongs to Daddy, 1942 (Siodmak 2, Dreier 4, Head 4)

My Heart Goes Crazy. *See* London Town, 1946

My Heart Is Calling, 1935 (Gilliat 4)

My Heart Is Calling. *See* Mein Herz ruft nach Dir, 1935

My Hero, 1912 (Griffith 2, Barrymore L. 3, Carey 3, Gish, D. 3, Bitzer 4)

My Hero. *See* Southern Yankee, 1948

My Hobo. *See* Burari burabura monogatari, 1962

My Home Is Copacabana. *See* Mitt hem ar Copacabana, 1965

My Husband Lies. *See* Hazasodik az uram, 1913

My Husband's Other Wife, 1919 (Blackton 2)

My Hustler, 1966 (Warhol 2)

My Irish Molly, 1939 (O'Hara 3)

My Kidnapper, My Love, 1980 (Rooney 3)

My Kingdom for a Cook, 1943 (Coburn, C. 3, Planer 4)

My Lady Incog, 1916 (Olcott 2)

My Lady of Whims, 1926 (Bow 3)

My Lady's Dress, 1917 (Cooper, Gladys 3)

My Lady's Garden, 1934 (Terry 4)

My Lady's Garter, 1920 (Tourneur, M. 2, Carré 4)

My Lady's Lips, 1925 (Bow 3, Powell, W. 3, Schulberg 4)

My Lady's Past, 1929 (Brown 3)

My Learned Friend, 1943 (Dearden 2, Hamer 2, Balcon 4)

My Life Story. *See* Mit livs eventyr, 1955 (Roos 2)

My Life to Live. *See* Vivre sa vie, 1962

My Life with Caroline, 1941 (Milestone 2, Colman 3, Miller, V. 4)

My Life with Mihály Károlyi. *See* Együtt Károlyi Mihállyal, 1973

My Life's Bright Day. *See* Waga shogai no kagayakeru hi, 1948

My Lips Betray, 1933 (Behrman 4, Friedhofer 4, Garmes 4, Kraly 4)

My Little Baby, 1916 (Bertini 3)

My Little Buckeroo, 1937 (Freleng 4)

My Little Chickadee, 1940 (Cody 3, Fields, W.C. 3, Meek 3, West 3)

My Little Duckaroo, 1954 (Jones 2)

My Little Sister, 1919 (Ruttenberg 4)

My Love. *See* Waga ai, 1960

My Love Burns. *See* Waga koi wa moenu, 1949

My Love Came Back, 1940 (De Havilland 3, Sakall 3, Wyman 3, Buckner 4, Orry-Kelly 4, Reisch 4, Rosher 4, Wallis 4)

My Love Has Been Burning. *See* Waga koi wa moenu, 1949

My Love Is Beyond the Mountain. *See* Waga ai wa yama no kanata ni, 1948

My Love is Like a Rose. *See* Min kara ar en ros, 1963

My Love to the Swallows. *See* . . . a pozdravuji vlaštovky, 1972

My Lover, My Son, 1970 (Schneider 3)

My Loving Child. *See* Itoshi no wagako, 1926

My Lucky Star, 1938 (Cook 3, Henie 3, Brown, Harry Joe 4)

My Madonna, 1915 (Guy 2)

My Man, 1928 (Zanuck 4)

My Man and I, 1952 (Wellman 2, Elam 3, Trevor 3, Winters 3, Basevi 4)

My Man Godfrey, 1936 (La Cava 2, Auer 3, Brady 3, Lombard 3, Powell, W. 3, Wyman 3, Banton 4, Ryskind 4)

My Man Godfrey, 1957 (Allyson 3, Niven 3, Daniels 4, Hunter 4)

My Marriage, 1936 (Trevor 3)

My Mother the General. *See* Imi Hageneralit, 1979

My Name is Joker. *See* Mera Naam Joker, 1970

My Name is Julia Ross, 1945 (Guffey 4)

My Name is Kerim. *See* Benim adim Kerim, 1967

My Name Is Mistress. *See* Watashi no na wa joufu, 1949

My Name Is Nobody, 1974 (Leone 2)

My Name Is Nobody. *See* Mio nome e nessuno, 1974

My Name is Puck. *See* Puck heter jag, 1951

My Neighbor's Wife, 1925 (Walker 4)

My New Gown. *See* Boogie Woogie Dream, 1942

My Night at Maud's. *See* Ma Nuit chez Maud, 1969

My Nights with Françoise. *See* Anatomy of a Marriage, 1964

My, nizhepodpisavshiesya . . ., 1980 (Yankovsky 3)

My Official Wife, 1914 (Valentino 3)

My Official Wife, 1926 (Blanke 4, Carré 4)

My Old China, 1931 (Balcon 4)

My Old Dutch, 1911 (Costello, M. 3)
My Old Dutch, 1926 (Hersholt 3)
My Old Dutch, 1934 (Balfour 3, Balcon 4)
My Old Kentucky Home, 1926 (Fleischer, M. and D. 2)
My Old Kentucky Home, 1946 (Terry 4)
My Old Man, 1979 (Oates 3)
My Old Man's Place, 1971 (Kennedy, A. 3)
My Other 'Husband', 1983 (Sarde 4)
My Outlaw Brother, 1951 (Preston 3, Rooney 3)
My Own Pal, 1926 (Mix 3)
My Own True Love, 1948 (Douglas, M. 3, Bumstead 4, Dreier 4, Head 4, Lang 4, Lewton 4)
My Pal Gus, 1952 (Widmark 3, Lemaire 4, Wheeler 4)
My Pal Paul, 1930 (Lantz 4)
My Pal, The King, 1932 (Mix 3, Rooney 3)
My Pal Trigger, 1946 (Rogers, R. 3)
My Pal, Wolf, 1944 (Paxton 4)
My Partner Mr. Davis, 1936 (Autant-Lara 2, Prévert 4)
My Partner Mr. Davis. See Mysterious Mr. Davis, 1936
My Past, 1931 (Blondell 3, Daniels 3, Stone 3)
My People Are Not Yours. See Mitt folk ar icke ditt, 1944
My Pony Boy, 1929 (Fleischer, M. and D. 2)
My Pop, My Pop, 1940 (Fleischer, M. and D. 2)
My Reputation, 1946 (Arden 3, Brent 3, Stanwyck 3, Blanke 4, Grot 4, Head 4, Howe 4, Steiner 4)
My Second Brother. See Nianchan, 1959
My 7 Little Sins. See J'avais sept filles, 1955
My Sin, 1930 (March 3, Green, J. 4)
My Sister, 1944 (Sircar 4)
My Sister and I. See Min syster och jag, 1950
My Sister Eileen, 1942 (Russell, R. 3, Three Stooges 3, Walker 4)
My Sister Eileen, 1955 (Edwards 2, Fosse 2, Leigh, J. 3, Lemmon 3, Duning 4, Wald 4)
My Sister, My Love. See Syskonbadd 1782, 1965
My Six Convicts, 1952 (Kramer, S. 2, Bronson 3, Anhalt 4, Tiomkin 4)
My Six Loves, 1963 (Reynolds, D. 3, Robertson 3, Cahn 4, Fulton 4, Head 4)
My Son, 1925 (Bennett C. 3, Bosworth 3, Nazimova 3)
My Son. See Moi syn, 1928
My Son. See Shodo satsujin: Musuko yo, 1979
My Son Is Guilty, 1939 (Carey 3, Ford, G. 3, Brown, K. 4)
My Son John, 1952 (McCarey 2, Heflin 3, Walker 3, Head 4, Mahin 4, Stradling 4)
My Son, My Son, 1940 (Vidor, C. 2, Carroll M. 3, Coffee 4, Stradling 4)
My Son, the Hero, 1943 (Ulmer 2)
My Son, the Hero. See Arrivano i Titani, 1962
My Son, the Hero. See Hermanos del hierro, 1963
My Son, The Vampire. See Old Mother Riley Meets the Vampire, 1952
My Song for You, 1934 (Junge 4)
My Song Goes Round the World, 1935 (Oswald 2)
My Son's Youth. See Musuko no seishun, 1952
My Stars, 1926 (Arbuckle 3)
My Stupid Brother. See Nisan no baka, 1932
My Tail's My Ticket, 1959 (Vukotić 4)
My Teenage Daughter, 1956 (Wilcox 2, Neagle 3)
My Tender Loving Beast. See Moi laskovyi i nezhnyi zver, 1978
My True Story, 1951 (Rooney 3)
My Twelve Fathers. See Tucet mých tatínku, 1959
My Two Husbands. See Too Many Husbands, 1940
My Universities. See Moi universiteti, 1940
My Valet, 1915 (Sennett 2, Normand 3)
My Way. See Waga michi, 1974
My Way Home. See Igy jottem, 1964
My Weakness, 1933 (Ayres 3, Langdon 3, Miller, A. 4)
My Widow and I. See Sbaglio di essere vivo, 1945
My Wife and I, 1925 (Bennett C. 3)
My Wife's Best Friend, 1952 (Baxter A. 3, Lemaire 4, Lennart 4)
My Wife's Enemy. See Nemico di mia moglie, 1959
My Wife's Family, 1941 (Greenwood 3)
My Wife's Gone to the Country, 1931 (Fleischer, M. and D. 2)
My Wife's Husband. See Cuisine au beurre, 1963
My Wife's Relations, 1922 (Keaton 2)

My Wild Irish Rose, 1947 (Edeson 4, Prinz 4, Steiner 4)
My Wonderful Yellow Car. See Fukeyo harukaze, 1953
Myohoin Kanpachi, 1939 (Shimura 3)
Myoreki meikenshi, 1934 (Hasegawa 3)
Myra Breckenridge, 1970 (Huston 2, Carradine 3, Welch 3, West 3, Head 4, Smith, J.M. 4, van Runkle 4)
Myriad Homes, 1953 (Lee, B. 3)
Myrt and Marge, 1933 (Three Stooges 3)
Myrte and the Demons. See Myrte en de demonen, 1949
Myrte en de demonen, 1949 (Haanstra 2)
Mystère Barton, 1948 (Rosay 3, Burel 4, Spaak 4)
Mystère de la chambre jaune, 1930 (L'Herbier 2, Burel 4, Meerson 4)
Mystère de la chambre jaune, 1948 (Modot 3, Reggiani 3, Douy 4)
Mystère de la Tour Eiffel, 1927 (Duvivier 2)
Mystère de l'atelier, 1957 (Marker 2)
Mystère de l'Atelier Quinze, 1957 (Resnais 2, Cloquet 4, Delerue 4)
Mystère du Palace Hôtel, 1953 (D'Eaubonne 4)
Mystère du Quai Conti, 1950 (Delerue 4)
Mystère Imberger, 1934 (Modot 3)
Mystère Koumiko, 1965 (Marker 2, Takemitsu 4)
Mystère Picasso, 1956 (Auric 4, Colpi 4, Renoir 4)
Mystère Saint-Val, 1945 (Fernandel 3)
Mystères d'Angkor. See Herrin der Welt, 1960
Mystères de Paris, 1922 (Fresnay 3, Modot 3)
Mystères de Paris, 1935 (Auric 4)
Mystères de Paris, 1943 (Barsacq 4, Burel 4)
Mysterians. See Chikyu boeigun, 1957
Mysteries, 1968 (Markopoulos 2)
Mysteries, 1978 (Rademakers 2)
Mysteries of India. See Indische Grabmal, 1921
Mysteries of New York. See Reggie Mixes In, 1916
Mysteries of the Novgorod Fair. See Taina niegorodskoi yamarki, 1915
Mysterious Avenger, 1936 (Rogers, R. 3)
Mysterious Box. See Boîte à malice, 1903
Mysterious Café, 1901 (Porter 2)
Mysterious Castle in the Carpathians. See Tajemstvi hradu v Karpatech, 1982
Mysterious Companion. See Mystiske Selskabsdame, 1916
Mysterious Cowboy, 1952 (Terry 4)
Mysterious Crossing, 1936 (Muse 3, Krasner 4)
Mysterious Desperado, 1949 (Musuraca 4)
Mysterious Dr. Fu Manchu, 1929 (Arthur 3, Johnson, N. 3, Oland 3)
Mysterious Island, 1926 (Tourneur, M. 2)
Mysterious Island, 1929 (Barrymore L. 3, Basevi 4, Gibbons 4)
Mysterious Island, 1952 (Katzman 4)
Mysterious Island, 1961 (Greenwood 3, Harryhausen 4, Herrmann 4)
Mysterious Island, 1973 (Bardem 2)
Mysterious Island. See Ile mystérieuse, 1973
Mysterious Jug, 1937 (Lantz 4)
Mysterious Lady, 1928 (Niblo 2, Garbo 3, Booth 4, Daniels 4, Gibbons 4, Meredyth 4)
Mysterious Lady. See Maaneprinsessen, 1916
Mysterious Lady's Companion. See Mystiske Selskabsdame, 1917
Mysterious Lodger, 1914 (Costello, M. 3, Talmadge, C. 3)
Mysterious Love of Mrs. White. See Hakufujin no yoren, 1956
Mysterious Miss Terry, 1917 (Burke 3)
Mysterious Mr. Davis, 1936 (Sim 3)
Mysterious Mr. Davis. See My Partner Mr. Davis, 1936
Mysterious Mr. Moto, 1938 (Lorre 3)
Mysterious Mr. Wong, 1935 (Lugosi 3)
Mysterious Mrs. M, 1917 (Weber 2)
Mysterious Mose, 1930 (Fleischer, M. and D. 2)
Mysterious Mystery, 1914 (Lawrence 3)
Mysterious Mystery, 1924 (Roach 4)
Mysterious Pilot, 1937 (Canutt 4)
Mysterious Portrait. See Portrait mystérieux, 1899
Mysterious Retort. See Alchimiste Prararafaragamus ou la Cornue infernale, 1906
Mysterious Rider, 1927 (Schulberg 4)
Mysterious Rider, 1938 (Head 4)
Mysterious Rider, 1943 (Crabbe 3)
Mysterious Rose, 1914 (Ford, J. 2)
Mysterious Shot, 1914 (Crisp 3, Gish, D. 3)

Mysterious Stranger, 1948 (Terry 4)
Mysterious X. *See* Hemmelighedsfulde X, 1913
Mystery at Monte Carlo. *See* Revenge at Monte Carlo, 1933
Mystery Club, 1926 (Oland 3)
Mystery House, 1938 (Sheridan 3)
Mystery in Mexico, 1948 (Wise 2)
Mystery in the Moonlight, 1948 (Terry 4)
Mystery Lake, 1953 (Crosby 4)
Mystery Man, 1923 (Roach 4)
Mystery Man, 1944 (Boyd 3)
Mystery Mountain, 1934 (Autry 3, Canutt 4, Eason 4)
Mystery of Blood. *See* Tajemství krve, 1953
Mystery of Brayton Court, 1914 (Costello, M. 3)
Mystery of Edwin Drood, 1935 (Rains 3, Balderston 4, D'Agostino 4,
    Fulton 4)
Mystery of Kaspar Hauser. *See* Jeder fur sich und Gott gegen alle, 1974
Mystery of Marie Roget, 1942 (Ouspenskaya 3, Salter 4)
Mystery of Mr. Wong, 1939 (Karloff 3)
Mystery of Mr. X, 1934 (Montgomery 3, Stone 3, Adrian 4)
Mystery of Monster Island. *See* Misterio en la isla de los monstruos,
    1980
Mystery of Oberwald. *See* Mistero di Oberwald, 1981
Mystery of Picasso. *See* Mystère Picasso, 1956
Mystery of Pine Tree Camp, 1913 (Olcott 2)
Mystery of Room 643, 1914 (Bushman 3)
Mystery of the Bermuda Triangle. *See* Triangulo diabolico de la
    Bermudas, 1977
Mystery of the Black Jungle. *See* Misteri della jungla nera, 1953
Mystery of the Blue Room. *See* Záhada modrého pokoje, 1933
Mystery of the Hindu Image, 1913 (Walsh 2)
Mystery of the Jewel Casket, 1905 (Bitzer 4)

Mystery of the Leaping Fish, 1916 (Browning 2, Fleming 2,
    Fairbanks, D. 3, Love 3, Brown, K. 4, Emerson 4)
Mystery of the Marie Celeste. *See* Phantom Ship, 1935
Mystery of the Museum. *See* Museumsmysteriet, 1909
Mystery of the Old Castle. *See* Tajemnica starego zamku, 1956
Mystery of the Poisoned Pool, 1914 (Rosher 4)
Mystery of the Sleeper Trunk, 1909 (Olcott 2)
Mystery of the Wax Museum, 1933 (Curtiz 2, Wray 3, Blanke 4,
    Grot 4, Orry-Kelly 4, Wallis 4)
Mystery of the Yellow Aster Mine, 1913 (Reid 3)
Mystery of the Yellow Room, 1919 (Von Sternberg 2)
Mystery of Wentworth Castle. *See* Doomed to Die, 1940
Mystery of Wickham Hall, 1914 (Meredyth 4)
Mystery Ranch, 1932 (Johnson, N. 3, August 4, Friedhofer 4)
Mystery Road, 1921 (Hitchcock 2)
Mystery Sea Raider, 1940 (Dmytryk 2, Dreier 4, Head 4)
Mystery Squadron, 1933 (Canutt 4)
Mystery Street, 1950 (Brooks, R. 2, Sturges, J. 2, Lanchester 3,
    Alton, J. 4)
Mystery Submarine, 1950 (Sirk 2, Boyle 4)
Mystery Woman, 1915 (Meredyth 4)
Mystery Woman, 1935 (Auer 3, Nichols 4)
Mystic, 1925 (Browning 2, Gibbons 4, Young, W. 4)
Mystic Pink, 1976 (McKimson 4)
Mystic Swing, 1900 (Porter 2)
Mystical Flame. *See* Flamme merveilleuse, 1903
Mystical Love-Making. *See* Drame chez les fantoches,
    1908
Mystical Maid of Jamasha Pass, 1912 (Dwan 2)
Mystike Fremmede, 1914 (Holger-Madsen 2)
Mystiske Selskabsdame, 1917 (Blom 2, Dreyer 2)

N

N.I. ni-c'est fini, 1908 (Cohl 2)
N.N., 1977 (Dovniković 4)
N.N. a halál angyala, 1970 (Gabór 3, Torocsik 3)
N. or N.W., 1938 (Cavalcanti 2, Lye 2)
N. P., 1972 (Thulin 3)
N.P. il segreto, 1971 (Papas 3)
N.U., 1948 (Antonioni 2, Fusco 4)
N.V.V. Congres, 1929–30 (Ivens 2)
N.Y. City Fire Dept., 1903 (Bitzer 4)
Na civot i smart, 1974 (Paskaleva 3)
Na estrada da vida, 1980 (Pereira Dos Santos 2)
Na kometě, 1970 (Zeman 2)
Na konci mesta, 1955 (Hrušínský 3)
Na krasnom fronte, 1920 (Kuleshov 2)
Na livadi, 1957 (Mimica 4)
Na Pražském hradě, 1932 (Hammid 2)
Na primavera da vida, 1926 (Mauro 2)
Na putl k Leninu. *See* Unterwegs zu Lenin, 1970
Na samotě u lesa, 1977 (Menzel 2)
Na semi vetrakh, 1962 (Tikhonov 3)
Na šivot i smart, 1974 (Danailov 3)
Na sluneční strane, 1933 (Stallich 4)
Na start!, 1935 (Ford, A. 2)
Na viershina slavy, 1916 (Mozhukin 3)
Naadige Frøken, 1911 (Blom 2)
Naaede Faergen, 1948 (Dreyer 2)
Naar Fruen gaar paa Eventyr, 1913 (Blom 2)
Naar Fruen skifter Pige. *See* Husassistenten, 1914
Naar man kun er ung, 1943 (Henning-Jensen 2)
Naaz, 1954 (Biswas 4)
Nabonga, 1944 (Crabbe 3)
Nacala, 1970 (Panfilov 2)

Načaloto na deňa, 1975 (Danailov 3)
Nacer en Leningrado, 1977 (Solás 2)
Naceradec, King of Kibitzers. *See* Načeradec, král kibicu, 1932
Načeradec, král kibicu, 1932 (Haas 3, Vích 4)
Nach dem Gesetz, 1919 (Nielsen 3)
Nach dem Sturm, 1950 (Schell, Maria 3)
Nach Meinem letzten Umzug, 1970 (Syberberg 2)
Nach zwanzig Jahren, 1918 (Jannings 3)
Nachalo, 1970 (Churikova 3)
Nachi chempiony. *See* Sportivnaya slava, 1950
Nacht auf Goldenhall, 1920 (Veidt 3)
Nacht der Einbrecher, 1921 (Planer 4)
Nacht der Entscheidung, 1931 (Tschechowa 3, Veidt 3)
Nacht der Entscheidung, 1938 (Negri 3)
Nacht der grossen Liebe, 1933 (Frohlich 3, Wagner 4)
Nacht der Königin Isabeau, 1920 (Wiene 2, Kortner 3)
Nacht der Medici, 1922 (Krauss 3)
Nacht der Verwandlung, 1935 (Frohlich 3, George, H. 3)
Nacht des Grauens, 1912 (Porten 3, Messter 4)
Nacht des Schreckens, 1929 (Kortner 3)
Nacht gehort uns, 1929 (Albers 3, Reisch 4)
Nacht im Grenzwald, 1968 (Hoppe 3)
Nacht im Paradies, 1932 (Ondra 3)
Nacht im Separée, 1950 (Tschechowa 3)
Nacht in London, 1928 (Pick 2, Warm 4)
Nacht in Venedig, 1934 (Gallone 2, Wiene 2)
Nacht mit dem Kaiser, 1936 (Warm 4)
Nacht unter Wolfen, 1963 (Geschonneck 3)
Nachtbesuch in der Northernbank, 1921 (Wagner 4)
Nachtdienst. *See* Milosierdzie platne z gory, 1975
Nachte am Bosporus. *See* Mann, der den Mord beging, 1931
Nachte des Cornelis Brouwer, 1921 (Basserman 3)

Nattvardsgasterna, 1963 (Bergman 2, Bjornstrand 3, Thulin 3, Von Sydow 3, Nykvist 4)
Natura e chimica, 1959 (Olmi 2)
Natural, 1984 (Duvall, R. 3, Redford 3, Towne 4)
Natural Born Salesman. *See* Earthworm Tractors, 1936
Natural Enemies, 1979 (Ferrer, J. 3)
Natural Wonders of the West, 1938 (Hoch 4)
Naturalisée, 1962 (Delerue 4)
Nature in the Wrong, 1933 (Roach 4)
Nature morte, 1966 (Guillemot 4)
Nature morte, 1970 (Lenica 2)
Nature of the Beast, 1919 (Hepworth 2)
Nature retrouvée, 1968 (Gélin 3)
Nature's Workshop, 1933 (Lantz 4)
Nau Do Gyarah, 1956 (Anand 3)
Naufrageurs, 1959 (Vanel 3, Cloquet 4)
Naughty Baby, 1929 (Leroy 2, Fort 4, Haller 4)
Naughty Blue Knickers. *See* Folies d'Elodie, 1981
Naughty Boy, 1962 (Burman 4)
Naughty But Mice, 1939 (Jones 2)
Naughty But Nice, 1927 (Moore, C. 3, Young, L. 3, Wilson, C. 4)
Naughty But Nice, 1939 (Pitts 3, Powell, D. 3, Reagan 3, Sheridan 3, Mercer 4, Wald 4)
Naughty Duck, 1950 (Popescu-Gopo 4)
Naughty Flirt, 1931 (Loy 3)
Naughty Marietta, 1935 (Van Dyke, W.S. 2, Eddy 3, Lanchester 3, MacDonald 3, Adrian 4, Daniels 4, Gibbons 4, Goodrich and Hackett 4, Mahin 4, Shearer 4, Stothart 4, Stromberg 4, Tiomkin 4)
Naughty Martine. *See* Mademoiselle Modiste, 1952
Naughty! Naughty!, 1918 (Barnes 4, Sullivan 4)
Naughty Neighbors, 1939 (Clampett 4)
Naughty Nineties, 1945 (Abbott and Costello 3, Johnson, B. 3)
Naughty Nurses. *See* Tender Loving Care, 1973
Nauka blizej zycic, 1951 (Munk 2)
Naukri, 1954 (Roy 2)
Naulahka, 1918 (Oland 3, Grot 4, Menzies 4, Miller, A. 4)
Nausicaa, 1970 (Varda 2)
Navajo, 1952 (Miller, V. 4)
Navajo Joe. *See* Dollaro a testa, 1966
Naval Bomber Fleet. *See* Kaigun bakugekitai, 1940
Nave Bianca, 1941 (Rossellini 2)
Navigation marchande, 1954 (Franju 2, Decaë 4)
Navigator, 1924 (Keaton 2, Crisp 3, Johnson, N. 3, Bruckman 4, Schenck 4)
Navire des hommes perdus. *See* Schiff der verlorene Menschen, 1929
Navire Night, 1978 (Duras 2)
Návrat domu, 1948 (Fric 2, Kopecký 3)
Návrat ztraceného syna, 1966 (Schorm 2, Brejchová 3)
Navy, 1930 (Lantz 4)
Navy Blue and Gold, 1937 (Wood 2, Barrymore L. 3, Burke 3, Stewart 3, Young, R. 3, Gibbons 4, Seitz 4)
Navy Blue Days, 1925 (Laurel 3)
Navy Blues, 1929 (Brown 2, Gibbons 4)
Navy Blues, 1941 (Bacon 2, Sheridan 3, Young, G. 3, Gaudio 4, Howe 4, Mercer 4, Polito 4, Wald 4, Wallis 4)
Navy Comes Through, 1942 (Sutherland 2, Cooper, J 3, O'Brien, P. 3, Dunn 4, Musuraca 4)
Navy Gravy, 1925 (Hardy 3)
Navy Secrets, 1939 (Wray 3)
Navy Steps Out. *See* Girl, a Guy, and a Gob, 1941
Navy Versus the Night Monsters, 1965 (Cortez 4)
Navy Wife, 1935 (Dwan 2, Darwell 3, Levien 4)
Navy Wife, 1956 (Bennett J. 3, Salter 4, Wanger 4)
Navy Wife. *See* Beauty's Daughter, 1935
Navy's Special Boy Sailors. *See* Kaigun tokubetsu nenshouhei, 1972
Naxalitees, 1980 (Patil 3)
Naya Zamana, 1971 (Burman 4)
Nayak, 1966 (Ray, S. 2, Chandragupta 4, Datta 4, Mitra 4)
Nayamashiki koro, 1926 (Tanaka 3)
Nayya, 1947 (Biswas 4)
Nazarín, 1958 (Buñuel 2, Figueroa 4)
Naze kanojo wa sonatta ka, 1956 (Kagawa 3)
Nazi Agent, 1942 (Dassin 2, Veidt 3, Schary 4, Stradling 4)

Nazis Strike, 1943 (Hornbeck 4, Veiller 4)
Nazraana, 1961 (Kapoor 2)
Nazty Nuisance, 1942 (Roach 4)
Ne bougeons plus, 1903 (Guy 2)
Ne compromettez pas vos loisirs, 1949 (Decaë 4)
Né de père inconnu, 1950 (Renoir 4)
Ne jouez pas avec les Martiens, 1967 (Broca 2)
Ne le criez pas sur des toits, 1942 (Fernandel 3, Burel 4)
Ne me demandez pas pourquoi. *See* Testament d'Orphée, 1960
Ne nado krovi, 1917 (Protazanov 2)
Ne nous fâchons pas, 1966 (Audiard 4)
Ne pleure pas, 1977 (Vanel 3)
Né pour la musique. *See* Nacido para la música, 1959
Ne tuez pas Dolly!, 1937 (Delannoy 2)
Néa, 1976 (Presle 3, Evein 4)
Neanderthal Man, 1953 (Dupont 2, Cortez 4)
Neapolitan Carousel. *See* Carosella napolitano, 1953
Neapolitan Mouse, 1953 (Hanna and Barbera 4)
Near and Far Away. *See* Långt Borta och Nära, 1976
Near Dublin, 1924 (Laurel 3, Roach 4)
Near to Earth, 1913 (Griffith 2, Barrymore L. 3, Bitzer 4)
Nearer My God to Thee, 1917 (Hepworth 2)
Nearly a Burglar's Bride, 1914 (Loos 4)
Nearly a King, 1916 (Barrymore J. 3, Menjou 3)
Nearly a Lady, 1915 (Bosworth 3, Marion 4)
Nearly Married, 1917 (Barthelmess 3, Edeson 4)
Near-Tragedy, 1911 (Sennett 2)
'Neath Brooklyn Bridge, 1942 (Katzman 4)
'Neath Canadian Skies, 1946 (Eason 4)
'Neath the Arizona Skies, 1934 (Wayne 3, Canutt 4)
Nebelnacht, 1967 (Hoppe 3)
Nebesnye lastochki, 1976 (Gurchenko 3)
Nebo zovet. *See* Battle Beyond the Sun, 1962
Nebraskan, 1953 (Van Cleef 3)
Necesito dinero, 1951 (Infante 3)
Nechci nic slyšet, 1978 (Brejchová 3)
Nechte to na mně, 1955 (Forman 2, Fric 2)
Neck and Neck, 1931 (Brennan 3, Fetchit 3)
Neck and Neck, 1942 (Terry 4)
Neck 'n Neck, 1927 (Disney 2)
Necklace, 1909 (Griffith 2, Lawrence 3, Pickford 3, Bitzer 4)
Necklace of Ramses, 1914 (Ingram 2)
Necklace of the Dead. *See* Dødes Halsbaand, 1910
Necromancy, 1973 (Welles 2, Hoch 4)
Ned Kelly, 1970 (Richardson 2, Fisher 4)
Ned McCobb's Daughter, 1929 (Lombard 3)
Ned med Vabnene, 1914 (Dreyer 2, Holger-Madsen 2)
Nedaa el Ochak, 1961 (Chahine 2)
Neděle ve všedni, 1962 (Brejchová 3)
Nederland, 1983 (Haanstra 2)
Nederland in 7 Lessen, 1948 (Hepburn, A. 3)
Nederlandse beeldhouw kunst tijdens de late Middeleeuwen, 1951 (Haanstra 2)
Nee kofun shicha iya yo, 1931 (Naruse 2)
Neecha Nagar, 1945 (Shankar 2)
Neel Akasher Neechey, 1959 (Sen 2)
Neel Kamal, 1947 (Kapoor 2)
Ne'er-Do-Well, 1916 (Selig 4)
Ne'er-Do-Well, 1923 (Haller 4)
Nefertite regina del Nilo, 1963 (Crain 3, Price 3)
Nefertiti, Queen of the Nile. *See* Nefertite regina del Nilo, 1963
Negatives, 1968 (Jackson 3)
Neglected. *See* Glaedens Dag, 1918
Neglected Wives, 1920 (Haller 4)
Negoto dorobo, 1964 (Iwashita 3)
Negra consentida, 1948 (Alcoriza 4)
Nègre blanc, 1912 (Gance 2)
Nègre blanc, 1925 (Meerson 4)
Negro Soldier, 1944 (Capra 2, Moss 4)
Negy lány egy udvarban, 1964 (Gábor 3, Torocsik 3)
Nehéz emberek, 1964 (Kovács 2)
Neige était sale, 1953 (Gélin 3)
Neiges, 1954 (Cloquet 4)

Neighbor Trouble, 1932 (Sennett 2)
Neighborhood House, 1936 (Roach 4)
Neighbors, 1907 (Bitzer 4)
Neighbors, 1911 (Sennett 2)
Neighbors, 1921 (Keaton 2)
Neighbors, 1952 (McLaren 2)
Neighbors. *See* Sujsedi, 1970
Neighbor's Wife and Mine. *See* Madamu to nyobo, 1931
Neighbors' Wives, 1933 (Eason 4)
Neigungsehe, 1944 (Porten 3)
Neigungsehe. *See* Familie Buchholz, 1944
Neither by Day nor Night, 1973 (Robinson, E. 3)
Nejlepší člověk, 1954 (Kopecký 3)
Nejlepší ženská mého života, 1968 (Fric 2)
Neko to Shozo to futari no onna, 1956 (Kagawa 3, Yamada 3)
Nekri Politeia, 1951 (Papas 3)
Nel blu dipinto di blu, 1959 (De Sica 2, Di Venanzo 4, Zavattini 4)
Nel gorgo della vita. *See* Lacrimae rerum, 1917
Nel nome del padre, 1971 (Bellocchio 2, Cristaldi 4)
Nel segno di Roma, 1958 (Leone 2, Cervi 3)
Nelken in Aspik, 1976 (Mueller-Stahl 3)
Nell Dale's Men Folks, 1924 (Bosworth 3)
Nell Gwyn, 1934 (Wilcox 2, Hardwicke 3, Neagle 3, Young, F. 4)
Nell Gwynne, 1926 (Wilcox 2, Gish, D. 3)
Nell of the Pampas, 1912 (Dwan 2)
Nell stretta morsa del ragno, 1971 (Kinski 3)
Nella città l'inferno, 1958 (Castellani 2, Magnani 3, Masina 3, Sordi 3, D'Amico 4)
Nella fornace, 1915 (Bertini 3)
Nella tormenta. *See* Tormenta, 1923
Nell'anno del signore, 1970 (Cardinale 3, Magnani 3, Manfredi 3)
Nelle luce di Roma, 1938 (Fusco 4)
Nellie, 1952 (King 2)
Nellie the Beautiful Cloak Model, 1924 (Bosworth 3)
Nell's Eugenic Wedding, 1914 (Loos 4)
Nell's Yells, 1939 (Iwerks 4)
Nelly la gigolette, 1914 (Bertini 3)
Nelly's Folly, 1962 (Jones 2)
Nelson, 1926 (Hardwicke 3)
Nelson Affair, 1973 (Dillon 4)
Nelson Affair. *See* Bequest to the Nation, 1973
Nelson Touch. *See* Corvette K-225, 1943
Nem, 1965 (Torocsik 3)
Nema kiáltás, 1982 (Mészáros 2)
N'embrassez pas votre bonne, 1909 (Linders 3)
Nemesis, 1921 (Gallone 2)
Nemesis. *See* Faedrenes Synd, 1914
Nemico di mia moglie, 1959 (De Sica 2, Mastroianni 3, Di Venanzo 4)
Nemrod et Compagnie, 1911 (Modot 3)
Nemureru bijo, 1968 (Yoshimura 2)
Nemuri Kyoshiro burai hikae: Majin jigoku, 1958 (Yamada 3)
Nemuri Kyoshiro no manji-giri, 1969 (Yoda 4)
Nene, 1924 (Modot 3)
Není stále zamrečeno, 1950 (Kachyna 2, Kučera 4)
Neobyčejná léta, 1952 (Kachyna 2)
Neobychainye priklucheniya Mistera Vesta v stranye bolshevikov, 1924 (Pudovkin 2, Kuleshov 2)
Neokonchennaya povest, 1955 (Ermler 2, Bondarchuk 3)
Neon Ceiling, 1971 (Grant, L. 3, Young, G. 3)
Neon Jungle. *See* Neon taiheiki-keieigaku nyumon, 1967
Neon taiheiki-keieigaku nyumon, 1967 (Imamura 2)
Neon Trifle. *See* Neonowa fraszka, 1959
Neonowa fraszka, 1959 (Giersz 4)
Neotpravlennoe pismo, 1958 (Samoilova 3, Smoktunovsky 3)
Nephew of Paris, 1934 (Garmes 4)
Nepokorenniye, 1945 (Donskoi 2)
Neppu, 1943 (Hara 3)
Neptune Disaster. *See* Neptune Factor, 1973
Neptune Factor, 1973 (Borgnine 3, Pidgeon 3, Schifrin 4)
Neptune's Daughter, 1912 (Bushman 3)
Neptune's Daughter, 1914 (Brenon 2)

Neptune's Daughter, 1949 (Williams 3, Wynn 3, Hanna and Barbera 4, Irene 4, Rosher 4)
Nerikej mi va siku, 1972 (Pojar 4)
Nero, 1944 (Sim 3)
Nero and the Burning of Rome, 1908 (Porter 2)
Nero Veneziamo, 1978 (Donaggio 4)
Nero Wolfe, 1977 (Baxter A. 3)
Nerone, 1930 (Blasetti 2)
Nerone e Messalina, 1953 (Cervi 3, Delli Colli 4)
Nero's Mistress. *See* Mio figlio Nerone, 1956
Nero's Weekend. *See* Mio figlio Nerone, 1956
Nertsery Rhymes, 1933 (Three Stooges 3)
Nerve and Gasoline, 1916 (Hardy 3)
Nervous Shakedown, 1947 (Bruckman 4)
Nervous Wreck, 1926 (Bosworth 3)
Nerze Nachts am Strassenrand, 1973 (Staudte 2)
Nesmotria ni na shto, 1972 (Ulyanov 3)
Nessa bala Rejal, 1952 (Chahine 2)
Nessa no byakuran, 1951 (Yamamura 3, Hayasaka 4)
Nessa no chikai, 1940 (Hasegawa 3, Shindo 3)
Nessuno o tutti — Matti da slegare, 1974 (Bellocchio 2)
Nessuno torna indietro, 1943 (Blasetti 2, De Sica 2, Germi 2, Cervi 3, Cortese 3, Vích 4)
Nest, 1927 (Stradling 4)
Nest, 1943 (Anger 2)
Nest. *See* Nid, 1926
Nest of Gentlefolk. *See* Dvoryanskoye gnezdo, 1969
Nesting, 1981 (Grahame 3)
Nesting. *See* Phobia, 1979
Net, 1952 (Asquith 2)
Net. *See* Red, 1953
Netherlands. *See* Nederland, 1983
Netherlands America, 1943 (Van Dongen 4)
Netsuaisha, 1961 (Yamamura 3)
Netsudeichi, 1950 (Ichikawa 2)
Netsujo no ichiya, 1929 (Gosho 2)
Nettezza urbana. *See* N.U., 1948
Nettoyage par le vide, 1908 (Feuillade 2)
Network, 1976 (Lumet 2, Dunaway 3, Duvall, R. 3, Finch 3, Holden 3, Chayefsky 4, Roizman 4)
Netz, 1975 (Ferrer, M. 3, Kinski 3)
Neue Dalila, 1918 (Gad 2)
Neues vom Hexer, 1965 (Kinski 3)
Neuf à trois, ou la journée d'une vedette, 1957 (Decaë 4)
Neuf étages tout acier, 1960 (Delerue 4, Kosma 4)
Neulovimie mstiteli, 1967 (Churikova 3)
99 Nacht, Nacht, 1919 (Albers 3)
1914 — die letzten Tage vor dem Weltbrand, 1931 (Oswald 2, Basserman 3, George, H. 3, Homolka 3)
Neunzig Nächte und ein Tag. *See* Sette contro la morte, 1964
Neúplné zatměni, 1982 (Jires 2)
Neutron Bomb Incident. *See* Teheran Incident, 1979
Neuvaine, 1914 (Feuillade 2)
Nevada, 1927 (Cooper, Gary 3, Powell, W. 3)
Nevada, 1934 (Crabbe 3)
Nevada, 1944 (Mitchum 3)
Nevada City, 1941 (Rogers, R. 3)
Nevada Kid. *See* Per una bara piena di dollari, 1970
Nevada Smith, 1966 (Hathaway 2, Cody 3, Kennedy, A. 3, Malden 3, Martin, S. 3, McQueen, S. 3, Ballard 4, Hayes 4, Head 4, Newman 4)
Nevada Smith, 1975 (Hayes 4)
Nevadan, 1950 (Malone 3, Scott, R. 3, Brown, Harry Joe 4)
Never a Dull Moment, 1943 (Salter 4)
Never a Dull Moment, 1950 (Dunne 3, MacMurray 3, Wood 3, Banton 4, Walker 4)
Never a Dull Moment, 1968 (Elam 3, Robinson, E. 3, Ellenshaw 4)
Never Again!, 1910 (Sennett 2, Pickford 3)
Never Again, 1915 (Mix 3)
Never Again, 1916 (Hardy 3)
Never Fear, 1950 (Lupino 3, Polglase 4)
Never Give a Sucker an Even Break, 1941 (Dumont 3, Fields, W.C. 3)
Never Give an Inch. *See* Sometimes a Great Notion, 1971

Never Kick a Woman, 1936 (Fleischer, M. and D. 2)
Never Let Go, 1960 (Sellers 3, Barry 4)
Never Let Me Go, 1953 (Brown 2, Daves 2, Gable 3, More 3,
    Tierney 3, Junge 4, Krasker 4)
Never Love a Stranger, 1957 (McQueen, S. 3, Garmes 4)
Never on Sunday. *See* Pote tin kyriaki, 1960
Never Say Die, 1939 (Hope 3, Dreier 4, Head 4)
Never Say Goodbye, 1946 (Flynn 3, McDaniel 3, Sakall 3, Diamond 4,
    Edeson 4, Grot 4)
Never Say Goodbye, 1956 (Sirk 2, Eastwood 3, Hudson 3, Sanders 3,
    Boyle 4)
Never Say Never, 1979 (Kennedy, G. 3)
Never Say Never Again, 1983 (Kershner 2, Connery 3, Von Sydow 3,
    Legrand 4, Semple 4, Slocombe 4)
Never Should Have Told You, 1937 (Fleischer, M. and D. 2)
Never So Few, 1959 (Sturges, J. 2, Bronson 3, Henreid 3,
    Lollobrigida 3, McQueen, S. 3, Sinatra 3, Daniels 4, Friedhofer 4,
    Rose 4)
Never Sock a Baby, 1939 (Fleischer, M. and D. 2)
Never Steal Anything Small, 1958 (Cagney 3, Jones S. 3, Lederer 4)
Never Strike a Woman, Even with a Flower. *See* Spadla s měsíce, 1966
Never Take Candy from a Stranger. *See* Never Take Sweets from a
    Stranger, 1960
Never Take No for an Answer, 1952 (Havelock-Allan 4)
Never Take No for an Answer, 1959 (Rota 4)
Never Take Sweets from a Stranger, 1960 (Francis 4)
Never the Twain Shall Meet, 1925 (Tourneur, M. 2, Karloff 3)
Never the Twain Shall Meet, 1931 (Van Dyke, W.S. 2, Howard, L. 3)
Never to Love. *See* Bill of Divorcement, 1940
Never Too Late, 1965 (O'Sullivan 3)
Never Too Old, 1919 (Sennett 2)
Never Too Old, 1926 (Laurel 3, Roach 4)
Never Touched Me, 1919 (Daniels 3, Lloyd 3, Roach 4)
Never Trouble Trouble, 1931 (Oberon 3)
Never Wave at a WAC, 1953 (McLeod 2, Beavers 3, Douglas, P. 3,
    Russell, R. 3, Bernstein 4, Daniels 4)
Never Weaken, 1921 (Lloyd 3, Roach 4)
Neveto Szaszkia, 1916 (Korda 2)
Neveu de Rameau, 1968 (Fresnay 3)
Nevideli jste Bobika, 1944 (Hrušínský 3)
Nevidimi chelovek, 1935 (Donskoi 2)
Neviditelní nepřátelé, 1950 (Brdečka 4)
Neviňátka, 1929 (Stallich 4)
Nevinost bez zaštite, 1968 (Makavejev 2)
Nevité o bytě, 1947 (Kadár 2, Kopecký 3)
Nevtelen vàr, 1920 (Lukas 3)
New Actors for the Classics, 1973 (Keach 3)
New Adventures of Dr. Fu Manchu, 1930 (Oland 3)
New Adventures of Don Juan. *See* Adventures of Don Juan, 1949
New Adventures of Get-Rich-Quick Wallingford, 1931 (Wood 2,
    Durante 3, MacArthur 4)
New Adventures of J. Rufus Wallingford, 1915 (Hardy 3)
New Adventures of Schweik. *See* Noviye pokhozdeniya Shveika, 1943
New Age of Fools. *See* Shin baka jidai, 1946
New Americans, 1945 (Vorkapich 3)
New Architecture. *See* Nieuwe architectur, 1929
New Aunt, 1929 (Sennett 2, Hornbeck 4)
New Baby, 1911 (Sennett 2)
New Baby, 1913 (Sennett 2)
New Babylon. *See* Novyi Vavilon, 1929
New Bankroll, 1929 (Sennett 2)
New Britain, 1940 (Alwyn 4)
New Brooms, 1925 (Love 3)
New Butler, 1915 (Hardy 3)
New Car, 1931 (Iwerks 4)
New Centurions, 1972 (Fleischer, R. 2, Keach 3, Scott, G. 3, Jones 4,
    Leven 4)
New Champion, 1925 (Eason 4)
New Church Organ, 1912 (Bushman 3)
New Commandment, 1925 (Sweet 3, Haller 4)
New Conductor, 1913 (Sennett 2)
New Cook. *See* Husassistenten, 1914
New Cowboy, 1911 (Ince 4)

New Cowpuncher, 1912 (Dwan 2)
New Daughters of Joshua Cabe, 1976 (Elam 3)
New Deal Money, 1934 (Temple 3)
New Deal Show, 1937 (Fleischer, M. and D. 2)
New Delhi Times, 1985 (Mitra 4)
New Domestic Animal. *See* Nova domaća zivotinja, 1964
New Dress, 1911 (Griffith 2, Bitzer 4)
New Earth. *See* Atarashiki tsuchi, 1937
New Earth. *See* Nieuwe gronden, 1934
New Enchantment. *See* Inhumaine, 1924
New England Idyll, 1914 (Ince 4)
New England Visions Past and Future, 1976 (Emshwiller 2)
New Exploits of Elaine, 1915 (White 3)
New Faces, 1954 (Ballard 4, Horner 4)
New Faces of 1937, 1937 (Miller 3, Epstein, J. & P. 4, Hunt 4,
    Polglase 4)
New Faith, 1911 (Bosworth 3)
New Frontier, 1935 (Wayne 3)
New Frontier, 1939 (Jones, J. 3, Wayne 3)
New Frontier, 1950 (Leacock 2)
New Frontiers, 1940 (Ivens 2)
New Generation, 1932 (Grierson 2)
New Gentlemen. *See* Nouveaux Messieurs, 1928
New Girl in Town. *See* Nashville Girl, 1976
New Gulliver. *See* Novy Gulliver, 1935
New Half-Back, 1929 (Sennett 2)
New Horizons. *See* Viborgskaya storona, 1939
New Horizons in Steel, 1977 (Benegal 2)
New House. *See* Novyi dom, 1947
New Improved Institutional Quality, 1975 (Landow 2)
New Interns, 1964 (Segal 3, Ballard 4)
New Janitor, 1914 (Chaplin 2, Sennett 2)
New Janko the Musician. *See* Nowy Janko muzykant, 1960
New Kids, 1985 (Schifrin 4)
New Kind of Love, 1963 (Chevalier 3, Newman 3, Ritter 3,
    Woodward 3, Head 4)
New Kind of Woman. *See* Shin josei kagami, 1929
New Klondike, 1926 (Milestone 2)
New Land. *See* Nybyggarna, 1972
New Leaf, 1971 (Matthau 3)
New Lord of the Village. *See* Nouveau Seigneur du village, 1908
New Lot, 1942 (Dickinson 2, Reed 2, Ustinov 3)
New Magdalene, 1910 (White 3)
New Manager, 1911 (Bushman 3)
New Mexico, 1951 (Aldrich 2, Ayres 3)
New Minister, 1910 (Lawrence 3)
New Monsters. *See* Nuovi mostri, 1977
New Moon, 1919 (Talmadge, N. 3)
New Moon, 1930 (Menjou 3, Adrian 4, Booth 4, Stothart 4)
New Moon, 1940 (Eddy 3, MacDonald 3, Adrian 4, Daniels 4,
    Stothart 4)
New Morals for Old, 1932 (Hersholt 3, Loy 3, Stone 3, Young, R. 3)
New Movietone Follies of 1930. *See* Fox Movietone Follies of 1930,
    1930
New Neighbor, 1912 (Sennett 2, Normand 3)
New Operator, 1932 (Grierson 2)
New Order at Sjogårda. *See* Nyordning på Sjogårda, 1944
New Orleans Adventure, 1950 (Presle 3)
New Orleans Uncensored, 1955 (Katzman 4)
New Rates, 1934 (Cavalcanti 2)
New School Teacher, 1924 (La Cava 2)
New Schoolmarm of Green River, 1913 (Anderson G. 3)
New Shawl, 1910 (Lawrence 3)
New Sheriff, 1913 (Anderson G. 3)
New Snow. *See* Shinsetsu,
New Stenographer, 1911 (Bunny 3, Costello, M. 3)
New Stenographer, 1914 (Blackton 2)
New Superintendent, 1911 (Bosworth 3)
New Tale of Heike. *See* Shin Heike monogatari, 1955
New Tale of the Taira Clan. *See* Shin Heike monogatari, 1955
New Teacher, 1915 (Beery 3)
New Teacher, 1941 (Cushing 3)
New Town. *See* Ville Nouvelle, 1980

Niente rose per OSS 117, 1968 (Delli Colli 4)
Niet!. *See* Habrichka el hashemersh, 1972
Niet genoeg. *See* Pas assez, 1968
Niet voor de poesen. *See* Because of the Cats, 1973
Nieuwe architectur, 1929 (Ivens 2)
Nieuwe gronden, 1934 (Ivens 2, Eisler 4, Van Dongen 4)
Nieuwe polders, 1931 (Van Dongen 4)
Niewinni czarodzieje, 1960 (Polanski 2, Skolimowski 2, Wajda 2, Cybulski 3, Lomnicki 3)
Niewolnica Zmyslow, 1914 (Negri 3)
Niger jeune république, 1961 (Jutra 2)
Nigeyuku Kodenji, 1930 (Yamada 3)
Niggard, 1914 (Reid 3)
Nigger, 1915 (Farnum 3)
Night, 1930 (Disney 2)
Night. *See* Notte, 1960
Night. *See* Yoru, 1923
Night Affair. *See* Désordre et la nuit, 1958
Night after Night, 1932 (Calhern 3, Raft 3, West 3, Banton 4, Haller 4, Plunkett 4)
Night Ambush. *See* Ill Met by Moonlight, 1957
Night and Day, 1946 (Curtiz 2, Arden 3, Grant, C. 3, Malone 3, Muse 3, Wyman 3, Prinz 4, Steiner 4)
Night and Day. *See* Jack's the Boy, 1932
Night and Fog. *See* Nuit et brouillard, 1955
Night and Fog in Japan. *See* Nihon no yoru to kiri, 1960
Night and the City, 1950 (Dassin 2, Tierney 3, Widmark 3, Lassally 4, Waxman 4)
Night Angel, 1931 (Goulding 2, March 3)
Night at Earl Carroll's, 1940 (Dreier 4, Head 4, Reynolds 4)
Night at Glimminge Castle. *See* Natt på Glimmingehus, 1954
Night at Karlstein. *See* Noc na Karlštejně, 1973
Night at the Biltmore Bowl, 1935 (Grable 3)
Night at the Crossroads. *See* Nuit du carrefour, 1932
Night at the Opera, 1935 (Wood 2, Dumont 3, Marx Brothers 3, Brown, N. 4, Carré 4, Freed 4, Gibbons 4, Kaper 4, Ryskind 4, Stothart 4, Thalberg 4)
Night Beat, 1948 (Francis 4, Vích 4)
Night Before. *See* No Time to Marry, 1938
Night Before Christian's Birthday. *See* Naten for Kristians Fodelsdag, 1908
Night Before Christmas, 1912 (Costello, M. 3)
Night Before Christmas, 1941 (Hanna and Barbera 4)
Night Before the Divorce, 1942 (Siodmak 2)
Night Before the War. *See* Laisen no zenya, 1943
Night Butterflies. *See* Yoru no cho, 1957
Night Call Nurses, 1972 (Corman 4)
Night Caller. *See* Peur sur la ville, 1975
Night Chase, 1970 (Cook 3)
Night Club, 1925 (Fazenda 3)
Night Club, 1928 (Florey 2)
Night Club Lady, 1932 (Menjou 3, Riskin 4)
Night Club Scandal, 1937 (Barrymore J. 3, Dreier 4, Head 4)
Night Court, 1932 (Van Dyke, W.S. 2, Hersholt 3, Huston 3, Raft 3, Stone 3)
Night Creature, 1977 (Pleasance 3)
Night Creatures. *See* Captain Clegg, 1962
Night Crossing, 1982 (Hurt, J. 3, Goldsmith 4)
Night Digger, 1971 (Herrmann 4)
Night Digger. *See* Road Builder, 1971
Night Drum. *See* Yoru no tsuzumi, 1958
Night Duty. *See* Milosierdzie platne z gory, 1975
Night Editor, 1946 (Guffey 4)
Night Fighters, 1960 (Mitchum 3)
Night Fighters. *See* Terrible Beauty, 1960
Night Flight, 1933 (Brown 2, Barrymore J. 3, Barrymore L. 3, Gable 3, Loy 3, Montgomery 3, Selznick 4, Stothart 4)
Night Flight. *See* Vol de nuit, 1978
Night Flight from Moscow. *See* Serpent, 1973
Night Flyer, 1928 (Daves 2, Boyd 3)
Night Freight, 1955 (Sanders 3)
Night Gallery, 1969 (Crawford, J. 3, Jaffe 3, McDowall 3)
Night Games, 1974 (Schifrin 4)

Night Games, 1979 (Vadim 2)
Night Games. *See* Nattlek, 1966
Night God Screamed, 1975 (Crain 3)
Night Has a Thousand Eyes, 1948 (Robinson, E. 3, Dreier 4, Head 4, Seitz 4, Young, V. 4)
Night Has Eyes, 1941 (Mason 3)
Night Hawk, 1924 (Carey 3, Stromberg 4)
Night Hawks, 1914 (Bushman 3)
Night Heaven Fell. *See* Bijoutiers du clair de lune, 1957
Night Holds Terror, 1955 (Cassavetes 2)
Night Horsemen, 1921 (Mix 3)
Night in a Dormitory, 1929 (Rogers, G. 3)
Night in Bangkok. *See* Bankokku no yuro, 1966
Night in Cairo. *See* Barbarian, 1933
Night in Casablanca, 1946 (Marx Brothers 3)
Night in Havana. *See* Big Boodle, 1957
Night in Hong Kong. *See* Honkon no yoru, 1961
Night in June. *See* Juninatten, 1940
Night in Karlstein. *See* Noc na Karlštejně, 1973
Night in London. *See* Nacht in London, 1928
Night in Marseilles, 1931 (Gilliat 4)
Night in Montmartre, 1931 (Balcon 4)
Night in New Orleans, 1942 (Johnson, N. 3, Dreier 4)
Night in Paradise, 1946 (Oberon 3, Banton 4, Wanger 4)
Night in the Harbor. *See* Natt i hamn, 1943
Night in the Show, 1915 (Chaplin 2, Purviance 3)
Night in Town, 1912–13 (White 3)
Night into Morning, 1951 (Milland 3, Basevi 4)
Night Invader, 1942 (Fisher 2)
Night Is Ending. *See* Paris after Dark, 1943
Night Is My Future. *See* Musik i morker, 1948
Night Is My Kingdom. *See* Nuit est mon royaume, 1951
Night Is the Phantom. *See* Frusta e il corpo, 1963
Night Is Young, 1935 (Horton 3, Merkel 3, Novarro 3, Russell, R. 3, Howe 4, Stothart 4)
Night Journey, 1960 (Hammid 2)
Night Journey. *See* Resa i natten, 1955
Night Key, 1937 (Bond 3, Karloff 3)
Night Kill, 1980 (Mitchum 3)
Night Life in the Army, 1942 (Terry 4)
Night Life of New York, 1925 (Dwan 2, Gish, D. 3)
Night Life of the Bugs, 1936 (Lantz 4)
Night Life of the Gods, 1935 (Fulton 4, Laemmle 4)
Night Light. *See* Natten ljus, 1957
Night Mail, 1936 (Cavalcanti 2, Grierson 2, Watt 2, Wright 2, Bennett 4)
Night Monster, 1942 (Lugosi 3, Salter 4)
Night Moves, 1975 (Penn 2, Hackman 3, Allen, D. 4, Jenkins 4)
Night Music. *See* Bartók Béla: az éjszaka zenéje, 1970
Night Must Fall, 1937 (Montgomery 3, Russell, R. 3, Stromberg 4)
Night Must Fall, 1964 (Reisz 2, Finney 3, Fisher 4, Francis 4)
Night My Number Came Up, 1955 (Redgrave, M. 3, Arnold 4, Balcon 4)
Night 'n' Gales, 1937 (Roach 4)
Night Nurse, 1931 (Wellman 2, Blondell 3, Gable 3, Stanwyck 3)
Night of January 16th, 1941 (Daves 2, Preston 3, Dreier 4, Head 4, Pirosh 4)
Night of June 13th, 1932 (Brook 3)
Night of Love, 1927 (Banky 3, Colman 3, Barnes 4, Coffee 4, Goldwyn 4)
Night of Love. *See* Tradita, 1954
Night of Mystery, 1928 (Menjou 3, Mankiewicz 4, Vajda 4)
Night of Mystery, 1937 (Dupont 2, Head 4)
Night of Nights, 1939 (Milestone 2, O'Brien, P. 3, Dreier 4, Head 4, Stewart 4, Young, V. 4)
Night of Passion. *See* Netsujo no ichiya, 1929
Night of Remembrance. *See* Celuloza, 1954
Night of San Lorenzo. *See* Notte di San Lorenzo, 1981
Night of Shame. *See* Marchandes d'illusions, 1954
Night of Terror, 1908 (Bitzer 4)
Night of Terror, 1933 (Lugosi 3)
Night of Terror, 1972 (Moorehead 3)
Night of the Askari. *See* Flusternde Tod, 1975

Niji ikutabi, 1956 (Kyo 3)
Niji o idaku shojo, 1948 (Takamine 3, Hayasaka 4)
Niji tatsu oka, 1938 (Takamine 3)
Nijinsky, 1980 (Bates 3, Slocombe 4)
Nijuissa no chichi, 1964 (Takemitsu 4)
Nijushi no hitomi, 1954 (Kinoshita 2, Takamine 3)
Nikai no himei, 1931 (Naruse 2)
Nikki, Wild Dog of the North, 1961 (Disney 2)
Niklashausen Journey. See Niklashauser Fahrt, 1970
Niklashauser Fahrt, 1970 (Fassbinder 2, Schygulla 3)
Nikolai Stavrogin, 1915 (Protazanov 2, Mozhukin 3)
Nikoniko taikai, 1946 (Tanaka 3)
Nikutai bi, 1928 (Ozu 2)
Nikutai no gakko, 1965 (Kishida 3, Yamamura 3)
Nikyho velebné dobrodružtvi, 1919 (Ondra 3)
Nile's Son. See Ibn el Nil, 1951
Nili, 1950 (Anand 3)
Nille, 1968 (Henning-Jensen 2)
Nilo di pietra, 1956 (Delli Colli 4)
Nils Holgerssons Underbara Resa, 1962 (Von Sydow 3)
Nina, 1956 (Aimée 3)
Nina, 1958 (D'Eaubonne 4)
Nina. See Hvide Slavehandel III, 1912
Nina B. Affair. See Affaire Nina B., 1962
Nina de Vanghel, 1952 (Schufftan 4)
Nina, The Flower Girl, 1917 (Love 3)
Nince ido, 1973 (Madaras 3)
Nine Days a Queen. See Tudor Rose, 1936
Nine Days of One Year. See Deviat dnei odnogo goda, 1962
Nine Guests for a Crime. See Nove ospiti per un delitto, 1976
Nine Hours to Live. See Nine Hours to Rama, 1963
Nine Hours to Rama, 1963 (Robson 2, Ferrer, J. 3, Arnold 4, Bass 4)
Nine Lives Are Not Enough, 1941 (Sutherland 2, Reagan 3, McCord 4)
9 Men, 1943 (Crichton 2, Watt 2, Balcon 4)
Nine Minutes. See Kilenc perc, 1960
Nine Months. See Kilenc hónap, 1976
Nine-Tenths of the Law, 1918 (Eason 4)
9/30/55, 1977 (Rosenman 4)
Nine till Six, 1932 (Dean 4, Reville 4)
Nine to Five, 1980 (Fonda, J. 3, Hayden 3)
9 Ways to Approach Helsinki. See Yhdeksan Tapaa Lahestya Helsinkia, 1982
1984, 1956 (O'Brien, E. 3, Pleasance 3, Redgrave, M. 3, Arnold 4)
1984, 1984 (Burton 3, Hurt, J. 3)
1941, 1979 (Fuller 2, Spielberg 2, Lee, C. 3, Mifune 3, Oates 3, Fraker 4, Willians, J. 4)
1914, die letzten Tage vor dem Weltbrand, 1931 (Oswald 2)
1900, 1976 (Bertolucci 2, Depardieu 3, Hayden 3, Sanda 3, Sutherland 3)
1900. See Novecento, 1976
Nineteen Nineteen, 1985 (Schell, Maria 3)
1919, A Russian Funeral, 1971 (Le Grice 2)
1963. julius 27. szombat, 1980 (Mészáros 2)
1933, 1967–68 (Wieland 2)
19th Hole Club, 1936 (Terry 4)
19th Spring. See Jukyu-sai no haru, 1933
Ninety and Nine, 1922 (Baxter W. 3, Moore, C. 3)
90 Degrees in the Shade. See Treicet jeona ve stinu, 1965
99. See Kilencvenkilenc, 1918
99 and 44/100% Dead!, 1974 (Frankenheimer 2, O'Brien, E. 3, Mancini 4)
99 River Street, 1953 (Planer 4)
99 Women. See 99 mujeres, 1969
92 in the Shade, 1975 (Fonda, P. 3, Meredith 3, Oates 3, Stanton 3)
Ningen, 1925 (Mizoguchi 2)
Ningen, 1962 (Shindo 2)
Ningen gyorai shutsugeki su, 1956 (Mori 3)
Ningen johatsu, 1967 (Imamura 2)
Ningen kakumei, 1973 (Muraki 4)
Ningen moyo, 1949 (Ichikawa 2)
Ningen no joken, 1961 (Kobayashi 2, Kishida 3, Ryu 3, Takamine 3, Yamamura 3)
Ningen no kabe, 1959 (Kagawa 3)

Ningen no shomei, 1977 (Crawford, B. 3, Kennedy, G. 3, Mifune 3)
Ninguém Duas Vezes, 1984 (Branco 4, de Almeida 4)
Ningyo bushi, 1928 (Hasegawa 3)
Nini Tirabuscio, la donna che incento la mossa, 1970 (Vitti 3)
Ninin sugata, 1942 (Yoda 4)
Ninja bugeicho, 1967 (Oshima 2)
Ninja III: The Domination, 1984 (Golan and Globus 4)
Ninja Sasuke Sarutobi of Sekigahara. See Ninjutsu Sekigahara Saruto Sasuke, 1938
Ninjo misui, 1957 (Hasegawa 3)
Ninjutsu, 1958 (Kagawa 3)
Ninjutsu. See Soryu hiken, 1958
Ninjutsu Sarutobi Sasuke, 1976 (Shimura 3)
Ninjutsu Sekigahara Sarutobi Sasuke, 1938 (Yoda 4)
Ninjutsu senshuken jiai, 1956 (Yoda 4)
Ninkyo Shimizu minato, 1957 (Shindo 3)
Niño y el muro, 1964 (Gélin 3)
Niño y la niebla, 1953 (Del Rio 3, Figueroa 4)
Ninotchka, 1939 (Lubitsch 2, Wilder 2, Douglas, M. 3, Garbo 3, Lugosi 3, Adrian 4, Brackett, C. 4, Daniels 4, Gibbons 4, Reisch
Ninth Configuration, 1979 (Keach 3)
Ninth of January. See Deviatoe yanvaria, 1926
Nip and Tuck, 1923 (Sennett 2)
Nipote Sabella, 1958 (Vích 4)
Nipped in the Bud, 1918 (Roach 4)
Nipper. See Brat, 1930
Nippon chinbotsu, 1973 (Muraki 4)
Nippon ichi dayo, 1962 (Kyo 3)
Nippon ichi no iro-otoko, 1963 (Muraki 4)
Nippon janjo, 1959 (Tsukasa 3)
Nippon kengo-den, 1945 (Hayasaka 4)
Nippon konchuki, 1963 (Imamura 2)
Nippon niju-roku seijin, 1931 (Yamada 3)
Nippon no ichiban nagai hi, 1967 (Mifune 3, Ryu 3, Shimura 3, Yamamura 3)
Nippon no obachan, 1962 (Imai 2)
Nippon sengoshi: Madame Omboro no seikatsu, 1970 (Imamura 2)
Nippon shunka-ko, 1967 (Toda 4)
Nippon tanjo, 1959 (Kagawa 3, Mifune 3, Tsuburaya 4)
Nippon yaburezu, 1954 (Yamamura 3)
Nippon-kai dai-kaisen, 1969 (Mifune 3)
Nippy's Nightmare, 1917 (O'Brien 4)
Nirala, 1950 (Anand 3)
Nirala Hindustan, 1938 (Biswas 3)
Nisan no baka, 1932 (Gosho 2, Tanaka 3)
Nishant, 1975 (Benegal 2, Azmi 3, Patil 3, Nihalani 4)
Nishi Ginza eki mae, 1958 (Imamura 2)
Nishi Ginza Station. See Nishi ginza eki mae, 1958
Nishi no taisho higashi no taisho, 1964 (Tsukasa 3)
Nishijin no shimai, 1952 (Yoshimura 2, Tanaka 3, Miyagawa 4)
Nishizumi sanshacho den, 1940 (Yoshimura 2)
Nisshoku no natsu, 1956 (Tsukasa 3, Yamamura 3)
Nitchevo, 1926 (Vanel 3)
Nitchevo, 1936 (Delannoy 2, Baur 3, Mozhukin 3, Honegger 4, Wakhévitch 4)
Nitwits, 1935 (Stevens 2, Grable 3, Cronjager 4, Polglase 4)
Nit-Witty Kitty, 1951 (Hanna and Barbera 4)
Niwa no kotori, 1922 (Kinugasa 2)
Niwatori wa futatabi naku, 1954 (Gosho 2)
Nix on Dames, 1929 (Beavers 3, Clarke, C.C. 4)
Nix on Hypnotricks, 1941 (Fleischer, M. and D. 2)
Nixchen, 1926 (Albers 3)
Njama nischto po-chubavo ot loschoto vreme, 1070 (Danailov 3)
Njepobedimye, 1943 (Babochkin 3)
Nju, 1924 (Czinner 2, Bergner 3, Jannings 3, Veidt 3)
No Barking, 1954 (Jones 2)
No basta ser charro, 1945 (Negrete 3)
No Biz Like Shoe Biz, 1960 (Hanna and Barbera 4)
No Blade of Grass, 1970 (Wilde 3)
No Brakes. See Oh, Yeah!, 1929
No Census, No Feelings, 1940 (Three Stooges 3)
No Children, 1921 (Roach 4)
No Clouds in the Sky. See Sora wa haretari, 1925

No Control, 1927 (Garnett 2)
No Defense, 1929 (Bacon 2)
No Deposit, No Return, 1975 (Niven 3)
No desearás la mujer de tu hijo, 1949 (Infante 3)
No Diamonds for Ursula. *See* Diamanti che nessuno voleva rubare, 1968
No Dough, Boys, 1944 (Three Stooges 3)
No Down Payment, 1957 (Hunter 3, Woodward 3, La Shelle 4, Lemaire 4, Wald 4, Wheeler 4)
No Drums, No Bugles, 1972 (Sheen 3)
No encontre rosas para mi madre, 1975 (Darrieux 3)
No es nada mama, solo un juego, 1973 (Valli 3)
No Escape, 1953 (Ayres 3, Bennett 4)
No Escape. *See* I Escaped from the Gestapo, 1943
No Escape. *See* Piège, 1958
No Exit. *See* Huis clos, 1954
No Eyes Today, 1929 (Fleischer, M. and D. 2)
No Father to Guide Him, 1925 (McCarey 2, Roach 4)
No Ford in the Fire. *See* V ogne broda net, 1968
No Funny Business, 1933 (Olivier 3)
No Greater Glory, 1934 (Borzage 2, August 4, Swerling 4)
No Greater Love, 1932 (Auer 3, Bosworth 3)
No Greater Love. *See* Ningen no joken, 1959
No Greater Love. *See* Ona zashchishchaet Rodinu, 1943
No Highway, 1951 (Dietrich 3, Hawkins 3, Love 3, More 3, Stewart 3, Périnal 4)
No Highway in the Sky. *See* No Highway, 1951
No Kidding, 1960 (Dillon 4)
No Leave, No Love, 1946 (Donen 2, Johnson, V. 3, Wynn 3, Ames 4, Irene 4, Pasternak 4, Rosson 4, Surtees 4)
No Limit, 1931 (Auer 3, Bow 3)
No Limit, 1935 (Formby 3, Dean 4)
No Love for Johnnie, 1961 (Finch 3, Holloway 3, Pleasance 3, Reed, O. 3, Arnold 4)
No Man is an Island, 1962 (Hunter 3)
No Man of Her Own, 1932 (Goulding 2, Ruggles 2, Gable 3, Lombard 3, Banton 4, Glazer 4)
No Man of Her Own, 1950 (Leisen 2, Stanwyck 3, Bumstead 4, Dreier 4, Friedhofer 4, Head 4)
No Man's Gold, 1926 (Mix 3)
No Man's Land, 1918 (Nilsson 3)
No Man's Land, 1978 (Richardson 3)
No Man's Land. *See* Branco di vigliacchi, 1962
No Man's Land. *See* Niemandsland, 1931
No Man's Law, 1927 (Stevens 2, Hardy 3)
No Man's Road, 1957 (Hopper 3)
No Man's Woman. *See* Ingens Mans Kvinna, 1953
No Marriage Ties, 1933 (Cronjager 4, Plunkett 4, Polglase 4, Steiner 4)
No matarás, 1943 (García 3)
No Minor Vices, 1948 (Aldrich 2, Milestone 2, Andrews D. 3, Jourdan 3, Waxman 4)
No Money, No Fight. *See* Musen fusen, 1924
No More Divorces. *See* Rozwodów nie bedzie, 1963
No More Ladies, 1935 (Cukor 2, Crawford, J. 3, Fontaine 3, Montgomery 3, Adrian 4, Stewart 4)
No More Orchids, 1932 (Lombard 3, August 4)
No More Women, 1924 (Walker 4)
No More Women, 1934 (Daves 2, McLaglen 3, Brown, Harry Joe 4)
No Mother to Guide Him, 1919 (Sennett 2)
No, My Darling Daughter, 1961 (Redgrave, M. 3)
No Name on the Bullet, 1959 (Murphy 3)
No! No! A Thousand Times No!, 1935 (Fleischer, M. and D. 2)
No, No, Lady, 1931 (Sennett 2)
No, No, Nanette, 1930 (Fazenda 3, Pitts 3, Grot 4, Polito 4)
No, No, Nanette, 1940 (Wilcox 2, Arden 3, Mature 3, Neagle 3, Pitts 3)
No Noise, 1923 (Roach 4)
No Nukes, 1980 (Wexler 4)
No odnoi planete, 1966 (Smoktunovsky 3)
No One Man, 1932 (Darwell 3, Lombard 3, Lukas 3, Buchman 4, Lang 4)
No One to Guide Him, 1916 (Sennett 2)
No Other One, 1936 (Fleischer, M. and D. 2)
No Other Woman, 1928 (Del Rio 3)

No Other Woman, 1933 (Dunne 3, Cronjager 4, Plunkett 4, Steiner 4, Vorkapich 4)
No oyes ladrar los perros?. *See* Entends-tu les chiens aboyer?, 1972
No Parking, 1937 (Reed 2)
No Parking Hare, 1954 (McKimson 4)
No Pets, 1923 (Roach 4)
No Place Like Jail, 1919 (Laurel 3, Roach 4)
No Place to Go, 1927 (Leroy 2, Astor 3)
No Place to Go, 1939 (Edeson 4)
No Place to Hide, 1974 (Stallone 3)
No Place to Hide, 1980 (Sangster 4)
No Place to Hide, 1983 (Sheen 3)
No Place to Land, 1958 (Ireland 3)
No Publicity, 1927 (Horton 3)
No Questions Asked, 1951 (Rose 4)
No Regrets for My Youth. *See* Waga seishun ni kuinashi, 1946
No Resting Place, 1951 (Alwyn 4)
No Return. *See* Kaeranu sasabue, 1926
No Return. *See* Okean, Vozvrata net, 1974
No Return. *See* Vozrata net, 1974
No Road Back, 1956 (Connery 3)
No Room for the Groom, 1952 (Sirk 2, Curtis 3)
No Sad Songs for Me, 1950 (Sullavan 3, Wood 3, Duning 4, Koch 4, Maté 4, Walker 4)
'No Sir, Orison', 1975 (Landow 2)
No Sleep for Percy, 1955 (Terry 4)
No Sleep on the Deep, 1934 (Langdon 3)
No Sleep till Dawn, 1957 (Wood 3)
No Sleep till Dawn. *See* Bombers B-25, 1957
No Small Affair, 1984 (Zsigmond 4)
No somos de piedra, 1967 (García Berlanga 2)
No Stop-Over, 1921 (Roach 4)
No Sun in Venice. *See* Sait-on jamais?, 1957
No te engañes corazón, 1936 (Cantinflas 3, García 3)
No Time for Comedy, 1940 (Beavers 3, Russell, R. 3, Stewart 3, Epstein, J. & P. 4, Haller 4, Orry-Kelly 4, Wallis 4)
No Time For Flowers, 1952 (Siegel 2)
No Time for Love, 1943 (Leisen 2, Colbert 3, Dreier 4, Head 4, Irene 4, Lang 4, Young, V. 4)
No Time for Pity. *See* Time Without Pity, 1957
No Time for Sergeants, 1958 (Leroy 2, Mahin 4, Rosson 4)
No Time for Tears, 1957 (Neagle 3, Quayle 3)
No Time for Tears. *See* Otoko arite, 1955
No Time to Die, 1958 (Mature 3, Box 4)
No Time to Kill. *See* Med mord i bagaget, 1961
No Time to Marry, 1938 (Arlen 3, Astor 3)
No Trees in the Street, 1959 (Holloway 3)
No Way Out, 1950 (Mankiewicz 2, Darnell 3, Poitier 3, Widmark 3, Krasner 4, Lemaire 4, Newman 4, Wheeler 4, Zanuck 4)
No Way to Treat a Lady, 1968 (Remick 3, Segal 3, Steiger 3, Jenkins 4)
No Woman Knows, 1921 (Browning 2)
Noah's Ark, 1928 (Curtiz 2, Costello, D. 3, Fazenda 3, Johnson, N. 3, Loy 3, Grot 4, Zanuck 4)
Noah's Ark, 1977 (Halas and Batchelor 2)
Noah's Ark. *See* Arche de Noë, 1946
Noah's Ark. *See* Arche de Noé, 1967
Noah's Lark, 1929 (Fleischer, M. and D. 2)
Noah's Outing, 1932 (Terry 4)
Nob Hill, 1945 (Hathaway 2, Bennett J. 3, Raft 3, Cronjager 4, Raine 4)
Nobi, 1959 (Ichikawa 2)
Nobody Home, 1919 (Garmes 4)
Nobody Lives Forever, 1946 (Negulesco 2, Brennan 3, Garfield 3, Burnett 4, Deutsch 4, Edeson 4)
Nobody Runs Away, 1956 (Cotten 3)
Nobody Runs Forever, 1968 (Delerue 4)
Nobody Said Nothing. *See* Nadie dijo nada, 1971
Nobody Shall Be Laughing, 1965 (Menzel 2)
Nobody's Baby, 1937 (Roach 4)
Nobody's Bride, 1923 (Miller, V. 4)
Nobody's Darling, 1943 (Mann 2, Calhern 3)
Nobody's Daughter. *See* Arvácska, 1975
Nobody's Daughter. *See* Syndens Datter, 1915

Nobody's Fool, 1921 (Glennon 4)
Nobody's Fool, 1936 (Horton 3)
Nobody's Kid, 1920 (Marsh 3)
Nobody's Son. See Senki fia, 1917
Nobody's Widow, 1927 (Crisp 3, Miller, A. 4)
Nobody's Women. See Femmes de personne, 1984
Noc na Karlštejně, 1973 (Brejchová 3, Kopecký 3, Kučera 4)
Noc nevěsty, 1967 (Kachyna 2, Brejchová 3)
Noc poslubna, 1959 (Andersson H. 3)
Noce au lac Saint-Fargeau, 1905 (Guy 2)
Noce i dnie, 1975 (Tyszkiewicz 3)
Noces d'argent, 1915 (Feuillade 2, Musidora 3)
Noces de sable, 1948 (Cocteau 2, Auric 4)
Noces rouges, 1973 (Chabrol 2, Audran 3, Piccoli 3, Rabier 4)
Noces sanglantes, 1916 (Feuillade 2)
Noces siciliennes, 1912 (Feuillade 2)
Noces vénitiennes. See Prima notte, 1958
Noche de los mayas, 1939 (Figueroa 4)
Noche de Reyes, 1947 (Rey 3)
Noche de sabado, 1950 (Félix 3)
Noche de tormenta, 1951 (Aimée 3)
Nochnoi gost, 1959 (Smoktunovsky 3)
Noční host, 1960 (Hrušínský 3)
Noční motýl, 1941 (Hrušínský 3)
Noční zkouška, 1980 (Schorm 2)
Noctem s belite kone, 1984 (Ivanov 3)
Nocturna, 1979 (Carradine 3)
Nocturne, 1919 (Feuillade 2)
Nocturne, 1946 (Raft 3, Boyle 4, Harrison 4)
Nocturne, 1954 (Alexeieff and Parker 2)
Nocturno, 1958 (Mimica 4)
Nocturno de amor, 1948 (Alcoriza 4)
Nocturno der Liebe, 1918 (Veidt 3)
Nodes, 1981 (Brakhage 2)
Nod-o-Nodi, 1954 (Sircar 4)
Noël de Francesca, 1912 (Feuillade 2)
Noël du poilu, 1915 (Feuillade 2)
Nogent, Eldorado du dimanche, 1929 (Carné 2)
Nogi Taisho to Kuma-san, 1926 (Mizoguchi 2)
Nogiku no gotoki kimi nariki, 1955 (Kinoshita 2)
Nogitsune Sanji, 1930 (Hasegawa 4, Tsuburaya 4)
No-Good Guy, 1916 (Sullivan 4)
No-Gun Man, 1924 (Arzner 2)
Noi donne siamo fatte cosí, 1971 (Risi 2, Scola 2, Vitti 3, Age and Scarpelli 4)
Noi due sole, 1953 (Rota 4)
Noi gangsters, 1959 (Cervi 3)
Noi non siamo angeli, 1975 (Ireland 3)
Noi siamo due evasi, 1959 (Tognazzi 3)
Noi siamo le colonne, 1956 (De Sica 2)
Noi vivi—addio Kira, 1942 (Brazzi 3)
Noia, 1963 (Davis 3, Guerra 4, Ponti 4)
Noire de . . ., 1966 (Sembene 2)
Noire et Caline, 1977 (Alekan 4)
Noise Annoys Ko-Ko, 1929 (Fleischer, M. and D. 2)
Noise from the Deep, 1913 (Sennett 2, Arbuckle 3, Normand 3)
Noise of Bombs, 1914 (Sennett 2)
Noisy Noises, 1929 (Roach 4)
Noisy Six, 1913 (Mix 3)
Noix de Coco, 1939 (Simon, M. 3, Achard 4)
Nomads of the North, 1920 (Chaney Lon 3, Stone 3)
Nommé La Rocca, 1961 (Belmondo 3, Cloquet 4)
Non c'è amore piu grande, 1955 (Cervi 3)
Non c'è pace tra gli ulivi, 1949 (De Santis 2)
Non coupable, 1947 (Simon, M. 3)
Non e mai troppe tardi, 1953 (Mastroianni 3)
Non me lo dire!, 1940 (Fellini 2)
Non perdiamo la test, 1959 (Tognazzi 3)
Non si servizia un paperino, 1972 (Papas 3)
Non sono superstirioso, ma . . .!, 1943 (De Sica 2)
Non stuzzicate la zanzara, 1967 (Wertmüller 2, Giannini 3, Masina 3)
Non ti conosco più, 1936 (De Sica 2)
Non toccate la donna bianca, 1973 (Ferreri 2, Fabrizi 3)

Non uccidere. See Tu ne tueras point, 1961
Nona, 1973 (Paskaleva 3)
Nona. See Statek na hranici, 1973
None But the Brave, 1965 (Sinatra 3, Daniels 4, Tsuburaya 4, Williams, J. 4)
None But the Brave. See Storm over the Nile, 1955
None But the Lonely Heart, 1944 (Barrymore E. 3, Duryea 3, Fitzgerald 3, Grant, C. 3, D'Agostino 4, Eisler 4)
None Shall Escape, 1944 (De Toth 2, Garmes 4)
None So Blind, 1923 (Costello, M. 3)
Nonki saiban, 1955 (Kagawa 3)
Nonna Sabella, 1957 (Risi 2, Delli Colli 4)
Nonsense Newsreel, 1954 (Terry 4)
Non-Skid Kid, 1922 (Roach 4)
Non-Stop Kid, 1918 (Daniels 3, Lloyd 3, Roach 4)
Non-Stop New York, 1937 (Siodmak 4)
Noon Whistle, 1923 (Laurel 3, Roach 4)
Noon Wine, 1966 (Peckinpah 2)
Noose, 1928 (Barthelmess 3)
Noose, 1948 (Holloway 3)
Noose Hangs High, 1948 (Abbott and Costello 3, Taradash 4)
Nor the Moon by Night, 1958 (Bernard 4)
Nora, 1923 (Kortner 3, Tschechowa 3, Pommer 4)
Nora Helmer, 1973 (Fassbinder 2)
Nora inu, 1949 (Kurosawa 2, Hayasaka 4)
Nora Prentiss, 1947 (Sheridan 3, Grot 4, Howe 4, Waxman 4)
Norainu, 1949 (Mifune 3, Shimura 4)
Nordlandrose, 1914 (Porten 3, Messter 4)
Noren, 1958 (Yamada 3)
Norliss Tapes, 1973 (Dickinson 3)
Norma Rae, 1979 (Ritt 2, Field 3, Alonzo 4, Ravetch 4)
Normal Young Man. See Giovane normale, 1969
Norman Conquests in the Bayeux Tapestry, 1967 (Evans 3)
Norman Jacobson, 1967 (Emshwiller 2)
Normandie-Niemen, 1959 (Spaak 4)
Noroît, 1976 (Rivette 2, Chaplin 3)
Norrlanningar, 1930 (Borgstrom 3)
Norseman, 1978 (Elam 3, Ferrer, M. 3, Wilde 3)
North Bridge. See Pont du nord, 1981
North by Northwest, 1959 (Hitchcock 2, Carroll L. 3, Grant, C. 3, Mason 3, Saint 3, Bass 4, Boyle 4, Herrmann 4, Lehman 4)
North Dallas Forty, 1978 (Nolte 3)
North of 50-50, 1924 (Roach 4)
North of 57, 1924 (Sennett 2)
North of Hudson Bay, 1923 (Ford, J. 2, Mix 3, Furthman 4)
North of Nevada, 1924 (Brown, Harry Joe 4)
North of the Border, 1946 (Eason 4)
North of the Great Divide, 1950 (Johnson, N. 3, Rogers, R. 3)
North of the Rio Grande, 1922 (Daniels 3)
North of the Rio Grande, 1937 (Boyd 3, Cobb 3, Head 4)
North of the Yukon. See North of Hudson Bay, 1923
North or North West. See N or NW, 1938
North Sea, 1938 (Cavalcanti 2, Watt 2)
North Sea Hijack. See Ffolkes, 1980
North Star, 1925 (Gable 3, Walker 4)
North Star, 1943 (Milestone 2, Von Stroheim 2, Andrews D. 3, Baxter A. 3, Brennan 3, Huston 3, Copland 4, Goldwyn 4, Howe 4, Mandell 4, Menzies 4)
North to Alaska, 1960 (Fleischer, R. 2, Hathaway 2, Granger 3, Wayne 3, Mahin 4, Shamroy 4, Smith, J.M. 4)
North to the Klondike, 1942 (Chaney Lon, Jr. 3, Crawford, B. 3, Salter 4)
North West Frontier, 1959 (More 3, Unsworth 4)
North West Mounted Police, 1940 (DeMille 2, Carroll M. 3, Chaney Lon, Jr. 3, Cody 3, Cooper, Gary 3, Goddard 3, Preston 3, Ryan 3, Dreier 4, Head 4, Sullivan 4, Young, V. 4)
North Woods, 1931 (Lantz 4)
Northern Bridge. See Pont du nord, 1981
Northern Frontier, 1935 (Brennan 3)
Northern Harbour. See Severní přístav, 1954
Northern Pursuit, 1943 (Walsh 2, Flynn 3, Deutsch 4)
Northern Star. See Etoile du nord, 1982
Northern Trail, 1921 (Stone 3)

Northwest. *See* Noroît, 1976
Northwest Hounded Police, 1946 (Avery 2)
Northwest Outpost, 1947 (Dwan 2, Eddy 3, Haas 3, Lanchester 3, Schildkraut 3, Canutt 4)
Northwest Passage, 1940 (Vidor, K. 2, Brennan 3, Tracy 3, Young, R. 3, Jennings 4, Stothart 4, Stromberg 4)
Northwest Rangers, 1942 (Carradine 3, Wynn 3, Schary 4)
Northwest Stampede, 1948 (Eason 4)
Northwest U.S.A.. *See* Pacific Northwest, 1944
Norvège, 1951 (Colpi 4)
Norway's Liv Ullman. *See* Look at Liv, 1977
Norwood, 1970 (Wallis 4)
Nos, 1971 (Komorowska 3)
Nos Bons Étudiants, 1903–04 (Guy 2)
Nos dicen los intocables, 1963 (García 3)
Nos lleva la tristeza, 1964 (García 3)
Nos Veremos en el cielo, 1950 (Armendáriz 3)
Nose. *See* Nez, 1963
Nosed Out, 1934 (Roach 4)
Nose's Story, 1911 (Gaudio 4)
Nosferatu, 1922 (Murnau 2, Galeen 4, Wagner 4)
Nosferatu—Phantom der Nacht, 1979 (Herzog 2, Adjani 3, Ganz 3, Kinski 3)
Nosferatu the Vampire. *See* Zwolfte Stunde—Eine Nacht des Grauens, 1930
Nosotros los pobres, 1947 (Infante 3)
Nostalgia, 1983 (Tarkovsky 2, Yankovsky 3, Guerra 4)
Nostalgie, 1937 (Baur 3, Manès 3, Annenkov 4, Wakhévitch 4)
Nostalgie. *See* Frühlingsrauschen, 1929
Nostra guerra, 1945 (Lattuada 2)
Nostradamus's Great Prophecy. *See* Nosutoradamusu no daiyogen, 1974
Nostri anna più belli. *See* Giorni più belli, 1956
Nostri figli. *See* Vinti, 1952
Nostri mariti, 1966 (Risi 2, Zampa 2, Sordi 3, Tognazzi 3, Age and Scarpelli 4)
Nostri sogni, 1943 (De Sica 2, Zavattini 4)
Nostro agente a Casablanca, 1966 (Fusco 4)
Nostros dos, 1954 (Fernández 2)
Noštta Sreštu 13-ti, 1961 (Karamitev 3)
Nosutoradamusu no daiyogen, 1974 (Tsukasa 3, Yamamura 3, Muraki 4)
Not a Drum Was Heard, 1924 (Wellman 2, August 4)
Not a Ladies' Man, 1942 (Wray 3)
Not as a Stranger, 1955 (Kramer, S. 2, Chaney Lon, Jr. 3, Crawford, B. 3, De Havilland 3, Grahame 3, Marvin 3, Mitchum 3, Sinatra 3, Anhalt 4, Planer 4)
Not as Wicked as That. *See* Pas si méchant que ça, 1975
Not Blood Relations. *See* Nasanu naka, 1932
Not Enough. *See* Pas assez, 1968
Not Exactly Gentlemen, 1931 (Wray 3, Nichols 4)
Not for Children. *See* Barnforbjudet, 1979
Not Guilty, 1908 (Méliès 2)
Not Guilty, 1921 (Franklin 2)
Not Guilty. *See* Non coupable, 1947
Not in Nottingham, 1963 (Hanna and Barbera 4)
Not Like Other Girls, 1912 (Lawrence 3)
Not My Kid, 1985 (Segal 3)
Not My Sister, 1916 (Sullivan 4)
Not Now, 1936 (Fleischer, M. and D. 2)
Not of This Earth, 1957 (Corman 4)
Not on Your Life. *See* Verdugo, 1963
Not One Shall Die, 1957 (Guffey 4)
Not Quite Decent, 1929 (Clarke, C.C. 4)
Not Reconciled. *See* Nicht versohnt oder Es hilft nur Gewalt, wo Gewalt herrscht, 1965
Not So Dumb, 1930 (Vidor, K. 2, Davies 3, Adrian 4, Gibbons 4, Stewart 4)
Not So Easy—Motorcycle Safety, 1973 (Fonda, P. 3)
Not So Long Ago, 1925 (Olcott 2, Howe 4)
Not So Quiet, 1930 (Lantz 4)
Not to Be Trusted, 1926 (Rooney 3)
Not Wanted, 1949 (Lupino 3)

Not Wanted on Voyage. *See* Treachery on the High Seas, 1938
Not with My Wife You Don't, 1966 (Curtis 3, Scott, G. 3, Bass 4, Head 4, Lang 4, Mercer 4, Panama 4, Williams, J. 4)
Notch pered Rozdestvom, 1913 (Mozhukin 3)
Note in the Shoe, 1909 (Griffith 2)
Notes for an African Oresteia. *See* Appunti per una Orestiade africana, 1969
Notes for Jerome, 1981 (Mekas 2)
Notes on a Green Revolution, 1972 (Benegal 2)
Notes on the Circus, 1966 (Mekas 2)
Notes on the Popular Arts, 1978 (Bass 4)
Notes to You, 1941 (Freleng 4)
Nothing But Pleasure, 1940 (Keaton 2, Bruckman 4)
Nothing But the Best, 1963 (Roeg 2, Bates 3, Raphael 4)
Nothing But the Night, 1972 (Cushing 3, Lee, C. 3)
Nothing But the Truth, 1929 (Cronjager 4)
Nothing But the Truth, 1941 (Goddard 3, Hope 3, Dreier 4, Head 4, Lang 4)
Nothing But the Truth. *See* Vérités et mensonges, 1973
Nothing But the Truth. *See* F for Fake, 1975
Nothing But Trouble, 1918 (Daniels 3, Lloyd 3, Roach 4)
Nothing But Trouble, 1945 (Laurel & Hardy 3, Irene 4)
Nothing Else Matters, 1920 (Pearson 2, Balfour 3)
Nothing in Common, 1986 (Alonzo 4)
Nothing Lasts Forever, 1980 (Jaffe 3)
Nothing Personal, 1980 (Sutherland 3)
Nothing Sacred, 1937 (Wellman 2, Lombard 3, March 3, McDaniel 3, Banton 4, Hecht 4, Plunkett 4, Selznick 4, Wheeler 4)
Nothing to Wear, 1928 (Walker 4)
Notorious, 1946 (Hitchcock 2, Bergman 3, Calhern 3, Grant, C. 3, Rains 3, D'Agostino 4, Head 4, Hecht 4)
Notorious Affair, 1930 (Bacon 2, Francis, K. 3, Rathbone 3, Grot 4, Haller 4)
Notorious But Nice, 1933 (Beavers 3)
Notorious Daughter of Fanny Hill, 1965 (Kovacs 4)
Notorious Elinor Lee, 1940 (Micheaux 2)
Notorious Gentleman. *See* Rake's Progress, 1945
Notorious Lady, 1927 (Stone 3, Gaudio 4, Murfin 4)
Notorious Landlady, 1962 (Edwards 2, Astaire 3, Lemmon 3, Novak 3, Duning 4)
Notorious Lone Wolf, 1946 (Guffey 4)
Notorious Sophie Lang, 1934 (Sheridan 3, Head 4, Veiller 4)
Notre histoire, 1984 (Evein 4)
Notre mariage, 1984 (Branco 4, de Almeida 4)
Notre pauvre coeur, 1916 (Feuillade 2)
Notre Dame, cathédrale de Paris, 1957 (Franju 2, Delerue 4, Fradetal 4)
Notre-Dame de Paris, 1931 (Epstein 2)
Notre-Dame de Paris, 1956 (Delannoy 2, Cuny 3, Lollobrigida 3, Aurenche 4, Auric 4, Prévert 4)
Notte, 1960 (Antonioni 2, Wicki 2, Mastroianni 3, Moreau 3, Vitti 3, Di Venanzo 4, Flaiano 4, Guerra 4)
Notte brava, 1959 (Bolognini 2, Pasolini 2)
Notte dei fiori, 1972 (Sanda 3)
Notte del nozze. *See* Tradita, 1954
Notte delle beffe, 1940 (Sordi 3, Amidei 4)
Notte di San Lorenzo, 1982 (Taviani, P. and V. 2, Guerra 4)
Notte di tempesta, 1945 (Castellani 2, Gherardi 4)
Notte porta consiglio. *See* Roma città libera, 1946
Notti bianche, 1957 (Visconti 2, Marais 3, Mastroianni 3, Schell, Maria 3, Cristaldi 4, D'Amico 4, Rota 4)
Notti di Cabiria, 1956 (Fellini 2, Pasolini 2, Masina 3, De Laurentiis 4, Flaiano 4, Gherardi 4, Pinelli 4, Rota 4)
Nous deux, 1979 (Lelouch 2)
Nous irons à Deauville, 1962 (Constantine 3)
Nous irons à Monte Carlo, 1951 (Dalio 3, Hepburn, A. 3)
Nous irons à Paris, 1949 (Raft 3)
Nous irons tous au paradis, 1977 (Gélin 3)
Nous les gosses, 1941 (Modot 3, Douy 4)
Nous les jeunes, 1938 (Barrault 3)
Nous les jeunes. *See* Altitude 3.200, 1938
Nous ne ferons jamais de cinéma, 1932 (Cavalcanti 2)
Nous ne sommes pas mariés, 1946 (Dauphin 3, Vích 4)

Nous ne sommes plus des enfants, 1934 (Dauphin 3, Stradling 4)
Nous n'irons plus au bois, 1951 (Sautet 2)
Nous n'irons plus au bois, 1963 (Carrière 4)
Nous sommes tous des assassins, 1952 (Cayatte 2, Spaak 4)
Nouveau Journal d'une femme en blanc, 1966 (Autant-Lara 2, Aurenche 4, Douy 4)
Nouveau Seigneur du village, 1908 (Méliès 2)
Nouveau Testament, 1936 (Guitry 2)
Nouveaux Messieurs, 1928 (Feyder 2, Meerson 4, Périnal 4, Spaak 4)
Nouveaux Misérables, 1947–51 (Verneuil 2)
Nouveaux riches, 1938 (Raimu 3, Simon, M. 3, Lourié 4)
Nouvelle mission de Judex, 1917 (Feuillade 2)
Nouvelles Luttes extravagantes, 1900 (Méliès 2)
Nova domaća zivotinja, 1964 (Makavejev 2)
Nova igračka, 1964 (Makavejev 2)
Nove ospiti per un delitto, 1976 (Kennedy, A. 3)
Novecento, 1976 (Bertolucci 2, Bertini 3, De Niro 3, Lancaster 3, Valli 3, Morricone 4, Storaro 4)
Novecento. See 1900, 1976
Novel with a Contrabass. See Román s basou, 1949
Novel: Yoshida School. See Shousetsu Yoshida gakkou, 1983
Novelletta, 1937 (Comencini 2)
November, 1921 (Fleischer, M. and D. 2)
November. See Listopad, 1934
Novembre à Paris, 1956 (Reichenbach 2, Braunberger 4, Delerue 4)
99 mujeres, 1969 (McCambridge 3, Schell, Maria 3)
Novia a la medida, 1949 (García 3)
Novice, 1911 (Bosworth 3)
Novices, 1970 (Bardot 3, Girardot 3, Gégauff 4)
Novio a la vista, 1953 (Bardem 2, García Berlanga 2)
Noviye pokhozdeniya Shveika, 1943 (Yutkevich 2)
Noviye rasskazy bravogo soldata Shveika, 1941 (Yutkevich 2)
Novosti dnia, 1944–54 (Vertov 2)
Novy Gulliver, 1935 (Ptushko 2)
Novyi dom, 1947 (Cherkassov 3)
Novyi Vavilon, 1929 (Gerasimov 2, Kozintsev 2, Enei 4, Moskvin 4, Shostakovich 4)
Now, 1965 (Alvarez 2)
Now, 1971–73 (Brocka 2)
Now about These Women. See For att inte tala om all dessa kvinnor, 1964
Now and Forever, 1934 (Hathaway 2, Cooper, Gary 3, Lombard 3, Temple 3, Banton 4, Dreier 4)
Now Barabbas, 1949 (Burton 3, Hardwicke 3, More 3, Adam 4, Wakhévitch 4)
Now Barabbas Was a Robber . . .. See Now Barabbas, 1949
Now Don't Get Excited. See Nee kofun shicha iya yo, 1931
Now Hare This, 1958 (McKimson 4)
Now Hear This, 1963 (Jones 2)
Now I'll Tell, 1934 (Faye 3, Tracy 3, Friedhofer 4)
Now I'll Tell One, 1926 (Laurel 3, Roach 4)
Now I'll Tell You, 1934 (Temple 3)
Now Is the Time, 1950–51 (McLaren 2)
Now It's Up to You. See Ustedes tienen la palabara, 1974
Now Let's Talk About Men. See Questa volta parliamo di uomini, 1965
Now or Never, 1921 (Lloyd 3, Roach 4)
Now That I Was Born a Woman. See Onna to umaretakaranya, 1934
Now, Voyager, 1942 (Cooper, Gladys 3, Davis 3, Henreid 3, Rains 3, Friedhofer 4, Orry-Kelly 4, Polito 4, Robinson 4, Steiner 4, Wallis 4)
Now We Will Call You Brother. See Ahora te vamos a llamar hermano, 1971
Now We're in the Air, 1927 (Beery 3, Brooks 3)
Now You're Talking, 1940 (Mills 3, Balcon 4)
Nowhere to Go, 1958 (Love 3, Smith 3)
Nowhere to Hide, 1977 (Van Cleef 3, Anhalt 4)
Nowy Janko muzykant, 1960 (Lenica 2)
Nož, 1967 (Marković 3, Samardžić 3)
Nóz w wodzie, 1962 (Polanski 2, Skolimowski 2)
Nozomi naki ni arazu, 1949 (Hayasaka 4)
Nseeb, 1981 (Bachchan 3)
N'te promène donc pas toute nue, 1906 (Feuillade 2)
Nth Commandment, 1923 (Borzage 2, Moore, C. 3, Marion 4)

Nu borjar livet, 1948 (Molander 2, Zetterling 2)
Nu går jag till Maxim, 1910 (Magnusson 4)
Nuage entre les dents, 1974 (Noiret 3)
Nude Bomb, 1980 (Gassman 3, Schifrin 4)
Nude in His Pocket. See Amour de poche, 1957
Nude Restaurant, 1967 (Warhol 2)
Nudo di donna, 1981 (Cassel 3, Manfredi 3, Age and Scarpelli 4)
Nuestra Natacha, 1936 (Rey 3)
Nuestras vidas, 1950 (Figueroa 4)
Nueva canción Chilena, 1972–73 (Ruiz 2)
Nueva cenicienta, 1964 (Rey 3)
Nuevitas, 1968 (Gómez, M. 2)
Nugget Jim's Pardner, 1916 (Borzage 2)
Nugget Nell, 1919 (Gish, D. 3, Garmes 4)
Nuisance, 1921 (Hardy 3)
Nuisance, 1933 (Toland 4)
Nuit à l'hôtel, 1931 (Dalio 3, Achard 4)
Nuit agitée, 1897 (Guy 2)
Nuit agitée, 1908 (Feuillade 2)
Nuit agitée, 1912 (Linders 3)
Nuit américaine, 1973 (Truffaut 2, Baye 3, Bisset 3, Léaud 3, Delerue 4)
Nuit américaine. See Day for Night, 1973
Nuit blanche, 1948 (Brasseur 3)
Nuit bulgare, 1969 (Vanel 3, Vierny 4)
Nuit d'or, 1976 (Blier 3, Kinski 3, Vanel 3)
Nuit de décembre, 1939 (Blier 3, Reggiani 3, D'Eaubonne 4, Jaubert 4)
Nuit de folies, 1934 (Fernandel 3)
Nuit de la revanche, 1924 (Duvivier 2, Vanel 3)
Nuit de la Saint-Jean. See Schweigen im Walde, 1929
Nuit de Sybille, 1946 (Gélin 3)
Nuit de Varennes, 1981 (Scola 2, Barrault 3, Gélin 3, Keitel 3, Mastroianni 3, Piccoli 3, Schygulla 3, Trintignant 3, Amidei 4)
Nuit des adieux, 1965 (Cherkassov 3)
Nuit du 11 Septembre, 1919 (Mozhukin 3)
Nuit du carrefour, 1932 (Becker 2, Renoir 2, Renoir 4)
Nuit est mon royaume, 1951 (Gabin 3, Spaak 4)
Nuit et brouillard, 1955 (Resnais 2, Cloquet 4, Colpi 4, Delerue 4, Eisler 4)
Nuit fantastique, 1942 (L'Herbier 2, Blier 3, Presle 3, Jeanson 4)
Nuit merveilleuse, 1940 (Fernandel 3, Vanel 3, Matras 4)
Nuit noire, Calcutta, 1964 (Duras 2)
Nuit sur le Mont Chauve, 1933 (Alexeieff and Parker 2)
Nuit terrible, 1896 (Méliès 2)
Nuit tous les chats sont gris, 1977 (Depardieu 3)
Nuits de feu, 1937 (L'Herbier 2, Annenkov 4, Lourié 4)
Nuits de Paris, 1951 (D'Eaubonne 4)
Nuits de prince, 1928 (L'Herbier 2, Manès 3, Burel 4)
Nuits moscovites, 1934 (Baur 3, Amidei 4, Andrejew 4, Annenkov 4, Jaubert 4, Planer 4)
Nuits rouges, 1974 (Franju 2)
Nukiashi sashiashi, 1934 (Yoshimura 2, Takamine 3)
Numazu Hei-gakko, 1939 (Imai 2)
Numazu Military Academy. See Numazu Hei-gakko, 1939
Number, 1979 (Boulting 2)
Number One, 1969 (Dern 3, Heston 3)
Number One, 1976 (Cannon 3)
Number, Please, 1920 (Lloyd 3, Roach 4)
Number, Please, 1931 (Bennett 4)
Number 17, 1932 (Hitchcock 2, Reville 4)
Number 13, 1922 (Hitchcock 2)
No. 2, 1940 (Sidney 2)
Numbered Men, 1930 (Leroy 2, Polito 4)
Numbered Woman, 1938 (Bond 3, Brown, K. 4)
Numéro deux, 1975 (Godard 2, de Beauregard 4)
Nun. See Suzanne Simonin, la religieuse de Denis Diderot, 1966
Nun's Night. See Noc nevěsty, 1967
Nun's Story, 1959 (Zinnemann 2, Evans 3, Finch 3, Hepburn, A. 3, Blanke 4, Planer 4, Trauner 4, Waxman 4)
Nunca pasa nada, 1963 (Bardem 2, Cassel 3, Delerue 4)
Nunzio, 1978 (Schifrin 4)
Nuovi angeli, 1961 (Delli Colli 4)
Nuovi mostri, 1977 (Monicelli 2, Risi 2, Scola 2, Gassman 3, Sordi 3, Tognazzi 3, Age and Scarpelli 4, Delli Colli 4)

Nuptiae, 1969 (Broughton 2)
. . . Nur ein Komodiant, 1935 (Henreid 3, Wegener 3)
Nur eine Tanzerin, 1926 (Planer 4)
Nur tote Zeugen schweigen, 1963 (Knef 3)
Nur um tausend Dollars, 1918 (Dupont 2)
Nur zum Spass—Nur zum Spiel. Kaleidoskop Valeska Gert, 1977
     (Schlondorff 2)
Nuregame Botan, 1961 (Kyo 3)
Nurekami kenka tabi, 1960 (Yamada 3)
Nuremburg Trials, 1946 (Lorentz 2)
Nuri the Flea. See Pire Nuri, 1968
Nurse. See Infermiera, 1975
Nurse Edith Cavell, 1939 (Wilcox 2, Neagle 3, Pitts 3, Sanders 3,
     August 4, Young, F. 4)
Nurse from Brooklyn, 1938 (Krasner 4)
Nurse Maid, 1932 (Iwerks 4)
Nurse Mates, 1940 (Fleischer, M. and D. 2)
Nurse Sisi, 1947 (Sircar 4)
Nurse to You, 1935 (Roach 4)
Nursery Crimes, 1943 (Fleischer, M. and D. 2)
Nursery Rhymes. See Ríkadla, 1949
Nursing a Viper, 1909 (Griffith 2, Sennett 2, Bitzer 4)
Nursing Sisters. See Sestřičky, 1983
Nusumareta koi, 1951 (Ichikawa 2, Mori 3)

Nusumareta yokujo, 1958 (Imamura 2)
Nut, 1921 (Chaplin 2, Fairbanks, D. 3)
Nut-Cracker, 1926 (Horton 3)
Nutcracker Fantasy, 1979 (Lee, C. 3, McDowall 3)
Nuts and Jolts, 1929 (Lantz 4)
Nuts and Volts, 1963 (Freleng 4)
Nuts in May, 1917 (Laurel 3)
Nutty But Nice, 1940 (Three Stooges 3, Bruckman 4)
Nutty Naughty Chateau. See Château en Suède, 1963
Nutty Network, 1939 (Terry 4)
Nutty Notes, 1929 (Lantz 4)
Nutty Professor, 1963 (Lewis 2, Head 4)
Nuuk 250 år, 1979 (Roos 2)
Nyan-nyan-myan-hoi, 1940 (Hayasaka 4)
Nyarsafton pa skanska slatten, 1961 (Troell 2)
Nybyggarna, 1972 (Troell 2, Ullmann 3, Von Sydow 3)
Nyckeln och ringen, 1947 (Borgstrom 3, Dahlbeck 3)
Nyobo funshitsu, 1928 (Ozu 2)
Nyobo gakko, 1961 (Mori 3)
8. szabad Május 1, 1952 (Jancsó 2)
Nyonin aishu, 1937 (Naruse 2)
Nyonin Mandara, 1933–4 (Yamada 3)
Nyordning på Sjogårda, 1944 (Bjornstrand 3)
Nyubo yo, eien nare, 1955 (Mori 3, Tanaka 3)

O

O canto do mar, 1953 (Cavalcanti 2)
O Circo, 1965 (Diegues 2)
O Dreamland, 1953 (Anderson 2)
O.H.M.S., 1937 (Walsh 2, Mills 3, Balcon 4)
O. Henry's Full House, 1952 (Hathaway 2, Hawks 2, King 2,
     Negulesco 2, Baxter A. 3, Crain 3, Laughton 3, Monroe 3,
     Widmark 3, Ballard 4, Johnson 4, Krasner 4, Lemaire 4,
     Newman 4, Trotti 4)
O.K. Connery, 1967 (Morricone 4)
O.K. Nerone, 1951 (Cervi 3)
O labuti, 1982 (Jires 2)
O liudiakh i atomakh, 1983 (Batalov 3)
O Lucky Man!, 1973 (Anderson 2, McDowell 3, Richardson 3,
     Roberts 3, Ondricek 4)
O lyubvi, 1971 (Yankovsky 3)
O Megalexandros, 1980 (Angelopoulos 2)
O Mimi san, 1914 (Hayakawa 3, Ince 4)
O mišu i satovima, 1969 (Grgić 4)
O něčem jiném, 1963 (Chytilová 2)
O.S.S., 1946 (Ladd 3, Dreier 4)
O saisons, o châteaux, 1957 (Varda 2, Braunberger 4)
O salto, 1967 (Broca 2)
O samon chelovekhnom, 1967 (Yutkevich 2)
O ševci Matoušovi, 1948 (Stallich 4)
O skleničku víc, 1953 (Trnka 2, Brdečka 4, Pojar 4)
O slavnosti a hostech, 1966 (Nemec 2, Schorm 2)
O sole mio, 1945 (Delli Colli 4)
O světle, 1953 (Brdečka 4)
O Thassios, 1975 (Angelopoulos 2)
O věcech nadpřirozených, 1958 (Kopecký 3)
Oasis, 1955 (Allégret, Y. 2, Morgan 3)
Oatari otoko ichidai, 1956 (Yamada 3)
Oath, 1913 (Anderson G. 3)
Oath, 1921 (Walsh 2, Nilsson 3, Menzies 4)
Oath and the Man, 1910 (Griffith 2, Bitzer 4)
Oath of a Viking, 1914 (Rosher 4)
Oath of His Office, 1912 (Anderson G. 3)
Oath of Vengeance, 1944 (Crabbe 3)
Oath of Youth. See Kliatva molodikh, 1944

Ob etom zabyvat nelzya, 1954 (Tikhonov 3)
Obaasan, 1944 (Takamine 3)
Oban: Kanketsu-hen, 1958 (Yamamura 3)
Občan Brych, 1958 (Kopecký 3)
Občan Karel Havlíček, 1966 (Jires 2)
Obchod na korze, 1965 (Kadár 2, Kroner 3)
Obedient Flame, 1939 (McLaren 2)
Oberdan, 1916 (Bertini 3)
Oberwachtmeister Schwenek, 1935 (Frohlich 3)
Oberwald Mystery. See Mistero di Oberwald, 1979
Obey the Law, 1933 (Bond 3)
Obič. See Mládi a láska, 1972
Object Alimony, 1929 (Walker 4)
Object Matrimony. See Help Wanted—Male, 1920
Objections Overruled, 1912 (Dwan 2)
Objectiv 500 millions, 1966 (de Beauregard 4)
Objective, Burma!, 1945 (Flynn 3, Howe 4, Wald 4, Waxman 4)
Oblačna priča, 1972 (Grgić 4)
Obliging Young Lady, 1941 (Arden 3, O'Brien, E. 3, Musuraca 4)
Oblomok imperii, 1929 (Ermler 2, Gerasimov 3, Enei 4)
Oblong Box, 1969 (Lee, C. 3, Price 3)
Obo Kissa, 1929 (Hasegawa 3)
Obocchan, 1926 (Tanaka 3)
Oboro kago, 1951 (Tanaka 3, Yamada 3, Yoda 4)
Oborona Sevastopolya, 1911 (Mozhukin 3)
Oborona Tsaritsina, 1942 (Vasiliev 2, Babochkin 3)
Oboroyo no onna, 1936 (Gosho 2)
Obráceni Ferdyše Pištory, 1931 (Haas 3, Stallich 4)
Obratnaya svyaz, 1977 (Gurchenko 3, Ulyanov 3, Yankovsky 3)
Obrazki z zycia, 1975 (Pszoniak 3)
Obryv, 1913 (Mozhukin 3)
Obsession, 1933 (Vanel 3, Jaubert 4)
Obsession, 1949 (Dmytryk 2, Baker S. 3, Adam 4, Rota 4)
Obsession, 1954 (Delannoy 2, Morgan 3)
Obsession, 1976 (De Palma 2, Schrader 2, Bujold 3, Robertson 3,
     Herrmann 4, Zsigmond 4)
Obsession. See Homme mysterieux, 1933
Obsession. See Junoon, 1978

Obuknovennoe utro, 1978 (Yankovsky 3)
Obǔsku, z pytle ven!, 1956 (Brdečka 4)
Obykhnovennyi fachizm, 1965 (Romm 2)
Obžalovaný, 1964 (Kadár 2)
Ocalenie, 1972 (Komorowska 3)
Occasional Work of a Female Slave. See Gelegenheitsarbeit einer
    Sklavin, 1973
Occhi freddi della paura, 1971 (Morricone 4)
Occhi, la bocca, 1983 (Piccoli 3)
Occhio alla penna, 1981 (Morricone 4)
Occhio del ragno, 1971 (Johnson, V. 3, Kinski 3)
Occhio nel labarinto, 1970 (Valli 3)
Occhio selvaggio, 1967 (Guerra 4)
Occident, 1938 (Berry 3, Vanel 3)
Occupe-toi d'Amélie, 1949 (Autant-Lara 2, Darrieux 3, Aurenche 4,
    Bost 4, Douy 4)
Ocean Breakers. See Branningar, 1935
Ocean Hop, 1927 (Disney 2)
Ocean in Flames. See Documents secrets, 1940
Ocean Swells, 1934 (Stevens 2)
Ocean Waif, 1916 (Guy 2)
Oceano, 1971 (Morricone 4)
Ocean's Eleven, 1960 (Milestone 2, Dickinson 3, MacLaine 3,
    Martin, D. 3, Raft 3, Sinatra 3, Bass 4, Brown, Harry 4, Cahn 4,
    Daniels 4, Lederer 4)
Ochazuke no aji, 1952 (Imamura 2, Ozu 2, Ryu 3)
Ochiba nikki, 1953 (Yamamura 3)
Ochimusha, 1925 (Tanaka 3)
Ochiyo toshigoro, 1937 (Miyagawa 4)
Ochiyo-gasa, 1935 (Miyagawa 4)
Ochiyo's Umbrella. See Ochiyo-gasa, 1935
800 Leguas por el Amazona, 1960 (Armendáriz 3)
Ochsenkrieg, 1920 (Planer 4)
OCIL 1958, 1958 (Delerue 4)
Očovské pastorále, 1973 (Kroner 3)
Octagon, 1980 (Van Cleef 3)
Octa-Man, 1970 (Baker 4)
October, 1982 (Bondarchuk 3)
October. See Oktiabr, 1928
October. See Oktiabr, 1967
October Days. See Oktiabr' dni, 1958
October Man, 1947 (Greenwood 3, Mills 3, Alwyn 4)
October Revolution, 1967 (Gielgud 3)
Octopussy, 1983 (Jourdan 3, Moore, R. 3, Barry 4)
Octubre de todos, 1977 (Alvarez 2)
Oczekiwanie, 1961 (Giersz 4)
Oda—vissza, 1962 (Gaál 2)
Odalisque, 1914 (Reid 3, Sweet 3, Walthall 3)
Odd Couple, 1968 (Lemmon 3, Matthau 3, Cahn 4, Westmore, W. 4)
Odd Job Man, 1912 (Dwan 2)
Odd Man Out, 1947 (Reed 2, Cusack 3, Mason 3, Alwyn 4, Krasker 4,
    Mathieson 4)
Odd Obsession. See Kagi, 1959
Oddinnadtsatii, 1928 (Vertov 2)
Odds Against Tomorrow, 1959 (Wise 2, Grahame 3, Ryan 3,
    Winters 3, Allen, D. 4)
Ode to Billy Joe, 1976 (Legrand 4)
Oden jigoku, 1960 (Kyo 3)
Odessa File, 1974 (Schell, Maria 3, Schell, Maximilian 3, Voight 3,
    Morris 4)
Odessa in fiamme, 1942 (Gallone 2)
Odette, 1927 (Bertini 3)
Odette, 1950 (Wilcox 2, Howard, T. 3, Neagle 3, Ustinov 3, Dehn 4)
Odeur des fauves, 1970 (De Sica 2, Lai 4)
Odin iz nas, 1971 (Gurchenko 3)
Odio per odio, 1967 (Ireland 3)
Odissea, 1968 (Papas 3)
Odkaz, 1965 (Schorm 2)
Odna, 1931 (Gerasimov 2, Kozintsev 2, Enei 4, Moskvin 4,
    Shostakovich 4)
Odna siemia, 1943 (Orlova 3)
Odongo, 1956 (Alwyn 4)
Odor-able Kitty, 1944 (Jones 2)

Odoriko, 1957 (Kyo 3)
Oduro Meikun, 1936 (Hasegawa 3)
Odwiedziny prezydenta, 1961 (Tyszkiewicz 3)
Odyssée du Capitaine Steve. See Walk into Paradise, 1955
Odyssée du Monsanto, 1981 (Cassel 3)
Odysseus, 1986 (Kučera 4)
Odysseus' Heimkehr, 1918 (Messter 4)
Odyssey of the North, 1914 (Franklin 2, Bosworth 3)
Oedipus Rex. See Edipo re, 1967
Oedipus the King, 1968 (Welles 2, Cusack 3, Sutherland 3, Lassally 4)
Oedo gonin otoko, 1951 (Yamada 3)
Oedo hara no yowa, 1938 (Shindo 3)
Oedo no kyoji, 1960 (Kagawa 3)
Oedo no oni, 1947 (Hasegawa 3, Takamine 3)
Oedo no saigon, 1928 (Tsuburaya 3)
Oeil du maître, 1957 (Resnais 2, Braunberger 4)
Oeil du malin, 1962 (Chabrol 2, Audran 3, de Beauregard 4, Ponti 4)
Oeil pour oeil, 1957 (Cayatte 2, Jurgens 3, Bost 4, Matras 4)
Oeil Torve. See Oko wykol, 1960
Oeil-du-Lynx, detective, 1936 (Kaufman 4)
Oen-dancho no koi, 1933 (Tanaka 3)
Oensan, 1955 (Tsukasa 3)
O'er Hill and Dale, 1932 (Grierson 2, Wright 2)
Oeufs brouillés, 1975 (Cassel 3, Karina 3, Carrière 4)
Oeufs de l'autruche, 1957 (Fresnay 3)
Oeuvre immortelle, 1924 (Duvivier 2)
Oeuvre scientifique de Pasteur, 1946 (Fradetal 4)
Oeyama Shuten-doji, 1960 (Hasegawa 3)
Of A Thousand Delights. See Vaghe stella dell'orsa, 1965
Of Cash and Hash, 1955 (Three Stooges 3)
Of Flesh and Blood. See Grands Chemins, 1962
Of Fox and Hounds, 1940 (Avery 2)
Of Great Events and Ordinary People. See De Grands Evènements et
    des gens ordinaires, 1979
Of Human Bondage, 1934 (Cromwell 2, Davis 3, Howard, L. 3,
    Berman 4, Plunkett 4, Polglase 4, Steiner 4)
Of Human Bondage, 1946 (Goulding 2, Gwenn 3, Henreid 3, Blanke 4,
    Friedhofer 4, Korngold 4)
Of Human Bondage, 1964 (Hathaway 2, Harvey 3, Novak 3, Box 4,
    Morris 4)
Of Human Hearts, 1938 (Brown 2, Bondi 3, Carradine 3, Coburn, C. 3,
    Huston 3, Stewart 3, Stothart 4, Vorkapich 4)
Of Human Rights, 1950 (Van Dongen 4)
Of Life and Love. See Questa è la vita, 1954
Of Love and Desire, 1963 (Jurgens 3, Oberon 3)
Of Men and Demons, 1969 (Hubley 4, Jones 4)
Of Men and Music, 1950 (Aldrich 2, Hammid 2, Crosby 4, Kurnitz 4,
    Paxton 4)
Of Mice and Ben. See O mišu i satovima, 1969
Of Mice and Men, 1939 (Milestone 2, Chaney Lon, Jr. 3, Meredith 3,
    Copland 4, Roach 4)
Of Mice and Men, 1981 (Ayres 3)
Of Pups and Puzzles, 1941 (Sidney 2)
Of Rice and Hen, 1953 (McKimson 4)
Of Stars and Men, 1961 (Hubley 4)
Of Thee I Sting, 1946 (Freleng 4)
Of Wayward Love. See Amore difficile, 1962
Off His Trolley, 1924 (Garnett 2, Sennett 2)
Off Limits, 1953 (Crosby 3, Hope 3, Rooney 3, Head 4)
Off the Dole, 1935 (Formby 3)
Off the Highway, 1925 (Stromberg 4)
Off the Record, 1939 (Blondell 3, O'Brien, P. 3, Deutsch 4, Rosher 4
Off the Trolley, 1919 (Daniels 3, Lloyd 3, Roach 4)
Off to China, 1936 (Terry 4)
Off to the Opera, 1952 (Terry 4)
Off to the Races, 1937 (Summerville 3)
Offbeat, 1960 (Zetterling 3)
Offence, 1972 (Lumet 2, Connery 3, Howard, T. 3, Fisher 4)
Offener Hass gegen Unbekannt, 1970 (Hauff 2)
Office Blues, 1930 (Rogers, G. 3)
Office Boy, 1932 (Iwerks 4)
Office Boy's Revenge, 103 (Porter 2)
Office Girl. See Sunshine Susie, 1931

Offbeat, 1960 (Zetterling 2)
Offence, 1972 (Lumet 2, Connery 3, Howard, T. 3, Fisher 4)
Offener Hass gegen Unbekannt, 1970 (Hauff 2)
Office Blues, 1930 (Rogers, G. 3)
Office Boy, 1932 (Iwerks 4)
Office Boy's Revenge, 1903 (Porter 2)
Office Girl. See Sunshine Susie, 1931
Office Wife, 1930 (Bacon 2, Blondell 3, Bosworth 3, Stone 3, Zanuck 4)
Officer and a Gentleman, 1982 (Gere 3, Gossett 3)
Officer Cupid, 1921 (Sennett 2)
Officer de police sans importance, 1972 (Denner 3)
Officer John Donovan, 1913 (Talmadge, N. 3)
Officer O'Brien, 1930 (Garnett 2, Boyd 3, Miller, A. 4)
Officer Pooch, 1941 (Hanna and Barbera 4)
Officer 666, 1915 (Niblo 2)
Officer Thirteen, 1932 (Rooney 3)
Officer's Mess, 1931 (Lanchester 3)
Official Officers, 1925 (Roach 4)
Offizierstragodie. See Rosenmontag, 1924
Off-Shore Pirate, 1921 (Young, W. 4)
Oficio más antiguo, 1968 (Alcoriza 4)
O'Flynn. See Fighting O'Flynn, 1948
Often an Orphan, 1949 (Jones 2)
Oggetti smarriti, 1979 (Ganz 2)
Oggi a me . . . domani a te!, 1968 (Argento 4)
Oggi, domani, dopodomani, 1965 (Ferreri 2, Mastroianni 3, Tognazzi 3, Di Venanzo 4, Ponti 4)
Ogin Sama, 1960 (Tanaka 3)
Ogin Sama, 1979 (Mifune 3, Okada 3, Shimura 3, Yoda 4)
Ogledalo, 1971 (Grgić 4)
Ognuno per se, 1968 (Heflin 3, Kinski 3)
Ogon, 1930 (Donskoi 2)
Ogro, 1979 (Pontecorvo 2, Cristaldi 4, Morricone 4)
Oh, 1968 (Vanderbeek 2)
Oh Amelia!. See Occupe-toi d'Amélie, 1949
Oh Dad, Poor Dad, 1967 (Mackendrick 2, Russell, R. 3, Stark 4, Unsworth 4)
Oh Daddy!, 1922 (Sennett 2)
Oh, Daddy!, 1935 (Balcon 4)
Oh, diese Jugend, 1963 (Domrose 3)
Oh, Doctor!, 1914 (Beery 3)
Oh, Doctor!, 1917 (Keaton 2, Arbuckle 3)
Oh, Doctor!, 1925 (Astor 3)
Oh, Doctor!, 1937 (Arden 3, Horton 3, Krasner 4)
Oh, For a Man, 1930 (Lugosi 3, MacDonald 3, Clarke, C.C. 4)
Oh! For a Man!. See Will Success Spoil Rock Hunter?, 1957
Oh Gentle Spring, 1942 (Terry 4)
Oh, God!, 1977 (Bellamy 3, Pleasance 3)
Oh! Heavenly Dog, 1980 (Sharif 3)
Oh! How I Hate to Get Up in the Morning, 1932 (Fleischer, M. and D. 2)
Oh, Jo! See Country Flapper, 1922
Oh, Johnny, How You Can Love!, 1940 (Meek 3, Krasner 4)
Oh, Kay!, 1928 (Leroy 2, Moore, C. 3, Wilson, C. 4)
Oh Lady, Lady, 1920 (Daniels 3)
Oh Life—A Woe Story—The A Test News, 1963 (Brakhage 2)
Oh, Mabel!, 1924 (Fleischer, M. and D. 2)
Oh, Men! Oh, Women!, 1957 (Dailey 3, Niven 3, Rogers, G. 3, Clarke, C.C. 4, Friedhofer 4, Johnson 4, Lemaire 4)
Oh Money, Money, 1951 (Coburn, C. 3)
Oh My Aunt, 1914 (Hepworth 2)
Oh! Oh! Cleopatra, 1931 (Farnum 3)
Oh, Promise Me, 1921 (Roach 4)
Oh! Que Mambo!, 1958 (Sordi 3)
Oh, Rosalinda!, 1955 (Powell and Pressburger 2, Schlesinger 2, Ferrer, M. 3, Quayle 3, Redgrave, M. 3, Walbrook 3)
Oh Serafina!. See Bruciati da cocente passione, 1976
Oh! Such a Night, 1910–11 (White 3)
Oh! Susanna, 1933 (Terry 4)
Oh! Susanna, 1936 (Autry 3)
Oh, Teacher, 1927 (Disney 2)
Oh, Those Eyes, 1911 (Sennett 2, Normand 3)

Oh, Uncle!, 1909 (Griffith 2, Pickford 3, Bitzer 4)
Oh, Uncle!, 1926 (Sennett 2)
Oh, What a Knight, 1928 (Disney 2)
Oh What a Knight, 1982 (Driessen 4)
Oh! What a Lovely War, 1969 (Attenborough 3, Bogarde 3, Cassel 3, Gielgud 3, Hawkins 3, Mills 3, More 3, Olivier 3, Redgrave, M. 3, Redgrave, V. 3, Richardson 3, Smith 3, York, S. 3)
Oh, What a Night!. See Rounders, 1914
Oh! What a Nurse!, 1926 (Zanuck 4)
Oh, Yeah!, 1929 (Garnett 2, Pitts 3, Miller, A. 4)
Oh, You Are Like a Rose. See Ack, du ar some en ros, 1967
Oh You Beautiful Doll, 1926 (Fleischer, M. and D. 2)
Oh You Beautiful Doll, 1929 (Fleischer, M. and D. 2)
Oh, You Beautiful Doll, 1949 (Stahl 2, Sakall 3, Lemaire 4, Newman 4, Steiner 4)
Oh! You Mummy!, 1912–13 (White 3)
Oh! You Pearl!, 1912–13 (White 3)
Oh! You Puppy!, 1912–13 (White 3)
Oh! You Scotch Lassie!, 1912–13 (White 3)
Oh, You Tony!, 1924 (Mix 3)
Oh, You Women!, 1919 (Emerson 4, Loos 4)
Ohanahan, 1966 (Iwashita 3)
O'Hara—Squatter and Philosopher, 1912 (Talmadge, N. 3)
Ohayo, 1959 (Ozu 2, Ryu 3)
Oh-Edo gonon otoko, 1951 (Yoda 4)
Ohitsu oharetsu Somekawa Shohachi, 1931 (Yamada 3)
Ohm Kruger, 1941 (Grundgens 3, Jannings 3, Wagner 4)
Ohne dich wird es Nacht, 1956 (Jurgens 3)
Ohne Zeugen, 1919 (Kortner 3)
Ohnivé léto, 1939 (Baarová 3)
Ohrfeigen, 1970 (Jurgens 3)
Ohtone no yogiri, 1950 (Kagawa 3)
Ohtoro-jo no hanayome, 1957 (Shimura 3, Shindo 3)
Oil and Water, 1913 (Griffith 2, Barrymore L. 3, Gish, D. 3, Gish, L. 3, Sweet 3, Walthall 3, Bitzer 4)
Oil Can Mystery, 1933 (Terry 4)
Oil for Aladdin's Lamp, 1942 (Ivens 2)
Oil for the Lamps of China, 1935 (Florey 2, Leroy 2, Crisp 3, O'Brien, P. 3, Gaudio 4)
Oil Hell of Killing Women. See Onna goroshi abura jigoku, 1949
Oil on Troubled Waters, 1913 (Dwan 2)
Oil Raider, 1934 (Crabbe 3)
Oilfield. See Olieveld, 1954
Oil's Well, 1929 (Lantz 4)
Oil's Well That Ends Well, 1958 (Three Stooges 3)
Oily American, 1954 (McKimson 4)
Oily Hare, 1952 (McKimson 4)
Oily Scoundrel, 1916 (Sennett 2)
Oily to Bed, Oily to Rise, 1939 (Three Stooges 3)
Oise mairi, 1939 (Yoda 4)
Oiseau de paradis, 1962 (Jarre 4)
Oiseau rare, 1935 (Brasseur 3, Prévert 4)
Oiseau rare, 1973 (Presle 3)
Oiseau s'en vole, 1960 (Alekan 4)
Oiseaux d'Afrique, 1961 (Braunberger 4)
Oiseaux vont mourir au Pérou, 1968 (Brasseur 3, Darrieux 3, Seberg 3, Matras 4)
Oito Universitários, 1967 (Diegues 2)
Ojciec krolowej, 1980 (Stawinsky 4)
Øjeblikket, 1980 (Henning-Jensen 2)
Ojo de la cerradura, 1964 (Torre-Nilsson 2)
Ojo Kichiza, 1926 (Kinugasa 2, Hasegawa 3)
Ojo Okichi, 1935 (Yamada 3)
Ojojoj eller sången om den eldroda hummern, 1965 (Fischer 4)
Ojos vendados, 1978 (Saura 2)
Ojosan, 1930 (Ozu 2, Tanaka 3)
Ojosan, 1937 (Takamine 3)
Ojosan kanpai, 1949 (Kinoshita 2, Shindo 2, Hara 3)
Ok ketten, 1977 (Mészáros 2, Nowicki 3)
Oka Oorie Katha, 1977 (Sen 2)
Oka wa hanazakari, 1952 (Yamamura 3)
O'Kalems' Visit to Killarney, 1912 (Olcott 2)
Okame, 1927 (Gosho 2)

Okanda, 1913 (Stiller 2)
Okarina, 1919 (Veidt 3)
Okasan, 1952 (Naruse 2, Kagawa 3, Okada 3, Tanaka 3)
Okay America, 1932 (Garnett 2, Ayres 3, Calhern 3, O'Sullivan 3, Miller, A. 4)
Okayo no kakugo, 1939 (Tanaka 3)
Okean, Vozvrata net, 1974 (Samoilova 3)
Okénko, 1933 (Baarová 3, Haas 3, Stallich 4)
Okiku to Harima, 1954 (Hasegawa 3)
Okinawa, 1952 (O'Brien, P. 3)
Okinawa Battles. See Okinawa kessen, 1971
Okinawa kessen, 1971 (Muraki 4)
Okinu to banto, 1940 (Tanaka 3)
Oklahoma!, 1955 (Zinnemann 2, Grahame 3, Jones S. 3, Steiger 3, Crosby 4, Deutsch 4, Levien 4, Orry-Kelly 4, Surtees 4)
Oklahoma Badlands, 1948 (Canutt 4)
Oklahoma Crude, 1973 (Kramer, S. 2, Dunaway 3, Mills 3, Palance 3, Scott, G. 3, Mancini 4, Surtees 4)
Oklahoma Kid, 1939 (Bacon 2, Bogart 3, Bond 3, Cagney 3, Crisp 3, Buckner 4, Deutsch 4, Friedhofer 4, Howe 4, Orry-Kelly 4, Steiner 4)
Oklahoma Outlaws, 1943 (Eason 4)
Oklahoma Renegades, 1940 (Canutt 4)
Oklahoma Woman, 1956 (Corman 2)
Oklahoman, 1957 (McCrea 3, Mirisch 4, Salter 4)
Okno, 1981 (Pszoniak 3)
Oko wykol, 1960 (Skolimowski 2)
Okomé, 1951 (Rabier 4)
Okos lány, 1955 (Macskássy 4)
Okoto and Sasuke. See Okoto to Sasuke, 1961
Okoto to Sasuke, 1935 (Tanaka 3)
Okoto to Sasuke, 1961 (Kinugasa 2)
Oktiabr, 1928 (Eisenstein 2, Tisse 4)
Oktiabr, 1967 (Shostakovich 4)
Oktiabr' dni, 1958 (Vasiliev 2)
Októberi vasárrap, 1979 (Kovács 2)
Okuman-choja, 1954 (Ichikawa 2, Okada 3, Yamada 3)
Okuni and Gohei. See Okuni to Gohei, 1952
Okuni to Gohei, 1952 (Naruse 2, Yamamura 3)
Okusama ni goyojin, 1950 (Mori 3, Tanaka 3)
Okusama shakuyosho, 1936 (Gosho 2)
Okusama wa daigaku-sei, 1956 (Kagawa 3)
Ol' Gray Hoss, 1928 (Roach 4)
Ol' Swimmin' 'ole, 1928 (Disney 2)
Ola and Julia. See Ola och Julia, 1967
Ola och Julia, 1967 (Fischer 4)
Olaf—An Atom, 1913 (Griffith 2, Carey 3, Bitzer 4)
Olaf Laughs Last, 1942 (Bruckman 4)
Olavi, 1920 (Lukas 3)
Old Acquaintance, 1943 (Davis 3, Hopkins, M. 3, Young, G. 3, Blanke 4, Coffee 4, Orry-Kelly 4, Polito 4, Waxman 4)
Old Actor, 1912 (Griffith 2, Marsh 3, Pickford 3, Bitzer 4)
Old Age Handicap, 1928 (Browning 2)
Old Age—The Wasted Years, 1966 (Leacock 2)
Old and New. See Staroie i novoie, 1929
Old and Young. See Oreg és fiatal, 1969
Old Barn, 1929 (Sennett 2, Hornbeck 4)
Old Barn Dance, 1938 (Autry 3, Rogers, R. 3)
Old Battersea House, 1961 (Russell 2)
Old Bill and Son, 1940 (Crichton 2, Mills 3, Dalrymple 4, Korda 4, Périnal 4)
Old Black Joe, 1926 (Fleischer, M. and D. 2)
Old Black Joe, 1929 (Fleischer, M. and D. 2)
Old Blackout Joe, 1940 (Hubley 4)
Old Bookkeeper, 1911 (Griffith 2, Bitzer 4)
Old Box, 1975 (Driessen 4)
Old Boyfriends, 1979 (Schrader 2, Fraker 4, Henry 4, Houseman 4)
Old Bull, 1932 (Pitts 3, Roach 4)
Old Chinese Opera. See Stará cínská opera, 1954
Old Chisholm Trail, 1942 (Salter 4)
Old Clothes, 1925 (Coogan 3, Crawford, J. 3)
Old Cobbler, 1914 (Chaney Lon 3)
Old Confectioner's Mistake, 1911 (Griffith 2, Bitzer 4)

Old Corral, 1936 (Autry 3, Chaney Lon, Jr. 3, Rogers, R. 3)
Old Cowboy. See Stary Kowboj, 1973
Old Czech Legends. See Staré povĕsti ceske, 1953
Old Dark House, 1932 (Whale 2, Douglas, M. 3, Karloff 3, Laughton 3, Massey 3, Edeson 4, Laemmle 4, Pierce 4)
Old Dog Tray, 1935 (Terry 4)
Old Doll, 1911 (Bunny 3)
Old Dracula. See Vampira, 1973
Old Dudino. See Granitsa, 1935
Old English, 1930 (Arliss 3)
'ld Fashioned Girl, 1915 (Crisp 3, Gish, D. 3)
Old Fashioned Way, 1934 (Fields, W.C. 3)
Old Fashioned World. See Piccolo mondo antico, 1941
Old Fire Horse, 1939 (Terry 4)
Old Fire Horse and the New Fire Chief, 1914 (Bunny 3)
Old Folk Song. See Hej, te eleven Fa . . . ., 1963
Old Folks at Home, 1924 (Fleischer, M. and D. 2)
Old Fool, 1923 (Fazenda 3)
Old Glory, 1939 (Jones 2)
Old Greatheart. See Way Back Home, 1931
Old Grey Hare, 1944 (Clampett 4)
Old Grey Manor, 1935 (Hope 3)
Old Guard, 1941 (Gerasimov 2)
Old Gun. See Vieux Fusil, 1975
Old Heads and Young Hearts, 1910 (Lawrence 3)
Old Heidelberg, 1915 (Von Stroheim 2, Gish, D. 3, Reid 3)
Old Home Week, 1925 (Heerman 4)
Old Homestead, 1922 (Cruze 2, Brown, K. 4)
Old Homestead, 1935 (Rogers, R. 3)
Old Hutch, 1936 (Beery 3, Meek 3)
Old Inhabitant. See Starozhil, 1962
Old Ironsides, 1926 (Arzner 2, Cruze 2, Arlen 3, Beery 3, Karloff 3, Schulberg 4)
Old Isaacs, the Pawnbroker, 1908 (Bitzer 4)
Old Lady 31, 1920 (Mathis 4)
Old Lantern. See Uta andon, 1960
Old Los Angeles, 1948 (Schildkraut 3)
Old Louisiana, 1937 (Hayworth 3)
Old Loves and New, 1926 (Tourneur, M. 2, Pidgeon 3, Stone 3)
Old Maid, 1914 (Sweet 3)
Old Maid, 1939 (Goulding 2, Brent 3, Crisp 3, Davis 3, Fazenda 3, Hopkins, M. 3, Blanke 4, Friedhofer 4, Gaudio 4, Orry-Kelly 4, Robinson 4, Steiner 4, Wallis 4)
Old Maid. See Vieille Fille, 1972
Old Maid's Baby, 1914 (Bunny 3)
Old Mammy's Secret Code, 1913 (Ince 4)
Old Man, 1914 (Gish, D. 3)
Old Man and the Sea, 1958 (Sturges, J. 2, Tracy 3, Crosby 4, Howe 4, Tiomkin 4)
Old Man Minick, 1932 (Beavers 3)
Old Man Motorcar. See Dĕdecek automobil, 1955
Old Man of the Mountain, 1931 (Fleischer, M. and D. 2)
Old Man Rhythm, 1935 (Ball 3, Grable 3, Meek 3, Mercer 4, Musuraca 4, Pan 4)
Old Man Who Cried Wolf, 1970 (Jaffe 3, Robinson, E. 3)
Old Man's Love Story, 1913 (Talmadge, N. 3)
Old Mansion. See Gunnar Hedes saga, 1922
Old Mill. See Gamla kvarnen, 1964
Old Mother Hubbard, 1935 (Iwerks 4)
Old Mother Riley Meets the Vampire, 1952 (Lugosi 3)
Old Oaken Bucket, 1941 (Terry 4)
Old Red Car. See Cervená aerovka, 1960
Old Reliable, 1914 (Talmadge, N. 3)
Old Rockin' Chair Tom, 1947 (Hanna and Barbera 4)
Old San Francisco, 1927 (Crosland 2, Costello, D. 3, Oland 3, Wong 3, Carré 4, Zanuck 4)
Old Sea Dogs, 1922 (Roach 4)
Old Shoes, 1925 (Pitts 3)
Old Soak, 1926 (Fazenda 3)
Old Soldiers, 1938 (Pearson 2)
Old South, 1940 (Zinnemann 2)
Old Spanish Custom. See Invader, 1935
Old Wedding Dress, 1912 (Bushman 3)

Old West, 1952 (Autry 3)
Old Wives for New, 1918 (DeMille 2, Boyd 3, Buckland 4, Macpherson 4)
Old Wives' Tales, 1946 (Halas and Batchelor 2)
Old Woman. *See* Öreg, 1971
Old Woman Ghost. *See* Yoba, 1976
Old Women of Japan. *See* Nippon no obachan, 1962
Old Writing Desk. *See* Chatollets Hemmelighed, 1913
Old Wyoming Trail, 1937 (Rogers, R. 3)
Old Yeller, 1957 (Disney 2, Canutt 4)
Oldás és kotés, 1963 (Jancsó 2, Latinovits 3)
Older Brother and Younger Sister. *See* Ani imoto, 1976
Older Brother, Younger Sister. *See* Ani imoto, 1953
Older Sister. *See* Starshaya sestra, 1967
Oldest Profession. *See* Plus Vieux Métier du monde, 1967
Öldurmek hakkimdir, 1968 (Guney 2)
Ole dole doff, 1968 (Troell 2)
Olevěný chléb, 1954 (Kopecký 3)
Olie op reis, 1957 (Haanstra 2)
Olieveld, 1954 (Haanstra 2)
Olimpiada 40, 1980 (Pszoniak 3)
Olimpiada en Mexico, 1968 (Lassally 4)
Olimpiadi dei mariti, 1960 (Cervi 3, Tognazzi 3)
Olive Oyl and Water Don't Mix, 1942 (Fleischer, M. and D. 2)
Olive Trees of Justice. *See* Oliviers de la justice, 1962
Oliver!, 1968 (Reed 2, Reed, O. 3, Box 4, Green, J. 4, Morris 4)
Oliver Twist, 1916 (Van Dyke, W.S. 2, Bosworth 3)
Oliver Twist, 1922 (Chaney Lon 3, Coogan 3)
Oliver Twist, 1933 (Brenon 2, Hunt 4)
Oliver Twist, 1948 (Lean 2, Guinness 3, Green, G. 4, Havelock-Allan 4, Mathieson 4, Morris 4)
Oliver Twist, 1982 (Scott, G. 3)
Oliver's Story, 1978 (Milland 3, Lai 4)
Olives and Their Oil, 1914 (Sennett 2)
Olive's Boithday Presink, 1941 (Fleischer, M. and D. 2)
Olive's Sweepstake Ticket, 1941 (Fleischer, M. and D. 2)
Olivia, 1950 (Feuillère 3, Noiret 3, Simon, S. 3, D'Eaubonne 4, Matras 4)
Oliviers de la justice, 1962 (Jarre 4)
Ollé torero, 1963 (Dovniković 4, Dragić 4)
Olly Olly Oxen Free, 1977 (Hepburn, K. 3, Head 4)
Olověný chléb, 1954 (Brejchová 3)
Ölprinz, 1965 (Granger 3)
Oltre d'amore, 1940 (Gallone 2)
Oltre la porta, 1982 (Mastroianni 3, Piccoli 3, Donaggio 4)
Oltre le legge, 1919 (Bertini 3)
Oltre l'oblio, 1948 (Antonioni 2)
Ölume yalniz gidilar, 1963 (Guney 2)
Olvidados, 1950 (Buñuel 2, Alcoriza 4, Figueroa 4)
Olvidados de dios, 1940 (Armendáriz 3)
Olyan, mint otthon, 1978 (Mészáros 2, Nowicki 3)
Olympia, 1930 (Feyder 2, Rosay 3, Daniels 4, Gibbons 4)
Olympia, 1938 (Riefenstahl 2, Herlth 4)
Olympia. *See* Breath of Scandal, 1960
Olympia 52, 1952 (Marker 2)
Olympic Games, 1927 (Roach 4)
Olympics in Mexico. *See* Olimpiada en Mexico, 1968
Omagatsuji's Duel. *See* Oumagatsuji no ketto, 1951
Omaha Trail, 1942 (Meek 3, Schary 4)
O'Malley of the Mounted, 1921 (Hart 3, August 4)
Omar Khayyam, 1957 (Massey 3, Wilde 3, Laszlo 4, Young, V. 4)
Omar Mukhtar, 1979 (Gielgud 3, Papas 3)
Omar the Tentmaker, 1922 (Karloff 3, Buckland 4)
Omatsuri Hanjiro, 1953 (Hasegawa 3)
Ombra, 1919 (Bertini 3)
Ombra, 1954 (Delli Colli 4)
Ombra di un trono, 1921 (Gallone 2)
Ombra nell' ombra, 1977 (Papas 3)
Ombre des châteaux, 1976 (Dalio 3)
Ombre et la nuit, 1977 (Alekan 4)
Ombre et lumière, 1950 (Signoret 3, Kosma 4)
Ombre rouge, 1981 (Baye 3)
Ombrellone, 1965 (Risi 2)

Ombres chinoises, 1982 (Ruiz 2)
Ombres du passé, 1926 (Musidora 3)
Ombres qui passent, 1924 (Mozhukin 3)
Ombyte fornojer, 1938 (Molander 2)
Omega Man, 1971 (Heston 3)
Omelette fantastique, 1909 (Cohl 2)
Omen, 1976 (Peck 3, Remick 3, Goldsmith 4)
Omens and Oracles, 1912 (Talmadge, N. 3)
Omicron, 1963 (Cristaldi 4)
Omlás, 1963 (Madaras 3)
Omokage, 1929 (Hasegawa 3)
Omokage, 1948 (Gosho 2)
Omokage no machi, 1942 (Hasegawa 3)
Omringade huset, 1922 (Sjostrom 2, Magnusson 4)
Omstridte Jord, 1915 (Holger-Madsen 2)
O-My the Tent Mover, 1917 (Pitts 3)
On, 1966 (Sjoberg 2, Andersson, B. 3)
On a Clear Day You Can See Forever, 1970 (Minnelli 2, Montand 3, Nicholson 3, Streisand 3, Beaton 4, Stradling 4)
On a Common Path. *See* Közos útan, 1953
On a jeho sestra, 1931 (Fric 2)
On a Summer's Day, 1921 (Sennett 2)
On a Sunday Afternoon, 1930 (Fleischer, M. and D. 2)
On a volé la cuisse de Jupiter, 1980 (Broca 2, Girardot 3, Noiret 3, Audiard 4)
On a volé la mer, 1962 (Delerue 4)
On a volé un homme, 1934 (Ophuls 2, Kaper 4, Pommer 4)
On Again—Off Again, 1937 (Polglase 4)
On an Island with You, 1948 (Charisse 3, Durante 3, Williams 3, Brown, N. 4, Irene 4, Pasternak 4, Rosher 4)
On Any Street. *See* Notte brava, 1959
On Any Sunday, 1971 (McQueen, S. 3)
On Approval, 1943 (Alwyn 4)
On aura tout vu!, 1976 (Sarde 4)
On Borrowed Time, 1939 (Franklin 2, Barrymore L. 3, Bondi 3, Hardwicke 3, Merkel 3, Ruttenberg 4, Waxman 4)
On Closer Inspection, 1953 (Foldès 4)
On Dangerous Ground, 1916 (Marion 4)
On Dangerous Ground, 1951 (Ray, N. 2, Bond 3, Lupino 3, Ryan 3, Herrmann 4, Houseman 4)
On démande un assassin, 1949 (Fernandel 3)
On demande un bandit, 1947–51 (Verneuil 2)
On demande une brute, 1934 (Tati 2)
On efface tout, 1978 (Presle 3)
On El Monte Ranch, 1912 (Anderson G. 3)
On est poivrot, mais on a du cœur, 1905 (Guy 2)
On Foreign Land. *See* Por la tierra ajena, 1932
On Golden Pond, 1981 (Fonda, H. 3, Fonda, J. 3, Hepburn, K. 3, Jeakins 4)
On Her Majesty's Secret Service, 1969 (Barry 4)
On His Wedding Day, 1913 (Sennett 2)
On Ice, 1933 (Langdon 3)
On ira lui porter des oranges, 1970 (Braunberger 4)
On ira tous au paradis, 1982 (Audran 3)
On Korkusuz adam, 1964 (Guney 2)
On Land, at Sea, and in the Air, 1980 (Driessen 4)
On Light. *See* O světle, 1953
On Location, 1921 (Roach 4)
On Moonlight Bay, 1951 (Day 3, Haller 4, Prinz 4, Steiner 4)
On My Way to the Crusades, I Met a Girl Who . . . *See* Cintura di castità, 1968
On n'a pas besoin d'argent, 1933 (Burel 4)
On n'aime qu'une fois, 1950 (Rosay 3, Audiard 4)
On n'arrête pas le printemps, 1971 (Braunberger 4)
On ne badine pas avec l'amour, 1952 (Evein 4)
On ne meurt pas comme ça, 1946 (Von Stroheim 2)
On ne meurt que deux foix, 1985 (Audiard 4)
On ne roule pas Antoinette, 1936 (Christian-Jaque 2, Kaufman 4)
On n'engraisse pas les cochons à l'eau claire, 1973 (Lefebvre 2)
On Our Merry Way, 1948 (Fonda, H. 3, Lamour 3, Laughton 3, MacMurray 3, Meredith 3, Stewart 3)
On Our Merry Way. *See* Miracle Can Happen, 1948
On Our Side. *See* Riadom s nami, 1931

On Patrol, 1922 (Sennett 2)
On peut le dire sans se fâcher!, 1978 (Legrand 4)
On Probation, 1912 (Cruze 2)
On purge Bébé, 1931 (Renoir 2, Fernandel 3, Simon, M. 3, Braunberger 4)
On Record, 1917 (Rosher 4)
On Roller Skates. See Rulleskøjterne, 1908
On Secret Service, 1912 (Ince 4)
On Seven Winds. See Na semi vetrakh, 1962
On Such a Night, 1937 (Dupont 2, Head 4)
On Such a Night, 1956 (Asquith 2, Dehn 4)
On Sundays, 1960–61 (Baillie 2)
On the Air Live with Captain Midnight, 1976 (Ireland 3)
On the Archipelago Boundary. See Havsbandet, 1971
On the Avenue, 1937 (Carroll M. 3, Faye 3, Fetchit 3, Powell, D. 3, Zanuck 4)
On the Banks of the Wabash, 1923 (Blackton 2, Musuraca 4)
On the Beach, 1959 (Kramer, S. 2, Astaire 3, Gardner 3, Peck 3, Perkins 3, Paxton 4)
On the Border, 1909 (Selig 4)
On the Border, 1913 (Dwan 2)
On the Brink, 1911 (Porter 2)
On the Cactus Trail, 1912 (Anderson G. 3)
On the Carpet. See Little Giant, 1946
On the Comet. See Na kometě, 1970
On the Desert's Edge, 1911 (Anderson G. 3)
On the Double, 1961 (Kaye 3, Rutherford 3, Head 4, Stradling 4, Unsworth 4)
On the Eagle Trail, 1915 (Mix 3, Selig 4)
On the Earth. See Chijo, 1957
On the Edge of Reality, 1977 (Lancaster 3)
On the Eve of Matriculation. See Před maturitou, 1932
On the Fiddle, 1961 (Connery 3, Holloway 3, Arnold 4)
On the Fire, 1918 (Daniels 3, Lloyd 3, Roach 4)
On the Firing Line, 1912 (Ince 4)
On the Front Page, 1926 (Laurel 3, Roach 4)
On the Harmfulness of Tobacco, 1959 (Newman 3)
On the High Seas, 1922 (Boyd 3)
On the Highway of Life. See Na estrada da vida, 1980
On the Jump, 1918 (Walsh 2, Daniels 3, Lloyd 3, Roach 4)
On the Level, 1930 (McLaglen 3, Nichols 4)
On the Line, 1977 (Torn 3)
On the Little Big Horn, 1910 (Mix 3, Selig 4)
On the Loose, 1932 (Pitts 3, Roach 4)
On the Loose, 1951 (Douglas, M. 3, Lederer 4)
On the Marriage Broker Joke, 1979 (Landow 2)
On the Moonlight Trail, 1912 (Anderson G. 3)
On the Move. See Utkosben, 1979
On the Night of the Fire, 1939 (Fisher 2, Richardson 3, Rozsa 4)
On the Night Stage, 1915 (Hart 3, August 4, Ince 4, Sullivan 4)
On the Old Spanish Trail, 1947 (Rogers, R. 3)
On the Other Side of the Araks. See Po tu storonu Araksa, 1946
On the Pole, 1960 (Leacock 2)
On the Quiet, 1918 (Barrymore J. 3)
On the Red Front. See Na krasnom fronte, 1920
On the Reef, 1909 (Griffith 2, Walthall 3, Bitzer 4)
On the Riviera, 1951 (Dalio 3, Kaye 3, Tierney 3, Cole 4, Lemaire 4, Newman 4, Shamroy 4)
On the Roads of Fate. See På livets odesvagar, 1913
On the Roofs of Budapest. See Pesti háztekök, 1961
On the Steep Cliff. See U Krutovo Yara, 1962
On the Sunny Side, 1942 (Darwell 3, McDowall 3)
On the Sunny Side. See På solsidan, 1936
On the Sunnyside. See Na sluneční strane, 1933
On the Swan. See O labuti, 1982
On the Threshold, 1925 (Walthall 3)
On the Threshold of Space, 1956 (Lemaire 4)
On the Town, 1949 (Donen 2, Kelly, Gene 3, Miller 3, Sinatra 3, Comden and Green 4, Edens 4, Freed 4, Gibbons 4, Rose 4, Rosson 4, Smith, J.M. 4)
On the Waterfront, 1954 (Kazan 2, Brando 3, Cobb 3, Malden 3, Saint 3, Steiger 3, Day 4, Kaufman 4, Spiegel 4)
On the Western Frontier, 1909 (Porter 2)

On the Wrong Trek, 1936 (Roach 4)
On Their Own, 1940 (Miller, A. 4)
On Their Way, 1921 (Roach 4)
On Their Wedding Eve, 1913 (Costello, M. 3)
On Thin Ice, 1925 (Zanuck 4)
On Time, 1924 (Fort 4)
On to Reno, 1927 (Cruze 2)
On Top of Old Smoky, 1953 (Autry 3)
On Trial. See Affaire Mauritzius, 1953
On with the Dance, 1920 (Miller, A. 4)
On with the New, 1938 (Fleischer, M. and D. 2)
On with the Show, 1929 (Crosland 2, Brown 3, Fazenda 3, Gaudio 4)
On Your Back, 1930 (August 4)
On Your Toes, 1939 (O'Connor 3, Howe 4, Orry-Kelly 4, Wald 4)
On ze Boulevard, 1927 (Adorée 3, Daniels 4, Gibbons 4)
Ona zashchishchayet rodinu, 1943 (Ermler 2, Maretskaya 3)
Onai goju-ryo, 1931 (Yamada 3)
Onatsu Seijuro, 1936 (Hasegawa 3, Tanaka 3)
Onatsu torimono-cho: Torima, 1960 (Yamada 3)
Onatsu torimono-cho: Tsukiyo ni kieta onna, 1959 (Yamada 3)
Once a Crook, 1941 (Cusack 3)
Once a Gentleman, 1930 (Cruze 2, Bushman 3, Horton 3)
Once a Hero, 1931 (Arbuckle 3)
Once a Hero. See It Happened in Hollywood, 1937
Once a Jolly Swagman, 1948 (Bogarde 3, Cusack 3, Dalrymple 4)
Once a Lady, 1931 (Novello 3, Akins 4, Banton 4, Hoffenstein 4, Lang 4)
Once a Rainy Day. See Akogare, 1966
Once a Sinner, 1931 (Brent 3, McCrea 3)
Once a Thief, 1935 (Pearson 2, Havelock-Allan 4)
Once a Thief, 1950 (Chaney Lon, Jr. 3, Clothier 4, Leven 4)
Once a Thief, 1965 (Delon 3, Heflin 3, Schifrin 4)
Once a Thief. See Tueurs de San Francisco, 1965
Once Every Ten Minutes, 1915 (Lloyd 3, Roach 4)
Once in a Blue Moon, 1935 (Garmes 4, Hecht 4, MacArthur 4)
Once in a Lifetime, 1932 (Fazenda 3, Ladd 3, Pitts 3, Laemmle 4)
Once Is Not Enough, 1975 (Douglas, K. 3, Mercouri 3, Alonzo 4, Epstein, J. & P. 4, Green, G. 4, Mancini 4)
Once More. See Ima hitotabi no, 1947
Once More, My Darling, 1949 (Montgomery 3, Harrison 4, Orry-Kelly 4, Planer 4)
Once More, with Feeling, 1960 (Donen 2, Brynner 3, Kurnitz 4, Périnal 4, Trauner 4)
Once Over, 1923 (Roach 4, Roach 4)
Once por cero, 1970 (Alvarez 2)
Once to Every Woman, 1920 (Valentino 3)
Once to Every Woman, 1934 (Bellamy 3, Darwell 3, Wray 3)
Once Upon a Dead Man, 1971 (Hudson 3)
Once Upon a Honeymoon, 1942 (McCarey 2, Basserman 3, Grant, C. 3, Rogers, G. 3)
Once upon a Scoundrel, 1973 (Figueroa 4, North 4)
Once upon a Spy, 1980 (Lee, C. 3, Sangster 4)
Once Upon a Thursday. See Affairs of Martha, 1942
Once Upon a Time, 1910 (Lawrence 3)
Once Upon a Time, 1944 (Grant, C. 3, Planer 4)
Once Upon a Time, 1957 (Ivanov-vano 4)
Once Upon a Time. See Byl sobie raz, 1957
Once Upon a Time. See C'era una volta, 1967
Once Upon a Time. See Var Engang, 1922
Once Upon a Time in America, 1984 (Leone 2, De Niro 3, Weld 3, Delli Colli 4, Morricone 4)
Once Upon a Time in the West, 1968 (Robards 3, Wynn 3)
Once Upon a Time in the West. See C'era una volta il West, 1968
Once Upon a Time . . . Is Now, 1977 (Hitchcock 2, Grant, C. 3, Grant, L. 3, Fisher 4)
Once Upon a Time There Was a Full Stop. See Bila jednom jedna točka, 1964
Once Upon a Time There Was a King. See Byl jednou jeden král, 195
Once Upon a Tractor, 1965 (Torre-Nilsson 2)
Oncle de Pekin, 1933 (Brasseur 3)
Onda, 1955 (Olmi 2)
Ondata di calore, 1970 (Seberg 3)
Ondamane, 1961 (Delerue 4)

One Night in Lisbon, 1941 (Burke 3, Carroll M. 3, Gwenn 3, MacMurray 3, Dreier 4, Glennon 4, Head 4)
One Night in the Tropics, 1940 (Sutherland 2, Abbott and Costello 3, Cummings 3)
One Night of Love, 1934 (Newman 4, Walker 4)
One Night of Passion. *See* Netsujo no ichiya, 1929
One Night Stand, 1915 (Sennett 2)
One Night Stand, 1918 (Roach 4)
One Night with You, 1948 (Holloway 3, Lee, C. 3)
One Note Tony, 1947 (Terry 4)
One of Nature's Noblemen, 1911 (Bosworth 3)
One of Our Aircraft Is Missing, 1942 (Lean 2, Powell and Pressburger 2, Ustinov 3, Green, G. 4, Krasker 4)
One of Our Dinosaurs Is Missing, 1976 (Ustinov 3)
One of Our Own, 1975 (Homolka 3, Martin, S. 3)
One of Our Spies is Missing, 1966 (Carroll L. 3)
One of the Best, 1927 (Lanchester 3, Balcon 4)
One of the Blood. *See* His Majesty, the American, 1919
One of the Discard, 1914 (Ince 4, Sullivan 4)
One of the Family, 1923 (Roach 4)
One of the Many. *See* En av de många, 1915
One of the Smiths, 1931 (Roach 4)
One of Them is Named Brett, 1965 (Baker S. 3)
One on Reno, 1911 (Lawrence 3)
One on Top of the Other. *See* Una sull'altra, 1969
One P.M., 1970 (Godard 2, Leacock 2)
One Parallel Movie. *See* One P.M., 1970
One Parisian 'Knight'. *See* Open All Night, 1924
One Piece Bathing Suit. *See* Million Dollar Mermaid, 1952
One Plus One, 1961 (Carroll L. 3)
One Plus One, 1968 (Godard 2, Guillemot 4)
One Plus One. *See* En och en, 1978
One Potato, 2 Potato . . .. *See* Eci, pec, pec, 1961
One Precious Year, 1933 (Rathbone 3)
One Punch O'Day, 1926 (Brown, Harry Joe 4)
One Quarter Inch, 1917 (Roach 4)
One Quiet Night, 1931 (Arbuckle 3)
One Rainy Afternoon, 1936 (Sturges, P. 2, Auer 3, Lupino 3, Meek 3, Day 4, Lasky 4, Newman 4)
One Romantic Night, 1930 (Dressler 3, Gish, L. 3, Menzies 4, Schenck 4, Struss 4)
One Round O'Brien, 1911 (Sennett 2)*
One Run Elmer, 1935 (Keaton 2)
One Russian Summer. *See* Giorno del furore, 1973
One Second in Montreal, 1968–69 (Snow 2)
One She Loved, 1912 (Griffith 2, Barrymore L. 3, Gish, L. 3, Pickford 3, Walthall 3, Bitzer 4)
One Shoe Makes It Murder, 1982 (Mitchum 3)
One Single Night. *See* Enda natt, 1938
One Sings, the Other Doesn't. *See* Une chante l'autre pas, 1977
One Spooky Night, 1924 (Sennett 2)
One Spy Too Many, 1966 (Carroll L. 3)
One Step to Hell, 1968 (Sanders 3)
One Step to Hell. *See* Rey de Africa, 1968
One Stolen Night, 1922 (Hardy 3)
One Summer Love, 1976 (Sarandon 3)
One Sunday Afternoon, 1933 (Cooper, Gary 3, Darwell 3, Wray 3, Dreier 4)
One Sunday Afternoon, 1948 (Walsh 2, Malone 3, Grot 4, Wald 4)
One Sunday Morning, 1926 (Arbuckle 3)
One Swallow Doesn't Make a Summer. *See* En fluga gor ingen sommar, 1947
One, Take Two, 1978 (Howard, T. 3)
One Terrible Day, 1922 (Roach 4)
One Third of a Nation, 1939 (Lumet 2, Sidney 3)
1001 Drawings, 1960 (Vukotić 4)
1001 Nights with Toho, 1947 (Yamada 3)
1001 Nights with Toho. *See* Toho sen-ichi-ya, 1947
$1000 a Touchdown, 1939 (Daves 2, Brown 3, Hayward 3, Dreier 4, Head 4)
One Too Many, 1916 (Hardy 3)
One Touch of Nature, 1908 (Griffith 2, Lawrence 3)

One Touch of Venus, 1948 (Tashlin 2, Arden 3, Gardner 3, Walker 3, Kurnitz 4, Orry-Kelly 4, Planer 4)
One Track Minds, 1933 (Pitts 3, Roach 4)
One Trick Pony, 1980 (Torn 3)
One Two Three, 1914 (Beery 3)
One, Two, Three, 1961 (Wilder 2, Cagney 3, Diamond 4, Mandell 4, Previn 4, Trauner 4)
One Two Three, 1975 (Popescu-Gopo 4)
One, Two, Three . . . *See* Számok története, 1962
1, 2, 3, 1912 (Dwan 3)
One Was Beautiful, 1940 (Burke 3)
One Way. *See* Senso unico, 1973
One Way or Another. *See* De cierta manera, 1977
One Way Passage, 1932 (Garnett 2, Francis, K. 3, Powell, W. 3, Grot 4, Orry-Kelly 4)
One Way Pendulum, 1964 (Yates 2)
One Way Street, 1925 (Nilsson 3, Edeson 4)
One Way Street, 1950 (Duryea 3, Elam 3, Hudson 3, Mason 3, Orry-Kelly 4)
One Way Ticket, 1936 (Schulberg 4)
One Way Ticket to Love. *See* Koi no katamichi kippu, 1960
One Week, 1920 (Keaton 2)
One Wild Oat, 1951 (Hepburn, A. 3, Holloway 3)
One Wild Ride, 1925 (Roach 4)
One Wild Week, 1921 (Daniels 3)
One Woman Idea, 1929 (Rosay 3)
One Woman's Story. *See* Passionate Friends, 1949
One Wonderful Night, 1914 (Bushman 3)
One Wonderful Sunday. *See* Subarashiki nichiyobi, 1947
One Yard to Go, 1931 (Sennett 2)
One Year Later, 1933 (Brennan 3)
Oneichan makari touru, 1959 (Muraki 4)
Onésime series, 1909-14 (Modot 3)
Onesta che uccide, 1914 (Bertini 3)
Ongaku dai-shingun, 1943 (Hasegawa 3)
Ongyilkos, 1970 (Macskássy 4)
Oni azami, 1926 (Kinugasa 2)
Oni azami, 1950 (Hasegawa 3)
Oni byli prervymi, 1956 (Ulyanov 3)
Oni no sumu yakata, 1969 (Takamine 3)
Oni srazhalis za rodinu, 1975 (Bondarchuk 3, Shukshin 3, Smoktunovsky 3, Tikhonov 3)
Oni znali Mayakovsky, 1955 (Cherkassov 3)
Onibaba, 1964 (Shindo 2)
Oni-kenji, 1963 (Yamamura 3)
Onion Pacific, 1940 (Fleischer, M. and D. 2)
Onionhead, 1958 (Taurog 2, Matthau 3, Rosson 4)
Oniromane, 1969 (Braunberger 4)
Onkel Brasig, 1936 (Rasp 3)
Onkel og Nevø. *See* Fader og Søn, 1911
Only a Dancing Girl. *See* Bara en danserska, 1927
Only A Farmer's Daughter, 1915 (Sennett 2)
Only a Farmer's Daughter. *See* Feathered Nest, 1916
Only a Janitor, 1919 (Beery 3)
Only A Messenger Boy, 1915 (Sennett 2)
Only a Mother. *See* Bara en mor, 1949
Only a Shop Girl, 1922 (Beery 3)
Only a Woman. *See* Ich bin auch nur eine Frau, 1962
Only Angels Have Wings, 1939 (Hawks 2, Arthur 3, Barthelmess 3, Grant, C. 3, Hayworth 3, Furthman 4, Tiomkin 4, Walker 4)
Only Count the Happy Moments. *See* Rakna de lyckliga stunderna blott, 1944
Only for Fun—Only for Play. Kaleidoscope Valeska Gert. *See* Nur zum Spass—Nur zum Spiel, 1977
Only Game in Town, 1970 (Stevens 2, Beatty 3, Taylor, E. 3, Decaë 4, Jarre 4)
Only Girl, 1933 (Boyer 3, Pommer 4, Waxman 4)
Only Girl. *See* Ich und die Kaiserin, 1933
Only One Night. *See* Enda natt, 1939
Only Saps Work, 1930 (Dmytryk 2, Mankiewicz 2, Arlen 3)
Only Son, 1914 (DeMille 2, Darwell 3)
Only Son, 1922 (Roach 4)
Only Son. *See* Hitori musuko, 1936

Orizzonte di sangue, 1942 (Cortese 3)
Orizzonte dipinto, 1940 (Cortese 3)
Orlacs Hande, 1924 (Wiene 2, Kortner 3, Veidt 3)
Orlando furioso, 1972 (Storaro 4)
Orlovi rano lete, 1966 (Samardžić 3)
Orme, 1974 (Kinski 3, Storaro 4)
Ormen, 1966 (Andersson H. 3)
Ornament des verliebten Herzens, 1919 (Reiniger 2)
Ornament of the Loving Heart. See Ornament des verliebten Herzens, 1919
Oro di Napoli, 1954 (De Sica 2, Loren 3, Mangano 3, De Laurentiis 4, Ponti 4, Zavattini 4)
Oro di Roma, 1961 (Fusco 4, Zavattini 4)
Oro per i Cesari, 1962 (De Toth 2, Hunter 3)
Örökbefogadás, 1975 (Mészáros 2)
Örokos, 1969 (Darvas 3, Latinovits 3)
Örökösök, 1970 (Kovács 2)
Orokség, 1980 (Mészáros 2, Huppert 3, Nowicki 3)
Oroku kanzashi, 1935 (Yamada 3)
Orologio a Cucù, 1938 (Castellani 2, De Sica 2)
Oros, 1960 (Guerra 2)
Oroszlán ugrani készul, 1969 (Madaras 3)
O'Rourke of the Royal Mounted. See Saskatchewan, 1954
Orphan, 1920 (Farnum 3)
Orphan Duck, 1939 (Terry 4)
Orphan Egg, 1953 (Terry 4)
Orphan Joyce, 1916 (Van Dyke, W.S. 2)
Orphan Mary. See Sirota Marija, 1968
Orphan of the Ring. See Kid from Kokomo, 1939
Orphan of the Sage, 1928 (Musuraca 4)
Orphan of the War, 1913 (Ince 4)
Orphan's Mine, 1913 (Dwan 2)
Orphans of the Storm, 1922 (Griffith 2, Gish, D. 3, Gish, L. 3, Schildkraut 3)
Orphan's Tragedy, 1955 (Lee, B. 3)
Orphée, 1950 (Cocteau 2, Melville 2, Marais 3, Auric 4, D'Eaubonne 4)
Orphelin de Paris, 1923 (Feuillade 2)
Orphelin du cirque, 1926 (Vanel 3)
Orpheline, 1921 (Clair 2, Feuillade 2, Florey 2)
Orpheus. See Orphée, 1950
Orpheus in der Unterwelt, 1974 (Hoppe 3)
Orpheus in the Underworld. See Urfeus i underjorden, 1910
Orrori del castello di Norimberga, 1972 (Cotten 3)
Orson Welles, 1966 (Reichenbach 2)
Országutak vándora, 1956 (Mészáros 2)
Orthopedic Paradise. See Paraiso ortopedico, 1969
Örult éjszaka, 1969 (Tyszkiewicz 3)
Orville and Wilbur, 1971 (Keach 3)
Orzowei, 1975 (Allégret, Y. 2, Baker S. 3)
Os filhos do medo, 1978 (Diegues 2)
Os herdeiros, 1969 (Diegues 2)
Osaka Elegy. See Naniwa ereji, 1936
Osaka monogatari, 1957 (Yoshimura 2, Yoda 4)
Osaka natsu no jin, 1937 (Kinugasa 2, Yamada 3)
Osaka no onna, 1958 (Kinugasa 2, Kyo 3)
Osaka no yado, 1954 (Gosho 2)
Osaka Story. See Osaka monogatari, 1957
Osaka Woman. See Naniwa onna, 1940
Osaka-jo monogatari, 1961 (Kagawa 3, Mifune 3, Shimura 3, Yamada 3, Tsuburaya 4)
Osaya koisugata, 1934 (Tanaka 3)
Osbemutató, 1974 (Szabó 2)
Oscar, 1966 (Borgnine 3, Brennan 3, Cotten 3, Crawford, B. 3, Hope 3, Oberon 3, Sinatra 3, Cahn 4, Delerue 4, Head 4, Ruttenberg 4, Wakhévitch 4, Westmore, W. 4)
Oscar, champion de tennis, 1932 (Tati 2)
Oscar per il Signor Rossi, 1960 (Bozzetto 4)
Oscar Wilde, 1960 (Richardson 3, Périnal 4)
Ose Hangoro, 1928 (Hasegawa 3, Tsuburaya 4)
Osen, 1940 (Ermler 2)
O'Shaughnessy's Boy, 1935 (Beery 3, Cooper, J 3, Muse 3, Howe 4)
Oshibka inzheneva Kochina, 1939 (Orlova 3)

Oshidori no aida, 1956 (Yamada 3)
Oshikiri shinkonki, 1930 (Naruse 2)
Osho ichidai, 1955 (Tanaka 3)
Oslerizing Papa, 1905 (Bitzer 4)
Oslo, 1963 (Roos 2)
Osman the Wanderer. See Piyade Osman, 1970
Osmjeh 61, 1961 (Makavejev 2)
Osmnáctiletá, 1939 (Stallich 4)
Osmonds series, 1973 (Halas and Batchelor 2)
Osmosis, 1948 (Kaufman 2)
Osmy dzien tygodnia, 1957 (Ford, A. 2, Cybulski 3, Lomnicki 3)
Osoba vizhnoe zadanie, 1980 (Gurchenko 3)
Osone-ke no asa, 1946 (Kinoshita 2)
Osore-zan no onna, 1964 (Gosho 2)
Ososhiki, 1985 (Ryu 3)
Ospedale del delitto, 1948 (Comencini 2)
Osram, 1957 (Alexeieff and Parker 2)
OSS 117 n'est pas mort, 1956 (D'Eaubonne 4)
Oss tjuvar emellan eller En burk ananas, 1945 (Dahlbeck 3)
Ossessione, 1942 (De Santis 2, Visconti 2)
Ossis Tagebuch, 1917 (Lubitsch 2)
Ossuary. See Kostnice, 1970
Ostanti liść, 1973 (Pszoniak 3)
Ostatni dzien lata, 1958 (Konwicki 4)
Ostatni etap, 1947 (Kawalerowicz 2)
Ostatni lisc, 1973 (Komorowska 3)
Ostende, reine des plages, 1930 (Storck 2, Jaubert 4)
Osterman Weekend, 1983 (Peckinpah 2, Hopper 3, Hurt, J. 3, Lancaster 3, Schifrin 4)
Ostia, 1969 (Pasolini 2)
'Ostler Joe, 1908 (Bitzer 4)
Ostře sledované vlaky, 1966 (Menzel 2, Brodský 3)
Ostrich Feathers, 1937 (Lantz 4)
Ostrich Has 2 Eggs. See Oeufs de l'autruche, 1957
Ostrov sokrovishch, 1937 (Cherkassov 3)
Ostrov stříbrných volavek, 1976 (Jires 2)
Ostrova okeane, 1978 (Gurchenko 3, Ulyanov 3)
Ostroznie yeti, 1960 (Polanski 2)
Osudy dobrého vojáka Svejkova, 1955 (Trnka 2, Pojar 4)
Osvetnik, 1958 (Vukotić 4)
Osvobozhdenie, 1940 (Dovzhenko 2)
Osvobozhdenie, 1972 (Olbrychski 3, Shukshin 3, Ulyanov 3)
Osvobozhdennaya Frantsei, 1944 (Yutkevich 2)
Oswego, 1943 (Van Dyke, W. 2)
Osynliga muren, 1944 (Molander 2, Borgstrom 3)
Osz Badacsonyban, 1954 (Jancsó 2)
Ot ništo nešto. See Z nepatrných přicin velké následky, 1979
Ot ora 40, 1939 (De Toth 2)
OTC, 1969 (Vukotić 4)
Otchen kharacho dziviosta. See Prostoi sluchai, 1932
Otec Kondelík a ženich Vejvara, 1926 (Vích 4)
Otello, 1955 (Yutkevich 2, Bondarchuk 3)
Otets i syn, 1917 (Mozhukin 3)
Otets Sergii, 1918 (Protazanov 2, Mozhukin 3)
Othello, 1922 (Jannings 3, Krauss 3)
Othello, 1952 (Welles 2, Bruce 3, Aldo 4, Trauner 4)
Othello, 1955 (Cotten 3, Fontaine 3)
Othello, 1966 (Olivier 3, Smith 3, Havelock-Allan 4, Unsworth 4)
Othello. See Otello, 1955
Othello—The Black Commando, 1982 (Curtis 3)
Other, 1972 (Mulligan 2, Goldsmith 4, Surtees 4)
Other, 1980 (Brakhage 2)
Other Crime, 1912 (Bitzer 4)
Other Fellow, 1912 (Bosworth 3)
Other Girl, 1914 (Bushman 3)
Other Girl, 1915 (Anderson G. 3)
Other Girl, 1917 (Hardy 3)
Other Half, 1912 (Cruze 2)
Other Half, 1919 (Vidor, K. 2, Pitts 3)
Other Half, 1947 (Stanwyck 3)
Other Half of the Sky, 1974 (MacLaine 3)
Other Love, 1947 (De Toth 2, Niven 3, Brown, Harry 4, Head 4, Rozsa 4)

Other Love. *See* Vot vspynulo utro, 1915
Other Man, 1914 (Bushman 3)
Other Man, 1916 (Sennett 2, Arbuckle 3)
Other Men's Wives, 1919 (Sullivan 4)
Other Men's Women, 1931 (Wellman 2, Blondell 3, Cagney 3)
Other Men's Women. *See* Steel Highway, 1931
Other Official Personages. *See* I drugie ofitsialyne litsa, 1976
Other One. *See* Une et l'autre, 1967
Other People's Business, 1914 (Sennett 2)
Other People's Money. *See* Argent des autres, 1978
Other People's Sins, 1931 (Dickinson 2)
Other People's Wives. *See* Home Breakers, 1915
Other Shore. *See* Chuzoi bereg, 1930
Other Side of Midnight, 1977 (Sarandon 3, Legrand 4, Taradash 4)
Other Side of Paradise. *See* Foxtrot, 1975
Other Side of the Wind, 1972 (Bogdanovich 2, Welles 2)
Other Tomorrow, 1930 (Bacon 2, Garmes 4)
Other Wise Man, 1912 (Dwan 2)
Other Woman, 1913 (Talmadge, N. 3)
Other Woman, 1921 (Gaudio 4)
Other Woman, 1954 (Haas 3)
Other Woman. *See* Tsuma to shite haha to shite, 1961
Othon, 1969 (Straub and Huillet 2)
Otklonenie, 1967 (Paskaleva 3)
Otkrytaya kniga, 1973 (Gurchenko 3, Yankovsky 3)
Otley, 1968 (Schneider 3, Dillon 4, Foreman 4)
Oto życie, 1969 (Giersz 4)
Ötödik pecsét, 1976 (Fábri 2, Latinovits 3)
Otoko arite, 1955 (Mifune 3, Shimura 3)
Otoko no hanamichi, 1941 (Hasegawa 3)
Otoko no Taiketsu, 1960 (Yamamura 3)
Otoko no tsugunai, 1936 (Tanaka 3)
Otoko o sabaku onna, 1948 (Yamamura 3, Miyagawa 4)
Otoko tai otoko, 1960 (Mifune 3, Shimura 3, Muraki 4)
Otoko wa tsuraiyo, 1972 (Kyo 3, Tanaka 3)
Otoko wa tsuraiyo: Torajiro koiuta, 1971 (Shimura 3)
Otoko wa tsuraiyo: Torajiro Haru no yume, 1979 (Kagawa 3)
Otoko-girai, 1964 (Mori 3)
Otokogokoro, 1925 (Gosho 2)
Otomar Korbelář, 1960 (Stallich 4)
Otøme-gokoro sannin shimai, 1935 (Naruse 2)
Otomi to Yosaburo, 1950 (Hasegawa 3, Yamada 3)
Otone no yogiri, 1950 (Yamamura 3)
Otoshi ana, 1962 (Teshigahara 2, Takemitsu 4)
Ototo, 1960 (Ichikawa 2, Kishida 3, Mori 3, Tanaka 3, Miyagawa 4)
Otra, 1946 (Del Rio 3)
Otrantský zámek, 1977 (Švankmajer 4)
Otrávene sevtlo, 1921 (Ondra 3)
Otre l'amore, 1940 (Valli 3)
Otro Cristobal, 1963 (Alekan 4)
Otsukisama niwa waruikedo, 1954 (Yamamura 3)
Otsuru junreika, 1937 (Yoda 4)
Otsuru's Pilgrim Song. *See* Otsuru junreika, 1937
Otsuya goroshi, 1951 (Yamada 3, Yoda 4)
Ottawa 80, 1980 (Patel 4)
Otto e mezzo, 1963 (Fellini 2, Wertmüller 2, Aimée 3, Cardinale 3, Mastroianni 3, Di Venanzo 4, Flaiano 4, Gherardi 4, Pinelli 4, Rota 4)
Otto e mezzo. *See* 8½, 1963
Otto ga mita, 1964 (Kishida 3)
Otto no teiso, 1937 (Takamine 3)
Oublie-moi Mandoline, 1975 (Delerue 4)
Oubliette, 1912 (Feuillade 2)
Oubliette, 1914 (Chaney Lon 3)
Ouch!, 1967 (Godfrey 4)
Oued, la ville aux mille coupoles, 1947 (Fradetal 4)
Ouija Board, 1920 (Fleischer, M. and D. 2)
Ouistiti de Toto, 1914 (Cohl 2)
Oumagatsuji no ketto, 1951 (Miyagawa 4)
Our Active Earth, 1972 (Heston 3)
Our Better Selves, 1919 (Miller, A. 4)
Our Betters, 1933 (Cukor 2, Bennett C. 3, Murfin 4, Rosher 4, Selznick 4, Steiner 4)

Our Blushing Brides, 1930 (Beavers 3, Crawford, J. 3, Montgomery 3, Adrian 4, Gibbons 4, Meredyth 4, Stromberg 4, Tiomkin 4)
Our Champions. *See* Sportivnaya slava, 1950
Our Children, 1913 (Sennett 2)
Our Combat, 1939 (Haas 3)
Our Congressman, 1924 (Rogers, W. 3, Roach 4)
Our Country, 1944 (Alwyn 4)
Our Country. *See* Strana rodnaya, 1946
Our Country Cousin, 1914 (Sennett 2, Arbuckle 3)
Our Country's Youth. *See* Molodost nashei strany, 1945
Our Crazy Family. *See* Naše bláznivá rodina, 1968
Our Daily Bread, 1921 (Garbo 3)
Our Daily Bread, 1930 (Murnau 2)
Our Daily Bread, 1934 (Mankiewicz 2, Vidor, K. 2, Newman 4)
Our Daily Bread. *See* Unser taglich Brot, 1949
Our Dancing Daughters, 1928 (Crawford, J. 3, Barnes 4, Day 4, Gibbons 4, Stromberg 4)
Our Dare Devil Chief, 1915 (Sennett 2)
Our Fair Play, 1914 (Talmadge, C. 3)
Our Father, 1985 (Rey 3)
Our Fighting Navy, 1937 (Wilcox 2)
Our Gang, 1922 (Roach 4)
Our Gang, 1929 (Cooper, J 3)
Our Gang Follies of 1936, 1935 (Roach 4)
Our Gang Follies of 1938, 1937 (Roach 4)
Our Girl Friday, 1953 (More 3)
Our Hearts Were Growing Up, 1946 (Dreier 4, Frank and Panama 4, Head 4, Young, V. 4)
Our Hearts Were Young and Gay, 1944 (Bondi 3, Gish, D. 3, Dreier 4, Head 4)
Our Hitler. *See* Hitler. Ein Film aus Deutschland, 1977
Our Hospitality, 1923 (Keaton 2, Bruckman 4, Schenck 4)
Our Husbands. *See* Nostri Mariti, 1966
Our Instructor. *See* Waga kyokan, 1939
Our Instructor. *See* Wareraga kyokan, 1939
Our Island Nation, 1937 (Holloway 3)
Our Land. *See* A mi Folkunk, 1959
Our Large Birds, 1914 (Sennett 2)
Our Last Spring. *See* Eroica, 1960
Our Leading Citizen, 1922 (Young, W. 4)
Our Leading Citizen, 1939 (Hayward 3, Head 4)
Our Little Girl, 1935 (McCrea 3, Temple 3, Seitz 4)
Our Little Nell, 1917 (Van Dyke, W.S. 2)
Our Little Nell, 1924 (Roach 4)
Our Little Red Riding Hood. *See* Naše Karkulka, 1960
Our Man Flint, 1966 (Cobb 3, Coburn, J. 3, Goldsmith 4, Reynolds 4, Smith, J.M. 4)
Our Man from Las Vegas. *See* They Came to Rob Las Vegas, 1968
Our Man in Havana, 1959 (Reed 2, Guinness 3, O'Hara 3, Richardson 3, Box 4, Coward 4, Morris 4)
Our Man in Marrakesh, 1966 (Kinski 3)
Our Marriage. *See* Watakushi-tachi no kekkon, 1962
Our Miss Brooks, 1956 (Arden 3, La Shelle 4)
Our Mr. Sun, 1956 (Capra 2)
Our Mrs. McChesney, 1918 (Barrymore E. 3)
Our Modern Maidens, 1929 (Crawford, J. 3, Fairbanks, D. Jr. 3, Adrian 4, Gibbons 4)
Our Mother's House, 1967 (Clayton 2, Bogarde 3, Delerue 4)
Our Neighbors, The Carters, 1939 (Bainter 3, Dreier 4, Head 4, Young, V. 4)
Our Parents-in-Law, 1912–13 (White 3)
Our Relations, 1936 (Laurel & Hardy 3, Maté 4, Roach 4)
Our Russian Front, 1941 (Ivens 2, Milestone 2, Huston 3, Eisler 4)
Our Story. *See* Notre histoire, 1984
Our Teacher. *See* Waga kyokan, 1939
Our Teacher. *See* Wareraga kyokan, 1939
Our Time, 1974 (Legrand 4)
Our Town, 1940 (Wood 2, Bainter 3, Bondi 3, Holden 3, Copland 4, Glennon 4, Horner 4, Menzies 4)
Our Very Own, 1950 (Wood 3, Day 4, Garmes 4, Goldwyn 4, Young, V. 4)
Our Vines Have Tender Grapes, 1945 (Moorehead 3, O'Brien, M. 3 Robinson, E. 3, Irene 4, Kaper 4, Surtees 4, Trumbo 4)

Outsiders. *See* Oka Oorie Katha, 1977
Outward Bound, 1930 (Fairbanks, D. Jr. 3, Howard, L. 3, Grot 4)
Outwitting Dad, 1914 (Hardy 3)
Ouvert pour cause d'inventaire, 1946 (Resnais 2)
Ouverture 2012, 1976 (Dragić 4)
Oveja negra, 1949 (Infante 3)
Over Again. *See* Punnascha, 1961
Over glas gesproken, 1958 (Haanstra 2)
Over Here, 1924 (Sennett 2)
Over Silent Paths, 1910 (Griffith 2, Bitzer 4)
Over the Andes, 1944 (Hoch 4)
Over the Brooklyn Bridge, 1984 (Gould 3, Donaggio 4, Golan and
    Globus 4)
Over the Counter, 1932 (Grable 3)
Over the Fence, 1917 (Daniels 3, Lloyd 3, Roach 4)
Over the Garden Wall, 1910 (Normand 3)
Over the Garden Wall, 1919 (Love 3)
Over the Goal, 1937 (McDaniel 3)
Over the Hill, 1922 (Ruttenberg 4)
Over the Hill, 1931 (King 2, Marsh 3, Furthman 4, Seitz 4)
Over the Hills to the Poorhouse, 1908 (Bitzer 4)
Over the Ledge, 1914 (Reid 3)
Over the Moon, 1937 (Howard 2, Harrison 3, Oberon 3, Biro 4,
    Hornbeck 4, Korda 4, Stradling 4, Wimperis 4)
Over the Wall, 1938 (Bond 3)
Over the Wire, 1921 (Ruggles 2)
Over There, 1917 (Nilsson 3)
Over There-Abouts, 1925 (Sennett 2)
Over 21, 1945 (Vidor, C. 2, Coburn, C. 3, Dunne 3, Buchman 4)
Overboard, 1978 (Dickinson 3, Robertson 3)
Overcoat. *See* Cappotto, 1952
Overcoat. *See* Shinel, 1926
Overcoat. *See* Shinel, 1960
Overland Mail, 1942 (Chaney Lon, Jr. 3)
Overland Red, 1920 (Carey 3)
Overland Riders, 1946 (Crabbe 3)
Overland Stage, 1927 (Brown, Harry Joe 4)
Overland Stage Raiders, 1938 (Brooks 3, Wayne 3, Canutt 4)
Overland Telegraph, 1951 (Hunt 4)
Overland Trail, 1927 (Polito 4)

Overland with Kit Carson, 1939 (Cody 3)
Overlanders, 1946 (Watt 2, Rafferty 3, Balcon 4)
Overnight. *See* That Night in London, 1933
Overnight Stay in the Tyrol. *See* Übernachtung in Tirol, 1974
Overtaking. *See* Sorpasso, 1962
Overtaxed. *See* Tartassati, 1959
Over-the-Hill Gang, 1969 (Brennan 3, Elam 3, O'Brien, P. 3,
    Friedhofer 4)
Over-The-Hill Gang Rides Again, 1970 (Astaire 3, Brennan 3, Raksin
    4)
Overture, 1958 (Dickinson 2)
Overval, 1962 (Haanstra 2)
Ovoce stromů rajských jíme, 1969 (Chytilová 2, Kučera 4)
Ovod, 1955 (Enei 4, Moskvin 4, Shostakovich 4)
Owen, 1975 (Black 3)
Owen Marshall, Counsellor at Law, 1981 (Sarandon 3, Bernstein 4)
Owl and the Pussy Cat, 1939 (Terry 4)
Owl and the Pussycat, 1934 (Terry 4)
Owl and the Pussycat, 1952 (Halas and Batchelor 2)
Owl and the Pussycat, 1970 (Segal 3, Streisand 3, Adam 4, Booth 4,
    Henry 4, Stark 4, Stradling 4)
Own Your Home, 1921 (Roach 4)
Oxalá, 1979 (Branco 4)
**Ox-Bow Incident, 1943 (Wellman 2, Andrews D. 3, Darwell 3,
    Fonda, H. 3, Quinn 3, Basevi 4, Day 4, Miller, A. 4, Trotti 4)**
Oxford and Cambridge Boat Race, 1898 (Hepworth 2)
Oxo Parade, 1948 (Halas and Batchelor 2)
Oyaji to sono ko, 1929 (Gosho 2)
Oyashiki-zame, 1959 (Hasegawa 3)
Oyster Dredger, 1915 (Chaney Lon 3)
Oyster Princess. *See* Austerprinzessin, 1919
Oysters, 1965 (Emshwiller 2)
Oyuki the Madonna. *See* Maria no Oyuki, 1935
Oyu-sama, 1951 (Mizoguchi 2, Shindo 3, Tanaka 3, Hayasaka 4,
    Miyagawa 4, Yoda 4)
Ozark Romance, 1918 (Daniels 3, Lloyd 3, Roach 4)
Ozvegy és a százados, 1967 (Darvas 3)
Ozzie of the Circus, 1929 (Lantz 4)
Ozzie of the Mounted, 1928 (Disney 2)
Ozzie Ostrich Comes to Town, 1937 (Terry 4)

P

P.C. Josser, 1931 (Balcon 4)
P.J., 1968 (Whitlock 4)
P . . . respecteuse, 1952 (Astruc 2, Auric 4, Bost 4, Schufftan 4)
P.T. Raiders. *See* Ship That Died of Shame, 1955
P.X., 1982 (Brocka 2)
På livets odesvagar, 1913 (Sjostrom 2, Jaenzon 4)
På livets odesvager, 1913 (Stiller 2)
Pa Says, 1913 (Barrymore L. 3, Gish, D. 3, Loos 4)
På solsidan, 1936 (Molander 2, Bergman 3)
På vej mod et job, 1953 (Carlsen 2)
Paa Besøg hos Kong Tingeling, 1947 (Roos 2)
Paa Livets Skyggeside, 1912 (Holger-Madsen 2)
Paamenento bruu: Manatsu no koi, 1976 (Okada 3)
Paapi, 1953 (Kapoor 2)
Pablo Casals Breaks His Journey, 1958 (Dickinson 2)
Pablo Casals Master Class, 1960 (Hammid 2)
Pablo Picasso: The Legacy of a Genius, 1982 (Segal 3)
Pablo y Carolina, 1955 (Infante 3)
Pace That Kills, 1928 (Laszlo 4)
Pace That Thrills, 1925 (Leroy 2, Astor 3, McCord 4)
Pacemaker series, 1925 (Garmes 4)
Pacemakers, 1925 (Gable 3)
Pacha, 1967 (Gabin 3, Audiard 4, D'Eaubonne 4)

Pacho, hybský zbojník, 1975 (Kroner 3)
Pacific Blackout, 1942 (Preston 3, Dreier 4, Siodmak 4)
Pacific Destiny, 1956 (Bernard 4)
Pacific Liner, 1939 (Fitzgerald 3, McLaglen 3, Musuraca 4)
Pacific Northwest, 1944 (Van Dyke, W. 2, Huston 3, Maddow 4)
Pacific Paradise, 1937 (Sidney 2)
Pacific Rendezvous, 1942 (Sidney 2, Kurnitz 4)
Pacifist. *See* Pacifista, 1970
Pacifista, 1970 (Jancsó 2, Olbrychski 3, Vitti 3)
Pack Train, 1953 (Autry 3)
Pack Up Your Troubles, 1926 (Fleischer, M. and D. 2)
Pack Up Your Troubles, 1932 (Goddard 3, Laurel & Hardy 3,
    Roach 4)
Pack Up Your Troubles, 1939 (Schildkraut 3, Day 4)
Packaging Story, 1964 (Bass 4)
Paco, 1975 (Ferrer, J. 3)
Pacsirta, 1964 (Darvas 3, Latinovits 3, Torocsik 3)
Pact with the Devil. *See* Pacto diabolico, 1968
Pacto diabolico, 1968 (Carradine 3)
Pad (and How to Use It), 1966 (Hunter 4)
Padatik, 1973 (Sen 2)
Paddy, 1969 (Corman 4)
Paddy O'Day, 1935 (Darwell 3, Hayworth 3, Miller, A. 4)

Paddy O'Hara, 1917 (Ince 4)
Paddy, The Next Best Thing, 1933 (Balfour 3, Baxter W. 3, Gaynor 3, Seitz 4)
Paddy-The-Next-Best-Thing, 1923 (Wilcox 2, Marsh 3)
Padella calibro 38, 1972 (Wynn 3)
Padeniye Berlina, 1949 (Shostakovich 4)
Padenye dinastii romanovykh, 1927 (Shub 2)
Padlocked, 1926 (Dwan 2, Arlen 3, Fairbanks, D. Jr. 3, Howe 4)
Padre, 1911 (Bosworth 3)
Padre, 1912 (Pastrone 2)
Padre de más de cuatro, 1938 (García 3, Figueroa 4)
Padre di famiglia, 1968 (Caron 3, Manfredi 3, Tognazzi 3)
Padre padrone, 1977 (Taviani, P. and V. 2)
Padrecito, 1964 (Cantinflas 3)
Padri e figli, 1957 (De Sica 2, Monicelli 2, Mastroianni 3, Age and Scarpelli 4, Gherardi 4)
Padrone del vapore, 1951 (Delli Colli 4)
Paese dei campanelli, 1953 (Loren 3)
Paese senza pace, 1943 (Delli Colli 4)
Pagan, 1929 (Van Dyke, W.S. 2, Adorée 3, Crisp 3, Novarro 3, Freed 4, Gibbons 4, La Shelle 4)
Pagan Lady, 1931 (Farnum 3)
Pagan Love Song, 1950 (Keel 3, Williams 3, Alton, R. 4, Brown, N. 4, Deutsch 4, Freed 4, Rose 4, Rosher 4)
Paganini, 1910 (Gance 2)
Paganini, 1923 (Veidt 3)
Page d'amour, 1977 (Aimée 3, Chaplin 3, Dalio 3)
Page de gloire, 1915 (Musidora 3)
Page Miss Glory, 1935 (Daves 2, Leroy 2, Astor 3, Davies 3, O'Brien, P. 3, Powell, D. 3, Orry-Kelly 4)
Page Mystery, 1917 (Edeson 4)
Page of Madness. See Kurutta ippeiji, 1926
Pages d'histoire, 1916 (Cohl 2)
Pages d'un catalogue, 1980 (Ruiz 2)
Pages from a Catalogue. See Pages d'un catalogue, 1980
Pages from the Story, 1956 (Bondarchuk 3)
Páginas del diario de José Martí, 1969 (Granados 3)
Pagliacci, 1936 (Eisler 4)
Pagliacci, 1943 (Valli 3)
Pagliacci, 1948 (Lollobrigida 3)
Pagliacci, 1970 (Wakhévitch 4)
Pagoda. See Goju-no to, 1944
Pagode, 1915 (Pick 2, Krauss 3)
Pagode, 1923 (Dieterle 2, Tschechowa 3)
Pahela Admi, 1950 (Roy 2, Sircar 4)
Pahli Nazar, 1945 (Biswas 4)
Paid, 1930 (Wood 2, Crawford, J. 3, Gibbons 4, MacArthur 4, Rosher 4)
Paid in Advance, 1919 (Chaney Lon 3)
Paid in Full, 1912 (Dwan 2)
Paid in Full, 1950 (Dieterle 2, Arden 3, Cummings 3, Dreier 4, Head 4, Schnee 4, Wallis 4, Young, V. 4)
Paid to Dance, 1937 (Hayworth 3)
Paid to Love, 1927 (Hawks 2, Powell, W. 3, Glazer 4, Miller, S. 4)
Paid with Interest, 1914 (Marsh 3)
Pain. See Aci, 1971
Pain de Barbarie, 1949 (Leenhardt 2)
Pain et le vin, 1964 (Cloquet 4)
Pain in the Pullman, 1936 (Three Stooges 3)
Painappuru butai, 1959 (Yamada 3)
Painel, 1951 (Cavalcanti 2)
Painless Dentistry. See Charlatan, 1901
Paint and Powder, 1921 (Roach 4)
Paint and Powder, 1925 (Polito 4, Stromberg 4)
Paint Pot Symphony, 1949 (Terry 4)
Paint Your Wagon, 1969 (Logan 2, Eastwood 3, Marvin 3, Seberg 3, Chayefsky 4, Fraker 4, Previn 4)
Painted Angel, 1929 (Seitz 4)
Painted Boats, 1945 (Crichton 2, Balcon 4)
Painted Desert, 1931 (Boyd 3, Farnum 3, Gable 3, La Shelle 4)
Painted Faces, 1929 (Brown 3)

Painted Lady, 1912 (Griffith 2, Sweet 3, Bitzer 4)
Painted Lady, 1914 (Gish, D. 3)
Painted Lady's Child, 1914 (Eason 4)
Painted Lips. See Boquitas pintadas, 1974
Painted Madonna, 1917 (Ruttenberg 4)
Painted People, 1924 (Moore, C. 3, Nilsson 3)
Painted Ponies, 1927 (Summerville 3, Eason 4)
Painted Post, 1928 (Mix 3)
Painted Soul, 1915 (Ince 4, Sullivan 4)
Painted Stallion, 1937 (Canutt 4)
Painted Veil, 1934 (Van Dyke, W.S. 2, Bondi 3, Brennan 3, Brent 3, Garbo 3, Hersholt 3, Marshall 3, Oland 3, Adrian 4, Daniels 4, Gibbons 4, Stothart 4, Stromberg 4)
Painted Woman, 1932 (Tracy 3, Friedhofer 4)
Painter and the Town. See Pintor e a cidade, 1956
Painter's Idyll, 1911 (Bosworth 3)
Painter's Revenge, 1908 (Porter 2)
Painters Painting, 1972 (de Antonio 2, Emshwiller 2)
Painting the Clouds with Sunshine, 1951 (Mayo 3, Sakall 3)
Paintings by Ed Emshwiller, 1955–58 (Emshwiller 2)
Pair of Cupids, 1918 (Bushman 3)
Pair of Silk Stockings, 1918 (Talmadge, C. 3)
Pair of Tights, 1928 (McCarey 2, Roach 4)
Paisà, 1946 (Fellini 2, Rossellini 2, Masina 3, Amidei 4)
Paisa hi paisa, 1956 (Biswas 4)
Paisan. See Paisà, 1946
Paix sur le Rhin, 1938 (Rosay 3)
Paja ubit ču te!, 1967 (Mimica 4)
Pajama Game, 1957 (Donen 2, Fosse 2, Day 3, Stradling 4)
Pajama Girl, 1903 (Bitzer 4)
Pajama Party, 1931 (Pitts 3, Roach 4)
Pajama Party, 1964 (Keaton 2, Lamour 3, Lanchester 3, Crosby 4)
Pajaro del faro, 1971 (Alvarez 2)
Pak slaag, 1979 (Haanstra 2)
Pal, Canine Detective, 1949 (Hunt 4)
Pal, Fugitive Dog, 1950 (Hunt 4)
Pal Joey, 1957 (Sidney 2, Hayworth 3, Novak 3, Sinatra 3, Cahn 4, Duning 4, Pan 4)
Pál utcai fiúk, 1968 (Fábri 2, Jancsó 2, Torocsik 3)
Palace of Nudes. See Crime au concert Mayol, 1954
Palace of Pleasure, 1926 (Glazer 4)
Palace of the Arabian Nights. See Palais des mille et une nuits, 1905
Palaces of Peking. See Pekingi palotái, 1957
Palais des mille et une nuits, 1905 (Méliès 2)
Palais-Royale, 1951 (Braunberger 4)
Palanquin. See Dochu sugoroku kago, 1926
Pale Flower. See Kawaita hana, 1963
Pale Rider, 1985 (Eastwood 3)
Paleface, 1922 (Keaton 2)
Paleface, 1948 (McLeod 2, Tashlin 2, Cody 3, Hope 3, Russell, J. 3, Dreier 4, Young, V. 4)
Pale-Face, 1933 (Iwerks 4)
Paleontologie, 1959 (Haanstra 2)
Palestine, 1912 (Olcott 2)
Palestinian, 1977 (Redgrave, V. 3)
Palindrome, 1969 (Frampton 2)
Palio, 1932 (Blasetti 2)
Palissades, 1962 (Delerue 4)
Pallard the Punter, 1919 (Pearson 2)
Palle alene i Verden, 1949 (Henning-Jensen 2)
Palle Alone in the World. See Palle alene i Verden, 1949
Palli Samai, 1932 (Sircar 4)
Palm Beach Girl, 1926 (Daniels 3, Banton 4, Garmes 4)
Palm Beach Story, 1942 (Sturges, P. 2, Astor 3, Colbert 3, McCrea 3, Dreier 4, Head 4, Irene 4, Young, V. 4)
Palm Springs, 1936 (Niven 3, Reynolds 4, Wanger 4)
Palm Springs Affair. See Palm Springs, 1936
Palm Springs Weekend, 1963 (Taurog 2)
Palmares des chansons, 1968 (Fernandel 3)
Palmes, 1951 (Rabier 4)
Palmier à l'huile, 1963 (Rouch 2)
Palmy Days, 1931 (Berkeley 2, Sutherland 2, Grable 3, Raft 3, Day 4, Goldwyn 4, Newman 4, Ryskind 4, Toland 4)

Parineeta, 1953 (Roy 2)
Paris, 1926 (Florey 2, Goulding 2, Crawford, J. 3, Gibbons 4)
Paris, 1929 (Buchanan 3, Pitts 3, Polito 4)
Paris, 1936 (Baur 3, Ibert 4)
Paris, 1951 (Cardiff 4)
Paris à l'automne, 1958 (Resnais 2)
Paris after Dark, 1943 (Dalio 3, Sanders 3, Basevi 4, Friedhofer 4)
Paris at Midnight, 1926 (Barrymore L. 3, Marion 4)
Paris au jour d'hiver, 1965 (Braunberger 4)
Paris au mois d'août, 1965 (Evein 4, Jeanson 4, Renoir 4)
Paris au temps des cerises: La Commune, 1967 (Delerue 4)
Paris—Béguin, 1931 (Fernandel 3, Gabin 3)
Paris Belongs to Us. See Paris nous appartient, 1961
Paris Blues, 1961 (Ritt 2, Poitier 3, Reggiani 3, Woodward 3, Matras 4, Trauner 4)
Paris Bound, 1929 (March 3)
Paris brûle-t-il?, 1966 (Clément 2, Belmondo 3, Brynner 3, Caron 3, Cassel 3, Dauphin 3, Delon 3, Douglas, K. 3, Ford, G. 3, Gélin 3, McDowall 3, Montand 3, Perkins 3, Piccoli 3, Signoret 3, Trintignant 3, Aurenche 4, Bost 4, Jarre 4)
Paris brûle-t-il?. See Is Paris Burning?, 1966
Paris Calling, 1941 (Bergner 3, Cobb 3, Rathbone 3, Scott, R. 3, Glazer 4, Krasner 4)
Paris canaille, 1955 (Gélin 3)
Paris chante toujours, 1950 (Montand 3)
Paris Commune. See Zori Parizha, 1936
Paris coquin. See Paris canaille, 1955
Paris—Deauville, 1935 (Delannoy 2)
Paris des mannequins, 1962 (Reichenbach 2, Braunberger 4)
Paris des photographes, 1962 (Reichenbach 2, Braunberger 4)
Paris d'hier et d'aujourd'hui, 1956 (Braunberger 4)
Paris 1900, 1947 (Resnais 2, Dauphin 3, Braunberger 4)
Paris Does Strange Things. See Élena et les hommes, 1956
Paris et le désert français, 1957 (Leenhardt 2)
Paris Exposition, 1900. See Exposition de 1900, 1900
Paris Express, 1953 (Aimée 3, Rains 3)
Paris Frills. See Falbalas, 1945
Paris Holiday, 1958 (Sturges, P. 2, Hope 3, Cahn 4, Wakhévitch 4)
Paris Honeymoon, 1939 (Crosby 3, Horton 3, Head 4, Struss 4)
Paris in Spring, 1935 (Lupino 3, Glazer 4, Hoffenstein 4)
Paris in the Month of August. See Paris au mois d'août, 1965
Paris in the Spring, 1935 (Milestone 2, Dreier 4)
Paris Interlude, 1934 (Merkel 3, Young, R. 3, Krasner 4)
Paris la belle, 1959 (Arletty 3, Colpi 4, Prévert 4)
Paris la nuit ou Exploits d'apaches à Montmartre, 1904 (Guy 2)
Paris mange son pain, 1958 (Grimault 4, Prévert 4)
Paris—Mediterranée, 1931 (Douy 4)
Paris mélodies, 1947–51 (Verneuil 2)
Paris, mes amours, 1935 (Fradetal 4)
Paris Model, 1953 (Goddard 3)
Paris—New York, 1939 (Von Stroheim 2, Berry 3, Dauphin 3, Simon 3, Andrejew 4)
Paris nous appartient, 1960 (Chabrol 2, Demy 2, Godard 2, Rivette 2)
Paris on Parade, 1938 (Cardiff 4)
Paris on the Seine, 1947 (Unsworth 4)
Paris på to måder, 1949 (Roos 2)
Paris Plane, 1933 (Bennett 4)
Paris qui dort, 1923 (Clair 2)
Paris qui ne dort pas, 1955 (Braunberger 4)
Paris Seen by . . . See Paris vu par . . ., 1964
Paris s'en va, 1981 (Rivette 2)
Paris soleil, 1932 (Dauphin 3)
Paris, Texas, 1983 (Stanton 3)
Paris Underground, 1945 (Bennett, C. 3, Fields, G. 3, Garmes 4)
Paris Underworld. See Apachen, 1919
Paris vu par . . ., 1965 (Chabrol 2, Godard 2, Rohmer 2, Rouch 2, Audran 3, Almendros 4, Rabier 4)
Paris Waltz. See Valse de Paris, 1949
Paris When It Sizzles, 1963 (Astaire 3, Curtis 3, Dietrich 3, Ferrer, M. 3, Hepburn, A. 3, Holden 3, Axelrod 4, Coward 4, D'Eaubonne 4, Lang 4)
Pariserinnen, 1921 (Rohrig 4, Herlth 4, Wagner 4)
Parisette, 1921 (Clair 2, Feuillade 2)

Parisian. See Mon gosse de père, 1930
Parisian Cobbler. See Parizhsky sapozhnik, 1928
Parisian Love, 1925 (Bow 3, Schulberg 4)
Parisian Nights, 1924 (Florey 2, Adorée 3, Karloff 3, Haller 4)
Parisian Romance, 1916 (Menjou 3)
Parisienne, 1957 (Bardot 3, Boyer 3)
Parisiennes, 1961 (Allégret, M. 2, Deneuve 3, Alekan 4)
Parisiskor, 1928 (Molander 2, Jaenzon 4)
Paris-Palace-Hôtel, 1956 (Verneuil 2, Boyer 3, D'Eaubonne 4, Spaak 4)
Paritran, 1951 (Sircar 4)
Parivar, 1956 (Roy 2)
Parivartan, 1949 (Kapoor 2)
Parizhsky sapozhnik, 1928 (Ermler 2)
Park Avenue Dame. See Murder in Greenwich Village, 1937
Park Avenue Girl. See Murder in Greenwich Village, 1937
Park Avenue Logger, 1937 (Bond 3)
Park Honeymooners, 1914 (Blackton 2)
Park Row, 1952 (Fuller 2)
Park Sands. See Jericho, 1937
Park Your Car, 1920 (Roach 4)
Parkettsessel 47, 1926 (Warm 4)
Parking Space, 1933 (Lantz 4)
Parkstrasse 13, 1939 (Tschechowa 3)
Parlementaire, 1916 (Mozhukin 3)
Parliamo tanto di me, 1967 (Zavattini 4)
Parlor, Bedroom & Bath, 1931 (Keaton 2)
Parlorna, 1922 (Molander 2)
Parmigiana, 1962 (Manfredi 3)
Parnell, 1937 (Stahl 2, Burke 3, Crisp 3, Gable 3, Gwenn 3, Loy 3, Meek 3, Adrian 4, Behrman 4, Freund 4)
Parole!, 1936 (Quinn 3)
Parole est au fleuve, 1961 (Delerue 4)
Parole Fixer, 1940 (Florey 2, Beavers 3, Quinn 3, Head 4)
Parole Girl, 1933 (Bellamy 3, Krasna 4)
Paroxismus, 1969 (Kinski 3)
Parque de Madrid, 1958 (Rey 3)
Parrish, 1961 (Daves 2, Colbert 3, Malden 3, Steiner 4, Stradling 4)
Parsifal, 1904 (Porter 2)
Parsifal, 1981 (Syberberg 2)
Parson of Panamint, 1941 (Schildkraut 3, Head 4)
Parson Who Fled West, 1915 (Mix 3)
Parson's Widow. See Prastankan, 1920
Parson's Wife, 1922 (Brook 3)
Part de l'ombre, 1945 (Delannoy 2, Barrault 3, Feuillère 3, Auric 4, Spaak 4)
Part du feu, 1977 (Cardinale 3, Piccoli 3)
Part Time Pal, 1946 (Hanna and Barbera 4)
Part Time Wife, 1930 (McCarey 2)
Parted Curtains, 1921 (Walthall 3, Glennon 4)
Partial Eclipse. See Neúplné zatměni, 1982
Particles in Space, 1961–66 (Lye 2)
Particular Men, 1972 (Keach 3)
Partie de campagne, 1946 (Becker 2, Renoir 2, Visconti 2, Braunberger 4, Kosma 4, Renoir 4)
Partie de plaisir, 1975 (Chabrol 2, Gégauff 4, Rabier 4)
Partie de tric-trac, 1895 (Lumière 2)
Partie d'écarté, 1895 (Lumière 2)
Parting Trails, 1911 (Dwan 2)
Partings. See Rozstanie, 1961
Partir, 1931 (Tourneur, M. 2, Douy 4)
Partir, 1971 (Reichenbach 2)
Partir, revenir, 1984 (Girardot 3, Piccoli 3, Trintignant 3)
Partire, 1938 (De Sica 2)
Partisan Squadron. See Partisanska eskadrila, 1979
Partisans in the Ukrainian Steppes. See Partizani v stepyakh Ukrainy, 1942
Partisanska eskadrila, 1979 (Samardžić 3)
Partizani, 1974 (Theodorakis 4)
Partizani v stepyakh Ukrainy, 1942 (Prokofiev 4)
Partner, 1968 (Bertolucci 2, Morricone 4)
Partners, 1982 (Hurt, J. 3, Delerue 4, Sylbert 4)
Partners Again, 1926 (King 2, Edeson 4, Goldwyn 4, Marion 4)

Passionate Stranger, 1956 (Richardson 3)
Passionate Thief. *See* Risate di gioia, 1960
Passione d'amore, 1981 (Scola 2, Blier 3)
Passione secondo San Matteo, 1949 (Cervi 3)
Passionels Tagebuch, 1916 (Jannings 3)
Passions, 1984 (Woodward 3)
Passions—He Had Three, 1913 (Sennett 2, Arbuckle 3)
Passions of the Sea. *See* Lost and Found on a South Sea Island, 1923
Passion's Playground, 1920 (Valentino 3)
Passover Plot, 1976 (Pleasance 3, Golan and Globus 4, North 4)
Passport Husband, 1938 (Chaney Lon, Jr. 3)
Passport to Destiny, 1944 (Lanchester 3)
Passport to Fame. *See* Whole Town's Talking, 1935
Passport to Heaven, 1943 (Basserman 3)
Passport to Hell, 1932 (Crisp 3, Lukas 3, Oland 3, Friedhofer 4, Seitz 4)
Passport to Pimlico, 1949 (Holloway 3, Rutherford 3, Auric 4, Balcon 4, Clarke, T.E.B. 4)
Passport to Shame, 1959 (Roeg 2, Caine 3, Constantine 3)
Passport to Suez, 1943 (De Toth 2)
Password Is Courage, 1962 (Bogarde 3)
Password: Korn, 1967 (Nowicki 3)
Past, 1950 (Fric 2)
Past and Present. *See* Passado e o presente, 1972
Past of Mary Holmes, 1933 (Arthur 3, Plunkett 4, Polglase 4, Rosher 4, Vorkapich 4)
Past Performance, 1955 (Jones 2)
Paste and Paper, 1922 (Roach 4)
Pasteur, 1922 (Benoit-Lévy 2, Epstein 2)
Pasteur, 1935 (Guitry 2)
Pasteur. *See* Oeuvre scientifique de Pasteur, 1946
Pastor Angelicus, 1942 (Flaiano 4)
Pastor Hall, 1940 (Boulting 2)
Pastoral, 1976 (Ioseliani 2)
Pastoral Symphony. *See* Denen Kokyogaku, 1938
Pastry Panic, 1951 (Terry 4)
Pat and Mike, 1952 (Cukor 2, Bronson 3, Gordon 3, Hepburn, K. 3, Tracy 3, Daniels 4, Kanin 4, Orry-Kelly 4, Raksin 4)
Pat Garrett and Billy the Kid, 1973 (Fernández 2, Peckinpah 2, Coburn, J. 3, Elam 3, Robards 3, Stanton 3)
Patate, 1964 (Darrieux 3, Marais 3, Douy 4)
Patates, 1969 (Autant-Lara 2, Aurenche 4, Douy 4)
Patch of Blue, 1965 (Poitier 3, Winters 3, Berman 4, Goldsmith 4, Green, G. 4)
Pâté kolo u vozu, 1958 (Stallich 4)
Patent Leather Kid, 1927 (Barthelmess 3, Edeson 4)
Pater, 1910 (Feuillade 2)
Páter Vojtěch, 1928 (Fric 2)
Páter Vojtěch, 1936 (Fric 2)
Paternity, 1981 (Reynolds, B. 3)
Path of Glory, 1949 (Bondarchuk 3)
Path of Hope. *See* Cammino della speranza, 1950
Pather Panchali, 1955 (Ray, S. 2, Chandragupta 4, Datta 4, Mitra 4, Shankar 4)
Pathetic Fallacy. *See* Ajantrik, 1958
Pathfinder, 1952 (Katzman 4)
Paths into the Night. *See* Wagen in der Nacht, 1979
Paths of Glory, 1957 (Kubrick 2, Douglas, K. 3, Menjou 3)
Pathway of Years, 1913 (Bushman 3)
Pathways of Life, 1913 (Gish, L. 3)
Patience, 1920 (Leni 2, Veidt 3, Hoffmann 4)
Patient in Room 18, 1938 (Sheridan 3)
Patient Vanishes. *See* This Man Is Dangerous, 1941
Patio, 1958 (Rocha 3)
Pâtisser et ramoneur, 1904 (Guy 2)
Patišta, 1960 (Karamitev 3)
Patita, 1953 (Anand 3)
Patjat minava prez Belovir. *See* Patišta, 1960
Patria, 1916 (Beery 3, Oland 3)
Patricia, 1916 (Valentino 3)
Patricia et Jean-Baptiste, 1966 (Lefebvre 2)
Patricia Neal Story, 1981 (Bogarde 3, Jackson 3)
Patricia of the Plains, 1910 (Anderson G. 3)
Patrick the Great, 1945 (Arden 3, O'Connor 3, Salter 4)

Patrie, 1945 (Annenkov 4, Bost 4, Spaak 4)
Patrimonio nacional, 1980 (García Berlanga 2)
Patriot, 1916 (Hart 3)
Patriot, 1928 (Lubitsch 2, Jannings 3, Stone 3, Clothier 4, Dreier 4, Glennon 4, Kraly 4)
Patriot and the Spy, 1915 (Cruze 2)
Patriote, 1938 (Tourneur, M. 2, Ibert 4, Jeanson 4)
Patrioten, 1937 (Baarová 3, Rohrig 4)
Patriotic Pooches, 1943 (Terry 4)
Patriotin, 1979 (Kluge 2, Jurgens 3)
Patriotism, 1964 (Wieland 2)
Patron est mort, 1938 (Storck 2)
Patrouille Blanche, 1941 (Hayakawa 3)
Patrouille des sables, 1954 (Dalio 3)
Patrullero 777, 1978 (Cantinflas 3)
Pat's Birthday, 1962 (Breer 2)
Pat's Day Off, 1912 (Sennett 2)
Patsy, 1921 (Pitts 3)
Patsy, 1928 (Vidor, K. 2, Davies 3, Dressler 3, Gibbons 4, Seitz 4)
Patsy, 1964 (Lewis 2, Carradine 3, Lorre 3, Raft 3, Sloane 3, Wynn 3, Head 3, Raksin 4)
Pattern for Plunder. *See* Bay of St. Michel, 1963
Pattern of Morality. *See* Owen Marshall, Counsellor at Law, 1981
Pattern of Supply. *See* Olie op reis, 1957
Patterns, 1956 (Heflin 3, Sloane 3, Kaufman 4)
Patterns of Power. *See* Patterns, 1956
Pattes blanches, 1949 (Grémillon 2, Barsacq 4)
Pattes de mouches, 1936 (Grémillon 2, Brasseur 3)
Pattes de velours. *See* Incantevole nemica, 1953
Patto col diavolo, 1949 (Amidei 4, D'Amico 4)
Patton, 1970 (Coppola 2, Schaffner 2, Malden 3, Scott, G. 3, Goldsmith 4)
Pattuglia di passo San Giacomo, 1954 (Olmi 2)
Pattuglia sperduta, 1954 (Cristaldi 4)
Paul and Michelle, 1973 (Renoir 4)
Paul Claudel, 1951 (Barrault 3, Honegger 4)
Paul Delvaux ou les femmes défendues, 1969–70 (Storck 2)
Paul Lawrence Dunbar, 1973 (Moss 4)
Paul Revere's Ride, 1910 (Walsh 2)
Paul Swan, 1965 (Warhol 2)
Paul Temple Returns, 1952 (Lee, C. 3)
Paul Valéry, 1959 (Leenhardt 2)
Paula, 1952 (Young, L. 3, Duning 4, Maté 4)
Paula. *See* Framed, 1947
Paule Paulander, 1975 (Hauff 2)
Paulina 1880, 1972 (Schell, Maximilian 3)
Pauline, 1914 (Warm 4)
Pauline à la plage, 1982 (Almendros 4)
Pauline at the Beach. *See* Pauline à la plage, 1982
Pauline Cushman, The Federal Spy, 1913 (Mix 3)
Paura. *See* Angst, 1954
Paura fa 90, 1951 (Tognazzi 3)
Pause, 1976 (Kubelka 2)
Pauvre John ou Les Aventures d'un buveur de whiskey, 1907 (Méliès 2)
Pauvre pompier, 1906 (Guy 2)
Pavé, 1905 (Guy 2)
Pavé de Paris, 1961 (Kosma 4)
Pavel Camrda's Career. *See* Kariera Pavla Čamrdy, 1931
Pavillon brûle, 1941 (Blier 3, Marais 3, Douy 4)
Pavillonens Hemmelighed, 1916 (Dreyer 2)
Pavlína, 1974 (Kachyna 2)
Pavle Pavlović, 1975 (Marković 3)
Paw, 1959 (Henning-Jensen 2)
Pawn of Fate, 1916 (Tourneur, M. 2, Carré 4)
Pawn Shop. *See* Stampen, 1955
Pawn Ticket 210, 1922 (Furthman 4)
Pawnbroker, 1965 (Lumet 2, Steiger 3, Jones 4, Kaufman 4, Rosenblum 4, Sylbert 4)
Pawnbroker's Heart, 1917 (Sennett 2)
Pawns of Destiny, 1914 (Lawrence 3)
Pawns of Passion. *See* Liebesholle, 1927
Pawnshop, 1916 (Chaplin 2, Purviance 3)

Paws of the Bear, 1917 (Ince 4)
Pax?, 1968 (Figueroa 4)
Pax Aeterna, 1916 (Holger-Madsen 2)
Pay as You Enter, 1928 (Bacon 2, Fazenda 3, Loy 3)
Pay As You Exit, 1936 (Roach 4)
Pay Attention. *See* Pazi, šta radiš, 1984
Pay Car, 1909 (Olcott 2)
Pay Day, 1922 (Chaplin 2, Fleischer, M. and D. 2, Purviance 3)
Pay Dirt, 1916 (King 2, Eason 4)
Pay Me, 1916 (Chaney Lon 3)
Pay Off, 1930 (Hunt 4, Murfin 4)
Pay or Die, 1960 (Borgnine 3, Ballard 4, Raksin 4)
Pay the Cashier, 1922 (Roach 4)
Pay the Devil, 1958 (Welles 2)
Pay the Devil. *See* Man in the Shadow, 1958
Pay Your Dues, 1919 (Daniels 3, Lloyd 3, Roach 4)
Payday, 1973 (Torn 3)
Paying Bay, 1964 (Halas and Batchelor 2)
Paying Guest, 1956 (Anand 3, Burman 4)
Paying the Penalty. *See* Underworld, 1927
Paying the Piper, 1921 (Miller, A. 4)
Paying the Piper, 1949 (McKimson 4)
Paymaster, 1906 (Bitzer 4)
Payment, 1916 (Sullivan 4)
Payment Deferred, 1932 (Laughton 3, Milland 3, O'Sullivan 3, Vajda 4)
Payment on Demand, 1951 (Davis 3, Head 4, Plunkett 4, Young, V. 4)
Pay-Off. *See* T-Bird Gang, 1959
Payoff, 1935 (Florey 2, Orry-Kelly 4)
Pays bleu, 1976 (Guillemot 4)
Pays de la terre sans arbre, 1979 (Perrault 2)
Pays d'où je viens, 1956 (Carné 2, Achard 4)
Pays sans bon sens, 1970 (Perrault 2)
Pays sans étoiles, 1946 (Brasseur 3, Philipe 3)
Pazi, šta radiš, 1984 (Samardžić 3)
Pazza di gioia, 1940 (De Sica 2, Fusco 4)
Pazzi della domenica, 1955–59 (Taviani, P. and V. 2)
PBL 2 and PBL 3, 1968 (Breer 2)
Peace Game. *See* Gladiatorerna, 1969
Peace to Your House, 1963 (Yutkevich 2)
Peace Tour. *See* Wyscig pokoju Warszawa-Berlin-Praga, 1952
Peace Will Win. *See* Pokoj zwyciezy swiat, 1951
Peaceable Kingdom, 1971 (Brakhage 2)
Peaceful Oscar, 1927 (Arbuckle 3)
Peacemaker, 1914 (Costello, M. 3, Talmadge, C. 3, Talmadge, N. 3)
Peace-Time Football, 1946 (Terry 4)
Peach Basket Hat, 1909 (Griffith 2, Lawrence 3, Pickford 3, Bitzer 4)
Peach Thief. *See* Kradetsat na praskovi, 1964
Peaches, 1964 (Ustinov 3, Lassally 4)
Peaches and Plumbers, 1927 (Sennett 2)
Peachy Cobbler, 1950 (Avery 2)
Peacock Alley, 1921 (Goulding 2)
Peacock Alley, 1930 (Wilson, C. 4)
Peaks of Zelengore, 1976 (Bondarchuk 3)
Peanut Vendor, 1931 (Fleischer, M. and D. 2)
Peanuts and Bullets, 1915 (Sennett 2)
Pearl. *See* Perla, 1945
Pearl and the Burglars, 1912–13 (White 3)
Pearl and the Poet, 1912–13 (White 3)
Pearl and the Tramp, 1912–13 (White 3)
Pearl As a Clairvoyant, 1912–13 (White 3)
Pearl As a Detective, 1912–13 (White 3)
Pearl of Death, 1944 (Bruce 3, Rathbone 3, Miller, V. 4, Salter 4)
Pearl of the Army, 1916 (White 3)
Pearl of the Punjab, 1914 (White 3)
Pearl of the South Pacific, 1955 (Dwan 2, Mayo 3, Alton, J. 4, Jennings 4, Polglase 4)
Pearl of Tlayucan. *See* Tlayucan, 1960
Pearl's Admirers, 1912–13 (White 3)
Pearl's Dilemma, 1912–13 (White 3)
Pearl's Hero, 1912–13 (White 3)
Pearl's Mistake, 1912–13 (White 3)
Pearls of the Crown. *See* Perles de la couronne, 1937

Pearls of the Deep. *See* Perličky na dně, 1964
Peasant Island, 1940 (Cardiff 4)
Peasants. *See* Krestyaniye, 1935
Peasant's Fate. *See* Krestyanskaya dolia, 1912
Peat and Repeat, 1931 (Arbuckle 3)
Peau d'âne, 1971 (Demy 2, Deneuve 3, Marais 3, Presle 3, Seyrig 3, Cloquet 4, Legrand 4)
Peau de banane, 1963 (Ophuls 2, Belmondo 3, Cuny 3, Moreau 3, Rabier 4, Wakhévitch 4)
Peau de l'ours, 1957 (Cassel 3)
Peau de Torpédo, 1969 (Delannoy 2, Audran 3, Kinski 3)
Peau d'espion, 1967 (Blier 3, Jourdan 3, O'Brien, E. 3)
Peau Douce, 1964 (Truffaut 2, Léaud 3, Coutard 4, Delerue 4)
Peau-de-pêche, 1925 (Benoit-Lévy 2)
Pecado, 1951 (Figueroa 4)
Pecado de una madre, 1960 (Del Rio 3)
Pečat, 1955 (Makavejev 2)
Peccati d'estate, 1962 (Vích 4)
Peccato, 1963 (Volonté 3)
Peccato che sia una canaglia, 1954 (Blasetti 2, De Sica 2, Loren 3, Mastroianni 3, D'Amico 4, Flaiano 4)
Peccato degli anni verdi, o L'assegno, 1961 (Valli 3)
Peccato di castità, 1956 (Age and Scarpelli 4, Amidei 4, Ponti 4)
Peccato di Rogelia Sanchez, 1939 (Fusco 4)
Peccato mortale, 1972 (Lollobrigida 3)
Peccato veniale, 1973 (Delli Colli 4)
Peccatrice, 1940 (De Sica 2, Cervi 3, Vích 4)
Pêche à la baleine, 1934 (Kosma 4)
Pêche au hareng, 1930 (Storck 2)
Pêche aux poissons rouges, (1815 (Dumière 2)
Péchés de jeunesse, 1941 (Tourneur, M. 2, Baur 3, Spaak 4)
Pêcheur dans le torrent, 1897 (Guy 2)
Pêcheur d'Islande, 1924 (Vanel 3)
Pêcheur d'Islande, 1958 (Vanel 3, Coutard 4, de Beauregard 4)
Pêcheurs du Niger, 1962 (Rouch 2)
Pechkolavochki, 1973 (Shukshin 3)
Pechmarie, (Staudte 2)
Peck o' Trouble, 1953 (McKimson 4)
Peck Up Your Troubles, 1945 (Freleng 4)
Peck's Bad Boy, 1921 (Wood 2, Coogan 3)
Peck's Bad Boy, 1934 (Cooper, J. 3)
Peck's Bad Boy with the Circus, 1939 (Beavers 3, Young, V. 4)
Peck's Bad Girl, 1918 (Normand 3)
Pecora nera, 1969 (Gassman 3)
Pecos Pest, 1953 (Hanna and Barbera 4)
Peculiar Patients' Pranks, 1915 (Lloyd 3, Roach 4)
Pedagogical Institution, 1940 (Fleischer, M. and D. 2)
Pedagoška bajka, 1961 (Makavejev 2)
Pedales sobre Cuba, 1965 (Alvarez 2)
Peddler, 1913 (Sennett 2, Arbuckle 3)
Peddler and the Lady. *See* Campo dei Fiori, 1943
Pedestrian. *See* Fussganger, 1974
Pedestrian. *See* Pješak, 1969
Pedro Páramo, 1966 (Figueroa 4)
Pedro Peramo, 1977 (Morricone 4)
Pedro soll hangen, 1941 (George, H. 3)
Pedro's Dilemma, 1912 (Sennett 2, Sennett 2, Normand 3)
Peeks at Hollywood, 1945 (Flynn 3)
Peep Show, 1958 (Russell 2)
Peeper, 1976 (Caine 3, Wood 3)
Peeper, about 1961 (Coppola 2)
Peeping Penguins, 1937 (Fleischer, M. and D. 2)
Peeping Pete, 1913 (Sennett 2, Arbuckle 3)
Peeping Tom, 1960 (Powell 2)
Peer Gynt, 1918 (Oswald 2, Veidt 3)
Peer Gynt, 1934 (Albers 3, Tschechowa 3, Hoffmann 4, Warm 4)
Peer Gynt, 1945 (Heston 3)
Peer Gynt, 1965 (Bushman 3, Heston 3)
Peg Leg Pete, 1932 (Terry 4)
Peg Leg Pete the Pirate, 1935 (Terry 4)
Peg o' My Heart, 1922 (Vidor, K. 2, Barnes 4)
Peg o' My Heart, 1933 (Davies 3, Adrian 4, Barnes 4, Booth 4, Brown, N. 4, Freed 4, Marion 4, Stothart 4)

Peg o' the Ring, 1916 (Ford, J. 2)
Peg of Old Drury, 1935 (Wilcox 2, Hardwicke 3, Hawkins 3, Neagle 3, Young, F. 4)
Peg Woffington, 1912 (Pearson 2)
Pegeen, 1919 (Love 3)
Peggy, 1916 (Burke 3, Ince 4, Sullivan 4)
Peggy, 1950 (Coburn, C. 3, Hudson 3)
Peggy on a Spree. See Peggy på vift, 1946
Peggy på vift, 1946 (Bjornstrand 3)
Peggy, Peg and Polly, 1950 (Fleischer, M. and D. 2)
Peggy, The Will o' th' Wisp, 1917 (Browning 2)
Peggy's Blue Skylight, 1964 (Wieland 2)
Pègre de Paris, 1906 (Guy 2)
Peine du talion, 1916 (Feuillade 2, Musidora 3)
Peintre et ivrogne, 1905 (Guy 2)
Peintre neo-impressioniste, 1910 (Cohl 2)
Peking Express, 1951 (Dieterle 2, Cotten 3, Gwenn 3, Furthman 4, Head 4, Lang 4, Tiomkin 4, Wallis 4)
Peking Remembered, 1966 (Henreid 3)
Pekingi palotái, 1957 (Jancsó 2)
Pelea cubana contra los demonios, 1971 (Gutiérrez 2)
Pèlerin de la beauce, 1950 (Fresnay 3)
Pelican's Bill, 1926 (Lantz 4)
Pelileo Earthquake, 1944–49 (Leacock 2)
Pelle, 1981 (Cardinale 3, Lancaster 3, Mastroianni 3, Schifrin 4)
Pellegrini d'amore, 1953 (Loren 3)
Pelliccia di visone, 1956 (Vitti 3, Age and Scarpelli 4, Amidei 4)
Pena de muerte, 1973 (Rey 3)
Penal Colony. See Colonia penal, 1971
Penalty, 1920 (Chaney Lon 3)
Penalty, 1941 (Barrymore L. 3, Rosson 4, Schary 4)
Penalty of Fame. See Gudernes Yndling, 1919
Penalty of Fame. See Okay America, 1932
Pencil and Rubber. See Ceruza és radír, 1960
Penderecki, Lutoslawa, 1977 (Zanussi 2)
Pendragon legenda, 1974 (Darvas 3, Latinovits 3)
Pendu, 1906 (Linders 3)
Pendulum, 1969 (Seberg 3)
Penelope, 1966 (Hiller 2, Falk 3, Wood 3, Ames 4, Head 4, Pasternak 4, Stradling 4, Williams, J. 4)
Penelope, folle de son corps, 1974 (Fradetal 4)
Pengar—en tragikomisk saga, 1946 (Dahlbeck 3)
Penge, 1916 (Dreyer 2)
Penge og økonomi, 1954 (Carlsen 2)
Pengene eller livet, 1982 (Carlsen 2)
Penguin. See Pingwin, 1965
Penguin Parade, 1938 (Avery 2)
Penguin Pool Murder, 1932 (MacGowan 4, Steiner 4)
Péniche tragique, 1924 (Pick 2)
Penitent, 1912 (Bushman 3)
Penitentiary, 1938 (Ballard 4, Miller, S. 4)
Peníze nebo život, 1932 (Vích 4)
Penn of Pennsylvania, 1941 (Kerr 3, Alwyn 4)
Penne nere, 1952 (Mastroianni 3)
Pennies for My Chocolate, 1976 (Jutra 2)
Pennies from Heaven, 1936 (McLeod 2, Crosby 3, Meek 3, Swerling 4)
Pennies from Heaven, 1981 (Adam 4, Willis 4)
Pennington's Choice, 1915 (Bushman 3, Loos 4)
Penny and the Pownall Case, 1948 (Lee, C. 3)
Penny Gold, 1973 (Cardiff 4)
Penny Journey, 1938 (Jennings 2)
Penny of Top Hill Trail, 1920 (Love 3)
Penny Paradise, 1938 (Dearden 2, Reed 2, Gwenn 3, Dean 4)
Penny Points to Paradise, 1951 (Sellers 3)
Penny Princess, 1952 (Bogarde 3, Unsworth 4)
Penny Serenade, 1941 (Stevens 2, Bondi 3, Dunne 3, Grant, C. 3, Ryskind 4, Walker 4)
Penny-in-the-Slot, 1921 (Roach 4)
Peñon de las ánimas, 1942 (Félix 3, Negrete 3)
Penrod, 1922 (Neilan 2)
Penrod and Sam, 1931 (Pitts 3, Young, W. 4)
Pensez à ceux qui sont en-dessous!, 1949 (Decaë 4)
Pension Groonen, 1924 (Wiene 2)

Pension Mimosas, 1935 (Feyder 2, Arletty 3, Rosay 3, Meerson 4, Spaak 4)
Pensioners, 1912 (Dwan 2)
Pensionnaire, 1953 (Spaak 4)
Pente, 1931 (Autant-Lara 2)
Pentecost Outing. See Pfingstausflug, 1978
Penthouse, 1933 (Van Dyke, W.S. 2, Baxter W. 3, Loy 3, Adrian 4, Goodrich and Hackett 4, Rosson 4, Stromberg 4)
Peony Lantern. See Botab dourou, 1968
People. See Ceddo, 1977
People Against O'Hara, 1951 (Sturges, J. 2, Bronson 3, Martin, S. 3, O'Brien, P. 3, Tracy 3, Alton, J. 4, Basevi 4, Rose 4)
People and Art. See Kié a müvészet, 1975
People and the Nile. See Nas wal Nil, 1968
People and Their Guns. See Peuple et ses fusils, 1969
People Are Bunny, 1959 (McKimson 4)
People Behind the Camera. See Lidé ze kamerou, 1961
People from the Metro. See Lidé z metra, 1974
People in the Subway. See Lidé z metra, 1974
People in the Sun, 1935 (Weiss 2)
People in the Town. See Machi no hitobito, 1926
People Like Maria, 1958 (Watt 2)
People Meet. See Mennesker modes och sod musik opstår a hjertet, 1967
People Next Door, 1970 (Wallach 3, Willis 4)
People of France. See Vie est à nous, 1936
People of One Heart. See Lidé jednoho srdce, 1953
People of Småland. See Smålanningar, 1935
People of the Cumberland, 1937 (Kazan 2, Maddow 4, North 4)
People of the Simlången Valley. See Folket i Simlångsdalen, 1947
People on a Glacier. See Lidé na kře, 1937
People on Sunday. See Menschen am Sonntag, 1929
People on Wheels. See Lidé z maringotek, 1966
People, People, People, 1975 (Hubley 4)
People Soup, 1969 (Arkin 3)
People Still Ask. See Még kér a nép, 1972
People vs. Dr. Kildare, 1941 (Ayres 3, Barrymore L. 3, Nilsson 3)
People Vs. John Doe, 1916 (Weber 2)
People vs. Nancy Preston, 1925 (Polito 4, Stromberg 4)
People, Watch Out! See Lidé bděte, 1961
People Will Talk, 1935 (Head 4)
People Will Talk, 1951 (Mankiewicz 2, Crain 3, Grant, C. 3, Krasner 4, Lemaire 4, Newman 4, Wheeler 4, Zanuck 4)
People's Enemy, 1935 (Coburn, C. 3, Douglas, M. 3, Ruttenberg 4)
People's Enemy. See Minshu no teki, 1946
People's Land, 1943 (Unsworth 4)
Peoples of Indonesia, 1943 (Van Dongen 4)
People's War, 1969 (Kramer, R. 2)
Pepe, 1960 (Sidney 2, Burke 3, Cantinflas 3, Chevalier 3, Coburn, C. 3, Crosby 3, Curtis 3, Dailey 3, Durante 3, Garland 3, Garson 3, Jones S. 3, Leigh, J. 3, Lemmon 3, Martin, D. 3, Novak 3, Reed, D. 3, Reynolds, D. 3, Robinson, E. 3, Sinatra 3, Green, J. 4, Head 4, Levien 4)
Pepe El Toro, 1952 (Infante 3)
Pépé et l'enfant, 1959 (Montand 3)
Pépé le Moko, 1937 (Duvivier 2, Dalio 3, Gabin 3, Modot 3, Jeanson 4)
Pepeljuga, 1979 (Grgić 4)
Pepina Rejholcová, 1932 (Stallich 4)
Pepita Jiménez, 1945 (Fernández 2)
Pepper, 1936 (Summerville 3, Trotti 4)
Peppermint frappé, 1967 (Saura 2, Chaplin 3)
Peppermint Freedom, 1984 (Fonda, P. 3)
Peppino e Violetta, 1951 (Rota 4)
Peppy Polly, 1919 (Barthelmess 3, Gish, D. 3)
Pequeno proscrito, 1955 (Armendáriz 3)
Pequeno proscrito. See Littlest Outlaw, 1954
Pequeno salvaje, 1959 (Armendáriz 3)
Per amare Ofelia, 1973 (Fabian 3)
Per amore, 1976 (Morricone 4)
Per amore . . . per magia, 1966 (Auer 3, Brazzi 3)
Per aspera ad astra, 1969 (Dragić 4)
Per grazia recevuta, 1971 (Manfredi 3)
Per il blasone, 1914 (Bertini 3)

er la sua gioia, 1913 (Bertini 3)
er le antiche scale, 1976 (Bolognini 2, Fabian 3, Mastroianni 3, Morricone 4, Pinelli 4)
er qualche dollaro in più, 1966 (Leone 2, Eastwood 3, Kinski 3, Van Cleef 3, Volonté 3, Morricone 4)
er un dollaro di gloria. See Escuadró de la muerte, 1966
er un pugno di dollari, 1964 (Leone 2, Volonté 3, Morricone 4)
er un pugno di dollari. See Fistful of Dollars, 1964
er una bara piena di dollari, 1970 (Kinski 3)
érák a SS, 1946 (Trnka 2, Brdečka 4, Hofman 4)
erceval, 1964–69 (Rohmer 2)
erceval le Gaullois, 1978 (Rohmer 2, Almendros 4)
erché pagare per essere felici!, 1970 (Ferreri 2)
erché si uccide un magistrato, 1974 (Fabian 3)
ercy, 1925 (Ince 4)
ercy's Progress, 1974 (Price 3)
erdido per cem, 1972 (Branco 4)
ère, 1971 (Fresnay 3)
ère de mademoiselle, 1953 (L'Herbier 2, Arletty 3)
ère Goriot, 1944 (Spaak 4)
ère Lampion, 1934 (Christian-Jaque 2, Kaufman 4)
ère Lebonnard, 1939 (Brasseur 3, Ibert 4)
ère Noel a les yeux bleus, 1964 (Almendros 4)
ère prématuré, 1933 (Delannoy 2)
ère Serge, 1945 (Annenkov 4, Ibert 4)
ère tranquille, 1946 (Clément 2, Renoir 4)
ered sudom istorii, 1967 (Ermler 2)
erfect, 1985 (Willis 4)
erfect Alibi. See Birds of Prey, 1930
erfect Clown, 1924 (Hardy 3)
erfect Couple, 1979 (Altman 2)
erfect Crime, 1921 (Dwan 2, Lombard 3, Buckland 4)
erfect Crime, 1928 (Brook 3, Glennon 4, Howe 4)
erfect Crime, 1957 (Hitchcock 2)
erfect Day, 1929 (Laurel and Hardy 3, Roach 4)
erfect Driver. See Kierowca doskonaly, 1971
erfect Flapper, 1924 (Moore, C. 3)
erfect Friday, 1970 (Baker S. 3)
erfect Furlough, 1958 (Edwards 2, Curtis 3, Dalio 3, Leigh, J. 3, Wynn 3)
erfect Gentleman, 1927 (Bruckman 4)
erfect Gentleman, 1935 (Clarke, C.C. 4, Kaper 4)
erfect Gentlemen, 1978 (Bacall 3, Gordon 3)
erfect Killer. See Quel pomeriggio maledetto, 1977
erfect Kiss, 1985 (Alekan 4)
erfect Lady, 1915 (Purviance 3)
erfect Lady, 1924 (Roach 4)
erfect Lady. See Woman, 1915
erfect Love, 1919 (Goulding 2)
erfect Marriage, 1946 (Niven 3, Pitts 3, Young, L. 3, Head 4, Wallis 4)
erfect Marriage. See Beau Mariage, 1982
erfect Match, 1980 (Sayles 4)
erfect Snob, 1941 (Quinn 3, Wilde 3, Clarke, C.C. 4)
erfect Specimen, 1937 (Curtiz 2, Blondell 3, Flynn 3, Horton 3, Brown, Harry Joe 4, Raine 4, Rosher 4, Wallis 4)
erfect Strangers, 1945 (Korda 2, Donat 3, Kerr 3, Moore, R. 3, Dalrymple 4, Korda 4, Périnal 4)
erfect Strangers, 1950 (Ritter 3, Rogers, G. 3, Wald 4)
erfect 36, 1918 (Normand 3)
erfect Understanding, 1933 (Dickinson 2, Olivier 3, Swanson 3, Courant 4)
erfect Weekend. See St. Louis Kid, 1934
erfect Woman, 1920 (Talmadge, C. 3, Emerson 4, Loos 4)
erfect Woman, 1949 (Holloway 3)
erfectionist. See Grand Patron, 1951
erfectionist gentleman, 1927 (Albers 3)
erfidy of Mary, 1913 (Griffith 2, Barrymore L. 3, Gish, D. 3, Bitzer 4)
erformance, 1970 (Roeg 2)
éril en la demeure, 1984 (Piccoli 3)
erilous Holiday, 1946 (O'Brien, P. 3)
erilous Journey, 1953 (Young, V. 4)
erilous Voyage, 1976 (Grant, L. 3)

Perils from the Planet Mongo. See Flash Gordon, 1936
Perils of Pauline, 1914 (White 3, Miller, A. 4)
Perils of Pauline, 1947 (Farnum 3, Hutton 3, Dreier 4, Head 4)
Perils of Pauline, 1967 (Horton 3)
Perils of Pearl Pureheart, 1949 (Terry 4)
Perils of Petersboro, 1926 (Sennett 2)
Perils of the Darkest Jungle. See Tiger Woman, 1944
Perils of the Park, 1916 (Sennett 2)
Perils of the White Lights, 1914 (Nilsson 3)
Perils of the Wind, 1925 (Karloff 3)
Period of Adjustment, 1962 (Hill, G.R. 2, Fonda, J. 3, Lennart 4)
Périscope, 1916 (Gance 2)
Perjura, 1938 (García 3)
Perjurer, 1957 (Ulmer 2)
Perjury, 1921 (Farnum 3)
Perkele! Kuvia Suomesta, 1971 (Donner 2)
Perla, 1945 (Fernández 2, Armendáriz 3, Figueroa 4)
Perla del cinema, 1916 (Bertini 3)
Perle, 1932 (Feuillère 3)
Perlenkette, 1951 (Tschechowa 3)
Perles de la couronne, 1937 (Christian-Jaque 2, Guitry 2, Arletty 3, Barrault 3, Dalio 3, Dauphin 3, Raimu 3)
Perličky na dně, 1964 (Chytilová 2, Jires 2, Nemec 2, Schorm 2, Kučera 4)
Permanent Wave, 1929 (Lantz 4)
Permette? Rocco Papaleo, 1971 (Scola 2, Mastroianni 3)
Permettete che ami vostre figlia?, 1974 (Fabrizi 3)
Permian Strata, 1969 (Conner 2)
Permission, 1968 (Van Peebles 2)
Permission to Kill, 1975 (Bogarde 3, Forrest 3, Gardner 3, Young, F. 4)
Perníková chaloupka, 1927 (Stallich 4)
Perníková chaloupka, 1951 (Trnka 2, Pojar 4)
Perón: actualización política y doctrinaria para la toma del poder, 1971 (Solanas and Getino 2)
Perón: La revolución justicialista, 1971 (Solanas and Getino 2)
Perpetua, 1922 (Hitchcock 2)
Perpetual Motion, 1920 (Fleischer, M. and D. 2)
Perpetual Motion, 1975 (Dinov 2)
Perpetuum & Mobile, Ltd., 1961 (Mimica 4)
Perplexed Bridegroom, 1913 (Costello, M. 3)
Perri, 1957 (Iwerks 4)
Perroquet vert, 1928 (D'Eaubonne 4)
Perros de Dios, 1973 (Figueroa 4)
Persecution, 1974 (Howard, T. 3, Turner, L. 3)
Persiane chiuse, 1951 (Comencini 2, Fellini 2, Masina 3, Solinas 4)
Persistent Lover, 1912 (Bunny 3)
Person to Bunny, 1959 (Freleng 4)
Persona, 1966 (Bergman 2, Andersson B. 3, Bjornstrand 3, Ullmann 3, Nykvist 4)
Personal, 1904 (Bitzer 4)
Personal Affair, 1932 (Vasiliev 2)
Personal Affair, 1953 (Tierney 3, Alwyn 4)
Personal Best, 1982 (Towne 4)
Personal Column. See Lured, 1947
Personal Column. See Pièges, 1939
Personal Introductions, 1914 (Bunny 3)
Personal Maid, 1931 (Meek 3, O'Brien, P. 3, Freund 4)
Personal Matter. See Personal Affair, 1932
Personal Property, 1937 (Van Dyke, W.S. 2, Harlow 3, Taylor, R. 3, Daniels 4, Vajda 4, Waxman 4)
Personal Secretary, 1938 (Cortez 4)
Personality, 1929 (Heerman 4)
Personality Kid, 1934 (Crosland 2, O'Brien, P. 3, Orry-Kelly 4)
Persons in Hiding, 1939 (Dreier 4, Head 4)
Persons Unknown. See Soliti ignoti, 1958
Perspective, 1941 (Cloquet 4)
Perspectrum, 1974 (Patel 4)
Peru—Istituto de Verano, 1956 (Olmi 2)
Pervaya liubov, 1968 (Smoktunovsky 3)
Pervaya lyubov, 1933 (Cherkassov 3)
Perversion. See Cosi dolce . . . cosi perversa, 1970
Perviat kurier, 1968 (Danailov 3)

Pervy posetitel, 1966 (Smoktunovsky 3)
Pervye eshelon, 1956 (Shostakovich 4)
Pervyi paren, 1958 (Paradzhanov 2)
Pesca a Mazzara del Vallo, 1949 (Di Venanzo 4)
Pescadores de perlas, 1938 (García 3)
Pescatorella, 1947 (Risi 2)
Peščeni grad, 1963 (Samardžić 3)
Pesen za Čoveka, 1954 (Karamitev 3)
Pesn o geroyazh, 1932 (Ivens 2, Eisler 4)
Pesnya katorzhanina, 1911 (Protazanov 2)
Pesnya o shchastye, 1934 (Donskoi 2)
Pest, 1917 (Hardy 3)
Pest, 1919 (Normand 3)
Pest, 1922 (Laurel 3)
Pest from the West, 1939 (Keaton 2, Bruckman 4)
Pest in the House, 1947 (Jones 2)
Pest Man Wins, 1951 (Three Stooges 3)
Pest of Friends, 1927 (Sennett 2)
Pest Pilot, 1941 (Fleischer, M. and D. 2)
Pest von Florenz, 1919 (Lang 2, Hoffmann 4, Pommer 4, Rohrig 4,
    Warm 4)
Pestalozzidorf, 1953 (Dahlbeck 3)
Pesti háztekok, 1961 (Kovács 2, Madaras 3)
Pesti Szerelenn, 1932 (Sakall 3)
Pests for Guests, 1954 (Freleng 4)
Pět holek na krku, 1966 (Schorm 2)
Pět hřišniku, 1964 (Hrušínský 3)
Pet Peeve, 1954 (Hanna and Barbera 4)
Pet Problems, 1954 (Terry 4)
Pet Pyar nur Paap, 1984 (Patil 3)
Pět z milionu, 1959 (Brodský 3)
Petal on the Current, 1919 (Browning 2, Young, W. 4)
Pete Hothead, 1952 (Burness 4)
Pete Kelly's Blues, 1955 (Leigh, J. 3, Mansfield 3, Marvin 3,
    O'Brien, E. 3, Cahn 4, Rosson 4)
Pete 'n' Tillie, 1972 (Ritt 2, Matthau 3, Page 3, Alonzo 4,
    Epstein, J. & P. 4, Head 4, Williams, J. 4)
Pete Roleum and His Cousins, 1939 (Losey 2, Eisler 4, Van Dongen 4)
Peter and Pavla. See Cerný Petr, 1963
Peter der Grosse, 1922 (Jannings 3, Kortner 3, Courant 4, Dreier 4)
Peter Ibbetson, 1935 (Hathaway 2, Cooper, Gary 3, Lupino 3, Meek 3,
    Dreier 4, Edouart 4, Head 4, Lang 4, Young, W. 4)
Peter Pan, 1924 (Brenon 2, Wong 3, Head 4, Howe 4)
Peter Pan, 1953 (Disney 2, Cahn 4)
Peter Pan, 1976 (Farrow 3, Kidd 4)
Peter Pan Handled, 1925 (Lantz 4)
Peter, Paul, und Nanette, 1934 (Warm 4)
Peter Schlemihl, 1915 (Wegener 3)
Peter Schlemihl, 1919 (Galeen 4)
Peter the Great. See Peter der Grosse, 1922
Peter the Great. See Piotr Pervyi, 1937–9
Peter the Pirate. See Pietro, der Korsar, 1925
Peter the Tramp. See Luffar-Petter, 1922
Peter Voss, der Millionendieb, 1932 (Dupont 2)
Peter Voss, Who Stole Millions. See Peter Voss, der Millionendieb,
    1932
Peterburgskaya noch, 1934 (Orlova 3)
Petering Out, 1927 (Lantz 4)
Peters Jugend, 1981 (Hoppe 3)
Petersburg Night. See Peterburgskaya noch, 1934
Petersburg Slums. See Petersburgskiye trushchobi, 1915
Petersburgskiye trushchobi, 1915 (Protazanov 2, Mozhukin 3)
Peterville Diamond, 1942 (Fisher 2)
Pete's Dragon, 1977 (Rooney 3, Winters 3)
Pete's Haunted House, 1926 (Lantz 4)
Petey and Johnny, 1961 (Leacock 2)
Peti, 1964 (Grgić 4)
Petipa. See Nuit des adieux, 1965
Pétistovka, 1949 (Fric 2)
Petit à petit, 1970 (Rouch 2, Braunberger 4)
Petit Babouin, 1932 (Grémillon 2)
Petit Bougnat, 1970 (Adjani 3, de Beauregard 4)
Petit Café, 1919 (Linders 3)

Petit Café, 1930 (Chevalier 3, Rosay 3)
Petit Café, 1962 (Reichenbach 2, Braunberger 4)
Petit Chantecler, 1910 (Cohl 2)
Petit Chaperon rouge, 1929 (Cavalcanti 2, Renoir 2, Jaubert 4)
Petit Chapiteau. See Circo mas pequeño, 1963
Petit Chasseur, 1961 (Fradetal 4)
Petit Chose, 1938 (Arletty 3)
Petit Cirque mexicain, 1975 (Reichenbach 2)
Petit Claus et le grand Claus, 1964 (Prévert 4)
Petit Discours de la méthode, 1963 (Jutra 2)
Petit frère et petite soeur, 1896-97 (Lumière 2)
Petit Garçon de l'ascenseur, 1961 (Dalio 3, Delerue 4)
Petit Hamlet. See Hamles, 1960
Petit Hotel à louer, 1923 (Modot 3)
Petit Jacques, 1922 (Fresnay 3)
Petit Jacques, 1934 (Burel 4, D'Eaubonne 4)
Petit Jeune Homme, 1909 (Linders 3)
Petit Jimmy. See Jimmy bruiteur, 1930
Petit Jour, 1964 (Godard 2, Karina 3, Coutard 4)
Petit Manuel d'histoire de France, 1979 (Ruiz 2)
Petit Marcel, 1975 (Huppert 3)
Petit Matin, 1971 (Lai 4)
Petit Monde de Don Camillo, 1951 (Duvivier 2, Cervi 3, Fernandel 3)
Petit Monde des étangs, 1952 (Colpi 4)
Petit Poucet, 1964 (Borowczyk 4)
Petit Poucet, 1973 (Lenica 2, Lai 4)
Petit riens, 1941 (Berry 3)
Petit Roi, 1933 (Duvivier 2, Jaubert 4)
Petit Soldat, 1947 (Grimault 4, Kosma 4, Prévert 4)
Petit Soldat, 1963 (Godard 2, Karina 3, Coutard 4, de Beauregard 4,
    Guillemot 4)
Petit Soldat qui devient Dieu, 1908 (Cohl 2)
Petit Théâtre de Jean Renoir, 1970 (Renoir 2, Moreau 3, Kosma 4)
Petit Trou pas cher, 1934 (Berry 3)
Petita Jimenez, 1976 (Baker S. 3)
Petite, 1978 (Malle 2)
Petite Andalouse, 1914 (Feuillade 2)
Petite Bonne du palace, 1926 (Balfour 3)
Petite Chocolatière, 1932 (Allégret, M. 2, Raimu 3, Simon, S. 3,
    Braunberger 4, Périnal 4)
Petite Chocolatière, 1949 (Dauphin 3)
Petite danseuse, 1913 (Feuillade 2)
Petite de Montparnasse, 1932 (Waxman 4)
Petite Diligence, 1951 (Cloquet 4)
Petite Femme dans le train, 1932 (Feuillère 3)
Petite Fille en velours bleu, 1978 (Cardinale 3, Piccoli 3, Delerue 4)
Petite Lise, 1930 (Grémillon 2, Douy 4, Spaak 4)
Petite magicienne, 1900 (Guy 2)
Petite Marchande d'allumettes, 1928 (Renoir 2)
Petite peste, 1938 (Presle 3)
Petite Refugiée, 1915 (Musidora 3)
Petite Republique, 1942 (Carroll M. 3)
Petite Rosse, 1909 (Linders 3)
Petite Sauvage, 1935 (Lourié 4)
Petite Vertu, 1967 (Brasseur 3, Audiard 4, Delerue 4, Rabier 4)
Petites Alliées, 1936 (Burel 4)
Petites Annonces, 1947 (Braunberger 4)
Petites apprenties, 1911 (Feuillade 2)
Petites du Quai aux Fleurs, 1943 (Allégret, M. 2, Blier 3, Gélin 3,
    Jourdan 3, Philipe 3, Achard 4, Alekan 4, Aurenche 4, Ibert 4)
Petites Filles modèles, 1952 (Rohmer 2)
Petites marionnettes, 1918 (Feuillade 2)
Petits Chats, 1959 (Deneuve 3)
Petits Coupeurs de bois vert, 1904 (Guy 2)
Petits Matins, 1961 (Arletty 3, Blier 3, Brasseur 3, Gélin 3)
Petits Riens, 1941 (Dauphin 3, Fernandel 3, Raimu 3, Auric 4)
Petorica odpisani, 1974 (Marković 3)
Petra, 1937–40 (Cardiff 4)
Petrified Dog, 1948 (Peterson 4)
Petrified Forest, 1936 (Daves 2, Bogart 3, Davis 3, Howard, L. 3,
    Blanke 4, Orry-Kelly 4, Polito 4)
Petrified Forest. See Kasekino mori, 1973
Pétrole de la Gironde, 1949 (Cloquet 4)

Pianos mécanicos, 1965 (Bardem 2, Delerue 4)
Pianos mécaniques, 1965 (Mason 3, Mercouri 3)
Pianos mécaniques. *See* Pianos mécanicos, 1965
Pianstvo i yevo pozledstvia, 1913 (Mozhukin 3)
Piat vecherov, 1978 (Gurchenko 3)
Piatka z ulicy Barskiej, 1954 (Ford, A. 2, Lomnicki 3)
Piatto piange, 1974 (Blier 3)
Piazza Pulita, 1972 (Papas 3)
Pibe cabeza, 1975 (Torre-Nilsson 2)
Pica sul Pacifico, 1959 (Tognazzi 3)
Picadilly Jim, 1920 (Ruggles 2)
Picador, 1932 (Dulac 2, Périnal 4)
Picador Porky, 1937 (Avery 2)
Picasso, 1955 (Amidei 4)
Picasso, romancero du picador, 1960 (Delerue 4)
Picasso Summer, 1972 (Brynner 3, Finney 3, Legrand 4, Zsigmond 4)
Piccadilly, 1929 (Dupont 2, Laughton 3, Wong 3, Junge 4)
Piccadilly Incident, 1946 (Wilcox 2, Moore, R. 3, Neagle 3)
Piccadilly Jim, 1936 (Burke 3, Montgomery 3, Brackett, C. 4, Hoffenstein 4, Ruttenberg 4)
Piccadilly null Uhr swolf, 1963 (Kinski 3)
Piccadilly Third Stop, 1960 (Zetterling 2)
Picciola, 1911 (Normand 3)
Piccioni di Piazza San Marco, 1980 (Belmondo 3)
Piccola posta, 1955 (Sordi 3, Delli Colli 4)
Piccolo, 1960 (Vukotić 4)
Piccolo fonte, 1918 (Bertini 3)
Piccolo mondo antico, 1941 (Lattuada 2, Risi 2, Valli 3, Ponti 4)
Piccolo mondo di Don Camillo. *See* Petit Monde de Don Camillo, 1951
Pick a Star, 1937 (Auer 3, Laurel & Hardy 3, Roach 4)
Pick and Shovel, 1923 (Laurel 3, Roach 4)
Pick Me Up, ur Flickorna Jackson, 1910 (Magnusson 4)
Pickaninny, 1921 (Roach 4)
Picket Guard, 1913 (Dwan 2, Reid 3)
Picking Peaches, 1924 (Capra 2, Sennett 2, Langdon 3)
Pickled Pink, 1965 (Freleng 4)
Pick-Me-Up est un sportman, 1912–14 (Cohl 2)
Pick-Necking, 1933 (Terry 4)
Pickpocket, 1913 (Bunny 3)
Pickpocket, 1959 (Bresson 2, Burel 4)
Pickup, 1951 (Haas 3)
Pick-Up, 1933 (Beavers 3, Raft 3, Sidney 3)
Pickup Alley. *See* Interpol, 1957
Pickup in Rome. *See* Giornata balorda, 1960
Pickup on 101, 1972 (Sheen 3)
Pickup on South Street, 1953 (Fuller 2, Ritter 3, Widmark 3, Lemaire 4, Wheeler 4)
Pickwick Papers, 1913 (Bunny 3)
Picnic, 1955 (Logan 2, Holden 3, Novak 3, Robertson 3, Russell, R. 3, Duning 4, Howe 4, Taradash 4, Wald 4, Wexler 4)
Picnic At Hanging Rock, 1975 (Weir 2, Roberts 3)
Picnic on the Grass. *See* Déjeuner sur l'herbe, 1959
Picnic with Papa, 1952 (Terry 4)
Picnic with Weisman. *See* Picnick mit Weisman, 1968
Picnick mit Weismann, 1968 (Švankmajer 4)
Picpus, 1942 (Andrejew 4)
Pictura, 1952 (Fonda, H. 3, Price 3, Haller 4)
Picture Mommy Dead, 1966 (Ameche 3)
Picture of Dorian Gray, 1913 (Reid 3)
Picture of Dorian Gray, 1945 (Hardwicke 3, Lansbury 3, Reed, D. 3, Sanders 3, Berman 4, Gibbons 4, Irene 4, Lewin 4, Stothart 4, Stradling 4)
Picture of Madame Yuki. *See* Yuki Fujin ezu, 1950
Picture of the Time. *See* Dr. Mabuse, der Spieler, 1921–22
Picture Snatcher, 1933 (Bacon 2, Bellamy 3, Cagney 3, Orry-Kelly 4, Polito 4)
Pictureland, 1911 (Gaudio 4)
Pictures at an Exhibition. *See* Egy kiállítás képei, 1954
Pictures at an Exhibition. *See* Tableaux d'une exposition, 1972
Pictures of My Brother Julio. *See* Pinturas de meu irmão Júlio, 1965
Picturesque South Africa, 1936 (Hoch 4)
Picturesque West, 1899 (Bitzer 4)
Pidgin Island, 1917 (Gaudio 4)

Pie Covered Wagon, 1932 (Temple 3)
Pie in the Sky, 1934 (Kazan 2)
Piebald. *See* Trápení, 1961
Piece of Pleasure. *See* Partie de plaisir, 1975
Piece of the Action, 1977 (Jones, J.E. 3, Poitier 3)
Pieces of Dog. *See* Psi kusy, 1971
Pieces of Dreams, 1970 (Legrand 4)
Pied Piper, 1924 (Lantz 4)
Pied Piper, 1942 (Preminger 2, Baxter A. 3, Dalio 3, McDowall 3, Cronjager 4, Johnson 4, Newman 4, Zanuck 4)
Pied Piper. *See* Pied Piper of Hamelin, 1972
Pied Piper Malone, 1924 (Haller 4)
Pied Piper of Guadalupe, 1960 (Freleng 4)
Pied Piper of Hamelin, 1961 (Reiniger 2, Johnson, V. 3, Rains 3)
Pied Piper of Hamelin, 1972 (Demy 2, Hurt, J. 3, Kaye 3, Pleasance 3
Pied Piper of Hamelin. *See* Rattenfanger von Hameln, 1918
Pied qui etreint, 1916 (Feyder 2, Musidora 3)
Piednadze albo zycie, 1961 (Skolimowski 2)
Piedra libre, 1976 (Torre-Nilsson 2)
Piedra sobre piedra, 1970 (Alvarez 2)
Pieds-Nickelés, 1964 (Broca 2, Denner 3, Presle 3)
Pie-Eyed, 1925 (Laurel 3)
Piège, 1958 (Vanel 3, Cloquet 4)
Piège à fourrure, 1977 (Robbe-Grillet 4)
Piège à pucelles, 1972 (Chabrol 2)
Piège pour Cendrillon, 1965 (Cayatte 2)
Pièges, 1939 (Siodmak 2, Von Stroheim 2, Chevalier 3, Fradetal 4, Wakhévitch 4)
Piel de verano, 1961 (Torre-Nilsson 2)
Pier 13, 1940 (Day 4, Miller, V. 4)
Pier 13. *See* Me and My Gal, 1932
Piera's Story. *See* Storia di Piera, 1983
Piernas de seda, 1935 (Hayworth 3)
Piero Gherardi, 1967 (Cardinale 3)
Pierre Boulez, 1965 (Braunberger 4)
Pierre dans la bouche, 1983 (Keitel 3, Alekan 4)
Pierre et Jean, 1943 (Cayatte 2)
Pierre et Paul, 1968 (Allio 2)
Pierre of the North, 1913 (Bosworth 3)
Pierre of the Plains, 1942 (Rosher 4)
Pierre philosophe, 1912 (Gance 2)
Pierre Vallières, 1972 (Wieland 2)
Pierres oubliées, 1952 (Grimault 4)
Pierrette No. 1, 1924 (Fischinger 2)
Pierrot assassin, 1903–04 (Guy 2)
Pierrot des bois, 1956 (Jutra 2)
Pierrot la tendresse, 1960 (Simon, M. 3)
Pierrot le fou, 1965 (Fuller 2, Godard 2, Belmondo 3, Karina 3, Léaud 3, Coutard 4, de Beauregard 4)
Pierrot Pierrette, 1924 (Feuillade 2)
Pierszwy dzien wolnosci, 1964 (Ford, A. 2)
Pierwsze lata, 1949 (Ivens 2)
Pierwszy dzień wolności, 1964 (Lomnicki 3, Tyszkiewicz 3)
Pies and Guys, 1958 (Three Stooges 3)
Pieta per chi cade, 1953 (Pinelli 4)
Pietro, der Korsar, 1925 (Robison 2, Pommer 4, Wagner 4)
Pietro Micca, 1938 (Amidei 4)
Piety. *See* Kegyelet, 1967
Piga blad pigor, 1924 (Magnusson 4)
Pigalle-Sainte-Germain-des-Prés, 1950 (Cassel 3, Moreau 3)
Pigen og skoene, 1959 (Karina 3)
Pigeon, 1969 (Malone 3)
Pigeon That Took Rome, 1962 (Heston 3, Head 4)
Pigpen. *See* Porcile, 1969
Pigs and Battleships. *See* Buta to gunkan, 1961
Pig's Curly Tail, 1926 (Lantz 4)
Pigs in a Polka, 1942 (Freleng 4)
Pigs Is Pigs, 1914 (Bunny 3)
Pigs Is Pigs, 1937 (Freleng 4)
Pigskin Capers, 1930 (Terry 4)
Pigskin Champions, 1937 (Clarke, C.C. 4)
Pigskin Parade, 1936 (Cook 3, Garland 3, Grable 3, Ladd 3, Miller, A. 4, Zanuck 4)

Piscina, 1976 (Bozzetto 4)
Piscine, 1969 (Delon 3, Schneider 3, Carrière 4, Legrand 4)
Piseň nemilovaného, 1980 (Brejchová 3)
Píseň o sietu, 1949 (Weiss 2)
Pisito, 1958 (Ferreri 2)
Pissarro, 1975 (Leenhardt 2)
Pissenlets par la racine, 1963 (Audiard 4)
Piste du nord. See Loi du nord, 1940
Piste du Sud, 1938 (Barrault 3, Matras 4, Renoir 4)
Pistol. See Pistolen, 1973
Pistol for Ringo. See Pistola per Ringo, 1965
Pistol Harvest, 1951 (Hunt 4)
Pistol Packin' Nitwits, 1945 (Langdon 3)
Pistola per Ringo, 1965 (Morricone 4)
Pistole per cento bare, 1968 (Ireland 3)
Pistolen, 1973 (Bjornstrand 3)
Pistolero of Red River. See Last Challenge, 1967
Pistoleros de Casa Grande, 1965 (Chase 4)
Pistols for Breakfast, 1919 (Daniels 3, Lloyd 3, Roach 4)
Pit, 1914 (Tourneur, M. 2, Carré 4)
Pit. See Ana, 1957
Pit and the Pendulum, 1913 (Guy 2)
Pit and the Pendulum, 1961 (Price 3, Corman 4, Crosby 4)
Pit and the Pendulum. See Puits et le pendule, 1963
Pit of Loneliness. See Olivia, 1950
Pit Stop, 1969 (Burstyn 3, Corman 4)
Pit, The Pendulum, and Hope. See Kyvadlo, jáma, a naděje, 1983
Pitchin' in the Kitchen, 1943 (Bruckman 4)
Pitfall, 1913 (Ince 4)
Pitfall, 1948 (De Toth 2)
Pitfall. See Otoshi ana, 1962
Pitfalls, 1948 (Powell, D. 3)
Pitfalls of a Big City, 1923 (Sennett 2)
Pittori in città, 1955–59 (Taviani, P. and V. 2)
Pittsburgh, 1942 (Dietrich 3, Howard, S. 3, Scott, R. 3, Wayne 3, Salter 4)
Pittsburgh Documents, 1971 (Brakhage 2)
Più bella serata della mia vita, 1972 (Scola 2, Brasseur 3, Dauphin 3, Simon, M. 3, Sordi 3, Vanel 3, Amidei 4)
Piu comico spettacolo del mondo, 1953 (Struss 4)
Piu forte ragazzi!, 1972 (Cusack 3)
Pivoine, 1929 (Simon, M. 3)
Pixilated, 1937 (Allyson 3)
Piyade Osman, 1970 (Guney 2)
Pizhon, 1929 (Donskoi 2)
Pizza Triangle. See Dramma della gelosia, 1970
Pizza Tweety-Pie, 1957 (Freleng 4)
Pizzicato Pussycat, 1953 (Freleng 4)
Pjervy vsvod, 1933 (Babochkin 3)
Pješak, 1969 (Dragić 4)
Place Beyond the Winds, 1916 (Chaney Lon 3)
Place de la Concorde, 1938 (Blier 3)
Place for Gold, 1960 (Wright 2, Bernard 4, Dehn 4)
Place for Lovers. See Amanti, 1968
Place in a Crowd, 1964 (Menzel 2)
Place in the Sun, 1951 (Stevens 2, Clift 3, Taylor, E. 3, Winters 3, Brown, Harry 4, Dreier 4, Head 4, Hornbeck 4, Waxman 4, Wilson, M. 4)
Place of One's Own, 1945 (Mason 3)
Place to Go, 1963 (Dearden 2)
Place to Live, 1941 (Maddow 4)
Places in the Heart, 1984 (Field 3, Almendros 4)
Plácido, 1961 (García Berlanga 2)
Placier est tenace, 1910 (Cohl 2)
Plage du désir. See Cafajestes, 1962
Plage privée, 1971 (Laguionie 4)
Plague Dogs, 1982 (Hurt, J. 3)
Plague in Florence. See Pest von Florenz, 1919
Plague of the Zombies, 1966 (Bernard 4)
Plain and Fancy Girls, 1925 (McCarey 2, Roach 4)
Plain aux As, 1939 (Modot 3)
Plain Clothes, 1925 (Capra 2, Sennett 2, Langdon 3)
Plain Girl's Love, 1912 (Bosworth 3)

Plain Jane, 1916 (Ince 4, Sullivan 4)
Plain Man's Guide to Advertising, 1962 (Godfrey 4)
Plain People. See Prostiye Lyudi, 1945
Plain Song, 1910 (Griffith 2, Pickford 3, Bitzer 4)
Plain Woman. See Okame, 1927
Plainsman, 1936 (DeMille 2, Arthur 3, Cody 3, Cooper, Gary 3, Quinn 3, Dreier 4, Prinz 4, Young, W. 4)
Plainsman, 1966 (Westmore, B. 4, Williams, J. 4)
Plainsman and the Lady, 1946 (Johnson, N. 3, Schildkraut 3)
Plaisir, 1952 (Ophuls 2, Brasseur 3, Darrieux 3, Dauphin 3, Gabin 3, Gélin 3, Simon, S. 3, Ustinov 3, Annenkov 4, D'Eaubonne 4, Matras 4)
Plaisir d'amour, 1968 (Braunberger 4)
Plaisir de plaire, 1960 (Delerue 4)
Plaisirs de Paris, 1932 (Wakhévitch 4)
Plaisirs de Paris, 1952 (D'Eaubonne 4)
Plaisirs défendus, 1933 (Cavalcanti 2)
Plan 9 from Outer Space, 1959 (Lugosi 3)
Plane Crazy, 1929 (Disney 2, Iwerks 4)
Plane Dippy, 1936 (Avery 2)
Plane Goofy, 1940 (Terry 4)
Plane Nuts, 1933 (Three Stooges 3)
Planet degli uomini spenti, 1960 (Rains 3)
Planet of Blood. See Queen of Blood, 1966
Planet of the Apes, 1968 (Schaffner 2, Heston 3, McDowall 3, Goldsmith 4, Shamroy 4, Smith, J.M. 4, Wilson, M. 4)
Planned Crops, 1943 (Lye 2)
Planter's Wife, 1908 (Griffith 2, Lawrence 3, Bitzer 4)
Planter's Wife, 1952 (Colbert 3, Hawkins 3, Unsworth 4)
Planton du colonel, 1897 (Guy 2)
Plastered in Paris, 1928 (Clarke, C.C. 4)
Plastic Age, 1925 (Ruggles 2, Bow 3, Gable 3, Walthall 3, Schulberg 4)
Plastic Dome of Norma Jean, 1970 (Legrand 4)
Plastic Surgery in Wartime, 1941 (Cardiff 4)
Plastiques, 1963 (Storck 2)
Plateau, 1905 (Guy 2)
Platinum Blonde, 1931 (Capra 2, Harlow 3, Young, L. 3, Riskin 4, Swerling 4, Walker 4)
Platinum High School, 1960 (Cook 3, Duryea 3, Rooney 3)
Platonische Ehe, 1919 (Leni 2)
Plato's Cave Inn, 1980 (Vanderbeek 2)
Play, 1962 (Vukotić 4)
Play Ball, 1932 (Terry 4)
Play Ball, 1933 (Iwerks 4)
Play Ball, 1937 (Terry 4)
Play Dirty, 1968 (De Toth 2, Caine 3, Legrand 4)
Play Girl, 1932 (Young, L. 3, Toland 4)
Play Girl, 1940 (Francis, K. 3, Musuraca 4)
Play It Again, Sam, 1972 (Allen 2, Keaton 3, Roizman 4)
Play It As It Lays, 1972 (Perkins 3, Weld 3)
Play It Safe, 1927 (Estabrook 4)
Play Misty for Me, 1971 (Siegel 2, Eastwood 3)
Play Safe, 1936 (Fleischer, M. and D. 2)
Play Square, 1921 (Howard 2)
Play Up the Band, 1935 (Holloway 3)
Playa prohibida, 1955 (Bardem 2)
Playboy. See Kicking the Moon Around, 1938
Playboy Adventure, 1936 (Havelock-Allan 4)
Playboy of Paris, 1930 (Chevalier 3)
Playboy of the Western World, 1962 (Unsworth 4)
Players, 1912 (Lawrence 3)
Players, 1979 (Schell, Maximilian 3, Goldsmith 4, Sylbert 4)
Playful Pest, 1943 (Fleischer, M. and D. 2)
Playful Polar Bears, 1938 (Fleischer, M. and D. 2)
Playful Pup, 1937 (Lantz 4)
Playful Puss, 1953 (Terry 4)
Playful Robot, 1956 (Vukotić 4)
Playgirl, 1954 (Winters 3)
Playgirl after Dark. See Too Hot to Handle, 1960
Playgirl and the War Minister. See Amorous Prawn, 1962
Playgrounds of the Mammals, 1932 (Sennett 2)
Playhouse, 1921 (Keaton 2)
Playing Around, 1930 (Leroy 2, Grot 4, Polito 4)

laying for Time, 1980 (Redgrave, V. 3)
laying on the Rainbow. *See* Lek på regnbågen, 1958
laying the Game, 1918 (Ince 4)
laying the Game. *See* Touchdown, 1931
laying the Ponies, 1937 (Three Stooges 3)
laying Truant. *See* Skola skolen, 1949
laying with Death. *See* Jugando con la muerte, 1982
laying with Fire. *See* Jeu avec le feu, 1974
laying with Souls, 1925 (Astor 3, Brook 3, Ince 4, Sullivan 4)
laying with the Devil. *See* Hrátky s čertem, 1956
laymates, 1918 (Hardy 3)
laymates, 1941 (Barrymore J. 3)
laymates, 1972 (Biroc 4)
laymates. *See* Lekkamraterna, 1914
lay's the Thing, 1914 (Ince 4)
laything, 1929 (Milland 3)
laytime, 1967 (Tati 2)
laytime. *See* Recreation, 1960
laytime in Hollywood, 1956 (Lancaster 3)
laza Suite, 1970 (Hiller 2, Grant, L. 3, Matthau 3, Jarre 4)
leasant Journey, 1923 (Roach 4)
leasantville, 1976 (Lassally 4)
lease, 1933 (Crosby 3)
lease Believe Me, 1950 (Taurog 2, Kerr 3, Walker 3, Irene 4, Lewton 4, Salter 4)
lease Don't Eat the Daisies, 1960 (Walters 2, Day 3, Niven 3, Lennart 4, Pasternak 4)
lease, Elephant. *See* Prosze slonia, 1978
lease Go 'way and Let Me Sleep, 1931 (Fleischer, M. and D. 2)
lease Keep Me in Your Dreams, 1937 (Fleischer, M. and D. 2)
lease, Mr. Balzac. *See* En effeuillant la Marguerite, 1956
lease Murder Me, 1956 (Lansbury 3)
lease, Not Now!. *See* Bride sur le cou, 1961
lease Turn Over, 1960 (Dillon 4)
leased to Meet Cha, 1935 (Fleischer, M. and D. 2)
leased to Mitt You, 1940 (Bruckman 4)
leasure Buyers, 1925 (Brook 3, Walker 4)
leasure Garden, 1926 (Hitchcock 2, Balcon 4)
leasure Garden, 1952 (Anderson 2, Lassally 4)
leasure Garden, 1953 (Broughton 2)
leasure Garden. *See* Lustgården, 1961
leasure Girls, 1965 (Kinski 3)
leasure Island, 1953 (Head 4)
leasure Mad, 1923 (Shearer 3)
leasure of His Company, 1961 (Seaton 2, Astaire 3, Reynolds, D. 3, Cahn 4, Edouart 4, Fulton 4, Head 4, Newman 4, Pan 4)
leasure Palace, 1980 (Ferrer, J. 3, Sharif 3)
leasure Party. *See* Partie de plaisir, 1975
leasure Seekers, 1964 (Negulesco 2, Tierney 3, Cahn 4, Smith, J.M. 4)
leasures of the Flesh. *See* Etsuraku, 1965
lebei, 1915 (Protazanov 2)
lebeian. *See* Plebei, 1915
lein aux as, 1933 (Fradetal 4)
lein de super, 1976 (Baye 3)
lein soleil, 1959 (Clément 2, Delon 3, Schneider 3, Decaë 4, Gégauff 4, Rota 4)
lein sud, 1980 (Moreau 3)
leins feux sur l'assassin, 1961 (Franju 2, Brasseur 3, Fradetal 4, Trintignant 3, Jarre 4)
leins feux sur Stanislas, 1965 (Delerue 4)
lenty, 1985 (Gielgud 3, Streep 3)
lenty Below Zero, 1943 (Fleischer, M. and D. 2)
lenty of Money and You, 1937 (Freleng 4)
les v dezju, 1961 (Chabrol 2)
leut sur Santiago, 1975 (Trintignant 3)
lombier amoureux, 1931 (Autant-Lara 4, Fairbanks, D. Jr. 3)
longée tragique, 1928 (Vanel 3)
lop Goes the Weasel, 1953 (McKimson 4)
lot, 1914 (Costello, M. 3)
lot. *See* Attendat, 1972
lot Against the Governor, 1913 (Cruze 2)
lot Thickens, 1936 (Pitts 3, Musuraca 4)

Plotzliche Reichtum der armen Leute von Kombach, 1970 (Fassbinder 2, Schlondorff 2, Von Trotta 2)
Plough and the Stars, 1936 (Ford, J. 2, Fitzgerald 3, Stanwyck 3, Nichols 4, Plunkett 4, Polglase 4)
Plow Boy, 1929 (Disney 2, Iwerks 4)
Plow Girl, 1916 (Rosher 4)
Plow That Broke the Plains, 1936 (Lorentz 2)
Pluck of the Irish. *See* Great Guy, 1936
Plucked. *See* Morte ha fatto l'uovo, 1967
Plum Tree, 1914 (Bushman 3)
Plumber, 1914 (Sennett 2)
Plumber, 1925 (Sennett 2)
Plumber, 1933 (Lantz 4)
Plumber, 1978 (Weir 2)
Plumber. *See* Work, 1915
Plumber and the Lady, 1933 (Sennett 2)
Plumber's Daughter, 1927 (Sennett 2)
Plumber's Helpers, 1953 (Terry 4)
Plumbing is a Pipe, 1938 (Fleischer, M. and D. 2)
Plumbing We Will Go, 1940 (Three Stooges 3)
Plunder, 1922 (White 3)
Plunder of the Sun, 1953 (Ford, G. 3, Friedhofer 4)
Plunder Road, 1957 (Cook 3, Haller 4)
Plunderer, 1915 (Farnum 3)
Plunderers, 1960 (Chandler 3, Rosenman 4)
Plus Beaux Jours, 1957 (Decaë 4)
Plus Belles Escroqueries du monde, 1964 (Chabrol 2, Godard 2, Polanski 2, Cassel 3, Deneuve 3, Denner 3, Coutard 4, Cristaldi 4, Delli Colli 4, Gégauff 4, Guillemot 4, Rabier 4)
Plus qu'on ne peut donner, 1963 (Braunberger 4)
Plus Vieux Métier du monde, 1967 (Autant-Lara 2, Bolognini 2, Broca 2, Godard 2, Dalio 3, Karina 3, Léaud 3, Moreau 3, Welch 3, Aurenche 4, Douy 4, Evein 4, Flaiano 4, Guillemot 4, Legrand 4)
Plus vite, 1965 (Foldès 4)
Plusz mínusz egy nap, 1973 (Fábri 2)
Plutocrat, 1931 (Rogers, W. 3)
Plymouth Adventure, 1952 (Brown 2, Johnson, V. 3, Tierney 3, Tracy 3, Daniels 4, Gillespie 4, Plunkett 4, Rozsa 4, Schary 4)
Po' di cielo, 1956 (Fabrizi 3)
Po di storia del caffe, 1954 (Fusco 4)
Po: forza 50.000, 1961 (Olmi 2)
Po išti poti se ne vračaj, 1965 (Samardžić 3)
Po stopach krve, 1970 (Hrušínský 3)
Po tu storonu Araksa, 1946 (Shub 2)
Po ulitsam komod volili, 1978 (Tikhonov 3)
Po zakonu, 1926 (Kuleshov 2)
Poachers. *See* Furtivos, 1975
Pobeda, 1938 (Pudovkin 2, Golovnya 4)
Pobeda na pravoberezhnoi Ukraine, 1945 (Dovzhenko 2)
Pobediteli nochi, 1927 (Moskvin 4)
Pobočník Jeho Výsosti, 1933 (Fric 2)
Pobre diablo, 1940 (Armendáriz 3)
Pobres millionarios, 1957 (García 3)
Pobres van al cielo, 1951 (Figueroa 4)
Počestné paní pardubické, 1944 (Fric 2)
Pocharde, 1952 (Brasseur 3)
Pociag, 1959 (Kawalerowicz 2, Cybulski 3)
Pocket Money, 1972 (Malick 2, Martin, S. 3, Marvin 3, Newman 3, Kovacs 4, North 4)
Pocket Policeman. *See* Agent de poche, 1909
Pocketful of Miracles, 1961 (Capra 2, Davis 3, Elam 3, Falk 3, Ford, G. 3, Horton 3, Cahn 4, Head 4, Plunkett 4)
Pocketmaar, 1956 (Anand 3)
Poczmistrs, 1967 (Stawinsky 4)
Pod gwiazda frygijska, 1954 (Kawalerowicz 2)
Pod Igoto, 1952 (Karamitev 3)
Pod jednou střechou, 1938 (Stallich 4)
Pod Jezevči, 1978 (Brejchová 3)
Pod kamennym nebom, 1974 (Yankovsky 3)
Podarta ksiażka, 1961 (Giersz 4)
Poder local, poder popular, 1970 (Gomez, S. 2)
Podkova pro štěsti, 1946 (Zeman 2)

Podne, 1968 (Samardžić 3)
Podor del deseo, 1976 (Bardem 2)
Podrugi, 1935 (Babochkin 3, Cherkassov 3, Shostakovich 4)
Podskalák, 1928 (Vích 4)
Podvig vo idach, 1928 (Vasiliev 2)
Poem Field, 1966 (Vanderbeek 2)
Poem of an Inland Sea. *See* Poema o more, 1958
Poema o more, 1958 (Dovzhenko 2)
Poemat symfoniczny 'Bajka' Stanislawa Moniuszki. *See* Bajka w Ursusie, 1952
Poet and Painter series, 1951 (Halas and Batchelor 2)
Poet and the Czar. *See* Poet i tsar, 1927
Poet i tsar, 1927 (Cherkassov 3)
Poet Iv Montan, 1957 (Yutkevich 2, Montand 3)
Poet na ekrane, 1973 (Yutkevich 2)
Poet of the Peaks, 1915 (Eason 4)
Poetate i djavolat, 1982 (Paskaleva 3)
Poète et sa folle amante, 1916 (Feuillade 2, Musidora 3)
Poet's Life, 1974 (Kawamoto 4)
Poet's London, 1959 (Russell 2)
Pogo Special Birthday Special, 1971 (Jones 2)
Pogón za Adamen, 1970 (Stawinsky 4)
Pohádka máje, 1926 (Vích 4)
Pohádka o Honzíkovi a Mařence, 1980 (Zeman 2)
Pohádky tisíce a jedné noci, 1974 (Zeman 2)
Poie pour l'ombre, 1960 (Gélin 3)
Poignard malais, 1930 (Douy 4)
Poignee de riz. *See* Handfull Ris, 1938
Poil de carotte, 1925 (Duvivier 2, Feyder 2)
Poil de carotte, 1932 (Duvivier 2, Baur 3, Jaubert 4)
Poil de carotte, 1973 (Noiret 3)
Poilus de la Neuvieme, 1910 (Modot 3)
Point Blank, 1967 (Boorman 2, Dickinson 3, Marvin 3, Wynn 3)
Point de fuite, 1983 (de Almeida 4)
Point de mire, 1977 (Dauphin 3, Girardot 3, Decaë 4, Delerue 4)
Point du jour, 1949 (Modot 3, Piccoli 3)
Point Loma, Old Town, 1912 (Dwan 2)
Point of Order, 1963 (de Antonio 2)
Point of Terror, 1971 (Fields 4)
Point of View, 1920 (Crosland 2)
Pointe courte, 1955 (Resnais 2, Varda 2, Noiret 3, Delerue 4)
Pointe de fuite, 1983 (Branco 4)
Pointed Heels, 1929 (Sutherland 2, Powell, W. 3, Wray 3)
Pointin', 1979 (Cusack 3)
Pointing Finger, 1919 (Browning 2)
Pointing Finger, 1933 (Pearson 2)
Points of Reference, 1959 (Leacock 2)
Poison, 1906 (Linders 3)
Poison, 1911 (Feuillade 2)
Poison, 1951 (Guitry 2)
Poison, 1958 (Hitchcock 2)
Poison Gas. *See* Giftgas, 1929
Poison Ivy. *See* Môme vert-de-gris, 1953
Poison of Gold. *See* Guldets Gift, 1916
Poison Pen, 1939 (McDowall 3)
Poisoned Paradise: The Forbidden Story of Monte Carlo, 1924 (Bow 4, Schulberg 4, Struss 4, Young, W. 4)
Poisoned Plume, 1911 (Dwan 2)
Poisonous Arrow. *See* Giftpilen, 1915
Poisonous Love. *See* Fader og Søn, 1911
Poisson, 1951 (Simon, M. 3)
Poisson Chinois. *See* Bataille silencieuse, 1937
Poisson d'avril, 1954 (Bourvil 3, Audiard 4)
Pojďte námi, 1938 (Hammid 2)
Pojdte, pane, budeme si hrát!, 1965-67 (Pojar 4)
Pojken i tradet, 1961 (Sucksdorff 2, Fischer 4, Jones 4)
Pojken och draken, 1962 (Troell 2, Widerberg 2)
Poker, 1920 (Fleischer, M. and D. 2)
Poker at Eight, 1935 (Roach 4)
Poker Faces, 1926 (Horton 3)
Poker Windows, 1931 (Sennett 2)
Pokerspiel, 1966 (Kluge 2)
Pókfoci, 1976 (Madaras 3)

Pókháló, 1973 (Madaras 3)
Pokhozdeniya Oktyabrini, 1924 (Kozintsev 2)
Pokkers Unger, 1947 (Henning-Jensen 2)
Poklad Ptačího ostrova, 1952 (Zeman 2)
Pokoj no 13, 1915 (Negri 3)
Pokoj zwyciezy swiat, 1951 (Ivens 2)
Pokolenie, 1955 (Polanski 2, Wajda 2, Cybulski 3, Lomnicki 3)
Pokolenie pobeditelie, 1936 (Maretskaya 3)
Pokorené rieky, 1961 (Kroner 3)
Pokrastvaneto, 1982 (Danailov 3)
Pokus o vraždu, 1973 (Brejchová 3)
Pokušení, 1957 (Kachyna 2)
Pokušení paní Antonie, 1934 (Vích 4)
Polar Pals, 1939 (Clampett 4)
Polar Pests, 1958 (Avery 2)
Pole neorané, 1953 (Kroner 3)
Polenblut, 1934 (Ondra 3)
Polenta, 1980 (Ganz 3)
Polety vo sne i naiavu, 1982 (Gurchenko 3, Yankovsky 3)
Polibek ze stadionu, 1948 (Fric 2)
Policarpo, ufficiale di scrittura, 1959 (Sordi 3, Age and Scarpelli 4)
Police!, 1916 (Chaplin 2, Purviance 3)
Police, 1985 (Depardieu 3)
Police Can't Move. *See* Polizia ha le mani legate, 1974
Police Car 17, 1933 (Bond 3)
Police Court, 1932 (Walthall 3)
Police Dog, 1955 (Fairbanks, D. Jr. 3)
Police Fang: Razor Hanzo's Torture in Hell. *See* Goyoukiba, 1973
Police Film. *See* Polizeifilm, 1970
Police mondaine, 1937 (Barrault 3, Vanel 3, D'Eaubonne 4)
Police Nr. 1111, 1915 (Kortner 3)
Police Python 357, 1976 (Montand 3, Delerue 4)
Police Story, 1973 (Goldsmith 4)
Policeman Hataoka. *See* Hataoka junsa, 1940
Poliche, 1929 (Tschechowa 3)
Poliche, 1934 (Gance 2, Meerson 4, Stradling 4)
Polijuschka, 1958 (Gallone 2)
Polin series, 1900–07 (Guy 2)
Polio and Communicable Diseases Hospital Trailer, 1949 (Grant, C. 3)
Polis Paulus påskasmall, 1924 (Molander 2)
Polishing Up, 1914 (Bunny 3)
Polite Invasion, 1960 (Zetterling 2)
Polite Flapper. *See* Patsy, 1928
Political Party, 1934 (Mills 3)
Political Pull, 1924 (Roach 4)
Political Theatre. *See* Soushi gekijou, 1946
Politician's Dream, 1911 (Bunny 3)
Politician's Love Story, 1909 (Griffith 2, Sennett 2, Bitzer 4)
Politics, 1931 (Dress!er 3)
Politics and the Press, 1914 (Talmadge, N. 3)
Politics Can Become a Habit, 1966 (Fonda, P. 3)
Politics Film, 1972 (Falk 3)
Politimesteren, 1911 (Blom 2)
Polizeiakte 909, 1933 (Wiene 2)
Polizeibericht meldet, 1933 (Tschechowa 3)
Polizeifilm, 1970 (Wenders 2)
Polizia accusa: il segreto uccide, 1974 (Ferrer, M. 3)
Polizia è al servizio del cittadino, 1973 (Gélin 3)
Polizia ha le mani legate, 1974 (Kennedy, A. 3)
Polizia incrimina, la legge assolve, 1973 (Rey 3)
Polizia ringrazia, 1972 (Cusack 3)
Polizia sta a guardare, 1973 (Cobb 3)
Polka des menottes, 1956 (Auer 3)
Polka-Dot Puss, 1948 (Hanna and Barbera 4)
Polkovnik v otstavke, 1976 (Yankovsky 3)
Pollo ruspante, 1962 (Tognazzi 3)
Polly Ann, 1917 (Love 3)
Polly Fulton. *See* B.F.'s Daughter, 1948
Polly of the Circus, 1917 (Marsh 3)
Polly of the Circus, 1932 (Davies 3, Gable 3, Milland 3, Adrian 4, Barnes 4, Wilson, C. 4)
Polly of the Follies, 1922 (Talmadge, C. 3, Emerson 4, Hunt 4, Loos 4, Schenck 4)

Polly of the Storm Country, 1920 (Rosson 4)
Polly Wants a Doctor, 1943 (Fleischer, M. and D. 2)
Polly with a Past, 1920 (Webb 3, Mathis 4)
Pollyanna, 1920 (Pickford 3, Marion 4, Rosher 4)
Pollyanna, 1960 (Disney 2, Crisp 3, Malden 3, Menjou 3, Moorehead 3, Wyman 3, Ellenshaw 4, Iwerks 4, Plunkett 4)
Polo, 1936 (Sidney 2)
Polo Games, Brooklyn, 1900 (Bitzer 4)
Polo Joe, 1936 (Brown 3, Wyman 3, Orry-Kelly 4)
Polo Substitute, 1912 (Bosworth 3)
Poločná omša, 1962 (Kroner 3)
Polowanie na muchy, 1969 (Wajda 2, Olbrychski 3)
Polská Krev. See Polenblut, 1934
Polska kronika filmowa nr 52 A–B, 1959. See Kronika jubileuszowa, 1959
Poltergeist, 1982 (Spielberg 2, Edlund 4, Goldsmith 4)
Poltergeist II, 1986 (Edlund 4, Goldsmith 4)
Polvere di stelle, 1973 (Sordi 3, Vitti 3)
Polvo rojo, 1981 (Villagra 3)
Polyecran for International Exposition of Labor Turin. See Polyekrán pro Mezinárodni výstavu práce Turin, 1961
Polyecran for the Brno Industrial Fair. See Polyekrán pro BVV, 1960
Polyekrán pro BVV, 1960 (Jires 2)
Polyekrán pro Mezinárodní výstavu práce Turin, 1961 (Jires 2)
Polygamous Polonius, 1958 (Godfrey 4)
Polygamous Polonius Revisited, 1985 (Godfrey 4)
Polyushko-pole, 1956 (Maretskaya 3)
Pomme d'amour, 1932 (Périnal 4)
Pommier, 1902 (Guy 2)
Pomodoro, 1961 (Olmi 2)
Pompadourtasken. See Naar Fruen gaar paa Eventyr, 1913
Pomperly's Kampf mit dem Schneeschuh, 1922 (Holger-Madsen 2)
Pompiers: Attaque du feu, 1895 (Lumière 2)
Pompon malencontreux, 1903–04 (Guy 2)
Pompon rouge, 1951 (Braunberger 4)
Pomsta, 1968 (Brdečka 4)
Ponedeljak ili utorak, 1966 (Mimica 4)
Ponedelnik sutrin, 1966 (Danailov 3, Paskaleva 3)
Ponjola, 1923 (Crisp 3, Nilsson 3)
Pont d'Iéna, 1900 (Lumière 2)
Pont de Tancarville, 1959 (Delerue 4)
Pont du nord, 1981 (Rivette 2)
Pont sur l'Abime, 1912 (Feuillade 2)
Pontcarral, Colonel d'empire, 1942 (Delannoy 2, Annenkov 4, Matras 4)
Ponti e porte de Roma, 1949 (Di Venanzo 4)
Pontius Pilate, 1962 (Rathbone 3)
Pontius Pilate. See Ponzio Pilato, 1962
Ponto di Vetro, 1940 (Brazzi 3)
Pony Express, 1909 (Porter 2)
Pony Express, 1925 (Cruze 2, Beery 3, Brown, K. 4)
Pony Express, 1952 (Heston 3, Head 4)
Pony Express Days, 1940 (Eason 4)
Pony Express Rider, 1910 (Anderson G. 3)
Pony Express Rider, 1916 (Mix 3)
Pony Express Rider, 1976 (Elam 3)
Pony Post, 1940 (Cody 3)
Pony Soldier, 1952 (Power 3, Newman 4, North 4, Wheeler 4)
Ponzio Pilato, 1962 (Crain 3, Marais 3)
Pooch, 1932 (Roach 4)
Pooja, 1940 (Biswas 4)
Pookie. See Sterile Cuckoo, 1969
Pool of London, 1950 (Dearden 2, Addison 4, Balcon 4)
Pool Sharks, 1915 (Fields, W.C. 3)
Pooly-tix in Washington, 1933 (Temple 3)
Poopdeck Pappy, 1940 (Fleischer, M. and D. 2)
Poopsie, 1974 (Loren 3, Mastroianni 3, Ponti 4)
Poor Boob, 1919 (Crisp 3)
Poor but Beautiful. See Poveri ma belli, 1956
Poor Cinderella, 1934 (Fleischer, M. and D. 2)
Poor Cow, 1967 (Loach 2, McDowell 3, Stamp 3)
Poor Devil, 1973 (Lee, C. 3)
Poor Fish, 1924 (McCarey 2, Roach 4)

Poor Fish, 1931 (Sennett 2)
Poor Girl. See Chudá holka, 1929
Poor Jake's Demise, 1913 (Chaney Lon 3)
Poor Little Chap He Was Only Dreaming, 1912–14 (Cohl 2)
Poor Little Peppina, 1916 (Olcott 2, Pickford 3)
Poor Little Rich Girl, 1917 (Tourneur, M. 2, Pickford 3, Carré 4, Marion 4)
Poor Little Rich Girl, 1936 (Darwell 3, Faye 3, Temple 3, Seitz 4)
Poor Little Rich Girl, 1965 (Warhol 2)
Poor Marja!. See Marja pieni!, 1972
Poor Men's Wives, 1923 (Pitts 3, Schulberg 4, Struss 4)
Poor Millionaire, 1941 (Nykvist 4)
Poor Millionaires. See Poveri milionari, 1958
Poor Nut, 1927 (Arthur 3)
Poor Old Fido, 1903 (Bitzer 4)
Poor Ones. See Zavallilar, 1975
Poor Papa, 1928 (Disney 2)
Poor People. See Chudí lidé, 1939
Poor Relation, 1913 (Cruze 2)
Poor Relation, 1921 (Rogers, W. 3)
Poor Relations, 1919 (Vidor, K. 2, Pitts 3)
Poor Rich, 1931 (Horton 3)
Poor Rich, 1934 (Bond 3)
Poor Rich Man, 1918 (Bushman 3)
Poor Simp, 1920 (Heerman 4)
Poovanam, 1969 (Benegal 2)
Pop, 1970 (Kuri 4)
Pop Always Pays, 1940 (Polglase 4)
Pop and Mom in Wild Oysters, 1941 (Fleischer, M. and D. 2)
Pop Buell, Hoosier Farmer in Laos, 1965 (Van Dyke, W. 2)
Pop Gear, 1965 (Unsworth 4)
Pop Goes the Easel, 1935 (Three Stooges 3)
Pop Goes the Easel, 1962 (Russell 2)
Pop Goes Your Heart, 1934 (Freleng 4)
Pop 'im Pop, 1950 (McKimson 4)
Popas in tabara de vara, 1958 (Mészáros 2)
Popcorn, 1931 (Terry 4)
Pope Joan, 1972 (De Havilland 3, Howard, T. 3, Schell, Maximilian 3, Ullmann 3, Jarre 4)
Pope John Paul II, 1984 (Finney 3)
Pope of Greenwich Village, 1984 (Page 3)
Popeye, 1980 (Altman 2, Duvall, S. 3)
Popeye series, 1955 (Halas and Batchelor 2)
Popeye series, from 1931 (Fleischer, M. and D. 2)
Popi, 1969 (Hiller 2, Arkin 3)
Popiól i diament, 1958 (Wajda 2, Cybulski 3)
Popioly, 1965 (Wajda 2, Nowicki 3, Olbrychski 3, Tyszkiewicz 3)
Poplach v oblacich, 1978 (Brejchová 3)
Popland. See Uno dos tres . . . al escondite inglés, 1969
Popo divorzieremo, 1940 (Amidei 4)
Popoli Morituri. See Sterbende Volker, 1922
Poppy, 1917 (Talmadge, N. 3, Banton 4)
Poppy, 1936 (Sutherland 2, Fields, W.C. 3, Dreier 4, Head 4, Young, W. 4)
Poppy. See Gubijinso, 1935
Poppy. See Gubijinso, 1941
Poppy Girl's Husband, 1919 (Hart 3, August 4, Sullivan 4)
Poppy Is Also a Flower, 1966 (Hayworth 3, Mastroianni 3, Quayle 3, Sharif 3, Wallach 3)
Poppy Is Also a Flower. See Danger Grows Wild, 1966
Poprigunya, 1955 (Bondarchuk 3)
Pop's Pal, 1933 (Langdon 3)
Popsy Pop, 1971 (Baker S. 3, Cardinale 3)
Popular Crafts. See Artesania popular, 1966
Popular Melodies, 1931 (Fleischer, M. and D. 2)
Popular Sin, 1926 (Brook 3, Banton 4, Garmes 4)
Por el mismo camino, 1952 (García 3)
Por ellas aunque mal paguen, 1952 (Infante 3)
Por la puerta falsa, 1950 (De Fuentes 2)
Por la tierra ajena (Littin 2)
Por mis pistolas, 1938 (García 3)
Por mis pistolas, 1968 (Cantinflas 3)
Por querer a una mujer, 1951 (Armendáriz 3)

Porcelaines tendres, 1909 (Cohl 2)
Porcile, 1969 (Ferreri 2, Pasolini 2, Léaud 3, Tognazzi 3, Delli Colli 4, Donati 4)
Porco mondo, 1978 (Kennedy, A. 3, Valli 3)
Porgi l'altra guancia, 1974 (Aumont 3)
Porgy and Bess, 1959 (Preminger 2, Dandridge 3, Muse 3, Poitier 3, Goldwyn 4, Mandell 4, Pan 4, Previn 4, Shamroy 4, Sharaff 4)
Pork Chop Hill, 1959 (Milestone 2, Peck 3, Torn 3, Rosenman 4)
Pork Chop Phooey, 1963 (Hanna and Barbera 4)
Porkala, 1956 (Donner 2)
Porky series, 1937–41 (Clampett 4)
Porky series, 1940 (Freleng 4)
Porky and Gabby, 1937 (Iwerks 4)
Porky the Rain Maker, 1936 (Avery 2)
Porky the Wrestler, 1936 (Avery 2)
Porky's Ant, 1941 (Jones 2)
Porky's Cafe, 1942 (Jones 2)
Porky's Duck Hunt, 1937 (Avery 2)
Porky's Garden, 1937 (Avery 2)
Porky's Midnight Matinee, 1941 (Jones 2)
Porky's Preview, 1941 (Avery 2)
Porky's Prize Pony, 1941 (Jones 2)
Porky's Super Service, 1937 (Iwerks 4)
Porno. See Porco mondo, 1978
Pornographers: Introduction to Anthropology. See Jinruigaku nyumon, 1966
Port Afrique, 1956 (Lee, C. 3, Arnold 4, Maté 4)
Port Arthur, 1936 (Darrieux 3, Vanel 3)
Port Arthur. See I Give My Life, 1936
Port Chicago, 1966 (Baillie 2)
Port de la tentation. See Temptation Harbour, 1946
Port du désir, 1954 (Gabin 3, Alekan 4, Kosma 4)
Port of Call. See Hamnstad, 1948
Port of Desire. See Fille de Hambourg, 1958
Port of Lost Dreams, 1935 (Boyd 3)
Port of Missing Girls, 1928 (Estabrook 4)
Port of Missing Girls, 1938 (Carey 3, Brown, K. 4)
Port of Missing Mice, 1945 (Terry 4)
Port of New York, 1949 (Brynner 3)
Port of 7 Seas, 1938 (Sturges, P. 2, Whale 2, Beery 3, O'Sullivan 3, Freund 4, Vorkapich 4, Waxman 4)
Port of Shadows. See Quai des brumes, 1938
Port Without a Sea. See Umi no nai minato, 1931
Porta del cielo, 1946 (De Sica 2, Zavattini 4)
Porte Chiuse, 1960 (Risi 2)
Porte d'Orient, 1950 (Dalio 3)
Porte de Lilas, 1957 (Clair 2, Brasseur 3, Barsacq 4)
Porte du large, 1936 (L'Herbier 2, Aumont 3, Francis, E. 3, Spaak 4)
Porter. See New Janitor, 1914
Portes claquent, 1960 (Deneuve 3, Legrand 4)
Portes de la maison, 1954 (Storck 2)
Portes de la nuit, 1946 (Carné 2, Brasseur 3, Montand 3, Reggiani 3, Kosma 4, Prévert 4, Trauner 4)
Porteuse de pain, 1906 (Feuillade 2)
Porteuse de pain, 1934 (Fernandel 3, Lourié 4, Stradling 4)
Porteuse de pain, 1963 (Noiret 3, Decaë 4)
Portia on Trial. See Trial of Portia Merriman, 1937
Portnoy's Complaint, 1972 (Black 3, Carradine 3, Clayburgh 3, Grant, L. 3, Boyle 4, Legrand 4, Lehman 4)
Portrait. See Shozo, 1948
Portrait de Barbara, 1978 (Reichenbach 2)
Portrait de Diane Dufresne, 1978 (Reichenbach 2)
Portrait de Hildegard Knef, 1974 (Reichenbach 2)
Portrait de Jacques Chirac, 1976 (Reichenbach 2)
Portrait de la France, 1957 (Delerue 4)
Portrait de Mireille, 1909 (Gance 2)
Portrait de son père, 1953 (Bardot 3)
Portrait d'Henri Goetz, 1947 (Resnais 2)
Portrait d'un assassin, 1949 (Von Stroheim 2, Arletty 3, Berry 3, Brasseur 3, Dalio 3, Spaak 4)
Portrait d'un novillero. See Lomelin, 1965
Portrait from Life, 1948 (Fisher 2, Zetterling 2)
Portrait in Black, 1960 (Quinn 3, Turner, L. 3, Wong 3, Hunter 4)

Portrait mystérieux, 1899 (Méliès 2)
Portrait of a Dead Girl. See McCloud: Who Killed Miss U.S.A.?, 1970
Portrait of a Girl. See Leányportre, 1971
Portrait of a Goon, 1959 (Russell 2)
Portrait of a Hit Man, 1983 (Palance 3)
Portrait of a Man. See Férfiarckép, 1964
Portrait of a Mobster, 1961 (Steiner 4)
Portrait of a Showgirl, 1982 (Curtis 3)
Portrait of a Sinner. See Rough and the Smooth, 1959
Portrait of a 60% Perfect Man, 1980 (Matthau 3)
Portrait of a Soviet Composer, 1961 (Russell 2)
Portrait of a Stripper, 1979 (Alonzo 4)
Portrait of a Woman, 1946 (Rosay 3)
Portrait of a Woman. See Femme disparaît, 1942
Portrait of a Woman, Nude. See Nudo di donna, 1981
Portrait of Alison, 1955 (Green, G. 4)
Portrait of an Escort, 1980 (Charisse 3)
Portrait of Chieko. See Chiekosho, 1967
Portrait of Fidel Castro, 1975 (Lollobrigida 3)
Portrait of Geza Anda, 1964 (Leacock 2)
Portrait of Innocence. See Nous les Gosses, 1941
Portrait of Jason, 1967 (Clarke 2)
Portrait of Jennie, 1948 (Dieterle 2, Barrymore E. 3, Cotten 3, Gish, L. 3, Jones, J. 3, August 4, Herrmann 4, Selznick 4, Tiomkin 4)
Portrait of Maria. See María Candelaria, 1943
Portrait of Paul Burkhard, 1964 (Leacock 2)
Portrait of Teresa. See Retrato de Teresa, 1979
Portrait of the Artist as a Young Man, 1979 (Strick 2, Gielgud 3)
Portrait of Van Cliburn, 1966 (Leacock 2)
Portrait spirite, 1903 (Méliès 2)
Portraits of Women. See Naisenkuvia, 1970
Porträt einer Bewährung, 1964 (Kluge 2)
Ports of Call, 1924 (Fort 4)
Ports of Industrial Scandinavia: Sweden's East Coast, 1949 (Fischer 4)
Ports of the Night. See Portes de la nuit, 1946
Poruchik Kizhe, 1934 (Prokofiev 4)
Poseidon Adventure, 1972 (Borgnine 3, Hackman 3, McDowall 3, Winters 3, Williams, J. 4)
Posesión, 1949 (Negrete 3)
Position Firing, 1944 (Hubley 4)
Position Wanted, 1924 (Roach 4)
Positive Negative Electronic Faces, 1973 (Emshwiller 2)
Posjet iz svemira, 1964 (Grgić 4)
Posledná bosorka, 1957 (Kroner 3)
Poslední bohém, 1931 (Stallich 4)
Poslední léto, 1937 (Hammid 2)
Poslední muž, 1934 (Fric 2, Haas 3)
Posledni trik pana Schwarzwaldea a pana Edgara, 1964 (Švankmajer 4)
Poslední výstřel, 1950 (Weiss 2)
Poslednii pobeg, 1981 (Ulyanov 3)
Poslizg, 1972 (Lomnicki 3)
Posljednji podvig diverzanta Oblaka, 1978 (Mimica 4)
Poslušně hlásím!, 1958 (Hrušínský 3)
Posse, 1975 (Dern 3, Douglas, K. 3, Jarre 4, Wheeler 4)
Posse Cat, 1952 (Hanna and Barbera 4)
Posse from Hell, 1961 (Murphy 3, Van Cleef 3)
Possédés, 1955 (Cloquet 4)
Possessed, 1931 (Brown 2, Crawford, J. 3, Gable 3, Coffee 4)
Possessed, 1947 (Crawford, J. 3, Heflin 3, Massey 3, Grot 4, Wald 4, Waxman 4)
Possessed, 1977 (Ford, H. 3)
Possession, 1929 (Bertini 3)
Possession, 1981 (Adjani 3)
Possession de l'enfant, 1909 (Feuillade 2)
Possession of Joel Delaney, 1972 (MacLaine 3)
Possessors. See Grandes Familles, 1958
Post Haste, 1934 (Grierson 2, Gilliat 4)
Post mortem Technique, 1951 (Carlsen 2)
Post No Bills, 1923 (Roach 4)
Post Office Europe. See Europa-Postlagernd, 1918
Post War Inventions, 1945 (Terry 4)

Practice Shots, 1931 (Fazenda 3)
Prade's Comet. *See* Savage Pampas, 1967
Praesidenten, 1919 (Dreyer 2)
Praesten i Vejlby, 1920 (Blom 2)
Praesten i Vejlby, 1931 (Holger-Madsen 2)
Praestens Datter, 1916 (Holger-Madsen 2)
Prague Castle. *See* Na Pražském hradě, 1932
Prague Nights. *See* Pražské noci, 1968
Prague Spring. *See* Jarov Praze, 1934
Prague War Secrecy. *See* Válečné tajnosti pražské, 1926
Prairie Badmen, 1946 (Crabbe 3)
Prairie Chickens, 1942 (Roach 4)
Prairie King, 1927 (Eason 4)
Prairie Law, 1940 (Hunt 4)
Prairie Moon, 1938 (Autry 3)
Prairie Pioneers, 1941 (Brown, K. 4, Canutt 4)
Prairie Pirate, 1925 (Carey 3)
Prairie Rustlers, 1945 (Crabbe 3)
Prairie Schooners, 1940 (Canutt 4)
Prairie Thunder, 1937 (Canutt 4, Eason 4)
Prairie Trails, 1920 (Mix 3)
Prairie Wife, 1925 (Karloff 3)
Prak a drak, 1960 (Brdečka 4)
Pram. *See* Barnvagnen, 1963
Pramen lásky, 1928 (Stallich 4)
Pramien auf den Tod, 1950 (Jurgens 3, Krauss 3)
Prangasiz mahkumlar, 1964 (Guney 2)
Pranke, 1931 (Rasp 3)
Prasident, 1928 (Mozhukin 3)
Prasident Barrada, 1920 (Courant 4)
Prästänkan, 1920 (Dreyer 2, Magnusson 4)
Prasten, 1914 (Sjostrom 2, Jaenzon 4, Magnusson 4)
Prasten i Uddarbo, 1957 (Von Sydow 3)
Prater, 1925 (Porten 3)
Praterherzen, 1953 (Jurgens 3)
Pratermizzi, 1926 (Ondra 3, Reisch 4)
Pratibad, 1948 (Sircar 4)
Pratidwandi, 1970 (Ray, S. 2, Datta 4)
Pratima, 1936 (Biswas 4)
Pratinidhi, 1964 (Sen 2)
Pratisruti, 1940 (Sircar 4)
Prato, 1979 (Taviani, P. and V. 2, Morricone 4)
Pravda, 1969 (Godard 2)
Právo na hřích, 1932 (Stallich 4)
Prawdziwy koniec wielkiej wojny, 1957 (Kawalerowicz 2)
Pray for the Wildcats, 1974 (Dickinson 3)
Prazdnik svyatovo Iorgena, 1930 (Protazanov 2)
Pražské noci, 1968 (Schorm 2, Kopecký 3, Brdečka 4)
Přchozi z temnot, 1921 (Ondra 3)
Precinct 45 Los Angeles Police. *See* New Centurions, 1972
Precious Green Mountains, 1958 (Zhao 3)
Precious Parcel, 1916 (Hardy 3)
Precipice. *See* Obryv, 1913
Precursores de la pintura argentina, 1957 (Torre-Nilsson 2)
Před maturitou, 1932 (Vích 4)
Preda, 1974 (Presle 3)
Predsedatel, 1964 (Ulyanov 3)
Predstava Hamleta u mrduši donjog, 1973 (Samardžić 3)
Predtucha, 1947 (Hrušínský 3, Stallich 4)
Preface to a Life, 1950 (Kaufman 4)
Prefetto di ferro, 1977 (Cardinale 3, Morricone 4)
Prega il morte e ammazza il vivo, 1970 (Kinski 3)
Prehistoric Perils, 1952 (Terry 4)
Prehistoric Poultry, 1917 (O'Brien 4)
Pre-hysterical Hare, 1958 (McKimson 4)
Preis fur Uberleben, 1979 (Piccoli 3, Lassally 4)
Prekobrojna, 1962 (Samardžić 3)
Prelude à l'apres-midi d'un faune, 1938 (Rossellini 2)
Prélude à l'Asie, 1960 (Braunberger 4)
Prélude à la gloire, 1949 (Renoir 4)
Prélude pour orchestre, voix, et caméra, 1959 (Delerue 4)
Prelude to Fame, 1950 (Lee, C. 3)

Prelude to War, 1942 (Huston 3, Friedhofer 4, Hornbeck 4, Newman 4, Veiller 4)
Preludio 11, 1964 (Mueller-Stahl 3)
Preludio d'amore, 1946 (Gassman 3)
Prem Bandhan, 1936 (Biswas 4)
Prem Murti. *See* Pratima, 1936
Prem Nagar, 1974 (Burman 4)
Prem Patra, 1962 (Roy 2)
Prem Pujari, 1970 (Anand 3, Burman 4)
Prem Rog, 1982 (Kapoor 2)
Prem Shastra, 1974 (Anand 3)
Premature Burial, 1962 (Coppola 2, Milland 3, Corman 4, Crosby 4)
Préméditation, 1912 (Feuillade 2)
Premier Bal, 1941 (Christian-Jaque 2, Blier 3, Spaak 4)
Premier Jour de Vacances de Poulot, 1912 (Cohl 2)
Premier May. *See* Festa di maggio, 1957
Premier Nuit, 1958 (Delerue 4)
Premier Pas, 1950 (Decaë 4)
Premier prix du conservatoire, 1942 (Decaë 4)
Premier rendezvous, 1941 (Darrieux 3, Gélin 3, Jourdan 3)
Premiere, 1936 (Planer 4)
Premiere. *See* Ösbemutató, 1974
Première Cigare d'un collégien, 1906 (Linders 3)
Première Cigarette, 1904 (Guy 2)
Première croisière, 1955 (Delerue 4)
Première Fois, 1976 (Denner 3, Trauner 4)
Première Gamelle, 1902 (Guy 2)
Première nuit, 1958 (Franju 2, Colpi 4)
Première Sortie d'un collégien, 1905 (Linders 3)
Premières Armes de Rocambole, 1922 (Fresnay 3)
Premiers pas de Bébé, 1896-97 (Lumière 2)
Premijera, 1957 (Mimica 4)
Premiya, 1974 (Yankovsky 3)
Prenez des gants, 1960 (Delerue 4)
Prenez Garde à la Peinture, 1935 (Simon, S. 3)
Prénom Carmen, 1983 (Coutard 4)
Préparez vos mouchoirs, 1977 (Blier 2, Depardieu 3, Delerue 4)
Prepotenti, 1958 (Fabrizi 3)
Prepotenti più di prima, 1959 (Fabrizi 3)
Pre-Production, 1973 (Le Grice 2)
Prés, 1971 (Torocsik 3)
Presagio, 1973 (Alcoriza 4, Figueroa 4)
Prescott Kid, 1936 (Brennan 3)
Prescription for Percy, 1954 (Terry 4)
Prescription for Romance, 1937 (Auer 3, Krasner 4)
Prescription: Murder, 1968 (Falk 3)
Presence, 1972 (Brakhage 2)
Presence. *See* Jelenlét, 1965
Présence au combat, 1945 (Dauphin 3)
Présence d'Albert Camus, 1962 (Jarre 4)
Present Arms. *See* Leathernecking, 1930
Present with a Future, 1943 (Davis 3, Haller 4)
Présentation ou Charlotte et son steak, 1951 (Godard 2, Rohmer 2, Audran 3, Karina 3)
Presentiment. *See* Predtucha, 1947
Presenting Lily Mars, 1943 (Taurog 2, Walters 2, Bainter 3, Garland 3, Heflin 3, Edens 4, Pasternak 4, Ruttenberg 4)
Presents, 1982 (Snow 2)
Preservation Man, 1962 (Russell 2)
President, 1937 (Sircar 4)
Président, 1960 (Verneuil 2, Blier 3, Gabin 3, Audiard 4, Jarre 4)
President. *See* Praesidenten, 1919
President. *See* Prasident, 1928
Président Haudecoeur, 1939 (Baur 3)
President McKinley's Inauguration, 1897 (Bitzer 4)
President T.R. Roosevelt, July 4th, 1903 (Bitzer 4)
President Vanishes, 1934 (Wellman 2, Russell, R. 3, Vorkapich 4, Wanger 4, Wilson, C. 4)
Presidente del Borgorosso Football Club, 1970 (Amidei 4)
Presidentessa, 1952 (Germi 2)
President's Analyst, 1967 (Coburn, J. 3, Fraker 4, Schifrin 4)
President's Death. *See* Śmierć Presydenta, 1977

esident's Lady, 1953 (Bainter 3, Hayward 3, Heston 3, Lemaire 4, Newman 4, Wheeler 4)
esident's Mistress, 1978 (Schifrin 4)
esident's Plane Is Missing, 1971 (Kennedy, A. 3, Massey 3, McCambridge 3, Torn 3)
esident's Women, 1977 (Rosenblum 4)
essens Magt, 1913 (Blom 2)
essing His Suit, 1914 (Roach 4)
essure of Guilt. See Shiro to kuro, 1963
essure Point, 1962 (Kramer, S. 2, Falk 3, Poitier 3, Hall 4, Haller 4)
estige, 1932 (Garnett 2, Douglas, M. 3, Menjou 3, Muse 3)
esto Change-O, 1939 (Jones 2)
estuplenie, 1976 (Gurchenko 3)
estuplenie i nakazanie, 1968 (Smoktunovsky 3)
ete, fai un miracolo, 1974 (D'Amico 4)
ête-moi ta femme, 1936 (Brasseur 3)
etender, 1947 (Alton, J. 4)
êtres interdits, 1973 (de Beauregard 4)
etty Baby, 1950 (Gwenn 3, Furthman 4, Kurnitz 4)
etty Baby, 1978 (Malle 2, Sarandon 3, Nykvist 4)
etty Boy Floyd, 1959 (Falk 3, Rosenblum 4)
etty Girl, 1950 (Duning 4)
etty Ladies, 1925 (Crawford, J. 3, Loy 3, Pitts 3, Shearer 3)
etty Maids All in a Row, 1971 (Vadim 2, Dickinson 3, Hudson 3, McDowall 3, Wynn 3, Schifrin 4)
etty Mrs. Smith, 1915 (Bosworth 3)
etty Poison, 1968 (Perkins 3, Weld 3, Semple 4, Smith, J.M. 4)
etty Polly, 1967 (Howard, T. 3, Green, G. 4, Legrand 4)
etty Sister of Jose, 1915 (Dwan 2)
etty Smooth, 1919 (Young, W. 4)
etzels, 1930 (Terry 4)
eussische Liebesgeschichte, 1950 (Baarová 3)
evailing Craze, 1914 (Beery 3)
eview Murder Mystery, 1936 (Florey 2, Dreier 4, Struss 4)
ežil isem svou smrt, 1960 (Kučera 4)
ezzo del potere, 1969 (Johnson, V. 3)
ice He Paid, 1912 (Bosworth 3)
ice of a Good Time, 1917 (Weber 2)
ice of a Party, 1924 (Astor 3, Seitz 4)
ice of a Song, 1935 (Powell 4)
ice of Beauty. See Farlige Alder, 1911
ice of Coal, 1977 (Loach 2)
ice of Death. See Venditore di morte, 1972
ice of Fear, 1956 (Oberon 3)
ice of Happiness, 1916 (Menjou 3)
ice of Man. See Tsena cheloveka, 1928
ice of Pleasure, 1925 (Fazenda 3)
ice of Power. See Prezzo del potere, 1969
ice of Pride, 1917 (Edeson 4)
ice of Redemption, 1920 (Polito 4)
ice of Silence, 1916 (Chaney Lon 3)
ice of Silence, 1917 (Farnum 3)
ice of Success, 1925 (Gaudio 4)
ice of the Necklace, 1914 (Ingram 2)
ice of Wisdom, 1935 (Havelock-Allan 4)
ichazeji z tmy, 1954 (Hrušínský 3)
ide and Prejudice, 1940 (Garson 3, Gwenn 3, O'Sullivan 3, Olivier 3, Adrian 4, Freund 4, Gibbons 4, Murfin 4, Stothart 4, Stromberg 4)
ide and the Man, 1916 (Borzage 2)
ide and the Passion, 1957 (Kramer, S. 2, Grant, C. 3, Loren 3, Sinatra 3, Anhalt 4, Bass 4, Planer 4)
ide of Bluegrass, 1939 (McCord 4)
ide of Jesse Hallam, 1981 (Wallach 3)
ide of Lonesome, 1913 (Reid 3)
ide of New York, 1918 (Walsh 2)
ide of Palomar, 1922 (Borzage 2, Oland 3)
ide of Pawnee, 1929 (Musuraca 4, Plunkett 4)
ide of Pickeville, 1927 (Sennett 2)
ide of Race. See Last of the Line, 1914
ide of St. Louis, 1952 (Dailey 3, Lemaire 4, Mankiewicz 4)
ide of the Bowery, 1941 (Katzman 4)
ide of the Clan, 1917 (Tourneur, M. 2, Pickford 3, Carré 4)
ide of the Marines, 1936 (Bond 3)

Pride of the Marines, 1942 (Mandell 4)
Pride of the Marines, 1945 (Daves 2, Garfield 3, Wald 4, Waxman 4)
Pride of the Plains, 1943 (Canutt 4)
Pride of the Range, 1910 (Mix 3)
Pride of the South, 1913 (Ince 4)
Pride of the West, 1938 (Boyd 3, Head 4)
Pride of the Yankees, 1942 (Wood 2, Brennan 3, Cooper, Gary 3, Duryea 3, Wright 3, Goldwyn 4, Mankiewicz 4, Maté 4, Menzies 4, Swerling 4)
Pride of the Yard, 1954 (Terry 4)
Prière, 1900–07 (Guy 2)
Priest. See Prasten, 1914
Priest and Empress. See Yoso, 1963
Priest Killer, 1971 (Kennedy, G. 3)
Priest of Love, 1981 (Gardner 3, Gielgud 3)
Priest of Wilderness, 1910 (Olcott 2)
Priest's End. See Farářuv konec, 1968
Priest's Wife. See Moglia del prete, 1970
Prigionera della torre del fuoco, 1952 (Brazzi 3, Manfredi 3)
Prigionieri del male, 1957 (Blier 3, Manfredi 3)
Prigioniero della montagna, 1955 (Pasolini 2)
Prigioniero di Santa Cruz, 1941 (Amidei 4)
Prima Angélica, 1974 (Saura 2)
Prima comunione, 1950 (Blasetti 2, Fabrizi 3, Zavattini 4)
Prima de Cantiflas, 1940 (Cantinflas 3)
Prima della rivoluzione, 1964 (Bertolucci 2, Morricone 4)
Prima donna che passa, 1940 (Valli 3)
Prima notte, 1958 (Cavalcanti 2, De Sica 2, Cardinale 3, Di Venanzo 4)
Prima notte di quiete, 1972 (Zurlini 2, Delon 3, Giannini 3, Valli 3)
Primal Call, 1911 (Griffith 2, Crisp 3, Bitzer 4)
Primal Lure, 1916 (Hart 3)
Primanerehe. See Boykott, 1930
Primanerliebe, 1927 (Albers 3, Kortner 3)
Primary, 1960 (Leacock 2)
Primate, 1974 (Wiseman 2)
Primavera del papa, 1949 (Di Venanzo 4)
Prime Cut, 1972 (Ritchie 2, Hackman 3, Marvin 3, Spacek 3, Schifrin 4)
Prime Minister, 1941 (Dickinson 2, Gielgud 3)
Prime of Life. See Toshigoro, 1968
Prime of Miss Jean Brodie, 1969 (Johnson, C. 3, Smith 3, Allen, J. 4)
Prime of Ochiyo's Life. See Ochiyo toshigoro, 1937
Prime Time, 1959 (Black 3)
Prime Time, 1977 (Oates 3)
Primer año, 1970 (Guzmán 2)
Primera carga al machete, 1969 (Gómez, M. 2, Herrera 4)
Primera fundación de Buenos Aires, 1959 (Birri 2)
Primerose, 1933 (Meerson 4)
Primitifs du XIII, 1960 (Arletty 3, Prévert 4)
Primitive Desires. See Montagna del dio cannibale, 1978
Primitive Love. See Amore primitivo, 1964
Primitive Lover, 1922 (Franklin 2, Talmadge, C. 3, Marion 4, Schenck 4)
Primitive Peoples: Australian Aborigines, 1949 (Finch 3)
Primitive Strain, 1916 (Van Dyke, W.S. 2)
Primo amore, 1941 (Gallone 2, Cortese 3, Vích 4)
Primo amore, 1958 (Age and Scarpelli 4, Delli Colli 4)
Primo amore, 1978 (Risi 2, Tognazzi 3, Delli Colli 4)
Primo Basilio, 1935 (Figueroa 4)
Primrose Path, 1925 (Bow 3)
Primrose Path, 1930 (Laszlo 4)
Primrose Path, 1940 (La Cava 2, McCrea 3, Rogers, G. 3, August 4, Polglase 4)
Primrose Ring, 1917 (Rosher 4)
Primula bianca, 1946 (Ponti 4)
Prince and Betty, 1919 (Karloff 3)
Prince and the Pauper, 1915 (Porter 2)
Prince and the Pauper, 1937 (Flynn 3, Rains 3, Friedhofer 4, Korngold 4, Polito 4, Wallis 4)
Prince and the Pauper, 1977 (Fleischer, R. 2, Borgnine 3, Harrison 3, Heston 3, Scott, G. 3, Jarre 4)
Prince and the Pauper. See Crossed Swords, 1977
Prince and the Pauper. See Seine Majestat das Bettelkind, 1920

Proud and the Profane, 1956 (Seaton 2, Holden 3, Kerr 3, Ritter 3, Head 4, Young, V. 4)
Proud City, 1945 (Alwyn 4)
Proud Flesh, 1925 (Vidor, K. 2, Crawford, J. 3)
Proud Nightgown. *See* Pyšné noční košilce, 1950
Proud Ones, 1956 (Brennan 3, Coogan 3, Hunter 3, Mayo 3, Ryan 3, Ballard 4, Lemaire 4)
Proud Rebel, 1958 (Curtiz 2, Carradine 3, De Havilland 3, Ladd 3, McCord 4)
Proud Stallion. *See* Trápení, 1961
Proud Valley, 1940 (Robeson 3, Balcon 4)
Prova d'orchestra, 1978 (Fellini 2, Rota 4)
Prova de Fogo, 1980 (Diegues 2)
Provaz z oběšence, 1927 (Stallich 4)
Provesso alla città, 1952 (D'Amico 4)
Provesso e morte di Socrate, 1940 (Brazzi 3)
Providence and Mrs. Urmy, 1915 (Bushman 3)
Providence, 1977 (Resnais 2, Bogarde 3, Burstyn 3, Dauphin 3, Gielgud 3, Rozsa 4)
Provinciale, 1953 (Lollobrigida 3, Aldo 4)
Provinciale, 1980 (Goretta 2, Baye 3, Ganz 3)
Provocation, 1970 (Marais 3)
Prowler, 1951 (Aldrich 2, Losey 2, Heflin 3, Leven 4, Miller, A. 4, Spiegel 4, Trumbo 4)
Prowlers of the Plains. *See* Knight of the Trails, 1915
Proxy Lover: A Fable of the Future, 1924 (Fleischer, M. and D. 2)
Proyekt inzhenera Praita, 1918 (Kuleshov 2)
Prozess, 1947 (Pabst 2)
Prozess der Kitty Kellermann. *See* Hokuspokus, 1930
Prozess Hauers, 1918 (Kraly 4)
Prstýnek, 1944 (Fric 2)
Prudence and the Pill, 1968 (Evans 3, Kerr 3, Niven 3, Williams, R. 4)
Prudence of Broadway, 1919 (Borzage 2)
Prude's Fall, 1924 (Hitchcock 2, Saville 2, Balcon 4)
Prunella, 1918 (Tourneur, M. 2, Carré 4)
Prussian Cur, 1918 (Walsh 2)
Prussian Spy, 1909 (Griffith 2, Bitzer 4)
První políbení, 1935 (Vích 4)
Przebudzenie, 1934 (Ford, A. 2)
Przedświateczny wieczór, 1965 (Cybulski 3, Stawinsky 4)
Przekladaniec, 1968 (Wajda 2)
Przemysl, 1966 (Zanussi 2)
Przeprowadzka, 1972 (Pszoniak 3)
Przeprowadzka Dominika, 1968 (Giersz 4)
Przhevalsky, 1951 (Yutkevich 2)
Przy Jaciel, 1960 (Skolimowski 2)
Przygody marynarza, 1958 (Giersz 4)
Przysiegam u Ziemi Polskiej, 1943 (Ford, A. 2)
Psalm. *See* Zalm, 1966
Pseudo Sultan, 1912 (Bunny 3)
Psi a lidé, 1970 (Schorm 2, Kučera 4)
Psi kusy, 1971 (Pojar 4)
Psí pohádka, 1959 (Hofman 4)
Psohlavci, 1931 (Vích 4)
Psohlavci, 1954 (Fric 2, Kopecký 3, Stallich 4)
Psyche 59, 1964 (Jurgens 3, Neal 3, Lassally 4)
Psychiatry in Russia, 1955 (Maysles A. 2)
Psycho, 1960 (Hitchcock 2, Leigh, J. 3, Perkins 3, Bass 4, Herrmann 4)
Psycho A Go-Go!, 1965 (Zsigmond 4)
Psycho A Go-Go!. *See* Blood of Ghastly Horror, 1965
Psycho Circus. *See* Circus of Fear, 1967
Psycho Killers. *See* Flesh and the Fiends, 1960
Psycho III, 1986 (Bumstead 4)
Psycho II, 1983 (Perkins 3, Goldsmith 4, Whitlock 4)
Psychocracy, or To See or Not to See, 1969 (Pojar 4)
Psychomania. *See* Living Dead, 1972
Psychopath, 1965 (Francis 4)
Psych-Out, 1968 (Dern 3, Nicholson 3, Kovacs 4)
Psychout for Murder. *See* Salvare la faccia, 1969
Psycosissimo, 1961 (Tognazzi 3)
PT 109, 1963 (Robertson 3, Surtees 4)
Ptica i crvek, 1977 (Grgić 4)

P'tite Lili, 1927 (Cavalcanti 2, Braunberger 4)
Puberty Blues, 1981 (Beresford 2)
Public Be Hanged. *See* World Gone Mad, 1933
Public Cowboy No. 1, 1937 (Autry 3, Farnum 3)
Public Deb No. 1, 1940 (Auer 3, Bellamy 3, Cook 3, Newman 4, Zanuck 4)
Public Defender, 1931 (Karloff 3, Cronjager 4, Steiner 4)
Public Enemy, 1931 (Wellman 2, Blondell 3, Cagney 3, Harlow 3, Zanuck 4)
Public Enemy's Wife, 1936 (O'Brien, P. 3, Haller 4)
Public Eye. *See* Follow Me, 1971
Public Ghost No. One, 1935 (Roach 4)
Public Hero No. 1, 1935 (Arthur 3, Barrymore L. 3, Stone 3, Toland 4)
Public Jitterbug No. 1, 1939 (Hutton 3)
Public Menace, 1935 (Arthur 3)
Public Opinion, 1916 (Sweet 3)
Public Pigeon No. 1, 1957 (McLeod 2)
Public Prosecutor. *See* Justic d'abord, 1919
Public Prosecutor. *See* Prokuror, 1917
Public Wedding, 1937 (Wyman 3)
Publicity Madness, 1927 (Loos 4)
Publicity Pays, 1924 (McCarey 2, Roach 4)
Pubs and Beaches, 1966 (Williams, R. 4)
Puccini, 1953 (Gallone 2, Renoir 4)
Puce à l'oreille, 1967 (Trauner 4)
Puce et le Privé, 1980 (Vanel 3)
Puce Moment, 1949 (Anger 2)
Puce Women, 1948 (Anger 2)
Pucérons, 1955 (Rabier 4)
Puces de sable, 1981 (Laguionie 4)
Puck heter jag, 1951 (Andersson H. 3)
Puddin' Head, 1941 (Summerville 3)
Puddle Pranks, 1931 (Iwerks 4)
Pudd'nhead Wilson, 1916 (Rosher 4)
Pudd'nhead Wilson, 1983 (Lassally 4)
Puddy the Pup series, 1936 (Terry 4)
Pudgy series, 1937-38 (Fleischer, M. and D. 2)
Pudr a benzin, 1931 (Vích 4)
Pueblerina, 1948 (Fernández 2, Figueroa 4)
Pueblito, 1961 (Fernández 2)
Pueblo armado. *See* Pueblos en armas, 1961
Pueblo, canto y esperanza, 1954 (Infante 3, Figueroa 4)
Pueblo Legend, 1912 (Griffith 2, Pickford 3, Bitzer 4)
Pueblo Terror, 1931 (Canutt 4)
Pueblos en armas, 1961 (Ivens 2)
Puente, 1977 (Bardem 2)
Puerta, 1968 (Alcoriza 4, Figueroa 4)
Puerta cerrada, 1939 (Alton, J. 4)
Puerta falsa, 1950 (Armendáriz 3)
Puerta . . . joven, 1949 (Cantinflas 3)
Puerto nuevo, 1936 (Alton, J. 4)
Pugilatori, 1951 (Zurlini 2)
Pugilist. *See* Knock Out, 1914
Pugni in tasca, 1965 (Bellocchio 2, Morricone 4)
Pugni, pupe e marinai, 1961 (Tognazzi 3)
Pugowitza, 1981 (Hoppe 3)
Puissance du travail, 1925 (Simon, M. 3)
Puits aux trois vérités, 1961 (Morgan 3, Jarre 4, Jeanson 4)
Puits et le pendule, 1963 (Astruc 2)
Puits fantastique, 1903 (Méliès 2)
Puits mitoyen, 1913 (Tourneur, M. 2)
Pujarin, 1936 (Sircar 4)
Pukar, 1983 (Bachchan 3)
Pukkelryggede. *See* Kaerligheds Laengsel, 1915
Pulcherie et ses meubles, 1916 (Cohl 2)
Pull My Daisy, 1958 (Seyrig 3)
Pullman Bride, 1917 (Sennett 2, Swanson 3)
Pulnoční příhoda, 1960 (Trnka 2, Pojar 4)
Pulp, 1972 (Caine 3, Rooney 3)
Pulpo humano, 1933 (García 3)
Pulsating Giant, 1971 (Benegal 2)
Pulse of Life, 1917 (Ingram 2)
Pulverschnee nach Ubersee, 1956 (Vích 4)

Q

Q Planes, 1939 (Olivier 3, Richardson 3, Dalrymple 4, Hornbeck 4, Korda 4, Mathieson 4, Stradling 4, Wimperis 4)
Qayamat, 1983 (Patil 3)
Q-bec My Love. *See* Successful commercial, 1970
Qingming Festival, 1936 (Zhao 3)
Quack, 1914 (Reid 3)
Quack, 1975 (Schell, Maria 3)
Quack Doctor, 1920 (Sennett 2)
Quack Quack, 1931 (Terry 4)
Quack Service, 1943 (Merkel 3)
Quack Shot, 1954 (McKimson 4)
Quackser Fortune Has a Cousin in the Bronx, 1970 (Wilder 3)
Quadrate, 1934 (Fischinger 2)
Quadriga, 1967 (Wicki 2)
Quadrille, 1938 (Guitry 2)
Quadrille, 1950 (Godard 2, Rivette 2)
Quadrille d'amour, 1934 (Brasseur 3)
Quadrille réaliste, 1902 (Guy 2)
Quaeta specie d'amore, 1972 (Seberg 3)
Quagmire, 1913 (Seitz 4)
Quai des blondes, 1953 (Audiard 4)
Quai des brumes, 1938 (Carné 2, Brasseur 3, Gabin 3, Morgan 3, Simon, M. 3, Alekan 4, Jaubert 4, Prévert 4, Schufftan 4, Trauner 4)
Quai des illusions, 1956 (Kosma 4)
Quai des Orfèvres, 1947 (Clouzot 2, Blier 3, Jouvet 3, Douy 4)
Quai Notre Dame, 1961 (Aimée 3)
Quail Hunt, 1935 (Lantz 4)
Quail Shooting, Pinehurst, 1905 (Bitzer 4)
Quakeress, 1913 (Ince 4)
Qualen der Nacht, 1926 (Dieterle 2, Rasp 3)
Quality Street, 1927 (Franklin 2, Davies 3, Gibbons 4, Kraly 4, Lewin 4)
Quality Street, 1937 (Stevens 2, Bainter 3, Fontaine 3, Hepburn, K. 3, Berman 4, Plunkett 4)
Qualsiasi prezzo, 1968 (Rowlands 3)
Quand la femme s'en mêle, 1957 (Allégret, Y. 2, Blier 3, Delon 3, Feuillère 3, D'Eaubonne 4, Spaak 4)
Quand la vie était belle, 1935 (Simon, M. 3, Lourié 4)
Quand la vie était belle. *See* Bébé de l'escadron, 1935
Quand le rideau se lève, 1957 (Lelouch 2)
Quand les feuilles tombent, 1911 (Feuillade 2)
Quand même, 1916 (Fresnay 3)
Quand midi sonne par la France, 1960 (Kosma 4)
Quand minuit sonna, 1914 (Feyder 2)
Quand minuit sonnera, 1936 (Dalio 3, Kaufman 4)
Quand on est belle, 1931 (Robison 2, Rosay 3)
Quand on est mort, c'est pour la vie, 1974 (Denner 3)
Quand passent les faisans, 1965 (Blier 3, Audiard 4, Legrand 4)
Quand sonnera midi, 1957 (Burel 4)
Quand tu liras cette lettre, 1953 (Melville 2, Alekan 4)
Quand tu nous tiens, amour, 1932 (Fernandel 3)
Quando l'amore è sensualità, 1972 (Morricone 4)
Quando le donne avevano la coda, 1970 (Morricone 4)
Quando le donne persero la coda, 1972 (Morricone 4)
Quando o Carnaval chegar, 1972 (Diegues 2)
Quando tramonta il sole, 1955 (Di Venanzo 4)
Quantez, 1957 (MacMurray 3, Malone 3)
Quanto costa morire, 1968 (Ireland 3)
Quara pagina, 1942 (Cortese 3)
Quarantane, 1923 (George, H. 3)
47 morto che parla, 1950 (Age and Scarpelli 4)

Quarante gradi all'ombra del'lenzuolo. *See* Quarante gradi sotto il lenzuolo, 1975
Quarante gradi sotto il lenzuolo, 1975 (Guerra 4)
48 heures d'amour, 1968 (de Beauregard 4)
Quarantièmes Rugissants, 1982 (Christie 3)
Quarantine, 1923 (Warm 4)
Quarantined, 1970 (Jaffe 3, Duning 4)
Quare Fellow, 1962 (Havelock-Allan 4)
Quark, 1981–83 (Bozzetto 4)
Quarrel, 1911 (White 3)
Quarrelsome Anglers, 1898 (Hepworth 2)
Quarry Mystery, 1914 (Hepworth 2)
Quarta pagina, 1942 (Fellini 2, Cervi 3, Zavattini 4)
Quarta parete, 1971 (Blier 3)
Quarterback, 1926 (Cronjager 4)
Quarterback, 1940 (Head 4, Pirosh 4)
Quartet, 1948 (Zetterling 2, Bogarde 3, Rosay 3)
Quartet, 1981 (Ivory 2, Adjani 3, Bates 3, Smith 3, Jhabvala 4)
Quartet That Split Up. *See* Kvartetten som sprangdes, 1950
Quartetto Pazzo, 1944 (Cervi 3, Magnani 3)
Quartier Chinois, 1947 (Hayakawa 3)
Quartier Latin, 1939 (Blier 3)
Quartieri alti, 1944 (Castellani 2)
Quarto d'Italia, 1960 (Zavattini 4)
Quatermass Experiment, 1955 (Bernard 4)
Quatermass II, 1957 (Bernard 4)
Quatorze juillet, 1932 (Clair 2, Modot 3, Jaubert 4, Meerson 4, Périnal 4, Trauner 4)
Quatorze juillet, 1954 (Gance 2)
Quatorze juillet, 1961 (Braunberger 4)
Quatre Cents Coups, 1959 (Broca 2, Demy 2, Truffaut 2, Léaud 3, Decaë 4, Evein 4)
400 Farces du Diable, 1906 (Meliès 2)
Quatre Charlots mousequetaires, 1973 (Douy 4)
4 Mouches de velours gris, 1972 (Lenica 2)
Quatre Nuits d'un rêveur, 1971 (Bresson 2)
Quatre Petits Tailleurs, 1910 (Cohl 2)
Quatre Temps, 1956 (Alexeieff and Parker 2)
Quatres Jambes, 1932 (Dalio 3)
Quatres Vagabonds, 1931 (Pick 2)
Quatres Vérités, 1962 (Clair 2, Blasetti 3, Brazzi 3, Caron 3, Karina 3, Vitti 3, Barsacq 4, D'Amico 4)
Quattro del getto tonante, 1955 (Fusco 4)
Quattro dell'ave Maria, 1968 (Wallach 3)
Quattro giornate de Napoli, 1962 (Volonté 3)
Quattro monaci, 1962 (Fabrizi 3)
Quattro mosche di velluto grigio, 1971 (Argento 4, Morricone 4)
Quattro moschettieri, 1963 (Fabrizi 3)
Quattro passi fra le nuvole, 1942 (Blasetti 2, Cervi 3, Zavattini 4)
Quattro passi fra le nuvole, 1949 (Vích 4)
Quattro ragazze sognano, 1943 (Cortese 3)
Quattro tassisti, 1964 (Fabrizi 3)
Que Dios me perdone, 1947 (Félix 3)
Que fait-on ce dimanche, 1977 (de Almeida 4)
Que Farei Eu Com Esta Espada, 1975 (de Almeida 4)
Que la bête meure, 1969 (Chabrol 2, Gégauff 4, Rabier 4)
Que la fête commence, 1975 (Tavernier 2, Dalio 3, Noiret 3, Aurenche 4)
Que les gros salaires lèvent le doigt!!!, 1982 (Piccoli 3)
Que peut-il avoir?, 1912 (Linders 3)
Que Viene mi marido, 1940 (Figueroa 4)
Que Viva Mexico!, 1931 (Tisse 4)
Québec-USA, 1962 (Jutra 2)

Queda, 1978 (Guerra 2)
Queen and the Cardinal. See Jérome Perreau, héros des barricades, 1936
Queen Bee, 1955 (Crawford, J. 3, Ireland 3, Wray 3, Duning 4, Lang 4, Wald 4)
Queen Bee. See Jo-bachi, 1978
Queen Bee. See Storia moderna, 1963
Queen Christina, 1933 (Mamoulian 2, Garbo 3, Gilbert 3, Stone 3, Adrian 4, Behrman 4, Daniels 4, Gibbons 4, Stothart 4, Wanger 4)
Queen Cotton, 1941 (Alwyn 4, Cardiff 4)
Queen Diamonds. See Three Musketeers, 1973
Queen Dorothy's Bow. See Luk královny Dorotky povikovy, 1970
Queen for a Day, 1911 (Bunny 3)
Queen for a Day, 1951 (Friedhofer 4, Miller, S. 4)
Queen High, 1930 (Rogers, G. 3, Green, J. 4)
Queen in Australia, 1955 (Finch 3)
Queen Kelly, 1928 (Von Stroheim 2, Swanson 3, Plunkett 4)
Queen Louise, 1928 (Bergner 3)
Queen Louise. See Konigin Luise, 1927
Queen of Apollo, 1970 (Leacock 2)
Queen of Blood, 1966 (Hopper 3, Rathbone 3, Corman 4)
Queen of Broadway, 1942 (Crabbe 3)
Queen of Destiny. See Sixty Glorious Years, 1938
Queen of Hearts, 1934 (Iwerks 4)
Queen of Hearts, 1936 (Fields, G. 3, Dean 4)
Queen of Modern Times. See Gendai no joo, 1924
Queen of Outer Space, 1958 (Hecht 4)
Queen of Sheba. See Regina di Saba, 1952
Queen of Spades, 1948 (Clayton 2, Dickinson 2, Evans 3, Walbrook 3, Adam 4, Auric 4)
Queen of Spades. See Pikovaya dama, 1916
Queen of Spies. See Joan of the Ozarks, 1942
Queen of the Band, 1915 (Browning 2)
Queen of the Circus. See Kyohubadan no joo, 1925
Queen of the Mob, 1940 (Bellamy 3, Ryan 3, Dreier 4, Head 4)
Queen of the Moulin Rouge, 1922 (Carré 4)
Queen of the Night Clubs, 1929 (Raft 3)
Queen of the Nile. See Nefertite—Regina del Nilo, 1961
Queen of the Quarry, 1909 (Olcott 2)
Queen of the Road, 1971 (Golan and Globus 4)
Queen Victoria. See Sixty Glorious Years, 1938
Queen X, 1917 (Polito 4)
Queenie, 1921 (Menjou 3)
Queenie of Hollywood, 1931 (Arbuckle 3)
Queens. See Fate, 1966
Queen's Affair, 1934 (Wilcox 2, Neagle 3, Raphaelson 4, Young, F. 4)
Queen's Diamonds. See Three Musketeers, 1973
Queen's Guards, 1961 (Powell 2, Massey 3)
Queen's Husband. See Royal Bed, 1930
Queen's Necklace. See Affaire du collier de la Reine, 1946
Queen's Secret. See Taina korolevy, 1918
Queens Up, 1920 (Roach 4)
Queer Quarantine, 1914 (Beery 3)
Queimada!, 1969 (Pontecorvo 2, Gherardi 4, Morricone 4, Solinas 4)
Queimada!. See Burn!, 1969
Quel bandito sono io!, 1949 (Ponti 4)
Quel caldo maledetto giorno di fuoco, 1968 (Ireland 3)
Quel pomeriggio maledetto, 1977 (Ireland 3)
Quelle drôle de blanchisserie, 1912 (Cohl 2)
Quelle drôle de gosse!, 1935 (Darrieux 3, Stradling 4)
Quelle joie de vivre, 1961 (Tognazzi 3)
Quelle joie de vivre. See Che gioia vivere, 1961
Quelle strane occasioni, 1976 (Comencini 2, Manfredi 3, Sordi 3)
Quelque part, quelqu'un, 1972 (Delerue 4)
Quelques pas dans la vie, 1953 (Simon, M. 3)
Quelqu'un a tue, 1933 (Modot 3, Wakhévitch 4)
Quelqu'un derrière la porte, 1971 (Bronson 3, Perkins 3)
Quem e beta, 1972 (Pereira Dos Santos 2)
Quemando tradiciones, 1971 (Alvarez 2)
Quentin Durward, 1955 (Taylor, R. 3, Berman 4)
Quentin Durward. See Adventures of Quentin Durward, 1955
Quentin Quail, 1945 (Jones 2)
Querelle, 1982 (Fassbinder 2, Moreau 3)

Querelle de, 1982 (Ruiz 2)
Querelle enfantine, 1895 (Lumière 2)
Queridísimos Verdugos, 1971 (de Almeida 4)
Quest, 1976 (Wynn 3)
Quest for Fire. See Guerre du feu, 1981
Quest of Life, 1916 (Goulding 2)
Questa è la vita, 1954 (Zampa 2, Fabrizi 3)
Questa specie d'amore, 1972 (Rey 3, Morricone 4)
Questa volta parliamo di uomini, 1965 (Wertmüller 2, Manfredi 3)
Qu'est-ce qui fait courir David?, 1982 (Aimée 3, Legrand 4)
Queste pazze, pazze, pazze donne, 1964 (Auer 3)
Questi fantasmi, 1967 (Castellani 2, Gassman 3, Loren 3, Mastroianni 3, Delli Colli 4, Ponti 4)
Questi ragazzi, 1937 (De Sica 2)
Question, 1967 (Halas and Batchelor 2)
Question, 1970 (Ghatak 4)
Question, 1977 (Tavernier 2)
Question d'assurance, 1959 (Delerue 4)
Question in Togoland, 1957 (Dickinson 2)
Question of Courage, 1914 (Crisp 3, Gish, D. 3)
Question of Guilt, 1980 (Weld 3)
Question of Honor, 1915 (Eason 4)
Question of Honor. See Questione d'onore, 1965
Question of Leadership, 1981 (Loach 2)
Question of Love, 1978 (Rowlands 3)
Question of Loyalty, 1957 (Hopper 3)
Question of Rape. See Viol, 1967
Questione d'onore, 1965 (Zampa 2, Blier 3)
Questor Tapes, 1974 (Whitlock 4)
Qui?, 1970 (Schneider 3, Gégauff 4)
Qui comincia l'avventura, 1975 (Cardinale 3, Cristaldi 4)
Qui commande aux fusils, 1969 (Ivens 2)
Qui êtes-vous, Polly Magoo?, 1966 (Noiret 3, Seyrig 3, Evein 4, Legrand 4)
Quick, 1932 (Siodmak 2, Albers 3, Berry 3, Brasseur 3, Pommer 4)
Quick, Before It Melts, 1965 (Ames 4)
Quick Billy, 1970 (Baillie 2)
Quick Gun, 1964 (Murphy 3)
Quick, Let's Get Married. See Confession, 1965
Quick Millions, 1931 (Raft 3, Tracy 3, August 4)
Quick Millions, 1939 (Day 4)
Quick Money, 1938 (Musuraca 4)
Quicker 'n a Wink, 1940 (Sidney 2)
Quicksand, 1950 (Elam 3, Lorre 3, Rooney 3, Leven 4)
Quicksands, 1914 (Gish, L. 3)
Quicksands, 1923 (Hawks 2, Arlen 3, Hersholt 3, Rosson 4)
Quién me quiere a mi?, 1936 (Buñuel 2)
Quien sabe?, 1967 (Kinski 3, Volonté 3, Morricone 4, Solinas 4)
Quien te quiere a ti?, 1941 (García 3)
Quiet Affair. See Stilla flirt, 1934
Quiet American, 1958 (Mankiewicz 2, Dauphin 3, Murphy 3, Redgrave, M. 3, Hornbeck 4, Krasker 4)
Quiet Duel. See Shizukanaru ketto, 1949
Quiet Fourth, 1935 (Grable 3)
Quiet Gun, 1957 (Van Cleef 3)
Quiet Little Wedding, 1913 (Sennett 2, Arbuckle 3)
Quiet Man, 1952 (Ford, J. 2, Bond 3, Fitzgerald 3, McLaglen 3, O'Hara 3, Wayne 3, Cooper 4, Hoch 4, Nugent 4, Young, V. 4)
Quiet Place in the Country. See Tranquillo posto di campagna, 1968
Quiet Place to Kill. See Paranoia, 1969
Quiet Please, 1933 (Stevens 2)
Quiet Please!, 1945 (Hanna and Barbera 4)
Quiet, Please, Murder, 1942 (Sanders 3, Day 4)
Quiet! Pleeze, 1941 (Fleischer, M. and D. 2)
Quiet Revolution, 1975 (Benegal 2)
Quiet Street, 1922 (Roach 4)
Quiet Takeover, 1963 (Emshwiller 2)
Quiet Wedding, 1941 (Asquith 2, Rutherford 3, Dillon 4)
Quiet Week in a House. See Tichý týden v domě, 1969
Quijote sin mancha, 1969 (Cantinflas 3)
Qu'il est joli garçon, l'assassin de papa, 1976 (Gélin 3)
Qu'il était bon mon petit français. See Como é gostoso o meu francês 1971

uille, 1961 (Guillemot 4)
uiller Memorandum, 1966 (Guinness 3, Sanders 3, Segal 3, Von
    Sydow 3, Barry 4, Pinter 4)
uincannon, Frontier Scout, 1956 (Biroc 4, Cahn 4)
uincy Adams Sawyer, 1922 (Chaney Lon 3, Fazenda 3, Sweet 3)
uintero. *See* Legge dei gangsters, 1969
uintet, 1979 (Altman 2, Andersson B. 3, Gassman 3, Newman 3,
    Rey 3)
5/18, 1973 (Akerman 2)
uirinale, 1947 (Delli Colli 4)

Quits, 1915 (Chaney Lon 3, Furthman 4)
Quitter, 1916 (Barrymore L. 3)
Quitter, 1929 (Walker 4)
Quixote, 1964–65 (Baillie 2)
Quiz Whiz, 1958 (Three Stooges 3)
Quo Vadis, 1901 (Zecca, 2)
Quo Vadis, 1923 (Jannings 3, Courant 4)
Quo Vadis, 1951 (Huston 2, Leroy 2, Kerr 3, Loren 3, Pidgeon 3,
    Taylor, E. 3, Taylor, R. 3, Ustinov 3, Behrman 4, Ellenshaw 4,
    Gibbons 4, Gillespie 4, Levien 4, Mahin 4, Rozsa 4, Surtees 4)

R

.F.D. 10,000 B.C., 1917 (O'Brien 4)
N 37, 1937 (Leenhardt 2)
.P.M., 1970 (Quinn 3)
aag Yaman Kalyan, 1972 (Benegal 2)
aaste Ka Patthar, 1972 (Bachchan 3)
aaste pyare ke, 1982 (Azmi 3)
aat Bhore, 1956 (Sen 2)
aawan, 1984 (Patil 3)
abaukenkabarett, 1961 (Hoffmann 3)
abbia, 1963 (Pasolini 2)
abbit Case. *See* Causa králík, 1979
abbit Every Monday, 1950 (Freleng 4)
abbit Fire, 1951 (Jones 2)
abbit Hood, 1949 (Jones 2)
abbit of Seville, 1950 (Jones 2)
abbit Punch, 1947 (Jones 2)
abbit Rampage, 1955 (Jones 2)
abbit Romeo, 1957 (McKimson 4)
abbit, Run, 1970 (Caan 3)
abbit Seasoning, 1952 (Jones 2)
abbit Stew and Rabbits Too, 1969 (McKimson 4)
abbit Test, 1978 (McDowall 3, Ballard 4)
abbit Transit, 1946 (Freleng 4)
abbit Trap, 1959 (Borgnine 3)
abbit's Feat, 1960 (Jones 2)
abbit's Kin, 1952 (McKimson 4)
abbit's Moon, 1971 (Anger 2)
abbit's Moon. *See* Lune des Lapins, 1950
abbitson Crusoe, 1955 (Freleng 4)
abindranath Tagore, 1961 (Ray, S. 2, Chandragupta 4, Datta 4)
ablélek, 1913 (Curtiz 2)
abochy posyolok, 1966 (Gurchenko 3)
abotchaia slobodka, 1912 (Mozhukin 3)
acconti d'estate, 1958 (Mastroianni 3, Morgan 3, Sordi 3, Amidei 4,
    Flaiano 4)
acconti di Canterbury, 1972 (Pasolini 2, Welles 2, Delli Colli 4,
    Donati 4, Morricone 4)
acconti romani, 1956 (De Sica 2, Age and Scarpelli 4, Amidei 4)
ace, 1914 (Sennett 2)
acconti romani di Pietro l'Aretino, 1972 (Cervi 3)
ace des 'Seigneurs', 1974 (Delon 3, Moreau 3, Sarde 4)
ace for a Bride, 1914 (Browning 2)
ace for a Gold Mine, 1915 (Mix 3)
ace for Life. *See* Mask of Dust, 1954
ace for Life. *See* Si tous les gars du monde, 1955
ace for the Yankee Zephyr, 1982 (Pleasance 3)
ace Gang. *See* Four Dark Hours, 1940
ace Gang. *See* Green Cockatoo, 1937
ace Street, 1948 (Bendix 3, Raft 3, Hunt 4)
ace Symphony. *See* Rennsymphonie, 1928–29
ace with the Devil, 1975 (Fonda, P. 3, Oates 3, Rosenman 4)
acers, 1955 (Hathaway 2, Cobb 3, Douglas, K. 3, Bass 4, North 4,
    Wheeler 4)

Racetrack, 1932 (Cruze 2)
Rache der Toten, 1917 (Oswald 2, Krauss 3)
Rache des Blutes, 1914 (Wegener 3)
Rache des Gefallenen, 1917 (Albers 3)
Rache einer Frau, 1921 (Wiene 2)
Rache ist mein, 1912 (Messter 4)
Rache ist mein, 1918 (Lang 2)
Rachel and the Stranger, 1948 (Holden 3, Mitchum 3, Young, L. 3,
    D'Agostino 4, Head 4, Salt 4)
Rachel, Rachel, 1968 (Newman 3, Woodward 3, Allen, D. 4)
Rachel's Man, 1975 (Rooney 3)
Rachel's Sin, 1911 (Hepworth 2)
Racher, 1960 (Kinski 3)
Racing Fool, 1927 (Brown, Harry Joe 4)
Racing Lady, 1937 (Carey 3, McDaniel 3)
Racing Luck, 1935 (Boyd 3)
Racing Luck, 1948 (Katzman 4)
Racing Luck. *See* Red Hot Tires, 1935
Racing Romance, 1926 (Brown, Harry Joe 4)
Racing Romeo, 1927 (Wood 2, Clarke, C.C. 4)
Racing Strain, 1918 (Marsh 3)
Racing the Chutes at Dreamland, 1904 (Bitzer 4)
Racing Youth, 1932 (Fazenda 3, Summerville 3)
Rack, 1916 (Brady 3, Carré 4)
Rack, 1956 (Marvin 3, Newman 3, O'Brien, E. 3, Pidgeon 3,
    Deutsch 4)
Racket, 1928 (Milestone 2, Gaudio 4)
Racket, 1951 (Cromwell 2, Mitchum 3, Ryan 3, Burnett 4)
Racket Buster, 1949 (Terry 4)
Racket Busters, 1938 (Rossen 2, Bogart 3, Brent 3, Deutsch 4,
    Edeson 4, Friedhofer 4)
Racket Cheers, 1930 (Sennett 2)
Racket Man, 1944 (Muse 3, Robinson 4)
Racketeer, 1929 (Lombard 3)
Racketeer Rabbit, 1946 (Freleng 4)
Racketeers in Exile, 1937 (Ballard 4)
Rackety Rax, 1932 (Bond 3, McLaglen 3)
Rács, 1970 (Macskássy 4)
Rad na otredjeno vreme, 1980 (Samardžić 3)
Radeau avec baigneurs, 1896-97 (Lumière 2)
Radha Krishna, 1954 (Burman 4)
Radio City Revels, 1938 (Miller 3, Hunt 4, Pan 4, Veiller 4)
Radio Dynamics, 1942 (Fischinger 2)
Radio Girl, 1932 (Terry 4)
Radio Kisses, 1930 (Sennett 2)
Radio Lover, 1936 (Dalrymple 4)
Radio Mad, 1924 (Roach 4)
Radio Philips, 1977 (Giersz 4)
Radio Ranch. *See* Phantom Empire, 1935
Radio Rhythm, 1931 (Lantz 4)
Radio Riot, 1930 (Fleischer, M. and D. 2)
Radioens Barndom, 1949 (Dreyer 2)
Radiografia di una Svastika, 1974 (Jurgens 3)

Radish and Carrot. *See* Daikon to ninjin, 1965
Raduga, 1944 (Donskoi 2)
Rafferty and the Gold Dust Twins, 1975 (Arkin 3, Stanton 3)
Raffles, Gentleman Burglar, 1914 (Sennett 2)
Raffles, the Amateur Cracksman, 1905 (Blackton 2)
Raffles, The Amateur Cracksman, 1917 (Barrymore J. 3)
Raffles, the American Cracksman, 1905 (Anderson G. 3)
Raffles, 1930 (d'Arrast 2, Colman 3, Francis, K. 3, Barnes 4,
    Goldwyn 4, Howard 4, Menzies 4, Toland 4)
Raffles, 1940 (Wood 2, De Havilland 3, Niven 3, Banton 4, Basevi 4,
    Goldwyn 4, Howard 4, Toland 4, Young, V. 4)
Rafle de chiens, 1904 (Guy 2)
Rafles sur la ville, 1954 (Manès 3, Piccoli 3, Vanel 3, Legrand 4)
Rafter Romance, 1933 (Rogers, G. 3, MacGowan 4, Plunkett 4,
    Polglase 4, Steiner 4)
Rag Man, 1925 (Coogan 3)
Raga and the Emotions, 1971 (Benegal 2)
Ragamuffin, 1916 (Sweet 3)
Ragamuffin. *See* Hoodlum, 1919
Ragazza che sapeva troppo, 1962 (Cortese 3)
Ragazza con la pistola, 1968 (Monicelli 2, Baker S. 3, Vitti 3)
Ragazza con la valigia, 1960 (Zurlini 2, Cardanale 3, Volonté 3)
Ragazza dal pigiami giallo, 1977 (Ferrer, M. 3, Milland 3)
Ragazza del bersagliere, 1967 (Blasetti 2, Brazzi 3)
Ragazza del Palio, 1957 (Zampa 2, Gassman 3)
Ragazza della Salina, 1957 (Mastroianni 3)
Ragazza di Bube, 1963 (Comencini 2, Cardinale 3, Cristaldi 4,
    Di Venanzo 4, Gherardi 4)
Ragazza di mille mesi, 1961 (Tognazzi 3)
Ragazza di Piazza S. Pietro, 1958 (De Sica 2)
Ragazza e il generale, 1967 (Steiger 3, Morricone 4)
Ragazza in prestito, 1964 (Brazzi 3, Girardot 3)
Ragazza in vetrina, 1961 (Pasolini 2, Flaiano 4)
Ragazze d'oggi, 1955 (Zampa 2, Ponti 3, Rosay 3)
Ragazze de marito, 1952 (Age and Scarpelli 4)
Ragazze delle nuvole, 1957 (Cervi 3)
Ragazze di Piazza di Spagna, 1952 (Mastroianni 3, Amidei 4)
Ragazze di San Frediano, 1954 (Zurlini 2, Di Venanzo 4)
Ragazze in bianco, 1949 (Antonioni 2)
Ragazzi dei paroli, 1959 (Manfredi 3)
Ragazzi della via Paal, 1935 (Monicelli 2)
Ragazzo di borgata, 1976 (Rota 4)
Rage, 1966 (Ford, G. 3)
Rage, 1972 (Scott, G. 3, Sheen 3, Schifrin 4)
Rage at Dawn, 1955 (Scott, R. 3)
Rage de dents, 1900 (Guy 2)
Rage in Heaven, 1941 (Van Dyke, W.S. 2, Bergman 3, Homolka 3,
    Montgomery 3, Sanders 3, Kaper 4)
Rage of Paris, 1938 (Auer 3, Darrieux 3, Fairbanks, D. Jr. 3, Salter 4)
Rage of the Buccaneer. *See* Gordon, il Pirato Nero, 1961
Rågens rike, 1929 (Borgstrom 3)
Rågens rike, 1950 (Nykvist 4)
Ragged Angels. *See* They Shall Have Music, 1939
Ragged Flag. *See* Ranru no hata, 1974
Ragged Heiress, 1922 (Furthman 4)
Raggedy Ann and Andy, 1941 (Fleischer, M. and D. 2)
Raggedy Ann and Andy, 1977 (Williams, R. 4)
Raggedy Man, 1981 (Spacek 3, Goldsmith 4)
Raggedy Rose, 1926 (Laurel 3, Normand 3)
Raggedy Rug, 1963 (Hanna and Barbera 4)
Raging Bull, 1979 (Schrader 2, Scorsese 2, De Niro 3)
Raging Moon, 1971 (McDowell 3)
Raging Tide, 1951 (Winters 3)
Raging Waters. *See* Green Promise, 1949
Ragione per vivere e una per morire, 1972 (Coburn, J. 3)
Rags, 1915 (Pickford 3)
Ragtime, 1981 (Forman 2, Cagney 3, Love 3, O'Brien, P. 3,
    O'Connor 3, Steenburgen 3, De Laurentiis 4, Ondricek 4)
Ragtime Bear, 1949 (Hubley 4)
Ragtime Romeo, 1931 (Iwerks 4)
Ragtime Snap Shots, 1915 (Lloyd 3, Roach 4)
Rahi, 1953 (Anand 3)
Raid, 1954 (Bancroft 3, Boone 3, Heflin 3, Marvin 3, Ballard 4)

Raid on Entebbe, 1976 (Kershner 2, Bronson 3, Finch 3, Sidney 3,
    Warden 3)
Raid on France, 1942 (Balcon 4)
Raid on Rommel, 1971 (Hathaway 2, Burton 3)
Raid Paris-Monte Carlo en deux heures, 1905 (Méliès 2)
Raider. *See* Western Approaches, 1944
Raiders, 1916 (Mix 3)
Raiders of Old California, 1957 (Van Cleef 3)
Raiders of San Joaquin, 1943 (Salter 4)
Raiders of the Desert, 1942 (Arlen 3, Salter 4)
**Raiders of the Lost Ark, 1981 (Lucas 2, Spielberg 2, Ford, H. 3,
    Burtt 4, Edlund 4, Slocombe 4, Williams, J. 4)**
Raiders of the Seven Seas, 1953 (Chaney Lon, Jr. 3, Reed, D. 3)
Raiding the Raiders, 1945 (Terry 4)
Raigeki tai shutsudo, 1944 (Tsuburaya 4)
Rail Rider, 1916 (Tourneur, M. 2, Carré 4)
Railroad Man. *See* Ferroviere, 1956
Railroaded, 1947 (Mann 2, Ireland 3)
Railroadin', 1929 (Roach 4)
Railrodder, 1965 (Keaton 2)
Rails into Laramie, 1954 (Duryea 3, Van Cleef 3)
Rails sous les palmiers, 1951 (Colpi 4)
Railwaymen. *See* Zeleznicáři, 1963
Rain, 1932 (Milestone 2, Bondi 3, Crawford, J. 3, Huston 3, Day 4,
    Newman 4)
Rain, 1940 (Eisler 4)
Rain. *See* Regen, 1929
Rain. *See* Sadie Thompson, 1928
Rain for a Dusty Summer, 1971 (Borgnine 3)
Rain Makers, 1951 (Terry 4)
Rain of Paris, 1980 (Dinov 4)
Rain or Shine, 1930 (Capra 2, Fazenda 3, Muse 3, Swerling 4,
    Walker 4)
Rain People, 1969 (Coppola 2, Caan 3, Duvall, R. 3, Murch 4)
Rainbow. *See* Raduga, 1944
Rainbow Dance, 1936 (Cavalcanti 2, Lye 2)
Rainbow Island, 1917 (Daniels 3, Lloyd 3, Roach 4)
Rainbow Island, 1944 (De Carlo 3, Lamour 3, Dreier 4, Head 4,
    Struss 4)
Rainbow Jacket, 1954 (Dearden 2, Alwyn 4, Clarke, T.E.B. 4)
Rainbow of This Sky. *See* Kono ten no niji, 1958
Rainbow on the River, 1936 (Beavers 3)
Rainbow over Texas, 1946 (Rogers, R. 3)
Rainbow Round My Shoulder, 1952 (Edwards 2)
Rainbow Trail, 1918 (Farnum 3)
Rainbow Trail, 1925 (Mix 3)
Rainbow Valley, 1935 (Wayne 3)
Raining in the Mountains. *See* K'ung shan ling yü, 1979
Rainmaker, 1956 (Hepburn, K. 3, Lancaster 3, Head 4, Lang 4, Nort
    4, Wallis 4)
Rainmakers, 1935 (McCord 4, Plunkett 4)
Rains Came, 1939 (Brown 2, Brent 3, Bruce 3, Darwell 3, Loy 3,
    Ouspenskaya 3, Power 3, Schildkraut 3, Brown, Harry Joe 4,
    Dunne 4, Glennon 4, Miller, A. 4, Newman 4, Zanuck 4)
Rain's Hat, 1978 (Zetterling 2)
Rains of Ranchipur, 1955 (Negulesco 2, Burton 3, MacMurray 3,
    Turner, L. 3, Friedhofer 4, Krasner 4, Lemaire 4, Rose 4)
Raintree County, 1957 (Dmytryk 2, Clift 3, Marvin 3, Moorehead 3,
    Saint 3, Taylor, E. 3, Green, J. 4, Plunkett 4, Surtees 4)
Rainy Day. *See* Deštivý den, 1963
Rainy Days, 1928 (Roach 4)
Rainy Knight, 1925 (Sennett 2)
Rainy Night Duel. *See* Kuroobi sangokushi, 1956
Raise Ravens. *See* Cria cuervos, 1975
Raise the Rent, 1920 (Roach 4)
Raise the Roof, 1930 (Balfour 3)
Raise the Titanic!, 1980 (Guinness 3, Robards 3, Barry 4)
Raisin in the Sun, 1961 (Gossett 3, Poitier 3)
Raising a Riot, 1954 (More 3, Dalrymple 4)
Raising the Wind, 1961 (Dillon 4)
Raison avant la passion, 1968–69 (Wieland 2)
Raison d'état, 1978 (Cayatte 2, Vitti 3)
Raison du plus fou est toujours la meilleure, 1972 (Reichenbach 2)

Rajah, 1919 (Daniels 3, Lloyd 3, Roach 4)
Rajat Jayanti, 1939 (Sircar 4)
Rajgi, 1937 (Burman 4)
Rajolfi Hayati, 1961 (Chahine 2)
Rajrani Meera, 1933 (Sircar 4)
Rajtunk is mulik, 1960 (Mészáros 2)
Raju aur Gangaram, 1964 (Biswas 4)
Rake's Progress, 1945 (Harrison 3, Alwyn 4, Gilliat 4, Mathieson 4)
Rakei kazoku, 1954 (Yamamura 3)
Rakkii-san, 1952 (Ichikawa 2)
Rakna de lyckliga stunderna blott, 1944 (Dahlbeck 3)
Rakoczy-Marsch, 1933 (Frohlich 3)
Rakudai wa shita keredo, 1930 (Ozu 2, Ryu 3, Tanaka 3)
Rakugaki kokuban, 1959 (Shindo 2)
Rakvičkárna, 1966 (Švankmajer 4)
Rallare, 1947 (Sjostrom 2)
Rally, 1980 (Lee, C. 3)
Rally Round the Flag, 1909 (Olcott 2)
Rally 'round the Flag, Boys!, 1958 (McCarey 2, Newman 3, Weld 3, Woodward 3, Lemaire 4, Shamroy 4, Wheeler 4)
Ram Balram, 1980 (Bachchan 3)
Rambles Through Hopland, 1913 (Pearson 2)
Ramblin' Kid, 1923 (Miller, V. 4)
Rambo: First Blood, Part II, 1985 (Stallone 3, Cardiff 4, Goldsmith 4)
'Rameau's Nephew' by Diderot, 1972 (Wieland 2)
Rameau's Nephew by Diderot (Thanx to Dennis Young) by Wilma Schoen, 1972–74 (Snow 2)
Ramer Sumati, 1947 (Sircar 4)
Ramkinkar, 1975 (Ghatak 4)
Ramona, 1910 (Griffith 2, Pickford 3, Walthall 3, Bitzer 4)
Ramona, 1916 (Crisp 3)
Ramona, 1928 (Baxter W. 3, Del Rio 3, D'Agostino 4)
Ramona, 1936 (King 2, Ameche 3, Carradine 3, Darwell 3, Young, L. 3, Trotti 4)
Ramoneur malgré lui, 1912 (Cohl 2)
Rampage, 1963 (Hathaway 2, Hawkins 3, Mitchum 3, Bernstein 4)
Rampage at Apache Wells. See Ölprinz, 1965
Ramparts We Watch, 1940 (de Rochemont 4)
Ramper, der Tiermensch, 1927 (Wegener 3)
Ramrod, 1947 (De Toth 2, Crisp 3, Lake 3, McCrea 3, Deutsch 4, Head 4)
Ramuntcho, 1938 (Jouvet 3, Rosay 3, Douy 4, Lourié 4)
Ramuntcho, 1958 (Broca 2, Coutard 4, de Beauregard 4)
Ramuru eteruneru, 1935 (Takamine 3)
Ramuz, passage d'un poete, 1959 (Tanner 2)
Ran, 1985 (Muraki 4, Takemitsu 4)
Ran Salu, 1967 (Peries 2)
Ranahansi, 1953 (Sircar 4)
Ranch Chicken, 1911 (Dwan 2)
Ranch Detective, 1912 (Dwan 2)
Ranch Feud, 1913 (Anderson G. 3)
Ranch Girl, 1911 (Dwan 2)
Ranch Girl's Legacy, 1910 (Anderson G. 3)
Ranch Girl's Mistake, 1912 (Anderson G. 3)
Ranch Girl's Partner, 1913 (Anderson G. 3)
Ranch Girl's Trial, 1912 (Anderson G. 3)
Ranch House Blues, 1930 (Burke 3)
Ranch Life in the Great Southwest, 1910 (Mix 3)
Ranch Life on the Range, 1912 (Dwan 2)
Ranch Romance, 1914 (Chaney Lon 3)
Ranch Tenor, 1911 (Dwan 2)
Ranchero's Revenge, 1913 (Griffith 2, Barrymore, L. 3, Carey 3, Bitzer 4)
Rancher's Failing, 1913 (Bosworth 3)
Ranchman's Anniversary, 1912 (Anderson G. 3)
Ranchman's Blunder, 1913 (Anderson G. 3)
Ranchman's Feud, 1910 (Anderson G. 3)
Ranchman's Marathon, 1912 (Dwan 2)
Ranchman's Nerve, 1911 (Dwan 2)
Ranchman's Rival, 1909 (Anderson G. 3)
Ranchman's Son, 1911 (Anderson G. 3)
Ranchman's Trust, 1912 (Anderson G. 3)
Rancho Deluxe, 1974 (Bridges 3, Stanton 3, Fraker 4)

Rancho Grande, 1940 (Autry 3)
Rancho Notorious, 1952 (Lang 2, Dietrich 3, Elam 3, Ferrer, M. 3, Kennedy, A. 3, Friedhofer 4, Taradash 4, Westmore, F. 4)
Rancid Ransom, 1962 (Hanna and Barbera 4)
Rancune. See Besuch, 1964
Randale, 1983 (Domrose 3)
Rande des Schreckens, 1960 (Rasp 3)
Randolph Family. See Dear Octopus, 1943
Random Harvest, 1942 (Franklin 2, Leroy 2, Colman 3, Garson 3, Ruttenberg 4, Stothart 4, Wimperis 4)
Randy Rides Alone, 1934 (Wayne 3, Canutt 4)
Randy Strikes Oil. See Fighting Texans, 1933
Range Boss, 1917 (Van Dyke, W.S. 2)
Range Defenders, 1937 (Canutt 4)
Range Feud, 1931 (Wayne 3)
Range Girl and the Cowboy, 1915 (Mix 3)
Range Law, 1913 (Mix 3)
Range Pals, 1911 (Bosworth 3)
Range Rider, 1910 (Mix 3)
Range War, 1939 (Boyd 3, Head 4, Young, V. 4)
Ranger and the Lady, 1940 (Johnson, N. 3, Rogers, R. 3, Canutt 4)
Ranger of Lonesome Gulf, 1913 (Seitz 4)
Ranger of the Big Pines, 1925 (Van Dyke, W.S. 2)
Ranger's Bride, 1910 (Anderson G. 3)
Rangers of Fortune, 1940 (Wood 2, MacMurray 3, Schildkraut 3, Dreier 4, Head 4)
Rangers of Yellowstone, 1963 (Fonda, H. 3)
Ranger's Romance, 1914 (Mix 3)
Rango, 1931 (Schoedsack 2)
Rangun, 1927 (Hasegawa 3, Tsuburaya 4)
Rank and File, 1971 (Loach 2)
Ranks and People. See Chiny i liudi, 1929
Ranny v lesie, 1964 (Olbrychski 3)
Ranru no hata, 1974 (Yoshimura 2, Shimura 3, Toda 4)
Ransom!, 1956 (Ford, G. 3, Reed, D. 3, Rose 4)
Ransom, 1928 (Walker 4)
Ransom, 1974 (Connery 3, Goldsmith 4, Nykvist 4)
Ransom. See Tengoku to jigoku, 1963
Ransom for a Dead Man, 1971 (Falk 3, Grant, L. 3)
Ranson's Folly, 1926 (Olcott 2, Barthelmess 3)
Rapaces diurnes et nocturnes, 1913 (Burel 4)
Rapa-Nui, 1928 (Andrejew 4)
Rape. See Because of the Cats, 1973
Rape of Czechoslovakia, 1939 (Weiss 2)
Rape of Malaya. See Town Like Alice, 1956
Rape of the Sabines. See Ratto delle Sabine, 1961
Raphael et Cacolet, 1938 (Fernandel 3)
Raphaël le Tatoué, 1938 (Christian-Jaque 2)
Raphaël ou Le Débauché, 1970 (Fabian 3)
Rapid Fire Romance, 1926 (Brown, Harry Joe 4)
Rapid Stream. See Honryu, 1926
Rápido de las 9.15, 1941 (Figueroa 4)
Rapids, 1922 (Astor 3)
Rappa to musume, 1933 (Takamine 3)
Rappel immédiat, 1939 (Von Stroheim 2)
Rappin', 1985 (Golan and Globus 4)
Rapporto segreto, 1967 (Storaro 4)
Rappresaglia, 1973 (Burton 3, Mastroianni 3, Morricone 4, Ponti 4)
Rapt, 1934 (Honegger 4)
Rapt d'enfant par les romanichels. See Volée par les bohémiens, 1904
Rapto, 1953 (Fernández 3, Félix 3, Negrete 3)
Rapture, 1965 (Douglas, M. 3, Delerue 4, Flaiano 4)
Rapunzel, 1897 (Messter 4)
Rare Breed, 1966 (Elam 3, Johnson, B. 3, O'Hara 3, Stewart 3, Clothier 4, Needham 4, Whitlock 4, Williams, J. 4)
Rascal, 1969 (Lanchester 3, Pidgeon 3)
Rascal. See Narazumono, 1956
Rascal of Wolfish Ways, 1915 (Sennett 4)
Rascals, 1938 (Cronjager 4)
Rascel Fifi, 1957 (Cristaldi 4, Di Venanzo 4)
Rascel Marine, 1959 (Cristaldi 4, Di Venanzo 4)
Rashomon, 1950 (Kurosawa 2, Kyo 3, Mifune 3, Mori 3, Shimura 3, Hayasaka 4, Miyagawa 4)

Red Ground. *See* Hakarka ha a dom, 1954
Red Hair, 1928 (Bow 3, Banton 4, Schulberg 4)
Red Headed Monkey, 1950 (Terry 4)
Red Heels. *See* Celimene, Poupee de Montmartre, 1925
Red, Hot, and Blue, 1949 (Hutton 3, Mature 3, Dreier 4, Head 4, Lederer 4)
Red Hot Hoofs, 1926 (Plunkett 4)
Red Hot Hottentots, 1920 (Roach 4)
Red Hot Mama, 1934 (Fleischer, M. and D. 2)
Red Hot Music, 1937 (Terry 4)
Red Hot Rangers, 1947 (Avery 2)
Red Hot Rhythm, 1929 (McCarey 2)
Red Hot Riding Hood, 1943 (Avery 2)
Red Hot Romance, 1913 (Sennett 2, Normand 3)
Red Hot Romance, 1922 (Fleming 2, Emerson 4, Loos 4)
Red Hot Tires, 1925 (Zanuck 4)
Red Hot Tires, 1935 (Astor 3, Grot 4, Schary 4)
Red House, 1947 (Daves 2, Anderson J. 3, Robinson, E. 3, Glennon 4, Rozsa 4)
Red Ink Tragedy, 1912 (Bunny 3)
Red Inn. *See* Auberge rouge, 1951
Red Kimono, 1925 (Arzner 2)
Red Kitchen Murder. *See* House on Greenapple Road, 1970
Red Lane, 1920 (Hersholt 3)
Red Lantern, 1919 (Nazimova 3, Wong 3, Mathis 4)
Red Light, 1949 (Mayo 3, Raft 3, Glennon 4, Tiomkin 4)
Red Light. *See* Spionen fra Tokio, 1910
Red Lights, 1923 (Hersholt 3, Wilson, C. 4)
Red Lily, 1924 (Niblo 2, Beery 3, Novarro 3, Carré 4, Meredyth 4)
Red Line 7000, 1965 (Hawks 2, Caan 3, Edouart 4, Head 4, Krasner 4)
Red Lion. *See* Akage, 1969
Red Mantle. *See* Rode kappe, 1967
Red Margaret, Moonshiner, 1913 (Dwan 2, Chaney Lon 3)
Red Mark, 1928 (Cruze 2, Daves 2)
Red May. *See* Vörös Május, 1968
Red Mill, 1927 (Arbuckle 3, Davies 3, Fazenda 3, Gibbons 4, Marion 4)
Red Mountain, 1951 (Dieterle 2, Cody 3, Ireland 3, Kennedy, A. 3, Ladd 3, Head 4, Lang 4, Wallis 4, Waxman 4)
Red Noses, 1932 (Pitts 3, Roach 4)
Red Pants. *See* Culottes rouges, 1962
Red Partisans. *See* Krasnye partizany, 1924
Red Peacock. *See* Arme Violetta, 1920
Red Peacock. *See* Camille, 1919
Red Pearls, 1930 (Gilliat 4)
Red Planet Mars, 1952 (Balderston 4, Biroc 4, Horner 4, Veiller 4)
Red Pony, 1949 (Aldrich 2, Milestone 2, Calhern 3, Loy 3, Mitchum 3, Copland 4, Gaudio 4)
Red Pony, 1973 (Elam 3, Fonda, H. 3, Johnson, B. 3, O'Hara 3, Goldsmith 4)
Red Psalm. *See* Még kér a nép, 1972
Red Raiders, 1927 (Brown, Harry Joe 4)
Red Riders of Canada, 1928 (Musuraca 4)
Red Riding Hood of the Hills, 1914 (Anderson G. 3)
Red Riding Hoodwinked, 1955 (Freleng 4)
Red River, 1948 (Hawks 2, Brennan 3, Carey 3, Clift 3, Ireland 3, Wayne 3, Winters 3, Chase 4, Schnee 4, Tiomkin 4)
Red River Range, 1938 (Wayne 3)
Red River Valley, 1936 (Autry 3, Eason 4)
Red River Valley, 1941 (Rogers, R. 3)
Red Roses for the Fuhrer. *See* Rose rosse per il Fuhrer, 1968
Red Salute, 1935 (Stanwyck 3, Young, R. 3)
Red Samson. *See* Vörös Sámson, 1917
Red Shoes, 1948 (Powell and Pressburger 2, Basserman 3, Walbrook 3, Cardiff 4)
Red Skies of Montana, 1952 (Hathaway 2, Boone 3, Bronson 3, Hunter 3, Widmark 3, Clarke, C.C. 4, Lemaire 4, Reynolds 4, Wheeler 4)
Red Sky at Morning, 1945 (Finch 3)
Red Sky at Morning, 1971 (Bloom 3, Martin, S. 3, Head 4, Wallis 4, Zsigmond 4)
Red Song. *See* Még kér a nép, 1972
Red Sonja, 1985 (De Laurentiis 4, Morricone 4, Whitlock 4)

Red Sport on the March. *See* Rotsport Marschiert, 1930
Red Stallion, 1947 (Darwell 3, Miller, V. 4)
Red Stallion in the Rockies, 1949 (Alton, J. 4, Canutt 4)
Red Sun. *See* Soleil rouge, 1971
Red Sundown, 1956 (Van Cleef 3, Salter 4)
Red Sword, 1929 (Musuraca 4, Plunkett 4)
Red Tent. *See* Krasnaya palatka, 1969
Red Tent. *See* Tenda rossa, 1969
Red Thorns, 1976 (Nowicki 3)
Red Throwing Knives. *See* Akai shuriken, 1965
Red Tomahawk, 1967 (Arlen 3, Crawford, B. 3, Keel 3)
Red Vase. *See* Kizil vazo, 1961
Red Viper, 1919 (Gilbert 3)
Red Wedding. *See* Noces rouges, 1973
Red White and Blue Blood, 1917 (Bushman 3)
Red Whitsun. *See* Olověný chléb, 1954
Red Widow, 1916 (Barrymore J. 3)
Redbird Wins, 1914 (Eason 4)
Redeemed Claim, 1913 (Anderson G. 3)
Redeemer, 1966 (Raksin 4)
Redeeming Sin, 1925 (Blackton 2, Nazimova 3)
Redeeming Sin, 1929 (Costello, D. 3)
Redemption of David Corson, 1914 (Farnum 3)
Redemption, 1930 (Niblo 2, Adorée 3, Gilbert 3, Adrian 4, Booth 4, Gibbons 4)
Redenzione, 1915 (Gallone 2)
Redes, 1934–35 (Zinnemann 2)
Red-Haired Alibi, 1932 (Temple 3)
Redhead, 1919 (Brady 3)
Redhead and the Cowboy, 1950 (Ford, G. 3, O'Brien, E. 3, Bumstead 4, Cody 4)
Redhead from Manhattan, 1943 (Velez 3)
Redhead from Wyoming, 1953 (O'Hara 3, Hoch 4)
Red-Headed Woman, 1932 (Boyer 3, Harlow 3, Merkel 3, Stone 3, Adrian 4, Lewin 4, Loos 4, Rosson 4)
Redheads on Parade, 1935 (McLeod 2, Lasky 4)
Red-man and the Child, 1908 (Griffith 2)
Redman's View, 1909 (Griffith 2, Bitzer 4)
Redmen and the Renegades, 1956 (Chaney Lon, Jr. 3)
Redneck County, 1979 (Winters 3)
Redoubtable Deceased. *See* Strasnia pokoynik, 1912
Reds, 1981 (Beatty 3, Hackman 3, Keaton 3, Love 3, Nicholson 3, Allen, D. 4, Russell 4, Storaro 4, Sylbert 4)
Redskin, 1929 (Hathaway 2, Johnson, N. 3, Cronjager 4)
Reducing, 1931 (Dressler 3)
Reducing Creme, 1934 (Iwerks 4)
Redwood Forest Trail, 1950 (Darwell 3)
Redwood Sap, 1951 (Lantz 4)
Reed: Insurgent Mexico. *See* Reed: México insurgente, 1973
Reed: México insurgente, 1973 (Leduc 2)
Reel Virginian, 1924 (Sennett 2)
Reflection. *See* Zrcadlení, 1965
Reflection of Fear, 1971 (Shaw 3, Fraker 4, Kovacs 4)
Reflections in a Golden Eye, 1967 (Coppola 2, Huston 2, Brando 3, Morris 3, Taylor, E. 3, Jenkins 4, Stark 4)
Reflections of Murder, 1974 (Weld 3, Leven 4)
Reflections on Black, 1955 (Brakhage 2)
Reflet de Claude Mercoeur, 1923 (Duvivier 2)
Reflexfilm, 1947 (Roos 2)
Reflux—L'Enfer au paradis, 1962 (Gégauff 4)
Reform School, 1939 (Beavers 3)
Reform School Girl, 1957 (Crosby 4)
Reformation. *See* Laereaar, 1914
Reformation of Sierra Smith, 1912 (Dwan 2)
Reformatory, 1938 (Bond 3)
Reformed Outlaw. *See* Scourge of the Desert, 1915
Reformed Santa Claus, 1912 (Costello, D. 3)
Reformed Wolf, 1954 (Terry 4)
Reformer and the Redhead, 1950 (Allyson 3, Frank and Panama 4, Powell, D. 3, Raksin 4, Rose 4)
Reformers, 1916 (Hardy 3)
Reformers or The Lost Art of Minding One's Business, 1913 (Griffith 2)

Refuge, 1923 (Schulberg 4)
Refuge. *See* Zuflucht, 1928
Refuge England, 1959 (Lassally 4)
Refugee, 1918 (Hepworth 2)
Refugee. *See* Three Faces West, 1940
Refugiados en Madrid, 1938 (Figueroa 4)
Regain, 1937 (Pagnol 2, Fernandel 3, Honegger 4)
Regal Cavalcade. *See* Royal Cavalcade, 1935
Regalo de Reyes, 1942 (García 3)
Regard sur la folie, 1961 (Colpi 4)
Regards sur l'Indochine, 1954 (Delerue 4)
Regards sur la Belgique ancienne, 1936 (Storck 2, Jaubert 4)
Régates de San Francisco, 1960 (Autant-Lara 2, Aurenche 4, Bost 4, Douy 4)
Regen, 1929 (Ivens 2, Van Dongen 4)
Regenerates, 1917 (August 4)
Regeneration, 1915 (Walsh 2, Nilsson 3, Reid 3)
Reggie Mixes In, 1916 (Fairbanks, D. 3, Love 3)
Reggimento Royal Cravate, 1922 (Gallone 2)
Régime sans pain, 1985 (de Almeida 4)
Régiment moderne, 1906 (Guy 2)
Regimentstochter, 1928 (Balfour 3)
Regina, 1982 (Gardner 3)
Regina della Scala, 1937 (Vích 4)
Regina di Navarra, 1941 (Gallone 2, Cervi 3, Cortese 3, Amidei 4)
Regina di Saba, 1952 (Cervi 3, Rota 4)
Regina von Emmertiz och Gustav II Adolf, 1910 (Jaenzon 4)
Regine, 1934 (Tschechowa 3)
Regine, 1955 (Herlth 4)
Regine, die Tragödie einer Frau, 1927 (Homolka 3, Junge 4)
Region centrale, 1970–71 (Snow 2)
Registered Nurse, 1934 (Florey 2, Beavers 3, Bondi 3, Daniels 3, Orry-Kelly 4)
Registered Woman. *See* Woman of Experience, 1931
Règle du jeu, 1939 (Becker 2, Renoir 2, Dalio 3, Modot 3, Douy 4, Kosma 4, Lourié 4)
Règlements de comptes, 1962 (Gélin 3)
Règne du jour, 1967 (Perrault 2)
Regreso al silencio, 1967 (Villagra 3)
Regreso de Martín Corona. *See* Enamorado, 1952
Regret. *See* Lítost, 1970
Regrets. *See* Miren, 1963
Regular Fellow, 1925 (Sutherland 2)
Regular Girl, 1919 (Goulding 2, Marion 4)
Regular Pal, 1920 (Roach 4)
Regular Scout, 1926 (Plunkett 4)
Réhabilitation, 1905 (Guy 2)
Rehearsal, 1974 (Dassin 2)
Rehearsal for Murder, 1982 (Preston 3)
Reifende Jugend, 1933 (George, H. 3)
Reifende Jugend, 1955 (Schell, Maximilian 3)
Reigen, 1920 (Oswald 2, Nielsen 3, Veidt 3, Dreier 4, Hoffmann 4)
Reign of Terror, 1949 (Mann 2, Bondi 3, Alton, J. 4, Menzies 4, Wanger 4)
Reign of Terror. *See* Black Book, 1949
Reign of the Vampire, 1970 (Le Grice 2)
Reijin, 1930 (Takamine 3)
Reijin, 1946 (Hara 3)
Reijin no bisho, 1931 (Takamine 3)
Reilly's Wash Day, 1919 (Sennett 2)
Reimei hachigatsu jugo-nichi, 1952 (Kagawa 3)
Reimei izen, 1931 (Kinugasa 2, Hasegawa 3)
Reina del mambo, 1950 (García 3)
Reina del Rio, 1940 (Armendáriz 3)
Reina Santa, 1947 (Rey 3)
Reincarnation. *See* Ujraélok, 1920
Réincarnation de Serge Renaudier, 1920 (Duvivier 2)
Reincarnation of Peter Proud, 1974 (Goldsmith 4, Smith, J.M. 4)
Reindeer People. *See* Sarvtid, 1943
Reine de Biarritz, 1934 (D'Eaubonne 4)
Reine des resquilleuses, 1936 (Brasseur 3)
Reine Margot, 1954 (Gance 2, Moreau 3, Rosay 3, Alekan 4)
Reine verte, 1964 (Carrière 4)

Re-Inforcer, 1949 (Lewis 2)
Reise in die Vergangenheit, 1943 (Tschechowa 3)
Reise ins Licht, 1977 (Fassbinder 2)
Reise nach Wien, 1973 (Kluge 2)
Reise um die Erde in 80 Tagen, 1919 (Oswald 2, Veidt 3)
Reise um die Welt. *See* Reise um die Erde in 80 Tagen, 1919
Reisenrad, 1961 (Schell, Maria 3)
Reiterate the Warning. *See* Varuj!, 1947
. . . reitet fur Deutschland, (Staudte 2)
Reivers, 1969 (McQueen, S. 3, Meredith 3, Ravetch 4, van Runkle 4, Williams, J. 4)
Rejected Woman, 1924 (Lugosi 3, Hunt 4)
Rejedor de Milagros, 1961 (Armendáriz 3)
Rejuvenation, 1912 (Cruze 2)
Reka, 1933 (Stallich 4)
Rekava, 1956 (Peries 2)
Rekolekcje, 1977 (Pszoniak 3)
Rekopis znaleziony w Saragossie, 1964 (Cybulski 3, Tyszkiewicz 3)
Relativity, 1966 (Emshwiller 2)
Relaxe toi, cheri, 1964 (Fernandel 3)
Relay Race. *See* Staféta, 1970
Relentless, 1948 (Young, R. 3, Cronjager 4)
Relentless Outlaw, 1912 (Dwan 2)
Relic of Old Japan, 1915 (Hayakawa 3, Ince 4)
Religieuse. *See* Suzanne Simonin, 1965
Religion and Gun Practice, 1913 (Mix 3)
Relitto, 1960 (Heflin 3, D'Amico 4)
Reluctant Astronaut, 1967 (Whitlock 4)
Reluctant Debutante, 1958 (Minnelli 2, Harrison 3, Lansbury 3, Berman 4, D'Eaubonne 4, Rose 4, Ruttenberg 4)
Reluctant Dragon, 1941 (Disney 2, Ladd 3, Glennon 4, Hoch 4, Iwerks 4)
Reluctant Heroes, 1971 (Oates 3)
Reluctant Millionaire. *See* Muž z neznáma, 1939
Reluctant Pup, 1953 (Terry 4)
Reluctant Saint, 1962 (Dmytryk 2, Schell, Maximilian 3, Rota 4)
Reluctant Widow, 1950 (Dillon 4)
Remains to Be Seen, 1953 (Allyson 3, Calhern 3, Dandridge 3, Johnson, V. 3, Lansbury 3, Rose 4)
Remarkable Andrew, 1942 (Holden 3, Head 4, Trumbo 4, Young, V. 4)
Remarkable Mr. Kipps. *See* Kipps, 1941
Remarkable Mr. Pennypacker, 1959 (Coburn, C. 3, Webb 3, Brackett, C. 4, Krasner 4, Lemaire 4, Reisch 4)
Rembrandt, 1936 (Korda 2, Lanchester 3, Laughton 3, Biro 4, Hornbeck 4, Korda 4, Krasker 4, Périnal 4)
Rembrandt, 1942 (Rohrig 4)
Rembrandt, Etc. and Jane, 1976 (Brakhage 2)
Rembrandt, Painter of Man. *See* Rembrandt, schilder van de mens, 1957
Rembrandt, schilder van de mens, 1957 (Haanstra 2)
Remedial Reading Comprehension, 1970 (Landow 2)
Remedy for Riches, 1940 (Hersholt 3, Alton, J. 4)
Remember?, 1939 (McLeod 2, Ayres 3, Burke 3, Garson 3, Taylor, R. 3, Gibbons 4)
Remember Last Night, 1935 (Whale 2, Young, R. 3, Laemmle 4, Waxman 4)
Remember Mary Magdalene, 1914 (Dwan 2, Chaney Lon 3)
Remember My Name, 1978 (Altman 2, Chaplin 3, Perkins 3)
Remember That Face. *See* Mob, 1951
Remember the Day, 1941 (King 2, Colbert 3, Day 4, Newman 4)
Remember the Night, 1940 (Leisen 2, Sturges, P. 2, Bondi 3, MacMurray 3, Stanwyck 3, Dreier 4, Head 4)
Remember Those Poker Playing Monkeys, 1977 (Rosenblum 4)
Remember When?, 1925 (Capra 2, Sennett 2, Langdon 3, Bruckman 4)
Remember When?, 1974 (Warden 3)
Remembrance, 1922 (Gibbons 4)
Remembrance of Love, 1982 (Douglas, K. 3)
Reminiscences of a Journey to Lithuania, 1972 (Mekas 2)
Remittance Woman, 1923 (Ruggles 2)
Re-mizeraburu, 1950 (Mori 3)
Remodeling Her Husband, 1920 (Gish, D. 3, Gish, L. 3)
Remontons les Champs-Elysées, 1938 (Guitry 2)

Remorques, 1941 (Cayatte 2, Grémillon 2, Cuny 3, Gabin 3, Morgan 3, Prévert 4, Spaak 4, Trauner 4)
Remote Control, 1930 (Gibbons 4)
Removal of Dominik. *See* Przeprowadzka Dominika, 1968
Remuemenage, 1981 (Presle 3)
Ren besked om snavs, 1962 (Carlsen 2)
Renacida, 1981 (Hopper 3)
Renai tokkyu, 1954 (Muraki 4)
Renaissance, 1963 (Borowczyk 4)
Renaissance du Havre, 1948 (Fradetal 4)
Renaissance du rail, 1949 (Dauphin 3)
Renaldo and Clara, 1978 (Stanton 3)
Renard et le corbeau, 1971 (Braunberger 4)
Renate im Quartett, 1939 (Frohlich 3)
Rencontre, 1914 (Feuillade 2)
Rencontre à Paris, 1956 (Matras 4, Spaak 4)
Rencontre avec le Président Ho Chi Minh, 1969 (Ivens 2)
Rencontre imprévue, 1908 (Linders 3)
Rencontres, 1962 (Brasseur 3, Morgan 3)
Rencontres sur le Rhin, 1953 (Colpi 4, Fradetal 4)
Rendezvous, 1923 (Neilan 2)
Rendez-vous, 1931 (Sakall 3)
Rendezvous, 1935 (Howard 2, Dumont 3, Powell, W. 3, Russell, R. 3, Daniels 4)
Rendez-vous, 1961 (Delannoy 2, Girardot 3, Noiret 3, Piccoli 3, Sanders 3, Aurenche 4, Bost 4)
Rendezvous, 1965 (Ghatak 4)
Rendez-vous, 1976 (Lelouch 2)
Rendezvous. *See* Darling, How Could You, 1951
Rendez-vous à Bray, 1971 (Karina 3, Cloquet 4)
Rendez-vous à Paris, 1946 (Dauphin 3)
Rendezvous at Midnight, 1935 (Bellamy 3)
Rendez-vous aux Champs-Elysées, 1937 (Berry 3)
Rendez-vous avec Maurice Chevalier, 1957 (Chevalier 3)
Rendez-vous d'Anna, 1978 (Akerman 2, Cassel 3)
Rendez-vous d'Asnières, 1962 (Delerue 4)
Rendez-vous de Cannes, 1929 (Becker 2)
Rendez-vous de juillet, 1949 (Becker 2, Gélin 3, Modot 3, Renoir 4)
Rendez-vous de minuit, 1961 (Leenhardt 2, Auric 4, Evein 4)
Rendez-vous de Noel, 1961 (Piccoli 3)
Rendezvous in Trieste. *See* Whisky und ein Sofa, 1963
Rendezvous with Annie, 1946 (Dwan 2)
Rendezvous with Dishonor. *See* Appuntamento col disonore, 1970
René la Canne, 1976 (Depardieu 3, Piccoli 3, Morricone 4)
Renegade, 1943 (Crabbe 3)
Renegade Ranger, 1938 (Hayworth 3)
Renegade Trail, 1939 (Boyd 3, Head 4)
Renegades, 1930 (Fleming 2, Baxter W. 3, Loy 3, Lugosi 3, Furthman 4)
Renegade's Heart, 1913 (Dwan 2)
Renegades of the West, 1932 (Steiner 4)
Rennen, 1961 (Kluge 2)
Rennfieber, 1917 (Dupont 2, Oswald 2)
Rennsymphonie, 1928–29 (Richter 2)
Ren-nyo: A Priest and His Mother, 1981 (Kawamoto 4)
Reno, 1939 (Hunt 4, Polglase 4)
Reno Romance, 1910 (Lawrence 3)
Renous, 1935 (Rosay 3)
Rent Collector, 1921 (Laurel 3)
Rent Free, 1922 (Reid 3)
Rent Jumpers, 1915 (Sennett 2)
Rentrée, 1964 (Braunberger 4)
Renunciation, 1909 (Griffith 2, Pickford 3, Bitzer 4)
Repaid, 1914 (Ince 4)
Repas de Bébé, 1895 (Lumière 2)
Repas des fauves, 1964 (Christian-Jaque 2, D'Eaubonne 4, Jeanson 4)
Repas en famille, 1896–97 (Lumière 2)
Repast. *See* Meshi, 1951
Repeat Performance, 1947 (Ireland 3)
Repeater, 1971 (Keach 3)
Repent at Leisure, 1941 (Musuraca 4)
Repérages, 1978 (Seyrig 3, Trintignant 3)
Répétition chez Jean-Louis Barrault, 1964 (Barrault 3)

Répétition dans un cirque, 1903 (Guy 2)
Re-Po Man, 1983 (Stanton 3)
Réponses de femmes, 1975 (Varda 2)
Report, 1963–67 (Conner 2)
Report from Lebiazhe. *See* Iz Lebiazhego soobshchaiut, 1960
Report from Millbrook, 1966 (Mekas 2)
Report from Miss Greer Garson, 1943 (Garson 3)
Report from the Aleutians, 1943 (Huston 2)
Report from the United States on President Theodore Roosevelt, 1907 (Jaenzon 4)
Report on China, 1963 (Massey 3)
Report on the Chairman of a Farmers' Co-Operative. *See* Riport egy TSZ-einokrol, 1960
Report on the Party and the Guests. *See* O slavnosti a hostech, 1966
Report to the Commissioner, 1975 (Gere 3, Bernstein 4)
Reportage sur Orly, 1964 (Godard 2)
Reportage sur 'Paris brûle-t-il?', 1966 (Reichenbach 2)
Reportaje, 1953 (Fernández 2, Armendáriz 3, Del Rio 3, Félix 3, Infante 3, Negrete 3)
Reporter, 1911 (Reid 3)
Reporters, 1981 (Kelly, Gene 3)
Repos du guerrier, 1962 (Vadim 2, Bardot 3)
Représentation au cinéma, 1905 (Linders 3)
Representative. *See* Pratinidhi, 1964
Reprieve. *See* Convicts Four, 1962
Reprieve. *See* Shikko yuyo, 1950
Répris de justice, 1954 (Cortese 3)
Reproduction interdite, 1956 (Girardot 3)
Réprouvés, 1936 (Modot 3, Matras 4)
Republic of Sin. *See* Ambiciosos, 1959
Republicans—The New Breed, 1964 (Leacock 2)
Repulsion, 1965 (Polanski 2, Deneuve 3)
Reputation. *See* Lady with a Past, 1932
Reqiem, 1981 (Fábri 2)
Requiem for a Heavyweight, 1962 (Quinn 3, Rooney 3, Smith, D. 4)
Requiem for a Secret Agent. *See* Requiem per un agent segreto, 1967
Requiem for a Snake. *See* Coplan sauve sa peau, 1967
Requiem for a Village, 1975 (Lassally 4, Lassally 4)
Requiem per un agent segreto, 1967 (Granger 3)
Requiescat, 1966, (Pasolini 2)
Requin, 1929 (Burel 4, Meerson 4)
Requins du pétrole, 1933 (Schufftan 4, Spiegel 4)
Réquisitoire, 1930 (Stradling 4)
Resa dei conti, 1967 (Van Cleef 3, Morricone 4, Solinas 4)
Resa di Titi, 1945 (Brazzi 3)
Resa i natten, 1955 (Dahlbeck 3)
Resa med far, 1968 (Sjoman 2)
Resan bort, 1945 (Sjoberg 2)
Rescate, 1974 (Alvarez 2)
Rescue, 1916 (Chaney Lon 3)
Rescue, 1929 (Brenon 2, Colman 3, Barnes 4, Goldwyn 4, Menzies 4)
Rescued by Her Lions, 1911 (Mix 3)
Rescued by Rover, 1905 (Hepworth 2)
Rescued from an Eagle's Nest, 1907 (Porter 2)
Rescuers, 1977 (Page 3)
Reserved for Ladies. *See* Service for Ladies, 1932
Reshma Aur Shera, 1971 (Bachchan 3)
Residencia para espias, 1967 (Constantine 3)
Resistance, 1976 (Burton 3)
Resourceful Lovers, 1911 (Sennett 2)
Respectable By Proxy, 1920 (Blackton 2)
Respectable Prostitute. *See* P . . . respecteuse, 1952
Response in October. *See* Respuesta de Octubre, 1972
Responsive Eye, 1966 (De Palma 2)
Respuesta de Octubre, 1972 (Guzmán 2)
Rest Resort, 1937 (Lantz 4)
Restaged. *See* Jeffries-Corbett Fight, 1903
Restaurant, 1920 (Fleischer, M. and D. 2)
Restaurant, 1965 (Warhol 2)
Restez diner, 1933 (Fernandel 3)
Restless, 1978 (Welch 3)
Restless. *See* Beloved, 1971
Restless. *See* Carne inquieta, 1952

Restless Breed, 1957 (Dwan 2, Bancroft 3)
Restless Knights, 1935 (Brennan 3, Three Stooges 3)
Restless Night. *See* Unruhige Nacht, 1958
Restless Ones, 1965 (Haller 4)
Restless Sex, 1920 (Davies 3, Shearer 3, Marion 4)
Restless Spirit, 1913 (Dwan 2)
Restless Wives, 1924 (La Cava 2)
Restless Years, 1958 (Wright 3, Anhalt 4, Hunter 4, Laszlo 4)
Restless Youth, 1928 (Walker 4)
Restoration, 1909 (Griffith 2, Pickford 3, Bitzer 4)
Resurrección, 1931 (Velez 3)
Resurrección, 1943 (García 3)
Resurrection, 1909 (Griffith 2, Lawrence 3, Bitzer 4)
Résurrection, 1923 (L'Herbier 2)
Resurrection, 1927 (Del Rio 3)
Resurrection, 1931 (Blasetti 2, Velez 3, Tiomkin 4)
Resurrection, 1980 (Burstyn 3, Jarre 4)
Resurrection. *See* Auferstehung, 1958
Resurrection. *See* Fukkatsu, 1950
Resurrection. *See* Opstandelse, 1914
Resurrection. *See* Vozrozhdennia, 1915
Resurrection of Bronco Billy, 1970 (Carpenter 2)
Resurrection of Love. *See* Ai ni yomigaeru hi, 1923
Resurrection of Zachary Wheeler, 1971 (Dickinson 3)
Resurrezione, 1958 (Castellani 2)
Retapeur de Cervelles, 1911 (Cohl 2)
Retour, 1961 (Goretta 2)
Retour à l'aube, 1938 (Darrieux 3, Burel 4)
Retour à la bien-aimée, 1978 (Ganz 3, Huppert 3)
Retour à la terre, 1938 (Tati 2)
Retour à la terre, 1976 (Perrault 2)
Retour à la vie, 1949 (Cayatte 2, Clouzot 2, Blier 3, Jouvet 3, Cloquet 4, Douy 4, Spaak 4)
Retour à la vie. *See* Achraroumès, 1978
Retour à Marseilles, 1980 (Allio 2)
Retour à New York, 1962 (Reichenbach 2, Braunberger 4)
Retour au bonheur, 1939 (Berry 3)
Retour au paradis, 1935 (Dauphin 3)
Retour d'Afrique, 1973 (Tanner 2)
Retour de Don Camillo, 1953 (Duvivier 2, Cervi 3, Fernandel 3)
Retour de Manivel, 1916 (Feuillade 2)
Retour de Manivelle, 1957 (Blier 3, Gélin 3, Morgan 3, Audiard 4)
Retour de Martin Guerre, 1981 (Baye 3, Depardieu 3, Carrière 4)
Retour des champs, 1899–1900 (Guy 2)
Retour du Capitaine Nemo, 1977 (Ferrer, M. 3)
Retour d'une promenade en mer, 1896-97 (Lumière 2)
Retour Madrid, 1967 (Haanstra 2)
Retrato, 1963 (Solás 2)
Retrato de Teresa, 1979 (Granados 3)
Retreat from Kiska. *See* Taiheiyo Kiseki no sakusen Kisuka, 1965
Retribution, 1913 (Nilsson 3)
Retroscena, 1939 (Blasetti 2, Germi 2, Vích 4)
Retten sejrer, 1917 (Holger-Madsen 2)
Return. *See* Kom tillbaka, 1962
Return Engagement, 1978 (Taylor, E. 3)
Return from the Ashes, 1965 (Schell, Maximilian 3, Thulin 3, Epstein, J. & P. 4)
Return from the Past. *See* Dr. Terror's Gallery of Horrors, 1967
Return from the Sun, 1956 (Lassally 4)
Return from Witch Mountain, 1978 (Davis 3, Schifrin 4)
Return of a Man Called Horse, 1976 (Kershner 2, Ròizman 4, Rosenman 4)
Return of a Stranger, 1961 (Ireland 3)
Return of Bulldog Drummond, 1934 (Richardson 3)
Return of Carol Deane, 1939 (Daniels 3)
Return of Chandu, 1934 (Lugosi 3)
Return of Dr. Fu Manchu, 1930 (Arthur 3, Oland 3)
Return of Dr. X, 1939 (Bogart 3, Westmore, P. 4)
Return of Don Camillo. *See* Retour de Don Camillo, 1953
Return of Draw Egan, 1916 (Hart 3, Sullivan 4)
Return of Eve, 1916 (Van Dyke, W.S. 2)

Return of Frank James, 1940 (Lang 2, Carradine 3, Cooper, J. 3, Fonda, H. 3, Meek 3, Tierney 3, Banton 4, Day 4, MacGowan 4, Zanuck 4)
Return of Helen Redmond, 1914 (Eason 4)
Return of Jack Slade, 1955 (Dickinson 3)
Return of Jesse James, 1950 (Ireland 3, Struss 4)
Return of Marcus Welby, M.D., 1984 (Rosenman 4)
Return of Martin Guerre. *See* Retour de Martin Guerre, 1981
Return of Maxim. *See* Vozvrashcheniye Maksima, 1937
Return of Mr. H. *See* Madmen of Mandoras, 1962
Return of Monte Cristo, 1946 (Siodmak 4)
Return of Nathan Becker. *See* Vosvraschtschenie Neitana Bebera, 1932
Return of Ninja. *See* Zoku shinobi no mono, 1963
Return of October, 1948 (Ford, G. 3, Duning 4, Frank and Panama 4, Maté 4)
Return of Peter Grimm, 1926 (Gaynor 3)
Return of Peter Grimm, 1935 (Barrymore L. 3, Meek 3, MacGowan 4, Plunkett 4, Polglase 4)
Return of Richard Neal, 1915 (Bushman 3)
Return of Sabata. *See* E tornato Sabata . . . hai chiuso, 1972
Return of Sherlock Holmes, 1929 (Brook 3, Crisp 3, Dean 4, Fort 4)
Return of Sophie Lang, 1936 (Milland 3, Head 4)
Return of the Ape Man, 1944 (Carradine 3, Lugosi 3, Katzman 4)
Return of the Bad Men, 1948 (Ryan 3, Scott, R. 3, Hunt 4)
Return of the Cisco Kid, 1939 (Baxter W. 3, Bond 3, Clarke, C.C. 4, Day 4, MacGowan 4, Zanuck 4)
Return of the Dragon, 1971 (Lee, B. 3)
Return of the Edge of the World, 1978 (Powell 2)
Return of the Fly, 1959 (Price 3)
Return of the Golem. *See* It!, 1967
Return of the Gunfighter, 1967 (Taylor, R. 3, Buckner 4, Salter 4)
Return of the Heroes. *See* Aslanlarin donusu, 1966
Return of the Jedi, 1983 (Lucas 2, Ford, H. 3, Jones, J.E. 3, Burtt 4, Edlund 4, Williams, J. 4)
Return of the Lost. *See* Povratak otpisani, 1977
Return of the Mohicans. *See* Last of the Mohicans, 1932
Return of the Pink Panther, 1974 (Edwards 2, Sellers 3, Mancini 4, Unsworth 4)
Return of the Plainsman. *See* Phantom Stockman, 1953
Return of the Prodigal Son. *See* Awdat al Ibn al Dal, 1976
Return of the Prodigal Son. *See* Návrat ztraceného syna, 1966
Return of the Rat, 1929 (Novello 3, Balcon 4)
Return of the Scarlet Pimpernel, 1937 (Mason 3, Biro 4, Hornbeck 4, Wimperis 4)
Return of the Secaucus Seven, 1980 (Sayles 4)
Return of the Seven, 1966 (Fernández 2, Brynner 3, Oates 3, Rey 3, Bernstein 4)
Return of the Soldier, 1982 (Bates 3, Christie 3, Jackson 3, Russell 4)
Return of the Terror, 1934 (Astor 3)
Return of the Texan, 1952 (Daves 2, Boone 3, Brennan 3, Ballard 4, Lemaire 4, Wheeler 4)
Return of the Vampire, 1944 (Lugosi 3)
Return of the Vikings, 1944 (Balcon 4)
Return of Vasili Bortnikov. *See* Vozvrachenia Vassilya Bortnikov, 1953
Return of 'Widow' Pogson's Husband, 1911 (Bunny 3)
Return of Wildfire, 1948 (Arlen 3)
Return of William Marr, 1912 (Bushman 3)
Return Ticket to Madrid. *See* Retour Madrid, 1967
Return to Earth, 1976 (Bellamy 3, Robertson 3)
Return to Fantasy Island, 1978 (Cotten 3)
Return to Glennascaul, 1951 (Welles 2)
Return to Life, 1937 (Kline 2, Maddow 4)
Return to Macon County, 1975 (Nolte 3)
Return to Oz, 1985 (Williamson 3, Murch 4, Vinton 4, Watkin 4)
Return to Paradise, 1953 (Robson 2, Cooper, Gary 3, Hoch 4, Mandell 4, Tiomkin 4)
Return to Peyton Place, 1961 (Astor 3, Chandler 3, Ferrer, J. 3, Weld 3, Clarke, C.C. 4, Smith, J.M. 4, Wald 4, Waxman 4)
Return to Treasure Island, 1954 (Dupont 2)
Return to Witch Mountain, 1978 (Lee, C. 3)
Return to Yesterday, 1940 (Brook 3, Balcon 4)

Reuben in the Subway, 1905 (Bitzer 4)
Reuben, Reuben, 1951 (Fleischer, M. and D. 2)
Reuben, Reuben, 1983 (Epstein, J. & P. 4)
Reunion, 1922 (Fleischer, M. and D. 2)
Reunion, 1936 (Taurog 2, Hersholt 3, McDaniel 3, Summerville 3, Levien 4)
Reunion, 1942 (Dassin 2, Carradine 3, Gardner 3)
Reunion. See Reunion in France, 1942
Reunion at Fairborough, 1985 (Kerr 3, Mitchum 3)
Réunion des artistes, 1963 (Alekan 4)
Reunion in France, 1942 (Mankiewicz 2, Basserman 3, Crawford, J. 3, Wayne 3, Irene 4, Waxman 4)
Reunion in France. See Reunion, 1942
Reunion in Rhythm, 1937 (Roach 4)
Reunion in Vienna, 1933 (Franklin 2, Barrymore J. 3, Merkel 3, Adrian 4, Vajda 4)
Revak, lo schiavo di Cartagine, 1960 (Maté 4)
Revanch, 1930 (Romm 2)
Revanche. See Revanch, 1930
Revanche de Baccarat, 1946 (Burel 4)
Revanche de Roger-la-Honte, 1946 (Cayatte 2, Spaak 4)
Rêve, 1930 (Douy 4)
Rêve, 1975 (Foldès 4)
Rêve blonde, 1931 (Brasseur 3)
Rêve dans la lune, 1904–05 (Zecca 2)
Rêve de Noël, 1900 (Méliès 2)
Rêve de singe, 1978 (Sarde 4)
Rêve d'horloger, 1904 (Méliès 2)
Rêve du chasseur, 1904 (Guy 2)
Rêve du garçon de café. See Songe d'un garçon de café, 1910
Rêve du maître de ballet, 1903 (Méliès 2)
Rêve d'un fumeur d'opium, 1908 (Méliès 2)
Rêve et réalité, 1901 (Zecca, 2)
Réveil, 1925 (Vanel 3)
Réveil du jardinier, 1904 (Guy 2)
Reveille, 1924 (Pearson 2, Balfour 3)
Reveille, das grosse Wecken, 1925 (Krauss 3)
Reveille with Beverly, 1943 (Miller 3, Sinatra 3)
Reveille-toi, chérie, 1960 (Gélin 3)
Revel Son, 1939 (Hornbeck 4)
Revelation, 1913 (Ince 4)
Revelation, 1918 (Nazimova 3)
Reveler, 1914 (Mix 3)
Revenant, 1903 (Méliès 2)
Revenant, 1913 (Feuillade 2)
Revenant, 1946 (Christian-Jaque 2, Jouvet 3, Honegger 4, Jeanson 4)
Revenge, 1918 (Browning 2)
Revenge, 1928 (Del Rio 3)
Revenge, 1955 (Hitchcock 2)
Revenge!, 1971 (Winters 3)
Revenge, 1979 (Wertmüller 2, Loren 3, Delli Colli 4)
Revenge. See Adauchi, 1964
Revenge. See Uomo ritorna, 1946
Revenge at Monte Carlo, 1933 (Eason 4)
Revenge Is Mine. See Rache ist mein, 1918
Revenge of Frankenstein, 1958 (Fisher 2, Sangster 4)
Revenge of Godzilla. See Gojira no gyakushu, 1955
Revenge of Hercules. See Vendetta di Ercole, 1960
Revenge of Milady. See Four Musketeers, 1974
Revenge of Suzenjinobaba. See Adauchi Suzenjinobaba, 1957
Revenge of the Colossal Beasts, (Carpenter 2)
Revenge of the Creature, 1955 (Eastwood 3)
Revenge of the Dead, 1975 (Lee, C. 3)
Revenge of the Jedi, 1983 (Guinness 3)
Revenge of the Ninja, 1983 (Golan and Globus 4)
Revenge of the Pink Panther, 1978 (Edwards 2, Cannon 3, Sellers 3, Mancini 4)
Revenge of the Zombies, 1944 (Carradine 3)
Revenge of Yukinojo. See Yukinojo henge, 1935
Revenge of Yukinojo. See Yukinojo henge, 1963
Revenger. See Osvetnik, 1958
Revengers, 1972 (Borgnine 3, Hayward 3, Holden 3)
Revenue Agent, 1915 (Anderson G. 3)

Revenue Agent, 1950 (Katzman 4)
Revenue Man and the Girl, 1911 (Bitzer 4)
Rêver ou Envol, 1971 (Reichenbach 2)
Reverberation, 1969 (Gehr 2)
Reverse of the Medal, 1923 (Brook 3)
Rêves d'amour, 1947 (Berry 3, Trauner 4)
Rêves de printemps. See Frühlingsrauschen, 1929
Rêves enfantins, 1910 (Cohl 2)
Revêtement des routes, 1923 (Grémillon 2)
Revêtements routiers, 1938 (Leenhardt 2)
Revisor, 1933 (Fric 2, Stallich 4)
Revnost, 1914 (Mozhukin 3)
Revolt, 1916 (Marion 4)
Revolt in Hungary. See Hungarn in Flammen, 1957
Revolt of Mamie Stover, 1956 (Walsh 2, Moorehead 3, Russell, J. 3, Friedhofer 4, Lemaire 4, Wheeler 4)
Revolt of the Mercenaries. See Rivolta dei Mercenari, 1962
Revolt of the Slaves. See Rivolta degli schiavi, 1961
Révolté, 1938 (Clouzot 2)
Revolte, 1969 (Hauff 2)
Révolte, 1971 (Braunberger 4)
Revolte dans la prison, 1930 (Boyer 3)
Révolte des vivants, 1939 (Von Stroheim 2)
Révolte des vivants. See Monde tremblera, 1939
Revolte im Erziehungshaus, 1930 (Baranovskaya 3, Homolka 3, Andrejew 4, Metzner 4)
Révolte sur la Volga. See Vendicatore, 1959
Révoltée, 1947 (L'Herbier 2, Matras 4)
Revolts in the Schoolhouse. See Revolte im Erziehungshaus, 1930
Revolución, 1932 (Figueroa 4)
Revoluční rok 1848, 1949 (Stallich 4)
Revolution Marriage. See Revolutionsbryllup, 1914
Revolutionary, 1970 (Duvall, R. 3, Voight 3)
Revolutionary Romance, 1911 (Guy 2)
Revolutionary Year 1848. See Revoluční rok 1848, 1949
Révolutionnaire, 1965 (Lefebvre 2)
Revolutionsbryllup, 1909 (Blom 2)
Revolutionsbryllup, 1914 (Blom 2)
Revolutionshochzeit, 1927 (Kortner 3)
Revolver, 1976 (Morricone 4)
Revolver. See Blood in the Streets, 1976
Revolver Bill. See 'Bad Buck' of Santa Ynez, 1915
Revue blanche, 1966 (Delerue 4)
Revue Man and the Girl, 1911 (Griffith 2)
Revue Montmartroise, 1932 (Cavalcanti 2)
Reward, 1965 (Fernández 2, Von Sydow 3, Bernstein 4, Boyle 4, Smith, J.M. 4)
Reward of Courage, 1913 (Dwan 2)
Reward of Patience, 1916 (Menjou 3)
Reward of the Faithless, 1917 (Ingram 2)
Reward of Valor, 1912 (Dwan 2)
Reward Unlimited, 1944 (Selznick 4)
Rex, King of the Wild Horses, 1923 (Hardy 3)
Rey de Africa, 1968 (Brazzi 3)
Rey de Mexico, 1955 (Alcoriza 4)
Rey que rabió, 1944 (Rey 3)
Rey se divierte, 1944 (De Fuentes 2)
Rezzou, 1934 (Leenhardt 2)
Rhapsodia del sangre, 1958 (Baarová 3)
Rhapsody, 1954 (Vidor, C. 2, Calhern 3, Gassman 3, Taylor, E. 3, Green, J. 4, Rose 4)
Rhapsody in Blue, 1945 (Basserman 3, Coburn, C. 3, Jolson 3, Grot 4, Haller 4, Koch 4, Lasky 4, Levien 4, Steiner 4)
Rhapsody in Brew, 1933 (Roach 4)
Rhapsody in Rivets, 1941 (Freleng 4)
Rhapsody in Wood, 1947 (Pal 2)
Rhapsody of Happiness, 1947 (Zhao 3)
Rhapsody Rabbit, 1946 (Freleng 4)
Rheinisches Madchen beim rheinischen Wein, 1927 (Reisch 4)
Rhinestone, 1984 (Stallone 3, van Runkle 4)
Rhino!, (Schifrin 4)
Rhinoceros, 1974 (Black 3, Wilder 3, Smith, J.M. 4)
Rhinoceroses. See Nashörner, 1963

hode Island Red, 1968 (Rainer 2)
hodes, 1936 (Homolka 3)
hodes of Africa, 1936 (Huston 3, Balcon 4)
hodes of Africa. See Rhodes, 1936
nubarb, 1951 (Seaton 2, Douglas, P. 3, Martin, S. 3, Ames 4, Head 4)
numba, 1935 (Banton 4)
nyme of Vengeance. See Akuma no temari-uta, 1977
nythm, 1953 (Lye 2)
nythm and Weep, 1946 (Three Stooges 3)
nythm in the Ranks, 1941 (Pal 2)
nythm of a City. See Manniskor i stad, 1947
nythm of the Range, 1936 (Struss 4)
nythm of the Rumba, 1944 (Prinz 4)
nythm of the Saddle, 1938 (Autry 3)
nythm on the Range, 1936 (Taurog 2, Crosby 3, Farmer 3,
    Rogers, R. 3, Glazer 4, Head 4, Mercer 4, Young, V. 4)
nythm on the Range. See Rootin' Tootin' Rhythm, 1937
nythm on the Reservation, 1939 (Fleischer, M. and D. 2)
nythm on the River, 1940 (Crosby 3, Rathbone 3, Head 4,
    Young, V. 4)
nythm on the River. See Freshman Love, 1935
nythm Parade, 1943 (De Carlo 3, Dumont 3, Foreman 4)
nythm Romance. See Some Like It Hot, 1939
nythmes de Paris, 1947–51 (Verneuil 2)
nythmus, 1921-25 (Richter 2)
adom s nami, 1931 (Romm 2)
adom s nami, 1958 (Smoktunovsky 3)
ba, 1976 (Grgić 4)
bolov, 1972 (Grgić 4)
bon o musubu fujin, 1939 (Hayasaka 4)
car bez Bronja, 1966 (Karamitev 3)
cco, 1973 (Kennedy, A. 3)
ce, 1964 (Van Dyke, W. 2)
ce. See Kome, 1957
ce Girl. See Risala, 1956
ce Packages. See Sengoku dawara, 1950
ch and Famous, 1981 (Cukor 2, Bisset 3, Delerue 4)
ch and Respectable. See Ab Morgen sind wir reich und ehrlich, 1977
ch and Strange, 1932 (Hitchcock 2, Reville 4)
ch Are Always With Us, 1932 (Brent 3, Davis 3, Haller 4, Orry-Kelly
    4)
ch Full Life. See Cynthia, 1947
ch Kids, 1979 (Altman 2)
ch Man, Poor Girl, 1938 (Ayres 3, Turner, L. 3, Young, R. 3)
ch Man, Poor Man, 1918 (Barthelmess 3)
ch Man, Poor Man, 1922 (Roach 4)
ch Man's Folly, 1931 (Cromwell 2, Laszlo 4)
ch Man's Son. See Pappas pojke, 1937
ch Men's Wives, 1922 (Schulberg 4, Struss 4)
ch People, 1929 (Bennett C. 3)
ch Revenge, 1910 (Griffith 2, Pickford 3, Bitzer 4)
ch, Young and Deadly. See Platinum High School, 1960
ch, Young, and Pretty, 1951 (Taurog 2, Dalio 3, Darrieux 3,
    Merkel 3, Cahn 4, Pasternak 4)
chard, 1972 (Carradine 3, Rooney 3)
chard III, 1908 (Costello, M. 3, Ince 4)
chard III, 1955 (Baker S. 3, Bloom 3, Gielgud 3, Hardwicke 3,
    Olivier 3, Richardson 3, Dillon 4)
chard Mortensens bevaegelige Maleri, 1944 (Roos 2)
chard Pryor Here and Now, 1983 (Pryor 3)
chard Pryor Is Back, 1979 (Pryor 3)
chard Pryor Live in Concert, 1978 (Pryor 3)
chard Pryor Live on the Sunset Strip, 1982 (Pryor 3, Wexler 4)
chard the Lion Hearted, 1923 (Walker 4)
chard Wagner, 1912 (Messter 4)
chard's Things, 1981 (Ullmann 3, Delerue 4, Raphael 4,
    Young, F. 4)
chelieu, 1914 (Dwan 2, Chaney Lon 3)
cher Than the Earth. See Whistle at Eaton Falls, 1951
ches and Rogues, 1913 (Hardwicke 3)
chest Girl in the World, 1934 (Hopkins, M. 3, McCrea 3, Wray 3,
    Berman 4, Krasna 4, Musuraca 4, Steiner 4)
chest Girl in the World, 1934 (Berman 4)

Richest Man in the World, 1930 (Wood 2)
Richest Man in the World. See Sins of the Children, 1930
Richter und sein Henker, 1975 (Ritt 2, Bisset 3, Dagover 3, Schell,
    Maximilian 3, Shaw 3, Sutherland 3, Voight 3, Goldman, B. 4)
Richter von Zalamea, 1921 (Dagover 3, Warm 4)
Rickety Gin, 1927 (Disney 2)
Rickshaw Man. See Muhomatsu no issho, 1958
Rickshaw Man. See Muhoumatsu no issho, 1943
Rid i natt, 1942 (Molander 2, Borgstrom 3, Dahlbeck 3)
Riddance. See Szabad lélegzet, 1973
Riddle Gawne, 1918 (Chaney Lon 3, Hart 3, August 4)
Riddle of Lumen, 1972 (Brakhage 2)
Riddle of the Sands, 1978 (York, M. 3)
Riddle Rider, 1924 (Canutt 4)
Ride a Crooked Mile, 1938 (Farmer 3, Head 4)
Ride a Crooked Trail, 1958 (Matthau 3, Murphy 3, Chase 4)
Ride a Northbound Horse, 1969 (Elam 3, Johnson, B. 3)
Ride a Wild Pony, 1976 (Addison 4, Cardiff 4)
Ride Back, 1957 (Aldrich 2, Quinn 3, Biroc 4)
Ride Beyond Vengeance, 1966 (Blondell 3, Grahame 3)
Ride Clear of Diablo, 1953 (Duryea 3, Elam 3, Murphy 3, Boyle 4)
Ride 'em Cowboy!, 1942 (Abbott and Costello 3, Cody 3)
Ride 'em Plow Boy!, 1928 (Disney 2)
Ride for a Bride, 1913 (Sennett 2, Arbuckle 3)
Ride for Your Life, 1924 (Miller, V. 4)
Ride Him Cowboy, 1932 (Walthall 3, Wayne 3, Krasner 4, McCord 4)
Ride in the Whirlwind, 1965 (Corman 4)
Ride, Kelly, Ride, 1941 (Miller, V. 4)
Ride Lonesome, 1959 (Boetticher 2, Coburn, J. 3, Van Cleef 3, Brown,
    Harry Joe 4)
Ride On, Vaquero, 1941 (Raksin 4)
Ride Out for Revenge, 1957 (Grahame 3, Crosby 4)
Ride, Ranger, Ride, 1936 (Autry 3)
Ride, Tenderfoot, Ride, 1940 (Autry 3)
Ride the High Country, 1962 (Peckinpah 2, McCrea 3, Oates 3,
    Scott, R. 3, Ballard 4)
Ride the Pink Horse, 1947 (Montgomery 3, Boyle 4, Harrison 4,
    Hecht 4, Lederer 4)
Ride the Whirlwind, 1966 (Nicholson 3)
Ride the Wild Surf, 1964 (Biroc 4)
Ride Tonight!. See Rid i natt, 1942
Ride, Vaquero!, 1953 (Elam 3, Gardner 3, Keel 3, Quinn 3,
    Taylor, R. 3, Kaper 4, Plunkett 4, Surtees 4)
Rideau cramoisi, 1953 (Astruc 2, Aimée 3, Cuny 3, Schufftan 4)
Rideau rouge, 1952 (Brasseur 3, Simon, M. 3, Kosma 4)
Rideaux blancs, 1965 (Franju 2)
Rider of Death Valley, 1932 (Mix 3)
Rider of the Law, 1919 (Ford, J. 2, Carey 3)
Rider of the Plains. See War Paint, 1926
Rider on the Rain. See Passager de la pluie, 1969
Ridere, ridere, ridere, 1954 (Tognazzi 3, Vitti 3)
Riders from Tucson, 1950 (Musuraca 4)
Riders in the Sky, 1949 (Autry 3)
Riders of Death Valley, 1941 (Chaney Lon, Jr. 3)
Riders of Destiny, 1933 (Wayne 3)
Riders of the Dark, 1927 (Van Dyke, W.S. 2)
Riders of the Dawn, 1937 (Canutt 4)
Riders of the Deadline, 1943 (Boyd 3, Mitchum 3)
Riders of the Golden Gulch, 1932 (Canutt 4)
Riders of the Kitchen Range, 1925 (Roach 4)
Riders of the Plains, 1924 (Karloff 3)
Riders of the Purple Cows, 1924 (Sennett 2)
Riders of the Purple Sage, 1918 (Farnum 3)
Riders of the Purple Sage, 1925 (Mix 3, Oland 3)
Riders of the Purple Sage, 1931 (Carré 4)
Riders of the Purple Sage, 1941 (Day 4)
Riders of the Range, 1949 (Hunt 4)
Riders of the Rockies, 1937 (Canutt 4)
Riders of the Storm, 1929 (Canutt 4)
Riders of the Timberline, 1941 (Boyd 3, Nilsson 3)
Riders of the Whistling Pines, 1949 (Autry 3)
Riders of the Whistling Skull, 1937 (Canutt 4)
Riders of Vengeance, 1919 (Ford, J. 2, Carey 3)

Riders to the Stars, 1953 (Marshall 3, Cortez 4, Siodmak 4)
Ridi, pagliaccio!, 1941 (Stallich 4)
Ridicule and Tears. See Löjen och tårar, 1913
Ridin' a Rainbow, 1941 (Autry 3)
Ridin' Down the Canyon, 1942 (Rogers, R. 3)
Ridin' for Love, 1926 (Wyler 2)
Ridin' Kid from Powder River, 1924 (Miller, V. 4)
Ridin' Law, 1930 (Canutt 4)
Ridin' Mad, 1924 (Canutt 4)
Ridin' Romeo, 1921 (Mix 3)
Ridin' Rowdy, 1927 (Brennan 3)
Ridin' Wild, 1922 (Miller, V. 4)
Ridin' Wild, 1925 (Miller, V. 4)
Riding de Trail, 1911 (Carey 3)
Riding for a Fall. See Manèges, 1950
Riding for Fame, 1928 (Summerville 3, Eason 4)
Riding High, 1943 (Lamour 3, Powell, D. 3, Dreier 4, Head 4, Struss 4, Young, V. 4)
Riding High, 1950 (Capra 2, Bond 3, Crosby 3, Hardy 3, Muse 3, Dreier 4, Head 4, Hornbeck 4, Laszlo 4, Young, V. 4)
Riding on Air, 1937 (Brown 3)
Riding Shotgun, 1954 (De Toth 2, Bronson 3, Scott, R. 3, Glennon 4)
Riding the Rails, 1938 (Fleischer, M. and D. 2)
Rien ne va plus, 1979 (Presle 3)
Rien n'est impossible à l'homme, 1910 (Cohl 2)
Rien que les heures, 1925 (Cavalcanti 2, Braunberger 4)
Riff Raff Girls. See Du Rififi chez les femmes, 1959
Riffraff, 1935 (Harlow 3, Merkel 3, Rooney 3, Tracy 3, Loos 4, Mahin 4, Marion 4)
Riff-Raff, 1947 (O'Brien, P. 3)
Riff-Raff. See Golfos, 1962
Rififi. See Du Rififi chez les hommes, 1955
Rififi à Tokyo, 1962 (Vanel 3, Delerue 4)
Rififi in Paris. See Du Rififi à Paname, 1966
Rififi in Tokyo. See Rififi à Tokyo, 1962
Right Bed, 1929 (Horton 3)
Right Cross, 1950 (Sturges, J. 2, Allyson 3, Barrymore L. 3, Monroe 3, Powell, D. 3, Raksin 4, Schnee 4)
Right Girl, 1910 (Lawrence 3)
Right Name But the Wrong Man, 1911 (Bosworth 3)
Right of Love, 1910 (Lawrence 3)
Right óf Man. See Propre de l'homme, 1960
Right of Way, 1914 (Talmadge, N. 3)
Right of Way, 1920 (Schenck 4)
Right of Way, 1931 (Young, L. 3)
Right of Way, 1983 (Davis 3, Stewart 3)
Right of Youth. See Ungdommens Ret, 1911
Right Sort. See Ugolok, 1916
Right That Failed, 1922 (Coffee 4)
Right to Happiness, 1915 (Eason 4)
Right to Kill, 1985 (Forrest 3)
Right to Lie, 1919 (Murfin 4)
Right to Live, 1935 (Brent 3. Carroll L. 3)
Right to Love, 1920 (Miller, A. 4)
Right to Love, 1930 (Lukas 3, Akins 4, Lang 4)
Right to Love. See Droit à aimer, 1972
Right to Love. See Ratten att Älska, 1956
Right to Love. See Recht auf Liebe, 1939
Right to Romance, 1933 (Young, R. 3, Buchman 4, Cooper 4, Plunkett 4, Steiner 4)
Right to the Heart, 1942 (Wilde 3, Miller, V. 4)
Right Way, 1913 (Bushman 3)
Right Way, 1921 (Olcott 2)
Rigolboche, 1936 (Christian-Jaque 2, Berry 3)
Rigoletto, 1922 (Brook 3)
Rigoletto, 1947 (Gallone 2)
Rika, the Mixed-Blood Girl. See Konketsuji Rika, 1973
Ríkadla, 1949 (Hofman 4)
Rikigun daikoshin, 1932 (Hasegawa 3)
Riki-Tiki-Tavi, 1973 (Batalov 3)
Riki-Tiki-Tavy, 1975 (Jones 2)
Riku no ooja, 1929 (Tanaka 3)
Rikugun, 1944 (Kinoshita 2, Tanaka 3)

Riley and Schultz, 1912 (Sennett 2)
Riley the Cop, 1928 (Ford, J. 2, Fazenda 3, Clarke, C.C. 4)
Rim of the Canyon, 1949 (Autry 3)
Rimal min Zahab, 1966 (Chahine 2)
Rime of the Ancient Mariner, 1968 (Burton 3)
Rimes, 1954 (Alexeieff and Parker 2)
Rimfire, 1949 (Eason 4)
Rimrock Jones, 1918 (Crisp 3, Reid 3)
Rimsky-Korsakov, 1952 (Cherkassov 3)
Rinaldo Rinaldina, 1927, (Albers 3)
Rincón cerca del cielo, 1952 (Infante 3)
Rinconcito madrileno, 1936 (Clothier 4)
Ring, 1912–13 (White 3)
Ring, 1927 (Hitchcock 2, Reville 4)
Ring, 1952 (Elam 3)
Ring. See Prstýnek, 1944
Ring der Giuditta Foscari, 1917 (Jannings 3)
Ring of a Spanish Grandee, 1912 (Cruze 2)
Ring of Bright Water, 1969 (Strick 2)
Ring of Fear, 1954 (O'Brien, P. 3)
Ring of Fire, 1961 (Clothier 4)
Ring of Steel, 1942 (Tracy 3, Kanin 4)
Ring Seller. See Baya el Khawatim, 1965
Ring Up the Curtain, 1919 (Daniels 3, Lloyd 3, Roach 4)
Ring Up the Curtain. See Broadway to Hollywood, 1933
Ring-a-Ding Rhythm. See It's Trad, Dad, 1962
Ringards, 1978 (Lai 4)
Ringer, 1931 (Balcon 4)
Ringer, 1952 (Zetterling 2, Arnold 4)
Ringo-en no shojo, 1952 (Yamamura 3)
Rings Around the World, 1966 (Ameche 3)
Rings on Her Fingers, 1942 (Mamoulian 2, Fonda, H. 3, Tierney 3, Day 4, Newman 4)
Ringside Maisie, 1941 (Sothern 3)
Rink, 1916 (Bacon 2, Chaplin 2, Purviance 3)
Rinty of the Desert, 1928 (Blanke 4)
Rinzo shusse-tabi, 1934 (Hasegawa 3)
Rio, 1939 (Negulesco 2, Cummings 3, McLaglen 4, Rathbone 3)
Rio Abajo, 1983 (Borau 2)
Rio Blanco, 1967 (Del Rio 3)
Rio Bravo, 1959 (Hawks 2, Bond 3, Brennan 3, Dickinson 3, Martin, D. 3, Wayne 3, Brackett, L. 4, Furthman 4, Tiomkin 4)
Rio Conchos, 1964 (Boone 3, O'Brien, E. 3, Goldsmith 4, Smith, J.M. 4)
Rio das Mortes, 1970 (Fassbinder 2, Schygulla 3)
Rio de Machado de Assis, 1964 (Pereira Dos Santos 2)
Río Escondido, 1947 (Fernández 2, Félix 3, Figueroa 4)
Rio, 40 Degrees. See Rio quarenta graus, 1955
Rio Grande, 1938 (Ballard 4)
Rio Grande, 1950 (Ford, J. 2, Johnson, B. 3, McLaglen 3, O'Hara 3, Wayne 3, Cooper 4, Glennon 4, Young, V. 4)
Rio Grande Patrol, 1950 (Hunt 4)
Rio Grande Romance, 1936 (Katzman 4)
Rio Hondo. See Comancho blanco, 1969
Rio Lobo, 1970 (Hawks 2, Elam 3, Wayne 3, Brackett, L. 4, Canutt 4, Clothier 4, Goldsmith 4)
Rio Negro, 1976 (Villagra 3)
Rio quarenta graus, 1955 (Pereira Dos Santos 2)
Rio Rita, 1929 (Daniels 3, Clothier 4, Steiner 4)
Rio Rita, 1942 (Abbott and Costello 3, Grayson 3, Berman 4, Stothart 4)
Rio '70, 1970 (Sanders 3)
Rio y la muerte, 1954 (Buñuel 2, Alcoriza 4)
Rio, zona norte, 1957 (Pereira Dos Santos 2)
Rio, zone nord. See Rio zona norte, 1957
Riom le beau, 1966 (Coutard 4)
Riot, 1913 (Arbuckle 2)
Riot, 1968 (Hackman 3)
Riot in Cell Block 11, 1954 (Siegel 2, Wanger 4)
Riot on Sunset Strip, 1967 (Katzman 4)
Rip & Stitch, Tailors, 1919 (Sennett 2, Fazenda 3)
Rip, Sew, and Stitch, 1953 (Three Stooges 3)
Rip Van Winkle, 1914 (Polito 4)

Rip Van Winkle, 1934 (Terry 4)
Rip Van Winkle, 1978 (Vinton 4)
Ripe Earth, 1938 (Boulting 2)
Riport egy TSZ-elnokrol, 1960 (Mészáros 2)
Ripoux, 1984 (Noiret 3, Lai 4)
Ripped-Off. See Uomo dalle pelle dura, 1971
Rip's Dream. See Légende de Rip van Winkle, 1905
Ripstitch the Tailor, 1930 (Crosby 3)
Riptide, 1934 (Goulding 2, Brennan 3, Marshall 3, Montgomery 3,
    Shearer 3, Adrian 4, Booth 4, Brown, N. 4, Freed 4, Stothart 4)
Riptide. See Si jolie petite plage, 1949
Risaia, 1965 (Ponti 4)
Risate di gioia, 1960 (Monicelli 2, Magnani 3, Age and Scarpelli 4,
    D'Amico 4, Gherardi 4)
Riscatto, 1953 (Flaiano 4, Pinelli 4)
Rise Against the Sword. See Abare Goemon, 1966
Rise and Fall of Emily Sprod, 1964 (Godfrey 4)
Rise and Fall of Horatio. See Horacijev uspon i pad, 1969
Rise and Fall of Legs Diamond, 1960 (Boetticher 2, Cannon 3, Oates 3,
    Ballard 4, Rosenman 4)
Rise and Fall of the Third Reich, 1968 (Schifrin 4)
Rise and Rise of Casanova. See Casanova & Co., 1977
Rise and Rise of Michael Rimmer, 1970 (Dillon 4)
Rise and Shine, 1941 (Dwan 2, Brennan 3, Darnell 3, Meek 3,
    Cronjager 4, Day 4, Mankiewicz 4, Pan 4)
Rise of Catherine the Great. See Catherine the Great, 1934
Rise of Helga. See Susan Lenox, Her Fall and Rise, 1931
Rise of Jenny Cushing, 1917 (Tourneur, M. 2, Carré 4)
Rise of Louis XIV. See Prise de pouvoir par Louis XIV, 1966
Rise of Michael Rimmer, 1970 (Pinter 4)
Rise of Susan, 1916 (Oland 3, Marion 4)
Risin' Comet, 1925 (Canutt 4)
Rising of the Moon, 1957 (Ford, J. 2, Cusack 3, Krasker 4)
Risk. See Suspect, 1960
Risky Business, 1926 (Pitts 3)
Risky Business, 1939 (Cortez 4)
Riso amaro, 1948 (De Santis 2, Gassman 3, Mangano 3, De
    Laurentiis 4)
Riso no otto, 1933 (Takamine 3)
Risque de vivre, 1979 (Braunberger 4)
Risques du métier, 1967 (Cayatte 2)
Risveglio di una città, 1933 (Zampa 2)
Rita. See Lettere di una novizia, 1960
Rita Hayworth, The Love Goddess, 1983 (Schifrin 4)
Rita la zanzara, 1966 (Wertmüller 2, Giannini 3)
Rita the Mosquito. See Rita la zanzara, 1966
Rite. See Riten, 1969
Riten, 1969 (Bergman 2, Bjornstrand 3, Thulin 3, Nykvist 4)
Ritorna Za-la-mort. See Fumeria d'oppio, 1947
Ritorno, 1940 (Brazzi 3)
Ritorno di Clint il solitario, 1972 (Kinski 3, Morricone 4)
Ritorno di Don Camillo. See Retour de Don Camillo, 1953
Ritratto dell'amata, 1912 (Bertini 3)
Ritter der Nacht, 1928 (Dieterle 2)
Rittmeister Wronski, 1954 (Tschechowa 3)
Ritual. See Riten, 1969
Ritual in Transfigured Time, 1946 (Deren 2, Hammid 2)
Ritual of Evil, 1970 (Baxter A. 3, Jourdan 3)
Ritz, 1976 (Lester 2, Love 3)
Ritzy, 1927 (Lang 4, Schulberg 4)
Riusciranno i nostri eroi a trovare l'amico misteriosamente
    scomparso in Africa?, 1968 (Scola 2, Blier 3, Manfredi 3,
    Sordi 3, Age and Scarpelli 4)
Rival. See Rivale, 1974
Rival Brother's Patriotism, 1911 (White 3)
Rival Demon. See Rural Demon, 1914
Rival Mashers. See Those Love Pangs, 1914
Rival Romeos, 1928 (Disney 2)
Rival Romeos, 1951 (Terry 4)
Rival Servants. See To Tjenestepiger, 1910
Rival Stage Lines, 1914 (Mix 3)
Rival Suitors. See Fatal Mallet, 1914
Rival World, 1955 (Haanstra 2)

Rivale, 1974 (Andersson B. 3)
Rivale dell'Imperatrice. See Shadow of the Eagle, 1950
Rivalen im Weltrekord, 1930 (Metzner 4)
Rivali, 1962 (Dragić 4)
Rivalry and War, 1914 (Beery 3)
Rivals, 1912 (Sennett 2, Bosworth 3, Normand 3)
Rivals, 1915 (Franklin 2, Nilsson 3)
Rivals. See Rivali, 1962
Rive gauche, 1931 (d'Arrast 2, Korda 2)
Rive Gauche. See Manner um Lucie, 1931
Rivelazione, 1956 (Blier 3)
River, 1929 (Borzage 2)
River, 1937 (Lorentz 2, Van Dyke, W. 2, Crosby 4)
River, 1951 (Renoir 2, Lourié 4, Renoir 4)
River, 1984 (Gibson 3, Spacek 3, Ondricek 4, Williams, J. 4, Zsigmond
    4)
River. See Reka, 1933
River and Death. See Rio y la muerte, 1954
River Ann. See Roadhouse Nights, 1930
River Beat, 1954 (Green, G. 4)
River Called Titas. See Tities Ekti Nadir Naam, 1973
River Fuefuki. See Fuefuki-gawa, 1960
River Gang, 1945 (Salter 4)
River Inn. See Roadhouse Nights, 1930
River Ki. See Kinokawa, 1966
River Lady, 1948 (De Carlo 3, Duryea 3)
River Melodies, 1948 (Fleischer, M. and D. 2)
River Music, 1961 (Hammid 2)
River Niger, 1976 (Gossett 3, Jones, J.E. 3)
River of Gold, 1971 (Milland 3)
River of Life and Death. See Reka života a smrti, 1939–40
River of Mystery, 1969 (O'Brien, E. 3)
River of No Return, 1954 (Preminger 2, Mitchum 3, Monroe 3, Cole 4,
    La Shelle 4, Lemaire 4, Wheeler 4)
River of Romance, 1916 (Gaudio 4)
River of Romance, 1929 (Cukor 2, Beery 3, Walthall 3)
River of Tears. See Namida-gawa, 1967
River Pirate, 1928 (Howard 2, Crisp 3, McLaglen 3, Carré 4)
River Pirates, 1905 (Bitzer 4)
River Solo Flows. See Bungawan Solo, 1951
River Speaks, 1957 (Lassally 4)
River Thames—Yesterday, 1937–40 (Cardiff 4)
River without Bridges. See Hashi no nai kawa, 1969–70
River Wolves, 1934 (Pearson 2, Mills 3)
River Woman, 1928 (Robinson 4)
Rivers and Landscapes. See Swiss Trip, 1934
River's Edge, 1957 (Dwan 2, Milland 3, Quinn 3, Polglase 4)
River's End, 1920 (Neilan 2, Stone 3, Carré 4)
River's End, 1930 (Curtiz 2, Pitts 3, Carré 4)
Riverside Murder, 1935 (Sim 3)
Rivolta degli schiavi, 1961 (Cervi 3, Rey 3)
Rivolta dei Mercenari, 1962 (Mayo 3)
Rivoluzione sessuale, 1968 (Argento 4)
Road Agent, 1941 (Salter 4)
Road Agent, 1952 (Hunt 4)
Road Agents, 1909 (Anderson G. 3)
Road Agent's Love, 1912 (Anderson G. 3)
Road Back, 1937 (Whale 2, Fazenda 3, Summerville 3, Tiomkin 4)
Road Builder, 1971 (Neal 3)
Road Builder. See Night Digger, 1971
Road Demon, 1921 (Mix 3)
Road Demon, 1938 (Chaney Lon, Jr. 3, Robinson, B. 3)
Road for Youth. See Droga mlodych, 1936
Road Gang, 1936 (Trumbo 4)
Road House, 1928 (Brown 3)
Road House, 1934 (Holloway 3, Balcon 4, Junge 4)
Road House, 1948 (Negulesco 2, Lupino 3, Widmark 3, Wilde 3,
    La Shelle 4, Lemaire 4)
Road I Travel with You. See Kimi to iku michi, 1936
Road in India, 1937–40 (Cardiff 4)
Road Movie, 1974 (Strick 2)
Road of the Dragon, 1932 (Cronjager 4)
Road of Truth, 1956 (Gerasimov 2)

Road Show, 1941 (Langdon 3, Menjou 3, Carmichael 4, Roach 4)
Road Show. See Chasing Rainbows, 1930
Road Through the Dark, 1918 (Edeson 4)
Road to Andalay, 1964 (Freleng 4)
Road to Arcady, 1921 (Haller 4)
Road to Bali, 1952 (Hope 3, Lamour 3, Martin, D. 3, Russell, J. 3, Head 4)
Road to Corinth. See Route de Corinthe, 1967
Road to Denver, 1955 (Cobb 3, Van Cleef 3)
Road to Frisco. See They Drive By Night, 1940
Road to Glory, 1926 (Hawks 2, Lombard 3, August 4)
Road to Glory, 1936 (Hawks 2, Barrymore L. 3, Baxter W. 3, March 3, Johnson 4, Toland 4, Zanuck 4)
Road to God. See Kami e no michi, 1928
Road to Happiness. See Goldene Schmetterling, 1926
Road to Happiness. See Lykken, 1916
Road to Heaven. See Himlaspelet, 1942
Road to Hollywood, 1946 (Crosby 3)
Road to Hong Kong, 1962 (Crosby 3, Hope 3, Lamour 3, Martin, D. 3, Niven 3, Sellers 3, Sinatra 3, Cahn 4, Fisher 4, Frank and Panama 4)
Road to Hope, 1951 (Ladd 3)
Road to Mandalay, 1926 (Browning 2, Chaney Lon 3, Walthall 3, Gibbons 4, Gillespie 4, Mankiewicz 4)
Road to Morocco, 1942 (Crosby 3, De Carlo 3, Hope 3, Lamour 3, Quinn 3, Dreier 4, Head 4, Young, V. 4)
Road to Nashville, 1966 (Arlen 3, Zsigmond 4)
Road to Paradise, 1930 (Young, L. 3, Seitz 4)
Road to Peace, 1949 (Crosby 3)
Road to Peace. See Béke utja, 1917
Road to Plaindale, 1914 (Loos 4, Loos 4)
Road to Reno, 1931 (Struss 4)
Road to Reno, 1938 (Scott, R. 3)
Road to Rio, 1947 (McLeod 2, Crosby 3, Hope 3, Lamour 3, Dreier 4, Head 4, Laszlo 4)
Road to Romance, 1927 (Novarro 3, Day 4, Gibbons 4)
Road to Ruin, 1913 (Dwan 2)
Road to Salina, 1971 (Hayworth 3)
Road to Singapore, 1931 (Calhern 3, Powell, W. 3)
Road to Singapore, 1940 (Coburn, C. 3, Crosby 3, Hope 3, Lamour 3, Quinn 3, Dreier 4, Head 4, Prinz 4, Young, V. 4)
Road to Success, 1913 (Dwan 2)
Road to the Barricades. See Cesta k barikádám, 1945
Road to the Heart, 1909 (Griffith 2, Lawrence 3)
Road to the Wall, 1962 (Cagney 3)
Road to Utopia, 1945 (Crosby 3, Hope 3, Lamour 3, Dreier 4, Frank and Panama 4, Head 4)
Road to Victory, 1944 (Crosby 3, Grant, C. 3, Sinatra 3)
Road to Yesterday, 1925 (DeMille 2, Boyd 3, Cody 3, Schildkraut 3, Grot 4, Macpherson 4)
Road to Zanzibar, 1941 (Crosby 3, Hope 3, Johnson, N. 3, Lamour 3, Merkel 3, Head 4, Prinz 4, Young, V. 4)
Road Warrior. See Mad Max 2, 1981
Roadblock, 1951 (Musuraca 4)
Roadgames, 1981 (Keach 3)
Roadhouse Murder, 1932 (Hunt 4)
Roadhouse Nights, 1930 (Durante 3, Fort 4, Hecht 4)
Roadhouse Queen, 1933 (Sennett 2)
Roads Across Britain, 1937 (Alwyn 4)
Roads to the South. See Routes du sud, 1978
Roadside Impressario, 1917 (Crisp 3)
Roadside Inn. See Hôtel des voyageurs de commerce, 1906
Roadways, 1937 (Cavalcanti 2)
Roamin' Holiday, 1937 (Roach 4)
Roamin' Vandals, 1934 (Roach 4)
Roaming Lady, 1936 (Bellamy 3, Wray 3)
Roaming Ranch. See Roaring Ranch, 1930
Roaming Romeo, 1933 (Langdon 3)
Roar, 1981 (Hedren 3)
Roar of the Dragon, 1932 (Ruggles 2, Horton 3, Pitts 3, Cooper 4, Selznick 4, Steiner 4)
Roar of the Iron Horse, 1951 (Katzman 4)
Roarin' Lead, 1936 (Canutt 4)

Roaring Rails, 1924 (Carey 3, Polito 4, Stromberg 4)
Roaring Ranch, 1930 (Eason 4)
Roaring Road, 1919 (Cruze 2, Reid 3)
Roaring Twenties, 1939 (Rossen 2, Walsh 2, Bogart 3, Cagney 3, Haller 4, Wald 4, Wallis 4)
Roaring Years. See Anni ruggenti, 1962
Roast-Beef and Movies, 1934 (Tiomkin 4)
Rob 'em Good, 1923 (Bruckman 4, Stromberg 4)
Rob Roy, The Highland Rogue, 1953 (Disney 2, Dillon 4, Ellenshaw 4, Green, G. 4)
Robber Spider. See Rovedderkoppen, 1916
Robber Symphony, 1935 (Wiene 2, Rosay 3, Metzner 4)
Robbers of the Sacred Mountain. See Falcon's Gold, 1982
Robber's Roost, 1933 (O'Sullivan 3, Nichols 4)
Robbers' Roost, 1955 (Boone 3)
Robber's Tale. See Loupežnická pohádka, 1964
Robbery, 1967 (Yates 2, Baker S. 3)
Robbery Under Arms, 1957 (Finch 3)
Robbing Cleopatra's Tomb. See Cléopâtre, 1899
Robby the Coward, 1911 (Griffith 2)
Robe, 1953 (Boone 3, Burton 3, Mature 3, Simmons 3, Dunne 4, Lemaire 4, Newman 4, Shamroy 4, Wheeler 4, Zanuck 4)
Robe. See Bhumika, 1978
Robert et Robert, 1978 (Lelouch 2, Denner 3, Morgan 3, Lai 4)
Robert Frost: A Lover's Quarrel with the World, 1963 (Clarke 2)
Robert Koch, 1939 (Jannings 3, Krauss 3, Wagner 4)
Robert Macaire et Bertrand, 1904 (Guy 2)
Robert McBryde and Robert Colquhoun, untitled, 1959 (Russell 2)
Robert und Bertram, 1915 (Lubitsch 2)
Roberta, 1935 (Astaire 3, Ball 3, Dunne 3, Rogers, G. 3, Scott, R. 3, Berman 4, Cronjager 4, Murfin 4, Pan 4, Polglase 4, Steiner 4)
Robert's Lesson, 1912–13 (White 3)
Robin and Marian, 1976 (Lester 2, Connery 3, Hepburn, A. 3, Shaw 3, Williamson 3, Barry 4, Watkin 4)
Robin and the Seven Hoods, 1964 (Crosby 3, Falk 3, Martin, D. 3, Robinson, E. 3, Sinatra 3, Cahn 4, Daniels 4)
Robin Hood, 1922 (Dwan 2, Florey 2, Beery 3, Fairbanks, D. 3, Buckland 4, Edeson 4, Florey 4, Grot 4, Menzies 4)
Robin Hood, 1933 (Terry 4)
Robin Hood, 1976 (Ustinov 3, Mercer 4)
Robin Hood and His Merrie Men, 1952 (Dillon 4)
Robin Hood Daffy, 1958 (Jones 2)
Robin Hood in an Arrow Escape, 1936 (Terry 4)
Robin Hood, Jr., 1934 (Iwerks 4)
Robin Hood Makes Good, 1939 (Jones 2)
Robin Hood of El Dorado, 1936 (Wellman 2, Baxter W. 3, Stothart 4)
Robin Hood of Texas, 1947 (Autry 3)
Robin Hood of the Pecos, 1941 (Rogers, R. 3)
Robin Hoodlum, 1948 (Hubley 4)
Robin Hoodwinked, 1957 (Hanna and Barbera 4)
Robinson, 1957 (Decaë 4, Rabier 4)
Robinson Crusoe, 1910 (Blom 2)
Robinson Crusoe, 1917 (Daniels 4)
Robinson Crusoe, 1925 (Lantz 4)
Robinson Crusoe, 1933 (Terry 4)
Robinson Crusoe Isle, 1935 (Lantz 4)
Robinson Crusoe, Jr., 1941 (Clampett 4)
Robinson Crusoe on Mars, 1964 (Hoch 4, Westmore, W. 4)
Robinson Crusoe-Land. See Atoll K, 1950
Robinson Crusoe's Broadcast, 1938 (Terry 4)
Robinson Girl. See Robinsonka, 1974
Robinson soll nicht sterben, 1957 (Schneider 3)
Robinsonka, 1974 (Kachyna 3)
Robo no ishi, 1955 (Yamada 3)
Robo no ishi, 1960 (Hara 3)
Robot, 1932 (Fleischer, M. and D. 2)
Robot Monster, 1953 (Bernstein 4)
Robot Rabbit, 1952 (Freleng 4)
Robust Romeo, 1914 (Sennett 2, Arbuckle 3)
Rocambole, 1946 (Brasseur 3, Burel 4)
Rocambole, 1962 (Fusco 4)
Roccia incantata, 1950 (Zavattini 4)
Rocco and His Brothers. See Rocco e i suoi fratelli, 1960

occo e i suoi fratelli, 1960 (Visconti 2, Cardinale 3, Delon 3, Girardot 3, D'Amico 4, Rota 4)
occo et ses frères. *See* Rocco e i suoi frattelli, 1960
occo Papaleo. *See* Permette? Rocco Papaleo, 1971
ock All Night, 1957 (Corman 4, Crosby 4)
ock Around the Clock, 1956 (Katzman 4)
ock 'n' Roll High School, 1979 (Bottin 4)
ock of Ages, 1902 (Porter 2)
ock of Riches, 1916 (Weber 2)
ock, Pretty Baby, 1956 (Mineo 3, Wray 3, Mancini 4)
ock, Rock, Rock, 1956 (Weld 3)
ockabye, 1932 (Cukor 2, Bennett C. 3, Lukas 3, McCrea 3, Pidgeon 3, Murfin 4, Rosher 4, Selznick 4, Steiner 4)
ock-a-Bye Baby, 1920 (Roach 4)
ock-a-Bye Baby, 1958 (Lewis 2, Sturges, P. 2, Tashlin 2, Cahn 4, Head 4)
ock-a-Bye Bear, 1952 (Avery 2)
ock-a-bye Cowboy, 1933 (Stevens 2)
ockabye Legend. *See* Chilly Willy in the Legend of Rockabye Point, 1955
ocket Busters, 1938 (Bacon 2)
ocket from Calabuch. *See* Calabuch, 1956
ocket Man, 1954 (Coburn, C. 3, Seitz 4)
ocket Ship X-M, 1950 (Struss 4)
ocket Squad, 1956 (Jones 2)
ocket-Bye Baby, 1956 (Jones 2)
ockets Galore, 1958 (Dearden 2)
ockin' in the Rockies, 1945 (Three Stooges 3)
ockin' Through the Rockies, 1940 (Three Stooges 3, Bruckman 4)
ocking Moon, 1926 (Clarke, C.C. 4, La Shelle 4)
ocking-Horse Winner, 1950 (Mills 3, Alwyn 4, Dillon 4)
ocky, 1948 (McDowall 3)
ocky, 1976 (Meredith 3, Stallone 3)
ocky IV, 1985 (Stallone 3)
ocky Horror Picture Show, 1975 (Sarandon 3)
ocky Mountain, 1950 (Flynn 3, Canutt 4, McCord 4, Steiner 4)
ocky Mountain Grandeur, 1937 (Hoch 4)
ocky Mountain Mystery, 1935 (Scott, R. 3, Sheridan 3)
ocky Rhodes, 1934 (McCord 4)
ocky Road, 1909 (Griffith 2, Bitzer 4)
ocky Road to Dublin, 1968 (Huston 2, Coutard 4)
ocky Road to Ruin, 1943 (Fleischer, M. and D. 2)
ocky III, 1982 (Meredith 3, Stallone 3)
ocky II, 1979 (Meredith 3, Stallone 3)
od Laver's Wimbledon, 1969 (Heston 3)
oda tornet, 1914 (Stiller 2, Jaenzon 4, Magnusson 4)
odan. *See* Sorano daikaijyu Rodan, 1956
øde Enke. *See* Rovedderkoppen, 1916
ode kappe, 1967 (Bjornstrand 3, Dahlbeck 3)
odedanska priča, 1969 (Grgić 4)
odelkavalier, 1918 (Lubitsch 2)
odeo, 1929 (Sennett 2, Hornbeck 4)
odeo, 1951 (Mirisch 4)
odinné trampoty oficiála Trísky, 1949 (Hrušínský 3)
odnoi brat, 1929 (Cherkassov 3)
odnye polia, 1944 (Babochkin 3)
odzina indonezyjska, 1973 (Giersz 4)
oei no uta, 1938 (Mizoguchi 2)
ogelia, 1962 (Rey 3)
oger Corman: Hollywood's Wild Angel, 1978 (Fonda, P. 3)
oger la Honte, 1966 (Papas 3)
oger Touhy, Gangster, 1944 (Florey 2, McLaglen 3, Quinn 3, Basevi 4, Friedhofer 4)
oger Wagner Chorale, 1954 (Krasner 4)
oger-la-Honte, 1946 (Cayatte 2)
ogopag, 1962 (Godard 2, Pasolini 2, Rossellini 2, Welles 2, Delli Colli 4, Donati 4, Guillemot 4, Rabier 4)
ogue, 1918 (Hardy 3)
ogue Cop, 1954 (Leigh, J. 3, Raft 3, Taylor, R. 3, Rose 4, Seitz 4)
ogue Male, 1975 (O'Toole 3, Sim 3)
ogue of the Rio Grande, 1930 (Loy 3)
ogue Regiment, 1948 (Florey 2)

Rogue Song, 1930 (Barrymore L. 3, Laurel & Hardy 3, Adrian 4, Booth 4, Gibbons 4, Marion 4, Shearer 4, Stothart 4, Tiomkin 4)
Rogues' Gallery, 1913 (Sennett 2)
Rogue's Gallery, 1967 (Hall 4)
Rogue's Gallery, 1968 (Arlen 3)
Rogues of Paris, 1913 (Guy 2)
Rogue's Regiment, 1948 (Powell, D. 3, Price 3, Buckner 4, Orry-Kelly 4)
Rogue's Romance, 1919 (Valentino 3)
Rogue's Tricks. *See* Douche d'eau bouillante, 1907
Roi, 1936 (Raimu 3)
Roi, 1949 (Chevalier 3)
Roi de Camambert, 1931 (Maté 4)
Roi de Camargue, 1934 (Vanel 3, Honegger 4)
Roi de coeur, 1966 (Broca 2, Brasseur 3, Bujold 3, Presle 3, Delerue 4)
Roi de coeur. *See* King of Hearts, 1966
Roi de Thulé, 1910 (Feuillade 2)
Roi des Champs-Elysées, 1934 (Delannoy 2, Keaton 2)
Roi des palaces, 1932 (Clouzot 2, Gallone 2, Berry 3, Simon, S. 3)
Roi des parfums, 1910 (Gance 2)
Roi du cirage, 1931 (Douy 4)
Roi du cirque. *See* Zirkuskonig, 1924
Roi du maquillage, 1904 (Méliès 2)
Roi du tiercé. *See* Gentleman d'Epsom, 1962
Roi et l'oiseau, 1980 (Grimault 4, Prévert 4)
Roi Lear au village, 1911 (Feuillade 2)
Roi Pandore, 1949 (Bourvil 3)
Roi Pelé, 1976 (Reichenbach 2)
Roi sans divertissement, 1963 (Vanel 3, Jarre 4)
Rois de la Flotte, 1938 (Renoir 4)
Rois du sport, 1937 (Berry 3, Fernandel 3, Raimu 3, Jeanson 4)
Rok ze samých pondělku, 1977 (Danailov 3)
Rokonok, 1954 (Darvas 3)
Rokujo yukiyama tsumugi, 1965 (Takamine 3)
Rola, 1971 (Zanussi 2)
Rolan i Francheska, 1961 (Gurchenko 3)
Role. *See* Bhumika, 1977
Roll on Texas Moon, 1946 (Rogers, R. 3)
Rolland Garros, 1975 (Reichenbach 2)
Rolle. *See* Rola, 1971
Rolled Stockings, 1927 (Arlen 3, Brooks 3, Banton 4, Schulberg 4)
Rollende Kugel, 1919 (Galeen 4, Messter 4)
Rollende Rad, 1934 (Reiniger 2)
Roller Skate. *See* Dance Movie, 1963
Rollerball, 1975 (Jewison 2, Caan 3, Richardson 3, Box 4, Houseman 4, Previn 4, Slocombe 4)
Rollercoaster, 1977 (Fonda, H. 3, Segal 3, Widmark 3, Schifrin 4)
Rollicking Adventures of Eliza Fraser. *See* Eliza Fraser, 1976
Rolling Down to Rio, 1947 (Bruckman 4)
Rolling Man, 1972 (Moorehead 3)
Rolling Road, 1927 (Balcon 4)
Rolling Sea. *See* Barande hav, 1951
Rolling Stones, 1936 (Terry 4)
Rolling Thunder, 1977 (Schrader 2)
Rollover, 1981 (Pakula 2, Fonda, J. 3, Jenkins 4)
Roma, 1972 (Fellini 2, Magnani 3, Donati 4, Rota 4)
Roma a mano armato, 1976 (Kennedy, A. 3)
Roma bene, 1971 (Manfredi 3, Papas 3)
Roma, città aperta, 1945 (Fellini 2, Rossellini 2, Fabrizi 3, Magnani 3, Amidei 4)
Roma città libera, 1946 (De Sica 2, Cortese 3, D'Amico 4, Flaiano 4, Rota 4, Zavattini 4)
Roma come Chicago, 1968 (Cassavetes 2, Morricone 4)
Roma—Montevideo, 1948 (Antonioni 2)
Roma ore undici, 1952 (De Santis 2, Petri 2, Barsacq 4, Zavattini 4)
Roma rivuole Cesare, 1974 (Jancsó 2, Olbrychski 3)
Roman, 1910 (Bosworth 3)
Roman aus den Bergen. *See* Geier-Wally, 1921
Roman Cowboy, 1917 (Mix 3)
Roman d'amour, 1904–05 (Zecca 2)
Roman d'amour . . . et d'aventures, 1918 (Guitry 2)
Roman de la midinette, 1915 (Musidora 3)
Roman de Soeur Louise, 1908 (Feuillade 2)

Rosen, die der Sturm entblattert, 1917 (Negri 3)
Rosen fur Bettina, 1956 (Pabst 2)
Rosen fur den Staatsanwalt, 1959 (Staudte 2)
Rosen im Herbst, 1955 (Wicki 2, Dagover 3)
Rosen in Tirol, 1940 (Herlth 4)
Rosen på Tistelon, 1916 (Sjostrom 2, Jaenzon 4, Magnusson 4)
Rosenkavalier, 1925 (Wiene 2)
Rosenkavalier, 1962 (Czinner 2)
Rosenkonig, 1984 (Branco 4)
Rosenmontag, 1924 (Warm 4)
Rosenmontag, 1930 (Herlth 4, Rohrig 4)
Rosen-resli, 1954 (Tschechowa 3)
Roses Are Red, 1947 (Chandler 3)
Roses for the Prosecutor. See Rosen fur den Staatsanwalt, 1959
Roses of Picardy, 1927 (Saville 2)
Roses of the South. See Minami no bara, 1950
Roses of Yesterday, 1913 (Selig 4)
Roses rouges et piments verts, 1975 (Lollobrigida 3)
Roses rouges et piments verts. See No encontre rosas para mi madre, 1975
Rose's Story, 1911 (Pickford 3)
Rosie, 1967 (Russell, R. 3, Hunter 4, Mercer 4)
Rosier de Madame Husson, 1932 (Fernandel 3, Rosay 3)
Rosier de Madame Husson, 1950 (Pagnol 2, Bourvil 3)
Rosier miraculeux, 1904 (Méliès 2)
Rosière des Halles, 1935 (Douy 4)
Rosie's Revenge, 1913 (Cruze 2)
Rosita, 1923 (Lubitsch 2, Pickford 3, Kraly 4, Menzies 4, Rosher 4)
Roslyn Romance, from 1971 (Baillie 2)
Rosmunda e Alboino, 1961 (Palance 3)
Rosolino Paternò, soldato, 1969 (Falk 3, Manfredi 3, Age and Scarpelli 4, Delli Colli 4)
Rossetto, 1960 (Germi 2, Fusco 4, Zavattini 4)
Rossiter Case, 1951 (Baker S. 3)
Rossiya Nikolaya II i Lev Tolstoi, 1928 (Shub 2)
Rosso e nero, 1954 (Delli Colli 4)
Rotagg, 1946 (Bjornstrand 3)
Rotation, 1949 (Staudte 2)
Rote Kreis, 1928 (Albers 3)
Rote Kreis, 1960 (Rasp 3)
Rote Maus, 1925 (Warm 4)
Rote Orchideen, 1938 (Tschechowa 3)
Rote Rausch, 1962 (Kinski 3)
Rote Rosen, rote Lippen, roter Wein, 1955 (Dagover 3)
Rote Streifen, 1916 (Gad 2)
Rote Tanzerin. See Mata Hari, 1927
Rothausgasse, 1928 (Oswald 2, Frohlich 3, Homolka 3, Planer 4)
Rothenburger, 1918 (Pick 2)
Rothschild, 1933 (Baur 3)
Roti, 1942 (Biswas 4)
Roti Kapada Aur Makaan, 1974 (Bachchan 3)
Rotsport Marschiert, 1930 (Dudow 2)
Rotten to the Core, 1965 (Boulting 2, Young, F. 4)
Rotterdam—Europoort, 1966 (Ivens 2)
Rotterdam—Europoort. See Rotterdam—Europoort, 1966
Rotters, 1921 (Holloway 3)
Roue, 1923 (Gance 2, Burel 4, Honegger 4)
Roue de la fortune, 1938 (Storck 2)
Roue tourne, 1941 (Allégret, Y. 2)
Roue's Heart, 1909 (Griffith 2, Bitzer 4)
Rouge aux lèvres, 1971 (Seyrig 3)
Rouge est mis, 1953 (Cocteau 3)
Rouge est mis, 1957 (Gabin 3, Girardot 3, Audiard 4)
Rouge et le blanc, 1971 (Autant-Lara 2)
Rouge et le noir, 1954 (Autant-Lara 2, Darrieux 3, Philipe 3, Sordi 3, Aurenche 4, Bost 4, Douy 4)
Rouge et le noir, 1976 (Gerasimov 2)
Rouge et le noir. See Geheime Kurier, 1928
Rouged Lips, 1923 (Bruckman 4)
Rough and Ready, 1918 (Farnum 3)
Rough and the Smooth, 1959 (Siodmak 2, Bendix 3, Adam 4, Mathieson 4)
Rough Company. See Violent Men, 1954

Rough Cut, 1980 (Niven 3, Reynolds, B. 3)
Rough Diamond, 1921 (Mix 3)
Rough Diamond. See Ganga bruta, 1932
Rough House, 1917 (Keaton 2, Arbuckle 3)
Rough House Rosie, 1927 (Bow 3, Rosson 4, Schulberg 4)
Rough Idea of Love, 1930 (Sennett 2)
Rough Night in Jericho, 1967 (Martin, D. 3, Simmons 3, Whitlock 4)
Rough on Romeo, 1922 (Roach 4)
Rough Riders, 1927 (Fleming 2, Hathaway 2, Astor 3, Howe 4, Schulberg 4)
Rough Riders' Roundup, 1939 (Rogers, R. 3)
Rough Ridin', 1924 (Haller 4)
Rough Ridin' Rangers, 1935 (Canutt 4)
Rough Ridin' Red, 1928 (Musuraca 4)
Rough Romance, 1930 (Wayne 3)
Rough Seas, 1921 (Roach 4)
Rough Shod, 1922 (Eason 4)
Rough Shoot, 1953 (Francis 4)
Rough Shoot. See Shoot First, 1953
Rough, Tough, and Ready, 1945 (McLaglen 3)
Rough Treatment. See Bez znieczuleniz, 1978
Roughest Africa, 1923 (Laurel 3, Roach 4)
Roughly Speaking, 1945 (Curtiz 2, Russell, R. 3, Blanke 4, Steiner 4, Walker 4, Waxman 4)
Roughly Squeaking, 1946 (Jones 2)
Roughneck, 1915 (Hart 3, Sullivan 4)
Roughneck. See Conversion of Frosty Blake, 1915
Rough-Riding Romance, 1919 (Mix 3)
Roughshod, 1949 (Robson 2, Grahame 3, Ireland 3, Biroc 4)
Rougoku no hanayome, 1939 (Miyagawa 4)
Roulement à billes, 1924 (Grémillon 2)
Rouletabille 2: Dernière incarnation de Larsan, 1914 (Tourneur, M. 2)
Rouletabille 1: Le Mystère de la chambre jaune, 1914 (Tourneur, M. 2)
Roulette, 1924 (Costello, M. 3, Selznick 4)
Rouli-Roulant, 1966 (Jutra 2, Denner 3)
Round Trip. See Volta redonda, 1952
Round Up, 1920 (Keaton 2, Sutherland 2)
Rounders, 1914 (Chaplin 2, Sennett 2, Arbuckle 2)
Rounders, 1964 (Fonda, H. 3, Fonda, P. 3, Ford, G. 3, Oates 3)
Roundup, 1920 (Arbuckle 3, Beery 3)
Roundup, 1941 (Head 4)
Round-Up. See Szegénylegények, 1965
Round-Up Time in Texas, 1937 (Autry 3)
Roustabout, 1922 (Roach 4)
Roustabout, 1964 (Presley 3, Stanwyck 3, Welch 3, Ballard 4, Head 4, Wallis 4)
Roustabout. See Property Man, 1914
Route de Corinthe, 1967 (Chabrol 2, Seberg 3, Rabier 4)
Route de Salina. See Road to Salina, 1971
Route du bagne, 1945 (Burel 4)
Route du bonheur, 1953 (Cassel 3)
Route d'un homme, 1967 (Barrault 3, Feuillère 3)
Route est belle, 1929 (Florey 2, Braunberger 4, Rosher 4)
Route heureuse, 1936 (Dauphin 3, Feuillère 3)
Route impériale, 1935 (L'Herbier 2, Francis, E. 3)
Route Napoléon, 1953 (Delannoy 2, Fresnay 3, Burel 4)
Route sans issue, 1947 (Dauphin 3, Spaak 4)
Route sans sillage, 1963 (Delerue 4)
Routes barrées, 1956 (Colpi 4)
Routes du sud, 1978 (Montand 3, Fisher 4, Legrand 4, Trauner 4)
Rovedderkoppen, 1916 (Blom 2, Dreyer 2)
Rover, 1967 (Hayworth 3, Quinn 3)
Rover's Rescue, 1940 (Terry 4)
Rover's Rival, 1937 (Clampett 4)
Rovin' Tumbleweeds, 1939 (Autry 3, Costello, M. 3, Farnum 3)
Row, Row, Row, 1930 (Fleischer, M. and D. 2)
Rowan and Martin at the Movies, 1969 (Heston 3)
Row-Boat Romance, 1914 (Sennett 2, Summerville 3)
Rower, 1955 (Polanski 2)
Rowing Across the Atlantic. See Traversée de l'Atlantique à la rame, 1978
Rowlandson's England, 1955 (Hamer 2, Guinness 3)

Roxie Hart, 1942 (Wellman 2, Bruce 3, Menjou 3, Rogers, G. 3, Day 4, Johnson 4, Shamroy 4)
Royal Affair. *See* Roi, 1949
Royal Affairs in Versailles. *See* Si Versailles m'était conté, 1953
Royal American, 1927 (Brown, Harry Joe 4)
Royal Ballet, 1959 (Czinner 2)
Royal Bed, 1930 (Astor 3)
Royal Blood, 1916 (Hardy 3)
Royal Box, 1914 (Selig 4)
Royal Cat Nap, 1957 (Hanna and Barbera 4)
Royal Cavalcade, 1935 (Brenon 2, Mills 3)
Royal Divorce, 1938 (Hawkins 3)
Royal Family of Broadway, 1930 (Cukor 2, Dmytryk 2, March 3, Banton 4, Mankiewicz 4)
Royal Flash, 1975 (Lester 2, Bates 3, McDowell 3, Reed, O. 3, Sim 3, Unsworth 4)
Royal Flush. *See* Two Guys from Milwaukee, 1946
Royal Four Flush, 1925 (Roach 4)
Royal Game. *See* Schachnovelle, 1960
Royal Heritage, 1952 (Alwyn 4)
Royal Hunt. *See* Kungajakt, 1944
Royal Hunt. *See* Mrigaya, 1976
Royal Hunt of the Sun, 1969 (Shaw 3, Lourié 4)
Royal Johansson. *See* Kungliga Johansson, 1933
Royal Oak, 1923 (Brook 3)
Royal Razz, 1924 (McCarey 2, Roach 4)
Royal Remembrances, 1929 (Hepworth 2)
Royal Rider, 1929 (Brown, Harry Joe 4, McCord 4)
Royal River. *See* Distant Thames, 1951
Royal Rogue, 1917 (Sennett 2)
Royal Romance, 1930 (Muse 3)
Royal Romance of Charles and Diana, 1982 (De Havilland 3, Granger 3, Milland 3)
Royal Scandal, 1945 (Preminger 2, Auer 3, Baxter A. 3, Coburn, C. 3, Price 3, Biro 4, Miller, A. 4, Newman 4)
Royal Scandal. *See* Hose, 1927
Royal Tour of New South Wales, 1956 (Finch 3)
Royal Waltz. *See* Konigswalzer, 1935
Royal Wedding, 1947 (Neagle 3)
Royal Wedding, 1951 (Donen 2, Astaire 3, Wynn 3, Freed 4, Green, J. 4, Smith, J.M. 4)
Royaume des Fées, 1903 (Méliès 2)
Royaume vous attend, 1976 (Perrault 2)
Roza, 1982 (Olbrychski 3)
Rozaniec z granatow, 1969 (Olbrychski 3)
Rozbijemy zabawe, 1957 (Polanski 2)
Rozbitkowie, 1969 (Giersz 4)
Rozdennie polzat utat ne mozet, 1914 (Mozhukin 3)
Rozeki mono, 1928 (Tsuburaya 4)
Rozhdennye burei, 1980 (Smoktunovsky 3)
Rozhovory, 1969 (Schorm 2)
Rozmarné léto, 1968 (Menzel 2, Brodský 3, Hrušínský 3)
Rozstanie, 1961 (Cybulski 3)
Roztržka, 1956 (Brejchová 3)
Rozum a cit, 1962 (Brdečka 4)
Rozwodów nie bedzie, 1963 (Cybulski 3, Stawinsky 4)
RPM, 1970 (Kramer, S. 2)
RR, 1981 (Brakhage 2)
Ruba al prossimo tuo, 1968 (Hudson 3, Cristaldi 4, Morricone 4)
Rubber Cement, 1975 (Breer 2)
Rubber Heels, 1927 (Heerman 4, Hunt 4)
Rubber Tires, 1927 (Garnett 2, Love 3)
Rubber Twice. *See* Dvakrát kauček, 1939–40
Rubberneck, 1924 (Roach 4)
Rube and the Baron, 1913 (Sennett 2, Normand 3)
Rube Brown in Town, 1907 (Bitzer 4)
Rubens, 1947–48 (Storck 2)
Rubezahls Hochzeit, 1916 (Reiniger 2, Wegener 3)
Ruby and Oswald, 1978 (Forrest 3)
Ruby Gentry, 1952 (Vidor, K. 2, Heston 3, Jones, J. 3, Malden 3, Head 4)
Ruby Keeler, 1928 (Keeler 3)
Ručak, 1972 (Grgić 4)

Ruckkehr der Truppen von der Fruhlingsparade, 1900 (Messter 4)
Ruckus, 1980 (Johnson, B. 3)
Rudá záře nad Kladnem, 1955 (Stallich 4)
Rudd Family Goes to Town. *See* Dad and Dave Come to Town, 1938
Ruddigore, 1964 (Halas and Batchelor 2)
Rude Hostess, 1909 (Griffith 2, Bitzer 4)
Rude journée pour la reine, 1973 (Allio 2, Depardieu 3, Signoret 3)
Rudolph, the Red-nosed Reindeer, 1948 (Fleischer, M. and D. 2)
Rudolph Valentino, 1938 (Negri 3)
Rudolph Valentino and His 88 American Beauties, 1923 (Selznick 4)
Rudy Vallee Melodies, 1932 (Fleischer, M. and D. 2)
Rudyard Kipling's Jungle Book, 1942 (Rozsa 4)
Rudyard Kipling's Jungle Book. *See* Jungle Book, 1942
Rue chinoise, 1956 (Delerue 4)
Rue de l'Estrapade, 1953 (Becker 2, Gélin 3, Jourdan 3, D'Eaubonne 4)
Rue des Prairies, 1959 (Gabin 3, Audiard 4)
Rue du Pied de Grue, 1979 (Tavernier 2)
Rue sans joie, 1938 (Auric 4)
Rues de Hong Kong, 1964 (Guillemot 4)
Ruf, 1949 (Kortner 3)
Ruf aus dem Äther, 1951 (Werner 3)
Ruf des Schicksals, 1922 (Kortner 3, Wagner 4)
Ruffian, 1982 (Morricone 4)
Rug Maker's Daughter, 1915 (Bosworth 3)
Rugged Water, 1925 (Baxter W. 3, Beery 3)
Ruggles of Red Gap, 1923 (Cruze 2, Horton 3, Brown, K. 4)
Ruggles of Red Gap, 1935 (Dmytryk 2, McCarey 2, Laughton 3, Pitts 3, Banton 4, Dreier 4, Head 4)
Ruines et des hommes, 1958 (Delerue 4)
Ruins. *See* Khandar, 1984
Ruins of Palmyra and Baalbek, 1937–40 (Cardiff 4)
Ruisseau, 1938 (Autant-Lara 2, Rosay 3, Simon, M. 3, Aurenche 4)
Ruka, 1965 (Trnka 2)
Ruler. *See* Herrscher, 1937
Rulers of the City. *See* Padroni della città, 1977
Rulers of the Sea, 1939 (Fairbanks, D. Jr. 3, Ladd 3, Dreier 4, Head 4, Jennings 4)
Rules of the Game. *See* Règle du jeu, 1939
Ruletero a toda marcha, 1962 (García 3)
Ruling Class, 1972 (O'Toole 3, Sim 3)
Ruling Passion, 1911 (Griffith 2, Bitzer 4)
Ruling Passion, 1916 (Brenon 2)
Ruling Passion, 1922 (Arliss 3)
Ruling Passion. *See* Reward of the Faithless, 1917
Ruling Passions, 1918 (Polito 4)
Ruling Voice, 1931 (Huston 3, Young, L. 3, Polito 4)
Rulleskøjterne, 1908 (Holger-Madsen 2)
Rum and Wall Paper, 1915 (Sennett 2, Arbuckle 3)
Rum Runner. *See* Boulevard du rhum, 1971
Rumaensk Blod or Søstrene Corrodi, 1913 (Christensen 2)
Rumba, 1935 (Lombard 3, Raft 3, Sheridan 3, Wyman 3, Dreier 4, Prinz 4)
Rumba, 1939–41 (McLaren 2)
Rumba. *See* Cuban Love Song, 1931
Rumble Fish, 1983 (Coppola 2, Hopper 3, Tavoularis 4)
Rumble on the Docks, 1956 (Katzman 4)
Rumiantsev Case. *See* Delo Rumiantseva, 1956
Rummelplatz der Liebe, 1954 (Wicki 2, Jurgens 3)
Rummy, 1933 (Roach 4)
Rumour of War, 1980 (Keach 3)
Rumpelstiltskin, 1915 (August 4)
Rumpus in the Harem, 1956 (Three Stooges 3)
Run a Crooked Mile, 1969 (Holloway 3, Jourdan 3)
Run for Cover, 1955 (Ray, N. 2, Borgnine 3, Cagney 3, Hersholt 3, Bumstead 4, Head 4, Ravetch 4)
Run for the Sun, 1956 (Boulting 2, Howard, T. 3, Widmark 3, La Shelle 4, Nichols 4)
Run for Your Money, 1949 (Guinness 3, Balcon 4, Slocombe 4)
Run for Your Wife. *See* Moglie americana, 1965
Run, Girl, Run, 1928 (Sennett 2, Lombard 3, Hornbeck 4)
Run Home Slow, 1966 (McCambridge 3)
Run Like a Thief, 1967 (Rey 3, Wynn 3)

Run, Man, Run. *See* Corri, uomo, corri, 1968
Run of the Arrow, 1957 (Fuller 2, Bronson 3, Cody 3, Dickinson 3, Steiger 3, Biroc 4, D'Agostino 4, Young, V. 4)
Run on Gold. *See* Midas Run, 1969
Run Silent, Run Deep, 1958 (Wise 2, Gable 3, Lancaster 3, Warden 3, Waxman 4)
Run, Simon, Run, 1970 (Reynolds, B. 3)
Run, Stranger, Run. *See* Happy Mother's Day—Love George, 1973
Run Wild, Run Free, 1969 (Mills 3)
Runaround, 1931 (Steiner 4)
Runaround, 1946 (Crawford, B. 3, Banton 4)
Runaway, 1924 (Fleischer, M. and D. 2)
Runaway, 1926 (Baxter W. 3, Bow 3, Powell, W. 3)
Runaway!, 1973 (Johnson, B. 3)
Runaway, 1984 (Alonzo 4, Goldsmith 4)
Runaway Barge, 1975 (Nolte 3)
Runaway Bride, 1930 (Astor 3, Crisp 3, Murfin 4)
Runaway Bus, 1954 (Rutherford 3)
Runaway Daughter. *See* Red Salute, 1935
Runaway Express, 1926 (Miller, V. 4)
Runaway Girls, 1928 (Sandrich 2)
Runaway Mouse, 1954 (Terry 4)
Runaway Princess, 1928 (Asquith 2)
Runaway Queen, 1934 (Young, F. 4)
Runaway Queen. *See* Queen's Affair, 1934
Runaway Romany, 1917 (Davies 3)
Runaway Train, 1985 (Voight 3, Golan and Globus 4)
Runaway Train. *See* Runaway!, 1973
Runaways, 1915 (Franklin 2)
Rund um eine Million, 1933 (Frohlich 3, Stradling 4)
Rund um Europa. *See* Rote Kreis, 1928
Runner Stumbles, 1979 (Kramer, S. 2, Kovacs 4)
Running after Luck. *See* Jagd nach dem Gluck, 1930
Running Fence, 1977 (Maysles A. and D. 2)
Running, Jumping, and Standing Still Film, 1960 (Lester 2, Sellers 3)
Running Man, 1963 (Reed 2, Bates 3, Harvey 3, Remick 3, Rey 3, Alwyn 4, Krasker 4, Mathieson 4)
Running Target, 1956 (Hall 4)
Running Wild, 1921 (Roach 4)
Running Wild, 1927 (La Cava 2, Fields, W.C. 3)
Running Wild, 1955 (Wynn 3, Boyle 4)
Runpen to sono musume, 1931 (Tanaka 3)
Runt, 1936 (Terry 4)
Runt Page, 1932 (Temple 3)
Runway. *See* Bari Theke Palive, 1959
Rupa, 1971 (Grgić 4)
Rupert of Cole Slaw, 1924 (Laurel 3, Roach 4)
Rupert of Hee-Haw. *See* Rupert of Cole Slaw, 1924
Rupert of Hentzau, 1923 (Bosworth 3, Menjou 3, Heerman 4)
Rupert the Runt, 1940 (Terry 4)
Rupkatha, 1950 (Sircar 4)
Ruplekha, 1934 (Sircar 4)
Rupture, 1961 (Carrière 4)
Rupture, 1970 (Chabrol 2, Audran 3, Cassel 3, Rabier 4)
Rural Community. *See* Gromada, 1952
Rural Conqueror, 1911 (Lawrence 3)
Rural Co-op, 1947 (Crosby 4)
Rural Demon, 1914 (Sennett 2, Arbuckle 3)
Rural Elopement, 1908 (Griffith 2, Bitzer 4)
Rural Hungary, 1939 (Hoch 4)
Rural Institute. *See* Selskaya uchitelnitsa, 1947
Rural School, 1940 (Pearson 2)
Rural Sweden, 1938 (Hoch 4)

Rural 3rd Degree, 1913 (Sennett 2)
Ruri no kishi, 1956 (Shindo 2)
Rusalka, 1962 (Stallich 4)
Ruscello di Ripasottile, 1941 (Rossellini 2)
Ruse, 1915 (Hart 3, August 4, Sullivan 4)
Ruses du Diable, 1965 (Piccoli 3)
Ruses, Rhymes, Roughnecks, 1915 (Lloyd 3, Roach 4)
Rush Hour, 1941 (Asquith 2)
Rush Orders, 1921 (Roach 4)
Rush to Judgment, 1966 (de Antonio 2)
Rushin' Ballet, 1937 (Roach 4)
Rushing Roulette, 1965 (McKimson 4)
Rusk. *See* Skorpan, 1957
Ruslan and Ludmila. *See* Ruslan i Ludmila, 1915
Ruslan i Ludmila, 1915 (Mozhukin 3)
Russia of Nicholas II and Lev Tolstoy. *See* Rossiya Nikolaya II i Lev Tolstoi, 1928
Russia—the Land of Oppression, 1910 (Porter 2)
Russian Lullaby, 1931 (Fleischer, M. and D. 2)
Russian Memory. *See* Russky suvenir, 1960
Russian Question. *See* Russkii vopros, 1948
Russian Rhapsody, 1944 (Clampett 4)
Russian Roulette, 1975 (Segal 3)
Russians Are Coming, The Russians Are Coming, 1966 (Ashby 2, Jewison 2, Arkin 3, Saint 3, Biroc 4, Boyle 4)
Russians at War, 1942 (Van Dongen 4)
Russkii vopros, 1948 (Romm 2)
Russky suvenir, 1960 (Orlova 3)
Rustle of Silk, 1923 (Brenon 2, Nilsson 3)
Rustler Sheriff, 1911 (Dwan 2)
Rustlers, 1919 (Ford, J. 2, Carey 3)
Rustlers, 1949 (Hunt 4)
Rustlers' Hideout, 1944 (Crabbe 3)
Rustlers' Paradise, 1935 (Carey 3)
Rustler's Rhapsody, 1985 (Rey 3)
Rustler's Roundup, 1933 (Mix 3)
Rustler's Spur, 1913 (Anderson G. 3)
Rustler's Step-Daughter, 1913 (Anderson G. 3)
Rustler's Valley, 1937 (Boyd 3, Cobb 3, Head 4)
Rusty Flame. *See* Sabita honoo, 1977
Rusty Romeos, 1957 (Three Stooges 3)
Ruten, 1956 (Kagawa 3)
Ruten, 1960 (Yamada 3)
Ruten Hiyoshimura, 1953 (Tanaka 3)
Ruten no oohi, 1960 (Kyo 3, Tanaka 3)
Ruth of the Range, 1922 (Van Dyke, W.S. 2)
Ruthless, 1948 (Ulmer 2, Greenstreet 3, Glennon 4)
Ruthless Four. *See* Ognuno per se, 1968
Ruthless Ones. *See* Ognuno per se, 1968
Rutschbahn, 1928 (George, H. 3, Sakall 3, Herlth 4, Rohrig 4)
Ruy Blas, 1909 (Costello, M. 3)
Ruy Blas, 1947 (Cocteau 2, Darrieux 3, Marais 3, Auric 4, Wakhévitch 4)
Ružové konbiné, 1932 (Stallich 4)
Ryan's Daughter, 1970 (Lean 2, Howard, T. 3, Mills 3, Mitchum 3, Havelock-Allan 4, Jarre 4, Young, F. 4)
Rynox, 1931 (Powell 2)
Ryoetsu daihyojo, 1937 (Shindo 3)
Ryoju, 1961 (Gosho 3)
Rysopis, 1964 (Skolimowski 2)
Rythmetic, 1956 (McLaren 2)
Ryuko sokitai, 1937 (Shimura 3)
Ryusei, 1949 (Yamamura 3)

S

Safety in Numbers, 1930 (Beavers 3, Lombard 3, Vorkapich 4)
Safety in Numbers, 1938 (Clarke, C.C. 4)
Safety Last, 1923 (Lloyd 3, Roach 4)
Safety Second, 1950 (Hanna and Barbera 4)
Safety Spin, 1953 (Burness 4)
Safety Worst, 1915 (Hardy 3)
S'affranchir, 1913 (Feuillade 2)
Sag det i toner, 1929 (Jaenzon 4)
Säg det med bloomer, 1952 (Bjornstrand 3)
Sag' die Wahrheit, 1946 (Frohlich 3)
Saga of Anatahan. *See* Anatahan, 1953
Saga of Death Valley, 1939 (Rogers, R. 3)
Saga of the Great Buddha. *See* Daibutsu kaigen, 1952
Saga of the Vagabonds. *See* Sengoku gunto-den, 1959
Saga of the Viking Women and Their Voyage to the Waters of the
     Great Sea Serpent, 1957 (Corman 4)
Sage vom Hund von Baskerville, 1915 (Oswald 2)
Sagebrush Phrenologist, 1911 (Dwan 2)
Sagebrush Sadie, 1928 (Disney 2)
Sagebrush Tom, 1915 (Mix 3)
Sagebrush Trail, 1922 (Beery 3)
Sagebrush Trail, 1933 (Wayne 3, Canutt 4)
Sagebrush Troubadour, 1935 (Autry 3)
Sagebrusher, 1920 (Seitz 4)
Sage-femme de première classe, 1902 (Guy 2)
Sage-femme, le curé et le bon dieu. *See* Jessica, 1962
Sagina, 1974 (Burman 4)
Saginaw Trail, 1953 (Autry 3)
Sagovor mjortvych, 1930 (Babochkin 3)
Sahara, 1919 (Sullivan 4)
Sahara, 1943 (Bogart 3, Duryea 3, Brown, Harry Joe 4, Lourié 4,
     Maté 4, Rozsa 4)
Sahara, 1984 (Golan and Globus 4, Morricone 4)
Sahara, an IV, 1960 (Delerue 4, Fradetal 4)
Sahara Hare, 1954 (Freleng 4)
Saheiji Finds a Way. *See* Bakumatsu Taiyoden, 1958
Sahib Bahadur, 1980 (Anand 3)
Sai cosa faceva Stalin alle donne, 1969 (Morricone 4)
Saigo ni warau otoko, 1949 (Kyo 3)
Saigo no shinpan, 1965 (Takemitsu 4)
Saigon, 1948 (Ladd 3, Lake 3, Bumstead 4, Dreier 4, Head 4, Seitz 4)
Saikai, 1953 (Mori 3)
**Saikaku ichidai onna, 1952 (Mizoguchi 2, Mifune 3, Shimura 3,
     Shindo 3, Tanaka 3, Yoda 4)**
Saikaku's Five Women. *See* Koushoku gonin onna, 1948
Sail a Crooked Ship, 1962 (Wagner 3, Biroc 4, Duning 4)
Sailboat, 1967–68 (Wieland 2)
Sailing Along, 1938 (Matthews 3, Sim 3, Junge 4)
Sailing with a Song, 1949 (Fleischer, M. and D. 2)
Sailing, Sailing Over the Bounding Main, 1926 (Fleischer, M. and D. 2)
Sailor and the Devil, 1967 (Williams, R. 4)
Sailor Be Good, 1933 (Cruze 2)
Sailor Beware, 1951 (Lewis 2, Dean 3, Hutton 3, Martin, D. 3,
     Head 4, Wallis 4)
Sailor Beware!, 1956 (Clayton 2, Slocombe 4)
Sailor from Gibraltar, 1967 (Richardson 2, Welles 2, Hurt, J. 3,
     Moreau 3, Redgrave, V. 3, Coutard 4)
Sailor Izzy Murphy, 1927 (Oland 3)
Sailor Jack's Reformation, 1911 (Olcott 2)
Sailor-Made Man, 1921 (Lloyd 3, Roach 4)
Sailor of the King, 1953 (Mathieson 4)
Sailor of the King. *See* Singlehanded, 1953
Sailor Papa, 1925 (Roach 4)
Sailor Takes a Wife, 1945 (Allyson 3, Nilsson 3, Walker 3, Green, J. 4,
     Irene 4)
Sailor Who Fell from Grace with the Sea, 1976 (Slocombe 4)
Sailor's Adventures. *See* Przygody marynarza, 1958
Sailors All, 1943 (Vorkapich 4)
Sailors Beware, 1927 (Laurel and Hardy 3, Velez 3, Roach 4)
Sailor's Consolation, 1951 (Holloway 3)
Sailor's Heart, 1912 (Sweet 3, Meredyth 4)
Sailor's Holiday, 1929 (Miller, A. 4)
Sailor's Holiday, 1944 (Winters 3, Guffey 4)

Sailor's Home, 1936 (Terry 4)
Sailor's Lady, 1940 (Dwan 2, Andrews D. 3, Crabbe 3)
Sailor's Luck, 1933 (Walsh 2, Carré 4, Miller, A. 4)
Sailor's Romance, 1927 (Fazenda 3)
Sailor's Sweetheart, 1927 (Bacon 2, Loy 3)
Sailor's 3 Crowns. *See* Trois Couronnes du matelot, 1982
Sailors' Wives, 1928 (Astor 3, Meredyth 4)
St. Benny the Dip, 1951 (Ulmer 2)
St. Elmo, 1923 (Baxter W. 3, Gilbert 3, Love 3, August 4, Furthman 4)
St. Elmo Murray. *See* St. Elmo, 1923
St. Helena and Its Man of Destiny, 1936 (Hoch 4)
Saint Ilario, 1921 (Rosher 4)
Saint in London, 1939 (Sanders 3)
Saint in New York, 1938 (Polglase 4)
Saint in Palm Springs, 1941 (Sanders 3)
St. Ives, 1976 (Bisset 3, Bronson 3, Cook 3, Schell, Maximilian 3,
     Ballard 4, Houseman 4, Schifrin 4)
Saint Jack, 1979 (Bogdanovich 2)
Saint Joan, 1957 (Preminger 2, Gielgud 3, Seberg 3, Walbrook 3,
     Widmark 3, Bass 4, Périnal 4)
St. Louis Blues, 1939 (Walsh 2, Lamour 3, Dreier 4, Head 4)
St. Louis Blues, 1958 (Head 4)
St. Louis Exposition, 1902 (Bitzer 4)
St. Louis Kid, 1934 (Cagney 3, Orry-Kelly 4)
St. Martin's Lane, 1938 (Hamer 2, Harrison 3, Laughton 3,
     Leigh, V. 3, Pommer 4)
St. Matthew's Passion, 1951 (Flaherty 2)
Saint Meets the Tiger, 1943 (Krasker 4)
Saint prend l'affût, 1966 (Christian-Jaque 2, Marais 3)
Saint Strikes Back, 1939 (Fitzgerald 3, Sanders 3)
Saint Takes Over, 1940 (Sanders 3)
St. Valentine's Day Massacre, 1967 (Dern 3, Robards 3, Segal 3,
     Corman 4, Krasner 4, Smith, J.M. 4)
St. Wenceslas. *See* Svatý Václav, 1929
Sainte et le fou. *See* Heilige und ihr Narr, 1928
Sainte Famille, 1972 (Thulin 3, Vierny 4)
Sainte Odile, 1915 (Musidora 3)
Sainted Devil, 1924 (Valentino 3, Westmore, M. 4)
Sainted Sisters, 1948 (Bondi 3, Fitzgerald 3, Lake 3, Bumstead 4,
     Dreier 4, Head 4)
Saintes Nitouches, 1962 (Blier 3)
Saint-Louis ou l'ange de la paix, 1950 (Philipe 3)
Saintly Sinner, 1917 (Hersholt 3)
Saint's Adventure, 1917 (Walthall 3)
Saint's Double Trouble, 1940 (Lugosi 3, Sanders 3, Hunt 4)
Saint-Tropez blues, 1960 (Chabrol 2, Audran 3)
Saint-Tropez, devoir de vacances, 1952 (Resnais 2, Brasseur 3, Gélin 3,
     Piccoli 3, Cloquet 4)
Sais seule que j'aime, 1938 (Presle 3)
Saison in Kairo, 1933 (Herlth 4, Hoffmann 4, Reisch 4, Rohrig 4)
Sait-on jamais?, 1957 (Vadim 2)
Sakai, 1953 (Hayasaka 4)
Sakanaka ronin, 1930 (Yamada 3)
Sakasu gonin-gumi, 1935 (Naruse 2)
Sakharov, 1984 (Jackson 3, Robards 3)
Sakiko-san chotto, 1963 (Yamada 3)
Sakujitsu kieta otoko, 1941 (Hasegawa 3, Takamine 3, Yamada 3)
Sakura Dance. *See* Sakura Ondo, 1934
Sakura no mori no mankai no shita, 1975 (Shinoda 2, Iwashita 3,
     Takemitsu 4)
Sakura Ondo, 1934 (Gosho 2, Tanaka 3)
Sakurada-mon, 1961 (Hasegawa 3)
Sakura-ondo: Kyo wa odotte, 1947 (Hasegawa 3)
Sal of Singapore, 1929 (Johnson, N. 3)
Sál ztracených kroku, 1960 (Jires 2)
Salación, 1966 (Herrera 4)
Saladin. *See* Naser Salah el Dine, 1963
Salaire de la peur, 1952 (Clouzot 2, Montand 3, Vanel 3)
Salaire du péché, 1956 (Darrieux 3, Moreau 3)
Salamander, 1981 (Cardinale 3, Lee, C. 3, Quinn 3, Wallach 3,
     Goldsmith 4)
Salamander. *See* Salamandre, 1971
Salamandre, 1971 (Tanner 2)

Samurai Rebellion. *See* Joiuchi, 1967
Samurai Saga. *See* Aru kengo no shogai, 1959
Samurai Song. *See* Samurai ondo, 1937
Samurai Spy, Sarutobi. *See* Ibun sarutobi sasuke, 1965
Samvetsomma Adolf, 1936 (Fischer 4, Jaenzon 4)
Samvittighedsnag. *See* Hvem var Forbryderen?, 1912
Samyi poslednii den, 1973 (Ulyanov 3)
San, 1966 (Samardžić 3)
San Antonio, 1945 (Walsh 2, Flynn 3, Sakall 3, Buckner 4, Burnett 4, Glennon 4, Steiner 4, Waxman 4)
San Antonio Rose, 1941 (Arden 3, Chaney Lon, Jr. 3, Howard, S. 3, Cortez 4)
San Babila ore 20: un delitto inutile, 1976 (Morricone 4)
San Demetrio London, 1943 (Hamer 2)
San Diego, 1912 (Dwan 2)
San Diego, I Love You, 1944 (Keaton 2, Horton 3, Muse 3, Salter 4)
San Domingo, 1970 (Syberberg 2)
San Fernando Valley, 1944 (Rogers, R. 3)
San Francisco, 1906 (Bitzer 4)
San Francisco, 1936 (Van Dyke, W.S. 2, Von Stroheim 2, Gable 3, MacDonald 3, Tracy 3, Brown, N. 4, Canutt 4, Edens 4, Emerson 4, Freed 4, Gibbons 4, Gillespie 4, Kaper 4, Loos 4, Shearer 4, Stothart 4)
San Francisco, 1945 (Van Dyke, W. 2)
San Francisco Celebration, 1913 (Sennett 2)
San Francisco Docks, 1940 (Fitzgerald 3, Meredith 3, Salter 4)
San Francisco International, 1970 (Johnson, V. 3)
San Francisco Story, 1952 (De Carlo 3, McCrea 3, Friedhofer 4, Jenkins 4, Seitz 4)
San Giovanni Decollato, 1940 (Zavattini 4)
San Massenza, 1955 (Olmi 2)
San Michele aveva un gallo, 1971 (Taviani, P. and V. 2)
San Miniato, luglio '44, 1954 (Taviani, P. and V. 2, Zavattini 4)
San Pietro, 1945 (Huston 2)
San Quentin, 1937 (Bacon 2, Bogart 3, O'Brien, P. 3, Sheridan 3, Raksin 4)
Sanam, 1951 (Anand 3)
Sanba, 1974 (Tanaka 3)
Sanbiki no tanuki, 1966 (Muraki 4)
Sanbyaku rokujugo-ya, 1948 (Ichikawa 2, Takamine 3)
Sanbyaku-rokuju-go-ya, 1962 (Yamada 3)
Sancta Simplicitas, 1968 (Popescu-Gopo 4)
Sanctuary, 1961 (Richardson 2, Martin, S. 3, Montand 3, Remick 3, North 4, Smith, J.M. 4)
Sanctuary. *See* Santuario, 1951
Sand, 1920 (Hart 3)
Sand, 1949 (Cody 3, Clarke, C.C. 4)
Sand of Gold. *See* Rimal min Zahab, 1966
Sand Pebbles, 1966 (Wise 2, Attenborough 3, McQueen, S. 3, Goldsmith 4, Leven 4, Reynolds 4)
Sanda tai Gailha. *See* Furankenshutain no kaiju—Sanda tai Gailah, 1966
Sandai kaiju chikyu saidai no kessen, 1965 (Okada 3, Shimura 3, Tsuburaya 4)
Sandakan hachi-ban shokan: Bokyo, 1974 (Tanaka 3)
Sandakan, House No. 8. *See* Sandakan hachi-ban shokan: Bokyo, 1974
Sande Kaerlighed, 1912 (Blom 2)
Sanders of the River, 1935 (Crichton 2, Robeson 3, Biro 4, Hornbeck 4, Korda 4, Périnal 4, Wimperis 4)
Sandesaya, 1960 (Peries 2)
Sandman, 1920 (Roach 4)
Sandokan, la tigre di Monpracem, 1963 (Fusco 4)
Sandor. *See* Zigeunerbaron, 1927
Sandpiper, 1965 (Minnelli 2, Bronson 3, Burton 3, O'Toole 3, Saint 3, Taylor, E. 3, Krasner 4, Sharaff 4, Trumbo 4, Wilson, M. 4)
Sandra. *See* Vaghe stelle dell'orsa, 1965
Sands of Dee, 1912 (Griffith 2, Marsh 3, Bitzer 4)
Sands of Fate, 1914 (Crisp 3, Gish, D. 3)
Sands of Iwo Jima, 1949 (Dwan 2, Wayne 3, Brown, Harry 4, Young, V. 4)
Sands of the Kalahari, 1965 (Baker S. 3, York, S. 3)
Sandwich, 1980 (Bozzetto 4)
Sandwich Man, 1968 (Holloway 3)

Sandy Claws, 1954 (Freleng 4)
Sandy Gets Her Man, 1940 (Merkel 3, Salter 4)
Sandy Is a Lady, 1940 (Auer 3, Krasner 4)
Sandy Steps Out, 1941 (Horton 3)
Sane Asylum, 1912 (Porter 2)
Sanfte Lauf, 1967 (Ganz 3)
Sang à la tête, 1955 (Gabin 3)
Sang d'Allah, 1922 (Modot 3)
Sang des autres, 1973 (Vanel 3)
Sang des bêtes, 1950 (Franju 2, Fradetal 4, Kosma 4)
Sang d'un poète, 1930 (Cocteau 2, Auric 4, D'Eaubonne 4, Périnal 4)
Sang et lumières, 1953 (Gélin 3)
Sanga ari, 1962 (Toda 4)
Sangaree, 1953 (Head 4)
Sången om den eldroda blommon, 1918 (Molander 2, Stiller 2, Jaenzon 4, Magnusson 4)
Sången om den eldroda blommon, 1934 (Jaenzon 4)
Sången om den eldroda blommon, 1957 (Molander 2)
Sången om Stockholm, 1947 (Borgstrom 3)
Sangre manda, 1933 (García 3)
Sangre y luces, 1953 (García Berlanga 2)
Sangue bleu, 1914 (Bertini 3)
Sangue Mineiro, 1929 (Mauro 2)
Sanitarium, 1910 (Arbuckle 3)
Sanitarium Scandal, 1916 (Eason 4)
Sanjaku Sagohei, 1944 (Takamine 3)
Sanjar, 1960 (Dragić 4)
Sanjog, 1972 (Bachchan 3)
Sanjuro, 1962 (Kurosawa 2, Muraki 4)
Sanjuro. *See* Tsubaki Sanjuro, 1962
Sanjusangendo toshiya monogatari, 1945 (Naruse 2, Hasegawa 3, Tanaka 3)
Sanka, 1972 (Shindo 2)
San-kyodai no ketto, 1960 (Hasegawa 3)
San-nin no kaoyaku, 1960 (Hasegawa 3, Kyo 3)
Sannin-musume kampai, 1962 (Iwashita 3)
Sanroku, 1962 (Yamada 3)
Sans famille, 1934 (Allégret, M. 2, Braunberger 4, Jaubert 4, Trauner 4)
Sans famille, 1958 (Blier 3, Brasseur 3, Cervi 3)
Sans laisser d'adresse, 1950 (Blier 3, Piccoli 3, Douy 4, Kosma 4)
Sans le joug, 1911 (Feuillade 2)
Sans lendemain, 1940 (Ophuls 2, Feuillère 3, Douy 4, Lourié 4, Schufftan 4)
Sans mobile apparent, 1971 (Audran 3, Sanda 3, Trintignant 3, Morricone 4)
Sans tambour ni trompette, 1950 (Berry 3)
Sans Tambour ni trompette, 1960 (Rosay 3)
Sansar Simante, 1966 (Ghatak 2)
Sanshiro of Ginza. *See* Ginza Sanshiro, 1950
Sanshiro Sugata. *See* Sugata Sanshiro, 1943
Sanshiro Sugata—Part 2. *See* Zoku Sugata Sanshiro, 1945
Sansho dayu, 1954 (Mizoguchi 2, Kagawa 3, Shindo 3, Tanaka 3, Hayasaka 4, Miyagawa 4, Yoda 4)
Sansho the Bailiff. *See* Sansho dayu, 1954
Sanskar, 1958 (Biswas 3)
Sånt händer inte här, 1950 (Bergman 2, Fischer 4)
Santa Catalina Islands, 1914 (Sennett 2)
Santa Catalina, Magic Isle of the Pacific, 1911 (Dwan 2)
Santa Claus: The Movie, 1985 (Meredith 3, Moore, D. 3, Mancini 4)
Santa Elena piccolo isola, 1942 (Sordi 3)
Santa Fe, 1951 (Scott, R. 3, Brown, Harry Joe 4)
Santa Fe Marshal, 1940 (Boyd 3, Head 4)
Santa Fe Scouts, 1943 (Canutt 4)
Santa Fe Stampede, 1938 (Farnum 3, Wayne 3, Canutt 4)
Santa Fe Trail, 1930 (Arlen 3, Head 4)
Santa Fe Trail, 1940 (Curtiz 2, Bond 3, De Havilland 3, Flynn 3, Heflin 3, Kennedy, A. 3, Massey 3, Reagan 3, Buckner 4, Friedhofer 4, Polito 4, Steiner 4, Wallis 4)
Santé à l'étable, 1957 (Braunberger 4)
Sante est malade ou Les Pauvres meurent les premiers. *See* Saluta e malato, 1971
Santee, 1972 (Ford, G. 3)

Savage, 1918 (Moore, C. 3)
Savage, 1926 (Murfin 4)
Savage, 1952 (Cody 3, Heston 3, Head 4, Seitz 4)
Savage. See Sauvage, 1975
Savage Bees, 1976 (Johnson, B. 3)
Savage Brigade. See Brigade sauvage, 1939
Savage Eye, 1960 (Strick 2, Fields 4, Maddow 4, Rosenman 4, Wexler 4)
Savage Guns. See Terra bruta, 1962
Savage Innocents, 1960 (Ray, N. 2, O'Toole 3, Quinn 3, Wong 3, Mathieson 4)
Savage Innocents. See Dents du diable, 1960
Savage Is Loose, 1974 (Scott, G. 3)
Savage/Love, 1981 (Clarke 2)
Savage Messiah, 1972 (Russell 2, Russell 4)
Savage Mutiny, 1953 (Weissmuller 3, Katzman 4)
Savage Pampas, 1967 (Taylor, R. 3)
Savage Sam, 1963 (Disney 2)
Savage Seven, 1968 (Kovacs 4)
Savage State. See Etat sauvage, 1978
Savage Triangle. See Garçon sauvage, 1951
Savage Woman, 1918 (Edeson 4)
Savages, 1972 (Ivory 2, Lassally 4)
Savant, 1974 (Fresnay 3)
Save Our Beach. See Sunset Cove, 1978
Save the Children Fund Film, 1971 (Loach 2)
Save the Ship, 1923 (Laurel 3, Roach 4)
Save the Tiger, 1973 (Lemmon 3)
Save Your Money, 1921 (Roach 4)
Saved by a Watch, 1914 (Mix 3)
Saved by Her Horse, 1915 (Mix 3)
Saved by Love, 1908 (Porter 2)
Saved by the Belle, 1939 (Three Stooges 3)
Saved by the Pony Express, 1913 (Mix 3)
Saved by Wireless, 1915 (Sennett 2)
Saved from Court Martial, 1912 (Nilsson 3)
Saved from Himself, 1911 (Griffith 2, Normand 3, Bitzer 4)
Saved from the Torrents, 1911 (Bushman 3)
Savetier et le financier, 1909 (Feuillade 2)
Saving Grace, 1914 (Gish, D. 3, Loos 4)
Saving of Bill Blewitt, 1936 (Cavalcanti 2, Grierson 2, Watt 2)
Saving Presence, 1914 (Loos 4)
Saving the Family Name, 1916 (Weber 2)
Savitri, 1961 (Biswas 4)
Savoy-Hotel 217, 1936 (Albers 3, Herlth 4, Rohrig 4, Wagner 4)
Saw Mill Mystery, 1937 (Terry 4)
Sawdust and Salome, 1914 (Talmadge, N. 3)
Sawdust and Tinsel. See Gycklarnas afton, 1953
Sawdust Paradise, 1928 (Bosworth 3, Rosson 4)
Sawdust Ring, 1917 (Love 3)
Sawdust Trail, 1924 (Miller, V. 4)
Sawmill, 1921 (Hardy 3)
Saxon Charm, 1948 (Hayward 3, Montgomery 3, Krasner 4)
Saxophon Susi, 1928 (Albers 3, Ondra 3)
Say Goodbye, Maggie Cole, 1972 (Hayward 3)
Say Hello to Yesterday, 1971 (Simmons 3)
Say It Again, 1926 (La Cava 2, Cronjager 4, Rosson 4)
Say It in French, 1938 (Milland 3, Head 4)
Say It With Babies, 1926 (Hardy 3, Roach 4)
Say It With Flowers, 1934 (Coburn, C. 3)
Say it With Flowers. See Sag det med bloomer, 1952
Say It with Music, 1933 (Wilcox 2)
Say It with Music. See Sag det i toner, 1929
Say It With Sables, 1928 (Capra 2, Bushman 3, Walker 4)
Say It with Songs, 1929 (Bacon 2, Jolson 3, Garmes 4, Zanuck 4)
Say One for Me, 1959 (Tashlin 2, Crosby 3, Reynolds, D. 3, Wagner 3, Cahn 4, Lemaire 4, Wheeler 4)
Say! Young Fellow, 1918 (Fairbanks, D. 3)
Sayat nova, 1972 (Paradzhanov 2)
Sayidet el Kitar, 1952 (Chahine 2)
Sayili kabadayilar, 1965 (Guney 2)
Sayonara, konnichiwa, 1959 (Ichikawa 2, Kyo 3)
Sayonara, 1957 (Logan 2, Brando 3, Hopper 3, Prinz 4, Waxman 4)

Saysons gais, 1930 (Rosay 3)
Saza, 1951 (Anand 3, Burman 4)
Sbaglio di essere vivo, 1945 (De Sica 2, Cervi 3)
Sbandati, 1955 (Birri 2, Di Venanzo 4, Fusco 4)
Sbarco di Anzio, 1968 (Dmytryk 2, Falk 3, Giannini 3, Kennedy, A. 3, Ryan 3, De Laurentiis 4)
Sbatti il mostro in prima pagina, 1972 (Bellocchio 2, Volonté 3)
Scabies, 1969 (Grgić 4)
Scacco tutto matto, 1968 (Robinson, E. 3)
Scalawag, 1973 (Douglas, K. 3, Cardiff 4)
Scalp Treatment, 1952 (Lantz 4)
Scalp Trouble, 1939 (Clampett 4)
Scalpel, Please. See Skalpel, prosím, 1985
Scalphunters, 1968 (Pollack 2, Lancaster 3, Winters 3, Bernstein 4)
Scamp, 1957 (Attenborough 3, Francis 4)
Scampolo, 1958 (Schneider 3)
Scampolo, ein Kind der Strasse, 1932 (Wilder 2, Courant 4)
Scampolo '53, 1953 (Rota 4)
Scandal, 1915 (Weber 2)
Scandal, 1917 (Talmadge, C. 3)
Scandal, 1929 (Ruggles 2)
Scandal. See Shubun, 1950
Scandal. See Skandalen, 1912
Scandal. See Sukyandaru, 1950
Scandal about Eva. See Skandal um Eva, 1930
Scandal at Scourie, 1953 (Negulesco 2, Garson 3, Moorehead 3, Pidgeon 3, Plunkett 4)
Scandal for Sale, 1932 (O'Brien, P. 3, Freund 4)
Scandal in Paris, 1946 (Sirk 2, Sanders 3, Eisler 4)
Scandal in Paris. See Frau auf der Folter, 1927
Scandal in Sorrento. See Pane, amore e . . ., 1955
Scandal Mongers, 1918 (Stahl 2, Weber 2)
Scandal of Colonel Redl. See Aféra plukovníka Redla, 1931
Scandal Sheet, 1931 (Cromwell 2, Brook 3, Francis, K. 3)
Scandal Sheet, 1938 (Head 4)
Scandal Sheet, 1952 (Fuller 2, Crawford, B. 3, Reed, D. 3, Duning 4, Guffey 4)
Scandal Sheet, 1985 (Lancaster 3)
Scandal Street, 1938 (Ayres 3, Beavers 3)
Scandale, 1934 (L'Herbier 2, Marais 3, Matras 4, Schufftan 4)
Scandale, 1948 (Jeanson 4)
Scandale, 1967 (Chabrol 2, Audran 3, Perkins 3, Gégauff 4, Rabier 4)
Scandale au village, 1913 (Feuillade 2)
Scandalo, 1966 (Aimée 3)
Scandalo, 1975 (Storaro 4)
Scandalous, 1983 (Gielgud 3, Cardiff 4)
Scandalous Adventures of Buraikan. See Buraikan, 1970
Scandalous Eva. See Skandal um Eva, 1930
Scanian Guerilla. See Snapphanar, 1942
Scanners, 1981 (Smith, D., 4)
Scapegoat, 1914 (Mix 3)
Scapegoat, 1958 (Hamer 2, Davis 3, Guinness 3, Balcon 4, Kaper 4)
Scape-Mates, 1972 (Emshwiller 2)
Scapolo, 1956 (Scola 2, Manfredi 3, Sordi 3, Di Venanzo 4)
Scar. See Hollow Triumph, 1948
Scar Hanan, 1925 (Canutt 4)
Scarab Murder Case, 1936 (Havelock-Allan 4)
Scarabea—Wieviel Erde braucht der Mensch?, 1968 (Syberberg 2)
Scaramouche, 1923 (Ingram 2, Tourneur, J., 2, Novarro 3, Stone 3, Seitz 4, Vorkapich 4)
Scaramouche, 1952 (Sidney 2, Ferrer, M. 3, Granger 3, Leigh, J. 3, Stone 3, Gibbons 4, Rosher 4, Wilson, C. 4, Young, V. 4)
Scarecrow, 1920 (Keaton 2)
Scarecrow, 1922 (Astor 3)
Scarecrow, 1973 (Pollack 2, Schatzberg 2, Hackman 3, Pacino 3, Wilder 3, Zsigmond 4)
Scarecrow, 1982 (Carradine 3)
Scarecrow. See Strašilo, 1957
Scared Crows, 1939 (Fleischer, M. and D. 2)
Scared Stiff, 1926 (Roach 4)
Scared Stiff, 1953 (Lewis 2, Crosby 3, Hope 3, Malone 3, Martin, D. 3, Miranda 3, Head 4, Laszlo 4, Wallis 4)
Scared to Death, 1947 (Lugosi 3)

Scaredy Cat, 1948 (Jones 2)
Scarem Much, 1924 (Sennett 2)
Scarf, 1951 (Dupont 2, Ireland 3, McCambridge 3, Planer 4)
Scarface, 1932 (Hawks 2, Karloff 3, Muni 3, Raft 3, Burnett 4, Garmes 4, Hecht 4, Mahin 4, Miller, S. 4, Westmore, M. 4)
Scarface, 1983 (De Palma 2, Pacino 3, Alonzo 4)
Scarface Mob, 1959 (Wynn 3)
Scarlet and the Black, 1983 (Gielgud 3, Peck 3, Morricone 4)
Scarlet Angel, 1952 (De Carlo 3, Hudson 3)
Scarlet Blade, 1963 (Reed, O. 3)
Scarlet Buccaneer. See Swashbuckler, 1976
Scarlet Camellia. See Goben no tsubaki, 1965
Scarlet Car, 1917 (Chaney Lon 3)
Scarlet Car, 1923 (Miller, V. 4)
Scarlet Claw, 1944 (Bruce 3, Rathbone 3, Salter 4)
Scarlet Coat, 1955 (Sturges, J. 2, Sanders 3, Wilde 3, Plunkett 4)
Scarlet Dawn, 1932 (Dieterle 2, Auer 3, Fairbanks, D. Jr. 3, Grot 4, Haller 4, Orry-Kelly 4)
Scarlet Days, 1919 (Griffith 2, Barthelmess 3, Bitzer 4)
Scarlet Drop, 1918 (Ford, J. 2, Carey 3)
Scarlet Empress, 1934 (Von Sternberg 2, Darwell 3, Dietrich 3, Jaffe 3, Banton 4, Dreier 4, Glennon 4)
Scarlet Fever. See Skarlatina, 1924
Scarlet Honeymoon, 1924 (Goulding 2)
Scarlet Hour, 1956 (Curtiz 2, Tashlin 2, Head 4)
Scarlet Lady, 1928 (Crosland 2, Oland 3, Meredyth 4)
Scarlet Letter, 1907 (Olcott 2)
Scarlet Letter, 1926 (Sjostrom 2, Cody 3, Gish, L. 3, Walthall 3, Gibbons 4, Marion 4)
Scarlet Letter, 1934 (Farnum 3, Moore, C. 3, Walthall 3)
Scarlet Letter. See Scharlachrote Buchstabe, 1972
Scarlet Lily, 1923 (Schulberg 4)
Scarlet Pimpernel, 1928 (Wilcox 2)
Scarlet Pimpernel, 1935 (Bruce 3, Howard, L. 3, Massey 3, Oberon 3, Behrman 4, Biro 4, Hornbeck 4, Korda 4, Mathieson 4, Meerson 4, Rosson 4, Sherwood 4, Wimperis 4)
Scarlet Pumpernickel, 1950 (Jones 2)
Scarlet River, 1933 (Chaney Lon, Jr. 3, McCrea 3, Canutt 4, Musuraca 4, Plunkett 4)
Scarlet Road, 1916 (Nilsson 3)
Scarlet Runner, 1916 (Menjou 3)
Scarlet Saint, 1925 (Astor 3)
Scarlet Seas, 1928 (Barthelmess 3, Young, L. 3, Polito 4)
Scarlet Sin, 1915 (Bosworth 3)
Scarlet Street, 1945 (Lang 2, Bennett J. 3, Duryea 3, Robinson, E. 3, Banton 4, Krasner 4, Nichols 4, Salter 4, Wanger 4)
Scarlet Thread, 1951 (Harvey 3)
Scarlet West, 1925 (Bow 3)
Scarlet Woman. See Femme écarlate, 1968
Scarlet Woman. See Scarlet Lady, 1928
Scars and Stripes, 1919 (Laurel 3)
Scars of Dracula, 1970 (Lee, C. 3, Bernard 4)
Scars of Possession, 1914 (Bushman 3)
Scary Time, 1960 (Clarke 2, Dickinson 2)
Scat Cats, 1956 (Hanna and Barbera 4)
Scatenato, 1967 (Gassman 3, Guerra 4)
Scattered Body and the World Upside Down. See Cuerpo repartido y el mundo al revés, 1975
Scattered Clouds. See Midaregumo, 1967
Scattergood Meets Broadway, 1941 (Tiomkin 4)
Scavenger Hunt, 1979 (Gordon 3, McDowall 3)
Scavengers, 1959 (Cromwell 2)
Scavengers. See Recuperanti, 1969
Sceicco bianco, 1952 (Fellini 2, Masina 3, Sordi 3, Flaiano 4, Pinelli 4, Rota 4)
Sceicco rosso, 1962 (Fusco 4)
Scélérats, 1960 (Morgan 3, Evein 4)
Scène d'escamotage, 1897–98 (Guy 2)
Scène en cabinet particulier vue à travers le trou de la serrure, 1902 (Guy 2)
Scene Nun, Take One, 1964 (York, S. 3)
Scene of the Crime, 1949 (Johnson, V. 3, Irene 4, Previn 4, Schnee 4)
Scenens Børn, 1913 (Christensen 2)

Scener ur ett aktenskap, 1973 (Bergman 2, Andersson B. 3, Ullmann 3, Nykvist 4)
Scenes de la vie cruelle, 1910 (Zecca 2)
Scènes de la vie de café. See Petit Café, 1962
Scènes de la vie parallèle. See Noroît, 1976
Scènes de ménage, 1954 (Blier 3, D'Eaubonne 4)
Scènes d'enfants, 1896–97 (Lumière 2)
Scènes directoire series, 1904 (Guy 2)
Scenes from a Marriage. See Scener ur ett aktenskap, 1973
Scenes from the Portuguese Class Struggle, 1977 (Kramer, R. 2)
Scenes from Under Childhood, 1970 (Brakhage 2)
Scenes in an Orphans' Asylum, 1903 (Porter 2)
Scent of a Woman. See Profumo di donna, 1974
Scent of Incense. See Koge, 1964
Scent of Mystery, 1960 (Lorre 3, Lukas 3, Taylor, E. 3, Cardiff 4, Korda 4)
Scent of the Matterhorn, 1961 (Jones 2)
Scent of Women. See Profumo di donna, 1974
Scenti-Mental Over You, 1946 (Jones 2)
Scent-Imental Romeao, 1951 (Jones 2)
Scenting a Terrible Crime, 1913 (Browning 2)
Sceriffa, 1959 (Tognazzi 3)
Schaatsenrijden, 1929 (Ivens 2)
Schachnovelle, 1960 (Bloom 3, Jurgens 3)
Schädel der Pharaonentochter, 1920 (Jannings 3, Kortner 3)
Schakel met het verleden. See Paleontologie, 1959
Scharlachrote Buchstabe, 1972 (Wenders 2, Vogler 3)
Scharlatan. See Namenlos, 1923
Scharloachrote Dschunke. See Scotland Yard jagt Doktor Mabuse, 1963
Schastlivogo plavaniya, 1949 (Cherkassov 3)
Schastye, 1932 (Cherkassov 3)
Schatten, 1918 (Dupont 2)
Schatten, 1922 (Robison 2, Kortner 3, Rasp 3, Wagner 4)
Schatten der Engel, 1976 (Fassbinder 2)
Schatten der Unterwelt, 1931 (Galeen 4)
Schatten der Vergangenheit, 1917 (Oswald 2)
Schatten des Meeres, 1912 (Porten 3, Messter 4)
Schatten uber den Insel, 1952 (Geschonneck 3)
Schatten uber St. Pauli, 1938 (Wagner 4)
Schattenkinder des Glucks, 1922 (Banky 3)
Schattered. See Scherben, 1921
Schatz, 1923 (Pabst 2, Krauss 3, Herlth 4, Rohrig 4)
Schatz der Azteken, 1965 (Siodmak 2)
Schatz der Gesine Jakobsen, 1923 (Wegener 3)
Schatz, mach kasse, 1926 (Albers 3, Planer 4)
Schatze des Teufels, 1955 (Porten 3)
Schatzsucher, 1979 (Hoppe 3)
Schauplätze, 1967 (Wenders 2)
Scheherazade. See Shéhérazade, 1963
Schéhérezade, 1963 (Godard 2, Rey 3)
Scheidungsgrund, 1937 (Ondra 3)
Scheintote Chinese, 1928 (Reiniger 2)
Schéma d'une identification, 1946 (Resnais 2, Philipe 3)
Schemers, 1913 (Bunny 3)
Schemers, 1916 (Hardy 3)
Scheming Gambler's Paradise. See Tripot clandestin, 1905
Scheming Schemers, 1956 (Three Stooges 3)
Scherben, 1921 (Pick 2, Krauss 3, Mayer 4)
Scherzo, 1932 (Cortez 4)
Scherzo, 1939–41 (McLaren 2)
Scheusal. See Dúval, 1959
Schiava del paradiso, 1967 (Brazzi 3)
Schicksal, 1924 (Veidt 3, Planer 4)
Schicksal, 1942 (George, H. 3)
Schicksal am Lenkrad, 1953 (Eisler 4)
Schicksal aus zweiter Hand, 1949 (Staudte 2)
Schicksal derer von Hapsburg, 1929 (Riefenstahl 2)
Schicksal einer schonen Frau, 1932 (Dagover 3)
Schielende Gluck. See Zezowate szczeście, 1960
Schiff der verlorene Menschen, 1929 (Tourneur, M. 2, Dietrich 3, Kortner 3, Modot 3)
Schiff in Not, 1925 (Frohlich 3)

Schiff in Not, 1936 (Ruttmann 2)
Schimbul de miine, 1959 (Mészáros 2)
Schinderhannes, 1927 (Homolka 3, Rasp 3)
Schinderhannes, 1958 (Jurgens 3, Schell, Maria 3)
Schirm mit dem Schwan, 1915 (Wiene 2, Messter 4)
Schizoid, 1980 (Kinski 3)
Schizoid. See Lucertola con la pelle di donna, 1971
Schlagende Wetter, 1923 (Metzner 4)
Schlagerparade, 1953 (Chevalier 3)
Schlange mit dem Madchenkopf, 1919 (Albers 3)
Schlangenei, 1977 (Bergman 2, De Laurentiis 4, Nykvist 4)
Schlangenei. See Serpent's Egg, 1977
Schlangengrube und das Pendel,.967 (Lee, C. 3)
Schlemihl, 1915 (Oswald 2, Pick 2, Schildkraut 3)
Schleppzug M 17, 1933 (George, H. 3)
Schlock, 1971 (Baker 4)
Schloss, 1968 (Schell, Maximilian 3)
Schloss Hubertus: Der Fischer von Heiligensee, 1955 (Dagover 3)
Schloss im Suden, 1933 (Wagner 4)
Schloss Vogelod, 1921 (Murnau 2, Tschechowa 3, Herlth 4, Mayer 4, Pommer 4, Wagner 4, Warm 4)
Schlosser und Katen, 1957 (Geschonneck 3)
Schlossherr von Hohenstein, 1917 (Oswald 2)
Schlussakkord, 1936 (Sirk 2, Dagover 3)
Schlussakkord, 1960 (Auric 4)
Schlussel, 1974 (Hoffmann 3)
Schmetterlingsschlacht, 1924 (Nielsen 3)
Schmuck des Rajah, 1918 (Gad 2)
Schneider's Anti-Noise Crusade, 1909 (Griffith 2)
Schnitz the Tailor, 1913 (Sennett 2)
Schody, 1964 (Hofman 4)
Scholar, 1918 (Hardy 3)
Schön muss man sein, 1951 (Ondra 3)
Schöne Abenteuer, 1924 (Albers 3, Banky 3)
Schöne Abenteuer, 1932 (Arletty 3, Wagner 4)
Schöne Abenteuer, 1959 (Herlth 4)
Schöne Lugnerin, 1959 (Schneider 3)
Schöne Prinzessin von China, 1916 (Reiniger 2)
Schöne Sunderin, 1915 (Oswald 2)
Schönen Tage von Aranjuez, 1933 (Grundgens 3)
Schöner Gigolo—armer Gigolo, 1978 (Dietrich 3, Jurgens 3, Schell, Maria 3)
Schönheitspflasterchen, 1937 (Dagover 3)
Schönste Geschenk, 1916 (Lubitsch 2)
Schönste tag meines Lebens, 1957 (Vích 4)
School. See Szkola, 1958
School Begins, 1928 (Roach 4)
School Birds, 1937 (Terry 4)
School Days, 1932 (Fleischer, M. and D. 2, Iwerks 4)
School Daze, 1942 (Terry 4)
School for Cats. See Kočičí škola, 1961
School for Deafmutes. See Escuela de sordomudos, 1967
School for Girls, 1934 (Farnum 3, Nilsson 3)
School for Husbands, 1937 (Harrison 3)
School for Love. See Futures vedettes, 1955
School for Sabotage. See They Came to Blow Up America, 1943
School for Scandal, 1923 (Rathbone 3)
School for Scandal, 1930 (Dickinson 2, Carroll M. 3, Harrison 3)
School for Scoundrels, 1960 (Hamer 2, Sim 3, Addison 4)
School for Secrets, 1946 (Richardson 3, Ustinov 3, Dillon 4)
School for Secrets. See Secret Flight, 1946
School for Sex. See Nikutai no gakko, 1965
School for Stars, 1935 (Havelock-Allan 4)
School for Wives, 1925 (Ruttenberg 4)
School Ma'am of Snake, 1911 (Dwan 2)
School of Echoes. See Yamabiko gakko, 1952
School of Freedom. See Jiyu gakko, 1951
School of Love. See Nikutai no gakko, 1965
School, the Basis of Life. See Skola, základ života, 1938
Schoolgirl Diary. See Ore nove lezione di chimica, 1941
Schoolmaster of Mariposa, 1911 (Mix 3)
Schoolmistress on the Spree. See Lararinna på vift, 1941
Schoolteacher and the Waif, 1912 (Griffith 2, Pickford 3, Bitzer 4)

Schornstein No. 4. See Voleuse, 1966
Schpountz, 1937 (Pagnol 2, Brasseur 3, Fernandel 3)
Schrage Vögel, 1968 (Von Trotta 2)
Schrecken. See Januskopf, 1920
Schreckensnacht in der Menagerie, 1921 (Hoffmann 4)
Schritt vom Wege, 1939 (Grundgens 3)
Schuberts unvollendete Symphonie. See Leise flehen meine Lieder, 1933
Schuhpalast Pinkus, 1916 (Lubitsch 2, Rasp 3, Kraly 4)
Schuld, 1918 (Porten 3)
Schuld der Lavinia Morland, 1920 (Leni 2)
Schuld und Sühne. See Raskolnikow, 1923
Schuldig, 1913 (Messter 4)
Schuldig, 1928 (Courant 4)
Schuldig?. See Édes Anna, 1957
Schuss am Nebelhorn, 1932 (Rasp 3)
Schuss aus dem Fenster, 1920 (Albers 3)
Schuss durchs Fenster, 1950 (Jurgens 3)
Schuss im Morgengrauen, 1932 (Lorre 3)
Schusse im 3/4-Takt, 1965 (Brejchová 3)
Schut, 1964 (Siodmak 2)
Schutzenliesl, 1926 (Reisch 4)
Schuzka se stiny, 1982 (Brejchová 3)
Schwabemädle, 1919 (Lubitsch 2)
Schwache Strunde, 1919 (Basserman 3)
Schwartze Schaf, 1960 (Rasp 3)
Schwarz und Weiss wie Tage und Nachte, 1978 (Ganz 3)
Schwarze Abt, 1963 (Kinski 3)
Schwarze Domino, 1929 (Reisch 4)
Schwarze Gesicht, 1922 (Planer 4)
Schwarze Husar, 1932 (Veidt 3, Herlth 4, Planer 4, Rohrig 4)
Schwarze Kobra, 1963 (Kinski 3)
Schwarze Moritz, 1915 (Lubitsch 2)
Schwarze Rosen, 1935 (Wagner 4)
Schwarze Walfisch, 1934 (Jannings 3)
Schwarzer Jager Johanna, 1934 (Staudte 2, Grundgens 3)
Schwarzwaldmadel, 1929 (Reisch 4)
Schwebende Jungfrau, 1931 (Sakall 3)
Schwechater, 1958 (Kubelka 2)
Schwedische Nachtigall, 1941 (Herlth 4)
Schweigen im Walde, 1929 (Dieterle 2, Pasternak 4)
Schweigende Mund, 1951 (Homolka 3, Jurgens 3)
Schweik in Russian Captivity. See Švejk v ruském zajetí, 1926
Schweik's New Adventures, 1943 (Attenborough 3)
Schwere Jungens—Leichte Madchen, 1927 (Frohlich 3)
Schweres Opfer, 1911 (Porten 3, Messter 4)
Schwester Osso, 1924 (Porten 3)
Schwestern oder Die Balance des Glücks, 1979 (Von Trotta 2)
Schwur des Peter Hergatz, 1921 (Jannings 3, Freund 4)
Science, 1911 (Pickford 3, Gaudio 4)
Science Friction, 1959 (Vanderbeek 2)
Science Goes With People. See Věda jde s lidem, 1952
Scientific Cardplayer. See Scopone scientifico, 1972
Scientists of Tomorrow, 1968 (Ghatak 4)
Scipio Africanus. See Scipione l'Africano, 1937
Scipio detto anche l'Africano, 1971 (Gassman 3, Mangano 3, Mastroianni 3)
Scipione l'Africano, 1937 (Gallone 2)
Scissors, 1962 (Ghatak 4)
Sciuscià, 1946 (De Sica 2, Amidei 4, Zavattini 4)
Scoffer, 1921 (Dwan 2)
Scolgiera del peccato, 1950 (Cervi 3)
Sconosciuto, 1979 (Schneider 3)
Sconosciuto di San Marino, 1947 (De Sica 2, Magnani 3, Zavattini 4)
Scoop. See Honor of the Press, 1932
Scooper Dooper, 1947 (Bruckman 4)
Scopone scientifico, 1972 (Comencini 2, Cotten 3, Davis 3, Mangano 3, Sordi 3)
Scorcher, 1927 (Brown, Harry Joe 4)
Scorching Sands, 1923 (Laurel 3, Roach 4)
Scorned and Swindled, 1984 (Weld 3)
Scorpio, 1972 (Delon 3, Lancaster 3, Mirisch 4)
Scorpio Rising, 1962–63 (Anger 2)

corpion. *See* Skorpió, 1918

cotch, 1930 (Sennett 2)

cotch Highball, 1930 (Terry 4)

cotched in Scotland, 1954 (Three Stooges 3)

cotland Yard, 1930 (Howard 2, Bennett J. 3, Crisp 3, Fort 4, Friedhofer 4)

cotland Yard, 1941 (Carroll L. 3, Gwenn 3, Balderston 4, Miller, V. 4)

cotland Yard Commands. *See* Lonely Road, 1936

cotland Yard Investigation, 1945 (Von Stroheim 2)

cotland Yard jagt Doktor Mabuse, 1963 (Kinski 3)

cott of the Antarctic, 1948 (Lee, C. 3, Mills 3, More 3, Balcon 4, Cardiff 4, Unsworth 4)

cottish Mazurka, 1943 (Cardiff 4)

coumoune, 1972 (Belmondo 3, Cardinale 3, Depardieu 3)

coundrel, 1935 (Coward 4, Garmes 4, Hecht 4, MacArthur 4)

coundrel. *See* Akuto, 1965

coundrel. *See* Mariés de l'an II, 1971

coundrel. *See* Narazumono, 1956

coundrel in White. *See* Docteur Popaul, 1972

coundrel's Toll, 1916 (Sennett 2)

courge of the Desert, 1915 (Hart 3)

couts to the Rescue, 1939 (Cooper, J 3)

cram, 1932 (Laurel & Hardy 3, Roach 4)

crambled Arches, 1957 (Jones 2)

crambled Brains, 1951 (Three Stooges 3)

crambles, 1963 (Emshwiller 2)

crap for Victory, 1943 (Terry 4)

crapper, 1917 (Ford, J. 2)

crapper, 1922 (Miller, V. 4)

cratch as Scratch Can, 1930 (Brennan 3)

cratch My Back, 1920 (Olcott 2)

cream. *See* Night God Screamed, 1975

cream and Scream Again, 1970 (Cushing 3, Lee, C. 3, Price 3)

cream in the Night, 1935 (Chaney Lon, Jr. 3)

cream of Fear. *See* Taste of Fear, 1961

cream, Pretty Peggy, 1973 (Davis 3)

creamers, 1980 (Cotten 3, Ferrer, M. 3)

creaming Lady, 1972 (Pidgeon 3)

creaming Mimi, 1958 (Brown, Harry Joe 4, Guffey 4)

creaming Skull, 1958 (Crosby 3)

creaming Woman, 1972 (Cotten 3, De Havilland 3, Head 4, Williams, J. 4)

creaming Woman. *See* Screaming Lady, 1972

creams from the Second Floor. *See* Nikai no himei, 1931

creen—Entrance Exit, 1974 (Le Grice 2)

creen of Death. *See* Clum perdesi, 1960

creen Snapshots, 1933 (Three Stooges 3)

creen Snapshots No. 8, 1931 (Brown 3, Love 3)

creen Snapshots No. 11, 1934 (Karloff 3)

creen Snapshots No. 5, 1930 (Brown 3)

creen Snapshots No. 9, 1939 (Three Stooges 3)

creen Snapshots No. 1, 1934 (Cagney 3)

creen Snapshots No. 107, 1942 (Barrymore J. 3)

creen Snapshots No. 103, 1943 (Dietrich 3)

creen Snapshots No. 6, 1935 (Three Stooges 3)

creen Snapshots No. 3, 1922 (Keaton 2)

creen Snapshots No. 206, 1952 (Baxter A. 3)

creen Snapshots No. 225, 1954 (Abbott and Costello 3)

creen Test I, 1965 (Warhol 2)

creen Test II, 1965 (Warhol 2)

crewball Football, 1939 (Avery 2)

crewdriver, 1941 (Lantz 2)

crew's Adventures. *See* Sroublkova dobrodružství, 1962

crewy Squirrel, 1944 (Avery 2)

crewy Truant, 1945 (Avery 2)

cribe, 1966 (Keaton 2)

crim, 1976 (Chaplin 3)

crooge, 1951 (Sim 3)

crooge, 1970 (Evans 3, Finney 3, Guinness 3, More 3, Morris 4)

crub Me Mama with a Boogie Beat, 1941 (Lantz 4)

crubbers, 1982 (Zetterling 2)

crublady, 1917 (Dressler 3)

Scruffy, 1938 (McDowall 3)

Scruggs, 1965 (York, S. 3, Coutard 4)

Scudda Hoo! Scudda Hay!, 1948 (Brennan 3, Monroe 3, Wood 3, Lemaire 4)

Sculptor's Nightmare, 1908 (Bitzer 4)

Sculptures au moyen-age, 1949 (Renoir 4)

Scuola dei timidi, 1942 (Zavattini 4)

Scuola di Severino, 1949 (Di Venanzo 4)

Scuola elementare, 1954 (Lattuada 2, Spaak 4)

Scusi, facciamo l'amore, 1968 (Cortese 3, Feuillère 3, Morricone 4)

Scusi, lei è contrario o favorevole. *See* Scusi, lei è favorevole o contrario, 1966

Scusi, lei è favorevole o contrario, 1966 (Andersson B. 3, Mangano 3, Sordi 3, Amidei 4)

Scuttlers, 1920 (Farnum 3)

Se incontri Sartana, prega per la tua morte. *See* Sartana, 1968

Se io fossi gnesto!, 1942 (De Sica 2)

Se ki, se be, 1919 (Korda 2)

Se le paso la mano, 1952 (Alcoriza 4)

Se permette parliamo di donne, 1964 (Scola 2, Gassman 3)

Se tutte le donne del mondo, 1966 (De Laurentiis 4, Gherardi 4)

Se vincessi 100 milioni, 1953 (Tognazzi 3)

Sea, 1954 (Halas and Batchelor 2)

Sea Bat, 1930 (Ruggles 2, Karloff 3, Gibbons 4, Meredyth 4, Shearer 4)

Sea Beast, 1926 (Barrymore J. 3, Costello, D. 3, Meredyth 4, Westmore, E. 4)

Sea Chase, 1955 (Turner, L. 3, Wayne 3, Clothier 4)

Sea Devil. *See* Havets Djavul, 1935–36

Sea Devils, 1937 (Lupino 3, McLaglen 3, August 4, Hunt 4, Polglase 4)

Sea Devils, 1953 (Walsh 2, De Carlo 3, Hudson 3, Chase 4)

Sea Dogs, 1916 (Hardy 3)

Sea Dog's Tale, 1926 (Sennett 2, Hardy 3)

Sea Eagle. *See* Rosen på Tistelon, 1916

Sea Fever. *See* En rade, 1927

Sea Fort, 1940 (Cavalcanti 2, Dalrymple 4)

Sea Fury, 1958 (Baker S. 3, McLaglen 3, Shaw 3)

Sea God, 1930 (Arlen 3, Wray 3)

Sea Going Birds, 1932 (Sennett 2)

Sea Gull, 1926 (Von Sternberg 2)

Sea Gull, 1968 (Lumet 2, Mason 3, Redgrave, V. 3, Signoret 3, Fisher 4)

Sea Gull. *See* Woman of the Sea, 1926

Sea Hawk, 1924 (Beery 3)

Sea Hawk, 1940 (Curtiz 2, Crisp 3, Flynn 3, Rains 3, Blanke 4, Friedhofer 4, Grot 4, Koch 4, Korngold 4, Miller, S. 4, Orry-Kelly 4, Polito 4, Wallis 4)

Sea Hornet, 1951 (Glennon 4)

Sea Horses, 1926 (Dwan 2, Powell, W. 3, Howe 4)

Sea Hound, 1947 (Crabbe 3)

Sea in Flames. *See* Documents secrets, 1940

Sea Legs, 1929 (Heerman 4)

Sea Lion, 1921 (Bosworth 3, Love 3)

Sea Nymphs, 1914 (Sennett 2, Arbuckle 3, Normand 3)

Sea of Grass, 1947 (Kazan 2, Carey 3, Douglas, M. 3, Hepburn, K. 3, Tracy 3, Walker 3, Berman 4, Plunkett 4, Stothart 4, Stradling 4)

Sea of Lost Ships, 1953 (Brennan 3, Raine 4)

Sea of Sand, 1958 (Attenborough 3, Green, G. 4, Mathieson 4)

Sea Shall Not Have Them, 1954 (Bogarde 3, Redgrave, M. 3, Arnold 4, Mathieson 4)

Sea Spoilers, 1936 (Wayne 3)

Sea Squaw, 1925 (Sennett 2)

Sea Squawk, 1925 (Capra 2, Langdon 3)

Sea Theme, 1949 (Hall 4)

Sea Tiger, 1927 (Astor 3, Wilson, C. 4)

Sea Urchin, 1913 (Chaney Lon 3)

Sea Urchin, 1926 (Balfour 3, Balcon 4)

Sea Wall. *See* Barrage contre le Pacifique, 1958

Sea Wall. *See* Diga sul Pacifico, 1958

Sea Wife, 1957 (Burton 3)

Sea Wolf, 1913 (Bosworth 3)

Sea Wolf, 1920 (Sutherland 2)

Sea Wolf, 1930 (Behrman 4)

Sea Wolf, 1941 (Curtiz 2, Rossen 2, Fitzgerald 3, Garfield 3, Lupino 3,

Robinson, E. 3, Blanke 4, Friedhofer 4, Grot 4, Korngold 4, Polito 4, Wallis 4)
Sea Wolves, 1981 (Howard, T. 3, Moore, R. 3, Niven 3, Peck 3)
Seafarers, 1953 (Kubrick 2)
Seagull. *See* Kaitchka, 1915
Seagull. *See* Woman of the Sea, 1926
Seagulls over Sorrento, 1954 (Boulting 2, Junge 4, Rozsa 4)
Seagulls over Sorrento. *See* Crest of the Wave, 1954
Seal. *See* Pečat, 1955
Seal of Silence, 1913 (Ince 4)
Seal Skinners, 1939 (Freleng 4)
Seal Skins, 1932 (Pitts 3)
Sealed Cargo, 1951 (Andrews D. 3, Rains 3)
Sealed Hearts, 1919 (Goulding 2)
Sealed Lips, 1925 (Gaudio 4)
Sealed Lips, 1928 (Young, W. 4)
Sealed Lips, 1941 (Cortez 4, Salter 4)
Sealed Lips. *See* After Tonight, 1933
Sealed Lips. *See* Forseglade lappar, 1927
Sealed Lips. *See* Lèvres closes, 1906
Sealed Room, 1909 (Griffith 2, Pickford 3, Walthall 3, Bitzer 4)
Sealed Verdict, 1948 (Crawford, B. 3, Milland 3, Dreier 4, Friedhofer 4, Head 4)
Seamstress. *See* Svadlenka, 1936
Séance de cinématographe, 1909 (Linders 3)
Seance on a Wet Afternoon, 1964 (Attenborough 3, Barry 4)
Seapower, 1965 (Ford, G. 3)
Search, 1947 (Zinnemann 2, Clift 3)
Search. *See* Probe, 1972
Search for Beauty, 1934 (Crabbe 3, Lupino 3, Sheridan 3, Banton 4, Prinz 4)
Search for Bridey Murphy, 1956 (Wright 3, Head 4)
Search for Danger, 1949 (Leven 4)
Search for Oil. *See* Opsporing van aardolie, 1954
Search for Paradise, 1957 (Tiomkin 4)
Search for the Evil One, 1967 (Fields 4)
Search for the Gods, 1975 (Bellamy 3)
Search into Darkness, 1962 (Van Dyke, W. 2)
Searchers, 1956 (Ford, J. 2, Bond 3, Cody 3, Hunter 3, Wayne 3, Wood 3, Basevi 4, Cooper 4, Hoch 4, Nugent 4, Steiner 4)
Searching Eye, 1964 (Bass 4)
Searching Wind, 1946 (Dieterle 2, Basserman 3, Sidney 3, Young, R. 3, Dreier 4, Garmes 4, Wallis 4, Young, V. 4)
Seas Beneath, 1931 (Ford, J. 2, August 4, Nichols 4)
Sea's Hold. *See* Havsbandet, 1971
Seashell and the Clergyman. *See* Coquille et le clergyman, 1927
Seashore Baby, 1904 (Bitzer 4)
Seashore Frolics, 1903 (Porter 2)
Seasick Sailors, 1951 (Terry 4)
Seaside Adventure, 1952 (Terry 4)
Seaside Girl, 1907 (Hepworth 2)
Season for Love. *See* Morte-saison des amours, 1960
Season of Passion, 1961 (Borgnine 3, Lansbury 3)
Season of Passion. *See* Summer of the Seventeenth Doll, 1959
Seasons, 1963 (Ivanov-Vano 4)
Season's Greetinks, 1931 (Fleischer, M. and D. 2)
Seasons of Meiji. *See* Meiji haruaki, 1968
Seasons We Walked Together. *See* Futari de aruita ikutoshitsuki, 1962
Seats of the Mighty, 1914 (Barrymore L. 3)
Seawards the Great Ships, 1959 (Grierson 2)
Seaweed Children, 1973 (Lassally 4)
Seawolf, 1973 (Staudte 2)
Sebastian, 1968 (Powell 2, Bogarde 3, Sutherland 3, York, S. 3, Fisher 4, Goldsmith 4)
Sécheresse. *See* Vidas sêcas, 1963
Sechs Tage Heimaturlaub, 1941 (Frohlich 3)
Sechs Wochen unter den Apachen. *See* Achtung Harry! Augen auf!!, 1926
Seclusion Near a Forest. *See* Na samotě u lesa, 1977
Second Awakening of Christa Klages. *See* Zweite Erwachen der Christa Klages, 1977
Second Best, 1972 (Bates 3)

Second Best Secret Agent in the Whole Wide World. *See* Licensed to Kill, 1965
Second Chance, 1953 (Darnell 3, Mitchum 3, Palance 3, D'Agostino 4, Maté 4)
Second Chance. *See* Si c'était à refaire, 1976
Second Chances. *See* Probation, 1932
Second Childhood, 1936 (Roach 4)
Second Choice, 1930 (Costello, D. 3)
Second Chorus, 1940 (Astaire 3, Goddard 3, Meredith 3, Leven 4, Mercer 4, Pan 4)
Second Class Passenger, 1973 (Dovniković 4)
Second Clue, 1914 (Eason 4)
Second Coming of Suzanne, 1974 (Dreyfuss 3)
Second Commandment, 1915 (Nilsson 3)
Second Face, 1950 (Darwell 3)
Second Fiddle, 1923 (Astor 3)
Second Fiddle, 1939 (Henie 3, Power 3, Glennon 4, Zanuck 4)
Second Greatest Sex, 1955 (Crain 3, Lahr 3)
Second Hand Hearts, 1981 (Ashby 2, Wexler 4)
Second Hand Love, 1923 (Wellman 2)
Second Hand Rose, 1922 (Sutherland 2)
Second Hand Wife, 1932 (Bellamy 3, Clarke, C.C. 4, Friedhofer 4)
Second Honeymoon, 1937 (Chaney Lon, Jr. 3, Power 3, Trevor 3, Young, L. 3)
Second Hundred Years, 1927 (McCarey 2, Laurel and Hardy 3)
Second in Command, 1915 (Bushman 3)
Second Mrs. Fenway. *See* Her Honor, The Governor, 1926
Second Mrs. Roebuck, 1914 (Reid 3, Sweet 3)
Second Shot. *See* Zweite Schuss, 1943
Second Sight, 1911 (Pickford 3, Gaudio 4)
Second Son Crow. *See* Jinanbou garasu, 1955
Second Thoughts, 1983 (Mancini 4)
Second Time Around, 1961 (Reynolds, D. 3, Ritter 3, Mancini 4, Smith, J.M. 4)
Second Touch. *See* Twee vrouwen, 1979
Second Tour. *See* Druhá směna, 1940
Second Victory Loan Campaign Fund, 1945 (Davis 3)
Second Wife, 1930 (Glennon 4, Plunkett 4)
Second Wife, 1936 (Bond 3, Musuraca 4)
Second Woman, 1951 (Young, R. 3, Leven 4)
Second Youth, 1924 (Hunt 4)
Seconde Vérité, 1966 (Christian-Jaque 2, Douy 4)
Seconds, 1966 (Frankenheimer 2, Hudson 3, Alonzo 4, Bass 4, Goldsmith 4, Howe 4)
Second-Story Murder, 1930 (Young, L. 3)
Secours aux naufragés, 1903–04 (Guy 2)
Secret, 1974 (Noiret 3, Trintignant 3, Morricone 4)
Secret Agent, 1936 (Hitchcock 2, Carroll M. 3, Gielgud 3, Lorre 3, Young, R. 3, Balcon 4, Bennett 4, Reville 4)
Secret Agent X-9, 1937 (Chaney Lon, Jr. 3)
Secret Agents. *See* Guerre secrète, 1965
Secret Beyond the Door, 1948 (Lang 2, Bennett J. 3, Redgrave, M. 3 Banton 4, Cortez 4, Rozsa 4, Wanger 4)
Secret Bride, 1934 (Dieterle 2, Stanwyck 3, Blanke 4, Grot 4, Orry-Kelly 4)
Secret Call, 1931 (Arlen 3)
Secret Ceremony, 1968 (Losey 2, Farrow 3, Mitchum 3, Taylor, E. 3, Fisher 4)
Secret Code, 1918 (Swanson 3)
Secret Command, 1944 (Sutherland 2, O'Brien, P. 3, Planer 4)
Secret de Delhia, 1929 (Burel 4)
Secret de Mayerling, 1949 (Delannoy 2, Marais 3)
Secret de Monte-Cristo, 1948 (Brasseur 3)
Secret de Polichinelle, 1936 (Raimu 3, Rosay 3, Spaak 4)
Secret de Soeur Angèle, 1955 (D'Eaubonne 4)
Secret de Woronzeff, 1934 (Robison 2)
Secret del Sacerdote, 1941 (Armendáriz 3)
Secret des hommes bleus, 1960 (Ferreri 2)
Secret Diary of Sigmund Freud, 1984 (Kinski 3)
Secret du Chevalier d'Eon, 1960 (Blier 3, Alekan 4, Trauner 4)
Secret du forçat, 1913 (Feuillade 2)
Secret Flight, 1946 (Attenborough 3)
Secret Flight. *See* School for Secrets, 1946

Septima's Ideal. *See* Idéal Septimy, 1938
Sequestrati di Altona, 1962 (De Sica 2, Loren 3, Schell, Maximilian 3, Wagner 3, Ponti 4, Rota 4, Shostakovich 4, Zavattini 4)
Séquestrée, 1908 (Cohl 2)
Sequoia, 1934 (Stothart 4, Wilson, C. 4)
Sera'a fil Mina, 1955 (Chahine 2, Sharif 3)
Sera'a fil Nil, 1959 (Sharif 3)
Sera'a fil Wadi, 1953 (Chahine 2, Sharif 3)
Serafino, 1968 (Germi 2, Pinelli 4)
Seraglio, 1958 (Reiniger 2)
Sérail, 1976 (Caron 3)
Séraphin, 1921 (Feuillade 2)
Seraphita's Diary, 1982 (Wiseman 2)
Serdtse betsia mor, 1960 (Gurchenko 3)
Serdtse materi, 1966 (Donskoi 2)
Serdtze betsya vnov, 1956 (Tikhonov 3)
Serenade, 1916 (Hardy 3)
Serenade, 1921 (Walsh 2, Johnson, N. 3, Menzies 4)
Serenade, 1927 (d'Arrast 2, Menjou 3, Vajda 4)
Sérénade, 1939 (Jouvet 3, Kaufman 4, Renoir 4, Wakhévitch 4)
Serenade, 1956 (Mann 2, Fontaine 3, Price 3, Blanke 4, Cahn 4)
Serenade. *See* Broadway Serenade, 1939
Sérénade aux nuages, 1946 (Cayatte 2, Wakhévitch 4)
Sérénade de Texas, 1958 (Bourvil 3)
Serenade einer grossen Liebe, 1958 (Maté 4)
Serenal, 1959 (McLaren 2)
Serene Siam, 1937 (Hoch 4)
Serene Velocity, 1970 (Gehr 2)
Serenity, 1955–61 (Markopoulos 2)
Serenyi, 1918 (Veidt 3)
Serge Panine, 1939 (Rosay 3)
Sergeant, 1968 (Steiger 3)
Sergeant. *See* Krek, 1967
Sergeant Berry, 1930 (Albers 3)
Sergeant Byrne of the N.W.M.P., 1912 (Selig 4)
Sergeant Deadhead, 1965 (Keaton 2, Taurog 2, Arden 3, Crosby 4)
Sergeant Madden, 1939 (Von Sternberg 2, Beery 3, Seitz 4)
Sergeant Murphy, 1938 (Crisp 3, Reagan 3, Eason 4, McCord 4)
Sergeant Pepper's Lonely Hearts Club Band, 1978 (Pleasance 3, Roizman 4)
Sergeant Rutledge, 1960 (Ford, J. 2, Burke 3, Hunter 3, Marsh 3, Glennon 4)
Sergeant Ryker, 1963 (Marvin 3, Williams, J. 4)
Sergeant York, 1941 (Hawks 2, Huston 2, Bond 3, Brennan 3, Cook 3, Cooper, Gary 3, Young, G. 3, Eason 4, Edeson 4, Friedhofer 4, Koch 4, Lasky 4, Polito 4, Steiner 4, Wallis 4)
Sergeant's Boy, 1912 (Ince 4)
Sergeants Three, 1962 (Sturges, J. 2, Martin, D. 3, Sinatra 3, Burnett 4, Hoch 4)
Sergent X, 1931 (Mozhukin 3)
Sergent X, 1959 (Auric 4, Renoir 4)
Sergo Ordzhonikidze, 1937 (Vertov 2)
Serial, 1980 (Lee, C. 3, Weld 3, Schifrin 4)
Série noire, 1955 (Von Stroheim 2, Audiard 4)
Série noire, 1979 (Blier 3)
Sérieux comme le plaisir, 1974 (Huppert 3, Carrière 4)
Serious Charge, 1959 (Périnal 4)
Serious Game. *See* Allvarsamme leken, 1945
Serious Sixteen, 1910 (Griffith 2, Bitzer 4)
Serp i molot, 1921 (Pudovkin 2, Tisse 4)
Serpe, 1919 (Bertini 2)
Serpent, 1916 (Walsh 2, Bara 3, Oland 3)
Serpent, 1972 (Verneuil 2, Bogarde 3, Brynner 3, Fonda, H. 3, Noiret 3, Morricone 4, Renoir 4)
Serpent. *See* Ormen, 1966
Serpent of the Nile, 1953 (Katzman 4)
Serpent's Egg, 1977 (Ullmann 3)
Serpent's Egg. *See* Schlangenei, 1977
Serpico, 1973 (Lumet 2, Pacino 3, Allen, D. 4, De Laurentiis 4, Mirisch 4, Salt 4, Theodorakis 4)
Serpico: The Deadly Game, 1976 (Bernstein 4)
Sertse byotsa vnov, 1956 (Gurchenko 3)
Servant, 1963 (Losey 2, Bogarde 3, Pinter 4, Slocombe 4)

Servant in the House, 1921 (Gilbert 3, Hersholt 3)
Servante, 1969 (Gélin 3)
Servants All, 1936 (Cusack 3)
Servants' Entrance, 1934 (Ayres 3, Gaynor 3, Friedhofer 4, Raphaelson 4)
Service de Luxe, 1938 (Auer 3, Bennett C. 3, Price 3)
Service de sauvetage sur la côte belge, 1930 (Storck 2)
Service for Ladies, 1927 (d'Arrast 2, Menjou 3, Glazer 4, Rosson 4, Vajda 4)
Service for Ladies, 1932 (Korda 2, Howard, L. 3, Oberon 3, Biro 4, Junge 4, Vajda 4)
Service précipité, 1903 (Guy 2)
Service with a Smile, 1937 (Fleischer, M. and D. 2)
Service with the Colors, 1940 (Eason 4)
Seryozha, 1960 (Bondarchuk 3)
Ses Ancêtres, 1915 (Cohl 2)
60 Minutos con el primer mundial de boxeo amateur, 1974 (Alvarez 2)
Sešir, 1976 (Grgić 4)
Sesso degli angeli, 1968 (Fusco 4)
Sesso di diavolo, 1970 (Brazzi 3)
Sesso e volentieri, 1982 (Risi 2)
Sesso in confessionale, 1974 (Morricone 4)
Sesso matto, 1973 (Risi 2, Giannini 3)
Šest medvědu s Cibulkou, 1972 (Kopecký 3)
Sest Mušketýru, 1925 (Ondra 3)
Sestra Angelika, 1932 (Fric 2, Haas 3)
Sestřičky, 1983 (Kachyna 2)
Sestry, 1970 (Schorm 2)
Set Free, 1918 (Browning 2)
Sete Balas para Selma, 1967 (de Almeida 4)
Setenta veces siete, 1961 (Torre-Nilsson 2)
Seth's Temptation, 1910 (Olcott 2)
Setkání v Bukurešti, 1954 (Stallich 4)
Setkání v červenci, 1977 (Kachyna 2)
Setkání v Lipsku, 1959 (Kučera 4)
Setouchi shounen yakyu-dan, 1984 (Miyagawa 4)
Setřelé písmo, 1920 (Ondra 3)
Sette canne e un vestito, 1950 (Antonioni 2)
Sette Contadini, 1957 (Petri 2)
Sette contro la morte, 1964 (Ulmer 2)
Sette dell'orsa maggiore, 1952 (Rota 4)
Sette donne per i MacGregor, 1966 (Morricone 4)
Sette donne per una strage. *See* Frauen, die durch die Holle gehen, 1966
Sette fratelli Cervi, 1967 (Reggiani 3, Volonté 3, Zavattini 4)
Sette monaci d'oro, 1966 (Fabrizi 3)
Sette peccati, 1942 (Zavattini 4)
Sette peccati capitali, 1920 (Bertini 3)
Sette peccati capitali, 1952 (Rossellini 2)
Sette pistole per i MacGregor, 1966 (Morricone 4)
Sette strani cadaveri. *See* Morte sorride all'assassino, 1973
Sette uomini e un cervello, 1968 (Brazzi 3)
Sette volte donna, 1967 (Zavattini 4)
Sette volte donna. *See* Woman Times Seven, 1967
Setting the Style, 1914 (Bunny 3)
Settled at the Seaside, 1915 (Sennett 2)
Settled Out of Court, 1925 (Buchanan 3)
Settlement of Love. *See* Aijo no kessan, 1956
Set-Up, 1949 (Wise 2, Ryan 3, D'Agostino 4, Krasner 4)
Seul Amour, 1943 (Presle 3, Honegger 4, Matras 4)
Seul dans la nuit, 1945 (Blier 3)
Seul dans Paris, 1951 (Bourvil 3)
Sève de la terre, 1955 (Alexeieff and Parker 2)
Seven Ages, 1905 (Porter 2)
Seven Ages of Man, 1906 (Ince 4)
Seven Angry Men, 1955 (Hunter 3, Massey 3)
Seven Arts, 1958 (Popescu-Gopo 4)
Seven Beauties, 1975 (Rey 3)
Seven Beauties. *See* Pasqualino Settebelleze, 1975
Seven Brides for Seven Brothers, 1954 (Donen 2, Keel 3, Nilsson 3, Deutsch 4, Gillespie 4, Goodrich and Hackett 4, Kidd 4, Mercer 4, Plunkett 4)

Seven Brothers and One Sister Meet Dracula. *See* Legend of the Seven Golden Vampires, 1974

Seven Brothers Meet Dracula. *See* Legend of the Seven Golden Vampires, 1974

Seven Capital Sins. *See* Sept Péchés Capitaux, 1951

Seven Capital Sins. *See* Sept Péchés capitaux, 1962

Seven Chances, 1925 (Keaton 2, Arthur 3, Bruckman 4, Schenck 4)

Seven Cities of Gold, 1955 (Hunter 3, Quinn 3, Ballard 4, Friedhofer 4, Lemaire 4, Smith, J.M. 4)

7 Colored Ring. *See* Nanairo yubi wa, 1918

Seven Days Ashore, 1944 (Dumont 3, Mayo 3)

Seven Days in January. *See* 7 Dias de enero, 1979

Seven Days in May, 1964 (Frankenheimer 2, Douglas, K. 3, Gardner 3, Lancaster 3, March 3, O'Brien, E. 3, Goldsmith 4, Houseman 4)

Seven Days Leave, 1930 (Cromwell 2, Hathaway 2, Cooper, Gary 3, Lang 4)

Seven Days' Leave, 1942 (Walters 2, Ball 3, Mature 3)

Seven Days . . . Seven Nights. *See* Moderato cantabile, 1960

Seven Days to Noon, 1950 (Boulting 2, Addison 4, Bernard 4, Dehn 4)

Seven Deadly Sins. *See* Sept Péchés capitaux, 1962

Seven Deadly Sins. *See* Sette peccati capitali, 1952

Seven Different Ways. *See* Confessions, 1964

Seven Faces, 1929 (Muni 3, August 4, Friedhofer 4)

7 Faces of Dr. Lao, 1964 (Pal 2)

Seven Footprints to Satan, 1929 (Christensen 2, Polito 4)

Seven from Heaven, 1979 (Palance 3)

Seven Guns for the MacGregors. *See* Sette pistole per i MacGregor, 1966

Seven Hills of Rome, 1957 (Delli Colli 4)

711 Ocean Drive, 1950 (O'Brien, E. 3, Planer 4)

Seven Keys to Baldpate, 1917 (Nilsson 3)

Seven Keys to Baldpate, 1929 (Cronjager 4, Murfin 4, Plunkett 4)

Seven Keys to Baldpate, 1935 (Brennan 3, Plunkett 4, Polglase 4, Veiller 4)

7 Kinds of Trouble. *See* Belanin yedi turlusu, 1969

Seven Little Foys, 1955 (Cagney 3, Hope 3, Head 4)

7 Madmen. *See* Siete Locos, 1973

Seven Magnificent Gladiators, 1984 (Golan and Globus 4, Morricone 4)

Seven Men from Now, 1956 (Boetticher 2, Marvin 3, Scott, R. 3, Clothier 4)

7 Miles from Alcatraz, 1942 (Dmytryk 2)

Seven Minutes, 1971 (Carradine 3, De Carlo 3)

Seven Nights in Japan, 1976 (York, M. 3, Decaë 4)

Seven No-goods. *See* Yedi belalilar, 1970

Seven of Clubs. *See* Makkhetes, 1916

Seven Pearls, 1917 (Grot 4)

Seven Samurai. *See* Shichinin no samurai, 1954

Seven Seas to Calais. *See* Dominatore dei sette mari, 1960

Seven Sinners, 1925 (Milestone 2, Brook 3)

Seven Sinners, 1936 (Balcon 4, Gilliat 4, Metzner 4)

Seven Sinners, 1940 (Garnett 2, Auer 3, Crawford, B. 3, Dietrich 3, Homolka 3, Wayne 3, Irene 4, Maté 4, Pasternak 4, Salter 4)

7 Sisters, 1915 (Olcott 2)

Seven Swans, 1917 (Barthelmess 3)

Seven Sweethearts, 1942 (Borzage 2, Beavers 3, Grayson 3, Heflin 3, Meek 3, Sakall 3, Pasternak 4, Reisch 4, Waxman 4)

Seven Thieves, 1960 (Hathaway 2, Robinson, E. 3, Steiger 3, Wallach 3, Wheeler 4)

7 Thunders, 1957 (Schlesinger 2)

Seven Till Five, 1934–35 (McLaren 2)

7 Waves Away. *See* Abandon Ship, 1956

Seven Ways from Sundown, 1960 (Murphy 3)

Seven Wild Lions. *See* Yedi dağin aslani, 1966

Seven Women from Hell, 1961 (Crosby 4)

Seven Women, 1965 (Ford, J. 2, Bancroft 3, Bernstein 4, La Shelle 4, Plunkett 4)

Seven Wonders of the World, 1955 (Garnett 2, Raksin 4)

Seven Year Itch, 1955 (Wilder 2, Homolka 3, Monroe 3, Axelrod 4, Bass 4, Cahn 4, Krasner 4, Lemaire 4, Newman 4, Wheeler 4)

Seven Years' Bad Luck, 1921 (Linders 3)

Seven-Per-Cent Solution, 1976 (Arkin 3, Duvall, R. 3, Olivier 3,

Redgrave, V. 3, Williamson 3, Adam 4, Addison 4, Morris 4, Reynolds 4)

Seventeen, 1940 (Cooper, J. 3, Dreier 4, Head 4)

Seventeen Moments in Spring. *See* Semnadtsat mnogovenii vesny, 1973

1776, 1909 (Griffith 2, Pickford 3, Bitzer 4)

1776, 1972 (Jenkins 4)

17th International Tournee of Animation, 1981 (Patel 4)

17th Parallel. *See* Dix-septième parallèle, 1968

Seventeen-Year-Olds. *See* Siebzehnjarigen, 1929

7th Age. *See* Gamle, 1947

7th Anniversary of the Red Army, 1925 (Vertov 2)

Seventh Bandit, 1926 (Carey 3, Polito 4)

Seventh Cavalry, 1955 (Scott, R. 3, Brown, Harry Joe 4)

Seventh Continent. *See* Sedmi kontinent, 1966

Seventh Cross, 1944 (Zinnemann 2, Moorehead 3, Tracy 3, Berman 4, Freund 4, Gibbons 4, Irene 4)

Seventh Dawn, 1964 (Holden 3, York, S. 3, Young, F. 4)

Seventh Day, 1909 (Griffith 2, Pickford 3, Bitzer 4)

7th Day, 1922 (Goulding 2, King 2, Barthelmess 3)

7th Day, 8th Night. *See* Den sedmý, osmá noc, 1969

Seventh Heaven, 1927 (Borzage 2, Gaynor 3, Glazer 4)

Seventh Heaven, 1937 (King 2, Hersholt 3, Simon, S. 3, Stewart 3, Zanuck 4)

Seventh Heaven. *See* Sjunde himlen, 1956

Seventh Juror. *See* Septième Juré, 1962

Seventh Man, 1943 (Lewton 4)

Seventh Seal. *See* Sjunde inseglet, 1957

Seventh Sin, 1957 (Franklin 2, Minnelli 2, Aumont 3, Rosay 3, Sanders 3, Rose 4, Rozsa 4)

Seventh Son, 1912 (Reid 3)

7th Survivor, 1941 (Fisher 2)

Seventh Veil, 1945 (Mason 3, Mathieson 4)

Seventh Victim, 1943 (Robson 2, Bodeen 4, D'Agostino 4, Musuraca 4)

Seventh Voyage of Sinbad, 1958 (Harryhausen 4, Herrmann 4)

Seventies People. *See* 70-Talets Människor, 1975

70, 1970 (Breer 2)

75 Years of Cinema Museum, 1972 (Daves 2, Hathaway 2)

79 Springtimes of Ho Chi Minh. *See* 79 Primaveras, 1969

77, 1977 (Breer 2)

70,000 Witnesses, 1932 (Fort 4, Krasner 4)

72 gradusa nizhe nulia, 1976 (Yankovsky 3)

Seven-Ups, 1973 (Scheider 3)

Severed Head, 1970 (Attenborough 3, Bloom 3, Remick 3, Raphael 4)

Severed Heads. *See* Cabezas cortadas, 1970

Severní přístav, 1954 (Kopecký 3, Brdečka 4)

Severnoe siianie, 1926 (Enei 4)

Severo Torelli, 1914 (Feuillade 2, Musidora 3)

Sevgili muhafizin, 1970 (Guney 2)

Sevillana, 1930 (Novarro 3)

Sevodiya, 1923–25 (Vertov 2)

Sevres Porcelain. *See* Porcelaines tendres, 1909

Sewak, 1975 (Azmi 3)

Sewer, 1912 (Guy 2)

Sex, 1920 (Niblo 2, Barnes 4, Sullivan 4)

Sex and the College Girl, 1970 (Arlen 3)

Sex and the Married Woman, 1977 (Wynn 3, Head 4)

Sex and the Single Girl, 1964 (Bacall 3, Curtis 3, Ferrer, M. 3, Fonda, H. 3, Horton 3, Wood 3, Head 4, Lang 4)

Sex and Violence. *See* Sesso e volentieri, 1982

Sex Hygiene, 1941 (Ford, J. 2)

Sex Kittens Go to College, 1960 (Carradine 3, Coogan 3, Weld 3)

Sex, Love and Marriage. *See* Love and Marriage, 1970

Sex O'Clock U.S.A., 1976 (Reichenbach 2, Braunberger 4)

Sex Power, 1970 (Vangelis 4)

Sex Quartet. *See* Fate, 1966

Sex Symbol, 1974 (Winters 3, Lai 4, Mancini 4)

Sex-Business—Made in Passing, 1969 (Syberberg 2)

Sex-Diary. *See* Letto in piazza, 1975

Sexe faible, 1933 (Siodmak 2, Brasseur 3)

Sexes enchaînés. *See* Geschlecht in Fesseln—Die Sexualnot der Gefangenen, 1928

Sexier Than Sex. *See* Baksmälla, 1973

Shanghai Drama. *See* Drame de Shanghai, 1938

Shanghai Express, 1932 (Hathaway 2, Von Sternberg 2, Brook 3, Dietrich 3, Oland 3, Wong 3, Banton 4, Dreier 4, Furthman 4, Garmes 4)

Shanghai Gesture, 1941 (Von Sternberg 2, Basserman 3, Dalio 3, Huston 3, Mature 3, Ouspenskaya 3, Tierney 3, Furthman 4, Leven 4)

Shanghai Madness, 1933 (Tracy 3, Wray 3, Garmes 4)

Shanghai Moon. *See* Shanhai no tsuki, 1941

Shanghai Orchid, 1134 (Florey 2)

Shanghai Story, 1954 (O'Brien, E. 3, Miller, S. 4)

Shanghaied, 1909 (Anderson G. 3)

Shanghaied, 1915 (Chaplin 2, Purviance 3)

Shanghaied, 1927 (Plunkett 4, Walker 4)

Shanghaied Jonah, 1917 (Sennett 2)

Shanghaied Ladies, 1924 (Sennett 2)

Shanghaied Lovers, 1924 (Capra 2, Langdon 3)

Shanhai gaeri no Riru, 1952 (Kagawa 3)

Shanhai no tsuki, 1941 (Naruse 2, Yamada 3)

Shanks, 1974 (Biroc 4, Leven 4, North 4)

Shannons of Broadway, 1929 (Brennan 3, Summerville 3)

Shantata, Court Chalu Ahe, 1970 (Nihalani 4)

Shape of Things to Come, 1968 (Van Dyke, W. 2)

Shape of Things to Come, 1979 (Ireland 3, Palance 3)

Shaque, 1977 (Azmi 3)

Sharabi, 1964 (Anand 3)

Sharad of Atlantis. *See* Undersea Kingdom, 1936

Sharada, 1958 (Kapoor 2)

Shards. *See* Cserepek, 1981

Share Cropper. *See* Hari Hondal Bargadar, 1980

Shark, 1920 (Ruttenberg 4)

Shark, 1970 (Kennedy, A. 3, Reynolds, B. 3)

Shark Monroe, 1918 (Hart 3, August 4, Sullivan 4)

Shark Reef. *See* She-Gods of Shark Reef, 1957

Shark River, 1953 (Cortez 4)

Sharkey's Machine, 1982 (Gassman 3, Reynolds, B. 3, Fraker 4)

Sharkfighters, 1956 (Mature 3, Garmes 4, Mandell 4)

Sharks' Cave. *See* Bermuda: la fossa maledetta, 1978

Shark's Treasure, 1975 (Wilde 3)

Sharmeelee, 1971 (Burman 4)

Sharon: Portrait of a Mistress, 1977 (Ferrer, M. 3)

Sharon vestida de rojo, 1968 (García Berlanga 2)

Sharp Shooters, 1928 (Scott, R. 3, Clarke, C.C. 4)

Sharpshooter, 1913 (Ince 4)

Shati el Asrar, 1957 (Sharif 3)

Shatranj Ke Khilari, 1977 (Ray, S. 2, Azmi 3, Datta 4)

Shatter. *See* Call Him Mr. Shatter, 1975

Shattered. *See* Scherben, 1921

Shattered Idols, 1921 (Gaudio 4)

Shattered Vase. *See* Razbitaya vaza, 1913

Shattered Vows, 1984 (Neal 3)

Shaughraun, 1908 (Lawrence 3)

Shaughraun, 1912 (Olcott 2)

Shayer, 1949 (Anand 3)

Shazka o spiatchek, 1914 (Mozhukin 3)

Shchit i mech, 1968 (Yankovsky 3)

Shchors, 1939 (Dovzhenko 2)

She, 1908 (Porter 2)

She, 1911 (Cruze 2)

She, 1935 (Bruce 3, Johnson, N. 3, Scott, R. 3, Cooper 4, Dunn 4, Hunt 4, Newman 4, Polglase 4, Steiner 4)

She, 1965 (Cushing 3, Lee, C. 3, Bernard 4)

She. *See* Kanojo, 1926

She and He. *See* Blaho lásky, 1965

She and He. *See* Kanojo to kare, 1963

She and the 3. *See* Sie und die Drei, 1922

She Asked for It, 1937 (Head 4, Schulberg 4, Shamroy 4)

She Conquered. *See* Hon segrade, 1916

She Couldn't Help It, 1921 (Daniels 3)

She Couldn't Say No, 1930 (Bacon 2, Beavers 3)

She Couldn't Say No, 1938 (Wyman 3)

She Couldn't Say No, 1941 (Arden 3, McCord 4)

She Couldn't Say No, 1954 (Bacon 2, Mitchum 3, Muse 3, Simmons 3, Orry-Kelly 4)

She Couldn't Take It, 1935 (Garnett 2, Bennett J. 3, Burke 3, Meek 3, Raft 3, Schulberg 4, Shamroy 4)

She Defends Her Country. *See* Ona zashchishchaet Rodinu, 1943

She Devil, 1957 (Struss 4)

She Done Him Wrong, 1933 (Beavers 3, Grant, C. 3, West 3, Head 4, Lang 4)

She Done Him Wrong. *See* Villain Still Pursued Her, 1940

She Fell Among Thieves, 1978 (McDowell 3)

She Fell Fainting in His Arms, 1903 (Bitzer 4)

She Fell from the Moon. *See* Spadla s měsíce, 1961

She Gets Her Man, 1935 (Bond 3, Carradine 3, Pitts 3, D'Agostino 4)

She Gets Her Man, 1945 (Bruckman 4)

She Goes to War, 1929 (King 2, D'Agostino 4, Estabrook 4, Fulton 4, Gaudio 4, Saunders 4)

She Got What She Wanted, 1930 (Cruze 2)

She Had to Choose, 1934 (Crabbe 3)

She Had to Say Yes, 1933 (Berkeley 2, Young, L. 3, Orry-Kelly 4)

She Has Lived Her Destiny. *See* Kanojo to unmei, 1924

She Knew All the Answers, 1941 (Arden 3, Bennett J. 3)

She Landed a Big One, 1914 (Beery 3)

She Learned About Sailors, 1934 (Ayres 3, Faye 3)

She Loved a Fireman, 1938 (Sheridan 3)

She Loved a Sailor, 1916 (Sennett 2)

She Loved Him Plenty, 1918 (Sennett 2)

She Loves and Lies, 1920 (Talmadge, N. 3)

She Loves Me Not, 1918 (Daniels 3, Lloyd 3, Roach 4)

She Loves Me Not, 1934 (Crosby 3, Hopkins, M. 3, Glazer 4, Lang 4, Prinz 4)

She Made Her Bed, 1934 (Arlen 3, Krasner 4, Robinson 4)

She Married an Artist, 1937 (Daves 2, Buchman 4)

She Married Her Boss, 1935 (La Cava 2, Colbert 3, Douglas, M. 3, Buchman 4, Shamroy 4)

She Needed a Doctor, 1917 (Sennett 2)

She Never Knew, 1915 (Eason 4)

She Played With Fire. *See* Fortune Is a Woman, 1957

She Reminds Me of You, 1934 (Fleischer, M. and D. 2)

She Sighed by the Seaside, 1921 (Sennett 2)

She Stayed for Breakfast, 1940 (Schulberg 4)

She Waits, 1971 (Bondi 3)

She Walketh Alone, 1915 (Eason 4)

She Wanted a Millionaire, 1932 (Bennett J. 3, Merkel 3, Tracy 3, Levien 4, Seitz 4)

She Was a Lady, 1934 (Glennon 4)

She Was an Acrobat's Daughter, 1937 (Freleng 4)

She Went to the Races, 1945 (Gardner 3, Gwenn 3, Irene 4)

She Wore a Yellow Ribbon, 1949 (Ford, J. 2, Cody 3, Johnson, B. 3, Johnson, N. 3, McLaglen 3, Wayne 3, Basevi 4, Cooper 4, Hoch 4, Nugent 4)

She Wouldn't Say Yes, 1945 (Muse 3, Russell, R. 3, Banton 4, Polglase 4, Walker 4)

She Wronged Him Right, 1934 (Fleischer, M. and D. 2)

She Wrote the Book, 1946 (Auer 3)

Sheba, 1919 (Hepworth 2, Colman 3)

Sheba. *See* Persecution, 1974

She-Devil, 1916 (Bara 3)

She-Devil, 1919 (Talmadge, C. 3)

Sheena, 1984 (Semple 4)

Sheep Ahoy, 1954 (Jones 2)

Sheep Has Five Legs. *See* Mouton à cinq pattes, 1953

Sheep in the Deep, 1962 (Jones 2)

Sheep in the Meadow, 1939 (Terry 4)

Sheep Stealers Anonymous, 1963 (Hanna and Barbera 4)

Sheepish Wolf, 1942 (Freleng 4)

Sheepman, 1958 (Ford, G. 3, MacLaine 3, Plunkett 4)

Sheepman's Daughter, 1911 (Dwan 2)

Sheepman's Escape, 1912 (Anderson G. 3)

Sheep's Clothing, 1914 (Bunny 3)

Sheer Madness. *See* Heller Wahn, 1982

She-Gods of Shark Reef, 1957 (Corman 4, Crosby 4)

Shéhérazade, 1929 (Litvak 2, Modot 3)

Shéhérazade, 1963 (Karina 3, Matras 4, Wakhévitch 4)

Sheik, 1921 (Brook 3, Menjou 3, Valentino 3)
Sheik Steps Out, 1937 (Novarro 3)
Sheila Levine Is Dead and Living in New York, 1975 (Scheider 3, Legrand 4)
Shelagh Delaney's Salford, 1960 (Russell 2)
Shell 43, 1916 (Gilbert 3, Sullivan 4)
She'll Have to Go, 1961 (Karina 3)
Shell-Shocked Egg, 1948 (McKimson 4)
Sheltered Daughters, 1922 (Baxter W. 3)
Shenandoah, 1913 (Nilsson 3)
Shenandoah, 1965 (Kennedy, G. 3, Martin, S. 3, Stewart 3, Clothier 4, Whitlock 4)
Shenandoah, 1977 (Lassally 4)
Shenanigans. See Great Georgia Bank Hoax, 1977
Shepherd of the Hills, 1928 (Polito 4)
Shepherd of the Hills, 1941 (Hathaway 2, Bond 3, Bondi 3, Carey 3, Wayne 3, Dreier 4, Head 4, Lang 4)
Shepherd of the Hills. See Thunder Mountain, 1964
Sher Ka Panja, 1936 (Biswas 4)
Sheriff, 1914 (Franklin 2)
Sheriff and His Man, 1912 (Anderson G. 3)
Sheriff and the Man, 1911 (Lawrence 3)
Sheriff and the Rustler, 1913 (Mix 3)
Sheriff Nell's Tussle, 1918 (Sennett 2)
Sheriff of Cimarron, 1945 (Canutt 4)
Sheriff of Cochise, 1913 (Anderson G. 3)
Sheriff of Fractured Jaw, 1958 (Walsh 2, Mansfield 3, More 3)
Sheriff of Sage Valley, 1942 (Crabbe 3)
Sheriff of Tombstone, 1941 (Rogers, R. 3)
Sheriff of Toulumne, 1911 (Bosworth 3)
Sheriff of Yawapai County, 1913 (Mix)
Sheriff's Adopted Child, 1912 (Ince 4)
Sheriff's Baby, 1913 (Griffith 2, Barrymore L. 3, Carey 3, Walthall 3, Bitzer 4)
Sheriff's Blunder, 1916 (Mix 3)
Sheriff's Brother, 1911 (Anderson G. 3)
Sheriff's Child, 1913 (Anderson G. 3)
Sheriff's Chum, 1911 (Anderson G. 3)
Sheriff's Decision, 1911 (Anderson G. 3)
Sheriff's Duty, 1916 (Mix 3)
Sheriff's Honeymoon, 1913 (Anderson G. 3)
Sheriff's Inheritance, 1912 (Anderson G. 3)
Sheriff's Luck, 1912 (Anderson G. 3)
Sheriff's Reward, 1914 (Mix 3)
Sheriff's Sacrifice, 1910 (Anderson G. 3)
Sheriff's Sisters, 1911 (Dwan 2)
Sheriff's Son, 1919 (Ince 4)
Sheriff's Story, 1913 (Anderson G. 3)
Sheriff's Streak of Yellow, 1915 (Hart 3)
Sherlock Brown, 1922 (Coffee 4)
Sherlock Holmes, 1908 (Holger-Madsen 2)
Sherlock Holmes, 1922 (Barrymore J. 3, Powell, W. 3, Hunt 4)
Sherlock Holmes, 1932 (Howard 2, Brook 3, Barnes 4, Friedhofer 4)
Sherlock Holmes. See Adventures of Sherlock Holmes, 1939
Sherlock Holmes and the Deadly Necklace, 1962 (Fisher 2)
Sherlock Holmes and the Deadly Necklace. See Sherlock Holmes und das Halsband des Todes, 1962
Sherlock Holmes and the Secret Code. See Dressed to Kill, 1945
Sherlock Holmes and the Secret Weapon, 1942 (Bruce 3, Rathbone 3, Salter 4)
Sherlock Holmes and the Spider Woman, 1943 (Bruce 3)
Sherlock Holmes and the Voice of Terror, 1942 (Bruce 3, Rathbone 3)
Sherlock Holmes Faces Death, 1943 (Bruce 3, Rathbone 3, Salter 4)
Sherlock Holmes in New York, 1976 (Huston 2, Coogan 3, Moore, R. 3, Young, G. 3)
Sherlock Holmes in Washington, 1943 (Bruce 3, Rathbone 3)
Sherlock Holmes Jr., 1911 (Porter 2)
Sherlock Holmes und das Halsband des Todes, 1962 (Fisher 2, Lee, C. 3, Siodmak 4)
Sherlock, Jr., 1924 (Keaton 2, Bruckman 4, Schenck 4)
Sherlock Pink, 1976 (McKimson 4)
Sherlock Sleuth, 1925 (Roach 4)
Sherman Said It, 1933 (Roach 4)

Sherman Was Right, 1932 (Terry 4)
She's a Sheik, 1927 (Arlen 3, Daniels 3, Powell, W. 3, Hunt 4)
She's a Soldier Too, 1944 (Bondi 3, Winters 3)
She's a Sweetheart, 1944 (Edwards 2, Darwell 3)
She's Back on Broadway, 1953 (Mayo 3, Blanke 4, Prinz 4)
She's Dangerous, 1937 (Brennan 3, Pidgeon 3, Krasner 4, Raksin 4)
She's Got Everything, 1938 (Sothern 3)
She's No Lady, 1937 (Vidor, C. 2, Head 4, Schulberg 4)
She's Oil Mine, 1941 (Keaton 2)
She's the Only One. See Hon den enda, 1926
She's Working Her Way through College, 1952 (Mayo 3, Reagan 3, Cahn 4, Prinz 4)
Shestaya chast' mira, 1926 (Vertov 2)
Shestdesyat dnei, 1943 (Cherkassov 3)
She-Wolf. See Lupa, 1953
SH-H-H-H-H, 1955 (Avery 2)
Shi no dangai, 1951 (Hayasaka 4)
Shiawase, 1974 (Takemitsu 4)
Shibaido, 1944 (Naruse 2, Hasegawa 3, Yamada 3)
Shichimencho no yukue, 1924 (Mizoguchi 2)
Shichi-nin no keiji: Onn o sagase, 1963 (Kagawa 3)
Shichinin no samurai, 1954 (Kurosawa 2, Mifune 3, Shimura 3, Hayasaka 4)
Shido monogatari, 1941 (Hayasaka 4)
Shield and Sword. See Shchit i mech, 1968
Shield for Murder, 1954 (O'Brien, E. 3)
Shifrovanny dokument, 1928 (Ptushko 2)
Shift, 1972–74 (Gehr 2)
Shifting Sands, 1918 (Swanson 3)
Shiga Naoya, 1958 (Hani 2)
Shigure-gasa, 1928 (Hasegawa 3)
Shiiku, 1961 (Oshima 2)
Shiinomi Gakuen, 1955 (Kagawa 3)
Shiju-hachi-nin me, 1936 (Yamada 3)
Shikamo karera wa yuku, 1931 (Mizoguchi 2)
Shikari, 1945 (Burman 4)
Shiki no aiyoku, 1958 (Yamada 3)
Shikko yuyo, 1950 (Hayasaka 4)
Shima to ratai jiken, 1931 (Gosho 2, Tanaka 3)
Shimai, 1931 (Tanaka 3)
Shima-sodachi, 1963 (Iwashita 3)
Shimau-boshi, 1950 (Yoda 4)
Shimizu no Jirocho Zen-den: Kohen Ashura fukushu no maki, 1926 (Tanaka 3)
Shimmy Lugano e tarantelle e vino, 1979 (Wertmüller 2, Loren 3, Mastroianni 3)
Shin baka jidai, 1946 (Mifune 3)
Shin Heike monogatari, 1955 (Mizoguchi 2, Kagawa 3, Kyo 3, Shindo 3, Takamine 3, Hayasaka 4, Miyagawa 4, Yoda 4)
Shin josei kagami, 1929 (Gosho 2, Tanaka 3)
Shin josei mondo, 1955 (Kyo 3)
Shin no shikotei, 1962 (Hasegawa 3, Kyo 3, Yamada 3)
Shin onna daigaku, 1960 (Tsukasa 3)
Shin ono ga tsumi, 1926 (Mizoguchi 2)
Shina no yoru, 1940 (Hasegawa 3)
Shinbone Alley, 1971 (Carradine 3)
Shindo, 1936 (Gosho 2, Takamine 3, Tanaka 3)
Shine 'em Up, 1922 (Roach 4)
Shine On, Harvest Moon, 1932 (Fleischer, M. and D. 2)
Shine On, Harvest Moon, 1938 (Farnum 3, Rogers, R. 3)
Shine On, Harvest Moon, 1944 (Sakall 3, Sheridan 3, Edeson 4, Prinz 4, Wald 4)
Shinel, 1926 (Gerasimov 2, Kozintsev 2, Enei 4, Moskvin 4)
Shinel, 1960 (Batalov 3)
Shingo jubanshobu, Part II, 1959 (Yamamura 3)
Shingun, 1930 (Tanaka 3)
Shining, 1980 (Kubrick 2, Duvall, S. 3, Nicholson 3)
Shining Future, 1944 (Crosby 3, Durbin 3, Grant, C. 3)
Shining Hour, 1938 (Borzage 2, Mankiewicz 2, Bainter 3, Crawford, J. 3, Douglas, M. 3, McDaniel 3, Young, R. 3, Adrian 4, Murfin 4, Waxman 4)
Shining in the Red Sunset. See Akai yuhi ni terasarete, 1925
Shining Season, 1979 (Torn 3)

Shining Star. *See* That's the Way of the World, 1975
Shining Sun Becomes Clouded. *See* Teru hi kumoru hi, 1926
Shining Victory, 1941 (Crisp 3, Davis 3, Howe 4, Koch 4, Steiner 4, Wallis 4)
Shinjitsu ichiro, 1954 (Yamamura 3)
Shinju fujin, 1927 (Tanaka 3)
Shinju fujin, 1933 (Yamada 3)
Shinju ten no amijima, 1969 (Shinoda 2, Iwashita 3, Takemitsu 4)
Shinju yoimachigusa, 1925 (Kinugasa 2)
Shinjuku dorobo nikki, 1969 (Oshima 2, Toda 4)
Shinkansen diabakuha, 1974 (Shimura 3)
Shinkei gyogun, 1956 (Oshima 2)
Shinkon-ryoko, 1934 (Tanaka 3)
Shinku chitai, 1952 (Okada 3)
Shinno Tsuruchiyo, 1935 (Yamada 3)
Shinobi no mono, 1962 (Kishida 3)
Shinpen bocchan, 1941 (Yamada 3)
Shinpen Tange Sazen, 1940 (Takamine 3)
Shinpen Tange Sazen: Sogan no maki, Koiguruma no maki, 1939 (Yamada 3)
Shinpen Tange Sazen: Yoto no maki, Futate no maki, 1938 (Yamada 3)
Shinrei Jakouneko, 1940 (Miyagawa 4)
Shinrun dorobom, 1952 (Yamamura 3)
Shinryu-ro, 1938 (Takamine 3)
Shinsen-gumi, 1969 (Mifune 3, Tsukasa 3)
Shinsetsu, 1942 (Gosho 2)
Shinshaku, 1938 (Tanaka 3)
Shinsho Taiheiki, 1953 (Tanaka 3)
Shiobara tasuke, 1930 (Tsuburaya 4)
Shiosai, 1954 (Mifune 3)
Ship. *See* Baten, 1961
Ship Ahoy, 1942 (Lahr 3, Powell, E. 3, Sinatra 3)
Ship Bound for India. *See* Skepp till Indialand, 1947
Ship Cafe, 1935 (Florey 2)
Ship Comes in, 1928 (Howard 2, Adrian 4, Grot 4, Levien 4)
Ship from Shanghai, 1930 (Gibbons 4)
Ship of Fools, 1965 (Kramer, S. 2, Ferrer, J. 3, Leigh, V. 3, Marvin 3, Segal 3, Signoret 3, Werner 3, Edouart 4, Laszlo 4, Tavoularis 4, Whitlock 4)
Ship of Lost Men. *See* Schiff der verlorene Menschen, 1929
Ship of Lost Souls. *See* Schiff der verlorene Menschen, 1929
Ship of Wanted Men, 1933 (Katzman 4)
Ship Safety. *See* Watertight, 1943
Ship Sails On. *See* E la nave va, 1983
Ship That Died of Shame, 1955 (Dearden 2, Attenborough 3, Alwyn 4)
Shipbuilders, 1943 (Brook 3)
Shipmates, 1931 (Daves 2, Bosworth 3, Montgomery 3)
Shipmates Forever, 1935 (Borzage 2, Daves 2, Keeler 3, Powell, D. 3, Stone 3, Orry-Kelly 4, Polito 4)
Shipmates o' Mine, 1936 (Pearson 2)
Ships Are Storming the Bastions, 1953 (Bondarchuk 3)
Ships Storm the Bastions. *See* Korabli shturmuiut bastioni, 1953
Ships with Wings, 1941 (Hamer 2, Balcon 4)
Shipwrecked, 1913 (Nilsson 3)
Shipwrecked, 1926 (Schildkraut 3)
Shipwrecked, 1931 (Lantz 4)
Shipyard Sally, 1939 (Fields, G. 3)
Shipyard Symphony, 1943 (Terry 4)
Shirai Gonpachi, 1928 (Hasegawa 3, Tsuburaya 4)
Shiralee, 1957 (Finch 3, Addison 4)
Shirasagi, 1941 (Hayasaka 4)
Shirasagi, 1957 (Kinugasa 2)
Shirayuri wa nageku, 1925 (Mizoguchi 2)
Shirazu no Yataro, 1954 (Hasegawa 3)
Shiriboe Sonichi, 1969 (Miyagawa 4)
Shirikurae Magoichi, 1969 (Miyagawa 4)
Shirley, 1922 (Brook 3)
Shiro to kuro, 1963 (Takemitsu 4)
Shiro Tokisada from Amakusa. *See* Amakusa shiro tokisada, 1962
Shiroi akuma, 1958 (Mori 3)
Shiroi ane, 1931 (Yoda 4)
Shiroi asa, 1964 (Teshigahara 2, Takemitsu 4)
Shiroi gake, 1960 (Imai 2)

Shiroi hekiga, 1942 (Tsuburaya 4)
Shiroi kiba, 1960 (Gosho 2)
Shiroi yaju, 1949 (Naruse 2, Yamamura 3)
Shishi no za, 1953 (Hasegawa 3, Tanaka 3)
Shishi-hen, 1937 (Hasegawa 3)
Shishkabugs, 1962 (Freleng 4)
Shitamachi, 1957 (Mifune 3, Yamada 3)
Shito no densetsu, 1963 (Kinoshita 2, Iwashita 3, Tanaka 3)
Shitoyakana kemono, 1963 (Shindo 2)
Shitto, 1949 (Shindo 2, Yoshimura 3)
Shitto, 1971 (Iwashita 3)
Shiva und die Galgenblume, 1945 (Albers 3)
Shiver and Shake, 1922 (Roach 4)
Shiver Me Timbers!, 1934 (Fleischer, M. and D. 2)
Shiver My Timbers, 1931 (Roach 4)
Shivering Shakespeare, 1929 (Roach 4)
Shivering Sherlocks, 1948 (Three Stooges 3)
Shivering Spooks, 1926 (Roach 4)
Shivers, 1934 (Langdon 3)
Shivoi trup. *See* Zhivoi trup, 1969
Shizen wa sabaku, 1925 (Tanaka 3)
Shizi jietou, 1937 (Zhao 3)
Shizuka gozen, 1938 (Yamada 3)
Shizukanaru ketto, 1949 (Kurosawa 2, Mifune 3, Shimura 3)
Shizukanaru kyodan, 1959 (Yamamura 3)
Shkval, 1916 (Mozhukin 3)
Shli soldaty, 1958 (Bondarchuk 3, Ulyanov 3)
Shlyapa, 1981 (Yankovsky 3)
Shobushi ro sono musume, 1959 (Shimura 3)
Shochiku biggu paredo, 1930 (Hasegawa 3)
Shock, 1923 (Chaney Lon 3)
Shock, 1946 (Price 3, Leven 4)
Shock. *See* Choc, 1982
Shock Corridor, 1963 (Fuller 2, Cortez 4, Lourié 4)
Shock Punch, 1925 (Saunders 4)
Shock Treatment, 1964 (Bacall 3, McDowall 3, Smith, J.M. 4)
Shock Troops. *See* Homme de trop, 1967
Shock Troops. *See* Homme qui ment, 1969
Shock Waves, 1975 (Carradine 3, Cushing 3)
Shocking Incident, 1903 (Bitzer 4)
Shocking Miss Pilgrim, 1947 (Goulding 2, Seaton 2, Grable 3, Basevi 4, Leven 4, Newman 4, Orry-Kelly 4, Raksin 4, Shamroy 4)
Shocking Pink, 1965 (Freleng 4)
Shockproof, 1949 (Fuller 2, Sirk 2, Wilde 3, Duning 4)
Shoddy the Tailor, 1915 (Hardy 3)
Shodo satsujin: Musukoyo, 1979 (Kinoshita 2, Takamine 3)
Shoein' Hosses, 1934 (Fleischer, M. and D. 2)
Shoemaker and the Hatter, 1949 (Halas and Batchelor 2)
Shoes, 1916 (Weber 2, Clarke, C.C. 4)
Shoes of the Fisherman, 1968 (De Sica 2, Gielgud 3, Olivier 3, Quinn 3, Werner 3, North 4)
Shoes That Danced, 1918 (Borzage 2)
Shoeshine. *See* Sciuscià, 1946
Shogun's Samurai. *See* Yagyu ichizoku no inbo, 1978
Shohin, 1924 (Kinugasa 2)
Shojo no shi, 1927 (Gosho 2)
Shojo nuyo, 1930 (Gosho 2)
Shojo yo sayonara, 1933 (Gosho 2)
Shojo-dakara, 1950 (Takamine 3, Yamamura 3)
Shokei no heya, 1956 (Ichikawa 2)
Shokei no shima, 1966 (Shinoda 2, Iwashita 3, Takemitsu 4, Toda 4)
Shokkaku, 1970 (Shindo 2)
Shokutaku no nai ie, 1985 (Takemitsu 4, Toda 4)
Sholay, 1975 (Bachchan 3)
Shonen, 1969 (Oshima 2, Toda 4)
Shonen ki, 1951 (Kinoshita 2)
Shonen shikei-shu, 1955 (Tanaka 3)
Shonen tanteidan, 1956–57 (Okada 3)
Shoot, 1976 (Borgnine 3, Robertson 3)
Shoot First, 1953 (McCrea 3)
Shoot First. *See* Rough Shoot, 1953
Shoot Loud, Louder . . . I Don't Understand. *See* Spara forte, più forte . . . non capisco, 1966

Shoot on Sight, 1920 (Roach 4)
Shoot Out, 1971 (Hathaway 2, Peck 3, Wallis 4)
Shoot Straight, 1923 (Roach 4)
Shoot the Moon, 1982 (Finney 3, Keaton 3, Goldman, B. 4)
Shoot the Piano Player. *See* Tirez sur le pianist, 1960
Shoot the Works, 1934 (Ruggles 2, Sheridan 3)
Shootin' for Love, 1923 (Miller, V. 4)
Shootin' Injuns, 1925 (Roach 4)
Shootin' Irons, 1927 (Schulberg 4)
Shootin' Mad, 1918 (Anderson G. 3)
Shooting, 1966 (Nicholson 3, Oates 3, Corman 4)
Shooting High, 1940 (Autry 3, Canutt 4, Day 4)
Shooting of Dan McGoo, 1945 (Avery 2)
Shooting Party, 1985 (Gielgud 3, Mason 3)
Shooting Stars, 1927 (Asquith 2)
Shooting Straight, 1930 (Cronjager 4)
Shooting Up the Movies, 1916 (Mix 3)
Shootist, 1976 (Siegel 2, Bacall 3, Boone 3, Carradine 3, Stewart 3, Wayne 3, Bernstein 4)
Shoot-Out at Medicine Bend, 1957 (Dickinson 3, Scott, R. 3)
Shootout in a One-Dog Town, 1974 (Elam 3)
Shop Around the Corner, 1940 (Lubitsch 2, Schildkraut 3, Stewart 3, Sullavan 3, Daniels 4, Raphaelson 4)
Shop at Sly Corner, 1946 (Homolka 3)
Shop Girls of Paris. *See* Au bonheur des Dames, 1943
Shop in the High Street. *See* Obchod na korze, 1965
Shop, Look, and Listen, 1940 (Freleng 4)
Shop on Main Street. *See* Obchod na korze, 1965
Shop Talk, 1936 (Hope 3)
Shopping with Wife, 1932 (Sennett 2)
Shopworn, 1932 (Pitts 3, Stanwyck 3, Riskin 4, Walker 4)
Shopworn Angel, 1928 (Hathaway 2, Cooper, Gary 3, Lukas 3, Estabrook 4, Lang 4)
Shopworn Angel, 1938 (Mankiewicz 2, McDaniel 3, Pidgeon 3, Stewart 3, Sullavan 3, Adrian 4, Ruttenberg 4, Salt 4, Vorkapich 4)
Shore Acres, 1920 (Ingram 2, Seitz 4)
Shore Leave, 1925 (Barthelmess 3)
Shores of Phos: A Fable, 1972 (Brakhage 2)
Shori no himade, 1945 (Naruse 2, Takamine 3)
Shori to haiboku, 1960 (Yamamura 3)
Short and Suite, 1959 (McLaren 2)
Short and Very Short Films, 1976 (Emshwiller 2)
Short Cut. *See* Postřižiny, 1980
Short Cut to Hell, 1957 (Head 4)
Short Films: 1975, 1975 (Brakhage 2)
Short Films: 1976, 1976 (Brakhage 2)
Short History, 1957 (Popescu-Gopo 4)
Short History of France. *See* Petit Manuel d'histoire de France, 1979
Short Is the Summer. *See* Kort ar sommaren, 1962
Short Kilts, 1924 (Laurel 3, Roach 4)
Short Memory. *See* Mémoire courte, 1978
Short Orders, 1923 (Laurel 3, Roach 4)
Short Shave, 1965 (Snow 2)
Short Tall Story, 1970 (Halas and Batchelor 2)
Short Vision, 1954 (Foldès 4)
Short Walk to Daylight, 1972 (Whitlock 4)
Shortest Day. *See* giorno piu corto, 1963
Shoshun, 1956 (Ryu 3)
Shot. *See* Skottet, 1914
Shot at Dawn. *See* Schuss im Morgengrauen, 1932
Shot in the Dark, 1914 (Nilsson 3)
Shot in the Dark, 1933 (Pearson 2, Hawkins 3)
Shot in the Dark, 1964 (Edwards 2, Sanders 3, Sellers 3, Mancini 4)
Shot in the Escape, 1943 (Bruckman 4)
Shot in the Excitement, 1914 (Sennett 2)
Shot in the Factory. *See* Laukaus Tehtaalla, 1973
Shot in the Frontier, 1954 (Three Stooges 3)
Shot in the Night. *See* Shot in the Dark, 1914
Shotgun, 1955 (De Carlo 3, Hayden 3)
Shotgun Jones, 1914 (Mix 3)
Shotgun Man and the Stage Driver, 1913 (Mix 3)
Shotgun Ranchman, 1912 (Anderson G. 3)
Shotguns That Kick, 1914 (Sennett 2, Arbuckle 3)

Should a Doctor Tell?, 1931 (Neagle 3)
Should a Husband Forgive, 1919 (Walsh 2)
Should a Mother Tell?, 1915 (Ingram 2)
Should a Woman Tell?, 1919 (Gilbert 3, Polito 4)
Should a Woman Tell? *See* Wandering Fires, 1925
Should Crooners Marry, 1933 (Stevens 2)
Should Husbands Be Watched?, 1925 (McCarey 2, Roach 4)
Should Husbands Marry, 1926 (Sennett 2)
Should Husbands Marry?, 1947 (Bruckman 4)
Should Ladies Behave?, 1933 (Barrymore L. 3, Brady 3)
Should Landlords Live?, 1924 (Roach 4)
Should Married Men Go Home?, 1928 (McCarey 2, Laurel and Hardy 3, Roach 4)
Should Men Walk Home?, 1926 (Hardy 3, Normand 3, Roach 4)
Should Sailors Marry?, 1925 (Hardy 3, Roach 4)
Should Sleepwalkers Marry, 1927 (Sennett 2)
Should Tall Men Marry?, 1926 (Laurel 3, Roach 4)
Should Women Drive?, 1928 (McCarey 2, Roach 4)
Shoulder, 1964 (Warhol 2)
Shoulder Arms, 1918 (Chaplin 2, Purviance 3)
Shouldn't Husbands Come First?, 1927 (Roach 4)
Shousetsu Yoshida gakkou, 1983 (Muraki 4)
Shout, 1978 (Skolimowski 2, Bates 3, Hurt, J. 3, York, S. 3)
Shout at the Devil, 1976 (Marvin 3, Moore, R. 3, Jarre 4)
Show, 1922 (Fleischer, M. and D. 2)
Show, 1927 (Browning 2, Adorée 3, Barrymore L. 3, Gilbert 3, Day 4, Gibbons 4, Young, W. 4)
Show Bardot. *See* Special Bardot, 1968
Show Biz Bugs, 1957 (Freleng 4)
Show Boat, 1929 (Fetchit 3, Schildkraut 3, Mandell 4)
Show Boat, 1936 (Whale 2, Dunne 3, Muse 3, Robeson 3, Laemmle 4, Prinz 4)
Show Boat, 1951 (Sidney 2, Brown 3, Gardner 3, Grayson 3, Keel 3, Moorehead 3, Nilsson 3, Alton, R. 4, Deutsch 4, Edens 4, Freed 4, Gibbons 4, Mahin 4, Plunkett 4, Rosher 4, Smith, J.M. 4)
Show Business, 1932 (Goddard 3, Pitts 3, Roach 4)
Show Business, 1944 (Malone 3, Duning 4)
Show Business, 1951 (Freleng 4)
Show Business at War, 1943 (Cagney 3, Hayworth 3, Loy 3)
Show Flat, 1936 (Havelock-Allan 4)
Show Folks, 1928 (Lombard 3)
Show Girl, 1928 (Grot 4, Polito 4)
Show Girl's Strategum, 1911 (Lawrence 3)
Show Goes On, 1937 (Fields, G. 3, Dean 4, Stallich 4)
Show Leader, 1966 (Baillie 2)
Show Me a Strong Town and I'll Show You a Strong Bank, 1966 (De Palma 2)
Show Me the Way to Go Home, 1932 (Fleischer, M. and D. 2)
Show of Shows, 1929 (Barrymore J. 3, Barthelmess 3, Bosworth 3, Buchanan 3, Costello, D. 3, Fairbanks, D. Jr. 3, Fazenda 3, Loy 3, Sothern 3, Young, L. 3)
Show People, 1928 (Chaplin 2, Vidor, K. 2, Adorée 3, Davies 3, Gilbert 3, Hart 3, Gibbons 4)
Show Them No Mercy, 1935 (Glennon 4, Zanuck 4)
Showa no inochi, 1968 (Okada 3)
Showa zankyo-den, 1969 (Shimura 3)
Showdown, 1917 (Hersholt 3, Young, W. 4)
Showdown, 1940 (Boyd 3, Head 4)
Showdown, 1950 (Brennan 3, Canutt 4)
Showdown, 1963 (Martin, S. 3, Murphy 3, Salter 4)
Showdown, 1973 (Seaton 2, Hudson 3, Martin, D. 3, Head 4, Laszlo 4)
Showdown at Boot Hill, 1958 (Bronson 3, Carradine 3)
Showdown at Ulcer Gulch, 1958 (Crosby 3, Hope 3)
Shower. *See* Shuu, 1956
Showgirl in Hollywood, 1930 (Leroy 2, Jolson 3, Pidgeon 3, Sweet 3, Polito 4)
Showing Up of Larry the Lamb, 1962 (Halas and Batchelor 2)
Showman, 1962 (Maysles A. and D. 2)
Show-Off, 1926 (Brooks 3, Garmes 4)
Show-Off, 1934 (Tracy 3, Howe 4, Mankiewicz 4)
Show-Off, 1946 (Ames 4)
Showtime. *See* Gaiety George, 1946
Shozo, 1948 (Kinoshita 2, Kurosawa 2)

Shri 420, 1955 (Kapoor 2)
Shriek, 1933 (Lantz 4)
Shriek in the Night, 1933 (Beavers 3, Rogers, G. 3)
Shriek of Araby, 1923 (Sennett 2, Hornbeck 4)
Shrike, 1955 (Allyson 3, Ferrer, J. 3, Bass 4, Daniels 4)
Shriman Satyavadi, 1960 (Kapoor 2)
Shrimp, 1930 (Langdon 3, Roach 4)
Shrimp Fisherman, 1953 (Hammid 2)
Shrimps for a Day, 1935 (Roach 4)
Shrine of Lorna Love. See Death at Love House, 1976
Shrine of Victory. See Greek Testament, 1942
Shriner's Daughter, 1913 (Eason 4)
Shrinking Corpse. See Blind Man's Bluff, 1971
Shrinking Rawhide, 1912 (Bosworth 3)
Shruti and Graces of Indian Music, 1972 (Benegal 2)
Shtorm, 1957 (Smoktunovsky 3)
Shu to midori, 1956 (Yamamura 3, Takemitsu 4)
Shubun, 1950 (Kurosawa 2, Mifune 3, Hayasaka 4)
Shubun. See Sukyandaru, 1950
Shujin-sen, 1956 (Mifune 3)
Shukujo to hige, 1931 (Ozu 2)
Shukujo wa nani o wasuretaka, 1937 (Ozu 2)
Shukuzu, 1953 (Shindo 2, Yamada 3, Yamamura 3)
Shunen, 1951 (Yoda 4)
Shunju-ittoryu, 1939 (Shimura 3)
Shunkin monogatari, 1954 (Kyo 3)
Shunkin-sho, 1935 (Tanaka 3)
Shunrai, 1939 (Tanaka 3)
Shunsetsu, 1950 (Yoshimura 2)
Shunsetsu shikakebari, 1974 (Iwashita 3)
Shuppatsu, 1938 (Tanaka 3)
Shura yako: Edo no hana-osho, 1936 (Shimura 3)
Shurajo hibun, 1952 (Kinugasa 2)
Shura-jo hibun: Soryu no maki, 1952 (Hasegawa 3)
Shura-zakura, 1959 (Yamada 3)
Shurochka, 1982 (Gurchenko 3)
Shusoku. See Shohin, 1924
Shusse Taikou-ki, 1938 (Miyagawa 4)
Shusse tohi, 1952 (Yamada 3)
Shut My Big Mouth, 1942 (Brown 3, Johnson, N. 3)
Shuto. See Shohin, 1924
Shutsugoku yonjuhachi jikan, 1969 (Miyagawa 4)
Shuttered Room, 1967 (Reed, O. 3, Young, G. 3)
Shuttle, 1918 (Talmadge, C. 3)
Shuu, 1956 (Naruse 2, Hara 3, Kagawa 3)
Shweik in the Concentration Camp. See Noviye rasskazy bravogo
    soldata Shveika, 1941
Shylock, 1910 (Baur 3)
Shylock von Krakau, 1913 (Warm 4)
Si c'était à refaire, 1976 (Lelouch 2, Aimée 3, Deneuve 3, Denner 3,
    Lai 4)
Si ça peut vous faire plaisir, 1948 (Fernandel 3)
Si ça vous chante, 1952 (Colpi 4)
Si Don Juan était une femme. See Don Juan 1973, 1973
Si j'avais quatre dromadaires, 1966 (Marker 2)
Si je suis comme ça, c'est la faute de papa, 1978 (Deneuve 3)
Si j'etais un espion, 1967 (Blier 2, Blier 3)
Si jeunesse savait, 1948 (Berry 3)
Si jolie petite plage, 1949 (Allégret, Y. 2, Philipe 3, Alekan 4)
Si le roi savait ça, 1957 (Delerue 4, Wakhévitch 4)
Si l'empereur savait ça!, 1930 (Feyder 2, Rosay 3, Daniels 4)
Si me han de matar mañana, 1946 (Infante 3)
Si me viera don Porfirio, 1950 (García 3, Alcoriza 4)
Si Paris nous était conté, 1955 (Guitry 2, Darrieux 3, Morgan 3,
    Philipe 3, Lourié 4)
Si puo fare . . . amigo, 1971 (Palance 3)
Si salvi chi vuole, 1980 (Cardinale 3, Morricone 4)
Si, Senor, 1919 (Daniels 3, Lloyd 3, Roach 4)
Si, Si Senor, 1930 (Arbuckle 3)
Si signora, 1942 (Lattuada 2)
Si te hubieses casado con migo, 1948 (Rey 3)
Si tous les gars du monde, 1955 (Christian-Jaque 2, Clouzot 2,
    Trintignant 3)

Si toutes les villes du monde . . ., 1951 (Kosma 4)
Si tu m'aimes, 1937 (Arletty 3, Simon, M. 3)
Si usted no puede, yo sí, 1950 (Buñuel 2)
Si Versailles m'était conté, 1953 (Guitry 2, Welles 2, Aumont 3,
    Bardot 3, Barrault 3, Bourvil 3, Cervi 3, Colbert 3, Gélin 3,
    Marais 3, Philipe 3, Presle 3, Vanel 3)
Si vous ne m'aimez pas, 1916 (Feuillade 2, Musidora 3)
Si yo fuera diputado, 1951 (Cantinflas 3)
Si yo fuera millionario, 1962 (Félix 3)
Siago no joui-tou, 1945 (Miyagawa 4)
Siamo donne, 1953 (Rossellini 2, Visconti 2, Zampa 2, Bergman 3,
    Magnani 3, D'Amico 4, Zavattini 4)
Siamo tutti in libertà provvisoria, 1972 (De Sica 2, Noiret 3)
Siamo tutti inquilini, 1953 (Fabrizi 3)
Siamo tutti milanesi, 1953 (Tognazzi 3)
Siberiad. See Siberiade, 1978
Siberiade, 1978 (Mikhalkov-Konchalovski 2, Gurchenko 3)
Siberians, 1940 (Kuleshov 2)
Sibirska Ledi Magbet, 1962 (Wajda 2)
Sic 'em Sam!, 1918 (Fairbanks, D. 3)
Sic 'em Towser, 1918 (Daniels 3, Lloyd 3, Roach 4)
Sicari di Hitler, 1960 (Cervi 3)
Sicario, 1961 (Germi 2, Zavattini 4)
Sićenik, 1966 (Marković 3)
Sich verkaufen, 1919 (Oswald 2)
Sicilian Clan. See Clan des Siciliens, 1969
Sicilian Cross. See Esecutori, 1976
Sick Abed, 1920 (Wood 2, Daniels 3, Reid 3)
Sickle and Hammer. See Serp i molot, 1921
Siddhartha, 1972 (Nykvist 4)
Side Lights of the Sawdust Ring. See Store Hjerte, 1924
Side Seat Paintings Slides Sound Film, 1970 (Snow 2)
Side Show, 1928 (Walker 4)
Side Show. See Two Flaming Youths, 1927
Side Show of Life, 1924 (Brenon 2, Nilsson 3, Howe 4)
Side Street, 1929 (Musuraca 4)
Side Street, 1934 (Grot 4, Orry-Kelly 4)
Side Street, 1950 (Mann 2, Ruttenberg 4)
Sidekicks, 1974 (Elam 3, Gossett 3)
Sideshow Wrestlers, 1908 (Méliès 2)
Sidetracked, 1916 (Hardy 3)
Sidewalks of London. See St. Martin's Lane, 1938
Sidewalks of New York, 1929 (Fleischer, M. and D. 2)
Sidewalks of New York, 1931 (Keaton 2)
Sidney's joujoux series, 1900 (Guy 2)
Sidonie Panache, 1934 (Artaud 3, Jeanson 4)
Sie kann nicht Nein sagen, 1914 (Oswald 2)
Sie sind frei, Dr. Korczak, 1973 (Ford, A. 2)
Sie und die Drei, 1922 (Dupont 2)
Sieben Affaren der Donna Juanita, 1973 (Mueller-Stahl 3)
Sieben Jahre Gluck, 1942 (Vích 4)
Sieben Tochter der Frau Gyurkovics, 1927 (Balfour 3, Hoffmann 4)
Siebzehnjarigen, 1929 (Baranovskaya 3)
Siècle a soif, 1958 (Colpi 4, Delerue 4)
Sieg des Glaubens, 1933 (Riefenstahl 2)
Siege, 1978 (Sidney 3)
Siege at Red River, 1954 (Boone 3, Johnson, V. 3, Cronjager 4,
    Lemaire 4, Maté 4, Wheeler 4)
Siege of Fort Bismark. See Chintao yosai bakugeki merrei, 1963
Siege of Petersburg, 1912 (Nilsson 3)
Siege of Pinchgut, 1959 (Watt 2)
Siege of Sidney Street, 1960 (Sangster 4)
Siege of Syracuse, 1960 (Brazzi 3)
Siege of Syracuse. See Assedio di siracusa, 1960
Sieger, 1932 (Albers 3)
Siegfrieds Tod. See Nibelungen, 1924
Siempre listo en las tinieblas, 1939 (Cantinflas 3)
Siempre tuya, 1950 (Fernández 2, Negrete 3, Figueroa 4)
Siero della verità, 1949 (Risi 2)
Sierra, 1950 (Curtis 3, Murphy 3, Boyle 4)
Sierra Jim's Reformation, 1914 (Reid 3)
Sierra Sue, 1941 (Autry 3)
Sieshum no yume ima izuko, 1932 (Ryu 3)

7 Dias de enero, 1979 (Bardem 2)
Siete Locos, 1973 (Torre-Nilsson 2)
Siete machos, 1950 (Cantinflas 3, Alcoriza 4)
79 Primaveras, 1969 (Alvarez 2)
Sight-Seeing Through Whiskey. *See* Pauvre John ou Les Aventures d'un buveur de whiskey, 1907
Sigillo rosso, 1950 (Cervi 3)
Sign Language. *See* Jelbeszéd, 1974
Sign of Four, 1932 (Dean 4)
Sign of Leo. *See* Signe du lion, 1959
Sign of the Claw, 1926 (Eason 4)
Sign of the Cross, 1914 (Farnum 3)
Sign of the Cross, 1932 (DeMille 2, Carradine 3, Colbert 3, Laughton 3, March 3, Buchman 4, Head 4, Prinz 4, Struss 4, Young, W. 4)
Sign of the Cross, 1944 (Nichols 4)
Sign of the Gladiator. *See* Nel segno di Roma, 1958
Sign of the Lion. *See* Signe du lion, 1959
Sign of the Pagan, 1954 (Sirk 2, Chandler 3, Palance 3, Salter 4)
Sign of the Ram, 1948 (Sturges, J. 2, Bennett 4, Guffey 4, Salter 4)
Sign of the Snake, 1913 (Ince 4)
Sign of the Wolf, 1941 (Beavers 3)
Sign of Venus. *See* Segno de Venere, 1955
Sign on the Door, 1921 (Brenon 2, Talmadge, N. 3, Hunt 4, Schenck 4)
Sign Please, 1933 (Gilliat 4)
Signal, 1918 (Tisse 4)
Signal Lights, 1912 (Bushman 3)
Signal Rouge, 1948 (Von Stroheim 2)
Signal Tower, 1924 (Brown 2, Beery 3)
Signals Office, 1940 (Balcon 4)
Signé Arsène Lupin, 1958 (Rappeneau 4)
Signe du lion, 1959 (Godard 2, Rohmer 2, Audran 3, Gégauff 4)
Signo de la muerte, 1939 (Cantinflas 3)
Signor Max, 1937 (De Sica 2)
Signor Rossi series, 1960–77 (Bozzetto 4)
Signora dalle camelie, 1915 (Bertini 3)
Signora dalle camelie, 1947 (Annenkov 4)
Signora degli Orrori, 1977 (Bolognini 2)
Signora della orroro, 1977 (Von Sydow 3)
Signora delle camelie, 1948 (Gallone 2, Cervi 3)
Signora dell'ouest, 1942 (Brazzi 3, Cortese 3)
Signora di tutti, 1934 (Ophuls 2)
Signora senza camelie, 1953 (Antonioni 2, Cervi 3, Cuny 3, D'Amico 4, Fusco 4)
Signore, 1960 (Guerra 4)
Signore and signorini, buonanotte, 1976 (Gassman 3)
Signore desidera?, 1933 (De Sica 2)
Signore e signori, 1965 (Germi 2, Age and Scarpelli 4)
Signore e signori, buonanotte, 1976 (Comencini 2, Monicelli 2, Scola 2, Manfredi 3, Mastroianni 3, Age and Scarpelli 4)
Signori in carrozza, 1951 (Zampa 2, Fabrizi 3, Age and Scarpelli 4)
Signorina, 1942 (Sordi 3)
Signorina madre di familglia, 1923 (Gallone 2)
Signorine della villa accanto, 1941 (Sordi 3)
Signorine dello 04, 1954 (Age and Scarpelli 4, Amidei 4, Delli Colli 4)
Signorinette, 1942 (Zampa 2)
Signpost to Murder, 1965 (Woodward 3)
Signs of Life. *See* Lebenszeichen, 1968
Sigpress contro Scotland Yard. *See* Mister Zehn Prozent—Miezen und Moneten, 1967
Sikátor, 1967 (Madaras 3, Torocsik 3)
Siker: Cirkusz, 1970 (Macskássy 4)
Sikkim, 1971 (Ray, S. 2, Datta 4)
S'il vous plait . . . la mer?, 1978 (Presle 3)
Silaha yeminliydim, 1965 (Guney 2)
Silahlarin kanunu, 1966 (Guney 2)
Silbermöwe, 1921 (Dieterle 2)
Silberne Kugel, 1915 (Oswald 2)
Silence, 1920 (Delluc 2, Francis, E. 3)
Silence, 1926 (Grot 4)
Silence, 1931 (Brook 3, Rosher 4)
Silence, 1975 (Jarre 4)
Silence. *See* Chinmoku, 1971

Silence. *See* Milczenie, 1963
Silence. *See* Tystnaden, 1963
Silence and Cry. *See* Csend es kiáltás, 1968
Silence . . . antenne, 1945 (Montand 3)
Silence dans la forêt. *See* Schweigen im Walde, 1929
Silence de la mer, 1948 (Melville 2, Decaë 4)
Silence est d'or, 1947 (Clair 2, Chevalier 3, Modot 3, Barsacq 4)
Silence of the Heart. *See* Golu Hadawatha, 1968
Silence of the North, 1981 (Burstyn 3)
Silence Will Reign. *See* Potem nastapi cisza, 1966
Silencers, 1966 (Charisse 3, Martin, D. 3, Bernstein 4, Guffey 4)
Silent Barriers, 1937 (Arlen 3)
Silent Barriers. *See* Great Barrier, 1937
Silent Battle, 1939 (Harrison 3, Havelock-Allan 4)
Silent Bell-Ringer, 1915 (Mozhukin 3)
Silent Call, 1921 (Murfin 4)
Silent Command, 1923 (Lugosi 3)
Silent Conflict, 1948 (Boyd 3)
Silent Cry. *See* Nema kiáltás, 1982
Silent Death, 1957 (Karloff 3)
Silent Duel. *See* Shizukanaru ketto, 1949
Silent Dust, 1948 (Auric 4)
Silent Enemy, 1957 (Harvey 3, Alwyn 4)
Silent Flute, 1978 (Lee, C. 3, McDowall 3)
Silent Flute. *See* Circle of Iron, 1978
Silent Lie, 1917 (Walsh 2)
Silent Lover, 1926 (Wilson, C. 4)
Silent Man, 1917 (Hart 3, August 4)
Silent Master, 1917 (Nilsson 3)
Silent Message, 1910 (Anderson G. 3)
Silent Movie, 1976 (Brooks, M. 2, Bancroft 3, Caan 3, Minnelli 3, Reynolds, B. 3)
Silent Night, Bloody Night, 1973 (Carradine 3)
Silent Night, Lonely Night, 1969 (Bridges 3, Jones S. 3)
Silent Partner, 1917 (Goulding 2, Neilan 2, Sweet 3)
Silent Partner, 1927 (Wyler 2)
Silent Partner, 1978 (Gould 3, York, S. 3)
Silent Passenger, 1935 (Dickinson 2, Stallich 4)
Silent Raid. *See* Overval, 1962
Silent Raiders, 1954 (Bernstein 4)
Silent Running, 1971 (Cimino 2, Dern 3, Trumbull 4)
Silent Sanderson, 1925 (Carey 3, Polito 4, Stromberg 4)
Silent Sandy, 1914 (Gish, D. 3, Gish, L. 3)
Silent Sentence, 1984 (Elam 3)
Silent Shelby, 1922 (Borzage 2)
Silent Shelby. *See* Land o' Lizards, 1916
Silent Signal, 1911 (Guy 2)
Silent Sound Sense Stars Subotnick and Sender, 1962 (Brakhage 2)
Silent Stranger, 1915 (August 4)
Silent Stranger, 1924 (Brown, Harry Joe 4)
Silent Stranger. *See* Man from Nowhere, 1915
Silent Village, 1943 (Jennings 2)
Silent Voice, 1915 (Bushman 3)
Silent Voice. *See* Man who Played God, 1932
Silent Watcher, 1924 (Bosworth 3, Love 3)
Silent Witness, 1932 (August 4)
Silent Witness, 1962 (Kennedy, G. 3)
Silent Witness, 1978 (More 3)
Silent Witnesses. *See* Rozdennie polzat utat ne mozet, 1914
Silent World. *See* Monde du silence, 1956
Silenzio, si gira, 1944 (Brazzi 3, Zavattini 4)
Silhouettes, 1936 (Reisch 4)
Silk Bouquet, 1926 (Wong 3)
Silk Express, 1933 (Gaudio 4, Orry-Kelly 4)
Silk Hat Kid, 1935 (Ayres 3, Schary 4)
Silk Hosiery, 1921 (Niblo 2, Barnes 4, Ince 4)
Silk Legs. *See* Piernas de seda, 1935
Silk Noose. *See* Noose, 1948
Silk Shadow. *See* Shadow of Silk Lennox, 1935
Silk Stocking Girl, 1924 (Browning 2)
Silk Stocking Sal. *See* Silk Stocking Girl, 1924
Silk Stockings, 1927 (Ruggles 2)

Silk Stockings, 1957 (Mamoulian 2, Astaire 3, Charisse 3, Lorre 3, Freed 4, Pan 4, Porter 4, Previn 4, Rose 4)
Silken Affair, 1956 (Niven 3)
Silken Spider, 1916 (Borzage 2)
Silks and Saddles, 1929 (Brennan 3, Mandell 4)
Silks and Saddles, 1938 (Katzman 4)
Silkwood, 1983 (Nichols 2, Streep 3, Delerue 4, Ondricek 4)
Silly Billies, 1936 (Hunt 4, Musuraca 4)
Silly Billy, 1948 (Burke 3)
Silly Scandals, 1931 (Fleischer, M. and D. 2)
Silly Younger Brother and Clever Elder Brother. See Gutei kenkei, 1931
Silnice spívá, 1937 (Hammid 2)
Silsila, 1981 (Bachchan 3)
Silver Bears, 1978 (Passer 2, Audran 3, Caine 3, Jourdan 3)
Silver Bullet, 1942 (Farnum 3, Salter 4)
Silver Canyon, 1951 (Autry 3)
Silver Chalice, 1954 (Saville 2, Mayo 3, Newman 3, Palance 3, Wood 3, Leven 4, Waxman 4)
Silver Cigarette Case, 1913 (Talmadge, N. 3)
Silver Circle. See Ginrin, 1955
Silver City, 1951 (Arlen 3, De Carlo 3, Fitzgerald 3, O'Brien, E. 3, Head 4)
Silver City, 1968 (Wenders 2)
Silver Cord, 1933 (Cromwell 2, Dunne 3, McCrea 3, Berman 4, Cooper 4, Murfin 4, Plunkett 4, Rosher 4, Steiner 4)
Silver Dollar, 1932 (Daniels 3, Robinson, E. 3)
Silver Double Suicide. See Gin-Shinju, 1956
Silver Fleet, 1943 (Richardson 3, Junge 4)
Silver Goat. See Ezust kecske, 1916
Silver Horde, 1930 (Arthur 3, McCrea 3, Sweet 3, Clothier 4)
Silver Lining, 1915 (Eason 4)
Silver Lining, 1932 (Crosland 2, O'Sullivan 3)
Silver Lode, 1954 (Dwan 2, Duryea 3, Alton, J. 4, Polglase 4)
Silver on the Sage, 1939 (Boyd 3, Head 4)
Silver Queen, 1942 (Bacon 2, Brent 3, Young, V. 4)
Silver River, 1948 (Walsh 2, Flynn 3, Sheridan 3, Steiner 4)
Silver Skies. See Stříbrná oblaka, 1938
Silver Spurs, 1943 (Carradine 3, Rogers, R. 3)
Silver Star, 1955 (Chaney Lon, Jr. 3)
Silver Streak, 1934 (Farnum 3, Hunt 4, Plunkett 4)
Silver Streak, 1945 (Terry 4)
Silver Streak, 1976 (Hiller 2, Clayburgh 3, Pryor 3, Wilder 3, Mancini 4)
Silver Valley, 1927 (Mix 3)
Silver Whip, 1953 (Wagner 3, Lemaire 4)
Silver Wings, 1922 (Ford, J. 2)
Silver-Plated Gun, 1913 (Dwan 2)
Silvestre, 1980 (Branco 4, de Almeida 4)
Simão o caolho, 1952 (Cavalcanti 2)
Simba, 1955 (Bogarde 3, Unsworth 4)
Simon, 1956 (Lassally 4)
Simon, 1961 (Delerue 4)
Simon, 1980 (Arkin 3, Green 4)
Simon and Laura, 1955 (Finch 3, Dillon 4)
Simon Bolivar, 1969 (Blasetti 2, Schell, Maximilian 3)
Simón Bolivar. See Life of Simon Bolivar, 1943
Simón del desierto, 1965 (Buñuel 2, Figueroa 4)
Simon i Backabo, 1934 (Borgstrom 3)
Simon, Simon, 1970 (Caine 3, Sellers 3)
Simon the Jester, 1925 (Walthall 3, Marion 4)
Simon the One-Eyed. See Simão o caolho, 1952
Simone Martini, 1957 (Fusco 4)
Simp and the Sophomores, 1915 (Hardy 3)
Simparele, 1974 (Solás 2)
Simple Case. See Prostoi sluchai, 1932
Simple Charity, 1910 (Griffith 2, Pickford 3, Bitzer 4)
Simple Life, 1905 (Bitzer 4)
Simple Love, 1912 (Dwan 2)
Simple People. See Prostiye Lyudi, 1945
Simple People. See Prostiye lyudi, 1956
Simple Simon, 1935 (Iwerks 4)
Simple Sis, 1927 (Fazenda 3, Loy 3)

Simple Souls, 1920 (Sweet 3)
Simple Story. See Histoire simple, 1978
Simple Story. See Prostaya istoriya, 1960
Simplet, 1942 (Andrejew 4)
Simpson and Godlee Story, 1956 (Lassally 4)
Sin, 1915 (Brenon 2, Bara 3, Oland 3)
Sin. See Beloved, 1971
Sin. See Grekh, 1916
Sin. See Hakai, 1962
Sin. See Synd, 1928
Sin Flood. See Way of All Men, 1930
Sin of Harold Diddlebock. See Mad Wednesday, 1947
Sin of Madelon Claudet, 1931 (Hersholt 3, Stone 3, Young, R. 3, MacArthur 4)
Sin of Martha Queed, 1921 (Dwan 2, Gaudio 4)
Sin of Nora Morgan, 1933 (Walthall 3)
Sin of Olga Brandt, 1915 (Chaney Lon 3)
Sin of Patricia. See Vita recominicia, 1945
Sin Ship, 1931 (Astor 3, Musuraca 4)
Sin Sister, 1929 (Clarke, C.C. 4)
Sin Takes a Holiday, 1930 (Bennett C. 3, Pitts 3, Rathbone 3, Mandell 4)
Sin That Was His, 1920 (Goulding 2)
Sin Town, 1929 (Howard 2)
Sin Town, 1942 (Brooks, R. 2, Bennett C. 3, Bond 3, Bosworth 3, Crawford, B. 3, Muse 3, Salter 4)
Sinatra in Israel, 1962 (Sinatra 3)
Sinbad and the Eye of the Tiger, 1977 (Harryhausen 4)
Sinbad the Sailor, 1935 (Iwerks 4)
Sinbad the Sailor, 1947 (Fairbanks, D. Jr. 3, O'Hara 3, Quinn 3)
Since You Went Away, 1944 (Cromwell 2, Barrymore L. 3, Basserman 3, Colbert 3, Cotten 3, Dandridge 3, Jones, J. 3, McDaniel 3, Moorehead 3, Nazimova 3, Temple 3, Walker 3, Wynn 3, Cortez 4, Garmes 4, Selznick 4, Steiner 4)
Sincere Heart. See Magokoro, 1953
Sincerely Charlotte, 1986 (Sarde 4)
Sincerely Yours, 1955 (Blanke 4, Clothier 4)
Sincerity, 1973 (Brakhage 4)
Sincerity. See Magokoro, 1939
Sincerity. See Magokoro, 1953
Sincerity V, 1980 (Brakhage 2)
Sincerity IV, 1980 (Brakhage 2)
Sincerity III, 1978 (Brakhage 2)
Sincerity II, 1975 (Brakhage 2)
Sinfonia d'amore—Schubert, 1954 (Age and Scarpelli 4, Pinelli 4)
Sinful Blood. See Hříšná krev, 1929
Sinful Davey, 1969 (Huston 2, Hurt, J. 3, Dillon 4, Mirisch 4, Young, F. 4)
Sing a Song, 1932 (Fleischer, M. and D. 2)
Sing a Song of Sex. See Nihon shunka-ko, 1967
Sing a Song of Six Pants, 1947 (Three Stooges 3)
Sing and Like It, 1934 (Horton 3, Pitts 3, Cooper 4, Musuraca 4, Plunkett 4, Steiner 4)
Sing Another Chorus, 1941 (Auer 3)
Sing as We Go, 1934 (Dickinson 2, Fields, G. 3, Holloway 3, Dean 4)
Sing, Babies, Sing, 1931 (Fleischer, M. and D. 2)
Sing, Baby, Sing, 1936 (Faye 3, Menjou 3, Zanuck 4)
Sing, Bing, Sing, 1933 (Sennett 2, Crosby 3)
Sing Boy Sing, 1958 (O'Brien, E. 3)
Sing for Sweetie, 1938 (Allyson 3)
Sing for Your Supper, 1941 (Arden 3, Cahn 4, Planer 4)
Sing Me a Love Song, 1936 (Pitts 3, Sheridan 3, Grot 4, Wald 4)
Sing Sing Prison, 1931 (Terry 4)
Sing, Sinner, Sing, 1933 (Brennan 3, Lukas 3)
Sing, Sister, Sing, 1935 (Roach 4)
Sing, Sisters, Sing!, 1931 (Fleischer, M. and D. 2)
Sing While You Work, 1948 (Fleischer, M. and D. 2)
Sing While You're Able, 1937 (Neilan 2)
Sing, You Sinners, 1938 (Ruggles 2, Crosby 3, MacMurray 3, O'Connor 3, Carmichael 4, Dreier 4, Head 4, Struss 4)
Sing, Young People!. See Utae, wakodo-tachi, 1963
Sing Your Troubles Away, 1942 (Lahr 3)
Sing Your Way Home, 1945 (Mann 2)

Sing Your Worries Away, 1942 (Sutherland 2, Dumont 3)
Singal l'antilope sacrée, 1967 (Coutard 4)
Singapore, 1947 (Gardner 3, MacMurray 3, Hornbeck 4, Miller, S. 4)
Singapore Sue, 1932 (Grant, C. 3)
Singapore Woman, 1941 (Negulesco 2, Deutsch 4, McCord 4)
Singaree, 1910 (Blom 2)
Singe en hiver, 1962 (Verneuil 2, Belmondo 3, Gabin 3, Audiard 4)
Singed, 1927 (Baxter W. 3, Sweet 3, Clarke, C.C. 4)
Singed Wings, 1922 (Daniels 3, Menjou 3)
Singende Haus, 1948 (Jurgens 3)
Singende Stadt, 1930 (Gallone 2, Courant 4)
Singer Jim McKee, 1924 (Hart 3)
Singer Not the Song, 1961 (Bogarde 3, Mills 3)
Singeries humaines, 1910 (Cohl 2)
Singin' in the Rain, 1952 (Donen 2, Charisse 3, Kelly, Gene 3, O'Connor 3, Reynolds, D. 3, Brown, N. 4, Comden and Green 4, Edens 4, Freed 4, Gibbons 4, Plunkett 4, Rosson 4)
Singin' the Blues, 1948 (Fleischer, M. and D. 2)
Singing Along, 1949 (Fleischer, M. and D. 2)
Singing Barbers, 1946 (Fleischer, M. and D. 2)
Singing Blacksmith, 1938 (Ulmer 2)
Singing Boxer, 1933 (Sennett 2)
Singing Cowboy, 1936 (Autry 3, Chaney Lon, Jr. 3)
Singing Fool, 1928 (Bacon 2, Johnson, V. 3)
Singing Guns, 1950 (Bond 3, Brennan 3)
Singing Hill, 1941 (Autry 3)
Singing in the Corn, 1946 (Duning 4)
Singing Kid, 1936 (Horton 3, Jolson 3, McDaniel 3, Barnes 4, Orry-Kelly 4)
Singing Lesson. See Raz, dwa, trzy, 1967
Singing Marine, 1937 (Berkeley 2, Daves 2, Darwell 3, Powell, D. 3, Wyman 3, Mercer 4, Orry-Kelly 4)
Singing Musketeer. See Three Musketeers, 1939
Singing Nun, 1966 (Garson 3, Moorehead 3, Reynolds, D. 3, Krasner 4)
Singing Plumber, 1932 (Sennett 2)
Singing Princess, 1967 (Andrews J. 3)
Singing River, 1921 (White 3, Furthman 4)
Singing Sap, 1930 (Lantz 4)
Singing Taxi Driver. See Taxi di notte, 1950
Singing Vagabond, 1935 (Autry 3)
Single Handed, 1923 (Miller, V. 4)
Single Man, 1929 (Adrian 4, Gibbons 4)
Single Room Furnished, 1967 (Mansfield 3, Kovacs 4)
Single Standard, 1929 (Garbo 3, McCrea 3, Adrian 4, Gibbons 4)
Single Wives, 1924 (Walthall 3)
Single-Handed, 1914 (Anderson G. 3)
Singlehanded, 1953 (Boulting 2, Schlesinger 2, Hiller 3, Hunter 3)
Singoalla, 1949 (Christian-Jaque 2, Matras 4)
Singular Cynic, 1914 (Lawrence 3)
Sinhalese Dance, 1950 (Peries 2)
Sinhasta or The Path to Immortality, 1968 (Benegal 2)
Sinister Hands, 1932 (Auer 3)
Sinister House. See Muss 'em Up, 1936
Sinister Journey, 1948 (Boyd 3)
Sink or Swim, 1921 (Roach 4)
Sink or Swim, 1952 (Terry 4)
Sink the Bismarck, 1960 (More 3)
Sinking of Japan. See Nippon chinbotsu, 1973
Sinking of the Lusitania, 1918 (McCay 2)
Sinless Sinner, 1919 (Brenon 2)
Sinner in Paradise. See Kaettekita yopparai, 1968
Sinner. See Sunderin, 1949 (Knef 3)
Sinners, 1920 (Brady 3)
Sinners. See Aux royaume des cieux, 1949
Sinners. See Piscine, 1968
Sinner's Holiday, 1930 (Cagney 3)
Sinner's Holiday. See Christmas Eve, 1947
Sinners in Heaven, 1924 (Crosland 2, Daniels 3)
Sinners in Love, 1928 (Plunkett 4)
Sinners in Paradise, 1938 (Whale 2)
Sinners in Silk, 1924 (Hersholt 3, Menjou 3, Glazer 4, Wilson, C. 4)

Sinners in the Sun, 1932 (Grant, C. 3, Lombard 3, Hoffenstein 4, Young, W. 4)
Sinners of Paris. See Rafles sur la ville, 1954
Sinners' Holiday, 1930 (Blondell 3)
Sins of Dorian Gray, 1983 (Perkins 3)
Sins of Jezebel, 1953 (Goddard 3)
Sins of Lola Montes. See Lola Montès, 1955
Sins of Man, 1936 (Ameche 3, Hersholt 3, Friedhofer 4, MacGowan 4, Zanuck 4)
Sins of Pompeii. See Derniers Jours de Pompéi, 1948
Sins of Rachel Cade, 1961 (Dickinson 3, Finch 3, Moore, R. 3, Anhalt 4, Blanke 4, Steiner 4)
Sins of Rose Bernd. See Rose Bernd, 1957
Sins of St. Anthony, 1920 (Cruze 2)
Sins of Society, 1916 (Polito 4)
Sins of the Borgias. See Lucrèce Borgia, 1952
Sins of the Children, 1930 (Wood 2, Montgomery 3, Day 4, Gibbons 4)
Sins of the Children. See In His Steps, 1936
Sins of the Children. See Børnenes Synd, 1916
Sins of the Fathers, 1928 (Arthur 3, Jannings 3, Pitts 3, Banton 4, Clothier 4)
Sins of the Parents, 1916 (Van Dyke, W.S. 2)
Sins of the Parents. See Sin of Martha Queed, 1921
Sin's Pay Day, 1932 (Rooney 3)
Sintflut, about 1927 (Fischinger 2)
Sioux City Sue, 1946 (Autry 3)
Sir Arne's Treasure. See Herr Arnes pengar, 1919
Sir Arne's Treasure. See Herr Arnes penningar, 1954
Sir Galahad of Twilight, 1914 (Eason 4)
Sir Henry at Rawlinson End, 1980 (Howard, T. 3)
Sir John greift ein!. See Mary, 1931
Sir Rupert's Wife, 1922 (Brook 3)
Sir Thomas Lipton Out West, 1913 (Sennett 2)
Sired Call, 1922 (Howe 4)
Siren, 1914 (Reid 3)
Siren of Atlantis, 1948 (Aumont 3, Struss 4)
Siren of Bagdad, 1953 (Henreid 3, Katzman 4)
Siren of Impulse, 1912 (Griffith 2, Bitzer 4)
Siren of Seville, 1924 (Polito 4, Stromberg 4)
Sirène, 1904 (Méliès 2)
Sirène, 1907 (Feuillade 2)
Sirène, 1962 (Braunberger 4)
Sirène des tropiques, 1927 (Buñuel 2)
Sirène du Mississippi, 1969 (Truffaut 2, Belmondo 3, Deneuve 3, Guillemot 4)
Sirens of the Sea, 1919 (Young, L. 3)
Siren's Reign, 1915 (Nilsson 3)
Siren's Song, 1919 (Bara 3)
Sirius Remembered, 1959 (Brakhage 2)
Sirocco, 1951 (Bogart 3, Cobb 3, Sloane 3, Guffey 4)
Sirocco. See Maison du Maltais, 1938
Sirocco d'hiver. See Sirokkó, 1969
Sirokkó, 1969 (Jancsó 2, Madaras 3)
Siroma sam, al sam besan, 1969 (Samardžić 3)
Sirota Marija, 1968 (Samardžić 3)
Sirtaki, 1966 (Storaro 4)
Sis Hopkins, 1919 (Normand 3)
Sis Hopkins, 1941 (Hayward 3)
Sisimiut, 1966 (Roos 2)
Siska, 1962 (Sjoman 2, Andersson H. 3, Fischer 4)
Sissi, 1932 (Reiniger 2)
Sissi, 1956 (Schneider 3)
Sissi—die junge Kaiserin, 1957 (Schneider 3)
Sissi—Schicksalsjahre einer Kaiserin, 1958 (Schneider 3)
Sissignora, 1941 (Ponti 4)
Sissignore, 1968 (Guerra 4)
Sista leken, 1984 (Andersson B. 3)
Sista paret ut, 1956 (Bergman 2, Sjoberg 2, Andersson B. 3, Andersson H. 3, Dahlbeck 3)
Sista ringen, 1955 (Nykvist 4)
Sista stegen, 1960 (Cromwell 2, Dahlbeck 3, Nykvist 4)
Sister, 1911 (Olcott 2)
Sister Against Sister, 1920 (Brenon 2)

Skies No Limit, 1984 (Jarre 4)
Skilsmissens Børn, 1939 (Christensen 2)
Skin. *See* Pelle, 1981
Skin Game, 1920 (Gwenn 3)
Skin Game, 1931 (Hitchcock 2, Gwenn 3, Reville 4)
Skin Game, 1971 (Gossett 3)
Skinner's Baby, 1917 (Coogan 3)
Skinners in Silk, 1925 (Sennett 2)
Skinny series, 1917 (Roach 4)
Skinny's Finish, 1908 (Porter 2)
Skip the Maloo, 1931 (Roach 4)
Skipalong Rosenbloom, 1951 (Coogan 3)
Skipper. *See* Todd Killings, 1971
Skipper & Co., 1974 (Henning-Jensen 2)
Skipper Next to God. *See* Maître après Dieu, 1950
Skipper of the Osprey, 1933 (Dean 4)
Skipper Surprised His Wife, 1950 (Walker 3, Kaper 4)
Skippy, 1931 (Mankiewicz 2, McLeod 2, Taurog 2, Cooper, J 3, Struss 4)
Skirmish on the Home Front, 1944 (Bendix 3, Hayward 3, Hopkins, M. 3, Hutton 3, Ladd 3, Brackett, C. 4)
Skirt Shy, 1929 (Roach 4)
Skirt Shy. *See* Leap Year, 1922
Skirts, 1921 (Summerville 3)
Skirts. *See* Little Bit of Fluff, 1928
Skirts Ahoy!, 1952 (Reynolds, D. 3, Williams 3, Lennart 4, Pasternak 4, Rose 4, Rose 4)
Skjulte Skat. *See* Dr. Nicola I, 1909
Sklaven der Sinne, 1920 (Nielsen 3)
Skok, 1969 (Olbrychski 3)
Skokie, 1981 (Kaye 3, Wallach 3)
Skola octu, 1957 (Hrušínský 3)
Skola skolen, 1949 (Bjornstrand 3)
Skola, základ života, 1938 (Fric 2, Stallich 4)
Skomakare bliv vid din last, 1915 (Sjostrom 2)
Sköna Helena, 1951 (Dahlbeck 3)
Skönhetsvård i djungeln, 1935–36 (Fejos 2)
Skonne Evelyn, 1916 (Dreyer 2)
Skorpan, 1957 (Bjornstrand 3)
Skorpió, 1918 (Curtiz 2)
Skorpion, panna, i lucznik, 1972 (Nowicki 3)
Skorpion srestu daga, 1969 (Paskaleva 3)
Skottet, 1914 (Stiller 2, Jaenzon 4)
Skřivánci na niti, 1969 (Menzel 2, Hrušínský 3)
Skřivánčí píseň, 1933 (Vích 4)
Skud i Mørket. *See* Truet Lykke, 1915
Skuggan, 1953 (Dahlbeck 3)
Skugger over snon, 1945 (Sucksdorff 2)
Skull, 1965 (Cushing 3, Lee, C. 3, Francis 4)
Skullduggery, 1960 (Vanderbeek 2)
Skullduggery, 1970 (Rafferty 3, Reynolds, B. 3, Head 4, Whitlock 4)
Skunked Again, 1936 (Terry 4)
Sky Bandits, 1986 (Watkin 4)
Sky Boy, 1929 (McCarey 2, Langdon 3, Roach 4)
Sky Bride, 1932 (Mankiewicz 2, Arlen 3, Scott, R. 3, Young, W. 4)
Sky Commando, 1953 (Duryea 3, Katzman 4)
Sky Devils, 1932 (Sutherland 2, Tracy 3, Gaudio 4, Newman 4)
Sky Full of Moon, 1952 (Wynn 3)
Sky Giant, 1938 (Carey 3, Fontaine 3)
Sky High, 1922 (Mix 3)
Sky is Clear. *See* Sora wa haretari, 1925
Sky Is Falling, 1947 (Terry 4)
Sky Is Red. *See* Cielo è rosso, 1950
Sky Larks, 1934 (Lantz 4)
Sky Murder, 1940 (Meek 3, Pidgeon 3)
Sky Party, 1965 (Corman 4)
Sky Patrol, 1939 (Coogan 3, Salter 4)
Sky Pilot, 1911 (Talmadge, N. 3)
Sky Pilot, 1921 (Vidor, K. 2, Moore, C. 3)
Sky Pilot, 1924 (Lantz 4)
Sky Pilot's Intemperance, 1911 (Dwan 2)
Sky Pirate, 1914 (Sennett 2, Arbuckle 3)
Sky Plumber, 1924 (Roach 4)

Sky Princess, 1942 (Pal 2)
Sky Riders, 1976 (York, S. 3, Schifrin 4)
Sky Scraping, 1930 (Fleischer, M. and D. 2)
Sky Scrappers, 1928 (Disney 2)
Sky Shines. *See* Sora wa haretari, 1925
Sky Ship, 1942 (Eason 4)
Sky Socialist, 1967 (Wieland 2)
Sky Terror. *See* Skyjacked, 1972
Sky, the Earth. *See* Ciel, la terre, 1966
Sky, West, and Crooked, 1966 (Mills 3, Arnold 4, Dillon 4)
Skyjacked, 1972 (Crain 3, Heston 3, Pidgeon 3)
Skylark, 1941 (Sandrich 2, Colbert 3, Milland 3, Dreier 4, Head 4, Irene 4, Lang 4, Young, V. 4)
Skylarking, 1923 (Sennett 2)
Skyldig—ikke skyldig, 1953 (Roos 2)
Skylight Sleep, 1916 (Roach 4)
Skyline, 1931 (Loy 3, O'Sullivan 3, Friedhofer 4, Nichols 4)
Skyrider, 1976 (Halas and Batchelor 2)
Skyriders, 1976 (Coburn, J. 3)
Skyrocket, 1926 (Neilan 2, Johnson, N. 3, Glazer 4)
Sky's the Limit, 1937 (Buchanan 3, Garmes 4)
Sky's the Limit, 1943 (Astaire 3, Ryan 3, Mercer 4)
Skyscraper, 1928 (Garnett 2, Boyd 3, Adrian 4)
Skyscraper, 1958 (Clarke 2, Van Dyke, W. 2)
Skyscraper Souls, 1932 (Hersholt 3, O'Sullivan 3, Daniels 4, Sullivan 4)
Skyscraper Symphony, 1928 (Florey 2)
Skyward, 1981 (Davis 3)
Skywayman, 1920 (Howard 2, Furthman 4)
Sladká Josefinka, 1927 (Ondra 3)
Sladkaya zhenzhchina, 1976 (Yankovsky 3)
Slady, 1974 (Giersz 4)
Slaedepatruljen Sirius, 1980 (Roos 2)
Släkten ar bast, 1944 (Borgstrom 3)
Slalom, 1965 (Gassman 3)
Slaměnný klobouk, 1971 (Kopecký 3, Kučera 4)
Slander, 1957 (Johnson, V. 3)
Slant, 1958 (Romero 2)
Slap. *See* Gifle, 1974
Slap Happy Hunters, 1941 (Terry 4)
Slap Happy Lion, 1947 (Avery 2)
Slap Happy Pappy, 1940 (Clampett 4)
Slap Shot, 1977 (Hill, G.R. 2, Martin, S. 3, Newman 3, Allen, D. 4, Bernstein 4)
Slap-Happy Sleuths, 1950 (Three Stooges 3)
Slap-Hoppy Mouse, 1956 (McKimson 4)
Slapstick, 1982 (Lewis 2)
Slashed Yosaburo. *See* Kirare Yosaburou, 1960
Slasti Otce vlasti, 1969 (Kopecký 3)
Slates of the Tenpyo Period. *See* Tenpyo no iraka, 1979
Slattery's Hurricane, 1949 (De Toth 2, Darnell 3, Lake 3, Widmark 3, Clarke, C.C. 4, Wheeler 4)
Slaughter, 1972 (Torn 3)
Slaughter Hotel. *See* Bestia uccide a sangue freddo, 1971
Slaughter on Tenth Avenue, 1957 (Duryea 3, Matthau 3)
Slaughter Trail, 1951 (Young, G. 3)
Slaughterhouse-5, 1972 (Hill, G.R. 2, Allen, D. 4, Bumstead 4, Ondricek 4)
Sláva, 1960 (Brdečka 4, Pojar 4)
Slava nam, smert vragam!, 1914 (Mozhukin 3)
Slava Sovetskim Geroiniam, 1938 (Vertov 2)
Slave, 1909 (Griffith 2, Sennett 2, Lawrence 3, Pickford 3, Bitzer 4)
Slave, 1917 (Hardy 3)
Slave Girl, 1915 (Browning 2)
Slave Girl, 1947 (Brent 3, Crawford, B. 3, De Carlo 3)
Slave of Desire, 1923 (Love 3)
Slave of Fashion, 1925 (Shearer 3, Gibbons 4, Meredyth 4, Murfin 4)
Slave Ship, 1937 (Garnett 2, Baxter W. 3, Beery 3, Chaney Lon, Jr. Darwell 3, Rooney 3, Sanders 3, Schildkraut 3, Johnson 4, Miller, V. 4, Newman 4, Trotti 4)
Slavenkönigin, 1924 (Curtiz 2)
Slavers, 1977 (Howard, T. 3, Milland 3)
Slave's Devotion, 1913 (Ince 4)
Slaves of Babylon, 1953 (Katzman 4)

Slaves of the Night. *See* Éjszaka rabjai, 1914
Slavey's Affinity, 1911 (Lawrence 3)
Slay It with Flowers, 1943 (Fleischer, M. and D. 2)
Slečna Golem, 1972 (Brejchová 3)
Slečna od vody, 1959 (Stallich 4)
Sledite ostavat, 1956 (Danailov 3)
Sleep, 1963 (Warhol 2)
Sleep, My Love, 1948 (Sirk 2, Ameche 3, Colbert 3, Cummings 3)
Sleeper, 1973 (Allen 2, Keaton 3, Rosenblum 4)
Sleeping Beauty, 1930 (Vasiliev 2)
Sleeping Beauty, 1954 (Reiniger 2)
Sleeping Beauty, 1958 (Disney 2, Iwerks 4)
Sleeping Beauty. *See* Nemureru bijo, 1968
Sleeping Beauty. *See* Shazka o spiatchek, 1914
Sleeping Car, 1933 (Litvak 2, Carroll M. 3, Holloway 3, Novello 3, Balcon 4, Junge 4)
Sleeping Car Murder. *See* Compartiment tueurs, 1965
Sleeping Dogs, 1977 (Oates 3)
Sleeping Ember. *See* Brasa dormida, 1928
Sleeping Tiger, 1954 (Losey 2, Bogarde 3, Arnold 4, Foreman 4)
Sleeping Words of the Bride. *See* Hanayome no negoto, 1933
Sleeping Words of the Bridegroom. *See* Hanamuko no negoto, 1935
Sleepless Night, 1948 (Terry 4)
Sleepy Head, 1921 (Roach 4)
Sleepy Time Down South, 1932 (Fleischer, M. and D. 2)
Sleepytime Gal, 1942 (Cook 3)
Sleepytime Possum, 1951 (McKimson 4)
Sleepy-Time Tom, 1951 (Hanna and Barbera 4)
Sleigh Bells, 1907 (Olcott 2)
Sleigh Bells, 1928 (Disney 2)
Slender Thread, 1965 (Pollack 2, Bancroft 3, Poitier 3, Head 4, Jones 4)
Slesar i kantzler, 1923 (Pudovkin 2)
Sleuth, 1922 (Roach 4)
Sleuth, 1925 (Laurel 3)
Sleuth, 1972 (Mankiewicz 2, Caine 3, Olivier 3, Adam 4, Addison 4, Morris 4)
Sleuths, 1918 (Sennett 2)
Sleuths at the Floral Parade, 1913 (Sennett 2, Normand 3)
Sleuth's Last Stand, 1913 (Sennett 2)
Slick Chick, 1962 (McKimson 4)
Slick Hare, 1946 (Freleng 4)
Slicked-Up Pup, 1951 (Hanna and Barbera 4)
Slide, Kelly, Slide, 1927 (Carey 3, Gibbons 4)
Slide, Speedy, Slide, 1931 (Sennett 2)
Slides, 1919 (Fleischer, M. and D. 2)
Slight Case of Larceny, 1953 (Rooney 3)
Slight Case of Murder, 1938 (Bacon 2, Robinson, E. 3, Wallis 4)
Slight Mistake, 1911 (Bunny 3)
Slightly Daffy, 1944 (Clampett 4)
Slightly Dangerous, 1943 (Ruggles 2, Bond 3, Brennan 3, Turner, L. 3, Young, R. 3, Berman 4, Irene 4, Kaper 4, Lederer 4, Rosson 4)
Slightly French, 1949 (Sirk 2, Ameche 3, Lamour 3, Duning 4)
Slightly Honorable, 1940 (Garnett 2, Arden 3, Crawford, B. 3, O'Brien, P. 3, Banton 4, Wanger 4)
Slightly Pregnant Man. *See* Evènement le plus important que l'homme a marché sur la lune, 1973
Slightly Scarlet, 1930 (Mankiewicz 2, Brook 3, Colbert 3, Lukas 3, Banton 4, Estabrook 4)
Slightly Scarlet, 1956 (Dwan 2, Alton, J. 4, Polglase 4)
Slightly Scarlet. *See* Enigmatique Monsieur Parkes, 1930
Slightly Static, 1935 (Rogers, R. 3, Roach 4)
Slightly Tempted, 1940 (Salter 4)
Slikovnica pčelara, 1958 (Makavejev 2)
Slim, 1937 (Daves 2, Fonda, H. 3, O'Brien, P. 3, Wyman 3, Steiner 4, Wallis 4)
Slim Carter, 1957 (Johnson, B. 3)
Slim Higgins, 1915 (Mix 3)
Slim Princess, 1915 (Beery 3, Bushman 3)
Slim Princess, 1920 (Normand 3)
Slim Shoulders, 1922 (Crosland 2)
Slinger. *See* Práce, 1960
Slingshot 6 7/8, 1951 (Lantz 4)

Slink Pink, 1967 (Freleng 4)
Slipper. *See* Tofflan-en lycklig komedi, 1967
Slipper and the Rose, 1976 (Evans 3, More 3)
Slipper Episode. *See* Voyage imprévu, 1934
Slippery Pearls, 1932 (Cooper, Gary 3, Fazenda 3)
Slippery Pearls. *See* Stolen Jools, 1932
Slippery Silks, 1936 (Three Stooges 3)
Slippery Slickers, 1920 (Roach 4)
Slippery Slippers, 1962 (Hanna and Barbera 4)
Slipping Wives, 1927 (Laurel and Hardy 3, Roach 4)
Slippy McGee, 1923 (Ruggles 2, Moore, C. 3, Clarke, C.C. 4)
Slither, 1973 (Caan 3, Kovacs 4)
Slivers, 1977 (Emshwiller 2)
Slocum Disaster, 1904 (Bitzer 4)
Slogan, 1969 (Gélin 3)
Sloppy Bill of the Rollicking R, 1911 (Dwan 2)
Sloppy Jalopy, 1952 (Burness 4, Hubley 4, Raksin 4)
Slot I Et Slot, 1954 (Dreyer 2)
Slóvce M, 1964 (Brdečka 2)
Slovo dlya zashchity, 1976 (Yankovsky 3)
Slow But Sure, 1934 (Terry 4)
Slow Motion. *See* Sauve qui peut (La Vie), 1979
Slučaj pospanog boksera, 1961 (Grgić 4)
Sluchai na stadione, 1929 (Ptushko 2)
Sluggard's Surprise, 1900 (Hepworth 2)
Slugger's Wife, 1985 (Booth 4, Stark 4)
Sluice, 1978 (Brakhage 2)
Slum, 1952 (Roos 2)
Slum Boy. *See* Ragazzo di borgata, 1976
Slumberland Express, 1936 (Lantz 4)
Slump Is Over. *See* Crise est finie, 1934
Slushaite, na toi storone, 1972 (Ulyanov 3)
Slut, 1966 (Fischer 4)
Sluzhili dva toverishcha, 1968 (Yankovsky 3)
Slzy, které svět nevidí, 1961 (Fric 2)
Smaa Landstrygere, 1908 (Holger-Madsen 2)
Smaeklaasen, 1908 (Holger-Madsen 2)
Smagliature. *See* Faille, 1975
Smålanningar, 1935 (Fischer 4, Jaenzon 4)
Small Adventure. *See* Chiisana boken ryoko, 1964
Small Back Room, 1949 (Powell and Pressburger 2, Cusack 3, Hawkins 3, Francis 4)
Small Change. *See* Argent de poche, 1976
Small Fry, 1939 (Fleischer, M. and D. 2)
Small Killing, 1981 (Sidney 3, Simmons 3)
Small Timers. *See* Ringards, 1978
Small Town Act, 1913 (Sennett 2)
Small Town Bully. *See* Little Teacher, 1915
Small Town Deb, 1939 (Darwell 3, Miller, V. 4)
Small Town Girl, 1914 (Dwan 2)
Small Town Girl, 1936 (Wellman 2, Gaynor 3, Stewart 3, Stone 3, Taylor, R. 3, Gibbons 4, Gillespie 4, Goodrich and Hackett 4, Mahin 4, Rosher 4, Stothart 4, Stromberg 4)
Small Town Girl, 1953 (Berkeley 2, Burke 3, Miller 3, Sakall 3, Wray 3, Pasternak 4, Previn 4, Rose 4, Ruttenberg 4)
Small Town Idol, 1921 (Sennett 2, Novarro 3, Hornbeck 4)
Small Town Princess, 1927 (Sennett 2)
Small Voice, 1948 (Keel 3, Havelock-Allan 4)
Small World, 1954 (Foldès 4)
Smallest Show on Earth, 1957 (Dearden 2, Rutherford 3, Sellers 3, Alwyn 4, Gilliat 4, Slocombe 4)
Smania addosso, 1963 (Cervi 3, Gassman 3)
Smart Alecks, 1942 (Katzman 4)
Smart Blonde, 1936 (Wyman 3)
Smart Girl, 1935 (Lupino 3, Wanger 4)
Smart Girls. *See* Dritte, 1958
Smart Girls Don't Talk, 1948 (Mayo 3, McCord 4)
Smart Money, 1931 (Cagney 3, Karloff 3, Robinson, E. 3, Zanuck 4)
Smart Set, 1928 (Bosworth 3, Gibbons 4)
Smart Woman, 1931 (La Cava 2, Astor 3, Horton 3, Musuraca 4)
Smart Woman, 1948 (Bennett C. 3, Adrian 4, Cortez 4)
Smart Work, 1931 (Arbuckle 3)
Smartest Girl in Town, 1936 (Sothern 3, Hunt 4)

Smarty, 1934 (Florey 2, Blondell 3, Horton 3, Barnes 4, Orry-Kelly 4)
Smarty Cat, 1954 (Hanna and Barbera 4)
Smash and Grab, 1937 (Buchanan 3)
Smash en direct, 1962 (Auric 4)
Smashing the Crime Syndicate. *See* Hell's Blood Devils, 1970
Smashing the Money Ring, 1939 (Reagan 3)
Smashing the Rackets, 1938 (Musuraca 4)
Smashing the Spy Ring, 1939 (Bellamy 3, Wray 3)
Smashing Through. *See* Cheyenne Cyclone, 1932
Smashing Time, 1967 (York, M. 3, Addison 4, Ponti 4)
Smash-Up, 1947 (Hayward 3, Banton 4, Cortez 4, Wanger 4)
S'matter, Pete?, 1927 (Lantz 4)
Smell of a Wild Flower. *See* Miris poljskog cveća, 1977
Smerti doma, 1915 (Mozhukin 3)
Směšný pán, 1969 (Kachyna 2)
Smetti di piovere. *See* Pacifista, 1971
Smic Smac Smoc, 1971 (Lelouch 2, Lai 4)
Śmierć Prezydenta, 1977 (Kawalerowicz 2)
Smierc prowincjala, 1966 (Zanussi 2)
Smil, 1916 (Holger-Madsen 2)
Smile, 1974 (Ritchie 2, Dern 3, Hall 4, Kidd 4)
Smile of a Child, 1911 (Griffith 2, Sweet 3, Bitzer 4)
Smile Please, 1924 (Capra 2, Sennett 2, Langdon 3)
Smile 61. *See* Osmjeh 61, 1961
Smile Wins, 1923 (Roach 4)
Smile Wins, 1927 (Roach 4)
Smiles, 1929 (Fleischer, M. and D. 2)
Smiles of a Summer Night. *See* Sommarnattens leende, 1955
Smiley, 1956 (Rafferty 3, Richardson 3, Alwyn 4)
Smiley Gets a Gun, 1958 (Rafferty 3)
Smilin' Guns, 1929 (Brennan 3)
Smilin' Through, 1922 (Franklin 2, Talmadge, N. 3, Hunt 4, Rosher 4, Schenck 4, Westmore, G. 4)
Smilin' Through, 1932 (Franklin 2, Howard, L. 3, March 3, Shearer 3, Adrian 4, Booth 4, Garmes 4, Stewart 4, Vajda 4)
Smilin' Through, 1941 (Borzage 2, Saville 2, MacDonald 3, Adrian 4, Balderston 4, Stewart 4, Stothart 4)
Smiling Again. *See* Ujra mosolyognak, 1954
Smiling All the Way, 1920 (Bushman 3)
Smiling Along. *See* Keep Smiling, 1938
Smiling Irish Eyes, 1929 (Moore, C. 3, Grot 4)
Smiling Lieutenant, 1931 (Lubitsch 2, Chevalier 3, Colbert 3, Hopkins, M. 3, Deutsch 4, Dreier 4, Green, J. 4, Raphaelson 4, Ruttenberg 4, Vajda 4)
Smiling Life. *See* Hohoemu jinsei, 1930
Smiling Madame Beudet. *See* Souriante Madame Beudet, 1923
Smith, 1939 (Richardson 3)
Smith!, 1969 (Ford, G. 3, George, Ch. D. 3, Oates 3, Wynn 3)
Smith series, 1926–28 (Sennett 2)
Smith series, 1928 (Hornbeck 2)
Smith, Our Friend, 1946 (Lassally 4)
Smith's Burglar. *See* Burglar, 1928
Smith's Pony, 1927 (Lombard 3)
Smithsonian Institution, 1965 (Bernstein 4)
Smithy, 1924 (Laurel 3, Roach 4)
Smithy, 1933 (Gwenn 3)
Smithy's Grandma's Party, 1913 (Beery 3)
Smitten Kitten, 1952 (Hanna and Barbera 4)
Smoke. *See* Fust, 1970
Smoke Bellew, 1915 (Franklin 2)
Smoke in the Wind, 1971 (Brennan 3)
Smoke Jumpers. *See* Red Skies of Montana, 1952
Smoke Menace, 1937 (Grierson 2, Wright 2)
Smoke of the 45, 1911 (Dwan 2)
Smoke Signal, 1955 (Andrews D. 3)
Smoked Husband, 1908 (Griffith 2, Lawrence 3, Bitzer 4)
Smoker, 1910 (Pickford 3)
Smokey and the Bandit, 1977 (Field 3, Reynolds, B. 3, Needham 4)
Smokey and the Bandit Ride Again. *See* Smokey and the Bandit II, 1980
Smokey and the Bandit III, 1983 (Reynolds, B. 3)
Smokey and the Bandit II, 1980 (Field 3, Reynolds, B. 3, Needham 4)
Smokey Bites the Dust, 1981 (Corman 4)

Smokey Joe, 1945 (Terry 4)
Smokey Smokes (and) Lampoons, 1920 (La Cava 2)
Smoking Guns, 1934 (McCord 4)
Smoking Lamp. *See* Lampe qui file, 1909
Smoky, 1946 (MacMurray 3, Clarke, C.C. 4, Raksin 4)
Smoky, 1966 (Smith, J.M. 4)
Smooth as Satin, 1925 (Berman 4)
Smorgasbord, 1982 (Lewis 2)
Smouldering Fires, 1924 (Brown 2)
Smouldering Spark, 1914 (Eason 4)
Smrt mouchy, 1975 (Kachyna 2, Kučera 4)
Smrt pana Baltisbergra, 1965 (Menzel 2)
Smrt si říká Engelchen, 1963 (Kadár 2)
Smuga cienia, 1976 (Wajda 2, Pszoniak 3)
Smuggler and the Girl, 1911 (Dwan 2)
Smugglers. *See* Man Within, 1947
Smugglers. *See* På livets odesvagar, 1913
Smuggler's Cave, 1915 (Eason 4)
Smuggler's Daughter, 1912 (Anderson G. 3)
Smuggler's Daughter, 1914 (Hardy 3, Meredyth 4)
Smuggler's Island, 1951 (Chandler 3)
Smugglers' Lass, 1915 (Rosher 4)
Smugglers of Death. *See* Král Sumavy, 1959
Smuggling Ship. *See* Mitsuyu-sen, 1954
Smultronstallet, 1957 (Bergman 2, Sjostrom 2, Andersson B. 3, Bjornstrand 3, Thulin 3, Von Sydow 3, Fischer 4)
Smurfs and the Magic Flute. *See* Flûte à six schtroumpfs, 1976
Snadný život, 1957 (Brdečka 4)
Snafu, 1946 (Planer 4)
Snaiper, 1932 (Enei 4)
Snake Pit, 1948 (Litvak 2, Bondi 3, De Havilland 3, Marsh 3, Lemaire 4, Newman 4, Wheeler 4, Zanuck 4)
Snake Princess. *See* Hebihime-sama, 1940
Snakes and Ladders. *See* Jeu de l'oie, 1980
Snapphanar, 1942 (Bjornstrand 3)
Snappy Salesman, 1930 (Lantz 4)
Snappy Snap Shots, 1953 (Terry 4)
Snappy Sneezer, 1929 (Roach 4)
Snapshots of the City, 1961 (Vanderbeek 2)
Snare of Fate, 1913 (Cruze 2)
Snare of Society, 1911 (Lawrence 3)
Snatched From a Burning Death, 1915 (Ingram 2)
Sneak Easily, 1933 (Pitts 3)
Sneak, Snoop and Snitch, 1940 (Fleischer, M. and D. 2)
Sneak, Snoop and Snitch in Triple Trouble, 1941 (Fleischer, M. and D. 2)
Sneaking. *See* Nukiashi sashiashi, 1934
Sneezing Breezes, 1925 (Sennett 2)
Sneezing Weasel, 1937 (Avery 2)
Sněhová královna, 1978 (Schorm 2)
Sniffles and the Bookworm, 1939 (Jones 2)
Sniffles Bells the Cat, 1940 (Jones 2)
Sniffles Takes a Trip, 1940 (Jones 2)
Snip and Snap series, 1960 (Halas and Batchelor 2)
Sniper, 1952 (Dmytryk 2, Kramer, S. 2, Menjou 3, Anhalt 4, Brown, Harry 4, Guffey 4)
Snitch in Time, 1950 (Three Stooges 3)
Snitching Hour, 1922 (Crosland 2)
Sno Fun', 1951 (Terry 4)
Snob, 1921 (Wood 2)
Snob, 1924 (Gilbert 3, Shearer 3, Gibbons 4)
Snobs, 1915 (DeMille 2)
Snobs, 1961 (Kosma 4)
Snoop Sisters, 1972 (Clayburgh 3, Goddard 3)
Snooper Service, 1945 (Langdon 3)
Snoopy Loopy, 1960 (Hanna and Barbera 4)
Snorkel, 1958 (Green, G. 4, Sangster 4)
Snotchak, 1912 (Mozhukin 3)
Snow Bride, 1923 (Brady 3, Levien 4)
Snow Carnival, 1949 (Cooper, Gary 3)
Snow Country. *See* Yukiguni, 1965
Snow Creature, 1954 (Crosby 4)
Snow Cure, 1916 (Sennett 2)

Snow Excuse, 1966 (McKimson 4)
Snow Festival. *See* Yuki matsuri, 1952
Snow Flurry. *See* Kazabana, 1959
Snow Hawk, 1925 (Garnett 2, Laurel 3)
Snow in the Desert, 1919 (Colman 3)
Snow Job, 1972 (De Sica 2)
Snow Maiden, 1952 (Ivanov-vano 4)
Snow Man, 1946 (Terry 4)
Snow Queen. *See* Sněhová královna, 1978
Snow Time for Comedy, 1941 (Jones 2)
Snow Time for Comedy. *See* Najveći snjegović, 1972
Snow Trail. *See* Ginrei no hate, 1947
Snow White, 1916 (Barthelmess 3)
Snow White, 1931 (Fleischer, M. and D. 2)
Snow White and Rose Red, 1953 (Reiniger 2)
Snow White and the 7 Dwarfs, 1937 (Disney 2)
Snow White and the Three Stooges, 1961 (Three Stooges 3, Shamroy 4, Smith, J.M. 4)
Snowball Berry Red. *See* Kalina krasnaya, 1974
Snowball Express, 1972 (Wynn 3)
Snowbeast, 1977 (Sidney 3)
Snowbird, 1916 (Cruze 2)
Snowblind, 1968 (Frampton 2)
Snowbound, 1948 (Dalio 3, Holloway 3)
Snowed Under, 1923 (Stromberg 4)
Snowed Under, 1936 (Brent 3, Orry-Kelly 4)
Snowfire, 1958 (Fields 4)
Snowman, 1908 (Bitzer 4)
Snowman, 1940 (Terry 4)
Snowman's Land, 1939 (Jones 2)
Snows of Kilimanjaro, 1952 (King 2, Carroll L. 3, Dalio 3, Gardner 3, Hayward 3, Knef 3, Peck 3, Herrmann 4, Lemaire 4, Newman 4, Robinson 4, Shamroy 4, Wheeler 4, Zanuck 4)
Snowtime, 1938 (Iwerks 4)
Snowy Heron. *See* Shirasagi, 1941
Snowy Heron. *See* Shirasagi, 1957
Snubbed by a Snob, 1940 (Fleischer, M. and D. 2)
Sny na neděli, 1959 (Kopecký 3)
So Alone, 1958 (Ford, J. 2)
So Big, 1924 (Beery 3, Hersholt 3, Moore, C. 3, McCord 4)
So Big, 1932 (Wellman 2, Brent 3, Davis 3, Stanwyck 3, Orry-Kelly 4)
So Big, 1953 (Wise 2, Hayden 3, Wyman 3, Blanke 4, Steiner 4)
So Bright the Flame. *See* Girl in White, 1952
So Close to Life. *See* Nara livet, 1958
So Dark the Night, 1946 (Friedhofer 4, Guffey 4)
So Dear to my Heart, 1948 (Disney 2, Bondi 3, Carey 3, Hoch 4)
So Does an Automobile, 1939 (Fleischer, M. and D. 2)
So ein Madel, 1920 (Gad 2)
So ein Madel vergisst man nicht, 1932 (Kortner 3)
So ein Theater, 1951 (Jurgens 3)
So Ended a Great Love. *See* So endete eine Liebe, 1934
So endete eine Liebe, 1934 (Grundgens 3, Planer 4)
So Ends Our Night, 1941 (Cromwell 2, Von Stroheim 2, Ford, G. 3, March 3, Sullavan 3, Daniels 4, Jennings 4, Lewin 4, Menzies 4, Reynolds 4)
So Evil My Love, 1948 (Carroll L. 3, Milland 3, Alwyn 4, Head 4, Wallis 4, Young, V. 4)
So Fine, 1981 (Warden 3, Morricone 4)
So Goes My Love, 1946 (Ameche 3, Loy 3, Salter 4)
So lang noch ein Walzer von Strauss erklingt, 1931 (Frohlich 3)
So lange Leben in mir ist, 1965 (Ulyanov 3)
So Little Time, 1952 (Schell, Maria 3, Morris 4)
So Long As You're Near Me. *See* Solange du da bist, 1953
So Long at the Fair, 1950 (Fisher 2, Bogarde 3, Simmons 3)
So Long Letty, 1920 (Moore, C. 3)
So Long Letty, 1929 (Bacon 2)
So Long, Mr. Chumps, 1941 (Three Stooges 3, Bruckman 4)
So Much for So Little, 1949 (Freleng 4)
So Near, Yet So Far, 1912 (Griffith 2, Barrymore L. 3, Pickford 3, Bitzer 4)
So oder so ist das Leben, 1976 (Schell, Maria 3)
So Proudly We Hail, 1943 (Sandrich 2, Colbert 3, De Carlo 3, Goddard 3, Lake 3, Dreier 4, Edouart 4, Lang 4, Rozsa 4)

So racht die Sonne, 1915 (Oswald 2)
So Red the Rose, 1935 (Vidor, K. 2, Cummings 3, Muse 3, Scott, R. 3, Sullavan 3, Banton 4, Dreier 4)
So Runs the Way, 1913 (Barrymore L. 3, Gish, L. 3)
So sind die Manner, 1922 (Dietrich 3)
So sind die Menschen. *See* Abschied, 1930
So Sweet . . . So Perverse. *See* Cosi dolce . . . cosi perversa, 1970
So That Men Are Free, 1962 (Van Dyke, W. 2)
So They Were Married. *See* Johnny Doesn't Live Here Anymore, 1944
So This Is Africa, 1933 (Krasna 4)
So This Is College, 1929 (Daves 2, Wood 2, McCrea 3, Montgomery 3, Gibbons 4)
So This Is Hamlet?, 1923 (La Cava 2)
So This Is Harris, 1932 (Sandrich 2, Glennon 4)
So This is Hollywood. *See* In Hollywood with Potash and Perlmutter, 1924
So This Is London, 1930 (O'Sullivan 3, Rogers, W. 3, Clarke, C.C. 4, Levien 4)
So This Is London, 1933 (Grierson 2)
So This Is London, 1939 (Granger 3, Sanders 3)
So This is Love, 1928 (Capra 2)
So This Is Love, 1953 (Grayson 3, Blanke 4, Prinz 4, Steiner 4)
So This Is Marriage, 1924 (Oland 3, Gibbons 4, Wilson, C. 4)
So This is New York, 1948 (Aldrich 2, Fleischer, R. 2, Kramer, S. 2, Foreman 4, Tiomkin 4)
So This Is Paris, 1926 (Lubitsch 2, Loy 3, Kraly 4)
So This Is Paris, 1954 (Curtis 3, Lourié 4)
So Well Remembered, 1947 (Dmytryk 2, Howard, T. 3, Mills 3, Eisler 4, Paxton 4, Young, F. 4)
So You Won't Squawk, 1941 (Keaton 2)
So You Won't Talk, 1940 (Brown 3)
So Young, So Bad, 1950 (Henreid 3)
Soak the Rich, 1936 (Hecht 4, MacArthur 4, Shamroy 4)
Soak the Sheik, 1922 (Roach 4)
Soaking the Clothes, 1914 (Roach 4)
Soap Bubbles. *See* Bulles de savon animées, 1906
Soap Opera. *See* Lester Persky Story, 1964
Soapsuds Lady, 1925 (Sennett 2)
Soapy Opera, 1953 (Terry 4)
Sobaka Baskervilei, 1981 (Yankovsky 3)
Sóbálvány, 1958 (Gabór 3)
Sobo, 1933 (Naruse 2)
Sobre el problema fronterizo, 1978 (Alvarez 2)
Sobre horas extras y trabajo voluntario, 1973 (Gomez, S. 2)
Sobre las olas, 1950 (Infante 3)
Sobrevivientes, 1979 (Gutiérrez 2)
Social Celebrity, 1926 (Brooks 3, Menjou 3, Garmes 4)
Social Club, 1916 (Sennett 2, Swanson 3)
Social Error, 1922 (La Cava 2)
Social Exile. *See* Déclassée, 1925
Social Gangster, 1915 (Lloyd 3, Roach 4)
Social Highwayman, 1916 (Marion 4)
Social Highwayman, 1926 (Zanuck 4)
Social Leper, 1917 (Edeson 4, Marion 4)
Social Lion, 1930 (Mankiewicz 2, Sutherland 2)
Social Quicksands, 1918 (Bushman 3)
Social Register, 1934 (Neilan 2, Moore, C. 3)
Social Secretary, 1916 (Fleming 2, Von Stroheim 2, Talmadge, N. 3, Emerson 4, Loos 4)
Socialist Realism. *See* Realismo socialista, 1972–73
Società Ovesticino-Dinamo, 1955 (Olmi 2)
Society, 1955 (Burman 4)
Society and Chaps, 1912 (Dwan 2)
Society Ballooning, 1906 (Bitzer 4)
Society Doctor, 1935 (Burke 3, Meek 3, Taylor, R. 3)
Society Exile, 1919 (Menzies 4, Miller, A. 4)
Society for Sale, 1918 (Borzage 2, Swanson 3)
Society Girl, 1932 (Tracy 3, Barnes 4)
Society Lawyer, 1939 (Pidgeon 3, Goodrich and Hackett 4)
Society Scandal, 1924 (Dwan 2, Swanson 3, Rosson 4)
Society Secrets, 1921 (Browning 2, McCarey 4)
Society Sensation, 1918 (Pitts 3, Valentino 3)
Society Sinner. *See* Tyven, 1910

Sock-a-Bye Baby, 1934 (Fleischer, M. and D. 2)
Sock-a-Bye Baby, 1942 (Three Stooges 3, Bruckman 4)
Sock-a-Doddle Do, 1952 (McKimson 4)
Sockeroo, 1940 (Eason 4)
Socrate, 1970 (Rossellini 2)
Socrates. *See* Socrate, 1970
Soda Squirt, 1933 (Iwerks 4)
Sodhbodh, 1942 (Sircar 4)
Sodom and Gomorrah. *See* Sodoma e Gomorra, 1962
Sodom und Gomorrah, 1922 (Curtiz 2)
Sodoma e Gomorra, 1962 (Aldrich 2, Leone 2, Aimée 3, Baker S. 3,
    Granger 3, Adam 4, Rozsa 4)
Sodrásban, 1964 (Gaál 2)
Soeurette, 1913 (Tourneur, M. 2)
Soeurs Brontë, 1978 (Adjani 3, Huppert 3, Sarde 4)
Soeurs ennemies, 1915 (Dulac 2)
Sofia, 1948 (Auer 3, Clothier 4)
Sofiya Perovskaya, 1967 (Shostakovich 4)
Sofka, 1948 (Marković 3)
Soft Ball Game, 1936 (Lantz 4)
Soft Beast. *See* Shitoyakana kemono, 1963
Soft Beds and Hard Battles, 1974 (Boulting 2, Jurgens 3, Sellers 3)
Soft Cushions, 1927 (Johnson, N. 3, Karloff 3, Carré 4)
Soft Living, 1928 (August 4)
Soft Money, 1919 (Daniels 3, Lloyd 3, Roach 4)
Soft Shoes, 1925 (Carey 3, Polito 4, Stromberg 4)
Soft Skin. *See* Peau Douce, 1964
Soft Tenderfoot, 1917 (Mix 3)
Soft-Boiled, 1923 (Mix 3)
Sogeki, 1968 (Mori 3)
Soggy Bottom, U.S.A., 1981 (Elam 3, Johnson, B. 3)
Sogni del Signor Rossi, 1977 (Bozzetto 4)
Sogni nel cassetto, 1957 (Castellani 2)
Sogno di Butterfly, 1939 (Gallone 2)
Sogno di tutti, 1941 (Cervi 3)
Sogno di Zorro, 1951 (Gassman 3, Loren 3)
Sohn der Hagar, 1927 (Freund 4)
Sohn der weissen Berge, 1930 (Planer 4)
Sohn des Hannibal, 1926 (Planer 4)
Sohn ohne Heimat, 1955 (Krauss 3)
Sohne der Nacht, 1921 (Albers 3)
Sohne des Grafen Dossy, 1920 (Basserman 3)
Sohne des Herrn Gaspary, 1948 (Dagover 3)
Soho Incident, 1956 (Adam 4)
Soif d'amour. *See* Fome de amor, 1968
Soif des bêtes, 1960 (Braunberger 4)
Soigne ton gauche, 1936 (Clément 2, Tati 2)
Soikina lyuböv, 1927 (Moskvin 4)
Soikin's Love. *See* Soikina lyubov, 1927
Soilers, 1923 (Laurel 3, Roach 4)
Soilers, 1932 (Pitts 3, Roach 4)
Soir à Tibériade, 1966 (Braunberger 4)
Soir de fête, 1956 (Braunberger 4)
Soir de notre vie, 1963 (Delerue 4)
Soir de rafle, 1931 (Clouzot 2, Gallone 2, Burel 4)
Soir de réveillon, 1933 (Arletty 3)
Soir . . . par hasard, 1964 (Brasseur 3)
Soir sur la plage, 1961 (Burel 4)
Soir, un train, 1968 (Aimée 3, Montand 3, Cloquet 4)
Soirée mondaine, 1917 (Chevalier 3)
Sois belle et tais-toi, 1958 (Allégret, M. 2, Belmondo 3, Delon 3)
Soiuzkinozhurnal No. 87, 1941 (Vertov 2)
Soiuzkinozhurnal No. 77, 1941 (Vertov 2)
Sok huség semmiert, 1966 (Darvas 3, Latinovits 3)
Sokakta kan vardi, 1965 (Guney 2)
Sokhranivshie ogon, 1970 (Yankovsky 3)
Sol, 1974 (Brakhage 2)
Sol Madrid, 1968 (Lukas 3, Torn 3, Schifrin 4)
Sol nad zlato, 1982 (Kroner 3)
Sol no se puede tapar con un dedo, 1976 (Alvarez 2)
Sol over Danmark, 1936 (Holger-Madsen 2)
Sol y ombra, 1922 (Musidora 3)
Sol ziemi czarnej, 1970 (Olbrychski 3)

Solang' es hubsche Madchen gibt, 1955 (Herlth 4)
Solange du da bist, 1953 (Schell, Maria 3)
Solange Leben in mir ist, 1965 (Hoffmann 3, Hoppe 3)
Solar Film, 1980 (Bass 4)
Solaris. *See* Solyaris, 1971
Sold, 1915 (Porter 2)
Sold at Auction, 1923 (Roach 4)
Sold for Marriage, 1916 (Gish, L. 3)
Sold to Thieves. *See* Smaa Landstrygere, 1908
Soldados do fogo, 1958 (Pereira Dos Santos 2)
Soldat Bom, 1948 (Bjornstrand 3, Fischer 4)
Soldat der Marie, 1926 (Albers 3)
Soldatesse, 1965 (Zurlini 2, Karina 3, Delli Colli 4, Solinas 4)
Soldati in città, 1953 (Zurlini 2)
Soldats d'eau douce, 1950 (Cloquet 4)
Soldaty, 1957 (Smoktunovsky 3)
Soldaty svobody, 1977 (Ulyanov 3)
Soldier, 1982 (Kinski 3)
Soldier. *See* Vojnik, 1966
Soldier and the Lady, 1936 (Bainter 3, Walbrook 3, August 4,
    Berman 4, Plunkett 4, Veiller 4)
Soldier Blue, 1970 (Pleasance 3)
Soldier Brothers of Suzanna, 1912 (Nilsson 3)
Soldier Has Come from the Front. *See* Prishell soldat s fronta, 1973
Soldier in the Rain, 1963 (Edwards 2, McQueen, S. 3, Weld 3,
    Mancini 4)
Soldier Man, 1926 (Capra 2, Sennett 2, Langdon 3, Hornbeck 4)
Soldier Marched. *See* Shli soldaty, 1958
Soldier of Fortune, 1955 (Dmytryk 2, Gable 3, Hayward 3, Duning 4,
    Friedhofer 4, Lemaire 4, Smith, J.M. 4)
Soldier of the Legion, (Johnson, N. 3)
Soldier—Sailor, 1944 (Alwyn 4)
Soldier Who Declared Peace. *See* Tribes, 1970
Soldiers and Other Cosmic Objects, 1977 (Brakhage 2)
Soldier's Duties. *See* Krigsmans erinran, 1947
Soldiers in White, 1941 (Eason 4)
Soldier's Oath, 1915 (Farnum 3)
Soldiers of Fortune, 1919 (Dwan 2, Beery 3, Nilsson 3, Polito 4)
Soldiers of Misfortune, 1914 (Sennett 2)
Soldiers of the King, 1933 (Horton 3, Balcon 4)
Soldier's Pay. *See* Soldier's Plaything, 1930
Soldier's Plaything, 1930 (Curtiz 2, Hersholt 3, Langdon 3)
Soldier's Prayer. *See* Kanetsu-hen, 1961
Soldier's Prayer. *See* Ningen no joken, 1961
Soldiers Three, 1951 (Garnett 2, Cusack 3, Granger 3, Niven 3,
    Pidgeon 3, Berman 4, Deutsch 4, Plunkett 4)
Sole, 1929 (Blasetti 2)
Sole di Montecassino, 1945 (Fusco 4)
Sole sorge ancora, 1946 (De Santis 2, Pontecorvo 2)
Soledad. *See* Fruits amers, 1966
Soledad. *See* Rebozo de Soledad, 1952
Soleil, 1966 (Braunberger 4)
Soleil a toujours raison, 1941 (Brasseur 3, Presle 3, Vanel 3, Kosma 4,
    Prévert 4, Trauner 4, Wakhévitch 4)
Soleil dans l'oeil, 1961 (Godard 2, Karina 3, Jarre 4)
Soleil de minuit, 1943 (Berry 3, Hayakawa 3)
Soleil de pierre, 1967 (Braunberger 4)
Soleil des voyous, 1967 (Delannoy 2, Gabin 3, Lai 4)
Soleil en face, 1979 (Audran 3, Cassel 3)
Soleil et ombre. *See* Sol y ombra, 1922
Soleil éteint, 1961 (Braunberger 4)
Soleil noir, 1918 (Gance 2)
Soleil noir, 1966 (Cortese 3, Gélin 3, Barsacq 4)
Soleil rouge, 1971 (Bronson 3, Delon 3, Mifune 3, Alekan 4, Jarre 4)
Soleils, 1960 (Rabier 4)
Soleils de l'Ile de Pâques, 1971 (Guerra 2)
Solid Gold Cadillac, 1956 (Douglas, P. 3, Holliday 3, Lang 4, Wald 4)
Solid Ivory, 1925 (Roach 4)
Solid Serenade, 1946 (Hanna and Barbera 4)
Solidaridad Cuba y Vietnam, 1965 (Alvarez 2)
Solidarity, 1973 (Wieland 2)
Soliloques du pauvre, 1954 (Brasseur 3)
Soliloquy, 1949 (Peries 2)

Solimani il conquistatore, 1961 (Mimica 4)
Solita de Cordoue, 1946 (Cuny 3)
Solitaire Man, 1933 (Marshall 3, Adrian 4)
Solitaires, 1913 (Talmadge, N. 3)
Soliti ignoti, 1958 (Monicelli 2, Cardinale 3, Gassman 3, Mastroianni 3,
    Age and Scarpelli 4, Cristaldi 4, D'Amico 4, Di Venanzo 4,
    Gherardi 4)
Soliti ignoti colpiscona ancore. See Ab Morgen sind wir reich und
    ehrlich, 1977
Solitude. See Lonesome, 1928
Solitude du chanteur de fond, 1974 (Montand 3)
Solkatten, 1948 (Borgstrom 3)
Soll man heiraten?, 1925 (Banky 3, Tschechowa 3, Warm 4)
Soll und haben, 1924 (George, H. 3, Tschechowa 3)
Solo for Sparrow, 1962 (Caine 3)
Sólo para maridos, 1952 (García 3)
Solo per te, 1938 (Gallone 2)
Solomennaya shliapka, 1974 (Gurchenko 3)
Solomon and Sheba, 1959 (Vidor, K. 2, Brynner 3, Lollobrigida 3,
    Sanders 3, Day 4, Veiller 4, Young, F. 4)
Solomon's Heart, 1932 (Gerasimov 2)
Solstik, 1953 (Henning-Jensen 2)
Soltanto un bacio, 1942 (Cortese 3, Fusco 4)
Soltero. See Scapolo, 1955
Solution of the Mystery, 1915 (Eason 4)
Solutions françaises, 1945 (Jaubert 4)
Solv, 1956 (Roos 2)
Solva Saal, 1958 (Burman 4)
Solvdaasen med Juvelerne, 1910 (Blom 2)
Solving the Puzzle. See Champion du jeu à la mode, 1910
Solwa Sal, 1959 (Anand 3)
Solyaris, 1971 (Tarkovsky 2)
Som en tjuv om natten, 1940 (Borgstrom 3)
Sombra verde, 1954 (Alcoriza 4)
Sombre dimanche, 1948 (Dalio 3)
Sombrero, 1953 (Charisse 3, De Carlo 3, Gassman 3, Pan 4, Rose 4)
Sombrero de tres picos. See Traviesa molinera, 1934
Some Baby, 1915 (Lloyd 3, Roach 4)
Some Baby, 1922 (Roach 4)
Some Bull's Daughter, 1914 (Loos 4)
Some Call It Loving, 1973 (Pryor 3)
Some Came Running, 1958 (Minnelli 2, Kennedy, A. 3, MacLaine 3,
    Martin, D. 3, Sinatra 3, Bernstein 4, Cahn 4, Daniels 4, Plunkett 4)
Some Collectors, 1912–13 (White 3)
Some Duel, 1916 (Mix 3)
Some Kind of a Nut, 1969 (Dickinson 3, Guffey 4, Kanin 4, Mirisch 4)
Some Kind of Hero, 1982 (Pryor 3)
Some Liar, 1919 (Furthman 4)
Some Like It Hot, 1939 (Dmytryk 2, Hope 3, Merkel 3, Dreier 4,
    Head 4, Struss 4)
**Some Like It Hot, 1959 (Wilder 2, Brown 3, Curtis 3, Lemmon 3,
    Monroe 3, O'Brien, P. 3, Raft 3, Cole 4, Deutsch 4, Diamond 4,
    Lang 4, Orry-Kelly 4)**
Some Like It Not. See I'm cold, 1955
Some Like It Rough, 1944 (Buchanan 3)
Some May Live, 1967 (Cotten 3, Cushing 3)
Some More of Samoa, 1941 (Three Stooges 3)
Some Nerve, 1913 (Sennett 2)
Some Nerve. See Gentleman of Nerve, 1914
Some of the Best, 1949 (Barrymore L. 3)
Some of Us May Die. See Journey, 1959
Some People, 1962 (More 3)
Some Sort of Cage, 1964 (Bernstein 4)
Some Steamer Snooping, 1913 (Costello, D. 3, Costello, M. 3)
Somebody Killed Her Husband, 1978 (Bridges 3, North 4)
Somebody Loves Me, 1952 (Seaton 2, Hutton 3, Head 4)
Somebody Stole My Gal, 1931 (Fleischer, M. and D. 2)
Somebody Up There Likes Me, 1956 (Wise 2, McQueen, S. 3,
    Mineo 3, Newman 3, Sloane 3, Cahn 4, Gibbons 4, Kaper 4,
    Lehman 4, Ruttenberg 4, Schnee 4)
Somebody's Darling, 1925 (Balfour 3)
Somebody's Stolen the Thigh of Jupiter. See On a vole la cuisse de
    Jupiter, 1980

Someday, 1935 (Powell 2)
Someone at the Door, 1936 (Brenon 2)
Someone Behind the Door. See Quelqu'un derrière la porte, 1971
Someone Else's Jacket, 1927 (Gerasimov 2)
Someone to Remember, 1943 (Siodmak 2)
Somersault of Life. See Jinsei tonbo-gaeri, 1946
Something Always Happens, 1928 (Auer 3, Johnson, N. 3, Hunt 4,
    Mankiewicz 4)
Something Always Happens, 1934 (Powell 2)
Something Big, 1971 (Johnson, B. 3, Martin, D. 3)
Something Different. See O něčem jiném, 1963
Something Else. See O něčem jiném, 1963
Something Evil, 1972 (Bellamy 3)
Something for a Lonely Man, 1968 (Oates 3)
Something for Everyone, 1970 (Lansbury 3, York, M. 3, Lassally 4,
    Rosenblum 4)
Something for Joey, 1977 (Page 3)
Something for Mrs. Gibbs, 1965 (Carradine 3)
Something for the Birds, 1952 (Wise 2, Gwenn 3, Mature 3, Neal 3,
    Diamond 4, La Shelle 4, Lemaire 4, Wheeler 4)
Something for the Boys, 1944 (Holliday 3, Miranda 3)
Something in Her Eye, 1915 (Hardy 3)
Something in the Wind, 1947 (Durbin 3, O'Connor 3, Green, J. 4,
    Krasner 4, Kurnitz 4, Orry-Kelly 4)
Something is Drifting on the Water. See Touha zvaná Anada, 1971
Something Money Can't Buy, 1952 (Rota 4)
Something of Value, 1957 (Brooks, R. 2, Hiller 3, Hudson 3, Poitier 3,
    Berman 4, Rose 4, Rozsa 4)
Something Short of Paradise, 1979 (Aumont 3, Sarandon 3, Lassally 4)
Something Simple, 1934 (Roach 4)
Something to Do, 1919 (Crisp 3)
Something to Hide, 1971 (Finch 3, Winters 3)
Something to Live For, 1952 (Stevens 2, Fontaine 3, Marshall 3,
    Milland 3, Wright 3, Head 4, Hornbeck 4, Young, V. 4)
Something to Shout About, 1943 (Ameche 3, Charisse 3, Planer 4,
    Porter 4)
Something to Sing About, 1937 (Cagney 3)
Something to Think About, 1920 (DeMille 2, Swanson 3,
    Macpherson 4, Struss 4)
Something Wicked This Way Comes, 1983 (Clayton 2, Robards 3)
Something Wild, 1961 (Baker C. 3, Bass 4, Copland 4, Day 4,
    Schufftan 4)
Something's Wrong, 1978 (Raphael 4)
Sometimes a Great Notion, 1971 (Fonda, H. 3, Newman 3, Remick 3,
    Head 4, Mancini 4)
Somewhere Beneath the Wide Sky. See Kono hiroi sora no dokoka ni,
    1954
Somewhere I'll Find You, 1942 (Ruggles 2, Gable 3, Johnson, V. 3,
    Turner, L. 3, Wynn 3, Berman 4, Kaper 4, Reisch 4, Rosson 4)
Somewhere in Dream Land, 1936 (Fleischer, M. and D. 2)
Somewhere in Egypt, 1943 (Terry 4)
Somewhere in France. See Foreman Went to France, 1941
Somewhere in Somewhere, 1925 (Roach 4)
Somewhere in Sonora, 1927 (Brown, Harry Joe 4, Polito 4)
Somewhere in Sonora, 1933 (Wayne 3, McCord 4)
Somewhere in the City. See Backfire, 1948
Somewhere in the Night, 1946 (Mankiewicz 2, Ireland 3, Kortner 3,
    Basevi 4)
Somewhere in the Pacific, 1942 (Terry 4)
Somewhere in Time, 1980 (Wright 3, Barry 4)
Somewhere in Turkey, 1918 (Daniels 3, Lloyd 3, Roach 4)
Somewhere in Wrong, 1925 (Garnett 2, Laurel 3)
Somewhere under the Broad Sky. See Kono hiroi sora no dokoka ni,
    1954
Sommaren med Monika, 1953 (Bergman 2, Andersson H. 3, Fischer 4)
Sommarlek, 1951 (Bergman 2, Fischer 4)
**Sommarnattens leende, 1955 (Bergman 2, Andersson B. 3,
    Andersson H. 3, Bjornstrand 3, Dahlbeck 3, Fischer 4)**
Sommarnoje sokes, 1957 (Andersson B. 3, Bjornstrand 3, Dahlbeck 3)
Sommarsaga, 1912 (Sjostrom 2, Borgstrom 3, Magnusson 4)
Sommartag, 1961 (Troell 2)
Sommeil d'Albertine, 1945 (Resnais 2)
Sommerfuglene, 1974 (Chaplin 3)

Sommergaste, 1975 (Ganz 3)
Sommernachtstraum, 1924 (Albers 3, Krauss 3, Rasp 3, Metzner 4)
Sommersaga, 1941 (Sucksdorff 2)
Somnambul, 1929 (Kortner 3)
Somnambulist. See Søvngaengersken, 1914 (Holger-Madsen 2)
Son altesse l'amour, 1931 (Courant 4)
Son autre amour, 1935 (Burel 4)
Son Comes Home, 1936 (Dupont 2)
Son Copain. See Inconnue de Montréal, 1950
Son Dernier Rôle, 1946 (Dalio 3)
Son dernier verdict, 1951 (Vanel 3)
Son et Lumière, 1961 (Delerue 4)
Son is Born, 1946 (Finch 3)
Son kizgin adam, 1970 (Guney 2)
Son nom de Venise dans Calcutta désert, 1976 (Duras 2, Seyrig 3)
Son of a Gun, 1919 (Anderson G. 3)
Son of a Gunfighter, 1966 (Rey 3)
Son of a Sailor, 1933 (Bacon 2, Brown 3, Grot 4, Orry-Kelly 4)
Son of a Samurai. See Samurai no ko, 1963
Son of Ali Baba, 1952 (Curtis 3)
Son of Captain Blood. See Figlio di Capitano Blood, 1962
Son of Cochise, 1953 (Sirk 2)
Son of David, 1919 (Colman 3)
Son of Destiny. See Madame de Thèbes, 1915
Son of Dracula, 1943 (Siodmak 2, Chaney Lon, Jr. 3, Salter 4, Siodmak 4)
Son of Dracula, 1974 (Francis 4)
Son of Fate. See Masterjuven, 1915
Son of Flubber, 1963 (Disney 2, MacMurray 3, Wynn 3, Ellenshaw 4)
Son of France, 1914 (Pearson 2)
Son of Frankenstein, 1939 (Karloff 3, Lugosi 3, Rathbone 3, Pierce 4)
Son of Fury, 1942 (Cromwell 2, Carradine 3, Farmer 3, Lanchester 3, McDowall 3, Power 3, Sanders 3, Tierney 3, Basevi 4, Day 4, Dunne 4, Newman 4, Zanuck 4)
Son of Godzilla. See Gojira no musuko, 1967
Son of His Father, 1925 (Fleming 2, Baxter W. 3, Love 3)
Son of India, 1931 (Feyder 2, Novarro 3, Rosson 3, Vajda 4)
Son of Kong, 1933 (Schoedsack 2, Johnson, N. 3, O'Brien 4, Steiner 4)
Son of Lassie, 1945 (Bruce 3, Crisp 3, Irene 4, Stothart 4)
Son of Lifeboat, 1949 (Lewis 2)
Son of Monte Cristo, 1940 (Bennett J. 3, Sanders 3)
Son of Paleface, 1952 (DeMille 2, Tashlin 2, Cody 3, Crosby 3, Hope 3, Rogers, R. 3, Russell, J. 3, Head 4)
Son of Satan, 1924 (Micheaux 2)
Son of Sinbad, 1955 (Novak 3, Price 3, Young, V. 4)
Son of Spellbound, 1949 (Lewis 2)
Son of Tarzan, 1921 (Clarke, C.C. 4)
Son of the Border, 1933 (Chaney Lon, Jr. 3, Musuraca 4, Steiner 4)
Son of the Gods, 1930 (Barthelmess 3, Bennett C. 3, Haller 4)
Son of the Golden West, 1928 (Mix 3, Plunkett 4)
Son of the Sheik, 1926 (Banky 3, Valentino 3, Young, L. 3, Barnes 4, Marion 4, Menzies 4, Westmore, M. 4)
Son of the 'Star'. See Hijo del crack, 1953
Son of Zorro, 1947 (Katzman 4)
Son oncle de Normandie, 1939 (Berry 3, Auric 4)
Son tornate a fiorire le rose, 1975 (Cortese 3)
Sonad oskuld, 1915 (Sjostrom 2)
Sonambulos, (Borau 2)
Sonar Kella, 1974 (Ray, S. 2, Chatterjee 3, Datta 4)
Sonatas, 1959 (Bardem 2, Félix 3, Rey 3, Figueroa 4)
Sonate à Kreutzer, 1956 (Rohmer 2)
Sondag i September, 1963 (Donner 2, Andersson H. 3)
Son-Daughter, 1932 (Brown 2, Novarro 3, Oland 3, Stone 3, Adrian 4, Booth 4, Stothart 4)
Sone, 1897 (Messter 4)
Sonezaki shinjuh, 1981 (Miyagawa 4)
Song, 1928 (George, H. 3, Wong 3)
Song a Day, 1936 (Fleischer, M. and D. 2)
Song About Flowers, 1959 (Ioseliani 2)
Song About Happiness. See Pesnya o shchastye, 1934
Song and Dance Man, 1926 (Brenon 2, Love 3, Howe 4)
Song and Dance Man, 1936 (Dwan 2, Dumont 3, Trevor 3)
Song for Prince Charlie, 1958 (Lassally 4)

Song for Tomorrow, 1948 (Fisher 2, Lee, C. 3)
Song from My Heart. See Waga koi waga uta, 1969
Song Is Born, 1947 (Hawks 2, Kaye 3, Mayo 3, Friedhofer 4, Goldwyn 4, Jenkins 4, Mandell 4, Sharaff 4, Toland 4)
Song Is Born. See Ball of Fire, 1941
Song Lantern. See Uta andon, 1943
Song o' My Heart, 1930 (Borzage 2, O'Sullivan 3, Levien 4)
Song of a Sad Country, 1937 (Weiss 2)
Song of Arizona, 1946 (Rogers, R. 3)
Song of Bernadette, 1943 (King 2, Seaton 2, Cobb 3, Cooper, Gladys 3, Dalio 3, Darnell 3, Jones, J. 3, Price 3, Basevi 4, La Shelle 4, Miller, A. 4, Newman 4, Zanuck 4)
Song of Bwana Toshi. See Bwana Toshi no uta, 1965
Song of Ceylon, 1934 (Cavalcanti 2, Grierson 2, Wright 2)
Song of Freedom, 1936 (Robeson 3)
Song of Hate, 1915 (Ingram 2)
Song of Heroes. See Pesn o geroyazh, 1932
Song of Home. See Furusato no uta, 1925
Song of Kentucky, 1929 (Clarke, C.C. 4)
Song of Life, 1922 (Stahl 2, Meredyth 4)
Song of Life. See Lied vom Leben, 1930
Song of Love, 1923 (Schildkraut 3, Talmadge, N. 3, Gaudio 4, Marion 4, Schenck 4)
Song of Love, 1929 (Arden 3, Walker 4)
Song of Love, 1947 (Brown 2, Carroll L. 3, Henreid 3, Hepburn, K. 3, Walker 3, Gibbons 4, Irene 4, Kaper 4, Plunkett 4, Stradling 4)
Song of Manshuk. See Pyesn o Manshuk, 1969
Song of Mexico, 1945 (Alton, J. 4)
Song of My Heart, 1947 (Hardwicke 3, Glazer 4)
Song of Nevada, 1944 (Rogers, R. 3)
Song of Norway, 1970 (Homolka 3, Robinson, E. 3)
Song of Paris, 1952 (Auer 3)
Song of Remembrance. See Chanson du souvenir, 1936
Song of Restoration. See Ishin no uta, 1938
Song of Russia, 1944 (Taylor, R. 3, Irene 4, Pasternak 4, Stothart 4, Stradling 4)
Song of Sadness. See Canto da saudade, 1952
Song of Scheherazade, 1947 (Arden 3, Aumont 3, De Carlo 3, Lourié 4, Reisch 4, Rozsa 4)
Song of Soho, 1930 (Wimperis 4)
Song of Songs, 1933 (Mamoulian 2, Dietrich 3, Banton 4, Dreier 4, Hoffenstein 4)
Song of Summer, 1968 (Russell 2)
Song of Surrender, 1949 (Leisen 2, Rains 3, Bumstead 4, Dreier 4, Head 4, Young, V. 4)
Song of Texas, 1943 (Rogers, R. 3, Canutt 4)
Song of the Birds, 1935 (Fleischer, M. and D. 2)
Song of the Caballero, 1930 (Brown, Harry Joe 4, McCord 4)
Song of the Camp. See Roei no uta, 1938
Song of the Cart. See Niguruma no uta, 1959
Song of the Eagle, 1933 (Arlen 3, Hersholt 3, Robinson 4)
Song of the Flame, 1930 (Crosland 2, Garmes 4, Grot 4)
Song of the Flower Basket. See Hanakago no 46 (Cuny 3)
Song of the Forge, 1937 (Holloway 3)
Song of the Godbody, 1977 (Broughton 2)
Song of the Heart. See Udari levego, 1917
Song of the Islands, 1942 (Grable 3, Mature 3, Day 4, Newman 4, Pan 4, Pirosh 4)
Song of the Meet, I and II. See Píseň o sletu I, II, 1949
Song of the Mountain Pass. See Toge no uta, 1924
Song of the Open Road, 1944 (Fields, W.C. 3)
Song of the Prairie. See Arie prérie, 1949
Song of the Rivers. See Lied der Strome, 1954
Song of the Scarlet Flower. See Sången om den eldroda blomman, 1918
Song of the Scarlet Flower. See Sången om den eldroda blomman, 1934
Song of the Scarlet Flower. See Sången om den eldroda blommon, 1957
Song of the Sea. See O canto do mar, 1953
Song of the Shirt, 1908 (Griffith 2, Sennett 2, Lawrence 3, Bitzer 4)
Song of the South, 1946 (Disney 2, McDaniel 3, Iwerks 4, Toland 4)
Song of the Streets. See Dans les rues, 1933
Song of the Thin Man, 1947 (Grahame 3, Loy 3, Powell, W. 3, Wynn 3, Irene 4, Rosher 4)
Song of the West, 1930 (Brown 3)

Soshu yakyoku. *See* Shina no yoru, 1940
Soshun, 1956 (Ozu 2, Yamamura 3)
Soshun, 1968 (Iwashita 3)
Sosie, 1915 (Feuillade 2, Musidora 3)
Sospetto, 1975 (Girardot.3, Volonté 3, Solinas 4)
Soster Cecilies Offer. *See* Hvor Sorgerne glemmes, 1916
Soster Karin, 1917 (Borgstrom 3)
Sostyazanie, 1964 (Gerasimov 2)
Sotelo, 1976 (Ruiz 2)
Sottaceti, 1971 (Bozzetto 4)
Sotto dieci bandiere, 1960 (Heflin 3, Laughton 3, Volonté 3, Gherardi 4, Rota 4)
Sotto gli occhi dell'assassino, 1982 (Argento 4)
Sotto il segno dello scorpione, 1969 (Taviani, P. and V. 2, Volonté 3)
Sotto il sole di Roma, 1948 (Castellani 2, Sordi 3, Amidei 4)
Soubrette and the Simp, 1914 (Hardy 3)
Souffle au coeur, 1971 (Malle 2, Gélin 3, Cristaldi 4)
Soufrière, 1977 (Herzog 2)
Sougandh, 1942 (Sircar 4)
Soul Astray, 1914 (Eason 4)
Soul Fire, 1925 (Love 3)
Soul Herder, 1917 (Ford, J. 2, Hersholt 3)
Soul Kill. *See* Lady's Morals, 1930
Soul Mate, 1914 (Mix 3)
Soul Mates, 1925 (Basevi 4, Gibbons 4, Wilson, C. 4)
Soul of a Monster, 1944 (Muse 3, Guffey 4)
Soul of a Thief, 1913 (Dwan 2)
Soul of Broadway, 1915 (Brenon 2)
Soul of Buddha, 1918 (Bara 3)
Soul of Honor, 1914 (Sweet 3, Walthall 3)
Soul of Kura-san, 1916 (Hayakawa 3)
Soul of Magdalen, 1917 (Barthelmess 3)
Soul of the Beast, 1923 (Sullivan 4)
Soul of the Sea. *See* Hai hun, 1957
Soulfire, 1925 (Barthelmess 3)
Soulier de satin, 1985 (Branco 4)
Soulier trop petit, 1909 (Linders 3)
Souliers de Saint-Pierre. *See* Shoes of the Fisherman, 1968
Souls Adrift, 1917 (Edeson 4)
Souls at Sea, 1937 (Hathaway 2, Carey 3, Cooper, Gary 3, Cummings 3, Raft 3, Schildkraut 3, Dreier 4, Head 4, Lang 4)
Souls for Sale, 1923 (Chaplin 2, Bosworth 3, Nilsson 3, Pitts 3)
Souls in Conflict, 1954 (Green, G. 4)
Souls in Pawn, 1917 (King 2, Furthman 4, Seitz 4)
Souls.óf Children. *See* Ames d'enfants, 1928
Souls Triumphant, 1915 (Gish, L. 3)
Sound and the Fury, 1959 (Ritt 2, Brynner 3, Rosay 3, Warden 3, Woodward 3, Cahn 4, Clarke, C.C. 4, North 4, Wald 4, Wheeler 4)
Sound Barrier, 1952 (Lean 2, Richardson 3, Arnold 4, Korda 4)
Sound of Fog. *See* Kiri no oto, 1956
Sound of Fury, 1950 (Friedhofer 4)
Sound of Music, 1965 (Wise 2, Andrews J. 3, Jeakins 4, Lehman 4, Leven 4, McCord 4, Reynolds 4)
Sound of the Mountain. *See* Yama no oto, 1954
Sound of the Violin. *See* Kunstners Gennembrud, 1915
Sound of Trumpets. *See* Posto, 1961
Sound Off, 1952 (Edwards 2, Rooney 3, Duning 4)
Sound Sleeper, 1909 (Griffith 2, Bitzer 4)
Sounder, 1971 (Ritt 2, Alonzo 4)
Sounds From the Mountains. *See* Yama no oto, 1954
Soup and Fish, 1934 (Roach 4)
Soup Song, 1931 (Iwerks 4)
Soup to Nuts, 1930 (Three Stooges 3)
Soupçons, 1956 (Kosma 4)
Soupirant, 1962 (Carrière 4)
Sour Grapes, 1950 (Terry 4)
Sour Puss, 1940 (Clampett 4)
Source, 1900 (Guy 2)
Source, 1918 (Cruze 2, Reid 3)
Source de beauté. *See* Fioritures, 1916
Source of Love. *See* Pramen lásky, 1928
Souriante Madame Beudet, 1923 (Dulac 2)
Souricière, 1950 (Blier 3)

Sourire, 1958 (Delerue 4)
Sourire aux lèvres. *See* Bonjour sourire, 1955
Sourire d'or. *See* Gyldne Smil, 1935
Sourire dans la tempête, 1951 (Jurgens 3, Werner 3)
Sourires de la destinée. *See* Vacances portugaises, 1963
Souris blanche, 1911 (Feuillade 2)
Souris chez les hommes, 1964 (Audiard 4)
Souris d'hôtel, 1928 (Meerson 4)
Sous la Griffe, 1912 (Modot 3)
Sous la griffe, 1935 (Christian-Jaque 2, Spaak 4)
Sous la signe de Monte-Cristo, 1968 (Brasseur 3)
Sous la signe du taureau, 1969 (Gabin 3, Audiard 4)
Sous la terre, 1931 (Matras 4)
Sous le Ciel d'Orient. *See* Shéhérazade, 1928
Sous le ciel de Paris, 1950 (Duvivier 2)
Sous le ciel de Provence, 1956 (Fernandel 3)
Sous les palmes de Marrakech, 1948 (Decaë 4)
Sous les ponts de Paris. *See* Clodoche, 1938
Sous les toits de Paris, 1930 (Clair 2, Modot 3, Meerson 4, Périnal 4, Trauner 4)
Sous les yeux d'Occident, 1936 (Allégret, M. 2, Barrault 3, Fresnay 3, Simon, M. 3, Auric 4, Lourié 4)
Sous un autre soleil, 1955 (Broca 2)
Soushi gekijou, 1946 (Miyagawa 4)
Sousto, 1960 (Nemec 2)
South Advancing Women. *See* Nanshin josei, 1939
South American George, 1941 (Formby 3)
South Limburg. *See* Zuid Limburg, 1929
South o' the North Pole, 1924 (Roach 4)
South of Algiers, 1952 (Heflin 3, Morris 4)
South of Caliente, 1951 (Rogers, R. 3)
South of Dixie, 1944 (Beavers 3, Bruckman 4)
South of Pago-Pago, 1940 (Farmer 3, McLaglen 3)
South of St. Louis, 1949 (Malone 3, McCrea 3, Freund 4, Steiner 4)
South of Santa Fe, 1932 (Glennon 4)
South of Santa Fe, 1942 (Rogers, R. 3)
South of Suez, 1940 (Brent 3)
South of Tahiti, 1941 (Crawford, B. 3, Boyle 4)
South of the Border, 1939 (Autry 3, Farnum 3)
South Pacific, 1958 (Logan 2, Brazzi 3, Jeakins 4, Newman 4, Prinz 4, Reynolds 4, Shamroy 4, Wheeler 4)
South Pole or Bust, 1934 (Terry 4)
South Riding, 1938 (Saville 2, Gwenn 3, Richardson 3, Dalrymple 4, Meerson 4, Stradling 4)
South Sea Bubble, 1928 (Novello 3, Balcon 4)
South Sea Love, 1927 (Musuraca 4)
South Sea Rose, 1929 (Dwan 2, Levien 4, Rosson 4)
South Sea Sinner, 1950 (Winters 3, Orry-Kelly 4)
South Sea Woman, 1953 (Lancaster 3, Martin, S. 3, Mayo 3, McCord 4)
South Seas Adventure, 1958 (Welles 2, North 4)
South Seas Bouquet. *See* Nankai no hanatabe, 1942
South to Karanga, 1940 (Salter 4)
South West Pacific, 1944 (Finch 3)
South Wind. *See* Minami ni kaze, 1942
South Wind and Waves. *See* Minami no kaze to nami, 1961
South Wind: Sequel. *See* Zoko minami no kaze, 1942
Southbound Duckling, 1954 (Hanna and Barbera 4)
Southern Cinderella, 1913 (Ince 4)
Southern Comfort, 1981 (Hill, W. 2)
Southern Exposure, 1935 (Roach 4)
Southern Fried Rabbit, 1952 (Freleng 4)
Southern Horse-pitality, 1935 (Terry 4)
Southern Justice, 1917 (Hersholt 3)
Southern Love, 1924 (Wilcox 2)
Southern Maid, 1933 (Daniels 3, Granger 3)
Southern Pride, 1917 (King 2)
Southern Rhythm, 1932 (Terry 4)
Southern Star, 1968 (Welles 2)
Southern Star. *See* Etoile du sud, 1969
Southern Yankee, 1948 (Ireland 3, Frank and Panama 4)
Southerner, 1931 (Booth 4, Stothart 4)
Southerner, 1945 (Aldrich 2, Renoir 2, Bondi 3, Lourié 4)

Southerner. *See* Prodigal, 1931
Southerners, 1914 (Ingram 2)
Southward Ho, 1939 (Rogers, R. 3)
Southwest, 1945 (Kaufman 4)
Southwest Passage, 1954 (Ireland 3)
Southwest to Sonora. *See* Appaloosa, 1966
Souvenir. *See* Aux yeux de souvenir, 1948
Souvenir d'Italie, 1957 (De Sica 2, Sordi 3, Age and Scarpelli 4)
Souvenir de Gilbralter, 1975 (Constantine 3)
Souvenir de Paris, 1955 (Guerra 2)
Souvenir of Paradise. *See* Vzpomínka na ráj, 1939–40
Souvenirs, 1938 (Pearson 2)
Souvenirs d'en France, 1975 (Moreau 3, Sarde 4)
Souvenirs from Sweden, 1960 (Carlsen 2)
Souvenirs perdus, 1950 (Christian-Jaque 2, Blier 3, Brasseur 3, Feuillère 3, Montand 3, Philipe 3, Jeanson 4, Kosma 4, Matras 4, Prévert 4)
Sovetskie igrushki, 1924 (Vertov 2)
Soviet Toys. *See* Sovetskie igrushki, 1924
Sovngaengersken, 1914 (Holger-Madsen 2)
Sovversivi, 1967 (Taviani, P. and V. 2, Fusco 4)
Sower Reaps, 1914 (Eason 4)
Sowers, 1916 (Sweet 3, Rosher 4)
Sowing the Wind, 1916 (Hepworth 2)
Sowing the Wind, 1920 (Stahl 3)
Soy charro de Rancho Grande, 1947 (Infante 3)
Soy Cuba. *See* Ya Cuba, 1964
Soy Mexico, 1970 (Reichenbach 2)
Soy puro mexicano, 1942 (Fernández 2, Armendáriz 3)
Soy un prófugo, 1946 (Cantinflas 3)
Soyez les bienvenus, 1940 (Berry 3, Gélin 3, Trauner 4)
Soyez ma femme. *See* Be My Wife, 1921
Soylent Green, 1973 (Fleischer, R. 2, Cotten 3, Heston 3, Robinson, E. 3, Westmore, B. 4)
Soyokaze chichi to tomoni, 1940 (Takamine 3)
Soyons doncs sportifs, 1909 (Cohl 2)
Soyons gai, 1931 (Menjou 3)
Soyuz Velikogo Dela. *See* S.V.D. 1927
Space, 1965 (Warhol 2)
Space Children, 1958 (Edouart 4, Laszlo 4)
Space Master X-7, 1958 (Howard, M. 3)
Space 1999, 1974 (Morricone 4)
Space Ship Sappy, 1957 (Three Stooges 3)
Space Works, 1981 (Strick 2)
SpaceCamp, 1986 (Fraker 4, Williams, J. 4)
Spacehunter: Adventures in the Forbidden Zone, 1983 (Bernstein 4)
Spaceman and King Arthur, 1979 (More 3)
Spacerek staromiejski, 1958 (Munk 2)
Spaceways, 1953 (Fisher 2)
Spadaccino di Siena, 1961 (Granger 3, Delli Colli 4)
Spade e la croce, 1958 (De Carlo 3)
Spades Are Trumps, 1915 (Talmadge, C. 3)
Spadla s měsíce, 1961 (Schorm 2, Brodský 3)
Spaedbarnet, 1953 (Roos 2)
Spaghetti, 1916 (Hardy 3)
Spaghetti a la Mode, 1915 (Hardy 3)
Spaghetti and Lottery, 1915 (Hardy 3)
Spaghetti House, 1982 (Manfredi 3)
Spain in Flames, 1936 (Van Dongen 4)
Spalíček, 1947 (Trnka 2, Pojar 4)
Spalovači mrtvol, 1968 (Hrušínský 3)
Span of Life, 1914 (Barrymore L. 3)
Spangles, 1926 (Bosworth 3)
Spaniard, 1925 (Walsh 2)
Spaniard and Indian, 1941 (Eisenstein 2)
Spanilá jízda, 1963 (Brdečka 4)
Spanish ABC, 1938 (Dickinson 2)
Spanish Affair, 1957 (Siegel 2)
Spanish Dancer, 1923 (Brenon 2, Beery 3, Menjou 3, Negri 3, Howe 4, Mathis 4)
Spanish Dilemma, 1912 (Sennett 2, Normand 3)
Spanish Earth, 1937 (Ivens 2, Renoir 2, Van Dongen 4)
Spanish Fiesta, 1941 (Haller 4)

Spanish Gardener, 1956 (Bogarde 3, Cusack 3)
Spanish Girl, 1909 (Anderson G. 3)
Spanish Gypsy, 1911 (Griffith 2, Bitzer 4, Macpherson 4)
Spanish Jade, 1922 (Hitchcock 2)
Spanish Main, 1945 (Borzage 2, Henreid 3, O'Hara 3, Eason 4, Eisler 4, Mankiewicz 4)
Spanish Onions, 1930 (Terry 4)
Spanish Shotgun. *See* Escopeta nacional, 1978
Spanish-American War Scenes, 1898 (Bitzer 4)
Spanking Breezes, 1926 (Sennett 2)
Spanky, 1932 (Roach 4)
Spara forte, più forte . . . non capisco, 1966 (Mastroianni 3, Welch 3, D'Amico 4, Rota 4)
Spara, gringo, spara, 1968 (Wynn 3)
Spara per primo vivrai di piú. *See* Consortium, 1968
Spare a Copper, 1940 (Dearden 2, Formby 3, Balcon 4)
Spare the Rod, 1954 (Terry 4)
Spare the Rod, 1961 (Pleasance 3)
Spare Time, 1939 (Cavalcanti 2, Jennings 2)
Spark. *See* Hibana, 1922
Spark. *See* Hibana, 1956
Spark of Manhood, 1914 (Reid 3)
Sparks of Fate, 1914 (Bushman 3)
Sparky the Firefly, 1953 (Terry 4)
Sparring at N.Y. Athletic Club, 1905 (Bitzer 4)
Sparring Partner, 1921 (Fleischer, M. and D. 2)
Sparrow. *See* Asfour, 1973
Sparrow of the Circus, 1914 (Eason 4)
Sparrows, 1926 (Pickford 3, Rosher 4, Struss 4, Sullivan 4)
Sparsh, 1984 (Azmi 3)
Spartacus, 1960 (Kubrick 2, Curtis 3, Douglas, K. 3, Ireland 3, Laughton 3, Olivier 3, Simmons 3, Ustinov 3, Bass 4, Canutt 4, Ellenshaw 4, North 4, Trumbo 4)
Spartakiad. *See* Spartakiáda, 1956
Spartakiáda, 1956 (Stallich 4)
Sparviero del Nilo, 1949 (Gassman 3)
Spasmo, 1974 (Morricone 4)
Spasms. *See* Death Bite, 1982
Spatně namalovaná slepice, 1963 (Brdečka 4)
Spawn of the North, 1938 (Hathaway 2, Barrymore J. 3, Fonda, H. 3, Lamour 3, Raft 3, Edouart 4, Furthman 4, Head 4, Jennings 4, Lang 4, Lewin 4, Tiomkin 4, Westmore, W. 4)
Speak Easily, 1932 (Keaton 2, Durante 3)
Speak Easy, 1919 (Sennett 2)
Speakeasy, 1929 (Walthall 3)
Speaking from America, 1939 (Cavalcanti 2, Jennings 2)
Speaking of Animals Down on the Farm, 1942 (Avery 2)
Speaking of Animals in a Pet Shop, 1942 (Avery 2)
Speaking of Animals in the Zoo, 1942 (Avery 2)
Speaking of Glass. *See* Over glas gesproken, 1958
Speaking of Murder. *See* Rouge est mis, 1957
Speaking of Relations, 1934 (Roach 4)
Spear Dance of 53 Stations. *See* Yari-odori gojusan-tsugi, 1946
Special Agent, 1935 (Davis 3, Orry-Kelly 4)
Special Bardot, 1968 (Reichenbach 2)
Special Boy Soldiers of the Navy. *See* Kaigun tokubetsu shonen hei, 1972
Special Day. *See* Giornata particolare, 1977
Special Day. *See* Giornata speciale, 1977
Special Delivery, 1927 (Arbuckle 3, Powell, W. 3, Schulberg 4)
Special Delivery, 1955 (Cotten 3)
Special Delivery, 1976 (Schifrin 4)
Special Education. *See* Spegalno vaspetanie, 1977
Special Inspector, 1939 (Hayworth 3)
Special Investigator, 1936 (Cronjager 4)
Special Section. *See* Section speciale, 1975
Specialist po Vsičko, 1962 (Karamitev 3)
Specialisti, 1969 (Fabian 3)
Specialists, 1975 (Coogan 3)
Species of a Mexican Man, (Johnson, N. 3)
Speckled Band, 1931 (Massey 3, Young, F. 4)
Spectacle Maker, 1934 (Stothart 4)
Specter of the Rose, 1946 (Anderson J. 3, Garmes 4, Hecht 4)

Spring Tonic, 1935 (Ayres 3, Pitts 3, Trevor 3, Bruckman 4)
Spring Wind on Venaya, 1959 (Bondarchuk 3)
Springende Hirsch, 1915 (Wiene 2)
Springer and the SS-Men. *See* Pérák a SS, 1946
Springfield Rifle, 1952 (De Toth 2, Chaney Lon, Jr. 3, Cooper, Gary 3, Steiner 4)
Springt die Ketten, 1930 (Dudow 2)
Springtime, 1920 (Hardy 3)
Springtime, 1929 (Iwerks 4)
Springtime for Henry, 1934 (Bruce 3, Lasky 4, Seitz 4)
Springtime for Thomas, 1946 (Hanna and Barbera 4)
Springtime in Budapest. *See* Budapesti tavasz, 1956
Springtime in the Rockage, 1940 (Fleischer, M. and D. 2)
Springtime in the Rockies, 1937 (Autry 3)
Springtime in the Rockies, 1942 (Grable 3, Horton 3, Miranda 3, Day 4, Newman 4, Pan 4)
Springtime in the Sierras, 1947 (Rogers, R. 3)
Springtime Serenade, 1935 (Lantz 4)
Sprucin' Up, 1935 (Roach 4)
Sprung ins Leben, 1924 (Dietrich 3, Wagner 4)
Spur des Falken, 1968 (Hoppe 3)
Spurs, 1930 (Eason 4)
Spurs and Saddles, 1927 (Wray 3)
Spurs of Sybil, 1918 (Brady 4)
Sputnik. *See* A pied, à cheval, et un sputnik, 1958
Sputnik Speaking, 1959 (Gerasimov 2)
Sputnik Speaks. *See* Sputnik Speaking, 1959
Spy, 1911 (Bosworth 3)
Spy, 1931 (Zinnemann 2)
Spy Against the World. *See* Spie contro il mondo, 1966
Spy Has Not Yet Died. *See* Kancho mada shinazu, 1942
Spy in Black, 1939 (Powell and Pressburger 2, Veidt 3, Hornbeck 4, Korda 4, Rozsa 4)
Spy in the Green Hat, 1964 (Cook 3)
Spy in the Pantry. *See* Ten Days in Paris, 1939
Spy in White. *See* Secret of Stambov, 1936
Spy in Your Eye. *See* Appuntamento per le spie, 1965
Spy Killer, 1969 (Sangster 4)
Spy of Napoleon, 1936 (Barthelmess 3, Courant 4)
Spy Ring, 1938 (Wyman 3)
Spy Smasher, 1942 (Canutt 4)
Spy 13. *See* Operator 13, 1934
Spy Who Came in from the Cold, 1966 (Ritt 2, Bloom 3, Burton 3, Cusack 3, Werner 3, Dehn 4, Morris 4)
Spy Who Loved Me, 1977 (Jurgens 3, Moore, R. 3, Adam 4, Renoir 4)
Spy With a Cold Nose, 1966 (Harvey 3, Williams, R. 4)
Spy with My Face, 1966 (Carroll L. 3)
Spy with the Green Hat, 1966 (Carroll L. 3)
Spylarks. *See* Intelligence Men, 1965
Spynx, 1917 (Lukas 3)
Spys, 1974 (Kershner 2, Gould 3, Sutherland 3, Fisher 4, Goldsmith 4)
Spy's Defeat, 1913 (Bushman 3)
Squabs and Squabbles, 1919 (Hardy 3)
Squadra antimafia, 1978 (Wallach 3)
Squadron, 1964 (Robertson 3)
Squadron Leader X, 1942 (Alwyn 4)
Squadron 992, 1940 (Cavalcanti 2, Watt 2)
Squadron of Doom. *See* Ace Drummond, 1936
Squadron of Honour, 1937 (Ballard 4)
Squall, 1929 (Korda 2, Loy 3, Pitts 3, Young, L. 3, Seitz 4)
Squall. *See* Shkval, 1916
Square. *See* Tér, 1971
Square Deal, 1917 (Edeson 4, Marion 4)
Square Deal. *See* Ruse, 1915
Square Deal Man, 1917 (Hart 3, August 4)
Square Deal Man. *See* Ruse, 1915
Square Deal Sanderson, 1919 (Hart 3, August 4)
Square Deceiver, 1917 (Gaudio 4)
Square Jungle, 1955 (Borgnine 3, Curtis 3)
Square Mile, 1953 (Guinness 3)
Square of Violence. *See* Nasilhe na trgu, 1961
Square Ring, 1953 (Dearden 2)
Square Shooter, 1927 (Wyler 2)

Squarehead. *See* Mabel's Married Life, 1914
Squareheads of the Round Table, 1948 (Three Stooges 3)
Squatter's Girl, 1914 (Anderson G. 3)
Squaw Man, 1914 (DeMille 2, Buckland 4)
Squaw Man, 1918 (DeMille 2, Buckland 4)
Squaw Man, 1931 (DeMille 2, Baxter W. 3, Velez 3, Adrian 4, Prinz 4, Rosson 4, Stothart 4)
Squaw Man's Son, 1917 (Reid 3)
Squawkin' Hawk, 1942 (Jones 2)
Squaw's Love, 1911 (Griffith 2, Normand 3, Bitzer 4)
Squeak in the Deep, 1966 (McKimson 4)
Squeaker, 1930 (Bruce 3)
Squeaker, 1937 (Howard 2, Sim 3, Korda 4, Krasker 4, Périnal 4, Rozsa 4)
Squeaker. *See* Zinker, 1963
Squeaks and Squawks, 1920 (Hardy 3)
Squealer, 1930 (Pitts 3, Brown, Harry Joe 4, Robinson 4)
Squeeze, 1977 (Keach 3)
Squeeze. *See* Controrapina, 1978
Squib Wins the Calcutta Sweep, 1922 (Pearson 2)
Squibs, 1921 (Pearson 2, Balfour 3)
Squibs, 1935 (Balfour 3, Holloway 3)
Squibs' Honeymoon, 1923 (Pearson 2, Balfour 3)
Squibs, M.P., 1923 (Pearson 2, Balfour 3)
Squibs Wins the Calcutta Sweep, 1922 (Balfour 3)
Squire's Son, 1914 (Ince 4)
Squirm, 1976 (Baker 4)
Squirrel Crazy, 1951 (Terry 4)
Srdce za písničku, 1933 (Stallich 4)
Srdečný pozdrav ze zeměkoule, 1982 (Kopecký 3)
Sreća u dvoje, 1969 (Grgić 4)
Sredi dobrykh lyudei, 1962 (Maretskaya 3)
Srestu vjatara, 1977 (Ivanov 3)
Sretlyi put, 1940 (Orlova 3)
Sroublkova dobrodružství, 1962 (Brdečka 4)
Srub, 1965 (Jires 2)
SS Ionian, 1939 (Jennings 2)
Ssaki, 1962 (Polanski 2)
SSSSSSS, 1973 (Martin, S. 3)
SST — Death Flight, 1977 (Meredith 3, Biroc 4)
SST — Disaster in the Sky. *See* SST — Death Flight, 1977
Staa tanjo, 1963 (Yamamura 3)
Staalkongens Vilje. *See* Mørke Punkt, 1913
Stability Versus Nobility, 1911 (Bosworth 3)
Stable Companions, 1922 (Brook 3)
Stablemates, 1938 (Wood 2, Beery 3, Rooney 3, Seitz 4)
Stachka, 1925 (Eisenstein 2, Tisse 4)
Stacked Cards, 1926 (Haller 4)
Stad, 1960 (Troell 2)
Staden vid vattnen, 1955 (Andersson B. 3)
Stadt Anatol, 1936 (Frohlich 3)
Stadt der tausend Freuden, 1927 (Gallone 2)
Stadt in Sicht, 1923 (Pick 2, Galeen 4)
Stadt ist voller Geheimnisse, 1955 (Kortner 3)
Stadt steht Kopf, 1932 (Grundgens 3, Sakall 3, Planer 4)
Stadt Stuttgart, 100. Cannstatter Volksfest, 1935 (Ruttmann 2)
Stadt vor Versuchung, 1925 (Tschechowa 3)
Stadtstreicher, 1965 (Fassbinder 2)
Staféta, 1970 (Kovács 2)
Staffs, about 1927 (Fischinger 2)
Staffs. *See* Orgelstabe, 1923–27
Stage, 1951 (Anand 3)
Stage Door, 1937 (La Cava 2, Arden 3, Ball 3, Hepburn, K. 3, Menjou 3, Miller 3, Rogers, G. 3, Berman 4, Polglase 4, Ryskind 4, Veiller 4)
Stage Door Canteen, 1943 (Borzage 2, Daves 2, Anderson J. 3, Bellamy 3, Darwell 3, Fields, G. 3, Hepburn, K. 3, Hersholt 3, Jaffe 3, Muni 3, Oberon 3, Raft 3, Weissmuller 3, Green, J. 4, Horner 4)
Stage Door Cartoon, 1944 (Freleng 4)
Stage Driver's Daughter, 1911 (Anderson G. 3)
Stage Fright, 1923 (Roach 4)

Stage Fright, 1950 (Hitchcock 2, Dietrich 3, Sim 3, Wyman 3, Reville 4)

Stage Hand, 1933 (Langdon 3)

Stage Hoax, 1952 (Lantz 4)

Stage Kisses, 1927 (Walker 4)

Stage Mother, 1933 (Brady 3, O'Sullivan 3, Adrian 4, Brown, N. 4, Freed 4)

Stage Note, 1910 (Lawrence 3)

Stage Robbers of San Juan, 1911 (Dwan 2)

Stage Romance, 1922 (Brenon 2, Farnum 3)

Stage Stars Off Screen, 1925 (Buchanan 3)

Stage Struck, 1917 (Gish, D. 3)

Stage Struck, 1922 (Roach 4)

Stage Struck, 1925 (Dwan 2, Swanson 3, Polglase 4)

Stage Struck, 1936 (Berkeley 2, Blondell 3, Powell, D. 3, Wyman 3, Orry-Kelly 4)

Stage Struck, 1951 (Terry 4)

Stage Struck, 1958 (Lumet 2, Fonda, H. 3, Greenwood 3, Marshall 3, North 4, Planer 4)

Stage Stunt, 1929 (Lantz 4)

Stage to Chino, 1940 (Hunt 4)

Stage to Thunder Rock, 1964 (Chaney Lon, Jr. 3, Wynn 3)

Stage to Tucson, 1950 (Brown, Harry Joe 4)

Stagecoach, 1939 (Ford, J. 2, Carradine 3, Cody 3, Meek 3, Trevor 3, Wayne 3, Canutt 4, Cooper 4, Glennon 4, Nichols 4, Plunkett 4, Wanger 4)

Stagecoach, 1966 (Crosby 3, Cummings 3, Heflin 3, Wynn 3, Clothier 4, Goldsmith 4, Smith, J.M. 4)

Stagecoach Buckaroo, 1942 (Salter 4)

Stagecoach Driver and the Girl, 1915 (Mix 3)

Stagecoach Guard, 1915 (Mix 3)

Stagecoach Kid, 1949 (Musuraca 4)

Stagecoach Outlaws, 1945 (Crabbe 3)

Stagecoach War, 1940 (Boyd 3, Head 4)

Stagione all'inferno, 1971 (Stamp 3, Jarre 4)

Stagione dei sensi, 1968 (Argento 4, Morricone 4)

Stagione dei sensi, 1968 (Vukotić 4)

Stain on the Conscience, 1968 (Vukotić 4)

Stained Glass at Fairford, 1955 (Wright 2, Donat 3)

Staircase, 1969 (Donen 2, Burton 3, Harrison 3, Moore, D. 3)

Stairs, 1953 (Maddow 4)

Stairs of Sand, 1929 (Arthur 3, Beery 3)

Stairway for a Star, 1947 (Wilde 3)

Stairway to Heaven. See Matter of Life and Death, 1946

Stajio wa tenya wanya, 1957 (Kyo 3)

Stake Uncle Sam to Play Your Hand, 1918 (Normand 3)

Stake-Out. See Police Story, 1973

Stakeout on Dope Street, 1958 (Kershner 2, Corman 4)

Staking His Life. See Conversion of Frosty Blake, 1915

Stalag 17, 1953 (Preminger 2, Wilder 2, Holden 3, Head 4, Laszlo 4, Waxman 4)

Stalingradskaya bitva, 1949 (Cherkassov 3)

Stalker, 1979 (Tarkovsky 2)

Stalking Moon, 1968 (Mulligan 2, Pakula 2, Peck 3, Saint 3, Jeakins 4, Lang 4, Sargent 4)

Stallion Road, 1947 (Walsh 2, Reagan 3, Edeson 4)

Stalowe serca, 1948 (Kawalerowicz 2, Lomnicki 3)

Stamboul Quest, 1934 (Wood 2, Auer 3, Brennan 3, Brent 3, Carroll L. 3, Loy 3, Howe 4, Mankiewicz 4, Stothart 4, Wanger 4)

Stammen Lever an, 1937–38 (Fejos 2)

Stamp Fantasia, 1961 (Kuri 4)

Stampede, 1911 (Guy 2, Pickford 3, Gaudio 4)

Stampede, 1949 (Edwards 2)

Stampeded. See Big Land, 1957

Stampen, 1955 (Bjornstrand 3, Fischer 4)

Stand and Deliver, 1928 (Crisp 3, Oland 3, Velez 3, Adrian 4, Grot 4)

Stand By for Action, 1942 (Brennan 3, Laughton 3, Taylor, R. 3, Balderston 4, Mankiewicz 4, Rosher 4)

Stand der Dinge, 1982 (Wenders 2, Alekan 4, Branco 4, Corman 4)

Stand Pat, 1922 (Roach 4)

Stand Up and Be Counted, 1972 (Bisset 3, Cooper, J 3, Wheeler 4)

Stand Up and Cheer, 1934 (Baxter W. 3, Bruce 3, Fetchit 3, Temple 3)

Stand Up and Fight, 1939 (Leroy 2, Van Dyke, W.S. 2, Beery 3, Taylor, R. 3, Murfin 4)

Standard Time, 1967 (Snow 2, Wieland 2)

Standarte, 1977 (Cushing 3, Dagover 3)

Standhafte Benjamin, 1917 (Wiene 2)

Stand-In, 1937 (Garnett 2, Blondell 3, Bogart 3, Howard, L. 3, Clarke, C.C. 4, Wanger 4)

Standing by the Treasury. See U pokladny stál, 1939

Standing Room Only, 1944 (De Carlo 3, Goddard 3, MacMurray 3, Dreier 4, Head 4, Lang 4)

Stanley and Livingstone, 1939 (King 2, Brennan 3, Coburn, C. 3, Hardwicke 3, Tracy 3, Dunne 4, MacGowan 4, Newman 4, Raksin 4, Zanuck 4)

Stanza del vescovo, 1977 (Risi 2, Tognazzi 3)

Staphylokok-faren, 1960 (Roos 2)

Star, 1952 (Davis 3, Hayden 3, Wood 3, Laszlo 4, Leven 4, Orry-Kelly 4, Young, V. 4)

Star!, 1968 (Wise 2, Andrews J. 3, Scheider 3, Cahn 4, Kidd 4, Laszlo 4, Leven 4, Reynolds 4)

Star Boarder, 1914 (Chaplin 2, Sennett 2)

Star Boarder, 1917 (Hardy 3)

Star Boarder, 1918 (Fazenda 3)

Star Boarder, 1920 (Sennett 2)

Star Child, 1983 (Corman 4)

Star Crash, 1979 (Barry 4)

Star Dust, 1940 (Darnell 3, Meek 3, Day 4, MacGowan 4, Zanuck 4)

Star 80, 1983 (Fosse 2, Baker C. 3, Robertson 3, Nykvist 4)

Star for a Night, 1936 (Darwell 3, McDaniel 3, Trevor 3)

Star Garden, 1974 (Brakhage 2)

Star in the Dust, 1956 (Boone 3, Eastwood 3)

Star in the Night, 1945 (Siegel 2)

Star Is Bored, 1956 (Freleng 4)

Star Is Born, 1937 (Fleming 2, Wellman 2, Gaynor 3, March 3, Menjou 3, Turner, L. 3, Selznick 4, Steiner 4, Wheeler 4)

Star Is Born, 1954 (Cukor 2, Bogart 3, Garland 3, Martin, S. 3, Mason 3, Edens 4, Sharaff 4)

Star Is Born, 1976 (Mazursky 2, Streisand 3, Surtees 4)

Star Is Born. See Birth of a Star, 1944

Star is Hatched, 1938 (Freleng 4)

Star Is Shorn, 1939 (Ballard 4)

Star Maker, 1939 (Crosby 3, Head 4, Newman 4, Struss 4)

Star Named Wormwood. See Hvězda zvaná Pelyněk, 1964

Star Night at the Cocoanut Grove, 1935 (Cooper, Gary 3, Crosby 3)

Star of Bethlehem, 1912 (Cruze 2)

Star of Bethlehem, 1956 (Reiniger 2)

Star of Hong Kong. See Honkon no hoshi, 1962

Star of India, 1913 (Guy 2)

Star of India, 1953 (Wilde 3, Adam 4, Rota 4)

Star of Married Couples. See Meoto boshi, 1926

Star of Midnight, 1935 (Powell, W. 3, Rogers, G. 3, Berman 4, Hunt 4, Polglase 4, Steiner 4, Veiller 4)

Star of the Circus, 1938 (Saunders 4)

Star of the Sea, 1915 (Chaney Lon 3)

Star Packer, 1934 (Wayne 3, Canutt 4)

Star Reporter, 1932 (Powell 2)

Star Rock. See Apple, 1980

Star Said No. See Callaway Went Thataway, 1951

Star Spangled Rhythm, 1942 (DeMille 2, Bendix 3, Crosby 3, Goddard 3, Hayward 3, Hope 3, Hutton 3, Ladd 3, Lake 3, Lamour 3, MacMurray 3, Milland 3, Powell, D. 3, Preston 3, Dreier 4, Frank and Panama 4, Head 4, Mercer 4)

Star Spangled Salesman, 1968 (Three Stooges 3)

Star, The Orphan, and the Butcher. See Evlalie quitte les champs, 1973

Star Trek: The Motion Picture, 1979 (Wise 2, Goldsmith 4, Serafine 4, Trumbull 4)

Star Trek III: The Search for Spock, 1984 (Anderson J. 3, Serafine 4)

Star Wars, 1977 (Lucas 2, Cushing 3, Ford, H. 3, Guinness 3, Jones, J.E. 3, Baker 4, Burtt 4, Edlund 4, Williams, J. 4)

Star Without Light. See Etoile sans lumière, 1945

Star Witness, 1931 (Wellman 2, Huston 3)

Stará čínská opera, 1954 (Kachyna 2)

Starci na chmelu, 1964 (Stallich 4, Stallich 4)

Stardoom, 1971–73 (Brocka 2)

Stardust Memories, 1980 (Allen 2, Willis 4)

Stardust on the Sage, 1942 (Autry 3)

Staré povĕsti české, 1953 (Trnka 2, Brdečka 4, Pojar 4)
Starets Vasili Gryaznov, 1924 (Tisse 4)
Starfish, 1950 (Schlesinger 2)
Starflight One: The Plane That Couldn't Land, 1983 (Schifrin 4)
Stark, 1985 (Hopper 3)
Stark Fear, 1963 (Williams, J. 4)
Stark Love, 1927 (Brown, K. 4)
Stark Mad, 1915 (Fazenda 3)
Stark Mad, 1929 (Bacon 2, Fazenda 3, Walthall 3)
Stark System, 1980 (Morricone 4)
Starkaste, 1929 (Sjoberg 2)
Starke Ferdinand, 1975 (Kluge 2)
Stärker als die Liebe, 1938 (Wegener 3)
Stärker als die Nacht, 1954 (Dudow 2)
Stärker als Paragraphen, (Staudte 2)
Stärkere, 1918 (Kortner 3)
Starlift, 1951 (Cagney 3, Cooper, Gary 3, Day 3, Mayo 3, Scott, R. 3,
    Wyman 3, McCord 4, Prinz 4)
Starlost. See Alien Oro, 1982
Starman, 1984 (Bridges 3)
Staroie i novoie, 1929 (Eisenstein 2, Tisse 4)
Staroye Dudino. See Granitsa, 1935
Starozhil, 1962 (Ermler 2)
Starring in Western Stuff, 1916 (Mix 3)
Stars. See Sterne, 1959
Stars and Bars, 1917 (Sennett 2)
Stars and Guitars. See Brazil, 1944
Stars and Stripes, 1939–41 (McLaren 2)
Stars and Stripes Forever, 1952 (Wagner 3, Webb 3, Clarke, C.C. 4,
    Jeakins 4, Lemaire 4, Newman 4, Trotti 4)
Stars Are Beautiful, 1974 (Brakhage 2)
Stars Are Singing, 1953 (Taurog 2, Bumstead 4, Head 4,
    Young, V. 4)
Stars in My Crown, 1950 (Tourneur, J. 2, McCrea 3, Stone 3,
    Deutsch 4, Plunkett 4)
Stars in the Backyard. See Paradise Alley, 1962
Stars Look Down, 1939 (Reed 2, Redgrave, M. 3)
Stars of Eger. See Egri csillagok, 1923
Stars on Horseback, 1943 (Davis 3)
Stars on the Wings. See Zvezdy na krylyakh, 1955
Stars over Broadway, 1935 (Berkeley 2, O'Brien, P. 3, Barnes 4,
    Epstein, J. & P. 4, Orry-Kelly 4, Wald 4)
Stars Their Courses Change, 1915 (Bushman 3)
Stars' War: The Flight of the Wild Geese, 1978 (Burton 3)
Starshaya sestra, 1967 (Churikova 3)
Starship Invasions. See Alien Encounter, 1976
Starsky and Hutch, 1975 (Schifrin 4)
Start Cheering, 1938 (Crawford, B. 3, Durante 3, Three Stooges 3,
    Green, J. 4, Walker 4)
Start in Life, 1943 (Alwyn 4)
Start the Revolution Without Me, 1970 (Welles 2, Sutherland 3,
    Wilder 3, Addison 4)
Start the Show, 1920 (Roach 4)
Starting Over, 1979 (Pakula 2, Clayburgh 3, Reynolds, B. 3, Jenkins 4,
    Nykvist 4)
Starvation Blues, 1925 (Roach 4)
Starving for Love, 1912–13 (White 3)
Stary Kowboj, 1973 (Giersz 4)
Starye steny, 1973 (Gurchenko 3)
Stasera alle undici, 1937 (Vích 4)
Stasera mi butto, 1967 (Giannini 3)
Stasera mi butto i due bagnani, 1968 (Giannini 3)
Stasera niente di nuovo, 1942 (Valli 3)
Stastie pride v nedelu, 1958 (Kroner 3)
Stastny lev, 1959 (Brdečka 4)
State Fair, 1933 (King 2, Ayres 3, Gaynor 3, Rogers, W. 3, Levien 4)
State Fair, 1945 (Andrews D. 3, Bainter 3, Crain 3, Meek 3, Levien 4,
    Newman 4, Shamroy 4)
State Fair, 1962 (Faye 3, Ferrer, J. 3, Brackett, C. 4, Newman 4,
    Smith, J.M. 4)
State Line, 1911 (Lawrence 3)
State of Siege. See Etat de siège, 1972
State of the Union, 1948 (Capra 2, Hepburn, K. 3, Johnson, V. 3,

Lansbury 3, Menjou 3, Stone 3, Tracy 3, Hornbeck 4, Irene 4,
    Veiller 4, Young, V. 4)
State of Things. See Stand der Dinge, 1982
State Penitentiary, 1950 (Baxter W. 3, Katzman 4)
State Secret, 1950 (Fairbanks, D. Jr. 3, Hawkins 3, Alwyn 4, Gilliat 4,
    Krasker 4)
State Street Sadie, 1928 (Loy 3, Zanuck 4)
State's Attorney, 1932 (Barrymore J. 3, Selznick 4, Steiner 4)
Statek na hranici, 1973 (Danailov 3)
Stateline Motel. See Ultima chance, 1973
States, 1967 (Frampton 2)
Station Content, 1918 (Swanson 3)
Station Master, 1917 (Hardy 3)
Station mondaine, 1951 (Braunberger 4)
Station Six Sahara, 1963 (Baker C. 3)
Station S-T-A-R, 1932 (Wayne 3)
Station West, 1948 (Moorehead 3, Powell, D. 3)
Stato interessante, 1977 (Morricone 4)
Statočný zlodej, 1958 (Kroner 3)
Statue, 1905 (Guy 2)
Statue, 1970 (Niven 3)
Statue. See Szobor, 1971
Statue animée, 1903 (Méliès 2)
Statues d'épouvante, 1953 (Cloquet 4)
Statues meurent aussi, 1953 (Marker 2, Resnais 2, Cloquet 4, Colpi 4)
Stavisky, 1974 (Resnais 2, Belmondo 3, Boyer 3, Depardieu 3,
    Vierny 4)
Stay As You Are. See Cosi come sei, 1978
Stay Away, Joe, 1968 (Blondell 3, Meredith 3, Presley 3)
Stay Hungry, 1976 (Rafelson 2, Bridges 3, Field 3)
Staying Alive, 1983 (Stallone 3)
Stazione Termini, 1953 (De Sica 2, Cervi 3, Jones, J. 3, Aldo 4, Cahn 4,
    Morris 4, Selznick 4, Zavattini 4)
Stazione Termini. See Indiscretion of an American Wife, 1953
Steady Company, 1915 (Chaney Lon 3, Furthman 4)
Steady Company, 1932 (Pitts 3)
Steagle, 1970 (Guffey 4)
Steak trop cuit, 1960 (Guillemot 4)
Steal Wool, 1957 (Jones 2)
Stealers, 1920 (Shearer 4)
Stealin' Ain't Honest, 1940 (Fleischer, M. and D. 2)
Steam Locomotive C-57. See Kikansha C-57, 1940
Steamboat Bill, Jr., 1928 (Keaton 2, Schenck 4)
Steamboat 'round the Bend, 1935 (Ford, J. 2, Bosworth 3, Fetchit 3,
    Rogers, W. 3, Nichols 4, Trotti 4)
Steamboat Willie, 1928 (Disney 2, Iwerks 4)
Steaming, 1985 (Redgrave, V. 3)
Steamroller and the Violin. See Katok i skripka, 1960
Steel, 1944 (Cardiff 4)
Steel, 1969 (Feries 2)
Steel: A Whole New Way of Life, 1971 (Benegal 2)
Steel Against the Sky, 1941 (Sutherland 2)
Steel Cage, 1954 (O'Sullivan 3, Alton, J. 4)
Steel Cowboy, 1978 (Martin, S. 3, Torn 3)
Steel Fist, 1951 (McDowall 3)
Steel Goes to War, 1941 (Alwyn 4)
Steel Hearts. See Stalowe serca, 1948
Steel Helmet, 1950 (Fuller 2)
Steel Highway, 1931 (Astor 3)
Steel King's Last Wish. See Mørke Punkt, 1913
Steel Lady, 1953 (Dupont 2, Crosby 4)
Steel Preferred, 1926 (Bosworth 3, Boyd 3)
Steel Rolling Mill, 1914 (Sennett 2)
Steel Town, 1952 (Sheridan 3, Hunter 4)
Steel Town. See Zocelení, 1950
Steel Trap, 1952 (Aldrich 2, Cotten 3, Wright 3, Laszlo 4, Tiomkin 4)
Steel Workers, 1937 (Lantz 4)
Steeltown, 1943 (Van Dyke, W. 2)
Steelyard Blues, 1972 (Fonda, J. 3, Sutherland 3, Kovacs 4)
Steeple Jacks, 1951 (Terry 4)
Stein Song, 1930 (Fleischer, M. and D. 2)
Stein unter Steinen, 1916 (Jannings 3)
Steinbruch, 1942 (Schell, Maria 3)

Steinerne Reiter, 1923 (Hoffmann 4, Pommer 4)
Stella, 1950 (Mature 3, Sheridan 3, Lemaire 4)
Stella, 1955 (Mercouri 3)
Stella, 1982 (Hoffmann 3)
Stella Dallas, 1925 (King 2, Colman 3, Fairbanks, D. Jr. 3, Hersholt 3,
    Edeson 4, Goldwyn 4, Marion 4, Westmore, P. 4)
Stella Dallas, 1937 (Vidor, K. 2, Stanwyck 3, Day 4, Goldwyn 4,
    Heerman 4, Maté 4, Newman 4)
Stella Maris, 1918 (Neilan 2, Pickford 3, Buckland 4, Marion 4)
Stella Parish, 1935 (Robinson 4)
Stem van het water, 1966 (Haanstra 2)
Stemning i April, 1947 (Henning-Jensen 2)
Sten Stensson Stéen från Eslov på nya aventyr, 1930 (Jaenzon 4)
Sten Stensson Stéen from Eslov on New Adventures. See Sten Stensson
    Stéen fran Eslov på nya aventyr, 1930
Stenata, 1957 (Forman 2, Brejchová 3, Kopecký 3)
Stenata, 1984 (Ivanov 3)
Stenographer Troubles, 1913 (Bunny 3)
Stenographer Wanted, 1912 (Bunny 3)
Step, 1977 (Smoktunovsky 3)
Step Forward, 1922 (Sennett 2)
Step Lively, 1918 (Lloyd 3, Roach 4)
Step Lively, 1944 (Menjou 3, Sinatra 3, Cahn 4)
Step on It, 1931 (Fleischer, M. and D. 2)
Step Out of Line, 1970 (Falk 3, Goldsmith 4)
Step-Brothers, 1913 (Eason 4)
Step-Brothers. See Ibo koudai, 1957
Stepen riska, 1969 (Smoktunovsky 3)
Stepford Wives, 1974 (Smith, D. , Goldman, W. 4, Roizman 4)
Stéphane et le garde chasse, 1966 (Braunberger 4)
Stephen Steps Out, 1923 (Fairbanks, D. Jr. 3)
Stepmother, 1912 (Dwan 2)
Stepmother, 1914 (Lawrence 3)
Stepmother. See Svend Dyrings Hus, 1908
Steppa, 1962 (Lattuada 2, Vanel 3, Donati 4, Pinelli 4)
Steppe, 1977 (Bondarchuk 3)
Steppe. See Step, 1977
Steppe. See Steppa, 1962
Steppenwolf, 1974 (Sanda 3, Von Sydow 3)
Steppin' in Society, 1945 (Horton 3)
Stepping Fast, 1923 (Mix 3)
Stepping into Society, 1936 (Fazenda 3)
Stepping Out, 1919 (Niblo 2, Barnes 4, Sullivan 4)
Stepping Out, 1923 (Roach 4)
Stepping Out, 1929 (Roach 4)
Stepping Stone, 1916 (Sullivan 4)
Steps. See Schody, 1964
Steps of Age, 1951 (Maddow 4)
Steps to the Moon. See Pasi spre luna, 1963
Stepsisters, 1910–11 (White 3)
Sterbende Modell, 1918 (Gad 2)
Sterbende Perlen, 1917 (Dupont 2)
Sterbende Volker, 1922 (Kortner 3, Wegener 3)
Sterile Cuckoo, 1969 (Pakula 2, Minnelli 3, Krasner 4, Sargent 4)
Sterimator Vesevo, 1920 (Gallone 2)
Sterling Metal. See Sporting Blood, 1940
Stern von Bethlehem, 1921 (Reiniger 2)
Stern von Damaskus, 1920 (Curtiz 2)
Sterne, 1959 (Wolf 2)
Sterne erloschern nie, 1957 (Albers 3)
Stet priklyuchenni, 1929 (Ptushko 2)
Steuerlos, 1924 (George, H. 3)
Steuermann Holck, 1920 (Nielsen 3, Wegener 3)
Stevedores, 1937 (Lantz 4)
Steven Donoghue Series, 1926 (Balcon 4)
Stevie, 1978 (Howard, T. 3, Jackson 3, Young, F. 4)
Stew in the Caribbean. See Estouffade à la Carabei, 1967
Stićenik, 1967 (Samardžić 3)
Stick, 1985 (Reynolds, B. 3, Segal 3)
Stick Around, 1925 (Hardy 3)
Stick, Start Beating!. See Obušku, z pytle ven!, 1956
Stick to Your Guns, 1941 (Boyd 3)
Stick to Your Story, 1926 (Brown, Harry Joe 4)

Sticky Affair, 1916 (Hardy 3)
Stier von Olivera, 1921 (Jannings 3, Messter 4, Metzner 4)
Stigma, 1913 (Bushman 3)
Stigmate, 1924 (Feuillade 2)
Stigmatized One. See Gezeichneten, 1922
Stiletto, 1969 (Scheider 3)
Still, 1969–71 (Gehr 2)
Still Alarm, 1903 (Porter 2)
Still Alarm, 1930 (Webb 3)
Still Life, 1966 (Baillie 2)
Still Life. See Stilleben, 1969
Still of the Night, 1982 (Scheider 3, Streep 3, Almendros 4)
Still We Live. See Dokkoi ikiteiru, 1951
Stilla flirt, 1934 (Molander 2)
Stilleben, 1969 (Lenica 2)
Stimme, 1920 (Basserman 3, Dreier 4)
Stimme des Anderen, 1952 (Kortner 3)
Stimme des Herzens, 1942 (Jurgens 3)
Stimulantia, 1967 (Bergman 2, Donner 2, Molander 2, Sjoman 2,
    Andersson H. 3, Bergman 3, Bjornstrand 3, Fischer 4)
Stín ve světle, 1928 (Stallich 4)
Sting, 1973 (Hill, G.R. 2, Newman 3, Redford 3, Shaw 3, Bumstead 4,
    Head 4, Reynolds 4, Surtees 4, Whitlock 4)
Sting of the Lash, 1921 (King 2)
Sting of Victory, 1916 (Walthall 3)
Sting II, 1983 (Malden 3, Reed, O. 3, Schifrin 4)
Stingaree, 1915 (Glennon 4)
Stingaree, 1934 (Wellman 2, Dunne 3, Berman 4, Cooper 4,
    Plunkett 4, Steiner 4)
Stips, 1951 (Frohlich 3)
Stir Crazy, 1980 (Poitier 3, Pryor 3, Wilder 3)
Stjaalne Ansigt, 1914 (Holger-Madsen 2)
Stjenka Rasin, 1936 (George, H. 3)
Sto dvadtsat tysyach v god, 1929 (Maretskaya 3)
Sto je radnički savjet?, 1959 (Makavejev 2)
Stockbroker. See For sin karleks skull, 1913
Stock-Cars. See A tout casser, 1953
Stockholm, Pride of Sweden, 1937 (Hoch 4)
Stockholm, 1977 (Zetterling 2)
Stocks and Blondes, 1928 (Berman 4, Miller, V. 4, Plunkett 4)
Stoj, 1965 (Roos 2)
Stolen Affections. See Révoltée, 1947
Stolen Airship. See Ukradená vzducholod, 1966
Stolen Assignment, 1955 (Fisher 2)
Stolen Birthright, 1914 (White 3)
Stolen Bride, 1913 (Gish, L. 3, Sweet 3)
Stolen Bride, 1927 (Korda 2, Wilson, C. 4)
Stolen by Gypsies, 1905 (Porter 2)
Stolen Desire. See Nusumareta yokujo, 1958
Stolen Face, 1952 (Fisher 2, Henreid 3)
Stolen Frontier. See Uloupená hranice, 1947
Stolen Glory, 1912 (Sennett 2, Normand 3)
Stolen Goods, 1915 (Sweet 3)
Stolen Goods, 1924 (McCarey 2, Roach 4)
Stolen Happiness. See Branningar, 1912
Stolen Harmony, 1935 (Raft 3, Wyman 3, Head 4)
Stolen Heart. See Gestohlene Herz, 1934
Stolen Heaven, 1931 (Calhern 3)
Stolen Heaven, 1938 (Stone 3, Dreier 4, Head 4)
Stolen Holiday, 1936 (Curtiz 2, Francis, K. 3, Rains 3, Grot 4,
    Orry-Kelly 4, Robinson 4, Wallis 4, Brown, Harry Joe)
Stolen Hours, 1963 (Hayward 3)
Stolen Jewels, 1908 (Griffith 2, Lawrence 3, Bitzer 4)
Stolen Jools, 1932 (Baxter W. 3, Beery 3, Brown 3, Chevalier 3,
    Dunne 3, Fairbanks, D. Jr. 3, Laurel and Hardy 3, Shearer 3)
Stolen Kisses. See Baisers volés, 1968
Stolen Life, 1939 (Czinner 2, Bergner 3, Redgrave, M. 3,
    Havelock-Allan 4)
Stolen Life, 1946 (Brennan 3, Davis 3, Ford, G. 3, Friedhofer 4,
    Haller 4, Orry-Kelly 4, Polito 4, Steiner 4)
Stolen Love, 1928 (Plunkett 4)
Stolen Love. See Nusumarata koi, 1951
Stolen Magic, 1915 (Sennett 2, Normand 3)

Stolen Masterpiece, 1914 (Loos 4)
Stolen Moccasins, 1913 (Mix 3)
Stolen Moments, 1920 (Valentino 3)
Stolen Paradise, 1917 (Edeson 4, Marion 4)
Stolen Purse, 1913 (Sennett 2)
Stolen Ranch, 1926 (Wyler 2)
Stolen Sweets, 1934 (Brown, K. 4)
Stolen Time, 1955 (Arlen 3)
Stolz der 3 Kompagnie, 1931 (Walbrook 3)
Stolz der Firma, 1914 (Lubitsch 2)
Stone Age, 1922 (Roach 4)
Stone Age, 1931 (Lantz 4)
Stone Age Romeos, 1955 (Three Stooges 3)
Stone Boy, 1984 (Duvall, R. 3, Forrest 3)
Stone Flower. See Kamenny tsvetok, 1946
Stone Killer, 1973 (Bronson 3, De Laurentiis 4)
Stone of River Creek, 1935 (McCord 4)
Stone Pillow, 1985 (Lassally 4)
Stones Cry Out. See Let Them Live!, 1937
Stooge, 1953 (Lewis 2, Taurog 2, Martin, D. 3, Head 4, Wallis 4)
Stooge for a Mouse, 1949 (Freleng 4)
Stooge to Conga, 1943 (Three Stooges 3)
Stool Pigeon, 1915 (Chaney Lon 3)
Stoopnocracy, 1931 (Fleischer, M. and D. 2)
Stop Kidding, 1921 (Roach 4)
Stop, Look, and Hasten!, 1954 (Jones 2)
Stop, Look, and Listen, 1926 (Hardy 3)
Stop, Look, and Listen, 1949 (Terry 4)
Stop Me Before I Kill, 1961 (Dauphin 3)
Stop Me Before I Kill. See Full Treatment, 1961
Stop Polio, 1981 (Jackson 3)
Stop Press Girl, 1949 (More 3)
Stop That Noise, 1935 (Fleischer, M. and D. 2)
Stop That Tank, 1941 (Iwerks 4)
Stop the Old Fox. See Kagero ezu, 1959
Stop the World—I Want to Get Off, 1966 (Morris 4)
Stop Train 349. See Verspatung in Marienborn, 1963
Stop, You're Killing Me, 1952 (Crawford, B. 3, Dumont 3, Trevor 3, McCord 4)
Stopover Tokyo, 1957 (O'Brien, E. 3, Wagner 3, Clarke, C.C. 4, Lemaire 4, Reisch 4, Wheeler 4)
Stopping the Show, 1932 (Fleischer, M. and D. 2, Chevalier 3)
Stopy, 1960 (Jires 2)
Stora aventyret, 1953 (Sucksdorff 2)
Stora famnen, 1939 (Jaenzon 4)
Stora skrallen, 1943 (Fischer 4)
Storch hat uns getraut, 1933 (Dagover 3)
Storch streikt, 1931 (Planer 4)
Store. See Floorwalker, 1916 (Chaplin 2)
Store Fald, 1911 (Holger-Madsen 2)
Store Flyver. See Aedel Daad, 1911
Store Hjerte, 1924 (Blom 2)
Store Klaus og Lille Klaus, 1913 (Christensen 2)
Store Magt, 1924 (Blom 2)
Store Middag, 1914 (Blom 2)
Storia de fratelli e de cortelli, 1973 (De Sica 2)
Storia dei tredici, 1916 (Gallone 2)
Storia del pugliato degli antichi ad oggi, 1974 (Brazzi 3)
Storia di Piera, 1982 (Ferreri 2, Mastroianni 3, Schygulla 3)
Storia di un peccato, 1918 (Gallone 2)
Storia di un quartiere, 1950 (Zurlini 2)
Storia di una donna, 1969 (Andersson B. 3, Girardot 3, Allen, D. 4, Williams, J. 4)
Storia milanese, 1962 (Olmi 2)
Storia moderna, 1963 (Ferreri 2, Tognazzi 3)
Storie d'amore, 1942 (Mastroianni 3)
Storie delle invenzioni, 1959 (Bozzetto 4)
Storie di ordinaria follia, 1981 (Amidei 4, Delli Colli 4)
Storie di ordinaria follia. See Tales of Ordinary Madness, 1981
Storie di ordinaria follia, 1981 (Sarde 4)
Storie di vita e malavita, 1975 (Morricone 4)
Storie scellerate, 1973 (Pasolini 2, Delli Colli 4)
Storie sulla sabbia, 1963 (Fusco 4)

Stories about Lenin. See Rasskazi o Lenine, 1957
Stories about Things. See April, 1961
Stories of Ordinary Madness. See Storie di ordinaria follia, 1981
Stork Bites Man, 1947 (Cooper, J 3)
Stork Club, 1945 (Fitzgerald 3, Hutton 3, Cahn 4, Carmichael 4, Dreier 4, Head 4, Lang 4)
Stork Naked, 1954 (Freleng 4)
Stork's Mistake, 1942 (Terry 4)
Storm, 1916 (Sweet 3)
Storm, 1925 (Fleischer, M. and D. 2)
Storm, 1930 (Huston 2, Wyler 2, Boyd 3, Velez 3)
Storm, 1938 (Krasner 4)
Storm. See Vihar, 1952
Storm at Balaton. See Ítél a Balaton, 1932
Storm at Daybreak, 1933 (Francis, K. 3, Huston 3, Adrian 4, Booth 4)
Storm Boy, 1917 (Hathaway 2)
Storm Center, 1956 (Davis 3, Bass 4, Duning 4, Guffey 4, Taradash 4)
Storm Fear, 1955 (Duryea 3, Grant, L. 3, Wilde 3, Bernstein 4, La Shelle 4)
Storm in a Teacup, 1937 (Saville 2, Harrison 3, Leigh, V. 3, Dalrymple 4, Hornbeck 4)
Storm in Tatra. See Bouře nad Tatrami, 1932
Storm of Passion. See Sturme der Leidenschaft, 1932
Storm of Strangers, 1970 (Maddow 4)
Storm of the Pacific. See Taiheiyo no arashi, 1960
Storm over Asia. See Potomok Chingis-khan, 1928
Storm over Bengal, 1938 (Canutt 4)
Storm over Lisbon, 1944 (Von Stroheim 2, Arlen 3, Alton, J. 4)
Storm over the Andes, 1935 (Schary 4)
Storm Over the Nile, 1955 (Harvey 3, Lee, C. 3, Wimperis 4)
Storm Over Tibet, 1951 (Martin, S. 3)
Storm over Tjuro, 1954 (Nykvist 4)
Storm over Wyoming, 1949 (Hunt 4)
Storm Warning, 1951 (Brooks, R. 2, Day 3, Reagan 3, Rogers, G. 3, Wald 4, Westmore, F. 4)
Storm Within. See Parents terribles, 1948
Stormfågeln, 1914 (Stiller 2, Jaenzon 4, Magnusson 4)
Storms of Life. See Livets Storme, 1910
Storms of Passion. See Sturme der Leidenschaft, 1931
Stormswept, 1923 (Beery 3)
Stormy Crossing, 1958 (Ireland 3)
Stormy Era. See Showa no inochi, 1968
Stormy Knight, 1917 (Young, W. 4)
Stormy Nights, 1917 (Hersholt 3)
Stormy Petrel. See Stormfågeln, 1914
Stormy Seas, 1932 (Iwerks 4)
Stormy, The Thoroughbred with an Inferiority Complex, 1953 (Crosby 4)
Stormy Waters. See Remorques, 1941
Stormy Weather, 1935 (Balcon 4)
Stormy Weather, 1943 (Horne 3, Robinson, B. 3, Basevi 4, Garmes 4, Rose 4, Shamroy 4)
Stormy Weather. See Remorques, 1941
Største i Verden, 1919 (Holger-Madsen 2)
Største Kaerlighed, 1914 (Blom 2)
Storstrømsbroen, 1950 (Dreyer 2)
Stortebeker, 1920 (Hoffmann 4)
Story for Echigo. See Echigo tsutsuishi oyashirazu, 1964
Story from Chikamatsu. See Chikamatsu monogatari, 1954
Story in Scarlet, 1973 (Nowicki 3)
Story in the Rocks. See Paleontologie, 1959
Story of a Cheat. See Roman d'un tricheur, 1936
Story of a Dog Who Had Fleas. See Historie blechatého psa, 1958
Story of a Girl, 1949 (Zhao 3)
Story of a Love Affair. See Cronaca di un amore, 1950
Story of a Man. See Historien om en Mand, 1944
Story of a Mosquito. See How a Mosquito Operates, 1912
Story of a Mother. See Historien om en moder, 1979
Story of a Patriot, 1957 (Seaton 2)
Story of a Penny. See Krajcár története, 1917
Story of a Potter. See Potterymaker, 1925
Story of a Real Man, 1948 (Bondarchuk 3)

Strange Alibi. *See* Strange Triangle, 1946
Strange Bedfellows, 1965 (Hudson 3, Lollobrigida 3, Young, G. 3, Frank 4)
Strange Bird, 1969 (Dovniković 4)
Strange Birds, 1930 (Sennett 2)
Strange Boarder, 1920 (Rogers, W. 3)
Strange Brew, 1983 (Von Sydow 3)
Strange Cargo, 1929 (Glazer 4, Miller, A. 4)
Strange Cargo, 1936 (Sanders 3)
Strange Cargo, 1940 (Borzage 2, Mankiewicz 2, Crawford, J. 3, Gable 3, Lorre 3, Lukas 3, Adrian 4, Waxman 4)
Strange Case of Captain Ramper. *See* Ramper, der Tiermensch, 1927
Strange Case of Clara Deane, 1932 (O'Brien, P. 3)
Strange Case of Dr. Jekyll and Mr. Hyde, 1968 (Homolka 3)
Strange Case of Dr. Rx, 1942 (Howard, S. 3, Salter 4)
Strange Case of Mary Page, 1916 (Walthall 3)
Strange Case of the Cosmic Rays, 1957 (Capra 2)
Strange Confession, 1944 (Chaney Lon, Jr. 3)
Strange Confession. *See* Imposter, 1944
Strange Conspiracy. *See* President Vanishes, 1934
Strange Death of Adolf Hitler, 1943 (Kortner 3, Salter 4)
Strange Deception. *See* Cristo proibito, 1951
Strange Door, 1951 (Karloff 3, Laughton 3, Salter 4)
Strange Evidence, 1933 (Biro 4)
Strange Experiment, 1937 (Sim 3)
Strange Fascination, 1952 (Haas 3)
Strange Gamble, 1948 (Boyd 3)
Strange Holiday, 1946 (Basserman 3, Rains 3)
Strange Idols, 1922 (Furthman 4)
Strange Illusion, 1945 (Ulmer 2)
Strange Impersonation, 1946 (Mann 2)
Strange Incident. *See* Ox-Bow Incident, 1943
Strange Interlude, 1932 (Gable 3, O'Sullivan 3, Walthall 3, Young, R. 3, Adrian 4, Booth 4, Garmes 4, Meredyth 4, Sullivan 4, Thalberg 4)
Strange Interval. *See* Strange Interlude, 1932
Strange Intruder, 1956 (Lupino 3)
Strange Invaders, 1982 (Addison 4)
Strange Lady in Town, 1955 (Leroy 2, Andrews D. 3, Garson 3, Rosson 4, Tiomkin 4)
Strange Love Affair, 1984 (Alekan 4)
Strange Love of Martha Ivers, 1946 (Aldrich 2, Edwards 2, Milestone 2, Rossen 2, Anderson J. 3, Douglas, K. 3, Heflin 3, Stanwyck 3, Dreier 4, Head 4, Rozsa 4, Wallis 4)
Strange Love of Molly Louvain, 1932 (Curtiz 2)
Strange Meeting, 1909 (Griffith 2, Pickford 3)
Strange New World, 1975 (Smith, J.M. 4)
Strange One, 1957 (Guffey 4, Spiegel 4)
Strange Passion of a Kiss. *See* Lyubov silna na strastyou potseluya, 1916
Strange People, 1933 (Brennan 3)
Strange People. *See* Strannye lyudi, 1969
Strange Possession of Mrs. Oliver, 1977 (Black 3)
Strange Rider, 1925 (Canutt 4)
Strange Triangle, 1946 (Basevi 4, Lemaire 4)
Strange Voyage, 1946 (Anhalt 4)
Strange Woman, 1946 (Ulmer 2, Lamarr 3, Sanders 3, Stromberg 4)
Stranger, 1910 (Olcott 2)
Stranger, 1917 (Hardy 3)
Stranger, 1924 (Stone 3)
Stranger, 1946 (Huston 2, Welles 2, Robinson, E. 3, Young, L. 3, D'Agostino 4, Kaper 4, Spiegel 4, Veiller 4)
Stranger. *See* Straniero, 1967
Stranger and the Gunfighter, 1976 (Van Cleef 3)
Stranger at Coyote, 1912 (Dwan 2)
Stranger Boarders, 1938 (Gilliat 4)
Stranger Came Home, 1954 (Fisher 2, Goddard 3)
Stranger from Venus, 1954 (Neal 3)
Stranger in Between. *See* Hunted, 1951
Stranger in My Arms, 1959 (Allyson 3, Astor 3, Chandler 3, Coburn, C. 3, Daniels 4, Hunter 4)
Stranger in the House, 1967 (Chaplin 3, Mason 3)
Stranger in Town, 1943 (Lennart 4, Schary 4)

Stranger in Town, 1969 (Chaney Lon, Jr. 3)
Stranger Is Watching, 1982 (Torn 3, Schifrin 4)
Stranger on Horseback, 1955 (Tourneur, J. 2, Carradine 3, McCrea 3)
Stranger on the Prowl, 1952 (Losey 2, Alekan 4)
Stranger on the Prowl. *See* Imbarco a mezzanotte, 1952
Stranger on the Run, 1967 (Siegel 2, Baxter A. 3, Duryea 3, Fonda, H. 3, Mineo 3)
Stranger on the Third Floor, 1940 (Cook 3, Lorre 3, D'Agostino 4, Musuraca 4, Polglase 4)
Stranger Rides Again, 1930 (Terry 4)
Stranger Than Fiction, 1921 (Schulberg 4)
Stranger Than Love. *See* Starker als die Liebe, 1938
Stranger Walked In. *See* Love from a Stranger, 1947
Stranger Within a Woman. *See* Onna no naka ni iru tanin, 1966
Stranger Wore a Gun, 1953 (De Toth 2, Borgnine 3, Marvin 3, Scott, R. 3, Trevor 3, Brown, Harry Joe 4)
Strangers, 1979 (Davis 3)
Strangers. *See* Viaggio in Italia, 1953
Strangers All, 1935 (Vidor, C. 2, Plunkett 4)
Stranger's Banquet, 1922 (Neilan 2, Bosworth 3, Hersholt 3)
Stranger's Hand. *See* Mano della straniero, 1953
Strangers in Love, 1932 (Francis, K. 3, March 3, Banton 4)
Strangers in 7A, 1972 (Lupino 3)
Strangers in the Night, 1944 (Mann 2)
Strangers May Kiss, 1931 (Montgomery 3, Shearer 3, Adrian 4, Daniels 4)
Strangers of the Evening, 1932 (Pitts 3, Edeson 4)
Strangers of the Night, 1923 (Niblo 2, Meredyth 4, Sullivan 4)
Strangers on a Train, 1951 (Hitchcock 2, Carroll L. 3, Walker 3, Chandler 4, Tiomkin 4)
Strangers on Honeymoon, 1936 (Balcon 4, Gilliat 4, Metzner 4)
Stranger's Return, 1933 (Vidor, K. 2, Barrymore L. 3, Bondi 3, Hopkins, M. 3, Adrian 4, Daniels 4)
Strangers: The Story of a Mother and Daughter, 1979 (Rowlands 3, Horner 4)
Strangers When We Meet, 1960 (Douglas, K. 3, Matthau 3, Novak 3, Duning 4, Lang 4)
Strangest Case. *See* Crime Doctor's Strangest Case, 1943
Strangled Eggs, 1961 (McKimson 4)
Strangler, 1962 (Lourié 4)
Strangler of the Swamp, 1945 (Edwards 2)
Strangler of Vienna. *See* Wuger kommt auf leisen Socken, 1972
Stranglers of Bombay, 1959 (Fisher 2, Bernard 4)
Strangling Threads, 1922 (Hepworth 2)
Straniero, 1967 (Visconti 2, Blier 3, Karina 3, Mastroianni 3, D'Amico 4, De Laurentiis 4)
Strannye lyudi, 1969 (Shukshin 3)
Straschnaia miest, 1913 (Mozhukin 3)
Strasilo, 1957 (Mimica 4)
Strasnia pokoynik, 1912 (Mozhukin 3)
Strass et compagnie, 1916 (Gance 2)
Strasse des Bosen. *See* Via Mala, 1948
Strategia del ragno, 1969 (Bertolucci 2, Valli 3, Storaro 4)
Strategic Air Command, 1955 (Mann 2, Allyson 3, Martin, S. 3, Stewart 3, Daniels 4, Head 4, Young, V. 4)
Stratená dolina, 1976 (Kroner 3)
Stratford Adventure, 1954 (Guinness 3)
Stratos-Fear, 1933 (Iwerks 4)
Stratton Story, 1949 (Wood 2, Allyson 3, Moorehead 3, Stewart 3, Deutsch 4, Rose 4, Rosson 4)
Strauberg ist Da, 1978 (Piccoli 3)
Strauss's Great Waltz. *See* Waltzes from Vienna, 1934
Stravinksy Portrait, 1964 (Leacock 2)
Straw Dogs, 1971 (Peckinpah 2, Hoffman 3)
Straw Hat. *See* Slaměnný klobouk, 1971
Straw Man, 1915 (Franklin 2)
Strawberry Blonde, 1941 (Walsh 2, Cagney 3, De Havilland 3, Hayworth 3, Epstein, J. & P. 4, Howe 4, Orry-Kelly 4, Wallis 4)
Strawberry Roan, 1933 (McCord 4)
Strawberry Roan, 1948 (Autry 3)
Strawberry Statement, 1970 (Ames 4)
Strawfire. *See* Strohfeuer, 1971
Straws in the Wind, 1924 (Matthews 3)

Stray Dog. *See* Norainu, 1949

Straziami ma di baci saziami, 1968 (Risi 2, Manfredi 3, Tognazzi 3, Age and Scarpelli 4)

Stream. *See* Sodrásban, 1964

Stream Line. *See* Linea del fiume, 1976

Streamers, 1983 (Altman 2)

Streamlined Greta Green, 1937 (Freleng 4)

Streamlined Swing, 1938 (Keaton 2)

Street Angel, 1928 (Borzage 2, Gaynor 3)

Street Angel. *See* Malu tianshi, 1937

Street Corner, 1948 (Miller, V. 4)

Street Corners, 1929 (Laszlo 4)

Street Girl, 1929 (Ruggles 2, Murfin 4, Plunkett 4)

Street Girls, 1974 (Corman 4)

Street Legion. *See* Legion ulicy, 1932

Street Meat, 1959 (Vanderbeek 2)

Street of Chance, 1930 (Cromwell 2, Cromwell 2, Arthur 3, Francis, K. 3, Powell, W. 3, Coffee 4, Estabrook 4, Lang 4, Selznick 4)

Street of Chance, 1942 (Meredith 3, Trevor 3, Dreier 4, Fort 4)

Street of Forgotten Men, 1925 (Brenon 2, Brooks 3, Rosson 4)

Street of Illusion, 1928 (Walker 4)

Street of Memories, 1940 (Clarke, C.C. 4, Day 4)

Street of Missing Men, 1939 (Carey 3)

Street of Shame. *See* Akasen chitai, 1956

Street of Sin, 1928 (Stiller 2, Jannings 3, Wray 3, Dreier 4, Glazer 4, Glennon 4, Schulberg 4)

Street of Sorrow. *See* Freudlose Gasse, 1925

Street of Women, 1932 (Beavers 3, Francis, K. 3)

Street People. *See* Esecutori, 1976

Street Photographer. *See* Minuteros, 1972–73

Street Scene, 1931 (Vidor, K. 2, Bondi 3, Sidney 3, Barnes 4, Day 4, Goldwyn 4, Newman 4)

Street Scene, 1970 (Keitel 3)

Street Singer, 1938 (Sircar 4)

Street Sketches. *See* Gaijo no suketchi, 1925

Street with No Name, 1948 (Widmark 3, Lemaire 4, Reynolds 4, Wheeler 4)

Street with the Cupola. *See* Kyupora no aru machi, 1962

Street Without End. *See* Kagirinaki hodo, 1934

Streetcar Named Desire, 1951 (Kazan 2, Brando 3, Leigh, V. 3, Malden 3, Day 4, North 4, Stradling 4)

Streetcar Named Sylvester, 1952 (Freleng 4)

Streetfighter. *See* Hard Times, 1975

Streets of Greenwood, 1963 (Emshwiller 2)

Streets of Illusion, 1917 (Barthelmess 3)

Streets of L.A., 1979 (Woodward 3)

Streets of Laredo, 1949 (Bendix 3, Holden 3, Dreier 4, Young, V. 4)

Streets of New York, 1939 (Cooper, J 3)

Streets of San Francisco, 1972 (Malden 3, Wagner 3)

Streets of Shanghai, 1927 (Wong 3)

Streets of Sorrow. *See* Freudlose Gasse, 1925

Strega in amore, 1966 (Volonté 3)

Streghe, 1967 (Bolognini 2, De Sica 2, Pasolini 2, Visconti 2, Eastwood 2, Girardot 3, Mangano 3, Sordi 3, Age and Scarpelli 4, De Laurentiis 4, Morricone 4, Zavattini 4)

Streit um den Knaben Jo, 1937 (Dagover 3)

Strejda, 1959 (Jires 2)

Strejken, 1915 (Sjostrom 2, Jaenzon 4, Magnusson 4)

Strength o' Ten, 1914 (Eason 4)

Strength of a Moustache. *See* Hige no chikara, 1931

Strength of the Hungarian Soil. *See* Magyar föld ereje, 1916

Strength of the Pines, 1922 (Polito 4)

Stresemann, 1956 (Aimée 3)

Stress es tres, tres, 1968 (Saura 2, Chaplin 3)

Stress is Three, Three. *See* Stress es tres, tres, 1968

Stress of Youth. *See* Trápení, 1961

Striapukha, 1966 (Churikova 3)

Stříbrná oblaka, 1938 (Stallich 4)

Stříbrný vítr, 1954 (Kopecký 3)

Strictly Business, 1912–13 (White 3)

Strictly Confidential. *See* Broadway Bill, 1934

Strictly Dishonorable, 1931 (Stahl 2, Sturges, P. 2, Lukas 3, Stone 3, Freund 4)

Strictly Dishonorable, 1951 (Sturges, P. 2, Leigh, J. 3, Frank and Panama 4, Rose 4)

Strictly Dynamite, 1934 (Durante 3, Velez 3, Cronjager 4, Plunkett 4, Steiner 4)

Strictly for Pleasure. *See* Perfect Furlough, 1958

Strictly in the Groove, 1943 (Howard, S. 3, O'Connor 3)

Strictly Modern, 1922 (Roach 4)

Strictly Personal, 1933 (Calhern 3, Head 4, Krasner 4, Robinson 4)

Strictly Secret Previews. *See* Přísně tajné premiéry, 1967

Strictly Unconventional, 1930 (Stone 3, Booth 4, Daniels 4, Gibbons 4)

Strictly Unreliable, 1932 (Pitts 3, Roach 4)

Stride, Soviet!. *See* Shagai, Soviet!, 1926

Striden går vidare, 1941 (Molander 2, Sjostrom 2, Borgstrom 3)

Strieborný Favorit, 1960 (Kroner 3)

Strife over the Boy Jo. *See* Streit um den Knaben Jo, 1937

Strife with Father, 1950 (McKimson 4)

Strijd zonder einde. *See* Rival World, 1955

Strike, 1909 (Porter 2)

Strike! See Red Ensign, 1934

Strike. *See* Stachka, 1925

Strike. *See* Strejken, 1915

Strike at the Little Johnny Mine, 1911 (Anderson G. 3)

Strike Force, 1975 (Gere 3)

Strike Me Pink, 1936 (Taurog 2, Alton, R. 4, Day 4, Goldwyn 4, Newman 4, Toland 4)

Strike the Monster on Page One. *See* Sbatti il mostro in prima pagina, 1972

Strike Up the Band, 1930 (Fleischer, M. and D. 2)

Strike Up the Band, 1940 (Berkeley 2, Garland 3, Rooney 3, Edens 4, Freed 4, Shearer 4)

String Bean Jack, 1938 (Terry 4)

String Beans, 1918 (Ince 4)

String of Pearls, 1911 (Griffith 2, Bitzer 4)

Stringent Prediction at the Early Hermaphroditic Stage, 1961 (Landow 2)

Strip, 1951 (Rooney 3, Pasternak 4, Rose 4, Surtees 4)

Stripes, 1981 (Oates 3, Bernstein 4)

Stripes and Stars, 1929 (Lantz 4)

Stripper, 1963 (Schaffner 2, Trevor 3, Woodward 3, Goldsmith 4, Smith, J.M. 4, Wald 4)

Strip-Tease, 1957 (Lenica 2, Borowczyk 4)

Strip-Tease, 1976 (Rey 3, Stamp 3)

Striptease. *See* Striptiz, 1969

Striptiz, 1969 (Dragić 4)

Strogoff, 1968 (Bergner 3)

Strogoscopes, 1963 (Borowczyk 4)

Strogovy, 1976 (Gurchenko 3)

Strohfeuer, 1971 (Schlondorff 2, Von Trotta 2)

Stroitsa most, 1966 (Gurchenko 3)

Stroke of Midnight. *See* Korkarlen, 1921

Stroker Ace, 1983 (Reynolds, B. 3, Needham 4)

Stromboli, 1949 (Rossellini 2, Bergman 3, Amidei 4)

Strømlinjede gris, 1952 (Roos 2)

Stromy a lidé, 1962 (Schorm 2)

Strong Boy, 1929 (Ford, J. 2, McLaglen 3, Summerville 3, August 4)

Strong Man, 1926 (Capra 2, Garnett 2, Langdon 3)

Strong Revenge, 1913 (Sennett 2, Normand 3)

Strong to the Finich, 1934 (Fleischer, M. and D. 2)

Strong Woman and Weak Man. *See* Tsuyomushi onna (&) yawamushi otoko, 1968

Stronger, 1976 (Grant, L. 3)

Stronger Love. *See* 'Tween Two Loves, 1911

Stronger Man, 1911 (Dwan 2)

Stronger Mind, 1915 (Chaney Lon 3)

Stronger Sex, 1931 (Lanchester 3, Balcon 4)

Stronger Than Death, 1915 (Chaney Lon 3)

Stronger Than Death, 1920 (Guy 2, Nazimova 3, Carré 4)

Stronger Than Desire, 1939 (Pidgeon 3, Daniels 4)

Stronger Than Fear. *See* Edge of Doom, 1950

Strongest, 1920 (Walsh 2, Adorée 3)

Strongest. *See* Starkaste, 1929

Strongheart, 1914 (Barrymore L. 3, Sweet 3, Walthall 3, Gaudio 4)
Stronghold, 1952 (Lake 3, Cortez 4)
Strongman Ferdinand. *See* Starke Ferdinand, 1975
Strop, 1962 (Chytilová 2)
Stroszek, 1977 (Herzog 2)
Structure of Crystals. *See* Struktura krsztalu, 1969
Struggle, 1913 (Anderson G. 3)
Struggle, 1931 (Griffith 2, Emerson 4, Loos 4, Ruttenberg 4)
Struggle. *See* Borza, 1935
Struggle Against Cancer. *See* Kampen Mod Kraeften, 1947
Struggle for His Heart. *See* Kampen om hans hjarta, 1916
Struggle in the Steeple. *See* Tools of Providence, 1915
Struggle in the Valley. *See* Sera'a fil Wadi, 1953
Struggle on the Pier. *See* Sera'a fil Mina, 1955
Struktura krsztalu, 1969 (Zanussi 2, Olbrychski 3)
Strýček z Ameriky, 1933 (Stallich 4)
Stubbs' New Servants, 1911 (Sennett 2)
Stubby. *See* Fimpen, 1974
Stuchis v lyubuyu dver, 1958 (Ulyanov 3)
Stud, 1978 (Cahn 4)
Stud. chem. Helene Willfuer, 1929 (Tschechowa 3, Planer 4)
Stud Farm. *See* A ménesgazda, 1978
Studenci, 1916 (Negri 3)
Student Mummy. *See* Studentská máma, 1935
Student Nurses, 1970 (Corman 4)
Student of Prague. *See* Student von Prag, 1926
Student of Prague. *See* Student von Prag, 1935
Student Prince, 1954 (Calhern 3, Gwenn 3, Sakall 3, Levien 4, Pan 4, Pasternak 4, Plunkett 4, Rose 4)
Student Prince. *See* Alt-Heidelberg, 1923
Student Prince in Old Heidelberg, 1927 (Lubitsch 2, Hersholt 3, Novarro 3, Shearer 3, Day 4, Dreier 4, Gibbons 4, Kraly 4)
Student Teachers, 1973 (Corman 4)
Student Tour, 1934 (Seaton 2, Auer 3, Durante 3, Eddy 3, Grable 3, Brown, N. 4, Dunne 4, Freed 4)
Student von Prag, 1913 (Wegener 3, Galeen 4)
Student von Prag, 1926 (Krauss 3, Veidt 3, Galeen 4, Warm 4)
Student von Prag, 1935 (Robison 2, Walbrook 3, Warm 4)
Studentská máma, 1935 (Vích 4)
Studies and Sketches, 1963–65 (Landow 2)
Studies for Louisiana Story, 1967 (Flaherty 2)
Studio en folie, 1947 (Bourvil 3)
Studio Girl, 1918 (Talmadge, C. 3)
Studio Murder Mystery, 1929 (Auer 3, March 3, Oland 3)
Studio Romance. *See* Satsueijo romansu: Renai annai, 1932
Studio Stoops, 1950 (Three Stooges 3)
Studs Lonigan, 1960 (Nicholson 3, Fields 4, Goldsmith 4, Wexler 4)
Studujeme za školou, 1939 (Hrušínský 3)
Study in Choreography for Camera, 1945 (Deren 2, Hammid 2)
Study in Scarlet, 1914 (Pearson 3)
Study in Scarlet, 1933 (Florey 2, Wong 3, Edeson 4)
Study in Terror, 1965 (Quayle 3)
Study in Tramps, 1915 (Talmadge, C. 3)
Study Opus I—Man, 1976 (Popescu-Gopo 4)
Study series, from 1929 (Fischinger 2)
Stuff Heroes Are Made Of, 1911 (Griffith 2, Bitzer 4)
Stuffie, 1940 (Zinnemann 2)
Stulen lycka. *See* Branningar, 1912
Stumme, 1975 (Schygulla 3)
Stunde der Versuchung, 1936 (Baarová 3, Frohlich 3, Wegener 3)
Stundenhotel von St. Pauli, 1970 (Jurgens 3)
Stunt Man, 1924 (Sennett 2)
Stunt Man, 1980 (O'Toole 3)
Stuntman, 1969 (Lollobrigida 3)
Stuntman. *See* Kaskader, 1972
Stunts Unlimited, 1980 (Needham 4)
Stupid Bom. *See* Dum-Bom, 1953
Stupid Young Brother and Wise Old Brother. *See* Gutei kenkei, 1931
Stupor Duck, 1956 (McKimson 4)
Sturm in Wasserglas. *See* Blumenfrau von Lindenau, 1931
Sturme der Leidenschaft, 1931 (Siodmak 2, Jannings 3, Pommer 4)
Sturme des Lebens, 1918 (Krauss 3)
Sturme uber dem Montblanc, 1930 (Riefenstahl 2)

Sturmflut, 1917 (Dupont 2)
Sturmfreie Junggeselle. *See* Moblierte Zimmer, 1929
Stuttgart, die Grossstadt zwischen Wald und Reben, 1935 (Ruttmann 2)
Stutzen der Gesellschaft, 1935 (Sirk 2, George, H. 3)
Štvaní lidé, 1933 (Stallich 4, Vích 4)
Stvoření světa, 1957 (Hofman 4)
Štvorylka, 1955 (Kroner 3)
Stydno skazat, 1930 (Maretskaya 3)
Su adorable majadero, 1938 (García 3)
Su exelencia, 1966 (Cantinflas 3)
Su última aventura, 1946 (Figueroa 4)
Sua Altezza ha detto: no!, 1953 (Tognazzi 3)
Sua Eccellenza si fermò a mangiare, 1961 (Tognazzi 3)
Subah, 1983 (Patil 3)
Subah Ka Tara, 1932 (Sircar 4)
Subarashii akujo, 1963 (Takemitsu 4)
Subarashiki musumetachi, 1959 (Tanaka 3)
Subarashiki nichiyobi, 1947 (Kurosawa 2)
Subduing of Mrs. Nag, 1911 (Bunny 3, Normand 3)
Sube y bajo, 1958 (Cantinflas 3)
Subida al cielo, 1951 (Buñuel 2)
Subject for a Short Story. *See* Siuzhet dliya nebolshogo rasskaza, 1969
Subject Was Roses, 1968 (Neal 3, Sheen 3, Jenkins 4)
Submarine, 1910 (Gaudio 4)
Submarine, 1928 (Capra 2, Walker 4)
Submarine Alert, 1943 (Arlen 3)
Submarine Command, 1951 (Bendix 3, Holden 3, Ames 4, Head 4)
Submarine Control, 1949 (Halas and Batchelor 2)
Submarine D-1, 1937 (Bacon 2, Brent 3, Crawford, B. 3, O'Brien, P. 3, Deutsch 4, Edeson 4, Steiner 4)
Submarine Patrol, 1938 (Ford, J. 2, Bond 3, Carradine 3, Chaney Lon, Jr. 3, Cook 3, Summerville 3, Miller, A. 4, Zanuck 4)
Submarine Pirate, 1915 (Sennett 2)
Submarine X-1, 1968 (Caan 3)
Submarine Zone, 1941 (Bennett C. 3)
Submarine Zone. *See* Escape to Glory, 1941
Submissive. *See* Untertan, 1949
Subpoena Server, 1906 (Bitzer 4)
Substitute Minister, 1915 (Eason 4)
Substitute Model, 1912 (Bosworth 3)
Substitute Wife, 1925 (Stradling 4)
Subterraneans, 1960 (Caron 3, McDowall 3, Freed 4, Previn 4, Ruttenberg 4)
Suburban House. *See* Dum na předměstí, 1933
Subway, 1985 (Trauner 4)
Subway Express, 1931 (Walker 4)
Subway in the Sky, 1959 (Johnson, V. 3, Knef 3)
Subway Sadie, 1926 (Edeson 4)
Succès commercial, 1970 (Lefebvre 2)
Success, 1923 (Astor 3)
Success. *See* American Success Company, 1979
Success. *See* Successo, 1963
Success at Any Price, 1934 (Fairbanks, D. Jr. 3, Horton 3, Moore, C. 3, Cooper 4, Plunkett 4, Steiner 4)
Success: The Circus. *See* Siker: Cirkusz, 1970
Successful Calamity, 1932 (Arliss 3, Astor 3, Scott, R. 3)
Successful Failure, 1913 (Beery 3)
Successo, 1963 (Risi 2, Aimée 3, Gassman 3, Trintignant 3, Morricone 4)
Such a Cook, 1914 (Sennett 2)
Such a Gorgeous Kid Like Me. *See* Belle Fille comme moi, 1972
Such a Hunter, 1914 (Bunny 3)
Such a Little Queen, 1914 (Porter 2, Crisp 3, Pickford 3)
Such a Little Queen, 1921 (Haller 4)
Such a Pretty Cloud, 1971 (Schell, Maria 3)
Such Good Friends, 1971 (Preminger 2, Cannon 3, Meredith 3, Bass 4)
Such High Mountains, 1974 (Bondarchuk 3)
Such Is Life, 1915 (Chaney Lon 3)
Such is Life. *See* Takový je zivot, 1930
Such Men Are Dangerous, 1930 (Baxter W. 3, Lugosi 3, Vajda 4)
Such Men Are Dangerous. *See* Racers, 1955
Such Women Are Dangerous, 1934 (Baxter W. 3)

Sucker. *See* Corniaud, 1965
Sucker. *See* Life of Jimmy Dolan, 1933
Sucker Money, 1933 (Auer 3)
Sucre, 1978 (Depardieu 3, Piccoli 3, Sarde 4)
Sud v Smolenske, 1946 (Shub 2)
Sudario a la medida. *See* Candidato per un assassino, 1969
Sudba cheloveka, 1959 (Bondarchuk 3)
Sudden Death, 1936 (Scott, R. 3)
Sudden Fear, 1952 (Crawford, J. 3, Grahame 3, Palance 3, Bernstein 4,
    Coffee 4, Lang 4, Leven 4)
Sudden Fortune of the Poor People of Kombach. *See* Plotzlicher
    Reichtum der armen Leute von Kombach, 1970
Sudden Impact, 1983 (Eastwood 3, Schifrin 4)
Sudden Money, 1939 (Crawford, B. 3, Head 4)
Sudden Rain. *See* Shu-u, 1956
Sudden Wealth of the Poor People of Kombach. *See* Plotzlicher
    Reichtum der armen Leute von Kombach, 1970
Suddenly, 1954 (Hayden 3, Sinatra 3, Clarke, C.C. 4, Raksin 4)
Suddenly Bad Names. *See* Akumyo niwaka, 1965
Suddenly it's Murder. *See* Crimen, 1960
Suddenly It's Spring, 1947 (Leisen 2, Goddard 3, MacMurray 3,
    Dreier 4, Young, V. 4)
Suddenly, Last Summer, 1959 (Mankiewicz 2, Clift 3, Hepburn, K. 3,
    McCambridge 3, Taylor, E. 3, Arnold 4, Fisher 4, Hornbeck 4,
    Spiegel 4)
Suddenly, Love, 1978 (Hunter 4)
Suddenly Single, 1971 (Moorehead 3)
Suds, 1920 (Pickford 3, Rosher 4, Young, W. 4)
Sue My Lawyer, 1938 (Langdon 3)
Sued for Libel, 1940 (Polglase 4)
Sueño del Pongo, 1970 (Alvarez 2)
Sueños de oro, 1956 (Figueroa 4)
Suez, 1938 (Dwan 2, Bruce 3, Power 3, Schildkraut 3, Young, L. 3,
    Clarke, C.C. 4, Dunne 4, Raksin 4, Zanuck 4)
Sufferin' Cats, 1943 (Hanna and Barbera 4)
Suffering of Susan, 1914 (Loos 4)
Suffering Shakespeare, 1924 (Roach 4)
Suffit d'une fois, 1946 (Feuillère 3)
Suffrageten, 1913 (Nielsen 3)
Suffragette, 1913 (Gad 2)
Suffragette. *See* Moderna suffragetten, 1913
Suffragette Battle of Nuttyville, 1914 (Gish, D. 3)
Suffragette Minstrels, 1913 (Barrymore L. 3, Gish, D. 3)
Sugar. *See* Sucre, 1978
Sugar. *See* Sukker, 1942
Sugar and Spice, 1930 (Balcon 4)
Sugar and Spies, 1966 (McKimson 4)
Sugar Cottage. *See* Cukrová bouda, 1980
Sugar Daddies, 1927 (Laurel and Hardy 3)
Sugar Plum Papa, 1930 (Sennett 2)
Sugarfoot, 1951 (Massey 3, Sakall 3, Scott, R. 3, Cahn 4, Steiner 4)
Sugarland Express, 1974 (Spielberg 2, Hawn 3, Johnson, B. 3, Fields 4,
    Williams, J. 4, Zsigmond 4)
Sugata Sanshiro, 1943 (Kurosawa 2, Shimura 3)
Sugata Sanshiro, 1955 (Yamamura 3)
Sugata Sanshiro, 1965 (Mifune 3, Okada 3)
Suhaag, 1979 (Bachchan 3)
Suicidate, mi amor, 1960 (Alcoriza 4)
Suicide, 1965 (Warhol 2)
Suicide Battalion, 1944 (Huston 3)
Suicide Battalion, 1958 (Crosby 4)
Suicide Club, 1909 (Griffith 2, Bitzer 4)
Suicide Club. *See* Klub nravstvennosti, 1915
Suicide Club. *See* Trouble for Two, 1936
Suicide de Lord Stilson, (Baur 3)
Suicide Fleet, 1931 (Boyd 3, Rogers, G. 3, Polito 4)
Suicide Pact, 1913 (Loos 4)
Suicide Squadron. *See* Dangerous Moonlight, 1941
Suicide Troops of the Watch Tower. *See* Boro no kesshitai, 1943
Suicide's Wife, 1979 (Dickinson 3)
Suikoden, 1942 (Takamine 3, Tsuburaya 4)
Suing Susan, 1912 (Bunny 3)
Suit of Armor, 1912 (Bunny 3)

Suitcase. *See* Kovčeg, 1968
Suitcase. *See* Maleta, 1960
Suite en si mineur, 1969 (Braunberger 4)
Suited to a T., 1931 (Fleischer, M. and D. 2)
Suitor. *See* Soupirant, 1962
Suivez cet homme!, 1953 (Blier 3)
Suivez l'oeuf, 1963 (Braunberger 4)
Suivez-moi, jeune homme, 1957 (Gélin 3)
Sujata, 1959 (Roy 2, Burman 4)
Sujsedi, 1970 (Dragić 4)
Sukinareba koso, 1928 (Gosho 2)
Sukker, 1942 (Henning-Jensen 2)
Sukovo trio, 1965 (Schorm 2)
Suk's Trio. *See* Sukovo trio, 1965
Sukyandaru, 1950 (Shimura 3)
Sul Ponte dei Sospiri, 1952 (Rosay 3)
Suleiman the Conqueror. *See* Solimani il conquistatore, 1961
Sullivans, 1944 (Baxter A. 3, Bond 3, Basevi 4, Newman 4)
Sullivan's Empire, 1967 (Schifrin 4)
**Sullivan's Travels, 1941 (Sturges, P. 2, Lake 3, McCrea 3, Edouart 4,
    Head 4, Seitz 4)**
Sult, 1966 (Carlsen 2)
Sultane de l'amour, 1919 (Modot 3)
Sultans, 1965 (Delannoy 2, Gélin 3, Jourdan 3, Lollobrigida 3,
    Noiret 3, Delli Colli 4)
Sultan's Birthday, 1944 (Terry 4)
Sultan's Cat, 1931 (Terry 4)
Sultan's Daughter, 1943 (Alton, J. 4)
Sultan's Wife, 1917 (Sennett 2, Swanson 3)
Sumka dipkuryera. *See* Teka dypkuryera, 1927
Summer, 1929 (Iwerks 4)
Summer. *See* Léto, 1949
Summer and Smoke, 1961 (Harvey 3, Merkel 3, Page 3, Bernstein 4,
    Head 4, Lang 4, Wallis 3)
Summer Bachelors, 1926 (Dwan 2, Ruttenberg 4)
Summer Battle of Osaka. *See* Osaka natsu no jin, 1937
Summer City, 1977 (Gibson 3)
Summer Clouds. *See* Bolond április, 1957
Summer Flirtation, 1910–11 (White 3)
Summer Girl, 1916 (Marion 4)
Summer Girls, 1918 (Sennett 2, Fazenda 3)
Summer Guests. *See* Sommergaste, 1975
Summer Holiday, 1948 (Mamoulian 2, Walters 2, Huston 3,
    Moorehead 3, Rooney 3, Freed 4, Goodrich and Hackett 4,
    Irene 4, Plunkett 4, Smith, J.M. 4)
Summer Holiday, 1962 (Yates 2)
Summer Holiday. *See* Always on Sunday, 1963
Summer Idyll, 1910 (Griffith 2, Walthall 3, Bitzer 4)
Summer in the City, 1970 (Wenders 2)
Summer in the Country. *See* Pastoral, 1976
Summer in the Fields, 1970 (Haanstra 2)
Summer Interlude. *See* Sommarlek, 1951
Summer Lightning. *See* Scudda Hoo! Scudda Hay!, 1948
Summer Lightning. *See* Strohfeuer, 1971
Summer Love, 1958 (Wray 3, Mancini 4, Salter 4)
Summer Madness, 1955 (Lean 2, Korda 4)
Summer Madness. *See* Summertime, 1955
Summer Magic, 1963 (Disney 2, Merkel 3, Ellenshaw 4)
Summer Manoeuvres. *See* Grandes Manoeuvres, 1955
Summer of '42, 1971 (Mulligan 2, Legrand 4, Surtees 4)
Summer of Silence. *See* Sommerfuglene, 1974
Summer of the Seventeenth Doll, 1959 (Baxter A. 3, Mills 3)
Summer on the Farm, 1943 (Alwyn 4)
Summer Paradise. *See* Paradistorg, 1976
Summer Place, 1959 (Daves 2, Bondi 3, Kennedy, A. 3, Steiner 4,
    Stradling 4)
Summer Place Wanted. *See* Sommarnoje sokes, 1957
Summer Rain. *See* Chuvas de verao, 1977
Summer Rain. *See* Zápor, 1960
Summer School Teachers, 1975 (Corman 4)
Summer Showers. *See* Chuvas de verao, 1977
Summer Sister. *See* Natsu no imoto, 1972
Summer Skin. *See* Piel de verano, 1961

Summer Soldiers, 1972 (Teshigahara 2, Takemitsu 4)
Summer Solstice, 1981 (Fonda, H. 3, Loy 3, Rosenblum 4)
Summer Stock, 1950 (Walters 2, Garland 3, Kelly, Gene 3, Green, J. 4, Pasternak 4, Plunkett 4, Rose 4, Smith, J.M. 4)
Summer Storm, 1944 (Sirk 2, Darnell 3, Haas 3, Horton 3, Sanders 3, Schufftan 4)
Summer Tale. *See* Sommarsaga, 1912
Summer Tales. *See* Racconti d'estate, 1958
Summer Train. *See* Sommartag, 1961
Summer Wishes, Winter Dreams, 1973 (Sidney 3, Woodward 3)
Summer with Monica. *See* Sommaren med Monika, 1953
Summer World, 1961 (Schaffner 2)
Summer's Tale. *See* Sommarsaga, 1941
Summertime, 1931 (Terry 4)
Summertime, 1935 (Iwerks 4)
Summertime, 1955 (Brazzi 3, Hepburn, K. 3)
Summertime. *See* Summer Madness, 1955
Summertime Killer, 1973 (Malden 3)
Summertree, 1971 (Warden 3)
Summit, 1961-62 (Vanderbeek 2)
Summit, 1968 (Volonté 3)
Summit of Mount Fuji. *See* Fuji sancho, 1948
Sumnjivo live, 1954 (Marković 3)
Sumo Festival. *See* Dohyou matsuri, 1944
Sumpf und Moral, 1925 (Dieterle 2)
Sumuru, 1967 (Kinski 3)
Sumuru, the Seven Secrets of Su-Muru. *See* Rio '70, 1970
Sumurun, 1920 (Lubitsch 2, Negri 3, Wegener 3, Kraly 4, Metzner 4)
Sun. *See* Nichirin, 1925
Sun Above, Death Below. *See* Sogeki, 1968
Sun Also Rises, 1957 (King 2, Dalio 3, Ferrer, M. 3, Flynn 3, Gardner 3, Power 3, Friedhofer 4, Lemaire 4, Wheeler 4, Zanuck 4)
Sun Comes Up, 1949 (MacDonald 3, Stone 3, Irene 4, Previn 4)
Sun Down Limited, 1924 (Roach 4)
Sun Legend of the Shogunate's Last Days. *See* Bakumatsu Taiyoden, 1958
Sun Never Sets, 1939 (Fairbanks, D. Jr. 3, Rathbone 3)
Sun Shines Bright, 1953 (Ford, J. 2, Darwell 3, Fetchit 3, Marsh 3, Muse 3, Cooper 4, Young, V. 4)
Sun Valley Cyclone, 1946 (Canutt 4)
Sun Valley Serenade, 1941 (Dandridge 3, Henie 3, Banton 4, Cronjager 4, Day 4, Pan 4)
Suna no onna, 1964 (Teshigahara 2, Kishida 3, Okada 3, Takemitsu 4)
Sunbeam, 1911 (Griffith 2, Bitzer 4)
Sunbonnet Blue, 1937 (Avery 2)
Sunburn, 1979 (Matthau 3, Wynn 3)
Sunday, 1961 (de Antonio 2)
Sunday Afternoon. *See* Tarde del domingo, 1957
Sunday, Bloody Sunday, 1971 (Schlesinger 2, Finch 3, Jackson 3, Love 3)
Sunday by the Sea, 1953 (Lassally 4)
Sunday Calm, 1923 (Roach 4)
Sunday Dinner for a Soldier, 1944 (Bacon 2, Baxter A. 3, Darwell 3, Newman 4)
Sunday Father, 1973 (Hoffman 3)
Sunday Go to Meetin' Time, 1936 (Freleng 4)
Sunday in August. *See* Domenica d'agosto, 1950
Sunday in New York, 1964 (Fonda, J. 3, Robertson 3, Krasna 4, Orry-Kelly 4)
Sunday in October. *See* Október vasárrap, 1979
Sunday in September. *See* Sondag i september, 1963
Sunday in the Country, 1975 (Borgnine 3)
Sunday in the Park, 1956 (Schlesinger 2)
Sunday Lovers, 1981 (Moore, R. 3, Tognazzi 3, Wilder 3, Age and Scarpelli 4, Delli Colli 4)
Sunday Morning. *See* Niedzielny poranek, 1955
Sunday Night at the Trocadero, 1937 (Sidney 2)
Sunday Punch, 1942 (Dailey 3, Gardner 3, Schary 4)
Sunday Woman. *See* Donna della domenica, 1975
Sundays and Cybele. *See* Cybèle, ou les dimanches de Ville d'Avray, 1961
Sunde, 1922 (Curtiz 2)

Sundelbabel, 1925 (Junge 4)
Sunden der Vater, 1913 (Gad 2, Nielsen 3)
Sundered Ties, 1912 (Ince 4)
Sunderin, 1949 (Frohlich 3, Knef 3, Vích 4)
Sundige Hof, 1932 (Rasp 3)
Sundige Mutter, 1921 (Oswald 2, Veidt 3)
Sundown, 1924 (Bosworth 3, Love 3, Marion 4)
Sundown, 1941 (Hathaway 2, Carey 3, Dandridge 3, Hardwicke 3, Sanders 3, Tierney 3, Irene 4, Lang 4, Plunkett 4, Rozsa 4, Wanger 4)
Sundown Rider, 1933 (Bond 3)
Sundown Slim, 1920 (Carey 3)
Sundown Trail, 1919 (Young, W. 4)
Sundown Trail, 1931 (Beavers 3, McCord 4)
Sundowners, 1949 (Elam 3, Preston 3, Hoch 4)
Sundowners, 1960 (Roeg 2, Zinnemann 2, Kerr 3, Mitchum 3, Rafferty 3, Ustinov 3, Fisher 4, Lennart 4, Tiomkin 4)
Sunehere Din, 1949 (Kapoor 2)
Sunflower. *See* Girasoli, 1970
Sunflower Girl. *See* Himawari-musume, 1953
Sunken. *See* Gesunkenen, 1925
Sunken Rocks, 1919 (Hepworth 2)
Sunken Treasure, 1936 (Terry 4)
Sunlight of Paris, 1924 (Pitts 3)
Sunny, 1930 (Haller 4)
Sunny, 1941 (Wilcox 2, Horton 3, Neagle 3)
Sunny Italy, 1951 (Terry 4)
Sunny Side of the Street, 1951 (Duning 4)
Sunny Side Up, 1926 (Crisp 3, Pitts 3)
Sunny Side Up, 1929 (Brown 3, Cooper, J 3, Gaynor 3, Friedhofer 4)
Sunny Skies, 1930 (Taurog 2)
Sunny South, 1931 (Lantz 4)
Sunny South, 1933 (Terry 4)
Sunny Spain, 1923 (Roach 4)
Sunnyside, 1919 (Chaplin 2, Purviance 3)
Sunrise, 1927 (Murnau 2, Gaynor 3, Mayer 4, Rosher 4, Struss 4)
Sunrise at Campobello, 1960 (Bellamy 3, Garson 3, Schary 4, Waxman 4)
Sun's Burial. *See* Taiyo no hakaba, 1960
Sunset Boulevard, 1950 (DeMille 2, Keaton 2, Von Stroheim 2, Wilder 2, Holden 3, Nilsson 3, Swanson 3, Brackett, C. 4, Dreier 4, Head 4, Seitz 4, Waxman 4)
Sunset Cove, 1978 (Carradine 3)
Sunset Derby, 1927 (Astor 3)
Sunset in El Dorado, 1945 (Dumont 3, Rogers, R. 3, Canutt 4)
Sunset in the West, 1950 (Rogers, R. 3)
Sunset in Vienna, 1938 (Wilcox 2)
Sunset in Wyoming, 1941 (Autry 3)
Sunset on the Desert, 1942 (Rogers, R. 3)
Sunset Pass, 1929 (Hathaway 2)
Sunset Pass, 1933 (Hathaway 2, Carey 3, Scott, R. 3)
Sunset Serenade, 1942 (Rogers, R. 3)
Sunset, Sunrise, 1973 (Rota 4)
Sunset Trail, 1932 (Eason 4)
Sunset Trail, 1939 (Boyd 3, Head 4)
Sunshine, 1916 (Sennett 2)
Sunshine Alley, 1917 (Marsh 3)
Sunshine and Gold, 1917 (King 2)
Sunshine and Shadow, 1914 (Talmadge, N. 3)
Sunshine Boys, 1975 (Matthau 3, Booth 4, Smith, D. 4, Stark 4)
Sunshine Christmas, 1977 (Head 4)
Sunshine Dad, 1916 (Browning 2)
Sunshine Follows Rain. *See* Driver dagg faller Regn, 1946
Sunshine in Poverty Row, 1910 (White 3)
Sunshine Molly, 1915 (Weber 2, Bosworth 3, Marion 4)
Sunshine Nan, 1918 (Barthelmess 3)
Sunshine Patriots, 1968 (Robertson 3, Sutherland 3)
Sunshine Sue, 1910 (Griffith 2, Crisp 3, Bitzer 4)
Sunshine Susie, 1931 (Saville 2, Balcon 4)
Sunshine Through the Dark, 1911 (Griffith 2, Bitzer 4)
Sunstone, 1979 (Emshwiller 2)
Sun-up, 1925 (Goulding 2)
Suo modo di fare, 1968 (Segal 3)

Suo nome faceva tremare . . . Interpol in allarme!. *See* Dio, sei proprio un padreterno, 1973
Suonatrice ambulante, 1912 (Bertini 3)
Suor Letizia, 1956 (Magnani 3, Di Venanzo 4, Zavattini 4)
Suor omicidi, 1978 (Valli 3)
Super Cops, 1974 (Semple 4)
Super Mouse Rides Again, 1943 (Terry 4)
Super Rabbit, 1943 (Jones 2)
Super Salesman, 1947 (Terry 4)
Super Secret Service, 1953 (Sellers 3)
Super Shylock. *See* Hendes Moders Løfte, 1916
Super Snooper, 1952 (McKimson 4)
Superchick, 1973 (Carradine 3)
Supercolpo da 7 miliard, 1966 (Andrews D. 3)
Superdome, 1978 (Johnson, V. 3)
Supergirl, 1970 (Fassbinder 2)
Supergirl, 1984 (Dunaway 3, Farrow 3, O'Toole 3, Goldsmith 4)
Super-Hooper-Dyne Lizzies, 1925 (Sennett 2)
Super-Imposition, 1968 (Vanderbeek 2)
Superman series, (Fleischer, M. and D. 2)
Superman, 1948 (Katzman 4)
Superman, 1978 (Brando 3, Cooper, J 3, Ford, G. 3, Hackman 3, Howard, T. 3, Schell, Maria 3, Stamp 3, York, S. 3, Unsworth 4, Williams, J. 4)
Superman II, 1981 (Lester 2, Cooper, J 3, Hackman 3, Stamp 3, York, S. 3, Unsworth 4)
Superman III, 1983 (Cooper, J 3, Hackman 3, Pryor 3)
Superman ki Wapasi, 1960 (Biswas 4)
Supernatural, 1933 (Farnum 3, Lombard 3, Scott, R. 3, Banton 4)
Super-Pacific, 1948 (Colpi 4)
Supersabio, 1948 (Cantinflas 3)
Super-Sleuth, 1937 (Sothern 3, August 4, Polglase 4)
Superstition, 1922 (Dwan 2)
Superstizione, 1949 (Antonioni 2) (Fusco 4)
Supertestimone, 1971 (Vitti 3, Guerra 4)
Supertrain, 1979 (Crawford, B. 3, Wynn 3, Lourié 4)
Supplice de Tantale, 1901 (Zecca, 2)
Support Your Local Gunfighter, 1971 (Blondell 3, Elam 3)
Support Your Local Sheriff, 1968 (Brennan 3, Dern 3, Elam 3)
Suppose They Gave a War and Nobody Came, 1970 (Ameche 3, Borgnine 3, Curtis 3, Guffey 4)
Suppressed Duck, 1965 (McKimson 4)
Suppressed Evidence, 1915 (Anderson G. 3)
Sur Faces, 1977 (Emshwiller 2)
Sur la barricade, 1907 (Guy 2)
Sur la route de Salina, 1971 (D'Eaubonne 4)
Sur la route de Salina. *See* Road to Salina, 1971
Sur le pont d'Avignon, 1956 (Franju 2, Fradetal 4, Jarre 4)
Sur le Sentier de la guerre, 1909 (Modot 3)
Sur les bords de la caméra, 1932 (Storck 2)
Sur les routes de l'été, 1936 (Storck 2)
Sur toute la gamme, 1954 (Chevalier 3)
Sur un air de Charleston, 1927 (Renoir 2, Braunberger 4)
Sur un arbre perché, 1971 (Chaplin 3)
Suraag, 1982 (Azmi 3)
Surcouf, 1924 (Artaud 3)
Sure Fire, 1921 (Ford, J. 2, Miller, V. 4)
Sure Shot Morgan, 1919 (Carey 3)
Sure-Mike, 1925 (Roach 4)
Surf. *See* Brannigar, 1935
Surf. *See* Shiosai, 1954
Surf Girl, 1916 (Sennett 2)
Surface Tension, 1968 (Frampton 2)
Surfacemen. *See* Pályamunkások, 1957
Surfacing, 1978 (Jutra 2)
Surgeon's Heroism, 1912 (Lawrence 3)
Suri Lanka no ai to wakare, 1976 (Kinoshita 2, Takamine 3, Muraki 4)
Surmenés, 1957 (Cassel 3, Braunberger 4, Delerue 4)
Suronin Chuya, 1930 (Yamada 3)
Surprise, 1923 (Fleischer, M. and D. 2)
Surprise-boogie, 1956 (Braunberger 4)
Surprise Package, 1960 (Donen 2, Brynner 3, Coward 4)
Surprise Packet. *See* Aegteskab og Pigesjov, 1914

Surprises de l'affichage, 1903–04 (Guy 2)
Surprises de la radio, 1940 (Dauphin 3, Gélin 3)
Surprises du sleeping, 1932 (Dauphin 3)
Surrender, 1927 (Mozhukin 3)
Surrender, 1931 (Howard 2, Baxter W. 3, Bellamy 3, Behrman 4, Grot 4, Howe 4, Levien 4)
Surrender, 1950 (Dwan 2, Brennan 3, Darwell 3)
Surrounded By Women. *See* Between Two Women, 1937
Surrounded House. *See* Omringade huset, 1922
Suru, 1978 (Guney 2)
Suruga yuhkyou-den: Yabure takka, 1964 (Miyagawa 4)
Surveillez votre tenue, 1949 (Decaë 4)
Survival. *See* Glanz und Elend der Kurtisanen, 1927
Survival. *See* Guide, 1965
Survival 67, 1967 (Dassin 2)
Survival Run, 1977 (Milland 3)
Surviving, 1985 (Burstyn 3)
Surviving Shinsengumi. *See* Ikinokata Shinsengumi, 1932
Survivor, 1981 (Cotten 3)
Survivors, 1983 (Ritchie 2, Matthau 3)
Survivors. *See* Sobrevivientes, 1979
Susan and God, 1940 (Cukor 2, Bruce 3, Crawford, J. 3, Dailey 3, Hayworth 3, March 3, Loos 4, Stothart 4, Stromberg 4)
Susan Lenox, Her Fall and Rise, 1931 (Gable 3, Garbo 3, Hersholt 3, Adrian 4, Booth 4, Daniels 4, Gibbons 4)
Susan Rocks the Boat, 1916 (Gish, D. 3)
Susan Slade, 1961 (Daves 2, Ballard 4, Steiner 4)
Susan Slept Here, 1954 (Tashlin 2, Powell, D. 3, Reynolds, D. 3, D'Agostino 4, Musuraca 4)
Susana, 1950 (Buñuel 2)
Susanna Pass, 1949 (Rogers, R. 3)
Susanna tutta panna, 1957 (Manfredi 3, Delli Colli 4, Ponti 4)
Susannah of the Mounties, 1939 (Scott, R. 3, Temple 3, MacGowan 4, Miller, A. 4, Zanuck 4)
Susanne im Bade, no date (Staudte 2)
Susanne macht Ordnung, 1931 (Sakall 3)
Susanne und der Zauberring, 1973 (Hoppe 3)
Susie Steps Out, 1946 (Dumont 3)
Suspect, 1945 (Siodmak 2, Laughton 3)
Suspect, 1960 (Boulting 2, Cushing 3, Pleasance 3)
Suspects, 1957 (Vanel 3)
Suspended Ordeal, 1914 (Sennett 2, Arbuckle 3)
Suspended Sentence, 1913 (Dwan 2)
Suspended Vocation. *See* Vocation suspendue, 1977
Suspense, 1946 (Struss 4)
Suspense au 2e Bureau, 1959 (D'Eaubonne 4)
Suspicion, 1918 (Stahl 2)
Suspicion, 1941 (Hitchcock 2, Bruce 3, Carroll L. 3, Fontaine 3, Grant, C. 3, Hardwicke 3, Harrison 4, Polglase 4, Raphaelson 4, Reville 4, Stradling 4, Waxman 4)
Suspicious Henry, 1913 (Bunny 3)
Suspicious Wives, 1922 (Stahl 3)
Suspiria, 1977 (Bennett J. 3, Valli 3, Argento 4)
Susret u snu, 1957 (Mimica 4)
Susse Madel, 1926 (Warm 4)
Sussie, 1945 (Bjornstrand 3)
Sussurro nel buio, 1976 (Cotten 3, Donaggio 4)
Susume dokuritsuki, 1943 (Kinugasa 2, Hasegawa 3, Mori 3)
Suszterherceq, 1916 (Sakall 3)
Sutekina konbanwa, 1965 (Iwashita 3)
Sutiejka, 1973 (Theodorakis 4)
Sutjeska, 1972 (Burton 3, Marković 3, Papas 3, Samardžić 3)
Sutter's Gold, 1936 (Cruze 2, Hawks 2, Carey 3, Waxman 4)
Suttobi kago, 1952 (Miyagawa 4)
Suvarna Rekha, 1963 (Ghatak 2)
Suvorov, 1941 (Pudovkin 2, Golovnya 4)
Suwanee River, 1925 (Fleischer, M. and D. 2)
Suzaku Gate. *See* Suzaku-mon, 1957
Suzaku-mon, 1957 (Miyagawa 4)
Suzanna, 1922 (Sennett 2, Normand 3, Hornbeck 4)
Suzanne au bain, 1930 (Storck 2)
Suzanne et ses brigands, 1948 (Burel 4)

Suzanne Simonin, 1966 (Rivette 2, Karina 3, Presle 3, de Beauregard 4)

Suzanne's Profession. *See* Carrière de Suzanne, 1963

Suzukake no sampomichi, 1959 (Mori 3, Tsukasa 3)

Suzukamori, 1937 (Hasegawa 3)

Suzy, 1936 (Grant, C. 3, Harlow 3, Stone 3, Coffee 4)

Sváb, 1947 (Brdečka 4)

Svadba, 1944 (Maretskaya 3)

Svadlenka, 1936 (Fric 2, Haas 3)

Svanger på slottet, 1959 (Bjornstrand 3)

Svarmor kommer, 1930 (Jaenzon 4)

Svarta Horisonter series, from 1935 (Fejos 2)

Svarta maskerna, 1912 (Sjostrom 2, Stiller 2, Jaenzon 4, Magnusson 4)

Svarta palmkronor, 1968 (Andersson B. 3, Von Sydow 3, Fischer 4)

Svarta rosor, 1932 (Molander 2)

Svarta rosor, 1945 (Dahlbeck 3)

Svarte fugler, 1983 (Andersson B. 3)

Svatba v Korálovém môri, 1943 (Hofman 4)

Svatbite na Joan Asen, 1975 (Karamitev 3)

Svatbite ne Joan Asen. *See* Pán a vládce, 1975

Svatby pana Voka, 1970 (Kopecký 3)

Svatý Václav, 1929 (Stallich 4, Vích 4)

Svegliati e uccidi, 1966 (Volonté 3, Morricone 4)

Švejk v ruském zajetí, 1926 (Vích 4)

Svend Dyrings Hus, 1908 (Holger-Madsen 2)

Svengali, 1927 (Wegener 3)

Svengali, 1931 (Barrymore J. 3, Crisp 3, Grot 4)

Svengali, 1954 (Knef 3, Alwyn 4)

Svengali, 1983 (O'Toole 3, Barry 4)

Svengali's Cat, 1946 (Terry 4)

Svensk tiger, 1948 (Bjornstrand 3)

Sverchok na Pechia, 1915 (Ouspenskaya 3)

Svesda plenitelnovo shchstia, 1976 (Smoktunovsky 3)

Svět Alfonso Muchy, 1980 (Jires 2)

Sǒvet, kde se žebra, 1938 (Haas 3, Stallich 4)

Svet nad Rossiei, 1947 (Yutkevich 2)

Svět otevřený náhodám, 1971 (Kopecký 3)

Svět patří nám, 1937 (Fric 2)

Svítalo celou noc, 1980 (Kučera 4)

Svítání, 1933 (Stallich 4)

Svoboda ili Smart, 1969 (Karamitev 3)

Svy Dager for Elisabeth, 1927 (Henie 3)

Swain, 1950 (Markopoulos 2)

Swallow the Leader, 1949 (McKimson 4)

Swami, 1977 (Azmi 3)

Swami Dada, 1982 (Anand 3)

Swamp, 1921 (Hayakawa 3, Love 3)

Swamp Fire, 1946 (Crabbe 3, Weissmuller 3)

Swamp Thing, 1982 (Jourdan 3)

Swamp Water, 1941 (Renoir 2, Andrews D. 3, Baxter A. 3, Bond 3, Brennan 3, Carradine 3, Huston 3, Day 4, Nichols 4)

Swamp Woman, 1956 (Corman 4)

Swan, 1925 (Menjou 3, Banton 4)

Swan, 1956 (Vidor, C. 2, Carroll L. 3, Guinness 3, Jourdan 3, Kelly, Grace 3, Moorehead 3, Gibbons 4, Kaper 4, Rose 4, Ruttenberg 4, Schary 4, Surtees 4)

Swan. *See* One Romantic Night, 1930

Swan Princess, 1928 (Sennett 2)

Swanee River, 1939 (Ameche 3, Jolson 3, Day 4, Dunne 4, Glennon 4, MacGowan 4, Zanuck 4)

Swann in Love, 1984 (Delon 3)

Swann in Love. *See* Amour de Swann, 1983

Swap, 1980 (De Niro 3)

Swaralipi, 1960 (Ghatak 4)

Swarg narak, 1978 (Azmi 3)

Swarm, 1978 (Caine 3, De Havilland 3, Ferrer, J. 3, Fonda, H. 3, Grant, L. 3, Johnson, B. 3, MacMurray 3, Widmark 3, Goldsmith 4)

Swash Buckled, 1962 (Hanna and Barbera 4)

Swashbuckler, 1976 (Bujold 3, Jones, J.E. 3, Shaw 3, Addison 4)

Swastika Savages. *See* Hell's Bloody Devils, 1970

Swat the Crook, 1919 (Daniels 3, Lloyd 3, Roach 4)

Swat the Fly, 1935 (Fleischer, M. and D. 2)

Sweater Girl, 1942 (Dreier 4, Young, V. 4)

Sweden, 1960 (Van Dyke, W. 2)

Swedenhielms, 1935 (Molander 2, Bergman 3)

Swedes in America, 1943 (Bergman 3)

Swedish Fly Girls. *See* Christa, 1970

Swedish Mistress. *See* Älskarinnan, 1962

Swedish Tiger. *See* Svensk tiger, 1948

Sweedie Goes to Gollege, 1915 (Swanson 3)

Sweedie series, 1914–16 (Beery 3)

Sweekar kiya maine, 1983 (Azmi 3)

Sweepings, 1933 (Cromwell 2, Barrymore L. 3, Cronjager 4, Plunkett 4, Selznick 4, Steiner 4)

Sweepstakes Winner, 1939 (Edeson 4)

Sweet Adeline, 1926 (Fleischer, M. and D. 2)

Sweet Adeline, 1935 (Leroy 2, Calhern 3, Dunne 3, Orry-Kelly 4, Polito 4, Wallis 4)

Sweet Aloes. *See* Give Me Your Heart, 1936

Sweet and Hot, 1958 (Three Stooges 3)

Sweet and Lowdown, 1944 (Darnell 3, Ballard 4)

Sweet and Sour. *See* Dragées au poivre, 1963

Sweet and Twenty, 1909 (Griffith 2, Pickford 3, Bitzer 4)

Sweet Bird of Youth, 1962 (Brooks, R. 2, Page 3, Torn 3, Berman 4, Krasner 4, Orry-Kelly 4)

Sweet Body of Deborah. *See* Dolce corpi di Deborah, 1968

Sweet By and By, 1921 (Roach 4)

Sweet Charity, 1968 (Fosse 2, MacLaine 3, Head 4, Surtees 4, Westmore, B. 4)

Sweet Cookie, 1921 (Garmes 4)

Sweet Cookie, 1933 (Sennett 2)

Sweet Daddies, 1926 (Edeson 4)

Sweet Daddy, 1924 (McCarey 2, Roach 4)

Sweet Devil, 1938 (Buchanan 3)

Sweet Dreams, 1985 (Lange 3)

Sweet Genevieve, 1947 (Katzman 4)

Sweet Hostage, 1975 (Sheen 3)

Sweet Hours. *See* Dulces horas, 1981

Sweet Hunters, 1969 (Guerra 2, Hayden 3, Evein 4)

Sweet Jenny Lee, 1932 (Fleischer, M. and D. 2)

Sweet Kill, 1972 (Crosby 4)

Sweet Kitty Bellairs, 1930 (Pidgeon 3)

Sweet Lavender, 1915 (Hepworth 2)

Sweet Light in the Dark Window. *See* Romeo, Julie a tma, 1960

Sweet Memories of Yesterday, 1911 (Pickford 3, Gaudio 4, Ince 4)

Sweet Movie, 1974 (Makavejev 2)

Sweet Music, 1935 (Gaudio 4, Wald 4)

Sweet November, 1968 (Legrand 4)

Sweet Pickle, 1925 (Sennett 2)

Sweet Revenge, 1909 (Griffith 2, Bitzer 4)

Sweet Revenge, 1913 (Beery 3)

Sweet Revenge, 1976 (Zsigmond 4)

Sweet Revenge. *See* Dandy, the All-American Girl, 1976

Sweet Ride, 1968 (Bisset 3, Day 4, Pasternak 4, Smith, J.M. 4)

Sweet Rosie O'Grady, 1943 (Grable 3, Menjou 3, Young, R. 3, Basevi 4, Pan 4)

Sweet Secret. *See* Amai himitsu, 1971

Sweet 17. *See* Susan Rocks the Boat, 1916

Sweet Sioux, 1937 (Freleng 4)

Sweet Sixteen. *See* Futures vedettes, 1954

Sweet Smell of Success, 1957 (Mackendrick 2, Curtis 3, Lancaster 3, Bernstein 4, Howe 4, Lehman 4)

Sweet Sweetback's Baadasssss Song, 1971 (Van Peebles 2)

Sweet Toronto, 1971 (Leacock 2)

Sweetheart. *See* Koibito, 1951

Sweetheart Days, 1921 (Sennett 2)

Sweetheart of Sigma Chi, 1933 (Crabbe 3, Grable 3)

Sweetheart of Sigma Chi, 1946 (Cahn 4, Hunter 4)

Sweetheart of the Campus, 1941 (Dmytryk 2, Keeler 3, Planer 4)

Sweethearts, 1938 (Van Dyke, W.S. 2, Auer 3, Eddy 3, MacDonald 3, Adrian 4, Stothart 4, Stromberg 4, Vorkapich 4)

Sweethearts and Wives, 1930 (Brook 3, Seitz 4)

Sweethearts of the U.S.A., 1944 (Merkel 3)

Sweethearts on Parade, 1930 (Neilan 2)

Sweethearts on Parade, 1953 (Dwan 2)

Sweets for the Sweet, 1903 (Bitzer 4)

Swell Guy, 1946 (Brooks, R. 2, Gaudio 4)

Swell-Head, 1929 (Love 3)

Swept Away by a Strange Destiny on an Azure August Sea. *See* Travolti da un insolito destino nell'azzurro mare d'agosto, 1974

Swift Current. *See* Gekiryu, 1952

Swim, Girl, Swim, 1927 (Daniels 3, Hunt 4, Schulberg 4)

Swim or Sink, 1932 (Fleischer, M. and D. 2)

Swim Princess, 1928 (Capra 2, Lombard 3, Hornbeck 4)

Swimmer, 1968 (Pollack 2, Lancaster 3, Perry 4, Wheeler 4)

Swimming Class, 1904 (Bitzer 4)

Swimming Pool. *See* Piscine, 1969

Swimmy, 1968 (Patel 4)

Swindlers. *See* Bidone, 1955

Swindlers. *See* Magliari, 1959

Swing, 1936 (Micheaux 2)

Swing Cleaning, 1941 (Fleischer, M. and D. 2)

Swing Ding Amigo, 1966 (McKimson 4)

Swing Fever, 1943 (Gardner 3, Horne 3, Brown, N. 4, Rosher 4)

Swing for Sale, 1937 (Allyson 3)

Swing Frolic, 1942 (Krasner 4)

Swing High, 1930 (Fetchit 3, Mandell 4)

Swing High, Swing Low, 1937 (Leisen 2, Lamour 3, Lombard 3, MacMurray 3, Quinn 3, Banton 4, Dreier 4, Young, V. 4)

Swing in the Saddle, 1944 (Summerville 3)

Swing It, 1936 (Cronjager 4)

Swing It, Professor, 1937 (Neilan 2)

Swing Out, Sister, 1945 (Burke 3)

Swing Parade of 1946, 1946 (Three Stooges 3)

Swing School, 1938 (Fleischer, M. and D. 2)

Swing Shift, 1983 (Demme 2, Hawn 3)

Swing Shift Cinderella, 1945 (Avery 2)

Swing Shift Maisie, 1943 (McLeod 2, Sothern 3, Irene 4, Stradling 4)

Swing, Teacher, Swing. *See* College Swing, 1938

Swing Time, 1936 (Stevens 2, Astaire 3, Rogers, G. 3, Berman 4, Pan 4, Polglase 4)

Swing with Bing, 1940 (Crosby 3)

Swing, You Sinner, 1930 (Fleischer, M. and D. 2)

Swing Your Baby, 1938 (Wallis 4)

Swing Your Lady, 1938 (Bogart 3, Fazenda 3, Reagan 3, Deutsch 4, Edeson 4, Friedhofer 4)

Swing Your Partners, 1918 (Lloyd 3, Roach 4)

Swinger, 1966 (Sidney 2, Biroc 4, Head 4, Previn 4)

Swingin' Maiden. *See* Iron Maiden, 1963

Swingin' on a Rainbow, 1945 (Langdon 3)

Swingin' Summer, 1965 (Welch 3)

Swinging at the Castle. *See* Svanger på slottet, 1959

Swinging the Lambeth Walk, 1939 (Lye 2)

Swingmen in Europe, 1977 (Rabier 4)

Swingtime Johnny, 1943 (Bruckman 4)

Swirl of Glory. *See* Sugarfoot, 1950

Swiss Army Knife with Rats and Pigeons, 1981 (Breer 2)

Swiss Cheese, 1930 (Terry 4)

Swiss Cheeze Family Robinson, 1947 (Terry 4)

Swiss Conspiracy, 1975 (Ireland 3, Milland 3)

Swiss Family Robinson, 1940 (Welles 2, Dunn 4, Musuraca 4)

Swiss Family Robinson, 1960 (Disney 2, Hayakawa 3, Mills 3, Alwyn 4, Ellenshaw 4)

Swiss Miss, 1938 (Negulesco 2, Laurel & Hardy 3, Roach 4)

Swiss Miss, 1951 (Terry 4)

Swiss Ski Yodelers, 1940 (Terry 4)

Swiss Tour. *See* Four Days' Leave, 1949

Swiss Trip, 1934 (Fischinger 2)

Switch, 1975 (Wagner 3)

Switch Tower, 1913 (Barrymore L. 3)

Switchboard Operator. *See* Ljubavni Slučaj, tragedija sluzbenice PTT, 1967

Switches and Sweeties, 1919 (Hardy 3)

Swooning the Swooners, 1945 (Terry 4)

Sword and Dice. *See* Kard és kocka, 1959

Sword and the Dragon, 1960 (Fields 4)

Sword and the Flute, 1960 (Ivory 2)

Sword and the Rose, 1953 (Disney 2, Dillon 4, Ellenshaw 4, Unsworth 4)

Sword and the Sorcerer, 1982 (Serafine 4)

Sword and the Sumo Ring. *See* Ippan gatana dohyoiri, 1934

Sword for Hire. *See* Sengoku-burai, 1952

Sword in the Desert, 1949 (Andrews D. 3, Chandler 3, Buckner 4)

Sword in the Stone, 1963 (Disney 2)

Sword of D'Artagnan, 1951 (Boetticher 2)

Sword of Doom. *See* Daibosatsu toge, 1966

Sword of Flying Dragon. *See* Hiryuh no ken, 1937

Sword of Lancelot. *See* Lancelot and Guinevere, 1963

Sword of Sherwood Forest, 1960 (Fisher 2, Cushing 3, Reed, O. 3)

Sword of the Conqueror. *See* Rosmunda e Alboino, 1961

Sword of the Valiant, 1983 (Cushing 3, Golan and Globus 4, Young, F. 4)

Swords and Hearts, 1911 (Griffith 2, Bitzer 4)

Swords of Blood. *See* Cartouche, 1961

Swordsman, 1947 (Friedhofer 4)

Swordsman of Siena. *See* Spadaccino di Siena, 1961

Sworn Enemy, 1936 (Quinn 3, Stone 3, Young, R. 3)

Syanhai no tsuki, 1941 (Tsuburaya 4)

Sybil, 1976 (Field 3, Woodward 3)

Sydenham Plan, 1949 (Ferrer, J. 3)

Sylvester, 1923 (Pick 2, Mayer 4)

Sylvia, 1965 (Baker C. 3, O'Brien, E. 3, Sothern 3, Head 4, Raksin 4, Ruttenberg 4)

Sylvia of the Secret Service, 1917 (Von Stroheim 2, Grot 4, Miller, A. 4)

Sylvia Scarlett, 1935 (Cukor 2, Grant, C. 3, Gwenn 3, Hepburn, K. 3, August 4, Berman 4, Plunkett 4, Polglase 4)

Sylvie and the Ghost. *See* Sylvie et le fantôme, 1944

Sylvie and the Phantom. *See* Sylvie et le fantôme, 1944

Sylvie et le fantôme, 1944 (Autant-Lara 2, Tati 2, Aurenche 4)

Symmetricks, 1972 (Vanderbeek 2)

Sympathy for the Devil. *See* One Plus One, 1968

Sympathy Sal, 1915 (Loos 4)

Symphonie d'amour. *See* Grand Refrain, 1936

Symphonie der Liebe. *See* Extase, 1933

Symphonie des brigands, 1936 (Schufftan 4)

Symphonie du travail, 1943 (Alekan 4)

Symphonie eines Lebens, 1942 (Baur 3, Porten 3, Hoffmann 4)

Symphonie fantastique, 1942 (Christian-Jaque 2, Barrault 3, Berry 3, Blier 3)

Symphonie industrielle. *See* Philips-Radio, 1931

Symphonie New York, 1956 (Braunberger 4)

Symphonie Nr. 3 in Es-dur, Opus 55, 'Eroica' von Ludwig von Beethoven, 1967 (Colpi 4)

Symphonie Nr. 7 von Ludwig von Beethoven, 1966 (Colpi 4)

Symphonie Nr. 9 von Franz Schubert, 1966 (Colpi 4)

Symphonie pastorale, 1946 (Delannoy 2, Morgan 3, Andrejew 4, Annenkov 4, Aurenche 4, Auric 4, Bost 4)

Symphonie paysanne, 1942–44 (Storck 2)

Symphonie pour un massacre, 1963 (Dauphin 3, Vanel 3, Barsacq 4, Renoir 4)

Symphony for a Massacre. *See* Symphonie pour un massacre, 1963

Symphony in Slang, 1951 (Avery 2)

Symphony in Two Flats, 1930 (Novello 3, Balcon 4)

Symphony of a City. *See* Manniskor i stad, 1947

Symphony of Six Million, 1932 (La Cava 2, Dunne 3, Berman 4, Selznick 4, Steiner 4)

Synanon, 1965 (O'Brien, E. 3, Stradling 4)

Synchromy, 1971 (McLaren 2)

Syncopated Sioux, 1940 (Lantz 4)

Syncopation, 1929 (Plunkett 4)

Syncopation, 1942 (Dieterle 2, Cooper, J 3, Menjou 3, Hunt 4)

Synd, 1928 (Molander 2, Manès 3, Jaenzon 4)

Synd, 1948 (Borgstrom 3)

Syndens Datter, 1915 (Blom 2)

Syndig Kaerlighed, 1915 (Blom 2)

Synnove Solbakken, 1934 (Sjostrom 2)

Synnove Solbakken, 1957 (Andersson H. 3, Nykvist 4)

Synteza, 1980's (Janda 3)

Synthetic Sin, 1928 (Moore, C. 3)

T

Tainu-ken no onna, 1948 (Yamamura 3)
Taiyo ni somuku mono, 1959 (Tanaka 3)
Taiyo no hakaba, 1960 (Oshima 2)
Taiyo no karyudo, 1970 (Takemitsu 4)
Taiyo to bara, 1956 (Kinoshita 2)
Taiyo wa higashi yori, 1932 (Tanaka 3)
Tajemnica dzikiego szybu, 1956 (Cybulski 3)
Tajemnica starego zamku, 1956 (Giersz 4)
Tajemství hradu v Karpatech, 1981 (Kopecký 3, Brdečka 4,
    Švankmajer 4)
Tajemství krve, 1953 (Fric 2, Brodský 3, Hrušínský 3, Kopecký 3,
    Stallich 4)
Tajemství velkého vypravěče, 1971 (Kachyna 2)
Tajiko mura, 1940 (Imai 2)
Tajiko Village. See Tajiko mura, 1940
Takadanobaba, 1944 (Yoda 4)
Takara no yama, 1929 (Ozu 2)
Take a Chance, 1918 (Daniels 3, Lloyd 3, Roach 4)
Take a Chance, 1933 (Lemaire 4)
Take a Giant Step, 1959 (Epstein, J. & P. 4)
Take a Girl Like You, 1970 (Reed, O. 3)
Take a Hard Ride, 1975 (Andrews D. 3, Van Cleef 3, Goldsmith 4)
Take a Letter, Darling, 1942 (Leisen 2, MacMurray 3, Russell, R. 3,
    Dreier 4, Irene 4, Young, V. 4)
Take a Trip, 1926 (Fleischer, M. and D. 2)
Take Care of My Little Girl, 1951 (Negulesco 2, Crain 3, Hunter 3,
    Epstein, J. & P. 4, Lemaire 4, Newman 4, Reynolds 4)
Take Cover, 1940 (Pearson 2)
Take 'em and Shake 'em, 1931 (Arbuckle 3)
Take Her, She's Mine, 1963 (Stewart 3, Ballard 4, Goldsmith 4,
    Johnson 4, Smith, J.M. 4)
Take It All. See A tout prendre, 1963
Take It or Leave It, 1944 (La Shelle 4)
Take Me Home, 1928 (Neilan 2, Brown 3, Daniels 3, Hunt 4)
Take Me Out to the Ball, 1910 (Anderson G. 3)
Take Me Out to the Ball Game, 1949 (Berkeley 2, Donen 2,
    Kelly, Gene 3, Sinatra 3, Williams 3, Comden and Green 4,
    Deutsch 4, Edens 4, Freed 4, Rose 4)
Take Me to Town, 1953 (Sirk 2, Hayden 3, Sheridan 3, Hunter 4)
Take My Life, 1947 (Alwyn 4, Green, G. 4, Havelock-Allan 4)
Take My Tip, 1937 (Gilliat 4, Metzner 4)
Take Next Car, 1922 (Roach 4)
Take One False Step, 1949 (Powell, W. 3, Winters 3, Orry-Kelly 4,
    Planer 4)
Take the 5:10 to Dreamland, 1976 (Conner 2)
Take the Air, 1923 (Roach 4)
Take the Air, 1940 (Eason 4)
Take the Heir, 1930 (Horton 3)
Take the High Ground, 1953 (Brooks, R. 2, Malden 3, Widmark 3,
    Alton, J. 4, Schary 4, Tiomkin 4)
Take the Money and Run, 1969 (Allen 2, Hill, W. 2, Rosenblum 4)
Take the Stage. See Curtain Call at Cactus Creek, 1950
Take This—My Body, 1974 (Baker C. 3)
Take Your Medicine, 1930 (Sennett 2)
Take Your Time, 1925 (Sennett 2)
Takekurabe, 1955 (Gosho 2, Yamada 3)
Taki no Shiraito, 1933 (Mizoguchi 2)
Taki no Shiraito, 1952 (Mori 3, Miyagawa 4, Yoda 4)
Taki no Shiraito, the Water Magician. See Taki no Shiraito, 1933
Takiji Kobayashi. See Kobayashi Takiji, 1974
Taking a Chance, 1912 (Lawrence 3)
Taking a Chance, 1916 (Mix 3)
Taking a Chance, 1928 (McLeod 2)
Taking His Medicine, 1911 (Sennett 2)
Taking of Luke McVane, 1915 (Hart 3)
Taking of Luke McVane. See Fugitive, 1915
Taking of Mustang Pete, 1915 (Mix 3)
Taking of Pelham One Two Three, 1974 (Matthau 3, Shaw 3,
    Roizman 4)
Taking Off, 1970 (Forman 2, Carrière 4, Henry 4)
Taking on the Bomb, 1983 (Christie 3)
Taking the Blame, 1935 (Fleischer, M. and D. 2)
Taki-no Shiraito, 1952 (Kyo 3)

Taková láska, 1959 (Weiss 2, Brdečka 4)
Takový je zivot, 1930 (Baranovskaya 3)
Tal des Lebens, 1913 (Porten 3, Messter 4)
Tal Farlow, 1980 (Lye 2)
Tal para cual, 1952 (Negrete 3)
Tal vez mañana. See Uomo dai calzoni corti, 1958
Tala and Rhythm, 1972 (Benegal 2)
Találkozás Lukács Gyorggyel, 1972 (Kovács 2)
Talash, 1969 (Burman 4)
Tale of a Dead Princess, 1953 (Ivanov-vano 4)
Tale of a Shirt, 1933 (Terry 4)
Tale of a Wolf, 1958 (Hanna and Barbera 4)
Tale of Africa. See Afurika monogatari, 1981
Tale of Archery at the Sanjusangendo. See Sanjusangendo toshiya
    monogatari, 1945
Tale of Czar Saltan, 1966 (Ptushko 2)
Tale of Five Cities, 1950 (Mastroianni 3)
Tale of Five Cities. See Passaporto per l'Oriente, 1951
Tale of Genji. See Genji monogatari, 1951
Tale of John and Mary. See Pohádka o Honzíkovi a Mařence, 1980
Tale of Lost Time, 1964 (Ptushko 2)
Tale of Tales, 1980 (Norstein 4)
Tale of the Black Eye, 1913 (Sennett 2)
Tale of the Fjords. See Dromda dalen, 1947
Tale of the Magician, 1964 (Halas and Batchelor 2)
Tale of the West, 1909 (Anderson G. 3)
Tale of the Wilderness, 1911 (Griffith 2, Bitzer 4)
Tale of Two Cities, 1911 (Costello, M. 3, Talmadge, N. 3)
Tale of Two Cities, 1917 (Dumont 3, Farnum 3)
Tale of Two Cities, 1922 (Brook 3)
Tale of two Cities, 1935 (Van Dyke, W.S. 2, Colman 3, Rathbone 3,
    Walthall 3, Behrman 4, Gibbons 4, Selznick 4, Stothart 4)
Tale of Two Cities, 1958 (Bogarde 3, Lee, C. 3, Pleasance 3,
    Clarke, T.E.B. 4, Dillon 4)
Tale of Two Cities, 1980 (Cushing 3, More 3)
Tale of Two Kitties, 1942 (Clampett 4)
Tale of Two Worlds, 1921 (Beery 3)
Talent Competition. See Konkurs, 1963
Talent for Loving, 1968 (Topol 3, Widmark 3)
Talent for Murder, 1983 (Olivier 3)
Tales by Capek. See Capkovy povídky, 1947
Tales from a Country by the Sea. See Kaikokuki, 1928
Tales from the Crypt, 1972 (Cushing 3, Richardson 3, Francis 4)
Tales from the Vienna Woods. See Geschichten aus dem Wienerwald,
    1981
Tales of a Long Journey. See Legenda a vonaton, 1962
Tales of a Salesman, 1965 (Zsigmond 4)
Tales of Adventure, 1954 (Chaney Lon, Jr. 3)
Tales of Hoffman, 1951 (Powell and Pressburger 2, Francis 4)
Tales of Hoffman. See Hoffmanns Erzahlungen, 1916
Tales of Hoffman. See Hoffmanovy povídky, 1962
Tales of Hoffnung series, 1964 (Halas and Batchelor 2)
Tales of Manhattan, 1942 (Duvivier 2, Boyer 3, Fonda, H. 3,
    Hayworth 3, Lanchester 3, Laughton 3, Marsh 3, Muse 3,
    Robeson 3, Robinson, E. 3, Rogers, G. 3, Sanders 3, Day 4,
    Hecht 4, Hoffenstein 4, Leven 4, Spiegel 4, Stewart 4, Trotti 4,
    Walker 4)
Tales of Mystery. See Histoires extraordinaires, 1968
Tales of Mystery. See Tre passi nel delirio, 1968
Tales of Ordinary Madness, 1981 (Ferreri 2)
Tales of Ordinary Madness. See Storia di ordinaria follia, 1981
Tales of Paris. See Parisiennes, 1961
Tales of Terror, 1962 (Lorre 3, Price 3, Rathbone 3, Corman 4,
    Crosby 4)
Tales That Witness Madness, 1973 (Hawkins 3, Novak 3, Pleasance 3,
    Francis 4)
Talíře nad Velkým Malíkovem, 1977 (Jires 2)
Talisman. See Amuletten, 1911
Talk about a Stranger, 1952 (Stone 3, Alton, J. 4)
Talk Between Men. See Muzhskoi Razgovor, 1969
Talk of Hollywood, 1929 (Sandrich 2)
Talk of the Devil, 1936 (Reed 2, Rutherford 3)
Talk of the Town, 1918 (Chaney Lon 3, Pitts 3)

Talk of the Town, 1942 (Stevens 2, Arthur 3, Colman 3, Grant, C. 3, Muse 3, Buchman 4, Irene 4)
Talker, 1925 (Nilsson 3, Stone 3, Edeson 4)
Talking Caftan. See Beszélo konto, 1968
Talking Magpies, 1946 (Terry 4)
Talking Through My Heart, 1936 (Fleischer, M. and D. 2)
Tall, 1967 (Le Grice 2)
Tall Blond Man with One Black Shoe. See Grand Blond avec une chaussure noire, 1972
Tall, Dark, and Gruesome, 1948 (Bruckman 4)
Tall Headlines, 1952 (Zetterling 2)
Tall in the Saddle, 1944 (Bond 3, Wayne 3)
Tall Lie. See For Men Only, 1951
Tall Man Riding, 1955 (Scott, R. 3)
Tall Men, 1955 (Walsh 2, Gable 3, Marsh 3, Russell, J. 3, Ryan 3, Lemaire 4, Nugent 4, Wheeler 4, Young, V. 4)
Tall Story, 1960 (Logan 2, Fonda, J. 3, Perkins 3, Epstein, J. & P. 4)
Tall Stranger, 1957 (Mayo 3, McCrea 3, Mirisch 4, Salter 4)
Tall T, 1957 (Boetticher 2, Boone 3, O'Sullivan 3, Scott, R. 3, Brown, Harry Joe 4)
Tall Tale Teller, 1954 (Terry 4)
Tall Tales, 1940 (Van Dyke, W. 2, Maddow 4)
Tall Target, 1951 (Mann 2, Menjou 3, Powell, D. 3, Gibbons 4)
Tall Texan, 1953 (Cobb 3, Biroc 4)
Tall Timber, 1928 (Disney 2)
Tall Timber. See Park Avenue Logger, 1937
Tall Timber Tale, 1951 (Terry 4)
Tall Trouble. See Outlaws, 1957
Tall Women. See Frauen, die durch die Holle gehen, 1966
Talto, Dalawa, Isa, 1974 (Brocka 2)
Tam Lin, 1971 (McDowall 3, Cusack 3)
Tam Lin. See Devil's Widow, 1971
Tam na horách, 1920 (Ondra 3)
Tam na konečné, 1957 (Kadár 2)
Tam Tam, 1954 (Vanel 3)
Tam Tam Mayumba, 1955 (Armendáriz 3, Mastroianni 3)
Tam za lesem, 1962 (Forman 2)
Tama no sanka, 1962 (Iwashita 3)
Tamahine, 1963 (Arnold 4, Unsworth 4)
Tamale Vendor, 1931 (Arbuckle 3)
Tamango, 1957 (Dandridge 3, Jurgens 3, Douy 4, Kosma 4, Wakhévitch 4)
Tamaño natural, 1973 (García Berlanga 2)
Tamara la complaisante, 1937 (Delannoy 2, Auric 4)
Tamarind Seed, 1974 (Edwards 2, Andrews J. 3, Homolka 3, Quayle 3, Sharif 3, Barry 4, Young, F. 4)
Tamasha, 1952 (Anand 3)
Tambari, 1977 (Geschonneck 3)
También de dolor se canta, 1950 (Infante 3)
Tambora, 1937–38 (Fejos 2)
Tambour, 1979 (Carrière 4)
Tambour battant, 1933 (Robison 2, Rosay 3)
Tambourin fantastique, 1908 (Méliès 2)
Tamburaši u Spejbla a Hurvínka, 1953 (Stallich 4)
Tame Men and Wild Women, 1925 (Roach 4)
Tamer of Wild Horses. See Krotitelj divljih konja, 1966
T'amerò sempre, 1943 (Berry 3, Cervi 3, Valli 3, Amidei 4)
Taming a Husband, 1910 (Griffith 2, Bitzer 4)
Taming Mrs. Shrew, 1912 (Porter 2)
Taming of Dorothy. See Her Favourite Husband, 1950
Taming of Grouchy Bill, 1916 (Mix 3)
Taming of Jane, 1910 (Lawrence 3)
Taming of Texas Pete, 1913 (Mix 3)
Taming of the Shrew, 1908 (Griffith 2, Lawrence 3, Bitzer 4)
Taming of the Shrew, 1929 (Fairbanks, D. 3, Pickford 3, Menzies 4, Struss 4)
Taming of the Shrew, 1967 (Zeffirelli 2, Burton 3, Cusack 3, Taylor, E. 3, York, M. 3, D'Amico 4, Dehn 4, Donati 4, Morris 4, Rota 4, Sharaff 4)
Taming of the Shrew. See Jajauma narashi, 1966
Taming of the Shrew. See Trold kan taemmes, 1914
Taming of the Snood, 1940 (Keaton 2, Bruckman 4)
Taming Target Center, 1917 (Sennett 2)

Taming the Cat, 1948 (Terry 4)
Taming the Four-Flusher. See Passing of Two-Gun Hicks, 1914
Taming the Mekong, 1965 (Van Dyke, W. 2)
Taming Wild Animals, 1910 (Mix 3)
T'ammazzo! Raccomandanti a Dio, 1968 (Ireland 3)
Tammy. See Tammy and the Bachelor, 1957
Tammy and the Bachelor, 1957 (Beavers 3, Brennan 3, Reynolds, D. 3, Wray 3, Hunter 4)
Tammy and the Doctor, 1963 (Bondi 3, Fonda, P. 3, Hunter 4)
Tammy Tell Me True, 1961 (Bondi 3, Hunter 4)
Tampico, 1944 (McLaglen 3, Robinson, E. 3, Basevi 4, Clarke, C.C. 4, Raksin 4)
Tampico. See Gran Casino, 1947
Tampon du capiston, 1950 (Braunberger 4)
Tang, 1970 (Douy 4)
Tanganyika, 1954 (De Toth 2, Heflin 3, Salter 4)
Tange Sazen, 1933 (Yamada 3)
Tange Sazen: Kenteki-hen, 1934 (Yamada 3)
Tangier, 1946 (Banton 4)
Tangier Assignment, 1955 (Rey 3)
Tangier Incident, 1953 (Brent 3)
Tangled Affair, 1913 (Sennett 2, Normand 3)
Tangled Fates, 1916 (Brady 3, Marion 4)
Tangled Hearts, 1916 (Chaney Lon 3)
Tangled Lives, 1911 (Olcott 2)
Tangled Marriage, 1912–13 (White 3)
Tangled Relations, 1912 (Lawrence 3)
Tangled Tangoists, 1914 (Bunny 3)
Tangled Travels, 1944 (Fleischer, M. and D. 2)
Tanglewood, Music School and Music Festival. See Tanglewood Story, 1950
Tanglewood Story, 1950 (Kaufman 4)
Tango del viudo, 1967 (Ruiz 2)
Tango fur dich, 1930 (Reisch 4)
Tango Notturno, 1938 (Negri 3, Wagner 4)
Tango Tangles, 1914 (Chaplin 2, Sennett 2, Arbuckle 3)
Tanin no kao, 1966 (Teshigahara 2, Kishida 3, Kyo 3, Okada 3, Takemitsu 4)
Tank, 1984 (Jones S. 3, Schifrin 4)
Tank Commando, 1959 (Corman 4)
Tank Commandos. See Tank Commando, 1959
Tank Force. See No Time to Die, 1958
Tank Tactics, 1942 (Dickinson 2)
Tanka—Traktirschitsa Protiv Otsa, 1929 (Ouspenskaya 3)
Tanks a Million, 1941 (Roach 4)
Tanks Are Coming, 1941 (Eason 4)
Tanks Are Coming, 1951 (Fuller 2)
Tanned Legs, 1929 (Neilan 2, Plunkett 4)
Tannenberg, (Staudte 2)
Tannhauser, 1913 (Cruze 2)
Tanoshiki kana jinsei, 1944 (Naruse 2)
Tansy, 1921 (Hepworth 2)
Tant d'amour perdu, 1958 (Fresnay 3)
Tant Grun, Tant Brun, och Tant Gredelin, 1945 (Fischer 4)
Tant que je vivrai, 1945 (Feuillère 3, Matras 4)
Tant que vous serez heureux, 1911 (Feuillade 2)
Tant qu'il est temps: le cancer, 1960 (Braunberger 4)
Tant qu'il y aura des femmes, 1955 (Burel 4)
Tant qu'on a la santé, 1965. See Nous n'irons plus au bois, 1963
Tantalizing Fly, 1919 (Fleischer, M. and D. 2)
Tanto va la gatta al lardo, 1978 (Cortese 3)
Tanuki, 1956 (Yoda 4)
Tanuki no kyujitsu, 1966 (Muraki 4)
Tanuki no taishou, 1965 (Muraki 4)
Tanulmány a nokrol, 1967 (Darvas 3, Latinovits 3)
Tanya's Island, 1981 (Bottin 4)
Tanyets smerti, 1916 (Mozhukin 3)
Tanz auf dem Vulkan, 1921 (Lugosi 3)
Tanz auf dem Vulkan, 1938 (Grundgens 3)
Tanz geht weiter, 1930 (Dieterle 2)
Tanz um Liebe und Gluck, 1921 (Krauss 3)
Tanzende Wien, 1927 (Andrejew 4)
Tanzer meiner Frau, 1925 (Korda 2, Leni 2)

Tanzerin Navarro, 1922 (Nielsen 3)
Tanzerin von Sanssouci, 1933 (Dagover 3)
Tap on the Shoulder, 1965 (Loach 2)
Tap Roots, 1948 (Bond 3, Hayward 3, Heflin 3, Karloff 3, Hoch 4, Wanger 4)
Tapis moquette, 1935 (Leenhardt 2)
Tapis volant, 1960 (Jarre 4)
Tapisserie au XXe siècle, 1955 (Kosma 4)
Tappa inte sugen, 1947 (Fischer 4)
Tappre soldaten Jonsson, 1956 (Nykvist 4)
Taps, 1981 (Scott, G. 3, Jarre 4, Roizman 4)
Tapum, la storia delle armi, 1958 (Bozzetto 4)
Tarahumara, 1965 (Alcoriza 4)
Tarakanova, 1930 (Artaud 3, D'Eaubonne 4, Wakhévitch 4)
Tarakanowa, 1938 (Magnani 3, Sordi 3, Andrejew 4, Annenkov 4, Courant 4, Jeanson 4)
Taran, 1951 (Biswas 4)
Tarantel, 1920 (Messter 4)
Tarantelle, 1900 (Guy 2)
Tarantola dal ventre nero, 1971 (Giannini 3, Morricone 4)
Tarantula, 1912 (Macpherson 4)
Tarantula, 1955 (Carroll L. 3, Eastwood 3, Mancini 4, Westmore, B. 4)
Taras Bulba, 1962 (Brynner 3, Curtis 3, Reynolds 4, Salt 4, Waxman 4)
Taras Shevchenko, 1951 (Bondarchuk 3)
Tarass Boulba, 1936 (Aumont 3, Baur 3, Darrieux 3, Andrejew 4, Planer 4)
Tarde del domingo, 1957 (Saura 2)
Tare, 1911 (Feuillade 2)
Tares, 1918 (Hepworth 2)
Target, 1916 (Bosworth 3)
Target, 1952 (Hunt 4)
Target, 1985 (Hackman 3)
Target Eagle. See Jugando con la muerte, 1982
Target for Killing. See Geheimnis der gelben Monche, 1966
Target for Scandal. See Washington Story, 1952
Target for Tonight, 1941 (Hitchcock 2, Watt 2, Dalrymple 4)
Target in the Sun. See Man Who Would Not Die, 1975
Target Risk, 1975 (Wynn 3)
Target Unknown, 1951 (Young, G. 3)
Target Zero, 1955 (Bronson 3, Martin, S. 3)
Targets, 1967 (Bogdanovich 2, Karloff 3, Corman 4, Fields 4, Kovacs 4)
Taris, 1931 (Vigo 2)
Taris roi de l'eau. See Taris, 1931
Tarka the Otter, 1978 (Ustinov 3)
Tarnish, 1924 (Boyd 3, Colman 3, Carré 4, Goldwyn 4, Marion 4, Miller, A. 4)
Tarnished Angel, 1938 (Miller 3, Musuraca 4, Polglase 4)
Tarnished Angels, 1957 (Sirk 2, Hudson 3, Malone 3)
Tarnished Lady, 1931 (Cukor 2, Brook 3, Banton 4, Stewart 4)
Tarnished Reputation, 1920 (Guy 2)
Tarnovskata zariza, 1980 (Danailov 3)
Tarot, 1973 (Grahame 3, Rey 3)
Tarps Elin, 1956 (Dahlbeck 3)
Tars and Spars, 1946 (Cahn 4, Walker 4, Westmore, F. 4)
Tars & Stripes, 1935 (Keaton 2)
Tartari, 1960 (Welles 2, Mature 3)
Tartarin de Tarascon, 1934 (Pagnol 2, Raimu 3, Douy 4)
Tartars. See Tartari, 1961
Tartassati, 1959 (Fabrizi 3)
Tartelette, 1968 (Grimault 4)
Tartu. See Adventures of Tartu, 1943
Tartuff, 1925 (Murnau 2, Dagover 3, Jannings 3, Krauss 3, Freund 4, Herlth 4, Mayer 4, Pommer 4, Rohrig 4)
Tartuffe. See Tartuff, 1925
Tarzan and His Mate, 1934 (O'Sullivan 3, Weissmuller 3, Clarke, C.C. 4, Gibbons 4, Gillespie 4)
Tarzan and Jane Regained . . . Sort Of, 1963 (Warhol 2, Hopper 3)
Tarzan and the Amazons, 1945 (Ouspenskaya 3, Weissmuller 3)
Tarzan and the Golden Lion, 1927 (Karloff 3, Walker 4)
Tarzan and the Huntress, 1947 (Weissmuller 3)
Tarzan and the Jungle Queen. See Tarzan's Peril, 1951
Tarzan and the Leopard Woman, 1946 (Weissmuller 3, Struss 4)

Tarzan and the Mermaids, 1948 (Florey 2, Weissmuller 3, Figueroa 4, Tiomkin 4)
Tarzan and the She Devil, 1953 (Struss 4)
Tarzan and the Slave Girl, 1950 (Horner 4)
Tarzan Escapes, 1936 (O'Sullivan 3, Weissmuller 3, Brown, K. 4)
Tarzan Finds a Son, 1939 (O'Sullivan 3, Weissmuller 3)
Tarzan, the Ape Man, 1932 (Van Dyke, W.S. 2, O'Sullivan 3, Weissmuller 3, Gillespie 4, Rosson 4)
Tarzan, The Ape Man, 1981 (Storaro 4)
Tarzan the Fearless, 1933 (Auer 3, Crabbe 3)
Tarzan Triumphs, 1943 (Weissmuller 3, Horner 4)
Tarzanova smrt, 1963 (Hrušínský 3)
Tarzan's Desert Mystery, 1943 (Weissmuller 3)
Tarzan's Greatest Adventure, 1959 (Connery 3, Quayle 3, Fisher 4)
Tarzan's Hidden Jungle, 1955 (Elam 3)
Tarzan's Magic Fountain, 1949 (Siodmak 4, Struss 4)
Tarzan's New York Adventure, 1942 (O'Sullivan 3, Weissmuller 3)
Tarzan's Peril, 1951 (Dandridge 3, Struss 4)
Tarzan's Savage Fury, 1952 (Struss 4)
Tarzan's Secret Treasure, 1941 (Fitzgerald 3, O'Sullivan 3, Weissmuller 3)
Tashkent—City of Bread. See Tashkent—gorod khlyebny, 1969
Tashkent—gorod khlyebny, 1969 (Mikhalkov-Konchalovski 2)
Task Force, 1949 (Daves 2, Brennan 3, Cooper, Gary 3, Wald 4, Waxman 4)
Tassels in the Air, 1938 (Three Stooges 3)
Taste for Women. See Aimez-vous des femmes, 1964
Taste of Catnip, 1966 (McKimson 4)
Taste of Evil, 1971 (McDowall 3, Stanwyck 3, Sangster 4)
Taste of Fear, 1961 (Lee, C. 3, Sangster 4, Slocombe 4)
Taste of Honey, 1961 (Richardson 2, Yates 2, Addison 4, Lassally 4)
Taste the Blood of Dracula, 1970 (Lee, C. 3, Bernard 4)
Tatárjárás, 1917 (Curtiz 2)
Tateshi Danpei, 1950 (Kurosawa 2, Yamada 3)
Tateshi Danpei, 1962 (Tanaka 3)
Tateshina no shiki, 1966 (Shindo 2)
Ta-ti nu-erh, 1964 (King Hu 2)
Tatjana, 1923 (Litvak 2, Tschechowa 3, Messter 4, Pommer 4)
Tatli-Bela, 1961 (Guney 2)
Tatooed Arm, 1913 (Reid 3)
Tatoué, 1968 (Gabin 3, Vierny 4)
Tatsu. See Toburoku no Tatsu, 1962
Tatsumaki bugyo, 1959 (Yamamura 3)
Tattered Dress, 1957 (Chandler 3, Crain 3)
Tattered Web, 1971 (Crawford, B. 3)
Tattle Television, 1940 (Hunt 4)
Tattoo, 1981 (Dern 3, Donaggio 4)
Tattoo. See Irezumi, 1966
Taugenichts, 1922 (Herlth 4)
Taumel. See Gehetzte Menschen, 1924
Tausend Augen des Dr. Mabuse, 1960 (Lang 2)
1001 Nacht, 1918 (Albers 3)
Tauw, 1970 (Sembene 2)
Tavasz a télben, 1917 (Curtiz 2)
Tavaszi zápor, 1932 (Fejos 2)
Tavaszni szerelem, 1921 (Banky 3)
Tavelure du pommier et du poirier, 1955 (Rabier 4)
Tavern Keeper's Daughter, 1908 (Griffith 2)
Tavern of Tragedy, 1914 (Crisp 3, Gish, D. 3)
Taverna rossa, 1939 (Valli 3)
Taverne du poisson couronne, 1947 (Berry 3, Simon, M. 3, Jeanson 4)
Tavola dei poveri, 1932 (Blasetti 2)
Taw. See Tauw, 1970
Taxi!, 1932 (Cagney 3, Raft 3, Young, L. 3)
Taxi, 1953 (Cassavetes 2, Dailey 3, Page 3, Krasner 4, Lemaire 4)
Taxi Barons, 1933 (Roach 4)
Taxi Beauties, 1928 (Sennett 2, Hornbeck 4)
Taxi Dancer, 1927 (Crawford, J. 3)
Taxi di notte, 1950 (Gallone 2, Aldo 4)
Taxi Dolls, 1929 (Sennett 2, Hornbeck 4)
Taxi Driver, 1927 (Gibbons 4)
Taxi Driver, 1954 (Anand 3, Burman 4)

Taxi Driver, 1976 (Schrader 2, Scorsese 2, De Niro 3, Keitel 3, Herrmann 4, Smith, D. 4)
Taxi for Tobruk. *See* Taxi pour Tobrouk, 1961
Taxi for Two, 1928 (Sennett 2, Hornbeck 4)
Taxi for Two, 1929 (Balcon 4)
Taxi mauve, 1977 (Astaire 3, Noiret 3, Ustinov 3, Delli Colli 4, Sarde 4)
Taxi, Mister, 1943 (Bendix 3, Roach 4)
Taxi pour Tobrouk, 1961 (Audiard 4)
Taxi Scandal, 1928 (Sennett 2, Hornbeck 4)
Taxi Spooks, 1929 (Sennett 2, Hornbeck 4)
Taxi Talks, 1930 (Tracy 3)
Taxi! Taxi!, 1927 (Horton 3)
Taxi 13, 1928 (Neilan 2, Berman 4)
Taxi Troubles, 1931 (Sennett 2)
Taxichauffeur Banz, 1957 (Schell, Maximilian 3)
Taylor Mead's Ass, 1964 (Warhol 2)
Taza, Son of Cochise, 1953 (Sirk 2, Hudson 3, Hunter 4)
Tažní ptáci, 1961 (Stallich 4)
T-Bird Gang, 1959 (Corman 4)
Tchaikovsky, 1968 (Tiomkin 4)
Tchaikovsky, 1970 (Harvey 3, Smoktunovsky 3)
Tchán Kondelík a zet Vejvara, 1929 (Vích 4)
Tchaz Boulat, 1913 (Mozhukin 3)
Tchékhov ou Le Miroir des vies perdues, 1965 (Goretta 2)
Tchin-Chao, the Chinese Conjurer. *See* Thaumaturge chinois, 1904
Te, 1963 (Szabó 2)
Te deum, 1973 (Palance 3)
Te o tsunagu kora, 1948 (Miyagawa 4)
Te o tsunagu kora, 1962 (Hani 2, Takemitsu 4)
Te quiero, 1978 (Figueroa 4)
Tea and Sympathy, 1956 (Minnelli 2, Kerr 3, Alton, J. 4, Berman 4, Deutsch 4, Rose 4)
Tea for Three, 1927 (Day 4, Gibbons 4)
Tea for Two, 1950 (Arden 3, Day 3, Sakall 3, Prinz 4)
Tea in the Garden, 1958 (Wieland 2)
Tea with a Kick, 1923 (Fazenda 3, Pitts 3)
Teacher. *See* Uchitel, 1939
Teacher and the Miracle. *See* Maestro, 1958
Teachers, 1984 (Grant, L. 3, Nolte 3)
Teacher's Beau, 1935 (Roach 4)
Teacher's Pest, 1931 (Fleischer, M. and D. 2)
Teacher's Pests, 1932 (Lantz 4)
Teacher's Pet, 1958 (Seaton 2, Day 3, Gable 3, Young, G. 3, Head 4)
Teaching Dad to Like Her, 1911 (Griffith 2, Bitzer 4)
Teaching of the Ittou Style. *See* Ittouryu shinan, 1936
Teaching the Teacher, 1921 (Roach 4)
Teachings of a Soviet Agricultural Deputation. *See* Szovjet mezőgazdasági hüldöttsek tanításai, 1951
Teahouse of the August Moon, 1956 (Brando 3, Ford, G. 3, Kyo 3, Alton, J. 4)
Teamwork, 1977 (Dunning 4)
Tear Me But Satiate Me with Your Kisses. *See* Straziami ma di baci saziami, 1968
Tear on the Page, 1915 (Loos 4)
Tear That Burned, 1914 (Gish, L. 3, Sweet 3)
Tearin' into Trouble, 1927 (Brennan 3)
Tearin' Loose, 1925 (Arthur 3)
Tears for Simon. *See* Lost, 1955
Tears of an Onion, 1938 (Fleischer, M. and D. 2)
Tears on the Lion's Mane. *See* Namidao Shishi no tategami no, 1962
Tears the World Can't See. *See* Slzy, které svět nevidí, 1961
Tease for Two, 1965 (McKimson 4)
Teaser, 1925 (Barnes 4)
Teatro Apolo, 1950 (Negrete 3)
Tebe, Front: Kazakhstan Front, 1943 (Vertov 2)
Tebukuro o nugasu otoko, 1946 (Miyagawa 4)
Técfica ed il rito, 1971 (Jancsó 2)
Technique and the Rite. *See* Técnica ed il rito, 1971
Techno-cracked, 1933 (Iwerks 4)
Techo de la ballena, 1982 (Ruiz 2, Alekan 4)
Teddy at the Throttle, 1917 (Sennett 2, Beery 3, Swanson 3)
Teddy Bears, 1907 (Porter 2)

Teddy-Bear Misha. *See* Míša Kulička, 1947
Tee for Two, 1925 (Sennett 2)
Tee for Two, 1945 (Hanna and Barbera 4)
Teen Deviyan, 1964 (Anand 3, Burman 4)
Teen Kanya, 1961 (Ray, S. 2, Chatterjee 3, Chandragupta 4, Datta 4)
Teenage Caveman, 1958 (Corman 4, Crosby 4)
Teenage Doll, 1957 (Corman 4)
Teenage Millionaire, 1962 (Pitts 3)
Teenage Rebel, 1956 (Goulding 2, Beavers 3, Rogers, G. 3, Brackett, C. 4, Lemaire 4, Reisch 4, Smith, J.M. 4, Wheeler 4)
Teenage Rebellion, 1967 (Donner 2)
Teesri Kasam, 1966 (Kapoor 2)
Teeth, 1924 (Mix 3)
Teeth of Steel, 1942 (Unsworth 4)
Teglafal mogott, 1979 (Torocsik 3)
Teheran 1943, 1979 (Jurgens 3)
Teheran 1943. *See* Teheran Incident, 1979
Teheran Incident, 1979 (Carradine 3, Delon 3)
Tehlikeli adam, 1965 (Guney 2)
Teilnehmer antwortet nicht, 1932 (Grundgens 3, Junge 4, Planer 4)
Teiva, enfant des îles, 1960 (Kosma 4)
Tejedor de milagros, 1961 (Figueroa 4)
Teka dypkuryera, 1927 (Dovzhenko 2)
Teketória, 1977 (Kroner 3, Torocsik 3)
Tekichu odan sanbyakuri, 1957 (Kurosawa 2)
Tekka bugyo, 1954 (Kinugasa 2, Hasegawa 3, Kagawa 3)
Tekken seisai, 1930 (Tanaka 3)
Tekki kushu, 1943 (Yoshimura 2, Tanaka 3)
Tel est pris qui croyait prendre, 1901 (Guy 2)
Telecouture sans fil, 1910 (Cohl 2)
Telefilm, 1928 (Fleischer, M. and D. 2)
Telefon, 1962 (Mimica 4)
Telefon, 1976 (Grgić 4)
Telefon, 1977 (Siegel 2, Bronson 3, Pleasance 3, Remick 3, Schifrin 4)
Telefoni bianchi, 1975 (Risi 2, Brazzi 3, Gassman 3, Tognazzi 3)
Telegram from New York. *See* New York expresz kabel, 1921
Telegraph Trail, 1933 (Wayne 3, Canutt 4, McCord 4)
Telephone, 1956 (Fernandel 3)
Telephone. *See* Telefon, 1962
Telephone. *See* Telefon, 1976
Telephone Belle, 1916 (Sutherland 2)
Telephone Engagement, 1912–13 (White 3)
Telephone Girl, 1912 (Reid 3)
Telephone Girl, 1927 (Brenon 2, Baxter W. 3)
Telephone Girl and the Lady, 1913 (Griffith 2, Barrymore L. 3, Marsh 3, Bitzer 4, Loos 4)
Telephone Girl series, 1924 (Garmes 4)
Telephone Rings in the Evening. *See* Denwa wa yugata ni naru, 1959
Telephone Workers, 1933 (Grierson 2)
Teletests, 1980 (Ruiz 2)
Telethon, 1978 (Leigh, J. 3)
Television Fan. *See* Zavada není na vašem přijímaci, 1961
Television Spy, 1939 (Dmytryk 2, Quinn 3, Head 4)
Telhetetlen méhecske, 1958 (Macskássy 4)
Teli sirokkó lek. *See* Sirokkó, 1969
Tell 'em Nothing, 1926 (McCarey 2, Roach 4)
Tell England, 1931 (Asquith 2)
Tell It to a Policeman, 1925 (Roach 4)
Tell It to Sweeney, 1927 (La Cava 2, Schulberg 4)
Tell It to the Judge, 1928 (McCarey 2, Roach 4)
Tell It to the Judge, 1949 (Beavers 3, Cummings 3, Russell, R. 3, Young, G. 3, Walker 4)
Tell It to the Marines, 1926 (Chaney Lon 3, Oland 3, Gibbons 4, Gillespie 4)
Tell Me a Riddle, 1980 (Douglas, M. 3, Grant, L. 3)
Tell Me Lies, 1968 (Jackson 3)
Tell Me That You Love Me, Junie Moon, 1970 (Preminger 2, Minnelli 3, Cortez 4, Kaufman 4, Wheeler 4)
Tell Me Tonight, 1932 (Gwenn 3)
Tell No Tales, 1939 (Douglas, M. 3, Ruttenberg 4)
Tell Tale Brother, 1912–13 (White 3)
Tell Tale Shells, 1912 (Dwan 2)
Tell Tale Wire, 1919 (Eason 4)

Ten Who Dared, 1960 (Disney 2, Johnson, B. 3, Iwerks 4)
10 Years of Cuba. *See* Tiz éves Kuba, 1969
Ten Years Old, 1927 (Roach 4)
Tenafly, 1973 (Ferrer, M. 3)
Tenant, 1976 (Dauphin 3, Douglas, M. 3, Winters 3)
Tenant. *See* Locataire, 1976
Tenda dos milagres, 1977 (Pereira Dos Santos 2)
Tenda rossa, 1969 (Connery 3)
Tenda rossa. *See* Krasnaya palatka, 1969
Tender Comrade, 1943 (Dmytryk 2, Darwell 3, Rogers, G. 3, Ryan 3,
    D'Agostino 4, Head 4, Trumbo 4)
Tender Dracula. *See* Tendre Dracula, 1974
Tender Enemy. *See* Tendre Ennemie, 1936
Tender Flesh. *See* Welcome to Arrow Beach, 1973
Tender Game, 1958 (Hubley 4)
Tender Hearted Boy, 1912 (Griffith 2, Barrymore L. 3, Bitzer 4)
Tender Hearts, 1909 (Griffith 2, Bitzer 4)
Tender Hour, 1927 (Wilson, C. 4)
Tender Is the Night, 1961 (King 2, Fontaine 3, Jones, J. 3, Lukas 3,
    Robards 3, Herrmann 4, Reynolds 4, Shamroy 4, Smith, J.M. 4)
Tender Loving Care, 1973 (Corman 4)
Tender Mercies, 1982 (Beresford 2, Duvall, R. 3)
Tender Scoundrel. *See* Tendre voyou, 1966
Tender Trap, 1955 (Walters 2, Reynolds, D. 3, Sinatra 3, Cahn 4,
    Epstein, J. & P. 4, Rose 4)
Tender Years, 1947 (Brown 3)
Tenderfoot, 1932 (Brown 3, Rogers, G. 3, Toland 4)
Tenderfoot Bob's Regeneration, 1912 (Bosworth 3)
Tenderfoot Courage, 1927 (Wyler 2)
Tenderfoot Days. *See* Kakedashi jidai, 1947
Tenderfoot Foreman, 1912 (Anderson G. 3)
Tenderfoot Messenger, 1910 (Anderson G. 3)
Tenderfoot Sheriff, 1913 (Anderson G. 3)
Tenderfoot's Triumph, 1915 (Mix 3)
Tenderloin, 1928 (Curtiz 2, Costello, D. 3, Zanuck 4)
Tenderloin Tragedy, 1907 (Bitzer 4)
Tenderly. *See* Suo modo di fare, 1968
Tenderness. *See* Hellyys, 1972
Tendon d'Achille, 1932 (Christian-Jaque 2)
Tendre Dracula, 1974 (Valli 3)
Tendre Dracula. *See* Grande Trouille, 1974
Tendre Ennemie, 1936 (Ophuls 2, Schufftan 4)
Tendre Poulet, 1977 (Broca 2, Girardot 3, Noiret 3, Audiard 4,
    Delerue 4)
Tendre voyou, 1966 (Belmondo 3, Dalio 3, Noiret 3, Audiard 4,
    Legrand 4, Wakhévitch 4)
Tendres requins. *See* Zarltiche Haie, 1966
Tendresse, 1931 (Christian-Jaque 2)
Tenebrae. *See* Sotto gli occhi dell'assassino, 1982
Tenente Craig, mio marito, 1950 (Fusco 4)
Ténériffe, 1932 (Allégret, Y. 2, Prévert 4)
Tengo fe en ti, 1979 (Alvarez 2)
Tengoku ni musubu koi, 1932 (Gosho 2, Takamine 3)
Tengoku to jigoku, 1963 (Kurosawa 2, Kagawa 3, Mifune 3, Shimura 3,
    Muraki 4)
Tengu-daoshi, 1944 (Kyo 3)
Teni zabytykh predkov, 1965 (Paradzhanov 2)
Tenichibo to iganosuke, 1933 (Kinugasa 2, Hasegawa 3)
Tenis, 1973 (Grgić 4)
Tenjodaifu, 1956 (Kagawa 3)
Tenka gomen, 1960 (Yamada 3)
Tenka no goikenban o Ikensuru otoko, 1947 (Yoda 4)
Tenka no igagoe, 1934 (Tsuburaya 4)
Tenka o nerau bishounen, 1955 (Miyagawa 4)
Tenka taihai, 1955 (Mifune 3, Tsukasa 3, Muraki 4)
Tenkrát o vánočích, 1958 (Kachyna 2)
Tennessee Champ, 1954 (Bronson 3, Winters 3, Wynn 3)
Tennessee Johnson, 1942 (Dieterle 2, Barrymore L. 3, Beavers 3,
    Farnum 3, Heflin 3, Balderston 4, Rosson 4, Stothart 4)
Tennessee's Partner, 1955 (Dwan 2, Dickinson 3, Reagan 3,
    Alton, J. 4, Polglase 4)
Tennis, 1949 (Cocteau 2)
Tennis. *See* Tenis, 1973

Tennis Chumps, 1949 (Hanna and Barbera 4)
Tennis Club, 1982 (Bozzetto 4)
Tennoji no harakiri, 1927 (Tanaka 3)
Tenpo hiken roku, 1927 (Tsuburaya 4)
Tenpo rokkasen: Jigokuno hanamichi, 1960 (Yamada 3)
Tenpo Yasubei, 1935 (Hasegawa 3)
Tenpyo no iraka, 1979 (Takemitsu 4, Yoda 4)
Tenryu shibuki, 1938 (Yoda 4)
Tensai sagishi monogatari: Tanuki no hanamichi, 1964 (Tsukasa 3)
Tense Alignment. *See* Blackbird Descending, 1977
Tension, 1949 (Charisse 3, Previn 4, Stradling 4)
Tension at Table Rock, 1956 (Dickinson 3, Malone 3, Biroc 4,
    Tiomkin 4)
Tent of Miracles. *See* Tenda dos milagres, 1977
Tentacles, 1977 (Huston 2, Winters 3)
Tentacles. *See* Shokkaku, 1970
Tentacles. *See* Tentacoli, 1976
Tentacles of the North, 1926 (Walker 4)
Tentacoli, 1976 (Fonda, H. 3)
Tentation de Barbizon, 1945 (Gélin 3)
Tentation de Saint-Antoine, 1898 (Méliès 2)
Tentative d'assassinat en chemin de fer, 1904 (Guy 2)
Tentative de films abstraits, 1930 (Storck 2)
Tentazioni proibite, 1963 (Bardot 3, De Carlo 3, Sordi 3)
Tenth Avenue, 1928 (Schildkraut 3)
Tenth Avenue, 1948 (Surtees 4)
Tenth Avenue Angel, 1947 (Lansbury 3, O'Brien, M. 3, Irene 4)
Tenth Victim. *See* Decima vittima, 1965
Tenth Warrant, (Johnson, N. 3)
10:30 P.M. Summer, 1966 (Dassin 2, Duras 2, Litvak 2, Finch 3,
    Mercouri 3, Schneider 3)
10,000 Kids and a Cop, 1948 (Stewart 3)
Tenting Tonight on the Old Camp Ground, 1943 (Salter 4)
Teodora, Imperatrice di Bisanzio, 1954 (Papas 3)
Teorema, 1968 (Pasolini 2, Mangano 3, Stamp 3, Morricone 4)
Tepepa, 1969 (Welles 2, Morricone 4, Solinas 4)
Tér, 1971 (Szabó 2)
Tercera palabra, 1955 (García 3, Infante 3, Alcoriza 4)
Tere Ghar Ke Samne, 1962 (Anand 3, Burman 4)
Tere Mere Sapne, 1971 (Anand 3, Burman 4)
Teresa, 1951 (Aldrich 2, Zinnemann 2, Steiger 3)
Teresa de Jesús, 1960 (Rey 3)
Teresa la ladra, 1972 (Vitti 3, Age and Scarpelli 4)
Teresa the Thief. *See* Teresa la ladra, 1972
Teresa Venerdi, 1941 (De Sica 2, Magnani 3, Zavattini 4)
Teri Ankhen, 1963 (Burman 4)
Terje vigen, 1917 (Molander 2, Sjostrom 2, Jaenzon 4, Magnusson 4)
Term of Trial, 1962 (Olivier 3, Signoret 3, Stamp 3, Morris 4)
Terminal Man, 1974 (Clayburgh 3, Segal 3)
Termination, 1966 (Baillie 2)
Terminus. 1961 (Schlesinger 2)
Termites of 1938, 1938 (Three Stooges 3)
Terms of Endearment, 1983 (MacLaine 3, Nicholson 3)
Terra bruta, 1962 (Sangster 4)
Terra di fuoco, 1938 (L'Herbier 2)
Terra em transe, 1967 (Diegues 2, Rocha 2)
Terra incognita, 1959 (Borowczyk 4)
Terra ladina, 1949 (Risi 2)
Terra madre, 1931 (Blasetti 2)
Terra promessa, 1913 (Bertini 3)
Terra sempere terra, 1951 (Cavalcanti 2)
Terra senza donne. *See* Land ohne Frauen, 1929
Terra straniera, 1953 (Di Venanzo 4)
Terra trema, 1947 (Rosi 2, Visconti 2, Aldo 4, Di Venanzo 4)
Terrace. *See* Terraza, 1962
Terrain vague, 1960 (Carné 2, Legrand 4, Renoir 4)
Terraza, 1962 (Torre-Nilsson 2, Tognazzi 3)
Terrazza, 1979 (Scola 2, Gassman 3, Mastroianni 3)
Terre, 1920 (Duvivier 2)
Terre d'amour, 1935 (Jaubert 4)
Terre de feu, 1938 (L'Herbier 2)
Terre de Flandre, 1938 (Storck 2)
Terre d'insectes, 1957 (Braunberger 4)

Terre d'oiseaux, 1957 (Braunberger 4)
Terre du Diable, 1922 (Modot 3)
Terre qui meurt, 1935 (Spaak 4)
Terre sous-marine, 1958 (Braunberger 4)
Terreur, 1924 (White 3)
Terreur de la Pampa, 1932 (Fernandel 3)
Terreur des Batignolles, 1931 (Clouzot 2)
Terreur en Oklahoma, 1951 (Piccoli 3, Douy 4)
Terreur sur la savane, 1962 (Allégret, Y. 2)
Terribile Teodoro, 1958 (Tognazzi 3)
Terrible Beauty, 1960 (Garnett 2, Cusack 3)
Terrible Beauty. See Night Fighters, 1960
Terrible Bout de papier, 1915 (Cohl 2)
Terrible Discovery, 1911 (Griffith 2, Bitzer 4)
Terrible Joe Moran, 1983 (Cagney 3)
Terrible Lesson, 1912 (Guy 2)
Terrible Night, 1912 (Guy 2)
Terrible Night. See Nuit terrible, 1896
Terrible Night. See Zlatcha notch, 1914
Terrible Ordeal. See Ildprøve, 1915
Terrible Ted, 1907 (Bitzer 4)
Terrible Teddy the Grizzly King, 1901 (Porter 2)
Terrible Toreador, 1929 (Disney 2, Iwerks 4)
Terrible Tragedy, 1916 (Hardy 3)
Terrible Troubadour, 1933 (Lantz 4)
Terrible Turkish Executioner. See Bourreau turc, 1904
Terrible Vengeance. See Straschnaia miest, 1913
Terribly Stuck Up, 1914 (Roach 4)
Terribly Talented, 1948 (Van Dyke, W. 2, Kaufman 4)
Terrier Stricken, 1952 (Jones 2)
Territoire, 1981 (Branco 4, de Almeida 4)
Territoire. See Territory, 1981
Territory, 1981 (Ruiz 2, Alekan 4)
Terror, (Johnson, N. 3)
Terror, 1917 (Hersholt 3)
Terror, 1920 (Mix 3)
Terror, 1928 (Fazenda 3, Horton 3, Musuraca 4)
Terror, 1938 (Sim 3)
Terror, 1963 (Coppola 2, Nicholson 3, Corman 4)
Terror Abroad, 1933 (Banton 4)
Terror at Black Falls, 1959 (Crosby 4)
Terror by Night, 1931 (Merkel 3)
Terror by Night, 1946 (Bruce 3, Rathbone 3, Salter 4)
Terror by Night. See Secret Witness, 1931
Terror from Space, 1962 (Carpenter 2)
Terror from the Year 5000, 1958 (Allen, D. 4)
Terror House. See Night Has Eyes, 1941
Terror in a Texas Town, 1958 (Hayden 3)
Terror in the Aisles, 1985 (Pleasance 3)
Terror in the City, 1966 (Grant, L. 3, Rosenblum 4)
Terror in the Crypt. See Cripta de l'incubo, 1963
Terror in the Midnight Sun. See Invasion of the Animal People, 1962
Terror in the Sky, 1971 (McDowall 3, Wynn 3)
Terror in the Wax Museum, 1973 (Carradine 3, Crawford, B. 3, Lanchester 3, Milland 3, Duning 4)
Terror Island, 1920 (Cruze 2)
Terror of Dr. Chaney. See Mansion of the Doomed, 1975
Terror of Sheba. See Persecution, 1974
Terror of the Tongs, 1961 (Lee, C. 3, Bernard 4, Sangster 4)
Terror on a Train. See Time Bomb, 1952
Terror Street. See Thirty-Six Hours, 1953
Terror Trail, 1933 (Mix 3)
Terror Train, 1979 (Johnson, B. 3)
Terrore dell 'Andalusia. See Carne de horca, 1954
Terrore sulla città, 1956 (Di Venanzo 4, Flaiano 4)
Terrorista, 1963 (Aimée 3, Volonté 3)
Terrorists. See Ransom, 1974
Terrors of Horseback, 1946 (Crabbe 3)
Terry Fox Story, 1983 (Hiller 2, Duvall, R. 3)
Teru kimuru hi, 1926 (Kinugasa 2)
Terza liceo, 1954 (Amidei 4)
T'es fou Marcel, 1974 (Montand 3)
Tesatura meccanica della linea a 220.000 volt, 1955 (Olmi 2)

Tesha, 1928 (Saville 2)
Tesla, 1979 (Welles 2)
Tesouro perdido. See Thesouro perdido, 1927
Tess, 1979 (Polanski 2, Cloquet 4, Sarde 4, Unsworth 4)
Tess of the D'Urbervilles, 1924 (Neilan 2, Sweet 3)
Tess of the Storm Country, 1914 (Porter 2, Pickford 3)
Tess of the Storm Country, 1922 (Hersholt 3, Pickford 3, Grot 4, Rosher 4)
Tess of the Storm Country, 1932 (Gaynor 3, Behrman 4, Levien 4)
Tess of the Storm Country, 1960 (Howe 4)
Test, 1909 (Griffith 2, Pickford 3, Bitzer 4)
Test, 1911 (Dwan 2, Lawrence 3)
Test, 1912 (Bosworth 3)
Test, 1914 (Reid 3)
Test. See False Bride, 1914
Test of Donald Norton, 1926 (Eason 4)
Test of Friendship, 1908 (Griffith 2, Lawrence 3, Bitzer 4)
Test of Honor, 1919 (Barrymore J. 3)
Test Pilot, 1938 (Fleming 2, Hawks 2, Barrymore L. 3, Gable 3, Loy 3, Merkel 3, Tracy 3, Gillespie 4, Vorkapich 4, Waxman 4, Young, W. 4)
Testa o croce, 1982 (Manfredi 3)
Testament, 1974 (Broughton 2)
Testament, 1975 (Cayatte 2, Loren 3, Ponti 4)
Testament, 1983 (Tavoularis 4)
Testament de Pierrot, 1904 (Guy 2)
Testament des Dr. Mabuse, 1933 (Lang 2, Von Harbou 4, Wagner 4)
Testament d'Orphée, 1960 (Cocteau 2, Bardot 3, Brynner 3, Gélin 3, Léaud 3, Marais 3, Auric 4)
Testament du Docteur Cordelier, 1959 (Renoir 2, Barrault 3, Modot 3, Kosma 4)
Testament du Docteur Cordelier, 1959 (Barrault 3)
Testament of Dr. Cordelier. See Testament du Docteur Cordelier, 1959
Testament of Dr. Mabuse. See Testament des Dr. Mabuse, 1933
Testament of Orpheus. See Testament d'Orphée, 1960
Testamentet. See Kaerlighedens Triumf, 1914
Testamentets Hemmelighed, 1916 (Holger-Madsen 2)
Testigos, 1968 (Villagra 3)
Testimone, 1946 (Germi 2, Zavattini 4)
Testimonies. See Vittnesbord om henne, 1962
Testing Block, 1920 (Hart 3, August 4)
Tête, 1973 (Grimault 4)
Tête blonde, 1950 (Berry 3)
Tête contre les murs, 1958 (Franju 2, Aimée 3, Brasseur 3, Jarre 4, Schufftan 4)
Tête coupée, 1915 (Feuillade 2)
Tête de turc, 1935 (Becker 2)
Tête d'horloge, 1969 (Fresnay 3)
Tête d'un homme, 1933 (Duvivier 2, Baur 3, Manès 3, Wakhévitch 4)
Tête qui rapporte. See Tête de turc, 1935
Têtes de femmes, femmes de tête, 1916 (Feyder 2)
Tetke pletke, 1969 (Grgić 4)
Tetno Polskiego Manchesteru, 1928 (Ford, A. 2)
Tetsu 'Jilba'. See Jiruba no Tetsu, 1950
Tetsu no shojo, 1928 (Tanaka 3)
Tetto, 1956 (De Sica 2, Zavattini 4)
Teufel, 1918 (Dupont 2)
Teufel fuhrt Regie. See Damonische Liebe, 1950
Teufel in Seide, 1956 (Jurgens 3, Herlth 4)
Teufel und die Madonna, 1919 (Dreier 4)
Teufels Advokat, 1977 (Audran 3)
Teufels General, 1955 (Jurgens 3)
Teufelsanbeter, 1920 (Lugosi 3)
Teufelskerl, 1935 (Baarová 3, Frohlich 3)
Teufelsreporter, 1929 (Wilder 2)
Teure Heimat, 1929 (Albers 3)
Teutonic Knights. See Krzyzacy, 1960
Tevye and His Seven Daughters. See Diamonds, 1975
Tex, 1982 (Johnson, B. 3, Donaggio 4)
Texan, 1920 (Mix 3, Furthman 4)
Texan, 1930 (Cromwell 2, Hathaway 2, Cooper, Gary 3, Wray 3, Canutt 4)
Texan Meets Calamity Jane, 1950 (Struss 4)

Texans, 1938 (Bennett J. 3, Brennan 3, Cummings 3, Scott, R. 3, Edouart 4, Head 4)
Texan's Honor, 1929 (Canutt 4)
Texans Never Cry, 1951 (Autry 3)
Texas, 1941 (Ford, G. 3, Holden 3, Trevor 3)
Texas Across the River, 1966 (Delon 3, Martin, D. 3, Cahn 4)
Texas Bad Man, 1932 (Mix 3)
Texas Bearcat, 1925 (Eason 4)
Texas, Brooklyn, and Heaven, 1948 (Murphy 3)
Texas Carnival, 1951 (Walters 2, Keel 3, Miller 3, Williams 3, Wynn 3, Pan 4, Rose 4)
Texas Chainsaw Massacre II, 1986 (Golan and Globus 4)
Texas Cyclone, 1932 (Brennan 3, Wayne 3)
Texas in 1999, 1931 (Fleischer, M. and D. 2)
Texas Kelly at Bay, 1913 (Ince 4)
Texas Kid, 1920 (Eason 4)
Texas Lady, 1955 (Colbert 3)
Texas Masquerade, 1944 (Boyd 3)
Texas Rangers, 1936 (Vidor, K. 2, MacMurray 3, Cronjager 4, Dreier 4, Head 4)
Texas Rangers Ride Again, 1940 (Crawford, B. 3, Quinn 3, Ryan 3, Head 4)
Texas Rose. See Return of Jack Slade, 1955
Texas Stampede, 1939 (Ballard 4)
Texas Steer, 1927 (Fairbanks, D. Jr. 3, Fazenda 3, Rogers, W. 3, Summerville 3)
Texas Terror, 1935 (Wayne 3)
Texas to Tokyo. See We've Never Been Licked, 1943
Texas Tom, 1950 (Hanna and Barbera 4)
Texas Tornado, 1928 (Berman 4)
Texas Tornado, 1934 (Canutt 4)
Texas Trail, 1925 (Carey 3)
Texas Trail, 1937 (Boyd 3, Head 4)
Texican, 1966 (Crawford, B. 3, Murphy 3)
Text of Light, 1974 (Brakhage 2)
Těžký život dobrodruha, 1941 (Fric 2, Hrušínský 3)
Thanatopsis, 1962 (Emshwiller 3)
Thank Heaven for Small Favors. See Drôle de paroissien, 1963
Thank You, 1925 (Ford, J. 2, Marion 4)
Thank You, Jeeves, 1936 (Niven 3)
Thank You Jesus for the Eternal Present: 1, 1973 (Landow 2)
Thank You Jesus for the Eternal Present: 2, 1974 (Landow 2)
Thank You Madame. See Im Sonnenschein, 1935
Thank You, Mr. Moto. 1937 (Carradine 3, Lorre 3, Miller, V. 4)
Thank Your Lucky Stars, 1943 (Bogart 3, Davis 3, De Havilland 3, Flynn 3, Garfield 3, Horton 3, Lupino 3, McDaniel 3, Sakall 3, Sheridan 3, Edeson 4, Frank and Panama 4, Grot 4, Prinz 4)
Thanks a Million, 1935 (Powell, D. 3, Johnson 4, Zanuck 4)
Thanks for Everything, 1938 (Menjou 3, Brown, Harry Joe 4, Zanuck 4)
Thanks for the Memory, 1938 (Fleischer, M. and D. 2, Hope 3, Dreier 4, Head 4, Struss 4)
Thark, 1932 (Wilcox 2)
That Awful Brother, 1911 (Lawrence 3)
That Cat. See Až přijde kocour, 1963
That Certain Age, 1938 (Cooper, J 3, Douglas, M. 3, Durbin 3, Pasternak 4)
That Certain Feeling, 1937 (Wallis 4)
That Certain Feeling, 1956 (Hope 3, Saint 3, Sanders 3, Bumstead 4, Diamond 4, Frank and Panama 4, Head 4)
That Certain Summer, 1972 (Sheen 3)
That Certain Thing, 1928 (Capra 2, Walker 4)
That Certain Woman, 1937 (Goulding 2, Crisp 3, Davis 3, Fonda, H. 3, Haller 4, Orry-Kelly 4, Steiner 4)
That Championship Season, 1982 (Dern 3, Keach 3, Mitchum 3, Sheen 3, Golan and Globus 4)
That Chink at Golden Gulch, 1910 (Griffith 2, Bitzer 4)
That Christmas. See Tenkrát o vánocích, 1958
That Cold Day in the Park, 1969 (Altman 2, Kovacs 4)
That Crying Baby, 1912–13 (White 3)
That Damned Hot Day of Fire. See Quel caldo maledetto giorno di fuoco, 1968
That Dangerous Age, 1950 (Loy 3, Périnal 4)

That Dare Devil, 1911 (Sennett 2)
That Darn Cat, 1965 (Disney 2, Lanchester 3, McDowall 3)
That Devil Bateese, 1918 (Chaney Lon 3)
That Female Scent. See Profumo di donna, 1974
That Forsyte Woman, 1949 (Flynn 3, Garson 3, Leigh, J. 3, Pidgeon 3 Young, R. 3, Kaper 4, Plunkett 4, Ruttenberg 4)
That Funny Feeling, 1965 (Carroll L. 3, O'Connor 3, Whitlock 4)
That Gal of Burke's, 1916 (Borzage 2)
That Gang of Mine, 1940 (Muse 3, Katzman 4)
That Girl from College. See Sorority House, 1939
That Girl from Paris, 1936 (Auer 3, Ball 3, Berman 4, Hunt 4)
That Girl Montana, 1921 (Sweet 3)
That Hagen Girl, 1947 (Reagan 3, Temple 3, Freund 4, Waxman 4)
That Hamilton Woman, 1941 (Korda 2, Guffey 4, Hornbeck 4, Reisch 4, Rozsa 4, Wheeler 4)
That Hamilton Woman. See Lady Hamilton, 1941
That Happy Couple. See Esa pareja feliz, 1951
That Happy Pair. See Esa pareja feliz, 1951
That House in the Outskirts. See Aquella casa en las afueras, 1980
That I May Live, 1937 (Dwan 2, Chaney Lon, Jr. 3)
That is the Port Light. See Are ga minato no tomoshibi da, 1961
That Joyous Eve . . .. See Makkers staakt uw wild geraas, 1960
That Kind of Girl. See Models, Inc., 1952
That Kind of Love. See Taková láska, 1959
That Kind of Woman, 1959 (Lumet 2, Loren 3, Sanders 3, Warden 3, Wynn 3, Head 4, Kaufman 4, Ponti 4)
That Lady, 1955 (De Havilland 3, Lee, C. 3, Rosay 3, Addison 4, Junge 4, Krasker 4, Veiller 4)
That Lady in Ermine, 1948 (Lubitsch 2, Preminger 2, Fairbanks, D. Jr. 3, Grable 3, Lemaire 4, Newman 4, Pan 4, Raphaelson 4, Shamroy 4, Wheeler 4)
That Little Band of Gold, 1915 (Sennett 2, Arbuckle 3, Fazenda 3, Normand 3)
That Little Big Fellow, 1927 (Fleischer, M. and D. 2)
That Lucky Touch, 1975 (Cobb 3, Moore, R. 3, Winters 3, York, S. 3
That Mad Mr Jones. See Fuller Brush Man, 1947
That Man from Rio. See Homme de Rio, 1964
That Man in Istanbul. See Estambul 65, 1965
That Man's Here Again, 1937 (Trumbo 4)
That Midnight Kiss, 1949 (Taurog 2, Barrymore E. 3, Grayson 3, Wynn 3, Ames 4, Pasternak 4, Surtees 4)
That Minstrel Man, 1914 (Sennett 2, Arbuckle 3)
That Model from Paris, 1926 (Florey 2)
That Most Important Thing: Love. See Important c'est aimer, 1974
That Mothers Might Live, 1938 (Zinnemann 2)
That Naughty Girl. See Cette sacrée gamine, 1956
That Navy Spirit. See Hold 'em Navy, 1937
That Night, 1917 (Sennett 2, Beery 3)
That Night, 1928 (McCarey 2, Roach 4)
That Night Adventure. See Sonoyo no bouken, 1948
That Night at Varennes. See Nuit de Varennes, 1981
That Night in London, 1932 (Donat 3, Wimperis 4)
That Night in Rio, 1941 (Seaton 2, Ameche 3, Faye 3, Miranda 3, Sakall 3, Banton 4, Day 4, Meredyth 4, Newman 4, Pan 4, Shamroy 4)
That Night with You, 1945 (Keaton 2, Salter 4)
That Noise, 1961 (Godfrey 4)
That Obscure Object of Desire. See Cet obscur objet de désir, 1977
That Old Gang of Mine, 1931 (Fleischer, M. and D. 2)
That Other Girl, 1912–13 (White 3)
That Other Woman, 1942 (Duryea 3, Day 4)
That Ragtime Band, 1913 (Sennett 2)
That Royle Girl, 1926 (Griffith 2, Fields, W.C. 3)
That Splendid November. See Bellissimo novembre, 1968
That Springtime Fellow, 1915 (Sennett 2)
That Tender Age. See Fleur de l'age ou Les Adolescentes, 1964
That They May Live. See J'accuse, 1937
That Touch of Mink, 1962 (Day 3, Grant, C. 3, Young, G. 3, Duning 4 Lourié 4, Westmore, B. 4)
That Uncertain Feeling, 1941 (Lubitsch 2, Arden 3, Douglas, M. 3, Meredith 3, Oberon 3, Irene 4, Reisch 4, Stewart 4)
That Way With Women, 1947 (Greenstreet 3, McCord 4)

That Wonderful Urge, 1948 (Power 3, Tierney 3, Clarke, C.C. 4, Lemaire 4, Newman 4)

That's a Good Girl, 1932 (Buchanan 3)

That's Dancing!, 1985 (Mancini 4)

That's Entertainment, 1974 (Astaire 3, Crosby 3, Kelly, Gene 3, Minnelli 3, Rooney 3, Sinatra 3, Stewart 3, Taylor, E. 3, Laszlo 4, Mancini 4)

That's Entertainment, Part II, 1976 (Astaire 3, Bass 4)

That's Him, 1918 (Lloyd 3, Roach 4)

That's Life. See Oto życie, 1969

That's Me, 1962 (Arkin 3)

That's My Baby, 1926 (Garnett 2)

That's my Baby, 1944 (Arlen 3)

That's My Boy, 1932 (Crabbe 3, Marsh 3, August 4, Krasna 4)

That's My Boy, 1951 (Lewis 2, Marsh 3, Martin, D. 3, Garmes 4, Head 4, Wallis 4)

That's My Line, 1931 (Arbuckle 3)

That's My Man, 1947 (Borzage 2, Ameche 3, Canutt 4, Gaudio 4, Salter 4)

That's My Meat, 1931 (Arbuckle 3)

That's My Mommy, 1955 (Hanna and Barbera 4)

That's My Pup, 1952 (Hanna and Barbera 4)

That's My Uncle, 1935 (Pearson 2)

That's My Wife, 1929 (Laurel and Hardy 3, Roach 4)

That's Right—Your're Wrong, 1939 (Ball 3, Horton 3, Menjou 3, Duning 4, Polglase 4)

That's the Spirit, 1945 (Keaton 2, Salter 4)

That's the Way of the World, 1975 (Keitel 3)

That's Where the Action Is, 1965 (de Antonio 2)

That's Worth While?, 1921 (Calhern 3)

Thau le pêcheur, 1957 (Coutard 4)

Thaumaturge chinois, 1904 (Méliès 2)

Thaumetopoea, 1960 (Guillemot 4)

Thé à la menthe, 1962 (Cybulski 3)

Thé chez la concierge, 1907 (Feuillade 2)

Theater in Trance, 1981 (Fassbinder 2)

Théâtre de Monsieur et Madame Kabal, 1965 (Borowczyk 4)

Théâtre National Populaire, 1956 (Franju 2, Philipe 3, Fradetal 4, Jarre 4)

Theatre of Blood, 1973 (Hawkins 3, Price 3)

Theatre of Death, 1967 (Lee, C. 3)

Theatre of Life. See Jinsei gekijo, 1952

Theatre of Life. See Jinsei gekijo seishun-hen, 1958

Theft of the Mona Lisa. See Raub der Mona Lisa, 1931

Their 1st Divorce, 1911 (Sennett 2)

Their 1st Divorce Case, 1911 (Sennett 2)

Their 1st Execution, 1913 (Sennett 2)

Their 1st Kidnapping Case, 1912 (Sennett 2)

Their Big Moment, 1934 (Cruze 2, Pitts 3, Summerville 3, Plunkett 4, Steiner 4)

Their Cheap Vacation, 1914 (Beery 3)

Their Compact, 1917 (Bushman 3)

Their Everyday Life. See Ich dzień powszedni, 1963

Their Fates Sealed, 1911 (Sennett 2)

Their First Acquaintance, 1914 (Crisp 3, Gish, D. 3)

Their First Mistake, 1932 (Laurel & Hardy 3, Roach 4)

Their First Misunderstanding, 1911 (Gaudio 4, Ince 4)

Their Hero Son, 1912 (Dwan 2)

Their Honeymoon, 1916 (Hardy 3)

Their Hour, 1915 (Meredyth 4)

Their Husbands, 1913 (Sennett 2)

Their Mad Moment, 1931 (Baxter W. 3, Pitts 3)

Their Masterpiece, 1913 (Dwan 2)

Their Own Desire, 1929 (Montgomery 3, Shearer 3, Stone 3, Adrian 4, Daniels 4, Day 4, Gibbons 4, Marion 4)

Their Promise, 1913 (Anderson G. 3)

Their Purple Moment, 1928 (Laurel and Hardy 3, Roach 4)

Their Secret Affair. See Top Secret Affair, 1957

Their Social Splash, 1915 (Sennett 2, Summerville 3)

Their Ups and Downs, 1914 (Sennett 2, Arbuckle 3)

Their Vacation, 1916 (Hardy 3)

Thelema Abbey, 1955 (Anger 2)

Thelma Jordan, 1950 (Young, V. 4)

Them, 1954 (Gwenn 3, Kaper 4)

Them Thar Hills, 1934 (Laurel & Hardy 3, Roach 4)

Them Was the Happy Days, 1916 (Lloyd 3, Roach 4)

Theme. See Tema, 1980

Thèmes et variations, 1928 (Dulac 2)

Themroc, 1973 (Piccoli 3)

Then Came Bronson, 1969 (Sheen 3)

Then I'll Come Back To You, 1916 (Brady 3, Marion 4)

Then kurote-gume, 1937 (Yamada 3)

Then There Were None, 1974 (Audran 3)

Theodor Hiernels oder: Wie man ehem. Hofkoch wird, 1972 (Syberberg 2)

Theodora Goes Wild, 1936 (Douglas, M. 3, Dunne 3, Buchman 4, Walker 4)

Théodore et Cie., 1933 (Raimu 3, Douy 4)

Theorum. See Teorema, 1968

There Ain't No Justice, 1939 (Balcon 4)

There Ain't No Santa Claus, 1926 (Roach 4)

There Are Mountains and Rivers. See Sanga ari, 1962

There Auto Be a Law, 1953 (McKimson 4)

There Burned a Flame. See Det brinner en eld, 1943

There Came a Man: A Man Named John. See E venne un uomo, 1965

There Goes My Girl, 1937 (Sothern 3, August 4, Musuraca 4, Walker 4)

There Goes My Heart, 1938 (McLeod 2, Langdon 3, March 3, Irene 4, Roach 4)

There Goes the Bride, 1925 (Roach 4)

There Goes the Bride, 1932 (Matthews 3, Balcon 4)

There Goes the Bride, 1980 (Crawford, B. 3)

There Goes the Groom, 1937 (Meredith 3, Sothern 3, Krasner 4)

There He Goes, 1925 (Capra 2, Sennett 3, Langdon 3)

There is a Season, 1953 (Van Dyke, W. 2)

There Is Another Sun, 1951 (Harvey 3)

There Is No Crossing Under Fire. See V ogne broda net, 1968

There is No Escape, 1952 (Henreid 3)

There Lived a Thrush. See Zil pevcij drozd, 1972

There They Go-Go-Go!, 1957 (Jones 2)

There Was a Crooked Man, 1960 (York, S. 3)

There Was a Crooked Man, 1970 (Mankiewicz 2, Douglas, K. 3, Fonda, H. 3, Grant, L. 3, Meredith 3, Oates 3, Westmore, P. 4, Westmore, W. 4)

There Was a Father. See Chichi ariki, 1942

There Was a Lad. See Zhivet takoi paren, 1964

There Was a Miller on the River. See Jsouc na rece mlynář jeden, 1971

There Was a Singing Blackbird. See Zil pevcij drozd, 1972

There Was Once a King. See Bly jednou jeden Král, 1955

There You Are!, 1926 (Garnett 2, Gibbons 4, Gillespie 4)

There's a Future in It, 1944 (Alwyn 4)

There's a Girl in My Heart, 1949 (Chaney Lon, Jr. 3)

There's a Girl in My Soup, 1970 (Boulting 2, Hawn 3, Sellers 3)

There's Always a Price Tag. See Retour de Manivelle, 1957

There's Always a Woman, 1938 (Astor 3, Blondell 3, Douglas, M. 3, Hayworth 3, Ryskind 4)

There's Always Tomorrow, 1934 (Taylor, R. 3)

There's Always Tomorrow, 1956 (Sirk 2, Bennett J. 3, Darwell 3, MacMurray 3, Stanwyck 3, Hunter 4)

There's Always Vanilla, 1972 (Romero 2)

There's Magic in Music, 1941 (Dreier 4, Head 4)

There's Music in the Hair, 1913 (Bunny 3)

There's No Business Like Show Business, 1954 (Dailey 3, Monroe 3, O'Connor 3, Alton, R. 4, Cole 4, Lemaire 4, Newman 4, Shamroy 4, Trotti 4, Wheeler 4)

There's No Place Like Home, 1917 (Weber 2)

There's One Born Every Minute, 1942 (Taylor, E. 3, Salter 4)

There's Something About a Soldier, 1934 (Fleischer, M. and D. 2)

There's Something About a Soldier, 1943 (Fleischer, M. and D. 2, Beavers 3)

There's That Woman Again, 1938 (Costello, M. 3, Douglas, M. 3, Epstein, J. & P. 4, Walker 4)

Therese, 1916 (Sjostrom 2, Jaenzon 4, Magnusson 4)

Therese. See Thérèse Desqueyroux, 1962

Thérèse and Isabelle, 1968 (Auric 4)

Thérèse Desqueyroux, 1962 (Franju 2, Noiret 3, Jarre 4, Matras 4)

Thérèse Martin, 1938 (Ibert 4)
Thérèse Raquin, 1928 (Feyder 2, Andrejew 4)
Thérèse Raquin, 1953 (Carné 2, Signoret 3, Spaak 4)
Thérèse Raquin. See Du sollst nicht Ehe brechen, 1928
Thermogenesis, 1972 (Emshwiller 2)
These Are the Damned. See Damned, 1963
These Children Are Safe, 1939 (Alwyn 4)
These Dangerous Years, 1957 (Wilcox 2, Neagle 3)
These Foolish Times. See Shin baka jidai, 1946
These Glamour Girls, 1939 (Ayres 3, Turner, L. 3, Walker 3)
These Kids Are Grown-Ups. See Sont grands ces petits, 1979
These Thousand Hills, 1958 (Fleischer, R. 2, Clarke, C.C. 4,
    Lemaire 4, Wheeler 4)
These Three, 1936 (Wyler 2, Brennan 3, Hopkins, M. 3, McCrea 3,
    Oberon 3, Day 4, Goldwyn 4, Mandell 4, Newman 4, Toland 4)
These Wilder Years, 1956 (Cagney 3, Pidgeon 3, Stanwyck 3, Ames 4,
    Rose 4)
Thesouro perdido, 1927 (Mauro 2)
They All Came Out, 1939 (Tourneur, J. 2)
They All Died Laughing. See Jolly Bad Fellow, 1963
They All Kissed the Bride, 1942 (Burke 3, Crawford, J. 3,
    Douglas, M. 3, Irene 4, Walker 4)
They All Laughed, 1983 (Bogdanovich 2, Hepburn, A. 3)
They Also Kill. See Some May Live, 1967
They Asked for It, 1939 (Cortez 4)
They Call It Sin, 1932 (Brent 3, Calhern 3, Merkel 3, Young, L. 3)
They Call Me Mister Tibbs!, 1970 (Poitier 3, Jones 4, Mirisch 4)
They Came by Night, 1940 (Gilliat 4)
They Came from Beyond Space, 1967 (Francis 4)
They Came to a City, 1944 (Dearden 2, Balcon 4)
They Came to Blow Up America, 1943 (Bond 3, Sanders 3, Basevi 4,
    Friedhofer 4)
They Came to Cordura, 1959 (Rossen 2, Cooper, Gary 3, Hayworth 3,
    Heflin 3, Cahn 4, Guffey 4)
They Came to Rob Las Vegas, 1968 (Cobb 3)
They Came to Rob Las Vegas. See Las Vegas 500 millones, 1968
They Caught the Ferry. See Naaede Faergen, 1948
They Dare Not Love, 1941 (Whale 2, Brent 3, Cushing 3, Lukas 3,
    Bennett 4, Planer 4, Vajda 4)
They Died With Their Boots On, 1941 (Walsh 2, Bosworth 3,
    Cody 3, De Havilland 3, Flynn 3, Greenstreet 3, Kennedy, A. 3,
    McDaniel 3, Quinn 3, Young, G. 3, Canutt 4, Eason 4, Glennon 4,
    Orry-Kelly 4, Steiner 4, Wallis 4)
They Done Him Right, 1933 (Lantz 4)
They Drive by Night, 1940 (Walsh 2, Bogart 3, Lupino 3, Raft 3,
    Sheridan 3, Deutsch 4, Edeson 4, Wald 4, Wallis 4)
They Flew Alone, 1942 (Wilcox 2, Neagle 3, Alwyn 4)
They Fought for the Fatherland. See Oni srazhalis za rodinu,
    1975
They Gave Him a Gun, 1937 (Van Dyke, W.S. 2, Tracy 3, Rosson 4)
They Go Boom, 1929 (Laurel and Hardy 3, Roach 4)
They Got Me Covered, 1942 (Preminger 2, Hope 3, Lamour 3, Meek 3,
    Goldwyn 4, Head 4, Kurnitz 4, Mandell 4, Maté 4, Mercer 4)
They Had to See Paris, 1929 (Borzage 2, Rogers, W. 3, Levien 4)
They Just Had to Get Married, 1933 (Pitts 3, Summerville 3)
They Knew Mayakovsky. See Oni znali Mayakovsky, 1955
They Knew Mr. Knight, 1945 (Greenwood 3)
They Knew What They Wanted, 1940 (Carey 3, Laughton 3,
    Lombard 3, Malden 3, Kanin 4, Newman 4, Polglase 4, Pommer 4,
    Stradling 4)
They Knew What They Wanted, 1941 (Stradling 4)
They Know What to Do. See Věděli si rady, 1950
They Leap Into Life. See Sprung ins Leben, 1924
They Learned About Women, 1930 (Wood 2, Love 3, Gibbons 4)
They Live Again, 1938 (Zinnemann 2)
They Live By Night, 1948 (Ray, N. 2, Houseman 4, Schary 4, Schnee 4)
They Loved Life. See Kanal[bl]p/, 1957
They Made Me a Criminal, 1939 (Berkeley 2, Bond 3, Garfield 3,
    Rains 3, Sheridan 3, Glazer 4, Grot 4, Howe 4, Steiner 4, Wallis 4)
They Made Me a Fugitive, 1947 (Cavalcanti 2, Howard, T. 3)
They Meet Again, 1941 (Hersholt 3)
They Met in a Taxi, 1936 (Bond 3, Wray 3)
They Met in Argentina, 1941 (O'Hara 3, Hunt 4)

They Met in Bombay, 1941 (Brown 2, Gable 3, Lorre 3, Russell, R. 3,
    Adrian 4, Daniels 4, Loos 4, Stothart 4, Stromberg 4)
They Met in the Dark, 1943 (Mason 3)
They Might Be Giants, 1971 (Scott, G. 3, Woodward 3, Barry 4)
They Only Come Out at Night, 1975 (Warden 3)
They Only Kill Their Masters, 1972 (Allyson 3, O'Brien, E. 3)
They Ran for Their Lives, 1968 (Carradine 3)
They Rode West, 1954 (Reed, D. 3, Nugent 4, Wald 4)
They Serve Abroad, 1942 (Boulting 2)
They Shall Have Music, 1939 (Brennan 3, McCrea 3, Goldwyn 4,
    Newman 4, Riskin 4, Toland 4)
They Shoot Horses, Don't They?, 1969 (Pollack 2, Dern 3, Fonda, J. 3,
    York, S. 3, Young, G. 3, Green, J. 4, Horner 4)
They Staked Their Lives. See Med livet som insats,
    1940
They Were Expendable, 1945 (Edwards 2, Ford, J. 2, Bond 3,
    Montgomery 3, Reed, D. 3, Wayne 3, August 4, Stothart 4)
They Were Five. See Belle equipe, 1936
They Were Not Divided, 1950 (Lee, C. 3)
They Were Sisters, 1945 (Mason 3)
They Who Dare, 1954 (Milestone 2, Bogarde 3)
They Who Step on the Tiger's Tail. See Tora no o o fumu otokotachi,
    1945
They Won't Believe Me, 1947 (Hayward 3, Young, R. 3, Boyle 4,
    Harrison 4)
They Won't Forget, 1937 (Leroy 2, Rossen 2, Cook 3, Rains 3,
    Turner, L. 3, Deutsch 4, Edeson 4)
They Would Elope, 1909 (Griffith 2, Pickford 3, Bitzer 4)
They're a Weird Mob, 1966 (Powell 2, Rafferty 3)
They're Off. See Straight, Place, and Show, 1938
They've Kidnapped Anne Benedict. See Abduction of Saint Anne,
    1975
Thicker Than Water, 1935 (Laurel & Hardy 3, Roach 4)
Thick-Walled Room. See Kabe atsuki heya, 1956
Thief, 1920 (White 3)
Thief, 1952 (Milland 3)
Thief, 1971 (Dickinson 3)
Thief, 1981 (Caan 3, Weld 3)
Thief. See Ladrone, 1979
Thief and the Cobbler, 1981 (Price 3)
Thief and the Girl, 1911 (Griffith 2, Bitzer 4)
Thief Catcher, 1914 (Sennett 2)
Thief Catcher. See Her Friend the Bandit, 1914
Thief in Paradise, 1925 (Colman 3, Goldwyn 4, Grot 4, Marion 4,
    Miller, A. 4)
Thief in the Dark, 1928 (Edeson 4)
Thief of Bagdad, 1924 (Walsh 2, Fairbanks, D. 3, Johnson, N. 3,
    Wong 3, Edeson 4, Grot 4, Menzies 4)
Thief of Bagdad, 1940 (Crichton 2, Powell and Pressburger 2, Veidt 3,
    Biro 4, Ellenshaw 4, Hornbeck 4, Korda 4, Krasker 4,
    Mathieson 4, Menzies 4, Périnal 4, Rozsa 4, Unsworth 4)
Thief of Bagdad, 1978 (McDowall 3, Stamp 3, Ustinov 3)
Thief of Bagdad. See Ladro di Bagdad, 1960
Thief of Damascus, 1952 (Chaney Lon, Jr. 3, Henreid 3, Katzman 4)
Thief of Hearts. See Hjertetyven, 1943
Thief of Paris, 1967 (Carrière 4)
Thief of Paris. See Voleur, 1967
Thief Who Came to Dinner, 1973 (Hill, W. 2, Bisset 3, Clayburgh 3,
    Oates 3, Mancini 4)
Thief's Wife, 1912 (Dwan 2)
Thieves, 1976 (Fosse 2, McCambridge 3)
Thieves Fall Out, 1941 (Darwell 3, Quinn 3)
Thieves' Gold, 1918 (Ford, J. 2, Carey 3)
Thieves' Highway, 1949 (Dassin 2, Cobb 3, Cortese 3, Lemaire 4,
    Newman 4, Wheeler 4)
Thieves Like Us, 1974 (Altman 2, Duvall, S. 3)
Thigh Line Lyre Triangular, 1961 (Brakhage 2)
Thin Air. See Body Stealers, 1969
Thin Ice, 1937 (Chaney Lon, Jr. 3, Henie 3, Power 3, Cronjager 4)
Thin Ice, 1981 (Gish, L. 3)
Thin Line. See Onna no naka ni iru tanin, 1966
**Thin Man, 1934 (Van Dyke, W.S. 2, Loy 3, O'Sullivan 3, Powell, W. 3,
    Gibbons 4, Goodrich and Hackett 4, Howe 4, Stromberg 4)**

Thin Man Goes Home, 1944 (Loy 3, Meek 3, Muse 3, Powell, W. 3, Freund 4, Irene 4, Kurnitz 4, Riskin 4)
Thin Red Line, 1964 (Warden 3, Arnold 4)
Thin Twins, 1929 (Roach 4)
Thing, 1951 (Hawks 2, D'Agostino 4, Dunn 4, Lederer 4, Tiomkin 4)
Thing, 1982 (Carpenter 2, Pleasance 3, Bottin 4, Morricone 4, Whitlock 4)
Thing from Another World. See Thing, 1951
Thing We Love, 1918 (Reid 3)
Thing with Two Heads, 1972 (Milland 3, Baker 4)
Things Are Looking Up, 1935 (Leigh, V. 3, Balcon 4)
Things Happen at Night, 1948 (Lassally 4)
Things in Life. See Choses de la vie, 1970
Things in Their Season, 1974 (Neal 3)
Things of Life. See Choses de la Vie, 1970
Things to Come, 1935 (Crichton 2, Hardwicke 3, Massey 3, Richardson 3, Hornbeck 4, Korda 4, Krasker 4, Mathieson 4, Menzies 4, Périnal 4)
Think, 1964 (Bernstein 4)
Think 20th, 1967 (Hayward 3, Heston 3)
Think Fast, Mr. Moto, 1937 (Lorre 3)
Think of a Number. See Taenk på ett tal, 1969
Third Alarm, 1930 (Bosworth 3, Hersholt 3)
Third Bad Name. See Daisan no Akumyo, 1963
Third Day, 1965 (Marshall 3, McDowall 3, Surtees 4)
Third Degree, 1926 (Curtiz 2, Costello, D. 3, Blanke 4)
Third Dimensional Murder, 1940 (Sidney 2)
Third Eye, 1920 (Oland 3)
Third Eye, 1969 (Meredith 3)
Third Finger, Left Hand, 1940 (Costello, M. 3, Douglas, M. 3, Loy 3, Meek 3)
Third Generation. See Dritte Generation, 1979
Third Girl from the Left, 1973 (Curtis 3, Novak 3)
Third Key. See Long Arm, 1956
Third Lover. See Oeil du malin, 1962
Third Man, 1949 (Reed 2, Welles 2, Cotten 3, Howard, T. 3, Valli 3, Korda 4, Krasker 4, Selznick 4)
Third Man on the Mountain, 1959 (Disney 2, Alwyn 4)
Third Part of the Night, 1971 (Nowicki 3)
Third Party Speculation. See Emily, 1979
Third Secret, 1964 (Crichton 2, Attenborough 3, Hawkins 3, Slocombe 4)
Third Squad. See Třetí rota, 1931
Third String, 1932 (Pearson 2)
Third Time Lucky, 1931 (Balcon 4)
Third Time Lucky, 1948 (Adam 4)
Third Voice, 1960 (O'Brien, E. 3, Haller 4)
Thirst, 1917 (Sennett 2)
Thirst. See Desert Nights, 1929
Thirst. See Törst, 1949
Thirst. See Zhazhda, 1959
13. See Trinadtsat, 1937
13 at Dinner, 1985 (Dunaway 3, Ustinov 3)
13 Chairs. See Tretton stolar, 1945
13 Down, 1915 (Bushman 3)
13 Ghosts, 1960 (Biroc 4)
13 Hours by Air, 1936 (Leisen 2, Bennett J. 3, MacMurray 3, Head 4)
Thirteen Men and a Girl. See Letzte Kompagnie, 1930
13 Most Beautiful Boys, 1965 (Warhol 2)
13 Most Beautiful Women, 1965 (Warhol 2)
13 Rue Madeleine, 1946 (Hathaway 2, Cagney 3, Jaffe 3, Malden 3, Basevi 4, de Rochemont 4, Newman 4, Zanuck 4)
Thirteen Steps to Death. See Why Must I Die?, 1960
Thirteen Trunks of Mr. O.F. See Koffer des Herrn O.F., 1931
13 Washington Square, 1928 (Hersholt 3, Pitts 3)
13 West Street, 1962 (Ladd 3, Steiger 3, Duning 4)
Thirteen Women, 1932 (Dunne 3, Loy 3, Steiner 4)
Thirteenth Chair, 1929 (Browning 2, Lugosi 3, Adrian 4, Day 4, Gibbons 4)
Thirteenth Chair, 1937 (Stone 3, Clarke, C.C. 4)
Thirteenth Commandment, 1920 (Nilsson 3)
Thirteenth Guest, 1932 (Rogers, G. 3)
Thirteenth Hour, 1927 (Barrymore L. 3)

Thirteenth Juror, 1927 (Bushman 3, Nilsson 3, Pidgeon 3)
Thirteenth Letter, 1950 (Preminger 2, Boyer 3, Darnell 3, Rosay 3, Koch 4, La Shelle 4, Lemaire 4, North 4, Wheeler 4)
13th Man, 1913 (Bushman 3)
Thirty Day Princess, 1934 (Sturges, P. 2, Grant, C. 3, Sidney 3, Schulberg 4, Shamroy 4)
Thirty Days, 1916 (Hardy 3)
Thirty Days, 1922 (Cruze 2, Reid 3, Brown, K. 4)
Thirty Days. See Silver Lining, 1932
35 Boulevard General Koenig, 1971 (Markopoulos 2)
30 Foot Bride of Candy Rock, 1957 (Costello 3)
30 Is a Dangerous Age, Cynthia, 1968 (Moore, D. 3)
39 Steps, 1935 (Hitchcock 2, Carroll M. 3, Donat 3, Balcon 4, Bennett 4, Reville 4)
39 Steps, 1960 (More 3)
39 Steps, 1979 (Mills 3)
Thirty Seconds Over Tokyo, 1944 (Edwards 2, Leroy 2, Johnson, V. 3, Mitchum 3, Tracy 3, Walker 3, Gibbons 4, Gillespie 4, Irene 4, Rosson 4, Shearer 4, Stothart 4, Surtees 4, Trumbo 4, Wheeler 4)
Thirty Six Chowringhee Lane, 1981 (Chandragupta 4)
36 Hours, 1953 (Duryea 3)
36 Hours, 1965 (Seaton 2, Saint 3, Head 4, Tiomkin 4)
36 Hours to Kill, 1936 (Fetchit 3, Burnett 4, Miller, A. 4)
Thirty three-go-sha oto nashi, 1955 (Tsukasa 3)
Thirty Times Your Money. See Heja Roland, 1966
32 Rue Montmartre. See Derrière la façade, 1939
Thirty Years of Fun, 1963 (Keaton 2)
This Above All, 1942 (Litvak 2, Bruce 3, Cooper, Gladys 3, Fontaine 3, Power 3, Day 4, Miller, A. 4, Newman 4, Zanuck 4)
This Ancient Law. See Alte Gesetz, 1923
This Angry Age. See Barrage contre le Pacifique, 1958
This Charming Couple, 1949 (Van Dyke, W. 2)
This Could Be the Night, 1957 (Wise 2, Douglas, P. 3, Pitts 3, Simmons 3, Cahn 4, Lennart 4, Pasternak 4)
This Day and Age, 1933 (DeMille 2, Carradine 3, Dreier 4)
This Doesn't Happen Here. See Sånt händer inte här, 1950
This Dusty World. See Jinkyo, 1924
This Earth Is Mine, 1959 (King 2, Hudson 3, Rains 3, Cahn 4, Friedhofer 4, Robinson 4)
This England, 1923 (Matthews 3)
This England, 1941 (McDowall 3)
This Freedom, 1923 (Brook 3)
This Girl for Hire, 1983 (Ferrer, J. 3)
This Greedy Old Skin. See Gametsui yatsu, 1960
This Gun for Hire, 1942 (De Carlo 3, Ladd 3, Lake 3, Preston 3, Burnett 4, Dreier 4, Head 4, Seitz 4)
This Happy Breed, 1944 (Lean 2, Holloway 3, Johnson, C. 3, Mills 3, Coward 4, Green, G. 4, Havelock-Allan 4)
This Happy Feeling, 1958 (Edwards 2, Astor 3, Jurgens 3, Reynolds, D. 3, Hunter 4)
This Happy Life. See Tanoshiki kana jinsei, 1944
This Hero Stuff, 1919 (Furthman 4)
This House Possessed, 1981 (Bennett J. 3)
This Is a Life?, 1955 (Freleng 4)
This Is Cinerama, 1952 (Schoedsack 2, Cooper 4, O'Brien 4, Steiner 4)
This Is Colour, 1942 (Cardiff 4)
This Is Dynamite, 1952 (Head 4)
This is England. See Heart of Britain, 1941
This is Heaven, 1929 (Banky 3, Barnes 4, Goldwyn 4, Toland 4)
This Is It, 1971 (Broughton 2)
This Is It, 1982 (Snow 2)
This is Korea!, 1951 (Ford, J. 2, Ireland 3)
This Is Lloyd's, 1962 (Quayle 3)
This is London, 1956 (Harrison 3)
This Is Me, 1979 (Patel 4)
This Is My Affair, 1937 (Carradine 3, McLaglen 3, Stanwyck 3, Taylor, R. 3, MacGowan 4, Trotti 4)
This Is My Affair. See I Can Get It for You Wholesale, 1951
This Is My Ducky Day, 1961 (Hanna and Barbera 4)
This Is My Love, 1954 (Darnell 3, Duryea 3, Reed, D. 3, Waxman 4)
This Is My Street, 1963 (Hurt, J. 3)
This Is Russia, 1957 (Wilson, C. 4)
This Is the Air Force, 1947 (Halas and Batchelor 2)

This is the Army, 1943 (Curtiz 2, Costello, D. 3, Merkel 3, Reagan 3, Glennon 4, Orry-Kelly 4, Polito 4, Prinz 4, Robinson 4, Steiner 4, Wallis 4)
This Is the Life, 1914 (Beery 3)
This Is the Life, 1917 (Walsh 2)
This Is the Life, 1933 (Milland 3)
This Is the Life, 1935 (Neilan 2, Trotti 4)
This Is the Life, 1944 (O'Connor 3, Wray 3)
This Is the Night, 1932 (Grant, C. 3)
This Island Earth, 1955 (Mancini 4, Salter 4)
This Kind of Love. See Quaeta specie d'amore, 1972
This Land is Full of Life. See Din tillvaros land, 1940
This Land Is Mine, 1943 (Renoir 2, Laughton 3, O'Hara 3, Sanders 3, D'Agostino 4, Lourié 4, Nichols 4)
This Land Is Mine, 1959 (Simmons 3)
This Life We Live, 1913 (Anderson G. 3)
This Little Piggie Went to Market, 1934 (Fleischer, M. and D. 2)
This Love of Ours, 1945 (Dieterle 2, Oberon 3, Rains 3, Ballard 4, Banton 4, Salter 4)
This Love Thing, 1970 (Halas and Batchelor 2)
This Mad World, 1930 (Rathbone 3, Adrian 4, Gibbons 4, Rosson 4)
This Man in Paris, 1939 (Sim 3, Havelock-Allan 4)
This Man Is Dangerous, 1941 (Mason 3)
This Man Is Dangerous, 1953 (Crawford, J. 3)
This Man is Dangerous. See Cet homme est dangereux, 1953
This Man Is Mine, 1934 (Bellamy 3, Dunne 3, Murfin 4, Plunkett 4, Polglase 4, Steiner 4)
This Man Is News, 1938 (Dearden 2, Sim 3, Havelock-Allan 4, Head 4)
This Man Must Die. See Que la bête meure, 1969
This Man Reuter. See Dispatch from Reuter's, 1940
This Man Stands Alone, 1979 (Gossett 3)
This Man's Navy, 1945 (Edwards 2, Wellman 2, Beery 3, Chase 4, Irene 4)
This Marriage Business, 1938 (August 4)
This Modern Age, 1931 (Bosworth 3, Crawford, J. 3, Rosher 4)
This Modern Age, No. 16. See British—Are They Artistic?, 1947
This Must Not Be Forgotten. See It Mustn't Be Forgotten, 1954
This Precious Freedom, 1942 (Surtees 4)
This Property Is Condemned, 1966 (Coppola 2, Pollack 2, Bronson 3, Redford 3, Wood 3, Edouart 4, Head 4, Houseman 4, Howe 4, Westmore, W. 4)
This Rebel Breed, 1960 (Cannon 3)
This Reckless Age, 1932 (Mankiewicz 2)
This Rugged Land, 1962 (Hiller 2, Bronson 3)
This Savage Land, 1969 (Scott, G. 3, Rosenman 4)
This Side of Heaven, 1934 (Howard 2, Bainter 3, Barrymore L. 3, Merkel 3, Rosson 4)
This Special Friendship. See Amitiés particulières, 1964
This Sporting Age, 1932 (Nichols 4)
This Sporting Life, 1963 (Anderson 2, Reisz 2, Jackson 3, Roberts 3)
This Strange Passion. See Gitana tenias que ser, 1953
This Thing Called Love, 1929 (Bennett C. 3, Harlow 3, Pitts 3)
This Thing Called Love, 1941 (Seaton 2, Cobb 3, Douglas, M. 3, Russell, R. 3, Walker 4)
This Time for Keeps, 1942 (Gardner 3)
This Time for Keeps, 1947 (Donen 2, Durante 3, Williams 3, Freund 4, Irene 4, Pasternak 4)
This Time Let's Talk About Men. See Questa volta parliamo di uomini, 1965
This Transient Life, 1971 (Okada 3)
This Was a Woman, 1947 (Adam 4, Lassally 4)
This Was Japan, 1945 (Wright 2)
This Way Out, 1915 (Hardy 3)
This Way Please, 1937 (Florey 2, Grable 3, Dreier 4, Head 4, Prinz 4)
This Way, That Way. See Ano te kono te, 1952
This Week of Grace, 1933 (Fields, G. 3)
This Woman, 1924 (Bow 3, Fazenda 3)
This Woman Is Dangerous, 1952 (McCord 4)
This Woman Is Mine, 1941 (Brennan 3, Bruce 3, Carroll L. 3, Krasner 4, Miller, S. 4)
This World. See Kataku, 1979
This Year's Love. See Kotoshi no koi, 1962
This'll Make You Whistle, 1937 (Wilcox 2, Buchanan 3)

Thodisi bewafai, 1980 (Azmi 3)
Thomas Crown Affair, 1968 (Ashby 2, Hill, W. 2, Jewison 2, Dunaway 3, McQueen, S. 3, Boyle 4, Legrand 4, van Runkle 4, Wexler 4)
Thomas Graals basta barn, 1914 (Sjostrom 2)
Thomas Graals basta barn, 1918 (Molander 2, Sjostrom 2, Stiller 2, Magnusson 4)
Thomas Graals basta film, 1917 (Molander 2, Sjostrom 2, Stiller 2, Magnusson 4)
Thomas Graal's Best Child. See Thomas Graals basta barn, 1918
Thomas Graal's Best Film. See Thomas Graals basta film, 1917
Thomas Graal's Best Picture. See Thomas Graals basta film, 1917
Thomas Graal's First Child. See Thomas Graals basta born, 1918
Thomas Graals myndling, 1922 (Molander 2)
Thomas Graal's Ward. See Thomas Graals myndling, 1922
Thomas l'imposteur, 1964 (Cocteau 2, Franju 2, Auric 4, Fradetal 4)
Thomas the Imposter. See Thomas l'imposteur, 1964
Thomasine and Bushrod, 1974 (Ballard 4)
Thompson's Night Out, 1908 (Bitzer 4)
Thorns and Orange Blossoms, 1922 (Schulberg 4, Struss 4)
Thoroughbred, 1916 (Sullivan 4)
Thoroughbreds. See Silks and Saddles, 1928
Thoroughbred's Don't Cry, 1937 (Garland 3, Rooney 3, Brown, N. 4)
Thoroughly Modern Millie, 1967 (Hill, G.R. 2, Andrews J. 3, Bernstein 4, Cahn 4, Hunter 4, Previn 4, Westmore, B. 4, Whitlock 4)
Thorvaldsen, 1949 (Dreyer 2)
Those Athletic Girls, 1918 (Sennett 2, Fazenda 3)
Those Awful Hats, 1909 (Griffith 2, Lawrence 3, Bitzer 4)
Those Beautiful Dames, 1934 (Freleng 4)
Those Bitter Sweets, 1915 (Sennett 2)
Those Blasted Kids. See Pokkers Unger, 1947
Those Boys, 1909 (Griffith 2, Bitzer 4)
Those Calloways, 1965 (Disney 2, Brennan 3, Steiner 4)
Those College Girls, 1915 (Sennett 2, Summerville 3)
Those Country Kids, 1914 (Sennett 2, Arbuckle 3, Normand 3)
Those Damned Savages. See Maudits sauvages, 1971
Those Daring Young Men in Their Jaunty Jalopies. See Monte Carlo or Bust, 1969
Those Endearing Young Charms, 1945 (Young, R. 3)
Those Gentlemen Who Have a Clean Sheet. See Herren mit der weissen Weste, 1970
Those Good Old Days, 1913 (Sennett 2, Normand 3)
Those Happy Days, 1914 (Sennett 2, Arbuckle 3)
Those Hicksville Boys, 1911 (Sennett 2)
Those High Grey Walls, 1939 (Vidor, C. 2)
Those Little Flowers, 1913 (Gish, D. 3)
Those Love Pangs, 1914 (Chaplin 2, Sennett 2)
Those Magnificent Men in Their Flying Machines, 1965 (Cassel 3, Sordi 3, Zanuck 4)
Those Redheads from Seattle, 1953 (Moorehead 3, Head 4, Mercer 4)
Those Three French Girls, 1930 (Freed 4, Gibbons 4)
Those Troublesome Tresses, 1913 (Bunny 3)
Those We Love, 1932 (Florey 2, Astor 3, Edeson 4)
Those Were the Days, 1934 (Mills 3)
Those Were the Days, 1940 (Holden 3, Ladd 3, Dreier 4, Head 4, Young, V. 4)
Those Were the Years. See C'eravamo tanti amati, 1974
Those Who Are Late. See Spóźnieni przechodnie, 1962
Those Who Dance, 1924 (Baxter W. 3, Love 3, Sweet 3)
Those Who Dance, 1930 (Boyd 3)
Those Who Make Tomorrow. See Asu o tsukuru hitobito, 1946
Those Who Pay, 1918 (Ince 4, Sullivan 4)
Those without Sin, 1917 (Neilan 2, Sweet 3)
Those Wonderful Men with a Crank. See Báječní muži s klikou, 1978
Thot Fal'n, 1978 (Brakhage 2)
Thou Shalt Honor Thy Wife. See Du Skal Aere Din Hustru, 1925
Thou Shalt Not, 1910 (Griffith 2, Walthall 3, Bitzer 4)
Thou Shalt Not Covet, 1912 (Bunny 3)
Thou Shalt Not Kill, 1982 (Grant, L. 3)
Thou Shalt Not Kill. See Tu ne tueras point, 1961
Thou Shalt Not Steal, 1917 (Ruttenberg 4)
Thought to Kill, 1953 (Fairbanks, D. Jr. 3)

Thousand and One Nights, 1945 (Wilde 3, Winters 3)
Thousand and One Nights. *See* Fiore delle mille e una notte, 1974
Thousand Carat Diamond. *See* Supercolpo da 7 miliard, 1966
Thousand Clowns, 1965 (Holliday 3, Robards 3, Rosenblum 4)
Thousand Cranes. *See* Senbazuru, 1969
Thousand Cranes. *See* Senba-zuru, 1953
Thousand Dollar Husband, 1916 (Sweet 3)
Thousand Eyes of Dr. Mabuse. *See* Tausend Augen des Dr. Mabuse, 1960
Thousand to One, 1920 (Bosworth 3)
Thousands Cheer, 1943 (Sidney 2, Allyson 3, Astor 3, Ball 3, Charisse 3, Garland 3, Grayson 3, Horne 3, Kelly, Gene 3, O'Brien, M. 3, Powell, E. 3, Reed, D. 3, Rooney 3, Sothern 3, Edens 4, Gibbons 4, Irene 4, Pasternak 4, Stothart 4)
Thread of Destiny, 1910 (Griffith 2, Pickford 3, Bitzer 4)
Thread of Life, 1912 (Dwan 2)
Threads of Fate, 1915 (Chaney Lon 3)
Threat, 1960 (Cronjager 4)
Threatening Sky, 1965 (Anderson 2)
Three. *See* Tri, 1967
Three Ages, 1923 (Keaton 2, Beery 3, Hardy 3, Bruckman 4, Schenck 4)
3 American Beauties, 1906 (Porter 2)
3 American LP's. *See* 3 amerikanische LPs, 1969
Three Apples, 1979 (Popescu-Gopo 4)
Three Arabian Nuts, 1951 (Three Stooges 3)
Three Bad Men, 1926 (Ford, J. 2)
Three Bad Men and a Girl, 1915 (Ford, J. 2)
Three Bad Men in a Hidden Fortress. *See* Kakushi toride no san-akunin, 1958
Three Badgers. *See* Sanbiki no tanuki, 1966
Three Bears, 1925 (Lantz 4)
Three Bears, 1934 (Terry 4)
Three Bears, 1935 (Iwerks 4)
Three Bears, 1939 (Terry 4)
Three Bites of the Apple, 1967 (Fabrizi 3)
Three Black Bags, 1913 (Bunny 3)
Three Blind Mice, 1938 (Cook 3, Darwell 3, McCrea 3, Niven 3, Young, L. 3, Zanuck 4)
Three Blind Mice, 1945 (Dunning 4)
Three Blondes in His Life, 1960 (Haller 4)
Three Brave Men, 1957 (Borgnine 3, Milland 3, Clarke, C.C. 4, Dunne 4, Lemaire 4, Salter 4)
Three Brothers, 1915 (Reid 3)
Three Brothers. *See* Tre fratelli, 1981
Three Caballeros, 1944 (Disney 2, Iwerks 4)
Three Came Home, 1950 (Negulesco 2, Colbert 3, Hayakawa 3, Clarke, C.C. 4, Friedhofer 4, Johnson 4, Krasner 4, Lemaire 4)
Three Cases of Murder, 1954 (Welles 2, Dalrymple 4, Mathieson 4, Périnal 4)
Three Cheers for Love, 1936 (Dmytryk 2, Cummings 3, Head 4, Young, V. 4)
Three Cheers for the Irish, 1940 (Bacon 2, Deutsch 4, Rosher 4, Wald 4, Wallis 4)
Three Chumps Ahead, 1934 (Roach 4)
Three Clear Sundays, 1965 (Loach 2)
Three Cockeyed Sailors. *See* Sailors Three, 1940
Three Coins in the Fountain, 1954 (Negulesco 2, Brazzi 3, Jourdan 3, Webb 3, Cahn 4, Jeakins 4, Krasner 4, Lemaire 4, Reynolds 4, Wheeler 4, Young, V. 4)
Three Comrades, 1938 (Borzage 2, Mankiewicz 2, Sullavan 3, Taylor, R. 3, Young, R. 3, Freund 4, Gibbons 4, Ruttenberg 4, Vorkapich 4, Waxman 4)
Three Comrades. *See* Tre Kammerater, 1912
Three-Cornered Hat. *See* It Happened in Spain, 1934
Three-Cornered Moon, 1933 (Arlen 3, Colbert 3, Banton 4, Schulberg 4, Shamroy 4)
Three Crosses. *See* Krizova trojka, 1948
Three Daring Daughters, 1948 (MacDonald 3, Ames 4, Irene 4, Levien 4, Pasternak 4, Stothart 4)
Three Dark Horses, 1952 (Three Stooges 3)
Three Daughters of the West, 1911 (Dwan 2)
Three Dawns to Sydney, 1948 (Alwyn 4)

Three Days of the Condor, 1975 (Pollack 2, Dunaway 3, Redford 3, Robertson 3, Von Sydow 3, De Laurentiis 4, Houseman 4, Roizman 4, Semple 4)
Three Days of Victor Chernyshev. *See* Tri dnia Viktora Chernysheva, 1968
Three Dumb Clucks, 1937 (Three Stooges 3, Bruckman 4)
Three Encounters. *See* Tri vstrechi, 1948
Three Fables of Love. *See* Quatre Vérités, 1962
Three Faces East, 1926 (Brook 3, Walthall 3, Sullivan 4)
Three Faces East, 1930 (Von Stroheim 2, Bennett C. 3)
Three Faces of Eve, 1957 (Cobb 3, Woodward 3, Cortez 4, Johnson 4, Lemaire 4, Wheeler 4)
Three Faces of Sin. *See* Puits aux trois verités, 1961
Three Faces West, 1940 (Coburn, C. 3, Wayne 3, Alton, J. 4, Young, V. 4)
Three Fat Men, 1965 (Batalov 3)
Three Foolish Wives, 1924 (Sennett 2)
Three for Bedroom C, 1952 (Dumont 3, Swanson 3, Laszlo 4)
Three for the Show, 1955 (Grable 3, Lemmon 3, Carmichael 4, Cole 4, Duning 4, Wald 4)
Three Forbidden Stories. *See* Tre storie proibite, 1952
Three Friends, 1912 (Griffith 2, Barrymore L. 3, Carey 3, Sweet 3, Walthall 3, Bitzer 4)
Three Gamblers, 1913 (Anderson G. 3)
Three Generations of Danjuro. *See* Danjuro sandai, 1944
Three Girls About Town, 1941 (Blondell 3, Planer 4)
Three Girls from Rome. *See* Ragazze di Piazza di Spagna, 1952
Three Girls Lost, 1931 (Wayne 3, Young, L. 3)
Three Godfathers, 1936 (Mankiewicz 2, Brennan 3, Stone 3, Ruttenberg 4)
Three Godfathers, 1948 (Ford, J. 2, Armendáriz 3, Bond 3, Darwell 3, Johnson, B. 3, Marsh 3, Wayne 3, Basevi 4, Cooper 4, Hoch 4, Nugent 4)
Three Gold Coins, 1920 (Mix 3)
Three Golden Hairs of Old Man Know-All. *See* Tři zlaté vlasy děda Vševěda, 1963
Three Guys Named Mike, 1951 (Walters 2, Johnson, V. 3, Keel 3, Wyman 3, Kaper 4)
Three Hams on Rye, 1950 (Three Stooges 3)
Three Ha'pence a Foot, 1936 (Holloway 3)
Three Hearts for Julia, 1943 (Douglas, M. 3, Sothern 3, Irene 4, Stothart 4)
Three Heroines. *See* Tri geroini, 1938
Three Hollywood Girls, 1930 (Arbuckle 3)
Three Hours, 1927 (Bosworth 3)
Three Hours. *See* Deserteur, 1938
Three Hours to Kill, 1954 (Andrews D. 3, Reed, D. 3, Brown, Harry Joe 4)
300 Miles through Enemy Lines. *See* Tekichu odan sanbyakuri, 1957
300 Din Ke Baad, 1938 (Biswas 4)
365 Days, 1922 (Roach 4)
365 Nights in Hollywood, 1934 (Faye 3)
365 Nights in Osaka. *See* Sanbyaku-rokujugo-ya: Osaka-hen, 1948
365 Nights in Tokyo. *See* Sanbyaku-rokujugo-ya Tokyo-hen, 1948
300 Spartans, 1961 (Richardson 3)
300 Spartans. *See* Lion of Sparta, 1961
Three Husbands, 1950 (Arden 3, Burke 3, Darwell 3, Planer 4)
Three in a Closet, 1920 (Bruckman 4)
Three Installations, 1952 (Anderson 2, Lassally 4)
Three into Two Won't Go, 1969 (Steiger 3, Bloom 3, Lai 4, Lassally 4)
Three Is a Crowd, 1951 (Terry 4)
Three Is a Family, 1944 (Bainter 3, McDaniel 3)
Three Jumps Ahead, 1923 (Ford, J. 2, Mix 3)
Three Keys, 1924 (Haller 4)
Three Kids and a Queen, 1935 (D'Agostino 4, Waxman 4)
Three Kings and a Queen, 1939 (Hutton 3)
Three Lazy Mice, 1935 (Lantz 4)
Three Legionnaires, 1937 (Meek 3)
Three Little Pigskins, 1934 (Three Stooges 3)
Three Little Beers, 1935 (Three Stooges 3, Bruckman 4)
Three Little Bops, 1956 (Freleng 4)
3 Ghosts, 1922 (Goulding 2)
Three Little Girls in Blue, 1946 (Newman 4)

Three Women, 1924 (Lubitsch 2, Blanke 4, Kraly 4)
Three Women, 1977 (Cromwell 2, Duvall, S. 3, Spacek 3)
Three Women Around Yoshinaka. *See* Yoshinaka o meguru sannin no onna, 1956
Three Women of France, 1917 (Meredyth 4)
Three Word Brand, 1921 (Hart 3, August 4)
Three Worlds of Gulliver, 1960 (Harryhausen 4, Herrmann 4)
Three X Gordon, 1918 (Gilbert 3)
Three Young Texans, 1953 (Lemaire 4)
Three's a Crowd, 1927 (Langdon 3)
Three's Company, 1953 (Fairbanks, D. Jr. 3)
Threshold, 1972 (Le Grice 2)
Threshold, 1981 (Sutherland 3)
Threshold. *See* Subah, 1983
Thrifty Cubs, 1953 (Terry 4)
Thrill Chaser, 1923 (Miller, V. 4)
Thrill of a Lifetime, 1937 (Crabbe 3, Grable 3, Lamour 3, Dreier 4, Head 4, Prinz 4, Young, V. 4)
Thrill of a Romance, 1945 (Walters 2, Johnson, V. 3, Williams 3, Cahn 4, Irene 4, Pasternak 4, Stradling 4)
Thrill of Brazil, 1946 (Miller 3, Wynn 3, Cole 4, Polglase 4)
Thrill of It All, 1963 (Jewison 2, Day 3, Pitts 3, Boyle 4, Hunter 4)
Thriller, 1984 (Price 3, Bernstein 4)
Thrilling, 1965 (Scola 2, Manfredi 3, Sordi 3)
Thrills and Chills, 1938 (Fleischer, M. and D. 2)
Thro' Life's Window, 1914 (Costello, M. 3)
Throne of Blood. *See* Kumonosujo, 1957
Throne of Fire. *See* Processo de las brujas, 1970
Through a Glass Darkly. *See* Såsom i en spegel, 1961
Through a Glass Window, 1922 (Rosson 4)
Through a Lens Brightly, 1966 (Markopoulos 2)
Through Austin Glen, 1906 (Bitzer 4)
Through Darkened Vales, 1911 (Griffith 2, Sweet 3, Bitzer 4)
Through Days and Months. *See* Hi mo tsuki mo, 1969
Through Dumb Luck, 1911 (Sennett 2)
Through Fire and Water, 1923 (Brook 3)
Through His Wife's Picture, 1911 (Sennett 2)
Through Jealous Eyes, 1911 (Lawrence 3)
Through the Back Door, 1921 (Menjou 3, Pickford 3, Rosher 4)
Through the Breakers, 1909 (Griffith 2, Bitzer 4)
Through the Dark, 1924 (Bosworth 3, Moore, C. 3, Marion 4)
Through the Storm, 1914 (Bushman 3)
Through the Storm. *See* Prairie Schooners, 1940
Through the Years, 1953 (Keel 3)
Through Thick and Thin, 1927 (Eason 3)
Through Trackless Sands, 1914 (Anderson G. 3)
Through Trials to Victory. *See* Gennem Kamp til Sejr, 1911
Throwing the Bull, 1946 (Terry 4)
Thrown Stone. *See* Feldobott ko, 1968
Thru Different Eyes, 1929 (Baxter W. 3, Fetchit 3, Sidney 3)
Thru Different Eyes, 1942 (Clarke, C.C. 4, Day 4, Raksin 4)
Thugs with Dirty Mugs, 1939 (Avery 2)
Thumb Fun, 1952 (McKimson 4)
Thumb Print, 1911 (Costello, M. 3, Talmadge, N. 3)
Thumb Tripping, 1972 (Dern 3)
Thumbelina, 1955 (Reiniger 2)
Thumbs Up, 1943 (Lanchester 3, Cahn 4)
Thunder, 1929 (Chaney Lon 3, Stromberg 4)
Thunder Across the Pacific. *See* Wild Blue Yonder, 1951
Thunder Afloat, 1939 (Beery 3, Seitz 4)
Thunder Alley, 1984 (Golan and Globus 4)
Thunder and Lightning, 1977 (Corman 4)
Thunder and Lightning. *See* Blixt och dunder, 1938
Thunder Bay, 1953 (Mann 2, Duryea 3, Stewart 3, Daniels 4, Hayes 4)
Thunder Below, 1932 (Lukas 3, Buchman 4, Lang 4)
Thunder Birds, 1942 (Wellman 2, Tierney 3, Basevi 4, Day 4)
Thunder County, 1973 (Rooney 3)
Thunder in the City, 1937 (Bruce 3, Richardson 3, Robinson, E. 3, Rozsa 4, Sherwood 4)
Thunder in the Dust. *See* Sundowners, 1949
Thunder in the East, 1953 (Vidor, C. 2, Boyer 3, Kerr 3, Ladd 3, Friedhofer 4, Garmes 4, Head 4, Swerling 4)
Thunder in the East. *See* Battle, 1934

Thunder in the Night, 1935 (Glennon 4)
Thunder in the Sun, 1959 (Chandler 3, Hayward 3, Cortez 4, Lemaire 4, Leven 4)
Thunder in the Valley, 1947 (Gwenn 3, Basevi 4, Clarke, C.C. 4, Lemaire 4)
Thunder Island, 1963 (Nicholson 3)
Thunder Mountain, 1925 (Pitts 3)
Thunder Mountain, 1964 (Arlen 3)
Thunder of Drums, 1961 (Boone 3, Bronson 3)
Thunder of the Sea, 1936 (Anhalt 4)
Thunder on the Hill, 1951 (Sirk 2, Colbert 3, Cooper, Gladys 3, Daniels 4, Salter 4)
Thunder Over Arizona, 1956 (Elam 3)
Thunder Over Mexico, 1933 (Eisenstein 2)
Thunder over Texas, 1934 (Ulmer 2)
Thunder over the Plains, 1953 (De Toth 2, Cook 3, Scott, R. 3, Glennon 4)
Thunder Pass, 1954 (Carradine 3)
Thunder Riders, 1928 (Wyler 2)
Thunder Road, 1958 (Mitchum 3)
Thunder Rock, 1942 (Boulting 2, Mason 3, Redgrave, M. 3)
Thunder Trail, 1937 (Head 4, Struss 4)
Thunderball, 1965 (Connery 3, Adam 4, Barry 4, Douy 4)
Thunderbirds, 1942 (Trotti 4, Zanuck 4)
Thunderbirds, 1952 (Bond 3, Young, V. 4)
Thunderbolt, 1912 (Cruze 2)
Thunderbolt, 1929 (Hathaway 2, Von Sternberg 2, Arlen 3, Wray 3, Dreier 4, Furthman 4, Mankiewicz 4)
Thunder-Bolt, 1947 (Wyler 2)
Thunderbolt and Lightfoot, 1974 (Cimino 2, Bridges 3, Eastwood 3, Kennedy, G. 3)
Thunderhead, Son of Flicka, 1945 (McDowall 3, Clarke, C.C. 4)
Thundering Dawn, 1923 (Nilsson 3, Wong 3, Coffee 4)
Thundering Fleas, 1926 (Hardy 3, Roach 4)
Thundering Gunslingers, 1944 (Crabbe 3)
Thundering Herd, 1925 (Hathaway 2, Howard 2, Cooper, Gary 3)
Thundering Herd, 1933 (Hathaway 2, Carey 3, Crabbe 3, Scott, R. 3)
Thundering Hoofs, 1941 (Hunt 4)
Thundering Landlords, 1925 (Roach 4)
Thundering Romance, 1924 (Arthur 3)
Thundering Taxis, 1933 (Roach 4)
Thundering Through, 1925 (Arthur 3)
Thundering Toupees, 1929 (Roach 4)
Thundering West, 1939 (Ballard 4)
Thunderstorm, 1957 (Lee, B. 3)
Thursday. *See* Giovedi, 1963
Thursday the Twelfth. *See* Pandemonium, 1982
Thursday's Child, 1943 (Granger 3)
Thursday's Child, 1983 (Rowlands 3)
Thursday's Children, 1953 (Anderson 2, Burton 3, Lassally 4)
Thursday's Game, 1974 (Burstyn 3, Wilder 3, Biroc 4)
Thursdays, Miracle. *See* Jueves, milagro, 1957
Thus Another Day. *See* Kyo mo mata kakute arinan, 1959
Thus Spake Theodor Herzl, 1967 (Cavalcanti 2)
Thus the Divine Wind Arrives. *See* Kakute kamikaze wa fuku, 1944
Thwarted Vengeance, 1911 (Anderson G. 3)
THX 1138, 1971 (Coppola 2, Lucas 2, Duvall, R. 3, Pleasance 3, Schifrin 4, Murch 4)
Thy Name Is Woman, 1924 (Niblo 2, Novarro 3, Carré 4, Meredyth 4)
Thy Neighbor's Wife, 1953 (Haas 3)
Thy Soul Shall Bear Witness. *See* Korkarlen, 1921
Ti attende una corda . . . Ringo. *See* Ritorno di Clint il solitario, 1972
Ti conosco, mascherina!, 1942 (Baarová 3)
Ti ho sempre amato, 1953 (Delli Colli 4)
Ti ho sposato per allegria, 1967 (Vitti 3, Age and Scarpelli 4)
Ti ritroverò, 1948 (Fusco 4)
Tiara Tahiti, 1962 (Dauphin 3, Mason 3, Mills 3)
Tiburoneros, 1962 (Alcoriza 4)
Tic, 1908 (Feuillade 2)
Tichý týden v domě, 1969 (Švankmajer 4)
Tick . . . Tick . . . Tick . . ., 1969 (March 3)
Tick Tock Tuckered, 1944 (Clampett 4)
Ticket of Leave, 1936 (Havelock-Allan 4)

Ticket of Leave Man, 1914 (White 3)
Ticket to Paradise. *See* Biljett till paradiset, 1962
Ticket to Tomahawk, 1950 (Baxter A. 3, Brennan 3, Dailey 3, Elam 3, Monroe 3, Lemaire 4)
Tickle Me, 1965 (Taurog 2, Presley 3)
Ticklish Affair, 1963 (Sidney 2, Jones S. 3, Young, G. 3, Gillespie 4, Krasner 4, Pasternak 4)
Tidal Wave. *See* Portrait of Jennie, 1949
Tide of Empire, 1929 (Dwan 2, Adorée 3, Gibbons 4, Young, W. 4)
Tide of Fortune, 1910 (Lawrence 3)
Tides of Barnegat, 1917 (Neilan 2, Sweet 3)
Tides of Passion, 1925 (Blackton 2, Marsh 3)
Tie That Binds, 1915 (Anderson G. 3)
Tied for Life, 1933 (Langdon 3)
Tief im Bohmerwald, 1908 (Porten 3, Messter 4)
Tiefe Furchen, 1965 (Geschonneck 3)
Tiefland, 1922 (Dagover 3)
Tiefland, 1954 (Riefenstahl 2)
Tiempo es el viento, 1976 (Alvarez 2)
Tiens, vous êtes à Poitiers?, 1916 (Feyder 2)
Tiera sedienta, 1945 (Rey 3)
Tierarzt Dr. Vlimmen, 1945 (Wegener 3)
Tierra baja, 1950 (Armendáriz 3)
Tierra brutal, 1962 (Rey 3)
Tierra de los toros, 1924 (Musidora 3)
Tierra de pasiónes, 1944 (Armendáriz 3, Negrete 3)
Tierra del Fuego se apaga, 1955 (Fernández 2, Figueroa 4)
Tierra prometida, 1972 (Littin 2, Villagra 3)
Tierra y el cielo, 1977 (Gómez, M. 2)
Ties. *See* Legato, 1977
Tieta d'agreste, 1981 (Loren 3)
Tifusari, 1963 (Mimica 4)
Tigar, 1978 (Samardžić 3)
Tiger, 1930 (Hoffmann 4)
Tiger. *See* Tigar, 1978
Tiger and the Flame. *See* Jhansi ri-rani, 1952
Tiger and the Pussycat. *See* Tigre, 1967
Tiger Bay, 1933 (Wong 3)
Tiger Bay, 1959 (Mills 3)
Tiger Hunt in Assam, 1958 (Van Dyke, W. 2)
Tiger in the Sky. *See* McConnell Story, 1955
Tiger in the Smoke, 1956 (Arnold 4)
Tiger Leaped and Killed, But He Will Die, He Will Die. *See* Tigre salto y mato . . . pero morira . . . morira, 1973
Tiger Likes Fresh Blood. *See* Tigre aime la chair fraiche, 1964
Tiger Love, 1924 (Hawks 2, Clarke, C.C. 4)
Tiger Makes Out, 1967 (Hiller 2, Hoffman 3, Wallach 3)
Tiger Man, 1918 (Hart 3, August 4)
Tiger Rose, 1923 (Franklin 2, Goulding 2, Rosher 4)
Tiger Rose, 1929 (MacMurray 3, Summerville 3, Velez 3, Gaudio 4)
Tiger Shark, 1932 (Hawks 2, Arlen 3, Robinson, E. 3, Gaudio 4, Orry-Kelly 4)
Tiger Thompson, 1924 (Carey 3, Eason 4, Stromberg 4)
Tiger Town, 1983 (Scheider 3)
Tiger von Eschnapur, 1952 (Lang 2)
Tiger Walks, 1964 (Disney 2, Merkel 3)
Tiger Woman, 1917 (Bara 3)
Tiger Woman, 1944 (Canutt 4)
Tiger's Club, 1920 (Ruttenberg 4)
Tiger's Cub, 1921 (White 3)
Tigerin, 1921 (Hoffmann 4)
Tigers Don't Cry, 1976 (Quinn 3)
Tight Little Island. *See* Whiskey Galore!, 1949
Tight Shoes, 1923 (Roach 4)
Tight Shoes, 1941 (Crawford, B. 3, Howard, S. 3, Salter 4)
Tight Spot, 1955 (Robinson, E. 3, Rogers, G. 3, Duning 4, Guffey 4, Wald 4)
Tightrope, 1984 (Bujold 3, Eastwood 3)
Tigra, 1953 (Torre-Nilsson 2)
Tigre, 1967 (Risi 2, Gassman 3, Age and Scarpelli 4)
Tigre aime la chair fraîche, 1964 (Chabrol 2, Audran 3, Rabier 4)
Tigre de Yautepec, 1933 (De Fuentes 2)
Tigre reale, 1916 (Pastrone 2)

Tigre salto y mato . . . pero morira . . . morira, 1973 (Alvarez 2)
Tigre se parfume à la dynamite, 1965 (Chabrol 2, Rabier 4)
Tigress, 1914 (Guy 2)
Tigress, 1927 (Walker 4)
Tigress. *See* Tigra, 1953
Tigullio minore, 1947 (Risi 2)
Tih Minh, 1918 (Feuillade 2)
Tijera de oro, 1958 (Alcoriza 4)
Tijuana Story, 1957 (Katzman 4)
Tikhy Don, 1957–58 (Gerasimov 2)
'Til We Meet Again, 1940 (Goulding 2, Oberon 3, Gaudio 4, Orry-Kelly 4)
Tilki Selim, 1966 (Guney 2)
Till Divorce Do You Part. *See* Castagne sono buone, 1970
Till Eulenspiegel, 1966 (Ophuls 2)
Till gladje, 1950 (Bergman 2, Sjostrom 2, Fischer 4)
Till I Come Back to You, 1918 (DeMille 2, Buckland 4, Rosher 4)
Till Osterland, 1926 (Molander 2, Jaenzon 4, Magnusson 4)
Till Sex Do Us Part. *See* Troll, 1971
Till the Clouds Roll By, 1946 (Minnelli 2, Allyson 3, Charisse 3, Garland 3, Heflin 3, Horne 3, Johnson, V. 3, Lansbury 3, Sinatra 3, Walker 3, Williams 3, Alton, R. 4, Freed 4, Irene 4, Rose 4, Stradling 4)
Till the End of Time, 1946 (Dmytryk 2, Edwards 2, Mitchum 3, D'Agostino 4, Schary 4)
Till Tomorrow Comes. *See* Asu aru kagiri, 1962
Till Victory. *See* Jusqu'à la victoire, 1970
Till We Meet Again, 1922 (Goulding 2, Marsh 3)
Till We Meet Again, 1936 (Florey 2, Marshall 3, O'Brien, P. 3, Head 4, Wallis 4)
Till We Meet Again, 1944 (Borzage 2, Milland 3, Coffee 4, Dreier 4, Head 4)
Tillie series, from 1914 (Dressler 3)
Tillie and Gus, 1933 (Fields, W.C. 3)
Tillie of the Nine Lives, 1917 (Pitts 3)
Tillie the Toiler, 1927 (Davies 3, Daniels 4, Day 4, Gibbons 4)
Tillie Wakes Up, 1917 (Marion 4)
Tillie's Nightmare. *See* Tillie's Punctured Romance, 1914
Tillie's Punctured Romance, 1914 (Chaplin 2, Sennett 2, Arbuckle 3, Normand 3, Summerville 3)
Tillie's Punctured Romance, 1928 (Sutherland 2, Fazenda 3, Fields, W.C. 3)
Tilly the Tomboy, 1909 (Hepworth 2)
Tilos a szerelem, 1965 (Torocsik 3)
Tim, 1981 (Gibson 3)
Timber, 1942 (Dailey 3, Salter 4)
Timber Industry. *See* Timmerfabriek, 1930
Timber Queen, 1922 (Roach 4)
Timber Queen, 1944 (Arlen 3)
Timber Tramps, 1972 (Garnett 2, Cotten 3)
Timber Wolf, 1925 (Van Dyke, W.S. 2)
Timberjack, 1954 (Cook 3, Hayden 3, Menjou 3, Carmichael 4, Mercer 4, Young, V. 4)
Timbuktu, 1959 (Tourneur, J. 2, De Carlo 3, Mature 3, Veiller 4)
Timbuktu. *See* Legend of the Lost, 1957
Time, 1967 (Vukotić 4)
Time & Fortune Vietnam Newsreel, 1969 (Mekas 2)
Time after Time, 1979 (McDowell 3, Steenburgen 3, Rozsa 4)
Time after Time, 1985 (Gielgud 3, Howard, T. 3)
Time and Tide, 1916 (Eason 4)
Time Bandits, 1981 (Connery 3, Duvall, S. 3, Richardson 3)
Time Bomb, 1952 (Ford, G. 3, Addison 4, Junge 4, Young, F. 4)
Time Bomb. *See* Vent se lève, 1959
Time for Action. *See* Tip on a Dead Jockey, 1957
Time for Dying, 1971 (Boetticher 2, Boetticher 2, Ballard 4)
Time for Killing, 1967 (Ford, G. 3, Ford, H. 3, Stanton 3, Anhalt 4, Brown, Harry Joe 4, Corman 4)
Time for Love, 1927 (Powell, W. 3)
Time for Love, 1935 (Fleischer, M. and D. 2)
Time for Loving, 1971 (Ferrer, M. 3, Noiret 3, Legrand 4)
Time for Miracles, 1980 (Aumont 3, Brazzi 3)
Time for Terror. *See* Flesh Feast, 1973
Time Gallops On, 1952 (Terry 4)

Time Gentlemen Please, 1952 (Grierson 2)
Time Has Stopped. *See* Tempo si è fermato, 1959
Time in the Sun, 1939 (Eisenstein 2)
Time Is Money, 1913 (Brenon 2)
Time Is Money, 1923 (Rasp 3)
Time is On Our Side, 1983 (Ashby 2)
Time Limit, 1957 (Malden 3, Torn 3, Widmark 3)
Time Lock, 1957 (Connery 3)
Time Lost and Time Remembered. *See* I Was Happy Here, 1966
Time Machine, 1959 (Pal 2)
Time of Indifference. *See* Indifferenti, 1963
Time of Kali. *See* Kaliyugaya, 1982
Time of Losing Faith. *See* Fushin no toki, 1986
Time of Reckoning. *See* Fushin no taki, 1968
Time of Reckoning. *See* Fushin no toki, 1986
Time of the Heathen, 1961 (Emshwiller 2)
Time of Their Lives, 1946 (Abbott and Costello 3)
Time of Your Life, 1948 (Bendix 3, Bond 3, Cagney 3, Crawford, B. 3, Darwell 3, Howe 4)
Time of Youth. *See* Seishun no koro, 1933
Time on My Hands, 1932 (Fleischer, M. and D. 2)
Time Out for Love. *See* Grandes Personnes, 1960
Time Out for Murder, 1938 (Darwell 3, Miller, V. 4)
Time Out for Rhythm, 1941 (Miller 3, Three Stooges 3, Cahn 4, Planer 4, Prinz 4)
Time Out for Romance, 1937 (Trevor 3)
Time Out of Mind, 1947 (Siodmak 2, Carroll L. 3, Rozsa 4)
Time Stood Still. *See* Tempo si è fermato, 1959
Time the Comedian, 1924 (Florey 2)
Time the Great Healer, 1914 (Hepworth 2)
Time, The Place, and the Girl, 1946 (Sakall 3, Edeson 4, Prinz 4)
Time to Die, 1983 (Morricone 4)
Time to Kill, 1942 (Clarke, C.C. 4, Day 4)
Time to Live, 1985 (Minnelli 3)
Time to Live, a Time to Die. *See* Feu follet, 1963
Time to Love, 1927 (Schulberg 4)
Time to Love and a Time to Die, 1958 (Sirk 2, Kinski 3, Wynn 3, Rozsa 4)
Time to Run. *See* Female Bunch, 1969
Time to Sing, 1968 (Katzman 4)
Time Travelers, 1964 (Kovacs 4, Zsigmond 4)
Time Travelers, 1976 (Lourié 4)
Time Without Memory. *See* Seigenki, 1972
Time Without Pity, 1957 (Losey 2, Cushing 3, Redgrave, M. 3, Francis 4)
Timely Interception, 1913 (Griffith 2, Barrymore L. 3, Gish, L. 3, Bitzer 4)
Times Gone By. *See* Altri tempi, 1952
Times of Joy and Sorrow. *See* Yorokobi mo kanashimi mo ikutoshituki, 1957
Times Square, 1929 (Robinson 4)
Times Square Lady, 1935 (Taylor, R. 3)
Times Square Playboy, 1936 (Orry-Kelly 4)
Timetable. *See* Gozenchu no jikanwari, 1972
Timid Rabbit, 1937 (Terry 4)
Timid Tabby, 1956 (Hanna and Barbera 4)
Timid Toreador, 1940 (Clampett 4)
Timid Young Man, 1935 (Keaton 2, Sennett 2)
Timidité vaincue, 1909 (Linders 3)
Timmerfabriek, 1930 (Ivens 2)
Timothy Dobbs, That's Me, 1916 (Beery 3)
Timothy's Quest, 1922 (Olcott 2)
Timothy's Quest, 1936 (Schary 4)
Timur's Oath, 1942 (Kuleshov 2)
Tin Can Tourist, 1937 (Terry 4)
Tin Drum. *See* Blechtrommel, 1979
Tin Gods, 1926 (Dwan 2, Adorée 3, Powell, W. 3)
Tin Hats, 1926 (Gibbons 4, Lewin 4)
Tin Man, 1935 (Roach 4)
Tin Pan Alley, 1940 (Cook 3, Faye 3, Grable 3, Banton 4, Day 4, MacGowan 4, Newman 4, Shamroy 4)
Tin Pan Alley Cats, 1943 (Clampett 4)

Tin Star, 1957 (Mann 2, Seaton 2, Fonda, H. 3, Perkins 3, Van Cleef 3, Bernstein 4, Head 4, Nichols 4)
Tin Woodman's Dream, 1967 (Smith 2)
Tindous, 1955 (Kosma 4)
Ting Yi-Shan, 1964 (King Hu 2)
Tingel-Tangel, 1927 (Reisch 4)
Tingler, 1960 (Price 3)
Tiniest of Stars, 1913 (Cruze 2)
Tinimbang ka Nguni't Kulang, 1974 (Brocka 2)
Tinkering with Trouble, 1915 (Lloyd 3, Roach 4)
Tinsel Tree, 1941–42 (Anger 2)
Tinted Venus, 1921 (Hepworth 2)
Tintin et le mystère de la Toison d'Or, 1961 (Vanel 3)
Tintomara, 1970 (Dahlbeck 3)
Tip, 1917 (Daniels 3, Lloyd 3, Roach 4)
Tip on a Dead Jockey, 1957 (Dalio 3, Malone 3, Taylor, R. 3, Lederer 4, Rose 4, Rozsa 4)
Tip Toes, 1927 (Wilcox 2, Gish, D. 3, Rogers, W. 3)
Tipi da spiaggia, 1959 (Tognazzi 3)
Tip-Off, 1931 (Rogers, G. 3)
Tip-Off Girls, 1938 (Quinn 3, Head 4)
Tire au flanc, 1928 (Renoir 2, Simon, M. 3, Braunberger 4)
Tire au flanc, 1933 (Simon, S. 3)
Tire-au-flanc 62, 1961 (Coutard 4)
Tire die, 1954 (Birri 2)
Tire Man, Spare My Tires, 1942 (Langdon 3)
Tire Trouble, 1942 (Terry 4)
Tire Troubles, 1923 (Roach 4)
Tired, Absent-Minded Man, 1911 (Bunny 3)
Tired Business Men, 1927 (Roach 4)
Tired Feet, 1933 (Langdon 3)
Tireman, Spare My Tires, 1942 (Bruckman 4)
Tirez s'il vous plait, 1908 (Berry 3)
Tirez sur le pianiste, 1960 (Truffaut 2, Braunberger 4, Coutard 4, Delerue 4)
Tiro a segno per uccidere. *See* Geheimnis der gelben Monche, 1966
Tirol in Waffen, 1914 (Porten 3, Messter 4)
Tis an Ill Wind That Blows No Good, 1909 (Griffith 2, Bitzer 4)
Tish, 1942 (Pitts 3)
Tishina, 1963 (Ulyanov 3)
Tisíčočná včela, 1983 (Kroner 3)
Tisza—Autumn Sketches. *See* Tisza—oszi vázlatok, 1962
Tisza—oszi vázlatok, 1962 (Gaál 2)
Tiszti kardbojt, 1915 (Korda 2)
Tit for Tat, 1935 (Laurel & Hardy 3, Roach 4)
Tit for Tat. *See* Bonne Farce avec ma tête, 1904
Titan Find, 1984 (Kinski 3)
Titan: The Story of Michelangelo, 1949 (Flaherty 2, March 3)
Titanic, 1953 (Negulesco 2, Ritter 3, Stanwyck 3, Wagner 3, Webb 3, Brackett, C. 4, Jeakins 4, Lemaire 4, Reisch 4, Wheeler 4)
Titans. *See* Arrivani i titani, 1961
Titfield Thunderbolt, 1952 (Crichton 2, Holloway 3, Auric 4, Clarke, T.E.B. 4, Slocombe 4)
Titicut Follies, 1967 (Wiseman 2)
Title for the Sin. *See* Právo na hřích, 1932
Title Match of Magic. *See* Ninjutsu senshuken jiai, 1956
Title Shot, 1979 (Curtis 3)
Titles Ekti Nadir Naam, 1973 (Ghatak 4)
Tito's Guitar, 1942 (Fleischer, M. and D. 2)
Tivoli, 1956 (Carlsen 2)
Tivoli Garden Games, 1954 (Henning-Jensen 2)
Tivoligarden spiller, 1954 (Henning-Jensen 2)
Tíz deka halhatatlanság, 1965 (Macskássy 4)
Tiz éves Kuba, 1969 (Gaál 2)
15 perc 15 évrol, 1965 (Mészáros 2)
Tizedes meg a tobbieg, 1965 (Darvas 3)
Tizoc, 1956 (Félix 3, Infante 3)
Tkada-no-baba, 1927 (Tanaka 3)
Tlatsche, 1939 (Ulmer 2)
Tlayucan, 1960 (Alcoriza 4)
T-Men, 1948 (Mann 2, Alton, J. 4)
TNT Jackson, 1974 (Corman 4)

To and Fro. *See* Oda—vissza, 1962
To Be a Crook. *See* Fille et des fusils, 1964
To be a Man. *See* Cry of Battle, 1963
To Be Alive!, 1962 (Hammid 2)
To Be Called For, 1914 (Mix 3)
To Be or Not to Be, 1942 (Lubitsch 2, Lombard 3, Irene 4, Korda 4, Maté 4, Plunkett 4)
To Be or Not to Be, 1983 (Brooks, M. 2, Bancroft 3, Ferrer, J. 3)
To Be Young. *See* Naar man kun er ung, 1943
To Beat the Band, 1935 (Mercer 4, Musuraca 4, Plunkett 4)
To Bed or Not to Bed. *See* Diavolo, 1963
To Catch a King, 1984 (Wagner 3)
To Catch a Thief, 1954 (Hitchcock 2, Grant, C. 3, Kelly, Grace 3, Vanel 3, Hayes 4, Head 4)
To Commit a Murder. *See* Peau d'espion, 1967
To Cover the World. *See* Lucky Devils, 1941
To Die in Madrid, 1967 (Gielgud 3)
To Die in Madrid. *See* Mourir à Madrid, 1962
To Die of Love. *See* Mourir d'aimer, 1970
To Dig a Pit. *See* Cavar un foso, 1966
To Dorothy, a Son, 1954 (Winters 3)
To Duck or Not to Duck, 1942 (Jones 2)
Tò, è morta la nonna!, 1969 (Monicelli 2, Cortese 3)
To Each His Own, 1946 (Leisen 2, De Havilland 3, Brackett, C. 4, Dreier 4, Head 4, Young, V. 4)
To Find a Man, 1970 (Booth 4)
To Fly, 1976 (Hammid 2)
To Hare is Human, 1957 (Jones 2)
To Have and Have Not, 1944 (Hawks 2, Bacall 3, Bogart 3, Brennan 3, Dalio 3, Carmichael 4, Furthman 4, Mercer 4, Waxman 4)
To Have and to Hold, 1916 (Reid 3)
To Have and to Hold, 1922 (Miller, A. 4)
To Hear Your Banjo Play, 1940 (Leacock 2, Van Dyke, W. 2)
To Heir Is Human, 1944 (Langdon 3, Merkel 3)
To Hell and Back, 1955 (Murphy 3)
To Hell with the Kaiser, 1918 (Mathis 4)
To Itch His Own, 1958 (Jones 2)
To John Bunny's, 1915 (Bunny 3)
To Joy. *See* Till gladje, 1950
To Kill a Clown, 1971 (Lassally 4)
To Kill a Cop, 1978 (Gossett 3)
To Kill a Mockingbird, 1962 (Mulligan 2, Pakula 2, Duvall, R. 3, Peck 3, Bernstein 4, Bumstead 4, Westmore, B. 4)
To Kill or to Die. *See* Mio nome è Shanghai Joe, 1973
To koritsi me ta mavra, 1955 (Lassally 4)
To Live. *See* Ikiru, 1952
To Live, Doomed. *See* Ikiru, 1952
To Live in Peace. *See* Vivere in pace, 1946
To Live One's Life. *See* Zít svuj život, 1963
To Love. *See* Att alska, 1964
To Love a Man. *See* Lyubit cheloveka, 1972
To Love Again. *See* Ai futatabi, 1972
To Love, Perhaps to Die, 1975 (Sordi 3)
To maend i ødemarken, 1972 (Roos 2)
To Mary—with Love, 1936 (Cromwell 2, Baxter W. 3, Loy 3, Trevor 3, MacGowan 4)
To Melody a Soul Responds, 1915 (Eason 4)
To New Shores. *See* Zu neuen Ufern, 1937
To Our Children's Children, 1969 (Halas and Batchelor 2)
To Paris with Love, 1954 (Hamer 2, Guinness 3, Buckner 4)
To Parsifal, 1963 (Baillie 2)
To Please a Lady, 1950 (Brown 2, Gable 3, Menjou 3, Stanwyck 3, Basevi 4, Kaper 4, Rose 4, Rosson 4)
To Please One Woman, 1921 (Weber 2)
To Rent—Furnished, 1915 (Eason 4)
To Sail Is Necessary. *See* Att Segla ar Nodvandigt, 1937–38
To Save Her Soul, 1909 (Griffith 2, Pickford 3, Bitzer 4)
To Sir with Love, 1967 (Poitier 3)
To telefteo psema, 1957 (Lassally 4)
To the Aid of Stonewall Jackson, 1911 (Olcott 2)
To the Devil a Daughter, 1976 (Lee, C. 3, Widmark 3, Watkin 4)
To the End of the Silver Mountains. *See* Ginrei no hate, 1947

To the Ends of the Earth, 1948 (Powell, D. 3, Buchman 4, Duning 4, Guffey 4)
To the Fair!, 1964 (Hammid 2)
To the Ladies, 1923 (Cruze 2, Astor 3, Horton 3, Brown, K. 4)
To the Last Man, 1923 (Fleming 2, Hathaway 2, Crabbe 3, Howe 4)
To the Last Man, 1933 (Hathaway 2, Carradine 3, Scott, R. 3, Temple 3)
To the Lord's Estate. *See* Do panského stavu, 1925
To the Moon and Beyond, 1964 (Trumbull 4)
To the North-West, 1934 (Zhao 3)
To the Orient. *See* Till Osterland, 1926
To the Public Danger, 1948 (Fisher 2)
To the Rescue, 1932 (Lantz 4)
To the Shores of Hell, 1966 (Arlen 3)
To the Shores of Tripoli, 1942 (O'Hara 3, Scott, R. 3, Cronjager 4, Newman 4, Trotti 4, Zanuck 4)
To the Victor, 1948 (Brooks, R. 2, Brooks, R. 2, Daves 2, Malone 3, Wald 4)
To the Western World, 1981 (Huston 2)
To Tjenestepiger, 1910 (Blom 2)
To Trap a Spy, 1964 (Carroll L. 3)
To Your Health, 1956 (Halas and Batchelor 2)
Toâ, 1949 (Guitry 2)
Toadstools. *See* Gljiva, 1972
Toast of New Orleans, 1950 (Taurog 2, Grayson 3, Niven 3, Cahn 4, Green, J. 4, Pasternak 4, Plunkett 4, Rose 4)
Toast of New York, 1937 (Farmer 3, Grant, C. 3, Meek 3, Nichols 4, Polglase 4)
Toast of Song, 1952 (Fleischer, M. and D. 2)
Toast of the Legion. *See* Kiss Me Again, 1931
Toast to a Young Miss. *See* Ojosan kanpai, 1949
Tobacco Road, 1941 (Ford, J. 2, Andrews D. 3, Bond 3, Summerville 3, Tierney 3, Banton 4, Basevi 4, Day 4, Johnson 4, La Shelle 4, Miller, A. 4, Newman 4, Zanuck 4)
Tobias Buntschuh, 1921 (Holger-Madsen 2)
Tobias Wants Out, 1913 (Mix 3)
Tobie est un ange, 1941 (Allégret, Y. 2, Alekan 4)
Tobira o hiraku onna, 1946 (Miyagawa 4, Yoda 4)
Tobisuke boken ryoko, 1949 (Hayasaka 4)
Tobisuke's Adventures. *See* Tobisuke boken ryoko, 1949
Toboggan, 1934 (Burel 4)
Tobruk, 1967 (Hiller 2, Hudson 3, Bumstead 4, Kaper 4, Whitlock 4)
Toburoku no Tatsu, 1962 (Mifune 3)
Toby and the Tall Corn, 1954 (Leacock 2, Van Dyke, W. 2)
Toby Tyler, or Ten Weeks with a Circus, 1959 (Disney 2, Iwerks 4)
Toccata for Toy Trains, 1957 (Bernstein 4)
Tochan no po ga kikoeru, 1971 (Tsukasa 3)
Tocher, 1937 (Reiniger 2)
Tochter der Landstrasse, 1914 (Gad 2, Nielsen 3)
Tochter des Bajazzo, 1919 (Albers 3)
Tochter des Mehemed, 1919 (Jannings 3)
Tochter des Regiments, 1933 (Ondra 3)
Tochter des Samurai. *See* Atarashiki tsuchi, 1937
Tochuken Kumoemon, 1936 (Naruse 2)
Tod in Sevilla, 1913 (Gad 2, Nielsen 3)
Tod ritt Dienstags. *See* Giorno dell'ira, 1967
Toda-ke no kyodai, 1941 (Ozu 2, Ryu 3)
Today, 1930 (D'Agostino 4, Howe 4, Miller, S. 4)
Today. *See* Segodnya, 1930
Today. *See* Sevodiya, 1923–25
Today and Tomorrow, 1945 (Alwyn 4)
Today and Tomorrow. *See* Ma es holnap, 1912
Today for the Last Time. *See* Dnes naposled, 1958
Today I Hang, 1942 (Farnum 3)
Today is Forever. *See* Griffin and Phoenix: A Love Story, 1976
Today It's Me—Tomorrow You. *See* Oggi a me . . . domani a te!, 196
Today Mexico, Tomorrow . . . the World, 1970 (Godfrey 4)
Today or Tomorrow. *See* Ma Vagy holnap, 1965
Today We Live, 1933 (Hawks 2, Cooper, Gary 3, Crawford, J. 3, Young, R. 3)
Todd Killings, 1971 (Grahame 3, Rosenman 4)
Todesreigen, 1921 (Tschechowa 3)
Todesritt in Riesenrad, 1912 (Planer 4)

Todessmaragd. *See* Knabe in Blau, 1919
Todlicher Irrtum, 1970 (Hoppe 3, Mueller-Stahl 3)
Todo es posible en Granada, 1954 (Oberon 3)
Todo modo, 1976 (Petri 2, Mastroianni 3, Piccoli 3, Volonté 3, Morricone 4)
Todoke haha no sakebi, 1959 (Yamada 3)
Todoke haha no uta, 1959 (Yoda 4)
Tofflan-en lycklig komedi, 1967 (Bjornstrand 3)
Toge no uta, 1924 (Mizoguchi 2)
Together, 1956 (Anderson 2, Lassally 4)
Together, 1976 (Broughton 2)
Together. *See* Amo non Amo, 1978
Together Again, 1944 (Vidor, C. 2, Boyer 3, Coburn, C. 3, Dunne 3, Polglase 4, Walker 4)
Together in the Weather, 1946 (Pal 2)
Togger, 1937 (Rasp 3)
Tohjin Okichi, 1935 (Hayakawa 3)
Toho senichiya, 1947 (Ichikawa 2, Hasegawa 3, Takamine 3, Yamada 3)
Toho shoboto, 1946 (Takamine 3)
Tohoku no zummu-tachi, 1957 (Ichikawa 2)
Toi kumo, 1955 (Kinoshita 2, Takamine 3)
Toi que j'adore, 1933 (Feuillère 3)
Toilers, 1919 (Colman 3)
Toilers, 1928 (Fairbanks, D. Jr. 3)
Toilet Section Chief. *See* Toiretto buchou, 1961
Toina no Ginpei, 1933 (Kinugasa 2)
Toiretto buchou, 1961 (Muraki 4)
Toît de la baleine, 1981 (Ruiz 3)
Tojin okichi, 1930 (Kinugasa 2, Mizoguchi 2)
Tojin Okichi, 1954 (Yamada 3)
Tojin Okichi, Funshin hen, 1938 (Tanaka 3)
Tojuro no koi, 1938 (Hasegawa 3)
Tojuro no koi, 1955 (Hasegawa 3, Kyo 3, Shindo 3, Yoda 4)
Toka kan no jinsei, 1941 (Tanaka 3)
Tokai kokyogaku, 1929 (Mizoguchi 2)
Tokaku omna to iu mono wa, 1932 (Yoda 4)
Toki no ujigami, 1932 (Mizoguchi 2)
Tokijiro of Katsukake. *See* Kutsukake Tokojiro, 1961
Tokkan kozo, 1929 (Ozu 2)
Tokyo Bay on Fire. *See* Tokyo-wan enjou, 1975
Tokyo boshoku, 1957 (Ozu 2, Hara 3, Ryu 3, Yamada 3, Yamamura 3)
Tokyo-ga, 1985 (Ryu 3)
Tokyo hika, 1951 (Mori 3)
Tokyo Joe, 1949 (Bogart 3, Hayakawa 3)
Tokyo koshinkyoko, 1927 (Gosho 2, Mizoguchi 2)
Tokyo March. *See* Tokyo koshinkyoko, 1927
Tokyo monogatari, 1953 (Imamura 2, Ozu 2, Hara 3, Kagawa 3, Ryu 3, Yamamura 3)
Tokyo mushuku, 1950 (Yamamura 3)
Tokyo 1958, 1958 (Teshigahara 2, Hani 2)
Tokyo no ekubo, 1952 (Takamine 3)
Tokyo no gassho, 1931 (Ozu 2, Takamine 3)
Tokyo no hiroin, 1950 (Mori 3)
Tokyo no koibito, 1952 (Mifune 3)
Tokyo no kyujitsu, 1958 (Hara 3, Kagawa 3, Mifune 3, Tsukasa 3)
Tokyo no onna, 1933 (Ozu 2, Tanaka 3)
Tokyo no sora no shita niwa, 1955 (Yamada 3)
Tokyo no yado, 1935 (Ozu 2)
Tokyo Olympiad. *See* Tokyo Orimpikku, 1965
Tokyo Orimpikku, 1965 (Ichikawa 2, Miyagawa 4)
Tokyo Rose, 1945 (Edwards 2)
Tokyo saiban, 1983 (Kobayashi 2, Takemitsu 4)
Tokyo senso sengo hiwa, 1970 (Oshima 2, Takemitsu 4, Toda 4)
Tokyo Story. *See* Tokyo monogatari, 1953
Tokyo Sweetheart. *See* Tokyo no koibito, 1952
Tokyo Trial. *See* Tokyo saiban, 1983
Tokyo Twilight. *See* Tokyo boshoku, 1957
Tokyo-wan enjou, 1975 (Muraki 4)
Tokyo yowa, 1961 (Kishida 3)
Tokyo's Chorus. *See* Tokyo no gassho, 1931
Tol'able David, 1921 (Goulding 2, King 2, Barthelmess 3)
Tol'able David, 1930 (Carradine 3, Walthall 3, Glazer 4)

Tol'able Romeo, 1926 (Roach 4)
Told at Twilight, 1917 (King 2)
Told in the Hills, 1919 (Howe 4)
Tolerance. *See* Tolerancija, 1967
Tolerancija, 1967 (Grgić 4)
Toll Bridge Troubles, 1942 (Fleischer, M. and D. 2)
Toll Gate, 1920 (Hart 3, Nilsson 3, August 4)
Toll Gate Raiders, 1912 (Nilsson 3)
Toll of the Marshes, 1913 (Bushman 3)
Toll of the Sea, 1922 (Wong 3, Marion 4)
Tolle Bomberg, 1957 (Albers 3, Vích 4)
Tolle Heirat von Laló, 1918 (Pick 2)
Tolle Miss. *See* Miss Hobbs, 1921
Tolle Nacht, 1927 (Oswald 2)
Tolle Nacht, 1943 (Frohlich 3)
Tolle Prinzessin. *See* Zopf und Schwert, 1926
Toller Einfall, 1932 (Kaper 4)
Toller hecht auf krummer tour, 1962 (Bendix 3)
Tolonc, 1914 (Curtiz 2)
Tom and Chérie, 1955 (Hanna and Barbera 4)
Tom and Jerry Cartoons, 1963–1966 (Jones 2)
Tom and Jerry Mix, 1917 (Mix 3)
Tom Brown of Culver, 1932 (Wyler 2, Power 3, Summerville 3)
Tom Brown's School Days, 1940 (Hardwicke 3, Biroc 4, Musuraca 4, Polglase 4)
Tom, Dick, and Harry, 1941 (Meredith 3, Rogers, G. 3, Kanin 4, Polglase 4)
Tom Horn, 1980 (Cook 3, McQueen, S. 3, Alonzo 4)
Tom Jones, 1963 (Richardson 2, Evans 3, Finney 3, Greenwood 3, York, S. 3, Addison 4, Lassally 4)
Tom Mix in Arabia, 1922 (Mix 3)
Tom Sawyer, 1930 (Cromwell 2, Coogan 3, Darwell 3, Lang 4)
Tom Sawyer, 1973 (Oates 3, Williams, J. 4)
Tom Sawyer, Detective, 1938 (O'Connor 3, Head 4)
Tom Thumb, 1936 (Iwerks 4)
Tom Thumb, 1958 (Pal 2, Matthews 3, Sellers 3, Périnal 4)
Tom Thumb in Trouble, 1940 (Jones 2)
Tom Tight et Dum Dum, 1903 (Méliès 2)
Tom, Tom the Piper's Son, 1934 (Terry 4)
Tom Tom Tomcat, 1952 (Freleng 4)
Tom Toms of Mayumba. *See* Tam Tam Mayumba, 1955
Tom Turk and Daffy, 1944 (Jones 2)
Tomahawk, 1951 (Cody 3, De Carlo 3, Heflin 3, Hudson 3, Salter 4)
Tomahawk and the Cross. *See* Pillars of the Sky, 1956
Tomalio, 1933 (Arbuckle 3)
Tomate, 1960 (Almendros 4)
Tomb of Ligeia, 1965 (Price 3, Corman 4, Towne 4)
Tombé du ciel, 1946 (Dauphin 3)
Tombeau sous l'Arc de Triomphe, 1927 (Wiene 2)
Tombeur, 1957 (Auer 3)
Tombola, paradiso nero, 1947 (Fabrizi 3)
Tomboy, 1909 (Olcott 2)
Tomboy and the Champ, 1960 (Johnson, B. 3, Clothier 4)
Tomboy Bessie, 1911 (Sennett 2, Normand 3)
Tomboy on Bar Z, 1912 (Anderson G. 3)
Tomboys, 1905 (Selig 4)
Tombs of Our Ancestors. *See* Våra Faders Gravar, 1935–36
Tombstone Terror, 1937 (Katzman 4)
Tomei ningen, 1954 (Tsuburaya 4)
Tomfoolery series, 1970 (Halas and Batchelor 2)
Tommy, 1931 (Protazanov 2)
Tommy, 1974 (Russell 2, Nicholson 3, Reed, O. 3, Russell 4)
Tommy Gets His Sister Married, 1910–11 (White 3)
Tommy Tucker's Tooth, 1923 (Disney 2)
Tomorrow, 1975 (Duvall, R. 3)
Tomorrow and Tomorrow, 1932 (Lukas 3, Lang 4)
Tomorrow at Eight, 1933 (Plunkett 4)
Tomorrow at Midnight. *See* For Love or Money, 1939
Tomorrow at Ten, 1963 (Shaw 3)
Tomorrow Begins Today: Industrial Research, 1976 (Benegal 2)
Tomorrow Is Another Day, 1951 (Blanke 4)
Tomorrow Is Forever, 1946 (Welles 2, Brent 3, Colbert 3, Wood 3, Coffee 4, Steiner 4)

Tomorrow Is My Turn. *See* Passage du Rhin, 1960
Tomorrow Is the Final Day. *See* Yarin son gundur, 1971
Tomorrow Mexico. *See* Jutra Meksyk, 1965
Tomorrow Never Comes, 1978 (Ireland 3, Pleasance 3, Reed, O. 3)
Tomorrow the World, 1944 (March 3, Moorehead 3, Lardner 4)
Tomorrow We Live, 1942 (Fisher 2, Ulmer 2)
Tomorrow's Dancers. *See* Asu no odoriko, 1939
Tomorrow's Island, 1968 (Crichton 2)
Tomorrow's Love, 1925 (Glennon 4)
Tomorrow's Youth, 1935 (Darwell 3)
Tomoshibi, 1954 (Kagawa 3)
Tom's Gang, 1927 (Musuraca 4)
Tom's Photo Finish, 1956 (Hanna and Barbera 4)
Tom's Sacrifice, 1916 (Mix 3)
Tom's Strategy, 1916 (Mix 3)
Tomuraishi tachi, 1968 (Miyagawa 4)
Ton ombre est la mienne, 1962 (Jarre 4)
Tonari no yane no shita, 1931 (Naruse 2)
Tondeur de chiens, 1899–1900 (Guy 2)
Tong Man, 1919 (Hayakawa 3)
Tongues of Flame, 1925 (Love 3)
Tongues of Scandal, 1927 (Laszlo 4, Shamroy 4)
Toni, 1928 (Buchanan 3)
Toni, 1935 (Becker 2, Renoir 2, Renoir 4)
Tonic, 1928 (Lanchester 3)
Tonight and Every Night, 1945 (Saville 2, Hayworth 3, Winters 3, Cahn 4, Cole 4, Maté 4)
Tonight at 8:30. *See* Meet Me Tonight, 1952
Tonight at Twelve, 1929 (Mandell 4)
Tonight Is Ours, 1933 (Leisen 2, Colbert 3, March 3, Struss 4)
Tonight Let's All Make Love in London, 1968 (Christie 3, Marvin 3, Redgrave, V. 3)
Tonight or Never, 1931 (Leroy 2, Douglas, M. 3, Karloff 3, Swanson 3, Goldwyn 4, Newman 4, Toland 4, Vajda 4)
Tonight or Never. *See* I natt eller aldrig, 1941
Tonight We Raid Calais, 1943 (Bondi 3, Cobb 3, Dalio 3, Ballard 4, Day 4, Salt 4)
Tonight We Sing, 1953 (Leisen 2, Bancroft 3, Kurnitz 4, Lemaire 4, Newman 4, Shamroy 4)
Tonight's the Night. *See* Happy Ever After, 1954
Tonio Kroger, 1964 (Flaiano 4)
Tonka, 1958 (Disney 2, Mineo 3)
Tonka sibenice. *See* Erlebnisse einer Nacht, 1930
Tonnelier, 1899–1900 (Guy 2)
Tonnerre, 1921 (Delluc 2, Epstein 2)
Tonnerre de Dieu, 1965 (Gabin 3)
Tonnerre de Jupiter, 1903 (Méliès 2)
Tonnèrre rouge. *See* Alien Thunder, 1973
Tontons flingueurs, 1973 (Blier 3, Audiard 4)
Tony Arzenta. *See* Big Guns, 1973
Tony Freunde, 1967 (Fassbinder 2)
Tony Rome, 1967 (Rowlands 3, Sinatra 3, Biroc 4, Smith, J.M. 4)
Tony Runs Wild, 1926 (Mix 3)
Tony the Fiddler, 1913 (Bushman 3)
Too Ardent Lover, 1903 (Bitzer 4)
Too Bad She's Bad. *See* Peccato che sia una canaglia, 1954
Too Busy to Work, 1932 (Beavers 3, Powell, D. 3, Rogers, W. 3, Clarke, C.C. 4)
Too Busy to Work, 1939 (Cronjager 4)
Too Far to Go, 1978 (Lassally 4)
Too Hop to Handle, 1956 (McKimson 4)
Too Hot to Handle, 1938 (Gable 3, Loy 3, Pidgeon 3, Mahin 4, Rosson 4, Waxman 4)
Too Hot to Handle, 1960 (Lee, C. 3, Mansfield 3)
Too Late Blues, 1961 (Cassavetes 2, Head 4, Raksin 4)
Too Late for Divorce, 1956 (Lee, B. 3)
Too Late for Tears, 1949 (Duryea 3, Kennedy, A. 3, Stromberg 4)
Too Late the Hero, 1970 (Aldrich 2, Caine 3, Fonda, H. 3, Robertson 3, Biroc 4)
Too Many Blondes, 1941 (Chaney Lon, Jr. 3, Howard, S. 3, Krasner 4)
Too Many Brides, 1914 (Sennett 2)
Too Many Burglars, 1911 (Sennett 2)
Too Many Chefs, 1916 (Mix 3)

Too Many Chefs. *See* Who Is Killing the Great Chefs of Europe?, 1978
Too Many Cooks, 1920 (Howard, L. 3)
Too Many Cooks, 1931 (Musuraca 4)
Too Many Crooks, 1930 (Olivier 3, Murfin 4)
Too Many Girls, 1910 (Porter 2)
Too Many Girls, 1940 (Ball 3, Johnson, V. 3, Miller 3, Polglase 4)
Too Many Highballs, 1933 (Sennett 2, Bruckman 4)
Too Many Husbands, 1931 (Sennett 2)
Too Many Husbands, 1940 (Ruggles 2, Arthur 3, Douglas, M. 3, MacMurray 3, Prinz 4, Walker 4)
Too Many Kisses, 1925 (Marx, H. 3, Powell, W. 3, Rosson 4, Saunders 4)
Too Many Mamas, 1924 (McCarey 2, Roach 4)
Too Many Millions, 1918 (Cruze 2, Reid 3, Rosher 4)
Too Many Parents, 1936 (Dmytryk 2, Farmer 3, Head 4, Struss 4)
Too Many Suspects. *See* Ellery Queen, 1975
Too Many Thieves, 1966 (Falk 3)
Too Many Too Soon, 1961 (Peries 2)
Too Many Wives, 1937 (Musuraca 4, Polglase 4)
Too Many Women, 1932 (Roach 4)
Too Many Women. *See* God's Gift to Women, 1931
Too Much Burglar, 1914 (Costello, D. 3, Costello, M. 3)
Too Much Business, 1922 (Horton 3)
Too Much for One Man. *See* Immorale, 1967
Too Much Harmony, 1933 (Mankiewicz 2, Sutherland 2, Crosby 3, Prinz 4)
Too Much Johnson, 1919 (Crisp 3)
Too Much Johnson, 1938 (Welles 2, Holliday 3)
Too Much Money, 1926 (Nilsson 3, Stone 3)
Too Much Speed, 1921 (Reid 3)
Too Much to Carry. *See* Kdo své nebe neunese, 1959
Too Much, Too Soon, 1958 (Flynn 3, Malone 3, Blanke 4, Musuraca 4, Orry-Kelly 4)
Too Soon To Love, 1959 (Nicholson 3)
Too Tough to Kill, 1935 (Bond 3)
Too Wise Wives, 1921 (Weber 2, Calhern 3)
Too Young for Love, 1959 (Head 4)
Too Young to Kiss, 1951 (Allyson 3, Johnson, V. 3, Young, G. 3, Goodrich and Hackett 4, Green, J. 4, Kaper 4, Rose 4, Ruttenberg 4)
Too Young to Know, 1945 (Malone 3)
Too Young to Love, 1959 (Love 3)
Too Young to Marry, 1931 (Leroy 2, Young, L. 3)
Tools of Providence, 1915 (Hart 3)
Toot! Toot!, 1926 (Fleischer, M. and D. 2)
Toote Khilone, 1978 (Azmi 3)
Tooth Will Out, 1951 (Three Stooges 3)
Tootsie, 1982 (Pollack 2, Hoffman 3, Lange 3, Roizman 4, Smith, D. 4)
Tootsie and Tamales, 1919 (Hardy 3)
Top Flat, 1935 (Roach 4)
Top Gun, 1955 (Hayden 3)
Top Hat, 1935 (Sandrich 2, Astaire 3, Ball 3, Horton 3, Meek 3, Rogers, G. 3, Berman 4, Pan 4, Polglase 4, Steiner 4)
Top Job. *See* Ad ogni costo, 1967
Top Man, 1943 (Beavers 3, Gish, L. 3, O'Connor 3)
Top o' the Morning, 1949 (Crosby 3, Fitzgerald 3, Bumstead 4, Dreier 4)
Top of New York, 1922 (Levien 4)
Top of the Bill, 1931 (Bosworth 3)
Top of the Hill, 1980 (Duning 4)
Top of the Town, 1937 (Auer 3)
Top of the World, 1925 (Nilsson 3, Clarke, C.C. 4)
Top of the World, 1955 (Clothier 4)
Top Priority, 1981 (Patel 4)
Top Secret, 1952 (Homolka 3, Lee, C. 3)
Top Secret, 1984 (Cushing 3, Sharif 3, Jarre 4)
Top Secret Affair, 1957 (Cromwell 2, Douglas, K. 3, Hayward 3, Cortez 4, Lemaire 4)
Top Sergeant, 1942 (Salter 4)
Top Speed, 1930 (Leroy 2, Brown 3, Grot 4)
Topaz, 1969 (Hitchcock 2, Piccoli 3, Bumstead 4, Head 4, Jarre 4, Whitlock 4)

Totò, Peppino, e Le fanatiche, 1958 (Age and Scarpelli 4)
Totò Tarzan, 1950 (Age and Scarpelli 4)
Totò terzo uomo, 1951 (Delli Colli 4)
Totò, Vittorio e la dottoressa, 1957 (De Sica 2)
Toto Wants a Home. *See* Totò cerca casa, 1950
Toton, 1919 (Borzage 2)
Toto's Troubles, 1919 (Roach 4)
Totsuguhi, 1956 (Yoshimura 2)
Totsuseki iseki, 1966 (Shindo 2)
Toubib, 1979 (Delon 3, Renoir 4, Sarde 4)
Touch. *See* Beroringen, 1971
Touch All the Bases, 1922 (Roach 4)
Touch and Go, 1955 (Hawkins 3, Love 3, Addison 4, Balcon 4,
    Slocombe 4)
Touch and Go. *See* Poudre d'escampette, 1971
Touch of a Child, 1918 (Hepworth 2)
Touch of Class, 1973 (Jackson 3, Segal 3, Cahn 4, Frank 4)
**Touch of Evil, 1958 (Welles 2, Cotten 3, Dietrich 3, Heston 3,
    Leigh, J. 3, McCambridge 3, Mancini 4)**
Touch of Hell. *See* Serious Charge, 1959
Touch of Larceny, 1960 (Mason 3, Sanders 3, Head 4)
Touch of Love, 1915 (Eason 4)
Touch of Scandal, 1984 (Dickinson 3)
Touch of the Sun, 1978 (Cushing 3, Wynn 3)
Touch of Zen. *See* Hsia nü, 1969
Touchdown, 1931 (McLeod 3, Arlen 3)
Touchdown Army, 1938 (Cummings 3, Head 4)
Touchdown Demons, 1940 (Terry 4)
Touche à tout, 1935 (Berry 3, Barsacq 4, Burel 4)
Touché and Go, 1957 (Jones 2)
Touche pas la femme blanche, 1974 (Cuny 3, Deneuve 3,
    Mastroianni 3, Noiret 3, Piccoli 3, Sarde 4)
Touche pas la femme blanche. *See* Non taccate la donna bianca, 1974
Touché, Pussy Cat, 1954 (Hanna and Barbera 4)
Touchez pas au Grisbi, 1953 (Becker 2, Gabin 3, Moreau 3,
    D'Eaubonne 4)
Tough as They Come, 1942 (Salter 4)
Tough Egg, 1936 (Terry 4)
Tough Enough, 1982 (Fleischer, R. 2, Oates 3)
Tough Game. *See* Hårda leken, 1955
Tough Guy, 1935 (Auer 3, Cooper, J 3, Hersholt 3)
Tough Kid's Waterloo, 1900 (Bitzer 4)
Tough Luck, 1920 (Roach 4)
Tough Winter, 1922 (Roach 4)
Tough Winter, 1930 (Roach 4)
Toughlove, 1985 (Dern 3, Remick 3)
Touha, 1958 (Brejchová 3, Kučera 4)
Touha zvaná Anada, 1971 (Kadár 2, Kroner 3, Marković 3)
Touiste encore, 1963 (Cloquet 4)
Toujin Okichi, 1955 (Yoda 4)
Toukai Suiko-den, 1945 (Miyagawa 4)
Toukai's Suiko Story. *See* Toukai Suiko-den, 1945
Toulouse-Lautrec, 1950 (Braunberger 4)
Tour, 1928 (Clair 2, Périnal 4)
Tour au large, 1926 (Grémillon 2)
Tour de Babel, 1951 (Honegger 4)
Tour de chant, 1933 (Cavalcanti 2)
Tour de cochon, 1934 (Wakhévitch 4)
Tour de Nèsle, 1955 (Gance 2, Brasseur 3)
Tour du monde en bateau-stop, 1954 (Storck 2)
Tour Eiffel, 1900 (Lumière 2)
Tourbiers, 1964 (Guillemot 4)
Tourbillon de Paris, 1928 (Duvivier 2, Dagover 3)
Toure une vie, 1974 (Lai 4)
Tourelle III, 1939 (Christian-Jaque 2, Blier 3)
Tourist, 1921 (Hardy 3)
Tourist, 1925 (Arbuckle 3)
Tourist. *See* Turista, 1961
Tourist Trap, 1979 (Donaggio 4)
Touristes revenant d'une excursion, 1896-97 (Lumière 2)
Tourists, 1911 (Sennett 2, Normand 3)
Tourment, 1912 (Feuillade 2)
Tournament. *See* Seishun, 1968

Tournament of Roses, 1954 (La Shelle 4)
Tournoi. *See* Tournoi dans la cité, 1928
Tournoi dans la cité, 1928 (Renoir 2)
Tous les chemins mènent à Rome, 1948 (Philipe 3, Presle 3, Barsacq 4,
    Matras 4)
Tous les deux, 1948 (Burel 4)
Tous les garçons s'appellent Patrick, 1957 (Braunberger 4)
Tous peuvent me tuer, 1957 (Broca 2, Aimée 3)
Tous vedettes, 1979 (Caron 3, Evein 4)
Tout ça ne vaut pas l'amour, 1931 (Tourneur, J. 2, Gabin 3)
Tout chante autour de moi, 1954 (Piccoli 3)
Tout dépend des filles, 1979 (Presle 3, de Beauregard 4)
Tout est à nous, 1979 (Chaplin 3)
Tout feu, tout flamme, 1982 (Adjani 3, Montand 3, Rappeneau 4)
Tout feu, tout flamme. *See* Ça va etre ta fête, 1961
Tout la mémoire du monde, 1956 (Cloquet 4)
Tout le monde il est beau, tout le monde il est gentil, 1972 (Blier 3)
Tout l'or du monde, 1961 (Clair 2, Bourvil 3, Noiret 3, Barsacq 4)
Tout Petit Faust, 1910 (Cohl 2)
Tout peut arriver, 1969 (Deneuve 3)
Tout pour l'amour, 1933 (Clouzot 2)
Tout pour le tout, 1958 (Guerra 2)
Tout pour rien, 1933 (Rosay 3, Douy 4)
Tout s'arrange, 1932 (Dauphin 3, Fradetal 4)
Tout va bien, 1972 (Godard 2, Fonda, J. 3, Montand 3)
Toutankhamon et son royaume, 1967 (Decaë 4)
Toute allure, 1981 (Kramer, R. 2)
Toute la mémoire du monde, 1956 (Resnais 2, Braunberger 4,
    Delerue 4, Jarre 4)
Toute la ville accuse, 1955 (Burel 4)
Toute la ville danse. *See* Great Waltz, 1938
Toute révolution est un coup de dés, 1977 (Straub and Huillet 2)
Toute sa vie, 1930 (Cavalcanti 2)
Toute une nuit, 1982 (Akerman 2)
Toute une vie, 1974 (Lelouch 2, Denner 3)
Toutes folles de lui, 1967 (Audiard 4, Wakhévitch 4)
Tout's Remembrance, 1910 (Anderson G. 3)
Tova se Sluči na Ulicata, 1956 (Karamitev 3)
Tovarich, 1937 (Litvak 2, Boyer 3, Colbert 3, Rathbone 3, Deutsch 4
    Grot 4, Lang 4, Orry-Kelly 4, Robinson 4, Steiner 4, Wallis 4)
Tovaritch, 1935 (Delannoy 2)
Toward the Decisive Battle in the Sky. *See* Kessen no ozura e, 1943
Toward the Unknown, 1956 (Leroy 2, Holden 3, Rosson 4)
Towards New Times. *See* Mot nua tider, 1939
Towards the Light. *See* Mod Lyset, 1918
Towed in a Hole, 1932 (Laurel & Hardy 3)
Tower of Jewels, 1920 (Costello, M. 3)
Tower of Lies, 1925 (Sjostrom 2, Chaney Lon 3, Shearer 3, Basevi 4,
    Gibbons 4)
Tower of Lilies. *See* Himeyuri no to, 1953
Tower of London, 1939 (Carroll L. 3, Karloff 3, Price 3, Rathbone 3
    Salter 4)
Tower of London, 1962 (Coppola 2, Price 3, Corman 4)
Towering Inferno, 1974 (Astaire 3, Dunaway 3, Holden 3, Jones J. 3
    McQueen, S. 3, Newman 3, Wagner 3, Biroc 4, Westmore, F. 4,
    Williams, J. 4)
Town, 1943–44 (Von Sternberg 2)
Town and Its Drains. *See* Machi to gesui, 1953
Town by the Sea. *See* Staden vid vattnen, 1955
Town Called Bastard, 1971 (Rey 3)
Town Called Bastard. *See* Town Called Hell, 1971
Town Called Hell, 1971 (Shaw 3)
Town in the Awkward Age. *See* Kamaszváros, 1962
Town Like Alice, 1956 (Finch 3, Unsworth 4)
Town of Love and Hope. *See* Ai to kibo no machi, 1959
Town of My Hope. *See* Město mé naděje, 1978
Town on Trial, 1957 (Coburn, C. 3, Mills 3)
Town on Trial. *See* Provesso alla città, 1952
Town People. *See* Machi no hitobito, 1926
Town Tamer, 1965 (Andrews D. 3, Arlen 3, Chaney Lon, Jr. 3,
    O'Brien, P. 3)
Town That Cried Terror. *See* Maniac, 1978
Town That Dreaded Sundown, 1977 (Johnson, B. 3)

Town That Forgot God, 1922 (Ruttenberg 4)
Town Went Wild, 1944 (Horton 3)
Town Without Pity, 1961 (Douglas, K. 3, Tiomkin 4, Trumbo 4)
Towne Hall Follies, 1935 (Avery 2, Lantz 4)
Toy, 1982 (Pryor 3, Booth 4, Kovacs 4)
Toy Grabbers. See Up Your Teddy Bear, 1970
Toy of Fate, 1917 (Sutherland 2)
Toy Parade, 1932 (Iwerks 4)
Toy Shoppe, 1934 (Lantz 4)
Toy Tiger, 1956 (Chandler 3)
Toy Town Hall, 1936 (Freleng 4)
Toy Trouble, 1941 (Jones 2)
Toy Wife, 1938 (Douglas, M. 3, Muse 3, Rainer 3, Young, R. 3,
    Adrian 4, Akins 4, Cooper 4)
Toyland, 1932 (Terry 4)
Toyland Premiere, 1934 (Lantz 4)
Toymaker on the Brink and the Devil, 1910 (Porter 2)
Toyo no haha, 1934 (Takamine 3, Tanaka 3)
Toyotomi's Record of Promotion. See Shusse Taikou-ki, 1938
Toys in the Attic, 1963 (Hill, G.R. 2, Hiller 3, Martin, D. 3, Page 3,
    Tierney 3, Biroc 4, Duning 4, Mirisch 4)
Toys of Fate, 1909 (Porter 2)
Toys of Fate, 1918 (Nazimova 3)
Tozi istinski mež, 1975 (Danailov 3)
Tra i gorghi, 1916 (Gallone 2)
Tra moglie e Mario, 1975 (Sordi 3)
Trachoma. See Trakom, 1964
Track of the Cat, 1954 (Wellman 2, Bondi 3, Mitchum 3, Wright 3,
    Clothier 4)
Track of Thunder, 1967 (Fields 4)
Trackdown: Finding the Goodbar Killer, 1983 (Segal 3)
Tracked by the Police, 1927 (Zanuck 4)
Tracked Down, 1912 (Bushman 3)
Tracking the Sleeping Death, 1938 (Zinnemann 2)
Tracks, 1922 (Johnson, N. 3)
Tracks, 1976 (Hopper 3)
Trade Gun Bullet, 1912 (Bosworth 3)
Trade Tattoo, 1937 (Grierson 2, Lye 2)
Trade Winds, 1938 (Garnett 2, Bellamy 3, Bennett J. 3, March 3,
    Sothern 3, Irene 4, Newman 4, Wanger 4)
Trader Horn, 1931 (Van Dyke, W.S. 2, Carey 3)
Tradewinds, 1938 (Maté 4)
Tradgårdsmastaren, 1912 (Sjostrom 2, Jaenzon 4, Magnusson 4)
Tradimento, 1951 (Monicelli 2, Gassman 3)
Trading Places, 1983 (Ameche 3, Bellamy 3, Bernstein 4)
Tradita, 1954 (Bardot 3, Delli Colli 4)
Tradition de minuit, 1939 (Dalio 3, Aurenche 4)
Traffic. See Trafic, 1971 (Tati 2)
Traffic in Soles, 1914 (Fazenda 3)
Traffic in Souls. See Cargaison blanche, 1937
Traffic Jam. See Ingorgo, 1979
Traffic Signs. See Saobraćajni znaci, 1968
Trafic, 1971 (Haanstra 2, Tati 2)
Trafiquant, 1911 (Feuillade 2)
Trafracken, 1966 (Bjornstrand 3)
Tragedia di un uomo ridicolo, 1981 (Bertolucci 2, Aimée 3, Tognazzi 3,
    Morricone 4)
Tragédie de Carmen, 1983 (Carrière 4, Nykvist 4, Wakhévitch 4)
Tragédie impériale, 1938 (L'Herbier 2, Baur 3, Lourié 4)
Tragedy of a Dress Suit, 1911 (Sennett 2)
Tragedy of a Ridiculous Man. See Tragedia di un uomo ridicolo, 1981
Tragedy of Carmen. See Tragédie de Carmen, 1983
Tragedy of Love. See Tragodie der Liebe, 1923
Tragedy of the Desert, 1912 (Olcott 2)
Tragedy of the Orient, 1914 (Hayakawa 3)
Tragedy of the Street. See Dirnentragodie, 1927
Tragedy of Whispering Creek, 1914 (Dwan 2, Chaney Lon 3)
Tragedy of Youth, 1928 (Baxter W. 3, Fetchit 3)
Tragic General, Yamashita Yasubumi. See Higegi no shogun
    Yamashita Yasubumi, 1953
Tragic Hunt. See Caccia tragica, 1947
Tragic Love, 1908 (Griffith 2, Bitzer 4)
Tragic Pursuit. See Caccia tragica, 1947

Tragic Ship. See Eld ombord, 1923
Tragic Symphony. See Song of My Heart, 1947
Tragico ritorno, 1952 (Mastroianni 3)
Tragikomodie, 1922 (Krauss 3)
Tragique Amour de Mona Lisa, 1910 (Gance 2)
Tragodie, 1925 (Porten 3)
Tragodie der Liebe, 1923 (Leni 2, Dietrich 3, Jannings 3)
Tragodie einer Leidenschaft, 1949 (Warm 4)
Tragodie eines Kindes. See Geheimnisse von London, 1920
Tragodie eines Verlorenen, 1927 (Junge 4)
Tragodie eines Verschollenen Fürstensohnes. See Versunkene
    Welt, 1922
Tragodie im Hause Habsburg, 1924 (Korda 2)
Tragoedia, 1976 (Brakhage 2)
Traidores de San Angel, 1966 (Torre-Nilsson 2)
Trail Beyond, 1934 (Wayne 3, Canutt 4)
Trail Drive, 1934 (McCord 4)
Trail Dust, 1936 (Boyd 3)
Trail Guide, 1952 (Musuraca 4)
Trail of '98, 1929 (Brown 2, Brown 2, Tourneur, J. 2, Carey 3,
    Del Rio 3, Gibbons 4, Glazer 4, Seitz 4, Young, W. 4)
Trail of Hate, 1917 (Ford, J. 2)
Trail of Robin Hood, 1950 (Rogers, R. 3)
Trail of the Books, 1911 (Griffith 2, Bitzer 4)
Trail of the Eucalyptus, 1911 (Dwan 2)
Trail of the Horse Thieves, 1929 (Musuraca 4)
Trail of the Law, 1924 (Shearer 3)
Trail of the Lonesome Pine, 1916 (DeMille 2, Buckland 4,
    Macpherson 4)
Trail of the Lonesome Pine, 1923 (Howe 4)
Trail of the Lonesome Pine, 1926 (Fleischer, M. and D. 2)
Trail of the Lonesome Pine, 1936 (Hathaway 2, Bondi 3, Bruce 3,
    Fonda, H. 3, MacMurray 3, Sidney 3, Canutt 4, Dreier 4,
    Friedhofer 4, Wanger 4)
Trail of the Pink Panther, 1982 (Sellers 3, Mancini 4)
Trail of the Snake Band, 1913 (Anderson G. 3)
Trail of the Swordfish, 1931 (Sennett 2)
Trail of the Vigilantes, 1940 (Dwan 2, Auer 3, Crawford, B. 3,
    Krasner 4, Salter 4)
Trail Rider, 1925 (Van Dyke, W.S. 2)
Trail Street, 1947 (Ryan 3, Scott, R. 3, Hunt 4)
Trail to San Antone, 1947 (Autry 3)
Trail to Yesterday, 1918 (Nilsson 3)
Trailed to the Hills. See Trailed to the West, 1910
Trailed to the West, 1910 (Anderson G. 3)
Trailer, 1959 (Breer 2)
Trailer Life, 1937 (Terry 4)
Trailer Thrills, 1937 (Lantz 4)
Trailin', 1921 (Mix 3)
Trailin' West, 1936 (McCord 4)
Trailin' West, 1949 (Elam 3)
Trailing the Counterfeit, 1911 (Sennett 2)
Train, 1964 (Frankenheimer 2, Lancaster 3, Moreau 3, Simon, M. 3,
    Jarre 4)
Train, 1973 (Schneider 3, Trintignant 3, Sarde 4)
Train de 8h 47, 1934 (Fernandel 3)
Train de la victoire. See Tren de la victoria, 1964
Train des suicides, 1931 (Fradetal 4)
Train en marche, 1973 (Marker 2)
Train of Events, 1949 (Crichton 2, Dearden 2, Finch 3, Balcon 4,
    Clarke, T.E.B. 4)
Train of Incidents, 1914 (Bunny 3)
Train on Jacob's Ladder, Mt. Washington, 1899 (Bitzer 4)
Train pour Venise, 1938 (D'Eaubonne 4)
Train Robbers, 1973 (Johnson, B. 3, Wayne 3, Clothier 4)
Train sans yeux, 1925 (Cavalcanti 2, Manès 3)
Train to Alcatraz, 1948 (Cody 3, Darwell 3)
Train to Heaven. See Vlak do stanice nebe, 1972
Train Trouble, 1940 (Halas and Batchelor 2)
Trained Nurse at Bar Z, 1911 (Dwan 2)
Training Pigeons, 1936 (Fleischer, M. and D. 2)
Trains de plaisir, 1930 (Storck 2)
Trains sans fumée, 1951 (Rabier 4)

Traitement de choc, 1972 (Delon 3, Girardot 3)
Traitor, 1914 (Weber 2, Bosworth 3, Marion 4)
Traitor to His Country. *See* Forraederen, 1910
Traitors, 1957 (Lee, C. 3)
Traitor's Gate, 1965 (Kinski 3, Francis 4)
Traitors of San Angel. *See* Traidores de San Angel, 1966
Traja svedkovia, 1968 (Kroner 3)
Trakom, 1964 (Troell 2)
Trame. *See* Après le vent des sables, 1974
Tramonte, 1913 (Bertini 3)
Tramp, 1915 (Bacon 2, Chaplin 2, Purviance 3)
Tramp and the Dog, 1896 (Selig 4)
Tramp and the Dog, 1906 (Selig 4)
Tramp and the Mattress-Makers. *See* Cardeuse de Matelas, 1906
Tramp, the Boys are Marching, 1926 (Fleischer, M. and D. 2)
Tramp, Tramp, Tramp, 1926 (Capra 2, Crawford, J. 3, Langdon 3)
Tramping Tramps, 1930 (Lantz 4)
Tramplers. *See* Uomini dal passo pesante, 1966
Tramps, 1915 (Hardy 3)
Tramp's Gratitude, 1912 (Dwan 2)
Tranen die ich dir geweint. *See* Frühlingsrauschen, 1929
Tranquillo posto di campagna, 1968 (Petri 2, Redgrave, V. 3, Guerra 4, Morricone 4)
Transatlantic, 1931 (Howard 2, Hersholt 3, Loy 3, Friedhofer 4, Howe 4)
Transatlantic Merry-Go-Round, 1934 (Newman 4)
Transatlantic Tunnel, 1935 (Arliss 3, Siodmak 4)
Transatlantic Tunnel. *See* Tunnel, 1935
Transatlantisches, 1926 (Amidei 4)
Trans-Europ Express, 1966 (Trintignant 3, Robbe-Grillet 4)
Transfigurations, 1909 (Cohl 2)
Transformation, 1959 (Emshwiller 2)
Transformation of Mike, 1911 (Griffith 2, Sweet 3, Bitzer 4)
Transformations, 1899–1900 (Guy 2)
Transformations, 1904 (Guy 2)
Transforms, 1970 (Vanderbeek 2)
Transfusion, 1910 (Lawrence 3)
Transgression, 1931 (Brenon 2, Francis, K. 3, Steiner 4)
Transgression of Manuel, 1913 (Dwan 2)
Transient Lady, 1935 (Carradine 3)
Transit, 1966 (Wicki 2)
Transmutations imperceptibles, 1904 (Méliès 2)
Transparency, 1969 (Gehr 2)
Transport from Paradise. *See* Mukl in transport z ráje, 1963
Transports urbains, 1948 (Braunberger 4)
Trap, 1913 (Chaney Lon 3)
Trap, 1918 (Brady 3)
Trap, 1922 (Chaney Lon 3, Miller, V. 4)
Trap, 1959 (Cobb 3, Widmark 3, Frank and Panama 4, Head 4)
Trap, 1966 (Reed, O. 3, Krasker 4)
Trap. *See* Fällen, 1975
Trap. *See* Past, 1950
Trap for Cinderella. *See* Piège pour Cendrillon, 1965
Trap for Santa Claus, 1909 (Griffith 2, Bitzer 4)
Trap for the General. *See* Klopka za generala, 1970
Trap Happy, 1946 (Hanna and Barbera 4)
Trap Happy Porky, 1945 (Jones 2)
Trapeni, 1961 (Kachyna 2)
Trapeze, 1956 (Reed 2, Curtis 3, Lancaster 3, Lollobrigida 3, Arnold 4, Krasker 4, Mankowitz 4)
Trapp Family, 1958 (Herlth 4)
Trapped, 1923 (Fleischer, M. and D. 2)
Trapped, 1949 (Fleischer, R. 2)
Trapped Beneath the Sea, 1974 (Cobb 3)
Trapped by Bloodhounds, or The Lynching at Cripple Creek, 1905 (Selig 4)
Trapped by Fear. *See* Distractions, 1960
Trapped by Television, 1936 (Astor 3)
Trapp-Familie, 1956 (Herlth 4)
Trapp-Familie in Amerika, 1958 (Herlth 4)
Traqué, 1950 (Signoret 3, Schufftan 4)
Traqué, 1974 (Renoir 4)
Traquenard. *See* Haine, 1979

Trash, 1970 (Warhol/Morrissey 2, Spacek 3)
Trás-os-Montes, 1976 (de Almeida 4)
Trastevere, 1971 (De Sica 2, Manfredi 3)
Tratta della bianche, 1952 (Comencini 2, Gassman 3, Loren 3, De Laurentis 4)
Traum des Hauptmann Loy, 1961 (Brejchová 3)
Trauma, 1979 (Cotten 3)
Traumende Mund, 1932 (Czinner 2, Bergner 3, Jaubert 4, Mayer 4)
Traumende Mund, 1939 (Czinner 2)
Traumende Mund, 1953 (Schell, Maria 3)
Traumkonig, 1925 (Dieterle 2)
Traumulus, 1936 (Jannings 3)
Travail, 1969 (Chabrol 2)
Travailleurs de la mer, 1918 (Duvivier 2)
Travaux du tunnel sous l'Escaut, 1932 (Storck 2, Kaufman 4)
Travel, 1973 (Kawamoto 4)
Travelin' Fast, 1924 (Arthur 3)
Travelin' On, 1914 (Carey 3)
Travelin' On, 1922 (Hart 3, August 4)
Traveling Actors. *See* Tabi yakusha, 1940
Traveling Executioner, 1970 (Keach 3, Goldsmith 4)
Traveling Husbands, 1931 (Steiner 4)
Traveling Saleslady, 1935 (Blondell 3, McDaniel 3, Barnes 4, Grot 4)
Traveling Salesman, 1921 (Arbuckle 3, Brown, K. 4)
Travelling Players. *See* O Thassios, 1975
Travels of Princess Snake. *See* Hebihime douchuh, 1949–50
Travels with Anita. *See* Viaggio con Anita, 1978
Travels With My Aunt, 1972 (Cukor 2, Gossett 3, Smith 3, Allen, J. 4, Box 4, Slocombe 4)
Traversata nera, 1939 (Amidei 4)
Traversée de l'Atlantique à la rame, 1978 (Laguionie 4)
Traversée de la France, 1961 (Leenhardt 2)
Traversée de Paris, 1956 (Autant-Lara 2, Bourvil 3, Gabin 3, Aurenche 4, Bost 4, Douy 4)
Travestis du diable, 1963 (Jarre 4)
Traviata, 1922 (Brook 3)
Traviata, 1982 (Zeffirelli 2)
Traviata. *See* Signora delle camelie, 1948
Traviata '53, 1953 (Fusco 4, Pinelli 4)
Traviesa molinera, 1934 (d'Arrast 2)
Travolti da un insolito destino nell'azzurro mare d'agosto, 1974 (Wertmüller 2, Giannini 3)
Tre acquilotta, 1942 (Rossellini 2, Sordi 3)
Tre corsari, 1952 (De Laurentiis 4, Delli Colli 4)
Tre eccetera del colonello. *See* Trois etc. . . . du colonel, 1959
Tre fili fino a Milano, 1958 (Olmi 2)
Tre fratelli, 1981 (Rosi 2, Noiret 3, Vane! 3)
Tre Kammerater, 1912 (Blom 2)
Tre ladri, 1954 (Simon, S. 3)
Tre nel mille, 1971 (Guerra 4, Morricone 4)
Tre notti d'amore, 1964 (Castellani 2, Comencini 2, Fusco 4, Gherardi 4)
Tre onskningar, 1960 (Dahlbeck 3)
Tre passi a nord, 1951 (Fabrizi 3)
Tre passi nel delirio, 1968 (Delon 3)
Tre piger i Paris, 1963 (Gélin 3)
Tre ragazze cercano marito, 1944 (Sordi 3)
Tre sergenti del Bengala, 1965 (Fusco 4)
Tre storie proibite, 1952 (Cervi 3, Aldo 4)
Tre straniere a Roma, 1958 (Cardinale 3)
Tre volti, 1965 (Antonioni 2, Bolognini 2, Sordi 3)
Tre volti della paura. *See* Black Sabbath, 1964
Treachery on the High Seas, 1938 (Daniels 3)
Treachery Within. *See* Double Crime sur la Ligne Maginot, 1938
Tread Softly Stranger, 1958 (Slocombe 4)
Treason, 1918 (Polito 4)
Treason. *See* Old Louisiana, 1937
Treasure. *See* Nidhanaya, 1970
Treasure. *See* Schatz, 1923
Treasure Blues, 1935 (Roach 4)
Treasure Island, 1917 (Franklin 2)
Treasure Island, 1920 (Tourneur, M. 2, Chaney Lon 3, Carré 4, Furthman 4)

Treasure Island, 1934 (Fleming 2, Barrymore L. 3, Beery 3, Bruce 3, Cooper, J 3, Stone 3, Mahin 4, Rosson 4, Stothart 4, Stromberg 4, Young, F. 4)
Treasure Island, 1950 (Disney 2, Ellenshaw 4)
Treasure Island, 1972 (Welles 2, Mankowitz 4)
Treasure Island. *See* Ostrov sokrovishch, 1937
Treasure of Bird Island. *See* Poklad Ptačího ostrova, 1952
Treasure of Kalifa. *See* Steel Lady, 1953
Treasure of Matecumbe, 1976 (Ustinov 3)
Treasure of Pancho Villa, 1955 (Winters 3)
Treasure of Ruby Hills, 1955 (Van Cleef 3)
Treasure of San Gennaro. *See* Operazione San Gennaro, 1966
Treasure of San Teresa, 1959 (Constantine 3, Lee, C. 3)
Treasure of the Four Crowns, 1983 (Morricone 4)
Treasure of the Golden Condor, 1953 (Daves 2, Bancroft 3, Carroll L. 3, Wilde 3, Wray 3, Cronjager 4, Jeakins 4, Lemaire 4, Newman 4, Wheeler 4)
Treasure of the Lost Canyon, 1951 (Powell, W. 3)
Treasure of the Sierra Madre, 1948 (Huston 2, Bogart 3, Huston 3, Sheridan 3, Blanke 4, McCord 4, Steiner 4)
Treasure of the Yankee Zephyr. *See* Race for the Yankee Zephyr, 1982
Treasure Trove, 1911 (Bunny 3)
Treasures of Satan. *See* Trésors de Satan, 1902
Treat 'em Rough, 1919 (Mix 3)
Treat 'em Rough, 1942 (Salter 4)
Treating 'em Rough, 1919 (Sennett 2, Fazenda 3)
Treatise on Japanese Bawdy Song. *See* Nihon shunka-ko, 1967
Treatise on Japanese Rowdy Songs. *See* Nippon shunka-ko, 1967
Trecassin, 1961 (Bourvil 3)
Tredie Magt, 1912 (Blom 2)
Tree for 2, 1943 (Fleischer, M. and D. 2)
Tree for Two, 1951 (Freleng 4)
Tree Grows in Brooklyn, 1945 (Kazan 2, Blondell 3, Marsh 3, Newman 4, Shamroy 4, Wheeler 4, Zanuck 4)
Tree Grows in Brooklyn, 1974 (Robertson 3, Goldsmith 4)
Tree in a Test Tube, 1943 (Laurel & Hardy 3)
Tree of Liberty. *See* Howards of Virginia, 1940
Tree of the Wooden Clogs. *See* Albero degli zoccoli, 1978
Tree Saps, 1931 (Fleischer, M. and D. 2)
Tree-Cornered Tweety, 1955 (Freleng 4)
Trees and People. *See* Stromy a lidé, 1962
Trèfle à cinq feuilles, 1972 (Noiret 3, Coutard 4)
Treize à table, 1955 (Auer 3, Girardot 3, Presle 3)
Treize jours en France, 1968 (Lelouch 2, Reichenbach 2, Lai 4)
Trelawney of the Wells, 1916 (Hepworth 2)
Trelawney of the Wells. *See* Actress, 1928
Tren de la victoria, 1964 (Ivens 2)
Trenchcoat, 1983 (Delli Colli 4)
Trenck, der Pandur, 1940 (Albers 3)
Trenck, 1932 (Tschechowa 3)
Treno crociato, 1942 (Brazzi 3)
Treno popolare, 1933 (Rota 4)
Trenta minuti d'amore, 1983 (Tognazzi 3, Vitti 3)
Trenta secondi d'amore, 1936 (Magnani 3)
Trente secondes d'amour. *See* Trenta secondi d'amore, 1936
33ème chambre, 1947–51 (Verneuil 2)
Trent's Last Case, 1920 (Brook 3)
Trent's Last Case, 1929 (Hawks 2, Crisp 3, Rosson 4)
Trent's Last Case, 1952 (Welles 2, Wilcox 2)
Trepadora, 1944 (García 3)
Trepidazione, 1946 (Delli Colli 4)
Tres alegres compadres, 1951 (Negrete 3)
Tres Berretines, 1933 (Alton, J. 4)
Tres calaveras, 1964 (Figueroa 4)
Tres cantos, 1948-49 (García Berlanga 2)
Tres citas con el destino, 1953 (De Fuentes 2)
Tres García, 1946 (García 3, Infante 3)
Tres huastecos, 1948 (Infante 3)
Tres mosqueteros, 1942 (Cantinflas 3, Figueroa 4)
Très Moutarde, 1908 (Linders 3)
Tres tristes tigres, 1968 (Ruiz 2, Villagra 3)
Trésor. *See* Bas de laine, 1911
Trésor de Cantenac, 1950 (Guitry 2)

Trésor des hommes bleus, 1961 (Kosma 4)
Trésor des Pieds-Nickelés, 1949 (Braunberger 4)
Trésor d'Ostende, 1955 (Storck 2, Kosma 4)
Trésors de Satan, 1902 (Méliès 2)
Trespasser, 1929 (Swanson 3, Walthall 3, Barnes 4, Toland 4)
Trespasser, 1947 (Alton, J. 4)
Trespasser. *See* Night Editor, 1946
Třetí rota, 1931 (Stallich 4)
33.333, 1924 (Molander 2)
Tretton stolar, 1945 (Nykvist 4)
Trêve, 1968 (Denner 3, Gélin 3, Guillemot 4)
Trevico-Torino . . . Viaggio nel Fiat Nam, 1973 (Scola 2)
Trevoschnaja mladost, 1955 (Babochkin 3)
Trewey: Under the Hat. *See* Chapeaux à transformations, 1895
Trey of Hearts, 1914 (Meredyth 4)
Tri, 1967 (Samardžić 3)
Tři čarovná péra, 1970 (Brdečka 4)
Tri dnia Viktora Chernysheva, 1968 (Shukshin 3)
Tri geroini, 1938 (Vertov 2)
Tri muzi ve snehu, 1936 (Haas 3)
Tri pensi o Lenine, 1934 (Vertov 2)
Tři přání, 1958 (Kadár 2)
Tři veteráni, 1983 (Švankmajer 4)
Tri vstrechi, 1948 (Ptushko 2, Pudovkin 2, Yutkevich 2)
Tři zlaté vlasy děda Vševěda, 1963 (Fric 2)
Triage, 1940 (Clément 2)
Trial, 1955 (Cook 3, Ford, G. 3, Kennedy, A. 3, Schary 4, Schnee 4)
Trial, 1962 (Welles 2, Moreau 3, Perkins 3)
Trial. *See* Procès, 1962
Trial. *See* Prozess, 1947
Trial and Error. *See* Dock Brief, 1962
Trial Balloons, 1982 (Breer 2)
Trial by Combat, 1976 (Cushing 3, Mills 3)
Trial by Combat. *See* Dirty Knights' Work, 1976
Trial in Smolensk. *See* Sud v Smolenske, 1946
Trial Marriage, 1921 (Berman 4)
Trial Marriage, 1929 (Levien 4, Walker 4)
Trial Marriages, 1906 (Bitzer 4)
Trial of Billy Jack, 1974 (Bernstein 4)
Trial of Joan of Arc. *See* Procès de Jeanne d'Arc, 1962
Trial of Mary Dugan, 1929 (Shearer 3, Stone 3, Adrian 4, Daniels 4, Gibbons 4)
Trial of Mary Dugan, 1941 (McLeod 2, Nilsson 3, Young, R. 3)
Trial of Mary Dugan. *See* Mordprozess Mary Dugan, 1931
Trial of Mironov. *See* Protess Mironova, 1919
Trial of Mr. Wolf, 1941 (Freleng 4)
Trial of Portia Merriman, 1937 (Bosworth 3)
Trial of the Catonsville Nine, 1972 (Peck 3, Wexler 4)
Trial of the Social Revolutionaries. *See* Protess Eserov, 1922
Trial of Vivienne Ware, 1932 (Howard 2, Bennett J. 3, Pitts 3, Friedhofer 4)
Trials of Celebrity. *See* Gudernes Yndling, 1919
Trials of Oscar Wilde, 1960 (Roeg 2, Finch 3, Mason 3, Adam 4)
Triangle, 1953 (Fairbanks, D. Jr. 3)
Triangle. *See* Idée fixe, 1962
Triangle: The Bermuda Mystery. *See* Triangulo diabolico de la Bermudas, 1977
Triangolo delle Bermude. *See* Triangulo diabolico de la Bermudas, 1977
Triangulo diabolico de la Bermudas, 1977 (Huston 2)
Tribal Law, 1912 (Reid 3)
Tribe Lives On. *See* Stammen Lever an, 1937–38
Tribes, 1970 (Day 4, Smith, J.M. 4)
Tribe's Penalty, 1911 (Anderson G. 3)
Tribu, 1934 (Fernández 2)
Tribulations d'un chinois en Chine, 1965 (Broca 2, Belmondo 3, Delerue 4)
Tribune film: Break and Build. *See* Tribune Film: Breken en bouwen, 1930
Tribune Film: Breken en bouwen, 1930 (Ivens 2)
Tribute, 1980 (Lemmon 3, Remick 3)
Tribute to a Bad Man, 1956 (Wise 2, Cagney 3, Papas 3, Van Cleef 3, Plunkett 4, Rozsa 4, Surtees 4)

Třicet jedna ve stínu, 1965 (Weiss 2, Hrušinský 3)
Tricheurs, 1958 (Carné 2, Belmondo 3, Renoir 4, Spaak 4)
Tricheurs, 1983 (Branco 4)
Trick for Trick, 1933 (Menzies 4)
Trick of Hearts, 1928 (Eason 4)
Trick or Tweet, 1958 (Freleng 4)
Trick That Failed, 1909 (Griffith 2, Pickford 3, Bitzer 4)
Tricking the Government, 1914 (Olcott 2)
Tricks, 1926 (Cooper, Gary 3)
Tricky Business, 1942 (Terry 4)
Tricky Dicks, 1953 (Three Stooges 3)
Tricky Girl. See Karakuri musume, 1927
Tricky Painter's Fate, 1908 (Méliès 2)
Tricorne. See Meunière débauchée, 1934
Triebmorder. See Bestaa uccide a sangue freddo, 1971
Tried for His Own Murder, 1915 (Costello, M. 3)
Trieste File, 1980 (Van Cleef 3)
Triflers, 1924 (Schulberg 4)
Trifling Women, 1922 (Ingram 2, Novarro 3, Stone 3, Seitz 4,
    Vorkapich 4)
Trifoliate Orange Diary. See Karatachi nikki, 1959
Trigger Finger, 1924 (Eason 4)
Trigger Happy. See Deadly Companions, 1961
Trigger, Jr., 1950 (Rogers, R. 3)
Trigger Tricks, 1930 (Eason 4)
Trikimia, 1974 (Powell 2)
Trilby, 1915 (Tourneur, M. 2)
Trilby, 1917 (Carré 4)
Trilby's Love Disaster, 1916 (Mix 3)
Trilogy, 1969 (Page 3, Perry 4, Rosenblum 4)
Trilogy of Terror, 1975 (Black 3)
Trimmed, 1922 (Polito 4)
Trimmed in Furs, 1934 (Langdon 3)
Trimmed in Gold, 1926 (Sennett 2)
Trimmed With Red. See Help Yourself, 1920
Trimming of Paradise Gulch, 1910 (Mix 3)
Třináctý. revír, 1945 (Fric 2, Stallich 4)
Trinadtsat, 1937 (Romm 2)
Trinkets of Tragedy, 1914 (Bushman 3)
Trio, 1950 (Simmons 3, Unsworth 4)
Trio, 1965 (Hofman 4)
Trio, 1976 (Brakhage 2)
Trio, 1978 (Grgić 4)
Trio Film, 1968 (Rainer 2)
Trio infernal, 1974 (Piccoli 3, Schneider 3, Morricone 4)
Trio: Rubinstein, Heifetz, and Piatigorsky, 1952 (Aldrich 2, Laszlo 4)
Triomphe de la vie. See Ich liebe für dich, 1929
Triomphe de Michel Strogoff, 1961 (Jurgens 3)
Trionfo di Ringo, 1965 (Morricone 4)
Trip, 1967 (Bogdanovich 2, Dern 3, Fonda, P. 3, Hopper 3,
    Nicholson 3)
Trip Around the World. See Put oko svijeta, 1964
Trip for Tat, 1960 (Freleng 4)
Trip Through a Hollywood Studio, 1935 (Cagney 3, Del Rio 3)
Trip to Bountiful, 1985 (Page 3)
Trip to Chinatown, 1926 (Wong 3)
Trip to Door, 1971 (Brakhage 2)
Trip to Mars. See Himmelskibet, 1917
Trip to Paradise, 1921 (Glazer 4, Mathis 4)
Trip to Terror. See Blood of the Iron Maiden, 1970
Trip to the Moon. See Voyage dans la lune, 1902
Triple Cross, 1966 (Brynner 3, Howard, T. 3, Schneider 3, Alekan 4)
Triple Crossed, 1958 (Three Stooges 3)
Triple Deception, 1956 (Buckner 4)
Triple Deception. See House of Secrets, 1956
Triple Echo, 1973 (Jackson 3, Reed, O. 3)
Triple Entente, 1915 (Musidora 3)
Triple Justice, 1940 (Hunt 4)
Triple Threat, 1948 (Katzman 4)
Triple Trouble, 1918 (Chaplin 2, Purviance 3)
Triple Trouble, 1948 (Terry 4)
Triple Trouble. See Kentucky Kernels, 1934
Triplet Trouble, 1952 (Hanna and Barbera 4)

Trip-Off Girls, 1938 (Crabbe 3)
Tripoli, 1950 (O'Hara 3, Howe 4)
Tripoli, bel suol d'amore, 1954 (Sordi 3)
Triporteur, 1957 (Legrand 4)
Tripot clandestin, 1905 (Méliès 2)
Trishul, 1978 (Bachchan 3)
Tristan and Isolde. See Tristan et Iseult, 1973
Tristan et Iseult, 1973 (Cusack 3)
Tristan Tzara, dadaismens fader, 1949 (Roos 2)
Tristana, 1970 (Buñuel 2, Deneuve 3, Rey 3)
Tristano e Isotta, 1911 (Bertini 3)
Triste Fin d'un vieux savant, 1904 (Guy 2)
Tristi amori, 1943 (Gallone 2, Berry 3, Cervi 3, Amidei 4)
Triumph, 1916 (Chaney Lon 3)
Triumph, 1924 (DeMille 2, Boyd 3, Pitts 3, Glennon 4, Macpherson 4)
Triumph des Lebens. See Ich lebe fur dich, 1929
Triumph des Willens, 1935 (Riefenstahl 2, Ruttmann 2)
Triumph eines Genies. See Friedrich Schiller, 1940
Triumph of Lester Snapwell, 1963 (Keaton 2)
Triumph of the Heart. See Hjartats triumf, 1929
Triumph of the Rat, 1926 (Novello 3, Balcon 4)
Triumph of the Will. See Triumph des Willens, 1935
Triumph of Will, 1940 (Buñuel 2)
Triumph Tiger '57. See Hempas bar, 1977
Trocadero, 1944 (Fleischer, M. and D. 2)
Trödler von Amsterdam, 1925 (Krauss 3, Andrejew 4)
Trofej, 1979 (Marković 3)
Trog, 1970 (Crawford, J. 3, Francis 4)
Troika, 1930 (Tschechowa 3)
Troika. See Vot mchitza troika potchtovaia, 1913
Troika sur la piste blanche, 1937 (Dalio 3, Vanel 3)
Trois Argentines à Montmartre, 1939 (Brasseur 3)
317e Section, 1964 (Coutard 4, de Beauregard 4)
Trois cents à l'heure, 1934 (Fradetal 4)
Trois Chambres à Manhattan, 1965 (Carné 2, Girardot 3, Barsacq 4,
    Schufftan 4)
Trois Chansons de la résistance, 1944 (Cavalcanti 2)
Trois Chants pour la France. See Trois Chansons de la résistance, 1944
Trois Couronnes danois de matelots. See Trois Couronnes du matelot,
    1982
Trois Couronnes du matelot, 1982 (Ruiz 2, Branco 4, Vierny 4)
Trois Enfants dans le dèsordre, 1966 (Bourvil 3)
Trois etc. . . . du colonel, 1959 (De Sica 2, Gélin 3)
Trois femmes, trois âmes, 1951 (Alekan 4)
Trois filles à Paris. See Tre piger i Paris, 1963
Trois font la paire, 1957 (Guitry 2, Simon, M. 3)
Trois Hommes a abattre, 1980 (Delon 3)
Trois hommes dur un cheval, 1969 (Braunberger 4)
Trois hommes en Corse, 1950 (Decaë 4)
Trois jours à vivre, 1957 (Gélin 3, Moreau 3, Audiard 4, Kosma 4)
Trois Masques, 1929 (Christian-Jaque 2)
Trois milliards sans ascenseur, 1972 (Reggiani 3)
Trois minutes—les saisons, 1938 (Auric 4)
Trois Mousquetaires, 1932 (Baur 3, Fradetal 4, Wakhévitch 4)
Trois Mousquetaires, 1953 (Bourvil 3, Cervi 3, Audiard 4)
Trois Pages d'un journal. See Tagebuch einer Verlorenen, 1929
Trois Passions. See Three Passions, 1929
Trois Rats, 1915 (Musidora 3)
Trois-six-neuf, 1937 (Blier 3, Barsacq 4)
Trois télégrammes, 1950 (Kosma 4)
Trois Themes, 1980 (Alexeieff and Parker 2)
Trois Valses, 1938 (Fresnay 3, D'Eaubonne 4, Schufftan 4)
Trois Vies une corde, 1933 (Storck 2, Jaubert 4)
Troisième Dalle, 1942 (Berry 3)
Troisième Larron, 1916 (Musidora 3)
Trois-Mâts, 1935 (Storck 2, Jaubert 4)
Trojan Horse, 1946 (Terry 4)
Trojan Women, 1971 (Bujold 3, Hepburn, K. 3, Papas 3,
    Redgrave, V. 3, Theodorakis 4)
Trold kan taemmes, 1914 (Holger-Madsen 2)
Troll, 1971 (Sjoman 2)
Trollenberg Terror, 1958 (Sangster 4)
Trolley Troubles, 1921 (Roach 4)

Trolley Troubles, 1927 (Disney 2)
Trollflöjten, 1975 (Bergman 2, Nykvist 4)
Troløs, 1913 (Blom 2)
Tromboni di Fra' Diavolo, 1962 (Tognazzi 3)
Trommelfeuer der Liebe, 1927 (Reisch 4)
Trommeln Asiens, 1921 (Planer 4)
Trompé mais content, 1902 (Guy 2)
Trompe-l'oeil, 1974 (Presle 3)
Trompette anti-neurasthenique, 1915 (Cohl 2)
Tron, 1982 (Bridges 3, Serafine 4)
Trône de France, 1937 (Alexeieff and Parker 2)
Trooper Hook, 1957 (McCrea 3, Stanwyck 3)
Trooper of Troop K, 1916 (Johnson, N. 3)
Trooper O'Neill, 1922 (Howard 2)
Troopers Three, 1930 (Taurog 2, Summerville 3, Eason 4)
Troopship. See Farewell Again, 1937
Trop aimée, 1909 (Linders 3)
Trop c'est trop, 1975 (Dalio 3, Gélin 3)
Trop crédules, 1908 (Chevalier 3)
Tropennachte, 1931 (Rasp 3)
Trophée du zouave, 1915 (Musidora 3)
Trophy. See Trofej, 1979
Tropic Fury, 1939 (Arlen 3, Johnson, N. 3)
Tropic Holiday, 1938 (Lamour 3, Milland 3, Head 4, Prinz 4)
Tropic Madness, 1928 (Musuraca 4, Plunkett 4)
Tropic of Cancer, 1970 (Strick 2, Burstyn 3, Torn 3)
Tropic Zone, 1953 (Reagan 3, Head 4)
Tropical Fish, 1933 (Terry 4)
Tropicana, 1943 (Planer 4)
Tropicana. See Heat's On, 1943
Tropisk Kaerlighed, 1911 (Blom 2)
Troppo bella. See Amante segreta, 1941
Troppo tardi t'ho conosciuta, 1939 (De Laurentiis 4)
Trots, 1952 (Molander 2, Sjoman 2, Andersson H. 3, Dahlbeck 3)
Trotta, 1971 (Schell, Maximilian 3)
Trötte Teodor, 1945 (Borgstrom 3)
Trottie True, 1949 (Lee, C. 3, Moore, R. 3)
Trotting Through Turkey, 1920 (Roach 4)
Trotz alledem!, 1972 (Hoffmann 3)
Trou, 1960 (Becker 2, Cloquet 4)
Trou dans le mur, 1930 (Brasseur 3)
Trou normand, 1952 (Bardot 3, Bourvil 3)
Troubador Girl. See Musume tabigeinin, 1941
Troubadour's Triumph, 1912 (Weber 2)
Trouble, 1922 (Beery 3, Coogan 3)
Trouble along the Way, 1953 (Curtiz 2, Coburn, C. 3, Reed, D. 3, Wayne 3, Steiner 4)
Trouble Back Stairs. See Krach im Hinterhaus, 1935
Trouble Brewing, 1939 (Formby 3)
Trouble Bruin, 1961 (Hanna and Barbera 4)
Trouble Enough, 1916 (Lloyd 3, Roach 4)
Trouble for Two, 1936 (Montgomery 3, Russell, R. 3, Clarke, C.C. 4, Waxman 4)
Trouble in Morocco, 1937 (Schoedsack 2)
Trouble in Panama. See Torchy Blane in Panama, 1938
Trouble in Paradise, 1932 (Lubitsch 2, Francis, K. 3, Hopkins, M. 3, Horton 3, Marshall 3, Banton 4, Dreier 4, Raphaelson 4)
Trouble in Store, 1953 (Rutherford 3)
Trouble in Sundown, 1939 (Bond 3)
Trouble in Texas, 1937 (Hayworth 3, Canutt 4)
Trouble in the Glen, 1954 (Welles 2, Wilcox 2, McLaglen 3, Nugent 4, Young, V. 4)
Trouble in the Morning. See Asa no hamon, 1952
Trouble in the Sky. See Cone of Silence, 1960
Trouble Indemnity, 1950 (Burness 4, Hubley 4)
Trouble Shooter, 1924 (Mix 3)
Trouble Shooter. See Man With the Gun, 1955
Trouble with Angels, 1966 (Lupino 3, Russell, R. 3, Goldsmith 4)
Trouble with Girls, 1969 (Carradine 3, Presley 3, Price 3)
Trouble with Harry, 1955 (Hitchcock 2, Gwenn 3, MacLaine 3, Hayes 4, Head 4, Herrmann 4)
Trouble with Women, 1947 (Milland 3, Dreier 4, Head 4, Young, V. 4)
Troubled Waters, 1936 (Mason 3, Rutherford 3, Sim 3)

Troublemaker, 1964 (Henry 4)
Troubles. See Making a Living, 1914
Troubles with Heat. See Klopoty z cieplem, 1964
Troublesome Satchel, 1909 (Griffith 2, Bitzer 4)
Troublesome Secretaries, 1911 (Normand 3)
Troublesome Stepdaughters, 1912 (Bunny 3, Talmadge, N. 3)
Trouper's Heart, 1911 (Dwan 2)
Trouping with Ellen, 1924 (Rathbone 3, Hunt 4)
Trousers. See Hose, 1927
Trout, 1982 (Losey 2, Huppert 3, Moreau 3, Alekan 4, Trauner 4)
Trout. See Truite, 1982
Trout Fishing, Rangeley Lakes, 1905 (Bitzer 4)
Trouvaille de Bûchu, 1917 (Feyder 2)
Trovatore, 1910 (Bertini 3)
Trovatore, 1949 (Gallone 2)
Truands, 1956 (Constantine 3, Modot 3)
Truant Soul, 1917 (Walthall 3)
Truants, 1907 (Bitzer 4)
Truba, 1976 (Grgić 4)
Trübe Wasser, 1959 (Eisler 4)
Truc du brésilien, 1932 (Cavalcanti 2, D'Eaubonne 4)
Truce Hurts, 1948 (Hanna and Barbera 4)
Truck Busters, 1943 (Eason 4)
Truck That Flew, 1943 (Pal 2)
Truckload of Trouble, 1949 (Terry 4)
Trude, die Sechzehnjahrige, 1926 (Ondra 3, Tschechowa 3)
Trudnoye shchastie, 1958 (Gurchenko 3)
True as Steel, 1924 (Fazenda 3)
True Blue, 1918 (Farnum 3)
True Chivalry, 1912–13 (White 3)
True Confession, 1937 (Ruggles 2, Barrymore J. 3, Lombard 3, MacMurray 3, McDaniel 3, Merkel 3, Dreier 4, Head 4, Lewin 4)
True Confessions, 1981 (Cusack 3, De Niro 3, Duvall, R. 3, Meredith 3, Delerue 4, Roizman 4)
True Glory, 1945 (Reed 2, Ustinov 3, Alwyn 4, Brown, Harry 4, Kanin 4)
True Grit, 1969 (Hathaway 2, Duvall, R. 3, Hopper 3, Martin, S. 3, Wayne 3, Ballard 4, Bernstein 4, Jeakins 4, Wallis 4)
True Grit, 1978 (Oates 3)
True Story of Camille. See Vera storia della Signora delle Camelie, 1981
True Story of Jesse James, 1957 (Ray, N. 2, Carradine 3, Hunter 3, Moorehead 3, Wagner 3)
True Story of Lilli Marlene, 1944 (Jennings 2)
True Story of Lynn Stuart, 1958 (Guffey 4)
True Story of the Civil War, 1956 (Massey 3)
True Story of the Lyons Mail, 1915 (Pearson 2)
True to Life, 1943 (De Carlo 3, Powell, D. 3, Carmichael 4, Dreier 4, Head 4, Lang 4, Mercer 4, Young, V. 4)
True to the Army, 1941 (Miller 3, Young, V. 4)
True to the Navy, 1930 (Bow 3, March 3, Mankiewicz 4)
True-Heart Susie, 1919 (Griffith 2, Gish, L. 3, Bitzer 4)
Truet Lykke, 1915 (Blom 2)
Truite, 1982 (Cassel 3)
Truman at Potsdam, 1976 (Houseman 4)
Trumpet. See Truba, 1976
Trumpet Blows, 1934 (Menjou 3, Raft 3)
Trumpet Call. See Rough Riders, 1927
Trumpet Island, 1920 (Haller 4)
Trunk Conveyor, 1952 (Anderson 2)
Trunk Crime, 1939 (Boulting 2)
Trunk Mystery, 1927 (Shamroy 4)
Trunk to Cairo, 1966 (Murphy 3, Sanders 3)
Trunk to Cairo. See Mivtza Kahir, 1966
Trust, 1911 (Feuillade 2)
Trust, 1915 (Chaney Lon 3)
Trusting Is Good, Shooting Is Better. See Fidarsi e benem sparare e meglio, 1967
Trusting Wives, 1929 (Horton 3)
Trut!, 1944 (Sucksdorff 2)
Truth, 1920 (Hunt 4)
Truth. See Great Problem, 1916
Truth. See Vérité, 1960

Truth about Spring, 1965 (Mills 3)
Truth about Women, 1957 (Zetterling 2, Harvey 3, Lee, C. 3, Beaton 4)
Truth about Youth, 1930 (Loy 3, Young, L. 3, Miller, A. 4)
Truth Juggler, 1922 (Roach 4)
Truthful Liar, 1924 (Rogers, W. 3, Roach 4)
Truthful Tulliver, 1917 (Hart 3, August 4)
Trutze von Trutzberg, 1921 (Planer 4)
Truxton King, 1923 (Gilbert 3, August 4)
Truxtonia. See Truxton King, 1923
Try and Get It, 1924 (Horton 3, Furthman 4)
Try and Get Me. See Sound of Fury, 1950
Try, Try Again, 1921 (Roach 4)
Trygon Factor, 1966 (Granger 3)
Trying to Fool, 1911 (Sennett 2)
Trying to Get Along, 1919 (Sennett 2)
Trying to Get Arrested, 1909 (Griffith 2)
Trying to Get Married, 1909 (Bitzer 4)
Tryout, 1916 (Hardy 3)
Tryst, 1929 (Gilliat 4)
Trzy koniety, 1957 (Lomnicki 3)
Trzy opowiesci, 1953 (Polanski 2)
Trzy starty, 1955 (Cybulski 3)
Tsena cheloveka, 1928 (Donskoi 2)
Tsirk, 1936 (Orlova 3)
Tsirk zazhigaet ogni, 1972 (Gurchenko 3)
Tsubaki Sanjuro, 1962 (Mifune 3, Shimura 3)
Tsubakuro-gasa, 1955 (Hasegawa 3)
Tsubasa no gaika, 1942 (Kurosawa 2)
Tsubasa wa kokoro ni tsukete, 1978 (Kagawa 3)
Tsuchiya Chikara: Rakka no make, 1937 (Hasegawa 3)
Tsujigahana, 1972 (Iwashita 3)
Tsuki kara kita otoko, 1951 (Hasegawa 3)
Tsuki no watari-dori, 1951 (Kinugasa 2, Hasegawa 3)
Tsuki wa noborinu, 1955 (Tanaka 3)
Tsukigata Hanpeita, 1925 (Kinugasa 2)
Tsukigata Hanpeita, 1929 (Hasegawa 3)
Tsukigata Hanpeita, 1933 (Yamada 3)
Tsukigata Hanpeita, 1934 (Hasegawa 3)
Tsukigata Hanpeita, 1952 (Yamada 3)
Tsukigata Hanpeita, 1956 (Kinugasa 2, Hasegawa 3, Kyo 3, Yamamura 3)
Tsukihime keizu, 1958 (Miyagawa 4)
Tsukimiso, 1959 (Oshima 2)
Tsukiwa noborinu, 1955 (Imamura 2)
Tsukiyo garasu, 1939 (Yoda 4)
Tsukiyo no kasa, 1955 (Tanaka 3)
Tsuma, 1953 (Naruse 2)
Tsuma no himitsu, 1924 (Kinugasa 2)
Tsuma no kokoro, 1956 (Naruse 2, Mifune 3, Takamine 3)
Tsuma to iu na no onnatachi, 1963 (Tsukasa 3)
Tsuma to onna no kisha, 1950 (Hayasaka 4)
Tsuma to onna no aida, 1976 (Ichikawa 2)
Tsuma to shite onna to shite, 1961 (Naruse 2, Mori 3, Takamine 3)
Tsuma yo bara no yo ni, 1935 (Naruse 2)
Tsurigane-so, 1940 (Takamine 3)
Tsurugi no ketsuen, 1928 (Hasegawa 3)
Tsurugi o koete, 1930 (Yamada 3)
Tsuruhachi and Tsurujiro. See Tsuruhachi tsurujiro, 1938
Tsuruhachi tsurujiro, 1938 (Naruse 2, Hasegawa 3, Yamada 3)
Tsuruhachi Tsurujiro, 1956 (Yamamura 3)
Tsuyomushi onna yawamushi otoko, 1968 (Shindo 2)
Tsuyu no atosaki, 1956 (Takemitsu 4)
Tsuzurikata kyodai, 1958 (Kagawa 3)
Tsuzurikata kyoshitsu, 1938 (Takamine 3)
Tsvetok na kamne, 1963 (Paradzhanov 2)
Tu che ne dici?, 1960 (Tognazzi 3)
Tu enfanteras sans douleur, 1956 (Delerue 4)
Tu es danse et vertige, 1967 (Coutard 4)
Tu m'appartiens, 1929 (Bertini 3)
Tu m'as sauvé la vie, 1950 (Guitry 2, Fernandel 3)
Tu ne tueras point, 1961 (Autant-Lara 2, Aurenche 4, Bost 4, Douy 4)

Tu n'epouseras jamais un avocat, 1914 (Musidora 3)
Tu seras vedette, 1942 (Alekan 4)
Tu, solo tu, 1949 (Alcoriza 4)
Tu ten kamen, 1923 (Ondra 3)
Tua donna, 1954 (Neal 3, Vích 4)
Tubby the Tuba, 1947 (Pal 2)
Tubina, 1941 (Hrušínský 3)
Tubog Sa Ginto, 1971–73 (Brocka 2)
Tucet Mých tatínku, 1959 (Brdečka 4, Hofman 4)
Tuchi nad Borskom, 1961 (Churikova 3)
Tudor Princess, 1913 (Ingram 2)
Tudor Rose, 1936 (Fisher 2, Hardwicke 3, Mills 3, Balcon 4)
Tuesday in November, 1945 (Houseman 4, Hubley 4, Koch 4)
Tueur, 1971 (Blier 3, Depardieu 3, Gabin 3, Renoir 4)
Tueurs de San Francisco, 1965 (Palance 3)
Tugboat Annie, 1933 (Leroy 2, Beery 3, Dressler 3, O'Sullivan 3, Young, R. 3, Raine 4, Toland 4)
Tugboat Annie Sails Again, 1940 (Reagan 3, Wyman 3, Deutsch 4, Edeson 4)
Tugboat Granny, 1956 (Freleng 4)
Tugboat Princess, 1936 (Trumbo 4)
Tugboat Romeos, 1916 (Sennett 2)
Tugthusfange No. 97, 1914 (Blom 2)
Tul a Kálvin-téren, 1955 (Mészáros 2)
Tulácka pohádka, 1972 (Hofman 4)
Tulip Time. See Seven Sweethearts, 1942
Tulipa, 1967 (Gómez, M. 2, Granados 3)
Tulipe noire, 1963 (Christian-Jaque 2, Delon 3, Decaë 4)
Tulips Shall Grow, 1942 (Pal 2)
Tull-Bom, 1951 (Bjornstrand 3)
Tulsa, 1949 (Armendáriz 3, Hayward 3, Preston 3, Fulton 4, Hoch 4, Nugent 4, Wanger 4)
Tumbleweed, 1953 (Murphy 3, Van Cleef 3, Hunter 4)
Tumbleweeds, 1925 (Hart 3, August 4, Sullivan 4)
Tumbling River, 1927 (Mix 3)
Tumbling Tumbleweeds, 1935 (Autry 3, Rogers, R. 3)
Tumultes, 1931 (Boyer 3)
Tuna Clipper, 1949 (McDowall 3)
Tune Up and Sing, 1934 (Fleischer, M. and D. 2)
Tunes of Glory, 1960 (Guinness 3, Mills 3, York, S. 3, Arnold 4)
Tung, 1966 (Baillie 2)
Tuning His Ivories. See Laughing Gas, 1914
Tunisian Victory, 1944 (Boulting 2, Capra 2, Huston 2, Meredith 3, Alwyn 4, Hornbeck 4, Veiller 4)
Tunnel, 1919 (Warm 4)
Tunnel, 1933 (Gabin 3, Grundgens 3, Hoffmann 4)
Tunnel, 1935 (Huston 3, Balcon 4, Metzner 4)
Tunnel. See Transatlantic Tunnel, 1935
Tunnel of Love, 1958 (Day 3, Kelly, Gene 3, Widmark 3, Young, G. 3, Rose 4)
Tunnel sous la manche ou Le Cauchemar franco-anglais, 1907 (Méliès 2)
Tunnel to the Sun. See Korube no taiyo, 1968
Tunnel 28, 1962 (Siodmak 2)
Tunnelling the English Channel. See Tunnel sous la manche, 1907
Tup-tup, 1972 (Dragić 4)
Tür mit den sieben Schlossern, 1962 (Kinski 3)
Turandot, princesse de Chine, 1934 (Dalio 3)
Turbina, 1940 (Baarová 3)
Turbina nr. 3, 1927 (Moskvin 4)
Turbine d'odio, 1914 (Gallone 2)
Turbine no. 3. See Turbina nr. 3, 1927
Turco napoletano, 1953 (Struss 4)
Turf Sensation. See Women First, 1924
Turista, 1961 (Schorm 2)
Turkey Dinner, 1936 (Lantz 4)
Turkey Hunt, Pinehurst, 1905 (Bitzer 4)
Turkey Time, 1933 (Balcon 4, Junge 4)
Turkeys in a Row. See Shichimencho no yukue, 1924
Turkish Delight, 1927 (Garnett 2, Sullivan 4)
Turm des Schweigens, 1924 (Pommer 4)
Turmoil, 1924 (Mandell 4)

Turn Back the Clock, 1933 (Three Stooges 3, Adrian 4, Gillespie 4, Hecht 4, Rosson 4, Stothart 4, Vorkapich 4)
Turn Back the Hours, 1928 (Loy 3, Pidgeon 3, Robinson 4)
Turn in the Road, 1919 (Vidor, K. 2)
Turn Off the Moon, 1937 (Dmytryk 2, Dreier 4, Head 4, Prinz 4, Young, V. 4)
Turn the Key Softly, 1953 (Unsworth 4)
Turn the Other Cheek. See Porgi l'altra guancia, 1974
Turn to the Right, 1922 (Ingram 2, Mathis 4, Seitz 4)
Turnabout, 1940 (Astor 3, Meek 3, Menjou 3, Roach 4)
Turned Out Nice Again, 1941 (Dearden 2, Hamer 2, Formby 3, Balcon 4)
Turner, 1972 (Rosenblum 4)
Turning Point, 1952 (Dieterle 2, Holden 3, O'Brien, E. 3, Head 4)
Turning Point, 1977 (Bancroft 3, MacLaine 3, Reynolds 4, Surtees 4)
Turning Point of Jim Malloy, 1975 (Young, G. 3)
Turning the Tables, 1919 (Gish, D. 3)
Turning to Hell. See Jigokuno magariko, 1959
Turno, 1981 (Gassman 3)
Turn-Tail Wolf, 1952 (McKimson 4)
Turtle Diary, 1985 (Jackson 3)
Tusalava, 1929 (Lye 2)
Tutta la città canta, 1943 (Fellini 2)
Tutta per la donna, 1939 (Zampa 2)
Tutti a casa, 1960 (Comencini 2, Reggiani 3, Sordi 3, Age and Scarpelli 4, De Laurentiis 4)
Tutti innamorati, 1959 (Mastroianni 3)
Tuttles of Tahiti, 1942 (Vidor, C. 2, Laughton 3, Musuraca 4)
Tutto a posto e niente in ordine, 1974 (Wertmüller 2)
Tutto per tutto, 1968 (Ireland 3)
Tütun zamani, 1959 (Guney 2)
Tutyu és Totyo, 1914 (Korda 2)
Tuxedo Warrior, 1982 (Lassally 4)
Tuya en cuerpo y alma, 1944 (García 3)
Tüzoltó utca 25, 1973 (Szabó 2, Geschonneck 3)
TV of Tomorrow, 1953 (Avery 2)
Två konungar, 1924 (Jaenzon 4)
Två kvinnor, 1947 (Bjornstrand 3, Dahlbeck 3)
Två kvinnor, 1975 (Andersson H. 3)
Två man om en anka, 1933 (Jaenzon 4)
Två människor, 1945 (Dreyer 2, Fischer 4)
Två Skona Juveler, 1954 (Thulin 3)
Två Svenska emigranters aventyr i Amerika, 1912 (Jaenzon 4, Magnusson 4)
Två trappor over gården, 1950 (Andersson H. 3)
Tvář, 1973 (Brdečka 4)
Tvärbalk, 1967 (Donner 2, Andersson H. 3)
Twarz aniola, 1970 (Pszoniak 3)
Twarza w twarz, 1968 (Zanussi 2)
'Twas Ever Thus, 1915 (Bosworth 3, Marion 4)
Twee vrouwen, 1979 (Andersson, B. 3, Perkins 3)
'Tween Two Loves, 1911 (Pickford 3)
Tweet and Lovely, 1959 (Freleng 4)
Tweet and Sour, 1955 (Freleng 4)
Tweet Dreams, 1959 (Freleng 4)
Tweetie Pie, 1946 (Freleng 4)
Tweety and the Beanstalk, 1956 (Freleng 4)
Tweety Zoo, 1956 (Freleng 4)
Tweety's Circus, 1954 (Freleng 4)
Tweety's SOS, 1950 (Freleng 4)
Twelfth Night, 1969 (Keach 3)
Twelfth Night. See Vizkereszet, 1967
Twelve Angry Men, 1957 (Lumet 2, Cobb 3, Fonda, H. 3, Warden 3, Kaufman 4)
Twelve Chairs, 1970 (Brooks, M. 2)
12 Chairs. See Doce sillas, 1962
12 Chairs. See Dvanáct křesel, 1933
12 Chapters on Women. See Josei ni kansuru juni-sho, 1954
Twelve Crowded Hours, 1939 (Ball 3, Fort 4, Musuraca 4)
12 Days of Christmas, 1956 (Peterson 2)
Twelve Good Men, 1936 (Gilliat 4)
Twelve Hours to Kill, 1960 (Crosby 4)
Twelve Miles Out, 1927 (Crawford, J. 3, Gilbert 3, Gibbons 4)

Twelve Months. See Dvanácti mèsíčkách, 1960
Twelve O'Clock and All Ain't Well, 1941 (Terry 4)
Twelve O'Clock High, 1949 (King 2, Douglas, P. 3, Peck 3, Newman 4, Shamroy 4, Wheeler 4, Zanuck 4)
12 Photographers. See Juninin no shashin-ka, 1953–57
Twelve Plus One. See Una su tredici, 1969
12 Tasks of Asterix, 1973 (Halas and Batchelor 2)
Twelve: Ten, 1919 (Brenon 2)
Twelve to the Moon, 1960 (Bushman 3, Alton, J. 4, Bodeen 4)
Twentieth Century, 1934 (Hawks 2, Barrymore J. 3, Lombard 3, August 4, Hecht 4, MacArthur 4)
$20 a Week, 1924 (Arliss 3, Colman 3)
25th Hour. See 25 Heure, 1967
25 Fireman's Street. See Tuzoltó utca 25, 1973
25 October, First Day, 1968 (Norstein 4)
24 Dollar Island, 1927 (Flaherty 2)
Twenty Four Eyes. See Nijushi no hitomi, 1954
24 Hours, 1931 (Brook 3, Francis, K. 3, Hopkins, M. 3, Haller 4)
24 Hours in an Underground Market. See Chikagai 24-jikan, 1947
24 Hours of a Secret Life. See Chikagai nijuyo-jikan, 1947
24 Hours of a Woman's Life, 1952 (Saville 2, Oberon 3, Francis 4)
24 Hours of Shanghai, 1933 (Zhao 3)
24 Hours of the Underground Street. See Chikagai nijuyo-jikan, 1947
Twenty-Four Hours to Kill, 1965 (Rooney 3)
Twenty Horses, 1932 (Johnson 4)
20 Hours. See Húsz óra, 1964
20 Legs Under the Sea, 1931 (Fleischer, M. and D. 2)
20,000,000 Dollar Mystery, 1915 (Cruze 2)
20,000,000 Miles to Earth, 1957 (Harryhausen 4)
Twenty Million Sweethearts, 1934 (O'Brien, P. 3, Powell, D. 3, Rogers, G. 3, Orry-Kelly 4, Wald 4)
Twenty Minutes at Warner Brothers Studios, 1927 (Barrymore J. 3)
20 Minutes of Love, 1914 (Chaplin 2, Sennett 2)
20 Mule Team, 1940 (Baxter A. 3, Beery 3)
Twenty-Nine, 1968 (Godfrey 4)
29 Nine Acacia Avenue, 1936 (Balfour 3)
Twenty One, 1923 (Barthelmess 3)
21 Carat Snatch. See Popsy Pop, 1971
21 Days, 1937 (Crichton 2, Leigh, V. 3, Olivier 3, Hornbeck 4, Korda 4)
21 Days. See First and the Last, 1937
21 Days Together. See First and the Last, 1937
$21 a Day Once a Month, 1941 (Lantz 4)
21 Hours at Munich, 1976 (Holden 3, Quayle 3)
21 Miles, 1942 (Watt 2)
Twenty Plus Two, 1961 (Crain 3, Moorehead 3)
20 Pounds a Ton, 1955 (Anderson 2)
27 Down, 1973 (Chandragupta 4)
Twenty Shades of Pink, 1976 (Wallach 3, Wynn 3)
20,000 Leagues under the Sea, 1954 (Disney 2, Fleischer, R. 2, Douglas, K. 3, Johnson, N. 3, Lorre 3, Lukas 3, Mason 3, Ellenshaw 4, Iwerks 4, Planer 4)
20,000 Men a Year, 1939 (Scott, R. 3)
20,000 Years in Sing Sing, 1933 (Curtiz 2, Calhern 3, Davis 3, Tracy 3, Grot 4, Orry-Kelly 4)
23½ Hours Leave, 1937 (Bond 3, Carré 4)
23 Paces to Baker Street, 1956 (Hathaway 2, Johnson, V. 3, Krasner 4, Lemaire 4)
22 Misfortunes, 1930 (Gerasimov 2)
22 Misfortunes. See Dvadzatdva neshchastia, 1930
22 Mishaps. See 22 Misfortunes, 1930
20 Years of Cinema. See Kino za XX liet, 1940
20 Years of Soviet Cinema. See Kino za XX liet, 1940
Twice a Man, 1963 (Markopoulos 2)
Twice a Woman. See Twee vrouwen, 1979
Twice Blessed, 1945 (Irene 4)
Twice Branded, 1936 (Mason 3)
Twice in a Lifetime, 1985 (Burstyn 3, Hackman 3)
Twice on a Certain Night. See Aruyo futatabi, 1956
Twice round the Daffodils, 1962 (Dillon 4)
Twice Two, 1920 (Howard, L. 3)
Twice Two, 1933 (Laurel & Hardy 3, Roach 4)

Twice Upon a Time, 1953 (Hawkins 3, Francis 4)
Twice-Told Tales, 1963 (Price 3)
Twiddle-Twiddle. *See* Klizi-puzi, 1968
Twilight, 1912 (Bushman 3)
Twilight. *See* Alkony, 1971
Twilight. *See* Belle Aventure, 1942
Twilight. *See* Duelle, 1976
Twilight and Dawn. *See* Alkonyok és hajnalok, 1961
Twilight for the Gods, 1958 (Charisse 3, Hudson 3, Kennedy, A. 3, Raksin 4)
Twilight in the Sierras, 1950 (Rogers, R. 3)
Twilight in Tokyo. *See* Tokyo boshoku, 1957
Twilight Meetings. *See* Moten i skymningen, 1957
Twilight of Honor, 1963 (Seaton 2, Rains 3, Green, J. 4)
Twilight on the Prairie, 1944 (Bruckman 4, Salter 4)
Twilight on the Rio Grande, 1947 (Autry 3, Canutt 4)
Twilight on the Trail, 1937 (Fleischer, M. and D. 2)
Twilight on the Trail, 1941 (Boyd 3)
Twilight Path. *See* Daikon to ninjin, 1965
Twilight Rendezvous. *See* Viaggiatori della sera, 1980
Twilight Time, 1983 (Malden 3)
Twilight Women. *See* Women of Twilight, 1952
Twilight Zone, 1983 (Miller 2, Spielberg 2, Bottin 4, Goldsmith 4)
Twilight's Last Gleaming, 1977 (Aldrich 2, Cotten 3, Douglas, M. 3, Lancaster 3, Widmark 3, Goldsmith 4)
Twin Beds, 1929 (Pitts 3, Polito 4)
Twin Beds, 1942 (Auer 3, Bennett J. 3, Brent 3, Merkel 3, Irene 4, Tiomkin 4)
Twin Brothers, 1909 (Griffith 2)
Twin Detectives, 1976 (Gish, L. 3)
Twin Flats, 1916 (Hardy 3)
Twin Kiddies, 1917 (King 2)
Twin Screws, 1933 (Roach 4)
Twin Sisters, 1915 (Hardy 3)
Twin Sisters. *See* Soseiji gakkyu, 1956
Twin Sisters of Kyoto. *See* Koto, 1963
Twin Triplets, 1935 (Roach 4)
Twinkle in God's Eye, 1955 (Rooney 3)
Twinkle Twinkle Killer Kane. *See* Ninth Configuration, 1979
Twinkletoes, 1926 (Leroy 2, Moore, C. 3, Oland 3)
Twinkletoes—Gets the Bird, 1941 (Fleischer, M. and D. 2)
Twinkletoes in Hat Stuff, 1941 (Fleischer, M. and D. 2)
Twinkletoes—Where He Goes Nobody Knows, 1941 (Fleischer, M. and D. 2)
Twinky, 1969 (Bronson 3, Hawkins 3, Howard, T. 3, Lassally 4)
Twins, 1916 (Sennett 2)
Twins, 1925 (Laurel 3)
Twins from Suffering Creek, 1920 (Wellman 2, Furthman 4)
Twins of Evil, 1971 (Cushing 3)
Twisker Pitcher, 1937 (Fleischer, M. and D. 2)
Twist. *See* Folies bourgeoises, 1976
Twist Around the Clock, 1961 (Katzman 4)
Twist, ninfette e vitelloni, 1962 (Fabrizi 3)
Twist of Fate, 1954 (Rogers, G. 3)
Twist of Fate. *See* Beautiful Stranger, 1954
Twisted Lives. *See* Menteurs, 1961
Twisted Nerve, 1968 (Boulting 2, Herrmann 4)
Twisted Road. *See* They Live By Night, 1948
Twisted Trail, 1910 (Griffith 2, Pickford 3, Bitzer 4)
Twisted Trails, 1916 (Mix 3)
Twisted Triggers, 1926 (Arthur 3)
Twixt Love and Fire, 1914 (Sennett 2, Arbuckle 3)
2 Acres of Land. *See* Do Bigha Zamin, 1953
Two Against the World, 1932 (Bennett C. 3, Orry-Kelly 4, Rosher 4)
Two Against the World, 1936 (Bogart 3)
Two Alone, 1934 (Bondi 3, Pitts 3, Steiner 4)
Two Americans, 1929 (Huston 3)
Two and Two Make Six, 1962 (Francis 4)
Two April Fools, 1954 (Bruckman 4)
Two Arabian Knights, 1927 (Milestone 2, Astor 3, Boyd 3, Karloff 3, August 4, Gaudio 4, Menzies 4)
Two Are Guilty. *See* Glaive et la balance, 1963
Two Bagatelles, 1952 (McLaren 2)

Two Barbers, 1944 (Terry 4)
Two Baroque Churches in Germany, 1959 (Bernstein 4)
Two Before Zero, 1962 (Rathbone 3)
Two Blondes and a Redhead, 1947 (Katzman 4)
Two Bottle Babies, 1904 (Bitzer 4)
2 Brave Men. *See* Ikisi de cesurdu, 1963
Two Brides, 1919 (Stone 3)
Two Bright Boys, 1939 (Cooper, J 3)
Two Brothers, 1910 (Griffith 2, Pickford 3, Bitzer 4)
Two Brothers. *See* Bruder Schellenberg, 1926
2 Brothers. *See* Matira Manisha, 1967
Two Can Play, 1926 (Bow 3)
2 Cents Worth of Hope. *See* Due Soldi di speranza, 1952
Two Centuries of Black American Art, 1976 (Moss 4)
Two Colonels. *See* Due colonelli, 1963
2 Convicts. *See* Eventyr paa Fodrejsen, 1911
Two: Creeley/McClure, 1965 (Brakhage 2)
2 Crooks, 1917 (Sennett 2)
2 Crowded Hours, 1931 (Powell 2)
Two Crows from Tacos, 1956 (Freleng 4)
Two Daughters. *See* Teen Kanya, 1961
Two Daughters of Eve, 1912 (Griffith 2, Gish, L. 3, Bitzer 4)
Two Dinky Dramas of a Non-Serious Kind, 1914 (Beery 3)
Two Dollar Bettor, 1951 (Leven 4)
Two Down, One to Go, 1945 (Capra 2, Hornbeck 4)
Two English Girls. *See* Deux Anglaises et le continent, 1971
2 Eyes. *See* Sobo, 1933
Two Faces of Dr. Jekyll, 1960 (Fisher 2, Lee, C. 3, Reed, O. 3, Mankowitz 4)
Two Fathers, 1911 (Lawrence 3)
Two Fathers, 1944 (Asquith 2)
Two Fedors. *See* Dva Fedora, 1959
2 Fisted, 1935 (Cruze 2)
Two Fisted Law, 1932 (Brennan 3, Wayne 3)
2 Fister, 1927 (Wyler 2)
Two Flags West, 1950 (Wise 2, Chandler 3, Cotten 3, Darnell 3, Wilde 3, Lemaire 4, Newman 4, Nugent 4, Robinson 4, Shamroy 4, Wheeler 4)
Two Flaming Youths, 1927 (Fields, W.C. 3, Mankiewicz 4)
Two Flats West, 1950 (Friedhofer 4)
2 Fools in a Canoe, 1898 (Hepworth 2)
Two for the Money, 1971 (Brennan 3, Dreyfuss 3, McCambridge 3)
Two for the Road, 1967 (Donen 2, Bisset 3, Dauphin 3, Finney 3, Hepburn, A. 3, Mancini 4, Raphael 4)
Two for the Seesaw, 1962 (Wise 2, MacLaine 3, Mitchum 3, Lennart 4, Leven 4, McCord 4, Mirisch 4, Orry-Kelly 4, Previn 4, Westmore, F. 4)
2 For the Zoo, 1941 (Fleischer, M. and D. 2)
Two for Tonight, 1935 (Bennett J. 3, Crosby 3, Head 4, Struss 4)
Two from One Housing Block. *See* Two from the Same Block, 1957
Two from the Same Block, 1957 (Bondarchuk 3)
2 Frosts. *See* Dva mrazíci, 1954
Two Fugitives, 1911 (Anderson G. 3)
Two Girls and a Sailor, 1944 (Allyson 3, Durante 3, Gardner 3, Horne 3, Johnson, V. 3, Meek 3, Irene 4, Pasternak 4, Surtees 4)
2 Girls of the Street. *See* Két lány az utcán, 1939
Two Girls on Broadway, 1940 (Goulding 2, Blondell 3, Turner, L. 3, Brown, N. 4, Freed 4)
Two Girls Wanted, 1927 (Gaynor 3, Miller, S. 4)
Two Grilled Fish, 1968 (Kuri 4)
Two Gun Hicks. *See* Passing of Two Gun Hicks, 1914
2 Gun Rusty, 1944 (Pal 2)
Two Guns, 1917 (Carey 3)
Two Guys Abroad, 1961 (Raft 3)
Two Guys from Milwaukee, 1946 (Bacall 3, Bogart 3, Sakall 3, Diamond 4, Edeson 4)
Two Guys from Texas, 1948 (Malone 3, Cahn 4, Diamond 4, Edeson 4)
Two Headed Giant, 1939 (Terry 4)
2 Hearts in Waltz Time, 1934 (Gallone 2)
Two Hearts that Beat as Ten, 1915 (Beery 3)
Two in a Crowd, 1936 (Bennett J. 3, Cook 3, McCrea 3, Meek 3)
2 in a Taxi, 1941 (Florey 2)
Two in Revolt, 1936 (Steiner 4)

Tycoon, 1947 (Anderson J. 3, Hardwicke 3, Quinn 3, Wayne 3, Chase 4, D'Agostino 4)
Type comme moi ne devrait jamais mourir, 1976 (Guillemot 4)
Typhoid. *See* Tifusari, 1963
Typhon sur Nagasaki, 1956 (Darrieux 3, Marais 3, Alekan 4)
Typhoon, 1914 (Hayakawa 3, Ince 4)
Typhoon, 1940 (Preston 3, Dreier 4, Head 4, Reynolds 4)
Typical Budget, 1925 (Buchanan 3)
Tyrannical Fiancée. *See* Tyranniske fastmannen, 1912
Tyranniske fastmannen, 1912 (Magnusson 2, Stiller 4)
Tyrant Is Dead, 1910 (Costello, M. 3)

Tyrant of Red Gulch, 1928 (Musuraca 4)
Tyrant of the Sea, 1950 (Katzman 4)
Tyrant of Toledo. *See* Amants de Tolède, 1953
Tyrant's Heart or Boccaccio in Hungary. *See* Zsarnok szíve avagy Boccaccio Magyarországon, 1981
Tyrtée, 1912 (Feuillade 2)
Tystnaden, 1963 (Bergman 2, Thulin 3, Nykvist 4)
Tyven, 1910 (Blom 2)
TZ, 1979 (Breer 2)
Tzveti Zepozclaliye, 1917 (Ouspenskaya 3)

U

U Krutovo Yara, 1962 (Gerasimov 2)
U.M.C., 1969 (Robinson, E. 3, La Shelle 4)
U oluji, 1952 (Mimica 4)
U ozera, 1969 (Gerasimov 2, Shukshin 3)
U pokladny stál, 1939 (Stallich 4)
U.S. Army in San Francisco, 1915 (Sennett 2)
U.S. Naval Militia, 1900 (Bitzer 4)
U.S.S. Maine, Havana Harbor, 1898 (Bitzer 4)
U.S.S. Tea Kettle. *See* You're in the Navy Now, 1951
U sněděného krámu, 1933 (Fric 2, Vích 4)
U sv. Matěje, 1928 (Stallich 4)
U svetého Antoníčka, 1933 (Vích 4)
U telefonu Martin, 1966 (Kopecký 3)
Uata no hanakago, 1946 (Tanaka 3)
Ubåt 39, 1952 (Andersson H. 3, Dahlbeck 3)
Uber Alles in der Welt, 1941 (Rohrig 4)
Uberfall, 1928 (Metzner 4)
Uberflussige Menschen, 1926 (George, H. 3, Krauss 3, Rasp 3, Andrejew 4)
Ubernachtung in Tirol, 1974 (Schlondorff 2, Von Trotta 2)
Ubiistvo na ulize Dante, 1956 (Romm 2)
Ubitzi vykhodyat na dorogu, 1942 (Pudovkin 2)
U-Boat. *See* Spy in Black, 1939
U-Boat 29, 1939 (Veidt 3)
U-Boat 29. *See* Spy in Black, 1939
U-boat 39. *See* Ubåt 39, 1952
U-Boat Prisoner, 1944 (Guffey 4)
Ubu and the Great Gidouille. *See* Ubu et la Grande Gidouille, 1979
Ubu et la Grande Gidouille, 1979 (Lenica 2)
Ubu Roi, 1976 (Lenica 2)
Uccellacci e uccellini, 1966 (Pasolini 2, Delli Colli 4, Donati 4, Morricone 4)
Uccello dalle piume di cristallo, 1969 (Argento 4, Morricone 4, Storaro 4)
Uccidere in silenzio, 1972 (Cervi 3)
Uccidete il vitello grasso ed arrostitelo, 1970 (Morricone 4)
Uchiiri zenya, 1941 (Shimura 3)
Uchitel, 1939 (Gerasimov 2)
Uchu daikaiju Dogora, 1964 (Tsuburaya 4)
Uchu daisensu, 1959 (Tsuburaya 4)
Uchveli uzh davno krisantemi v sadu, 1916 (Mozhukin 3)
Ucunuzu de mihlarim, 1965 (Guney 2)
Udarat, 1983 (Ivanov 3)
Udari levego, 1917 (Lukas 3)
Udayer Pathey, 1944 (Roy 2, Sircar 4)
Udbrudte Slave. *See* Eventyr paa Fodrejsen, 1911
Uddhar, 1949 (Anand 3)
Ude ippon, 1930 (Yamada 3)
Uden Faedreland. *See* Forviste, 1914
Udflytterne, 1972 (Roos 2)
Udienza, 1971 (Ferreri 2, Cardinale 3, Cuny 3, Gassman 3, Piccoli 3, Cristaldi 4)

Uemon torimono-cho: Uemon Edo-sugata, 1940 (Shimura 3)
UFO Incident, 1975 (Jones, J.E. 3)
UFOria, 1982 (Stanton 3)
Ugetsu. *See* Ugetsu monogatari, 1953
Ugetsu monogatari, 1953 (Mizoguchi 2, Kyo 3, Mori 3, Tanaka 3, Hayasaka 4, Miyagawa 4, Yoda 4)
Ugly American, 1963 (Brando 3, Okada 3)
Ugly Boy. *See* Csunya fiu, 1918
Ugly Dachshund, 1966 (Disney 2)
Ugly Dino, 1940 (Fleischer, M. and D. 2)
Ugly Man. *See* Bir cirkin adam, 1969
Ugly Village. *See* Skaredá dědina, 1975
Ugolok, 1916 (Mozhukin 3)
Uhuka, a kis bagoly, 1969 (Macskássy 4)
Uijin, 1933 (Hasegawa 3)
Uj Gilgames, 1963 (Darvas 3)
Ujra mosolyognak, 1954 (Mészáros 2)
Ujraélok, 1920 (Fejos 2)
Ujszulott, 1916 (Sakall 3)
Ukagusa, 1959 (Ryu 3)
Ukelele Sheiks, 1926 (Roach 4)
Ukhod velikovo startza, 1912 (Protazanov 2)
Ukhodi-ukhodi, 1978 (Gurchenko 3)
Ukifune, 1957 (Kinugasa 2)
Ukigumo, 1955 (Naruse 2, Mori 3, Takamine 3)
Ukigusa, 1959 (Ozu 2, Kyo 3, Miyagawa 4)
Ukigusa monogatari, 1934 (Ozu 2)
Ukiyo-buro, 1929 (Gosho 2)
Ukiyo kouji, 1939 (Yoda 4)
Ukjent mann, 1952 (Henning-Jensen 2)
Uklady a láska, 1972 (Schorm 2)
Ukradená vzducholod, 1966 (Zeman 2)
Ukraine in Flames. *See* Nezabivaemoe, 1968
Ukrainian Rhapsody. *See* Ukrainskaia rapsodiia, 1961
Ukrainskaia rapsodiia, 1961 (Paradzhanov 2)
Ukroshchenie ognia, 1971 (Smoktunovsky 3)
Ukrotiteli velosipedov, 1964 (Gurchenko 3)
Ulica graniczna, 1949 (Ford, A. 2)
Ulička v ráji, 1936 (Fric 2, Haas 3)
Ulisse, 1954 (Douglas, K. 3, Mangano 3, Quinn 3, De Laurentiis 4, Hecht 4, Ponti 4, Rosson 4, Schufftan 4)
Ulla, min Ulla, 1930 (Jaenzon 4)
Ulla, My Ulla. *See* Ulla, min Ulla, 1930
Uloupená hranice, 1947 (Weiss 2, Brodský 3)
Ulrik fortaeller en historie, 1972 (Roos 2)
Ultima carrozzella, 1943 (Fellini 2, Fabrizi 3, Magnani 3)
Última cena, 1976 (Gutiérrez 2, Villagra 3)
Ultima chance, 1973 (Wallach 3)
Ultima donna, 1976 (Ferreri 2, Baye 3, Depardieu 3, Piccoli 3, Sarde 4)
Ultima fiamma, 1940 (Vích 4)
Ultima nemica, 1938 (Valli 3)
Ultima Sentenza. *See* Son dernier verdict, 1951

Ultima Thule, 1968 (Roos 2)
Ultimate Solution of Grace Quigley, 1983 (Hepburn, K. 3, Nolte 3, Addison 4, Golan and Globus 4)
Ultimate Warrior, 1975 (Brynner 3, Von Sydow 3)
Ultimatum, 1938 (Siodmak 2, Von Stroheim 2, Wiene 2, Fradetal 4)
Ultimatum, 1971 (Lefebvre 2)
Ultimatum. See Ultimatum alla città, 1975
Ultimatum alla città, 1975 (Cobb 3)
Ultimi angeli, 1977 (Kennedy, A. 3)
Ultimi cinque minuti, 1955 (De Sica 2, Brazzi 3, Darnell 3)
Ultimi filibustieri, 1943 (Amidei 4)
Ultimi giorni di Pompei, 1959 (Leone 2)
Ultimi giorni di Pompei. See Derniers Jours de Pompéi, 1948
Ultimi giorni di Pompeii, 1926 (Gallone 2)
Ultimi zar, 1928 (Amidei 4)
Ultimo addio, 1942 (Cervi 3, Vích 4)
Ultimo amante, 1955 (Ponti 4)
Ultimo amore, 1946 (De Santis 2)
Ultimo ballo, 1941 (Amidei 4)
Ultimo dia de la guerra, 1969 (Bardem 2)
Ultimo incontro, 1952 (Aumont 3, Valli 3)
Ultimo Lord. See Femme en homme, 1931
Ultimo paradiso, 1946 (Flaiano 4)
Ultimo sogno, 1921 (Bertini 3)
Ultimo tango a Parigi, 1972 (Bertolucci 2, Brando 3, Léaud 3, Storaro 4)
Ultimo treno della notte, 1975 (Morricone 4)
Ultimo uomo della terra, 1964 (Price 3)
Ultimo uomo di Sara, 1972 (Morricone 45
Ultimos de Filipinas, 1945 (Rey 3)
Ultimos dias de Pompeya, 1960 (Rey 3)
Ultraman, 1967 (Tsuburaya 4)
Ultus series, 1915-17 (Pearson 2)
Ulysse ou Les Mauvaises rencontres, 1949 (Astruc 2)
Ulysses, 1967 (Strick 2)
Ulysses. See Ulisse, 1954
Ulzana, 1974 (Hoppe 3)
Ulzana's Raid, 1972 (Aldrich 2, Lancaster 3, Biroc 4)
Um Adeus Português, 1985 (de Almeida 4)
Um das Lacheln einer Frau, 1919 (Wiene 2)
Um Haaresbreite, 1913 (Porten 3, Messter 4)
Um Liebe und Thron, 1922 (Planer 4)
Um seine Ehre. See Perfekt gentleman, 1927
Um Thron und Liebe. See Sarajewo, 1955
Uma, 1941 (Kurosawa 2, Takamine 3)
Umanità, 1946 (Cervi 3)
Umanoide, 1979 (Kennedy, A. 3, Morricone 4)
Umarete wa mita keredo, 1932 (Ozu 2, Ryu 3)
Umarmungen und andere Sachen, 1976 (Léaud 3)
Umbartha. See Subah, 1983
Umberto D, 1952 (De Sica 2, Aldo 4, Zavattini 4)
Umbracle, 1970 (Lee, C. 3)
Umbrellas of Cherbourg. See Parapluies de Cherbourg, 1964
Umbrellas to Men, or Mr. Niceman's Umbrella, 1912 (Bunny 3)
Umi no bara, 1945 (Kinugasa 2)
Umi no hanabi, 1951 (Kinoshita 2, Yamada 3)
Umi no nai minato, 1931 (Yoda 4)
Umi no yaju, 1949 (Yamamura 3)
Umi no yarodomo, 1957 (Shindo 2)
Umi o wataru sairei, 1941 (Shimura 3)
Umi o yuku bushi, 1939 (Yoda 4)
Umi wa ikiteiru, 1958 (Hani 2)
Umirai samo v kraen slutschai, 1978 (Danailov 3)
Umon torimonocho: Harebare gojusan-tsugi, 1936 (Shimura 3)
Umut, 1970 (Guney 2)
Umutsuzlar, 1971 (Guney 2)
Umweg zur Ehe, 1918 (Wiene 2)
Umwege zum Gluck, 1939 (Dagover 3)
Un de la Canebière, 1938 (D'Eaubonne 4)
Un de la Légion, 1936 (Christian-Jaque 2)
Un, deux, trois . . ., 1974 (Grimault 4)
Un, deux, trois, quatre, 1960 (Chevalier 3)

Un, Deux, trois, quatre . . . See Collants noirs, 1960
Un Dollaro per 7 vigliacchi, 1967 (Hoffman 3)
Un genio, due compari, un pollo, 1975 (Leone 2, Kinski 3, Morricone 4)
Un novio para dos hermanos, 1967 (García 3)
Una su tredici, 1969 (De Sica 2, Welles 2, Gassman 3)
Una sull'altra, 1969 (Ireland 3)
Unaccustomed as We Are, 1929 (Stevens 2, Laurel and Hardy 3, Roach 4)
Unafraid, 1915 (DeMille 2, Buckland 4, Macpherson 4)
Unafraid, 1918 (King 2)
Unashamed, 1932 (Beavers 3, Hersholt 3, Stone 3, Young, R. 3, Adrian 4)
Unbandiges Spanien, 1962 (Eisler 4)
Unbearable Bear, 1943 (Jones 2)
Unbekannte, 1936 (Jurgens 3)
Unbekannte Gast, 1931 (Sakall 3, Metzner 4)
Unbekannte Morgen, 1923 (Korda 2, Krauss 3, Lukas 3)
Unbeliever, 1918 (Crosland 2, Von Stroheim 2)
Unbesiegbaren, 1953 (Geschonneck 3)
Unbezahmbare Leni Peickert, 1969 (Kluge 2)
Uncanny, 1977 (Cushing 3, Greenwood 3, Milland 3, Pleasance 3)
Uncensored, 1942 (Asquith 2)
Uncensored Movies, 1923 (Rogers, W. 3, Roach 4)
Uncertain Glory, 1944 (Walsh 2, Flynn 3, Lukas 3, Buckner 4, Deutsch 4)
Uncertain Lady, 1934 (Horton 3, Freund 4)
Unchained, 1955 (Miller, V. 4, North 4)
Unchained Goddess, 1958 (Capra 2)
Unchanging Sea, 1910 (Griffith 2, Pickford 3, Bitzer 4)
Uncharted Channels, 1920 (King 2)
Uncharted Seas, 1921 (Ruggles 2, Valentino 3, Seitz 4)
Uncharted Waters, 1933 (Grierson 2)
Unchastened Woman, 1925 (Bara 3)
Uncivil War Brides, 1946 (Bruckman 4)
Uncivil Warbirds, 1946 (Three Stooges 3)
Uncivil Warriors, 1935 (Three Stooges 3)
Uncle. See Strejda, 1959
Uncle Bill, 1914 (Talmadge, C. 3)
Uncle from America. See Strýček z Ameriky, 1933
Uncle Harry, 1945 (Siodmak 2, Sanders 3, Harrison 4, Lourié 4)
Uncle Harry. See Strange Affair of Uncle Harry, 1945
Uncle Jake, 1933 (Sennett 2)
Uncle Joey, 1941 (Terry 4)
Uncle Joey Comes to Town, 1941 (Terry 4)
Uncle John's Arrival in Stockholm. See Farbror Johannes ankomst till Stockholm, 1912
Uncle Josh at the Moving Picture Show, 1902 (Porter 2)
Uncle Sam's Songs, 1951 (Fleischer, M. and D. 2)
Uncle Silas, 1947 (Simmons 3, Krasker 4)
Uncle Tom, 1929 (Sennett 2, Hornbeck 4)
Uncle Tom Without the Cabin, 1919 (Sennett 2)
Uncle Tom's Bungalow, 1937 (Avery 2)
Uncle Tom's Cabana, 1947 (Avery 2)
Uncle Tom's Cabin, 1903 (Porter 2)
Uncle Tom's Cabin, 1910 (Costello, M. 3, Talmadge, N. 3)
Uncle Tom's Cabin, 1913 (Nilsson 3)
Uncle Tom's Cabin, 1927 (Beavers 3, Mandell 4)
Uncle Tom's Cabin, 1957 (Massey 3)
Uncle Tom's Uncle, 1926 (Roach 4)
Uncle Vanya. See Dyadya Vanya, 1970
Uncle Was a Vampire. See Tempi duri vampiri, 1959
Uncle Yanco, 1967 (Varda 2)
Uncommon Valor, 1983 (Hackman 3)
Unconquerable. See Invincible, 1943
Unconquerable. See Njepobedimye, 1943
Unconquered, 1917 (Bosworth 3)
Unconquered, 1947 (DeMille 2, Bond 3, Cody 3, Cooper, Gary 3, Goddard 3, Johnson, N. 3, Karloff 3, Bennett 4, Dreier 4, Edouart 4, Westmore, F. 4, Young, V. 4)
Unconquered. See Nepokorenniye, 1945
Unconventional Linda. See Holiday, 1938
Uncovered Wagon, 1923 (Roach 4)

Und das am Montagmorgen, 1959 (Comencini 2)
Und deine Liebe auch, 1962 (Mueller-Stahl 3)
. . . und fuhre uns nicht an Versuchung, 1957 (Herlth 4)
Und uber uns der Himmel, 1947 (Albers 3, Pommer 4)
Und wandern sollst du ruhelos . . ., 1915 (Oswald 2, Pommer 4)
Undead, 1956 (Corman 4)
Undefeated, 1969 (Hudson 3, Johnson, B. 3, Wayne 3, Clothier 4,
   Needham 4)
Under a Flag of Truce, 1912 (Nilsson 3)
Under a Shadow, 1915 (Chaney Lon 3)
Under a Texas Moon, 1930 (Curtiz 2, Loy 3)
Under Age, 1941 (Dmytryk 2)
Under Burning Skies, 1912 (Griffith 2, Sweet 3, Bitzer 4)
Under California Skies, 1948 (Rogers, R. 3)
Under Capricorn, 1949 (Hitchcock 2, Bergman 3, Cotten 3, Cardiff 4)
Under Cover of Night, 1937 (Clarke, C.C. 4)
Under Crimson Skies, 1920 (Ingram 2, Johnson, N. 3)
Under False Colors, 1914 (Talmadge, N. 3)
Under False Colours. See Under falsk flagg, 1935
Under False Pretences, 1912 (Dwan 2)
Under falsk flagg, 1935 (Molander 2)
Under Fiesta Stars, 1941 (Autry 3, Brown, K. 4)
Under Fire, 1926 (Arthur 3)
Under Fire, 1983 (Hackman 3, Nolte 3, Trintignant 3, Goldsmith 4)
Under Handicap, 1917 (Gaudio 4)
Under Kaerlighedens Aag. See Skaebnes Veje, 1913
Under Mexican Skies, 1912 (Anderson G. 3)
Under Milk Wood, 1971 (Burton 3, O'Toole 3, Taylor, E. 3)
Under Mindernes Trae, 1913 (Holger-Madsen 2)
Under Montana Skies, 1930 (Summerville 3)
Under My Skin, 1950 (Negulesco 2, Garfield 3, Presle 3, La Shelle 4,
   Lemaire 4, Robinson 4)
Under Nevada Skies, 1946 (Rogers, R. 3, Canutt 4)
Under Pesten. See Mens Pesten raserr, 1913
Under Pressure, 1935 (Walsh 2, McLaglen 3, Chase 4)
Under Royal Patronage, 1914 (Bushman 3)
Under Savklingens Taender, 1913 (Holger-Madsen 2)
Under Sheriff, 1914 (Sennett 2, Arbuckle 3)
Under Sodra Korset, 1952 (Nykvist 3)
Under Suspicion, 1918 (Bushman 3)
Under Suspicion, 1931 (Brent 3)
Under Suspicion. See Garde a vue, 1980
Under Ten Flags. See Sotto diece bandiero, 1960
Under Texas Skies, 1940 (Canutt 4)
Under the Bamboo Tree, 1905 (Bitzer 4)
Under the Banner of Samurai. See Furin kaza, 1969
Under the Big Top, 1938 (Brown, K. 4)
Under the Black Eagle, 1927 (Van Dyke, W.S. 2)
Under the Blue Sky. See Neel Akasher Neechey, 1959
Under the Cherry Blossoms. See Sakura no mori no mankai no shita,
   1975
Under the Cherry Moon, 1986 (Sylbert 4)
Under the Clock. See Clock, 1945
Under the Daisies, 1913 (Talmadge, N. 3)
Under the Gaslight, 1914 (Barrymore L. 3)
Under the Gun, 1950 (Jaffe 3, Orry-Kelly 4)
Under the Lash, 1921 (Wood 2, Swanson 3)
Under the Military Flag. See Gunki hatameku shitani, 1972
Under the Neighbor's Roof. See Tonari no yane no shita, 1931
Under the Old Apple Tree, 1907 (Bitzer 4)
Under the Olive Tree. See Non c'è pace tra gli ulivi, 1949
Under the Pampas Moon, 1935 (Baxter W. 3, Hayworth 3)
Under the Phrygian Star. See Pod gwiazda frygijska, 1954
Under the Rainbow, 1981 (Arden 3)
Under the Red Robe, 1923 (Crosland 2, Powell, W. 3)
Under the Red Robe, 1937 (Sjostrom 2, Massey 3, Veidt 3, Biro 4,
   Howe 4, Périnal 4, Wimperis 4)
Under the Roofs of Paris. See Sous les Toits de Paris, 1930
Under the Sign of Scorpio. See Sotto il segno dello scorpione, 1969
Under the Southern Cross. See Under Sodra Korset, 1952
Under the Sun of Rome. See Sotto il sole di Roma, 1948
Under the Tonto Rim, 1928 (Hathaway 2, Arlen 3, Schulberg 4)
Under the Tonto Rim, 1933 (Hathaway 2)

Under the Tonto Rim, 1947 (Hunt 4)
Under the Top, 1918 (Cruze 2, Crisp 3, Emerson 4, Loos 4)
Under the Volcano, 1984 (Bisset 3, Finney 3, Figueroa 4, North 4)
Under the Yoke, 1918 (Bara 3)
Under the Yoke of Sin. See Vo vlasti gretcha, 1915
Under the Yum Yum Tree, 1963 (Lemmon 3, Biroc 4, Cahn 4)
Under Two Flags, 1916 (Bara 3)
Under Two Flags, 1922 (Browning 2)
Under Two Flags, 1936 (Bruce 3, Carradine 3, Colbert 3, Colman 3,
   McLaglen 3, Russell, R. 3, Meredyth 4, Zanuck 4)
Under Two Jags, 1923 (Laurel 3, Roach 4)
Under Western Skies, 1910 (Anderson G. 3)
Under Western Skies, 1926 (Miller, V. 4)
Under Western Skies, 1945 (Bruckman 4)
Under Western Stars, 1938 (Rogers, R. 3)
Under Your Hat, 1940 (Henreid 3)
Under Your Spell, 1936 (Preminger 2)
Underbara lognen, 1955 (Nykvist 4)
Underbare Luge der Nina Petrowna, 1929 (Pommer 4)
Undercover, 1943 (Baker S. 3, Balcon 4)
Undercover Doctor, 1939 (Crawford, B. 3, Head 4)
Undercover Hero. See Soft Beds and Hard Battles, 1974
Undercover Maisie, 1947 (Sothern 3, Irene 4)
Undercover Man, 1932 (Raft 3, Fort 4, Head 4)
Undercover Man, 1942 (Boyd 3)
Undercover Man, 1949 (Rossen 2, Ford, G. 3, Ireland 3, Duning 4,
   Guffey 4)
Undercurrent, 1946 (Minnelli 2, Gwenn 3, Hepburn, K. 3, Mitchum
   Taylor, R. 3, Berman 4, Freund 4, Irene 4, Previn 4, Stothart 4)
Undercurrent. See Yoru no kawa, 1956
Underdog, 1932 (Lantz 4)
Underground, 1928 (Asquith 2)
Underground, 1941 (Deutsch 4, Wallis 4)
Underground, 1976 (de Antonio 2, Wexler 4)
Underground. See Undercover, 1943
Underground Guerrillas. See Undercover, 1943
Underpup, 1939 (Bondi 3, Cummings 3, Pasternak 3)
Undersea Kingdom, 1936 (Chaney Lon, Jr. 3, Farnum 3, Eason 4)
Understanding Heart, 1927 (Crawford, J. 3, Gibbons 4)
Understudy, 1912 (Bushman 3)
Understudy, 1915 (Costello, M. 3)
Undertakers. See Tomuraishi tachi, 1968
Undertow, 1930 (Mandell 4)
Undertow, 1949 (Hudson 3, Orry-Kelly 4)
Underwater, 1955 (Sturges, J. 2, Russell, J. 3, D'Agostino 4)
Underwater Odyssey. See Neptune Factor, 1973
Underwater Warrior, 1958 (Dailey 3, Biroc 4)
**Underworld, 1927 (Hathaway 2, Hawks 2, Von Sternberg 2, Brook 3,
   Clothier 4, Dreier 4, Glennon 4, Hecht 4)**
Underworld, 1934 (Orry-Kelly 4)
Underworld, 1936 (Micheaux 2)
Underworld. See Ankoku-gai, 1956
Underworld. See Bas-Fonds, 1936
Underworld Story, 1950 (Duryea 3, Marshall 3, Cortez 4)
Underworld U.S.A., 1961 (Fuller 2, Robertson 3)
Undici moschettieri, 1952 (Delli Colli 4)
Undine, 1912 (Cruze 2)
Undying Flame, 1917 (Tourneur, M. 2, Carré 4)
Undying Monster, 1942 (Ballard 4, Day 4, Raksin 4)
Une chante l'autre pas, 1977 (Varda 2)
Une et l'autre, 1967 (Allio 2, Dauphin 3, Noiret 3)
Une Java, 1927 (Christan-Jaque 2)
Unearthly, 1957 (Carradine 3)
Uneasy Moment. See Unheimlicher Moment, 1970
Uneasy Money, 1917 (Pitts 3)
Uneasy 3, 1925 (McCarey 2, Roach 4)
Unendliche Fahrt—aber begrenzt, 1965 (Kluge 2)
Unexpected Father, 1932 (Pitts 3, Summerville 3)
Unexpected Father, 1939 (Auer 3, Darwell 3)
Unexpected Fireworks. See Feu d'artifice improvisé, 1905
Unexpected Guest, 1947 (Boyd 3)
Unexpected Help, 1910 (Griffith 2, Bitzer 4)
Unexpected Pest, 1956 (McKimson 4)

Unexpected Review, 1911 (Bunny 3)
Unexpected Romance, 1915 (Anderson G. 3)
Unexpected Santa Claus, 1908 (Porter 2)
Unexpected Uncle, 1941 (Daves 2, Garnett 2, Coburn, C. 3)
Unfaithful, 1931 (Cromwell 2, Lukas 3, Lang 4)
Unfaithful, 1947 (Arden 3, Ayres 3, Sheridan 3, Haller 4, Steiner 4, Wald 4)
Unfaithful. See Utro, 1966
Unfaithful Wife, 1903 (Bitzer 4)
Unfaithful Wife. See Femme infidèle, 1969
Unfaithfully Yours, 1948 (Sturges, P. 2, Darnell 3, Harrison 3, Lemaire 4, Newman 4, Wheeler 4, Zanuck 4)
Unfaithfully Yours, 1985 (Moore, D. 3)
Unfinished Business, 1941 (La Cava 2, Dunne 3, Montgomery 3, Waxman 4)
Unfinished Dance, 1947 (Charisse 3, O'Brien, M. 3, Irene 4, Pasternak 4, Rose 4, Stothart 4, Surtees 4)
Unfinished Journey, 1943 (Gielgud 3)
Unfinished Love Song, 1919 (Kuleshov 2)
Unfinished Rainbows, 1941 (Ladd 3)
Unfinished Story. See Ek Adhuri Kahani, 1972
Unfinished Story. See Neokonchennaya povest, 1955
Unfinished Symphony, 1934 (Asquith 2)
Unfinished Symphony. See Leise flehen meine Lieder, 1933
Unfinished Tale. See Neokonchennaya povest, 1955
Unfit or The Strength of the Weak, 1914 (Hepworth 2)
Unfoldment, 1922 (Lawrence 3)
Unforeseen Complication, 1911 (White 3)
Unforeseen Metamorphosis, 1912–14 (Cohl 2)
Unforgettable. See Nezabivaemoe, 1968
Unforgettable Year 1919. See Nezabyvayemyi 1919-god, 1952
Unforgiven, 1960 (Huston 2, Gish, L. 3, Hepburn, A. 3, Lancaster 3, Murphy 3, Jeakins 4, Maddow 4, Planer 4, Tiomkin 4)
Unfriendly Enemies, 1925 (Laurel 3, Roach 4)
Unfriendly Fruit, 1916 (Lloyd 3)
Unfug der Liebe, 1928 (Wiene 2)
Ung flukt, 1959 (Ullmann 3)
Ungarische Rhapsodie, 1913 (Porten 3, Messter 4)
Ungarische Rhapsodie, 1928 (Dagover 3, Hoffmann 4, Pommer 4)
Ungarmadel. See Zigeunerblut, 1934
Ungarn in Flammen, 1957 (Schell, Maria 3)
Ungdom og Letsind. See Ekspeditricen, 1911
Ungdommens Ret, 1911 (Blom 2)
Unge Blod, 1915 (Holger-Madsen 2)
Ungekusst soll man nicht schlaten geh'n, 1936 (Stradling 4)
Ungkarlspappan, 1934 (Molander 2)
Unglassed Windows Cast a Terrible Reflection, 1953 (Brakhage 2)
Unguarded Hour, 1936 (Wood 2, Stone 3, Young, L. 3, Irene 4)
Unguarded Moment, 1956 (Russell, R. 3, Williams 3, Daniels 4)
Unguarded Women, 1924 (Crosland 2, Astor 3, Daniels 3)
Unhappy Finish, 1921 (Sennett 2)
Unheilbar, 1916 (Jannings 3)
Unheimliche Gast, 1922 (Duvivier 2)
Unheimliche Geschichten, 1919 (Oswald 2, Veidt 3, Hoffmann 4)
Unheimliche Geschichten, 1932 (Oswald 2, Wegener 3)
Unheimliche Haus, 1916 (Oswald 2)
Unheimlichen Wunsche, 1939 (Tschechowa 3)
Unheimlicher Moment, 1970 (Schlondorff 2)
Unholy Desire. See Akai satsui, 1964
Unholy Four. See Stranger Came Home, 1954
Unholy Garden, 1931 (Auer 3, Colman 3, Wray 3, Barnes 4, Day 4, Goldwyn 4, Hecht 4, MacArthur 4, Newman 4, Toland 4)
Unholy Love. See Alraune, 1927
Unholy Night, 1929 (Barrymore L. 3, Karloff 3, Adrian 4, Day 4, Gibbons 4, Hecht 4)
Unholy Night. See Spectre vert, 1930
Unholy Partners, 1941 (Leroy 2, Dalio 3, Robinson, E. 3, Gibbons 4)
Unholy Rollers, 1972 (Corman 4)
Unholy Three, 1925 (Browning 2, Chaney Lon 3, McLaglen 3, Gibbons 4, Young, W. 4)
Unholy Three, 1930 (Chaney Lon 3, Gibbons 4, Shearer 4)
Unholy Wife, 1957 (Bondi 3, Steiger 3, Ballard 4, D'Agostino 4)
Unicorn. See Enhorningen, 1955

Unicorn in the Garden, 1953 (Raksin 4)
Unidentified Flying Oddball. See Spaceman and King Arthur, 1979
Uniform Lovers. See Hold 'em Yale, 1935
Uniformes et grandes manoeuvres, 1950 (Fernandel 3)
Uninhibited. See Pianos mécanicos, 1965
Uninvited, 1944 (Crisp 3, Milland 3, Brackett, C. 4, Dreier 4, Head 4, Lang 4, Young, V. 4)
Uninvited Pests, 1946 (Terry 4)
Union Depot, 1932 (Blondell 3, Fairbanks, D. Jr. 3, Polito 4)
Union Pacific, 1939 (DeMille 2, Chaney Lon, Jr. 3, Cody 3, McCrea 3, Preston 3, Quinn 3, Stanwyck 3, Dreier 4, Edouart 4, Head 4, Sullivan 4)
Union Pacific Railroad Scenes, 1901 (Bitzer 4)
Union Pacific Railroad Shots, 1899 (Bitzer 4)
Union sacrée, 1915 (Feuillade 2, Musidora 3)
Union Square, 1950 (Fitzgerald 3)
Union Station, 1950 (Holden 3, Dreier 4, Maté 4)
United Action, 1940 (Maddow 4)
United States Mail. See Appointment with Danger, 1951
United States Smith, 1928 (Robinson 4)
Univermag, 1922 (Vertov 2)
Universe, 1961 (Meredith 3)
Universe d'Utrillo, 1954 (Jarre 4)
Unjustly Accused. See Ballettens Datter, 1913
Unkissed Man, 1929 (McCarey 2, Harlow 3)
Unknown, 1927 (Browning 2, Chaney Lon 3, Crawford, J. 3, Day 4, Gibbons 4, Young, W. 4)
Unknown Cavalier, 1926 (Brown, Harry Joe 4, Polito 4)
Unknown Claim, 1910 (Anderson G. 3)
Unknown Guest, 1943 (Tiomkin 4)
Unknown Man, 1951 (Nilsson 3, Pidgeon 3, Stone 3, Rose 4)
Unknown Man. See Ukjent mann, 1952
Unknown Purple, 1923 (Walthall 3)
Unknown Soldier, 1926 (Walthall 3)
Unknown Terror, 1957 (Biroc 4)
Unknown To-morrow. See Unbekannte Morgen, 1923
Unknown Valley, 1933 (Bond 3)
Unknown Violinist, 1912 (Bunny 3)
Unknown Woman. See Okanda, 1913
Unlawful Trade, 1914 (Dwan 2, Chaney Lon 3)
Unlucky Woman. See Boogie Woogie Dream, 1942
Unman, Wittering, and Zigo, 1971 (Unsworth 4)
Unmarried, 1920 (Cooper, Gladys 3, Gwenn 3)
Unmarried, 1939 (Crabbe 3, O'Connor 3, Dreier 4, Head 4)
Unmarried. See Glasberget, 1953
Unmarried Bachelor, 1941 (Young, R. 3)
Unmarried Woman, 1978 (Mazursky 2, Bates 3, Clayburgh 3)
Unmensch. See Homo immanis, 1919
Unmentionables, 1963 (Freleng 4)
Unmogliche Frau, 1936 (Frohlich 3, Von Harbou 4)
Unmogliche Liebe, 1932 (Nielsen 3)
Uno dos tres . . . al escondite inglés, 1969 (Borau 2)
Uno tra la folla, 1946 (Fusco 4)
Unos, 1952 (Kadár 2, Hrušínský 3, Kopecký 3)
Unos bankéře Fuxe, 1922 (Ondra 3, Vích 4)
Unpainted Woman, 1919 (Browning 2, Young, W. 4)
Unpardonable Sin, 1916 (Gaudio 4)
Unpardonable Sin, 1919 (Neilan 2, Beery 3, Sweet 3)
Unplanned Elopement, 1914 (Bushman 3)
Unpopular Mechanic, 1936 (Lantz 4)
Unprotected, 1916 (Sweet 3)
Unprotected Female, 1903 (Bitzer 4)
Unpublished Story, 1942 (Dillon 4, Havelock-Allan 4)
Unrecorded Victory. See Spring Offensive, 1939
Unruhige Nacht, 1958 (Wicki 2)
Uns et les autres, 1981 (Lelouch 2, Caan 3, Chaplin 3, Olbrychski 3, Lai 4)
Unscrupulous Ones. See Cafajestes, 1962
Unseeing Eyes, 1923 (Barrymore L. 3)
Unseen, 1945 (Marshall 3, McCrea 3, Chandler 4, Dreier 4, Houseman 4, Seitz 4)
Unseen Defense, 1913 (Bosworth 3)

Unseen Enemy, 1912 (Griffith 2, Carey 3, Gish, D. 3, Gish, L. 3, Bitzer 4)
Unseen Forces, 1920 (Franklin 2)
Unseen Hands, 1924 (Beery 3)
Unseen Heroes. *See* Battle of the V 1, 1958
Unseen Vengeance, 1914 (Eason 4)
Unsent Letter. *See* Neotpravlennoe pismo, 1960
Unser stiller Mann, 1976 (Hoppe 3)
Unser taglich Brot, 1949 (Dudow 2, Eisler 4)
Unsere Afrikareise, 1961–66 (Kubelka 2)
Unsichtbare Front, 1932 (Pasternak 4)
Unsichtbare Gegner, 1933 (Homolka 3, Lorre 3, Spiegel 4)
Unsinkable Molly Brown, 1964 (Walters 2, Reynolds, D. 3, Ames 4, Edens 4, Gillespie 4)
Unsterbliche Herz, 1939 (George, H. 3, Wegener 3, Warm 4)
Unsterbliche Lump, 1930 (Frohlich 3, Herlth 4, Hoffmann 4, Rohrig 4)
Unsuspected, 1947 (Curtiz 2, Bennett C. 3, Rains 3, Grot 4, Meredyth 4, Waxman 4)
Untamable Whiskers. *See* Roi du maquillage, 1904
Untamed, 1920 (Mix 3)
Untamed, 1929 (Crawford, J. 3, Montgomery 3, Brown, N. 4, Day 4, Freed 4, Gibbons 4, Polglase 4)
Untamed, 1940 (Darwell 3, Milland 3, Dreier 4, Head 4, Young, V. 4)
Untamed, 1955 (King 2, Hayward 3, Moorehead 3, Power 3, Jennings 4, Waxman 4)
Untamed. *See* Arakure, 1957
Untamed Breed, 1948 (Brown, Harry Joe 4, Duning 4)
Untamed Frontier, 1952 (Cotten 3, Van Cleef 3, Winters 3, Salter 4)
Untamed Lady, 1926 (Swanson 3)
Untel père et fils, 1940 (Duvivier 2, Jourdan 3, Jouvet 3, Morgan 3, Raimu 3, Achard 4, Spaak 4)
Unter Ausschluss der Offentlichkeit, 1927 (Dieterle 2, Krauss 3)
Unter Ausschluss der Offentlichkeit, 1937 (Baarová 3, Tschechowa 3, Wegener 3)
Unter den Brucken, 1945 (Knef 3)
Unter falscher Flagge, 1932 (Frohlich 3, Pasternak 4)
Unter Geiern, 1964 (Granger 3)
Unter heissem Himmel, 1936 (Albers 3, Herlth 4, Rohrig 4, Wagner 4)
Unter Palmen am blauen Meer, 1957 (Dagover 3)
Unter Raubern und Bestien, 1921 (Hoffmann 4)
Untergang der Emma, 1974 (Geschonneck 3)
Untermann—Obermann, 1969 (Hauff 2)
Untern Birnbaum, 1973 (Domrose 3)
Unternehmen Michael, 1937 (George, H. 3, Rohrig 4)
Untertan, 1949 (Staudte 2)
Unterwegs nach Atlantis, 1977 (Hoppe 3)
Unterwegs zu Lenin, 1970 (Ulyanov 3)
Until September, 1984 (Barry 4)
Until the Day We Meet Again. *See* Mata au hi made, 1950
Until They Get Me, 1917 (Borzage 2)
Until They Sail, 1957 (Wise 2, Fontaine 3, Newman 3, Simmons 3, Cahn 4, Raksin 4, Ruttenberg 4, Schnee 4)
Until Victory Day. *See* Shori no hi made, 1945
Until We Meet Again. *See* Mata au hi made, 1950
Until You Have Mamma. *See* Dokud máš maminku, 1934
Untitled Film of Geoffery Holder's Wedding, 1955 (Brakhage 2)
Unto the Third Generation, 1913 (Lawrence 3)
Unusual Years. *See* Neobyčejná léta, 1952
Unvanquished. *See* Nepokorenniye, 1945
Unveiling, 1911 (Griffith 2, Bitzer 4)
Unwelcome Children. *See* Kreuzzug des Weibes, 1926
Unwelcome Guest, 1912 (Griffith 2, Carey 3, Gish, L. 3, Pickford 3, Bitzer 4)
Unwelcome Mrs. Hatch, 1914 (Dwan 2)
Unwiderstehliche, 1937 (Ondra 3)
Unwilling Hero, 1921 (Gibbons 4)
Unwilling Sinner. *See* Sjaeletyven, 1915
Unwritten Code, 1944 (Edwards 2, Guffey 4)
Unwritten Law, 1932 (Auer 3, Fazenda 3)
Uogashi shunjitsu, 1952 (Yamamura 3)
Uomini che mascalzoni, 1953 (Age and Scarpelli 4, Rota 4)
Uomini . . . che mascalzoni, 1932 (De Sica 2)
Uomini contro, 1970 (Rosi 2, Cuny 3, Volonté 3, Guerra 4)

Uomini dal passo pesante, 1966 (Cotten 3)
Uomini e lupi, 1956 (De Santis 2, Petri 2, Armendáriz 3, Mangano 3, Montand 3, Guerra 4, Zavattini 4)
Uomini e no, 1980 (Morricone 2)
Uomini e nobiluomini, 1959 (De Sica 2)
Uomini in più, 1950 (Antonioni 2)
Uomini nella nebbia, 1955 (Fusco 4)
Uomini non guardano il cielo, 1951 (De Sica 2)
Uomini non sono ingrati, 1937 (Cervi 3)
Uomini sono nemici, 1948 (Cortese 3, Mangano 3)
Uomo a metà, 1966 (Morricone 4)
Uomo che sorride, 1936 (De Sica 2)
Uomo che viene de lontano, 1968 (Van Cleef 3)
Uomo da bruciare, 1962 (Taviani, P. and V. 3, Volonté 3)
Uomo da rispettare, 1973 (Douglas, K. 3, Delli Colli 4, Morricone 4)
Uomo dagli occhi di ghiaccio, 1971 (Wynn 3)
Uomo dai calzoni corti, 1958 (Bardem 2, Valli 3)
Uomo dai cinque palloni, 1965 (Mastroianni 3)
Uomo dalle due ombre, 1971 (Mason 3)
Uomo dalle pelle dura, 1971 (Borgnine 3)
Uomo della croce, 1943 (Rossellini 2)
Uomo di Corleone, 1977 (Papas 3)
Uomo di paglia, 1957 (Germi 2, Cristaldi 4)
Uomo e il suo mondo, 1967 (Bozzetto 4)
Uomo, la bestia e la virtu, 1953 (Welles 2)
Uomo, l'orgoglio, la vendetta, 1967 (Kinski 3, D'Amico 4)
Uomo ritorna, 1946 (Cervi 3, Magnani 3)
Uomo senza domenica, 1957 (De Santis 2, Petri 2)
Uomo, una città, 1974 (Fabian 3)
Uomo venuto dal mare, 1941 (Fusco 4)
Up a Tree, 1930 (Arbuckle 3)
Up and at 'em, 1924 (Roach 4)
Up and Going, 1922 (Mix 3)
Up for Murder, 1931 (Ayres 3, Beavers 3, Freund 4)
Up from the Beach, 1965 (Crawford, B. 3, Robertson 3, Rosay 3)
Up Goes Maisie, 1946 (Sothern 3, Irene 4)
Up in Alf's Place, 1919 (Sennett 2)
Up in Arms, 1944 (Andrews D. 3, Calhern 3, Cook 3, Dumont 3, Kaye 3, Mayo 3, Day 4, Goldwyn 4, Mandell 4, Pirosh 4)
Up in Central Park, 1948 (Durbin 3, Price 3, Green, J. 4, Krasner 4)
Up in Daisy's Penthouse, 1953 (Three Stooges 3, Bruckman 4)
Up in Mabel's Room, 1926 (Garnett 2, Rosson 4)
Up in Mabel's Room, 1944 (Dwan 2, Auer 3)
Up in Smoke, 1978 (Keach 3, Martin, S. 3)
Up in the Clouds. *See* Akash Kusum, 1965
Up Periscope!, 1959 (Oates 3, O'Brien, E. 3)
Up Pops the Devil, 1931 (Sutherland 2, Lombard 3, Banton 4, Struss 4)
Up Pops the Duke, 1931 (Arbuckle 3)
Up Romance Road, 1918 (King 2)
Up San Juan Hill, 1909 (Bosworth 3, Mix 3, Selig 4)
Up She Goes. *See* Up Goes Maisie, 1945
Up the Creek, 1958 (Sellers 3)
Up the Down Staircase, 1967 (Mulligan 2, Pakula 2, Jenkins 4)
Up the Front, 1972 (Holloway 3)
Up the Junction, 1965 (Loach 2)
Up the Junction, 1968 (Havelock-Allan 4)
Up the MacGregors. *See* Sette donne per i MacGregor, 1966
Up the River, 1930 (Ford, J. 2, Bogart 3, Brown 3, Tracy 3, August 4)
Up the River, 1938 (Darwell 3, Robinson, B. 3, Summerville 3)
Up the Road with Sallie, 1918 (Talmadge, C. 3)
Up the Sandbox, 1972 (Kershner 2, Streisand 3, Horner 4, Willis 4)
Up the Thames to Westminster, 1910 (Olcott 2)
Up to His Ears. *See* Tribulations d'un chinois de Chine, 1965
Up to Mars, 1930 (Fleischer, M. and D. 2)
Up with the Green Lift. *See* Oppåt med grona hissen, 1952
Up Your Anchor. *See* Eskimo Ohgen, 1985
Up Your Teddy Bear, 1970 (Jones 4)
Upheaval, 1916 (Barrymore L. 3)
Upholding the Law, 1917 (August 4)
Upkeep, 1973 (Hubley 4)
Upland Rider, 1928 (Brown, Harry Joe 4, McCord 4)
Upon This Rock, 1969 (Bogarde 3, Evans 3)
Uppbrott, 1948 (Sucksdorff 2)

Uppehall i Myrlandet. *See* 4 x 4, 1965
Upper Crust, 1981 (Crawford, B. 3)
Upper Hand, 1914 (Ingram 2)
Upper Hand. *See* Du Rififi à Paname, 1966
Upper Underworld, 1931 (Polito 4)
Uppercut, 1922 (Roach 4)
Uppercut O'Brien, 1929 (Sennett 2)
Upperworld, 1934 (Astor 3, Rogers, G. 3, Rooney 3, Gaudio 4, Grot 4, Hecht 4)
Upright and Wrong, 1947 (Dunning 4)
Upright Sinner. *See* Brave Sunder, 1931
Ups and Downs, 1911 (Bunny 3)
Ups and Downs, 1914 (Beery 3)
Ups and Downs, 1915 (Hardy 3)
Upstage, 1926 (Shearer 3, Gaudio 4, Gibbons 4, Gillespie 4)
Upstairs, 1919 (Normand 3)
Upstairs and Downstairs, 1959 (Cardinale 3)
Upstanding Sitter, 1948 (McKimson 4)
Upstream, 1927 (Ford, J. 2, Johnson, N. 3, Clarke, C.C. 4)
Upstream, 1931 (Grierson 2)
Upswept Hare, 1953 (McKimson 4)
Uptight, 1968 (Dassin 2, Hubley 4, Kaufman 4, Trauner 4)
Up-To-Date Conjurer. *See* Impressioniste fin de siècle, 1899
Uptown Saturday Night, 1974 (Poitier 3, Pryor 3)
Upturned Glass, 1947 (Mason 3)
Uragirareta mono, 1926 (Tanaka 3)
Urakaidan, 1965 (Tsukasa 3)
Uranium Boom, 1956 (Katzman 4)
Uranium Conspiracy, 1977 (Golan and Globus 4)
Urashima Taro no koei, 1946 (Naruse 2, Takamine 3)
Urbanisme africain, 1962 (Rouch 2)
Urbanissimo, 1966 (Hubley 4)
Urchins. *See* Golfos, 1962
Ureshii koro, 1934 (Yamada 3)
Urfeus i underjorden, 1910 (Magnusson 4)
Urgano sul Po, 1955 (Schell, Maria 3)
Uriel Acosta, 1920 (Hoffmann 4)
Urlaub und Ehrenwort, 1937 (Rohrig 4)
Urlo, 1965 (Storaro 4)
Urodziny Matyldy, 1974 (Stawinsky 4)
Urodziny mlodego warszawiaka, 1980 (Stawinsky 4)
Ursula, 1978 (Hoffmann 3)
Ursule et Grelu, 1973 (Dalio 3, Girardot 3)
Uruhashiki ai, 1931 (Takamine 3)
Uruhashiki shuppatsu, 1939 (Takamine 3)
Uruwashiki saigetsu, 1955 (Kobayashi 2)
US, 1968 (Hammid 2)
US Killer Force. *See* Diamond Mercenaries, 1975
Us Paar, 1974 (Burman 4)
Us Two. *See* A nous deux, 1979
USA en vrac, 1953 (Lelouch 2)
Used Cars, 1980 (Warden 3)

Useful Sheep, 1912 (Sennett 2)
Users, 1978 (Curtis 3, Fontaine 3, Jarre 4)
Usne Kaha Tha, 1960 (Roy 2)
Uso, 1963 (Kinugasa 2)
Ustedes los ricos, 1948 (Infante 3)
Ustedes tienen la palabara, 1974 (Gómez, M. 2)
Usual Way, 1913 (Beery 3)
Usurer, 1910 (Griffith 2, Walthall 3, Bitzer 4)
Usurer's Son. *See* Under Savklingens Taender, 1913
Ut Mine Stromtid, 1920 (Dreier 4)
Uta andon, 1943 (Naruse 2, Yamada 3)
Uta andon, 1960 (Kinugasa 2)
Utae wakodo-tachi, 1963 (Kinoshita 2, Iwashita 3)
Utage, 1967 (Gosho 2, Iwashita 3)
Utah, 1945 (Rogers, R. 3)
Utah Blaine, 1956 (Katzman 4)
Utah Kid, 1930 (Karloff 3)
Uta-kichi andon, 1938 (Yamada 3)
Utamaro and Five Women. *See* Utamaro o mehuru go-nin no onna, 1946
Utamaro o meguru gonin no onna, 1946 (Mizoguchi 2, Tanaka 3, Yoda 4)
Utamaro o meguru gonin no onna, 1959 (Hasegawa 3)
Utazás a koponyám korul, 1971 (Latinovits 3, Torocsik 3)
Útěky domu, 1980 (Jires 2, Schorm 2, Brejchová 3, Kopecký 3)
Utkozben, 1979 (Mészáros 2, Nowicki 3, Tyszkiewicz 3)
Utolsó bohém, 1912 (Curtiz 2)
Utolsó hajnal, 1917 (Curtiz 2)
Utolsó vacsora, 1962 (Gábor 3)
Utopia, 1978 (Sanda 3)
Utopia. *See* Atoll K, 1950
Utopia. *See* Cuerpo repartido y el mundo al revés, 1975
Utószezon, 1967 (Fábri 2)
Utro, 1966 (Henning-Jensen 2)
Utro nad Rodinata, 1951 (Karamitev 3)
Utsukishisa to kanashimi to, 1965 (Yamamura 3)
Utsukushii hito, 1954 (Kagawa 3)
Utsukushiki batsu, 1949 (Yamamura 3)
Utsukushisa to kanashimi to, 1965 (Shinoda 2, Takemitsu 4)
Utvandrarna, 1971 (Troell 2, Ullmann 3, Von Sydow 3)
U-47: Kapitänleutnant Prien, 1958 (Tschechova 3)
Uvodní slovo pronese, 1964 (Pojar 4)
Uwaki no susume, 1960 (Iwashita 3)
Uwaki wa kisha ni notte, 1931 (Naruse 2)
Uwasa no musume, 1935 (Naruse 2)
Uwasa no onna, 1954 (Mizoguchi 2, Shindo 3, Tanaka 3, Miyagawa 4, Yoda 4)
Uwayaku shitayaku godouyaku, 1959 (Muraki 4)
Už je ráno, 1956 (Hofman 4)
Už zase skáču přes kaluže, 1970 (Kachyna 2)
Uže, 1976 (Grgić 4)
Uzu, 1961 (Iwashita 3)

V

V Blouznĕni, 1928 (Stallich 4)
V bolshom gorode, 1927 (Donskoi 2)
V boynoi slepote strastei, 1916 (Mozhukin 3)
V chetverg i bolshe nikogda, 1977 (Smoktunovsky 3)
V dni borbi, 1920 (Pudovkin 2)
V for Victory, 1941 (McLaren 2)
V gorakh Ala-Tau, 1944 (Vertov 2)
V hlavní roli Oldřich Nový, 1980 (Kopecký 3)
V mirnye dni, 1950 (Tikhonov 3)
V ogne broda net, 1968 (Panfilov 2, Churikova 3)
V 1, 1944 (Jennings 2)

V polnotch na kladbische, 1914 (Mozhukin 3)
V prachu hvezd, 1975 (Brejchová 3)
V roukatch bespotchadnogo roka, 1914 (Mozhukin 3)
V tom domečku pod Emauzy, 1933 (Vích 4)
V tylu u belych, 1925 (Enei 4)
V.G.E. *See* Valérie Giscard d'Estaing au Mexique, 1979
V.I.P.s, 1963 (Asquith 2, Welles 2, Burton 3, Jourdan 3, Rutherford 3, Smith 3, Taylor, E. 3, Booth 4, Fisher 4, Rozsa 4)
Va banque, 1930 (Dagover 3, Grundgens 3, Reisch 4)
Va voir maman, papa travaille, 1977 (Presle 3)
Vacances, 1938 (Storck 2)

Vacances conjugales, 1933 (Brasseur 3)
Vacances de Monsieur Hulot, 1953 (Tati 2, Grimault 4)
Vacances du diable, 1930 (Cavalcanti 2)
Vacances du diable. *See* Devil's Holiday, 1930
Vacances en enfer, 1961 (Fradetal 4)
Vacances explosives, 1956 (Arletty 3)
Vacances portugaises, 1962 (Wicki 2, Aumont 3, Deneuve 3, Gélin 3, Coutard 4)
Vacanza, 1969 (Redgrave, V. 3)
Vacanza del divolo. *See* Devil's Holiday, 1930
Vacanze a Ischia, 1957 (De Sica 2)
Vacanze col gangster, 1952 (Risi 2)
Vacanze d'inverno, 1959 (De Sica 2, Morgan 3, Sordi 3)
Vacation, 1924 (Fleischer, M. and D. 2)
Vacation. *See* Vacanza, 1969
Vacation Days, 1947 (Katzman 4)
Vacation from Love, 1938 (Adrian 4)
Vacation from Marriage. *See* Perfect Strangers, 1945
Vacation Loves, 1930 (Sennett 2)
Vacation with a Gangster. *See* Vacanze col gangster, 1952
Vache et le prisonnier, 1959 (Verneuil 2, Fernandel 3, Jeanson 4)
Vacuum Cleaner, 1982 (Grgić 4)
Vad veta val mannen, 1933 (Borgstrom 3, Jaenzon 4)
Vae maraculeuse de Thérèse Eartan, 1928 (Christian-Baque 2)
Vaeddeloberen, 1919 (Schenstrom 3)
Vagabond, 1916 (Bacon 2, Chaplin 2, Purviance 3)
Vagabond. *See* Awara, 1951 (Kapoor 2)
Vagabond Cub, 1929 (Miller, V. 4)
Vagabond King, 1930 (MacDonald 3, Oland 3, Banton 4, Mankiewicz 4)
Vagabond King, 1956 (Curtiz 2, Grayson 3, Hardwicke 3, Price 3, Bumstead 4, Young, V. 4)
Vagabond Lady, 1935 (Young, R. 3, Roach 4)
Vagabond Loafers, 1949 (Three Stooges 3)
Vagabond Lover, 1929 (Neilan 2, Dressler 3, Plunkett 4)
Vagabond Queen, 1929 (Balfour 3, Rosher 4)
Vagabond Trail, 1924 (Wellman 2, August 4)
Vagabond Violinist, 1934 (Oberon 3)
Vagabonda, 1918 (Musidora 3)
Vagabonde, 1931 (Fradetal 4)
Vagabonds, 1912 (Olcott 2)
Vagabonds du rêve, 1949 (Rosay 3)
Vagabond's Galoshes. *See* Kolingens galoscher, 1912
Vagen till Kolckrike, 1953 (Nykvist 4)
Vägen till mannens hjarta, 1914 (Borgstrom 3)
Vaghe stelle dell'orsa, 1965 (Visconti 2, Cristaldi 4)
Vagrant. *See* Tolonc, 1914
Vagrant's Tale. *See* Tulácka pohádka, 1972
Vagues, 1901 (Guy 2)
Vainqueur de la course pédestre, 1909 (Feuillade 2)
Vakzal dlia dvoikh, 1982 (Gurchenko 3)
Val d'enfer, 1943 (Tourneur, M. 2)
Valachi Papers, 1972 (Bronson 3)
Valadão, o cratera, 1925 (Mauro 2)
Valadao the Disaster. *See* Valadão, o cratera, 1925
Valahol Európában, 1947 (Gabór 3)
Választás elótt, 1953 (Jancsó 2)
Valborgsmassoafton, 1935 (Sjostrom 2, Bergman 3)
Valdez Horses. *See* Valdez il mezzosangue, 1973
Valdez il mezzosangue, 1973 (Sturges, J. 2, Bronson 3)
Valdez Is Coming, 1971 (Lancaster 3)
Valdez the Halfbreed. *See* Valdez il mezzosanque, 1973
Válečné tajnosti pražské, 1926 (Vích 4)
Valencia, 1926 (Karloff 3, Gibbons 4, Gillespie 4)
Valentin De Las Sierras, 1967 (Baillie 2)
Valentina, 1938 (Negrete 3)
Valentina, 1965 (Félix 3)
Valentina, 1981 (Panfilov 2, Churikova 3, Quinn 3)
Valentina—The Virgin Wife. *See* Moglie virgine, 1976
Valentine Girl, 1917 (Barthelmess 3, Menjou 3)
Valentino, 1951 (Banton 4, Mandell 4, Stradling 4)
Valentino, 1977 (Russell 2, Caron 3, Russell 4)
Valentino en Angleterre, 1923 (Florey 2)

Valerie, 1957 (Hayden 3, Laszlo 4)
Valerie a týden divu, 1970 (Jires 2)
Valerie and a Week of Wonders. *See* Valerie a týden divu, 1970 (Jires 2)
Valérie Giscard d'Estaing au Mexique, 1979 (Reichenbach 2)
Valet's Wife, 1908 (Lawrence 3, Bitzer 4)
Valfangare, 1939 (Fischer 4, Jaenzon 4)
Valiant, 1929 (Howard 2, Muni 3, Carré 4)
Valiant, 1962 (Mills 3, Shaw 3)
Valiant Is the Word for Carrie, 1936 (Ruggles 2, Carey 3, McDaniel 3, Banton 4)
Valiant Ones. *See* Chung lieh t'u, 1975
Valiant Tailor, 1934 (Iwerks 4)
Valientes no mueren, 1961 (Armendáriz 3)
Valigia dei sogni, 1953 (Comencini 2, Vích 4)
Valise, 1974 (Sarde 4)
Valise diplomatique, 1909 (Cohl 2)
Valise enchantée, 1903 (Guy 2)
Valle de las espadas, 1963 (Rey 3, Valli 3)
Vallée, 1972 (Almendros 4, Gégauff 4)
Vallée aux loups, 1966 (Fresnay 3)
Valley. *See* Vallée, 1972
Valley Between Love and Death. *See* Ai to shi no tanima, 1954
Valley Forge, 1974 (Fonda, H. 3)
Valley Girl, 1983 (Forrest 3)
Valley of Decision, 1915 (Bennett C. 3, Bennett J. 3)
Valley of Decision, 1945 (Garnett 2, Barrymore L. 3, Cooper, Gladys 3, Crisp 3, Duryea 3, Garson 3, Nilsson 3, Peck 3, Gillespie 4, Irene 4, Ruttenberg 4, Stothart 4)
Valley of Esopus, 1906 (Bitzer 4)
Valley of Fire, 1951 (Autry 3)
Valley of Gwangi, 1969 (Harryhausen 4)
Valley of Head Hunters, 1953 (Weissmuller 3)
Valley of Hell, 1927 (Stevens 2)
Valley of Night, 1919 (Barrymore L. 3)
Valley of Silent Men, 1922 (Borzage 2)
Valley of Song, 1952 (Roberts 3)
Valley of the Dolls, 1967 (Robson 2, Dreyfuss 3, Grant, L. 3, Hayward 3, Previn 4, Smith, J.M. 4, Williams, J. 4)
Valley of the Dolls, 1981 (Simmons 3)
Valley of the Eagles, 1951 (Lee, C. 3, Rota 4)
Valley of the Giants, 1919 (Cruze 2, Reid 3)
Valley of the Giants, 1927 (McCord 4)
Valley of the Giants, 1938 (Crisp 3, Trevor 3, Friedhofer 4, Miller, S. 4, Polito 4)
Valley of the Head Hunters, 1953 (Katzman 4)
Valley of the Kings, 1954 (Taylor, R. 3, Pirosh 4, Plunkett 4, Rozsa 4, Smith, J.M. 4, Surtees 4)
Valley of the Moon, 1914 (Bosworth 3)
Valley of the Sun, 1942 (Ball 3, Cody 3, Hardwicke 3)
Valley of the Tennessee, 1944 (Hammid 2)
Valley of Tomorrow, 1920 (Furthman 4)
Valley of Vanishing Men, 1942 (Summerville 3)
Valley of Vengeance, 1944 (Crabbe 3)
Valley Town, 1940 (Van Dyke, W. 2, Maddow 4)
Vallfarten till Kevlar, 1921 (Magnusson 4)
Valmiki, 1946 (Kapoor 2)
Valparaiso, Valparaiso, 1971 (Cuny 3)
Valse brillante, 1936 (Ophuls 2, Planer 4)
Valse brillante, 1949 (Annenkov 4, Burel 4)
Valse de Paris, 1949 (Astruc 2, Fresnay 3, Achard 4, Matras 4)
Valse du gorille, 1959 (Vanel 3, Renoir 4)
Valse eternelle, 1936 (Brasseur 3)
Valse renversante, 1914 (Chevalier 3)
Valse royale, 1935 (Grémillon 2)
Valse Triste, 1977 (Conner 2)
Valseuses, 1973 (Blier 2, Depardieu 3, Huppert 3, Moreau 3)
Value for Money, 1955 (Pleasance 3, Arnold 4, Unsworth 4)
Valvaire d'Amour, 1923 (Vanel 3)
Vámamos con Pancho Villa, 1935 (De Fuentes 2, Figueroa 4)
Vámhatár, 1977 (Gaál 2)
Vamos a matar, compañeros!, 1970 (Palance 3, Rey 3, Morricone 4)
Vamp, 1918 (Barnes 4, Ince 4, Sullivan 4)

Vamp till Ready, 1936 (Roach 4)
Vamping Venus, 1928 (Fazenda 3)
Vamping Venus. *See* Property Man, 1914
Vampir, 1969 (Lee, C. 3)
Vampira, 1973 (Niven 3)
Vampiras, 1969 (Carradine 3)
Vampire, 1915 (Guy 2)
Vampire. *See* Vampyren, 1912
Vampire Ambrose, 1916 (Sennett 2)
Vampire Bat, 1933 (Douglas, M. 3, Wray 3)
Vampire Beast Craves Blood. *See* Blood Beast Terror, 1968
Vampire Dancer. *See* Vampyrdanserinden, 1911
Vampire Happening. *See* Gebissen wird nur Nachts—Happening der Vampire, 1971
Vampire Hookers, 1978 (Carradine 3)
Vampire Lovers, 1970 (Cushing 3)
Vampire Men of the Lost Planet. *See* Horror of the Blood Monsters, 1970
Vampire over London. *See* Old Mother Riley Meets the Vampire, 1952
Vampires, 1915 (Feyder 2, Musidora 3)
Vampires. *See* Vampiras, 1969
Vampire's Ghost, 1945 (Brackett, L. 4)
Vampyr, 1932 (Dreyer 2, Fradetal 4, Maté 4, Warm 4)
Vampyrdanserinden, 1911 (Blom 2)
Vampyren, 1912 (Sjostrom 2, Stiller 2, Jaenzon 4, Magnusson 4)
Vampyres, 1975 (Love 3)
Vampyres, Daughters of Darkness. *See* Vampyres, 1975
Van Gogh, 1948 (Resnais 2, Dauphin 3, Braunberger 4)
Vancouver, 1979 (Duras 2)
Vanderbeekiana, 1968 (Vanderbeek 2)
Vanderbilt Cup Auto Race, 1904 (Bitzer 4)
Vandet På Låndet, 1946 (Dreyer 2)
Vanessa, 1935 (Howard 2, Crisp 3, Montgomery 3, Stone 3, Coffee 4, Selznick 4, Stothart 4)
Vangelo '70. *See* Amore e rabbia, 1969
Vangelo secondo Matteo, 1964 (Pasolini 2, Delli Colli 4, Donati 4)
Vanina, 1922 (Nielsen 3, Wegener 3, Mayer 4, Pommer 4)
Vanina Vanini, 1961 (Rossellini 2, Solinas 4)
Vanina Vanini. *See* Vanina, 1922
Vanish, 1978 (Kuri 4)
Vanished, 1971 (Widmark 3, Young, R. 3)
Vanishing American, 1925–26 (Cooper, Gary 3)
Vanishing American, 1955 (Van Cleef 3)
Vanishing Body. *See* Black Cat, 1934
Vanishing Cornwall, 1958 (Redgrave, M. 3)
Vanishing Corporal. *See* Caporal épinglé, 1962
Vanishing Duck, 1957 (Hanna and Barbera 4)
Vanishing Frontier, 1932 (Pitts 3)
Vanishing Lady. *See* Escamotage d'une dame chez Robert-Houdin, 1896
Vanishing Legion, 1931 (Carey 3, Canutt 4)
Vanishing Pioneer, 1928 (Powell, W. 3)
Vanishing Point, 1970 (Alonzo 4)
Vanishing Prairie, 1954 (Iwerks 4)
Vanishing Race, 1912 (Dwan 2)
Vanishing Rider, 1928 (Karloff 3)
Vanishing Shadow, 1934 (Cobb 3)
Vanishing Vault, 1915 (Talmadge, C. 3)
Vanishing Virginian, 1942 (Borzage 2, Beavers 3, Grayson 3)
Vanishing West, 1928 (Canutt 4)
Vanity, 1927 (Crisp 3, Johnson, N. 3, Adrian 4, Grot 4, Miller, A. 4, Sullivan 4)
Vanity and Its Cure, 1911 (Lawrence 3)
Vanity Fair, 1911 (Bunny 3)
Vanity Fair, 1922 (Brook 3)
Vanity Fair, 1923 (Bosworth 3)
Vanity Fair, 1932 (Loy 3)
Vanity Pool, 1918 (Nilsson 3)
Vanity Street, 1932 (August 4)
Vanity's Price, 1924 (Von Sternberg 2, Nilsson 3)
Vánoce s Alžbětou, 1968 (Kachyna 2)
Vánočni, 1946 (Zeman 2)
Vanquished, 1953 (Head 4)

Vanquished. *See* Vinti, 1952
Vanskeligt Valg. *See* Guldet og vort Hjerte, 1913
Vantande vatten, 1965 (Fischer 4)
Vaquero's Vow, 1908 (Griffith 2, Lawrence 3, Bitzer 4)
Var Engang, 1922 (Dreyer 2)
Var i Dalby hage, 1962 (Troell 2)
Var sin vag, 1948 (Bjornstrand 3, Borgstrom 3, Dahlbeck 3)
Våra Faders Gravar, 1935–36 (Fejos 2)
Varakozok, 1975 (Komorowska 3, Torocsik 3)
Varan the Unbelievable. *See* Daikaiju Baran, 1958
Varázskeringo, 1918 (Curtiz 2)
Vargtimmen, 1968 (Bergman 2, Thulin 3, Ullmann 3, Von Sydow 3, Nykvist 4)
Varhaník v sv. Víta, 1929 (Fric 2)
Variable Studies, 1960–61 (Emshwiller 2)
Variációk egy témára, 1961 (Szabó 2)
Variaciones, 1963 (Solás 2)
Variation sur le geste, 1962 (Storck 2)
Variations, 1965 (Vanderbeek 2)
Variations on a Mechanical Theme, 1959 (Russell 2)
Variations on a Theme. *See* Variációk egy témára, 1961
Variété, 1925 (Dupont 2, Jannings 3, Freund 4, Pommer 4, Schufftan 4)
Variétés, 1935 (Albers 3, Gabin 3)
Variétés, 1947–51 (Verneuil 2)
Varietes, 1971 (Bardem 2)
Variety. *See* Variété, 1925
Variety Girl, 1947 (DeMille 2, Tashlin 2, Bendix 3, Cooper, Gary 3, Crosby 3, Fitzgerald 3, Goddard 3, Hayden 3, Holden 3, Hope 3, Ladd 3, Lake 3, Lamour 3, Lancaster 3, Milland 3, Preston 3, Stanwyck 3, Head 4)
Variety Lights. *See* Luci del varietà, 1950
Variola vera, 1983 (Marković 3)
Världens mest Anvandbara Trad, 1935–36 (Fejos 2)
Var-matin, 1976 (Leenhardt 2)
Varmlanningarna, 1921 (Nilsson 3)
Varmlanningarna, 1932 (Borgstrom 3)
Varmlanningarne, 1909 (Magnusson 4)
Várostérkép, 1977 (Szabó 2)
Varsity, 1928 (Estabrook 4)
Varsity Girl. *See* Fair Co-ed, 1927
Varsity Show, 1937 (Berkeley 2, Powell, D. 3, Mercer 4, Polito 4, Wald 4)
Varsoí Világifjusági Találkozo I–III. *See* Varsoí vit, 1955
Varsoí vit, 1955 (Jancsó 2)
Vart hjarta har sin saga, 1948 (Borgstrom 3)
Varuj!, 1947 (Fric 2)
Varvara. *See* Selskaya uchitelnitsa, 1947
Vásárhelyi szinek, 1961 (Mészáros 2)
Vášeň, 1961 (Trnka 2)
Vasens Hemmelighed, 1913 (Blom 2)
Vases of Hymen, 1914 (Bunny 3)
Vash syn i brat, 1965 (Shukshin 3)
Vasha znakomaya, 1927 (Kuleshov 2)
Vassa, 1981 (Panfilov 2, Churikova 3)
Vassira, 1958 (Torocsik 3)
Vas-y maman, 1978 (Girardot 3)
Vasya the Reformer. *See* Vasya-reformator, 1926
Vasya-reformator, 1926 (Dovzhenko 2)
Vatan, 1938 (Biswas 4)
Vater und Sohn, 1918 (Basserman 3)
Vater werden ist nicht schwer . . ., 1926 (Wagner 4)
Vatican Affair. *See* A qualsiasi prezzo, 1968
Vatican Pimpernel, 1982 (Gielgud 3)
Vatican Story. *See* A qualsiasi prezzo, 1968
Vaticano de Pio XII, 1940 (Buñuel 2)
Vaudeville, 1924 (Fleischer, M. and D. 2)
Vaudeville. *See* Variété, 1925
Vault of Horror, 1973 (Jurgens 3)
Vautrin, 1943 (Simon, M. 3)
Vautrin the Thief. *See* Vautrin, 1943
Vavasour Ball, 1914 (Talmadge, N. 3)
Vdavky Nanynky Kulichovy, 1925 (Ondra 3)

Ve dvou se to lépe táhne, 1928 (Vích 4)
Veau, 1908 (Cohl 2)
Veau gras, 1939 (Kaufman 4)
Vecchia guardia, 1934 (Blasetti 2)
Vecchia signora, 1932 (De Sica 2)
Večery s Jindřichem Plachtou, 1954 (Stallich 4)
Ved Faengslets Port, 1911 (Blom 2)
Věda jde s lidem, 1952 (Kachyna 2)
Věděli si rady, 1950 (Kachyna 2)
Vedi come soi . . . lo vedi come sei?!, 1939 (Fellini 2)
Vedo Nudo, 1969 (Risi 2, Manfredi 3, Vitti 3)
Vedova, 1957 (Milestone 2)
Vedova scaltra, 1922 (Gallone 2)
Vedovo, 1959 (Risi 2, Sordi 3)
Vedovo allegro, 1949 (Age and Scarpelli 4)
Veena, 1948 (Biswas 4)
Veera Puran Appu, 1979 (Peries 2)
Vegas, 1978 (Allyson 3, Curtis 3)
Vegas Strip War, 1984 (Hudson 3, Jones, J.E. 3)
Vegetarian's Dream, 1912–14 (Cohl 2)
Végul, 1973 (Kroner 3, Torocsik 3)
Veilchenfresser, 1926 (Dagover 3, Andrejew 4)
Veiled Adventure, 1919 (Talmadge, C. 3)
Veiled Lady, 1912–13 (White 3)
Veiled Lady. See For sin Faders Skyld, 1916
Veiled Woman, 1929 (Lugosi 3, Clarke, C.C. 4)
Veille d'Armes, 1926 (Modot 3)
Veille d'armes, 1935 (L'Herbier 2, Francis, E. 3, Spaak 4)
Veils of Baghdad, 1953 (Mature 3)
Vein, 1965 (Brakhage 2)
Vein of Gold, 1910 (Anderson G. 3)
Vein Stripping, 1952 (Peterson 2)
Veinard, 1975 (Cassel 3)
Veinards, 1962 (Broca 2)
Veine d'Anatole. See Gros Lot, 1933
Vel' d'hiv', 1960 (Audiard 4, Jarre 4)
Velbloud uchem jehly, 1936 (Haas 3)
Velbound uchem jehly, 1926 (Ondra 3)
Veleno della parole, 1914 (Bertini 3)
Velha a Fiar, 1964 (Mauro 2)
Veli Jože, 1980 (Grgić 4)
Velikaya sila, 1950 (Ermler 2, Babochkin 3)
Veliki strah, 1958 (Vukotić 4)
Velikii grazhdanin, 1938-39 (Shostakovich 4)
Velikii grazhdanin: Part I, 1938 (Ermler 2)
Velikii grazhdanin: Part II, 1939 (Ermler 2)
Velikii perelom, 1946 (Ermler 2)
Velikii uteshitel, 1933 (Kuleshov 2)
Velikiy voin Albanii Skanderberg, 1953 (Yutkevich 2)
Veliky put', 1927 (Shub 2)
Velká prehrada, 1942 (Hrušínský 3)
Velké dobrodružství, 1952 (Kopecký 3, Brdečka 4)
Velkommen til Vendsyssel, 1954 (Carlsen 2)
Velorenè Schatten, 1921 (Wegener 3)
Velvet Fingers, 1920 (Grot 4)
Velvet Paw, 1916 (Tourneur, M. 2, Carré 4)
Velvet Touch, 1948 (Greenstreet 3, Russell, R. 3, Trevor 3, Banton 4, Walker 4)
Velvet Underground, 1966 (Warhol 2)
Velvet Vampire, 1971 (Corman 4)
Vem domer, 1922 (Sjostrom 2, Jaenzon 4, Magnusson 4)
Vem skot?, 1916 (Magnusson 4)
Vena d'oro, 1955 (Bolognini 2)
Vendanges, 1922 (Epstein 2)
Vendémiaire, 1918 (Feuillade 2)
Vendetta, 1920 (Jannings 3, Negri 3)
Vendetta, 1946 (Ophuls 2)
Vendetta, 1950 (Sturges, P. 2, Bruce 3, Haas 3, Burnett 4, Planer 4)
Vendetta. See Joaquin Murieta, 1964
Vendetta del corsaro, 1951 (Aumont 3)
Vendetta della signora. See Besuch, 1964
Vendetta di Aquila Nera, 1951 (Brazzi 3)
Vendetta di Ercole, 1960 (Crawford, B. 3)

Vendetta di una pazza, 1951 (Baarová 3)
Vendetta e un piatto che si serve freddo, 1971 (Kinski 3)
Vendetta en Camargue, 1950 (Kosma 4)
Vendetta nel sole, 1947 (Lollobrigida 3)
Vendetta of Samurai. See Ketto kagiya no tsuji, 1952
Vendicatore, 1959 (Dieterle 2)
Venditore di morte, 1972 (Kinski 3)
Venditore di palloncini, 1974 (Cobb 3, Cusack 3)
Venere imperiale, 1962 (Castellani 2, Delannoy 2, Lollobrigida 3, Presle 3, Aurenche 4)
Venetian Affair, 1967 (Karloff 3, Krasner 4, Schifrin 4)
Venetian Bird, 1952 (Rota 4)
Venetian Lies. See Footloose, 1979
Venezia città minore, 1958 (Olmi 2)
Venezia, la luna, e tu, 1958 (Risi 2, Manfredi 3, Sordi 3)
Venezia, una Mostra per il cinema, 1982 (Blasetti 2)
Venezianische Nacht, 1914 (Freund 4)
Venga a prendere il caffè . . . da noi, 1970 (Lattuada 2, Tognazzi 3)
Venganza, 1957 (Bardem 2, Rey 3)
Venganza de Heraclio Bernal, 1957 (Figueroa 4)
Vengeance, 1962 (Francis 4)
Vengeance. See Haevnet, 1911
Vengeance. See Noroît, 1976
Vengeance. See Pomsta, 1968
Vengeance. See Venganza, 1957
Vengeance d'Edgar Poe, 1912 (Gance 2)
Vengeance d'une orpheline russe, 1965 (Braunberger 4)
Vengeance de Riri, 1908 (Cohl 2)
Vengeance des esprits, 1911 (Cohl 2)
Vengeance du domestique, 1912 (Linders 3)
Vengeance du sergent de ville, 1913 (Feuillade 2)
Vengeance du sicilien. See Torino nera, 1972
Vengeance Is Mine, 1917 (Miller, A. 4)
Vengeance is Mine. See Fukushu suruwa wareni ari, 1979
Vengeance of Fate, 1912 (Ince 2)
Vengeance of Fu Manchu, 1967 (Lee, C. 3)
Vengeance of Galora, 1913 (Barrymore L. 3, Gish, D. 3)
Vengeance of the Deep, 1923 (Arlen 3)
Vengeance of the 47 Ronin. See Chushingura, 1932
Vengeance of the West, 1916 (Chaney Lon 3)
Vengeance that Failed, 1912 (Dwan 2)
Vengeance Trail. See Vendetta e un piatto che si serve freddo, 1971
Vengeance Valley, 1951 (Ireland 3, Lancaster 3, Walker 3, Plunkett 4, Ravetch 4)
Venice, the Moon, and You. See Venezia, la luna e tu, 1958
Venice: Theme and Variations, 1957 (Ivory 2)
Venir du Havre, 1962 (Braunberger 4)
Venise et ses amants, 1950 (Cocteau 2)
Venom, 1982 (Hayden 3, Kinski 3, Reed, O. 3, Williamson 3)
Venoušek a Stázička, 1922 (Vích 4)
Venski Les, 1963 (Gerasimov 2)
Vent 'anni, 1949 (Zavattini 4)
Vent d'est, 1970 (Ferreri 2, Godard 2, Volonté 3)
Vent se lève, 1959 (Jurgens 3, Bost 4)
Vent souffle oú il veut. See Condamné à mort s'est échappé, 1956
Vento del sud, 1960 (Cardinale 3, Cristaldi 4)
Vento dell'est. See Vent d'est, 1970
Vento mi ha cantato una canzone, 1948 (Sordi 3)
Ventriloquist Cat, 1950 (Avery 2)
Ventriloquist's Trunk, 1911 (Bunny 3)
Venus, 1929 (Talmadge, C. 3, Burel 4)
Vénus aveugle, 1941 (Gance 2, Alekan 4, Burel 4)
Vénus de l'or, 1938 (Delannoy 2)
Vénus et Adonis series, 1900 (Guy 2)
Vénus impériale. See Venere imperiale, 1962
Venus in Furs. See Paroxismus, 1969
Venus in the East, 1918 (Crisp 3, Nilsson 3)
Venus Makes Trouble, 1937 (Ballard 4)
Venus Model, 1918 (Normand 3)
Venus of Venice, 1927 (Neilan 2, Talmadge, C. 3, Barnes 4, Schenck 4)
Venus Victrix, 1916 (Dulac 2)
Venus von Montmartre, 1925 (Albers 3, Tschechowa 3)

Vestire gli ignudi, 1953 (Brasseur 3, Flaiano 4, Spaak 4)
Vesuvius Express, 1953 (Clarke, C.C. 4)
Vesyoly musikanty, 1937 (Ptushko 2)
Veszelyban a pokol, 1921 (Banky 3)
Veszprém—Town of Bells. *See* Harangok városa—Veszprém, 1965
Vêtements Sigrand, 1938 (Alexeieff and Parker 2)
Vetrná hora, 1956 (Hrušínský 3)
Vetta, 1957 (Donner 2)
Veuve Couderc, 1971 (Delon 3, Signoret 3)
Veuve en or, 1969 (Audiard 4)
Veuve joyeuse, 1934 (Achard 4)
Veuves de quinze ans. *See* Fleur de l'âge ou les adolescents, 1964
Vezelay, 1950 (Fresnay 3)
Vežen no Bezdĕze, 1932 (Stallich 4)
Vi går landsvagen, 1937 (Jaenzon 4)
Vi haenger i en tråd, 1962 (Roos 2)
Vi har manje namn, 1976 (Zetterling 2)
Vi som går koksvagen, 1932 (Molander 2)
Vi som går scenvagen, 1938 (Bjornstrand 3)
Vi tre debutera, 1953 (Bjornstrand 3, Fischer 4)
Vi två, 1939 (Bjornstrand 3)
Via Cabaret, 1913 (Reid 3)
Via Crucis, 1918 (Blom 2)
Via Fast Freight. *See* Fast Freight, 1921
Via lattea. *See* Voie lactée, 1969
Via libre a la zafra del '64, 1964 (Alvarez 2)
Via Mala, 1945 (Hoffmann 4, Rohrig 4, Von Harbou 4)
Via Padova 46, 1954 (Sordi 3, Rota 4)
Via Pony Express, 1933 (Canutt 4)
Viaccia, 1961 (Bolognini 2, Germi 2, Belmondo 3, Cardinale 3)
Viager, 1972 (Depardieu 3)
Viaggiatori della sera, 1980 (Tognazzi 3)
Viaggio, 1974 (De Sica 2, Attenborough 3, Burton 3, Loren 3, Ponti 4)
Viaggio con Anita, 1978 (Monicelli 2, Hawn 3, Morricone 4, Pinelli 4)
Viaggio de lavoro, 1968 (Mangano 3)
Viaggio in Italia, 1953 (Rossellini 2, Bergman 3)
Viaggio in Italy. *See* Journey to Italy, 1953
Viaggio nella vertigini,, 1975 (Thulin 3)
Viaje al centro de la tierra, 1977 (More 3)
Viale della speranza, 1953 (Risi 2, Mastroianni 3)
Vibes 1-2-3, 1971 (Foldès 4)
Vicar of Bray, 1937 (Holloway 3)
Vicar of Vejlby. *See* Praesten i Vejlby, 1920
Vice and Virtue. *See* Vice et la vertu, 1962
Vice et la vertu, 1962 (Vadim 2, Deneuve 3, Girardot 3, Gégauff 4)
Vice Raid, 1959 (Cortez 4)
Vice Squad, 1931 (Cromwell 2, Francis, K. 3, Lukas 3, Lang 4)
Vice Squad, 1953 (Goddard 3, Robinson, E. 3, Van Cleef 3, Biroc 4)
Vice Versa, 1947 (Ustinov 3)
Vicenta, 1920 (Musidora 3)
Vices and Pleasures. *See* Vizi privati, pubbliche virtú, 1976
Vichy 1969. *See* A fleur d'eau, 1969
Vicious Circle, 1948 (Kortner 3)
Vicious Circle. *See* Circle, 1957
Vicious Years, 1950 (Florey 3)
Vicki, 1953 (Boone 3, Crain 3, Horner 4, Krasner 4)
Vicomte de Bragelonne, 1954 (Astruc 2)
Vicomte règle ses comptes, 1967 (O'Brien, E. 3, Rey 3)
Victim, 1914 (Marsh 3)
Victim, 1961 (Dearden 2, Bogarde 3)
Victim, 1972 (Bumstead 4)
Victim 5, 1964 (Roeg 2)
Victim of a Character. *See* Potifars Hustru, 1911
Victim of Circumstances, 1911 (Sennett 2)
Victim of Jealousy, 1910 (Griffith 2, Pickford 3, Bitzer 4)
Víctimas del pecado, 1950 (Fernández 2, Figueroa 4)
Victimes de l'alcoolisme, 1902 (Zecca, 2)
Victims, 1982 (Schifrin 4)
Victims of Terror, 1967 (Lee, C. 3)
Victims of the Beyond. *See* Sucker Money, 1933
Victims of the Mormon. *See* Mormonens Offer, 1911
Victims of Vesuvius. *See* Victims of Terror, 1967
Victor, 1915 (Beery 3)

Victor, 1951 (Gabin 3)
Victor Hugo, 1951 (Leenhardt 2)
Victor I, 1968 (Wenders 2)
Victor/Victoria, 1982 (Edwards 2, Andrews J. 3, Preston 3, Mancini 4)
Victoria, 1979 (Widerberg 2)
Victoria Cross, 1912 (Reid 3)
Victoria Cross, 1917 (Hayakawa 3)
Victoria the Great, 1937 (Wilcox 2, Henreid 3, Neagle 3, Walbrook 3, Young, F. 4)
Victorine, 1915 (Gish, D. 3)
Victors, 1963 (Finney 3, Fonda, P. 3, Mercouri 3, Moreau 3, Schneider 3, Wallach 3, Bass 4, Foreman 4)
Victor's Egg-o-mat. *See* Viktorov jajomat, 1969
Victory, 1919 (Tourneur, M. 2, Beery 3, Chaney Lon 3, Carré 4, Furthman 4)
Victory, 1940 (Cromwell 2, Hardwicke 3, March 3, Balderston 4, Head 4, Veiller 4)
Victory, 1981 (Huston 2, Caine 3, Stallone 3, Von Sydow 3)
Victory. *See* Pobeda, 1938
Victory and Peace, 1918 (Brenon 2)
Victory at Entebbe, 1976 (Douglas, K. 3, Dreyfuss 3, Hopkins, A. 3, Lancaster 3, Taylor, E. 3)
Victory at Yorktown, 1965 (Hawkins 3)
Victory in the Dark. *See* Seger i morker, 1954
Victory of the Faith. *See* Sieg des Glaubens, 1933
Victory of the Night. *See* Pobediteli nochi, 1927
Victory of Women. *See* Josei no shori, 1946
Victory Song. *See* Hisshoka, 1945
Victory through Air Power, 1943 (Disney 2)
Victory Wedding, 1944 (Matthews 3, Mills 3)
Victuailles de Gretchen se revoltent, 1916 (Cohl 2)
Vida cambia, 1976 (Figueroa 4)
Vida Criminal de Archibaldo de La Cruz. *See* Ensayo de un crimen, 1955
Vida de Pedro Infante, 1963 (García 3)
Vida es magnifica. *See* Voleur du Tibidabo, 1964
Vida no vale nada, 1954 (Infante 3, Alcoriza 4)
Vidas, 1983 (Branco 4, de Almeida 4)
Vidas sêcas, 1963 (Pereira Dos Santos 2)
Videodrome, 1983 (Baker 4)
Videospace, 1972 (Vanderbeek 2)
Vidya, 1948 (Anand 3, Burman 4)
Vidyapati, 1937 (Sircar 4)
Vie, 1958 (Astruc 2, Schell, Maria 3, Renoir 4)
Vie. *See* Sauve qui peut, 1980
Vie à deux, 1958 (Guitry 2, Brasseur 3, Darrieux 3, Fernandel 3, Feuillère 3, Philipe 3)
Vie à l'envers, 1964 (Denner 3)
Vie chantée, 1950 (Burel 4)
Vie commence demain, 1950 (Aumont 3)
Vie conjugale, 1964 (Cayatte 2)
Vie continue, 1982 (Cassel 3, Girardot 3)
Vie continue. *See* Vie devant soi, 1977
Vie dans l'herbe, 1957 (Braunberger 4)
Vie de Bohème, 1916 (Carré 4, Marion 4)
Vie de Bohème, 1943 (L'Herbier 2, Jourdan 3, Wakhévitch 4)
Vie de château, 1966 (Brasseur 3, Deneuve 3, Noiret 3, Borowczyk 4, Legrand 4, Rappeneau 4)
Vie de chien, 1941 (Fernandel 3)
Vie de Jésus, 1951 (Braunberger 4)
Vie de plaisir, 1943 (Spaak 4)
Vie de Polichinelle, 1905 (Linders 3)
Vie de Raimu, 1948 (Raimu 3)
Vie del Petrolio, 1965–66 (Bertolucci 2)
Vie des oiseaux en Mauritanie, 1963 (Braunberger 4)
Vie des termites, 1958 (Braunberger 4)
Vie des travailleurs italiens en France, 1926 (Grémillon 2)
Vie devant moi. *See* Madame Rosa, 1977
Vie devant soi, 1977 (Costa-Gavras 2, Almendros 4, Evein 4, Sarde 4)
Vie du Christ, 1899–1900 (Guy 2)
Vie du Christ, 1906 (Guy 2)
Vie du marin, 1906 (Guy 2)

Vie du moyen age, 1955 (Rabier 4)
Vie d'un fleuve: La Seine, 1932 (Jaubert 4, Kaufman 4)
Vie d'un grand journal, 1934 (Epstein 2)
Vie d'un homme, 1938 (Auric 4)
Vie d'un honnête homme, 1953 (Guitry 2, Simon, M. 3)
Vie d'un joueur, 1903 (Zecca, 2)
Vie d'un poète. *See* Sang d'un poète, 1930
Vie d'une femme, 1920 (Gallone 2)
Vie en rose, 1948 (Jeanson 4)
Vie est à nous, 1936 (Becker 2, Renoir 2, Modot 3, Eisler 4, Renoir 4)
Vie est un roman, 1984 (Resnais 2, Chaplin 3, Gassman 3)
Vie, l'amour, la mort, 1969 (Lelouch 2, Girardot 3, Lai 4)
Vie miraculeuse de Thérèse Martin, 1929 (Duvivier 2)
Vie ou la mort, 1912 (Feuillade 2)
Vie parisienne, 1936 (Siodmak 2, Morgan 3, Jaubert 4)
Vie privée, 1962 (Malle 2, Bardot 3, Mastroianni 3, Evein 4, Rappeneau 4)
Vie sans joie. *See* Catherine, 1927
Vie sentimentale de Georges le Tueur, 1971 (Braunberger 4)
Vieil Homme et l'enfant, 1966 (Denner 3, Simon, M. 3)
Vieille Dame indigne, 1965 (Allio 2)
Vieille Fille, 1972 (Girardot 3, Noiret 3, Legrand 4)
Vieilles estampes series, 1904 (Guy 2)
Vieilles Femmes de l'Hospice, 1917 (Feyder 2)
Vielgeliebtes Sternchen, 1959 (Domrose 3)
Vienna Burgtheater. *See* Burgtheater, 1936
Vienna Waltzes. *See* Wien tantz, 1951
Vienna Woods. *See* Venski Les, 1963
Viennese Nights, 1930 (Crosland 2, Fazenda 3, Hersholt 3, Lugosi 3, Pidgeon 3)
Vient de paraître, 1949 (Fresnay 3)
Viento norte, 1937 (Alton, J. 4)
Vier ein halb Musketiere, 1935 (Sakall 3)
Vier gesellen, 1938 (Bergman 3)
Vier um die Frau. *See* Kampfende Herzen, 1920
24 Stunden aus dem Leben einer Frau, 1931 (Porten 3)
Vier vom Bob, 1931 (Rasp 3)
Vierge d'Argos, 1911 (Feuillade 2)
Vierge du Rhin, 1953 (Gabin 3)
Vierge folle, 1928 (Fresnay 3)
Vièrges, 1962 (Schufftan 4)
Viernes de la eternidad, 1981 (Schifrin 4)
Vierte Gebot, 1920, (Oswald 2)
Vierte kommt nicht, 1939 (Wagner 4)
Viertelstunde Grossstadtstatistik, 1933 (Fischinger 2)
Vierzehn Menschenleben. *See* Életjel, 1954
Vietnam! Vietnam!, 1971 (Ford, J. 2, Heston 3)
Vieux Chaland, 1932 (Epstein 2)
Vieux de la vieille, 1960 (Fresnay 3, Gabin 3, Audiard 4)
Vieux Fusil, 1975 (Noiret 3, Schneider 3)
Vieux garçon, 1931 (Tourneur, J. 2)
Vieux Pays ou Rimbaud est mort, 1977 (Lefebvre 2)
View from Pompey's Head, 1955 (Bernstein 4, Dunne 4, Lemaire 4)
View from the Bridge, 1962 (Lumet 2)
View from the Bridge. *See* Vu du pont, 1962
View to a Kill, 1985 (Moore, R. 3, Barry 4)
Viewing Sherman Institute for Indians at Riverside, 1915 (Sennett 2)
Vig ozvegy, 1918 (Curtiz 2)
Vigil, 1914 (Hayakawa 3, Ince 4)
Vigil in the Night, 1939 (Newman 4, Plunkett 4)
Vigil in the Night, 1940 (Stevens 2, Cushing 3, Lombard 3, Polglase 4)
Vigilantes Are Coming, 1936 (Farnum 3, Canutt 4)
Vigilantes Return, 1947 (Miller, V. 4)
Vigile, 1960 (De Sica 2, Zampa 2, Sordi 3)
Vigilia di natale, 1913 (Bertini 3)
Vignes du seigneur, 1958 (Fernandel 3)
Vihar, 1952 (Fábri 2)
Vijaya, 1942 (Biswas 4)
Vijeta, 1983 (Nihalani 4)
Viking, 1929 (Crisp 3)
Viking Women. *See* Saga of the Viking Women, 1957
Viking Women and the Sea Serpent. *See* Saga of the Viking Women, 1957

Vikings, 1958 (Fleischer, R. 2, Welles 2, Borgnine 3, Curtis 3, Douglas, K. 3, Leigh, J. 3, Cardiff 4)
Viking's Daughter, 1908 (Lawrence 3)
Viktor und Viktoria, 1933 (Walbrook 3)
Viktoria, 1934 (Hoffmann 4)
Viktorov jajomat, 1969 (Grgić 4)
Vilaine histoire, 1934 (Christian-Jaque 2)
Vildfagel, 1921 (Magnusson 4)
Vildfåglar, 1955 (Sjoberg 2)
Vildledt Elskov, 1911 (Blom 2)
Vildmarkens sång, 1940 (Borgstrom 3)
Viled Adventure, 1919 (Sutherland 2)
Villa Borghese, 1953 (De Sica 2, Presle 3, Amidei 4, Flaiano 4)
Villa dei mostri, 1950 (Antonioni 2, Fusco 4)
Villa des mille joies, 1928 (Modot 3)
Villa Destin, 1921 (Autant-Lara 2, L'Herbier 2)
Villa dévalisée, 1905 (Guy 2)
Villa Falconieri, 1928 (Oswald 2)
Villa im Tiergarten, 1926 (Albers 3)
Villa Miranda, 1971–73 (Brocka 2)
Villa of the Movies, 1917 (Sennett 2, Summerville 3)
Villa Rides, 1968 (Bronson 3, Brynner 3, Ireland 3, Mitchum 3, Rey 3, Jarre 4, Towne 4)
Villa Santo-Sospir, 1952 (Cocteau 2)
Villa vuelve, 1949 (Armendáriz 3)
Village. *See* Pestalozzidorf, 1953
Village Barber, 1931 (Iwerks 4)
Village Blacksmith, 1916 (Sennett 2)
Village Blacksmith, 1922 (Ford, J. 2, Love 3)
Village Blacksmith, 1933 (Terry 4)
Village Blacksmith, 1938 (Terry 4)
Village Blacksmith. *See* Song of the Forge, 1937
Village Bride. *See* Mura na hanayome, 1928
Village Chestnut, 1918 (Sennett 2, Fazenda 3)
Village Cut-Up, 1906 (Bitzer 4)
Village dans Paris, 1939 (Clair 2)
Village dans Paris: Montmartre, 1940 (Jaubert 4)
Village Festival. *See* Fidlovačka, 1930
Village Hero, 1911 (Sennett 2)
Village in India, 1937–40 (Cardiff 4)
Village in the Jungle. *See* Baddegama, 1980
Village magique, 1954 (Kosma 4)
Village Mill. *See* Gromada, 1952
Village Near the Pleasant Fountain. *See* Byn vid den Trivsamma Brunnen, 1937–38
Village of Tajiko. *See* Tajiko mura, 1940
Village of the Damned, 1960 (Sanders 3)
Village of the Giants, 1965 (Edouart 4)
Village on the Frontier. *See* Ves v pohraničí, 1948
Village on the River. *See* Dorp aan de rivier, 1958
Village perdu, 1947 (Honegger 4)
Village Romance, 1912 (Lawrence 3)
Village Scandal, 1915 (Sennett 2, Arbuckle 3)
Village School of Emperor Supporters. *See* Sonnou sonjuku, 1939
Village School-teacher. *See* Selskaya uchitelnitsa, 1947
Village Smithy, 1919 (Sennett 2, Fazenda 3)
Village Smithy, 1936 (Avery 2)
Village Smitty, 1931 (Iwerks 4)
Village Specialist, 1932 (Iwerks 4)
Village Squire, 1935 (Leigh, V. 3, Havelock-Allan 4)
Village Tale, 1935 (Meek 3, Scott, R. 3, Musuraca 4, Plunkett 4, Polglase 4)
Village Vampire, 1916 (Sennett 2)
Villain, 1917 (Hardy 3)
Villain, 1971 (Burton 3)
Villain, 1979 (Douglas, K. 3, Elam 3, Martin, S. 3)
Villain Foiled, 1911 (Sennett 2)
Villain Still Pursued Her, 1937 (Terry 4)
Villain Still Pursued Her, 1940 (Keaton 2, Farnum 3, Ballard 4)
Villain's Curse, 1932 (Terry 4)
Villanelle des Rubans, 1932 (Epstein 2)
Ville a Chandigarh, 1966 (Tanner 2)
Ville accuse. *See* Polizia accusa: il segreto uccide, 1974

Ville Bidon, 1975 (Cloquet 4)
Ville de Madame Tango, 1914 (Musidora 3)
Ville de pirates, 1984 (Branco 4, de Almeida 4)
Ville de silences, 1979 (Cassel 3)
Ville della Brianza, 1955–59 (Taviani, P. and V. 2)
Ville Nouvelle, 1980 (Ruiz 2)
Vilna zona, 1975 (Paskaleva 3)
Vim, Vigor and Vitaliky, 1936 (Fleischer, M. and D. 2)
Vina Vladimira Olmera, 1956 (Brejchová 3)
Vinata, 1976 (Danailov 3, Paskaleva 3)
Vince il sistema, 1949 (Risi 2)
Vincent, François, Paul and the Others. See Vincent, François, Paul,
    et les autres, 1974
Vincent, François, Paul, et les autres, 1974 (Sautet 2, Audran 3,
    Depardieu 3, Montand 3, Piccoli 3, Reggiani 3, Sarde 4)
Vincent Lopez and His Orchestra, 1939 (Hutton 3)
Vincent the Dutchman, 1971 (Zetterling 2)
Vinden från våster, 1943 (Sucksdorff 2)
Vinden och floden, 1951 (Sucksdorff 2)
Vindicta, 1923 (Feuillade 2)
Vine Bridge, 1965 (Zetterling 2)
Vine Bridge. See Lianbron, 1965
Vine Garden. See Lianbron, 1965
Vingar Kring fyren, 1938 (Borgstrom 3)
Vingarne, 1916 (Stiller 2, Jaenzon 4, Magnusson 4)
Vingeskudt, 1913 (Christensen 2)
Vingt-cinq ans de l'Olympia, 1979 (Reichenbach 2)
25e Heure, 1967 (Verneuil 2, Dalio 3, Reggiani 3, Quinn 3, Rosay 3,
    Mankowitz 4, Ponti 4)
24 heures d'amant, 1964 (Lelouch 2)
Vingt-quatre heures de la vie d'un clown, 1946 (Melville 2)
Vingt-quatre heures de la vie d'une femme, 1968 (Darrieux 3)
Vingt-quatre heures de perm', 1945 (Wakhévitch 4)
Vingt-quatre heures en trente minutes, 1928 (Kaufman 4)
Vintage, 1957 (Ferrer, M. 3, Morgan 3, Raksin 4, Ruttenberg 4)
Vintage of Fate, 1912 (Bosworth 3)
Vinterbørn, 1978 (Henning-Jensen 2)
Vinti, 1952 (Antonioni 2, Rosi 2, Fusco 4)
Vinyl, 1965 (Warhol 2)
Viol, 1967 (Andersson B. 3)
Violanta, 1977 (Depardieu 3)
Violantha, 1927 (Dieterle 2, Porten 3)
Violence. See Boryoku, 1952
Violence at Noon. See Hakuchu no torima, 1966
Violence in the Cinema: Part I, 1971 (Miller 2)
Violence sur Houston, 1969 (Reichenbach 2)
Violent City. See Città violenta, 1970
Violent Four. See Banditi a Milano, 1968
Violent Hour. See Dial 1119, 1950
Violent Is the Word for Curly, 1938 (Three Stooges 3, Ballard 4)
Violent Journey, 1966 (Jeakins 4)
Violent Men, 1955 (Ford, G. 3, Robinson, E. 3, Stanwyck 3, Guffey 4,
    Maté 4, Steiner 4, Wald 4)
Violent Playground, 1958 (Dearden 2, Baker S. 3, Cushing 3)
Violent Saturday, 1955 (Fleischer, R. 2, Borgnine 3, Marvin 3,
    Mature 3, Sidney 3, Clarke, C.C. 4, Friedhofer 4, Lemaire 4,
    Wheeler 4)
Violent Streets. See Thief, 1981
Violent Summer. See Estate violenta, 1959
Violents, 1957 (Fabian 3)
Violenza segreta, 1962 (Fusco 4, Gherardi 4)
Violenza: quinto potere, 1972 (Morricone 4)
Violette. See Violette Nozière, 1978
Violette and François. See Violette et François, 1977
Violette et François, 1977 (Adjani 3, Reggiani 3, Sarde 4)
Violette Nozière, 1978 (Chabrol 2, Audran 3, Huppert 3, Rabier 4)
Violettes impériales, 1952 (Barsacq 4, Matras 4)
Violin Concert. See Houslový koncert, 1962
Violin Maker, 1915 (Chaney Lon 3)
Violin Maker of Cremona, 1909 (Griffith 2, Pickford 3, Bitzer 4)
Violin Maker of Nuremberg, 1911 (Guy 2)
Violinist of Florence. See Geiger von Florenz, 1926
Violon et agent. See Violoniste, 1908

Violoniste, 1908 (Cohl 2)
Violons d'Ingres, 1940 (Jaubert 4)
Violons du bal, 1974 (Trintignant 3)
Violons parfois, 1977 (Guillemot 4)
Vip mio fratello superuomo, 1968 (Bozzetto 4)
Vipères, 1911 (Feuillade 2)
Virgen de medianoche, 1942 (Figueroa 4)
Virgen que forjó una Patria, 1942 (Novarro 3, Figueroa 4)
Virgin, Goodbye. See Shojo yo sayonara, 1933
Virgin Island, 1958 (Cassavetes 2, Poitier 3, Francis 4, Lardner 4)
Virgin Lips, 1928 (Walker 4)
Virgin of Stamboul, 1920 (Browning 2, Beery 3)
Virgin Paradise, 1920 (White 3)
Virgin Paradise, 1921 (Ruttenberg 4)
Virgin Queen, 1923 (Blackton 2)
Virgin Queen, 1955 (Davis 3, Marshall 3, Brackett, C. 4, Brown,
    Harry 4, Clarke, C.C. 4, Lemaire 4, Waxman 4)
Virgin Soldiers, 1970 (Foreman 4)
Virgin Spring. See Jungfrukallan, 1960
Virgin Wanted. See Shojo nyuyo, 1930
Virgin Who Embraces a Rainbow. See Niji o idaku shojo, 1948
Virginia, 1941 (Beavers 3, Carroll M. 3, Hayden 3, MacMurray 3,
    Edouart 4, Glennon 4, Head 4, Young, V. 4)
Virginia City, 1940 (Curtiz 2, Bogart 3, Bond 3, Flynn 3,
    Hopkins, M. 3, Scott, R. 3, Buckner 4, Canutt 4, Friedhofer 4,
    Polito 4, Steiner 4, Wallis 4)
Virginia Courtship, 1922 (Rosson 4)
Virginia Hill Story, 1974 (Cannon 3, Keitel 3)
Virginia Judge, 1935 (Cummings 3, Fetchit 3, Krasner 4)
Virginia Romance, 1916 (Bushman 3)
Virginian, 1914 (DeMille 2, Buckland 4)
Virginian, 1923 (Lang 4, Schulberg 4)
Virginian, 1929 (Fleming 2, Hathaway 2, Arlen 3, Cooper, Gary 3,
    Huston 3, Scott, R. 3, Estabrook 4, Head 4, Hunt 4)
Virginian, 1946 (Bainter 3, McCrea 3, Edouart 4, Goodrich and
    Hackett 4, Head 4)
Virginie, 1962 (Braunberger 4, Matras 4)
Virginity. See Panenstvi, 1937
Viridiana, 1961 (Bardem 2, Buñuel 2, Rey 3)
Virtue, 1932 (Bond 3, Lombard 3, O'Brien, P. 3, Riskin 4, Walker 4)
Virtue Is Its Own Reward, 1914 (Chaney Lon 3)
Virtue of Rage, 1912 (Bushman 3)
Virtuous Bigamist. See Era du venerdi 17, 1956
Virtuous Bigamist. See Sous le ciel de Provence, 1956
Virtuous Dames of Pardubice. See Počestné paní pardubické, 1944
Virtuous Husband, 1931 (Arthur 3)
Virtuous Liars, 1924 (Costello, M. 3)
Virtuous Scoundrel. See Vie d'un honnête homme, 1952
Virtuous Sin, 1930 (Cukor 2, Francis, K. 3, Huston 3)
Virtuous Sinners, 1919 (Valentino 3)
Virtuous Thief, 1919 (Niblo 2, Barnes 4, Sullivan 4)
Virtuous Vamp, 1919 (Talmadge, C. 3, Emerson 4, Loos 4)
Visage, 1975 (Foldès 4)
Visage mysterieux d'Océanie, 1970 (Braunberger 4)
Visages d'enfants, 1925 (Feyder 2, Burel 4)
Visages de femmes, 1939 (Brasseur 3)
Visages de femmes, 1969 (Foldès 4)
Visages de France, 1936 (Honegger 4)
Visages de Paris, 1955 (Reichenbach 2, Braunberger 4)
Viscount. See Vicomte règle ses comptes, 1967
Vishnu Priva, 1949 (Sircar 4)
Vishwasghaat, 1976 (Azmi 3)
Visible Manifestations, 1961 (Dunning 4)
Vision Beautiful, 1912 (Bosworth 3)
Vision Quest, 1985 (Roizman 4)
Visioniii, 1958 (Vanderbeek 2)
Visions of 8, 1973 (Forman 2, Ichikawa 2, Lelouch 2, Penn 2,
    Schlesinger 2, Zetterling 2, Allen, D. 4, Lassally 4, Mancini 4)
Visit. See Besuch, 1964
Visit from Space, 1964 (Vukotić 4)
Visit from Space. See Posjet iz svemira, 1964
Visit to a Chief's Son, 1974 (Lai 4)
Visit to a Foreign Country. See Québec-USA, 1962

Voyage d'agrément, 1935 (Christian-Jaque 2)
Voyage dans la lune, 1902 (Méliès 2)
Voyage de Brigitte Bardot aux U.S.A., 1966 (Reichenbach 2)
Voyage de Monsieur Perrichon, 1933 (Arletty 3, Wakhévitch 4)
Voyage de noces, 1932 (Brasseur 3)
Voyage de noces, 1975 (Baye 3, Trintignant 3)
Voyage de noces. *See* Jalousie 1976, 1976
Voyage de noces. *See* Voyage de noces en Espagne, 1912
Voyage de noces en Espagne, 1912 (Linders 3)
Voyage des comédiens. *See* O Thassios, 1975
Voyage du père, 1966 (Fernandel 3, Noiret 3)
Voyage du silence. *See* O salto, 1967
Voyage en Amérique, 1951 (Fresnay 3, Alekan 4)
Voyage en Amérique, 1975 (Seyrig 3)
Voyage en Boscavie, 1958 (Guillemot 4)
Voyage en Camardie, 1971 (Braunberger 4)
Voyage en douce, 1981 (Chaplin 3, Sanda 3)
Voyage en Espagne series, 1906 (Guy 2)
Voyage imaginaire, 1925 (Clair 2)
Voyage imprévu, 1934 (Dauphin 3, Spaak 4)
Voyage of the Damned, 1976 (Welles 2, Dunaway 3, Ferrer, J. 3,
    Grant, L. 3, Hiller 3, McDowell 3, Rey 3, Schell, Maria 3,
    Von Sydow 3, Werner 3, Schifrin 4)
Voyage round My Father, 1982 (Bates 3, Olivier 3)
Voyage sans espoir, 1943 (Christian-Jaque 2, Marais 3)
Voyage to a Prehistoric Planet, 1967 (Rathbone 3)
Voyage to America, 1964 (Houseman 4)
Voyage to America. *See* Voyage en Amérique, 1951
Voyage to Italy. *See* Viaggio in Italia, 1953
Voyage to Next, 1974 (Hubley 4)
Voyage to the Bottom of the Sea, 1961 (Fontaine 3, Lorre 3, Pidgeon 3,
    Bennett 4, Hoch 4, Smith, J.M. 4)
Voyage to the Planet of the Prehistoric Women, 1966 (Bogdanovich 2)
Voyager, 1911 (Bosworth 3)
Voyage-surprise, 1946 (Kosma 4, Prévert 4, Trauner 4)
Voyageur de la Toussaint, 1943 (Berry 3, Reggiani 3)
Voyageur sans bagage, 1943 (Fresnay 3, Matras 4)
Voyante, 1923 (Baur 3)
Voyou, 1970 (Lelouch 2, Denner 3, Trintignant 3, Lai 4)
Vozrata net, 1974 (Batalov 3)
Vozrozhdennia, 1915 (Mozhukin 3)
Vozvrachenia Vassilya Bortnikov, 1953 (Pudovkin 2)
Vozvrashcheniye Maksima, 1937 (Kozintsev 2, Enei 4, Moskvin 4,
    Shostakovich 4)
Vragi, 1977 (Smoktunovsky 3)
Vrah skrývá tvář, 1966 (Hrušínský 3)
Vrai Visage de Thérèse de Lisieux, 1961 (Grimault 4)

Vrata, 1971 (Grgić 4)
Vražda po česku, 1966 (Hrušínský 3)
Vražda po našem, 1966 (Weiss 2)
Vražda v hotelu Excelsior, 1971 (Kopecký 3)
Vražda v Ostrovní ulici, 1933 (Vích 4)
Vredens Dag, 1943 (Dreyer 2)
Vroeger kon je lachen, 1983 (Haanstra 2)
Vsadniki vetra, 1930 (Cherkassov 3)
Vse ostaetsia lyudyam, 1963 (Cherkassov 3)
Vše pro lásku, 1930 (Fric 2)
Vserusski starets Kalinin, 1920 (Vertov 2)
Všichni dobři rodáci, 1968 (Kučera 4)
Vsicki i nikoj, 1978 (Paskaleva 3)
Vsicko e ljubov, 1979 (Ivanov 3)
Vskrytie moschei Sergeia Radonezhskogo, 1919 (Vertov 2)
Vsorvanny ad, 1968 (Gurchenko 3)
Vstanou noví bojovníci, 1950 (Weiss 2)
Vstrecha na Elba, 1949 (Orlova 3, Shostakovich 4, Tisse 4)
Vstrecha s Frantsei, 1960 (Yutkevich 2)
Vstrechnyi, 1932 (Ermler 2, Yutkevich 2, Shostakovich 4)
Vsyou zhizn pod maskoi, 1915 (Mozhukin 3)
VTIK Train, Agit-Train of the Central Committee. *See* Agitpoezd
    VTsIK, 1921
Vu du pont, 1962 (Aurenche 4)
Vucko series, 1983 (Dragić 4)
Vuelo de la muerte, 1933 (García 3)
Vuelven los García, 1946 (García 3, Infante 3)
Vulcan Entertains. *See* Hell's Fire, 1934
Vulcano, 1941 (Magnani 3)
Vulcano, 1949 (Dieterle 2, Brazzi 3)
Vulture, 1966 (Crawford, B. 3)
Vultures and Doves, 1912 (Costello, D. 3)
Vultures of the Sea, 1928 (Karloff 3)
Vurguncular, 1971 (Guney 2)
VVVC Journal, 1931 (Ivens 2)
Vybor tseli, 1975 (Smoktunovsky 3, Ulyanov 3)
Vyborg Side. *See* Vyborgskaya storona, 1939
Vyborgskaya storona, 1939 (Gerasimov 2, Kozintsev 2, Moskvin 4,
    Shostakovich 4)
Vynález zkázy, 1958 (Zeman 2, Brdečka 4)
Vysoká zed, 1964 (Kachyna 2)
Vyšši princip, 1960 (Brejchová 3)
Výstřely ve 3/4 taktu. *See* Schusse im 3/4-Takt, 1965
Vzorná výchova, 1953 (Stallich 4)
Vzpomínka na ráj, 1939–40 (Hammid 2)
Vzucholod a láska, 1947 (Brdečka 4)

W

W, 1974 (Ferrer, M. 3)
W dźungli, 1957 (Giersz 4)
W piaskach pustyni, 1963 (Giersz 4)
W Plan, 1930 (Saville 2, Carroll M. 3, Young, F. 4)
W.C. Fields and Me, 1976 (Hiller 2, Steiger 3, Head 4, Mancini 4)
W.R.: Misterije organizma, 1971 (Makavejev 2)
W.R.: Mysteries of the Organism. *See* W.R.: Misterije organizma,
    1971
W.S.P., 1974 (Lassally 4)
W.V.S., 1942 (Alwyn 4)
W.W. and the Dixie Dancekings, 1975 (Reynolds, B. 3)
Wabash Avenue, 1950 (Grable 3, Mature 3, Lederer 4, Lemaire 4)
Wabbit Twouble, 1941 (Clampett 4)
Wabbit Who Came to Supper, 1941 (Freleng 4)
Wachsfigurenkabinett, 1924 (Dieterle 2, Leni 2, Wiene 2, Jannings 3,
    Krauss 3, Veidt 3, Galeen 4, Junge 4)

Wackiest Ship in the Army, 1960 (Lemmon 3, Rafferty 3, Duning 4)
Wackiki Wabbit, 1943 (Jones 2)
Wacky Blackout, 1942 (Clampett 4)
Wacky Wabbit, 1942 (Clampett 4)
Wacky Wild Life, 1940 (Avery 2)
Wacky World of Mother Goose, 1967 (Rutherford 3)
Wacky Worm, 1941 (Jones 2, Freleng 4)
Waco, 1966 (Arlen 3, Keel 3, Russell, J. 3, Head 4)
Wadaat Hobak, 1957 (Chahine 2)
Wade Brent Pays, 1914 (Mix 3)
Waffen der Jugend, 1912 (Wiene 2)
Waffenkammern Deutschland. *See* Deutsche Waffenschmiede, 1940
Waga ai, 1960 (Gosho 2)
Waga ai wa yama no kanata ni, 1948 (Hayasaka 4)
Waga haha no sho, 1936 (Tanaka 3)
Waga koi no tabiji, 1961 (Shinoda 2, Iwashita 3, Yamamura 3)

Waga koi wa moenu, 1949 (Mizoguchi 2, Shindo 2, Tanaka 3, Yoda 4)
Waga koi waga uta, 1969 (Iwashita 3)
Waga koiseshi otome, 1946 (Kinoshita 2, Hara 3)
Waga kyokan, 1939 (Imai 2)
Waga michi, 1974 (Shindo 2)
Waga seishun ni kuinashi, 1946 (Kurosawa 2, Hara 3, Shimura 3)
Waga shogai no kagayakeru hi, 1948 (Shindo 2, Yoshimura 2, Mori 3)
Wagahai wa neko de aru, 1975 (Ichikawa 2)
Wagaya wa tanoshi, 1951 (Takamine 3, Yamada 3)
Wagen in der Nacht, 1979 (Zanussi 2, Komorowska 3)
Wager. See Kaerligheds-Vaeddemaalet, 1914
Wages for Wives, 1925 (Borzage 2, Pitts 3)
Wages of Fear. See Salaire de la peur, 1952
Wages of Fear. See Sorcerer, 1977
Wages of Sin, 1903 (Bitzer 4)
Wages of Tin, 1924 (Roach 4)
Wages of Virtue, 1924 (Dwan 2, Swanson 3)
Waggily Tale, 1957 (Freleng 4)
Wagner, 1983 (Burton 3, Gielgud 3, Olivier 3, Redgrave, V. 3,
    Richardson 3, Russell 4, Storaro 4)
Wagon Heels, 1945 (Clampett 4)
Wagon Master, 1929 (Brown, Harry Joe 4, McCord 4)
Wagon Show, 1928 (Costello, M. 3, Brown, Harry Joe 4)
Wagon Team, 1952 (Autry 3)
Wagon Tracks, 1919 (Hart 3, August 4, Ince 4, Sullivan 4)
Wagon Trail, 1935 (Carey 3)
Wagon Train, 1940 (Cody 3, Polglase 4)
Wagon Wheels, 1934 (Scott, R. 3, Sheridan 3)
Wagon Wheels West, 1943 (Eason 4)
Wagonmaster, 1950 (Ford, J. 2, Bond 3, Cody 3, Darwell 3,
    Johnson, B. 3, Basevi 4, Cooper 4, Glennon 4, Nugent 4)
Wagons Roll at Night, 1941 (Bogart 3, Sidney 3, Wallis 4)
Wags to Riches, 1949 (Avery 2)
Wahlverwandschaften, 1974 (Tyszkiewicz 3)
Wahnsinn, 1919 (Veidt 3, Hoffmann 4)
Wahrheit uber Rosemarie, 1959 (Warm 4)
Waikiki Wedding, 1937 (Crosby 3, Quinn 3, Head 4, Prinz 4, Struss 4,
    Young, V. 4)
Wail. See Dokoku, 1952
Waise von Lowood, 1926 (Rasp 3)
Waisenhauskind, 1917 (Nielsen 3)
Wait, 1968 (Gehr 2)
Wait a Second! See Alljon meg á menet!, 1973
Wait 'til the Sun Shines, 1952 (King 2)
Wait Till the Sun Shines, Nellie, 1932 (Fleischer, M. and D. 2)
Wait till the Sun Shines, Nellie, 1952 (Lemaire 4, Newman 4,
    Shamroy 4)
Wait until Dark, 1967 (Arkin 3, Ferrer, M. 3, Hepburn, A. 3,
    Jenkins 4, Lang 4, Mancini 4)
Waiter from the Ritz, 1926 (Cruze 2)
Waiter No. 5, 1910 (Griffith 2, Pickford 3, Bitzer 4)
Waiters' Ball, 1916 (Sennett 2, Arbuckle 3)
Waiters' Picnic, 1913 (Sennett 2, Arbuckle 3)
Waiting for the Rain. See Cekání na déšť, 1978
Waiting Water. See Vantande vatten, 1965
Waiting Women. See Kvinnors vantan, 1952
Wakai hito, 1952 (Ichikawa 2)
Wakai hitotachi, 1954 (Yoshimura 2)
Wakai koibito-tachi, 1959 (Tsukasa 3)
Wakai sensei, 1941 (Hayasaka 4)
Wakaki hi, 1929 (Ozu 2)
Wakaki hi no chuji, 1925 (Kinugasa 2)
Wakaki hi no kangeki, 1931 (Gosho 2)
Wakaki ushio, 1955 (Yamada 3)
Wakamono yo naze naku ka, 1930 (Tanaka 3)
Wakare, 1959 (Yamada 3)
Wakare-gumo, 1951 (Gosho 2)
Wakaret ikiru toki mo, 1961 (Tanaka 3, Tsukasa 3)
Wakasama zamurai torimonocho: Nazo no noh-men yashiki, 1950
    (Kagawa 3)
Wakasama zamurai torimonocho: Noroi no ningyo-shi, 1951
    (Kagawa 3)
Wake in Fright, 1971 (Rafferty 3)

Wake Island, 1942 (Bendix 3, Preston 3, Burnett 4, Dreier 4, Head 4)
Wake Me When It's Over, 1960 (Leroy 2, Warden 3, Cahn 4,
    Shamroy 4, Wheeler 4)
Wake of the Red Witch, 1948 (Wayne 3, Young, G. 3, Brown, Harry 4)
Wake Up and Die. See Svegliati e uccidi, 1966
Wake Up and Dream, 1934 (Darwell 3, Mandell 4)
Wake Up and Dream, 1946 (Bacon 2, Ireland 3, Wheeler 4)
Wake Up and Live, 1937 (Faye 3, Cronjager 4, MacGowan 4,
    Zanuck 4)
Wake Up Lenochka. See Razbudite Lenochky, 1933
Wakefield Express, 1952 (Anderson 2, Lassally 4)
Wakiki hi no yorokobi, 1943 (Takamine 3)
Waking Up the Town, 1925 (Cruze 2, Shearer 3, Edeson 4)
Wakodo no yume, 1928 (Ozu 2, Ryu 3)
Wak–Wak, ein Marchenzauber. See Geschichte des Prinzen Achmed,
    1923–26
Walden, 1968 (Mekas 2)
Waldwinter, 1956 (Kinski 3)
Wales—Green Mountain, Black Mountain, 1942 (Alwyn 4)
Walk a Tightrope, 1963 (Duryea 3)
Walk, Don't Run, 1966 (Walters 2, Grant, C. 3, Jones 4, Stradling 4)
Walk East on Beacon, 1952 (Hill, G.R. 2, de Rochemont 4)
Walk in the Forest, 1975 (Friedhofer 4)
Walk in the Old City of Warsaw. See Spacerek staromiejski, 1958
Walk in the Shadow. See Life for Ruth, 1962
Walk in the Spring Rain, 1970 (Bergman 3, Quinn 3, Bernstein 4,
    Green, G. 4, Lang 4)
Walk in the Sun, 1946 (Milestone 2, Rossen 2, Andrews D. 3,
    Ireland 3)
Walk into Hell. See Walk into Paradise, 1956
Walk into Paradise, 1955 (Rafferty 3, Auric 4, Guillemot 4)
Walk on the Wild Side, 1962 (Dmytryk 2, Edwards 2, Baxter A. 3,
    Fonda, J. 3, Harvey 3, Stanwyck 3, Bass 4, Bernstein 4, Lemaire 4
    Sylbert 4)
Walk Softly, Stranger, 1950 (Cotten 3, Valli 3, Schary 4)
Walk Tall, 1960 (Crosby 4)
Walk the Proud Land, 1956 (Bancroft 3, Murphy 3, Salter 4)
Walk with Love and Death, 1969 (Huston 2, Delerue 4)
Walkabout, 1971 (Roeg 2, Barry 4)
Walking Along the Main Road. See Vi går landsvagen, 1937
Walking Back, 1928 (Adrian 4, Grot 4)
Walking Dead, 1936 (Curtiz 2, Gwenn 3, Karloff 3, Orry-Kelly 4,
    Westmore, P. 4)
Walking Down Broadway, 1933 (Von Stroheim 2)
Walking Down Broadway, 1938 (Chaney Lon, Jr. 3, Trevor 3,
    Miller, V. 4)
Walking Down Broadway. See Hello, Sister!, 1933
Walking Hills, 1949 (Sturges, J. 2, Ireland 3, Kennedy, A. 3,
    Scott, R. 3, Brown, Harry Joe 4)
Walking My Baby Back Home, 1953 (Bacon 2, Leigh, J. 3,
    O'Connor 3)
Walking on Air, 1936 (Sothern 3, Hunt 4)
Walking Trip of Revenge. See Adauchi hizakurige, 1936
Walking Walking. See Camminacammina, 1983
Walking Woman Work. See New York Eye and Ear Control, 1964
Walkout, 1923 (Roach 4)
Walkover. See Walkower, 1965
Walkower, 1965 (Skolimowski 2)
Walky Talky Hawky, 1946 (McKimson 4)
Wall, 1982 (Roberts 3, Wallach 3, Rosenman 4)
Wall. See Mur, 1982
Wall. See Muro, 1947
Wall Between, 1916 (Bushman 3)
Wall in Jerusalem, 1972 (Burton 3)
Wall of Death. See There Is Another Sun, 1951
Wall of Money, 1913 (Dwan 2, Reid 3)
Wall of Noise, 1963 (Ballard 4)
Wall Street, 1929 (Beavers 3)
Wall Street Blues, 1924 (Sennett 2)
Wall Street Cowboy, 1939 (Rogers, R. 3)
Wall Walls. See Mur Murs, 1980
Wallenberg: A Hero's Story, 1985 (Andersson B. 3)
Wallflower, 1922 (Moore, C. 3)

Wallflower, 1948 (Freund 4)
Wallflowers, 1928 (Arthur 3, Plunkett 4)
Wallop, 1921 (Ford, J. 2, Carey 3, Johnson, N. 3)
Walls. See Falak, 1968
Walls of Fire, 1974 (Kline 2)
Walls of Jericho, 1948 (Stahl 2, Baxter A. 3, Darnell 3, Douglas, K. 3,
    Wilde 3, Lemaire 4, Miller, A. 4, Newman 4, Trotti 4)
Walls of Malapaga. See Au-delà des grilles, 1949
Walls of Malapaga. See Mura di Malapaga, 1949
Walpurgis Night. See Valborgsmassoafton, 1935
Walter brani Sarajevo, 1972 (Marković 3, Samardžić 3)
Walter Defends Sarajevo. See Walter brani Sarajevo, 1972
Walter Wanger's Vogues of 1938. See Vogues of 1938, 1937
Walternacht, 1917 (Kraly 4)
Waltz at Noon. See Mahiru no enbukyoku, 1949
Waltz Dream. See Walzertraum, 1925
Waltz Me Around, 1920 (Roach 4)
Waltz of the Toreadors, 1962 (Cusack 3, Sellers 3, Mankowitz 4,
    Mathieson 4)
Waltz Time, 1933 (Junge 4)
Waltz Time in Vienna, 1933 (Walbrook 3)
Waltz Time in Vienna. See Walzerkrieg, 1933
Waltz War. See Walzerkrieg, 1933
Waltzes from Vienna, 1934 (Hitchcock 2, Gwenn 3, Matthews 3,
    Junge 4, Reville 4)
Walzer um den Stephansturm, 1935 (Tschechowa 3)
Walzer von Strauss, 1925 (Reisch 4)
Walzerkönig. See Heut Spielt der Strauss, 1928
Walzerkrieg, 1933 (Arletty 3, Walbrook 3, Herlth 4, Hoffmann 4,
    Rohrig 4)
Walzerparadies, 1932 (Sakall 3)
Walzertraum, 1925 (Pommer 4, Schufftan 4)
Wanda la peccatrice, 1952 (Rosay 3, Pinelli 4)
Wanda Nevada, 1979 (Fonda, H. 3, Fonda, P. 3)
Wanderer, 1912 (Dwan 2)
Wanderer, 1913 (Griffith 2, Barrymore L. 3, Walthall 3, Bitzer 4)
Wanderer, 1926 (Walsh 2, Beery 3, Carey 3, Head 4, Menzies 4)
Wanderer of the Wasteland, 1934 (Crabbe 3, Nilsson 3)
Wanderers. See Girovaghi, 1956
Wanderers. See Matatabi, 1973
Wanderer's Notebook. See Horoki, 1962
Wanderers of the Desert, 1937–40 (Cardiff 4)
Wandering, 1965 (Menzel 2)
Wandering. See Bloudĕni, 1965
Wandering Daughters, 1923 (Coffee 4)
Wandering Fires, 1925 (Bennett C. 3, Stradling 4)
Wandering Gypsy, 1912 (Dwan 2)
Wandering Husbands, 1924 (Sullivan 4)
Wandering Image. See Wandernde Bild, 1920
Wandering Jew, 1908 (Schildkraut 3)
Wandering Jew, 1933 (Veidt 3)
Wandering Jew. See Juif errant, 1904
Wandering on Highways. See Országutak vándora, 1956
Wandering Papas, 1925 (Hardy 3, Laurel 3, Roach 4)
Wandering Willies, 1926 (Sennett 2)
Wanderlust. See Mary Jane's Pa, 1935
Wandernde Bild, 1920 (Lang 2, Von Harbou 4)
Wandernde Licht, 1915 (Porten 3)
Wandernde Licht, 1916 (Wiene 2, Messter 4)
Wandernder Held. See Wandernde Bild, 1920
Waning Sex, 1926 (Shearer 3, Gibbons 4)
Wanted, 1937 (Pitts 3)
Wanted: A Baby. See Bachelor's Baby, 1927
Wanted—A Bad Man, 1917 (Hardy 3)
Wanted, A Child, 1909 (Griffith 2, Bitzer 4)
Wanted, A Grandmother, 1912 (Costello, D. 3)
Wanted—a Husband, 1919 (Burke 3)
Wanted: Babysitter. See Baby-Sitter, 1975
Wanted—$5000, 1918 (Daniels 3, Lloyd 3, Roach 4)
Wanted for Murder, 1946 (Holloway 3)
Wanted Men. See Wolves, 1930
Wanted: Perfect Mother, 1970 (Brocka 2)
Wanters, 1923 (Stahl 2, Fazenda 3, Shearer 3)

Wanton Countess. See Senso, 1954
War Against Mrs. Hadley, 1942 (Bainter 3, Johnson, V. 3, Freund 4,
    Schary 4)
War and Peace, 1956 (Vidor, K. 2, Ferrer, M. 3, Fonda, H. 3,
    Gassman 3, Hepburn, A. 3, Homolka 3, Mills 3, Cardiff 4,
    De Laurentiis 4, Gherardi 4, Ponti 4, Rota 4)
War and Peace, 1983 (Schlondorff 2)
War and Peace. See Krieg und Frieden, 1983
War and Peace. See Voina i mir, 1912
War and Peace. See Voina i mir, 1915
War and Peace. See Voina i mir, 1967
War Arrow, 1954 (Chandler 3, O'Hara 3, Daniels 4, Hayes 4)
War at Sea from Hawaii to Malaya. See Hawai-Marei oki kaisen, 1942
War Babies, 1932 (Temple 3)
War Between Men and Women, 1972 (Lemmon 3, Robards 3)
War Between the Tates, 1977 (Barry 4)
War Bonnet. See Savage, 1952
War Brides, 1916 (Brenon 2, Barthelmess 3, Nazimova 3, Hunt 4)
War Comes to America, 1945 (Huston 3, Hornbeck 4, Veiller 4)
War Correspondent, 1932 (Swerling 4)
War Correspondent. See Krigskorrespondenten, 1913
War Dogs, 1943 (Hanna and Barbera 4)
War Drums, 1956 (Johnson, B. 3)
War Feathers, 1926 (Roach 4)
War Game, 1961 (Zetterling 2)
War Game, 1966 (Watkins 2)
War Games. See Suppose They gave a War and Nobody Came?, 1970
War Gods of the Deep, 1965 (Tourneur, J. 2)
War Gods of the Deep. See City under the Sea, 1965
War Hunt, 1962 (Pollack 2, Redford 3, McCord 4)
War in the Mediterranean, 1943 (Howard, L. 3)
War is Over. See Guerre est finie, 1966
War, Italian Style. See Due Marines e un Generale, 1967
War Lord, 1965 (Schaffner 2, Boone 3, Heston 3, Bumstead 4, Salter 4,
    Westmore, B. 4, Whitlock 4)
War Lord. See West of Shanghai, 1937
War Lover, 1962 (McQueen, S. 3, Wagner 3, Koch 4, Mathieson 4)
War Mamas, 1931 (Pitts 3, Roach 4)
War Nurse, 1930 (Montgomery 3, Pitts 3, Gibbons 4, Rosher 4)
War of the Gardens. See Querelle de, 1982
War of the Gargantuas. See Furankenshutain no kaiju—Sanda tai
    Gailah, 1966
War of the Satellites, 1958 (Corman 4, Crosby 4)
War of the Wildcats. See In Old Oklahoma, 1943
War of the Worlds, 1953 (Pal 2, Hardwicke 3, Head 4)
War on the Plains, 1912 (Ince 4)
War Paint, 1926 (Van Dyke, W.S. 2, Cody 3)
War Relief, 1917 (Fairbanks, D. 3)
War Shock. See Woman's Devotion, 1956
War Wagon, 1967 (Fernández 2, Dern 3, Douglas, K. 3, Keel 3,
    Wayne 3, Wynn 3, Clothier 4, Needham 4, Tiomkin 4,
    Westmore, B. 4, Whitlock 4)
Ward of the King, 1913 (Cruze 2)
Wardrobe, 1958 (Dunning 4)
Ware Case, 1938 (Brook 3, Balcon 4)
Ware hitotsubu no mugi naredo, 1965 (Takamine 3)
Ware nakinurete, 1948 (Mori 3)
Warenhausprinzessin, 1926 (Albers 3)
Warera sarariiman, 1963 (Tsukasa 3)
Wareraga kyokan, 1939 (Takamine 3)
WarGames, 1983 (Burtt 4, Fraker 4)
Waris, 1954 (Biswas 4)
Warlock, 1959 (Dmytryk 2, Arlen 3, Fonda, H. 3, Malone 3, Quinn 3,
    Widmark 3, Lemaire 4)
Warlords of Atlantis, 1978 (Charisse 3)
Warm Corner, 1930 (Saville 2, Balcon 4, Wimperis 4)
Warm Current. See Danryu, 1939
Warm December, 1973 (Poitier 3)
Warm Reception, 1916 (Hardy 3)
Warmakers, 1913 (Costello, M. 3)
Warming up, 1928 (Arthur 3, Cronjager 4)
Warn London, 1934 (Gwenn 3, Bennett 4)
Warning, 1914 (Anderson G. 3, Crisp 3, Gish, D. 3, White 3)

Warning, 1927 (Walker 4)
Warning, 1982 (Bardem 2)
Warning!. *See* Varuj!, 1947
Warning Hand, 1912 (Bushman 3)
Warning Shadows. *See* Schatten, 1922
Warning Shot, 1967 (Gish, L. 3, Pidgeon 3, Sanders 3, Wynn 3,
     Biroc 4, Edouart 4, Head 4, Goldsmith 4)
Warnung vor einer heiligen Nutte, 1970 (Fassbinder 2, Constantine 3,
     Schygulla 3)
Warpath, 1951 (O'Brien, E. 3)
Warrant, 1975 (Anand 3)
Warrant Officer Panin. *See* Michman Panin, 1960
Warrens of Virginia, 1915 (DeMille 2, Sweet 3, Buckland 4)
Warrior and the Demon, 1962 and afte (Carpenter 2)
Warrior of the Lost Word, 1984 (Pleasance 3)
Warrior Who Crosses the Sea. *See* Umi o yuku bushi, 1939
Warriors, 1979 (Hill, W. 2)
Warriors. *See* Dark Avengers, 1955
Warriors 5. *See* Guerra continua, 1961
Warrior's Husband, 1933 (Levien 4)
Warriors of Faith. *See* Jan Roháč z dubé, 1947
Warrior's Rest. *See* Repos du guerrier, 1962
War's Havoc, 1912 (Nilsson 3)
Wars of the Primal Tribes. *See* In Prehistoric Days, 1913
Warsaw World Youth Meeting I–III. *See* Varsoí vit, 1955
Warschauer Zitadelle, 1937 (Warm 4)
Wartezimmer zum Jenseits, 1964 (Kinski 3, Knef 3)
Warui yatsu hodo yoku nemuru, 1960 (Kurosawa 2, Kagawa 3,
     Mifune 3, Mori 3, Ryu 3, Shimura 3, Muraki 4)
Warum die Ufos unseren Salat klauen, 1980 (Jurgens 3)
Warum lauft Herr R amok?, 1969 (Fassbinder 2, Schygulla 3)
Warum sind sie gegen uns?, 1958 (Wicki 2)
Was bin ich ohne Dich?, 1934 (Tschechowa 3, Von Harbou 4)
Was es der im dritten Stock?, 1938 (Porten 3)
Was Frauen traumen, 1933 (Wilder 2, Frohlich 3, Lorre 3)
Was geschah in dieser Nacht, 1941 (Wagner 4)
Was He a Coward?, 1911 (Griffith 2, Sweet 3, Bitzer 4)
Was ist los mit Nanette, 1928 (Holger-Madsen 2)
Was Justice Served?, 1909 (Griffith 2, Bitzer 4)
Wasei kenka tomodachi, 1929 (Ozu 2)
Washed Ashore, 1922 (Roach 4)
Washee Ironee, 1934 (Roach 4)
Washington at Valley Forge, 1908 (Olcott 2)
Washington Cowboy. *See* Rovin' Tumbleweeds, 1939
Washington Masquerade, 1932 (Barrymore L. 3, McDaniel 3,
     Adrian 4, Toland 4)
Washington Melodrama, 1941 (Dailey 3, Rosson 4)
Washington Merry-Go-Round, 1932 (Cruze 2, Muse 3, Swerling 4,
     Wanger 4)
Washington Story, 1952 (Calhern 3, Johnson, V. 3, Neal 3, Alton, J. 4,
     Pirosh 4, Rose 4, Schary 4)
Wasp, 1915 (Eason 4)
Wasp Woman, 1959 (Corman 4)
Wasser fur Canitoga, 1939 (Albers 3)
Wasted Love, 1930 (Wong 3)
Wasted Night, 1972 (Nowicki 3)
Wastrel. *See* Relitto, 1960
Wasureenu bojo, 1956 (Yamamura 3)
Wasyatnama, 1945 (Sircar 4)
Watakushi-tachi no kekkon, 1962 (Shinoda 2)
Wataridori itsukaeru, 1955 (Takamine 3, Tanaka 3)
Watashi niwa otto ga aru, 1940 (Tanaka 3)
Watashi no na wa joufu, 1949 (Yoda 4)
Watashi no niisan, 1934 (Hasegawa 3, Tanaka 3)
Watashi no papa-san mamaga suki, 1931 (Takamine 3)
Watashi no subete o, 1954 (Ichikawa 3)
Watashi wa Bellet, 1964 (Oshima 2)
Watashi wa kai ni naritai, 1959 (Muraki 4)
Watashi wa nisai, 1962 (Ichikawa 2, Kishida 3)
Watch Dog, 1923 (Roach 4)
Watch Dog, 1945 (Terry 4)
Watch on the Lime, 1949 (Lewis 2)
Watch on the Rhine, 1943 (Bondi 3, Davis 3, Lukas 3, Muse 3,

Friedhofer 4, Orry-Kelly 4, Steiner 4, Wallis 4)
Watch Out, 1924 (Sennett 2)
Watch Out, Ward Round!. *See* Pozor, vizita!, 1980
Watch the Birdie, 1935 (Hope 3)
Watch the Birdie, 1950 (Miller 3)
Watch the Birdie, 1954 (Godfrey 4)
Watch the Birdie, 1963 (Russell 2)
Watch the Birdie! See Zaostřit prosím, 1956
Watch Your Neighbors, 1918 (Sennett 2)
Watch Your Stern, 1960 (Dillon 4)
Watch Your Wife, 1922 (Roach 4)
Watch Your Wife, 1926 (Cooper, Gary 3)
Watcha Watchin', 1962 (Hanna and Barbera 4)
Watchdog, 1939 (Terry 4)
Watched, 1974 (Keach 3)
Watcher in the Woods, 1980 (Baker C. 3, Davis 3)
Watchtower over Tomorrow, 1945 (Hecht 4)
Water, 1985 (Slocombe 4)
Water. *See* Vetta, 1957
Water Babies, 1978 (Greenwood 3)
Water Circle, 1975 (Broughton 2)
Water Cure, 1916 (Hardy 3)
Water Dog, 1914 (Sennett 2, Arbuckle 3)
Water Duel, 1900 (Bitzer 4)
Water for Fire Fighting, 1948 (Halas and Batchelor 2)
Water from the Land. *See* Vandet På Låndet, 1946
Water Gipsies, 1932 (Dean 4, Reville 4)
Water Hole, 1928 (Mankiewicz 4)
Water in Our Life. *See* Seikatsu to mizu, 1952
Water Magician. *See* Taki no shiraito, 1952
Water Nymph, 1912 (Sennett 2, Normand 3)
Water Wagons, 1925 (Sennett 2)
Water War, 1911 (Dwan 2)
Water, Water Every Hare, 1952 (Jones 2)
Water, Water Everywhere, 1920 (Rogers, W. 3)
Watercolor, 1958 (Ioseliani 2)
Waterfront, 1928 (Garmes 4, Robinson 4)
Waterfront, 1939 (Bond 3)
Waterfront, 1944 (Carradine 3)
Waterfront, 1950 (Burton 3, Mathieson 4)
Waterfront Lady, 1935 (Bond 3)
Waterfront Women. *See* Waterfront, 1950
Waterhole No. 3, 1967 (Blondell 3, Coburn, J. 3, Dern 3)
Waterloo, 1928 (Wagner 4, Vanel 3)
Waterloo, 1970 (Welles 2, Bondarchuk 3, Hawkins 3, Steiger 3,
     De Laurentiis 4, Rota 4)
Waterloo Bridge, 1931 (Whale 2, Davis 3, Edeson 4, Fulton 4,
     Laemmle 4)
Waterloo Bridge, 1940 (Franklin 2, Leroy 2, Carroll L. 3, Leigh, V. 3,
     Ouspenskaya 3, Taylor, R. 3, Adrian 4, Behrman 4, Gillespie 4,
     Ruttenberg 4, Stothart 4)
Waterloo Road, 1944 (Granger 3, Gilliat 4)
Waterloo Road, 1945 (Mills 3, Sim 3)
Watermelon Man, 1970 (Van Peebles 2)
Waters of Time, 1950 (Wright 2, Dehn 4)
Watersark, 1964–65 (Wieland 2)
Watership Down, 1978 (Hurt, J. 3, Richardson 3)
Water-Sprite's Tale. *See* Vodnická pohádka, 1973
Watertight, 1943 (Cavalcanti 2)
Wattstax, 1973 (Pryor 3)
Wave. *See* Redes, 1934–35
Wavelength, 1967 (Snow 2, Wieland 2)
Wavelength, 1983 (Wynn 3)
Wavell's 30,000, 1942 (Dalrymple 4)
Wax Experiments, 1921–26 (Fischinger 2)
Wax Works, 1934 (Lantz 4)
Waxworks. *See* Wachsfigurenkabinett, 1924
Way. *See* Yol, 1981
Way Ahead, 1944 (Reed 2, Holloway 3, Howard, T. 3, Niven 3,
     Ustinov 3, Alwyn 4, Green, G. 4, Mathieson 4)
Way Back Home, 1931 (Davis 3, Berman 4, Hunt 4, Murfin 4,
     Steiner 4, Westmore, E. 4)
Way Back When series, 1940 (Fleischer, M. and D. 2)

Wedding, 1978 (Altman 2, Cromwell 2, Chaplin 3, Farrow 3, Gassman 3, Gish, L. 3)
Wedding. *See* Svadba, 1944
Wedding. *See* Wesele, 1972
Wedding at Ulfåsa. *See* Brollopet på Ulfåsa, 1911
Wedding Bells, 1921 (Talmadge, C. 3, Schenck 4)
Wedding Bells, 1927 (Schulberg 4)
Wedding Bells. *See* Royal Wedding, 1951
Wedding Bells Out of Tune, 1921 (Sennett 2)
Wedding Belts, 1940 (Fleischer, M. and D. 2)
Wedding Breakfast. *See* Catered Affair, 1956
Wedding Day. *See* Baishey Shravana, 1960
Wedding Day. *See* Brollopsdagen, 1960
Wedding Day. *See* Jour des noces, 1970
Wedding Dress, 1912 (Dwan 2)
Wedding During the French Revolution. *See* Revolutionsbryllup, 1909
Wedding Gown, 1913 (Loos 4)
Wedding Group, 1936 (Sim 3)
Wedding in Blood. *See* Noces rouges, 1973
Wedding in Monaco, 1956 (Kelly, Grace 3)
Wedding in the Eccentric Club. *See* Hochzeit im Ekzentrik Klub, 1917
Wedding in Toprin. *See* Toprini nász, 1939
Wedding in White, 1973 (Pleasance 3)
Wedding March, 1928 (Von Stroheim 2, Pitts 3, Wray 3, Day 4)
Wedding March. *See* Kekkon koshinkyoku, 1951
Wedding Night, 1935 (Vidor, K. 2, Bellamy 3, Brennan 3, Cooper, Gary 3, Goldwyn 4, Newman 4, Toland 4)
Wedding Night. *See* Noc poslubna, 1959
Wedding of Jack and Jill, 1930 (Garland 3)
Wedding Party, 1969 (De Palma 2, Clayburgh 3, De Niro 3)
Wedding Present, 1936 (Bennett J. 3, Grant, C. 3, Dreier 4, Head 4, Schulberg 4, Shamroy 4)
Wedding Rehearsal, 1932 (Korda 2, Oberon 3, Biro 4, Korda 4, Wimperis 4)
Wedding Ring. *See* Prstýnek, 1944
Wedding Rings, 1929 (Haller 4)
Wedlock, 1918 (Gilbert 3)
Wedlock Deadlock, 1947 (Bruckman 4)
Wedlock House, 1959 (Brakhage 2)
Wednesday, 1974 (Lemmon 3)
Wednesday's Child, 1934 (Berman 4, MacGowan 4, Plunkett 4, Steiner 4)
Wednesday's Luck, 1936 (Pearson 2, Havelock-Allan 4)
Wee Geordie. *See* Geordie, 1955
Wee Lady Betty, 1917 (Borzage 2, Love 3)
Wee MacGregor's Sweetheart, 1922 (Pearson 2, Balfour 3)
Wee Sandy, 1962 (Reiniger 2)
Wee Wee Monsieur, 1938 (Three Stooges 3)
Wee Willie Winkie, 1937 (Ford, J. 2, McLaglen 3, Temple 3, Miller, A. 4, Newman 4, Zanuck 4)
Week End Husbands, 1924 (Costello, M. 3)
Week Ends Only, 1932 (Crosland 2, Bennett J. 3)
Weekend, 1930 (Ruttmann 2)
Week-end, 1967 (Godard 2, Léaud 3, Coutard 4, Gégauff 4, Guillemot 4)
Week-end à Zuydcoote, 1964 (Verneuil 2, Belmondo 3, Decaë 4, Jarre 4)
Week-end at Dunkirk. *See* Week-end à Zuydcoote, 1964
Weekend at the Waldorf, 1945 (Walters 2, Johnson, V. 3, Pidgeon 3, Rogers, G. 3, Turner, L. 3, Wynn 3, Green, J. 4, Irene 4)
Week-end en mer, 1962 (Reichenbach 2)
Weekend for Three, 1941 (Garnett 2, Horton 3, Pitts 3)
Weekend in Havana, 1941 (Faye 3, Miranda 3, Day 4, Newman 4, Pan 4)
Weekend Italian Style. *See* Ombrellone, 1965
Week-End Marriage, 1932 (Brent 3, Young, L. 3, Orry-Kelly 4)
Weekend Murders. *See* Concerto per pistola solista, 1970
Weekend Nun, 1972 (Sothern 3)
Weekend of a Champion, 1972 (Polanski 2)
Week-End Party, 1922 (Laurel 3)
Week-end Pass, 1944 (Bruckman 4)
Week-end total, 1965 (Braunberger 4)
Weekend with Father, 1951 (Sirk 2, Heflin 3, Neal 3, Boyle 4)

Weekend Wives. *See* Ombrellone, 1965
Weekly Reels. *See* Kino-Nedelia, 1918–19
Week's Holiday. *See* Semaine de vacances, 1980
Weg der ins Verdergen fuhrt. *See* Berlin W., 1920
Weg, der zur Verdammnis fuhrt, 1918 (Hoffmann 4)
Weg des Todes, 1917 (Veidt 3)
Weg ins Freie, 1918 (Oswald 2)
Weg zum Nachbarn, 1966 (Lenica 2)
Wege des Schreckens, 1921 (Curtiz 2)
Wege im Zwielicht, 1948 (Frohlich 3)
Wege nach Rio, 1931 (Homolka 3)
Wege ubers Land, 1968 (Domrose 3)
Wege zu Kraft und Schonheit, 1925 (Pommer 4)
Wege zur guten Ehe, 1933 (Tschechowa 3)
Wehe, wenn sie losgelassen, 1926 (Porten 3, Courant 4)
Weib des Pharao, 1922 (Lubitsch 2, Basserman 3, Jannings 3, Wegener 3, Kraly 4, Metzner 4)
Weib in Flammen, 1928 (Albers 3, Planer 4)
Weibchen, 1970 (Fabian 3)
Weighing the Baby, 1903 (Bitzer 4)
Weil du arm bist, musst du früher sterben, 1956 (Wicki 2)
Weird Woman, 1944 (Chaney Lon, Jr. 3, Miller, V. 4, Salter 4)
Weir-Falcon Saga, 1970 (Brakhage 2)
Weiss Rausch, 1931 (Riefenstahl 2)
Weisse Abenteuer, 1951 (Herlth 4)
Weisse Damon, 1932 (Albers 3, Lorre 3, Hoffmann 4)
Weisse Holle vom Piz Palu, 1929 (Pabst 2, Riefenstahl 2, Metzner 4)
Weisse Pfau, 1920 (Dupont 2, Leni 2)
Weisse Rosen, 1914 (Gad 2, Nielsen 3, Kraly 4)
Weisse Stadion, 1928 (Ruttmann 2)
Weisse Teufel, 1930 (Litvak 2, Dagover 3, Mozhukin 3, Courant 4)
Weisse Wolfe, 1969 (Hoppe 3)
Weissen Rosen von Ravensberg, 1929 (Warm 4)
Weite Strassen—stille Liebe, 1969 (Hoffmann 3)
Welcome Burglar, 1908 (Griffith 2, Bitzer 4)
Welcome Danger, 1929 (Lloyd 3, Bruckman 4)
Welcome Home, 1925 (Cruze 2, Baxter W. 3, Brown, K. 4)
Welcome Home, 1935 (Miller, A. 4)
Welcome Home. *See* Vlast vítá, 1945
Welcome Home, Johnny Bristol, 1972 (O'Brien, P. 3, Sheen 3, Schifrin 4)
Welcome Intruder, 1913 (Griffith 2, Barrymore L. 3, Bitzer 4)
Welcome Little Stranger, 1941 (Terry 4)
Welcome, Mr. Marshall!. *See* Bienvenido, Mr. Marshall!, 1952
Welcome Stranger, 1947 (Crosby 3, Fitzgerald 3, Dreier 4, Head 4)
Welcome to Arrow Beach, 1973 (Harvey 3, Ireland 3)
Welcome to Blood City, 1977 (Palance 3)
Welcome to Britain, 1943 (Asquith 2, Hope 3, Meredith 3, Alwyn 4)
Welcome to Hard Times, 1967 (Chaney Lon, Jr. 3, Cook 3, Fonda, H. 3, Oates 3, Wynn 3)
Welcome to L.A., 1976 (Altman 2, Chaplin 3, Keitel 3, Spacek 3)
Welcome to the Club, 1971 (Warden 3)
Welfare, 1975 (Wiseman 2)
Welfare of the Workers, 1940 (Jennings 2)
Well, 1913 (Barrymore L. 3)
Well, 1951 (Laszlo 4, Tiomkin 4)
We'll Meet in the Gallery. *See* Ci troviamo in Galleria, 1953
Well Paid Stroll. *See* Dobře placená procházka, 1965
We'll Survive until Monday. *See* dozhivem do ponedelnika, 1968
Well Well Well. *See* Ojojoj eller sången om den eldroda hummern, 1965
Well Worn Daffy, 1965 (McKimson 4)
Well-Digger's Daughter. *See* Fille du puisatier, 1940
Well-Filled Day. *See* Journée bien remplie, 1972
Well-Groomed Bride, 1946 (De Havilland 3, Milland 3, Dreier 4, Head 4, Seitz 4)
Wellington Mystery. *See* Wellingtoni rejtély, 1918
Wellingtoni rejtély, 1918 (Curtiz 2)
Wells Fargo, 1937 (Cummings 3, McCrea 3, Dreier 4, Estabrook 4, Head 4, Young, V. 4)
Well-To-Do Gentleman. *See* Lepší pán, 1971
Welsh Singer, 1915 (Evans 3)
Welt am Draht, 1973 (Fassbinder 2)

Welt ohne Maske, 1934 (Tschechowa 3)
Welt ohne Waffen, 1918 (Wegener 3)
Welt will belogen sein, 1926 (Courant 4)
Weltbrand, 1920 (Gad 2, Kortner 3)
Weltrekord im Seitensprung, 1940 (Jurgens 3)
Weltspiegel, 1918 (Pick 2)
Weltstrasse See—Welthafen Hamburg, 1938 (Ruttmann 2)
Wem Gehört die Welt?. See Kuhle Wampe, 1930
Wen kummert's . . ., 1960 (Schlondorff 3)
Wenn am Sonntagabend die Dorfmusik spielt, 1933 (Warm 4)
Wenn das Herz in Hass ergluht, 1918 (Negri 3)
Wenn der Hahn kraht, 1936 (George, H. 3)
Wenn der junge Wein bluht, 1943 (Porten 3)
Wenn der weisse Flieder wieder bluht, 1953 (Schneider 3)
Wenn des Herz der Jugend spricht, 1926 (Basserman 3)
Wenn die Gotter Lieben, 1942 (Jurgens 3)
Wenn die Maske fallt, 1912 (Gad 2, Nielsen 3)
Wenn die Musik nicht war, 1935 (Gallone 2)
Wenn die Schwalben heimwarts ziehn, 1928 (Frohlich 3)
Wenn die Sonne wieder scheint, 1943 (Wegener 3, Herlth 4)
Wenn du einmal dein Herz verschenkst, 1929 (Wagner 4)
Wenn du zu mir haltst, 1962 (Domrose 3)
Wenn ein Weib den Weg verliert. See Café Electric, 1927
Wenn Frauen lieben und hassen, 1917 (Krauss 3)
Wenn ich Konig war!, 1934 (Warm 4)
Wenn Manner Schlange stehen. See Chikita, 1961
Wenn Tote sprechen, 1917 (Veidt 3)
Wenn vier dasselbe Tun, 1917 (Lubitsch 2, Jannings 3)
Went the Day Well?, 1942 (Cavalcanti 2, Balcon 4)
Wer das Scheiden hat erfunden, 1928 (Albers 3)
Wer nimmt die Liebe ernst?, 1931 (Courant 4)
Werdegang. See Reigen, 1920
We're All Gamblers, 1927 (Cruze, Glennon 4)
We're Going to Be Rich, 1938 (Fields, G. 3, McLaglen 3)
We're in the Army Now. See Pack Up Your Troubles, 1939
We're in the Money, 1935 (Blondell 3, Brown, Harry Joe 4)
We're in the Navy Now, 1926 (Sutherland 2, Beery 3, Schulberg 4)
We're No Angels, 1955 (Curtiz 2, Bennett J. 3, Bogart 3, Carroll L. 3,
    Rathbone 3, Ustinov 3)
We're No Angels. See Noi non siamo angeli, 1975
We're Not Dressing, 1934 (Taurog 2, Crosby 3, Lombard 3, Milland 3,
    Dreier 4, Glazer 4, Lang 4)
We're Not Married, 1952 (Goulding 2, Arden 3, Calhern 3, Darwell 3,
    Douglas, P. 3, Marvin 3, Monroe 3, Rogers, G. 3, Johnson 4,
    Lemaire 4)
We're Off!. See Hotovo, jedem!, 1947
We're on the Jury, 1937 (Musuraca 4)
We're Only Human, 1936 (Auer 3, Darwell 3, Hunt 4)
We're Ready, Let's Go. See Hotovo, jedem, 1947
We're Rich Again, 1934 (Burke 3, Crabbe 3, Musuraca 4, Plunkett 4,
    Steiner 4)
Werewolf, 1956 (Katzman 4)
Werewolf of London, 1935 (Oland 3, D'Agostino 4, Fulton 4, Pierce 4)
Werk seines Lebens, 1919 (Basserman 3)
Werther, 1922 (Dulac 2)
Werther, 1938 (Ophuls 2, Douy 4, Lourié 4)
Wesele, 1972 (Wajda 2, Komorowska 3, Olbrychski 3, Pszoniak 3)
West and Soda, 1965 (Bozzetto 4)
West is West, 1920 (Carey 3)
West of Broadway, 1931 (Bellamy 3, Gilbert 3, Meredyth 4)
West of Chicago, 1922 (Adorée 3)
West of Hot Dog, 1924 (Laurel 3)
West of Shanghai, 1937 (Karloff 3)
West of the Divide, 1934 (Wayne 3, Canutt 4)
West of the Pecos, 1934 (Beavers 3)
West of the Pecos, 1945 (Mitchum 3)
West of the Pesos, 1960 (McKimson 4)
West of the Water Tower, 1924 (Pitts 3)
West of Zanzibar, 1928 (Browning 2, Baxter W. 3, Chaney Lon 3,
    Johnson, N. 3, Day 4, Gibbons 4, Young, W. 4)
West of Zanzibar, 1954 (Watt 2)
West Point, 1927 (Dwan 2, Crawford, J. 3)
West Point of the Air, 1935 (Beery 3, O'Sullivan 3, Russell, R. 3,

Stone 3, Taylor, R. 3, Young, R. 3, Saunders 4)
West Point Story, 1950 (Cagney 3, Day 3, Mayo 3, Cahn 4, Prinz 4)
West Point Widow, 1941 (Siodmak 2, Dreier 4, Head 4, Kraly 4)
West Side Story, 1961 (Wise 2, Wood 3, Bass 4, Dunn 4, Green, J. 4,
    Lehman 4, Leven 4, Mirisch 4, Sharaff 4)
West Virginian. See Reel Virginian, 1924
Westbound, 1959 (Boetticher 2, Mayo 3, Scott, R. 3, Blanke 4)
Western Approaches, 1944 (Cardiff 4)
Western Blood, 1918 (Mix 3)
Western Chivalry, 1910 (Anderson G. 3)
Western Code, 1933 (Auer 3)
Western Courage, 1935 (Bond 3)
Western Cyclone, 1943 (Crabbe 3)
Western Daze, 1941 (Pal 3)
Western Doctor's Peril, 1911 (Dwan 2)
Western Dreamer, 1911 (Dwan 2)
Western Girls, 1912 (Anderson G. 3)
Western Girl's Sacrifice, 1911 (Anderson G. 3)
Western Governor's Humanity, (Johnson, N. 3)
Western Hearts, 1911 (Mix 3)
Western Hearts, 1912 (Anderson G. 3)
Western History, 1971 (Brakhage 2)
Western Isles, 1941 (Alwyn 4, Cardiff 4)
Western Jamboree, 1938 (Autry 3)
Western Justice, 1907 (Anderson G. 3, Selig 4)
Western Justice, 1937 (Katzman 4)
Western Law That Failed, 1913 (Anderson G. 3)
Western Love, 1913 (Guy 2)
Western Maid, 1910 (Anderson G. 3)
Western Masquerade, 1916 (Mix 3)
Western Redemption, 1911 (Anderson G. 3)
Western Sister's Devotion, 1913 (Anderson G. 3)
Western Story. See Gal Who Took the West, 1949
Western Trail, 1936 (Terry 4)
Western Union, 1941 (Lang 2, Carradine 3, Cody 3, Scott, R. 3,
    Summerville 3, Young, R. 3, Banton 4, Brown, Harry Joe 4,
    Canutt 4, Cronjager 4, Day 4)
Western Waif, 1911 (Dwan 2)
Western Way, 1915 (Anderson G. 3)
Western Woman's Way, 1910 (Anderson G. 3)
Westerner, 1940 (Wyler 2, Andrews D. 3, Brennan 3, Cooper, Gary 3,
    Basevi 4, Goldwyn 4, Mandell 4, Newman 4, Swerling 4,
    Tiomkin 4, Toland 4)
Westerners, 1919 (Seitz 4)
Westerner's Way, 1910 (Anderson G. 3)
Westfront 1918, 1930 (Pabst 2, Metzner 4, Wagner 4)
Westinghouse A.B.C., 1965 (Bernstein 4)
Westward Bound, 1930 (Canutt 4)
Westward Ho, 1935 (Wayne 3, Canutt 4)
Westward Ho! 1940, 1940 (Dickinson 2)
Westward Ho the Wagons!, 1956 (De Toth 2, Disney 2, Cody 3,
    Iwerks 4)
Westward Passage, 1932 (Olivier 3, Pitts 3, Selznick 4, Steiner 4)
Westward the Wagon. See Hitched, 1971
Westward the Women, 1951 (Capra 2, Wellman 2, Taylor, R. 3,
    Plunkett 4, Schary 4, Schnee 4)
Westworld, 1973 (Brynner 3)
Wet Hare, 1962 (McKimson 4)
Wet Knight, 1932 (Lantz 4)
Wet Parade, 1932 (Fleming 2, Durante 3, Huston 3, Loy 3, Muse 3,
    Stone 3, Young, R. 3, Adrian 4, Barnes 4, Mahin 4, Stromberg 4)
Wet Saturday, 1956 (Hitchcock 2)
Wet Weather, 1922 (Roach 4)
Wetherby, 1985 (Redgrave, V. 3)
Wetterleuchten, 1925 (Dieterle 2)
Wetterwart, 1923 (Pommer 4)
We've Come a Long Way, 1952 (Halas and Batchelor 2)
We've Come a Long, Long Way, 1943 (Horne 3)
We've Never Been Licked, 1943 (Mitchum 3, Krasner 4, Raine 4,
    Wanger 4)
Whale for the Killing, 1981 (Widmark 3, Lourié 4)
Whale of a Time, 1971 (Arlen 3)
Whalers. See Valfångare, 1939

Whale's Roof. *See* Toît de la baleine, 1981
Wham Bam Slam, 1955 (Three Stooges 3, Bruckman 4)
Wharf, 1968 (Le Grice 2)
Wharf Angel, 1934 (Auer 3, McLaglen 3, Hoffenstein 4, Menzies 4)
Wharf Rat, 1916 (Marsh 3, Loos 4)
What?, 1971 (Breer 2)
What?, 1973 (Polanski 2)
What?. *See* Che?, 1972
What!. *See* Frusta e il corpo, 1963
What a Blonde, 1945 (Hunt 4)
What a Bozo, 1931 (Roach 4)
What a Carve Up!, 1961 (Pleasance 3)
What a Cinch, 1915 (Hardy 3)
What a Life, 1932 (Iwerks 4)
What a Life, 1939 (Wilder 2, Cooper, J 3, Dreier 4, Head 4)
What a Lion!, 1938 (Hanna and Barbera 4)
What a Little Sneeze Will Do, 1941 (Terry 4)
What a Man. *See* Never Give a Sucker an Even Break, 1941
What a Night, 1935 (Terry 4)
What a Night!, 1928 (Sutherland 2, Daniels 3, Cronjager 4, Mankiewicz 4)
What a Way to Go!, 1964 (Smith, D. , Cummings 3, Dumont 3, Kelly, Gene 3, MacLaine 3, Martin, D. 3, Mitchum 3, Newman 3, Comden and Green 4, Head 4, Shamroy 4, Smith, J.M. 4, Westmore, F. 4)
What a Whopper, 1921 (Roach 4)
What a Widow!, 1930 (Dwan 2, Swanson 3, Barnes 4)
What a Woman!, 1943 (Russell, R. 3, Winters 3, Banton 4, Polglase 4, Walker 4)
What a Woman Can Do, 1911 (Anderson G. 3)
What Are Best Friends For?, 1973 (Grant, L. 3, Lourié 4)
What Came to Bar Q, 1914 (Anderson G. 3)
What Demoralized the Barber Shop, 1901 (Porter 2)
What Did You Do in the War, Daddy?, 1966 (Edwards 2, Coburn, J. 3, Dunn 4, Mancini 4)
What Do Men Know? See Vad veta val mannen?, 1932
What Do Men Want?, 1921 (Weber 2)
What Does Dorrie Want?, 1982 (Keaton 3)
What Drink Did, 1909 (Griffith 2, Bitzer 4)
What Ever Happened to Uncle Fred?, 1967 (Godfrey 4)
What Every Iceman Knows, 1927 (Roach 4)
What Every Woman Knows, 1934 (La Cava 2, Carroll L. 3, Crisp 3, Meek 3, Adrian 4, Lewin 4, Rosher 4, Stothart 4)
What Every Woman Learns, 1919 (Niblo 2, Barnes 4)
What Exploded? See Co to bouchlo?, 1970
What Father Saw, 1913 (Sennett 2)
What Fools Men, 1925 (Stone 3)
What Fools Men Are, 1922 (Carré 4)
What Happened to Father?, 1927 (Oland 3)
What Happened to Jones, 1920 (Cruze 2)
What Happened to Jones, 1926 (Pitts 3)
What Happened to Rosa?, 1921 (Menjou 3, Normand 3)
What Happens at Night, 1941 (Terry 4)
What He Forgot, 1915 (Hardy 3)
What I Didn't Say to the Prince, 1975 (Brdečka 4)
What Is a Computer?, 1967 (Halas and Batchelor 2)
What is a Workers' Council?. *See* Sto je radnički savjet?, 1959
What Is It Like, The Sea? See Kakoe, ono, more?, 1965
What Kind of Fool Am I?, 1961 (Godfrey 4)
What Lola Wants. *See* Damn Yankees, 1958
What Love Forgives, 1919 (Polito 4)
What Love Will Do, 1921 (Howard 2)
What Makes David Run?. *See* Qu'est-ce qui fait courir David?, 1982
What Makes Lizzy Dizzy?, 1942 (Langdon 3)
What Money Can Buy, 1928 (Carroll M. 3)
What Money Can't Buy, 1917 (Cruze 2, Bosworth 3)
What Next, Corporal Hargrove, 1945 (Edwards 2, Haas 3, Walker 3, Irene 4, Irene 4, Kurnitz 4)
What! No Beer?, 1933 (Keaton 2, Durante 3, Wilson, C. 4)
What No Spinach?, 1936 (Fleischer, M. and D. 2)
What Papa Got, 1912–13 (White 3)
What Pearl's Pearl Did, 1912–13 (White 3)
What Price Beauty, 1928 (Loy 3, Adrian 4, Menzies 4)

What Price Fame? See Hollywood Hoodlum, 1934
What Price Fleadom, 1948 (Avery 2)
What Price Glory, 1926 (Walsh 2, Del Rio 3, McLaglen 3)
What Price Glory, 1952 (Ford, J. 2, Cagney 3, Dailey 3, Wagner 3, Lemaire 4, Newman 4)
What Price Goofy?, 1925 (McCarey 2, Roach 4)
What Price Hollywood?, 1932 (Cukor 2, Beavers 3, Bennett C. 3, Berman 4, Murfin 4, Rosher 4, Selznick 4, Steiner 4, Vorkapich 4)
What Price Innocence, 1933 (Beavers 3, Grable 3)
What Price Melody? See Lord Byron of Broadway, 1930
What Price Taxi, 1932 (Roach 4)
What Sex Am I?, 1985 (Grant, L. 3)
What Shall I Do?, 1924 (Walker 4)
What Shall We Do with Our Old?, 1910 (Griffith 2, Crisp 3, Bitzer 4)
What the Birds Knew. *See* Ikimono no kiroku, 1955
What the Daisy Said, 1910 (Griffith 2, Pickford 3, Bitzer 4)
What the Doctor Ordered, 1911 (Sennett 2)
What the Scotch Started, 1933 (Harlow 3)
What Who How, 1957 (Vanderbeek 2)
What Will People Say?, 1916 (Guy 2)
What Women Did for Me, 1927 (Velez 3, Roach 4)
What Women Dream. *See* Was Frauen traumen, 1933
What Women Will Do, 1921 (Nilsson 3, Hunt 4)
Whatever Happened to Aunt Alice?, 1969 (Aldrich 2, Gordon 3, Page 3, Biroc 4)
Whatever Happened to Baby Jane?, 1962 (Aldrich 2, Crawford, J. 3, Davis 3, Haller 4)
Whatever Happened to Baby Toto?, 1964 (Auer 3)
Whatever Happened to Green Valley?, 1973 (Weir 2)
What's a Nice Girl Like You . . .?, 1971 (McDowall 3, O'Brien, E. 3, Price 3, Warden 3)
What's a Nice Girl Like You Doing in a Place Like This?, 1963 (Scorsese 2)
What's Brewin' Bruin, 1947 (Jones 2)
What's Buzzin', Buzzard?, 1943 (Avery 2)
What's Buzzin' Cousin?, 1943 (Miller 3, Walker 4)
What's Cookin', 1942 (Burke 3, O'Connor 3)
What's Cookin', Doc?, 1944 (Clampett 4)
What's Cooking?, 1947 (Halas and Batchelor 2)
What's Good for the Goose, 1969 (Golan and Globus 4)
What's Happened to Sugar, 1945 (Flaherty 2)
What's Happening: The Beatles in the USA, 1964 (Maysles A. and D. 2)
What's His Name, 1914 (DeMille 2, Buckland 4)
What's in a Number, 1948 (Lassally 4)
What's My Lion?, 1961 (McKimson 4)
What's New Pussycat?, 1965 (Allen 2, Burton 3, O'Toole 3, Schneider 3, Sellers 3, Sylbert 4, Williams, R. 4)
What's Opera, Doc?, 1957 (Jones 2)
What's Sauce for the Goose, 1916 (Hardy 3)
What's So Bad about Feeling Good?, 1968 (Seaton 2, Ritter 3, Bumstead 4, Head 4, Pirosh 4)
What's the Matador?, 1942 (Three Stooges 3)
What's the Matter with Helen?, 1971 (Moorehead 3, Reynolds, D. 3, Winters 3, Ballard 4, Lourié 4, Raksin 4, Reynolds 4)
What's the World Coming To?, 1926 (Roach 4)
What's Up Doc?, 1950 (McKimson 4)
What's Up, Doc?, 1972 (Bogdanovich 2, Streisand 3, Fields 4, Henry 4, Kovacs 4)
What's Up Front, 1964 (Zsigmond 4)
What's Up, Tiger Lily?, 1966 (Allen 2)
What's Worth While, 1921 (Weber 2)
What's Wrong with the Women?, 1922 (Bennett C. 3)
What's Wrong with This Picture?, 1971–72 (Landow 2)
What's Your Daughter Doing? See Daughters of Today, 1924
What's Your Hurry, 1909 (Griffith 2, Pickford 3, Bitzer 4)
What's Your Hurry?, 1920 (Wood 2, Reid 3)
What's Your I.Q.?, 1940 (Sidney 2)
Wheeeeels, 1958 (Vanderbeek 2)
Wheel of Chance, 1928 (Barthelmess 3, Oland 3, Haller 4)
Wheel of Fate. *See* Bhagyachakra, 1935
Wheel of Fortune. *See* Man Betrayed, 1941
Wheel of Life, 1914 (Reid 3)

Wheel of Life, 1929 (Cronjager 4)
Wheelchair. *See* Cochecito, 1960
Wheeler & Murdoch, 1972 (Warden 3)
Wheeler Dealers, 1963 (Hiller 2, Remick 3, Lang 4)
Wheels of Destiny, 1934 (McCord 4)
Wheels of Justice, 1911 (Mix 3)
Wheels of Time. *See* Idö kereke, 1961
When a Feller Needs a Friend, 1932 (Cooper, J. 3, Rosson 4)
When a Girl Loves, 1919 (Weber 2)
When a Man Loves, 1910 (Griffith 2, Pickford 3, Bitzer 4)
When a Man Loves, 1927 (Crosland 2, Barrymore J. 3, Costello, D. 3, Johnson, N. 3, Oland 3, Carré 4, Meredyth 4)
When a Man Rides Alone, 1919 (King 2, Furthman 4)
When a Man Sees Red, 1917 (Farnum 3)
When a Man Sees Red, 1934 (McCord 4)
When a Man's a Prince, 1926 (Sennett 2)
When a Stranger Calls, 1979 (Roberts 3)
When a Woman Ascends the Stairs. *See* Onna ga kaidan o agaru toki, 1960
When a Woman Guides, 1914 (Loos 4)
When a Woman Loses Her Way. *See* Café Electric, 1927
When a Woman Loves. *See* Waga ai, 1960
When a Woman Sins, 1918 (Bara 3)
When a Woman Won't, 1913 (Dwan 2)
When Ambrose Dared Walrus, 1915 (Sennett 2)
When Angels Fall. *See* Gdy spadaja anioly, 1959
When Artists Love. *See* Nar konstnarer alska, 1914
When Bearcat Went Dry, 1919 (Chaney Lon 3)
When Bess Got in Wrong, 1914 (Meredyth 4)
When Boys Leave Home. *See* Downhill, 1927
When Carnival Comes. *See* Quando o Carnaval chegar, 1972
When Comedy was King, 1960 (Keaton 2)
When Cupid Slipped, 1916 (Mix 3)
When Dawn Came, 1920 (Moore, C. 3)
When Do We Eat?, 1918 (Niblo 2, Barnes 4, Ince 4)
When Doctors Disagree, 1919 (Normand 3)
When Dreams Come True, 1913 (Sennett 2)
When East Comes West, 1911 (Dwan 2)
When East Comes West, 1922 (Eason 4)
When Edith Played Judge and Jury, 1912 (Bosworth 3)
When Eight Bells Toll, 1971 (Hawkins 3, Hopkins, A. 3)
When Empty Hearts Are Filled, 1915 (Eason 4)
When He Wants a Dog He Wants a Dog, 1912–14 (Cohl 2)
When Hell Broke Loose, 1958 (Bronson 3)
When Hell Was in Season, 1979 (Saint 3)
When Husbands Flirt, 1925 (Arzner 2, Wellman 2)
When I Grow Up, 1951 (Preston 3, Laszlo 4, Spiegel 4)
When I Was a Kid, I Didn't Dare. *See* Si je suis comme ça, c'est la faute de papa, 1978
When I Yoo Hoo, 1936 (Freleng 4)
When in Rome, 1952 (Brown 2, Douglas, P. 3, Johnson, V. 3, Buckner 4, Daniels 4, Schnee 4)
When Jim Returned, 1913 (Reid 3)
When Johnny Comes Marching Home, 1943 (O'Connor 3)
When Kings Were the Law, 1912 (Griffith 2, Crisp 3, Bitzer 4)
When Knighthood Was in Flower, 1922 (Davies 3, Powell, W. 3)
When Knights Were Bold, 1908 (Bitzer 4)
When Knights Were Bold, 1936 (Buchanan 3, Fitzgerald 3, Wray 3, Young, F. 4)
When Knights Were Bold, 1941 (Terry 4)
When Knights Were Cold, 1922 (Laurel 3)
When Ladies Meet, 1933 (Brady 3, Loy 3, Montgomery 3, Adrian 4)
When Ladies Meet, 1941 (Crawford, J. 3, Garson 3, Marshall 3, Taylor, R. 3, Adrian 4, Kaper 4, Loos 4)
When Leaves Fall. *See* Listopad, 1966
When Lee Surrenders, 1912 (Ince 4)
When Lilacs Blossom. *See* Nar syrenerna blommar, 1952
When Love and Honor Called, 1911 (Anderson G. 3)
When Love and Honor Called, 1915 (Anderson G. 3)
When Love Grows Cold, 1925 (Brook 3)
When Love is Blind, 1919 (Sennett 2)
When Love Is Young, 1912–13 (White 3)
When Love is Young, 1937 (Brennan 3)

When Love Kills. *See* Nar karleken dodar, 1913
When Love Took Wings, 1915 (Sennett 2, Arbuckle 3)
When Luck Changes, 1913 (Dwan 2, Reid 3)
When Men Desire, 1919 (Bara 3)
When Men Would Kill, 1914 (Olcott 2)
When Mercy Tempers Justice, 1912 (Cruze 2)
When Money Comes, 1929 (McCarey 2, Roach 4)
When Mousehood Was in Flower, 1953 (Terry 4)
When My Baby Smiles At Me, 1948 (Arlen 3, Dailey 3, Grable 3, Lemaire 4, Newman 4, Trotti 4)
When My Ship Comes in, 1934 (Fleischer, M. and D. 2)
When Passion Blinds Honesty. *See* Hulda Rasmussen, 1911
When Reuben Fooled the Bandits, 1914 (Sennett 2)
When Romance Rides, 1922 (Hersholt 3)
When Ruben Fooled the Bandits. *See* When Reuben Fooled the Bandits, 1914
When She Says No, 1984 (Torn 3)
When Soul Meets Soul, 1913 (Bushman 3)
When Strangers Marry, 1944 (Mitchum 3, Tiomkin 4)
When Strangers Meet, 1933 (Bond 3)
When Strangers Meet. *See* Einer frisst den anderern, 1964
When Sugar-Cookies are Broken. *See* Sato-gashi ga kazureru toki, 1967
When Summer Comes, 1922 (Sennett 2)
When the Alarm Bell Rings. *See* Nar larmhlockan ljuder, 1913
When the Boys Meet the Girls, 1965 (Katzman 4)
When the Cat's Away, 1929 (Disney 2, Iwerks 4)
When the Chrysanthemums Fade. *See* Uchveli uzh davno krisantemi v sadu, 1916
When the Clouds Roll By, 1919 (Fleming 2, Fairbanks, D. 3)
When the Cook Fell Ill, 1914 (Mix 3)
When the Cookie Crumbles. *See* Sato-gashi ga kazureru toki, 1967
When the Daltons Rode, 1940 (Crawford, B. 3, Francis, K. 3, Scott, R. 3)
When the Dead Return, 1911 (Olcott 2)
When the Desert Calls, 1922 (Carré 4)
When the Door Opened. *See* Escape, 1940
When the Fire Bells Rang, 1911 (Sennett 2)
When the Girls Take Over, 1962 (Coogan 3)
When the Gods Played a Badger Game, 1915 (Chaney Lon 3)
When the Law Rides, 1928 (Musuraca 4, Plunkett 4)
When the Legends Die, 1972 (Forrest 3, Widmark 3)
When the Light Fades, 1913 (Dwan 2)
When the Lights Go on Again, 1944 (Howard 2)
When the Mother-in-Law Reigns. *See* Nar svarmor regerar, 1912
When the Pie Was Opened, 1941 (Lye 2)
When the Poppies Bloom Again. *See* Dokter Pulder zaait papavers, 1975
When the Press Speaks, 1913 (Bunny 3)
When the Red Red Robin Comes Bob Bob Bobbin' Along, 1932 (Fleischer, M. and D. 2)
When the Redskins Rode, 1951 (Katzman 4)
When the Studio Burned, 1913 (Cruze 2)
When the Trees Were Tall. *See* Kogda derevya byli bolshimi, 1962
When the Violin Sighs. *See* Když struny lkají, 1930
When the Wind Blows, 1920 (Roach 4)
When the Wind Blows, 1930 (Roach 4)
When the Wind Blows. *See* Make Way for Tomorrow, 1937
When Thief Meets Thief, 1937 (Walsh 2)
When Thief Meets Thief. *See* Jump for Glory, 1937
When Time Ran Out, 1980 (Bisset 3, Borgnine 3, Cortese 3, Holden 3, Meredith 3, Newman 3, Foreman 4, Schifrin 4)
When Tomorrow Comes, 1939 (Stahl 2, Boyer 3, Dunne 3, Orry-Kelly 4)
When Villains Wait, 1914 (Sennett 2)
When We Were in Our Teens, 1910 (Pickford 3)
When We Were 21, 1921 (King 2)
When Wealth Torments, 1912 (Bushman 3)
When Were You Born?, 1938 (Wong 3)
When Wifey Holds the Purse Strings, 1911 (Sennett 2)
When Willie Comes Marching Home, 1950 (Ford, J. 2, Dailey 3, Marsh 3, Lemaire 4, Newman 4, Wheeler 4)
When Women Lie. *See* Uso, 1963

When Worlds Collide, 1951 (Pal 2, Edouart 4, Head 4, Maté 4, Seitz 4)
When You and I Were Young, 1917 (Guy 2)
When You Comin' Back, Red Ryder?, 1978 (Grant, L. 3)
When You're in Love, 1937 (Brooks 3, Grant, C. 3, Newman 4, Riskin 4, Walker 4)
When You're Married. *See* Mabel's Married Life, 1914
When Yuba Plays the Rumba on the Tuba, 1931 (Fleischer, M. and D. 2)
When's Your Birthday, 1936 (Clampett 4)
When's Your Birthday?, 1937 (Brown 3)
Whence and Where To. *See* Kudy kam, 1956
Where Am I?, 1923 (Roach 4)
Where Angels Go . . . Trouble Follows, 1968 (Johnson, V. 3, Russell, R. 3, Taylor, R. 3, Schifrin 4, Wheeler 4)
Where Are My Children?, 1915 (Weber 2)
Where Are the Dreams of Youth? See Sieshum no yume ima izuko, 1932
Where Are You Maxim? See Gde ty teper, Maxim?, 1965
Where Are Your Children?, 1943 (Cooper, J 3)
Where Broadway Meets the Mountains, 1912 (Dwan 2)
Where Charity Begins, 1912–13 (White 3)
Where Chimneys Are Seen. *See* Entotsu no mieru basho, 1953
Where Danger Lives, 1950 (Mitchum 3, O'Sullivan 3, Rains 3, Bennett 4, Musuraca 4)
Where Destiny Guides, 1913 (Dwan 2)
Where Did You Get That Girl?, 1941 (Salter 4)
Where Do We Go from Here?, 1945 (Preminger 2, MacMurray 3, Quinn 3, Raksin 4, Ryskind 4, Shamroy 4)
Where Does It Hurt?, 1972 (Sellers 3)
Where Eagles Dare, 1968 (Burton 3, Eastwood 3, Canutt 4)
Where East Is East, 1929 (Browning 2, Chaney Lon 3, Velez 3, Gibbons 4, Young, W. 4)
Where Hazel Met the Villain, 1914 (Sennett 2)
Where History Has Been Written, 1913 (Pearson 2)
Where is My Wandering Boy This Evening, 1923 (Sennett 2)
Where is Parsifal, 1984 (Curtis 3)
Where It's At, 1969 (Kanin 4, Guffey 4)
Where Lights Are Low, 1921 (Hayakawa 3)
Where Love Has Gone, 1964 (Dmytryk 2, Davis 3, Hayward 3, Cahn 4, Hayes 4, Head 4)
Where Mountains Float. *See* Hvor bjergene sejler, 1955
Where No Vultures Fly, 1951 (Watt 2, Balcon 4)
Where Now Are the Dreams of Youth? See Seishun no yume ima izuko, 1932
Where Sinners Meet, 1934 (Brook 3, Burke 3, Biroc 4, Musuraca 4, Plunkett 4, Steiner 4)
Where the Boys Are, 1960 (Ames 4, Pasternak 4)
Where the Breakers Roar, 1908 (Griffith 2, Lawrence 3, Bitzer 4)
Where the Devil Cannot Get. *See* Kam čert nemuže, 1970
Where the Forest Ends, 1915 (Chaney Lon 3)
Where the Ganges Flows. *See* Jis Desh Me Ganga Behti Hai, 1960
Where the Hot Wind Blows. *See* Loi, 1959
Where the Ladies Go, 1980 (Black 3)
Where the Lilies Bloom, 1974 (Stanton 3)
Where the Mountains Meet, 1913 (Anderson G. 3)
Where the Pavement Ends, 1923 (Ingram 2, Novarro 3, Seitz 4)
Where the River Bends. *See* Bend of the River, 1952
Where the Sidewalk Ends, 1950 (Preminger 2, Andrews D. 3, Malden 3, Tierney 3, Hecht 4, La Shelle 4, Lemaire 4, Wheeler 4)
Where the Spies Are, 1965 (Cusack 3, Niven 3, Mankowitz 4)
Where the West Begins, 1919 (King 2, Furthman 4)
Where There's a Heart, 1912 (Dwan 2)
Where There's a Will, 1936 (Fisher 2, Balcon 4, Gilliat 4)
Where There's Life, 1947 (Bendix 3, Hope 3, Dreier 4, Head 4, Lang 4)
Where There's Smoke. *See* Il n'y a pas de fumée sans feu, 1973
Where Were You When the Lights Went Out?, 1968 (Day 3)
Where's Charley, 1952 (Kidd 4)
Where's Jack, 1969 (Baker S. 3, Bernstein 4)
Where's Misha? See Kde je Míša?, 1954
Where's Poppa?, 1970 (Gordon 3, Segal 3)
Where's the Fire?, 1921 (Roach 4)
Which is Which. *See* Hans rigtige Kone, 1916

Which Is Witch?, 1948 (Freleng 4)
Which Way Did He Go?, 1913 (Bunny 3)
Which Way Is Up?, 1977 (Pryor 3, Alonzo 4)
Which Way to the Front?, 1970 (Lewis 2)
Which Woman, 1918 (Browning 2)
Whiffs, 1975 (Gould 3, Cahn 4)
While America Sleeps, 1939 (Zinnemann 2)
While I Run This Race, 1966 (Heston 3)
While Paris Sleeps, 1923 (Tourneur, M. 2, Chaney Lon 3, Gilbert 3)
While Paris Sleeps, 1932 (Dwan 2, McLaglen 3)
While the Cat's Away, 1911 (Pickford 3, Gaudio 4)
While the City Sleeps, 1928 (Chaney Lon 3, Day 4, Gibbons 4)
While the City Sleeps, 1956 (Lang 2, Andrews D. 3, Lupino 3, Marsh 3, Price 3, Sanders 3, Fields 4, Laszlo 4, Robinson 4)
While the City Sleeps. *See* Medan staden sover, 1950
While the Door Was Locked. *See* Medan porten var stangd, 1946
While the Patient Slept, 1935 (Brown, Harry Joe 4, Edeson 4)
While the Sun Shines, 1947 (Asquith 2, Rutherford 3)
While There's War, There's Hope. *See* Finche c'è guerra c'è speranza, 1974
Whimsical Illusions. *See* Illusions fantaisistes, 1910
Whip, 1917 (Tourneur, M. 2, Carré 4)
Whip, 1928 (Nilsson 3)
Whip Hand, 1913 (Bushman 3)
Whip Hand, 1951 (Menzies 4, Musuraca 4)
Whip Saw, 1936 (Wood 2)
Whip Woman, 1928 (Young, L. 3, Haller 4)
Whiplash, 1948 (Arden 3, Sakall 3, Waxman 4)
Whipped. *See* Underworld Story, 1950
Whipsaw, 1935 (Loy 3, Tracy 3, Howe 4)
Whirl of Life, 1915 (Gordon 3)
Whirlpool, 1918 (Crosland 2, Brady 3)
Whirlpool, 1934 (Arthur 3, Bond 3)
Whirlpool, 1949 (Ferrer, J. 3, Tierney 3)
Whirlpool, 1950 (Preminger 2, Hecht 4, Lemaire 4, Miller, A. 4, Newman 4, Raksin 4, Wheeler 4)
Whirlpool, 1959 (Unsworth 4)
Whirls and Girls, 1929 (Sennett 2)
Whirlwind, 1951 (Autry 3)
Whirlwind. *See* Dai tatsumaki, 1964
Whirlwind of Youth, 1927 (Schulberg 4)
Whisky Galore!, 1949 (Mackendrick 2, Greenwood 3, Balcon 4)
Whisky und ein Sofa, 1963 (Schell, Maria 3)
Whisper in the Dark. *See* Sussurro nel buio, 1976
Whisperers, 1967 (Evans 3, Barry 4)
Whispering, 1922 (Wilcox 2, Brook 3)
Whispering Chorus, 1918 (DeMille 2, Buckland 4, Macpherson 4)
Whispering City, 1947 (Lukas 3)
Whispering Death, 1975 (Lee, C. 3)
Whispering Death. *See* Flusternde Tod, 1975
Whispering Devils, 1920 (Gaudio 4)
Whispering Enemies, 1939 (Costello, D. 3)
Whispering Ghosts, 1942 (Carradine 3, Ballard 4, Day 4, Raksin 4)
Whispering Shadows, 1933 (Lugosi 3, Walthall 3)
Whispering Smith, 1926 (Clarke, C.C. 4, La Shelle 4)
Whispering Smith, 1948 (Crisp 3, Ladd 3, Preston 3, Deutsch 4, Dreier 4, Head 4)
Whispering Smith Hits London, 1952 (Baker S. 3)
Whispering Smith Vs. Scotland Yard. *See* Whispering Smith Hits London, 1952
Whispering Tongues, 1934 (Pearson 2)
Whispering Whiskers, 1926 (Sennett 2)
Whispers in the Dark, 1937 (Fleischer, M. and D. 2)
Whistle, 1921 (Hart 3, August 4)
Whistle at Eaton Falls, 1951 (Siodmak 2, Borgnine 3, Gish, D. 3, de Rochemont 4)
Whistle Down the Wind, 1961 (Attenborough 3, Bates 3, Arnold 4)
Whistle in My Heart. *See* Kotan no kuchibue, 1959
Whistle Stop, 1946 (Gardner 3, McLaglen 3, Raft 3, Tiomkin 4)
Whistler, 1949 (Lewis 2)
Whistling in Brooklyn, 1943 (Irene 4)
Whistling in Kotan. *See* Kotan no kuchibue, 1959
Whistling in the Dark, 1933 (Merkel 3)

Whistling in the Dark, 1941 (Arden 3, Veidt 3, Kaper 4)
Whitchurch Down, 1972 (Le Grice 2)
White Angel, 1936 (Dieterle 2, Bruce 3, Crisp 3, Francis, K. 3, Blanke 4, Gaudio 4, Grot 4, Orry-Kelly 4)
White Banners, 1938 (Goulding 2, Bainter 3, Cooper, J 3, Rains 3, Blanke 4, Rosher 4, Steiner 4, Wallis 4)
White Beast. See Shiroi yaju, 1949
White Bim with the Black Ear. See Belyi Bim Chernoe Ukho, 1977
White Black Sheep, 1926 (Olcott 2, Barthelmess 3)
White Blacksmith, 1922 (Roach 4)
White Buffalo, 1977 (Bronson 3, Carradine 3, Novak 3, Warden 3, Barry 4, De Laurentiis 4)
White Bus, 1967 (Anderson 2, Hopkins, A. 3, Ondricek 4)
White Caps, 1905 (Porter 2)
White Cargo, 1942 (Saville 2, Lamarr 3, Pidgeon 3, Kaper 4, Stradling 4)
White Cat. See Vita katten, 1950
White Christmas, 1954 (Curtiz 2, Crosby 3, Kaye 3, Alton, R. 4, Frank and Panama 4, Head 4, Krasna 4)
White Circle, 1920 (Tourneur, M. 2, Gilbert 3, Furthman 4)
White Cliff. See Shiroi gake, 1960
White Cliffs of Dover, 1944 (Brown 2, Franklin 2, Cooper, Gladys 3, Dunne 3, Johnson, V. 3, McDowall 3, Taylor, E. 3, Gillespie 4, Irene 4, Stothart 4)
White Cockatoo, 1935 (Crosland 2, Blanke 4, Gaudio 4)
White Comanche. See Comancho blanco, 1969
White Cradle Inn, 1947 (Carroll M. 3, Dillon 4)
White Dawn, 1974 (Gossett 3, Oates 3, Mancini 4)
White Demon. See Weisse Damon, 1932
White Devil. See Hvide Djœvel, 1916
White Devil. See Weisse Teufel, 1930
White Dove, 1920 (King 2)
White Eagle, 1922 (Van Dyke, W.S. 2)
White Eagle, 1941 (Howard, L. 3, Canutt 4)
White Eagle. See Byelyi orel, 1928
White Eagles, 1932 (Bond 3)
White Elder Sister. See Shiroi ane, 1931
White Face, 1932 (Balcon 4)
White Fang, 1925 (Murfin 4)
White Fang, 1936 (Carradine 3, Darwell 3, Summerville 3, Friedhofer 4, Miller, A. 4, Zanuck 4)
White Fangs. See Shiroi kiba, 1960
White Feather, 1955 (Daves 2, Cody 3, Hunter 3, Wagner 3, Ballard 4, Friedhofer 4, Smith, J.M. 4)
White Field Duration, 1972 (Le Grice 2)
White Flannels, 1927 (Bacon 2)
White Flood, 1940 (Eisler 4, Maddow 4)
White Flowers for the Dead. See Ahasin Polawatha, 1978
White Game. See Vita sporten, 1969
White Ghost. See Hvide Dame, 1913
White Gold, 1927 (Garnett 2, Howard 2, Fort 4, Grot 4, Sullivan 4)
White Grass. See Bela Trave, 1976
White Hands, 1922 (Bosworth 3, Sullivan 4)
White Harvest. See Bestia, 1978
White Heat, 1934 (Weber 2)
White Heat, 1949 (Walsh 2, Cagney 3, Mayo 3, O'Brien, E. 3, Steiner 4)
White Heather, 1919 (Tourneur, M. 2, Gilbert 3, Carré 4)
White Hell of Piz Palu. See Weisse Holle von Piz Palu, 1929
White Heron. See Shirasagi, 1957
White Horses of Summer. See Bianchi cavalli d'Agosto, 1975
White Hunter, 1936 (Baxter W. 3)
White Legion, 1936 (Brown, K. 4)
White Lies, 1934 (Wray 3)
White Lightning, 1953 (Van Cleef 3)
White Lightning, 1973 (Reynolds, B. 3)
White Lily Laments. See Shirayuri wa nageku, 1925
White Line. See Cuori senza frontiere, 1950
White Mama, 1980 (Cooper, J 3, Davis 3)
White Man, 1924 (Gable 3, Schulberg 4, Struss 4)
White Man. See Squaw Man, 1914
White Man. See Squaw Man, 1931
White Man's Law, 1918 (Hayakawa 3, Rosher 4)

White Medicine Man, 1911 (Bosworth 3)
White Mice, 1926 (Powell, W. 3)
White Moll, 1920 (White 3)
White Moor. See De-as fi Harap Alb, 1965
White Morning. See Shiroi asa, 1964
White Moth, 1924 (Tourneur, M. 2)
White Mouse, 1914 (Mix 3)
White Mouse, 1921 (Stone 3)
White Nights, 1985 (Page 3, Watkin 4)
White Nights. See Notti bianche, 1957
White Oak, 1921 (Hart 3, August 4)
White Orchid of the Heating Desert. See Nessa no byakuran, 1951
White Outlaw, 1929 (Laszlo 4)
White Parade, 1934 (Darwell 3, Young, L. 3, La Shelle 4, Lasky 4, Levien 4, Miller, A. 4)
White Peacock. See Weisse Pfau, 1920
White Plague. See Bila nemoc, 1937
White Raven, 1917 (Barrymore E. 3)
White Raven. See Belaya vorona, 1941
White Red Man, 1911 (Porter 2)
White Rider. See White Thunder, 1925
White Rock, 1976 (Coburn, J. 3)
White Rocker, 1949 (Peterson 2)
White Rose, 1913 (Bushman 3)
White Rose, 1923 (Griffith 2, Marsh 3, Merkel 3, Novello 3, Bitzer 4)
White Rose, 1967 (Conner 2)
White Rose of the Wilds, 1911 (Griffith 2, Sennett 2, Sweet 3, Bitzer 4)
White Roses, 1911 (Bushman 3, Pickford 3)
White Savage, 1943 (Brooks, R. 2)
White Savage. See South of Tahiti, 1943
White Scar, 1915 (Bosworth 3)
White Sea of Yushima. See Yushima no shiraume, 1955
White Shadow, 1924 (Hitchcock 2, Saville 2, Brook 3, Balcon 4)
White Shadows. See White Shadow, 1924
White Shadows in the South Seas, 1928 (Van Dyke, W.S. 2, Stromberg 4)
White Sheep, 1924 (Stevens 2, Roach 4)
White Sheik. See Sceicco bianco, 1952
White Shoulders, 1922 (Schulberg 4)
White Shoulders, 1931 (Astor 3)
White Sister, 1923 (King 2, Colman 3, Gish, L. 3)
White Sister, 1933 (Fleming 2, Gable 3, Stone 3, Adrian 4, Booth 4, Daniels 4, Stewart 4, Stothart 4, Stromberg 4)
White Sister. See Bianco, rosso, e . . ., 1972
White Slave. See Hvide Slavehandel I, 1910
White Slave Catchers, 1914 (Browning 2, Loos 4)
White Slave Trade. See Tratta della bianche, 1952
White Slide. See Bílá spona, 1960
White Stallion, 1984 (Borgnine 3)
White Telephones. See Telefoni bianchi, 1975
White Thread of the Waterfall. See Taki no shiraito, 1952
White Thunder, 1925 (Canutt 4)
White Tie and Tails, 1946 (Bendix 3, Duryea 3)
White Tiger, 1923 (Browning 2, Beery 3)
White Tower, 1950 (Aldrich 2, Ford, G. 3, Hardwicke 3, Homolka 3, Rains 3, Valli 3)
White Treachery, 1912 (Dwan 2)
White Unicorn, 1947 (Greenwood 3)
White Voices. See Voci bianche, 1964
White Widow. See Rovedderkoppen, 1916
White Wilderness, 1958 (Iwerks 4)
White Wings, 1922 (Laurel 3, Roach 4)
White Wings. See Yankee Clipper, 1927
White Wing's Bride, 1925 (Capra 2, Langdon 3)
White Witch Doctor, 1953 (Hathaway 2, Hayward 3, Mitchum 3, Herrmann 4, Jeakins 4, Lemaire 4, Shamroy 4, Wheeler 4)
White Woman, 1933 (Johnson, N. 3, Laughton 3, Lombard 3, Dreier 4, Head 4, Hoffenstein 4, Raine 4)
White Zombie, 1932 (Lugosi 3, Muse 3)
Whitechapel, 1920 (Dupont 2)
Whitsun Outing. See Pfingstausflug, 1978
Whity, 1970 (Fassbinder 2, Schygulla 3)
Who?, 1974 (Gould 3, Howard, T. 3)

Who Are My Parents?, 1922 (Ruttenberg 4)
Who Are We?, 1975 (Grgić 4)
Who Believes in the Stork. See Kto wierzy w bociany, 1971
Who Cares . . . . See Wen kummert's . . ., 1960
Who Cares?, 1919 (Talmadge, C. 3)
Who Dares Wins. See Final Option, 1982
Who Do I Dream Those Dreams, 1934 (Freleng 4)
Who Done It?, 1942 (Abbott and Costello 3, Bendix 3, Salter 4)
Who Done It?, 1949 (Three Stooges 3)
Who Done It?, 1955 (Dearden 2, Clarke, T.E.B. 4)
Who Goes Next?, 1938 (Hawkins 3, Dillon 4)
Who Goes There, 1952 (Mathieson 4)
Who Got Stung?. See Caught in the Rain, 1914
Who Got the Reward, 1911 (Sennett 2)
Who Has Been Rocking My Dream Boat, 1941 (Anger 2)
Who Has Seen the Wind?, 1965 (Baker S. 3, Head 4)
Who Has Seen the Wind?, 1977 (Ferrer, J. 3)
Who Ho Ray, 1972 (Vanderbeek 2)
Who I Kissed Yesterday. See Koho jsem včera líbal, 1935
Who is Harry Kellerman and Why Is He Saying Those Terrible Things
    About Me, 1971 (Hoffman 3, Warden 3, Horner 4, Smith, D. 4)
Who Is Hope Schuyler?, 1942 (Miller, V. 4, Raksin 4)
Who Is in the Box?, 1912-13 (White 3)
Who is Killing the Great Chefs of Europe?, 1978 (Bisset 3, Cassel 3,
    Noiret 3, Segal 3, Mancini 4)
Who Is the Black Dahlia?, 1975 (McCambridge 3)
Who Is the Man?, 1924 (Gielgud 3)
Who Is to Blame?, 1918 (Borzage 2)
Who Killed Barno O'Neal. See Nattens Mysterium, 1916
Who Killed Cock Robin?, 1933 (Terry 4)
Who Killed Doc Robbin, 1948 (Roach 4)
Who Killed Doc Robin?, 1931 (Balcon 4)
Who Killed Doc Robin?. See Dangerous Game, 1941
Who Killed Gail Preston?, 1938 (Hayworth 3)
Who Killed Santa Claus?. See Assassinat du Père Noël, 1941
Who Killed Teddy Bear?, 1965 (Mineo 3)
Who Killed Who?, 1943 (Avery 2)
Who Knows, 1916 (Eason 4)
Who Know's a Woman's Heart. See Onna-gokoro dare ga shiru, 1951
Who Loved Him Best, 1918 (Polito 4)
Who Pays?, 1915 (King 2)
Who Pays My Wife's Bill? See Be My Wife, 1921
Who Pulled the Trigger, (Johnson, N. 3)
Who Saw Him Die?. See Ole dole doff, 1968
Who Scent You?, 1960 (Jones 2)
Who Seeks the Gold Bottom. See Kdo hledá zlaté dno, 1975
Who Slew Auntie Roo?, 1971 (Richardson 3, Winters 3, Sangster 4)
Who So Diggeth a Pit, 1914 (Reid 3)
Who So Loveth His Father's Honor. See Hvo som elsker sin Fader or
    Faklen, 1915
Who Stole Bunny's Umbrella, 1912 (Bunny 3)
Who Stole the Doggies?, 1915 (Hardy 3)
Who Stole the Shah's Jewels?, 1974 (Kinski 3)
Who Was That Lady?, 1960 (Sidney 2, Curtis 3, Leigh, J. 3,
    Martin, D. 3, Cahn 4, Krasna 4, Previn 4, Stradling 4)
Who Was the Goat?, 1912-13 (White 3)
Who Will Love My Children, 1983 (Forrest 3)
Who Will Marry Me?, 1919 (Levien 4)
Who Writes to Switzerland, 1937 (Cavalcanti 2)
Whoa, Begone!, 1958 (Jones 2)
Whole Family Works. See Hataraku ikka, 1939
Whole Town's Talking, 1926 (Del Rio 3, Horton 3)
Whole Town's Talking, 1935 (Ford, J. 2, Arthur 3, Ball 3, Meek 3,
    Robinson, E. 3, August 4, Burnett 4, Riskin 4, Swerling 4)
Whole Truth, 1923 (Laurel 3)
Whole Truth, 1958 (Clayton 2, Granger 3, Reed, D. 3, Sanders 3)
Whole Truth, 1964 (Loach 2)
Who'll Save Our Children?, 1978 (Jones S. 3)
Who'll Stop the Rain, 1978 (Reisz 2, Nolte 3, Weld 3)
Wholly Moses!, 1980 (Moore, D. 3, Pryor 3, Houseman 4)
Whom God Hath Joined, 1912 (Cruze 2)
Whom the Gods Destroy, 1916 (Blackton 2, Brenon 2)
Whom the Gods Destroy, 1919 (Borzage 2)

Whom the Gods Destroy, 1934 (Bosworth 3, Young, R. 3, Buchman 4)
Whom the Gods Love, 1936 (Dickinson 2, Andrejew 4, Dean 4,
    Stallich 4)
Whoopee!, 1930 (Berkeley 2, Grable 3, Sothern 3, Brown, N. 4, Day 4,
    Garmes 4, Goldwyn 4, Hackett 4, Newman 4, Toland 4)
Whoops! I'm a Cowboy, 1937 (Fleischer, M. and D. 2)
Whoops! I'm an Indian, 1936 (Three Stooges 3, Bruckman 4)
Who's Afraid of the Avant-Garde, 1968 (Leacock 2)
Who's Afraid of Virginia Woolf?, 1966 (Nichols 2, Burton 3, Segal 3,
    Taylor, E. 3, Lehman 4, North 4, Sharaff 4, Sylbert 4, Wexler 4)
Who's Been Sleeping in My Bed?, 1963 (Martin, D. 3, Duning 4,
    Head 4, Ruttenberg 4)
Who's Got the Action?, 1962 (Martin, D. 3, Matthau 3, Turner, L. 3,
    Duning 4, Head 4, Ruttenberg 4)
Who's Got the Black Box?. See Route de Corinthe, 1967
Who's Guilty?, 1916 (Nilsson 3)
Who's Kitten Who?, 1952 (McKimson 4)
Who's Minding the Mint?, 1967 (Brennan 3, Biroc 4, Schifrin 4)
Who's Minding the Store?, 1963 (Lewis 2, Tashlin 2, Moorehead 3,
    Head 4)
Who's That Knocking at My Door?, 1968 (Scorsese 2, Keitel 3)
Who's To Win, 1912 (Bunny 3)
Who's Who, 1906 (Selig 4)
Who's Who in the Jungle, 1945 (Terry 4)
Who's Who in the Zoo, 1931 (Sennett 2)
Who's Your Father?, 1918 (Mix 3)
Who's Your Friend, 1925 (Garnett 2)
Who's Your Lady Friend?, 1937 (Reed 2)
Whose Baby, 1916 (Sennett 2)
Whose Baby? See Nick of Time Baby, 1916
Whose Life Is It Anyway?, 1981 (Dreyfuss 3)
Whose Little Girl Are You? See Better Late Than Never, 1982
Whose Little Wife Are You, 1918 (Sennett 2)
Whose Wife?, 1917 (Seitz 4)
Whose Zoo, 1918 (Laurel 3)
Why?, 1972 (Garmes 4)
Why?. See Detenuto in attesa di giudizio, 1971
Why?. See Proč, 1964
Why Albert Pinto Is Angry. See Albert Pinto ko gussa kyon aata hai,
    1981
Why Announce Your Marriage?, 1922 (Crosland 2)
Why Be Good?, 1929 (Moore, C. 3, Grot 4, Wilson, C. 4)
Why Beaches Are Popular, 1919 (Sennett 2)
Why Birds Sit on Telegraph Wires. See Pročsedají ptáci na
    telegrafní dráty, 1948
Why Bother to Knock. See Don't Bother to Knock, 1961
Why Bri?, 1961 (Lassally 4)
Why Bring That Up?, 1929 (Hunt 4)
Why Change Your Wife?, 1920 (DeMille 2, Boyd 3, Daniels 3,
    Swanson 3)
Why Do You Smile, Mona Lisa?. See Proč se usmíváš, Mono Liso?,
    1966
Why Does Mr. R Run Amok? See Warum lauft Herr R amok?, 1969
Why Foxy Grandpa Escaped Ducking, 1903 (Bitzer 4)
Why Girls Go Back Home, 1926 (Brook 3, Loy 3, Levien 4)
Why Girls Leave Home, 1921 (Nilsson 3)
Why Girls Leave Home, 1945 (Cook 3)
Why Girls Love Sailors, 1927 (Laurel and Hardy 3, Roach 4)
Why Girls Say No, 1927 (Hardy 3, Roach 4)
Why Go Home?, 1920 (Roach 4)
Why He Gave Up, 1911 (Sennett 2)
Why Husbands Go Mad, 1924 (McCarey 2, Roach 4)
Why Is a Plumber?, 1929 (McCarey 2, Roach 4)
Why Man Creates, 1968 (Bass 4)
Why Men Leave Home, 1924 (Stahl 2, Stone 3, Booth 4, Polito 4)
Why Men Work, 1924 (McCarey 2, Roach 4)
Why Mrs. Jones Got a Divorce, 1900 (Porter 2)
Why Mules Leave Home, 1934 (Terry 4)
Why Must I Die?, 1960 (Haller 4)
Why Not?. See Eijanaika, 1980
Why Pick on Me?, 1918 (Daniels 3, Lloyd 3, Roach 4)
Why Reginald Reformed, 1914 (Cruze 2)
Why Sailors Go Wrong, 1928 (Johnson, N. 3)

Why Smith Left Home, 1919 (Crisp 3)
Why the Actor Was Late, 1908 (Méliès 2)
Why the Sheriff Is a Bachelor, 1914 (Mix 3)
Why They Left Home, 1917 (Pitts 3)
Why UNESCO?. *See* Proč UNESCO?, 1958
Why We Fight series, 1942–45 (Capra 2, Litvak 2, Tiomkin 4)
Why Women Love, 1925 (Sweet 3)
Why Worry?, 1923 (Lloyd 3, Roach 4)
Wiano, 1964 (Lomnicki 3)
Wichita, 1955 (Tourneur, J. 2, Elam 3, McCrea 3, Mirisch 4, Salter 4)
Wicked, 1931 (Dwan 2, McLaglen 3, Merkel 3)
Wicked As They Come, 1956 (Marshall 3, Arnold 4)
Wicked Darling, 1919 (Browning 2, Chaney Lon 3)
Wicked Dreams of Paula Schultz, 1968 (Lewin 4)
Wicked Lady, 1945 (Fisher 2, Mason 3)
Wicked Lady, 1983 (Bates 3, Dunaway 3, Gielgud 3, Cardiff 4, Golan and Globus 4)
Wicked West, 1929 (Lantz 4)
Wicked Wolf, 1946 (Terry 4)
Wicked Woman, 1934 (Taylor, R. 3)
Wickedness Preferred, 1928 (Day 4, Gibbons 4)
Wicker Man, 1973 (Lee, C. 3)
Wicket Wacky, 1951 (Lantz 4)
Wicky-Wacky Romance, 1939 (Terry 4)
Wide Angle Saxon, 1975 (Landow 2)
Wide Open, 1930 (Beavers 3, Fazenda 3, Horton 3)
Wide Open Faces, 1938 (Brown 3, Wyman 3)
Wide Open Spaces, 1924 (Laurel 3, Roach 4)
Wide Open Spaces, 1932 (Farnum 3)
Wide Open Spaces, 1950 (Terry 4)
Wide Open Spaces, about 1961 (Coppola 2)
Wide Open Town, 1941 (Boyd 3, Head 4)
Wideo Wabbit, 1956 (McKimson 4)
Widow, 1903 (Bitzer 4)
Widow, 1910 (Lawrence 3)
Widow. *See* Vedova, 1957
Widow and the Only Man, 1904 (Bitzer 4)
Widow by Proxy, 1919 (Gilbert 3)
Widow Couderc. *See* Veuve Couderc, 1971
Widow from Chicago, 1930 (Robinson, E. 3, Polito 4)
Widow from Monte Carlo, 1936 (Del Rio 3, Fazenda 3, Orry-Kelly 4)
Widow of Nevada, 1913 (Anderson G. 3)
Widow Visits Sprigtown, 1911 (Bunny 3)
Widower. *See* Samma no aji, 1962
Widower. *See* Vedovo, 1959
Widower's Tango. *See* Tango del viudo, 1967
Widow's Kids, 1913 (Gish, D. 3, Loos 4)
Widow's Might, 1918 (Rosher 4)
Widow's Nest, 1977 (Cortese 3, Neal 3)
Widow's Nest. *See* Nido de viudas, 1977
Wie bliebe ich jung und schön, 1926 (Dieterle 2)
Wie der Berliner Arbeiter wohnt, 1930 (Dudow 2)
Wie ein Vogel auf dem Draht, 1974 (Fassbinder 2)
Wie einst im Mai, 1926 (Leni 2)
Wie futtert man einen Esel, 1974 (Hoppe 3)
Wie heirate ich meinen Chef, 1927 (Planer 4)
Wie Ich Ermordert Wurde, 1915 (Lubitsch 2)
Wie kommt ein so reizendes Madchen zu diesem Gewerbe?, 1970 (Crawford, B. 3, Kinski 3)
Wie konntest du, Veronika?, 1940 (Von Harbou 4)
Wie sag ich's meinem Mann, 1932 (Hoffmann 4)
Wie totet man eine Dame. *See* Geheimnis der gelben Monche, 1966
Wie werde ich reich und glucklich?, 1930 (Reisch 4)
Wiegenlied, 1908 (Porten 3, Messter 4)
Wielka miłość Balzaca, 1973 (Tyszkiewicz 3)
Wielki Szu, 1983 (Nowicki 3)
Wien 1910, 1942 (Dagover 3, George, H. 3)
Wien, du Stadt der Lieder, 1930 (Oswald 2)
Wien tantz, 1951 (Walbrook 3)
Wiener Blut, 1942 (Stallich 4)
Wiener Herzen. *See* Familie Schimeck, 1926
Wiener Madeln, 1945 (Jurgens 3, Stallich 4)
Wife, 1914 (Gish, D. 3, Gish, L. 3)

Wife. *See* Tsuma, 1953
Wife Against Wife, 1921 (Haller 4)
Wife and Auto Troubles, 1916 (Sennett 2)
Wife and Woman Journalist. *See* Tsuma to onna kisha, 1950
Wife, Doctor, and Nurse, 1937 (Baxter W. 3, Chaney Lon, Jr. 3, Cook 3, Darwell 3, Young, L. 3, Cronjager 4, Trotti 4)
Wife for a Night. *See* Moglie per una notte, 1952
Wife, Husband, and Friend, 1939 (Baxter W. 3, Young, L. 3, Johnson 4, Zanuck 4)
Wife in Love. *See* Koisuru tsuma, 1947
Wife in Name Only, 1923 (Carré 4)
Wife of Monte Cristo, 1946 (Ulmer 2, Kortner 3)
Wife of Seishu Hanaoka. *See* Hanaoka Seishu no tsuma, 1967
Wife of the Centaur, 1925 (Vidor, K. 2, Gilbert 3, Gibbons 4)
Wife of the Hills, 1912 (Anderson G. 3)
Wife on a Wager, 1914 (Reid 3)
Wife or Country, 1918 (Swanson 3)
Wife Savers, 1928 (Beery 3, Pitts 3, Schulberg 4)
Wife Takes a Flyer, 1942 (Bennett J. 3, Planer 4, Schulberg 4)
Wife Tamers, 1926 (Barrymore L. 3, Roach 4)
Wife vs. Secretary, 1936 (Brown 2, Gable 3, Harlow 3, Loy 3, Stewart 3, Gibbons 4, Krasna 4, Mahin 4, Stothart 4, Stromberg 4)
Wife Wanted, 1907 (Bitzer 4)
Wife Wanted, 1913 (Sennett 2)
Wife Wanted, 1946 (Francis, K. 3)
Wife Who Wasn't Wanted, 1925 (Meredyth 4)
Wifemistress. *See* Mogliamante, 1977
Wife's Awakening, 1911 (Lawrence 3)
Wife's Heart. *See* Tsuma no kokoro, 1956
Wiggle Your Ears, 1929 (Roach 4)
Wiggs Takes the Rest Cure, 1914 (Mix 3)
Wij bouwen, 1929 (Ivens 2, Van Dongen 4)
Wilbur Crawfords wundersames Abenteuer. *See* Seine Frau, die Unbekannte, 1923
Wilbur the Lion, 1947 (Pal 2)
Wilby Conspiracy, 1975 (Caine 3, Poitier 3, Williamson 3)
Wild About Hurry, 1960 (Jones 2)
Wild Affair, 1963 (Love 3, Box 4)
Wild and the Innocent, 1959 (Martin, S. 3, Murphy 3, Salter 4)
Wild and the Willing, 1962 (Hurt, J. 3)
Wild and Wonderful, 1964 (Curtis 3, Dalio 3, La Shelle 4, Salt 4)
Wild and Woolfy, 1945 (Avery 2)
Wild and Woolly, 1917 (Fairbanks, D. 3, Edeson 4, Emerson 4, Loos 4)
Wild and Woolly, 1932 (Lantz 4)
Wild and Wooly, 1937 (Brennan 3, Chaney Lon, Jr. 3)
Wild and Wooly Hare, 1959 (Freleng 4)
Wild Angels, 1966 (Bogdanovich 2, Dern 3, Fonda, P. 3, Corman 4)
Wild Babies, 1932 (Roach 4)
Wild Beasts. *See* Dravci, 1948
Wild Bill Hiccup, 1923 (Laurel 3)
Wild Bill Hickok, 1923 (Hart 3)
Wild Bill Hickok Rides, 1941 (Bennett C. 3, Bond 3, McCord 4)
Wild Birds. *See* Vildfåglar, 1955
Wild Blue Yonder, 1951 (Dwan 2, Brennan 3, Young, V. 4)
Wild Boss. *See* Abarenbou taishou, 1960
Wild Boy, 1934 (Balcon 4, Junge 4)
Wild Boys of the Road, 1933 (Wellman 2, Bond 3)
Wild Brian Kent, 1936 (Bellamy 3)
Wild Bunch, 1969 (Fernández 2, Peckinpah 2, Borgnine 3, Holden 3, Johnson, B. 3, Martin, S. 3, O'Brien, E. 3, Oates 3, Ryan 3, Ballard 4)
Wild Cat. *See* Wildcat Trooper, 1936
Wild Chase, 1965 (Freleng 4)
Wild Child. *See* Enfant sauvage, 1969
Wild Company, 1930 (McCarey 2, Lugosi 3)
Wild Country, 1970 (Elam 3)
Wild Dakotas, 1956 (Cody 3)
Wild Duck, 1984 (Ullmann 3)
Wild Duck. *See* Wildente, 1976
Wild Elephinks, 1931 (Fleischer, M. and D. 2)
Wild Eye. *See* Occhio selvaggio, 1967
Wild Flowers. *See* Fleurs sauvages, 1981

Wild for Kicks. *See* Beat Girl, 1960
Wild Game. *See* Wildwechsel, 1972
Wild Geese, 1978 (Burton 3, Granger 3, Moore, R. 3)
Wild Geese Calling, 1941 (Bennett J. 3, Fonda, H. 3, Ballard 4,
    Banton 4, Brown, Harry Joe 4, Day 4, Newman 4)
Wild Geese Five. *See* Codename Wildgeese, 1984
Wild Girl, 1914 (Browning 2)
Wild Girl, 1932 (Walsh 2, Beavers 3, Bellamy 3, Bennett J. 3)
Wild Girl from the Hills, 1915 (Marion 4)
Wild Girl of the Sierras, 1916 (Marsh 3, Loos 4)
Wild Gold, 1934 (Trevor 3, Nichols 4, Trotti 4)
Wild Goose Chase, 1915 (DeMille 2, Buckland 4)
Wild Goose Chase. *See* Course a l'echalote, 1975
Wild Goose Chaser, 1925 (Sennett 2)
Wild Guys. *See* Grandes Gueules, 1965
Wild Hare, 1940 (Avery 2)
Wild Harvest, 1947 (Garnett 2, Ladd 3, Lamour 3, Preston 3, Dreier 4,
    Friedhofer 4, Head 4, Seitz 4)
Wild Heart, 1950 (Jones, J. 3)
Wild Heart. *See* Gone to Earth, 1950
Wild Heather, 1921 (Hepworth 2)
Wild Heritage, 1958 (O'Sullivan 3, Boyle 4)
Wild Honey, 1922 (Ruggles 2, Beery 3)
Wild Horse, 1931 (Fetchit 3)
Wild Horse Mesa, 1925 (Hathaway 2, Cooper, Gary 3,
    Fairbanks, D. Jr. 3, Glennon 4)
Wild Horse Mesa, 1932 (Hathaway 2, Scott, R. 3)
Wild Horse Phantom, 1944 (Crabbe 3)
Wild Horse Rodeo, 1937 (Rogers, R. 3)
Wild Horse Stampede, 1926 (Wray 3)
Wild in the Country, 1961 (Ireland 3, Presley 3, Weld 3, Ames 4,
    Dunne 4, Smith, J.M. 4, Wald 4)
Wild in the Sky, 1972 (Wynn 3)
Wild in the Streets, 1968 (Pryor 3, Winters 3)
Wild is the Wind, 1957 (Cukor 2, Magnani 3, Quinn 3, Head 4, Lang 4,
    Tiomkin 4, Trumbo 4, Wallis 4)
Wild Justice, 1925 (Sullivan 4)
Wild Love. *See* Innamorati, 1955
Wild Main Line. *See* Abarenbou kaido, 1957
Wild Man of Borneo, 1941 (Mankiewicz 2, Burke 3, Dailey 3, Meek 3,
    Salt 4)
Wild Money, 1937 (Horton 3, Head 4)
Wild Mustangs, 1935 (Carey 3)
Wild North, 1952 (Charisse 3, Granger 3, Kaper 4, Surtees 4)
Wild Oats Lane, 1926 (Neilan 2, Glazer 4)
Wild One, 1954 (Kramer, S. 2, Brando 3, Marvin 3, Paxton 4)
Wild Open Faces, 1926 (Sennett 2)
Wild Oranges, 1924 (Vidor, K. 2)
Wild Orchids, 1929 (Franklin 2, Garbo 3, Stone 3, Adrian 4, Daniels 4,
    Gibbons 4, Kraly 4)
Wild Over You, 1953 (Jones 2)
Wild Papa, 1925 (Roach 4)
Wild Party, 1929 (Arzner 2, Bow 3, March 3, Banton 4)
Wild Party, 1956 (Quinn 3, Horner 4)
Wild Party, 1974 (Ivory 2, Welch 3, Lassally 4)
Wild Poses, 1933 (Roach 4)
Wild Racers, 1967 (Almendros 4, Corman 4, Fields 4)
Wild Ride, 1958 (Nicholson 3, Corman 4)
Wild River, 1960 (Kazan 2, Clift 3, Dern 3, Remick 3, Reynolds 4,
    Wheeler 4)
Wild Rovers, 1971 (Edwards 2, Holden 3, Malden 3, Roberts 3,
    Goldsmith 4)
Wild Seed, 1964 (Fraker 4)
Wild Seed. *See* Fargo, 1965
Wild Stallion, 1952 (Johnson, B. 3, Mirisch 4)
Wild Strawberries. *See* Smultronstallet, 1957
Wild Times, 1980 (Hopper 3)
Wild West Days, 1937 (Cody 3)
Wild West Days. *See* Pony Express Days, 1940
Wild West Love, 1914 (Sennett 2)
Wild Westerners, 1962 (Katzman 4)
Wild Wicked, 1923 (La Cava 2)
Wild Wife, 1954 (McKimson 4)

Wild, Wild Susan, 1925 (Sutherland 2, Daniels 3, Hunt 4)
Wild, Wild Women. *See* Nella città l'inferno, 1958
Wild, Wild World of Jayne Mansfield, 1967 (Mansfield 3)
Wild, Wild World, 1960 (McKimson 4)
Wild Women, 1918 (Ford, J. 2, Carey 3)
Wild Youth, 1918 (Cruze 2)
Wildcat, 1942 (Arlen 3, Cook 3, Crabbe 3)
Wildcat. *See* Bergkatze, 1921
Wildcat. *See* Verkenningsboring, 1954
Wildcat Bus, 1940 (Ladd 3, Wray 3)
Wildcat Trooper, 1936 (Bosworth 3, Canutt 4)
Wildcatter, 1937 (Bond 3, McDaniel 3, Cortez 4)
Wildcatters, 1980 (Malden 3)
Wildente, 1976 (Ganz 3, Seberg 3)
Wildente. *See* Haus der Luge, 1925
Wildentes, 1925 (Rasp 3)
Wilderness Mail, 1914 (Mix 3)
Wilderness Trail, 1919 (Mix 3, Moore, C. 3)
Wilderness Woman, 1926 (Haller 4)
Wildfire, 1915 (Barrymore L. 3, Edeson 4)
Wildfire, 1925 (Hunt 4)
Wildfire, 1945 (Farnum 3)
Wildflower, 1914 (Dwan 2)
Wildwechsel, 1972 (Fassbinder 2, Schygulla 3)
Wilfredo Lam, 1978 (Solás 2)
Wilful Ambrose, 1915 (Sennett 2, Fazenda 3)
Wilful Peggy, 1910 (Griffith 2, Pickford 3, Bitzer 4)
Wilhelm Busch Album series, 1977 (Halas and Batchelor 2)
Wilhelm Tell, 1923 (Veidt 3)
Wilhelm Tell, 1934 (Veidt 3)
Wilhelm von Kobell, 1966 (Syberberg 2)
Will, 1968 (Vanderbeek 2)
Will He Conquer Dempsey?, 1923 (Selznick 4)
Will of His Grace. *See* Hans nåds testamente, 1919
Will of James Waldron, 1912 (Dwan 2)
Will Penny, 1967 (Dern 3, Heston 3, Johnson, B. 3, Pleasance 3,
    Ballard 4, Raksin 4, Westmore, W. 4)
Will Power, 1912–13 (White 3)
Will Rogers series, 1927–1928 (Rogers, W. 3)
Will Success Spoil Rock Hunter?, 1957 (Tashlin 2, Blondell 3,
    Mansfield 3, Marx, G. 3, Axelrod 4, Lemaire 4, Wheeler 4)
Will There Really Be a Morning, 1983 (Grant, L. 3)
Will Tomorrow Ever Come?. *See* That's My Man, 1947
Willa, 1979 (Barry 4)
Willard, 1971 (Borgnine 3, Lanchester 3, North 4)
Willful Willie, 1942 (Terry 4)
Willi eine Zauberposse. *See* Also es war so . . ., 1976
Willi Tobler and the Wreck of the 6th Fleet. *See* Willi Tobler und der
    Untergang der 6. Flotte, 1971
Willi Tobler und der Untergang der 6. Flotte, 1971 (Kluge 2)
William McKinley at Canton, Ohio, 1896 (Bitzer 4)
William Tell, 1934 (Lantz 4)
William Tell. *See* Guglielmo Tell, 1949
Williamsburg, 1957 (Seaton 2, Herrmann 4)
Willie, 1914 (Roach 4)
Willie and Phil, 1980 (Mazursky 2, Wood 3)
Willie and the Mouse, 1941 (Sidney 2)
Willie Becomes An Artist, 1911 (Sennett 2)
Willie Goes to Sea, 1914 (Roach 4)
Willie Minds the Dog, 1913 (Sennett 2)
Willie Walrus and the Awful Confession, 1914 (Meredyth 4)
Willie's Camera, 1903 (Bitzer 4)
Willie's Disguise, 1912–13 (White 3)
Willie's Great Scheme, 1912–13 (White 3)
Willie's Haircut, 1914 (Roach 4)
Willoughby's Magic Hat, 1943 (Fleischer, M. and D. 2)
Willow Tree in the Ginza. *See* Ginza no yanagi, 1932
Willy and Phil, 1980 (Nykvist 4)
Willy Wonka and the Chocolate Factory, 1971 (Wilder 3)
Wilmar 8, 1980 (Grant, L. 3)
Wilson, 1944 (King 2, Bushman 3, Coburn, C. 3, Dalio 3, Hardwicke 3,
    Price 3, Basevi 4, Newman 4, Shamroy 4, Trotti 4, Zanuck 4)
Wily Weasel, 1937 (Lantz 4)

Wimmin Hadn't Oughta Drive, 1940 (Fleischer, M. and D. 2)
Wimmin Is a Myskery, 1940 (Fleischer, M. and D. 2)
Winchester '73, 1950 (Mann 2, Curtis 3, Duryea 3, Hudson 3, Stewart 3, Winters 3, Chase 4, Daniels 4)
Winchester '73, 1967 (Blondell 3, Duryea 3)
Winchester Woman, 1919 (Ruggles 2)
Wind, 1928 (Sjostrom 2, Gish, L. 3, Gibbons 4, Marion 4)
Wind Across the Everglades, 1958 (Ray, N. 2, Falk 3, Sylbert 4)
Wind and the Lion, 1975 (Huston 2, Milius 2, Connery 3, Goldsmith 4)
Wind and the River. See Vinden och floden, 1951
Wind Cannot Read, 1958 (Bogarde 3, Pleasance 3)
Wind from the East. See Vent d'est, 1970
Wind from the West. See Vinden från våster, 1943
Wind Is My Lover. See Singoalla, 1949
Wind of Change, 1961 (Pleasance 3)
Wind Rose, 1956 (Signoret 3)
Wind Rose. See Windrose, 1956
Windbag the Sailor, 1936 (Fisher 2, Balcon 4)
Windblown Hare, 1949 (McKimson 4)
Winding Stair, 1925 (Oland 3, Struss 4)
Windjammer, 1926 (Brown, Harry Joe 4)
Windjammer, 1958 (de Rochemont 4)
Windmill in Barbados, 1933 (Cavalcanti 2, Grierson 2, Wright 2)
Windmill Revels, 1937 (More 3)
Windom's Way, 1957 (Finch 3, Bernard 4)
Window, 1949 (Kennedy, A. 3, D'Agostino 4)
Window, 1965 (Kuri 4)
Window, 1976 (Brakhage 2)
Window Dummy, 1925 (Sennett 2)
Window in London, 1939 (Redgrave, M. 3, Dalrymple 4)
Window Water Baby Moving, 1959 (Brakhage 2)
Windowmobile, 1977 (Broughton 2)
Windows, 1980 (Morricone 4, Willis 4)
Windrose, 1956 (Cavalcanti 2, Ivens 2, Pontecorvo 2, Alekan 4, Solinas 4)
Winds of Autumn, 1976 (Elam 3)
Winds of Chance, 1925 (Bosworth 3, McLaglen 3, Nilsson 3)
Winds of Change, 1978 (Ustinov 3)
Winds of the Wasteland, 1936 (Wayne 3, Canutt 4)
Windwalker, 1981 (Howard, T. 3)
Windy Day, 1968 (Hubley 4)
Windy Riley Goes Hollywood, 1931 (Arbuckle 3, Brooks 3)
Windy Story. See Vjetrovita priča, 1969
Wine, 1913 (Sennett 2)
Wine, 1924 (Florey 2, Bow 3)
Wine of Life, 1924 (Brook 3)
Wine of Youth, 1924 (Vidor, K. 2, Pitts 3, Wilson, C. 4)
Wine Opener, 1905 (Bitzer 4)
Wine, Women and Song, 1915 (Anderson G. 3)
Wine, Women and Song, 1933 (Brenon 2)
Wine, Women, and Horses, 1937 (Sheridan 3)
Wing and a Prayer, 1944 (Edwards 2, Hathaway 2, Ameche 3, Andrews D. 3, Hardwicke 3, Friedhofer 4, Wheeler 4)
Winged Horse, 1932 (Lantz 4)
Winged Horseman, 1929 (Eason 4)
Winged Idol, 1915 (Ince 4, Sullivan 4)
Winged Victory, 1944 (Cukor 2, Ritt 2, Cobb 3, Crain 3, Holliday 3, Malden 3, O'Brien, E. 3, Horner 4, Wheeler 4, Zanuck 4)
Wings, 1927 (Wellman 2, Arlen 3, Bow 3, Cooper, Gary 3, Walthall 3, Clothier 4, Head 4, Saunders 4)
Wings. See Vingarna, 1916
Wings and the Woman. See They Flew Alone, 1942
Wings and Wheels, 1916 (Sennett 2)
Wings for the Eagle, 1942 (Bacon 2, Sheridan 3, Gaudio 4)
Wings in the Dark, 1935 (Grant, C. 3, Loy 3, Dreier 4, Head 4)
Wings of a Serf. See Krylya kholopa, 1926
Wings of Danger, 1952 (Fisher 2)
Wings of Eagles, 1957 (Ford, J. 2, Bond 3, Dailey 3, Marsh 3, O'Hara 3, Wayne 3, Plunkett 4, Schnee 4)
Wings of Fire, 1967 (Bellamy 3)
Wings of Steel, 1941 (Eason 4)
Wings of the Hawk, 1953 (Boetticher 2, Heflin 3)
Wings of the Morning, 1919 (Farnum 3)

Wings of the Morning, 1937 (Fonda, H. 3, Cardiff 4)
Wings of the Navy, 1939 (Bacon 2, Brent 3, De Havilland 3, Edeson 4, Mercer 4, Orry-Kelly 4, Wallis 4)
Wings over Empire, 1937 (Alwyn 4)
Wings over Everest, 1934 (Balcon 4)
Wings over Honolulu, 1937 (Beavers 3, Milland 3, Raksin 4)
Wings Up, 1944 (Gable 3)
Winifred Wagner und die Geschichte des Hauses Wahnfried von 1914–1975, 1975 (Syberberg 2)
Win(k)some Widow, 1914 (Blackton 2)
Winner, 1914 (Beery 3)
Winner, 1926 (Brown, Harry Joe 4)
Winner. See Coeur gros comme ça, 1961
Winner Take All, 1924 (Van Dyke, W.S. 2, Roach 4)
Winner Take All, 1932 (Cagney 3, Muse 3, Orry-Kelly 4)
Winner Take All, 1939 (Summerville 3, Cronjager 4)
Winner Take All, 1975 (Blondell 3, Jones S. 3, Sidney 3)
Winners of the Wilderness, 1927 (Van Dyke, W.S. 2, Crawford, J. 3)
Winnetou: II Teil, 1964 (Kinski 3)
Winning, 1969 (Newman 3, Wagner 3, Woodward 3, Head 4)
Winning a Widow, 1912 (Olcott 2)
Winning Back His Love, 1910 (Griffith 2, Crisp 3, Bitzer 4, Macpherson 4)
Winning Boat, 1909 (Olcott 2)
Winning Coat, 1909 (Griffith 2, Lawrence 3, Bitzer 4)
Winning His Stripes. See High and Handsome, 1925
Winning of Barbara Worth, 1926 (King 2, Banky 3, Colman 3, Cooper, Gary 3, Barnes 4, Goldwyn 4, Marion 4)
Winning of Denise, 1914 (Ince 4)
Winning of La Mesa, 1912 (Dwan 2)
Winning of the West, 1953 (Autry 3)
Winning of Wonega, 1911 (Ince 4)
Winning Punch, 1910 (Lawrence 3)
Winning Punch, 1916 (Sennett 2, Summerville 3)
Winning Team, 1952 (Day 3, Reagan 3)
Winning the Futurity, 1926 (Stromberg 4)
Winning the West, 1946 (Terry 4)
Winning Ticket, 1935 (Seaton 2, Fazenda 3, Clarke, C.C. 4, Pirosh 4)
Winning Way. See All-American, 1953
Winning Your Wings, 1942 (Stewart 3)
Winonah's Vengeance, 1911 (White 3)
Wins Out, 1932 (Lantz 4)
Winslow Boy, 1948 (Asquith 2, Donat 3, Hardwicke 3, Holloway 3, Alwyn 4, Andrejew 4, Young, F. 4)
Winter Carnival, 1939 (Sheridan 3, Walker 3, Wanger 4)
Winter Children. See Vinterbørn, 1978
Winter Kill, 1974 (Nolte 3, Goldsmith 4)
Winter Kills, 1979 (Huston 2, Boone 3, Bridges 3, Hayden 3, Malone 3, Mifune 3, Perkins 3, Taylor, E. 3, Wallach 3, Jarre 4, Zsigmond 4)
Winter Light. See Nattsvardsgasterna, 1963
Winter Meeting, 1948 (Davis 3, Blanke 4, Haller 4, Steiner 4)
Winter of Our Discontent, 1983 (Sutherland 3, Weld 3)
Winter on the Farm, 1942 (Alwyn 4)
Winter Sirocco. See Sirokkó, 1969
Winter Sports and Pastimes of Coronado Beach, 1912 (Dwan 2)
Winter Sports Champions. See Mistři zimních sportu, 1954
Winter Wind. See Sirokkó, 1969
Winter Wonderland, 1947 (Alton, J. 4)
Winterhawk, 1975 (Cook 3)
Winter's Tale, 1968 (Harvey 3, Keach 3, Morris 4)
Winterset, 1936 (Auer 3, Ball 3, Carradine 3, Meredith 3, Berman 4, Polglase 4, Steiner 4, Veiller 4)
Wintertime, 1943 (Henie 3, Sakall 3, Wilde 3, Basevi 4, Brown, N. 4, Clarke, C.C. 4, Friedhofer 4, Newman 4)
Wiosenne przygody krasnala, 1959 (Giersz 4)
Wiping Something Off the Slate, 1900 (Hepworth 2)
Wir brauchen kein Geld. See Man braucht kein Geld, 1931
Wir kaufen eine Feuerwehr, 1970 (Geschonneck 3)
Wir schalten um auf Hollywood, 1931 (George, H. 3)
Wir sind vom K. und K. Infanterie-Regiment, 1926 (Oswald 2, Albers 3)
Wir um schalten auf Hollywood, 1931 (Menjou 3)

Wir verbauen 3 X 27 Milliarden Dollar in einen Angriffsschlachter, 1971 (Kluge 2)
Wirtshaus im Spessart, 1957 (Herlth 4)
Wise Aristotle Gets Still Wiser. *See* Jak se moudrý Aristoteles stal jěstě moudřejšim, 1970
Wise Blood, 1979 (Huston 2, Stanton 3, North 4)
Wise Flies, 1930 (Fleischer, M. and D. 2)
Wise Fool, 1921 (Boyd 3)
Wise Girl, 1937 (Dumont 3, Hopkins, M. 3, Milland 3)
Wise Girls, 1929 (Booth 4, Daniels 4, Day 4, Gibbons 4)
Wise Guy, 1926 (Astor 3, Furthman 4)
Wise Guys. *See* Grandes Gueules, 1965
Wise Guys Prefer Brunettes, 1926 (Laurel 3, Roach 4)
Wise Kid, 1922 (Browning 2)
Wise Old Elephant, 1913 (Bosworth 3)
Wise Owl, 1940 (Iwerks 4)
Wise Quackers, 1947 (Freleng 4)
Wise Quacking Duck, 1943 (Clampett 4)
Wise Quacks, 1939 (Clampett 4)
Wise Quacks, 1953 (Terry 4)
Wise Virgin, 1924 (Walker 4)
Wise Wife, 1927 (Garnett 2, Adrian 4)
Wiser Age. *See* Onna no za, 1962
Wiser Sex, 1932 (Zinnemann 2, Colbert 3, Douglas, M. 3, Green, J. 4)
Wish-Fulfillment. *See* Ichhapuran, 1970
Wishing Ring, 1914 (Tourneur, M. 2, Carré 4)
Wishing Ring Man, 1919 (Love 3)
Wishing Seat, 1913 (Dwan 2)
Wistful Widow. *See* Wistful Widow of Wagon Gap, 1947
Wistful Widow of Wagon Gap, 1947 (Abbott and Costello 3)
Witch. *See* Fée caraboose ou le Poignard fatal, 1906
Witch. *See* Strega in amore, 1966
Witch of Salem, 1913 (Ince 4, Sullivan 4)
Witch of the Range, 1911 (Dwan 2)
Witch Without a Broom. *See* Bruja sin esoba, 1966
Witch Woman. *See* Prästänkan, 1920
Witchcraft, 1964 (Chaney Lon, Jr. 3)
Witchcraft Through the Ages. *See* Häxan, 1922
Witches, 1966 (Fontaine 3)
Witches. *See* Streghe, 1967
Witches' Cradle, 1943 (Deren 2)
Witches of Salem. *See* Sorcières de Salem, 1956
Witchfinder General. *See* Conqueror Worm, 1968
Witching Hour, 1921 (Sutherland 2)
Witching Hour, 1934 (Hathaway 2, Head 4)
Witch's Cat, 1948 (Terry 4)
Witch's Revenge. *See* Sorcier, 1903
With a Kodak, 1911 (Sennett 2)
With a Smile. *See* Avec le sourire, 1936
With a Song in My Heart, 1952 (Hayward 3, Merkel 3, Ritter 3, Wagner 3, Lemaire 4, Newman 4, Shamroy 4, Trotti 4)
With Baited Breath. *See* Col cuore in gola, 1967
With Beauty and Sorrow. *See* Utsukishisa to kanashimi to, 1965
With General Pancho Villa in Mexico, 1914 (Rosher 4)
With Her Card, 1909 (Griffith 2, Bitzer 4)
With Her Rival's Help, 1912–13 (White 3)
With Hoops of Steel, 1919 (Walthall 3)
With Intent to Kill, 1984 (Malden 3)
With Lee in Virginia, 1913 (Ince 4)
With Love. *See* Z lásky, 1928
With Love and Hisses, 1927 (Laurel and Hardy 3, Roach 4)
With Love From Truman, 1966 (Maysles A. and D. 2)
With Neatness and Dispatch, 1918 (Bushman 3)
With Potash and Perlmutter. *See* Partners Again, 1926
With Six You Get Egg Roll, 1968 (Day 3)
With the Aid of the Law, 1915 (Mix 3)
With the Blood of Others. *See* Par le sang des autres, 1974
With the Enemy's Help, 1912 (Pickford 3, Sweet 3)
Within Hail. *See* Bilocation, 1973
Within Man's Power, 1954 (Kaufman 4)
Within Our Gates, 1920 (Micheaux 2)
Within the Law, 1923 (Talmadge, N. 3, Gaudio 4, Marion 4, Schenck 4)

Within the Law, 1939 (Lederer 4)
Within the Rock. *See* Marriage Bargain, 1935
Without a Country. *See* Forviste, 1914
Without Anesthetic. *See* Bez znieczulenia, 1978
Without Apparent Motive. *See* Sans mobile apparent, 1971
Without Benefit of Clergy, 1921 (Karloff 3)
Without Compromise, 1922 (Farnum 3)
Without Dowry. *See* Bespridannitsa, 1937
Without Each Other, 1961 (Tiomkin 4)
Without Honor, 1950 (Moorehead 3, Steiner 4)
Without Honors, 1932 (Carey 3)
Without Limit, 1921 (Nilsson 3)
Without Love, 1945 (Ball 3, Grahame 3, Hepburn, K. 3, Tracy 3, Wynn 3, Freund 4, Irene 4, Kaper 4, Stewart 4)
Without Mercy, 1925 (Clarke, C.C. 4)
Without Orders, 1936 (Bond 3, Hunt 4)
Without Pity. *See* Senza pietà, 1948
Without Regret, 1935 (Niven 3, Brackett, C. 4)
Without Reservations, 1946 (Leroy 2, Colbert 3, Grant, C. 3, Wayne 3, Krasner 4, Lasky 4)
Without Title, 1964 (Dovniković 4)
Without Warning, 1952 (Biroc 4)
Without Warning, 1980 (Palance 3)
Without Warning. *See* Invisible Menace, 1938
Witness, 1985 (Ford, H. 3, Jarre 4)
Witness. *See* Temoin, 1978
Witness. *See* Temps du ghetto, 1961
Witness for the Defense, 1919 (Oland 3, Menzies 4, Miller, A. 4)
Witness for the Prosecution, 1957 (Wilder 2, Dietrich 3, Lanchester 3, Laughton 3, Power 3, Head 4, Kurnitz 4, Mandell 4, Trauner 4)
Witness for the Prosecution, 1982 (Hiller 3, Kerr 3, Pleasance 3, Richardson 3)
Witness Out of Hell. *See* Gorge trave, 1965
Witness to Murder, 1954 (Sanders 3, Stanwyck 3, Alton, J. 4)
Witness to the Will, 1914 (Ingram 2)
Witnesses. *See* Temps du ghetto, 1961
Wives and Lovers, 1963 (Johnson, V. 3, Leigh, J. 3, Winters 3, Anhalt 4, Ballard 4, Head 4, Wallis 4)
Wives and Other Wives, 1918 (Furthman 4)
Wives Beware. *See* Two White Arms, 1932
Wives Never Know, 1936 (Beavers 3, Menjou 3, Head 4)
Wives of Jamestown, 1913 (Olcott 2)
Wives of Men, 1918 (Stahl 2)
Wives of the Prophet, 1926 (Costello, M. 3)
Wives Under Suspicion, 1938 (Whale 2)
Wiz, 1978 (Lumet 2, Horne 3, Pryor 3, Allen, D. 4, Jones 4, Morris 4, Whitlock 4)
Wizard of Arts, 1941 (Fleischer, M. and D. 2)
Wizard of Babylon, 1983 (Moreau 3)
Wizard of Baghdad, 1960 (Katzman 4)
Wizard of Mars, 1965 (Carradine 3)
Wizard of Oz, 1910 (Selig 4)
Wizard of Oz, 1924 (Hardy 3)
Wizard of Oz, 1939 (Fleming 2, Leroy 2, Burke 3, Garland 3, Lahr 3, Adrian 4, Edens 4, Freed 4, Gibbons 4, Gillespie 4, Rosson 4, Smith, J.M. 4, Stothart 4)
Wizard of the Saddle, 1928 (Plunkett 4)
Wizards, 1977 (Bakshi 2)
Wizja Lokalna—1901, 1981 (Olbrychski 3)
Wo ist Coletti?, 1913 (Warm 4)
Wo ist Herr Belling?, 1944 (Jannings 3)
Wo ist mein Schatz?, 1916 (Lubitsch 2)
Wochenende. *See* Weekend, 1930
Woe Oh Ho No, 1972 (Emshwiller 2)
Woes of a Waitress, 1914 (Costello, M. 3)
Woes of a Wealthy Lady, 1911 (Bunny 3)
Woes of Roller Skates, 1908 (Méliès 2)
Wojna swiatownastepne, 1980's (Janda 3)
Wold Shadow, 1972 (Brakhage 2)
Wolf. *See* Farkas, 1916
Wolf, Are You There? See Loup y es-tu?, 1983
Wolf Dog, 1933 (Walthall 3, Canutt 4)
Wolf Fangs, 1927 (Miller, S. 4)

Wolf Hounded, 1958 (Hanna and Barbera 4)
Wolf Hunters, 1949 (Boetticher 2)
Wolf in Cheap Clothing, 1936 (Terry 4)
Wolf in Sheepdog's Clothing, 1963 (Hanna and Barbera 4)
Wolf Larsen, 1958 (Crosby 4)
Wolf Lowry, 1917 (Hart 3, August 4)
Wolf Man, 1924 (Gilbert 3, Shearer 3)
Wolf Man, 1941 (Bellamy 3, Chaney Lon, Jr. 3, Lugosi 3,
    Ouspenskaya 3, Rains 3, Pierce 4, Salter 4, Siodmak 4)
Wolf Song, 1929 (Fleming 2, Hathaway 2, Boyd 3, Cody 3,
    Cooper, Gary 3, Velez 3, Head 4)
Wolf Trap. See Vlčí jáma, 1957
Wolf unter Wolfen, 1965 (Mueller-Stahl 3)
Wolf with Child. See Kozure ohkami, 1972
Wolf! Wolf!, 1934 (Lantz 4)
Wolf! Wolf!, 1944 (Terry 4)
Wolf Woman, 1916 (Sullivan 4)
Wolfen, 1981 (Finney 3)
Wolfhound, 1916 (Terry 4)
Wolf's Pardon, 1947 (Terry 4)
Wolf's Side of the Story, 1938 (Terry 4)
Wolf's Tale, 1944 (Terry 4)
Wolga-Wolga, 1928 (Andrejew 4, Planer 4)
Wolkenbau und Flimmerstern, 1919 (Lang 2)
Wolves, 1930 (Gish, D. 3, Laughton 3)
Wolves. See Volki, 1925
Wolves. See Ookami, 1955
Wolves of the Air, 1927 (Boyd 3, Costello, M. 3)
Wolves of the Night, 1919 (Farnum 3)
Wolves of the Rail, 1918 (August 4)
Wolves of the Road, 1925 (Canutt 4)
Wolves of the Sea, 1938 (Bosworth 3)
Wolves of the Trail, 1918 (Hart 3)
Woman, 1915 (Chaplin 2, Purviance 3)
Woman, 1918 (Tourneur, M. 2, Carré 4)
Woman, 1939 (Stromberg 4)
Woman. See Amore, 1948
Woman. See Onna, 1948
Woman, A Man, A City. See Mujer, un hombre, una ciudad, 1978
Woman Accused, 1933 (Calhern 3, Grant, C. 3, Struss 4)
Woman Against Woman, 1938 (Astor 3)
Woman Alone, 1917 (Brady 3, Edeson 4, Marion 4)
Woman Alone, 1937 (Sidney 3)
Woman Alone. See Sabatage, 1936
Woman and Bean Soup. See Onna no misoshiru, 1968
Woman and Pirates. See Onna to kauzoku, 1959
Woman and the Hunter, 1957 (Sheridan 3)
Woman and the Law, 1918 (Walsh 2)
Woman and Wife, 1918 (Brady 3)
Woman at Her Window. See Femme à sa fenêtre, 1976
Woman Between, 1931 (Hunt 4)
Woman Between. See Woman I Love, 1937
Woman Chases Man, 1937 (Crawford, B. 3, Hopkins, M. 3, McCrea 3,
    Day 4, Goldwyn 4, Mandell 4, Newman 4, Toland 4)
Woman Commands, 1932 (Negri 3, Rathbone 3, Brown, N. 4,
    Krasner 4, Mandell 4)
Woman Conquers, 1922 (Karloff 3, Schulberg 4)
Woman Destroyed. See Smash-Up, 1947
Woman Disputed, 1928 (Florey 2, King 2, Talmadge, N. 3, Menzies 4,
    Schenck 4, Sullivan 4)
Woman, Don't Make Your Name Dirty. See Onna yo, kini no na o
    kegasu nakare, 1930
Woman from Headquarters, 1950 (Salter 4)
Woman from Hell, 1929 (Astor 3, Carré 4)
Woman from Mellon's, 1909 (Griffith 2, Pickford 3, Bitzer 4)
Woman from Monte Carlo, 1932 (Curtiz 2, Dagover 3, Huston 3,
    Muse 3, Haller 4)
Woman from Moscow, 1928 (Lukas 3, Negri 3)
Woman from Warren's, 1915 (Browning 2)
Woman Gives, 1920 (Talmadge, N. 3)
Woman God Forgot, 1917 (DeMille 2, Bosworth 3, Reid 3,
    Buckland 4, Macpherson 4)
Woman Hater, 1925 (Brook 3)

Woman Hater, 1948 (Feuillère 3, Granger 3, Dillon 4)
Woman Haters, 1913 (Sennett 2, Arbuckle 3)
Woman Haters, 1934 (Brennan 3, Three Stooges 3)
Woman He Loved, 1922 (Sutherland 2, Gaudio 4)
Woman He Married, 1922 (Niblo 2, Meredyth 4)
Woman He Scorned, 1930 (Czinner 2, Negri 3)
Woman Hungry, 1931 (Polito 4)
Woman Hunt, 1961 (Crosby 4)
Woman Hunt, 1974 (Corman 4)
Woman Hunt. See Au royaume des cieux, 1947
Woman Hunter, 1972 (Duning 4)
Woman I Love, 1929 (Miller, V. 4, Plunkett 4)
Woman I Love, 1937 (Litvak 2, Hopkins, M. 3, Muni 3, Plunkett 4,
    Polglase 4, Rosher 4, Veiller 4)
Woman I Love, 1971 (Dunaway 3)
Woman I Stole, 1933 (Wray 3)
Woman in a Dressing Gown, 1957 (Quayle 3)
Woman in a Leopardskin Coat. See Kvinna i leopard, 1958
Woman in Black, 1914 (Barrymore L. 3, Gaudio 4)
Woman in Bondage. See Impassive Footman, 1932
Woman in Brown. See Vicious Circle, 1948
Woman in Command. See Soldiers of the King, 1933
Woman in 47, 1916 (Brady 3)
Woman in Green, 1945 (Bruce 3, Rathbone 3, Miller, V. 4, Salter 4)
Woman in Her Thirties. See Side Streets, 1934
Woman in Hiding, 1949 (Lupino 3, Daniels 4, Orry-Kelly 4)
Woman in His House, 1920 (Stahl 2)
Woman in His House. See Animal Kingdom, 1932
Woman in His Life, 1933 (Adrian 4)
Woman in Leopardskin. See Kvinna i leopard, 1958
Woman in Question, 1950 (Asquith 2, Bogarde 3, Dillon 4)
Woman in Red, 1935 (Florey 2, Stanwyck 3, Brown, Harry Joe 4,
    Orry-Kelly 4, Polito 4)
Woman in Red, 1984 (Wilder 3)
Woman in Room 13, 1932 (King 2, Bellamy 3, Loy 3, Friedhofer 4,
    Seitz 4)
Woman in the Case. See Allotment Wives, 1945
Woman in the Dark, 1934 (Bellamy 3, Douglas, M. 3, Wray 3,
    Plunkett 4)
Woman in the Dunes. See Suna no onna, 1963
Woman in the Hall, 1947 (Simmons 3, Dalrymple 4, Mathieson 4)
Woman in the Moon. See Frau im Mond, 1929
Woman in the Night. See Tesha, 1928
Woman in the Suitcase, 1919 (Niblo 2, Barnes 4, Ince 4)
Woman in the Ultimate, 1913 (Gish, L. 3)
Woman in the Window, 1944 (Lang 2, Bennett J. 3, Duryea 3,
    Massey 3, Robinson, E. 3, Fields 4, Friedhofer 4, Johnson 4,
    Krasner 4)
Woman in White, 1927 (Sweet 3)
Woman in White, 1929 (Wilcox 2)
Woman in White, 1948 (Greenstreet 3, Moorehead 3, Young, G. 3,
    Blanke 4, Steiner 4)
Woman in White. See Journal d'une femme en blanc, 1965
Woman in White. See Kvinna i vitt, 1949
Woman Inside, 1981 (Blondell 3)
Woman Is a Woman. See Femme est une femme, 1961
Woman Is the Judge, 1939 (Brown, K. 4)
Woman Like Satan. See Femme et le pantin, 1958
Woman Named En. See En to iu onna, 1971
Woman Next Door. See Femme d'à côte, 1981
Woman Obsessed, 1959 (Hathaway 2, Hayward 3, Friedhofer 4,
    Lemaire 4, Smith, J.M. 4, Wheeler 4)
Woman of a Misty Moonlight. See Oboroyo no onna, 1936
Woman of Affairs, 1928 (Brown 2, Bosworth 3, Fairbanks, D. Jr. 3,
    Garbo 3, Gilbert 3, Stone 3, Adrian 4, Daniels 4, Gibbons 4,
    Meredyth 4)
Woman of Arizona, 1912 (Anderson G. 3)
Woman of Bronze, 1923 (Vidor, K. 2)
Woman of Distinction, 1950 (Ball 3, Gwenn 3, Milland 3, Russell, R. 3,
    Walker 4)
Woman of Experience, 1931 (Pitts 3, Brown, Harry Joe 4)
Woman of Mystery, 1914 (Guy 2)
Woman of No Importance. See Frau ohne Bedeutung, 1936

Woman of Osaka. *See* Osaka no onna, 1958
Woman of Otowi Crossing, 1974 (Koch 4)
Woman of Pale Night. *See* Oboroyo no onna, 1936
Woman of Paris, 1923 (Chaplin 2, Menjou 3, Purviance 3)
Woman of Pleasure, 1919 (Sweet 3)
Woman of Plesure. *See* Kanraku no onna, 1924
Woman of Rome. *See* Romana, 1954
Woman of Rumors. *See* Uwasa no onna, 1954
Woman of Sin. *See* Woman Scorned, 1911
Woman of Straw, 1964 (Dearden 2, Connery 3, Lollobrigida 3, Richardson 3, Adam 4, Mathieson 4)
Woman of Summer. *See* Stripper, 1963
Woman of the Circus. *See* Carola Lamberti — Eine vom Zirkus, 1954
Woman of the Dunes. *See* Suna no onna, 1963
Woman of the Jury, 1924 (Love 3)
Woman of the North Country, 1952 (Raine 4)
Woman of the Osore Mountains. *See* Osore-zan no onna, 1964
Woman of the People. *See* Kvinde af Folket, 1909
Woman of the River. *See* Donna del fiume, 1954
Woman of the Sea, 1926 (Chaplin 2, Purviance 3)
Woman of the Sea. *See* Sea Gull, 1926
Woman of the Sleeping Forest. *See* Sleeping Beauty, 1930
Woman of the Town, 1943 (Trevor 3, Rozsa 4)
Woman of the World, 1925 (Negri 3, Glennon 4)
Woman of the World. *See* Outcast Lady, 1934
Woman of the Year, 1942 (Mankiewicz 2, Stevens 2, Bainter 3, Bendix 3, Hepburn, K. 3, Tracy 3, Adrian 4, Lardner 4, Ruttenberg 4, Waxman 4)
Woman of the Year, 1976 (Ames 4)
Woman of Tomorrow. *See* Zhemtsina zavtrastchevo dnia, 1914
Woman on Pier 13, 1949 (Ryan 3, Musuraca 4)
Woman on the Beach, 1947 (Renoir 2, Bennett J. 3, Ryan 3, D'Agostino 4, Eisler 4)
Woman on the Jury, 1924 (Bosworth 3, Hersholt 3, Walthall 3)
Woman on the Run, 1950 (Sheridan 3, Leven 4)
Woman on Trial, 1927 (Stiller 2, Negri 3, Glennon 4, Schulberg 4)
Woman One Longs For. *See* Frau, nach der Man sich sehnt, 1929
Woman Opening a Door. *See* Tobira o hiraku onna, 1946
Woman Pays, 1914 (Cruze 2)
Woman Possessed, 1958 (Roeg 2)
Woman Racket, 1930 (Sweet 3, Gibbons 4)
Woman Racket. *See* Cargaison blanche, 1937
Woman Rebels, 1936 (Sandrich 2, Crisp 3, Heflin 3, Hepburn, K. 3, Marshall 3, Berman 4, Polglase 4, Vajda 4, Veiller 4)
Woman Scorned, 1911 (Griffith 2, Sweet 3, Bitzer 4)
Woman Tamer. *See* She Couldn't Take It, 1935
Woman Tempted Me. *See* Frelsende Film, 1915
Woman the Flower. *See* Femme-Fleur, 1965
Woman There Was, 1919 (Bara 3)
Woman They Almost Lynched, 1953 (Dwan 2)
Woman Times Seven, 1967 (De Sica 2, Arkin 3, Caine 3, Gassman 3, MacLaíne 3, Noiret 3, Sellers 3, Evein 4)
Woman Times Seven. *See* Sept fois femme, 1967
Woman to Woman, 1923 (Hitchcock 2, Saville 2, Brook 3, Balcon 4, Reville 4)
Woman to Woman, 1929 (Saville 2, Balcon 4)
Woman Trap, 1929 (Wellman 2)
Woman Trap, 1936 (Brackett, C. 4, Head 4)
Woman Under Oath, 1919 (Stahl 2)
Woman Under the Influence, 1974 (Cassavetes 2, Falk 3, Rowlands 3)
Woman Using a Small Sword. *See* Kodachi o tsukau onna, 1944
Woman Using a Small Sword. *See* Kodachi o tsukau onna, 1961
Woman, Wake Up!, 1922 (Vidor, K. 2, Calhern 3, Barnes 4)
Woman Wanted, 1935 (Calhern 3, McCrea 3, O'Sullivan 3, Stone 3, Clarke, C.C. 4)
Woman Who Convicts Men. *See* Otoko o sabaku onna, 1948
Woman Who Did. *See* Frau mit dem schlechten Ruf, 1924
Woman Who Did Not Care, 1913 (Cruze 2)
Woman Who Gave, 1918 (Ruttenberg 4)
Woman Who is Waiting. *See* Machiboke no onna, 1946
Woman Who Killed a Vulture. *See* Geier-Wally, 1921
Woman Who Knows What She Wants. *See* Zena, která ví co chce, 1934
Woman Who Touched Legs. *See* Ashi ni sawatta onna, 1952

Woman Who Walked Alone, 1922 (Glennon 4, Howe 4)
Woman Who Wouldn't Die, 1965 (Andrews D. 3)
Woman Wise, 1928 (Pidgeon 3)
Woman with a Dagger. *See* Zhenshchina s kinzhalom, 1916
Woman with Four Faces, 1923 (Brenon 2, Howe 4)
Woman with No Name, 1950 (Burton 3)
Woman with the Orchid. *See* Frau mit den Orchiden, 1919
Woman Without a Face. *See* Kvinna utan ansikte, 1947
Womanhandled, 1925 (La Cava 2, Cronjager 4)
Womanhood, or The Glory of a Nation, 1917 (Blackton 2)
Woman-Proof, 1923 (Astor 3, Haller 4)
Woman's Decision. *See* Bilans kwartalny, 1975
Woman's Decoration. *See* Onna no kunsho, 1961
Woman's Descent. *See* Onna no saka, 1960
Woman's Devotion, 1956 (Henreid 3)
Woman's Face, 1941 (Cukor 2, Saville 2, Basserman 3, Crawford, J. 3, Douglas, M. 3, Farnum 3, Meek 3, Veidt 3, Adrian 4, Kaper 4, Stewart 4)
Woman's Face. *See* Kvinnas ansikte, 1938
Woman's Face. *See* Onna no kao, 1949
Woman's Faith, 1925 (Hersholt 3, Pitts 3)
Woman's Fool, 1918 (Ford, J. 2, Carey 3)
Woman's Heart. *See* Onnagokoru, 1959
Woman's Heresy. *See* Jashumon no onna, 1924
Woman's Honor, 1913 (Dwan 2)
Woman's Life. *See* Onna no rekishi, 1963
Woman's Past, 1915 (Ingram 2)
Woman's Place, 1921 (Fleming 2, Talmadge, C. 3, Emerson 4, Hunt 4, Loos 4, Schenck 4)
Woman's Place, 1956 (Peterson 2)
Woman's Revenge, 1912–13 (White 3)
Woman's Secret, 1924 (Marsh 3)
Woman's Secret, 1949 (Ray, N. 2, Douglas, M. 3, Grahame 3, O'Hara.3, Mankiewicz 4)
Woman's Secret. *See* Fujinkai no himitsu, 1959
Woman's Side, 1922 (Schulberg 4)
Woman's Sorrows. *See* Nyonin aishu, 1937
Woman's Status. *See* Onna no za, 1962
Woman's Story. *See* Onna no rekishi, 1963
Woman's Testament, Part 2: Women Who Sell Things at High Prices. *See* Jokyo II, 1959
Woman's Touch. *See* Woman Chases Man, 1937
Woman's Vengeance, 1947 (Boyer 3, Hardwicke 3, Lourié 4, Orry-Kelly 4, Rozsa 4)
Woman's Way, 1908 (Griffith 2, Lawrence 3)
Woman's Way, 1916 (Marion 4)
Woman's Way, 1928 (Baxter W. 3)
Woman's Woman, 1922 (Hackett 4)
Woman's World, 1954 (Negulesco 2, Allyson 3, Bacall 3, Heflin 3, MacMurray 3, Webb 3, Wilde 3, Brackett, C. 4, Lemaire 4)
Woman-Wise, 1937 (Dwan 2)
Womb of Power, 1979 (Nihalani 4)
Women, 1939 (Cukor 2, Franklin 2, Crawford, J. 3, Dumont 3, Fontaine 3, Goddard 3, McQueen, B. 3, Russell, R. 3, Shearer 3, Adrian 4, Loos 4, Murfin 4, Ruttenberg 4)
Women, 1973 (Brakhage 2)
Women Against Women, 1938 (Marshall 3)
Women and Gold, 1925 (Daniels 4)
Women and Miso Soup. *See* Onna no misoshiru, 1968
Women and Roses, 1914 (Reid 3)
Women and War, 1913 (Dwan 2)
Women and War. *See* Arêtez les tambours, 1961
Women Are Like That, 1938 (Francis, K. 3, O'Brien, P. 3, Orry-Kelly 4)
Women Are Strong. *See* Josei wa tsuyoshi, 1924
Women Are Weak. *See* Faibles femmes, 1959
Women Condemned, 1934 (Auer 3)
Women Defend the Home!. *See* Onna koso ie o momore, 1939
Women, Do Not Shame Your Names. *See* Onna yo, kini no na o kegasu nakare, 1930
Women Everywhere, 1930 (Korda 2, Biro 4)
Women Family. *See* Jokei kazoku, 1963
Women First, 1924 (Eason 4)

Women in Cages, 1971 (Corman 4)
Women in Chains, 1972 (Lupino 3)
Women in His Life, 1933 (Merkel 3)
Women in Love, 1969 (Russell 2, Bates 3, Jackson 3, Reed, O. 3, Delerue 4, Russell 4)
Women in New York. *See* Frauen in New York, 1977
Women in Our Time, 1948 (Arnold 4)
Women in Prison. *See* Joshu to tomoni, 1957
Women in Revolt, 1972 (Warhol/Morrissey 2)
Women in the Spinnery. *See* Lorinci fonóban, 1971
Women in the Wind, 1939 (Arden 3, Francis, K. 3, Orry-Kelly 4)
Women in War, 1940 (Cushing 3)
Women Left Alone, 1913 (Dwan 2)
Women Love Diamonds, 1927 (Goulding 2, Barrymore L. 3, Fairbanks, D. Jr. 3, Gibbons 4, Gillespie 4, Young, W. 4)
Women Love Once, 1931 (Auer 3, Lukas 3, Akins 4, Struss 4)
Women Men Forget, 1920 (Stahl 2)
Women Men Marry, 1931 (Scott, R. 3, Shamroy 4)
Women Must Dress, 1935 (Krasner 4)
Women of all Nations, 1931 (Walsh 2, Bogart 3, Lugosi 3, McLaglen 3, Carré 4)
Women of Dolwyn. *See* Last Days of Dolwyn, 1948
Women of Glamour, 1937 (Douglas, M. 3)
Women of Paris. *See* Parisiskor, 1928
Women of the Ginza. *See* Ginza no onna, 1955
Women of the Night. *See* Yoru no onna tachi, 1948
Women of the World. *See* Donna del mondo, 1963
Women of Twilight, 1952 (Harvey 3)
Women Should Stay at Home. *See* Onna koso ie o momore, 1939
Women: So We Are Made. *See* Noi donne siamo fatte cosi, 1971
Women Tend to . . . *See* Tokaku omna to iu mono wa, 1932
Women They Talk About, 1928 (Bacon 2)
Women Trouble. *See* Molti sogni per le strade, 1948
Women Unveiled. *See* Onnade arukoto, 1958
Women Who Give, 1924 (Adorée 3)
Women Without Men. *See* Dirnentragodie, 1927
Women without Men. *See* Nessa bala Rejal, 1952
Women without Names, 1940 (Florey 2, Beavers 3, Dreier 4, Head 4, Lang 4)
Women without Names. *See* Donne senza nome, 1949
Women, Women, 1918 (Ruttenberg 4)
Women Won't Tell, 1933 (Darwell 3)
Women's Origin. *See* Fukeizu, 1962
Women's Prison, 1955 (Lupino 3)
Women's Room, 1980 (Remick 3)
Women's Scroll. *See* Jokei, 1960
Women's Street. *See* Onna no machi, 1940
Women's Town. *See* Onna no machi, 1940
Won by a Fish, 1911 (Sennett 2, Pickford 3)
Won by a Foot, 1916 (Sutherland 2)
Won By a Neck, 1930 (Arbuckle 3)
Won in a Closet, 1914 (Sennett 2, Normand 3)
Won Through a Medium, 1911 (Sennett 2)
Won Ton Ton, The Dog Who Saved Hollywood, 1976 (Arlen 3, Blondell 3, Borgnine 3, Carradine 3, Charisse 3, Coogan 3, Crawford, B. 3, De Carlo 3, Dern 3, Faye 3, Mature 3, Mayo 3, Pidgeon 3, Weissmuller 3)
Wonder Bar, 1934 (Bacon 2, Berkeley 2, Darwell 3, Del Rio 3, Fazenda 3, Francis, K. 3, Jolson 3, Powell, D. 3, Orry-Kelly 4, Polito 4)
Wonder Boy. *See* Wunder unserer Tage, 1951
Wonder Kid, 1950 (Krasker 4)
Wonder Kid. *See* Wunder unserer Tage, 1951
Wonder Man, 1945 (Kaye 3, Mayo 3, Sakall 3, Banton 4, Fulton 4, Goldwyn 4, Mandell 4)
Wonder of the Dust. *See* Divota prašine, 1975
Wonder of Women, 1929 (Brown 2, Stone 3, Day 4, Gibbons 4, Meredyth 4)
Wonder of Wool, 1960 (Halas and Batchelor 2)
Wonder Ring, 1955 (Brakhage 2)
Wonder Woman, 1974 (Biroc 4)
Wonder World, 1972 (Takemitsu 4)
Wonderful Adventure, 1915 (Ingram 2, Farnum 3)

Wonderful Adventures of Herr Munchhausen. *See* Monsieur de Crac, 1910
Wonderful Bad Woman. *See* Subarashii akujo, 1963
Wonderful Chance, 1920 (Valentino 3)
Wonderful Country, 1959 (Armendáriz 3, Mitchum 3, Crosby 4, Horner 4, North 4)
Wonderful Crook. *See* Pas si méchant que ça, 1975
Wonderful Eye, 1911 (Sennett 2)
Wonderful Lie of Nina Petrovna. *See* Wunderbare Luge der Nina Petrowna, 1929
Wonderful Living Fan. *See* Merveilleux éventail vivant, 1904
Wonderful Nights of Peter Kinema, 1913 (Pearson 2)
Wonderful Rose Tree. *See* Rosier miraculeux, 1904
Wonderful Statue, 1913 (Bunny 3)
Wonderful Story, 1922 (Wilcox 2)
Wonderful Sunday. *See* Subarashiki nichiyobi, 1947
Wonderful Thing, 1921 (Brenon 2, Talmadge, N. 3, Carré 4, Schenck 4)
Wonderful Things, 1958 (Wilcox 2, Neagle 3)
Wonderful to Be Young. *See* Young Ones, 1961
Wonderful World of Jack Paar, 1959 (McLaren 2)
Wonderful World of the Brothers Grimm, 1962 (Pal 2, Bloom 3, Bondi 3, Harvey 3, Homolka 3)
Wonderful Years, 1958 (Wright 3)
Wonderful Years. *See* Restless Years, 1958
Wonderland, 1931 (Lantz 4)
Wonders of Aladdin. *See* Meraviglie di Aladino, 1961
Wood and Stone. *See* Mokuseki, 1940
Wooden Head. *See* Mokuseki, 1940
Wooden Horse, 1950 (Finch 3, Dalrymple 4)
Wooden Indian, 1949 (Terry 4)
Wooden Leg, 1909 (Griffith 2, Bitzer 4)
Woodland, 1932 (Terry 4)
Woodman Spare That Tree, 1951 (Terry 4)
Woodpecker in the Rough, 1952 (Lantz 4)
Woods. *See* Forest, 1931
Woody Woodpecker, 1941 (Lantz 4)
Woody Woodpecker Polka, 1951 (Lantz 4)
Wooers of Mountain Kate, 1912 (Dwan 2)
Wooing of Miles Standish, 1908 (Olcott 2)
Wooing of Winifred, 1911 (Costello, M. 3)
Woolen Under Where, 1963 (Jones 2)
Word, 1978 (Chaplin 3, Williamson 3)
Word. *See* Ordet, 1943
Word. *See* Ordet, 1955
Word of Honor, 1981 (Malden 3)
Wordless Message, 1912 (Dwan 2, Mix 3)
Words and Music, 1929 (Bond 3, Wayne 3, Clarke, C.C. 4)
Words and Music, 1948 (Taurog 2, Allyson 3, Charisse 3, Garland 3, Horne 3, Kelly, Gene 3, Leigh, J. 3, Rooney 3, Sothern 3, Alton, R. 4, Edens 4, Freed 4, Rose 4, Rosher 4, Smith, J.M. 4, Stradling 4)
Words for Battle, 1941 (Jennings 2, Olivier 3)
Work, 1915 (Chaplin 2, Purviance 3)
Work or Profession?. *See* Munka vagy hivatás?, 1963
Work Party, 1942 (Lye 2)
Worker and Warfront series, 1945 (Alwyn 4)
Workers' Quarters. *See* Rabotchaia slobodka, 1912
Working and Playing to Health, 1953 (Van Dyke, W. 2)
Working Class Goes to Paradise. *See* Classe operaia va in paradiso, 1971
Working for Hubby, 1912 (Bunny 3)
Working Girls, 1931 (Arzner 2, Lukas 3, Akins 4)
Working Man, 1933 (Arliss 3, Davis 3, Orry-Kelly 4)
Working Trip. *See* Komandirovka, 1962
Works and Days, 1969 (Frampton 2)
Workshop for Peace, 1954 (Hammid 2)
Workshop for Peace, 1959 (Dickinson 2)
World According to Garp, 1982 (Hill, G.R. 2, Bumstead 4, Ondricek 4, Tesich 4)
World Against Him, 1916 (Polito 4)
World and His Wife, 1920 (Marion 4)
World and His Wife. *See* State of the Union, 1948

World and Its Women, 1919 (Gibbons 4)
World and the Flesh, 1932 (Cromwell 2, Hopkins, M. 3, Struss 4)
World Apart, 1917 (Reid 3)
World at Her Feet, 1927 (Schulberg 4)
World Cafe. *See* Automat Svět, 1965
World Championship of Air Models. *See* Mistrovstvĭ světa leteckych modelářu, 1957
World Changes, 1933 (Leroy 2, Astor 3, Muni 3, Nilsson 3, Rooney 3, Gaudio 4, Orry-Kelly 4, Wallis 4)
World Flier, 1931 (Sennett 2)
World for Ransom, 1954 (Aldrich 2, Bruce 3, Duryea 3)
World for Sale, 1918 (Blackton 2)
World Gardens, 1942 (Unsworth 4)
World Gone Mad, 1933 (Calhern 3, O'Brien, P. 3)
World in Flames, 1940 (Head 4)
World in his Arms, 1952 (Walsh 2, Peck 3, Quinn 3, Chase 4)
World in My Corner, 1956 (Murphy 3)
World in My Pocket, 1961 (Steiger 3)
World in My Pocket. *See* An einem Freitag um halb zwolf . . ., 1961
World Is Full of Married Men, 1979 (Baker C. 3)
World is Ours. *See* Svět patří nám, 1937
World Is Peaceful. *See* Tenka taihei, 1955
World Melody. *See* Melodie der Welt, 1929
World Moves On, 1934 (Ford, J. 2, Carroll M. 3, Fetchit 3, Friedhofer 4, Steiner 4)
World of Abbott and Costello, 1965 (Abbott and Costello 3)
World of Alphonse Mucha. *See* Svět Alfonso Muchy, 1980
World of Andrew Wyeth, 1977 (Fonda, H. 3)
World of Apu. *See* Apur Sansar, 1959
World of Dong Kingman. *See* Dong Kingman, 1955
World of Henry Orient, 1964 (Hill, G.R. 2, Lansbury 3, Sellers 3, Bernstein 4, Johnson 4, Kaufman 4, Smith, D. 4)
World of Ingmar Bergman, 1975 (Donner 2)
World of Little Ig, 1956 (Halas and Batchelor 2)
World of Plenty, 1943 (Alwyn 4, Mayer 4)
World of Sport Fishing, 1972 (Crosby 3)
World of Suzie Wong, 1960 (Holden 3, Box 4, Cahn 4, Duning 4, Stark 4, Unsworth 4)
World of Wall Street, 1929 (Lukas 3)
World on a Wire. *See* Welt am Draht, 1973
World Premiere, 1941 (Barrymore J. 3, Farmer 3, Head 4)
World, the Flesh, and the Devil, 1959 (Ferrer, M. 3, Rozsa 4)
World to Live In, 1919 (Brady 3)
World War III, 1982 (Hudson 3)
World Was His Jury, 1958 (O'Brien, E. 3, Katzman 4)
World Window Documentaries, 1937–40 (Cardiff 4)
World Without End, 1953 (Wright 2)
World Youth Festival in Warsaw. *See* Varsoí vit, 1955
Worldly Goods, 1924 (Glennon 4)
Worldly Madonna, 1922 (Edeson 4)
Worlds Apart, 1921 (Crosland 3)
World's Applause, 1923 (Daniels 3, Menjou 3, Stone 3)
World's Best Bride. *See* Hanayome san wa sekai-ichi, 1959
World's Champion, 1922 (Reid 3)
World's Greatest Athlete, 1974 (Muse 3)
World's Greatest Lover, 1977 (Wilder 3)
Worlds in Struggle. *See* Kämpfende Welten, 1922
World's Oldest Living Thing, 1914 (Sennett 2)
Worse You Are the Better You Sleep. *See* Warui yatsu hodo yoku nemuru, 1960
Worst of Farm Disasters, 1941 (Ivens 2)
Worst of Friends, 1916 (Sennett 2)
Worst Woman in Paris?, 1933 (Menjou 3)
Worth of a Life, 1914 (Ince 4)
Wot Dot, 1970 (Halas and Batchelor 2)
Wotan's Wake, 1962 (De Palma 2)
Wot's All th' Shootin' Fer, 1940 (Terry 4)
Wotta Nitemare, 1939 (Fleischer, M. and D. 2)
Would You Believe It?, 1929 (Gilliat 4)
Would You Forgive?, 1920 (Furthman 4)
Would-Be Heir, 1912 (Dwan 2)
Would-Be Shriner, 1912 (Sennett 2)
Wounded in Honour. *See* Mimì metallurgio ferito nell'onore, 1972

Wounded in the Forest. *See* Ranny v lesie, 1964
Wow, 1969 (Jutra 2)
Woyzeck, 1979 (Herzog 2, Kinski 3)
Wozzeck, 1947 (Warm 4)
Wraki, 1957 (Polanski 2, Cybulski 3)
Wrath of God, 1972 (Hayworth 3, Mitchum 3, Schifrin 4)
Wrath of the Gods, 1914 (Hayakawa 3, Ince 4)
Wreath in Time, 1908 (Griffith 2, Bitzer 4)
Wreath of Orange Blossoms, 1910 (Griffith 2, Crisp 3, Bitzer 4)
Wreck of the Hesperus, 1927 (Adrian 4)
Wreck of the Hesperus, 1944 (Terry 4)
Wreck of the Mary Deare, 1959 (Cooper, Gary 3, Heston 3, Redgrave, M. 3, Duning 4, Ruttenberg 4, Young, F. 4)
Wrecker, 1928 (Balcon 4)
Wrecker, 1933 (Bond 3, Muse 3)
Wreckety Wrecks, 1933 (Roach 4)
Wrecking Crew, 1942 (Arlen 3)
Wrecking Crew, 1969 (Lee, B. 3, Martin, D. 3)
Wrecks. *See* Wraki, 1957
Wrestlers, 1933 (Sennett 2)
Wrestler's Bride. *See* Wrestlers, 1933
Wrestling. *See* Lutte, 1961
Wrestling, N.Y. Athletic Club, 1905 (Bitzer 4)
Wrestling Sextette. *See* Nouvelles Luttes extravagantes, 1900
Wrestling Swordfish, 1931 (Sennett 2)
Wringing Good Joke, 1900 (Porter 2)
Written Law, 1931 (Carroll M. 3)
Written on the Wind, 1956 (Sirk 2, Bacall 3, Hudson 3, Malone 3, Cahn 4)
Wrong Again, 1929 (McCarey 2, Laurel and Hardy 3)
Wrong All Around, 1914 (Browning 2)
Wrong Arm of the Law, 1962 (Caine 3, Sellers 3)
Wrong Box, 1966 (Caine 3, Mills 3, Moore, D. 3, Richardson 3, Sellers 3, Barry 4)
Wrong Is Right, 1982 (Brooks, R. 2, Connery 3)
Wrong Man, 1956 (Hitchcock 2, Fonda, H. 3, Quayle 3, Herrmann 4)
Wrong Move. *See* Falsche Bewegung, 1974
Wrong Movement. *See* Falsche Bewegung, 1974
Wrong Mr. Wright, 1927 (Hersholt 3)
Wrong Patient, 1911 (Bunny 3)
Wrong Road, 1937 (Cruze 2)
Wrong Room, 1939 (Lake 3)
Wrongdoers, 1925 (Barrymore L. 3)
Wrongdoers. *See* Vurguncular, 1971
Wspanialu marsz, 1970 (Giersz 4)
Wspólny pokój, 1959 (Tyszkiewicz 3)
Wszystko na sprzedaz, 1968 (Wajda 2, Olbrychski 3, Tyszkiewicz 3)
Wu Li Chang, 1930 (Gibbons 4, Marion 4)
Wüger kommt auf leisen Socken, 1972 (Ireland 3)
Wunder des Malachias, 1961 (Wicki 2)
Wunder unserer Tage, 1951 (Werner 3)
Wunderbare Luge der Nina Petrowna, 1929 (Herlth 4, Hoffmann 4, Jaubert 4, Pommer 4, Rohrig 4)
Wunderbarer Sommer. *See* Gluck auf der Alm, 1958
Würger der Welt, 1919 (Dupont 2)
WUSA, 1970 (Harvey 3, Newman 3, Perkins 3, Woodward 3, Schifrin 4)
Wuthering Heights, 1939 (Wyler 2, Carroll L. 3, Crisp 3, Niven 3, Oberon 3, Olivier 3, Basevi 4, Goldwyn 4, Hecht 4, MacArthur 4, Mandell 4, Newman 4, Toland 4)
Wuthering Heights, 1970 (Legrand 4)
Wuya yu Maque, 1948 (Zhao 3)
Wycieczka za miasto, 1968 (Giersz 4)
Wyoming, 1928 (Van Dyke, W.S. 2, Selznick 4)
Wyoming, 1940 (Beery 3)
Wyoming, 1947 (Ouspenskaya 3, Alton, J. 4, Canutt 4)
Wyoming Kid. *See* Cheyenne, 1947
Wyoming Outlaw, 1939 (Wayne 3, Canutt 4)
Wyoming Whirlwind, 1932 (Canutt 4)
Wyscig pokoju Warszawa-Berlin-Praga, 1952 (Ivens 2)

X

X, 1963 (Corman 4, Crosby 4)
X—The Man with the X-Ray Eyes, 1963 (Milland 3)
X—The Unknown, 1956 (Bernard 4, Sangster 4)
X, Y, and Zee, 1972 (Taylor, E. 3)
X, Y, and Zee. *See* Zee and Co., 1972
Xala, 1974 (Sembene 2)
Xanadu, 1980 (Kelly, Gene 3)

X-Diagnosis. *See* Diagnoza X, 1933
Xiao Lingzi, 1936 (Zhao 3)
Xica. *See* Xica da Silva, 1976
Xica da Silva, 1976 (Diegues 2)
Xochimilco. *See* María Candelária, 1943
X-Ray Glasses. *See* Lunettes féeriques, 1909

Y

Y el cielo fue tomado por asalto, 1973 (Alvarez 2)
Y el projimo?, 1973 (Chaplin 3)
. . . Y mañana seran mujeres!, 1954 (Alcoriza 4)
Y tenemos sabor, 1967 (Gomez, S. 2)
Ya Cuba, 1964 (Corrieri 3)
Ya, Frantsisk Skorina, 1970 (Yankovsky 3)
Ya k vam lechu vospominaniem, I s vamy snova ya, Osen, 1977–82 (Smoktunovsky 3)
Ya shagal po Moskva, 1964 (Churikova 3)
Yaarana, 1981 (Bachchan 3)
Yaban gulu, 1961 (Guney 2)
Yabu no naka no kuroneko, 1968 (Shindo 2)
Yabure amigasa, 1927 (Hasegawa 3)
Yabure daiko, 1949 (Kinoshita 2, Mori 3)
Yabure kabure, 1930 (Kyo 3)
Yacht on the High Seas, 1955 (Lemaire 4)
Yagodki lyubvi. *See* Yahidka kokhannya, 1926
Yagua, 1940–41 (Fejos 2)
Yagui, 1916 (Bosworth 3)
Yagyu bugei-cho, 1957 (Kagawa 3, Mifune 3)
Yagyu ichizoku no inbo, 1978 (Yamada 3)
Yahidka kokhannya, 1926 (Dovzhenko 2)
Yahudi, 1958 (Roy 2)
Yahudi Ki Ladki, 1933 (Sircar 4)
Yaji Kita, 1933 (Hasegawa 3)
Yaji Kita bijin sodo, 1932 (Hasegawa 3)
Yakko Kagami-san, 1934 (Hasegawa 3)
Yakko no Koman, 1927 (Tanaka 3)
Yakoman and Tetsu. *See* Yakoman to Tetsu, 1949
Yakoman to Tetsu, 1949 (Kurosawa 2)
Yakov Sverdlov, 1940 (Yutkevich 2)
Yakuza, 1975 (Pollack 2, Schrader 2, Mitchum 3, Towne 4)
Yakuza kiji, 1937 (Shindo 3)
Yale Laundry, 1907 (Bitzer 4)
Yalis, la vergine del Roncador. *See* Vergine del Roncador, 1953
Yalta Conference, 1944 (Gerasimov 2)
Yama no gaika, 1929 (Tanaka 3)
Yama no oto, 1954 (Naruse 2, Hara 3, Yamamura 3)
Yama no sanka, 1962 (Shinoda 2, Yamada 3, Yamamura 3)
Yamabiko gakko, 1952 (Imai 2, Okada 3)
Yamada Nagamasa Oja no tsurugi, 1959 (Hasegawa 3)
Yamamoto Isoroku, 1968 (Mifune 3, Mori 3, Tsukasa 3, Tsuburaya 4)
Yamaneko rei jou, 1948 (Yoda 4)
Yamaneko Tomi no hanashi, 1943 (Takamine 3)
Yamata, 1919 (Korda 2)

Yami no Kageboushi, 1938 (Miyagawa 4)
Yami o yokogire, 1959 (Yamamura 3)
Yamile sous les cèdres, 1940 (Francis, E. 3, Vanel 3)
Yamiuchi tosei, 1932 (Yamada 3)
Yanapanacuna, 1970 (Alvarez 2)
Yaneura no onnatachi, 1956 (Kishida 3)
Yang-tse Incident, 1957 (Wilcox 2)
Yangyu. *See* Yagyu bugei-cho, 1957
Yank at Eton, 1942 (Taurog 2, Gwenn 3, Rooney 3, Freund 4, Kaper 4)
Yank at Oxford, 1938 (Barrymore L. 3, Gwenn 3, Leigh, V. 3, O'Sullivan 3, Taylor, R. 3, Balcon 4, Booth 4, Gilliat 4, Rosson 4, Saunders 4)
Yank Came Back, 1947 (Meredith 3)
Yank in Dutch. *See* Wife Takes a Flyer, 1942
Yank in Indo-China, 1952 (Katzman 4)
Yank in Korea, 1951 (Katzman 4)
Yank in London, 1945 (Darwell 3)
Yank in London. *See* I Live in Grosvenor Square, 1945
Yank in Rome. *See* Americano in vacanza, 1945
Yank in the R.A.F., 1941 (King 2, Grable 3, Power 3, Banton 4, Basevi 4, Day 4, Newman 4, Shamroy 4, Zanuck 4)
Yank on the Burma Road, 1942 (Schary 4)
Yankee at King Arthur's Court. *See* Connecticut Yankee, 1931
Yankee Buccaneer, 1952 (Chandler 3, Boyle 4)
Yankee Clipper, 1927 (Boyd 3, Fort 4, Sullivan 4)
Yankee Dood It, 1956 (Freleng 4)
Yankee Doodle Andy, 1941 (Bruckman 4)
Yankee Doodle Boy, 1929 (Fleischer, M. and D. 2)
Yankee Doodle Bugs, 1954 (Freleng 4)
Yankee Doodle Cricket, 1974 (Jones 2)
Yankee Doodle Daffy, 1943 (Freleng 4)
Yankee Doodle Dandy, 1942 (Curtiz 2, Cagney 3, Huston 3, Sakall 3, Buckner 4, Howe 4, Prinz 4, Wallis 4)
Yankee Doodle Dixie, 1913 (Bosworth 3)
Yankee Doodle Dude, 1926 (Sennett 2)
Yankee Doodle in Berlin, 1919 (Sennett 2)
Yankee Doodle Mouse, 1944 (Hanna and Barbera 4)
Yankee from the West, 1915 (Reid 3)
Yankee Girl, 1910 (White 3)
Yankee Girl, 1915 (Bosworth 3)
Yankee in King Arthur's Court. *See* Connecticut Yankee in King Arthur's Court, 1949
Yankee Pasha, 1954 (Chandler 3, Cobb 3, Salter 4)
Yankee Princess, 1919 (Love 3)

Yankee Senor, 1926 (Mix 3)
Yanks, 1979 (Schlesinger 2, Gere 3, Redgrave, V. 3, Roberts 3, Russell 4)
Yanks Ahoy, 1942 (Roach 4)
Yanqui No, 1960 (Leacock 2)
Yaps and Yokels, 1919 (Hardy 3)
Yaqui Cur, 1913 (Griffith 2, Barrymore L. 3, Bitzer 4)
Yarali kartal, 1965 (Guney 2)
Yari no Gonza, 1985 (Miyagawa 4, Takemitsu 4)
Yari no Gonzo, 1929 (Hasegawa 3)
Yarin son gundur, 1971 (Guney 2)
Yari-odori gojusan-tsugi, 1946 (Miyagawa 4)
Yarn about Yarn, 1941 (Terry 4)
Yashagaike, 1979 (Shinoda 2)
Yashu Honno-ji, 1934 (Hasegawa 3)
Yataro-gasa, 1955 (Yamada 3)
Yataro-gasa: Kyorai no maki, Dokuho no maki, 1932 (Yamada 3)
Yato kaze no naka o hashiru, 1961 (Ryu 3)
Yatrik, 1952 (Sircar 4)
Yatsu no hajiki wa jigoku daze, 1958 (Yamamura 3)
Ye Happy Pilgrims, 1934 (Lantz 4)
Ye Olde Melodies, 1929 (Fleischer, M. and D. 2)
Ye Olde Saw Mill, 1935 (Sennett 2)
Ye Olde Songs, 1932 (Terry 4)
Ye Olde Swap Shoppe, 1940 (Iwerks 4)
Ye Olde Toy Shop, 1935 (Terry 4)
Ye Olden Grafter, 1915 (Sennett 2)
Year Around, 1948 (Fleischer, M. and D. 2)
Year of Living Dangerously, 1982 (Weir 2, Gibson 3, Jarre 4)
Year of the Dragon, 1985 (De Laurentiis 4)
Year of the Horse, 1966 (Hubley 4)
Year of the Woman, 1973 (Beatty 3)
Yearling, 1946 (Brown 2, Franklin 2, Peck 3, Wyman 3, Gibbons 4, Irene 4, Rosher 4, Stothart 4)
Yearning. See Akogare, 1935
Yearning. See Midareru, 1964
Years Are So Long. See Make Way for Tomorrow, 1937
Years Between, 1946 (Redgrave, M. 3)
Years of Change, 1950 (Van Dyke, W. 2)
Years of Change. See New Frontier, 1950
Years to Come, 1922 (Roach 4)
Years Without Days. See Castle on the Hudson, 1940
Yedi belalilar, 1970 (Guney 2)
Yedi dağin aslani, 1966 (Guney 2)
Yeh Gulistan Hamara, 1973 (Anand 3, Burman 4)
Yeh kaisa insaaf, 1980 (Azmi 3)
Yehudi Menuhin—Chemin de lumière, 1970 (Reichenbach 2)
Yehudi Menuhin—Road of Light. See Yehudi Menuhin—Chemin de lumière, 1970
Yehudi Menuhin Story. See Yehudi Menuhin—Chemin de lumière, 1970
Yellow Arm, 1921 (Oland 3)
Yellow Balloon, 1952 (More 3)
Yellow Cab Man, 1950 (Deutsch 4, Stradling 4)
Yellow Caesar, 1940 (Cavalcanti 2, Crichton 2)
Yellow Canary, 1943 (Wilcox 2, Neagle 3, Rutherford 3, Bodeen 4)
Yellow Canary, 1963 (Crosby 4)
Yellow Contraband, 1928 (Johnson, N. 3)
Yellow Crow. See Kiiroi karasu, 1957
Yellow Dust, 1936 (Cronjager 4)
Yellow Headed Summer, 1974 (Pidgeon 3)
Yellow Horse, 1965 (Baillie 2)
Yellow Jack, 1938 (Coburn, C. 3, Montgomery 3, Stone 3, Vorkapich 4)
Yellow Lily, 1928 (Korda 2, Brook 3, Biro 4, Garmes 4, Meredyth 4)
Yellow Men and Gold, 1922 (Gibbons 4)
Yellow Mountain, 1954 (Hunter 4)
Yellow Passport, 1916 (Marion 4)
Yellow Passport, 1931 (Olivier 3)
Yellow Passport. See Yellow Ticket, 1931
Yellow Pawn, 1916 (Reid 3)
Yellow Peril, 1908 (Bitzer 4)
Yellow Robe. See Ran Salu, 1967

Yellow Rolls-Royce, 1964 (Asquith 2, Bergman 3, Delon 3, Harrison 3, MacLaine 3, Moreau 3, Scott, G. 3, Sharif 3, Fisher 4, Head 4, Korda 4)
Yellow Rose of Texas, 1944 (Rogers, R. 3)
Yellow Sands, 1938 (Brenon 2, McDowall 3)
Yellow Sky, 1948 (Wellman 2, Baxter A. 3, Peck 3, Widmark 3, Burnett 4, Lemaire 4, Newman 4, Trotti 4, Zanuck 4)
Yellow Stain, 1922 (Gilbert 3, Furthman 4)
Yellow Streak, 1915 (Barrymore L. 3)
Yellow Submarine, 1968 (Dunning 4)
Yellow Ticket, 1918 (Oland 3)
Yellow Ticket, 1931 (Walsh 2, Auer 3, Barrymore L. 3, Karloff 3, Friedhofer 4, Furthman 4, Howe 4)
Yellow Ticket. See Gelbe Schein, 1918
Yellow Ticket. See Yellow Passport, 1931
Yellow Tomahawk, 1954 (Van Cleef 3)
Yellow Traffic, 1914 (Guy 2)
Yellowbeard, 1983 (Mason 3, York, S. 3, Reynolds 4)
Yellowstone, 1936 (Krasner 4)
Yellowstone Kelly, 1959 (Oates 3)
Yentl, 1983 (Streisand 3, Legrand 4, Watkin 4)
Yes, Giorgio, 1982 (Schaffner 2, Williams, J. 4)
Yes Mr. Brown, 1932 (Buchanan 3)
Yes, My Darling Daughter, 1939 (Bainter 3, Robinson 4, Rosher 4, Wallis 4)
Yes No Maybe Maybenot, 1967 (Le Grice 2)
Yes or No, 1920 (Talmadge, N. 3, Haller 4)
Yes or No?, 1915 (Eason 4)
Yes Sir, That's My Baby, 1949 (Coburn, C. 3, O'Connor 3)
Yes! We Have No Bananas, 1930 (Fleischer, M. and D. 2)
Yes, We Have no Bonanza, 1939 (Three Stooges 3)
Yes, Yes, Nanette, 1925 (Hardy 3, Laurel 3, Roach 4)
Yesterday Girl. See Abschied von Gestern, 1966
Yesterday Is Over Your Shoulder, 1940 (Dickinson 2)
Yesterday, Today, and Tomorrow. See Ieri, oggi, domani, 1963
Yesterday's Child, 1977 (Jones S. 3)
Yesterday's Enemy, 1959 (Baker S. 3)
Yesterday's Heroes, 1940 (Clarke, C.C. 4, Day 4)
Yesterday's Tomorrow. See Zwischengleis, 1978
Yet, 1957–58 (Vanderbeek 2)
Yet Spies Haven't Died. See Kancho mada shinazu, 1942
Yeux cernés, 1964 (Morgan 3)
Yeux d'Elstir, 1967 (Fradetal 4)
Yeux de l'amour, 1959 (Blier 3, Darrieux 3)
Yeux fermés, 1971 (Dalio 3)
Yeux, la bouche, 1983 (Bellocchio 2)
Yeux ne veulent pas en tout temps se fermer. See Othon, 1969
Yeux noirs, 1935 (Aumont 3, Baur 3, Simon, S. 3, Andrejew 4, Lourié 4)
Yeux ouverts, 1913 (Feuillade 2)
Yeux qui fascinent, 1916 (Feuillade 2)
Yeux qui meurent, 1912 (Feuillade 2)
Yeux sans visage, 1960 (Franju 2, Valli 3, Jarre 4)
Yeux sans visages, 1960 (Brasseur 3, Schufftan 4)
Yevo prevosoditelstvo, 1927 (Donskoi 2, Cherkassov 3)
Yevo prizyv, 1925 (Protazanov 2)
Yhdeksan Tapaa Lahestya Helsinkia, 1982 (Donner 2)
Yiddisher Cowboy, 1911 (Dwan 2)
Yiğit yarali olur, 1966 (Guney 2)
Yin and Yang of Mr. Go, 1970 (Bridges 3)
Ying and the Yang. See Third Eye, 1969
Ying-ch'un ko chih feng-po, 1973 (King Hu 2)
Yip, Yip, Yippy, 1939 (Fleischer, M. and D. 2)
Yo pecador, 1959 (Armendáriz 3, García 3)
Yo quiero ser hombre, 1949 (García 3, Alcoriza 4)
Yo quiero ser tonta, 1950 (García 3)
Yoake mae, 1953 (Yoshimura 2)
Yoba, 1976 (Imai 2, Kyo 3, Miyagawa 4)
Yodelin' Kid from Pine Ridge, 1937 (Autry 3)
Yogen, 1982 (Takemitsu 4)
Yoghl, 1916 (Wegener 3)
Yogiri no ketto, 1959 (Mori 3)
Yogoreta hanazono, 1948 (Yoda 4)

Yogoto no yume, 1933 (Naruse 2)
Yoidore bayashi, 1955 (Yoda 4)
Yoidore nito-ryu, 1954 (Hasegawa 3)
Yoidore tenshi, 1948 (Kurosawa 2, Mifune 3, Shimura 3, Shindo 3, Hayasaka 4)
Yoiyami semareba, 1969 (Oshima 2)
Yojimbo, 1961 (Kurosawa 2, Mifune 3, Shimura 3, Tsukasa 3, Yamada 3, Miyagawa 4, Muraki 4)
Yokaren monogatari: Konpeki no sora toku, 1960 (Yamada 3)
Yokel. See Boob, 1926
Yokel Boy Makes Good, 1938 (Lantz 4)
Yokel Duck Makes Good, 1943 (Terry 4)
Yoke's on Me, 1944 (Three Stooges 3, Bruckman 4)
Yoki na onna, 1946 (Takamine 3)
Yokihi, 1955 (Mizoguchi 2, Kyo 3, Mori 3, Shindo 3, Yamamura 3, Hayasaka 4, Yoda 4)
Yokina ojo-san, 1932 (Takamine 3)
Yokina uramachi, 1939 (Yoshimura 2)
Yokina uta, 1929 (Tanaka 3)
Yokino-jo henge, 1935 (Hasegawa 3)
Yoki-no-jo henge, 1963 (Hasegawa 3)
Yokino-jo henge: Kaiketsu-hen, 1936 (Hasegawa 3)
Yokmok, 1963 (Tyszkiewicz 3)
Yokohama Yankee, 1955 (Terry 4)
Yoku, 1958 (Gosho 3)
Yokubo, 1953 (Yoshimura 2)
Yol, 1981 (Guney 2)
Yolanda, 1924 (Davies 3, Barnes 4)
Yolanda and the Thief, 1945 (Minnelli 2, Astaire 3, Edens 4, Freed 4, Gibbons 4, Gillespie 4, Irene 4, Rosher 4, Sharaff 4, Smith, J.M. 4)
Yoma Kidan, 1929 (Tsuburaya 4)
Yomeiri mae, 1933 (Tanaka 3)
Yomigaeru daichi, 1971 (Okada 3, Tsukasa 3, Takemitsu 4)
Yonjuhachi-sai no teiko, 1956 (Yoshimura 2, Yamamura 3)
Yonkers, Hanging Out. See Hanging Out—Yonkers, 1973
Yopparai tengoku, 1962 (Yamamura 3)
Yorck, 1931 (Grundgens 3, Krauss 3, Herlth 4, Hoffmann 4, Rohrig 4)
Yorokobi mo kanashimi mo ikutoshituki, 1957 (Kinoshita 2, Takamine 3)
Yoru, 1923 (Mizoguchi 2)
Yoru hiraku, 1931 (Gosho 2)
Yoru no cho, 1957 (Yoshimura 2, Kyo 3, Miyagawa 4)
Yoru no haiyaku, 1959 (Yamamura 3)
Yoru no kawa, 1956 (Yoshimura 2, Miyagawa 4)
Yoru no keisha, 1962 (Tsukasa 3)
Yoru no kyoja, 1927 (Tanaka 3)
Yoru no mesuneko, 1929 (Gosho 2)
Yoru no mibojin, 1951 (Tanaka 3)
Yoru no nagare, 1960 (Naruse 2, Tsukasa 3, Yamada 3)
Yoru no onnatachi, 1948 (Mizoguchi 2, Tanaka 3, Yoda 4)
Yoru no sugao, 1958 (Yoshimura 2, Kyo 3)
Yoru no togyo, 1959 (Kyo 3)
Yoru no tsuzumi, 1958 (Imai 2, Shindo 2, Mori 3)
Yoruno cho, 1957 (Yamamura 3)
Yosei Gorasu. See Yosei Gorath, 1962
Yosei Gorath, 1962 (Shimura 3, Tsuburaya 4)
Yosei wa hana no nioi ga suru, 1953 (Mori 3)
Yosemite, 1914 (Sennett 2)
Yoshia goten, 1937 (Yamada 3)
Yoshinaka o meguru sannin no onna, 1956 (Kinugasa 2, Hasegawa 3, Kyo 3)
Yoshiwara, 1937 (Ophuls 2, Hayakawa 3, Barsacq 4, Schufftan 4)
Yoso, 1963 (Kinugasa 2)
Yotamono to kyakusen-bi, 1933 (Takamine 3)
Yoto, 1926 (Tanaka 3)
Yotsuya Ghost Story. See Yotsuya kaidan, 1949
Yotsuya kaidan, 1949 (Kinoshita 2, Tanaka 3)
Yotsuya kaidan, 1959 (Hasegawa 3)
Yotsuya kaidan, 1965 (Takemitsu 4)
Yottsu no kekkon, 1944 (Takamine 3, Yamada 3)
Yottsu no koi no monogatari, 1947 (Kinugasa 2, Kurosawa 2, Naruse 2, Hayasaka 4)
Yotz 'im Kavua, 1979 (Golan and Globus 4)

You . . .. See Te, 1963
You and Me, 1938 (Lang 2, Carey 3, Cummings 3, Raft 3, Sidney 3, Dreier 4, Head 4, Krasna 4, Lang 4)
You and Me Together, 1979 (Welch 3)
You Are in Danger. See Girl Next Door, 1923
You Are My Adventure. See Du ar mitt aventyr, 1958
You Are My Love. See Inta Habibi, 1956
You Are Stupid, My Brother. See Niisan no baka, 1932
You Are Weighed in the Balance But Are Found Lacking. See Tinimbang ka Nguni't Kulang, 1974
You Belong to Me, 1934 (Sheridan 3, Head 4, Prinz 4)
You Belong to Me, 1941 (Ruggles 2, Fonda, H. 3, Stanwyck 3, Head 4, Trumbo 4, Walker 4)
You Belong to My Heart. See Mr. Imperium, 1950
You Bring the Ducks, 1934 (Roach 4)
You Came Along, 1945 (Cummings 3, Dreier 4, Head 4, Wallis 4, Young, V. 4)
You Came to My Rescue, 1937 (Fleischer, M. and D. 2)
You Can Change the World, 1949 (Crosby 3)
You Can Draw, 1938 (Van Dongen 2)
You Can't Beat Love, 1937 (Fontaine 3)
You Can't Believe Everything, 1918 (Swanson 3)
You Can't Buy Everything, 1934 (Stone 3, Nichols 4, Trotti 4)
You Can't Buy Luck, 1937 (Hunt 4)
You Can't Cheat an Honest Man, 1939 (Fields, W.C. 3, Krasner 4)
You Can't Do That to Me. See Maisie Goes to Reno, 1944
You Can't Do Without Love. See One Exciting Night, 1944
You Can't Escape, 1942 (Deutsch 4)
You Can't Escape Forever, 1942 (Brent 3, Gaudio 4)
You Can't Fool Your Wife, 1923 (Stone 3, Glennon 4, Young, W. 4)
You Can't Fool Your Wife, 1940 (Ball 3, Hunt 4, Polglase 4)
You Can't Get Away with Murder, 1939 (Bogart 3, Buckner 4, Friedhofer 4, Polito 4)
You Can't Go Home Again, 1975 (Ray, N. 2)
You Can't Go Home Again, 1979 (Grant, L. 3)
You Can't Have Everything, 1937 (Taurog 2, Ameche 3, Faye 3)
You Can't Ration Love, 1944 (Dreier 4, Head 4)
You Can't Run Away from It, 1956 (Allyson 3, Beavers 3, Lemmon 3, Powell, D. 3, Duning 4, Mercer 4, Wald 4)
You Can't Shoe a Horsefly, 1940 (Fleischer, M. and D. 2)
You Can't Sleep Here. See I Was A Male War Bride, 1949
You Can't Take It With You, 1938 (Capra 2, Arthur 3, Auer 3, Barrymore L. 3, Meek 3, Miller 3, Stewart 3, Irene 4, Riskin 4, Tiomkin 4, Walker 4)
You Can't Win 'em All, 1970 (Bronson 3, Curtis 3, Mathieson 4)
You Do, I Do, We Do, 1972 (Vanderbeek 2)
You Don't Need Pajamas at Rosie's. See First Time, 1969
You for Me, 1952 (Young, G. 3)
You Gotta Be a Football Hero, 1935 (Fleischer, M. and D. 2)
You Gotta Stay Happy, 1948 (Fontaine 3, Stewart 3)
You, John Jones, 1943 (Cagney 3)
You Know What Sailors Are, 1954 (Arnold 4)
You Leave Me Breathless, 1938 (Fleischer, M. and D. 2)
You Lie So Deep, My Love, 1975 (Pidgeon 3)
You May be Next, 1935 (Sothern 3)
You May Be Next. See Panic on the Air, 1935
You Must Be Joking, 1965 (Godfrey 4, Unsworth 4)
You Nazty Spy, 1940 (Three Stooges 3, Bruckman 4)
You Never Can Tell, 1920 (Daniels 3)
You Never Can Tell, 1951 (Powell, D. 3, Salter 4)
You Never Know. See You Never Can Tell, 1951
You Never Know Women, 1926 (Wellman 2, Brook 3, Glazer 4, Vajda 4)
You Only Live Once, 1937 (Lang 2, Bond 3, Fonda, H. 3, Sidney 3, Mandell 4, Newman 4, Shamroy 4, Wanger 4)
You Only Live Twice, 1967 (Connery 3, Pleasance 3, Adam 4, Barry 4, Young, F. 4)
You Ought to Be in Pictures, 1940 (Freleng 4)
You Remember Ellen?, 1911 (Olcott 2)
You Said a Hatful!, 1934 (Roach 4)
You Said a Mouthful, 1932 (Bacon 2, Brown 3, Rogers, G. 3, Orry-Kelly 4)
You Shouldn't Die. See Kimi shinitamau koto nakare, 1954

You Took the Words Right Out of My Heart, 1938 (Fleischer, M. and D. 2)
You Try Somebody Else, 1932 (Fleischer, M. and D. 2)
You Were Like a Wild Chrysanthemum. *See* Nogiku no gotoki kimi nariki, 1955
You Were Meant For Me, 1948 (Bacon 2, Crain 3, Dailey 3, Lemaire 4, Reynolds 4)
You Were Never Duckier, 1948 (Jones 2)
You Were Never Lovelier, 1942 (Daves 2, Astaire 3, Hayworth 3, Menjou 3, Irene 4, Mercer 4)
You Who Are About to Enter . . . *See* I som har intraden . . . 1945
You Will Remember, 1940 (McDowall 3)
You Will Send Me to Bed, Eh?, 1903 (Bitzer 4)
You Wouldn't Believe It, 1920 (Sennett 2)
You'd Be Surprised!, 1930 (Gilliat 4)
You'd Be Surprised, 1926 (Furthman 4, Schulberg 4)
Youki no seidayo, 1932 (Yoda 4)
You'll Find Out, 1940 (Karloff 3, Lorre 3, Lugosi 3, Mercer 4, Polglase 4)
You'll Never Get Rich, 1941 (Astaire 3, Hayworth 3, Alton, R. 4, Porter 4)
You'll Never Walk Alone, 1952 (Keel 3)
Young America, 1932 (Borzage 2, Beavers 3, Bellamy 3, Tracy 3)
Young America, 1942 (Darwell 3)
Young America Flies, 1940 (Daves 2, Eason 4)
Young and Beautiful, 1934 (Schary 4)
Young and Eager. *See* Claudelle Inglish, 1961
Young and Innocent, 1937 (Hitchcock 2, Bennett 4, Junge 4, Reville 4)
Young and Innocent. *See* Girl Was Young, 1937
Young and the Brave, 1963 (Arlen 3, Bendix 3)
Young and the Damned. *See* Olvidados, 1950
Young and the Passionate. *See* Vitelloni, 1953
Young and Willing, 1943 (Hayward 3, Holden 3, Dreier 4, Head 4, Young, V. 4)
Young and Willing. *See* Weak and the Wicked, 1953
Young and Willing. *See* Wild and the Willing, 1962
Young April, 1926 (Crisp 3, Love 3, Schildkraut 3, Adrian 4, Grot 4, Macpherson 4)
Young as You Feel, 1931 (Borzage 2, Rogers, W. 3)
Young As You Feel, 1940 (Lake 3, Clarke, C.C. 4)
Young at Heart, 1938 (Burke 3, Gaynor 3)
Young at Heart, 1954 (Barrymore E. 3, Day 3, Malone 3, Sinatra 3, Young, G. 3, Blanke 4, Coffee 4, Epstein, J. & P. 4, McCord 4)
Young Bess, 1953 (Franklin 2, Sidney 2, Carroll L. 3, Granger 3, Kerr 3, Laughton 3, Simmons 3, Plunkett 4, Rosher 4, Rozsa 4, Wimperis 4)
Young Bill Hickok, 1940 (Rogers, R. 3, Canutt 4)
Young Billy Young, 1969 (Dickinson 3, Mitchum 3)
Young Bride, 1932 (Fort 4, Miller, A. 4, Murfin 4, Steiner 4)
Young Buffalo Bill, 1940 (Rogers, R. 3)
Young Captives, 1959 (Kershner 2, Head 4)
Young Cassidy, 1965 (Ford, J. 2, Christie 3, Evans 3, Redgrave, M. 3, Smith 3, Cardiff 4)
Young Country, 1970 (Brennan 3)
Young Days. *See* Mladé dny, 1956
Young Diana, 1922 (Davies 3)
Young Dillinger, 1965 (Cortez 4)
Young Doctor Kildare, 1938 (Ayres 3, Barrymore, L. 3, Seitz 4)
Young Doctors, 1961 (Ashby 2, March 3, Segal 3, Bernstein 4, Sylbert 4)
Young Doctors in Love, 1982 (Stanton 3, Jarre 4)
Young Donovan's Kid, 1931 (Karloff 3, Cronjager 4, Steiner 4)
Young Donovan's Kid. *See* Donovan's Kid, 1931
Young Don't Cry, 1957 (Mineo 3, Haller 4)
Young Eagles, 1930 (Wellman 2, Arthur 3, Lukas 3)
Young Frankenstein, 1974 (Brooks, M. 2, Hackman 3, Wilder 3, Jeakins 4)
Young Fugitives, 1938 (Salter 4)
Young Fury, 1965 (Arlen 3, Bendix 3, Chaney Lon, Jr. 3, Mayo 3)
Young Generation. *See* Wakai hito, 1952
Young Girl at the University, 1959 (Daigaku no oneichan, 1959
Young Girl Dares to Pass. *See* Oneichan makari touru, 1959
Young Girls Beware. *See* Méfiez-vous fillettes, 1957

Young Girls of Rochefort, 1967 (Kelly, Gene 3)
Young Girls of Rochefort. *See* Demoiselles de Rochefort, 1967
Young Guard, 1948 (Bondarchuk 3)
Young Guard. *See* Molodaya gvardiya, 1947
Young Guns, 1959 (Fraker 4)
Young Have No Morals. *See* Dragueurs, 1959
Young Husbands. *See* Giovani mariti, 1957
Young Ideas, 1943 (Dassin 2, Astor 3, Gardner 3, Marshall 3, Schary 4)
Young in Heart, 1938 (Fairbanks, D. Jr. 3, Goddard 3, Bennett 4, Menzies 4, Selznick 4, Shamroy 4, Waxman 4, Wheeler 4)
Young Invaders. *See* Darby's Rangers, 1958
Young Ironsides, 1932 (Goddard 3, Roach 4)
Young Joe, The Forgotten Kennedy, 1977 (Barry 4)
Young Ladies of Wilko. *See* Panny z Wilka, 1979
Young Lady from the Riverside. *See* Slečna od vody, 1959
Young Lady in a Dream. *See* Yume no naka no ojousan, 1934
Young Land, 1957 (Hopper 3, Hoch 4, Tiomkin 4)
Young Lawyers, 1969 (Pryor 3, Wynn 3, Schifrin 4)
Young Lions, 1958 (Dmytryk 2, Brando 3, Clift 3, Martin, D. 3, Schell, Maximilian 3, Van Cleef 3, Anhalt 4, Friedhofer 4, Lemaire 4, Wheeler 4)
Young Lord. *See* Bonchi, 1960
Young Lovers, 1954 (Asquith 2, Havelock-Allan 4)
Young Lovers, 1964 (Fonda, P. 3, Biroc 4)
Young Lovers. *See* Never Fear, 1950
Young Man and Moby Dick. *See* Mladý muž a bílá velryba, 1978
Young Man and the White Whale. *See* Mladý muž a bílá velryba, 1978
Young Man of Manhattan, 1930 (Colbert 3, Rogers, G. 3)
Young Man of Music. *See* Young Man with a Horn, 1950
Young Man Who Figgered, 1915 (Talmadge, C. 3)
Young Man with a Horn, 1950 (Curtiz 2, Bacall 3, Day 3, Douglas, K. 3, Cahn 4, Carmichael 4, Foreman 4, McCord 4, Wald 4)
Young Man with Ideas, 1952 (Leisen 2, Ford, G. 3, Ruttenberg 4)
Young Man's Fancy, 1920 (Sennett 2)
Young Man's Fancy, 1939 (Balcon 4)
Young Master Feng, 1925 (Zhao 3)
Young Mr. Jazz, 1919 (Daniels 3, Lloyd 3, Roach 4)
Young Mr. Lincoln, 1939 (Ford, J. 2, Bond 3, Brady 3, Fonda, H. 3, Meek 3, Day 4, Glennon 4, MacGowan 4, Newman 4, Trotti 4, Zanuck 4)
Young Mr. Pitt, 1942 (Reed 2, Donat 3, Mills 3, Beaton 4, Gilliat 4, Young, F. 4)
Young Mrs. Eames, 1913 (Bosworth 3)
Young Nowheres, 1929 (Barthelmess 3, Haller 4)
Young Nurses, 1972 (Corman 4)
Young Oldfield, 1924 (McCarey 2, Roach 4)
Young One, 1960 (Buñuel 2)
Young Ones, 1961 (Figueroa 4, Slocombe 4)
Young Onions, 1932 (Sennett 2)
Young Painter, 1922 (Astor 3)
Young People, 1940 (Dwan 2, Marsh 3, Temple 3, Brown, Harry Joe 4, Cronjager 4, Day 4, Newman 4)
Young People. *See* Wakai hito, 1952
Young People. *See* Wakai hitotachi, 1954
Young People, Remember. *See* Emlékezz, ifjúság, 1955
Young Philadelphians, 1959 (Burke 3, Newman 3, Stradling 4)
Young Racers, 1963 (Coppola 2, Corman 4, Crosby 4, Golan and Globus 4)
Young Rajah, 1922 (Boyd 3, Valentino 3, Mathis 4)
Young Rebel. *See* Cervantes, 1968
Young Rebel/Cervantes. *See* Avventure e gli amori di Miguel Cervantes, 1968
Young Runaways, 1968 (Dreyfuss 3, Katzman 4)
Young Samurai. *See* Samurai no ko, 1963
Young Savages, 1961 (Frankenheimer 2, Pollack 2, Lancaster 3, Winters 3, Anhalt 4)
Young Scarface. *See* Brighton Rock, 1947
Young Sherlocks, 1922 (Roach 4)
Young Sinners, 1931 (Seitz 4)
Young Sinners. *See* High School Big Shot, 1959
Young Stranger, 1957 (Frankenheimer 2, Bass 4, Rosenman 4)
Young Teacher. *See* Wakai sensei, 1941

Young Tom Edison, 1940 (Taurog 2, Bainter 3, Rooney 3, Schary 4)
Young Torless. See Junge Torless, 1966
Young Veteran, 1941 (Cavalcanti 2, Crichton 2, Dearden 2)
Young Whirlwind, 1928 (Miller, V. 4)
Young Widow, 1946 (De Toth 2, Beavers 3, Russell, J. 3, Garmes 4, Stromberg 4)
Young Winston, 1972 (Attenborough 3, Bancroft 3, Hawkins 3, Hopkins, A. 3, Mills 3, Shaw 3, Foreman 4)
Young Wives' Tale, 1951 (Greenwood 3, Hepburn, A. 3)
Young Wolves. See Jeunes Loups, 1967
Young Woodley, 1930 (Carroll M. 3)
Young World. See Mondo nuovo, 1965
Youngblood Hawke, 1964 (Daves 2, Astor 3, Steiner 4)
Younger Generation, 1929 (Capra 2, Hersholt 3, Levien 4)
Youngest Profession, 1943 (Garson 3, Moorehead 3, Pidgeon 3, Powell, W. 3, Taylor, R. 3, Turner, L. 3, Irene 4, Lederer 4, Schary 4)
Youngsters. See Stěňata, 1957
Your Acquaintance. See Vasha znakomaya, 1927
Your Beer. See Anata no biru, 1954
Your Cheatin' Heart, 1964 (Katzman 4)
Your Children and You, 1946 (Alwyn 4)
Your Children's Ears, 1945 (Alwyn 4)
Your Children's Eyes, 1944 (Alwyn 4)
Your Children's Sleep, 1948 (Alwyn 4)
Your Children's Teeth, 1945 (Alwyn 4)
Your Girl and Mine, 1914 (Mix 3)
Your Highness. See Kakka, 1940
Your Husband's Past, 1926 (Roach 4)
Your Key to the Future, 1956 (Kidd 4)
Your Last Act, 1941 (Zinnemann 2)
Your Lips No. 1, 1970 (Le Grice 2)
Your Lips 3, 1971 (Le Grice 2)
Your Money or Your Life. See Peníze nebo život, 1932
Your Own Back Yard, 1925 (Roach 4)
Your Own Land. See Din tillvaros land, 1940
Your Past Is Showing. See Naked Truth, 1958
Your Red Wagon. See They Live by Night, 1948
Your Son and Brother. See Vash syn i brat, 1965
Your Ticket Is No Longer Valid, 1980 (Moreau 3)
Your Time on Earth. See Din stund på jorden, 1972
Your Turn, Darling. See A toi de faire, Mignonne, 1963
Your Turn, Darling. See Femmes d'abord, 1963
Your Turn, My Turn. See Va voir Maman . . . Papa travaille, 1977
Your Uncle Dudley, 1935 (Horton 3, Schary 4)
Your Witness, 1950 (Baker S. 3, Montgomery 3, Adam 4, Arnold 4, Harrison 4)
You're a Big Boy Now, 1966 (Coppola 2, Black 3, Page 3, Torn 3)
You're a Lucky Fellow, Mr. Smith, 1943 (Burke 3)
You're a Sweetheart, 1937 (Faye 3, Meek 3)
You're Darn Tootin', 1928 (Laurel and Hardy 3, Roach 4)
You're Driving Me Crazy, 1931 (Fleischer, M. and D. 2)
You're Fired, 1919 (Cruze 2, Reid 3)
You're in the Army Now, 1941 (Durante 3, Young, G. 3)
You're in the Army Now. See O.H.M.S., 1937
You're in the Navy Now, 1941 (Wyman 3)
You're in the Navy Now, 1951 (Hathaway 2, Bronson 3, Cooper, Gary 3, Marvin 3, Warden 3, Lemaire 4, Wheeler 4)
You're Lying. See Ni ljuger, 1969
You're My Everything, 1949 (Keaton 2, Baxter A. 3, Dailey 3, Lemaire 4, Newman 4, Trotti 4)
You're Never Too Young, 1955 (Lewis 2, Taurog 2, Martin, D. 3, Cahn 4, Head 4)
You're Next, 1921 (Roach 4)
You're Not Built That Way, 1936 (Fleischer, M. and D. 2)
You're Not So Tough, 1940 (Salter 4)
You're Only Young Once, 1938 (Rooney 3, Stone 3)
You're Only Young Twice, 1952 (Grierson 2)
You're Pinched, 1920 (Roach 4)
You're Telling Me!, 1932 (Roach 4)
You're Telling Me!, 1941 (Gilliat 4, Salter 4)
Your'e Telling Me, 1934 (Crabbe 3, Fields, W.C. 3, Banton 4)
You're the One, 1941 (Horton 3, Head 4, Mercer 4)
Yours for the Asking, 1936 (Costello, D. 3, Lupino 3, Raft 3, Banton 4, Dreier 4)

Yours, Mine, and Ours, 1968 (Ball 3, Fonda, H. 3, Johnson, V. 3)
Youth. See Jugend, 1938
Youth. See Seishun, 1925
Youth. See Seishun, 1968
Youth and His Amulet. See Gen to Fudo-myoh, 1961
Youth and Jealousy, 1913 (Dwan 2, Reid 3)
Youth Gets a Break, 1941 (Losey 2)
Youth in Fury. See Kawaita mizuumi, 1960
Youth in Poland, 1957 (Maysles A. and D. 2)
Youth in Revolt. See Altitude 3200, 1938
Youth of Chopin. See Mlodosc Chopina, 1952
Youth of Heiji Zenigata. See Seishun Zenigata Heiji, 1953
Youth of Japan. See Nihon no seishun, 1968
Youth of Maxim. See Yunost Maksima, 1935
Youth of 'The Land of Angels'. See Angyalföldi fiatalok, 1955
Youth on Parade, 1943 (De Carlo 3, Cahn 4)
Youth on Parole, 1938 (Dumont 3)
Youth on Trial, 1944 (Boetticher 2)
Youth Runs Wild, 1944 (Kline 2, Robson 2, Lewton 4)
Youth Speaks. See Pesn o Gerojach, 1932
Youth Takes a Fling, 1938 (McCrea 3, Maté 4, Pasternak 4)
Youth to Youth, 1922 (Pitts 3)
Youth Will Be Served, 1940 (Darwell 3, Cronjager 4, Day 4)
Youthful Folly, 1920 (Crosland 2)
Youthful Sinners. See Tricheurs, 1958
Youth's Gamble, 1925 (Brown, Harry Joe 4)
Youth's Oath. See Kliatva molodikh, 1944
You've Got to Walk It Like You Talk It or You'll Lose That Beat, 1971 (Pryor 3)
Yovita. See Jowita, 1967
Yoyo, 1964 (Carrière 4)
Yuganthayo, 1983 (Peries 2)
Yugato, 1953 (Kagawa 3)
Yuhi ni akai ore no kao, 1961 (Shinoda 2)
Yuhrei ressha, 1949 (Miyagawa 4)
Yuhu ni ore no akai kao, 1961 (Iwashita 3)
Yukan naru koi, 1925 (Tanaka 3)
Yuki Fujin ezu, 1950 (Mizoguchi 2, Yamamura 3, Hayasaka 4, Yoda 4)
Yuki matsuri, 1952 (Hani 2)
Yuki no honoo, 1955 (Tsukasa 3, Yamamura 3)
Yuki no wataridori, 1957 (Hasegawa 3)
Yuki no yo ketto, 1954 (Kinugasa 2)
Yukiguni, 1965 (Iwashita 3)
Yukiko, 1955 (Imai 2)
Yukiko to Natsuko, 1941 (Yamada 3)
Yukinojo henge, 1935 (Kinugasa 2)
Yukinojo henge, 1963 (Ichikawa 2)
Yukinojo's Disguise. See Yukinojo henge, 1935
Yukinojo's Revenge. See Yukinojo henge, 1935
Yukon Jake, 1924 (Sennett 2)
Yukovsky, 1950 (Pudovkin 2, Golovnya)
Yukubo, 1953 (Miyagawa 4)
Yukyo gonin otoko, 1958 (Hasegawa 3)
Yukyo no mure, 1948 (Hasegawa 3, Yamamura 3)
Yul 871, 1966 (Denner 3)
Yuma, 1971 (Duning 4)
Yume de aritai, 1962 (Yamamura 3)
Yume no naka no ojousan, 1934 (Yoda 4)
Yume Utsutsu, 1935 (Tanaka 3)
Yumrutzi i presta, 1980 (Ivanov 3)
Yunbogi no nikki, 1965 (Oshima 2)
Yunost Maksima, 1935 (Kozintsev 2, Enei 4, Moskvin 4, Shostakovich 4)
Yurakucho de aimasho, 1958 (Kyo 3)
Yurei akatsuki ni shisu, 1948 (Hasegawa 3)
Yurei hanjo-ki, 1960 (Kagawa 3)
Yushima no shiraume, 1955 (Kinugasa 2, Mori 3)
Yuwaku, 1948 (Shindo 2, Yoshimura 2, Hara 3)
Yuyake-gumo, 1956 (Kinoshita 2, Yamada 3)
Yves Montand chante en U.R.S.S. See Poet Iv Montan, 1957
Yves Montand Sings. See Poet Iv Montan, 1957
Yvette, 1927 (Cavalcanti 2, Braunberger 4)
Yvonne la nuit, 1949 (Cervi 3)

Z

Z, 1969 (Costa-Gavras 2, Denner 3, Montand 3, Papas 3, Trintignant 3, Coutard 4, Theodorakis 4)
'Z', 1972 (Grgić 4)
Z bláta do louže, 1934 (Stallich 4)
Z ceskych mlynu, 1925 (Haas 3)
Z čínskěo zápisníku, 1954 (Kachyna 2)
Z lásky, 1928 (Vích 4)
Z mého života, 1970 (Schorm 2)
Z nepatrných přicin velké následky, 1979 (Danailov 3)
Z.P.G., 1971 (Chaplin 3, Reed, O. 3)
Za rodnou hroudu, 1930 (Stallich 4, Vích 4)
Za sciana, 1971 (Zanussi 2, Komorowska 3)
Za trnkovým keřem, 1979 (Brejchová 3)
Za život radostný, 1951 (Kachyna 2, Kučera 4)
Zaak M.P., 1960 (Haanstra 2)
Zaarden, 1918 (Basserman 3)
Zabijaka, 1967 (Stawinsky 4)
Zabil jsem Einsteina pánové, 1969 (Brejchová 3, Kopecký 3)
Zabriskie Point, 1970 (Antonioni 2, Ford, H. 3, Guerra 4, Ponti 4, Tavoularis 4)
Zacharovannaya Desna, 1965 (Dovzhenko 2)
Zaczarowany rower, 1955 (Polanski 2)
Zaczelo sie w Hiszpanii, 1950 (Munk 2)
Zadnuszki, 1961 (Tyszkiewicz 3, Konwicki 4)
Zadzwoncie do mojej zony, 1958 (Polanski 2)
Zagranichnii pokhod sudov Baltiiskogo flota kreisere 'Aurora' i uchebnogo sudna 'Komsomolts', 1925 (Vertov 2)
Zagreb '74, 1974 (Dragić 4)
Záhada modrého pokoje, 1933 (Stallich 4)
Zahrada, 1968 (Švankmajer 4)
Zahradu, 1975 (Pojar 4)
Zaida, die Tragodie eines Modells, 1923 (Holger-Madsen 2)
Zajtra bude neskoro . . ., 1972 (Kroner 3)
Zakazane piosenki, 1947 (Kawalerowicz 2)
Zakázaný výlet, 1981 (Kopecký 3)
Zakoni Bolshoi zemli. See alitet ukhodit v gory, 1949
Zakroichik iz Torzhka, 1925 (Protazanov 2, Maretskaya 3)
Zaliczenie, 1969 (Zanussi 2)
Zalm, 1966 (Schorm 2)
Zaloga-Crew, 1952 (Lomnicki 3)
Zalzala, 1952 (Anand 3)
Zamach, 1959 (Lomnicki 3, Stawinsky 4)
Zamanat, 1977 (Azmi 3)
Zameer, 1975 (Bachchan 3)
Zámek Gripsholm, 1960 (Brejchová 3)
Zampó y yo, 1965 (Rey 3)
Zander the Great, 1925 (Daves 2, Bosworth 3, Davies 3, Barnes 4, Marion 4)
Zandunga, 1937 (De Fuentes 2, Velez 3)
Zandy's Bride, 1974 (Troell 2, Hackman 3, Ullmann 3)
Zange no yaiba, 1927 (Ozu 2)
Zangiku monogatari, 1939 (Mizoguchi 2, Yoda 4)
Zangiku monogatari, 1956 (Hasegawa 3, Yoda 4)
Zánik domu Usheru, 1981 (Švankmajer 4)
Zánik samoty Berhof, 1983 (Brejchová 3)
Zanjeer, 1973 (Bachchan 3)
Zanna bianca, 1973 (Rey 3)
Zansho, 1978 (Tsukasa 3)
Zany Adventures of Robin Hood, 1984 (McDowall 3, Segal 3)
Zanzibar, 1940 (Muse 3, Krasner 4, Salter 4)
Zaostřit prosím, 1956 (Fric 2)
Zapadli vlastenci, 1932 (Haas 3)
Zapatas Bande, 1914 (Gad 2, Nielsen 3, Freund 4)

Zapfenstreich am Rhein, 1930 (Planer 4)
Zápisník zmizelého, 1979 (Jires 2)
Zápor, 1960 (Kovács 2)
Zaporosch Sa Dunayem, 1938 (Ulmer 2)
Zapotecan Village, 1941 (Eisenstein 2)
Zaproszenie do wnetrza, 1978 (Wajda 2)
Zarak, 1957 (Mature 3, Alwyn 4, Box 4)
Zarco, 1957 (Armendáriz 3)
Zarco—The Bandit. See Zarco, 1957
Zardoz, 1973 (Boorman 2, Connery 3, Unsworth 4)
Záře nad Drávou, 1974 (Danailov 3)
Zarevo nad Drava. See Záře nad Drávou, 1974
Zářijové noci, 1957 (Brodský 3, Kučera 4)
Zärltiche Haie, 1966 (Karina 3)
Zärtlichen Verwandten, 1930 (Oswald 2)
Zärtlichkeit der Wolfe, 1973 (Fassbinder 2)
Zasadil dědek řepu, 1945 (Trnka 2, Hofman 4)
Zásah odbornika, 1978 (Danailov 3)
Zatoichi , 1970 (Mori 3)
Zatoichi hatashi-jo, 1968 (Shimura 3)
Zatoichi Meets Yojimbo. See Zatoichi to Yojimbo, 1970
Zatoichi to Yojimbo, 1970 (Mifune 3, Miyagawa 4)
Zatoichi's Conspiracy, 1973 (Okada 3, Shimura 3)
Zatoichi's Song Is Heard. See Zatouichi no uta ga kikoeru, 1966
Zatouichi: A Thousand Dollar Price on His Head. See Zatouichi senryo kubi, 1964
Zatouichi abare himatsuri, 1970 (Miyagawa 4)
Zatouichi Breaking Out of Prison. See Zatouichi rouyaburi, 1967
Zatouichi Challenge Letter. See Zatouichi hatashijou, 1968
Zatouichi hatashijou, 1968 (Miyagawa 4)
Zatouichi no uta ga kikoeru, 1966 (Miyagawa 4)
Zatouichi rouyaburi, 1967 (Miyagawa 4)
Zatouichi senryo kubi, 1964 (Miyagawa 4)
Zatouichi: Wild Fire Festival. See Zatouichi abare himatsuri, 1970
Zavada není na vašem přijímaci, 1961 (Brdečka 4)
Zavallilar, 1975 (Guney 2)
Závodník, 1948 (Hofman 4)
Závrat, 1962 (Kachyna 2)
Zaza, 1915 (Porter 2)
Zaza, 1923 (Dwan 2, Swanson 3, Rosson 4)
Zaza, 1939 (Cukor 2, Dmytryk 2, Colbert 3, Lahr 3, Marshall 3, Nazimova 3, Akins 4, Dreier 4, Head 4, Lang 4, Lewin 4)
Zaza, 1942 (Castellani 2, Rota 4)
Zazhivo Pogrebennii, 1919 (Ouspenskaya 3)
Zazie. See Zazie dans le Métro, 1960
Zazie dans le métro, 1960 (Malle 2, Noiret 3, Evein 4, Rappeneau 4)
Zbabělec, 1962 (Weiss 2)
Zbohom, sladké driemoty, 1983 (Kopecký 3)
Zbrodniarz i panna, 1963 (Cybulski 3)
Zdjecia, 1976 (Olbrychski 3)
Zdravstvuitye deti, 1962 (Donskoi 2)
Zdravstvuy Moskva!, 1945 (Yutkevich 2)
Ze soboty na neděli, 1931 (Hammid 2, Vích 4)
Ze světa lesních samot, 1933 (Vích 4)
Zeb vs. Paprika, 1924 (Laurel 3, Roach 4)
Zeder: Voices from Darkness, 1983 (Delli Colli 4)
Zee and Co., 1972 (Caine 3, York, S. 3)
Zeedijk—Filmstudie, 1927 (Ivens 2)
Zehn Minuten Mozart, 1930 (Reiniger 2)
Zehnte Pavillon der Zitadelle, 1916 (Jannings 3)
Zeichen des Ersten, 1969 (Domrose 3)
Zeit der Einsamkeit, 1984 (Hoffmann 3)
Zeit zu leben, 1969 (Hoffmann 3)

Zoku shacho hanjo-ki, 1968 (Tsukasa 3)
Zoku shacho ninpo-cho, 1965 (Tsukasa 3)
Zoku shacho sandai-ki, 1958 (Tsukasa 3)
Zoku shacho sen-ichiya, 1967 (Tsukasa 3)
Zoku shacho shinshiroku, 1964 (Tsukasa 3)
Zoku shinobi no mono, 1963 (Yamamura 3)
Zoku Sugata Sanshiro, 1945 (Kurosawa 2, Mori 3)
Zöldár, 1965 (Gaál 2)
Zolinierz zwyciestwa, 1953 (Lomnicki 3)
Zolotoi eshelon, 1959 (Shukshin 3)
Zolotoi klyuchik, 1939 (Ptushko 2)
Zolotye vorota, 1969 (Dovzhenko 2)
Zoltan . . . Hound of Dracula, 1977 (Ferrer, J. 3)
Zombie, 1978 (Romero 2, Argento 4)
Zombies of Mora Tau, 1957 (Katzman 4)
Zombies on Broadway, 1945 (Lugosi 3, D'Agostino 4)
Zona, 1916 (Negri 3)
Zona roja, 1975 (Fernández 2)
Zone, 1928 (Périnal 4)
Zone de la mort, 1917 (Gance 2, Modot 3, Burel 4)
Zone Moment, 1956 (Brakhage 2)
Zoo, 1933 (Lantz 4)
Zoo, 1962 (Haanstra 2)
Zoo. See Chiriakhana, 1967
Zoo and You, 1938 (Alwyn 4)
Zoo Babies, 1938 (Alwyn 4)
Zoo in Budapest, 1933 (Young, L. 3, Friedhofer 4, Garmes 4, Lasky 4)
Zoo Is Company, 1961 (Hanna and Barbera 4)
Zoo Story. See Dobutsuen nikki, 1956
Zoo zéro, 1978 (Kinski 3, Valli 3)
Zoom and Bored, 1957 (Jones 2)
Zoom at the Top, 1962 (Jones 2)
Zoot Cat, 1944 (Hanna and Barbera 4)
Zopf und Schwert, 1926 (Dieterle 2)
Zora. See Silent Night, Bloody Night, 1973
Zorba the Greek, 1964 (Bates 3, Papas 3, Quinn 3, Lassally 4)
Zori Parizha, 1936 (Maretskaya 3)
Zorn's Lemma, 1970 (Frampton 2)
Zorro, 1975 (Baker S. 3, Delon 3)
Zorro Rides Again, 1937 (Canutt 4)
Zorro's Black Whip, 1944 (Canutt 4)
Zorro's Fighting Legion, 1939 (Canutt 4)
Zotz!, 1962 (Dumont 3)
Zouhei monogatari, 1963 (Miyagawa 4)
Zouzou, 1934 (Allégret, M. 2, Gabin 3, Douy 4, Kaufman 4, Meerson 4)
Zoya, 1944 (Shostakovich 4)
Zoya, 1954 (Batalov 3)
Zpěv zlata, 1920 (Ondra 3)
Zpívající pudřenka, 1959 (Kopecký 3)
Zrak, 1978 (Grgić 4)
Zralé víno, 1981 (Kopecký 3)
Zrcadlení, 1965 (Schorm 2)
Zsarnok szíve avagy Boccaccio Magyarországon, 1981 (Jancsó 2)
Zsigmond Moricz 1879–1942. See Móricz Zsigmond, 1956
Ztracená stopa, 1956 (Kachyna 2, Kučera 4)
Ztracená tvář, 1965 (Brejchová 3)
Ztracená varta, 1956 (Brdečka 4)
Ztracenci, 1957 (Brdečka 4)
'Zu böser Schlacht schleich'ich heut' Nacht so bang', 1977 (Kluge 2)
Zu jedem kommt einmal die Liebe. See Alte Lied, 1930
Zu neuen Ufern, 1937 (Sirk 2, Jurgens 3)
Zu spat, 1911 (Messter 4)
Zucker und Zimt, 1915 (Lubitsch 2)
Zuckerkandl!, 1968 (Hubley 4)
Zudora, 1914 (Cruze 2)

Zudora Mystery. See Zudora, 1914
Zuflucht, 1928 (Porten 3)
Zugelloses Blut, 1917 (Negri 3)
Zuid Limburg, 1929 (Ivens 2)
Zuider-zee Dike, 1931 (Van Dongen 4)
Zula Hula, 1937 (Fleischer, M. and D. 2)
Zulu, 1963 (Baker S. 3, Burton 3, Caine 3, Hawkins 3, Barry 4)
Zulu Dawn, 1979 (Lancaster 3, Mills 3, O'Toole 3, Bernstein 4)
Zulu-Land, 1911 (Selig 4)
Zulu's Heart, 1908 (Griffith 2, Lawrence 3, Bitzer 4)
Zum Goldenen Anker, 1931 (Korda 2, Basserman 3)
Zum Paradies der Damen, 1922 (Pick 2)
Zum Tee bei Dr. Borsig, 1963 (Herlth 4)
Zum Tode gehetz, 1912 (Gad 2, Nielsen 3)
Zündschnüre, 1974 (Hauff 2)
Zur Chronik von Grieshuus, 1925 (Dagover 3, Herlth 4, Rohrig 4, Von Harbou 4, Wagner 4)
Zürcher Verlobung, 1957 (Wicki 2, Ondra 3)
Zurnál FAMU, 1961 (Schorm 2)
Zut, chien des rues, 1955 (Kosma 4)
Zuyderzee, 1933 (Ivens 2, Van Dongen 4)
Zuzu the Band Leader, 1913 (Sennett 2, Normand 3)
Zvanyi uzhin, 1962 (Ermler 2)
Zvenigora. See Zvenyhora, 1928
Zvenyhora, 1928 (Dovzhenko 2)
Zvezda plenitelnogo schastya, 1975 (Batalov 3, Yankovsky 3)
Zvezdi i kosite, salzi v ocite, 1977 (Paskaleva 3)
Zvezdy na krylyakh, 1955 (Tikhonov 3)
Zvířátka a Petrovští, 1946 (Trnka 2, Hofman 4, Pojar 4)
20 Juli, 1955 (Schell, Maximilian 3)
Zwei Frauen, 1911 (Porten 3, Messter 4)
Zwei Frauen, 1938 (Tschechowa 3)
Zwei ganze tage, 1971 (Ophuls 2)
Zwei Girls vom roten Stern, 1965 (Gélin 3, Jurgens 3)
Zwei Herzen im 3/4 Takt, 1930 (Sakall 3, Reisch 4)
Zwei in einem Anzug, 1950 (Tschechowa 3)
Zwei in einer grosser Stadt, 1942 (Hoffmann 4)
Zwei Kinder, 1924 (Courant 4)
Zwei Krawatten, 1930 (Tschechowa 3, Metzner 4)
Zwei Menschen, 1930 (Frohlich 3, Pasternak 4)
Zwei rote Rosen, 1928 (Andrejew 4)
Zwei Welten, 1930 (Dupont 2)
Zwei Welten, 1940 (Grundgens 3)
Zweigroschenzauber, 1928–29 (Richter 2)
Zweite Erwachen der Christa Klages, 1977 (Von Trotta 2)
Zweite Frau, 1917 (Oswald 2)
Zweite Fruhling, 1975 (Jurgens 3)
Zweite Leben, 1916 (Kortner 3)
Zweite Leben, 1954 (Wicki 2)
Zweite Leben des Friederich Wilhelm Georg Platow, 1973 (Hoppe 3
Zweite Schuss, 1923 (Dieterle 2)
Zweite Schuss, 1943 (Fric 2)
Zwielicht, 1940 (Wegener 3)
Zwischen Abends und Morgens, 1923 (Robison 2, Krauss 3, Rasp 3, Wagner 4)
Zwischen Gestern und Morgen, 1947 (Knef 3, Herlth 4, Pommer 4)
Zwischen Himmel und Erde, 1942 (Krauss 3)
Zwischen Nacht und Morgen, 1931 (Homolka 3)
Zwischen Nacht und Morgen, 1944 (Wegener 3)
Zwischen Tag und Nacht, 1975 (Hoppe 3)
Zwischen zwei Herzen, 1934 (Tschechowa 3)
Zwischengleis, 1978 (Staudte 2, Ferrer, M. 3)
Zwolfte Stunde—Eine Nacht des Grauens, 1930 (Murnau 2)
Zycie raz jeszcze, 1965 (Lomnicki 3)
Zycie rodzinne, 1970 (Zanussi 2, Komorowska 3, Nowicki 3, Olbrychski 3)